The Power of
Attraction

By Saffi Crawford and Geraldine Sullivan

THE POWER OF BIRTHDAYS, STARS, AND NUMBERS:
The Complete Personology Reference Guide

THE POWER OF ATTRACTION:
The Astrological Guide to Personal Success, Prosperity, and Happy Relationships

The Power of Attraction

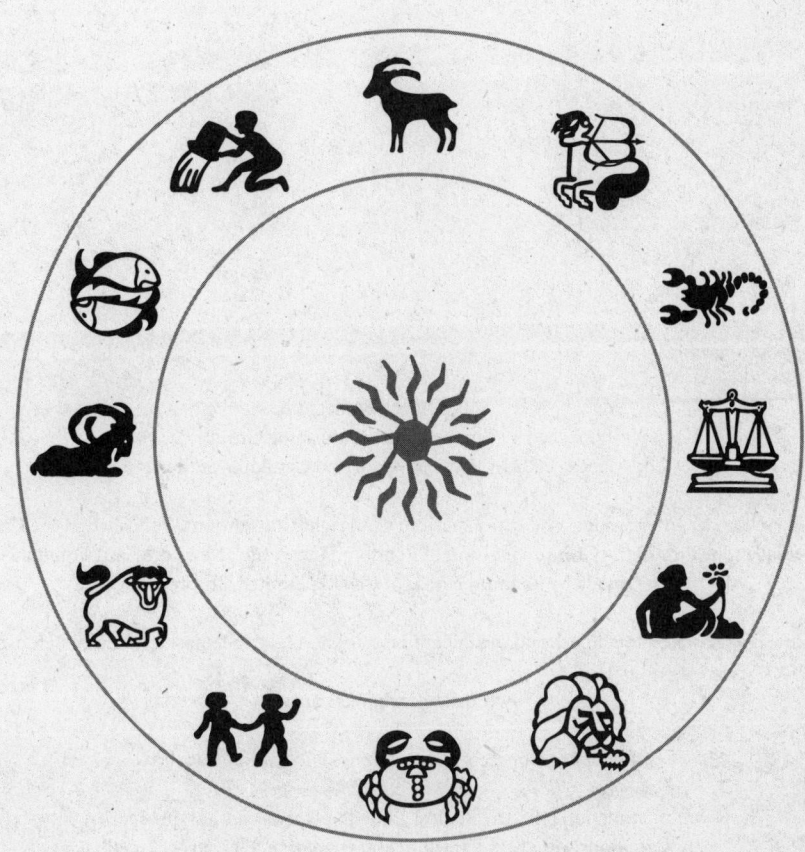

THE ASTROLOGICAL GUIDE TO PERSONAL SUCCESS,
PROSPERITY, AND HAPPY RELATIONSHIPS

Saffi Crawford and Geraldine Sullivan

BALLANTINE BOOKS · NEW YORK

A Ballantine Book
Published by The Ballantine Publishing Group
Copyright © 2002 by Saffi Crawford and Geraldine Sullivan

www.ballantinebooks.com

Library of Congress Cataloging-in-Publication Data
Crawford, Saffi.
The power of attraction : the astrological guide to personal success, prosperity, and
happy relationships / Saffi Crawford and Geraldine Sullivan.— 1st ed.
p.   cm.
1. Success—Miscellanea.   2. Astrology and personal finance.   3. Interpersonal relations—Miscellanea.
I. Sullivan, Geraldine.   II. Title.
BF1729.S88 C73 2002

133.5'81581—dc21   2001043934

ISBN 0-345-44351-9

Text design by Holly Johnson

Cover illustration by Rodica Prato

Manufactured in the United States of America

First Edition: February 2002

10   9   8   7   6   5   4   3   2   1

Contents

Acknowledgments

We would like to thank all those
who made this project possible, in particular,
Julie Castiglia, Leslie Meredith, Jeremie Ruby-Strauss,
Melissa Belle Crawford, Kristina Grushko, Hazel Aldred,
Margaret Sullivan, Cleo Foulcer, Kevin Sullivan, Chuck Wein,
Emma Aldred, Tom Sullivan, Ricky Foulcer, Darren Dickson,
Jonathan Creighton, John Badger, and Rebecca Aldred.

Introduction

The Power of Attraction is an astrological book designed especially for you. It is a comprehensive volume of astrological data that is a follow-up to our last book, *The Power of Birthdays, Stars and Numbers*. The purpose of our previous book was to create a personality profile for each of the 366 days of the year by synthesizing knowledge of astrology, numerology, and fixed stars. The intention of this new book is to take you a step further in your journey of self-discovery by including your year of birth. The knowledge gained from your full birth date can deepen your understanding and enhance your ability to gain personal success, prosperity, and happy relationships.

In your individual birthday entry and in Section Two, you will find information relating to your unique powers of attraction. You will discover how the planets Venus and Mars can enhance your personal appeal. This will enable you to carefully assess your true desires and what really motivates you.

The Power of Attraction also provides for the first time a rare system of astrological data in the form of a personalized timetable for each birthday entry. Professional astrologers work out the geometrical relationships between planets from complicated astronomical tables (the ephemeris). These geometrical connections are called aspects in the case of people, or transits when predicting a particular period of time. In this book we have simplified this complex process and have listed both aspects and transits of your Sun to the Outer Planets. Hence you will find on your birthday pages an easy-to-read timetable especially created for you. This timetable will be a key to unlocking the many interpretations listed in Section Three, "Empowerment and the Outer Planets." With no previous astrological experience, you will be able to utilize your personal timetable and make predictions like a professional astrologer.

Each birthday timetable focuses on the unique relationships between the Sun and the Outer Planets: Jupiter, Saturn, Uranus, Neptune, and Pluto. Learning about these planets and their powers will help you to understand the events and influences that affect your life. All the information for each planet is arranged simply in three categories: Beneficial, Challenging, and Special. You will be able to utilize this timetable in a number of ways to gain information about yourself and others as well as predict what the future may bring.

Your special timetable will also prove to be a valuable source of knowledge when dealing with relationships and individuals to whom you are attracted. By looking up on your own timetable the birth dates of lovers, friends, family members, or people you have just met, you will be able to gain deeper insights into your relationships.

Once you have mastered working with your own personalized timetable, you can visit the timetables of those you know. You can check whether your date of birth appears on their pages and find out more about your relationships with others.

Your Personal Profile

Each birthday profile consists of two pages. The entry for each day contains specific insight into your special characteristics, love and relationships, and potential for prosperity.

The first page is divided into three parts. The first part is "Your Personal Powers" and describes the personality traits of your particular birthday. This part lists attributes linked to your Sun's degree and decanate. The decanate further individualizes your Sun sign by adding the subinfluence of another sign and planet.

The second part of your birthday page is "Your Powers of Attraction in Relationships" and focuses on your love life. From a Venus/Mars influence it describes what motivates and inspires you in relationships. You will be able to discover the type of romance you desire and attract into your life.

The last part is "Your Venus Power." According to your full birth date (month, day, and year of birth), your individual Venus sign describes in greater detail your powers of attraction in relationships. To find your individual Venus sign you need to go to Section Two of the book. There you will not only find your Venus table but also your Mars table and interpretation.

The second page for each birthday entry consists of a personalized timetable that is based on your Sun's degree. This unique timetable begins in 1938 and continues until 2012. It provides information on the positions of the Outer Planets, Jupiter, Saturn, Uranus, Neptune, and Pluto, and their different relationships to your Sun degree. By interpreting the effect of these planets, you will be able to understand in greater depth what you are attracting into your life.

You will be able to discover:

- How your Sun interacts with the Outer Planets.
- How your Sun interacts with the Outer Planets of other people.
- How to use your Sun interaction with the Outer Planets to predict the future.

Although your personalized timetable may look complex at first glance, it is in fact easy to use, just as easy as a calendar. Your timetable will be a guide to unlocking the many interpretations listed in Section Two. These interpretations will prove particularly helpful when you wish to discover what is beneficial, challenging, or special in your quest for happiness, prosperity, and success.

You can use these interpretations of the Outer Planets linked to your Sun degree to find out:

- In Chapter 1: What are the Outer Planets saying about you?
- In Chapter 2: What type of relationships are the Outer Planets attracting into your life? Are they challenging, beneficial, or special?
- In Chapter 3: When are you likely to encounter periods of challenge and when are you likely to attract periods of opportunity and success?

Introduction to Astrology

Astrology is a method of exploring the relationship between humankind and the Universe. The tenets of astrology maintain that cosmic forces, rhythms, and cycles of nature exert an influence on every living organism, and proponents of astrology believe that life can be better understood through the knowledge of the signs of the zodiac and the interaction of the planets. Accurate astrological practices are based on a single moment in space and time, making each astrology chart symbolically unique. Although astrologers require the exact time, place, and complete date of birth in order to construct a horoscope wheel, popular astrology usually only refers to the division of the year into twelve monthly categories called signs of the zodiac. This division, along with the planets, can be viewed as the basis of astrological studies. In this book we have synthesized many years of astrological experience and research to provide you with an easy-to-read comprehensive day, month, and year reference tool. We hope this book will help you to increase your powers of attraction and success as well as deepen your understanding of yourself and others.

The Sun's Yearly Cycle

The Sun is the center of our solar system, and the planets, including Earth, travel and orbit around it. In addition to its counterclockwise path around the Sun, the Earth also rotates on an axis; this is what brings about the cycles of day and night. From a geocentric view—that is, from Earth's point of view—the Sun appears to cross the sky from the eastern horizon to the western horizon. The Sun's apparent journey against the backdrop of the stars in the twelve constellations marks a path around the Earth called the ecliptic. The Earth's axis is not only rotating but tilting, with the North Pole facing the Sun and away from the Sun at different times of the year to produce the four climate variations we know as the four seasons—winter, spring, summer, and fall. Each of the seasons is marked by a point in the Sun's travels. They are commonly called the spring and autumnal equinoxes and the summer and winter solstices. In astrology, these four divisions of the year are called the four cardinal points of the 360-degree zodiacal wheel. The astrological year begins in the spring at 0 degrees Aries; the summer solstice is marked as 0 degrees Cancer; the autumn is at 0 degrees Libra; and the winter solstice is at 0 degrees Capricorn. Since the zodiacal wheel is divided into twelve equal parts of 30 degrees arc each, these four cardinal, or dynamic, signs of the zodiacal wheel are followed by the four fixed signs of Taurus, Leo, Scorpio, and Aquarius. The four mutable, or changeable, signs of Gemini, Virgo, Sagittarius, and Pisces complete the twelve signs of the zodiac wheel.

As the Sun returns to approximately the same degree every year, astrologers refer to a person's birthday as a Solar Return. While the zodiac is divided into twelve distinct signs, in advanced astrological practice those signs are divided further into thirds called decanates. Each of these decanates is associated with an additional sign and planet and is listed on your personal page.

The Sun

The Sun, the energy center of our solar system, radiates the power of light and vitality and is thought of in many cultures as a life-giving force. In astrology, the Sun represents the energy source of all living things and gives a forceful assertion of individuality. It signifies the center of our being, our sense of identity and ego. The Sun's glyph, or symbol, is a circle with a point in the center, indicating the heart of our physical universe. In esoteric symbolism, this circle represents the totality of infinity or eternity and the dot in the middle signifies a particular point in time and space within that totality. Willpower, energy, strength, and self-expression are just some of the Sun's attributes. It also stands for ambition and pride, consciousness, self-confidence, and is a metaphor for the father or the masculine archetype. In mythology, kings and heroes are frequently associated with Helios, the Sun, which rules the zodiac sign of Leo.

Attractive qualities: vitality, magnetism, creativity, vigor, willpower, inspiration, self-confidence, charisma

Less attractive qualities: egotistical, self-centered, proud, arrogant, overbearing, dominating

The Twelve Astrological Signs

Aries

1ST SIGN
CARDINAL/FIRE
RULING PLANET: MARS
BODY PART: HEAD

Since Arians are the pioneers and leaders of the zodiac, even the quieter among you secretly want to be "number one" or first at something. The men of this sign love to play knight-errant and the women may appear forceful and assertive.

The attractive qualities of the sign of Aries indicate that you are bold and confident by nature, highly spirited, and enthusiastic. You probably hold a genuine belief that the world is yours to explore and conquer. As the first fire sign of the zodiac, you are able to forge ahead with endless projects and activities. Being energetic, you love to initiate new enterprises, and with your competitive spirit are also keen on winning. Ruled by the planet Mars, you are a doer and very rarely sit around twiddling your thumbs. Combining a daring character and enterprising spirit, you usually seek to be in the forefront of any activity. Frequently courageous and passionate, you can also be idealistic, chivalrous, and fiercely loyal to the people you love. You like to talk about your latest achievements and new projects, but are equally supportive of your partners if you truly believe in them. The less attractive attributes of the Sun in Aries suggest that patience is not your strongest point. Although you are quick to anger and eager to express your opinions, you are just as likely to quickly forgive and forget.

Although you are often recognized by your direct approach or decisive actions, you can lack subtlety. The drive of your ruling planet, Mars, indicates that lack of composure can also make you intolerant or impulsive. This may lead you to do something rash on a moment's notice. As an Arian, however, you respond well to crisis, have the ability to meet challenges head on, and can face difficult situations courageously. Fired with enthusiasm but often impatient with detail, you work better at initiating or launching new projects. Refusing to be put down, dynamic and generous, your Aries spirit lives to fight another day.

Despite opposing public opinion, you will usually refuse to compromise your ideals, even if it gets you into trouble or into a confrontation. Eventually, as you mature, you learn the value of diplomacy and compromise.

Although it is generally known that as a fire sign you are compatible with Leo and Sagittarius, in this book you will find that Venus, Mars, and the Outer Planets have an important influence on your relationships and powers of attraction.

Aries attractive qualities: independent, daring, courageous, intelligent, pioneering, bold, action-oriented

Aries less attractive qualities: aggressive, self-centered, headstrong, impulsive, competitive, bossy

Taurus

2ND SIGN
FIXED/EARTH
RULING PLANET: VENUS
BODY PART: THROAT AND NECK
SYMBOL: BULL
KEYWORDS: ENDURANCE, PERSISTENCE, SENSUALITY

As a sensible Taurean you are a quietly determined individual who very rarely gives up. With patience and resolution you continue on even when all others have fallen by the wayside. Your warm, seemingly calm and easygoing manner reflects your enjoyment of the simple pleasures in life.

As a Taurean you do not like to rush into things: you make decisions carefully and deliberately with security and financial issues very much to the fore. With Venus as your ruling planet you are often magnetic, sensual, and can be extremely attractive to the opposite sex. The Venus influence also bestows an enhanced love of beauty, interest in the arts, and a highly refined sense of touch.

Being a practical Earth sign, the basic securities of life are especially important to you. With a need for comfort and luxury, good food is part of your well-being, but guard against a tendency to overindulge. You often become an expert at culinary skills, a connoisseur of wine, and love entertaining. More commonly, your Sun sign is associated with the established world of finance. As a Taurean you like to know exactly were your money went, and make careful lists of all your financial dealings.

When charged with being materialistic, you will defend yourself by replying that you are merely being sensible and looking for "value for money." You can therefore become an expert at evaluating everything, from money matters and property to people. As a Taurean, through your desires to build a solid foundation in life, you can attract and achieve success.

Although you are often generous with your loved ones, you may have to avoid being overpossessive. Among some of your attractive qualities are your reliability, loyalty, and devotion. In fact, you can suffer in silence in order to keep the peace, but if pushed too far you are notorious for being obstinate. This stubbornness is one of your less attractive qualities. Since you need to feel grounded and stable, you are often drawn to individuals who are dependable and traditional, preferring to keep things the way they are. In times of change and instability you may have difficulty in adapting to new situations. Happily, you can always find comfort through a love of art and creativity, the joys of nature or music.

As a Taurean you usually have an attractive speaking or singing voice. If stressed, however, illness may affect your

throat. Nevertheless, Taurus, ruled by the bull, is renowned for being the sign of strength.

Although it is generally known that as an earth sign you are compatible with Virgo and Capricorn, in this book you will find that Venus, Mars, and the Outer Planets have an important influence on your relationships and powers of attraction.

Taurus attractive qualities: loyal, artistic, determined, persevering, stable, sensual, enduring, practical, musical

Taurus less attractive qualities: stubborn, materialistic, possessive, indulgent

Gemini

3RD SIGN
MUTABLE/AIR
RULING PLANET: MERCURY
BODY PARTS: LUNGS, ARMS, HANDS
SYMBOL: TWINS
KEYWORDS: VERSATILITY, TALKATIVE, INGENUITY

Your attractive qualities are your flexibility, versatility, and adaptable nature. Like the twins, Geminis are renowned for being able to do more than one thing at a time. Having more than one interest, however, suggests that you must guard against scattering your energies in too many directions. You are often seen as the child of the zodiac, always in a state of wonder. As a natural communicator with a never-ending thirst for knowledge, your Gemini character is that of the eternal student or one of youthfulness.

Being the first of the air signs suggests that you are astute and often on the move, ever satisfying your curiosity. Being extremely quick at picking out the salient points of any subject, you usually acquire a great deal of information, which you also like to share with others. It is often through mental discipline and learning that you develop a greater depth of thought and realize your true mental powers. As a Gemini you can also be friendly, bright, and multitalented.

Linked to the planet Mercury, you often have an androgynous quality, with a slim and youthful body. As you enjoy entertaining others with your wealth of ideas or stories, you frequently let your mercurial spirit soar. This also suggests that you usually have bright facial expressions and enjoy using your hands when conveying your ideas A love of talking indicates that you can chat on for hours; unfortunately, this can also turn into one of your less attractive qualities. To master the art of conversation, however, you may need to develop your listening skills.

Although your airy, sophisticated Gemini nature does not like to be pinned down, you usually make sure you are never bored or boring. Not known for consistency, you can nevertheless adapt and move with the times. As a Gemini you are generally intellectual and more interested in a stimulating mental challenge than earthly passion. Yet with a sensitive nervous system, your Gemini nature needs to guard against a tendency to worry.

Light and sociable, you often have an easy rapport with others and are more than willing to share the veritable mine of information you have at your disposal. With your youthful charm and natural quick wit, is it any wonder that you can be the most delightful friend and companion.

Although it is generally known that as an air sign you are compatible with Libra and Aquarius, in this book you will find that Venus, Mars, and the Outer Planets have an important influence on your relationships and powers of attraction.

Gemini attractive qualities: curious, informed, clever, good conversationalist, friendly, and sociable

Gemini less attractive qualities: inconsistent, superficial, too talkative, nervous

Cancer

4TH SIGN
CARDINAL/WATER
RULING PLANET: MOON
BODY PARTS: BREASTS AND STOMACH
SYMBOL: CRAB
KEYWORDS: SENSITIVITY, SYMPATHETIC, AFFECTIONATE

Emotional and sensitive, as a Cancerian you are ruled by your feelings. Like your guiding planet the Moon, you are able to run through the whole gamut of emotions that come with the changing tides. You possess the power of the deepest ocean and the vulnerability of a solitary crab on an empty beach. Like that crab, you have a protective shell of shyness to hide your great sensitivity and caution. This should not be interpreted as a weakness, however, as you often withdraw to gather strength.

Your most attractive qualities are your sympathetic and kind nature. You have a strong need to nurture, so you often take the role of mother, caretaker, or therapist. Having a protective streak implies that you will defend your loved ones against all odds. It is hardly surprising that home and family play an important role in establishing your security. Being generally domesticated you also show a natural flair for good food and cooking.

Despite your many changing moods, you are naturally affectionate and caring. With all your protective love and devotion, however, you may need to guard against one of your less attractive qualities—that of becoming too emotionally involved. You may benefit from learning about tough love since at times others can take advantage of your caring nature. As a Water sign, you are often shy, have sentimental tendencies, and are inclined to hang on to the past. This can be the reason why you care about family heirlooms such as photos and let-

ters or become a collector of antiquities. Security conscious, you also have a talent for hanging on to money, which you like to store in savings accounts for a rainy day.

As a Cancerian you are more likely to have a complex personality and be a master in the art of passive resistance. On the one hand you may appear to be a tower of strength, yet on the other hand you seem to have the vulnerability of a child.

With the Moon coloring your responses, you are naturally intuitive or mediumistic, but you may also need to resist the tendency to be easily hurt. Your powerful imagination and sensitive understanding frequently find an avenue of expression through the creative and artistic worlds. Yet above all, once you trust someone enough to show them your feelings, you can be loyal and devoted.

Although it is generally known that as a water sign you are compatible with Scorpio and Pisces, in this book you will find that Venus, Mars, and the Outer Planets have an important influence on your relationships and powers of attraction.

Cancer attractive qualities: caring, understanding, imaginative, intuitive, good parent, sensitive

Cancer less attractive qualities: moody, insecure, oversensitive, living in the past

---

Leo

5TH SIGN
FIXED/FIRE
RULING PLANET: SUN
BODY PART: HEART
SYMBOL: LION
KEYWORDS: VITALITY, CONFIDENCE, SELF-EXPRESSION

As a Leo you are generous and warm with a loving nature. Like the Sun, your personality shines brightly. Some of your attractive attributes are your kindness and generosity. Your magnanimous gestures usually come from a love of the dramatic. Usually not bashful, you enjoy playing to the crowd and feel happiest with an appreciative audience. Luckily, to compensate for the likelihood of your grabbing center stage, you can also be attentive to others. You may shower them with compliments on their talents or make them feel appreciated. As a Leo you also possess a lovable, childlike playfulness and a strong creative need for self-expression. Since Leo is a sign associated with rulers and kings, you probably seek a leading role rather than one in the chorus.

Some of the less attractive characteristics of your sign are linked to vanity and pride, while flattery can leave you open to manipulation. Belonging to the fixed group of signs, you may find it hard to admit that you are wrong. Nevertheless, you can easily compensate for any failings with your warm personality and sense of fun. With your playful and gre-

garious outlook on life, you can be the ideal partner for social events or the life and soul of the party. Alternatively, you can be keen on the theater, games, and entertainment.

A desire to shine, combined with your ability to take charge, often brings you to positions of authority, where you can show your excellent leadership skills. Although you possess inborn executive abilities, one of your less attractive qualities is that you may become too bossy. Generally, however, you work extremely hard to fulfill your responsibilities. Known for your courage, integrity, and self-respect, you would much rather act assured than appear weak and defenseless. If you are too afraid to fulfill your high calling you may alternate between arrogance and self-doubt. Aware of the effect you have on others, your pride also suggests that it is important for you to make a good impression on people and be popular. As a Leo you love to love and be loved.

Although it is generally known that as a fire sign you are compatible with Sagittarius and Aries, in this book you will find that Venus, Mars, and the Outer Planets have an important influence on your relationships and powers of attraction.

Leo attractive qualities: generous, kind, warmhearted, fun-loving, creative, entertaining, courageous, leadership

Leo less attractive qualities: arrogant, bossy, stubborn, vain, self-centered

---

Virgo

6TH SIGN
MUTABLE/EARTH
RULING PLANET: MERCURY
BODY PART: INTESTINES
SYMBOL: VIRGIN
KEYWORDS: DISCRIMINATING, EFFICIENT, SERVICE

Analytical and efficient, you have a strong work ethic. As a Virgo you need an ordered life and want things done in a methodical way. One of your attractive qualities is your ability to be of service to others. Possessing natural organizational skills, reliability, and accuracy, you are an asset to any establishment. With your penetrating mind you constantly reexamine and refine in order to improve existing systems. Unfortunately, this perfectionism may point to one of your less attractive qualities. You can become your own worst critic, or criticize your environment and the people around you. Nevertheless, your ability to admit to your own failings can make you modest and unassuming.

Being ruled by the planet Mercury suggests that you are intelligent and articulate with a discriminating mind. The added element of Earth in your sign also indicates that you are practical and responsible. Although you are economical and prudent with money, your less attractive attributes manifest

when you worry or keep a tight hold on your purse strings. Nevertheless, you can be more than generous with time and money should anybody need assistance. You will, however, expect the people you help to make an effort to help themselves.

As a rule, you do not respond well to stupidity or vulgarity and your logical mind instinctively wants to bring order to any confusion. Since you are likely to analyze the smallest of details, you must guard against going over and over the same issues and lose sight of the big picture.

With your high standards, you can be extra fastidious in certain areas. Often interested in cleanliness and nutrition, you may advocate regular exercise and a healthy lifestyle. Despite this, you are susceptible to stress and tension, occasionally becoming overanxious. This may frequently be due to the pressures of work and your strong sense of obligation and duty.

Although it is generally known that as an earth sign you are compatible with Capricorn and Taurus, in this book you will find that Venus, Mars, and the Outer Planets have an important influence on your relationships and powers of attraction.

Virgo attractive qualities: precise, efficient, helpful, dutiful, discriminating, practical, dependable

Virgo less attractive qualities: worry, critical, cynical, lost in the detail, anxious

---

Libra

7TH SIGN
CARDINAL/AIR
RULING PLANET: VENUS
BODY PART: KIDNEYS
SYMBOL: SCALES
KEYWORDS: BALANCE, DIPLOMACY, RELATIONSHIP

Your charm, captivating smile, and gracious attitude usually attract people. Affectionate and refined, with a need to be popular, you often present a friendly, warm, and intelligent personality to others. As an air sign, you often utilize your diplomatic and social skills to keep life peaceful and harmonious.

Ruled by Venus and keenly aware of relationships, you are always able to see things from another person's point of view. An expert at being just and fair, you weigh everything carefully before making a decision. You can discuss the pros and cons of any situation or problem with amazing logic and discerning definition. This ability ensures your skill at the art of compromise and negotiation. In excess, however, this constant weighing of opposites may lead to the less attractive qualities of indecisiveness and an inability to arrive at a final conclusion.

Maintaining a balance is essential to keep your positive powers of attraction working for you. To avoid going too far or becoming too reliant on others, you need to work on your self-awareness. By learning to stand up for yourself even when it creates conflict, you become strong and assertive.

Ruled by Venus, you have a natural eye for color and need to be surrounded by tasteful, luxurious, and harmonious surroundings. You are likely to have an attractive home and be naturally good at some form of artistic expression. Your love of beauty can often be seen in your stylish appearance.

Courteous and amiable, you usually enjoy playing host or hostess. With a talent for making people feel special, you can be popular and have many friends. Since you usually prefer to be in a partnership, you need someone who can share your romantic soul.

Although it is generally known that as an air sign you are compatible with Aquarius and Gemini, in this book you will find that Venus, Mars, and the Outer Planets have an important influence on your relationships and powers of attraction.

Libra attractive qualities: diplomatic, charming, social skills, stylish, artistic, fair

Libra less attractive qualities: indecisive, self-indulgent, vain, codependent

---

Scorpio

8TH SIGN
FIXED/WATER
RULING PLANET: PLUTO
BODY PART: THE SEX ORGANS
SYMBOL: SCORPION
KEYWORDS: REGENERATION, SECRECY, POWER

As a magnetic Scorpio you belong to the most passionate sign of the zodiac. People are attracted to your power and intriguing personality. There is nothing half-hearted about you, with your strong will and "all or nothing" attitude.

Belonging to a Water sign, you prefer to investigate life at a deeper emotional level. Just as your ruling planet Pluto governs the underworld and all that is hidden, you unconsciously pick up the feelings of others. Like a detective or psychologist you may ask probing questions without revealing your own thoughts. As you feel deeply and can be painfully hurt, you prefer to be in control.

You have a powerful sex drive and people are often drawn to your seductive appeal. Although others can find you fascinating, one of your less attractive qualities may be that your passionate nature can lead to jealousy or misplaced desires.

Transformation is a powerful force that you are not afraid to experience. Not scared to let go, there will be times when you are willing to walk away from everything and start all over again. Yet once you have decided to start a project you can be determined and uncompromising, persevering with a situation until the bitter end.

You are usually competitive and do not like losing. One of your less attractive qualities is that once defeated you will remember and wait until you can get even at a later date. On the other hand you can be loyal and loving, totally giving of yourself regardless of effort or sacrifice.

Although it is generally known that as a water sign you are compatible with Pisces and Cancer, in this book you will find that Venus, Mars, and the Outer Planets have an important influence on your relationships and powers of attraction.

Scorpio attractive qualities: sensitive, powerful, focused, passionate, loyal, determined

Scorpio less attractive qualities: revengeful, stubborn, too passionate, secretive, intense

---

Sagittarius

9TH SIGN
MUTABLE/FIRE
RULING PLANET: JUPITER
BODY PARTS: HIPS AND THIGHS
SYMBOL: CENTAUR
KEYWORDS: EXPANSION, HONESTY, EXPLORATION, IDEALISM

You are friendly, optimistic, and easygoing and others are attracted by your free spirit. With a love of truth, honesty, and justice you have a philosophical approach to life. Being very independent, you dislike restrictions and usually look to expand your horizons and improve your lot.

People are impressed by your ability to see the larger picture. With your positive outlook you are usually looking at some future scheme or project. This may lead you to expand your mind through study or travel. Placing a high value on knowledge, you usually love to come up with inspired ideas whether for yourself or for others.

Although you genuinely desire to uplift people, sometimes you may upset them instead. Your less attractive qualities are your outspoken opinions or tactless comments. As you possess a sincere attitude, however, your naive quality indicates that your comments were not intended to offend.

Among your many interests you may enjoy exploring subjects such as religion, philosophy, or law. Alternatively, you may be interested in travel and other cultures or be keen on sport rather than intellectual pursuits, getting your excitement from being competitive and playing games. Usually lucky, you also love to take risks in one form or another and may be drawn to gambling or speculations. Whatever you do, you like to do it in style. While you enjoy the good things in life and indulge in the best, resist carrying your extravagant streak too far.

Since you love the freedom to move around, you prefer to leave your options open. Enthusiastic, warm, and generous, people are attracted to your good-humored and direct approach to life.

Although it is generally known that as a fire sign you are compatible with Aries and Leo, in this book you will find that Venus, Mars, and the Outer Planets have an important influence on your relationships and powers of attraction.

Sagittarius attractive qualities: optimistic, frank, enthusiastic, adventurous, open, idealistic

Sagittarius less attractive qualities: tactless, arrogant, fearful of commitment, self-indulgent

---

Capricorn

10TH SIGN
CARDINAL/EARTH
RULING PLANET: SATURN
BODY PARTS: KNEES, SKELETAL BONES
SYMBOL: GOAT
KEYWORDS: AMBITIOUS, CONSCIENTIOUS, DILIGENT

As a realistic Capricorn you know full well there is no gain without hard work. You have a strong sense of duty and are willing to wait patiently in order to accomplish your goals.

People are attracted to the fact that you are diligent and determined. You need to have a sense of purpose or a definite goal. Usually preferring a strategy rather than acting on a whim, you desire order and structure to make yourself feel complete. Security is important to you, and like your ruling planet, Saturn, you take a cautious and conservative approach to life. You show a great respect for authority and admire the wisdom of age and experience. This extends to your work, for when you execute a job you are usually very conscientious. However, the less attractive side of Capricorn can be cold and calculating. It is better to use the toughness of your ruling planet, Saturn, for self-discipline rather than controlling others.

The economical, practical, and thrifty characteristics of your earthly element blend well with your desire for status and prestige. Able to persevere, you can rise to positions of power. Although one of your better qualities is your realistic outlook, there is a danger that this can turn into pessimism. In order to be more attractive to others you may need to develop a more optimistic and positive perspective. When you doubt yourself and your abilities, you can give up without even trying. When given the security of a firm foundation, however, you are relentless in your drive for success.

People are attracted by your willingness to help, your reliability, and your pragmatic approach. Yet beneath your slightly shy and reserved exterior is a wonderful dry sense of humor and a tenacity that comes from inner discipline.

Although it is generally known that as an earth sign you are compatible with Virgo and Taurus, in this book you will find that Venus, Mars, and the Outer Planets have an important influence on your relationships and powers of attraction.

Capricorn attractive qualities: hardworking, responsible, practical, realistic, disciplined, loyal

Capricorn less attractive qualities: pessimistic, selfish, calculating, hard, depressive, controlling

Aquarius

11TH SIGN
FIXED/AIR
RULING PLANET: URANUS
BODY PARTS: ANKLES AND CALVES
SYMBOL: WATER BEARER
KEYWORDS: DETACHMENT, HUMANITARIAN, INDEPENDENT

Original and unconventional, you are a progressive and independent thinker. Usually playing the detached observer, you are able to take an impersonal and unemotional view on life. This detached tendency links you to group awareness, as you realize that separate individuals operate within a larger whole. One of your most attractive qualities is your lack of separatism, making you friendly and liberal. This humanitarian viewpoint may lead you to universal or philanthropic interests or to campaign for just causes.

The Aquarian rebel streak originates with your ruling planet, Uranus. This planet bestows the ability to perceive future trends and indicates a love of freedom. You do not like to take orders, so you need the autonomy to think for yourself and to do things in your own unique style. Too much insistence from others on following a certain way will cause you to do the opposite. The combination of your strong contrary streak with your fixed sign can bring out your less attractive quality of being awkward. Fortunately, you are always willing to listen to an alternative viewpoint as long as it is presented in an objective way.

The futuristic outlook of Aquarius enables you to embrace technology and all new and exciting innovations without being intimidated. Like Uranus, you possess an electrical quality, which can manifest as a form of mental intuition. This can often produce the "eureka" effect when you suddenly know something to be true. Your zany genius can make you volatile or unpredictable but also highly inventive. Even if the rest of the world does not understand you today, anything you are doing now others will be doing tomorrow.

Although it is generally known that as an air sign you are compatible with Libra and Gemini, in this book you will find that Venus, Mars, and the Outer Planets have an important influence on your relationships and powers of attraction.

Aquarius attractive qualities: independent, intelligent, inventive, good psychologist

Aquarius less attractive qualities: stubborn, eccentric, too detached, rebellious, unpredictable

Pisces

12TH SIGN
MUTABLE/WATER
RULING PLANET: NEPTUNE
BODY PART: FEET
SYMBOL: FISH
KEYWORDS: COMPASSIONATE, RECEPTIVE, IMAGINATIVE

As a sensitive Piscean you are constantly receiving impressions from your outer environment, yet you are also acutely aware of your inner feelings. Your powerful private dream world is a place into which you can retreat to enjoy the musings of your wondrous imagination or escape from dealing with the harsher realities of life. The symbol for Pisces is two fish swimming in opposite directions, indicating a dual personality of extremes. At times you can drift through life; at other times you can be efficient, precise, and extremely hardworking.

Psychically open to all the more subtle emotions, you attract people with your generosity and compassion for others. As you sometimes do not have strong boundaries, you can often dissolve yourself in other people's needs. Taken to extremes, this can lead to the less attractive qualities of no self-worth or being a martyr. Generally, you need reassurance to boost your confidence. Yet at other times you can be quite stubborn, not allowing anyone to influence you. The least selfish sign of the zodiac, you can be extremely patient and hold your feelings within; however, if provoked, you can become highly emotional, letting your feelings overflow and appearing surprisingly aggressive.

Being imaginative and sensitive, you may be good at different forms of healing, music, art, drama, photography, and subjects of a spiritual nature. The less attractive quality of your sensitivity is your openness to mood swings. Sometimes you will be extremely optimistic; at other times you can be vague or become an escapist. Being naturally idealistic, it is also especially important for you to avoid projecting your high expectations and dreams onto others.

Fortunately, you can use your natural psychic ability to plug directly into the collective consciousness of all humanity. You are a visionary who cannot help but attract others with your humor, charm, and empathy.

Although it is generally known that as a water sign you are compatible with Cancer and Scorpio, in this book you will find that Venus, Mars, and the Outer Planets have an important influence on your relationships and powers of attraction.

Pisces attractive qualities: imaginative, sensitive, compassionate, subtle, visionary, idealistic, adaptable

Pisces less attractive qualities: vague, weak, escapist, impractical, easily discouraged

The Outer Planets

The Planet Jupiter

♃ Jupiter, the fifth planet from the Sun, is the largest planet in our solar system. Named after the ruler of the Roman pantheon (known as Zeus to the Greeks), Jupiter was mythologically associated with wisdom, victory, and justice. In keeping with its large size, Jupiter expands or exaggerates. It represents the ability to reach beyond our present horizons and look for the "bigger plan" or grander vision, and it carries with it the optimism and confidence to carry this through.

The desire to discover meaning in circumstance and "a greater truth" means that Jupiter approaches life philosophically. This desire for greater knowledge inspires higher learning and is linked to universities or spiritual teachers. In addition, Jupiter as the Lord of Truth is often associated with the judicial system, courts, and law and order.

Analogous with the urge to grow mentally, emotionally, and spiritually, Jupiter is often associated with good fortune and plenty. The best of Jupiter brings the attractive qualities of generosity and good humor. This planet also stimulates a yearning for numerous experiences and travel to distant and exotic places. Excessive expansion, however, can bring the less attractive qualities of greed and an inflated ego. Nevertheless, Jupiter can represent idealists who have the faith and wisdom to make their large schemes a reality. Jupiter rules the sign of Sagittarius.

Attractive qualities: desire for truth, generosity, idealism, optimism, long journeys, higher learning

Less attractive qualities: exaggeration, overexpansion, insincerity, false optimism

The Planet Saturn

♄ In mythology Saturn is Old Father Time, the Reaper. In Greek and Roman times he was the god of social order and was shown as the harvester with a sickle. Symbolic of "that which we sow we shall also reap," Saturn represents perfect justice or the law of cause and effect.

Psychologically, Saturn is the archetype of the wise old teacher. By accepting the responsibility and discipline of self-realization we become older and wiser. The hard work and training suggested by Saturn's restrictive influence is ultimately worthwhile, as it is the only way to learn. To balance the expansiveness of Jupiter we have the curtailing influence of Saturn, which can positively restrain overinflation and maintain order.

The positive qualities of Saturn enable us to create structure or work with space and form. He defines boundaries in order to produce control, regulation, and security. This planet requires us to face up to our responsibilities and duties. Saturn is totally fair and just: whatever work has been put in will be repaid exactly. Nevertheless, his lessons are sometimes uncomfortable. The unattractive qualities of Saturn can cause pessimism, fear or denial, and overseriousness.

With Saturn you cannot expect to get something for nothing. Yet he will reward you if you develop the determination and the perseverance to succeed. Saturn also represents anything "hard," such as bones and teeth or when we need to be "hard" with ourselves. Saturn governs the sign of Capricorn.

The attractive attributes of Saturn are the ability to concentrate and to demonstrate our willpower and self-reliance. With the assistance of Saturn we develop patience and perseverance. Since Saturn represents order and authority, this planet helps us become realistic and efficient.

Attractive qualities: honorable, sense of duty, determination, self-control, patience, dedication, perseverance

Less attractive qualities: difficulties and challenges, melancholy, inhibition, suspicion, cold, unfeeling

The Planet Uranus

♅ The ancient Greek name for Uranus was Heaven or Night Sky, and in mythology Uranus was the father of Saturn. The vastness of the heavens symbolizes our ability to open our minds to the universal. Uranus brings enlightenment and freedom of spirit by breaking away from the restriction and safety of Saturn. This kind of freedom involves leaving a space in our life for the unexpected, or daring to express our own individuality despite the pressures of conformity. If we push this too far, however, we are in danger of becoming rebellious for the sake of it.

Psychologically, through Uranus we can widen our point of view to the universal, and comprehend humankind as a family of brothers and sisters. Uranus is willing to fight for human rights and the freedom to express oneself.

Uranus governs electrical energy of all types: television and radio waves, magnetic fields, lasers, computers, and new technology. Always looking to the future and being able to think in a symbolic and abstract way, Uranus helps to develop intuition and inventive abilities. These qualities make individuals very attractive, since they are able to stand ahead of society and freely express themselves in their own unique style. If there is an excess of Uranian energy, however, the desire to express one's individuality at all costs can lead to the less attractive qualities of stubborn defiance or a wild eccentricity. Uranus governs the sign of Aquarius.

Attractive qualities: freedom, humanitarianism, detachment, objectivity, originality

Less attractive qualities: rebellion, revolutionary tendencies, obstinacy

The Planet Neptune

♆ In mythology Neptune is the god of the sea—deep, unfathomable, and mysterious. Just as the ocean can dissolve rocks into sand, so Neptune can slowly and subtly dissolve the barriers the ego creates and release us into mystical experience. The mist that hangs over the seashore is representative of the mists that surround this planet, where nothing is solid and everything is illusionary and enigmatic.

Psychologically, Neptune's function is to help us transcend our limitations by refining and purifying our emotional nature. Unlike Saturn, it knows of no boundaries and feels a sense of oneness with all things. This ability to blend with everything, however, can also give a sense of vagueness. Neptune's extreme sensitivity to everything can confer great compassion for the suffering of mankind as well as the ability to "lose oneself" in inspired creative endeavors, such as art, music, or drama. It can give an artist the inspiration and imagination for what is possible.

The attractive qualities of Neptune are universal love, compassion, and willingness to sacrifice something of ourselves. Working with Neptune's influence positively means we are able to hold on to the vision of our ideal in order to fulfill our dreams. Neptune also heightens our perception and can help develop mediumistic and psychic abilities. The unattractive qualities of Neptune suggest escapism into a world of fantasy; it can also lead to drug or alcohol abuse or indulgence in self-deception. Neptune governs the sign of Pisces.

Attractive qualities: sensitivity, vision, compassion, inspiration, idealism

Less attractive qualities: illusion, deception, escapism, confusion, vagueness

The Planet Pluto

♇ Mythologically Pluto, the god of the underworld, represents transformation, death, and rebirth. Signifying deep change, Pluto's energy is intense and powerful. With this planet's influence we are able to penetrate or read the subconscious from subliminal signals, particularly through body language. This can be used positively in subjects like depth psychology, but can also be abused to control others.

The discovery of Pluto was simultaneous to the discovery of the nuclear subatomic level and Jung's theory of the unconscious. Whether governing shady underworld characters, fanatics, and terrorists or major transformers of society for good, Pluto's energy is extreme in its nature.

It can also provoke the same level of intensity within us. Pluto often symbolizes the "all or nothing" response. As part of our continuing self-improvement program there will be times when we must leave the old behind with no guarantees for the future. It is this death and rebirth energy that is powerfully symbolized by Pluto. With Pluto's help we accept the forthcoming changes in our life. When the time is right we learn to let go of the past or anything we have outgrown. Pluto teaches us that every ending has a new beginning and life goes on.

If you connect strongly with Pluto (for example, if you are a Scorpio or have Pluto beneficial, special, or challenging links in your personalized timetable), you possess the attractive qualities of being a strong person who is willing to put yourself through powerful changes in your desire for personal transformation. You would know it was essential to leave situations where you no longer grow as a person even though it is a challenge to make changes. If Pluto is working negatively in your life, you may project the less attractive qualities of being overly intense or be unable to let go of people or situations. Pluto governs the sign of Scorpio.

Attractive qualities: powerful, good psychologist, desire for transformation, determined

Less attractive qualities: abuse of power, obsessive, compulsive, vengeful

A Brief Overview of How to Use This Book

Let's use Judy, who was born on May 28, 1979, as our example. First, Judy turns to the page marked May 28, where she reads about her day, learns some of her attractive qualities, and discovers what she finds attractive in others. On that page she also finds four different Venus interpretations, one of which is her personal Venus according to her year of birth. To find out which of the four interpretations is hers, Judy turns to Section Two, where she finds the Venus table from 1938 to 2012.

In this section of the book, Judy can also find her personal Mars sign according to her year of birth and twelve interpretations both for men and women.

Next, Judy returns to her personal birthday profile page to look at her personalized timetable. Judy's unique timetable is the key to unlocking all the information in Section Three. With this information she can discover a great deal about three major categories in her life.

- In the first category, Judy discovers more about herself. She can find out whether she has beneficial qualities or challenging or special aspects in relation to her own Gemini Sun degree.
- In the second category, Judy finds what type of relationships she is attracting into her life. She learns what influences are affecting those relationships. Are they beneficial, challenging, or special?
- In the third category, Judy can learn about the time periods in her life. In beneficial periods she can expect good opportunities to come her way. In challenging times she has the opportunity to overcome certain tests that will benefit her at a later date. Alternatively, Judy can find out about special times in her life that may come only once or twice.

A full step-by-step guide to how Judy uses this book appears in Section Three: Empowerment and the Outer Planets.

The 366 Birthdays of the Year

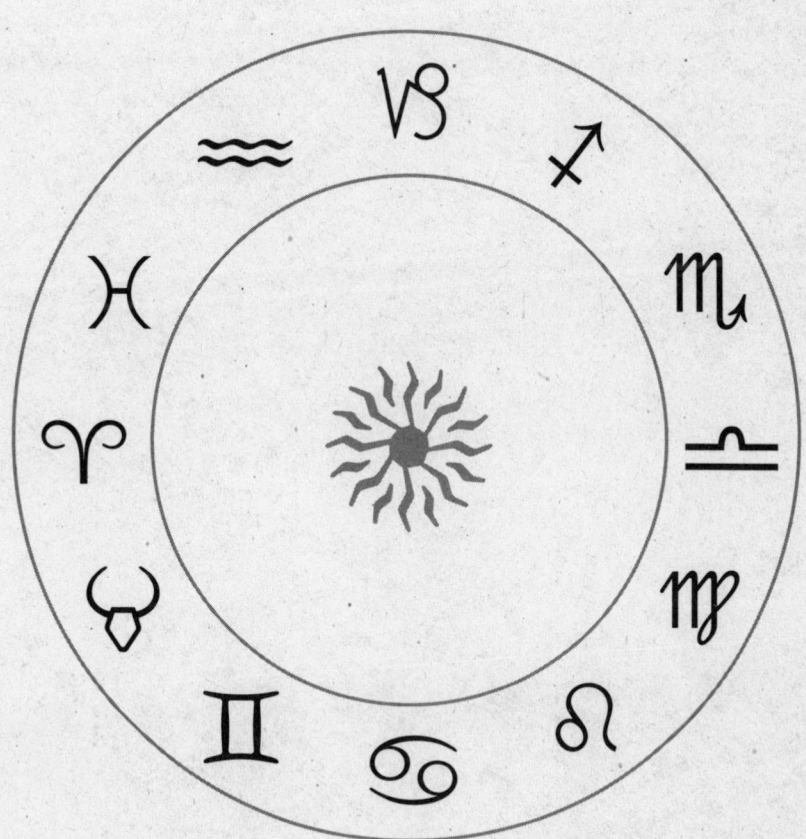

Aries

March 21 – April 20

March 21

Your Personal Powers

Your personal powers include both the sensitivity and imagination of Pisces and the dynamic drive and enthusiasm of Aries. Others are attracted by your ability to combine socializing with hard work and your flair for dealing with people. Assertive yet friendly, your quick instincts can always recognize a good business idea and your talent for making contacts always stands you in good stead. If you become too fearful, however, this can cause you to lose power by overcompensating and becoming too tough or selfish. Even though you are often driven by ambition and a need for personal recognition, you have a very caring and generous nature. It is particularly through your relationships with others that you learn to balance your practical skills with your idealism. Your fast responses and creative ideas also blend well with your innate sixth sense. Being a visionary with determination and dynamic drive, you usually succeed most when you see a clear picture of what you want to achieve before you move into action.

Your Powers of Attraction in Relationships

Magnetic and sociable with strong convictions, you know how to impress others with your enthusiasm and creative ideas. Being determined, you often get what you want. Yet behind your powerful desires and independent manner there is a strong need for the harmony of a loving home and a good relationship. Although you are often attracted to partners with strong individuality who can inspire you, avoid clashing wills or power struggles. You may encounter a pull between your desire for freedom and your need for a relationship. It is important not to waste your generosity on those who do not deserve it. In order to avoid self-delusion you need to clearly see when others are being honest with you. With your ability to turn on the charm, however, you have no trouble attracting others.

Your attractive qualities: enthusiastic, hardworking, people skills, friendly, determined, dynamic, inspired, fun-loving, original, charming, intuitive, creative, independent spirit, idealistic, gregarious, imaginative, strong, cooperative, courageous

Your less attractive qualities: selfish, dependent, too reserved, bossy, stubborn, harsh, fearful about money or change, argumentative, materialistic, envious, inactive, anxious, critical, impatient

Your Venus Power

The planet Venus has a great deal of influence on your powers of attraction. Below are four possible Venus types for women and men. To find your Venus you need to go to page 771, where you will find the Venus table and extra information. The planet Mars also affects your powers of attraction. To find your Mars table and interpretation go to page 761.

WOMEN WITH VENUS IN AQUARIUS: You attract and impress others with your friendly approach and progressive ideas. As you are usually independent and easygoing, you value freedom within a relationship. A good companion with a sense of your own person, you enjoy socializing, especially with people who are original, cosmopolitan, and have a strong sense of individuality. Although being friendly and detached usually serves you well, avoid losing touch with your emotions. You usually prefer the company of those who have innovative or progressive views.

MEN WITH VENUS IN AQUARIUS: Friendly and honest, you attract people with your broad-minded approach to life. You usually possess an objective and slightly detached attitude to affairs of the heart. If you are too removed, however, others can misinterpret your behavior as uncaring. It is often more important to you that your love relationships are based on friendship and honesty than intense passion. As you are generally tolerant and liberal you may be drawn to less conventional relationships.

WOMEN WITH VENUS IN PISCES: In love, you are sensitive, tender, and affectionate, experiencing your partner's feelings almost as strongly as your own. Being imaginative and visionary, you also possess the capabilities to develop creative gifts as well as deep compassion for others. Idealistic when in love, you usually prefer to see only your partner's good points, but be careful that your high expectations do not bring disappointment if you avoid being realistic. Nevertheless, in your relationships with others, you can be devoted, loving, and positively enchanting.

MEN WITH VENUS IN PISCES: The combination of your emotional subtlety and charm can make you very alluring when dealing with affairs of the heart. Perceptive and impressionable, you have an easygoing style in your relationships, usually preferring to avoid ugly confrontation. You are drawn to a woman who has a touch of glamour and is sensitive to the needs of others. Alternatively, she can be a visionary with a rich imagination, like your own, and can keep you enchanted.

WOMEN WITH VENUS IN ARIES: Idealistic, passionate, and adventurous, you are direct in your dealings with others. When you are attracted to a person, you usually take the initiative and use your people skills to make things happen. In close relationships you are not afraid to confront your other half. This self-assertiveness is positive if differences can be brought into the open through diplomacy and compromise. Independent and spirited, you enjoy your freedom.

MEN WITH VENUS IN ARIES: You are usually drawn to courageous or assertive women who possess strong personal magnetism. Therefore, you find those who seem to be independent or action-oriented very attractive. Your own eagerness and need for activity suggest that you start relationships with great enthusiasm, especially if they offer you excitement or adventures. The challenge is often to maintain relationships and not get bored too easily.

WOMEN WITH VENUS IN TAURUS: Being physically attractive you can make a good impression on the opposite sex. As security and stability in relationships are very important to you, you usually want a partner who is not only attractive but also reliable and a good provider. Being sensual or tactile you need a lover who is affectionate, but beware that your lover does not show signs of possessiveness or jealousy. Your own sense of style and love of beauty imply that you can be attracted to creative people, especially those in art and music.

MEN WITH VENUS IN TAURUS: As well as attracting people with your warm personality, you also possess an innate sense of the value of material possessions. Keeping yourself stylish and having an attractive appearance can also be important to you. You are naturally attracted to practical yet sensual women who understand your need for comfort, security, and the pleasures and luxuries of life. Naturally affectionate, you enjoy socializing but can make a loyal and loving partner.

To read all about your Outer Planets and work out how to use your personalized timetable, go to Section Three, page 789.

To read all about your Outer Planets and work out how to use your personalized timetable, go to Section Three, page 789.

Your Personalized Timetable

JUPITER BENEFICIAL
1941 5/5 – 6/17
1942 9/28 – 12/27
1943 5/21 – 8/7
1947 1/11 – 11/30
1949 3/10 – 8/6
1949 10/31 – 12/25
1953 4/18 – 5/31
1954 9/3 – until 1955 2/6
1955 4/24 – 7/21
1958 12/22 – until 1959 7/19
1959 7/22 – 11/14
1961 2/18 – 4/19
1961 7/1 – 12/6
1964 8/21 – 10/9
1965 3/30 – 5/15
1966 8/15 – until 1967 7/5
1970 12/5 – until 1971 10/28
1973 2/1 – 3/21
1973 8/16 – 11/10
1976 7/17 – 11/25
1977 3/6 – 4/28
1978 7/29 – 11/2
1978 12/19 – until 1979 6/17
1982 11/19 – until 1983 2/12
1983 5/11 – 10/9
1985 1/16 – 3/1
1988 6/26 – 8/31
1988 10/19 – until 1989 4/9
1990 7/13 – 9/30
1991 2/1 – 5/26
1994 11/3 – until 1995 1/19
1995 6/20 – 9/13
1996 12/31 – until 1997 2/12
2000 6/8 – 7/27
2000 12/5 – until 2001 3/16
2002 6/27 – 9/9
2003 3/29 – 4/10
2006 10/19 – 12/31
2008 12/15 – until 2009 1/27
2012 5/21 – 7/5

SATURN BENEFICIAL
1941 7/8 – 11/16
1942 3/28 – 6/18
1945 9/11 – until 1946 1/3
1946 5/30 – 10/23
1946 12/19 – until 1947 7/2
1955 11/2 – until 1956 12/21
1957 7/19 – 9/4
1961 2/18 – 8/8
1961 11/15 – until 1962 2/16
1962 9/18 – 10/30
1971 5/11 – 8/10
1971 10/29 – until 1972 4/23
1975 7/12 – until 1976 8/10
1984 12/7 – until 1985 6/26
1985 8/23 – until 1986 2/3
1986 5/3 – 10/30
1990 4/19 – 5/20
1990 12/27 – until 1991 3/31
1991 7/4 – 12/25
2000 6/17 – 12/21
2001 2/28 – 5/31
2004 8/20 – until 2005 2/5
2005 5/5 – 9/22
2006 1/24 – 6/12

URANUS BENEFICIAL
1940 7/13 – until 1944 3/10
1953 9/12 – until 1958 5/22
1979 11/27 – until 1983 11/12
1994 3/7 – until 1997 11/14

NEPTUNE BENEFICIAL
1966 2/11 – until 1974 10/29
1995 3/20 – until 2000 12/26

PLUTO BENEFICIAL
1938 1/1 – until 1945 5/23
1992 1/2 – until 1999 9/26

JUPITER CHALLENGING
1942 5/5 – 7/16

1944 11/12 – until 1945 3/16
1945 7/11 – 10/2
1948 2/5 – 6/30
1948 9/30 – 12/22
1953 8/22 – 12/8
1954 4/13 – 6/29
1956 10/22 – until 1957 5/5
1957 6/1 – 9/17
1960 1/17 – 12/5
1965 7/30 – until 1966 1/23
1966 3/10 – 6/13
1968 10/5 – until 1969 8/31
1971 12/31 – until 1972 4/14
1972 5/5 – 11/17
1977 7/11 – until 1978 5/27
1980 9/19 – 12/17
1981 3/4 – 8/13
1983 12/15 – until 1984 3/3
1984 6/29 – 10/27
1989 6/25 – 9/17
1989 12/9 – until 1990 5/7
1992 9/4 – 11/21
1993 4/12 – 7/20
1995 11/29 – until 1996 2/10
1996 8/20 – 9/17
2001 6/8 – 8/21
2002 1/20 – 4/10
2004 8/19 – 11/2
2007 11/13 – until 2008 1/23

SATURN CHALLENGING
1943 7/27 – 12/28
1944 4/13 – 8/29
1944 12/19 – until 1945 5/16
1950 9/11 – until 1951 10/21
1958 1/26 – 6/17
1958 10/26 – until 1959 12/20
1973 5/31 – until 1974 6/29
1979 10/21 – until 1980 4/2
1980 7/10 – 12/6
1981 3/4 – 8/27
1987 12/3 – until 1989 1/23
1989 8/9 – 10/13
2002 7/8 – until 2003 8/7
2004 1/21 – 4/22
2009 8/25 – until 2010 10/4

URANUS CHALLENGING
1947 6/17 – until 1951 6/6
1966 10/18 – until 1970 9/16
1986 3/4 – until 1990 12/4

NEPTUNE CHALLENGING
1938 10/19 – until 1947 7/10
1980 2/9 – until 1988 11/9

PLUTO CHALLENGING
1967 11/4 – until 1975 9/6
2004 3/5 – until 2012 11/27

JUPITER SPECIAL
1939 4/5 – 7/10
1939 8/18 – until 1940 2/12
1951 3/19 – 6/1
1951 10/10 – until 1952 1/18
1963 3/2 – 5/10
1975 2/13 – 4/21
1986 6/21 – 8/2
1987 1/26 – 4/5
1998 5/15 – 9/23
1999 1/2 – 3/20
2010 4/23 – until 2011 3/2

SATURN SPECIAL
1938 1/1 – 3/30
1966 3/29 – until 1967 5/11
1967 10/14 – until 1968 2/1
1995 5/9 – 9/4
1996 2/1 – until 1997 3/14

URANUS SPECIAL
2008 5/22 – Continues

March 22

Your Personal Powers

Strong-willed, independent, and hardworking, you are usually purposeful and imaginative. You gain power from your natural foresight, leadership skills, and ability to overcome challenges. Often able you to sense success, you can accomplish much by paying attention to your inner voice when spotting opportunities or initiating new projects. Once committed, you pursue your goals with drive and courage. As determined as you are, it is in your own best interest to utilize your innate diplomatic skills. Although you are resolute and determined you may lose some of your power if you force your will onto others, causing resentment or arguments. Nevertheless, charismatic and adventurous, you usually impress people with your honest and forthright approach. An idealistic side to your personality and genuine interest in others usually urges you to accomplish for the benefit of all. You gain power from being flexible and cooperative rather than selfish or stubborn. You possess outstanding potential for success if you stay focused, innovative, and think big.

Your Powers of Attraction in Relationships

Your friendly manner and natural people skills usually attract friends and admirers. Although you are direct and feel strongly about those you love, you sometimes appear impatient or impulsive. Nevertheless, being pragmatic, you are usually well aware of the practical advantages to be gained from a successful relationship and can give generously of your time and love. You particularly seek partners who can deal with your changing emotions and prefer those who can inspire you to explore new and stimulating experiences. If your partner is not exciting enough for you or leaves you doubting, you need to creatively challenge yourself to avoid boredom or restlessness. Your desire to constantly better your life implies that you frequently analyze yourself and your partner in the hope of improving personal relationships.

Your attractive qualities: strong-willed, intelligent, good leader, highly intuitive, practical, dynamic, sociable, enthusiastic, daring, hardworking, builder, universal realist, problem solver, achiever, innovative, original, creative, adventurous

Your less attractive qualities: impulsive, nervous, inferiority complex, bossy, lack of vision, lazy, get-rich-quick schemes, impatient, restless, greedy, egotistical, selfish

Your Venus Power

The planet Venus has a great deal of influence on your powers of attraction. Below are four possible Venus types for women and men. To find your Venus you need to go to page 771, where you will find the Venus table and extra information. The planet Mars also affects your powers of attraction. To find your Mars table and interpretation go to page 761.

WOMEN WITH VENUS IN AQUARIUS: When it comes to relationships, others are attracted to your honest and friendly approach. You enjoy social interaction and have a genuine concern for others. In fact, at times, your friends may be just as important as your partner. You usually present a tolerant and reasonable front in love situations and attempt to view your relationships objectively. If partners become too demanding, however, you can become stubborn or awkward. Nevertheless, inventive and progressive, you enjoy the company of like-minded people who can share your original ideas.

MEN WITH VENUS IN AQUARIUS: You are sociable and open-minded, and people are attracted by your friendly and easygoing style. Being independent, you value freedom-loving partners who give you the space to be yourself. Other people can sometimes interpret your detachment as being emotionally cool, but they admire your objectivity and humanitarian inclinations. You are attracted to intelligent individuals who are as truthful and as direct as you, but above all they must be true friends. Ideally your partner shares your liberal views on life and possesses a strong sense of individuality.

WOMEN WITH VENUS IN PISCES: Being sensitive to affairs of the heart, when you care for someone you can feel their emotions and sense their every mood. Their goals can even become as important to you as your own. This empathy indicates that you can love on an unselfish level, but you may have to guard against giving too much, especially to those who do not reciprocate. As you are seductive and captivating, partners can be fascinated by your subtle charms and attracted by your caring and affectionate nature.

MEN WITH VENUS IN PISCES: Romantic and idealistic when in love, you can be a sensitive and responsive lover. Being pliant and flexible with an impressionable nature helps you to adapt to the needs of others. In your desire to blend with those you love, however, you need to guard against not clearly defining your own boundaries. With your affectionate and sentimental nature, you are often attracted to those who understand your sensitivity and share your vision.

Women with Venus in Aries: With your strong desires and enthusiastic nature you can be a passionate lover. Although idealistic and single-minded, you need to avoid unnecessary conflicts in your relationships by being more patient and less headstrong. Although at times others can accuse you of being bossy or impulsive, you possess a great deal of warmth and charm. When necessary, you can disarm others by making them feel important.

Men with Venus in Aries: You are usually inclined to seek a partner who is active, goal-oriented, or decisive. Not known for your patience, you probably seek relationships early in life. You may find that you are attracted more to women who have a daring or adventurous spirit, but in your close relationships you may encounter rivalry or find that both you and your partner want to lead or be the boss. Although you may act rashly, you possess a great deal of magnetism and are capable of demonstrating your love and affection.

Women with Venus in Taurus: For your ideal relationship, you seek partners who are both financially secure and demonstrative with their affections. With these thoughts in mind, you are likely to also want a partner who is refined yet pragmatic or someone concerned with safeguarding your future. Although you have a stubborn streak you can be loving and affectionate in your relationships. With your good sense of style you may have an attraction for the arts, music, or luxury items.

Men with Venus in Taurus: Although you are usually drawn to sensual and physically beautiful individuals, you want a partner who is also reliable and loyal. When in love you enjoy buying your partner things of quality that will grow in value or useful things of a practical nature. You also love to socialize and entertain, particularly in luxurious surroundings. Affectionate and caring, you are often attracted to creative people or those with artistic talents.

To read all about your Outer Planets and work out how to use your personalized timetable, go to Section Three, page 789.

♈

Your Personalized Timetable

Jupiter Beneficial
1941 5/10 – 6/22
1942 10/7 – 12/18
1943 5/27 – 8/11
1947 1/18 – 5/10
1947 9/17 – 12/4
1949 3/16 – 7/29
1949 11/7 – 12/30
1953 4/22 – 6/4
1954 9/9 – until **1955** 1/29
1955 5/2 – 7/26
1958 12/27 – until **1959** 6/24
1959 8/15 – 11/19
1961 2/23 – 4/30
1961 6/20 – 12/11
1965 4/4 – 5/19
1966 8/20 – until **1967** 7/10
1970 12/9 – until **1971** 11/2
1973 2/5 – 3/27
1973 8/7 – 11/17
1976 7/23 – 11/18
1977 3/13 – 5/2
1978 8/3 – until **1979** 6/22
1982 11/23 – until **1983** 2/21
1983 5/1 – 10/15
1985 1/21 – 3/6
1988 7/1 – until **1989** 1/16
1989 1/24 – 4/14
1990 7/18 – 10/6
1991 1/24 – 6/1
1994 11/8 – until **1995** 1/24
1995 6/12 – 9/21
1997 1/5 – 2/17
2000 6/12 – 8/2
2000 11/28 – until **2001** 3/23
2002 7/1 – 9/14
2003 3/9 – 4/30
2006 10/23 – until **2007** 1/5
2008 12/19 – until **2009** 1/31
2012 5/26 – 7/10

Saturn Beneficial
1941 7/19 – 11/4
1942 4/6 – 6/26
1943 1/13 – 3/2
1945 9/23 – 12/21
1946 6/8 – until **1947** 7/10
1955 11/11 – until **1956** 12/30
1957 6/29 – 9/23
1961 2/28 – 7/25
1961 11/27 – until **1962** 2/25
1962 8/28 – 11/19
1971 5/19 – 8/29
1971 10/9 – until **1972** 5/1
1975 7/20 – until **1976** 8/18
1984 12/16 – until **1985** 6/8
1985 9/9 – until **1986** 2/21
1986 4/14 – 11/8
1991 1/5 – 4/17
1991 6/16 – until **1992** 1/3
2000 6/26 – 12/6
2001 3/14 – 6/8
2004 8/29 – until **2005** 1/23
2005 5/17 – 10/3
2006 1/12 – 6/21

Uranus Beneficial
1940 8/26 – until **1944** 4/8
1954 7/12 – until **1958** 6/16
1979 12/14 – until **1983** 11/28
1994 4/8 – until **1997** 12/12

Neptune Beneficial
1966 12/18 – until **1975** 9/10
1996 2/9 – until **2001** 11/9

Pluto Beneficial
1938 1/1 – until **1945** 7/8
1992 11/21 – until **1999** 10/31

Jupiter Challenging
1942 5/10 – 7/20
1944 11/18 – until **1945** 3/9
1945 7/18 – 10/7
1948 2/11 – 6/22
1948 10/7 – 12/26
1953 8/29 – 11/30
1954 4/19 – 7/4
1956 10/28 – until **1957** 4/19
1957 6/17 – 9/21
1960 1/21 – 12/10
1965 8/4 – until **1966** 1/12
1966 3/21 – 6/18
1968 10/10 – until **1969** 9/5
1972 1/4 – 11/22
1977 7/16 – until **1978** 6/1
1980 9/24 – 12/27
1981 2/22 – 8/18
1983 12/19 – until **1984** 3/9
1984 6/21 – 11/2
1989 6/29 – 9/25
1989 11/30 – until **1990** 5/13
1992 9/8 – 11/27
1993 4/4 – 7/27
1995 12/4 – until **1996** 2/15
1996 8/5 – 10/2
2001 6/12 – 8/27
2002 1/12 – 4/18
2004 8/24 – 11/8
2005 5/24 – 6/16
2007 11/18 – until **2008** 1/28

Saturn Challenging
1943 8/6 – 12/16
1944 4/23 – 9/10
1944 12/5 – until **1945** 5/25
1950 9/19 – until **1951** 10/29
1952 5/7 – 7/14
1958 2/6 – 6/4
1958 11/5 – until **1959** 12/29
1973 6/7 – until **1974** 7/6
1979 10/30 – until **1980** 3/20
1980 7/22 – 12/22
1981 2/14 – 9/5
1987 12/12 – until **1989** 2/1
1989 7/23 – 10/29
2002 7/16 – until **2003** 1/20
2003 3/27 – 8/16
2004 1/8 – 5/4
2009 9/2 – until **2010** 10/12

Uranus Challenging
1947 7/4 – until **1951** 6/23
1966 11/6 – until **1970** 10/1
1986 12/24 – until **1990** 12/22

Neptune Challenging
1938 11/29 – until **1947** 8/25
1981 1/3 – until **1988** 12/10

Pluto Challenging
1968 9/28 – until **1976** 7/16
2005 1/12 – until **2012** 12/26

Jupiter Special
1939 4/9 – until **1940** 2/17
1951 3/23 – 6/7
1951 10/3 – until **1952** 1/24
1963 3/6 – 5/14
1975 2/17 – 4/26
1987 1/31 – 4/9
1998 5/21 – 9/15
1999 1/8 – 3/24
2010 4/27 – until **2011** 3/7

Saturn Special
1938 1/1 – 4/7
1966 4/6 – 11/11
1966 12/12 – until **1967** 5/21
1967 10/1 – until **1968** 2/11
1995 5/22 – 8/21
1996 2/10 – until **1997** 3/22

Uranus Special
2009 3/22 – Continues

March 23

Your Personal Powers

Intelligent and independent, with courage and drive, you possess great potential for success. Usually conscientious and responsible, you are a natural leader who can rise to positions of authority. Astute, with quick responses, you gain power from your perseverance, determination, and ability to work hard. You can lose power, however, if you become too bossy or impatient. Friendly yet competitive, you think independently and are especially enthusiastic when initiating new ideas. Usually hardworking and productive, you can be both a traditionalist and a nonconformist. Even if you are a woman, you have a forceful approach, preferring to take the initiative rather than be passive. Education, or keeping yourself up to date, can help you make the most of your innate talents. With your inventive or unusual approach and a need to keep mentally stimulated, you particularly enjoy debates or testing your wits with a little friendly banter. Adventurous and spirited when inspired, you empower yourself by leading an active life and being versatile.

Your Powers of Attraction in Relationships

Other people admire your quick intelligence, communication skills, and ability to lead. Although in relationships you like to be in control, you gain from honestly expressing your feelings, especially your fears, rather than resorting to manipulative measures. You are nevertheless well aware of the advantages of working cooperatively with others, either in partnerships or team efforts, and can be diplomatic when necessary. Although you can be fortunate in marriage or lasting relationships, freedom is important to you, and usually you want a certain amount of autonomy within a partnership. You are attracted to partners who do not become insecure or intimidated by your powerful mind and strong will. By learning to be more compassionate and tolerant you increase your chances for success in your dealings with partners.

Your attractive qualities: intelligent, responsible, friendly, creative, pioneering, quick thinker, natural authority, loyal, intuitive, hardworking, conscientious, enthusiastic, diplomatic, good judgment, original, versatile, idealist, leader, practical, strong-willed, adaptable

Your less attractive qualities: domineering, intolerant, argumentative, arrogant, tactless, uncompromising, manipulative, autocratic, selfish, impulsive, restless, emotionally insecure

Your Venus Power

The planet Venus has a great deal of influence on your powers of attraction. Below are four possible Venus types for women and men. To find your Venus you need to go to page 771, where you will find the Venus table and extra information. The planet Mars also affects your powers of attraction. To find your Mars table and interpretation go to page 761.

WOMEN WITH VENUS IN AQUARIUS: When it comes to relationships, others are attracted to your honest, friendly, and easygoing approach. You enjoy social interaction and have a genuine concern for others. In fact, at times, your friends may be just as important as your partner. You usually present a tolerant and reasonable front in love situations and attempt to view your relationships objectively. If partners become too demanding, however, you can become stubborn or awkward. Nevertheless, inventive and progressive, you enjoy the company of like-minded people who can share your original ideas.

MEN WITH VENUS IN AQUARIUS: Friendly and honest, you attract people with your broad-minded approach to life. You usually possess an objective and slightly detached attitude to affairs of the heart. If you are too removed, however, others can misinterpret your behavior as uncaring. It is often more important to you that your love relationships are based on friendship and honesty than on intense passion. As you are generally tolerant and liberal, you may be drawn to less conventional relationships.

WOMEN WITH VENUS IN PISCES: Being sensitive to affairs of the heart, when you care for someone you can feel their emotions and sense their every mood. Their goals can even become as important as your own. This empathy indicates that you can love on an unselfish level, but you may have to guard against giving too much, especially to those who do not reciprocate. As you are seductive and captivating, partners can be fascinated by your subtle charms and attracted by your caring and affectionate nature.

MEN WITH VENUS IN PISCES: Romantic and idealistic when in love, you can be a sensitive and responsive lover. Being pliant and flexible with an impressionable nature helps you to adapt to the needs of others. In your desire to blend with

those you love, however, you need to guard against not clearly defining your own boundaries. With your affectionate and sentimental nature, you are often attracted to those who understand your sensitivity and share your vision.

WOMEN WITH VENUS IN ARIES: Self-reliant and strong, you usually want things your way. This can present problems if you refuse to compromise with your partners. Your life lessons in the area of love and relationships often involve patience and learning to trust. When you project the full power of your Venus, however, you can radiate a charismatic and captivating energy and make a strong impression on others. Independence is often high on your relationship agenda.

MEN WITH VENUS IN ARIES: You are drawn to strong, independent women who can stand up to you. Although you can enthusiastically follow the object of your desire, you may lose power if you allow your forceful emotions to become too dominant. Warm and passionate, you have a side to your nature that longs for new adventures. Romantic and chivalrous, you really enjoy the excitement of the initial chase, but unless you keep the enthusiasm alive and avoid falling into a rut you may become easily bored.

WOMEN WITH VENUS IN TAURUS: Warm and affectionate, you are naturally tactile with a love of sensual pleasures. With a streak of the conventional you love the simple pleasures of life: good food, close friends, and happy relationships. Having an inner strength, you can express genuine patience and are often a pillar of support for loved ones and friends. Although you possess endurance, be careful not to let this turn to plain stubbornness.

MEN WITH VENUS IN TAURUS: As you yourself may be attractive to the opposite sex, you desire a partner who is sensual and loving or has physical beauty. Needing stability, when faced with changes that are out of your control you may become insecure or possessive. Reassuring and loyal, you can be affectionate, tactile, and constant in your love. Your own sense of style and your love of beauty imply that you can be attracted to creative people, especially those in art and music.

To read all about your Outer Planets and work out how to use your personalized timetable, go to Section Three, page 789.

go to Section Three, page 789.

Your Personalized Timetable

JUPITER BENEFICIAL
1941 5/14 – 6/26
1942 10/17 – 12/8
1943 6/1 – 8/16
1947 1/25 – 5/2
1947 9/23 – 12/9
1949 3/22 – 7/21
1949 11/14 – until **1950** 1/3
1953 4/27 – 6/9
1954 9/14 – until **1955** 1/21
1955 5/9 – 7/30
1959 1/1 – 6/13
1959 8/26 – 11/23
1961 2/28 – 5/22
1961 5/29 – 12/16
1965 4/9 – 5/23
1966 8/25 – until **1967** 7/15
1970 12/14 – until **1971** 11/7
1973 2/10 – 4/2
1973 7/31 – 11/23
1976 7/30 – 11/10
1977 3/19 – 5/7
1978 8/7 – until **1979** 6/27
1982 11/28 – until **1983** 3/5
1983 4/19 – 10/20
1985 1/25 – 3/11
1988 7/6 – 12/26
1989 2/14 – 4/19
1990 7/22 – 10/13
1991 1/17 – 6/7
1994 11/12 – until **1995** 1/30
1995 6/4 – 9/28
1997 1/9 – 2/21
2000 6/17 – 8/8
2000 11/20 – until **2001** 3/29
2002 7/6 – 9/19
2003 2/26 – 5/11
2006 10/28 – until **2007** 1/10
2007 7/27 – 8/17
2008 12/24 – until **2009** 2/4
2012 5/30 – 7/15

SATURN BENEFICIAL
1941 8/1 – 10/21
1942 4/15 – 7/4
1942 12/26 – until **1943** 3/19
1945 10/8 – 12/5
1946 6/17 – until **1947** 7/18
1955 11/19 – until **1957** 1/8
1957 6/14 – 10/7
1961 3/11 – 7/11
1961 12/8 – until **1962** 3/7
1962 8/13 – 12/2
1971 5/26 – until **1972** 5/9
1975 7/28 – until **1976** 8/26
1977 3/28 – 4/24
1984 12/25 – until **1985** 5/25
1985 9/22 – until **1986** 11/17
1991 1/13 – until **1992** 1/12
2000 7/5 – 11/24
2001 3/25 – 6/16
2004 9/8 – until **2005** 1/11
2005 5/27 – 10/17
2005 12/28 – until **2006** 6/30

URANUS BENEFICIAL
1941 6/2 – until **1944** 4/28
1954 7/29 – until **1958** 7/5
1980 1/2 – until **1984** 9/24
1995 1/29 – until **1998** 1/1

NEPTUNE BENEFICIAL
1967 1/27 – until **1975** 10/26
1996 3/12 – until **2001** 12/22

PLUTO BENEFICIAL
1938 1/1 – until **1946** 6/18
1992 12/17 – until **1999** 11/27

JUPITER CHALLENGING
1942 5/14 – 7/25
1944 11/25 – until **1945** 3/1
1945 7/24 – 10/11

1948 2/17 – 6/14
1948 10/14 – 12/30
1953 9/6 – 11/22
1954 4/24 – 7/8
1956 11/2 – until **1957** 4/9
1957 6/28 – 9/26
1960 1/26 – 8/6
1960 9/4 – 12/14
1965 8/10 – until **1966** 1/3
1966 3/30 – 6/22
1968 10/15 – until **1969** 9/10
1972 1/9 – 11/27
1977 7/21 – until **1978** 6/5
1980 9/29 – until **1981** 1/12
1981 2/6 – 8/24
1983 12/24 – until **1984** 3/17
1984 6/13 – 11/8
1989 7/3 – 10/7
1989 11/19 – until **1990** 5/18
1992 9/13 – 12/3
1993 3/27 – 8/3
1995 12/8 – until **1996** 2/20
1996 7/26 – 10/12
2001 6/17 – 9/2
2002 1/5 – 4/25
2004 8/28 – 11/13
2005 5/8 – 7/3
2007 11/22 – until **2008** 2/2

SATURN CHALLENGING
1943 8/16 – 12/3
1944 5/3 – 9/26
1944 11/19 – until **1945** 6/3
1950 9/27 – until **1951** 11/7
1952 4/21 – 7/29
1958 2/19 – 5/20
1958 11/15 – until **1960** 1/6
1973 6/15 – until **1974** 7/14
1979 11/9 – until **1980** 3/8
1980 8/1 – until **1981** 9/13
1987 12/20 – until **1989** 2/11
1989 7/9 – 11/10
2002 7/25 – until **2003** 1/5
2003 4/10 – 8/26
2003 12/27 – until **2004** 5/14
2009 9/10 – until **2010** 10/20

URANUS CHALLENGING
1947 7/22 – until **1952** 4/9
1966 12/5 – until **1971** 7/27
1987 1/10 – until **1991** 10/15

NEPTUNE CHALLENGING
1939 10/16 – until **1947** 9/23
1981 2/3 – until **1989** 11/3

PLUTO CHALLENGING
1968 10/27 – until **1976** 8/25
2005 2/17 – Continues

JUPITER SPECIAL
1939 4/13 – until **1940** 2/21
1951 3/27 – 6/13
1951 9/25 – until **1952** 1/30
1963 3/10 – 5/19
1963 11/17 – 12/23
1975 2/22 – 4/30
1987 2/4 – 4/13
1998 5/28 – 9/8
1999 1/14 – 3/28
2010 5/2 – 10/30
2010 12/7 – until **2011** 3/11

SATURN SPECIAL
1938 1/1 – 4/15
1966 4/15 – 10/19
1967 1/2 – 6/1
1967 9/18 – until **1968** 2/21
1995 6/9 – 8/3
1996 2/19 – until **1997** 3/29

URANUS SPECIAL
2009 4/9 – Continues

March 24

SUN: ARIES • DECANATE: ARIES/MARS • DEGREE: 2°5–3°5 ARIES • MODE: CARDINAL • ELEMENT: FIRE

Your Personal Powers

Confident and intelligent, your fast mental responses, honesty, and a direct approach are among your many personal qualities. Ambitious and determined, with a stream of creative ideas, you gain power from your competitive edge. You also benefit from intellectual pursuits, improving your knowledge or broadening your horizon. Beneath your bold exterior lies an inner sensitivity that suggests a strong intuitive sense and a need for emotional self-expression. If blocked, these emotions can cause you to lose some of your power through stubbornness, intolerance, or self-pity. Usually mentally dynamic and enthusiastic, the mixture of your insight and common sense is likely to lead you to positions of trust and authority. Your enterprising and practical approach also provides you with a good business sense and attracts many opportunities for material success. Nonetheless, you may find greater satisfaction from combining your organizational skills and commercial acumen with some form of service to others. Sociable and charming, you can gain from being generous and helpful.

Your Powers of Attraction in Relationships

Your friendly, confident manner and impressive intelligence attract others. With your quick comprehension and sharp insight into human nature, you can quickly assess others. You therefore need a partner who can mentally keep up with you and stop you from becoming bored. With a strong need for a secure home, you can also be a devoted spouse or parent. People are drawn to your generosity and ability to make them feel special. You generally admire people who are courageous, adventurous, and creative. You often find new opportunities attractive, particularly travel with your partner. Although you are usually sociable, dependable, and direct with others, sometimes you can become changeable and dramatic, leaving others unsure of where they stand. Nevertheless, with your special awareness and helpful and kind nature you will always attract admirers.

Your attractive qualities: creative, intelligent, clever, generous, helpful, kind, sociable, honest, hardworking, determined, practical, active, good judgment, generous, leadership ability, enthusiastic, conscientious, practical, enterprising, pioneering, responsible

Your less attractive qualities: stubborn, restless, martyr, impatient, revengeful, jealous, materialistic, lazy, selfish, suspicious, manipulative

Your Venus Power

The planet Venus has a great deal of influence on your powers of attraction. Below are four possible Venus types for women and men. To find your Venus you need to go to page 771, where you will find the Venus table and extra information. The planet Mars also affects your powers of attraction. To find your Mars table and interpretation go to page 761.

WOMEN WITH VENUS IN AQUARIUS: Sociable and gracious, you are usually sincere and capable of showing tolerance and liberalism. Although you are keen on forming relationships, you also like to have freedom and act independently. Your intimate partnerships need to be founded on true friendship. Full of bright and progressive ideas, you can express yourself better when you are free and unrestricted. An ability to think in a dispassionate way suggests that you can stay detached. Your love of freedom also implies that you can be loving and loyal without smothering your partner.

MEN WITH VENUS IN AQUARIUS: Although independent, you often enjoy being part of a group. The partners you frequently attract are often nonconformists or free spirits. As an individualist, you may not find it easy to settle into a routine or an entirely mundane type of relationship. You value your freedom and can sometimes be cool and detached. Friendship is important to you as you enjoy sharing your progressive ideas.

WOMEN WITH VENUS IN PISCES: Idealistic and impressionable, when in love you are romantic. Being sensitive to other people you are receptive to their moods and feelings. This affinity indicates that although you can be selfless, you may have to guard against being too sentimental or overly romantic, especially with those who can take advantage of your kindness. Nevertheless, your partners can be allured by your seductiveness and intrigued by your poetic soul or mysterious nature.

MEN WITH VENUS IN PISCES: Being adaptable and sensitive, you are able to intuitively feel the moods of those you love. Although you are receptive to others, you can sometimes be ambiguous about your own feelings toward your partner. Romantic and kindhearted, you long to be loved but you need to be realistic about your relationships in order to avoid disap-

pointments. When in love, you may idealize your partners and fail to see any faults in their personality.

WOMEN WITH VENUS IN ARIES: You gain power from your strong individuality, energy, and enthusiasm. Your young-at-heart and spirited approach to relationships adds to your appeal. If you become too impatient or self-absorbed, however, your partnerships are likely to suffer. Nevertheless, you can be creative, sharp, and quick, especially when you are able to share new and exciting projects with your partners. Mischievous, with a love of action, you may even incite them to a playful fight.

MEN WITH VENUS IN ARIES: As you often have the courage and strength to initiate situations, you like to take the lead and let others follow. With your unconscious desire for conquest you may also have to beware of being competitive with your partners. Nevertheless, you are drawn to direct and strong-willed women who can share your love of action and enthusiasm for life. When you are feeling good you can be charming and enthusiastic in romantic situations with an entertaining and spontaneous spirit.

WOMEN WITH VENUS IN TAURUS: Good-natured and romantic, you have a highly developed sense of touch that particularly responds to massage, hugs, and all things physical. Being friendly and affectionate you enjoy socializing and are able to put others at their ease. Although you can be lavish toward your partners, you may have to be careful that you do not overdo things. With your natural sense of beauty and harmony, your charm can always attract others.

MEN WITH VENUS IN TAURUS: Attractive and affectionate, in relationships you are often faithful with a conservative approach. You are usually drawn to warmhearted partners with whom you can share a familiar routine as well as life's pleasures and comforts. Seeking a partner who is dependable or reassuring, you often put security high on your priority list when looking for love. Your sociability and friendliness usually make you popular, and partners often admire your practicality and good sense of values.

To read all about your Outer Planets and work out how to use your personalized timetable, go to Section Three, page 789.

♈

Your Personalized Timetable

JUPITER BENEFICIAL
1938 1/1 – 1/24
1941 5/18 – 7/1
1942 11/4 – 11/20
1943 6/7 – 8/20
1947 2/2 – 4/24
1947 9/28 – 12/13
1949 3/29 – 7/13
1949 11/20 – until 1950 1/8
1953 5/1 – 6/13
1954 9/21 – until 1955 1/14
1955 5/16 – 8/4
1959 1/7 – 6/4
1959 9/4 – 11/27
1961 3/5 – 9/1
1961 10/15 – 12/21
1965 4/13 – 5/28
1966 8/30 – until 1967 2/28
1967 4/11 – 7/19
1970 12/19 – until 1971 11/11
1973 2/14 – 4/8
1973 7/23 – 11/30
1976 8/6 – 11/3
1977 3/24 – 5/11
1978 8/12 – until 1979 7/2
1982 12/2 – until 1983 10/25
1985 1/29 – 3/16
1985 9/8 – 10/27
1988 7/11 – 12/16
1989 2/24 – 4/24
1990 7/27 – 10/21
1991 1/9 – 6/13
1994 11/17 – until 1995 2/6
1995 5/27 – 10/5
1997 1/13 – 2/25
2000 6/21 – 8/15
2000 11/13 – until 2001 4/3
2002 7/10 – 9/25
2003 2/17 – 5/19
2006 11/2 – until 2007 1/15
2007 7/10 – 9/4
2008 12/28 – until 2009 2/9
2012 6/3 – Continues

SATURN BENEFICIAL
1941 8/19 – 10/2
1942 4/23 – 7/13
1942 12/13 – until 1943 3/31
1946 6/25 – until 1947 7/26
1955 11/28 – until 1957 1/19
1957 5/31 – 10/18
1961 3/23 – 6/27
1961 12/17 – until 1962 3/17
1962 7/31 – 12/14
1971 6/3 – until 1972 5/17
1975 8/4 – until 1976 9/4
1977 3/5 – 5/17
1985 1/5 – 5/11
1985 10/3 – until 1986 11/25
1991 1/21 – until 1992 1/20
2000 7/16 – 11/11
2001 4/4 – 6/24
2002 1/29 – 2/16
2004 9/19 – 12/29
2005 6/6 – 11/8
2005 12/6 – until 2006 7/8

URANUS BENEFICIAL
1941 6/20 – until 1944 5/16
1954 8/15 – until 1958 7/21
1980 1/28 – until 1984 10/19
1995 2/15 – until 1998 1/18

NEPTUNE BENEFICIAL
1967 12/15 – until 1975 11/23
1997 2/4 – until 2002 1/19

PLUTO BENEFICIAL
1938 1/1 – until 1947 5/18
1993 1/20 – until 2000 10/20

JUPITER CHALLENGING
1942 5/19 – 7/29

1944 12/3 – until 1945 2/20
1945 7/30 – 10/16
1948 2/24 – 6/7
1948 10/20 – until 1949 1/4
1953 9/16 – 11/12
1954 4/30 – 7/12
1956 11/8 – until 1957 3/31
1957 7/6 – 9/30
1960 2/1 – 7/22
1960 9/19 – 12/19
1965 8/15 – 12/26
1966 4/6 – 6/26
1968 10/20 – until 1969 9/15
1972 1/13 – 12/2
1977 7/25 – until 1978 6/10
1980 10/3 – until 1981 8/29
1983 12/28 – until 1984 3/26
1984 6/3 – 11/13
1989 7/8 – until 1990 5/23
1992 9/17 – 12/10
1993 3/20 – 8/9
1995 12/12 – until 1996 2/26
1996 7/17 – 10/20
2001 6/21 – 9/8
2001 12/28 – until 2002 5/2
2004 9/2 – 11/18
2005 4/27 – 7/14
2007 11/27 – until 2008 2/6

SATURN CHALLENGING
1943 8/29 – 11/20
1944 5/12 – until 1945 6/11
1950 10/5 – until 1951 11/17
1952 4/8 – 8/10
1958 3/9 – 5/1
1958 11/24 – until 1960 1/15
1973 6/23 – until 1974 7/22
1979 11/21 – until 1980 2/23
1980 8/11 – until 1981 9/22
1987 12/29 – until 1989 2/21
1989 6/25 – 11/21
2002 8/3 – 12/23
2003 4/21 – 9/6
2003 12/15 – until 2004 5/23
2009 9/18 – until 2010 10/28
2011 5/15 – 7/11

URANUS CHALLENGING
1947 8/13 – until 1952 5/10
1967 9/23 – until 1971 8/20
1987 1/28 – until 1991 11/14

NEPTUNE CHALLENGING
1939 11/20 – until 1948 8/19
1981 12/31 – until 1989 12/7

PLUTO CHALLENGING
1969 9/23 – until 1976 9/22
2006 1/7 – Continues

JUPITER SPECIAL
1939 4/18 – until 1940 2/26
1951 3/31 – 6/20
1951 9/18 – until 1952 2/5
1963 3/14 – 5/24
1963 11/4 – until 1964 1/4
1975 2/26 – 5/4
1987 2/9 – 4/18
1998 6/4 – 8/31
1999 1/20 – 4/1
2010 5/7 – 10/18
2010 12/19 – until 2011 3/15

SATURN SPECIAL
1938 1/1 – 4/23
1966 4/24 – 10/4
1967 1/16 – 6/14
1967 9/4 – until 1968 3/1
1996 2/27 – until 1997 4/6

URANUS SPECIAL
2009 4/29 – Continues

11

March 25

Your Personal Powers

Clever and naturally talented, you usually possess a progressive outlook and express yourself in an original way. Hidden behind your bright exterior is a wealth of emotional power, inner sensitivity, and creative abilities or ideas. Confident and ambitious, you usually gain power when you apply your practical skills to your ingenious theories. Being mentally quick with an active mind, you need new and exciting opportunities or experiences to stop you from becoming bored. If you become impatient, too restless, or carried away with unrealistic schemes, however, you are likely to lose some of your power. Ardent and enthusiastic when involved with a project or new venture, your natural idealism and youthful optimism can carry you far. Thoughtful and determined, you are usually willing to work hard for your objectives. Your fine mind, dramatic flair, and natural leadership skills also indicate that you can achieve outstanding success if you are willing to develop the perseverance and responsibility needed to bring your natural talents to their full potential.

Your Powers of Attraction in Relationships

You can attract others with your natural social skills and talent for communication. Usually you can be entertaining, loving, and charming, but at times you may have trouble expressing your feelings or giving and receiving affection. Although you usually enjoy sharing your thoughts with a partner, you need to have freedom within your relationship. Ideally, your partner can rise to your mental level, share your sense of humor, and keep up with your sharp mental repartee. Being a fiery and daring person, you may rush into love, your passions fully aroused. Be careful, however, that your initial enthusiasm does not backfire, leaving you feeling isolated or alone. Often chivalrous or idealistic when in love, communication is a vital key to a healthy relationship.

Your attractive qualities: sociable, intuitive, perfectionist, perceptive, creative, good communicator, enthusiastic, loving, intelligent, entertaining, original, youthful, sensitive, idealistic, responsible, rational, spontaneous

Your less attractive qualities: impulsive, stubborn, impatient, irresponsible, restless, overly emotional, bossy, immature, jealous, uncommunicative, critical, nervous

Your Venus Power

The planet Venus has a great deal of influence on your powers of attraction. Below are four possible Venus types for women and men. To find your Venus you need to go to page 771, where you will find the Venus table and extra information. The planet Mars also affects your powers of attraction. To find your Mars table and interpretation go to page 761.

WOMEN WITH VENUS IN AQUARIUS: Sociable and gracious, you are usually sincere and are capable of showing tolerance and liberalism. Although you are keen on forming relationships, you also like to have freedom and act independently. Your intimate partnerships need to be founded on true friendship. Full of bright and progressive ideas, you can express yourself better when you are free and unrestricted. An ability to think in a dispassionate way suggests that you can stay detached. Your love of freedom also implies that you can be loving and loyal without smothering your partner.

MEN WITH VENUS IN AQUARIUS: Although independent, you often enjoy being part of a group. The partners you frequently attract are themselves nonconformists or free spirits. As an individual, you may not find it easy to settle into a routine or an entirely mundane type of relationship. You may have some unconventional views on the traditional marriage or your partner may hold such views. Often original and ahead of your time, you may also be interested in alternative lifestyles, such as collective living.

WOMEN WITH VENUS IN PISCES: Romantic and impressionable, you are a caring and loving individual with a dreamy nature. In relationships you are often attracted to idealistic, compassionate, or sympathetic individuals who have imagination or a strong romantic sense. A tendency to be sensitive to others suggests that you are intuitive and aware of people's inner feelings. Be careful therefore not to get caught in other people's dramas or play the rescuer too often.

MEN WITH VENUS IN PISCES: As a romantic and generous person you are attracted to imaginative or artistic partners who can be sensitive and generous. While you are willing to make allowances for your loved ones, playing the martyr in relationships can lead to allowing others to take advantage of your kind nature. Nevertheless, giving and loving, you are usually willing to forgive your partner's shortcomings.

WOMEN WITH VENUS IN ARIES: With your strong desires and enthusiastic nature you can be a passionate lover. Although idealistic and single-minded, you need to avoid un-

necessary conflicts in your relationships by being more patient and less headstrong. Although at times others can accuse you of being bossy or impulsive, you possess a great deal of warmth and charm. When necessary you can disarm others by making them feel important.

MEN WITH VENUS IN ARIES: You are usually drawn to courageous or assertive women who possess strong personal magnetism. You might therefore find those who seem to be independent or action-oriented very attractive. Your own eagerness and need for activity suggests that you start relationships with great enthusiasm, especially if they offer you excitement or adventure. The challenge is often to maintain relationships and not become bored too easily.

WOMEN WITH VENUS IN TAURUS: Warm and affectionate, you are naturally tactile with a love of sensual pleasures. With a streak of the conventional you love the simple pleasures of life: good food, close friends, and happy relationships. Having an inner strength, you can express genuine patience and are often a pillar of support for loved ones and friends. Although you possess endurance, be careful not to let this turn to plain stubbornness.

MEN WITH VENUS IN TAURUS: As you yourself may be attractive to the opposite sex, you desire a partner who is sensual and loving or who has physical beauty. Needing stability when faced with changes that are out of your control, you may become insecure or possessive. Faithful and loyal, you can be affectionate, tactile, and constant in your love. Your own sense of style and your love of beauty imply that you can be attracted to creative people, especially those in art and music.

To read all about your Outer Planets and work out how to use your personalized timetable, go to Section Three, page 789.

Your Personalized Timetable

JUPITER BENEFICIAL
1938 1/1 – 1/28
1941 5/22 – 7/5
1943 6/12 – 8/25
1947 2/11 – 4/14
1947 10/4 – 12/18
1949 4/5 – 7/5
1949 11/25 – until 1950 1/12
1953 5/5 – 6/17
1954 9/27 – until 1955 1/6
1955 5/22 – 8/8
1959 1/13 – 5/26
1959 9/11 – 12/2
1961 3/10 – 8/20
1961 10/27 – 12/25
1965 4/18 – 6/1
1966 9/4 – until 1967 2/16
1967 4/23 – 7/24
1970 12/24 – until 1971 11/16
1973 2/19 – 4/16
1973 7/15 – 12/5
1976 8/14 – 10/25
1977 3/30 – 5/15
1978 8/17 – until 1979 7/7
1982 12/7 – until 1983 10/30
1985 2/2 – 3/21
1985 8/28 – 11/7
1988 7/17 – 12/7
1989 3/4 – 4/28
1990 7/31 – 10/30
1990 12/30 – until 1991 6/19
1994 11/21 – until 1995 2/13
1995 5/19 – 10/11
1997 1/17 – 3/2
2000 6/26 – 8/24
2000 11/4 – until 2001 4/9
2002 7/15 – 9/30
2003 2/9 – 5/27
2006 11/6 – until 2007 1/21
2007 6/29 – 9/14
2009 1/1 – 2/13
2012 6/7 – Continues

SATURN BENEFICIAL
1942 5/1 – 7/23
1942 12/1 – until 1943 4/11
1946 7/3 – until 1947 8/3
1955 12/6 – until 1957 1/30
1957 5/17 – 10/28
1961 4/9 – 6/9
1961 12/26 – until 1962 3/28
1962 7/17 – 12/24
1971 6/11 – until 1972 5/24
1975 8/12 – until 1976 3/19
1976 4/6 – 9/12
1977 2/19 – 5/31
1985 1/16 – 4/28
1985 10/13 – until 1986 12/3
1991 1/30 – until 1992 1/28
2000 7/27 – 10/29
2001 4/13 – 7/2
2002 1/4 – 3/14
2004 10/2 – 12/15
2005 6/15 – until 2006 7/16

URANUS BENEFICIAL
1941 7/11 – until 1945 2/14
1954 9/3 – until 1958 8/7
1980 11/22 – until 1984 11/7
1995 3/7 – until 1998 11/14

NEPTUNE BENEFICIAL
1968 1/19 – until 1976 10/21
1997 3/6 – until 2002 12/17

PLUTO BENEFICIAL
1938 1/1 – until 1947 7/7
1993 12/4 – until 2000 11/18

JUPITER CHALLENGING
1942 5/24 – 8/3
1944 12/13 – until 1945 2/10
1945 8/5 – 10/21
1948 3/2 – 5/29

1948 10/26 – until 1949 1/8
1953 9/30 – 10/29
1954 5/5 – 7/17
1956 11/14 – until 1957 3/23
1957 7/13 – 10/5
1960 2/6 – 7/11
1960 9/29 – 12/23
1965 8/21 – 12/19
1966 4/13 – 7/1
1968 10/25 – until 1969 9/19
1972 1/18 – 12/6
1977 7/30 – until 1978 2/17
1978 2/23 – 6/14
1980 10/8 – until 1981 9/3
1984 1/1 – 4/6
1984 5/23 – 11/19
1989 7/12 – until 1990 5/28
1992 9/22 – 12/18
1993 3/11 – 8/15
1995 12/17 – until 1996 3/3
1996 7/9 – 10/27
2001 6/25 – 9/15
2001 12/21 – until 2002 5/8
2004 9/7 – 11/24
2005 4/18 – 7/22
2007 12/1 – until 2008 2/11

SATURN CHALLENGING
1943 9/15 – 11/2
1944 5/20 – until 1945 6/19
1950 10/14 – until 1951 5/3
1951 6/23 – 11/27
1952 3/26 – 8/21
1958 12/3 – until 1960 1/23
1960 8/28 – 10/4
1973 6/30 – until 1974 7/30
1975 3/1 – 3/27
1979 12/6 – until 1980 2/8
1980 8/20 – until 1981 9/30
1988 1/6 – 8/15
1988 9/14 – until 1989 3/6
1989 6/11 – 12/1
2002 8/13 – 12/11
2003 5/1 – 9/20
2003 11/30 – until 2004 6/1
2009 9/26 – until 2010 11/6
2011 4/28 – 7/28

URANUS CHALLENGING
1947 9/20 – until 1952 5/31
1967 10/9 – until 1971 9/7
1987 2/22 – until 1991 12/4

NEPTUNE CHALLENGING
1940 10/11 – until 1948 9/19
1982 1/29 – until 1990 10/27

PLUTO CHALLENGING
1969 10/21 – until 1977 8/11
2006 2/8 – Continues

JUPITER SPECIAL
1939 4/22 – until 1940 3/1
1951 4/4 – 6/29
1951 9/9 – until 1952 2/10
1963 3/19 – 5/29
1963 10/26 – until 1964 1/13
1975 3/2 – 5/9
1987 2/13 – 4/22
1998 6/12 – 8/22
1999 1/25 – 4/5
2010 5/13 – 10/9
2010 12/28 – until 2011 3/19

SATURN SPECIAL
1938 1/1 – 5/2
1938 11/13 – until 1939 1/14
1966 5/4 – 9/21
1967 1/27 – 7/4
1967 8/14 – until 1968 3/9
1996 3/6 – until 1997 4/14

URANUS SPECIAL
2009 5/26 – Continues

☐

13

March 26

Your Personal Powers

Your natural warmth, dynamic drive, and sharp intellect are just some of your many personal powers. Your ruling planet, Mars, indicates that you also possess courage and energy. Natural organizational or managerial abilities and problem-solving skills can help you in your rise to success. You gain power by being direct, friendly, and generous. As a spirited individual with a need for self-expression, you are likely to excel at initiating projects. Although you prefer to be up front with people, be careful not to lose some of your power by being bossy or difficult. Enthusiastic and determined, however, you are able to utilize your keen intelligence and excellent social skills to draw people toward you and encourage them with your natural charm. Since your eagerness is not something you can fake, it is important that you find work or projects that inspire you in order to achieve personal success. By adding patience and discipline to your ambition and determination, you are able to enhance your personal powers and achieve outstanding results.

Your Powers of Attraction in Relationships

Your strong personality and good social skills can act as a magnet to attract others. An interesting mixture of opposites, at times you can be sensitive, supportive, and generous and on other occasions you can show your less attractive qualities by being selfish, overbearing, or controlling. A strong need for a relationship and a secure home suggest, however, that you are usually willing to make a real commitment in order to secure your long-term relationship. It is important that your partner is able to handle your strong and independent spirit and understands your passion and dedication to your work and/or career. If not, you may feel bored and restricted by their demands or indecisive about your feelings. Women of this birthday are particularly drawn to powerful men they can respect.

Your attractive qualities: daring, creative, intelligent, practical, caring, responsible, honest, proud, enthusiastic, courageous, dynamic, home-loving, confident, ambitious, affectionate, leader, conscientious, powerful, determined, dependable

Your less attractive qualities: bossy, stubborn, selfish, rebellious, lack of drive, inconsistent, give up too easily, overly ambitious, materialistic, unstable, compulsive

Your Venus Power

The planet Venus has a great deal of influence on your powers of attraction. Below are four possible Venus types for women and men. To find your Venus you need to go to page 771, where you will find the Venus table and extra information. The planet Mars also affects your powers of attraction. To find your Mars table and interpretation go to page 761.

WOMEN WITH VENUS IN AQUARIUS: When it comes to relationships, others are attracted to your honest, friendly, and easygoing approach. You really enjoy social interaction with others and may develop a genuine concern for humanity. Usually you present a tolerant and reasonable front in love situations and attempt to view your relationships objectively. If partners become too demanding, however, you can become stubborn and fixed. Friendship may be even more important for you than sexual compatibility.

MEN WITH VENUS IN AQUARIUS: You are sociable and open-minded and people are attracted by your friendly and relaxed style. Being independent, you value freedom-loving partners who give you the space to be yourself. Others sometimes interpret your detachment as being emotionally cool, but they may not understand your progressive views on relationships. Friendship can sometimes be even more important than earthly passion. Ideally, your partners can share your ideas on life and possess as strong a sense of originality as your own. Not easily ruffled, you can deal well with difficult situations or moody partners.

WOMEN WITH VENUS IN PISCES: Romantic and idealistic when in love, you can be a sensitive and responsive lover. With your affectionate and impressionable nature you are often attracted to those who understand your sensitivity and share your vision. Being flexible with an impressionable nature helps you to adapt to the needs of others. In your desire to blend with those you love, guard against giving too much of yourself by not defining your boundaries clearly.

MEN WITH VENUS IN PISCES: The combination of your emotional subtlety and charm can make you very alluring when dealing with affairs of the heart. Perceptive and impressionable, you have an easygoing style in your relationships, usually preferring to avoid ugly confrontation. You are drawn to a partner who has a touch of glamour and is sensitive to the needs of others. Alternatively, your partner could be a visionary with a rich imagination, like you, and can keep you en-

chanted. With your insight you have the ability to observe the subtle moods of your partner.

WOMEN WITH VENUS IN ARIES: You gain power from your strong individuality, energy, and enthusiasm. Your young-at-heart and spirited approach to relationships adds to your appeal. If you become too impatient or self-absorbed, however, your partnerships are likely to suffer. Nevertheless, you can be creative, sharp, and quick, especially when you are able to share new and exciting projects with your partners. Mischievous, with a love of action, you may even incite them to a playful fight.

MEN WITH VENUS IN ARIES: You are drawn to strong, independent women who can stand up to you. Although you can enthusiastically follow the object of your desire, you may lose power if you allow your forceful emotions to become too dominant. Warm and passionate, you have a side to your nature that longs for new adventures. Romantic and chivalrous, you really enjoy the excitement of the initial chase, but unless you keep the enthusiasm alive and avoid falling into a rut, you may become easily bored.

WOMEN WITH VENUS IN TAURUS: Good-natured and romantic, you have a highly developed sense of touch that particularly responds to massage, hugs, and all things physical. Being friendly and affectionate you enjoy socializing and are able to put others at their ease. Although you can be lavish toward your partners you may have to be careful that you do not overdo things. With your natural sense of beauty and harmony, your natural charm can always attract others.

MEN WITH VENUS IN TAURUS: Attractive and affectionate, in relationships you are often faithful with a conservative approach. You are usually drawn to warmhearted partners with whom you can share a familiar routine as well as life's pleasures and comforts. Seeking a partner who is dependable or reassuring, you often put security high on your priority list when looking for love. Your sociability and friendliness usually make you popular and partners often admire your practicality and good sense of values.

To read all about your Outer Planets and work out how to use your personalized timetable, go to Section Three, page 789.

Your Personalized Timetable

JUPITER BENEFICIAL
1938 1/1 – 2/1
1941 5/26 – 7/10
1943 6/17 – 8/29
1947 2/25 – 3/31
1947 10/9 – 12/22
1949 4/13 – 6/26
1949 12/1 – until 1950 1/16
1953 5/10 – 6/22
1954 10/5 – 12/29
1955 5/28 – 8/13
1959 1/19 – 5/19
1959 9/18 – 12/6
1961 3/15 – 8/11
1961 11/4 – 12/30
1965 4/23 – 6/5
1966 9/10 – until 1967 2/7
1967 5/2 – 7/28
1970 12/29 – until 1971 7/6
1971 8/11 – 11/20
1973 2/23 – 4/24
1973 7/6 – 12/10
1976 8/24 – 10/15
1977 4/4 – 5/20
1978 8/21 – until 1979 7/12
1982 12/12 – until 1983 11/4
1985 2/7 – 3/27
1985 8/19 – 11/15
1988 7/22 – 11/30
1989 3/11 – 5/3
1990 8/4 – 11/12
1990 12/17 – until 1991 6/24
1994 11/26 – until 1995 2/21
1995 5/11 – 10/16
1997 1/22 – 3/7
2000 6/30 – 9/3
2000 10/25 – until 2001 4/14
2002 7/19 – 10/7
2003 2/2 – 6/3
2006 11/11 – until 2007 1/26
2007 6/20 – 9/22
2009 1/6 – 2/17
2012 6/12 – Continues

SATURN BENEFICIAL
1942 5/9 – 8/3
1942 11/18 – until 1943 4/20
1946 7/11 – until 1947 8/10
1955 12/15 – until 1956 6/26
1956 9/2 – until 1957 2/13
1957 5/2 – 11/7
1962 1/4 – 4/11
1962 7/2 – until 1963 1/2
1971 6/19 – until 1972 1/8
1972 2/23 – 6/1
1975 8/21 – until 1976 2/22
1976 5/1 – 9/22
1977 2/6 – 6/11
1985 1/31 – 4/12
1985 10/22 – until 1986 12/12
1991 2/7 – until 1992 2/6
2000 8/12 – 10/14
2001 4/21 – 7/11
2001 12/21 – until 2002 3/28
2004 10/23 – 11/24
2005 6/23 – until 2006 7/24

URANUS BENEFICIAL
1941 8/12 – until 1945 4/5
1954 9/27 – until 1959 6/4
1980 12/8 – until 1984 11/24
1995 4/5 – until 1998 12/14

NEPTUNE BENEFICIAL
1968 12/11 – until 1976 11/19
1998 1/31 – until 2003 1/15

PLUTO BENEFICIAL
1938 1/1 – until 1948 6/13
1994 1/1 – until 2001 10/8

JUPITER CHALLENGING
1942 5/28 – 8/8

1944 12/27 – until 1945 1/27
1945 8/10 – 10/25
1948 3/11 – 5/20
1948 10/31 – until 1949 1/12
1954 5/10 – 7/21
1956 11/20 – until 1957 3/16
1957 7/20 – 10/10
1960 2/12 – 7/3
1960 10/7 – 12/27
1965 8/28 – 12/12
1966 4/19 – 7/5
1968 10/30 – until 1969 4/27
1969 6/18 – 9/24
1972 1/23 – 12/11
1977 8/4 – until 1978 1/26
1978 3/17 – 6/19
1980 10/13 – until 1981 9/8
1984 1/6 – 11/23
1989 7/17 – until 1990 6/2
1992 9/27 – 12/27
1993 3/2 – 8/21
1995 12/21 – until 1996 3/9
1996 7/1 – 11/2
2001 6/30 – 9/22
2001 12/13 – until 2002 5/13
2004 9/11 – 11/30
2005 4/10 – 7/30
2007 12/6 – until 2008 2/16
2008 8/20 – 9/26

SATURN CHALLENGING
1944 5/28 – until 1945 6/27
1950 10/22 – until 1951 4/15
1951 7/11 – 12/9
1952 3/12 – 8/30
1958 12/11 – until 1960 2/1
1960 8/6 – 10/25
1973 7/8 – until 1974 8/7
1975 2/6 – 4/18
1980 8/28 – until 1981 10/8
1988 1/15 – 7/22
1988 10/7 – until 1989 3/22
1989 5/25 – 12/10
2002 8/25 – 11/28
2003 5/10 – 10/13
2003 11/6 – until 2004 6/9
2009 10/4 – until 2010 11/15
2011 4/14 – 8/10

URANUS CHALLENGING
1948 6/30 – until 1952 6/17
1967 10/26 – until 1971 9/24
1987 12/22 – until 1991 12/22

NEPTUNE CHALLENGING
1940 11/13 – until 1949 8/14
1982 12/28 – until 1990 12/3

PLUTO CHALLENGING
1969 11/28 – until 1977 9/11
2007 1/2 – Continues

JUPITER SPECIAL
1939 4/27 – until 1940 3/6
1951 4/9 – 7/9
1951 8/30 – until 1952 2/15
1963 3/23 – 6/4
1963 10/18 – until 1964 1/21
1975 3/6 – 5/13
1987 2/18 – 4/26
1998 6/23 – 8/11
1999 1/30 – 4/9
2010 5/18 – 10/1
2011 1/4 – 3/23

SATURN SPECIAL
1938 1/1 – 5/11
1938 10/28 – until 1939 1/29
1966 5/15 – 9/8
1967 2/6 – until 1968 3/18
1996 3/14 – until 1997 4/22

URANUS SPECIAL
2010 3/26 – Continues

15

March 27

SUN: ARIES • DECANATE: ARIES/MARS • DEGREE: 5°5–6°5 ARIES • MODE: CARDINAL • ELEMENT: FIRE

Your Personal Powers

Intelligent and direct, your personal powers include creativity, strong instincts, and an ability to quickly assess people or situations. Your ruling planet, Mars, indicates that you can be courageous and dynamic with a pioneering spirit. Although you have a good deal of energy and original ideas, you also need patience to turn your inspired thoughts into a tangible reality. You empower yourself by being confident, generous, warm, and kind. If you do not stay positively focused, however, you may lose power to negative thinking, frustration, or discouragement. Nevertheless, people recognize that you are usually enthusiastic and charitable with a sympathetic and understanding nature. Although you possess strong emotions it is often through developing your perseverance and tolerance that you gain power and avoid anxiety. Usually an idealist with a broad-minded or philanthropic approach, you benefit from expanding your knowledge, improving your skills, and building a definite belief system. By combining discipline with your enterprising spirit you can achieve satisfaction and success.

Your Powers of Attraction in Relationships

People are attracted to your quick intelligence, unusual approach, and sociable nature. You are dramatic and sensitive, and romantic relationships can be particularly important to you. Generous and kind, you are attracted to those who can inspire or encourage you and give you the emotional support you need. Desiring harmony, peace, and security, you also need a partner who can share your strong need for a stable home. Once married, you are usually a dutiful and responsible partner. With an awareness of your responsibilities you can also be a very caring parent. Nevertheless, it is important for you to keep the balance of power in your relationships. Working on the basis of give and take, you can avoid becoming too dependent on your partner. Communicating your feelings in a diplomatic way can greatly aid your relationships.

Your attractive qualities: honest, kind, broad-minded, generous, versatile, imaginative, creative, courageous, mentally quick, humanitarian, philanthropic, inventive, idealistic, sensitive, intelligent, direct, people skills, love, knowledge

Your less attractive qualities: too forceful, inner tensions, argumentative, restless, nervous, frustration, mistrusting, disappointment, oversensitive, impulsive, restlessness, impatience

Your Venus Power

The planet Venus has a great deal of influence on your powers of attraction. Below are four possible Venus types for women and men. To find your Venus you need to go to page 771, where you will find the Venus table and extra information. The planet Mars also affects your powers of attraction. To find your Mars table and interpretation go to page 761.

WOMEN WITH VENUS IN AQUARIUS: You attract and impress others with your friendly approach and progressive ideas. As you are usually independent and easygoing, you value freedom within a relationship. A good companion, with a sense of your own person, you enjoy socializing, especially with people who are original, cosmopolitan, and have a strong sense of individuality. Although being friendly and detached usually serves you well, avoid losing touch with your emotions. You usually prefer the company of those who have innovative or progressive views.

MEN WITH VENUS IN AQUARIUS: Although independent, you often enjoy being part of a group. The partners you frequently attract are often nonconformists or free spirits. As an individualist, you may not find it easy to settle into a routine or an entirely mundane type of relationship. You value your freedom and can sometimes be cool and detached. Friendship is important to you as you enjoy sharing your progressive ideas.

WOMEN WITH VENUS IN PISCES: As a romantic and idealistic individual you can be both loving and giving. In relationships you may need to balance the practical with the charitable. While making allowances and sacrifices is understandable in a loving relationship, playing the martyr is often a state of romantic illusion that can lead to self-deception. Your benevolence and sacrifices in the right relationship nonetheless make you a partner who is devoted, kind, and compassionate. Subtle, sensitive, and alluring, you make a sensual and caring partner.

MEN WITH VENUS IN PISCES: In love you are sensitive, tender, and affectionate, experiencing your partner's feelings almost as strongly as your own. Being also imaginative and visionary, you possess the capability to develop deep compassion for others. As you are idealistic when in love, you usually

prefer to see only your partner's good points, but be careful that your high expectations do not bring disappointment if you avoid harsh reality. Nevertheless, in your relationships with others, you can be devoted, loving, and positively enchanting.

WOMEN WITH VENUS IN ARIES: Idealistic, passionate, and adventurous, you are direct in your dealings with others. When you are attracted to a person you usually take the initiative and use your people skills to make things happen. In close relationships you are not afraid to confront your other half. This self-assertiveness is positive if differences can be brought into the open through diplomacy and compromise. Independent and spirited, you enjoy your freedom.

MEN WITH VENUS IN ARIES: As you often have the courage and strength to initiate situations, you like to take the lead and let others follow. With your unconscious desire for conquest you may also have to beware of being competitive with your partners. Nevertheless, you are drawn to direct and strong-willed women who can share your love of action and enthusiasm for life. When you are feeling good you can be charming and enthusiastic in romantic situations with an entertaining and spontaneous spirit.

WOMEN WITH VENUS IN TAURUS: Good-natured and romantic, you have a highly developed sense of touch that particularly responds to massage, hugs, and all things physical. Being friendly and affectionate you enjoy socializing and are able to put others at their ease. Although you can be lavish toward your partners, you may have to be careful that you do not overdo things. With your inborn sense of beauty and harmony, your natural charm can always attract others.

MEN WITH VENUS IN TAURUS: Attractive and affectionate, in relationships you are often faithful with a conservative approach. You are usually drawn to warmhearted partners with whom you can share a familiar routine as well as life's pleasures and comforts. Seeking a partner who is dependable or reassuring, you often put security high on your priority list when looking for love. Your sociability and friendliness usually make you popular, and partners often admire your practicality and good sense of values.

To read all about your Outer Planets and work out how to use your personalized timetable, go to Section Three, page 789.

To read all about your Outer Planets and work out how to use your personalized timetable, go to Section Three, page 789.

Your Personalized Timetable

JUPITER BENEFICIAL
1938 1/1 – 2/6
1941 5/31 – 7/15
1943 6/21 – 9/3
1947 10/14 – 12/27
1949 4/24 – 6/16
1949 12/6 – until 1950 1/20
1953 5/14 – 6/26
1954 10/13 – 12/21
1955 6/2 – 8/17
1959 1/26 – 5/11
1959 9/24 – 12/11
1961 3/21 – 8/3
1961 11/12 – until 1962 1/3
1965 4/27 – 6/9
1966 9/15 – until 1967 1/30
1967 5/10 – 8/2
1971 1/3 – 6/23
1971 8/25 – 11/25
1973 2/28 – 5/5
1973 6/25 – 12/16
1976 9/11 – 9/28
1977 4/9 – 5/24
1978 8/26 – until 1979 7/17
1982 12/16 – until 1983 11/9
1985 2/11 – 4/1
1985 8/11 – 11/22
1988 7/28 – 11/22
1989 3/18 – 5/7
1990 8/9 – until 1991 6/29
1994 11/30 – until 1995 3/3
1995 4/30 – 10/22
1997 1/26 – 3/11
2000 7/5 – 9/20
2000 10/8 – until 2001 4/19
2002 7/24 – 10/13
2003 1/25 – 6/9
2006 11/15 – until 2007 2/1
2007 6/12 – 9/29
2009 1/10 – 2/22
2012 6/16 – Continues

SATURN BENEFICIAL
1942 5/17 – 8/15
1942 11/5 – until 1943 4/29
1946 7/18 – until 1947 8/18
1955 12/24 – until 1956 6/9
1956 9/18 – until 1957 3/8
1957 4/9 – 11/16
1962 1/13 – 5/2
1962 6/10 – until 1963 1/11
1971 6/27 – 12/21
1972 3/12 – 6/9
1975 8/29 – until 1976 2/7
1976 5/15 – 10/2
1977 1/25 – 6/21
1985 3/1 – 3/13
1985 10/31 – until 1986 12/20
1991 2/16 – 9/1
1991 11/6 – until 1992 2/14
2001 4/29 – 7/20
2001 12/8 – until 2002 4/8
2005 7/1 – until 2006 8/1

URANUS BENEFICIAL
1942 6/2 – until 1945 4/27
1955 7/23 – until 1959 6/26
1980 12/25 – until 1985 9/8
1996 1/30 – until 1999 1/3

NEPTUNE BENEFICIAL
1969 1/12 – until 1977 10/16
1998 3/1 – until 2003 12/11

PLUTO BENEFICIAL
1938 1/1 – until 1948 7/22
1994 11/23 – until 2001 11/9

JUPITER CHALLENGING
1942 6/1 – 8/12
1945 8/15 – 10/30

1948 3/22 – 5/8
1948 11/5 – until 1949 1/17
1954 5/15 – 7/26
1956 11/27 – until 1957 3/8
1957 7/26 – 10/14
1960 2/17 – 6/25
1960 10/14 – until 1961 1/1
1965 9/4 – 12/4
1966 4/25 – 7/10
1968 11/5 – until 1969 4/16
1969 6/29 – 9/29
1972 1/28 – 12/15
1977 8/9 – until 1978 1/15
1978 3/27 – 6/23
1980 10/17 – until 1981 9/12
1984 1/10 – 11/28
1989 7/21 – until 1990 6/7
1992 10/1 – until 1993 1/9
1993 2/17 – 8/26
1995 12/25 – until 1996 3/16
1996 6/24 – 11/8
2001 7/4 – 10/1
2001 12/4 – until 2002 5/19
2004 9/16 – 12/6
2005 4/2 – 8/6
2007 12/10 – until 2008 2/21
2008 8/7 – 10/9

SATURN CHALLENGING
1944 6/5 – until 1945 7/4
1950 10/31 – until 1951 4/1
1951 7/24 – 12/24
1952 2/25 – 9/8
1958 12/20 – until 1960 2/11
1960 7/21 – 11/8
1973 7/16 – until 1974 2/10
1974 3/17 – 8/16
1975 1/23 – 5/2
1980 9/5 – until 1981 10/16
1988 1/24 – 7/6
1988 10/21 – until 1989 12/19
2002 9/8 – 11/13
2003 5/19 – until 2004 6/17
2009 10/13 – until 2010 5/13
2010 6/16 – 11/25
2011 4/1 – 8/21

URANUS CHALLENGING
1948 7/18 – until 1952 7/4
1967 11/15 – until 1971 10/10
1988 1/8 – until 1992 10/2

NEPTUNE CHALLENGING
1941 10/8 – until 1949 9/15
1983 1/25 – until 1991 10/15

PLUTO CHALLENGING
1970 10/14 – until 1978 7/20
2007 2/2 – Continues

JUPITER SPECIAL
1939 5/2 – until 1940 3/10
1951 4/13 – 7/28
1951 8/10 – until 1952 2/20
1963 3/27 – 6/10
1963 10/11 – until 1964 1/27
1975 3/10 – 5/18
1987 2/22 – 4/30
1999 2/4 – 4/13
2010 5/24 – 9/23
2011 1/11 – 3/27

SATURN SPECIAL
1938 1/1 – 5/20
1938 10/15 – until 1939 2/10
1966 5/28 – 8/25
1967 2/15 – until 1968 3/25
1996 3/22 – until 1997 5/1
1997 11/21 – until 1998 1/9

URANUS SPECIAL
2010 4/13 – Continues

March 28

SUN: ARIES • DECANATE: ARIES/MARS • DEGREE: 6°5–7°5 ARIES • MODE: CARDINAL • ELEMENT: FIRE

Your Personal Powers

Independent and direct, among your many personal powers are your keen mental insight, quick comprehension, and strong will. Your ruling planet, Mars, indicates that you can be daring, energetic, and idealistic. Although you are a visionary with a powerful imagination, your life lessons often revolve around how you handle financial matters, status, and power. Enthusiastic and action-oriented by nature, your projects and plans may encounter setbacks until you are able to apply methodology and process to your inspired ideas and handle your challenges with calmness. By using your foresight you can resist striving too hard for success or being overdependent on others. Clever and intuitive, however, you gain power from your natural sixth sense and intellectual prowess. Although you are ambitious and determined, you need to maintain your patience and stay focused on your goals in order to make the most of your natural talents. Being a good strategist with an innate business sense you also gain from initiating projects that can place you in leadership positions.

Your Powers of Attraction in Relationships

People are attracted to your sharp perceptions, creative imagination, and good mind. Although you can sometimes be bossy, you can also be diplomatic and persuasive. Your strong need for love and affection can lead you to different emotional experiences, but as family and home life are important to you, you usually look for the security of a stable relationship. You may nevertheless encounter a strong pull between wanting independence and being in a partnership. In love, others admire the fact that you can be both strong-willed and determined yet sensitive and tender. You attract others with your direct approach and elegant manner. With your strong imagination, however, be careful of deception or escapism. When inspired, you can project love so powerfully that you can enchant and delight others.

Your attractive qualities: intelligent, sensitive, inspired, daring, creative, idealistic, ambitious, hardworking, determined, diplomatic, imaginative, communication skills, mental power, visionary, compassion, strong-willed, persuasive, intuitive, leadership, success-oriented

Your less attractive qualities: fantasist, tactless, overemotional, dependent, selfish, bossy, contentious, escapist, lacking confidence, unmotivated, deceptive

Your Venus Power

The planet Venus has a great deal of influence on your powers of attraction. Below are four possible Venus types for women and men. To find your Venus you need to go to page 771, where you will find the Venus table and extra information. The planet Mars also affects your powers of attraction. To find your Mars table and interpretation go to page 761.

WOMEN WITH VENUS IN AQUARIUS: Usually you have a modern outlook on love and are open to new or current lifestyles. Your intuitive abilities, communal sense, and people skills often allow you to see deeper into human intentions and read telepathically other people's thoughts. Although you are usually group-oriented, you are drawn to strong individuals within the group who are independent and self-motivated. You are more inclined to choose a partner who is unconventional and/or freedom-loving. Conscious of your social standing, however, you want someone who can relate well to your friends.

MEN WITH VENUS IN AQUARIUS: Sociable and open-minded, you attract people with your friendly and easygoing style. Being independent, you value freedom-loving partners who give you the space to be yourself. Other people can sometimes interpret your detachment as being emotionally cool, but they admire your objectivity and humanitarian inclinations. You are attracted to intelligent individuals who are as truthful and direct as you, but above all they must be true friends. Ideally, your partner shares your liberal views on life and possesses a strong sense of individuality.

WOMEN WITH VENUS IN PISCES: Idealistic and impressionable, in love you are romantic. Being sensitive to other people, you are receptive to their moods and feelings. This affinity indicates that although you can be selfless you may have to guard against being too sentimental or overly romantic, especially with those who can take advantage of your kindness. Nevertheless, alluring and seductive, you can intrigue your partners with your poetic soul or mysterious nature.

MEN WITH VENUS IN PISCES: The combination of your emotional subtlety and charm can make you very alluring when dealing with affairs of the heart. Perceptive and impres-

sionable, you have an easygoing style in your relationships, usually preferring to avoid ugly confrontation. You are drawn to a woman who has a touch of glamour and is sensitive to the needs of others. Alternatively, she can be a visionary with a rich imagination, like your own, who will keep you enchanted.

WOMEN WITH VENUS IN ARIES: Idealistic, passionate, and adventurous, you are direct in your dealings with others. When you are attracted to a person you usually take the initiative and use your people skills to make things happen. In close relationships you are not afraid to confront your other half. This self-assertiveness is positive if differences can be brought into the open through diplomacy and compromise. Independent and spirited, you enjoy your freedom.

MEN WITH VENUS IN ARIES: As you often have the courage and strength to initiate situations, you like to take the lead and let others follow. With your unconscious desire for conquest you may also have to beware of being competitive with your partners. Nevertheless, you are drawn to direct and strong-willed women who can share your love of action and enthusiasm for life. When you are feeling good you can be charming and enthusiastic in romantic situations with an entertaining and spontaneous spirit.

WOMEN WITH VENUS IN TAURUS: For your ideal relationship you seek partners who are both financially secure and demonstrative with their affections. With these thoughts in mind, you are likely to also want a partner who is refined yet pragmatic or someone concerned with safeguarding your future. Although you have a stubborn streak you can be loving and affectionate in your relationships. With your good sense of style you may also have an attraction for the arts, music, or luxury items.

MEN WITH VENUS IN TAURUS: Although you are usually drawn to sensual and physically beautiful individuals, you want a partner who is also reliable and loyal. When in love, you enjoy buying your partner things of quality that will grow in value or useful things of a practical nature. You also love to socialize and entertain, especially in luxurious surroundings. Affectionate and caring, you are often attracted to creative people or those with artistic talents.

To read all about your Outer Planets and work out how to use your personalized timetable, go to Section Three, page 789.

To read all about your Outer Planets and work out how to use your personalized timetable, go to Section Three, page 789.

Your Personalized Timetable

JUPITER BENEFICIAL
1938 1/1 – 2/10
1941 6/4 – 7/20
1942 1/16 – 2/25
1943 6/26 – 9/8
1947 10/19 – 12/31
1949 5/13 – 5/27
1949 12/11 – until **1950** 1/25
1953 5/18 – 6/30
1954 10/25 – 12/9
1955 6/8 – 8/22
1959 2/2 – 5/3
1959 9/30 – 12/15
1961 3/27 – 7/26
1961 11/18 – until **1962** 1/8
1965 5/1 – 6/14
1966 9/21 – until **1967** 1/23
1967 5/17 – 8/6
1971 1/9 – 6/13
1971 9/4 – 11/29
1973 3/5 – 5/26
1973 6/5 – 12/20
1977 4/13 – 5/28
1978 8/31 – until **1979** 3/19
1979 3/31 – 7/21
1982 12/21 – until **1983** 11/13
1985 2/15 – 4/8
1985 8/4 – 11/29
1988 8/4 – 11/15
1989 3/24 – 5/12
1990 8/14 – until **1991** 7/4
1994 12/5 – until **1995** 3/18
1995 4/15 – 10/27
1997 1/30 – 3/16
2000 7/10 – until **2001** 1/2
2001 2/17 – 4/24
2002 7/28 – 10/21
2003 1/18 – 6/15
2006 11/20 – until **2007** 2/7
2007 6/4 – 10/6
2009 1/14 – 2/26
2012 6/21 – Continues

SATURN BENEFICIAL
1942 5/24 – 9/3
1942 10/17 – until **1943** 5/7
1946 7/26 – until **1947** 8/26
1956 1/2 – 5/26
1956 9/30 – until **1957** 11/24
1962 1/21 – until **1963** 1/19
1971 7/6 – 12/7
1972 3/24 – 6/16
1975 9/7 – until **1976** 1/25
1976 5/26 – 10/14
1977 1/12 – 6/30
1985 11/9 – until **1986** 12/29
1987 7/24 – 9/14
1991 2/25 – 8/16
1991 11/22 – until **1992** 2/23
1992 9/28 – 11/2
2001 5/7 – 7/30
2001 11/26 – until **2002** 4/18
2005 7/9 – until **2006** 8/9

URANUS BENEFICIAL
1942 6/20 – until **1945** 5/15
1955 8/8 – until **1959** 7/14
1981 1/15 – until **1985** 10/13
1996 2/17 – until **1999** 1/21

NEPTUNE BENEFICIAL
1969 12/8 – until **1977** 11/16
1998 4/16 – until **2004** 1/12

PLUTO BENEFICIAL
1938 7/1 – until **1949** 7/1
1994 12/19 – until **2002** 9/20

JUPITER CHALLENGING
1942 6/6 – 8/17
1945 8/20 – 11/4

1948 11/10 – until **1949** 1/21
1954 5/19 – 7/30
1956 12/4 – until **1957** 2/28
1957 8/1 – 10/19
1960 2/24 – 6/17
1960 10/20 – until **1961** 1/5
1965 9/12 – 11/26
1966 4/30 – 7/14
1968 11/10 – until **1969** 4/7
1969 7/8 – 10/3
1972 2/2 – 8/6
1972 9/13 – 12/20
1977 8/15 – until **1978** 1/7
1978 4/5 – 6/28
1980 10/22 – until **1981** 9/17
1984 1/15 – 12/3
1989 7/26 – until **1990** 6/11
1992 10/6 – until **1993** 8/31
1995 12/30 – until **1996** 3/24
1996 6/15 – 11/14
2001 7/8 – 10/14
2001 11/21 – until **2002** 5/24
2004 9/20 – 12/13
2005 3/25 – 8/12
2007 12/14 – until **2008** 2/27
2008 7/28 – 10/18

SATURN CHALLENGING
1944 6/13 – until **1945** 7/12
1950 11/10 – until **1951** 3/19
1951 8/4 – until **1952** 9/17
1958 12/28 – until **1960** 2/21
1960 7/8 – 11/20
1973 7/24 – until **1974** 1/20
1974 4/6 – 8/25
1975 1/10 – 5/13
1980 9/14 – until **1981** 10/24
1988 2/3 – 6/22
1988 11/2 – until **1989** 12/27
2002 10/7 – 10/16
2003 5/27 – until **2004** 6/25
2009 10/21 – until **2010** 4/21
2010 7/8 – 12/7
2011 3/19 – 8/31

URANUS CHALLENGING
1948 8/6 – until **1953** 4/30
1967 12/18 – until **1972** 8/6
1988 1/26 – until **1992** 11/11

NEPTUNE CHALLENGING
1941 11/8 – until **1950** 8/9
1983 3/8 – until **1991** 11/29

PLUTO CHALLENGING
1970 11/15 – until **1978** 8/30
2007 12/30 – Continues

JUPITER SPECIAL
1939 5/7 – 11/14
1939 12/5 – until **1940** 3/14
1951 4/17 – until **1952** 2/24
1963 3/31 – 6/16
1963 10/3 – until **1964** 2/2
1975 3/14 – 5/23
1975 11/27 – 12/24
1987 2/26 – 5/5
1999 2/8 – 4/17
2010 5/30 – 9/16
2011 1/17 – 3/31

SATURN SPECIAL
1938 1/1 – 5/30
1938 10/2 – until **1939** 2/20
1966 6/14 – 8/7
1967 2/24 – until **1968** 4/2
1996 3/30 – until **1997** 5/10
1997 11/3 – until **1998** 1/27

URANUS SPECIAL
2010 5/3 – Continues

19

March 29

SUN: ARIES • DECANATE: ARIES/MARS • DEGREE: 7.5°–8.5 °ARIES • MODE: CARDINAL • ELEMENT: FIRE

Your Personal Powers

Assertive and direct, you can use your insight, quick comprehension, and discriminating mind to achieve success. Your ruling planet, Mars, indicates that you can be daring and enthusiastic with many innovative ideas. Ambitious and determined, your competitive spirit implies that you usually work best when you rise to a challenge and show your courage. Generally thoughtful and reserved, you possess an intuitive sensitivity that works well with your imagination and enterprising plans. You gain power by combining your knowledge, energy, and drive. Your dedication and hard work often result in your being placed in leadership positions. When you lose faith and succumb to worry or skepticism, however, you can become critical or confused and lose some of your power. By staying focused and purposeful you are able to utilize your vision and innate business ability to win friends and achieve material success. Being an idealist, money just for its own sake will not be fulfilling enough for you without projects that stimulate your remarkable mental potential.

Your Powers of Attraction in Relationships

People are drawn to your friendly personality, quick mind, and natural enthusiasm. Although you are often highly sensitive and intuitive, you usually protect yourself by concealing it from others. With a need to be popular, you enjoy social situations and collaborating with people. You may be particularly drawn to hardworking individuals with a sense of the dramatic, or those who possess deep insight. Women can also prove to be especially helpful to you. In relationships, slowly build up trust with others to avoid vacillating between idealistic naivete and skepticism. You can be strong-willed with a need to do things your way and need to beware of a stubborn streak. By developing your patience you are able to establish loving relationships. Usually considerate and supportive, you can attract others with your generosity and passion.

Your attractive qualities: intelligent, knowledgeable, visionary, dynamic, faithful, spiritual, analytical, generous, thoughtful, humanitarian, shrewd, creative, intuitive, inspired, spontaneous, leadership potential, loving, determined, idealistic, passionate

Your less attractive qualities: insecure, nervous, moody, oversensitive, bossy, critical, opinionated, stubborn, selfish, isolated, frustrated, worried, too passionate, confused, skeptical

Your Venus Power

The planet Venus has a great deal of influence on your powers of attraction. Below are four possible Venus types for women and men. To find your Venus you need to go to page 771, where you will find the Venus table and extra information. The planet Mars also affects your powers of attraction. To find your Mars table and interpretation go to page 761.

WOMEN WITH VENUS IN AQUARIUS: When it comes to relationships, others are attracted to your honest, friendly, and easygoing approach. You really enjoy social interaction with others and may develop a genuine concern for humanity. You usually present a tolerant and reasonable front in love situations and attempt to view your relationships objectively. If partners become too demanding, however, you can become stubborn and fixed. Friendship may be even more important for you than sexual compatibility.

MEN WITH VENUS IN AQUARIUS: You are friendly and honest, and people are attracted to your broad-minded approach to life. You usually possess an objective and slightly detached attitude to affairs of the heart. If you are too removed, however, others can misinterpret your behavior as uncaring. It is often more important to you that your love relationships are based on friendship and honesty than intense passion. As you are generally tolerant and liberal, you may be drawn toward less conventional relationships.

WOMEN WITH VENUS IN PISCES: Romantic and idealistic when in love, you can be a sensitive and responsive lover. With your affectionate and impressionable nature you are often attracted to those who understand your sensitivity and share your vision. Being flexible with an impressionable nature helps you to adapt to the needs of others. In your desire to blend with those you love, guard against giving too much of yourself by not defining your boundaries clearly.

MEN WITH VENUS IN PISCES: Romantic and idealistic when in love, you can be a sensitive and responsive lover. Being pliant and flexible with an impressionable nature helps you to adapt to the needs of others. In your desire to blend with those you love, however, guard against not clearly defining your own boundaries. With your affectionate and senti-

mental nature you are often attracted to those who understand your sensitivity and share your vision.

WOMEN WITH VENUS IN ARIES: Self-reliant and strong, you usually want things your way. This can present problems if you refuse to compromise with your partners. Your life lessons in the area of love and relationships often involve patience and learning to trust. When you project the full power of your Venus, you can radiate a charismatic and captivating energy and make a strong impression on others. Independence is often high on your relationship agenda.

MEN WITH VENUS IN ARIES: You are usually inclined to seek a partner who is active, goal-oriented, or decisive. Not known for your patience, you probably seek relationships from youth. You may find that you are more attracted to women who have a daring or adventurous spirit, but in your close relationships you may encounter rivalry or find that both you and your partner want to lead or be the boss. Although you may act rashly, you possess a great deal of magnetism and are capable of demonstrating your love and affection.

WOMEN WITH VENUS IN TAURUS: Warm and affectionate, you are naturally tactile with a love of sensual pleasures. With a streak of the conventional, you love the simple pleasures of life: good food, close friends, and happy relationships. Having an inner strength you can express genuine patience and are often a pillar of support for loved ones and friends. Although you possess endurance be careful not to let this turn to plain stubbornness.

MEN WITH VENUS IN TAURUS: As you yourself may be attractive to the opposite sex, you desire a partner who is sensual and loving or has physical beauty. Needing stability, when faced with changes that are out of your control you may become insecure or possessive. Faithful and loyal, however, you can be affectionate, tactile, and constant in your love. Your own sense of style and love of beauty imply that you can be attracted to creative people, especially in art and music.

To read all about your Outer Planets and work out how to use your personalized timetable, go to Section Three, page 789.

Your Personalized Timetable

JUPITER BENEFICIAL
1938 1/2 – 2/14
1941 6/8 – 7/25
1942 1/4 – 3/9
1943 7/1 – 9/13
1947 10/24 – until 1948 1/5
1949 12/16 – until 1950 1/29
1953 5/22 – 7/5
1955 6/13 – 8/27
1959 2/11 – 4/23
1959 10/5 – 12/19
1961 4/3 – 7/19
1961 11/24 – until 1962 1/12
1965 5/6 – 6/18
1966 9/28 – until 1967 1/15
1967 5/23 – 8/11
1971 1/14 – 6/4
1971 9/12 – 12/4
1973 3/10 – 9/6
1973 10/20 – 12/25
1977 4/18 – 6/1
1978 9/5 – until 1979 2/28
1979 4/21 – 7/26
1982 12/26 – until 1983 11/18
1985 2/20 – 4/14
1985 7/27 – 12/5
1988 8/11 – 11/7
1989 3/29 – 5/16
1990 8/18 – until 1991 7/9
1994 12/9 – until 1995 11/1
1997 2/3 – 3/21
1997 9/13 – 11/1
2000 7/15 – 12/22
2001 2/28 – 4/28
2002 8/2 – 10/29
2003 1/9 – 6/20
2006 11/24 – until 2007 2/14
2007 5/27 – 10/12
2009 1/18 – 3/2
2012 6/25 – Continues

SATURN BENEFICIAL
1942 6/1 – until 1943 5/15
1946 8/3 – until 1947 9/3
1948 3/29 – 5/5
1956 1/13 – 5/13
1956 10/11 – until 1957 12/3
1962 1/29 – until 1963 1/28
1971 7/16 – 11/25
1972 4/4 – 6/24
1975 9/17 – until 1976 1/13
1976 6/5 – 10/29
1976 12/27 – until 1977 7/9
1985 11/17 – until 1987 1/7
1987 7/5 – 10/2
1991 3/7 – 8/2
1991 12/4 – until 1992 3/2
1992 9/6 – 11/23
2001 5/15 – 8/11
2001 11/13 – until 2002 4/27
2005 7/17 – until 2006 8/17

URANUS BENEFICIAL
1942 7/10 – until 1945 6/1
1955 8/26 – until 1959 7/31
1981 2/23 – until 1985 11/3
1996 3/7 – until 1999 11/13

NEPTUNE BENEFICIAL
1970 1/7 – until 1978 10/11
1999 2/24 – until 2004 12/3

PLUTO BENEFICIAL
1938 8/6 – until 1950 6/3
1995 1/20 – until 2002 11/1

JUPITER CHALLENGING
1942 6/10 – 8/22
1943 2/16 – 4/4

1945 8/25 – 11/9
1948 11/15 – until 1949 1/25
1954 5/24 – 8/4
1956 12/13 – until 1957 2/19
1957 8/7 – 10/23
1960 3/2 – 6/9
1960 10/26 – until 1961 1/9
1965 9/22 – 11/16
1966 5/5 – 7/18
1968 11/16 – until 1969 3/30
1969 7/16 – 10/8
1972 2/7 – 7/24
1972 9/26 – 12/24
1977 8/21 – 12/30
1978 4/12 – 7/2
1980 10/27 – until 1981 9/22
1984 1/19 – 12/8
1989 7/31 – until 1990 6/16
1992 10/10 – until 1993 9/5
1996 1/3 – 4/2
1996 6/6 – 11/19
2001 7/13 – until 2002 5/29
2004 9/25 – 12/20
2005 3/17 – 8/18
2007 12/19 – until 2008 3/3
2008 7/20 – 10/26

SATURN CHALLENGING
1944 6/20 – until 1945 7/19
1950 11/21 – until 1951 3/6
1951 8/14 – until 1952 9/25
1959 1/6 – until 1960 3/3
1960 6/24 – 11/30
1973 8/2 – until 1974 1/7
1974 4/19 – 9/4
1974 12/29 – until 1975 5/23
1980 9/22 – until 1981 11/2
1982 5/23 – 7/14
1988 2/14 – 6/9
1988 11/13 – until 1990 1/4
2003 6/4 – until 2004 7/2
2009 10/30 – until 2010 4/6
2010 7/22 – 12/20
2011 3/4 – 9/9

URANUS CHALLENGING
1948 9/1 – until 1953 5/24
1968 9/29 – until 1972 8/28
1988 2/16 – until 1992 12/3

NEPTUNE CHALLENGING
1942 10/5 – until 1950 9/12
1984 1/21 – until 1991 12/27

PLUTO CHALLENGING
1971 10/7 – until 1978 9/26
2008 1/28 – Continues

JUPITER SPECIAL
1939 5/11 – 10/29
1939 12/21 – until 1940 3/18
1951 4/21 – until 1952 2/29
1963 4/4 – 6/23
1963 9/26 – until 1964 2/8
1975 3/19 – 5/28
1975 11/12 – until 1976 1/7
1987 3/3 – 5/9
1999 2/13 – 4/22
2010 6/6 – 9/8
2011 1/23 – 4/5

SATURN SPECIAL
1938 1/15 – 6/11
1938 9/19 – until 1939 3/2
1967 3/4 – until 1968 4/10
1996 4/7 – until 1997 5/19
1997 10/21 – until 1998 2/8

URANUS SPECIAL
2010 5/30 – Continues

♈

March 30

SUN: ARIES • DECANATE: ARIES/MARS • DEGREE: 8°5–9°5 ARIES • MODE: CARDINAL • ELEMENT: FIRE

Your Personal Powers

Sociable and energized, you can be direct, daring, and keen on initiating new projects. You gain power from your enthusiasm, sharp intelligence, and talent for communication. This also suggests that you can sell your many creative ideas or keep people entertained. Although you have natural leadership ability, you also recognize the value of working cooperatively with others and therefore are a good team member. You impress others with your easygoing style but you can lose some of your power if you become stubborn or difficult. Although generally hardworking, you enjoy people and the good life. Your conscientious nature implies that when you evade your responsibilities you are subjecting yourself to worry and anxiety. Ambitious with strong opinions, however, you take pleasure in mental pursuits and work best by following your own unique vision. Blessed with the ability to make important contacts you can succeed in people-related careers. With your strong determination, once you are set on a course of action your inner power comes to the fore.

Your Powers of Attraction in Relationships

Dramatic and stylish, your amiable charm is a quality others find attractive. You need partners who are creative or accomplished in their own right and who share your need for a secure home base. Usually you are friendly, loving, and affectionate, but if your powerful need for love is not fulfilled, resist feeling downhearted and don't resort to escapism or overindulgence in order to compensate. A good conversationalist, you are admired for your sociable and intelligent approach as well your ability to be entertaining. Although you usually enjoy the excitement of the chase in a new relationship, once you settle down you can be loving and caring. With your keen mentality, imagination, and gift for self-expression you have no problem attracting admirers.

Your attractive qualities: creative, leader, fun-loving, loyal, friendly, optimistic, artistic, affectionate, worldly, intuitive, intelligent, responsible, hardworking, generous, perceptive, gift with words, charismatic

Your less attractive qualities: worrier, selfish, lazy, obstinate, inactive, impatient, escapist, nervous, avoider, insecure, depressive, jealous, self-pity, scattered, overindulgent

Your Venus Power

The planet Venus has a great deal of influence on your powers of attraction. Below are four possible Venus types for women and men. To find your Venus you need to go to page 771, where you will find the Venus table and extra information. The planet Mars also affects your powers of attraction. To find your Mars table and interpretation go to page 761.

WOMEN WITH VENUS IN AQUARIUS: When it comes to relationships others are attracted to your honest, friendly, and easygoing approach. You enjoy social interaction and have a genuine concern for others. In fact, at times, your friends may be just as important as your partner. You usually present a tolerant and reasonable front in love situations and attempt to view your relationships objectively. If your partner becomes too demanding, however, you can become stubborn or awkward. Nevertheless, inventive and progressive, you enjoy the company of like-minded people who can share your original ideas.

MEN WITH VENUS IN AQUARIUS: Ideally, in your relationships your lover is also your best friend. Since freedom of expression is a prerequisite to your well-being, you fare better when left alone to do your own thing. You also need a partner who recognizes and appreciates your need for independence. Although usually friendly, at times you can be stubborn or your cool detachment can appear to others as distant or impersonal. Very sociable, however, you particularly enjoy the company of those who share your original, fair-minded, and progressive views.

WOMEN WITH VENUS IN PISCES: In love you are sensitive, tender, and affectionate, experiencing your partner's feelings almost as strongly as your own. Being also imaginative and a visionary, you possess the capabilities to develop both creative gifts as well as deep compassion for others. As you are idealistic when in love, you usually prefer to see only your partner's good points, but be careful that your high expectations do not bring disappointment if you avoid being realistic. Nevertheless, in your relationships with others you can be devoted, loving, and positively enchanting.

MEN WITH VENUS IN PISCES: Being adaptable and sensitive, you are able to intuitively feel the moods of those you love. Although you are receptive to others you can be ambiguous about your own feelings toward your partner. Romantic and kindhearted, you long to be loved but you need to be realistic about your relationships in order to avoid disappoint-

ments. When in love you may idealize your partners and fail to see any faults in their personalities.

WOMEN WITH VENUS IN ARIES: You gain power from your strong individuality, energy, and enthusiasm. Your young-at-heart and spirited approach to relationships adds to your appeal. If you become too impatient or self-absorbed, however, your partnerships are likely to suffer. Nevertheless, you can be creative, sharp, and quick, especially when you are able to share new and exciting projects with your partners. Mischievous, with a love of action, you may even incite them to a playful fight.

MEN WITH VENUS IN ARIES: You are drawn to strong, independent women who can stand up to you. Although you can enthusiastically follow the object of your desire, you may lose power if you allow your forceful emotions to become too dominant. Warm and passionate, you have a side to your nature that longs for new adventures. Romantic and chivalrous, you really enjoy the excitement of the initial chase, but unless you keep the enthusiasm alive and avoid falling into a rut you may become easily bored.

WOMEN WITH VENUS IN TAURUS: Good-natured and romantic, you have a highly developed sense of touch that particularly responds to massage, hugs, and all things physical. Being friendly and affectionate, you enjoy socializing and are able to put others at their ease. Although you can be lavish toward your partners you may have to be careful that you do not overdo things. With your natural sense of beauty and harmony, your charm can always attract others.

MEN WITH VENUS IN TAURUS: Attractive and affectionate, in relationships you are often faithful with a conservative approach. You are usually drawn to warmhearted partners with whom you can share a familiar routine as well as life's pleasures and comforts. Seeking a partner who is dependable or reassuring, you often put security high on your priority list when looking for love. Your sociability and friendliness usually make you popular and partners often admire your practicality and good sense of values.

To read all about your Outer Planets and work out how to use your personalized timetable, go to Section Three, page 789.

To read all about your Outer Planets and work out how to use your personalized timetable, go to Section Three, page 789.

♈

Your Personalized Timetable

JUPITER BENEFICIAL
1938 1/7 – 2/18
1941 6/12 – 7/30
1941 12/26 – until 1942 3/18
1943 7/5 – 9/18
1944 4/10 – 4/13
1947 10/29 – until 1948 1/10
1949 12/20 – until 1950 2/2
1953 5/26 – 7/10
1955 6/18 – 8/31
1959 2/22 – 4/12
1959 10/11 – 12/24
1961 4/10 – 7/11
1961 11/30 – until 1962 1/16
1965 5/10 – 6/22
1966 10/4 – until 1967 1/8
1967 5/29 – 8/15
1971 1/20 – 5/27
1971 9/19 – 12/8
1973 3/15 – 8/26
1973 10/31 – 12/30
1977 4/23 – 6/6
1978 9/11 – until 1979 2/17
1979 5/1 – 7/30
1982 12/31 – until 1983 11/22
1985 2/24 – 4/22
1985 7/19 – 12/10
1988 8/19 – 10/30
1989 4/4 – 5/21
1990 8/23 – until 1991 7/14
1994 12/14 – until 1995 11/6
1997 2/7 – 3/26
1997 9/2 – 11/12
2000 7/21 – 12/14
2001 3/8 – 5/3
2002 8/6 – 11/9
2002 12/29 – until 2003 6/26
2006 11/28 – until 2007 2/22
2007 5/19 – 10/18
2009 1/22 – 3/7
2012 6/30 – Continues

SATURN BENEFICIAL
1942 6/9 – until 1943 5/23
1946 8/10 – until 1947 9/11
1948 3/9 – 5/25
1956 1/25 – 4/29
1956 10/21 – until 1957 12/11
1962 2/7 – until 1963 2/5
1971 7/27 – 11/13
1972 4/13 – 7/2
1973 1/23 – 3/6
1975 9/29 – until 1976 1/1
1976 6/15 – until 1977 7/17
1985 11/25 – until 1987 1/16
1987 6/20 – 10/15
1991 3/18 – 7/19
1991 12/14 – until 1992 3/12
1992 8/22 – 12/7
2001 5/23 – 8/26
2001 10/29 – until 2002 5/5
2005 7/24 – until 2006 8/24

URANUS BENEFICIAL
1942 8/5 – until 1946 3/30
1955 9/14 – until 1960 5/10
1981 12/3 – until 1985 11/21
1996 4/2 – until 1999 12/16

NEPTUNE BENEFICIAL
1970 12/4 – until 1978 11/13
1999 4/3 – until 2005 1/7

PLUTO BENEFICIAL
1938 9/16 – until 1950 7/16
1995 12/7 – until 2002 11/29

JUPITER CHALLENGING
1942 6/15 – 8/28
1943 2/5 – 4/15
1945 8/30 – 11/14
1948 11/20 – until 1949 1/30

1954 5/29 – 8/8
1956 12/25 – until 1957 2/7
1957 8/12 – 10/28
1960 3/9 – 6/1
1960 11/1 – until 1961 1/13
1965 10/7 – 11/1
1966 5/11 – 7/23
1968 11/22 – until 1969 3/22
1969 7/22 – 10/12
1972 2/12 – 7/14
1972 10/5 – 12/28
1977 8/27 – 12/23
1978 4/19 – 7/7
1980 11/1 – until 1981 5/7
1981 6/16 – 9/27
1984 1/24 – 12/12
1989 8/5 – until 1990 2/12
1990 3/8 – 6/20
1992 10/15 – until 1993 9/10
1996 1/8 – 4/15
1996 5/24 – 11/24
2001 7/17 – until 2002 6/3
2004 9/30 – 12/29
2005 3/8 – 8/24
2007 12/23 – until 2008 3/9
2008 7/12 – 11/2

SATURN CHALLENGING
1944 6/28 – until 1945 7/27
1950 12/4 – until 1951 2/20
1951 8/23 – until 1952 10/3
1959 1/14 – 8/8
1959 10/1 – until 1960 3/17
1960 6/9 – 12/9
1973 8/11 – 12/25
1974 4/30 – 9/16
1974 12/16 – until 1975 6/1
1980 9/29 – until 1981 11/10
1982 5/4 – 8/1
1988 2/27 – 5/25
1988 11/22 – until 1990 1/13
2003 6/12 – until 2004 7/10
2009 11/8 – until 2010 3/25
2010 8/2 – until 2011 1/12
2011 2/9 – 9/17

URANUS CHALLENGING
1949 6/27 – until 1953 6/12
1968 10/15 – until 1972 9/15
1988 12/20 – until 1992 12/21

NEPTUNE CHALLENGING
1942 11/3 – until 1951 8/1
1984 2/26 – until 1992 11/23

PLUTO CHALLENGING
1971 11/4 – until 1979 8/14
2008 3/14 – Continues

JUPITER SPECIAL
1939 5/17 – 10/19
1939 12/31 – until 1940 3/23
1951 4/26 – until 1952 3/5
1963 4/8 – 7/1
1963 9/18 – until 1964 2/13
1975 3/23 – 6/2
1975 11/3 – until 1976 1/16
1987 3/7 – 5/14
1999 2/17 – 4/26
2010 6/14 – 8/31
2011 1/28 – 4/9

SATURN SPECIAL
1938 1/27 – 6/26
1938 9/3 – until 1939 3/10
1967 3/12 – until 1968 4/18
1996 4/16 – 11/11
1996 12/25 – until 1997 5/29
1997 10/8 – until 1998 2/19

URANUS SPECIAL
2011 3/30 – Continues

March 31

SUN: ARIES · DECANATE: LEO/SUN · DEGREE: 9.5°–10.5 ARIES° · MODE: CARDINAL · ELEMENT: FIRE

Your Personal Powers

Energetic and discerning, you are able to impress others with your pragmatic skills, determination, and assertive personality. Strong-willed with quick instincts you are also daring and keen on acquiring practical knowledge. With your need for self-expression you gain power from your good conversation skills and constructive approach. Usually you are able to combine your organizational abilities and decisive manner to appear confident. Inner insecurities imply that you lose some of your power to a hidden need for approval or respect. When inspired and positive you can be versatile and productive with an ability to extensively educate yourself in your particular field of interest. In order to keep yourself mentally stimulated and to stop from being bored, you need to channel your dynamic energies into projects that involve variety or opportunities to explore new territories. When you become restless and impatient, however, this may cause you to lose power to arrogance or stubbornness. Full of original ideas, if you patiently adhere to a set goal or course of action you can achieve prosperity and succeed.

Your Powers of Attraction in Relationships

People are attracted to your sociable personality, your quick intelligence, and your ability to relate to people on their own level. Although you can be open about your beliefs, you are often more discreet about your personal relationships. Being restless, you may encounter a conflict between your desire for personal freedom and your determination to build a solid foundation in life. This can sometimes lead to your having many friends but few committed relationships. You are usually attracted to strong-willed individuals with sharp insight. Marriage usually works better for you if you find someone who is independent and enterprising. Interested in improvements, you may be drawn to those who are working on their own self-development. Usually sincere and helpful, your enthusiastic approach to life will always attract others.

Your attractive qualities: practical, energetic, clever, creative, hardworking, good organizer, self-assured, persevering, responsible, enduring, good conversationalist, responsible, successful in business, adventurous, daring, versatile, flexible, agreeable

Your less attractive qualities: impatient, cynical, selfish, insecure, suspicious, discouraged, lack of ambition, restless, dogmatic, possessive, stubborn, jealous, unforgiving

Your Venus Power

The planet Venus has a great deal of influence on your powers of attraction. Below are four possible Venus types for women and men. To find your Venus you need to go to page 771, where you will find the Venus table and extra information. The planet Mars also affects your powers of attraction. To find your Mars table and interpretation go to page 761.

WOMEN WITH VENUS IN AQUARIUS: Sociable and gracious, you are usually sincere and are capable of showing attributes of real tolerance and liberalism. Although you are keen on forming relationships you also like to have freedom and act independently. Your intimate partnerships need to be founded on true friendship. Full of bright and progressive ideas, you can express yourself better when you are free and unrestricted. An ability to think in a dispassionate way suggests that you can stay detached. Your love of freedom also implies that you can be loving and loyal without smothering your partner.

MEN WITH VENUS IN AQUARIUS: You are sociable and open-minded, and people are attracted by your friendly and relaxed style. Being independent, you value freedom-loving partners who give you the space to be yourself. Others sometimes interpret your detachment as being emotionally cool, but they may not understand your progressive views on relationships. Friendship can sometimes be even more important than earthly passion. Ideally your partners can share your ideas on life and possess as strong a sense of originality as your own. Not easily ruffled, you can deal well with difficult situations or moody partners.

WOMEN WITH VENUS IN PISCES: As a romantic and idealistic individual you can be both loving and giving. In relationships you may need to balance the practical with the charitable. While making allowances and sacrifices is understandable in a loving relationship, playing the martyr is often a state of romantic illusion that can lead to self-deception. Your benevolence and sacrifices in the right relationship nonetheless make you a partner who is devoted, kind, and compassionate. Subtle, sensitive, and alluring, you make a sensual and caring partner.

MEN WITH VENUS IN PISCES: As a romantic and generous person you are attracted to imaginative or artistic part-

ners who can be sensitive and generous. While you are willing to make allowances for your loved ones, playing the martyr in relationships can lead to allowing others to take advantage of your kind nature. Nevertheless, giving and loving, you are usually willing to forgive your partner's shortcomings.

WOMEN WITH VENUS IN ARIES: Idealistic, passionate, and adventurous, you are direct in your dealings with others. When you are attracted to a person you usually take the initiative and use your people skills to make things happen. In close relationships you are not afraid to confront your other half. This self-assertiveness is positive if differences can be brought into the open through diplomacy and compromise. Independent and spirited, you enjoy your freedom.

MEN WITH VENUS IN ARIES: As you often have the courage and strength to initiate situations, you like to take the lead and let others follow. With your unconscious desire for conquest you may also have to beware of being competitive with your partners. Nevertheless, you are drawn to direct and strong-willed women who can share your love of action and enthusiasm for life. When you are feeling good, you can be charming and enthusiastic in romantic situations with an entertaining and spontaneous spirit.

WOMEN WITH VENUS IN TAURUS: Warm and affectionate, you are drawn to partners with whom you can share life's simple comforts. With a need for stability and security or an appreciation of earthly pleasures you may have to avoid overindulgence or becoming too preoccupied with material concerns. Nevertheless, your sociability and friendliness usually makes you popular. You need a partner who can also share your appreciation of beauty and style.

MEN WITH VENUS IN TAURUS: As well as attracting people with your warm personality, you possess an innate sense of the value of material possessions. Keeping yourself stylish and having an attractive home can therefore be important to you. You are naturally attracted to practical yet sensual women who understand your need for comfort, security, and the pleasures and luxuries of life. Naturally affectionate, you enjoy socializing but can make a loyal and loving partner.

To read all about your Outer Planets and work out how to use your personalized timetable, go to Section Three, page 789.

Your Personalized Timetable

JUPITER BENEFICIAL
1938 1/11 – 2/22
1941 6/17 – 8/5
1941 12/18 – until 1942 3/25
1943 7/10 – 9/23
1944 3/18 – 5/8
1947 11/2 – until 1948 1/14
1949 12/25 – until 1950 2/6
1953 5/31 – 7/14
1955 6/23 – 9/5
1959 10/16 – 12/28
1961 4/18 – 7/2
1961 12/5 – until 1962 1/20
1965 5/14 – 6/27
1966 10/12 – 12/30
1967 6/4 – 8/20
1971 1/27 – 5/19
1971 9/25 – 12/12
1973 3/20 – 8/16
1973 11/9 – until 1974 1/3
1977 4/27 – 6/10
1978 9/16 – until 1979 2/9
1979 5/10 – 8/4
1983 1/5 – 7/3
1983 8/23 – 11/27
1985 3/1 – 4/30
1985 7/10 – 12/16
1988 8/29 – 10/20
1989 4/9 – 5/25
1990 8/28 – until 1991 7/19
1994 12/19 – until 1995 11/10
1997 2/12 – 4/1
1997 8/25 – 11/20
2000 7/26 – 12/6
2001 3/15 – 5/8
2002 8/11 – 11/29
2002 12/10 – until 2003 7/1
2006 12/3 – until 2007 3/3
2007 5/10 – 10/23
2009 1/27 – 3/11
2012 7/4 – Continues

SATURN BENEFICIAL
1942 6/17 – until 1943 5/31
1946 8/18 – until 1947 3/25
1947 4/13 – 9/20
1948 2/24 – 6/8
1956 2/10 – 4/12
1956 10/30 – until 1957 12/19
1962 2/15 – 9/21
1962 10/27 – until 1963 2/13
1971 8/8 – 10/30
1972 4/22 – 7/10
1973 1/4 – 3/24
1975 10/13 – 12/17
1976 6/23 – until 1977 7/25
1985 12/4 – until 1987 1/26
1987 6/6 – 10/26
1991 3/30 – 7/5
1991 12/24 – until 1992 3/22
1992 8/8 – 12/18
2001 5/30 – until 2002 5/13
2005 8/1 – until 2006 9/1

URANUS BENEFICIAL
1943 6/2 – until 1946 4/24
1955 10/14 – until 1960 6/14
1981 12/20 – until 1985 12/7
1997 1/31 – until 2000 1/5

NEPTUNE BENEFICIAL
1971 1/2 – until 1979 10/3
2000 2/20 – until 2005 11/23

PLUTO BENEFICIAL
1939 8/30 – until 1951 6/22
1996 1/3 – until 2003 10/23

JUPITER CHALLENGING
1942 6/19 – 9/2
1943 1/27 – 4/24

1945 9/4 – 11/19
1946 5/26 – 7/4
1948 11/25 – until 1949 2/3
1954 6/2 – 8/13
1957 8/18 – 11/2
1960 3/19 – 5/22
1960 11/6 – until 1961 1/18
1966 5/16 – 7/27
1968 11/29 – until 1969 3/15
1969 7/29 – 10/17
1972 2/18 – 7/6
1972 10/13 – until 1973 1/1
1977 9/2 – 12/15
1978 4/25 – 7/11
1980 11/7 – until 1981 4/24
1981 6/29 – 10/1
1984 1/29 – 12/17
1989 8/10 – until 1990 1/28
1990 3/24 – 6/25
1992 10/20 – until 1993 9/15
1996 1/12 – 11/29
2001 7/22 – until 2002 6/8
2004 10/4 – until 2005 1/10
2005 2/24 – 8/29
2007 12/27 – until 2008 3/16
2008 7/4 – 11/8

SATURN CHALLENGING
1944 7/6 – until 1945 8/4
1946 3/11 – 3/29
1950 12/24 – until 1951 1/31
1951 9/1 – until 1952 10/12
1959 1/23 – 7/20
1959 10/19 – until 1960 4/5
1960 5/19 – 12/18
1973 8/22 – 12/13
1974 5/10 – 9/30
1974 12/1 – until 1975 6/10
1980 10/8 – until 1981 11/19
1982 4/20 – 8/14
1988 3/17 – 5/6
1988 12/1 – until 1990 1/21
2003 6/19 – until 2004 7/18
2009 11/19 – until 2010 3/12
2010 8/12 – until 2011 9/26

URANUS CHALLENGING
1949 7/14 – until 1953 6/29
1968 11/2 – until 1972 10/1
1989 1/5 – until 1993 1/7

NEPTUNE CHALLENGING
1942 12/26 – until 1951 9/8
1985 1/16 – until 1992 12/23

PLUTO CHALLENGING
1971 12/29 – until 1979 9/14
2009 1/23 – Continues

JUPITER SPECIAL
1939 5/22 – 10/11
1940 1/7 – 3/27
1951 4/30 – until 1952 3/9
1963 4/12 – 7/10
1963 9/8 – until 1964 2/18
1975 3/27 – 6/8
1975 10/25 – until 1976 1/24
1987 3/11 – 5/18
1999 2/22 – 4/30
2010 6/24 – 8/21
2011 2/2 – 4/13

SATURN SPECIAL
1938 2/6 – 7/31
1938 8/2 – until 1939 3/18
1967 3/20 – until 1968 4/26
1996 4/25 – 10/23
1997 1/12 – 6/9
1997 9/25 – until 1998 2/28

URANUS SPECIAL
2011 4/17 – Continues

♈

25

April 1

Your Personal Powers

Intelligent and creative, your personal powers include a fine mind and good intuition. Your ruling planet, Mars, indicates that although you are introspective you prefer to keep active and enjoy exploring new interests or projects. Ambitious and goal-oriented yet sensitive, you gain power by developing your independent attitude and original ideas. Empowering yourself to express your ideas confidently and build a strong sense of self-identity can be a major part of your life lessons. This confidence can also help you reach out for leadership positions. Others usually respect you for your capable and determined approach to life. You also possess inner wisdom and natural organizational or administrative abilities that can bring you recognition and success. If you become too self-centered, skeptical, or critical, however, you can lose some of your charm and undermine your achievements. Developing more faith and trust in your spirit enables you to flow more easily with what life has to offer. Through patience, calmness, and thoughtfulness you are able to impress others with your many gifts and talents.

Your Powers of Attraction in Relationships

Others are attracted to your responsible attitude and sharp awareness. Being sensitive, you can often work quietly behind the scenes, but you really attract others when you push yourself out into the limelight. You usually admire those with good intelligence who can hold their own in a serious conversation. As you seek a partner you can admire and respect, it is also important that this person be strong-willed and confident. You may, however, need to avoid using your own will to become bossy or impatient. With your keen, discerning nature and love of the original, your relationships may be connected to your stimulating interests. Although you can be very sensitive, at times you may repress your feelings and become undemonstrative or withdraw. Nevertheless, you can be a firm and loyal friend and build lasting relationships.

Your attractive qualities: intelligent, creative, progressive, forceful, optimistic, strong convictions, competitive, freedom-loving, sociable, leader, independent, knowledgeable, insightful, analytical, friendly, sensitive

Your less attractive qualities: dependent, egocentric, cynical, domineering, jealous, fearful, prideful, cold, argumentative, withdrawn, obstinate, weak, unstable, impatient

Your Venus Power

The planet Venus has a great deal of influence on your powers of attraction. Below are four possible Venus types for women and men. To find your Venus you need to go to page 771, where you will find the Venus table and extra information. The planet Mars also affects your powers of attraction. To find your Mars table and interpretation go to page 761.

WOMEN WITH VENUS IN AQUARIUS: You usually have a modern outlook on love and are open to new or current lifestyles. Your intuitive abilities, communal sense, and people skills often allow you to see deeper into human intentions and read telepathically other people's thoughts. Although you are usually group-oriented, you are drawn to strong individuals within the group who are independent and self-motivated. You are more inclined to choose a partner who is unconventional or freedom-loving. Conscious of your social standing, however, you want someone who can relate well to your friends.

MEN WITH VENUS IN AQUARIUS: Although independent, you often enjoy being part of a group. The partners you frequently attract are often nonconformists or free spirits. As an individualist you may not find it easy to settle into a routine or an entirely mundane type of relationship. You value your freedom and can sometimes be cool and detached. Friendship is important to you as you enjoy sharing your progressive ideas.

WOMEN WITH VENUS IN PISCES: Being sensitive to affairs of the heart, when you care for someone you can feel their emotions and sense their every mood. Their goals can even become as important as your own. This empathy indicates that you can love on an unselfish level, but you may have to guard against giving too much, especially to those who do not reciprocate. As you are seductive and captivating, partners can be fascinated by your subtle charms and attracted by your caring and affectionate nature.

MEN WITH VENUS IN PISCES: The combination of your emotional subtlety and charm can make you very alluring when dealing with affairs of the heart. Perceptive and impressionable, you have an easygoing style in your relationships, usually preferring to avoid ugly confrontation. You are drawn

to partners who have a touch of glamour and are sensitive to the needs of others. Alternatively, they could be visionaries with a rich imagination, like yours, who will know how to keep you enchanted. With your insight you have the ability to observe the subtle moods of your partner.

WOMEN WITH VENUS IN ARIES: Idealistic, passionate, and adventurous, you are direct in your dealings with others. When you are attracted to a person, you usually take the initiative and use your people skills to make things happen. In close relationships you are not afraid to confront your other half. This self-assertiveness is positive if differences can be brought into the open through diplomacy and compromise. Independent and spirited, you enjoy your freedom.

MEN WITH VENUS IN ARIES: You are usually inclined to seek a partner who is active, goal-oriented, or decisive. Not known for your patience, you probably seek relationships early in life. You may find that you are attracted more to women who have a daring or adventurous spirit, but in your close relationships you may encounter rivalry or find that both you and your partner want to lead or be the boss. Although you may act rashly, you possess a great deal of magnetism and are capable of demonstrating your love and affection.

WOMEN WITH VENUS IN TAURUS: Demonstrative and affectionate, you are naturally tactile with a love of sensual pleasures. With a streak of the conventional, you love the simple pleasures of life: good food, close friends, and happy relationships. Although you possess endurance be careful not to let this turn into plain stubbornness. Having inner strength, you can express genuine patience and are often a pillar of support for loved ones and friends.

MEN WITH VENUS IN TAURUS: Although you are usually drawn to sensual and physically beautiful individuals, you also want a partner who is reliable and loyal. When in love you enjoy buying your partner things of quality that will grow in value or useful things of a practical nature. You also love to socialize and entertain, particularly in luxurious surroundings. Affectionate and caring, you are often attracted to people who are creative or have artistic talents.

To read all about your Outer Planets and work out how to use your personalized timetable, go to Section Three, page 789.

Your Personalized Timetable

JUPITER BENEFICIAL
1938 1/15 – 2/27
1941 6/21 – 8/10
1941 12/11 – until 1942 4/1
1943 7/14 – 9/28
1944 3/7 – 5/19
1947 11/7 – until 1948 1/19
1949 12/29 – until 1950 2/10
1953 6/4 – 7/19
1955 6/28 – 9/10
1959 10/21 – until 1960 1/2
1961 4/29 – 6/21
1961 12/10 – until 1962 1/25
1965 5/19 – 7/1
1966 10/22 – 12/21
1967 6/9 – 8/24
1971 2/3 – 5/11
1971 10/1 – 12/17
1973 3/26 – 8/8
1973 11/16 – until 1974 1/8
1977 5/2 – 6/14
1978 9/22 – until 1979 2/1
1979 5/17 – 8/8
1983 1/10 – 6/22
1983 9/3 – 12/1
1985 3/6 – 5/11
1985 6/29 – 12/21
1988 9/17 – 10/1
1989 4/14 – 5/29
1990 9/2 – until 1991 7/23
1994 12/23 – until 1995 11/15
1997 2/16 – 4/6
1997 8/17 – 11/27
2000 8/1 – 11/29
2001 3/22 – 5/12
2002 8/15 – until 2003 7/6
2006 12/7 – until 2007 3/15
2007 4/27 – 10/29
2009 1/31 – 3/16
2012 7/9 – Continues

SATURN BENEFICIAL
1942 6/25 – until 1943 1/15
1943 2/27 – 6/7
1946 8/27 – until 1947 2/27
1947 5/8 – 9/29
1948 2/11 – 6/19
1956 11/7 – until 1957 12/28
1962 2/24 – 8/30
1962 11/17 – until 1963 2/22
1971 8/26 – 10/12
1972 4/30 – 7/19
1972 12/22 – until 1973 4/6
1976 7/1 – until 1977 8/2
1985 12/12 – until 1987 2/7
1987 5/24 – 11/5
1991 4/15 – 6/18
1992 1/2 – 4/2
1992 7/26 – 12/28
2001 6/7 – until 2002 5/21
2005 8/9 – until 2006 9/9
2007 3/19 – 5/21

URANUS BENEFICIAL
1943 6/19 – until 1946 5/13
1956 8/1 – until 1960 7/4
1982 1/7 – until 1986 10/6
1997 2/17 – until 2000 1/23

NEPTUNE BENEFICIAL
1971 2/21 – until 1979 11/10
2000 3/24 – until 2006 1/2

PLUTO BENEFICIAL
1940 8/14 – until 1951 7/28
1996 2/17 – until 2003 11/22

JUPITER CHALLENGING
1942 6/23 – 9/8

JUPITER BENEFICIAL (cont.)
1943 1/20 – 5/2
1945 9/8 – 11/24
1946 5/13 – 7/17
1948 11/29 – until 1949 2/8
1954 6/7 – 8/18
1957 8/23 – 11/7
1960 4/1 – 5/9
1960 11/11 – until 1961 1/22
1966 5/20 – 8/1
1968 12/6 – until 1969 3/7
1969 8/4 – 10/22
1972 2/24 – 6/28
1972 10/20 – until 1973 1/6
1977 9/9 – 12/8
1978 4/30 – 7/15
1980 11/12 – until 1981 4/15
1981 7/9 – 10/6
1984 2/3 – 12/21
1989 8/15 – until 1990 1/18
1990 4/3 – 6/29
1992 10/25 – until 1993 9/20
1996 1/16 – 12/7
2001 7/26 – until 2002 6/12
2004 10/9 – until 2005 9/3
2008 1/1 – 3/23
2008 6/26 – 11/14

SATURN CHALLENGING
1944 7/13 – until 1945 8/12
1946 2/13 – 4/23
1951 9/9 – until 1952 10/20
1959 2/2 – 7/6
1959 11/1 – until 1960 12/27
1973 9/3 – 11/30
1974 5/19 – until 1975 6/18
1980 10/16 – until 1981 5/31
1981 6/10 – 11/29
1982 4/7 – 8/25
1988 12/10 – until 1990 1/30
1990 9/3 – 10/12
2003 6/27 – until 2004 7/25
2009 12/1 – until 2010 2/26
2010 8/22 – until 2011 10/4

URANUS CHALLENGING
1949 8/1 – until 1954 4/3
1968 11/23 – until 1973 7/11
1989 1/23 – until 1993 11/10

NEPTUNE CHALLENGING
1943 10/30 – until 1952 7/18
1985 2/17 – until 1993 11/18

PLUTO CHALLENGING
1972 10/25 – until 1980 7/12
2009 3/3 – Continues

JUPITER SPECIAL
1939 5/28 – 10/3
1940 1/14 – 3/31
1951 5/5 – until 1952 3/13
1963 4/17 – 7/24
1963 8/26 – until 1964 2/23
1975 3/31 – 6/23
1975 10/18 – until 1976 1/31
1987 3/15 – 5/23
1999 2/26 – 5/4
2010 7/8 – 8/7
2011 2/7 – 4/17

SATURN SPECIAL
1938 2/16 – until 1939 3/27
1967 3/28 – until 1968 5/4
1968 12/2 – until 1969 1/9
1996 5/4 – 10/9
1997 1/25 – 6/22
1997 9/11 – until 1998 3/9

URANUS SPECIAL
2011 5/7 – Continues

♈

27

April 2

Your Personal Powers

Among your personal powers are originality and a progressive attitude. You gain power by combining your unique awareness, charming personality, and sensitivity with your ambitious nature. Your ruling planet, Mars, indicates that you enjoy exploring new interests and do not like to be tied down. Although adventurous and pioneering, with a need for action and excitement, you equally possess a strong desire for peace and harmony that can leave you just as happy to stay at home in congenial surroundings. If this dichotomy becomes too difficult it can lead to your losing power through anxiety, restlessness, or verbally taking out your frustrations on others. With a desire for worldly achievement, you can utilize your personal powers of perseverance, creativity, and mental quickness to achieve success. Beneath your fair and amiable exterior, you can be hardworking and determined. Since collaborating with others is essential to your success, you empower yourself by using your people skills and diplomacy. With self-discipline and patience, however, you are able to make the most of your exceptional potential.

Your Powers of Attraction in Relationships

Others are attracted to your firm strength and receptive personality. A good team member, you attract others with your ability to be considerate, friendly, and generous. You fare well in partnerships or cooperative ventures where you are able to utilize your innate understanding of people. Although being sympathetic to the needs of others can make you popular, avoid dependent situations as they can make you feel frustrated or disappointed. You tend to admire those who are mentally sharp and success-oriented as they stimulate your natural enthusiasm. With your strong need for love and security you require a partner who understands your desire for a stable and harmonious home environment. Showing willingness to work at your relationships, your sensitivity and idealism can make you caring and responsible.

Your attractive qualities: popular, kindhearted, subtle, enterprising, tactful, strong-willed, clever, responsible, hardworking, considerate, home-loving, astute, intuitive, refined, caring, sensitive, creative, active, sociable

Your less attractive qualities: egotistical, problems with confidence, lethargic, restless, moody, oversensitive, stubborn, interfering, arrogant, discouraged, impatient, headstrong

Your Venus Power

The planet Venus has a great deal of influence on your powers of attraction. Below are four possible Venus types for women and men. To find your Venus you need to go to page 771, where you will find the Venus table and extra information. The planet Mars also affects your powers of attraction. To find your Mars table and interpretation go to page 761.

WOMEN WITH VENUS IN AQUARIUS: You attract and impress others with your friendly approach and progressive ideas. As you are usually independent and easygoing, you value freedom within a relationship. A good companion, with a sense of your own person, you enjoy socializing, especially with people who are original, cosmopolitan, and have a strong sense of individuality. Although being friendly and detached usually serves you well, avoid losing touch with your emotions. You usually prefer the company of those who have innovative or progressive views.

MEN WITH VENUS IN AQUARIUS: Sociable and open-minded, you attract people with your friendly and easygoing style. Being independent, you value freedom-loving partners who give you the space to be yourself. Other people can sometimes interpret your detachment as being emotionally cool, but they admire your objectivity and humanitarian inclinations. You are attracted to intelligent individuals who are as truthful and direct as you, but above all they must be true friends. Ideally your partner shares your liberal views on life and possesses a strong sense of individuality.

WOMEN WITH VENUS IN PISCES: Romantic and impressionable, you are a caring and loving individual with a dreamy nature. In relationships you are often attracted to idealistic, compassionate, or sympathetic individuals who have imagination or a strong romantic sense. A tendency to be sensitive to others suggests that you are intuitive and aware of people's inner feelings. Be careful therefore not to get caught in other people's dramas or play the rescuer too often.

MEN WITH VENUS IN PISCES: In love you are sensitive, tender, and affectionate, experiencing your partner's feelings almost as strongly as your own. Being also imaginative and visionary, you possess the capability to develop deep compas-

sion for others. As you are idealistic when in love, you usually prefer to see only your partner's good points, but be careful that your high expectations do not bring disappointment if you avoid harsh reality. Nevertheless, in your relationships with others, you can be devoted, loving, and positively enchanting.

WOMEN WITH VENUS IN ARIES: You gain power from your strong individuality, energy, and enthusiasm. Your young-at-heart and spirited approach to relationships adds to your appeal. If you become too impatient or self-absorbed, however, your partnerships are likely to suffer. Nevertheless, you can be creative, sharp, and quick, especially when you are able to share new and exciting projects with your partners. Mischievous, with a love of action, you may even incite them to a playful fight.

MEN WITH VENUS IN ARIES: You are drawn to strong, independent women who can stand up to you. Although you can enthusiastically follow the object of your desire, you may lose power if you allow your forceful emotions to become too dominant. Warm and passionate, you have a side to your nature that longs for new adventures. Romantic and chivalrous, you really enjoy the excitement of the initial chase, but unless you keep the enthusiasm alive and avoid falling into a rut you may become easily bored.

WOMEN WITH VENUS IN TAURUS: For your ideal relationship you seek partners who are both financially secure and demonstrative with their affections. With these thoughts in mind, you are likely to also want a partner who is refined yet pragmatic, or someone concerned with safeguarding your future. Although you have a stubborn streak, you can be loving and affectionate in your relationships. With your good sense of style, you may be attracted to the arts, music, and luxury items.

MEN WITH VENUS IN TAURUS: As you yourself may be attractive to the opposite sex, you desire a partner who is sensual and loving or who has physical beauty. Needing stability, when faced with changes that are out of your control you may become insecure or possessive. Your own sense of style and your love of beauty imply that you can be attracted to creative people, especially those in art and music. Faithful and loyal, you can be affectionate, tactile, and constant in your love.

To read all about your Outer Planets and work out how to use your personalized timetable, go to Section Three, page 789.

Your Personalized Timetable

JUPITER BENEFICIAL
1938 1/19 – 3/3
1941 6/26 – 8/17
1941 12/4 – until 1942 4/7
1943 7/19 – 10/4
1944 2/28 – 5/28
1947 11/11 – until 1948 1/24
1948 7/22 – 9/9
1950 1/3 – 2/14
1953 6/8 – 7/24
1954 1/22 – 3/1
1955 7/2 – 9/14
1959 10/26 – until 1960 1/6
1961 5/16 – 6/3
1961 12/15 – until 1962 1/29
1965 5/23 – 7/5
1966 11/4 – 12/8
1967 6/15 – 8/29
1971 2/11 – 5/3
1971 10/7 – 12/21
1973 4/1 – 8/1
1973 11/23 – until 1974 1/12
1977 5/6 – 6/18
1978 9/28 – until 1979 1/24
1979 5/24 – 8/13
1983 1/16 – 6/13
1983 9/12 – 12/6
1985 3/10 – 12/26
1989 4/19 – 6/2
1990 9/7 – until 1991 3/13
1991 4/16 – 7/28
1994 12/28 – until 1995 11/20
1997 2/20 – 4/13
1997 8/9 – 12/3
2000 8/7 – 11/21
2001 3/28 – 5/17
2002 8/20 – until 2003 7/11
2006 12/12 – until 2007 11/3
2009 2/4 – 3/21
2012 7/14 – Continues

SATURN BENEFICIAL
1942 7/3 – 12/28
1943 3/17 – 6/15
1946 9/4 – until 1947 2/13
1947 5/22 – 10/10
1948 1/30 – 6/29
1956 11/16 – until 1958 1/6
1958 7/20 – 9/26
1962 3/5 – 8/15
1962 12/1 – until 1963 3/2
1963 9/25 – 11/16
1972 5/8 – 7/29
1972 12/10 – until 1973 4/17
1976 7/9 – until 1977 8/10
1985 12/21 – until 1986 7/3
1986 9/10 – until 1987 2/21
1987 5/8 – 11/15
1992 1/11 – 4/15
1992 7/11 – until 1993 1/7
2001 6/15 – until 2002 5/29
2005 8/16 – until 2006 9/18
2007 3/3 – 6/5

URANUS BENEFICIAL
1943 7/8 – until 1946 5/30
1956 8/17 – until 1960 7/22
1982 1/31 – until 1986 10/30
1997 3/9 – until 2000 11/11

NEPTUNE BENEFICIAL
1971 12/29 – until 1980 9/20
2001 2/15 – until 2006 1/30

PLUTO BENEFICIAL
1940 9/27 – until 1952 7/5
1996 12/21 – until 2004 10/11

JUPITER CHALLENGING
1942 6/28 – 9/14

1943 1/12 – 5/8
1945 9/13 – 11/30
1946 5/3 – 7/27
1948 12/4 – until **1949** 2/12
1954 6/11 – 8/23
1955 3/8 – 3/25
1957 8/28 – 11/11
1960 11/16 – until **1961** 1/26
1966 5/25 – 8/5
1968 12/15 – until **1969** 2/26
1969 8/9 – 10/26
1972 3/1 – 6/20
1972 10/26 – until **1973** 1/10
1977 9/17 – 11/29
1978 5/6 – 7/20
1980 11/18 – until **1981** 4/6
1981 7/17 – 10/10
1984 2/8 – 8/6
1984 9/22 – 12/25
1989 8/21 – until **1990** 1/10
1990 4/11 – 7/4
1992 10/30 – until **1993** 9/25
1996 1/21 – 12/8
2001 7/31 – until **2002** 6/17
2004 10/13 – until **2005** 9/8
2008 1/5 – 3/31
2008 6/18 – 11/19

SATURN CHALLENGING
1944 7/21 – until **1945** 2/20
1945 3/19 – 8/21
1946 1/30 – 5/7
1951 9/17 – until **1952** 10/28
1959 2/12 – 6/22
1959 11/12 – until **1961** 1/4
1973 9/18 – 11/14
1974 5/27 – until **1975** 6/26
1980 10/24 – until **1981** 4/30
1981 7/10 – 12/10
1982 3/25 – 9/4
1988 12/18 – until **1990** 2/8
1990 8/12 – 11/2
2003 7/5 – until **2004** 8/2
2009 12/18 – until **2010** 2/9
2010 8/31 – until **2011** 10/12

URANUS CHALLENGING
1949 8/23 – until **1954** 5/15
1969 9/21 – until **1973** 8/16
1989 2/12 – until **1993** 12/3

NEPTUNE CHALLENGING
1943 12/8 – until **1952** 9/3
1986 1/12 – until **1993** 12/19

PLUTO CHALLENGING
1972 11/29 – until **1980** 8/30
2010 1/21 – Continues

JUPITER SPECIAL
1939 6/3 – 9/26
1940 1/20 – 4/4
1951 5/10 – until **1952** 3/18
1963 4/21 – until **1964** 2/28
1975 4/4 – 6/20
1975 10/10 – until **1976** 2/6
1987 3/19 – 5/28
1987 12/4 – 12/27
1999 3/2 – 5/9
2011 2/12 – 4/21

SATURN SPECIAL
1938 2/24 – until **1939** 4/3
1967 4/5 – until **1968** 5/13
1968 11/12 – until **1969** 1/28
1996 5/14 – 9/26
1997 2/5 – 7/12
1997 8/21 – until **1998** 3/17

URANUS SPECIAL
2011 6/2 – Continues

April 3

Your Personal Powers

Dynamic, friendly, and sociable, your personal powers include a vibrant presence, enthusiasm, and creative talents. With a strong drive and a need for new and exciting experiences, you enjoy facing life with a spirit of adventure. With all your natural gifts, success is guaranteed if you are willing to focus patiently on your goals and work hard. Blessed with charisma and eagerness, you gain power from your persuasive charm and talent with words. Adding your vivid imagination and sense of the dramatic to your good communication skills can help you in your climb to the top. When you become restless, impatient, or bored, however, you can scatter your energy in too many directions and lose some of your power or undermine your chances. Fortunately, with your desire for change, you quickly adapt to new circumstances and make new opportunities work in your favor. Your warm heart, decisive actions, and amusing personality can assist when you are facing challenges or in your reach for success.

Your Powers of Attraction in Relationships

Your friendly and fun-loving personality attracts others. When positive, you can radiate with enthusiasm and be a good companion. You can be particularly attracted to clever people with a broad-minded approach. Although you are romantic, in your personal relationships you may have some testing experiences where you can learn about detachment. If you do not learn how to let go, you may hold on to disappointment from the past. You usually display an attractive generosity and dynamic warmth that others find appealing. Being bold and passionate as well as idealistic, you may have to resist rushing into relationships, playing the rescuer, or idealizing your partner. Nevertheless, generally you are entertaining and popular, so you have no trouble attracting partners or admirers.

Your attractive qualities: friendly, amusing, enthusiastic, daring, creative, witty, persuasive, a talent with words, imaginative, optimistic, artistic, joyful, organized, pioneering, love travel, sense of humor, visionary, determined, versatile

Your less attractive qualities: bored, worried, conceited, insecure, idle, self-pitying, selfish, arrogant, escapist, restless, exaggerate, vain, indecisive, scattered, stubborn, tactless, impatient

Your Venus Power

The planet Venus has a great deal of influence on your powers of attraction. Below are four possible Venus types for women and men. To find your Venus you need to go to page 771, where you will find the Venus table and extra information. The planet Mars also affects your powers of attraction. To find your Mars table and interpretation go to page 761.

WOMEN WITH VENUS IN AQUARIUS: When it comes to relationships others are attracted to your honest, friendly, and easygoing attitude. You enjoy social interaction and have a genuine concern for others. In fact, at times, your friends may be just as important as your partner. You usually present a tolerant and reasonable front in love situations and attempt to view your relationships objectively. If partners become too demanding, however, you can become stubborn or awkward. Nevertheless, inventive and progressive, you enjoy the company of like-minded people who can share your original ideas.

MEN WITH VENUS IN AQUARIUS: People are attracted to your friendliness, honesty, and broad-minded approach to life. You usually possess an objective and slightly detached attitude to affairs of the heart. If you are too removed, however, others can misinterpret your behavior as uncaring. It is often more important to you that your love relationships are based on friendship and honesty than intense passion. As you are generally tolerant and liberal, you may be drawn toward less conventional relationships.

WOMEN WITH VENUS IN PISCES: As a romantic and idealistic individual you can be both loving and giving. In relationships you may need to balance the practical with the charitable. While making allowances and sacrifices is understandable in a loving relationship, playing the martyr is often a state of romantic illusion that can lead to self-deception. Your benevolence and sacrifices in the right relationship nonetheless make you a partner who is devoted, kind, and compassionate. Subtle, sensitive, and alluring, you make a sensual and caring partner.

MEN WITH VENUS IN PISCES: The combination of your emotional subtlety and charm can make you very alluring when dealing with affairs of the heart. Perceptive and impressionable, you have an easygoing style in your relationships, usually preferring to avoid ugly confrontation. You are drawn to a partner who has a touch of glamour and is sensitive to the needs of others. Alternatively, your partner can be a visionary with a rich imagination, like your own, who will keep you enchanted.

WOMEN WITH VENUS IN ARIES: Self-reliant and strong, you usually want things your own way. This can present problems if you refuse to compromise with your partner. Your life lessons in the area of love and relationships often involve patience and learning to trust. When you project the full power of your Venus you can radiate a charismatic and captivating energy and make a strong impression on others. Independence is often high on your relationship agenda.

MEN WITH VENUS IN ARIES: As you often have the courage and strength to initiate situations, you like to take the lead and let others follow. With your unconscious desire for conquest you may also have to beware of being competitive with your partners. Nevertheless, you are drawn to direct and strong-willed women who can share your love of action and enthusiasm for life. When you are feeling good you can be charming and enthusiastic in romantic situations with an entertaining and spontaneous spirit.

WOMEN WITH VENUS IN TAURUS: Good-natured and romantic, you have a highly developed sense of touch that particularly responds to massage, hugs, and all things physical. With a streak of the conventional you love the simple pleasures of life: good food, close friends, and happy relationships. With your natural sense of beauty and harmony you are likely to have an attractive voice, beautiful home, or a strong link to nature. You may have to be careful of becoming too extravagant, as often your taste is more expensive than what you are able to afford.

MEN WITH VENUS IN TAURUS: Attractive and affectionate, in relationships you are often faithful with a conservative approach. You are usually drawn to warmhearted partners with whom you can share a familiar routine as well as life's pleasures and comforts. Seeking a partner who is dependable or reassuring you often put security high on your priority list when looking for love. Your sociability and friendliness usually make you popular and partners often admire your practicality and good sense of values.

To read all about your Outer Planets and work out how to use your personalized timetable, go to Section Three, page 789.

Your Personalized Timetable

JUPITER BENEFICIAL
1938 1/24 – 3/7
1941 6/30 – 8/24
1941 11/26 – until 1942 4/13
1943 7/23 – 10/9
1944 2/20 – 6/5
1947 11/16 – until 1948 1/30
1948 7/11 – 9/20
1950 1/7 – 2/18
1953 6/12 – 7/29
1954 1/10 – 3/13
1955 7/7 – 9/19
1959 10/30 – until 1960 1/11
1961 12/20 – until 1962 2/2
1965 5/27 – 7/10
1967 6/20 – 9/2
1971 2/20 – 4/23
1971 10/12 – 12/25
1973 4/8 – 7/24
1973 11/29 – until 1974 1/16
1977 5/11 – 6/23
1978 10/4 – until 1979 1/17
1979 5/30 – 8/17
1983 1/22 – 6/5
1983 9/19 – 12/10
1985 3/15 – 9/10
1985 10/26 – 12/30
1989 4/23 – 6/7
1990 9/12 – until 1991 2/28
1991 4/30 – 8/1
1995 1/2 – 11/24
1997 2/25 – 4/19
1997 8/1 – 12/9
2000 8/14 – 11/14
2001 4/3 – 5/21
2002 8/24 – until 2003 7/16
2006 12/16 – until 2007 11/7
2009 2/8 – 3/26
2009 9/20 – 11/4
2012 7/19 – 12/29

SATURN BENEFICIAL
1942 7/12 – 12/14
1943 3/30 – 6/23
1946 9/13 – until 1947 1/31
1947 6/3 – 10/22
1948 1/17 – 7/8
1956 11/24 – until 1958 1/15
1958 7/3 – 10/12
1962 3/16 – 8/1
1962 12/12 – until 1963 3/11
1963 9/7 – 12/3
1972 5/16 – 8/8
1972 11/28 – until 1973 4/26
1976 7/17 – until 1977 8/18
1985 12/30 – until 1986 6/16
1986 9/26 – until 1987 3/17
1987 4/14 – 11/23
1992 1/19 – 5/4
1992 6/22 – until 1993 1/15
2001 6/23 – until 2002 6/6
2005 8/25 – until 2006 3/10
2006 5/1 – 9/27
2007 2/18 – 6/17

URANUS BENEFICIAL
1943 7/31 – until 1947 3/20
1956 9/4 – until 1960 8/7
1982 2/4 – until 1986 11/18
1997 4/2 – until 2000 12/17

NEPTUNE BENEFICIAL
1972 2/6 – until 1980 11/5
2001 3/17 – until 2006 12/28

PLUTO BENEFICIAL
1941 9/6 – until 1953 6/1
1997 1/21 – until 2004 11/15

JUPITER CHALLENGING
1942 7/2 – 9/20

1943 1/5 – 5/15
1945 9/18 – 12/5
1946 4/24 – 8/4
1948 12/8 – until 1949 2/17
1954 6/15 – 8/28
1955 2/18 – 4/12
1957 9/2 – 11/16
1960 11/21 – until 1961 1/30
1966 5/30 – 8/10
1968 12/25 – until 1969 2/15
1969 8/15 – 10/31
1972 3/8 – 6/12
1972 11/1 – until 1973 1/14
1977 9/27 – 11/19
1978 5/11 – 7/24
1980 11/24 – until 1981 3/30
1981 7/24 – 10/15
1984 2/13 – 7/25
1984 10/3 – 12/30
1989 8/26 – until 1990 1/2
1990 4/18 – 7/8
1992 11/4 – until 1993 5/19
1993 6/13 – 9/29
1996 1/26 – 12/13
2001 8/5 – until 2002 6/22
2004 10/18 – until 2005 9/13
2008 1/9 – 4/9
2008 6/8 – 11/25

SATURN CHALLENGING
1944 7/30 – until 1945 1/28
1945 4/10 – 8/30
1946 1/17 – 5/19
1951 9/25 – until 1952 11/5
1953 5/31 – 7/16
1959 2/24 – 6/9
1959 11/22 – until 1961 1/13
1974 6/4 – until 1975 7/4
1980 11/2 – until 1981 4/15
1981 7/24 – 12/24
1982 3/10 – 9/13
1988 12/27 – until 1990 2/17
1990 7/28 – 11/16
2003 7/12 – until 2004 8/10
2005 2/24 – 4/16
2010 9/8 – until 2011 10/20

URANUS CHALLENGING
1949 10/4 – until 1954 6/5
1969 10/7 – until 1973 9/6
1989 3/12 – until 1993 12/21

NEPTUNE CHALLENGING
1944 10/25 – until 1952 10/2
1986 2/11 – until 1994 11/10

PLUTO CHALLENGING
1973 10/16 – until 1980 9/27
2010 2/26 – Continues

JUPITER SPECIAL
1939 6/10 – 9/18
1940 1/26 – 4/8
1951 5/15 – 11/9
1951 12/20 – until 1952 3/22
1963 4/25 – until 1964 3/4
1975 4/8 – 6/26
1975 10/3 – until 1976 2/12
1987 3/23 – 6/2
1987 11/18 – until 1988 1/11
1999 3/6 – 5/13
2011 2/16 – 4/25

SATURN SPECIAL
1938 3/5 – until 1939 4/11
1967 4/13 – until 1968 5/22
1968 10/29 – until 1969 2/10
1996 5/25 – 9/13
1997 2/14 – until 1998 3/25

URANUS SPECIAL
2012 4/2 – Continues

April 4

Your Personal Powers

Friendly, purposeful, and down to earth, among your many personal powers are an open and direct manner and constructive attitude. Your ruling planet, Mars, indicates that you can be courageous and enthusiastic. Independent with an astute mind, you gain power from your dynamic yet practical approach to life. You usually have good taste and appreciate beauty and luxury. Ambitious and security conscious, you are generally willing to work hard in order to create a solid material base for yourself. Fortunately, your personal powers include good organizational skills and an innate business sense that can ensure definite financial success if you are productive and self-disciplined. Although you are determined and assertive, if you are too direct or controlling you are likely to lose some of your power by becoming bossy or stubborn. Nevertheless, focused and tenacious when you have a goal in mind, you can utilize your natural energy and drive to achieve results and enjoy life to the full.

Your Powers of Attraction in Relationships

Being honest yet charming, you can use your personal magnetism and strong will to win people over or get your own way. Others admire your warm generosity and friendly manner. As you enjoy power and prestige, you often make good social connections. You are usually attracted to successful and wealthy individuals with glamorous personalities. You feel contented, however, when you realize that money does not always bring you happiness. Being independent, you do not enjoy being with a domineering partner yet you need to resist being bossy or controlling yourself. With your daring nature and enthusiasm, you need partners who can share your love of travel and adventure. Proud and magnanimous, you are often sincere with others and can make a loyal friend or partner.

Your attractive qualities: honest, popular, friendly, enthusiastic, down to earth, practical, hardworking, disciplined, kind, ambitious, stable, fair, organized, constructive, kind, noble, loyal, generous, dynamic, determined, self-reliant, problem solver, good conversationalist, witty

Your less attractive qualities: overindulgent, repressed, resentful, lazy, too tough, conceited, bossy, rigid, hidden affections, too outspoken, inflexible, overbearing, stubborn, dogmatic

Your Venus Power

The planet Venus has a great deal of influence on your powers of attraction. Below are four possible Venus types for women and men. To find your Venus you need to go to page 771, where you will find the Venus table and extra information. The planet Mars also affects your powers of attraction. To find your Mars table and interpretation go to page 761.

WOMEN WITH VENUS IN AQUARIUS: Sociable and gracious, you are usually sincere and capable of showing attributes of real tolerance and liberalism. Although you are keen on forming relationships, you also like to have your freedom and act independently. Your intimate partnerships need to be founded on true friendships. Full of bright and progressive ideas, you can express yourself better when you are free and unrestricted. An ability to think in a dispassionate way suggests that you can stay detached. Your love of freedom also implies that you can be loving and loyal without smothering your partner.

MEN WITH VENUS IN AQUARIUS: Ideally, in your relationships your lover is also your best friend. Since freedom of expression is a prerequisite to your well-being, you fare better when left alone to do your own thing. You also need a partner who recognizes and appreciates your need for independence. Although usually friendly, at times you can be stubborn or your cool detachment can appear to others as distant or impersonal. Very sociable, however, you particularly enjoy the company of those who share your original, fair-minded, and progressive views.

WOMEN WITH VENUS IN PISCES: As a romantic and idealistic individual you can be both loving and giving. In relationships you may need to balance the practical with the charitable. While making allowances and sacrifices is understandable in a loving relationship, playing the martyr is often a state of romantic illusion that can lead to self-deception. Your benevolence and sacrifices in the right relationship nonetheless make you a partner who is devoted, kind, and compassionate. Subtle, sensitive, and alluring, you make a sensual and caring partner.

MEN WITH VENUS IN PISCES: The combination of your emotional subtlety and charm can make you very alluring when dealing with affairs of the heart. Perceptive and impressionable, you have an easygoing style in your relationships, usually preferring to avoid ugly confrontation. You are drawn to a partner who has a touch of glamour and is sensitive to the

needs of others. Alternatively, your partner can be a visionary with a rich imagination, like your own, who will keep you enchanted.

WOMEN WITH VENUS IN ARIES: You gain power from your strong individuality, energy, and enthusiasm. Your young-at-heart and spirited approach to relationships adds to your appeal. If you become too impatient or self-absorbed, however, your partnerships are likely to suffer. Nevertheless, you can be creative, sharp, and quick, especially when you are able to share new and exciting projects with your partners. Mischievous, with a love of action, you may even incite them to a playful fight.

MEN WITH VENUS IN ARIES: Friendly, sociable, and expressive with your feelings, you can become easily aroused and animated when involved with a person who is close to your heart. Although you can enthusiastically follow the object of your desire, you may lose power if you allow your forceful emotions to become too dominant or if you go for instant gratification. You are drawn to women who can match you in quickness and boldness. Warm and passionate, a side to your nature longs for excitement and new adventures.

WOMEN WITH VENUS IN TAURUS: Warm and affectionate, you are drawn to partners with whom you can share life's simple comforts. With a need for stability and security or an appreciation of earthly pleasures, you may have to avoid over-indulgence or becoming too preoccupied with material concerns. Nevertheless, your sociability and friendliness usually make you popular. You need a partner who can share your appreciation of beauty and style.

MEN WITH VENUS IN TAURUS: As well as attracting people with your warm personality, you also possess an innate sense of the value of material possessions. Keeping yourself stylish and having an attractive home can therefore be important to you. You are naturally attracted to practical yet sensual women who understand your need for comfort, security, and the pleasures and luxuries of life. Naturally affectionate, you enjoy socializing but can make a loyal and loving partner.

To read all about your Outer Planets and work out how to use your personalized timetable, go to Section Three, page 789.

♈

Your Personalized Timetable

JUPITER BENEFICIAL
1938 1/28 – 3/12
1941 7/5 – 8/31
1941 11/18 – until **1942** 4/19
1943 7/28 – 10/15
1944 2/12 – 6/11
1947 11/20 – until **1948** 2/4
1948 7/2 – 9/29
1950 1/11 – 2/23
1953 6/17 – 8/3
1954 1/1 – 3/22
1955 7/12 – 9/24
1956 3/31 – 5/5
1959 11/4 – until **1960** 1/16
1961 12/25 – until **1962** 2/6
1965 5/31 – 7/14
1967 6/25 – 9/7
1971 3/6 – 4/9
1971 10/17 – 12/30
1973 4/15 – 7/16
1973 12/4 – until **1974** 1/21
1977 5/15 – 6/27
1978 10/12 – until **1979** 1/9
1979 6/5 – 8/22
1983 1/28 – 5/28
1983 9/26 – 12/14
1985 3/21 – until 8/29
1985 11/6 – until **1986** 1/4
1989 4/28 – 6/11
1990 9/17 – until **1991** 2/18
1991 5/9 – 8/6
1995 1/7 – 7/16
1995 8/19 – 11/29
1997 3/1 – 4/26
1997 7/24 – 12/15
2000 8/22 – 11/5
2001 4/8 – 5/25
2002 8/29 – until **2003** 7/21
2006 12/21 – until **2007** 11/12
2009 2/12 – 3/31
2009 9/9 – 11/15
2012 7/24 – 12/20

SATURN BENEFICIAL
1942 7/21 – 12/2
1943 4/10 – 6/30
1946 9/23 – until **1947** 1/19
1947 6/13 – 11/7
1947 12/31 – until **1948** 7/16
1956 12/3 – until **1958** 1/25
1958 6/19 – 10/24
1962 3/27 – 7/19
1962 12/23 – until **1963** 3/21
1963 8/23 – 12/16
1972 5/23 – 8/20
1972 11/14 – until **1973** 5/5
1976 7/25 – until **1977** 8/25
1986 1/9 – 6/2
1986 10/8 – until **1987** 12/2
1992 1/27 – until **1993** 1/24
2001 7/1 – until **2002** 1/6
2002 3/12 – 6/13
2005 9/2 – until **2006** 2/21
2006 5/18 – 10/7
2007 2/6 – 6/27

URANUS BENEFICIAL
1944 5/31 – until **1947** 4/20
1956 9/25 – until **1961** 5/24
1982 12/26 – until **1986** 12/5
1998 2/2 – until **2001** 1/7

NEPTUNE BENEFICIAL
1972 12/24 – until **1980** 12/3
2002 2/11 – until **2007** 1/26

PLUTO BENEFICIAL
1942 8/20 – until **1953** 7/16
1997 12/10 – until **2005** 9/26

JUPITER CHALLENGING
1942 7/6 – 9/27
1942 12/28 – until **1943** 5/21

1945 9/22 – 12/11
1946 4/16 – 8/11
1948 12/12 – until **1949** 2/22
1954 6/20 – 9/2
1955 2/8 – 4/22
1957 9/6 – 11/21
1958 6/7 – 7/1
1960 11/26 – until **1961** 2/4
1966 6/3 – 8/15
1969 1/14 – 1/26
1969 8/20 – 11/4
1972 3/16 – 6/3
1972 11/6 – until **1973** 1/18
1977 10/15 – 11/2
1978 5/16 – 7/29
1980 11/30 – until **1981** 3/22
1981 7/31 – 10/19
1984 2/19 – 7/16
1984 10/12 – until **1985** 1/3
1989 9/1 – 12/26
1990 4/25 – 7/13
1992 11/9 – until **1993** 5/3
1993 6/30 – 10/4
1996 1/30 – 12/18
2001 8/10 – until **2002** 2/15
2002 3/16 – 6/26
2004 10/23 – until **2005** 9/18
2008 1/14 – 4/24
2008 5/24 – 11/30

SATURN CHALLENGING
1944 8/7 – until **1945** 1/14
1945 4/24 – 9/9
1946 1/5 – 5/29
1951 10/3 – until **1952** 11/14
1953 5/11 – 8/5
1959 3/11 – 5/24
1959 12/1 – until **1961** 1/21
1974 6/12 – until **1975** 7/11
1980 11/11 – until **1981** 4/2
1981 8/5 – until **1982** 1/14
1982 2/17 – 9/22
1989 1/4 – until **1990** 2/27
1990 7/15 – 11/27
2003 7/20 – until **2004** 8/19
2005 2/7 – 5/3
2010 9/16 – until **2011** 10/28

URANUS CHALLENGING
1950 7/10 – until **1954** 6/23
1969 10/23 – until **1973** 9/23
1990 1/4 – until **1994** 1/7

NEPTUNE CHALLENGING
1944 11/28 – until **1953** 8/30
1987 1/8 – until **1994** 12/15

PLUTO CHALLENGING
1973 11/15 – until **1981** 8/10
2011 1/19 – Continues

JUPITER SPECIAL
1939 6/17 – 9/10
1940 2/1 – 4/12
1951 5/20 – 10/28
1952 1/1 – 3/26
1963 4/30 – until **1964** 3/8
1975 4/12 – 7/4
1975 9/25 – until **1976** 2/17
1987 3/27 – 6/7
1987 11/8 – until **1988** 1/20
1999 3/11 – 5/17
2011 2/21 – 4/29

SATURN SPECIAL
1938 3/13 – until **1939** 4/19
1967 4/21 – 11/20
1967 12/28 – until **1968** 6/1
1968 10/16 – until **1969** 2/21
1996 6/7 – 8/30
1997 2/23 – until **1998** 4/2

URANUS SPECIAL
2012 4/20 – Continues

33

April 5

SUN: ARIES • DECANATE: LEO/SUN • DEGREE: 14.5°–15.5° ARIES • MODE: CARDINAL • ELEMENT: FIRE

Your Personal Powers

Versatile and charismatic, you have the ability to accomplish and succeed when you act decisively. An inner desire for change or the determination to make headway indicates that you enjoy initiating new projects and being creative. A dynamic and strong-willed individual, you empower yourself when you take advantage of new opportunities and overcome inner fears or skepticism about future transformation. If, on the other hand, you initiate changes too frequently, you may lose some of your resolve and feel impatient or unsettled. By persevering and being accountable for your actions, you develop the diligence necessary to succeed. Your confidence and inner faith can also improve your attitude toward life's challenges. Although you may appear to be concerned with financial issues, your heart usually tells you that wisdom and experience cannot be replaced by money. The driving force that often leads you stems from your need to express yourself; therefore, you do better when you can find a constructive way to channel your sensitive emotions.

Your Powers of Attraction in Relationships

You are instinctive and enterprising, and people admire your initiative and resourcefulness. Sociable and charming, you can attract all types of friends. You may need, on occasion, to be discriminating in your choice of partners. A tendency to fluctuate between feeling altruistic and warm to being unsympathetic or self-seeking indicates that you can be prone to mood swings. Other people usually find you less attractive if you project your insecurities and uncertainty about your resources, direction, or money issues. Since you are attracted to self-assured individuals who are astute yet thoughtful, you enjoy sharing your ideas and interests with others. To secure long-lasting relationships you may need to be more consistent, trusting, and open with your feelings. The more cooperative and thoughtful you are the more attractive you are to others.

Your attractive qualities: creative, industrious, patient, consistent, focused, direct, assertive, objective, versatile, adaptable, ambitious, determined, progressive, strong instincts, magnetic, tolerant, diligent, bold, confident, diplomatic, thoughtful, spiritual, sociable, loyal, persistent

Your less attractive qualities: restless, dissatisfied, frustrated, irritable, inconsistent, stubborn, scattered, indecisive, worried, overconfident, moody, headstrong, indecisive, bossy, too demanding, hasty

Your Venus Power

The planet Venus has a great deal of influence on your powers of attraction. Below are four possible Venus types for women and men. To find your Venus you need to go to page 771, where you will find the Venus table and extra information. The planet Mars also affects your powers of attraction. To find your Mars table and interpretation go to page 761.

WOMEN WITH VENUS IN AQUARIUS: When it comes to relationships, others are attracted to your honest, friendly, and easygoing attitude. You really enjoy social interaction with others and may develop a genuine concern for humanity. You usually present a tolerant and reasonable front in love situations and attempt to view your relationships objectively. If partners become too demanding, however, you can become stubborn and fixed. Friendship may be even more important for you than sexual compatibility.

MEN WITH VENUS IN AQUARIUS: People are attracted by your sociability, open-mindedness, and your friendly and relaxed style. Being independent, you value freedom-loving partners who give you the space to be yourself. Others sometimes interpret your detachment as being emotionally cool, but they may not understand your progressive views on relationships. Friendship can sometimes be even more important than earthly passion. Ideally your partners can share your ideas on life and possess as strong a sense of originality as your own. Not easily ruffled, you can deal well with difficult situations or moody partners.

WOMEN WITH VENUS IN PISCES: Romantic and impressionable, you are a caring and loving individual with a dreamy nature. In relationships you are often attracted to idealistic, compassionate, or sympathetic individuals who are imaginative or have a strong romantic sense. A tendency to be sensitive to others suggests that you are intuitive and aware of people's inner feelings. Be careful therefore not to get caught in other people's dramas or play the rescuer too often.

MEN WITH VENUS IN PISCES: Romantic and idealistic when in love, you can be a sensitive and responsive lover. Being pliant and flexible with an impressionable nature helps you to adapt to the needs of others. In your desire to

blend with those you love, however, guard against not clearly defining your own boundaries. With your affectionate and sentimental nature, you are often attracted to those who understand your sensitivity and share your vision.

WOMEN WITH VENUS IN ARIES: Idealistic, passionate, and adventurous, you are direct in your dealings with others. When you are attracted to a person you usually take the initiative and use your people skills to make things happen. In close relationships you are not afraid to confront your other half. This self-assertiveness is positive if differences can be brought out in the open through diplomacy and compromise. Independent and spirited, you enjoy your freedom.

MEN WITH VENUS IN ARIES: As you often have the courage and strength to initiate situations, you like to take the lead and let others follow. With your unconscious desire for conquest you may also have to beware of being competitive with your partners. Nevertheless, you are drawn to direct and strong-willed women who can share your love of action and enthusiasm for life. When you are feeling good, you can be charming and enthusiastic in romantic situations with an entertaining and spontaneous spirit.

WOMEN WITH VENUS IN TAURUS: Demonstrative and affectionate, you are naturally tactile with a love of sensual pleasures. With a streak of the conventional you love the simple pleasures of life: good food, close friends, and happy relationships. Although you possess endurance, be careful not to let this turn into plain stubbornness. Having inner strength, you can express genuine patience and are often a pillar of support for loved ones and friends.

MEN WITH VENUS IN TAURUS: Although you are usually drawn to sensual and physically beautiful individuals, you also want a partner who is reliable and loyal. When in love, you enjoy buying your partner things of quality that will grow in value or useful things of a practical nature. You also love to socialize and entertain, especially in luxurious surroundings. Affectionate and caring, you are often attracted to creative people and those with artistic talents.

To read all about your Outer Planets and work out how to use your personalized timetable, go to Section Three, page 789.

♈

35

Your Personalized Timetable

JUPITER BENEFICIAL
1938 2/1 – 3/16
1941 7/9 – 9/10
1941 11/9 – until 1942 4/24
1943 8/1 – 10/22
1944 2/5 – 6/18
1947 11/25 – until 1948 2/10
1948 6/24 – 10/6
1950 1/16 – 2/27
1953 6/21 – 8/9
1953 12/24 – until 1954 3/30
1955 7/16 – 9/30
1956 3/17 – 5/19
1959 11/9 – until 1960 1/21
1961 12/29 – until 1962 2/10
1965 6/4 – 7/19
1967 6/29 – 9/12
1971 10/22 – until 1972 1/3
1973 4/23 – 7/7
1973 12/10 – until 1974 1/25
1977 5/19 – 7/1
1978 10/20 – until 1979 1/1
1979 6/11 – 8/26
1983 2/3 – 5/20
1983 10/2 – 12/19
1985 3/26 – 8/20
1985 11/14 – until 1986 1/8
1989 5/2 – 6/15
1990 9/23 – until 1991 2/10
1991 5/17 – 8/10
1995 1/12 – 7/2
1995 9/2 – 12/3
1997 3/6 – 5/5
1997 7/16 – 12/20
2000 9/1 – 10/27
2001 4/13 – 5/30
2002 9/3 – until 2003 7/25
2006 12/26 – until 2007 11/17
2009 2/17 – 4/5
2009 8/31 – 11/24
2012 7/30 – 12/13

SATURN BENEFICIAL
1942 8/1 – 11/20
1943 4/19 – 7/8
1944 2/3 – 3/8
1946 10/5 – until 1947 1/6
1947 6/22 – until 1948 7/24
1956 12/11 – until 1958 2/4
1958 6/6 – 11/4
1962 4/9 – 7/4
1963 1/1 – 3/31
1963 8/10 – 12/27
1972 5/31 – 9/6
1972 10/28 – until 1973 5/13
1976 8/1 – until 1977 9/2
1986 1/19 – 5/20
1986 10/18 – until 1987 12/10
1992 2/5 – until 1993 2/1
2001 7/9 – 12/22
2002 3/26 – 6/21
2005 9/11 – until 2006 2/8
2006 5/30 – 10/18
2007 1/25 – 7/7

URANUS BENEFICIAL
1944 6/17 – until 1947 5/10
1956 11/5 – until 1961 6/23
1983 1/1 – until 1987 9/25
1998 2/19 – until 2001 1/25

NEPTUNE BENEFICIAL
1973 1/27 – until 1981 10/31
2002 3/12 – until 2007 12/22

PLUTO BENEFICIAL
1942 10/3 – until 1954 6/17
1998 1/7 – until 2005 11/8

JUPITER CHALLENGING
1942 7/11 – 10/5
1942 12/20 – until 1943 5/26

1945 9/27 – 12/18
1946 4/9 – 8/18
1948 12/17 – until 1949 2/27
1949 8/29 – 10/8
1954 6/24 – 9/8
1955 1/30 – 5/1
1957 9/11 – 11/26
1958 5/21 – 7/17
1960 11/30 – until 1961 2/8
1966 6/8 – 8/19
1969 8/25 – 11/9
1972 3/26 – 5/24
1972 11/12 – until 1973 1/23
1978 5/21 – 8/2
1980 12/7 – until 1981 3/14
1981 8/6 – 10/24
1984 2/24 – 7/8
1984 10/19 – until 1985 1/7
1989 9/8 – 12/19
1990 5/1 – 7/17
1992 11/14 – until 1993 4/22
1993 7/10 – 10/8
1996 2/4 – 12/22
2001 8/15 – until 2002 2/1
2002 3/30 – 7/1
2004 10/28 – until 2005 9/23
2008 1/18 – 12/4

SATURN CHALLENGING
1944 8/16 – until 1945 1/2
1945 5/5 – 9/21
1945 12/23 – until 1946 6/7
1951 10/11 – until 1952 11/23
1953 4/27 – 8/18
1959 4/6 – 4/27
1959 12/10 – until 1961 1/29
1974 6/20 – until 1975 7/19
1980 11/22 – until 1981 3/20
1981 8/16 – until 1982 9/30
1989 1/12 – until 1990 3/10
1990 7/1 – 12/7
2003 7/28 – until 2004 2/9
2004 4/3 – 8/27
2005 1/25 – 5/15
2010 9/24 – until 2011 11/6
2012 6/9 – 7/11

URANUS CHALLENGING
1950 7/27 – until 1954 7/10
1969 11/9 – until 1973 10/9
1990 1/21 – until 1994 11/8

NEPTUNE CHALLENGING
1945 10/21 – until 1953 9/29
1987 2/6 – until 1995 10/31

PLUTO CHALLENGING
1974 10/7 – until 1981 9/13
2011 2/22 – Continues

JUPITER SPECIAL
1939 6/25 – 9/1
1940 2/6 – 4/16
1951 5/25 – 10/20
1952 1/9 – 3/30
1963 5/4 – until 1964 3/13
1975 4/16 – 7/12
1975 9/16 – until 1976 2/22
1987 3/31 – 6/12
1987 10/31 – until 1988 1/28
1999 3/15 – 5/22
2011 2/25 – 5/3

SATURN SPECIAL
1938 3/21 – until 1939 4/27
1967 4/30 – 10/30
1968 1/17 – 6/11
1968 10/4 – until 1969 3/3
1996 6/26 – 8/10
1997 3/4 – until 1998 4/10

URANUS SPECIAL
2012 5/10 – Continues

April 6

SUN: ARIES • DECANATE: LEO/SUN • DEGREE: 15°5–16°5 ARIES • MODE: CARDINAL • ELEMENT: FIRE

Your Personal Powers

As a determined and intuitive individual, you are likely to be both practical and astute. A serious side to your nature indicates that you possess determination and inner strength. You gain power when you are willing to compromise and create harmony around you. Although your independence can be very important to you, your personal powers increase when you accept the responsibilities that come from being disciplined or committed to others. You can also succeed admirably when you show your sincerity, charm, and generosity. Financial rewards usually come from perseverance, hard work, and collaborating with others. People admire your relaxed manner, initiative, and drive. If you become overindulgent or controlling, however, you can show your less attractive qualities and lose your popularity or personal power. This can also cause misunderstandings, lead to confrontations, and deny you the support you want from those around you. Since you desire to create stability, you gain power by developing your tact and diplomacy. With your natural grace and entertaining manner, however, you can become popular and successful.

Your Powers of Attraction in Relationships

Sociable and charismatic, you gain the admiration of other people by being warmhearted and altruistic. Friendly, you often achieve popularity, and if you can resist an inclination to overindulge, you can be liked for your taste and refined manners. You are usually attracted to enterprising individuals who are ambitious and success-oriented. Although you are at times autonomous or stubborn, once you are committed you can be dedicated and reliable and gain the loyalty of loved ones. Long-term relationships are usually successful if everything is shared equally and you do not feel used or controlled. You display your less attractive qualities when you become overbearing rather than gracious and sincere. Leading a well-balanced life may be a vital key to your happiness.

Your attractive qualities: responsible, optimistic, enterprising, friendly, generous, affectionate, confident, diplomatic, idealistic, sociable, creative, compassionate, charismatic, poised, kind, congenial, stylish, refined, understanding, popular, supportive, humanitarian, artistic, happy

Your less attractive qualities: discontented, anxious, extravagant, excessive, outspoken, indulgent, disharmonious, dependent, self-centered, perfectionist, anxious, restless, domineering, misplaced sympathy, vain, cynical, lazy

Your Venus Power

The planet Venus has a great deal of influence on your powers of attraction. Below are four possible Venus types for women and men. To find your Venus you need to go to page 771, where you will find the Venus table and extra information. The planet Mars also affects your powers of attraction. To find your Mars table and interpretation go to page 761.

WOMEN WITH VENUS IN PISCES: When in love, you are sensitive, tender, and affectionate, experiencing your partner's feelings almost as strongly as your own. Being also imaginative and visionary, you possess the capabilities to develop both creative gifts as well as deep compassion for others. As you are idealistic when in love, you usually prefer to see only your partner's good points, but be careful that your high expectations do not bring disappointment if you avoid being realistic. Nevertheless, in your relationships with others, you can be devoted, loving, and positively enchanting.

MEN WITH VENUS IN PISCES: Being adaptable and sensitive, you are able to intuitively feel the moods of those you love. Although you are receptive to others, you can be ambiguous about your own feelings toward your partner. Romantic and kindhearted, you long to be loved but you need to be realistic about your relationships in order to avoid disappointments. When in love you may idealize your partners and fail to see any faults in their personality.

WOMEN WITH VENUS IN ARIES: Idealistic, passionate, and adventurous, you are direct in your dealings with others. When you are attracted to a person, you usually take the initiative and use your people skills to make things happen. In close relationships you are not afraid to confront your other half. This self-assertiveness is positive if differences can be brought out in the open through diplomacy and compromise. Independent and spirited, you enjoy your freedom.

MEN WITH VENUS IN ARIES: You are usually inclined to seek a partner who is active, goal-oriented, and/or decisive. Not known for your patience, you probably seek relationships early in life. You may find that you are attracted more to women who have a daring or adventurous spirit, but in your close relationships you may encounter rivalry or find

that both you and your partner want to lead or be the boss. Although you may act rashly, you possess a great deal of magnetism and are capable of demonstrating your love and affection.

WOMEN WITH VENUS IN TAURUS: For your ideal relationship, you seek a partner who is both financially secure and demonstrative with his affections. With these thoughts in mind you are likely to also want a partner who is refined yet pragmatic or someone concerned with safeguarding your future. Although you have a stubborn streak you can be loving and affectionate in your relationships, and with your good sense of style you may be attracted to the arts, music, or luxury items.

MEN WITH VENUS IN TAURUS: As you yourself may be attractive to the opposite sex, you desire a partner who is sensual and loving or who has physical beauty. Needing stability, when faced with changes that are out of your control you may become insecure or possessive. Your own sense of style and your love of beauty implies that you can be attracted to creative people, especially in art and music. Faithful or loyal, you can be affectionate, tactile, and constant in your love.

WOMEN WITH VENUS IN GEMINI: In relationships you need intellectual stimulation and usually prefer to keep things light. Certainly not boring, you love to talk and are at your best being witty and entertaining. Although your easygoing approach to relationships is very attractive, guard against losing touch with your emotions. You prefer a partner who can keep up with your fast stream of ideas, and if you have shared interests then so much the better.

MEN WITH VENUS IN GEMINI: Charming, amusing, and adaptable, you attract others with your natural communication skills and friendly personality. You have a wonderful childlike quality and love to keep life playful, but a reluctance to contact your deeper feelings may cause you to avoid serious commitment. With your need for variety and intellectual stimulation, you are attracted to clever and amusing partners who have many interesting sides to their personalities.

To read all about your Outer Planets and work out how to use your personalized timetable, go to Section Three, page 789.

♈

Your Personalized Timetable

JUPITER BENEFICIAL
1938 2/5 – 3/21
1941 7/14 – 9/23
1941 10/27 – until 1942 4/29
1943 8/6 – 10/29
1944 1/28 – 6/24
1947 11/29 – until 1948 2/16
1948 6/16 – 10/13
1950 1/20 – 3/3
1953 6/25 – 8/15
1953 12/17 – until 1954 4/6
1955 7/21 – 10/5
1956 3/7 – 5/28
1959 11/13 – until 1960 1/26
1960 8/10 – 8/31
1962 1/3 – 2/14
1965 6/9 – 7/24
1967 7/4 – 9/17
1971 10/27 – until 1972 1/8
1973 5/3 – 6/27
1973 12/15 – until 1974 1/29
1977 5/23 – 7/6
1978 10/30 – 12/21
1979 6/16 – 8/31
1983 2/11 – 5/12
1983 10/8 – 12/23
1985 4/1 – 8/12
1985 11/22 – until 1986 1/13
1989 5/7 – 6/19
1990 9/28 – until 1991 2/2
1991 5/25 – 8/15
1995 1/17 – 6/22
1995 9/12 – 12/7
1997 3/11 – 5/16
1997 7/4 – 12/25
2000 9/17 – 10/12
2001 4/18 – 6/3
2002 9/8 – until 2003 7/30
2006 12/30 – until 2007 11/21
2009 2/21 – 4/11
2009 8/23 – 12/1
2012 8/5 – 12/5

SATURN BENEFICIAL
1942 8/14 – 11/6
1943 4/28 – 7/17
1944 1/13 – 3/28
1946 10/19 – 12/22
1947 6/30 – until 1948 8/1
1956 12/19 – until 1957 7/24
1957 8/30 – until 1958 2/17
1958 5/23 – 11/13
1962 4/28 – 6/14
1963 1/10 – 4/12
1963 7/27 – until 1964 1/6
1972 6/8 – until 1973 5/21
1976 8/9 – until 1977 9/10
1978 4/7 – 5/13
1986 2/1 – 5/6
1986 10/28 – until 1987 12/19
1992 2/13 – until 1993 2/9
2001 7/19 – 12/10
2002 4/6 – 6/28
2005 9/20 – until 2006 1/26
2006 6/10 – 11/1
2007 1/10 – 7/15

URANUS BENEFICIAL
1944 7/5 – until 1947 5/28
1957 8/10 – until 1961 7/13
1983 1/21 – until 1987 10/26
1998 3/10 – until 2001 11/9

NEPTUNE BENEFICIAL
1973 12/21 – until 1981 11/30
2002 5/4 – until 2008 1/21

PLUTO BENEFICIAL
1943 9/9 – until 1954 7/25
1998 2/20 – until 2005 12/6

JUPITER CHALLENGING
1942 7/15 – 10/15
1942 12/10 – until 1943 6/1

1945 10/1 – 12/25
1946 4/1 – 8/24
1948 12/21 – until 1949 3/4
1949 8/17 – 10/20
1954 6/28 – 9/13
1955 1/23 – 5/8
1957 9/16 – 12/2
1958 5/11 – 7/28
1960 12/5 – until 1961 2/13
1966 6/12 – 8/24
1969 8/30 – 11/14
1972 4/9 – 5/10
1972 11/17 – until 1973 1/27
1978 5/26 – 8/7
1980 12/15 – until 1981 3/6
1981 8/12 – 10/29
1984 3/1 – 6/30
1984 10/26 – until 1985 1/11
1989 9/15 – 12/11
1990 5/6 – 7/21
1992 11/20 – until 1993 4/14
1993 7/18 – 10/13
1996 2/9 – 8/25
1996 9/12 – 12/26
2001 8/20 – until 2002 1/22
2002 4/9 – 7/5
2004 11/2 – until 2005 9/28
2008 1/22 – 12/9

SATURN CHALLENGING
1944 8/27 – 12/21
1945 5/15 – 10/5
1945 12/8 – until 1946 6/15
1951 10/19 – until 1952 12/3
1953 4/14 – 8/29
1959 12/19 – until 1961 2/7
1961 8/28 – 10/27
1974 6/27 – until 1975 7/26
1980 12/3 – until 1981 3/7
1981 8/25 – until 1982 10/8
1989 1/21 – 8/13
1989 10/9 – until 1990 3/24
1990 6/16 – 12/16
2003 8/6 – until 2004 1/24
2004 4/19 – 9/6
2005 1/13 – 5/26
2010 10/2 – until 2011 11/14
2012 5/17 – 8/2

URANUS CHALLENGING
1950 8/16 – until 1955 4/29
1969 12/1 – until 1974 7/27
1990 2/9 – until 1994 12/3

NEPTUNE CHALLENGING
1945 11/22 – until 1954 8/25
1987 3/28 – until 1995 12/11

PLUTO CHALLENGING
1974 11/3 – until 1981 10/9
2012 1/19 – Continues

JUPITER SPECIAL
1939 7/7 – 8/21
1940 2/11 – 4/20
1951 5/31 – 10/12
1952 1/17 – 4/3
1963 5/9 – until 1964 3/17
1975 4/20 – 7/24
1975 9/5 – until 1976 2/27
1987 4/4 – 6/18
1987 10/24 – until 1988 2/4
1999 3/19 – 5/27
2011 3/1 – 5/8

SATURN SPECIAL
1938 3/29 – until 1939 5/5
1967 5/9 – 10/16
1968 1/30 – 6/24
1968 9/20 – until 1969 3/12
1997 3/12 – until 1998 4/18

URANUS SPECIAL
2012 6/5 – Continues

April 7

SUN: ARIES • DECANATE: LEO/SUN • DEGREE: 16°5–17°5 ARIES • MODE: CARDINAL • ELEMENT: FIRE

Your Personal Powers

Motivated and inspired, your independent spirit is alert and ambitious, yet your bright personality can conceal a sensitive individual. Since you usually rely on hard work and determination to succeed, you gain power when you let your perception and inner wisdom be your guiding light in life. You can also increase your power if you learn to utilize your discrimination when making important decisions or to quickly assess situations. You may also surprise people with your ingenuity and foresight. Others admire your practical approach, willpower, and ability to persevere. By being cheerful and relaxed you can achieve remarkable results. Being analytical and thoughtful can cause you to be introspective and self-absorbed. If taken to extremes, it can also cause inner tension and unnecessary stress or anxiety. You can therefore lose your power if you over-rationalize issues or overburden your mind with unimportant issues. An increase in your confidence is often due to your calm approach and tactful manner.

Your Powers of Attraction in Relationships

People are attracted to your natural creative flow, spontaneity, and inspired actions. They also admire your ability to stay assured and calm under pressure. Being intelligent and witty, you may enjoy socializing or entertaining people. Charming yet inquisitive, you can ask subtle questions without letting anyone know what you think. In your close relationships do not let inhibitions and indecision cloud your judgment; stay open and use your communication skills to air any burdens you might suppress inside. Since you desire to feel secure and loved, loyalty and stability are often what you seek in a partner. Avoid giving the impression of being too detached simply because you like to think and act independently. Capable of being loyal and caring, you need a partner who understands your moods and shares your high ideals.

Your attractive qualities: observant, independent, well-informed, trusting, meticulous, spiritual, idealistic, honest, analytical, intuitive, reflective, methodical, pioneering, enthusiastic, original, sympathetic, spontaneous, practical, enterprising, detached, communicative, compromising

Your less attractive qualities: concealing, skeptical, nervous, too serious, uncommunicative, loner, stubborn, critical, unfeeling, argumentative, misunderstood, moody, impulsive actions, resentful, pessimistic

Your Venus Power

The planet Venus has a great deal of influence on your powers of attraction. Below are four possible Venus types for women and men. To find your Venus you need to go to page 771, where you will find the Venus table and extra information. The planet Mars also affects your powers of attraction. To find your Mars table and interpretation go to page 761.

WOMEN WITH VENUS IN PISCES: Idealistic and impressionable, in love you are romantic. Being sensitive to other people you are receptive to their moods and feelings. This affinity indicates that, although you can be selfless, you may have to guard against being too sentimental or overly romantic, especially with those who can take advantage of your kindness. You are alluring and seductive, and your partners can be intrigued by your poetic soul or mysterious nature.

MEN WITH VENUS IN PISCES: As a romantic and generous person, you are attracted to imaginative or artistic partners who can be sensitive and generous. While you are willing to make allowances for your loved ones, playing the martyr in relationships can lead to allowing others to take advantage of your kind nature. Nevertheless, giving and loving, you are usually willing to forgive your partner's shortcomings.

WOMEN WITH VENUS IN ARIES: Idealistic, passionate, and adventurous, you are direct in your dealings with others. When you are attracted to a person you usually take the initiative and use your people skills to make things happen. In close relationships you are not afraid to confront your other half. This self-assertiveness is positive if differences can be brought into the open through diplomacy and compromise. Independent and spirited, you enjoy your freedom.

MEN WITH VENUS IN ARIES: As you often have the courage and strength to initiate situations, you like to take the lead and let others follow. With your unconscious desire for conquest you may have to beware of being competitive with your partners. Nevertheless, you are drawn to direct and strong-willed women who can share your love of action and enthusiasm for life. When you're feeling good, you can be charming and enthusiastic in romantic situations, with an entertaining and spontaneous spirit.

WOMEN WITH VENUS IN TAURUS: Good-natured and ro-

mantic, you have a highly developed sense of touch that particularly responds to massage, hugs, and all things physical. With a streak of the conventional you love the simple pleasures of life: good food, close friends, and happy relationships. With your natural sense of beauty and harmony, you are likely to have an attractive voice, beautiful home, or a strong link to nature. You may have to be careful of becoming too extravagant as often your taste is more expensive than what you are able to afford.

MEN WITH VENUS IN TAURUS: Attractive and affectionate, in relationships you are often down-to-earth, with a conservative approach. You are usually drawn to warmhearted partners with whom you can share a familiar routine as well as life's pleasures and comforts. Seeking a partner who is dependable or reassuring, you often put security high on your priority list when looking for love. Your sociability and friendliness usually make you popular and partners often admire your practicality and good sense of values.

WOMEN WITH VENUS IN GEMINI: Curious, with a bright and animated approach to life, you are attracted to those who are clever or sophisticated. Your love of variety and desire for knowledge suggests that you need a partner and friends who can keep you mentally stimulated. Although witty and a good conversationalist, you may need to keep in touch with your deeper feelings. Nevertheless, intelligent and friendly, you possess a youthful sense of wonder and seek a playmate who can keep you from becoming bored.

MEN WITH VENUS IN GEMINI: Friendly and sociable, you attract others with your clever and amusing conversation. Drawn to partners who can match you in wit and intelligence, you usually prefer to keep relationships light rather than emotionally intense. With your youthful charm and desire for knowledge and new experiences you usually have many friends and a low boredom threshold.

To read all about your Outer Planets and work out how to use your personalized timetable, go to Section Three, page 789.

Your Personalized Timetable

JUPITER BENEFICIAL
1938 2/9 – 3/26
1941 7/19 – until 1942 1/18
1942 2/23 – 5/4
1943 8/10 – 11/7
1944 1/19 – 6/29
1947 12/4 – until 1948 2/23
1948 6/8 – 10/19
1950 1/24 – 3/7
1953 6/30 – 8/21
1953 12/9 – until 1954 4/12
1955 7/25 – 10/11
1956 2/28 – 6/5
1959 11/18 – until 1960 1/31
1960 7/24 – 9/17
1962 1/7 – 2/18
1965 6/13 – 7/29
1966 1/26 – 3/7
1967 7/9 – 9/21
1971 11/1 – until 1972 1/12
1973 5/20 – 6/10
1973 12/20 – until 1974 2/2
1977 5/28 – 7/10
1978 11/18 – 12/3
1979 6/21 – 9/4
1983 2/19 – 5/3
1983 10/14 – 12/27
1985 4/7 – 8/5
1985 11/28 – until 1986 1/17
1989 5/11 – 6/24
1990 10/5 – until 1991 1/26
1991 5/31 – 8/19
1995 1/23 – 6/14
1995 9/20 – 12/12
1997 3/15 – 12/30
2001 4/23 – 6/7
2002 9/13 – until 2003 3/11
2003 4/27 – 8/4
2007 1/4 – 11/26
2009 2/25 – 4/17
2009 8/15 – 12/7
2012 8/11 – 11/28

SATURN BENEFICIAL
1942 8/30 – 10/20
1943 5/6 – 7/25
1943 12/31 – until 1944 4/11
1947 7/9 – until 1948 8/9
1956 12/28 – until 1957 7/2
1957 9/20 – until 1958 3/5
1958 5/6 – 11/23
1963 1/18 – 4/26
1963 7/12 – until 1964 1/15
1972 6/15 – until 1973 5/29
1976 8/17 – until 1977 9/18
1978 3/17 – 6/3
1986 2/17 – 4/19
1986 11/6 – until 1987 12/27
1992 2/21 – 10/4
1992 10/27 – until 1993 2/18
2001 7/29 – 11/28
2002 4/16 – 7/6
2005 10/1 – until 2006 1/14
2006 6/19 – 11/24
2006 12/17 – until 2007 7/24

URANUS BENEFICIAL
1944 7/26 – until 1947 6/14
1957 8/27 – until 1961 7/30
1983 2/23 – until 1987 11/15
1998 4/3 – until 2001 12/19

NEPTUNE BENEFICIAL
1974 1/21 – until 1982 10/25
2003 3/7 – until 2008 12/13

PLUTO BENEFICIAL
1944 8/21 – until 1955 6/28
1998 12/27 – until 2006 11/1

JUPITER CHALLENGING
1942 7/19 – 10/30

1942 11/25 – until 1943 6/6
1945 10/6 – until 1946 1/2
1946 3/23 – 8/29
1948 12/25 – until 1949 3/9
1949 8/8 – 10/29
1954 7/3 – 9/19
1955 1/15 – 5/15
1957 9/20 – 12/7
1958 5/2 – 8/5
1960 12/9 – until 1961 2/17
1966 6/17 – 8/29
1967 3/3 – 4/8
1969 9/4 – 11/19
1972 11/21 – until 1973 1/31
1978 5/31 – 8/11
1980 12/25 – until 1981 2/24
1981 8/17 – 11/2
1984 3/8 – 6/22
1984 11/1 – until 1985 1/15
1989 9/24 – 12/2
1990 5/12 – 7/26
1992 11/26 – until 1993 4/6
1993 7/26 – 10/17
1996 2/14 – 8/7
1996 9/30 – 12/31
2001 8/26 – until 2002 1/14
2002 4/17 – 7/10
2004 11/7 – until 2005 10/2
2008 1/27 – 12/14

SATURN CHALLENGING
1944 9/7 – 12/8
1945 5/24 – until 1946 6/23
1951 10/28 – until 1952 5/11
1952 7/10 – 12/14
1953 4/1 – 9/8
1959 12/27 – until 1961 2/16
1961 8/11 – 11/12
1974 7/5 – until 1975 8/3
1980 12/19 – until 1981 2/18
1981 9/3 – until 1982 10/17
1989 1/30 – 7/26
1989 10/26 – until 1990 4/13
1990 5/27 – 12/25
2003 8/15 – until 2004 1/11
2004 5/1 – 9/17
2004 12/31 – until 2005 6/4
2010 10/10 – until 2011 11/23
2012 5/2 – until 2012 8/16

URANUS CHALLENGING
1950 9/10 – until 1955 5/27
1970 9/28 – until 1974 8/26
1990 3/5 – until 1994 12/22

NEPTUNE CHALLENGING
1946 10/17 – until 1954 9/26
1988 2/1 – until 1996 1/7

PLUTO CHALLENGING
1974 12/9 – until 1982 8/28
2012 2/21 – Continues

JUPITER SPECIAL
1940 2/16 – 4/24
1951 6/5 – 10/4
1952 1/23 – 4/7
1963 5/13 – until 1964 3/21
1975 4/25 – until 1976 3/3
1987 4/8 – 6/24
1987 10/16 – until 1988 2/10
1999 3/23 – 5/31
2011 3/6 – 5/12

SATURN SPECIAL
1938 4/6 – until 1939 5/13
1939 12/4 – until 1940 1/20
1967 5/19 – 10/3
1968 2/9 – 7/11
1968 9/2 – until 1969 3/20
1997 3/20 – until 1998 4/26

April 8

Your Personal Powers

Your ambition and creative drive indicate that you are constantly looking for ways to express yourself. Often enthusiastic and inquisitive, you are a discerning learner. Having a keen eye and a good sense of values makes you a shrewd assessor of people and situations. Your ruling planet, Mars, endows you with plenty of energy; if inspired, you are willing to put in a great deal of work or are able to produce on a prolific scale. Self-reliant and daring, your forceful personality also indicates that you have the initiative to take the lead. You can, however, lose some of your power by being impetuous, scattered, or indecisive. The problem usually arises when you attempt to do too many things and overload yourself with commitments. Proud and bold by nature, you often conceal your vulnerability and insecurities, yet if you act in a bossy or controlling manner you can lose some of your charm and dignity. You gain power by being methodical, enterprising, and decisive.

Your Powers of Attraction in Relationships

Being friendly and sociable, you enjoy exchanging ideas with others or working with people who share your enthusiasm and aspirations. Although you may appear cool and in control, underneath your seemingly unconcerned exterior lie deep and intense emotions that indicate your true sensitivity or inner tensions. Being inquisitive and keen on learning, you also like to join different groups and take pleasure from being involved in all types of activity. Other people find you easy to talk to as you are often well-informed and willing to share your wisdom and knowledge . Nevertheless, you usually prefer like-minded people who are interested in progress or those who can inspire you to be mentally creative. Since you can be objective, honest, and idealistic, your most attractive qualities can be your daring personality and willingness to fight for your beliefs.

Your attractive qualities: authoritative, common sense, love of knowledge, thoroughness, hardworking, warmhearted, generous, progressive, artistic, organizational skills, protective, determined, creative, good judge of values, cautious, persevering

Your less attractive qualities: impatient, restless, workaholic, power struggles, easily discouraged, tactless, domineering, quick temper, lack of planning, controlling, stubborn, easily bored, dislike criticism

Your Venus Power

The planet Venus has a great deal of influence on your powers of attraction. Below are four possible Venus types for women and men. To find your Venus you need to go to page 771, where you will find the Venus table and extra information. The planet Mars also affects your powers of attraction. To find your Mars table and interpretation go to page 761.

WOMEN WITH VENUS IN PISCES: Being sensitive to affairs of the heart, when you care for someone you can feel their emotions and sense their every mood. Their goals can even become as important as your own. This empathy indicates that you can love on an unselfish level, but you may have to guard against giving too much, especially to those who do not reciprocate. You are seductive and captivating, and partners can be fascinated by your subtle charms and attracted by your caring and affectionate nature.

MEN WITH VENUS IN PISCES: The combination of your emotional subtlety and charm can make you very alluring when dealing with affairs of the heart. Perceptive and impressionable, you have an easygoing style in your relationships, usually preferring to avoid ugly confrontation. You are drawn to a partner who has a touch of glamour and is sensitive to the needs of others. Alternatively, your partner could be visionary with a rich imagination, like your own, who will keep you enchanted. With your insight you have the ability to observe the subtle moods of your partner.

WOMEN WITH VENUS IN ARIES: Self-reliant and strong, you usually want things your own way. This can present problems if you refuse to compromise with your partners. Your life lessons in the area of love and relationships often involve patience and learning to trust. When you project the full power of your Venus, you can radiate a charismatic and captivating energy and make a strong impression on others. Independence is often high on your relationship agenda.

MEN WITH VENUS IN ARIES: You are drawn to strong, independent women who can stand up to you. Although you can enthusiastically follow the object of your desire, you may lose power if you allow your forceful emotions to become too dominant. Warm and passionate, you have a side to your na-

ture that longs for new adventures. Romantic and chivalrous, you really enjoy the excitement of the initial chase, but unless you keep the enthusiasm alive and avoid falling into a rut you may become easily bored.

WOMEN WITH VENUS IN TAURUS: Warm and affectionate, you are drawn to partners with whom you can share life's simple comforts. With a need for stability and security or an appreciation of earthly pleasures, you may have to avoid overindulgence or becoming too preoccupied with material concerns. Nevertheless, your sociability and friendliness usually make you popular. You need a partner who can also share your appreciation of beauty and style.

MEN WITH VENUS IN TAURUS: As well as attracting people with your warm personality, you also possess an innate sense of the value of material possessions. Keeping yourself stylish and having an attractive home can therefore be important to you. You are naturally attracted to practical yet sensual women who understand your need for comfort, security, and the pleasures and luxuries of life. Naturally affectionate, you enjoy socializing but can make a loyal and loving partner.

WOMEN WITH VENUS IN GEMINI: By nature you are young at heart, adaptable, and sociable. Being curious and willing to cooperate makes you a good team player. You are usually drawn to articulate people who have charm and flair or sharp wit. With a need to expand your knowledge you also look for a partner who can challenge or stimulate you intellectually. Although you love to talk with all types of people you may need to develop your listening skills and tune into your feelings in order to build better communication in your relationships.

MEN WITH VENUS IN GEMINI: Adaptable yet often flirtatious, you enjoy mixing with people who are quick-minded and versatile. Since you can learn a great deal through interacting with others, you are often attracted to intelligent partners who have comprehensive knowledge or good ideas. One of your less attractive qualities is your tendency to get bored or be inconsistent. Having an adaptable partner is important to you, therefore it must be someone who can offer you different options and keep you interested.

To read all about your Outer Planets and work out how to use your personalized timetable, go to Section Three, page 789.

Your Personalized Timetable

JUPITER BENEFICIAL
1938 2/13 – 3/31
1938 10/1 – 11/5
1941 7/24 – until 1942 1/6
1942 3/8 – 5/9
1943 8/15 – 11/17
1944 1/9 – 7/5
1947 12/8 – until 1948 3/1
1948 5/31 – 10/25
1950 1/28 – 3/12
1953 7/4 – 8/28
1953 12/2 – until 1954 4/18
1955 7/30 – 10/16
1956 2/20 – 6/13
1959 11/22 – until 1960 2/5
1960 7/13 – 9/27
1962 1/11 – 2/23
1965 6/17 – 8/3
1966 1/14 – 3/19
1967 7/14 – 9/26
1968 4/14 – 4/29
1971 11/6 – until 1972 1/17
1973 12/25 – until 1974 2/6
1977 6/1 – 7/15
1979 6/26 – 9/9
1983 3/2 – 4/22
1983 10/19 – until 1984 1/1
1985 4/13 – 7/28
1985 12/4 – until 1986 1/21
1989 5/16 – 6/28
1990 10/11 – until 1991 1/18
1991 6/6 – 8/24
1995 1/29 – 6/6
1995 9/27 – 12/16
1997 3/20 – 9/15
1997 10/30 – until 1998 1/4
2001 4/28 – 6/11
2002 9/18 – until 2003 2/28
2003 5/9 – 8/8
2007 1/9 – 11/30
2009 3/2 – 4/23
2009 8/8 – 12/13
2012 8/18 – 11/20

SATURN BENEFICIAL
1943 5/14 – 8/4
1943 12/18 – until 1944 4/21
1947 7/17 – until 1948 8/17
1957 1/6 – 6/17
1957 10/4 – until 1958 12/1
1963 1/26 – 5/19
1963 6/18 – until 1964 1/23
1972 6/23 – until 1973 6/6
1976 8/25 – until 1977 9/27
1978 3/3 – 6/16
1986 11/15 – until 1988 1/5
1992 3/1 – 9/8
1992 11/21 – until 1993 2/26
2001 8/9 – 11/15
2002 4/25 – 7/14
2003 1/24 – 3/23
2005 10/14 – 12/31
2006 6/28 – until 2007 8/1

URANUS BENEFICIAL
1944 8/27 – until 1948 4/12
1957 9/14 – until 1961 8/15
1983 12/11 – until 1987 12/3
1999 2/4 – until 2002 1/10

NEPTUNE BENEFICIAL
1974 12/17 – until 1982 11/26
2003 4/14 – until 2009 1/16

PLUTO BENEFICIAL
1944 10/2 – until 1955 8/3
1999 1/27 – until 2006 12/2

JUPITER CHALLENGING
1942 7/24 – until 1943 6/11

1945 10/11 – until 1946 1/11
1946 3/14 – 9/4
1948 12/30 – until 1949 3/15
1949 7/30 – 11/6
1954 7/7 – 9/26
1955 1/8 – 5/21
1957 9/25 – 12/13
1958 4/24 – 8/13
1960 12/13 – until 1961 2/22
1966 6/21 – 9/3
1967 2/18 – 4/21
1969 9/9 – 11/24
1972 11/26 – until 1973 2/4
1978 6/4 – 8/16
1981 1/7 – 2/10
1981 8/22 – 11/7
1984 3/15 – 6/14
1984 11/7 – until 1985 1/20
1989 10/4 – 11/22
1990 5/17 – 7/30
1992 12/2 – until 1993 3/29
1993 8/2 – 10/22
1996 2/19 – 7/28
1996 10/10 – until 1997 1/4
2001 8/31 – until 2002 1/6
2002 4/24 – 7/14
2004 11/12 – until 2005 5/10
2005 7/1 – 10/7
2008 2/1 – 12/18

SATURN CHALLENGING
1944 9/22 – 11/23
1945 6/1 – until 1946 7/1
1951 11/5 – until 1952 4/24
1952 7/26 – 12/27
1953 3/18 – 9/17
1960 1/4 – until 1961 2/26
1961 7/27 – 11/25
1974 7/12 – until 1975 8/11
1981 9/12 – until 1982 10/25
1989 2/9 – 7/12
1989 11/8 – until 1991 1/3
2003 8/24 – 12/29
2004 5/12 – 9/29
2004 12/18 – until 2005 6/13
2010 10/18 – until 2011 12/3
2012 4/19 – 8/28

URANUS CHALLENGING
1951 7/6 – until 1955 6/16
1970 10/14 – until 1974 9/15
1991 1/4 – until 1995 1/8

NEPTUNE CHALLENGING
1946 11/16 – until 1955 8/18
1988 3/11 – until 1996 12/5

PLUTO CHALLENGING
1975 10/23 – until 1982 9/26

JUPITER SPECIAL
1940 2/20 – 4/28
1951 6/12 – 9/27
1952 1/29 – 4/11
1963 5/18 – 11/20
1963 12/20 – until 1964 3/26
1975 4/29 – until 1976 3/8
1987 4/13 – 6/30
1987 10/9 – until 1988 2/16
1999 3/27 – 6/5
1999 11/27 – until 2000 1/12
2011 3/10 – 5/16

SATURN SPECIAL
1938 4/14 – until 1939 5/22
1939 11/16 – until 1940 2/7
1967 5/29 – 9/21
1968 2/19 – until 1969 3/28
1997 3/28 – until 1998 5/4

♈

April 9

SUN: ARIES • DECANATE: LEO/MARS • DEGREE: 18°5–19°5 ARIES • MODE: CARDINAL • ELEMENT: FIRE

Your Personal Powers

Industrious and pragmatic, you have an ability to concentrate on your goals as your journey to success calls for steady advancement. As a forceful character you prefer to be your own boss or be placed in a managerial post rather than be subservient to others. You gain power when you overcome your inborn tendency to worry or be indecisive about money matters. When you see the benefits that come from staying open-minded and being universal in your attitude, you can be more successful. Learning how to budget and manage your finances can be one of your keys to prosperity. You can lose power by being disorganized, too obstinate, or suspicious of others. By being methodical and learning to stay detached you empower yourself and gain the respect you desire. Your ability to think objectively and learn new subjects quickly also indicates that you need to put your fine mind to good use in order to feel successful.

Your Powers of Attraction in Relationships

Self-assured and friendly, you gain the admiration of others when you show your more liberal or humanitarian attitude. Your generosity and enterprising nature usually attract others. Although you can be witty and entertaining, a tendency to be argumentative or too headstrong may cause anxiety in your personal relationships. You are intelligent and creative with an ability to grasp ideas quickly and other people admire your practical skills and often think of you as clever and talented. Usually you are attracted to creative or ambitious people who can inspire you to express yourself or be adventurous. Although you need love and affection, your indecisiveness or alternating moods can cause misunderstandings, especially if you allow money issues to create tension or conflict in your personal relationships. Staying detached and keeping yourself purposeful increases your confidence and inspires you to be more altruistic.

Your attractive qualities: idealistic, humanitarian, creative, sensitive, astute, hardworking, ambitious, good business acumen, generous, charismatic, detached, enterprising, resourceful, inner strength, proud, receptive, sensitive, intuitive, dynamic, philanthropic, diligent, dependable

Your less attractive qualities: easily frustrated, nervous, unsure, selfish, impractical, materialistic, uneconomical, indulgent, hasty actions, impatient, critical, bossy, demanding, temperamental, uncommunicative

Your Venus Power

The planet Venus has a great deal of influence on your powers of attraction. Below are four possible Venus types for women and men. To find your Venus you need to go to page 771, where you will find the Venus table and extra information. The planet Mars also affects your powers of attraction. To find your Mars table and interpretation go to page 761.

WOMEN WITH VENUS IN PISCES: Romantic and idealistic when in love, you can be a sensitive and responsive lover. With your affectionate and impressionable nature you are often attracted to those who understand your sensitivity and share your vision. Being flexible with an impressionable nature helps you to adapt to the needs of others. In your desire to blend with those you love, guard against giving too much of yourself by not defining your boundaries clearly.

MEN WITH VENUS IN PISCES: In love you are sensitive, tender, and affectionate, experiencing your partner's feelings almost as strongly as your own. Being also imaginative and visionary, you possess the capability to develop deep compassion for others. As you are idealistic when in love, you usually prefer to see only your partner's good points, but be careful that your high expectations do not bring disappointment if you avoid harsh reality. Nevertheless, in your relationships with others you can be devoted, loving, and positively enchanting.

WOMEN WITH VENUS IN ARIES: You gain power from your strong individuality, energy, and enthusiasm. Your young-at-heart and spirited approach to relationships adds to your appeal. If you become too impatient or self-absorbed, however, your partnerships are likely to suffer. Nevertheless, you can be creative, sharp, and quick, especially when you are able to share new and exciting projects with your partners. Mischievous, with a love of action, you may even incite them to a playful fight.

MEN WITH VENUS IN ARIES: Friendly, sociable, and expressive with your feelings, you can become easily aroused and animated when involved with a person who is close to your heart. Although you can enthusiastically follow the object of your desire, you may lose power if you allow your forceful emotions to become too dominant or go for instant gratifica-

tion. You are drawn to women who can match you in quickness and boldness. Warm and passionate, a side to your nature longs for excitement and new adventures.

WOMEN WITH VENUS IN TAURUS: Demonstrative and affectionate, you are naturally tactile with a love of sensual pleasures. With a streak of the conventional, you love the simple pleasures of life: good food, close friends, and happy relationships. Although you possess endurance be careful not to let this turn into plain stubbornness. Having inner strength, you can express genuine patience and are often a pillar of support for loved ones and friends.

MEN WITH VENUS IN TAURUS: Although you are usually drawn to sensual and physically beautiful individuals, you want a partner who is also reliable and loyal. When in love, you enjoy buying your partner things of quality that will grow in value or useful things of a practical nature. You also love to socialize and entertain, especially in luxurious surroundings. Affectionate and caring, you are often attracted to creative people or those with artistic talents.

WOMEN WITH VENUS IN GEMINI: Charming and usually easygoing, you like to talk to people who are intelligent and witty. With a good social sense and a desire for mental expansion, you need a partner who is informed and has good ideas. Although you enjoy having different experiences, you need to resist your tendencies to become bored too quickly or be too talkative. As you enjoy sharing and learning new things, you usually prefer being with someone rather than operating alone.

MEN WITH VENUS IN GEMINI: Informed and curious, charming and friendly, you seek a partner who shares your interests or enjoys your witty remarks. Although a good communicator, you have an inborn tendency to be lighthearted and less profound about deep emotional commitment. Although you are keen on experiences that bring variety into your life, boredom or scattering your energies in too many directions is probably your biggest handicap in relationships. Nevertheless you are attracted to intelligent partners who can match your lively banter.

To read all about your Outer Planets and work out how to use your personalized timetable, go to Section Three, page 789.

Your Personalized Timetable

JUPITER BENEFICIAL
1938 2/17 – 4/5
1938 9/18 – 11/18
1941 7/29 – 12/27
1942 3/17 – 5/13
1943 8/19 – 12/4
1943 12/23 – until 1944 7/10
1947 12/12 – until 1948 3/9
1948 5/22 – 10/30
1950 2/1 – 3/16
1953 7/9 – 9/4
1953 11/24 – until 1954 4/23
1955 8/3 – 10/23
1956 2/13 – 6/19
1959 11/27 – until 1960 2/10
1960 7/4 – 10/5
1962 1/16 – 2/27
1965 6/21 – 8/8
1966 1/5 – 3/28
1967 7/18 – 10/2
1968 3/26 – 5/18
1971 11/10 – until 1972 1/22
1973 12/29 – until 1974 2/10
1977 6/5 – 7/19
1979 7/1 – 9/14
1983 3/26 – 3/30
1983 10/24 – until 1984 1/5
1985 4/20 – 7/20
1985 12/10 – until 1986 1/26
1989 5/29 – 7/2
1990 10/19 – until 1991 1/10
1991 6/12 – 8/28
1995 2/4 – 5/29
1995 10/3 – 12/20
1997 3/26 – 9/4
1997 11/10 – until 1998 1/8
2001 5/2 – 6/16
2002 9/23 – until 2003 2/19
2003 5/18 – 8/13
2007 1/14 – 7/12
2007 9/1 – 12/5
2009 3/6 – 5/1
2009 7/31 – 12/19
2012 8/26 – 11/12

SATURN BENEFICIAL
1943 5/22 – 8/14
1943 12/6 – until 1944 5/1
1947 7/24 – until 1948 8/25
1957 1/16 – 6/3
1957 10/16 – until 1958 12/10
1963 2/4 – until 1964 2/1
1972 7/1 – until 1973 1/27
1973 3/2 – 6/13
1976 9/2 – until 1977 3/9
1977 5/13 – 10/7
1978 2/19 – 6/27
1986 11/23 – until 1988 1/13
1988 7/25 – 10/4
1992 3/10 – 8/24
1992 12/5 – until 1993 3/6
1993 10/10 – 11/14
2001 8/23 – 10/31
2002 5/4 – 7/23
2003 1/8 – 4/7
2005 11/1 – 12/13
2006 7/7 – until 2007 8/9

URANUS BENEFICIAL
1945 6/15 – until 1948 5/5
1957 10/7 – until 1962 6/7
1983 12/27 – until 1987 12/19
1999 2/22 – until 2002 1/28

NEPTUNE BENEFICIAL
1975 1/15 – until 1983 10/18
2004 3/1 – until 2009 12/2

PLUTO BENEFICIAL
1945 9/8 – until 1956 7/6
1999 12/17 – until 2007 10/25

JUPITER CHALLENGING
1942 7/28 – until 1943 6/16
1945 10/15 – until 1946 1/25
1946 2/28 – 9/9
1949 1/3 – 3/21
1949 7/23 – 11/12
1954 7/11 – 10/3
1954 12/31 – until 1955 5/27
1957 9/29 – 12/20
1958 4/16 – 8/19
1960 12/18 – until 1961 2/27
1966 6/25 – 9/9
1967 2/9 – 5/1
1969 9/14 – 11/29
1970 5/30 – 7/17
1972 12/1 – until 1973 2/9
1978 6/9 – 8/20
1981 8/28 – 11/11
1984 3/24 – 6/6
1984 11/12 – until 1985 1/24
1990 5/22 – 8/4
1992 12/9 – until 1993 3/21
1993 8/8 – 10/26
1996 2/25 – 7/19
1996 10/18 – until 1997 1/8
2001 9/7 – 12/30
2002 4/30 – 7/18
2004 11/17 – until 2005 4/29
2005 7/12 – 10/11
2008 2/5 – 12/23

SATURN CHALLENGING
1945 6/9 – until 1946 7/9
1951 11/14 – until 1952 4/10
1952 8/8 – until 1953 1/15
1953 2/26 – 9/26
1960 1/13 – until 1961 3/8
1961 7/14 – 12/6
1974 7/20 – until 1975 8/19
1976 2/25 – 4/28
1981 9/20 – until 1982 11/2
1989 2/19 – 6/28
1989 11/19 – until 1991 1/11
2003 9/4 – 12/17
2004 5/21 – 10/17
2004 11/30 – until 2005 6/21
2010 10/27 – until 2011 5/20
2011 7/6 – 12/13
2012 4/6 – 9/7

URANUS CHALLENGING
1951 7/22 – until 1955 7/3
1970 10/30 – until 1974 10/2
1991 1/20 – until 1995 11/5

NEPTUNE CHALLENGING
1947 10/14 – until 1955 9/22
1989 1/27 – until 1997 1/3

PLUTO CHALLENGING
1975 11/22 – until 1983 8/2

JUPITER SPECIAL
1940 2/25 – 5/3
1951 6/19 – 9/19
1952 2/3 – 4/16
1963 5/23 – 11/7
1964 1/2 – 3/30
1975 5/3 – until 1976 3/12
1987 4/17 – 7/8
1987 10/1 – until 1988 2/21
1999 3/31 – 6/10
1999 11/16 – until 2000 1/23
2011 3/14 – 5/21

SATURN SPECIAL
1938 4/22 – until 1939 5/31
1939 11/2 – until 1940 2/19
1967 6/11 – 9/7
1968 2/28 – until 1969 4/5
1997 4/5 – until 1998 5/12
1998 12/18 – until 1999 1/10

April 10

SUN: ARIES • DECANATE: SAGITTARIUS/JUPITER • DEGREE: 19°5–20°5 ARIES • MODE: CARDINAL • ELEMENT: FIRE

Your Personal Powers

Enthusiastic and intelligent, you are a highly motivated individual with idealistic convictions and ambition to succeed. Being youthful and adventurous, your ruling plant, Mars, endows you with vitality and a daring spirit. Keen to explore different experiences in life, you are usually enthusiastic and optimistic, but you may lose some of your power if you vacillate between faith and self-doubt. Although you are determined to make headway and enjoy the good things in life, you gain power when you are able to create a balance between what inspires you intellectually and what you desire materially. Shrewd and purposeful, you are excellent at problem solving, and by concentrating on your goals, you are able to achieve favorable results. Although you have an astute mind, nervous sensitivity or a reluctance to be serious indicates that you may lose some of your power if you act on impulse or refuse to take responsibility for your actions. Adopting a mature perspective therefore can enhance your chances for true success.

Your Powers of Attraction in Relationships

With your enthusiasm, charm, and personal magnetism, you attract many friends and admirers. Although you need to act independently or be self-sufficient, you benefit from partnerships and collaborating with other people. You are often attracted to idealistic or romantic individuals who are artistic and generous. Alternatively, practical, steady, and solid individuals who can provide you with security can attract you. As a romantic and sensitive individual, you can charm your partner to forgive you any of your shortcomings, yet to gain the respect or support of others you need to stay calm, act responsibly, and deliver what you promise. When your ideas and beliefs inspire your actions, other people appreciate your foresight and practical idealism.

Your attractive qualities: energetic, optimistic, determined, responsible, ambitious, creative, progressive, forceful, strong convictions, leader, competitive, independent, gregarious, intuitive, charming, intelligent, youthful, entertaining, generous, daring, enthusiastic, enterprising

Your less attractive qualities: impatient, restless, selfish, overbearing, pretentious, bossy, too competitive, materialistic, indulgent, lazy, unmotivated, dissatisfied, give up without a fight, take the easy option, temperamental, stubborn

Your Venus Power

The planet Venus has a great deal of influence on your powers of attraction. Below are four possible Venus types for women and men. To find your Venus you need to go to page 771, where you will find the Venus table and extra information. The planet Mars also affects your powers of attraction. To find your Mars table and interpretation go to page 761.

WOMEN WITH VENUS IN PISCES: Romantic and impressionable, you are a caring and loving individual with a dreamy nature. In relationships you are often attracted to idealistic, compassionate, or sympathetic individuals who have imagination or a strong romantic sense. A tendency to be sensitive to others suggests that you are intuitive and aware of people's inner feelings. Be careful therefore not to get caught in other people's dramas or play the rescuer too often.

MEN WITH VENUS IN PISCES: The combination of your emotional subtlety and charm can make you very alluring when dealing with affairs of the heart. Perceptive and impressionable, you have an easygoing style in your relationships, usually preferring to avoid ugly confrontation. You are drawn to a partner who has a touch of glamour and is sensitive to the needs of others. Alternatively, your partner can be a visionary with a rich imagination, like your own, who will keep you enchanted.

WOMEN WITH VENUS IN ARIES: Idealistic, passionate, and adventurous, you are direct in your dealings with others. When you are attracted to a person you usually take the initiative and use your people skills to make things happen. In close relationships you are not afraid to confront your other half. This self-assertiveness is positive if differences can be brought into the open through diplomacy and compromise. Independent and spirited, you enjoy your freedom.

MEN WITH VENUS IN ARIES: As you often have the courage and strength to initiate situations, you like to take the lead and let others follow. With your unconscious desire for conquest, you may also have to beware of being competitive with your partners. Nevertheless, you are drawn to direct and strong-willed women who can share your love of action and

enthusiasm for life. When you are feeling good you can be charming and enthusiastic in romantic situations with an entertaining and spontaneous spirit.

WOMEN WITH VENUS IN TAURUS: For your ideal relationship you seek a partner who is both financially secure and demonstrative with his affections. With these thoughts in mind, you are likely to also want a partner who is refined yet pragmatic or someone concerned with safeguarding your future. Although you have a stubborn streak, you can be loving and affectionate in your relationships, and with your good sense of style you may be attracted to the arts, music, or luxury items.

MEN WITH VENUS IN TAURUS: As you yourself may be attractive to the opposite sex, you desire a partner who is sensual and loving or who has physical beauty. Needing stability, when faced with changes that are out of your control, you may become insecure or possessive. Your own sense of style and love of beauty imply that you can be attracted to creative people, especially in art and music. Faithful and/or loyal, you can be affectionate, tactile, and constant in your love.

WOMEN WITH VENUS IN GEMINI: In relationships, you need intellectual stimulation and usually prefer to keep things light. Certainly not boring, you love to talk and are at your best being witty and entertaining. Although your easygoing approach to relationships is very attractive, guard against losing touch with your emotions. You prefer a partner who can keep up with your fast stream of ideas, and if you have shared interests then so much the better.

MEN WITH VENUS IN GEMINI: Charming, amusing, and adaptable, you attract others with your natural communication skills and friendly personality. You have a wonderful childlike quality and love to keep life playful, but a reluctance to contact your deeper feelings may cause you to avoid serious commitment. With your need for variety and intellectual stimulation, you are attracted to clever and amusing partners who have many interesting sides to their personalities.

To read all about your Outer Planets and work out how to use your personalized timetable, go to Section Three, page 789.

Your Personalized Timetable

JUPITER BENEFICIAL
1938 2/22 – 4/10
1938 9/9 – 11/27
1941 8/4 – 12/19
1942 3/24 – 5/18
1943 8/24 – until 1944 7/15
1947 12/17 – until 1948 3/20
1948 5/11 – 11/4
1950 2/5 – 3/21
1953 7/13 – 9/13
1953 11/15 – until 1954 4/29
1955 8/7 – 10/30
1956 2/5 – 6/25
1959 12/1 – until 1960 2/16
1960 6/26 – 10/12
1962 1/20 – 3/3
1965 6/26 – 8/14
1965 12/28 – until 1966 4/5
1967 7/23 – 10/7
1968 3/16 – 5/29
1971 11/15 – until 1972 1/27
1974 1/3 – 2/15
1977 6/9 – 7/24
1979 7/6 – 9/18
1983 10/29 – until 1984 1/9
1985 4/29 – 7/11
1985 12/15 – until 1986 1/30
1989 5/24 – 7/7
1990 10/28 – until 1991 1/1
1991 6/17 – 9/2
1995 2/11 – 5/21
1995 10/9 – 12/25
1997 3/31 – 8/26
1997 11/19 – until 1998 1/13
2001 5/7 – 6/20
2002 9/29 – until 2003 2/11
2003 5/25 – 8/17
2007 1/19 – 7/1
2007 9/12 – 12/9
2009 3/11 – 5/9
2009 7/22 – 12/24
2012 9/4 – 11/3

SATURN BENEFICIAL
1943 5/30 – 8/26
1943 11/23 – until 1944 5/10
1947 8/1 – until 1948 9/2
1957 1/27 – 5/21
1957 10/26 – until 1958 12/18
1963 2/12 – until 1964 2/9
1972 7/9 – until 1973 1/7
1973 3/22 – 6/21
1976 9/10 – until 1977 2/22
1977 5/28 – 10/17
1978 2/6 – 7/7
1986 12/2 – until 1988 1/22
1988 7/9 – 10/19
1992 3/20 – 8/10
1992 12/17 – until 1993 3/15
1993 9/18 – 12/5
2001 9/17 – 10/5
2002 5/12 – 8/1
2002 12/26 – until 2003 4/19
2006 7/15 – until 2007 8/16

URANUS BENEFICIAL
1945 7/3 – until 1948 5/24
1958 8/3 – until 1962 7/2
1984 1/15 – until 1988 10/20
1999 3/12 – until 2002 2/14

NEPTUNE BENEFICIAL
1975 12/14 – until 1983 11/22
2004 4/4 – until 2010 1/10

PLUTO BENEFICIAL
1946 8/20 – until 1956 8/8
2000 1/14 – until 2007 11/27

JUPITER CHALLENGING
1942 8/2 – until 1943 6/20

1945 10/20 – until 1946 9/14
1949 1/7 – 3/27
1949 7/15 – 11/18
1954 7/16 – 10/11
1954 12/23 – until 1955 6/1
1957 10/4 – 12/26
1958 4/8 – 8/26
1960 12/22 – until 1961 3/4
1961 9/4 – 10/12
1966 6/30 – 9/14
1967 2/1 – 5/8
1969 9/18 – 12/4
1970 5/19 – 7/28
1972 12/5 – until 1973 2/13
1978 6/13 – 8/25
1981 9/2 – 11/16
1984 4/3 – 5/26
1984 11/17 – until 1985 1/28
1990 5/27 – 8/8
1992 12/16 – until 1993 3/13
1993 8/14 – 10/31
1996 3/1 – 7/11
1996 10/25 – until 1997 1/12
2001 9/13 – 12/22
2002 5/6 – 7/23
2004 11/23 – until 2005 4/20
2005 7/21 – 10/16
2008 2/10 – 12/27

SATURN CHALLENGING
1945 6/17 – until 1946 7/17
1951 11/24 – until 1952 3/29
1952 8/19 – until 1953 10/5
1960 1/21 – 9/7
1960 9/24 – until 1961 3/20
1961 6/30 – 12/15
1974 7/28 – until 1975 8/28
1976 2/10 – 5/12
1981 9/28 – until 1982 11/10
1983 6/17 – 7/15
1989 3/3 – 6/14
1989 11/29 – until 1991 1/19
2003 9/17 – 12/4
2004 5/30 – until 2005 6/29
2010 11/4 – until 2011 5/1
2011 7/25 – 12/26
2012 3/23 – 9/17

URANUS CHALLENGING
1951 8/9 – until 1955 7/20
1970 11/17 – until 1974 10/17
1991 2/8 – until 1995 12/3

NEPTUNE CHALLENGING
1947 11/11 – until 1956 8/8
1989 3/2 – until 1997 11/29

PLUTO CHALLENGING
1938 3/28 – 4/24
1976 10/12 – until 1983 9/11

JUPITER SPECIAL
1940 2/29 – 5/7
1951 6/27 – 9/11
1952 2/9 – 4/20
1963 5/28 – 10/28
1964 1/11 – 4/3
1975 5/8 – until 1976 3/17
1987 4/21 – 7/16
1987 9/22 – until 1988 2/27
1999 4/4 – 6/16
1999 11/8 – until 2000 1/31
2011 3/18 – 5/25

SATURN SPECIAL
1938 4/30 – 11/17
1939 1/10 – 6/10
1939 10/21 – until 1940 2/29
1967 6/29 – 8/20
1968 3/7 – until 1969 4/13
1997 4/13 – until 1998 5/20
1998 11/24 – until 1999 2/2

April 11

SUN: ARIES • DECANATE: SAGITTARIUS/JUPITER • DEGREE: 20°5–21°5 ARIES • MODE: CARDINAL • ELEMENT: FIRE

Your Personal Powers

Optimistic, enterprising, and ambitious, you are motivated by success and inspired by new opportunities to widen your horizons. Your ruling plant, Mars, endows you with courage, dynamic drive, and a daring or enterprising nature. Being persuasive with excellent organizational skills, you can inspire others to follow your latest scheme or exciting idea. Goal-oriented, you are usually aiming for the top and prefer to think on a large scale. You gain power when you realize that success is often a spark of inspiration and a great deal of hard work and determination. In order to succeed, therefore, and make use of some of the excellent opportunities granted to you, you must apply self-discipline, dedication, and perseverance. You may lose some of your power when you agree to take unnecessary chances or when you rush into speculative ventures without thinking them through first. Fortunately, as an astute and intuitive individual, you learn quickly how to take advantage of some of the opportunities that life has to offer you.

Your Powers of Attraction in Relationships

You can attract other people with your confidence, generosity, optimism, and determination. You gain the support and respect you want when you use tact and diplomacy to convey your ideas. You are usually attracted to dynamic or freedom-loving individuals with integrity. Although you can be friendly and cooperative, you can sometimes irritate others by being impatient and impulsive. When you balance your priorities and do not let your appetite for success interfere with your desire for true love and affection, you can establish long-term relationships. As you dislike taking orders yourself, you may need to be more sensitive to others and resist a temptation to be arrogant or bossy. Nevertheless, your charismatic appeal is likely to make you popular and provide you with many social and romantic opportunities.

Your attractive qualities: dynamic, adventurous, determined, resourceful, methodical, attention to detail, think big, generous, objective, intuitive, enthusiastic, foresightful, inventive, persuasive, quick-minded, business acumen, diplomatic, idealistic, intelligent, sociable, inspired

Your less attractive qualities: extravagant, restless, inconsistent, speculative, materialistic, domineering, selfish, too idealistic, impractical, overly ambitious, impatient, speculative, scattered, unorganized, closed to criticism

Your Venus Power

The planet Venus has a great deal of influence on your powers of attraction. Below are four possible Venus types for women and men. To find your Venus you need to go to page 771, where you will find the Venus table and extra information. The planet Mars also affects your powers of attraction. To find your Mars table and interpretation go to page 761.

WOMEN WITH VENUS IN PISCES: As a romantic and idealistic individual you can be both loving and giving. In relationships you may need to balance the practical with the charitable. While making allowances and sacrifices is understandable in a loving relationship, playing the martyr is often a state of romantic illusion that can lead to self-deception. Your benevolence and sacrifices in the right relationship nonetheless make you a partner who is devoted, kind, and compassionate. Subtle, sensitive, and alluring, you make a sensual and caring partner.

MEN WITH VENUS IN PISCES: Romantic and idealistic when in love, you can be a sensitive and responsive lover. Being pliant and flexible with an impressionable nature helps you to adapt to the needs of others. In your desire to blend with those you love, however, guard against not clearly defining your own boundaries. With your affectionate and sentimental nature, you are often attracted to those who understand your sensitivity and share your vision.

WOMEN WITH VENUS IN ARIES: Idealistic, passionate, and adventurous, you are direct in your dealings with others. When you are attracted to a person, you usually take the initiative and use your people skills to make things happen. In close relationships, you are not afraid to confront your other half. This self-assertiveness is positive if differences can be brought into the open through diplomacy and compromise. Independent and spirited, you enjoy your freedom.

MEN WITH VENUS IN ARIES: You are usually inclined to seek a partner who is active, goal-oriented, and/or decisive. Not known for your patience, you probably seek relationships early in life. You may find that you are attracted more to women who have a daring or adventurous spirit, but in your

close relationships you may encounter rivalry or find that both you and your partner want to lead or be the boss. Although you may act rashly you possess a great deal of magnetism and are capable of demonstrating your love and affection.

WOMEN WITH VENUS IN TAURUS: Good-natured and romantic, you have a highly developed sense of touch that particularly responds to massage, hugs, and all things physical. With a streak of the conventional you love the simple pleasures of life: good food, close friends, and happy relationships. With your natural sense of beauty and harmony you are likely to have an attractive voice, beautiful home, or a strong link to nature. You may have to be careful of becoming too extravagant, as often your taste is more expensive than what you are able to afford.

MEN WITH VENUS IN TAURUS: Attractive and affectionate in relationships you are often down-to-earth, with a conservative approach. You are usually drawn to warmhearted partners with whom you can share a familiar routine as well as life's pleasures and comforts. Seeking a partner who is dependable or reassuring you often put security high on your priority list when looking for love. Your sociability and friendliness usually make you popular, and partners often admire your practicality and good sense of values.

WOMEN WITH VENUS IN GEMINI: Curious, with a bright and animated approach to life, you are attracted to those who are clever or sophisticated. Your love of variety and desire for knowledge suggest that you need a partner and friends who can keep you mentally stimulated. Although witty and a good conversationalist, you may need to keep in touch with your deeper feelings. Nevertheless, intelligent and friendly, you possess a youthful sense of wonder and seek a playmate who can keep you from becoming bored.

MEN WITH VENUS IN GEMINI: Friendly and sociable, you attract others with your clever and amusing conversation. Drawn to partners who can match you in wit and intelligence, you usually prefer to keep relationships light rather than emotionally intense. With your youthful charm and desire for knowledge and new experiences you usually have many friends and a low boredom threshold.

To read all about your Outer Planets and work out how to use your personalized timetable, go to Section Three, page 789.

♈

Your Personalized Timetable

JUPITER BENEFICIAL
1938 2/26 – 4/15
1938 9/1 – 12/4
1941 8/10 – 12/12
1942 3/31 – 5/22
1943 8/28 – until 1944 7/20
1947 12/21 – until 1948 4/9
1948 4/21 – 11/9
1950 2/9 – 3/25
1953 7/18 – 9/26
1953 11/3 – until 1954 5/4
1955 8/12 – 11/6
1956 1/28 – 7/1
1959 12/5 – until 1960 2/22
1960 6/19 – 10/19
1962 1/24 – 3/7
1965 6/30 – 8/20
1965 12/21 – until 1966 4/11
1967 7/27 – 10/12
1968 3/7 – 6/7
1971 11/19 – until 1972 1/31
1972 8/10 – 9/9
1974 1/7 – 2/19
1977 6/14 – 7/29
1979 7/11 – 9/23
1983 11/3 – until 1984 1/14
1985 5/9 – 7/1
1985 12/20 – until 1986 2/3
1989 5/29 – 7/11
1990 11/9 – 12/21
1991 6/23 – 9/7
1995 2/19 – 5/13
1995 10/15 – 12/29
1997 4/6 – 8/18
1997 11/26 – until 1998 1/17
2001 11/5 – 6/24
2002 10/5 – until 2003 2/4
2003 6/1 – 8/22
2007 1/25 – 6/22
2007 9/20 – 12/13
2009 3/15 – 5/19
2009 7/12 – 12/29
2012 9/17 – 10/21

SATURN BENEFICIAL
1943 6/6 – 9/10
1943 11/7 – until 1944 5/18
1947 8/9 – until 1948 9/9
1957 2/10 – 5/6
1957 11/5 – until 1958 12/26
1963 2/20 – until 1964 2/17
1972 7/18 – 12/24
1973 4/4 – 6/28
1976 9/19 – until 1977 2/9
1977 6/9 – 10/29
1978 1/24 – 7/16
1986 12/10 – until 1988 2/1
1988 6/25 – 10/31
1992 3/31 – 7/28
1992 12/27 – until 1993 3/24
1993 9/3 – 12/19
2002 5/20 – 8/11
2002 12/14 – until 2003 4/29
2006 7/23 – until 2007 8/24

URANUS BENEFICIAL
1945 7/22 – until 1948 6/10
1958 8/19 – until 1962 7/21
1984 2/7 – until 1988 11/11
1999 4/4 – until 2002 12/22

NEPTUNE BENEFICIAL
1976 1/11 – until 1984 10/7
2005 2/25 – until 2010 2/7

PLUTO BENEFICIAL
1946 9/28 – until 1957 7/13
2000 3/5 – until 2008 10/16

JUPITER CHALLENGING
1942 8/7 – until 1943 6/25
1945 10/24 – until 1946 9/19

1949 1/11 – 4/3
1949 7/7 – 11/24
1954 7/20 – 10/22
1954 12/12 – until 1955 6/7
1957 10/9 – until 1958 1/3
1958 3/31 – 8/31
1960 12/26 – until 1961 3/9
1961 8/23 – 10/24
1966 7/4 – 9/20
1967 1/24 – 5/15
1969 9/23 – 12/10
1970 5/9 – 0 8/6
1972 12/10 – until 1973 2/18
1978 6/18 – 8/30
1981 9/7 – 11/21
1984 4/22 – 5/6
1984 11/22 – until 1985 2/1
1990 6/1 – 8/13
1992 12/25 – until 1993 3/4
1993 8/19 – 11/5
1996 3/8 – 7/3
1996 11/1 – until 1997 1/16
2001 9/21 – 12/15
2002 5/12 – 7/27
2004 11/28 – until 2005 4/12
2005 7/28 – 10/20
2008 2/15 – 8/25
2008 9/22 – 12/31

SATURN CHALLENGING
1945 6/25 – until 1946 7/24
1951 12/6 – until 1952 3/16
1952 8/28 – until 1953 10/13
1960 1/30 – 8/10
1960 10/21 – until 1961 4/4
1961 6/14 – 12/24
1974 8/5 – until 1975 2/10
1975 4/15 – 9/5
1976 1/28 – 5/24
1981 10/6 – until 1982 11/19
1983 5/24 – 8/8
1989 3/17 – 5/30
1989 12/8 – until 1991 1/28
2003 10/6 – 11/14
2004 6/7 – until 2005 7/7
2010 11/13 – until 2011 4/17
2011 8/7 – until 2012 1/11
2012 3/5 – 9/26

URANUS CHALLENGING
1951 8/30 – until 1956 5/13
1970 12/10 – until 1975 8/10
1991 3/1 – until 1995 12/23

NEPTUNE CHALLENGING
1947 12/25 – until 1956 9/17
1990 1/23 – until 1997 12/29

PLUTO CHALLENGING
1938 1/25 – 6/22
1976 11/7 – until 1983 10/8

JUPITER SPECIAL
1940 3/5 – 5/11
1951 7/6 – 9/1
1952 2/14 – 4/24
1963 6/3 – 10/20
1964 1/19 – 4/7
1975 5/12 – until 1976 3/21
1987 4/25 – 7/27
1987 9/11 – until 1988 3/3
1999 4/8 – 6/21
1999 10/31 – until 2000 2/7
2011 3/22 – 5/30

SATURN SPECIAL
1938 5/9 – 10/31
1939 1/26 – 6/20
1939 10/8 – until 1940 3/10
1968 3/16 – until 1969 4/21
1997 4/21 – until 1998 5/29
1998 11/9 – until 1999 2/16

April 12

SUN: ARIES • DECANATE: SAGITTARIUS/JUPITER • DEGREE: 21°5–22°5 ARIES • MODE: CARDINAL • ELEMENT: FIRE

Your Personal Powers

Your energy and drive indicate that you possess the courage to achieve your goals if you employ good planning and perseverance. As a practical and analytical individual you gain power when you think intuitively, act decisively, and use your ingenuity. Although your idealistic or chivalrous nature encourages you to make magnanimous or spontaneous gestures, you also possess business acumen and a strong sense of values. Your ruling planet, Mars, urges you to think and act independently, but you can lose power if you behave in an obstinate, impatient, or compulsive manner. This may occur if you feel insecure, unhappy, or dissatisfied. Since you have a great deal of vitality, you have to channel your enthusiasm in a constructive way. You empower yourself when you learn that as life is unpredictable, in order to enjoy the fortunate periods you need to make provision for when your luck lets you down. Nevertheless, you thrive on mental stimulation and often seek a rewarding life full of activity or adventure.

Your Powers of Attraction in Relationships

When you feel positive, others appreciate your understanding, kind words, and good advice. They may not, however, value your tendency to be too opinionated or too controlling. You are usually attracted to intelligent individuals you trust and with whom you can communicate. Although you are confident and self-assured, at times inner fears or self-doubts can make you feel vulnerable. From time to time other people may criticize your abilities, and although you may benefit from their opinions, you should never let them undermine your high spirits. Since you want intimacy with your partners, you need to be straightforward and open about your feelings, doubts, or worries. Good at casual banter, your sense of humor and generosity suggest that you can be mentally stimulating and witty. You usually feel at ease with others or when socializing and you have no difficulties making friends.

Your attractive qualities: pragmatic, disciplined, generous, spontaneous, quick perception, sociable, good economist, knowledgeable, affectionate, quick wit, entertaining, creative, attractive, initiative, persuasive, energetic, humanitarian, intuitive, pioneering, compassionate

Your less attractive qualities: moody, bossy, compulsive, restless, extravagant, hasty, oversensitive, lacking in self-esteem, financial worries, easily bored, takes unnecessary risks, too demanding

Your Venus Power

The planet Venus has a great deal of influence on your powers of attraction. Below are four possible Venus types for women and men. To find your Venus you need to go to page 771, where you will find the Venus table and extra information. The planet Mars also affects your powers of attraction. To find your Mars table and interpretation go to page 761.

WOMEN WITH VENUS IN PISCES: Idealistic and impressionable, in love you are romantic. Being sensitive to other people, you are receptive to their moods and feelings. This affinity indicates that although you can be selfless, you may have to guard against being too sentimental or overly romantic, especially with those who can take advantage of your kindness. Nevertheless, as you are alluring and seductive, your partners can be intrigued by your poetic soul or mysterious nature.

MEN WITH VENUS IN PISCES: Being adaptable and sensitive, you are able to intuitively feel the moods of those you love. Although you are receptive to others you can be ambiguous about your own feelings toward your partner. Romantic and kindhearted, you long to be loved, but you need to be realistic about your relationships in order to avoid disappointments. When in love you may idealize your partners, but you can be loving and giving.

WOMEN WITH VENUS IN ARIES: Self-reliant and strong, you usually want things your own way. This can present problems if you refuse to compromise with your partners. Your life lessons in the area of love and relationships often involve patience and learning to trust. When you project the full power of your Venus you can radiate a charismatic and captivating energy and make a strong impression on others. Independence is often high on your relationship agenda.

MEN WITH VENUS IN ARIES: You are drawn to strong, independent women who can stand up to you. Although you can enthusiastically follow the object of your desire, you may lose power if you allow your forceful emotions to become too dominant. Warm and passionate, you have a side to your nature that longs for new adventures. Romantic and chivalrous, you really enjoy the excitement of the initial chase, but unless you keep the enthusiasm alive and avoid falling into a rut you may become easily bored.

WOMEN WITH VENUS IN TAURUS: Demonstrative and affectionate, you are naturally tactile with a love of sensual pleasures. With a streak of the conventional you love the simple pleasures of life: good food, close friends, and happy relationships. Although you possess endurance be careful not to let this turn into plain stubbornness. Having inner strength you can express genuine patience and are often a pillar of support for loved ones and friends.

MEN WITH VENUS IN TAURUS: Although you are usually drawn to sensual and physically beautiful individuals, you want a partner who is also reliable and loyal. When in love, you enjoy buying your partner things of quality that will grow in value or useful things of a practical nature. You also love to socialize and entertain, especially in luxurious surroundings. Affectionate and caring, you are often attracted to creative people or those with artistic talents.

WOMEN WITH VENUS IN GEMINI: Charming and usually easygoing, you like to talk to people who are intelligent and witty. With a good social sense and a desire for mental expansion, you need a partner who is informed and has good ideas. Although you enjoy having different experiences you need to resist your tendencies to become bored quickly or be too talkative. As you enjoy sharing and learning new things, you usually prefer being with someone rather than operating alone.

MEN WITH VENUS IN GEMINI: Informed and curious yet charming and friendly, you seek a partner who shares your interests or enjoys your witty remarks. Although a good communicator, you have an inborn tendency to be lighthearted and less profound about deep emotional commitment. Although you are keen on experiences that bring variety into your life, boredom or scattering your energies in too many directions is probably your biggest handicap in relationships. Nevertheless, you are attracted to intelligent partners who can match your lively banter.

To read all about your Outer Planets and work out how to use your personalized timetable, go to Section Three, page 789.

Your Personalized Timetable

JUPITER BENEFICIAL
1938 3/2 – 4/21
1938 8/24 – 12/11
1941 8/16 – 12/5
1942 4/6 – 5/27
1943 9/2 – until **1944** 7/25
1947 12/26 – until **1948** 11/14
1950 2/14 – 3/30
1953 7/23 – until **1954** 1/25
1954 2/26 – 5/9
1955 8/16 – 11/15
1956 1/19 – 7/6
1959 12/10 – until **1960** 2/29
1960 6/11 – 10/25
1962 1/28 – 3/11
1965 7/5 – 8/26
1965 12/13 – until **1966** 4/17
1967 8/1 – 10/18
1968 2/28 – 6/14
1971 11/24 – until **1972** 2/6
1972 7/26 – 9/23
1974 1/11 – 2/23
1977 6/18 – 8/3
1978 1/29 – 3/13
1979 7/15 – 9/28
1983 11/7 – until **1984** 1/18
1985 5/27 – 6/12
1985 12/25 – until **1986** 2/7
1989 6/2 – 7/16
1991 6/28 – 9/11
1995 2/28 – 5/3
1995 10/20 – until **1996** 1/2
1997 4/11 – 8/10
1997 12/2 – until **1998** 1/21
2001 5/16 – 6/29
2002 10/12 – until **2003** 1/27
2003 6/7 – 8/26
2007 1/31 – 6/14
2007 9/28 – 12/18
2009 3/20 – 6/5
2009 6/25 – until **2010** 1/3

SATURN BENEFICIAL
1943 6/14 – until **1944** 5/26
1947 8/16 – until **1948** 9/17
1949 4/6 – 5/26
1957 2/28 – 4/16
1957 11/14 – until **1959** 1/4
1963 3/1 – 9/29
1963 11/12 – until **1964** 2/25
1972 7/27 – 12/12
1973 4/15 – 7/6
1976 9/29 – until **1977** 1/28
1977 6/19 – 11/14
1978 1/8 – 7/25
1986 12/18 – until **1988** 2/12
1988 6/12 – 11/10
1992 4/13 – 7/14
1993 1/5 – 4/3
1993 8/21 – 12/30
2002 5/28 – 8/21
2002 12/2 – until **2003** 5/8
2006 7/30 – until **2007** 9/1

URANUS BENEFICIAL
1945 8/16 – until **1949** 4/1
1958 9/5 – until **1988** 11/30
2000 2/7 – until **2003** 1/13

NEPTUNE BENEFICIAL
1976 2/24 – until **1984** 11/16
2005 3/27 – until **2011** 1/4

PLUTO BENEFICIAL
1947 9/5 – until **1958** 5/28
2001 1/3 – until **2008** 11/22

JUPITER CHALLENGING
1942 8/11 – until **1943** 6/30
1945 10/29 – until **1946** 9/24

1949 1/16 – 4/11
1949 6/29 – 11/30
1954 7/25 – 11/9
1954 11/24 – until **1955** 6/12
1957 10/13 – until **1958** 1/12
1958 3/22 – 9/6
1960 12/31 – until **1961** 3/14
1961 8/13 – 11/2
1966 7/8 – 9/26
1967 1/17 – 5/22
1969 9/28 – 12/15
1970 5/1 – 8/14
1972 12/14 – until **1973** 2/22
1978 6/22 – 9/4
1979 3/3 – 4/18
1981 9/11 – 11/26
1984 11/27 – until **1985** 2/6
1990 6/5 – 8/17
1993 1/5 – 2/21
1993 8/25 – 11/9
1996 3/14 – 6/25
1996 11/7 – until **1997** 1/21
2001 9/29 – 12/6
2002 5/17 – 8/1
2004 12/4 – until **2005** 4/4
2005 8/4 – 10/25
2008 2/20 – 8/10
2008 10/7 – until **2009** 1/5

SATURN CHALLENGING
1945 7/2 – until **1946** 8/1
1951 12/20 – until **1952** 3/1
1952 9/6 – until **1953** 10/21
1960 2/8 – 7/25
1960 11/5 – until **1961** 5/8
1961 5/10 – until **1962** 1/2
1974 8/13 – until **1975** 1/26
1975 4/29 – 9/15
1976 1/16 – 6/3
1981 10/14 – until **1982** 11/28
1983 5/8 – 8/22
1989 4/13 – 5/2
1989 12/17 – until **1991** 2/5
2004 6/15 – until **2005** 7/15
2010 11/23 – until **2011** 4/4
2011 8/18 – until **2012** 10/4

URANUS CHALLENGING
1951 10/2 – until **1956** 6/7
1971 10/6 – until **1975** 9/5
1992 1/3 – until **1996** 1/9

NEPTUNE CHALLENGING
1948 11/6 – until **1957** 7/20
1990 2/23 – until **1998** 11/21

PLUTO CHALLENGING
1938 1/1 – until **1939** 6/7
1976 12/13 – until **1984** 8/22

JUPITER SPECIAL
1940 3/9 – 5/15
1951 7/21 – 8/18
1952 2/19 – 4/28
1963 6/8 – 10/12
1964 1/26 – 4/11
1975 5/17 – until **1976** 3/25
1987 4/29 – until **1988** 3/7
1999 4/12 – 6/27
1999 10/24 – until **2000** 2/13
2011 3/26 – 6/3

SATURN SPECIAL
1938 5/18 – 10/18
1939 2/8 – 7/4
1939 9/24 – until **1940** 3/19
1968 3/24 – until **1969** 4/28
1997 4/29 – 11/28
1998 1/3 – 6/7
1998 10/27 – until **1999** 2/27

♈

April 13

Your Personal Powers

Your strong nature indicates that you are ambitious, determined, and adventurous. Your ruling planet, Mars, grants you courage, willpower, and a commanding personality. Often willing to work hard in order to achieve your objectives, you enjoy power and responsibilities. Alternatively, your leadership or executive abilities can inspire you to be creative and pioneer new ideas or enterprises. Although you gain power by being focused, efficient, and structured, you also learn by trusting your personal experience and innate wisdom. You lose power if you use your natural talents and versatility solely for your own benefit by being controlling, too competitive, or domineering. Nevertheless, you usually possess a natural business sense and seek financial security by building a strong foundation, but be careful of becoming enmeshed in materialism. You empower yourself when you recognize the value of knowledge and take the time to express your sensitivity and finer feelings as well as master your skills.

Your Powers of Attraction in Relationships

As a sociable individual, you can be friendly, generous, and entertaining. When you are decisive and enthusiastic, people admire your spontaneity, optimism, and determination. Usually you are attracted to creative and mentally quick individuals who have a charismatic or romantic personality. Although you often appear decisive about your career, you can be less sure about your emotional needs. Nevertheless, your generosity and willingness to make a commitment to those you love suggest that you are serious and purposeful. You can, however, upset people if you behave in a selfish manner. In close relationships your inner doubts or suspicions can cause you worry and make you indecisive. By making sure that you are contented with what you've got, you can resist anxieties or disappointment. Once you make a firm commitment you are likely to work hard to make the relationship work.

Your attractive qualities: ambitious, hardworking, determined, pioneering, daring, strong sense of values, freedom-loving, creative self-expression, initiative, determined, confident, businesslike, helpful, innately wise, enthusiastic, decisive, efficient, executive or leadership skills

Your less attractive qualities: impulsive, bossy, cynical, too competitive, extravagant, selfish, materialistic, controlling, temperamental, obstinate, too demanding, critical, dissatisfied, moody, restless, impractical, argumentative, irresponsible, stubborn

Your Venus Power

The planet Venus has a great deal of influence on your powers of attraction. Below are four possible Venus types for women and men. To find your Venus you need to go to page 771, where you will find the Venus table and extra information. The planet Mars also affects your powers of attraction. To find your Mars table and interpretation go to page 761.

WOMEN WITH VENUS IN PISCES: In love you are sensitive, tender, and affectionate, experiencing your partner's feelings almost as strongly as your own. Being also imaginative and visionary, you possess the capabilities to develop creative gifts as well as deep compassion for others. As you are idealistic when in love you usually prefer to see only your partner's good points, but be careful that your high expectations do not bring disappointment if you avoid being realistic. Nevertheless, in your relationships with others, you can be devoted, loving, and positively enchanting.

MEN WITH VENUS IN PISCES: As a romantic and generous person, you are attracted to imaginative or artistic partners who can be sensitive and generous. While you are willing to make allowances for your loved ones, playing the martyr in relationships can lead to allowing others to take advantage of your kind nature. Nevertheless, giving and loving, you are usually willing to forgive your partner's shortcomings.

WOMEN WITH VENUS IN ARIES: You gain power from your strong individuality, energy, and enthusiasm. Your young-at-heart and spirited approach to relationships adds to your appeal. If you become too impatient or self-absorbed, however, your partnerships are likely to suffer. Nevertheless, you can be creative, sharp, and quick, especially when you are able to share new and exciting projects with your partners. Mischievous, with a love of action, you may even incite them to a playful fight.

MEN WITH VENUS IN ARIES: Friendly, sociable, and expressive with your feelings, you can become easily aroused and animated when involved with a person who is close to your heart. Although you can enthusiastically follow the object of your desire, you may lose power if you allow your forceful emotions to become too dominant or go for instant gratifica-

tion. You are drawn to women who can match you in quickness and boldness. Warm and passionate, a side to your nature longs for excitement and new adventures.

WOMEN WITH VENUS IN TAURUS: Warm and affectionate, you are drawn to partners with whom you can share life's simple comforts. With a need for stability and security or an appreciation of earthly pleasures, you may have to avoid overindulgence or becoming too preoccupied with material concerns. Nevertheless, your sociability and friendliness usually make you popular. You need a partner who can also share your appreciation of beauty and style.

MEN WITH VENUS IN TAURUS: As well as attracting people with your warm personality, you also possess an innate sense of the value of material possessions. Keeping yourself stylish and having an attractive home can therefore be important to you. You are naturally attracted to practical yet sensual women who understand your need for comfort, security, and the pleasures and luxuries of life. Naturally affectionate, you enjoy socializing but can make a loyal and loving partner.

WOMEN WITH VENUS IN GEMINI: In relationships you need intellectual stimulation and usually prefer to keep things light. Certainly not boring, you love to talk and are at your best being witty and entertaining. Although your easygoing approach to relationships is very attractive, guard against losing touch with your emotions. You prefer a partner who can keep up with your fast stream of ideas, and if you have shared interests then so much the better.

MEN WITH VENUS IN GEMINI: Charming, amusing, and adaptable, you attract others with your natural communication skills and friendly personality. You have a wonderful childlike quality and love to keep life playful, but a reluctance to contact your deeper feelings may cause you to avoid serious commitment. With your need for variety and intellectual stimulation, you are attracted to clever and amusing partners who have many interesting sides to their personalities.

To read all about your Outer Planets and work out how to use your personalized timetable, go to Section Three, page 789.

Your Personalized Timetable

JUPITER BENEFICIAL
1938 3/7 – 4/28
1938 8/16 – 12/17
1941 8/22 – 11/27
1942 4/12 – 5/31
1943 9/7 – until 1944 7/30
1947 12/30 – until 1948 11/19
1950 2/18 – 4/4
1950 10/12 – 11/4
1953 7/28 – until 1954 1/12
1954 3/11 – 5/13
1955 8/21 – 11/27
1956 1/7 – 7/12
1959 12/14 – until 1960 3/8
1960 6/3 – 10/30
1962 2/1 – 3/16
1965 7/9 – 9/2
1965 12/6 – until 1966 4/23
1967 8/5 – 10/24
1968 2/20 – 6/21
1971 11/28 – until 1972 2/11
1972 7/16 – 10/3
1974 1/16 – 2/27
1977 6/22 – 8/8
1978 1/18 – 3/25
1979 7/20 – 10/3
1980 4/7 – 5/15
1983 11/12 – until 1984 1/23
1985 12/30 – until 1986 2/11
1989 6/6 – 7/20
1991 7/3 – 9/16
1995 3/13 – 4/20
1995 10/26 – until 1996 1/7
1997 4/18 – 8/3
1997 12/8 – until 1998 1/26
2001 5/20 – 7/3
2002 10/19 – until 2003 1/20
2003 6/13 – 8/31
2007 2/6 – 6/6
2007 10/4 – 12/22
2009 3/25 – 9/23
2009 11/2 – until 2010 1/8

SATURN BENEFICIAL
1943 6/21 – until 1944 6/3
1947 8/24 – until 1948 9/26
1949 3/19 – 6/12
1957 11/22 – until 1959 1/12
1959 8/14 – 9/26
1963 3/10 – 9/9
1963 12/1 – until 1964 3/5
1972 8/6 – 11/30
1973 4/25 – 7/14
1974 2/21 – 3/6
1976 10/10 – until 1977 1/15
1977 6/28 – until 1978 8/2
1986 12/27 – until 1987 7/31
1987 9/7 – until 1988 2/24
1988 5/29 – 11/20
1992 4/30 – 6/26
1993 1/14 – 4/14
1993 8/8 – until 1994 1/9
2002 6/4 – 9/4
2002 11/18 – until 2003 5/17
2006 8/7 – until 2007 9/9

URANUS BENEFICIAL
1946 6/13 – until 1949 4/30
1958 9/23 – until 1962 8/23
1984 12/22 – until 1988 12/16
2000 2/24 – until 2003 1/31

NEPTUNE BENEFICIAL
1977 1/6 – until 1984 12/14
2006 2/20 – until 2011 2/2

PLUTO BENEFICIAL
1947 10/25 – until 1958 7/18
2001 2/6 – until 2009 10/7

JUPITER CHALLENGING
1942 8/16 – until 1943 7/4

1945 11/3 – until 1946 9/29
1949 1/20 – 4/21
1949 6/19 – 12/5
1954 7/29 – until 1955 6/17
1957 10/18 – until 1958 1/23
1958 3/10 – 9/11
1961 1/4 – 3/20
1961 8/5 – 11/10
1966 7/13 – 10/3
1967 1/9 – 5/28
1969 10/2 – 12/21
1970 4/23 – 8/21
1972 12/19 – until 1973 2/27
1978 6/27 – 9/9
1979 2/19 – 4/29
1981 9/16 – 12/1
1982 6/11 – 7/14
1984 12/2 – until 1985 2/10
1990 6/10 – 8/22
1993 8/30 – 11/14
1996 3/22 – 6/17
1996 11/12 – until 1997 1/25
2001 10/10 – 11/25
2002 5/23 – 8/5
2004 12/11 – until 2005 3/27
2005 8/11 – 10/29
2008 2/25 – 7/31
2008 10/16 – until 2009 1/9

SATURN CHALLENGING
1945 7/10 – until 1946 8/9
1952 1/12 – 2/6
1952 9/15 – until 1953 10/29
1960 2/18 – 7/11
1960 11/17 – until 1962 1/10
1974 8/22 – until 1975 1/13
1975 5/11 – 9/26
1976 1/4 – 6/12
1981 10/22 – until 1982 12/7
1983 4/25 – 9/3
1989 12/25 – until 1991 2/14
1991 9/7 – 11/1
2004 6/23 – until 2005 7/22
2010 12/4 – until 2011 3/22
2011 8/28 – until 2012 10/12

URANUS CHALLENGING
1952 7/16 – until 1956 6/25
1971 10/21 – until 1975 9/24
1992 1/20 – until 1996 10/30

NEPTUNE CHALLENGING
1948 12/12 – until 1957 9/12
1991 1/20 – until 1998 12/25

PLUTO CHALLENGING
1938 1/1 – until 1940 5/15
1977 10/26 – until 1984 9/23

JUPITER SPECIAL
1940 3/13 – 5/20
1952 2/23 – 5/2
1963 6/15 – 10/5
1964 2/1 – 4/15
1975 5/22 – 12/4
1975 12/17 – until 1976 3/30
1987 5/4 – until 1988 3/12
1999 4/16 – 7/3
1999 10/17 – until 2000 2/19
2011 3/30 – 6/8
2011 12/9 – until 2012 1/11

SATURN SPECIAL
1938 5/28 – 10/5
1939 2/18 – 7/22
1939 9/5 – until 1940 3/27
1968 3/31 – until 1969 5/6
1997 5/7 – 11/7
1998 1/23 – 6/18
1998 10/15 – until 1999 3/9

♈

April 14

Your Personal Powers

Although you can be hardworking and competitive, your sense of duty and reserved nature indicate that you are more sensitive than you would like others to believe. You gain power when you learn to value yourself and balance the extreme sides of your nature. Often genuine, determined, and enterprising, your pragmatic approach indicates that you can achieve success. You can, however, lose some of your power when you let overidealism influence your judgment. Equally, by resisting a tendency to be overly serious or inflexible, you can empower yourself and avoid disappointments. You also gain power when you know exactly what you want or what can make you happy. You are often rewarded for your efforts, but at times you may be tested as to how far you are willing to compromise your own needs in order to get the recognition or respect you want. Often the key to your success lies in your faith and trust, learning to take life as it comes and letting go of what is outside your control.

Your Powers of Attraction in Relationships

Although you can be practical or matter-of-fact, inwardly you are highly idealistic, sensitive, and romantic. You gain other people's admiration when you are willing to compromise and show how caring and forgiving you can be. Your enthusiasm and spontaneity also attracts people. If you overreact or behave in a controlling manner, however, you exhibit your less attractive qualities. You may also put other people off with your bold attitude or lack of sympathy. On the positive side, however, you can be generous and charming. You are often drawn to friendly, creative, and enterprising partners who express themselves openly. In close relationships, rather than build up resentment you need to let others know where you stand, what you think, or how you feel. Staying detached can also help you express your feelings calmly.

Your attractive qualities: astute, magnetic, decisive, energetic, ambitious, hardworking, creative, witty, pragmatic, dutiful, imaginative, industrious, intellectual, determined, focused, loyal, reserved, generous, charming, compromising, communicative, expressive, stable, resourceful, informed, generous

Your less attractive qualities: impatient, calculating, impulsive, unstable, frustrated, worry, controlling, bossy, restless, jealous, pessimistic, unorganized, careless, lazy, too idealistic, selfish, stubborn, critical

Your Venus Power

The planet Venus has a great deal of influence on your powers of attraction. Below are four possible Venus types for women and men. To find your Venus you need to go to page 771, where you will find the Venus table and extra information. The planet Mars also affects your powers of attraction. To find your Mars table and interpretation go to page 761.

WOMEN WITH VENUS IN PISCES: Romantic and idealistic when in love, you can be a sensitive and responsive lover. With your affectionate and impressionable nature you are often attracted to those who understand your sensitivity and share your vision. Being flexible with an impressionable nature helps you to adapt to the needs of others. In your desire to blend with those you love, guard against giving too much of yourself by not clearly defining your boundaries.

MEN WITH VENUS IN PISCES: The combination of your emotional subtlety and charm can make you very alluring when dealing with affairs of the heart. Perceptive and impressionable, you have an easygoing style in your relationships, usually preferring to avoid ugly confrontation. You are drawn to partners who have a touch of glamour and are sensitive to the needs of others. Alternatively, like you, they could be visionaries with a rich imagination who know how to keep you enchanted. With your insight you have the ability to observe the subtle moods of your partner.

WOMEN WITH VENUS IN ARIES: You gain power from your strong individuality, energy, and enthusiasm. Your young-at-heart and spirited approach to relationships adds to your appeal. If you become too impatient or self-absorbed, however, your partnerships are likely to suffer. Nevertheless, you can be creative, sharp, and quick, especially when you are able to share new and exciting projects with your partners. Mischievous, with a love of action, you may even incite them to a playful fight.

MEN WITH VENUS IN ARIES: As you often have the courage and strength to initiate situations, you like to take the lead and let others follow. With your unconscious desire for conquest you may also have to beware of being competitive with your partners. Nevertheless, you are drawn to direct and strong-willed women who can share your love of action and

enthusiasm for life. When you are feeling good you can be charming and enthusiastic in romantic situations with an entertaining and spontaneous spirit.

WOMEN WITH VENUS IN TAURUS: Good-natured and romantic, you have a highly developed sense of touch that particularly responds to massage, hugs, and all things physical. With a streak of the conventional you love the simple pleasures of life: good food, close friends, and happy relationships. With your natural sense of beauty and harmony you are likely to have an attractive voice, beautiful home, or a strong link to nature. You may have to be careful of becoming too extravagant, as often your taste is more expensive than what you are able to afford.

MEN WITH VENUS IN TAURUS: Attractive and affectionate, in relationships you are often down-to-earth with a conservative approach. You are usually drawn to warmhearted partners with whom you can share a familiar routine as well as life's pleasures and comforts. Seeking a partner who is dependable or reassuring, you often put security high on your priority list when looking for love. Your sociability and friendliness usually make you popular and partners often admire your practicality and good sense of values.

WOMEN WITH VENUS IN GEMINI: Curious, with a bright and animated approach to life, you are attracted to those who are clever and/or sophisticated. Your love of variety and desire for knowledge suggest that you need a partner and friends who can keep you mentally stimulated. Although witty and a good conversationalist, you may need to keep in touch with your deeper feelings. Nevertheless, intelligent and friendly, you possess a youthful sense of wonder and seek a playmate who can keep you from becoming bored.

MEN WITH VENUS IN GEMINI: Friendly and sociable, you attract others with your clever and amusing conversation. Drawn to partners who can match you in wit and intelligence, you usually prefer to keep relationships light rather than emotionally intense. With your youthful charm and desire for knowledge and new experiences you usually have many friends and a low boredom threshold.

To read all about your Outer Planets and work out how to use your personalized timetable, go to Section Three, page 789.

Your Personalized Timetable

JUPITER BENEFICIAL
1938 3/11 – 5/4
1938 8/9 – 12/23
1941 8/30 – 11/20
1942 4/18 – 6/5
1943 9/11 – until 1944 8/3
1948 1/4 – 11/24
1950 2/22 – 4/9
1950 9/27 – 11/20
1953 8/2 – until 1954 1/2
1954 3/21 – 5/18
1955 8/25 – until 1956 7/17
1959 12/18 – until 1960 3/16
1960 5/24 – 11/5
1962 2/5 – 3/20
1965 7/14 – 9/9
1965 11/28 – until 1966 4/29
1967 8/10 – 10/31
1968 2/13 – 6/27
1971 12/3 – until 1972 2/16
1972 7/7 – 10/11
1974 1/20 – 3/3
1977 6/26 – 8/13
1978 1/9 – 4/3
1979 7/25 – 10/8
1980 3/25 – 5/28
1983 11/17 – until 1984 1/28
1986 1/3 – 2/15
1989 6/10 – 7/25
1991 7/8 – 9/20
1995 10/31 – until 1996 1/11
1997 4/25 – 7/26
1997 12/14 – until 1998 1/30
2001 5/25 – 7/7
2002 10/27 – until 2003 1/11
2003 6/19 – 9/4
2007 2/12 – 5/29
2007 10/11 – 12/26
2009 3/30 – 9/11
2009 11/13 – until 2010 1/12

SATURN BENEFICIAL
1943 6/29 – until 1944 6/11
1947 9/1 – until 1948 4/10
1948 4/24 – 10/5
1949 3/6 – 6/25
1957 12/1 – until 1959 1/21
1959 7/24 – 10/16
1963 3/19 – 8/26
1963 12/14 – until 1964 3/13
1964 10/9 – 11/25
1972 8/18 – 11/17
1973 5/3 – 7/22
1974 1/25 – 4/2
1976 10/24 – until 1977 1/1
1977 7/7 – until 1978 8/10
1987 1/4 – 7/9
1987 9/28 – until 1988 3/12
1988 5/11 – 11/29
1993 1/22 – 4/27
1993 7/24 – until 1994 1/18
2002 6/12 – 9/24
2002 10/28 – until 2003 5/25
2006 8/15 – until 2007 9/17
2008 4/21 – 5/14

URANUS BENEFICIAL
1946 6/30 – until 1949 5/20
1958 10/18 – until 1963 6/17
1985 1/9 – until 1989 10/13
2000 3/13 – until 2003 2/17

NEPTUNE BENEFICIAL
1977 2/11 – until 1985 11/11
2006 3/21 – until 2011 12/29

PLUTO BENEFICIAL
1948 9/20 – until 1959 6/6
2001 12/25 – until 2009 11/18

JUPITER CHALLENGING
1942 8/21 – until 1943 2/20
1943 3/31 – 7/9
1945 11/8 – until 1946 10/4
1949 1/24 – 5/5
1949 6/4 – 12/10
1954 8/3 – until 1955 6/22
1957 10/22 – until 1958 9/17
1961 1/8 – 3/26
1961 7/28 – 11/17
1966 7/17 – 10/10
1967 1/1 – 6/3
1969 10/7 – 12/28
1970 4/16 – 8/27
1972 12/23 – until 1973 3/4
1978 7/1 – 9/15
1979 2/11 – 5/8
1981 9/21 – 12/6
1982 5/28 – 7/28
1984 12/6 – until 1985 2/14
1990 6/15 – 8/27
1993 9/4 – 11/19
1996 3/30 – 6/8
1996 11/18 – until 1997 1/29
2002 5/28 – 8/9
2004 12/18 – until 2005 3/19
2005 8/16 – 11/3
2008 3/2 – 7/22
2008 10/24 – until 2009 1/13

SATURN CHALLENGING
1945 7/17 – until 1946 8/17
1952 9/23 – until 1953 11/6
1960 2/29 – 6/27
1960 11/27 – until 1962 1/19
1974 9/1 – until 1975 1/1
1975 5/21 – 10/10
1975 12/20 – until 1976 6/21
1981 10/30 – until 1982 5/30
1982 7/7 – 12/18
1983 4/12 – 9/13
1990 1/2 – until 1991 2/23
1991 8/20 – 11/18
2004 6/30 – until 2005 7/30
2010 12/17 – until 2011 3/8
2011 9/6 – until 2012 10/21

URANUS CHALLENGING
1952 8/2 – until 1956 7/12
1971 11/7 – until 1975 10/10
1992 2/6 – until 1996 12/2

NEPTUNE CHALLENGING
1949 11/2 – until 1957 10/11
1991 2/17 – until 1999 11/11

PLUTO CHALLENGING
1938 1/1 – until 1940 7/1
1977 11/24 – until 1984 10/18

JUPITER SPECIAL
1940 3/17 – 5/24
1952 2/28 – 5/6
1963 6/21 – 9/28
1964 2/7 – 4/19
1975 5/27 – 11/15
1976 1/4 – 4/3
1987 5/8 – until 1988 3/17
1999 4/20 – 7/10
1999 10/9 – until 2000 2/25
2011 4/3 – 6/13
2011 11/26 – until 2012 1/24

SATURN SPECIAL
1938 6/8 – 9/22
1939 2/27 – until 1940 4/4
1968 4/8 – until 1969 5/14
1997 5/16 – 10/24
1998 2/5 – 6/30
1998 10/2 – until 1999 3/18

April 15

Your Personal Powers

The right mixture of inspiration and determination often guarantees your success. Although you are creative and enterprising with many ideas and plans, you need to persevere and stay realistic if you want to achieve your goals. Your ruling planet, Mars, grants you stamina and enthusiasm and also helps you to remain optimistic in times of adversity. Idealistic, you empower yourself by structuring the right set of values and presenting yourself as a modest yet confident individual. Keeping your sense of humor also helps you to stay mentally and emotionally balanced. Although usually sympathetic and helpful, if you neglect your responsibilities you can lose power to overindulgence, becoming idle or experiencing mental frustration. Since your success usually depends on the amount of effort you have put in, achievement and victory often come after a struggle or when you've proved how conscientious you are. Blessed with talents and a fortunate financial streak, however, you possess much potential for achievement and financial rewards.

Your Powers of Attraction in Relationships

Charismatic and gregarious, you enjoy having fun and being sociable. Other people are attracted to your enthusiastic and direct approach. Usually you are drawn to glamorous and creative people who are confident, enterprising, and generous. Also attracted by those who are success-oriented, you are bighearted and have a lot of love to give. As a caring and compassionate individual you can attract people who want your support, so you need to be discriminating with your time and energy. To avoid getting caught up in other people's dramas it may be necessary for you to stay focused on your own objectives and many talents. Since you have powerful emotions it is also vital that you stay coolheaded if you wish to make your point clear. With your strong interest in home and family, you can be a devoted partner or parent.

Your attractive qualities: generous, enthusiastic, responsible, kind, cooperative, inspired, appreciative, creative, optimistic, organized, versatile, spontaneous, determined, friendly, charismatic, realistic, sensitive, charming, imaginative, persevering, resilient, persuasive

Your less attractive qualities: easily discouraged, inactive, extravagant, arrogant, restless, self-centered, stubborn, too serious, anxious, materialistic, inner tensions, moody, over-indulgent, critical, bossy

Your Venus Power

The planet Venus has a great deal of influence on your powers of attraction. Below are four possible Venus types for women and men. To find your Venus you need to go to page 771, where you will find the Venus table and extra information. The planet Mars also affects your powers of attraction. To find your Mars table and interpretation go to page 761.

WOMEN WITH VENUS IN PISCES: Being sensitive to affairs of the heart, when you care for someone you can feel their emotions and sense their every mood. Their goals can even become as important as your own. This empathy indicates that you can love on an unselfish level, but you may have to guard against giving too much, especially to those who do not reciprocate. Seductive and captivating, you can fascinate partners with your subtle charms and attract them with your caring and affectionate nature.

MEN WITH VENUS IN PISCES: In love you are sensitive, tender, and affectionate, experiencing your partner's feelings almost as strongly as your own. Being also imaginative and visionary, you possess the capability to develop deep compassion for others. As you are idealistic when in love, you usually prefer to see only your partner's good points, but be careful that your high expectations do not bring disappointment if you avoid harsh reality. Nevertheless, in your relationships with others, you can be devoted, loving, and positively enchanting.

WOMEN WITH VENUS IN ARIES: Idealistic, passionate, and adventurous, you are direct in your dealings with others. When you are attracted to a person you usually take the initiative and use your people skills to make things happen. In close relationships, you are not afraid to confront your other half. This self-assertiveness is positive if differences can be brought into the open through diplomacy and compromise. Independent and spirited, you enjoy your freedom.

MEN WITH VENUS IN ARIES: You are usually inclined to seek a partner who is active, goal-oriented, or decisive. Not known for your patience, you probably seek relationships early in life. You may find that you are attracted more to women who have a daring or adventurous spirit, but in your close relationships you may encounter rivalry or find that both you and your partner want to lead or be the

boss. Although you may act rashly, you possess a great deal of magnetism and are capable of demonstrating your love and affection.

WOMEN WITH VENUS IN TAURUS: For your ideal relationship you seek a partner who is both financially secure and demonstrative with his affections. With these thoughts in mind you are likely to also want a partner who is refined yet pragmatic or someone concerned with safeguarding your future. Although you have a stubborn streak you can be loving and affectionate in your relationships and with your good sense of style may be attracted to the arts, music, or luxury items.

MEN WITH VENUS IN TAURUS: As you yourself may be attractive to the opposite sex, you desire a partner who is sensual and loving or has physical beauty. Needing stability, when faced with changes that are out of your control you may become insecure or possessive. Your own sense of style and love of beauty imply that you can be attracted to creative people, especially in art and music. Faithful and/or loyal, you can be affectionate, tactile, and constant in your love.

WOMEN WITH VENUS IN GEMINI: By nature you are young at heart, adaptable, and sociable. Being curious and willing to cooperate makes you a good team player. You are usually drawn to articulate people who have charm and flair or sharp wit. With a need to expand your knowledge you also look for a partner who can challenge or stimulate you intellectually. Although you love to talk with all types of people you may need to develop your listening skills and tune into your feelings in order to build better communication in your relationships.

MEN WITH VENUS IN GEMINI: Adaptable yet often flirtatious, you enjoy mixing with people who are quick-minded and versatile. Since you can learn a great deal through interacting with others you are often attracted to intelligent partners who have comprehensive knowledge or good ideas. One of your less attractive qualities is your tendency to get bored or be inconsistent. Having an adaptable partner is important to you; therefore it must be someone who can offer you many different options and keep you interested.

To read all about your Outer Planets and work out how to use your personalized timetable, go to Section Three, page 789.

To read all about your Outer Planets and work out how to use your personalized timetable, go to Section Three, page 789.

Your Personalized Timetable

JUPITER BENEFICIAL
1938 3/16 – 5/12
1938 7/31 – 12/28
1941 9/8 – 11/11
1942 4/23 – 6/9
1943 9/16 – until 1944 8/8
1948 1/8 – 11/28
1950 2/26 – 4/14
1950 9/17 – 11/29
1953 8/8 – 12/25
1954 3/29 – 5/23
1955 8/30 – until 1956 7/22
1959 12/23 – until 1960 3/28
1960 5/13 – 11/10
1962 2/9 – 2 3/25
1965 7/18 – 9/19
1965 11/19 – until 1966 5/4
1967 8/14 – 11/7
1968 2/5 – 7/3
1971 12/7 – until 1972 2/22
1972 6/30 – 10/18
1974 1/24 – 3/7
1977 7/1 – 8/19
1978 1/1 – 4/10
1979 7/29 – 10/14
1980 3/15 – 6/7
1983 11/21 – until 1984 2/2
1986 1/8 – 2/19
1989 6/14 – 7/30
1991 7/13 – 9/25
1995 11/4 – until 1996 1/15
1997 5/3 – 7/17
1997 12/19 – until 1998 2/3
2001 5/29 – 7/12
2002 11/5 – until 2003 1/2
2003 6/24 – 9/9
2007 2/20 – 5/21
2007 10/16 – 12/31
2009 4/4 – 9/1
2009 11/22 – until 2010 1/17

SATURN BENEFICIAL
1943 7/7 – until 1944 2/10
1944 3/1 – 6/18
1947 9/9 – until 1948 3/13
1948 5/21 – 10/14
1949 2/21 – 7/6
1957 12/9 – until 1959 1/31
1959 7/9 – 10/29
1963 3/29 – 8/12
1963 12/25 – until 1964 3/22
1964 9/20 – 12/13
1972 9/2 – 11/1
1973 5/12 – 7/31
1974 1/10 – 4/16
1976 11/18 – 12/7
1977 7/15 – until 1978 8/18
1987 1/14 – 6/24
1987 10/12 – until 1988 12/8
1993 1/31 – 5/15
1993 7/6 – until 1994 1/27
2002 6/19 – until 2003 6/2
2006 8/22 – until 2007 9/25
2008 3/28 – 6/8

URANUS BENEFICIAL
1946 7/18 – until 1949 6/6
1959 8/11 – until 1963 7/11
1985 1/29 – until 1989 11/8
2000 4/4 – until 2003 12/24

NEPTUNE BENEFICIAL
1978 1/2 – until 1985 12/10
2006 5/13 – until 2012 1/29

PLUTO BENEFICIAL
1949 8/29 – until 1959 7/23
2002 1/24 – until 2010 9/14

JUPITER CHALLENGING
1942 8/26 – until 1943 2/8

1943 4/13 – 7/13
1945 11/12 – until 1946 10/8
1949 1/29 – 12/14
1954 8/7 – until 1955 6/26
1957 10/27 – until 1958 9/22
1961 1/12 – 4/1
1961 7/21 – 11/23
1966 7/22 – 10/19
1966 12/23 – until 1967 6/8
1969 10/11 – until 1970 1/4
1970 4/8 – 9/2
1972 12/27 – until 1973 3/9
1973 9/11 – 10/16
1978 7/5 – 9/20
1979 2/3 – 5/16
1981 9/25 – 12/11
1982 5/18 – 8/7
1984 12/11 – until 1985 2/19
1990 6/19 – 8/31
1993 9/9 – 11/23
1996 4/11 – 5/28
1996 11/23 – until 1997 2/2
2002 6/2 – 8/14
2004 12/27 – until 2005 3/11
2005 8/22 – 11/8
2008 3/8 – 7/14
2008 10/31 – until 2009 1/17

SATURN CHALLENGING
1945 7/25 – until 1946 8/25
1947 3/4 – 5/4
1952 10/1 – until 1953 11/15
1954 6/23 – 7/19
1960 3/13 – 6/13
1960 12/7 – until 1962 1/27
1974 9/12 – 12/20
1975 5/30 – 11/1
1975 11/28 – until 1976 6/29
1981 11/8 – until 1982 5/9
1982 7/28 – 12/30
1983 3/29 – 9/22
1990 1/11 – until 1991 3/4
1991 8/5 – 12/1
2004 7/8 – until 2005 8/7
2011 1/4 – 2/17
2011 9/15 – until 2012 10/29

URANUS CHALLENGING
1952 8/20 – until 1956 7/28
1971 11/25 – until 1975 10/26
1992 2/27 – until 1996 12/23

NEPTUNE CHALLENGING
1949 12/4 – until 1958 9/7
1992 1/16 – until 1999 12/20

PLUTO CHALLENGING
1938 1/1 – until 1941 6/15
1978 10/15 – until 1985 9/6

JUPITER SPECIAL
1940 3/21 – 5/28
1952 3/3 – 5/10
1963 6/29 – 9/20
1964 2/12 – 4/23
1975 6/1 – 11/5
1976 1/14 – 4/7
1987 5/12 – until 1988 3/21
1999 4/25 – 7/18
1999 10/1 – until 2000 3/1
2011 4/8 – 6/18
2011 11/17 – until 2012 2/2

SATURN SPECIAL
1938 6/22 – 9/8
1939 3/8 – until 1940 4/12
1968 4/16 – until 1969 5/22
1969 12/6 – until 1970 1/31
1997 5/26 – 10/11
1998 2/16 – 7/15
1998 9/16 – until 1999 3/26

April 16

Your Personal Powers

Your desire for diversity suggests that you want to experience many different things in life; however, it also indicates that you can encounter periods of change or instability. Your ruling planet, Mars, grants you tenacity and a love for adventure. You can succeed admirably when you persevere and accept that in order to fulfill your wonderful plans you need to be both patient and methodical. You gain power by blending your visionary foresight with your ability to think and learn quickly. Although you are not likely to stick with a plan that lacks financial rewards, you often lose power when you act impulsively or expect your material needs to be met instantaneously. As an independent, carefree, and generous individual you need to minimize fluctuations in your financial circumstances by resisting an inclination to be extravagant. Nevertheless, you are likely to enjoy an active life full of excitement and variety. Unexpected opportunities or luck through travel can often change your fortunes for the better. With your fast responses and original approach, through perseverance you can definitely achieve outstanding success.

Your Powers of Attraction in Relationships

Quick-witted, astute, and charming, other people enjoy your lighthearted manner and friendly personality. When you are inspired you can impress others with your ingenuity and dedication as well as your good social skills, allowing you to mix in different social circles. Although you can be spontaneous and generous with those you love, by taking your responsibilities seriously and avoiding a tendency to be argumentative you can diffuse charged-up situations. Your sensitive side, however, can make you a tender and caring lover. Attracted to those who can inspire you mentally as well as emotionally in your personal relationships, it is often necessary to maintain good communications or have shared interests. Clever but quick-witted, your sense of humor can usually get you out of tight spots.

Your attractive qualities: astute, enterprising, daring, quick learner, intuitive, hardworking, clever, integrity, sociable, cooperative, insightful, thoughtful, creative, caring, resourceful, witty, generous, confident, original, ambitious, compassionate, enthusiastic, instinctive

Your less attractive qualities: insecure, opinionated, dissatisfied, impatient, skeptical, irresponsible, too idealistic, unsympathetic, critical, irritable, restless, selfish, impractical, lacks perseverance

Your Venus Power

The planet Venus has a great deal of influence on your powers of attraction. Below are four possible Venus types for women and men. To find your Venus you need to go to page 771, where you will find the Venus table and extra information. The planet Mars also affects your powers of attraction. To find your Mars table and interpretation go to page 761.

WOMEN WITH VENUS IN PISCES: Romantic and idealistic when in love, you can be a sensitive and responsive lover. With your affectionate and impressionable nature you are often attracted to those who understand your sensitivity and share your vision. Being flexible with an impressionable nature helps you to adapt to the needs of others. In your desire to blend with those you love, guard against giving too much of yourself by not clearly defining your boundaries.

MEN WITH VENUS IN PISCES: The combination of your emotional subtlety and charm can make you very alluring when dealing with affairs of the heart. Perceptive and impressionable you have an easygoing style in your relationships, usually preferring to avoid ugly confrontation. You are drawn to a partner who has a touch of glamour and is sensitive to the needs of others. Alternatively, your partner can be a visionary with a rich imagination, like your own, who will and can keep you enchanted.

WOMEN WITH VENUS IN ARIES: Idealistic, passionate, and adventurous, you are direct in your dealings with others. When you are attracted to a person you usually take the initiative and use your people skills to make things happen. In close relationships you are not afraid to confront your other half. This self-assertiveness is positive if differences can be brought out in the open through diplomacy and compromise. Independent and spirited, you enjoy your freedom.

MEN WITH VENUS IN ARIES: You are drawn to strong, independent women who can stand up to you. Although you can enthusiastically follow the object of your desire you may lose power if you allow your forceful emotions to become too dominant. Warm and passionate, you have a side to your nature that longs for new adventures. Romantic and chivalrous, you really enjoy the excitement of the initial chase, but unless

you keep the enthusiasm alive and avoid falling into a rut you may become easily bored.

WOMEN WITH VENUS IN TAURUS: Demonstrative and affectionate, you are naturally tactile with a love of sensual pleasures. With a streak of the conventional you love the simple pleasures of life: good food, close friends, and happy relationships. Although you possess endurance be careful not to let this turn into plain stubbornness. Having inner strength, you can express genuine patience and are often a pillar of support for loved ones and friends.

MEN WITH VENUS IN TAURUS: Although you are usually drawn to sensual and physically beautiful individuals, you want a partner who is also reliable and loyal. When in love you enjoy buying your partner things of quality that will grow in value or useful things of a practical nature. You also love to socialize and entertain, especially in luxurious surroundings. Affectionate and caring, you are often attracted to creative people or those with artistic talents.

WOMEN WITH VENUS IN GEMINI: Charming and usually easygoing, you like to talk to people who are intelligent and witty. With a good social sense and a desire for mental expansion, you need a partner who is informed and has good ideas. Although you enjoy having different experiences you need to resist your tendencies to become bored too quickly or be too talkative. As you enjoy sharing and learning new things you usually prefer being with someone rather than operating alone.

MEN WITH VENUS IN GEMINI: Informed and curious yet charming and friendly, you seek a partner who shares your interests or enjoys your witty remarks. Although a good communicator, you have an inborn tendency to be lighthearted and less profound about deep emotional commitment. Although you are keen on experiences that bring variety into your life, boredom or scattering your energies in too many directions is probably your biggest handicap in relationships. Nevertheless you are attracted to intelligent partners who can match your lively banter.

To read all about your Outer Planets and work out how to use your personalized timetable, go to Section Three, page 789.

Your Personalized Timetable

JUPITER BENEFICIAL
1938 3/20 – 5/21
1938 7/22 – until 1939 1/2
1941 9/20 – 10/30
1942 4/28 – 6/13
1943 9/21 – until 1944 3/22
1944 5/4 – 8/13
1948 1/13 – 12/3
1950 3/2 – 4/19
1950 9/8 – 12/7
1953 8/14 – 12/18
1954 4/4 – 5/27
1955 9/4 – until 1956 7/27
1959 12/27 – until 1960 11/15
1962 2/14 – 3/29
1965 7/23 – 10/1
1965 11/6 – until 1966 5/9
1967 8/19 – 11/15
1968 1/27 – 7/9
1971 12/11 – until 1972 2/28
1972 6/22 – 10/24
1974 1/28 – 3/11
1977 7/5 – 8/25
1977 12/25 – until 1978 4/17
1979 8/3 – 10/19
1980 3/7 – 6/15
1983 11/26 – until 1984 2/7
1984 8/9 – 9/19
1986 1/12 – 2/23
1989 6/19 – 8/3
1991 7/17 – 9/30
1995 11/9 – until 1996 1/20
1997 5/13 – 7/7
1997 12/24 – until 1998 2/7
2001 6/2 – 7/16
2002 11/20 – 12/18
2003 6/30 – 9/13
2007 2/28 – 5/12
2007 10/22 – until 2008 1/4
2009 4/10 – 8/24
2009 11/29 – until 2010 1/21

SATURN BENEFICIAL
1943 7/15 – until 1944 1/16
1944 3/25 – 6/26
1947 9/18 – until 1948 2/27
1948 6/4 – 10/25
1949 2/9 – 7/15
1957 12/17 – until 1959 2/10
1959 6/26 – 11/10
1963 4/9 – 7/30
1964 1/4 – 3/31
1964 9/5 – 12/26
1973 5/20 – 8/9
1973 12/29 – until 1974 4/27
1977 7/23 – until 1978 8/26
1987 1/24 – 6/10
1987 10/23 – until 1988 12/16
1993 2/8 – until 1994 2/4
2002 6/27 – until 2003 6/10
2006 8/30 – until 2007 10/4
2008 3/13 – 6/22

URANUS BENEFICIAL
1946 8/9 – until 1949 6/23
1959 8/27 – until 1963 7/29
1985 3/1 – until 1989 11/28
2000 5/14 – until 2004 1/16

NEPTUNE BENEFICIAL
1978 2/4 – until 1986 11/6
2007 3/15 – until 2012 12/19

PLUTO BENEFICIAL
1949 10/7 – until 1960 6/10
2002 12/18 – until 2010 11/16

JUPITER CHALLENGING
1942 8/31 – until 1943 1/30

1943 4/22 – 7/18
1945 11/18 – until 1946 5/31
1946 6/29 – 10/13
1949 2/2 – 12/19
1954 8/12 – until 1955 7/1
1957 10/31 – until 1958 9/26
1961 1/16 – 4/8
1961 7/13 – 11/28
1966 7/26 – 10/31
1966 12/12 – until 1967 6/13
1969 10/16 – until 1970 1/12
1970 3/30 – 9/8
1972 12/31 – until 1973 3/14
1973 8/28 – 10/28
1978 7/10 – 9/26
1979 1/26 – 5/22
1981 9/30 – 12/17
1982 5/9 – 8/15
1984 12/15 – until 1985 2/23
1990 6/24 – 9/5
1991 3/18 – 4/11
1993 9/14 – 11/28
1996 11/28 – until 1997 2/6
2002 6/6 – 8/19
2005 1/6 – 2/28
2005 8/28 – 11/12
2008 3/14 – 7/7
2008 11/6 – until 2009 1/21

SATURN CHALLENGING
1945 8/2 – until 1946 9/2
1947 2/16 – 5/19
1952 10/9 – until 1953 11/23
1954 5/29 – 8/13
1960 3/30 – 5/26
1960 12/16 – until 1962 2/4
1974 9/26 – 12/6
1975 6/7 – until 1976 7/7
1981 11/17 – until 1982 4/24
1982 8/11 – until 1983 1/15
1983 3/12 – 10/1
1990 1/19 – until 1991 3/14
1991 7/23 – 12/12
2004 7/15 – until 2005 8/14
2011 9/23 – until 2012 11/6

URANUS CHALLENGING
1952 9/12 – until 1957 5/26
1971 12/19 – until 1976 8/21
1992 3/29 – until 1997 1/9

NEPTUNE CHALLENGING
1950 10/29 – until 1958 10/8
1992 2/12 – until 2000 1/17

PLUTO CHALLENGING
1938 1/1 – until 1942 5/24
1978 11/9 – until 1985 10/5

JUPITER SPECIAL
1940 3/26 – 6/2
1952 3/8 – 5/14
1963 7/7 – 9/11
1964 2/17 – 4/28
1975 6/6 – 10/28
1976 1/22 – 4/11
1987 5/17 – until 1988 3/26
1999 4/29 – 7/28
1999 9/21 – until 2000 3/6
2011 4/12 – 6/24
2011 11/9 – until 2012 2/9

SATURN SPECIAL
1938 7/13 – 8/17
1939 3/16 – until 1940 4/20
1968 4/24 – until 1969 5/31
1969 11/20 – until 1970 2/16
1997 6/6 – 9/29
1998 2/25 – until 1999 4/3

April 17

SUN: ARIES • DECANATE: SAGITTARIUS/JUPITER • DEGREE: 26°5–27°5 ARIES • MODE: CARDINAL • ELEMENT: FIRE

Your Personal Powers

Resourceful and idealistic, you like to think independently or create your own vision and dreams. Your ruling planet, Mars, endows you with vitality and courage. Since you want both excitement and stability, you gain power when you combine your inspired ideas with your pragmatic approach and your innate sense of duty. You also possess the capacity to think creatively and cope with challenging situations by solving your problems with the power of intuitive realization. New possibilities often arise from taking up some type of study or higher education. Since a part of you yearns for adventure, new experiences, and variety, you need to avoid becoming bored. You lose power when you settle into a situation that is too predictable or restrictive. If material considerations repress your need for self-expression, you may lose power by feeling restless or dissatisfied without realizing why. Nevertheless, many fine opportunities for enterprise and success may be presented to you in life if you are not afraid of hard work and responsibility.

Your Powers of Attraction in Relationships

Although you may be reserved by nature, other people usually admire your practical and analytical abilities and your straightforward approach. To keep your home life peaceful and congenial you need to avoid being sarcastic and occasionally take time out alone to regenerate your energies. When you are warm and sympathetic people are drawn to your natural charm. Since you are likely to have a refined mind and emotional sensitivity, try to resist a tendency to be moody by expressing your feelings honestly. Although pragmatic, when you love, you possess powerful and deep emotions. You are usually attracted to strong, determined, or purposeful individuals but be careful of clashing wills. Keeping your spirit of adventure alive can help you and your partner to feel happy or emotionally satisfied.

Your attractive qualities: independent, thoughtful, shrewd, analytical, generous, determined, instinctive, foresight, business sense, strategist, precise, methodical, diplomatic, kind, sociable, consistent, retrospective, communicative, responsible, hardworking, pragmatic, observant

Your less attractive qualities: careless, moody, impatient, bossy, stubborn, oversensitive, critical, sulky, frustrated, materialistic, extravagant, restless, anxious, arrogant, vain, overindulgent, escapist

Your Venus Power

The planet Venus has a great deal of influence on your powers of attraction. Below are four possible Venus types for women and men. To find your Venus you need to go to page 771, where you will find the Venus table and extra information. The planet Mars also affects your powers of attraction. To find your Mars table and interpretation go to page 761.

WOMEN WITH VENUS IN PISCES: As a romantic and idealistic individual you can be both loving and giving. In relationships you may need to balance the practical with the charitable. While making allowances and sacrifices is understandable in a loving relationship, playing the martyr is often a state of romantic illusion that can lead to self-deception. Your benevolence and sacrifices in the right relationship nonetheless make you a partner who is devoted, kind, and compassionate. Subtle, sensitive, and alluring, you make a sensual and caring partner.

MEN WITH VENUS IN PISCES: Romantic and idealistic when in love, you can be a sensitive and responsive lover. Being pliant and flexible with an impressionable nature helps you to adapt to the needs of others. In your desire to blend with those you love, guard against not clearly defining your own boundaries. With your affectionate and sentimental nature you are often attracted to those who understand your sensitivity and share your vision.

WOMEN WITH VENUS IN ARIES: Self-reliant and strong, you usually want things your own way. This can present problems if you refuse to compromise with your partners. Your life lessons in the area of love and relationships often involve patience and learning to trust. When you project the full power of your Venus you can radiate a charismatic and captivating energy and make a strong impression on others. Independence is often high on your relationship agenda.

MEN WITH VENUS IN ARIES: Friendly, sociable, and expressive with your feelings, you can become easily aroused and animated when involved with a person who is close to your heart. Although you can enthusiastically follow the object of your desire, you may lose power if you allow your forceful emotions to become too dominant or go for instant gratification. You are drawn to women who can match you in quick-

ness and boldness. Warm and passionate, a side to your nature longs for excitement and new adventures.

WOMEN WITH VENUS IN TAURUS: Warm and affectionate, you are drawn to partners with whom you can share life's simple comforts. With a need for stability and security or an appreciation of earthly pleasures, you may have to avoid overindulgence or becoming too preoccupied with material concerns. Nevertheless, your sociability and friendliness usually make you popular. You need a partner who can share your appreciation of beauty and style.

MEN WITH VENUS IN TAURUS: As well as attracting people with your warm personality, you possess an innate sense of the value of material possessions. Keeping yourself stylish and having an attractive home can therefore be important to you. You are naturally attracted to practical yet sensual women who understand your need for comfort, security, and the pleasures and luxuries of life. Naturally affectionate, you enjoy socializing but can be a loyal and loving partner.

WOMEN WITH VENUS IN GEMINI: In relationships you need intellectual stimulation and usually prefer to keep things light. Certainly not boring, you love to talk and are at your best being witty and entertaining. Although your easygoing approach to relationships is very attractive, guard against losing touch with your deeper emotions. You prefer a partner who can keep up with your fast stream of ideas, and if you have shared interests then so much the better.

MEN WITH VENUS IN GEMINI: Charming, amusing, and adaptable, you attract others with your natural communication skills and friendly personality. You have a wonderful childlike quality and love to keep life playful, but a reluctance to contact your deeper feelings may cause you to avoid serious commitment. With your need for variety and intellectual stimulation, you are attracted to clever and amusing partners who have many interesting sides to their personalities.

To read all about your Outer Planets and work out how to use your personalized timetable, go to Section Three, page 789.

Your Personalized Timetable

JUPITER BENEFICIAL
1938 3/25 – 6/4
1938 7/9 – until 1939 1/7
1942 5/3 – 6/18
1943 9/27 – until 1944 3/10
1944 5/17 – 8/17
1948 1/18 – 12/7
1950 3/6 – 4/25
1950 8/31 – 12/14
1953 8/20 – 12/11
1954 4/11 – 6/1
1955 9/8 – until 1956 8/1
1960 1/1 – 11/20
1962 2/18 – 4/3
1965 7/28 – until 1966 1/29
1966 3/4 – 5/14
1967 8/23 – 11/26
1968 1/17 – 7/14
1971 12/16 – until 1972 3/6
1972 6/14 – 10/30
1974 2/1 – 3/16
1977 7/9 – 8/31
1977 12/18 – until 1978 4/23
1979 8/7 – 10/25
1980 2/28 – 6/22
1983 11/30 – until 1984 2/12
1984 7/28 – 10/1
1986 1/16 – 2/27
1989 6/23 – 8/8
1990 2/1 – 3/20
1991 7/22 – 10/5
1992 4/22 – 5/8
1995 11/14 – until 1996 1/24
1997 5/30 – 6/20
1997 12/29 – until 1998 2/11
2001 6/6 – 7/21
2003 7/5 – 9/18
2007 3/11 – 5/2
2007 10/27 – until 2008 1/8
2009 4/16 – 8/17
2009 12/6 – until 2010 1/25

SATURN BENEFICIAL
1943 7/24 – until 1944 1/2
1944 4/8 – 7/3
1947 9/27 – until 1948 2/15
1948 6/16 – 11/6
1949 1/26 – 7/24
1957 12/26 – until 1959 2/21
1959 6/12 – 11/20
1963 4/23 – 7/15
1964 1/13 – 4/10
1964 8/23 – until 1965 1/5
1973 5/28 – 8/19
1973 12/17 – until 1974 5/7
1977 7/31 – until 1978 9/2
1987 2/4 – 5/28
1987 11/2 – until 1988 12/24
1993 2/16 – until 1994 2/12
2002 7/5 – until 2003 6/17
2006 9/7 – until 2007 3/25
2007 5/15 – 10/13
2008 2/29 – 7/3

URANUS BENEFICIAL
1946 9/17 – until 1950 4/22
1959 9/13 – until 1963 8/15
1985 12/19 – until 1989 12/15
2001 2/25 – until 2004 2/3

NEPTUNE BENEFICIAL
1978 12/29 – until 1986 12/6
2007 4/22 – Continues

PLUTO BENEFICIAL
1950 9/11 – until 1960 7/25
2003 1/14 – until 2010 12/15

JUPITER CHALLENGING
1942 9/6 – until 1943 1/22

1943 4/30 – 7/22
1945 11/23 – until 1946 5/16
1946 7/14 – 10/17
1949 2/6 – 12/24
1954 8/17 – until 1955 7/6
1957 11/5 – until 1958 10/1
1961 1/21 – 4/16
1961 7/5 – 12/4
1966 7/30 – until 1967 6/18
1969 10/20 – until 1970 1/22
1970 3/20 – 9/13
1973 1/5 – 3/19
1973 8/19 – 11/7
1978 7/14 – 10/3
1979 1/19 – 5/29
1981 10/4 – 12/23
1982 5/1 – 8/22
1984 12/20 – until 1985 2/28
1990 6/28 – 9/10
1991 3/3 – 4/27
1993 9/18 – 12/3
1996 12/3 – until 1997 2/10
2002 6/11 – 8/23
2005 1/24 – 2/10
2005 9/2 – 11/17
2008 3/21 – 6/29
2008 11/12 – until 2009 1/25

SATURN CHALLENGING
1945 8/10 – until 1946 2/18
1946 4/18 – 9/11
1947 2/3 – 5/31
1952 10/17 – until 1953 12/2
1954 5/14 – 8/27
1960 12/24 – until 1962 2/13
1974 10/18 – 11/13
1975 6/16 – until 1976 7/15
1981 11/26 – until 1982 4/11
1982 8/22 – until 1983 10/10
1990 1/27 – 9/16
1990 9/29 – until 1991 3/26
1991 7/9 – 12/21
2004 7/23 – until 2005 8/22
2006 3/16 – 4/25
2011 10/2 – until 2012 11/14

URANUS CHALLENGING
1953 7/11 – until 1957 6/16
1972 10/12 – until 1976 9/13
1993 1/19 – until 1997 10/18

NEPTUNE CHALLENGING
1950 11/28 – until 1959 9/1
1992 3/23 – until 2000 12/14

PLUTO CHALLENGING
1938 1/1 – until 1942 7/7
1978 12/12 – until 1986 8/11

JUPITER SPECIAL
1940 3/30 – 6/7
1952 3/12 – 5/19
1963 7/19 – 8/30
1964 2/22 – 5/2
1975 6/12 – 10/20
1976 1/29 – 4/15
1987 5/22 – until 1988 3/30
1999 5/3 – 8/13
1999 9/5 – until 2000 3/11
2011 4/16 – 6/30
2011 11/2 – until 2012 2/16

SATURN SPECIAL
1939 3/24 – until 1940 4/27
1968 5/2 – 12/14
1968 12/28 – until 1969 6/9
1969 11/7 – until 1970 2/28
1997 6/18 – 9/15
1998 3/6 – until 1999 4/11

April 18

SUN: ARIES · DECANATE: SAGITTARIUS/JUPITER · DEGREE: 27°5–28°5 ARIES · MODE: CARDINAL · ELEMENT: FIRE

Your Personal Powers

Intelligent, resourceful, and intuitive, you can express yourself in unique and original ways. Your ruling planet, Mars, encourages you to take the lead or initiate new projects. Capable of seeing numerous sides to every situation, when faced with a problem you can usually come up with a good strategy or a new solution. A good psychologist, you gain power when you can articulate your original ideas and are flexible enough to accommodate others in your plans. You can, however, lose power if you become bossy or scatter your energies. Nevertheless, astute and witty, you can impress others and be very persuasive. A need for material security is often an important issue for you, but you may lose some of your power if you worry about it. You also lose power when you are indecisive or overly serious about financial or emotional matters. Yet your determination to move forward and achieve indicates that you should not settle for a routine that restricts or stifles your outstanding mental creativity.

Your Powers of Attraction in Relationships

Other people admire your integrity and direct approach. Clever, kindhearted, and sympathetic, you are often able to advise those who need your help. If, on the other hand, you are too self-absorbed, you can be oblivious to what happens around you and appear too detached or uncaring. Sometimes you may have to balance your need to solve problems with your partner's need for understanding and love. You are usually attracted to cultured and intelligent people with graceful expression. Concerns over your long-term security, however, may at times cause you to come into conflict with your partner. Nevertheless, being idealistic, honest, and sincere implies that once you realize you are in the wrong you want to make amends and do your fair share or show your willingness to make sacrifices.

Your attractive qualities: progressive, creative, decisive, industrious, assertive, methodical, intuitive, daring, resolute, original, pioneering, business acumen, shrewd, inventive, bright ideas, well-informed, idealistic, sociable, communicative, enterprising, spontaneous, supportive, loving

Your less attractive qualities: indecisive, fluctuating moods, unfeeling, extreme reactions, controlling, worry about lack of resources or failure, unmotivated, reckless, oversensitive, self-doubt, pessimistic, anxious, too serious, uncompromising

Your Venus Power

The planet Venus has a great deal of influence on your powers of attraction. Below are four possible Venus types for women and men. To find your Venus you need to go to page 771, where you will find the Venus table and extra information. The planet Mars also affects your powers of attraction. To find your Mars table and interpretation go to page 761.

WOMEN WITH VENUS IN PISCES: Being sensitive to affairs of the heart, when you care for someone you can feel their emotions and sense their every mood. Their goals can even become as important as your own. This empathy indicates that you can love on an unselfish level, but you may have to guard against giving too much, especially to those who do not reciprocate. You are seductive and captivating, and partners can be fascinated by your subtle charms and attracted by your caring and affectionate nature.

MEN WITH VENUS IN PISCES: Being adaptable and sensitive, you are able to intuitively feel the moods of those you love. Although you are receptive to others you can be ambiguous about your own feelings toward your partner. Romantic and kindhearted, you long to be loved but you need to be realistic about your relationships in order to avoid disappointments. When in love you may idealize your partners and fail to see any faults in their personality.

WOMEN WITH VENUS IN ARIES: Idealistic, passionate, and adventurous, you are direct in your dealings with others. When you are attracted to a person you usually take the initiative and use your people skills to make things happen. In close relationships you are not afraid to confront your other half. This self-assertiveness is positive if differences can be brought into the open through diplomacy and compromise. Independent and spirited, you enjoy your freedom.

MEN WITH VENUS IN ARIES: You are usually inclined to seek a partner who is active, goal-oriented, or decisive. Not known for your patience, you probably seek relationships early in life. You may find that you are attracted more to women who have a daring or adventurous spirit, but in your close relationships you may encounter rivalry or find that both you and your partner want to lead or be the boss. Although you may act rashly you possess a great deal of

magnetism and are capable of demonstrating your love and affection.

WOMEN WITH VENUS IN TAURUS: Good-natured and romantic, you have a highly developed sense of touch that particularly responds to massage, hugs, and all things physical. With a streak of the conventional you love the simple pleasures of life: good food, close friends, and happy relationships. With your natural sense of beauty and harmony, you are likely to have an attractive voice, beautiful home, or a strong link to nature. You may have to be careful of becoming too extravagant, as often your taste is more expensive than what you are able to afford.

MEN WITH VENUS IN TAURUS: Attractive and affectionate, in relationships you are often faithful with a conservative approach. You are usually drawn to warmhearted partners with whom you can share a familiar routine as well as life's pleasures and comforts. Seeking a partner who is dependable or reassuring, you often put security high on your priority list when looking for love. Your sociability and friendliness usually make you popular and partners often admire your practicality and good sense of values.

WOMEN WITH VENUS IN GEMINI: Curious, with a bright and animated approach to life, you are attracted to those who are clever and/or sophisticated. Your love of variety and desire for knowledge suggest that you need a partner and friends who can keep you mentally stimulated. Although witty and a good conversationalist, you may need to keep in touch with your deeper feelings. Nevertheless, intelligent and friendly, you possess a youthful sense of wonder and seek a playmate who can keep you from becoming bored.

MEN WITH VENUS IN GEMINI: Friendly and sociable, you attract others with your clever and amusing conversation. Drawn to partners who can match you in wit and intelligence, you usually prefer to keep relationships light rather than emotionally intense. With your youthful charm and desire for knowledge and new experiences you usually have many friends and a low boredom threshold.

To read all about your Outer Planets and work out how to use your personalized timetable, go to Section Three, page 789.

Your Personalized Timetable

JUPITER BENEFICIAL
1938 3/30 – 10/5
1938 11/2 – until 1939 1/12
1942 5/8 – 6/22
1943 10/2 – until 1944 3/1
1944 5/26 – 8/22
1948 1/23 – 7/27
1948 9/4 – 12/11
1950 3/11 – 5/1
1950 8/24 – 12/20
1953 8/26 – 12/3
1954 4/17 – 6/5
1955 9/13 – until 1956 8/5
1960 1/5 – 11/24
1962 2/22 – 4/7
1965 8/2 – until 1966 1/16
1966 3/17 – 5/19
1967 8/28 – 12/14
1967 12/30 – until 1968 7/19
1971 12/20 – until 1972 3/14
1972 6/6 – 11/5
1974 2/6 – 3/20
1977 7/14 – 9/7
1977 12/10 – until 1978 4/29
1979 8/12 – 11/1
1980 2/21 – 6/28
1983 12/4 – until 1984 2/17
1984 7/18 – 10/10
1986 1/21 – 3/4
1989 6/27 – 8/13
1990 1/21 – 3/31
1991 7/26 – 10/10
1992 4/4 – 5/27
1995 11/18 – until 1996 1/29
1998 1/3 – 2/15
2001 6/11 – 7/25
2003 7/10 – 9/23
2007 4/1 – 4/11
2007 11/1 – until 2008 1/12
2009 4/22 – 8/9
2009 12/12 – until 2010 1/30

SATURN BENEFICIAL
1943 8/2 – 12/21
1944 4/19 – 7/11
1947 10/7 – until 1948 2/3
1948 6/26 – 11/24
1949 1/8 – 8/2
1958 1/3 – 7/26
1958 9/20 – until 1959 3/6
1959 5/28 – 11/29
1963 5/12 – 6/25
1964 1/22 – 4/21
1964 8/10 – until 1965 1/15
1973 6/4 – 8/30
1973 12/5 – until 1974 5/16
1977 8/8 – until 1978 9/10
1987 2/17 – 5/13
1987 11/12 – until 1989 1/2
1993 2/24 – until 1994 2/20
2002 7/13 – until 2003 1/28
2003 3/19 – 6/25
2006 9/15 – until 2007 3/7
2007 6/1 – 10/23
2008 2/17 – 7/13

URANUS BENEFICIAL
1947 6/27 – until 1950 5/14
1959 10/2 – until 1963 8/30
1986 1/4 – until 1990 10/1
2001 3/15 – until 2004 2/21

NEPTUNE BENEFICIAL
1979 1/28 – until 1987 10/30
2008 3/9 – Continues

PLUTO BENEFICIAL
1950 10/29 – until 1961 6/13
2003 2/22 – until 2011 11/13

JUPITER CHALLENGING
1942 9/12 – until 1943 1/14
1943 5/7 – 7/27
1945 11/28 – until 1946 5/5
1946 7/24 – 10/22
1949 2/11 – 12/28
1954 8/21 – until 1955 7/10
1957 11/10 – until 1958 10/6
1961 1/25 – 4/25
1961 6/25 – 12/9
1966 8/4 – until 1967 6/23
1969 10/25 – until 1970 2/7
1970 3/4 – 9/19
1973 1/9 – 3/24
1973 8/11 – 11/14
1978 7/18 – 10/10
1979 1/11 – 6/4
1981 10/9 – 12/29
1982 4/23 – 8/29
1984 12/24 – until 1985 3/4
1990 7/2 – 9/16
1991 2/21 – 5/7
1993 9/23 – 12/8
1994 6/6 – 7/27
1996 12/7 – until 1997 2/15
2002 6/16 – 8/28
2005 9/7 – 11/21
2008 3/28 – 6/21
2008 11/18 – until 2009 1/30

SATURN CHALLENGING
1945 8/18 – until 1946 2/3
1946 5/4 – 9/21
1947 1/22 – 6/10
1952 10/25 – until 1953 12/12
1954 5/1 – 9/8
1961 1/2 – until 1962 2/21
1962 9/4 – 11/12
1975 6/24 – until 1976 7/23
1981 12/7 – until 1982 3/29
1982 9/1 – until 1983 10/18
1990 2/5 – 8/18
1990 10/28 – until 1991 4/9
1991 6/24 – 12/30
2004 7/31 – until 2005 8/31
2006 2/25 – 5/14
2011 10/10 – until 2012 11/23

URANUS CHALLENGING
1953 7/27 – until 1957 7/4
1972 10/28 – until 1976 10/2
1993 2/5 – until 1997 12/2

NEPTUNE CHALLENGING
1951 10/25 – until 1959 10/4
1993 2/7 – until 2001 1/11

PLUTO CHALLENGING
1938 1/1 – until 1943 6/19
1979 10/28 – until 1986 9/19

JUPITER SPECIAL
1940 4/3 – 6/11
1940 12/27 – until 1941 1/4
1952 3/16 – 5/23
1964 2/27 – 5/6
1975 6/18 – 10/13
1976 2/4 – 4/19
1987 5/26 – until 1988 4/3
1999 5/7 – until 2000 3/16
2011 4/20 – 7/6
2011 10/25 – until 2012 2/22

SATURN SPECIAL
1939 4/1 – until 1940 5/5
1968 5/10 – 11/17
1969 1/24 – 6/19
1969 10/25 – until 1970 3/10
1997 7/5 – 8/29
1998 3/15 – until 1999 4/19

April 19

SUN: ARIES • DECANATE: SAGITTARIUS/JUPITER • DEGREE: 28°5–29°5 ARIES • MODE: CARDINAL • ELEMENT: FIRE

Your Personal Powers

Bold and determined, you are usually motivated by strong desires to accomplish much. Being independent and enterprising, if you believe in a cause you can be quite forceful and persuasive. Although you have the dynamic drive to achieve substantial results materially, your adventurous spirit seeks emotional fulfillment. You gain power when you can balance your idealistic notions with a need to be practical about money and career. You lose power when you alienate yourself from others or when you are unwilling to compromise in order to keep the peace. Capable of hard work, your idealistic and energetic personality can impress others. As a good strategist with a flair for socializing, you are also an excellent networker who can mix business with pleasure. You excel at all types of work that demand courage and decisive action. Equally, you can use your people skills and act as a mediator or you can promote your ideas with great enthusiasm.

Your Powers of Attraction in Relationships

Being charismatic and outgoing indicates that you are sociable and friendly. Often daring, other people are attracted to your resolute nature and pioneering spirit. Although you like to be the boss or work independently, you benefit from working in collaboration with others. By taking responsibility for your own financial affairs, you can avoid conflicts or misunderstandings with other people. Generous to those you love, other people admire your passionate idealism. Although you appear as a strong individual your inner sensitivity implies that you also care deeply about what others think or say. You are usually attracted to intelligent and imaginative individuals who have integrity and strong principles. In your close relationships, however, you may need to resist being arrogant, impulsive, or bossy. Dramatic and independent, you need a partner who is as mentally determined as yourself.

Your attractive qualities: dynamic, resourceful, optimistic, independent, enterprising, strong convictions, progressive, imaginative, cooperative, diplomatic, ethical, gregarious, networker, intuitive, generous, calm, observant, good business sense, flexible, responsive, friendly, kind

Your less attractive qualities: stubborn, moody, self-centered, impatient, careless, tactless, indulgent, inconsistent, dissatisfied, insecure, fearful of rejection, materialistic, bossy, speculative, restless, arrogant, too competitive

Your Venus Power

The planet Venus has a great deal of influence on your powers of attraction. Below are four possible Venus types for women and men. To find your Venus you need to go to page 771, where you will find the Venus table and extra information. The planet Mars also affects your powers of attraction. To find your Mars table and interpretation go to page 761.

WOMEN WITH VENUS IN PISCES: In love you are sensitive, tender, and affectionate, experiencing your partner's feelings almost as strongly as your own. Being also imaginative and visionary, you possess the capabilities to develop both creative gifts as well as deep compassion for others. As you are idealistic when in love, you usually prefer to see only your partner's good points, but be careful that your high expectations do not bring disappointment if you avoid being realistic. Nevertheless, in your relationships with others, you can be devoted, loving, and positively enchanting.

MEN WITH VENUS IN PISCES: As a romantic and generous person you are attracted to imaginative or artistic partners who can be sensitive and generous. While you are willing to make allowances for your loved ones, playing the martyr in relationships can lead to allowing others to take advantage of your kind nature. Nevertheless, giving and loving, you are usually willing to forgive your partner's shortcomings.

WOMEN WITH VENUS IN ARIES: Idealistic, passionate, and adventurous, you are direct in your dealings with others. When you are attracted to a person, you usually take the initiative and use your people skills to make things happen. In close relationships you are not afraid to confront your other half. This self-assertiveness is positive if differences can be brought out in the open through diplomacy and compromise. Independent and spirited, you enjoy your freedom.

MEN WITH VENUS IN ARIES: You are drawn to strong and independent women who can stand up to you. Although you can enthusiastically follow the object of your desire, you may lose power if you allow your forceful emotions to become too dominant. Warm and passionate, you have a side to your that nature longs for new adventures. Romantic and chivalrous, you really enjoy the excitement of the initial chase, but

unless you keep the enthusiasm alive and avoid falling into a rut you may become easily bored.

WOMEN WITH VENUS IN TAURUS: For your ideal relationship, you seek a partner who is both financially secure and demonstrative with his affections. With these thoughts in mind, you are likely to also want a partner who is refined yet pragmatic or someone concerned with safeguarding your future. Although you have a stubborn streak you can be loving and affectionate in your relationships and with your good sense of style may be attracted to the arts, music, and luxury items.

MEN WITH VENUS IN TAURUS: As you yourself may be attractive to the opposite sex, you desire a partner who is sensual and loving or who has physical beauty. Needing stability, when faced with changes that are out of your control you may become insecure or possessive. Your own sense of style and love of beauty imply that you can be attracted to creative people, especially in art and music. Faithful and/or loyal, you can be affectionate, tactile, and constant in your love.

WOMEN WITH VENUS IN GEMINI: By nature you are young at heart, adaptable, and sociable. Being curious and willing to cooperate makes you a good team player. You are usually drawn to articulate people who have charm and flair or sharp wit. With a need to expand your knowledge, you also look for a partner who can challenge or stimulate you intellectually. Although you love to talk with all types of people, you may need to develop your listening skills and tune into your feelings in order to build better communication in your relationships.

MEN WITH VENUS IN GEMINI: Adaptable yet often flirtatious, you enjoy mixing with people who are quick-minded and versatile. Since you can learn a great deal through interacting with others you are often attracted to intelligent partners who have comprehensive knowledge or good ideas. One of your less attractive qualities is your tendency to get bored or be inconsistent. Having an adaptable partner is important to you, therefore it must be someone who can offer you different options and keep you interested.

To read all about your Outer Planets and work out how to use your personalized timetable, go to Section Three, page 789.

To read all about your Outer Planets and work out how to use your personalized timetable, go to Section Three, page 789.

Your Personalized Timetable

JUPITER BENEFICIAL
1938 4/4 – 9/20
1938 11/16 – until 1939 1/16
1942 5/12 – 6/26
1943 10/8 – until 1944 2/22
1944 6/2 – 8/26
1948 1/28 – 7/14
1948 9/17 – 12/16
1950 3/15 – 5/8
1950 8/16 – 12/26
1953 9/3 – 11/26
1954 4/22 – 6/10
1955 9/18 – until 1956 8/10
1960 1/10 – 11/29
1962 2/26 – 4/12
1962 10/6 – 11/21
1965 8/7 – until 1966 1/7
1966 3/26 – 5/24
1967 9/1 – until 1968 7/24
1971 12/24 – until 1972 3/23
1972 5/27 – 11/10
1974 2/10 – 3/24
1977 7/19 – 9/15
1977 12/2 – until 1978 5/4
1979 8/16 – 11/8
1980 2/13 – 7/5
1983 12/9 – until 1984 2/23
1984 7/10 – 10/17
1986 1/25 – 3/8
1989 7/2 – 8/19
1990 1/12 – 4/9
1991 7/31 – 10/15
1992 3/24 – 6/7
1995 11/23 – until 1996 2/3
1998 1/7 – 2/19
2001 6/15 – 7/30
2003 7/14 – 9/27
2007 11/6 – until 2008 1/17
2009 4/29 – 8/1
2009 12/18 – until 2010 2/3

SATURN BENEFICIAL
1943 8/12 – 12/9
1944 4/29 – 7/19
1947 10/18 – until 1948 1/21
1948 7/5 – until 1949 8/10
1958 1/12 – 7/8
1958 10/8 – until 1959 3/26
1959 5/7 – 12/8
1964 1/30 – 5/5
1964 7/26 – until 1965 1/24
1973 6/12 – 9/13
1973 11/20 – until 1974 5/24
1977 8/15 – until 1978 9/18
1987 3/7 – 4/23
1987 11/21 – until 1989 1/10
1993 3/5 – 10/19
1993 11/5 – until 1994 2/28
2002 7/21 – until 2003 1/11
2003 4/4 – 7/2
2006 9/24 – until 2007 2/22
2007 6/14 – 11/3
2008 4/4 – 7/22

URANUS BENEFICIAL
1947 7/14 – until 1950 6/2
1959 10/29 – until 1990 11/5
2001 4/6 – until 2004 12/26

NEPTUNE BENEFICIAL
1979 12/26 – until 1987 12/2
2008 4/11 – Continues

PLUTO BENEFICIAL
1951 9/23 – until 1961 7/27
2004 1/6 – until 2011 12/14

JUPITER CHALLENGING
1942 9/18 – until 1943 1/7
1943 5/13 – 7/31

JUPITER BENEFICIAL (continued)
1945 12/4 – until 1946 4/27
1946 8/2 – 10/26
1949 2/16 – until 1950 1/1
1954 8/26 – until 1955 2/22
1955 4/8 – 7/15
1957 11/15 – until 1958 10/11
1961 1/29 – 5/8
1961 6/11 – 12/14
1966 8/8 – until 1967 6/28
1969 10/29 – until 1970 9/24
1973 1/13 – 3/30
1973 8/3 – 11/21
1978 7/23 – 10/17
1979 1/3 – 6/9
1981 10/14 – until 1982 1/5
1982 4/16 – 9/4
1984 12/28 – until 1985 3/9
1990 7/7 – 9/21
1991 2/12 – 5/15
1993 9/28 – 12/13
1994 5/26 – 8/7
1996 12/12 – until 1997 2/19
2002 6/20 – 9/2
2005 9/12 – 11/26
2008 4/6 – 6/11
2008 11/23 – until 2009 2/3

SATURN CHALLENGING
1945 8/27 – until 1946 1/21
1946 5/16 – 10/1
1947 1/10 – 6/19
1952 11/3 – until 1953 6/10
1953 7/7 – 12/22
1954 4/18 – 9/18
1961 1/10 – until 1962 3/2
1962 8/19 – until 1962 11/27
1975 7/1 – until 1976 7/30
1981 12/19 – until 1982 3/15
1982 9/10 – until 1983 10/26
1990 2/14 – 8/2
1990 11/12 – until 1991 5/4
1991 5/30 – until 1992 1/8
2004 8/8 – until 2005 3/4
2005 4/9 – 9/8
2006 2/11 – 5/27
2011 10/18 – until 2012 12/1

URANUS CHALLENGING
1953 8/13 – until 1957 7/21
1972 11/13 – until 1976 10/18
1993 2/24 – until 1997 12/24

NEPTUNE CHALLENGING
1951 11/23 – until 1960 8/22
1993 3/13 – until 2001 12/7

PLUTO CHALLENGING
1938 1/1 – until 1944 5/25
1979 11/24 – until 1986 10/16

JUPITER SPECIAL
1940 4/7 – 6/16
1940 12/6 – until 1941 1/24
1952 3/21 – 5/27
1964 3/2 – 5/10
1975 6/24 – 10/5
1976 2/10 – 4/23
1987 5/31 – 11/22
1988 1/7 – 4/7
1999 5/12 – until 2000 3/20
2011 4/24 – 7/12
2011 10/18 – until 2012 2/28

SATURN SPECIAL
1939 4/9 – until 1940 5/13
1968 5/19 – 11/2
1969 2/7 – 6/30
1969 10/13 – until 1970 3/19
1998 3/23 – until 1999 4/27

April 20

SUN: ARIES/TAURUS CUSP • DECANATE: SAGITTARIUS/JUPITER • DEGREE: 29°5 ARIES–00°5 TAURUS • MODE: CARDINAL • ELEMENT: FIRE

Your Personal Powers

Born on the cusp of Aries and Taurus, you are both idealistic and determined with powerful emotions. Usually you have a natural flair for dealing with people, and being instinctive can help you quickly assess situations. You gain power when you initiate projects that you really believe in, especially while collaborating with others. Since at times you may be unsure of how you feel or what you want, you may then lose power to an inner conflict between your vision and the reality of your circumstances. Nevertheless, by being disciplined, hardworking, and realistic you can achieve admirable results. When positive, your strong convictions and desire for success can bring you definite results. However, if you use power tactics and show an unwillingness to compromise, you can lose power to opposition from others. Your power to resist and personal magnetism often help you to overcome any obstacles in your path and your intuition frequently comes to your aid.

Your Powers of Attraction in Relationships

Relationship is an area where you can particularly gain, since you learn a great deal about yourself through your everyday encounters with other people. You are kindhearted and altruistic, and people admire your visionary ideas and generosity. They may, however, resent you if you become too intense or demanding. You are usually drawn to mentally quick and versatile people who are bold and/or enterprising. Not so keen on being alone, you usually prefer to spend your time with others and are likely to have an active social life. Nevertheless, your sensitivity or restlessness implies that you can be easily hurt or susceptible to other people's criticism. Although you are romantic at heart, you are prone to changing your feelings. Therefore you need to take your time before committing to a long-term relationship.

Your attractive qualities: cooperative, dynamic, idealistic, generous, tactful, enthusiastic, assertive, receptive, intuitive, practical, leadership, considerate, calm, strong instincts, inspired, sociable, diplomatic, persuasive, progressive, negotiating skills, enterprising

Your less attractive qualities: impatient, unsettled, suspicious, lack of confidence, oversensitive, dissatisfied, selfish, impulsive, materialistic, indecisive, worried, unrealistic, bossy, too demanding, mistrustful, intense, headstrong

Your Venus Power

The planet Venus has a great deal of influence on your powers of attraction. Below are four possible Venus types for women and men. To find your Venus you need to go to page 771, where you will find the Venus table and extra information. The planet Mars also affects your powers of attraction. To find your Mars table and interpretation go to page 761.

WOMEN WITH VENUS IN PISCES: Idealistic and impressionable, in love you are romantic. Being sensitive to other people you are receptive to their moods and feelings. This affinity indicates that although you can be selfless you may have to guard against being too sentimental or overly romantic, especially of those who can take advantage of your kindness. Nevertheless, your partners can be allured by your seductiveness and intrigued by your poetic soul or mysterious nature.

MEN WITH VENUS IN PISCES: The combination of your emotional subtlety and charm can make you very alluring when dealing with affairs of the heart. Perceptive and impressionable, you have an easygoing style in your relationships, usually preferring to avoid ugly confrontation. You are drawn to a partner who has a touch of glamour and is sensitive to the needs of others. Alternatively, your partner could be visionary with a rich imagination, like your own, who will keep you enchanted. With your insight you have the ability to observe the subtle moods of your partner.

WOMEN WITH VENUS IN ARIES: Self-reliant and strong, you usually want things your own way. This can present problems if you refuse to compromise with your partners. Your life lessons in the area of love and relationships often involve patience and learning to trust. When you project the full power of your Venus you can radiate a charismatic and captivating energy and make a strong impression on others. Independence is often high on your relationship agenda.

MEN WITH VENUS IN ARIES: Friendly, sociable, and expressive with your feelings, you can become easily aroused and animated when involved with a person who is close to your heart. Although you can enthusiastically follow the object of your desire you may lose power if you allow your forceful emotions to become too dominant or go for instant gratification. You are drawn to women who can match you in quickness and boldness. Warm and passionate, a side to your nature longs for excitement and new adventures.

WOMEN WITH VENUS IN TAURUS: Demonstrative and affectionate, you are naturally tactile with a love of sensual plea-

sures. With a streak of the conventional you love the simple pleasures of life: good food, close friends, and happy relationships. Although you possess endurance be careful not to let this turn to plain stubbornness. Having inner strength you can express genuine patience and are often a pillar of support for loved ones and friends.

MEN WITH VENUS IN TAURUS: Although you are usually drawn to sensual and physically beautiful individuals, you want a partner who is also reliable and loyal. When in love you enjoy buying your partner things of quality that will grow in value or useful things of a practical nature. You also love to socialize and entertain, especially in luxurious surroundings. Affectionate and caring, often you are attracted to creative people or those with artistic talents.

WOMEN WITH VENUS IN GEMINI: Charming and usually easygoing, you like to talk to people who are intelligent and witty. With a good social sense and a desire for mental expansion, you need a partner who is informed and has good ideas. Although you enjoy having different experiences you need to resist your tendencies to become bored quickly or be too talkative. As you enjoy sharing and learning new things, you usually prefer being with someone rather than operating alone.

MEN WITH VENUS IN GEMINI: Informed and curious yet charming and friendly, you seek a partner who shares your interests or enjoys your witty remarks. Although a good communicator, there is an inborn tendency to be lighthearted and less profound about deep emotional commitment. Although you are keen on experiences that bring variety into your life, boredom or scattering your energies in too many directions is probably your biggest handicap in relationships. Nevertheless you are attracted to intelligent partners who can match your lively banter.

To read all about your Outer Planets and work out how to use your personalized timetable, go to Section Three, page 789.

To read all about your Outer Planets and work out how to use your personalized timetable, go to Section Three, page 789.

Your Personalized Timetable

JUPITER BENEFICIAL
1938 4/9 – 9/11
1938 11/25 – until 1939 1/21
1942 5/17 – 7/1
1943 10/14 – until 1944 2/15
1944 6/9 – 8/31
1948 2/2 – 7/4
1948 9/26 – 12/20
1950 3/20 – 5/15
1950 8/9 – 12/31
1953 9/11 – 11/17
1954 4/27 – 6/14
1955 9/23 – until 1956 4/7
1956 4/28 – 8/15
1960 1/14 – 12/3
1962 3/2 – 4/17
1962 9/25 – 12/1
1965 8/13 – 12/30
1966 4/3 – 5/28
1967 9/6 – until 1968 7/29
1971 12/29 – until 1972 4/4
1972 5/15 – 11/15
1974 2/14 – 3/29
1977 7/23 – 9/24
1977 11/23 – until 1978 5/9
1979 8/20 – 11/15
1980 2/5 – 7/10
1983 12/13 – until 1984 2/29
1984 7/2 – 10/24
1986 1/29 – 3/12
1989 7/6 – 8/24
1990 1/5 – 4/16
1991 8/4 – 10/21
1992 3/15 – 6/16
1995 11/27 – until 1996 2/8
1998 1/12 – 2/24
2001 6/19 – 8/3
2003 7/19 – 10/2
2007 11/11 – until 2008 1/21
2009 5/7 – 7/24
2009 12/23 – until 2010 2/7

SATURN BENEFICIAL
1943 8/23 – 11/26
1944 5/8 – 7/27
1945 2/3 – 4/5
1947 11/1 – until 1948 1/6
1948 7/14 – until 1949 8/18
1958 1/21 – 6/24
1958 10/21 – until 1959 12/16
1964 2/7 – 5/25
1964 7/6 – until 1965 2/2
1973 6/19 – 10/8
1973 10/25 – until 1974 6/1
1977 8/23 – until 1978 9/26
1979 4/13 – 6/5
1987 11/29 – until 1989 1/19
1989 8/20 – 10/2
1993 3/13 – 9/22
1993 12/2 – until 1994 3/8
2002 7/30 – 12/29
2003 4/17 – 7/10
2006 10/4 – until 2007 2/10
2007 6/24 – 11/18
2008 1/20 – 7/31

URANUS BENEFICIAL
1947 8/3 – until 1950 6/18
1960 8/18 – until 1964 7/17
1986 2/15 – until 1990 11/26
2001 5/10 – until 2005 1/18

NEPTUNE BENEFICIAL
1980 1/23 – until 1988 10/19
2009 3/4 – Continues

PLUTO BENEFICIAL
1952 8/29 – until 1962 6/13
2004 2/8 – until 2012 11/10

JUPITER CHALLENGING
1938 1/1 – 1/22

1942 9/25 – 12/31
1943 5/19 – 8/4
1945 12/9 – until 1946 4/19
1946 8/9 – 10/31
1949 2/20 – until 1950 1/6
1954 9/1 – until 1955 2/11
1955 4/20 – 7/19
1957 11/20 – until 1958 10/15
1961 2/2 – 12/19
1966 8/13 – until 1967 7/3
1969 11/3 – until 1970 9/29
1973 1/17 – 4/5
1973 7/26 – 11/27
1978 7/27 – 10/27
1978 12/25 – until 1979 6/15
1981 10/18 – until 1982 1/13
1982 4/7 – 9/10
1985 1/1 – 3/14
1985 9/15 – 10/21
1990 7/11 – 9/27
1991 2/4 – 5/23
1993 10/2 – 12/19
1994 5/17 – 8/16
1996 12/16 – until 1997 2/23
2002 6/25 – 9/6
2005 9/17 – 12/1
2008 4/18 – 5/30
2008 11/28 – until 2009 2/7

SATURN CHALLENGING
1945 9/6 – until 1946 1/9
1946 5/26 – 10/15
1946 12/27 – until 1947 6/28
1952 11/11 – until 1953 5/17
1953 7/30 – until 1954 1/3
1954 4/4 – 9/28
1961 1/18 – until 1962 3/12
1962 8/6 – 12/9
1975 7/9 – until 1976 8/7
1982 1/5 – 2/25
1982 9/19 – until 1983 11/3
1990 2/24 – 7/19
1990 11/24 – until 1992 1/16
2004 8/16 – until 2005 2/12
2005 4/28 – 9/18
2006 1/30 – 6/7
2011 10/26 – until 2012 12/11

URANUS CHALLENGING
1953 9/1 – until 1958 5/2
1972 12/2 – until 1976 11/2
1993 3/22 – until 1998 1/11

NEPTUNE CHALLENGING
1952 1/13 – until 1960 9/28
1994 2/2 – until 2002 1/7

PLUTO CHALLENGING
1938 1/1 – until 1944 7/8
1980 1/6 – until 1987 8/30

JUPITER SPECIAL
1940 4/11 – 6/21
1940 11/26 – until 1941 2/3
1952 3/25 – 6/1
1964 3/7 – 5/14
1975 7/1 – 9/28
1976 2/15 – 4/27
1987 6/5 – 11/11
1988 1/18 – 4/11
1999 5/16 – until 2000 3/25
2011 4/28 – 7/20
2011 10/10 – until 2012 3/4

SATURN SPECIAL
1939 4/17 – until 1940 5/21
1968 5/28 – 10/20
1969 2/18 – 7/13
1969 9/29 – until 1970 3/28
1998 3/31 – until 1999 5/4

Aries Timetable

X-Special · X-Beneficial · X-Challenging

March 21
URANUS X-SPECIAL
2010 4/14 – until **2012** 2/9
PLUTO X-CHALLENGING
2007 2/3 – until **2009** 11/29

March 22
URANUS X-SPECIAL
2010 5/4 – until **2012** 2/29
PLUTO X-CHALLENGING
2007 12/31 – until **2010** 10/20

March 23
URANUS X-SPECIAL
2010 6/1 – until **2012** 3/18
PLUTO X CHALLENGING
2008 1/30 – until **2010** 11/27

March 24
URANUS X-SPECIAL
2011 3/31 – until **2013** 1/16
PLUTO X-CHALLENGING
2008 3/22 – until **2011** 10/16

March 25
URANUS X-SPECIAL
2011 4/18 – until **2013** 2/12
PLUTO X CHALLENGING
2009 1/25 – until **2011** 11/26

March 26
URANUS X-SPECIAL
2011 5/9 – until **2013** 3/4
PLUTO X CHALLENGING
2009 3/8 – until **2012** 10/11

March 27
URANUS X-SPECIAL
2011 6/5 – until **2013** 3/22
NEPTUNE X-BENEFICIAL
2001 1/1 – until **2002** 1/18
PLUTO X CHALLENGING
2010 1/23 – until **2012** 11/25

March 28
URANUS X-SPECIAL
2012 4/3 – until **2013** 4/8
NEPTUNE X-BENEFICIAL
2001 1/1 – until **2002** 12/16
PLUTO X CHALLENGING
2010 3/2 – until **2012** 12/25

March 29
URANUS X-SPECIAL
2012 4/21 – until **2013** 4/26

NEPTUNE X-BENEFICIAL
2001 1/21 – until **2003** 1/15
PLUTO X CHALLENGING
2011 1/22 – until **2013** 1/22

March 30
URANUS X-SPECIAL
2012 5/11 – until **2013** 5/16
NEPTUNE X-BENEFICIAL
2001 2/16 – until **2003** 12/10
PLUTO X CHALLENGING
2011 2/26 – until **2013** 2/26

March 31
URANUS X-SPECIAL
2012 6/7 – until **2013** 6/13
NEPTUNE X-BENEFICIAL
2001 3/19 – until **2004** 1/11
PLUTO X CHALLENGING
2012 1/21 – Continues

April 1
NEPTUNE X-BENEFICIAL
2002 2/12 – until **2004** 12/2
PLUTO X-BENEFICIAL
2001 7/10 – until **2002** 9/14

April 2
NEPTUNE X-BENEFICIAL
2002 3/13 – until **2005** 1/5
PLUTO X-BENEFICIAL
2001 7/10 – until **2002** 9/14

April 3
NEPTUNE X-BENEFICIAL
2003 2/8 – until **2005** 11/21
PLUTO X-BENEFICIAL
2001 4/19 – until **2002** 9/14

April 4
NEPTUNE X-BENEFICIAL
2003 3/8 – until **2006** 1/1
PLUTO X-BENEFICIAL
2001 1/1 – until **2002** 10/30

April 5
NEPTUNE X-BENEFICIAL
2003 4/17 – until **2006** 1/28
PLUTO X-BENEFICIAL
2000 12/16 – until **2002** 11/27

April 6
NEPTUNE X-BENEFICIAL
2004 3/3 – until **2006** 12/26

PLUTO X-BENEFICIAL
2001 1/6 – until **2003** 10/20

April 7
NEPTUNE X-BENEFICIAL
2004 4/6 – until **2007** 1/24
PLUTO X-BENEFICIAL
2001 2/11 – until **2003** 11/20

April 8
NEPTUNE X-BENEFICIAL
2005 2/26 – until **2007** 12/20
PLUTO X-BENEFICIAL
2001 12/28 – until **2004** 10/7

April 9
NEPTUNE X-BENEFICIAL
2005 3/29 – until **2008** 1/20
PLUTO X-BENEFICIAL
2002 1/28 – until **2004** 11/12

April 10
NEPTUNE X-BENEFICIAL
2006 2/22 – until **2008** 12/10
PLUTO X-BENEFICIAL
2002 12/21 – until **2005** 9/17

April 11
URANUS X-BENEFICIAL
2001 1/5 – until **2002** 1/9
NEPTUNE X-BENEFICIAL
2006 3/23 – until **2009** 1/14
PLUTO X-BENEFICIAL
2003 1/18 – until **2005** 11/5

April 12
URANUS X-BENEFICIAL
2001 1/23 – until **2002** 1/27
NEPTUNE X-BENEFICIAL
2007 2/17 – until **2009** 11/28
PLUTO X-BENEFICIAL
2003 3/4 – until **2005** 12/4

April 13
URANUS X-BENEFICIAL
2001 2/9 – until **2002** 2/13
NEPTUNE X-BENEFICIAL
2007 3/17 – until **2010** 1/9
PLUTO X-BENEFICIAL
2004 1/10 – until **2006** 10/28

April 14
URANUS X-BENEFICIAL
2001 2/26 – until **2002** 12/20

NEPTUNE X-BENEFICIAL
2007 4/26 – until **2010** 2/5
PLUTO X-BENEFICIAL
2004 2/13 – until **2006** 11/28

April 15
URANUS X-BENEFICIAL
2001 3/17 – until **2003** 1/12
NEPTUNE X-BENEFICIAL
2008 3/11 – until **2011** 1/2
PLUTO X-BENEFICIAL
2005 1/2 – until **2007** 10/20

April 16
URANUS X-BENEFICIAL
2001 4/7 – until **2003** 1/30
NEPTUNE X-BENEFICIAL
2008 4/14 – until **2011** 2/1
PLUTO X-BENEFICIAL
2005 2/2 – until **2007** 11/24

April 17
URANUS X-BENEFICIAL
2001 5/15 – until **2003** 2/16
NEPTUNE X-BENEFICIAL
2009 3/6 – until **2011** 12/26
PLUTO X-BENEFICIAL
2005 12/28 – until **2008** 10/10

April 18
URANUS X-BENEFICIAL
2002 3/1 – until **2003** 12/23
NEPTUNE X-BENEFICIAL
2009 4/5 – until **2012** 1/27
PLUTO X-BENEFICIAL
2006 1/25 – until **2008** 11/18

April 19
URANUS X-BENEFICIAL
2002 3/19 – until **2004** 1/15
NEPTUNE X-BENEFICIAL
2010 3/1 – until **2012** 12/15
PLUTO X-BENEFICIAL
2006 3/15 – until **2009** 9/24

April 20
URANUS X-BENEFICIAL
2002 4/9 – until **2004** 2/2
NEPTUNE X-BENEFICIAL
2010 3/29 – until **2013** 1/20
PLUTO X-BENEFICIAL
2007 1/19 – until **2009** 11/14

Taurus

April 21–May 21

April 21

SUN: TAURUS/ARIES CUSP • DECANATE: TAURUS/VENUS • DEGREE: 0°–1°5 TAURUS • MODE: FIXED • ELEMENT: EARTH

Your Personal Powers

Practical and analytical, you need to be mentally stimulated or challenged in order to extend your personal powers. Being born on the cusp of Aries and Taurus means that you are daring, independent, and resourceful. You gain power when you learn to persevere and accept slow but steady progress. As an astute, versatile, and creative individual, you benefit from expanding your knowledge and expressing your individuality. Intelligent and inventive, you empower yourself when you share your ideas with others or show willingness to advise those who seek your help. Personal power also comes from developing your executive skills, talent with words, or your ability to project your authority with reassuring calmness. This provides opportunities to display your capacity for taking responsibility and being hardworking or productive. Nevertheless, you can lose some of your power if you become stubborn or rebellious. Although you usually project a bold and assertive front, others rarely see your more sensitive inner idealist.

Your Powers of Attraction in Relationships

Other people are attracted to your honesty, sharp intellect, and strong sense of loyalty. Often self-assured and usually strong-minded, you are not afraid to confront others. Generous with those you care for, you will do your utmost to please loved ones. Your partner, however, may resent your tendency to be critical or domineering. You may therefore need to learn how to resist a tendency to be uncompromising. Being intelligent and loving, you prefer to be with bright or creative individuals who can keep you mentally stimulated. Since stability and security are usually important to you, you may prefer a reliable or practical individual whom you can count on. Alternatively, in your close relationships you may be attracted to a partner who is sincere, warmhearted, and supportive, and who can accept your strength and idealism yet be receptive to your hidden sensitivity.

Your attractive qualities: resourceful, inspired, thoughtful, self-assured, charming, patient, methodical, reliable, flair for mixing business with pleasure, industrious, persistent, sociable, compassionate, astute, mental creativity, enduring, problem-solving, disciplined, enterprising

Your less attractive qualities: codependent, insecure, worried, indecisive, moody, restless, bossy, materialistic, indulgent, nervous, oversensitive, extravagant, vain, undemonstrative, stubborn, hidden fears

Your Venus Power

The planet Venus has a great deal of influence on your powers of attraction. Below are four possible Venus types for women and men. To find your Venus you need to go to page 771, where you will find the Venus table and extra information. The planet Mars also affects your powers of attraction. To find your Mars table and interpretation go to page 761.

WOMEN WITH VENUS IN PISCES: Being sensitive to affairs of the heart, when you care for someone you can feel their emotions and sense their every mood. This empathy indicates that you can love on an unselfish level, but you may have to guard against giving too much, especially to those who do not reciprocate. Partners can be fascinated by your subtle charms, captivated by your seductiveness, and attracted by your caring and affectionate nature.

MEN WITH VENUS IN PISCES: The combination of your emotional subtlety and charm can make you very alluring when dealing with affairs of the heart. Perceptive and impressionable you have an easygoing style in your relationships, usually preferring to avoid ugly confrontation. You are drawn to a partner who has a touch of glamour and is sensitive to the needs of others. Alternatively, your partner can be a visionary with a rich imagination, like your own, who will keep you enchanted.

WOMEN WITH VENUS IN ARIES: You gain power from your strong individuality, energy, and enthusiasm. Your young-at-heart and spirited approach to relationships adds to your appeal. But if you become too impatient or self-absorbed your partnerships are likely to suffer. Nevertheless, you can be creative, sharp, and quick, especially when you are able to share new and exciting projects with your partners. Mischievous, with a love of action, you may even incite them to a playful fight.

MEN WITH VENUS IN ARIES: You are drawn to strong, independent women who can stand up to you. Although you can enthusiastically follow the object of your desire, you may lose power if you allow your forceful emotions to become too dominant. Warm and passionate, you have a side to your nature that longs for new adventures. Romantic and chivalrous,

you really enjoy the excitement of the initial chase, but unless you keep the enthusiasm alive and avoid falling into a rut you may become easily bored.

WOMEN WITH VENUS IN TAURUS: Being physically attractive, you can make a good impression on the opposite sex. As security and stability in relationships is very important to you, you usually want a partner who is not only attractive but also reliable and a good provider. Being sensual or tactile you also need a lover who is affectionate, but beware that your love does not show signs of possessiveness or jealousy. Your own sense of style and love of beauty implies that you can be attracted to creative people, especially in art and music.

MEN WITH VENUS IN TAURUS: Attractive and affectionate, in relationships you are often down-to-earth, with a conservative outlook. You are drawn to warmhearted partners with whom you can share a familiar routine as well as life's pleasures and comforts. Seeking a partner who is dependable or reassuring, you often put security high on your priority list when looking for love. Your sociability and friendliness usually make you popular and partners often admire your good sense of values and practical skills.

WOMEN WITH VENUS IN GEMINI: Curious, with a bright, animated approach to life, you are attracted to those who are clever and/or sophisticated. Your love of variety and desire for knowledge suggests that you need a partner and friends who keep you mentally stimulated. Although witty and a good conversationalist, you may need to keep in touch with your deeper feelings. Nevertheless, intelligent and friendly, you possess a youthful sense of wonder and seek a playmate who can keep you from becoming bored.

MEN WITH VENUS IN GEMINI: Charming, amusing, and adaptable, you attract others with your natural communication skills and friendly personality. You have a wonderful childlike quality and love to keep life playful, but a reluctance to contact your deeper feelings may cause you to avoid serious commitment. With your need for variety and intellectual stimulation you are attracted to clever and amusing partners who have many interesting sides to their personalities.

To read all about your Outer Planets and work out how to use your personalized timetable, go to Section Three, page 789.

Your Personalized Timetable

JUPITER BENEFICIAL
1938 4/14 – 9/2
1938 12/3 – until 1939 1/25
1942 5/21 – 7/5
1943 10/20 – until 1944 2/7
1944 6/16 – 9/4
1948 2/8 – 6/26
1948 10/4 – 12/24
1950 3/24 – 5/24
1950 7/31 – until 1951 1/6
1953 9/22 – 11/6
1954 5/3 – 6/18
1955 9/28 – until 1956 3/21
1956 5/15 – 8/19
1960 1/19 – 12/8
1962 3/6 – 4/23
1962 9/16 – 12/10
1965 8/18 – 12/22
1966 4/10 – 6/2
1967 9/10 – until 1968 8/3
1972 1/2 – 11/20
1974 2/18 – 4/2
1977 11/10 – 1978 7/27
1979 8/25 – 11/24
1980 1/27 – 7/16
1983 12/17 – until 1984 3/6
1984 6/25 – 10/30
1986 2/2 – 3/16
1989 7/10 – 8/30
1989 12/28 – until 1990 4/23
1991 8/9 – 10/27
1992 3/7 – 6/23
1995 12/1 – until 1996 2/12
1996 8/11 – 9/26
1998 1/16 – 2/28
2001 6/23 – 8/8
2002 2/25 – 3/5
2003 7/24 – 10/7
2007 11/15 – until 2008 1/26
2009 5/16 – 7/14
2009 12/28 – until 2010 2/11

SATURN BENEFICIAL
1943 9/6 – 11/11
1944 5/16 – 8/4
1945 1/19 – 4/20
1947 11/30 – 12/9
1948 7/22 – until 1949 8/26
1958 2/1 – 6/10
1958 10/31 – until 1959 12/25
1964 2/15 – until 1965 2/10
1973 6/27 – until 1974 6/9
1977 8/31 – until 1978 10/4
1979 3/26 – 6/21
1987 12/8 – until 1989 1/27
1989 7/31 – 10/22
1993 3/22 – 9/6
1993 12/16 – until 1994 3/17
2002 8/8 – 12/17
2003 4/27 – 7/18
2006 10/14 – until 2007 1/29
2007 7/4 – until 2008 8/8

URANUS BENEFICIAL
1947 8/28 – until 1951 4/7
1960 9/3 – until 1964 8/4
1986 12/16 – until 1990 12/13
2002 2/28 – until 2005 2/5

NEPTUNE BENEFICIAL
1980 3/16 – until 1988 11/26
2009 4/3 – until 2012 12/13

PLUTO BENEFICIAL
1952 10/4 – until 1962 7/28
2004 12/30 – until 2012 12/12

JUPITER CHALLENGING
1942 10/2 – 12/23
1943 5/24 – 8/9

1945 12/16 – until 1946 4/11
1946 8/15 – 11/4
1949 2/25 – 9/5
1949 10/2 – until 1950 1/10
1954 9/6 – until 1955 2/2
1955 4/28 – 7/24
1957 11/25 – until 1958 5/25
1958 7/13 – 10/20
1961 2/7 – 12/23
1966 8/18 – until 1967 7/8
1969 11/8 – until 1970 10/3
1973 1/21 – 4/12
1973 7/19 – 12/3
1978 8/1 – 11/10
1978 12/11 – until 1979 6/20
1981 10/23 – until 1982 1/22
1982 3/29 – 9/15
1985 1/6 – 3/19
1985 9/2 – 11/3
1990 7/16 – 10/3
1991 1/28 – 5/29
1993 10/7 – 12/25
1994 5/9 – 8/24
1996 12/20 – until 1997 2/28
2002 6/29 – 9/11
2003 3/16 – 4/23
2005 9/21 – 12/6
2008 12/3 – until 2009 2/11

SATURN CHALLENGING
1945 9/17 – 12/28
1946 6/4 – 11/4
1946 12/6 – until 1947 7/6
1952 11/20 – until 1953 5/1
1953 8/14 – until 1954 1/19
1954 3/18 – 10/6
1961 1/27 – until 1962 3/23
1962 7/23 – 12/19
1975 7/16 – until 1976 8/15
1982 9/28 – until 1983 11/12
1990 3/7 – 7/6
1990 12/4 – until 1992 1/25
2004 8/24 – until 2005 1/29
2005 5/12 – 9/28
2006 1/18 – 6/17
2011 11/3 – until 2012 12/21

URANUS CHALLENGING
1953 9/27 – until 1958 6/5
1972 12/28 – until 1977 9/2
1994 1/19 – until 1998 1/28

NEPTUNE CHALLENGING
1952 11/17 – until 1961 8/10
1994 3/5 – until 2002 11/30

PLUTO CHALLENGING
1938 8/29 – until 1945 6/19
1980 11/8 – until 1987 10/1

JUPITER SPECIAL
1940 4/15 – 6/27
1940 11/18 – until 1941 2/11
1952 3/29 – 6/5
1964 3/11 – 5/18
1975 7/9 – 9/19
1976 2/21 – 5/2
1987 6/10 – 11/3
1988 1/26 – 4/16
1999 5/20 – until 2000 3/29
2011 5/2 – 7/28
2011 10/1 – until 2012 3/9

SATURN SPECIAL
1939 4/24 – until 1940 5/29
1940 12/11 – until 1941 2/7
1968 6/8 – 10/8
1969 2/28 – 8/3
1969 9/8 – until 1970 4/5
1998 4/8 – until 1999 5/12

April 22

Your Personal Powers

As a determined, competent, and highly intuitive individual you are a quick thinker and a good evaluator. Although you are sensitive to others, you have the confidence to lead or take on big responsibilities. You can gain power and achieve success when you believe in your convictions and capabilities. The influence of your ruling planet, Venus, indicates that you are also refined, artistic, sympathetic, and kindhearted. Although you can assess situations quickly, you lose some of your power by acting obstinately or hastily. By recognizing that ultimately it is your knowledge or wisdom that gains you the most power, you become self-assured and recognize your own true strength. In order to create prosperity and wealth, you may need to abandon the safe route, be more enterprising, and learn to trust your intuition. Usually you disarm others with your charm and straightforward approach. Being intelligent and a good organizer greatly aids your success, especially when you are able to utilize your excellent people skills.

Your Powers of Attraction in Relationships

Other people admire your confidence and determination. Gregarious, you may particularly enjoy groups where you can share your interests, expand your knowledge, and improve your skills. You are usually attracted to enterprising and clever people with a pleasing manner. You also admire innovative and pragmatic partners who show a talent for making money. Astute or quick, you do not suffer fools gladly, and although you can be sensitive to others, resist a tendency to be irritable, sarcastic, or too anxious. Nevertheless, a witty and good conversationalist, you can uplift others with your optimism and humorous remarks. Although you are loyal and willing to make sacrifices for those you love, resist taking on too many responsibilities or martyring yourself. With your sharp intelligence and warm manner you may find others coming to you for advice and help.

Your attractive qualities: resolute, quick perception, determined, pragmatic, direct, highly intuitive, hardworking, good judgment, impressive speech, ambitious, well-informed, sociable, decisive, creative, skillful, organized, inspired yet realistic, maker of big plans, achiever

Your less attractive qualities: materialistic, impatient, overconfident, unmotivated, critical, nervous, insecure, indecisive, extravagant, stubborn, bossy, unreliable, too sensitive, argumentative, irritable, impulsive

Your Venus Power

The planet Venus has a great deal of influence on your powers of attraction. Below are four possible Venus types for women and men. To find your Venus you need to go to page 771, where you will find the Venus table and extra information. The planet Mars also affects your powers of attraction. To find your Mars table and interpretation go to page 761.

WOMEN WITH VENUS IN PISCES: Romantic and idealistic, you can be both loving and giving. In relationships you may need to balance the practical with the charitable. While making allowances and sacrifices is understandable in a relationship, avoid playing the martyr. Your benevolence and generosity in the right relationship nonetheless makes you a partner who is devoted, kind, and compassionate. Subtle, sensitive, and alluring, you make a sensual and caring partner.

MEN WITH VENUS IN PISCES: Romantic and idealistic when in love, you can be a sensitive and responsive lover. Being pliant and flexible with an impressionable nature helps you to adapt to the needs of others. In your desire to blend with those you love, however, guard against not clearly defining your own boundaries. With your affectionate and sentimental nature you are often attracted to those who understand your sensitivity and share your vision.

WOMEN WITH VENUS IN ARIES: Idealistic, passionate, and adventurous, you are direct in your dealings with others. When you are attracted to a person, you usually take the initiative and use your people skills to make things happen. In close relationships, you are not afraid to confront your other half. This self-assertiveness is positive if differences can be aired in the open through diplomacy and compromise.

MEN WITH VENUS IN ARIES: As you often have the courage and strength to initiate situations, you like to take the lead and let others follow. With your unconscious desire for conquest you may also have to beware of being competitive with your partners. Nevertheless, you are drawn to a direct and strong-willed partner who can share your love of action and enthusiasm for life. When you are feeling good, you can be charming and enthusiastic in romantic situations as you have an entertaining and spontaneous spirit.

WOMEN WITH VENUS IN TAURUS: For your ideal rela-

tionship you seek a partner who is both financially secure and demonstrative with his affections. With these thoughts in mind, you are likely to want a partner who is refined yet pragmatic or someone concerned with safeguarding your future. Your stubborn streak suggests that even when you know you are in the wrong, you are reluctant to give way. Attracted to people with a good sense of style, you can succeed in all kinds of business partnerships, especially those involving the arts, music, or luxury goods.

MEN WITH VENUS IN TAURUS: As well as attracting people with your warm personality, you possess an innate sense of the value of material possessions. Keeping yourself stylish and having an attractive appearance can also be important to you. You are naturally attracted to practical yet sensual women who understand your need for comfort, security, and the pleasures and luxuries of life. Naturally affectionate, you enjoy socializing but can make a loyal and loving partner.

WOMEN WITH VENUS IN GEMINI: In relationships you need intellectual stimulation and usually prefer to keep things light. Certainly not boring, you love to talk and are at your best being witty and entertaining. Although your easygoing approach to relationships is very attractive, guard against losing touch with your emotions. You prefer a partner who can keep up with your fast stream of ideas, and if you have shared interests then so much the better.

MEN WITH VENUS IN GEMINI: Adaptable yet often flirtatious, you enjoy mixing with people who are quick-minded and versatile. Since you can learn a great deal through interacting with others, you are often attracted to intelligent partners who have comprehensive knowledge or good ideas. One of your less attractive qualities is your tendency to become bored or be inconsistent. Having an adaptable partner is therefore important to you; it must be someone who can offer you different options and keep you interested.

To read all about your Outer Planets and work out how to use your personalized timetable, go to Section Three, page 789.

To read all about your Outer Planets and work out how to use your personalized timetable, go to Section Three, page 789.

Your Personalized Timetable

JUPITER BENEFICIAL
1938 4/20 – 8/26
1938 12/10 – until 1939 1/30
1942 5/26 – 7/9
1943 10/27 – until 1944 1/31
1944 6/22 – 9/9
1948 2/14 – 6/18
1948 10/11 – 12/28
1950 3/29 – 6/4
1950 7/19 – until 1951 1/10
1954 5/7 – 6/23
1955 10/3 – until 1956 3/10
1956 5/25 – 8/24
1960 1/24 – 12/12
1962 3/10 – 4/28
1962 9/8 – 12/17
1965 8/24 – 12/15
1966 4/16 – 6/6
1967 9/15 – until 1968 8/8
1972 1/6 – 11/25
1974 2/22 – 4/7
1977 8/2 – until 1978 2/2
1978 3/10 – 5/19
1979 8/29 – 12/7
1980 1/15 – 7/21
1983 12/21 – until 1984 3/13
1984 6/17 – 11/5
1986 2/6 – 3/20
1989 7/15 – 9/6
1989 12/21 – until 1990 4/29
1991 8/13 – 11/2
1992 2/29 – 6/30
1995 12/6 – until 1996 2/18
1996 7/31 – 10/7
1998 1/21 – 3/4
2001 6/28 – 8/13
2002 2/4 – 3/26
2003 7/29 – 10/12
2004 4/13 – 5/26
2007 11/20 – until 2008 1/30
2009 5/31 – 6/30
2010 1/2 – 2/15

SATURN BENEFICIAL
1944 5/24 – 8/13
1945 1/6 – 5/1
1948 7/30 – until 1949 9/2
1958 2/12 – 5/28
1958 11/10 – until 1960 1/2
1964 2/23 – until 1965 2/18
1973 7/4 – until 1974 6/17
1977 9/7 – until 1978 10/13
1979 3/13 – 7/4
1987 12/16 – until 1989 2/6
1989 7/16 – 11/4
1993 4/1 – 8/24
1993 12/28 – until 1994 3/25
1994 10/6 – 12/12
2002 8/19 – 12/5
2003 5/6 – 7/25
2004 2/17 – 3/26
2006 10/27 – until 2007 1/15
2007 7/13 – until 2008 8/16

URANUS BENEFICIAL
1948 6/22 – until 1951 5/7
1960 9/20 – until 1964 8/20
1987 1/1 – until 1990 12/30
2002 3/18 – until 2005 2/23

NEPTUNE BENEFICIAL
1981 1/17 – until 1989 9/29
2010 2/27 – Continues

PLUTO BENEFICIAL
1953 9/7 – until 1963 6/9
2005 1/28 – Continues

JUPITER CHALLENGING
1942 10/11 – 12/14

1943 5/30 – 8/13
1945 12/22 – until 1946 4/4
1946 8/22 – 11/9
1949 3/2 – 8/21
1949 10/17 – until 1950 1/14
1954 9/11 – until 1955 1/25
1955 5/6 – 7/28
1957 11/30 – until 1958 5/14
1958 7/25 – 10/24
1961 2/11 – until 1961 12/28
1966 8/22 – until 1967 7/12
1969 11/12 – until 1970 10/8
1973 1/25 – 4/20
1973 7/10 – 12/8
1978 8/5 – until 1979 6/25
1981 10/27 – until 1982 2/3
1982 3/17 – 9/21
1985 1/10 – 3/24
1985 8/23 – 11/12
1990 7/20 – 10/9
1991 1/21 – 6/4
1993 10/11 – 12/31
1994 5/1 – 8/30
1996 12/25 – until 1997 3/4
2002 7/4 – 9/16
2003 3/3 – 5/6
2005 9/26 – 12/11
2006 6/15 – 7/27
2008 12/8 – until 2009 2/15

SATURN CHALLENGING
1945 9/30 – 12/14
1946 6/13 – until 1947 7/14
1952 11/29 – until 1953 4/18
1953 8/26 – until 1954 10/15
1961 2/4 – 9/5
1961 10/19 – until 1962 4/4
1962 7/9 – 12/29
1975 7/24 – until 1976 8/22
1982 10/6 – until 1983 11/20
1990 3/19 – 6/22
1990 12/13 – until 1992 2/2
2004 9/3 – until 2005 1/17
2005 5/22 – 10/10
2006 1/5 – 6/26
2011 11/11 – until 2012 5/23
2012 7/27 – Continues

URANUS CHALLENGING
1954 7/20 – until 1958 6/25
1973 10/20 – until 1977 9/23
1994 2/5 – until 1998 12/2

NEPTUNE CHALLENGING
1952 12/26 – until 1961 9/24
1995 1/29 – until 2003 1/2

PLUTO CHALLENGING
1939 8/14 – until 1946 5/21
1980 12/8 – until 1987 10/27

JUPITER SPECIAL
1940 4/19 – 7/2
1940 11/10 – until 1941 2/18
1952 4/2 – 6/10
1964 3/16 – 5/22
1975 7/20 – 9/9
1976 2/26 – 5/6
1987 6/16 – 10/26
1988 2/2 – 4/20
1999 5/25 – until 2000 4/3
2011 5/6 – 8/9
2011 9/20 – until 2012 3/14

SATURN SPECIAL
1939 5/2 – until 1940 6/6
1940 11/25 – until 1941 2/22
1968 6/19 – 9/25
1969 3/9 – until 1970 4/13
1998 4/15 – until 1999 5/20

April 23

Your Personal Powers

Sociable and receptive to new ideas, your enthusiastic nature indicates that you gain power by using your discerning abilities and acquiring knowledge. Influenced by your ruling planet, Venus, you can empower yourself by expressing your creativity, wit, and refined taste. Being astute and original, you also enjoy expressing your individuality. Being a strong and forceful individual you may resent criticism and lose some of your charm if you become impatient or anxious. As an industrious and sociable individual, you can often accomplish more through your willingness to collaborate and your persuasive charm. Since you are likely to maintain your youthful spirit, you are able to see opportunities or new ways to expand your horizons and succeed. In order to build on something solid and enduring in life, you will also have to remain receptive and focused on your goals. A strong need to feel secure indicates that your resources and financial matters may be a priority and it encourages you to use your creative ideas in an enterprising way.

Your Powers of Attraction in Relationships

Affectionate and charming, you can be charismatic and persuasive. Other people are also drawn to your lighthearted qualities. Being sociable, you enjoy mixing with people who can inspire you with their idealism and originality. You are usually attracted to clever, independent people with whom you feel a special bond. Although you can be affectionate, in your close relationships you may need to guard against letting your inner tensions get the better of you and cause you vacillating moods. If you're inconsistent you may sometimes appear irresponsible or uncaring. Nonetheless when you feel optimistic you can be inspiring and uplift others. Being romantic and loyal suggests that you can be a devoted and loving partner.

Your attractive qualities: independent thinker, friendly, intelligent, loyal, responsible, youthful, organized, communicative, intuitive, creative, versatile, trustworthy, educated, patient, astute, sociable, business acumen, enduring, resourceful, enthusiastic, charming, enterprising, witty

Your less attractive qualities: restless, uncompromising, irresponsible, impatient, extravagant, materialistic, impressionable, insecure, nervous, stressed, opinionated, faultfinding, give up easily, stubborn

Your Venus Power

The planet Venus has a great deal of influence on your powers of attraction. Below are four possible Venus types for women and men. To find your Venus you need to go to page 771, where you will find the Venus table and extra information. The planet Mars also affects your powers of attraction. To find your Mars table and interpretation go to page 761.

WOMEN WITH VENUS IN PISCES: Being sensitive to affairs of the heart, when you care for someone you can feel their emotions and sense their every mood. This empathy means you can love on an unselfish level, but you may have to guard against giving too much, especially to those who do not reciprocate. Partners can be fascinated by your subtle charms, captivated by your seductiveness, and attracted by your caring and affectionate nature.

MEN WITH VENUS IN PISCES: Romantic and idealistic when in love, you can be a sensitive and responsive lover. Being pliant and flexible with an impressionable nature helps you to adapt to the needs of others. In your desire to blend with those you love, however, guard against not clearly defining your own boundaries. With your affectionate and sentimental nature, you are often attracted to those who understand your sensitivity and share your vision.

WOMEN WITH VENUS IN ARIES: Idealistic, passionate, and adventurous, you are direct in your dealings with others. When you are attracted to a person you usually take the initiative and use your people skills to make things happen. In close relationships you are not afraid to confront your other half. This self-assertiveness is positive if differences can be brought into the open through diplomacy and compromise.

MEN WITH VENUS IN ARIES: As you often have the courage and strength to initiate situations, you like to take the lead and let others follow. With your unconscious desire for conquest you may also have to beware of being competitive with your partners. Nevertheless, you are drawn to a direct and strong-willed partner who can share your love of action and enthusiasm for life. When you are feeling good you can be charming and enthusiastic in romantic situations with an entertaining and spontaneous spirit.

WOMEN WITH VENUS IN TAURUS: Being physically attractive, you can make a good impression on the opposite sex. Security and stability in relationships are very important to you, so you usually want a partner who is not only attractive but also reliable and a good provider. Being sensual or tactile,

you also need a lover who is affectionate, but beware that your love does not show signs of possessiveness or jealousy. Your own sense of style and love of beauty imply that you can be attracted to creative people, especially in art and music.

MEN WITH VENUS IN TAURUS: Warm and affectionate, you are naturally tactile with a love of sensual pleasures. With a streak of the conventional you love the simple pleasures of life: good food, close friends, and happy relationships. Having an inner strength you can express genuine patience and are often a pillar of support for loved ones and friends. Although you possess endurance be careful not to let this turn into plain stubbornness.

WOMEN WITH VENUS IN GEMINI: By nature you are young at heart, adaptable, and sociable. Being curious and willing to cooperate makes you a good team player. You are usually drawn to articulate people who have charm and flair or sharp wit. With a need to expand your knowledge, you also look for a partner who can challenge or stimulate you intellectually. Although you love to talk with all types of people, you may need to develop your listening skills in order to build better communication in your relationships.

MEN WITH VENUS IN GEMINI: Charming, amusing, and adaptable, you attract others with your natural communication skills and friendly personality. You have a wonderful child-like quality and love to keep life playful, but a reluctance to contact your deeper feelings may cause you to avoid serious commitment. With your need for variety and intellectual stimulation you are attracted to clever and amusing partners who have many interesting sides to their personalities.

To read all about your Outer Planets and work out how to use your personalized timetable, go to Section Three, page 789.

Your Personalized Timetable

JUPITER BENEFICIAL
1938 4/26 – 8/18
1938 12/16 – 2/3
1942 5/30 – 7/13
1943 11/4 – until 1944 1/22
1944 6/27 – 9/13
1948 2/20 – 6/11
1948 10/17 – until 1949 1/2
1950 4/3 – 10/23
1950 10/25 – until 1951 1/15
1954 5/12 – 6/27
1955 10/9 – until 1956 3/2
1956 6/3 – 8/28
1960 1/29 – 7/28
1960 9/12 – 12/16
1962 3/15 – 5/4
1962 9/1 – 12/23
1965 8/31 – 12/8
1966 4/22 – 6/11
1967 9/20 – until 1968 8/13
1972 1/11 – 11/29
1974 2/26 – 4/11
1977 8/7 – until 1978 1/20
1978 3/22 – 5/24
1979 9/3 – until 1980 7/26
1983 12/26 – until 1984 3/21
1984 6/8 – 11/11
1986 2/10 – 3/24
1989 7/19 – 9/12
1989 12/14 – until 1990 5/4
1991 8/18 – 11/8
1992 2/21 – 7/6
1995 12/10 – until 1996 2/23
1996 7/21 – 10/16
1998 1/25 – 3/8
2001 7/2 – 8/18
2002 1/25 – 4/6
2003 8/2 – 10/17
2004 4/1 – 6/8
2007 11/24 – until 2008 2/4
2010 1/7 – 2/19

SATURN BENEFICIAL
1944 6/1 – 8/23
1944 12/25 – until 1945 5/11
1948 8/7 – until 1949 9/10
1958 2/27 – 5/12
1958 11/20 – until 1960 1/10
1964 3/3 – until 1965 2/26
1973 7/12 – until 1974 6/24
1977 9/16 – until 1978 3/23
1978 5/28 – 10/23
1979 3/1 – 7/15
1987 12/24 – until 1989 2/16
1989 7/2 – 11/16
1993 4/11 – 8/11
1994 1/7 – 4/3
1994 9/20 – 12/27
2002 8/31 – 11/21
2003 5/15 – 8/3
2004 1/29 – 4/14
2006 11/13 – 12/28
2007 7/21 – until 2008 8/24

URANUS BENEFICIAL
1948 7/9 – until 1951 5/27
1960 10/10 – until 1964 9/5
1987 1/18 – until 1991 11/1
2002 4/7 – until 2005 12/28

NEPTUNE BENEFICIAL
1981 2/25 – until 1989 11/21
2010 3/27 – Continues

PLUTO BENEFICIAL
1953 10/16 – until 1963 7/27
2005 12/24 – Continues

JUPITER CHALLENGING
1942 10/24 – 12/2
1943 6/4 – 8/18

1945 12/30 – until 1946 3/26
1946 8/27 – 11/13
1949 3/7 – 8/11
1949 10/26 – until 1950 1/18
1954 9/17 – until 1955 1/18
1955 5/13 – 8/2
1957 12/6 – until 1958 5/5
1958 8/3 – 10/29
1961 2/16 – until 1962 1/1
1966 8/27 – until 1967 3/11
1967 3/31 – 7/17
1969 11/17 – until 1970 10/13
1973 1/30 – 4/29
1973 7/1 – 12/13
1978 8/10 – until 1979 6/30
1981 11/1 – until 1982 9/26
1985 1/14 – 3/30
1985 8/15 – 11/19
1990 7/24 – 10/17
1991 1/13 – 6/10
1993 10/16 – until 1994 1/6
1994 4/23 – 9/6
1996 12/29 – until 1997 3/9
2002 7/8 – 9/22
2003 2/22 – 5/15
2005 10/1 – 12/16
2006 6/3 – 8/8
2008 12/12 – until 2009 2/19

SATURN CHALLENGING
1945 10/20 – 11/24
1946 6/21 – until 1947 7/22
1952 12/10 – until 1953 4/5
1953 9/5 – until 1954 10/23
1961 2/13 – 8/16
1961 11/7 – until 1962 4/20
1962 6/22 – until 1963 1/7
1975 7/31 – until 1976 8/30
1977 3/15 – 5/8
1982 10/14 – until 1983 11/28
1984 6/9 – 8/15
1990 4/4 – 6/4
1990 12/22 – until 1992 2/10
2004 9/13 – until 2005 1/5
2005 6/1 – 10/25
2005 12/20 – until 2006 7/4
2011 11/20 – until 2012 5/7
2012 8/12 – Continues

URANUS CHALLENGING
1954 8/6 – until 1958 7/13
1973 11/4 – until 1977 10/11
1994 2/23 – until 1998 12/24

NEPTUNE CHALLENGING
1953 11/13 – until 1961 10/22
1995 2/27 – until 2003 11/18

PLUTO CHALLENGING
1939 9/27 – until 1946 7/7
1981 10/26 – until 1988 9/13

JUPITER SPECIAL
1940 4/23 – 7/8
1940 11/3 – until 1941 2/25
1952 4/6 – 6/14
1964 3/20 – 5/27
1975 8/7 – 8/21
1976 3/1 – 5/10
1987 6/22 – 10/19
1988 2/8 – 4/24
1999 5/30 – until 2000 4/7
2011 5/10 – until 2012 3/19

SATURN SPECIAL
1939 5/10 – 12/14
1940 1/11 – 6/15
1940 11/12 – until 1941 3/6
1968 7/4 – 9/9
1969 3/17 – until 1970 4/21
1998 4/23 – until 1999 5/28
1999 12/25 – until 2000 1/30

73

April 24

SUN: TAURUS • DECANATE: TAURUS/VENUS • DEGREE: 3°–4° TAURUS • MODE: FIXED • ELEMENT: EARTH

Your Personal Powers

As a practical yet sensitive individual with an inquisitive mind, you want to shine in your own right. Your ruling plant, Venus, endows you with charm and creative abilities, yet it also indicates that a search for self-expression is often uppermost in your mind. When you are happy you can be sociable, charming, and amusing. You gain power by being self-assured, determined, and working hard for what you believe in. You lose some of your power, however, if you appear arrogant or too opinionated. Nevertheless, when you feel enthusiastic about an idea or a project, you are often willing to persevere until you achieve a result. Although you really value your independence and freethinking, your sensitivity indicates that you also need other people to collaborate or work with. If you lack self-confidence or are feeling restricted, however, you may become emotionally unsettled and express your discontent by being moody or stubborn. Fortunately, with your cerebral spark and strong willpower, you can develop the necessary self-discipline in order to succeed admirably.

Your Powers of Attraction in Relationships

Other people are attracted to your charismatic personality, generosity, and imaginative mind. They also admire your intelligence and practical skills as well as your ability to work with others. Although you usually want people to see you as strong and independent, they are often attracted to your sympathetic, kind, and sensitive side. You are usually drawn to individuals who have achieved success by their own efforts or those who are resourceful, authoritative, and commanding. Being a strong-willed person, you should be careful not to become too demanding or discontented as this can distance you from those you love. When positive, you can inspire and uplift people with your words of wisdom. Loving and appreciative, with an ability for hard work, you can be helpful and a devoted partner or parent.

Your attractive qualities: practical, intelligent, responsible, determined, supportive, hardworking, fair, common sense, assertive, inner faith, energetic, generous, optimistic, loyal, creative, idealistic, receptive, responsible, frank, philanthropic, enterprising, leader

Your less attractive qualities: hasty judgment, stubborn, bossy, too demanding, lazy, too serious, controlling, critical, provocative, lack of faith, easily discouraged, manipulative, materialistic, too economical, restless

Your Venus Power

The planet Venus has a great deal of influence on your powers of attraction. Below are four possible Venus types for women and men. To find your Venus you need to go to page 771, where you will find the Venus table and extra information. The planet Mars also affects your powers of attraction. To find your Mars table and interpretation go to page 761.

WOMEN WITH VENUS IN PISCES: In love you are sensitive, tender, and affectionate, experiencing your partner's feelings almost as strongly as your own. Being also imaginative and visionary, you possess the capabilities to develop both creative gifts as well as deep compassion for others. As you are idealistic when in love, you usually prefer to see only your partner's good points, but be careful that your high expectations do not bring disappointment if you avoid being realistic. Nevertheless, in your relationships with others you can be devoted, loving, and positively enchanting.

MEN WITH VENUS IN PISCES: The combination of your emotional subtlety and charm can make you very alluring when dealing with affairs of the heart. Perceptive and impressionable, you have an easygoing style in your relationships, usually preferring to avoid ugly confrontation. You are drawn to a partner who has a touch of glamour and is sensitive to the needs of others. Alternatively, your partner can be a visionary with a rich imagination, like your own, who will keep you enchanted.

WOMEN WITH VENUS IN ARIES: With your strong desires and enthusiastic nature you can be a passionate lover. Although idealistic and single-minded, you need to avoid unnecessary conflicts in your relationships by being more patient and less headstrong. Although at times others can accuse you of being bossy or impulsive, you possess a great deal of warmth and charm. When necessary you can disarm others by making them feel important.

MEN WITH VENUS IN ARIES: You are drawn to strong, independent women who can stand up to you. Although you can enthusiastically follow the object of your desire, you may lose power if you allow your forceful emotions to become too dominant. Warm and passionate, you have a side to your nature that longs for new adventures. Romantic and chivalrous,

you really enjoy the excitement of the initial chase, but unless you keep the enthusiasm alive and avoid falling into a rut you may become easily bored.

WOMEN WITH VENUS IN TAURUS: Good-natured and romantic, you have a highly developed sense of touch that particularly responds to massage, hugs, and all things physical. Being friendly, you enjoy socializing and are able to put others at their ease. With your innate sense of beauty and harmony, your natural charm can attract others. Although you can be lavish toward your partner you may have to be careful that you do not overdo things.

MEN WITH VENUS IN TAURUS: As you yourself may be attractive to the opposite sex, you desire a partner who is sensual and loving or possesses physical beauty. Needing stability, when faced with changes that are out of your control you may become insecure or worried about your future. Reassuring and loyal, you usually hang on to relationships but may display controlling tendencies. Your own sense of style and your love of beauty implies that you can be attracted to creative people, especially those in art and music.

WOMEN WITH VENUS IN GEMINI: Curious, with a bright and animated approach to life, you are attracted to those who are clever or sophisticated. Your love of variety and desire for knowledge suggest that you need a partner and friends who keep you mentally stimulated. Although witty and a good conversationalist you may need to keep in touch with your deeper feelings. Nevertheless, intelligent and friendly, you possess a youthful sense of wonder and seek a playmate who can keep you from becoming bored.

MEN WITH VENUS IN GEMINI: Adaptable yet often flirtatious, you enjoy mixing with people who are quick-minded and versatile. Since you can learn a great deal through interacting with others, you are often attracted to intelligent partners who have comprehensive knowledge or good ideas. One of your less attractive qualities is your tendency to become bored or be inconsistent. Having an adaptable partner, therefore, is important to you; it must be someone who can offer you different options and keep you interested.

To read all about your Outer Planets and work out how to use your personalized timetable, go to Section Three, page 789.

To read all about your Outer Planets and work out how to use your personalized timetable, go to Section Three, page 789.

Your Personalized Timetable

JUPITER BENEFICIAL
1938 5/3 – 8/11
1938 12/22 – until 1939 2/7
1942 6/4 – 7/18
1943 11/13 – until 1944 1/13
1944 7/3 – 9/18
1948 2/27 – 6/3
1948 10/23 – until 1949 1/6
1950 4/7 – 9/30
1950 11/17 – until 1951 1/20
1954 5/17 – 7/1
1955 10/14 – until 1956 2/23
1956 6/10 – 9/2
1960 2/3 – 7/17
1960 9/24 – 12/21
1962 3/19 – 5/11
1962 8/25 – 12/29
1965 9/7 – 11/30
1966 4/27 – 6/15
1967 9/25 – until 1968 8/17
1972 1/15 – 12/4
1974 3/2 – 4/16
1974 10/15 – 11/21
1977 8/12 – until 1978 1/11
1978 4/1 – 5/29
1979 9/7 – until 1980 7/31
1983 12/30 – until 1984 3/30
1984 5/30 – 11/16
1986 2/14 – 3/29
1989 7/24 – 9/20
1989 12/6 – until 1990 5/10
1991 8/22 – 11/16
1992 2/14 – 7/12
1995 12/14 – until 1996 2/29
1996 7/13 – 10/23
1998 1/29 – 3/12
2001 7/6 – 8/24
2002 1/17 – 4/14
2003 8/7 – 10/23
2004 3/23 – 6/17
2007 11/29 – until 2008 2/9
2010 1/11 – 2/23

SATURN BENEFICIAL
1944 6/9 – 9/3
1944 12/13 – until 1945 5/20
1948 8/14 – until 1949 9/18
1958 3/23 – 4/17
1958 11/28 – until 1960 1/19
1964 3/11 – 10/16
1964 11/18 – until 1965 3/6
1973 7/20 – until 1974 1/29
1974 3/29 – 7/2
1977 9/24 – until 1978 3/8
1978 6/12 – 11/2
1979 2/16 – 7/24
1988 1/2 – until 1989 2/27
1989 6/19 – 11/26
1993 4/24 – 7/28
1994 1/16 – 4/13
1994 9/7 – until 1995 1/7
2002 9/18 – 11/4
2003 5/23 – 8/11
2004 1/15 – 4/27
2007 7/29 – until 2008 9/1

URANUS BENEFICIAL
1948 7/27 – until 1951 6/13
1960 11/9 – until 1965 7/2
1987 2/8 – until 1991 11/24
2002 5/9 – until 2006 1/21

NEPTUNE BENEFICIAL
1982 1/13 – until 1989 12/20
2010 5/10 – Continues

PLUTO BENEFICIAL
1954 9/16 – until 1963 8/26
2006 1/21 – Continues

JUPITER CHALLENGING
1938 1/5 – 2/8

1943 6/9 – 8/22
1946 1/8 – 3/17
1946 9/2 – 11/18
1949 3/13 – 8/2
1949 11/3 – until 1950 1/22
1954 9/24 – until 1955 1/10
1955 5/19 – 8/6
1957 12/11 – until 1958 4/26
1958 8/10 – 11/2
1961 2/20 – until 1962 1/6
1966 9/1 – until 1967 2/22
1967 4/17 – 7/21
1969 11/22 – until 1970 10/17
1973 2/3 – 5/12
1973 6/18 – 12/18
1978 8/14 – until 1979 7/4
1981 11/5 – until 1982 10/1
1985 1/18 – 4/4
1985 8/8 – 11/26
1990 7/29 – 10/25
1991 1/4 – 6/16
1993 10/20 – until 1994 1/14
1994 4/15 – 9/11
1997 1/2 – 3/14
2002 7/12 – 9/27
2003 2/14 – 5/23
2005 10/5 – 12/21
2006 5/24 – 8/17
2008 12/17 – until 2009 2/24

SATURN CHALLENGING
1946 6/29 – until 1947 7/30
1952 12/22 – until 1953 3/23
1953 9/14 – until 1954 10/31
1961 2/22 – 8/1
1961 11/21 – until 1963 1/15
1975 8/8 – until 1976 9/8
1977 2/26 – 5/24
1982 10/22 – until 1983 12/7
1984 5/24 – 8/31
1990 12/31 – until 1992 2/18
2004 9/24 – 12/23
2005 6/10 – until 2006 7/12
2011 11/29 – until 2012 4/23
2012 8/24 – Continues

URANUS CHALLENGING
1954 8/23 – until 1958 7/29
1973 11/21 – until 1977 10/27
1994 3/18 – until 1999 1/12

NEPTUNE CHALLENGING
1953 12/16 – until 1962 9/19
1996 1/24 – until 2003 12/28

PLUTO CHALLENGING
1938 1/1 – until 1947 6/15
1981 11/20 – until 1988 10/12

JUPITER SPECIAL
1940 4/27 – 7/14
1940 10/27 – until 1941 3/2
1952 4/10 – 6/19
1952 12/17 – until 1953 1/23
1964 3/24 – 5/31
1976 3/6 – 5/14
1987 6/28 – 10/11
1988 2/14 – 4/28
1999 6/3 – 12/2
2000 1/7 – 4/11
2011 5/15 – until 2012 3/23

SATURN SPECIAL
1939 5/19 – 11/21
1940 2/1 – 6/25
1940 10/31 – until 1941 3/16
1969 3/25 – until 1970 4/28
1998 5/1 – until 1999 6/5
1999 12/5 – until 2000 2/18

April 25

SUN: TAURUS • DECANATE: TAURUS/VENUS • DEGREE: 4°–5° TAURUS • MODE: FIXED • ELEMENT: EARTH

Your Personal Powers

Bright and alert, you are full of creative ideas and have an original approach to life. Often gifted with artistic talents, your ruling plant, Venus, grants you physical attractiveness, love of nature, and charm. Being pragmatic, hardworking, yet idealistic, you gain power when you dedicate yourself to projects and interests that you enjoy. If you are passionate about what you do you can inspire others with your enthusiasm. Being a perfectionist implies that although you are inquisitive you are generally keener on acquiring skills that can improve your practical abilities. When you apply self-discipline to your latent talents you are also able to express yourself in a spectacular way. Although you are intellectually bright, you can lose some of your power by thinking negatively or becoming frustrated. In order to succeed you may need to persevere rather than be impatient or make impulsive decisions. People, nevertheless, warm to your generosity and wonderful ideas and respond well to your loving and affectionate nature.

Your Powers of Attraction in Relationships

Other people are attracted to your intelligence, charm, and charismatic personality. Sociable and friendly, you enjoy captivating others with your charm and witty conversations. By communicating your feelings in a cool or dispassionate way you can establish a good rapport with those you love and avoid letting emotional tension creep into your relationships. You are usually attracted to people who have a positive outlook or philosophy of life or those who understand your sensitivity and can shower you with encouragement and love. Although other people admire your spontaneity, your discontentment or uncommunicative behavior may sometimes put them off. You therefore need to stay honest and sincere with your partners. Two of the attractive qualities you bring to your relationships are your compassion and generosity.

Attractive qualities: intuitive, realistic, resourceful, mentally quick, well-informed, creative ideas, skillful, educated, generous, spontaneous, methodical, perfectionist, perceptive, multitalented, sensitive, idealistic, sociable, caring, affectionate, communicative, persevering

Less attractive qualities: stubborn, impulsive, impatient, overemotional, possessive, extravagant, critical, withdrawn, moody, disappointed, negative thinking, worry, inhibited, dissatisfied

Your Venus Power

The planet Venus has a great deal of influence on your powers of attraction. Below are four possible Venus types for women and men. To find your Venus you need to go to page 771, where you will find the Venus table and extra information. The planet Mars also affects your powers of attraction. To find your Mars table and interpretation go to page 761.

WOMEN WITH VENUS IN PISCES: Romantic and idealistic, you can be both loving and giving. In relationships you may need to balance the practical with the charitable. While making allowances and sacrifices is understandable in a relationship, avoid playing the martyr. Your benevolence and generosity in the right relationship nonetheless makes you a partner who is devoted, kind, and compassionate. Subtle, sensitive, and alluring, you make a sensual and caring partner.

MEN WITH VENUS IN PISCES: The combination of your emotional subtlety and charm can make you very alluring when dealing with affairs of the heart. Perceptive and impressionable, you have an easygoing style in your relationships, usually preferring to avoid ugly confrontation. You are drawn to a partner who has a touch of glamour and is sensitive to the needs of others. Alternatively, your partner can be a visionary with a rich imagination, like your own, who will keep you enchanted.

WOMEN WITH VENUS IN ARIES: With your strong desires and enthusiastic nature you can be a passionate lover. Although idealistic and single-minded, you need to avoid unnecessary conflicts in your relationships by being more patient and less headstrong. Although at times others can accuse you of being bossy or impulsive, you possess a great deal of warmth and charm. When necessary you can disarm others by making them feel important.

MEN WITH VENUS IN ARIES: As you often have the courage and strength to initiate situations, you like to take the lead and let others follow. With your unconscious desire for conquest you may also have to beware of being competitive with your partners. Nevertheless, you are drawn to a direct and strong-willed partner who can share your love of action

and enthusiasm for life. When you are feeling good you can be charming and enthusiastic in romantic situations with an entertaining and spontaneous spirit.

WOMEN WITH VENUS IN TAURUS: For your ideal relationship you seek a partner who is both financially secure and demonstrative with his affections. With these thoughts in mind, you are likely to want a partner who is refined yet pragmatic, or someone concerned with safeguarding your future. A stubborn streak suggests that even when you know you are in the wrong you are reluctant to give way. Attracted to people with a good sense of style, you can succeed in all kinds of business partnerships, especially those involving the arts, music, and luxury goods.

MEN WITH VENUS IN TAURUS: Attractive and affectionate, in relationships you are often down with a conservative outlook. You are drawn to warmhearted partners with whom you can share a familiar routine as well as life's pleasures and comforts. Seeking a partner who is dependable or reassuring, you often put security high on your priority list when looking for love. Your sociability and friendliness usually make you popular and partners often admire your good sense of values and practical skills.

WOMEN WITH VENUS IN GEMINI: Curious, with a bright and animated approach to life, you are attracted to those who are clever or sophisticated. Your love of variety and desire for knowledge suggest that you need a partner and friends who keep you mentally stimulated. Although witty and a good conversationalist you may need to keep in touch with your deeper feelings. Nevertheless, intelligent and friendly, you possess a youthful sense of wonder and seek a playmate who can keep you from becoming bored.

MEN WITH VENUS IN GEMINI: Adaptable yet often flirtatious, you enjoy mixing with people who are quick-minded and versatile. Since you can learn a great deal through interacting with others, you are often attracted to intelligent partners who have comprehensive knowledge or good ideas. One of your less attractive qualities is your tendency to become bored or be inconsistent. Having an adaptable partner is therefore important to you; it must be someone who can offer you different options and keep you interested.

To read all about your Outer Planets and work out how to use your personalized timetable, go to Section Three, page 789.

Your Personalized Timetable

JUPITER BENEFICIAL
1938 5/10 – 8/3
1938 12/27 – until 1939 2/11
1942 6/8 – 7/22
1943 11/26 – 12/31
1944 7/8 – 9/22
1948 3/6 – 5/25
1948 10/28 – until 1949 1/10
1950 4/13 – 9/19
1950 11/27 – until 1951 1/24
1954 5/22 – 7/5
1955 10/20 – until 1956 2/16
1956 6/17 – 9/6
1960 2/8 – 7/7
1960 10/2 – 12/25
1962 3/23 – 5/18
1962 8/17 – until 1963 1/4
1965 9/16 – 11/21
1966 5/3 – 6/19
1967 9/30 – until 1968 3/31
1968 5/13 – 8/22
1972 1/20 – 12/8
1974 3/6 – 4/21
1974 10/3 – 12/4
1977 8/18 – until 1978 1/3
1978 4/8 – 6/3
1979 9/12 – until 1980 8/5
1984 1/3 – 4/13
1984 5/15 – 11/21
1986 2/18 – 4/2
1989 7/28 – 9/30
1989 11/26 – until 1990 5/15
1991 8/27 – 11/24
1992 2/5 – 7/18
1995 12/19 – until 1996 3/6
1996 7/6 – 10/30
1998 2/2 – 3/16
2001 7/11 – 8/29
2002 1/9 – 4/21
2003 8/11 – 10/28
2004 3/15 – 6/25
2007 12/3 – until 2008 2/13
2008 9/7 – 9/10
2010 1/16 – 2/27

SATURN BENEFICIAL
1944 6/16 – 9/16
1944 11/29 – until 1945 5/29
1948 8/22 – until 1949 9/26
1958 12/7 – until 1960 1/27
1960 8/16 – 10/15
1964 3/20 – 9/24
1964 12/9 – until 1965 3/14
1973 7/29 – until 1974 1/13
1974 4/13 – 7/9
1977 10/3 – until 1978 2/23
1978 6/23 – 11/15
1979 2/2 – 8/2
1988 1/10 – 8/2
1988 9/27 – until 1989 3/12
1989 6/4 – 12/5
1993 5/10 – 7/11
1994 1/25 – 4/23
1994 8/25 – until 1995 1/17
2003 5/31 – 8/20
2004 1/3 – 5/8
2007 8/6 – until 2008 9/9

URANUS BENEFICIAL
1948 8/17 – until 1951 6/30
1961 8/25 – until 1965 7/24
1987 3/12 – until 1991 12/12
2003 3/2 – until 2006 2/8

NEPTUNE BENEFICIAL
1982 2/15 – until 1990 11/15
2011 3/21 – Continues

PLUTO BENEFICIAL
1954 10/28 – until 1964 7/24
2006 3/2 – Continues

JUPITER CHALLENGING
1938 1/1 – 2/12

1943 6/14 – 8/27
1946 1/19 – 3/6
1946 9/7 – 11/22
1949 3/19 – 7/25
1949 11/10 – until 1950 1/27
1954 10/1 – until 1955 1/3
1955 5/25 – 8/10
1957 12/17 – until 1958 4/19
1958 8/17 – 11/7
1961 2/25 – until 1962 1/10
1966 9/7 – until 1967 2/12
1967 4/27 – 7/26
1969 11/27 – until 1970 6/5
1970 7/11 – 10/22
1973 2/7 – 12/23
1978 8/19 – until 1979 7/9
1981 11/10 – until 1982 10/5
1985 1/22 – 4/11
1985 7/31 – 12/2
1990 8/2 – 11/4
1990 12/25 – until 1991 6/21
1993 10/25 – until 1994 1/22
1994 4/7 – 9/17
1997 1/6 – 3/19
1997 9/21 – 10/24
2002 7/17 – 10/3
2003 2/6 – 5/30
2005 10/10 – 12/27
2006 5/16 – 8/25
2008 12/21 – until 2009 2/28

SATURN CHALLENGING
1946 7/6 – until 1947 8/6
1953 1/6 – 3/6
1953 9/23 – until 1954 11/8
1961 3/4 – 7/19
1961 12/2 – until 1963 1/23
1975 8/16 – until 1976 3/3
1976 4/20 – 9/16
1977 2/13 – 6/5
1982 10/30 – until 1983 12/17
1984 5/10 – 9/12
1991 1/8 – until 1992 2/27
1992 9/16 – 11/14
2004 10/10 – 12/7
2005 6/18 – until 2006 7/20
2011 12/9 – until 2012 4/10
2012 9/4 – Continues

URANUS CHALLENGING
1954 9/12 – until 1959 5/17
1973 12/10 – until 1978 8/13
1995 1/19 – until 1999 1/29

NEPTUNE CHALLENGING
1954 11/9 – until 1962 10/19
1996 2/21 – until 2004 1/25

PLUTO CHALLENGING
1938 1/1 – until 1947 7/23
1981 12/24 – until 1989 8/17

JUPITER SPECIAL
1940 5/1 – 7/21
1940 10/19 – until 1941 3/8
1952 4/14 – 6/24
1952 12/5 – until 1953 2/4
1964 3/28 – 6/4
1976 3/11 – 5/18
1987 7/5 – 10/4
1988 2/20 – 5/2
1999 6/8 – 11/20
2000 1/19 – 4/15
2011 5/19 – until 2012 3/28

SATURN SPECIAL
1939 5/27 – 11/7
1940 2/15 – 7/6
1940 10/19 – until 1941 3/25
1969 4/2 – until 1970 5/6
1998 5/9 – until 1999 6/14
1999 11/21 – until 2000 3/2

April 26

Your Personal Powers

Driven by your inspired ideas, you are an imaginative and sensitive individual who needs to put your talents to some practical use. You gain power when you let your idealism and vision motivate you into action, making you industrious and determined. You also possess artistic or musical gifts and are receptive to color, form, and sound. An ability to learn new concepts quickly indicates that you also are an analytical and intuitive thinker with an ability to be spontaneous and enthusiastic. Very capable in practical, managerial, or organizational matters, you can handle large projects efficiently. Nonetheless, you also gain power by being open and honest with your feelings toward others. Although you need to stay true to your ideals, you may lose some of your powers by longing for the impossible or sticking too rigidly to what you want without showing flexibility. Ambitious and dependable, however, you can particularly attract success when you add self-discipline to your energy, confidence, and mentally sharp personality.

Your Powers of Attraction in Relationships

Other people admire your responsible attitude and idealistic nature. As an affectionate person, you are drawn to people who are passionate and loving. Equally, you admire sincere individuals with an honest and direct manner or big plans. Mentally quick and security conscious, you want to feel secure and confident with your partner before you commit yourself wholeheartedly. Since you are likely to have high ideals about love, if your partner does not fulfill your expectations you may become overcritical or cynical. Although you do not want to offend those you love, by telling the truth rather than being manipulative you can often avoid misunderstandings or power struggles. When you fall in love, however, you do so with enthusiasm and can be a loyal friend and partner.

Your attractive qualities: resourceful, practical, visionary, enthusiastic, charismatic, sociable, generous, stylish, ethical, organized, ambitious, business sense, confident, productive, creative, intuitive, imaginative, caring, responsible, direct, supportive, determined, persuasive

Your less attractive qualities: obstinate, unfulfilled plans, argumentative, misdirected, vain, extravagant, overindulgent, unmotivated, lack of persistence, irritable, materialistic, vain, sincere, stubborn, obstinate, dogmatic

Your Venus Power

The planet Venus has a great deal of influence on your powers of attraction. Below are four possible Venus types for women and men. To find your Venus you need to go to page 771, where you will find the Venus table and extra information. The planet Mars also affects your powers of attraction. To find your Mars table and interpretation go to page 761.

WOMEN WITH VENUS IN PISCES: Romantic and impressionable, you are a caring and loving individual with a dreamy nature. In relationships you are often attracted to idealistic, compassionate, or sympathetic individuals who have imagination or a strong romantic sense. A tendency to be sensitive to others suggests that you are intuitive and aware of people's inner feelings. Be careful therefore not to get caught in other people's dramas or play the rescuer too often.

MEN WITH VENUS IN PISCES: As a romantic and generous person you are attracted to imaginative or artistic partners who can be sensitive and generous. While you are willing to make allowances for your loved ones, playing the martyr in relationships can lead to allowing others to take advantage of your kind nature. Nevertheless, giving and loving, you are usually willing to forgive your partner's shortcomings.

WOMEN WITH VENUS IN ARIES: You gain power from your strong individuality, energy, and enthusiasm. Your young-at-heart and spirited approach to relationships adds to your appeal. If you become too impatient or self-absorbed, however, your partnerships are likely to suffer. Nevertheless, you can be creative, sharp, and quick, especially when you are able to share new and exciting projects with your partners. Mischievous with a love of action, you may even incite them to a playful fight.

MEN WITH VENUS IN ARIES: You are drawn to strong, independent women who can stand up to you. Although you can enthusiastically follow the object of your desire, you may lose power if you allow your forceful emotions to become too dominant. Warm and passionate, you have a side to your nature that longs for new adventures. Romantic and chivalrous, you really enjoy the excitement of the initial chase, but unless you keep the enthusiasm alive and avoid falling into a rut you may become easily bored.

WOMEN WITH VENUS IN TAURUS: For your ideal relationship, you seek a partner who is both financially secure and demonstrative with his affections. With these thoughts in mind, you are likely to want a partner who is refined yet prag-

matic, or someone concerned with safeguarding your future. Although you are affectionate and caring, a stubborn streak suggests that even when you know you are in the wrong, you are reluctant to give way. Attracted to people with a good sense of style, you can succeed in all kinds of business partnerships, especially those involving the arts, music, and luxury goods.

MEN WITH VENUS IN TAURUS: As well as attracting people with your warm personality, you possess an innate sense of the value of material possessions. Keeping yourself stylish and having an attractive appearance can also be important to you. You are naturally attracted to practical yet sensual women who understand your need for comfort, security, and the pleasures and luxuries of life. Naturally affectionate, you enjoy socializing but can be a loyal and loving partner.

WOMEN WITH VENUS IN GEMINI: By nature you are young at heart, adaptable, and sociable. Being curious and willing to cooperate makes you a good team player. You are usually drawn to articulate people who have charm and flair or sharp wit. With a need to expand your knowledge you also look for a partner who can challenge or stimulate you intellectually. Although you love to talk with all types of people you may need to develop your listening skills in order to build better communication in your relationships.

MEN WITH VENUS IN GEMINI: Informed and curious yet charming and friendly, you seek a partner who shares your interests and/or enjoys your witty remarks. Although you are a good communicator you have an inborn tendency to be lighthearted and less profound about deep emotional commitment. While you are keen on experiences that bring variety into your life, boredom or scattering your energies in too many directions is probably your biggest handicap in relationships. Nevertheless you are attracted to intelligent partners who can match your lively banter.

To read all about your Outer Planets and work out how to use your personalized timetable, go to Section Three, page 789.

Your Personalized Timetable

JUPITER BENEFICIAL
1938 5/19 – 7/25
1939 1/1 – 2/15
1942 6/12 – 7/27
1944 7/13 – 9/27
1948 3/15 – 5/15
1948 11/2 – until 1949 1/14
1950 4/18 – 9/10
1950 12/6 – until 1951 1/29
1954 5/26 – 7/10
1955 10/27 – until 1956 2/8
1956 6/23 – 9/11
1960 2/14 – 6/29
1960 10/10 – 12/29
1962 3/28 – 5/26
1962 8/8 – until 1963 1/9
1965 9/27 – 11/10
1966 5/8 – 6/24
1967 10/5 – until 1968 3/19
1968 5/25 – 8/26
1972 1/25 – 12/13
1974 3/10 – 4/26
1974 9/24 – 12/12
1977 8/23 – 12/27
1978 4/15 – 6/7
1979 9/17 – until 1980 8/10
1984 1/8 – 11/26
1986 2/22 – 4/7
1989 8/2 – 10/14
1989 11/12 – until 1990 5/20
1991 8/31 – 12/4
1992 1/26 – 7/23
1995 12/23 – until 1996 3/12
1996 6/28 – 11/5
1998 2/6 – 3/20
2001 7/15 – 9/4
2002 1/2 – 4/28
2003 8/16 – 11/3
2004 3/7 – 7/2
2007 12/8 – until 2008 2/18
2008 8/14 – 10/3
2010 1/20 – 3/3

SATURN BENEFICIAL
1944 6/24 – 10/6
1944 11/8 – until 1945 6/6
1948 8/30 – until 1949 10/4
1950 4/11 – 6/17
1958 12/15 – until 1960 2/5
1960 7/30 – 11/1
1964 3/29 – 9/9
1964 12/23 – until 1965 3/22
1965 11/8 – 11/19
1973 8/6 – until 1974 1/1
1974 4/24 – 7/17
1977 10/13 – until 1978 2/11
1978 7/4 – 12/3
1979 1/15 – 8/11
1988 1/19 – 7/15
1988 10/14 – until 1989 4/1
1989 5/15 – 12/14
1994 2/2 – 5/5
1994 8/12 – until 1995 1/27
2003 6/8 – 8/31
2003 12/22 – until 2004 5/18
2007 8/14 – until 2008 9/16

URANUS BENEFICIAL
1948 9/25 – until 1952 4/24
1961 9/10 – until 1965 8/11
1987 12/29 – until 1991 12/29
2003 3/20 – until 2006 2/26

NEPTUNE BENEFICIAL
1983 1/8 – until 1990 12/16
2011 4/25 – Continues

PLUTO BENEFICIAL
1955 9/23 – until 1964 8/24
2007 1/15 – Continues

JUPITER CHALLENGING
1938 1/1 – 2/16

1943 6/19 – 8/31
1946 9/12 – 11/27
1949 3/25 – 7/18
1949 11/16 – until 1950 1/31
1954 10/8 – 12/26
1955 5/30 – 8/15
1957 12/24 – until 1958 4/11
1958 8/23 – 11/11
1961 3/2 – 9/12
1961 10/4 – until 1962 1/14
1966 9/12 – until 1967 2/4
1967 5/6 – 7/30
1969 12/2 – until 1970 5/23
1970 7/24 – 10/26
1973 2/12 – 12/27
1978 8/23 – until 1979 7/14
1981 11/14 – until 1982 10/10
1985 1/26 – 4/17
1985 7/23 – 12/7
1990 8/6 – 11/24
1990 12/6 – until 1991 6/26
1993 10/29 – until 1994 2/1
1994 3/27 – 9/22
1997 1/11 – 3/24
1997 9/8 – 11/6
2002 7/21 – 10/9
2003 1/30 – 6/5
2005 10/14 – until 2006 1/2
2006 5/8 – 9/1
2008 12/25 – until 2009 3/4

SATURN CHALLENGING
1946 7/14 – until 1947 8/14
1953 10/1 – until 1954 11/17
1961 3/16 – 7/5
1961 12/12 – until 1963 2/1
1975 8/24 – until 1976 2/15
1976 5/7 – 9/26
1977 2/1 – 6/16
1982 11/7 – until 1983 12/27
1984 4/27 – 9/22
1991 1/16 – until 1992 3/7
1992 8/30 – 11/30
2005 6/26 – until 2006 7/28
2011 12/21 – until 2012 3/28
2012 9/13 – Continues

URANUS CHALLENGING
1954 10/14 – until 1959 6/14
1974 1/8 – until 1978 9/13
1995 2/5 – until 1999 12/1

NEPTUNE CHALLENGING
1954 12/9 – until 1963 9/13
1996 3/31 – until 2004 12/21

PLUTO CHALLENGING
1938 1/1 – until 1948 7/1
1982 11/6 – until 1989 9/26

JUPITER SPECIAL
1940 5/5 – 7/29
1940 10/11 – until 1941 3/13
1952 4/18 – 6/29
1952 11/26 – until 1953 2/13
1964 4/1 – 6/9
1976 3/15 – 5/22
1987 7/13 – 9/26
1988 2/25 – 5/6
1999 6/14 – 11/11
2000 1/28 – 4/19
2011 5/23 – until 2012 4/1

SATURN SPECIAL
1939 6/6 – 10/25
1940 2/26 – 7/20
1940 10/4 – until 1941 4/3
1969 4/10 – until 1970 5/13
1998 5/17 – 11/30
1999 1/27 – 6/23
1999 11/8 – until 2000 3/13

April 27

SUN: TAURUS • DECANATE: TAURUS/VENUS • DEGREE: 6°–7° TAURUS • MODE: FIXED • ELEMENT: EARTH

Your Personal Powers

Pragmatic and discriminating, you are a determined individual who can evaluate situations with remarkable accuracy. The influence of your ruling planet, Venus, suggests that you possess charm, refined taste, and an appreciation of art, music, and literature. It also implies that you have an inclination to indulge in the luxuries of life. In order to achieve prosperity and success, you must be disciplined, dedicated, and believe in the work you do. Although you have a fine mind and sensitive perceptions, you may need to refrain from negative thinking by focusing on your creative self-expression. You gain power, however, when you trust your intuition and think independently. Although you enjoy learning and acquiring knowledge, you can at times, be skeptical and lose some of your personal charm through self-doubt or suspicion. If unsure, you are also likely to become inflexible and unyielding. When you act with authority, however, your persistence and originality can impress others. You can also be very persuasive when you want to achieve your objectives.

Your Powers of Attraction in Relationships

Usually ambitious, you are drawn to strong individuals who are determined and purposeful. You also admire independent and hardworking people who achieve success by their own merit. Mentally quick, you enjoy lively discussions or friendly banter where you can test your mental agility and sharp wit. Sociable and amusing, your grace and enthusiasm suggest you can turn on the charm whenever you need to impress others. When you feel restricted, however, you may retaliate or appear irritable. Although very sensitive, if you show a reluctance to disclose your deeper feelings you may find it hard to get close to your partner. By being honest and direct, you can build long-lasting ties based on trust. If you have a common goal with your partner it can strengthen your relationship.

Your attractive qualities: shrewd, intuitive, inventive, resolute, enduring, persevering, independent, thoughtful, methodical, versatile, sociable, imaginative, daring, practical, business acumen, responsible, hardworking, witty, spiritual potential, mental strength

Your less attractive qualities: disagreeable, irritable, stubborn, worried, rebellious, skeptical, restless, irresponsible, indecisive, tense, mistrusting, secretive, argumentative, nervous, lack of inner faith, anxious

Your Venus Power

The planet Venus has a great deal of influence on your powers of attraction. Below are four possible Venus types for women and men. To find your Venus you need to go to page 771, where you will find the Venus table and extra information. The planet Mars also affects your powers of attraction. To find your Mars table and interpretation go to page 761.

WOMEN WITH VENUS IN PISCES: Being sensitive to other people, you are receptive to their moods and feelings. This affinity indicates that although you can be selfless, you may have to guard against being too sentimental or overly romantic, especially with those who can take advantage of your kindness. Nevertheless, you are alluring and seductive, and your partners can be intrigued by your poetic soul or mysterious nature.

MEN WITH VENUS IN PISCES: Being adaptable and sensitive, you are able to intuitively feel the moods of those you love. Although you are receptive to others, you can sometimes be ambiguous about your own feelings toward your partner. Romantic and kindhearted, you long to be loved but you need to be realistic about your relationships in order to avoid disappointments. When in love, you may idealize your partners and fail to see any faults in their personality.

WOMEN WITH VENUS IN ARIES: Idealistic, passionate, and adventurous, you are direct in your dealings with others. When you are attracted to a person, you usually take the initiative and use your people skills to make things happen. In close relationships, you are not afraid to confront your other half. This self-assertiveness is positive if differences can be aired out in the open through diplomacy and compromise.

MEN WITH VENUS IN ARIES: As you often have the courage and strength to initiate situations, you like to take the lead and let others follow. With your unconscious desire for conquest you may also have to beware of being competitive with your partners. Nevertheless, you are drawn to a direct and strong-willed partner who can share your love of action and enthusiasm for life. When you are feeling good, you can be charming and enthusiastic in romantic situations with an entertaining and spontaneous spirit.

WOMEN WITH VENUS IN TAURUS: Good-natured and romantic, you have a highly developed sense of touch that particularly responds to massage, hugs, and all things physical. Being friendly, you enjoy socializing and are able to put others at their ease. With your natural sense of beauty and harmony, your natural charm can attract others. Although you can be lavish toward your partner you may have to be careful that you do not overdo things.

MEN WITH VENUS IN TAURUS: As you yourself may be attractive to the opposite sex, you desire a partner who is sensual and loving or possesses physical beauty. Needing stability, when faced with changes that are out of your control, you may become insecure or worried about your future. Reassuring and loyal, you usually hang on to relationships but may display controlling tendencies. Your own sense of style and your love of beauty implies that you can be attracted to creative people, especially those in art and music.

WOMEN WITH VENUS IN GEMINI: Articulate, versatile, and youthful, your personal magnetism is often linked to your charm, wit, and communication skills. You seek a partner who is clever, who can communicate with you at ease and share your thoughts and interests. Since you find it easy to mix with people, you have many friends. When you do find someone you can communicate with, you can easily lose yourself in long conversations.

MEN WITH VENUS IN GEMINI: Charming, amusing, and adaptable, you attract others with your natural communication skills and friendly personality. You have a wonderful child-like quality and love to keep life playful, but a reluctance to contact your deeper feelings may cause you to avoid serious commitment. With your need for variety and intellectual stimulation, you are attracted to clever and amusing partners who have many interesting sides to their personalities.

To read all about your Outer Planets and work out how to use your personalized timetable, go to Section Three, page 789.

Your Personalized Timetable

JUPITER BENEFICIAL
1938 5/30 – 7/13
1939 1/6 – 2/19
1942 6/17 – 7/31
1944 7/18 – 10/2
1948 3/29 – 5/2
1948 11/7 – until 1949 1/18
1950 4/23 – 9/2
1950 12/12 – until 1951 2/2
1954 5/31 – 7/14
1955 11/3 – until 1956 1/31
1956 6/29 – 9/15
1960 2/20 – 6/22
1960 10/16 – until 1961 1/2
1962 4/1 – 6/4
1962 7/29 – until 1963 1/14
1966 5/13 – 6/28
1967 10/10 – until 1968 3/10
1968 6/3 – 8/31
1972 1/30 – 12/17
1974 3/14 – 5/2
1974 9/16 – 12/20
1977 8/29 – 12/19
1978 4/21 – 6/12
1979 9/21 – until 1980 8/15
1984 1/12 – 11/30
1986 2/26 – 4/11
1989 8/7 – until 1990 2/4
1990 3/17 – 5/25
1991 9/5 – 12/22
1992 1/8 – 7/28
1995 12/27 – until 1996 3/19
1996 6/20 – 11/11
1998 2/10 – 3/24
2001 7/19 – 9/10
2001 12/25 – until 2002 5/4
2003 8/20 – 11/10
2004 2/29 – 7/8
2007 12/12 – until 2008 2/23
2008 8/3 – 10/13
2010 1/24 – 3/7

SATURN BENEFICIAL
1944 7/1 – until 1945 6/14
1948 9/6 – until 1949 10/13
1950 3/27 – 7/2
1958 12/23 – until 1960 2/15
1960 7/15 – 11/13
1964 4/7 – 8/27
1965 1/3 – 3/31
1965 10/10 – 12/18
1973 8/16 – 12/20
1974 5/4 – 7/25
1977 10/24 – until 1978 1/29
1978 7/13 – until 1979 8/19
1988 1/28 – 6/30
1988 10/27 – until 1989 12/22
1994 2/10 – 5/20
1994 7/26 – until 1995 2/4
2003 6/15 – 9/11
2003 12/9 – until 2004 5/26
2007 8/21 – until 2008 9/24

URANUS BENEFICIAL
1949 7/5 – until 1952 5/19
1961 9/27 – until 1965 8/27
1988 1/15 – until 1992 10/25
2003 4/10 – until 2006 12/30

NEPTUNE BENEFICIAL
1983 2/8 – until 1991 11/8
2012 3/14 – Continues

PLUTO BENEFICIAL
1955 11/9 – until 1965 7/21
2007 2/18 – Continues

JUPITER CHALLENGING
1938 1/1 – 2/20
1943 6/23 – 9/5
1946 9/17 – 12/1

1949 3/31 – 7/10
1949 11/22 – until 1950 2/4
1954 10/18 – 12/16
1955 6/5 – 8/19
1957 12/31 – until 1958 4/3
1958 8/29 – 11/15
1961 3/7 – 8/27
1961 10/20 – until 1962 1/18
1966 9/18 – until 1967 1/27
1967 5/13 – 8/4
1969 12/8 – until 1970 5/13
1970 8/3 – 10/31
1973 2/16 – until 1974 1/1
1978 8/28 – until 1979 7/18
1981 11/19 – until 1982 10/15
1985 1/31 – 4/25
1985 7/15 – 12/13
1990 8/11 – until 1991 7/1
1993 11/3 – until 1994 2/19
1994 3/10 – 9/28
1997 1/15 – 3/29
1997 8/29 – 11/15
2002 7/26 – 10/16
2003 1/22 – 6/11
2005 10/19 – until 2006 1/8
2006 4/30 – 9/8
2008 12/30 – until 2009 3/9

SATURN CHALLENGING
1946 7/21 – until 1947 8/21
1953 10/10 – until 1954 11/25
1961 3/29 – 6/21
1961 12/21 – until 1963 2/9
1975 9/2 – until 1976 2/2
1976 5/20 – 10/6
1977 1/20 – 6/25
1982 11/15 – until 1983 5/31
1983 8/1 – until 1984 1/8
1984 4/13 – until 1984 10/2
1991 1/25 – until 1992 3/16
1992 8/16 – 12/12
2005 7/4 – until 2006 8/4
2012 1/4 – 3/13
2012 9/22 – Continues

URANUS CHALLENGING
1955 7/30 – until 1959 7/4
1974 10/27 – until 1978 10/3
1995 2/23 – until 1999 12/26

NEPTUNE CHALLENGING
1955 11/5 – until 1963 10/15
1997 2/15 – Continues

PLUTO CHALLENGING
1938 1/1 – until 1949 6/4
1982 12/3 – until 1989 10/23

JUPITER SPECIAL
1940 5/9 – 8/8
1940 10/1 – until 1941 3/18
1952 4/22 – 7/5
1952 11/18 – until 1953 2/21
1964 4/6 – 6/13
1976 3/19 – 5/26
1987 7/23 – 9/16
1988 3/1 – 5/10
1999 6/19 – 11/3
2000 2/4 – 4/23
2011 5/28 – until 2012 4/6

SATURN SPECIAL
1939 6/16 – 10/13
1940 3/6 – 8/9
1940 9/14 – until 1941 4/11
1969 4/18 – until 1970 5/21
1998 5/25 – 11/14
1999 2/11 – 7/4
1999 10/27 – until 2000 3/22

URANUS SPECIAL
1938 1/1 – until 1939 3/2

81

April 28

SUN: TAURUS • DECANATE: TAURUS/VENUS • DEGREE: 7°–8° TAURUS • MODE: FIXED • ELEMENT: EARTH

Your Personal Powers

Direct and enterprising, your ambition and enthusiasm imply that you have business acumen and are purposeful in your approach. Usually you prefer to rely on your own efforts in order to advance in life. As an alert and inquisitive individual you are constantly looking for new challenges. When you are inspired by something fresh, you show eagerness and commitment. If you become too intense, however, you can lose some of your charm. Although your ruling planet, Venus, can add fuel to your passion, it can also tempt you to overindulge in the good life and distract you from accomplishing your big dreams. By taking responsibility for your actions and finding the balance between duty and pleasure, you can empower yourself and make the best of your creative talents. Analytical and multitalented, you enjoy exploring or learning different subjects. You gain power by sharing and working with people who have interests similar to yours. Astute about material affairs, you have an innate ability to form useful contacts and make money from your many talents.

Your Powers of Attraction in Relationships

Seeking harmony and security, you are usually drawn to sensitive individuals who can show you much love and affection. Passionate by nature, other people admire your determination and high ideals. You may, however, need to resist the temptation to get carried away and overwhelm others with your strong opinions. You usually seek a partner who can stimulate you mentally or who shares your interests and enthusiasm. A touch of the dramatic implies that you can make an impression on people and your creativity can inspire others. In order to achieve congeniality in your personal relationships you may need to tone down your pent-up feelings and use your emotions in a more composed way. Nevertheless, intelligent and thoughtful, you can be stimulating company and a loyal friend.

Your attractive qualities: idealistic, imaginative, creative, ambitious, hardworking, sensual, persistent, resolute, enthusiastic, enterprising, practical visionary, wealth of feelings, friendly, kindhearted, supportive, cautious, foresight, self-restrained, disciplined, security conscious, strong-willed

Your less attractive qualities: unrealistic, dissatisfied, self-doubting, too intense, worry, moody, mistrusting, indulgent, stubborn, procrastinating, demanding, selfish, rash, impulsive, unmotivated, argumentative, bossy, irritable, lacks compassion, escapist

Your Venus Power

The planet Venus has a great deal of influence on your powers of attraction. Below are four possible Venus types for women and men. To find your Venus you need to go to page 771, where you will find the Venus table and extra information. The planet Mars also affects your powers of attraction. To find your Mars table and interpretation go to page 761.

WOMEN WITH VENUS IN PISCES: Being sensitive to other people you are receptive to their moods and feelings. This affinity indicates that although you can be selfless, you may have to guard against being too sentimental or overly romantic, especially with those who can take advantage of your kindness. Nevertheless, you are alluring and seductive, and your partners can be intrigued by your poetic soul or mysterious nature.

MEN WITH VENUS IN PISCES: Being adaptable and sensitive, you are able to intuitively feel the moods of those you love. Although you are receptive to others, you can be ambiguous about your own feelings toward your partner. Romantic and kindhearted, you long to be loved but you need to be realistic about your relationships in order to avoid disappointments. When in love you may idealize your partners and fail to see any faults in their personality.

WOMEN WITH VENUS IN ARIES: With your strong desires and enthusiastic nature you can be a passionate lover. Although idealistic and single-minded, you need to avoid unnecessary conflicts in your relationships by being more patient and less headstrong. Although at times others can accuse you of being bossy or impulsive, you possess a great deal of warmth and charm. When necessary, you can disarm others by making them feel important.

MEN WITH VENUS IN ARIES: You are usually drawn to courageous or assertive women who possess strong personal magnetism. Therefore, you find those who seem to be independent or action-oriented very attractive. Your own eagerness and need for activity suggest that you start relationships with great enthusiasm, especially if they offer you excitement or adventures. The challenge is often to maintain relationships and not get bored too easily.

WOMEN WITH VENUS IN TAURUS: Warm and affectionate, you are naturally tactile with a love of sensual pleasures. With a streak of the conventional you love the simple pleasures of life: good food, close friends, and happy relationships. Having an inner strength you can express genuine patience and are often a pillar of support for loved ones and friends. Although you possess endurance be careful not to let this turn to plain stubbornness.

MEN WITH VENUS IN TAURUS: Although you are usually drawn to sensual and physically beautiful individuals, you want a partner who is reliable and loyal. When in love you enjoy buying your partner things of quality that will grow in value or useful things of a practical nature. You also love to socialize and entertain, especially in luxurious surroundings. You are often attracted to creative people or those with artistic talents.

WOMEN WITH VENUS IN GEMINI: In relationships you need intellectual stimulation and usually prefer to keep things light. Certainly not boring, you love to talk and are at your best being witty and entertaining. Although your easygoing approach to relationships is very attractive, guard against losing touch with your deeper emotions. You prefer a partner who can keep up with your fast stream of ideas, and if you have shared interests then so much the better.

MEN WITH VENUS IN GEMINI: Adaptable yet often flirtatious, you enjoy mixing with people who are quick-minded and versatile. Since you can learn a great deal through interacting with others, you are often attracted to intelligent partners who have comprehensive knowledge or good ideas. One of your less attractive qualities is your tendency to become bored or be inconsistent. Having an adaptable partner is therefore important to you; it must be someone who can offer you different options and keep you interested.

To read all about your Outer Planets and work out how to use your personalized timetable, go to Section Three, page 789.

Your Personalized Timetable

JUPITER BENEFICIAL
1939 1/11 – 2/23
1942 6/21 – 8/5
1944 7/23 – 10/6
1948 11/12 – until 1949 1/23
1950 4/29 – 8/26
1950 12/19 – until 1951 2/6
1954 6/4 – 7/18
1955 11/12 – until 1956 1/23
1956 7/4 – 9/20
1960 2/26 – 6/14
1960 10/22 – until 1961 1/6
1962 4/6 – 6/21
1962 7/13 – until 1963 1/18
1966 5/18 – 7/2
1967 10/16 – until 1968 3/2
1968 6/11 – 9/4
1972 2/4 – 7/31
1972 9/19 – 12/21
1974 3/19 – 5/8
1974 9/9 – 12/26
1977 9/5 – 12/12
1978 4/27 – 6/16
1979 9/26 – until 1980 8/19
1984 1/17 – 12/5
1986 3/3 – 4/16
1989 8/12 – until 1990 1/23
1990 3/29 – 5/30
1991 9/9 – until 1992 8/2
1996 1/1 – 3/27
1996 6/12 – 11/16
1998 2/14 – 3/28
2001 7/24 – 9/17
2001 12/18 – until 2002 5/10
2003 8/24 – 11/17
2004 2/21 – 7/14
2007 12/16 – until 2008 2/29
2008 7/25 – 10/22
2010 1/28 – 3/11

SATURN BENEFICIAL
1944 7/9 – until 1945 6/22
1948 9/14 – until 1949 4/18
1949 5/14 – 10/22
1950 3/14 – 7/14
1959 1/1 – until 1960 2/25
1960 7/2 – 11/24
1964 4/18 – 8/14
1965 1/13 – 4/9
1965 9/24 – until 1966 1/1
1973 8/27 – 12/8
1974 5/14 – 8/2
1975 2/18 – 4/7
1977 11/7 – until 1978 1/15
1978 7/21 – until 1979 8/27
1988 2/8 – 6/17
1988 11/6 – until 1989 12/30
1994 2/18 – until 1995 2/13
2003 6/23 – 9/27
2003 11/24 – until 2004 6/4
2007 8/29 – until 2008 10/2
2009 4/21 – 6/11

URANUS BENEFICIAL
1949 7/22 – until 1952 6/6
1961 10/18 – until 1965 9/11
1988 2/3 – until 1992 11/21
2003 5/9 – until 2007 1/23

NEPTUNE BENEFICIAL
1984 1/4 – until 1991 12/11
2012 4/15 – Continues

PLUTO BENEFICIAL
1956 9/28 – until 1965 8/22
2008 1/10 – Continues

JUPITER CHALLENGING
1938 1/1 – 2/24
1943 6/28 – 9/10
1946 9/22 – 12/6

1949 4/8 – 7/2
1949 11/27 – until 1950 2/8
1954 10/31 – 12/3
1955 6/10 – 8/24
1958 1/8 – 3/26
1958 9/4 – 11/20
1961 3/12 – 8/17
1961 10/30 – until 1962 1/22
1966 9/24 – until 1967 1/20
1967 5/19 – 8/8
1969 12/13 – until 1970 5/4
1970 8/11 – 11/4
1973 2/20 – until 1974 1/5
1978 9/2 – until 1979 3/9
1979 4/11 – 7/23
1981 11/24 – until 1982 10/19
1985 2/4 – 5/4
1985 7/5 – 12/18
1990 8/15 – until 1991 7/6
1993 11/7 – until 1994 10/3
1997 1/19 – 4/3
1997 8/21 – 11/23
2002 7/30 – 10/24
2003 1/14 – 6/17
2005 10/23 – until 2006 1/15
2006 4/22 – 9/14
2009 1/3 – 3/13

SATURN CHALLENGING
1946 7/29 – until 1947 8/29
1953 10/18 – until 1954 12/3
1955 6/14 – 8/23
1961 4/17 – 5/31
1961 12/30 – until 1963 2/17
1975 9/11 – until 1976 1/21
1976 5/30 – 10/19
1977 1/6 – 7/4
1982 11/24 – until 1983 5/14
1983 8/17 – until 1984 1/22
1984 3/28 – 10/11
1991 2/2 – until 1992 3/26
1992 8/2 – 12/23
2005 7/12 – until 2006 8/12
2012 2/1 – 2/14
2012 10/1 – Continues

URANUS CHALLENGING
1955 8/15 – until 1959 7/21
1974 11/12 – until 1978 10/20
1995 3/16 – until 2000 1/14

NEPTUNE CHALLENGING
1955 12/4 – until 1964 9/4
1997 3/20 – until 2005 12/14

PLUTO CHALLENGING
1938 7/15 – until 1949 7/16
1983 1/18 – until 1990 9/6

JUPITER SPECIAL
1940 5/14 – 8/24
1940 9/15 – until 1941 3/23
1952 4/26 – 7/10
1952 11/11 – until 1953 2/27
1964 4/10 – 6/18
1976 3/24 – 5/31
1987 8/7 – 9/1
1988 3/6 – 5/14
1999 6/25 – 10/27
2000 2/11 – 4/28
2011 6/2 – until 2012 4/10

SATURN SPECIAL
1939 6/28 – 9/30
1940 3/15 – until 1941 4/19
1969 4/25 – until 1970 5/29
1998 6/4 – 11/1
1999 2/23 – 7/16
1999 10/14 – until 2000 3/31

URANUS SPECIAL
1938 1/1 – until 1939 3/26

April 29

Your Personal Powers

Your ability to think quickly and act spontaneously suggest that you like a fast pace and are often one step ahead of everyone else. Your ruling planet, Venus, indicates that your sensual nature appreciates harmony and beauty but warns against overindulgence and emotional restlessness. Your enterprising spirit and natural business sense mean you can succeed when collaborating with others. You gain power by being direct and honest in your approach. Equally, your abilities to assess situations intuitively or make instant decisions indicate that you can gain from your fast instincts. Although you have a sharp mind, you may be prone to emotional discontentment. If you fail to control your restlessness you may lose some of your power and become easily bored or scatter your energies by initiating plans that you fail to finish. For success and prosperity, you may need to focus your mental energy on only a few worthwhile projects. Alternatively, in order to avoid boredom, you may need to seek a challenge that will keep you constantly engaged.

Your Powers of Attraction in Relationships

Sociable and astute, you can be charming and entertaining company. Your feelings often run deep and you may be reluctant to express what you really perceive or think. Being enterprising, you can inspire others to join or support your ventures. You are usually drawn to charismatic, strong-willed, or idealistic individuals who share your enthusiasm or unusual interests. Although you rely on your pragmatic approach and analytical skills to assess situations, when you are attracted to a partner you are inclined to be infatuated rather than cautious. In order to achieve harmony and security in relationships you need to create a balance between being too fixed and being flexible and communicative. You are aware and sensitive, and others will always be attracted to your youthful qualities and agile mind.

Your attractive qualities: focused, intuitive, astute, direct, inspired, enterprising, practical, assertive, security conscious, disciplined, persistent, determined, generous, foresight, optimistic, methodical, dependable, organized, strategist, determined, realistic, industrious

Your less attractive qualities: distrusting, stubborn, unfocused, uncommunicative, reserved, inefficient, skeptical, pessimistic, restless, nervous, moody, too sensitive, tactless, willful, scattered, impatient, lack of persistence, inhibited

Your Venus Power

The planet Venus has a great deal of influence on your powers of attraction. Below are four possible Venus types for women and men. To find your Venus you need to go to page 771, where you will find the Venus table and extra information. The planet Mars also affects your powers of attraction. To find your Mars table and interpretation go to page 761.

WOMEN WITH VENUS IN PISCES: Romantic and idealistic, you can be both loving and giving. In relationships you may need to balance the practical with the charitable. While making allowances and sacrifices is understandable in a relationship, avoid playing the martyr. Your benevolence and generosity in the right relationship nonetheless makes you a partner who is devoted, kind, and compassionate. Subtle, sensitive, and alluring, you make a sensual and caring partner.

MEN WITH VENUS IN PISCES: The combination of your emotional subtlety and charm can make you very alluring when dealing with affairs of the heart. Perceptive and impressionable you have an easygoing style in your relationships, usually preferring to avoid ugly confrontation. You are drawn to a partner who has a touch of glamour and is sensitive to the needs of others. Alternatively, your partner can be a visionary with a rich imagination, like your own, who will keep you enchanted.

WOMEN WITH VENUS IN ARIES: Idealistic, passionate, and adventurous, you are direct in your dealings with others. When you are attracted to a person you usually take the initiative and use your people skills to make things happen. In close relationships you are not afraid to confront your other half. This self-assertiveness is positive if differences can be brought into the open through diplomacy and compromise.

MEN WITH VENUS IN ARIES: As you often have the courage and strength to initiate situations, you like to take the lead and let others follow. With your unconscious desire for conquest you may also have to beware of being competitive with your partners. Nevertheless, you are drawn to a direct and strong-willed partner who can share your love of action and enthusiasm for life. When you are feeling good, you can be charming and enthusiastic in romantic situations with an entertaining and spontaneous spirit.

WOMEN WITH VENUS IN TAURUS: Being physically attractive you can make a good impression on the opposite sex. As security and stability in relationships is very important to you, you usually want a partner who is not only attractive but also reliable and a good provider. Being sensual or tactile you also need a lover who is affectionate, but beware that your love does not show signs of possessiveness or jealousy. Your own sense of style and your love of beauty imply that you can be attracted to creative people, especially those in art and music.

MEN WITH VENUS IN TAURUS: As you yourself may be attractive to the opposite sex, you desire a partner who is sensual and loving or possesses physical beauty. Needing stability, when faced with changes that are out of your control you may become insecure or worried about your future. Reassuring and loyal, you usually hang on to relationships but may display controlling tendencies. Your own sense of style and your love of beauty imply that you can be attracted to creative people, especially those in art and music.

WOMEN WITH VENUS IN GEMINI: Curious, with a bright and animated approach to life, you are attracted to those who are clever or sophisticated. Your love of variety and desire for knowledge suggest that you need a partner and friends who keep you mentally stimulated. Although witty and a good conversationalist you may need to keep in touch with your deeper feelings. Nevertheless, intelligent and friendly, you possess a youthful sense of wonder and seek a playmate who can keep you from becoming bored.

MEN WITH VENUS IN GEMINI: Charming, amusing, and adaptable, you attract others with your natural communication skills and friendly personality. You have a wonderful child-like quality and love to keep life playful, but a reluctance to contact your deeper feelings may cause you to avoid serious commitment. With your need for variety and intellectual stimulation, you are attracted to clever and amusing partners who have many interesting sides to their personalities.

To read all about your Outer Planets and work out how to use your personalized timetable, go to Section Three, page 789.

To read all about your Outer Planets and work out how to use your personalized timetable, go to Section Three, page 789.

Your Personalized Timetable

JUPITER BENEFICIAL
1939 1/15 – 2/27
1942 6/25 – 8/9
1944 7/28 – 10/11
1948 11/17 – until **1949** 1/27
1950 5/6 – 8/19
1950 12/25 – until **1951** 2/10
1954 6/8 – 7/23
1955 11/22 – until **1956** 1/12
1956 7/10 – 9/24
1960 3/4 – 6/6
1960 10/28 – until **1961** 1/11
1962 4/11 – 10/10
1962 11/17 – until **1963** 1/23
1966 5/22 – 7/7
1967 10/22 – until **1968** 2/23
1968 6/18 – 9/9
1972 2/9 – 7/20
1972 9/30 – 12/26
1974 3/23 – 5/14
1974 9/1 – until **1975** 1/1
1977 9/12 – 12/4
1978 5/3 – 6/20
1979 10/1 – until **1980** 4/15
1980 5/7 – 8/24
1984 1/21 – 12/9
1986 3/7 – 4/21
1986 10/23 – 11/25
1989 8/17 – until **1990** 1/14
1990 4/6 – 6/4
1991 9/14 – until **1992** 8/7
1996 1/5 – 4/6
1996 6/1 – 11/21
1998 2/18 – 4/2
2001 7/28 – 9/25
2001 12/10 – until **2002** 5/15
2003 8/29 – 11/24
2004 2/13 – 7/20
2007 12/20 – until **2008** 3/5
2008 7/17 – 10/29
2010 2/2 – 3/15

SATURN BENEFICIAL
1944 7/17 – until **1945** 6/29
1948 9/22 – until **1949** 3/26
1949 6/6 – 10/31
1950 3/2 – 7/24
1959 1/9 – until **1960** 3/8
1960 6/18 – 12/3
1964 5/1 – 7/31
1965 1/22 – 4/18
1965 9/11 – until **1966** 1/12
1973 9/9 – 11/24
1974 5/22 – 8/10
1975 2/1 – 4/24
1977 12/1 – 12/21
1978 7/30 – until **1979** 9/4
1988 2/19 – 6/3
1988 11/16 – until **1990** 1/8
1994 2/26 – until **1995** 2/21
2003 6/30 – until **2004** 6/12
2007 9/6 – until **2008** 10/11
2009 4/3 – 6/28

URANUS BENEFICIAL
1949 8/10 – until **1952** 6/23
1961 11/21 – until **1966** 7/9
1988 2/27 – until **1992** 12/10
2004 3/4 – until **2007** 2/11

NEPTUNE BENEFICIAL
1984 2/1 – until **1992** 10/28

PLUTO BENEFICIAL
1956 11/25 – until **1966** 7/16
2008 2/10 – Continues

JUPITER CHALLENGING
1938 1/1 – 2/28
1943 7/2 – 9/15
1946 9/27 – 12/11

1949 4/17 – 6/23
1949 12/3 – until **1950** 2/12
1955 6/15 – 8/28
1958 1/18 – 3/15
1958 9/9 – 11/24
1961 3/17 – 8/8
1961 11/7 – until **1962** 1/26
1966 9/30 – until **1967** 1/12
1967 5/26 – 8/12
1969 12/19 – until **1970** 4/26
1970 8/18 – 11/9
1973 2/25 – until **1974** 1/10
1978 9/7 – until **1979** 2/24
1979 4/25 – 7/27
1981 11/29 – until **1982** 10/24
1985 2/8 – 5/18
1985 6/22 – 12/23
1990 8/20 – until **1991** 7/11
1993 11/12 – until **1994** 10/7
1997 1/23 – 4/9
1997 8/13 – 11/30
2002 8/3 – 11/2
2003 1/5 – 6/22
2005 10/28 – until **2006** 1/23
2006 4/14 – 9/19
2009 1/7 – 3/18

SATURN CHALLENGING
1946 8/6 – until **1947** 9/6
1948 3/20 – 5/14
1953 10/26 – until **1954** 12/12
1955 5/29 – 9/7
1962 1/7 – until **1963** 2/25
1975 9/22 – until **1976** 1/9
1976 6/9 – 11/6
1976 12/19 – until **1977** 7/12
1982 12/3 – until **1983** 4/30
1983 8/29 – until **1984** 10/20
1991 2/10 – 9/17
1991 10/22 – until **1992** 4/7
1992 7/20 – until **1993** 1/1
2005 7/19 – until **2006** 8/19
2012 10/9 – Continues

URANUS CHALLENGING
1955 9/2 – until **1959** 8/6
1974 11/29 – until **1978** 11/5
1995 4/26 – until **2000** 1/31

NEPTUNE CHALLENGING
1956 10/31 – until **1964** 10/9
1998 2/10 – until **2006** 1/14

PLUTO CHALLENGING
1938 8/20 – until **1950** 6/22
1983 11/17 – until **1990** 10/8

JUPITER SPECIAL
1940 5/18 – until **1941** 3/28
1952 4/30 – 7/17
1952 11/4 – until **1953** 3/5
1964 4/14 – 6/23
1964 12/27 – until **1965** 1/24
1976 3/28 – 6/4
1988 3/10 – 5/18
1999 7/1 – 10/20
2000 2/17 – 5/2
2011 6/6 – 12/19
2011 12/31 – until **2012** 4/14

SATURN SPECIAL
1939 7/14 – 9/14
1940 3/24 – until **1941** 4/26
1969 5/3 – until **1970** 6/6
1970 12/20 – until **1971** 2/14
1998 6/13 – 10/20
1999 3/5 – 8/1
1999 9/28 – until **2000** 4/9

URANUS SPECIAL
1938 1/1 – until **1939** 4/14

85

April 30

Your Personal Powers

Your quick mind and ability to deal with problems creatively indicate that you are versatile with common sense. With your refined artistic taste you often have a gift with words. Although you appear to be pragmatic and hardworking, your need for emotional satisfaction or self-expression suggest that you are also an idealist with powerful emotions. As an independent thinker, however, you may at times be obstinate or lose some of your power through worry and indecision. In order to achieve harmony and tranquillity you may need to be more patient or tolerant and use your gift for diplomacy and gentle persuasion. Having many inspired ideas that can turn out to be commercially feasible implies that your mental creativity can make you successful and wealthy. Although you often have good business plans you need to apply yourself to hard work, be practical, and avoid extravagant dreams. A natural ability to sell others your ideas or make business contacts guarantees that you are enterprising and can often see good financial opportunities.

Your Powers of Attraction in Relationships

Others are attracted to your creative ideas and direct or unique approach. Naturally intelligent and charming, you enjoy sharp wit and the company of clever and successful people. Your enthusiastic and youthful optimism can enchant many admirers. As you are likely to be constantly seeking mental fulfillment, it is important to find a partner who can share some of your interests and beliefs or who can inspire your idealistic nature. Rarely swept off your feet by emotions, you may need to learn about love or how to get in touch with your deeper feelings. Communicating these feelings as freely as your thoughts and ideas can really help your relationships. With a bit of encouragement from others, however, your fun-loving nature can emerge to delight everyone with your natural spontaneity.

Your attractive qualities: determined, idealistic, enterprising, enthusiastic, wealth of ideas, practical, creative, problem-solving, organized, energetic, honorable, witty, independent, daring, loyal, friendly, persuasive, inner peace, confident, sensual, versatile, enduring

Your less attractive qualities: obstinate, impatient, restless, stubborn, rebellious, scattered, overindulgent, lazy, worry, emotionally insecure, mistrusting, impulsive, intolerant, extravagant, hasty, or premature actions

Your Venus Power

The planet Venus has a great deal of influence on your powers of attraction. Below are four possible Venus types for women and men. To find your Venus you need to go to page 771, where you will find the Venus table and extra information. The planet Mars also affects your powers of attraction. To find your Mars table and interpretation go to page 761.

WOMEN WITH VENUS IN PISCES: Being sensitive to affairs of the heart, when you care for someone you can feel their emotions and sense their every mood. This empathy means you can love on an unselfish level, but you may have to guard against giving too much, especially to those who do not reciprocate. You are seductive and captivating, and partners can be fascinated by your subtle charms and attracted by your caring and affectionate nature.

MEN WITH VENUS IN PISCES: Romantic and idealistic when in love, you can be a sensitive and responsive lover. Being pliant and flexible with an impressionable nature helps you to adapt to the needs of others. In your desire to blend with those you love, however, guard against not clearly defining your own boundaries. With your affectionate and sentimental nature, you are often attracted to those who understand your sensitivity and share your vision.

WOMEN WITH VENUS IN ARIES: With your strong desires and enthusiastic nature you can be a passionate lover. Although idealistic and single-minded, you need to avoid unnecessary conflicts in your relationships by being more patient and less headstrong. Although at times others can accuse you of being bossy or impulsive, you possess a great deal of warmth and charm. When necessary, you can disarm others by making them feel important.

MEN WITH VENUS IN ARIES: You are usually inclined to seek a partner who is active, goal-oriented, or decisive. Not known for your patience, you probably seek relationships early in youth. You may find that you are attracted more to women who have a daring or adventurous spirit, but in your close relationships you may encounter rivalry or find that both you and your partner want to lead or be the boss. Although you

may act rashly, you possess a great deal of magnetism and are capable of demonstrating your love and affection.

WOMEN WITH VENUS IN TAURUS: For your ideal relationship you seek a partner who is both financially secure and demonstrative with his affections. With these thoughts in mind you are likely to want a partner who is refined yet pragmatic or someone concerned with safeguarding your future. Although you are affectionate and caring, a stubborn streak suggests that even when you know you are in the wrong, you are reluctant to give way. Attracted to people with a good sense of style, you can succeed in all kinds of business partnerships, especially those involving the arts, music, and luxury goods.

MEN WITH VENUS IN TAURUS: Although you are usually drawn to sensual and physically beautiful individuals you want a partner who is reliable and loyal. When in love you enjoy buying your partner things of quality that will grow in value or useful things of a practical nature. You also love to socialize and entertain, especially in luxurious surroundings. Often you are attracted to creative people or those with artistic talents.

WOMEN WITH VENUS IN GEMINI: By nature you are young at heart, adaptable, and sociable. Being curious and willing to cooperate makes you a good team player. You are usually drawn to articulate people who have charm and flair or sharp wit. With a need to expand your knowledge, you also look for a partner who can challenge or stimulate you intellectually. Although you love to talk with all types of people, you may need to develop your listening skills in order to build better communication in your relationships.

MEN WITH VENUS IN GEMINI: Friendly and sociable, you attract others with your clever and amusing conversation. Drawn to people who can match you in wit and intelligence, you usually prefer to keep relationships light rather than emotionally intense. With your youthful charm and desire for knowledge and new experiences you usually have many friends and a low boredom threshold.

To read all about your Outer Planets and work out how to use your personalized timetable, go to Section Three, page 789.

Your Personalized Timetable

JUPITER BENEFICIAL
1939 1/20 – 3/3
1942 6/29 – 8/14
1944 8/1 – 10/16
1948 11/22 – until 1949 1/31
1950 5/13 – 8/11
1950 12/30 – until 1951 2/15
1954 6/13 – 7/27
1955 12/11 – 12/25
1956 7/15 – 9/29
1960 3/13 – 5/28
1960 11/3 – until 1961 1/15
1962 4/16 – 9/28
1962 11/29 – until 1963 1/28
1966 5/27 – 7/11
1967 10/28 – until 1968 2/16
1968 6/25 – 9/13
1972 2/14 – 7/11
1972 10/8 – 12/30
1974 3/27 – 5/20
1974 8/25 – until 1975 1/7
1977 9/21 – 11/26
1978 5/8 – 6/25
1979 10/6 – until 1980 3/29
1980 5/24 – 8/28
1984 1/26 – 12/14
1986 3/11 – 4/26
1986 10/10 – 12/7
1989 8/23 – until 1990 1/7
1990 4/14 – 6/8
1991 9/19 – until 1992 8/12
1996 1/9 – 4/22
1996 5/16 – 11/26
1998 2/22 – 4/6
2001 8/2 – 10/5
2001 11/30 – until 2002 5/20
2003 9/2 – 12/4
2004 2/3 – 7/25
2007 12/25 – until 2008 3/11
2008 7/9 – 11/4
2010 2/6 – 3/19

SATURN BENEFICIAL
1944 7/25 – until 1945 2/9
1945 3/30 – 7/7
1948 10/1 – until 1949 3/11
1949 6/20 – 11/12
1950 2/17 – 8/2
1959 1/18 – 8/1
1959 10/9 – until 1960 3/23
1960 6/2 – 12/13
1964 5/18 – 7/13
1965 1/30 – 4/29
1965 8/29 – until 1966 1/22
1973 9/28 – 11/5
1974 5/30 – 8/18
1975 1/18 – 5/6
1978 8/7 – until 1979 9/11
1988 3/4 – 5/19
1988 11/25 – until 1990 1/16
1994 3/6 – until 1995 3/1
2003 7/8 – until 2004 6/19
2007 9/13 – until 2008 10/20
2009 3/21 – 7/11

URANUS BENEFICIAL
1949 9/3 – until 1952 7/9
1962 9/1 – until 1966 7/31
1988 12/26 – until 1992 12/27
2004 3/22 – until 2007 2/28

NEPTUNE BENEFICIAL
1984 3/27 – until 1992 12/5

PLUTO BENEFICIAL
1957 10/3 – until 1966 8/18
2009 1/5 – Continues

JUPITER CHALLENGING
1938 1/1 – 3/5
1943 7/7 – 9/20

1944 3/28 – 4/28
1946 10/2 – 12/16
1949 4/28 – 6/11
1949 12/8 – until 1950 2/16
1955 6/20 – 9/2
1958 2/3 – 2/27
1958 9/14 – 11/29
1961 3/23 – 7/31
1961 11/14 – until 1962 1/31
1966 10/7 – until 1967 1/5
1967 5/31 – 8/17
1969 12/25 – until 1970 4/19
1970 8/25 – 11/13
1973 3/2 – until 1974 1/14
1978 9/12 – until 1979 2/14
1979 5/5 – 8/1
1981 12/4 – until 1982 6/2
1982 7/23 – 10/28
1985 2/12 – 12/28
1990 8/25 – until 1991 7/16
1993 11/17 – until 1994 10/12
1997 1/27 – 4/15
1997 8/6 – 12/6
2002 8/8 – 11/13
2002 12/25 – until 2003 6/28
2005 11/1 – until 2006 2/2
2006 4/4 – 9/25
2009 1/11 – 3/23
2009 10/1 – 10/24

SATURN CHALLENGING
1946 8/13 – until 1947 9/15
1948 3/3 – 5/31
1953 11/3 – until 1954 12/22
1955 5/15 – 9/19
1962 1/15 – until 1963 3/6
1963 9/17 – 11/24
1975 10/4 – 12/26
1976 6/18 – until 1977 7/20
1982 12/13 – until 1983 4/18
1983 9/9 – until 1984 10/28
1991 2/19 – 8/26
1991 11/12 – until 1992 4/22
1992 7/4 – until 1993 1/10
2005 7/27 – until 2006 8/27
2012 10/17 – Continues

URANUS CHALLENGING
1955 9/23 – until 1960 5/27
1974 12/19 – until 1979 8/29
1996 2/5 – until 2000 11/30

NEPTUNE CHALLENGING
1956 11/27 – until 1965 8/24
1998 3/12 – until 2006 12/5

PLUTO CHALLENGING
1938 10/12 – until 1950 7/28
1983 12/16 – until 1990 11/3

JUPITER SPECIAL
1940 5/22 – until 1941 4/1
1952 5/4 – 7/23
1952 10/28 – until 1953 3/11
1964 4/18 – 6/28
1964 12/13 – until 1965 2/7
1976 4/1 – 6/8
1988 3/15 – 5/22
1999 7/7 – 10/12
2000 2/23 – 5/6
2011 6/11 – 12/1
2012 1/19 – 4/19

SATURN SPECIAL
1940 4/1 – until 1941 5/4
1969 5/11 – until 1970 6/14
1970 12/4 – until 1971 3/2
1998 6/25 – 10/7
1999 3/14 – until 2000 4/17

URANUS SPECIAL
1938 1/1 – until 1939 5/2

May 1

SUN: TAURUS • DECANATE: VIRGO/MERCURY • DEGREE: 9°5–11° TAURUS • MODE: FIXED • ELEMENT: EARTH

Your Personal Powers

As an astute individual with strong instincts, you like to be active and have many interests. As well as a need for variety, you possess warmth, charm, and refined artistic taste. You gain power when you use your determination and purposeful nature to express your natural creativity. Since you are driven by strong desires it is crucial that you find a form of self-expression other than just seeking fulfillment in financial interests. A definite life plan is an essential element to your success and prosperity. You lose some of your power when you lack purpose or a strategy for action. You may also need to resist getting caught up in other people's emotional dramas. When you develop your powers of patience and perseverance, you can overcome a tendency to be restless or desire instant satisfaction. By being intuitive and learning to trust your own perceptions you usually discover that you are at the right place, at the right time, making the right decision.

Your Powers of Attraction in Relationships

You are charismatic and enterprising, and others admire your positive determination. You are usually attracted to intelligent people who are optimistic, loyal, and hardworking. Your emotional sensitivity indicates that as you are highly idealistic about relationships, you are likely to wait for real love. Nevertheless, avoid the disappointments that come from having too many expectations. Being single-minded and sometimes stubborn means that others may sometimes feel undermined if you are selfish or too critical. By learning to accept your partner's little faults, you can express more affection and the humanitarian side of your nature. Nevertheless, once you find someone you can truly love, you can be devoted and loyal. You are youthful and enthusiastic, and people are usually drawn to your magnetic charm.

Your attractive qualities: gregarious, creative, instinctive, versatile, astute, practical, focused, charismatic, forceful, optimistic, warmhearted, independent, disciplined, diligent, sociable, diplomatic, confident, enthusiastic, cooperative, imaginative, determined, enterprising

Your less attractive qualities: dissatisfied, stubborn, impatient, overbearing, inner tension, tactless, irritable, fluctuating moods, too detached, egotistical, easily discouraged, impulsive, overindulgent, lack of restraint, selfish, restless

Your Venus Power

The planet Venus has a great deal of influence on your powers of attraction. Below are four possible Venus types for women and men. To find your Venus you need to go to page 771, where you will find the Venus table and extra information. The planet Mars also affects your powers of attraction. To find your Mars table and interpretation go to page 761.

WOMEN WITH VENUS IN PISCES: As a romantic and idealistic individual you can be both loving and giving. While making allowances and sacrifices is understandable in a loving relationship, playing the martyr is often a state of romantic illusion that can lead to self-deception. In relationships you need to balance the practical with the charitable and not allow relationships to get into a vicious circle. Nevertheless, your benevolence and sacrifices in the right relationship make you a partner who is devoted and kind.

MEN WITH VENUS IN PISCES: Romantic and idealistic when in love, you can be a sensitive and responsive lover. Being pliant and flexible with an impressionable nature helps you to adapt to the needs of others. In your desire to blend with those you love, however, guard against not clearly defining your own boundaries. With your affectionate and sentimental nature, you are often attracted to those who understand your sensitivity and share your vision.

WOMEN WITH VENUS IN ARIES: You gain power from your strong individuality, energy, and enthusiasm. Your young-at-heart and spirited approach to relationships adds to your appeal. If you become too impatient or self-absorbed, however, your partnerships are likely to suffer. Nevertheless, you can be creative, sharp, and quick, especially when you are able to share new and exciting projects with your partners. Mischievous, with a love of action, you may even incite them to a playful fight.

MEN WITH VENUS IN ARIES: You are drawn to strong, independent women who can stand up to you. Although you can enthusiastically follow the object of your desire, you may lose power if you allow your forceful emotions to become too dominant. Warm and passionate, you have a side to your nature that longs for new adventures. Romantic and chivalrous,

you really enjoy the excitement of the initial chase, but unless you keep the enthusiasm alive and avoid falling into a rut you may become easily bored.

WOMEN WITH VENUS IN TAURUS: Good-natured and romantic, you have a highly developed sense of touch that particularly responds to massage, hugs, and all things physical. Being friendly you enjoy socializing and are able to put others at their ease. With your innate sense of beauty and harmony, your natural charm can attract others. Although you can be lavish toward your partner you may have to be careful that you do not overdo things.

MEN WITH VENUS IN TAURUS: As well as attracting people with your warm personality, you also possess an innate sense of the value of material possessions. Keeping yourself stylish and having an attractive appearance can also be important to you. You are naturally attracted to practical yet sensual women who understand your need for comfort, security, and the pleasures and luxuries of life. Naturally affectionate, you enjoy socializing but can be a loyal and loving partner.

WOMEN WITH VENUS IN GEMINI: By nature you are young at heart, adaptable, and sociable. Being curious and willing to cooperate makes you a good team player. You are usually drawn to articulate people who have charm and flair or sharp wit. With a need to expand your knowledge you also look for a partner who can challenge or stimulate you intellectually. Although you love to talk with all types of people, you may need to develop your listening skills in order to build better communication in your relationships.

MEN WITH VENUS IN GEMINI: Friendly and sociable, you attract others with your clever and amusing conversation. Drawn to partners who can match you in wit and intelligence, you usually prefer to keep relationships light rather than emotionally intense. With your youthful charm and desire for knowledge and new experiences you usually have many friends and a low boredom threshold.

To read all about your Outer Planets and work out how to use your personalized timetable, go to Section Three, page 789.

Your Personalized Timetable

JUPITER BENEFICIAL
1939 1/24 – 3/7
1942 7/4 – 8/19
1943 3/1 – 3/23
1944 8/6 – 10/21
1945 4/21 – 6/7
1948 11/26 – until **1949** 2/5
1950 5/21 – 8/2
1951 1/4 – 2/19
1954 6/17 – 8/1
1956 7/20 – 10/4
1960 3/22 – 5/18
1960 11/8 – until **1961** 1/19
1962 4/21 – 9/19
1962 12/8 – until **1963** 2/1
1966 5/31 – 7/15
1967 11/4 – until **1968** 2/8
1968 7/1 – 9/18
1972 2/20 – 7/3
1972 10/15 – until **1973** 1/3
1974 4/1 – 5/28
1974 8/16 – until **1975** 1/12
1977 10/3 – 11/14
1978 5/13 – 6/29
1979 10/12 – until **1980** 3/19
1980 6/3 – 9/2
1984 1/31 – 12/18
1986 3/15 – 5/1
1986 9/30 – 12/16
1989 8/29 – 12/30
1990 4/21 – 6/13
1991 9/23 – until **1992** 8/17
1996 1/14 – 12/1
1998 2/26 – 4/10
2001 8/7 – 10/20
2001 11/15 – until **2002** 5/25
2003 9/7 – 12/17
2004 1/21 – 7/31
2007 12/29 – until **2008** 3/18
2008 7/2 – 11/10
2010 2/10 – 3/24

SATURN BENEFICIAL
1944 8/2 – until **1945** 1/22
1945 4/16 – 7/14
1948 10/10 – until **1949** 2/26
1949 7/1 – 11/26
1950 2/2 – 8/11
1959 1/27 – 7/15
1959 10/24 – until **1960** 4/20
1960 5/4 – 12/21
1965 2/8 – 5/11
1965 8/16 – until **1966** 2/1
1974 6/7 – 8/28
1975 1/7 – 5/17
1978 8/15 – until **1979** 9/19
1988 3/28 – 4/25
1988 12/4 – until **1990** 1/24
1994 3/14 – until **1995** 3/9
2003 7/15 – until **2004** 6/27
2007 9/22 – until **2008** 4/4
2008 5/31 – 10/29
2009 3/8 – 7/22

URANUS BENEFICIAL
1950 6/30 – until **1953** 5/8
1962 9/17 – until **1966** 8/17
1989 1/11 – until **1993** 10/16
2004 4/11 – until **2008** 1/1

NEPTUNE BENEFICIAL
1938 5/22 – 6/8
1985 1/26 – until **1993** 10/4

PLUTO BENEFICIAL
1958 9/5 – until **1967** 7/8
2009 2/3 – Continues

JUPITER CHALLENGING
1938 1/1 – 3/9
1943 7/11 – 9/25
1944 3/14 – 5/12

1946 10/6 – 12/21
1947 6/24 – 8/6
1949 12/12 – until **1950** 2/20
1955 6/24 – 9/7
1958 9/20 – 12/3
1961 3/29 – 7/24
1961 11/20 – until **1962** 2/4
1966 10/15 – 12/27
1967 6/6 – 8/21
1970 1/1 – 4/11
1970 8/31 – 11/17
1973 3/6 – 9/21
1973 10/5 – until **1974** 1/18
1978 9/18 – until **1979** 2/6
1979 5/12 – 8/5
1981 12/9 – until **1982** 5/22
1982 8/3 – 11/2
1985 2/17 – until **1986** 1/1
1990 8/29 – until **1991** 7/20
1993 11/21 – until **1994** 10/17
1997 1/31 – 4/22
1997 7/29 – 12/12
2002 8/12 – until **2003** 7/3
2005 11/6 – until **2006** 2/15
2006 3/22 – 9/30
2009 1/15 – 3/28
2009 9/15 – 11/9

SATURN CHALLENGING
1946 8/21 – until **1947** 3/13
1947 4/25 – 9/23
1948 2/19 – 6/12
1953 11/11 – until **1955** 1/1
1955 5/2 – 9/29
1962 1/24 – until **1963** 3/15
1963 9/1 – 12/9
1975 10/20 – 12/10
1976 6/26 – until **1977** 7/28
1982 12/25 – until **1983** 4/4
1983 9/19 – until **1984** 11/5
1991 2/28 – 8/11
1991 11/26 – until **1992** 5/17
1992 6/8 – until **1993** 1/19
2005 8/4 – until **2006** 9/4
2007 4/4 – 5/5
2012 10/25 – Continues

URANUS CHALLENGING
1956 7/21 – until **1960** 6/21
1975 1/23 – until **1979** 9/23
1996 2/23 – until **2000** 12/26

NEPTUNE CHALLENGING
1957 1/6 – until **1965** 10/5
1999 2/5 – until **2007** 1/9

PLUTO CHALLENGING
1939 9/14 – until **1951** 7/6
1984 11/2 – until **1991** 9/21

JUPITER SPECIAL
1940 5/26 – until **1941** 4/6
1952 5/8 – 7/31
1952 10/20 – until **1953** 3/16
1964 4/22 – 7/3
1964 12/4 – until **1965** 2/16
1976 4/5 – 6/13
1988 3/19 – 5/27
1999 7/15 – 10/4
2000 2/28 – 5/10
2011 6/16 – 11/21
2012 1/29 – 4/23

SATURN SPECIAL
1940 4/9 – until **1941** 5/11
1969 5/19 – 12/16
1970 1/22 – 6/23
1970 11/21 – until **1971** 3/13
1998 7/8 – 9/23
1999 3/23 – until **2000** 4/24

URANUS SPECIAL
1938 1/1 – until **1940** 2/26

May 2

SUN: TAURUS • DECANATE: VIRGO/MERCURY • DEGREE: 10°5–12° TAURUS • MODE: FIXED • ELEMENT: EARTH

Your Personal Powers

Being receptive and adept at understanding others, you can be sympathetic and enjoy being popular. You can therefore present a friendly image to the world and achieve success through collaboration with others. Although your ruling planet, Venus, grants you graceful charm, it may also influence you to be extravagant or indulgent. Nevertheless, being naturally inquisitive and impressionable implies that you are also gifted with psychic abilities. You empower yourself when you establish order and stability yet let your intuitive feelings guide you. With natural analytical and practical skills you can succeed admirably when you apply your business acumen and turn your visions into reality. Alternatively, you may find that your interests lie in more mystical or spiritual subjects. Although you are often blessed with a comfortable life you accomplish more through hard work, calm determination, and your resolution to succeed. Being resourceful can counterbalance any tendency to be overly concerned about money. Often you find inner contentment comes after first establishing a stable environment.

Your Powers of Attraction in Relationships

Having magnetic charm ensures that you can be popular and have many friends. Although with your easygoing approach you are concerned with making people happy, you need to guard against becoming overly dependent in relationships. You are usually attracted to ambitious or enterprising people or those with status. Although you know how to have a good time, a tendency for self-indulgence, extravagance, or being stubborn could possibly become a bone of contention in close relationships. Usually friendly and helpful, you can be generous and kind with those you love. Even though you like to be honest and direct, when you utilize your natural tact you can captivate other people with your affectionate and warmhearted nature. Others also admire your loyalty and friendly consideration.

Your attractive qualities: cooperative, generous, charming, enterprising, considerate, hardworking, refined, tactful, receptive, intuitive, sociable, business sense, pragmatic, dependable, good evaluator, entertaining, harmonious, diplomatic, determined, receptive, stylish, versatile, honest

Your less attractive qualities: oversensitive, vain, overindulgent, extravagant, lazy, mistrusting, suspicious, materialistic, dependent, conceited, subservient, dissatisfied

Your Venus Power

The planet Venus has a great deal of influence on your powers of attraction. Below are four possible Venus types for women and men. To find your Venus you need to go to page 771, where you will find the Venus table and extra information. The planet Mars also affects your powers of attraction. To find your Mars table and interpretation go to page 761.

WOMEN WITH VENUS IN PISCES: In love you are sensitive, tender, and affectionate, experiencing your partner's feelings almost as strongly as your own. Being also imaginative and visionary, you possess the capabilities to develop both creative gifts as well as deep compassion for others. As you are idealistic when in love, you usually prefer to see only your partner's good points, but be careful that your high expectations do not bring disappointment if you avoid being realistic. Nevertheless, in your relationships with others you can be devoted, loving, and positively enchanting.

MEN WITH VENUS IN PISCES: The combination of your emotional subtlety and charm can make you very alluring when dealing with affairs of the heart. Perceptive and impressionable, you have an easygoing style in your relationships usually preferring to avoid ugly confrontation. You are drawn to a partner who has a touch of glamour and is sensitive to the needs of others. Alternatively, your partner can be a visionary with a rich imagination, like your own, who will keep you enchanted.

WOMEN WITH VENUS IN ARIES: Idealistic, passionate, and adventurous, you are direct in your dealings with others. When you are attracted to a person you usually take the initiative and use your people skills to make things happen. In close relationships you are not afraid to confront your other half. This self-assertiveness is positive if differences can be brought into the open through diplomacy and compromise.

MEN WITH VENUS IN ARIES: As you often have the courage and strength to initiate situations, you like to take the lead and let others follow. With your unconscious desire for conquest you may also have to beware of being competitive with your partners. Nevertheless, you are drawn to a direct and strong-willed partner who can share your love of action and enthusiasm for life. When you are feeling good you can be charming and enthusiastic in romantic situations with an entertaining and spontaneous spirit.

WOMEN WITH VENUS IN TAURUS: Good-natured and romantic, you have a highly developed sense of touch that par-

ticularly responds to massage, hugs, and all things physical. Being friendly, you enjoy socializing and are able to put others at their ease. With your innate sense of beauty and harmony, your natural charm can attract others. Although you can be lavish toward your partner, you may have to be careful that you do not overdo things.

MEN WITH VENUS IN TAURUS: Attractive and affectionate, in relationships you are often faithful with a conservative outlook. You are drawn to warmhearted partners with whom you can share a familiar routine as well as life's pleasures and comforts. Seeking a partner who is dependable or reassuring you often put security high on your priority list when looking for love. Your sociability and friendliness usually make you popular and partners often admire your good sense of values and practical skills.

WOMEN WITH VENUS IN GEMINI: In relationships you need intellectual stimulation and usually prefer to keep things light. Certainly not boring, you love to talk and are at your best being witty and entertaining. Although your easygoing approach to relationships is very attractive, guard against losing touch with your emotions. You prefer a partner who can keep up with your fast stream of ideas, and if you have shared interests then so much the better.

MEN WITH VENUS IN GEMINI: Charming, amusing, and adaptable, you attract others with your natural communication skills and friendly personality. You have a wonderful childlike quality and love to keep life playful, but a reluctance to contact your deeper feelings may cause you to avoid serious commitment. With your need for variety and intellectual stimulation, you are attracted to clever and amusing partners who have many interesting sides to their personalities.

To read all about your Outer Planets and work out how to use your personalized timetable, go to Section Three, page 789.

Your Personalized Timetable

JUPITER BENEFICIAL
1939 1/28 – 3/12
1942 7/8 – 8/24
1943 2/13 – 4/8
1944 8/11 – 10/26
1945 4/9 – 6/19
1948 12/1 – until **1949** 2/9
1950 5/31 – 7/23
1951 1/9 – 2/23
1954 6/21 – 8/5
1956 7/25 – 10/8
1960 4/7 – 5/3
1960 11/13 – until **1961** 1/23
1962 4/27 – 9/11
1962 12/15 – until **1963** 2/5
1966 6/5 – 7/20
1967 11/12 – until **1968** 1/31
1968 7/6 – 9/22
1972 2/26 – 6/25
1972 10/22 – until **1973** 1/7
1974 4/5 – 6/6
1974 8/7 – until **1975** 1/17
1978 5/18 – 7/3
1979 10/17 – until **1980** 3/10
1980 6/12 – 9/6
1984 2/4 – 8/18
1984 9/10 – 12/22
1986 3/19 – 5/6
1986 9/22 – 12/24
1989 9/4 – 12/23
1990 4/27 – 6/17
1991 9/28 – until **1992** 8/21
1996 1/18 – 12/5
1998 3/2 – 4/15
2001 8/12 – until **2002** 2/8
2002 3/22 – 5/30
2003 9/11 – until **2004** 8/5
2008 1/2 – 3/25
2008 6/24 – 11/16
2010 2/14 – 3/28

SATURN BENEFICIAL
1944 8/11 – until **1945** 1/9
1945 4/28 – 7/22
1948 10/20 – until **1949** 2/14
1949 7/11 – 12/20
1950 1/8 – 8/20
1959 2/5 – 7/1
1959 11/5 – until **1960** 12/30
1965 2/16 – 5/26
1965 7/31 – until **1966** 2/9
1974 6/15 – 9/7
1974 12/26 – until **1975** 5/26
1978 8/22 – until **1979** 9/27
1988 12/13 – until **1990** 2/2
1990 8/25 – 10/21
1994 3/23 – 10/12
1994 12/7 – until **1995** 3/17
2003 7/23 – until **2004** 2/28
2004 3/16 – 7/5
2007 9/30 – until **2008** 3/19
2008 6/16 – 11/9
2009 2/24 – 7/31

URANUS BENEFICIAL
1950 7/17 – until **1953** 5/30
1962 10/4 – until **1966** 9/2
1989 1/29 – until **1993** 11/18
2004 5/8 – until **2008** 1/26

NEPTUNE BENEFICIAL
1938 3/26 – 8/1
1985 3/5 – until **1993** 11/29

PLUTO BENEFICIAL
1958 10/7 – until **1967** 8/13
2010 1/2 – Continues

JUPITER CHALLENGING
1938 1/4 – 3/14
1943 7/16 – 9/30

1944 3/4 – 5/22
1946 10/11 – 12/26
1947 6/12 – 8/18
1949 12/17 – until **1950** 2/24
1955 6/29 – 9/11
1958 9/24 – 12/8
1961 4/5 – 7/16
1961 11/26 – until **1962** 2/8
1966 10/25 – 12/17
1967 6/11 – 8/26
1970 1/9 – 4/3
1970 9/6 – 11/22
1973 3/11 – 9/2
1973 10/24 – until **1974** 1/22
1978 9/24 – until **1979** 1/29
1979 5/20 – 8/10
1981 12/15 – until **1982** 5/13
1982 8/12 – 11/6
1985 2/21 – until **1986** 1/6
1990 9/3 – until **1991** 7/25
1993 11/26 – until **1994** 10/21
1997 2/4 – 4/29
1997 7/21 – 12/17
2002 8/17 – until **2003** 7/8
2005 11/10 – until **2006** 10/5
2009 1/19 – 4/2
2009 9/5 – 11/18

SATURN CHALLENGING
1946 8/29 – until **1947** 2/22
1947 5/13 – 10/3
1948 2/7 – 6/22
1953 11/19 – until **1954** 6/6
1954 8/5 – until **1955** 1/13
1955 4/18 – 10/9
1962 2/1 – until **1963** 3/24
1963 8/18 – 12/20
1976 7/4 – until **1977** 8/5
1983 1/8 – 3/20
1983 9/28 – until **1984** 11/13
1991 3/10 – 7/29
1991 12/7 – until **1993** 1/27
2005 8/11 – until **2006** 9/12
2007 3/13 – 5/26
2012 11/2 – Continues

URANUS CHALLENGING
1956 8/6 – until **1960** 7/10
1975 11/4 – until **1979** 10/12
1996 3/14 – until **2001** 1/14

NEPTUNE CHALLENGING
1957 11/23 – until **1965** 11/2
1999 3/5 – until **2007** 11/20

PLUTO CHALLENGING
1940 8/26 – until **1952** 6/3
1984 11/27 – until **1991** 10/20

JUPITER SPECIAL
1940 5/31 – until **1941** 4/10
1952 5/13 – 8/9
1952 10/11 – until **1953** 3/21
1964 4/26 – 7/8
1964 11/26 – until **1965** 2/24
1976 4/9 – 6/17
1988 3/24 – 5/31
1999 7/24 – 9/25
2000 3/4 – 5/14
2011 6/21 – 11/12
2012 2/6 – 4/27

SATURN SPECIAL
1940 4/16 – until **1941** 5/19
1969 5/27 – 11/26
1970 2/10 – 7/3
1970 11/9 – until **1971** 3/23
1998 7/29 – 9/2
1999 3/31 – until **2000** 5/2

URANUS SPECIAL
1938 1/1 – until **1940** 3/24

May 3

SUN: TAURUS • DECANATE: VIRGO/MERCURY • DEGREE: 11°5–13° TAURUS • MODE: FIXED • ELEMENT: EARTH

Your Personal Powers

Your ability to be both creative and practical implies that you are friendly and original with exceptional gifts. Your ruling planet, Venus, grants you warm charm, artistic appreciation or talents, and a love of nature. Easygoing but determined, you gain power when you stay focused rather than taking on too much. Although you are multitalented and show remarkable qualities you can lose some of your creative power if you become upset or frustrated due to worry and indecision. Be careful that emotional stress does not affect your health. Your personal powers are enhanced when you have faith in what you are trying to achieve or when you listen to your inner voice and trust your intuition. Although you usually find yourself through your work, you also possess an inherent spiritual side, which, if taken further, could aid you in your quest for greater understanding of yourself and your destiny. Being persuasive with good people skills, you need only apply hard work and integrity to achieve in an outstanding way or inspire others with your dreams.

Your Powers of Attraction in Relationships

Friendly and sensitive, you are a romantic and outgoing individual who is keen on mixing with different types of people. A good conversationalist, you are attracted to intelligent people with strong opinions. Your relationships can be an especially valuable tool for learning about yourself and what motivates others. As a practical idealist, you often seek an almost spiritual bond with your partner. Being generous and affectionate indicates that if you do not apply discrimination, you can sometimes attract individuals who lack integrity and make demands on your time and money. By learning to trust your intuition, however, you can usually sense if someone is sincere. When you are positive and purposeful, you can inspire others with your honesty and creative ideas.

Your attractive qualities: charismatic, versatile, decisive, friendly, productive, patient, sense of duty, honorable, agile mind, responsible, enterprising, confident, persevering, kind, hardworking, serious, focused, creative, artistic, balanced, independent, modest, calm, sensual

Your less attractive qualities: stubborn, worry, discontented, rebellious, vain, indecision, overimaginative, critical, exaggerates, possessive, extravagant, overindulgent, lazy, hypocritical, deceptive

Your Venus Power

The planet Venus has a great deal of influence on your powers of attraction. Below are four possible Venus types for women and men. To find your Venus you need to go to page 771, where you will find the Venus table and extra information. The planet Mars also affects your powers of attraction. To find your Mars table and interpretation go to page 761.

WOMEN WITH VENUS IN PISCES: Romantic and idealistic, you can be both loving and giving. In relationships you may need to balance the practical with the charitable. While making allowances and sacrifices is understandable in a relationship, avoid playing the martyr. Your benevolence and generosity in the right relationship nonetheless makes you a partner who is devoted, kind, compassionate. Subtle, sensitive, and alluring, you make a sensual and caring partner.

MEN WITH VENUS IN PISCES: In love you are sensitive, tender, and affectionate, experiencing your partner's feelings almost as strongly as your own. Being also imaginative and visionary, you possess the capability to develop deep compassion for others. As you are idealistic when in love, you usually prefer to see only your partner's good points, but be careful that your high expectations do not bring disappointment if you avoid harsh reality. Nevertheless, in your relationships with others you can be devoted, loving, and positively enchanting.

WOMEN WITH VENUS IN ARIES: With your strong desires and enthusiastic nature you can be a passionate lover. Although idealistic and single-minded, you need to avoid unnecessary conflicts in your relationships by being more patient and less headstrong. Although at times others can accuse you of being bossy or impulsive, you possess a great deal of warmth and charm. When necessary, you can disarm others by making them feel important.

MEN WITH VENUS IN ARIES: As you often have the courage and strength to initiate situations, you like to take the lead and let others follow. With your unconscious desire for conquest you may also have to beware of being competitive with your partners. Nevertheless, you are drawn to a direct and strong-willed partner who can share your love of action

and enthusiasm for life. When you are feeling good, you can be charming and enthusiastic in romantic situations with an entertaining and spontaneous spirit.

WOMEN WITH VENUS IN TAURUS: For your ideal relationship you seek a partner who is both financially secure and demonstrative with his affections. With these thoughts in mind you are likely to want a partner who is refined yet pragmatic or someone concerned with safeguarding your future. Attracted to people with a good sense of style, you can succeed in all kinds of business partnerships, especially those involving the arts, music, and luxury goods. Although a stubborn streak suggests that even when you know you are in the wrong you are reluctant to give way, you can be affectionate and caring.

MEN WITH VENUS IN TAURUS: As you yourself may be attractive to the opposite sex, you desire a partner who is sensual and loving or possesses physical beauty. Needing stability, when faced with changes that are out of your control you may become insecure or worried about your future. Faithful and/or loyal, you usually hang on to relationships but may display controlling tendencies. Your own sense of style and love of beauty imply that you can be attracted to creative people, especially those in art and music.

WOMEN WITH VENUS IN GEMINI: Curious, with a bright and animated approach to life, you are attracted to those who are clever and/or sophisticated. Your love of variety and desire for knowledge suggest that you need a partner and friends who keep you mentally stimulated. Although witty and a good conversationalist, you may need to keep in touch with your deeper feelings. Nevertheless, intelligent and friendly, you possess a youthful sense of wonder and seek a playmate who can keep you from becoming bored.

MEN WITH VENUS IN GEMINI: Friendly and sociable, you attract others with your clever and amusing conversation. Drawn to people who can match you in wit and intelligence, you usually prefer to keep relationships light rather than emotionally intense. With your youthful charm and desire for knowledge and new experiences, you usually have many friends and a low boredom threshold.

To read all about your Outer Planets and work out how to use your personalized timetable, go to Section Three, page 789.

Your Personalized Timetable

JUPITER BENEFICIAL
1939 2/2 – 3/16
1942 7/12 – 8/29
1943 2/3 – 4/18
1944 8/15 – 11/1
1945 3/31 – 6/28
1948 12/5 – until 1949 2/14
1950 6/18 – 7/5
1951 1/14 – 2/27
1954 6/26 – 8/10
1956 7/30 – 10/13
1960 11/18 – until 1961 1/27
1962 5/2 – 9/3
1962 12/21 – until 1963 2/10
1966 6/9 – 7/24
1967 11/21 – until 1968 1/22
1968 7/12 – 9/27
1972 3/3 – 6/17
1972 10/28 – until 1973 1/11
1974 4/10 – 6/19
1974 7/25 – until 1975 1/22
1978 5/23 – 7/8
1979 10/23 – until 1980 3/3
1980 6/19 – 9/11
1984 2/10 – 8/2
1984 9/26 – 12/27
1986 3/23 – 5/12
1986 9/15 – 12/30
1989 9/10 – 12/16
1990 5/3 – 6/22
1991 10/3 – until 1992 8/26
1996 1/22 – 12/10
1998 3/7 – 4/20
2001 8/17 – until 2002 1/28
2002 4/3 – 6/4
2003 9/16 – until 2004 8/10
2008 1/6 – 4/2
2008 6/15 – 11/21
2010 2/18 – 4/1

SATURN BENEFICIAL
1944 8/20 – 12/29
1945 5/9 – 7/29
1948 11/1 – until 1949 2/2
1949 7/20 – until 1950 8/28
1959 2/16 – 6/18
1959 11/15 – until 1961 1/7
1965 2/24 – until 1966 2/18
1974 6/22 – 9/19
1974 12/13 – until 1975 6/4
1978 8/30 – until 1979 10/5
1980 5/10 – 6/3
1988 12/21 – until 1990 2/11
1990 8/7 – 11/7
1994 4/1 – 9/25
1994 12/23 – until 1995 3/25
2003 7/31 – until 2004 2/2
2004 4/10 – 7/12
2007 10/9 – until 2008 3/5
2008 6/28 – 11/21
2009 2/10 – 8/9

URANUS BENEFICIAL
1950 8/3 – until 1953 6/17
1962 10/25 – until 1967 6/7
1989 2/19 – until 1993 12/9
2005 3/7 – until 2008 2/14

NEPTUNE BENEFICIAL
1938 2/19 – 8/30
1986 1/21 – until 1993 12/28

PLUTO BENEFICIAL
1959 9/8 – until 1968 6/24
2010 1/30 – Continues

JUPITER CHALLENGING
1938 1/8 – 3/18
1943 7/20 – 10/5
1944 2/25 – 5/31

1946 10/15 – 12/31
1947 6/2 – 8/27
1949 12/22 – until 1950 2/28
1955 7/4 – 9/16
1958 9/29 – 12/13
1961 4/12 – 7/8
1961 12/1 – until 1962 2/12
1966 11/12 – 11/30
1967 6/16 – 8/30
1970 1/18 – 3/24
1970 9/11 – 11/26
1973 3/17 – 8/23
1973 11/3 – until 1974 1/26
1978 9/30 – until 1979 1/22
1979 5/26 – 8/14
1981 12/20 – until 1982 5/5
1982 8/19 – 11/11
1985 2/26 – until 1986 1/10
1990 9/8 – until 1991 3/8
1991 4/21 – 7/29
1993 12/1 – until 1994 10/26
1997 2/9 – 5/8
1997 7/12 – 12/22
2002 8/21 – until 2003 7/13
2005 11/15 – until 2006 10/10
2009 1/24 – 4/7
2009 8/28 – 11/26

SATURN CHALLENGING
1946 9/7 – until 1947 2/9
1947 5/26 – 10/13
1948 1/26 – 7/2
1953 11/28 – until 1954 5/20
1954 8/21 – until 1955 1/28
1955 4/2 – 10/18
1962 2/9 – until 1963 4/4
1963 8/5 – 12/31
1976 7/12 – until 1977 8/12
1983 2/1 – 2/23
1983 10/6 – until 1984 11/21
1991 3/21 – 7/15
1991 12/17 – until 1993 2/4
2005 8/19 – until 2006 9/21
2007 2/27 – 6/9
2012 11/10 – Continues

URANUS CHALLENGING
1956 8/23 – until 1960 7/27
1975 11/20 – until 1979 10/29
1996 4/13 – until 2001 2/1

NEPTUNE CHALLENGING
1957 12/26 – until 1966 9/29
1999 4/24 – until 2008 1/3

PLUTO CHALLENGING
1940 10/27 – until 1952 7/16
1984 12/30 – until 1992 8/24

JUPITER SPECIAL
1940 6/4 – until 1941 4/15
1952 5/17 – 8/20
1952 9/29 – until 1953 3/26
1964 4/30 – 7/14
1964 11/18 – until 1965 3/3
1976 4/13 – 6/22
1988 3/28 – 6/4
1999 8/5 – 9/14
2000 3/9 – 5/18
2011 6/27 – 11/5
2012 2/13 – 5/1

SATURN SPECIAL
1940 4/24 – until 1941 5/27
1969 6/5 – 11/12
1970 2/23 – 7/14
1970 10/27 – until 1971 4/1
1999 4/8 – until 2000 5/9

URANUS SPECIAL
1938 1/1 – until 1940 4/13

May 4

Your Personal Powers

Practical and down-to-earth, you are an astute and imaginative individual who grasps information quickly, usually preferring to make up your own mind. In order to succeed, however, you usually need ideals that can inspire and motivate you to act. Your ruling planet, Venus, grants you grace and a love of harmony. Having a strong sense of responsibility you empower yourself when you are willing to work hard for what you believe in. Your personal powers are also enhanced when you are prepared to cooperate with others, especially on an equal footing. You lose some of your power, however, when you behave in a stubborn or bossy manner. The serenity and security that you seek from your environment and personal relationships may also be undermined if you allow inner fears to make you moody or tense. With good mental capabilities, however, you are often committed to your work. Your ingenuity and intuitive sense also suggest that you can surprise people with your ability to be inventive and original.

Your Powers of Attraction in Relationships

Your powers of perception indicate that you have an innate understanding of human nature. Being both delicate and strong, you are constantly trying to balance the two poles of your personality. You are usually drawn to enterprising people who are determined, innovating, and imaginative. You are also influenced by your strong need for security. Although you do not like to be restricted or dictated to, working collaborations with others can help you understand how to create harmony in your personal relationships. Having a talent for giving others personal attention, you are excellent at relating to people on a one-to-one basis. If you display a self-willed stubbornness, however, other people will oppose you and create conflict in your life. Learning the art of gentle persuasion and diplomatic negotiation is the key to success in all your people-related activities.

Your attractive qualities: well-organized, positive, confident, conscientious, practical, idealistic, imaginative, sensual, honorable, disciplined, steady, responsible, hardworking, skilled, pragmatic, common sense, enduring, determined, trusting, exact, balanced, intuitive

Your less attractive qualities: self-doubt, moody, lacks structure, stubborn, rigid, secretive, uncommunicative, arrogant, repressed, unfeeling, procrastinating, too economical, bossy, lazy, anxious, resentful, escapist

Your Venus Power

The planet Venus has a great deal of influence on your powers of attraction. Below are four possible Venus types for women and men. To find your Venus you need to go to page 771, where you will find the Venus table and extra information. The planet Mars also affects your powers of attraction. To find your Mars table and interpretation go to page 761.

WOMEN WITH VENUS IN PISCES: Romantic and impressionable, you are a caring and loving individual with a dreamy nature. In relationships you are often attracted to idealistic, compassionate, or sympathetic individuals who have imagination or a strong romantic sense. A tendency to be sensitive to others suggests that you are intuitive and aware of people's inner feelings. Be careful therefore not to get caught in other people's dramas or play the rescuer too often.

MEN WITH VENUS IN PISCES: Romantic and idealistic when in love, you can be a sensitive and responsive lover. With your affectionate and impressionable nature you are often attracted to those who understand your sensitivity and share your vision. Being flexible with an impressionable nature helps you to adapt to the needs of others. In your desire to blend with those you love, guard against giving too much of yourself by not clearly defining your boundaries.

WOMEN WITH VENUS IN ARIES: You gain power from your strong individuality, energy, and enthusiasm. Your young-at-heart and spirited approach to relationships adds to your appeal. If you become too impatient or self-absorbed, however, your partnerships are likely to suffer. Nevertheless, you can be creative, sharp, and quick, especially when you are able to share new and exciting projects with your partners. Mischievous, with a love of action, you may even incite them to a playful fight.

MEN WITH VENUS IN ARIES: As you often have the courage and strength to initiate situations, you like to take the lead and let others follow. With your unconscious desire for conquest you may also have to beware of being competitive with your partners. Nevertheless, you are drawn to a direct and strong-willed partner who can share your love of action

and enthusiasm for life. When you are feeling good you can be charming and enthusiastic in romantic situations with an entertaining and spontaneous spirit.

WOMEN WITH VENUS IN TAURUS: For your ideal relationship you seek a partner who is both financially secure and demonstrative with his affections. With these thoughts in mind, you are likely to want a partner who is refined yet pragmatic, or someone concerned with safeguarding your future. Although you are loving and caring, a stubborn streak suggests that even when you know you are in the wrong you are reluctant to give way. Attracted to people with a good sense of style, you can succeed in all kinds of business partnerships, especially those involving the arts, music, and luxury goods.

MEN WITH VENUS IN TAURUS: As well as attracting people with your warm personality, you possess an innate sense of the value of material possessions. Keeping yourself stylish and having an attractive appearance can also be important to you. You are naturally attracted to practical yet sensual women who understand your need for comfort, security, and the pleasures and luxuries of life. Naturally affectionate, you enjoy socializing but can be a loyal and loving partner.

WOMEN WITH VENUS IN GEMINI: By nature you are young at heart, adaptable, and sociable. Being curious and willing to cooperate makes you a good team player. Usually you are drawn to articulate people who have charm and flair or sharp wit. With a need to expand your knowledge you also look for a partner who can challenge or stimulate you intellectually. Although you love to talk with all types of people, you may need to develop your listening skills in order to build better communication in your relationships.

MEN WITH VENUS IN GEMINI: Informed and curious yet charming and friendly, you seek a partner who shares your interests or enjoys your witty remarks. Although a good communicator, you have an inborn tendency to be lighthearted and less profound about deep emotional commitment. Although you are keen on experiences that bring variety into your life, boredom or scattering your energies in too many directions is probably your biggest handicap in relationships. Nevertheless, you are attracted to intelligent partners who can match your lively banter.

To read all about your Outer Planets and work out how to use your personalized timetable, go to Section Three, page 789.

Your Personalized Timetable

JUPITER BENEFICIAL
1939 2/6 – 3/20
1942 7/17 – 9/3
1943 1/25 – 4/26
1944 8/20 – 11/6
1945 3/23 – 7/5
1948 12/9 – until **1949** 2/18
1951 1/18 – 3/3
1954 6/30 – 8/14
1956 8/3 – 10/18
1960 11/22 – until **1961** 2/1
1962 5/9 – 8/27
1962 12/27 – until **1963** 2/14
1966 6/14 – 7/28
1967 12/4 – until **1968** 1/9
1968 7/17 – 10/1
1972 3/10 – 6/10
1972 11/2 – until **1973** 1/15
1974 4/15 – 10/21
1974 11/16 – until **1975** 1/27
1978 5/28 – 7/12
1979 10/29 – until **1980** 2/24
1980 6/26 – 9/15
1984 2/15 – 7/22
1984 10/6 – 12/31
1986 3/28 – 5/18
1986 9/7 – until **1987** 1/5
1989 9/18 – 12/8
1990 5/8 – 6/26
1991 10/8 – until **1992** 4/10
1992 5/21 – 8/31
1996 1/27 – 12/14
1998 3/11 – 4/24
1998 11/5 – 11/21
2001 8/22 – until **2002** 1/19
2002 4/12 – 6/9
2003 9/21 – until **2004** 8/15
2008 1/11 – 4/13
2008 6/4 – 11/26
2010 2/22 – 4/5

SATURN BENEFICIAL
1944 8/30 – 12/17
1945 5/18 – 8/6
1946 3/1 – 4/8
1948 11/15 – until **1949** 1/17
1949 7/29 – until **1950** 9/5
1959 2/28 – 6/4
1959 11/25 – until **1961** 1/15
1965 3/4 – until **1966** 2/26
1974 6/30 – 10/6
1974 11/26 – until **1975** 6/12
1978 9/7 – until **1979** 10/13
1980 4/16 – 6/27
1988 12/29 – until **1990** 2/20
1990 7/24 – 11/19
1994 4/10 – 9/11
1995 1/4 – 4/2
1995 11/3 – 12/9
2003 8/9 – until **2004** 1/19
2004 4/24 – 7/20
2007 10/18 – until **2008** 2/22
2008 7/9 – 12/9
2009 1/23 – 8/18

URANUS BENEFICIAL
1950 8/23 – until **1953** 7/3
1962 12/7 – until **1967** 7/16
1989 3/31 – until **1993** 12/27
2005 3/24 – until **2008** 3/2

NEPTUNE BENEFICIAL
1938 1/1 – until **1939** 7/25
1986 2/23 – until **1994** 11/23

PLUTO BENEFICIAL
1959 10/10 – until **1968** 8/6
2010 3/16 – Continues

JUPITER CHALLENGING
1938 1/12 – 3/23

1943 7/25 – 10/11
1944 2/17 – 6/7
1946 10/20 – until **1947** 1/6
1947 5/25 – 9/4
1949 12/26 – until **1950** 3/5
1955 7/8 – 9/21
1958 10/4 – 12/18
1961 4/21 – 6/29
1961 12/7 – until **1962** 2/16
1967 6/21 – 9/4
1970 1/30 – 3/12
1970 9/16 – 12/1
1973 3/22 – 8/14
1973 11/11 – until **1974** 1/31
1978 10/6 – until **1979** 1/15
1979 6/1 – 8/19
1981 12/26 – until **1982** 4/27
1982 8/26 – 11/15
1985 3/2 – until **1986** 1/14
1990 9/13 – until **1991** 2/25
1991 5/3 – until **1991** 8/3
1993 12/6 – until **1994** 6/13
1994 7/20 – 10/30
1997 2/13 – 5/20
1997 6/30 – 12/27
2002 8/26 – until **2003** 7/17
2005 11/19 – until **2006** 10/15
2009 1/28 – 4/13
2009 8/20 – 12/3

SATURN CHALLENGING
1946 9/16 – until **1947** 1/28
1947 6/6 – 10/26
1948 1/13 – 7/10
1953 12/7 – until **1954** 5/6
1954 9/3 – until **1955** 10/26
1962 2/17 – 9/14
1962 11/3 – until **1963** 4/16
1963 7/22 – until **1964** 1/9
1976 7/19 – until **1977** 8/20
1983 10/15 – until **1984** 11/30
1991 4/3 – 7/1
1991 12/26 – until **1993** 2/12
2005 8/27 – until **2006** 3/4
2006 5/7 – 9/30
2007 2/15 – Continues

URANUS CHALLENGING
1956 9/10 – until **1960** 8/12
1975 12/7 – until **1979** 11/14
1997 2/5 – until **2001** 11/29

NEPTUNE CHALLENGING
1958 11/18 – until **1966** 10/29
2000 2/27 – until **2008** 1/30

PLUTO CHALLENGING
1941 9/19 – until **1953** 6/18
1985 11/12 – until **1992** 10/4

JUPITER SPECIAL
1940 6/9 – until **1941** 4/19
1952 5/21 – until **1953** 3/31
1964 5/4 – 7/20
1964 11/11 – until **1965** 3/9
1976 4/17 – 6/27
1977 1/7 – 1/23
1988 4/1 – 6/8
2000 3/14 – 5/22
2011 7/3 – 10/29
2012 2/19 – 5/5

SATURN SPECIAL
1940 5/1 – until **1941** 6/3
1969 6/14 – 10/31
1970 3/6 – 7/27
1970 10/14 – until **1971** 4/10
1999 4/16 – until **2000** 5/17

URANUS SPECIAL
1938 1/1 – until **1940** 4/30

May 5

Your Personal Powers

Mentally sharp with strong instincts, you have a determined and adventurous nature. Ambitious, with a sense of initiative, you gain power from your inner strength and ability to persevere in challenging situations. With your unique perception and need for variety in life, you constantly seek new experiences to keep you motivated. Although you can be charming and friendly, you also possess the necessary endurance and toughness to be in leadership positions. Enterprising and hardworking, you like to be in control and do a job well. By keeping busy, productive, and focused, you empower yourself and develop your sense of purpose. Having a philosophical outlook on life and displaying your unusual sense of humor can help you overcome a tendency to be overly serious, bossy, or stubborn. Although you can be practical and realistic, you also possess an innate intuitive talent that helps you to make accurate first impressions of others. By trusting your sixth sense you can also develop your inner faith and resolve.

Your attractive qualities: willpower, hardworking, mentally sharp, creative talents, analytical, loving, practical, compassionate, discipline, instinctive, adaptable, progressive, daring, witty, sociable, magnetic, intuitive, versatile, responsible, confident, sympathetic

Your less attractive qualities: selfishness, indulgence, self-pity, resentful, unreliable, materialistic, irresponsible, cold, willful, depressive, inconsistent, headstrong, moody, overconfident, emotional disappointment, withdrawn, restlessness

Your Powers of Attraction in Relationships

You are astute and quick and your strong instincts ensure that your first impressions about people are often right. As your sensitivity and aspirations are usually concealed behind your pragmatic manner, others may find it hard to pin you down or live up to your high ideals. People admire your self-confidence, enthusiasm, and ability to act spontaneously. They may find you less appealing when you are too serious or self-centered. By using your dry humor, you have the ability to deal with difficult issues or situations in a detached way. Usually you are attracted to idealistic individuals who hold strong beliefs. Dynamic and action-oriented partners may also inspire you or suit your busy lifestyle. A need for freedom and room to make changes indicates that you want a partner who can be loving yet not too demanding.

Your Venus Power

The planet Venus has a great deal of influence on your powers of attraction. Below are four possible Venus types for women and men. To find your Venus you need to go to page 771, where you will find the Venus table and extra information. The planet Mars also affects your powers of attraction. To find your Mars table and interpretation go to page 761.

WOMEN WITH VENUS IN PISCES: Romantic and idealistic, you can be both loving and giving. In relationships you may need to balance the practical with the charitable. While making allowances and sacrifices is understandable in a relationship, avoid playing the martyr. Your benevolence and generosity in the right relationship nonetheless makes you a partner who is devoted, kind, and compassionate. Subtle, sensitive, and alluring, you make a sensual and caring partner.

MEN WITH VENUS IN PISCES: In love you are sensitive, tender, and affectionate, experiencing your partner's feelings almost as strongly as your own. Being also imaginative and visionary, you possess the ability to develop deep compassion for others. As you are idealistic when in love you usually prefer to see only your partner's good points, but be careful that your high expectations do not bring disappointment if you avoid harsh reality. Nevertheless, in your relationships with others you can be devoted, loving, and positively enchanting.

WOMEN WITH VENUS IN ARIES: With your strong desires and enthusiastic nature you can be a passionate lover. Although idealistic and single-minded, you need to avoid unnecessary conflicts in your relationships by being more patient and less headstrong. Although at times others can accuse you of being bossy or impulsive, you possess a great deal of warmth and charm. When necessary you can disarm others by making them feel important.

MEN WITH VENUS IN ARIES: As you often have the courage and strength to initiate situations, you like to take the lead and let others follow. With your unconscious desire for conquest you may also have to beware of being competitive with your partners. Nevertheless, you are drawn to a direct and strong-willed partner who can share your love of action and enthusiasm for life. When you are feeling good you can be

charming and enthusiastic in romantic situations with an entertaining and spontaneous spirit.

WOMEN WITH VENUS IN TAURUS: Good-natured and romantic, you have a highly developed sense of touch that particularly responds to massage, hugs, and all things physical. Being friendly, you enjoy socializing and are able to put others at their ease. With your innate sense of beauty and harmony, your natural charm can attract others. Although you can be lavish toward your partner you may have to be careful that you do not overdo things.

MEN WITH VENUS IN TAURUS: Attractive and affectionate, in relationships you are often faithful with a conservative outlook. You are drawn to warmhearted partners with whom you can share a familiar routine as well as life's pleasures and comforts. Seeking a partner who is dependable or reassuring, you often put security high on your priority list when looking for love. Your sociability and friendliness usually make you popular, and partners often admire your good sense of values and practical skills.

WOMEN WITH VENUS IN GEMINI: In relationships you need intellectual stimulation and usually prefer to keep things light. Certainly not boring, you love to talk and are at your best being witty and entertaining. Although your easygoing approach to relationships is very attractive, guard against losing touch with your emotions. You prefer a partner who can keep up with your fast stream of ideas, and if you have shared interests then so much the better.

MEN WITH VENUS IN GEMINI: Charming, amusing, and adaptable, you attract others with your natural communication skills and friendly personality. You have a wonderful child-like quality and love to keep life playful, but a reluctance to contact your deeper feelings may cause you to avoid serious commitment. With your need for variety and intellectual stimulation, you are attracted to clever and amusing partners who have many interesting sides to their personalities.

To read all about your Outer Planets and work out how to use your personalized timetable, go to Section Three, page 789.

Your Personalized Timetable

JUPITER BENEFICIAL
1939 2/10 – 3/24
1942 7/21 – 9/9
1943 1/18 – 5/3
1944 8/24 – 11/12
1945 3/15 – 7/12
1948 12/14 – until **1949** 2/23
1951 1/23 – 3/7
1954 7/4 – 8/19
1956 8/8 – 10/23
1957 5/2 – 6/4
1960 11/27 – until **1961** 2/5
1962 5/15 – 8/19
1963 1/2 – 2/18
1966 6/18 – 8/2
1968 7/22 – 10/6
1972 3/19 – 6/1
1972 11/8 – until **1973** 1/20
1974 4/20 – 10/6
1974 12/1 – until **1975** 1/31
1978 6/1 – 7/16
1979 11/4 – until **1980** 2/17
1980 7/2 – 9/20
1984 2/20 – 7/14
1984 10/14 – until **1985** 1/4
1986 4/1 – 5/25
1986 8/31 – until **1987** 1/11
1989 9/27 – 11/29
1990 5/14 – 6/30
1991 10/13 – until **1992** 3/29
1992 6/3 – 9/4
1996 2/1 – 12/19
1998 3/15 – 4/29
1998 10/19 – 12/9
2001 8/28 – until **2002** 1/11
2002 4/19 – 6/14
2003 9/25 – until **2004** 8/19
2008 1/15 – 5/2
2008 5/17 – 12/1
2010 2/26 – 4/9

SATURN BENEFICIAL
1944 9/11 – 12/3
1945 5/26 – 8/14
1946 2/9 – 4/27
1949 8/6 – until **1950** 9/12
1959 3/16 – 5/18
1959 12/4 – until **1961** 1/23
1963 3/12 – until **1966** 3/5
1974 7/7 – until **1975** 6/20
1978 9/14 – until **1979** 10/22
1980 4/1 – 7/11
1989 1/6 – until **1990** 3/2
1990 7/11 – 11/30
1994 4/20 – 8/29
1995 1/14 – 4/10
1995 10/13 – 12/29
2003 8/18 – until **2004** 1/7
2004 5/5 – 7/27
2007 10/29 – until **2008** 2/10
2008 7/18 – until **2009** 8/26

URANUS BENEFICIAL
1950 9/23 – until **1954** 4/20
1963 9/8 – until **1967** 8/6
1990 1/9 – until **1994** 1/12
2005 4/13 – until **2009** 1/1

NEPTUNE BENEFICIAL
1938 1/1 – until **1939** 8/25
1987 1/16 – until **1994** 12/23

PLUTO BENEFICIAL
1960 9/9 – until **1968** 9/4
2011 1/28 – Continues

JUPITER CHALLENGING
1938 1/16 – 3/27
1943 7/29 – 10/17
1944 2/10 – 6/13
1946 10/24 – until **1947** 1/12

1947 5/17 – 9/11
1949 12/30 – until **1950** 3/9
1955 7/13 – 9/26
1956 3/26 – 5/10
1958 10/9 – 12/23
1959 7/11 – 7/29
1961 5/1 – 6/18
1961 12/12 – until **1962** 2/20
1967 6/26 – 9/8
1970 9/21 – 12/5
1973 3/27 – 8/6
1973 11/18 – until **1974** 2/4
1978 10/14 – until **1979** 1/7
1979 6/7 – 8/23
1982 1/2 – 4/19
1982 9/1 – 11/19
1985 3/7 – until **1986** 1/19
1990 9/19 – until **1991** 2/16
1991 5/12 – 8/7
1993 12/11 – until **1994** 5/31
1994 8/3 – 11/4
1997 2/17 – until **1998** 1/1
2002 8/30 – until **2003** 7/22
2005 11/24 – until **2006** 10/19
2009 2/1 – 4/19
2009 8/13 – 12/9

SATURN CHALLENGING
1946 9/26 – until **1947** 1/16
1947 6/15 – 11/13
1947 12/25 – until **1948** 7/19
1953 12/17 – until **1954** 4/23
1954 9/14 – until **1955** 11/4
1962 2/26 – 8/26
1962 11/21 – until **1963** 5/2
1963 7/6 – until **1964** 1/18
1976 7/27 – until **1977** 8/27
1983 10/23 – until **1984** 12/8
1985 6/24 – 8/26
1991 4/20 – 6/13
1992 1/4 – until **1993** 2/20
2005 9/4 – until **2006** 2/17
2006 5/22 – 10/10
2007 2/3 – 6/30
2012 11/27 – Continues

URANUS CHALLENGING
1956 10/3 – until **1961** 6/5
1975 12/28 – until **1980** 9/10
1997 2/22 – until **2001** 12/27

NEPTUNE CHALLENGING
1958 12/19 – until **1967** 9/23
2000 4/4 – until **2008** 12/26

PLUTO CHALLENGING
1942 8/30 – until **1953** 7/25
1985 12/8 – until **1992** 10/30

JUPITER SPECIAL
1940 6/14 – 12/12
1941 1/18 – 4/23
1952 5/25 – until **1953** 4/5
1964 5/8 – 7/26
1964 11/4 – until **1965** 3/15
1976 4/22 – 7/1
1976 12/21 – until **1977** 2/9
1988 4/5 – 6/13
2000 3/18 – 5/26
2011 7/9 – 10/21
2012 2/25 – 5/9

SATURN SPECIAL
1940 5/9 – until **1941** 6/11
1941 12/28 – until **1942** 2/18
1969 6/25 – 10/19
1970 3/15 – 8/15
1970 9/24 – until **1971** 4/18
1999 4/23 – until **2000** 5/25

URANUS SPECIAL
1938 1/1 – until **1941** 2/14

May 6

SUN: TAURUS · DECANATE: VIRGO/MERCURY · DEGREE: 14°5–16° TAURUS · MODE: FIXED · ELEMENT: EARTH

Your Personal Powers

Intuition, rationality, and good communication skills are among your many personal powers. Keen on creating a harmonious atmosphere, you can be friendly and charming. Although you are easygoing and receptive to others, you also possess leadership potential. Your practical skills imply that you are particularly assertive when you are involved in monetary pursuits. Learning quickly and being a good psychologist, you have the ability to rapidly assess people and situations. You gain power by combining your innate business sense and your ability to make contacts with your natural expertise at dealing with others. You can, however, lose power when you become unfocused, worried, or anxious, especially about making decisions. By developing your sense of responsibility and your inner faith in your own capabilities, you are able to make the most of your outstanding natural talents. You can succeed admirably when you turn your inspired ideas into concrete accomplishments. Humanitarian service can also bring you extra material and spiritual rewards. Through combining your natural creativity with decisive action and self-discipline, you get the recognition you deserve.

Your Powers of Attraction in Relationships

People are attracted to your intelligence, social skills, and ability to turn on the charm. With your natural diplomacy, you usually appear easygoing and confident. Active and independent, you generally seek clever and bold partners who possess practical skills and foresight. Although others admire your strength, avoid an inclination to be bossy or stubborn with your friends or lovers. In relationships you can be very caring and supportive. Usually you need someone who will understand the importance home and security play in your life. Although you may want to share the good things in life with your partner, you may need to avoid overindulgence. Being a good conversationalist with a sharp mind, you choose friends who are interesting and mentally stimulating.

Your attractive qualities: talented, clever, friendly, sociable, good psychologist, dependable, sympathetic, creative, leadership, restless, natural business sense, independent, inspired ideas, considerate, insightful, loving, idealistic, humanitarian, understanding, caring

Your less attractive qualities: worry, selfishness, cynical, indecision, anxiety, shy, self-centered, overindulgent, perfectionist, unreasonable, extravagant, resentment, interfering, outspoken, lack of responsibility, domineering, critical, dissatisfied, stubborn

Your Venus Power

The planet Venus has a great deal of influence on your powers of attraction. Below are four possible Venus types for women and men. To find your Venus you need to go to page 771, where you will find the Venus table and extra information. The planet Mars also affects your powers of attraction. To find your Mars table and interpretation go to page 761.

WOMEN WITH VENUS IN PISCES: Being sensitive to affairs of the heart, when you care for someone you can feel their emotions and sense their every mood. This empathy indicates that you can love on an unselfish level, but you may have to guard against giving too much, especially to those who do not reciprocate. You are seductive and captivating, and partners can be fascinated by your subtle charms and attracted by your caring and affectionate nature.

MEN WITH VENUS IN PISCES: As a romantic and generous person you are attracted to imaginative or artistic partners who can be sensitive and generous. While you are willing to make allowances for your loved ones, playing the martyr in relationships can lead to allowing others to take advantage of your kind nature. Nevertheless, giving and loving, you are usually willing to forgive your partner's shortcomings.

WOMEN WITH VENUS IN ARIES: You gain power from your strong individuality, energy, and enthusiasm. Your young-at-heart and spirited approach to relationships adds to your appeal. If you become too impatient or self-absorbed, however, your partnerships are likely to suffer. Nevertheless, you can be creative, sharp, and quick, especially when you are able to share new and exciting projects with your partners. Mischievous, with a love of action, you may even incite them to a playful fight.

MEN WITH VENUS IN ARIES: As you often have the courage and strength to initiate situations, you like to take the lead and let others follow. With your unconscious desire for conquest you may also have to beware of being competitive with your partners. Nevertheless, you are drawn to a direct and strong-willed partner who can share your love of action and enthusiasm for life. When you are feeling good you can be

charming and enthusiastic in romantic situations with an entertaining and spontaneous spirit.

WOMEN WITH VENUS IN TAURUS: Warm and affectionate, you are naturally tactile with a love of sensual pleasures. With a streak of the conventional you love the simple pleasures of life: good food, close friends, and happy relationships. Having an inner strength, you can express genuine patience and are often a pillar of support for loved ones and friends. Although you possess endurance be careful not to let this turn into plain stubbornness.

MEN WITH VENUS IN TAURUS: Although you are usually drawn to sensual and physically beautiful individuals, you want a partner who is reliable and loyal. When in love, you enjoy buying your partner things of quality that will grow in value or useful things of a practical nature. You also love to socialize and entertain, especially in luxurious surroundings. Often, you are attracted to creative people or those with artistic talents.

WOMEN WITH VENUS IN GEMINI: By nature you are young at heart, adaptable, and sociable. Being curious and willing to cooperate makes you a good team player. You are usually drawn to articulate people who have charm and flair or sharp wit. With a need to expand your knowledge you also look for a partner who can challenge or stimulate you intellectually. Although you love to talk with all types of people, you may need to develop your listening skills in order to build better communication in your relationships.

MEN WITH VENUS IN GEMINI: Adaptable yet often flirtatious, you enjoy mixing with people who are quick-minded and versatile. Since you can learn a great deal through interacting with others, you are often attracted to intelligent partners who have comprehensive knowledge or good ideas. One of your less attractive qualities is your tendency to become bored or be inconsistent. Having an adaptable partner is important to you, therefore it must be someone who can offer you different options and keep you interested.

To read all about your Outer Planets and work out how to use your personalized timetable, go to Section Three, page 789.

Your Personalized Timetable

JUPITER BENEFICIAL
1939 2/14 – 3/28
1942 7/25 – 9/15
1943 1/11 – 5/10
1944 8/29 – 11/19
1945 3/8 – 7/19
1948 12/18 – until 1949 2/28
1949 8/26 – 10/12
1951 1/27 – 3/11
1954 7/8 – 8/24
1955 3/2 – 3/31
1956 8/13 – 10/28
1957 4/18 – 6/19
1960 12/1 – until 1961 2/9
1962 5/23 – 8/11
1963 1/7 – 2/22
1966 6/22 – 8/6
1968 7/27 – 10/11
1972 3/29 – 5/21
1972 11/13 – until 1973 1/24
1974 4/25 – 9/27
1974 12/10 – until 1975 2/5
1978 6/6 – 7/21
1979 11/12 – until 1980 2/9
1980 7/8 – 9/24
1984 2/26 – 7/6
1984 10/21 – until 1985 1/8
1986 4/5 – 6/1
1986 8/23 – until 1987 1/16
1989 10/9 – 11/17
1990 5/19 – 7/5
1991 10/18 – until 1992 3/19
1992 6/12 – 9/9
1996 2/5 – 12/23
1998 3/19 – 5/4
1998 10/8 – 12/18
2001 9/2 – until 2002 1/4
2002 4/26 – 6/18
2003 9/30 – until 2004 8/24
2008 1/19 – 12/6
2010 3/2 – 4/14

SATURN BENEFICIAL
1944 9/28 – 11/16
1945 6/4 – 8/23
1946 1/27 – 5/10
1949 8/14 – until 1950 9/20
1959 12/13 – until 1961 2/1
1965 3/20 – until 1966 3/13
1974 7/15 – until 1975 6/28
1978 9/22 – until 1979 4/26
1979 5/22 – 10/31
1980 3/19 – 7/23
1989 1/15 – until 1990 3/14
1990 6/28 – 12/10
1994 5/1 – 8/16
1995 1/24 – 4/19
1995 9/29 – until 1996 1/12
2003 8/27 – 12/26
2004 5/15 – 8/4
2007 11/11 – until 2008 1/27
2008 7/27 – until 2009 9/3

URANUS BENEFICIAL
1951 7/11 – until 1954 5/20
1963 9/24 – until 1967 8/23
1990 1/26 – until 1994 11/16
2005 5/9 – until 2009 1/27

NEPTUNE BENEFICIAL
1938 1/1 – until 1940 7/17
1987 2/15 – until 1995 11/14

PLUTO BENEFICIAL
1960 10/10 – until 1969 7/29
2011 3/7 – Continues

JUPITER CHALLENGING
1938 1/20 – 4/1
1938 9/26 – 11/10

1943 8/2 – 10/24
1944 2/3 – 6/19
1946 10/29 – until 1947 1/18
1947 5/10 – 9/17
1950 1/4 – 3/13
1955 7/17 – 10/1
1956 3/14 – 5/21
1958 10/13 – 12/28
1959 6/23 – 8/16
1961 12/16 – until 1962 2/24
1967 7/1 – 9/13
1970 9/26 – 12/10
1973 4/2 – 7/30
1973 11/24 – until 1974 2/8
1978 10/22 – 12/29
1979 6/12 – 8/28
1982 1/9 – 4/11
1982 9/7 – 11/24
1985 3/12 – 9/25
1985 10/10 – until 1986 1/23
1990 9/24 – until 1991 2/8
1991 5/19 – 8/12
1993 12/16 – until 1994 5/21
1994 8/12 – 11/8
1997 2/21 – until 1998 1/5
2002 9/4 – until 2003 7/27
2005 11/29 – until 2006 10/24
2009 2/5 – 4/26
2009 8/5 – 12/15

SATURN CHALLENGING
1946 10/8 – until 1947 1/3
1947 6/24 – until 1948 7/27
1953 12/28 – until 1954 4/10
1954 9/23 – until 1955 11/12
1962 3/8 – 8/12
1962 12/4 – until 1964 1/26
1976 8/3 – until 1977 9/4
1983 10/31 – until 1984 12/17
1985 6/7 – 9/11
1992 1/13 – until 1993 2/28
2005 9/13 – until 2006 2/4
2006 6/2 – 10/21
2007 1/21 – 7/9
2012 12/6 – Continues

URANUS CHALLENGING
1957 7/29 – until 1961 6/29
1976 10/26 – until 1980 10/3
1997 3/13 – until 2002 1/16

NEPTUNE CHALLENGING
1959 11/14 – until 1967 10/25
2001 2/21 – until 2009 1/24

PLUTO CHALLENGING
1942 10/28 – until 1954 6/29
1986 1/19 – until 1993 9/14

JUPITER SPECIAL
1940 6/19 – 11/30
1941 1/30 – 4/27
1952 5/30 – until 1953 4/9
1964 5/12 – 8/2
1964 10/27 – until 1965 3/20
1976 4/26 – 7/6
1976 12/11 – until 1977 2/19
1988 4/10 – 6/17
2000 3/23 – 5/30
2011 7/16 – 10/14
2012 3/2 – 5/13

SATURN SPECIAL
1940 5/17 – until 1941 6/20
1941 12/11 – until 1942 3/6
1969 7/7 – 10/6
1970 3/24 – until 1971 4/26
1999 5/1 – until 2000 6/1

URANUS SPECIAL
1938 1/1 – until 1941 3/21

May 7

Your Personal Powers

Friendly and persuasive, your personal powers include a thoughtful approach and good communication skills. Possessing a practical mind and good judgment, you are usually capable of evaluating and organizing others. This talent gives you the potential to rise to positions of leadership or to stimulate a more humanitarian side to your nature. Being persistent and decisive, you gain power when you display your tenacity and determination. If you are not careful, however, these qualities can also make you stubborn and headstrong. You can lose some of your power if you become withdrawn, too cynical, or skeptical. Your natural talents are likely to include an innate business sense, dramatic or creative gifts, and the capacity for inspiring others. Although you possess a natural expertise in gaining material assets, you undermine your potential if you become anxious or too security-conscious. Developing faith in your talents or fighting for others aids your success. Nevertheless, with your discernment abilities and shrewd practicality you possess the capacity for outstanding achievements.

Your Powers of Attraction in Relationships

Your ability to turn on the charm implies that people are attracted to your warm and friendly personality. Being security conscious, you usually prefer a solid relationship based on trust. If you are indecisive, you tend to worry about your love life. Creative, loving, and sociable, you usually seek a gregarious partner who can be an asset in social situations. A more uncertain side to your nature, however, indicates that you could also become oversensitive or insecure if you do not receive the love you desire. Nevertheless, being generous, with expensive taste, you usually enjoy spending or sharing your money with your loved ones. In your personal relationships you can be happier if you keep a light attitude and resist getting overly serious or intense. When you develop detachment, you often establish better personal relationships.

Your attractive qualities: thoughtful, generous, methodical, loving, communication or writing skills, idealistic, honest, strong-willed, problem solver, loves beauty, scientific, organized, clever, freedom fighter, humanitarian potential, reformer, rational, reflective

Your less attractive qualities: extravagant, critical, self-absorbed, worry, critical, cold, frustrated, self-indulgence, too perfectionist, skeptical, anxious, confused, stubborn, bossy

Your Venus Power

The planet Venus has a great deal of influence on your powers of attraction. Below are four possible Venus types for women and men. To find your Venus you need to go to page 771, where you will find the Venus table and extra information. The planet Mars also affects your powers of attraction. To find your Mars table and interpretation go to page 761.

WOMEN WITH VENUS IN ARIES: With your strong desires and enthusiastic nature, you can be a passionate lover. Although idealistic and single-minded, you need to avoid unnecessary conflicts in your relationships by being more patient and less headstrong. Although at times others can accuse you of being bossy or impulsive, you possess a great deal of warmth and charm. When necessary you can disarm others by making them feel important.

MEN WITH VENUS IN ARIES: You are usually inclined to seek a partner who is active, goal-oriented, or decisive. Not known for your patience, you probably seek relationships early in life. You may find that you are attracted more to women who have a daring or adventurous spirit, but in your close relationships you may encounter rivalry or find that both you and your partner want to lead or be the boss. Although you may act rashly, you possess a great deal of magnetism and are capable of demonstrating your love and affection.

WOMEN WITH VENUS IN TAURUS: Good-natured and romantic, you have a highly developed sense of touch that particularly responds to massage, hugs, and all things physical. Being friendly, you enjoy socializing and are able to put others at their ease. With your innate sense of beauty and harmony, your natural charm can attract others. Although you can be lavish toward your partner, you may have to be careful that you do not overdo things.

MEN WITH VENUS IN TAURUS: Attractive and affectionate, in relationships you are often down-to-earth, with a conservative outlook. You are drawn to warmhearted partners with whom you can share a familiar routine as well as life's pleasures and comforts. Seeking a partner who is dependable or reassuring, you often put security high on your priority list

when looking for love. Your sociability and friendliness usually make you popular and partners often admire your good sense of values and practical skills.

WOMEN WITH VENUS IN GEMINI: Curious, with a bright and animated approach to life, you are attracted to those who are clever or sophisticated. Your love of variety and desire for knowledge suggest that you need a partner and friends who keep you mentally stimulated. Although witty and a good conversationalist, you may need to keep in touch with your deeper feelings. Nevertheless, intelligent and friendly, you possess a youthful sense of wonder and seek a playmate who can keep you from becoming bored.

MEN WITH VENUS IN GEMINI: Informed and curious yet charming and friendly, you seek a partner who shares your interests or enjoys your witty remarks. Although a good communicator, there is an inborn tendency to be lighthearted and less profound about deep emotional commitment. Although you are keen on experiences that bring variety into your life, boredom or scattering your energies in too many directions is probably your biggest handicap in relationships. Nevertheless, you are attracted to intelligent partners who can match your lively banter.

WOMEN WITH VENUS IN CANCER: Gentle and tender, you are romantic by nature. You possess a strong need for security and usually you help others feel safe or protected. This preservation is especially centered around the home, which is your haven from life's storm. Although your maternal instincts are strong, avoid making sacrifices for others at your own expense. Nevertheless, affectionate and caring, once committed to a relationship, your loyalty and devotion to your partner is very strong.

MEN WITH VENUS IN CANCER: Being emotionally receptive, you can be a sensitive lover. With your desire to care for and protect others you are likely to have strong family connections. Love is often tied in with being attentive to the needs of others and you may find yourself attracted to individuals who have sympathetic or maternal qualities. Security-conscious, you need a loyal partner who can offer you support and ideally be a good cook and homemaker.

To read all about your Outer Planets and work out how to use your personalized timetable, go to Section Three, page 789.

To read all about your Outer Planets and work out how to use your personalized timetable, go to Section Three, page 789.

Your Personalized Timetable

JUPITER BENEFICIAL
1939 2/18 – 4/1
1942 7/30 – 9/21
1943 1/3 – 5/16
1944 9/2 – 11/26
1945 2/28 – 7/25
1948 12/22 – until 1949 3/5
1949 8/15 – 10/23
1951 2/1 – 3/15
1954 7/13 – 8/29
1955 2/16 – 4/14
1956 8/17 – 11/2
1957 4/8 – 6/28
1960 12/6 – until 1961 2/14
1962 6/1 – 8/2
1963 1/12 – 2/26
1966 6/27 – 8/11
1968 8/1 – 10/15
1972 4/16 – 5/3
1972 11/18 – until 1973 1/28
1974 4/30 – 9/18
1974 12/18 – until 1975 2/9
1978 6/10 – 7/25
1979 11/20 – until 1980 1/31
1980 7/13 – 9/29
1984 3/3 – 6/28
1984 10/28 – until 1985 1/12
1986 4/10 – 6/10
1986 8/14 – until 1987 1/21
1990 5/24 – 7/9
1991 10/24 – until 1992 3/11
1992 6/20 – 9/13
1996 2/10 – 8/19
1996 9/18 – 12/27
1998 3/23 – 5/10
1998 9/30 – 12/26
2001 9/9 – 12/28
2002 5/2 – 6/23
2003 10/5 – until 2004 8/29
2008 1/24 – 12/10
2010 3/6 – 4/18

SATURN BENEFICIAL
1945 6/12 – 9/1
1946 1/15 – 5/21
1949 8/22 – until 1950 9/28
1959 12/21 – until 1961 2/9
1961 8/23 – 11/1
1965 3/28 – 10/16
1965 12/12 – until 1966 3/21
1974 7/22 – until 1975 7/5
1978 9/30 – until 1979 4/3
1979 6/14 – 11/10
1980 3/7 – 8/2
1989 1/23 – 8/8
1989 10/14 – until 1990 3/28
1990 6/12 – 12/19
1994 5/15 – 8/1
1995 2/2 – 4/29
1995 9/16 – until 1996 1/23
2003 9/7 – 12/13
2004 5/24 – 8/12
2005 2/20 – 4/20
2007 11/29 – until 2008 1/8
2008 8/4 – until 2009 9/11

URANUS BENEFICIAL
1951 7/28 – until 1954 6/9
1963 10/11 – until 1967 9/8
1990 2/14 – until 1994 12/8
2006 3/9 – until 2009 2/15

NEPTUNE BENEFICIAL
1938 1/1 – until 1940 8/20
1988 1/12 – until 1995 12/18

PLUTO BENEFICIAL
1961 9/10 – until 1969 8/28
2012 1/26 – Continues

JUPITER CHALLENGING
1938 1/24 – 4/6
1938 9/15 – 11/21
1943 8/7 – 10/31

1944 1/26 – 6/25
1946 11/2 – until 1947 1/25
1947 5/2 – 9/23
1950 1/8 – 3/17
1955 7/22 – 10/6
1956 3/5 – 5/30
1958 10/18 – until 1959 1/2
1959 6/12 – 8/27
1961 12/21 – until 1962 2/28
1967 7/5 – 9/18
1970 10/1 – 12/15
1973 4/9 – 7/22
1973 11/30 – until 1974 2/12
1978 11/2 – 12/18
1979 6/17 – 9/1
1982 1/17 – 4/3
1982 9/13 – 11/28
1985 3/16 – 9/7
1985 10/29 – until 1986 1/27
1990 9/30 – until 1991 1/31
1991 5/26 – 8/16
1993 12/22 – until 1994 5/13
1994 8/20 – 11/13
1997 2/26 – until 1998 1/10
2002 9/9 – until 2003 3/26
2003 4/12 – 7/31
2005 12/4 – until 2006 10/28
2009 2/9 – 5/3
2009 7/28 – 12/20

SATURN CHALLENGING
1946 10/24 – 12/18
1947 7/2 – until 1948 8/3
1954 1/11 – 3/26
1954 10/2 – until 1955 11/20
1962 3/18 – 7/30
1962 12/15 – until 1964 2/3
1976 8/11 – until 1977 9/12
1978 3/31 – 5/20
1983 11/8 – until 1984 12/26
1985 5/24 – 9/23
1992 1/21 – until 1993 3/9
1993 10/2 – 11/22
2005 9/23 – until 2006 1/23
2006 6/12 – 11/5
2007 1/6 – 7/18
2012 12/16 – Continues

URANUS CHALLENGING
1957 8/14 – until 1961 7/18
1976 11/11 – until 1980 10/21
1997 4/9 – until 2002 2/2

NEPTUNE CHALLENGING
1959 12/13 – until 1968 9/14
2001 3/25 – until 2009 12/17

PLUTO CHALLENGING
1943 9/20 – until 1954 8/2
1986 11/22 – until 1993 10/16

JUPITER SPECIAL
1940 6/24 – 11/21
1941 2/8 – 5/1
1952 6/3 – until 1953 4/14
1964 5/16 – 8/11
1964 10/19 – until 1965 3/25
1976 4/30 – 7/12
1976 12/2 – until 1977 2/27
1988 4/14 – 6/22
2000 3/27 – 6/4
2011 7/24 – 10/6
2012 3/7 – 5/17

SATURN SPECIAL
1940 5/25 – 12/22
1941 1/27 – 6/29
1941 11/28 – until 1942 3/18
1969 7/22 – 9/19
1970 4/1 – until 1971 5/4
1999 5/8 – until 2000 6/9
2001 1/13 – 2/6

URANUS SPECIAL
1938 1/1 – until 1941 4/11

May 8

SUN: TAURUS • DECANATE: VIRGO/MERCURY • DEGREE: 16°5–18° TAURUS • MODE: FIXED • ELEMENT: EARTH

Your Personal Powers

Your natural magnetism, warmth, and sociable nature add to your charm and personal powers. Your ruling planet, Venus, indicates that you appreciate beauty and have style as well as good taste. Your pragmatic approach to life endows you with a natural business sense and an ability to be of practical use to others. You gain power when you strive to attain your goals and ideals rather than get sidetracked by recreational diversions or material distractions. Innovative and resourceful with a sharp yet imaginative mind, you have original ideas and excellent plans. Aware of image, you can impress others with your analytical skills and eye for detail. Although clever and articulate, a desire to rise above the ordinary can lead you to explore unusual or mystical experiences. You may, however, need to resist getting carried away with fantasies or escaping from your responsibilities. Nevertheless, your power and confidence can increase when you develop your organizational skills and capacity for successfully dealing with monetary situations. Friendly and charming, you also benefit from your social contacts and people skills.

Your Powers of Attraction in Relationships

Charming and enthusiastic, your kind and affectionate ways, coupled with your refined manner, make you attractive to others. Often honest and direct with others, you are drawn to sincere and frank individuals. Although you possess lofty ideas and a strong urge for freedom, you also hold a strong need for security. You are usually attracted to shrewd people with common sense or those who can materially help or advise you. Sociable and friendly, you know how to enjoy yourself and be entertaining. Although you possess a playful side to your nature, if you also avoid responsibility, you will shy away from making a strong commitment to your lover. Once you decide to settle down, however, your idealism and practical considerations ensure that you are a romantic and loyal partner.

Your attractive qualities: spontaneous, determined, leadership, playful, hardworking, artistic, creative, idealistic, youthful, smart, loving, ambitious, charming, loves beauty, articulate, good evaluator, direct, business sense, executive skills, sociable, freedom-loving

Your less attractive qualities: intolerant, restless, workaholic, domineering, impatient, power issues, immature, mate-rialistic, easily discouraged, lack of planning, critical, controlling, too security conscious, escapist

Your Venus Power

The planet Venus has a great deal of influence on your powers of attraction. Below are four possible Venus types for women and men. To find your Venus you need to go to page 771, where you will find the Venus table and extra information. The planet Mars also affects your powers of attraction. To find your Mars table and interpretation go to page 761.

WOMEN WITH VENUS IN ARIES: Idealistic, passionate, and adventurous, you are direct in your dealings with others. When you are attracted to a person you usually take the initiative and use your people skills to make things happen. In close relationships you are not afraid to confront your other half. This self-assertiveness is positive if differences can be brought into the open through diplomacy and compromise.

MEN WITH VENUS IN ARIES: You are drawn to strong, independent women who can stand up to you. Although you can enthusiastically follow the object of your desire, you may lose power if you allow your forceful emotions to become too dominant. Warm and passionate, you have a side to your nature that longs for new adventures. Romantic and chivalrous, you really enjoy the excitement of the initial chase, but unless you keep the enthusiasm alive and avoid falling into a rut you may become easily bored.

WOMEN WITH VENUS IN TAURUS: Being physically attractive, you can make a good impression on the opposite sex. As security and stability in relationships are very important to you, you usually want a partner who is not only attractive but also reliable and a good provider. Being sensual or tactile, you also need a lover who is affectionate, but beware that your love does not show signs of possessiveness or jealousy. Your own sense of style and love of beauty imply that you can be attracted to creative people, especially those in art and music.

MEN WITH VENUS IN TAURUS: As well as attracting people with your warm personality you also possess an innate sense of the value of material possessions. Keeping yourself stylish and having an attractive appearance can also be important to you. You are naturally attracted to practical yet sensual women who understand your need for comfort, security, and the pleasures and luxuries of life. Naturally affectionate, you enjoy socializing but can make a loyal and loving partner.

WOMEN WITH VENUS IN GEMINI: Articulate, versatile, and youthful, your personal magnetism is often linked to your charm, wit, and communication skills. You seek a partner who is clever, can communicate with you at ease, and share your thoughts and interests. Since you find it easy to mix with people, you have many friends. When you do find someone you can communicate with, you can easily lose yourself in long conversations.

MEN WITH VENUS IN GEMINI: Charming, amusing, and adaptable, you attract others with your natural communication skills and friendly personality. You have a wonderful child-like quality and love to keep life playful, but a reluctance to contact your deeper feelings may cause you to avoid serious commitment. With your need for variety and intellectual stimulation, you are attracted to clever and amusing partners who have many interesting sides to their personalities.

WOMEN WITH VENUS IN CANCER: Possessing a soft femininity, you have tender and sensitive emotions. Sympathetic and caring, you often mother those in your care by making sure they are comfortable and have plenty to eat. When you feel hurt or insecure in relationships, you are likely to cover your feelings by being defensive or appearing tough on the outside while on the inside you are feeling vulnerable. Affectionate and romantic, you make a faithful and devoted partner.

MEN WITH VENUS IN CANCER: Being caring and sensitive, you probably seek a nurturing partner who can provide you with emotional security and a sense of belonging in a loving and safe environment. Receptive to others, at times you find it hard to be direct or confrontational in relationships. Usually you deal indirectly with what is causing you concern, and although you are willing to make sacrifices for dear ones, resist the temptation to be exploited by those you love.

To read all about your Outer Planets and work out how to use your personalized timetable, go to Section Three, page 789.

Your Personalized Timetable

JUPITER BENEFICIAL
1939 2/22 – 4/5
1942 8/3 – 9/28
1942 12/27 – until 1943 5/22
1944 9/7 – 12/4
1945 2/20 – 7/30
1948 12/26 – until 1949 3/11
1949 8/6 – 10/31
1951 2/5 – 3/19
1954 7/17 – 9/3
1955 2/6 – 4/24
1956 8/22 – 11/8
1957 3/31 – 7/6
1960 12/10 – until 1961 2/18
1962 6/14 – 7/20
1963 1/17 – 3/2
1966 7/1 – 8/15
1968 8/6 – 10/20
1972 11/23 – until 1973 2/1
1974 5/6 – 9/11
1974 12/24 – until 1975 2/13
1978 6/15 – 7/29
1979 11/30 – until 1980 1/21
1980 7/19 – 10/3
1984 3/10 – 6/21
1984 11/2 – until 1985 1/16
1986 4/14 – 6/22
1986 8/2 – until 1987 1/26
1990 5/28 – 7/13
1991 10/30 – until 1992 3/3
1992 6/27 – 9/18
1996 2/15 – 8/5
1996 10/2 – until 1997 1/1
1998 3/27 – 5/15
1998 9/22 – until 1999 1/2
2001 9/15 – 12/20
2002 5/8 – 6/27
2003 10/10 – until 2004 4/22
2004 5/17 – 9/2
2008 1/28 – 12/15
2010 3/10 – 4/23

SATURN BENEFICIAL
1945 6/19 – 9/11
1946 1/3 – 5/30
1949 8/30 – until 1950 10/6
1959 12/29 – until 1961 2/18
1961 8/7 – 11/15
1965 4/6 – 9/29
1965 12/28 – until 1966 3/29
1974 7/30 – until 1975 2/27
1975 3/29 – 7/13
1978 10/9 – until 1979 3/19
1979 6/28 – 11/22
1980 2/23 – 8/11
1989 2/1 – 7/23
1989 10/29 – until 1990 4/20
1990 5/19 – 12/27
1994 6/6 – 7/9
1995 2/10 – 5/10
1995 9/3 – until 1996 2/1
2003 9/21 – 11/29
2004 6/1 – 8/20
2005 2/4 – 5/5
2008 8/13 – until 2009 9/19

URANUS BENEFICIAL
1951 8/15 – until 1954 6/26
1963 11/1 – until 1968 6/16
1990 3/13 – until 1994 12/26
2006 3/27 – until 2009 3/5

NEPTUNE BENEFICIAL
1938 1/1 – until 1941 7/6
1988 2/9 – until 1996 11/1

PLUTO BENEFICIAL
1961 10/11 – until 1970 7/18
2012 3/2 – Continues

JUPITER CHALLENGING
1938 1/28 – 4/11
1938 9/6 – 11/29

1943 8/11 – 11/9
1944 1/17 – 7/1
1946 11/7 – until 1947 2/2
1947 4/23 – 9/29
1950 1/12 – 3/22
1955 7/26 – 10/12
1956 2/26 – 6/7
1958 10/22 – until 1959 1/7
1959 6/3 – 9/4
1961 12/26 – until 1962 3/4
1967 7/10 – 9/23
1970 10/6 – 12/19
1973 4/16 – 7/14
1973 12/5 – until 1974 2/16
1979 6/22 – 9/6
1982 1/27 – 3/23
1982 9/18 – 12/3
1985 3/22 – 8/28
1985 11/8 – until 1986 1/31
1990 10/6 – until 1991 1/24
1991 6/2 – 8/20
1993 12/28 – until 1994 5/5
1994 8/27 – 11/17
1997 3/2 – until 1998 1/14
2002 9/14 – until 2003 3/8
2003 4/30 – 8/5
2005 12/8 – until 2006 6/25
2006 7/17 – 11/2
2009 2/13 – 5/11
2009 7/20 – 12/25

SATURN CHALLENGING
1947 7/10 – until 1948 8/11
1954 2/2 – 3/3
1954 10/11 – until 1955 11/28
1962 3/29 – 7/16
1962 12/24 – until 1964 2/11
1976 8/19 – until 1977 9/20
1978 3/14 – 6/6
1983 11/16 – until 1985 1/5
1985 5/11 – 10/4
1992 1/29 – until 1993 3/18
1993 9/14 – 12/9
2005 10/4 – until 2006 1/11
2006 6/21 – until 2007 7/26
2012 12/27 – Continues

URANUS CHALLENGING
1957 8/31 – until 1961 8/3
1976 11/27 – until 1980 11/6
1998 2/5 – until 2002 11/28

NEPTUNE CHALLENGING
1960 11/9 – until 1968 10/19
2002 2/16 – until 2010 1/19

PLUTO CHALLENGING
1944 8/29 – until 1955 7/7
1986 12/21 – until 1993 11/11

JUPITER SPECIAL
1940 6/29 – 11/14
1941 2/15 – 5/6
1952 6/7 – until 1953 4/18
1964 5/20 – 8/21
1964 10/8 – until 1965 3/30
1976 5/4 – 7/17
1976 11/25 – until 1977 3/6
1988 4/18 – 6/26
2000 3/31 – 6/8
2011 8/3 – 9/26
2012 3/12 – 5/21

SATURN SPECIAL
1940 6/2 – 12/2
1941 2/15 – 7/8
1941 11/16 – until 1942 3/28
1970 4/9 – until 1971 5/11
1999 5/16 – until 2000 6/17
2000 12/21 – until 2001 2/28

URANUS SPECIAL
1938 1/1 – until 1941 4/29

May 9

SUN: TAURUS • DECANATE: VIRGO/MERCURY • DEGREE: 17°5–19° TAURUS • MODE: FIXED • ELEMENT: EARTH

Your Personal Powers

Ambitious, clever, and independent, you are a warmhearted individual with a generous spirit. As your personal powers include an optimistic nature and natural business sense, you often have in mind some project or plan of action. Quick to recognize opportunities, you can be enterprising and ambitious. Even though you are determined and resourceful, you can lose some of your power if you do not discipline yourself to follow through with plans and turn them to reality. Your self-assured charm can certainly help you capitalize on your assets as well as help you mix with people from all walks of life. Articulate, with analytical ability and foresight, you often have inventive ideas that are ahead of their time. Nevertheless, you may find the greatest rewards by following your ideals rather than pursuing projects for pure capital gains. You empower yourself by combining your intelligence, intuitive abilities, and ideals with your practical skills. When you put all your natural talents to good use, you possess all the qualities needed for success.

Your Powers of Attraction in Relationships

Your warmth and friendly manner attract others. With your strong views you need a partner who can understand your ambition and motivation. Although you can be very generous and loving, an extreme behavioral pattern implies that you can also possess a selfish side to your nature. Regardless, you enjoy being amorous and can be a good lover or loving companion. You are usually attracted to strong, determined individuals with a sense of the dramatic. Naturally gregarious and quick at assessing people, you can be enchanting, witty, and entertaining. If a materialistic streak in your nature is channeled into a more humanitarian or philanthropic approach, this can help you avoid restlessness or indecision in your relationships. Nevertheless, sensual and loving, with good people skills, you will always be attractive to others.

Your attractive qualities: mental agility, success-oriented, idealistic, creative, sensitive, good organizer, generous, drive, motivated, magnetic, analytical, giving, detached, shrewd, freedom-loving, humanitarian potential, fortunate, popular

Your less attractive qualities: frustrated, nervous, selfish, impractical, easily led, inferiority complex, self-centered, materialistic, obstinate, disappointed, fears, worry, stuck in a rut

Your Venus Power

The planet Venus has a great deal of influence on your powers of attraction. Below are four possible Venus types for women and men. To find your Venus you need to go to page 771, where you will find the Venus table and extra information. The planet Mars also affects your powers of attraction. To find your Mars table and interpretation go to page 761.

WOMEN WITH VENUS IN ARIES: Idealistic, passionate, and adventurous, you are direct in your dealings with others. When you are attracted to a person you usually take the initiative and use your people skills to make things happen. In close relationships you are not afraid to confront your other half. This self-assertiveness can be bossy but is positive if differences can be brought into the open through diplomacy and compromise.

MEN WITH VENUS IN ARIES: As you often have the courage and strength to initiate situations, you like to take the lead. With your unconscious desire for conquest you may also have to beware of being competitive with your partners. Nevertheless, you are drawn to a direct and strong-willed partner who can share your love of action and enthusiasm for life. When you are feeling good you can be charming and enthusiastic in romantic situations with an entertaining and spontaneous spirit.

WOMEN WITH VENUS IN TAURUS: For your ideal relationship, you seek a partner who is both financially secure and demonstrative with his affections. With these thoughts in mind, you are likely to want a partner who is refined yet pragmatic or someone concerned with safeguarding your future. Your stubborn streak suggests that even when you know you are in the wrong, you are reluctant to give way. Attracted to people with a good sense of style, you can succeed in all kinds of business partnerships, especially those involving the arts, music, and luxury goods.

MEN WITH VENUS IN TAURUS: Attractive and affectionate, in relationships you are often faithful with a conservative outlook. You are drawn to warmhearted partners with whom you can share a familiar routine as well as life's pleasures and comforts. Seeking a partner who is dependable or reassuring, you often put security high on your priority list when looking for love. Your sociability and friendliness usually make you popular, and partners often admire your good sense of values and practical skills.

WOMEN WITH VENUS IN GEMINI: In relationships you

need intellectual stimulation and usually prefer to keep things light. Certainly not boring, you love to talk and are at your best being witty and entertaining. Although your easygoing approach to relationships is very attractive, guard against losing touch with your emotions. You prefer a partner who can keep up with your fast stream of ideas, and if you have shared interests then so much the better.

MEN WITH VENUS IN GEMINI: Adaptable yet often flirtatious, you enjoy mixing with people who are quick-minded and versatile. Since you can learn a great deal through interacting with others, you are often attracted to intelligent partners who have comprehensive knowledge or good ideas. One of your less attractive qualities is your tendency to become bored or be inconsistent. Having an adaptable partner is important to you; therefore it must be someone who can offer you different options and keep you interested.

WOMEN WITH VENUS IN CANCER: With your intuitive abilities and sympathetic nature, you are usually supportive to those you love. Impressionable and empathetic, your receptivity allows you to quickly pick up on the moods of people, and you are especially aware of the emotional changes in your close partner. As you often display true maternal tendencies toward those you know, you want a partner who is considerate and sensitive.

MEN WITH VENUS IN CANCER: You seek a partner who is sympathetic, caring, and protective. Able to be forgiving and compassionate, you want a secure emotional bond in your close relationships. Usually you are drawn to partners who are maternal, unselfish, or demonstrative with their feelings. Although you can sometimes appear to others as impressionable, you have powerful emotions and inner strength.

To read all about your Outer Planets and work out how to use your personalized timetable, go to Section Three, page 789.

Your Personalized Timetable

JUPITER BENEFICIAL
1939 2/26 – 4/9
1942 8/8 – 10/7
1942 12/18 – until 1943 5/27
1944 9/11 – 12/13
1945 2/10 – 8/5
1948 12/31 – until 1949 3/16
1949 7/29 – 11/7
1951 2/9 – 3/23
1954 7/21 – 9/9
1955 1/29 – 5/2
1956 8/26 – 11/14
1957 3/23 – 7/14
1960 12/14 – until 1961 2/23
1963 1/22 – 3/6
1966 7/5 – 8/20
1968 8/10 – 10/25
1969 5/19 – 5/27
1972 11/27 – until 1973 2/5
1974 5/12 – 9/3
1974 12/30 – until 1975 2/17
1978 6/19 – 8/3
1979 12/18 – until 1980 1/3
1980 7/24 – 10/8
1984 3/17 – 6/13
1984 11/8 – until 1985 1/21
1986 4/19 – 10/30
1986 11/18 – until 1987 1/31
1990 6/2 – 7/18
1991 11/5 – until 1992 2/25
1992 7/3 – 9/22
1996 2/20 – 7/26
1996 10/12 – until 1997 1/5
1998 3/31 – 5/21
1998 9/15 – until 1999 1/8
2001 9/23 – 12/12
2002 5/14 – 7/1
2003 10/15 – until 2004 4/6
2004 6/2 – 9/7
2008 2/2 – 12/19
2010 3/14 – 4/27

SATURN BENEFICIAL
1945 6/27 – 9/23
1945 12/21 – until 1946 6/8
1949 9/6 – until 1950 10/14
1951 5/2 – 6/24
1960 1/6 – until 1961 2/28
1961 7/25 – 11/27
1965 4/15 – 9/15
1966 1/9 – 4/6
1966 11/11 – 12/12
1974 8/7 – until 1975 2/5
1975 4/19 – 7/20
1978 10/18 – until 1979 3/6
1979 7/10 – 12/6
1980 2/7 – 8/20
1989 2/11 – 7/9
1989 11/10 – until 1991 1/5
1995 2/18 – 5/22
1995 8/21 – until 1996 2/10
2003 10/15 – 11/5
2004 6/9 – 8/29
2005 1/23 – 5/17
2008 8/20 – until 2009 9/26

URANUS BENEFICIAL
1951 9/6 – until 1954 7/12
1964 8/29 – until 1968 7/21
1991 1/7 – until 1995 1/12
2006 4/15 – until 2010 1/2

NEPTUNE BENEFICIAL
1938 1/1 – until 1941 8/15
1988 3/28 – until 1996 12/11

PLUTO BENEFICIAL
1962 9/10 – until 1970 8/21

JUPITER CHALLENGING
1938 2/2 – 4/17
1938 8/29 – 12/6
1943 8/16 – 11/20

JUPITER BENEFICIAL (continued)
1944 1/6 – 7/6
1946 11/11 – until 1947 2/11
1947 4/14 – 10/4
1950 1/16 – 3/26
1955 7/30 – 10/18
1956 2/19 – 6/14
1958 10/27 – until 1959 1/13
1959 5/26 – 9/11
1961 12/30 – until 1962 3/8
1967 7/15 – 9/28
1968 4/8 – 5/5
1970 10/11 – 12/24
1973 4/24 – 7/6
1973 12/11 – until 1974 2/20
1979 6/27 – 9/10
1982 2/13 – 3/6
1982 9/23 – 12/7
1985 3/27 – 8/19
1985 11/16 – until 1986 2/4
1990 10/13 – until 1991 1/17
1991 6/7 – 8/25
1994 1/3 – 4/27
1994 9/3 – 11/21
1997 3/7 – until 1998 1/18
2002 9/19 – until 2003 2/26
2003 5/11 – 8/9
2005 12/13 – until 2006 6/8
2006 8/3 – 11/6
2009 2/17 – 5/22
2009 7/8 – 12/30

SATURN CHALLENGING
1947 7/18 – until 1948 8/19
1954 10/19 – until 1955 12/6
1962 4/12 – 7/1
1963 1/2 – until 1964 2/19
1976 8/26 – until 1977 3/28
1977 4/25 – 9/29
1978 2/28 – 6/19
1983 11/24 – until 1984 6/20
1984 8/5 – until 1985 1/17
1985 4/27 – 10/13
1992 2/6 – until 1993 3/27
1993 8/31 – 12/22
2005 10/17 – 12/28
2006 6/30 – until 2007 8/3

URANUS CHALLENGING
1957 9/18 – until 1961 8/19
1976 12/15 – until 1981 8/18
1998 2/22 – until 2002 12/28

NEPTUNE CHALLENGING
1960 12/6 – until 1969 9/3
2002 3/17 – until 2010 12/4

PLUTO CHALLENGING
1944 10/18 – until 1956 5/19
1987 11/8 – until 1994 9/30

JUPITER SPECIAL
1940 7/5 – 11/6
1941 2/22 – 5/10
1952 6/12 – until 1953 4/22
1964 5/25 – until 1965 4/4
1976 5/8 – 7/23
1976 11/18 – until 1977 3/13
1988 4/22 – 7/1
1989 1/16 – 1/24
2000 4/5 – 6/12
2011 8/19 – 9/10
2012 3/17 – 5/26

SATURN SPECIAL
1940 6/11 – 11/18
1941 2/28 – 7/19
1941 11/4 – until 1942 4/6
1970 4/17 – until 1971 5/19
1999 5/24 – until 2000 6/26
2000 12/6 – until 2001 3/14

URANUS SPECIAL
1938 2/18 – until 1941 5/16

105

May 10

SUN: TAURUS • DECANATE: VIRGO/MERCURY • DEGREE: 18°5–20° TAURUS • MODE: FIXED • ELEMENT: EARTH

Your Personal Powers

Ambitious and persistent, your sharp intelligence and enterprising nature are constantly looking for new ways to achieve success. You gain power when you display the generous side of your personality. Being independent and broad-minded, you prefer the freedom to work in your own unique way. Inventive and creative, you empower yourself by initiating new projects rather than staying with the tried and tested methods. When you feel assured and enthusiastic you have the ability to inspire others. You may lose some of your power if you become stubborn, rebellious, or overly serious. Being both imaginative and down to earth, you can be a practical visionary and a good strategist. If life does not meet your high ideals or expectations, avoid surrendering your power to frustration or disappointment by not losing sight of your sense of humor. With your excellent mental potential and natural psychological skills, you have a talent for quickly evaluating situations. When all this is combined with your flair for dealing with people, you possess excellent potential for achieving success.

Your Powers of Attraction in Relationships

People are attracted to your independent style and original approach. Your good communication skills also attract the admiration of others. You usually enjoy friendly mental jesting with friends and partners, using your sharp awareness of human behavior. Although outwardly confident or cool and objective, hidden fears can sometimes undermine your close relationships. Before you know how to handle your partner, you may need to first experience lessons concerning loss or detachment. Nevertheless, when positive, you can be generous, caring, and giving. Being intelligent, you are looking for partners with whom you can share some mental rapport, preferably those who can keep you on your toes. Although you often have unconventional or unusual views, you also seek the security of a long-lasting marriage or traditional relationship.

Your attractive qualities: leadership ability, intelligent, self-confidence, willpower, creative, progressive, broadminded, idealistic, optimistic, practical, daring, sensual, independent, enthusiastic, gregarious, humanitarian, objective, humorous, ambitious, imaginative

Your less attractive qualities: bossy, compulsive, jealous, frustrated, egotistical, rebellious, too proud, overindulgent, antagonistic, hidden insecurities, stubborn, selfish, weak, unstable, extravagant, impatient

Your Venus Power

The planet Venus has a great deal of influence on your powers of attraction. Below are four possible Venus types for women and men. To find your Venus you need to go to page 771, where you will find the Venus table and extra information. The planet Mars also affects your powers of attraction. To find your Mars table and interpretation go to page 761.

WOMEN WITH VENUS IN ARIES: You gain power from your strong individuality, energy, and enthusiasm. Your young-at-heart and spirited approach to relationships adds to your appeal. If you become too impatient or self-absorbed, however, your partnerships are likely to suffer. Nevertheless, you can be creative, sharp, and quick, especially when you are able to share new and exciting projects with your partners. Mischievous, with a love of action, you may even incite them to a playful fight.

MEN WITH VENUS IN ARIES: As you often have the courage and strength to initiate situations, you like to take the lead. With your unconscious desire for conquest you may also have to beware of being competitive with your partners. Nevertheless, you are drawn to a direct and strong-willed partner who can share your love of action and enthusiasm for life. When you are feeling good you can be charming and enthusiastic in romantic situations with an entertaining and spontaneous spirit.

WOMEN WITH VENUS IN TAURUS: Being physically attractive you can make a good impression on the opposite sex. As security and stability in relationships are very important to you, you usually want a partner who is not only attractive but also reliable and a good provider. Being sensual or tactile you also need a lover who is affectionate, but beware that your love does not show signs of possessiveness or jealousy. Your own sense of style and love of beauty imply that you can be attracted to creative people, especially those in art and music.

MEN WITH VENUS IN TAURUS: Attractive and affectionate, in relationships you are often faithful with a conservative outlook. You are drawn to warmhearted partners with whom you can share a familiar routine as well as life's pleasures and comforts. Seeking a partner who is dependable or reassuring, you often put security high on your priority list when looking

for love. Your sociability and friendliness usually make you popular and partners often admire your good sense of values and practical skills.

WOMEN WITH VENUS IN GEMINI: Curious, with a bright and animated approach to life, you are attracted to those who are clever or sophisticated. Your love of variety and desire for knowledge suggest that you need a partner and friends who keep you mentally stimulated. Although witty and a good conversationalist, you may need to keep in touch with your deeper feelings. Nevertheless, intelligent and friendly, you possess a youthful sense of wonder and seek a playmate who can keep you from becoming bored.

MEN WITH VENUS IN GEMINI: Adaptable yet often flirtatious, you enjoy mixing with people who are quick-minded and versatile. Since you can learn a great deal through interacting with others, you are often attracted to intelligent partners who have comprehensive knowledge or good ideas. One of your less attractive qualities is your tendency to become bored or be inconsistent. Having an adaptable partner is, therefore, important to you, and it must be someone who can offer you different options and keep you interested.

WOMEN WITH VENUS IN CANCER: Gentle and tender, you are romantic by nature. You possess a strong need for security and usually you help others feel safe or protected. This preservation is especially centered around the home, which is your haven from life's storm. Although your maternal instincts are strong, avoid making sacrifices for others at your own expense. Nevertheless, affectionate and caring, once committed to a relationship your loyalty and devotion to your partner are very strong.

MEN WITH VENUS IN CANCER: You seek a partner who is sympathetic, caring, and protective. Able to be forgiving and compassionate, you want a secure emotional bond in your close relationships. You are usually drawn to partners who are maternal, unselfish, or demonstrative with their feelings. Although you can sometimes appear to others as shy or impressionable, you have powerful emotions and inner strength.

To read all about your Outer Planets and work out how to use your personalized timetable, go to Section Three, page 789.

To read all about your Outer Planets and work out how to use your personalized timetable, go to Section Three, page 789.

Your Personalized Timetable

JUPITER BENEFICIAL
1939 3/2 – 4/13
1942 8/13 – 10/17
1942 12/8 – until **1943** 6/1
1944 9/15 – 12/27
1945 1/27 – 8/10
1949 1/4 – 3/22
1949 7/21 – 11/14
1951 2/13 – 3/27
1954 7/26 – 9/14
1955 1/21 – 5/9
1956 8/31 – 11/20
1957 3/16 – 7/20
1960 12/19 – until **1961** 2/28
1963 1/26 – 3/10
1966 7/10 – 8/25
1968 8/15 – 10/30
1969 4/27 – 6/18
1972 12/2 – until **1973** 2/10
1974 5/18 – 8/27
1975 1/5 – 2/22
1978 6/23 – 8/7
1980 7/29 – 10/13
1984 3/25 – 6/4
1984 11/13 – until **1985** 1/25
1986 4/24 – 10/13
1986 12/4 – until **1987** 2/4
1990 6/7 – 7/22
1991 11/12 – until **1992** 2/18
1992 7/9 – 9/27
1996 2/26 – 7/17
1996 10/20 – until **1997** 1/9
1998 4/5 – 5/27
1998 9/8 – until **1999** 1/14
2001 10/2 – 12/3
2002 5/19 – 7/6
2003 10/20 – until **2004** 3/27
2004 6/13 – 9/11
2008 2/6 – 12/24
2010 3/18 – 5/2
2010 10/31 – 12/7

SATURN BENEFICIAL
1945 7/4 – 10/8
1945 12/6 – until **1946** 6/17
1949 9/14 – until **1950** 10/22
1951 4/15 – 7/11
1960 1/15 – until **1961** 3/10
1961 7/11 – 12/8
1965 4/25 – 9/3
1966 1/19 – 4/15
1966 10/20 – until **1967** 1/2
1974 8/16 – until **1975** 1/22
1975 5/2 – 7/28
1978 10/28 – until **1979** 2/22
1979 7/20 – until **1980** 8/28
1989 2/21 – 6/26
1989 11/21 – until **1991** 1/13
1995 2/26 – 6/8
1995 8/3 – until **1996** 2/19
2004 6/17 – 9/7
2005 1/11 – 5/27
2008 8/28 – until **2009** 10/4

URANUS BENEFICIAL
1952 7/4 – until **1955** 5/5
1964 9/13 – until **1968** 8/11
1991 1/24 – until **1995** 11/12
2006 5/10 – until **2010** 1/29

NEPTUNE BENEFICIAL
1938 1/1 – until **1942** 6/13
1989 2/2 – until **1997** 1/8

PLUTO BENEFICIAL
1962 10/10 – until **1971** 6/28

JUPITER CHALLENGING
1938 2/6 – 4/23
1938 8/22 – 12/13
1943 8/20 – until **1944** 7/11
1946 11/16 – until **1947** 2/25

1947 3/31 – 10/9
1950 1/20 – 3/31
1955 8/4 – 10/24
1956 2/11 – 6/20
1958 10/31 – until **1959** 1/19
1959 5/19 – 9/18
1962 1/3 – 3/12
1967 7/19 – 10/3
1968 3/24 – 5/21
1970 10/15 – 12/29
1971 7/6 – 8/11
1973 5/5 – 6/25
1973 12/16 – until **1974** 2/24
1979 7/2 – 9/15
1982 9/28 – 12/12
1985 4/2 – 8/11
1985 11/23 – until **1986** 2/8
1990 10/21 – until **1991** 1/9
1991 6/13 – 8/29
1994 1/10 – 4/19
1994 9/9 – 11/26
1997 3/11 – until **1998** 1/23
2002 9/25 – until **2003** 2/17
2003 5/19 – 8/14
2005 12/19 – until **2006** 5/28
2006 8/13 – 11/11
2009 2/22 – until **2010** 1/4

SATURN CHALLENGING
1947 7/26 – until **1948** 8/26
1954 10/27 – until **1955** 12/15
1956 6/26 – 9/2
1962 5/3 – 6/9
1963 1/11 – until **1964** 2/27
1976 9/4 – until **1977** 3/6
1977 5/17 – 10/8
1978 2/16 – 6/29
1983 12/3 – until **1984** 5/31
1984 8/24 – until **1985** 1/31
1985 4/12 – 10/22
1992 2/14 – until **1993** 4/6
1993 8/18 – until **1994** 1/2
2005 11/7 – 12/7
2006 7/8 – until **2007** 8/10

URANUS CHALLENGING
1957 10/13 – until **1962** 6/13
1977 1/7 – until **1981** 9/23
1998 3/13 – until **2003** 1/18

NEPTUNE CHALLENGING
1961 1/15 – until **1969** 10/14
2003 2/11 – until **2011** 1/13

PLUTO CHALLENGING
1945 9/17 – until **1956** 7/13
1987 12/3 – until **1994** 10/29

JUPITER SPECIAL
1940 7/11 – 10/30
1941 2/28 – 5/14
1952 6/17 – 12/28
1953 1/13 – 4/27
1964 5/29 – until **1965** 4/9
1976 5/12 – 7/29
1976 11/11 – until **1977** 3/18
1988 4/26 – 7/6
1988 12/26 – until **1989** 2/13
2000 4/9 – 6/16
2012 3/21 – 5/30

SATURN SPECIAL
1940 6/20 – 11/6
1941 3/11 – 7/31
1941 10/22 – until **1942** 4/15
1970 4/25 – until **1971** 5/26
1999 6/1 – 12/13
2000 2/10 – 7/5
2000 11/24 – until **2001** 3/25

URANUS SPECIAL
1938 3/17 – until **1942** 3/17

107

May 11

SUN: TAURUS • DECANATE: CAPRICORN/SATURN • DEGREE: 19°5–21° TAURUS • MODE: FIXED • ELEMENT: EARTH

Your Personal Powers

Determined, pragmatic, and self-willed, your purposeful nature suggests that although you can be very ambitious you also possess a personable charm and emotional sensitivity. Your sharp mind does not miss a trick, and with your forceful personality you prefer to deal with people directly. As you often enjoy power and have a strong sense of the dramatic, you prefer working independently rather than in subservient positions. Having both good organizational skills and intuitive insight can certainly help you in your climb to the top. You gain power from your ability to keep active and you work hard on achieving your goals. You may, however, lose power if you become too skeptical or selfish. You usually achieve more when you create harmony around you and cooperate with others. You are capable of outstanding achievements when you work with dedication and perseverance on your original and innovative ideas. Inspired by knowledge, you empower yourself when you apply the information at your disposal in a practical way.

Your Powers of Attraction in Relationships

Others admire your natural blend of strong will and imaginative sensitivity. Although you possess an independent spirit, you also realize the advantages of working cooperatively with others. You may, however, have to compromise some of your strong views to achieve accord. Sociable and affectionate, you need the admiration and respect of others. You may sometimes encounter indecision in your relationships or take a long time before making a commitment. Loyal, loving, and reliable, you will often do your utmost for those you love. Although your enthusiasm and charm bring you admirers, your worrisome nature and insecurities can cause you to be bossy or jealous. By avoiding stress and anxiety or power struggles with others, you are able to establish peace and harmony in your relationships.

Your attractive qualities: determined, perceptive, practical, focused, objective, enthusiastic, inspired, spiritual potential, idealistic, intuitive, intelligent, outgoing, inventive, artistic, confident, humanitarian, psychic, energetic, affectionate, sensual

Your less attractive qualities: superiority complex or lack of confidence, aimless, mistrusting, overemotional, overindulgent, easily hurt, irritable, obstinate, mean, highly strung, critical, selfish, lack of clarity, dominating

Your Venus Power

The planet Venus has a great deal of influence on your powers of attraction. Below are four possible Venus types for women and men. To find your Venus you need to go to page 771, where you will find the Venus table and extra information. The planet Mars also affects your powers of attraction. To find your Mars table and interpretation go to page 761.

WOMEN WITH VENUS IN ARIES: With your strong desires and enthusiastic nature, you can be a passionate lover. Although idealistic and single-minded, you need to avoid unnecessary conflicts in your relationships by being more patient and less headstrong. Although at times others can accuse you of being bossy or impulsive, you possess a great deal of warmth and charm. When necessary, you can disarm others by making them feel important.

MEN WITH VENUS IN ARIES: You are usually drawn to courageous or assertive women who possess strong personal magnetism. Therefore you find those who seem to be independent or action-oriented very attractive. Your own eagerness and need for activity suggest that you start relationships with great enthusiasm, especially if they offer you excitement or adventure. The challenge is often to maintain relationships and not get bored too easily.

WOMEN WITH VENUS IN TAURUS: Warm and affectionate, you are naturally tactile with a love of sensual pleasures. With a streak of the conventional you love the simple pleasures of life: good food, close friends, and happy relationships. Having an inner strength, you can express genuine patience and are often a pillar of support for loved ones and friends. Although you possess endurance, be careful not to let this turn into plain stubbornness.

MEN WITH VENUS IN TAURUS: As you yourself may be attractive to the opposite sex, you desire a partner who is sensual and loving or possesses physical beauty. Needing stability, when faced with changes that are out of your control you may become insecure or worried about your future. Faithful and loyal, you usually hang on to relationships but may display controlling tendencies. Your own sense of style and love of beauty imply that you can be attracted to creative people, especially those in art and music.

WOMEN WITH VENUS IN GEMINI: By nature you are young at heart, adaptable, and sociable. Being curious and willing to cooperate make you a good team player. You are usually drawn to articulate people who have charm and flair

or sharp wit. With a need to expand your knowledge you also look for a partner who can challenge or stimulate you intellectually. Although you love to talk with all types of people, you may need to develop your listening skills in order to build better communication in your relationships.

MEN WITH VENUS IN GEMINI: Friendly and sociable, you attract others with your clever and amusing conversation. Drawn to people who can match you in wit and intelligence, you usually prefer to keep relationships light rather than emotionally intense. With your youthful charm and desire for knowledge and new experiences, you usually have many friends and a low boredom threshold.

WOMEN WITH VENUS IN CANCER: Possessing a soft femininity, you have tender and sensitive emotions. Sympathetic and caring, you often mother those in your care by making sure they are comfortable and have plenty to eat. When you feel hurt or insecure in relationships you are likely to cover your feelings by being defensive or appearing tough on the outside while on the inside you are feeling vulnerable. Affectionate and romantic, you make a faithful and devoted partner.

MEN WITH VENUS IN CANCER: Being emotionally receptive, you can be a sensitive lover. With your desire to care for and protect others, you are likely to have strong family connections. Love is often tied in with being attentive to the needs of others, and you may find yourself attracted to individuals who have sympathetic or maternal qualities. Security-conscious, you need a loyal partner who can offer you support and ideally be a good cook and homemaker.

To read all about your Outer Planets and work out how to use your personalized timetable, go to Section Three, page 789.

Your Personalized Timetable

JUPITER BENEFICIAL
1939 3/6 – 4/18
1942 8/17 – 11/2
1942 11/22 – until **1943** 6/6
1944 9/20 – until **1945** 8/15
1949 1/8 – 3/28
1949 7/14 – 11/20
1951 2/17 – 3/31
1954 7/30 – 9/20
1955 1/14 – 5/16
1956 9/4 – 11/27
1957 3/8 – 7/26
1960 12/23 – until **1961** 3/5
1961 9/2 – 10/15
1963 1/31 – 3/14
1966 7/14 – 8/30
1967 3/1 – 4/10
1968 8/19 – 11/4
1969 4/16 – 6/29
1972 12/6 – until **1973** 2/14
1974 5/26 – 8/19
1975 1/10 – 2/26
1978 6/28 – 8/12
1980 8/3 – 10/17
1984 4/5 – 5/23
1984 11/18 – until **1985** 1/29
1986 4/29 – 10/3
1986 12/13 – until **1987** 2/9
1990 6/11 – 7/26
1991 11/19 – until **1992** 2/9
1992 7/15 – 10/1
1996 3/3 – 7/9
1996 10/27 – until **1997** 1/13
1998 4/9 – 6/3
1998 8/31 – until **1999** 1/19
2001 10/14 – 11/21
2002 5/24 – 7/10
2003 10/26 – until **2004** 3/19
2004 6/21 – 9/16
2008 2/11 – 12/28
2010 3/22 – 5/7
2010 10/18 – 12/19

SATURN BENEFICIAL
1945 7/12 – until **1946** 6/25
1949 9/22 – until **1950** 10/31
1951 4/1 – 7/24
1960 1/23 – 8/29
1960 10/3 – until **1961** 3/23
1961 6/28 – 12/17
1965 5/7 – 8/20
1966 1/29 – 4/24
1966 10/5 – until **1967** 1/15
1974 8/25 – until **1975** 1/10
1975 5/13 – 8/4
1978 11/8 – until **1979** 2/9
1979 7/29 – until **1980** 9/5
1989 3/5 – 6/12
1989 11/30 – until **1991** 1/21
1995 3/6 – until **1996** 2/27
2004 6/25 – 9/18
2004 12/30 – until **2005** 6/5
2008 9/5 – until **2009** 10/12
2010 5/14 – 6/16

URANUS BENEFICIAL
1952 7/20 – until **1955** 5/30
1964 9/29 – until **1968** 8/28
1991 2/11 – until **1995** 12/7
2007 3/12 – until **2010** 2/18

NEPTUNE BENEFICIAL
1938 1/1 – until **1942** 8/9
1989 3/11 – until **1997** 12/5

PLUTO BENEFICIAL
1962 11/26 – until **1971** 8/12

JUPITER CHALLENGING
1938 2/10 – 4/29
1938 8/15 – 12/19
1943 8/25 – until **1944** 7/16

1946 11/20 – until **1947** 10/14
1950 1/24 – 4/5
1950 10/7 – 11/9
1955 8/8 – 10/31
1956 2/4 – 6/26
1958 11/4 – until **1959** 1/26
1959 5/11 – 9/24
1962 1/8 – 3/17
1967 7/24 – 10/8
1968 3/14 – 5/31
1970 10/20 – until **1971** 1/3
1971 6/23 – 8/25
1973 5/25 – 6/5
1973 12/20 – until **1974** 2/28
1979 7/7 – 9/19
1982 10/3 – 12/16
1985 4/7 – 8/4
1985 11/29 – until **1986** 2/12
1990 10/30 – 12/31
1991 6/18 – 9/3
1994 1/17 – 4/11
1994 9/14 – 11/30
1997 3/16 – until **1998** 1/27
2002 9/30 – until **2003** 2/10
2003 5/27 – 8/18
2005 12/24 – until **2006** 5/20
2006 8/22 – 11/15
2009 2/26 – until **2010** 1/9

SATURN CHALLENGING
1947 8/2 – until **1948** 9/3
1954 11/4 – until **1955** 12/24
1956 6/9 – 9/18
1963 1/19 – until **1964** 3/7
1977 5/31 – 10/19
1978 2/4 – 7/9
1983 12/12 – until **1984** 5/17
1984 9/6 – until **1985** 2/27
1985 3/15 – 10/31
1992 2/22 – 9/28
1992 11/1 – until **1993** 4/17
1993 8/4 – until **1994** 1/11
2006 7/16 – until **2007** 8/18

URANUS CHALLENGING
1958 8/6 – until **1962** 7/6
1977 11/3 – until **1981** 10/14
1998 4/6 – until **2003** 2/5

NEPTUNE CHALLENGING
1961 12/1 – until **1969** 11/11
2003 3/11 – until **2011** 2/9

PLUTO CHALLENGING
1946 8/27 – until **1957** 6/2
1988 1/3 – until **1995** 9/7

JUPITER SPECIAL
1940 7/18 – 10/23
1941 3/5 – 5/18
1952 6/22 – 12/11
1953 1/30 – 5/1
1964 6/2 – until **1965** 4/13
1976 5/16 – 8/5
1976 11/3 – until **1977** 3/24
1988 4/30 – 7/11
1988 12/16 – until **1989** 2/23
2000 4/13 – 6/21
2012 3/26 – 6/3

SATURN SPECIAL
1940 7/1 – 10/25
1941 3/20 – 8/18
1941 10/3 – until **1942** 4/23
1970 5/2 – until **1971** 6/3
1999 6/9 – 11/27
2000 2/25 – 7/15
2000 11/12 – until **2001** 4/3

URANUS SPECIAL
1938 4/5 – until **1942** 4/9

May 12

Your Personal Powers

Friendly and thoughtful, you can be an understanding, warm, and charming individual. Your ruling planet, Venus, indicates that you possess an aesthetic sense and artistic potential. Usually you appreciate beauty, luxury, and comfort. As a practical and responsible individual, you carry out your commitments efficiently and can be supportive. Your natural people skills help you gain power in business or work situations. Since you are usually willing to work hard to achieve your goals, security and faithfulness are very important to you. Although you can be tactful and cooperative with others, you lose some of your power if you alternate between being caring and being too tough. A need for harmony and tranquillity indicates that your love of nature can usually be a great antidote to stressful situations. A strong desire to express yourself or define your identity may lead you to creative ventures and artistic pursuits. You gain power by combining your affectionate nature and pragmatic perspective with your focused attention on your goals.

Your Powers of Attraction in Relationships

Warm and friendly, you attract others with your kindness and sensitivity. Romantic and charming as well as idealistic, you possess a strong desire to love and be loved. Although a serious and realistic part of your nature can make you responsible and loyal, if carried too far you could become worried or insecure. By developing faith in yourself and ensuring that your partnerships are fair and equal, you can avoid feeling disappointed with others or sorry for yourself. You are usually drawn to creative or youthful individuals or those who can inspire you to be lighthearted and spontaneous. Alternatively, you may be attracted to clever and emotionally sensitive people with a sense of the dramatic. When in love you can be supportive emotionally and materially as a parent, partner, or friend.

Your attractive qualities: hardworking, creative, precise, warm, innovative, responsible, spiritual potential, good concentration, easygoing, spontaneous, dutiful, disciplined, friendly, charming, caring, artistic, love of nature, supportive, humanitarian, affectionate, solid, loving

Your less attractive qualities: self-pity, too sensitive, lack of self-worth, withdrawn, misplaced sympathy, too serious, stubborn, suspicious, depressive, doubting, inflexible, self-indulgent

Your Venus Power

The planet Venus has a great deal of influence on your powers of attraction. Below are four possible Venus types for women and men. To find your Venus you need to go to page 771, where you will find the Venus table and extra information. The planet Mars also affects your powers of attraction. To find your Mars table and interpretation go to page 761.

WOMEN WITH VENUS IN ARIES: Idealistic, passionate, and adventurous, you are direct in your dealings with others. When you are attracted to a person you usually take the initiative and use your people skills to make things happen. In close relationships you are not afraid to confront your other half. This self-assertiveness is positive if differences can be brought into the open through diplomacy and compromise.

MEN WITH VENUS IN ARIES: Usually you are inclined to seek a partner who is active, goal-oriented, or decisive. Not known for your patience, you probably seek relationships from youth. You may find that you are attracted more to women who have a daring or adventurous spirit, but in your close relationships you may encounter rivalry or find that both you and your partner want to lead or be the boss. Although you may act rashly, you possess a great deal of magnetism and are capable of demonstrating your love and affection.

WOMEN WITH VENUS IN TAURUS: Being physically attractive, you can make a good impression on the opposite sex. As security and stability in relationships are very important to you, you want a partner who is not only attractive but also reliable and a good provider. Being sensual or tactile, you also need a lover who is affectionate, but beware that your love does not show signs of possessiveness or jealousy. Your own sense of style and love of beauty imply that you can be attracted to creative people, especially those in art and music.

MEN WITH VENUS IN TAURUS: As well as attracting people with your warm personality, you also possess an innate sense of the value of material possessions. Keeping yourself stylish and having an attractive appearance can also be important to you. You are naturally attracted to practical yet sensual

women who understand your need for comfort, security, and the pleasures and luxuries of life. Naturally affectionate, you enjoy socializing but can be a loyal and loving partner.

WOMEN WITH VENUS IN GEMINI: By nature you are young at heart, adaptable, and sociable. Being curious and willing to cooperate makes you a good team player. You are usually drawn to articulate people who have charm and flair or sharp wit. With a need to expand your knowledge you also look for a partner who can challenge or stimulate you intellectually. Although you love to talk with all types of people, you may need to develop your listening skills in order to build better communication in your relationships.

MEN WITH VENUS IN GEMINI: Informed and curious yet charming and friendly, you seek a partner who shares your interests or enjoys your witty remarks. Although a good communicator, you have an inborn tendency to be lighthearted and less profound about deep emotional commitment. Although you are keen on experiences that bring variety into your life, boredom or scattering your energies in too many directions is probably your biggest handicap in relationships. Nevertheless you are attracted to intelligent partners who can match your lively banter.

WOMEN WITH VENUS IN CANCER: Possessing a soft femininity, you have tender and sensitive emotions. Sympathetic and caring, you often mother those in your care by making sure they are comfortable and have plenty to eat. When you feel hurt or insecure in relationships you are likely to cover your feelings by being defensive or appearing tough on the outside while on the inside you are feeling vulnerable. Affectionate and romantic, you make a faithful and devoted partner.

MEN WITH VENUS IN CANCER: Affectionate with a strong sensitive streak, you can love very deeply. You may find yourself drawn to sympathetic partners who can tune in to your moods and feelings as well as be reassuring and supportive. Family links are especially important to you and the more positive these relationships are the more confident and safe you feel.

To read all about your Outer Planets and work out how to use your personalized timetable, go to Section Three, page 789.

Your Personalized Timetable

JUPITER BENEFICIAL
1939 3/10 – 4/22
1942 8/22 – until 1943 2/17
1943 4/4 – 6/11
1944 9/25 – until 1945 8/20
1949 1/12 – 4/4
1949 7/6 – 11/25
1951 2/21 – 4/4
1954 8/4 – 9/27
1955 1/7 – 5/22
1956 9/9 – 12/4
1957 2/28 – 8/1
1960 12/27 – until 1961 3/10
1961 8/21 – 10/26
1963 2/4 – 3/18
1966 7/18 – 9/4
1967 2/17 – 4/22
1968 8/24 – 11/10
1969 4/7 – 7/8
1972 12/11 – until 1973 2/18
1974 6/3 – 8/10
1975 1/15 – 3/2
1978 7/2 – 8/16
1980 8/8 – 10/22
1984 11/23 – until 1985 2/2
1986 5/4 – 9/25
1986 12/21 – until 1987 2/13
1990 6/16 – 7/31
1991 11/29 – until 1992 1/31
1992 7/20 – 10/6
1996 3/9 – 7/2
1996 11/2 – until 1997 1/17
1998 4/13 – 6/12
1998 8/23 – until 1999 1/24
2002 5/29 – 7/14
2003 10/31 – until 2004 3/11
2004 6/28 – 9/20
2008 2/16 – 8/21
2008 9/25 – until 2009 1/1
2010 3/26 – 5/12
2010 10/10 – 12/27

SATURN BENEFICIAL
1945 7/19 – until 1946 7/2
1949 9/30 – until 1950 4/22
1950 6/7 – 11/10
1951 3/19 – 8/4
1960 2/1 – 8/7
1960 10/24 – until 1961 4/7
1961 6/11 – 12/26
1965 5/21 – 8/6
1966 2/6 – 5/3
1966 9/22 – until 1967 1/26
1974 9/4 – 12/30
1975 5/23 – 8/12
1976 3/29 – 3/30
1978 11/23 – until 1979 1/25
1979 8/7 – until 1980 9/13
1989 3/20 – 5/26
1989 12/9 – until 1991 1/29
1995 3/14 – until 1996 3/6
2004 7/2 – 10/1
2004 12/16 – until 2005 6/14
2008 9/12 – until 2009 10/21
2010 4/22 – 7/7

URANUS BENEFICIAL
1952 8/6 – until 1955 6/18
1964 10/16 – until 1968 9/13
1991 3/6 – until 1995 12/26
2007 3/29 – until 2010 3/7

NEPTUNE BENEFICIAL
1938 1/1 – until 1942 9/7
1990 1/28 – until 1998 1/3

PLUTO BENEFICIAL
1963 10/8 – until 1971 9/9

JUPITER CHALLENGING
1938 2/14 – 5/6
1938 8/7 – 12/24

1943 8/29 – until 1944 7/21
1946 11/25 – until 1947 10/19
1950 1/29 – 4/10
1950 9/24 – 11/22
1955 8/13 – 11/8
1956 1/27 – 7/2
1958 11/9 – until 1959 2/2
1959 5/3 – 9/30
1962 1/12 – 3/21
1967 7/28 – 10/13
1968 3/5 – 6/8
1970 10/24 – until 1971 1/8
1971 6/13 – 9/3
1973 12/25 – until 1974 3/4
1979 7/12 – 9/24
1982 10/8 – 12/21
1985 4/14 – 7/27
1985 12/5 – until 1986 2/16
1990 11/11 – 12/18
1991 6/24 – 9/7
1994 1/27 – 4/2
1994 9/20 – 12/5
1997 3/21 – 9/14
1997 11/1 – until 1998 1/31
2002 10/6 – until 2003 2/2
2003 6/2 – 8/23
2005 12/30 – until 2006 5/12
2006 8/29 – 11/19
2009 3/2 – until 2010 1/13

SATURN CHALLENGING
1947 8/10 – until 1948 9/11
1954 11/13 – until 1956 1/2
1956 5/27 – 9/30
1963 1/27 – until 1964 3/15
1964 10/4 – 11/30
1976 9/21 – until 1977 2/7
1977 6/11 – 10/31
1978 1/22 – 7/18
1983 12/22 – until 1984 5/4
1984 9/17 – until 1985 11/8
1992 3/2 – 9/6
1992 11/23 – until 1993 5/1
1993 7/21 – until 1994 1/20
2006 7/24 – until 2007 8/25

URANUS CHALLENGING
1958 8/22 – until 1962 7/24
1977 11/19 – until 1981 10/31
1999 2/6 – until 2003 11/26

NEPTUNE CHALLENGING
1962 1/4 – until 1970 10/8
2003 4/22 – until 2012 1/6

PLUTO CHALLENGING
1946 10/7 – until 1957 7/19
1988 11/17 – until 1995 10/15

JUPITER SPECIAL
1940 7/25 – 10/15
1941 3/11 – 5/22
1952 6/27 – 12/1
1953 2/9 – 5/5
1964 6/7 – until 1965 4/18
1976 5/20 – 8/13
1976 10/26 – until 1977 3/29
1988 5/4 – 7/16
1988 12/8 – until 1989 3/4
2000 4/17 – 6/25
2012 3/30 – 6/7

SATURN SPECIAL
1940 7/12 – 10/12
1941 3/29 – until 1942 5/1
1970 5/10 – until 1971 6/10
1999 6/18 – 11/14
2000 3/8 – 7/26
2000 10/30 – until 2001 4/12

URANUS SPECIAL
1938 4/23 – until 1942 4/28

May 13

Your Personal Powers

Your personal powers include practicality, warmth, and a friendly manner. As truth is important to you, you prefer to deal with people in an honest and direct way, although you can soften this with kindness. As material security, status, and physical comfort are often high on your agenda, you are usually willing to be responsible and work hard to achieve your goals. Clever, sympathetic, and benevolent, you gain power when you help others with your practical, down-to-earth approach. Although generally patient and easygoing, you lose power if you allow your frustration or disappointment with others to manifest as irritability or discouragement. With your natural sense of harmony, you usually love peace or are particularly attracted to music, art, interior design, or gardening. Another side to your personality, however, is often willing to fight for the rights of others. Intelligent yet unpretentious, you gain power from the expression of your good taste, fine mind, or creative talents.

Your Powers of Attraction in Relationships

People are attracted to the combination of your practicality, graciousness, and friendly charm. With your natural sensuality and sense of style you usually have no trouble attracting admirers. Once committed to a relationship you are loyal and supportive. Prospective partners will have to understand the high level of importance you place on security, home, and family. You are often drawn to those who are success-oriented or who seem to possess outstanding potential. Avoid dwelling on dissatisfaction or being frustrated if partners are not able to live up to your expectations. By being motivated on your own projects, you enhance your confidence and become clearer about your relationships. Charismatic and persuasive, you have the ability to mix with people from all levels.

Your attractive qualities: charming, frank, responsible, clever, intuitive, imaginative, kindly, versatile, hardworking, artistic, gracious, creative, philosophical, ambitious, stylish, broadminded, courteous, humanitarian, dependable, sincere, loyal, expressive, modest, realistic

Your less attractive qualities: anxious, obstinate, critical, indecisive, lack of confidence, rebellious, irritability, unstable, frustration, dissatisfaction, overly serious, stubborn, stuck in rut, feels restricted, overindulgent, demanding

Your Venus Power

The planet Venus has a great deal of influence on your powers of attraction. Below are four possible Venus types for women and men. To find your Venus you need to go to page 771, where you will find the Venus table and extra information. The planet Mars also affects your powers of attraction. To find your Mars table and interpretation go to page 761.

WOMEN WITH VENUS IN ARIES: You gain power from your strong individuality, energy, and enthusiasm. Your young-at-heart and spirited approach to relationships adds to your appeal. If you become too impatient or self-absorbed, however, your partnerships are likely to suffer. Nevertheless, you can be creative, sharp, and quick, especially when you are able to share new and exciting projects with your partners. Mischievous, with a love of action, you may even incite them to a playful fight.

MEN WITH VENUS IN ARIES: As you often have the courage and strength to initiate situations, you like to take the lead. With your unconscious desire for conquest you may also have to beware of being competitive with your partners. Nevertheless, you are drawn to a direct and strong-willed partner who can share your love of action and enthusiasm for life. When you are feeling good you can be charming and enthusiastic in romantic situations with an entertaining and spontaneous spirit.

WOMEN WITH VENUS IN TAURUS: Good-natured and romantic, you have a highly developed sense of touch that particularly responds to massage, hugs, and all things physical. Being friendly, you enjoy socializing and are able to put others at their ease. With your innate sense of beauty and harmony, your natural charm can attract others. Although you can be lavish toward your partner you may have to be careful that you do not overdo things.

MEN WITH VENUS IN TAURUS: Attractive and affectionate, in relationships you are often faithful with a conservative outlook. You are drawn to warmhearted partners with whom you can share a familiar routine as well as life's pleasures and comforts. Seeking a partner who is dependable or reassuring, you often put security high on your priority list when looking

for love. Your sociability and friendliness usually make you popular and partners often admire your good sense of values and practical skills.

WOMEN WITH VENUS IN GEMINI: By nature you are young at heart, adaptable, and sociable. Being curious and willing to cooperate makes you a good team player. You are usually drawn to articulate people who have charm and flair or sharp wit. With a need to expand your knowledge, you also look for a partner who can challenge or stimulate you intellectually. Although you love to talk with all types of people you may need to develop your listening skills in order to build better communication in your relationships.

MEN WITH VENUS IN GEMINI: Charming, amusing, and adaptable, you attract others with your natural communication skills and friendly personality. You have a wonderful childlike quality and love to keep life playful, but a reluctance to contact your deeper feelings may cause you to avoid serious commitment. With your need for variety and intellectual stimulation, you are attracted to clever and amusing partners who have many interesting sides to their personalities.

WOMEN WITH VENUS IN CANCER: Possessing a soft femininity, you have tender and sensitive emotions. Sympathetic and caring, you often mother those in your care by making sure they are comfortable with plenty to eat. When you feel hurt or insecure in relationships, you are likely to cover your feelings by being defensive or appearing tough on the outside while on the inside you are feeling vulnerable. Affectionate and romantic, you make a faithful and devoted partner.

MEN WITH VENUS IN CANCER: You seek a partner who is sympathetic, caring, and protective. Able to be forgiving and compassionate, you want a secure emotional bond in your close relationships. Usually you are drawn to partners who are maternal, unselfish, or demonstrative with their feelings. Although you can sometimes appear to others as impressionable, you have powerful emotions and inner strength.

To read all about your Outer Planets and work out how to use your personalized timetable, go to Section Three, page 789.

Your Personalized Timetable

JUPITER BENEFICIAL
1939 3/14 – 4/27
1942 8/27 – until 1943 2/6
1943 4/15 – 6/16
1944 9/29 – until 1945 8/25
1949 1/16 – 4/12
1949 6/27 – 11/30
1951 2/25 – 4/8
1954 8/8 – 10/4
1954 12/30 – until 1955 5/27
1956 9/13 – 12/13
1957 2/19 – 8/7
1960 12/31 – until 1961 3/15
1961 8/12 – 11/4
1963 2/8 – 3/22
1966 7/23 – 9/9
1967 2/8 – 5/1
1968 8/29 – 11/16
1969 3/30 – 7/15
1972 12/15 – until 1973 2/23
1974 6/14 – 7/30
1975 1/20 – 3/6
1978 7/6 – 8/21
1980 8/12 – 10/27
1984 11/28 – until 1985 2/6
1986 5/10 – 9/17
1986 12/28 – until 1987 2/17
1990 6/20 – 8/4
1991 12/11 – until 1992 1/19
1992 7/26 – 10/10
1996 3/15 – 6/24
1996 11/8 – until 1997 1/21
1998 4/18 – 6/22
1998 8/12 – until 1999 1/29
2002 6/3 – 7/19
2003 11/6 – until 2004 3/3
2004 7/5 – 9/25
2008 2/21 – 8/8
2008 10/8 – until 2009 1/5
2010 3/30 – 5/18
2010 10/2 – until 2011 1/4

SATURN BENEFICIAL
1945 7/27 – until 1946 7/10
1949 10/8 – until 1950 4/3
1950 6/25 – 11/20
1951 3/7 – 8/13
1960 2/10 – 7/22
1960 11/7 – until 1962 1/3
1965 6/12 – 7/14
1966 2/15 – 5/14
1966 9/10 – until 1967 2/5
1974 9/15 – 12/17
1975 6/1 – 8/20
1976 2/23 – 4/29
1979 8/15 – until 1980 9/21
1989 12/18 – until 1991 2/6
1995 3/22 – until 1996 3/14
2004 7/10 – 10/20
2004 11/27 – until 2005 6/22
2008 9/20 – until 2009 10/29
2010 4/7 – 7/21

URANUS BENEFICIAL
1952 8/25 – until 1955 7/5
1964 11/7 – until 1969 6/24
1992 1/6 – until 1996 1/12
2007 4/17 – until 2011 1/2

NEPTUNE BENEFICIAL
1938 1/1 – until 1943 8/2
1990 3/1 – until 1998 11/27

PLUTO BENEFICIAL
1963 11/18 – until 1972 7/30

JUPITER CHALLENGING
1938 2/18 – 5/14
1938 7/30 – 12/29
1943 9/3 – until 1944 7/26
1946 11/29 – until 1947 10/24

1950 2/2 – 4/15
1950 9/15 – 12/1
1955 8/17 – 11/17
1956 1/18 – 7/7
1958 11/13 – until 1959 2/10
1959 4/24 – 10/5
1962 1/16 – 3/25
1967 8/1 – 10/19
1968 2/27 – 6/15
1970 10/29 – until 1971 1/14
1971 6/5 – 9/11
1973 12/30 – until 1974 3/8
1979 7/16 – 9/29
1982 10/12 – 12/26
1985 4/21 – 7/19
1985 12/10 – until 1986 2/20
1991 6/29 – 9/12
1994 2/8 – 3/20
1994 9/25 – 12/9
1997 3/26 – 9/3
1997 11/11 – until 1998 2/4
2002 10/13 – until 2003 1/26
2003 6/8 – 8/27
2006 1/5 – 5/4
2006 9/5 – 11/24
2009 3/7 – until 2010 1/18

SATURN CHALLENGING
1947 8/17 – until 1948 9/19
1949 4/3 – 5/29
1954 11/21 – until 1956 1/12
1956 5/14 – 10/10
1963 2/4 – until 1964 3/24
1964 9/16 – 12/16
1976 10/1 – until 1977 1/26
1977 6/20 – 11/17
1978 1/4 – 7/26
1984 1/1 – 4/21
1984 9/27 – until 1985 11/17
1992 3/11 – 8/23
1992 12/6 – until 1993 5/21
1993 6/30 – until 1994 1/29
2006 7/31 – until 2007 9/2

URANUS CHALLENGING
1958 9/7 – until 1962 8/10
1977 12/5 – until 1981 11/16
1999 2/23 – until 2003 12/30

NEPTUNE CHALLENGING
1962 11/27 – until 1970 11/6
2004 3/4 – until 2012 2/3

PLUTO CHALLENGING
1947 9/11 – until 1958 6/10
1988 12/13 – until 1995 11/10

JUPITER SPECIAL
1940 8/3 – 10/6
1941 3/16 – 5/26
1952 7/2 – 11/22
1953 2/17 – 5/9
1964 6/11 – until 1965 4/22
1976 5/24 – 8/23
1976 10/16 – until 1977 4/3
1988 5/8 – 7/22
1988 11/30 – until 1989 3/11
2000 4/21 – 6/30
2012 4/4 – 6/11

SATURN SPECIAL
1940 7/28 – 9/26
1941 4/7 – until 1942 5/8
1970 5/17 – until 1971 6/18
1972 1/10 – 2/21
1999 6/28 – 11/2
2000 3/18 – 8/10
2000 10/15 – until 2001 4/20

URANUS SPECIAL
1938 5/10 – until 1942 5/15

May 14

SUN: TAURUS • DECANATE: CAPRICORN/SATURN • DEGREE: 22°–23°5 TAURUS • MODE: FIXED • ELEMENT: EARTH

Your Personal Powers

Imaginative yet practical, your personal powers include a shrewd business sense and quick reactions. Your ruling planet, Venus, indicates that you possess an appreciation of beauty, art, and nature as well as a love for the good things in life. Being sociable and engaging, you can uplift others with your youthful charm or work well with the public. Ambitious and intelligent, when you are interested in a subject your quick comprehension indicates that you learn fast and you show a willingness to work hard. As you sometimes enjoy taking a risk, it may be necessary for you to balance your ability to be reliable, security-conscious, and home-loving with your desire for adventure or change. You gain power when you develop your perseverance and concentration. You lose some of your power by being restless or impatient. Nevertheless, resourceful and innovative, you gain confidence and success when you stay detached and apply your intuitive insight to problem solving. Inspired by knowledge, you also empower yourself through education, travel, or manifesting your strong visions.

Your Powers of Attraction in Relationships

You usually like to present a good image and attract people with your sense of style and tactful manner. When you feel confident you can be humorous and amusing, with the ability to keep others entertained. Astute and curious, you are attracted to partners who can keep you mentally interested as well as share your desire for a good time. Although you can be unsettled and freedom-loving, you also possess a strong need for loyalty and a secure relationship. At times this can prove challenging, therefore your relationships fare better when you honestly express your deeper feelings rather than let your repressed emotions cause you frustration. Nevertheless, romantic, sensual, and generous, you may be particularly attracted to smart or creative people with good communication skills.

Your attractive qualities: imaginative, perceptive, intelligent, hardworking, determined, people skills, confident, adventurous, pragmatic, loyal, freedom-loving, romantic, giving, quick instincts, creative, intuitive, sensitive, risk-taking, sensual, visionary, decisive actions

Your less attractive qualities: stubbornness, avoidance, frustrated, overindulgent, oversensitive, worried, extravagant, too cautious or too impulsive, bored, escapist, fear about money, too serious, distracted, insecure, impatient

Your Venus Power

The planet Venus has a great deal of influence on your powers of attraction. Below are four possible Venus types for women and men. To find your Venus you need to go to page 771, where you will find the Venus table and extra information. The planet Mars also affects your powers of attraction. To find your Mars table and interpretation go to page 761.

WOMEN WITH VENUS IN ARIES: Self-reliant and strong, you usually want things your own way. This can present problems if you refuse to compromise with your partners. Your life lessons in the area of love and relationships often involve patience and learning to trust. When you project the full power of your Venus, however, you can radiate a charismatic and captivating energy and make a strong impression on others. Independence is often high on your relationship agenda.

MEN WITH VENUS IN ARIES: Usually you are drawn to courageous or assertive women who possess strong personal magnetism. Therefore you find those who seem to be independent or action-oriented very attractive. Your own eagerness and need for activity suggest that you start relationships with great enthusiasm, especially if they offer you excitement or adventures. The challenge is often to maintain relationships and not get bored too easily.

WOMEN WITH VENUS IN TAURUS: For your ideal relationship you seek a partner who is both financially secure and demonstrative with his affections. With these thoughts in mind you are likely to want a partner who is refined yet pragmatic or someone concerned with safeguarding your future. Your stubborn streak suggests that even when you know you are in the wrong, you are reluctant to give way. Attracted to people with a good sense of style, you can succeed in all kinds of business partnerships, especially those involving the arts, music, and luxury goods.

MEN WITH VENUS IN TAURUS: Attractive and affectionate, in relationships you are often faithful with a conservative outlook. You are drawn to warmhearted partners with whom you can share a familiar routine as well as life's pleasures and comforts. Seeking a partner who is dependable or reassuring, you often put security high on your priority list when looking for love. Your sociability and friendliness usually make you

popular and partners often admire your good sense of values and practical skills.

WOMEN WITH VENUS IN GEMINI: Curious, with a bright and animated approach to life, you are attracted to those who are clever and/or sophisticated. Your love of variety and desire for knowledge suggest that you need a partner and friends who keep you mentally stimulated. Although witty and a good conversationalist, you may need to keep in touch with your deeper feelings. Nevertheless, intelligent and friendly, you possess a youthful sense of wonder and seek a playmate who can keep you from becoming bored.

MEN WITH VENUS IN GEMINI: Friendly and sociable, you attract others with your clever and amusing conversation. Drawn to people who can match you in wit and intelligence, you usually prefer to keep relationships light rather than emotionally intense. With your youthful charm and desire for knowledge and new experiences you usually have many friends and a low boredom threshold.

WOMEN WITH VENUS IN CANCER: Gentle and tender, you are romantic by nature. You possess a strong need for security and usually you help others feel safe or protected. This preservation is especially centered around the home, which is your haven from life's storm. Although your maternal instincts are strong, avoid making sacrifices for others at your own expense. Nevertheless, affectionate and caring, once committed to a relationship, your loyalty and devotion to your partner is very strong.

MEN WITH VENUS IN CANCER: Being emotionally receptive you can be a sensitive lover. With your desire to care for and protect others, you are likely to have strong family connections. Love is often tied in with being attentive to the needs of others and you may find yourself attracted to individuals who have sympathetic or maternal qualities. Security conscious, you need a loyal partner who can offer you support and ideally be a good cook and homemaker.

To read all about your Outer Planets and work out how to use your personalized timetable, go to Section Three, page 789.

Your Personalized Timetable

JUPITER BENEFICIAL
1939 3/18 – 5/1
1942 9/2 – until **1943** 1/28
1943 4/24 – 6/21
1944 10/4 – until **1945** 8/30
1949 1/20 – 4/22
1949 6/17 – 12/5
1951 3/1 – 4/12
1954 8/13 – 10/12
1954 12/22 – until **1955** 6/2
1956 9/18 – 12/24
1957 2/8 – 8/12
1961 1/4 – 3/20
1961 8/4 – 11/11
1963 2/12 – 3/26
1966 7/27 – 9/15
1967 1/31 – 5/9
1968 9/2 – 11/22
1969 3/23 – 7/22
1972 12/19 – until **1973** 2/28
1975 1/25 – 3/10
1978 7/11 – 8/26
1980 8/17 – 11/1
1981 5/9 – 6/15
1984 12/3 – until **1985** 2/10
1986 5/16 – 9/10
1987 1/3 – 2/22
1990 6/25 – 8/8
1992 7/31 – 10/15
1996 3/23 – 6/16
1996 11/13 – until **1997** 1/25
1998 4/23 – 7/11
1998 7/24 – until **1999** 2/3
2002 6/7 – 7/23
2003 11/13 – until **2004** 2/25
2004 7/11 – 9/29
2008 2/26 – 7/29
2008 10/17 – until **2009** 1/9
2010 4/4 – 5/23
2010 9/24 – until **2011** 1/10

SATURN BENEFICIAL
1945 8/4 – until **1946** 3/17
1946 3/22 – 7/17
1949 10/17 – until **1950** 3/21
1950 7/8 – 12/3
1951 2/21 – 8/22
1960 2/20 – 7/9
1960 11/18 – until **1962** 1/12
1966 2/23 – 5/26
1966 8/27 – until **1967** 2/14
1974 9/29 – 12/2
1975 6/9 – 8/28
1976 2/9 – 5/13
1979 8/23 – until **1980** 9/29
1989 12/26 – until **1991** 2/15
1991 9/4 – 11/4
1995 3/30 – until **1996** 3/21
2004 7/17 – until **2005** 6/30
2008 9/28 – until **2009** 5/10
2009 5/24 – 11/8
2010 3/26 – 8/1

URANUS BENEFICIAL
1952 9/18 – until **1955** 7/21
1965 9/3 – until **1969** 7/27
1992 1/22 – until **1996** 11/6
2007 5/11 – until **2011** 1/31

NEPTUNE BENEFICIAL
1938 1/1 – until **1943** 9/2
1991 1/23 – until **1998** 12/29

PLUTO BENEFICIAL
1938 3/18 – 5/4
1964 10/5 – until **1972** 8/30

JUPITER CHALLENGING
1938 2/22 – 5/24
1938 7/20 – until **1939** 1/3

1943 9/7 – until **1944** 7/30
1946 12/4 – until **1947** 10/28
1950 2/6 – 4/20
1950 9/7 – 12/9
1955 8/21 – 11/29
1956 1/5 – 7/13
1958 11/18 – until **1959** 2/21
1959 4/13 – 10/10
1962 1/20 – 3/30
1967 8/6 – 10/25
1968 2/19 – 6/22
1970 11/2 – until **1971** 1/20
1971 5/28 – 9/18
1974 1/3 – 3/12
1979 7/21 – 10/4
1980 4/4 – 5/18
1982 10/17 – 12/30
1985 4/29 – 7/11
1985 12/15 – until **1986** 2/24
1991 7/4 – 9/16
1994 9/30 – 12/13
1997 3/31 – 8/25
1997 11/19 – until **1998** 2/8
2002 10/20 – until **2003** 1/19
2003 6/14 – 8/31
2006 1/12 – 4/26
2006 9/11 – 11/28
2009 3/11 – until **2010** 1/22

SATURN CHALLENGING
1947 8/25 – until **1948** 9/27
1949 3/17 – 6/14
1954 11/29 – until **1955** 6/25
1955 8/12 – until **1956** 1/24
1956 4/30 – 10/20
1963 2/13 – until **1964** 4/2
1964 9/3 – 12/28
1976 10/12 – until **1977** 1/14
1977 6/29 – until **1978** 8/3
1984 1/14 – 4/6
1984 10/6 – until **1985** 11/25
1992 3/21 – 8/9
1992 12/18 – until **1994** 2/6
2006 8/8 – until **2007** 9/10

URANUS CHALLENGING
1958 9/26 – until **1962** 8/25
1977 12/24 – until **1982** 9/8
1999 3/14 – until **2004** 1/20

NEPTUNE CHALLENGING
1962 12/27 – until **1971** 10/1
2004 4/7 – until **2012** 12/27

PLUTO CHALLENGING
1948 8/20 – until **1958** 7/23
1989 1/20 – until **1996** 9/27

JUPITER SPECIAL
1940 8/14 – 9/25
1941 3/21 – 5/30
1952 7/7 – 11/15
1953 2/24 – 5/13
1964 6/16 – until **1965** 4/26
1976 5/28 – 9/7
1976 10/1 – until **1977** 4/8
1988 5/12 – 7/27
1988 11/23 – until **1989** 3/17
2000 4/25 – 7/5
2012 4/8 – 6/16

SATURN SPECIAL
1941 4/14 – until **1942** 5/16
1970 5/25 – until **1971** 6/26
1971 12/23 – until **1972** 3/10
1999 7/9 – 10/21
2000 3/27 – 9/10
2000 9/14 – until **2001** 4/28

URANUS SPECIAL
1938 5/27 – until **1943** 3/9

May 15

SUN: TAURUS • DECANATE: CAPRICORN/SATURN • DEGREE: 23°–24°5 TAURUS • MODE: FIXED • ELEMENT: EARTH

Your Personal Powers

Down to earth and methodical, yet quick to grasp what life has to offer, you possess a pragmatic and steady nature. Your ruling planet, Venus, enhances your charm, sense of style, and sociability. You also possess a love of beauty and luxury. You empower yourself by blending your sensitivity with your common sense. Hardworking and reliable, you seek material security and job satisfaction. Although you can be cautious and practical, your natural business sense implies that you are quick to see opportunities for progress and improvement. As your work is important to you, you gain power when you feel you are doing your job professionally. Although you need routine or a goal to aspire to, you also seek adventure and excitement. If you become bored or stuck in a rut you may become restless or moody. Warm and friendly, however, you like to be straight and sincere with others. Emotionally perceptive with a powerful imagination, you benefit substantially from trusting your intuitive feelings whether in your personal life or in your work.

Your Powers of Attraction in Relationships

Your direct manner and natural charm indicate that you enjoy meeting people and are likely to have many friends. With your powerful emotions and strong willpower, in relationships you can be romantic and magnetic yet determined to get your own way. Sensitive and generous, you can be kind and affectionate with the one you love. Although you are often drawn to forceful individuals, resist being stubborn and avoid emotional power struggles. Even though you enjoy being independent you are willing to work very hard to keep up your responsibilities to home and family. As you possess a strong desire for material security as well as an inner restlessness, you may experience inner tensions in your relationships until you find an outlet for change and adventure in your life.

Your attractive qualities: responsible, sincere, generous, warm, perceptive, sensible, kind, cooperative, strong instincts, high ideals, creative ideas, love of beauty and nature, imaginative, common sense, friendly, supportive, sensitive, sympathetic, organized

Your less attractive qualities: stubborn, restless, moody, irresponsible, overindulgent, self-centered, fearful of change, obstinate, worry, too sensitive, dissatisfied, impatient, pessimist, too serious, materialistic, escapism

Your Venus Power

The planet Venus has a great deal of influence on your powers of attraction. Below are four possible Venus types for women and men. To find your Venus you need to go to page 771, where you will find the Venus table and extra information. The planet Mars also affects your powers of attraction. To find your Mars table and interpretation go to page 761.

WOMEN WITH VENUS IN ARIES: You gain power from your strong individuality, energy, and enthusiasm. Your young-at-heart and spirited approach to relationships adds to your appeal. If you become too impatient or self-absorbed, however, your partnerships are likely to suffer. Nevertheless, you can be creative, sharp, and quick, especially when you are able to share new and exciting projects with your partners. Mischievous, with a love of action, you may even incite them to a playful fight.

MEN WITH VENUS IN ARIES: Usually you are inclined to seek a partner who is active, goal-oriented, or decisive. Not known for your patience, you probably seek relationships from youth. You may find that you are attracted more to women who have a daring or adventurous spirit, but in your close relationships you may encounter rivalry or find that both you and your partner want to lead or be the boss. Although you may act rashly, you possess a great deal of magnetism and are capable of demonstrating your love and affection.

WOMEN WITH VENUS IN TAURUS: Being physically attractive you can make a good impression on the opposite sex. As security and stability in relationships are very important to you, you usually want a partner who is not only attractive but also reliable and a good provider. Being sensual or tactile, you also need a lover who is affectionate, but beware that your love does not show signs of possessiveness or jealousy. Your own sense of style and love of beauty imply that you can be attracted to creative people, especially those in art and music.

MEN WITH VENUS IN TAURUS: Attractive and affectionate, in relationships you are often faithful with a conservative outlook. You are drawn to warmhearted partners with whom you can share a familiar routine as well as life's pleasures and

comforts. Seeking a partner who is dependable or reassuring, you often put security high on your priority list when looking for love. Your sociability and friendliness usually make you popular and partners often admire your good sense of values and practical skills.

WOMEN WITH VENUS IN GEMINI: By nature you are young at heart, adaptable, and sociable. Being curious and willing to cooperate makes you a good team player. You are usually drawn to articulate people who have charm and flair or sharp wit. With a need to expand your knowledge you also look for a partner who can challenge or stimulate you intellectually. Although you love to talk with all types of people, you may need to develop your listening skills in order to build better communication in your relationships.

MEN WITH VENUS IN GEMINI: Informed and curious yet charming and friendly, you seek a partner who shares your interests or enjoys your witty remarks. Although a good communicator, you have an inborn tendency to be lighthearted and less profound about deep emotional commitment. Although you are keen on experiences that bring variety into your life, boredom or scattering your energies in too many directions is probably your biggest handicap in relationships. Nevertheless you are attracted to intelligent partners who can match your lively banter.

WOMEN WITH VENUS IN CANCER: Possessing a soft femininity, you have tender and sensitive emotions. Sympathetic and caring, you often mother those in your care by making sure they are comfortable and have plenty to eat. When you feel hurt or insecure in relationships you are likely to cover your feelings by being defensive or appearing tough on the outside while on the inside you are feeling vulnerable. Affectionate and romantic, you make a faithful and devoted partner.

MEN WITH VENUS IN CANCER: Although you are usually drawn to sensual and physically beautiful individuals, you want a partner who is reliable and loyal. When in love, you enjoy spending money on your partner by buying things of quality that will grow in value or useful things of a practical nature. You also love to socialize and entertain, especially in luxurious surroundings. Often you are attracted to creative people or those with artistic talents.

To read all about your Outer Planets and work out how to use your personalized timetable, go to Section Three, page 789.

Your Personalized Timetable

JUPITER BENEFICIAL
1939 3/22 – 5/6
1939 11/19 – 11/29
1942 9/7 – until 1943 1/20
1943 5/1 – 6/25
1944 10/9 – until 1945 9/3
1949 1/25 – 5/8
1949 6/1 – 12/10
1951 3/5 – 4/16
1954 8/17 – 10/23
1954 12/11 – until 1955 6/7
1956 9/22 – until 1957 8/17
1961 1/8 – 3/26
1961 7/27 – 11/17
1963 2/17 – 3/30
1966 7/31 – 9/20
1967 1/24 – 5/16
1968 9/6 – 11/28
1969 3/15 – 7/28
1972 12/23 – until 1973 3/4
1975 1/30 – 3/14
1978 7/15 – 8/30
1980 8/21 – 11/6
1981 4/26 – 6/28
1984 12/7 – until 1985 2/15
1986 5/22 – 9/2
1987 1/9 – 2/26
1990 6/29 – 8/13
1992 8/5 – 10/19
1996 4/1 – 6/7
1996 11/18 – until 1997 1/29
1998 4/27 – 10/23
1998 12/4 – until 1999 2/8
2002 6/12 – 7/27
2003 11/20 – until 2004 2/17
2004 7/17 – 10/4
2008 3/2 – 7/21
2008 10/25 – until 2009 1/13
2010 4/8 – 5/29
2010 9/17 – until 2011 1/16

SATURN BENEFICIAL
1945 8/12 – until 1946 2/15
1946 4/22 – 7/25
1949 10/26 – until 1950 3/8
1950 7/19 – 12/21
1951 2/2 – 8/31
1960 3/1 – 6/26
1960 11/29 – until 1962 1/20
1966 3/3 – 6/11
1966 8/10 – until 1967 2/22
1975 6/17 – 9/6
1976 1/27 – 5/25
1979 8/31 – until 1980 10/7
1990 1/3 – until 1991 2/24
1991 8/18 – 11/20
1995 4/7 – 10/19
1995 12/24 – until 1996 3/29
2004 7/24 – until 2005 7/8
2008 10/6 – until 2009 4/12
2009 6/20 – 11/18
2010 3/13 – 8/11

URANUS BENEFICIAL
1953 7/14 – until 1956 5/15
1965 9/19 – until 1969 8/17
1992 2/9 – until 1996 12/5
2008 3/13 – until 2011 2/20

NEPTUNE BENEFICIAL
1938 1/1 – until 1944 7/24
1991 2/22 – until 1999 11/18

PLUTO BENEFICIAL
1938 1/22 – 6/25
1964 11/10 – until 1973 7/12

JUPITER CHALLENGING
1938 2/26 – 6/7
1938 7/5 – until 1939 1/8
1943 9/12 – until 1944 8/4

1946 12/8 – until 1947 11/2
1950 2/10 – 4/26
1950 8/30 – 12/15
1955 8/26 – until 1956 7/18
1958 11/22 – until 1959 3/13
1959 3/24 – 10/15
1962 1/24 – 4/4
1967 8/10 – 11/1
1968 2/12 – 6/28
1970 11/6 – until 1971 1/26
1971 5/20 – 9/24
1974 1/7 – 3/16
1979 7/25 – 10/9
1980 3/24 – 5/30
1982 10/22 – until 1983 1/4
1983 7/5 – 8/22
1985 5/10 – 6/30
1985 12/20 – until 1986 2/28
1991 7/8 – 9/21
1994 10/5 – 12/18
1997 4/6 – 8/17
1997 11/26 – until 1998 2/12
2002 10/28 – until 2003 1/10
2003 6/20 – 9/5
2006 1/19 – 4/19
2006 9/16 – 12/2
2009 3/16 – until 2010 1/26

SATURN CHALLENGING
1947 9/2 – until 1948 4/3
1948 4/30 – 10/6
1949 3/4 – 6/26
1954 12/8 – until 1955 6/6
1955 8/30 – until 1956 2/8
1956 4/14 – 10/29
1963 2/21 – until 1964 4/12
1964 8/21 – until 1965 1/7
1976 10/26 – 12/30
1977 7/8 – until 1978 8/11
1984 2/1 – 3/18
1984 10/15 – until 1985 12/3
1992 4/1 – 7/27
1992 12/27 – until 1994 2/14
2006 8/15 – until 2007 9/18
2008 4/16 – 5/19

URANUS CHALLENGING
1958 10/22 – until 1963 6/20
1978 1/18 – until 1982 10/5
1999 4/5 – until 2004 2/7

NEPTUNE CHALLENGING
1963 11/23 – until 1971 11/2
2005 2/26 – Continues

PLUTO CHALLENGING
1948 9/25 – until 1959 6/15
1989 11/28 – until 1996 10/28

JUPITER SPECIAL
1941 3/25 – 6/3
1952 7/13 – 11/8
1953 3/2 – 5/17
1964 6/20 – until 1965 5/1
1976 6/2 – until 1977 4/13
1988 5/16 – 8/3
1988 11/16 – until 1989 3/23
2000 4/30 – 7/9
2001 1/4 – 2/15
2012 4/12 – 6/20

SATURN SPECIAL
1941 4/22 – until 1942 5/23
1970 6/2 – until 1971 1/2
1971 2/2 – until 1971 7/5
1971 12/9 – until 1972 3/22
1999 7/23 – 10/7
2000 4/4 – until 2001 5/6

URANUS SPECIAL
1938 6/14 – until 1943 4/6

May 16

Your Personal Powers

Friendly and creative with an original outlook or ideas, your personal powers include charm and keen intelligence. Your ruling planet, Venus, indicates that you love beauty, harmony, and the good things of life. Intuitive and receptive, you gain power from your natural insight and innate psychological skills. Ambitious with a sharp business sense, you can be determined, focused, and hardworking when you have a goal or a project. Thoughtful, mentally alert, and inventive, you may also have philosophical or humanitarian inclinations. A talent with words and an ability to solve problems imply that you also have creative or technical gifts. Although you are usually confident, you can lose some of your power when you experience times of sudden insecurity. This can especially happen if you worry or become too indecisive. You gain power if you do not become overly serious but are detached and able express the lighter side of your personality. Regardless, your fine mind, innovative approach, and creative abilities have the potential to bring you outstanding success.

Your Powers of Attraction in Relationships

Kind and thoughtful, your amiable charm and ability to make a good impression can attract others. Personable and stylish, with your flair for people you can mix easily in many social circles, although you also need time alone to reflect or for self-analysis. Although you can experience times of inner joy, your major tests in life usually involve your idealistic beliefs and relationships. It is important for you to get the balance right between being romantic and practical. By having faith in yourself and life in general, you can stay open and loving no matter what challenges you encounter. If you withdraw, however, you can appear disinterested and lose your spontaneity. Being independent, freedom is important to you, therefore you need a partner who is supportive yet liberal.

Your attractive qualities: creative, original, practical, leadership, responsible, integrity, intuitive, thoughtful, visionary, sociable, cooperative, insightful, humanitarian, witty, love of beauty, ambitious, kind, business sense, artistic, sensitive, perfectionist, spiritual, versatile

Your less attractive qualities: selfish, worry, indecisive, overconfident or self-doubt, never satisfied, contrary, withdrawn, irresponsible, stingy, obstinate, impatient, scattered, jealous, opinionated, skeptical

Your Venus Power

The planet Venus has a great deal of influence on your powers of attraction. Below are four possible Venus types for women and men. To find your Venus you need to go to page 771, where you will find the Venus table and extra information. The planet Mars also affects your powers of attraction. To find your Mars table and interpretation go to page 761.

WOMEN WITH VENUS IN ARIES: Self-reliant and strong, you usually want things your own way. This can present problems if you refuse to compromise with your partners. Your life lessons in the area of love and relationships often involve patience and learning to trust. When you project the full power of your Venus, however, you can radiate a charismatic and captivating energy and make a strong impression on others. Independence is often high on your relationship agenda.

MEN WITH VENUS IN ARIES: As you often have the courage and strength to initiate situations, you like to take the lead. With your unconscious desire for conquest you may also have to beware of being competitive with your partners. Nevertheless, you are drawn to a direct and strong-willed partner who can share your love of action and enthusiasm for life. When you are feeling good you can be charming and enthusiastic in romantic situations with an entertaining and spontaneous spirit.

WOMEN WITH VENUS IN TAURUS: Warm and affectionate, you are naturally tactile with a love of sensual pleasures. With a streak of the conventional you love the simple pleasures of life: good food, close friends, and happy relationships. Having an inner strength you can express genuine patience and are often a pillar of support for loved ones and friends. Although you possess endurance, be careful not to let this turn into plain stubbornness.

MEN WITH VENUS IN TAURUS: As well as attracting people with your warm personality, you also possess an innate sense of the value of material possessions. Keeping yourself stylish and having an attractive appearance can also be important to you. You are naturally attracted to practical yet sensual women who understand your need for comfort, security, and the pleasures and luxuries of life. Naturally affectionate, you enjoy socializing but can make a loyal and loving partner.

WOMEN WITH VENUS IN GEMINI: In relationships you need intellectual stimulation and usually prefer to keep things light. Certainly not boring, you love to talk and are at your best being witty and entertaining. Although your easygoing approach to relationships is very attractive, guard against losing touch with your emotions. You prefer a partner who can keep up with your fast stream of ideas, and if you have shared interests then so much the better.

MEN WITH VENUS IN GEMINI: Charming, amusing, and adaptable, you attract others with your natural communication skills and friendly personality. You have a wonderful child-like quality and love to keep life playful, but a reluctance to contact your deeper feelings may cause you to avoid serious commitment. With your need for variety and intellectual stimulation, you are attracted to clever and amusing partners who have many interesting sides to their personalities.

WOMEN WITH VENUS IN CANCER: Good-natured and romantic, you have a highly developed sense of touch that particularly responds to massage, hugs, and all things physical. Being friendly, you enjoy socializing and are able to put others at their ease. With your innate sense of beauty and harmony, your natural charm can attract others. Although you can be lavish toward your partner, you may have to be careful that you do not overdo things.

MEN WITH VENUS IN CANCER: You seek a partner who is sympathetic, caring, and protective. Able to be forgiving and compassionate, you want a secure emotional bond in your close relationships. Usually you are drawn to partners who are maternal, unselfish, or demonstrative with their feelings. Although you can sometimes appear to others as shy or impressionable, you have powerful emotions and inner strength.

To read all about your Outer Planets and work out how to use your personalized timetable, go to Section Three, page 789.

Your Personalized Timetable

JUPITER BENEFICIAL
1938 1/1 – until **1939** 5/11
1939 10/31 – 12/19
1942 9/13 – until **1943** 1/13
1943 5/8 – 6/30
1944 10/13 – until **1945** 9/8
1949 1/29 – 12/15
1951 3/9 – 4/21
1954 8/22 – 11/12
1954 11/21 – until **1955** 3/14
1955 3/16 – 6/12
1956 9/27 – until **1957** 8/22
1961 1/13 – 4/2
1961 7/20 – 11/23
1963 2/21 – 4/3
1966 8/5 – 9/26
1967 1/16 – 5/22
1968 9/11 – 12/5
1969 3/8 – 8/3
1972 12/28 – until **1973** 3/9
1973 9/9 – 10/17
1975 2/3 – 3/18
1978 7/19 – 9/4
1979 3/2 – 4/18
1980 8/26 – 11/11
1981 4/16 – 7/8
1984 12/11 – until **1985** 2/19
1986 5/29 – 8/26
1987 1/14 – 3/2
1990 7/3 – 8/17
1992 8/9 – 10/24
1996 4/12 – 5/26
1996 11/23 – until **1997** 2/3
1998 5/2 – 10/12
1998 12/15 – until **1999** 2/12
2002 6/17 – 8/1
2003 11/28 – until **2004** 2/9
2004 7/22 – 10/8
2008 3/8 – 7/13
2008 11/1 – until **2009** 1/18
2010 4/12 – 6/5
2010 9/10 – until **2011** 1/22

SATURN BENEFICIAL
1945 8/20 – until **1946** 1/31
1946 5/6 – 8/1
1949 11/6 – until **1950** 2/24
1950 7/28 – until **1951** 9/8
1960 3/14 – 6/11
1960 12/8 – until **1962** 1/28
1966 3/11 – until **1967** 3/3
1975 6/25 – 9/16
1976 1/15 – 6/4
1979 9/7 – until **1980** 10/15
1990 1/11 – until **1991** 3/5
1991 8/4 – 12/2
1995 4/16 – 10/4
1996 1/7 – 4/6
2004 8/1 – until **2005** 7/15
2008 10/15 – until **2009** 3/28
2009 7/5 – 11/29
2010 2/28 – 8/21

URANUS BENEFICIAL
1953 7/30 – until **1956** 6/7
1965 10/5 – until **1969** 9/3
1992 2/29 – until **1996** 12/25
2008 3/31 – until **2011** 3/10

NEPTUNE BENEFICIAL
1938 1/1 – until **1944** 8/27
1992 1/18 – until **1999** 12/23

PLUTO BENEFICIAL
1938 1/1 – until **1939** 6/9
1965 10/1 – until **1973** 8/20

JUPITER CHALLENGING
1938 3/2 – until **1939** 1/13
1943 9/17 – until **1944** 8/8

JUPITER BENEFICIAL (continued)
1946 12/13 – until **1947** 11/6
1950 2/14 – 5/2
1950 8/23 – 12/21
1955 8/30 – until **1956** 7/23
1958 11/26 – until **1959** 10/20
1962 1/28 – 4/8
1962 10/23 – 11/4
1967 8/15 – 11/8
1968 2/4 – 7/4
1970 11/11 – until **1971** 2/2
1971 5/13 – 9/30
1974 1/12 – 3/21
1979 7/30 – 10/14
1980 3/14 – 6/8
1982 10/26 – until **1983** 1/10
1983 6/24 – 9/2
1985 5/29 – 6/11
1985 12/25 – until **1986** 3/4
1991 7/13 – 9/26
1994 10/10 – 12/23
1997 4/12 – 8/10
1997 12/3 – until **1998** 2/16
2002 11/7 – 12/31
2003 6/25 – 9/9
2006 1/27 – 4/10
2006 9/22 – 12/7
2009 3/20 – until **2010** 1/30

SATURN CHALLENGING
1947 9/10 – until **1948** 3/12
1948 5/23 – 10/15
1949 2/20 – 7/7
1954 12/17 – until **1955** 5/22
1955 9/13 – until **1956** 11/6
1963 3/1 – 9/28
1963 11/13 – until **1964** 4/24
1964 8/8 – until **1965** 1/17
1977 7/16 – until **1978** 8/19
1984 10/23 – until **1985** 12/11
1992 4/13 – 7/13
1993 1/6 – until **1994** 2/22
2006 8/23 – until **2007** 9/26
2008 3/26 – 6/9

URANUS CHALLENGING
1959 8/13 – until **1963** 7/13
1978 11/12 – until **1982** 10/24
2000 2/7 – until **2004** 11/18

NEPTUNE CHALLENGING
1963 12/21 – until **1972** 9/22
2005 3/29 – Continues

PLUTO CHALLENGING
1949 9/1 – until **1959** 7/26
1989 12/25 – until **1997** 8/28

JUPITER SPECIAL
1941 3/30 – 6/7
1952 7/20 – 11/1
1953 3/8 – 5/22
1964 6/25 – 12/20
1965 1/31 – 5/5
1976 6/6 – until **1977** 4/17
1988 5/20 – 8/9
1988 11/9 – until **1989** 3/28
2000 5/4 – 7/14
2000 12/24 – until **2001** 2/26
2012 4/16 – 6/24

SATURN SPECIAL
1941 4/30 – until **1942** 5/31
1970 6/10 – 12/12
1971 2/22 – 7/14
1971 11/27 – until **1972** 4/2
1999 8/12 – 9/16
2000 4/12 – until **2001** 5/14

URANUS SPECIAL
1938 7/7 – until **1943** 4/25

119

May 17

SUN: TAURUS • DECANATE: CAPRICORN/SATURN • DEGREE: 25°–26°5 TAURUS • MODE: FIXED • ELEMENT: EARTH

Your Personal Powers

Practical yet idealistic, your personal charm and friendly manner often counterbalance your tough and disciplined nature. You gain power when you positively combine your determination with your sensitivity, kindness, and foresight. Your ruling planet, Venus, ensures that you can be warm and affectionate with a love of beauty and luxury. Usually ambitious and responsible, you empower yourself when you focus on your goals, especially your long-term plans. Although you can lose power by being stubborn, the combination of your tenacious staying power and intuitive receptivity can help you in your climb to success. As an enthusiastic individual with networking skills, you excel at making contacts. When you are confident about a project you are also good at promoting it or mixing business and pleasure. A need for security and recognition can drive you on, but be careful not to lose power to ungrounded fears about money. Usually resourceful and talented, you are nearly always able to turn situations to your advantage and win success through perseverance.

Your Powers of Attraction in Relationships

You usually attract others through your skill at dealing with people on a personal level. Although you are independent, you also realize the benefits of working cooperatively with others, either in partnerships or in a team. You usually admire strong characters or those of power and influence. With two sides to your nature, in relationships you can either go after a partner with the same determination and drive you use to manifest your goals or, alternatively, be sensitive and detached with a philosophical or accepting attitude. By staying balanced you avoid becoming too dependent on your partner or attracting the wrong type of relationship. Once committed, you are loyal and supportive, generously donating your time and energy to those you love.

Your attractive qualities: idealistic, thoughtful, specialist, good strategist, business sense, attracts money, social skills, individual thinker, resolute, fun-loving, disciplined, precise, technical or scientific, loves beauty, determined, focused, spiritual potential, kind, caring

Your less attractive qualities: materialistic, tough, detached, impatient, lonely, stubborn, too serious, moody, overindulgent, skeptical, insensitive, suspicious, critical, depressive, isolated, anxious

Your Venus Power

The planet Venus has a great deal of influence on your powers of attraction. Below are four possible Venus types for women and men. To find your Venus you need to go to page 771, where you will find the Venus table and extra information. The planet Mars also affects your powers of attraction. To find your Mars table and interpretation go to page 761.

WOMEN WITH VENUS IN ARIES: Idealistic, passionate, and adventurous, you are direct in your dealings with others. When you are attracted to a person you usually take the initiative and use your people skills to make things happen. In close relationships you are not afraid to confront your other half. This self-assertiveness is positive if differences can be brought into the open through diplomacy and compromise.

MEN WITH VENUS IN ARIES: You are drawn to strong, independent women who can stand up to you. Although you can enthusiastically follow the object of your desire, you may lose power if you allow your forceful emotions to become too dominant. Warm and passionate, you have a side to your nature that longs for new adventures. Romantic and chivalrous, you really enjoy the excitement of the initial chase, but unless you keep the enthusiasm alive and avoid falling into a rut you may become easily bored.

WOMEN WITH VENUS IN TAURUS: Being physically attractive you can make a good impression on the opposite sex. As security and stability in relationships are very important to you, you usually want a partner who is not only attractive but also reliable and a good provider. Being sensual or tactile, you also need a lover who is affectionate, but beware that your love does not show signs of possessiveness or jealousy. Your own sense of style and love of beauty imply that you are attracted to creative people, especially those in art and music.

MEN WITH VENUS IN TAURUS: Attractive and affectionate, in relationships you are often faithful with a conservative outlook. You are drawn to warmhearted partners with whom you can share a familiar routine as well as life's pleasures and comforts. Seeking a partner who is dependable or reassuring, you often put security high on your priority list when looking for love. Your sociability and friendliness usually make you

popular, and partners often admire your good sense of values and practical skills.

WOMEN WITH VENUS IN GEMINI: Curious, with a bright and animated approach to life, you are attracted to those who are clever and/or sophisticated. Your love of variety and desire for knowledge suggest that you need a partner and friends who keep you mentally stimulated. Although witty and a good conversationalist, you may need to keep in touch with your deeper feelings. Nevertheless, intelligent and friendly, you possess a youthful sense of wonder and seek a playmate who can keep you from becoming bored.

MEN WITH VENUS IN GEMINI: Charming, amusing, and adaptable, you attract others with your natural communication skills and friendly personality. You have a wonderful childlike quality and love to keep life playful, but a reluctance to contact your deeper feelings may cause you to avoid serious commitment. With your need for variety and intellectual stimulation, you are attracted to clever and amusing partners who have many interesting sides to their personalities.

WOMEN WITH VENUS IN CANCER: With your intuitive abilities and sympathetic nature, you are usually supportive of those you love. Impressionable and empathetic, your receptivity allows you to quickly pick up on the moods of people, and you are especially aware of the emotional changes in your close partner. As you often display true maternal tendencies toward those you know, you want a partner who is considerate and sensitive.

MEN WITH VENUS IN CANCER: As well as attracting people with your warm personality, you possess an innate sense of the value of material possessions. Keeping yourself stylish and having an attractive appearance can also be important to you. You are naturally attracted to practical yet sensual women who understand your need for comfort, security, and the pleasures and luxuries of life. Naturally affectionate, you enjoy socializing but can be a loyal and loving partner.

To read all about your Outer Planets and work out how to use your personalized timetable, go to Section Three, page 789.

Your Personalized Timetable

JUPITER BENEFICIAL
1939 3/30 – 5/16
1939 10/21 – 12/29
1942 9/19 – until 1943 1/6
1943 5/14 – 7/4
1944 10/18 – until 1945 4/30
1945 5/29 – 9/12
1949 2/2 – 12/19
1951 3/13 – 4/25
1954 8/27 – until 1955 2/20
1955 4/10 – 6/17
1956 10/1 – until 1957 8/27
1961 1/17 – 4/8
1961 7/12 – 11/29
1963 2/25 – 4/7
1966 8/9 – 10/3
1967 1/9 – 5/28
1968 9/15 – 12/13
1969 2/27 – 8/9
1973 1/1 – 3/14
1973 8/28 – 10/29
1975 2/7 – 3/22
1978 7/24 – 9/9
1979 2/19 – 4/29
1980 8/31 – 11/17
1981 4/8 – 7/16
1984 12/16 – until 1985 2/23
1986 6/7 – 8/17
1987 1/19 – 3/6
1990 7/7 – 8/22
1992 8/14 – 10/29
1996 11/28 – until 1997 2/7
1998 5/8 – 10/3
1998 12/24 – until 1999 2/16
2002 6/21 – 8/5
2003 12/9 – until 2004 1/29
2004 7/28 – 10/13
2008 3/14 – 7/6
2008 11/7 – until 2009 1/22
2010 4/17 – 6/13
2010 9/2 – until 2011 1/27

SATURN BENEFICIAL
1945 8/29 – until 1946 1/19
1946 5/17 – 8/9
1949 11/18 – until 1950 2/11
1950 8/6 – until 1951 9/16
1960 4/1 – 5/24
1960 12/17 – until 1962 2/5
1966 3/18 – until 1967 3/10
1975 7/2 – 9/27
1976 1/3 – 6/13
1979 9/15 – until 1980 10/23
1981 5/3 – 7/7
1990 1/20 – until 1991 3/15
1991 7/22 – 12/12
1995 4/25 – 9/20
1996 1/19 – 4/14
1996 11/17 – 12/19
2004 8/9 – until 2005 2/27
2005 4/13 – 7/23
2008 10/24 – until 2009 3/15
2009 7/16 – 12/14
2010 2/12 – 8/29

URANUS BENEFICIAL
1953 8/16 – until 1956 6/26
1965 10/22 – until 1969 9/19
1992 4/2 – until 1997 1/11
2008 4/18 – until 2012 1/1

NEPTUNE BENEFICIAL
1938 1/1 – until 1945 7/12
1992 2/15 – until 2000 10/30

PLUTO BENEFICIAL
1938 1/1 – until 1940 5/16
1965 11/3 – until 1973 9/16

JUPITER CHALLENGING
1938 3/7 – until 1939 1/17
1943 9/22 – until 1944 3/21

1944 5/6 – 8/13
1946 12/18 – until 1947 7/6
1947 7/25 – 11/11
1950 2/18 – 5/9
1950 8/15 – 12/27
1955 9/4 – until 1956 7/27
1958 12/1 – until 1959 10/25
1962 2/1 – 4/13
1962 10/4 – 11/23
1967 8/19 – 11/16
1968 1/27 – 7/9
1970 11/15 – until 1971 2/9
1971 5/4 – 10/6
1974 1/16 – 3/25
1979 8/3 – 10/20
1980 3/6 – 6/16
1982 10/30 – until 1983 1/15
1983 6/14 – 9/11
1985 12/30 – until 1986 3/8
1991 7/18 – 9/30
1994 10/14 – 12/27
1997 4/18 – 8/2
1997 12/9 – until 1998 2/20
2002 11/22 – 12/16
2003 6/30 – 9/14
2006 2/7 – 3/30
2006 9/27 – 12/11
2009 3/25 – 9/22
2009 11/2 – until 2010 2/3

SATURN CHALLENGING
1947 9/18 – until 1948 2/26
1948 6/5 – 10/26
1949 2/8 – 7/16
1954 12/26 – until 1955 5/9
1955 9/24 – until 1956 11/15
1963 3/10 – 9/9
1963 12/1 – until 1964 5/8
1964 7/24 – until 1965 1/26
1977 7/24 – until 1978 8/26
1984 11/1 – until 1985 12/20
1986 7/6 – 9/7
1992 4/30 – 6/25
1993 1/14 – until 1994 3/2
2006 8/31 – until 2007 10/4
2008 3/12 – 6/23

URANUS CHALLENGING
1959 8/29 – until 1963 7/31
1978 11/27 – until 1982 11/10
2000 2/24 – until 2004 12/30

NEPTUNE CHALLENGING
1964 11/17 – until 1972 10/27
2006 2/21 – Continues

PLUTO CHALLENGING
1949 10/12 – until 1960 6/17
1990 11/14 – until 1997 10/14

JUPITER SPECIAL
1941 4/3 – 6/12
1952 7/27 – 10/24
1953 3/13 – 5/26
1964 6/30 – 12/9
1965 2/11 – 5/9
1976 6/10 – until 1977 4/22
1988 5/24 – 8/17
1988 11/1 – until 1989 4/3
2000 5/8 – 7/20
2000 12/15 – until 2001 3/7
2012 4/21 – 6/29

SATURN SPECIAL
1941 5/7 – until 1942 6/7
1970 6/19 – 11/28
1971 3/7 – 7/25
1971 11/15 – until 1972 4/11
2000 4/20 – until 2001 5/21

URANUS SPECIAL
1939 5/9 – until 1943 5/13

May 18

SUN: TAURUS • DECANATE: CAPRICORN/ SATURN • DEGREE: 26°–27°5 TAURUS • MODE: FIXED • ELEMENT: EARTH

Your Personal Powers

Practical and hardworking, your personal powers include the willpower and endurance for outstanding accomplishment in the material world. As your ruling planet is Venus, you can also be kind and affectionate with a love for beauty and luxury. You gain power from your strong individuality and ability to initiate new projects, often placing you in positions of leadership. Ambitious and determined with natural business acumen and evaluation skills, you are usually willing to work hard to achieve your goals. You may, however, lose power if you become impatient with those around you or use your forceful will to dominate others. You gain power from making the best out of opportunities, utilizing your natural negotiation skills and your friendly approach to make useful contacts. Although down to earth, your idealism can inspire you to help others whether through practical support or compassionate causes. Being an active person you always like to keep busy, but you also know how to relax and enjoy the finer things of life.

Your Powers of Attraction in Relationships

You attract others with your open and direct approach, friendly manner, and strong will. Although you are independent and usually prefer to lead, you realize the advantages of working cooperatively with others and therefore can be diplomatic when necessary. With a powerful need to give and receive love, your personal relationships can be especially important to you, but your partners may experience your restless spirit and changing moods. You can be loyal and extremely generous, but on some occasions may be demanding or stubborn. Although your practical side still weighs up the pros and cons of every relationship, you are usually idealistic about love. You may attract partners who are distant from you or meet someone through travel. Developing patience and your communication skills can help you establish loving unions.

Your attractive qualities: leadership skills, honest, energetic, idealistic, hardworking, people skills, decisive, friendly, business sense, creative, visionary, determined, humanitarian, precise, spiritual potential, organizational skills, kind, progressive, assertive, intuitive, daring

Your less attractive qualities: too material, selfish, bossy, impatient, moody, overindulgent, disorderly, restless, deceitful, obstinate, uncommunicative, overemotional, lazy, unfeeling

Your Venus Power

The planet Venus has a great deal of influence on your powers of attraction. Below are four possible Venus types for women and men. To find your Venus you need to go to page 771, where you will find the Venus table and extra information. The planet Mars also affects your powers of attraction. To find your Mars table and interpretation go to page 761.

WOMEN WITH VENUS IN ARIES: With your strong desires and enthusiastic nature you can be a passionate lover. Although idealistic and single-minded, you need to avoid unnecessary conflicts in your relationships by being more patient and less headstrong. Although at times others can accuse you of being bossy or impulsive, you possess a great deal of warmth and charm. When necessary, you can disarm others by making them feel important.

MEN WITH VENUS IN ARIES: You are drawn to strong, independent women who can stand up to you. Although you can enthusiastically follow the object of your desire, you may lose power if you allow your forceful emotions to become too dominant. Warm and passionate, you have a side to your nature that longs for new adventures. Romantic and chivalrous, you really enjoy the excitement of the initial chase, but unless you keep the enthusiasm alive and avoid falling into a rut you may become easily bored.

WOMEN WITH VENUS IN TAURUS: Good-natured and romantic, you have a highly developed sense of touch that particularly responds to massage, hugs, and all things physical. Being friendly, you enjoy socializing and are able to put others at their ease. With your innate sense of beauty and harmony, your natural charm can attract others. Although you can be lavish toward your partner, you may have to be careful that you do not overdo things.

MEN WITH VENUS IN TAURUS: As you yourself may be attractive to the opposite sex, you desire a partner who is sensual and loving or possesses physical beauty. Needing stability, when faced with changes that are out of your control you may become insecure or worried about your future. Faithful and/or loyal, you usually hang on to relationships but may

display controlling tendencies. Your own sense of style and love of beauty imply that you can be attracted to creative people, especially those in art and music.

WOMEN WITH VENUS IN GEMINI: By nature you are young at heart, adaptable, and sociable. Being curious and willing to cooperate makes you a good team player. Usually you are drawn to articulate people who have charm and flair or sharp wit. With a need to expand your knowledge, you also look for a partner who can challenge or stimulate you intellectually. Although you love to talk with all types of people, you may need to develop your listening skills in order to build better communication in your relationships.

MEN WITH VENUS IN GEMINI: Informed and curious yet charming and friendly, you seek a partner who shares your interests or enjoys your witty remarks. Although a good communicator, you have an inborn tendency to be lighthearted and less profound about deep emotional commitment. Although you are keen on experiences that bring variety into your life, boredom or scattering your energies in too many directions is probably your biggest handicap in relationships. Nevertheless you are attracted to intelligent partners who can match your lively banter.

WOMEN WITH VENUS IN CANCER: Good-natured and romantic, you have a highly developed sense of touch that particularly responds to massage, hugs, and all things physical. Being friendly, you enjoy socializing and are able to put others at their ease. With your natural sense of beauty and harmony, your natural charm can attract others. Although you can be lavish toward your partner you may have to be careful that you do not overdo things.

MEN WITH VENUS IN CANCER: Being emotionally receptive you can make a sensitive lover. With your desire to care for and protect others you are likely to have strong family connections. Love is often tied in with being attentive to the needs of others and you may find yourself attracted to individuals who have sympathetic or maternal qualities. Security-conscious, you need a loyal partner who can offer you support and ideally be a good cook and homemaker.

To read all about your Outer Planets and work out how to use your personalized timetable, go to Section Three, page 789.

Your Personalized Timetable

JUPITER BENEFICIAL
1939 4/3 – 5/21
1939 10/12 – until **1940** 1/6
1942 9/26 – 12/30
1943 5/20 – 7/9
1944 10/23 – until **1945** 4/15
1945 6/13 – 9/17
1949 2/7 – 12/24
1951 3/17 – 4/29
1954 9/1 – until **1955** 2/9
1955 4/21 – 6/22
1956 10/6 – until **1957** 9/1
1961 1/21 – 4/16
1961 7/4 – 12/4
1963 3/1 – 4/11
1966 8/14 – 10/10
1967 1/1 – 6/3
1968 9/20 – 12/23
1969 2/17 – 8/14
1973 1/5 – 3/19
1973 8/18 – 11/7
1975 2/12 – 3/26
1978 7/28 – 9/15
1979 2/10 – 5/8
1980 9/4 – 11/23
1981 3/31 – 7/23
1984 12/20 – until **1985** 2/28
1986 6/17 – 8/7
1987 1/24 – 3/10
1990 7/12 – 8/27
1992 8/19 – 11/3
1993 5/25 – 6/6
1996 12/3 – until **1997** 2/11
1998 5/13 – 9/25
1998 12/31 – until **1999** 2/21
2002 6/25 – 8/10
2003 12/28 – until **2004** 1/10
2004 8/2 – 10/17
2008 3/21 – 6/28
2008 11/13 – until **2009** 1/26
2010 4/21 – 6/21
2010 8/24 – until **2011** 2/1

SATURN BENEFICIAL
1945 9/7 – until **1946** 1/7
1946 5/27 – 8/17
1949 12/4 – until **1950** 1/25
1950 8/15 – until **1951** 9/24
1960 12/25 – until **1962** 2/13
1962 10/1 – 10/17
1966 3/26 – until **1967** 3/18
1975 7/10 – 10/10
1975 12/20 – until **1976** 6/21
1979 9/23 – until **1980** 10/31
1981 4/17 – 7/22
1990 1/28 – 9/11
1990 10/4 – until **1991** 3/27
1991 7/8 – 12/22
1995 5/6 – 9/8
1996 1/29 – 4/23
1996 10/26 – until **1997** 1/9
2004 8/17 – until **2005** 2/9
2005 5/1 – 7/30
2008 11/3 – until **2009** 3/3
2009 7/26 – until **2010** 9/7

URANUS BENEFICIAL
1953 9/4 – until **1956** 7/12
1965 11/13 – until **1970** 7/1
1993 1/20 – until **1997** 10/28
2008 5/12 – until **2012** 2/1

NEPTUNE BENEFICIAL
1938 1/1 – until **1945** 8/22
1992 3/29 – until **2000** 12/16

PLUTO BENEFICIAL
1938 1/1 – until **1940** 7/1
1966 9/27 – until **1974** 8/7

JUPITER CHALLENGING
1938 3/11 – until **1939** 1/22

JUPITER BENEFICIAL *(continued)*
1943 9/27 – until **1944** 3/9
1944 5/17 – 8/17
1946 12/23 – until **1947** 6/18
1947 8/12 – 11/15
1950 2/22 – 5/16
1950 8/7 – until **1951** 1/1
1955 9/9 – until **1956** 8/1
1958 12/6 – until **1959** 10/30
1962 2/5 – 4/18
1962 9/24 – 12/3
1967 8/23 – 11/27
1968 1/16 – 7/14
1970 11/19 – until **1971** 2/18
1971 4/25 – 10/11
1974 1/20 – 3/29
1979 8/7 – 10/26
1980 2/28 – 6/22
1982 11/4 – until **1983** 1/21
1983 6/6 – 9/18
1986 1/3 – 3/12
1991 7/22 – 10/5
1992 4/20 – 5/11
1994 10/19 – until **1995** 1/1
1997 4/25 – 7/26
1997 12/14 – until **1998** 2/24
2003 7/5 – 9/18
2006 2/28 – 3/9
2006 10/2 – 12/16
2009 3/30 – 9/11
2009 11/13 – until **2010** 2/8

SATURN CHALLENGING
1947 9/27 – until **1948** 2/14
1948 6/17 – 11/7
1949 1/25 – 7/25
1955 1/6 – 4/26
1955 10/4 – until **1956** 11/23
1963 3/19 – 8/25
1963 12/14 – until **1964** 5/30
1964 7/1 – until **1965** 2/3
1977 7/31 – until **1978** 9/3
1984 11/9 – until **1985** 12/28
1986 6/19 – 9/23
1993 1/23 – until **1994** 3/10
2006 9/8 – until **2007** 3/23
2007 5/17 – 10/13
2008 2/28 – 7/4

URANUS CHALLENGING
1959 9/14 – until **1963** 8/16
1978 12/14 – until **1982** 11/26
2000 3/13 – until **2005** 1/21

NEPTUNE CHALLENGING
1964 12/15 – until **1973** 9/9
2006 3/21 – Continues

PLUTO CHALLENGING
1950 9/13 – until **1960** 7/27
1990 12/8 – until **1997** 11/11

JUPITER SPECIAL
1941 4/8 – 6/16
1952 8/3 – 10/16
1953 3/19 – 5/30
1964 7/5 – 11/30
1965 2/20 – 5/13
1976 6/15 – until **1977** 4/26
1988 5/29 – 8/27
1988 10/22 – until **1989** 4/8
2000 5/12 – 7/25
2000 12/8 – until **2001** 3/14
2012 4/25 – 7/3

SATURN SPECIAL
1941 5/15 – until **1942** 6/15
1970 6/28 – 11/15
1971 3/18 – 8/5
1971 11/3 – until **1972** 4/20
2000 4/28 – until **2001** 5/29

URANUS SPECIAL
1939 5/26 – until **1943** 5/29

123

May 19

SUN: TAURUS · DECANATE: CAPRICORN/SATURN · DEGREE: 27°–28°5 TAURUS · MODE: FIXED · ELEMENT: EARTH

Your Personal Powers

Your personal powers include keen intelligence and a sense of the dramatic. Your ruling planet, Venus, indicates that you possess good style, social skills, and a love of beauty or luxury. Naturally gifted, you strike others as confident with a strong presence. Although a natural leader, you are aware of the importance of teamwork or group efforts. Possessing practical common sense, you usually work hard and take your responsibilities seriously. You may lose power, however, if you use your natural authority to become arrogant or overbearing. Although prestige, material security, and respect are important to you, an unconventional side to your personality and a natural interest in people may draw you to new and innovative ideas or humanitarian causes. Honest and perceptive, you empower yourself by using your persuasive charm, direct communication skills, and standing up for your ideals. Intuitive, strong, and influential, you can obtain more satisfaction when being of service to others. Although sometimes obstinate, your ability to persist and endure can help you make the most of your outstanding talents.

Your Powers of Attraction in Relationships

Others are attracted to your strong individuality and clever ideas. Your understanding of human nature also makes you witty and popular with others. You usually prefer to be in a long-term relationship and are attracted to loyal and honest individuals with common sense. Since you enjoy using your mind for playful competitiveness, you are also attracted to those who can keep up with you mentally or those who do not find your intelligence threatening. With your strong need for material security, avoid too fixed a routine. You may experience a pull between your need for a relationship and your desire for freedom. If you pick a partner who gives you a fairly free reign, you can achieve a harmonious balance. Once committed, you can be protective of those you love.

Your attractive qualities: intelligent, self-assured, dynamic, intuitive, progressive, optimistic, competitive, independent, artistic, sociable, hardworking, creative ideas, leader, honest, disciplined, strong opinions, humanitarian, enthusiastic, ambitious, tenacious

Your less attractive qualities: overbearing, too proud, egotistical, worry, fear of rejection, unstable, materialistic, stubborn, impatient, unsympathetic, overindulgent, arrogant, restless, inner tensions

Your Venus Power

The planet Venus has a great deal of influence on your powers of attraction. Below are four possible Venus types for women and men. To find your Venus you need to go to page 771, where you will find the Venus table and extra information. The planet Mars also affects your powers of attraction. To find your Mars table and interpretation go to page 761.

WOMEN WITH VENUS IN ARIES: You gain power from your strong individuality, energy, and enthusiasm. Your young-at-heart and spirited approach to relationships adds to your appeal. If you become too impatient or self-absorbed, however, your partnerships are likely to suffer. Nevertheless, you can be creative, sharp, and quick, especially when you are able to share new and exciting projects with your partners. Mischievous, with a love of action, you may even incite them to a playful fight.

MEN WITH VENUS IN ARIES: As you often have the courage and strength to initiate situations, you like to take the lead and let others follow. With your unconscious desire for conquest you may also have to beware of being competitive with your partners. Nevertheless, you are drawn to direct and strong-willed women who can share your love of action and enthusiasm for life. When you are feeling good you can be charming and enthusiastic in romantic situations with an entertaining and spontaneous spirit.

WOMEN WITH VENUS IN TAURUS: Warm and affectionate, you are naturally tactile with a love of sensual pleasures. With a streak of the conventional, you love the simple pleasures of life: good food, close friends, and happy relationships. Having an inner strength you can express genuine patience and are often a pillar of support for loved ones and friends. Although you possess endurance be careful not to let this turn into plain stubbornness.

MEN WITH VENUS IN TAURUS: As well as attracting people with your warm personality, you possess an innate sense of the value of material possessions. Keeping yourself stylish and having an attractive appearance can also be important to you. You are naturally attracted to practical yet sensual women who understand your need for comfort, security, and the plea-

sures and luxuries of life. Naturally affectionate, you enjoy socializing but can make a loyal and loving partner.

WOMEN WITH VENUS IN GEMINI: In relationships you need intellectual stimulation and usually prefer to keep things light. Certainly not boring, you love to talk and are at your best being witty and entertaining. Although your easygoing approach to relationships is very attractive, guard against losing touch with your emotions. You prefer a partner who can keep up with your fast stream of ideas, and if you have shared interests then so much the better.

MEN WITH VENUS IN GEMINI: Informed and curious yet charming and friendly, you seek a partner who shares your interests or enjoys your witty remarks. Although a good communicator, you have an inborn tendency to be lighthearted and less profound about deep emotional commitment. Although you are keen on experiences that bring variety into your life, boredom or scattering your energies in too many directions is probably your biggest handicap in relationships. Nevertheless you are attracted to intelligent partners who can match your lively banter.

WOMEN WITH VENUS IN CANCER: Possessing a soft femininity, you have tender and sensitive emotions. Sympathetic and caring, you often mother those in your care by making sure that they are comfortable and have plenty to eat. When you feel hurt or insecure in relationships, you are likely to cover your feelings by being defensive or appearing tough on the outside while on the inside you are feeling vulnerable. Affectionate and romantic, you make a faithful and devoted partner.

MEN WITH VENUS IN CANCER: Attractive and affectionate, in relationships you are often family oriented with a conservative outlook. You are drawn to warmhearted partners with whom you can share a familiar routine as well as life's pleasures and comforts. Seeking a partner who is dependable or reassuring, you often put security high on your priority list when looking for love. Your sociability and friendliness usually makes you popular and partners often admire your good sense of values and practical skills.

To read all about your Outer Planets and work out how to use your personalized timetable, go to Section Three, page 789.

Your Personalized Timetable

JUPITER BENEFICIAL
1939 4/8 – 5/26
1939 10/5 – until 1940 1/13
1942 10/4 – 12/22
1943 5/25 – 7/13
1944 10/29 – until 1945 4/5
1945 6/23 – 9/21
1949 2/11 – 12/28
1951 3/21 – 5/4
1954 9/7 – until 1955 2/1
1955 4/29 – 6/26
1956 10/10 – until 1957 9/5
1961 1/25 – 4/26
1961 6/24 – 12/9
1963 3/5 – 4/15
1966 8/18 – 10/19
1966 12/23 – until 1967 6/8
1968 9/24 – until 1969 1/7
1969 2/2 – 8/19
1973 1/9 – 3/25
1973 8/10 – 11/15
1975 2/16 – 3/30
1978 8/1 – 9/20
1979 2/3 – 5/16
1980 9/8 – 11/29
1981 3/23 – 7/29
1984 12/24 – until 1985 3/4
1986 7/6 – 7/18
1987 1/29 – 3/14
1990 7/16 – 8/31
1992 8/23 – 11/8
1993 5/5 – 6/27
1996 12/7 – until 1997 2/15
1998 5/19 – 9/18
1999 1/6 – 2/25
2002 6/30 – 8/14
2004 8/7 – 10/22
2008 3/29 – 6/20
2008 11/18 – until 2009 1/30
2010 4/26 – 7/4
2010 8/11 – until 2011 2/6

SATURN BENEFICIAL
1945 9/18 – 12/26
1946 6/5 – 8/25
1947 3/4 – 5/4
1950 8/23 – until 1951 10/1
1961 1/2 – until 1962 2/22
1962 9/3 – 11/13
1966 4/3 – until 1967 3/26
1975 7/17 – 10/31
1975 11/28 – until 1976 6/29
1979 9/30 – until 1980 11/9
1981 4/4 – 8/3
1990 2/6 – 8/17
1990 10/29 – until 1991 4/10
1991 6/23 – 12/31
1995 5/17 – 8/26
1996 2/7 – 5/1
1996 10/12 – until 1997 1/22
2004 8/26 – until 2005 1/27
2005 5/13 – 8/7
2008 11/14 – until 2009 2/18
2009 8/5 – until 2010 9/15

URANUS BENEFICIAL
1953 10/3 – until 1956 7/28
1966 9/9 – until 1970 8/2
1993 2/6 – until 1997 12/3
2009 3/16 – until 2012 2/22

NEPTUNE BENEFICIAL
1938 1/1 – until 1945 9/19
1993 2/8 – until 2001 1/13

PLUTO BENEFICIAL
1938 1/1 – until 1941 6/14
1966 10/27 – until 1974 9/6

JUPITER CHALLENGING
1938 3/15 – until 1939 1/26
1943 10/2 – until 1944 3/1

1944 5/26 – 8/22
1946 12/28 – until 1947 6/7
1947 8/22 – 11/19
1950 2/26 – 5/25
1950 7/29 – until 1951 1/6
1955 9/13 – until 1956 8/6
1958 12/10 – until 1959 11/3
1962 2/9 – 4/23
1962 9/15 – 12/11
1967 8/28 – 12/17
1967 12/27 – until 1968 7/20
1970 11/24 – until 1971 3/2
1971 4/13 – 10/16
1974 1/24 – 4/3
1979 8/12 – 11/1
1980 2/21 – 6/29
1982 11/8 – until 1983 1/26
1983 5/30 – 9/25
1986 1/8 – 3/17
1991 7/27 – 10/10
1992 4/3 – 5/28
1994 10/23 – until 1995 1/6
1995 7/21 – 8/15
1997 5/3 – 7/17
1997 12/19 – until 1998 2/28
2003 7/10 – 9/23
2006 10/7 – 12/20
2009 4/4 – 9/1
2009 11/22 – until 2010 2/12

SATURN CHALLENGING
1947 10/7 – until 1948 2/2
1948 6/26 – 11/25
1949 1/7 – 8/2
1955 1/19 – 4/12
1955 10/13 – until 1956 12/1
1963 3/29 – 8/12
1963 12/25 – until 1965 2/11
1977 8/8 – until 1978 9/10
1984 11/17 – until 1986 1/7
1986 6/5 – 10/5
1993 1/31 – until 1994 3/18
1994 10/29 – 11/19
2006 9/16 – until 2007 3/6
2007 6/2 – 10/23
2008 2/16 – 7/14

URANUS CHALLENGING
1959 10/4 – until 1963 8/31
1979 1/2 – until 1983 9/24
2000 4/4 – until 2005 2/8

NEPTUNE CHALLENGING
1965 1/23 – until 1973 10/21
2006 5/12 – Continues

PLUTO CHALLENGING
1950 11/4 – until 1961 6/17
1991 1/8 – until 1998 9/27

JUPITER SPECIAL
1941 4/12 – 6/20
1952 8/13 – 10/6
1953 3/24 – 6/3
1964 7/11 – 11/22
1965 2/27 – 5/18
1976 6/19 – until 1977 5/1
1988 6/2 – 9/10
1988 10/8 – until 1989 4/13
2000 5/16 – 7/31
2000 11/30 – until 2001 3/20
2012 4/29 – 7/8

SATURN SPECIAL
1941 5/22 – until 1942 6/23
1943 1/23 – 2/20
1970 7/8 – 11/3
1971 3/27 – 8/21
1971 10/18 – until 1972 4/28
2000 5/5 – until 2001 6/5

URANUS SPECIAL
1939 6/13 – until 1944 3/30

125

May 20

SUN: TAURUS • DECANATE: CAPRICORN/SATURN • DEGREE: 28°–29°5 TAURUS • MODE: FIXED • ELEMENT: EARTH

Your Personal Powers

Among the most noticeable of your personal powers are your quick intelligence and friendly manner. Your ruling planet, Venus, indicates that you possess creative potential and usually appreciate beauty, harmony, and the finer things of life. Honest and sincere, you like to be direct and to the point. Diplomatic and sensitive, you can deliver your message in a considerate and agreeable way. If you become overemotional or impatient, however, your tact and gracious manner soon vanish and you lose some of your charm or power. Your restlessness can also lead to irritability and caustic comments or self-pity. Nevertheless, you are generally cheerful and bright, gaining power from your people skills, natural optimism, and common sense. Being responsible, you work hard and can be tenacious in achieving your goals. Quick with penetrating intellect, you need to be active and constantly improving yourself through learning in order to avoid boredom. As you like to think big, faith and self-discipline are vital keys to keep you focused on your plans and inspired ideals.

Your Powers of Attraction in Relationships

People are attracted to your warm personality and ability to move in different social circles with ease. With the people you love, you can be very generous and supportive. Verbally skilled with the ability to grasp concepts quickly, you need intelligent and communicative friends and lovers with whom to share your witty and insightful comments. Being sensitive, in close relationships you fare better when you reveal your feelings and clearly express your needs to others. If not, you run the risk of playing the martyr or becoming insecure. Even if you are in a partnership, you need regular time alone to sort out your thoughts and emotions. Although independent, you enjoy group activities and are a good friend. You are naturally gifted and have a sense of the dramatic. You can attract others with your personal charm and fun-loving personality.

Your attractive qualities: intelligent, generous, creative, diplomatic, artistic, kind, friendly, frank, tactful, dignified, receptive, sensual, intuitive, organizational skills, considerate, independent, harmonious, agreeable, amicable, honest, sincere, enthusiastic, witty

Your less attractive qualities: moody, too materialistic, suspicious, overemotional, too serious, bossy, lack of confidence, impulsiveness, caustic, overindulgent, dependent, selfish, martyr, opinionated, obstinate

Your Venus Power

The planet Venus has a great deal of influence on your powers of attraction. Below are four possible Venus types for women and men. To find your Venus you need to go to page 771, where you will find the Venus table and extra information. The planet Mars also affects your powers of attraction. To find your Mars table and interpretation go to page 761.

WOMEN WITH VENUS IN ARIES: With your strong desires and enthusiastic nature, you can be a passionate lover. Although idealistic and single-minded, you need to avoid unnecessary conflicts in your relationships by being more patient and less headstrong. Although at times others can accuse you of being bossy or impulsive, you possess a great deal of warmth and charm. When necessary you can disarm others by making them feel important.

MEN WITH VENUS IN ARIES: You are drawn to strong, independent women who can stand up to you. Although you can enthusiastically follow the object of your desire, you may lose power if you allow your forceful emotions to become too dominant. Warm and passionate, you have a side to your nature that longs for new adventures. Romantic and chivalrous, you really enjoy the excitement of the initial chase, but unless you keep the enthusiasm alive and avoid falling into a rut you may become easily bored.

WOMEN WITH VENUS IN TAURUS: For your ideal relationship you seek a partner who is both financially secure and demonstrative with his affections. With these thoughts in mind, you are likely to want a partner who is refined yet pragmatic or someone concerned with safeguarding your future. Although you have a stubborn streak, you can be loving and affectionate. Attracted to people with a good sense of style, you can succeed in all kinds of business partnerships, especially those involving the arts, music, and luxury goods.

MEN WITH VENUS IN TAURUS: Attractive and affectionate, in relationships you are often faithful with a conservative outlook. You are drawn to warmhearted partners with whom you can share a familiar routine as well as life's pleasures and comforts. Seeking a partner who is dependable or reassuring,

you often put security high on your priority list when looking for love. Your sociability and friendliness usually make you popular and partners often admire your good sense of values and practical skills.

WOMEN WITH VENUS IN GEMINI: Curious, with a bright and animated approach to life, you are attracted to those who are clever or sophisticated. Your love of variety and desire for knowledge suggest that you need a partner and friends who can keep you mentally stimulated. Although witty and a good conversationalist you may need to keep in touch with your deeper feelings. Nevertheless, intelligent and friendly, you possess a youthful sense of wonder and seek a playmate who can keep you from becoming bored.

MEN WITH VENUS IN GEMINI: Charming, amusing, and adaptable, you attract others with your natural communication skills and friendly personality. You have a wonderful child-like quality and love to keep life playful, but a reluctance to contact your deeper feelings may cause you to avoid serious commitment. With your need for variety and intellectual stimulation, you are attracted to clever and amusing partners who have many interesting sides to their personalities.

WOMEN WITH VENUS IN CANCER: Possessing a soft femininity, you have tender and sensitive emotions. Sympathetic and caring, you often mother those in your care by making sure they are comfortable and have plenty to eat. When you feel hurt or insecure in relationships you are likely to cover your feelings by being defensive or appearing tough on the outside while on the inside you are feeling vulnerable. Affectionate and romantic, you make a faithful and devoted partner.

MEN WITH VENUS IN CANCER: You seek a partner who is sympathetic, caring, and protective. Able to be forgiving and compassionate, you want a secure emotional bond in your close relationships. Usually you are drawn to partners who are maternal, unselfish, or demonstrative with their feelings. Although you sometimes appear shy and/or impressionable, you have powerful emotions and inner strength.

To read all about your Outer Planets and work out how to use your personalized timetable, go to Section Three, page 789.

Your Personalized Timetable

JUPITER BENEFICIAL
1939 4/12 – 6/1
1939 9/28 – until 1940 1/19
1942 10/13 – 12/12
1943 5/30 – 7/18
1944 11/3 – until 1945 3/27
1945 7/1 – 9/26
1949 2/16 – until 1950 1/2
1951 3/25 – 5/9
1954 9/12 – until 1955 1/24
1955 5/7 – 7/1
1956 10/15 – until 1957 9/10
1961 1/29 – 5/9
1961 6/10 – 12/14
1963 3/9 – 4/20
1966 8/23 – 10/31
1966 12/12 – until 1967 6/13
1968 9/29 – until 1969 8/24
1973 1/13 – 3/30
1973 8/3 – 11/21
1975 2/20 – 4/3
1978 8/6 – 9/26
1979 1/26 – 5/22
1980 9/13 – 12/6
1981 3/16 – 8/4
1984 12/28 – until 1985 3/9
1987 2/3 – 3/18
1990 7/20 – 9/5
1991 3/19 – 4/10
1992 8/28 – 11/13
1993 4/25 – 7/8
1996 12/12 – until 1997 2/19
1998 5/25 – 9/10
1999 1/12 – 3/1
2002 7/4 – 8/18
2004 8/12 – 10/27
2008 4/7 – 6/11
2008 11/23 – until 2009 2/3
2010 4/30 – 11/7
2010 11/30 – until 2011 2/10

SATURN BENEFICIAL
1945 10/1 – 12/12
1946 6/14 – 9/2
1947 2/16 – 5/19
1950 8/31 – until 1951 10/9
1961 1/10 – until 1962 3/3
1962 8/19 – 11/28
1966 4/12 – 10/26
1966 12/27 – until 1967 4/3
1975 7/25 – until 1976 7/7
1979 10/9 – until 1980 4/27
1980 6/17 – 11/19
1981 3/23 – 8/13
1990 2/15 – 8/1
1990 11/12 – until 1991 5/6
1991 5/27 – until 1992 1/8
1995 6/1 – 8/10
1996 2/16 – 5/11
1996 9/29 – until 1997 2/2
2004 9/4 – until 2005 1/15
2005 5/24 – 8/14
2008 11/28 – until 2009 2/3
2009 8/13 – until 2010 9/22

URANUS BENEFICIAL
1954 7/22 – until 1957 5/25
1966 9/24 – until 1970 8/22
1993 2/25 – until 1997 12/24
2009 4/2 – until 2012 3/11

NEPTUNE BENEFICIAL
1938 1/1 – until 1946 8/15
1993 3/15 – until 2001 12/9

PLUTO BENEFICIAL
1938 1/1 – until 1942 5/22
1967 9/22 – until 1975 7/18

JUPITER CHALLENGING
1938 3/20 – until 1939 1/30

1943 10/8 – until 1944 2/22
1944 6/3 – 8/26
1947 1/3 – 5/30
1947 8/31 – 11/24
1950 3/2 – 6/6
1950 7/18 – until 1951 1/11
1955 9/18 – until 1956 8/10
1958 12/15 – until 1959 11/8
1962 2/13 – 4/29
1962 9/8 – 12/18
1967 9/1 – until 1968 7/25
1970 11/28 – until 1971 10/21
1974 1/28 – 4/7
1979 8/16 – 11/8
1980 2/13 – 7/5
1982 11/13 – until 1983 2/2
1983 5/22 – 10/1
1986 1/12 – 3/21
1991 7/31 – 10/16
1992 3/24 – 6/7
1994 10/28 – until 1995 1/11
1995 7/5 – 8/31
1997 5/13 – 7/7
1997 12/24 – until 1998 3/4
2003 7/15 – 9/28
2006 10/12 – 12/25
2009 4/10 – 8/25
2009 11/29 – until 2010 2/16

SATURN CHALLENGING
1947 10/19 – until 1948 1/21
1948 7/5 – until 1949 8/10
1955 2/7 – 3/23
1955 10/21 – until 1956 12/9
1963 4/9 – 7/30
1964 1/4 – until 1965 2/19
1977 8/16 – until 1978 9/18
1984 11/25 – until 1986 1/17
1986 5/23 – 10/16
1993 2/8 – until 1994 3/26
1994 10/4 – 12/14
2006 9/25 – until 2007 2/21
2007 6/14 – 11/4
2008 2/3 – 7/23

URANUS CHALLENGING
1959 10/31 – until 1964 6/26
1979 2/1 – until 1983 10/17
2000 5/11 – until 2005 2/25

NEPTUNE CHALLENGING
1965 12/10 – until 1973 11/18
2007 3/15 – Continues

PLUTO CHALLENGING
1951 9/25 – until 1961 7/28
1991 11/24 – until 1998 10/30

JUPITER SPECIAL
1941 4/16 – 6/24
1952 8/29 – 9/21
1953 3/28 – 6/7
1964 7/16 – 11/15
1965 3/5 – 5/22
1976 6/24 – until 1977 5/5
1988 6/6 – until 1989 4/17
2000 5/20 – 8/6
2000 11/23 – until 2001 3/26
2012 5/3 – 7/13

SATURN SPECIAL
1941 5/30 – until 1942 7/1
1943 1/1 – 3/13
1970 7/19 – 10/22
1971 4/5 – until 1972 5/6
2000 5/13 – until 2001 6/13

URANUS SPECIAL
1939 7/4 – until 1944 4/21

May 21

Your Personal Powers

Clever and outspoken, your keen intelligence and ambitious nature usually keep you active and determined. Your ruling planet, Venus, indicates that you possess good people skills and an artistic eye for things of quality and beauty. Among your many personal powers is your ability to grasp ideas quickly and make the most of opportunities. Practical and resourceful, you possess natural business acumen and are usually responsible and hardworking. You are likely to be gifted with organizational abilities and a spirit of enterprise. Although your strong individuality and tenacious attitude can help you make headway, you may lose some of your power if you become too rebellious and obstinate. Concern over money and security can also cause you anxiety and stress. In contrast, you gain power from the enthusiastic and creative way you can express your thoughts and ideas. Possessing personal charisma and a sharp mind, you have a gift for persuading others to see your point of view. You win success through combining your playful charm with a disciplined approach to life.

Your Powers of Attraction in Relationships

Others are attracted to your friendly and sociable nature. Usually you like to mix with people from different social circles. Being dramatic, your gift for being witty and entertaining can also attract admirers. You can find close relationships more challenging if others cannot reach your high standards. Your practical and down-to-earth approach and strong sense of security imply that you may end up compromising some of your ideals for partnership. If you feel insecure, you may have to overcome issues concerning feeling lonely or abandoned. Although you are independent, your need for devotion to a partner implies that once committed, you can be caring and dependable. You are particularly attracted to clever or wise individuals who can stimulate your mind and increase your faith and spontaneity.

Your attractive qualities: loyal, creative ideas, friendly, talent with words, intelligent, kind, ambitious, responsible, hardworking, frank, honest, enthusiastic, inspired, sensual, good communication skills, business acumen, charm, people skills, talented, enthusiastic

Your less attractive qualities: materialistic, irresponsible, overindulgent, moody, unstable, dependent, obstinate, nervous, overemotional, stubborn, disappointed, fearful of change

Your Venus Power

The planet Venus has a great deal of influence on your powers of attraction. Below are four possible Venus types for women and men. To find your Venus you need to go to page 771, where you will find the Venus table and extra information. The planet Mars also affects your powers of attraction. To find your Mars table and interpretation go to page 761.

WOMEN WITH VENUS IN ARIES: Idealistic, passionate, and adventurous, you are direct in your dealings with others. When you are attracted to a person you usually take the initiative and use your people skills to make things happen. In close relationships you are not afraid to confront your other half. This self-assertiveness is positive if differences can be brought into the open through diplomacy and compromise.

MEN WITH VENUS IN ARIES: You are usually drawn to courageous or assertive women who possess strong personal magnetism. Therefore you find those who seem to be independent or action-oriented very attractive. Your own eagerness and need for activity suggest that you start relationships with great enthusiasm, especially if they offer you excitement or adventures. The challenge is often to maintain relationships and not get bored.

WOMEN WITH VENUS IN TAURUS: Being physically attractive, you can make a good impression on the opposite sex. As security and stability in relationships are very important to you, you usually want a partner who is not only attractive but also reliable and a good provider. Being sensual or tactile, you also need a lover who is affectionate, but beware that your love does not show signs of possessiveness or jealousy. Your own sense of style and love of beauty imply that you can be attracted to creative people, especially those in art and music.

MEN WITH VENUS IN TAURUS: Attractive and affectionate, in relationships you are often faithful with a conservative outlook. You are drawn to warmhearted partners with whom you can share a familiar routine as well as life's pleasures and comforts. Seeking a partner who is dependable or reassuring, you often put security high on your priority list when looking for love. Your sociability and friendliness usually make you popular and partners often admire your good sense of values and practical skills.

WOMEN WITH VENUS IN GEMINI: In relationships you need intellectual stimulation and usually prefer to keep things light. Certainly not boring, you love to talk and are at your best being witty and entertaining. Although your easygoing approach to relationships is very attractive, guard against losing touch with your deeper emotions. You prefer a partner who can keep up with your fast stream of ideas, and if you have shared interests then so much the better.

MEN WITH VENUS IN GEMINI: Informed and curious yet charming and friendly, you seek a partner who shares your interests or enjoys your witty remarks. Although a good communicator, you have an inborn tendency to be lighthearted and less profound about deep emotional commitment. Although you are keen on experiences that bring variety into your life, boredom or scattering your energies in too many directions is probably your biggest handicap in relationships. Nevertheless, you are attracted to intelligent partners who can match your lively banter.

WOMEN WITH VENUS IN CANCER: Gentle and tender, you are romantic by nature. You possess a strong need for security and you usually help others feel safe and protected. This preservation is especially centered around the home, which is your haven from life's storm. Although your maternal instincts are strong, avoid making sacrifices for others at your own expense. Nevertheless, affectionate and caring, once committed to a relationship, your loyalty and devotion to your partner are very strong.

MEN WITH VENUS IN CANCER: Being emotionally receptive you can be a sensitive lover. With your desire to care for and protect others, you are likely to have strong family connections. Love is often tied in with being attentive to the needs of others and you may find yourself attracted to individuals who have sympathetic or maternal qualities. Security-conscious, you need a loyal partner who can offer you support and ideally be a good cook and homemaker.

To read all about your Outer Planets and work out how to use your personalized timetable, go to Section Three, page 789.

Your Personalized Timetable

JUPITER BENEFICIAL
1939 4/16 – 6/7
1939 9/20 – until 1940 1/25
1942 10/25 – 11/30
1943 6/4 – 7/22
1944 11/9 – until 1945 3/20
1945 7/8 – 9/30
1949 2/20 – until 1950 1/6
1951 3/29 – 5/13
1951 11/13 – 12/16
1954 9/18 – until 1955 1/17
1955 5/13 – 7/6
1956 10/20 – until 1957 9/15
1961 2/3 – 12/19
1963 3/13 – 4/24
1966 8/28 – until 1967 3/8
1967 4/3 – 6/18
1968 10/3 – until 1969 8/29
1973 1/17 – 4/6
1973 7/26 – 11/27
1975 2/24 – 4/7
1978 8/10 – 10/2
1979 1/19 – 5/28
1980 9/17 – 12/13
1981 3/8 – 8/10
1985 1/2 – 3/14
1985 9/14 – 10/22
1987 2/7 – 3/22
1990 7/25 – 9/10
1991 3/3 – 4/26
1992 9/2 – 11/18
1993 4/16 – 7/16
1996 12/16 – until 1997 2/24
1998 6/1 – 9/3
1999 1/17 – 3/5
2002 7/9 – 8/23
2004 8/17 – 10/31
2008 4/19 – 5/29
2008 11/28 – until 2009 2/7
2010 5/5 – 10/23
2010 12/15 – until 2011 2/15

SATURN BENEFICIAL
1938 1/1 – 3/2
1945 10/23 – 11/20
1946 6/22 – 9/11
1947 2/4 – 5/30
1950 9/8 – until 1951 10/17
1961 1/19 – until 1962 3/12
1962 8/5 – 12/9
1966 4/20 – 10/10
1967 1/11 – 4/11
1975 8/1 – until 1976 7/15
1979 10/17 – until 1980 4/9
1980 7/4 – 11/30
1981 3/10 – 8/23
1990 2/24 – 7/19
1990 11/24 – until 1992 1/17
1995 6/29 – 7/13
1996 2/24 – 5/21
1996 9/17 – until 1997 2/12
2004 9/14 – until 2005 1/3
2005 6/2 – 8/22
2006 3/17 – 4/24
2008 12/24 – until 2009 1/8
2009 8/21 – until 2010 9/30

URANUS BENEFICIAL
1954 8/7 – until 1957 6/16
1966 10/10 – until 1970 9/8
1993 3/23 – until 1998 1/11
2009 4/20 – until 2012 12/27

NEPTUNE BENEFICIAL
1938 10/7 – until 1946 9/14
1994 2/3 – until 2002 1/8

PLUTO BENEFICIAL
1938 1/1 – until 1942 7/5
1967 10/20 – until 1975 8/25

JUPITER CHALLENGING
1938 3/25 – until 1939 2/3

1943 10/14 – until 1944 2/14
1944 6/9 – 8/31
1947 1/8 – 5/22
1947 9/7 – 11/28
1950 3/6 – until 1951 1/16
1955 9/23 – until 1956 4/6
1956 4/29 – 8/15
1958 12/20 – until 1959 11/12
1962 2/17 – 5/5
1962 8/31 – 12/24
1967 9/6 – until 1968 7/29
1970 12/3 – until 1971 10/26
1974 2/1 – 4/12
1979 8/21 – 11/15
1980 2/5 – 7/10
1982 11/17 – until 1983 2/9
1983 5/14 – 10/7
1986 1/16 – 3/25
1991 8/5 – 10/21
1992 3/15 – 6/16
1994 11/1 – until 1995 1/16
1995 6/25 – 9/10
1997 5/29 – 6/21
1997 12/29 – until 1998 3/8
2003 7/19 – 10/2
2006 10/17 – 12/29
2009 4/15 – 8/17
2009 12/6 – until 2010 2/20

SATURN CHALLENGING
1947 11/2 – until 1948 1/6
1948 7/14 – until 1949 8/18
1955 10/30 – until 1956 12/17
1957 8/6 – 8/16
1963 4/22 – 7/16
1964 1/13 – until 1965 2/27
1977 8/23 – until 1978 9/26
1979 4/12 – 6/5
1984 12/3 – until 1985 7/8
1985 8/11 – until 1986 1/28
1986 5/10 – 10/26
1993 2/16 – until 1994 4/4
1994 9/19 – 12/28
2006 10/4 – until 2007 2/10
2007 6/24 – 11/19
2008 1/19 – 7/31

URANUS CHALLENGING
1960 8/19 – until 1964 7/18
1979 11/20 – until 1983 11/4
2001 2/25 – until 2005 12/31

NEPTUNE CHALLENGING
1966 1/12 – until 1974 10/15
2007 4/20 – Continues

PLUTO CHALLENGING
1952 8/30 – until 1962 6/15
1991 12/20 – until 1998 11/24

JUPITER SPECIAL
1941 4/21 – 6/29
1953 4/2 – 6/11
1964 7/22 – 11/8
1965 3/11 – 5/26
1976 6/29 – 12/28
1977 2/2 – 5/9
1988 6/10 – until 1989 4/22
2000 5/24 – 8/12
2000 11/16 – until 2001 4/1
2012 5/7 – 7/17

SATURN SPECIAL
1941 6/7 – until 1942 1/14
1942 1/31 – 7/9
1942 12/18 – until 1943 3/26
1970 8/3 – 10/7
1971 4/13 – until 1972 5/13
2000 5/20 – until 2001 6/20

URANUS SPECIAL
1939 8/3 – until 1944 5/9

129

Taurus Timetable
X-Special · X-Beneficial · X-Challenging

April 21
URANUS X-BENEFICIAL
2002 5/13 – until **2004** 2/19
NEPTUNE X-BENEFICIAL
2010 5/18 – Continues
PLUTO X-BENEFICIAL
2007 2/26 – until **2009** 12/13

April 22
URANUS X-BENEFICIAL
2003 3/4 – until **2004** 12/24
NEPTUNE X-BENEFICIAL
2011 3/23 – Continues
PLUTO X-BENEFICIAL
2008 1/14 – until **2010** 11/11

April 23
URANUS X-BENEFICIAL
2003 3/22 – until **2005** 1/16
NEPTUNE X-BENEFICIAL
2011 4/29 – Continues
PLUTO X-BENEFICIAL
2008 2/17 – until **2010** 12/11

April 24
URANUS X-BENEFICIAL
2003 4/11 – until **2005** 2/4
NEPTUNE X-BENEFICIAL
2012 3/17 – Continues
PLUTO X-BENEFICIAL
2009 1/10 – until **2011** 11/7

April 25
URANUS X-BENEFICIAL
2003 5/12 – until **2005** 2/21
NEPTUNE X-CHALLENGING
2000 11/11 – until **2001** 12/2
NEPTUNE X-BENEFICIAL
2012 4/18 – Continues
PLUTO X-BENEFICIAL
2009 2/10 – until **2011** 12/10

April 26
URANUS X-BENEFICIAL
2004 3/6 – until **2005** 12/26
NEPTUNE X-CHALLENGING
2000 11/11 – until **2002** 1/3
PLUTO X-BENEFICIAL
2010 1/7 – Continues

April 27
URANUS X-BENEFICIAL
2004 3/23 – until **2006** 1/19
NEPTUNE X-CHALLENGING
2000 11/11 – until **2002** 11/22
PLUTO X-BENEFICIAL
2010 2/5 – until **2012** 12/8

April 28
URANUS X-BENEFICIAL
2004 4/13 – until **2006** 2/7
NEPTUNE X-CHALLENGING
2001 1/5 – until **2002** 12/29
PLUTO X-BENEFICIAL
2011 1/4 – Continues

April 29
URANUS X-BENEFICIAL
2004 5/12 – until **2006** 2/24
NEPTUNE X-CHALLENGING
2001 1/30 – until **2003** 11/3
PLUTO X-BENEFICIAL
2011 2/2 – Continues

April 30
URANUS X-BENEFICIAL
2005 3/8 – until **2006** 12/28
NEPTUNE X-CHALLENGING
2001 2/26 – until **2003** 12/23
PLUTO X-BENEFICIAL
2011 3/21 – until **2012** 8/5

May 1
URANUS X-BENEFICIAL
2005 3/26 – until **2007** 1/21
NEPTUNE X-CHALLENGING
2001 4/2 – until **2004** 1/20
PLUTO X-BENEFICIAL
2012 2/1 – Continues

May 2
URANUS X-BENEFICIAL
2005 4/15 – until **2007** 2/10
NEPTUNE X-CHALLENGING
2002 2/21 – until **2004** 12/15
PLUTO X-BENEFICIAL
2012 3/13 – Continues

May 3
URANUS X-BENEFICIAL
2005 5/12 – until **2007** 2/27
NEPTUNE X-CHALLENGING
2002 3/24 – until **2005** 1/14

May 4
URANUS X-BENEFICIAL
2006 3/11 – until **2007** 12/29
NEPTUNE X-CHALLENGING
2003 2/16 – until **2005** 12/7

May 5
URANUS X-BENEFICIAL
2006 3/29 – until **2008** 1/24
NEPTUNE X-CHALLENGING
2003 3/17 – until **2006** 1/9

May 6
URANUS X-BENEFICIAL
2006 4/17 – until **2008** 2/12
NEPTUNE X-CHALLENGING
2004 2/12 – until **2006** 11/24

May 7
URANUS X-BENEFICIAL
2006 5/14 – until **2008** 3/1
NEPTUNE X-CHALLENGING
2004 3/10 – until **2007** 1/3

May 8
URANUS X-BENEFICIAL
2007 3/14 – until **2008** 12/29
NEPTUNE X-CHALLENGING
2004 4/18 – until **2007** 1/30

May 9
URANUS X-BENEFICIAL
2007 3/31 – until **2009** 1/25
NEPTUNE X-CHALLENGING
2005 3/4 – until **2007** 12/27

May 10
URANUS X-CHALLENGING
2000 12/18 – until **2001** 11/21
URANUS X-BENEFICIAL
2007 4/20 – until **2009** 2/14
NEPTUNE X-CHALLENGING
2005 4/6 – until **2008** 1/25

May 11
URANUS X-CHALLENGING
2000 12/18 – until **2001** 12/23
URANUS X-BENEFICIAL
2007 5/15 – until **2009** 3/3
NEPTUNE X-CHALLENGING
2006 2/27 – until **2008** 12/18

May 12
URANUS X-CHALLENGING
2001 1/8 – until **2002** 1/12
URANUS X-BENEFICIAL
2008 3/15 – until **2009** 12/29
NEPTUNE X-CHALLENGING
2006 3/29 – until **2009** 1/19

May 13
URANUS X-CHALLENGING
2001 1/26 – until **2002** 1/30
URANUS X-BENEFICIAL
2008 4/2 – until **2010** 1/27
NEPTUNE X-CHALLENGING
2007 2/21 – until **2009** 12/7

May 14
URANUS X-CHALLENGING
2001 2/12 – until **2002** 11/15

URANUS X-BENEFICIAL
2008 4/21 – until **2010** 2/16
NEPTUNE X-CHALLENGING
2007 3/21 – until **2010** 1/13

May 15
URANUS X-CHALLENGING
2001 2/28 – until **2002** 12/23
URANUS X-BENEFICIAL
2008 5/15 – until **2010** 3/6
NEPTUNE X-CHALLENGING
2007 5/5 – until **2010** 11/13

May 16
URANUS X-CHALLENGING
2001 3/19 – until **2003** 1/14
URANUS X-BENEFICIAL
2009 3/18 – until **2010** 12/28
NEPTUNE X-CHALLENGING
2008 3/14 – until **2011** 1/6

May 17
URANUS X-CHALLENGING
2001 4/10 – until **2003** 2/1
URANUS X-BENEFICIAL
2009 4/4 – until **2011** 1/28
NEPTUNE X-CHALLENGING
2008 4/18 – until **2011** 2/3

May 18
URANUS X-CHALLENGING
2001 5/23 – until **2003** 2/18
URANUS X-BENEFICIAL
2009 4/23 – until **2011** 2/18
NEPTUNE X-CHALLENGING
2009 3/8 – until **2011** 12/29

May 19
URANUS X-CHALLENGING
2002 3/2 – until **2003** 12/24
URANUS X-BENEFICIAL
2009 5/16 – until **2011** 3/8
NEPTUNE X-CHALLENGING
2009 4/8 – until **2012** 1/28

May 20
URANUS X-CHALLENGING
2002 3/20 – until **2004** 1/15
URANUS X-BENEFICIAL
2010 3/20 – until **2011** 12/25
NEPTUNE X-CHALLENGING
2010 3/2 – until **2012** 12/18

May 21
URANUS X-CHALLENGING
2002 4/10 – until **2004** 2/3
URANUS X-BENEFICIAL
2010 4/6 – until **2012** 1/30
NEPTUNE X-CHALLENGING
2010 3/30 – Continues

Gemini

May 22–June 21

May 22

SUN: GEMINI/TAURUS CUSP • DECANATE: GEMINI/MERCURY • DEGREE: 00°–01°5 GEMINI • MODE: MUTABLE • ELEMENT: AIR

Your Personal Powers

As a perceptive and intuitive individual your assessment of others is generally reliable. You usually work better when you trust your first instincts about people and situations. Your personal powers include a quick mind, persuasive charm, and friendly approach. Social skills come naturally to you, as you have the ability to talk to people from all walks of life. You gain power when you develop the necessary self-discipline to put your ideas into action. You can, however, lose some of your power if you argue or just talk about your aspirations or dreams. Being ambitious, with natural leadership skills and big plans, you need projects into which you can channel all your enthusiasm and determination. Without these, there is a danger you may become bored and obstinate. Fortunately, you possess an innate common sense and a creative imagination that helps you solve problems and achieve success. Possessing a natural sixth sense, you are able to recognize opportunities or turn situations to your advantage. Being proud and intelligent, you fare better in life when you identify with success.

Your Powers of Attraction in Relationships

Others are attracted to your quick responses and gregarious personality. You usually have a plan going to improve your situation and you prefer a hardworking partner by your side to share your dreams and/or responsibilities. Although often friendly yet reserved, you possess insight into people's motivation and can show a caring concern for the welfare of others. You are attracted to clever and industrious people who have achieved or been successful in life. Equally, you admire those who possess astute perceptiveness mixed with common sense. There is, however, a danger that you may be drawn to bossy people or may be the demanding partner yourself. Being a pragmatist yourself, you prefer your partner to be direct and take a realistic stand.

Your attractive qualities: clever, positive vitality, creative mind, frank, enthusiastic, universal, highly intuitive, pragmatic, charm, success-oriented, proud, leader, good organizer, realist, honest, problem solver, ambitious, charismatic, practical

Your less attractive qualities: bossy, arrogant, nervous, moody, obstinate, materialistic, rebellious, egotistical, restless, underachievement, curtness, lazy, nervous, impatient, too talkative, lack of confidence, restless

Your Venus Power

The planet Venus has a great deal of influence on your powers of attraction. Below are four possible Venus types for women and men. To find your Venus you need to go to page 771, where you will find the Venus table and extra information. The planet Mars also affects your powers of attraction. To find your Mars table and interpretation go to page 761.

WOMEN WITH VENUS IN ARIES: Idealistic, passionate, and adventurous, you are direct in your dealings with others. When you are attracted to a person you usually take the initiative and use your people skills to make things happen. In close relationships you are not afraid to confront your other half. This self-assertiveness is positive if differences can be brought into the open through diplomacy and compromise. Independent and spirited, you enjoy your freedom.

MEN WITH VENUS IN ARIES: You are usually drawn to courageous or assertive women who possess strong personal magnetism. Therefore you find those who seem to be independent or action-oriented very attractive. Your own eagerness and need for activity suggest that you start relationships with great enthusiasm, especially if they offer you excitement or adventures. The challenge is often to maintain relationships and not get bored too easily.

WOMEN WITH VENUS IN TAURUS: Being physically attractive, you can make a good impression on the opposite sex. As security and stability in relationships are very important to you, you usually want a partner who is not only attractive but also reliable and a good provider. Being sensual or tactile, you also need a lover who is affectionate, but beware that your love does not show signs of possessiveness or jealousy. Your own sense of style and love of beauty imply that you can be attracted to creative people, especially those in art and music.

MEN WITH VENUS IN TAURUS: As well as attracting people with your warm personality, you also possess an innate sense of the value of material possessions. Keeping yourself stylish and having an attractive appearance can also be important to you. You are naturally attracted to practical yet sensual women who understand your need for comfort, security, and the pleasures and luxuries of life. Naturally affectionate, you enjoy socializing but can be a loyal and loving partner.

WOMEN WITH VENUS IN GEMINI: In relationships you need intellectual stimulation and usually prefer to keep things light. Certainly not boring, you love to talk and are at your best being witty and entertaining. Although your easygoing

approach to relationships is very attractive, guard against losing touch with your deeper emotions. You prefer a partner who can keep up with your fast stream of ideas, and if you have shared interests then so much the better.

MEN WITH VENUS IN GEMINI: Charming, amusing, and adaptable, you attract others with your natural communication skills and friendly personality. You have a wonderful child-like quality and love to keep life playful, but a reluctance to contact your deeper feelings may cause you to avoid serious commitment. With your need for variety and intellectual stimulation, you are attracted to clever and amusing partners who have many interesting sides to their personalities.

WOMEN WITH VENUS IN CANCER: Gentle and tender, you are romantic by nature. You possess a strong need for security and usually help others feel safe and protected. This preservation especially centers around the home, which is your haven from life's storm. Although your maternal instincts are strong, avoid making too many sacrifices for others at your own expense. Nevertheless, affectionate and caring, once committed to a relationship, your loyalty and devotion to your partner are very strong.

MEN WITH VENUS IN CANCER: Affectionate with a strong sensitive streak, you can love very deeply. You may find yourself drawn to sympathetic partners who can tune in to your moods and feelings as well as be reassuring and supportive. Family links are especially important to you and the more positive these relationships are the more confident and safe you feel.

To read all about your Outer Planets and work out how to use your personalized timetable, go to Section Three, page 789.

Your Personalized Timetable

JUPITER BENEFICIAL
1938 1/1 – until **1939** 6/14
1939 9/13 – until **1940** 1/30
1943 6/9 – 7/26
1944 11/15 – until **1945** 3/12
1945 7/15 – 10/5
1949 2/25 – 9/4
1949 10/2 – until **1950** 1/10
1951 4/2 – 5/18
1951 11/1 – 12/29
1954 9/24 – until **1955** 1/10
1955 5/19 – 7/10
1956 10/25 – until **1957** 4/25
1957 6/11 – 9/19
1961 2/7 – 12/23
1963 3/17 – 4/28
1966 9/2 – until **1967** 2/21
1967 4/18 – 6/23
1968 10/8 – until **1969** 9/3
1973 1/21 – 4/12
1973 7/19 – 12/3
1975 2/28 – 4/11
1978 8/15 – 10/9
1979 1/12 – 6/3
1980 9/22 – 12/22
1981 2/27 – 8/16
1985 1/6 – 3/19
1985 9/2 – 11/3
1987 2/11 – 3/26
1990 7/29 – 9/15
1991 2/21 – 5/7
1992 9/6 – 11/24
1993 4/8 – 7/24
1996 12/21 – until **1997** 2/28
1998 6/8 – 8/26
1999 1/22 – 3/9
2002 7/13 – 8/28
2004 8/21 – 11/5
2008 12/3 – until **2009** 2/11
2010 5/10 – 10/13
2010 12/24 – until **2011** 2/19

SATURN BENEFICIAL
1938 1/1 – until **1946** 9/20
1947 1/23 – 6/10
1950 9/16 – until **1951** 10/25
1952 5/17 – 7/4
1961 1/27 – until **1962** 3/23
1962 7/23 – 12/19
1966 4/30 – 9/27
1967 1/22 – 4/19
1967 12/4 – 12/13
1975 8/9 – until **1976** 7/22
1979 10/26 – until **1980** 3/26
1980 7/16 – 12/14
1981 2/23 – 9/1
1990 3/7 – 7/5
1990 12/4 – until **1992** 1/25
1996 3/3 – 6/2
1996 9/3 – until **1997** 2/21
2004 9/26 – 12/22
2005 6/11 – 8/30
2006 2/26 – 5/13
2009 8/30 – until **2010** 10/8

URANUS BENEFICIAL
1954 8/25 – until **1957** 7/3
1966 10/28 – until **1970** 9/24
1994 1/19 – until **1998** 1/28
2009 5/13 – Continues

NEPTUNE BENEFICIAL
1938 11/7 – until **1947** 8/8
1994 3/6 – until **2002** 11/30

PLUTO BENEFICIAL
1938 1/1 – until **1943** 6/17
1967 11/30 – until **1975** 9/21

JUPITER CHALLENGING
1938 3/29 – 10/6
1938 10/31 – until **1939** 2/7

1943 10/20 – until **1944** 2/7
1944 6/16 – 9/4
1947 1/14 – 5/14
1947 9/14 – 12/2
1950 3/11 – until **1951** 1/20
1955 9/28 – until **1956** 3/20
1956 5/15 – 8/19
1958 12/25 – until **1959** 7/1
1959 8/8 – 11/17
1962 2/22 – 5/11
1962 8/24 – 12/30
1967 9/10 – until **1968** 8/3
1970 12/7 – until **1971** 10/31
1974 2/5 – 4/17
1974 10/14 – 11/23
1979 8/25 – 11/25
1980 1/27 – 7/16
1982 11/21 – until **1983** 2/17
1983 5/6 – 10/12
1986 1/20 – 3/29
1991 8/9 – 10/27
1992 3/7 – 6/23
1994 11/6 – until **1995** 1/22
1995 6/16 – 9/18
1998 1/3 – 3/12
2003 7/24 – 10/7
2006 10/21 – until **2007** 1/3
2009 4/22 – 8/10
2009 12/12 – until **2010** 2/24

SATURN CHALLENGING
1947 12/2 – 12/3
1948 7/22 – until **1949** 8/26
1955 11/7 – until **1956** 12/26
1957 7/7 – 9/16
1963 5/11 – 6/26
1964 1/21 – until **1965** 3/7
1977 8/31 – until **1978** 10/5
1979 3/26 – 6/22
1984 12/12 – until **1985** 6/16
1985 9/2 – until **1986** 2/12
1986 4/24 – 11/4
1993 2/24 – until **1994** 4/14
1994 9/6 – until **1995** 1/8
2006 10/14 – until **2007** 1/28
2007 7/4 – until **2008** 8/8

URANUS CHALLENGING
1960 9/3 – until **1964** 8/4
1979 12/6 – until **1983** 11/20
2001 3/14 – until **2006** 1/22

NEPTUNE CHALLENGING
1966 12/5 – until **1974** 11/13
2008 3/7 – Continues

PLUTO CHALLENGING
1952 10/5 – until **1962** 7/28
1992 1/24 – until **1999** 10/17

JUPITER SPECIAL
1941 4/25 – 7/3
1953 4/7 – 6/15
1964 7/29 – 11/1
1965 3/17 – 5/30
1976 7/4 – 12/16
1977 2/14 – 5/13
1988 6/15 – until **1989** 4/26
2000 5/28 – 8/20
2000 11/8 – until **2001** 4/6
2012 5/11 – Continues

SATURN SPECIAL
1941 6/15 – 12/20
1942 2/25 – 7/18
1942 12/6 – until **1943** 4/6
1971 4/21 – until **1972** 5/21
2000 5/28 – until **2001** 6/28
2002 1/12 – 3/6

URANUS SPECIAL
1940 5/24 – until **1944** 5/26

♊

May 23

SUN: GEMINI • DECANATE: GEMINI/MERCURY • DEGREE: 1°–2° GEMINI • MODE: MUTABLE • ELEMENT: AIR

Your Personal Powers

Clever, with quick comprehension and responses, you like to keep yourself informed. Talkative, broad-minded, and analytical, you enjoy debating or communicating with others. Being versatile and mentally curious, you usually like discussions on world affairs. Your ruling planet, Mercury, indicates that you possess an active mind and a wealth of ideas. You gain power by combining your love for knowledge with your fertile imagination and creative ideas. Usually you prefer an honest and direct approach when dealing with others. Although you are usually loyal and responsible, you can also be spontaneous and youthful in your attitude or outer appearance. You may lose power, however, if you become obstinate or let frustration turn into nervous tension. Gracious and caring, nonetheless, you can be kind and generous with your time and resources. Being sensitive, mentally restless, and creative, you need to find avenues of expression for your many bright ideas and talents. Although you like to keep active it is essential for you to feel that you are constantly learning and expanding your horizons.

Your Powers of Attraction in Relationships

Your quick perception, intelligence, and kindhearted personality attract others. Although you have a strong sense of duty and responsibility, if you get into a rut you can also suffer from discontentment or impatience. Often thrifty with yourself but generous and caring with others, you can be a loyal and responsible partner. As you are willing to make sacrifices for those you love, you need a partner who can offer you a strong and stable home base to make you feel protected. Since your relationships are especially important to you, you may sometimes experience disappointment, especially if you have high expectations of others. As you are charitable, be careful to balance the "give and take" in your relationships or you may give too much and become dependent on your partner.

Your attractive qualities: kind, friendly, honest, loyal, intelligent, responsible, generous, creative, communicative, intuitive, versatile, sincere, altruistic, trustworthy, broad-minded, charitable, just, humanitarian, good adviser, common sense, universal, fair

Your less attractive qualities: stubborn, nervous, insecure, arrogant, too talkative, vain, frustrating, uncompromising, restless, faultfinding, disappointed, prejudiced, impatient, irritable, negative thinker

Your Venus Power

The planet Venus has a great deal of influence on your powers of attraction. Below are four possible Venus types for women and men. To find your Venus you need to go to page 771, where you will find the Venus table and extra information. The planet Mars also affects your powers of attraction. To find your Mars table and interpretation go to page 761.

WOMEN WITH VENUS IN ARIES: With your strong desires and enthusiastic nature you can be a passionate lover. Although idealistic and single-minded, you need to avoid unnecessary conflicts in your relationships by being more patient and less headstrong. Although at times others can accuse you of being bossy or impulsive, you possess a great deal of warmth and charm. When necessary you can disarm others by making them feel important.

MEN WITH VENUS IN ARIES: You are usually inclined to seek a partner who is active, goal-oriented, or decisive. Not known for your patience, you probably seek relationships from youth. You may find that you are attracted more to women who have a daring or adventurous spirit, but in your close relationships you may encounter rivalry or find that both you and your partner want to lead or be the boss. Although you may act rashly you possess a great deal of magnetism and are capable of demonstrating your love and affection.

WOMEN WITH VENUS IN TAURUS: For your ideal relationship you seek a partner who is both financially secure and demonstrative with his affections. With these thoughts in mind you are likely to also want a partner who is refined yet pragmatic, or someone concerned with safeguarding your future. Although you have a stubborn streak you can be loving and affectionate in your relationships, and with your good sense of style may have an attraction for the arts, music, or luxury items.

MEN WITH VENUS IN TAURUS: Although you are usually drawn to sensual and physically beautiful individuals, you want a partner who is also reliable and loyal. When in love you enjoy buying your partner things of quality that will grow in value or useful things of a practical nature. You also love to so-

cialize and entertain, particularly in luxurious surroundings. Affectionate and caring you are often attracted to creative people or those with artistic talents.

WOMEN WITH VENUS IN GEMINI: In relationships you need intellectual stimulation and usually prefer to keep things light. Certainly not boring, you love to talk and are at your best being witty and entertaining. Although your easygoing approach to relationships is very attractive, guard against losing touch with your deeper emotions. You prefer a partner who can keep up with your fast stream of ideas, and if you have shared interests then so much the better.

MEN WITH VENUS IN GEMINI: Charming, amusing, and adaptable, you attract others with your natural communication skills and friendly personality. You have a wonderful childlike quality and love to keep life playful, but a reluctance to contact your deeper feelings may cause you to avoid serious commitment. With your need for variety and intellectual stimulation, you are attracted to clever and amusing partners who have many interesting sides to their personalities.

WOMEN WITH VENUS IN CANCER: Possessing a soft femininity, you have tender and sensitive emotions. Sympathetic and caring, you often mother those in your care by making sure that they are comfortable and have plenty to eat. When you feel hurt or insecure in relationships you are likely to cover your feelings by being defensive or appearing tough on the outside while on the inside you are feeling vulnerable. Affectionate and romantic, you make a faithful and devoted partner.

MEN WITH VENUS IN CANCER: Being emotionally receptive you can be a sensitive lover. With your desire to care for and protect others you are likely to have strong family connections. Love is often tied in with being attentive to the needs of others and you may find yourself attracted to individuals who have sympathetic or maternal qualities. Security-conscious, you need a loyal partner who can offer you support and ideally be a good cook and homemaker.

To read all about your Outer Planets and work out how to use your personalized timetable, go to Section Three, page 789.

To read all about your Outer Planets and work out how to use your personalized timetable, go to Section Three, page 789.

Your Personalized Timetable

JUPITER BENEFICIAL
1939 4/25 – 6/22
1939 9/5 – until 1940 2/4
1943 6/14 – 7/31
1944 11/21 – until 1945 3/5
1945 7/21 – 10/9
1949 3/2 – 8/21
1949 10/17 – until 1950 1/14
1951 4/7 – 5/23
1951 10/22 – until 1952 1/7
1954 10/1 – until 1955 1/2
1955 5/25 – 7/14
1956 10/30 – until 1957 4/14
1957 6/23 – 9/24
1961 2/11 – 12/28
1963 3/21 – 5/2
1966 9/7 – until 1967 2/11
1967 4/28 – 6/28
1968 10/13 – until 1969 9/8
1973 1/25 – 4/20
1973 7/10 – 12/8
1975 3/4 – 4/15
1978 8/19 – 10/17
1979 1/4 – 6/9
1980 9/26 – until 1981 1/3
1981 2/15 – 8/21
1985 1/10 – 3/24
1985 8/23 – 11/12
1987 2/16 – 3/30
1990 8/2 – 9/21
1991 2/13 – 5/15
1992 9/10 – 11/30
1993 3/31 – 7/31
1996 12/25 – until 1997 3/4
1998 6/18 – 8/16
1999 1/27 – 3/13
2002 7/17 – 9/1
2004 8/26 – 11/10
2005 5/14 – 6/26
2008 12/8 – until 2009 2/15
2010 5/16 – 10/5
2011 1/1 – 2/24

SATURN BENEFICIAL
1938 1/1 – 3/18
1946 7/7 – 10/1
1947 1/11 – 6/19
1950 9/23 – until 1951 11/3
1952 4/28 – 7/22
1961 2/4 – 9/5
1961 10/19 – until 1962 4/4
1962 7/9 – 12/29
1966 5/10 – 9/14
1967 2/1 – 4/27
1967 11/5 – until 1968 1/11
1975 8/17 – until 1976 3/2
1976 4/22 – 7/30
1979 11/4 – until 1980 3/14
1980 7/27 – until 1981 1/5
1981 1/31 – 9/9
1990 3/19 – 6/21
1990 12/13 – until 1992 2/2
1996 3/11 – 6/18
1996 8/18 – until 1997 3/1
2004 10/11 – 12/6
2005 6/19 – 9/8
2006 2/12 – 5/26
2009 9/6 – until 2010 10/16

URANUS BENEFICIAL
1954 9/14 – until 1957 7/20
1966 11/18 – until 1971 7/8
1994 2/5 – until 1998 12/2
2010 3/18 – Continues

NEPTUNE BENEFICIAL
1939 10/2 – until 1947 9/9
1995 1/29 – until 2003 1/2

PLUTO BENEFICIAL
1938 1/1 – until 1944 5/20
1968 10/12 – until 1976 8/9

JUPITER CHALLENGING
1938 4/3 – 9/21
1938 11/15 – until 1939 2/12
1943 10/27 – until 1944 1/31
1944 6/22 – 9/9
1947 1/21 – 5/7
1947 9/20 – 12/7
1950 3/15 – until 1951 1/25
1955 10/3 – until 1956 3/10
1956 5/25 – 8/24
1958 12/30 – until 1959 6/18
1959 8/21 – 11/21
1962 2/26 – 5/18
1962 8/16 – until 1963 1/4
1967 9/15 – until 1968 8/8
1970 12/12 – until 1971 11/4
1974 2/9 – 4/22
1974 10/2 – 12/4
1979 8/29 – 12/7
1980 1/15 – 7/21
1982 11/26 – until 1983 2/27
1983 4/26 – 10/17
1986 1/24 – 4/3
1991 8/13 – 11/2
1992 2/29 – 6/30
1994 11/10 – until 1995 1/27
1995 6/8 – 9/25
1998 1/7 – 3/16
2003 7/29 – 10/12
2004 4/13 – 5/26
2006 10/26 – until 2007 1/8
2009 4/28 – 8/2
2009 12/17 – until 2010 2/28

SATURN CHALLENGING
1948 7/30 – until 1949 9/2
1955 11/15 – until 1957 1/4
1957 6/21 – 10/1
1964 1/29 – until 1965 3/15
1977 9/7 – until 1978 10/13
1979 3/13 – 7/4
1984 12/21 – until 1985 6/1
1985 9/16 – until 1986 3/10
1986 3/28 – 11/12
1993 3/4 – until 1994 4/24
1994 8/24 – until 1995 1/18
2006 10/27 – until 2007 1/15
2007 7/13 – until 2008 8/16

URANUS CHALLENGING
1960 9/20 – until 1964 8/20
1979 12/23 – until 1984 9/1
2001 4/4 – until 2006 2/10

NEPTUNE CHALLENGING
1967 1/4 – until 1975 10/8
2008 4/8 – Continues

PLUTO CHALLENGING
1953 9/7 – until 1963 6/9
1992 12/4 – until 1999 11/14

JUPITER SPECIAL
1941 4/29 – 7/8
1953 4/11 – 6/20
1964 8/6 – 10/24
1965 3/22 – 6/3
1976 7/9 – 12/7
1977 2/23 – 5/18
1988 6/19 – until 1989 5/1
2000 6/1 – 8/29
2000 10/30 – until 2001 4/11
2012 5/15 – Continues

SATURN SPECIAL
1941 6/23 – 12/6
1942 3/11 – 7/28
1942 11/24 – until 1943 4/16
1971 4/29 – until 1972 5/28
2000 6/5 – until 2001 7/6
2001 12/27 – until 2002 3/21

URANUS SPECIAL
1940 6/10 – until 1945 3/22

May 24

SUN: GEMINI • DECANATE: GEMINI/MERCURY • DEGREE: 2°–3° GEMINI • MODE: MUTABLE • ELEMENT: AIR

Your Personal Powers

Quick comprehension, keen intelligence, excellent communication skills, and vivid imagination are just some of your personal powers. Your ruling planet, Mercury, indicates that you possess a talent for critical analysis and skills in expressing your ideas in writing or verbally. As you are likely to be versatile, resist scattering your energy in many directions. You gain power when you combine your foresight with self-discipline and remain focused on a few goals. Although you can be very idealistic, you possess an innate common sense that inspires you to seek the truth. Nevertheless, impressionable and visionary, you thrive on inspiration, but you must beware of losing some of your power to fantasy or escapism. Fortunately, you are also ambitious with the ability to quickly recognize opportunities or turn situations to your advantage. This is aided by your good sense of structure, natural business sense, and organizational skills. As a practical visionary you can be very determined when you set on a course of action, often willing to take a risk to achieve your objectives.

Your Powers of Attraction in Relationships

People are attracted to your sharp insight and subtle perceptivity. Being fair-minded, you usually believe that actions speak louder than words. Sociable and clever, you are able to impress others with kindness and generosity. Although sensitive and emotional, you may vacillate between being aloof on the one hand and caring or tender on the other. Being highly intuitive you usually work best in relationships when you trust your own instincts and are totally honest with your partners. You are attracted to individuals who are straightforward and direct or those who can match you in shrewdness and intelligence. To create harmony in your close relationships you need to resist power struggles or being stubborn. Although independent, you can still work well with others, sometimes acting as a spokesperson or peacemaker.

Your attractive qualities: energy, communication skills, business sense, idealist, practical, strong determination, caring, compassionate, talent for writing, sensitive, honest, frank, popular, fair, spiritual, generous, love of home, active, kind, visionary

Your less attractive qualities: manipulative, escapist, materialistic, restless, opinionated, nervous, stubborn, undemonstrative, fixed ideas, repressed, get-rich-quick schemes, controlling

Your Venus Power

The planet Venus has a great deal of influence on your powers of attraction. Below are four possible Venus types for women and men. To find your Venus you need to go to page 771, where you will find the Venus table and extra information. The planet Mars also affects your powers of attraction. To find your Mars table and interpretation go to page 761.

WOMEN WITH VENUS IN ARIES: Self-reliant and strong, you usually want things your own way. This can present problems if you refuse to compromise with your partners. Your life lessons in the area of love and relationships often involve patience and learning to trust. When you project the full power of your Venus, however, you can radiate a charismatic and captivating energy and make a strong impression on others. Independence is often high on your relationship agenda.

MEN WITH VENUS IN ARIES: You are drawn to strong, independent women who can stand up to you. Although you can enthusiastically follow the object of your desire, you may lose power if you allow your forceful emotions to become too dominant. Warm and passionate, you have a side to your nature that longs for new adventures. Romantic and chivalrous, you really enjoy the excitement of the initial chase but unless you keep the enthusiasm alive and avoid falling into a rut you may become easily bored.

WOMEN WITH VENUS IN TAURUS: Warm and affectionate, you are naturally tactile with a love of sensual pleasures. With a streak of the conventional you love the simple pleasures of life: good food, close friends, and happy relationships. Having an inner strength you can express genuine patience and are often a pillar of support for loved ones and friends. Although you possess endurance be careful not to let this turn into plain stubbornness.

MEN WITH VENUS IN TAURUS: As you yourself may be attractive to the opposite sex, you desire a partner who is sensual and loving or who has physical beauty. Needing stability, when faced with changes that are out of your control you may become insecure or possessive. Faithful and reassuring, however, you can be affectionate, tactile, and constant in your love. Your own sense of style and love of beauty imply that you can be attracted to creative people, especially in art and music.

WOMEN WITH VENUS IN GEMINI: Curious, with a bright and animated approach to life, you are attracted to those who are clever or sophisticated. Your love of variety and desire for knowledge suggest that you need a partner and friends who can keep you mentally stimulated. Although witty and a good conversationalist, you may need to keep in touch with your deeper feelings. Nevertheless, intelligent and friendly, you possess a youthful sense of wonder and seek a playmate who can keep you from becoming bored.

MEN WITH VENUS IN GEMINI: Friendly and sociable, you attract others with your clever and amusing conversation. Drawn to people who can match you in wit and intelligence, you usually prefer to keep relationships light rather than emotionally intense. With your youthful charm and desire for knowledge and new experiences you usually have many friends and a low boredom threshold.

WOMEN WITH VENUS IN CANCER: With your intuitive abilities and sympathetic nature, you are usually supportive of those you love. Impressionable and empathetic, your receptivity allows you to quickly pick up on the moods of others, making you especially aware of the emotional changes in your close partner. As you often display true maternal tendencies toward those you know, you want a partner who is considerate and sensitive.

MEN WITH VENUS IN CANCER: Being caring and sensitive, you probably seek a nurturing partner who could provide you with emotional security and a sense of belonging in a loving and safe environment. Receptive to others, at times you find it hard to be direct or confrontational in relationships. Usually you deal indirectly with what is causing you concern, and although you are willing to make sacrifices for dear ones, resist the temptation to be exploited by those you love.

To read all about your Outer Planets and work out how to use your personalized timetable, go to Section Three, page 789.

Your Personalized Timetable

JUPITER BENEFICIAL
1938 1/1 – until 1939 7/2
1939 8/26 – until 1940 2/9
1943 6/19 – 8/4
1944 11/29 – until 1945 2/25
1945 7/27 – 10/14
1949 3/7 – 8/11
1949 10/26 – until 1950 1/18
1951 4/11 – 5/28
1951 10/15 – until 1952 1/14
1954 10/9 – 12/25
1955 5/31 – 7/19
1956 11/5 – until 1957 4/5
1957 7/2 – 9/28
1961 2/16 – until 1962 1/1
1963 3/25 – 5/7
1966 9/12 – until 1967 2/3
1967 5/6 – 7/3
1968 10/17 – until 1969 9/12
1973 1/30 – 4/29
1973 7/1 – 12/13
1975 3/8 – 4/19
1978 8/24 – 10/26
1978 12/26 – until 1979 6/14
1980 10/1 – until 1981 8/26
1985 1/14 – 3/30
1985 8/15 – 11/19
1987 2/20 – 4/3
1990 8/7 – 9/26
1991 2/5 – 5/22
1992 9/15 – 12/7
1993 3/24 – 8/6
1996 12/29 – until 1997 3/9
1998 7/1 – 8/3
1999 2/1 – 3/17
2002 7/21 – 9/6
2004 8/30 – 11/15
2005 5/2 – 7/9
2008 12/12 – until 2009 2/19
2010 5/21 – 9/27
2011 1/8 – 2/28

SATURN BENEFICIAL
1938 1/1 – 3/26
1946 7/14 – 10/13
1946 12/28 – until 1947 6/27
1950 10/1 – until 1951 11/11
1952 4/15 – 8/4
1961 2/13 – 8/16
1961 11/7 – until 1962 4/20
1962 6/23 – until 1963 1/6
1966 5/21 – 9/2
1967 2/11 – 5/5
1967 10/21 – until 1968 1/25
1975 8/25 – until 1976 2/14
1976 5/8 – 8/6
1979 11/14 – until 1980 3/2
1980 8/6 – until 1981 9/17
1990 4/4 – 6/4
1990 12/22 – until 1992 2/10
1996 3/18 – until 1997 3/9
2005 6/27 – 9/17
2006 1/31 – 6/6
2009 9/14 – until 2010 10/24
2011 5/31 – 6/26

URANUS BENEFICIAL
1954 10/18 – until 1958 4/26
1967 9/14 – until 1971 8/8
1994 2/23 – until 1998 12/24
2010 4/4 – Continues

NEPTUNE BENEFICIAL
1939 10/31 – until 1948 7/29
1995 2/26 – until 2003 11/18

PLUTO BENEFICIAL
1938 1/1 – until 1944 7/5
1968 11/14 – until 1976 9/8

JUPITER CHALLENGING
1938 4/8 – 9/11
1938 11/24 – until 1939 2/16

1943 11/3 – until 1944 1/22
1944 6/27 – 9/13
1947 1/28 – 4/29
1947 9/25 – 12/11
1950 3/19 – until 1951 1/29
1955 10/9 – until 1956 3/2
1956 6/3 – 8/28
1959 1/4 – 6/8
1959 8/30 – 11/25
1962 3/2 – 5/26
1962 8/8 – until 1963 1/9
1967 9/20 – until 1968 8/12
1970 12/16 – until 1971 11/9
1974 2/13 – 4/27
1974 9/23 – 12/13
1979 9/3 – until 1980 7/26
1982 11/30 – until 1983 3/13
1983 4/11 – 10/22
1986 1/29 – 4/7
1991 8/18 – 11/8
1992 2/22 – 7/6
1994 11/14 – until 1995 2/2
1995 5/31 – 10/1
1998 1/11 – 3/20
2003 8/2 – 10/17
2004 4/1 – 6/8
2006 10/30 – until 2007 1/13
2007 7/17 – 8/27
2009 5/6 – 7/25
2009 12/22 – until 2010 3/4

SATURN CHALLENGING
1948 8/7 – until 1949 9/10
1955 11/23 – until 1957 1/13
1957 6/7 – 10/12
1964 2/7 – until 1965 3/23
1965 11/3 – 11/24
1977 9/15 – until 1978 3/23
1978 5/28 – 10/23
1979 3/1 – 7/15
1984 12/30 – until 1985 5/19
1985 9/28 – until 1986 11/21
1993 3/12 – 9/24
1993 11/30 – until 1994 5/6
1994 8/11 – until 1995 1/27
2006 11/13 – 12/28
2007 7/21 – until 2008 8/24

URANUS CHALLENGING
1960 10/9 – until 1964 9/5
1980 1/13 – until 1984 10/7
2001 5/5 – until 2006 2/27

NEPTUNE CHALLENGING
1967 11/30 – until 1975 11/9
2009 3/1 – Continues

PLUTO CHALLENGING
1953 10/15 – until 1963 7/27
1992 12/31 – until 2000 9/29

JUPITER SPECIAL
1941 5/3 – 7/12
1953 4/15 – 6/24
1964 8/15 – 10/15
1965 3/27 – 6/7
1976 7/14 – 11/29
1977 3/2 – 5/22
1988 6/24 – until 1989 5/5
2000 6/5 – 9/10
2000 10/19 – until 2001 4/16
2012 5/19 – Continues

SATURN SPECIAL
1941 7/2 – 11/23
1942 3/22 – 8/9
1942 11/12 – until 1943 4/25
1971 5/7 – until 1972 6/5
2000 6/12 – until 2001 1/1
2001 2/17 – 7/15
2001 12/14 – until 2002 4/2

URANUS SPECIAL
1940 6/30 – until 1945 4/16

May 25

Your Personal Powers

Friendly and intelligent, your personal powers show you to be mentally sharp, intuitive, and spontaneous. Your ruling planet, Mercury, enhances your youthful quality and communication skills. You gain power when you combine your enterprising spirit with your astute perception. Being daring and competitive you enjoy adventures or trying out new ideas. Although you grasp concepts very quickly with your agile mind, you lose some of your power when your desire for speed turns into restlessness. Even though you gain power from your inner strength and determination, resist an inclination to be obstinate. A natural gift for business or material achievement indicates that you can attain success as long as you have inner faith and show willingness to put in the necessary work. Innovative, you can be witty and inspired with possible writing or musical gifts. Perceptive and discerning, you possess strong insight and a desire for freedom. Your ability to push relentlessly forward toward your goal can help your overall success.

Your Powers of Attraction in Relationships

Your intelligence, youthful charm, and thoughtfulness often attract others. Not one to give your heart immediately, you often weigh your desire for freedom with your need for caution and security. You are usually attracted to hard-working, straightforward, and successful people who possess a natural sense of authority. Your emotional sensitivity, sincerity, and spontaneity attract others. Issues of trust indicate that you need to find ways to express yourself freely before you give your heart away. When in love, you can be quietly dramatic and sensitive, even though you make attempts to appear in control, cool, and collected. Although you are independent and success-oriented, make time for regular rest or self-analysis to help bring your dynamic drive and inspiration into your relationships.

Your attractive qualities: intelligent, highly intuitive, spontaneous, people skills, perfectionist, perceptive, witty, innovative, creative mind, playful, freedom-loving, business ability, confident, thoughtful, inventive, spiritual, ambitious, popular, communication skills

Your less attractive qualities: nervous, lack of faith, impatient, too serious, impulsive, irresponsible, over-emotional, doubting, rebellious, obstinate, irritable, argumentative, self-centered, dissatisfaction, critical

Your Venus Power

The planet Venus has a great deal of influence on your powers of attraction. Below are four possible Venus types for women and men. To find your Venus you need to go to page 771, where you will find the Venus table and extra information. The planet Mars also affects your powers of attraction. To find your Mars table and interpretation go to page 761.

WOMEN WITH VENUS IN ARIES: You gain power from your strong individuality, energy, and enthusiasm. Your young-at-heart and spirited approach to relationships adds to your appeal. If you become too impatient or self-absorbed, however, your partnerships are likely to suffer. Nevertheless, you can be creative, sharp, and quick, especially when you are able to share new and exciting projects with your partners. Mischievous, with a love of action, you may even incite them to a playful fight.

MEN WITH VENUS IN ARIES: As you often have the courage and strength to initiate situations, you like to take the lead. With your unconscious desire for conquest you may also have to beware of being competitive with your partners. Nevertheless, you are drawn to direct and strong-willed women who can share your love of action and enthusiasm for life. When you are feeling good you can be charming and enthusiastic in romantic situations with an entertaining and spontaneous spirit.

WOMEN WITH VENUS IN TAURUS: Warm and affectionate, you are naturally tactile with a love of sensual pleasures. With a streak of the conventional you love the simple pleasures of life: good food, close friends, and happy relationships. Having an inner strength you can express genuine patience and are often a pillar of support for loved ones and friends. Although you possess endurance be careful not to let this turn into plain stubbornness.

MEN WITH VENUS IN TAURUS: As you yourself may be attractive to the opposite sex, you desire a partner who is sensual and loving or who has physical beauty. Needing stability, when faced with changes that are out of your control you may become insecure or possessive. Reliable and reassuring, however, you can be affectionate, tactile, and constant in your love.

Your own sense of style and love of beauty imply that you can be attracted to creative people, especially in art and music.

WOMEN WITH VENUS IN GEMINI: By nature you are young at heart, adaptable, and sociable. Being curious and willing to cooperate makes you a good team player. Usually you are drawn to articulate people who have charm and flair or sharp wit. With a need to expand your knowledge you also look for a partner who can challenge or stimulate you intellectually. Although you love to talk with all types of people, you may need to develop your listening skills and tune in to your feelings in order to build better communication in your relationships.

MEN WITH VENUS IN GEMINI: Adaptable yet often flirtatious, you enjoy mixing with people who are quick-minded and versatile. Since you can learn a great deal through interacting with others, you are often attracted to intelligent partners who have comprehensive knowledge or good ideas. One of your less attractive qualities is your tendency to get bored or be inconsistent. Having an adaptable partner is important to you, therefore it must be someone who can offer you different options and keep you interested.

WOMEN WITH VENUS IN CANCER: Sensitive and understanding, you are sympathetic to other people's emotions and needs. Protective toward those you love, close relationships with your partner, relatives, and friends are important to your sense of well-being. Aware of how easy it is to hurt other people's feelings you are often indirect and approach delicate issues in a roundabout way. Nevertheless, learning to face facts and not allowing others to exploit your good nature is a valuable lesson.

MEN WITH VENUS IN CANCER: You seek a partner who is sympathetic, caring, and protective. Able to be forgiving and compassionate, you want a secure emotional bond in your close relationships. Usually you are drawn to partners who are maternal, unselfish, or demonstrative with their feelings. Although you can sometimes appear to others as impressionable, you have powerful emotions and inner strength.

To read all about your Outer Planets and work out how to use your personalized timetable, go to Section Three, page 789.

II

Your Personalized Timetable

JUPITER BENEFICIAL
1938 1/1 – 2/7
1939 5/4 – 7/17
1939 8/10 – until 1940 2/14
1943 6/24 – 8/8
1944 12/7 – until 1945 2/16
1945 8/1 – 10/18
1949 3/13 – 8/2
1949 11/3 – until 1950 1/22
1951 4/15 – 6/3
1951 10/7 – until 1952 1/21
1954 10/18 – 12/16
1955 6/5 – 7/23
1956 11/10 – until 1957 3/28
1957 7/9 – 10/2
1961 2/20 – until 1962 1/5
1963 3/29 – 5/11
1966 9/18 – until 1967 1/27
1967 5/13 – 7/7
1968 10/22 – until 1969 9/17
1973 2/3 – 5/12
1973 6/19 – 12/18
1975 3/12 – 4/23
1978 8/29 – 11/8
1978 12/13 – until 1979 6/19
1980 10/5 – until 1981 8/31
1985 1/18 – 4/4
1985 8/8 – 11/26
1987 2/24 – 4/7
1990 8/11 – 10/2
1991 1/29 – 5/29
1992 9/19 – 12/14
1993 3/16 – 8/12
1997 1/2 – 3/14
1999 2/6 – 3/21
2002 7/26 – 9/11
2003 3/17 – 4/21
2004 9/4 – 11/21
2005 4/23 – 7/18
2008 12/17 – until 2009 2/24
2010 5/27 – 9/20
2011 1/14 – 3/4

SATURN BENEFICIAL
1938 1/1 – 4/3
1946 7/22 – 11/1
1946 12/9 – until 1947 7/5
1950 10/9 – until 1951 5/27
1951 5/31 – 11/21
1952 4/2 – 8/15
1961 2/22 – 8/2
1961 11/20 – until 1963 1/15
1966 6/4 – 8/18
1967 2/19 – 5/15
1967 10/8 – until 1968 2/5
1975 9/2 – until 1976 2/1
1976 5/21 – 8/14
1979 11/27 – until 1980 2/17
1980 8/15 – until 1981 9/25
1990 12/31 – until 1992 2/18
1996 3/26 – until 1997 3/17
2005 7/5 – 9/27
2006 1/19 – 6/16
2009 9/22 – until 2010 11/1
2011 5/7 – 7/20

URANUS BENEFICIAL
1955 7/30 – until 1958 6/2
1967 9/30 – until 1999 1/12
2010 4/22 – until 1938 1/1

NEPTUNE BENEFICIAL
1940 9/26 – until 1948 9/3
1996 1/24 – until 2003 12/27

PLUTO BENEFICIAL
1938 1/1 – until 1945 6/14
1969 10/4 – until 1977 7/14

JUPITER CHALLENGING
1938 4/14 – 9/3
1938 12/2 – until 1939 2/20

1943 11/13 – until 1944 1/13
1944 7/3 – 9/18
1947 2/6 – 4/20
1947 10/1 – 12/15
1950 3/24 – until 1951 2/2
1955 10/14 – until 1956 2/23
1956 6/10 – 9/2
1959 1/10 – 5/31
1959 9/7 – 11/29
1962 3/6 – 6/5
1962 7/29 – until 1963 1/14
1967 9/25 – until 1968 8/17
1970 12/21 – until 1971 11/13
1974 2/17 – 5/2
1974 9/16 – 12/20
1979 9/7 – until 1980 7/31
1982 12/4 – until 1983 10/27
1986 2/2 – 4/11
1991 8/22 – 11/15
1992 2/14 – 7/12
1994 11/19 – until 1995 2/9
1995 5/24 – 10/7
1998 1/16 – 3/24
2003 8/6 – 10/23
2004 3/23 – 6/17
2006 11/4 – until 2007 1/18
2007 7/5 – 9/8
2009 5/15 – 7/15
2009 12/27 – until 2010 3/8

SATURN CHALLENGING
1948 8/14 – until 1949 9/18
1955 12/1 – until 1957 1/24
1957 5/25 – 10/23
1964 2/15 – until 1965 3/31
1965 10/9 – 12/19
1977 9/24 – until 1978 3/8
1978 6/11 – 11/2
1979 2/16 – 7/24
1985 1/10 – 5/6
1985 10/8 – until 1986 11/29
1993 3/21 – 9/8
1993 12/15 – until 1994 5/22
1994 7/25 – until 1995 2/5
2007 7/29 – until 2008 9/1

URANUS CHALLENGING
1960 11/7 – until 1965 7/2
1980 2/23 – until 1984 10/28
2002 2/26 – until 2007 1/1

NEPTUNE CHALLENGING
1967 12/29 – until 1976 9/28
2009 3/30 – Continues

PLUTO CHALLENGING
1954 9/15 – until 1963 8/26
1993 11/20 – until 2000 11/2

JUPITER SPECIAL
1941 5/7 – 7/17
1942 1/26 – 2/14
1953 4/20 – 6/28
1964 8/27 – 10/3
1965 4/1 – 6/11
1976 7/20 – 11/22
1977 3/9 – 5/26
1988 6/28 – until 1989 5/10
2000 6/10 – until 2001 4/21
2012 5/23 – Continues

SATURN SPECIAL
1941 7/12 – 11/11
1942 4/1 – 8/23
1942 10/28 – until 1943 5/3
1971 5/14 – until 1972 6/12
2000 6/21 – 12/14
2001 3/6 – 7/25
2001 12/2 – until 2002 4/13

URANUS SPECIAL
1940 7/25 – until 1945 5/5

May 26

SUN: GEMINI • DECANATE: GEMINI/MERCURY • DEGREE: 3°5–5° GEMINI • MODE: MUTABLE • ELEMENT: AIR

Your Personal Powers

Your amiable charm, creativity, and agile mind mark you as someone special. Usually you like to express your individuality and have a flair for the dramatic. You also possess a youthful spirit and the potential to develop your writing skills or artistic talents. Being intellectually bright and observant, you grasp ideas or subjects very quickly. Usually you are well-informed or knowledgeable about many topics. Talkative, your gift for communication implies that you enjoy intellectual debates, discussion, and friendly chats. You gain power when you combine your unique vision, discipline, and hard-working attitude with determination and perseverance. You can lose some of your power if you abandon your plans, avoid your responsibilities, or let idleness undermine your determination. Fortunately, you are usually conscientious with a sensible approach to life and a good business sense. You enjoy power and usually prefer to be in control, as indicated by your inborn executive or organizational abilities, but your love of harmony emphasizes the importance of your home in your priorities.

Your Powers of Attraction in Relationships

People are attracted to your quick intelligence and friendly personality. A need to be popular suggests that you are likely to have many friends. Although in relationships you need a certain amount of control, resist going to extremes by being too dominant or too passive. Romantic and dramatic in love, however, you can be generous and affectionate. When your support is needed you can be a tower of strength for others; you are willing to support friends and family or make sacrifices for those you love. If insecurity starts affecting your relationships, however, you are likely to become overemotional or stubborn. You are attracted to partners who are success-oriented yet emotionally sensitive. You can especially benefit from partnerships and cooperative efforts.

Your attractive qualities: good communication skills, practical, caring, responsible, home-loving, aesthetic sense, imaginative, disciplined, idealistic, tenacious, enthusiastic, perceptive, adviser, intuitive, creative talents, determined, writing potential, courage, strategist

Your less attractive qualities: stubborn, anxious, rebellious, escapist, melancholy, materialistic, lack of persistence, inertia, stressed, avoidance, restless, manipulative, unstable

Your Venus Power

The planet Venus has a great deal of influence on your powers of attraction. Below are four possible Venus types for women and men. To find your Venus you need to go to page 771, where you will find the Venus table and extra information. The planet Mars also affects your powers of attraction. To find your Mars table and interpretation go to page 761.

WOMEN WITH VENUS IN ARIES: With your strong desires and enthusiastic nature you can be a passionate lover. Although idealistic and single-minded, you need to avoid unnecessary conflicts in your relationships by being more patient and less headstrong. Although at times others can accuse you of being bossy or impulsive, you possess a great deal of warmth and charm. When necessary you can disarm others by making them feel important.

MEN WITH VENUS IN ARIES: Usually you are drawn to courageous or assertive women who possess strong personal magnetism. You might therefore find those who seem to be independent or action-oriented very attractive. Your own eagerness and need for activity suggest that you start relationships with great enthusiasm, especially if they offer you excitement or adventures. The challenge is often to maintain relationships and not get bored too easily.

WOMEN WITH VENUS IN TAURUS: For your ideal relationship you seek a partner who is both financially secure and demonstrative with his affections. With these thoughts in mind you are likely to also want a partner who is refined yet pragmatic, or someone concerned with safeguarding your future. Although you have a stubborn streak you can be loving and affectionate in your relationships, and with your good sense of style may have an attraction for the arts, music, or luxury items.

MEN WITH VENUS IN TAURUS: Although you are usually drawn to sensual and physically beautiful individuals, you want a partner who is also reliable and loyal. When in love you enjoy buying your partner things of quality that will grow in value or useful things of a practical nature. You also love to socialize and entertain, especially in luxurious surroundings. Affectionate and caring, you are often attracted to creative people or those with artistic talents.

WOMEN WITH VENUS IN GEMINI: Charming and usually easygoing, you like to talk to people who are intelligent and witty. With a good social sense and a desire for mental expansion, you need a partner who is informed and who has good

ideas. Although you enjoy having different experiences, you need to resist your tendencies to become bored too quickly or be too talkative. As you enjoy sharing and learning new things, you usually prefer being with someone rather than operating alone.

MEN WITH VENUS IN GEMINI: Informed and curious yet charming and friendly, you seek a partner who shares your interests or enjoys your witty remarks. Although a good communicator, you have an inborn tendency to be lighthearted and less profound about deep emotional commitment. Although you are keen on experiences that bring variety into your life, boredom or scattering your energies in too many directions is probably your biggest handicap in relationships. Nevertheless you are attracted to intelligent partners who can match your lively banter.

WOMEN WITH VENUS IN CANCER: Gentle and tender, you are romantic by nature. You possess a strong need for security and usually help others feel safe and protected. This preservation is especially centered around the home, which your haven from life's storm. Although your maternal instincts are strong, avoid making too many sacrifices for others at your own expense. Nevertheless, affectionate and caring, once committed to a relationship your loyalty and devotion to your partner are very strong.

MEN WITH VENUS IN CANCER: Affectionate with a strong sensitive streak, you can love very deeply. You may find yourself drawn to sympathetic partners who can tune in to your moods and feelings as well as be reassuring and supportive. Family links are especially important to you and the more positive these relationships are the more confident and safe you feel.

To read all about your Outer Planets and work out how to use your personalized timetable, go to Section Three, page 789.

Your Personalized Timetable

JUPITER BENEFICIAL
1938 1/1 – 2/12
1939 5/9 – 11/5
1939 12/14 – until 1940 2/18
1943 6/28 – 8/13
1944 12/18 – until 1945 2/6
1945 8/7 – 10/23
1949 3/18 – 7/26
1949 11/10 – until 1950 1/26
1951 4/19 – 6/9
1951 9/30 – until 1952 1/26
1954 11/1 – 12/2
1955 6/10 – 7/28
1956 11/16 – until 1957 3/20
1957 7/16 – 10/7
1961 2/25 – until 1962 1/10
1963 4/2 – 5/16
1966 9/24 – until 1967 1/19
1967 5/20 – 7/12
1968 10/27 – until 1969 5/7
1969 6/8 – 9/21
1973 2/7 – 12/23
1975 3/16 – 4/27
1978 9/2 – until 1979 3/8
1979 4/12 – 6/24
1980 10/10 – until 1981 9/5
1985 1/22 – 4/10
1985 7/31 – 12/2
1987 2/28 – 4/11
1990 8/16 – 10/8
1991 1/22 – 6/4
1992 9/24 – 12/22
1993 3/8 – 8/17
1997 1/6 – 3/18
1997 9/22 – 10/23
1999 2/10 – 3/25
2002 7/30 – 9/16
2003 3/4 – 5/5
2004 9/9 – 11/26
2005 4/15 – 7/26
2008 12/21 – until 2009 2/28
2010 6/2 – 9/13
2011 1/19 – 3/8

SATURN BENEFICIAL
1938 1/7 – 4/10
1946 7/29 – until 1947 7/13
1950 10/17 – until 1951 4/24
1951 7/2 – 12/1
1952 3/20 – 8/25
1961 3/4 – 7/19
1961 12/1 – until 1963 1/23
1966 6/27 – 7/26
1967 2/27 – 5/25
1967 9/26 – until 1968 2/15
1975 9/12 – until 1976 1/20
1976 5/31 – 8/21
1979 12/14 – until 1980 1/30
1980 8/23 – until 1981 10/3
1991 1/8 – until 1992 2/26
1992 9/17 – 11/13
1996 4/3 – until 1997 3/25
2005 7/12 – 10/8
2006 1/6 – 6/25
2009 9/30 – until 2010 11/10
2011 4/22 – 8/3

URANUS BENEFICIAL
1955 8/16 – until 1958 6/23
1967 10/15 – until 1971 9/14
1995 1/18 – until 1999 1/28
2010 5/14 – Continues

NEPTUNE BENEFICIAL
1940 10/24 – until 1949 7/14
1996 2/20 – until 2004 1/24

PLUTO BENEFICIAL
1938 7/17 – until 1946 5/10
1969 11/3 – until 1977 8/25

JUPITER CHALLENGING
1938 4/19 – 8/27

1938 12/9 – until 1939 2/24
1943 11/25 – until 1944 1/1
1944 7/8 – 9/22
1947 2/16 – 4/9
1947 10/6 – 12/20
1950 3/28 – until 1951 2/6
1955 10/20 – until 1956 2/16
1956 6/16 – 9/6
1959 1/15 – 5/23
1959 9/14 – 12/4
1962 3/10 – 6/22
1962 7/12 – until 1963 1/19
1967 9/30 – until 1968 4/1
1968 5/13 – 8/22
1970 12/26 – until 1971 11/18
1974 2/21 – 5/8
1974 9/8 – 12/27
1979 9/12 – until 1980 8/5
1982 12/9 – until 1983 11/1
1986 2/6 – 4/16
1991 8/27 – 11/23
1992 2/5 – 7/17
1994 11/23 – until 1995 2/16
1995 5/16 – 10/13
1998 1/20 – 3/29
2003 8/11 – 10/28
2004 3/15 – 6/24
2006 11/8 – until 2007 1/23
2007 6/25 – 9/18
2009 5/28 – 7/2
2010 1/1 – 3/12

SATURN CHALLENGING
1948 8/22 – until 1949 9/26
1955 12/10 – until 1956 7/10
1956 8/20 – until 1957 2/4
1957 5/11 – 11/1
1964 2/22 – until 1965 4/9
1965 9/24 – until 1966 1/2
1977 10/3 – until 1978 2/23
1978 6/23 – 11/15
1979 2/3 – 8/2
1985 1/22 – 4/22
1985 10/17 – until 1986 12/7
1993 3/31 – 8/25
1993 12/26 – until 1995 2/13
2007 8/6 – until 2008 9/8

URANUS CHALLENGING
1961 8/25 – until 1965 7/23
1980 11/28 – until 1984 11/14
2002 3/15 – until 2007 1/24

NEPTUNE CHALLENGING
1968 2/19 – until 1976 11/3
2010 2/24 – Continues

PLUTO CHALLENGING
1954 10/25 – until 1964 7/23
1993 12/15 – until 2000 11/28

JUPITER SPECIAL
1941 5/11 – 7/22
1942 1/10 – 3/3
1953 4/24 – 7/2
1965 4/6 – 6/15
1976 7/26 – 11/15
1977 3/15 – 5/30
1988 7/3 – until 1989 1/4
1989 2/4 – 5/14
2000 6/14 – until 2001 4/26
2012 5/27 – Continues

SATURN SPECIAL
1941 7/23 – 10/30
1942 4/10 – 9/22
1942 9/26 – until 1943 5/11
1971 5/22 – until 1972 6/20
2000 6/29 – 12/1
2001 3/18 – 8/4
2001 11/20 – until 2002 4/22

URANUS SPECIAL
1941 5/23 – until 1945 5/23

May 27

SUN: GEMINI · DECANATE: GEMINI/MERCURY · DEGREE: 4°5–6° GEMINI · MODE: MUTABLE · ELEMENT: AIR

Your Personal Powers

Enterprising, intelligent, and versatile, you are an alert and friendly individual. Mercury, your ruling planet, grants you a love of variety and excellent communication skills. You may also possess a talent for writing. Although your original ideas and creative mind can inspire you to be adventurous, you gain power by utilizing your knowledge in a practical way. Your speed of thought warns that you can lose some of your power by being impatient or not developing your listening skills. Interested in many subjects and not wanting to be bored, you can benefit from all types of study and exploring many subjects can broaden your horizon. Your intuition and quick instincts grant you keen insight into people. Generally optimistic and enthusiastic, you have a dynamic approach to life that can take you far. Although a pragmatic and resourceful strategist, you also possess an inner sensitivity you may sometimes keep hidden. Courageous and idealistic, you have opportunities in life to enjoy different experiences or to travel.

Your Powers of Attraction in Relationships

Your fast responses, intelligence, and broad-minded approach to life attract others. Being sensitive often allows you to recognize the feelings and hidden motives of others and enhances your compassion. The same sensitivity may cause you to conceal your own emotions or make you reluctant to express your thoughts. Usually you are sociable and work well with others, preferring to use persuasion rather than confrontation. Strong-willed individuals, particularly those with natural leadership ability, often attract you. Restless and sometimes a little skeptical about people, you need to take your time to get to know your partner. Nevertheless, being idealistic, you can be supportive and generous with those you love. The more secure you feel within yourself the better you relate to others.

Your attractive qualities: mental strength, fast responses, versatile, imaginative, creative, resoluteness, bravery, idealistic, enterprising, rational, spiritual potential, inventive, detached, love of travel, communication skills, entrepreneurial spirit, original ideas

Your less attractive qualities: restless, argumentative, skeptical, too talkative, tense, nervous, impulsive, mistrust-ing, stubborn, secretive, bored, cynical, overemotional, high-strung

Your Venus Power

The planet Venus has a great deal of influence on your powers of attraction. Below are four possible Venus types for women and men. To find your Venus you need to go to page 771, where you will find the Venus table and extra information. The planet Mars also affects your powers of attraction. To find your Mars table and interpretation go to page 761.

WOMEN WITH VENUS IN ARIES: You gain power from your strong individuality, energy, and enthusiasm. Your young-at-heart and spirited approach to relationships adds to your appeal. If you become too impatient or self-absorbed, however, your partnerships are likely to suffer. Nevertheless you can be creative, sharp, and quick, especially when you are able to share new and exciting projects with your partners. Mischievous, with a love of action, you may even incite them to a playful fight.

MEN WITH VENUS IN ARIES: You are drawn to strong, independent women who can stand up to you. Although you can enthusiastically follow the object of your desire, you may lose power if you allow your forceful emotions to become too dominant. Warm and passionate, you have a side to your nature that longs for new adventures. Romantic and chivalrous, you really enjoy the excitement of the initial chase, but unless you keep the enthusiasm alive and avoid falling into a rut you may become easily bored.

WOMEN WITH VENUS IN TAURUS: Warm and affectionate, you are drawn to partners with whom you can share life's simple comforts. With a need for stability and security or an appreciation of earthly pleasures, you may have to avoid overindulgence or becoming too preoccupied with material concerns. Nevertheless, your sociability and friendliness usually make you popular. You need a partner who can also share your appreciation of beauty and style.

MEN WITH VENUS IN TAURUS: As well as attracting people with your warm personality, you also possess an innate sense of the value of material possessions. Keeping yourself stylish and having an attractive home can therefore be important to you. You are naturally attracted to practical yet sensual women who understand your need for comfort, security, and

the pleasures and luxuries of life. Naturally affectionate, you enjoy socializing but can make a loyal and loving partner.

WOMEN WITH VENUS IN GEMINI: In relationships you need intellectual stimulation and usually prefer to keep things light. Certainly not boring, you love to talk and are at your best being witty and entertaining. Although your easygoing approach to relationships is very attractive, guard against losing touch with your deeper emotions. You prefer a partner who can keep up with your fast stream of ideas, and if you have shared interests then so much the better.

MEN WITH VENUS IN GEMINI: Charming, amusing, and adaptable, you attract others with your natural communication skills and friendly personality. You have a wonderful child-like quality and love to keep life playful, but a reluctance to contact your deeper feelings may cause you to avoid serious commitment. With your need for variety and intellectual stimulation you are attracted to clever and amusing partners who have many interesting sides to their personalities.

WOMEN WITH VENUS IN CANCER: Possessing a soft femininity, you have tender and sensitive emotions. Sympathetic and caring, you often mother those in your care by making sure that they are comfortable and have plenty to eat. When you feel hurt or insecure in relationships you are likely to cover your feelings by being defensive or appearing tough on the outside while on the inside you are feeling vulnerable. Affectionate and romantic, you make a faithful and devoted partner.

MEN WITH VENUS IN CANCER: Being emotionally receptive, you can be a sensitive lover. With your desire to care for and protect others you are likely to have strong family connections. Love is often tied in with being attentive to the needs of others and you may find yourself attracted to individuals who have sympathetic or maternal qualities. Security-conscious, you need a loyal partner who can offer you support and ideally be a good cook and homemaker.

To read all about your Outer Planets and work out how to use your personalized timetable, go to Section Three, page 789.

Ⅱ

Your Personalized Timetable

JUPITER BENEFICIAL
1938 1/1 – 2/16
1939 5/14 – 10/24
1939 12/25 – until 1940 2/23
1943 7/3 – 8/17
1945 1/8 – 1/15
1945 8/12 – 10/27
1949 3/24 – 7/18
1949 11/16 – until 1950 1/30
1951 4/23 – 6/16
1951 9/23 – until 1952 2/1
1955 6/15 – 8/1
1956 11/22 – until 1957 3/13
1957 7/23 – 10/11
1961 3/2 – 9/14
1961 10/3 – until 1962 1/14
1963 4/6 – 5/21
1963 11/12 – 12/28
1966 9/30 – until 1967 1/12
1967 5/26 – 7/16
1968 11/1 – until 1969 4/23
1969 6/22 – 9/26
1973 2/11 – 12/27
1975 3/20 – 5/1
1978 9/7 – until 1979 2/23
1979 4/25 – 6/29
1980 10/14 – until 1981 9/10
1985 1/26 – 4/17
1985 7/24 – 12/7
1987 3/4 – 4/15
1990 8/20 – 10/15
1991 1/14 – 6/9
1992 9/28 – until 1993 1/1
1993 2/26 – 8/23
1997 1/10 – 3/23
1997 9/8 – 11/6
1999 2/15 – 3/29
2002 8/3 – 9/21
2003 2/23 – 5/14
2004 9/13 – 12/2
2005 4/7 – 8/2
2008 12/25 – until 2009 3/4
2010 6/9 – 9/5
2011 1/25 – 3/12

SATURN BENEFICIAL
1938 1/20 – 4/18
1946 8/6 – until 1947 7/21
1950 10/26 – until 1951 4/9
1951 7/16 – 12/14
1952 3/7 – 9/3
1961 3/15 – 7/6
1961 12/11 – until 1963 1/31
1967 3/7 – 6/5
1967 9/13 – until 1968 2/24
1975 9/22 – until 1976 1/8
1976 6/9 – 8/29
1977 3/18 – 5/5
1980 8/31 – until 1981 10/11
1991 1/16 – until 1992 3/6
1992 8/30 – 11/29
1996 4/11 – until 1997 4/1
2005 7/20 – 10/23
2005 12/22 – until 2006 7/3
2009 10/7 – until 2010 11/19
2011 4/9 – 8/14

URANUS BENEFICIAL
1955 9/2 – until 1958 7/11
1967 11/2 – until 1971 9/30
1995 2/4 – until 1999 11/30
2010 6/18 – until 1938 1/1

NEPTUNE BENEFICIAL
1940 12/1 – until 1949 8/28
1996 3/28 – until 2004 12/19

PLUTO BENEFICIAL
1938 8/21 – until 1946 7/2
1970 9/27 – until 1977 9/21

JUPITER CHALLENGING
1938 4/25 – 8/19

JUPITER BENEFICIAL (right column continued)
1938 12/15 – until 1939 2/28
1944 7/13 – 9/27
1947 3/7 – 3/21
1947 10/11 – 12/24
1950 4/2 – until 1951 2/11
1955 10/27 – until 1956 2/9
1956 6/23 – 9/11
1959 1/21 – 5/16
1959 9/20 – 12/8
1962 3/14 – until 1963 1/23
1967 10/5 – until 1968 3/20
1968 5/25 – 8/26
1970 12/31 – until 1971 6/30
1971 8/17 – 11/22
1974 2/25 – 5/14
1974 9/1 – until 1975 1/1
1979 9/16 – until 1980 8/10
1982 12/13 – until 1983 11/6
1986 2/10 – 4/21
1986 10/22 – 11/25
1991 8/31 – 12/3
1992 1/26 – 7/23
1994 11/27 – until 1995 2/25
1995 5/7 – 10/18
1998 1/24 – 4/2
2003 8/15 – 11/3
2004 3/8 – 7/1
2006 11/12 – until 2007 1/28
2007 6/17 – 9/25
2010 1/6 – 3/16

SATURN CHALLENGING
1948 8/29 – until 1949 10/4
1950 4/12 – 6/16
1955 12/18 – until 1956 6/19
1956 9/9 – until 1957 2/20
1957 4/25 – 11/10
1964 3/2 – until 1965 4/19
1965 9/11 – until 1966 1/13
1977 10/12 – until 1978 2/12
1978 7/3 – 12/2
1979 1/16 – 8/10
1985 2/7 – 4/4
1985 10/26 – until 1986 12/15
1993 4/10 – 8/13
1994 1/5 – until 1995 2/21
2007 8/13 – until 2008 9/16

URANUS CHALLENGING
1961 9/9 – until 1965 8/10
1980 12/14 – until 1984 11/30
2002 4/4 – until 2007 2/12

NEPTUNE CHALLENGING
1968 12/22 – until 1977 9/13
2010 3/23 – Continues

PLUTO CHALLENGING
1955 9/21 – until 1964 8/22
1994 1/15 – until 2001 10/22

JUPITER SPECIAL
1941 5/15 – 7/27
1941 12/31 – until 1942 3/13
1953 4/28 – 7/7
1965 4/10 – 6/20
1976 8/1 – 11/8
1977 3/21 – 6/3
1988 7/8 – 12/22
1989 2/17 – 5/18
2000 6/18 – until 2001 4/30
2012 5/31 – Continues

SATURN SPECIAL
1941 8/6 – 10/15
1942 4/18 – until 1943 5/19
1971 5/29 – until 1972 6/27
2000 7/9 – 11/19
2001 3/28 – 8/16
2001 11/7 – until 2002 4/30

URANUS SPECIAL
1941 6/8 – until 1946 3/3

143

May 28

Your Personal Powers

Articulate and direct, your personal powers include extraordinary mental energy and keen insight into people or situations. You also possess a youthful spirit and the potential for developing your writing or creative gifts. Resourceful and independent, you gain power when you combine your charm with your strategic capabilities and sharp communication skills. Although you have a very fast mind, you may lose some of your power if you become impatient or intolerant with those who do not share your quick instincts. Inspired by wisdom, you are constantly seeking knowledge. You empower yourself when you establish a belief system that can provide you with security and peace of mind. Your innate common sense and an entrepreneurial business spirit indicate that you are inventive yet unconventional. You gain power when you use your enthusiasm to promote exciting projects that can be both educational and profitable. Travel may also play a strong part in your life. Although you possess a determined and adventurous spirit, you find inner contentment when you focus on peace and harmony in your life.

Your Powers of Attraction in Relationships

Others are attracted to your honest, straightforward manner and quick intelligence. Needing mental stimulation you are often attracted to clever and dramatic individuals. Use discrimination, however, to make sure that their cleverness is used for noble aims. For you, partnerships can be particularly important, as it is here that you learn to become selfless and altruistic. You may find it hard to express your deeper feelings, so look for those with special insight into your motives or actions. Being independent, you need much freedom within a relationship or you may become restless and impatient. Idealistic with sound common sense, you seek romance but are also very aware of the practicalities. Being home-loving and security conscious, you need a loyal and hardworking partner who can fulfill responsibilities.

Your attractive qualities: good planner, inspired, strategist, progressive, daring, artistic, idealistic, compassionate, ambitious, sensitive, hardworking, responsible, shrewd, leadership, stable home life, determined, confident, well-informed, intuitive, creative, communication skills

Your less attractive qualities: intolerant, impatient, bossy, escapist, unmotivated, lack of compassion, unrealistic, lack of judgment, dependent, anxious, argumentative, stressed, too proud

Your Venus Power

The planet Venus has a great deal of influence on your powers of attraction. Below are four possible Venus types for women and men. To find your Venus you need to go to page 771, where you will find the Venus table and extra information. The planet Mars also affects your powers of attraction. To find your Mars table and interpretation go to page 761.

WOMEN WITH VENUS IN ARIES: Idealistic, passionate, and adventurous, you are direct in your dealings with others. When you are attracted to a person you usually take the initiative and use your people skills to make things happen. In close relationships you are not afraid to confront your other half. This self-assertiveness is positive if differences can be brought into the open through diplomacy and compromise. Independent and spirited, you enjoy your freedom.

MEN WITH VENUS IN ARIES: As you often have the courage and strength to initiate situations, you like to take the lead and let others follow. With your unconscious desire for conquest you may also have to beware of being competitive with your partners. Nevertheless, you are drawn to direct and strong-willed women who can share your love of action and enthusiasm for life. When you are feeling good, you can be charming and enthusiastic in romantic situations with an entertaining and spontaneous spirit.

WOMEN WITH VENUS IN TAURUS: Demonstrative and affectionate, you are naturally tactile with a love of sensual pleasures. With a streak of the conventional you love the simple pleasures of life: good food, close friends, and happy relationships. Although you possess endurance be careful not to let this turn into plain stubbornness. Having inner strength, you can express genuine patience and are often a pillar of support for loved ones and friends.

MEN WITH VENUS IN TAURUS: Although you are usually drawn to sensual and physically beautiful individuals, you want a partner who is also reliable and loyal. When in love you enjoy buying your parter things of quality that will grow in value or useful things of a practical nature. You also love to so-

cialize and entertain, especially in luxurious surroundings. Affectionate and caring, you are often attracted to creative people or those with artistic talents.

WOMEN WITH VENUS IN GEMINI: Curious, with a bright and animated approach to life, you are attracted to those who are clever or sophisticated. Your love of variety and desire for knowledge suggest that you need a partner and friends who can keep you mentally stimulated. Although witty and a good conversationalist, you may need to keep in touch with your deeper feelings. Nevertheless, intelligent and friendly, you possess a youthful sense of wonder and seek a playmate who can keep you from becoming bored.

MEN WITH VENUS IN GEMINI: Friendly and sociable, you attract others with your clever and amusing conversation. Drawn to people who can match you in wit and intelligence, you usually prefer to keep relationships light rather than emotionally intense. With your youthful charm and desire for knowledge and new experiences you usually have many friends and a low boredom threshold.

WOMEN WITH VENUS IN CANCER: With your intuitive abilities and sympathetic nature, you are usually supportive of those you love. Impressionable and empathetic, your receptivity allows you to quickly pick up on the moods of others, making you especially aware of the emotional changes in your close partner. As you often display true maternal tendencies toward those you know, you want a partner who is considerate and sensitive.

MEN WITH VENUS IN CANCER: Being caring and sensitive, you probably seek a nurturing partner who could provide you with emotional security and a sense of belonging in a loving and safe environment. Receptive to others, at times you find it hard to be direct or confrontational in relationships. Usually you deal indirectly with what is causing you concern, and although you are willing to make sacrifices for dear ones, resist the temptation to be exploited by those you love.

To read all about your Outer Planets and work out how to use your personalized timetable, go to Section Three, page 789.

II

Your Personalized Timetable

JUPITER BENEFICIAL
1938 1/1 – 2/20
1939 5/19 – 10/16
1940 1/3 – 2/27
1943 7/7 – 8/22
1945 8/17 – 11/1
1949 3/31 – 7/11
1949 11/22 – until 1950 2/3
1951 4/28 – 6/23
1951 9/15 – until 1952 2/6
1955 6/20 – 8/5
1956 11/29 – until 1957 3/5
1957 7/29 – 10/16
1961 3/6 – 8/28
1961 10/19 – until 1962 1/18
1963 4/10 – 5/26
1963 11/1 – until 1964 1/8
1966 10/7 – until 1967 1/5
1967 5/31 – 7/21
1968 11/6 – until 1969 4/13
1969 7/2 – 9/30
1973 2/16 – until 1974 1/1
1975 3/24 – 5/6
1978 9/13 – until 1979 2/14
1979 5/5 – 7/4
1980 10/19 – until 1981 9/14
1985 1/30 – 4/25
1985 7/16 – 12/12
1987 3/8 – 4/19
1990 8/25 – 10/23
1991 1/6 – 6/15
1992 10/3 – until 1993 1/16
1993 2/10 – 8/28
1997 1/15 – 3/28
1997 8/30 – 11/15
1999 2/19 – 4/2
2002 8/8 – 9/27
2003 2/15 – 5/22
2004 9/17 – 12/8
2005 3/31 – 8/8
2008 12/29 – until 2009 3/9
2010 6/18 – 8/27
2011 1/30 – 3/16

SATURN BENEFICIAL
1938 1/31 – 4/26
1938 11/30 – 12/29
1946 8/13 – until 1947 7/28
1950 11/4 – until 1951 3/27
1951 7/28 – 12/31
1952 2/18 – 9/11
1961 3/28 – 6/22
1961 12/20 – until 1963 2/8
1967 3/15 – 6/20
1967 8/29 – until 1968 3/4
1975 10/4 – 12/26
1976 6/18 – 9/6
1977 2/28 – 5/22
1980 9/8 – until 1981 10/19
1991 1/24 – until 1992 3/15
1992 8/16 – 12/12
1996 4/19 – 11/2
1997 1/2 – 4/9
2005 7/27 – until 2006 7/11
2009 10/15 – until 2010 5/4
2010 6/26 – 11/29
2011 3/27 – 8/24

URANUS BENEFICIAL
1955 9/24 – until 1958 7/27
1967 11/24 – until 1972 7/14
1995 2/21 – until 1999 12/24
2011 4/6 – Continues

NEPTUNE BENEFICIAL
1941 10/18 – until 1949 9/25
1997 2/13 – until 2005 1/17

PLUTO BENEFICIAL
1938 10/14 – until 1947 6/8
1970 10/24 – until 1978 8/7

JUPITER CHALLENGING
1938 5/2 – 8/12

1938 12/21 – until 1939 3/4
1944 7/18 – 10/1
1947 10/16 – 12/28
1950 4/7 – 10/1
1950 11/15 – until 1951 2/15
1955 11/3 – until 1956 2/1
1956 6/28 – 9/15
1959 1/28 – 5/8
1959 9/26 – 12/12
1962 3/18 – until 1963 1/28
1967 10/10 – until 1968 3/10
1968 6/3 – 8/31
1971 1/5 – 6/19
1971 8/29 – 11/26
1974 3/1 – 5/21
1974 8/24 – until 1975 1/7
1979 9/21 – until 1980 8/14
1982 12/18 – until 1983 11/10
1986 2/14 – 4/26
1986 10/9 – 12/7
1991 9/4 – 12/20
1992 1/10 – 7/28
1994 12/2 – until 1995 3/7
1995 4/26 – 10/23
1998 1/28 – 4/6
2003 8/20 – 11/9
2004 2/29 – 7/8
2006 11/17 – until 2007 2/3
2007 6/9 – 10/2
2010 1/10 – 3/20

SATURN CHALLENGING
1948 9/6 – until 1949 10/12
1950 3/28 – 7/1
1955 12/27 – until 1956 6/4
1956 9/22 – until 1957 11/19
1964 3/10 – 10/23
1964 11/11 – until 1965 4/29
1965 8/29 – until 1966 1/23
1977 10/23 – until 1978 1/30
1978 7/12 – until 1979 8/18
1985 11/3 – until 1986 12/23
1993 4/22 – 7/30
1994 1/15 – until 1995 3/1
2007 8/21 – until 2008 9/24

URANUS CHALLENGING
1961 9/26 – until 1965 8/26
1981 1/1 – until 1985 9/25
2002 5/2 – until 2007 3/1

NEPTUNE CHALLENGING
1969 1/28 – until 1977 10/28
2010 4/30 – Continues

PLUTO CHALLENGING
1955 11/4 – until 1965 7/19
1994 12/2 – until 2001 11/19

JUPITER SPECIAL
1941 5/19 – 8/1
1941 12/23 – until 1942 3/21
1953 5/2 – 7/11
1965 4/15 – 6/24
1976 8/8 – 10/31
1977 3/26 – 6/7
1988 7/13 – 12/13
1989 2/27 – 5/22
2000 6/23 – until 2001 5/5
2012 6/4 – Continues

SATURN SPECIAL
1941 8/30 – 9/21
1942 4/26 – until 1943 5/26
1971 6/6 – until 1972 7/5
1973 1/15 – 3/14
2000 7/19 – 11/7
2001 4/7 – 9/2
2001 10/21 – until 2002 5/8

URANUS SPECIAL
1941 6/27 – until 1946 4/10

145

May 29

SUN: GEMINI • DECANATE: GEMINI/MERCURY • DEGREE: 6°5–8° GEMINI • MODE: MUTABLE • ELEMENT: AIR

Your Personal Powers

Intuitive, mentally sharp, and multitalented, you are a gifted individual with a charismatic nature. Charming, persuasive, and communicative, you may have a creative approach to words and humor. Your keen intellect and desire for knowledge can lead you to become absorbed in many types of diverse activities. With your delicate nervous system, however, you lose power if you scatter your energies or become indecisive. By increasing your awareness and developing your self-expression you become more confident, self-assured, and able to attract success. Naturally dramatic and emotional, you can appear confident, witty, and perceptive, with a zest for life. If stressed and unfocused, however, you may suffer from worry and a lack of faith in your own abilities. By avoiding distractions and using your inherent strategic skills to reach definite goals, you can be disciplined and determined. You gain power when you are optimistic and enthusiastic, utilizing your creative spark to inspire both yourself and others.

Your Powers of Attraction in Relationships

Your friendly manner, sociability, and good conversational skills are very attractive to others. When positive, you can be charming and entertaining with remarkable powers of persuasion. Being idealistic with a romantic heart, you seek the pleasures of relationship, but your need for variety and new experiences may sometimes leave you uncertain about making serious commitment. Being a creative individual you often seek the company of enterprising and imaginative people who can inspire you. When in love you can be magnetic, affectionate, and generous with others. At these times you have the spontaneity to know when to go with the flow and live in the moment. If you lose faith or become indecisive, however, you can withdraw or become overly serious. You are attracted to partners who can be warmhearted and sensitive yet also detached and independent.

Your attractive qualities: friendly, inspirational, charming, inspired, balanced, popular, generous, successful, creative, intuitive, joyful, interest in the arts, mystical potential, worldly, faith, sensitive, inner nobility, business sense, talent with words

Your less attractive qualities: worry, scattered, insecure, nervous, moody, difficult, extremist, inconsiderate, dreamer, restless, lack of purpose, indecisive, impatient, isolated, too sensitive, extravagant

Your Venus Power

The planet Venus has a great deal of influence on your powers of attraction. Below are four possible Venus types for women and men. To find your Venus you need to go to page 771, where you will find the Venus table and extra information. The planet Mars also affects your powers of attraction. To find your Mars table and interpretation go to page 761.

WOMEN WITH VENUS IN ARIES: Idealistic, passionate, and adventurous, you are direct in your dealings with others. When you are attracted to a person you usually take the initiative and use your people skills to make things happen. In close relationships you are not afraid to confront your other half. This self-assertiveness is positive if differences can be brought into the open through diplomacy and compromise. Independent and spirited, you enjoy your freedom.

MEN WITH VENUS IN ARIES: As you often have the courage and strength to initiate situations, you like to take the lead. With your unconscious desire for conquest you may also have to beware of being competitive with your partners. Nevertheless, you are drawn to direct and strong-willed women who can share your love of action and enthusiasm for life. When you are feeling good you can be charming and enthusiastic in romantic situations with an entertaining and spontaneous spirit.

WOMEN WITH VENUS IN TAURUS: For your ideal relationship you seek a partner who is both financially secure and demonstrative with his affections. With these thoughts in mind, you are likely to also want a partner who is refined yet pragmatic or someone concerned with safeguarding your future. Although you have a stubborn streak, you can be loving and affectionate in your relationships and with your good sense of style may have an attraction for the arts, music, or luxury items.

MEN WITH VENUS IN TAURUS: As you yourself may be attractive to the opposite sex, you desire a partner who is sensual and loving or who has physical beauty. Needing stability, when faced with changes that are out of your control you may become insecure or possessive. Your own sense of style and

love of beauty imply that you can be attracted to creative people, especially those in art and music. Faithful and/or loyal, you can be affectionate, tactile, and constant in your love.

WOMEN WITH VENUS IN GEMINI: Charming and usually easygoing, you like to talk to people who are intelligent and witty. With a good social sense and a desire for mental expansion, you need a partner who is informed and has good ideas. Although you enjoy having different experiences, you need to resist your tendencies to become bored too quickly or be too talkative. As you enjoy sharing and learning new things, you usually prefer being with someone rather than operating alone.

MEN WITH VENUS IN GEMINI: Informed and curious yet charming and friendly, you seek a partner who shares your interests or enjoys your witty remarks. Although a good communicator, you have an inborn tendency to be lighthearted and less profound about deep emotional commitment. Although you are keen on experiences that bring variety into your life, boredom or scattering your energies in too many directions is probably your biggest handicap in relationships. Nevertheless you are attracted to intelligent partners who can match your lively banter.

WOMEN WITH VENUS IN CANCER: Sensitive and understanding, you are sympathetic to other people's emotions and needs. Protective toward those you love, close relationships with your partner, relatives, and friends are important to your sense of well-being. Aware of how easy it is to hurt other people's feelings, you are often indirect and approach delicate issues in a roundabout way. Nevertheless, learning to face facts and not allowing others to exploit your good nature is a valuable lesson.

MEN WITH VENUS IN CANCER: You seek a partner who is sympathetic, caring, and protective. Able to be forgiving and compassionate, you want a secure emotional bond in your close relationships. Usually you are drawn to partners who are maternal, unselfish, or demonstrative with their feelings. Although you can sometimes appear to others as impressionable, you have powerful emotions and inner strength.

To read all about your Outer Planets and work out how to use your personalized timetable, go to Section Three, page 789.

To read all about your Outer Planets and work out how to use your personalized timetable, go to Section Three, page 789.

♊

Your Personalized Timetable

JUPITER BENEFICIAL
1938 1/1 – 2/24
1939 5/24 – 10/8
1940 1/10 – 3/2
1943 7/11 – 8/26
1945 8/22 – 11/5
1949 4/7 – 7/3
1949 11/27 – until 1950 2/7
1951 5/2 – 7/1
1951 9/6 – until 1952 2/11
1955 6/24 – 8/10
1956 12/7 – until 1957 2/25
1957 8/3 – 10/20
1961 3/12 – 8/18
1961 10/29 – until 1962 1/22
1963 4/14 – 5/31
1963 10/24 – until 1964 1/16
1966 10/16 – 12/27
1967 6/6 – 7/25
1968 11/12 – until 1969 4/4
1969 7/10 – 10/5
1973 2/20 – until 1974 1/5
1975 3/28 – 5/10
1978 9/18 – until 1979 2/6
1979 5/13 – 7/8
1980 10/24 – until 1981 9/19
1985 2/4 – 5/4
1985 7/6 – 12/18
1987 3/12 – 4/23
1990 8/29 – 11/2
1990 12/27 – until 1991 6/20
1992 10/7 – until 1993 9/2
1997 1/19 – 4/3
1997 8/22 – 11/22
1999 2/23 – 4/6
2002 8/12 – 10/2
2003 2/7 – 5/29
2004 9/22 – 12/15
2005 3/23 – 8/14
2009 1/3 – 3/13
2010 6/28 – 8/17
2011 2/4 – 3/20

SATURN BENEFICIAL
1938 2/10 – 5/4
1938 11/8 – until 1939 1/19
1946 8/21 – until 1947 3/12
1947 4/25 – 8/5
1950 11/13 – until 1951 3/15
1951 8/7 – until 1952 9/20
1961 4/15 – 6/2
1961 12/29 – until 1963 2/16
1967 3/23 – 7/16
1967 8/3 – until 1968 3/12
1975 10/20 – 12/10
1976 6/26 – 9/15
1977 2/15 – 6/3
1980 9/16 – until 1981 10/27
1991 2/1 – until 1992 3/26
1992 8/4 – 12/22
1996 4/28 – 10/17
1997 1/17 – 4/17
2005 8/4 – until 2006 7/19
2009 10/24 – until 2010 4/16
2010 7/13 – 12/11
2011 3/14 – 9/2

URANUS BENEFICIAL
1956 7/21 – until 1959 5/9
1968 9/19 – until 1972 8/13
1995 3/14 – until 2000 1/12
2011 4/24 – Continues

NEPTUNE BENEFICIAL
1941 11/20 – until 1950 8/21
1997 3/17 – until 2005 12/11

PLUTO BENEFICIAL
1939 9/15 – until 1947 7/17
1970 11/29 – until 1978 9/8

JUPITER CHALLENGING
1938 5/9 – 8/4

1938 12/26 – until 1939 3/8
1944 7/23 – 10/6
1947 10/21 – until 1948 1/2
1950 4/12 – 9/20
1950 11/26 – until 1951 2/19
1955 11/11 – until 1956 1/24
1956 7/4 – 9/20
1959 2/5 – 4/30
1959 10/2 – 12/16
1962 3/23 – until 1963 2/1
1967 10/15 – until 1968 3/3
1968 6/11 – 9/4
1971 1/10 – 6/10
1971 9/6 – 12/1
1974 3/5 – 5/28
1974 8/16 – until 1975 1/12
1979 9/26 – until 1980 8/19
1982 12/23 – until 1983 11/15
1986 2/18 – 5/1
1986 9/30 – 12/16
1991 9/9 – until 1992 8/2
1994 12/6 – until 1995 10/28
1998 2/1 – 4/10
2003 8/24 – 11/16
2004 2/22 – 7/14
2006 11/21 – until 2007 2/10
2007 6/2 – 10/8
2010 1/15 – 3/24

SATURN CHALLENGING
1948 9/14 – until 1949 4/22
1949 5/10 – 10/21
1950 3/15 – 7/13
1956 1/6 – 5/22
1956 10/4 – until 1957 11/27
1964 3/18 – 9/27
1964 12/6 – until 1965 5/11
1965 8/16 – until 1966 2/1
1977 11/5 – until 1978 1/16
1978 7/21 – until 1979 8/26
1985 11/11 – until 1987 1/1
1987 7/17 – 9/21
1993 5/7 – 7/14
1994 1/23 – until 1995 3/9
2007 8/28 – until 2008 10/2
2009 4/23 – 6/9

URANUS CHALLENGING
1961 10/16 – until 1965 9/10
1981 1/23 – until 1985 10/21
2003 2/28 – until 2008 1/1

NEPTUNE CHALLENGING
1969 12/16 – until 1977 11/25
2011 3/16 – Continues

PLUTO CHALLENGING
1956 9/25 – until 1965 8/19
1994 12/28 – until 2002 10/8

JUPITER SPECIAL
1941 5/23 – 8/7
1941 12/16 – until 1942 3/28
1953 5/7 – 7/16
1965 4/19 – 6/28
1976 8/17 – 10/23
1977 3/31 – 6/11
1988 7/18 – 12/5
1989 3/6 – 5/26
2000 6/27 – until 2001 5/9
2012 6/9 – Continues

SATURN SPECIAL
1942 5/4 – until 1943 6/2
1971 6/13 – until 1972 7/14
1972 12/30 – until 1973 3/29
2000 7/31 – 10/25
2001 4/15 – until 2002 5/16

URANUS SPECIAL
1941 7/19 – until 1946 5/1

May 30

Your Personal Powers

Clever and bright with an astute mind, you can be friendly and sociable. Your ruling planet, Mercury, indicates that you possess a special talent for communication through speaking or writing. You gain power when you combine your natural psychological skills with your keen insight and sensitivity to increase your awareness. Although your quick instincts also give you speedy responses in competitive situations, you lose some of your power by being argumentative or too provocative. Besides being a shrewd observer, you have powerful emotions and a strong need for self-expression. You empower yourself when you combine your creativity with your ability to synthesize knowledge and information. You lose some of your power if you take life too seriously and become frustrated. By adopting a more philosophical view you can appreciate your special gift for understanding the joy of life. You can also express your personal awareness through your unique sense of humor, which enables you to explore the light and dark sides of any situation.

Your Powers of Attraction in Relationships

Friendly and bright, you attract others by your ability to shine in social situations. With your skill in fast verbal retorts or witty repartee, you particularly enjoy personal relationships with those who can keep up with your quick mind. Although you are articulate and enjoy a good debate, avoid going too far and becoming antagonistic or sarcastic. By using your innate diplomacy and charm, you have an ability to make people feel special and keep them happy. As you usually do better in a relationship than being alone, finding the right partner can be an essential requirement. Choose carefully, rather than acting on impulse, to avoid indecision later. With a sense of the dramatic you are often attracted to those with a strong self-identity or a creative spirit.

Your attractive qualities: creative, loyal, friendly, mentally quick, dramatic, versatile, fun-loving, talent with words, wise, sharp intellect, humorous, tact, diplomacy, good instincts, generous, insightful, sociable, clever, determined, psychic, expressive

Your less attractive qualities: lazy, obstinate, worry, indecisive, erratic, impatient, too talkative, insecure, scattered, provocative, argumentative, overindulgent, jealous, restless, unsettled, doubting, irritable

Your Venus Power

The planet Venus has a great deal of influence on your powers of attraction. Below are four possible Venus types for women and men. To find your Venus you need to go to page 771, where you will find the Venus table and extra information. The planet Mars also affects your powers of attraction. To find your Mars table and interpretation go to page 761.

WOMEN WITH VENUS IN ARIES: Self-reliant and strong, you usually want things your own way. This can present problems if you refuse to compromise with your partners. Your life lessons in the area of love and relationships often involve patience and learning to trust. When you project the full power of your Venus you can radiate a charismatic and captivating energy and make a strong impression on others. Independence is often high on your relationship agenda.

MEN WITH VENUS IN ARIES: You are usually inclined to seek a partner who is active, goal-oriented or decisive. Not known for your patience, you probably seek relationships from youth. You may find that you are attracted more to women who have a daring or adventurous spirit, but in your close relationships you may encounter rivalry or find that both you and your partner want to lead or be the boss. Although you may act rashly, you possess a great deal of magnetism and are capable of demonstrating your love and affection.

WOMEN WITH VENUS IN TAURUS: Good-natured and romantic, you have a highly developed sense of touch that particularly responds to massage, hugs, and all things physical. With a streak of the conventional you love the simple pleasures of life: good food, close friends, and happy relationships. With your natural sense of beauty and harmony you are likely to have an attractive voice, beautiful home, or a strong link to nature. You may have to be careful of becoming too extravagant, as often your taste is more expensive than what you are able to afford.

MEN WITH VENUS IN TAURUS: Attractive and affectionate, in relationships you are often down-to-earth, with a conservative approach. You are usually drawn to warmhearted partners with whom you can share a familiar routine as well as life's pleasures and comforts. Seeking a partner who is dependable or reassuring, you often put security high on your priority list when looking for love. Your sociability and friendliness usually make you popular and partners often admire your practicality and good sense of values.

WOMEN WITH VENUS IN GEMINI: Charming and usually easygoing, you like to talk to people who are intelligent and witty. With a good social sense and a desire for mental expansion, you need a partner who is informed and has good ideas. Although you enjoy having different experiences you need to resist your tendencies to become bored too quickly or be too talkative. As you enjoy sharing and learning new things, you usually prefer being with someone rather than operating alone.

MEN WITH VENUS IN GEMINI: Informed and curious, yet charming and friendly, you seek a partner who shares your interests or enjoys your witty remarks. Although a good communicator, you have an inborn tendency to be lighthearted and less profound about deep emotional commitment. Although you are keen on experiences that bring variety into your life, boredom or scattering your energies in too many directions is probably your biggest handicap in relationships. Nevertheless you are attracted to intelligent partners who can match your lively banter.

WOMEN WITH VENUS IN CANCER: Gentle and tender, you are romantic by nature. You possess a strong need for security and usually help others feel safe and protected. This preservation is especially centered around your home, which is your haven from life's storm. Although your maternal instincts are strong, avoid making too many sacrifices for others at your own expense. Nevertheless, affectionate and caring, once committed to a relationship your loyalty and devotion to your partner are very strong.

MEN WITH VENUS IN CANCER: Affectionate with a strong sensitive streak, you can love very deeply. You may find yourself drawn to sympathetic partners who can tune in to your moods and feelings as well as be reassuring and supportive. Family links are especially important to you and the more positive these relationships are the more confident and safe you feel.

To read all about your Outer Planets and work out how to use your personalized timetable, go to Section Three, page 789.

♊

Your Personalized Timetable

JUPITER BENEFICIAL
1938 1/1 – 2/28
1939 5/30 – 9/30
1940 1/16 – 3/7
1943 7/16 – 8/31
1945 8/27 – 11/10
1949 4/16 – 6/24
1949 12/2 – until **1950** 2/11
1951 5/7 – 7/12
1951 8/26 – until **1952** 2/16
1955 6/29 – 8/14
1956 12/16 – until **1957** 2/15
1957 8/9 – 10/25
1961 3/17 – 8/9
1961 11/6 – until **1962** 1/26
1963 4/18 – 6/5
1963 10/16 – until **1964** 1/22
1966 10/25 – 12/17
1967 6/11 – 7/29
1968 11/18 – until **1969** 3/28
1969 7/18 – 10/9
1973 2/25 – until **1974** 1/9
1975 4/1 – 5/15
1978 9/24 – until **1979** 1/29
1979 5/19 – 7/13
1980 10/29 – until **1981** 9/23
1985 2/8 – 5/16
1985 6/24 – 12/22
1987 3/16 – 4/27
1990 9/3 – 11/18
1990 12/12 – until **1991** 6/25
1992 10/12 – until **1993** 9/7
1997 1/23 – 4/8
1997 8/14 – 11/29
1999 2/27 – 4/10
2002 8/17 – 10/8
2003 1/31 – 6/4
2004 9/26 – 12/23
2005 3/15 – 8/20
2009 1/7 – 3/18
2010 7/18 – 7/28
2011 2/8 – 3/24

SATURN BENEFICIAL
1938 2/19 – 5/13
1938 10/24 – until **1939** 2/2
1946 8/29 – until **1947** 2/22
1947 5/13 – 8/12
1950 11/25 – until **1951** 3/2
1951 8/17 – until **1952** 9/28
1962 1/6 – until **1963** 2/24
1967 3/31 – until **1968** 3/20
1976 7/4 – 9/24
1977 2/3 – 6/14
1980 9/24 – until **1981** 11/4
1982 5/17 – 7/20
1991 2/9 – 9/21
1991 10/18 – until **1992** 4/6
1992 7/21 – 12/31
1996 5/7 – 10/4
1997 1/29 – 4/25
2005 8/11 – until **2006** 7/26
2009 11/2 – until **2010** 4/3
2010 7/25 – 12/25
2011 2/27 – 9/11

URANUS BENEFICIAL
1956 8/6 – until **1959** 6/10
1968 10/4 – until **1972** 9/2
1995 4/18 – until **2000** 1/29
2011 5/15 – Continues

NEPTUNE BENEFICIAL
1942 10/13 – until **1950** 9/20
1998 2/7 – until **2006** 1/11

PLUTO BENEFICIAL
1940 8/26 – until **1948** 6/24
1971 10/14 – until **1978** 10/3

JUPITER CHALLENGING
1938 5/17 – 7/26

1938 12/31 – until **1939** 3/11
1944 7/27 – 10/11
1947 10/25 – until **1948** 1/6
1950 4/17 – 9/12
1950 12/4 – until **1951** 2/23
1955 11/21 – until **1956** 1/13
1956 7/9 – 9/24
1959 2/14 – 4/21
1959 10/7 – 12/21
1962 3/27 – until **1963** 2/5
1967 10/21 – until **1968** 2/24
1968 6/18 – 9/8
1971 1/16 – 6/2
1971 9/14 – 12/5
1974 3/10 – 6/6
1974 8/7 – until **1975** 1/17
1979 10/1 – until **1980** 4/18
1980 5/4 – 8/23
1982 12/27 – until **1983** 11/19
1986 2/22 – 5/6
1986 9/22 – 12/24
1991 9/13 – until **1992** 8/7
1994 12/11 – until **1995** 11/2
1998 2/5 – 4/15
2003 8/29 – 11/24
2004 2/14 – 7/19
2006 11/25 – until **2007** 2/16
2007 5/25 – 10/14
2010 1/19 – 3/28

SATURN CHALLENGING
1948 9/22 – until **1949** 3/27
1949 6/5 – 10/31
1950 3/3 – 7/23
1956 1/16 – 5/9
1956 10/14 – until **1957** 12/5
1964 3/27 – 9/11
1964 12/20 – until **1965** 5/26
1965 7/31 – until **1966** 2/9
1977 11/27 – 12/25
1978 7/29 – until **1979** 9/3
1985 11/20 – until **1987** 1/9
1987 6/30 – 10/6
1994 2/1 – until **1995** 3/17
2007 9/5 – until **2008** 10/10
2009 4/5 – 6/27

URANUS CHALLENGING
1961 11/15 – until **1966** 7/7
1981 11/22 – until **1985** 11/8
2003 3/17 – until **2008** 1/26

NEPTUNE CHALLENGING
1970 1/18 – until **1978** 10/22
2011 4/17 – Continues

PLUTO CHALLENGING
1956 11/11 – until **1966** 7/12
1995 2/2 – until **2002** 11/10

JUPITER SPECIAL
1941 5/28 – 8/12
1941 12/9 – until **1942** 4/3
1953 5/11 – 7/21
1965 4/24 – 7/2
1976 8/28 – 10/12
1977 4/5 – 6/16
1988 7/24 – 11/28
1989 3/13 – 5/31
2000 7/2 – until **2001** 5/14
2012 6/13 – Continues

SATURN SPECIAL
1942 5/11 – until **1943** 6/10
1971 6/21 – until **1972** 1/2
1972 2/29 – 7/22
1972 12/18 – until **1973** 4/10
2000 8/17 – 10/9
2001 4/23 – until **2002** 5/24

URANUS SPECIAL
1942 5/21 – until **1946** 5/19

May 31

SUN: GEMINI • DECANATE: GEMINI/MERCURY • DEGREE: 8°5–10° GEMINI • MODE: MUTABLE • ELEMENT: AIR

Your Personal Powers

Courageous, determined, and intelligent, you are a dynamic individual with charming manners and a charismatic personality. Your ruling planet, Mercury, indicates that you also possess a youthful quality that will stay with you throughout your life. You gain power when you combine your thirst for knowledge with your original ideas and conversational skills. The alliance of your strong willpower, practicality, and intuitive understanding adds up to a powerful mixture for success. Versatile and rational with an interest in many different subjects, you are usually the initiator or leader of ideas. Idealistic with an inner sensitivity, you need beauty and harmony to balance your intellectual talents. Although you usually love to share your knowledge with others, you lose some of your power if you scatter yourself in too many directions. When you organize your good ideas into a solid form, you are able to achieve success. Although you are often aware of the advantages of working cooperatively with others, you usually like to do things in your own individual style.

Your Powers of Attraction in Relationships

Your determination, strong willpower, and sharp intelligence attract others. Being sociable, with a flair for dealing with people, you are usually popular. Although you are likely to be active and industrious, being in a secure and loving relationship is often essential to your well-being. Usually you are attracted to partners who are disciplined and hardworking or those who are successful through their own efforts. Although you seem very independent, being romantic and idealistic, you are constantly looking for the perfect partner. Once committed to a relationship, you are loyal and supportive. In order to keep the peace you are usually willing to make sacrifices for others. Resist going too far, however, as you may hold resentment or feel jealous. Nevertheless, with your natural diplomatic skills, you can be very loving and giving.

Your attractive qualities: creative, strong willpower, independent, original, hardworking, good teacher, idealistic, constructive, talent with words, determination, persistence, practical, good conversationalist, intuitive, organizational skills, responsible, quick mind

Your less attractive qualities: insecure, impatient, bossy, vain, nervous, suspicious, easily discouraged, jealous, scattered, extravagant, temperamental, dependent, indulgent, lack of ambition, selfish, stubborn

Your Venus Power

The planet Venus has a great deal of influence on your powers of attraction. Below are four possible Venus types for women and men. To find your Venus you need to go to page 771, where you will find the Venus table and extra information. The planet Mars also affects your powers of attraction. To find your Mars table and interpretation go to page 761.

WOMEN WITH VENUS IN ARIES: You gain power from your strong individuality, energy, and enthusiasm. Your young-at-heart and spirited approach to relationships adds to your appeal. If you become too impatient or self-absorbed, however, your partnerships are likely to suffer. Nevertheless, you can be creative, sharp, and quick, especially when you are able to share new and exciting projects with your partners. Mischievous, with a love of action, you may even incite them to a playful fight.

MEN WITH VENUS IN ARIES: You are drawn to strong, independent women who can stand up to you. Although you can enthusiastically follow the object of your desire, you may lose power if you allow your forceful emotions to become too dominant. Warm and passionate, you have a side to your nature that longs for new adventures. Romantic and chivalrous, you really enjoy the excitement of the initial chase, but unless you keep the enthusiasm alive and avoid falling into a rut you may become easily bored.

WOMEN WITH VENUS IN TAURUS: Warm and affectionate, you are drawn to partners with whom you can share life's simple comforts. With a need for stability and security or an appreciation of earthly pleasures, you may have to avoid overindulgence or becoming too preoccupied with material concerns. Nevertheless, your sociability and friendliness usually make you popular. You need a partner who can also share your appreciation of beauty and style.

MEN WITH VENUS IN TAURUS: As well as attracting people with your warm personality, you also possess an innate sense of the value of material possessions. Keeping yourself stylish and having an attractive home can therefore be important to you. You are naturally attracted to practical yet sensual

women who understand your need for comfort, security, and the pleasures and luxuries of life. Naturally affectionate, you enjoy socializing but can be a loyal and loving partner.

WOMEN WITH VENUS IN GEMINI: In relationships you need intellectual stimulation and usually prefer to keep things light. Certainly not boring, you love to talk and are at your best being witty and entertaining. Although your easygoing approach to relationships is very attractive, guard against losing touch with your deeper emotions. You prefer a partner who can keep up with your fast stream of ideas, and if you have shared interests then so much the better.

MEN WITH VENUS IN GEMINI: Charming, amusing, and adaptable, you attract others with your natural communication skills and friendly personality. You have a wonderful childlike quality and love to keep life playful, but a reluctance to contact your deeper feelings may cause you to avoid serious commitment. With your need for variety and intellectual stimulation you are attracted to clever and amusing partners who have many interesting sides to their personalities.

WOMEN WITH VENUS IN CANCER: Possessing a soft femininity, you have tender and sensitive emotions. Sympathetic and caring, you often mother those in your care by making sure that they are comfortable and have plenty to eat. When you feel hurt or insecure in relationships you are likely to cover your feelings by being defensive or appearing tough on the outside while on the inside you are feeling vulnerable. Affectionate and romantic, you make a faithful and devoted partner.

MEN WITH VENUS IN CANCER: Being emotionally receptive you can make a sensitive lover. With your desire to care for and protect others you are likely to have strong family connections. Love is often tied in with being attentive to the needs of others and you may find yourself attracted to individuals who have sympathetic or maternal qualities. Security-conscious, you need a loyal partner who can offer you support and ideally be a good cook and homemaker.

To read all about your Outer Planets and work out how to use your personalized timetable, go to Section Three, page 789.

♊

Your Personalized Timetable

JUPITER BENEFICIAL
1938 1/1 – 3/4
1939 6/5 – 9/23
1940 1/22 – 3/11
1943 7/20 – 9/4
1945 8/31 – 11/15
1949 4/27 – 6/13
1949 12/7 – until **1950** 2/15
1951 5/11 – 11/25
1951 12/5 – until **1952** 2/21
1955 7/4 – 8/18
1956 12/30 – until **1957** 2/2
1957 8/14 – 10/29
1961 3/22 – 8/1
1961 11/13 – until **1962** 1/30
1963 4/22 – 6/11
1963 10/9 – until **1964** 1/29
1966 11/11 – 12/1
1967 6/16 – 8/3
1968 11/24 – until **1969** 3/20
1969 7/24 – 10/14
1973 3/1 – until **1974** 1/13
1975 4/5 – 5/19
1978 9/30 – until **1979** 1/22
1979 5/26 – 7/18
1980 11/3 – until **1981** 5/3
1981 6/20 – 9/28
1985 2/12 – 12/27
1987 3/20 – 5/1
1990 9/8 – until **1991** 3/8
1991 4/21 – 6/30
1992 10/16 – until **1993** 9/11
1997 1/27 – 4/14
1997 8/7 – 12/5
1999 3/4 – 4/14
2002 8/21 – 10/15
2003 1/24 – 6/10
2004 10/1 – until **2005** 1/1
2005 3/5 – 8/25
2009 1/11 – 3/22
2009 10/4 – 10/21
2011 2/13 – 3/28

SATURN BENEFICIAL
1938 2/27 – 5/22
1938 10/12 – until **1939** 2/12
1946 9/7 – until **1947** 2/9
1947 5/26 – 8/20
1950 12/8 – until **1951** 2/16
1951 8/25 – until **1952** 10/6
1962 1/14 – until **1963** 3/5
1963 9/19 – 11/22
1967 4/7 – until **1968** 3/27
1976 7/12 – 10/4
1977 1/22 – 6/23
1980 10/2 – until **1981** 11/13
1982 4/30 – 8/5
1991 2/18 – 8/28
1991 11/10 – until **1992** 4/20
1992 7/6 – until **1993** 1/9
1996 5/17 – 9/22
1997 2/8 – 5/3
1997 11/16 – until **1998** 1/14
2005 8/19 – until **2006** 8/3
2009 11/11 – until **2010** 3/21
2010 8/5 – until **2011** 9/20

URANUS BENEFICIAL
1956 8/22 – until **1959** 6/30
1968 10/20 – until **1972** 9/19
1996 2/3 – until **2000** 11/26
2011 6/14 – Continues

NEPTUNE BENEFICIAL
1942 11/12 – until **1951** 8/13
1998 3/8 – until **2006** 11/29

PLUTO BENEFICIAL
1940 10/24 – until **1949** 5/22
1971 11/13 – until **1979** 8/23

JUPITER CHALLENGING
1938 5/28 – 7/15

1939 1/5 – 3/15
1944 8/1 – 10/16
1947 10/30 – until **1948** 1/11
1950 4/22 – 9/4
1950 12/11 – until **1951** 2/27
1955 12/7 – 12/28
1956 7/14 – 9/29
1959 2/26 – 4/8
1959 10/12 – 12/25
1962 4/1 – until **1963** 2/10
1967 10/27 – until **1968** 2/17
1968 6/24 – 9/13
1971 1/22 – 5/25
1971 9/20 – 12/9
1974 3/14 – 6/19
1974 7/26 – until **1975** 1/22
1979 10/6 – until **1980** 3/31
1980 5/22 – 8/28
1983 1/1 – 7/17
1983 8/10 – 11/23
1986 2/26 – 5/12
1986 9/15 – 12/30
1991 9/18 – until **1992** 8/11
1994 12/15 – until **1995** 11/7
1998 2/9 – 4/19
2003 9/2 – 12/2
2004 2/4 – 7/25
2006 11/30 – until **2007** 2/24
2007 5/17 – 10/19
2010 1/23 – 4/1

SATURN CHALLENGING
1948 9/30 – until **1949** 3/12
1949 6/19 – 11/10
1950 2/19 – 8/1
1956 1/29 – 4/25
1956 10/23 – until **1957** 12/13
1964 4/6 – 8/29
1965 1/1 – until **1966** 2/17
1978 8/6 – until **1979** 9/11
1985 11/28 – until **1987** 1/19
1987 6/16 – 10/18
1994 2/9 – until **1995** 3/24
2007 9/13 – until **2008** 10/19
2009 3/22 – 7/10

URANUS CHALLENGING
1962 8/31 – until **1966** 7/29
1981 12/7 – until **1985** 11/25
2003 4/5 – until **2008** 2/14

NEPTUNE CHALLENGING
1970 12/11 – until **1978** 11/20
2012 3/9 – Continues

PLUTO CHALLENGING
1957 9/29 – until **1966** 8/15
1995 12/14 – until **2003** 9/14

JUPITER SPECIAL
1941 6/1 – 8/19
1941 12/1 – until **1942** 4/9
1953 5/15 – 7/25
1954 1/18 – 3/5
1965 4/28 – 7/7
1977 4/10 – 6/20
1988 7/30 – 11/21
1989 3/19 – 6/4
2000 7/6 – until **2001** 1/17
2001 2/2 – 5/18
2012 6/17 – Continues

SATURN SPECIAL
1942 5/19 – until **1943** 6/17
1971 6/29 – 12/18
1972 3/15 – 8/1
1972 12/6 – until **1973** 4/20
2001 5/1 – until **2002** 5/31

URANUS SPECIAL
1942 6/6 – until **1946** 6/4

June 1

SUN: GEMINI · DECANATE: LIBRA/VENUS · DEGREE: 9°5–11° GEMINI · MODE: MUTABLE · ELEMENT: AIR

Your Personal Powers

Intelligent, persuasive, and charming, you are a versatile and imaginative individual with innovative and artistic talents. Among your other personal powers are individualism and a pioneering spirit that can inspire you to positions of leadership. Your ruling planet, Mercury, provides you with a youthful look and an ability to grasp concepts very quickly. Your sharp intellect and desire to increase your knowledge may lead to your exploring many different avenues of activity. You gain power when you direct your strong will and mental determination toward achieving your goals. You can lose power, however, if you become too domineering, self-centered, or scatter your energies on too many interests. Nevertheless, usually courageous and energetic, with an ability to work well with others, you are quick to see and take advantage of opportunities. Your mental agility and strong need for self-expression can manifest in an enterprising venture or dedication to an ideal. Your visionary sense can be a positive force to see your way into the future.

Your Powers of Attraction in Relationships

With personal magnetism and the ability to turn on the charm, you have no problem attracting others. Your need for variety implies that you are likely to seek different types of people for relationships or partners in your life. In many of your enterprises, women can prove to be especially fortunate for you. You are usually attracted to creative individuals who share your interests or who match your intelligence. A tendency to blow hot and cold, however, may spoil some of your more attractive qualities. Idealistic and romantic, you often seek a special connection or a spiritual link with your partner. If your partner cannot live up to your high expectations, you may go to extremes by being moody or critical. Nevertheless you are usually bright and friendly, especially when you share your interests with your partner.

Your attractive qualities: clever, leadership, charismatic, creative, sociable, progressive, forceful, optimistic, strong convictions, patient, caring, talent with words, affectionate, insightful, competitive, youthful, enthusiastic, artistic or musical, self-starter, independent, imaginative

Your less attractive qualities: overbearing, impatient, jealous, self-centered, too proud, too sensitive, opinionated, antagonistic, indecisive, intolerant, lacks restraint, escapist

Your Venus Power

The planet Venus has a great deal of influence on your powers of attraction. Below are four possible Venus types for women and men. To find your Venus you need to go to page 771, where you will find the Venus table and extra information. The planet Mars also affects your powers of attraction. To find your Mars table and interpretation go to page 761.

WOMEN WITH VENUS IN ARIES: Idealistic, passionate, and adventurous, you are direct in your dealings with others. When you are attracted to a person you usually take the initiative and use your people skills to make things happen. In close relationships you are not afraid to confront your other half. This self-assertiveness is positive if differences can be brought into the open through diplomacy and compromise. Independent and spirited, you enjoy your freedom.

MEN WITH VENUS IN ARIES: As you often have the courage and strength to initiate situations, you like to take the lead. With your unconscious desire for conquest you may also have to beware of being competitive with your partners. Nevertheless you are drawn to direct and strong-willed women who can share your love of action and enthusiasm for life. When you are feeling good you can be charming and enthusiastic in romantic situations with an entertaining and spontaneous spirit.

WOMEN WITH VENUS IN TAURUS: Demonstrative and affectionate, you are naturally tactile with a love of sensual pleasures. With a streak of the conventional you love the simple pleasures of life: good food, close friends, and happy relationships. Although you possess endurance be careful not to let this turn into plain stubbornness. Having inner strength, you can express genuine patience and are often a pillar of support for loved ones and friends.

MEN WITH VENUS IN TAURUS: Although you are usually drawn to sensual and physically beautiful individuals, you want a partner who is also reliable and loyal. When in love you enjoy buying your partner things of quality that will grow in value or useful things of a practical nature. You also love to socialize and entertain, especially in luxurious surroundings. Affectionate and caring, you are often attracted to creative people or those with artistic talents.

WOMEN WITH VENUS IN GEMINI: Curious, with a bright and animated approach to life, you are attracted to those who are clever and/or sophisticated. Your love of variety and desire for knowledge suggest that you need a partner and friends who can keep you mentally stimulated. Although witty and a good conversationalist, you may need to keep in touch with your deeper feelings. Nevertheless, intelligent and friendly, you possess a youthful sense of wonder and seek a playmate who can keep you from becoming bored.

MEN WITH VENUS IN GEMINI: Friendly and sociable, you attract others with your clever and amusing conversation. Drawn to people who can match you in wit and intelligence, you usually prefer to keep relationships light rather than emotionally intense. With your youthful charm and desire for knowledge and new experiences you usually have many friends and a low boredom threshold.

WOMEN WITH VENUS IN CANCER: With your intuitive abilities and sympathetic nature you are usually supportive of those you love. Impressionable and empathetic, your receptivity allows you to quickly pick up on the moods of others, making you especially aware of the emotional changes in your close partner. As you often display true maternal tendencies toward those you know, you want a partner who is considerate and sensitive.

MEN WITH VENUS IN CANCER: Being affectionate, you probably seek a nurturing partner who could provide you with emotional security and a sense of belonging in a loving and safe home. A sensitive side to your nature is often expressed through your relationships with others. When positive and confident, you can be sympathetic, caring, and loving.

To read all about your Outer Planets and work out how to use your personalized timetable, go to Section Three, page 789.

To read all about your Outer Planets and work out how to use your personalized timetable, go to Section Three, page 789.

Your Personalized Timetable

JUPITER BENEFICIAL
1938 1/1 – 3/9
1939 6/11 – 9/16
1940 1/28 – 3/15
1943 7/25 – 9/9
1945 9/5 – 11/20
1946 5/22 – 7/8
1949 12/12 – until 1950 2/20
1951 5/16 – 11/5
1951 12/24 – until 1952 2/25
1955 7/8 – 8/23
1957 8/19 – 11/3
1961 3/28 – 7/25
1961 11/19 – until 1962 2/3
1963 4/26 – 6/17
1963 10/2 – until 1964 2/4
1967 6/21 – 8/7
1968 11/30 – until 1969 3/13
1969 7/30 – 10/18
1973 3/6 – until 1974 1/18
1975 4/9 – 5/24
1975 11/23 – 12/27
1978 10/6 – until 1979 1/15
1979 6/1 – 7/22
1980 11/8 – until 1981 4/22
1981 7/2 – 10/2
1985 2/16 – until 1986 1/1
1987 3/24 – 5/5
1990 9/13 – until 1991 2/25
1991 5/3 – 7/5
1992 10/21 – until 1993 9/16
1997 1/31 – 4/21
1997 7/30 – 12/11
1999 3/8 – 4/18
2002 8/26 – 10/22
2003 1/16 – 6/16
2004 10/5 – until 2005 1/13
2005 2/21 – 8/30
2009 1/15 – 3/27
2009 9/17 – 11/7
2011 2/17 – 4/1

SATURN BENEFICIAL
1938 3/7 – 6/2
1938 9/30 – until 1939 2/22
1946 9/16 – until 1947 1/28
1947 6/5 – 8/28
1951 1/1 – 1/22
1951 9/3 – until 1952 10/13
1962 1/23 – until 1963 3/14
1963 9/2 – 12/7
1967 4/15 – until 1968 4/4
1976 7/19 – 10/16
1977 1/9 – 7/2
1980 10/9 – until 1981 11/22
1982 4/17 – 8/17
1991 2/27 – 8/13
1991 11/24 – until 1992 5/12
1992 6/13 – until 1993 1/18
1996 5/28 – 9/9
1997 2/17 – 5/11
1997 11/1 – until 1998 1/29
2005 8/27 – until 2006 3/5
2006 5/7 – 8/10
2009 11/22 – until 2010 3/9
2010 8/15 – until 2011 9/28

URANUS BENEFICIAL
1956 9/9 – until 1959 7/17
1968 11/6 – until 1972 10/5
1996 2/20 – until 2000 12/23
2012 4/7 – Continues

NEPTUNE BENEFICIAL
1943 10/8 – until 1951 9/15
1999 2/2 – until 2007 1/5

PLUTO BENEFICIAL
1941 9/18 – until 1949 7/8
1972 10/4 – until 1979 9/20

JUPITER CHALLENGING
1939 1/10 – 3/19

1944 8/5 – 10/20
1945 4/22 – 6/6
1947 11/3 – until 1948 1/16
1950 4/28 – 8/27
1950 12/17 – until 1951 3/3
1956 7/19 – 10/3
1959 10/17 – 12/29
1962 4/5 – until 1963 2/14
1967 11/3 – until 1968 2/9
1968 6/30 – 9/17
1971 1/28 – 5/18
1971 9/27 – 12/13
1974 3/18 – until 1975 1/26
1979 10/11 – until 1980 3/20
1980 6/2 – 9/1
1983 1/6 – 7/1
1983 8/26 – 11/28
1986 3/2 – 5/18
1986 9/7 – until 1987 1/5
1991 9/23 – until 1992 8/16
1994 12/20 – until 1995 11/11
1998 2/13 – 4/24
1998 11/6 – 11/20
2003 9/6 – 12/15
2004 1/23 – 7/30
2006 12/4 – until 2007 3/5
2007 5/7 – 10/25
2010 1/28 – 4/5

SATURN CHALLENGING
1948 10/9 – until 1949 2/28
1949 6/30 – 11/24
1950 2/4 – 8/10
1956 2/15 – 4/6
1956 11/1 – until 1957 12/21
1964 4/16 – 8/16
1965 1/11 – until 1966 2/25
1978 8/14 – until 1979 9/18
1985 12/6 – until 1987 1/29
1987 6/3 – 10/29
1994 2/17 – until 1995 4/2
1995 11/4 – 12/8
2007 9/21 – until 2008 4/7
2008 5/28 – 10/28
2009 3/10 – 7/21

URANUS CHALLENGING
1962 9/15 – until 1966 8/15
1981 12/24 – until 1985 12/11
2003 5/1 – until 2008 3/2

NEPTUNE CHALLENGING
1971 1/10 – until 1979 10/14
2012 4/7 – Continues

PLUTO CHALLENGING
1957 11/18 – until 1967 7/2
1996 1/11 – until 2003 10/31

JUPITER SPECIAL
1941 6/5 – 8/26
1941 11/24 – until 1942 4/15
1953 5/19 – 7/30
1954 1/7 – 3/16
1965 5/2 – 7/11
1977 4/14 – 6/24
1988 8/5 – 11/14
1989 3/25 – 6/8
2000 7/11 – 12/31
2001 2/19 – 5/22
2012 6/21 – Continues

SATURN SPECIAL
1942 5/26 – until 1943 6/25
1971 7/8 – 12/5
1972 3/26 – 8/11
1972 11/24 – until 1973 4/29
2001 5/9 – until 2002 6/8

URANUS SPECIAL
1942 6/24 – until 1947 3/31

♊

153

June 2

Your Personal Powers

Clever and imaginative with charming manners, you possess a strong sixth sense and practical skills. Your ruling planet, Mercury, grants you an exceptional talent for communication, through speech or writing, and creative talents. You gain power from the combination of your strong mental energy and innate diplomatic skills. Usually sensitive to the needs of others, you can display a courteous and thoughtful nature, although you also like to be in control. You empower yourself by being adaptable and understanding. Usually you enjoy cooperative activities where you can display your quick perception and original ideas. As a networker you can excel at making useful contacts or linking people together. When inspired you are willing to work hard and take on a great deal of responsibility. Although as an articulate mediator you like to keep situations amicable, you lose power if you allow an inner stubbornness or rebelliousness to surface. With dignity and a sense of style, you gain confidence from trusting your powerful intuition and by truly believing in your success.

Your Powers of Attraction in Relationships

Amiable and popular, your people skills and personal charm make you attractive to others. With a strong need to be part of a team, you usually operate better when working cooperatively with others. You are happier when the balance of power is equal in your close relationships. Therefore, in your hope to please your partner avoid going too far and allowing yourself to become too dependent. With your desire for harmony, however, you usually prefer to keep the peace and do better with a partner who understands your need for a safe, secure, and attractive home. Usually you are attracted to loyal and hardworking individuals who will stand by you. Alternatively, you may be drawn to intelligent and mentally stimulating partners who can inspire you with their creative ideas and beliefs.

Your attractive qualities: tactful, receptive, intuitive, kind, gentle, compassionate, hardworking, mentally agile, good partnerships, considerate, artistic or musical, visionary, adaptable, negotiator, harmonious, agreeable, diplomatic, articulate, intelligent, courteous

Your less attractive qualities: suspicious, obstinate, lack of confidence, irritable, subservient, opinionated, too sensitive, lazy, social excesses, moody, selfish, controlling, rebellious, overdependent

Your Venus Power

The planet Venus has a great deal of influence on your powers of attraction. Below are four possible Venus types for women and men. To find your Venus you need to go to page 771, where you will find the Venus table and extra information. The planet Mars also affects your powers of attraction. To find your Mars table and interpretation go to page 761.

WOMEN WITH VENUS IN ARIES: Idealistic, passionate, and adventurous, you are direct in your dealings with others. When you are attracted to a person you usually take the initiative and use your people skills to make things happen. In close relationships you are not afraid to confront your other half. This self-assertiveness is positive if differences can be brought into the open through diplomacy and compromise. Independent and spirited, you enjoy your freedom.

MEN WITH VENUS IN ARIES: As you often have the courage and strength to initiate situations, you like to take the lead. With your unconscious desire for conquest you may also have to beware of being competitive with your partners. Nevertheless you are drawn to direct and strong-willed women who can share your love of action and enthusiasm for life. When you are feeling good you can be charming and enthusiastic in romantic situations with an entertaining and spontaneous spirit.

WOMEN WITH VENUS IN TAURUS: Good-natured and romantic, you have a highly developed sense of touch that particularly responds to massage, hugs, and all things physical. With a streak of the conventional you love the simple pleasures of life: good food, close friends, and happy relationships. With your natural sense of beauty and harmony you are likely to have an attractive voice, beautiful home, or a strong link to nature. You may have to be careful of becoming too extravagant, as often your taste is more expensive than what you are able to afford.

MEN WITH VENUS IN TAURUS: Attractive and affectionate, in relationships you are often faithful with a conservative approach. You are usually drawn to warmhearted partners with whom you can share a familiar routine as well as life's pleasures and comforts. Seeking a partner who is dependable or reassuring, you often put security high on your priority list

154

when looking for love. Your sociability and friendliness usually make you popular and partners often admire your practicality and good sense of values.

WOMEN WITH VENUS IN GEMINI: By nature you are young at heart, adaptable, and sociable. Being curious and willing to cooperate makes you a good team player. Usually you are drawn to articulate people who have charm and flair or sharp wit. With a need to expand your knowledge, you also look for a partner who can challenge or stimulate you intellectually. Although you love to talk with all types of people you may need to develop your listening skills and tune in to your feelings in order to build better communication in your relationships.

MEN WITH VENUS IN GEMINI: Adaptable yet often flirtatious, you enjoy mixing with people who are quick-minded and versatile. Since you can learn a great deal through interacting with others, you are often attracted to intelligent partners who have comprehensive knowledge or good ideas. One of your less attractive qualities is your tendency to get bored or be inconsistent. Having an adaptable partner is important to you, therefore it must be someone who can offer you many different options and keep you interested.

WOMEN WITH VENUS IN CANCER: Sensitive and understanding, you are sympathetic to other people's emotions and needs. Protective toward those you love, close relationships with your partner, relatives, and friends are important to your sense of well-being. Aware of how easy it is to hurt other people's feelings, you are often indirect and approach delicate issues in a roundabout way. Nevertheless, learning to face facts and not allowing others to exploit your good nature is a valuable lesson.

MEN WITH VENUS IN CANCER: You seek a partner who is sympathetic, caring, and protective. Able to be forgiving and compassionate, you want a secure emotional bond in your close relationships. Usually you are drawn to partners who are maternal, unselfish, or affectionate with their feelings. Although you can sometimes appear to others as shy or impressionable, you have powerful emotions and inner strength.

To read all about your Outer Planets and work out how to use your personalized timetable, go to Section Three, page 789.

Ⅱ

Your Personalized Timetable

JUPITER BENEFICIAL
1938 1/3 – 3/13
1939 6/19 – 9/8
1940 2/2 – 3/19
1943 7/29 – 9/14
1945 9/9 – 11/25
1946 5/10 – 7/19
1949 12/16 – until 1950 2/24
1951 5/21 – 10/26
1952 1/3 – 3/1
1955 7/13 – 8/27
1957 8/24 – 11/7
1961 4/4 – 7/17
1961 11/25 – until 1962 2/7
1963 5/1 – 6/24
1963 9/24 – until 1964 2/9
1967 6/26 – 8/11
1968 12/8 – until 1969 3/5
1969 8/5 – 10/22
1973 3/11 – 9/4
1973 10/22 – until 1974 1/22
1975 4/13 – 5/29
1975 11/10 – until 1976 1/9
1978 10/14 – until 1979 1/7
1979 6/6 – 7/26
1980 11/13 – until 1981 4/13
1981 7/11 – 10/7
1985 2/21 – until 1986 1/5
1987 3/28 – 5/10
1990 9/18 – until 1991 2/16
1991 5/12 – 7/10
1992 10/26 – until 1993 9/21
1997 2/4 – 4/28
1997 7/22 – 12/16
1999 3/12 – 4/22
2002 8/30 – 10/30
2003 1/8 – 6/21
2004 10/10 – until 2005 9/4
2009 1/19 – 4/1
2009 9/7 – 11/17
2011 2/22 – 4/5

SATURN BENEFICIAL
1938 3/15 – 6/13
1938 9/17 – until 1939 3/3
1946 9/26 – until 1947 1/16
1947 6/15 – 9/4
1948 3/25 – 5/10
1951 9/11 – until 1952 10/21
1962 1/31 – until 1963 3/23
1963 8/20 – 12/19
1967 4/23 – 11/13
1968 1/3 – 4/11
1976 7/27 – 11/1
1976 12/24 – until 1977 7/10
1980 10/17 – until 1981 5/19
1981 6/21 – 12/1
1982 4/5 – 8/27
1991 3/9 – 7/30
1991 12/6 – until 1993 1/26
1996 6/11 – 8/26
1997 2/25 – 5/20
1997 10/18 – until 1998 2/10
2005 9/4 – until 2006 2/17
2006 5/21 – 8/18
2009 12/4 – until 2010 2/23
2010 8/24 – until 2011 10/6

URANUS BENEFICIAL
1956 10/1 – until 1959 8/2
1968 11/28 – until 1973 7/22
1996 2/27 – until 2001 1/12
2012 4/24 – Continues

NEPTUNE BENEFICIAL
1943 11/5 – until 1952 8/2
1999 3/1 – until 2007 2/1

PLUTO BENEFICIAL
1942 8/29 – until 1950 6/12
1972 10/31 – until 1980 7/29

JUPITER CHALLENGING
1939 1/14 – 3/23

1944 8/10 – 10/26
1945 4/10 – 6/17
1947 11/8 – until 1948 1/20
1948 8/7 – 8/24
1950 5/4 – 8/20
1950 12/23 – until 1951 3/7
1956 7/24 – 10/8
1959 10/22 – until 1960 1/3
1962 4/10 – 10/14
1962 11/13 – until 1963 2/18
1967 11/11 – until 1968 2/1
1968 7/5 – 9/22
1971 2/4 – 5/10
1971 10/2 – 12/18
1974 3/22 – until 1975 1/31
1979 10/16 – until 1980 3/12
1980 6/11 – 9/6
1983 1/11 – 6/20
1983 9/5 – 12/2
1986 3/6 – 5/24
1986 8/31 – until 1987 1/11
1991 9/27 – until 1992 8/21
1994 12/24 – until 1995 11/16
1998 2/17 – 4/29
1998 10/19 – 12/8
2003 9/11 – until 2004 8/4
2006 12/8 – until 2007 3/18
2007 4/24 – 10/30
2010 2/1 – 4/9

SATURN CHALLENGING
1948 10/19 – until 1949 2/16
1949 7/10 – 12/15
1950 1/14 – 8/18
1956 11/9 – until 1957 12/30
1958 8/11 – 9/5
1964 4/28 – 8/3
1965 1/20 – until 1966 3/5
1978 8/21 – until 1979 9/26
1985 12/14 – until 1986 7/24
1986 8/21 – until 1987 2/10
1987 5/21 – 11/7
1994 2/24 – until 1995 4/10
1995 10/14 – 12/29
2007 9/29 – until 2008 3/21
2008 6/14 – 11/7
2009 2/26 – 7/30

URANUS CHALLENGING
1962 10/2 – until 1966 8/31
1982 1/11 – until 1986 10/12
2004 2/29 – until 2008 12/31

NEPTUNE CHALLENGING
1938 3/31 – 7/27
1971 12/7 – until 1979 11/16

PLUTO CHALLENGING
1958 10/2 – until 1967 8/9
1996 11/30 – until 2003 11/28

JUPITER SPECIAL
1941 6/9 – 9/2
1941 11/16 – until 1942 4/20
1953 5/23 – 8/5
1953 12/30 – until 1954 3/24
1965 5/6 – 7/16
1977 4/19 – 6/28
1988 8/12 – 11/6
1989 3/30 – 6/12
2000 7/16 – 12/21
2001 3/1 – 5/26
2012 6/26 – Continues

SATURN SPECIAL
1942 6/2 – until 1943 7/2
1971 7/18 – 11/23
1972 4/5 – 8/24
1972 11/11 – until 1973 5/7
2001 5/16 – until 2002 6/15

URANUS SPECIAL
1942 7/13 – until 1947 4/25

June 3

Your Personal Powers

Strong-willed and determined yet friendly and creative, you are an astute and highly intuitive individual. Your ruling planet, Mercury, grants you quick comprehension and excellent communication skills. Possessing strong individuality and the potential to be very disciplined or focused, you usually work hard to achieve your goals. Although your quick and inventive mind has a shrewd perceptiveness that helps you think creatively, it also warns against losing some of your power to worry by imagining the worst or being negative. Your deeper insight can work well, however, for understanding others or exploring more profound subjects. When you become absorbed in a topic, you can reach to the depth of the matter and gain greater understanding. Nevertheless, by resisting too much self-analysis, you think less and act more decisively. Usually sociable and charming, you gain power from the positive expression of your inspired wisdom and sense of the dramatic. Your unique brand of humor can also help keep you happy. Being talented, you need to work hard, particularly when initiating new and exciting projects.

Your Powers of Attraction in Relationships

Clever and charming, you have no trouble attracting admirers. Sociable, you need outlets for your self-expression, through like-minded friends or sharing creative endeavors. With your sensitivity you are often an idealist when it comes to relationships. It may take you a while to learn to express your deeper feelings, but once you become more spontaneous and true to yourself, you can truly enjoy your close relationships. If you have been hurt in the past you may need to learn to let go, otherwise you can hold on to your sentimental feelings. Usually, you seek intelligent people with insight who can handle your strong will and not be intimidated. You can be especially attractive when you display the generous and affectionate side to your personality.

Your attractive qualities: strong-willed, hardworking, original, responsible, dedicated, happy, determined, friendly, productive, creative, persistent, understanding, caring, artistic, freedom-loving, a talent with words, clever, fertile imagination, communication skills

Your less attractive qualities: bossy, insecure, secretive, vain, worried, self-involved, overimaginative, cold, jealous, indecisive, self-indulgent, bored, depressed, irritable, self-absorbed, extravagant, self-indulgent

Your Venus Power

The planet Venus has a great deal of influence on your powers of attraction. Below are four possible Venus types for women and men. To find your Venus you need to go to page 771, where you will find the Venus table and extra information. The planet Mars also affects your powers of attraction. To find your Mars table and interpretation go to page 761.

WOMEN WITH VENUS IN ARIES: Idealistic, passionate, and adventurous, you are direct in your dealings with others. When you are attracted to a person you usually take the initiative and use your people skills to make things happen. In close relationships you are not afraid to confront your other half. This self-assertiveness is positive if differences can be brought into the open through diplomacy and compromise. Independent and spirited, you enjoy your freedom.

MEN WITH VENUS IN ARIES: As you often have the courage and strength to initiate situations, you like to take the lead. With your unconscious desire for conquest you may also have to beware of being competitive with your partners. Nevertheless, you are drawn to direct and strong-willed women who can share your love of action and enthusiasm for life. When you are feeling good you can be charming and enthusiastic in romantic situations with an entertaining and spontaneous spirit.

WOMEN WITH VENUS IN TAURUS: Warm and affectionate, you are drawn to partners with whom you can share life's simple comforts. With a need for stability and security or an appreciation of earthly pleasures, you may have to avoid overindulgence or becoming too preoccupied with material concerns. Nevertheless, your sociability and friendliness usually make you popular. You need a partner who can also share your appreciation of beauty and style.

MEN WITH VENUS IN TAURUS: As well as attracting people with your warm personality, you also possess an innate sense of the value of material possessions. Keeping yourself stylish and having an attractive home can therefore be important to you. You are naturally attracted to practical yet sensual women who understand your need for comfort, security, and the pleasures and luxuries of life. Naturally affectionate you enjoy socializing but can make a loyal and loving partner.

WOMEN WITH VENUS IN GEMINI: Charming and usually easygoing, you like to talk to people who are intelligent and witty. With a good social sense and a desire for mental expansion, you need a partner who is informed and who has good ideas. Although you enjoy having different experiences you need to resist your tendency to become bored too quickly or be too talkative. As you enjoy sharing and learning new things, you usually prefer being with someone rather than operating alone.

MEN WITH VENUS IN GEMINI: Informed and curious yet charming and friendly, you seek a partner who shares your interests or enjoys your witty remarks. Although a good communicator, you have an inborn tendency to be lighthearted and less profound about deep emotional commitment. Although you are keen on experiences that bring variety into your life, boredom or scattering your energies in too many directions is probably your biggest handicap in relationships. Nevertheless you are attracted to intelligent partners who can match your lively banter.

WOMEN WITH VENUS IN CANCER: Gentle and tender, you are romantic by nature. You possess a strong need for security and usually help others feel safe and protected. This preservation is especially centered around the home, which is your haven from life's storm. Although your maternal instincts are strong, avoid making too many sacrifices for others at your own expense. Nevertheless, affectionate and caring, once committed to a relationship your loyalty and devotion to your partner are very strong.

MEN WITH VENUS IN CANCER: Affectionate with a strong sensitive streak, you can love very deeply. You may find yourself drawn to sympathetic partners who can tune in to your moods and feelings as well as be reassuring and supportive. Family links are especially important to you and the more positive these relationships are the more confident and safe you feel.

To read all about your Outer Planets and work out how to use your personalized timetable, go to Section Three, page 789.

♊

Your Personalized Timetable

JUPITER BENEFICIAL
1938 1/7 – 3/17
1939 6/28 – 8/30
1940 2/7 – 3/23
1943 8/2 – 9/18
1944 4/3 – 4/22
1945 9/14 – 12/1
1946 5/1 – 7/28
1949 12/21 – until **1950** 2/28
1951 5/26 – 10/18
1952 1/11 – 3/5
1955 7/17 – 9/1
1957 8/29 – 11/12
1961 4/11 – 7/9
1961 12/1 – until **1962** 2/11
1963 5/5 – 7/2
1963 9/16 – until **1964** 2/14
1967 7/1 – 8/16
1968 12/16 – until **1969** 2/24
1969 8/10 – 10/27
1973 3/16 – 8/24
1973 11/1 – until **1974** 1/26
1975 4/17 – 6/3
1975 11/1 – until **1976** 1/17
1978 10/22 – 12/30
1979 6/12 – 7/31
1980 11/19 – until **1981** 4/5
1981 7/18 – 10/11
1985 2/25 – until **1986** 1/9
1987 4/1 – 5/14
1990 9/24 – until **1991** 2/8
1991 5/19 – 7/14
1992 10/31 – until **1993** 9/25
1997 2/8 – 5/7
1997 7/13 – 12/21
1999 3/16 – 4/26
2002 9/4 – 11/10
2002 12/28 – until **2003** 6/27
2004 10/14 – until **2005** 9/9
2009 1/23 – 4/6
2009 8/29 – 11/25
2011 2/26 – 4/9

SATURN BENEFICIAL
1938 3/23 – 6/29
1938 9/1 – until **1939** 3/11
1946 10/8 – until **1947** 1/3
1947 6/24 – 9/13
1948 3/7 – 5/27
1951 9/19 – until **1952** 10/29
1962 2/8 – until **1963** 4/2
1963 8/7 – 12/29
1967 5/2 – 10/27
1968 1/20 – 4/19
1976 8/3 – until **1977** 7/18
1980 10/26 – until **1981** 4/27
1981 7/13 – 12/13
1982 3/23 – 9/5
1991 3/19 – 7/17
1991 12/16 – until **1993** 2/3
1996 7/2 – 8/3
1997 3/6 – 5/30
1997 10/6 – until **1998** 2/20
2005 9/13 – until **2006** 2/5
2006 6/2 – 8/25
2009 12/21 – until **2010** 2/5
2010 9/1 – until **2011** 10/13

URANUS BENEFICIAL
1957 7/29 – until **1960** 6/13
1969 9/24 – until **1973** 8/20
1996 4/7 – until **2001** 1/29
2012 5/14 – Continues

NEPTUNE BENEFICIAL
1943 12/22 – until **1952** 9/9
1999 4/11 – until **2007** 12/29

PLUTO BENEFICIAL
1942 10/21 – until **1950** 7/20
1972 12/8 – until **1980** 9/4

JUPITER CHALLENGING
1939 1/19 – 3/27

1944 8/14 – 10/31
1945 4/1 – 6/27
1947 11/12 – until **1948** 1/25
1948 7/20 – 9/11
1950 5/11 – 8/13
1950 12/29 – until **1951** 3/11
1956 7/29 – 10/12
1959 10/27 – until **1960** 1/7
1962 4/15 – 9/30
1962 11/27 – until **1963** 2/22
1967 11/19 – until **1968** 1/23
1968 7/11 – 9/26
1971 2/12 – 5/1
1971 10/8 – 12/22
1974 3/26 – until **1975** 2/4
1979 10/22 – until **1980** 3/4
1980 6/18 – 9/10
1983 1/17 – 6/12
1983 9/13 – 12/6
1986 3/10 – 6/1
1986 8/23 – until **1987** 1/16
1991 10/2 – until **1992** 8/25
1994 12/29 – until **1995** 11/20
1998 2/21 – 5/4
1998 10/9 – 12/18
2003 9/15 – until **2004** 8/9
2006 12/13 – until **2007** 11/3
2010 2/5 – 4/14

SATURN CHALLENGING
1948 10/30 – until **1949** 2/4
1949 7/19 – until **1950** 8/26
1956 11/17 – until **1958** 1/7
1958 7/17 – 9/30
1964 5/13 – 7/18
1965 1/28 – until **1966** 3/13
1978 8/29 – until **1979** 10/4
1985 12/22 – until **1986** 6/30
1986 9/13 – until **1987** 2/24
1987 5/5 – 11/16
1994 3/4 – until **1995** 4/19
1995 9/30 – until **1996** 1/11
2007 10/7 – until **2008** 3/7
2008 6/27 – 11/19
2009 2/12 – 8/8

URANUS CHALLENGING
1962 10/22 – until **1966** 9/15
1982 2/6 – until **1986** 11/3
2004 3/17 – until **2009** 1/26

NEPTUNE CHALLENGING
1938 1/1 – 8/26
1972 1/3 – until **1980** 10/2

PLUTO CHALLENGING
1958 11/23 – until **1968** 6/5
1996 12/26 – until **2004** 10/18

JUPITER SPECIAL
1941 6/13 – 9/12
1941 11/6 – until **1942** 4/25
1953 5/27 – 8/10
1953 12/22 – until **1954** 3/31
1965 5/11 – 7/20
1977 4/23 – 7/2
1988 8/20 – 10/29
1989 4/4 – 6/16
2000 7/21 – 12/13
2001 3/9 – 5/31
2012 6/30 – Continues

SATURN SPECIAL
1942 6/10 – until **1943** 7/10
1944 1/28 – 3/14
1971 7/28 – 11/11
1972 4/14 – 9/11
1972 10/23 – until **1973** 5/15
2001 5/24 – until **2002** 6/22

URANUS SPECIAL
1942 8/10 – until **1947** 5/14

June 4

SUN: GEMINI • DECANATE: LIBRA/VENUS • DEGREE: 12°5–14° GEMINI • MODE: MUTABLE • ELEMENT: AIR

Your Personal Powers

Intelligence, friendly charm, and a creative mind are just some of your personal powers. Your ruling planet, Mercury, enhances your communication skills. Possessing a practical approach and an objective viewpoint, you gain power through your expertise in evaluating people or situations. Your keen intellect and need to expand your knowledge may place you in leadership positions or find you exploring many different types of subjects or experiences. You have a gift with words and for synthesizing information that may make you an especially good conversationalist or writer. With your highly tuned nervous system, you gain power when you stay focused and determined, but you may lose some of your power if you become indecisive, worried, or scatter your energies. Usually fair and direct, you need to express your strong individuality and experiment with new ideas. Often impatient, though you may hide it well, you gain better results from having faith in yourself, being persuasive, and using your innate diplomatic skills rather than being too forceful.

Your Powers of Attraction in Relationships

Your good social skills and confident personality can charm others and enable you to mix with people from all walks of life. Warm and generous with those you love, your open and easygoing style can make you attractive to the opposite sex. Being intelligent, you are drawn to clever and ambitious people who have positive plans for the future. You may even choose to work with your partner. Honesty is also high on your relationship agenda. Although you appear self-assured, inner insecurities or a need to be popular can suggest that you need the approval of others. Being very independent, however, you want freedom within a relationship. With your hidden sensitivity, valuing the power of love in your life can help you create positive relationships.

Your attractive qualities: leadership skills, clever, independent, creative, sociable, business sense, humanitarian, insightful, direct, talent with words, advisory skills, artistic, practical, self-disciplined, steady, hardworking, organized, exact, inspired, people skills, good psychologist

Your less attractive qualities: stubborn, scattered, indecisive, vain, self-doubt, too strict, critical, repressed, lazy, self-indulgent, arrogant, unfeeling, procrastinating, bossy, resentful, nervous

Your Venus Power

The planet Venus has a great deal of influence on your powers of attraction. Below are four possible Venus types for women and men. To find your Venus you need to go to page 771, where you will find the Venus table and extra information. The planet Mars also affects your powers of attraction. To find your Mars table and interpretation go to page 761.

WOMEN WITH VENUS IN ARIES: Idealistic, passionate, and adventurous, you are direct in your dealings with others. When you are attracted to a person you usually take the initiative and use your people skills to make things happen. In close relationships you are not afraid to confront your other half. This self-assertiveness is positive if differences can be brought into the open through diplomacy and compromise. Independent and spirited, you enjoy your freedom.

MEN WITH VENUS IN ARIES: You are usually inclined to seek a partner who is active, goal-oriented, or decisive. Not known for your patience, you probably seek relationships early in life. You may find that you are attracted more to women who have a daring or adventurous spirit, but in your close relationships you may encounter rivalry or find that both you and your partner want to lead or be the boss. Although you may act rashly, you possess a great deal of magnetism and are capable of demonstrating your love and affection.

WOMEN WITH VENUS IN TAURUS: Demonstrative and affectionate, you are naturally tactile with a love of sensual pleasures. With a streak of the conventional you love the simple pleasures of life: good food, close friends, and happy relationships. Although you possess endurance be careful not to let this turn into plain stubbornness. Having inner strength, you can express genuine patience and are often a pillar of support for loved ones and friends.

MEN WITH VENUS IN TAURUS: Although you are usually drawn to sensual and physically beautiful individuals, you want a partner who is also reliable and loyal. When in love you enjoy buying your partner things of quality that will grow in value or useful things of a practical nature. You also love to socialize and entertain, especially in luxurious surroundings. Af-

fectionate and caring, you are often attracted to creative people or those with artistic talents.

WOMEN WITH VENUS IN GEMINI: In relationships you need intellectual stimulation and usually prefer to keep things light. Certainly not boring, you love to talk and are at your best being witty and entertaining. Although your easygoing approach to relationships is very attractive, guard against losing touch with your deeper emotions. You prefer a partner who can keep up with your fast stream of ideas, and if you have shared interests then so much the better.

MEN WITH VENUS IN GEMINI: Charming, amusing, and adaptable, you attract others with your natural communication skills and friendly personality. You have a wonderful childlike quality and love to keep life playful, but a reluctance to contact your deeper feelings may cause you to avoid serious commitment. With your need for variety and intellectual stimulation you are attracted to clever and amusing partners who have many interesting sides to their personalities.

WOMEN WITH VENUS IN CANCER: Possessing a soft femininity, you have tender and sensitive emotions. Sympathetic and caring, you often mother those in your care by making sure that they are comfortable and have plenty to eat. When you feel hurt or insecure in relationships you are likely to cover your feelings by being defensive or appearing tough on the outside while on the inside you are feeling vulnerable. Affectionate and romantic, you make a faithful and devoted partner.

MEN WITH VENUS IN CANCER: Being emotionally receptive you can make a sensitive lover. With your desire to care for and protect others you are likely to have strong family connections. Love is often tied in with being attentive to the needs of others and you may find yourself attracted to individuals who have sympathetic or maternal qualities. Security-conscious, you need a loyal partner who can offer you support and ideally be a good cook and homemaker.

To read all about your Outer Planets and work out how to use your personalized timetable, go to Section Three, page 789.

♊

Your Personalized Timetable

JUPITER BENEFICIAL
1938 1/11 – 3/22
1939 7/10 – 8/18
1940 2/12 – 3/27
1943 8/7 – 9/23
1944 3/17 – 5/10
1945 9/18 – 12/6
1946 4/23 – 8/5
1949 12/25 – until **1950** 3/4
1951 6/1 – 10/10
1952 1/18 – 3/9
1955 7/21 – 9/5
1957 9/2 – 11/17
1961 4/19 – 7/1
1961 12/6 – until **1962** 2/15
1963 5/10 – 7/11
1963 9/7 – until **1964** 2/19
1967 7/5 – 8/20
1968 12/27 – until **1969** 2/13
1969 8/16 – 10/31
1973 3/21 – 8/16
1973 11/10 – until **1974** 1/30
1975 4/21 – 6/8
1975 10/25 – until **1976** 1/25
1978 11/2 – 12/19
1979 6/17 – 8/4
1980 11/25 – until **1981** 3/28
1981 7/25 – 10/16
1985 3/1 – until **1986** 1/14
1987 4/5 – 5/19
1990 9/30 – until **1991** 2/1
1991 5/26 – 7/19
1992 11/4 – until **1993** 5/16
1993 6/16 – 9/30
1997 2/12 – 5/18
1997 7/2 – 12/26
1999 3/20 – 4/30
2002 9/9 – until **2003** 3/29
2003 4/10 – 7/2
2004 10/19 – until **2005** 9/14
2009 1/27 – 4/12
2009 8/21 – 12/2
2011 3/2 – 4/13

SATURN BENEFICIAL
1938 3/30 – until **1939** 3/19
1946 10/23 – 12/19
1947 7/2 – 9/21
1948 2/22 – 6/9
1951 9/26 – until **1952** 11/6
1953 5/27 – 7/20
1962 2/16 – 9/18
1962 10/30 – until **1963** 4/14
1963 7/25 – until **1964** 1/8
1967 5/11 – 10/14
1968 2/1 – 4/27
1976 8/10 – until **1977** 7/26
1980 11/3 – until **1981** 4/13
1981 7/26 – 12/26
1982 3/8 – 9/14
1991 3/31 – 7/4
1991 12/25 – until **1993** 2/11
1997 3/14 – 6/10
1997 9/24 – until **1998** 3/1
2005 9/22 – until **2006** 1/24
2006 6/12 – 9/2
2010 9/9 – until **2011** 10/21

URANUS BENEFICIAL
1957 8/13 – until **1960** 6/16
1969 10/9 – until **1973** 9/8
1997 2/2 – until **2001** 11/23
2012 6/11 – Continues

NEPTUNE BENEFICIAL
1944 10/29 – until **1953** 7/13
2000 2/23 – until **2008** 1/26

PLUTO BENEFICIAL
1943 9/18 – until **1951** 6/26
1973 10/20 – until **1980** 9/30

JUPITER CHALLENGING
1939 1/23 – 4/1

1944 8/19 – 11/5
1945 3/24 – 7/4
1947 11/17 – until **1948** 1/30
1948 7/9 – 9/21
1950 5/19 – 8/4
1951 1/3 – 3/15
1956 8/3 – 10/17
1959 10/31 – until **1960** 1/12
1962 4/20 – 9/21
1962 12/6 – until **1963** 2/26
1967 12/1 – until **1968** 1/12
1968 7/16 – 10/1
1971 2/22 – 4/21
1971 10/13 – 12/26
1974 3/31 – until **1975** 2/9
1979 10/28 – until **1980** 2/25
1980 6/25 – 9/15
1983 1/23 – 6/4
1983 9/20 – 12/10
1986 3/14 – 6/9
1986 8/14 – until **1987** 1/21
1991 10/7 – until **1992** 4/12
1992 5/19 – 8/30
1995 1/3 – 11/25
1998 2/25 – 5/9
1998 9/30 – 12/26
2003 9/20 – until **2004** 8/14
2006 12/17 – until **2007** 11/8
2010 2/9 – 4/18

SATURN CHALLENGING
1948 11/12 – until **1949** 1/20
1949 7/28 – until **1950** 9/3
1956 11/25 – until **1958** 1/16
1958 7/1 – 10/14
1965 2/6 – until **1966** 3/21
1978 9/5 – until **1979** 10/12
1980 4/18 – 6/25
1985 12/31 – until **1986** 6/14
1986 9/27 – until **1987** 3/27
1987 4/4 – 11/25
1994 3/12 – until **1995** 4/28
1995 9/17 – until **1996** 1/22
2007 10/17 – until **2008** 2/24
2008 7/7 – 12/5
2009 1/27 – 8/17

URANUS CHALLENGING
1962 11/22 – until **1967** 7/12
1982 12/1 – until **1986** 11/20
2004 4/5 – until **2009** 2/14

NEPTUNE CHALLENGING
1938 1/1 – until **1939** 7/19
1972 2/16 – until **1980** 11/9

PLUTO CHALLENGING
1959 10/4 – until **1968** 8/1
1997 1/27 – until **2004** 11/19

JUPITER SPECIAL
1941 6/17 – 9/27
1941 10/23 – until **1942** 4/30
1953 5/31 – 8/16
1953 12/15 – until **1954** 4/7
1965 5/15 – 7/25
1977 4/28 – 7/7
1988 8/31 – 10/19
1989 4/9 – 6/20
2000 7/27 – 12/5
2001 3/16 – 6/4
2012 7/5 – Continues

SATURN SPECIAL
1942 6/18 – until **1943** 7/18
1944 1/11 – 3/31
1971 8/10 – 10/29
1972 4/23 – until **1973** 5/23
2001 5/31 – until **2002** 6/30

URANUS SPECIAL
1943 6/4 – until **1947** 5/31

June 5

Your Personal Powers

Forceful with quick comprehension and strong instincts, you are a resourceful individual with ambition and charm. Mercury, your ruling planet, grants you versatility, a rational mind, and good communication skills. Enterprising and determined, you can be very hardworking and diligent when you have a definite goal to focus on. Although you gain power from your courage and independent spirit, you may lose some of your power, if you allow your desire for material security to override your enthusiasm for new and progressive ideas. Usually freedom is high on your agenda, so you often show a willingness to fight for your rights. When positive you can be generous with a lively touch of the dramatic. With a good understanding of structure and organization, you can be businesslike and precise in your approach. With your spirit of adventure, you can be quick to see opportunities and take action. Besides your people and business skills, equally important is your natural aesthetic sense that can enrich your creative abilities and give you a love of beauty and luxury.

Your Powers of Attraction in Relationships

Friendly and sociable, you are good with people and can attract others with your gregarious personality and entertaining manner. Although you seem independent and self-reliant, relationships are very important to you. In love matters, pride and indecision may cause you some delays. You are better off keeping a light and detached attitude toward your partnerships in order to avoid worry or disappointment. You can be particularly attracted to creative and sociable people who stimulate your own imagination and talents. With your strong opinions, you like to be direct with others, but be careful of being too frank and forthright. Instead of being headstrong, you usually get better results by being persuasive and diplomatic. Nevertheless you can be a loyal friend, and very generous and loving with those you care for.

Your attractive qualities: clever, quick responses, witty, creative, common sense, good organizational skills, direct, deep thinker, business sense, reformer, philosophical, persistent, artistic, inventive, determined, leadership skills, adaptable, versatile, observant, assertive

Your less attractive qualities: bossy, inconsistent, too talkative, short-tempered, verbally cutting, extravagant, restless, unpredictable, excessive, willful, obstinate, materialistic, overconfident, headstrong, impatient

Your Venus Power

The planet Venus has a great deal of influence on your powers of attraction. Below are four possible Venus types for women and men. To find your Venus you need to go to page 771, where you will find the Venus table and extra information. The planet Mars also affects your powers of attraction. To find your Mars table and interpretation go to page 761.

WOMEN WITH VENUS IN ARIES: You gain power from your strong individuality, energy, and enthusiasm. Your young-at-heart and spirited approach to relationships adds to your appeal. If you become too impatient or self-absorbed, however, your partnerships are likely to suffer. Nevertheless, you can be creative, sharp, and quick, especially when you are able to share new and exciting projects with your partners. Mischievous, with a love of action, you may even incite them to a playful fight.

MEN WITH VENUS IN ARIES: You are drawn to strong, independent women who can stand up to you. Although you can enthusiastically follow the object of your desire, you may lose power if you allow your forceful emotions to become too dominant. Warm and passionate, you have a side to your nature that longs for new adventures. Romantic and chivalrous, you really enjoy the excitement of the initial chase, but unless you keep the enthusiasm alive and avoid falling into a rut you may become easily bored.

WOMEN WITH VENUS IN TAURUS: For your ideal relationship you seek a partner who is both financially secure and demonstrative with his affections. With these thoughts in mind, you are likely to also want a partner who is refined yet pragmatic or someone concerned with safeguarding your future. Although you have a stubborn streak you can be loving and affectionate in your relationships, and with your good sense of style you may have an attraction for the arts, music, or luxury items.

MEN WITH VENUS IN TAURUS: As you yourself may be attractive to the opposite sex, you desire a partner who is sensual and loving or who has physical beauty. Needing stability, when faced with changes that are out of your control you may become insecure or possessive. Your own sense of style and love of beauty imply that you can be attracted to creative peo-

ple, especially those in art and music. Faithful and/or loyal, you can be affectionate, tactile, and constant in your love.

WOMEN WITH VENUS IN GEMINI: Curious, with a bright and animated approach to life, you are attracted to those who are clever and/or sophisticated. Your love of variety and desire for knowledge suggest that you need a partner and friends who can keep you mentally stimulated. Although witty and a good conversationalist, you may need to keep in touch with your deeper feelings. Nevertheless, intelligent and friendly, you possess a youthful sense of wonder and seek a playmate who can keep you from becoming bored.

MEN WITH VENUS IN GEMINI: Friendly and sociable, you attract others with your clever and amusing conversation. Drawn to people who can match you in wit and intelligence, you usually prefer to keep relationships light rather than emotionally intense. With your youthful charm and desire for knowledge and new experiences you usually have many friends and a low boredom threshold.

WOMEN WITH VENUS IN CANCER: With your intuitive abilities and sympathetic nature you are usually supportive of those you love. Impressionable and empathetic, your receptivity allows you to quickly pick up on the moods of others, making you especially aware of the emotional changes in your close partner. As you often display true maternal tendencies toward those you know, you want a partner who is considerate and sensitive.

MEN WITH VENUS IN CANCER: Being caring and sensitive, you probably seek a nurturing partner who could provide you with emotional security and a sense of belonging in a loving environment. Receptive to others, at times you may find it hard to be direct or confrontational in relationships. You may find yourself drawn to partners who are affectionate and sympathetic like yourself. You are lucky to have strong family links.

To read all about your Outer Planets and work out how to use your personalized timetable, go to Section Three, page 789.

To read all about your Outer Planets and work out how to use your personalized timetable, go to Section Three, page 789.

Your Personalized Timetable

JUPITER BENEFICIAL
1938 1/15 – 3/27
1940 2/16 – 3/31
1943 8/11 – 9/29
1944 3/7 – 5/20
1945 9/23 – 12/12
1946 4/16 – 8/12
1949 12/30 – until 1950 3/8
1951 6/6 – 10/3
1952 1/24 – 3/14
1955 7/26 – 9/10
1957 9/7 – 11/22
1958 6/4 – 7/3
1961 4/29 – 6/20
1961 12/11 – until 1962 2/19
1963 5/14 – 7/25
1963 8/24 – until 1964 2/24
1967 7/10 – 8/25
1969 8/21 – 11/5
1973 3/26 – 8/8
1973 11/17 – until 1974 2/3
1975 4/25 – 6/14
1975 10/17 – until 1976 1/31
1979 6/22 – 8/9
1980 12/1 – until 1981 3/21
1981 7/31 – 10/20
1985 3/6 – until 1986 1/18
1987 4/9 – 5/23
1990 10/6 – until 1991 1/25
1991 6/1 – 7/24
1992 11/10 – until 1993 5/2
1993 7/1 – 10/4
1997 2/16 – 12/31
1999 3/24 – 5/5
2002 9/14 – until 2003 3/9
2003 4/30 – 7/6
2004 10/23 – until 2005 9/19
2009 1/31 – 4/18
2009 8/14 – 12/8
2011 3/6 – 4/17

SATURN BENEFICIAL
1938 4/7 – until 1939 3/27
1947 7/10 – 9/30
1948 2/10 – 6/19
1951 10/4 – until 1952 11/15
1953 5/10 – 8/6
1962 2/25 – 8/29
1962 11/19 – until 1963 4/29
1963 7/9 – until 1964 1/16
1967 5/20 – 10/1
1968 2/11 – 5/5
1968 11/30 – until 1969 1/11
1976 8/18 – until 1977 8/3
1980 11/12 – until 1981 3/31
1981 8/7 – until 1982 1/18
1982 2/12 – 9/23
1991 4/16 – 6/16
1992 1/3 – until 1993 2/19
1997 3/21 – 6/23
1997 9/10 – until 1998 3/9
2005 10/3 – until 2006 1/12
2006 6/21 – 9/10
2007 3/18 – 5/22
2010 9/17 – until 2011 10/29

URANUS BENEFICIAL
1957 8/29 – until 1960 7/6
1969 10/25 – until 1973 9/25
1997 2/19 – until 2001 12/23

NEPTUNE BENEFICIAL
1944 12/4 – until 1953 9/3
2000 3/27 – until 2008 12/19

PLUTO BENEFICIAL
1944 8/27 – until 1952 5/5
1973 11/19 – until 1981 8/15

JUPITER CHALLENGING
1939 1/27 – 4/5
1944 8/23 – 11/11

1945 3/17 – 7/11
1947 11/21 – until 1948 2/5
1948 7/1 – 9/30
1950 5/28 – 7/26
1951 1/8 – 3/19
1956 8/7 – 10/22
1957 5/6 – 5/31
1959 11/5 – until 1960 1/16
1962 4/25 – 9/13
1962 12/13 – until 1963 3/2
1968 7/21 – 10/5
1971 3/8 – 4/7
1971 10/18 – 12/30
1974 4/4 – until 1975 2/13
1979 11/3 – until 1980 2/18
1980 7/1 – 9/19
1983 1/29 – 5/27
1983 9/27 – 12/15
1986 3/18 – 6/21
1986 8/3 – until 1987 1/26
1991 10/12 – until 1992 3/30
1992 6/1 – 9/3
1995 1/8 – 7/14
1995 8/22 – 11/29
1998 3/1 – 5/15
1998 9/23 – until 1999 1/2
2003 9/24 – until 2004 8/18
2006 12/22 – until 2007 11/13
2010 2/13 – 4/22

SATURN CHALLENGING
1948 12/6 – 12/27
1949 8/5 – until 1950 9/11
1956 12/3 – until 1958 1/26
1958 6/18 – 10/25
1965 2/14 – until 1966 3/29
1978 9/13 – until 1979 10/20
1980 4/3 – 7/9
1986 1/10 – 6/1
1986 10/9 – until 1987 12/3
1994 3/21 – 10/18
1994 12/1 – until 1995 5/9
1995 9/4 – until 1996 2/1
2007 10/27 – until 2008 2/12
2008 7/17 – until 2009 8/25

URANUS CHALLENGING
1963 9/5 – until 1967 8/3
1982 12/17 – until 1986 12/7
2004 4/29 – until 2009 3/4

NEPTUNE CHALLENGING
1938 1/1 – until 1939 8/21
1972 12/27 – until 1981 9/9

PLUTO CHALLENGING
1959 11/22 – until 1968 8/30
1997 12/13 – until 2005 10/4

JUPITER SPECIAL
1941 6/21 – until 1942 5/5
1953 6/4 – 8/22
1953 12/8 – until 1954 4/13
1965 5/19 – 7/30
1966 1/23 – 3/9
1977 5/2 – 7/11
1988 9/20 – 9/28
1989 4/14 – 6/24
2000 8/2 – 11/28
2001 3/22 – 6/8
2012 7/9 – Continues

SATURN SPECIAL
1942 6/25 – until 1943 1/14
1943 3/1 – 7/27
1943 12/28 – until 1944 4/12
1971 8/28 – 10/10
1972 5/1 – until 1973 5/30
2001 6/8 – until 2002 7/8

URANUS SPECIAL
1943 6/21 – until 1947 6/16

Ⅱ

June 6

Your Personal Powers

Versatile and imaginative, you have a bright and alert mind. Your enterprising personality indicates that you are buoyant and enthusiastic with a zest for life. You empower yourself when you take your responsibilities seriously and trust your intuition. Your ruling planet, Mercury, grants you communication skills, a talent for business, and a cheerful nature. Although you may be inspired by idealism, a desire for material comforts indicates that you can be decisive and hardworking. You gain power when your objective and resourceful nature has a sense of purpose and a clear goal. Being people-oriented and sociable, your interest in human relationships and your persuasive charm can help you make influential friends or be popular. Yet you can lose some of your power when you become nervous, sensitive, or too easily influenced by others. Nevertheless, having a gregarious and charismatic personality indicates that you are going to remain lively and youthful in spirit until late in life.

Your Powers of Attraction in Relationships

Your humanitarian and sociable personality implies that you have a talent for making people feel at ease. Others are attracted to your inspired ideas and liberal outlook. Although you may have a tendency to talk a great deal, you can motivate others with your wonderful plans and imaginative ideas. A need to be popular and liked suggests that sharing and being a part of a group is usually very important to you. Often you are attracted to confident people who are idealistic and charitable. Alternatively, you may seek the company of intelligent people who can stimulate your imagination or offer you practical support. The key to your success in partnerships often lies in your ability to keep the peace, negotiate, and compromise. Often willing to help and assist others, you know how to entertain and make people happy.

Your attractive qualities: disciplined, quick learner, articulate, youthful, communicative, witty, poised, dependable, organized, well-informed, inspired ideas, compassionate, friendly, focused, understanding, idealistic, enterprising, determined, purposeful, artistic, generous, intuitive

Your less attractive qualities: materialistic, discontented, unrealistic, stubborn, anxious, moody, self-centered, inertia, indulgent, lack of determination, speculative, domineering, suspicious, critical

Your Venus Power

The planet Venus has a great deal of influence on your powers of attraction. Below are four possible Venus types for women and men. To find your Venus you need to go to page 771, where you will find the Venus table and extra information. The planet Mars also affects your powers of attraction. To find your Mars table and interpretation go to page 761.

WOMEN WITH VENUS IN ARIES: Self-reliant and strong, you usually want things your own way. This can present problems if you refuse to compromise with your partners. Your life lessons in the area of love and relationships often involve patience and learning to trust. When you project the full power of your Venus, you can radiate a charismatic and captivating energy and make a strong impression on others. Independence is often high on your relationship agenda.

MEN WITH VENUS IN ARIES: As you often have the courage and strength to initiate situations, you like to take the lead. With your unconscious desire for conquest you may also have to beware of being competitive with your partners. Nevertheless, you are drawn to direct and strong-willed women who can share your love of action and enthusiasm for life. When you are feeling good you can be charming and enthusiastic in romantic situations with an entertaining and spontaneous spirit.

WOMEN WITH VENUS IN TAURUS: Good-natured and romantic, you have a highly developed sense of touch that particularly responds to massage, hugs, and all things physical. With a streak of the conventional, you love the simple pleasures of life: good food, close friends, and happy relationships. With your natural sense of beauty and harmony you are likely to have an attractive voice, beautiful home, or a strong link to nature. You may have to be careful of becoming too extravagant, as often your taste is more expensive than what you are able to afford.

MEN WITH VENUS IN TAURUS: Attractive and affectionate, in relationships you are often faithful with a conservative approach. You are usually drawn to warmhearted partners with whom you can share a familiar routine as well as life's

pleasures and comforts. Seeking a partner who is dependable or reassuring, you often put security high on your priority list when looking for love. Your sociability and friendliness usually make you popular and partners often admire your practicality and good sense of values.

WOMEN WITH VENUS IN GEMINI: By nature you are young at heart, adaptable, and sociable. Being curious and willing to cooperate makes you a good team player. Usually you are drawn to articulate people who have charm and flair or sharp wit. With a need to expand your knowledge you also look for a partner who can challenge or stimulate you intellectually. Although you love to talk with all types of people, you may need to develop your listening skills and tune in to your feelings in order to build better communication in your relationships.

MEN WITH VENUS IN GEMINI: Adaptable yet often flirtatious, you enjoy mixing with people who are quick-minded and versatile. Since you can learn a great deal through interacting with others, you are often attracted to intelligent partners who have comprehensive knowledge or good ideas. One of your less attractive qualities is your tendency to get bored or be inconsistent. Having an adaptable partner is important to you, therefore it must be someone who can offer you different options and keep you interested.

WOMEN WITH VENUS IN CANCER: Sensitive and understanding, you are sympathetic to other people's emotions and needs. Protective toward those you love, close relationships with your partner, relatives, and friends are important to your sense of well-being. Aware of how easy it is to hurt other people's feelings, you are often indirect and approach delicate issues in a roundabout way. Nevertheless, learning to face facts and not allowing others to exploit your good nature is a valuable lesson.

MEN WITH VENUS IN CANCER: You seek a partner who is sympathetic, caring, and protective. Able to be forgiving and compassionate, you want a secure emotional bond in your close relationships. Usually you are drawn to partners who are maternal, unselfish, or demonstrative with their feelings. Although you can sometimes appear to others as impressionable, you have powerful emotions and inner strength.

To read all about your Outer Planets and work out how to use your personalized timetable, go to Section Three, page 789.

♊

Your Personalized Timetable

JUPITER BENEFICIAL
1938 1/20 – 3/31
1938 9/29 – 11/8
1940 2/21 – 4/4
1943 8/15 – 10/4
1944 2/27 – 5/28
1945 9/27 – 12/18
1946 4/8 – 8/18
1950 1/3 – 3/12
1951 6/13 – 9/26
1952 1/30 – 3/18
1955 7/30 – 9/15
1957 9/11 – 11/27
1958 5/20 – 7/18
1961 5/18 – 6/1
1961 12/16 – until **1962** 2/23
1963 5/19 – 11/18
1963 12/22 – until **1964** 2/28
1967 7/14 – 8/29
1969 8/26 – 11/10
1973 4/1 – 7/31
1973 11/23 – until **1974** 2/7
1975 4/30 – 6/20
1975 10/10 – until **1976** 2/6
1979 6/27 – 8/13
1980 12/8 – until **1981** 3/13
1981 8/6 – 10/24
1985 3/11 – until **1986** 1/22
1987 4/13 – 5/28
1987 12/2 – 12/28
1990 10/12 – until **1991** 1/17
1991 6/7 – 7/28
1992 11/15 – until **1993** 4/22
1993 7/11 – 10/9
1997 2/21 – until **1998** 1/4
1999 3/28 – 5/9
2002 9/19 – until **2003** 2/27
2003 5/10 – 7/11
2004 10/28 – until **2005** 9/23
2009 2/4 – 4/24
2009 8/7 – 12/14
2011 3/10 – 4/21

SATURN BENEFICIAL
1938 4/15 – until **1939** 4/4
1947 7/18 – 10/10
1948 1/30 – 6/29
1951 10/12 – until **1952** 11/24
1953 4/26 – 8/19
1962 3/6 – 8/14
1962 12/2 – until **1963** 5/26
1963 6/11 – until **1964** 1/25
1967 5/31 – 9/19
1968 2/20 – 5/13
1968 11/11 – until **1969** 1/29
1976 8/26 – until **1977** 4/1
1977 4/21 – 8/10
1980 11/23 – until **1981** 3/19
1981 8/17 – until **1982** 10/1
1992 1/11 – until **1993** 2/27
1997 3/29 – 7/14
1997 8/20 – until **1998** 3/18
2005 10/16 – 12/29
2006 6/29 – 9/18
2007 3/3 – 6/6
2010 9/25 – until **2011** 11/6
2012 6/6 – 7/13

URANUS BENEFICIAL
1957 9/17 – until **1960** 7/23
1969 11/11 – until **1973** 10/10
1997 3/10 – until **2002** 1/13

NEPTUNE BENEFICIAL
1945 10/23 – until **1953** 10/1
2001 2/16 – until **2009** 1/19

PLUTO BENEFICIAL
1944 10/11 – until **1952** 7/6
1974 10/9 – until **1981** 9/16

JUPITER CHALLENGING
1939 2/1 – 4/9
1944 8/28 – 11/18
1945 3/9 – 7/18
1947 11/25 – until **1948** 2/10
1948 6/23 – 10/7
1950 6/11 – 7/12
1951 1/13 – 3/23
1956 8/12 – 10/27
1957 4/20 – 6/16
1959 11/9 – until **1960** 1/21
1962 5/1 – 9/5
1962 12/20 – until **1963** 3/6
1968 7/26 – 10/10
1971 10/23 – until **1972** 1/4
1974 4/9 – until **1975** 2/17
1979 11/10 – until **1980** 2/11
1980 7/7 – 9/24
1983 2/4 – 5/20
1983 10/3 – 12/19
1986 3/22 – until **1987** 1/30
1991 10/17 – until **1992** 3/21
1992 6/10 – 9/8
1995 1/13 – 7/1
1995 9/3 – 12/3
1998 3/5 – 5/20
1998 9/16 – until **1999** 1/8
2003 9/29 – until **2004** 8/23
2006 12/26 – until **2007** 11/17
2010 2/17 – 4/27

SATURN CHALLENGING
1949 8/13 – until **1950** 9/19
1956 12/12 – until **1958** 2/5
1958 6/5 – 11/5
1965 2/22 – until **1966** 4/6
1966 11/14 – 12/8
1978 9/21 – until **1979** 10/29
1980 3/21 – 7/21
1986 1/20 – 5/19
1986 10/19 – until **1987** 12/11
1994 3/29 – 9/29
1994 12/19 – until **1995** 5/21
1995 8/22 – until **1996** 2/9
2007 11/8 – until **2008** 1/30
2008 7/26 – until **2009** 9/2

URANUS CHALLENGING
1963 9/21 – until **1967** 8/20
1983 1/3 – until **1987** 9/29
2005 3/2 – until **2009** 12/30

NEPTUNE CHALLENGING
1938 1/1 – until **1940** 7/8
1973 1/31 – until **1981** 11/3

PLUTO CHALLENGING
1960 10/4 – until **1969** 7/22
1998 1/10 – until **2005** 11/11

JUPITER SPECIAL
1941 6/26 – until **1942** 5/9
1953 6/8 – 8/29
1953 12/1 – until **1954** 4/19
1965 5/23 – 8/4
1966 1/13 – 3/20
1977 5/6 – 7/16
1989 4/19 – 6/29
2000 8/8 – 11/21
2001 3/28 – 6/12
2012 7/14 – Continues

SATURN SPECIAL
1942 7/4 – 12/27
1943 3/18 – 8/5
1943 12/17 – until **1944** 4/23
1972 5/8 – until **1973** 6/7
2001 6/15 – until **2002** 7/15
2003 1/21 – 3/25

URANUS SPECIAL
1943 7/9 – until **1948** 4/16

June 7

Your Personal Powers

Analytical, tactful, and charming, your ability to make many contacts and quickly judge people or situations implies that you are an astute and accomplished individual. Full of ideas and plans, you gain power when you let your imaginative and optimistic nature inspire you or others. Your ruling planet, Mercury, grants you a love of variety or change and a talent for business. When your need for expansion and determination are combined, you can become an unstoppable force. Original and receptive, your awareness and resourcefulness suggest that you can often turn your knowledge into profit. Since making money can become a preoccupation, you also need to learn that it cannot replace emotional fulfillment and happiness. By learning to trust your intuition and overcoming your tendency to be skeptical or restless, your chances for success are often outstanding. Although large projects with big rewards probably inspire you most, a need for mental stimulation is crucial if you want to stay interested in a project for long.

Your Powers of Attraction in Relationships

Charming and a good conversationalist, you can be very entertaining and witty when you want to impress others. Although you are often persuasive, capable, and determined, your impatience or restless nature can create tension in your close relationships. Usually you are drawn to the company of smart, creative, or intelligent people who have vitality or forceful personalities. Being friendly, you can show willingness to assist others with practical advice or encouragement. As generosity can also be one of your attractive attributes, your partners usually appreciate your spontaneity and grand gestures. If your success becomes a focal point, it is possible that you may experience a pull between your need for close and loving relationships and your quest for material accomplishment. Others are usually attracted to your spirit of enterprise and wonderful ideas.

Your attractive qualities: intelligent, optimistic, confident, inner faith, versatile, diplomatic, independent, trusting, charismatic, enterprising, methodical, persuasive, communicative, direct, meticulous, idealistic, thoughtful, receptive, rational, reflective, shrewd, observant, articulate

Your less attractive qualities: materialistic, indulgent, skeptical, overly ambitious, unfocused, impatient, critical, too idealistic, cynical, intolerant, argumentative, cold, self-absorbed, bored easily, lack of determination

Your Venus Power

The planet Venus has a great deal of influence on your powers of attraction. Below are four possible Venus types for women and men. To find your Venus you need to go to page 771, where you will find the Venus table and extra information. The planet Mars also affects your powers of attraction. To find your Mars table and interpretation go to page 761.

WOMEN WITH VENUS IN TAURUS: Good-natured and romantic, you have a highly developed sense of touch that particularly responds to massage, hugs, and all things physical. With a streak of the conventional you love the simple pleasures of life: good food, close friends, and happy relationships. With your natural sense of beauty and harmony, you are likely to have an attractive voice, beautiful home, or a strong link to nature. You may have to be careful of becoming too extravagant, as often your taste is more expensive than what you are able to afford.

MEN WITH VENUS IN TAURUS: Attractive and affectionate, in relationships you are often faithful with a conservative approach. You are usually drawn to warmhearted partners with whom you can share a familiar routine as well as life's pleasures and comforts. Seeking a partner who is dependable or reassuring, you often put security high on your priority list when looking for love. Your sociability and friendliness usually make you popular and partners often admire your practicality and good sense of values.

WOMEN WITH VENUS IN GEMINI: Charming and usually easygoing, you like to talk to people who are intelligent and witty. With a good social sense and a desire for mental expansion, you need a partner who is informed and has good ideas. Although you enjoy having different experiences, you need to resist your tendencies to become bored too quickly or be too talkative. As you enjoy sharing and learning new things, you usually prefer being with someone rather than operating alone.

MEN WITH VENUS IN GEMINI: Informed and curious yet charming and friendly, you seek a partner who shares your interests or enjoys your witty remarks. Although a good communicator, you have an inborn tendency to be lighthearted and

less profound about deep emotional commitment. Although you are keen on experiences that bring variety into your life, boredom or scattering your energies in too many directions is probably your biggest handicap in relationships. Nevertheless, you are attracted to intelligent partners who can match your lively banter.

WOMEN WITH VENUS IN CANCER: Gentle and tender, you are romantic by nature. You possess a strong need for security and usually you help others feel safe or protected. This preservation is especially centered around the home, which is your haven from life's storm. Although your maternal instincts are strong, avoid making too many sacrifices for others at your own expense. Nevertheless, affectionate and caring, once committed to a relationship your loyalty and devotion to your partner are very strong.

MEN WITH VENUS IN CANCER: Affectionate with a strong sensitive streak, you can love very deeply. You may find yourself drawn to sympathetic partners who can tune in to your moods and feelings as well as be reassuring and supportive. Family links are especially important to you and the more positive these relationships are the more confident and safe you feel.

WOMEN WITH VENUS IN LEO: You possess the wonderful ability to project your warm and sunny personality and keep others happily entertained. Loving attention yourself, you seek a partner who can appreciate you, be supportive, and give you positive feedback. Proud, with a natural regal air, you expect respect from your partners but are willing to be loyal and supportive in exchange. Although sometimes a little self-centered, you know how to make your partner feel special.

MEN WITH VENUS IN LEO: Enthusiastic, playful, and kind, you can be benevolent with those you love. Warm, romantic, and self-expressive, you adore the drama of love or having fun with your friends. Usually you are attracted to partners with a warm and generous nature. Although you can be a confident and charismatic partner yourself, you may need to develop humility in order to stop pride or arrogance from marring your relationships.

To read all about your Outer Planets and work out how to use your personalized timetable, go to Section Three, page 789.

♊

165

Your Personalized Timetable

JUPITER BENEFICIAL
1938 1/24 – 4/5
1938 9/17 – 11/19
1940 2/25 – 4/8
1943 8/20 – 10/9
1944 2/20 – 6/5
1945 10/2 – 12/25
1946 3/31 – 8/24
1950 1/7 – 3/17
1951 6/20 – 9/18
1952 2/4 – 3/22
1955 8/3 – 9/19
1957 9/16 – 12/2
1958 5/10 – 7/28
1961 12/20 – until 1962 2/27
1963 5/24 – 11/5
1964 1/3 – 3/4
1967 7/19 – 9/3
1969 8/31 – 11/14
1973 4/8 – 7/24
1973 11/29 – until 1974 2/11
1975 5/4 – 6/26
1975 10/3 – until 1976 2/12
1979 7/2 – 8/17
1980 12/16 – until 1981 3/5
1981 8/12 – 10/29
1985 3/16 – 9/9
1985 10/26 – until 1986 1/26
1987 4/17 – 6/2
1987 11/18 – until 1988 1/11
1990 10/20 – until 1991 1/10
1991 6/13 – 8/1
1992 11/20 – until 1993 4/13
1993 7/19 – 10/13
1997 2/25 – until 1998 1/9
1999 4/1 – 5/13
2002 9/24 – until 2003 2/18
2003 5/19 – 7/16
2004 11/2 – until 2005 9/28
2009 2/8 – 5/1
2009 7/30 – 12/19
2011 3/15 – 4/25

SATURN BENEFICIAL
1938 4/23 – until 1939 4/11
1947 7/25 – 10/22
1948 1/17 – 7/8
1951 10/20 – until 1952 12/3
1953 4/13 – 8/30
1962 3/16 – 8/1
1962 12/13 – until 1964 2/2
1967 6/13 – 9/5
1968 2/29 – 5/22
1968 10/29 – until 1969 2/10
1976 9/3 – until 1977 3/7
1977 5/15 – 8/18
1980 12/4 – until 1981 3/6
1981 8/26 – until 1982 10/9
1992 1/19 – until 1993 3/7
1993 10/7 – 11/18
1997 4/6 – until 1998 3/25
2005 11/4 – 12/9
2006 7/7 – 9/27
2007 2/18 – 6/17
2010 10/3 – until 2011 11/15
2012 5/16 – 8/3

URANUS BENEFICIAL
1957 10/10 – until 1960 8/7
1969 12/3 – until 1974 7/30
1997 4/3 – until 2002 1/30

NEPTUNE BENEFICIAL
1945 11/24 – until 1954 8/27
2001 3/18 – until 2009 12/8

PLUTO BENEFICIAL
1945 9/13 – until 1953 6/2
1974 11/5 – until 1981 10/11

JUPITER CHALLENGING
1939 2/5 – until 1945 7/24

1947 11/29 – until 1948 2/16
1948 6/15 – 10/13
1951 1/17 – 3/27
1956 8/16 – 11/1
1957 4/10 – 6/27
1959 11/14 – until 1960 1/26
1960 8/8 – 9/1
1962 5/7 – 8/29
1962 12/26 – until 1963 3/10
1968 7/31 – 10/14
1971 10/28 – until 1972 1/8
1974 4/13 – 11/1
1974 11/6 – until 1975 2/21
1979 11/18 – until 1980 2/2
1980 7/12 – 9/28
1983 2/11 – 5/12
1983 10/8 – 12/23
1986 3/26 – until 1987 2/4
1991 10/23 – until 1992 3/13
1992 6/18 – 9/12
1995 1/18 – 6/22
1995 9/12 – 12/8
1998 3/9 – 5/27
1998 9/8 – until 1999 1/13
2003 10/4 – until 2004 8/28
2006 12/31 – until 2007 11/22
2010 2/21 – 5/2
2010 11/1 – 12/5

SATURN CHALLENGING
1949 8/21 – until 1950 9/26
1956 12/20 – until 1957 7/22
1957 9/1 – until 1958 2/17
1958 5/22 – 11/14
1965 3/1 – until 1966 4/14
1966 10/21 – 12/31
1978 9/29 – until 1979 4/6
1979 6/11 – 11/8
1980 3/9 – 7/31
1986 2/2 – 5/5
1986 10/29 – until 1987 12/19
1994 4/7 – 9/15
1995 1/1 – 6/6
1995 8/5 – until 1996 2/18
2007 11/25 – until 2008 1/13
2008 8/3 – until 2009 9/9

URANUS CHALLENGING
1963 10/8 – until 1967 9/5
1983 1/23 – until 1987 10/27
2005 3/19 – until 2010 1/27

NEPTUNE CHALLENGING
1938 1/1 – until 1940 8/14
1973 12/22 – until 1981 12/1

PLUTO CHALLENGING
1960 11/19 – until 1969 8/23
1998 2/26 – until 2005 12/8

JUPITER SPECIAL
1941 6/30 – until 1942 5/14
1953 6/12 – 9/5
1953 11/23 – until 1954 4/24
1965 5/27 – 8/9
1966 1/4 – 3/29
1977 5/11 – 7/20
1989 4/23 – 7/3
2000 8/15 – 11/14
2001 4/3 – 6/16
2012 7/19 – 12/29

SATURN SPECIAL
1942 7/12 – 12/14
1943 3/30 – 8/15
1943 12/5 – until 1944 5/2
1972 5/16 – until 1973 6/14
2001 6/23 – until 2002 7/24
2003 1/6 – 4/9

URANUS SPECIAL
1943 8/1 – until 1948 5/7

June 8

Your Personal Powers

Ambitious and determined, your courage indicates that you can be a decisive and resolute individual with extraordinary power for achievement. Mentally quick and flexible, you need to have variety in your life to keep you from becoming bored or restless. Your ruling planet, Mercury, grants you versatility, business acumen, and a friendly nature. You gain power when you stay balanced and positive, resisting the temptation to act in a compulsive or erratic manner. Being both liberal and a good communicator, you have a charismatic charm and a flair for dealing with people. You lose power when you let your inner discontent lead you to be extravagant or impulsive. Although you have executive skills and a sixth sense for making money, you may experience fluctuating finances at different periods in your life. Nevertheless, knowing how to spot a good investment, you can experience unexpected good fortune. Being resourceful and analytical, you can combine your exceptional evaluating skills, experience, and intuition to achieve excellent results.

Your Powers of Attraction in Relationships

Intelligent and accomplished, you can inspire others with your knowledge and discriminative powers. Your resourcefulness and resolute determination also impress people. When you feel relaxed and confident, you can be witty and entertain others with your quick repartee. Although you are often dynamic and persuasive, the key to successful relationships often lies in your ability to keep a good balance of power. Occasionally, however, inner tensions can cause you to become dominating or nervous. Being energetic indicates that you need a partner who can offer you variety in your everyday life yet at the same time have a calming influence on you. Generosity is often one of your attractive qualities, and other people respond well to your kind gestures.

Your attractive qualities: quick intelligence, sound judgment, energetic, generous, ambitious, enterprising, hardworking, natural psychologist, humorous, intuitive, well-informed, persuasive, independent, sociable, generous, supportive, liberal, insight, business acumen, strong values

Your less attractive qualities: impulsive actions, bossy, intolerant, impatient, controlling, easily bored or discouraged, too demanding, restless, frustrated, materialistic, overly enthusiastic, disappointed, insecure

Your Venus Power

The planet Venus has a great deal of influence on your powers of attraction. Below are four possible Venus types for women and men. To find your Venus you need to go to page 771, where you will find the Venus table and extra information. The planet Mars also affects your powers of attraction. To find your Mars table and interpretation go to page 761.

WOMEN WITH VENUS IN TAURUS: Demonstrative and affectionate, you are naturally tactile with a love of sensual pleasures. With a streak of the conventional, you love the simple pleasures of life: good food, close friends, and happy relationships. Although you possess endurance, be careful not to let this turn into plain stubbornness. Having inner strength, you can express genuine patience and are often a pillar of support for loved ones and friends.

MEN WITH VENUS IN TAURUS: Although you are usually drawn to sensual and physically beautiful individuals, you want a partner who is also reliable and loyal. When in love you enjoy buying your partner things of quality that will grow in value or useful things of a practical nature. You also love to socialize and entertain, especially in luxurious surroundings. Affectionate and caring, you are often attracted to creative people or those with artistic talents.

WOMEN WITH VENUS IN GEMINI: In relationships you need intellectual stimulation and usually prefer to keep things light. Certainly not boring, you love to talk and are at your best being witty and entertaining. Although your easygoing approach to relationships is very attractive, guard against losing touch with your deeper emotions. You prefer a partner who can keep up with your fast stream of ideas, and if you have shared interests then so much the better.

MEN WITH VENUS IN GEMINI: Charming, amusing, and adaptable, you attract others with your natural communication skills and friendly personality. You have a wonderful childlike quality and love to keep life playful, but a reluctance to contact your deeper feelings may cause you to avoid serious commitment. With your need for variety and intellectual stimulation, you are attracted to clever and amusing partners who have many interesting sides to their personalities.

WOMEN WITH VENUS IN CANCER: Possessing a soft femininity, you have tender and sensitive emotions. Sympathetic and caring, you often mother those in your care by making sure that they are comfortable and have plenty to eat. When you feel hurt or insecure in relationships you are likely to cover your feelings by being defensive or appearing tough on the outside while on the inside you are feeling vulnerable. Affectionate and romantic, you make a faithful and devoted partner.

MEN WITH VENUS IN CANCER: Being emotionally receptive you can make a sensitive lover. With your desire to care for and protect others you are likely to have strong family connections. Love is often tied in with being attentive to the needs of others and you may find yourself attracted to individuals who have sympathetic or maternal qualities. Security-conscious, you need a loyal partner who can offer you support and ideally be a good cook and homemaker.

WOMEN WITH VENUS IN LEO: Warm and playful with a touch of the dramatic, you enjoy the company of generous or strong individuals who can share your sense of fun. Although there are advantages to your being strong-willed, in your relationships you need to resist being bossy as it can cause resentment. With your wonderful mixture of regal authority and childlike wonder, you love to keep others entertained and amused.

MEN WITH VENUS IN LEO: Sociable and outgoing, you are kind and generous with those you love. Looking for a relationship that can be fun and entertaining, you need a playmate who can share your enthusiasm and high spirits. Your pride, however, often stops you from associating with lovers or partners whom you see as beneath you. As you desire someone who can appreciate your sense of the dramatic, you are often attracted to people with strong personalities.

To read all about your Outer Planets and work out how to use your personalized timetable, go to Section Three, page 789.

♊

Your Personalized Timetable

JUPITER BENEFICIAL
1938 1/28 – 4/10	**1944** 9/6 – 12/2
1938 9/8 – 11/28	**1945** 2/22 – 7/29
1940 3/1 – 4/12	**1947** 12/4 – until **1948** 2/23
1943 8/24 – 10/15	**1948** 6/8 – 10/19
1944 2/12 – 6/11	**1951** 1/22 – 3/31
1945 10/6 – until **1946** 1/2	**1956** 8/21 – 11/7
1946 3/23 – 8/30	**1957** 4/1 – 7/5
1950 1/11 – 3/21	**1959** 11/18 – until **1960** 1/31
1951 6/27 – 9/10	**1960** 7/23 – 9/17
1952 2/9 – 3/26	**1962** 5/13 – 8/22
1955 8/8 – 9/24	**1962** 12/31 – until **1963** 3/14
1956 3/31 – 5/5	**1968** 8/5 – 10/19
1957 9/20 – 12/8	**1971** 11/1 – until **1972** 1/13
1958 5/1 – 8/6	**1974** 4/18 – 10/10
1961 12/25 – until **1962** 3/3	**1974** 11/27 – until **1975** 2/25
1963 5/29 – 10/27	**1979** 11/28 – until **1980** 1/23
1964 1/12 – 3/8	**1980** 7/18 – 10/3
1967 7/23 – 9/7	**1983** 2/20 – 5/3
1969 9/4 – 11/19	**1983** 10/14 – 12/27
1973 4/15 – 7/16	**1986** 3/31 – until **1987** 2/8
1973 12/4 – until **1974** 2/15	**1991** 10/29 – until **1992** 3/5
1975 5/8 – 7/4	**1992** 6/25 – 9/17
1975 9/25 – until **1976** 2/17	**1995** 1/23 – 6/13
1979 7/6 – 8/22	**1995** 9/20 – 12/12
1980 12/25 – until **1981** 2/24	**1998** 3/13 – 6/3
1981 8/17 – 11/2	**1998** 9/1 – until **1999** 1/19
1985 3/21 – 8/30	**2003** 10/9 – until **2004** 4/30
1985 11/6 – until **1986** 1/30	**2004** 5/10 – 9/1
1987 4/21 – 6/7	**2007** 1/4 – 11/26
1987 11/8 – until **1988** 1/20	**2010** 2/25 – 5/7
1990 10/29 – until **1991** 1/1	**2010** 10/20 – 12/18
1991 6/18 – 8/6	
1992 11/26 – until **1993** 4/6	**SATURN CHALLENGING**
1993 7/26 – 10/18	**1949** 8/28 – until **1950** 10/4
1997 3/1 – until **1998** 1/13	**1956** 12/29 – until **1957** 7/1
1999 4/5 – 5/17	**1957** 9/21 – until **1958** 3/5
2002 9/30 – until **2003** 2/10	**1958** 5/5 – 11/23
2003 5/26 – 7/21	**1965** 3/9 – until **1966** 4/23
2004 11/7 – until **2005** 5/31	**1966** 10/6 – until **1967** 1/14
2005 6/9 – 10/2	**1978** 10/7 – until **1979** 3/22
2009 2/12 – 5/9	**1979** 6/26 – 11/19
2009 7/21 – 12/24	**1980** 2/25 – 8/9
2011 3/19 – 4/29	**1986** 2/17 – 4/18

SATURN BENEFICIAL
1938 5/1 – 11/15	**1986** 11/6 – until **1987** 12/27
1939 1/12 – 4/19	**1994** 4/17 – 9/2
1947 8/2 – 11/7	**1995** 1/11 – until **1996** 2/26
1948 1/1 – 7/16	**2008** 8/11 – until **2009** 9/17
1951 10/28 – until **1952** 5/10	
1952 7/11 – 12/14	**URANUS CHALLENGING**
1953 4/1 – 9/8	**1963** 10/27 – until **1967** 9/20
1962 3/27 – 7/19	**1983** 2/25 – until **1987** 11/16
1962 12/22 – until **1964** 2/10	**2005** 4/7 – until **2010** 2/16
1967 7/1 – 8/18	
1968 3/8 – 5/31	**NEPTUNE CHALLENGING**
1968 10/16 – until **1969** 2/21	**1938** 1/1 – until **1941** 6/20
1976 9/11 – until **1977** 2/21	**1974** 1/22 – until **1982** 10/27
1977 5/29 – 8/25	
1980 12/19 – until **1981** 2/18	**PLUTO CHALLENGING**
1981 9/3 – until **1982** 10/17	**1961** 10/4 – until **1970** 7/8
1992 1/27 – until **1993** 3/16	**1998** 12/27 – until **2006** 11/2
1993 9/17 – 12/7	
1997 4/13 – until **1998** 4/2	**JUPITER SPECIAL**
2006 7/15 – 10/7	**1941** 7/5 – until **1942** 5/18
2007 2/6 – 6/27	**1953** 6/17 – 9/14
2010 10/11 – until **2011** 11/23	**1953** 11/14 – until **1954** 4/29
2012 5/1 – 8/17	**1965** 5/31 – 8/14
	1965 12/27 – until **1966** 4/5
URANUS BENEFICIAL	**1977** 5/15 – 7/25
1958 8/4 – until **1961** 5/25	**1989** 4/28 – 7/7
1970 9/29 – until **1974** 8/26	**2000** 8/22 – 11/6
1998 2/2 – until **2002** 11/15	**2001** 4/8 – 6/20
	2012 7/24 – 12/21
NEPTUNE BENEFICIAL	
1946 10/18 – until **1954** 9/27	**SATURN SPECIAL**
2002 2/11 – until **2010** 1/13	**1942** 7/21 – 12/2
	1943 4/9 – 8/27
PLUTO BENEFICIAL	**1943** 11/22 – until **1944** 5/11
1946 8/23 – until **1953** 7/15	**1972** 5/23 – until **1973** 6/21
1974 12/11 – until **1982** 8/29	**2001** 7/1 – until **2002** 1/7
	2002 3/11 – 8/2
JUPITER CHALLENGING	**2002** 12/25 – until **2003** 4/20
1939 2/9 – 4/17	
	URANUS SPECIAL
	1944 5/31 – until **1948** 5/25

June 9

SUN: GEMINI • DECANATE: LIBRA/VENUS • DEGREE: 17°–18°5 GEMINI • MODE: MUTABLE • ELEMENT: AIR

Your Personal Powers

Astute and intuitive, you are an intelligent and mentally sharp individual who can comprehend knowledge quickly and benefit from what you learn. Your ruling planet, Mercury, grants you versatility, talent for business, and an inquisitive nature. As a sensitive person on an inner level, you usually seek peace of mind and emotional security. You may, however, have to overcome a tendency to worry or be skeptical, so you therefore gain power when you act with confidence and purpose. Usually you are determined and hardworking; at other times, however, you may decide to free yourself from restrictions and find projects that are more creative or emotionally rewarding. Since you like to be in charge, you are often willing to take responsibilities. In order to lead, you may need to develop patience and resist the temptation to be too domineering. You lose power and create mental stress when you are drawn into disputes with others and act in an obstinate or rebellious way. By staying focused and disciplined, however, you can overcome the obstacles set in your way and win admirably with little struggle.

Your Powers of Attraction in Relationships

Often inspired by new and exciting ideas or projects, other people admire your enthusiasm and love of knowledge. Usually you are attracted to mentally creative individuals who can inspire or encourage you to express yourself. If you are constantly seeking excitement or emotionally fulfilling experiences, you can become restless or easily bored. Since you can be amusing and sociable, you attract friends with ease, especially if you share the same interests. Hidden insecurities sometimes cause you to become overly serious or argumentative, leaving you to display some of your less attractive qualities. In order to establish happy and successful relationships or partnerships you may need to develop a more detached attitude or show willingness to compromise.

Your attractive qualities: quick comprehension, determined, loyal, inquisitive mind, intuitive, idealistic, receptive, imaginative, sensitive, generous, magnetic, charitable, detached, popular, tolerant, focused, thoughtful, calm, self-confident, hardworking, business sense, optimistic, benevolent, kind

Your less attractive qualities: argumentative, indecisive, frustrated, nervous, impractical, moody, critical, skeptical, indifferent, inner fears or insecurity, materialistic, bossy, isolated, lack of interest, self-doubt, unfocused

Your Venus Power

The planet Venus has a great deal of influence on your powers of attraction. Below are four possible Venus types for women and men. To find your Venus you need to go to page 771, where you will find the Venus table and extra information. The planet Mars also affects your powers of attraction. To find your Mars table and interpretation go to page 761.

WOMEN WITH VENUS IN TAURUS: Warm and affectionate, you are drawn to partners with whom you can share life's simple comforts. With a need for stability and security or an appreciation of earthly pleasures, you may have to avoid overindulgence or becoming too preoccupied with material concerns. Nevertheless, your sociability and friendliness usually make you popular. You need a partner who can share your appreciation of beauty and style.

MEN WITH VENUS IN TAURUS: As well as attracting people with your warm personality, you also possess an innate sense of the value of material possessions. Keeping yourself stylish and having an attractive home can therefore be important to you. You are naturally attracted to practical yet sensual women who understand your need for comfort, security, and the pleasures and luxuries of life. Naturally affectionate, you enjoy socializing but can be a loyal and loving partner.

WOMEN WITH VENUS IN GEMINI: Curious, with a bright and animated approach to life, you are attracted to those who are clever or sophisticated. Your love of variety and desire for knowledge suggest that you need a partner and friends who can keep you mentally stimulated. Although witty and a good conversationalist, you may need to keep in touch with your deeper feelings. Nevertheless, intelligent and friendly, you possess a youthful sense of wonder and seek a playmate who can keep you from becoming bored.

MEN WITH VENUS IN GEMINI: Friendly and sociable, you attract others with your clever and amusing conversation. Drawn to people who can match you in wit and intelligence, you usually prefer to keep relationships light rather than emotionally intense. With your youthful charm and desire for knowledge and new experiences you usually have many friends and a low boredom threshold.

WOMEN WITH VENUS IN CANCER: With your intuitive abilities and sympathetic nature, you are usually supportive of those you love. Impressionable and empathetic, your receptivity allows you to quickly pick up on the moods of others, making you especially aware of the emotional changes in your close partner. As you often display true maternal tendencies toward those you know, you want a partner who is considerate and sensitive.

MEN WITH VENUS IN CANCER: Being caring and sensitive, you probably seek a nurturing partner who could provide you with emotional security and a sense of belonging in a loving and safe environment. Receptive to others, at times you find it hard to be direct or confrontational in relationships. You may find yourself drawn to affectionate and sympathetic partners like yourself. You are also likely to have strong family links.

WOMEN WITH VENUS IN LEO: As someone who wants to radiate in your own right, you are likely to desire partners you can be proud of. Usually you are attracted to fun-loving, warm, and generous individuals. If self-expression is important to you, you will probably seek the company of creative people such as artists, musicians, or those with a flair for acting. Romantic and dignified, with a regal air, you can project confidence and success to attract others.

MEN WITH VENUS IN LEO: Generous, animated, and pleasure-seeking, you can be very entertaining and fun to be with. Usually you are attracted to extroverted and benevolent individuals with a sunny personality. If ambitious, you are drawn to a partner who shows leadership qualities or one who is highly motivated. Your less attractive qualities are your tendencies to be bossy or vain. With a sense of the dramatic, however, you can be the life and soul of the party and inspire those around you.

To read all about your Outer Planets and work out how to use your personalized timetable, go to Section Three, page 789.

♊

Your Personalized Timetable

JUPITER BENEFICIAL
1938 2/4 – 4/20
1938 8/25 – 12/10
1940 3/8 – 4/19
1943 9/1 – 10/27
1944 1/30 – 6/22
1945 10/14 – until 1946 1/21
1946 3/4 – 9/8
1950 1/18 – 3/29
1951 7/17 – 8/22
1952 2/18 – 4/2
1955 8/15 – 10/3
1956 3/10 – 5/25
1957 9/28 – 12/18
1958 4/18 – 8/18
1962 1/1 – 3/11
1963 6/7 – 10/14
1964 1/24 – 3/16
1967 7/31 – 9/15
1969 9/13 – 11/28
1970 6/3 – 7/13
1973 4/30 – 6/30
1973 12/13 – until 1974 2/22
1975 5/16 – 7/20
1975 9/9 – until 1976 2/26
1979 7/14 – 8/29
1981 8/26 – 11/10
1985 3/30 – 8/15
1985 11/20 – until 1986 2/6
1987 4/28 – 6/16
1987 10/26 – until 1988 2/2
1991 6/27 – 8/14
1992 12/7 – until 1993 3/23
1993 8/6 – 10/25
1997 3/9 – until 1998 1/21
1999 4/11 – 5/25
2002 10/10 – until 2003 1/29
2003 6/6 – 7/29
2004 11/16 – until 2005 5/2
2005 7/9 – 10/10
2009 2/20 – 5/31
2009 6/30 – until 2010 1/2
2011 3/26 – 5/6

SATURN BENEFICIAL
1938 5/16 – 10/20
1939 2/5 – 5/2
1947 8/15 – until 1948 7/30
1951 11/12 – until 1952 4/14
1952 8/5 – until 1953 1/9
1953 3/4 – 9/24
1962 4/21 – 6/21
1963 1/7 – until 1964 2/24
1968 3/22 – 6/20
1968 9/24 – until 1969 3/9
1976 9/27 – until 1977 1/30
1977 6/17 – 9/8
1978 4/25 – 4/25
1981 9/18 – until 1982 10/31
1992 2/10 – until 1993 4/1
1993 8/24 – 12/28
1997 4/27 – 12/5
1997 12/27 – until 1998 4/15
2006 7/29 – 10/27
2007 1/15 – 7/13
2010 10/24 – until 2011 5/28
2011 6/28 – 12/10
2012 4/9 – 9/5

URANUS BENEFICIAL
1958 9/1 – until 1961 7/8
1970 10/26 – until 1974 9/27
1998 3/4 – until 2003 1/9

NEPTUNE BENEFICIAL
1946 12/20 – until 1955 9/14
2002 4/8 – until 2010 12/29

PLUTO BENEFICIAL
1947 8/29 – until 1954 7/15
1975 11/13 – until 1982 10/15

JUPITER CHALLENGING
1939 2/16 – 4/25

1944 9/13 – 12/20
1945 2/4 – 8/8
1947 12/11 – until 1948 3/7
1948 5/24 – 10/29
1951 1/29 – 4/7
1956 8/29 – 11/17
1957 3/19 – 7/17
1959 11/25 – until 1960 2/9
1960 7/7 – 10/3
1962 5/27 – 8/7
1963 1/9 – 3/21
1968 8/13 – 10/28
1969 5/4 – 6/11
1971 11/9 – until 1972 1/21
1974 4/27 – 9/23
1974 12/13 – until 1975 3/4
1980 7/26 – 10/11
1983 3/14 – 4/9
1983 10/23 – until 1984 1/4
1986 4/7 – until 1987 2/16
1991 11/9 – until 1992 2/21
1992 7/6 – 9/24
1995 2/3 – 5/31
1995 10/2 – 12/19
1998 3/21 – 6/18
1998 8/16 – until 1999 1/28
2003 10/18 – until 2004 4/1
2004 6/8 – 9/9
2007 1/13 – 7/16
2007 8/28 – 12/4
2010 3/4 – 5/16
2010 10/4 – until 2011 1/1

SATURN CHALLENGING
1949 9/11 – until 1950 10/18
1951 4/22 – 7/4
1957 1/14 – 6/6
1957 10/13 – until 1958 12/8
1965 3/23 – 10/31
1965 11/27 – until 1966 5/10
1966 9/14 – until 1967 2/2
1978 10/23 – until 1979 2/28
1979 7/15 – 12/17
1980 1/26 – 8/24
1986 11/21 – until 1988 1/11
1988 7/31 – 9/29
1994 5/7 – 8/10
1995 1/28 – until 1996 3/11
2008 8/25 – until 2009 10/1

URANUS CHALLENGING
1964 9/6 – until 1968 8/2
1983 12/23 – until 1987 12/15
2005 5/29 – until 2010 3/18

NEPTUNE CHALLENGING
1938 1/1 – until 1941 8/30
1975 1/7 – until 1983 10/4

PLUTO CHALLENGING
1962 9/26 – until 1970 9/5
1999 12/11 – until 2007 10/14

JUPITER SPECIAL
1941 7/13 – until 1942 5/26
1953 6/24 – until 1954 5/8
1965 6/7 – 8/25
1965 12/15 – until 1966 4/16
1977 5/22 – 8/2
1978 2/1 – 3/10
1989 5/6 – 7/15
2000 9/11 – 10/18
2001 4/17 – 6/28
2012 8/3 – 12/7

SATURN SPECIAL
1942 8/9 – 11/11
1943 4/25 – until 1944 5/25
1972 6/5 – until 1973 7/5
2001 7/16 – 12/13
2002 4/3 – 8/19
2002 12/4 – until 2003 5/6

URANUS SPECIAL
1944 6/29 – until 1949 3/23

June 10

Your Personal Powers

Intuitive and responsible, your strong determination and willingness to learn suggest that you are quietly ambitious. Although you can appear detached, underneath you are usually sensitive with deep feelings. Your ruling planet, Mercury, grants you versatility, communication skills, and quick intelligence. Your desire to achieve materially and your sense of duty are often challenged by your quest for love and affection or emotional satisfaction. You gain power when you can balance between your need for independence and your need for intimacy. Although you are enterprising and ambitious, you gain power when you combine your liberal attitude and inspiration with practical skills and strong sense of responsibility. It is often your need for diversity and self-fulfillment that encourages you to be creative and seek different experiences in life. Able to persevere, you gain power from your ability to overcome challenges. When you are true to yourself, life often rewards you for your hard efforts and dedication. You can be undermined by fears or frustration; however, you gain power when you learn to manage your own affairs with confidence. You also benefit from being spontaneous.

Your Powers of Attraction in Relationships

You are kind and caring, and people warm to your sunny and idealistic personality. Although you can be spontaneous and generous, when you take life too seriously others can find you too intense. An inclination to see things in black and white also implies that in relationships you can be all or nothing. Since relationships can cause you to feel extreme emotions, you may swing from being enthusiastic and spontaneous to being bored, disinterested, or cold. Although you can be tolerant and show willingness to make sacrifices for the one you love, the key to happy or successful relationships often lies in taking your time, being cautious, and keeping the balance of power between giving and taking. Nevertheless, caring and considerate, you can be a faithful and supportive partner or friend.

Your attractive qualities: forceful, independent, determined, progressive, ambitious, optimistic trustworthy, direct, quick comprehension, inquisitive mind, responsible, strong convictions, inventive, gregarious, pioneering, loyal, tolerant, sympathetic, cooperative, calm, contented

Your less attractive qualities: argumentative, indecisive, overbearing, egotistical, lack of restraint, vacillating moods, impatient, critical, too ambitious, materialistic, run hot and cold, one-sided, indifferent, too proud, antagonistic, codependent, resentful

Your Venus Power

The planet Venus has a great deal of influence on your powers of attraction. Below are four possible Venus types for women and men. To find your Venus you need to go to page 771, where you will find the Venus table and extra information. The planet Mars also affects your powers of attraction. To find your Mars table and interpretation go to page 761.

WOMEN WITH VENUS IN TAURUS: Good-natured and romantic, you have a highly developed sense of touch that particularly responds to massage, hugs, and all things physical. With a streak of the conventional, you love the simple pleasures of life: good food, close friends, and happy relationships. With your natural sense of beauty and harmony you are likely to have an attractive voice, beautiful home, or a strong link to nature. You may have to be careful of becoming too extravagant, as often your taste is more expensive than what you are able to afford.

MEN WITH VENUS IN TAURUS: Attractive and affectionate, in relationships you are often faithful with a conservative approach. You are usually drawn to warmhearted partners with whom you can share a familiar routine as well as life's pleasures and comforts. Seeking a partner who is dependable or reassuring, you often put security high on your priority list when looking for love. Your sociability and friendliness usually make you popular and partners often admire your practicality and good sense of values.

WOMEN WITH VENUS IN GEMINI: By nature you are young at heart, adaptable, and sociable. Being curious and willing to cooperate makes you a good team player. Usually you are drawn to articulate people who have charm and flair or sharp wit. With a need to expand your knowledge, you also look for a partner who can challenge or stimulate you intellectually. Although you love to talk with all types of people, you may need to develop your listening skills and tune in to your feelings in order to build better communication in your relationships.

MEN WITH VENUS IN GEMINI: Adaptable yet often flirtatious, you enjoy mixing with people who are quick-minded

and versatile. Since you can learn a great deal through interacting with others, you are often attracted to intelligent partners who have comprehensive knowledge or good ideas. One of your less attractive qualities is your tendency to become bored or be inconsistent. Having an adaptable partner is important to you, therefore it must be someone who can offer you different options and keep you interested.

WOMEN WITH VENUS IN CANCER: Sensitive and understanding, you are sympathetic to other people's emotions and needs. You are protective toward those you love; close relationships with your partner, relatives, and friends are important to your sense of well-being. Aware of how easy it is to hurt other people's feelings, you are often indirect and approach delicate issues in a roundabout way. Nevertheless, learning to face facts and not allowing others to exploit your good nature is a valuable lesson.

MEN WITH VENUS IN CANCER: You seek a partner who is sympathetic, caring, and protective. Able to be forgiving and compassionate, you want a secure emotional bond in your close relationships. Usually you are drawn to partners who are maternal, unselfish, or demonstrative with their feelings. Although you can sometimes appear to others as shy or impressionable, you have powerful emotions and inner strength.

WOMEN WITH VENUS IN LEO: Your friendly and sunny personality often makes you stand out in a crowd. Generous and giving, you know how to make your partner feel special. As you often expect loyalty and devotion from your partner in return, you can become easily offended if they ignore you or behave in an inconsiderate manner. Charming and kind, when you are in love you can be romantic, dramatic, and passionate.

MEN WITH VENUS IN LEO: As an extrovert you enjoy being involved in all types of activities where you can assert yourself and show your talents and abilities. Your childlike nature suggests that you are versatile and keen on games or being entertained. You are usually attracted to vivacious partners with a benevolent nature. Others may recognize your inborn tendencies to lead but are also aware of your vanity or pride. Nevertheless, generous, kind, and caring, you often show compassion to those less fortunate than yourself.

To read all about your Outer Planets and work out how to use your personalized timetable, go to Section Three, page 789.

To read all about your Outer Planets and work out how to use your personalized timetable, go to Section Three, page 789.

Your Personalized Timetable

JUPITER BENEFICIAL
1938 2/5 – 4/21
1938 8/24 – 12/11
1940 3/9 – 4/20
1943 9/2 – 10/29
1944 1/28 – 6/23
1945 10/15 – until **1946** 1/25
1946 2/28 – 9/9
1950 1/19 – 3/30
1951 7/22 – 8/17
1952 2/19 – 4/3
1955 8/17 – 10/5
1956 3/8 – 5/28
1957 9/29 – 12/19
1958 4/16 – 8/19
1962 1/2 – 3/12
1963 6/9 – 10/12
1964 1/26 – 3/17
1967 8/1 – 9/16
1969 9/14 – 11/29
1970 5/31 – 7/16
1973 5/2 – 6/28
1973 12/15 – until **1974** 2/23
1975 5/17 – 7/23
1975 9/5 – until **1976** 2/27
1979 7/16 – 8/31
1981 8/27 – 11/11
1985 3/31 – 8/13
1985 11/21 – until **1986** 2/7
1987 4/29 – 6/17
1987 10/24 – until **1988** 2/4
1991 6/28 – 8/15
1992 12/9 – until **1993** 3/22
1993 8/8 – 10/26
1997 3/10 – until **1998** 1/22
1999 4/12 – 5/26
2002 10/12 – until **2003** 1/27
2003 6/8 – 7/30
2004 11/17 – until **2005** 4/29
2005 7/12 – 10/11
2009 2/21 – 6/6
2009 6/24 – until **2010** 1/3
2011 3/27 – 5/7

SATURN BENEFICIAL
1938 5/18 – 10/17
1939 2/8 – 5/4
1947 8/17 – until **1948** 8/1
1951 11/14 – until **1952** 4/11
1952 8/8 – until **1953** 1/14
1953 2/26 – 9/26
1962 4/26 – 6/16
1963 1/9 – until **1964** 2/26
1968 3/24 – 6/23
1968 9/21 – until **1969** 3/11
1976 9/30 – until **1977** 1/27
1977 6/19 – 9/10
1978 4/9 – 5/11
1981 9/20 – until **1982** 11/2
1992 2/12 – until **1993** 4/4
1993 8/20 – 12/30
1997 4/29 – 11/26
1998 1/4 – 4/17
2006 7/30 – 10/31
2007 1/11 – 7/15
2010 10/26 – until **2011** 5/21
2011 7/6 – 12/13
2012 4/6 – 9/7

URANUS BENEFICIAL
1958 9/5 – until **1961** 7/12
1970 10/30 – until **1974** 10/1
1998 3/9 – until **2003** 1/14

NEPTUNE BENEFICIAL
1947 10/13 – until **1955** 9/21
2002 4/24 – until **2011** 1/6

PLUTO BENEFICIAL
1947 9/6 – until **1954** 7/23
1975 11/21 – until **1983** 8/1

JUPITER CHALLENGING
1939 2/17 – 4/26

1944 9/14 – 12/23
1945 1/31 – 8/9
1947 12/12 – until **1948** 3/9
1948 5/22 – 10/30
1951 1/30 – 4/8
1956 8/30 – 11/19
1957 3/17 – 7/19
1959 11/26 – until **1960** 2/10
1960 7/4 – 10/5
1962 5/29 – 8/5
1963 1/11 – 3/22
1968 8/14 – 10/29
1969 4/30 – 6/15
1971 11/10 – until **1972** 1/22
1974 4/28 – 9/21
1974 12/15 – until **1975** 3/5
1980 7/28 – 10/12
1983 3/23 – 3/31
1983 10/24 – until **1984** 1/5
1986 4/8 – until **1987** 2/17
1991 11/10 – until **1992** 2/19
1992 7/8 – 9/26
1995 2/4 – 5/29
1995 10/3 – 12/20
1998 3/22 – 6/21
1998 8/14 – until **1999** 1/29
2003 10/19 – until **2004** 3/29
2004 6/10 – 9/10
2007 1/14 – 7/13
2007 8/31 – 12/5
2010 3/5 – 5/17
2010 10/3 – until **2011** 1/3

SATURN CHALLENGING
1949 9/12 – until **1950** 10/20
1951 4/18 – 7/8
1957 1/16 – 6/3
1957 10/16 – until **1958** 12/10
1965 3/25 – 10/23
1965 12/5 – until **1966** 5/12
1966 9/11 – until **1967** 2/4
1978 10/26 – until **1979** 2/25
1979 7/18 – 12/25
1980 1/18 – 8/26
1986 11/23 – until **1988** 1/13
1988 7/26 – 10/3
1994 5/10 – 8/6
1995 1/30 – until **1996** 3/13
2008 8/26 – until **2009** 10/3

URANUS CHALLENGING
1964 9/9 – until **1968** 8/7
1983 12/27 – until **1987** 12/19
2006 3/4 – until **2010** 12/28

NEPTUNE CHALLENGING
1938 1/1 – until **1941** 9/5
1975 1/15 – until **1983** 10/17

PLUTO CHALLENGING
1962 10/3 – until **1970** 9/11
1999 12/17 – until **2007** 10/24

JUPITER SPECIAL
1941 7/14 – until **1942** 5/27
1953 6/25 – until **1954** 5/9
1965 6/8 – 8/26
1965 12/13 – until **1966** 4/18
1977 5/23 – 8/3
1978 1/29 – 3/14
1989 5/7 – 7/16
2000 9/15 – 10/13
2001 4/18 – 6/29
2012 8/4 – 12/6

SATURN SPECIAL
1942 8/13 – 11/8
1943 4/27 – until **1944** 5/27
1972 6/7 – until **1973** 7/6
2001 7/18 – 12/10
2002 4/6 – 8/22
2002 12/1 – until **2003** 5/9

URANUS SPECIAL
1944 7/4 – until **1949** 4/3

June 11

SUN: GEMINI • DECANATE: AQUARIUS/URANUS • DEGREE: 19°–21°5 GEMINI • MODE: MUTABLE • ELEMENT: AIR

Your Personal Powers

Mentally creative, you are usually inspired by a wealth of ideas, and with your innate common sense you can achieve a great deal. Although you are usually caring, friendly, and idealistic, your practical attitude indicates that you possess a rational and discerning mind. Besides a bright outlook, your ruling planet, Mercury, grants you versatility, quick judgment, and business acumen. Having powerful emotions and strong desires also implies that although you are idealistic you can be determined and ambitious. This is especially evident when you find ways to express yourself creatively. You can succeed admirably if you do not let your tendency to be impatient or frustrated with setbacks get in the way. You gain power when you allow your intuition and innovation to guide and motivate you to work hard. Although you are often a multitalented individual, you empower yourself when you stay focused on a few goals. You gain power when you trust your abilities and act with certainty and confidence.

Your Powers of Attraction in Relationships

As a benevolent and warm individual, your success in dealing with people often comes naturally. With your charismatic and friendly approach, you can also make friends easily. You are usually drawn to sincere people who are plain-speaking or creative and enthusiastic individuals. Success-oriented people also attract you. Since you possess abilities to comfort people or make them feel emotionally secure, you attract people to your supportive ways. Be careful, however, that others do not become dependent upon your kindness. It is therefore necessary to establish your personal relationships on an equal give-and-take basis. Having high expectations from relationships, you are attracted to partners who can offer you material security and provide you with much love and attention. A tendency to be impatient, however, suggests that you may need to take your time when choosing a partner.

Your attractive qualities: inspired, objective, creative, focused, enthusiastic, idealistic, inner faith, intuitive, intelligent, inventive, original self-expression, methodical, articulate, realistic, versatile, humanitarian, astute, gregarious, discerning, quick wit, communicative, charismatic

Your less attractive qualities: indulgent, too proud, inner tensions, selfish, lack of clarity, bossy, irritable, discontented, frustrated, overly optimistic, easily discouraged, inertia, blocked creativity, too proud, emotional ups and downs

Your Venus Power

The planet Venus has a great deal of influence on your powers of attraction. Below are four possible Venus types for women and men. To find your Venus you need to go to page 771, where you will find the Venus table and extra information. The planet Mars also affects your powers of attraction. To find your Mars table and interpretation go to page 761.

WOMEN WITH VENUS IN TAURUS: For your ideal relationship you need to seek a partner who is both financially secure and demonstrative with his affections. With these thoughts in mind, you are also likely to want a partner who is refined yet pragmatic or someone concerned with safeguarding your future. Although you have a stubborn streak, you can be loving and affectionate in your relationships, and with your good sense of style you may have an attraction for the arts, music, or luxury items.

MEN WITH VENUS IN TAURUS: As you yourself may be attractive to the opposite sex, you desire a partner who is sensual and loving or who has physical beauty. Needing stability, when faced with changes that are out of your control you may become insecure or possessive. Your own sense of style and love of beauty imply that you can be attracted to creative people, especially those in art and music. Reliable and reassuring, you can be affectionate, tactile, and constant in your love.

WOMEN WITH VENUS IN GEMINI: Charming and usually easygoing, you like to talk to people who are intelligent and witty. With a good social sense and a desire for mental expansion, you need a partner who is informed and has good ideas. Although you enjoy having different experiences, you need to resist your tendencies to become bored too quickly or be too talkative. As you enjoy sharing and learning new things, you usually prefer being with someone rather than operating alone.

MEN WITH VENUS IN GEMINI: Informed and curious yet charming and friendly, you seek a partner who shares your interests or enjoys your witty remarks. Although a good communicator, you have an inborn tendency to be lighthearted and less profound about deep emotional commitment. Although you are keen on experiences that bring variety into your life, boredom or scattering your energies in too many di-

rections is probably your biggest handicap in relationships. Nevertheless you are attracted to intelligent partners who can match your lively banter.

WOMEN WITH VENUS IN CANCER: Gentle and tender, you are romantic by nature. You possess a strong need for security and usually you help others feel safe and protected. This preservation is especially centered around the home, which is your haven from life's storm. Although your maternal instincts are strong, avoid making too many sacrifices for others at your own expense. Nevertheless, affectionate and caring, once committed to a relationship your loyalty and devotion to your partner are very strong.

MEN WITH VENUS IN CANCER: Affectionate with a strong sensitive streak, you can love very deeply. You may find yourself drawn to sympathetic partners who can tune in to your moods and feelings as well as be reassuring and supportive. Family links are especially important to you, and the more positive these relationships are the more confident and safe you feel.

WOMEN WITH VENUS IN LEO: You possess the wonderful ability to project your warm and sunny personality and keep others happily entertained. Loving attention yourself, you seek a partner who can appreciate you, be supportive, and give you positive feedback. Proud, with a natural regal air, you expect respect from your partners but are willing to be loyal and supportive in exchange. Although sometimes a little self-centered, you know how to make your partner feel special.

MEN WITH VENUS IN LEO: Enthusiastic, playful, and kind, you can be benevolent with those you love. Warm, romantic, and self-expressive, you adore the drama of love or having fun with your friends. Usually you are attracted to partners with a warm and generous nature. Although you can be a confident and charismatic partner yourself, you may need to develop humility in order to stop pride or arrogance from marring your relationships.

To read all about your Outer Planets and work out how to use your personalized timetable, go to Section Three, page 789.

♊

Your Personalized Timetable

JUPITER BENEFICIAL
1938 2/9 – 4/28
1938 8/16 – 12/17
1940 3/13 – 4/24
1943 9/7 – 11/6
1944 1/20 – 6/29
1945 10/19 – until 1946 9/14
1950 1/24 – 4/4
1950 10/12 – 11/5
1952 2/23 – 4/7
1955 8/21 – 10/10
1956 2/29 – 6/5
1957 10/4 – 12/26
1958 4/9 – 8/25
1962 1/7 – 3/16
1963 6/15 – 10/5
1964 2/1 – 3/21
1967 8/5 – 9/21
1969 9/18 – 12/4
1970 5/19 – 7/28
1973 5/17 – 6/13
1973 12/19 – until 1974 2/27
1975 5/22 – 12/3
1975 12/17 – until 1976 3/2
1979 7/20 – 9/4
1981 9/1 – 11/16
1985 4/6 – 8/6
1985 11/27 – until 1986 2/11
1987 5/4 – 6/23
1987 10/17 – until 1988 2/10
1991 7/3 – 8/19
1992 12/16 – until 1993 3/14
1993 8/13 – 10/31
1997 3/15 – until 1998 1/26
1999 4/16 – 5/31
2002 10/19 – until 2003 1/20
2003 6/13 – 8/3
2004 11/22 – until 2005 4/20
2005 7/20 – 10/16
2009 2/25 – until 2010 1/8
2011 3/30 – 5/11

SATURN BENEFICIAL
1938 5/28 – 10/5
1939 2/18 – 5/12
1939 12/6 – until 1940 1/18
1947 8/24 – until 1948 8/9
1951 11/24 – until 1952 3/29
1952 8/18 – until 1953 10/4
1963 1/17 – until 1964 3/5
1968 3/19 – 7/9
1968 9/5 – until 1969 3/19
1976 10/11 – until 1977 1/15
1977 6/28 – 9/18
1978 3/19 – 6/1
1981 9/28 – until 1982 11/10
1983 6/19 – 7/13
1992 2/20 – 10/12
1992 10/20 – until 1993 4/14
1993 8/8 – until 1994 1/9
1997 5/7 – 11/7
1998 1/23 – 4/25
2006 8/7 – 11/20
2006 12/21 – until 2007 7/23
2010 11/4 – until 2011 5/2
2011 7/24 – 12/25
2012 3/24 – 9/16

URANUS BENEFICIAL
1958 9/24 – until 1961 7/29
1970 11/16 – until 1974 10/17
1998 3/31 – until 2003 1/31

NEPTUNE BENEFICIAL
1947 11/10 – until 1956 8/5
2003 3/4 – until 2011 2/3

PLUTO BENEFICIAL
1947 10/25 – until 1955 6/24
1976 10/11 – until 1983 9/10

JUPITER CHALLENGING
1939 2/21 – 4/30

1944 9/19 – until 1945 8/14
1947 12/16 – until 1948 3/19
1948 5/12 – 11/4
1951 2/4 – 4/12
1956 9/3 – 11/25
1957 3/10 – 7/25
1959 12/1 – until 1960 2/16
1960 6/27 – 10/12
1962 6/9 – 7/25
1963 1/15 – 3/26
1968 8/18 – 11/3
1969 4/19 – 6/26
1971 11/15 – until 1972 1/26
1974 5/4 – 9/13
1974 12/22 – until 1975 3/9
1980 8/2 – 10/16
1983 10/29 – until 1984 1/9
1986 4/13 – until 1987 2/21
1991 11/18 – until 1992 2/11
1992 7/14 – 9/30
1995 2/11 – 5/21
1995 10/9 – 12/24
1998 3/26 – 7/6
1998 7/29 – until 1999 2/2
2003 10/24 – until 2004 3/21
2004 6/19 – 9/15
2007 1/19 – 7/2
2007 9/11 – 12/9
2010 3/9 – 5/23
2010 9/25 – until 2011 1/9

SATURN CHALLENGING
1949 9/20 – until 1950 10/29
1951 4/4 – 7/21
1957 1/27 – 5/21
1957 10/26 – until 1958 12/18
1965 4/3 – 10/4
1965 12/23 – until 1966 5/24
1966 8/29 – until 1967 2/13
1978 11/6 – until 1979 2/13
1979 7/27 – until 1980 9/3
1986 12/1 – until 1988 1/22
1988 7/10 – 10/18
1994 5/28 – 7/19
1995 2/7 – until 1996 3/20
2008 9/3 – until 2009 10/10
2010 5/30 – 6/2

URANUS CHALLENGING
1964 9/25 – until 1968 8/24
1984 1/14 – until 1988 10/18
2006 3/21 – until 2011 1/28

NEPTUNE CHALLENGING
1938 1/1 – until 1942 8/1
1975 12/13 – until 1983 11/21

PLUTO CHALLENGING
1962 11/10 – until 1971 8/4
2000 1/13 – until 2007 11/26

JUPITER SPECIAL
1941 7/18 – until 1942 1/20
1942 2/21 – 5/31
1953 6/29 – until 1954 5/13
1965 6/13 – 9/2
1965 12/6 – until 1966 4/23
1977 5/27 – 8/8
1978 1/18 – 3/25
1989 5/11 – 7/20
2001 4/23 – 7/3
2012 8/10 – 11/29

SATURN SPECIAL
1942 8/28 – 10/22
1943 5/5 – until 1944 6/3
1972 6/14 – until 1973 7/14
1974 2/20 – 3/7
2001 7/28 – 11/29
2002 4/15 – 9/4
2002 11/18 – until 2003 5/17

URANUS SPECIAL
1944 7/24 – until 1949 4/30

June 12

SUN: GEMINI • DECANATE: AQUARIUS/URANUS • DEGREE: 20°–21°5 GEMINI • MODE: MUTABLE • ELEMENT: AIR

Your Personal Powers

Astute and inquisitive, you are an enterprising individual with foresight and youthful idealism. Your ruling planet, Mercury, grants you good communication skills, flexibility, and a talent for business. Although at times you may be unclear about your direction, your strong instincts and motivation often turn you into a determined and security-conscious individual. When you believe in an idea and overcome your tendency to be impulsive, you show the willingness to put into your project the necessary effort and time. You gain power by persevering and being purposeful. Once you become focused and make up your mind, you can become highly successful and achieve admirable results in a short span of time. If you have an extravagant streak or mismanage your financial affairs, you may need to learn how to be more practical or cautious. You lose power when you lack confidence in your abilities or when you fail to accept your responsibilities. In spite of this, when you utilize your quick instincts and ability to adapt, you often attract wonderful opportunities to prosper.

Your Powers of Attraction in Relationships

Usually other people admire your generosity, optimism, and charm. Witty and observant, your quick grasp of ideas implies that you can be engaging and entertaining. Although you may be independent by nature, you enjoy collaborating with others. Conscious of your image, you like to make a good impression on others, especially with your good conversational skills. Being intelligent and curious, you prefer to mix with like-minded people who can inspire you with their knowledge or stimulate your imagination. You therefore often seek a versatile and intelligent partner who has many interests or ideas. The key to successful relationships often lies in your being discriminating or taking a responsible attitude toward your partners. Making sure that your finances are in order usually alleviates the tension between you and your partner.

Your attractive qualities: quick comprehension, original thoughts, creative, strategist, persevering, gift with words, friendly, idealistic, entertaining, hardworking, determined, intelligent, focused, skilled, adaptable, versatile, independent, articulate, well-informed, communicative, witty

Your less attractive qualities: restless, too sensitive, lack of self-esteem, worry, frustration, anxious, easily bored, dislike routine, moody, indecisive, impatient, extravagant, materialistic, argumentative, worried

Your Venus Power

The planet Venus has a great deal of influence on your powers of attraction. Below are four possible Venus types for women and men. To find your Venus you need to go to page 771, where you will find the Venus table and extra information. The planet Mars also affects your powers of attraction. To find your Mars table and interpretation go to page 761.

WOMEN WITH VENUS IN TAURUS: Demonstrative and affectionate, you are naturally tactile with a love of sensual pleasures. With a streak of the conventional you love the simple pleasures of life: good food, close friends, and happy relationships. Although you possess endurance be careful not to let this turn into plain stubbornness. Having inner strength, you can express genuine patience and are often a pillar of support for loved ones and friends.

MEN WITH VENUS IN TAURUS: Although usually you are drawn to sensual and physically beautiful individuals, you want a partner who is also reliable and loyal. When in love you enjoy buying your partner things of quality that will grow in value or useful things of a practical nature. You also love to socialize and entertain, especially in luxurious surroundings. Affectionate and caring, you are often attracted to creative people or those with artistic talents.

WOMEN WITH VENUS IN GEMINI: Curious, with a bright and animated approach to life, you are attracted to those who are clever and/or sophisticated. Your love of variety and desire for knowledge suggest that you need a partner and friends who can keep you mentally stimulated. Although witty and a good conversationalist, you may need to keep in touch with your deeper feelings. Nevertheless, intelligent and friendly, you possess a youthful sense of wonder and seek a playmate who can keep you from becoming bored.

MEN WITH VENUS IN GEMINI: Charming, amusing, and adaptable, you attract others with your natural communication skills and friendly personality. You have a wonderful childlike quality and love to keep life playful, but a reluctance to contact your deeper feelings may cause you to avoid serious commitment. With your need for variety and intellectual stimulation, you are attracted to clever and amusing partners who have many interesting sides to their personalities.

WOMEN WITH VENUS IN CANCER: Possessing a soft femininity, you have tender and sensitive emotions. Sympathetic and caring, you often mother those in your care by making sure that they are comfortable and have plenty to eat. When you feel hurt or insecure in relationships, you are likely to cover your feelings by being defensive or appearing tough on the outside while on the inside you are feeling vulnerable. Affectionate and romantic, you make a faithful and devoted partner.

MEN WITH VENUS IN CANCER: Being emotionally receptive you can make a sensitive lover. With your desire to care for and protect others, you are likely to have strong family connections. Love is often tied in with being attentive to the needs of others and you may find yourself attracted to individuals who have sympathetic or maternal qualities. Security-conscious, you need a loyal partner who can offer you support and ideally be a good cook and homemaker.

WOMEN WITH VENUS IN LEO: Warm and playful with a touch of the dramatic, you enjoy the company of generous or strong individuals who can share your sense of fun. Although there are advantages to your being strong-willed, in your relationships you need to resist being bossy as it can cause resentment. With your wonderful mixture of regal authority and childlike wonder, you love to keep others entertained and amused.

MEN WITH VENUS IN LEO: Sociable and outgoing, you are kind and generous with those you love. Looking for a relationship that can be fun and entertaining, you need a playmate who can share your enthusiasm and high spirits. Your pride, however, often stops you from associating with lovers or partners whom you see as beneath you. As you desire someone who can appreciate your sense of the dramatic, you are often attracted to people with strong personalities.

To read all about your Outer Planets and work out how to use your personalized timetable, go to Section Three, page 789.

Your Personalized Timetable

JUPITER BENEFICIAL
1938 2/13 – 5/4
1938 8/9 – 12/23
1940 3/17 – 4/28
1943 9/11 – 11/15
1944 1/11 – 7/4
1945 10/24 – until **1946** 9/19
1950 1/28 – 4/9
1950 9/27 – 11/20
1952 2/28 – 4/11
1955 8/25 – 10/16
1956 2/21 – 6/12
1957 10/8 – until **1958** 1/2
1958 4/1 – 8/31
1962 1/11 – 3/20
1963 6/21 – 9/28
1964 2/6 – 3/25
1967 8/10 – 9/26
1969 9/23 – 12/9
1970 5/10 – 8/6
1973 12/24 – until **1974** 3/3
1975 5/27 – 11/15
1976 1/4 – 3/7
1979 7/24 – 9/8
1981 9/6 – 11/21
1985 4/12 – 7/29
1985 12/3 – until **1986** 2/15
1987 5/8 – 6/30
1987 10/10 – until **1988** 2/15
1991 7/8 – 8/23
1992 12/24 – until **1993** 3/5
1993 8/19 – 11/4
1997 3/20 – 9/17
1997 10/28 – until **1998** 1/30
1999 4/20 – 6/5
1999 11/29 – until **2000** 1/11
2002 10/27 – until **2003** 1/11
2003 6/19 – 8/8
2004 11/28 – until **2005** 4/12
2005 7/28 – 10/20
2009 3/1 – until **2010** 1/12
2011 4/3 – 5/16

SATURN BENEFICIAL
1938 6/8 – 9/23
1939 2/27 – 5/21
1939 11/18 – until **1940** 2/5
1947 9/1 – until **1948** 4/11
1948 4/22 – 8/16
1951 12/5 – until **1952** 3/17
1952 8/28 – until **1953** 10/12
1963 1/25 – until **1964** 3/13
1964 10/9 – 11/24
1968 4/8 – until **1969** 3/27
1976 10/24 – until **1977** 1/1
1977 7/7 – 9/26
1978 3/5 – 6/15
1981 10/5 – until **1982** 11/18
1983 5/25 – 8/6
1992 2/29 – 9/11
1992 11/19 – until **1993** 4/27
1993 7/25 – until **1994** 1/18
1997 5/16 – 10/24
1998 2/5 – 5/3
2006 8/14 – until **2007** 7/31
2010 11/13 – until **2011** 4/18
2011 8/6 – until **2012** 1/10
2012 3/7 – 9/25

URANUS BENEFICIAL
1958 10/18 – until **1961** 8/13
1970 12/8 – until **1975** 8/7
1999 2/2 – until **2003** 2/17

NEPTUNE BENEFICIAL
1947 12/19 – until **1956** 9/15
2003 4/8 – until **2011** 12/28

PLUTO BENEFICIAL
1948 9/19 – until **1955** 7/29
1976 11/5 – until **1983** 10/6

JUPITER CHALLENGING
1939 2/25 – 5/5

1944 9/23 – until **1945** 8/19
1947 12/21 – until **1948** 4/5
1948 4/24 – 11/9
1951 2/8 – 4/16
1956 9/7 – 12/2
1957 3/2 – 7/31
1959 12/5 – until **1960** 2/22
1960 6/19 – 10/18
1963 1/20 – 3/30
1968 8/23 – 11/9
1969 4/9 – 7/5
1971 11/19 – until **1972** 1/31
1972 8/11 – 9/8
1974 5/10 – 9/6
1974 12/28 – until **1975** 3/13
1980 8/6 – 10/21
1983 11/2 – until **1984** 1/14
1986 4/17 – until **1987** 2/25
1991 11/26 – until **1992** 2/3
1992 7/19 – 10/4
1995 2/18 – 5/13
1995 10/15 – 12/29
1998 3/30 – until **1999** 2/7
2003 10/30 – until **2004** 3/13
2004 6/26 – 9/19
2007 1/25 – 6/23
2007 9/20 – 12/13
2010 3/13 – 5/29
2010 9/18 – until **2011** 1/15

SATURN CHALLENGING
1949 9/28 – until **1950** 4/29
1950 5/31 – 11/7
1951 3/23 – 8/1
1957 2/9 – 5/7
1957 11/4 – until **1958** 12/26
1965 4/12 – 9/20
1966 1/5 – 6/8
1966 8/13 – until **1967** 2/21
1978 11/19 – until **1979** 1/30
1979 8/4 – until **1980** 9/11
1986 12/9 – until **1988** 1/31
1988 6/26 – 10/30
1995 2/15 – until **1996** 3/28
2008 9/11 – until **2009** 10/19
2010 4/26 – 7/3

URANUS CHALLENGING
1964 10/12 – until **1968** 9/9
1984 2/5 – until **1988** 11/10
2006 4/8 – until **2011** 2/17

NEPTUNE CHALLENGING
1938 1/1 – until **1942** 8/31
1976 1/9 – until **1984** 10/2

PLUTO CHALLENGING
1963 10/1 – until **1971** 9/2
2000 2/25 – until **2008** 10/12

JUPITER SPECIAL
1941 7/23 – until **1942** 1/7
1942 3/6 – 6/5
1953 7/4 – until **1954** 5/18
1965 6/17 – 9/9
1965 11/28 – until **1966** 4/29
1977 5/31 – 8/13
1978 1/9 – 4/2
1989 5/15 – 7/25
2001 4/27 – 7/7
2012 8/17 – 11/21

SATURN SPECIAL
1943 5/13 – until **1944** 6/11
1972 6/22 – until **1973** 7/22
1974 1/25 – 4/2
2001 8/7 – 11/17
2002 4/24 – 9/23
2002 10/29 – until **2003** 5/25

URANUS SPECIAL
1944 8/21 – until **1949** 5/19

June 13

Your Personal Powers

Although you are imaginative and idealistic, your strong sense of values and astute mind indicate that you possess good common sense and a practical outlook on life. When you are inspired by an idea, you are willing to work diligently and be dedicated in order to achieve results. Your ruling planet, Mercury, grants you quick comprehension, original thoughts, and a talent for business. You gain power when you take pride in your work or when you find a goal to focus on. Since there is a strong emphasis on enterprise in your life, you are likely to see good financial results from your concerted efforts. You lose power when your restless nature challenges your need for stability and you cannot find contentment in the work you do. Nevertheless, as a sociable and fun-loving person, you cannot afford to bury yourself in work, and by finding the correct balance between fun and duty you can relax and succeed at the same time.

Your Powers of Attraction in Relationships

Other people are often impressed by your powers of perception and insight. They are also attracted to you when you think creatively and act with optimism. Being sociable and friendly, you enjoy mixing with people, especially those who are charismatic or creative. Usually you are drawn to partners with strong personalities or powerful emotions. Often romantic and generous with your friends or partners, you know how to make others feel loved. Since one of your less attractive qualities is a tendency to worry or think the worst, avoid putting others off with pessimistic thoughts. As you are usually attracted to forceful individuals resist becoming involved in disputes that can cause you stress. The key to successful relationships often lies in your ability to establish emotional stability and overcome a tendency to be dissatisfied or easily bored.

Your attractive qualities: inventive, pragmatic, articulate, versatile, responsible, friendly, witty, dutiful, cooperative, compassionate, hardworking, enthusiastic, inspired, resourceful, creative, methodical, ambitious, freedom-loving, self-expressive, initiative, adaptable, imaginative, communicative

Your less attractive qualities: obstinate, too serious, dissatisfied, bossy, unsettled, nervous, escapist, indulgent, selfish, unsympathetic, impulsive, indecisive, scattered, unemotional, rebellious, moody, restless, anxious

Your Venus Power

The planet Venus has a great deal of influence on your powers of attraction. Below are four possible Venus types for women and men. To find your Venus you need to go to page 771, where you will find the Venus table and extra information. The planet Mars also affects your powers of attraction. To find your Mars table and interpretation go to page 761.

WOMEN WITH VENUS IN TAURUS: Warm and affectionate, you are drawn to partners with whom you can share life's simple comforts. With a need for stability and security or an appreciation of earthly pleasures, you may have to avoid overindulgence or becoming too preoccupied with material concerns. Nevertheless, your sociability and friendliness usually make you popular. You need a partner who can also share your appreciation of beauty and style.

MEN WITH VENUS IN TAURUS: As well as attracting people with your warm personality, you also possess an innate sense of the value of material possessions. Keeping yourself stylish and having an attractive home can therefore be important to you. You are naturally attracted to practical yet sensual women who understand your need for comfort, security, and the pleasures and luxuries of life. Naturally affectionate, you enjoy socializing but can make a loyal and loving partner.

WOMEN WITH VENUS IN GEMINI: In relationships you need intellectual stimulation and usually prefer to keep things light. Certainly not boring, you love to talk and are at your best being witty and entertaining. Although your easygoing approach to relationships is very attractive, guard against losing touch with your deeper emotions. You prefer a partner who can keep up with your fast stream of ideas, and if you have shared interests then so much the better.

MEN WITH VENUS IN GEMINI: Charming, amusing, and adaptable, you attract others with your natural communication skills and friendly personality. You have a wonderful childlike quality and love to keep life playful, but a reluctance to contact your deeper feelings may cause you to avoid serious commitment. With your need for variety and intellectual stimulation, you are attracted to clever and amusing partners who have many interesting sides to their personalities.

WOMEN WITH VENUS IN CANCER: With your intuitive abilities and sympathetic nature, you are usually supportive of those you love. Impressionable and empathetic, your receptivity allows you to quickly pick up on the moods of others, making you especially aware of the emotional changes in your close partner. As you often display true maternal tendencies toward those you know, you want a partner who is considerate and sensitive.

MEN WITH VENUS IN CANCER: Being caring and sensitive, you probably seek a nurturing partner who could provide you with emotional security and a sense of belonging in a loving and safe environment. Receptive to others, at times you find it hard to be direct or confrontational in relationships. You may find yourself drawn to an affectionate and sympathetic partner like yourself. You are likely to have strong family links.

WOMEN WITH VENUS IN LEO: As someone who wants to radiate in your own right, you are likely to desire partners you can be proud of. Usually you are attracted to fun-loving, warm, and generous individuals. If self-expression is important to you, you will probably seek the company of creative people such as artists, musicians, or those with a flair for acting. Romantic and dignified, with a regal air, you can project confidence and success to attract others.

MEN WITH VENUS IN LEO: Generous, animated, and pleasure-seeking, you can be very entertaining and fun to be with. Usually you are attracted to extroverted and benevolent individuals with a sunny personality. If ambitious, you are drawn to a partner who shows leadership qualities or one who is highly motivated. Your less attractive qualities are your tendencies to be bossy or vain. With a sense of the dramatic, however, you can be the life and soul of the party and inspire those around you.

To read all about your Outer Planets and work out how to use your personalized timetable, go to Section Three, page 789.

♊

Your Personalized Timetable

JUPITER BENEFICIAL
1938 2/17 – 5/12
1938 8/1 – 12/28
1940 3/21 – 5/2
1943 9/16 – 11/30
1943 12/27 – until 1944 7/9
1945 10/29 – until 1946 9/24
1950 2/1 – 4/14
1950 9/17 – 11/29
1952 3/3 – 4/15
1955 8/30 – 10/22
1956 2/14 – 6/18
1957 10/13 – until 1958 1/11
1958 3/23 – 9/5
1962 1/15 – 3/24
1963 6/28 – 9/20
1964 2/12 – 3/29
1967 8/14 – 10/1
1968 3/28 – 5/16
1969 9/27 – 12/15
1970 5/2 – 8/13
1973 12/28 – until 1974 3/7
1975 6/1 – 11/5
1976 1/14 – 3/11
1979 7/29 – 9/13
1981 9/11 – 11/25
1985 4/19 – 7/21
1985 12/9 – until 1986 2/19
1987 5/12 – 7/7
1987 10/2 – until 1988 2/21
1991 7/12 – 8/28
1993 1/4 – 2/22
1993 8/24 – 11/9
1997 3/25 – 9/6
1997 11/9 – until 1998 2/3
1999 4/24 – 6/9
1999 11/18 – until 2000 1/21
2002 11/5 – until 2003 1/2
2003 6/24 – 8/12
2004 12/4 – until 2005 4/5
2005 8/4 – 10/25
2009 3/5 – until 2010 1/16
2011 4/7 – 5/20

SATURN BENEFICIAL
1938 6/21 – 9/8
1939 3/8 – 5/29
1939 11/4 – until 1940 2/17
1947 9/9 – until 1948 3/14
1948 5/20 – 8/24
1951 12/18 – until 1952 3/2
1952 9/5 – until 1953 10/20
1963 2/2 – until 1964 3/21
1964 9/20 – 12/12
1968 4/16 – until 1969 4/4
1976 11/16 – 12/9
1977 7/15 – 10/5
1978 2/20 – 6/26
1981 10/13 – until 1982 11/27
1983 5/10 – 8/21
1992 3/9 – 8/26
1992 12/3 – until 1993 5/14
1993 7/7 – until 1994 1/26
1997 5/26 – 10/12
1998 2/15 – 5/10
2006 8/22 – until 2007 8/7
2010 11/22 – until 2011 4/5
2011 8/17 – until 2012 10/3

URANUS BENEFICIAL
1959 8/11 – until 1962 6/1
1971 10/4 – until 1975 9/2
1999 2/19 – until 2003 12/23

NEPTUNE BENEFICIAL
1948 11/3 – until 1956 10/12
2004 2/26 – until 2012 1/27

PLUTO BENEFICIAL
1949 8/28 – until 1956 6/29
1976 12/8 – until 1984 8/17

JUPITER CHALLENGING
1939 3/1 – 5/10

1939 11/2 – 12/17
1944 9/28 – until 1945 8/24
1947 12/25 – until 1948 11/14
1951 2/12 – 4/20
1956 9/12 – 12/10
1957 2/22 – 8/5
1959 12/9 – until 1960 2/28
1960 6/12 – 10/24
1963 1/25 – 4/3
1968 8/27 – 11/14
1969 4/1 – 7/13
1971 11/23 – until 1972 2/5
1972 7/27 – 9/22
1974 5/16 – 8/30
1975 1/3 – 3/17
1980 8/11 – 10/26
1983 11/7 – until 1984 1/18
1986 4/22 – 10/18
1986 11/29 – until 1987 3/1
1991 12/7 – until 1992 1/23
1992 7/24 – 10/9
1995 2/27 – 5/4
1995 10/20 – until 1996 1/2
1998 4/3 – until 1999 2/11
2003 11/5 – until 2004 3/5
2004 7/3 – 9/24
2007 1/30 – 6/15
2007 9/27 – 12/17
2010 3/17 – 6/4
2010 9/11 – until 2011 1/21

SATURN CHALLENGING
1949 10/6 – until 1950 4/7
1950 6/21 – 11/17
1951 3/10 – 8/11
1957 2/26 – 4/19
1957 11/13 – until 1959 1/3
1965 4/22 – 9/7
1966 1/16 – until 1967 3/1
1978 12/10 – until 1979 1/7
1979 8/13 – until 1980 9/19
1986 12/17 – until 1988 2/11
1988 6/13 – 11/9
1995 2/23 – until 1996 4/5
2008 9/18 – until 2009 10/27
2010 4/11 – 7/18

URANUS CHALLENGING
1964 11/1 – until 1968 9/24
1984 12/5 – until 1988 11/28
2006 4/30 – until 2011 3/7

NEPTUNE CHALLENGING
1938 1/1 – until 1943 7/23
1976 2/16 – until 1984 11/13

PLUTO CHALLENGING
1963 11/4 – until 1972 7/19
2000 12/31 – until 2008 11/19

JUPITER SPECIAL
1941 7/28 – 12/29
1942 3/15 – 6/9
1953 7/8 – until 1954 5/23
1965 6/21 – 9/18
1965 11/19 – until 1966 5/4
1977 6/4 – 8/19
1978 1/1 – 4/10
1989 5/19 – 7/29
2001 5/2 – 7/11
2012 8/24 – 11/14

SATURN SPECIAL
1943 5/21 – until 1944 6/18
1972 6/30 – until 1973 2/2
1973 2/24 – 7/30
1974 1/11 – 4/15
2001 8/20 – 11/3
2002 5/3 – until 2003 6/2

URANUS SPECIAL
1945 6/13 – until 1949 6/5

June 14

SUN: GEMINI • DECANATE: AQUARIUS/URANUS • DEGREE: 22°–23°5 GEMINI • MODE: MUTABLE • ELEMENT: AIR

Your Personal Powers

As an intuitive individual with a talent for being innovative, you possess an astute mind. Articulate and quick-witted, your ruling planet, Mercury, grants you original thoughts and a talent for business. Although you usually present yourself in a lighthearted way, underneath you have a serious side that is shrewd and resourceful. You are capable of finding quick solutions to difficult problems. You gain power when you combine your talent for dealing with people with your free-flowing inspiration and unique ideas. When you feel apprehensive, however, you can lose some of your power and scatter your energies by letting indecisiveness or worries take control. Nevertheless, clever and articulate, once you are clear about what you are doing you can communicate your ideas with enthusiasm and sincerity. Although you can be mentally sharp with strong instincts, you are very sensitive to discord or disharmony. You increase your power when you establish balance and equilibrium and refrain from worrying about money.

Your Powers of Attraction in Relationships

Your joie de vivre and quick wit often make you very attractive to people. Caring, friendly, and generous, you are willing to help others if they turn to you for practical advice or assistance. Partners often admire your shrewd business sense and ability to articulate your thoughts. Prone to changing moods, however, you may waver between being friendly, spontaneous, and affectionate, and appearing detached or withdrawn. Being idealistic and sensitive, you may be looking for a partner who can fulfill your dreams. This high calling may be difficult for anyone to live up to. If, on the other hand, you accept your partner's shortcomings, your inner dissatisfaction may diminish. Your naturally friendly personality nevertheless ensures that you are easy to talk to and have many friends.

Your attractive qualities: wealth of ideas, creative spark, objective, inventive, decisive actions, hardworking, creative, pragmatic, imaginative, articulate, common sense, industrious, unusual interests, versatile, intuitive, intelligent, shrewd business sense, independent, instinctive

Your less attractive qualities: scattered, stubborn, skeptical, uncommunicative, moody, irritable, restless, indecisive, insecure, arrogant, anxious, too idealistic, impulsive, materialistic, critical, bossy, inconsistent, nervous

Your Venus Power

The planet Venus has a great deal of influence on your powers of attraction. Below are four possible Venus types for women and men. To find your Venus you need to go to page 771, where you will find the Venus table and extra information. The planet Mars also affects your powers of attraction. To find your Mars table and interpretation go to page 761.

WOMEN WITH VENUS IN TAURUS: Good-natured and romantic, you have a highly developed sense of touch that particularly responds to massage, hugs, and all things physical. With a streak of the conventional, you love the simple pleasures of life: good food, close friends, and happy relationships. With your natural sense of beauty and harmony you are likely to have an attractive voice, beautiful home, or a strong link to nature. You may have to be careful of becoming too extravagant, as often your taste is more expensive than what you are able to afford.

MEN WITH VENUS IN TAURUS: Attractive and affectionate, in relationships you are often down-to-earth, with a conservative approach. You are usually drawn to warmhearted partners with whom you can share a familiar routine as well as life's pleasures and comforts. Seeking a partner who is dependable or reassuring, you often put security high on your priority list when looking for love. Your sociability and friendliness usually make you popular and partners often admire your practicality and good sense of values.

WOMEN WITH VENUS IN GEMINI: Curious, with a bright and animated approach to life, you are attracted to those who are clever and/or sophisticated. Your love of variety and desire for knowledge suggest that you need a partner and friends who can keep you mentally stimulated. Although witty and a good conversationalist, you may need to keep in touch with your deeper feelings. Nevertheless, intelligent and friendly, you possess a youthful sense of wonder and seek a playmate who can keep you from becoming bored.

MEN WITH VENUS IN GEMINI: Friendly and sociable, you attract others with your clever and amusing conversation. Drawn to people who can match you in wit and intelligence, you usually prefer to keep relationships light rather than emotionally intense. With your youthful charm and desire for

knowledge and new experiences you usually have many friends and a low boredom threshold.

WOMEN WITH VENUS IN CANCER: Sensitive and understanding, you are sympathetic to other people's emotions and needs. You are protective toward those you love; close relationships with your partner, relatives, and friends are important to your sense of well-being. Aware of how easy it is to hurt other people's feelings, you are often indirect and approach delicate issues in a roundabout way. Nevertheless, learning to face facts and not allowing others to exploit your good nature is a valuable lesson.

MEN WITH VENUS IN CANCER: You seek a partner who is sympathetic, caring, and protective. Able to be forgiving and compassionate, you want a secure emotional bond in your close relationships. Usually you are drawn to partners who are maternal, unselfish, or demonstrative with their feelings. Although you can sometimes appear to others as impressionable, you have powerful emotions and inner strength.

WOMEN WITH VENUS IN LEO: Your friendly and sunny personality often makes you stand out in a crowd. Generous and giving, you know how to make your partner feel special. As you often expect loyalty and devotion from your partner in return, you can become easily offended if they ignore you or behave in an inconsiderate manner. Charming and kind, when you are in love, you can be romantic, dramatic, and passionate.

MEN WITH VENUS IN LEO: As an extrovert you enjoy being involved in all types of activities where you can assert yourself and show your talents and abilities. A childlike nature suggests that you are versatile and keen on games or being entertained. You are usually attracted to vivacious partners with a benevolent nature. Others may recognize your inborn tendencies to lead but are also aware of your vanity or pride. Nevertheless, generous, kind, and caring, you often show compassion to those less fortunate than yourself.

To read all about your Outer Planets and work out how to use your personalized timetable, go to Section Three, page 789.

To read all about your Outer Planets and work out how to use your personalized timetable, go to Section Three, page 789.

♊

Your Personalized Timetable

JUPITER BENEFICIAL
1938 2/21 – 5/21
1938 7/23 – until **1939** 1/2
1940 3/25 – 5/6
1943 9/21 – until **1944** 3/23
1944 5/3 – 7/14
1945 11/2 – until **1946** 9/28
1950 2/5 – 4/19
1950 9/9 – 12/7
1952 3/7 – 4/19
1955 9/3 – 10/28
1956 2/7 – 6/24
1957 10/17 – until **1958** 1/21
1958 3/12 – 9/11
1962 1/19 – 3/29
1963 7/7 – 9/11
1964 2/17 – 4/2
1967 8/18 – 10/6
1968 3/17 – 5/27
1969 10/2 – 12/21
1970 4/24 – 8/20
1974 1/2 – 3/11
1975 6/6 – 10/28
1976 1/22 – 3/16
1979 8/2 – 9/18
1981 9/16 – 11/30
1982 6/14 – 7/10
1985 4/27 – 7/13
1985 12/14 – until **1986** 2/23
1987 5/17 – 7/15
1987 9/24 – until **1988** 2/26
1991 7/17 – 9/1
1993 8/29 – 11/13
1997 3/30 – 8/27
1997 11/17 – until **1998** 2/7
1999 4/29 – 6/15
1999 11/9 – until **2000** 1/30
2002 11/19 – 12/19
2003 6/29 – 8/16
2004 12/10 – until **2005** 3/28
2005 8/10 – 10/29
2009 3/10 – until **2010** 1/21
2011 4/11 – 5/24

SATURN BENEFICIAL
1938 7/11 – 8/19
1939 3/16 – 6/8
1939 10/23 – until **1940** 2/28
1947 9/17 – until **1948** 2/28
1948 6/3 – 8/31
1952 1/7 – 2/11
1952 9/14 – until **1953** 10/28
1963 2/10 – until **1964** 3/30
1964 9/6 – 12/25
1968 4/23 – until **1969** 4/11
1977 7/23 – 10/15
1978 2/9 – 7/5
1981 10/21 – until **1982** 12/6
1983 4/27 – 9/1
1992 3/18 – 8/13
1992 12/15 – until **1994** 2/4
1997 6/5 – 9/30
1998 2/25 – 5/18
1998 11/27 – until **1999** 1/30
2006 8/30 – until **2007** 8/15
2010 12/2 – until **2011** 3/24
2011 8/27 – until **2012** 10/11

URANUS BENEFICIAL
1959 8/26 – until **1962** 6/28
1971 10/19 – until **1975** 9/21
1999 3/8 – until **2004** 1/15

NEPTUNE BENEFICIAL
1948 12/6 – until **1957** 9/8
2004 3/27 – until **2012** 12/16

PLUTO BENEFICIAL
1949 10/4 – until **1956** 8/3
1977 10/23 – until **1984** 9/19

JUPITER CHALLENGING
1939 3/5 – 5/15

1939 10/22 – 12/27
1944 10/3 – until **1945** 8/28
1947 12/30 – until **1948** 11/18
1951 2/16 – 4/24
1956 9/16 – 12/21
1957 2/11 – 8/10
1959 12/13 – until **1960** 3/7
1960 6/4 – 10/30
1963 1/29 – 4/7
1968 9/1 – 11/20
1969 3/25 – 7/20
1971 11/28 – until **1972** 2/10
1972 7/17 – 10/2
1974 5/23 – 8/22
1975 1/8 – 3/21
1980 8/16 – 10/31
1981 5/15 – 6/9
1983 11/12 – until **1984** 1/23
1986 4/27 – 10/6
1986 12/10 – until **1987** 3/5
1992 7/29 – 10/13
1995 3/11 – 4/22
1995 10/25 – until **1996** 1/6
1998 4/7 – until **1999** 2/16
2003 11/11 – until **2004** 2/27
2004 7/9 – 9/28
2007 2/5 – 6/7
2007 10/4 – 12/21
2010 3/21 – 6/11
2010 9/3 – until **2011** 1/26

SATURN CHALLENGING
1949 10/15 – until **1950** 3/24
1950 7/5 – 11/29
1951 2/25 – 8/20
1957 11/21 – until **1959** 1/11
1959 8/18 – 9/22
1965 5/2 – 8/25
1966 1/25 – until **1967** 3/9
1979 8/21 – until **1980** 9/27
1986 12/26 – until **1987** 8/4
1987 9/2 – until **1988** 2/23
1988 5/31 – 11/19
1995 3/3 – until **1996** 4/13
1996 11/23 – 12/13
2008 9/26 – until **2009** 11/5
2010 3/29 – 7/30

URANUS CHALLENGING
1964 12/3 – until **1969** 7/21
1984 12/20 – until **1988** 12/14
2006 6/12 – until **2011** 12/22

NEPTUNE CHALLENGING
1938 1/1 – until **1943** 8/26
1977 1/2 – until **1984** 12/11

PLUTO CHALLENGING
1964 9/27 – until **1972** 8/23
2001 1/31 – until **2009** 9/24

JUPITER SPECIAL
1941 8/3 – 12/21
1942 3/23 – 6/13
1953 7/13 – until **1954** 5/27
1965 6/25 – 9/30
1965 11/7 – until **1966** 5/9
1977 6/9 – 8/24
1977 12/25 – until **1978** 4/16
1989 5/23 – 8/3
2001 5/6 – 7/16
2012 9/2 – 11/5

SATURN SPECIAL
1943 5/28 – until **1944** 6/25
1972 7/8 – until **1973** 1/10
1973 3/19 – 8/8
1973 12/30 – until **1974** 4/26
2001 9/10 – 10/13
2002 5/11 – until **2003** 6/9

URANUS SPECIAL
1945 6/29 – until **1949** 6/22

June 15

Your Personal Powers

Knowing how to utilize your intuitive powers, you are fast at recognizing opportunities when they arise. Your ruling planet, Mercury, grants you good communication skills, quick comprehension, and a talent for selling others your ideas. Although you often want to be independent, your personal touch and a talent for public relations indicate that you are usually drawn to working with people. In fact, your willingness to share and collaborate is often a key factor in your achievement and success. You gain power when you pursue your ideals with pragmatism and dedication. Being persuasive, you can convince others to support you; alternatively, you can inspire people with your enterprising spirit. You can lose some of your power, however, when you allow your domineering tendencies to spoil the equilibrium of any association. Nevertheless, your mental creativity points to a shrewd individual who can be determined and dynamic. You gain power by overcoming your sense of limitation or by finding ways to freely express your creativity and feelings.

Your Powers of Attraction in Relationships

Enthusiastic and friendly, other people usually find you easy to talk to. Being aware of the advantages of working cooperatively, you attract others by using your diplomacy and persuasive charm. You are frequently attracted to partners who are enterprising, purposeful, and optimistic with creative ideas. Alternatively, you can be drawn to people who have a vision that inspires you or appeals to your idealistic nature. If you mix business and pleasure you often achieve good results. Since you are also likely to possess a stubborn streak, other people may find your tendency to argue less attractive. Nevertheless, you are often very generous with those you love and your sense of fair play indicates that you like to reward kindness with kindness.

Your attractive qualities: intelligent, intuitive, perceptive, sincere, direct, persuasive, balanced, generous, strategic abilities, enterprising, business sense, responsible, enduring, energetic, cooperative, appreciative, creative ideas, sociable, networker, practical, idealistic

Your less attractive qualities: extremist, stubborn, restless, frustrated, inertia, anxious, indecisive, materialistic, unfounded fear about lack of resources, impatient, too idealistic, unsettled, moody

Your Venus Power

The planet Venus has a great deal of influence on your powers of attraction. Below are four possible Venus types for women and men. To find your Venus you need to go to page 771, where you will find the Venus table and extra information. The planet Mars also affects your powers of attraction. To find your Mars table and interpretation go to page 761.

WOMEN WITH VENUS IN TAURUS: For your ideal relationship, you seek a partner who is both financially secure and demonstrative with his affections. With these thoughts in mind you are likely to also want a partner who is refined yet pragmatic or someone concerned with safeguarding your future. Although you have a stubborn streak you can be loving and affectionate in your relationships, and with your good sense of style may have an attraction for the arts, music, or luxury items.

MEN WITH VENUS IN TAURUS: As you yourself may be attractive to the opposite sex, you desire a partner who is sensual and loving or who has physical beauty. Needing stability, when faced with changes that are out of your control you may become insecure or possessive. Your own sense of style and love of beauty imply that you can be attracted to creative people, especially those in art and music. Reliable and reassuring, you can be affectionate, tactile, and constant in your love.

WOMEN WITH VENUS IN GEMINI: By nature you are young at heart, adaptable, and sociable. Being curious and willing to cooperate makes you a good team player. Usually you are drawn to articulate people who have charm and flair or sharp wit. With a need to expand your knowledge, you also look for a partner who can challenge or stimulate you intellectually. Although you love to talk with all types of people, you may need to develop your listening skills and tune in to your deeper feelings in order to build better communication in your relationships.

MEN WITH VENUS IN GEMINI: Adaptable yet often flirtatious, you enjoy mixing with people who are quick-minded and versatile. Since you can learn a great deal through interacting with others, you are often attracted to intelligent partners who have comprehensive knowledge or good ideas. One

of your less attractive qualities is your tendency to become bored or be inconsistent. Having an adaptable partner is important to you; therefore it must be someone who can offer you different options and keep you interested.

WOMEN WITH VENUS IN CANCER: Gentle and tender, you are romantic by nature. You possess a strong need for security and usually help others feel safe and protected. This preservation is especially centered around the home, which is your haven from life's storm. Although your maternal instincts are strong, avoid making too many sacrifices for others at your own expense. Nevertheless, affectionate and caring, once committed to a relationship, your loyalty and devotion to your partner are very strong.

MEN WITH VENUS IN CANCER: Affectionate with a strong sensitive streak, you can love very deeply. You may find yourself drawn to sympathetic partners who can tune in to your moods and feelings as well as be reassuring and supportive. Family links are especially important to you and the more positive these relationships are the more confident and safe you feel.

WOMEN WITH VENUS IN LEO: Warm and playful with a touch of the dramatic, you enjoy the company of generous or strong individuals who can share your sense of fun. Although there are advantages to your being strong-willed, in your relationships you need to resist being bossy as it can cause resentment. With your wonderful mixture of regal authority and childlike wonder, you love to keep others entertained and amused.

MEN WITH VENUS IN LEO: Sociable and outgoing, you are kind and generous with those you love. Looking for a relationship that can be fun and entertaining, you need a playmate who can share your enthusiasm and high spirits. Your pride, however, often stops you from associating with lovers or partners whom you see as beneath you. As you desire someone who can appreciate your sense of the dramatic, you are often attracted to people with strong personalities.

To read all about your Outer Planets and work out how to use your personalized timetable, go to Section Three, page 789.

To read all about your Outer Planets and work out how to use your personalized timetable, go to Section Three, page 789.

Your Personalized Timetable

JUPITER BENEFICIAL
1938 2/25 – 6/2
1938 7/10 – until 1939 1/7
1940 3/29 – 5/10
1943 9/26 – until 1944 3/11
1944 5/16 – 7/19
1945 11/7 – until 1946 10/3
1950 2/9 – 4/24
1950 9/1 – 12/14
1952 3/12 – 4/23
1955 9/8 – 11/5
1956 1/30 – 6/30
1957 10/22 – until 1958 9/16
1962 1/23 – 4/2
1963 7/18 – 8/31
1964 2/22 – 4/6
1967 8/23 – 10/11
1968 3/9 – 6/5
1969 10/6 – 12/27
1970 4/17 – 8/26
1974 1/6 – 3/15
1975 6/11 – 10/21
1976 1/28 – 3/20
1979 8/7 – 9/22
1981 9/20 – 12/5
1982 5/30 – 7/26
1985 5/7 – 7/3
1985 12/19 – until 1986 2/27
1987 5/21 – 7/25
1987 9/14 – until 1988 3/2
1991 7/21 – 9/6
1993 9/3 – 11/18
1997 4/4 – 8/20
1997 11/25 – until 1998 2/11
1999 5/3 – 6/20
1999 11/2 – until 2000 2/6
2003 7/4 – 8/21
2004 12/17 – until 2005 3/21
2005 8/16 – 11/2
2009 3/14 – until 2010 1/25
2011 4/15 – 5/29

SATURN BENEFICIAL
1939 3/24 – 6/18
1939 10/11 – until 1940 3/8
1947 9/26 – until 1948 2/16
1948 6/15 – 9/8
1952 9/22 – until 1953 11/5
1963 2/18 – until 1964 4/9
1964 8/24 – until 1965 1/5
1968 5/1 – until 1969 4/19
1977 7/30 – 10/26
1978 1/27 – 7/14
1981 10/29 – until 1982 6/4
1982 7/2 – 12/16
1983 4/14 – 9/12
1992 3/29 – 7/31
1992 12/25 – until 1994 2/12
1997 6/17 – 9/16
1998 3/6 – 5/27
1998 11/12 – until 1999 2/13
2006 9/6 – until 2007 3/27
2007 5/13 – 8/23
2010 12/14 – until 2011 3/10
2011 9/5 – until 2012 10/19

URANUS BENEFICIAL
1959 9/12 – until 1962 7/18
1971 11/4 – until 1975 10/8
1999 3/29 – until 2004 2/2

NEPTUNE BENEFICIAL
1949 10/28 – until 1957 10/7
2005 2/19 – Continues

PLUTO BENEFICIAL
1950 9/8 – until 1957 7/5
1977 11/19 – until 1984 10/15

JUPITER CHALLENGING
1939 3/9 – 5/20

1939 10/14 – until 1940 1/5
1944 10/7 – until 1945 9/2
1948 1/3 – 11/23
1951 2/20 – 4/29
1956 9/21 – until 1957 1/7
1957 1/25 – 8/16
1959 12/18 – until 1960 3/15
1960 5/26 – 11/4
1963 2/2 – 4/11
1968 9/5 – 11/26
1969 3/18 – 7/26
1971 12/2 – until 1972 2/16
1972 7/9 – 10/10
1974 5/31 – 8/14
1975 1/14 – 3/25
1980 8/20 – 11/5
1981 4/29 – 6/25
1983 11/16 – until 1984 1/27
1986 5/2 – 9/28
1986 12/18 – until 1987 3/9
1992 8/3 – 10/18
1995 10/30 – until 1996 1/10
1998 4/12 – until 1999 2/20
2003 11/18 – until 2004 2/19
2004 7/15 – 10/2
2007 2/11 – 5/31
2007 10/10 – 12/26
2010 3/25 – 6/20
2010 8/25 – until 2011 1/31

SATURN CHALLENGING
1949 10/24 – until 1950 3/12
1950 7/16 – 12/15
1951 2/9 – 8/28
1957 11/29 – until 1959 1/20
1959 7/27 – 10/13
1965 5/15 – 8/12
1966 2/3 – until 1967 3/17
1979 8/28 – until 1980 10/4
1987 1/3 – 7/12
1987 9/25 – until 1988 3/9
1988 5/14 – 11/28
1995 3/11 – until 1996 4/21
1996 10/29 – until 1997 1/6
2008 10/4 – until 2009 4/17
2009 6/15 – 11/15
2010 3/17 – 8/9

URANUS CHALLENGING
1965 9/15 – until 1969 8/12
1985 1/6 – until 1989 10/7
2007 3/22 – until 2012 1/28

NEPTUNE CHALLENGING
1938 1/1 – until 1944 7/9
1977 2/4 – until 1985 11/6

PLUTO CHALLENGING
1964 10/29 – until 1972 9/18
2001 12/21 – until 2009 11/14

JUPITER SPECIAL
1941 8/8 – 12/14
1942 3/30 – 6/17
1953 7/17 – until 1954 5/31
1965 6/29 – until 1966 5/14
1977 6/13 – 8/30
1977 12/18 – until 1978 4/22
1989 5/28 – 8/8
1990 2/2 – 3/19
2001 5/11 – 7/20
2012 9/13 – 10/25

SATURN SPECIAL
1943 6/5 – until 1944 7/3
1972 7/16 – 12/27
1973 4/2 – 8/18
1973 12/18 – until 1974 5/6
2002 5/18 – until 2003 6/17

URANUS SPECIAL
1945 7/18 – until 1950 4/19

II

181

June 16

SUN: GEMINI • DECANATE: AQUARIUS/URANUS • DEGREE: 24°–25° GEMINI • MODE: MUTABLE • ELEMENT: AIR

Your Personal Powers

With your enthusiasm, willpower, and determination, you have the tenacity to make your ideas a reality. Mentally quick and decisive, your insight and practical approach indicate that you can initiate new ideas or projects. Your ruling planet, Mercury, grants you foresight, communication skills, and a talent for business. You gain power when you focus on your goals and are clear and purposeful about what it is you want. You can lose some of your power when you vacillate between strong desires for material betterment and your idealistic beliefs. If you feel restless you can throw caution to the wind and fail to take your responsibilities seriously. Nevertheless, since no one can negotiate or make things happen as quickly as you, you are an excellent strategist with practical common sense. As an independent thinker, you can also evaluate people and circumstances quickly and empower yourself by finding new opportunities and advantages in any given situation. Although you are self-reliant and usually a strong individual, you gain power by resisting being bossy and by using your energy for the good of others.

Your Powers of Attraction in Relationships

Forceful and enterprising, other people admire your ability to initiate new ideas by thinking creatively and quickly. They are also attracted to your diplomatic but no-nonsense approach. You may, however, need to resist an inclination to feel restless or anxious. Being a pragmatist you are usually drawn to articulate, intelligent, and hardworking individuals who have good common sense. As a person with strong convictions, you may at times display an obstinate streak or be too demanding. Nevertheless, naturally congenial and generous, you have an easy way with people and an excellent ability to spot others' talents. The key to successful close relationships often lies in your ability to maintain your freedom and be an equal partner.

Your attractive qualities: broad-minded, imaginative, independent, generous, mentally sharp, energetic, receptive, decisive, enterprising, enthusiastic, idealistic, a talent for spotting opportunities, intuitive, sociable, helpful, cooperative, intelligent, articulate, integrity, kind

Your less attractive qualities: inner tensions, too impressionable, impulsive, overbearing, anxious, dissatisfied, restless, irresponsible, self-promoting, opinionated, skeptical, indecisive, irritable, pessimistic, unrealistic, uncommunicative, speculative, too demanding

Your Venus Power

The planet Venus has a great deal of influence on your powers of attraction. Below are four possible Venus types for women and men. To find your Venus you need to go to page 771, where you will find the Venus table and extra information. The planet Mars also affects your powers of attraction. To find your Mars table and interpretation go to page 761.

WOMEN WITH VENUS IN TAURUS: Demonstrative and affectionate, you are naturally tactile with a love of sensual pleasures. With a streak of the conventional, you love the simple pleasures of life: good food, close friends, and happy relationships. Although you possess endurance be careful not to let this turn into plain stubbornness. Having inner strength, you can express genuine patience and are often a pillar of support for loved ones and friends.

MEN WITH VENUS IN TAURUS: Although you are usually drawn to sensual and physically beautiful individuals, you want a partner who is also reliable and loyal. When in love you enjoy buying your partner things of quality that will grow in value or useful things of a practical nature. You also love to socialize and entertain, especially in luxurious surroundings. Affectionate and caring, you are often attracted to creative people or those with artistic talents.

WOMEN WITH VENUS IN GEMINI: Charming and usually easygoing, you like to talk to people who are intelligent and witty. With a good social sense and a desire for mental expansion, you need a partner who is informed and who has good ideas. Although you enjoy having different experiences, you need to resist your tendencies to become bored too quickly or be too talkative. As you enjoy sharing and learning new things, you usually prefer being with someone rather than operating alone.

MEN WITH VENUS IN GEMINI: Informed and curious yet charming and friendly, you seek a partner who shares your interests or enjoys your witty remarks. Although a good communicator, you have an inborn tendency to be lighthearted and less profound about deep emotional commitment. Although you are keen on experiences that bring variety into your life, boredom or scattering your energies in too many di-

rections is probably your biggest handicap in relationships. Nevertheless you are attracted to intelligent partners who can match your lively banter.

WOMEN WITH VENUS IN CANCER: Possessing a soft femininity, you have tender and sensitive emotions. Sympathetic and caring, you often mother those in your care by making sure that they are comfortable and have plenty to eat. When you feel hurt or insecure in relationships, you are likely to cover your feelings by being defensive or appearing tough on the outside while on the inside you are feeling vulnerable. Affectionate and romantic, you make a faithful and devoted partner.

MEN WITH VENUS IN CANCER: Being emotionally receptive, you can make a sensitive lover. With your desire to care for and protect others, you are likely to have strong family connections. Love is often tied in with being attentive to the needs of others and you may find yourself attracted to individuals who have sympathetic or maternal qualities. Security-conscious, you need a loyal partner who can offer you support and ideally be a good cook and homemaker.

WOMEN WITH VENUS IN LEO: As someone who wants to radiate in your own right, you are likely to desire partners you can be proud of. Usually you are attracted to fun-loving, warm, and generous individuals. If self-expression is important to you, you will probably seek the company of creative people such as artists, musicians, or those with a flair for acting. Romantic and dignified, with a regal air, you can project confidence and success to attract others.

MEN WITH VENUS IN LEO: Generous, animated, and pleasure-seeking, you can be very entertaining and fun to be with. You are usually attracted to extroverted and benevolent individuals with a sunny personality. If ambitious, you are drawn to a partner who shows leadership qualities or one who is highly motivated. Your less attractive qualities are your tendencies to be bossy or vain. With a sense of the dramatic, however, you can be the life and soul of the party and inspire those around you.

To read all about your Outer Planets and work out how to use your personalized timetable, go to Section Three, page 789.

Your Personalized Timetable

JUPITER BENEFICIAL
1938 3/1 – until **1939** 1/11
1940 4/2 – 5/14
1943 10/1 – until **1944** 3/2
1944 5/25 – 7/24
1945 11/12 – until **1946** 10/8
1950 2/13 – 4/30
1950 8/25 – 12/20
1952 3/16 – 4/27
1955 9/12 – 11/13
1956 1/21 – 7/5
1957 10/26 – until **1958** 9/21
1962 1/27 – 4/7
1964 2/26 – 4/10
1967 8/27 – 10/17
1968 3/1 – 6/12
1969 10/10 – until **1970** 1/3
1970 4/9 – 9/1
1974 1/10 – 3/19
1975 6/17 – 10/13
1976 2/4 – 3/24
1979 8/11 – 9/27
1981 9/25 – 12/11
1982 5/19 – 8/5
1985 5/21 – 6/19
1985 12/24 – until **1986** 3/3
1987 5/26 – 8/11
1987 8/27 – until **1988** 3/6
1991 7/26 – 9/10
1993 9/8 – 11/22
1997 4/10 – 8/12
1997 12/1 – until **1998** 2/15
1999 5/7 – 6/26
1999 10/26 – until **2000** 2/12
2003 7/9 – 8/25
2004 12/25 – until **2005** 3/12
2005 8/21 – 11/7
2009 3/19 – until **2010** 1/29
2011 4/19 – 6/2

SATURN BENEFICIAL
1939 3/31 – 6/30
1939 9/28 – until **1940** 3/17
1947 10/6 – until **1948** 2/4
1948 6/25 – 9/16
1949 4/12 – 5/19
1952 9/30 – until **1953** 11/13
1963 2/27 – 10/7
1963 11/4 – until **1964** 4/20
1964 8/12 – until **1965** 1/14
1968 5/9 – 11/19
1969 1/22 – 4/26
1977 8/7 – 11/9
1978 1/12 – 7/23
1981 11/6 – until **1982** 5/11
1982 7/25 – 12/28
1983 4/1 – 9/21
1992 4/9 – 7/17
1993 1/3 – until **1994** 2/19
1997 7/3 – 8/31
1998 3/14 – 6/5
1998 10/30 – until **1999** 2/25
2006 9/15 – until **2007** 3/9
2007 5/31 – 8/30
2010 12/31 – until **2011** 2/21
2011 9/14 – until **2012** 10/27

URANUS BENEFICIAL
1959 9/30 – until **1962** 8/3
1971 11/22 – until **1975** 10/23
1999 5/1 – until **2004** 2/19

NEPTUNE BENEFICIAL
1949 11/28 – until **1958** 8/31
2005 3/19 – Continues

PLUTO BENEFICIAL
1950 10/20 – until **1957** 8/7
1978 1/2 – until **1985** 8/31

JUPITER CHALLENGING
1939 3/13 – 5/25
1939 10/6 – until **1940** 1/12
1944 10/12 – until **1945** 9/6
1948 1/8 – 11/27
1951 2/24 – 5/3
1956 9/25 – until **1957** 8/21
1959 12/22 – until **1960** 3/25
1960 5/15 – 11/9
1963 2/7 – 4/15
1968 9/10 – 12/3
1969 3/10 – 8/1
1971 12/6 – until **1972** 2/21
1972 7/1 – 10/17
1974 6/9 – 8/4
1975 1/18 – 3/29
1980 8/25 – 11/10
1981 4/19 – 7/5
1983 11/20 – until **1984** 2/1
1986 5/8 – 9/20
1986 12/26 – until **1987** 3/13
1992 8/8 – 10/23
1995 11/3 – until **1996** 1/15
1998 4/16 – until **1999** 2/24
2003 11/26 – until **2004** 2/11
2004 7/21 – 10/7
2007 2/18 – 5/23
2007 10/15 – 12/30
2010 3/29 – 7/1
2010 8/14 – until **2011** 2/5

SATURN CHALLENGING
1949 11/2 – until **1950** 2/28
1950 7/26 – until **1951** 9/6
1957 12/7 – until **1959** 1/29
1959 7/12 – 10/27
1965 6/1 – 7/25
1966 2/12 – until **1967** 3/25
1979 9/5 – until **1980** 10/12
1987 1/12 – 6/26
1987 10/10 – until **1988** 12/6
1995 3/19 – until **1996** 4/30
1996 10/14 – until **1997** 1/20
2008 10/12 – until **2009** 4/1
2009 7/1 – 11/26
2010 3/4 – 8/18

URANUS CHALLENGING
1965 9/30 – until **1969** 8/29
1985 1/25 – until **1989** 11/4
2007 4/9 – until **2012** 2/19

NEPTUNE CHALLENGING
1938 1/1 – until **1944** 8/19
1977 12/28 – until **1985** 12/6

PLUTO CHALLENGING
1965 9/23 – until **1973** 8/11
2002 1/18 – until **2009** 12/12

JUPITER SPECIAL
1941 8/14 – 12/7
1942 4/5 – 6/21
1953 7/22 – until **1954** 1/31
1954 2/20 – 6/5
1965 7/4 – until **1966** 5/18
1977 6/17 – 9/6
1977 12/11 – until **1978** 4/28
1989 6/1 – 8/13
1990 1/22 – 3/30
2001 5/15 – 7/25

SATURN SPECIAL
1943 6/12 – until **1944** 7/10
1972 7/25 – 12/14
1973 4/13 – 8/28
1973 12/6 – until **1974** 5/15
2002 5/26 – until **2003** 6/24

URANUS SPECIAL
1945 8/9 – until **1950** 5/12

♊

June 17

Your Personal Powers

By recognizing that ultimately it is your knowledge that gains you most power, you become more self-assured as you get older. As a quick and independent thinker, you develop the clear perception that can help you to assess people and situations without prejudice. Your ruling planet, Mercury, grants you communication skills, powers of concentration, and business acumen. Discerning, you gain power and are capable of accomplishing a great deal when you combine your inventive mind, intuition, and determination. As a serious or hardworking person, you show your talent for leadership when you share your wisdom with others and guide those who seek your help. You can lose some of your charm and influence, however, if you insist that others do things your way. Although you have high regard for your freedom and opinions, your sensitivity indicates that you need other people's reassurance and usually seek to establish harmony and stability in your environment.

Your Powers of Attraction in Relationships

Usually friendly and genuine, you attract other people with your direct and forceful personality. Being outspoken and persuasive, you are attracted to loyal and reliable people who show a caring and sensitive side to their nature. Alternatively, you may find creative and imaginative individuals very attractive. You show your pleasing qualities when you cooperate with others on an equal footing. Although people admire your powers of perception, they often like you more when you are flexible and adaptable. Your hidden sensitivity implies that in close relationships you must not lose sight of your sense of humor. By staying independent, detached, and composed rather than becoming critical or doubting, you can avoid power struggles and arguments. Loyal and generous, you are often very supportive of those you love.

Your attractive qualities: individual thinker, methodical, persuasive, self-reliant, considerate, generous, authoritative, good business sense, knowledgeable, determined, skilled, inquisitive, well-informed, idealistic, progressive, objective, direct, dignified, articulate, straightforward

Your less attractive qualities: detached, skeptical, critical, dissatisfied, self-doubting, moody, stubborn, careless, uncommunicative, too sensitive, inner fears, anxious, worried, suspicious, controlling, rebellious, argumentative

Your Venus Power

The planet Venus has a great deal of influence on your powers of attraction. Below are four possible Venus types for women and men. To find your Venus you need to go to page 771, where you will find the Venus table and extra information. The planet Mars also affects your powers of attraction. To find your Mars table and interpretation go to page 761.

WOMEN WITH VENUS IN TAURUS: Warm and affectionate, you are drawn to partners with whom you can share life's simple comforts. With a need for stability and security or an appreciation of earthly pleasures, you may have to avoid overindulgence or becoming too preoccupied with material concerns. Nevertheless, your sociability and friendliness usually make you popular. You need a partner who can also share your appreciation of beauty and style.

MEN WITH VENUS IN TAURUS: As well as attracting people with your warm personality, you possess an innate sense of the value of material possessions. Keeping yourself stylish and having an attractive home can therefore be important to you. You are naturally attracted to practical yet sensual women who understand your need for comfort, security, and the pleasures and luxuries of life. Naturally affectionate, you enjoy socializing but can be a loyal and loving partner.

WOMEN WITH VENUS IN GEMINI: In relationships you need intellectual stimulation and usually prefer to keep things light. Certainly not boring, you love to talk and are at your best being witty and entertaining. Although your easygoing approach to relationships is very attractive, guard against losing touch with your deeper emotions. You prefer a partner who can keep up with your fast stream of ideas, and if you have shared interests then so much the better.

MEN WITH VENUS IN GEMINI: Charming, amusing, and adaptable, you attract others with your natural communication skills and friendly personality. You have a wonderful childlike quality and love to keep life playful, but a reluctance to contact your deeper feelings may cause you to avoid serious commitment. With your need for variety and intellectual stimulation, you are attracted to clever and amusing partners who have many interesting sides to their personalities.

WOMEN WITH VENUS IN CANCER: With your intuitive abilities and sympathetic nature, you are usually supportive of those you love. Impressionable and empathetic, your receptivity allows you to quickly pick up on the moods of others, making you especially aware of the emotional changes in your close partner. As you often display true maternal tendencies toward those you know, you want a partner who is considerate and sensitive.

MEN WITH VENUS IN CANCER: Being caring and sensitive, you probably seek a nurturing partner who could provide you with emotional security and a sense of belonging in a loving and safe environment. Receptive to others, at times you find it hard to be direct or confrontational in relationships. You may find yourself drawn to affectionate and sympathetic partners like yourself. You are lucky to have a strong family link.

WOMEN WITH VENUS IN LEO: Your friendly and sunny personality often makes you stand out in a crowd. Generous and giving, you know how to make your partner feel special. As you often expect loyalty and devotion from your partner in return, you can become easily offended if they ignore you or behave in an inconsiderate manner. Charming and kind, when you are in love, you can be romantic, dramatic, and passionate.

MEN WITH VENUS IN LEO: As an extrovert you enjoy being involved in all types of activities where you can assert yourself and show your talents and abilities. A childlike nature suggests that you are versatile and keen on games or being entertained. You are usually attracted to vivacious partners with a benevolent nature. Others may recognize your inborn tendencies to lead but are also aware of your vanity or pride. Nevertheless, generous, kind, and caring, you often show compassion to those less fortunate than yourself.

To read all about your Outer Planets and work out how to use your personalized timetable, go to Section Three, page 789.

To read all about your Outer Planets and work out how to use your personalized timetable, go to Section Three, page 789.

Your Personalized Timetable

JUPITER BENEFICIAL
1938 3/5 – until **1939** 1/16
1940 4/6 – 5/18
1943 10/7 – until **1944** 2/23
1944 6/1 – 7/28
1945 11/16 – until **1946** 6/6
1946 6/23 – 10/12
1950 2/17 – 5/7
1950 8/17 – 12/25
1952 3/20 – 5/1
1955 9/17 – 11/24
1956 1/11 – 7/10
1957 10/31 – until **1958** 9/26
1962 1/31 – 4/12
1962 10/8 – 11/19
1964 3/2 – 4/14
1967 8/31 – 10/23
1968 2/22 – 6/19
1969 10/15 – until **1970** 1/11
1970 4/1 – 9/7
1974 1/15 – 3/24
1975 6/23 – 10/6
1976 2/9 – 3/28
1979 8/15 – 10/2
1980 4/12 – 5/10
1981 9/29 – 12/16
1982 5/11 – 8/13
1985 12/28 – until **1986** 3/7
1987 5/30 – 11/23
1988 1/6 – 3/11
1991 7/30 – 9/15
1993 9/13 – 11/27
1997 4/16 – 8/5
1997 12/7 – until **1998** 2/19
1999 5/11 – 7/2
1999 10/19 – until **2000** 2/18
2003 7/14 – 8/30
2005 1/4 – 3/2
2005 8/26 – 11/11
2009 3/24 – 9/27
2009 10/28 – until **2010** 2/2
2011 4/23 – 6/7
2011 12/15 – until **2012** 1/5

SATURN BENEFICIAL
1939 4/8 – 7/16
1939 9/11 – until **1940** 3/25
1947 10/16 – until **1948** 1/23
1948 7/4 – 9/24
1949 3/23 – 6/8
1952 10/8 – until **1953** 11/21
1954 6/2 – 8/9
1963 3/7 – 9/14
1963 11/27 – until **1964** 5/3
1964 7/29 – until **1965** 1/23
1968 5/18 – 11/4
1969 2/5 – 5/4
1977 8/14 – until **1978** 7/31
1981 11/15 – until **1982** 4/27
1982 8/8 – until **1983** 1/11
1983 3/16 – 9/30
1992 4/25 – 7/1
1993 1/12 – until **1994** 2/27
1998 3/22 – 6/15
1998 10/18 – until **1999** 3/6
2006 9/23 – until **2007** 2/24
2007 6/12 – 9/7
2011 9/22 – until **2012** 11/4

URANUS BENEFICIAL
1959 10/25 – until **1962** 8/19
1971 12/13 – until **1976** 8/15
2000 2/19 – until **2004** 12/22

NEPTUNE BENEFICIAL
1950 10/23 – until **1958** 10/2
2005 5/9 – Continues

PLUTO BENEFICIAL
1951 9/18 – until **1958** 7/9
1978 11/4 – until **1985** 9/29

JUPITER CHALLENGING
1939 3/17 – 5/31
1939 9/29 – until **1940** 1/18
1944 10/17 – until **1945** 5/10
1945 5/19 – 9/11
1948 1/12 – 12/2
1951 2/28 – 5/8
1956 9/30 – until **1957** 8/25
1959 12/26 – until **1960** 4/16
1960 4/24 – 11/14
1963 2/11 – 4/19
1968 9/14 – 12/11
1969 3/2 – 8/7
1971 12/10 – until **1972** 2/27
1972 6/23 – 10/23
1974 6/24 – 7/20
1975 1/23 – 4/2
1980 8/29 – 11/15
1981 4/10 – 7/14
1983 11/25 – until **1984** 2/6
1984 8/13 – 9/15
1986 5/13 – 9/13
1987 1/1 – 3/17
1992 8/13 – 10/27
1995 11/8 – until **1996** 1/19
1998 4/21 – until **1999** 2/28
2003 12/5 – until **2004** 2/2
2004 7/26 – 10/11
2007 2/26 – 5/14
2007 10/21 – until **2008** 1/3
2010 4/2 – until **2011** 2/9

SATURN CHALLENGING
1949 11/14 – until **1950** 2/15
1950 8/4 – until **1951** 9/13
1957 12/15 – until **1959** 2/8
1959 6/28 – 11/7
1966 2/20 – until **1967** 4/1
1979 9/13 – until **1980** 10/20
1981 5/9 – until **1981** 7/1
1987 1/22 – 6/13
1987 10/21 – until **1988** 12/14
1995 3/27 – until **1996** 5/9
1996 10/1 – until **1997** 1/31
2008 10/21 – until **2009** 3/19
2009 7/13 – 12/9
2010 2/18 – 8/27

URANUS CHALLENGING
1965 10/17 – until **1969** 9/14
1985 2/20 – until **1989** 11/24
2007 5/1 – until **2012** 3/8

NEPTUNE CHALLENGING
1938 1/1 – until **1944** 9/16
1978 1/27 – until **1986** 10/29

PLUTO CHALLENGING
1965 10/23 – until **1973** 9/8
2002 3/6 – until **2010** 11/8

JUPITER SPECIAL
1941 8/21 – 11/29
1942 4/11 – 6/26
1953 7/27 – until **1954** 1/15
1954 3/9 – 6/9
1965 7/8 – until **1966** 5/23
1977 6/21 – 9/13
1977 12/3 – until **1978** 5/3
1989 6/5 – 8/18
1990 1/13 – 4/8
2001 5/19 – 7/29

SATURN SPECIAL
1943 6/19 – until **1944** 7/18
1972 8/4 – 12/3
1973 4/22 – 9/11
1973 11/22 – until **1974** 5/23
2002 6/2 – until **2003** 7/1

URANUS SPECIAL
1946 6/9 – until **1950** 5/30

II

June 18

Your Personal Powers

Cerebral and insightful, you are an intuitive thinker and a purposeful individual. Your personality projects assertiveness and you are usually resourceful, direct, and sincere. Your ruling planet, Mercury, grants you quick understanding, good communication skills, and creative ideas. As you are not afraid to take on responsibilities and think on a grand scale, you often rise to executive positions. Although you are by nature proud and independent, you benefit from listening or taking advice from others. Do not therefore allow a stubborn streak to undermine your efforts or cause you to lose power. Your sensitive inner nature often needs emotional reassurance and avenues for self-expression. You gain power when you are decisive and sure of your feelings. You may need to ensure, however, that your desire for success or monetary gains does not impair your pursuit of happiness. You empower yourself when you are disciplined and combine your communication skill with your leadership abilities. Usually you can be persuasive and impress others with your skills and many talents.

Your Powers of Attraction in Relationships

Friendly and sociable, other people admire your astute perceptions. Although you usually have many opportunities for love and romance, you can be cautious about making a serious commitment. You may be particularly drawn to individuals who are ambitious, intelligent, and enterprising. Mentally quick, you need people who can appreciate your sharp wit and fast repartee. As you are usually sympathetic and understanding, others may come to you for support and practical advice. A responsible and hardworking individual, you may need to take time out in order to avoid tension in your relationships. A tendency to be impatient suggests that you do not suffer fools gladly and a lack of mental stimulation can also make you restless or bored. With your love of variety, you need a partner who has diverse interests and enjoys socializing.

Your attractive qualities: progressive, astute, determined, original, humanitarian, executive abilities, intuitive, think big, articulate, intelligent, assertive, efficient, sharp wit, enterprising, love of learning, persuasive, friendly, considerate, resolute, creative, versatile, patient, sociable

Your less attractive qualities: doubtful, critical, rash or impatient, mentally restless, stubborn, moody, lazy, lack of order, selfish, callous, anxious, materialistic, frustrated, temperamental, intense, argumentative, dissatisfied, irritable

Your Venus Power

The planet Venus has a great deal of influence on your powers of attraction. Below are four possible Venus types for women and men. To find your Venus you need to go to page 771, where you will find the Venus table and extra information. The planet Mars also affects your powers of attraction. To find your Mars table and interpretation go to page 761.

WOMEN WITH VENUS IN TAURUS: Good-natured and romantic, you have a highly developed sense of touch that particularly responds to massage, hugs, and all things physical. With a streak of the conventional, you love the simple pleasures of life: good food, close friends, and happy relationships. With your innate sense of beauty and harmony you are likely to have an attractive voice, beautiful home, or a strong link to nature. You may have to be careful of becoming too extravagant, as often your taste is more expensive than what you are able to afford.

MEN WITH VENUS IN TAURUS: Attractive and affectionate, in relationships you are often faithful with a conservative approach. You are usually drawn to warmhearted partners with whom you can share a familiar routine as well as life's pleasures and comforts. Seeking a partner who is dependable or reassuring, you often put security high on your priority list when looking for love. Your sociability and friendliness usually make you popular and partners often admire your practicality and good sense of values.

WOMEN WITH VENUS IN GEMINI: Curious, with a bright and animated approach to life, you are attracted to those who are clever and sophisticated. Your love of variety and desire for knowledge suggest that you need a partner and friends who can keep you mentally stimulated. Although witty and a good conversationalist, you may need to keep in touch with your deeper feelings. Nevertheless, intelligent and friendly, you possess a youthful sense of wonder and seek a playmate who can keep you from becoming bored.

MEN WITH VENUS IN GEMINI: Friendly and sociable, you attract others with your clever and amusing conversation. Drawn to people who can match you in wit and intelligence, you usually prefer to keep relationships light rather than emotionally intense. With your youthful charm and desire for

knowledge and new experiences you usually have many friends and a low boredom threshold.

WOMEN WITH VENUS IN CANCER: Sensitive and understanding, you are sympathetic to other people's emotions and needs. Protective toward those you love, close relationships with your partner, relatives, and friends are important to your sense of well-being. Aware of how easy it is to hurt other people's feelings, you are often indirect and approach delicate issues in a roundabout way. Nevertheless, learning to face facts and not allowing others to exploit your good nature is a valuable lesson.

MEN WITH VENUS IN CANCER: You seek a partner who is sympathetic, caring, and protective. Able to be forgiving and compassionate, you want a secure emotional bond in your close relationships. Usually you are drawn to partners who are maternal, unselfish, or demonstrative with their feelings. Although you can sometimes appear to others as impressionable, you have powerful emotions and inner strength.

WOMEN WITH VENUS IN LEO: You possess the wonderful ability to project your warm and sunny personality and keep others happily entertained. Loving attention yourself, you seek a partner who can appreciate you, be supportive, and give you positive feedback. Proud, with a natural regal air, you expect respect from your partners but are willing to be loyal and supportive in exchange. Although sometimes a little self-centered, you know how to make your partner feel special.

MEN WITH VENUS IN LEO: Enthusiastic, playful, and kind, you can be benevolent with those you love. Warm, romantic, and self-expressive, you adore the drama of love or having fun with your friends. Usually you are attracted to partners with a warm and generous nature. Although you can be a confident and charismatic partner yourself, you may need to develop humility in order to stop pride or arrogance from marring your relationships.

To read all about your Outer Planets and work out how to use your personalized timetable, go to Section Three, page 789.

go to Section Three, page 789.

Your Personalized Timetable

JUPITER BENEFICIAL
1938 3/10 – until **1939** 1/20
1940 4/10 – 5/23
1943 10/13 – until **1944** 2/16
1944 6/8 – 8/2
1945 11/21 – until **1946** 5/19
1946 7/11 – 10/16
1950 2/21 – 5/14
1950 8/10 – 12/31
1952 3/24 – 5/5
1955 9/22 – until **1956** 4/13
1956 4/21 – 7/15
1957 11/4 – until **1958** 9/30
1962 2/4 – 4/17
1962 9/27 – 11/30
1964 3/6 – 4/18
1967 9/5 – 10/29
1968 2/15 – 6/25
1969 10/19 – until **1970** 1/20
1970 3/22 – 9/12
1974 1/19 – 3/28
1975 6/30 – 9/29
1976 2/15 – 4/2
1979 8/20 – 10/7
1980 3/28 – 5/25
1981 10/3 – 12/22
1982 5/3 – 8/21
1986 1/2 – 3/11
1987 6/4 – 11/13
1988 1/16 – 3/15
1991 8/4 – 9/19
1993 9/17 – 12/2
1997 4/23 – 7/28
1997 12/12 – until **1998** 2/23
1999 5/15 – 7/8
1999 10/11 – until **2000** 2/23
2003 7/18 – 9/3
2005 1/18 – 2/16
2005 9/1 – 11/16
2009 3/29 – 9/14
2009 11/11 – until **2010** 2/6
2011 4/27 – 6/12
2011 11/29 – until **2012** 1/20

SATURN BENEFICIAL
1939 4/15 – until **1940** 4/2
1947 10/30 – until **1948** 1/9
1948 7/12 – 10/2
1949 3/9 – 6/21
1952 10/16 – until **1953** 11/30
1954 5/17 – 8/24
1963 3/16 – 8/30
1963 12/11 – until **1964** 5/21
1964 7/10 – until **1965** 1/31
1968 5/27 – 10/22
1969 2/16 – 5/12
1977 8/22 – until **1978** 8/8
1981 11/24 – until **1982** 4/14
1982 8/19 – until **1983** 10/8
1993 1/20 – until **1994** 3/7
1998 3/30 – 6/26
1998 10/6 – until **1999** 3/15
2006 10/2 – until **2007** 2/12
2007 6/23 – 9/14
2011 9/30 – until **2012** 11/12

URANUS BENEFICIAL
1960 8/16 – until **1963** 6/7
1972 10/9 – until **1976** 9/9
2000 3/8 – until **2005** 1/15

NEPTUNE BENEFICIAL
1950 11/20 – until **1959** 8/21
2006 3/12 – Continues

PLUTO BENEFICIAL
1951 11/13 – until **1958** 8/10
1978 12/3 – until **1985** 10/24

JUPITER CHALLENGING
1939 3/21 – 6/6

1939 9/22 – until **1940** 1/24
1944 10/22 – until **1945** 4/19
1945 6/9 – 9/15
1948 1/17 – 12/6
1951 3/4 – 5/12
1951 11/17 – 12/12
1956 10/4 – until **1957** 8/30
1959 12/31 – until **1960** 11/19
1963 2/15 – 4/23
1968 9/18 – 12/20
1969 2/20 – 8/12
1971 12/15 – until **1972** 3/5
1972 6/16 – 10/29
1975 1/28 – 4/6
1980 9/3 – 11/21
1981 4/2 – 7/21
1983 11/29 – until **1984** 2/11
1984 7/30 – 9/28
1986 5/19 – 9/5
1987 1/7 – 3/21
1992 8/17 – 11/1
1995 11/13 – until **1996** 1/23
1998 4/25 – 10/30
1998 11/27 – until **1999** 3/4
2003 12/20 – until **2004** 1/19
2004 7/31 – 10/16
2007 3/8 – 5/4
2007 10/26 – until **2008** 1/7
2010 4/6 – until **2011** 2/14

SATURN CHALLENGING
1949 11/28 – until **1950** 1/31
1950 8/12 – until **1951** 9/21
1957 12/24 – until **1959** 2/18
1959 6/15 – 11/18
1966 2/27 – until **1967** 4/9
1979 9/20 – until **1980** 10/29
1981 4/22 – 7/18
1987 2/1 – 5/31
1987 10/31 – until **1988** 12/23
1995 4/4 – 10/28
1995 12/16 – until **1996** 5/19
1996 9/19 – until **1997** 2/10
2008 10/31 – until **2009** 3/7
2009 7/23 – until **2010** 1/2
2010 1/25 – 9/4

URANUS CHALLENGING
1965 11/5 – until **1969** 9/29
1985 12/15 – until **1989** 12/11
2007 6/3 – until **2012** 3/25

NEPTUNE CHALLENGING
1938 1/1 – until **1945** 8/12
1978 12/23 – until **1986** 11/30

PLUTO CHALLENGING
1966 9/19 – until **1974** 7/25
2003 1/8 – until **2010** 12/9

JUPITER SPECIAL
1941 8/28 – 11/22
1942 4/16 – 6/30
1953 8/1 – until **1954** 1/5
1954 3/18 – 6/13
1965 7/12 – until **1966** 5/27
1977 6/25 – 9/22
1977 11/24 – until **1978** 5/9
1989 6/9 – 8/23
1990 1/6 – 4/15
2001 5/23 – 8/3

SATURN SPECIAL
1943 6/27 – until **1944** 7/26
1945 2/6 – 4/2
1972 8/14 – 11/21
1973 5/1 – 10/1
1973 11/1 – until **1974** 5/31
2002 6/10 – until **2003** 7/9

URANUS SPECIAL
1946 6/25 – until **1950** 6/16

II

June 19

SUN: GEMINI • DECANATE: AQUARIUS/URANUS • DEGREE: 27°–28° GEMINI • MODE: MUTABLE • ELEMENT: AIR

Your Personal Powers

Often gifted with words, your strong instincts and creative ideas give you an edge in life. Quick to comprehend ideas, you are an enthusiastic individual with a progressive outlook and business acumen. Your ruling planet, Mercury, grants you youthful charm, quick perceptions, and powers of concentration. Being lighthearted and idealistic, you gain power when you feel inspired or share your knowledge with others. It is often your spirit of enterprise that motivates you to be ambitious and hardworking. Frustration or fluctuating financial circumstances, however, may occur if you act rashly or impulsively. Nevertheless, benefits that come from perseverance and determination allow you to achieve on a large scale. Although your strong desire to establish an individual identity implies that you often hold on to your strong opinions and beliefs, you gain your power when you learn that diplomacy is the art of listening and being objective with your communication.

Your Powers of Attraction in Relationships

You are charming and friendly, and other people admire your direct approach and optimistic outlook. Although you like to be spontaneous, your feelings may alter and you can, at times, confuse others by appearing moody or indifferent. Being idealistic, you often seek a special bond with your partner, but if your expectations are unrealistic you may experience some disappointment. By staying open-minded or frank about your feelings you can avoid misunderstanding with partners. In personal relationships you are frequently in tune with the feelings of your partner, and although you can be sympathetic and understanding, monetary worries or unresolved inner tensions may cause you emotional ups and downs. The key to happy relationships often lies in your ability to maintain the balance of power and build a partnership based on faith and trust.

Your attractive qualities: dynamic, youthful, enterprising, sociable, persuasive powers, kind, articulate, quick mind, generous heart, independent, centered, creative, progressive, optimistic, strong convictions, instinctive, intuitive, assertive, independent, gregarious, witty, clever, communication skills

Your less attractive qualities: headstrong, irresponsible, impatient, moody, stubborn, nervous, anxious, restless, easily bored, materialistic, inconsistent, too idealistic, selfish, indecisive, make hasty decision, speculative

Your Venus Power

The planet Venus has a great deal of influence on your powers of attraction. Below are four possible Venus types for women and men. To find your Venus you need to go to page 771, where you will find the Venus table and extra information. The planet Mars also affects your powers of attraction. To find your Mars table and interpretation go to page 761.

WOMEN WITH VENUS IN TAURUS: For your ideal relationship, you seek a partner who is both financially secure and demonstrative with his affections. With these thoughts in mind, you are likely to also want a partner who is refined yet pragmatic or someone concerned with safeguarding your future. Although you have a stubborn streak, you can be loving and affectionate in your relationships and with your good sense of style may have an attraction for the arts, music, or luxury items.

MEN WITH VENUS IN TAURUS: As you yourself may be attractive to the opposite sex, you desire a partner who is sensual and loving or who has physical beauty. Needing stability, when faced with changes that are out of your control you may become insecure or possessive. Your own sense of style and love of beauty imply that you can be attracted to creative people, especially those in art and music. Reliable and reassuring, you can be affectionate, tactile, and constant in your love.

WOMEN WITH VENUS IN GEMINI: By nature you are young at heart, adaptable, and sociable. Being curious and willing to cooperate makes you a good team player. Usually you are drawn to articulate people who have charm and flair or sharp wit. With a need to expand your knowledge, you also look for a partner who can challenge or stimulate you intellectually. Although you love to talk with all types of people, you may need to develop your listening skills and tune in to your feelings in order to build better communication in your relationships.

MEN WITH VENUS IN GEMINI: Adaptable yet often flirtatious, you enjoy mixing with people who are quick-minded and versatile. Since you can learn a great deal through interacting with others, you are often attracted to intelligent part-

ners who have comprehensive knowledge or good ideas. One of your less attractive qualities is your tendency to become bored or be inconsistent. Having an adaptable partner is important to you; therefore it must be someone who can offer you different options and keep you interested.

WOMEN WITH VENUS IN CANCER: Gentle and tender, you are romantic by nature. You possess a strong need for security and usually you help others feel safe and protected. This preservation is especially centered around the home, which is your haven from life's storm. Although your maternal instincts are strong, avoid making too many sacrifices for others at your own expense. Nevertheless, affectionate and caring, once committed to a relationship, your loyalty and devotion to your partner are very strong.

MEN WITH VENUS IN CANCER: Affectionate with a strong sensitive streak, you can love very deeply. You may find yourself drawn to sympathetic partners who can tune in to your moods and feelings as well as be reassuring and supportive. Family links are especially important to you and the more positive these relationships are the more confident and safe you feel.

WOMEN WITH VENUS IN LEO: You possess the wonderful ability to project your warm and sunny personality and keep others happily entertained. Loving attention yourself, you seek a partner who can appreciate you, be supportive, and give you positive feedback. Proud, with a natural regal air, you expect respect from your partners but are willing to be loyal and supportive in exchange. Although sometimes a little self-centered, you know how to make your partner feel special.

MEN WITH VENUS IN LEO: Enthusiastic, playful, and kind, you can be benevolent with those you love. Warm, romantic, and self-expressive, you adore the drama of love or having fun with your friends. Usually you are attracted to partners with a warm and generous nature. Although you can be a confident and charismatic partner yourself, you may need to develop humility in order to stop pride or arrogance from marring your relationships.

To read all about your Outer Planets and work out how to use your personalized timetable, go to Section Three, page 789.

Ⅱ

Your Personalized Timetable

JUPITER BENEFICIAL
1938   3/14 – until **1939** 1/25
1940   4/14 – 5/27
1943   10/19 – until **1944** 2/8
1944   6/15 – 8/7
1945   11/27 – until **1946** 5/8
1946   7/22 – 10/21
1950   2/25 – 5/22
1950   8/1 – until **1951** 1/5
1952   3/28 – 5/9
1955   9/27 – until **1956** 3/23
1956   5/13 – 7/20
1957   11/9 – until **1958** 10/5
1962   2/8 – 4/22
1962   9/18 – 12/8
1964   3/11 – 4/22
1967   9/9 – 11/5
1968   2/8 – 7/1
1969   10/24 – until **1970** 2/2
1970   3/9 – 9/17
1974   1/23 – 4/1
1975   7/8 – 9/21
1976   2/20 – 4/6
1979   8/24 – 10/12
1980   3/18 – 6/4
1981   10/8 – 12/28
1982   4/25 – 8/27
1986   1/6 – 3/15
1987   6/9 – 11/4
1988   1/25 – 3/20
1991   8/8 – 9/24
1993   9/22 – 12/7
1994   6/10 – 7/23
1997   4/30 – 7/20
1997   12/18 – until **1998** 2/27
1999   5/20 – 7/16
1999   10/3 – until **2000** 2/29
2003   7/23 – 9/7
2005   9/6 – 11/20
2009   4/3 – 9/4
2009   11/20 – until **2010** 2/10
2011   5/1 – 6/17
2011   11/20 – until **2012** 1/30

SATURN BENEFICIAL
1939   4/23 – until **1940** 4/9
1947   11/20 – 12/18
1948   7/20 – 10/11
1949   2/25 – 7/2
1952   10/23 – until **1953** 12/9
1954   5/4 – 9/5
1963   3/26 – 8/17
1963   12/22 – until **1965** 2/9
1968   6/6 – 10/10
1969   2/26 – 5/20
1969   12/13 – until **1970** 1/25
1977   8/29 – until **1978** 8/15
1981   12/4 – until **1982** 4/1
1982   8/30 – until **1983** 10/16
1993   1/28 – until **1994** 3/15
1998   4/6 – 7/10
1998   9/21 – until **1999** 3/24
2006   10/12 – until **2007** 1/31
2007   7/2 – 9/22
2008   4/2 – 6/2
2011   10/8 – until **2012** 11/20

URANUS BENEFICIAL
1960   8/31 – until **1963** 7/4
1972   10/24 – until **1976** 9/27
2000   4/3 – until **2005** 2/2

NEPTUNE BENEFICIAL
1951   1/7 – until **1959** 9/26
2006   4/17 – Continues

PLUTO BENEFICIAL
1952   9/27 – until **1959** 7/11
1979   10/21 – until **1986** 9/12

JUPITER CHALLENGING
1939   3/25 – 6/13

1939   9/14 – until **1940** 1/29
1944   10/27 – until **1945** 4/8
1945   6/20 – 9/20
1948   1/22 – 7/31
1948   8/31 – 12/10
1951   3/8 – 5/17
1951   11/3 – 12/27
1956   10/9 – until **1957** 9/4
1960   1/4 – 11/23
1963   2/19 – 4/27
1968   9/23 – until **1969** 1/1
1969   2/8 – 8/18
1971   12/19 – until **1972** 3/12
1972   6/8 – 11/3
1975   2/1 – 4/10
1980   9/7 – 11/27
1981   3/26 – 7/27
1983   12/3 – until **1984** 2/16
1984   7/21 – 10/8
1986   5/26 – 8/29
1987   1/12 – 3/25
1992   8/22 – 11/6
1993   5/10 – 6/23
1995   11/17 – until **1996** 1/28
1998   4/30 – 10/16
1998   12/11 – until **1999** 3/9
2004   8/5 – 10/20
2007   3/23 – 4/19
2007   10/31 – until **2008** 1/11
2010   4/10 – until **2011** 2/18

SATURN CHALLENGING
1950   8/21 – until **1951** 9/29
1958   1/1 – 8/2
1958   9/14 – until **1959** 3/3
1959   6/1 – 11/27
1966   3/7 – until **1967** 4/17
1979   9/28 – until **1980** 11/6
1981   4/8 – 7/31
1987   2/13 – 5/17
1987   11/10 – until **1988** 12/31
1995   4/12 – 10/10
1996   1/2 – 5/31
1996   9/6 – until **1997** 2/19
2008   11/10 – until **2009** 2/22
2009   8/2 – until **2010** 9/12

URANUS CHALLENGING
1965   12/7 – until **1970** 7/26
1985   12/31 – until **1989** 12/27
2008   3/23 – Continues

NEPTUNE CHALLENGING
1938   1/1 – until **1945** 9/10
1979   1/20 – until **1987** 10/17

PLUTO CHALLENGING
1966   10/17 – until **1974** 8/28
2003   2/10 – until **2011** 11/4

JUPITER SPECIAL
1941   9/5 – 11/14
1942   4/21 – 7/4
1953   8/6 – 12/28
1954   3/26 – 6/18
1965   7/17 – until **1966** 6/1
1977   6/29 – 10/4
1977   11/13 – until **1978** 5/14
1989   6/13 – 8/29
1989   12/30 – until **1990** 4/21
2001   5/28 – 8/7

SATURN SPECIAL
1943   7/4 – until **1944** 8/3
1945   1/21 – 4/17
1972   8/28 – 11/7
1973   5/9 – until **1974** 6/8
2002   6/17 – until **2003** 7/16

URANUS SPECIAL
1946   7/12 – until **1951** 3/27

189

June 20

Your Personal Powers

Determined and analytical, you are an observant person who has an interest in human relationships. Your ruling planet, Mercury, grants you a quick mind, an inquiring nature, and good communication skills. Usually ambitious and innovative, you are able think independently and turn your knowledge and original ideas into a profitable commodity. By combining your expertise with your ability to connect on a personal level, you also benefit from collaborating with others. Although successful partnerships can often advance your position, you lose some of your power when you fail to maintain balance, focusing too much on others at your own expense. Being shrewd and pragmatic, you gain power when you learn self-discipline and honestly face your own failings. An inability to discipline yourself, however, can result in a lack of inner faith, underachieving, or scattering your energies in too many directions. Innate intuitive abilities and good organizational skills also suggest that you are able to trust your own instincts in order to fulfill your goals or objectives.

Your Powers of Attraction in Relationships

Being charismatic and charming, you know how to enjoy yourself and keep people entertained. A flair for dealing effortlessly with others indicates that you are also very persuasive. Usually you are attracted to exceptional people or strong individuals who seem to know how to take control of situations. In your desire to emulate them resist a temptation to become too demanding or insensitive. Nevertheless, people are usually attracted to your inner strength, creativity, and genuine enthusiasm. In order to establish harmonious unions you may have to resist a tendency to waver between being warm and caring, and moody and critical. In your personal relationships you need to stay bright and optimistic and avoid becoming overly serious or bossy. A need for mental stimulation and a love of knowledge implies that you seek a partner who is both intelligent and versatile.

Your attractive qualities: determined, astute, inquiring, intuitive, adaptable, energetic, good strategist, think big, tactful, persuasive, generous, authoritative, agreeable, articulate, gentle, collaborative, good listener, receptive, optimistic, communication skills, understanding, assertive, patient, observant

Your less attractive qualities: suspicious, insecure, manipulative, hasty actions, stubborn, restless, impatient, demanding, argumentative, too sensitive, emotional, sensitive to criticism or easily hurt, tactless, self-absorbed, moody, lack of stamina

Your Venus Power

The planet Venus has a great deal of influence on your powers of attraction. Below are four possible Venus types for women and men. To find your Venus you need to go to page 771, where you will find the Venus table and extra information. The planet Mars also affects your powers of attraction. To find your Mars table and interpretation go to page 761.

WOMEN WITH VENUS IN TAURUS: Demonstrative and affectionate, you are naturally tactile with a love of sensual pleasures. With a streak of the conventional, you love the simple pleasures of life: good food, close friends, and happy relationships. Although you possess endurance be careful not to let this turn into plain stubbornness. Having inner strength, you can express genuine patience and are often a pillar of support for loved ones and friends.

MEN WITH VENUS IN TAURUS: Although usually you are drawn to sensual and physically beautiful individuals, you want a partner who is also reliable and loyal. When in love you enjoy buying your partner things of quality that will grow in value or useful things of a practical nature. You also love to socialize and entertain, especially in luxurious surroundings. Affectionate and caring, often you are attracted to creative people or those with artistic talents.

WOMEN WITH VENUS IN GEMINI: Charming and usually easygoing, you like to talk to people who are intelligent and witty. With a good social sense and a desire for mental expansion, you need a partner who is informed and has good ideas. Although you enjoy having different experiences, you need to resist your tendencies to become bored too quickly or be too talkative. As you enjoy sharing and learning new things, you usually prefer being with someone rather than operating alone.

MEN WITH VENUS IN GEMINI: Informed and curious yet charming and friendly, you seek a partner who shares your interests or enjoys your witty remarks. Although a good communicator, you have an inborn tendency to be lighthearted and less profound about deep emotional commitment. Although you are keen on experiences that bring variety into

your life, boredom or scattering your energies in too many directions is probably your biggest handicap in relationships. Nevertheless you are attracted to intelligent partners who can match your lively banter.

WOMEN WITH VENUS IN CANCER: Possessing a soft femininity, you have tender and sensitive emotions. Sympathetic and caring, you often mother those in your care by making sure they are comfortable and have plenty to eat. When you feel hurt or insecure in relationships, you are likely to cover your feelings by being defensive or appearing tough on the outside while on the inside you are feeling vulnerable. Affectionate and romantic, you make a faithful and devoted partner.

MEN WITH VENUS IN CANCER: Being emotionally receptive you can make a sensitive lover. With your desire to care for and protect others, you are likely to have strong family connections. Love is often tied in with being attentive to the needs of others, and you may find yourself attracted to individuals who have sympathetic or maternal qualities. Security conscious, you need a loyal partner who can offer you support and ideally be a good cook and homemaker.

WOMEN WITH VENUS IN LEO: As a person who wants to radiate in your own right, you are likely to desire partners you can be proud of. Usually you are attracted to fun-loving, warm, and generous individuals. If self-expression is important to you, you will probably seek the company of creative people such as artists, musicians, or those with a flair for acting. Romantic and dignified, with a regal air, you can project confidence and success to attract others.

MEN WITH VENUS IN LEO: Generous, animated, and pleasure-seeking, you can be very entertaining and fun to be with. You are usually attracted to extroverted and benevolent individuals with a sunny personality. If ambitious, you are drawn to a partner who shows leadership qualities or one who is highly motivated. Your less attractive qualities are your tendencies to be bossy or vain. With a sense of the dramatic, however, you can be the life and soul of the party and inspire those around you.

To read all about your Outer Planets and work out how to use your personalized timetable, go to Section Three, page 789.

To read all about your Outer Planets and work out how to use your personalized timetable, go to Section Three, page 789.

Your Personalized Timetable

JUPITER BENEFICIAL
1938 3/19 – until 1939 1/29
1940 4/18 – 5/31
1943 10/25 – until 1944 2/1
1944 6/21 – 8/11
1945 12/2 – until 1946 4/29
1946 7/30 – 10/25
1950 3/1 – 6/1
1950 7/22 – until 1951 1/10
1952 4/1 – 5/13
1955 10/2 – until 1956 3/12
1956 5/23 – 7/25
1957 11/13 – until 1958 10/9
1962 2/12 – 4/27
1962 9/10 – 12/15
1964 3/15 – 4/26
1967 9/14 – 11/12
1968 1/31 – 7/7
1969 10/28 – until 1970 9/22
1974 1/27 – 4/6
1975 7/17 – 9/11
1976 2/25 – 4/10
1979 8/28 – 10/18
1980 3/10 – 6/12
1981 10/12 – until 1982 1/3
1982 4/18 – 9/2
1986 1/10 – 3/19
1987 6/15 – 10/27
1988 2/1 – 3/24
1991 8/13 – 9/28
1993 9/27 – 12/12
1994 5/29 – 8/4
1997 5/10 – 7/11
1997 12/23 – until 1998 3/3
1999 5/24 – 7/25
1999 9/24 – until 2000 3/4
2003 7/28 – 9/12
2005 9/10 – 11/25
2009 4/8 – 8/27
2009 11/27 – until 2010 2/14
2011 5/5 – 6/22
2011 11/12 – until 2012 2/7

SATURN BENEFICIAL
1939 5/1 – until 1940 4/17
1948 7/28 – 10/21
1949 2/13 – 7/12
1952 10/31 – until 1953 12/19
1954 4/21 – 9/15
1963 4/5 – 8/4
1964 1/1 – until 1965 2/16
1968 6/17 – 9/27
1969 3/7 – 5/28
1969 11/25 – until 1970 2/11
1977 9/6 – until 1978 8/23
1981 12/16 – until 1982 3/19
1982 9/8 – until 1983 10/24
1993 2/5 – until 1994 3/24
1994 10/10 – 12/8
1998 4/14 – 8/1
1998 8/30 – until 1999 4/1
2006 10/24 – until 2007 1/18
2007 7/11 – 10/1
2008 3/17 – 6/17
2011 10/15 – until 2012 11/29

URANUS BENEFICIAL
1960 9/16 – until 1963 7/23
1972 11/9 – until 1976 10/13
2000 4/24 – until 2005 2/19

NEPTUNE BENEFICIAL
1951 11/14 – until 1960 8/3
2007 3/5 – Continues

PLUTO BENEFICIAL
1953 9/1 – until 1959 8/12
1979 11/16 – until 1986 10/9

JUPITER CHALLENGING
1939 3/29 – 6/21
1939 9/6 – until 1940 2/3

1944 11/1 – until 1945 3/30
1945 6/29 – 9/24
1948 1/27 – 7/17
1948 9/14 – 12/14
1951 3/12 – 5/22
1951 10/24 – until 1952 1/5
1956 10/14 – until 1957 9/9
1960 1/8 – 11/28
1963 2/23 – 5/2
1968 9/27 – until 1969 8/23
1971 12/23 – until 1972 3/20
1972 5/30 – 11/9
1975 2/6 – 4/14
1980 9/11 – 12/3
1981 3/18 – 8/3
1983 12/7 – until 1984 2/21
1984 7/12 – 10/16
1986 6/3 – 8/21
1987 1/17 – 3/29
1992 8/27 – 11/11
1993 4/28 – 7/5
1995 11/22 – until 1996 2/1
1998 5/5 – 10/6
1998 12/20 – until 1999 3/13
2004 8/10 – 10/25
2007 11/5 – until 2008 1/16
2010 4/15 – until 2011 2/23

SATURN CHALLENGING
1950 8/29 – until 1951 10/7
1958 1/10 – 7/12
1958 10/4 – until 1959 3/20
1959 5/14 – 12/5
1966 3/15 – until 1967 4/25
1967 11/9 – until 1968 1/7
1979 10/6 – until 1980 5/5
1980 6/8 – 11/16
1981 3/27 – 8/10
1987 3/1 – until 1987 4/30
1987 11/18 – until 1989 1/8
1995 4/21 – 9/26
1996 1/14 – 6/14
1996 8/22 – until 1997 2/27
2008 11/23 – until 2009 2/9
2009 8/10 – until 2010 9/20

URANUS CHALLENGING
1966 9/19 – until 1970 8/16
1986 1/18 – until 1990 10/29
2008 4/10 – Continues

NEPTUNE CHALLENGING
1938 1/1 – until 1946 8/4
1979 3/8 – until 1987 11/24

PLUTO CHALLENGING
1966 11/26 – until 1974 9/23
2003 12/30 – until 2011 12/6

JUPITER SPECIAL
1941 9/15 – 11/3
1942 4/26 – 7/8
1953 8/11 – 12/20
1954 4/2 – 6/22
1965 7/21 – until 1966 6/5
1977 7/4 – until 1978 5/18
1989 6/17 – 9/4
1989 12/23 – until 1990 4/27
2001 6/1 – 8/12
2002 2/7 – 3/23

SATURN SPECIAL
1943 7/12 – until 1944 1/23
1944 3/20 – 8/11
1945 1/8 – 4/29
1972 9/19 – 10/15
1973 5/17 – until 1974 6/15
2002 6/24 – until 2003 7/24
2004 2/24 – 3/19

URANUS SPECIAL
1946 8/1 – until 1951 5/2

Ⅱ

191

June 21

Your Personal Powers

Mentally quick and creative, you need to express your versatility and put your imaginative ideas to good use. Mercury, your ruling planet, grants you excellent communication skills and an inquiring nature. Usually you are an astute and intuitive individual with a progressive outlook on life. You may lose some of your power when you let your inner restlessness cause you to feel dissatisfied or pessimistic. You gain power when you are willing to discipline your exceptional mind. Being able to channel your powerful emotions into worthwhile projects usually uplifts your spirits, increasing your faith and confidence. You empower yourself by being patient and resisting a tendency to act on impulse. If you are facing obstacles do not let frustration undermine your determination. Even though you benefit from collaborating with others you are likely to want to achieve something by your own efforts. Maintaining a positive outlook or persevering usually assures your success. Enterprising, you enjoy new experiences and therefore should avoid getting stuck in a rut.

Your Powers of Attraction in Relationships

Social and friendly, you are a gregarious individual who needs to be popular and liked. Usually sensitive and kindhearted, your generous nature shows how much you care about and love those around you. A good conversationalist, you attract people with your enthusiastic and altruistic nature. Although you usually have many friends and acquaintances, it is through periods of difficulties that you find who your true friends are. Since close personal relationships and security are very important to you, it is vital in partnerships that you maintain some independence, resisting any tendencies to become dependent on partners. The key to successful relationships often lies in your ability to communicate your feelings and take responsibility for your own emotional fulfillment. You are often willing to make sacrifices for loved ones.

Your attractive qualities: inspired, imaginative, realistic, well-informed, loyal, responsible, witty, economical, disciplined, original ideas, independent, creative, enduring, intuitive, affectionate, practical, objective, good sense of values, talent with words, focused, optimistic, selfless, generous, tender

Your less attractive qualities: codependent, nervous, frustrated, dissatisfied, irritable, temperamental, insecure, impulsive, worry, insecure, negative thinking, anxious, lack of vision, too idealistic, critical

Your Venus Power

The planet Venus has a great deal of influence on your powers of attraction. Below are four possible Venus types for women and men. To find your Venus you need to go to page 771, where you will find the Venus table and extra information. The planet Mars also affects your powers of attraction. To find your Mars table and interpretation go to page 761.

WOMEN WITH VENUS IN TAURUS: Warm and affectionate, you are drawn to partners with whom you can share life's simple comforts. With a need for stability and security or an appreciation of earthly pleasures, you may have to avoid overindulgence or becoming too preoccupied with material concerns. Nevertheless, your sociability and friendliness usually make you popular. You need a partner who can also share your appreciation of beauty and style.

MEN WITH VENUS IN TAURUS: As well as attracting people with your warm personality, you possess an innate sense of the value of material possessions. Keeping yourself stylish and having an attractive home can therefore be important to you. You are naturally attracted to practical yet sensual women who understand your need for comfort, security, and the pleasures and luxuries of life. Naturally affectionate, you enjoy socializing but can be a loyal and loving partner.

WOMEN WITH VENUS IN GEMINI: Articulate, versatile, and youthful, your personal magnetism is often linked to your charm, wit, and communication skills. You seek a partner who is clever, can communicate with you at ease, and can share your thoughts and interests. Since you find it easy to mix with people you usually have many friends. When you do find someone you can communicate with, you can easily lose yourself in long conversations.

MEN WITH VENUS IN GEMINI: Friendly and sociable, you attract others with your clever and amusing conversation. Drawn to people who can match you in wit and intelligence, you usually prefer to keep relationships light rather than too emotionally intense. With your youthful charm and desire for knowledge and new experiences, you usually have many friends and a low boredom threshold.

WOMEN WITH VENUS IN CANCER: With your intuitive

abilities and sympathetic nature, you are usually supportive of those you love. Impressionable and empathetic, your receptivity allows you to quickly pick up on the moods of others, making you especially aware of the emotional changes in your partner. As you often display true maternal tendencies toward those you know, you want a partner who is considerate and sensitive.

MEN WITH VENUS IN CANCER: Being caring and sensitive, you probably seek a nurturing partner who could provide you with emotional security and a sense of belonging in a loving and safe environment. Receptive to others, at times you find it hard to be direct or confrontational in relationships. You may find yourself drawn to affectionate and sympathetic partners like yourself. You are also likely to have strong family links.

WOMEN WITH VENUS IN LEO: Your friendly and sunny personality often makes you stand out in a crowd. Generous and giving, you know how to make your partner feel special. As you often expect loyalty and devotion from your partner in return, you can become easily offended if they ignore you or behave in an inconsiderate manner. Charming and kind, when you are in love, you can be romantic, dramatic, and passionate.

MEN WITH VENUS IN LEO: As an extrovert you enjoy being involved in all types of activities where you can assert yourself and show your talents and abilities. A childlike nature suggests that you are versatile and keen on games or being entertained. You are usually attracted to vivacious partners with a benevolent nature. Others may recognize your inborn tendencies to lead but are also aware of your vanity or pride. Nevertheless, generous, kind, and caring, you often show compassion to those less fortunate than yourself.

To read all about your Outer Planets and work out how to use your personalized timetable, go to Section Three, page 789.

To read all about your Outer Planets and work out how to use your personalized timetable, go to Section Three, page 789.

Your Personalized Timetable

JUPITER BENEFICIAL
1938 3/23 – until 1939 2/2
1940 4/22 – 6/5
1943 11/2 – until 1944 1/24
1944 6/26 – 8/15
1945 12/8 – until 1946 4/21
1946 8/7 – 10/30
1950 3/5 – 6/21
1950 7/2 – until 1951 1/14
1952 4/5 – 5/17
1955 10/7 – until 1956 3/4
1956 6/1 – 7/30
1957 11/18 – until 1958 10/14
1962 2/16 – 5/3
1962 9/3 – 12/22
1964 3/19 – 4/30
1967 9/19 – 11/22
1968 1/21 – 7/12
1969 11/2 – until 1970 9/27
1974 1/31 – 4/10
1975 8/1 – 8/28
1976 2/29 – 4/14
1979 9/2 – 10/23
1980 3/2 – 6/19
1981 10/17 – until 1982 1/10
1982 4/10 – 9/8
1986 1/15 – 3/24
1987 6/21 – 10/20
1988 2/7 – 3/28
1991 8/17 – 10/3
1993 10/1 – 12/17
1994 5/20 – 8/14
1997 5/22 – 6/28
1997 12/27 – until 1998 3/7
1999 5/29 – 8/6
1999 9/12 – until 2000 3/9
2003 8/1 – 9/16
2005 9/15 – 11/29
2009 4/13 – 8/20
2009 12/4 – until 2010 2/18
2011 5/10 – 6/27
2011 11/4 – until 2012 2/14

SATURN BENEFICIAL
1939 5/9 – until 1940 4/24
1948 8/5 – 11/1
1949 2/1 – 7/21
1952 11/9 – until 1953 5/22
1953 7/25 – 12/30
1954 4/8 – 9/25
1963 4/17 – 7/21
1964 1/10 – until 1965 2/24
1968 7/1 – 9/13
1969 3/15 – 6/6
1969 11/11 – until 1970 2/24
1977 9/14 – until 1978 3/27
1978 5/24 – 8/30
1981 12/31 – until 1982 3/3
1982 9/17 – until 1983 11/1
1993 2/13 – until 1994 4/1
1994 9/24 – 12/24
1998 4/21 – until 1999 4/8
2006 11/9 – until 2007 1/2
2007 7/19 – 10/9
2008 3/5 – 6/29
2011 10/23 – until 2012 12/8

URANUS BENEFICIAL
1960 10/5 – until 1963 8/9
1972 11/26 – until 1976 10/29
2001 2/19 – until 2005 12/21

NEPTUNE BENEFICIAL
1951 12/21 – until 1960 9/19
2007 4/5 – Continues

PLUTO BENEFICIAL
1953 10/6 – until 1960 7/12
1979 12/19 – until 1987 8/16

JUPITER CHALLENGING
1939 4/2 – 6/30

JUPITER BENEFICIAL (continued, right column)
1939 8/28 – until 1940 2/8
1944 11/7 – until 1945 3/22
1945 7/6 – 9/29
1948 2/1 – 7/7
1948 9/24 – 12/19
1951 3/16 – 5/27
1951 10/16 – until 1952 1/12
1956 10/19 – until 1957 9/13
1960 1/13 – 12/2
1963 2/27 – 5/6
1968 10/2 – until 1969 8/27
1971 12/27 – until 1972 3/31
1972 5/19 – 11/14
1975 2/10 – 4/18
1980 9/16 – 12/11
1981 3/11 – 8/8
1983 12/12 – until 1984 2/27
1984 7/5 – 10/22
1986 6/12 – 8/12
1987 1/22 – 4/2
1992 8/31 – 11/17
1993 4/19 – 7/14
1995 11/26 – until 1996 2/6
1998 5/11 – 9/28
1998 12/28 – until 1999 3/17
2004 8/15 – 10/30
2007 11/9 – until 2008 1/20
2010 4/19 – until 2011 2/27

SATURN CHALLENGING
1938 1/1 – 3/24
1950 9/5 – until 1951 10/15
1958 1/19 – 6/28
1958 10/17 – until 1959 12/14
1966 3/23 – until 1967 5/4
1967 10/24 – until 1968 1/23
1979 10/14 – until 1980 4/14
1980 6/29 – 11/26
1981 3/14 – 8/20
1987 11/27 – until 1989 1/16
1989 9/1 – 9/21
1995 5/1 – 9/14
1996 1/24 – 7/15
1996 7/20 – until 1997 3/7
2008 12/11 – until 2009 1/21
2009 8/19 – until 2010 9/28

URANUS CHALLENGING
1966 10/5 – until 1970 9/3
1986 2/7 – until 1990 11/20
2008 4/30 – Continues

NEPTUNE CHALLENGING
1938 9/28 – until 1946 9/5
1980 1/14 – until 1987 12/21

PLUTO CHALLENGING
1967 10/10 – until 1975 8/14
2004 1/28 – until 2012 10/29

JUPITER SPECIAL
1941 10/5 – 10/15
1942 5/1 – 7/12
1953 8/17 – 12/13
1954 4/8 – 6/26
1965 7/26 – until 1966 2/6
1966 2/24 – 6/10
1977 7/8 – until 1978 5/23
1989 6/21 – 9/11
1989 12/15 – until 1990 5/3
2001 6/5 – 8/17
2002 1/27 – 4/4

SATURN SPECIAL
1943 7/20 – until 1944 1/7
1944 4/4 – 8/21
1944 12/28 – until 1945 5/9
1973 5/25 – until 1974 6/23
2002 7/2 – until 2003 8/1
2004 2/1 – 4/11

URANUS SPECIAL
1946 8/28 – until 1951 5/23

Gemini Timetable
X-Special · X-Beneficial · X-Challenging

May 22
URANUS X-CHALLENGING
2002 5/14 – until 2004 2/20
URANUS X-BENEFICIAL
2010 4/24 – until 2012 2/20
NEPTUNE X-CHALLENGING
2010 5/20 – until 2013 2/17

May 23
URANUS X-CHALLENGING
2003 3/4 – until 2004 12/24
URANUS X-BENEFICIAL
2010 5/17 – until 2012 3/9
NEPTUNE X-CHALLENGING
2011 3/23 – until 2013 3/14

May 24
URANUS X-CHALLENGING
2003 3/21 – until 2005 1/16
URANUS X-BENEFICIAL
2011 3/22 – until 2012 3/26
NEPTUNE X-CHALLENGING
2011 4/29 – until 2013 4/13

May 25
URANUS X-CHALLENGING
2003 4/11 – until 2005 2/4
URANUS X-BENEFICIAL
2011 4/8 – until 2013 1/29
NEPTUNE X-CHALLENGING
2012 3/16 – Continues

May 26
URANUS X-CHALLENGING
2003 5/10 – until 2005 2/21
URANUS X-BENEFICIAL
2011 4/26 – until 2013 2/20
NEPTUNE X-CHALLENGING
2012 4/16 – Continues

May 27
URANUS X-CHALLENGING
2003 5/10 – until 2005 2/21
URANUS X-BENEFICIAL
2011 4/26 – until 2013 2/20
NEPTUNE X-CHALLENGING
2012 4/16 – Continues

May 28
URANUS X-CHALLENGING
2004 3/22 – until 2006 1/17
URANUS X-BENEFICIAL
2011 6/22 – until 2013 3/28
NEPTUNE X-BENEFICIAL
2000 2/20 – until 2002 11/18

May 29
URANUS X-CHALLENGING
2004 4/11 – until 2006 2/5
URANUS X-BENEFICIAL
2012 4/9 – until 2013 4/14
NEPTUNE X-BENEFICIAL
2001 1/2 – until 2002 12/26

May 30
URANUS X-CHALLENGING
2004 5/8 – until 2006 2/23

(col 2)
URANUS X-BENEFICIAL
2012 4/27 – Continues
NEPTUNE X-BENEFICIAL
2001 1/28 – until 2003 1/22

May 31
URANUS X-CHALLENGING
2005 3/6 – until 2006 12/24
URANUS X-BENEFICIAL
2012 5/17 – until 2013 5/22
NEPTUNE X-BENEFICIAL
2001 2/23 – until 2003 12/19

June 1
URANUS X-CHALLENGING
2005 3/24 – until 2007 1/19
URANUS X-BENEFICIAL
2012 6/17 – until 2013 6/22
NEPTUNE X-BENEFICIAL
2001 3/28 – until 2004 1/17

June 2
URANUS X-CHALLENGING
2005 4/12 – until 2007 2/7
NEPTUNE X-BENEFICIAL
2002 2/18 – until 2004 12/10

June 3
URANUS X-CHALLENGING
2005 5/7 – until 2007 2/24
NEPTUNE X-BENEFICIAL
2002 3/19 – until 2005 1/10

June 4
URANUS X-CHALLENGING
2006 3/8 – until 2007 12/23
NEPTUNE X-BENEFICIAL
2003 2/12 – until 2005 11/29
PLUTO X-CHALLENGING
2000 12/20 – until 2002 9/24

June 5
URANUS X-CHALLENGING
2006 3/26 – until 2008 1/20
NEPTUNE X-BENEFICIAL
2003 3/12 – until 2006 1/4
PLUTO X-CHALLENGING
2000 11/19 – until 2002 11/2

June 6
URANUS X-CHALLENGING
2006 4/13 – until 2008 2/9
NEPTUNE X-BENEFICIAL
2003 4/24 – until 2006 11/7
PLUTO X-CHALLENGING
2000 11/19 – until 2002 11/29

June 7
URANUS X-CHALLENGING
2006 5/7 – until 2008 2/26
NEPTUNE X-BENEFICIAL
2004 3/4 – until 2006 12/28
PLUTO X-CHALLENGING
2001 1/8 – until 2003 10/22

June 8
URANUS X-CHALLENGING
2007 3/10 – until 2008 12/20
NEPTUNE X-BENEFICIAL
2004 4/7 – until 2007 1/25
PLUTO X-CHALLENGING
2001 2/13 – until 2003 11/21

June 9
URANUS X-CHALLENGING
2007 4/10 – until 2009 2/5
NEPTUNE X-BENEFICIAL
2005 3/20 – until 2008 1/13
PLUTO X-CHALLENGING
2002 1/19 – until 2004 11/4

June 10
URANUS X-CHALLENGING
2007 4/10 – until 2009 2/5
NEPTUNE X-BENEFICIAL
2005 3/20 – until 2008 1/13
PLUTO X-CHALLENGING
2002 1/19 – until 2004 11/4

June 11
URANUS X-CHALLENGING
2007 5/8 – until 2009 2/27
NEPTUNE X-BENEFICIAL
2006 2/20 – until 2008 12/8
PLUTO X-CHALLENGING
2002 12/20 – until 2005 9/9

June 12
URANUS X-BENEFICIAL
2001 1/3 – until 2002 1/8
URANUS X-CHALLENGING
2008 3/11 – until 2009 12/16
NEPTUNE X-BENEFICIAL
2006 3/20 – until 2009 1/12
PLUTO X-CHALLENGING
2003 1/16 – until 2005 11/2

June 13
URANUS X-BENEFICIAL
2001 1/21 – until 2002 1/26
URANUS X-CHALLENGING
2008 3/28 – until 2010 1/21
NEPTUNE X-BENEFICIAL
2006 5/7 – until 2009 11/19
PLUTO X-CHALLENGING
2003 2/24 – until 2005 12/1

June 14
URANUS X-BENEFICIAL
2001 1/21 – until 2002 1/26
URANUS X-CHALLENGING
2008 3/28 – until 2010 1/21
NEPTUNE X-BENEFICIAL
2006 5/7 – until 2009 11/19
PLUTO X-CHALLENGING
2003 2/24 – until 2005 12/1

June 15
URANUS X-BENEFICIAL
2001 1/21 – until 2002 1/26

June 16
URANUS X-BENEFICIAL
2001 3/13 – until 2003 1/8
URANUS X-CHALLENGING
2008 6/17 – until 2010 3/18
NEPTUNE X-BENEFICIAL
2008 3/6 – until 2010 12/27
PLUTO X-CHALLENGING
2004 12/29 – until 2007 10/12

June 17
URANUS X-BENEFICIAL
2001 4/2 – until 2003 1/27
URANUS X-CHALLENGING
2009 3/30 – until 2011 1/21
NEPTUNE X-BENEFICIAL
2008 4/6 – until 2011 1/26
PLUTO X-CHALLENGING
2005 1/26 – until 2007 11/18

June 18
URANUS X-BENEFICIAL
2001 5/2 – until 2003 2/13
URANUS X-CHALLENGING
2009 4/17 – until 2011 2/12
NEPTUNE X-BENEFICIAL
2009 2/28 – until 2011 12/16
PLUTO X-CHALLENGING
2005 12/22 – until 2008 9/19

June 19
URANUS X-BENEFICIAL
2002 2/25 – until 2003 12/15
URANUS X-CHALLENGING
2009 5/8 – until 2011 3/2
NEPTUNE X-BENEFICIAL
2009 3/28 – until 2012 1/20
PLUTO X-CHALLENGING
2006 1/18 – until 2008 11/10

June 20
URANUS X-BENEFICIAL
2002 3/14 – until 2004 1/9
URANUS X-CHALLENGING
2009 6/9 – until 2011 3/19
NEPTUNE X-BENEFICIAL
2009 5/17 – until 2012 11/27
PLUTO X-CHALLENGING
2006 2/23 – until 2008 12/9

June 21
URANUS X-BENEFICIAL
2002 4/3 – until 2004 1/28
URANUS X-CHALLENGING
2010 3/31 – until 2012 1/21
NEPTUNE X-BENEFICIAL
2010 3/20 – until 2013 1/11
PLUTO X-CHALLENGING
2007 1/11 – until 2009 11/4

Cancer

June 22–July 22

June 22

Your Personal Powers

Highly intuitive and idealistic, you are often a sympathetic individual with strong convictions. Having practical abilities and a sincere approach suggests that you are reliable and honest in your dealing with others. Your ruler, the Moon, grants you sensitivity, a strong sixth sense, and inspired ideas. Caring by nature with an innate business sense, your acute awareness also indicates that you can become successful in all types of people-related activities. Often supportive to those around you, you gain power when you feel secure in your knowledge and act upon your beliefs. Although you find your strength in your convictions, you can lose some of your power when you become too single-minded or inflexible. Visionary by nature, you are also concerned with the emotional value of your actions. Once you make a commitment, however, you can be inspired, hardworking, and dedicated. Being methodical and keen on details, your desire for knowledge and mental stimulation suggest that you are a quick learner with excellent potential to excel in any field of interest you choose.

Your Powers of Attraction in Relationships

Good-natured and affectionate, you have a natural talent for making people feel at ease. Others are attracted to your sincere and friendly personality and unusual approach. As you like to know where you stand with your partners, you are usually attracted to practical, honest, or hardworking individuals who can make you feel emotionally and materially secure. Generous with those you love, you are a sympathetic and supportive friend. Although you have your own visions and opinions you benefit from working with others or entering business partnerships. In your dealings with others, however, you need to stay objective or detached and overcome a tendency to be stubborn or oversensitive. You need a clever and solid partner with whom you can share your unique thoughts and ideals.

Your attractive qualities: inner strength, intuitive, caring, sensitive, versatile, inspired, imaginative, powerful emotions, sympathetic, protective, pragmatic, purposeful, motivated, practical, common sense, capable, hardworking, good organizer, enterprising, security-conscious, problem solver

Your less attractive qualities: nervous tension, moody, stubborn, manipulative, self-doubt, materialistic, too outspoken, dominating, unrealistic, domineering, power games, suspicious, cynical, interfering, escapist, lack of inner faith

Your Venus Power

The planet Venus has a great deal of influence on your powers of attraction. Below are four possible Venus types for women and men. To find your Venus you need to go to page 771, where you will find the Venus table and extra information. The planet Mars also affects your powers of attraction. To find your Mars table and interpretation go to page 761.

WOMEN WITH VENUS IN TAURUS: Being physically attractive, you can make a good impression on the opposite sex. As security and stability in relationships are very important to you, you usually want a partner who is not only attractive but also reliable and a good provider. Being sensual or tactile you also need a lover who is affectionate, but beware that your love does not show signs of possessiveness or jealousy. Your own sense of style and love of beauty imply that you can be attracted to creative people, especially those in art and music.

MEN WITH VENUS IN TAURUS: Attractive and affectionate, in relationships you are often down-to-earth, with a conservative outlook. You are drawn to warmhearted partners with whom you can share a familiar routine as well as life's pleasures and comforts. Seeking a partner who is dependable or reassuring, you often put security high on your priority list when looking for love. Your sociability and friendliness usually make you popular and partners often admire your good sense of values and practical skills.

WOMEN WITH VENUS IN GEMINI: In relationships you need intellectual stimulation and usually prefer to keep things light. Certainly not boring, you love to talk and are at your best being witty and entertaining. Although your easygoing approach to relationships is very attractive, guard against losing touch with your deeper emotions. You prefer a partner who can keep up with your fast stream of ideas, and if you have shared interests then so much the better.

MEN WITH VENUS IN GEMINI: Informed and curious yet charming and friendly, you seek a partner who shares your interests or enjoys your witty remarks. Although a good communicator, you have an inborn tendency to be lighthearted and less profound about deep emotional commitment. Although you are keen on experiences that bring variety into

your life, boredom or scattering your energies in too many directions is probably your biggest handicap in relationships. Nevertheless you are attracted to intelligent partners who can match your lively banter.

WOMEN WITH VENUS IN CANCER: With your intuitive abilities and sympathetic nature you are usually supportive of those you love. Impressionable and empathetic, your receptivity allows you to quickly pick up on the moods of people and you are especially aware of the emotional changes in your close partner. As you often display true maternal tendencies toward those you know, you want a partner who is considerate and sensitive.

MEN WITH VENUS IN CANCER: You seek a partner who is sympathetic, caring, and protective. Able to be forgiving and compassionate, you want a secure emotional bond in your close relationships. You are usually drawn to partners who are maternal, unselfish, or demonstrative with their feelings. Although you can sometimes appear to others as impressionable, you have powerful emotions and inner strength.

WOMEN WITH VENUS IN LEO: As a person who wants to radiate in their own right, you are likely to desire partners you can be proud of. Usually you are attracted to fun-loving, warm, and generous individuals. If self-expression is important to you, you will probably seek the company of creative people such as artists, musicians, or those with a flair for acting. Alternatively, you may be drawn to people who are dignified, regal, or who have already achieved success.

MEN WITH VENUS IN LEO: Enthusiastic, playful, and kind, you can be benevolent with those you love. Warm, romantic, and self-expressive, you adore the drama of love or having fun with your friends. Usually you are attracted to partners with a warm and generous nature. Although you can be a confident and charismatic partner, you may need to develop humility to stop pride or arrogance from marring your relationships.

To read all about your Outer Planets and work out how to use your personalized timetable, go to Section Three, page 789.

To read all about your Outer Planets and work out how to use your personalized timetable, go to Section Three, page 789.

Your Personalized Timetable

JUPITER BENEFICIAL
1938 3/28 – until 1939 2/6
1940 4/26 – 6/9
1943 11/10 – until 1944 1/15
1944 7/1 – 8/20
1945 12/14 – until 1946 4/14
1946 8/13 – 11/3
1950 3/9 – until 1951 1/19
1952 4/9 – 5/21
1955 10/13 – until 1956 2/25
1956 6/8 – 8/4
1957 11/23 – until 1958 5/30
1958 7/8 – 10/18
1962 2/20 – 5/9
1962 8/26 – 12/28
1964 3/23 – 5/4
1967 9/24 – 12/4
1968 1/8 – 7/17
1969 11/6 – until 1970 10/2
1974 2/4 – 4/15
1974 10/20 – 11/17
1976 3/5 – 4/18
1979 9/6 – 10/29
1980 2/24 – 6/26
1981 10/21 – until 1982 1/19
1982 4/1 – 9/14
1986 1/19 – 3/28
1987 6/27 – 10/13
1988 2/13 – 4/1
1991 8/21 – 10/8
1992 4/9 – 5/22
1993 10/5 – 12/23
1994 5/11 – 8/21
1998 1/1 – 3/11
1999 6/2 – 12/6
2000 1/3 – 3/14
2003 8/6 – 9/21
2005 9/20 – 12/4
2009 4/19 – 8/12
2009 12/10 – until 2010 2/22
2011 5/14 – 7/3
2011 10/28 – until 2012 2/20

SATURN BENEFICIAL
1939 5/17 – 11/25
1940 1/28 – 5/2
1948 8/12 – 11/16
1949 1/16 – 7/29
1952 11/17 – until 1953 5/6
1953 8/10 – until 1954 1/14
1954 3/24 – 10/4
1963 5/3 – 7/4
1964 1/18 – until 1965 3/4
1968 7/22 – 8/22
1969 3/23 – 6/15
1969 10/30 – until 1970 3/6
1977 9/22 – until 1978 3/11
1978 6/9 – 9/7
1982 9/25 – until 1983 11/9
1993 2/21 – until 1994 4/10
1994 9/10 – until 1995 1/5
1998 4/29 – until 1999 4/16
2007 7/27 – 10/19
2008 2/22 – 7/9
2011 10/31 – until 2012 12/18

URANUS BENEFICIAL
1960 10/30 – until 1963 8/24
1972 12/18 – until 1977 8/24
2001 3/8 – until 2006 1/16

NEPTUNE BENEFICIAL
1952 11/8 – until 1960 10/18
2008 2/27 – Continues

PLUTO BENEFICIAL
1954 9/8 – until 1960 8/13
1980 10/31 – until 1987 9/22

JUPITER CHALLENGING
1939 4/6 – 7/13
1939 8/15 – until 1940 2/13

1944 11/13 – until 1945 3/15
1945 7/13 – 10/3
1948 2/6 – 6/29
1948 10/1 – 12/23
1951 3/20 – 6/2
1951 10/9 – until 1952 1/19
1956 10/23 – until 1957 4/30
1957 6/6 – 9/18
1960 1/18 – 12/6
1963 3/3 – 5/10
1968 10/6 – until 1969 9/1
1972 1/1 – 11/19
1975 2/14 – 4/22
1980 9/20 – 12/19
1981 3/2 – 8/14
1983 12/16 – until 1984 3/4
1984 6/27 – 10/28
1986 6/24 – 7/30
1987 1/27 – 4/6
1992 9/5 – 11/22
1993 4/11 – 7/21
1995 11/30 – until 1996 2/11
1996 8/16 – 9/21
1998 5/16 – 9/21
1999 1/3 – 3/20
2004 8/20 – 11/4
2007 11/14 – until 2008 1/24
2010 4/24 – until 2011 3/3

SATURN CHALLENGING
1938 1/1 – 4/1
1950 9/13 – until 1951 10/23
1952 5/28 – 6/23
1958 1/28 – 6/15
1958 10/28 – until 1959 12/22
1966 3/31 – until 1967 5/13
1967 10/11 – until 1968 2/3
1979 10/23 – until 1980 3/31
1980 7/12 – 12/9
1981 3/1 – 8/29
1987 12/5 – until 1989 1/24
1989 8/5 – 10/17
1995 5/12 – 9/1
1996 2/3 – until 1997 3/15
2009 8/27 – until 2010 10/5

URANUS CHALLENGING
1966 10/21 – until 1970 9/19
1986 3/19 – until 1990 12/8
2008 5/30 – Continues

NEPTUNE CHALLENGING
1938 10/26 – until 1947 7/24
1980 2/19 – until 1988 11/16

PLUTO CHALLENGING
1967 11/12 – until 1975 9/12
2004 12/21 – until 2012 12/3

JUPITER SPECIAL
1942 5/6 – 7/17
1953 8/24 – 12/6
1954 4/14 – 6/30
1965 7/31 – until 1966 1/20
1966 3/13 – 6/14
1977 7/12 – until 1978 5/28
1989 6/26 – 9/18
1989 12/8 – until 1990 5/9
2001 6/9 – 8/22
2002 1/18 – 4/12

SATURN SPECIAL
1943 7/29 – 12/25
1944 4/15 – 8/31
1944 12/16 – until 1945 5/18
1973 6/1 – until 1974 6/30
2002 7/10 – until 2003 2/7
2003 3/8 – 8/9
2004 1/18 – 4/24

URANUS SPECIAL
1947 6/20 – until 1951 6/9

June 23

Your Personal Powers

Intuitive and pragmatic, you are a mentally alert individual who likes to keep occupied and well-informed. As well as being clever, you possess emotional sensitivity and can strengthen your potential by developing your innate psychic powers. By learning to channel your intuition, thoughts, and feelings toward a practical goal, you can also overcome bouts of frustration and emotional fluctuations. Although you have tender feelings, your ability to endure indicates that you have survival instincts and an ability to adapt to situations. You gain power when you use your nervous energy to withstand difficulties. Usually you empower yourself when you combine your discerning mind, insight, and versatility with your professional sensibility. Although you possess inner determination, you lose some of your power when you let strong emotional tensions cause you stress or stir up your restlessness. By developing your self-confidence more and allowing yourself to be guided by your inner faith, you can become resolute and create inner peace of mind.

Your Powers of Attraction in Relationships

People are often attracted to your warmth and quick mind. With your sensitivity you can often feel or read other people's emotions and thoughts. Usually you are attracted to enterprising partners or independent people who are intelligent and well-informed. Alternatively, you may be drawn to ambitious or career-oriented individuals who are hardworking. Although you can be very loving and caring, an impatient streak suggests that you need to be patient and sure before you settle down or commit to long-term relationships. Although you can be spontaneous and fun-loving, your tendency to take things too seriously also implies that you need to avoid becoming stressed or worried. You may therefore be better off with a partner who is calm and easygoing or one who can understand your sensitivity and changing moods.

Your attractive qualities: loyal, responsible, intelligent, communicative, instinctive, creative, caring, sociable, versatile, trustworthy, spontaneous, sympathetic, receptive, shrewd, sociable, hardworking, inner wisdom, determined, love of learning, business sense, cooperative, enterprising

Your less attractive qualities: uncertain, skeptical, worries, moody, lose faith, uncommunicative, selfish, insecure, manipulative, stubborn, uncompromising, withdrawn, bossy, too demanding, restless, impatient, intense emotions, critical

Your Venus Power

The planet Venus has a great deal of influence on your powers of attraction. Below are four possible Venus types for women and men. To find your Venus you need to go to page 771, where you will find the Venus table and extra information. The planet Mars also affects your powers of attraction. To find your Mars table and interpretation go to page 761.

WOMEN WITH VENUS IN TAURUS: Being physically attractive, you can make a good impression on the opposite sex. As security and stability in relationships is very important to you, you usually want a partner who is not only attractive but also reliable and a good provider. Being sensual or tactile, you also need a lover who is affectionate, but beware that your love does not show signs of possessiveness or jealousy. Your own sense of style and your love of beauty imply that you can be attracted to creative people, especially in the arts and music.

MEN WITH VENUS IN TAURUS: Attractive and affectionate, in relationships you are often down-to-earth, with a conservative outlook. You are drawn to warmhearted partners with whom you can share a familiar routine as well as life's pleasures and comforts. Seeking a partner who is dependable or reassuring, you often put security high on your priority list when looking for love. Your sociability and friendliness usually make you popular and partners often admire your good sense of values and practical outlook.

WOMEN WITH VENUS IN GEMINI: By nature you are young at heart, adaptable, and sociable. Being curious and willing to cooperate makes you a good team player. Usually you are drawn to articulate people who have charm and flair or sharp wit. With a need to expand your knowledge, you also look for a partner who can challenge or stimulate you intellectually. Although you love to talk with all types of people, you may need to develop your listening skills in order to build better communication in your relationships.

MEN WITH VENUS IN GEMINI: Informed and curious yet charming and friendly, you seek a partner who shares your interests or enjoys your witty remarks. Although a good communicator, you have in inborn tendency to be lighthearted and less profound about deep emotional commitment. Although you are keen on experiences that bring variety into

your life, boredom or scattering your energies in too many directions is probably your biggest handicap in relationships. Nevertheless you are attracted to intelligent partners who can match your lively banter.

WOMEN WITH VENUS IN CANCER: Good-natured and romantic, you have a highly developed sense of touch that particularly responds to massage, hugs, and all things physical. Being friendly, you enjoy socializing and are able to put others at their ease. With your natural sense of beauty and harmony, your natural charm can attract others. Although you can be lavish toward your partner you may have to be careful that you do not overdo things.

MEN WITH VENUS IN CANCER: Being emotionally receptive you can make a sensitive lover. With your desire to care for and protect others, you are likely to have strong family connections. Love is often tied in with being attentive to the needs of others and you may find yourself attracted to individuals who have sympathetic or maternal qualities. Security-conscious, you need a loyal partner who can offer you support and ideally be a good cook and homemaker.

WOMEN WITH VENUS IN LEO: Warm and playful with a touch of the dramatic, you enjoy the company of generous or strong individuals who can share your sense of fun. Although there are advantages to your being strong-willed, in your relationships you need to resist being bossy as it can cause resentment. With your wonderful mixture of regal authority and childlike wonder, you love to keep others entertained and amused.

MEN WITH VENUS IN LEO: Generous, animated, and pleasure-seeking, you can be very entertaining and fun to be with. You are usually attracted to extroverted and benevolent individuals with a sunny personality. If ambitious, you are drawn to a partner who shows leadership qualities or one who is highly motivated. Your less attractive qualities are your tendencies to be bossy or vain. With a sense of the dramatic, however, you can be the life and soul of the party and inspire those around you.

To read all about your Outer Planets and work out how to use your personalized timetable, go to Section Three, page 789.

Your Personalized Timetable

JUPITER BENEFICIAL
1938 4/2 – 9/25	1944 11/19 – until 1945 3/7
1938 11/11 – until 1939 2/10	1945 7/19 – 10/8
1940 4/30 – 6/14	1948 2/12 – 6/21
1940 12/12 – until 1941 1/18	1948 10/8 – 12/27
1943 11/22 – until 1944 1/4	1951 3/24 – 6/8
1944 7/7 – 8/24	1951 10/2 – until 1952 1/25
1945 12/20 – until 1946 4/6	1956 10/28 – until 1957 4/17
1946 8/20 – 11/7	1957 6/19 – 9/22
1950 3/13 – until 1951 1/23	1960 1/22 – 12/11
1952 4/13 – 5/25	1963 3/7 – 5/15
1955 10/19 – until 1956 2/18	1968 10/11 – until 1969 9/6
1956 6/15 – 8/8	1972 1/5 – 11/23
1957 11/28 – until 1958 5/17	1975 2/18 – 4/26
1958 7/21 – 10/23	1980 9/25 – 12/29
1962 2/24 – 5/16	1981 2/20 – 8/19
1962 8/19 – until 1963 1/2	1983 12/20 – until 1984 3/10
1964 3/27 – 5/8	1984 6/20 – 11/3
1967 9/28 – until 1968 4/4	1987 2/1 – 4/10
1968 5/9 – 7/22	1992 9/9 – 11/28
1969 11/11 – until 1970 10/7	1993 4/3 – 7/28
1974 2/8 – 4/20	1995 12/4 – until 1996 2/16
1974 10/6 – 12/1	1996 8/3 – 10/4
1976 3/9 – 4/22	1998 5/22 – 9/14
1979 9/11 – 11/5	1999 1/9 – 3/24
1980 2/17 – 7/2	2004 8/24 – 11/8
1981 10/25 – until 1982 1/29	2005 5/21 – 6/20
1982 3/22 – 9/19	2007 11/18 – until 2008 1/29
1986 1/23 – 4/1	2010 4/28 – until 2011 3/7
1987 7/3 – 10/6	
1988 2/18 – 4/6	**SATURN CHALLENGING**
1991 8/26 – 10/13	1938 1/1 – 4/9
1992 3/28 – 6/3	1950 9/21 – until 1951 10/31
1993 10/10 – 12/29	1952 5/4 – 7/17
1994 5/4 – 8/28	1958 2/8 – 6/1
1998 1/5 – 3/15	1958 11/7 – until 1959 12/30
1999 6/7 – 11/23	1966 4/8 – 11/6
2000 1/17 – 3/18	1966 12/17 – until 1967 5/22
2003 8/10 – 9/25	1967 9/29 – until 1968 2/13
2005 9/24 – 12/9	1979 11/1 – until 1980 3/18
2006 6/22 – 7/20	1980 7/24 – 12/26
2009 4/26 – 8/5	1981 2/11 – 9/6
2009 12/15 – until 2010 2/26	1987 12/13 – until 1989 2/2
2011 5/18 – 7/9	1989 7/21 – 10/31
2011 10/21 – until 2012 2/25	1995 5/25 – 8/18
	1996 2/12 – until 1997 3/23
SATURN BENEFICIAL	2009 9/4 – until 2010 10/13
1939 5/25 – 11/10	
1940 2/12 – 5/9	**URANUS CHALLENGING**
1948 8/20 – until 1949 8/7	1966 11/10 – until 1970 10/4
1952 11/26 – until 1953 4/23	1986 12/26 – until 1990 12/24
1953 8/22 – until 1954 2/9	2009 3/25 – Continues
1954 2/24 – 10/12	
1964 1/27 – until 1965 3/12	**NEPTUNE CHALLENGING**
1969 3/31 – 6/25	1938 12/14 – until 1947 8/30
1969 10/18 – until 1970 3/15	1981 1/7 – until 1988 12/15
1977 10/1 – until 1978 2/26	
1978 6/21 – 9/15	**PLUTO CHALLENGING**
1982 10/3 – until 1983 11/17	1968 10/2 – until 1976 7/25
1993 3/1 – until 1994 4/20	2005 1/17 – until 2012 12/31
1994 8/28 – until 1995 1/15	
1998 5/7 – until 1999 4/23	**JUPITER SPECIAL**
2007 8/4 – 10/29	1942 5/10 – 7/21
2008 2/10 – 7/19	1953 8/30 – 11/29
2011 11/8 – until 2012 5/30	1954 4/20 – 7/4
2012 7/20 – 12/29	1965 8/5 – until 1966 1/10
	1966 3/23 – 6/18
URANUS BENEFICIAL	1977 7/17 – until 1978 6/1
1961 8/21 – until 1964 6/11	1989 6/30 – 9/27
1973 10/14 – until 1977 9/16	1989 11/29 – until 1990 5/14
2001 3/27 – until 2006 2/4	2001 6/13 – 8/28
	2002 1/11 – 4/19
NEPTUNE BENEFICIAL	
1952 12/9 – until 1961 9/12	**SATURN SPECIAL**
2008 3/27 – Continues	1943 8/7 – 12/14
	1944 4/25 – 9/12
PLUTO BENEFICIAL	1944 12/3 – until 1945 5/27
1954 10/14 – until 1961 7/12	1973 6/9 – until 1974 7/7
1980 11/26 – until 1987 10/18	2002 7/18 – until 2003 1/17
	2003 3/29 – 8/18
JUPITER CHALLENGING	2004 1/6 – 5/5
1939 4/10 – until 1940 2/17	
	URANUS SPECIAL
	1947 7/7 – until 1951 6/25

♋

June 24

SUN: CANCER • DECANATE: CANCER/ MOON • DEGREE: 1.5°–3° CANCER • MODE: CARDINAL • ELEMENT: WATER

Your Personal Powers

Receptive and intuitive, you are a caring and sensitive individual with strong determination. You gain power when you feel secure with your knowledge or within your family environment. Inspired by wisdom, you need to keep your mind active and creative. Your ruler, the Moon, grants you emotional sensitivity and a strong sixth sense. Although you have a discerning mind and a responsible nature, you lose some of your power through a tendency to be anxious or uncertain. If worry about your security or financial matters undermine your efforts, you can let inertia challenge your otherwise ambitious nature. Nevertheless, by combining your determination, powers of concentration, and pragmatic approach, you can be very resourceful, hardworking, and dedicated. Since your success often depends not only on your willingness to work hard but also on collaborative efforts, you gain power when you realize that you can achieve more by being flexible and showing tolerance toward others. As you often seek harmony and balance, resist conflicts in order to gain the support you need.

Your Powers of Attraction in Relationships

Other people are drawn to your charming, friendly, and sympathetic nature. With strong feelings and parental instincts you can be a passionate and loving partner or a devoted parent. Quietly dramatic and emotionally sensitive, you are happy when you can express your feelings and affections openly. Although you can be very supportive of those you love, avoid an inclination to be bossy or oversensitive. Usually you are drawn to intelligent people who are confident and enterprising. Although your need for self-expression can also draw you to dynamic individuals, you may need to resist a tendency to be too intense or melodramatic in your everyday life. Being sociable, you enjoy the company of active people who can inspire you to be more motivated.

Your attractive qualities: friendly, caring, love of learning, energetic, strong sense of duty, idealist, practical, determined, sincere, generous, love of home, active, responsible, motivated, business sense, skillful, easygoing, diplomatic, good mediator, sociable, organized, ambitious

Your less attractive qualities: materialistic, inactive, worried, unsympathetic, too economical, bossy, discontented, irresponsible, disorganized, intense, stubborn, mistrusting, demanding, resentful, interfering

Your Venus Power

The planet Venus has a great deal of influence on your powers of attraction. Below are four possible Venus types for women and men. To find your Venus you need to go to page 771, where you will find the Venus table and extra information. The planet Mars also affects your powers of attraction. To find your Mars table and interpretation go to page 761.

WOMEN WITH VENUS IN TAURUS: Warm and affectionate, you are naturally tactile with a love of sensual pleasures. With a streak of the conventional, you love the simple pleasures of life: good food, close friends, and happy relationships. Having an inner strength, you can express genuine patience and are often a pillar of support for loved ones and friends. Although you possess endurance, be careful not to let this turn into plain stubbornness.

MEN WITH VENUS IN TAURUS: As well as attracting people with your warm personality, you possess an innate sense of the value of material possessions. Keeping yourself stylish and having an attractive appearance can also be important to you. You are naturally attracted to practical yet sensual women who understand your need for comfort, security, and the pleasures and luxuries of life. Naturally affectionate, you enjoy socializing but can make a loyal and loving partner.

WOMEN WITH VENUS IN GEMINI: In relationships you need intellectual stimulation and usually prefer to keep things light. Certainly not boring, you love to talk and are at your best being witty and entertaining. Although your easygoing approach to relationships is very attractive, guard against losing touch with your deeper emotions. You prefer a partner who can keep up with your fast stream of ideas, and if you have shared interests then so much the better.

MEN WITH VENUS IN GEMINI: Informed and curious yet charming and friendly, you seek a partner who shares your interests or enjoys your witty remarks. Although a good communicator, you have an inborn tendency to be lighthearted and less profound about deep emotional commitment. Although you are keen on experiences that bring variety into your life, boredom or scattering your energies in too many di-

rections is probably your biggest handicap in relationships. Nevertheless you are attracted to intelligent partners who can match your lively banter.

WOMEN WITH VENUS IN CANCER: Gentle and tender, you are romantic by nature. You possess a strong need for security and usually help others feel safe and protected. This preservation is especially centered around the home, which is your haven from life's storm. Although your maternal instincts are strong, avoid making sacrifices for others at your own expense. Nevertheless, affectionate and caring, once committed to a relationship your loyalty and devotion to your partner are very strong.

MEN WITH VENUS IN CANCER: Being emotionally receptive you can make a sensitive lover. With your desire to care for and protect others, you are likely to have strong family connections. Love is often tied in with being attentive to the needs of others and you may find yourself attracted to individuals who have sympathetic or maternal qualities. Security-conscious, you need a loyal partner who can offer you support and ideally be a good cook and homemaker.

WOMEN WITH VENUS IN LEO: As someone who wants to radiate in her own right, you are likely to desire partners you can be proud of. You are usually attracted to fun-loving, warm and generous individuals. If self-expression is important to you, you will probably seek the company of creative people such as artists, musicians, or those with a flair for acting. Alternatively, you may be drawn to people who are dignified, regal, or have already achieved success.

MEN WITH VENUS IN LEO: A childlike nature suggests that you are versatile and keen on games or being entertained. You are usually attracted to vivacious partners with a benevolent nature. As an extrovert you enjoy being involved in all types of activities where you can assert yourself and show your talents and abilities. Others may recognize your inborn tendencies to lead but are also aware of your vanity or pride. Nevertheless, generous and caring, you often show more compassion to those less fortunate than yourself.

To read all about your Outer Planets and work out how to use your personalized timetable, go to Section Three, page 789.

Your Personalized Timetable

JUPITER BENEFICIAL
1938 4/7 – 9/15
1938 11/21 – until 1939 2/14
1940 5/4 – 6/19
1940 11/30 – until 1941 1/30
1944 7/12 – 8/29
1945 12/27 – until 1946 3/29
1946 8/25 – 11/12
1950 3/18 – until 1951 1/27
1952 4/17 – 5/30
1955 10/25 – until 1956 2/10
1956 6/21 – 8/13
1957 12/4 – until 1958 5/8
1958 7/31 – 10/27
1962 2/28 – 5/23
1962 8/11 – until 1963 1/7
1964 3/31 – 5/12
1967 10/3 – until 1968 3/22
1968 5/22 – 7/27
1969 11/15 – until 1970 10/11
1974 2/12 – 4/25
1974 9/26 – 12/10
1976 3/14 – 4/26
1979 9/15 – 11/12
1980 2/9 – 7/8
1981 10/30 – until 1982 2/17
1982 3/3 – 9/24
1986 1/27 – 4/5
1987 7/11 – 9/28
1988 2/23 – 4/10
1991 8/30 – 10/18
1992 3/19 – 6/12
1993 10/14 – until 1994 1/4
1994 4/26 – 9/3
1998 1/10 – 3/19
1999 6/12 – 11/13
2000 1/26 – 3/23
2003 8/14 – 9/30
2005 9/29 – 12/14
2006 6/6 – 8/4
2009 5/3 – 7/28
2009 12/21 – until 2010 3/2
2011 5/22 – 7/16
2011 10/14 – until 2012 3/2

SATURN BENEFICIAL
1939 6/3 – 10/29
1940 2/23 – 5/17
1948 8/27 – until 1949 8/14
1952 12/6 – until 1953 4/10
1953 9/1 – until 1954 10/20
1964 2/4 – until 1965 3/20
1969 4/8 – 7/7
1969 10/5 – until 1970 3/24
1977 10/10 – until 1978 2/14
1978 7/1 – 9/22
1979 4/25 – 5/23
1982 10/11 – until 1983 11/25
1984 6/17 – 8/8
1993 3/9 – 10/1
1993 11/23 – until 1994 5/2
1994 8/16 – until 1995 1/24
1998 5/15 – 12/6
1999 1/21 – 5/1
2007 8/11 – 11/11
2008 1/27 – 7/27
2011 11/17 – until 2012 5/12
2012 8/7 – Continues

URANUS BENEFICIAL
1961 9/6 – until 1964 7/8
1973 10/30 – until 1977 10/4
2001 4/21 – until 2006 2/21

NEPTUNE BENEFICIAL
1953 11/3 – until 1961 10/13
2008 5/24 – Continues

PLUTO BENEFICIAL
1955 9/13 – until 1961 8/13
1981 1/9 – until 1988 8/30

JUPITER CHALLENGING
1939 4/14 – until 1940 2/22

1944 11/26 – until 1945 2/28
1945 7/25 – 10/12
1948 2/18 – 6/13
1948 10/15 – 12/31
1951 3/28 – 6/14
1951 9/24 – until 1952 1/31
1956 11/3 – until 1957 4/8
1957 6/29 – 9/26
1960 1/27 – 8/3
1960 9/7 – 12/15
1963 3/11 – 5/20
1963 11/15 – 12/25
1968 10/16 – until 1969 9/11
1972 1/9 – 11/28
1975 2/22 – 5/1
1980 9/29 – until 1981 1/16
1981 2/3 – 8/24
1983 12/24 – until 1984 3/18
1984 6/12 – 11/9
1987 2/5 – 4/14
1992 9/13 – 12/4
1993 3/27 – 8/4
1995 12/9 – until 1996 2/21
1996 7/25 – 10/13
1998 5/28 – 9/7
1999 1/15 – 3/28
2004 8/29 – 11/13
2005 5/6 – 7/5
2007 11/23 – until 2008 2/2
2010 5/3 – 10/28
2010 12/9 – until 2011 3/11

SATURN CHALLENGING
1938 1/1 – 4/16
1950 9/28 – until 1951 11/8
1952 4/19 – 7/31
1958 2/21 – 5/18
1958 11/16 – until 1960 1/7
1966 4/16 – 10/17
1967 1/4 – 6/2
1967 9/16 – until 1968 2/22
1979 11/11 – until 1980 3/6
1980 8/2 – until 1981 9/14
1987 12/21 – until 1989 2/12
1989 7/7 – 11/12
1995 6/11 – 7/31
1996 2/20 – until 1997 3/30
2009 9/11 – until 2010 10/21

URANUS CHALLENGING
1966 12/11 – until 1971 7/31
1987 1/12 – until 1991 10/20
2009 4/11 – Continues

NEPTUNE CHALLENGING
1939 10/20 – until 1948 7/2
1981 2/8 – until 1989 11/9

PLUTO CHALLENGING
1968 11/1 – until 1976 8/29
2005 2/24 – Continues

JUPITER SPECIAL
1942 5/15 – 7/25
1953 9/7 – 11/21
1954 4/25 – 7/9
1965 8/10 – until 1966 1/2
1966 3/31 – 6/23
1977 7/21 – until 1978 6/6
1989 7/4 – 10/9
1989 11/17 – until 1990 5/19
2001 6/17 – 9/2
2002 1/4 – 4/26

SATURN SPECIAL
1943 8/18 – 12/2
1944 5/4 – 9/29
1944 11/16 – until 1945 6/4
1973 6/16 – until 1974 7/15
2002 7/26 – until 2003 1/3
2003 4/12 – 8/28
2003 12/25 – until 2004 5/15

URANUS SPECIAL
1947 7/25 – until 1952 4/15

June 25

SUN: CANCER · DECANATE: CANCER/MOON · DEGREE: 2°5–4° CANCER · MODE: CARDINAL · ELEMENT: WATER

Your Personal Powers

Although you are sensitive with a caring nature, your astute mind and quick perceptions urge you to be active and enterprising. Practical yet enthusiastic, you thrive on mental stimulation, and diversity. An ability to concentrate on a single issue indicates that you enjoy a mental challenge or problem solving. Your ruler, the Moon, grants you natural psychic abilities. You gain power when you combine your strong instincts and innate common sense. Since you often have many inspired ideas, it is vital that you keep yourself busy yet focused. You lose some of your powers when you permit skepticism or inner restlessness to cause you emotional discontentment. Usually you prefer to trust your own intuition or your own belief system. You generally gain more knowledge through practical application than mere theory. In order to achieve success, however, you may need to find an interest that can challenge you mentally or one that can truly inspire your imagination and creativity. You empower yourself when you become open-minded, objective, and thoughtful.

Your Powers of Attraction in Relationships

Protective and caring, you are usually a loyal and trustworthy partner. You can be good company, especially when you blend your quick perceptions with your unique sense of humor. Other people are drawn to your warmth and inspiring personality. Usually you admire enterprising or independent people who act with spontaneity. Even though you are usually sociable and charming with friends, at times you can be shy or reserved and may need to learn to express your feelings more openly. Although you can be tolerant, you display your less attractive qualities when you become moody or impatient. Romantic, you may need to take your time before you commit yourself to a serious relationship. Nevertheless, being idealistic with powerful emotions, you particularly show your strength by being supportive in family matters.

Your attractive qualities: astute, common sense, self-discipline, enthusiastic, direct, sensitive, highly intuitive, perfectionist, perceptive, creative, spontaneous, alert, caring, sociable, tolerant, self-reliant, analytical, instinctive, eye for detail, good concentration, enterprising, quick learner

Your less attractive qualities: mentally restless, careless, impulsive, irritable, irresponsible, overemotional, jealous, withdrawn, critical, moody, impatient, nervous, easily bored, discontented, worried or anxious, skeptical

Your Venus Power

The planet Venus has a great deal of influence on your powers of attraction. Below are four possible Venus types for women and men. To find your Venus you need to go to page 771, where you will find the Venus table and extra information. The planet Mars also affects your powers of attraction. To find your Mars table and interpretation go to page 761.

WOMEN WITH VENUS IN TAURUS: Being physically attractive, you can make a good impression on the opposite sex. As security and stability in relationships are very important to you, you usually want a partner who is not only attractive but also reliable and a good provider. Being sensual or tactile, you also need a lover who is affectionate, but beware that your love does not show signs of possessiveness or jealousy. Your own sense of style and love of beauty imply that you can be attracted to creative people, especially those in art and music.

MEN WITH VENUS IN TAURUS: Attractive and affectionate, in relationships you are often down-to-earth, with a conservative outlook. You are drawn to warmhearted partners with whom you can share a familiar routine as well as life's pleasures and comforts. Seeking a partner who is dependable or reassuring, you often put security high on your priority list when looking for love. Your sociability and friendliness usually make you popular and partners often admire your good sense of values and practical outlook.

WOMEN WITH VENUS IN GEMINI: By nature you are young at heart, adaptable, and sociable. Being curious and willing to cooperate makes you a good team player. Usually you are drawn to articulate people who have charm and flair or sharp wit. With a need to expand your knowledge you also look for a partner who can challenge or stimulate you intellectually. Although you love to talk with all types of people, you may need to develop your listening skills in order to build better communication in your relationships.

MEN WITH VENUS IN GEMINI: Charming, amusing, and adaptable, you attract others with your natural communication skills and friendly personality. You have a wonderful childlike quality and love to keep life playful, but a reluctance to contact your deeper feelings may cause you to avoid serious commitment. With your need for variety and intellectual

stimulation you are attracted to clever and amusing partners who have many interesting sides to their personalities.

WOMEN WITH VENUS IN CANCER: With your intuitive abilities and sympathetic nature, you are usually supportive of those you love. Impressionable and empathetic, your receptivity allows you to quickly pick up on the moods of people and you are especially aware of the emotional changes in your close partner. As you often display true maternal tendencies toward those you know, you want a partner who is considerate and sensitive.

MEN WITH VENUS IN CANCER: You seek a partner who is sympathetic, caring, and protective. Able to be forgiving and compassionate, you want a secure emotional bond in your close relationships. Usually you are drawn to partners who are maternal, unselfish, or demonstrative with their feelings. Although you can sometimes appear to others as impressionable, you have powerful emotions and inner strength.

WOMEN WITH VENUS IN LEO: You possess the wonderful ability to project your warm and sunny personality and keep others happily entertained. Loving attention yourself, you seek a partner who can appreciate you and be supportive and give you positive feedback. Proud, with a natural regal air, you expect respect from your partners but are willing to be loyal and supportive in exchange. Although sometimes a little self-centered, you know how to make your partner feel special.

MEN WITH VENUS IN LEO: Generous, animated, and pleasure-seeking, you can be very entertaining and fun to be with. Usually you are attracted to extroverted and benevolent individuals with a sunny personality. If ambitious, you are drawn to a partner who shows leadership qualities or one who is highly motivated. Your less attractive qualities are your tendencies to be bossy or vain. With a sense of the dramatic, however, you can be the life and soul of the party and inspire those around you.

To read all about your Outer Planets and work out how to use your personalized timetable, go to Section Three, page 789.

Your Personalized Timetable

JUPITER BENEFICIAL
1938 4/12 – 9/6
1938 11/30 – until **1939** 2/18
1940 5/8 – 6/24
1940 11/21 – until **1941** 2/8
1944 7/17 – 9/2
1946 1/4 – 3/21
1946 8/31 – 11/16
1950 3/22 – until **1951** 2/1
1952 4/21 – 6/3
1955 11/1 – until **1956** 2/3
1956 6/27 – 8/17
1957 12/9 – until **1958** 4/29
1958 8/7 – 10/31
1962 3/4 – 6/1
1962 8/2 – until **1963** 1/12
1964 4/4 – 5/16
1967 10/9 – until **1968** 3/12
1968 6/1 – 8/1
1969 11/20 – until **1970** 10/16
1974 2/16 – 4/30
1974 9/18 – 12/18
1976 3/18 – 4/30
1979 9/20 – 11/20
1980 1/31 – 7/13
1981 11/3 – until **1982** 9/29
1986 1/31 – 4/10
1987 7/20 – 9/19
1988 2/28 – 4/14
1991 9/3 – 10/24
1992 3/11 – 6/20
1993 10/19 – until **1994** 1/11
1994 4/19 – 9/9
1998 1/14 – 3/23
1999 6/17 – 11/5
2000 2/2 – 3/27
2003 8/19 – 10/5
2005 10/4 – 12/19
2006 5/27 – 8/14
2009 5/12 – 7/19
2009 12/26 – until **2010** 3/6
2011 5/27 – 7/24
2011 10/6 – until **2012** 3/7

SATURN BENEFICIAL
1939 6/13 – 10/17
1940 3/4 – 5/25
1940 12/22 – until **1941** 1/27
1948 9/4 – until **1949** 8/22
1952 12/17 – until **1953** 3/28
1953 9/11 – until **1954** 10/28
1964 2/12 – until **1965** 3/28
1965 10/16 – 12/12
1969 4/15 – 7/22
1969 9/19 – until **1970** 4/1
1977 10/20 – until **1978** 2/2
1978 7/10 – 9/30
1979 4/3 – 6/14
1982 10/19 – until **1983** 12/4
1984 5/29 – 8/25
1993 3/18 – 9/13
1993 12/10 – until **1994** 5/15
1994 8/1 – until **1995** 2/2
1998 5/23 – 11/18
1999 2/7 – 5/8
2007 8/19 – 11/30
2008 1/8 – 8/5
2011 11/26 – until **2012** 4/28
2012 8/20 – Continues

URANUS BENEFICIAL
1961 9/22 – until **1964** 7/27
1973 11/14 – until **1977** 10/21
2002 2/20 – until **2006** 12/20

NEPTUNE BENEFICIAL
1953 12/2 – until **1962** 9/4
2009 3/19 – Continues

PLUTO BENEFICIAL
1955 10/21 – until **1962** 7/11
1981 11/10 – until **1988** 10/2

JUPITER CHALLENGING
1939 4/18 – until **1940** 2/26
1944 12/4 – until **1945** 2/20
1945 7/30 – 10/16
1948 2/24 – 6/6
1948 10/21 – until **1949** 1/4
1951 4/1 – 6/21
1951 9/17 – until **1952** 2/5
1956 11/8 – until **1957** 3/31
1957 7/7 – 10/1
1960 2/1 – 7/21
1960 9/20 – 12/19
1963 3/15 – 5/25
1963 11/3 – until **1964** 1/5
1968 10/20 – until **1969** 9/15
1972 1/14 – 12/2
1975 2/26 – 5/5
1980 10/4 – until **1981** 8/29
1983 12/28 – until **1984** 3/26
1984 6/2 – 11/14
1987 2/9 – 4/18
1992 9/18 – 12/11
1993 3/19 – 8/10
1995 12/13 – until **1996** 2/26
1996 7/16 – 10/21
1998 6/5 – 8/30
1999 1/20 – 4/1
2004 9/2 – 11/19
2005 4/26 – 7/15
2007 11/27 – until **2008** 2/7
2010 5/8 – 10/17
2010 12/20 – until **2011** 3/15

SATURN CHALLENGING
1938 1/1 – 4/24
1950 10/6 – until **1951** 11/17
1952 4/6 – 8/11
1958 3/11 – 4/29
1958 11/25 – until **1960** 1/15
1966 4/25 – 10/3
1967 1/17 – 6/16
1967 9/2 – until **1968** 3/2
1979 11/22 – until **1980** 2/22
1980 8/12 – until **1981** 9/22
1987 12/29 – until **1989** 2/22
1989 6/24 – 11/22
1996 2/28 – until **1997** 4/7
2009 9/19 – until **2010** 10/29
2011 5/13 – 7/13

URANUS CHALLENGING
1967 9/24 – until **1971** 8/22
1987 1/30 – until **1991** 11/16
2009 5/1 – Continues

NEPTUNE CHALLENGING
1939 11/25 – until **1948** 8/22
1982 1/2 – until **1989** 12/9

PLUTO CHALLENGING
1969 9/25 – until **1976** 9/24
2006 1/9 – Continues

JUPITER SPECIAL
1942 5/19 – 7/30
1953 9/17 – 11/11
1954 4/30 – 7/13
1965 8/16 – 12/26
1966 4/7 – 6/27
1977 7/26 – until **1978** 6/10
1989 7/8 – until **1990** 5/24
2001 6/21 – 9/9
2001 12/28 – until **2002** 5/2

SATURN SPECIAL
1943 8/30 – 11/19
1944 5/13 – until **1945** 6/12
1973 6/23 – until **1974** 7/22
2002 8/4 – 12/22
2003 4/22 – 9/8
2003 12/13 – until **2004** 5/24

URANUS SPECIAL
1947 8/15 – until **1952** 5/12

203

June 26

SUN: CANCER • DECANATE: CANCER/MOON • DEGREE: 3°5–5° CANCER • MODE: CARDINAL • ELEMENT: WATER

Your Personal Powers

Intuitive and astute, you are an instinctive and observant individual with strong premonitions. Sensitive, your caring nature is often concerned with the welfare of other people. As an enthusiastic individual you enjoy being active and purposeful. Your ruler, the Moon, grants you sensitivity, insight, strong feelings, and an affectionate nature. Since security and stability are very important to your peace of mind, you work toward creating harmony in your home or working environment. Versatile and creative, you gain power when you trust your own judgment and present to the world a confident and assertive front. With good organizational skills and a natural business sense, you are often an intuitive strategist who can solve problems by using your knowledge in a constructive way. You also gain power by using your innate wisdom, diplomacy, and powers of persuasion. You may lose some of your power, however, if you let fluctuating moods or restlessness cloud your decision-making or affect your common sense. Since you constantly want to widen your horizons, you benefit greatly from any form of learning or higher education.

Your Powers of Attraction in Relationships

Affectionate and sociable, others admire your friendly and sympathetic nature. You are likely to have many friends and usually keep in close touch with other family members. Since you need the affections of those you love, you often go to great lengths to make everyone happy. Although you usually have good intentions, you need to guard against stretching yourself too far trying to please all and ending by pleasing no one. Being romantic and idealistic you may be drawn to unconventional or unusual individuals or relationships. Although you need to feel secure in a family or loving environment, a side to your nature dreams of freedom and independence. Your key to successful relationships is often in your ability to compromise and be flexible.

Your attractive qualities: friendly, sensitive, considerate, practical, responsible, good negotiator, educated, inquisitive, quick comprehension, common sense, creative, caring, imaginative, strategist, enthusiastic, determined, organized, enterprising, business sense, security conscious, tolerant, kind

Your less attractive qualities: unsympathetic, opinionated, mistrusting, worried, stubborn, restless, intolerant, impatient, bored easily, insecure, uncaring, unenthusiastic, overanxious, too emotional, inner tensions, lack of purpose

Your Venus Power

The planet Venus has a great deal of influence on your powers of attraction. Below are four possible Venus types for women and men. To find your Venus you need to go to page 771, where you will find the Venus table and extra information. The planet Mars also affects your powers of attraction. To find your Mars table and interpretation go to page 761.

WOMEN WITH VENUS IN TAURUS: Good-natured and romantic, you have a highly developed sense of touch that particularly responds to massage, hugs, and all things physical. Being friendly, you enjoy socializing and are able to put others at their ease. With your innate sense of beauty and harmony, your natural charm can attract others. Although you can be lavish toward your partner you may have to be careful that you do not overdo things.

MEN WITH VENUS IN TAURUS: Attractive and affectionate, in relationships you are often down-to-earth, with a conservative outlook. You are drawn to warmhearted partners with whom you can share a familiar routine as well as life's pleasures and comforts. Seeking a partner who is dependable or reassuring, you often put security high on your priority list when looking for love. Your sociability and friendliness usually make you popular and partners often admire your good sense of values and practical skills.

WOMEN WITH VENUS IN GEMINI: In relationships you need intellectual stimulation and usually prefer to keep things light. Certainly not boring, you love to talk and are at your best being witty and entertaining. Although your easygoing approach to relationships is very attractive, guard against losing touch with your deeper emotions. You prefer a partner who can keep up with your fast stream of ideas, and if you have shared interests then so much the better.

MEN WITH VENUS IN GEMINI: Charming, amusing, and adaptable, you attract others with your natural communication skills and friendly personality. You have a wonderful childlike quality and love to keep life playful, but a reluctance to contact your deeper feelings may cause you to avoid serious commitment. With your need for variety and intellectual stimulation, you are attracted to clever and amusing partners who have many interesting sides to their personalities.

WOMEN WITH VENUS IN CANCER: Gentle and tender, you are romantic by nature. You possess a strong need for security and usually help others feel safe and protected. This preservation is especially centered around the home, which is your haven from life's storm. Although your maternal instincts are strong, avoid making sacrifices for others at your own expense. Nevertheless, affectionate and caring, once committed to a relationship, your loyalty and devotion to your partner are very strong.

MEN WITH VENUS IN CANCER: You seek a partner who is sympathetic, caring, and protective. Able to be forgiving and compassionate, you want a secure emotional bond in your close relationships. Usually you are drawn to partners who are maternal, unselfish, or demonstrative with their feelings. Although you can sometimes appear to others as impressionable, you have powerful emotions and inner strength.

WOMEN WITH VENUS IN LEO: You possess the wonderful ability to project your warm and sunny personality and keep others happily entertained. Loving attention yourself, you seek a partner who can appreciate you, be supportive, and give you positive feedback. Proud with a natural regal air, you expect respect from your partners but are willing to be loyal and supportive in exchange. Although sometimes a little self-centered, you know how to make your partner feel special.

MEN WITH VENUS IN LEO: Enthusiastic, playful, and kind, you can be benevolent with those you love. Warm, romantic, and self-expressive, you adore the drama of love or having fun with your friends. Usually you are attracted to partners with a warm and generous nature. Although you can be a confident and charismatic partner, you may need to develop humility to stop pride or arrogance from marring your relationships.

To read all about your Outer Planets and work out how to use your personalized timetable, go to Section Three, page 789.

To read all about your Outer Planets and work out how to use your personalized timetable, go to Section Three, page 789.

Your Personalized Timetable

JUPITER BENEFICIAL
1938 4/17 – 8/29
1938 12/7 – until 1939 2/22
1940 5/12 – 6/29
1940 11/14 – until 1941 2/15
1944 7/21 – 9/6
1946 1/14 – 3/11
1946 9/5 – 11/20
1950 3/27 – until 1951 2/5
1952 4/25 – 6/7
1955 11/9 – until 1956 1/26
1956 7/3 – 8/22
1957 12/15 – until 1958 4/22
1958 8/14 – 11/5
1962 3/8 – 6/14
1962 7/20 – until 1963 1/17
1964 4/8 – 5/20
1967 10/14 – until 1968 3/4
1968 6/9 – 8/6
1969 11/25 – until 1970 6/16
1970 6/30 – 10/20
1974 2/20 – 5/6
1974 9/11 – 12/24
1976 3/22 – 5/4
1979 9/25 – 11/30
1980 1/21 – 7/19
1981 11/8 – until 1982 10/3
1986 2/4 – 4/14
1987 8/1 – 9/7
1988 3/4 – 4/18
1991 9/8 – 10/30
1992 3/4 – 6/27
1993 10/23 – until 1994 1/18
1994 4/10 – 9/15
1998 1/18 – 3/27
1999 6/23 – 10/29
2000 2/9 – 3/31
2003 8/23 – 10/10
2004 4/23 – 5/17
2005 10/8 – 12/25
2006 5/19 – 8/22
2009 5/23 – 7/8
2009 12/31 – until 2010 3/10
2011 5/31 – 8/3
2011 9/26 – until 2012 3/12

SATURN BENEFICIAL
1939 6/24 – 10/4
1940 3/13 – 6/2
1940 12/2 – until 1941 2/15
1948 9/12 – until 1949 8/30
1952 12/30 – until 1953 3/14
1953 9/19 – until 1954 11/5
1964 2/20 – until 1965 4/6
1965 9/29 – 12/28
1969 4/23 – until 1970 4/9
1977 11/2 – until 1978 1/20
1978 7/19 – 10/9
1979 3/19 – 6/28
1982 10/27 – until 1983 12/13
1984 5/15 – 9/7
1993 3/27 – 8/30
1993 12/22 – until 1994 6/6
1994 7/10 – until 1995 2/10
1998 6/1 – 11/5
1999 2/19 – 5/16
2007 8/26 – until 2008 8/12
2011 12/5 – until 2012 4/16
2012 8/31 – Continues

URANUS BENEFICIAL
1961 10/11 – until 1964 8/13
1973 12/2 – until 1977 11/5
2002 3/9 – until 2007 1/16

NEPTUNE BENEFICIAL
1954 10/29 – until 1962 10/7
2009 4/24 – Continues

PLUTO BENEFICIAL
1956 9/17 – until 1962 8/13
1981 12/8 – until 1988 10/27

JUPITER CHALLENGING
1939 4/23 – until 1940 3/1
1944 12/13 – until 1945 2/10

1945 8/5 – 10/21
1948 3/3 – 5/29
1948 10/26 – until 1949 1/8
1951 4/5 – 6/29
1951 9/9 – until 1952 2/10
1956 11/14 – until 1957 3/23
1957 7/14 – 10/5
1960 2/6 – 7/11
1960 9/29 – 12/23
1963 3/19 – 5/30
1963 10/26 – until 1964 1/14
1968 10/25 – until 1969 5/18
1969 5/28 – 9/20
1972 1/18 – 12/7
1975 3/2 – 5/9
1980 10/8 – until 1981 9/3
1984 1/2 – 4/7
1984 5/22 – 11/19
1987 2/14 – 4/22
1992 9/22 – 12/19
1993 3/11 – 8/15
1995 12/17 – until 1996 3/3
1996 7/9 – 10/27
1998 6/13 – 8/21
1999 1/25 – 4/5
2004 9/7 – 11/24
2005 4/18 – 7/23
2007 12/1 – until 2008 2/11
2010 5/13 – 10/8
2010 12/28 – until 2011 3/19

SATURN CHALLENGING
1938 1/1 – 5/2
1938 11/12 – until 1939 1/15
1950 10/14 – until 1951 5/2
1951 6/25 – 11/27
1952 3/25 – 8/21
1958 12/3 – until 1960 1/24
1960 8/26 – 10/6
1966 5/5 – 9/21
1967 1/28 – 7/6
1967 8/12 – until 1968 3/10
1979 12/7 – until 1980 2/7
1980 8/20 – until 1981 9/30
1988 1/7 – 8/13
1988 9/15 – until 1989 3/6
1989 6/10 – 12/1
1996 3/7 – until 1997 4/15
2009 9/27 – until 2010 11/7
2011 4/27 – 7/29

URANUS CHALLENGING
1967 10/9 – until 1971 9/8
1987 2/23 – until 1991 12/5
2009 5/28 – Continues

NEPTUNE CHALLENGING
1940 10/13 – until 1948 9/20
1982 1/31 – until 1990 10/29

PLUTO CHALLENGING
1969 10/22 – until 1977 8/13
2006 2/10 – Continues

JUPITER SPECIAL
1942 5/24 – 8/3
1953 10/1 – 10/28
1954 5/5 – 7/17
1965 8/21 – 12/19
1966 4/13 – 7/1
1977 7/30 – until 1978 2/13
1978 2/26 – 6/15
1989 7/12 – until 1990 5/28
2001 6/26 – 9/15
2001 12/20 – until 2002 5/8

SATURN SPECIAL
1943 9/17 – 11/1
1944 5/21 – until 1945 6/19
1973 7/1 – until 1974 7/30
1975 2/27 – 3/29
2002 8/14 – 12/10
2003 5/2 – 9/21
2003 11/29 – until 2004 6/1

URANUS SPECIAL
1947 9/27 – until 1952 6/1

205

June 27

Your Personal Powers

In your quest for diversity and mental stimulation, you may seek different experiences that can enrich your life. Your ruler, the Moon, grants you emotional receptivity, natural psychic abilities, and an affectionate nature. As a caring person and good conversationalist, you inspire others with your idealism and witty repartee. Being sympathetic to others, you are often a good listener. Nevertheless, sensitive and intuitive, you may prefer to remain reserved until you make up your own mind. You lose some of your power, however, if you allow doubts or indecisiveness to deplete your energies. You gain power when you develop the necessary patience to plan ahead or develop a long-term strategy. With self-discipline, your ability to endure and your enterprising nature can bring you good results. You also empower yourself when you have purpose or a goal that inspires you to express your natural creativity and versatility. Your highly developed perception suggests that you are good at assessing situations and recognizing the strengths and weaknesses in others.

Your Powers of Attraction in Relationships

Other people are drawn to your friendly nature and often admire your quick mental approach. Idealistic and romantic, you can be very affectionate toward your partner. A love of fun or excitement often inspires you to be sociable, yet a tendency to feel moody implies that you may alternate from appearing warm one minute to cold the next. Your sensitivity indicates that you are drawn to people who can inspire you to express your thoughts and creative ideas. Nevertheless, your paternal instincts and caring nature suggest that you are usually protective toward your partners and show a willingness to make sacrifices for those you love. Your excellent sense of humor and witty repartee indicate that usually you are good company. Personal relationships work better if both of you are generous, sympathetic, and communicative.

Your attractive qualities: intellectually bright, versatile, decisive, focused, psychic, analytical, gregarious, sensitive, imaginative, enterprising, resolute, idealistic, harmonious, creative, tolerant, understanding, compassionate, proud, witty, dignified, practical, inventive, quick perceptions

Your less attractive qualities: disagreeable, arrogant, indecisive, moody, uncaring, manipulative, indulgent, easily offended, argumentative, mistrusting, high-strung, tense, worried, self-doubt, resentful, uncommunicative

Your Venus Power

The planet Venus has a great deal of influence on your powers of attraction. Below are four possible Venus types for women and men. To find your Venus you need to go to page 771, where you will find the Venus table and extra information. The planet Mars also affects your powers of attraction. To find your Mars table and interpretation go to page 761.

WOMEN WITH VENUS IN TAURUS: For your ideal relationship, you seek a partner who is both financially secure and demonstrative with his affections. With these thoughts in mind you are likely to want a partner who is refined yet pragmatic or someone concerned with safeguarding your future. Your stubborn streak suggests that even when you know you are in the wrong you are reluctant to give way. Attracted to people with a good sense of style, you can succeed in all kinds of business partnerships, especially those involving the arts, music, and luxury goods.

MEN WITH VENUS IN TAURUS: Attractive and affectionate, in relationships you are often down-to-earth, with a conservative outlook. You are drawn to warmhearted partners with whom you can share a familiar routine as well as life's pleasures and comforts. Seeking a partner who is dependable or reassuring, you often put security high on your priority list when looking for love. Your sociability and friendliness usually make you popular and partners often admire your good sense of values and practical outlook.

WOMEN WITH VENUS IN GEMINI: Articulate, versatile, and youthful, your personal magnetism is often linked to your charm, wit, and communication skills. You seek a partner who is clever, can communicate with you at ease, and can share your thoughts and interests. Since you find it easy to mix with people you have many friends. When you do find someone you can communicate with, you can easily lose yourself in long conversations.

MEN WITH VENUS IN GEMINI: Charming, amusing, and adaptable, you attract others with your natural communication skills and friendly personality. You have a wonderful childlike quality and love to keep life playful, but a reluctance to contact your deeper feelings may cause you to avoid serious commitment. With your need for variety and intellectual

stimulation, you are attracted to clever and amusing partners who have many interesting sides to their personalities.

WOMEN WITH VENUS IN CANCER: With your intuitive abilities and sympathetic nature, you are usually supportive of those you love. Impressionable and empathetic, your receptivity allows you to quickly pick up on people's moods and you are especially aware of the emotional changes in your close partner. As you often display true maternal tendencies toward those you know, you want a partner who is considerate and sensitive.

MEN WITH VENUS IN CANCER: As well as attracting people with your warm personality, you possess an innate sense of the value of material possessions. Keeping yourself stylish and having an attractive appearance can also be important to you. You are naturally attracted to practical yet sensual women who understand your need for comfort, security, and the pleasures and luxuries of life. Naturally affectionate, you enjoy socializing but can be a loyal and loving partner.

WOMEN WITH VENUS IN LEO: As a person who wants to radiate in their own right, you are likely to desire partners you can be proud of. Usually you are attracted to fun-loving, warm, and generous individuals. If self-expression is important to you, you will probably seek the company of creative people such as artists, musicians, or those with a flair for acting. Alternatively, you may be drawn to people who are dignified, regal, or have already achieved success.

MEN WITH VENUS IN LEO: Sociable and outgoing, you are kind and generous with those you love. Looking for a relationship that can be fun and entertaining, you need a playmate who can share your enthusiasm and high spirits. Your pride, however, often stops you from associating with lovers or partners you see as beneath you. As you desire someone who can appreciate your sense of the dramatic, you are often attracted to people with strong personalities.

To read all about your Outer Planets and work out how to use your personalized timetable, go to Section Three, page 789.

To read all about your Outer Planets and work out how to use your personalized timetable, go to Section Three, page 789.

♋

Your Personalized Timetable

JUPITER BENEFICIAL
1938   4/23 – 8/22
1938   12/13 – until 1939 2/26
1940   5/16 – 7/5
1940   11/6 – until 1941 2/21
1944   7/26 – 9/11
1946   1/29 – 2/23
1946   9/10 – 11/25
1950   3/31 – until 1951 2/9
1952   4/29 – 6/12
1955   11/18 – until 1956 1/16
1956   7/8 – 8/26
1957   12/21 – until 1958 4/14
1958   8/21 – 11/9
1962   3/13 – until 1963 1/22
1964   4/12 – 5/24
1967   10/20 – until 1968 2/26
1968   6/16 – 8/10
1969   11/30 – until 1970 5/28
1970   7/19 – 10/24
1974   2/24 – 5/12
1974   9/4 – 12/30
1976   3/26 – 5/8
1979   9/30 – 12/17
1980   1/4 – 7/24
1981   11/12 – until 1982 10/8
1986   2/8 – 4/19
1986   10/30 – 11/17
1988   3/9 – 4/22
1991   9/12 – 11/5
1992   2/25 – 7/3
1993   10/27 – until 1994 1/27
1994   4/1 – 9/20
1998   1/23 – 3/31
1999   6/29 – 10/22
2000   2/15 – 4/5
2003   8/27 – 10/15
2004   4/7 – 6/2
2005   10/12 – 12/30
2006   5/11 – 8/29
2010   1/4 – 3/14
2011   6/5 – 8/18
2011   9/11 – until 2012 3/16

SATURN BENEFICIAL
1939   7/8 – 9/20
1940   3/21 – 6/11
1940   11/19 – until 1941 2/28
1948   9/20 – until 1949 4/1
1949   5/31 – 9/6
1953   1/21 – 2/19
1953   9/28 – until 1954 11/13
1964   2/27 – until 1965 4/15
1965   9/16 – until 1966 1/9
1969   4/30 – until 1970 4/17
1977   11/20 – until 1978 1/2
1978   7/27 – 10/18
1979   3/7 – 7/10
1982   11/4 – until 1983 12/22
1984   5/3 – 9/18
1993   4/6 – 8/17
1994   1/2 – until 1995 2/18
1998   6/10 – 10/24
1999   3/2 – until 1999 5/24
2007   9/3 – until 2008 8/20
2011   12/16 – until 2012 4/3
2012   9/9 – Continues

URANUS BENEFICIAL
1938   1/1 – 2/17
1961   11/5 – until 1964 8/28
1973   12/25 – until 1978 9/2
2002   3/27 – until 2007 2/5

NEPTUNE BENEFICIAL
1954   11/25 – until 1963 8/23
2010   3/12 – Continues

PLUTO BENEFICIAL
1956   10/26 – until 1963 7/8
1982   10/26 – until 1989 9/12

JUPITER CHALLENGING
1939   4/27 – until 1940 3/6

1944   12/27 – until 1945 1/27
1945   8/10 – 10/25
1948   3/11 – 5/20
1948   10/31 – until 1949 1/12
1951   4/9 – 7/9
1951   8/29 – until 1952 2/15
1956   11/20 – until 1957 3/16
1957   7/20 – 10/10
1960   2/12 – 7/3
1960   10/7 – 12/27
1963   3/23 – 6/4
1963   10/18 – until 1964 1/21
1968   10/30 – until 1969 4/27
1969   6/18 – 9/24
1972   1/23 – 12/11
1975   3/6 – 5/14
1980   10/13 – until 1981 9/8
1984   1/6 – 11/24
1987   2/18 – 4/26
1992   9/27 – 12/27
1993   3/2 – 8/21
1995   12/21 – until 1996 3/9
1996   7/1 – 11/2
1998   6/23 – 8/11
1999   1/30 – 4/9
2004   9/11 – 11/30
2005   4/10 – 7/30
2007   12/6 – until 2008 2/16
2008   8/20 – 9/27
2010   5/18 – 10/1
2011   1/5 – 3/23

SATURN CHALLENGING
1938   1/1 – 5/11
1938   10/28 – until 1939 1/30
1950   10/22 – until 1951 4/14
1951   7/11 – 12/9
1952   3/12 – 8/31
1958   12/12 – until 1960 2/1
1960   8/5 – 10/26
1966   5/15 – 9/8
1967   2/6 – until 1968 3/18
1980   8/28 – until 1981 10/8
1988   1/15 – 7/22
1988   10/7 – until 1989 3/22
1989   5/25 – 12/10
1996   3/14 – until 1997 4/23
2009   10/4 – until 2010 11/15
2011   4/14 – 8/10

URANUS CHALLENGING
1967   10/26 – until 1971 9/24
1987   12/22 – until 1991 12/22
2010   3/26 – Continues

NEPTUNE CHALLENGING
1940   11/14 – until 1949 8/15
1982   12/28 – until 1990 12/4

PLUTO CHALLENGING
1969   11/28 – until 1977 9/12
2007   1/3 – Continues

JUPITER SPECIAL
1942   5/28 – 8/8
1954   5/10 – 7/21
1965   8/28 – 12/11
1966   4/19 – 7/5
1977   8/4 – until 1978 1/26
1978   3/17 – 6/19
1989   7/17 – until 1990 6/2
2001   6/30 – 9/23
2001   12/13 – until 2002 5/13

SATURN SPECIAL
1944   5/28 – until 1945 6/27
1973   7/8 – until 1974 8/7
1975   2/6 – 4/19
2002   8/25 – 11/28
2003   5/11 – 10/14
2003   11/6 – until 2004 6/9

URANUS SPECIAL
1948   7/1 – until 1952 6/18

207

June 28

Your Personal Powers

Astute and sensitive, you are an observant and highly intuitive individual with powerful emotions and quick perceptions. Your ruler, the Moon, grants you depth of feeling, a strong sixth sense, and good imagination. As a dynamic and enterprising person, you succeed admirably when you incorporate your people skills or ability to communicate with others on a personal level and your need to accomplish. Often presenting a confident front, you can usually hide your inner doubts and fears from other people by appearing proud and assertive. Although you may prefer diplomacy to direct confrontation, you lose some of your power if you fail to relate your true thoughts and feelings. Nevertheless, you are a persuasive communicator and can empower yourself if you remain detached and rational. Your ability to persevere indicates that you can also be tenacious and determined. Although you enjoy collaborating with others, your natural leadership ability suggests you usually want a central role or to work for yourself. Usually charismatic and friendly, you can be witty and entertaining.

Your Powers of Attraction in Relationships

Other people find your charming and friendly manner engaging, and with your ability to make other people feel special you often make a good impression. Usually you are attracted to enterprising or optimistic individuals who can respond to your witty banter. You also enjoy being with intelligent people with whom you can have intellectual conversations. Being sentimental, however, means that holding on to old memories or partners can create obstacles to the formation of new relationships. Although you are reluctant to show your true sensitivity out of fear of losing the upper hand, other people often prefer your openness and sincerity. By learning to cooperate with others without becoming overly dependent or too serious with your partner you can achieve the right balance in your close relationships.

Your attractive qualities: self-reliant, collaborative, entertaining, witty, articulate, compromising, generous, enterprising, intuitive, communicative, people skills, pragmatic, determined, charismatic, independent, idealistic, compassionate, progressive, creative, hardworking, persuasive, caring

Your less attractive qualities: impressionable, manipulative, intolerant, too proud, moody, too sensitive, self-doubts, argumentative, unrealistic, bossy, easily bored, restless, sarcastic, codependent

Your Venus Power

The planet Venus has a great deal of influence on your powers of attraction. Below are four possible Venus types for women and men. To find your Venus you need to go to page 771, where you will find the Venus table and extra information. The planet Mars also affects your powers of attraction. To find your Mars table and interpretation go to page 761.

WOMEN WITH VENUS IN TAURUS: Warm and affectionate, you are naturally tactile with a love of sensual pleasures. With a streak of the conventional, you love the simple pleasures of life: good food, close friends, and happy relationships. Having an inner strength, you can express genuine patience and are often a pillar of support for loved ones and friends. Although you possess endurance, be careful not to let this turn into plain stubbornness.

MEN WITH VENUS IN TAURUS: As well as attracting people with your warm personality, you possess an innate sense of the value of material possessions. Keeping yourself stylish and having an attractive appearance can also be important to you. You are naturally attracted to practical yet sensual women who understand your need for comfort, security, and the pleasures and luxuries of life. Naturally affectionate, you enjoy socializing but can be a loyal and loving partner.

WOMEN WITH VENUS IN GEMINI: By nature you are young at heart, adaptable, and sociable. Being curious and willing to cooperate makes you a good team player. Usually you are drawn to articulate people who have charm and flair or sharp wit. With a need to expand your knowledge you also look for a partner who can challenge or stimulate you intellectually. Although you love to talk with all types of people, you may need to develop your listening skills in order to build better communication in your relationships.

MEN WITH VENUS IN GEMINI: Informed and curious yet charming and friendly, you seek a partner who shares your interests or enjoys your witty remarks. Although a good communicator, you have an inborn tendency to be lighthearted and less profound about deep emotional commitment. Although you are keen on experiences that bring variety into your life, boredom or scattering your energies in too many directions is probably your biggest handicap in relationships.

Nevertheless, you are attracted to intelligent partners who can match your lively banter.

WOMEN WITH VENUS IN CANCER: Possessing a soft femininity, you have tender and sensitive emotions. Sympathetic and caring, you often mother those in your care by making sure they are comfortable and have plenty to eat. When you feel hurt or insecure in relationships you are likely to cover your feelings by being defensive or appearing tough on the outside while on the inside you are feeling vulnerable. Affectionate and romantic, you make a faithful and devoted partner.

MEN WITH VENUS IN CANCER: Affectionate with a strong sensitive streak, you can love very deeply. You may find yourself drawn to sympathetic partners who can tune in to your moods and feelings as well as be reassuring and supportive. Family links are especially important to you, and the more positive these relationships are the more confident and safe you feel.

WOMEN WITH VENUS IN LEO: Warm and playful with a touch of the dramatic, you enjoy the company of generous or strong individuals who can share your sense of fun. Although there are advantages to your being strong-willed, in your relationships you need to resist being bossy as it can cause resentment. With your wonderful mixture of regal authority and childlike wonder, you love to keep others entertained and amused.

MEN WITH VENUS IN LEO: Your friendly and sunny personality often makes you stand out in a crowd. Generous and giving, you know how to make your partner feel special. As you often expect loyalty and devotion from your partners in return, you can become easily offended if they ignore you or behave in an inconsiderate manner. Charming and kind, when you are in love you can be romantic, dramatic, and passionate.

To read all about your Outer Planets and work out how to use your personalized timetable, go to Section Three, page 789.

Your Personalized Timetable

JUPITER BENEFICIAL
1938 4/29 – 8/15
1938 12/19 – until **1939** 3/2
1940 5/21 – 7/11
1940 10/30 – until **1941** 2/27
1944 7/31 – 9/15
1946 9/15 – 11/29
1950 4/5 – 10/7
1950 11/9 – until **1951** 2/13
1952 5/3 – 6/17
1952 12/29 – until **1953** 1/11
1955 12/1 – until **1956** 1/3
1956 7/13 – 8/30
1957 12/28 – until **1958** 4/7
1958 8/27 – 11/13
1962 3/17 – until **1963** 1/26
1964 4/16 – 5/29
1967 10/26 – until **1968** 2/19
1968 6/22 – 8/15
1969 12/5 – until **1970** 5/17
1970 7/30 – 10/29
1974 2/28 – 5/18
1974 8/27 – until **1975** 1/5
1976 3/31 – 5/12
1979 10/5 – until **1980** 4/3
1980 5/19 – 7/29
1981 11/17 – until **1982** 10/13
1986 2/12 – 4/24
1986 10/13 – 12/3
1988 3/13 – 4/26
1991 9/17 – 11/12
1992 2/18 – 7/9
1993 11/1 – until **1994** 2/9
1994 3/19 – 9/25
1998 1/27 – 4/4
1999 7/5 – 10/15
2000 2/21 – 4/9
2003 9/1 – 10/20
2004 3/28 – 6/12
2005 10/17 – until **2006** 1/5
2006 5/4 – 9/5
2010 1/9 – 3/18
2011 6/9 – 12/5
2012 1/14 – 3/21

SATURN BENEFICIAL
1939 7/30 – 8/29
1940 3/29 – 6/20
1940 11/6 – until **1941** 3/11
1948 9/28 – until **1949** 3/16
1949 6/15 – 9/14
1953 10/6 – until **1954** 11/21
1964 3/7 – until **1965** 4/25
1965 9/3 – until **1966** 1/19
1969 5/8 – until **1970** 4/24
1978 8/4 – 10/28
1979 2/23 – 7/19
1982 11/12 – until **1983** 6/11
1983 7/21 – until **1984** 1/2
1984 4/20 – 9/28
1993 4/17 – 8/5
1994 1/11 – until **1995** 2/26
1998 6/20 – 10/12
1999 3/11 – 6/1
1999 12/14 – until **2000** 2/10
2007 9/11 – until **2008** 8/28
2011 12/28 – until **2012** 3/20
2012 9/18 – Continues

URANUS BENEFICIAL
1938 1/1 – 3/16
1962 8/27 – until **1965** 6/16
1974 10/20 – until **1978** 9/24
2002 4/20 – until **2007** 2/22

NEPTUNE BENEFICIAL
1955 1/5 – until **1963** 10/2
2010 4/12 – Continues

PLUTO BENEFICIAL
1957 9/21 – until **1963** 8/11
1982 11/20 – until **1989** 10/11

JUPITER CHALLENGING
1939 5/2 – until **1940** 3/10

1945 8/15 – 10/30
1948 3/22 – 5/9
1948 11/5 – until **1949** 1/17
1951 4/13 – 7/27
1951 8/11 – until **1952** 2/20
1956 11/27 – until **1957** 3/8
1957 7/26 – 10/14
1960 2/17 – 6/25
1960 10/13 – 12/31
1963 3/27 – 6/10
1963 10/11 – until **1964** 1/27
1968 11/4 – until **1969** 4/16
1969 6/29 – 9/29
1972 1/27 – 12/15
1975 3/10 – 5/18
1980 10/17 – until **1981** 9/12
1984 1/10 – 11/28
1987 2/22 – 4/30
1992 10/1 – until **1993** 1/9
1993 2/17 – 8/26
1995 12/25 – until **1996** 3/16
1996 6/24 – 11/8
1999 2/4 – 4/13
2004 9/16 – 12/6
2005 4/2 – 8/6
2007 12/10 – until **2008** 2/21
2008 8/7 – 10/9
2010 5/24 – 9/23
2011 1/11 – 3/27

SATURN CHALLENGING
1938 1/1 – 5/20
1938 10/15 – until **1939** 2/10
1950 10/31 – until **1951** 4/1
1951 7/24 – 12/23
1952 2/26 – 9/8
1958 12/20 – until **1960** 2/10
1960 7/22 – 11/8
1966 5/27 – 8/26
1967 2/15 – until **1968** 3/25
1980 9/5 – until **1981** 10/16
1988 1/24 – 7/6
1988 10/21 – until **1989** 12/18
1996 3/22 – until **1997** 5/1
1997 11/22 – until **1998** 1/9
2009 10/12 – until **2010** 5/14
2010 6/16 – 11/25
2011 4/1 – 8/20

URANUS CHALLENGING
1967 11/14 – until **1971** 10/9
1988 1/7 – until **1992** 9/29
2010 4/13 – Continues

NEPTUNE CHALLENGING
1941 10/8 – until **1949** 9/15
1983 1/24 – until **1991** 10/12

PLUTO CHALLENGING
1970 10/13 – until **1978** 7/18
2007 2/1 – Continues

JUPITER SPECIAL
1942 6/1 – 8/12
1954 5/15 – 7/26
1965 9/4 – 12/4
1966 4/25 – 7/9
1977 8/9 – until **1978** 1/16
1978 3/27 – 6/23
1989 7/21 – until **1990** 6/6
2001 7/4 – 10/1
2001 12/4 – until **2002** 5/19

SATURN SPECIAL
1944 6/5 – until **1945** 7/4
1973 7/16 – until **1974** 2/10
1974 3/16 – 8/15
1975 1/23 – 5/2
2002 9/8 – 11/14
2003 5/19 – until **2004** 6/17

URANUS SPECIAL
1948 7/17 – until **1952** 7/4

June 29

SUN: CANCER • DECANATE: CANCER/MOON • DEGREE: 6°–7°5 CANCER • MODE: CARDINAL • ELEMENT: WATER

Your Personal Powers

Receptive, graceful, and mentally quick, you possess a natural ability to assess people. With the addition of your heightened sensitivity, you can usually sense what others feel or think. Your ruler, the Moon, grants you depth of feelings, natural intuition, and a strong sixth sense. Although you project a strong personality, inwardly you are often romantic, idealistic, and softhearted. Personal relationships therefore figure high on your list of priorities. Although you can be quite resolute, a tendency to act on impulse also implies that you can be hasty and sometimes jump into action without thinking. Curious and intelligent, you like to be well-informed. You gain power when you are inspired to become involved in the pursuit of a particular field of study. If you regularly change your goals, however, you may lose some of your power. With your natural leadership ability, if something really captures your imagination you can become an expert or a leading authority in your area of interest.

Your Powers of Attraction in Relationships

Usually your social skills are impeccable and your responses are quick and witty. Being concerned for the welfare of others, you can easily attract people with your friendly manner and lighthearted nature. Drawn to forceful characters, you usually admire accomplished or determined people who are intelligent and hardworking. Alternatively, you can establish a strong bond with people who share your interests and ideals. Caring and understanding, you often show true devotion and compassion to those you love and often do your utmost to help those around you. Although you appear resourceful and self-contained on the outside, a dislike for being alone indicates that on an inner level you usually feel complete when you are in a secure relationship. In personal relationships you need to give and receive in equal measures.

Your attractive qualities: discerning, good memory, idealistic, practical, charismatic, forceful, diplomatic, well-informed, affectionate, love of knowledge, progressive, innovative, optimistic, capable, intuitive, agreeable, sensitive, intelligent, generous, leadership abilities, inspired, creative

Your less attractive qualities: insecure, jealous, bossy, unfocused, nervous, extremist, critical, inconsiderate, isolated, too sensitive, moody, doubting, cold, vain, pessimistic, dependent on others, overemotional

Your Venus Power

The planet Venus has a great deal of influence on your powers of attraction. Below are four possible Venus types for women and men. To find your Venus you need to go to page 771, where you will find the Venus table and extra information. The planet Mars also affects your powers of attraction. To find your Mars table and interpretation go to page 761.

WOMEN WITH VENUS IN TAURUS: For your ideal relationship you seek a partner who is both financially secure and demonstrative with his affections. With these thoughts in mind, you are likely to want a partner who is refined yet pragmatic or someone concerned with safeguarding your future. Although stubborn, you can be loving and affectionate. Attracted to people with a good sense of style, you can succeed in all kinds of business partnerships, especially those involving the arts, music, and luxury goods.

MEN WITH VENUS IN TAURUS: Attractive and affectionate, in relationships you are often faithful with a conservative outlook. You are drawn to warmhearted partners with whom you can share a familiar routine as well as life's pleasures and comforts. Seeking a partner who is dependable or reassuring, you often put security high on your priority list when looking for love. Your sociability and friendliness usually make you popular and partners often admire your good sense of values and practical skills.

WOMEN WITH VENUS IN GEMINI: Articulate, versatile, and youthful, your personal magnetism is often linked to your charm, wit, and communication skills. You seek a partner who is clever, can communicate with you at ease, and can share your thoughts and interests. Since you find it easy to mix with people you have many friends. When you find someone you can communicate with, you can easily lose yourself in long conversations.

MEN WITH VENUS IN GEMINI: Charming, amusing, and adaptable, you attract others with your natural communication skills and friendly personality. You have a wonderful childlike quality and love to keep life playful, but a reluctance to contact your deeper feelings may cause you to avoid serious commitment. With your need for variety and intellectual

stimulation, you are attracted to clever and amusing partners who have many interesting sides to their personalities.

WOMEN WITH VENUS IN CANCER: Gentle and tender, you are romantic by nature. You possess a strong need for security and usually help others feel safe and protected. This preservation is especially centered around the home, which is your haven from life's storm. Although your maternal instincts are strong, avoid making sacrifices for others at your own expense. Nevertheless, affectionate and caring, once committed to a relationship your loyalty and devotion to your partner are very strong.

MEN WITH VENUS IN CANCER: Being emotionally receptive you can make a sensitive lover. With your desire to care for and protect others, you are likely to have strong family connections. Love is often tied in with being attentive to the needs of others and you may find yourself attracted to individuals who have sympathetic or maternal qualities. Security-conscious, you need a loyal partner who can offer you support and ideally be a good cook and homemaker.

WOMEN WITH VENUS IN LEO: As a person who wants to radiate in their own right, you are likely to desire partners you can be proud of. Usually you are attracted to fun-loving, warm, and generous individuals. If self-expression is important to you, you will probably seek the company of creative people such as artists, musicians, or those with a flair for acting. Alternatively, you may be drawn to people who are dignified, regal, or have already achieved success.

MEN WITH VENUS IN LEO: Generous, animated, and pleasure-seeking, you can be very entertaining and fun to be with. Usually you are attracted to extroverted and benevolent individuals with a sunny personality. If ambitious, you are drawn to a partner who shows leadership qualities or one who is highly motivated. Your less attractive qualities are your tendencies to be bossy or vain. With a sense of the dramatic, however, you can be the life and soul of the party and inspire those around you.

To read all about your Outer Planets and work out how to use your personalized timetable, go to Section Three, page 789.

Your Personalized Timetable

JUPITER BENEFICIAL
1938 5/6 – 8/7
1938 12/24 – until 1939 3/6
1940 5/25 – 7/17
1940 10/23 – until 1941 3/5
1944 8/4 – 9/20
1946 9/20 – 12/4
1950 4/10 – 9/24
1950 11/22 – until 1951 2/17
1952 5/7 – 6/21
1952 12/11 – until 1953 1/29
1956 7/18 – 9/4
1958 1/4 – 3/30
1958 9/1 – 11/18
1962 3/21 – until 1963 1/30
1964 4/20 – 6/2
1967 11/1 – until 1968 2/11
1968 6/28 – 8/19
1969 12/10 – until 1970 5/8
1970 8/8 – 11/2
1974 3/4 – 5/25
1974 8/20 – until 1975 1/10
1976 4/4 – 5/16
1979 10/10 – until 1980 3/23
1980 5/31 – 8/2
1981 11/22 – until 1982 10/17
1986 2/16 – 4/29
1986 10/3 – 12/13
1988 3/18 – 4/30
1991 9/21 – 11/19
1992 2/10 – 7/15
1993 11/5 – until 1994 9/30
1998 1/31 – 4/9
1999 7/12 – 10/7
2000 2/26 – 4/13
2003 9/5 – 10/25
2004 3/19 – 6/21
2005 10/21 – until 2006 1/12
2006 4/26 – 9/11
2010 1/13 – 3/22
2011 6/14 – 11/24
2012 1/26 – until 2012 3/26

SATURN BENEFICIAL
1940 4/6 – 6/30
1940 10/25 – until 1941 3/20
1948 10/7 – until 1949 3/3
1949 6/27 – 9/22
1953 10/14 – until 1954 11/29
1955 6/24 – 8/13
1964 3/15 – 10/4
1964 11/29 – until 1965 5/6
1965 8/21 – until 1966 1/28
1969 5/16 – until 1970 5/2
1978 8/12 – 11/8
1979 2/10 – 7/28
1982 11/20 – until 1983 5/21
1983 8/10 – until 1984 1/15
1984 4/5 – 10/7
1993 4/30 – 7/21
1994 1/20 – until 1995 3/6
1998 7/3 – 9/29
1999 3/20 – 6/9
1999 11/28 – until 2000 2/24
2007 9/18 – until 2008 4/13
2008 5/22 – 9/4
2012 1/15 – 3/2
2012 9/27 – Continues

URANUS BENEFICIAL
1938 1/1 – 4/5
1962 9/11 – until 1965 7/13
1974 11/5 – until 1978 10/12
2003 2/21 – until 2007 12/18

NEPTUNE BENEFICIAL
1955 11/19 – until 1963 10/29
2011 3/6 – Continues

PLUTO BENEFICIAL
1957 10/30 – until 1964 7/3
1982 12/21 – until 1990 8/8

JUPITER CHALLENGING
1939 5/6 – 11/16
1939 12/3 – until 1940 3/14
1945 8/20 – 11/4
1948 11/10 – until 1949 1/21
1951 4/17 – until 1952 2/24
1956 12/4 – until 1957 2/28
1957 8/1 – 10/19
1960 2/23 – 6/17
1960 10/20 – until 1961 1/5
1963 3/31 – 6/16
1963 10/4 – until 1964 2/2
1968 11/10 – until 1969 4/8
1969 7/7 – 10/3
1972 2/1 – 8/7
1972 9/12 – 12/19
1975 3/14 – 5/23
1975 11/28 – 12/22
1980 10/22 – until 1981 9/17
1984 1/15 – 12/3
1987 2/26 – 5/4
1992 10/5 – until 1993 8/31
1995 12/30 – until 1996 3/23
1996 6/16 – 11/13
1999 2/8 – 4/17
2004 9/20 – 12/12
2005 3/26 – 8/12
2007 12/14 – until 2008 2/26
2008 7/29 – 10/18
2010 5/30 – 9/16
2011 1/17 – 3/31

SATURN CHALLENGING
1938 1/1 – 5/30
1938 10/3 – until 1939 2/20
1950 11/9 – until 1951 3/20
1951 8/3 – until 1952 9/17
1958 12/28 – until 1960 2/20
1960 7/8 – 11/19
1966 6/13 – 8/9
1967 2/23 – until 1968 4/2
1980 9/13 – until 1981 10/24
1988 2/3 – 6/23
1988 11/2 – until 1989 12/27
1996 3/30 – until 1997 5/9
1997 11/4 – until 1998 9/16
2009 10/20 – until 2010 4/22
2010 7/7 – 12/6
2011 3/20 – 8/30

URANUS CHALLENGING
1967 12/14 – until 1972 8/4
1988 1/25 – until 1992 11/10
2010 5/2 – Continues

NEPTUNE CHALLENGING
1941 11/6 – until 1950 8/6
1983 3/4 – until 1991 11/27

PLUTO CHALLENGING
1970 11/13 – until 1978 8/28
2007 12/28 – Continues

JUPITER SPECIAL
1942 6/6 – 8/17
1954 5/19 – 7/30
1965 9/11 – 11/26
1966 4/30 – 7/14
1977 8/14 – until 1978 1/7
1978 4/4 – 6/28
1989 7/26 – until 1990 6/11
2001 7/8 – 10/13
2001 11/22 – until 2002 5/24

SATURN SPECIAL
1944 6/12 – until 1945 7/11
1973 7/24 – until 1974 1/21
1974 4/5 – 8/24
1975 1/11 – 5/13
2002 10/3 – 10/19
2003 5/27 – until 2004 6/24

URANUS SPECIAL
1948 8/5 – until 1953 4/28

June 30

SUN: CANCER • DECANATE: CANCER/MOON • DEGREE: 7°–8°5 CANCER • MODE: CARDINAL • ELEMENT: WATER

Your Personal Powers

Charged by powerful emotions, your resolute and enterprising nature indicates that you often succeed by sheer determination. Able to quickly assess people and situations, you empower yourself when you use your persuasive speech and charm. Although strong-willed, you may, however, need to resist displaying your frustration or irritability through being obstinate. Nevertheless, kind and caring, you often express yourself by being spontaneous and generous. Possessing natural leadership skills, when you apply your touch of the dramatic you can be quite impressive. Your ruler, the Moon, grants you intuitive feelings, emotional depth, and an affectionate nature. Often ruled by passion, your sensitivity implies that you can lose some of your power if you become selfish or negate your personal needs. You gain power when you combine your sharp discrimination with perseverance and hard work in order to achieve your ambition or goals. Self-expression and creative pursuits can inspire you to be imaginative and allow you to display your finer points.

Your Powers of Attraction in Relationships

Sociable and friendly, you enjoy entertaining and meeting people. A good conversationalist, you attract others with your sincere, loyal, and caring nature. Capable of showing true compassion, you can be a pillar of strength to those you love. Often you are drawn to warm and compassionate or idealistic people who have an affectionate character. Although you possess deep and powerful emotions, guard against becoming overly serious with your partners or secretive about the way you feel. Protective and generous toward those you love, you have strong parental instincts and place your home high on your priority list. An inclination to being sentimental implies you are romantic at heart but can also hold on to the past. Since your dynamic emotions can be your greatest asset you can show your strength of character by uplifting yourself and others.

Your attractive qualities: emotional strength, dynamic, charismatic, persuasive, diplomatic, proud, loyal, hardworking, altruistic, intuitive, creative, sense of the dramatic, direct, dignified, friendly, courageous, supportive, imaginative, talent with words, fun-loving, articulate, generous, tolerant

Your less attractive qualities: selfish, bossy, moody, frustrated, uncaring, obstinate, demanding, too sentimental, impatient, discontented, lack of self-expression, overworked, pessimistic, insecure, deceitful, lazy, indulgent, withdrawn, too serious

Your Venus Power

The planet Venus has a great deal of influence on your powers of attraction. Below are four possible Venus types for women and men. To find your Venus you need to go to page 771, where you will find the Venus table and extra information. The planet Mars also affects your powers of attraction. To find your Mars table and interpretation go to page 761.

WOMEN WITH VENUS IN TAURUS: For your ideal relationship you seek a partner who is both financially secure and demonstrative with his affections. With these thoughts in mind you are likely to want a partner who is refined yet pragmatic or someone concerned with safeguarding your future. Although stubborn, you can be loving and affectionate. Attracted to people with a good sense of style, you can succeed in all kinds of business partnerships especially those involving the arts, music, and luxury goods.

MEN WITH VENUS IN TAURUS: As well as attracting people with your warm personality, you possess an innate sense of the value of material possessions. Keeping yourself stylish and having an attractive appearance can also be important to you. You are naturally attracted to practical yet sensual women who understand your need for comfort, security, and the pleasures and luxuries of life. Naturally affectionate, you enjoy socializing but can be a loyal and loving partner.

WOMEN WITH VENUS IN GEMINI: In relationships you need intellectual stimulation and usually prefer to keep things light. Certainly not boring, you love to talk and are at your best being witty and entertaining. Although your easygoing approach to relationships is very attractive, guard against losing touch with your deeper emotions. You prefer a partner who can keep up with your fast stream of ideas, and if you have shared interests then so much the better.

MEN WITH VENUS IN GEMINI: Charming, amusing, and adaptable, you attract others with your natural communication skills and friendly personality. You have a wonderful childlike quality and love to keep life playful, but a reluctance to contact your deeper feelings may cause you to avoid serious commitment. With your need for variety and intellectual

stimulation you are attracted to clever and amusing partners who have many interesting sides to their personalities.

WOMEN WITH VENUS IN CANCER: With your intuitive abilities and sympathetic nature you are usually supportive of those you love. Impressionable and empathetic, your receptivity allows you to quickly pick up on the moods of people and you are especially aware of the emotional changes in your close partner. As you often display true maternal tendencies toward those you know, you want a partner who is considerate and sensitive.

MEN WITH VENUS IN CANCER: As well as attracting people with your warm personality, you possess an innate sense of the value of material possessions. Keeping yourself stylish and having an attractive appearance can also be important to you. You are naturally attracted to practical yet sensual women who understand your need for comfort, security, and the pleasures and luxuries of life. Naturally affectionate, you enjoy socializing but can be a loyal and loving partner.

WOMEN WITH VENUS IN LEO: You possess the wonderful ability to project your warm and sunny personality and keep others happily entertained. Loving attention yourself, you seek a partner who can appreciate you and be supportive and give you positive feedback. Proud, with a natural regal air, you expect respect from your partners but are willing to be loyal and supportive in exchange. Although sometimes a little self-centered, you know how to make your partner feel special.

MEN WITH VENUS IN LEO: Enthusiastic, playful, and kind, you can be benevolent with those you love. Warm, romantic, and self-expressive, you adore the drama of love or having fun with your friends. Usually you are attracted to partners with a warm and generous nature. Although you can be a confident and charismatic partner, you may need to develop humility to stop pride or arrogance from marring your relationships.

To read all about your Outer Planets and work out how to use your personalized timetable, go to Section Three, page 789.

To read all about your Outer Planets and work out how to use your personalized timetable, go to Section Three, page 789.

Your Personalized Timetable

JUPITER BENEFICIAL
1938 5/14 – 7/30
1938 12/29 – until 1939 3/10
1940 5/29 – 7/25
1940 10/16 – until 1941 3/10
1944 8/9 – 9/24
1946 9/25 – 12/9
1950 4/15 – 9/15
1950 12/1 – until 1951 2/21
1952 5/11 – 6/26
1952 12/1 – until 1953 2/8
1956 7/23 – 9/8
1958 1/13 – 3/21
1958 9/7 – 11/22
1962 3/25 – until 1963 2/4
1964 4/24 – 6/6
1967 11/8 – until 1968 2/4
1968 7/4 – 8/24
1969 12/16 – until 1970 4/30
1970 8/15 – 11/7
1974 3/8 – 6/2
1974 8/11 – until 1975 1/15
1976 4/8 – 5/20
1979 10/15 – until 1980 3/14
1980 6/8 – 8/7
1981 11/27 – until 1982 10/22
1986 2/20 – 5/4
1986 9/25 – 12/21
1988 3/22 – 5/4
1991 9/26 – 11/28
1992 2/1 – 7/20
1993 11/10 – until 1994 10/5
1998 2/4 – 4/13
1999 7/20 – 9/29
2000 3/2 – 4/17
2003 9/10 – 10/31
2004 3/11 – 6/28
2005 10/26 – until 2006 1/19
2006 4/18 – 9/17
2010 1/17 – 3/26
2011 6/19 – 11/15
2012 2/3 – 3/30

SATURN BENEFICIAL
1940 4/13 – 7/12
1940 10/13 – until 1941 3/29
1948 10/16 – until 1949 2/19
1949 7/7 – 9/29
1950 4/24 – 6/5
1953 10/22 – until 1954 12/8
1955 6/5 – 8/31
1964 3/23 – 9/17
1964 12/15 – until 1965 5/20
1965 8/7 – until 1966 2/6
1969 5/24 – 12/2
1970 2/4 – 5/9
1978 8/19 – 11/22
1979 1/26 – 8/6
1982 11/29 – until 1983 5/7
1983 8/24 – until 1984 2/2
1984 3/17 – 10/15
1993 5/20 – 7/1
1994 1/28 – until 1995 3/13
1998 7/19 – 9/12
1999 3/28 – 6/18
1999 11/15 – until 2000 3/7
2007 9/27 – until 2008 3/24
2008 6/11 – 9/12
2012 10/5 – Continues

URANUS BENEFICIAL
1938 1/1 – 4/22
1962 9/27 – until 1965 8/1
1974 11/20 – until 1978 10/28
2003 3/10 – until 2008 1/17

NEPTUNE BENEFICIAL
1955 12/23 – until 1964 9/24
2011 4/3 – Continues

PLUTO BENEFICIAL
1958 9/24 – until 1964 8/7
1983 11/5 – until 1990 9/24

JUPITER CHALLENGING
1939 5/11 – 10/30
1939 12/20 – until 1940 3/18
1945 8/25 – 11/8
1948 11/15 – until 1949 1/25
1951 4/21 – until 1952 2/29
1956 12/12 – until 1957 2/19
1957 8/6 – 10/23
1960 3/1 – 6/10
1960 10/25 – until 1961 1/9
1963 4/4 – 6/22
1963 9/26 – until 1964 2/7
1968 11/15 – until 1969 3/31
1969 7/15 – 10/7
1972 2/6 – 7/25
1972 9/25 – 12/24
1975 3/18 – 5/28
1975 11/13 – until 1976 1/6
1980 10/27 – until 1981 9/22
1984 1/19 – 12/7
1987 3/2 – 5/9
1992 10/10 – until 1993 9/5
1996 1/3 – 4/1
1996 6/7 – 11/19
1999 2/12 – 4/21
2004 9/25 – 12/20
2005 3/18 – 8/17
2007 12/18 – until 2008 3/3
2008 7/21 – 10/25
2010 6/6 – 9/9
2011 1/22 – 4/4

SATURN CHALLENGING
1938 1/13 – 6/10
1938 9/20 – until 1939 3/1
1950 11/20 – until 1951 3/7
1951 8/13 – until 1952 9/25
1959 1/5 – until 1960 3/2
1960 6/25 – 11/29
1967 3/3 – until 1968 4/9
1980 9/21 – until 1981 11/1
1982 5/25 – 7/12
1988 2/13 – 6/10
1988 11/12 – until 1990 1/4
1996 4/7 – until 1997 5/18
1997 10/22 – until 1998 2/7
2009 10/29 – until 2010 4/8
2010 7/21 – 12/19
2011 3/5 – 9/8

URANUS CHALLENGING
1968 9/28 – until 1972 8/26
1988 2/14 – until 1992 12/1
2010 5/27 – Continues

NEPTUNE CHALLENGING
1942 10/2 – until 1950 9/9
1984 1/18 – until 1991 12/25

PLUTO CHALLENGING
1971 10/4 – until 1978 9/24
2008 1/25 – Continues

JUPITER SPECIAL
1942 6/10 – 8/22
1943 2/18 – 4/3
1954 5/24 – 8/3
1965 9/20 – 11/17
1966 5/5 – 7/18
1977 8/20 – 12/31
1978 4/11 – 7/2
1989 7/30 – until 1990 6/15
2001 7/12 – until 2002 5/29

SATURN SPECIAL
1944 6/20 – until 1945 7/19
1973 8/1 – until 1974 1/8
1974 4/18 – 9/3
1974 12/30 – until 1975 5/22
2003 6/3 – until 2004 7/2

URANUS SPECIAL
1948 8/29 – until 1953 5/22

July 1

Your Personal Powers

Caring and receptive, you are an idealist who shows true compassion toward others. Yet underneath your warm exterior and smiling face lies a forceful character that has true determination and natural leadership skills. Your ruler, the Moon, grants you depth of feeling and imaginative sensitivity. You empower yourself when you follow your strong instincts and let your profound intuition guide you toward self-mastery or independence. You lose some of your power, however, when you indulge in doubts or become indecisive. Although you can achieve much through hard work, your sensitive emotions can at times cause fluctuating moods, especially if you feel insecure or are involved in personal conflict. Avoid therefore becoming entangled in situations that create disharmonious environments around you. Your resolute nature not only gives you the courage to overcome obstacles but also proves to strengthen your character in the process. Keen on new beginnings, in order to change your circumstances, you may need to make a clean break from the past or let go of situations that are outside your control.

Your Powers of Attraction in Relationships

Sensitive and romantic, you are usually idealistic about relationships. You are drawn to a partner you can rely on to provide you with emotional and material security. An inclination to be reserved or shy implies that loyalty and trust play an important role in close friendships. If you are ambitious, your family life and parental responsibilities may at times oppose your personal aspirations. Having strong feelings toward people indicates that although you like to make your own decisions, you can be sympathetic and supportive to others. Being an extremist by nature, you sometimes experience relationships that are on an all-or-nothing basis. You are more suited to someone who can understand your deep sensitivity and shares your high ideals and aspirations.

Your attractive qualities: independent, authoritative, receptive, optimistic, idealistic, enterprising, enthusiastic, intuitive, tolerant, ambitious, sensitive, protective, gentle, confident, tenacious, insightful, caring, loving, courageous, romantic, compassionate, affectionate, progressive, forceful, gregarious

Your less attractive qualities: moody, depressed, too impressionable, inner conflict, resentful, selfish, impatient, suspicious, stubborn, frustrated, indulgent, codependent, indecisive, bossy, fear of being alone or abandoned, arrogant, too sensitive, insecure

Your Venus Power

The planet Venus has a great deal of influence on your powers of attraction. Below are four possible Venus types for women and men. To find your Venus you need to go to page 771, where you will find the Venus table and extra information. The planet Mars also affects your powers of attraction. To find your Mars table and interpretation go to page 761.

WOMEN WITH VENUS IN TAURUS: For your ideal relationship, you seek a partner who is both financially secure and demonstrative with his affections. With these thoughts in mind, you are likely to want a partner who is refined yet pragmatic or someone concerned with safeguarding your future. Although stubborn, you can be loving and affectionate. Attracted to people with a good sense of style, you can succeed in all kinds of business partnerships, especially those involving the arts, music, and luxury goods.

MEN WITH VENUS IN TAURUS: As well as attracting people with your warm personality, you possess an innate sense of the value of material possessions. Keeping yourself stylish and having an attractive appearance can also be important to you. You are naturally attracted to practical yet sensual women who understand your need for comfort, security, and the pleasures and luxuries of life. Naturally affectionate, you enjoy socializing but can be a loyal and loving partner.

WOMEN WITH VENUS IN GEMINI: By nature you are young at heart, adaptable, and sociable. Being curious and willing to cooperate makes you a good team player. Usually you are drawn to articulate people who have charm and flair or sharp wit. With a need to expand your knowledge, you also look for a partner who can challenge or stimulate you intellectually. Although you love to talk with all types of people, you may need to develop your listening skills in order to build better communication in your relationships.

MEN WITH VENUS IN GEMINI: Charming, amusing, and adaptable, you attract others with your natural communication skills and friendly personality. You have a wonderful childlike quality and love to keep life playful, but a reluctance to contact your deeper feelings may cause you to avoid serious commitment. With your need for variety and intellectual

stimulation, you are attracted to clever and amusing partners who have many interesting sides to their personalities.

WOMEN WITH VENUS IN CANCER: Gentle and tender, you are romantic by nature. You possess a strong need for security and usually help others feel safe and protected. This preservation is especially centered around the home, which is your haven from life's storm. Although your maternal instincts are strong, avoid making sacrifices for others at your own expense. Nevertheless, affectionate and caring, once committed to a relationship, your loyalty and devotion to your partner are very strong.

MEN WITH VENUS IN CANCER: Being emotionally receptive you can make a sensitive lover. With your desire to care and protect others, you are likely to have strong family connections. Love is often tied in with being attentive to the needs of others and you may find yourself attracted to individuals who have sympathetic or maternal qualities. Security conscious, you need a loyal partner who can offer you support and ideally be a good cook and homemaker.

WOMEN WITH VENUS IN LEO: Sociable and outgoing, you are kind and generous with those you love. Looking for a relationship that can be fun and entertaining, you need a playmate who can share your enthusiasm and high spirits. Your pride, however, often stops you from associating with lovers or partners you see as beneath you. As you desire someone who can appreciate your sense of the dramatic, you are often attracted to people with strong personalities.

MEN WITH VENUS IN LEO: Generous, animated, and pleasure-seeking, you can be very entertaining and fun to be with. Usually, you are attracted to extrovert and benevolent individuals with sunny personalities. If ambitious, you are drawn toward a partner who shows leadership qualities or one who is highly motivated. Your less attractive qualities are your tendencies to be bossy or vain. With your sense of the dramatic, however, you can be the life and soul of the party and inspire those around you.

To read all about your Outer Planets and work out how to use your personalized timetable, go to Section Three, page 789.

go to Section Three, page 789.

Your Personalized Timetable

JUPITER BENEFICIAL
1938 5/23 – 7/20
1939 1/3 – 3/14
1940 6/3 – 8/2
1940 10/7 – until 1941 3/15
1944 8/13 – 9/29
1946 9/29 – 12/13
1950 4/20 – 9/7
1950 12/8 – until 1951 2/25
1952 5/15 – 7/1
1952 11/23 – until 1953 2/16
1956 7/28 – 9/13
1958 1/25 – 3/9
1958 9/12 – 11/27
1962 3/30 – until 1963 2/8
1964 4/28 – 6/11
1967 11/17 – until 1968 1/26
1968 7/10 – 8/28
1969 12/22 – until 1970 4/23
1970 8/22 – 11/11
1974 3/12 – 6/13
1974 7/31 – until 1975 1/20
1976 4/12 – 5/24
1979 10/20 – until 1980 3/6
1980 6/16 – 8/12
1981 12/1 – until 1982 6/9
1982 7/15 – 10/26
1986 2/24 – 5/9
1986 9/18 – 12/28
1988 3/26 – 5/8
1991 10/1 – 12/9
1992 1/20 – 7/25
1993 11/14 – until 1994 10/10
1998 2/8 – 4/18
1999 7/30 – 9/19
2000 3/7 – 4/21
2003 9/14 – 11/6
2004 3/4 – 7/4
2005 10/30 – until 2006 1/28
2006 4/9 – 9/22
2010 1/22 – 3/30
2011 6/25 – 11/8
2012 2/10 – 4/3

SATURN BENEFICIAL
1940 4/21 – 7/27
1940 9/27 – until 1941 4/6
1948 10/27 – until 1949 2/7
1949 7/17 – 10/8
1950 4/5 – 6/24
1953 10/30 – until 1954 12/17
1955 5/22 – 9/13
1964 4/2 – 9/3
1964 12/27 – until 1965 6/9
1965 7/16 – until 1966 2/14
1969 6/1 – 11/17
1970 2/18 – 5/17
1978 8/27 – 12/23
1978 12/27 – until 1979 8/14
1982 12/8 – until 1983 4/24
1983 9/4 – until 1984 10/24
1994 2/5 – until 1995 3/21
1999 4/5 – 6/27
1999 11/3 – until 2000 3/17
2007 10/5 – until 2008 3/11
2008 6/24 – 9/20
2012 10/13 – Continues

URANUS BENEFICIAL
1938 1/1 – until 1939 2/5
1962 10/16 – until 1965 8/18
1974 12/8 – until 2008 2/6

NEPTUNE BENEFICIAL
1956 11/13 – until 1964 10/23
2011 5/31 – Continues

PLUTO BENEFICIAL
1958 11/2 – until 1965 6/24
1983 11/30 – until 1990 10/21

JUPITER CHALLENGING
1939 5/16 – 10/20
1939 12/29 – until 1940 3/22

1945 8/29 – 11/13
1948 11/19 – until 1949 1/29
1951 4/25 – until 1952 3/4
1956 12/23 – until 1957 2/8
1957 8/12 – 10/27
1960 3/8 – 6/2
1960 10/31 – until 1961 1/13
1963 4/8 – 6/30
1963 9/19 – until 1964 2/13
1968 11/21 – until 1969 3/23
1969 7/22 – 10/12
1972 2/11 – 7/15
1972 10/4 – 12/28
1975 3/22 – 6/2
1975 11/4 – until 1976 1/15
1980 11/1 – until 1981 5/10
1981 6/14 – 9/26
1984 1/24 – 12/12
1987 3/6 – 5/13
1992 10/15 – until 1993 9/10
1996 1/7 – 4/13
1996 5/26 – 11/24
1999 2/17 – 4/25
2004 9/29 – 12/28
2005 3/9 – 8/23
2007 12/22 – until 2008 3/8
2008 7/13 – 11/1
2010 6/13 – 9/1
2011 1/27 – 4/8

SATURN CHALLENGING
1938 1/25 – 6/24
1938 9/6 – until 1939 3/9
1950 12/2 – until 1951 2/25
1951 8/22 – until 1952 10/2
1959 1/13 – 8/11
1959 9/28 – until 1960 3/15
1960 6/11 – 12/8
1967 3/11 – until 1968 4/17
1980 9/28 – until 1981 11/9
1982 5/6 – 7/30
1988 2/26 – 5/27
1988 11/21 – until 1990 1/12
1996 4/15 – 11/14
1996 12/21 – until 1997 5/27
1997 10/10 – until 1998 2/17
2009 11/7 – until 2010 3/26
2010 8/1 – until 2011 1/8
2011 2/13 – 9/16

URANUS CHALLENGING
1968 10/13 – until 1972 9/12
1988 3/19 – until 1992 12/19
2011 3/28 – Continues

NEPTUNE CHALLENGING
1942 10/30 – until 1951 7/24
1984 2/20 – until 1992 11/19

PLUTO CHALLENGING
1971 10/31 – until 1979 8/8
2008 3/4 – Continues

JUPITER SPECIAL
1942 6/14 – 8/27
1943 2/7 – 4/14
1954 5/28 – 8/8
1965 10/4 – 11/3
1966 5/10 – 7/22
1977 8/26 – 12/24
1978 4/18 – 7/6
1989 8/4 – until 1990 2/17
1990 3/4 – 6/20
2001 7/17 – until 2002 6/2

SATURN SPECIAL
1944 6/27 – until 1945 7/26
1973 8/10 – 12/27
1974 4/29 – 9/14
1974 12/18 – until 1975 5/31
2003 6/11 – until 2004 7/9

URANUS SPECIAL
1949 6/25 – until 1953 6/10

July 2

Your Personal Powers

Thoughtful, diplomatic, and friendly, your sensitivity and strong emotions are usually hidden behind your gracious personality. Your ruler, the Moon, provides you with a strong sixth sense and an affectionate nature, but you may need to resist letting others discourage you from doing what you think is right. You gain power when you combine your inborn people skills with your intuition and common sense. You lose power by being restless and impatient or by getting bored easily. Although you possess a strong need to express yourself creatively, your pragmatic nature indicates that you have business acumen and good negotiating skills. You can also lose some of your power by allowing doubts and indecision to undermine your purposeful nature. Usually determined and hardworking, however, you empower yourself through accumulating knowledge or making sensible decisions based on your good evaluation skills. Self-aware, with natural leadership skills, you can greatly benefit from interacting and working cooperatively with others.

Your Powers of Attraction in Relationships

Charismatic and friendly, you can often make useful contacts that bring you new opportunities. As an excellent networker, you have a flair for combining business and pleasure and may even work together with your partner. Other people are drawn to your sympathetic nature and open-minded attitude. You are usually attracted to intelligent and mentally stimulating individuals who can inspire you to be creative. Alternatively, you may be interested in practical partners who are security-conscious and reassuring but have big plans. Helpful by nature, you are usually willing to assist others. You may, however, find it hard to say no to the people you care about. Although your inner strength shows stamina, guard against being too intense or bossy. Loyalty and trust are important factors when it comes to choosing a partner.

Your attractive qualities: idealistic, assertive, motivated, inspired, compassionate, keen business sense, sociable, tactful, networker, intuitive, direct, decisive, natural psychologist, methodical, communicative, impressive, realistic, optimistic, collaborative, harmonious, composed, gentle

Your less attractive qualities: indecisive, worry, indulgent, submissive, critical, overrationalize, oversensitive, tactless, bossy, doubtful, being undermined, indulgent, discontented, materialistic

Your Venus Power

The planet Venus has a great deal of influence on your powers of attraction. Below are four possible Venus types for women and men. To find your Venus you need to go to page 771, where you will find the Venus table and extra information. The planet Mars also affects your powers of attraction. To find your Mars table and interpretation go to page 761.

WOMEN WITH VENUS IN TAURUS: Warm and affectionate, you are naturally tactile with a love of sensual pleasures. With a streak of the conventional, you love the simple pleasures of life: good food, close friends, and happy relationships. Having an inner strength, you can express genuine patience and are often a pillar of support for loved ones and friends. Although you possess endurance, be careful not to let this turn into plain stubbornness.

MEN WITH VENUS IN TAURUS: Although usually you are drawn to sensual and physically beautiful individuals, you want a partner who is reliable and loyal. When in love you enjoy buying your partner things of quality that will grow in value or useful things of a practical nature. You also love to socialize and entertain, especially in luxurious surroundings. Often you are attracted to creative people or those with artistic talents.

WOMEN WITH VENUS IN GEMINI: Articulate, versatile, and youthful, your personal magnetism is often linked to your charm, wit, and communication skills. You seek a partner who is clever, can communicate with you at ease, and can share your thoughts and interests. Since you find it easy to mix with people you have many friends. When you find someone you can communicate with, you can easily lose yourself in long conversations.

MEN WITH VENUS IN GEMINI: Charming, amusing, and adaptable, you attract others with your natural communication skills and friendly personality. You have a wonderful childlike quality and love to keep life playful, but a reluctance to contact your deeper feelings may cause you to avoid serious commitment. With your need for variety and intellectual stimulation, you are attracted to clever and amusing partners who have many interesting sides to their personalities.

WOMEN WITH VENUS IN CANCER: Possessing a soft femi-

ninity, you have tender and sensitive emotions. Sympathetic and caring, you often mother those in your care by making sure that they are comfortable and have plenty to eat. When you feel hurt or insecure in relationships you are likely to cover your feelings by being defensive or appearing tough on the outside while on the inside you are feeling vulnerable. Affectionate and romantic, you make a faithful and devoted partner.

MEN WITH VENUS IN CANCER: Being caring and sensitive, you probably seek a nurturing partner who could provide you with emotional security and a sense of belonging in a loving and safe environment. Receptive to others, at times you find it hard to be direct or confrontational in relationships. You may find yourself drawn to affectionate and sympathetic partners like yourself. You are also likely to have strong family links.

WOMEN WITH VENUS IN LEO: As a person who wants to radiate in their own right, you are likely to desire partners you can be proud of. Usually you are attracted to fun-loving, warm, and generous individuals. If self-expression is important to you, you will probably seek the company of creative people such as artists, musicians, or those with a flair for acting. Alternatively, you may be drawn to people who are dignified, regal, or have already achieved success.

MEN WITH VENUS IN LEO: A childlike nature suggests that you are versatile and keen on games or being entertained. You are usually attracted to vivacious partners with a benevolent nature. As an extrovert you enjoy being involved in all types of activities where you can assert yourself and show your talents and abilities. Others may recognize your inborn tendencies to lead but are also aware of your vanity or pride. Nevertheless, generous and caring, you often show more compassion to those less fortunate than yourself.

To read all about your Outer Planets and work out how to use your personalized timetable, go to Section Three, page 789.

Your Personalized Timetable

JUPITER BENEFICIAL
1938 6/6 – 7/6
1939 1/8 – 3/18
1940 6/7 – 8/13
1940 9/26 – until 1941 3/20
1944 8/18 – 10/3
1946 10/4 – 12/18
1947 7/5 – 7/26
1950 4/26 – 8/30
1950 12/15 – until 1951 3/1
1952 5/19 – 7/7
1952 11/16 – until 1953 2/23
1956 8/1 – 9/17
1958 9/17 – 12/1
1962 4/3 – until 1963 2/12
1964 5/2 – 6/15
1967 11/27 – until 1968 1/15
1968 7/15 – 9/2
1969 12/28 – until 1970 4/15
1970 8/28 – 11/15
1974 3/16 – until 1975 1/25
1976 4/16 – 5/28
1979 10/26 – until 1980 2/27
1980 6/23 – 8/16
1981 12/6 – until 1982 5/27
1982 7/29 – 10/31
1986 2/28 – 5/15
1986 9/10 – until 1987 1/3
1988 3/30 – 5/12
1991 10/6 – until 1992 4/18
1992 5/13 – 7/30
1993 11/19 – until 1994 10/14
1998 2/12 – 4/22
1999 8/17 – 9/1
2000 3/12 – 4/25
2003 9/19 – 11/12
2004 2/26 – 7/10
2005 11/3 – until 2006 2/7
2006 3/30 – 9/27
2010 1/26 – 4/3
2011 6/30 – 11/1
2012 2/17 – 4/8

SATURN BENEFICIAL
1940 4/28 – until 1941 4/14
1948 11/8 – until 1949 1/24
1949 7/25 – 10/16
1950 3/22 – 7/7
1953 11/7 – until 1954 12/27
1955 5/9 – 9/24
1964 4/12 – 8/22
1965 1/7 – until 1966 2/22
1969 6/10 – 11/5
1970 3/1 – 5/24
1978 9/3 – until 1979 8/22
1982 12/19 – until 1983 4/11
1983 9/14 – until 1984 11/1
1994 2/13 – until 1995 3/29
1999 4/12 – 7/8
1999 10/22 – until 2000 3/26
2007 10/14 – until 2008 2/27
2008 7/4 – 9/27
2012 10/21 – Continues

URANUS BENEFICIAL
1938 1/1 – until 1939 3/13
1962 11/11 – until 1965 9/2
1975 1/1 – until 1979 9/12
2003 4/19 – until 2008 2/24

NEPTUNE BENEFICIAL
1956 12/13 – until 1965 9/17
2012 3/26 – Continues

PLUTO BENEFICIAL
1959 9/25 – until 1965 8/4
1984 1/6 – until 1991 8/31

JUPITER CHALLENGING
1939 5/21 – 10/12
1940 1/6 – 3/26

1945 9/3 – 11/18
1946 5/29 – 7/1
1948 11/24 – until 1949 2/2
1951 4/30 – until 1952 3/8
1957 8/17 – 11/1
1960 3/17 – 5/24
1960 11/5 – until 1961 1/17
1963 4/12 – 7/8
1963 9/10 – until 1964 2/18
1968 11/28 – until 1969 3/16
1969 7/28 – 10/16
1972 2/17 – 7/7
1972 10/12 – until 1973 1/1
1975 3/26 – 6/7
1975 10/27 – until 1976 1/23
1980 11/6 – until 1981 4/26
1981 6/28 – 9/30
1984 1/28 – 12/16
1987 3/10 – 5/17
1992 10/19 – until 1993 9/14
1996 1/11 – 11/28
1999 2/21 – 4/29
2004 10/3 – until 2005 1/8
2005 2/27 – 8/28
2007 12/27 – until 2008 3/15
2008 7/6 – 1/7
2010 6/22 – 8/23
2011 2/1 – 4/12

SATURN CHALLENGING
1938 2/5 – 7/17
1938 8/13 – until 1939 3/17
1950 12/20 – until 1952 2/4
1951 8/30 – until 1952 10/10
1959 1/22 – 7/23
1959 10/17 – until 1960 4/1
1960 5/24 – 12/17
1967 3/19 – until 1968 4/25
1980 10/6 – until 1981 11/18
1982 4/22 – 8/12
1988 3/13 – 5/10
1988 11/30 – until 1990 1/20
1996 4/23 – 10/25
1997 1/10 – 6/7
1997 9/27 – until 1998 2/27
2009 11/17 – until 2010 3/14
2010 8/11 – until 2011 9/24

URANUS CHALLENGING
1968 10/30 – until 1972 9/28
1989 1/3 – until 1993 1/4
2011 4/14 – Continues

NEPTUNE CHALLENGING
1942 12/9 – until 1945 9/3
1985 1/11 – until 1992 12/19

PLUTO CHALLENGING
1971 12/11 – until 1979 9/10
2009 1/18 – Continues

JUPITER SPECIAL
1942 6/18 – 9/1
1943 1/29 – 4/23
1954 6/1 – 8/12
1966 5/15 – 7/26
1977 9/1 – 12/17
1978 4/24 – 7/10
1989 8/9 – until 1990 1/30
1990 3/22 – 6/24
2001 7/21 – until 2002 6/7

SATURN SPECIAL
1944 7/4 – until 1945 8/3
1973 8/20 – 12/15
1974 5/8 – 9/28
1974 12/4 – until 1975 6/8
2003 6/18 – until 2004 7/16

URANUS SPECIAL
1949 7/11 – until 1953 6/26

July 3

SUN: CANCER • DECANATE: SCORPIO/PLUTO • DEGREE: 10°45–12° CANCER • MODE: CARDINAL • ELEMENT: WATER

Your Personal Powers

Ambitious and single-minded, your determination to succeed often conceals your sensitivity, idealism, and powerful emotions. Although you are resourceful and possess great courage, you may need to resist being stubborn or too critical. Your ruler, the Moon, grants you receptivity and a sympathetic nature. You gain power when you combine your pragmatic approach to life with your creativity and imagination. Security conscious, you empower yourself when you follow your strong instincts and let money matters take care of themselves. Being versatile and enterprising, however, you can turn your ideas or talents into moneymaking ventures, usually ensuring that your material needs are taken care of. You empower yourself when you show determination and the fortitude to endure until you reach your objectives. You lose power by scattering your creative energies in too many directions or by being indecisive. When inspired, however, you have the talent to achieve a great deal and are willing work hard for what you believe in.

Your Powers of Attraction in Relationships

Altruistic, you like to show your affection by being generous and are usually keen to support and help those you love or admire. Other people admire your endurance, inner strength, and ability to overcome obstacles. Often you are attracted to mentally sharp, purposeful, and enterprising people who show enthusiasm and initiative. You may also be drawn to creative individuals. Changes in circumstances or worries about money and career indicate that if you do not budget your finances well money can become a bone of contention in your personal relationships. Although you are usually proud and confident, at other times you can become insecure or impulsive. If you are unsure about commitment and close relationships, your restlessness would suggest that you have had a change of heart, but once you settle down you can be very loyal and caring.

Your attractive qualities: determined, persevering, charitable, intuitive, generous, sensitive, dynamic, persuasive, friendly, articulate, authoritative, good sense of money and values, organized, productive, altruistic, versatile, enthusiastic, analytical, inquisitive, quick comprehension, caring

Your less attractive qualities: critical, emotionally intense, extravagant, possessive, insecure, materialistic, too sentimental, skeptical, indulgent, bossy, mistrusting, moody, manipulative, preoccupied, stubborn, impractical, too sensitive

Your Venus Power

The planet Venus has a great deal of influence on your powers of attraction. Below are four possible Venus types for women and men. To find your Venus you need to go to page 771, where you will find the Venus table and extra information. The planet Mars also affects your powers of attraction. To find your Mars table and interpretation go to page 761.

WOMEN WITH VENUS IN TAURUS: Good-natured and romantic, you have a highly developed sense of touch that particularly responds to massage, hugs, and all things physical. Being friendly, you enjoy socializing and are able to put others at their ease. With your innate sense of beauty and harmony, your natural charm can attract others. Although you can be lavish to your partner you may have to be careful that you do not overdo things.

MEN WITH VENUS IN TAURUS: Attractive and affectionate, in relationships you are often down-to-earth, with a conservative outlook. You are drawn to warmhearted partners with whom you can share a familiar routine as well as life's pleasures and comforts. Seeking a partner who is dependable or reassuring, you often put security high on your priority list when looking for love. Your sociability and friendliness usually make you popular and partners often admire your good sense of values and practical outlook.

WOMEN WITH VENUS IN GEMINI: By nature you are young at heart, adaptable, and sociable. Being curious and willing to cooperate makes you a good team player. You are usually drawn to articulate people who have charm and flair or sharp wit. With a need to expand your knowledge you also look for a partner who can challenge or stimulate you intellectually. Although you love to talk with all types of people, you may need to develop your listening skills in order to build better communication in your relationships.

MEN WITH VENUS IN GEMINI: Charming, amusing, and adaptable, you attract others with your natural communication skills and friendly personality. You have a wonderful childlike quality and love to keep life playful, but a reluctance to contact your deeper feelings may cause you to avoid serious commitment. With your need for variety and intellectual

stimulation, you are attracted to clever and amusing partners who have many interesting sides to their personalities.

WOMEN WITH VENUS IN CANCER: With your intuitive abilities and sympathetic nature, you are usually supportive of those you love. Impressionable and empathetic, your receptivity allows you to quickly pick up on people's moods and you are especially aware of the emotional changes in your close partner. As you often display true maternal tendencies toward those you know, you want a partner who is considerate and sensitive.

MEN WITH VENUS IN CANCER: As well as attracting people with your warm personality, you possess an innate sense of the value of material possessions. Keeping yourself stylish and having an attractive appearance can also be important to you. You are naturally attracted to practical yet sensual women who understand your need for comfort, security, and the pleasures and luxuries of life. Naturally affectionate, you enjoy socializing but can be a loyal and loving partner.

WOMEN WITH VENUS IN LEO: Your friendly and sunny personality often makes you stand out in a crowd. Generous and giving you know how to make your partner feel special. As you often expect loyalty and devotion from your partner in return, you can become easily offended if they ignore you or behave in an inconsiderate manner. Charming and kind, when you are in love you can be romantic, dramatic, and passionate.

MEN WITH VENUS IN LEO: Sociable and outgoing, you are kind and generous with those you love. Looking for a relationship that can be fun and entertaining, you need a playmate who can share your enthusiasm and high spirits. Your pride, however, often stops you from associating with lovers or partners you see as beneath you. As you desire someone who can appreciate your sense of the dramatic, you are often attracted to people with strong personalities.

To read all about your Outer Planets and work out how to use your personalized timetable, go to Section Three, page 789.

Your Personalized Timetable

JUPITER BENEFICIAL
1939	1/12 – 3/22
1940	6/12 – 12/22
1941	1/9 – 3/25
1944	8/22 – 10/8
1946	10/9 – 12/23
1947	6/18 – 8/12
1950	5/2 – 8/23
1950	12/21 – until **1951** 3/5
1952	5/23 – 7/13
1952	11/9 – until **1953** 3/2
1956	8/6 – 9/22
1958	9/22 – 12/6
1962	4/8 – 10/28
1962	10/31 – until **1963** 2/16
1964	5/6 – 6/20
1968	7/20 – 9/6
1970	1/4 – 4/7
1970	9/3 – 11/20
1974	3/20 – until **1975** 1/29
1976	4/20 – 6/1
1979	11/1 – until **1980** 2/20
1980	6/29 – 8/21
1981	12/12 – until **1982** 5/17
1982	8/7 – 11/4
1986	3/4 – 5/22
1986	9/3 – until **1987** 1/8
1988	4/4 – 5/16
1991	10/11 – until **1992** 4/2
1992	5/29 – 8/4
1993	11/23 – until **1994** 10/19
1998	2/16 – 4/27
1998	10/24 – 12/3
2000	3/16 – 4/29
2003	9/23 – 11/19
2004	2/18 – 7/16
2005	11/8 – until **2006** 2/28
2006	3/8 – 10/2
2010	1/30 – 4/7
2011	7/6 – 10/25
2012	2/23 – 4/12

SATURN BENEFICIAL
1940	5/6 – until **1941** 4/21
1948	11/27 – until **1949** 1/6
1949	8/3 – 10/25
1950	3/10 – 7/18
1953	11/15 – until **1954** 6/21
1954	7/21 – until **1955** 1/6
1955	4/26 – 10/4
1964	4/23 – 8/9
1965	1/16 – until **1966** 3/2
1969	6/20 – 10/24
1970	3/11 – 6/1
1971	1/5 – 1/29
1978	9/11 – until **1979** 8/30
1982	12/31 – until **1983** 3/29
1983	9/23 – until **1984** 11/9
1994	2/21 – until **1995** 4/7
1995	10/21 – 12/22
1999	4/20 – 7/21
1999	10/9 – until **2000** 4/3
2007	10/24 – until **2008** 2/16
2008	7/14 – 10/5
2009	4/13 – 6/18
2012	10/29 – Continues

URANUS BENEFICIAL
1938	1/1 – until **1939** 4/3
1963	9/1 – until **1966** 6/20
1975	10/27 – until **1979** 10/3
2004	2/22 – until **2008** 12/12

NEPTUNE BENEFICIAL
1957	11/8 – until **1965** 10/18
2012	5/1 – Continues

PLUTO BENEFICIAL
1959	11/2 – until **1966** 6/5
1984	11/13 – until **1991** 10/5

JUPITER CHALLENGING
1939	5/27 – 10/4
1940	1/13 – 3/30
1945	9/8 – 11/23
1946	5/15 – 7/15
1948	11/28 – until **1949** 2/7
1951	5/4 – until **1952** 3/12
1957	8/22 – 11/6
1960	3/28 – 5/12
1960	11/10 – until **1961** 1/21
1963	4/16 – 7/20
1963	8/29 – until **1964** 2/22
1968	12/5 – until **1969** 3/8
1969	8/3 – 10/21
1972	2/22 – 6/29
1972	10/18 – until **1973** 1/5
1975	3/30 – 6/12
1975	10/19 – until **1976** 1/29
1980	11/11 – until **1981** 4/17
1981	7/7 – 10/5
1984	2/2 – 12/20
1987	3/14 – 5/22
1992	10/24 – until **1993** 9/19
1996	1/16 – 12/3
1999	2/25 – 5/3
2004	10/8 – until **2005** 1/30
2005	2/4 – 9/2
2007	12/31 – until **2008** 3/21
2008	6/28 – 11/13
2010	7/4 – 8/11
2011	2/6 – 4/16

SATURN CHALLENGING
1938	2/14 – until **1939** 3/25
1951	9/7 – until **1952** 10/18
1959	1/31 – 7/9
1959	10/30 – until **1960** 12/25
1967	3/26 – until **1968** 5/3
1968	12/9 – until **1969** 1/2
1980	10/14 – until **1981** 11/27
1982	4/10 – 8/23
1988	12/8 – until **1990** 1/28
1990	9/10 – 10/5
1996	5/2 – 10/11
1997	1/23 – 6/19
1997	9/14 – until **1998** 3/7
2009	11/29 – until **2010** 3/1
2010	8/20 – until **2011** 10/2

URANUS CHALLENGING
1968	11/18 – until **1972** 10/14
1989	1/19 – until **1993** 11/4
2011	5/3 – Continues

NEPTUNE CHALLENGING
1943	10/24 – until **1951** 10/1
1985	2/10 – until **1993** 11/9

PLUTO CHALLENGING
1972	10/19 – until **1979** 10/5
2009	2/21 – Continues

JUPITER SPECIAL
1942	6/22 – 9/7
1943	1/21 – 4/30
1954	6/6 – 8/17
1966	5/19 – 7/31
1977	9/8 – 12/9
1978	4/29 – 7/14
1989	8/14 – until **1990** 1/20
1990	4/1 – 6/28
2001	7/26 – until **2002** 6/12

SATURN SPECIAL
1944	7/12 – until **1945** 8/11
1946	2/17 – 4/20
1973	8/31 – 12/3
1974	5/17 – 10/22
1974	11/9 – until **1975** 6/16
2003	6/26 – until **2004** 7/24

URANUS SPECIAL
1949	7/29 – until **1953** 7/12

♋

219

July 4

Your Personal Powers

Intuitive, intelligent, and resourceful, you have an enthusiastic nature and a youthful quality about you that can be idealistic and enterprising. The Moon, your ruler, gives you emotional sensitivity and a sympathetic nature. You gain power when you realize that knowledge and education or gaining skills is as important as being security-conscious. Even though you may appear carefree and lighthearted, a more ambitious side to your nature suggests that under your easygoing exterior lies a determined and aware individual. Although you may change direction or take your time deciding what you really want to accomplish, you lose power if you shy away from your responsibilities or waste your time on trivial pursuits. You are particularly likely to gain through your work, so you need to find something that really interests you. When you are inspired, you can easily become capable and industrious, gaining much through cooperative efforts. Insightful with personal charisma, your people skills greatly aid your success.

Your Powers of Attraction in Relationships

Your youthful attitude and warm personality attract others. Although you are independent, you are more inclined to team efforts. In order to make your business partnerships successful you need to resist power struggles and arguments. Usually helpful, sincere, and sympathetic, you have no problem attracting friends and admirers. Being enthusiastic and entertaining, you are fun and delightful company at any social event. Although you are likely to be actively sociable, home and family are just as important to your well-being. Security-conscious, you are often attracted to straightforward people who are established and stable. Nevertheless, romantic and idealistic by nature, it may be necessary for you to take your time in choosing your partner. You are likely to receive assistance from your friends or benefit from close partnerships.

Your attractive qualities: idealistic, good sense of values, responsible, hardworking, informed or educated, steady progress, productive, practical, intuitive, discriminative, friendly, spontaneous, adaptable, social skills, sensitive, youthful, tenacious, security-conscious, trusting, disciplined

Your less attractive qualities: stubborn, extravagant, mistrusting, inner tension, worry, indecisive, moody, repressed, bossy, uncaring, opportunistic, lazy, materialistic, restless, resentful, strict,

Your Venus Power

The planet Venus has a great deal of influence on your powers of attraction. Below are four possible Venus types for women and men. To find your Venus you need to go to page 771, where you will find the Venus table and extra information. The planet Mars also affects your powers of attraction. To find your Mars table and interpretation go to page 761.

WOMEN WITH VENUS IN TAURUS: Good-natured and romantic, you have a highly developed sense of touch that particularly responds to massage, hugs, and all things physical. Being friendly, you enjoy socializing and are able to put others at their ease. With your innate sense of beauty and harmony, your natural charm can attract others. Although you can be lavish to your partner you may have to be careful that you do not overdo things.

MEN WITH VENUS IN TAURUS: Attractive and affectionate, in relationships you are often down-to-earth, with a conservative outlook. You are drawn to warmhearted partners with whom you can share a familiar routine as well as life's pleasures and comforts. Seeking a partner who is dependable or reassuring, you often put security high on your priority list when looking for love. Your sociability and friendliness usually make you popular and partners often admire your good sense of values and practical outlook.

WOMEN WITH VENUS IN GEMINI: By nature you are young at heart, adaptable, and sociable. Being curious and willing to cooperate makes you a good team player. Usually you are drawn to articulate people who have charm and flair or sharp wit. With a need to expand your knowledge, you also look for a partner who can challenge or stimulate you intellectually. Although you love to talk with all types of people, you may need to develop your listening skills in order to build better communication in your relationships.

MEN WITH VENUS IN GEMINI: Adaptable yet often flirtatious, you enjoy mixing with people who are quick-minded and versatile. Since you can learn a great deal through interacting with others, you are often attracted to intelligent partners who have comprehensive knowledge or good ideas. One of your less attractive qualities is your tendency to become

bored or be inconsistent. Having an adaptable partner is important to you; therefore it must be someone who can offer you different options and keep you interested.

WOMEN WITH VENUS IN CANCER: Good-natured and romantic, you have a highly developed sense of touch that particularly responds to massage, hugs, and all things physical. Being friendly, you enjoy socializing and are able to put others at their ease. With your natural sense of beauty and harmony, your natural charm can attract others. Although you can be lavish to your partner you may have to be careful that you do not overdo things.

MEN WITH VENUS IN CANCER: You seek a partner who is sympathetic, caring, and protective. Able to be forgiving and compassionate, you want a secure emotional bond in your close relationships. Usually you are drawn to partners who are maternal, unselfish, or demonstrative with their feelings. Although you can sometimes appear to others as impressionable, you have powerful emotions and inner strength.

WOMEN WITH VENUS IN LEO: You possess the wonderful ability to project your warm and sunny personality and keep others happily entertained. Loving attention yourself, you seek a partner who can appreciate you and be supportive and give you positive feedback. Proud, with a natural regal air, you expect respect from your partners but are willing to be loyal and supportive in exchange. Although sometimes a little self-centered, you know how to make your partner feel special.

MEN WITH VENUS IN LEO: Generous, animated, and pleasure-seeking, you can be very entertaining and fun to be with. Usually you are attracted to extroverted and benevolent individuals with a sunny personality. If ambitious, you are drawn to a partner who shows leadership qualities or one who is highly motivated. Your less attractive qualities are your tendencies to be bossy or vain. With a sense of the dramatic, however, you can be the life and soul of the party and inspire those around you.

To read all about your Outer Planets and work out how to use your personalized timetable, go to Section Three, page 789.

To read all about your Outer Planets and work out how to use your personalized timetable, go to Section Three, page 789.

Your Personalized Timetable

JUPITER BENEFICIAL
1939 1/17 – 3/26
1940 6/17 – 12/5
1941 1/25 – 3/29
1944 8/27 – 10/13
1946 10/13 – 12/28
1947 6/7 – 8/22
1950 5/8 – 8/16
1950 12/27 – until 1951 3/9
1952 5/28 – 7/19
1952 11/1 – until 1953 3/7
1956 8/11 – 9/26
1958 9/27 – 12/10
1962 4/13 – 10/5
1962 11/22 – until 1963 2/20
1964 5/10 – 6/24
1964 12/21 – until 1965 1/30
1968 7/25 – 9/10
1970 1/12 – 3/30
1970 9/8 – 11/24
1974 3/25 – until 1975 2/3
1976 4/24 – 6/5
1979 11/8 – until 1980 2/13
1980 7/5 – 8/26
1981 12/17 – until 1982 5/9
1982 8/15 – 11/8
1986 3/8 – 5/28
1986 8/27 – until 1987 1/14
1988 4/8 – 5/20
1991 10/16 – until 1992 3/23
1992 6/8 – 8/9
1993 11/28 – until 1994 10/23
1998 2/20 – 5/2
1998 10/13 – 12/14
2000 3/21 – 5/3
2003 9/28 – 11/27
2004 2/10 – 7/22
2005 11/12 – until 2006 10/7
2010 2/3 – 4/12
2011 7/13 – 10/17
2012 2/28 – 4/16

SATURN BENEFICIAL
1940 5/13 – until 1941 4/29
1949 8/11 – 11/4
1950 2/25 – 7/27
1953 11/23 – until 1954 5/29
1954 8/13 – until 1955 1/19
1955 4/12 – 10/13
1964 5/6 – 7/25
1965 1/25 – until 1966 3/10
1969 7/1 – 10/12
1970 3/20 – 6/9
1970 12/13 – until 1971 2/20
1978 9/19 – until 1979 9/6
1983 1/16 – 3/12
1983 10/2 – until 1984 11/17
1994 3/1 – until 1995 4/15
1995 10/5 – until 1996 1/6
1999 4/27 – 8/9
1999 9/20 – until 2000 4/11
2007 11/4 – until 2008 2/3
2008 7/23 – 10/14
2009 3/29 – 7/3
2012 11/6 – Continues

URANUS BENEFICIAL
1938 1/1 – until 1939 4/21
1963 9/16 – until 1966 7/18
1975 11/11 – until 1979 10/20
2004 3/10 – until 2009 1/16

NEPTUNE BENEFICIAL
1957 12/6 – until 1966 9/7

PLUTO BENEFICIAL
1960 9/25 – until 1966 7/29
1984 12/10 – until 1991 10/31

JUPITER CHALLENGING
1939 6/1 – 9/27

1940 1/19 – 4/3
1945 9/12 – 11/28
1946 5/5 – 7/25
1948 12/3 – until 1949 2/11
1951 5/9 – until 1952 3/17
1957 8/27 – 11/10
1960 11/15 – until 1961 1/25
1963 4/20 – until 1964 2/27
1968 12/12 – until 1969 2/28
1969 8/8 – 10/25
1972 2/29 – 6/22
1972 10/25 – until 1973 1/9
1975 4/3 – 6/18
1975 10/12 – until 1976 2/5
1980 11/16 – until 1981 4/8
1981 7/15 – 10/9
1984 2/7 – 8/9
1984 9/19 – 12/24
1987 3/18 – 5/27
1987 12/13 – 12/17
1992 10/29 – until 1993 9/23
1996 1/20 – 12/7
1999 3/1 – 5/8
2004 10/12 – until 2005 9/7
2008 1/4 – 3/29
2008 6/20 – 11/18
2011 2/10 – 4/20

SATURN CHALLENGING
1938 2/22 – until 1939 4/2
1951 9/15 – until 1952 10/26
1959 2/10 – 6/25
1959 11/10 – until 1961 1/2
1967 4/3 – until 1968 5/11
1968 11/16 – until 1969 1/25
1980 10/22 – until 1981 5/5
1981 7/5 – 12/8
1982 3/28 – 9/2
1988 12/16 – until 1990 2/6
1990 8/17 – 10/29
1996 5/11 – 9/29
1997 2/2 – until 1997 7/6
1997 8/27 – until 1998 3/15
2009 12/13 – until 2010 2/14
2010 8/29 – until 2011 10/10

URANUS CHALLENGING
1968 12/17 – until 1973 8/10
1989 2/7 – until 1993 11/28
2011 5/26 – Continues

NEPTUNE CHALLENGING
1943 11/26 – until 1952 8/27
1986 1/6 – until 1993 12/13

PLUTO CHALLENGING
1972 11/19 – until 1980 8/22
2010 1/14 – Continues

JUPITER SPECIAL
1942 6/27 – 9/12
1943 1/14 – 5/7
1954 6/10 – 8/22
1966 5/24 – 8/4
1977 9/15 – 12/1
1978 5/5 – 7/19
1989 8/19 – until 1990 1/12
1990 4/9 – 7/3
2001 7/30 – until 2002 6/16

SATURN SPECIAL
1944 7/19 – until 1945 8/19
1946 2/2 – 5/4
1973 9/14 – 11/18
1974 5/25 – until 1975 6/24
2003 7/3 – until 2004 7/31

URANUS SPECIAL
1949 8/17 – until 1954 5/9

July 5

SUN: CANCER • DECANATE: SCORPIO/PLUTO • DEGREE: 12°45–14° CANCER • MODE: CARDINAL • ELEMENT: WATER

Your Personal Powers

Intelligent, intuitive, and ambitious, you usually possess both practical awareness and high ideals. Your ruler, the Moon, endows you with emotional receptivity and a strong sixth sense. Since you want to achieve a great deal in life you are likely to seek opportunities to expand. Being capable and determined, you can use events to your advantage and make real changes in order to achieve your goals if you only apply self-discipline. You gain power from developing your inner faith or optimism and staying focused. By trusting your quick comprehension or intuition you are able to see the larger picture. You lose some of your power, however, when you let fear of the unknown undermine your progress. Fortunately, many opportunities will present themselves throughout your life and you will benefit greatly if you approach them with hope rather than skepticism. Although you probably believe in the power of wealth, a failure to see beyond material riches may result in not realizing what is truly valuable in life.

Your Powers of Attraction in Relationships

Friendly and gregarious, you like to socialize and have fun. Usually you are kind and generous to those you love. People admire your ability to think quickly and utilize information in a practical way. Although you are capable and confident, you attract others by being caring and liberal. A tendency to be impulsive or excessive suggests that others may be put off if you behave in an extravagant or self-indulgent manner. Having fast instincts and superior intuition suggests that you can quickly assess others. A stubborn streak, however, implies that reluctance on your part to take advice or to compromise can mean confrontations or setbacks in relationships. Usually drawn to intelligent or clever people, you prefer to be associated with enterprising and powerful individuals who can inspire you both creatively and mentally.

Your attractive qualities: optimistic, intelligent, intuitive, sensitive, strong instincts, dignified, versatile, imaginative, practical, shrewd, business sense, persevering, enterprising, kind, witty, disciplined, foresight, progressive, confident, generous, supportive, adaptable, contented

Your less attractive qualities: extravagant, materialistic, dissatisfied, unreliable, restless, lack of purpose, speculative, opportunistic, uncompromising, sentimental, stubborn, inconsistent, intense, bossy, manipulative, easily bored, moody

Your Venus Power

The planet Venus has a great deal of influence on your powers of attraction. Below are four possible Venus types for women and men. To find your Venus you need to go to page 771, where you will find the Venus table and extra information. The planet Mars also affects your powers of attraction. To find your Mars table and interpretation go to page 761.

WOMEN WITH VENUS IN TAURUS: For your ideal relationship you seek a partner who is both financially secure and demonstrative with his affections. With these thoughts in mind you are likely to want a partner who is refined yet pragmatic or someone concerned with safeguarding your future. Although stubborn, you can be affectionate and loving. Attracted to people with a good sense of style, you can succeed in all kinds of business partnerships, especially those involving the arts, music, and luxury goods.

MEN WITH VENUS IN TAURUS: Although you are usually drawn to sensual and physically beautiful individuals, you want a partner who is reliable and loyal. When in love you enjoy buying your partner things of quality that will grow in value or useful things of a practical nature. You also love to socialize and entertain, especially in luxurious surroundings. You are often attracted to creative people or those with artistic talents.

WOMEN WITH VENUS IN GEMINI: Curious, with a bright and animated approach to life, you are attracted to those who are clever or sophisticated. Your love of variety and desire for knowledge suggest that you need a partner and friends who keep you mentally stimulated. Although witty and a good conversationalist, you may need to keep in touch with your deeper feelings. Nevertheless, intelligent and friendly, you possess a youthful sense of wonder and seek a playmate who can keep you from becoming bored.

MEN WITH VENUS IN GEMINI: Friendly and sociable, you attract others with your clever and amusing conversation. Drawn to partners who can match you in wit and intelligence, you usually prefer to keep relationships light rather than emotionally intense. With your youthful charm and desire for

knowledge and new experiences you usually have many friends and a low boredom threshold.

WOMEN WITH VENUS IN CANCER: Gentle and tender, you are romantic by nature. You possess a strong need for security and usually help others feel safe and protected. This preservation is especially centered around the home, which is your haven from life's storm. Although your maternal instincts are strong, avoid making sacrifices for others at your own expense. Nevertheless, affectionate and caring, once committed to a relationship your loyalty and devotion to your partner is very strong.

MEN WITH VENUS IN CANCER: Being emotionally receptive, you can make a sensitive lover. With your desire to care for and protect others you are likely to have strong family connections. Love is often tied in with being attentive to the needs of others and you may find yourself attracted to individuals who have sympathetic or maternal qualities. Security-conscious, you need a loyal partner who can offer you support and ideally be a good cook and homemaker.

WOMEN WITH VENUS IN LEO: Your friendly and sunny personality often makes you stand out in a crowd. Generous and giving, you know how to make your partner feel special. As you often expect loyalty and devotion from your partner in return, you can become easily offended if they ignore you or behave in an inconsiderate manner. Charming and kind, when you are in love you can be romantic, dramatic, and passionate.

MEN WITH VENUS IN LEO: Enthusiastic, playful, and kind, you can be benevolent with those you love. Warm, romantic, and self-expressive, you adore the drama of love or having fun with your friends. Usually you are attracted to partners with a warm and generous nature. Although you can be a confident and charismatic partner, you may need to develop humility to stop pride or arrogance from marring your relationships.

To read all about your Outer Planets and work out how to use your personalized timetable, go to Section Three, page 789.

Your Personalized Timetable

JUPITER BENEFICIAL
1939 1/21 – 3/30
1940 6/22 – 11/25
1941 2/4 – 4/3
1944 8/31 – 10/18
1945 5/3 – 5/26
1946 10/17 – until **1947** 1/3
1947 5/30 – 8/31
1950 5/15 – 8/8
1951 1/1 – 3/13
1952 6/1 – 7/26
1952 10/25 – until **1953** 3/13
1956 8/15 – 10/1
1958 10/1 – 12/15
1962 4/18 – 9/24
1962 12/2 – until **1963** 2/24
1964 5/14 – 6/29
1964 12/10 – until **1965** 2/10
1968 7/30 – 9/15
1970 1/22 – 3/20
1970 9/13 – 11/28
1974 3/29 – until **1975** 2/7
1976 4/28 – 6/10
1979 11/16 – until **1980** 2/5
1980 7/11 – 8/30
1981 12/23 – until **1982** 5/1
1982 8/22 – 11/13
1986 3/12 – 6/5
1986 8/18 – until **1987** 1/19
1988 4/12 – 5/24
1991 10/21 – until **1992** 3/15
1992 6/16 – 8/14
1993 12/3 – until **1994** 10/28
1998 2/24 – 5/7
1998 10/4 – 12/23
2000 3/25 – 5/7
2003 10/3 – 12/7
2004 1/31 – 7/27
2005 11/17 – until **2006** 10/12
2010 2/7 – 4/16
2011 7/20 – 10/10
2012 3/4 – 4/20

SATURN BENEFICIAL
1940 5/21 – until **1941** 5/6
1949 8/18 – 11/16
1950 2/13 – 8/5
1953 12/2 – until **1954** 5/14
1954 8/27 – until **1955** 2/6
1955 3/24 – 10/21
1964 5/27 – 7/4
1965 2/2 – until **1966** 3/17
1969 7/14 – 9/28
1970 3/28 – 6/17
1970 11/29 – until **1971** 3/6
1978 9/26 – until **1979** 4/11
1979 6/6 – 9/14
1983 10/10 – until **1984** 11/25
1994 3/9 – until **1995** 4/24
1995 9/22 – until **1996** 1/18
1999 5/5 – until **2000** 4/19
2007 11/19 – until **2008** 1/18
2008 8/1 – 10/23
2009 3/16 – 7/15
2012 11/14 – Continues

URANUS BENEFICIAL
1938 1/1 – until **1939** 5/7
1963 10/3 – until **1966** 8/6
1975 11/27 – until **1979** 11/5
2004 3/28 – until **2009** 2/7

NEPTUNE BENEFICIAL
1958 1/24 – until **1966** 10/13

PLUTO BENEFICIAL
1960 11/1 – until **1966** 8/28
1985 2/1 – until **1992** 9/15

JUPITER CHALLENGING
1939 6/8 – 9/20

1940 1/25 – 4/7
1945 9/16 – 12/4
1946 4/27 – 8/2
1948 12/7 – until **1949** 2/16
1951 5/13 – 11/13
1951 12/16 – until **1952** 3/21
1957 8/31 – 11/15
1960 11/20 – until **1961** 1/29
1963 4/24 – until **1964** 3/3
1968 12/22 – until **1969** 2/18
1969 8/14 – 10/30
1972 3/6 – 6/14
1972 10/30 – until **1973** 1/13
1975 4/7 – 6/24
1975 10/5 – until **1976** 2/10
1980 11/22 – until **1981** 4/1
1981 7/22 – 10/14
1984 2/12 – 7/28
1984 10/1 – 12/28
1987 3/22 – 5/31
1987 11/21 – until **1988** 1/8
1992 11/2 – until **1993** 9/28
1996 1/24 – 12/12
1999 3/5 – 5/12
2004 10/17 – until **2005** 9/12
2008 1/8 – 4/7
2008 6/11 – 11/23
2011 2/15 – 4/24

SATURN CHALLENGING
1938 3/3 – 4/9
1951 9/23 – until **1952** 11/3
1953 6/8 – 7/8
1959 2/21 – 6/12
1959 11/20 – until **1961** 1/10
1967 4/11 – until **1968** 5/19
1968 11/1 – until **1969** 2/7
1980 10/31 – until **1981** 4/19
1981 7/21 – 12/20
1982 3/15 – 9/11
1988 12/24 – until **1990** 2/15
1990 8/1 – 11/12
1996 5/22 – 9/16
1997 2/12 – until **1998** 3/23
2010 9/6 – until **2011** 10/18

URANUS CHALLENGING
1969 10/3 – until **1973** 9/1
1989 3/3 – until **1993** 12/17
2012 3/28 – Continues

NEPTUNE CHALLENGING
1944 10/17 – until **1952** 9/25
1986 2/2 – until **1994** 10/26

PLUTO CHALLENGING
1973 10/9 – until **1980** 9/20
2010 2/14 – Continues

JUPITER SPECIAL
1942 7/1 – 9/18
1943 1/7 – 5/13
1954 6/14 – 8/27
1955 2/21 – 4/9
1966 5/28 – 8/9
1977 9/25 – 11/22
1978 5/10 – 7/23
1989 8/25 – until **1990** 1/4
1990 4/16 – 7/7
2001 8/4 – until **2002** 6/20

SATURN SPECIAL
1944 7/27 – until **1945** 2/2
1945 4/6 – 8/28
1946 1/20 – 5/16
1973 10/14 – 10/19
1974 6/2 – until **1975** 7/2
2003 7/10 – until **2004** 8/8
2005 3/2 – 4/10

URANUS SPECIAL
1949 9/16 – until **1954** 5/31

223

July 6

Your Personal Powers

Friendly and broad-minded, your caring nature and optimism indicate that you can be a kind individual with a responsible attitude and high ideals. Your superior intellect blends well with your imagination, making you a practical visionary. Often generous, you gain power when you overcome a tendency to become emotionally intense or overly critical. You lose power, however, when you relinquish your wonderful sense of humor by becoming frustrated or disappointed. As you are likely to be security-conscious, how well you manage your financial affairs or assets may be key to your success. You empower yourself when you consider your long-term options and plan for the future. Although you may experience fluctuations in your income, just when you think the worst, your circumstances can change for the better. Although capable and talented, be careful of an extravagant streak. By trusting your highly developed intuition and acting rationally, you can succeed admirably.

Your Powers of Attraction in Relationships

Outgoing and friendly, you enjoy mixing with people and socializing. Entertaining and witty, you can draw people with your lively style. Being independent, however, you do not like to be restrained by others. Nevertheless, generous and caring, you show your love by being liberal, affectionate, and encouraging. People also admire your special insight and purposeful nature. Keen on communicating, you seek relationships that can be mentally stimulating or inspiring. Usually you want a partner who can share your interests and be sympathetic to your needs. Although you often have strong opinions, avoid being confrontational or argumentative, particularly if inner fears cause you to become bossy or interfering. When you are positive and optimistic, however, you can uplift others with your kind gestures and support. Persuasive and charming, you usually get your own way by appealing to your partner's better nature.

Your attractive qualities: balanced, friendly, enthusiastic, intuitive, intellectual, liberal, caring, humanitarian, methodical, responsible, sense of values, generous, entrepreneurial, insight, home-loving, sympathetic, trusting, compassionate, dependable, understanding, humorous, affectionate

Your less attractive qualities: interfering, skeptical, uncar-ing, sarcastic, agitated, dissatisfied, restless, anxious, insecure, stubborn, outspoken, disappointed, impulsive, disharmonious, too sensitive, suspicious, bossy

Your Venus Power

The planet Venus has a great deal of influence on your powers of attraction. Below are four possible Venus types for women and men. To find your Venus you need to go to page 771, where you will find the Venus table and extra information. The planet Mars also affects your powers of attraction. To find your Mars table and interpretation go to page 761.

WOMEN WITH VENUS IN TAURUS: For your ideal relationship you seek a partner who is both financially secure and demonstrative with his affections. With these thoughts in mind, you are likely to want a partner who is refined yet pragmatic or someone concerned with safeguarding your future. Although stubborn, you can be affectionate and loving. Attracted to people with a good sense of style, you can succeed in all kinds of business partnerships, especially those involving the arts, music, and luxury goods.

MEN WITH VENUS IN TAURUS: As well as attracting people with your warm personality, you possess an innate sense of the value of material possessions. Keeping yourself stylish and having an attractive appearance can also be important to you. You are naturally attracted to practical yet sensual women who understand your need for comfort, security, and the pleasures and luxuries of life. Naturally affectionate, you enjoy socializing but can be a loyal and loving partner.

WOMEN WITH VENUS IN GEMINI: In relationships you need intellectual stimulation and usually prefer to keep things light. Certainly not boring, you love to talk and are at your best being witty and entertaining. Although your easygoing approach to relationships is very attractive, guard against losing touch with your deeper emotions. You prefer a partner who can keep up with your fast stream of ideas, and if you have shared interests then so much the better.

MEN WITH VENUS IN GEMINI: Adaptable yet often flirtatious, you enjoy mixing with people who are quick-minded and versatile. Since you can learn a great deal through interacting with others, you are often attracted to intelligent partners who have comprehensive knowledge or good ideas. One of your less attractive qualities is your tendency to become bored or be inconsistent. Having an adaptable partner is im-

portant to you; therefore it must be someone who can offer you different options and keep you interested.

WOMEN WITH VENUS IN CANCER: Possessing a soft femininity, you have tender and sensitive emotions. Sympathetic and caring, you often mother those in your care by making sure they are comfortable and have plenty to eat. When you feel hurt or insecure in relationships you are likely to cover your feelings by being defensive or appearing tough on the outside while on the inside you are feeling vulnerable. Affectionate and romantic, you make a faithful and devoted partner.

MEN WITH VENUS IN CANCER: Affectionate with a strong sensitive streak, you can love very deeply. You may find yourself drawn to sympathetic partners who can tune in to your moods and feelings as well as be reassuring and supportive. Family links are especially important to you and the more positive these relationships are the more confident and safe you feel.

WOMEN WITH VENUS IN LEO: You possess the wonderful ability to project your warm and sunny personality and keep others happily entertained. Loving attention yourself, you seek a partner who can appreciate you and be supportive and give you positive feedback. Proud, with a natural regal air, you expect respect from your partners but are willing to be loyal and supportive in exchange. Although sometimes a little self-centered, you know how to make your partner feel special.

MEN WITH VENUS IN LEO: Generous, animated, and pleasure-seeking, you can be very entertaining and fun to be with. Usually you are attracted to extroverted and benevolent individuals with a sunny personality. If ambitious, you are drawn to a partner who shows leadership qualities or one who is highly motivated. Your less attractive qualities are your tendencies to be bossy or vain. With a sense of the dramatic, however, you can be the life and soul of the party and inspire those around you.

To read all about your Outer Planets and work out how to use your personalized timetable, go to Section Three, page 789.

Your Personalized Timetable

JUPITER BENEFICIAL
1939 1/26 – 4/3
1940 6/27 – 11/17
1941 2/12 – 4/7
1944 9/4 – 10/23
1945 4/16 – 6/11
1946 10/22 – until 1947 1/8
1947 5/22 – 9/7
1950 5/24 – 7/30
1951 1/6 – 3/17
1952 6/5 – 8/2
1952 10/17 – until 1953 3/18
1956 8/19 – 10/5
1958 10/6 – 12/20
1962 4/23 – 9/16
1962 12/10 – until 1963 2/28
1964 5/18 – 7/4
1964 12/1 – until 1965 2/19
1968 8/3 – 9/19
1970 2/7 – 3/4
1970 9/18 – 12/3
1974 4/2 – until 1975 2/11
1976 5/2 – 6/14
1979 11/25 – until 1980 1/26
1980 7/16 – 9/3
1981 12/29 – until 1982 4/24
1982 8/29 – 11/17
1986 3/16 – 6/15
1986 8/8 – until 1987 1/24
1988 4/16 – 5/28
1991 10/27 – until 1992 3/7
1992 6/23 – 8/18
1993 12/8 – until 1994 6/7
1994 7/27 – 11/1
1998 2/28 – 5/12
1998 9/26 – 12/30
2000 3/29 – 5/11
2003 10/7 – 12/23
2004 1/15 – 8/1
2005 11/21 – until 2006 10/17
2010 2/11 – 4/20
2011 7/29 – 10/1
2012 3/9 – 4/24

SATURN BENEFICIAL
1940 5/29 – 12/10
1941 2/7 – 5/14
1949 8/26 – 12/1
1950 1/28 – 8/14
1953 12/11 – until 1954 5/1
1954 9/7 – until 1955 10/30
1965 2/10 – until 1966 3/25
1969 8/4 – 9/7
1970 4/5 – 6/26
1970 11/17 – until 1971 3/17
1978 10/5 – until 1979 3/26
1979 6/22 – 9/22
1983 10/18 – until 1984 12/3
1985 7/9 – 8/11
1994 3/17 – 11/6
1994 11/11 – until 1995 5/4
1995 9/10 – until 1996 1/28
1999 5/12 – until 2000 4/27
2008 8/9 – 11/1
2009 3/4 – 7/25
2012 11/22 – Continues

URANUS BENEFICIAL
1938 1/1 – until 1940 3/7
1963 10/21 – until 1966 8/22
1975 12/15 – until 1980 8/20
2004 4/18 – until 2009 2/24

NEPTUNE BENEFICIAL
1938 4/24 – until 1938 7/4
1958 11/30 – until 1967 8/23

PLUTO BENEFICIAL
1961 9/25 – until 1967 7/22
1985 11/22 – until 1992 10/15

JUPITER CHALLENGING
1939 6/15 – 9/13

1940 1/30 – 4/11
1945 9/21 – 12/10
1946 4/19 – 8/9
1948 12/11 – until 1949 2/20
1951 5/18 – 10/31
1951 12/29 – until 1952 3/25
1957 9/5 – 11/20
1960 11/24 – until 1961 2/3
1963 4/28 – until 1964 3/7
1969 1/5 – 2/4
1969 8/19 – 11/3
1972 3/14 – 6/6
1972 11/5 – until 1973 1/17
1975 4/11 – 7/1
1975 9/28 – until 1976 2/15
1980 11/28 – until 1981 3/24
1981 7/29 – 10/18
1984 2/17 – 7/19
1984 10/10 – until 1985 1/2
1987 3/26 – 6/5
1987 11/11 – until 1988 1/18
1992 11/7 – until 1993 5/7
1993 6/26 – 10/2
1996 1/29 – 12/16
1999 3/9 – 5/16
2004 10/21 – until 2005 9/17
2008 1/12 – 4/19
2008 5/30 – 11/28
2011 2/19 – 4/28

SATURN CHALLENGING
1938 3/11 – until 1939 4/17
1951 10/1 – until 1952 11/11
1953 5/16 – 7/31
1959 3/6 – 5/29
1959 11/29 – until 1961 1/18
1967 4/19 – 12/3
1967 12/15 – until 1968 5/29
1968 10/20 – until 1969 2/18
1980 11/8 – until 1981 4/5
1981 8/2 – until 1982 1/6
1982 2/25 – 9/19
1989 1/1 – until 1990 2/24
1990 7/19 – 11/24
1996 6/3 – 9/3
1997 2/21 – until 1998 3/31
2010 9/14 – until 2011 10/26

URANUS CHALLENGING
1969 10/18 – until 1973 9/18
1989 12/31 – until 1994 1/2
2012 4/14 – Continues

NEPTUNE CHALLENGING
1944 11/16 – until 1953 8/19
1986 3/18 – until 1994 12/6

PLUTO CHALLENGING
1973 11/5 – until 1981 7/25
2011 1/11 – Continues

JUPITER SPECIAL
1942 7/5 – 9/25
1942 12/31 – until 1943 5/19
1954 6/18 – 9/1
1955 2/11 – 4/20
1966 6/2 – 8/13
1977 10/8 – 11/9
1978 5/15 – 7/27
1989 8/30 – 12/28
1990 4/23 – 7/11
2001 8/8 – until 2002 2/24
2002 3/7 – 6/25

SATURN SPECIAL
1944 8/5 – until 1945 1/18
1945 4/20 – 9/6
1946 1/9 – 5/26
1974 6/10 – until 1975 7/9
2003 7/18 – until 2004 8/16
2005 2/11 – 4/29

URANUS SPECIAL
1950 7/5 – until 1954 6/18

225

July 7

SUN: CANCER • DECANATE: SCORPIO/PLUTO • DEGREE: 14°5–16°5 CANCER • MODE: CARDINAL • ELEMENT: WATER

Your Personal Powers

Intuitive, mentally sharp, and hardworking, you can be a determined and strong-willed individual. The Moon, your ruler, indicates that you are extremely sensitive although you may hide it behind a proud exterior. Although you are thoughtful and impressionable, you gain power from you innate intuition, inner strength, and pragmatic approach. You possess a strong drive for success and financial security but you also like the freedom to act independently. Straightforward and persistent, you enjoy power or being in control, and unless you are learning new skills you often resent taking orders from others. Be careful not to go too far, however, and appear defiant to the point of severing your communication with others. Nonetheless, with your innate organizational abilities, you often possess a good business sense and can be very focused in achieving your goals. Although you are noble with strong opinions, you lose power if you become too headstrong or impatient. Being a quick and astute observer, however, you usually enjoy playful banter.

Your Powers of Attraction in Relationships

Your enthusiasm, strong will, and sociable personality draw others toward you. Being tenacious and independent, you are often attracted by those who can emotionally express themselves and are creative. Although you appear very confident, in relationships you sometimes have doubts or experience insecurities. You may then vacillate between being a tower of strength for those you love and feeling sensitive or vulnerable. By keeping yourself busy and creative you reassure yourself and possibly avoid indecision regarding your partners. Nevertheless, fiercely protective of those in your care, you enhance your persuasion skills by using your discreet approach and collaborating with others. By having faith in yourself and your talents you can positively channel your strong inner power to transform yourself and your relationships.

Your attractive qualities: determined, honest, imaginative, faithful, responsible, happy, enterprising, creative, sincere, sympathetic, generous, committed, perseverance, fastidious, idealistic, psychic, independent, kind, scientific, self-awareness, sensible, reflective

Your less attractive qualities: frustrated, bossy, concealing, unfriendly, secretive, skeptical, self-doubt, confused, too proud, oversensitive, cold, discontented

Your Venus Power

The planet Venus has a great deal of influence on your powers of attraction. Below are four possible Venus types for women and men. To find your Venus you need to go to page 771, where you will find the Venus table and extra information. The planet Mars also affects your powers of attraction. To find your Mars table and interpretation go to page 761.

WOMEN WITH VENUS IN GEMINI: By nature you are young at heart, adaptable, and sociable. Being curious and willing to cooperate makes you a good team player. Usually you are drawn to articulate people who have charm and flair or sharp wit. With a need to expand your knowledge, you also look for a partner who can challenge or stimulate you intellectually. Although you love to talk with all types of people you may need to develop your listening skills in order to build better communication in your relationships.

MEN WITH VENUS IN GEMINI: Charming, amusing, and adaptable, you attract others with your natural communication skills and friendly personality. You have a wonderful childlike quality and love to keep life playful, but a reluctance to contact your deeper feelings may cause you to avoid serious commitment. With your need for variety and intellectual stimulation, you are attracted to clever and amusing partners who have many interesting sides to their personalities.

WOMEN WITH VENUS IN CANCER: Gentle and tender, you are romantic by nature. You possess a strong need for security and usually help others feel safe and protected. This preservation is especially centered around the home, which is your haven from life's storm. Although your maternal instincts are strong, avoid making sacrifices for others at your own expense. Nevertheless, affectionate and caring, once committed to a relationship your loyalty and devotion to your partner is very strong.

MEN WITH VENUS IN CANCER: Being emotionally receptive, you can make a sensitive lover. With your desire to care for and protect others, you are likely to have strong family connections. Love is often tied in with being attentive to the needs of others and you may find yourself attracted to individuals who have sympathetic or maternal qualities. Security-

conscious, you need a loyal partner who can offer you support and ideally be a good cook and homemaker.

WOMEN WITH VENUS IN LEO: Your friendly and sunny personality often makes you stand out in a crowd. Generous and giving, you know how to make your partners feel special. As you often expect loyalty and devotion from your partners in return, you can become easily offended if they ignore you or behave in an inconsiderate manner. Charming and kind when you are in love, you can be romantic, dramatic and passionate.

MEN WITH VENUS IN LEO: Warm and playful with a touch of the dramatic, you enjoy the company of generous or strong individuals who can share your sense of fun. Although there are advantages to your being strong-willed, in your relationships you need to resist being bossy as it can cause resentment. With your wonderful mixture of regal authority and childlike wonder, you love to keep others entertained and amused.

WOMEN WITH VENUS IN VIRGO: In relationships you can be modest and unassuming but desire perfection. You usually analyze your partnerships until you feel you have understood them to the last little detail in order to improve them. A problem usually arises when you become too critical either of partners or yourself and indulge in being skeptical or fault-finding. As you are modest, others may not be aware of the strong sensuality beneath your well-groomed exterior.

MEN WITH VENUS IN VIRGO: Practical, idealistic, and perfectionist, you seek a relationship with an intelligent and hardworking partner who can inspire you to be more industrious and well-ordered. At times you can come across as a sympathetic and caring person and at other times you may appear pragmatic and very businesslike. This may sometimes lead to unclear communication between you and your partner. Usually helpful and caring, however, you like to analyze the faults in your relationships and then work methodically to improve them.

To read all about your Outer Planets and work out how to use your personalized timetable, go to Section Three, page 789.

Your Personalized Timetable

JUPITER BENEFICIAL
1939 1/30 – 4/7
1940 7/2 – 11/10
1941 2/18 – 4/12
1944 9/9 – 10/28
1945 4/6 – 6/22
1946 10/26 – until **1947** 1/14
1947 5/14 – 9/13
1950 6/4 – 7/19
1951 1/11 – 3/21
1952 6/10 – 8/12
1952 10/8 – until **1953** 3/23
1956 8/24 – 10/10
1958 10/10 – 12/25
1959 7/1 – 8/7
1962 4/28 – 9/8
1962 12/17 – until **1963** 3/4
1964 5/22 – 7/10
1964 11/23 – until **1965** 2/26
1968 8/8 – 9/24
1970 9/23 – 12/7
1974 4/7 – until **1975** 2/15
1976 5/6 – 6/19
1979 12/7 – until **1980** 1/14
1980 7/21 – 9/8
1982 1/5 – 4/16
1982 9/4 – 11/21
1986 3/20 – 7/1
1986 7/23 – until **1987** 1/28
1988 4/20 – 6/1
1991 11/2 – until **1992** 2/29
1992 6/30 – 8/23
1993 12/13 – until **1994** 5/27
1994 8/7 – 11/6
1998 3/4 – 5/18
1998 9/19 – until **1999** 1/5
2000 4/3 – 5/15
2003 10/12 – until **2004** 4/13
2004 5/27 – 8/6
2005 11/26 – until **2006** 10/21
2010 2/15 – 4/25
2011 8/9 – 9/20
2012 3/14 – 4/28

SATURN BENEFICIAL
1940 6/6 – 11/25
1941 2/22 – 5/21
1949 9/3 – until **1950** 8/22
1953 12/21 – until **1954** 4/18
1954 9/17 – until **1955** 11/7
1965 2/18 – until **1966** 4/2
1970 4/13 – 7/6
1970 11/5 – until **1971** 3/26
1978 10/13 – until **1979** 3/13
1979 7/4 – 9/29
1983 10/26 – until **1984** 12/11
1985 6/16 – 9/2
1994 3/25 – 10/6
1994 12/12 – until **1995** 5/16
1995 8/28 – until **1996** 2/6
1999 5/20 – until **2000** 5/4
2008 8/16 – 11/12
2009 2/20 – 8/3
2012 12/1 – Continues

URANUS BENEFICIAL
1938 1/1 – until **1940** 3/30
1963 11/16 – until **1966** 9/7
1976 1/9 – until **1980** 9/20
2004 5/22 – until **2009** 3/13

NEPTUNE BENEFICIAL
1938 3/15 – 8/10
1959 1/5 – until **1967** 10/7

PLUTO BENEFICIAL
1961 10/30 – until **1967** 8/22
1985 12/21 – until **1992** 11/9

JUPITER CHALLENGING
1939 6/23 – 9/4
1940 2/4 – 4/15

1945 9/25 – 12/16
1946 4/11 – 8/15
1948 12/15 – until **1949** 2/25
1949 9/5 – 10/2
1951 5/23 – 10/22
1952 1/7 – 3/29
1957 9/10 – 11/25
1958 5/25 – 7/13
1960 11/29 – until **1961** 2/7
1963 5/3 – until **1964** 3/11
1969 8/24 – 11/8
1972 3/22 – 5/28
1972 11/10 – until **1973** 1/21
1975 4/15 – 7/9
1975 9/19 – until **1976** 2/21
1980 12/5 – until **1981** 3/17
1981 8/4 – 10/22
1984 2/22 – 7/11
1984 10/17 – until **1985** 1/6
1987 3/30 – 6/10
1987 11/3 – until **1988** 1/26
1992 11/13 – until **1993** 4/26
1993 7/7 – 10/7
1996 2/2 – 12/20
1999 3/13 – 5/20
2004 10/26 – until **2005** 9/21
2008 1/17 – 12/3
2011 2/24 – 5/2

SATURN CHALLENGING
1938 3/18 – until **1939** 4/24
1951 10/8 – until **1952** 11/20
1953 5/1 – 8/14
1959 3/25 – 5/9
1959 12/7 – until **1961** 1/27
1967 4/27 – 11/5
1968 1/11 – 6/8
1968 10/8 – until **1969** 2/28
1980 11/18 – until **1981** 3/24
1981 8/12 – until **1982** 9/27
1989 1/10 – until **1990** 3/7
1990 7/6 – 12/4
1996 6/18 – 8/18
1997 3/1 – until **1998** 4/8
2010 9/22 – until **2011** 11/3

URANUS CHALLENGING
1969 11/3 – until **1973** 10/4
1990 1/16 – until **1994** 10/26
2012 5/3 – until **2012** 9/26

NEPTUNE CHALLENGING
1945 10/12 – until **1953** 9/20
1987 1/27 – until **1995** 1/3

PLUTO CHALLENGING
1973 12/15 – until **1981** 9/4
2011 2/10 – Continues

JUPITER SPECIAL
1942 7/9 – 10/2
1942 12/23 – until **1943** 5/24
1954 6/23 – 9/6
1955 2/2 – 4/28
1966 6/6 – 8/18
1978 5/20 – 8/1
1989 9/6 – 12/21
1990 4/29 – 7/15
2001 8/13 – until **2002** 2/4
2002 3/26 – 6/29

SATURN SPECIAL
1944 8/13 – until **1945** 1/6
1945 5/1 – 9/17
1945 12/28 – until **1946** 6/4
1974 6/17 – until **1975** 7/16
2003 7/26 – until **2004** 2/17
2004 3/27 – until **2004** 8/24
2005 1/29 – until **2005** 5/12

URANUS SPECIAL
1950 7/22 – until **1954** 7/4

July 8

SUN: CANCER • DECANATE: SCORPIO/PLUTO • DEGREE: 15°5–17° CANCER • MODE: CARDINAL • ELEMENT: WATER

Your Personal Powers

You can really succeed in life by combining your natural charm, ambition, and determination with your innate understanding of money and values. Although the Moon, your ruler, indicates that you are both receptive and impressionable, your tenacity and perseverance are important keys to your accomplishments. Hardworking and sociable with business acumen, you possess the ability to mix work and pleasure. Although you are sensitive and caring, you enjoy being in control or in charge of situations; therefore you gain power from your quick judgment and drive. You empower yourself when you can integrate the spontaneous and creative side of your nature with your serious outlook and forceful nature. You lose some of your power when you become critical, too serious, or withdrawn. Kind and responsible, however, you have innate organizational and executive skills that make you highly disciplined. Besides being perceptive and imaginative, you also have high ideals and an inner dramatic sense that seeks self-expression.

Your Powers of Attraction in Relationships

With your ability to feel other people's problems as if they are your own, others are attracted by your sympathetic nature. Very protective of lovers, family, and friends, you are often willing to make sacrifices for those you love. In your attempt to support or help your partner, avoid martyring yourself or becoming too controlling. In love situations generally you can be generous and loving, placing a great value on your relationships. As you are youthful and idealistic, you may even be attracted to someone of a different age group. Being romantic, you may seek a more spiritual partnership, but unless you develop a detached attitude, you may find that your partner cannot live up to your high expectations. Nonetheless, affectionate and loving, you possess a strong inner power that can help you transform any difficulties in your relationships into strengths.

Your attractive qualities: leadership, generous, thoroughness, hardworking, protective, sensitive, responsible, good judge of values, idealistic, commitment, faithful, light-hearted, spontaneous, practical, receptive, business sense, creative, charming, imaginative

Your less attractive qualities: impatient, intolerant, workaholic, domineering, easily discouraged, critical, too serious, cold, dissatisfied, frustration, power challenges, controlling

Your Venus Power

The planet Venus has a great deal of influence on your powers of attraction. Below are four possible Venus types for women and men. To find your Venus you need to go to page 771, where you will find the Venus table and extra information. The planet Mars also affects your powers of attraction. To find your Mars table and interpretation go to page 761.

WOMEN WITH VENUS IN GEMINI: In relationships you need intellectual stimulation and usually prefer to keep things light. Certainly not boring, you love to talk and are at your best being witty and entertaining. Although your easygoing approach to relationships is very attractive, guard against losing touch with your emotions. You prefer a partner who can keep up with your fast stream of ideas, and if you have shared interests then so much the better.

MEN WITH VENUS IN GEMINI: Adaptable yet often flirtatious, you enjoy mixing with people who are quick-minded and versatile. Since you can learn a great deal through interacting with others, you are often attracted to intelligent partners who have comprehensive knowledge or good ideas. One of your less attractive qualities is your tendency to become bored or be inconsistent. Having an adaptable partner is important to you; therefore it must be someone who can offer you different options and keep you interested.

WOMEN WITH VENUS IN CANCER: Possessing a soft femininity, you have tender and sensitive emotions. Sympathetic and caring, you often mother those in your care by making sure they are comfortable and have plenty to eat. When you feel hurt or insecure in relationships you are likely to cover your feelings by being defensive or appearing tough on the outside while on the inside you are feeling vulnerable. Affectionate and romantic, you make a faithful and devoted partner.

MEN WITH VENUS IN CANCER: Being emotionally receptive, you can make a sensitive lover. With your desire to care for and protect others, you are likely to have strong family connections. Love is often tied in with being attentive to the needs of others and you may find yourself attracted to indi-

viduals who have sympathetic or maternal qualities. Security-conscious, you need a loyal partner who can offer you support and ideally be a good cook and homemaker.

WOMEN WITH VENUS IN LEO: You possess the wonderful ability to project your warm and sunny personality and keep others happily entertained. Loving attention yourself, you seek a partner who can appreciate you, be supportive, and give you positive feedback. Proud, with a natural regal air, you expect respect from your partners but are willing to be loyal and supportive in exchange. Although sometimes a little self-centered, you know how to make your partner feel special.

MEN WITH VENUS IN LEO: Sociable and outgoing, you are kind and generous with those you love. Looking for a relationship that can be fun and entertaining, you need a playmate who can share your enthusiasm and high spirits. Your pride, however, often stops you from associating with lovers or partners you see as beneath you. As you desire someone who can appreciate your sense of the dramatic, you are often attracted to people with strong personalities.

WOMEN WITH VENUS IN VIRGO: Articulate and straightforward in your relationships, you attract others with your genuine concern for their well-being. By being understanding and a good listener, you are able to show your love and friendship. With your analytical approach to relationships, however, you may have to be careful of becoming too matter-of-fact. You often display your concern for the welfare of others by your willingness to offer practical help and assistance. You usually seek a partner who is willing to work as hard on relationships as you are.

MEN WITH VENUS IN VIRGO: Although you are constantly analyzing your relationships in order to understand and improve them, you may nevertheless need to refrain from continuously mulling over issues that can cause anxiety. You are happiest when you are able to help your loved ones in practical ways and forget yourself in your willingness to be of service to others. You seek a partner who has high standards and can be as pragmatic and hardworking as yourself. Ideally they should also be impeccably dressed with a fine analytical mind.

To read all about your Outer Planets and work out how to use your personalized timetable, go to Section Three, page 789.

Your Personalized Timetable

JUPITER BENEFICIAL
1939 2/3 – 4/11
1940 7/8 – 11/3
1941 2/25 – 4/16
1944 9/13 – 11/2
1945 3/29 – 6/30
1946 10/31 – until 1947 1/21
1947 5/7 – 9/19
1951 1/15 – 3/25
1952 6/14 – 8/25
1952 9/24 – until 1953 3/28
1956 8/28 – 10/15
1958 10/15 – 12/30
1959 6/18 – 8/20
1962 5/4 – 9/1
1962 12/23 – until 1963 3/8
1964 5/27 – 7/15
1964 11/16 – until 1965 3/4
1968 8/13 – 9/28
1970 9/28 – 12/12
1974 4/11 – until 1975 2/19
1976 5/10 – 6/23
1980 7/26 – 9/12
1982 1/12 – 4/8
1982 9/9 – 11/26
1986 3/24 – until 1987 2/2
1988 4/24 – 6/5
1991 11/8 – until 1992 2/21
1992 7/6 – 8/27
1993 12/19 – until 1994 5/18
1994 8/15 – 11/10
1998 3/8 – 5/24
1998 9/12 – until 1999 1/11
2000 4/7 – 5/19
2003 10/17 – until 2004 4/1
2004 6/8 – 8/11
2005 12/1 – until 2006 10/26
2010 2/19 – 4/30
2010 11/11 – 11/25
2012 3/19 – 5/2

SATURN BENEFICIAL
1940 6/15 – 11/12
1941 3/6 – 5/29
1949 9/10 – until 1950 8/30
1954 1/2 – 4/5
1954 9/27 – until 1955 11/15
1965 2/26 – until 1966 4/10
1966 10/29 – 12/24
1970 4/21 – 7/17
1970 10/24 – until 1971 4/4
1978 10/23 – until 1979 3/1
1979 7/15 – 10/7
1980 4/30 – 6/13
1983 11/3 – until 1984 12/20
1985 6/1 – 9/16
1994 4/3 – 9/20
1994 12/27 – until 1995 5/29
1995 8/13 – until 1996 2/14
1999 5/28 – 12/25
2000 1/30 – 5/12
2008 8/24 – 11/25
2009 2/6 – 8/12
2012 12/10 – Continues

URANUS BENEFICIAL
1938 3/4 – until 1940 4/18
1964 9/5 – until 1967 6/24
1976 11/1 – until 1980 10/10
2005 3/12 – until 2010 1/17

NEPTUNE BENEFICIAL
1938 2/7 – until 1939 6/16
1959 11/24 – until 1967 11/4

PLUTO BENEFICIAL
1962 9/24 – until 1968 7/10
1986 11/7 – until 1993 9/28

JUPITER CHALLENGING
1939 7/2 – 8/25
1940 2/9 – 4/19

1945 9/30 – 12/22
1946 4/4 – 8/21
1948 12/20 – until 1949 3/2
1949 8/21 – 10/16
1951 5/29 – 10/14
1952 1/14 – 4/2
1957 9/14 – 11/30
1958 5/14 – 7/24
1960 12/3 – until 1961 2/11
1963 5/7 – until 1964 3/16
1969 8/29 – 11/12
1972 4/3 – 5/16
1972 11/15 – until 1973 1/25
1975 4/19 – 7/19
1975 9/9 – until 1976 2/25
1980 12/12 – until 1981 3/9
1981 8/10 – 10/27
1984 2/28 – 7/3
1984 10/24 – until 1985 1/10
1987 4/3 – 6/16
1987 10/26 – until 1988 2/2
1992 11/18 – until 1993 4/17
1993 7/16 – 10/11
1996 2/7 – 12/25
1999 3/17 – 5/25
2004 10/31 – until 2005 9/26
2008 1/21 – 12/7
2011 2/28 – 5/6

SATURN CHALLENGING
1938 3/26 – until 1939 5/2
1951 10/16 – until 1952 11/29
1953 4/19 – 8/25
1959 12/16 – until 1961 2/4
1961 9/6 – 10/18
1967 5/6 – 10/21
1968 1/25 – 6/19
1968 9/25 – until 1969 3/8
1980 11/29 – until 1981 3/11
1981 8/22 – until 1982 10/5
1989 1/18 – 8/23
1989 9/30 – until 1990 3/19
1990 6/22 – 12/13
1997 3/9 – until 1998 4/15
2010 9/29 – until 2011 11/11
2012 5/24 – 7/27

URANUS CHALLENGING
1969 11/23 – until 1973 10/19
1990 2/2 – until 1994 11/25
2012 5/25 – Continues

NEPTUNE CHALLENGING
1945 11/9 – until 1954 8/8
1987 3/2 – until 1995 11/29

PLUTO CHALLENGING
1974 10/24 – until 1981 9/30
2012 1/8 – Continues

JUPITER SPECIAL
1942 7/13 – 10/11
1942 12/14 – until 1943 5/30
1954 6/27 – 9/11
1955 1/25 – 5/6
1966 6/11 – 8/22
1978 5/24 – 8/5
1989 9/12 – 12/14
1990 5/4 – 7/20
2001 8/18 – until 2002 1/25
2002 4/6 – 7/4

SATURN SPECIAL
1944 8/23 – 12/25
1945 5/11 – 9/29
1945 12/14 – until 1946 6/12
1974 6/24 – until 1975 7/24
2003 8/3 – until 2004 1/29
2004 4/14 – 9/2
2005 1/17 – 5/22

URANUS SPECIAL
1950 8/8 – until 1955 4/3

229

July 9

SUN: CANCER • DECANATE: SCORPIO/PLUTO • DEGREE: 16°5–17°5 CANCER • MODE: CARDINAL • ELEMENT: WATER

Your Personal Powers

With your caring nature, quick wit, warmth, and charm, you have a wonderful gift for dealing with people. The Moon, your ruler, indicates that you possess powerful emotions and a strong need for security. You gain power when you use your intuitive insight and sympathetic understanding for the needs of others. Not lacking in common sense, your enterprising nature and enthusiasm imply that you like to be honest and direct in your dealings with people. With your natural sense of fair play, you often have strong opinions and are willing to fight for your ideals. Your strong sense of values and a special gift for understanding others can make you a good psychologist or a leader in your field of expertise. You may lose power, however, if you allow self-doubt, anxiety, or frustration to block your personal self-expression. Being imaginative with an aesthetic sense, you can create harmony or express your innate artistic or creative gifts. Your home and security are likely to be extremely high on your priority list, so your family in particular will benefit from your responsible and generous nature.

Your Powers of Attraction in Relationships

Charismatic, friendly, and sociable, you can attract others with your warm and gregarious personality and good sense of humor. Being responsible and caring, you can be very protective of loved ones and need a partner who values home and family. Although you desire peace and harmony, if you avoid confrontation, hidden resentments are likely to surface as irritation or frustration. To overcome emotional outbursts or being taken for granted, you may need to develop your own self-esteem and focus on your creative self-expression. When positive, you can magnetize and enchant others by your powerful projection of love. You are particularly attracted to people who seem to possess the potential for success or those who can provide you with the love and security that you need. With your strong sense of justice, you value loyalty and fair play in your relationships.

Your attractive qualities: sociable, idealistic, common sense, creative, sensitive, generous, magnetic, sincere, detached, fortunate, popular, artistic, enduring, kind, thoughtful, astute, considerate, compassionate, determined, responsible, committed, persevering

Your less attractive qualities: frustration, discontent, nervous, unsure, insecure, resentment, lack of confidence, too sensitive, worried, isolated, aggressive, anxious, irritable, intolerant

Your Venus Power

The planet Venus has a great deal of influence on your powers of attraction. Below are four possible Venus types for women and men. To find your Venus you need to go to page 771, where you will find the Venus table and extra information. The planet Mars also affects your powers of attraction. To find your Mars table and interpretation go to page 761.

WOMEN WITH VENUS IN GEMINI: By nature you are young at heart, adaptable, and sociable. Being curious and willing to cooperate makes you a good team player. Usually you are drawn to articulate people who have charm and flair or sharp wit. With a need to expand your knowledge, you also look for a partner who can challenge or stimulate you intellectually. Although you love to talk with all types of people, you may need to develop your listening skills in order to build better communication in your relationships.

MEN WITH VENUS IN GEMINI: Charming, amusing, and adaptable, you attract others with your natural communication skills and friendly personality. You have a wonderful childlike quality and love to keep life playful, but a reluctance to contact your deeper feelings may cause you to avoid serious commitment. With your need for variety and intellectual stimulation, you are attracted to clever and amusing partners who have many interesting sides to their personalities.

WOMEN WITH VENUS IN CANCER: Gentle and tender, you are romantic by nature. You possess a strong need for security and usually help others feel safe and protected. This preservation is especially centered around the home, which is your haven from life's storm. Although your maternal instincts are strong, avoid making sacrifices for others at your own expense. Nevertheless, affectionate and caring, once committed to a relationship, your loyalty and devotion to your partner are very strong.

MEN WITH VENUS IN CANCER: Being emotionally receptive, you can make a sensitive lover. With your desire to care for and protect others, you are likely to have strong family connections. Love is often tied in with being attentive to the needs of others and you may find yourself attracted to individuals who have sympathetic or maternal qualities. Security-

230

conscious, you need a loyal partner who can offer you support and ideally be a good cook and homemaker.

WOMEN WITH VENUS IN LEO: Warm and playful with a touch of the dramatic, you enjoy the company of generous or strong individuals who can share your sense of fun. Although there are advantages to your being strong-willed, in your relationships you need to resist being bossy as it can cause resentment. With your wonderful mixture of regal authority and childlike wonder, you love to keep others entertained and amused.

MEN WITH VENUS IN LEO: A childlike nature suggests that you are versatile and keen on games or being entertained. You are usually attracted to vivacious partners with a benevolent nature. As an extrovert you enjoy being involved in all types of activities where you can assert yourself and show your talents and abilities. Others may recognize your inborn tendencies to lead but are also aware of your vanity or pride. Nevertheless, generous and caring, you often show more compassion to those less fortunate than yourself.

WOMEN WITH VENUS IN VIRGO: Articulate and straightforward in your relationships, you attract others with your genuine concern for their well-being. By being understanding and a good listener, you are able to show your love and friendship. With your analytical approach to relationships, however, you may have to be careful of becoming too matter-of-fact. You often display your concern for the welfare of others by your willingness to offer practical help and assistance. You usually seek a partner who is willing to work as hard on relationships as you are.

MEN WITH VENUS IN VIRGO: Industrious and well-ordered, you relate to others in a considerate and down-to-earth way. You enjoy giving practical advice and being of service to those you love even in small ways. Being a perfectionist, you are drawn to partners with high morals or a strong work ethic. Partners who have strong analytical minds are very attractive to you, particularly if they are also clean and meticulously dressed.

To read all about your Outer Planets and work out how to use your personalized timetable, go to Section Three, page 789.

♋

Your Personalized Timetable

JUPITER BENEFICIAL
1939 2/7 – 4/15
1940 7/14 – 10/27
1941 3/2 – 4/20
1944 9/18 – 11/8
1945 3/21 – 7/7
1946 11/4 – until **1947** 1/28
1947 4/29 – 9/25
1951 1/20 – 3/29
1952 6/19 – 12/18
1953 1/23 – 4/1
1956 9/2 – 10/19
1958 10/19 – until **1959** 1/4
1959 6/9 – 8/30
1962 5/10 – 8/25
1962 12/29 – until **1963** 3/12
1964 5/31 – 7/21
1964 11/9 – until **1965** 3/10
1968 8/17 – 10/3
1970 10/3 – 12/16
1974 4/16 – 10/16
1974 11/21 – until **1975** 2/24
1976 5/14 – 6/28
1977 1/1 – 1/30
1980 7/31 – 9/17
1982 1/21 – 3/30
1982 9/15 – 11/30
1986 3/29 – until **1987** 2/6
1988 4/28 – 6/10
1991 11/15 – until **1992** 2/14
1992 7/12 – 9/1
1993 12/24 – until **1994** 5/10
1994 8/23 – 11/14
1998 3/12 – 5/31
1998 9/4 – until **1999** 1/16
2000 4/11 – 5/23
2003 10/23 – until **2004** 3/23
2004 6/17 – 8/16
2005 12/5 – until **2006** 10/30
2010 2/23 – 5/4
2010 10/24 – 12/13
2012 3/23 – 5/6

SATURN BENEFICIAL
1940 6/25 – 10/31
1941 3/16 – 6/6
1949 9/18 – until **1950** 9/7
1954 1/17 – 3/20
1954 10/6 – until **1955** 11/23
1965 3/6 – until **1966** 4/19
1966 10/12 – until **1967** 1/9
1970 4/28 – 7/31
1970 10/9 – until **1971** 4/12
1978 11/2 – until **1979** 2/16
1979 7/24 – 10/15
1980 4/11 – 7/2
1983 11/11 – until **1984** 12/30
1985 5/19 – 9/27
1994 4/12 – 9/7
1995 1/7 – 6/21
1995 7/21 – until **1996** 2/22
1999 6/5 – 12/5
2000 2/18 – 5/19
2008 9/1 – 12/16
2009 1/15 – 8/20

URANUS BENEFICIAL
1938 3/26 – until **1940** 5/5
1964 9/20 – until **1967** 7/22
1976 11/17 – until **1980** 10/27
2005 3/29 – until **2010** 2/8

NEPTUNE BENEFICIAL
1938 1/1 – until **1939** 8/4
1959 12/26 – until **1968** 9/29

PLUTO BENEFICIAL
1962 10/27 – until **1968** 8/14
1986 12/2 – until **1993** 10/26

JUPITER CHALLENGING
1939 7/17 – 8/10
1940 2/14 – 4/23
1945 10/4 – 12/30
1946 3/27 – 8/27
1948 12/24 – until **1949** 3/7
1949 8/11 – 10/26
1951 6/3 – 10/7
1952 1/21 – 4/6
1957 9/19 – 12/5
1958 5/5 – 8/2
1960 12/7 – until **1961** 2/16
1963 5/11 – until **1964** 3/20
1969 9/2 – 11/17
1972 11/20 – until **1973** 1/29
1975 4/23 – 8/5
1975 8/23 – until **1976** 3/1
1980 12/21 – until **1981** 2/28
1981 8/15 – 10/31
1984 3/5 – 6/25
1984 10/30 – until **1985** 1/14
1987 4/7 – 6/22
1987 10/19 – until **1988** 2/8
1992 11/23 – until **1993** 4/9
1993 7/23 – 10/16
1996 2/12 – 8/13
1996 9/25 – 12/29
1999 3/21 – 5/29
2004 11/5 – until **2005** 9/30
2008 1/25 – 12/12
2011 3/4 – 5/10

SATURN CHALLENGING
1938 4/3 – until **1939** 5/10
1939 12/16 – until **1940** 1/9
1951 10/24 – until **1952** 5/20
1952 7/1 – 12/9
1953 4/6 – 9/4
1959 12/24 – until **1961** 2/12
1961 8/17 – 11/7
1967 5/15 – 10/8
1968 2/5 – 7/3
1968 9/10 – until **1969** 3/17
1980 12/12 – until **1981** 2/25
1981 8/31 – until **1982** 10/13
1989 1/26 – 8/1
1989 10/20 – until **1990** 4/3
1990 6/5 – 12/22
1997 3/17 – until **1998** 4/23
2010 10/7 – until **2011** 11/20
2012 5/7 – 8/11

URANUS CHALLENGING
1969 12/22 – until **1974** 8/16
1990 2/23 – until **1994** 12/15

NEPTUNE CHALLENGING
1945 12/26 – until **1954** 9/14
1988 1/21 – until **1995** 12/28

PLUTO CHALLENGING
1974 11/23 – until **1982** 8/13
2012 2/6 – Continues

JUPITER SPECIAL
1942 7/18 – 10/23
1942 12/2 – until **1943** 6/4
1954 7/1 – 9/17
1955 1/18 – 5/12
1966 6/15 – 8/27
1967 3/12 – 3/29
1978 5/29 – 8/9
1989 9/20 – 12/6
1990 5/10 – 7/24
2001 8/24 – until **2002** 1/17
2002 4/14 – 7/8

SATURN SPECIAL
1944 9/2 – 12/13
1945 5/20 – 10/18
1945 11/25 – until **1946** 6/20
1974 7/2 – until **1975** 7/31
2003 8/11 – until **2004** 1/15
2004 4/27 – 9/12
2005 1/5 – 6/1

URANUS SPECIAL
1950 8/30 – until **1955** 5/18

231

July 10

SUN: CANCER • DECANATE: SCORPIO/PLUTO • DEGREE: 17°5–18°5 CANCER • MODE: CARDINAL • ELEMENT: WATER

Your Personal Powers

Deeply sensitive yet ambitious and self-assured, your personal powers include an active and innovative approach to life. Your ruler, the Moon, indicates that you possess a psychic awareness about people or situations. Although you have strong emotions and a need for security, your spirited nature craves variety and adventure. In your attempt to improve your circumstances, you are sometimes willing to take the opportunities to travel or make total transformations in your life. You may lose some of your power, however, if you allow restlessness or impatience to distract you from the discipline needed to fulfill your high potential. You empower yourself when you combine your strong imagination and visionary ability with your receptivity, intuition, and creativity. Clever, gifted, and versatile, you learn quickly and can display an astute objective view on most subjects. Your pioneering spirit and love of freedom can provide you with the necessary determination and drive to succeed. Your confidence is increased when you know that your instinctive feelings are usually right.

Your Powers of Attraction in Relationships

Others are attracted to your enthusiasm, willpower, and quick mind. An idealistic side to your nature suggests that you enjoy giving and sharing with others. Although home and family can be very important to you, your independent attitude suggests that you also need freedom for self-expression. An ideal relationship is one that does not totally confine you but leaves you some license to explore life. You are usually attracted to those who are clever and entertaining. With your shrewd and perceptive understanding of people you can be an amusing companion. An inner restlessness and desire for instant rewards, however, may cause you to hesitate when you are faced with the reality, commitment, and work of a long-term relationship. By taking a responsible attitude while not compromising your principles, you can build good relationships.

Your attractive qualities: leadership, progressive, intelligent, forceful, optimistic, strong convictions, competitive, open-minded, creative talents, sensitive, independent, musical, gregarious, articulate, good intuition, idealistic, visionary, sociable

Your less attractive qualities: restless, overbearing, jealous, too sensitive, egotistical, too proud, antagonistic, boredom, lack of self-confidence, selfish, frustrated, unstable, lazy, vacillating, impatient

Your Venus Power

The planet Venus has a great deal of influence on your powers of attraction. Below are four possible Venus types for women and men. To find your Venus you need to go to page 771, where you will find the Venus table and extra information. The planet Mars also affects your powers of attraction. To find your Mars table and interpretation go to page 761.

WOMEN WITH VENUS IN GEMINI: By nature you are young at heart, adaptable, and sociable. Being curious and willing to cooperate makes you a good team player. Usually you are drawn to articulate people who have charm and flair or sharp wit. With a need to expand your knowledge you also look for a partner who can challenge or stimulate you intellectually. Although you love to talk with all types of people, you may need to develop your listening skills in order to build better communication in your relationships.

MEN WITH VENUS IN GEMINI: Informed and curious yet charming and friendly, you seek a partner who shares your interests or enjoys your witty remarks. Although a good communicator, you have an inborn tendency to be lighthearted and less profound about deep emotional commitment. Although you are keen on experiences that bring variety into your life, boredom or scattering your energies in too many directions is probably your biggest handicap in relationships. Nevertheless, you are attracted to intelligent partners who can match your lively banter.

WOMEN WITH VENUS IN CANCER: Gentle and tender, you are romantic by nature. You possess a strong need for security and usually help others feel safe and protected. This preservation is especially centered around the home, which is your haven from life's storm. Although your maternal instincts are strong, avoid making sacrifices for others at your own expense. Nevertheless, affectionate and caring, once committed to a relationship, your loyalty and devotion to your partner are very strong.

MEN WITH VENUS IN CANCER: Being emotionally receptive, you can make a sensitive lover. With your desire to care for and protect others, you are likely to have strong family connections. Love is often tied in with being attentive to the needs of others and you may find yourself attracted to indi-

viduals who have sympathetic or maternal qualities. Security-conscious, you need a loyal partner who can offer you support and ideally be a good cook and homemaker.

WOMEN WITH VENUS IN LEO: A childlike nature suggests that you are versatile and keen on games or being entertained. You are usually attracted to vivacious partners with a benevolent nature. As an extrovert you enjoy being involved in all types of activities where you can assert yourself and show your talents and abilities. Others may recognize your inborn tendencies to lead but are also aware of your vanity or pride. Nevertheless, generous and caring, you often show more compassion to those less fortunate than yourself.

MEN WITH VENUS IN LEO: Sociable and outgoing, you are kind and generous with those you love. You look for relationships that can be fun and entertaining and need a playmate that can share your enthusiasm and high spirits. Your pride, however, often stops you from associating with lovers or partners whom you see as beneath you. As you desire someone who can appreciate your sense of the dramatic, you are often attracted to people with strong personalities.

WOMEN WITH VENUS IN VIRGO: In relationships you can be modest and unassuming but desire perfection. You usually analyze your partnerships until you feel you have understood them to the last little detail in order to improve them. A problem usually arises when you become too critical either of partners or yourself and indulge in being skeptical or faultfinding. As you are modest, others may not be aware of the strong sensuality beneath your well-groomed exterior.

MEN WITH VENUS IN VIRGO: Although you are constantly analyzing your relationships in order to understand and improve them, you may nevertheless need to refrain from continuously mulling over issues that can cause anxiety. You are happiest when you are able to help loved ones in practical ways and forget yourself in your willingness to be of service to others. You seek a partner who has high standards and can be as pragmatic and hardworking as yourself. Ideally they should also be impeccably dressed with a fine analytical mind.

To read all about your Outer Planets and work out how to use your personalized timetable, go to Section Three, page 789.

Your Personalized Timetable

JUPITER BENEFICIAL
1939 2/11 – 4/20
1940 7/21 – 10/19
1941 3/8 – 4/24
1944 9/22 – 11/14
1945 3/14 – 7/14
1946 11/8 – until **1947** 2/5
1947 4/20 – 10/1
1951 1/24 – 4/2
1952 6/24 – 12/6
1953 2/4 – 4/6
1956 9/6 – 10/24
1957 4/28 – 6/9
1958 10/24 – until **1959** 1/9
1959 5/31 – 9/7
1962 5/17 – 8/17
1963 1/3 – 3/16
1964 6/4 – 7/28
1964 11/2 – until **1965** 3/16
1968 8/22 – 10/7
1970 10/8 – 12/21
1974 4/21 – 10/4
1974 12/3 – until **1975** 2/28
1976 5/18 – 7/3
1976 12/18 – until **1977** 2/12
1980 8/5 – 9/21
1982 2/1 – 3/19
1982 9/20 – 12/4
1986 4/2 – until **1987** 2/11
1988 5/2 – 6/14
1991 11/23 – until **1992** 2/5
1992 7/17 – 9/5
1993 12/30 – until **1994** 5/2
1994 8/30 – 11/19
1998 3/16 – 6/7
1998 8/27 – until **1999** 1/22
2000 4/15 – 5/27
2003 10/28 – until **2004** 3/15
2004 6/24 – 8/20
2005 12/10 – until **2006** 6/17
2006 7/25 – 11/3
2010 2/27 – 5/9
2010 10/14 – 12/23
2012 3/28 – 5/10

SATURN BENEFICIAL
1940 7/6 – 10/19
1941 3/25 – 6/14
1941 12/23 – until **1942** 2/22
1949 9/26 – until **1950** 9/14
1954 10/14 – until **1955** 12/1
1965 3/14 – until **1966** 4/28
1966 9/29 – until **1967** 1/20
1970 5/5 – 8/24
1970 9/15 – until **1971** 4/20
1978 11/14 – until **1979** 2/3
1979 8/2 – 10/24
1980 3/28 – 7/15
1983 11/19 – until **1985** 1/9
1985 5/6 – 10/7
1994 4/23 – 8/26
1995 1/17 – until **1996** 3/1
1999 6/13 – 11/21
2000 3/2 – 5/27
2008 9/8 – until **2009** 8/28

URANUS BENEFICIAL
1938 4/14 – until **1941** 2/27
1964 10/7 – until **1967** 8/10
1976 12/3 – until **1980** 11/12
2005 4/19 – until **2010** 2/26

NEPTUNE BENEFICIAL
1938 1/1 – until **1939** 9/1
1960 11/18 – until **1968** 10/29

PLUTO BENEFICIAL
1963 9/22 – until **1969** 6/21
1987 1/3 – until **1994** 9/3

JUPITER CHALLENGING
1940 2/18 – 4/27

1945 10/9 – until **1946** 1/7
1946 3/18 – 9/2
1948 12/28 – until **1949** 3/12
1949 8/3 – 11/3
1951 6/9 – 9/30
1952 1/26 – 4/10
1957 9/23 – 12/11
1958 4/27 – 8/10
1960 12/12 – until **1961** 2/20
1963 5/16 – until **1964** 3/24
1969 9/7 – 11/22
1972 11/24 – until **1973** 2/3
1975 4/27 – until **1976** 3/6
1981 1/1 – 2/17
1981 8/20 – 11/5
1984 3/12 – 6/18
1984 11/4 – until **1985** 1/18
1987 4/11 – 6/28
1987 10/12 – until **1988** 2/14
1992 11/29 – until **1993** 4/1
1993 7/30 – 10/20
1996 2/17 – 8/1
1996 10/6 – until **1997** 1/2
1999 3/25 – 6/3
1999 12/4 – until **2000** 1/6
2004 11/10 – until **2005** 5/16
2005 6/24 – 10/5
2008 1/30 – 12/16
2011 3/8 – 5/14

SATURN CHALLENGING
1938 4/10 – until **1939** 5/18
1939 11/22 – until **1940** 1/31
1951 11/2 – until **1952** 4/30
1952 7/20 – 12/21
1953 3/24 – 9/13
1960 1/1 – until **1961** 2/22
1961 8/2 – 11/20
1967 5/25 – 9/26
1968 2/15 – 7/31
1968 8/14 – until **1969** 3/25
1981 1/1 – 2/5
1981 9/8 – until **1982** 10/21
1989 2/4 – 7/17
1989 11/3 – until **1990** 12/30
1997 3/25 – until **1998** 4/30
2010 10/15 – until **2011** 11/29
2012 4/24 – 8/23

URANUS CHALLENGING
1970 10/7 – until **1974** 9/7
1990 3/31 – until **1995** 1/1

NEPTUNE CHALLENGING
1946 11/3 – until **1955** 7/20
1988 2/21 – until **1996** 11/19

PLUTO CHALLENGING
1975 10/12 – until **1982** 9/15
2012 3/27 – Continues

JUPITER SPECIAL
1942 7/22 – until **1943** 6/9
1954 7/5 – 9/23
1955 1/11 – 5/18
1966 6/19 – 9/1
1967 2/23 – 4/16
1978 6/2 – 8/14
1989 9/30 – 11/26
1990 5/15 – 7/28
2001 8/29 – until **2002** 1/9
2002 4/21 – 7/12

SATURN SPECIAL
1944 9/15 – 11/30
1945 5/29 – until **1946** 6/28
1974 7/9 – until **1975** 8/8
2003 8/20 – until **2004** 1/4
2004 5/8 – 9/24
2004 12/24 – until **2005** 6/9

URANUS SPECIAL
1951 6/29 – until **1955** 6/8

July 11

Your Personal Powers

Your personal powers include both a practical and down-to-earth approach and an impressionable sensitivity. With your strong emotions you are quick to pick up on the feelings and motivations of others. You gain power from your keen intelligence and straightforward manner. Although you are sensible and pragmatic, you can also be idealistic and inspired. Perceptive and imaginative, you may develop your emotional awareness for creative reasons. Alternatively, your psychic abilities can provide you with very accurate first impressions of people or situations. With a need for security, you are usually responsible and outspoken with a strong sense of duty. Innovative, proud, and efficient, you can be productive and organized, preferring to do a professional job. Although your work can be especially important to you, if you deny an inner desire for adventure and change, you may lose some of your power to restlessness or escapism. Being a gifted perfectionist, you need only apply the necessary focus and application in order to succeed.

Your Powers of Attraction in Relationships

With the ability to charm others, you can attract many admirers. Although you may have been reserved earlier in your life, you enjoy meeting people and being sociable. Even though you can love deeply and powerfully, your strong sensitivity and inner restlessness can sometimes leave you discontented or moody. Relationships usually involve responsibilities that may challenge your inner need for adventure. Nevertheless, your pragmatic qualities and desire for security usually win over, highlighting your sense of obligation or commitment. Although strong-willed individuals attract you, avoid getting involved in power struggles or being stubborn. You are most content when you can maintain a happy home yet be creative and inspired.

Your attractive qualities: focused, objective, direct, enthusiastic, inspirational, spiritual potential, idealistic, intelligent, outgoing, inventive, artistic, humanitarian, psychic, thrifty, organizational skills, persistence, determination, pragmatic, enduring, communicative, practical

Your less attractive qualities: stubborn, overemotional, easily hurt, high-strung, insecure or overconfident, selfish, lack of clarity, moody, dominating, impatient, too self-sacrificing, escapist, pessimistic, stressed

Your Venus Power

The planet Venus has a great deal of influence on your powers of attraction. Below are four possible Venus types for women and men. To find your Venus you need to go to page 771, where you will find the Venus table and extra information. The planet Mars also affects your powers of attraction. To find your Mars table and interpretation go to page 761.

WOMEN WITH VENUS IN GEMINI: In relationships you need intellectual stimulation and usually prefer to keep things light. Certainly not boring, you love to talk and are at your best being witty and entertaining. Although your easygoing approach to relationships is very attractive, guard against losing touch with your emotions. You prefer a partner who can keep up with your fast stream of ideas, and if you have shared interests then so much the better.

MEN WITH VENUS IN GEMINI: Adaptable yet often flirtatious, you enjoy mixing with people who are quick-minded and versatile. Since you can learn a great deal through interacting with others, you are often attracted to intelligent partners who have comprehensive knowledge or good ideas. One of your less attractive qualities is your tendency to become bored or be inconsistent. Having an adaptable partner is important to you; therefore it must be someone who can offer you different options and keep you interested.

WOMEN WITH VENUS IN CANCER: Possessing a soft femininity, you have tender and sensitive emotions. Sympathetic and caring, you often mother those in your care by making sure that they are comfortable and have plenty to eat. When you feel hurt or insecure in relationships you are likely to cover your feelings by being defensive or appearing tough on the outside while on the inside you are feeling vulnerable. Affectionate and romantic, you make a faithful and devoted partner.

MEN WITH VENUS IN CANCER: Attractive and affectionate, in relationships you are often faithful with a conservative outlook. You are drawn to warmhearted partners with whom you can share a familiar routine as well as life's pleasures and comforts. Seeking a partner who is dependable or reassuring, you often put security high on your priority list when looking for love. Your sociability and friendliness usually make you popular and partners often admire your good sense of values and practical skills.

WOMEN WITH VENUS IN LEO: As a person who wants to radiate in their own right, you are likely to desire partners you

can be proud of. You are usually attracted to fun-loving, warm, and generous individuals. If self-expression is important to you, you will probably seek the company of creative people such as artists, musicians, or those with a flair for acting. Alternatively, you may be drawn to people who are dignified, regal, or have already achieved success.

MEN WITH VENUS IN LEO: Sociable and outgoing, you are kind and generous with those you love. Looking for a relationship that can be fun and entertaining, you need a playmate who can share your enthusiasm and high spirits. Your pride, however, often stops you from associating with lovers or partners you see as beneath you. As you desire someone who can appreciate your sense of the dramatic, you are often attracted to people with strong personalities.

WOMEN WITH VENUS IN VIRGO: Polite, refined, and organized, you are attracted to articulate and intelligent people. Since you are caring, concerned, and want to be of practical help to others, you can be an asset to any partnership. By being too analytical, exacting, or faultfinding, however, a doubting element can creep into your relationships. By expressing your feelings in a positive way you can become more decisive and improve on how you relate to your loved ones.

MEN WITH VENUS IN VIRGO: Practical, idealistic, and a perfectionist, you seek a relationship with an intelligent and hardworking partner who can inspire you to be more industrious and well-ordered. At times you can come across as a sympathetic and caring person and at other times you may appear pragmatic and very businesslike. This may sometimes lead to unclear communication between you and your partner. Usually helpful and caring, however, you like to analyze the faults in your relationships and then work methodically to improve them.

To read all about your Outer Planets and work out how to use your personalized timetable, go to Section Three, page 789.

Your Personalized Timetable

JUPITER BENEFICIAL
1939 2/15 – 4/24
1940 7/29 – 10/11
1941 3/13 – 4/28
1944 9/27 – 11/20
1945 3/6 – 7/20
1946 11/13 – until 1947 2/15
1947 4/10 – 10/6
1951 1/28 – 4/6
1952 6/29 – 11/27
1953 2/13 – 4/10
1956 9/11 – 10/29
1957 4/15 – 6/21
1958 10/28 – until 1959 1/15
1959 5/24 – 9/14
1962 5/25 – 8/9
1963 1/8 – 3/20
1964 6/8 – 8/4
1964 10/25 – until 1965 3/21
1968 8/26 – 10/12
1970 10/12 – 12/26
1974 4/26 – 9/25
1974 12/12 – until 1975 3/4
1976 5/22 – 7/8
1976 12/9 – until 1977 2/21
1980 8/10 – 9/25
1982 9/25 – 12/9
1986 4/6 – until 1987 2/15
1988 5/6 – 6/18
1991 12/3 – until 1992 1/26
1992 7/23 – 9/10
1994 1/5 – 4/25
1994 9/5 – 11/23
1998 3/20 – 6/16
1998 8/18 – until 1999 1/27
2000 4/19 – 5/31
2003 11/3 – until 2004 3/8
2004 7/1 – 8/25
2005 12/15 – until 2006 6/4
2006 8/7 – 11/8
2010 3/3 – 5/15
2010 10/6 – 12/31
2012 4/1 – 5/14

SATURN BENEFICIAL
1940 7/19 – 10/5
1941 4/2 – 6/22
1941 12/8 – until 1942 3/9
1949 10/4 – until 1950 4/13
1950 6/16 – 9/22
1954 10/22 – until 1955 12/9
1956 7/11 – 8/18
1965 3/22 – until 1966 5/8
1966 9/17 – until 1967 1/31
1970 5/13 – until 1971 4/28
1978 12/2 – until 1979 1/16
1979 8/10 – 11/2
1980 3/16 – 7/25
1983 11/27 – until 1984 6/12
1984 8/12 – until 1985 1/21
1985 4/22 – 10/17
1994 5/4 – 8/12
1995 1/26 – until 1996 3/9
1999 6/23 – 11/9
2000 3/12 – 6/3
2008 9/16 – until 2009 9/5

URANUS BENEFICIAL
1938 4/30 – until 1941 3/27
1964 10/25 – until 1967 8/27
1976 12/22 – until 1981 9/4
2005 5/18 – until 2010 3/15

NEPTUNE BENEFICIAL
1938 5/11 – until 1940 7/26
1960 12/17 – until 1969 9/21

PLUTO BENEFICIAL
1963 10/23 – until 1969 8/6
1987 11/16 – until 1994 10/11

JUPITER CHALLENGING
1940 2/23 – 5/1

1945 10/13 – until 1946 1/18
1946 3/7 – 9/7
1949 1/1 – 3/18
1949 7/26 – 11/9
1951 6/16 – 9/23
1952 2/1 – 4/14
1957 9/27 – 12/17
1958 4/19 – 8/16
1960 12/16 – until 1961 2/25
1963 5/21 – 11/12
1963 12/28 – until 1964 3/28
1969 9/12 – 11/27
1970 6/7 – 7/9
1972 11/29 – until 1973 2/7
1975 5/1 – until 1976 3/10
1981 8/25 – 11/9
1984 3/20 – 6/10
1984 11/10 – until 1985 1/22
1987 4/15 – 7/4
1987 10/5 – until 1988 2/19
1992 12/6 – until 1993 3/25
1993 8/5 – 10/24
1996 2/22 – 7/23
1996 10/15 – until 1997 1/6
1999 3/29 – 6/8
1999 11/21 – until 2000 1/18
2004 11/15 – until 2005 5/4
2005 7/7 – 10/9
2008 2/3 – 12/21
2011 3/12 – 5/19

SATURN CHALLENGING
1938 4/18 – until 1939 5/27
1939 11/8 – until 1940 2/14
1951 11/10 – until 1952 4/16
1952 8/2 – until 1953 1/5
1953 3/8 – 9/22
1960 1/9 – until 1961 3/3
1961 7/20 – 12/1
1967 6/5 – 9/13
1968 2/24 – until 1969 4/2
1981 9/16 – until 1982 10/29
1989 2/14 – 7/4
1989 11/14 – until 1991 1/7
1997 4/1 – until 1998 5/8
2010 10/23 – until 2011 6/10
2011 6/16 – 12/8
2012 4/12 – 9/3

URANUS CHALLENGING
1970 10/23 – until 1974 9/24
1991 1/13 – until 1995 1/17

NEPTUNE CHALLENGING
1946 12/8 – until 1955 9/8
1989 1/15 – until 1996 12/21

PLUTO CHALLENGING
1975 11/7 – until 1982 10/10

JUPITER SPECIAL
1942 7/26 – until 1943 6/13
1954 7/9 – 9/30
1955 1/4 – 5/24
1966 6/23 – 9/6
1967 2/13 – 4/27
1978 6/7 – 8/18
1989 10/13 – 11/13
1990 5/20 – 8/2
2001 9/4 – until 2002 1/2
2002 4/27 – 7/16

SATURN SPECIAL
1944 10/4 – 11/10
1945 6/6 – until 1946 7/6
1974 7/17 – until 1975 8/15
1976 3/6 – 4/18
2003 8/30 – 12/23
2004 5/17 – 10/8
2004 12/9 – until 2005 6/18

URANUS SPECIAL
1951 7/15 – until 1955 6/26

235

July 12

Your Personal Powers

A friendly, helpful manner and easygoing charm mark you as someone special. Your ruler, the Moon, enhances your psychic abilities and emphasizes your need for security. Being intuitive and clever, you gain power from using your emotional awareness and good psychological skills to understand others. Idealistic yet practical and direct, you have many original ideas and a gift with words. Inwardly, you are very sensitive with a need for peace, harmony, and emotional self-expression. You may lose power, however, if you abandon your usual faith and objectivity and become worried and indecisive. Ordinarily you are innovative and enterprising, with an optimistic, confident, and creative approach to life. Your protective nature may even have you fighting for a just cause or an ideal. With your imagination and shrewd business sense, your home is an important symbol of emotional and material security. You gain power by combining your natural diplomacy and social skills with the dedication and exceptional gifts you possess.

Your Powers of Attraction in Relationships

Your keen intelligence, caring, and supportive attitude can attract others. As you possess a friendly personality and natural social skills, you are sure to have many friends. Although on the outside you appear confident and tenacious, you need a partner who understands your inner vulnerability and sensitive emotions. Your partners also need to be smart enough to keep up with your bright ideas and challenge you to have faith in yourself. In love situations you may have an idealized picture of a romantic partner, almost seeking a perfect bond with someone else. Naturally, if you pick partners who do not live up to this high ideal, you can become cynical or withdrawn or appear cold. It is important to keep an emotional balance so that you can express your loving and affectionate nature but also experience an equal give-and-take relationship with others.

Your attractive qualities: keen intelligence, persistence, sensitive, pragmatic, determination, common sense, artistic pursuits, articulate, love of music, creative talents, initiative, disciplinarian, objective thinker, original, idealistic, humanitarian, tenacious, focused

Your less attractive qualities: self-doubt, pessimistic, scattered, hypersensitive, arrogant, lack of self-esteem, reserved, too shy, moody, worried, selfish, eccentric, uncooperative, too sensitive

Your Venus Power

The planet Venus has a great deal of influence on your powers of attraction. Below are four possible Venus types for women and men. To find your Venus you need to go to page 771, where you will find the Venus table and extra information. The planet Mars also affects your powers of attraction. To find your Mars table and interpretation go to page 761.

WOMEN WITH VENUS IN GEMINI: In relationships you need intellectual stimulation and usually prefer to keep things light. Certainly not boring, you love to talk and are at your best being witty and entertaining. Although your easygoing approach to relationships is very attractive, guard against losing touch with your emotions. You prefer a partner who can keep up with your fast stream of ideas, and if you have shared interests then so much the better.

MEN WITH VENUS IN GEMINI: Informed and curious yet charming and friendly, you seek a partner who shares your interests or enjoys your witty remarks. Although a good communicator, you have an inborn tendency to be lighthearted and less profound about deep emotional commitment. Although you are keen on experiences that bring variety into your life, boredom or scattering your energies in too many directions is probably your biggest handicap in relationships. Nevertheless, you are attracted to intelligent partners who can match your lively banter.

WOMEN WITH VENUS IN CANCER: Possessing a soft femininity, you have tender and sensitive emotions. Sympathetic and caring, you often mother those in your care by making sure they are comfortable and have plenty to eat. When you feel hurt or insecure in relationships you are likely to cover your feelings by being defensive or appearing tough on the outside while on the inside you are feeling vulnerable. Affectionate and romantic, you make a faithful and devoted partner.

MEN WITH VENUS IN CANCER: Attractive and affectionate, in relationships you are often faithful with a conservative outlook. You are drawn to warmhearted partners with whom you can share a familiar routine as well as life's pleasures and comforts. Seeking a partner who is dependable or reassuring, you often put security high on your priority list when looking

for love. Your sociability and friendliness usually make you popular and partners often admire your good sense of values and practical skills.

WOMEN WITH VENUS IN LEO: Your friendly and sunny personality often makes you stand out in a crowd. Generous and giving, you know how to make your partner feel special. As you often expect loyalty and devotion from your partner in return, you can become easily offended if they ignore you or behave in an inconsiderate manner. Charming and kind, when you are in love you can be romantic, dramatic, and passionate.

MEN WITH VENUS IN LEO: Enthusiastic, playful, and kind, you can be benevolent with those you love. Warm, romantic, and self-expressive, you adore the drama of love or having fun with your friends. Usually you are attracted to partners with a warm and generous nature. Although you can be a confident and charismatic partner, you may need to develop humility to stop pride or arrogance from marring your relationships.

WOMEN WITH VENUS IN VIRGO: Articulate and straightforward in your relationships, you attract others with your genuine concern for their well-being. By being understanding and a good listener, you are able to show your love and friendship. With your analytical approach to relationships, however, you may have to be careful of becoming too matter-of-fact. You often display your concern for the welfare of others by your willingness to offer practical help and assistance. You usually seek a partner who is willing to work as hard on relationships as you are.

MEN WITH VENUS IN VIRGO: Industrious and well-ordered, you relate to others in a considerate and down-to-earth way. You enjoy giving practical advice and being of service to those your love, even in small ways. Being a perfectionist, you are drawn to partners with high morals or a strong work ethic. Partners who have strong analytical minds are very attractive to you, particularly if they are also clean and meticulously dressed.

To read all about your Outer Planets and work out how to use your personalized timetable, go to Section Three, page 789.

To read all about your Outer Planets and work out how to use your personalized timetable, go to Section Three, page 789.

Your Personalized Timetable

JUPITER BENEFICIAL
1939 2/19 – 4/28
1940 8/7 – 10/2
1941 3/18 – 5/2
1944 10/1 – 11/27
1945 2/27 – 7/26
1946 11/17 – until **1947** 3/4
1947 3/23 – 10/11
1951 2/2 – 4/10
1952 7/4 – 11/19
1953 2/20 – 4/15
1956 9/15 – 11/4
1957 4/6 – 6/30
1958 11/1 – until **1959** 1/21
1959 5/16 – 9/20
1962 6/4 – 7/30
1963 1/13 – 3/24
1964 6/13 – 8/13
1964 10/17 – until **1965** 3/26
1968 8/30 – 10/16
1970 10/17 – 12/31
1971 7/1 – 8/17
1974 5/1 – 9/17
1974 12/19 – until **1975** 3/8
1976 5/26 – 7/13
1976 12/1 – until **1977** 3/1
1980 8/14 – 9/30
1982 9/30 – 12/13
1986 4/11 – until **1987** 2/19
1988 5/10 – 6/23
1991 12/19 – until **1992** 1/10
1992 7/28 – 9/14
1994 1/12 – 4/17
1994 9/11 – 11/27
1998 3/24 – 6/28
1998 8/6 – until **1999** 1/31
2000 4/23 – 6/5
2003 11/9 – until **2004** 2/29
2004 7/8 – 8/30
2005 12/20 – until **2006** 5/26
2006 8/16 – 11/12
2010 3/7 – 5/20
2010 9/28 – until **2011** 1/7
2012 4/5 – 5/18

SATURN BENEFICIAL
1940 8/6 – 9/16
1941 4/10 – 7/1
1941 11/25 – until **1942** 3/20
1949 10/12 – until **1950** 3/28
1950 7/1 – 9/30
1954 10/30 – until **1955** 12/18
1956 6/20 – 9/8
1965 3/30 – 10/11
1965 12/16 – until **1966** 5/19
1966 9/4 – until **1967** 2/9
1970 5/20 – until **1971** 5/5
1979 8/18 – 11/12
1980 3/4 – 8/4
1983 12/6 – until **1984** 5/26
1984 8/29 – until **1985** 2/6
1985 4/5 – 10/25
1994 5/19 – 7/28
1995 2/4 – until **1996** 3/17
1999 7/3 – 10/28
2000 3/22 – 6/11
2001 1/5 – 2/13
2008 9/24 – until **2009** 9/13

URANUS BENEFICIAL
1938 5/17 – until **1941** 4/16
1964 11/20 – until **1967** 9/12
1977 1/17 – until **1981** 9/30
2006 3/13 – until **2011** 1/17

NEPTUNE BENEFICIAL
1938 1/1 – until **1940** 8/26
1961 11/13 – until **1969** 10/23

PLUTO BENEFICIAL
1964 9/18 – until **1969** 9/4
1987 12/12 – until **1994** 11/6

JUPITER CHALLENGING
1940 2/27 – 5/5
1945 10/17 – until **1946** 9/12
1949 1/5 – 3/24
1949 7/19 – 11/16
1951 6/23 – 9/15
1952 2/6 – 4/18
1957 10/2 – 12/23
1958 4/12 – 8/23
1960 12/20 – until **1961** 3/1
1961 9/16 – 9/30
1963 5/26 – 11/1
1964 1/7 – 4/1
1969 9/16 – 12/2
1970 5/24 – 7/23
1972 12/3 – until **1973** 2/11
1975 5/6 – until **1976** 3/14
1981 8/30 – 11/14
1984 3/29 – 5/31
1984 11/15 – until **1985** 1/26
1987 4/19 – 7/12
1987 9/27 – until **1988** 2/24
1992 12/13 – until **1993** 3/17
1993 8/11 – 10/29
1996 2/28 – 7/15
1996 10/22 – until **1997** 1/10
1999 4/2 – 6/13
1999 11/12 – until **2000** 1/27
2004 11/20 – until **2005** 4/24
2005 7/17 – 10/14
2008 2/8 – 12/25
2011 3/16 – 5/23

SATURN CHALLENGING
1938 4/26 – 11/30
1938 12/28 – until **1939** 6/5
1939 10/27 – until **1940** 2/25
1951 11/19 – until **1952** 4/4
1952 8/14 – until **1953** 10/1
1960 1/17 – until **1961** 3/14
1961 7/7 – 12/11
1967 6/19 – 8/29
1968 3/3 – until **1969** 4/9
1981 9/24 – until **1982** 11/6
1989 2/25 – 6/21
1989 11/24 – until **1991** 1/15
1997 4/9 – until **1998** 5/16
1998 12/3 – until **1999** 1/25
2010 10/31 – until **2011** 5/9
2011 7/17 – 12/19
2012 3/30 – 9/12

URANUS CHALLENGING
1970 11/8 – until **1974** 10/10
1991 1/30 – until **1995** 11/21

NEPTUNE CHALLENGING
1947 10/28 – until **1955** 10/7
1989 2/12 – until **1997** 11/7

PLUTO CHALLENGING
1975 12/13 – until **1983** 8/27

JUPITER SPECIAL
1942 7/31 – until **1943** 6/18
1954 7/14 – 10/7
1954 12/27 – until **1955** 5/30
1966 6/28 – 9/11
1967 2/5 – 5/5
1978 6/11 – 8/23
1990 5/25 – 8/6
2001 9/10 – 12/26
2002 5/3 – 7/21

SATURN SPECIAL
1945 6/13 – until **1946** 7/13
1974 7/24 – until **1975** 8/23
1976 2/16 – 5/6
2003 9/10 – 12/10
2004 5/26 – until **2005** 6/26

URANUS SPECIAL
1951 7/31 – until **1955** 7/12

237

July 13

Your Personal Powers

Ambitious and versatile, among your many personal powers are a friendly manner and a natural flair for people-related activities. Although you can be forceful, your intuitive and receptive nature indicates that you are idealistic, sensitive, with a strong sixth sense. Your inner dynamism and strong convictions often motivate you to initiate projects or create new opportunities for success. As you thrive on a good mental challenge to keep you active and alert, you need definite goals. In particular, you gain power from your relationship skills and ability to make easy contacts. Even though you have a strong need to be independent and self-reliant, as a natural negotiator you benefit and gain success especially in cooperative endeavors. With your powerful emotions and imagination, it is important that you remain positive and focused to achieve success. You may lose some of your power to moods or an unrealistic fear of not having enough money. Through the combination of your ambition, original ideas, and hard work, however, you can really achieve success.

Your Powers of Attraction in Relationships

Your charming and fun-loving personality attracts others. Generous and affectionate with those you love, you can be reassuring and supportive. Sociable with a wide circle of friends, you are attracted to determined and strong-willed individuals. You also enjoy the company of people who possess strong mental power and definite opinions. Romantic and idealistic, you can also be protective of those you admire. As you need recognition from others, be careful in relationships not to give too much. If you lose your individuality you may vacillate between being passive or being too demanding. You need a partner who can share your love of home and family and understand your need for security. Although you can sometimes display your stubborn side, you are usually warm, kind, and cooperative.

Your attractive qualities: determination, ambitious, artistic pursuits, convincing, intuitive, love of music, creative talents, keen intelligence, fair, direct, wit, courageous, competitive, subtle, sensitive, creative, freedom-loving, self-expressive, initiative, idealistic

Your less attractive qualities: stubborn, anxious, materialistic, martyr, pessimistic, lazy, hypersensitive, escapist, arrogant, fooling yourself, impulsive, quarrelsome, selfish, moody, impulsive, indecisive, bossy, unemotional, rebellious

Your Venus Power

The planet Venus has a great deal of influence on your powers of attraction. Below are four possible Venus types for women and men. To find your Venus you need to go to page 771, where you will find the Venus table and extra information. The planet Mars also affects your powers of attraction. To find your Mars table and interpretation go to page 761.

WOMEN WITH VENUS IN GEMINI: Curious, with a bright and animated approach to life, you are attracted to those who are clever and/or sophisticated. Your love of variety and desire for knowledge suggest that you need a partner and friends who can keep you mentally stimulated. Although witty and a good conversationalist, you may need to keep in touch with your deeper feelings. Nevertheless, intelligent and friendly, you possess a youthful sense of wonder and seek a playmate who can keep you from becoming bored.

MEN WITH VENUS IN GEMINI: Charming, amusing, and adaptable, you attract others with your natural communication skills and friendly personality. You have a wonderful childlike quality and love to keep life playful, but a reluctance to contact your deeper feelings may cause you to avoid serious commitment. With your need for variety and intellectual stimulation, you are attracted to clever and amusing partners who have many interesting sides to their personalities.

WOMEN WITH VENUS IN CANCER: Possessing a soft femininity, you have tender and sensitive emotions. Sympathetic and caring, you often mother those in your care by making sure they are comfortable and have plenty to eat. When you feel hurt or insecure in relationships, you are likely to cover your feelings by being defensive or appearing tough on the outside when inside you are feeling vulnerable. Affectionate and romantic, you make a faithful and devoted partner.

MEN WITH VENUS IN CANCER: Affectionate with a strong sensitive streak, you can love very deeply. You may find yourself drawn to sympathetic partners who can tune in to your moods and feelings as well as be reassuring and supportive. Family links are especially important to you, and the more positive these relationships are, the more confident and safe you feel.

WOMEN WITH VENUS IN LEO: As a person who wants to

radiate in their own right, you are likely to desire partners you can be proud of. Usually you are attracted to fun-loving, warm, and generous individuals. If self-expression is important to you, you will probably seek the company of creative people such as artists, musicians, or those with a flair for acting. Alternatively, you may be drawn to people who are dignified, regal, or have already achieved success.

MEN WITH VENUS IN LEO: Generous, animated, and pleasure-seeking, you can be very entertaining and fun to be with. Usually you are attracted to extroverted and benevolent individuals with a sunny personality. If ambitious, you are drawn to a partner who shows leadership qualities or one who is highly motivated. Your less attractive qualities are your tendencies to be bossy or vain. With a sense of the dramatic, however, you can be the life and soul of the party and inspire those around you.

WOMEN WITH VENUS IN VIRGO: In relationships, you can be modest and unassuming but desire perfection. You usually analyze your partnerships until you feel you have understood them to the last little detail in order to improve them. A problem usually arises when you become too critical either of partners or yourself and indulge in being skeptical or faultfinding. As you are modest, others may not be aware of the strong sensuality beneath your well-groomed exterior.

MEN WITH VENUS IN VIRGO: Although you are constantly analyzing your relationships in order to understand and improve them, you may nevertheless need to refrain from continuously mulling over issues that can cause anxiety. You are happiest when you are able to help your loved ones in practical ways and forget yourself in your willingness to be of service to others. You seek a partner who has high standards and can be as pragmatic and hardworking as yourself. Ideally they should also be impeccably dressed with a fine analytical mind.

To read all about your Outer planets and work out how to use your personalized timetable, go to Section Three, page 789.

Your Personalized Timetable

JUPITER BENEFICIAL
1939 2/23 – 5/3
1940 8/22 – 9/18
1941 3/23 – 5/6
1944 10/6 – 12/5
1945 2/18 – 7/31
1946 11/21 – until 1947 10/16
1951 2/6 – 4/14
1952 7/10 – 11/12
1953 2/27 – 4/19
1956 9/19 – 11/9
1957 3/29 – 7/8
1958 11/6 – until 1959 1/28
1959 5/8 – 9/26
1962 6/18 – 7/16
1963 1/18 – 3/28
1964 6/18 – 8/24
1964 10/6 – until 1965 3/31
1968 9/4 – 10/21
1970 10/21 – until 1971 1/5
1971 6/20 – 8/28
1974 5/7 – 9/9
1974 12/26 – until 1975 3/12
1976 5/30 – 7/18
1976 11/23 – until 1977 3/8
1980 8/19 – 10/4
1982 10/5 – 12/18
1986 4/15 – until 1987 2/23
1988 5/14 – 6/27
1992 8/2 – 9/19
1994 1/20 – 4/8
1994 9/16 – 12/2
1998 3/28 – until 1999 2/5
2000 4/27 – 6/9
2003 11/16 – until 2004 2/22
2004 7/14 – 9/3
2005 12/26 – until 2006 5/17
2006 8/24 – 11/16
2010 3/11 – 5/26
2010 9/21 – until 2011 1/13
2012 4/10 – 5/22

SATURN BENEFICIAL
1941 4/18 – 7/10
1941 11/14 – until 1942 3/30
1949 10/21 – until 1950 3/15
1950 7/13 – 10/7
1954 11/7 – until 1955 12/26
1956 6/5 – 9/22
1965 4/8 – 9/26
1965 12/31 – until 1966 6/1
1966 8/21 – until 1967 2/18
1970 5/28 – until 1971 5/13
1979 8/26 – 11/24
1980 2/20 – 8/13
1983 12/15 – until 1984 5/12
1984 9/10 – until 1985 11/3
1994 6/17 – 6/29
1995 2/12 – until 1996 3/25
1999 7/14 – 10/15
2000 3/30 – 6/19
2000 12/17 – until 2001 3/3
2008 10/2 – until 2009 4/24
2009 6/9 – 9/20

URANUS BENEFICIAL
1938 6/3 – until 1941 5/3
1965 9/10 – until 1968 6/27
1977 11/8 – until 1981 10/19
2006 3/31 – until 2011 2/9

NEPTUNE BENEFICIAL
1938 1/1 – until 1941 7/17
1961 12/10 – until 1970 9/9

PLUTO BENEFICIAL
1964 10/18 – until 1970 7/26
1988 1/18 – until 1995 9/22

JUPITER CHALLENGING
1940 3/2 – 5/9
1945 10/22 – until 1946 9/17
1949 1/9 – 3/30
1949 7/11 – 11/21

1951 7/1 – 9/6
1952 2/11 – 4/22
1957 10/6 – 12/30
1958 4/4 – 8/29
1960 12/24 – until 1961 3/6
1961 8/28 – 10/19
1963 5/31 – 10/24
1964 1/15 – 4/5
1969 9/21 – 12/7
1970 5/14 – 8/2
1972 12/8 – until 1973 2/15
1975 5/10 – until 1976 3/19
1981 9/4 – 11/19
1984 4/10 – 5/19
1984 11/20 – until 1985 1/30
1987 4/23 – 7/21
1987 9/17 – until 1988 2/29
1992 12/20 – until 1993 3/9
1993 8/17 – 11/2
1996 3/4 – 7/7
1996 10/29 – until 1997 1/14
1999 4/6 – 6/18
1999 11/4 – until 2000 2/4
2004 11/25 – until 2005 4/16
2005 7/25 – 10/18
2008 2/12 – 12/29
2011 3/20 – 5/27

SATURN CHALLENGING
1938 5/4 – 11/8
1939 1/19 – 6/15
1939 10/15 – until 1940 3/5
1951 11/30 – until 1952 3/22
1952 8/23 – until 1953 10/9
1960 1/26 – 8/20
1960 10/11 – until 1961 3/27
1961 6/23 – 12/20
1967 7/15 – 8/4
1968 3/12 – until 1969 4/17
1981 10/2 – until 1982 11/14
1983 6/3 – 7/29
1989 3/9 – 6/7
1989 12/3 – until 1991 1/23
1997 4/17 – until 1998 5/24
1998 11/16 – until 1999 2/9
2010 11/9 – until 2011 4/24
2011 8/1 – until 2012 1/2
2012 3/15 – 9/21

URANUS CHALLENGING
1970 11/28 – until 1975 7/11
1991 2/17 – until 1995 12/13

NEPTUNE CHALLENGING
1947 11/28 – until 1956 8/31
1989 4/7 – until 1997 12/15

PLUTO CHALLENGING
1976 10/24 – until 1983 9/25

JUPITER SPECIAL
1942 8/4 – until 1943 6/23
1954 7/18 – 10/16
1954 12/18 – until 1955 6/4
1966 7/2 – 9/17
1967 1/28 – 5/12
1978 6/16 – 8/28
1990 5/29 – 8/10
2001 9/17 – 12/19
2002 5/9 – 7/25

SATURN SPECIAL
1945 6/21 – until 1946 7/21
1974 8/1 – until 1975 2/21
1975 4/4 – 9/1
1976 2/3 – 5/18
2003 9/25 – 11/26
2004 6/3 – until 2005 7/3

URANUS SPECIAL
1951 8/19 – until 1956 4/23

PLUTO SPECIAL
1938 2/18 – until 1938 5/31

July 14

Your Personal Powers

Motivated by a strong combination of practicality, idealism, and keen intelligence, you have the potential to achieve remarkable results. Being mentally sharp and forceful with an excellent ability to deal with people implies that you aim for leadership positions. Once you have decided upon a course of action, you gain power from your strong determination to succeed. Although you project a confident persona to the world, underneath you have sensitive and idealistic emotions and a strong need for security. Although you can be very generous and accommodating with those you admire, you can lose some of your power if you become too bossy and inflexible. Willing to fight for others, however, you are able to work very hard for a cause. With your excellent business sense and pragmatic approach, you empower yourself when you combine your ability to quickly spot opportunities with your natural executive skills and strong intuition. As an imaginative individual and a good organizer you can also succeed by being entrepreneurial

Your Powers of Attraction in Relationships

Your dynamic willpower and ability to achieve your objectives attract others. Although you often put your work first, to those you love and admire you will give generously of your time and resources. With your dramatic sense and kind heart you can be a strong supporter of others. If you become impatient or frustrated you may show your domineering or obstinate nature. Attracted by individuals with an adventurous spirit, you need a partner who can handle your changing moods. Although independent, your powerful desire for security and affection implies that you also recognize the advantages of being in a partnership. Being safety-conscious, you like to build a strong foundation for yourself and your family. Magnanimous and frank, you usually have happier relationships when you utilize your persuasive charm and retain some personal freedom.

Your attractive qualities: decisive actions, direct, hardworking, idealistic, active, creative, pragmatic, imaginative, honest, kind, caring, leadership skills, clever, humanitarian streak, competitive, subtle, self-sacrificing, practical, sensitive, energetic, enthusiastic, protective

Your less attractive qualities: bossy, materialistic, obstinate, impatient, moody, controlling, selfish, overly cautious or impulsive, demanding, thoughtless, stubborn

Your Venus Power

The planet Venus has a great deal of influence on your powers of attraction. Below are four possible Venus types for women and men. To find your Venus you need to go to page 771, where you will find the Venus table and extra information. The planet Mars also affects your powers of attraction. To find your Mars table and interpretation go to page 761.

WOMEN WITH VENUS IN GEMINI: By nature you are young at heart, adaptable, and sociable. Being curious and willing to cooperate makes you a good team player. Usually you are drawn to articulate people who have charm and flair or sharp wit. With a need to expand your knowledge you also look for a partner who can challenge or stimulate you intellectually. Although you love to talk with all types of people you may need to develop your listening skills in order to build better communication in your relationships.

MEN WITH VENUS IN GEMINI: Informed and curious yet charming and friendly, you seek a partner who shares your interests or enjoys your witty remarks. Although a good communicator, you have an inborn tendency to be lighthearted and less profound about deep emotional commitment. Although you are keen on experiences that bring variety into your life, boredom or scattering your energies in too many directions is probably your biggest handicap in relationships. Nevertheless, you are attracted to intelligent partners who can match your lively banter.

WOMEN WITH VENUS IN CANCER: Possessing a soft femininity, you have tender and sensitive emotions. Sympathetic and caring, you often mother those in your care by making sure they are comfortable and have plenty to eat. When you feel hurt or insecure in relationships you are likely to cover your feelings by being defensive or appearing tough on the outside while on the inside you are feeling vulnerable. Affectionate and romantic, you make a faithful and devoted partner.

MEN WITH VENUS IN CANCER: Being emotionally receptive, you can make a sensitive lover. With your desire to care for and protect others, you are likely to have strong family connections. Love is often tied in with being attentive to the needs of others and you may find yourself attracted to individuals who have sympathetic or maternal qualities. Security-conscious, you need a loyal partner who can offer you support and ideally be a good cook and homemaker.

WOMEN WITH VENUS IN LEO: Your friendly and sunny

personality often makes you stand out in a crowd. Generous and giving, you know how to make your partner feel special. As you often expect loyalty and devotion from your partner in return, you can become easily offended if they ignore you or behave in an inconsiderate manner. Charming and kind, when you are in love you can be romantic, dramatic, and passionate.

MEN WITH VENUS IN LEO: Generous, animated, and pleasure-seeking, you can be very entertaining and fun to be with. You are usually attracted to extroverted and benevolent individuals with a sunny personality. If ambitious, you are drawn to a partner who shows leadership qualities or one who is highly motivated. Your less attractive qualities are your tendencies to be bossy or vain. With a sense of the dramatic, however, you can be the life and soul of the party and inspire those around you.

WOMEN WITH VENUS IN VIRGO: Articulate and straightforward in your relationships, you attract others with your genuine concern for their well-being. By being understanding and a good listener, you are able to show your love and friendship. With your analytical approach to relationships, however, you may have to be careful of becoming too matter-of-fact. You often display your concern for the welfare of others by your willingness to offer practical help and assistance. You usually seek a partner who is willing to work as hard on relationships as you are.

MEN WITH VENUS IN VIRGO: Although you are constantly analyzing your relationships in order to understand and improve them, you may nevertheless need to refrain from continuously mulling over issues that can cause anxiety. You are happiest when you are able to help your loved ones in practical ways and forget yourself in your willingness to be of service to others. You seek a partner who has high standards and can be as pragmatic and hardworking as yourself. Ideally they should also be impeccably dressed with a fine analytical mind.

To read all about your Outer Planets and work out how to use your personalized timetable, go to Section Three, page 789.

♋

Your Personalized Timetable

JUPITER BENEFICIAL
1939 2/27 – 5/8
1939 11/8 – 12/10
1941 3/27 – 5/10
1944 10/11 – 12/15
1945 2/8 – 8/6
1946 11/26 – until 1947 10/20
1951 2/10 – 4/18
1952 7/16 – 11/5
1953 3/5 – 4/23
1956 9/24 – 11/15
1957 3/22 – 7/15
1958 11/10 – until 1959 2/4
1959 4/30 – 10/1
1963 1/23 – 4/1
1964 6/22 – 12/30
1965 1/21 – 4/5
1968 9/8 – 10/26
1969 5/11 – 6/4
1970 10/25 – until 1971 1/10
1971 6/10 – 9/6
1974 5/13 – 9/2
1975 1/1 – 3/15
1976 6/3 – 7/24
1976 11/16 – until 1977 3/14
1980 8/23 – 10/9
1982 10/9 – 12/22
1986 4/20 – 10/25
1986 11/22 – until 1987 2/27
1988 5/18 – 7/2
1989 1/9 – 1/31
1992 8/7 – 9/23
1994 1/30 – 3/30
1994 9/21 – 12/6
1998 4/1 – until 1999 2/9
2000 5/1 – 6/13
2003 11/23 – until 2004 2/14
2004 7/19 – 9/8
2006 1/1 – 5/9
2006 8/31 – 11/21
2010 3/15 – 6/1
2010 9/14 – until 2011 1/18
2012 4/14 – 5/26

SATURN BENEFICIAL
1941 4/25 – 7/21
1941 11/1 – until 1942 4/8
1949 10/30 – until 1950 3/3
1950 7/23 – 10/15
1951 4/28 – 6/28
1954 11/15 – until 1956 1/5
1956 5/23 – 10/3
1965 4/17 – 9/13
1966 1/11 – 6/20
1966 8/1 – until 1967 2/26
1970 6/5 – 12/22
1971 2/12 – 5/20
1979 9/3 – 12/10
1980 2/3 – 8/22
1983 12/25 – until 1984 4/30
1984 9/20 – until 1985 11/11
1995 2/20 – until 1996 4/1
1999 7/29 – 9/30
2000 4/8 – 6/28
2000 12/4 – until 2001 3/16
2008 10/10 – until 2009 4/5
2009 6/27 – 9/28

URANUS BENEFICIAL
1938 6/23 – until 1941 5/19
1965 9/25 – until 1968 7/26
1977 11/24 – until 1981 11/5
2006 4/19 – until 2011 2/27

NEPTUNE BENEFICIAL
1938 1/1 – until 1941 8/20
1962 1/20 – until 1970 10/18

PLUTO BENEFICIAL
1964 12/14 – until 1970 8/26
1988 11/25 – until 1995 10/23

JUPITER CHALLENGING
1940 3/7 – 5/13

1945 10/26 – until 1946 9/22
1949 1/13 – 4/7
1949 7/3 – 11/27
1951 7/12 – 8/27
1952 2/16 – 4/26
1957 10/11 – until 1958 1/7
1958 3/27 – 9/3
1960 12/28 – until 1961 3/11
1961 8/18 – 10/29
1963 6/5 – 10/16
1964 1/22 – 4/9
1969 9/25 – 12/12
1970 5/5 – 8/10
1972 12/12 – until 1973 2/20
1975 5/15 – until 1976 3/23
1981 9/9 – 11/23
1984 11/25 – until 1985 2/3
1987 4/27 – 8/4
1987 9/4 – until 1988 3/5
1992 12/30 – until 1993 2/27
1993 8/22 – 11/7
1996 3/11 – 6/30
1996 11/4 – until 1997 1/18
1999 4/10 – 6/24
1999 10/28 – until 2000 2/10
2004 12/1 – until 2005 4/8
2005 8/1 – 10/23
2008 2/17 – 8/17
2008 9/30 – until 2009 1/2
2011 3/24 – 6/1

SATURN CHALLENGING
1938 5/13 – 10/25
1939 2/1 – 6/26
1939 10/2 – until 1940 3/14
1951 12/12 – until 1952 3/9
1952 9/2 – until 1953 10/17
1960 2/3 – 8/2
1960 10/29 – until 1961 4/14
1961 6/4 – 12/28
1968 3/19 – until 1969 4/24
1981 10/10 – until 1982 11/23
1983 5/16 – 8/15
1989 3/26 – 5/20
1989 12/12 – until 1991 2/1
1997 4/24 – until 1998 6/2
1998 11/3 – until 1999 2/21
2010 11/18 – until 2011 4/11
2011 8/12 – until 2012 1/24
2012 2/22 – 9/30

URANUS CHALLENGING
1970 12/26 – until 1975 8/23
1991 3/15 – until 1995 12/31

NEPTUNE CHALLENGING
1948 10/22 – until 1956 9/30
1990 2/5 – until 1998 1/11

PLUTO CHALLENGING
1976 11/21 – until 1984 7/13

JUPITER SPECIAL
1942 8/9 – until 1943 6/27
1954 7/22 – 10/28
1954 12/6 – until 1955 6/9
1966 7/6 – 9/23
1967 1/21 – 5/18
1978 6/20 – 9/1
1979 3/12 – 4/8
1990 6/3 – 8/15
2001 9/24 – 12/11
2002 5/15 – 7/29

SATURN SPECIAL
1945 6/28 – until 1946 7/28
1974 8/9 – until 1975 2/2
1975 4/22 – 9/10
1976 1/22 – 5/29
2004 6/11 – until 2005 7/11

URANUS SPECIAL
1951 9/11 – until 1956 5/26

PLUTO SPECIAL
1938 1/5 – until 1939 5/4

241

July 15

SUN: CANCER • DECANATE: PISCES/NEPTUNE • DEGREE: 22°–23° CANCER • MODE: CARDINAL • ELEMENT: WATER

Your Personal Powers

Astute and instinctive, among your many personal powers are a quick, incisive mind and strong imagination. Your ruler, the Moon, indicates that you possess deep feelings and a desire for emotional security. Impressionable and sympathetic, you are able to put yourself in the position of others, yet it is your keen intelligence that makes you stand out from the crowd. Although very sensitive, you can also be strong and authoritative with a touch of the dramatic. With strong premonitions and good perception, you gain power from the combination of your inborn intuition and good reasoning powers. Although you can appear proud and confident, you can sometimes lose power to insecurity or self-doubt. Nevertheless, you have the perseverance and determination to keep going regardless. Drawing on the power of knowledge, you like to keep well-informed, respecting both tradition and new and inventive ideas. Your sensitive leadership, personal charisma, and capacity to work hard and take responsibility ensure your potential for outstanding success.

Your Powers of Attraction in Relationships

Your intelligence and air of strength can win you many admirers. You are drawn to partners who can be direct and honest. You also want a partner who is solid and stable. Strong convictions and a stubborn streak suggest you stand your ground and usually like to confront situations to clear the air. Determined and assertive, your sensitive and vulnerable nature is often concealed behind a tough exterior. Your need for security emphasizes the importance of your family and establishing a secure home. Despite being self-reliant, you realize the advantages of cooperative endeavors when you receive help from others. Although you are very protective, caring, and supportive of loved ones, avoid taking charge or appearing bossy. You can attract others with your sharp wit and amiable personality.

Your attractive qualities: intelligent, commanding, intuitive, responsible, idealistic, generous, kind, cooperative, imaginative, determination, independent, appreciative, caring, home-loving, relentless, confident, creative ideas, multi-talented, enthusiastic, knowledgeable

Your less attractive qualities: restless, dominating, arrogant, unhelpful, impatient, dependent, worry, insecure, too sensitive, uncompromising, skeptical, power battles, underachiever

Your Venus Power

The planet Venus has a great deal of influence on your powers of attraction. Below are four possible Venus types for women and men. To find your Venus you need to go to page 771, where you will find the Venus table and extra information. The planet Mars also affects your powers of attraction. To find your Mars table and interpretation go to page 761.

WOMEN WITH VENUS IN GEMINI: By nature you are young at heart, adaptable, and sociable. Being curious and willing to cooperate makes you a good team player. Usually you are drawn to articulate people who have charm and flair or sharp wit. With a need to expand your knowledge, you also look for a partner who can challenge or stimulate you intellectually. Although you love to talk with all types of people, you may need to develop your listening skills in order to build better communication in your relationships.

MEN WITH VENUS IN GEMINI: Informed and curious yet charming and friendly, you seek a partner who shares your interests or enjoys your witty remarks. Although a good communicator, you have an inborn tendency to be lighthearted and less profound about deep emotional commitment. Although you are keen on experiences that bring variety into your life, boredom or scattering your energies in too many directions is probably your biggest handicap in relationships. Nevertheless you are attracted to intelligent partners who can match your lively banter.

WOMEN WITH VENUS IN CANCER: Gentle and tender, you are romantic by nature. You possess a strong need for security and usually help others feel safe and protected. This preservation is especially centered around the home, which is your haven from life's storm. Although your maternal instincts are strong, avoid making sacrifices for others at your own expense. Nevertheless, affectionate and caring, once committed to a relationship your loyalty and devotion to your partner are very strong.

MEN WITH VENUS IN CANCER: You seek a partner who is sympathetic, caring, and protective. Able to be forgiving and compassionate, you want a secure emotional bond in your close relationships. Usually you are drawn to partners who are maternal, unselfish, or demonstrative with their feelings. Al-

though you can sometimes appear to others as shy or impressionable, you have powerful emotions and inner strength.

Women with Venus in Leo: As a person who wants to radiate in their own right, you are likely to desire partners you can be proud of. You are usually attracted to fun-loving, warm, and generous individuals. If self-expression is important to you, you will probably seek the company of creative people such as artists, musicians, or those with a flair for acting. Alternatively, you may be drawn to people who are dignified, regal, or have already achieved success.

Men with Venus in Leo: Generous, animated, and pleasure-seeking, you can be very entertaining and fun to be with. Usually you are attracted to extroverted and benevolent individuals with a sunny personality. If ambitious, you are drawn to a partner who shows leadership qualities or one who is highly motivated. Your less attractive qualities are your tendencies to be bossy or vain. With a sense of the dramatic, however, you can be the life and soul of the party and inspire those around you.

Women with Venus in Virgo: Intelligent and discriminating, you are usually drawn to polite and refined individuals. As a perfectionist, you may be keen to analyze and criticize yourself, but be careful of continually going over your partner's shortcomings. By focusing on how you can make positive improvements in yourself and in your relationships, you avoid becoming skeptical or confused. You empower yourself when you display your kind and caring concern for the well-being of your loved ones and spontaneously offer your practical assistance.

Men with Venus in Virgo: A love of order usually indicates that you are attracted to refined individuals with analytical or practical abilities. You and your partner may be working together or serving similar causes. As you constantly analyze partnerships in order to improve them, you are likely to use former relationships as a point of reference and compare them to your present partner. Because you are helpful and kind, others usually rely on your good judgment and often turn to you for advice or practical assistance.

To read all about your Outer Planets and work out how to use your personalized timetable, go to Section Three, page 789.

Your Personalized Timetable

JUPITER BENEFICIAL
1939 3/3 – 5/13
1939 10/27 – 12/23
1941 4/1 – 5/15
1944 10/15 – until 1944 12/31
1945 1/23 – 8/11
1946 11/30 – until 1947 10/25
1951 2/14 – 4/22
1952 7/22 – 10/29
1953 3/10 – 4/27
1956 9/28 – 11/21
1957 3/14 – 7/21
1958 11/14 – until 1959 2/13
1959 4/21 – 10/7
1963 1/27 – 4/5
1964 6/27 – 12/15
1965 2/5 – 4/9
1968 9/13 – 10/31
1969 4/25 – 6/20
1970 10/30 – until 1971 1/16
1971 6/2 – 9/13
1974 5/19 – 8/26
1975 1/6 – 3/19
1976 6/8 – 7/31
1976 11/9 – until 1977 3/19
1980 8/28 – 10/13
1982 10/14 – 12/27
1986 4/25 – 10/11
1986 12/6 – until 1987 3/3
1988 5/22 – 7/7
1988 12/24 – until 1989 2/15
1992 8/11 – 9/27
1994 2/13 – 3/16
1994 9/26 – 12/10
1998 4/5 – until 1999 2/14
2000 5/5 – 6/17
2003 12/2 – until 2004 2/5
2004 7/25 – 9/12
2006 1/7 – 5/2
2006 9/6 – 11/25
2010 3/19 – 6/8
2010 9/7 – until 2011 1/24
2012 4/18 – 5/30

SATURN BENEFICIAL
1938 1/1 – 1/18
1941 5/3 – 8/3
1941 10/19 – until 1942 4/16
1949 11/10 – until 1950 2/19
1950 8/1 – 10/24
1951 4/12 – 7/14
1954 11/23 – until 1956 1/16
1956 5/10 – 10/13
1965 4/27 – 8/31
1966 1/21 – until 1967 3/6
1970 6/13 – 12/6
1971 2/28 – 5/27
1979 9/10 – until 1980 8/30
1984 1/5 – 4/17
1984 9/30 – until 1985 11/19
1995 2/28 – until 1996 4/9
2000 4/15 – 7/7
2000 11/22 – until 2001 3/26
2008 10/18 – until 2009 3/22
2009 7/9 – 10/6

URANUS BENEFICIAL
1938 7/18 – until 1942 3/22
1965 10/11 – until 1968 8/14
1977 12/10 – until 1981 11/21
2006 5/16 – until 2011 3/16

NEPTUNE BENEFICIAL
1938 1/1 – until 1942 7/4
1962 12/5 – until 1970 11/14

PLUTO BENEFICIAL
1965 10/13 – until 1971 7/10
1988 12/22 – until 1995 11/17

JUPITER CHALLENGING
1940 3/11 – 5/17

1945 10/31 – until 1946 9/26
1949 1/17 – 4/15
1949 6/25 – 12/2
1952 2/21 – 4/30
1957 10/15 – until 1958 1/16
1958 3/17 – 9/8
1961 1/1 – 3/16
1961 8/10 – 11/6
1963 6/11 – 10/9
1964 1/29 – 4/13
1969 9/30 – 12/18
1970 4/28 – 8/17
1972 12/16 – until 1973 2/24
1975 5/19 – until 1976 3/27
1981 9/13 – 11/28
1984 11/29 – until 1985 2/7
1987 5/1 – until 1988 3/10
1993 1/12 – 2/13
1993 8/27 – 11/11
1996 3/17 – 6/22
1996 11/9 – until 1997 1/22
1999 4/14 – 6/30
1999 10/21 – until 2000 2/16
2004 12/7 – until 2005 4/1
2005 8/7 – 10/27
2008 2/22 – 8/5
2008 10/11 – until 2009 1/6
2011 3/28 – 6/6

SATURN CHALLENGING
1938 5/22 – 10/12
1939 2/12 – 7/10
1939 9/17 – until 1940 3/22
1951 12/27 – until 1952 2/22
1952 9/10 – until 1953 10/24
1960 2/13 – 7/18
1960 11/10 – until 1962 1/6
1968 3/27 – until 1969 5/2
1981 10/18 – until 1982 12/2
1983 5/3 – 8/27
1989 12/20 – until 1991 2/9
1991 9/25 – 10/15
1997 5/2 – 11/17
1998 1/14 – 6/12
1998 10/22 – until 1999 3/3
2010 11/27 – until 2011 3/29
2011 8/23 – until 2012 10/8

URANUS CHALLENGING
1971 10/13 – until 1975 9/13
1992 1/11 – until 1996 1/17

NEPTUNE CHALLENGING
1948 11/19 – until 1957 8/22
1990 3/14 – until 1998 12/8

PLUTO CHALLENGING
1977 10/12 – until 1984 9/6

JUPITER SPECIAL
1942 8/13 – until 1943 7/2
1954 7/27 – until 1955 6/14
1966 7/10 – 9/29
1967 1/14 – 5/25
1978 6/24 – 9/6
1979 2/25 – 4/23
1990 6/8 – 8/19
2001 10/4 – 12/1
2002 5/20 – 8/3

SATURN SPECIAL
1945 7/6 – until 1946 8/4
1974 8/17 – until 1975 1/20
1975 5/5 – 9/20
1976 1/11 – 6/7
2004 6/18 – until 2005 7/18

URANUS SPECIAL
1952 7/7 – until 1956 6/15

PLUTO SPECIAL
1938 1/1 – until 1939 6/25

July 16

Your Personal Powers

Thoughtful, intuitive, and mentally bright, your personal powers include quick comprehension, foresight, and sensitive awareness of people. Your ruler, the Moon, can provide you with powerful emotions, a sixth sense, and creativity. Being imaginative and determined suggest that you possess a strong sense of vision and willingness to work hard to achieve your dreams. When you are focused, your good organizational skills and the ability to think big may place you in leadership positions. Astute and responsive, you also enjoy a mental challenge and like to be well-informed. You empower yourself by combining your sensitive and caring nature with the ability to be of practical help to others. You may lose some of your power if you become impatient, intolerant, or frustrated. Although you are often drawn to education and knowledge, you can excel equally in expressing your thoughts and ideas through writing, art, and drama. Sociable and kind, you gain from your honest and direct approach and your natural generosity. Multitalented or motivated, you have the potential for outstanding success.

Your Powers of Attraction in Relationships

You attract others with your refined manners and helpful attitude. Being clever, you seek a partner who can keep up with your sharp intellect and stop you from being bored. You usually enjoy challenges, variety, or travel and prefer to share your experiences with quick-witted individuals. Being independent, you may experience tension between your responsibility to others and personal needs. Nevertheless, you attract people with your caring and generous nature, often going out of your way to be accommodating. Although you are kind and thoughtful, your sensitivity indicates that you sometimes have difficulty expressing your feelings. A stubborn streak can also cause you to feel misunderstood or close your mind to advice from others. Nevertheless, you like to socialize with interesting people who can keep you mentally stimulated.

Your attractive qualities: sensitive, intelligent, caring, common sense, leadership ability, intuitive, friendly, responsible, receptive, integrity, intuitive, sociable, generous, kind, knowledgeable, sixth sense, gifted, cooperative, insightful, creative, protective

Your less attractive qualities: worried, impatient, dissatisfied, opinionated, skeptical, insecure, isolated, too sensitive, self-pity, intolerant, interfering, irritable, martyr, self-centered, stubborn

Your Venus Power

The planet Venus has a great deal of influence on your powers of attraction. Below are four possible Venus types for women and men. To find your Venus you need to go to page 771, where you will find the Venus table and extra information. The planet Mars also affects your powers of attraction. To find your Mars table and interpretation go to page 761.

WOMEN WITH VENUS IN GEMINI: Curious, with a bright and animated approach to life, you are attracted to those who are clever and/or sophisticated. Your love of variety and desire for knowledge suggest that you need a partner and friends who keep you mentally stimulated. Although witty and a good conversationalist, you may need to keep in touch with your deeper feelings. Nevertheless, intelligent and friendly, you possess a youthful sense of wonder and seek a playmate who can keep you from becoming bored.

MEN WITH VENUS IN GEMINI: Adaptable yet often flirtatious, you enjoy mixing with people who are quick-minded and versatile. Since you can learn a great deal through interacting with others, you are often attracted to intelligent partners who have comprehensive knowledge or good ideas. One of your less attractive qualities is your tendency to become bored or be inconsistent. Having an adaptable partner is important to you; therefore it must be someone who can offer you different options and keep you interested.

WOMEN WITH VENUS IN CANCER: Possessing a soft femininity, you have tender and sensitive emotions. Sympathetic and caring, you often mother those in your care by making sure they are comfortable and have plenty to eat. When you feel hurt or insecure in relationships you are likely to cover your feelings by being defensive or appearing tough on the outside while on the inside you are feeling vulnerable. Affectionate and romantic, you make a faithful and devoted partner.

MEN WITH VENUS IN CANCER: Being emotionally receptive you can make a sensitive lover. With your desire to care for and protect others, you are likely to have strong family connections. Love is often tied in with being attentive to the needs of others and you may find yourself attracted to individuals

who have sympathetic or maternal qualities. Security-conscious, you need a loyal partner who can offer you support and ideally be a good cook and homemaker.

WOMEN WITH VENUS IN LEO: Warm and playful with a touch of the dramatic, you enjoy the company of generous or strong individuals who can share your sense of fun. Although there are advantages to your being strong-willed, in your relationships you need to resist being bossy as it can cause resentment. With your wonderful mixture of regal authority and childlike wonder, you love to keep others entertained and amused.

MEN WITH VENUS IN LEO: Sociable and outgoing, you are kind and generous with those you love. Looking for a relationship that can be fun and entertaining, you need a playmate who can share your enthusiasm and high spirits. Your pride, however, often stops you from associating with lovers or partners you see as beneath you. As you desire someone who can appreciate your sense of the dramatic, you are often attracted to people with strong personalities.

WOMEN WITH VENUS IN VIRGO: In relationships, you can be modest and unassuming but desire perfection. You usually analyze your partnerships until you feel you have understood them to the last little detail in order to improve them. A problem usually arises when you become too critical either of partners or yourself and indulge in being skeptical or faultfinding. As you are modest, others may not be aware of the strong sensuality beneath your well-groomed exterior.

MEN WITH VENUS IN VIRGO: Industrious and well-ordered, you relate to others in a considerate and down-to-earth way. You enjoy giving practical advice and being of service to those you love, even in small ways. Being a perfectionist, you are drawn to partners with high morals or a strong work ethic. Partners who have strong analytical minds are very attractive to you, particularly if they are also clean and meticulously dressed.

To read all about your Outer Planets and work out how to use your personalized timetable, go to Section Three, page 789.

To read all about your Outer Planets and work out how to use your personalized timetable, go to Section Three, page 789.

Your Personalized Timetable

JUPITER BENEFICIAL
1939 3/7 – 5/18
1939 10/17 – until 1940 1/1
1941 4/5 – 5/19
1944 10/20 – until 1945 4/23
1945 6/5 – 8/16
1946 12/5 – until 1947 10/30
1951 2/18 – 4/27
1952 7/29 – 10/21
1953 3/15 – 5/2
1956 10/3 – 11/28
1957 3/7 – 7/27
1958 11/19 – until 1959 2/24
1959 4/9 – 10/12
1963 1/31 – 4/9
1964 7/2 – 12/5
1965 2/15 – until 1965 4/14
1968 9/17 – 11/5
1969 4/15 – 6/30
1970 11/3 – until 1971 1/21
1971 5/26 – 9/20
1974 5/27 – 8/18
1975 1/11 – 3/23
1976 6/12 – 8/7
1976 11/2 – until 1977 3/25
1980 9/1 – 10/18
1982 10/18 – until 1983 1/1
1983 7/19 – 8/8
1986 4/30 – 10/1
1986 12/15 – until 1987 3/7
1988 5/26 – 7/12
1988 12/15 – until 1989 2/25
1992 8/16 – 10/2
1994 10/1 – 12/15
1998 4/10 – until 1999 2/18
2000 5/9 – 6/22
2003 12/14 – until 2004 1/24
2004 7/30 – 9/16
2006 1/14 – 4/24
2006 9/12 – 11/29
2010 3/23 – 6/16
2010 8/29 – until 2011 1/29
2012 4/22 – 6/4

SATURN BENEFICIAL
1938 1/1 – 1/29
1941 5/10 – 8/23
1941 9/29 – until 1942 4/24
1949 11/23 – until 1950 2/5
1950 8/10 – 11/2
1951 3/30 – 7/26
1954 12/1 – until 1955 6/19
1955 8/18 – until 1956 1/28
1956 4/26 – 10/22
1965 5/9 – 8/18
1966 1/30 – until 1967 3/13
1970 6/22 – 11/23
1971 3/12 – 6/4
1979 9/18 – until 1980 9/7
1984 1/18 – 4/2
1984 10/9 – until 1985 11/27
1995 3/7 – until 1996 4/17
1996 11/6 – 12/29
2000 4/23 – 7/17
2000 11/10 – until 2001 4/5
2008 10/27 – until 2009 3/10
2009 7/20 – 10/14
2010 5/9 – 6/21

URANUS BENEFICIAL
1939 5/16 – until 1942 4/12
1965 10/30 – until 1968 8/31
1977 12/30 – until 1982 9/17
2007 3/15 – until 2012 1/16

NEPTUNE BENEFICIAL
1938 1/1 – until 1942 8/14
1963 1/7 – until 1971 10/11

PLUTO BENEFICIAL
1965 11/21 – until 1971 8/17
1989 11/10 – until 1996 10/7

JUPITER CHALLENGING
1940 3/15 – 5/21

1945 11/5 – until 1946 10/1
1949 1/22 – 4/26
1949 6/14 – 12/7
1952 2/25 – 5/4
1957 10/20 – until 1958 1/30
1958 3/4 – 9/14
1961 1/5 – 3/22
1961 8/2 – 11/13
1963 6/17 – 10/2
1964 2/3 – 4/17
1969 10/4 – 12/24
1970 4/20 – 8/24
1972 12/20 – until 1973 3/1
1975 5/24 – 11/24
1975 12/26 – until 1976 3/31
1981 9/18 – 12/3
1982 6/4 – 7/21
1984 12/4 – until 1985 2/12
1987 5/5 – until 1988 3/14
1993 9/1 – 11/16
1996 3/25 – 6/14
1996 11/15 – until 1997 1/26
1999 4/18 – 7/6
1999 10/14 – until 2000 2/22
2004 12/14 – until 2005 3/24
2005 8/13 – 10/31
2008 2/28 – 7/27
2008 10/20 – until 2009 1/10
2011 4/1 – 6/10
2011 12/3 – until 2012 1/17

SATURN CHALLENGING
1938 6/1 – 9/30
1939 2/22 – 8/7
1939 8/19 – until 1940 3/30
1952 9/18 – until 1953 11/1
1960 2/22 – 7/5
1960 11/21 – until 1962 1/14
1968 4/4 – until 1969 5/9
1981 10/25 – until 1982 12/11
1983 4/20 – until 1983 9/7
1989 12/28 – until 1991 2/17
1991 8/29 – 11/9
1997 5/11 – 11/1
1998 1/29 – 6/22
1998 10/10 – until 1999 3/13
2010 12/9 – until 2011 3/17
2011 9/1 – until 2012 10/16

URANUS CHALLENGING
1971 10/28 – until 1975 10/1
1992 1/27 – until 1996 11/16

NEPTUNE CHALLENGING
1949 10/17 – until 1957 9/25
1991 1/31 – until 1999 1/5

PLUTO CHALLENGING
1977 11/6 – until 1984 10/4

JUPITER SPECIAL
1942 8/18 – until 1943 3/7
1943 3/17 – 7/6
1954 7/31 – until 1955 6/19
1966 7/15 – 10/6
1967 1/6 – 5/30
1978 6/28 – 9/11
1979 2/16 – 5/3
1990 6/12 – 8/24
2001 10/16 – 11/19
2002 5/25 – 8/7

SATURN SPECIAL
1945 7/13 – until 1946 8/12
1974 8/26 – until 1975 1/8
1975 5/15 – 10/1
1975 12/29 – until 1976 6/16
2004 6/26 – until 2005 7/26

URANUS SPECIAL
1952 7/23 – until 1956 7/2

PLUTO SPECIAL
1938 1/1 – until 1940 6/7

245

July 17

Your Personal Powers

A keen mind, natural charm, and emotional common sense are just some of your personal powers. Your ruler, the Moon, indicates that you also possess a strong sixth sense and powerful emotions. Being sensitive and impressionable empowers you with imagination and enables you to empathize with the feelings of others. Independent, determined, and ambitious with a need to succeed and accomplish, you gain power from your depth of thought and natural analytical skills. Even though you are intelligent, you usually learn more from personal experience. You can be very persuasive when you feel confident and enthusiastic. Although you are very shrewd about money, you can lose some of your power if you compromise your high ideals for material security. Although you can be sociable and entertaining with a youthful charm, you also possess a side to your character that is more serious and reserved. With your strong feelings and individuality you have a big heart, firm opinions, and the determination to succeed.

Your Powers of Attraction in Relationships

People are attracted to your strong character, natural talents, and thoughtful approach. Although you have a charming, dramatic, fun-loving, and sociable nature, you can also be reserved and private. You are usually attracted to intelligent individuals with whom you can have stimulating conversations or share interests. Although you may encounter some issues regarding secrecy or loneliness in relationships, you can be loving and romantic. When committed to a partner, you can give much of yourself without expecting much in return. Although you are more sensitive than you appear, you prefer to be direct and honest with your feelings. If you are hurt, however, you may withdraw and appear cold. You need your own time for contemplation and renewal, in order to balance your partner's needs with your own.

Your attractive qualities: decisive actions, clever, sociable, multitalented, hardworking, creative, pragmatic, charming, analytical, imaginative, independent, endurance, honest, subtle, thoughtful, intelligent, entertaining, sensitive, well-informed, idealistic, spontaneous

Your less attractive qualities: impulsive, aggressive, competitive, selfish, too self-sacrificing, cold, withdrawn, bossy, moody, opinionated, secretive, too security conscious, cynical, stubborn, skeptical, uncommunicative

Your Venus Power

The planet Venus has a great deal of influence on your powers of attraction. Below are four possible Venus types for women and men. To find your Venus you need to go to page 771, where you will find the Venus table and extra information. The planet Mars also affects your powers of attraction. To find your Mars table and interpretation go to page 761.

WOMEN WITH VENUS IN GEMINI: By nature you are young at heart, adaptable, and sociable. Being curious and willing to cooperate makes you a good team player. Usually you are drawn to articulate people who have charm and flair or sharp wit. With a need to expand your knowledge you also look for a partner who can challenge or stimulate you intellectually. Although you love to talk with all types of people you may need to develop your listening skills in order to build better communication in your relationships.

MEN WITH VENUS IN GEMINI: Adaptable yet often flirtatious, you enjoy mixing with people who are quick-minded and versatile. Since you can learn a great deal by interacting with others, you are often attracted to intelligent partners who have comprehensive knowledge or good ideas. One of your less attractive qualities is your tendency to become bored or be inconsistent. Having an adaptable partner is important to you, therefore it must be someone who can offer you different options and keep you interested.

WOMEN WITH VENUS IN CANCER: Possessing a soft femininity, you have tender and sensitive emotions. Sympathetic and caring, you often mother those in your care by making sure they are comfortable and have plenty to eat. When you feel hurt or insecure in relationships you are likely to cover your feelings by being defensive or appearing tough on the outside while on the inside you are feeling vulnerable. Affectionate and romantic, you make a faithful and devoted partner.

MEN WITH VENUS IN CANCER: You seek a partner who is sympathetic, caring, and protective. Able to be forgiving and compassionate, you want a secure emotional bond in your close relationships. Usually you are drawn to partners who are maternal, unselfish, or demonstrative with their feelings. Al-

though you can sometimes appear to others as shy or impressionable, you have powerful emotions and inner strength.

WOMEN WITH VENUS IN LEO: Warm and playful with a touch of the dramatic, you enjoy the company of generous or strong individuals who can share your sense of fun. Although there are advantages to your being strong-willed, in your relationships you need to resist being bossy as it can cause resentment. With your wonderful mixture of regal authority and childlike wonder, you love to keep others entertained and amused.

MEN WITH VENUS IN LEO: Generous, animated, and pleasure-seeking, you can be very entertaining and fun to be with. Usually you are attracted to extroverted and benevolent individuals with a sunny personality. If ambitious, you are drawn to a partner who shows leadership qualities or one who is highly motivated. Your less attractive qualities are your tendencies to be bossy or vain. With a sense of the dramatic, however, you can be the life and soul of the party and inspire those around you.

WOMEN WITH VENUS IN VIRGO: Articulate and straightforward in your relationships, you attract others with your genuine concern for their well-being. By being understanding and a good listener, you are able to show your love and friendship. With your analytical approach to relationships, however, you may have to be careful of becoming too matter-of-fact. You often display your concern for the welfare of others by your willingness to offer practical help and assistance. You usually seek a partner who is willing to work as hard on relationships as you are.

MEN WITH VENUS IN VIRGO: Although you are constantly analyzing your relationships in order to understand and improve them, you may nevertheless need to refrain from continuously mulling over issues that can cause anxiety. You are happiest when you are able to help your loved ones in practical ways and forget yourself in your willingness to be of service to others. You seek a partner who has high standards and can be as pragmatic and hardworking as yourself. Ideally they should also be impeccably dressed with a fine analytical mind.

To read all about your Outer Planets and work out how to use your personalized timetable, go to Section Three, page 789.

Your Personalized Timetable

JUPITER BENEFICIAL
1939 3/11 – 5/23
1939 10/9 – until 1940 1/9
1941 4/9 – 5/23
1944 10/25 – until 1945 4/11
1945 6/17 – 8/21
1946 12/10 – until 1947 11/3
1951 2/22 – 5/1
1952 8/7 – 10/13
1953 3/20 – 5/6
1956 10/8 – 12/5
1957 2/27 – 8/2
1958 11/23 – until 1959 10/17
1963 2/5 – 4/13
1964 7/7 – 11/27
1965 2/23 – 4/18
1968 9/22 – 11/11
1969 4/6 – 7/9
1970 11/8 – until 1971 1/28
1971 5/18 – 9/26
1974 6/4 – 8/9
1975 1/16 – 3/27
1976 6/16 – 8/15
1976 10/25 – until 1977 3/30
1980 9/6 – 10/23
1982 10/23 – until 1983 1/6
1983 7/2 – 8/25
1986 5/5 – 9/23
1986 12/23 – until 1987 3/11
1988 5/30 – 7/17
1988 12/7 – until 1989 3/5
1992 8/21 – 10/6
1994 10/6 – 12/19
1998 4/14 – until 1999 2/22
2000 5/13 – 6/26
2004 8/4 – 9/21
2006 1/21 – 4/16
2006 9/18 – 12/4
2010 3/27 – 6/26
2010 8/19 – until 2011 2/3
2012 4/26 – 6/8

SATURN BENEFICIAL
1938 1/1 – 2/8
1941 5/18 – until 1942 5/2
1949 12/13 – until 1950 1/15
1950 8/18 – 11/11
1951 3/18 – 8/5
1954 12/10 – until 1955 6/1
1955 9/3 – until 1956 2/13
1956 4/8 – 10/31
1965 5/23 – 8/3
1966 2/8 – until 1967 3/21
1970 7/1 – 11/11
1971 3/22 – 6/12
1979 9/26 – until 1980 9/14
1984 2/9 – 3/10
1984 10/17 – until 1985 12/5
1995 3/15 – until 1996 4/26
1996 10/20 – until 1997 1/14
2000 5/1 – 7/28
2000 10/28 – until 2001 4/13
2008 11/7 – until 2009 2/26
2009 7/30 – 10/22
2010 4/19 – 7/10

URANUS BENEFICIAL
1939 6/2 – until 1942 4/30
1965 11/24 – until 1968 9/15
1978 1/28 – until 1982 10/11
2007 4/1 – until 2012 2/10

NEPTUNE BENEFICIAL
1938 1/1 – until 1942 9/11
1963 11/30 – until 1971 11/9

PLUTO BENEFICIAL
1966 10/7 – until 1971 9/13
1989 12/4 – until 1996 11/4

JUPITER CHALLENGING
1940 3/19 – 5/26

1945 11/9 – until 1946 10/5
1949 1/26 – 12/11
1952 3/1 – 5/8
1957 10/24 – until 1958 9/19
1961 1/10 – 3/28
1961 7/25 – 11/19
1963 6/24 – 9/25
1964 2/9 – 4/21
1969 10/8 – 12/31
1970 4/13 – 8/30
1972 12/24 – until 1973 3/5
1975 5/29 – 11/11
1976 1/8 – 4/4
1981 9/23 – 12/8
1982 5/24 – 8/1
1984 12/8 – until 1985 2/16
1987 5/10 – until 1988 3/18
1993 9/6 – 11/20
1996 4/3 – 6/4
1996 11/20 – until 1997 1/30
1999 4/22 – 7/13
1999 10/6 – until 2000 2/27
2004 12/21 – until 2005 3/16
2005 8/19 – 11/5
2008 3/4 – 7/19
2008 10/27 – until 2009 1/15
2011 4/5 – 6/15
2011 11/22 – until 2012 1/27

SATURN CHALLENGING
1938 6/13 – 9/17
1939 3/3 – until 1940 4/7
1952 9/26 – until 1953 11/9
1960 3/5 – 6/22
1960 12/1 – until 1962 1/22
1968 4/11 – until 1969 5/17
1969 12/23 – until 1970 1/15
1981 11/3 – until 1982 5/20
1982 7/17 – 12/22
1983 4/7 – 9/17
1990 1/5 – until 1991 2/26
1991 8/14 – 11/23
1997 5/20 – 10/19
1998 2/9 – 7/5
1998 9/26 – until 1999 3/21
2010 12/22 – until 2011 3/2
2011 9/10 – until 2012 10/24

URANUS CHALLENGING
1971 11/13 – until 1975 10/16
1992 2/14 – until 1996 12/10

NEPTUNE CHALLENGING
1949 11/13 – until 1958 8/8
1991 3/3 – until 1999 11/29

PLUTO CHALLENGING
1977 12/8 – until 1985 8/11

JUPITER SPECIAL
1942 8/23 – until 1943 2/15
1943 4/6 – 7/11
1954 8/4 – until 1955 6/23
1966 7/19 – 10/14
1966 12/29 – until 1967 6/5
1978 7/3 – 9/17
1979 2/7 – 5/11
1990 6/16 – 8/28
2002 5/30 – 8/11

SATURN SPECIAL
1945 7/20 – until 1946 8/20
1947 3/18 – 4/19
1974 9/5 – 12/28
1975 5/24 – 10/16
1975 12/14 – until 1976 6/24
2004 7/3 – until 2005 8/2

URANUS SPECIAL
1952 8/9 – until 1956 7/18

PLUTO SPECIAL
1938 1/1 – until 1941 5/11

July 18

SUN: CANCER • DECANATE: PISCES/NEPTUNE • DEGREE: 25°–26° CANCER • MODE: CARDINAL • ELEMENT: WATER

Your Personal Powers

Persistent and resourceful, among your many personal powers is a determination to continue until you succeed. Combined with your magnetic charm and inherent leadership skills, you possess a natural advantage over others. Your ruler, the Moon, also grants you imagination and strong intuition. You gain power from the use of your organizational skills and foresight. Your shrewd perception also enables you to utilize opportunities for advancement and success. Although you are assertive and mentally sharp, you can lose power if you become controlling, argumentative, or stubborn. Intelligent and highly intuitive, you can enjoy your power when you learn to use it creatively. Although your fast responses can make you decisive, if they turn into intolerance or impatience others may resent you. Nevertheless, as you are responsible and hardworking, your natural sensitivity gives you the ability to identify with others. This often places you in an advisory capacity where you can be of help. Besides your persuasive manner, you can also succeed through your natural business sense, pragmatic attitude, and strong convictions.

Your Powers of Attraction in Relationships

Your individualism and determination can attract friends and admirers. Affectionate and enthusiastic when positive, you are likely to inspire others to follow you. With your strong opinions and resolute nature, you want a hardworking partner who can stand up to you. Although enterprising and creative, you especially value the importance of home and family. Though you are very protective of those in your care, you need variety in your life to keep you from becoming bored or restless. Being generous, however, once you find something inspiring, you willingly share it with loved ones. With your sixth sense about people, it pays for you to trust your first instincts or go by your first impressions.

Your attractive qualities: determination, capable, enthusiasm, charismatic, independent, ambitious, assertive, progressive, intuitive, responsible, courageous, resolute, efficient, advisory skill, dynamic drive, magnetic

Your less attractive qualities: bossy, lazy, stubborn, argumentative, selfish, power issues, underachiever, overemotional, arrogant, daredevil, procrastinator, restless, secretive

Your Venus Power

The planet Venus has a great deal of influence on your powers of attraction. Below are four possible Venus types for women and men. To find your Venus you need to go to page 771, where you will find the Venus table and extra information. The planet Mars also affects your powers of attraction. To find your Mars table and interpretation go to page 761.

WOMEN WITH VENUS IN GEMINI: Curious, with a bright and animated approach to life, you are attracted to those who are clever and/or sophisticated. Your love of variety and desire for knowledge suggest that you need a partner and friends who keep you mentally stimulated. Although witty and a good conversationalist, you may need to keep in touch with your deeper feelings. Nevertheless, intelligent and friendly, you possess a youthful sense of wonder and seek a playmate who can keep you from becoming bored.

MEN WITH VENUS IN GEMINI: Charming, amusing, and adaptable, you attract others with your natural communication skills and friendly personality. You have a wonderful childlike quality and love to keep life playful, but a reluctance to contact your deeper feelings may cause you to avoid serious commitment. With your need for variety and intellectual stimulation, you are attracted to clever and amusing partners who have many interesting sides to their personalities.

WOMEN WITH VENUS IN CANCER: Good-natured and romantic, you have a highly developed sense of touch that particularly responds to massage, hugs, and all things physical. Being friendly, you enjoy socializing and are able to put others at their ease. With your natural sense of beauty and harmony, your natural charm can attract others. Although you can be lavish toward your partner you may have to be careful that you do not overdo things.

MEN WITH VENUS IN CANCER: Being emotionally receptive, you can make a sensitive lover. With your desire to care for and protect others, you are likely to have strong family connections. Love is often tied in with being attentive to the needs of others and you may find yourself attracted to individuals who have sympathetic or maternal qualities. Security-conscious, you need a loyal partner who can offer you support and ideally be a good cook and homemaker.

WOMEN WITH VENUS IN LEO: As a person who wants to radiate in their own right, you are likely to desire partners you can be proud of. Usually you are attracted to fun-loving,

warm, and generous individuals. If self-expression is important to you, you will probably seek the company of creative people such as artists, musicians, or those with a flair for acting. Alternatively, you may be drawn to people who are dignified, regal, or have already achieved success.

MEN WITH VENUS IN LEO: A childlike nature suggests that you are versatile and keen on games or being entertained. You are usually attracted to vivacious partners with a benevolent nature. As an extrovert you enjoy being involved in all types of activities where you can assert yourself and show your talents and abilities. Others may recognize your inborn tendencies to lead but are also aware of your vanity or pride. Nevertheless, generous and caring, you often show more compassion to those less fortunate than yourself.

WOMEN WITH VENUS IN VIRGO: Polite, refined, and organized, you are attracted to articulate and intelligent people. Since you are caring, concerned, and want to be of practical help to others, you can be an asset to any partnership. By being too analytical, exacting, or faultfinding, however, a doubting element can creep into your relationships. By expressing your feelings in a positive way you can become more decisive and improve on how you relate to your loved ones.

MEN WITH VENUS IN VIRGO: Industrious and well-ordered, you relate to others in a considerate and down-to-earth way. You enjoy giving practical advice and being of service to those you love, even in small ways. Being a perfectionist you are drawn to partners with high morals or a strong work ethic. Partners who have strong analytical minds are very attractive to you, particularly if they are also clean and meticulously dressed.

To read all about your Outer Planets and work out how to use your personalized timetable, go to Section Three, page 789.

To read all about your Outer Planets and work out how to use your personalized timetable, go to Section Three, page 789.

Your Personalized Timetable

JUPITER BENEFICIAL
1939 3/15 – 5/28
1939 10/2 – until 1940 1/15
1941 4/14 – 5/27
1944 10/31 – until 1945 4/2
1945 6/26 – 8/25
1946 12/14 – until 1947 11/7
1951 2/26 – 5/6
1952 8/18 – 10/2
1953 3/25 – 5/10
1956 10/12 – 12/14
1957 2/18 – 8/7
1958 11/28 – until 1959 10/21
1963 2/9 – 4/17
1964 7/13 – 11/20
1965 3/1 – 4/23
1968 9/26 – 11/16
1969 3/29 – 7/16
1970 11/12 – until 1971 2/4
1971 5/11 – 10/2
1974 6/16 – 7/28
1975 1/21 – 3/31
1976 6/21 – 8/25
1976 10/15 – until 1977 4/4
1980 9/10 – 10/28
1982 10/27 – until 1983 1/11
1983 6/21 – 9/4
1986 5/11 – 9/16
1986 12/29 – until 1987 3/15
1988 6/3 – 7/22
1988 11/29 – until 1989 3/12
1992 8/25 – 10/11
1994 10/11 – 12/24
1998 4/19 – until 1999 2/27
2000 5/17 – 7/1
2004 8/9 – 9/25
2006 1/30 – 4/7
2006 9/23 – 12/8
2010 3/31 – 7/11
2010 8/4 – until 2011 2/7
2012 4/30 – 6/12

SATURN BENEFICIAL
1938 1/1 – 2/17
1941 5/25 – until 1942 5/9
1950 8/26 – 11/22
1951 3/5 – 8/15
1954 12/19 – until 1955 5/19
1955 9/15 – until 1956 11/8
1965 6/18 – 7/7
1966 2/16 – until 1967 3/29
1970 7/12 – 10/30
1971 3/31 – 6/19
1972 1/7 – 2/24
1979 10/3 – until 1980 9/22
1984 10/26 – until 1985 12/13
1986 7/28 – 8/16
1995 3/23 – until 1996 5/5
1996 10/7 – until 1997 1/26
2000 5/8 – 8/12
2000 10/13 – until 2001 4/22
2008 11/18 – until 2009 2/13
2009 8/8 – 10/31
2010 4/5 – 7/23

URANUS BENEFICIAL
1939 6/20 – until 1942 5/17
1966 9/15 – until 1969 7/1
1978 11/16 – until 1982 10/29
2007 4/20 – until 2012 2/29

NEPTUNE BENEFICIAL
1938 1/1 – until 1943 8/7
1963 12/30 – until 1972 10/2

PLUTO BENEFICIAL
1966 11/10 – until 1972 8/4
1990 1/3 – until 1997 9/15

JUPITER CHALLENGING
1940 3/23 – 5/30
1945 11/14 – until 1946 10/10

1949 1/30 – 12/16
1952 3/5 – 5/12
1957 10/28 – until 1958 9/23
1961 1/14 – 4/3
1961 7/18 – 11/25
1963 7/2 – 9/17
1964 2/14 – 4/25
1969 10/13 – until 1970 1/7
1970 4/5 – 9/4
1972 12/29 – until 1973 3/10
1973 9/5 – 10/21
1975 6/3 – 11/2
1976 1/17 – 4/8
1981 9/27 – 12/13
1982 5/15 – 8/10
1984 12/13 – until 1985 2/20
1987 5/14 – until 1988 3/23
1993 9/11 – 11/25
1996 4/16 – 5/22
1996 11/25 – until 1997 2/4
1999 4/26 – 7/22
1999 9/28 – until 2000 3/3
2004 12/30 – until 2005 3/7
2005 8/24 – 11/9
2008 3/10 – 7/11
2008 11/2 – until 2009 1/19
2011 4/9 – 6/20
2011 11/14 – until 2012 2/4

SATURN CHALLENGING
1938 6/28 – 9/2
1939 3/11 – until 1940 4/15
1952 10/4 – until 1953 11/18
1954 6/12 – 7/31
1960 3/18 – 6/7
1960 12/10 – until 1962 1/30
1968 4/19 – until 1969 5/25
1969 11/30 – until 1970 2/7
1981 11/11 – until 1982 5/3
1982 8/2 – until 1983 1/4
1983 3/24 – 9/26
1990 1/14 – until 1991 3/8
1991 8/1 – 12/5
1997 5/30 – 10/7
1998 2/19 – 7/23
1998 9/8 – until 1999 3/29
2011 1/16 – 2/4
2011 9/18 – until 2012 11/1

URANUS CHALLENGING
1971 12/3 – until 1976 7/26
1992 3/7 – until 1996 12/29

NEPTUNE CHALLENGING
1949 12/22 – until 1958 9/19
1992 1/25 – until 1999 12/30

PLUTO CHALLENGING
1978 10/24 – until 1985 9/17

JUPITER SPECIAL
1942 8/28 – until 1943 2/4
1943 4/16 – 7/15
1954 8/9 – until 1955 6/28
1966 7/23 – 10/23
1966 12/20 – until 1967 6/10
1978 7/7 – 9/22
1979 1/31 – 5/18
1990 6/21 – 9/2
2002 6/3 – 8/16

SATURN SPECIAL
1945 7/28 – until 1946 8/28
1947 2/26 – 5/10
1974 9/17 – 12/15
1975 6/2 – until 1976 7/2
2004 7/11 – until 2005 8/9

URANUS SPECIAL
1952 8/28 – until 1957 5/5

PLUTO SPECIAL
1938 1/1 – until 1941 6/29

249

July 19

SUN: CANCER • DECANATE: PISCES/NEPTUNE • DEGREE: 26°–27° CANCER • MODE: CARDINAL • ELEMENT: WATER

Your Personal Powers

Forceful, astute, and intuitive, you present a friendly and caring yet dynamic personality. Your ruler, the Moon, suggests that you possess deep emotions and a natural sixth sense. Dramatic and creative, when you feel optimistic you can uplift others with your personal philosophy and spirited approach. Alternatively, your sensitive imagination and idealism can inspire you to pursue your artistic or musical inclinations. Often original and clever, you gain power by combining your natural people skills with your love of knowledge. Honest and fair, you possess executive ability even though you may at times use an unconventional approach. Being naturally sympathetic, idealistic, and broad-minded, you also make a good adviser to others. You may lose power, however, if you forfeit your usual detached perspective and allow negative thinking or impatience to cloud your sharp awareness and rational view. Generous and humane, however, your wealth of feelings and mental creativity endow you with a kind heart and a desire to succeed.

Your Powers of Attraction in Relationships

Your quick comprehension and friendly personality attract others. With your strong feelings you can be sensitive and romantic in love situations. Once committed to a long-term relationship, you are usually loyal and generous. Although you can be very protective of those you love, avoid becoming bossy, interfering, or taking things too much to heart. Security-conscious, you are attracted by those who can give you emotional and financial support. In return you can be tolerant, dutiful, and affectionate. Being too sentimental means that you need to avoid holding on to the past or harboring old resentments. By staying detached and philosophical, you can make sure that you maintain equal rights in your partnerships and avoid situations of dependency in the future.

Your attractive qualities: clever, resourceful, dynamic, proud, centered, creative, leader, progressive, optimistic, sensitive, philosophical, strong convictions, unusual talents, humanitarian, loyal, sixth sense, competitive, independent, courage, gregarious

Your less attractive qualities: self-centered, depressive, disappointment, fear of rejection, moody, negative thinking, anxious, frustration, worrisome, materialistic, impatient

Your Venus Power

The planet Venus has a great deal of influence on your powers of attraction. Below are four possible Venus types for women and men. To find your Venus you need to go to page 771, where you will find the Venus table and extra information. The planet Mars also affects your powers of attraction. To find your Mars table and interpretation go to page 761.

WOMEN WITH VENUS IN GEMINI: Curious, with a bright and animated approach to life, you are attracted to those who are clever and/or sophisticated. Your love of variety and desire for knowledge suggest that you need a partner and friends who can keep you mentally stimulated. Although witty and a good conversationalist, you may need to keep in touch with your deeper feelings. Nevertheless, intelligent and friendly, you possess a youthful sense of wonder and seek a playmate who can keep you from becoming bored.

MEN WITH VENUS IN GEMINI: Adaptable yet often flirtatious, you enjoy mixing with people who are quick-minded and versatile. Since you can learn a great deal through interacting with others, you are often attracted to intelligent partners who have comprehensive knowledge or good ideas. One of your less attractive qualities is your tendency to become bored or be inconsistent. Having an adaptable partner is important to you; therefore it must be someone who can offer you different options and keep you interested.

WOMEN WITH VENUS IN CANCER: Good-natured and romantic, you have a highly developed sense of touch that particularly responds to massage, hugs, and all things physical. Being friendly, you enjoy socializing and are able to put others at their ease. With your natural sense of beauty and harmony, your natural charm can attract others. Although you can be lavish toward your partner you may have to be careful that you do not overdo things.

MEN WITH VENUS IN CANCER: Being emotionally receptive you can make a sensitive lover. With your desire to care for and protect others, you are likely to have strong family connections. Love is often tied in with being attentive to the needs of others and you may find yourself attracted to individuals who have sympathetic or maternal qualities. Security-conscious, you need a loyal partner who can offer you support and ideally be a good cook and homemaker.

WOMEN WITH VENUS IN LEO: Your friendly and sunny personality often make you stand out in a crowd. Generous and giving, you know how to make your partner feel special.

As you often expect loyalty and devotion from your partners in return, you can become easily offended if they ignore you or behave in an inconsiderate manner. Charming and kind, when you are in love you can be romantic, dramatic, and passionate.

Men with Venus in Leo: Warm and playful with a touch of the dramatic, you enjoy the company of generous or strong individuals who can share your sense of fun. Although there are advantages to your being strong-willed, in your relationships you need to resist being bossy as it can cause resentment. With your wonderful mixture of regal authority and childlike wonder, you love to keep others entertained and amused.

Women with Venus in Virgo: In relationships you can be modest and unassuming but desire perfection. You usually analyze your partnerships until you feel you have understood them to the last little detail in order to improve them. A problem usually arises when you become too critical either of partners or yourself and indulge in being skeptical or faultfinding. As you are modest, others may not be aware of the strong sensuality beneath your well-groomed exterior.

Men with Venus in Virgo: Practical, idealistic, and perfectionist, you seek a relationship with an intelligent and hardworking partner who can inspire you to be more industrious and well-ordered. At times you can come across as a sympathetic and caring person and at other times you may appear pragmatic and very businesslike. This may sometimes lead to unclear communication between you and your partner. Usually helpful and caring, however, you like to analyze the faults in your relationships and then work methodically to improve them.

To read all about your Outer Planets and work out how to use your personalized timetable, go to Section Three, page 789.

To read all about your Outer Planets and work out how to use your personalized timetable, go to Section Three, page 789.

Your Personalized Timetable

JUPITER BENEFICIAL
1939   3/19 – 6/3
1939   9/25 – until 1940 1/21
1941   4/18 – 5/31
1944   11/5 – until 1945 3/25
1945   7/4 – 8/30
1946   12/19 – until 1947 6/29
1947   7/31 – 11/12
1951   3/2 – 5/10
1953   3/30 – 5/14
1956   10/17 – 12/26
1957   2/6 – 8/13
1958   12/2 – until 1959 10/26
1963   2/13 – 4/21
1964   7/18 – 11/13
1965   3/8 – 4/27
1968   9/30 – 11/22
1969   3/22 – 7/23
1970   11/16 – until 1971 2/11
1971   5/2 – 10/7
1975   1/26 – 4/4
1976   6/26 – 9/12
1976   9/27 – until 1977 4/9
1980   9/15 – 11/2
1981   5/7 – 6/17
1982   11/1 – until 1983 1/16
1983   6/12 – 9/13
1986   5/17 – 9/9
1987   1/4 – 3/19
1988   6/7 – 7/28
1988   11/22 – until 1989 3/18
1992   8/30 – 10/15
1994   10/15 – 12/28
1998   4/23 – until 1999 3/3
2000   5/21 – 7/5
2004   8/14 – 9/30
2006   2/10 – 3/26
2006   9/28 – 12/12
2010   4/4 – until 2011 2/12
2012   5/4 – 6/16

SATURN BENEFICIAL
1938   1/1 – 2/25
1941   6/2 – until 1942 5/17
1950   9/3 – 12/5
1951   2/19 – 8/23
1954   12/29 – until 1955 5/6
1955   9/26 – until 1956 11/17
1966   2/24 – until 1967 4/6
1970   7/24 – 10/17
1971   4/8 – 6/28
1971   12/21 – until 1972 3/12
1979   10/11 – until 1980 4/19
1980   6/24 – 9/30
1984   11/3 – until 1985 12/22
1986   7/1 – 9/12
1995   3/31 – 11/11
1995   12/1 – until 1996 5/14
1996   9/25 – until 1997 2/6
2000   5/15 – until 2001 4/29
2008   12/4 – until 2009 1/28
2009   8/16 – 11/9
2010   3/24 – 8/3

URANUS BENEFICIAL
1939   7/13 – until 1943 3/14
1966   9/30 – until 1969 7/30
1978   12/1 – until 1982 11/14
2007   5/15 – until 2012 3/17

NEPTUNE BENEFICIAL
1938   1/1 – until 1943 9/6
1964   11/24 – until 1972 11/2

PLUTO BENEFICIAL
1967   10/2 – until 1972 9/3
1990   11/19 – until 1997 10/21

JUPITER CHALLENGING
1940   3/27 – 6/3
1945   11/19 – until 1946 5/25

JUPITER BENEFICIAL (cont.)
1946   7/5 – 10/14
1949   2/3 – 12/21
1952   3/9 – 5/16
1957   11/2 – until 1958 9/28
1961   1/18 – 4/10
1961   7/10 – 11/30
1963   7/11 – 9/7
1964   2/19 – 4/29
1969   10/17 – until 1970 1/15
1970   3/27 – 9/10
1973   1/2 – 3/15
1973   8/25 – 11/1
1975   6/8 – 10/25
1976   1/24 – 4/12
1981   10/1 – 12/19
1982   5/6 – 8/18
1984   12/17 – until 1985 2/25
1987   5/18 – until 1988 3/27
1993   9/15 – 11/30
1996   11/29 – until 1997 2/8
1999   4/30 – 8/1
1999   9/17 – until 2000 3/8
2005   1/10 – 2/24
2005   8/29 – 11/14
2008   3/16 – 7/4
2008   11/8 – until 2009 1/23
2011   4/13 – 6/26
2011   11/7 – until 2012 2/11

SATURN CHALLENGING
1939   3/19 – until 1940 4/22
1952   10/12 – until 1953 11/26
1954   5/24 – 8/18
1960   4/7 – 5/18
1960   12/19 – until 1962 2/7
1968   4/27 – until 1969 6/3
1969   11/15 – until 1970 2/20
1981   11/20 – until 1982 4/19
1982   8/15 – until 1983 1/23
1983   3/4 – 10/4
1990   1/22 – until 1991 3/18
1991   7/19 – 12/15
1997   6/9 – 9/24
1998   2/28 – until 1999 4/6
2011   9/26 – until 2012 11/8

URANUS CHALLENGING
1972   1/1 – until 1976 8/30
1993   1/8 – until 1997 1/15

NEPTUNE CHALLENGING
1950   11/7 – until 1958 10/17
1992   2/23 – until 2000 11/17

PLUTO CHALLENGING
1978   11/19 – until 1985 10/13

JUPITER SPECIAL
1942   9/2 – until 1943 1/27
1943   4/25 – 7/19
1954   8/13 – until 1955 7/3
1966   7/27 – 11/6
1966   12/6 – until 1967 6/15
1978   7/11 – 9/28
1979   1/24 – 5/24
1990   6/25 – 9/7
1991   3/12 – 4/18
2002   6/8 – 8/20

SATURN SPECIAL
1945   8/5 – until 1946 3/8
1946   4/1 – 9/5
1947   2/12 – 5/23
1974   10/1 – 11/30
1975   6/10 – until 1976 7/10
2004   7/18 – until 2005 8/17

URANUS SPECIAL
1952   9/23 – until 1957 6/3

PLUTO SPECIAL
1938   1/1 – until 1942 6/10

251

July 20

Your Personal Powers

Your personal powers are enhanced by the combination of your superb intellect and intuitive sensitivity. Although determined with a natural business sense, you are often an idealist who seeks harmony and inspiration. Your ruler, the Moon, implies that although you can be sensitive, receptive, and gracious, you enjoy a mental challenge. In your attempt to test your wits and intelligence, resist being manipulative or getting involved in mental power games. Along with your vivid imagination you possess strong insight and vision that you can utilize in new opportunities. You will lose some of your power, however, if you use your imagination to overfantasize or indulge in escapism. Nevertheless, as a practical visionary, you gain power from the active use of your versatility, people skills, and inspired actions. Aware of the benefits that come from working with others, you usually enjoy shared activities where you can interact and learn from those around you. As a clever and purposeful idealist, you need only discipline yourself to manifest your wonderful dreams.

Your Powers of Attraction in Relationships

Affectionate and sensitive, you can attract others by being caring, courteous, and charming. You are drawn to honest and straightforward individuals or those who possess common sense. Being smart, you also appreciate those who can match your wits and keep you mentally on your toes. Receptive to your environment, you enjoy the stability of home and family and usually pay much attention to friends and loved ones. With your extreme sensitivity to the feelings of others, you can also be tender and very affectionate. In your relationships, however, you may have to avoid an inclination to martyr yourself or become dependent on others. Very sociable, you usually fare better in partnerships or group efforts than in individual enterprises.

Your attractive qualities: powerful mind, gentle, charming, tactful, receptive, intuitive, considerate, determined, practical, harmonious, agreeable, amicable, business sense, harmonious, subtle, social skills, drive, receptive, good partnerships, friendly

Your less attractive qualities: lack of confidence, suspicious, lazy, shy, too sensitive, selfish, secretive, impatient, restless, escapist, power games, calculating, dependent, moody, stubborn

Your Venus Power

The planet Venus has a great deal of influence on your powers of attraction. Below are four possible Venus types for women and men. To find your Venus you need to go to page 771, where you will find the Venus table and extra information. The planet Mars also affects your powers of attraction. To find your Mars table and interpretation go to page 761.

WOMEN WITH VENUS IN GEMINI: By nature you are young at heart, adaptable, and sociable. Being curious and willing to cooperate makes you a good team player. Usually you are drawn to articulate people who have charm and flair or sharp wit. With a need to expand your knowledge you also look for a partner who can challenge or stimulate you intellectually. Although you love to talk with all types of people, you may need to develop your listening skills in order to build better communication in your relationships.

MEN WITH VENUS IN GEMINI: Informed and curious yet charming and friendly, you seek a partner who shares your interests or enjoys your witty remarks. Although a good communicator, you have an inborn tendency to be lighthearted and less profound about deep emotional commitment. Although you are keen on experiences that bring variety into your life, boredom or scattering your energies in too many directions is probably your biggest handicap in relationships. Nevertheless, you are attracted to intelligent partners who can match your lively banter.

WOMEN WITH VENUS IN CANCER: Possessing a soft femininity, you have tender and sensitive emotions. Sympathetic and caring, you often mother those in your care by making sure they are comfortable and have plenty to eat. When you feel hurt or insecure in relationships you are likely to cover your feelings by being defensive or appearing tough on the outside while on the inside you are feeling vulnerable. Affectionate and romantic, you make a faithful and devoted partner.

MEN WITH VENUS IN CANCER: Being caring and sensitive, you probably seek a nurturing partner who could provide you with emotional security and a sense of belonging in a loving and safe environment. Receptive to others, at times you

find it hard to be direct or confrontational in relationships. You may find yourself drawn to affectionate and sympathetic partners like yourself. You are also likely to have strong family links.

WOMEN WITH VENUS IN LEO: Warm and playful with a touch of the dramatic, you enjoy the company of generous or strong individuals who can share your sense of fun. Although there are advantages to your being strong-willed, in your relationships you need to resist being bossy as it can cause resentment. With your wonderful mixture of regal authority and childlike wonder, you love to keep others entertained and amused.

MEN WITH VENUS IN LEO: Sociable and outgoing, you are kind and generous with those you love. Looking for a relationship that can be fun and entertaining, you need a playmate who can share your enthusiasm and high spirits. Your pride, however, often stops you from associating with lovers or partners you see as beneath you. As you desire someone who can appreciate your sense of the dramatic, you are often attracted to people with strong personalities.

WOMEN WITH VENUS IN VIRGO: Intelligent and discriminating, you are usually drawn to polite and refined individuals. As a perfectionist you may be keen to analyze and criticize yourself, but be careful of continually going over your partner's shortcomings. By focusing on how you can make positive improvements in yourself and in your relationships, you avoid becoming skeptical or confused. You empower yourself when you display your kind and caring concern for the well-being of your loved ones and spontaneously offer your practical assistance.

MEN WITH VENUS IN VIRGO: A love of order usually indicates that you are attracted to refined individuals with analytical or practical abilities. You and your partner may be working together or serving similar causes. As you constantly analyze partnerships in order to improve them, you are likely to use former relationships as a point of reference and compare them to your present partner. Because you are helpful and kind, others usually rely on your good judgment and often turn to you for advice or practical assistance.

To read all about your Outer Planets and work out how to use your personalized timetable, go to Section Three, page 789.

⊙

Your Personalized Timetable

JUPITER BENEFICIAL
1939 3/23 – 6/10
1939 9/18 – until 1940 1/27
1941 4/22 – 6/4
1944 11/11 – until 1945 3/17
1945 7/11 – 9/4
1946 12/24 – until 1947 6/15
1947 8/15 – 11/16
1951 3/6 – 5/15
1951 11/8 – 12/21
1953 4/4 – 5/18
1956 10/22 – until 1957 5/7
1957 5/30 – 8/18
1958 12/7 – until 1959 10/31
1963 2/17 – 4/25
1964 7/25 – 11/6
1965 3/13 – 5/1
1968 10/5 – 11/29
1969 3/14 – 7/29
1970 11/21 – until 1971 2/21
1971 4/22 – 10/13
1975 1/30 – 4/8
1976 6/30 – 12/24
1977 2/7 – 4/13
1980 9/19 – 11/7
1981 4/24 – 6/30
1982 11/5 – until 1983 1/22
1983 6/5 – 9/20
1986 5/23 – 9/1
1987 1/10 – 3/23
1988 6/12 – 8/3
1988 11/15 – until 1989 3/24
1992 9/3 – 10/20
1994 10/20 – until 1995 1/2
1998 4/28 – 10/21
1998 12/6 – until 1999 3/7
2000 5/25 – 7/10
2001 1/2 – 2/16
2004 8/18 – 10/4
2006 10/3 – 12/17
2010 4/8 – until 2011 2/16
2012 5/8 – 6/20

SATURN BENEFICIAL
1938 1/1 – 3/5
1941 6/10 – until 1942 1/2
1942 2/13 – 5/24
1950 9/11 – 12/24
1951 1/30 – 9/1
1955 1/9 – 4/23
1955 10/6 – until 1956 11/25
1966 3/4 – until 1967 4/13
1970 8/10 – 9/30
1971 4/16 – 7/6
1971 12/8 – until 1972 3/24
1979 10/20 – until 1980 4/4
1980 7/9 – 10/8
1984 11/11 – until 1985 12/30
1986 6/16 – 9/26
1995 4/8 – 10/17
1995 12/26 – until 1996 5/25
1996 9/12 – until 1997 2/15
2000 5/23 – until 2001 5/7
2009 8/24 – 11/19
2010 3/12 – 8/13

URANUS BENEFICIAL
1940 5/13 – until 1943 4/8
1966 10/16 – until 1969 8/19
1978 12/18 – until 1982 11/30
2008 3/15 – Continues

NEPTUNE BENEFICIAL
1938 10/16 – until 1944 7/29
1964 12/22 – until 1973 9/23

PLUTO BENEFICIAL
1967 10/31 – until 1973 7/19
1990 12/15 – until 1997 11/16

JUPITER CHALLENGING
1940 3/31 – 6/8

1945 11/24 – until 1946 5/12
1946 7/17 – 10/19
1949 2/8 – 12/25
1952 3/13 – 5/20
1957 11/7 – until 1958 10/3
1961 1/22 – 4/18
1961 7/2 – 12/5
1963 7/24 – 8/25
1964 2/23 – 5/3
1969 10/22 – until 1970 1/26
1970 3/16 – 9/15
1973 1/6 – 3/20
1973 8/16 – 11/9
1975 6/14 – 10/18
1976 1/31 – 4/16
1981 10/6 – 12/25
1982 4/29 – 8/24
1984 12/21 – until 1985 3/1
1987 5/23 – until 1988 3/31
1993 9/20 – 12/5
1994 6/18 – 7/15
1996 12/4 – until 1997 2/12
1999 5/4 – until 2000 3/12
2005 9/3 – 11/18
2008 3/23 – 6/26
2008 11/14 – until 2009 1/27
2011 4/17 – 7/1
2011 10/30 – until 2012 2/18

SATURN CHALLENGING
1939 3/27 – until 1940 4/30
1952 10/20 – until 1953 12/5
1954 5/10 – 8/31
1960 12/27 – until 1962 2/15
1962 9/21 – 10/27
1968 5/5 – 12/2
1969 1/9 – 6/12
1969 11/3 – until 1970 3/3
1981 11/29 – until 1982 4/7
1982 8/25 – until 1983 10/12
1990 1/30 – 9/2
1990 10/13 – until 1991 3/30
1991 7/5 – 12/24
1997 6/23 – 9/10
1998 3/9 – until 1999 4/14
2011 10/4 – until 2012 11/17

URANUS CHALLENGING
1972 10/17 – until 1976 9/19
1993 1/24 – until 1997 11/10

NEPTUNE CHALLENGING
1950 12/10 – until 1959 9/12
1993 1/19 – until 2000 12/23

PLUTO CHALLENGING
1978 12/28 – until 1986 8/26

JUPITER SPECIAL
1942 9/8 – until 1943 1/19
1943 5/2 – 7/24
1954 8/18 – until 1955 7/7
1966 8/1 – until 1967 6/20
1978 7/15 – 10/5
1979 1/17 – 5/30
1990 6/29 – 9/12
1991 2/27 – 4/30
2002 6/13 – 8/25

SATURN SPECIAL
1945 8/13 – until 1946 2/13
1946 4/24 – 9/14
1947 1/31 – 6/3
1975 6/18 – until 1976 7/17
2004 7/25 – until 2005 8/25
2006 3/9 – 5/2

URANUS SPECIAL
1953 7/16 – until 1957 6/22

PLUTO SPECIAL
1938 1/1 – until 1943 5/11

July 21

SUN: CANCER • DECANATE: PISCES/NEPTUNE • DEGREE: 28°–29° CANCER • MODE: CARDINAL • ELEMENT: WATER

Your Personal Powers

Charismatic, original, and intuitive, your personal powers include emotional sensitivity and discerning insight. Your ruler, the Moon, also points to your close family ties and innate receptivity to other people. You empower yourself when you combine your strong instincts and acute awareness with your competitive nature and enjoyment of challenges. Although you have many creative ideas and an optimistic or enthusiastic outlook, be careful not to lose some of your power by scattering your energies in too many directions. The mixture of your strong imagination and your spontaneity, however, can bestow on you a gift for words, whether through writing or conversation. Innovative and independent, your strong individuality needs some form of creative self-expression that includes both the conventional and nonconformist sides of your personality. Although generally cheerful, you lose some of your power if you abandon your inner faith and trust. Worry often sucks your energy and causes stress and anxiety. Fortunately, you possess a strong inner determination, and sense of values that can help you succeed.

Your Powers of Attraction in Relationships

Although you may sometimes still retain an inner shyness, you are usually friendly and gregarious with the ability to attract others. Quick to assess what motivates people, you are able to express your strong feelings. With so much emotion, however, you may sometimes experience rapid highs and lows. Nevertheless, your sensitivity can also make you affectionate, loving, and supportive of others. You are attracted to hardworking individuals or those with shrewd insight and a sense of the dramatic. Usually you need to relate to others while maintaining your independent spirit. Being perceptive and intelligent, you need clever partners who can match your conversational skills and appreciate your thoughtful qualities. Creative with an ability to turn on the charm, you can also be very generous with those you love.

Your attractive qualities: inspiration, creativity, imaginative, courage, self-assured, productive, intuitive, shrewd, good with words, ambitious, sensitive, independent, daring, resourceful, knowledgeable, psychic, intelligent, sixth sense

Your less attractive qualities: skeptical, worry, nervous, too sensitive, lazy, lack of vision, irresponsible, dependency, easily discouraged, fear of change, cold, impulsive, lack of faith, quarrelsome, stubborn

Your Venus Power

The planet Venus has a great deal of influence on your powers of attraction. Below are four possible Venus types for women and men. To find your Venus you need to go to page 771, where you will find the Venus table and extra information. The planet Mars also affects your powers of attraction. To find your Mars table and interpretation go to page 761.

WOMEN WITH VENUS IN GEMINI: Curious, with a bright and animated approach to life, you are attracted to those who are clever or sophisticated. Your love of variety and desire for knowledge suggest that you need a partner and friends who can keep you mentally stimulated. Although witty and a good conversationalist, you may need to keep in touch with your deeper feelings. Nevertheless, intelligent and friendly, you possess a youthful sense of wonder and seek a playmate who can keep you from becoming bored.

MEN WITH VENUS IN GEMINI: Charming, amusing, and adaptable, you attract others with your natural communication skills and friendly personality. You have a wonderful childlike quality and love to keep life playful, but a reluctance to contact your deeper feelings may cause you to avoid serious commitment. With your need for variety and intellectual stimulation, you are attracted to a clever and amusing partners who have many interesting sides to their personalities.

WOMEN WITH VENUS IN CANCER: Possessing a soft femininity, you have tender and sensitive emotions. Sympathetic and caring, you often mother those in your care by making sure they are comfortable and have plenty to eat. When you feel hurt or insecure in relationships you are likely to cover your feelings by being defensive or appearing tough on the outside while on the inside you are feeling vulnerable. Affectionate and romantic, you make a faithful and devoted partner.

MEN WITH VENUS IN CANCER: Affectionate with a strong sensitive streak, you can love very deeply. You may find yourself drawn to sympathetic partners who can tune into your moods and feelings as well as be reassuring and supportive. Family links are especially important to you and the more

positive these relationships are the more confident and safe you feel.

WOMEN WITH VENUS IN LEO: As a person who wants to radiate in their own right, you are likely to desire partners you can be proud of. Usually you are attracted to fun-loving, warm, and generous individuals. If self-expression is important to you, you will probably seek the company of creative people such as artists, musicians, or those with a flair for acting. Alternatively, you may be drawn to people who are dignified, regal, or have already achieved success.

MEN WITH VENUS IN LEO: Generous, animated, and pleasure-seeking, you can be very entertaining and fun to be with. Usually you are attracted to extroverted and benevolent individuals with a sunny personality. If ambitious, you are drawn to a partner who shows leadership qualities or one who is highly motivated. Your less attractive qualities are your tendencies to be bossy or vain. With a sense of the dramatic, however, you can be the life and soul of the party and inspire those around you.

WOMEN WITH VENUS IN VIRGO: Polite, refined, and organized, you are attracted to articulate and intelligent people. Since you are caring, concerned, and want to be of practical help to others, you can be an asset to any partnership. By being too analytical, exacting, or faultfinding, however, a doubting element can creep into your relationships. By expressing your feelings in a positive way you can become more decisive and improve on how you relate to your loved ones.

MEN WITH VENUS IN VIRGO: Practical, idealistic, and perfectionist, you seek a relationship with an intelligent and hardworking partner who can inspire you to be more industrious and well-ordered. At times you can come across as a sympathetic and caring person and at other times you may appear pragmatic and very businesslike. This may sometimes lead to unclear communication between you and your partner. Usually helpful and caring, however, you like to analyze the faults in your relationships and then work methodically to improve them.

To read all about your Outer Planets and work out how to use your personalized timetable, go to Section Three, page 789.

♋

Your Personalized Timetable

JUPITER BENEFICIAL
1939 3/27 – 6/17
1939 9/10 – until 1940 2/1
1941 4/26 – 6/8
1944 11/17 – until 1945 3/10
1945 7/17 – 9/8
1946 12/30 – until 1947 6/5
1947 8/24 – 11/20
1951 3/10 – 5/20
1951 10/28 – until 1952 1/1
1953 4/8 – 5/22
1956 10/27 – until 1957 4/21
1957 6/16 – 8/23
1958 12/11 – until 1959 11/4
1963 2/21 – 4/30
1964 8/1 – until 1964 10/29
1965 3/19 – 5/5
1968 10/10 – 12/6
1969 3/7 – 8/4
1970 11/25 – until 1971 3/6
1971 4/9 – 10/18
1975 2/4 – 4/12
1976 7/5 – 12/13
1977 2/17 – 4/18
1980 9/23 – 11/12
1981 4/15 – 7/9
1982 11/9 – until 1983 1/28
1983 5/28 – 9/26
1986 5/30 – 8/25
1987 1/15 – 3/27
1988 6/16 – 8/10
1988 11/8 – until 1989 3/29
1992 9/8 – 10/25
1994 10/24 – until 1995 1/7
1995 7/16 – 8/20
1998 5/3 – 10/11
1998 12/16 – until 1999 3/11
2000 5/29 – 7/15
2000 12/23 – until 2001 2/27
2004 8/23 – 10/9
2006 10/8 – 12/21
2010 4/13 – until 2011 2/21
2012 5/12 – until 2012 6/25

SATURN BENEFICIAL
1938 1/1 – 3/13
1941 6/18 – 12/15
1942 3/3 – 6/1
1950 9/18 – until 1951 9/9
1955 1/23 – 4/8
1955 10/15 – until 1956 12/3
1966 3/11 – until 1967 4/21
1967 11/19 – 12/28
1971 4/24 – 7/15
1971 11/26 – until 1972 4/3
1979 10/29 – until 1980 3/22
1980 7/20 – 10/15
1984 11/19 – until 1986 1/9
1986 6/2 – 10/8
1995 4/17 – 10/2
1996 1/9 – 6/7
1996 8/29 – until 1997 2/24
2000 5/30 – until 2001 5/15
2009 9/1 – 12/1
2010 2/27 – 8/22

URANUS BENEFICIAL
1940 5/30 – until 1943 4/27
1966 11/3 – until 1969 9/5
1979 1/8 – until 1983 9/30
2008 4/2 – Continues

NEPTUNE BENEFICIAL
1938 11/21 – until 1944 8/31
1965 2/15 – until 1973 10/28

PLUTO BENEFICIAL
1968 9/24 – until 1973 8/23
1991 1/17 – until 1998 10/6

JUPITER CHALLENGING
1940 4/4 – 6/13

1940 12/17 – until 1941 1/13
1945 11/30 – until 1946 5/3
1946 7/27 – 10/23
1949 2/12 – 12/29
1952 3/18 – 5/24
1957 11/11 – until 1958 10/7
1961 1/26 – 4/28
1961 6/22 – 12/10
1964 2/28 – 5/7
1969 10/26 – until 1970 9/20
1973 1/10 – 3/26
1973 8/8 – 11/16
1975 6/19 – 10/11
1976 2/6 – 4/20
1981 10/10 – 12/31
1982 4/21 – 8/31
1984 12/25 – until 1985 3/6
1987 5/28 – 12/4
1987 12/26 – until 1988 4/4
1993 9/24 – 12/10
1994 6/3 – 7/31
1996 12/8 – until 1997 2/16
1999 5/8 – until 2000 3/17
2005 9/8 – 11/23
2008 3/31 – 6/18
2008 11/19 – until 2009 1/31
2011 4/21 – 7/7
2011 10/23 – until 2012 2/24

SATURN CHALLENGING
1939 4/3 – until 1940 5/7
1952 10/28 – until 1953 12/14
1954 4/27 – 9/11
1961 1/4 – until 1962 2/24
1962 8/30 – 11/17
1968 5/13 – 11/12
1969 1/28 – 6/22
1969 10/22 – until 1970 3/13
1981 12/10 – until 1982 3/25
1982 9/4 – until 1983 10/21
1990 2/8 – 8/13
1990 11/2 – until 1991 4/15
1991 6/19 – until 1992 1/2
1997 7/12 – 8/22
1998 3/17 – until 1999 4/21
2011 10/12 – until 2012 11/25

URANUS CHALLENGING
1972 11/1 – until 1976 10/6
1993 2/10 – until 1997 12/9

NEPTUNE CHALLENGING
1951 11/2 – until 1959 10/12
1993 2/15 – until 2001 10/23

PLUTO CHALLENGING
1979 11/4 – until 1986 9/27

JUPITER SPECIAL
1942 9/14 – until 1943 1/12
1943 5/8 – 7/28
1954 8/23 – until 1955 3/8
1955 3/24 – 7/12
1966 8/5 – until 1967 6/25
1978 7/20 – 10/12
1979 1/9 – 6/5
1990 7/4 – 9/17
1991 2/18 – 5/10
2002 6/17 – 8/29

SATURN SPECIAL
1945 8/21 – until 1946 1/30
1946 5/7 – 9/24
1947 1/19 – 6/13
1975 6/26 – until 1976 7/25
2004 8/2 – until 2005 9/2
2006 2/21 – 5/18

URANUS SPECIAL
1953 7/31 – until 1957 7/9

PLUTO SPECIAL
1938 1/1 – until 1943 6/30

July 22

SUN: CANCER • DECANATE: PISCES • DEGREE: 29° CANCER–0° LEO • MODE: CARDINAL • ELEMENT: WATER

Your Personal Powers

Gregarious and amiable yet practical and direct, you gain power and success by combining your creative vision with your pragmatism and ambition. Being born on the cusp of Cancer and Leo indicates that you also possess a remarkably perceptive mind, imagination, and strong feelings. Being clever, you are usually well-informed in your areas of interest and have the inherent strategic skills to manifest your plans. Emotionally sensitive and considerate yet firm and resolute, you can blend your charm and quiet determination to be persuasive and persistent. You lose some of your power, however, if you undermine your great potential through avoidance, escapism, or inertia. When you feel inspired, however, you work hard to achieve your goals and are able to commercialize your talents. You often gain power from your ability to make contacts and combine business with pleasure. Impressionable yet assertive, you fare best when you have both the securities of home and the competitive edge and recognition that come from your work.

Your Powers of Attraction in Relationships

Your geniality, quick understanding, and ability to turn on the charm can give you a magnetic presence that attracts others. You usually admire those who have strong personalities and are motivated by success. Although independent, you work well in collaboration with others and understand the benefits of partnerships, team efforts, and making contacts. Avoid displaying your less attractive qualities when you become anxious, insecure, or overly serious. Often unorthodox in your approach, your love life can be a dramatic area for you. With your powerful desire for love or romance, you generally seek partners who enjoy social activities and have the ability to win friends and admirers. You also possess a more conventional side that seeks the stability and security of home and family and has a caring concern for loved ones.

Your attractive qualities: clever, highly intuitive, practical, skillful, builder, good organizer, ambitious, friendly, problem solver, achiever, perfectionist, knowledgeable, sensitive, proud, assertive, director, imaginative, determination, visionary, business sense, home-loving

Your less attractive qualities: nervous, inertia, anxious, insecure, bossy, avoider, materialistic, worry, escapist, lack of vision, moody, lazy, egotistical, fear about money, too security-conscious

Your Venus Power

The planet Venus has a great deal of influence on your powers of attraction. Below are four possible Venus types for women and men. To find your Venus you need to go to page 771, where you will find the Venus table and extra information. The planet Mars also affects your powers of attraction. To find your Mars table and interpretation go to page 761.

WOMEN WITH VENUS IN GEMINI: Articulate, versatile, and youthful, your personal magnetism is often linked to your charm, wit, and communication skills. You seek a partner who is clever, can communicate easily with you, and can share your thoughts and interests. Since you find it easy to mix with people, you have many friends. When you do find someone you can communicate with, you can easily lose yourself in long conversations.

MEN WITH VENUS IN GEMINI: Charming, amusing, and adaptable, you attract others with your natural communication skills and friendly personality. You have a wonderful childlike quality and love to keep life playful, but a reluctance to contact your deeper feelings may cause you to avoid serious commitment. With your need for variety and intellectual stimulation, you are attracted to clever and amusing partners who have many interesting sides to their personalities.

WOMEN WITH VENUS IN CANCER: Possessing a soft femininity, you have tender and sensitive emotions. Sympathetic and caring, you often mother those in your care by making sure they are comfortable and have plenty to eat. When you feel hurt or insecure in relationships you are likely to cover your feelings by being defensive or appearing tough on the outside while on the inside you are feeling vulnerable. Affectionate and romantic, you make a faithful and devoted partner.

MEN WITH VENUS IN CANCER: You seek a partner who is sympathetic, caring, and protective. Able to be forgiving and compassionate, you want a secure emotional bond in your close relationships. Usually you are drawn to partners who are maternal, unselfish, or demonstrative with their feelings. Although you can sometimes appear to others as shy or impressionable, you have powerful emotions and inner strength.

WOMEN WITH VENUS IN LEO: You possess the wonderful

ability to project your warm and sunny personality and keep others happily entertained. Loving attention yourself, you seek a partner who can appreciate you and be supportive and give you positive feedback. Proud, with a natural regal air, you expect respect from your partners but are willing to be loyal and supportive in exchange. Although sometimes a little self-centered, you know how to make your partner feel special.

MEN WITH VENUS IN LEO: A childlike nature suggests that you are versatile and keen on games or being entertained. You are usually attracted to vivacious partners with a benevolent nature. As an extrovert you enjoy being involved in all types of activities where you can assert yourself and show your talents and abilities. Others may recognize your inborn tendencies to lead but are also aware of your vanity or pride. Nevertheless, generous and caring, you often show more compassion to those less fortunate than yourself.

WOMEN WITH VENUS IN VIRGO: In relationships, you can be modest and unassuming but desire perfection. You usually analyze your partnerships until you feel you have understood them to the last little detail in order to improve them. A problem usually arises when you become too critical either of partners or yourself and indulge in being skeptical or faultfinding. As you are modest, others may not be aware of the strong sensuality beneath your well-groomed exterior.

MEN WITH VENUS IN VIRGO: Industrious and well-ordered, you relate to others in a considerate and down-to-earth way. You enjoy giving practical advice and being of service to those you love, even in small ways. Being a perfectionist, you are drawn to partners with high morals or a strong work ethic. Partners who have strong analytical minds are very attractive to you, particularly if they are also clean and meticulously dressed.

To read all about your Outer Planets and work out how to use your personalized timetable, go to Section Three, page 789.

Your Personalized Timetable

JUPITER BENEFICIAL
1939 3/31 – 6/25
1939 9/1 – until 1940 2/6
1941 4/30 – 6/12
1944 11/24 – until 1945 3/2
1945 7/23 – 9/13
1947 1/4 – 5/28
1947 9/1 – 11/25
1951 3/14 – 5/25
1951 10/20 – until 1952 1/9
1953 4/13 – 5/26
1956 11/1 – until 1957 4/11
1957 6/26 – 8/27
1958 12/16 – until 1959 11/9
1963 2/25 – 5/4
1964 8/8 – 10/21
1965 3/24 – 5/10
1968 10/14 – 12/14
1969 2/26 – 8/9
1970 11/29 – until 1971 10/22
1975 2/8 – 4/16
1976 7/10 – 12/4
1977 2/25 – 4/22
1980 9/28 – 11/17
1981 4/7 – 7/17
1982 11/14 – until 1983 2/3
1983 5/20 – 10/2
1986 6/8 – 8/16
1987 1/20 – 3/31
1988 6/20 – 8/18
1988 10/31 – until 1989 4/3
1992 9/12 – 10/29
1994 10/29 – until 1995 1/12
1995 7/2 – 9/2
1998 5/8 – 10/2
1998 12/24 – until 1999 3/15
2000 6/3 – 7/20
2000 12/14 – until 2001 3/7
2004 8/27 – 10/13
2006 10/13 – 12/26
2010 4/17 – until 2011 2/25
2012 5/16 – 6/29

SATURN BENEFICIAL
1938 1/1 – 3/21
1941 6/26 – 12/1
1942 3/15 – 6/8
1950 9/26 – until 1951 9/17
1955 2/13 – 3/17
1955 10/23 – until 1956 12/11
1966 3/19 – until 1967 4/30
1967 10/31 – until 1968 1/16
1971 5/2 – 7/26
1971 11/14 – until 1972 4/12
1979 11/7 – until 1980 3/10
1980 7/31 – 10/24
1981 5/1 – 7/9
1984 11/27 – until 1986 1/19
1986 5/20 – 10/18
1995 4/26 – 9/19
1996 1/20 – 6/25
1996 8/10 – until 1997 3/4
2000 6/7 – until 2001 5/22
2009 9/9 – 12/16
2010 2/10 – 8/30

URANUS BENEFICIAL
1940 6/17 – until 1943 5/14
1966 11/28 – until 1969 9/20
1979 2/14 – until 1983 10/21
2008 4/20 – Continues

NEPTUNE BENEFICIAL
1939 10/11 – until 1945 7/18
1965 12/16 – until 1974 9/7

PLUTO BENEFICIAL
1968 10/22 – until 1973 9/18
1991 11/29 – until 1998 11/5

JUPITER CHALLENGING
1940 4/8 – 6/17

1940 12/3 – until 1941 1/27
1945 12/5 – until 1946 4/25
1946 8/4 – 10/28
1949 2/17 – until 1950 1/3
1952 3/22 – 5/28
1957 11/16 – until 1958 10/12
1961 1/30 – 5/14
1961 6/5 – 12/15
1964 3/4 – 5/11
1969 10/31 – until 1970 9/25
1973 1/14 – 4/1
1973 8/1 – 11/22
1975 6/26 – 10/3
1976 2/11 – 4/24
1981 10/15 – until 1982 1/7
1982 4/14 – 9/5
1984 12/29 – until 1985 3/10
1987 6/1 – 11/19
1988 1/10 – 4/8
1993 9/29 – 12/15
1994 5/24 – 8/10
1996 12/13 – until 1997 2/20
1999 5/13 – until 2000 3/21
2005 9/13 – 11/27
2008 4/9 – 6/8
2008 11/24 – until 2009 2/4
2011 4/25 – 7/14
2011 10/16 – 2/29

SATURN CHALLENGING
1939 4/11 – until 1940 5/15
1952 11/5 – until 1953 6/1
1953 7/15 – 12/25
1954 4/14 – 9/21
1961 1/12 – until 1962 3/5
1962 8/16 – 11/30
1968 5/21 – 10/29
1969 2/10 – 7/3
1969 10/9 – until 1970 3/21
1981 12/23 – until 1982 3/11
1982 9/13 – until 1983 10/28
1990 2/17 – 7/29
1990 11/15 – until 1992 1/10
1998 3/25 – until 1999 4/29
2011 10/20 – until 2012 12/4

URANUS CHALLENGING
1972 11/18 – until 1976 10/22
1993 3/2 – until 1997 12/28

NEPTUNE CHALLENGING
1951 12/2 – until 1960 9/3
1993 3/27 – until 2001 12/16

PLUTO CHALLENGING
1979 12/2 – until 1986 10/22

JUPITER SPECIAL
1942 9/20 – until 1943 1/5
1943 5/14 – 8/1
1954 8/28 – until 1955 2/19
1955 4/12 – 7/16
1966 8/10 – until 1967 6/29
1978 7/24 – 10/20
1979 1/1 – 6/11
1990 7/8 – 9/22
1991 2/10 – 5/17
2002 6/21 – 9/3

SATURN SPECIAL
1945 8/30 – until 1946 1/18
1946 5/18 – 10/5
1947 1/7 – 6/22
1975 7/3 – until 1976 8/1
2004 8/10 – until 2005 2/25
2005 4/15 – 9/11
2006 2/8 – 5/30

URANUS SPECIAL
1953 8/18 – until 1957 7/25

PLUTO SPECIAL
1938 1/1 – until 1944 6/8

Cancer Timetable

X-Special · X-Beneficial · X-Challenging

June 22
URANUS X-BENEFICIAL
2002 4/29 – until 2004 2/14
URANUS X-CHALLENGING
2010 4/18 – until 2012 2/13
NEPTUNE X-BENEFICIAL
2010 4/25 – until 2013 2/8
PLUTO X-CHALLENGING
2007 2/11 – until 2009 12/5

June 23
URANUS X-BENEFICIAL
2003 2/26 – until 2004 12/13
URANUS X-CHALLENGING
2010 5/8 – until 2012 3/3
NEPTUNE X-BENEFICIAL
2011 3/14 – Continues
PLUTO X-CHALLENGING
2008 1/5 – until 2010 10/28

June 24
URANUS X-BENEFICIAL
2003 3/15 – until 2005 1/9
URANUS X-CHALLENGING
2010 6/6 – until 2012 3/20
NEPTUNE X-BENEFICIAL
2011 4/13 – Continues
PLUTO X-CHALLENGING
2008 2/3 – until 2010 12/1

June 25
URANUS X-BENEFICIAL
2003 4/3 – until 2005 1/28
URANUS X-CHALLENGING
2011 4/2 – Continues
NEPTUNE X-BENEFICIAL
2012 3/6 – Continues
PLUTO X-CHALLENGING
2008 12/30 – until 2011 10/21

June 26
URANUS X-BENEFICIAL
2003 4/27 – until 2005 2/14
URANUS X-CHALLENGING
2011 4/19 – until 2013 2/13

NEPTUNE X-BENEFICIAL
2012 4/3 – Continues
PLUTO X-CHALLENGING
2009 1/27 – until 2011 11/28

June 27
URANUS X-BENEFICIAL
2004 2/27 – until 2005 12/10
URANUS X-CHALLENGING
2011 5/9 – until 2012 5/13
NEPTUNE X-BENEFICIAL
2012 5/23 – Continues
PLUTO X-CHALLENGING
2009 3/9 – Continues

June 28
URANUS X-BENEFICIAL
2004 3/15 – until 2006 1/9
URANUS X-CHALLENGING
2011 6/4 – until 2013 3/21
PLUTO X-CHALLENGING
2010 1/22 – until 2012 11/24

June 29
URANUS X-BENEFICIAL
2004 4/3 – until 2006 1/29
URANUS X-CHALLENGING
2012 4/2 – Continues
PLUTO X-CHALLENGING
2010 2/26 – Continues

June 30
URANUS X-BENEFICIAL
2004 4/26 – until 2006 2/16
URANUS X-CHALLENGING
2012 4/19 – Continues
PLUTO X-CHALLENGING
2011 1/19 – Continues

July 1
URANUS X-BENEFICIAL
2005 2/28 – until 2006 12/6
URANUS X-CHALLENGING
2012 5/9 – Continues
PLUTO X-CHALLENGING
2011 2/20 – Continues

July 2
URANUS X-BENEFICIAL
2005 3/17 – until 2007 1/10
URANUS X-CHALLENGING
2012 6/2 – Continues
PLUTO X-CHALLENGING
2012 1/16 – Continues

July 3
URANUS X-BENEFICIAL
2005 4/4 – until 2007 1/31
PLUTO X-CHALLENGING
2012 2/16 – Continues

July 4
URANUS X-BENEFICIAL
2005 4/26 – until 2007 2/17

July 5
URANUS X-BENEFICIAL
2005 6/7 – until 2007 3/6

July 6
URANUS X-BENEFICIAL
2006 3/18 – until 2008 1/10

July 7
URANUS X-BENEFICIAL
2006 4/5 – until 2008 2/1

July 8
URANUS X-BENEFICIAL
2006 4/26 – until 2008 2/19

July 9
URANUS X-BENEFICIAL
2006 5/29 – until 2008 3/7

July 10
URANUS X-BENEFICIAL
2007 3/20 – until 2009 1/9

July 11
URANUS X-BENEFICIAL
2007 4/6 – until 2009 2/1

July 12
URANUS X-BENEFICIAL
2007 4/27 – until 2009 2/19

July 13
URANUS X-BENEFICIAL
2007 5/26 – until 2009 3/8

July 14
URANUS X-BENEFICIAL
2008 3/20 – until 2010 1/9

July 15
URANUS X-BENEFICIAL
2008 4/7 – until 2010 2/2

July 16
URANUS X-BENEFICIAL
2008 4/27 – until 2010 2/21

July 17
URANUS X-BENEFICIAL
2008 5/23 – until 2010 3/10

July 18
URANUS X-BENEFICIAL
2009 3/22 – until 2011 1/8

July 19
URANUS X-BENEFICIAL
2009 4/8 – until 2011 2/3

July 20
URANUS X-BENEFICIAL
2009 4/28 – until 2011 2/22

July 21
URANUS X-BENEFICIAL
2009 5/22 – until 2011 3/12

July 22
URANUS X-BENEFICIAL
2010 3/24 – until 2012 1/6

Leo

July 23–August 22

July 23

SUN: LEO/CANCER CUSP • DECANATE: LEO/SUN • DEGREE: 29°5 CANCER–1° LEO • MODE: FIXED • ELEMENT: FIRE

Your Personal Powers

With your quick comprehension, intelligence, and adventurous spirit you are usually open to new interests and experiences. Your ruler, the Sun, indicates that you can be enterprising and creative with a confident personality. You gain power from your quick instincts, inquiring mind, and willingness to learn or improve your skills. Although you are fast and versatile, be careful not to lose some of your power by becoming bored and impatient or acting too impulsively. Dramatically dignified and proud, your daring energy and love of freedom give you many lucky breaks and an enthusiasm for life. Idealistic and optimistic, you are often ready to take a risk to achieve your dreams. Besides being resourceful and ingenious, you can also be sensitive and creative with a need for self-expression. Since you also possess a practical sense and shrewdness about money, you gain the most when you are direct, honest, and have a definite plan of action. Alternatively, you may pursue knowledge and education in order to advance and broaden your horizons.

Your Powers of Attraction in Relationships

Enthusiastic and kind with an entertaining manner, you are likely to have many friends and admirers. Adaptable and progressive, you work extremely well with others. In intimate relationships, however, you may experience inner doubts or be more sensitive than you care to show. Although you are very sociable and a delightful companion, a restless side to your nature may resist the routine and responsibility needed for a long-term relationship. As love and friendships are of major importance to you, you are very likely to make that commitment. An element of secrecy around your relationships warns against rushing too quickly into them. You are drawn to strong-willed or very focused individuals. Loving variety, your ideal partner is someone with whom you can travel or share exciting adventures.

Your attractive qualities: fast mind, loyal, adventurous, proud, quick instincts, enterprising, intelligent, sensitive, responsible, industrious, methodical, kind, generous, entertaining, communicative, intuitive, creative, versatile, lucky, trustworthy, dignified, witty, kind

Your less attractive qualities: selfish, insecure, restless, impatient, stubborn, uncompromising, faultfinding, withdrawn, bored, impulsive, self-doubt, prejudiced, too proud, impulsive

Your Venus Power

The planet Venus has a great deal of influence on your powers of attraction. Below are four possible Venus types for women and men. To find your Venus you need to go to page 771, where you will find the Venus table and extra information. The planet Mars also affects your powers of attraction. To find your Mars table and interpretation go to page 761.

WOMEN WITH VENUS IN GEMINI: In relationships you need intellectual stimulation and usually prefer to keep things light. Certainly not boring, you love to talk and are at your best being witty and entertaining. Although your easygoing approach to relationships is very attractive, guard against losing touch with your deeper emotions. You prefer a partner who can keep up with your fast stream of ideas, and if you have shared interests then so much the better.

MEN WITH VENUS IN GEMINI: Informed and curious yet charming and friendly, you seek a partner who shares your interests or enjoys your witty remarks. Although a good communicator, you have an inborn tendency to be lighthearted and less profound about deep emotional commitment. Although you are keen on experiences that bring variety into your life, boredom or scattering your energies in too many directions is probably your biggest handicap in relationships. Nevertheless, you are attracted to intelligent partners who can match your lively banter.

WOMEN WITH VENUS IN CANCER: Gentle and tender, you are romantic by nature. You possess a strong need for security and usually help others feel safe and protected. This preservation is especially centered in the home, which is your haven from life's storm. Although your maternal instincts are strong, avoid making sacrifices for others at your own expense. Nevertheless, affectionate and caring, once committed to a relationship, your loyalty and devotion to your partner are very strong.

MEN WITH VENUS IN CANCER: Being emotionally receptive, you can make a sensitive lover. With your desire to care for and protect others, you are likely to have strong family connections. Love is often tied in with being attentive to the needs of others and you may find yourself attracted to individuals who have sympathetic or maternal qualities. Security-

conscious, you need a loyal partner who can offer you support and ideally be a good cook and homemaker.

WOMEN WITH VENUS IN LEO: You possess the wonderful ability to project your warm and sunny personality and keep others happily entertained. Loving attention yourself, you seek a partner who can appreciate you and be supportive and give you positive feedback. Proud, with a natural regal air, you expect respect from your partners but are willing to be loyal and supportive in exchange. Although sometimes a little self-centered, you know how to make your partner feel special.

MEN WITH VENUS IN LEO: Enthusiastic, playful, and kind, you can be benevolent with those you love. Warm, romantic, and self-expressive, you adore the drama of love or having fun with your friends. You are usually attracted to partners with a warm and generous nature. Although you can be a confident and charismatic partner, you may need to develop humility to stop pride or arrogance from marring your relationships.

WOMEN WITH VENUS IN VIRGO: Polite, refined, and organized, you are attracted to articulate and intelligent people. Since you are caring, concerned, and want to be of practical help to others, you can be an asset to any partnership. By being too analytical, exacting, or faultfinding, however, a doubting element can creep into your relationships. By expressing your feelings in a positive way you can become more decisive and improve how you relate to your loved ones.

MEN WITH VENUS IN VIRGO: A love of order usually indicates that you are attracted to refined individuals with analytical or practical abilities. You and your partner may be working together or serving similar causes. As you constantly analyze partnerships in order to improve them, you are likely to use former relationships as a point of reference and compare them to your present partner. Because you are helpful and kind, others usually rely on your good judgment and often turn to you for advice or practical assistance.

To read all about your Outer Planets and work out how to use your personalized timetable, go to Section Three, page 789.

♌

Your Personalized Timetable

JUPITER BENEFICIAL
1939 4/4 – 7/6
1939 8/22 – until 1940 2/11
1941 5/4 – 6/16
1944 12/1 – until 1945 2/22
1945 7/29 – 9/17
1947 1/10 – 5/20
1947 9/8 – 11/29
1951 3/18 – 5/30
1951 10/12 – until 1952 1/16
1953 4/17 – 5/30
1956 11/6 – until 1957 4/2
1957 7/4 – 9/1
1958 12/21 – until 1959 11/13
1963 3/1 – 5/8
1964 8/18 – 10/11
1965 3/29 – 5/14
1968 10/19 – 12/24
1969 2/16 – 8/14
1970 12/4 – until 1971 10/27
1975 2/12 – 4/20
1976 7/16 – 11/27
1977 3/4 – 4/27
1980 10/2 – 11/23
1981 3/30 – 7/23
1982 11/18 – until 1983 2/10
1983 5/12 – 10/8
1986 6/18 – 8/6
1987 1/25 – 4/4
1988 6/25 – 8/28
1988 10/21 – until 1989 4/8
1992 9/16 – 11/3
1993 5/22 – 6/10
1994 11/2 – until 1995 1/17
1995 6/23 – 9/12
1998 5/14 – 9/24
1998 12/31 – until 1999 3/19
2000 6/7 – 7/25
2000 12/7 – until 2001 3/15
2004 9/1 – 10/18
2006 10/18 – 12/30
2010 4/22 – until 2011 3/1
2012 5/20 – 7/4

SATURN BENEFICIAL
1938 1/1 – 3/28
1941 7/6 – 11/19
1942 3/25 – 6/16
1950 10/4 – until 1951 9/24
1955 11/1 – until 1956 12/19
1957 7/26 – 8/28
1966 3/27 – until 1967 5/8
1967 10/17 – until 1968 1/29
1971 5/9 – 8/7
1971 11/1 – until 1972 4/21
1979 11/18 – until 1980 2/26
1980 8/9 – 11/1
1981 4/16 – 7/23
1984 12/5 – until 1985 7/2
1985 8/18 – until 1986 1/31
1986 5/7 – 10/28
1995 5/7 – 9/7
1996 1/30 – until 1997 3/12
2000 6/15 – 12/25
2001 2/24 – 5/29
2009 9/17 – until 2010 9/7

URANUS BENEFICIAL
1940 7/7 – until 1944 2/25
1967 9/19 – until 1970 7/6
1979 11/24 – until 1983 11/8
2008 5/14 – Continues

NEPTUNE BENEFICIAL
1939 11/11 – until 1945 8/25
1966 1/22 – until 1974 10/22

PLUTO BENEFICIAL
1968 12/1 – until 1974 8/10
1991 12/26 – until 1999 9/12

JUPITER CHALLENGING
1940 4/12 – 6/22
1940 11/24 – until 1941 2/5

1945 12/11 – until 1946 4/17
1946 8/10 – 11/1
1949 2/21 – until 1950 1/7
1952 3/26 – 6/2
1957 11/21 – until 1958 6/9
1958 6/28 – 10/16
1961 2/3 – 12/20
1964 3/8 – 5/15
1969 11/4 – until 1970 9/30
1973 1/18 – 4/7
1973 7/25 – 11/28
1975 7/3 – 9/26
1976 2/17 – 4/28
1981 10/19 – until 1982 1/15
1982 4/5 – 9/11
1985 1/2 – 3/15
1985 9/11 – 10/25
1987 6/6 – 11/9
1988 1/20 – 4/12
1993 10/3 – 12/20
1994 5/15 – 8/18
1996 12/17 – until 1997 2/24
1999 5/17 – until 2000 3/26
2005 9/18 – 12/2
2008 4/22 – 5/26
2008 11/29 – until 2009 2/8
2011 4/29 – 7/22
2011 10/8 – until 2012 3/5

SATURN CHALLENGING
1939 4/18 – until 1940 5/22
1941 1/6 – 1/12
1952 11/13 – until 1953 5/13
1953 8/3 – until 1954 1/7
1954 3/31 – 9/30
1961 1/20 – until 1962 3/15
1962 8/2 – 12/12
1968 5/31 – 10/17
1969 2/20 – 7/17
1969 9/25 – until 1970 3/30
1982 1/11 – 2/19
1982 9/21 – until 1983 11/5
1990 2/26 – 7/16
1990 11/26 – until 1992 1/18
1998 4/2 – until 1999 5/6
2011 10/28 – until 2012 12/13

URANUS CHALLENGING
1972 12/7 – until 1977 8/7
1993 3/31 – until 1998 1/15

NEPTUNE CHALLENGING
1952 10/27 – until 1960 10/5
1994 2/9 – until 2002 1/13

PLUTO CHALLENGING
1980 10/20 – until 1987 9/8

JUPITER SPECIAL
1942 9/27 – 12/29
1943 5/20 – 8/6
1954 9/2 – until 1955 2/8
1955 4/22 – 7/20
1966 8/14 – until 1967 7/4
1978 7/28 – 10/30
1978 12/22 – until 1979 6/16
1990 7/12 – 9/28
1991 2/3 – 5/24
2002 6/26 – 9/8

SATURN SPECIAL
1945 9/8 – until 1946 1/6
1946 5/28 – 10/19
1946 12/23 – until 1947 6/30
1975 7/11 – until 1976 8/9
2004 8/18 – until 2005 2/8
2005 5/2 – 9/20
2006 1/27 – 6/9

URANUS SPECIAL
1953 9/6 – until 1958 5/14

PLUTO SPECIAL
1938 1/1 – until 1945 4/19

261

July 24

Your Personal Powers

Honest and direct, you take an enthusiastic but practical approach to life. You gain power by combining your idealism and determination with your forward thinking and ability to plan. With self-discipline and a well-organized routine you can achieve remarkable results. Your ruler, the Sun, enhances your sense of the dramatic and creative problem solving. Proud and dignified yet able to be witty and entertaining, you are usually an optimistic thinker. Versatile and generous with a desire for knowledge, you like to use your polished common sense to build a solid foundation in life. Being helpful, you are quite willing to share your insights with anothers or be an adviser. Ambitious and responsible, you have many money-making ideas and the courage to pursue your goals. Although you are usually purposeful and enterprising, be careful that in your desire for fast action you do not lose some of your power to stubbornness, impatience, or intolerance. Although you are very independent, a knack for making contacts and working cooperatively with others can particularly help you succeed.

Your Powers of Attraction in Relationships

Clever and straightforward, you attract others with your friendly personality. Action-oriented and trusting, you can work well with others, but avoid individuals who seem interesting yet are not entirely honorable. As you usually have a practical approach to life, you are drawn to hardworking or professional people. Although you want to express your love and sensitivity in relationships, you may repress some of your feelings. Nevertheless, generous and caring, you need a partner who understands that at home you find security and inner peace. Although you can be a devoted partner, if you become overanxious you can be critical, stubborn, or bossy. You are particularly attracted to those who seem to have some inner knowledge or wisdom as well as those who are clever or original.

Your attractive qualities: idealistic, honest, practical, determination, creative, frank, fair, kind, generous, direct, home-loving, pragmatic, loyal, hardworking, active, energetic, good business sense, creative, responsible, philosophical, insight, well-informed

Your less attractive qualities: bossy, materialistic, bored, too economical, restless, impatient, ruthless, anxious, interfering, intolerant, lazy, too proud, critical, stubborn

Your Venus Power

The planet Venus has a great deal of influence on your powers of attraction. Below are four possible Venus types for women and men. To find your Venus you need to go to page 771, where you will find the Venus table and extra information. The planet Mars also affects your powers of attraction. To find your Mars table and interpretation go to page 761.

WOMEN WITH VENUS IN GEMINI: Articulate, versatile, and youthful, your personal magnetism is often linked to your charm, wit, and communication skills. You seek a partner who is clever, can communicate with you at ease, and can share your thoughts and interests. Since you find it easy to mix with people you have many friends. When you do find someone you can communicate with you can easily lose yourself in long conversations.

MEN WITH VENUS IN GEMINI: Charming, amusing, and adaptable, you attract others with your natural communication skills and friendly personality. You have a wonderful childlike quality and love to keep life playful, but a reluctance to contact your deeper feelings may cause you to avoid serious commitment. With your need for variety and intellectual stimulation, you are attracted to clever and amusing partners who have many interesting sides to their personalities.

WOMEN WITH VENUS IN CANCER: Gentle and tender, you are romantic by nature. You possess a strong need for security and usually help others feel safe and protected. This preservation is especially centered in the home, which is your haven from life's storm. Although your maternal instincts are strong, avoid making sacrifices for others at your own expense. Nevertheless, affectionate and caring, once committed to a relationship, your loyalty and devotion to your partner are very strong.

MEN WITH VENUS IN CANCER: You seek a partner who is sympathetic, caring, and protective. Able to be forgiving and compassionate, you want a secure emotional bond in your close relationships. Usually you are drawn to partners who are maternal, unselfish, or demonstrative with their feelings. Although you can sometimes appear to others as impressionable, you have powerful emotions and inner strength.

WOMEN WITH VENUS IN LEO: As a person who wants to

radiate in her own right, you are likely to desire partners you can be proud of. Usually you are attracted to fun-loving, warm, and generous individuals. If self-expression is important to you, you will probably seek the company of creative people such as artists, musicians, or those with a flair for acting. Alternatively, you may be drawn to people who are dignified, regal, or have already achieved success.

MEN WITH VENUS IN LEO: A childlike nature suggests that you are versatile and keen on games or being entertained. You are usually attracted to vivacious partners with a benevolent nature. As an extrovert you enjoy being involved in all types of activities where you can assert yourself and show your talents and abilities. Others may recognize your inborn tendencies to lead but are also aware of your vanity or pride. Nevertheless, generous and caring, you often show more compassion to those less fortunate than yourself.

WOMEN WITH VENUS IN VIRGO: Articulate and straightforward in your relationships, you attract others with your genuine concern for their well-being. By being understanding and a good listener, you are able to show your love and friendship. With your analytical approach to relationships, however, you may have to be careful of becoming too matter-of-fact. You often display your concern for the welfare of others by your willingness to offer practical help and assistance. You usually seek a partner who is willing to work as hard on relationships as you are.

MEN WITH VENUS IN VIRGO: Practical, idealistic, and a perfectionist, you seek a relationship with an intelligent and hardworking partner who can inspire you to be more industrious and well-ordered. At times you can come across as a sympathetic and caring person and at other times you may appear pragmatic and very businesslike. This may sometimes lead to unclear communication between you and your partner. Usually helpful and caring, however, you like to analyze the faults in your relationships and then work methodically to improve them.

To read all about your Outer Planets and work out how to use your personalized timetable, go to Section Three, page 789.

go to Section Three, page 789.

♌

Your Personalized Timetable

JUPITER BENEFICIAL
1939 4/8 – until **1940** 2/15
1941 5/9 – 6/20
1944 12/10 – until **1945** 2/13
1945 8/3 – 9/22
1947 1/16 – 5/13
1947 9/15 – 12/3
1951 3/22 – 6/5
1951 10/5 – 1/23
1953 4/21 – 6/3
1956 11/12 – until **1957** 3/25
1957 7/12 – 9/6
1958 12/26 – until **1959** 6/28
1959 8/11 – 11/17
1963 3/5 – 5/13
1964 9/2 – 9/26
1965 4/3 – 5/18
1968 10/24 – until **1969** 1/10
1969 1/31 – 8/20
1970 12/8 – until **1971** 11/1
1975 2/16 – 4/24
1976 7/21 – 11/20
1977 3/11 – 5/1
1980 10/7 – 11/29
1981 3/23 – 7/30
1982 11/22 – until **1983** 2/19
1983 5/4 – 10/13
1987 1/29 – 4/8
1988 6/30 – 9/12
1988 10/6 – until **1989** 4/13
1992 9/21 – 11/8
1993 5/4 – 6/28
1994 11/7 – until **1995** 1/23
1995 6/14 – 9/19
1998 5/19 – 9/17
1999 1/7 – 3/23
2000 6/11 – 7/31
2000 11/30 – until **2001** 3/21
2004 9/5 – 10/22
2006 10/22 – until **2007** 1/4
2010 4/26 – until **2011** 3/5
2012 5/24 – 7/8

SATURN BENEFICIAL
1938 1/1 – 4/5
1941 7/16 – 11/7
1942 4/4 – 6/23
1943 1/20 – 2/23
1950 10/12 – until **1951** 5/9
1951 6/17 – 10/2
1955 11/9 – until **1956** 12/28
1957 7/3 – 9/19
1966 4/4 – until **1967** 5/18
1967 10/4 – until **1968** 2/9
1971 5/17 – 8/23
1971 10/16 – until **1972** 4/29
1979 12/2 – until **1980** 2/12
1980 8/18 – 11/10
1981 4/3 – 8/4
1984 12/13 – until **1985** 6/12
1985 9/5 – until **1986** 2/15
1986 4/20 – 11/5
1995 5/18 – 8/25
1996 2/8 – until **1997** 3/19
2000 6/23 – 12/10
2001 3/10 – 6/6
2009 9/24 – until **2010** 9/15

URANUS BENEFICIAL
1940 8/6 – until **1944** 4/1
1967 10/5 – until **1970** 8/4
1979 12/9 – until **1983** 11/24
2009 3/17 – Continues

NEPTUNE BENEFICIAL
1940 10/5 – until **1946** 6/26
1966 12/10 – until **1974** 11/19

PLUTO BENEFICIAL
1969 10/13 – until **1974** 9/8
1992 2/7 – until **1999** 10/23

JUPITER CHALLENGING
1940 4/16 – 6/28
1940 11/16 – until **1941** 2/13

1945 12/17 – until **1946** 4/10
1946 8/17 – 11/5
1949 2/26 – 8/31
1949 10/6 – until **1950** 1/11
1952 3/30 – 6/6
1957 11/26 – until **1958** 5/22
1958 7/16 – 10/21
1961 2/8 – 12/24
1964 3/12 – 5/19
1969 11/9 – until **1970** 10/4
1973 1/22 – 4/14
1973 7/17 – 12/4
1975 7/11 – 9/17
1976 2/22 – 5/2
1981 10/23 – until **1982** 1/24
1982 3/27 – 9/16
1985 1/7 – 3/20
1985 8/31 – 11/5
1987 6/12 – 11/1
1988 1/28 – 4/16
1993 10/8 – 12/26
1994 5/7 – 8/25
1996 12/21 – until **1997** 3/1
1999 5/21 – until **2000** 3/30
2005 9/22 – 12/7
2008 12/4 – until **2009** 2/12
2011 5/3 – 7/31
2011 9/29 – until **2012** 3/10

SATURN CHALLENGING
1939 4/26 – until **1940** 5/31
1940 12/7 – until **1941** 2/11
1952 11/22 – until **1953** 4/28
1953 8/17 – until **1954** 1/24
1954 3/13 – 10/8
1961 1/28 – until **1962** 3/25
1962 7/20 – 12/21
1968 6/10 – 10/5
1969 3/2 – 8/11
1969 8/30 – until **1970** 4/7
1982 9/29 – until **1983** 11/13
1990 3/9 – 7/3
1990 12/6 – until **1992** 1/26
1998 4/9 – until **1999** 5/14
2011 11/5 – until **2012** 6/14
2012 7/5 – 12/23

URANUS CHALLENGING
1973 1/6 – until **1977** 9/7
1994 1/22 – until **1998** 10/29

NEPTUNE CHALLENGING
1952 11/24 – until **1961** 8/24
1994 3/14 – until **2002** 12/8

PLUTO CHALLENGING
1980 11/14 – until **1987** 10/7

JUPITER SPECIAL
1942 10/4 – 12/21
1943 5/26 – 8/10
1954 9/7 – until **1955** 1/31
1955 4/30 – 7/25
1966 8/19 – until **1967** 7/9
1978 8/2 – 11/15
1978 12/6 – until **1979** 6/21
1990 7/16 – 10/4
1991 1/26 – 5/31
2002 6/30 – 9/12
2003 3/12 – 4/26

SATURN SPECIAL
1945 9/19 – 12/25
1946 6/6 – 11/16
1946 11/25 – until **1947** 7/8
1975 7/18 – until **1976** 8/16
2004 8/26 – until **2005** 1/26
2005 5/14 – 9/30
2006 1/15 – 6/19

URANUS SPECIAL
1953 10/6 – until **1958** 6/10

PLUTO SPECIAL
1938 1/1 – until **1945** 6/27

263

July 25

SUN: LEO • DECANATE: LEO/SUN • DEGREE: 1°45–3° LEO • MODE: FIXED • ELEMENT: FIRE

Your Personal Powers

Instinctive and shrewd, among your many personal powers are quick perception, a creative approach to life, and good people skills. You gain power from your dynamic charm and ability to instantly appraise people and circumstances. Although you can be confident, as a perfectionist you may need to overcome indecision, frustration, or self-doubt. In your desire for success you usually seek new and exciting experiences to keep you alert and enthusiastic. When positive, you can express the joy of life and be a source of inspiration to others. You are likely to have many creative ideas and a gift with words. Clever and intuitive, you can capitalize on your talents with your innate business sense, but you may lose some of your power to worry, impatience, or hesitation. Dignified, thoughtful, and perceptive, however, you can be warm, sociable, and generous with your time and energy. Naturally dramatic and talented, you need to stay disciplined and focused if you want to make the most of your outstanding talents.

Your Powers of Attraction in Relationships

Being naturally charming, thoughtful, and well-mannered ensures your success in attracting others. Creative and magnetic, you feel deeply and have a romantic soul. When you have faith and trust in your partner you can reveal your love and sensitive feelings. Usually you are looking for a partner who can be generous and emotionally open. On occasion, your personal frustrations may spill over into your relationships and you may become overly serious or withdrawn. In order to move on it may be necessary to let go of past disappointments and show your generosity and compassion. As you often look for inspiration, you usually love fun and romance but your need for variety can sometimes lead to indecision. The more detached and philosophical your attitude, the better your relationships become.

Your attractive qualities: warm, perfectionist, quick intelligence, kind, perceptive, creative mind, highly intuitive, dramatic gifts, drive, enthusiasm, generous, people skills, inspired ideas, happy, entertaining, introspective, versatile, good strategist, enterprising

Your less attractive qualities: impulsive, impatient, irresponsible, worried, overemotional, jealous, secretive, extrava-gant, scattered, moody, changeable, frustration, calculating, confusing, critical

Your Venus Power

The planet Venus has a great deal of influence on your powers of attraction. Below are four possible Venus types for women and men. To find your Venus you need to go to page 771, where you will find the Venus table and extra information. The planet Mars also affects your powers of attraction. To find your Mars table and interpretation go to page 761.

WOMEN WITH VENUS IN GEMINI: By nature you are young at heart, adaptable, and sociable. Being curious and willing to cooperate makes you a good team player. Usually you are drawn to articulate people who have charm and flair or sharp wit. With a need to expand your knowledge you also look for a partner who can challenge or stimulate you intellectually. Although you love to talk with all types of people, you may need to develop your listening skills in order to build better communication in your relationships.

MEN WITH VENUS IN GEMINI: Charming, amusing, and adaptable, you attract others with your natural communication skills and friendly personality. You have a wonderful childlike quality and love to keep life playful but in love a reluctance to contact your deeper feelings may cause you to avoid serious commitment. With your need for variety and intellectual stimulation, you are attracted to clever and amusing partners who have many interesting sides to their personalities.

WOMEN WITH VENUS IN CANCER: With your intuitive abilities and sympathetic nature you are usually supportive of those you love. Impressionable and empathetic, your receptivity allows you to quickly pick up on the moods of people and you are especially aware of the emotional changes in your close partner. As you often display true maternal tendencies toward those you know, you want a partner who is considerate and sensitive.

MEN WITH VENUS IN CANCER: Affectionate with a strong sensitive streak, you can love very deeply. You may find yourself drawn toward sympathetic and supportive partners who can tune in to your moods and feelings. Family links are especially important to you, and the more positive these relationships are, the more confident and safe you feel. Being emotionally receptive can make you a caring and responsive lover.

WOMEN WITH VENUS IN LEO: Your friendly and sunny personality often makes you stand out in a crowd. Generous and giving, you know how to make your partner feel special. As you often expect loyalty and devotion from your partner in return, you can become easily offended if they ignore you or behave in an inconsiderate manner. Charming and kind, when you are in love you can be romantic, dramatic, and passionate.

MEN WITH VENUS IN LEO: Sociable and outgoing, you are kind and generous with those you love. Looking for a relationship that can be fun and entertaining, you need a playmate who can share your enthusiasm and high spirits. Your pride, however, often stops you from associating with lovers or partners you see as beneath you. As you desire someone who can appreciate your sense of the dramatic, you are often attracted to people with strong personalities.

WOMEN WITH VENUS IN VIRGO: In relationships you can be modest and unassuming but desire perfection. You usually analyze your partnerships until you feel you have understood them to the last little detail in order to improve them. A problem usually arises when you become too critical either of partners or yourself and indulge in being skeptical or fault-finding. As you are modest, others may not be aware of the strong sensuality beneath your well-groomed exterior.

MEN WITH VENUS IN VIRGO: Industrious and well-ordered, you relate to others in a considerate and down-to-earth way. You enjoy giving practical advice and being of service to those you love, even in small ways. Being a perfectionist, you are drawn to partners with high morals or a strong work ethic. Partners who have strong analytical minds are very attractive to you, particularly if they are also clean and meticulously dressed.

To read all about your Outer Planets and work out how to use your personalized timetable, go to Section Three, page 789.

♌

265

Your Personalized Timetable

JUPITER BENEFICIAL
1939 4/12 – until 1940 2/20
1941 5/13 – 6/25
1944 12/22 – until 1945 2/1
1945 8/8 – 9/26
1947 1/22 – 5/5
1947 9/21 – 12/7
1951 3/26 – 6/11
1951 9/28 – until 1952 1/28
1953 4/25 – 6/7
1956 11/18 – until 1957 3/18
1957 7/18 – 9/10
1958 12/31 – until 1959 6/16
1959 8/23 – 11/22
1963 3/9 – 5/18
1963 11/23 – 12/18
1965 4/7 – 5/22
1968 10/29 – until 1969 5/1
1969 6/14 – 8/25
1970 12/13 – until 1971 11/5
1975 2/20 – 4/29
1976 7/28 – 11/13
1977 3/17 – 5/5
1980 10/11 – 12/6
1981 3/15 – 8/5
1982 11/27 – until 1983 3/1
1983 4/23 – 10/18
1987 2/3 – 4/12
1988 7/4 – 12/30
1989 2/9 – 4/18
1992 9/25 – 11/13
1993 4/24 – 7/9
1994 11/11 – until 1995 1/28
1995 6/7 – 9/26
1998 5/25 – 9/10
1999 1/12 – 3/27
2000 6/15 – 8/6
2000 11/23 – until 2001 3/27
2004 9/10 – 10/27
2006 10/27 – until 2007 1/9
2010 5/1 – 11/5
2010 12/2 – until 2011 3/9
2012 5/29 – 7/13

SATURN BENEFICIAL
1938 1/1 – 4/13
1941 7/27 – 10/26
1942 4/12 – 7/1
1942 12/31 – until 1943 3/14
1950 10/20 – until 1951 4/19
1951 7/7 – 10/10
1955 11/17 – until 1957 1/5
1957 6/18 – 10/3
1966 4/12 – 10/25
1966 12/28 – until 1967 5/28
1967 9/22 – until 1968 2/18
1971 5/24 – until 1972 5/6
1979 12/23 – until 1980 1/21
1980 8/26 – 11/20
1981 3/22 – 8/14
1984 12/22 – until 1985 5/29
1985 9/19 – until 1986 11/14
1995 6/2 – 8/9
1996 2/16 – until 1997 3/27
2000 7/2 – 11/27
2001 3/22 – 6/13
2009 10/2 – until 2010 9/23

URANUS BENEFICIAL
1941 5/28 – until 1944 4/22
1967 10/21 – until 1970 8/24
1979 12/27 – until 1984 9/12
2009 4/3 – Continues

NEPTUNE BENEFICIAL
1940 11/3 – until 1946 8/18
1967 1/12 – until 1975 10/15

PLUTO BENEFICIAL
1969 11/14 – until 1975 7/22
1992 12/9 – until 1999 11/19

JUPITER CHALLENGING
1940 4/20 – 7/3
1940 11/9 – until 1941 2/20

1945 12/24 – until 1946 4/2
1946 8/23 – 11/10
1949 3/3 – 8/19
1949 10/19 – until 1950 1/15
1952 4/3 – 6/11
1957 12/1 – until 1958 5/12
1958 7/27 – 10/25
1961 2/12 – 12/29
1964 3/16 – 5/23
1969 11/13 – until 1970 10/9
1973 1/26 – 4/22
1973 7/9 – 12/9
1975 7/22 – 9/6
1976 2/26 – 5/6
1981 10/28 – until 1982 2/6
1982 3/14 – 9/22
1985 1/11 – 3/25
1985 8/22 – 11/13
1987 6/17 – 10/25
1988 2/3 – 4/21
1993 10/12 – until 1994 1/1
1994 4/30 – 9/1
1996 12/26 – until 1997 3/5
1999 5/26 – until 2000 4/3
2005 9/27 – 12/12
2006 6/12 – 7/30
2008 12/9 – until 2009 2/16
2011 5/7 – 8/12
2011 9/17 – until 2012 3/15

SATURN CHALLENGING
1939 5/4 – until 1940 6/8
1940 11/23 – until 1941 2/24
1952 12/1 – until 1953 4/16
1953 8/28 – until 1954 10/17
1961 2/6 – 8/31
1961 10/24 – until 1962 4/7
1962 7/6 – 12/30
1968 6/22 – 9/22
1969 3/10 – until 1970 4/14
1982 10/7 – until 1983 11/21
1984 7/1 – 7/25
1990 3/22 – 6/19
1990 12/15 – until 1992 2/3
1998 4/17 – until 1999 5/21
2011 11/13 – until 2012 5/19
2012 7/31 – Continues

URANUS CHALLENGING
1938 1/2 – 2/2
1973 10/23 – until 1977 9/27
1994 2/8 – until 1998 12/7

NEPTUNE CHALLENGING
1953 1/10 – until 1961 9/30
1995 2/3 – until 2003 1/8

PLUTO CHALLENGING
1980 12/15 – until 1988 8/3

JUPITER SPECIAL
1942 10/13 – 12/12
1943 5/31 – 8/14
1954 9/13 – until 1955 1/24
1955 5/7 – 7/29
1966 8/23 – until 1967 7/13
1978 8/6 – until 1979 6/26
1990 7/21 – 10/11
1991 1/19 – 6/6
2002 7/5 – 9/18
2003 3/1 – 5/8

SATURN SPECIAL
1945 10/3 – 12/11
1946 6/14 – until 1947 7/16
1975 7/25 – until 1976 8/24
2004 9/5 – until 2005 1/14
2005 5/24 – 10/12
2006 1/2 – 6/27

URANUS SPECIAL
1954 7/24 – until 1958 6/29

PLUTO SPECIAL
1938 1/1 – until 1946 6/3

July 26

SUN: LEO • DECANATE: LEO/SUN • DEGREE: 2°45–3°5 LEO • MODE: FIXED • ELEMENT: FIRE

Your Personal Powers

Your confident front, charm, and natural enthusiasm are just some of your many personal powers. Often cheerful with a sharp intellect and acute awareness, you can be a master of quick insight and retort. Warm and generous, you are a natural psychologist and gain power from your developed social skills. Ruled by the Sun, you love attention and can be dramatic and creative. Being ambitious with natural organizational abilities indicates you are usually willing to work hard to achieve your goals or reach leadership positions. Naturally forceful and sometimes provocative, you may lose some of your power if you become too obstinate, impatient, or arrogant. Although your shrewd intellect gives you a pragmatic approach to life, you also gain power from your natural sense of the dramatic or the ridiculous. When not used for sarcasm, your humor allows you to extricate yourself from difficult situations and enlighten others. Clever, conscientious, and capable, you have a great potential for success and a gift for influencing people.

Your Powers of Attraction in Relationships

Charming and verbally persuasive, you are an engaging individual with a charismatic personality. Although independent, you realize the advantages of working with others. You can also attract people with your strong will and determination. Being clever and sociable, you seek the company of other lively minds to keep you mentally stimulated and entertained. In your close relationships you may need to find a balance between your own needs and your commitments to others. Being proud, you may not take criticism easily. You are attracted to those who have a dramatic or creative streak and those who possess a youthful spirit. In close relationships, avoid being rebellious or antagonistic. Nevertheless, being bighearted, you can be very supportive of those you love.

Your attractive qualities: creative, practical, mentally sharp, good psychologist, executive ability, proud of family, cheerful, enthusiastic, courageous, charming, generous, kind, hardworking, responsible, good business sense, persuasive, tenacious, persistent, sociable, dignified

Your less attractive qualities: stubborn, headstrong, materialistic, obstinate, impatient, bossy, rebellious, unstable relationships, unenthusiastic, lack of persistence, sarcastic, arrogant, provocative

Your Venus Power

The planet Venus has a great deal of influence on your powers of attraction. Below are four possible Venus types for women and men. To find your Venus you need to go to page 771, where you will find the Venus table and extra information. The planet Mars also affects your powers of attraction. To find your Mars table and interpretation go to page 761.

WOMEN WITH VENUS IN GEMINI: By nature you are young at heart, adaptable, and sociable. Being curious and willing to cooperate makes you a good team player. Usually you are drawn to articulate people who have charm and flair or sharp wit. With a need to expand your knowledge you also look for a partner who can challenge or stimulate you intellectually. Although you love to talk with all types of people, you may need to develop your listening skills in order to build better communication in your relationships.

MEN WITH VENUS IN GEMINI: Charming, amusing, and adaptable, you attract others with your natural communication skills and friendly personality. You have a wonderful childlike quality and love to keep life playful, but a reluctance to contact your deeper feelings may cause you to avoid serious commitment. With your need for variety and intellectual stimulation, you are attracted to clever and amusing partners who have many interesting sides to their personalities.

WOMEN WITH VENUS IN CANCER: Good-natured and romantic, you have a highly developed sense of touch that particularly responds to massage, hugs, and all things physical. Being friendly, you enjoy socializing and are able to put others at their ease. Your natural sense of beauty and harmony and your natural charm can attract others. Although you can be lavish toward your partner you may have to be careful that you do not overdo things.

MEN WITH VENUS IN CANCER: You seek a partner who is sympathetic, caring, and protective. Able to be forgiving and compassionate, you want a secure emotional bond in your close relationships. You are usually drawn to partners who are maternal, unselfish, or demonstrative with their feelings. Although you can sometimes appear to others as impressionable, you have powerful emotions and inner strength.

WOMEN WITH VENUS IN LEO: Your friendly and sunny personality often makes you stand out in a crowd. Generous and giving, you know how to make your partner feel special. As you often expect loyalty and devotion from your partners in return, you can become easily offended if they ignore you or behave in an inconsiderate manner. Charming and kind, when you're in love you can be romantic, dramatic, and passionate.

MEN WITH VENUS IN LEO: Enthusiastic, playful, and kind, you can be benevolent with those you love. Warm, romantic, and self-expressive, you adore the drama of love or having fun with your friends. Usually you are attracted to partners with a warm and generous nature. Although you can be a confident and charismatic partner, you may need to develop humility to stop pride or arrogance from marring your relationships.

WOMEN WITH VENUS IN VIRGO: Intelligent and discriminating, you are usually drawn to polite and refined individuals. As a perfectionist, you may be keen to analyze and criticize yourself but be careful of continually going over your partner's shortcomings. By focusing on how you can make positive improvements in yourself and in your relationships, you avoid becoming skeptical or confused. You empower yourself when you display kind and caring concern for the well-being of loved ones and spontaneously offer your practical assistance.

MEN WITH VENUS IN VIRGO: Although you are constantly analyzing your relationships in order to understand and improve them, you may nevertheless need to refrain from continuously mulling over issues that can cause anxiety. You are happiest when you are able to help your loved ones in practical ways and forget yourself in your willingness to be of service to others. You seek a partner who has high standards and can be as pragmatic and hardworking as yourself. Ideally they should also be impeccably dressed with a fine analytical mind.

To read all about your Outer Planets and work out how to use your personalized timetable, go to Section Three, page 789.

To read all about your Outer Planets and work out how to use your personalized timetable, go to Section Three, page 789.

Your Personalized Timetable

JUPITER BENEFICIAL
1939 4/16 – until 1940 2/24
1941 5/17 – 6/29
1945 8/13 – 10/1
1947 1/30 – 4/27
1947 9/26 – 12/12
1951 3/30 – 6/18
1951 9/20 – until 1952 2/3
1953 4/30 – 6/11
1956 11/25 – until 1957 3/10
1957 7/24 – 9/15
1959 1/5 – 6/7
1959 9/1 – 11/26
1963 3/13 – 5/22
1963 11/8 – until 1964 1/1
1965 4/12 – 5/26
1968 11/3 – until 1969 4/19
1969 6/26 – 8/29
1970 12/17 – until 1971 11/10
1975 2/24 – 5/3
1976 8/3 – 11/5
1977 3/22 – 5/10
1980 10/16 – 12/14
1981 3/7 – 8/11
1982 12/1 – until 1983 3/18
1983 4/6 – 10/23
1987 2/7 – 4/16
1988 7/9 – 12/19
1989 2/21 – 4/22
1992 9/30 – 11/19
1993 4/15 – 7/17
1994 11/15 – until 1995 2/4
1995 5/30 – 10/3
1998 6/1 – 9/2
1999 1/18 – 3/31
2000 6/19 – 8/13
2000 11/15 – until 2001 4/1
2004 9/14 – 11/1
2006 10/31 – until 2007 1/14
2007 7/14 – 8/30
2010 5/6 – 10/22
2010 12/16 – until 2011 3/13
2012 6/2 – 7/18

SATURN BENEFICIAL
1938 1/1 – 4/21
1941 8/12 – 10/10
1942 4/20 – 7/10
1942 12/17 – until 1943 3/27
1950 10/28 – until 1951 4/5
1951 7/20 – 10/18
1955 11/25 – until 1957 1/15
1957 6/5 – 10/14
1966 4/21 – 10/9
1967 1/12 – 6/9
1967 9/9 – until 1968 2/27
1971 5/31 – until 1972 5/14
1980 9/3 – 12/1
1981 3/9 – 8/24
1985 1/1 – 5/16
1985 9/30 – until 1986 11/22
1996 2/24 – until 1997 4/4
2000 7/12 – 11/16
2001 3/31 – 6/21
2009 10/10 – until 2010 10/1

URANUS BENEFICIAL
1941 6/14 – until 1944 5/10
1967 11/8 – until 1970 9/10
1980 1/18 – until 1984 10/11
2009 4/22 – Continues

NEPTUNE BENEFICIAL
1941 9/30 – until 1946 9/16
1967 12/5 – until 1975 11/14

PLUTO BENEFICIAL
1970 10/5 – until 1975 8/27
1993 1/6 – until 2000 10/7

JUPITER CHALLENGING
1938 1/1 – 2/4
1940 4/24 – 7/9
1940 11/1 – until 1941 2/26

1945 12/31 – until 1946 3/25
1946 8/28 – 11/14
1949 3/8 – 8/9
1949 10/28 – until 1950 1/19
1952 4/7 – 6/15
1957 12/7 – until 1958 5/3
1958 8/4 – 10/29
1961 2/17 – until 1962 1/2
1964 3/21 – 5/27
1969 11/18 – until 1970 10/14
1973 1/30 – 5/1
1973 6/29 – 12/14
1976 3/2 – 5/10
1981 11/1 – until 1982 9/26
1985 1/15 – 3/31
1985 8/14 – 11/20
1987 6/23 – 10/17
1988 2/9 – 4/25
1993 10/17 – until 1994 1/8
1994 4/22 – 9/7
1996 12/30 – until 1997 3/10
1999 5/31 – until 2000 4/8
2005 10/1 – 12/17
2006 6/1 – 8/10
2008 12/13 – until 2009 2/20
2011 5/11 – until 2012 3/20

SATURN CHALLENGING
1939 5/12 – 12/8
1940 1/16 – 6/17
1940 11/10 – until 1941 3/8
1952 12/12 – until 1953 4/3
1953 9/6 – until 1954 10/25
1961 2/15 – 8/13
1961 11/10 – until 1962 4/24
1962 6/19 – until 1963 1/8
1968 7/8 – 9/6
1969 3/19 – until 1970 4/22
1982 10/15 – until 1983 11/30
1984 6/6 – 8/18
1990 4/8 – 5/31
1990 12/24 – until 1992 2/11
1998 4/24 – until 1999 5/29
1999 12/20 – until 2000 2/3
2011 11/22 – Continues

URANUS CHALLENGING
1973 11/7 – until 1977 10/13
1994 2/27 – until 1998 12/28

NEPTUNE CHALLENGING
1953 11/18 – until 1962 8/6
1995 3/5 – until 2003 11/28

PLUTO CHALLENGING
1981 10/30 – until 1988 9/19

JUPITER SPECIAL
1942 10/26 – 11/29
1943 6/5 – 8/19
1954 9/18 – until 1955 1/16
1955 5/14 – 8/2
1966 8/28 – until 1967 3/6
1967 4/5 – 7/18
1978 8/10 – until 1979 7/1
1990 7/25 – 10/18
1991 1/12 – 6/11
2002 7/9 – 9/23
2003 2/20 – 5/17

SATURN SPECIAL
1945 10/26 – 11/17
1946 6/22 – until 1947 7/23
1975 8/2 – until 1976 9/1
1977 3/11 – 5/11
2004 9/15 – until 2005 1/2
2005 6/3 – 10/29
2005 12/16 – until 2006 7/6

URANUS SPECIAL
1954 8/9 – until 1958 7/16

PLUTO SPECIAL
1938 1/1 – until 1946 7/13

267

July 27

Your Personal Powers

Friendly and enthusiastic, your personal powers include courage, a good mind, creative ideas, and an eagerness to gain greater understanding. You are often commanding and determined but can also be equally receptive and sensitive. Being observant, you can analyze and assess the finer points of situations. You empower yourself when you combine your inquiring mind with your sharp receptivity and desire for knowledge. Although you are usually quick to come to conclusions, you can lose some of your power if you act in haste. Nevertheless, your judgment is often accurate if you avoid skepticism and suspicion. You gain power by synthesizing your idealism, progressive thinking, and ability to communicate your ideas to others. A need to be well-informed indicates that you are likely to read avidly or be interested in new ways of learning. Although you are proud, strong, and independent, you can also be warm, caring, and creatively inspired. Ambitious and innovative, you often achieve the most success when you are mentally stimulated and initiating new or original ventures.

Your Powers of Attraction in Relationships

Sociable and persuasive, you can attract others with your intelligence and broad-minded approach. Often you possess an inner desire to love and be loved, and your greatest pleasure comes from sharing with others. Being idealistic and romantic, you seek deep and meaningful relationships. Being extremely sensitive to others makes you compassionate and caring, but avoid losing your free spirit by becoming involved in dependent situations. You are particularly attracted to individuals who have won success through their hard-earned efforts or those who think big. Although you are usually warm and loving, at times you can experience inner tensions that cause you to withdraw or appear cold. As you possess deep feelings that need to be expressed, you want an open and sincere relationship.

Your attractive qualities: versatile, leadership skills, imaginative, creative, resolute, brave, good understanding, sixth sense, mentally capable, spiritual, inventive, good teacher, caring, artistic, musical or writing ability, clever, intuitive, innovative, mental strength, ambitious

Your less attractive qualities: disagreeable, bossy, easily offended, skeptical, restless, opinionated, quarrelsome, egotistical, codependent, nervous, mistrusting, overemotional, tense

Your Venus Power

The planet Venus has a great deal of influence on your powers of attraction. Below are four possible Venus types for women and men. To find your Venus you need to go to page 771, where you will find the Venus table and extra information. The planet Mars also affects your powers of attraction. To find your Mars table and interpretation go to page 761.

WOMEN WITH VENUS IN GEMINI: Curious, with a bright and animated approach to life, you are attracted to those who are clever or sophisticated. Your love of variety and desire for knowledge suggest that you need a partner and friends who keep you mentally stimulated. Although witty and a good conversationalist, you may need to keep in touch with your deeper feelings. Nevertheless, intelligent and friendly, you possess a youthful sense of wonder and seek a playmate who can keep you from becoming bored.

MEN WITH VENUS IN GEMINI: Friendly and sociable, you attract others with your clever and amusing conversation. Drawn to people who can match you in wit and intelligence, you usually prefer to keep relationships light rather than emotionally intense. With your youthful charm and desire for knowledge and new experiences you usually have many friends and a low boredom threshold.

WOMEN WITH VENUS IN CANCER: Possessing a soft femininity, you have tender and sensitive emotions. Sympathetic and caring, you often mother those in your care by making sure they are comfortable and have plenty to eat. When you feel hurt or insecure in relationships you are likely to cover your feelings by being defensive or appearing tough on the outside while on the inside you are feeling vulnerable. Affectionate and romantic, you make a faithful and devoted partner.

MEN WITH VENUS IN CANCER: Affectionate with a strong sensitive streak, you can love very deeply. You may find yourself drawn to sympathetic partners who can tune in to your moods and feelings as well as be reassuring and supportive. Family links are especially important to you and the more positive these relationships are, the more confident and safe you feel.

WOMEN WITH VENUS IN LEO: You possess the wonderful

ability to project your warm and sunny personality and keep others happily entertained. Loving attention yourself, you seek a partner who can appreciate you, be supportive, and give you positive feedback. Proud, with a natural regal air, you expect respect from your partners but are willing to be loyal and supportive in exchange. Although sometimes a little self-centered, you know how to make your partner feel special.

MEN WITH VENUS IN LEO: Generous, animated, and pleasure-seeking, you can be very entertaining and fun to be with. Usually you are attracted to extroverted and benevolent individuals with a sunny personality. If ambitious, you are drawn to a partner who shows leadership qualities or one who is highly motivated. Your less attractive qualities are your tendencies to be bossy or vain. With a sense of the dramatic, however, you can be the life and soul of the party and inspire those around you.

WOMEN WITH VENUS IN VIRGO: Polite, refined, and organized, you are attracted to articulate and intelligent people. Since you are caring, concerned, and want to be of practical help to others, you can be an asset to any partnership. By being too analytical, exacting, or faultfinding, however, a doubting element can creep into your relationships. By expressing your feelings in a positive way you can become more decisive and improve on how you relate to your loved ones.

MEN WITH VENUS IN VIRGO: A love of order usually indicates that you are attracted to refined individuals with analytical or practical abilities. You and your partner may be working together or serving similar causes. As you constantly analyze partnerships in order to improve them, you are likely to use former relationships as a point of reference and compare them to your present partner. Because you are helpful and kind, others usually rely on your good judgment and often turn to you for advice or practical assistance.

To read all about your Outer Planets and work out how to use your personalized timetable, go to Section Three, page 789.

page 789.

Your Personalized Timetable

JUPITER BENEFICIAL
1939 4/21 – until **1940** 2/29
1941 5/21 – 7/3
1945 8/18 – 10/5
1947 2/7 – 4/18
1947 10/2 – 12/16
1951 4/3 – 6/25
1951 9/12 – until **1952** 2/8
1953 5/4 – 6/16
1956 12/2 – until **1957** 3/3
1957 7/30 – 9/19
1959 1/11 – 5/30
1959 9/8 – 11/30
1963 3/17 – 5/27
1963 10/29 – until **1964** 1/10
1965 4/16 – 5/30
1968 11/8 – until **1969** 4/10
1969 7/5 – 9/3
1970 12/22 – until **1971** 11/14
1975 2/28 – 5/7
1976 8/11 – 10/29
1977 3/28 – 5/14
1980 10/21 – 12/22
1981 2/26 – 8/16
1982 12/5 – until **1983** 10/28
1987 2/12 – 4/20
1988 7/14 – 12/10
1989 3/1 – 4/27
1992 10/4 – 11/24
1993 4/7 – 7/24
1994 11/20 – until **1995** 2/10
1995 5/22 – 10/8
1998 6/9 – 8/25
1999 1/23 – 4/4
2000 6/24 – 8/20
2000 11/8 – until **2001** 4/7
2004 9/19 – 11/6
2006 11/4 – until **2007** 1/19
2007 7/3 – 9/10
2010 5/11 – 10/12
2010 12/25 – until **2011** 3/18
2012 6/6 – Continues

SATURN BENEFICIAL
1938 1/1 – 4/29
1938 11/21 – until **1939** 1/7
1942 4/28 – 7/19
1942 12/5 – until **1943** 4/7
1950 11/7 – until **1951** 3/23
1951 7/31 – 10/26
1952 5/16 – 7/5
1955 12/3 – until **1957** 1/26
1957 5/23 – 10/25
1966 4/30 – 9/26
1967 1/23 – 6/25
1967 8/23 – until **1968** 3/6
1971 6/8 – until **1972** 5/21
1980 9/11 – 12/15
1981 2/22 – 9/1
1985 1/12 – 5/3
1985 10/9 – until **1986** 11/30
1996 3/3 – until **1997** 4/11
2000 7/23 – 11/3
2001 4/9 – 6/29
2002 1/11 – 3/7
2009 10/18 – until **2010** 4/27
2010 7/2 – 10/9

URANUS BENEFICIAL
1941 7/3 – until **1944** 5/27
1967 12/3 – until **1970** 9/25
1980 11/16 – until **1984** 10/31
2009 5/14 – Continues

NEPTUNE BENEFICIAL
1941 10/27 – until **1947** 8/10
1968 1/4 – until **1976** 10/6

PLUTO BENEFICIAL
1970 11/2 – until **1975** 9/22
1993 11/25 – until **2000** 11/7

JUPITER CHALLENGING
1940 4/28 – 7/15

1940 10/25 – until **1941** 3/3
1946 1/9 – 3/16
1946 9/3 – 11/18
1949 3/14 – 8/1
1949 11/4 – until **1950** 1/23
1952 4/11 – 6/20
1952 12/15 – until **1953** 1/26
1957 12/12 – until **1958** 4/25
1958 8/11 – 11/3
1961 2/21 – until **1962** 1/6
1964 3/25 – 6/1
1969 11/23 – until **1970** 10/18
1973 2/4 – 5/15
1973 6/15 – 12/19
1976 3/7 – 5/14
1981 11/6 – until **1982** 10/1
1985 1/19 – 4/5
1985 8/6 – 11/27
1987 6/29 – 10/10
1988 2/15 – 4/29
1993 10/21 – until **1994** 1/15
1994 4/14 – 9/12
1997 1/3 – 3/14
1999 6/4 – 11/30
2000 1/9 – 4/12
2005 10/6 – 12/22
2006 5/23 – 8/19
2008 12/17 – until **2009** 2/24
2011 5/15 – until **2012** 3/24

SATURN CHALLENGING
1939 5/20 – 11/19
1940 2/4 – 6/27
1940 10/29 – until **1941** 3/17
1952 12/24 – until **1953** 3/21
1953 9/16 – until **1954** 11/2
1961 2/24 – 7/30
1961 11/23 – until **1963** 1/16
1969 3/27 – until **1970** 4/29
1982 10/23 – until **1983** 12/9
1984 5/21 – 9/2
1991 1/1 – until **1992** 2/20
1998 5/2 – until **1999** 6/6
1999 12/2 – until **2000** 2/21
2011 12/1 – until **2012** 4/21
2012 8/26 – Continues

URANUS CHALLENGING
1973 11/24 – until **1977** 10/29
1994 3/23 – until **1999** 1/15

NEPTUNE CHALLENGING
1953 12/24 – until **1962** 9/24
1996 1/28 – until **2004** 1/2

PLUTO CHALLENGING
1981 11/25 – until **1988** 10/16

JUPITER SPECIAL
1943 6/10 – 8/23
1954 9/25 – until **1955** 1/9
1955 5/20 – 8/7
1966 9/2 – until **1967** 2/20
1967 4/19 – 7/22
1978 8/15 – until **1979** 7/5
1990 7/29 – 10/26
1991 1/3 – 6/17
2002 7/13 – 9/28
2003 2/12 – 5/24

SATURN SPECIAL
1946 6/30 – until **1947** 7/31
1975 8/9 – until **1976** 9/9
1977 2/24 – 5/26
2004 9/27 – 12/21
2005 6/11 – until **2006** 7/13

URANUS SPECIAL
1954 8/26 – until **1958** 7/31

PLUTO SPECIAL
1938 1/1 – until **1947** 6/22

♌

269

July 28

SUN: SUN • DECANATE: LEO/SUN • DEGREE: 4°45–5°5 LEO • MODE: FIXED • ELEMENT: FIRE

Your Personal Powers

Warm, kind, and sociable with a dramatic personality, your natural creativity and determination mark you as someone special. Diplomatic and charismatic, you gain power from your dynamic emotional strength, stamina, and fast responses. Highly intuitive and sensitive, you possess a good understanding of people. If you extend this awareness to some form of humanitarian service it can bring you extra spiritual and material rewards. With your enterprising spirit and ability to lead, you can rise to positions of power and receive recognition for your hard work or dedication. Although your ambition and determination can inspire you to work hard, a desire for the good things in life implies that you can play equally hard. Just be careful not to lose some of your power to escapism or indulgence by socializing too much. With self-discipline and perseverance, however, you can develop your outstanding talents. Fortunately, your endurance, courage, natural creativity, and strong individuality show your potential for outstanding achievement in life.

Your Powers of Attraction in Relationships

With your confident image, quick wit, and ability to entertain, you will always attract popularity. Highly persuasive, you can also influence others with your charm. Although independent, your biggest rewards often come through partnerships or associations with others. If female, you may have to balance your forceful nature with sensitivity to keep your partnerships working successfully. You admire honest and direct individuals and those who can provide you with emotional security. You need a responsible and solid partner who can also be supportive and affectionate. As you do not like to be alone, you may compromise for peace, home, and family. Sometimes bossy or selfish, especially if frustrated, you also need a partner who is not intimidated by your headstrong personality. Loving and generous, you can be a devoted partner or parent.

Your attractive qualities: leadership skills, progressive, courageous, artistic, creative, idealistic, ambitious, talented, popular, compassionate, hardworking, humanitarian, generous, stable home life, enterprising, kind, humorous, strong-willed, determined, loving, direct

Your less attractive qualities: escapist, selfish, unmotivated, lack of compassion, bossy, intolerant, too sensual, under- or overconfident, obstinate, argumentative, frustrated, prideful, underachieving, living in fantasy, dependent on others

Your Venus Power

The planet Venus has a great deal of influence on your powers of attraction. Below are four possible Venus types for women and men. To find your Venus you need to go to page 771, where you will find the Venus table and extra information. The planet Mars also affects your powers of attraction. To find your Mars table and interpretation go to page 761.

WOMEN WITH VENUS IN GEMINI: In relationships you need intellectual stimulation and usually prefer to keep things light. Certainly not boring, you love to talk and are at your best being witty and entertaining. Although your easygoing approach to relationships is very attractive, guard against losing touch with your deeper emotions. You prefer a partner who can keep up with your fast stream of ideas, and if you have shared interests then so much the better.

MEN WITH VENUS IN GEMINI: Informed and curious yet charming and friendly, you seek a partner who shares your interests or enjoys your witty remarks. Although a good communicator, you have an inborn tendency to be lighthearted and less profound about deep emotional commitment. Although you are keen on experiences that bring variety into your life, boredom or scattering your energies in too many directions is probably your biggest handicap in relationships. Nevertheless you are attracted to intelligent partners who can match your lively banter.

WOMEN WITH VENUS IN CANCER: Possessing a soft femininity, you have tender and sensitive emotions. Sympathetic and caring, you often mother those in your care by making sure they are comfortable and have plenty to eat. When you feel hurt or insecure in relationships you are likely to cover your feelings by being defensive or appearing tough on the outside while on the inside you are feeling vulnerable. Affectionate and romantic, you make a faithful and devoted partner.

MEN WITH VENUS IN CANCER: Being emotionally receptive, you can be a sensitive lover. With your desire to care and protect others, you are likely to have strong family connections. Love is often tied in with being attentive to the needs of others, and you may find yourself attracted to individuals who have sympathetic or maternal qualities. Security-conscious,

you need a loyal partner who can offer you support and ideally be a good cook and homemaker.

WOMEN WITH VENUS IN LEO: Your friendly and sunny personality often makes you stand out in a crowd. Generous and giving, you know how to make your partner feel special. As you often expect loyalty and devotion from your partner in return, you can become easily offended if they ignore you or behave in an inconsiderate manner. Charming and kind, when you're in love you can be romantic, dramatic, and passionate.

MEN WITH VENUS IN LEO: Enthusiastic, playful, and kind, you can be benevolent with those you love. Warm, romantic, and self-expressive, you adore the drama of love or having fun with your friends. Usually you are attracted to partners with a warm and generous nature. Although you can be a confident and charismatic partner, you may need to develop humility to stop pride or arrogance from marring your relationships.

WOMEN WITH VENUS IN VIRGO: Articulate and straightforward in your relationships, you attract others with your genuine concern for their well-being. By being understanding and a good listener, you are able to show your love and friendship. With your analytical approach to relationships, however, you may have to be careful of becoming too matter-of-fact. You often display your concern for the welfare of others by your willingness to offer practical help and assistance. You usually seek a partner who is willing to work as hard on relationships as you are.

MEN WITH VENUS IN VIRGO: Industrious and well-ordered, you relate to others in a considerate and down-to-earth way. You enjoy giving practical advice and being of service to those you love, even in small ways. Being a perfectionist you are drawn to partners with high morals or a strong work ethic. Partners who have strong analytical minds are very attractive to you, particularly if they are also clean and meticulously dressed.

To read all about your Outer Planets and work out how to use your personalized timetable, go to Section Three, page 789.

go to Section Three, page 789.

Your Personalized Timetable

JUPITER BENEFICIAL
1939 4/25 – until **1940** 3/4
1941 5/25 – 7/8
1945 8/23 – 10/9
1947 2/18 – 4/7
1947 10/7 – 12/20
1951 4/7 – 7/4
1951 9/3 – until **1952** 2/13
1953 5/8 – 6/20
1956 12/10 – until **1957** 2/22
1957 8/5 – 9/24
1959 1/16 – 5/22
1959 9/15 – 12/4
1963 3/21 – 6/2
1963 10/21 – until **1964** 1/18
1965 4/21 – 6/3
1968 11/14 – until **1969** 4/2
1969 7/13 – 9/8
1970 12/27 – until **1971** 7/17
1971 7/31 – 11/19
1975 3/4 – 5/12
1976 8/20 – 10/20
1977 4/2 – 5/18
1980 10/25 – until **1981** 1/3
1981 2/14 – 8/21
1982 12/10 – until **1983** 11/2
1987 2/16 – 4/24
1988 7/20 – 12/3
1989 3/8 – 5/1
1992 10/9 – 11/30
1993 3/31 – 7/31
1994 11/24 – until **1995** 2/18
1995 5/14 – 10/14
1998 6/18 – 8/16
1999 1/28 – 4/7
2000 6/28 – 8/29
2000 10/30 – until **2001** 4/12
2004 9/23 – 11/10
2005 5/14 – 6/27
2006 11/9 – until **2007** 1/24
2007 6/24 – 9/19
2010 5/16 – 10/4
2011 1/1 – 3/22
2012 6/10 – 7/28

SATURN BENEFICIAL
1938 1/1 – until **1939** 1/24
1942 5/6 – 7/29
1942 11/23 – until **1943** 4/16
1950 11/17 – until **1951** 3/11
1951 8/10 – 11/3
1952 4/28 – 7/23
1955 12/11 – until **1956** 7/5
1956 8/24 – until **1957** 2/7
1957 5/9 – 11/3
1966 5/10 – 9/14
1967 2/2 – until **1968** 3/14
1971 6/16 – until **1972** 1/21
1972 2/10 – 5/29
1980 9/18 – until **1981** 1/8
1981 1/28 – 9/10
1985 1/25 – 4/19
1985 10/19 – until **1986** 12/8
1996 3/11 – until **1997** 4/19
2000 8/5 – 10/21
2001 4/18 – 7/7
2001 12/26 – until **2002** 3/22
2009 10/26 – until **2010** 4/12
2010 7/17 – 10/16

URANUS BENEFICIAL
1941 7/27 – until **1945** 3/24
1968 9/23 – until **1971** 7/11
1980 12/1 – until **1984** 11/17
2010 3/19 – Continues

NEPTUNE BENEFICIAL
1941 12/6 – until **1947** 9/11
1968 11/29 – until **1976** 11/8

PLUTO BENEFICIAL
1970 12/24 – until **1976** 8/11
1993 12/20 – until **2001** 9/15

JUPITER CHALLENGING
1938 1/1 – 2/12

1940 5/2 – 7/22
1940 10/18 – until **1941** 3/9
1946 1/21 – 3/4
1946 9/8 – 11/23
1949 3/19 – 7/24
1949 11/11 – until **1950** 1/27
1952 4/15 – 6/25
1952 12/4 – until **1953** 2/6
1957 12/18 – until **1958** 4/18
1958 8/18 – 11/7
1961 2/26 – until **1962** 1/10
1964 3/29 – 6/5
1969 11/28 – until **1970** 6/3
1970 7/13 – 10/23
1973 2/8 – 12/23
1976 3/11 – 5/19
1981 11/10 – until **1982** 10/6
1985 1/23 – 4/12
1985 7/30 – 12/3
1987 7/6 – 10/3
1988 2/20 – 5/3
1993 10/25 – until **1994** 1/23
1994 4/5 – 9/18
1997 1/7 – 3/19
1997 9/19 – 10/27
1999 6/9 – 11/19
2000 1/21 – 4/16
2005 10/10 – 12/28
2006 5/15 – 8/26
2008 12/22 – until **2009** 3/1
2011 5/20 – until **2012** 3/29

SATURN CHALLENGING
1939 5/29 – 11/5
1940 2/16 – 7/8
1940 10/17 – until **1941** 3/26
1953 1/9 – 3/3
1953 9/24 – until **1954** 11/10
1961 3/6 – 7/17
1961 12/3 – until **1963** 1/24
1969 4/3 – until **1970** 5/7
1982 10/31 – until **1983** 12/18
1984 5/8 – 9/13
1991 1/9 – until **1992** 2/28
1992 9/13 – 11/17
1998 5/10 – until **1999** 6/15
1999 11/19 – until **2000** 3/4
2011 12/11 – until **2012** 4/9
2012 9/5 – Continues

URANUS CHALLENGING
1973 12/14 – until **1978** 8/19
1995 1/21 – until **1999** 1/31

NEPTUNE CHALLENGING
1954 11/13 – until **1962** 10/22
1996 2/25 – until **2004** 11/10

PLUTO CHALLENGING
1982 1/1 – until **1989** 8/25

JUPITER SPECIAL
1943 6/15 – 8/27
1954 10/2 – until **1955** 1/2
1955 5/25 – 8/11
1966 9/7 – until **1967** 2/11
1967 4/29 – 7/26
1978 8/19 – until **1979** 7/10
1990 8/3 – 11/6
1990 12/23 – until **1991** 6/22
2002 7/17 – 10/4
2003 2/5 – 5/31

SATURN SPECIAL
1946 7/7 – until **1947** 8/7
1975 8/17 – until **1976** 2/29
1976 4/23 – 9/18
1977 2/11 – 6/7
2004 10/12 – 12/4
2005 6/20 – until **2006** 7/21

URANUS SPECIAL
1954 9/16 – until **1959** 5/22

PLUTO SPECIAL
1938 1/1 – until **1948** 5/18

♌

271

July 29

SUN: LEO · DECANATE: LEO/SUN · DEGREE: 5°5–6°5 LEO · MODE: FIXED · ELEMENT: FIRE

Your Personal Powers

Sensitive yet dramatic, your strong emotions, imagination, and unique personality mark you out as having remarkable potential for achievement. Your sign ruler, the Sun, indicates that you can also be creative, kind, and warmhearted. Proud and strong-willed, you gain power from your dynamic motivation and idealism. This can endow you with visionary ability and the enthusiasm to carry your dreams through. Besides being very sensitive, at the other extreme, you can be tough, businesslike, and uncompromising with an innate sense of authority. You may, however, lose some of your power if you do not stay emotionally balanced and relaxed. A tendency to become emotionally excited can also cause you to be excessive, moody, or discontented. Nevertheless, the combination of your natural leadership ability, personal charm, and inspired ideas can help you accomplish things in a big way. You empower yourself when you have a sense of purpose and show your determination to achieve success. If this purpose is linked to inspiring others or improving society then so much the better.

Your Powers of Attraction in Relationships

With your strong emotions and individuality you can radiate charm and charisma. Imaginative and creative, you often inspire others by example and work well in a team effort. Although idealistic in love, you are attracted to power and influence and a partner who is confident and determined to succeed. Being very romantic and sensitive, you can give much in the way of love and friendship. Be careful, however, not to give too much or do things in excess. As a true dreamer your relationships get better when you are actively expressing some of your natural talents rather than thinking about them. The more confident you are about your sense of self-identity the happier you are to help others and build positive relationships.

Your attractive qualities: inspirational, charismatic, leadership ability, confident, strong, talented, very sensitive, humanitarian, honest, inner peace, determined, generous, charm, compassionate, successful, creative, intuitive, mystical, worldly, faith, artistic, kind

Your less attractive qualities: unfocused, insecure, nervous, selfish, vain, moody, extremist, melodramatic, inconsiderate, bossy, worry, escapist, frustration, arrogant, disappointed, martyr, lazy, temperamental, too sensitive

Your Venus Power

The planet Venus has a great deal of influence on your powers of attraction. Below are four possible Venus types for women and men. To find your Venus you need to go to page 771, where you will find the Venus table and extra information. The planet Mars also affects your powers of attraction. To find your Mars table and interpretation go to page 761.

WOMEN WITH VENUS IN GEMINI: Articulate, versatile, and youthful, your personal magnetism is often linked to your charm, wit, and communication skills. You seek a partner who is clever, can communicate with you at ease, and can share your thoughts and interests. Since you find it easy to mix with people you have many friends. When you do find someone you can communicate with you can easily lose yourself in long conversations.

MEN WITH VENUS IN GEMINI: Charming, amusing, and adaptable, you attract others with your natural communication skills and friendly personality. You have a wonderful childlike quality and love to keep life playful, but a reluctance to contact your deeper feelings may cause you to avoid serious commitment. With your need for variety and intellectual stimulation, you are attracted to clever and amusing partners who have many interesting sides to their personalities.

WOMEN WITH VENUS IN CANCER: Possessing a soft femininity, you have tender and sensitive emotions. Sympathetic and caring, you often mother those in your care by making sure they are comfortable and have plenty to eat. When you feel hurt or insecure in relationships you are likely to cover your feelings by being defensive or appearing tough on the outside while on the inside you are feeling vulnerable. Affectionate and romantic, you make a faithful and devoted partner.

MEN WITH VENUS IN CANCER: You seek a partner who is sympathetic, caring, and protective. You are forgiving and compassionate and want a secure emotional bond in your close relationships. Usually you are drawn toward partners who are maternal, unselfish, or demonstrative with their feelings. Although you can sometimes appear to others

as impressionable, you have powerful emotions and inner strength.

. **WOMEN WITH VENUS IN LEO:** Warm and playful with a touch of the dramatic, you enjoy the company of generous or strong individuals who can share your sense of fun. Although there are advantages to your being strong-willed, in your relationships you need to resist being bossy as it can cause resentment. With your wonderful mixture of regal authority and childlike wonder, you love to keep others entertained and amused.

MEN WITH VENUS IN LEO: Generous, animated, and pleasure-seeking, you can be very entertaining and fun to be with. Usually you are attracted to extroverted and benevolent individuals with sunny personalities. If ambitious, you are drawn to a partner who shows leadership qualities or one who is highly motivated. Your less attractive qualities are your tendencies to be bossy or vain. With a sense of the dramatic, however, you can be the life and soul of the party and inspire those around you.

WOMEN WITH VENUS IN VIRGO: Polite, refined, and organized, you are attracted to articulate and intelligent people. Since you are caring, concerned, and want to be of practical help to others, you can be an asset to any partnership. By being too analytical, exacting, or faultfinding, however, a doubting element can creep into your relationships. By expressing your feelings in a positive way you can become more decisive and improve on how you relate to your loved ones.

MEN WITH VENUS IN VIRGO: Practical, idealistic, and a perfectionist, you seek a relationship with an intelligent and hardworking partner who can inspire you to be more industrious and well-ordered. At times you can come across as a sympathetic and caring person and at other times you may appear pragmatic and very businesslike. This may sometimes lead to unclear communication between you and your partner. Usually helpful and caring, however, you like to analyze the faults in your relationships and then work methodically to improve them.

To read all about your Outer Planets and work out how to use your personalized timetable, go to Section Three, page 789.

♌

Your Personalized Timetable

JUPITER BENEFICIAL
1939 4/30 – until **1940** 3/8
1941 5/29 – 7/13
1945 8/28 – 10/14
1947 10/12 – 12/25
1951 4/11 – 7/17
1951 8/22 – until **1952** 2/18
1953 5/12 – 6/24
1956 12/20 – until **1957** 2/12
1957 8/10 – 9/28
1959 1/23 – 5/14
1959 9/21 – 12/9
1963 3/25 – 6/7
1963 10/14 – until **1964** 1/24
1965 4/25 – 6/7
1968 11/19 – until **1969** 3/25
1969 7/20 – 9/12
1971 1/1 – 6/28
1971 8/20 – 11/23
1975 3/8 – 5/16
1976 9/1 – 10/7
1977 4/6 – 5/22
1980 10/30 – until **1981** 5/16
1981 6/7 – 8/26
1982 12/14 – until **1983** 11/6
1987 2/20 – 4/28
1988 7/25 – 11/26
1989 3/15 – 5/5
1992 10/13 – 12/7
1993 3/23 – 8/6
1994 11/28 – until **1995** 2/26
1995 5/5 – 10/19
1998 7/2 – 8/2
1999 2/1 – 4/11
2000 7/3 – 9/10
2000 10/18 – until **2001** 4/17
2004 9/28 – 11/16
2005 5/2 – 7/9
2006 11/13 – until **2007** 1/29
2007 6/16 – 9/26
2010 5/21 – 9/27
2011 1/8 – 3/25
2012 6/14 – Continues

SATURN BENEFICIAL
1938 1/1 – 5/16
1938 10/20 – until **1939** 2/5
1942 5/13 – 8/9
1942 11/11 – until **1943** 4/25
1950 11/28 – until **1951** 2/26
1951 8/19 – 11/12
1952 4/14 – 8/5
1955 12/20 – until **1956** 6/16
1956 9/12 – until **1957** 2/23
1957 4/21 – 11/12
1966 5/22 – 9/1
1967 2/11 – until **1968** 3/22
1971 6/24 – 12/28
1972 3/5 – 6/5
1980 9/26 – until **1981** 9/18
1985 2/11 – 3/31
1985 10/27 – until **1986** 12/16
1996 3/19 – until **1997** 4/27
1997 12/6 – 12/26
2000 8/24 – 10/1
2001 4/26 – 7/16
2001 12/13 – until **2002** 4/3
2009 11/4 – until **2010** 3/30
2010 7/29 – 10/24
2011 5/29 – 6/28

URANUS BENEFICIAL
1942 5/26 – until **1945** 4/18
1968 10/9 – until **1971** 8/10
1980 12/17 – until **1984** 12/3
2010 4/5 – Continues

NEPTUNE BENEFICIAL
1942 10/21 – until **1948** 7/31
1968 12/27 – until **1977** 9/26

PLUTO BENEFICIAL
1971 10/23 – until **1976** 9/9
1994 1/22 – until **2001** 10/27

JUPITER CHALLENGING
1938 1/1 – 2/16
1940 5/6 – 7/30
1940 10/10 – until **1941** 3/14
1946 9/13 – 11/27
1949 3/26 – 7/17
1949 11/17 – until **1950** 1/31
1952 4/19 – 6/30
1952 11/25 – until **1953** 2/14
1957 12/25 – until **1958** 4/10
1958 8/24 – 11/12
1961 3/2 – 9/9
1961 10/7 – until **1962** 1/15
1964 4/2 – 6/9
1969 12/3 – until **1970** 5/21
1970 7/26 – 10/27
1973 2/12 – 12/28
1976 3/16 – 5/23
1981 11/15 – until **1982** 10/11
1985 1/27 – 4/18
1985 7/22 – 12/8
1987 7/14 – 9/25
1988 2/25 – 5/7
1993 10/30 – until **1994** 2/3
1994 3/26 – 9/23
1997 1/11 – 3/24
1997 9/7 – 11/8
1999 6/14 – 11/10
2000 1/29 – 4/20
2005 10/15 – until **2006** 1/3
2006 5/7 – 9/2
2008 12/26 – until **2009** 3/5
2011 5/24 – until **2012** 4/2

SATURN CHALLENGING
1939 6/7 – 10/24
1940 2/27 – 7/22
1940 10/2 – until **1941** 4/3
1953 10/2 – until **1954** 11/18
1961 3/17 – 7/4
1961 12/13 – until **1963** 2/1
1969 4/11 – until **1970** 5/14
1982 11/8 – until **1983** 12/28
1984 4/25 – 9/24
1991 1/17 – until **1992** 3/8
1992 8/28 – 12/2
1998 5/18 – 11/28
1999 1/29 – 6/24
1999 11/7 – until **2000** 3/14
2011 12/22 – until **2012** 3/27
2012 9/14 – Continues

URANUS CHALLENGING
1974 1/15 – until **1978** 9/15
1995 2/7 – until **1999** 12/5

NEPTUNE CHALLENGING
1954 12/14 – until **1963** 9/17
1996 4/9 – until **2004** 12/25

PLUTO CHALLENGING
1982 11/9 – until **1989** 9/30

JUPITER SPECIAL
1943 6/19 – 9/1
1954 10/9 – 12/25
1955 5/31 – 8/15
1966 9/13 – until **1967** 2/3
1967 5/7 – 7/31
1978 8/24 – until **1979** 7/14
1990 8/7 – until **1991** 6/27
2002 7/22 – 10/10
2003 1/29 – 6/6

SATURN SPECIAL
1946 7/15 – until **1947** 8/15
1975 8/25 – until **1976** 2/13
1976 5/9 – 9/27
1977 1/30 – 6/17
2005 6/27 – until **2006** 7/29

URANUS SPECIAL
1954 10/23 – until **1959** 6/17

PLUTO SPECIAL
1938 1/1 – until **1948** 7/6

273

July 30

SUN: LEO • DECANATE: LEO/SUN • DEGREE: 6°5–8° LEO • MODE: FIXED • ELEMENT: FIRE

Your Personal Powers

Original, sociable, and friendly, you are a gregarious individual with a receptive mind and strong determination. Possessing strong feelings, you can be warmhearted, kind, and exceptionally loving. Being charismatic, you gain power from your own unique dramatic style and innate creative talents. As you often have a strong need for self-expression, you may be drawn to activities such as drama, art, writing, or music. Dignified and proud, you usually project confidence and people often place you in leadership positions. Independent and enterprising, you may prefer to work for yourself. Although strong-willed, be careful not to get carried away and lose some of your power to arrogance or temperamental moods. At the other extreme, your confidence can sometimes disguise hidden insecurities or worries that can undermine your remarkable potential. Nevertheless, idealistic and inspired, you can also be ambitious with good business acumen. Naturally generous and giving, you can gain a great deal of satisfaction when you use your outstanding sensitivity and talents to help and uplift others.

Your Powers of Attraction in Relationships

Creative, entertaining, and a good conversationalist, you have star quality. When positive, your gestures of generosity indicate that you attract others by projecting love and warmth. Appearing confident yet reserved, you have many admirers. Although you can be a leader among your crowd, in your love life you may have to learn detachment. Although usually optimistic and friendly, if you find yourself getting too serious or intense you may need to back away and review the situation. Idealistic and romantic in relationships, you are attracted by thoughtful and detached individuals or those who have special talents or insight. Affectionate and loyal, you often attract others with your broad-minded and sympathetic understanding.

Your attractive qualities: loyal, friendly, creative, generous, original, fun-loving, talent with words, creative, intuitive, strong feelings, sociable, kind, loving, frankness, enterprising, strong will, openness, multitalented, generous, loving, sympathetic, sensitive, youthful

Your less attractive qualities: obstinate, erratic, worry, impatient, overindulgent, insecure, indifferent, scattered, self-pity, egotistical, arrogant, jealous, competitive, lazy, excessive, temperamental, stubborn, skeptical, escapist

Your Venus Power

The planet Venus has a great deal of influence on your powers of attraction. Below are four possible Venus types for women and men. To find your Venus you need to go to page 771, where you will find the Venus table and extra information. The planet Mars also affects your powers of attraction. To find your Mars table and interpretation go to page 761.

WOMEN WITH VENUS IN GEMINI: By nature you are young at heart, adaptable, and sociable. Being curious and willing to cooperate makes you a good team player. Usually you are drawn to articulate people who have charm and flair or sharp wit. With a need to expand your knowledge you also look for a partner who can challenge or stimulate you intellectually. Although you love to talk with all types of people, you may need to develop your listening skills in order to build better communication in your relationships.

MEN WITH VENUS IN GEMINI: Adaptable yet often flirtatious, you enjoy mixing with people who are quick-minded and versatile. Since you can learn a great deal through interacting with others, you are often attracted to intelligent partners who have comprehensive knowledge or good ideas. One of your less attractive qualities is your tendency to get bored or be inconsistent. Having an adaptable partner is important to you; therefore it must be someone who can offer you different options and keep you interested.

WOMEN WITH VENUS IN CANCER: Possessing a soft femininity, you have tender and sensitive emotions. Sympathetic and caring, you often mother those in your care by making sure they are comfortable and have plenty to eat. When you feel hurt or insecure in relationships you are likely to cover your feelings by being defensive or appearing tough on the outside while on the inside you are feeling vulnerable. Affectionate and romantic, you make a faithful and devoted partner.

MEN WITH VENUS IN CANCER: You seek a partner who is sympathetic, caring, and protective. You are forgiving and compassionate, and want a secure emotional bond in your close relationships. Usually you are drawn toward partners who are maternal, unselfish, or demonstrative with their feelings. Although you can sometimes appear to others

as impressionable, you have powerful emotions and inner strength.

WOMEN WITH VENUS IN LEO: As a person who wants to radiate in their own right, you are likely to desire partners you can be proud of. You are usually attracted to fun-loving, warm, and generous individuals. If self-expression is important to you, you will probably seek the company of creative people such as artists, musicians, or those with a flair for acting. Alternatively, you may be drawn to people who are dignified, regal, or have already achieved success.

MEN WITH VENUS IN LEO: Generous, animated, and pleasure-seeking, you can be very entertaining and fun to be with. Usually you are attracted to extroverted and benevolent individuals with sunny personalities. If ambitious, you are drawn to a partner who shows leadership qualities or one who is highly motivated. Your less attractive qualities are your tendencies to be bossy or vain. With a sense of the dramatic, however, you can be the life and soul of the party and inspire those around you.

WOMEN WITH VENUS IN VIRGO: In relationships you can be modest and unassuming but desire perfection. You usually analyze your partnerships until you feel you have understood them to the last little detail in order to improve them. A problem usually arises when you become too critical either of partners or yourself and indulge in being skeptical or faultfinding. Being modest, others may not be aware of the strong sensuality beneath your well-groomed exterior.

MEN WITH VENUS IN VIRGO: Although you are constantly analyzing your relationships in order to understand and improve them, you may nevertheless need to refrain from continuously mulling over issues that can cause anxiety. You are happiest when you are able to help your loved ones in practical ways and forget yourself in your willingness to be of service to others. You seek a partner who has high standards and can be as pragmatic and hardworking as yourself. Ideally they should also be impeccably dressed with a fine analytical mind.

To read all about your Outer Planets and work out how to use your personalized timetable, go to Section Three, page 789.

♌

Your Personalized Timetable

JUPITER BENEFICIAL
1939 5/4 – until **1940** 3/12
1941 6/2 – 7/17
1942 1/25 – 2/16
1945 9/2 – 10/18
1947 10/17 – 12/29
1951 4/15 – until **1952** 2/22
1953 5/16 – 6/28
1957 1/5 – 1/27
1957 8/15 – 10/3
1959 1/29 – 5/7
1959 9/27 – 12/13
1963 3/29 – 6/13
1963 10/7 – until **1964** 1/30
1965 4/29 – 6/11
1968 11/26 – until **1969** 3/18
1969 7/26 – 9/17
1971 1/6 – 6/17
1971 8/30 – 11/27
1975 3/12 – 5/21
1977 4/11 – 5/26
1980 11/4 – until **1981** 4/30
1981 6/24 – 8/31
1982 12/19 – until **1983** 11/11
1987 2/24 – 5/3
1988 7/31 – 11/19
1989 3/21 – 5/10
1992 10/18 – 12/14
1993 3/16 – 3 8/12
1994 12/3 – until **1995** 3/10
1995 4/24 – 10/24
1999 2/6 – 4/15
2000 7/8 – until **2001** 1/10
2001 2/9 – 4/21
2004 10/2 – 11/21
2005 4/22 – 7/18
2006 11/17 – until **2007** 2/4
2007 6/8 – 10/3
2010 5/27 – 9/19
2011 1/14 – 3/29
2012 6/18 – Continues

SATURN BENEFICIAL
1938 1/1 – 5/25
1938 10/8 – until **1939** 2/16
1942 5/21 – 8/24
1942 10/27 – until **1943** 5/3
1950 12/14 – until **1951** 2/10
1951 8/28 – 11/21
1952 4/1 – 8/15
1955 12/29 – until **1956** 6/2
1956 9/25 – until **1957** 11/20
1966 6/5 – 8/17
1967 2/20 – until **1968** 3/30
1971 7/2 – 12/13
1972 3/18 – 6/13
1980 10/4 – until **1981** 9/26
1985 11/5 – until **1986** 12/25
1987 8/10 – 8/27
1996 3/26 – until **1997** 5/5
1997 11/11 – until **1998** 1/19
2001 5/3 – 7/25
2001 12/2 – until **2002** 4/13
2009 11/14 – until **2010** 3/18
2010 8/8 – 11/2
2011 5/6 – 7/20

URANUS BENEFICIAL
1942 6/11 – until **1945** 5/6
1968 10/25 – until **1971** 8/29
1981 1/4 – until **1985** 9/30
2010 4/23 – Continues

NEPTUNE BENEFICIAL
1942 11/24 – until **1948** 9/4
1969 2/9 – until **1977** 11/2

PLUTO BENEFICIAL
1971 11/25 – until **1977** 7/18
1994 12/6 – until **2001** 11/23

JUPITER CHALLENGING
1938 1/1 – 2/20
1940 5/10 – 8/9
1940 9/30 – until **1941** 3/19

1946 9/18 – 12/2
1949 4/1 – 7/9
1949 11/23 – until **1950** 2/4
1952 4/23 – 7/5
1952 11/18 – until **1953** 2/21
1958 1/1 – 4/2
1958 8/30 – 11/16
1961 3/7 – 8/26
1961 10/21 – until **1962** 1/19
1964 4/6 – 6/14
1969 12/8 – until **1970** 5/12
1970 8/4 – 10/31
1973 2/16 – until **1974** 1/1
1976 3/20 – 5/27
1981 11/20 – until **1982** 10/15
1985 1/31 – 4/26
1985 7/14 – 12/13
1987 7/24 – 9/15
1988 3/1 – 5/11
1993 11/3 – until **1994** 2/22
1994 3/5 – 9/28
1997 1/15 – 3/29
1997 8/28 – 11/16
1999 6/20 – 11/2
2000 2/5 – 4/24
2005 10/19 – until **2006** 1/9
2006 4/29 – 9/8
2008 12/30 – until **2009** 3/9
2011 5/28 – until **2012** 4/6

SATURN CHALLENGING
1939 6/17 – 10/12
1940 3/7 – 8/12
1940 9/10 – until **1941** 4/11
1953 10/11 – until **1954** 11/26
1955 7/9 – 7/29
1961 3/31 – 6/19
1961 12/22 – until **1963** 2/9
1969 4/18 – until **1970** 5/22
1982 11/16 – until **1983** 5/29
1983 8/3 – until **1984** 1/9
1984 4/12 – 10/3
1991 1/25 – until **1992** 3/17
1992 8/14 – 12/13
1998 5/26 – 11/13
1999 2/12 – 7/5
1999 10/26 – until **2000** 3/23
2012 1/6 – 3/11
2012 9/23 – Continues

URANUS CHALLENGING
1938 1/1 – until **1939** 3/5
1974 10/29 – until **1978** 10/4
1995 2/25 – until **1999** 12/28

NEPTUNE CHALLENGING
1955 11/7 – until **1963** 10/17
1997 2/17 – until **2005** 1/22

PLUTO CHALLENGING
1982 12/6 – until **1989** 10/25

JUPITER SPECIAL
1943 6/24 – 9/6
1954 10/19 – 12/15
1955 6/5 – 8/20
1966 9/18 – until **1967** 1/26
1967 5/14 – 8/4
1978 8/29 – until **1979** 7/19
1990 8/11 – until **1991** 7/2
2002 7/26 – 10/17
2003 1/22 – 6/12

SATURN SPECIAL
1946 7/22 – until **1947** 8/22
1975 9/3 – until **1976** 1/31
1976 5/21 – 10/8
1977 1/18 – 6/26
2005 7/5 – until **2006** 8/5

URANUS SPECIAL
1955 7/31 – until **1959** 7/6

PLUTO SPECIAL
1938 1/1 – until **1949** 6/10

275

July 31

SUN: LEO • DECANATE: LEO /SUN • DEGREE: 7°5–8°5 LEO • MODE: FIXED • ELEMENT: FIRE

Your Personal Powers

Sociable yet determined, you are a constructive and dignified individual with powerful emotions and enhanced sensitivity. Keen to express your thoughts and feelings, you gain power by combining your personal charm and friendly personality with your strong will and tenacity. Your ruler, the Sun, adds a sense of drama to your good-hearted nature. Your persuasive manner implies that you have the ability to communicate to others in a direct and unpretentious way. Often gifted with words and common sense, you can achieve a great deal when you recognize your special talents. Although you usually project a proud and confident front, you may lose some of your power if you allow your changing moods, worries, or insecurities to undermine your outstanding potential. You make the most of your organizational and leadership abilities by having a good plan of action. Being idealistic as well as ambitious, if your work can inspire or encourage people then so much the better. With your keen intellect, practical attitude, and inner faith, you can impress others and attain recognition.

Your Powers of Attraction in Relationships

As you are usually generous and kind, success with people is a foregone conclusion. Friendly and charismatic, you attract others with your passionate and understanding nature. Honest and frank, you like to speak your mind and be open about your feelings. Often popular and inspired by intelligence, you are drawn to individuals with strong awareness or powerful and determined character who mean business. Although usually sincere, avoid being stubborn with your partners or getting involved in power dramas. With your extreme sensitivity you can be kind and considerate, although an inner youthful quality can also suggest an immature streak. With your strong need for love, your relationships are particularly important to you. Talking about your feelings and especially your insecurities often clears the air and rectifies misunderstandings in your close relationships.

Your attractive qualities: creative, leadership, original, generous, constructive, tenacious, practical, proud, good conversationalist, ambitious, responsible, lucky, thoughtful, visionary, idealistic, independent, hardworking, spirit of enterprise, frank, fair, entertaining, sensitive

Your less attractive qualities: insecure, impatient, suspicious, opinionated, easily discouraged, restlessness, worry, lack of ambition, lazy, selfish, stubborn, moody, vain

Your Venus Power

The planet Venus has a great deal of influence on your powers of attraction. Below are four possible Venus types for women and men. To find your Venus you need to go to page 771, where you will find the Venus table and extra information. The planet Mars also affects your powers of attraction. To find your Mars table and interpretation go to page 761.

WOMEN WITH VENUS IN GEMINI: Curious, with a bright and animated approach to life, you are attracted to those who are clever and/or sophisticated. Your love of variety and desire for knowledge suggest that you need a partner and friends who keep you mentally stimulated. Although witty and a good conversationalist, you may need to keep in touch with your deeper feelings. Nevertheless, intelligent and friendly, you possess a youthful sense of wonder and seek a playmate who can keep you from becoming bored.

MEN WITH VENUS IN GEMINI: Friendly and sociable, you attract others with your clever and amusing conversation. Drawn to partners who can match you in wit and intelligence, you usually prefer to keep relationships light rather than emotionally intense. With your youthful charm and desire for knowledge and new experiences you usually have many friends and a low boredom threshold.

WOMEN WITH VENUS IN CANCER: Possessing a soft femininity, you have tender and sensitive emotions. Sympathetic and caring, you often mother those in your care by making sure they are comfortable and have plenty to eat. When you feel hurt or insecure in relationships, you are likely to cover your feelings by being defensive or appearing tough on the outside while on the inside you are feeling vulnerable. Affectionate and romantic, you make a faithful and devoted partner.

MEN WITH VENUS IN CANCER: Being emotionally receptive, you can make a sensitive lover. With your desire to care for and protect others, you are likely to have strong family connections. Love is often tied in with being attentive to the needs of others and you may find yourself attracted to individuals who have sympathetic or maternal qualities. Security-conscious, you need a loyal partner who can offer you support and ideally be a good cook and homemaker.

WOMEN WITH VENUS IN LEO: Your friendly and sunny personality often makes you stand out in a crowd. Generous and giving, you know how to make your partner feel special. As you often expect loyalty and devotion from your partner in return, you can become easily offended if they ignore you or behave in an inconsiderate manner. Charming and kind, when you are in love you can be romantic, dramatic, and passionate.

MEN WITH VENUS IN LEO: Generous, animated, and pleasure-seeking, you can be very entertaining and fun to be with. Usually you are attracted to extroverted and benevolent individuals with sunny personalities. If ambitious, you are drawn to a partner who shows leadership qualities or one who is highly motivated. Your less attractive qualities are your tendencies to be bossy or vain. With a sense of the dramatic, however, you can be the life and soul of the party and inspire those around you.

WOMEN WITH VENUS IN VIRGO: Articulate and straightforward in your relationships, you attract others with your genuine concern for their well-being. By being understanding and a good listener you are able to show your love and friendship. With your analytical approach to relationships, however, you may have to be careful of becoming too matter-of-fact. You often display your concern for the welfare of others by your willingness to offer practical help and assistance. You usually seek a partner who is willing to work as hard on relationships as you are.

MEN WITH VENUS IN VIRGO: Although you are constantly analyzing your relationships in order to understand and improve them, you may nevertheless need to refrain from continuously mulling over issues that can cause anxiety. You are happiest when you are able to help your loved ones in practical ways and forget yourself in your willingness to be of service to others. You seek a partner who has high standards and can be as pragmatic and hardworking as yourself. Ideally they should also be impeccably dressed with a fine analytical mind.

To read all about your Outer Planets and work out how to use your personalized timetable, go to Section Three, page 789.

Your Personalized Timetable

JUPITER BENEFICIAL
1939 5/9 – 11/5
1939 12/14 – until 1940 3/16
1941 6/6 – 7/22
1942 1/10 – 3/4
1945 9/6 – 10/23
1947 10/21 – until 1948 1/3
1951 4/19 – until 1952 2/27
1953 5/20 – 7/3
1957 8/20 – 10/7
1959 2/6 – 4/28
1959 10/3 – 12/17
1963 4/2 – 6/19
1963 9/30 – until 1964 2/5
1965 5/4 – 6/16
1968 12/2 – until 1969 3/10
1969 8/1 – 9/22
1971 1/11 – 6/8
1971 9/8 – 12/1
1975 3/16 – 5/25
1975 11/18 – until 1976 1/1
1977 4/16 – 5/30
1980 11/9 – until 1981 4/19
1981 7/5 – 9/5
1982 12/23 – until 1983 11/15
1987 2/28 – 5/7
1988 8/7 – 11/11
1989 3/26 – 5/14
1992 10/22 – 12/22
1993 3/7 – 8/18
1994 12/7 – until 1995 10/29
1999 2/11 – 4/19
2000 7/13 – 12/27
2001 2/22 – 4/26
2004 10/7 – 11/26
2005 4/14 – 7/26
2006 11/22 – until 2007 2/11
2007 5/31 – 10/9
2010 6/3 – 9/12
2011 1/20 – 4/2
2012 6/23 – Continues

SATURN BENEFICIAL
1938 1/7 – 6/5
1938 9/26 – until 1939 2/25
1942 5/28 – until 1943 5/11
1951 9/5 – 12/2
1952 3/20 – 8/25
1956 1/7 – 5/20
1956 10/5 – until 1957 11/28
1966 6/29 – 7/23
1967 2/28 – until 1968 4/6
1971 7/11 – 12/1
1972 3/29 – 6/20
1980 10/12 – until 1981 10/3
1985 11/13 – until 1987 1/2
1987 7/13 – 9/24
1996 4/3 – until 1997 5/14
1997 10/27 – until 1998 2/2
2001 5/11 – 8/4
2001 11/20 – until 2002 4/22
2009 11/25 – until 2010 3/5
2010 8/17 – 11/10
2011 4/21 – 8/3

URANUS BENEFICIAL
1942 6/29 – until 1945 5/23
1968 11/12 – until 1971 9/15
1981 1/28 – until 1985 10/24
2010 5/15 – Continues

NEPTUNE BENEFICIAL
1943 10/16 – until 1949 7/18
1969 12/21 – until 1978 9/1

PLUTO BENEFICIAL
1972 10/12 – until 1977 8/26
1995 1/2 – until 2002 10/14

JUPITER CHALLENGING
1938 1/1 – 2/25
1940 5/14 – 8/27

1940 9/12 – until 1941 3/23
1946 9/23 – 12/7
1949 4/9 – 7/1
1949 11/28 – until 1950 2/8
1952 4/27 – 7/11
1952 11/11 – until 1953 2/28
1958 1/9 – 3/25
1958 9/4 – 11/20
1961 3/12 – 8/16
1961 10/31 – until 1962 1/23
1964 4/10 – 6/18
1969 12/14 – until 1970 5/3
1970 8/12 – 11/5
1973 2/21 – until 1974 1/6
1976 3/24 – 5/31
1981 11/24 – until 1982 10/20
1985 2/4 – 5/5
1985 7/5 – 12/18
1987 8/9 – 8/29
1988 3/6 – 5/15
1993 11/8 – until 1994 10/3
1997 1/19 – 4/4
1997 8/20 – 11/24
1999 6/25 – 10/26
2000 2/12 – 4/28
2005 10/24 – until 2006 1/16
2006 4/22 – 9/14
2009 1/3 – 3/14
2011 6/2 – until 2012 4/11

SATURN CHALLENGING
1939 6/29 – 9/29
1940 3/16 – until 1941 4/19
1953 10/19 – until 1954 12/4
1955 6/12 – 8/24
1961 4/20 – 5/28
1961 12/30 – until 1963 2/18
1969 4/26 – until 1970 5/30
1982 11/25 – until 1983 5/13
1983 8/18 – until 1984 1/24
1984 3/27 – 10/12
1991 2/2 – until 1992 3/27
1992 8/1 – 12/24
1998 6/4 – 10/31
1999 2/24 – 7/17
1999 10/13 – Continues

URANUS CHALLENGING
1938 1/1 – until 1939 3/28
1974 10/4 – until 1978 10/21
1995 3/18 – until 2000 1/15

NEPTUNE CHALLENGING
1955 12/6 – until 1964 9/8
1997 3/24 – until 2005 12/17

PLUTO CHALLENGING
1983 10/25 – until 1990 9/9

JUPITER SPECIAL
1943 6/28 – 9/10
1954 11/1 – 12/2
1955 6/10 – 8/24
1966 9/24 – until 1967 1/19
1967 5/20 – 8/8
1978 9/3 – until 1979 3/7
1979 4/13 – 7/23
1990 8/16 – until 1991 7/6
2002 7/30 – 10/24
2003 1/14 – 6/18

SATURN SPECIAL
1946 7/30 – until 1947 8/30
1975 9/12 – until 1976 1/20
1976 5/31 – 10/20
1977 1/5 – 7/5
2005 7/13 – until 2006 8/13

URANUS SPECIAL
1955 8/16 – until 1959 7/22

PLUTO SPECIAL
1938 7/18 – until 1949 7/19

August 1

SUN: LEO • DECANATE: LEO/ SUN • DEGREE: 8°5–9°5 LEO • MODE: FIXED • ELEMENT: FIRE

Your Personal Powers

Proud and astute, with strong willpower and original ideas, you stand out from the crowd. As an independent thinker you gain power from your quick responses and creative approach to life. Your ruler, the Sun, grants you ambition, a kindhearted nature, and a sense of the dramatic. You possess natural leadership abilities and your keen intelligence stimulates you to constantly seek opportunities for success. In your desire to be honest and direct be careful not to lose some of your power by being too outspoken or verbally cutting. Being courageous, innovative, and action-oriented, however, you can be adventurous, pioneering, and good at standing up for the rights of others. Although usually detached, avoid losing your energy to unnecessary frustration, worry, or indecision about finances. You have the potential to achieve outstanding results once you are focused on a course of action. Your natural generosity and people skills can certainly help you in your climb up the ladder of success.

Your Powers of Attraction in Relationships

Others admire your strong individuality and creative ideas. Being sociable with the ability to turn on the charm, you can always attract relationships, but with them you can also experience a certain amount of worry or indecision. Along with your need to be independent is your desire to be loved. You generally do better with a partner who is both supportive and undemanding or one who is liberal and freedom-loving. Being creative, you can be particularly drawn to those who stimulate your imagination and sense of the dramatic. Alternatively, you may prefer a partner who shares your strong desire for material success. Determined and strong-willed, however, you may have to resist being overbearing or critical. Fortunately, you can also be fair and just, gaining the respect of others with your generosity and kindness.

Your attractive qualities: strong-willed, leadership potential, kind, progressive, creative, optimistic, strong convictions, organizational skills, courageous, humanitarian, competitive, direct, independent, enthusiastic, gregarious, enterprising, freedom fighter, generous

Your less attractive qualities: jealous, competitive, too proud, antagonistic, frustration, bossy, impatience, selfish, restlessness, self-centered, too outspoken, worry, extravagant, impatient, stubborn

Your Venus Power

The planet Venus has a great deal of influence on your powers of attraction. Below are four possible Venus types for women and men. To find your Venus you need to go to page 771, where you will find the Venus table and extra information. The planet Mars also affects your powers of attraction. To find your Mars table and interpretation go to page 761.

WOMEN WITH VENUS IN GEMINI: In relationships you need intellectual stimulation and usually prefer to keep things light. Certainly not boring, you love to talk and are at your best being witty and entertaining. Although your easygoing approach to relationships is very attractive, guard against losing touch with your deeper emotions. You prefer a partner who can keep up with your fast stream of ideas, and if you have shared interests then so much the better.

MEN WITH VENUS IN GEMINI: Informed and curious yet charming and friendly, you seek a partner who shares your interests or enjoys your witty remarks. Although a good communicator, you have an inborn tendency to be lighthearted and less profound about deep emotional commitment. Although you are keen on experiences that bring variety into your life, boredom or scattering your energies in too many directions is probably your biggest handicap in relationships. Nevertheless you are attracted to intelligent partners who can match your lively banter.

WOMEN WITH VENUS IN CANCER: Gentle and tender, you are romantic by nature. You possess a strong need for security and usually help others feel safe and protected. This preservation is especially centered in the home, which is your haven from life's storm. Although your maternal instincts are strong, avoid making sacrifices for others at your own expense. Nevertheless, affectionate and caring, once committed to a relationship, your loyalty and devotion to your partner are very strong.

MEN WITH VENUS IN CANCER: You seek a partner who is sympathetic, caring, and protective. Able to be forgiving and compassionate, you want a secure emotional bond in your close relationships. Usually you are drawn to partners who are maternal, unselfish, or demonstrative with their feelings. Al-

though you can sometimes appear to others as impressionable, you have powerful emotions and inner strength.

WOMEN WITH VENUS IN LEO: As a person who wants to radiate in their own right, you are likely to desire partners you can be proud of. You are usually attracted to fun-loving, warm, and generous individuals. If self-expression is important to you, you will probably seek the company of creative people such as artists, musicians, or those with a flair for acting. Alternatively, you may be drawn to people who are dignified, regal, or have already achieved success.

MEN WITH VENUS IN LEO: Generous, animated, and pleasure-seeking, you can be very entertaining and fun to be with. Usually you are attracted to extroverted and benevolent individuals with a sunny personality. If ambitious, you are drawn to a partner who shows leadership qualities or one who is highly motivated. Your less attractive qualities are your tendencies to be bossy or vain. With a sense of the dramatic, however, you can be the life and soul of the party and inspire those around you.

WOMEN WITH VENUS IN VIRGO: Intelligent and discriminative, you are usually drawn to polite and refined individuals. As a perfectionist, you may be keen to analyze and criticize yourself but be careful of continually going over your partner's shortcomings. By focusing on how you can make positive improvements in yourself and in your relationships, you avoid becoming skeptical or confused. You empower yourself when you display your kind and caring concern for the well-being of loved ones and spontaneously offer your practical assistance.

MEN WITH VENUS IN VIRGO: A love of order usually indicates that you are attracted to refined individuals with analytical or practical abilities. You and your partner may be working together or serving similar causes. As you constantly analyze partnerships in order to improve them, you are likely to use former relationships as a point of reference and compare them to your present partner. Because you are helpful and kind, others usually rely on your good judgment and often turn to you for advice or practical assistance.

To read all about your Outer Planets and work out how to use your personalized timetable, go to Section Three, page 789.

♌

Your Personalized Timetable

JUPITER BENEFICIAL
1939 5/14 – 10/24
1939 12/26 – until 1940 3/20
1941 6/10 – 7/27
1941 12/31 – until 1942 3/13
1945 9/11 – 10/27
1947 10/26 – until 1948 1/7
1951 4/23 – until 1952 3/2
1953 5/24 – 7/7
1957 8/25 – 10/12
1959 2/15 – 4/19
1959 10/8 – 12/21
1963 4/6 – 6/26
1963 9/22 – until 1964 2/10
1965 5/8 – 6/20
1968 12/10 – until 1969 3/2
1969 8/7 – 9/26
1971 1/17 – 5/31
1971 9/15 – 12/6
1975 3/20 – 5/30
1975 11/8 – until 1976 1/11
1977 4/20 – 6/3
1980 11/15 – until 1981 4/11
1981 7/13 – 9/10
1982 12/28 – until 1983 11/20
1987 3/4 – 5/11
1988 8/14 – 11/4
1989 4/1 – 5/18
1992 10/27 – until 1993 1/1
1993 2/25 – 8/23
1994 12/11 – until 1995 11/3
1999 2/15 – 4/23
2000 7/18 – 12/18
2001 3/4 – 5/1
2004 10/11 – 12/2
2005 4/7 – 8/2
2006 11/26 – until 2007 2/18
2007 5/24 – 10/15
2010 6/10 – 9/5
2011 1/25 – 4/6
2012 6/27 – Continues

SATURN BENEFICIAL
1938 1/20 – 6/18
1938 9/12 – until 1939 3/5
1942 6/5 – until 1943 5/19
1951 9/13 – 12/14
1952 3/6 – 9/3
1956 1/18 – 5/7
1956 10/15 – until 1957 12/6
1967 3/8 – until 1968 4/14
1971 7/21 – 11/20
1972 4/8 – 6/28
1980 10/20 – until 1981 5/11
1981 6/29 – 10/11
1985 11/21 – until 1987 1/11
1987 6/28 – 10/8
1996 4/11 – until 1997 5/23
1997 10/15 – until 1998 2/13
2001 5/18 – 8/17
2001 11/7 – until 2002 5/1
2009 12/8 – until 2010 2/19
2010 8/26 – 11/19
2011 4/8 – 8/15

URANUS BENEFICIAL
1942 7/20 – until 1946 3/7
1968 12/6 – until 1971 9/30
1981 11/24 – until 1985 11/11
2010 6/21 – Continues

NEPTUNE BENEFICIAL
1943 11/15 – until 1949 8/29
1970 1/25 – until 1978 10/27

PLUTO BENEFICIAL
1972 11/9 – until 1977 9/22
1995 2/14 – until 2002 11/14

JUPITER CHALLENGING
1938 1/1 – 3/1
1940 5/18 – until 1941 3/28
1946 9/27 – 12/11
1949 4/17 – 6/22

1949 12/3 – until 1950 2/12
1952 5/1 – 7/17
1952 11/4 – until 1953 3/6
1958 1/19 – 3/14
1958 9/10 – 11/25
1961 3/18 – 8/8
1961 11/8 – until 1962 1/27
1964 4/14 – 6/23
1964 12/26 – until 1965 1/25
1969 12/19 – until 1970 4/26
1970 8/19 – 11/9
1973 2/25 – until 1974 1/10
1976 3/28 – 6/4
1981 11/29 – until 1982 6/21
1982 7/3 – 10/24
1985 2/8 – 5/19
1985 6/21 – 12/23
1988 3/11 – 5/19
1993 11/12 – until 1994 10/8
1997 1/23 – 4/9
1997 8/13 – 11/30
1999 7/1 – 10/19
2000 2/17 – 5/2
2005 10/28 – until 2006 1/24
2006 4/13 – 9/20
2009 1/7 – 3/18
2011 6/7 – 12/17
2012 1/3 – 4/15

SATURN CHALLENGING
1939 7/15 – 9/12
1940 3/24 – until 1941 4/27
1953 10/26 – until 1954 12/13
1955 5/28 – 9/8
1962 1/8 – until 1963 2/26
1963 10/13 – 10/30
1969 5/4 – until 1970 6/7
1970 12/18 – until 1971 2/16
1982 12/4 – until 1983 4/29
1983 8/30 – until 1984 10/20
1991 2/11 – 9/15
1991 10/24 – until 1992 4/8
1992 7/19 – until 1993 1/2
1998 6/14 – 10/19
1999 3/6 – 8/2
1999 9/26 – until 2000 4/9
2012 10/10 – Continues

URANUS CHALLENGING
1938 1/1 – until 1939 4/16
1974 11/30 – until 1978 11/6
1996 1/21 – until 2000 2/1

NEPTUNE CHALLENGING
1956 11/2 – until 1964 10/11
1998 2/12 – until 2006 1/16

PLUTO CHALLENGING
1983 11/19 – until 1990 10/10

JUPITER SPECIAL
1943 7/3 – 9/15
1955 6/15 – 8/29
1966 10/1 – until 1967 1/12
1967 5/26 – 8/13
1978 9/8 – until 1979 2/23
1979 4/26 – 7/28
1990 8/20 – until 1991 7/11
2002 8/4 – 11/2
2003 1/5 – 6/23

SATURN SPECIAL
1946 8/6 – until 1947 9/7
1948 3/19 – 5/16
1975 9/22 – until 1976 1/8
1976 6/10 – 11/8
1976 12/17 – until 1977 7/13
2005 7/20 – until 2006 8/20

URANUS SPECIAL
1955 9/3 – until 1959 8/7

PLUTO SPECIAL
1938 8/23 – until 1950 6/25

279

August 2

Your Personal Powers

Sociable, sensitive, and intellectually bright, you are a receptive and astute individual with strong determination. Your ruler, the Sun, bestows you with pride, strong individuality, and a creative approach to life. Highly spirited, you love freedom and are an interesting blend of materialism and idealism. Your confidence is often increased through higher learning, gaining information, or perfecting your skills. Friendly, charismatic, and group aware, you gain power from your ability to mix with people from all walks of life. Although you usually appear confident, if you become insecure you may lose some of your power to worry, occasional moods, or escapism. When you are able to positively express yourself, however, you can be enthusiastic, original, and ahead of your time with creative talents. Ambitious and determined, you also possess a practical side to your nature that learns quickly and has a strong desire for material gains. By adding responsibility to your spontaneous, youthful, and entertaining personality, you have the potential to achieve outstanding success.

Your Powers of Attraction in Relationships

Being dramatic and very sociable, you can attract others with your entertaining ways. Considerate, courteous, and diplomatic, you can particularly enjoy and gain from cooperative activities where you can interact with others. You need a down-to-earth partner who can be practical, supportive, direct, and honest. Although you need a certain amount of freedom, as you are very sensitive to others, your relationships can be an especially important part of your life. As you may sometimes vacillate between being overconfident and insecure, avoid becoming codependent on your partner. An immature streak can also stop you from making long-term commitments. Nonetheless, being affectionate and responsive suggests that you can also be warm and romantic. With your personal magnetism, creativity, and witty personality you should have no trouble in attracting admirers.

Your attractive qualities: social skills, warm, friendly, ambitious, good partnerships, gentle, tactful, receptive, individuality, intuitive, spontaneous, charismatic, intelligent, playful, charming, determined, considerate, harmonious, youthful, diplomatic, optimistic, entertaining

Your less attractive qualities: moody, over- or under-confident, too dependent, too sensitive, perfectionist, critical, selfish, materialistic, immature, easily hurt, temperamental, escapist, worry, confusion

Your Venus Power

The planet Venus has a great deal of influence on your powers of attraction. Below are four possible Venus types for women and men. To find your Venus you need to go to page 771, where you will find the Venus table and extra information. The planet Mars also affects your powers of attraction. To find your Mars table and interpretation go to page 761.

WOMEN WITH VENUS IN GEMINI: By nature you are young at heart, adaptable, and sociable. Being curious and willing to cooperate makes you a good team player. Usually you are drawn to articulate people who have charm and flair or sharp wit. With a need to expand your knowledge, you also look for a partner who can challenge or stimulate you intellectually. Although you love to talk with all types of people, you may need to develop your listening skills in order to build better communication in your relationships.

MEN WITH VENUS IN GEMINI: Charming, amusing, and adaptable, you attract others with your natural communication skills and friendly personality. You have a wonderful childlike quality and love to keep life playful, but a reluctance to contact your deeper feelings may cause you to avoid serious commitment. With your need for variety and intellectual stimulation, you are attracted to clever and amusing partners who have many interesting sides to their personalities.

WOMEN WITH VENUS IN CANCER: Possessing a soft femininity, you have tender and sensitive emotions. Sympathetic and caring, you often mother those in your care by making sure they are comfortable and have plenty to eat. When you feel hurt or insecure in relationships, you are likely to cover your feelings by being defensive or appearing tough on the outside while on the inside you are feeling vulnerable. Affectionate and romantic, you make a faithful and devoted partner.

MEN WITH VENUS IN CANCER: Being emotionally receptive, you can make a sensitive lover. With your desire to care for and protect others, you are likely to have strong family connections. Love is often tied in with being attentive to the needs of others and you may find yourself attracted to individuals who have sympathetic or maternal qualities. Security-

conscious, you need a loyal partner who can offer you support and ideally be a good cook and homemaker.

WOMEN WITH VENUS IN LEO: Warm and playful with a touch of the dramatic, you enjoy the company of generous or strong individuals who can share your sense of fun. Although there are advantages to your being strong-willed, in your relationships you need to resist being bossy as it can cause resentment. With your wonderful mixture of regal authority and childlike wonder, you love to keep others entertained and amused.

MEN WITH VENUS IN LEO: Sociable and outgoing, you are kind and generous with those you love. Looking for a relationship that can be fun and entertaining, you need a playmate who can share your enthusiasm and high spirits. Your pride, however, often stops you from associating with lovers or partners you see as beneath you. As you desire someone who can appreciate your sense of the dramatic, you are often attracted to people with strong personalities.

WOMEN WITH VENUS IN VIRGO: In relationships you can be modest and unassuming but desire perfection. You usually analyze your partnerships until you feel you have understood them to the last little detail in order to improve them. A problem usually arises when you become too critical either of partners or yourself and indulge in being skeptical or fault-finding. Because you are modest, others may not be aware of the strong sensuality beneath your well-groomed exterior.

MEN WITH VENUS IN VIRGO: Industrious and well-ordered, you relate to others in a considerate and down-to-earth way. You enjoy giving practical advice and being of service to those you love even in small ways. Being a perfectionist you are drawn to partners with high morals or a strong work ethic. Partners who have strong analytical minds are very attractive to you, particularly if they are also clean and meticulously dressed.

To read all about your Outer Planets and work out how to use your personalized timetable, go to Section Three, page 789.

♌

Your Personalized Timetable

JUPITER BENEFICIAL
1939   5/19 – 10/15
1940   1/3 – 3/24
1941   6/14 – 8/1
1941   12/23 – until **1942** 3/21
1945   9/15 – 11/1
1947   10/31 – until **1948** 1/12
1951   4/28 – until **1952** 3/6
1953   5/28 – 7/11
1957   8/30 – 10/16
1959   2/28 – 4/6
1959   10/13 – 12/26
1963   4/10 – 7/5
1963   9/14 – until **1964** 2/16
1965   5/12 – 6/24
1968   12/19 – until **1969** 2/21
1969   8/12 – 9/30
1971   1/23 – 5/24
1971   9/21 – 12/10
1975   3/24 – 6/4
1975   10/30 – until **1976** 1/20
1977   4/25 – 6/7
1980   11/21 – until **1981** 4/3
1981   7/20 – 9/14
1983   1/2 – 7/13
1983   8/14 – 11/24
1987   3/8 – 5/15
1988   8/23 – 10/26
1989   4/6 – 5/22
1992   11/1 – until **1993** 1/17
1993   2/9 – 8/28
1994   12/16 – until **1995** 11/8
1999   2/19 – 4/28
2000   7/23 – 12/10
2001   3/11 – 5/5
2004   10/16 – 12/9
2005   3/30 – 8/8
2006   11/30 – until **2007** 2/25
2007   5/15 – 10/20
2010   6/18 – 8/27
2011   1/30 – 4/10
2012   7/2 – 8/31
2012   11/7 – Continues

SATURN BENEFICIAL
1938   1/31 – 7/4
1938   8/26 – until **1939** 3/14
1942   6/12 – until **1943** 5/26
1951   9/21 – 12/31
1952   2/17 – 9/12
1956   1/31 – 4/22
1956   10/24 – until **1957** 12/15
1967   3/15 – until **1968** 4/21
1971   8/1 – 11/7
1972   4/17 – 7/6
1973   1/14 – 3/15
1980   10/28 – until **1981** 4/23
1981   7/17 – 10/19
1985   11/29 – until **1987** 1/20
1987   6/14 – 10/20
1996   4/19 – 11/2
1997   1/3 – 6/2
1997   10/3 – until **1998** 2/23
2001   5/26 – 9/3
2001   10/20 – until **2002** 5/9
2009   12/30 – until **2010** 1/27
2010   9/4 – 11/29
2011   3/27 – 8/25

URANUS BENEFICIAL
1942   8/24 – until **1946** 4/11
1969   9/28 – until **1972** 7/16
1981   12/10 – until **1985** 11/28
2011   4/6 – Continues

NEPTUNE BENEFICIAL
1944   10/10 – until **1949** 9/26
1970   12/16 – until **1978** 11/25

PLUTO BENEFICIAL
1973   10/2 – until **1978** 8/8
1995   12/18 – until **2003** 9/27

JUPITER CHALLENGING
1938   1/1 – 3/5

1940   5/22 – until **1941** 4/2
1946   10/2 – 12/16
1949   4/29 – 6/10
1949   12/8 – until **1950** 2/16
1952   5/5 – 7/24
1952   10/27 – until **1953** 3/11
1958   2/4 – 2/26
1958   9/15 – 11/29
1961   3/23 – 7/31
1961   11/14 – until **1962** 1/31
1964   4/18 – 6/28
1964   12/13 – until **1965** 2/7
1969   12/26 – until **1970** 4/18
1970   8/25 – 11/13
1973   3/2 – until **1974** 1/14
1976   4/1 – 6/8
1981   12/4 – until **1982** 6/1
1982   7/24 – 10/29
1985   2/13 – 12/28
1988   3/15 – 5/23
1993   11/17 – until **1994** 10/12
1997   1/27 – 4/15
1997   8/6 – 12/6
1999   7/8 – 10/12
2000   2/23 – 5/6
2005   11/1 – until **2006** 2/2
2006   4/4 – 9/25
2009   1/11 – 3/23
2009   9/29 – 10/26
2011   6/11 – 11/30
2012   1/20 – 4/19

SATURN CHALLENGING
1940   4/1 – until **1941** 5/4
1953   11/3 – until **1954** 12/22
1955   5/14 – 9/19
1962   1/16 – until **1963** 3/6
1963   9/16 – 11/25
1969   5/11 – until **1970** 6/15
1970   12/3 – until **1971** 3/2
1982   12/14 – until **1983** 4/17
1983   9/10 – until **1984** 10/28
1991   2/19 – 8/25
1991   11/13 – until **1992** 4/23
1992   7/3 – until **1993** 1/11
1998   6/25 – 10/7
1999   3/15 – until **2000** 4/17
2012   10/18 – Continues

URANUS CHALLENGING
1938   1/1 – until **1939** 5/3
1974   12/20 – until **1979** 8/31
1996   2/6 – until **2000** 12/2

NEPTUNE CHALLENGING
1956   11/29 – until **1965** 8/28
1998   3/14 – until **2006** 12/7

PLUTO CHALLENGING
1983   12/18 – until **1990** 11/4

JUPITER SPECIAL
1943   7/7 – 9/20
1944   3/27 – 4/29
1955   6/20 – 9/2
1966   10/8 – until **1967** 1/4
1967   6/1 – 8/17
1978   9/13 – until **1979** 2/13
1979   5/5 – 8/1
1990   8/25 – until **1991** 7/16
2002   8/8 – 11/14
2002   12/24 – until **2003** 6/28

SATURN SPECIAL
1946   8/14 – until **1947** 9/15
1948   3/3 – 5/31
1975   10/5 – 12/26
1976   6/18 – until **1977** 7/21
2005   7/27 – until **2006** 8/28

URANUS SPECIAL
1955   9/25 – until **1960** 5/29

PLUTO SPECIAL
1938   10/19 – until **1951** 5/14

August 3

Your Personal Powers

Personal charm, enthusiasm, and a friendly manner are just some of the qualities listed among your personal powers. Ambitious and smart with good communication skills, you can quickly evaluate people and situations. Versatile with an ability to think big, you gain power by combining your adventurous nature with your inborn business acumen, but you must also be aware that money does not necessarily buy happiness. Usually optimistic and creative, you possess a strong need to achieve success. You may lose some of your power, however, if you become overly confident or follow unrealistic or poorly thought out plans. Although your optimism and bright intellect often keep you positive, be careful that inner dissatisfaction does not bring out a rebellious streak hidden within you. Nevertheless, you possess innate organizational abilities and the capacity to shine in leadership positions. Inventive and persuasive with a generous and fun-loving nature, you are usually able to use your popularity and personal charisma to help promote your personal success.

Your Powers of Attraction in Relationships

Optimistic and sociable, you can charm others and gain their affections. With your easygoing manner and good sense of humor, you are able to utilize your people skills both in your personal and work life. You have an enormous amount of love to give as long as you do not become too self-absorbed. You enjoy being the center of attention but you usually work hard to keep others entertained. A tendency to be indecisive or worried can undermine your confidence at handling people. Nevertheless, you can be a generous partner who enjoys love and romance. Your need for emotional self-expression can lead you to explore many different kinds of relationship before you finally settle down. If you are spiritually aware, you can be a channel of inspiration for others.

Your attractive qualities: friendly, courageous, multi-talented, productive, creative, inspired, business acumen, insightful, leadership ability, humorous, organizational skills, inventive, happy, freedom-loving, shrewd judge of character, expressive, lucky, a talent with words

Your less attractive qualities: vain, exaggerates, easily bored, worry, boastful, takes the easy way out, lazy, insecure, selfish, indecisive, extravagant, rebellious, self-indulgent

Your Venus Power

The planet Venus has a great deal of influence on your powers of attraction. Below are four possible Venus types for women and men. To find your Venus you need to go to page 771, where you will find the Venus table and extra information. The planet Mars also affects your powers of attraction. To find your Mars table and interpretation go to page 761.

WOMEN WITH VENUS IN GEMINI: In relationships you need intellectual stimulation and usually prefer to keep things light. Certainly not boring, you love to talk and are at your best being witty and entertaining. Although your easygoing approach to relationships is very attractive, guard against losing touch with your deeper emotions. You prefer a partner who can keep up with your fast stream of ideas, and if you have shared interests then so much the better.

MEN WITH VENUS IN GEMINI: Adaptable yet often flirtatious, you enjoy mixing with people who are quick-minded and versatile. Since you can learn a great deal through interacting with others, you are often attracted to intelligent partners who have comprehensive knowledge or good ideas. One of your less attractive qualities is your tendency to get bored or be inconsistent. Having an adaptable partner is important to you; therefore it must be someone who can offer you different options and keep you interested.

WOMEN WITH VENUS IN CANCER: Possessing a soft femininity, you have tender and sensitive emotions. Sympathetic and caring, you often mother those in your care by making sure they are comfortable and have plenty to eat. When you feel hurt or insecure in relationships you are likely to cover your feelings by being defensive or appearing tough on the outside while on the inside you are feeling vulnerable. Affectionate and romantic, you make a faithful and devoted partner.

MEN WITH VENUS IN CANCER: You seek a partner who is sympathetic, caring, and protective. Able to be forgiving and compassionate, you want a secure emotional bond in your close relationships. Usually you are drawn to partners who are maternal, unselfish, or demonstrative with their feelings. Although you can sometimes appear to others as impressionable, you have powerful emotions and inner strength.

WOMEN WITH VENUS IN LEO: Warm and playful with a touch of the dramatic, you enjoy the company of generous or strong individuals who can share your sense of fun. Although there are advantages to your being strong-willed, in your rela-

tionships you need to resist being bossy as it can cause resentment. With your wonderful mixture of regal authority and childlike wonder, you love to keep others entertained and amused.

MEN WITH VENUS IN LEO: Generous, animated, and pleasure-seeking, you can be very entertaining and fun to be with. You are usually attracted to extroverted and benevolent individuals with sunny personalities. If ambitious, you are drawn to a partner who shows leadership qualities or one who is highly motivated. Your less attractive qualities are your tendencies to be bossy or vain. With a sense of the dramatic, however, you can be the life and soul of the party and inspire those around you.

WOMEN WITH VENUS IN VIRGO: You are articulate and straightforward in your relationships, and others are attracted by your genuine concern for their well-being. By being understanding and a good listener you are able to show your love and friendship. With your analytical approach to relationships, however, you may have to be careful of becoming too matter-of-fact. You often display your concern for the welfare of others by your willingness to offer practical help and assistance. You usually seek a partner who is willing to work as hard on relationships as you are.

MEN WITH VENUS IN VIRGO: Although you are constantly analyzing your relationships in order to understand and improve them, you may nevertheless need to refrain from continuously mulling over issues that can cause anxiety. You are happiest when you are able to help your loved ones in practical ways and forget yourself in your willingness to be of service to others. You seek a partner who has high standards and can be as pragmatic and hardworking as yourself. Ideally they should also be impeccably dressed with a fine analytical mind.

To read all about your Outer Planets and work out how to use your personalized timetable, go to Section Three, page 789.

Your Personalized Timetable

JUPITER BENEFICIAL
1939 5/24 – 10/8
1940 1/10 – 3/28
1941 6/19 – 8/7
1941 12/15 – until 1942 3/28
1945 9/20 – 11/6
1947 11/4 – until 1948 1/16
1951 5/2 – until 1952 3/11
1953 6/1 – 7/16
1957 9/4 – 10/20
1959 10/18 – 12/30
1963 4/14 – 7/15
1963 9/4 – until 1964 2/20
1965 5/16 – 6/28
1968 12/31 – until 1969 2/9
1969 8/17 – 10/5
1971 1/29 – 5/16
1971 9/28 – 12/14
1975 3/28 – 6/10
1975 10/22 – until 1976 1/27
1977 4/29 – 6/12
1980 11/27 – until 1981 3/26
1981 7/27 – 9/19
1983 1/7 – 6/29
1983 8/28 – 11/28
1987 3/12 – 5/20
1988 9/4 – 10/14
1989 4/11 – 5/27
1992 11/6 – until 1993 5/11
1993 6/22 – 9/2
1994 12/20 – until 1995 11/12
1999 2/23 – 5/2
2000 7/28 – 12/3
2001 3/18 – 5/9
2004 10/20 – 12/15
2005 3/23 – 8/14
2006 12/5 – until 2007 3/7
2007 5/5 – 10/25
2010 6/28 – 8/17
2011 2/4 – 4/14
2012 7/6 – 9/10
2012 10/28 – Continues

SATURN BENEFICIAL
1938 2/10 – until 1939 3/22
1942 6/20 – until 1943 6/3
1951 9/29 – until 1952 9/20
1956 2/19 – 4/2
1956 11/2 – until 1957 12/23
1967 3/23 – until 1968 4/29
1971 8/14 – 10/24
1972 4/25 – 7/14
1972 12/30 – until 1973 3/30
1980 11/6 – until 1981 4/9
1981 7/30 – 10/27
1985 12/7 – until 1987 1/31
1987 6/1 – 10/30
1996 4/28 – 10/17
1997 1/18 – 6/14
1997 9/20 – until 1998 3/4
2001 6/2 – until 2002 5/16
2010 9/12 – 12/11
2011 3/14 – 9/3

URANUS BENEFICIAL
1943 6/9 – until 1946 5/2
1969 10/14 – until 1972 8/14
1981 12/27 – until 1986 9/9
2011 4/24 – Continues

NEPTUNE BENEFICIAL
1944 11/7 – until 1950 8/22
1971 1/16 – until 1979 10/20

PLUTO BENEFICIAL
1973 10/28 – until 1978 9/9
1996 1/16 – until 2003 11/5

JUPITER CHALLENGING
1940 5/27 – until 1941 4/6
1946 10/7 – 12/21
1947 6/23 – 8/7

1949 12/13 – until 1950 2/20
1952 5/9 – 7/31
1952 10/20 – until 1953 3/16
1958 9/20 – 12/4
1961 3/29 – 7/24
1961 11/21 – until 1962 2/4
1964 4/22 – 7/3
1964 12/3 – until 1965 2/17
1970 1/1 – 4/11
1970 8/31 – 11/18
1973 3/7 – 9/19
1973 10/7 – until 1974 1/18
1976 4/5 – 6/13
1981 12/9 – until 1982 5/21
1982 8/4 – 11/2
1985 2/17 – until 1986 1/1
1988 3/19 – 5/27
1993 11/22 – until 1994 10/17
1997 2/1 – 4/22
1997 7/29 – 12/12
1999 7/15 – 10/4
2000 2/28 – 5/10
2005 11/6 – until 2006 2/16
2006 3/21 – 9/30
2009 1/16 – 3/28
2009 9/15 – 11/9
2011 6/16 – 11/20
2012 1/30 – 4/23

SATURN CHALLENGING
1940 4/9 – until 1941 5/12
1953 11/11 – until 1955 1/2
1955 5/1 – 9/30
1962 1/24 – until 1963 3/15
1963 8/31 – 12/9
1969 5/19 – 12/14
1970 1/23 – 6/24
1970 11/20 – until 1971 3/14
1982 12/25 – until 1983 4/4
1983 9/19 – until 1984 11/5
1991 2/28 – 8/10
1991 11/26 – until 1992 5/19
1992 6/5 – until 1993 1/19
1998 7/9 – 9/22
1999 3/23 – until 2000 4/25

URANUS CHALLENGING
1938 1/1 – until 1940 2/27
1975 1/27 – until 1979 9/24
1996 2/23 – until 2000 12/27

NEPTUNE CHALLENGING
1957 1/9 – until 1965 10/6
1999 2/6 – until 2007 1/10

PLUTO CHALLENGING
1984 11/3 – until 1991 9/23

JUPITER SPECIAL
1943 7/12 – 9/25
1944 3/14 – 5/13
1955 6/25 – 9/7
1966 10/16 – 12/27
1967 6/6 – 8/22
1978 9/18 – until 1979 2/5
1979 5/13 – 8/6
1990 8/30 – until 1991 7/20
2002 8/12 – until 2003 7/3

SATURN SPECIAL
1946 8/22 – until 1947 3/11
1947 4/26 – 9/24
1948 2/19 – 6/12
1975 10/21 – 12/9
1976 6/26 – until 1977 7/28
2005 8/4 – until 2006 9/4
2007 4/2 – 5/7

URANUS SPECIAL
1956 7/22 – until 1960 6/22

PLUTO SPECIAL
1939 9/17 – until 1951 7/7

♌

283

August 4

SUN: LEO · DECANATE: SAGITTARIUS/JUPITER · DEGREE: 11°–12°5 LEO · MODE: FIXED · ELEMENT: FIRE

Your Personal Powers

Intelligent and thoughtful, with good reasoning powers, you are a broad-minded individual with an honest and direct approach. You gain power by combining your psychological insight with your practical common sense. Your ruler, the Sun, grants you personal pride and a magnanimous attitude toward others, although you may sometimes have to avoid being bossy. Usually generous with your time and energy, you can project a friendly and optimistic personality, but you may lose some of your power if you allow disappointment and frustration to dissipate your outstanding potential. Independent with natural leadership abilities, you usually prefer to give the orders or be allowed to work in your own individual way. You can also gain power from your unusual and detached perspective that can often see the humor in difficult situations. Although you are security-conscious, do not permit worries or uncertainties about money to undermine your positivity. A good planner and visionary with original and creative ideas, you have the potential to attract success and inspire others.

Your Powers of Attraction in Relationships

Friendly and cheerful, you can attract others with your clever comments and dry wit. Honest and direct, you have good conversational and social skills and the ability to quickly evaluate people. You are attracted to those who can match your quick mental responses. Conscientious and dependable, you like to be of practical help to others. In relationships you are usually security-conscious and take your responsibilities seriously. Often you prefer the more traditional approach. Although rational and detached, you also possess imagination and sensitivity but worry may repress some of your feelings. If you learn to talk about your fears and emotions rather than keeping them hidden, you can keep a fractious element from creeping into your relationships. Nevertheless, you are a loving and loyal partner and a devoted parent.

Your attractive qualities: honest, intelligent, common sense, good psychologist, humorous, organized, disciplined, hardworking, friendly, craftsman, courage, detachment, kind, persistence, practical, trusting, determined, humanitarian, creative, kind, leader, generous

Your less attractive qualities: bossy, stubborn, uncommunicative, repressed, lazy, unfeeling, rash, too strict, procrastination, financial instability or worry, pessimism, frustration

Your Venus Power

The planet Venus has a great deal of influence on your powers of attraction. Below are four possible Venus types for women and men. To find your Venus you need to go to page 771, where you will find the Venus table and extra information. The planet Mars also affects your powers of attraction. To find your Mars table and interpretation go to page 761.

WOMEN WITH VENUS IN GEMINI: In relationships you need intellectual stimulation and usually prefer to keep things light. Certainly not boring, you love to talk and are at your best being witty and entertaining. Although your easygoing approach to relationships is very attractive, guard against losing touch with your emotions. You prefer a partner who can keep up with your fast stream of ideas, and if you have shared interests then so much the better.

MEN WITH VENUS IN GEMINI: Informed and curious yet charming and friendly, you seek a partner who shares your interests or enjoys your witty remarks. Although a good communicator, you have an inborn tendency to be lighthearted and less profound about deep emotional commitment. Although you are keen on experiences that bring variety into your life, boredom or scattering your energies in too many directions is probably your biggest handicap in relationships. Nevertheless, you are attracted to intelligent partners who can match your lively banter.

WOMEN WITH VENUS IN CANCER: Good-natured and romantic, you have a highly developed sense of touch that particularly responds to massage, hugs, and all things physical. Being friendly, you enjoy socializing and are able to put others at their ease. With your natural sense of beauty and harmony your natural charm can attract others. Although you can be lavish toward your partner you may have to be careful that you do not overdo things.

MEN WITH VENUS IN CANCER: Being emotionally receptive, you can make a sensitive lover. With your desire to care for and protect others, you are likely to have strong family connections. Love is often tied in with being attentive to the needs of others and you may find yourself attracted to individuals who have sympathetic or maternal qualities. Security

conscious, you need a loyal partner who can offer you support and ideally be a good cook and homemaker.

WOMEN WITH VENUS IN LEO: As a person who wants to radiate in her own right, you are likely to desire partners you can be proud of. Usually you are attracted to fun-loving, warm, and generous individuals. If self-expression is important to you, you will probably seek the company of creative people such as artists, musicians, or those with a flair for acting. Alternatively, you may be drawn to people who are dignified, regal, or have already achieved success.

MEN WITH VENUS IN LEO: A childlike nature suggests that you are versatile and keen on games or being entertained. You are usually attracted to vivacious partners with a benevolent nature. As an extrovert, you enjoy being involved in all types of activities where you can assert yourself and show your talents and abilities. Others may recognize your inborn tendencies to lead but are also aware of your vanity or pride. Nevertheless, generous and caring, you often show more compassion to those less fortunate than yourself.

WOMEN WITH VENUS IN VIRGO: Polite, refined, and organized, you are attracted to articulate and intelligent people. Since you are caring, concerned, and want to be of practical help to others, you can be an asset to any partnership. By being too analytical, exacting, or faultfinding, however, a doubting element can creep into your relationships. By expressing your feelings in a positive way you can become more decisive and improve on how you relate to loved ones.

MEN WITH VENUS IN VIRGO: Industrious and well-ordered, you relate to others in a considerate and down-to-earth way. You enjoy giving practical advice and being of service to those you love even in small ways. Being a perfectionist you are drawn to partners with high morals or a strong work ethic. Partners who have strong analytical minds are very attractive to you, particularly if they are also clean and meticulously dressed.

To read all about your Outer Planets and work out how to use your personalized timetable, go to Section Three, page 789.

go to Section Three, page 789.

♌

Your Personalized Timetable

JUPITER BENEFICIAL
1939 5/30 – 9/30
1940 1/17 – 4/1
1941 6/23 – 8/13
1941 12/8 – until 1942 4/3
1945 9/24 – 11/10
1947 11/9 – until 1948 1/21
1948 8/2 – 8/29
1951 5/7 – until 1952 3/15
1953 6/5 – 7/21
1957 9/8 – 10/25
1959 10/23 – until 1960 1/4
1963 4/18 – 8/2
1963 8/16 – until 1964 2/25
1965 5/20 – 7/3
1969 8/22 – 10/9
1971 2/5 – 5/8
1971 10/3 – 12/18
1975 4/1 – 6/16
1975 10/15 – until 1976 2/2
1977 5/3 – 6/16
1980 12/3 – until 1981 3/19
1981 8/2 – 9/23
1983 1/12 – 6/19
1983 9/7 – 12/3
1987 3/16 – 5/25
1989 4/16 – 5/31
1992 11/11 – until 1993 4/28
1993 7/4 – 9/7
1994 12/25 – until 1995 11/17
1999 2/28 – 5/6
2000 8/3 – 11/26
2001 3/24 – 5/14
2004 10/25 – 12/23
2005 3/15 – 8/20
2006 12/9 – until 2007 3/21
2007 4/21 – 10/30
2010 7/20 – 7/23
2011 2/9 – 4/18
2012 7/11 – Continues

SATURN BENEFICIAL
1938 2/19 – until 1939 3/29
1942 6/28 – until 1943 1/8
1943 3/7 – 6/10
1951 10/6 – until 1952 9/28
1956 11/10 – until 1957 12/31
1958 8/5 – 9/11
1967 3/31 – until 1968 5/7
1968 11/23 – until 1969 1/17
1971 9/6 – 10/1
1972 5/3 – 7/23
1972 12/17 – until 1973 4/10
1980 11/15 – until 1981 3/27
1981 8/10 – 11/4
1982 5/16 – 7/21
1985 12/15 – until 1986 7/18
1986 8/27 – until 1987 2/12
1987 5/19 – 11/9
1996 5/7 – 10/4
1997 1/29 – 6/28
1997 9/5 – until 1998 3/12
2001 6/10 – until 2002 5/24
2010 9/19 – 12/26
2011 2/26 – 9/11

URANUS BENEFICIAL
1943 6/26 – until 1946 5/19
1969 10/30 – until 1972 9/3
1982 1/15 – until 1986 10/16
2011 5/15 – Continues

NEPTUNE BENEFICIAL
1944 12/25 – until 1950 9/21
1971 12/11 – until 1979 11/20

PLUTO BENEFICIAL
1973 11/30 – until 1978 10/4
1996 12/4 – until 2003 12/2

JUPITER CHALLENGING
1938 1/4 – 3/14
1940 5/31 – until 1941 4/10

1946 10/11 – 12/26
1947 6/12 – 8/18
1949 12/17 – until 1950 2/24
1952 5/13 – 8/9
1952 10/11 – until 1953 3/21
1958 9/25 – 12/8
1961 4/5 – 7/16
1961 11/26 – until 1962 2/8
1964 4/26 – 7/8
1964 11/25 – until 1965 2/24
1970 1/9 – 4/2
1970 9/6 – 11/22
1973 3/12 – 9/2
1973 10/24 – until 1974 1/22
1976 4/9 – 6/17
1981 12/15 – until 1982 5/12
1982 8/12 – 11/6
1985 2/21 – until 1986 1/6
1988 3/24 – 5/31
1993 11/26 – until 1994 10/22
1997 2/5 – 4/30
1997 7/21 – 12/17
1999 7/24 – 9/25
2000 3/4 – 5/14
2005 11/10 – until 2006 10/5
2009 1/20 – 4/2
2009 9/5 – 11/19
2011 6/22 – 11/12
2012 2/6 – 4/27

SATURN CHALLENGING
1940 4/16 – until 1941 5/19
1953 11/20 – until 1954 6/6
1954 8/5 – until 1955 1/13
1955 4/18 – 10/9
1962 2/1 – until 1963 3/25
1963 8/18 – 12/21
1969 5/27 – 11/25
1970 2/11 – 7/3
1970 11/8 – until 1971 3/24
1983 1/8 – 3/20
1983 9/28 – until 1984 11/13
1991 3/10 – 7/28
1991 12/7 – until 1993 1/27
1998 7/30 – 9/1
1999 3/31 – until 2000 5/2

URANUS CHALLENGING
1938 1/1 – until 1940 3/25
1975 11/4 – until 1979 10/13
1996 3/15 – until 2001 1/15

NEPTUNE CHALLENGING
1957 11/23 – until 1965 11/2
1999 3/6 – until 2007 11/22

PLUTO CHALLENGING
1984 11/28 – until 1991 10/21

JUPITER SPECIAL
1943 7/16 – 9/30
1944 3/4 – 5/23
1955 6/29 – 9/11
1966 10/26 – 12/17
1967 6/11 – 8/26
1978 9/24 – until 1979 1/29
1979 5/20 – 8/10
1990 9/3 – until 1991 7/25
2002 8/17 – until 2003 7/8

SATURN SPECIAL
1946 8/30 – until 1947 2/22
1947 5/14 – 10/3
1948 2/7 – 6/22
1976 7/4 – until 1977 8/5
2005 8/11 – until 2006 9/12
2007 3/13 – 5/27

URANUS SPECIAL
1956 8/7 – until 1960 7/11

PLUTO SPECIAL
1940 8/28 – until 1952 6/5

August 5

Your Personal Powers

Determined and forceful when set on a course of action, you are an individual with fast instincts and natural enthusiasm. Your ruler, the Sun, grants you strong pride, creative ideas, and innate leadership skills. You gain power from your resolve, common sense, and natural organizational abilities. You may have to beware of losing what you have built up through impatience or stubbornness. Usually you do not like to take orders from others but you may lose some of your power if you become overbearing or bossy. Nevertheless, purposeful, hardworking, and generous, you can establish a solid foundation for yourself and others. Courageous and adventurous with strong opinions, you like the honest and direct approach, but being blunt, cynical, or headstrong can undermine your wonderful potential. By challenging yourself to be daring and spontaneous or trust your intuition, you can add to your personal powers. The combination of your good business sense, progressive ideas, and strong drive for material achievement adds to your opportunities for success.

Your Powers of Attraction in Relationships

Your tenacious personality and sociable manner can attract others. Although you can appear strong on the outside you possess an inner emotional sensitivity that can highlight the extremes of your character. Since you may experience uncertainty about your relationships, you may sometimes become controlling or find it difficult to expose your inner vulnerability. Nevertheless, you can be very loyal and willing to make great sacrifices for those you love. Generous to your partner, you are attracted to lighthearted and cheerful individuals or those who can uplift you emotionally. With your strong need for emotional expression you are often drawn to those who can stimulate your creativity. Your relationships with clever women can prove to be especially beneficial. Magnetic and warm, you enjoy socializing and meeting others.

Your attractive qualities: versatile, adaptable, mentally quick, progressive, strong instincts, magnetic, warm, generous, daring, freedom-loving, pragmatic, determined, proud, creative, leadership ability, patience, curious, sociable, common sense, hardworking, business sense

Your less attractive qualities: unreliable, changeable, bossy, restlessness, procrastinator, arrogant, power tactics, overconfident, rebellious, headstrong, mistrustful, impatient, materialistic, opinionated

Your Venus Power

The planet Venus has a great deal of influence on your powers of attraction. Below are four possible Venus types for women and men. To find your Venus you need to go to page 771, where you will find the Venus table and extra information. The planet Mars also affects your powers of attraction. To find your Mars table and interpretation go to page 761.

WOMEN WITH VENUS IN GEMINI: Curious, with a bright and animated approach to life, you are attracted to those who are clever and/or sophisticated. Your love of variety and desire for knowledge suggest that you need a partner and friends who keep you mentally stimulated. Although witty and a good conversationalist, you may need to keep in touch with your deeper feelings. Nevertheless, intelligent and friendly, you possess a youthful sense of wonder and seek a playmate who can keep you from becoming bored.

MEN WITH VENUS IN GEMINI: Adaptable yet often flirtatious, you enjoy mixing with people who are quick-minded and versatile. Since you can learn a great deal through interacting with others, you are often attracted to intelligent partners who have comprehensive knowledge or good ideas. One of your less attractive qualities is your tendency to become bored or be inconsistent. Having an adaptable partner is important to you; therefore it must be someone who can offer you different options and keep you interested.

WOMEN WITH VENUS IN CANCER: Good-natured and romantic, you have a highly developed sense of touch that particularly responds to massage, hugs, and all things physical. Being friendly, you enjoy socializing and are able to put others at their ease. With your natural sense of beauty and harmony, you can attract others. Although you can be lavish toward your partner you may have to be careful that you do not overdo things.

MEN WITH VENUS IN CANCER: Being emotionally receptive, you can make a sensitive lover. With your desire to care for and protect others, you are likely to have strong family connections. Love is often tied in with being attentive to the needs of others and you may find yourself attracted to indi-

viduals who have sympathetic or maternal qualities. Security-conscious, you need a loyal partner who can offer you support and ideally be a good cook and homemaker.

WOMEN WITH VENUS IN LEO: Your friendly and sunny personality often makes you stand out in a crowd. Generous and giving, you know how to make your partners feel special. As you often expect loyalty and devotion from your partner in return, you can become easily offended if they ignore you or behave in an inconsiderate manner. Charming and kind, when you are in love you can be romantic, dramatic, and passionate.

MEN WITH VENUS IN LEO: Warm and playful with a touch of the dramatic, you enjoy the company of generous or strong individuals who can share your sense of fun. Although there are advantages to being strong-willed, in your relationships you need to resist being bossy as it can cause resentment. With your wonderful mixture of regal authority and childlike wonder, you love to keep others entertained and amused.

WOMEN WITH VENUS IN VIRGO: In relationships you can be modest and unassuming but desire perfection. You usually analyze your partnerships until you feel you have understood them to the last little detail in order to improve them. A problem usually arises when you become too critical either of partners or yourself and indulge in being skeptical or faultfinding. As you are modest, others may not be aware of the strong sensuality beneath your well-groomed exterior.

MEN WITH VENUS IN VIRGO: Practical, idealistic, and a perfectionist, you seek a relationship with an intelligent and hardworking partner who can inspire you to be more industrious and well-ordered. At times you can come across as a sympathetic and caring person and at other times you may appear pragmatic and very businesslike. This may sometimes lead to unclear communication between you and your partner. Usually helpful and caring, however, you like to analyze the faults in your relationships and then work methodically to improve them.

To read all about your Outer Planets and work out how to use your personalized timetable, go to Section Three, page 789.

♌

To read all about your Outer Planets and work out how to use your personalized timetable, go to Section Three, page 789.

Your Personalized Timetable

JUPITER BENEFICIAL
1939 6/5 – 9/23
1940 1/22 – 4/5
1941 6/27 – 8/19
1941 12/1 – until 1942 4/9
1945 9/29 – 11/15
1947 11/13 – until 1948 1/26
1948 7/18 – 9/13
1951 5/11 – 11/23
1951 12/6 – until 1952 3/19
1953 6/10 – 7/26
1954 1/18 – 3/6
1957 9/13 – 10/29
1959 10/27 – until 1960 1/8
1963 4/22 – until 1964 3/1
1965 5/24 – 7/7
1969 8/27 – 10/14
1971 2/14 – 4/30
1971 10/9 – 12/23
1975 4/5 – 6/22
1975 10/8 – until 1976 2/8
1977 5/8 – 6/20
1980 12/10 – until 1981 3/11
1981 8/8 – 9/28
1983 1/18 – 6/10
1983 9/15 – 12/7
1987 3/20 – 5/29
1987 11/27 – until 1988 1/2
1989 4/20 – 6/4
1992 11/16 – until 1993 4/19
1993 7/13 – 9/12
1994 12/30 – until 1995 11/21
1999 3/4 – 5/10
2000 8/10 – 11/19
2001 3/30 – 5/18
2004 10/29 – until 2005 1/1
2005 3/5 – 8/25
2006 12/13 – until 2007 11/4
2011 2/13 – 4/22
2012 7/16 – Continues

SATURN BENEFICIAL
1938 2/27 – until 1939 4/6
1942 7/6 – 12/23
1943 3/22 – 6/18
1951 10/14 – until 1952 10/6
1956 11/19 – until 1958 1/9
1958 7/14 – 10/2
1967 4/8 – until 1968 5/16
1968 11/7 – until 1969 2/2
1972 5/11 – 8/1
1972 12/6 – until 1973 4/20
1980 11/26 – until 1981 3/15
1981 8/19 – 11/13
1982 4/30 – 8/5
1985 12/24 – until 1986 6/27
1986 9/16 – until 1987 2/27
1987 5/2 – 11/18
1996 5/17 – 9/22
1997 2/8 – 7/28
1997 8/6 – until 1998 3/20
2001 6/17 – until 2002 5/31
2010 9/27 – until 2011 9/20

URANUS BENEFICIAL
1943 7/15 – until 1946 6/5
1969 11/17 – until 1972 9/20
1982 2/12 – until 1986 11/6
2011 6/16 – Continues

NEPTUNE BENEFICIAL
1945 11/1 – until 1951 8/15
1972 1/8 – until 1980 10/11

PLUTO BENEFICIAL
1974 10/17 – until 1979 8/24
1996 12/30 – until 2004 10/24

JUPITER CHALLENGING
1938 1/8 – 3/18
1940 6/5 – until 1941 4/15
1946 10/16 – 12/31

1947 6/2 – 8/27
1949 12/22 – until 1950 2/28
1952 5/17 – 8/21
1952 9/29 – until 1953 3/26
1958 9/29 – 12/13
1961 4/12 – 7/8
1961 12/2 – until 1962 2/12
1964 4/30 – 7/14
1964 11/18 – until 1965 3/3
1970 1/18 – 3/24
1970 9/11 – 11/26
1973 3/17 – 8/23
1973 11/3 – until 1974 1/26
1976 4/13 – 6/22
1981 12/20 – until 1982 5/4
1982 8/19 – 11/11
1985 2/26 – until 1986 1/10
1988 3/28 – 6/4
1993 12/1 – until 1994 10/26
1997 2/9 – 5/9
1997 7/12 – 12/22
1999 8/5 – 9/13
2000 3/9 – 5/18
2005 11/15 – until 2006 10/10
2009 1/24 – 4/7
2009 8/28 – 11/26
2011 6/27 – 11/5
2012 2/13 – 5/1

SATURN CHALLENGING
1940 4/24 – until 1941 5/27
1953 11/28 – until 1954 5/20
1954 8/21 – until 1955 1/29
1955 4/2 – 10/18
1962 2/9 – until 1963 4/4
1963 8/5 – 12/31
1969 6/5 – 11/12
1970 2/23 – 7/14
1970 10/27 – until 1971 4/2
1983 2/2 – 2/22
1983 10/6 – until 1984 11/21
1991 3/21 – 7/15
1991 12/17 – until 1993 2/4
1999 4/8 – until 2000 5/10

URANUS CHALLENGING
1938 1/1 – until 1940 4/13
1975 11/20 – until 1979 10/29
1996 4/14 – until 2001 2/1

NEPTUNE CHALLENGING
1957 12/27 – until 1966 9/30
1999 4/27 – until 2008 1/3

PLUTO CHALLENGING
1984 12/31 – until 1992 8/25

JUPITER SPECIAL
1943 7/20 – 10/5
1944 2/25 – 5/31
1955 7/4 – 9/16
1966 11/12 – 11/30
1967 6/16 – 8/30
1978 9/30 – until 1979 1/22
1979 5/26 – 8/14
1990 9/8 – until 1991 3/8
1991 4/22 – 7/29
2002 8/21 – until 2003 7/13

SATURN SPECIAL
1946 9/7 – until 1947 2/8
1947 5/26 – 10/14
1948 1/26 – 7/2
1976 7/12 – until 1977 8/12
2005 8/19 – until 2006 9/21
2007 2/27 – 6/9

URANUS SPECIAL
1956 8/23 – until 1960 7/27

PLUTO SPECIAL
1941 8/11 – until 1952 7/17

August 6

Your Personal Powers

Charming but strong-willed, your personal powers include ambition, enthusiasm, and excellent people skills. Your ruler, the Sun, suggests that you are proud and creative with a strong need for love and attention. As you usually show willingness to be responsible and hardworking in order to achieve your goals, you gain power from your ability to combine business and pleasure. Although you can be persevering and dutiful, you may lose some of your power if you are too critical and tough on yourself or others. At the other extreme you can be warm and magnanimous, with a kind heart and a caring and compassionate nature. Possessing an inner emotional sensitivity and idealism, you seek inspiration, gaining your greatest rewards when you are able to be of help to others. You lose power, however, when your strong emotions become too intense and lead you to frustration or disappointment. When you are selfless, however, your creative vitality can act as a beacon of light for others to follow.

Your Powers of Attraction in Relationships

Gregarious and sociable, you should find it easy to make friends and gain admirers. Your desire to love and be loved implies that you can be charming, romantic, and sensitive to others. Being idealistic, the expression of love is likely to be extra important to you. Hardworking and disciplined yet sensitive and caring, the extremes of your nature show that you may sometimes have a conflict between work and relationship. By obtaining a balance between your own needs and giving to others, you can avoid becoming bossy or feeling sorry for yourself. You need a partner who is emotionally giving and supportive or who brings out your spontaneity. You are a supportive and devoted lover or parent, and you want a partner who understands the importance of home and family to your security.

Your attractive qualities: determined, worldly, friendly, creative, compassionate, dependable, understanding, patient, disciplined, direct, sympathetic, artistic talents, pragmatic, idealistic, home-loving, humanitarian, creative, balanced, clever, good social skills

Your less attractive qualities: discontented, anxious, stubborn, outspoken, perfectionist, interfering, bossy, denial, worry, insecurity, rigid, materialistic, rebellious, self-centered, suspicious, too tough

Your Venus Power

The planet Venus has a great deal of influence on your powers of attraction. Below are four possible Venus types for women and men. To find your Venus you need to go to page 771, where you will find the Venus table and extra information. The planet Mars also affects your powers of attraction. To find your Mars table and interpretation go to page 761.

WOMEN WITH VENUS IN GEMINI: By nature you are young at heart, adaptable, and sociable. Being curious and willing to cooperate makes you a good team player. You are usually drawn to articulate people who have charm and flair or sharp wit. With a need to expand your knowledge you also look for a partner who can challenge or stimulate you intellectually. Although you love to talk with all types of people, you may need to develop your listening skills in order to build better communication in your relationships.

MEN WITH VENUS IN GEMINI: Informed and curious yet charming and friendly, you seek a partner who shares your interests or enjoys your witty remarks. Although a good communicator, you have an inborn tendency to be lighthearted and less profound about deep emotional commitment. Although you are keen on experiences that bring variety into your life, boredom or scattering your energies in too many directions is probably your biggest handicap in relationships. Nevertheless, you are attracted to intelligent partners who can match your lively banter.

WOMEN WITH VENUS IN CANCER: Possessing a soft femininity, you have tender and sensitive emotions. Sympathetic and caring, you often mother those in your care by making sure they are comfortable and have plenty to eat. When you feel hurt or insecure in relationships you are likely to cover your feelings by being defensive or appearing tough on the outside while on the inside you are feeling vulnerable. Affectionate and romantic, you make a faithful and devoted partner.

MEN WITH VENUS IN CANCER: Being caring and sensitive, you probably seek a nurturing partner who could provide you with emotional security and a sense of belonging in a loving and safe environment. Receptive to others, at times you

find it hard to be direct or confrontational in relationships. You are caring and affectionate with loved ones, and family links are important to you.

WOMEN WITH VENUS IN LEO: Warm and playful with a touch of the dramatic, you enjoy the company of generous or strong individuals who can share your sense of fun. Although there are advantages to your being strong-willed, in your relationships you need to resist being bossy as it can cause resentment. With your wonderful mixture of regal authority and childlike wonder, you love to keep others entertained and amused.

MEN WITH VENUS IN LEO: Sociable and outgoing, you are kind and generous with those you love. Looking for a relationship that can be fun and entertaining, you need a playmate who can share your enthusiasm and high spirits. Your pride, however, often stops you from associating with lovers or partners you see as beneath you. As you desire someone who can appreciate your sense of the dramatic, you are often attracted to people with strong personalities.

WOMEN WITH VENUS IN VIRGO: Intelligent and discriminating, you are usually drawn to polite and refined individuals. As a perfectionist you may be keen to analyze and criticize yourself, but be careful of continually going over your partner's shortcomings. By focusing on how you can make positive improvements in yourself and in your relationships, you avoid becoming skeptical or confused. You empower yourself when you display kind and caring concern for the well-being of loved ones and spontaneously offer your practical assistance.

MEN WITH VENUS IN VIRGO: A love of order usually indicates that you are attracted to refined individuals with analytical or practical abilities. You and your partner may be working together or serving similar causes. As you constantly analyze partnerships in order to improve them, you are likely to use former relationships as a point of reference and compare them to your present partner. As you are helpful and kind, others usually rely on your good judgment and often turn to you for advice or practical assistance.

To read all about your Outer Planets and work out how to use your personalized timetable, go to Section Three, page 789.

♌

289

Your Personalized Timetable

JUPITER BENEFICIAL
1939 6/12 – 9/16
1940 1/28 – 4/9
1941 7/1 – 8/26
1941 11/24 – until 1942 4/15
1945 10/3 – 11/20
1946 5/21 – 7/8
1947 11/17 – until 1948 1/31
1948 7/8 – 9/23
1951 5/16 – 11/5
1951 12/25 – until 1952 3/23
1953 6/14 – 7/31
1954 1/7 – 3/16
1957 9/17 – 11/3
1959 11/1 – until 1960 1/12
1963 4/26 – until 1964 3/5
1965 5/28 – 7/11
1969 9/1 – 10/18
1971 2/24 – 4/20
1971 10/14 – 12/27
1975 4/9 – 6/28
1975 10/1 – until 1976 2/13
1977 5/12 – 6/24
1980 12/18 – until 1981 3/3
1981 8/14 – 10/2
1983 1/23 – 6/2
1983 9/22 – 12/11
1987 3/24 – 6/3
1987 11/15 – until 1988 1/14
1989 4/25 – 6/8
1992 11/22 – until 1993 4/11
1993 7/21 – 9/16
1995 1/3 – 11/25
1999 3/8 – 5/14
2000 8/17 – 11/11
2001 4/4 – 5/22
2004 11/3 – until 2005 1/14
2005 2/20 – 8/30
2006 12/18 – until 2007 11/9
2011 2/18 – 4/26
2012 7/21 – 12/26

SATURN BENEFICIAL
1938 3/7 – until 1939 4/14
1942 7/15 – 12/10
1943 4/2 – 6/25
1951 10/22 – until 1952 5/30
1952 6/21 – 10/14
1956 11/27 – until 1958 1/18
1958 6/29 – 10/16
1967 4/15 – until 1968 5/25
1968 10/25 – until 1969 2/14
1972 5/18 – 8/12
1972 11/24 – until 1973 4/29
1980 12/8 – until 1981 3/1
1981 8/28 – 11/22
1982 4/17 – 8/17
1986 1/2 – 6/12
1986 9/30 – until 1987 11/26
1996 5/28 – 9/9
1997 2/17 – until 1998 3/28
2001 6/25 – until 2002 1/22
2002 2/24 – 6/8
2010 10/5 – until 2011 9/28

URANUS BENEFICIAL
1943 8/9 – until 1947 4/1
1969 12/11 – until 1972 10/5
1982 12/4 – until 1986 11/23

NEPTUNE BENEFICIAL
1945 12/7 – until 1951 9/16
1972 12/5 – until 1980 11/14

PLUTO BENEFICIAL
1974 11/14 – until 1979 9/21
1997 2/4 – until 2004 11/23

JUPITER CHALLENGING
1938 1/12 – 3/23
1940 6/9 – until 1941 4/19

1946 10/20 – until 1947 1/6
1947 5/25 – 9/4
1949 12/26 – until 1950 3/5
1952 5/21 – until 1953 3/31
1958 10/4 – 12/18
1961 4/21 – 6/29
1961 12/7 – until 1962 2/16
1964 5/4 – 7/20
1964 11/11 – until 1965 3/9
1970 1/30 – 3/12
1970 9/16 – 12/1
1973 3/22 – 8/14
1973 11/11 – until 1974 1/31
1976 4/18 – 6/27
1977 1/7 – 1/23
1981 12/26 – until 1982 4/27
1982 8/26 – 11/15
1985 3/2 – until 1986 1/14
1988 4/1 – 6/8
1993 12/6 – until 1994 6/13
1994 7/20 – 10/30
1997 2/13 – 5/20
1997 6/30 – 12/27
2000 3/14 – 5/22
2005 11/19 – until 2006 10/15
2009 1/28 – 4/13
2009 8/20 – 12/3
2011 7/3 – 10/29
2012 2/19 – 5/5

SATURN CHALLENGING
1940 5/2 – until 1941 6/3
1953 12/7 – until 1954 5/6
1954 9/3 – until 1955 10/26
1962 2/18 – 9/14
1962 11/3 – until 1963 4/16
1963 7/22 – until 1964 1/9
1969 6/14 – 10/31
1970 3/6 – 7/27
1970 10/14 – until 1971 4/10
1983 10/15 – until 1984 11/30
1991 4/3 – 7/1
1991 12/26 – until 1993 2/12
1999 4/16 – until 2000 5/17

URANUS CHALLENGING
1938 1/1 – until 1940 4/30
1975 12/7 – until 1979 11/14
1997 2/5 – until 2001 11/30

NEPTUNE CHALLENGING
1958 11/18 – until 1966 10/29
2000 2/28 – until 2008 1/31

PLUTO CHALLENGING
1985 11/12 – until 1992 10/4

JUPITER SPECIAL
1943 7/25 – 10/11
1944 2/17 – 6/7
1955 7/8 – 9/21
1967 6/21 – 9/4
1978 10/7 – until 1979 1/15
1979 6/1 – 8/19
1990 9/13 – until 1991 2/25
1991 5/3 – 8/3
2002 8/26 – until 2003 7/17

SATURN SPECIAL
1946 9/16 – until 1947 1/27
1947 6/6 – 10/26
1948 1/13 – until 1948 7/10
1976 7/19 – until 1977 8/20
2005 8/27 – until 2006 3/4
2006 5/7 – 9/30
2007 2/15 – 6/20

URANUS SPECIAL
1956 9/10 – until 1960 8/12

PLUTO SPECIAL
1941 9/20 – until 1953 6/18

August 7

SUN: LEO • DECANATE: SAGITTARIUS/JUPITER • DEGREE: 14°–15°5 LEO • MODE: FIXED • ELEMENT: FIRE

Your Personal Powers

Intelligent and optimistic with a wealth of ideas and confidence in yourself, you are a determined individual with innate common sense. Although you appear dynamic and vivacious, you can be a sensitive and caring individual. Your ruler, the Sun, grants you energy, pride, and creativity. You gain power when you combine your practical skills and your creativity. Although you are often a sympathetic and compassionate listener, your pride implies that you can lose some of your power when you overreact to situations. Being spirited and full of hope, you can also make the most of your talents. Your success usually depends on your positive frame of mind or trusting what you believe in. In order to maximize your potential for success you may need to overcome a fear of failure and develop your perseverance. You lose power by being skeptical or by allowing emotional frustration to build from within. Nevertheless your intuition and business acumen suggest that it would only take a spark to light up your fiery spirit.

Your Powers of Attraction in Relationships

Thoughtful and charismatic, you are affectionate and usually sociable and fun-loving. Other people are drawn to your generous personality. Although you are idealistic, your all-or-nothing attitude can sometimes make you impatient. Your sense of justice indicates that you can be especially kind to people less fortunate than you. Since you thrive on praise, you prefer the company of enthusiastic individuals who can offer you support and encouragement. Usually you are drawn to enterprising partners who are ambitious and creative. Wanting the best that life can offer, your high expectations meet with disappointment if you do not tolerate criticism, exercise patience, and persist. Nevertheless, you are warm and understanding, and your nobility and strong convictions imply that you are loyal and compassionate.

Your attractive qualities: creative, dramatic, artistic, intuitive, generous, genuine, charismatic, considerate, confident, determined, hardworking, sociable, honorable, charming, common sense, economical, optimistic, persuasive, trusting, meticulous, idealistic, honest, compassionate

Your less attractive qualities: lethargic, fixed, stubborn, arrogant, extravagant, self-righteous, pessimistic, easily discouraged, drifts aimlessly, overemotional, skeptical, too demanding, critical, frustrated, discontented

Your Venus Power

The planet Venus has a great deal of influence on your powers of attraction. Below are four possible Venus types for women and men. To find your Venus you need to go to page 771, where you will find the Venus table and extra information. The planet Mars also affects your powers of attraction. To find your Mars table and interpretation go to page 761.

WOMEN WITH VENUS IN CANCER: Possessing a soft femininity, you have tender and sensitive emotions. Sympathetic and caring, you often mother those in your care by making sure they are comfortable and have plenty to eat. When you feel hurt or insecure in relationships you are likely to cover your feelings by being defensive or appearing tough on the outside while on the inside you are feeling vulnerable. Affectionate and romantic, you make a faithful and devoted partner.

MEN WITH VENUS IN CANCER: Affectionate with a strong sensitive streak, you can love very deeply. You may find yourself drawn to sympathetic partners who can tune into your moods and feelings as well as be reassuring and supportive. Family links are especially important to you and the more positive these relationships are the more confident and safe you feel.

WOMEN WITH VENUS IN LEO: As a person who wants to radiate in her own right, you are likely to desire partners you can be proud of. Usually you are attracted to fun-loving, warm, and generous individuals. If self-expression is important to you, you will probably seek the company of creative people such as artists, musicians, or those with a flair for acting. Alternatively, you may be drawn to people who are dignified, regal, or have already achieved success.

MEN WITH VENUS IN LEO: Generous, animated, and pleasure-seeking, you can be very entertaining and fun to be with. Usually you are attracted to extroverted and benevolent individuals with sunny personalities. If ambitious, you are drawn to a partner who shows leadership qualities or one who is highly motivated. Your less attractive qualities are your tendencies to be bossy or vain. With a sense of the dramatic, however, you can be the life and soul of the party and inspire those around you.

WOMEN WITH VENUS IN VIRGO: Polite, refined, and organized, you are attracted to articulate and intelligent people. Since you are caring, concerned, and want to be of practical help to others, you can be an asset to any partnership. By being too analytical, exacting, or faultfinding, however, a doubting element can creep into your relationships. By expressing your feelings in a positive way you can become more decisive and improve on how you relate to your loved ones.

MEN WITH VENUS IN VIRGO: Practical, idealistic, and a perfectionist, you seek a relationship with an intelligent and hardworking partner who can inspire you to be more industrious and well-ordered. At times you can come across as a sympathetic and caring person and at other times you may appear pragmatic and very businesslike. This may sometimes lead to unclear communication between you and your partner. Usually helpful and caring, however, you like to analyze the faults in your relationships and then work methodically to improve them.

WOMEN WITH VENUS IN LIBRA: Gracious, charming, and sociable with a sense of style, you have no trouble attracting admirers. With your natural diplomatic skills and desire for harmony you usually like to keep the peace and avoid confrontations, but be careful of failing to make a stand when it is necessary. Romantic and easygoing yourself, you are attracted to affectionate and refined individuals who share your love of peace, justice, and fair play.

MEN WITH VENUS IN LIBRA: You are such good company, people are naturally drawn to you and especially appreciate your talent for making them feel special. You find status in your social contacts and place importance on your relationships. Being clever and a charming companion, you will go out of your way to keep situations peaceful and harmonious. In relationships, however, be careful of indecision or compromising too much. Nevertheless, others are attracted by your natural refinement and good taste, which is reflected in your sense of style.

To read all about your Outer Planets and work out how to use your personalized timetable, go to Section Three, page 789.

♌

Your Personalized Timetable

JUPITER BENEFICIAL
1939 6/19 – 9/8
1940 2/2 – 4/13
1941 7/6 – 9/3
1941 11/16 – until 1942 4/20
1945 10/7 – 11/25
1946 5/10 – 7/20
1947 11/22 – until 1948 2/6
1948 6/29 – 10/1
1951 5/21 – 10/26
1952 1/3 – 3/27
1953 6/18 – 8/5
1953 12/30 – until 1954 3/24
1957 9/22 – 11/8
1959 11/5 – until 1960 1/17
1963 5/1 – until 1964 3/10
1965 6/1 – 7/16
1969 9/6 – 10/23
1971 3/12 – 4/3
1971 10/19 – 12/31
1975 4/13 – 7/6
1975 9/23 – until 1976 2/18
1977 5/16 – 6/28
1980 12/28 – until 1981 2/20
1981 8/19 – 10/7
1983 1/30 – 5/26
1983 9/28 – 12/15
1987 3/28 – 6/8
1987 11/6 – until 1988 1/23
1989 4/29 – 6/12
1992 11/28 – until 1993 4/3
1993 7/28 – 9/21
1995 1/8 – 7/11
1995 8/24 – 11/30
1999 3/12 – 5/19
2000 8/25 – 11/3
2001 4/10 – 5/27
2004 11/8 – until 2005 5/21
2005 6/19 – 9/4
2006 12/22 – until 2007 11/14
2011 2/22 – 4/30
2012 7/26 – 12/18

SATURN BENEFICIAL
1938 3/15 – until 1939 4/21
1942 7/24 – 11/29
1943 4/12 – 7/3
1951 10/30 – until 1952 5/5
1952 7/16 – 10/22
1956 12/5 – until 1958 1/27
1958 6/16 – 10/27
1967 4/24 – 11/13
1968 1/4 – 6/3
1968 10/13 – until 1969 2/24
1972 5/26 – 8/24
1972 11/10 – until 1973 5/7
1980 12/25 – until 1981 2/12
1981 9/6 – 12/2
1982 4/4 – 8/27
1986 1/12 – 5/30
1986 10/11 – until 1987 12/4
1996 6/11 – 8/25
1997 2/26 – until 1998 4/4
2001 7/3 – until 2002 1/2
2002 3/16 – 6/15
2010 10/13 – until 2011 10/6

URANUS BENEFICIAL
1944 6/5 – until 1947 4/26
1970 10/3 – until 1973 7/24
1982 12/20 – until 1986 12/9
2012 4/25 – Continues

NEPTUNE BENEFICIAL
1946 10/26 – until 1952 8/4
1973 1/1 – until 1981 9/28

PLUTO BENEFICIAL
1975 10/6 – until 1980 7/31
1997 12/18 – until 2005 10/12

JUPITER CHALLENGING
1938 1/16 – 3/27
1940 6/14 – 12/13

1941 1/18 – 4/23
1946 10/24 – until 1947 1/12
1947 5/17 – 9/11
1949 12/30 – until 1950 3/9
1952 5/25 – until 1953 4/5
1958 10/9 – 12/22
1959 7/11 – 7/29
1961 5/1 – 6/18
1961 12/12 – until 1962 2/20
1964 5/8 – 7/26
1964 11/4 – until 1965 3/15
1970 9/21 – 12/5
1973 3/27 – 8/6
1973 11/18 – until 1974 2/4
1976 4/22 – 7/1
1976 12/21 – until 1977 2/9
1982 1/2 – 4/19
1982 9/1 – 11/19
1985 3/7 – until 1986 1/19
1988 4/5 – 6/13
1993 12/11 – until 1994 5/31
1994 8/3 – 11/4
1997 2/17 – until 1998 1/1
2000 3/18 – 5/26
2005 11/24 – until 2006 10/19
2009 2/1 – 4/19
2009 8/13 – 12/9
2011 7/9 – 10/21
2012 2/25 – 5/9

SATURN CHALLENGING
1940 5/9 – until 1941 6/11
1941 12/28 – until 1942 2/18
1953 12/17 – until 1954 4/23
1954 9/13 – until 1955 11/3
1962 2/26 – 8/26
1962 11/21 – until 1963 5/2
1963 7/6 – until 1964 1/18
1969 6/25 – 10/19
1970 3/15 – 8/15
1970 9/24 – until 1971 4/18
1983 10/23 – until 1984 12/8
1985 6/24 – 8/26
1991 4/20 – 6/13
1992 1/4 – until 1993 2/20
1999 4/23 – until 2000 5/25

URANUS CHALLENGING
1938 1/1 – until 1941 2/14
1975 12/28 – until 1980 9/10
1997 2/22 – until 2001 12/27

NEPTUNE CHALLENGING
1958 12/19 – until 1967 9/23
2000 4/4 – until 2008 12/25

PLUTO CHALLENGING
1985 12/8 – until 1992 10/30

JUPITER SPECIAL
1943 7/29 – 10/17
1944 2/10 – 6/13
1955 7/13 – 9/26
1956 3/26 – 5/10
1967 6/26 – 9/8
1978 10/14 – until 1979 1/7
1979 6/7 – 8/23
1990 9/19 – until 1991 2/16
1991 5/12 – 8/7
2002 8/30 – until 2003 7/22

SATURN SPECIAL
1946 9/26 – until 1947 1/16
1947 6/15 – 11/13
1947 12/25 – until 1948 7/19
1976 7/27 – until 1977 8/27
2005 9/4 – until 2006 2/17
2006 5/22 – 10/10
2007 2/3 – 6/30

URANUS SPECIAL
1956 10/2 – until 1961 6/5

PLUTO SPECIAL
1942 8/30 – until 1953 7/25

291

August 8

Your Personal Powers

Dynamic and determined, you are an ambitious and purposeful individual who is full of vitality. Your ruler, the Sun, grants you energy, pride, confidence, and creativity. Eager to make quick progress in life, you can empower yourself by being decisive, methodical, and patient. Astute and intuitive, you also achieve good results when you combine your original or imaginative ideas with your intuition and knowledge. Your business acumen indicates that you can succeed admirably in the world of commerce. You lose some of your power when you allow pride, restlessness, or frustration to undermine your efforts. Fluctuations in your financial circumstances or changes in career plans suggest that taking responsibility or making long-term investments can help you feel more settled and contented. Staying focused can also increase your self-esteem. Although you should avoid getting stuck in a rut by being versatile and enterprising, your strength increases when you accept that everything does not happen momentarily and adopt a more cautious approach.

Your Powers of Attraction in Relationships

Youthful, lively, and naturally charismatic, you can attract many friends and admirers. Wanting to live well, you can be generous with your friends or loved ones. A tendency to be hasty suggests that you need to take your time in choosing your partners, otherwise you may later regret making rash decisions. Usually you are attracted to creative and intelligent people who can inspire you and keep you mentally stimulated. Alternatively, since you frequently associate success with money and wealth, you are drawn to partners who are professional or financially secure. You are naturally enthusiastic, and others admire your spirit of enterprise and determination. Even though you are often independent and strong-willed, in personal relationships do not let pride get in the way of your attitude to your partner.

Your attractive qualities: authoritative, thorough, hardworking, efficient, protective, good judge of values, idealistic, careful planner, enthusiastic, creative ideas, imaginative, practical, structured, productive, courageous, astute, great accomplishment, quick perceptions

Your less attractive qualities: materialistic, impatient, stressed, intolerant, impatient, easily discouraged, lack of planning, controlling behavior, unfocused, unfinished projects, inactive, vain, too dominant, restless

Your Venus Power

The planet Venus has a great deal of influence on your powers of attraction. Below are four possible Venus types for women and men. To find your Venus you need to go to page 771, where you will find the Venus table and extra information. The planet Mars also affects your powers of attraction. To find your Mars table and interpretation go to page 761.

WOMEN WITH VENUS IN CANCER: Possessing a soft femininity, you have tender and sensitive emotions. Sympathetic and caring, you often mother those in your care by making sure they are comfortable and have plenty to eat. When you feel hurt or insecure in relationships you are likely to cover your feelings by being defensive or appearing tough on the outside while on the inside you are feeling vulnerable. Affectionate and romantic, you make a faithful and devoted partner.

MEN WITH VENUS IN CANCER: You seek a partner who is sympathetic, caring, and protective. Able to be forgiving and compassionate, you want a secure emotional bond in your close relationships. Usually you are drawn to partners who are maternal, unselfish, or demonstrative with their feelings. Although you can sometimes appear to others as impressionable, you have powerful emotions and inner strength.

WOMEN WITH VENUS IN LEO: You possess the wonderful ability to project your warm and sunny personality and keep others happily entertained. Loving attention yourself, you seek a partner who can appreciate you, be supportive, and give you positive feedback. Proud, with a natural regal air, you expect respect from your partners but are willing to be loyal and supportive in exchange. Although sometimes a little self-centered, you know how to make your partner feel special.

MEN WITH VENUS IN LEO: A childlike nature suggests that you are versatile and keen on games or being entertained. You are usually attracted to vivacious partners with a benevolent nature. As an extrovert you enjoy being involved in all types of activities where you can assert yourself and show your talents and abilities. Others may recognize your inborn tendencies to lead but are also aware of your vanity or pride. Nevertheless, generous and caring, you often show more compassion to those less fortunate than yourself.

WOMEN WITH VENUS IN VIRGO: In relationships, you can be modest and unassuming but desire perfection. You usually analyze your partnerships until you feel you have understood them to the last little detail in order to improve them. A problem usually arises when you become too critical either of partners or yourself and indulge in being skeptical or faultfinding. As you are modest, others may not be aware of the strong sensuality beneath your well-groomed exterior.

MEN WITH VENUS IN VIRGO: Industrious and well-ordered, you relate to others in a considerate and down-to-earth way. You enjoy giving practical advice and being of service to those you love, even in small ways. Being a perfectionist you are drawn to partners with high morals or a strong work ethic. Partners who have strong analytical minds are very attractive to you, particularly if they are also clean and meticulously dressed.

WOMEN WITH VENUS IN LIBRA: Attractive, refined, and conscious of the needs of others, you usually desire harmonious relationships. As a peacemaker with good negotiating skills, you can smooth out difficulties with others, but your dislike of confrontation may sometimes leave you refusing to make a stand or compromising too many of your own needs. Courteous, stylish, and charming with polished social skills, you are an expert at relating to others in a gracious and civilized manner.

MEN WITH VENUS IN LIBRA: As a sociable and friendly individual with an eye for beauty, you are amorous and charming. You are a natural gentleman and your ideal partner usually has an elegant appearance, artistic appreciation, and good taste. Your relationships benefit when you resist the temptation to take the easy way out or put too much emphasis on vanity and high living. Intellectual and naturally refined, you seek a loving partner who can share your romantic and sophisticated aspirations.

To read all about your Outer Planets and work out how to use your personalized timetable, go to Section Three, page 789.

go to Section Three, page 789.

Your Personalized Timetable

JUPITER BENEFICIAL
1939 6/28 – 8/30
1940 2/7 – 4/17
1941 7/10 – 9/12
1941 11/6 – until 1942 4/25
1945 10/12 – 12/1
1946 5/1 – 7/29
1947 11/26 – until 1948 2/11
1948 6/22 – 10/8
1951 5/26 – 10/18
1952 1/11 – 3/31
1953 6/22 – 8/10
1953 12/22 – until 1954 4/1
1957 9/26 – 11/12
1959 11/10 – until 1960 1/22
1963 5/5 – until 1964 3/14
1965 6/6 – 7/20
1969 9/10 – 10/27
1971 10/24 – until 1972 1/4
1975 4/17 – 7/15
1975 9/14 – until 1976 2/23
1977 5/20 – 7/3
1981 1/14 – 2/4
1981 8/24 – 10/11
1983 2/5 – 5/18
1983 10/4 – 12/20
1987 4/1 – 6/14
1987 10/29 – until 1988 1/30
1989 5/4 – 6/16
1992 12/4 – until 1993 3/27
1993 8/4 – 9/26
1995 1/13 – 6/30
1995 9/5 – 12/4
1999 3/16 – 5/23
2000 9/4 – 10/24
2001 4/15 – 5/31
2004 11/13 – until 2005 5/6
2005 7/5 – 9/9
2006 12/27 – until 2007 11/18
2011 2/26 – 5/4
2012 7/31 – 12/11

SATURN BENEFICIAL
1938 3/23 – until 1939 4/29
1942 8/4 – 11/17
1943 4/21 – 7/10
1944 1/27 – 3/15
1951 11/8 – until 1952 4/20
1952 7/30 – 10/30
1956 12/13 – until 1958 2/7
1958 6/3 – 11/6
1967 5/2 – 10/27
1968 1/20 – 6/14
1968 9/30 – until 1969 3/5
1972 6/2 – 9/12
1972 10/22 – until 1973 5/15
1981 9/14 – 12/13
1982 3/22 – 9/6
1986 1/22 – 5/17
1986 10/21 – until 1987 12/12
1996 7/4 – 8/2
1997 3/6 – until 1998 4/12
2001 7/12 – 12/19
2002 3/29 – 6/23
2010 10/21 – until 2011 10/14

URANUS BENEFICIAL
1944 6/21 – until 1947 5/15
1970 10/19 – until 1973 8/21
1983 1/6 – until 1987 10/5
2012 5/15 – Continues

NEPTUNE BENEFICIAL
1946 11/27 – until 1952 9/10
1973 2/9 – until 1981 11/8

PLUTO BENEFICIAL
1975 10/31 – until 1980 9/5
1998 1/15 – until 2005 11/16

JUPITER CHALLENGING
1938 1/20 – 4/1

1938 9/26 – 11/10
1940 6/19 – 11/30
1941 1/30 – 4/27
1946 10/29 – until 1947 1/18
1947 5/10 – 9/17
1950 1/4 – 3/13
1952 5/30 – until 1953 4/9
1958 10/13 – 12/28
1959 6/23 – 8/16
1961 12/16 – until 1962 2/24
1964 5/12 – 8/2
1964 10/27 – until 1965 3/20
1970 9/26 – 12/10
1973 4/2 – 7/30
1973 11/24 – until 1974 2/8
1976 4/26 – 7/6
1976 12/11 – until 1977 2/19
1982 1/9 – 4/11
1982 9/7 – 11/24
1985 3/11 – 9/26
1985 10/10 – until 1986 1/23
1988 4/9 – 6/17
1993 12/16 – until 1994 5/21
1994 8/12 – 11/8
1997 2/21 – until 1998 1/5
2000 3/23 – 5/30
2005 11/29 – until 2006 10/24
2009 2/5 – 4/25
2009 8/5 – 12/15
2011 7/16 – 10/14
2012 3/2 – 5/13

SATURN CHALLENGING
1940 5/17 – until 1941 6/20
1941 12/11 – until 1942 3/6
1953 12/28 – until 1954 4/10
1954 9/23 – until 1955 11/12
1962 3/7 – 8/12
1962 12/4 – until 1964 1/26
1969 7/7 – 10/6
1970 3/24 – until 1971 4/26
1983 10/31 – until 1984 12/17
1985 6/7 – 9/11
1992 1/12 – until 1993 2/28
1999 5/1 – until 2000 6/1

URANUS CHALLENGING
1938 1/1 – until 1941 3/21
1976 10/26 – until 1980 10/3
1997 3/13 – until 2002 1/16

NEPTUNE CHALLENGING
1959 11/13 – until 1967 10/24
2001 2/21 – until 2009 1/24

PLUTO CHALLENGING
1986 1/18 – until 1993 9/14

JUPITER SPECIAL
1943 8/2 – 10/24
1944 2/3 – 6/19
1955 7/17 – 10/1
1956 3/14 – 5/21
1967 7/1 – 9/13
1978 10/22 – 12/29
1979 6/12 – 8/27
1990 9/24 – until 1991 2/8
1991 5/19 – 8/12
2002 9/4 – until 2003 7/27

SATURN SPECIAL
1946 10/8 – until 1947 1/3
1947 6/24 – until 1948 7/27
1976 8/3 – until 1977 9/4
2005 9/13 – until 2006 2/4
2006 6/2 – 10/21
2007 1/21 – 7/9

URANUS SPECIAL
1957 7/29 – until 1961 6/29

PLUTO SPECIAL
1942 10/26 – until 1954 6/28

♌

293

August 9

Your Personal Powers

Creative and sensitive, you are a bright and imaginative individual with strong instincts and powerful emotions. Your ruler, the Sun, grants you energy, pride, optimism, and creativity. You gain power when you stay focused and let your idealism and intuition guide you. Your need for self-expression and fulfillment implies that you thrive on being active or planning for a brighter future. As you often take pride in your work, your self-respect and personal achievement are important factors in your overall success. You need therefore to avoid monotonous work that does not offer a sense of accomplishment. If you fail to find job satisfaction you can become discontented and resort to different forms of escapism. Your common sense and practical outlook indicate that your financial problems are often temporary and that you can usually bounce back or overcome challenges in your path. You empower yourself when you are willing to work hard and develop or perfect your unique skills.

Your Powers of Attraction in Relationships

You are charming and warm, and people are drawn to your friendly and self-assured personality. Although your romantic nature suggests that you have a great deal of love to give, you need to stay practical and cautious before entering long-term partnerships. Creative individuals who can fire your imagination and expand your knowledge often inspire your idyllic notions. A tendency to fluctuate emotionally, however, warns that if you do not channel your emotions positively you can change from being warm and generous to overly serious, irritable, and restless. When you become moody you display your less appealing qualities and express your disappointment with your partner. By developing your inner faith and staying mentally creative, you can remain lighthearted, loving, and achieve the happiness you seek.

Your attractive qualities: magnetic, charitable, ambitious, intuitive, creative, imaginative, pragmatic, responsible, strong-willed, noble, dynamic, gregarious, inspired, enthusiastic, kind, perfectionist, confident, charming, generous, sensitive, methodical, idealistic, humanitarian

Your less attractive qualities: rigid, stubborn, discontented, restless, emotional ups and downs, frustrated, nervous, unsure, selfish, impractical, too proud, arrogant, prone to flattery, indulgent, too economical, lack of motivation

Your Venus Power

The planet Venus has a great deal of influence on your powers of attraction. Below are four possible Venus types for women and men. To find your Venus you need to go to page 771, where you will find the Venus table and extra information. The planet Mars also affects your powers of attraction. To find your Mars table and interpretation go to page 761.

WOMEN WITH VENUS IN CANCER: With your intuitive abilities and sympathetic nature you are usually supportive to those you love. Impressionable and intuitive, your receptivity allows you to quickly pick up on the moods of people and you are especially aware of the emotional changes in your partner. As you often display true maternal tendencies toward those you know, you want a partner who is considerate and sensitive.

MEN WITH VENUS IN CANCER: You seek a partner who is sympathetic, caring, and protective. You are forgiving and compassionate and want a secure emotional bond in your close relationships. Usually you are drawn toward partners who are maternal, unselfish, or demonstrative with their feelings. Although you can sometimes appear to others as impressionable, you have powerful emotions and inner strength.

WOMEN WITH VENUS IN LEO: You possess the wonderful ability to project your warm and sunny personality and keep others happily entertained. Loving attention yourself, you seek a partner who can appreciate you, be supportive, and give you positive feedback. Proud, with a natural regal air, you expect respect from your partners but are willing to be loyal and supportive in exchange. Although sometimes a little self-centered, you know how to make your partner feel special.

MEN WITH VENUS IN LEO: Generous, animated, and pleasure-seeking, you can be very entertaining and fun to be with. You are usually attracted to extroverted and benevolent individuals with sunny personalities. If ambitious, you are drawn to a partner who shows leadership qualities or one who is highly motivated. Your less attractive qualities are your tendencies to be bossy or vain. With a sense of the dramatic, however, you can be the life and soul of the party and inspire those around you.

WOMEN WITH VENUS IN VIRGO: In relationships you can be modest and unassuming but desire perfection. You usually analyze your partnerships until you feel you have understood them to the last little detail in order to improve them. A problem usually arises when you become too critical either of part-

ners or yourself and indulge in being skeptical or faultfinding. As you are modest, others may not be aware of the strong sensuality beneath your well-groomed exterior.

MEN WITH VENUS IN VIRGO: Practical, idealistic, and a perfectionist, you seek a relationship with an intelligent and hardworking partner who can inspire you to be more industrious and well-ordered. At times you can come across as a sympathetic and caring person and at other times you may appear pragmatic and very businesslike. This may sometimes lead to unclear communication between you and your partner. Usually helpful and caring, however, you like to analyze the faults in your relationships and then work methodically to improve them.

WOMEN WITH VENUS IN LIBRA: A natural romantic with good social skills, you love to entertain or put people at ease by projecting a warm and gracious manner. Elegant and fair with a touch of glamour, you are also adept at dealing with people in delicate situations or conflicts. You seek refinement and will go out of your way to achieve harmony and keep the peace. For you, relationships are so important you may need to guard against becoming dependent on others for approval. With your friendly personality and inherent charm, however, you will always be popular and loved.

MEN WITH VENUS IN LIBRA: Your good social skills, charming personality, and refined manner usually make you attractive to the opposite sex. Equally, you desire a sophisticated partner with grace, elegance, and a strong sense of style. Although you have the ability to be persuasive and irresistible to others, avoid manipulative love games. Nevertheless, your natural diplomacy and sense of fair play help you to relate to people in all social situations. With your love for balance and harmony, you seek a partner who is also moderate, easygoing, and loving.

To read all about your Outer Planets and work out how to use your personalized timetable, go to Section Three, page 789.

go to Section Three, page 789.

♌

295

Your Personalized Timetable

JUPITER BENEFICIAL
1939 7/10 – 8/18
1940 2/12 – 4/21
1941 7/15 – 9/28
1941 10/22 – until **1942** 4/30
1945 10/16 – 12/6
1946 4/23 – 8/5
1947 11/30 – until **1948** 2/17
1948 6/14 – 10/14
1951 6/1 – 10/10
1952 1/18 – 4/4
1953 6/26 – 8/16
1953 12/15 – until **1954** 4/7
1957 10/1 – 11/17
1959 11/14 – until **1960** 1/27
1960 8/5 – 9/5
1963 5/10 – until **1964** 3/18
1965 6/10 – 7/25
1969 9/15 – 11/1
1971 10/28 – until **1972** 1/9
1975 4/21 – 7/28
1975 9/1 – until **1976** 2/28
1977 5/24 – 7/7
1981 8/29 – 10/16
1983 2/13 – 5/10
1983 10/9 – 12/24
1987 4/5 – 6/19
1987 10/22 – until **1988** 2/6
1989 5/8 – 6/20
1992 12/11 – until **1993** 3/19
1993 8/10 – 9/30
1995 1/19 – 6/20
1995 9/14 – 12/8
1999 3/20 – 5/28
2000 9/24 – 10/4
2001 4/19 – 6/4
2004 11/19 – until **2005** 4/26
2005 7/14 – 9/14
2006 12/31 – until **2007** 11/22
2011 3/2 – 5/9
2012 8/6 – 12/4

SATURN BENEFICIAL
1938 3/31 – until **1939** 5/7
1942 8/17 – 11/3
1943 4/30 – 7/19
1944 1/10 – 4/1
1951 11/17 – until **1952** 4/7
1952 8/11 – 11/7
1953 5/27 – 7/21
1956 12/21 – until **1957** 7/18
1957 9/5 – until **1958** 2/20
1958 5/19 – 11/16
1967 5/11 – 10/13
1968 2/1 – 6/27
1968 9/17 – until **1969** 3/14
1972 6/9 – until **1973** 5/23
1981 9/22 – 12/27
1982 3/7 – 9/15
1986 2/4 – 5/2
1986 10/30 – until **1987** 12/21
1997 3/14 – until **1998** 4/20
2001 7/21 – 12/7
2002 4/9 – 6/30
2010 10/29 – until **2011** 5/14
2011 7/12 – 10/22

URANUS BENEFICIAL
1944 7/9 – until **1947** 6/1
1970 11/4 – until **1973** 9/9
1983 1/27 – until **1987** 10/31
2012 6/13 – Continues

NEPTUNE BENEFICIAL
1947 10/21 – until **1953** 7/18
1973 12/27 – until **1981** 12/6

PLUTO BENEFICIAL
1975 12/2 – until **1980** 10/1
1998 12/6 – until **2006** 9/23

JUPITER CHALLENGING
1938 1/24 – 4/6
1938 9/15 – 11/21
1940 6/24 – 11/22

1941 2/7 – 5/1
1946 11/2 – until **1947** 1/25
1947 5/2 – 9/23
1950 1/8 – 3/17
1952 6/3 – until **1953** 4/14
1958 10/18 – until **1959** 1/2
1959 6/12 – 8/26
1961 12/21 – until **1962** 2/28
1964 5/16 – 8/10
1964 10/19 – until **1965** 3/25
1970 10/1 – 12/14
1973 4/9 – 7/23
1973 11/30 – until **1974** 2/12
1976 4/30 – 7/12
1976 12/3 – until **1977** 2/27
1982 1/17 – 4/3
1982 9/13 – 11/28
1985 3/16 – 9/7
1985 10/28 – until **1986** 1/27
1988 4/14 – 6/22
1993 12/22 – until **1994** 5/13
1994 8/20 – 11/13
1997 2/26 – until **1998** 1/10
2000 3/27 – 6/3
2005 12/3 – until **2006** 10/28
2009 2/9 – 5/3
2009 7/29 – 12/20
2011 7/24 – 10/6
2012 3/7 – 5/17

SATURN CHALLENGING
1940 5/25 – 12/23
1941 1/26 – 6/28
1941 11/28 – until **1942** 3/17
1954 1/11 – 3/27
1954 10/2 – until **1955** 11/20
1962 3/17 – 7/30
1962 12/14 – until **1964** 2/3
1969 7/22 – 9/20
1970 4/1 – until **1971** 5/3
1983 11/8 – until **1984** 12/26
1985 5/24 – 9/23
1992 1/21 – until **1993** 3/9
1993 10/2 – 11/22
1999 5/8 – until **2000** 6/9
2001 1/14 – 2/4

URANUS CHALLENGING
1938 1/1 – until **1941** 4/11
1976 11/10 – until **1980** 10/21
1997 4/8 – until **2002** 2/2

NEPTUNE CHALLENGING
1959 12/12 – until **1968** 9/13
2001 3/24 – until **2009** 12/16

PLUTO CHALLENGING
1986 11/22 – until **1993** 10/16

JUPITER SPECIAL
1943 8/7 – 10/31
1944 1/26 – 6/25
1955 7/22 – 10/6
1956 3/5 – 5/30
1967 7/5 – 9/18
1978 11/2 – 12/19
1979 6/17 – 9/1
1990 9/30 – until **1991** 2/1
1991 5/26 – 8/16
2002 9/9 – until **2003** 3/27
2003 4/11 – 7/31

SATURN SPECIAL
1946 10/23 – 12/18
1947 7/2 – until **1948** 8/3
1976 8/11 – until **1977** 9/12
1978 4/1 – 5/19
2005 9/23 – until **2006** 1/24
2006 6/12 – 11/5
2007 1/6 – 7/17

URANUS SPECIAL
1957 8/14 – until **1961** 7/17

PLUTO SPECIAL
1943 9/19 – until **1954** 8/2

August 10

Your Personal Powers

Ambitious and independent, you are a talented individual with a forceful personality and strong determination. Your ruler, the Sun, grants you vitality, confidence, and creativity. Although you are usually objective and pragmatic, a tendency to overanalyze situations suggests that you lose power when you allow indecisiveness and worry to cloud your rational thinking. Often direct in your dealings with others, you prefer to be forthright and honest. Your original thoughts or unique talents indicate that you have an unusual approach to solving problems. As a determined and security-conscious individual, your accomplishment usually comes from being enterprising, using your foresight and creative ideas. Since your ambitious or radical plans are often thought-provoking, you need to apply tact and diplomacy if you want to instigate changes or influence others. Although you enjoy planning or initiating new projects, it may be best to exercise some caution, especially if you are taking risks in order to be successful. Industrious and methodical, however, you empower yourself using your ingenuity and common sense.

Your Powers of Attraction in Relationships

You are friendly and sociable, and your charm ensures that you can attract people from all walks of life, but in particular those who are creative and enterprising like yourself. Romantic, you are usually drawn to highly idealistic individuals who have strong conviction or principals. Although you may have high standards, you can often be loving and generous. A stubborn streak warns that you may need to guard against becoming withdrawn or being critical. If you stay open-minded and receptive in matters of love and romance, you can be very spontaneous and passionate. If you become overly serious or preoccupied with career and money matters, your personal relationships may be affected. Nevertheless, benevolent and progressive as you are, when you believe in someone you can be very supportive and encouraging.

Your attractive qualities: dramatic, innovative, multi-talented, courageous, enthusiastic, focused, determined, pragmatic, frank, instinctive, direct, idealistic, creative, forceful, philanthropist, independent, optimistic, progressive, gregarious, thoughtful, responsible

Your less attractive qualities: doubtful, reckless, worry about money or the lack of it, selfish, impatient, too ambitious, indulgent, overbearing, jealous, arrogant, bossy, egotistical, too proud, antagonistic, disorganized, too competitive

Your Venus Power

The planet Venus has a great deal of influence on your powers of attraction. Below are four possible Venus types for women and men. To find your Venus you need to go to page 771, where you will find the Venus table and extra information. The planet Mars also affects your powers of attraction. To find your Mars table and interpretation go to page 761.

WOMEN WITH VENUS IN CANCER: Possessing a soft femininity, you have tender and sensitive emotions. Sympathetic and caring, you often mother those in your care by making sure they are comfortable and have plenty to eat. When you feel hurt or insecure in relationships you are likely to cover your feelings by being defensive or appearing tough on the outside while on the inside you are feeling vulnerable. Affectionate and romantic, you make a faithful and devoted partner.

MEN WITH VENUS IN CANCER: Being emotionally receptive, you can make a sensitive lover. With your desire to care for and protect others, you are likely to have strong family connections. Love is often tied in with being attentive to the needs of others and you may find yourself attracted to individuals who have sympathetic or maternal qualities. Security conscious, you need a loyal partner who can offer you support and ideally be a good cook and homemaker.

WOMEN WITH VENUS IN LEO: You possess the wonderful ability to project your warm and sunny personality and keep others happily entertained. Loving attention yourself, you seek a partner who can appreciate you and be supportive and give you positive feedback. Proud, with a natural regal air, you expect respect from your partners but are willing to be loyal and supportive in exchange. Although sometimes a little self-centered, you know how to make your partner feel special.

MEN WITH VENUS IN LEO: Sociable and outgoing, you are kind and generous with those you love. Looking for a relationship that can be fun and entertaining, you need a playmate who can share your enthusiasm and high spirits. Your pride, however, often stops you from associating with lovers or

partners you see as beneath you. As you desire someone who can appreciate your sense of the dramatic, you are often attracted to people with strong personalities.

WOMEN WITH VENUS IN VIRGO: Articulate and straightforward in your relationships, you attract others with your genuine concern for their well-being. By being understanding and a good listener, you are able to show your love and friendship. With your analytical approach to relationships, however, you may have to be careful of becoming too matter-of-fact. You often display your concern for the welfare of others by your willingness to offer practical help and assistance. You usually seek a partner who is willing to work as hard on relationships as you are.

MEN WITH VENUS IN VIRGO: Although you are constantly analyzing your relationships in order to understand and improve them, you may nevertheless need to refrain from continuously mulling over issues that can cause anxiety. You are happiest when you are able to help your loved ones in practical ways and forget yourself in your willingness to be of service to others. You seek a partner who has high standards and can be as pragmatic and hardworking as yourself. Ideally they should also be impeccably dressed with a fine analytical mind.

WOMEN WITH VENUS IN LIBRA: Gracious, charming, and sociable with a sense of style, you have no trouble attracting admirers. With your natural diplomatic skills and desire for harmony you usually like to keep the peace and avoid confrontations but be careful of failing to make a stand when it is necessary. Romantic and easygoing yourself, you are attracted to affectionate and refined individuals who share your love of peace, justice, and fair play.

MEN WITH VENUS IN LIBRA: You are such good company, people are naturally drawn to you and especially appreciate your talent for making them feel special. You find status in your social contacts and place importance on your relationships. Being clever and a charming companion, you will go out of your way to keep situations peaceful and harmonious. In relationships, however, be careful of indecision or compromising too much. Nevertheless, others are attracted by your natural refinement and good taste, which is reflected in your sense of style.

To read all about your Outer Planets and work out how to use your personalized timetable, go to Section Three, page 789.

To read all about your Outer Planets and work out how to use your personalized timetable, go to Section Three, page 789.

♌

Your Personalized Timetable

JUPITER BENEFICIAL
1940 2/17 – 4/25
1941 7/20 – until 1942 1/15
1942 2/26 – 5/5
1945 10/21 – 12/12
1946 4/15 – 8/12
1947 12/4 – until 1948 2/24
1948 6/6 – 10/20
1951 6/7 – 10/3
1952 1/24 – 4/8
1953 7/1 – 8/22
1953 12/8 – until 1954 4/13
1957 10/5 – 11/22
1958 6/3 – 7/4
1959 11/19 – until 1960 2/1
1960 7/21 – 9/19
1963 5/14 – until 1964 3/22
1965 6/14 – 7/30
1966 1/23 – 3/10
1969 9/20 – 11/5
1971 11/2 – until 1972 1/13
1975 4/26 – until 1976 3/4
1977 5/28 – 7/11
1981 9/3 – 10/20
1983 2/21 – 5/1
1983 10/15 – 12/28
1987 4/9 – 6/25
1987 10/15 – until 1988 2/11
1989 5/12 – 6/25
1992 12/18 – until 1993 3/11
1993 8/15 – 10/4
1995 1/24 – 6/12
1995 9/21 – 12/12
1999 3/24 – 6/1
1999 12/12 – 12/28
2001 4/24 – 6/8
2004 11/24 – until 2005 4/18
2005 7/23 – 9/19
2007 1/5 – 11/27
2011 3/7 – 5/13
2012 8/12 – 11/26

SATURN BENEFICIAL
1938 4/7 – until 1939 5/15
1939 11/29 – until 1940 1/24
1942 9/4 – 10/15
1943 5/8 – 7/27
1943 12/28 – until 1944 4/13
1951 11/27 – until 1952 3/25
1952 8/21 – 11/15
1953 5/9 – 8/7
1956 12/30 – until 1957 6/29
1957 9/23 – until 1958 3/9
1958 5/1 – 11/24
1967 5/21 – 10/1
1968 2/11 – 7/16
1968 8/29 – until 1969 3/22
1972 6/17 – until 1973 5/31
1981 9/30 – until 1982 1/20
1982 2/11 – 9/23
1986 2/21 – 4/14
1986 11/8 – until 1987 12/29
1997 3/22 – until 1998 4/27
2001 7/31 – 11/25
2002 4/18 – 7/8
2010 11/6 – until 2011 4/27
2011 7/28 – 10/30

URANUS BENEFICIAL
1944 7/31 – until 1948 3/7
1970 11/22 – until 1973 9/26
1983 11/28 – until 1987 11/19

NEPTUNE BENEFICIAL
1947 11/19 – until 1953 9/4
1974 1/29 – until 1982 11/2

PLUTO BENEFICIAL
1976 10/18 – until 1981 8/17
1999 1/1 – until 2006 11/8

JUPITER CHALLENGING
1938 1/28 – 4/11
1938 9/7 – 11/29

1940 6/29 – 11/14
1941 2/15 – 5/5
1946 11/7 – until 1947 2/2
1947 4/24 – 9/28
1950 1/12 – 3/22
1952 6/7 – until 1953 4/18
1958 10/22 – until 1959 1/7
1959 6/4 – 9/4
1961 12/25 – until 1962 3/4
1964 5/20 – 8/21
1964 10/9 – until 1965 3/30
1970 10/6 – 12/19
1973 4/16 – 7/15
1973 12/5 – until 1974 2/16
1976 5/4 – 7/17
1976 11/25 – until 1977 3/6
1982 1/27 – 3/24
1982 9/18 – 12/3
1985 3/21 – 8/28
1985 11/7 – until 1986 1/31
1988 4/18 – 6/26
1993 12/28 – until 1994 5/5
1994 8/27 – 11/17
1997 3/2 – until 1998 1/14
2000 3/31 – 6/8
2005 12/8 – until 2006 6/26
2006 7/16 – 11/2
2009 2/13 – 5/11
2009 7/20 – 12/25
2011 8/3 – 9/26
2012 3/12 – 5/21

SATURN CHALLENGING
1940 6/2 – 12/3
1941 2/15 – 7/8
1941 11/16 – until 1942 3/28
1954 2/1 – 3/4
1954 10/11 – until 1955 11/28
1962 3/29 – 7/17
1962 12/24 – until 1964 2/11
1970 4/9 – until 1971 5/11
1983 11/16 – until 1985 1/5
1985 5/11 – 10/3
1992 1/29 – until 1993 3/17
1993 9/14 – 12/9
1999 5/16 – until 2000 6/17
2000 12/21 – until 2001 2/28

URANUS CHALLENGING
1938 1/1 – until 1941 4/29
1976 11/26 – until 1980 11/6
1998 2/5 – until 2002 11/27

NEPTUNE CHALLENGING
1960 2/7 – until 1968 10/18
2002 2/15 – until 2010 1/18

PLUTO CHALLENGING
1986 12/20 – until 1993 11/10

JUPITER SPECIAL
1943 8/11 – 11/8
1944 1/18 – 6/30
1955 7/26 – 10/12
1956 2/27 – 6/7
1967 7/10 – 9/22
1979 6/22 – 9/5
1990 10/6 – until 1991 1/24
1991 6/1 – 8/20
2002 9/14 – until 2003 3/9
2003 4/30 – 8/5

SATURN SPECIAL
1947 7/10 – until 1948 8/11
1976 8/18 – until 1977 9/20
1978 3/14 – 6/6
2005 10/3 – until 2006 1/12
2006 6/21 – until 2007 7/25

URANUS SPECIAL
1957 8/30 – until 1961 8/3

PLUTO SPECIAL
1944 8/28 – until 1955 7/6

August 11

Your Personal Powers

Dynamic and inspired, and determined, you can be both idealistic and pragmatic. Often proud and confident, you enjoy being active and use your vitality and forceful nature in a productive manner. Since there is a need to create harmony and keep your desires on an even keel, you gain power when you balance your ambitious plans with your ideals. You lose some of your power when you act on impulse or show single-minded stubbornness. Although you may be tempted to achieve things single-handed, you benefit from collaborating with others and using your powers of gentle persuasion. As a good strategist with business acumen you can often achieve success in careers that involve mixing commerce with creativity. It is often your associations with others that bring you new opportunities and financial gains. You are therefore likely to find that true emotional fulfillment comes from doing things that can also benefit others. Although talented, it is often through endurance, hard work, and self-discipline that you achieve your goals.

Your Powers of Attraction in Relationships

Being energetic, you usually have a full and active social life. Creative and dynamic, your extrovert character indicates that you can attract others with your optimism and charismatic personality. You are usually attracted to powerful individuals who possess a strong identity. Alternatively, you may be attracted to creative and enterprising people who are full of bright ideas and can impress and inspire you. Being ambitious and people-oriented, you enjoy interacting with others, especially if there is a business angle to your associations. Although becoming involved with people who possess strong character may encourage you to test your own willpower and inner strength, avoid acting in an obstinate manner. Nevertheless, you can be extremely generous and very supportive of those you love, often turning new friendships into useful contacts.

Your attractive qualities: extrovert, determined, harmonious, objective, diplomatic, intuitive, compromising, peaceful, contented, entertaining, sociable, generous, idealistic, business acumen, inspired, focused, artistic, executive abilities, enthusiastic, intelligent, inspired, humanitarian

Your less attractive qualities: materialistic or worried about money, anxious, moody, extremist, impractical, arrogant, inertia, overemotional, easily hurt, selfish, unmotivated, too serious, extravagant, boastful, bossy

Your Venus Power

The planet Venus has a great deal of influence on your powers of attraction. Below are four possible Venus types for women and men. To find your Venus you need to go to page 771, where you will find the Venus table and extra information. The planet Mars also affects your powers of attraction. To find your Mars table and interpretation go to page 761.

WOMEN WITH VENUS IN CANCER: Gentle and tender, you are romantic by nature. You possess a strong need for security and usually help others feel safe and protected. This preservation is especially centered in the home, which is your haven from life's storm. Although your maternal instincts are strong, avoid making sacrifices for others at your own expense. Nevertheless, affectionate and caring, once committed to a relationship your loyalty and devotion to your partner is very strong.

MEN WITH VENUS IN CANCER: Being emotionally receptive, you can make a sensitive lover. With your desire to care for and protect others, you are likely to have strong family connections. Love is often tied in with being attentive to the needs of others and you may find yourself attracted to individuals who have sympathetic or maternal qualities. Security conscious, you need a loyal partner who can offer you support and ideally be a good cook and homemaker.

WOMEN WITH VENUS IN LEO: Warm and playful with a touch of the dramatic, you enjoy the company of generous or strong individuals who can share your sense of fun. Although there are advantages to your being strong-willed, in your relationships you need to resist being bossy as it can cause resentment. With your wonderful mixture of regal authority and childlike wonder, you love to keep others entertained and amused.

MEN WITH VENUS IN LEO: A childlike nature suggests that you are versatile and keen on games or being entertained. You are usually attracted to vivacious partners with a benevolent nature. As an extrovert you enjoy being involved in all types of activities where you can assert yourself and show your talents and abilities. Others may recognize your inborn tendencies to lead but are also aware of your vanity or pride.

Nevertheless, generous and caring, you often show more compassion to those less fortunate than yourself.

WOMEN WITH VENUS IN VIRGO: Articulate and straightforward in your relationships, you attract others with your genuine concern for their well-being. By being understanding and a good listener, you are able to show your love and friendship. With your analytical approach to relationships, however, you may have to be careful of becoming too matter-of-fact. You often display your concern for the welfare of others by your willingness to offer practical help and assistance. You usually seek a partner who is willing to work as hard on relationships as you are.

MEN WITH VENUS IN VIRGO: Industrious and well-ordered, you relate to others in a considerate and down-to-earth way. You enjoy giving practical advice and being of service to those you love, even in small ways. Being a perfectionist you are drawn to partners with high morals or a strong work ethic. Partners who have strong analytical minds are very attractive to you, particularly if they are also clean and meticulously dressed.

WOMEN WITH VENUS IN LIBRA: Attractive refined and conscious of the needs of others, you usually desire harmonious relationships. As a peacemaker with good negotiating skills, you can smooth out difficulties with others but your dislike of confrontation may sometimes leave you refusing to take a stand or compromising many of your own needs. Courteous, stylish, and charming with polished social skills, you are an expert at relating to others in a gracious and civilized manner.

MEN WITH VENUS IN LIBRA: Courteous and refined, you are attracted to beautiful and elegant people. You are looking for a partner who can share your natural good taste and enjoy an intellectual conversation. Disliking conflict, you may have to be careful not to go along with others just to keep the peace. Your ideal partner will appreciate beauty and the little luxuries of life as well as possess good social skills. You have a strong sense of social etiquette yourself so you need an intelligent and sophisticated partner.

To read all about your Outer Planets and work out how to use your personalized timetable, go to Section Three, page 789.

♌

Your Personalized Timetable

JUPITER BENEFICIAL
1940 2/21 – 4/29
1941 7/25 – until **1942** 1/4
1942 3/9 – 5/9
1945 10/25 – 12/19
1946 4/8 – 8/18
1947 12/9 – until **1948** 3/2
1948 5/29 – 10/26
1951 6/13 – 9/26
1952 1/30 – 4/12
1953 7/5 – 8/29
1953 12/1 – until **1954** 4/19
1957 10/10 – 11/27
1958 5/19 – 7/19
1959 11/23 – until **1960** 2/6
1960 7/11 – 9/28
1963 5/19 – 11/17
1963 12/23 – until **1964** 3/26
1965 6/18 – 8/4
1966 1/12 – 3/21
1969 9/24 – 11/10
1971 11/7 – until **1972** 1/18
1975 4/30 – until **1976** 3/8
1977 6/2 – 7/16
1981 9/8 – 10/25
1983 3/5 – 4/20
1983 10/20 – until **1984** 1/1
1987 4/13 – 7/2
1987 10/7 – until **1988** 2/17
1989 5/16 – 6/29
1992 12/27 – until **1993** 3/2
1993 8/21 – 10/9
1995 1/30 – 6/4
1995 9/28 – 12/17
1999 3/28 – 6/6
1999 11/25 – until **2000** 1/14
2001 4/29 – 6/12
2004 11/30 – until **2005** 4/10
2005 7/30 – 9/24
2007 1/10 – 7/28
2007 8/16 – 12/1
2011 3/11 – 5/17
2012 8/19 – 11/19

SATURN BENEFICIAL
1938 4/15 – until **1939** 5/23
1939 11/13 – until **1940** 2/9
1943 5/16 – 8/5
1943 12/16 – until **1944** 4/23
1951 12/9 – until **1952** 3/12
1952 8/30 – 11/24
1953 4/25 – 8/19
1957 1/8 – 6/14
1957 10/6 – until **1958** 12/3
1967 6/1 – 9/18
1968 2/21 – until **1969** 3/30
1972 6/24 – until **1973** 6/7
1981 10/8 – until **1982** 10/1
1986 11/16 – until **1988** 1/6
1988 8/16 – 9/13
1997 3/29 – until **1998** 5/5
2001 8/11 – 11/13
2002 4/27 – 7/16
2003 1/20 – 3/26
2010 11/15 – until **2011** 4/14
2011 8/10 – 11/7
2012 6/5 – 7/15

URANUS BENEFICIAL
1944 9/9 – until **1948** 4/17
1970 12/17 – until **1973** 10/11
1983 12/14 – until **1987** 12/6

NEPTUNE BENEFICIAL
1948 10/15 – until **1953** 10/3
1974 12/22 – until **1982** 12/1

PLUTO BENEFICIAL
1976 11/14 – until **1981** 9/17
1999 2/4 – until **2006** 12/6

JUPITER CHALLENGING
1938 2/1 – 4/17
1938 8/30 – 12/6
1940 7/5 – 11/7

1941 2/21 – 5/10
1946 11/11 – until **1947** 2/11
1947 4/14 – 10/4
1950 1/16 – 3/26
1952 6/12 – until **1953** 4/22
1958 10/26 – until **1959** 1/13
1959 5/27 – 9/11
1961 12/30 – until **1962** 3/8
1964 5/24 – 9/11
1964 9/17 – until **1965** 4/4
1970 10/10 – 12/24
1973 4/24 – 7/6
1973 12/10 – until **1974** 2/20
1976 5/8 – 7/23
1976 11/18 – until **1977** 3/12
1982 2/12 – 3/8
1982 9/23 – 12/7
1985 3/27 – 8/19
1985 11/15 – until **1986** 2/4
1988 4/22 – 7/1
1994 1/3 – 4/27
1994 9/2 – 11/21
1997 3/7 – until **1998** 1/18
2000 4/5 – 6/12
2005 12/13 – until **2006** 6/9
2006 8/2 – 11/6
2009 2/17 – 5/22
2009 7/9 – 12/30
2011 8/18 – 9/11
2012 3/16 – 5/25

SATURN CHALLENGING
1940 6/10 – 11/19
1941 2/28 – 7/18
1941 11/4 – until **1942** 4/6
1954 10/19 – until **1955** 12/6
1962 4/11 – 7/2
1963 1/2 – until **1964** 2/19
1970 4/17 – until **1971** 5/18
1983 11/24 – until **1984** 6/21
1984 8/4 – until **1985** 1/16
1985 4/28 – 10/13
1992 2/6 – until **1993** 3/26
1993 8/31 – 12/21
1999 5/24 – until **2000** 6/26
2000 12/7 – until **2001** 3/13

URANUS CHALLENGING
1938 2/16 – until **1941** 5/15
1976 12/14 – until **1981** 8/13
1998 2/22 – until **2002** 12/28

NEPTUNE CHALLENGING
1960 12/5 – until **1969** 8/31
2002 3/16 – until **2010** 12/2

PLUTO CHALLENGING
1987 11/7 – until **1994** 9/29

JUPITER SPECIAL
1943 8/15 – 11/19
1944 1/7 – 7/6
1955 7/30 – 10/18
1956 2/19 – 6/14
1967 7/14 – 9/27
1968 4/9 – 5/4
1979 6/27 – 9/10
1990 10/13 – until **1991** 1/17
1991 6/7 – 8/25
2002 9/19 – until **2003** 2/26
2003 5/10 – 8/9

SATURN SPECIAL
1947 7/18 – until **1948** 8/18
1976 8/26 – until **1977** 3/29
1977 4/23 – 9/29
1978 3/1 – 6/18
2005 10/16 – 12/29
2006 6/30 – until **2007** 8/2

URANUS SPECIAL
1957 9/17 – until **1961** 8/18

PLUTO SPECIAL
1944 10/14 – until **1955** 8/8

August 12

SUN: LEO · DECANATE: SAGITTARIUS/JUPITER · DEGREE: 19°–20° LEO · MODE: FIXED · ELEMENT: FIRE

Your Personal Powers

Idealistic and purposeful, you have tremendous energy and motivation to achieve success. Your ruler, the Sun, grants you a dramatic character, executive abilities, vitality, and self-confidence. Having natural business acumen and good social skills implies that you benefit from associations that involve financial dealings. You gain power, therefore, when you initiate or create new ideas or promote those you find inspiring or creative. You lose some of your power, however, when you let fear or worries about your finances undermine your great potential. Being proud, you are likely to hold on to your strong convictions and at times appear stubborn or uncompromising. Bold and energetic, however, you can create a strong impact on others. In addition, you can be charming and generous, empowering yourself by showing your benevolent nature. By being liberal or taking a more detached view you learn to accept other people's ideas and resolve conflict. The combination of your many creative ideas and determination can bring you much success.

Your Powers of Attraction in Relationships

You are sociable and gregarious, and other people are attracted to your enthusiastic and good-natured manner. Fun-loving and adventurous, you want a busy life with plenty of opportunities to meet new people. Proud and independent, you need a supportive partner who can give you the freedom to express yourself. You are usually attracted to creative, enterprising, and determined individuals. Although generally warm and caring you can, at times, display selfish and domineering behavior with your loved ones. Being affectionate and optimistic, your eagerness and sense of urgency implies that you may rush into relationships. A tendency to change your mind warns, however, that unless you feel certain about long-term commitments you need to be careful and take your time in choosing your partner.

Your attractive qualities: dynamic, courageous, idealistic, objective, ambitious, uplifting, direct, diplomatic, persuasive, negotiating skills, motivated, philanthropist, intuitive, assertive, forceful, alert, strategic skills, creative, attractive, disciplined, dignified, magnanimous, cooperative

Your less attractive qualities: domineering, restless, moody, indecisive, materialistic, impatient, arrogant, prideful, snobbish, selfish, uncooperative, too sensitive, lack of self-esteem, pushy, uncompromising

Your Venus Power

The planet Venus has a great deal of influence on your powers of attraction. Below are four possible Venus types for women and men. To find your Venus you need to go to page 771, where you will find the Venus table and extra information. The planet Mars also affects your powers of attraction. To find your Mars table and interpretation go to page 761.

WOMEN WITH VENUS IN CANCER: Gentle and tender, you are romantic by nature. You possess a strong need for security and usually help others feel safe and protected. This preservation is especially centered in the home, which is your haven from life's storm. Although your maternal instincts are strong, avoid making sacrifices for others at your own expense. Nevertheless, affectionate and caring, once committed to a relationship your loyalty and devotion to your partner is very strong.

MEN WITH VENUS IN CANCER: Being emotionally receptive, you can make a sensitive lover. With your desire to care for and protect others, you are likely to have strong family connections. Love is often tied in with being attentive to the needs of others and you may find yourself attracted to individuals who have sympathetic or maternal qualities. Security conscious, you need a loyal partner who can offer you support and ideally be a good cook and homemaker.

WOMEN WITH VENUS IN LEO: You possess the wonderful ability to project your warm and sunny personality and keep others happily entertained. Loving attention yourself, you seek a partner who can appreciate you and be supportive and give you positive feedback. Proud, with a natural regal air, you expect respect from your partners but are willing to be loyal and supportive in exchange. Although sometimes a little self-centered, you know how to make your partner feel special.

MEN WITH VENUS IN LEO: A childlike nature suggests that you are versatile and keen on games or being entertained. You are usually attracted to vivacious partners with a benevolent nature. As an extrovert you enjoy being involved in all types of activities where you can assert yourself and show your talents and abilities. Others may recognize your inborn tendencies to lead but are also aware of your vanity or pride.

Nevertheless, generous and caring, you often show more compassion to those less fortunate than yourself.

WOMEN WITH VENUS IN VIRGO: In relationships you can be modest and unassuming but desire perfection. You usually analyze your partnerships until you feel you have understood them to the last little detail in order to improve them. A problem usually arises when you become too critical either of partners or yourself and indulge in being skeptical or faultfinding. As you are modest, others may not be aware of the strong sensuality beneath your well-groomed exterior.

MEN WITH VENUS IN VIRGO: Although you are constantly analyzing your relationships in order to understand and improve them, you may nevertheless need to refrain from continuously mulling over issues that can cause anxiety. You are happiest when you are able to help your loved ones in practical ways and forget yourself in your willingness to be of service to others. You seek partners who have high standards and can be as pragmatic and hardworking as yourself. Ideally they should also be impeccably dressed with a fine analytical mind.

WOMEN WITH VENUS IN LIBRA: Usually you are attractive and sociable with an easygoing manner. Your love of beauty, harmony, and pleasure implies that you are a romantic with a desire for love and affection. Once in a relationship you need to learn to negotiate your position rather than adapt to the wishes of others and compromise just to keep the peace. Nevertheless, your advanced social skills and strong sense of fair play can help you succeed in any social or romantic situation.

MEN WITH VENUS IN LIBRA: As a sociable and friendly individual with an eye for beauty, you are amorous and charming. You are a natural gentleman and your ideal partner usually has an elegant appearance, artistic appreciation, and good taste. Your relationships benefit when you resist the temptation to take the easy way out or put too much emphasis on vanity and high living. Intellectual and naturally refined, you seek a loving partner who can share your romantic and sophisticated aspirations.

To read all about your Outer Planets and work out how to use your personalized timetable, go to Section Three, page 789.

Your Personalized Timetable

JUPITER BENEFICIAL
1940 2/25 – 5/3
1941 7/30 – 12/26
1942 3/18 – 5/14
1945 10/30 – 12/26
1946 3/31 – 8/24
1947 12/13 – until 1948 3/11
1948 5/20 – 10/31
1951 6/20 – 9/18
1952 2/4 – 4/16
1953 7/10 – 9/6
1953 11/23 – until 1954 4/24
1957 10/14 – 12/2
1958 5/10 – 7/29
1959 11/27 – until 1960 2/11
1960 7/3 – 10/6
1963 5/24 – 11/5
1964 1/4 – 3/30
1965 6/22 – 8/9
1966 1/4 – 3/29
1969 9/29 – 11/14
1971 11/11 – until 1972 1/22
1975 5/4 – until 1976 3/13
1977 6/6 – 7/20
1981 9/12 – 10/29
1983 10/25 – until 1984 1/6
1987 4/17 – 7/9
1987 9/30 – until 1988 2/22
1989 5/21 – 7/3
1993 1/9 – 2/18
1993 8/26 – 10/13
1995 2/5 – 5/28
1995 10/4 – 12/21
1999 4/1 – 6/11
1999 11/15 – until 2000 1/24
2001 5/3 – 6/16
2004 12/6 – until 2005 4/3
2005 8/6 – 9/28
2007 1/15 – 7/10
2007 9/3 – 12/5
2011 3/15 – 5/21
2012 8/27 – 11/11

SATURN BENEFICIAL
1938 4/23 – until 1939 6/1
1939 10/31 – until 1940 2/21
1943 5/23 – 8/16
1943 12/4 – until 1944 5/2
1951 12/23 – until 1952 2/26
1952 9/8 – 12/4
1953 4/13 – 8/30
1957 1/18 – 6/1
1957 10/17 – until 1958 12/11
1967 6/13 – 9/5
1968 2/29 – until 1969 4/6
1972 7/2 – until 1973 1/23
1973 3/6 – 6/14
1981 10/16 – until 1982 10/9
1986 11/24 – until 1988 1/15
1988 7/23 – 10/6
1997 4/6 – until 1998 5/13
1998 12/12 – until 1999 1/15
2001 8/26 – 10/29
2002 5/5 – 7/24
2003 1/6 – 4/9
2010 11/25 – until 2011 4/1
2011 8/20 – 11/15
2012 5/15 – 8/4

URANUS BENEFICIAL
1945 6/18 – until 1948 5/8
1971 10/9 – until 1974 8/1
1983 12/30 – until 1988 9/8

NEPTUNE BENEFICIAL
1948 11/12 – until 1954 8/28
1975 1/21 – until 1983 10/25

PLUTO BENEFICIAL
1976 12/26 – until 1981 10/12
1999 12/21 – until 2007 10/31

JUPITER CHALLENGING
1938 2/5 – 4/23
1938 8/22 – 12/12
1940 7/11 – 10/30

1941 2/27 – 5/14
1946 11/15 – until 1947 2/24
1947 4/1 – 10/9
1950 1/20 – 3/31
1952 6/17 – 12/29
1953 1/11 – 4/26
1958 10/31 – until 1959 1/19
1959 5/19 – 9/18
1962 1/3 – 3/12
1964 5/29 – until 1965 4/8
1970 10/15 – 12/29
1971 7/7 – 8/11
1973 5/4 – 6/26
1973 12/15 – until 1974 2/24
1976 5/12 – 7/29
1976 11/11 – until 1977 3/18
1982 9/28 – 12/11
1985 4/1 – 8/12
1985 11/22 – until 1986 2/8
1988 4/26 – 7/6
1988 12/27 – until 1989 2/13
1994 1/10 – 4/20
1994 9/8 – 11/26
1997 3/11 – until 1998 1/22
2000 4/9 – 6/16
2005 12/18 – until 2006 5/29
2006 8/13 – 11/10
2009 2/21 – until 2010 1/4
2012 3/21 – 5/30

SATURN CHALLENGING
1940 6/20 – 11/7
1941 3/11 – 7/31
1941 10/22 – until 1942 4/14
1954 10/27 – until 1955 12/14
1956 6/26 – 9/2
1962 5/1 – 6/11
1963 1/11 – until 1964 2/27
1970 4/24 – until 1971 5/26
1983 12/2 – until 1984 6/1
1984 8/23 – until 1985 1/30
1985 4/13 – 10/22
1992 2/14 – until 1993 4/5
1993 8/18 – until 1994 1/1
1999 6/1 – 12/14
2000 2/9 – 7/5
2000 11/24 – until 2001 3/24

URANUS CHALLENGING
1938 3/16 – until 1942 3/16
1977 1/5 – until 1981 9/22
1998 3/12 – until 2003 1/17

NEPTUNE CHALLENGING
1961 1/12 – until 1969 10/12
2003 2/10 – until 2011 1/11

PLUTO CHALLENGING
1987 12/2 – until 1994 10/28

JUPITER SPECIAL
1943 8/20 – 12/13
1943 12/15 – until 1944 7/11
1955 8/4 – 10/24
1956 2/12 – 6/20
1967 7/19 – 10/2
1968 3/24 – 5/20
1979 7/2 – 9/14
1990 10/20 – until 1991 1/9
1991 6/13 – 8/29
2002 9/24 – until 2003 2/18
2003 5/19 – 8/13

SATURN SPECIAL
1947 7/25 – until 1948 8/26
1976 9/3 – until 1977 3/6
1977 5/16 – 10/8
1978 2/17 – 6/29
2005 11/6 – 12/8
2006 7/8 – until 2007 8/10

URANUS SPECIAL
1957 10/11 – until 1962 6/12

PLUTO SPECIAL
1945 9/15 – until 1956 7/12

♌

August 13

Your Personal Powers

Inventive, creative, and intelligent, you are a resourceful individual with a forceful personality. Proud and hardworking, your perseverance and commanding manner suggest that you are able to rise to positions of authority. Your ruler, the Sun, grants you self-confidence, executive abilities, and vitality. Although you may feel at times inwardly vulnerable, you present an assured and assertive front. You gain power when you utilize your quick comprehension to acquire knowledge and skills. You also empower yourself when you combine your leadership ability and persuasive charm to advance in the world, especially in education or business. Alternatively, being intelligent and articulate, you can succeed in pursuing your creative talents especially in writing and management. Although you are by nature pragmatic, the idealistic part of your nature can make you altruistic toward others. You gain power when you show your warm and loving spirit or when you campaign for justice and reforms.

Your Powers of Attraction in Relationships

Magnanimous and dynamic, your strong presence and fine mind usually attract other people's admiration. Dramatic and direct, you like to take the initiative and be in command. Although others recognize your powers of reasoning, guard against displaying your less appealing qualities by being pretentious or bossy. Usually you seek a loving partner who can be both supportive and practical. Loving and passionate, you can be very romantic with your partner or lover. Since you also like to provide a secure environment for loved ones, you can be very protective toward the people you care about. Since feeling secure in a loving environment is also important to you, you are more likely to form long-lasting and stable relationships with those who can provide you with stability.

Your attractive qualities: ambitious, intelligent, responsible, hardworking, shrewd, analytical, persistent, determined, creative, dry humor, supportive, rational, knowledgeable, assertive, common sense, disciplined, romantic, charming, generous, reassuring, initiative, diplomatic, idealistic

Your less attractive qualities: stubborn, domineering, uncompromising, controlling, arrogant, unemotional, self-doubting, power struggles, cynical, critical, bossy, impulsive, indecisive, rebellious, opinionated

Your Venus Power

The planet Venus has a great deal of influence on your powers of attraction. Below are four possible Venus types for women and men. To find your Venus you need to go to page 771, where you will find the Venus table and extra information. The planet Mars also affects your powers of attraction. To find your Mars table and interpretation go to page 761.

WOMEN WITH VENUS IN CANCER: Possessing a soft femininity, you have tender and sensitive emotions. Sympathetic and caring, you often mother those in your care by making sure they are comfortable and have plenty to eat. When you feel hurt or insecure in relationships, you are likely to cover your feelings by being defensive or appearing tough on the outside while on the inside you are feeling vulnerable. Affectionate and romantic, you make a faithful and devoted partner.

MEN WITH VENUS IN CANCER: Affectionate with a strong sensitive streak, you can love very deeply. You may find yourself drawn toward sympathetic and supportive partners who can tune in to your moods and feelings. Family links are especially important to you and the more positive these relationships are, the more confident and safe you feel. Being emotionally receptive can make you a caring and responsive lover.

WOMEN WITH VENUS IN LEO: Your friendly and sunny personality often makes you stand out in a crowd. Generous and giving, you know how to make your partners feel special. As you often expect loyalty and devotion from your partner in return, you can become easily offended if they ignore you or behave in an inconsiderate manner. Charming and kind, when you are in love you can be romantic, dramatic, and passionate.

MEN WITH VENUS IN LEO: Enthusiastic, playful, and kind, you can be benevolent with those you love. Warm, romantic, and self-expressive, you adore the drama of love or having fun with your friends. Usually you are attracted to partners with a warm and generous nature. Although you can be a confident and charismatic partner, you may need to develop humility to stop pride or arrogance from marring your relationships.

WOMEN WITH VENUS IN VIRGO: In relationships you can be modest and unassuming but desire perfection. You usually analyze your partnerships until you feel you have understood them to the last little detail in order to improve them. A problem usually arises when you become too critical either of part-

ners or yourself and indulge in being skeptical or faultfinding. As you are modest, others may not be aware of the strong sensuality beneath your well-groomed exterior.

MEN WITH VENUS IN VIRGO: Although you are constantly analyzing your relationships in order to understand and improve them, you may nevertheless need to refrain from continuously mulling over issues that can cause anxiety. You are happiest when you are able to help your loved ones in practical ways and forget yourself in your willingness to be of service to others. You seek a partner who has high standards and can be as pragmatic and hardworking as yourself. Ideally they should also be impeccably dressed with a fine analytical mind.

WOMEN WITH VENUS IN LIBRA: Gracious, charming, and sociable with a sense of style, you have no trouble attracting admirers. With your natural diplomatic skills and desire for harmony, you usually like to keep the peace and avoid confrontations, but be careful of failing to make a stand when it is necessary. Romantic and easygoing yourself, you are attracted to affectionate and refined individuals who share your love of peace, justice, and fair play.

MEN WITH VENUS IN LIBRA: Your good social skills, charming personality, and refined manner usually make you attractive to the opposite sex. Equally, you desire a sophisticated partner with grace, elegance, and a strong sense of style. Although you have the ability to be persuasive and irresistible to others, avoid manipulative love games. Nevertheless, your natural diplomacy and sense of fair play help you to relate to people in all social situations. With your love for balance and harmony, you seek a partner who is also moderate, easygoing, and loving.

To read all about your Outer Planets and work out how to use your personalized timetable, go to Section Three, page 789.

Your Personalized Timetable

JUPITER BENEFICIAL
1940 3/1 – 5/7
1941 8/4 – 12/18
1942 3/25 – 5/19
1945 11/4 – until 1946 1/2
1946 3/23 – 8/30
1947 12/17 – until 1948 3/22
1948 5/9 – 11/5
1951 6/28 – 9/10
1952 2/9 – 4/20
1953 7/14 – 9/15
1953 11/13 – until 1954 4/29
1957 10/19 – 12/8
1958 5/1 – 8/6
1959 12/1 – until 1960 2/17
1960 6/25 – 10/13
1963 5/29 – 10/27
1964 1/13 – 4/3
1965 6/26 – 8/15
1965 12/27 – until 1966 4/5
1969 10/3 – 11/19
1971 11/15 – until 1972 1/27
1975 5/8 – until 1976 3/17
1977 6/10 – 7/25
1981 9/17 – 11/2
1983 10/30 – until 1984 1/10
1987 4/21 – 7/18
1987 9/21 – until 1988 2/27
1989 5/25 – 7/7
1993 8/31 – 10/18
1995 2/12 – 5/20
1995 10/10 – 12/25
1999 4/5 – 6/16
1999 11/7 – until 2000 2/1
2001 5/8 – 6/21
2004 12/12 – until 2005 3/26
2005 8/12 – 10/3
2007 1/20 – 6/30
2007 9/13 – 12/10
2011 3/19 – 5/26
2012 9/5 – 11/2

SATURN BENEFICIAL
1938 5/1 – 11/15
1939 1/13 – 6/11
1939 10/19 – until 1940 3/2
1943 5/31 – 8/28
1943 11/21 – until 1944 5/11
1952 9/16 – 12/15
1953 3/31 – 9/9
1957 1/29 – 5/19
1957 10/27 – until 1958 12/19
1967 7/2 – 8/17
1968 3/9 – until 1969 4/14
1972 7/10 – until 1973 1/5
1973 3/24 – 6/22
1981 10/24 – until 1982 10/17
1986 12/3 – until 1988 1/24
1988 7/7 – 10/21
1997 4/14 – until 1998 5/21
1998 11/22 – until 1999 2/4
2002 5/13 – 8/2
2002 12/24 – until 2003 4/20
2010 12/6 – until 2011 3/20
2011 8/30 – 11/24
2012 5/1 – 8/17

URANUS BENEFICIAL
1945 7/5 – until 1948 5/26
1971 10/24 – until 1974 8/27
1984 1/17 – until 1988 10/23

NEPTUNE BENEFICIAL
1948 12/23 – until 1954 9/28
1975 12/17 – until 1983 11/26

PLUTO BENEFICIAL
1977 10/31 – until 1982 8/31
2000 1/18 – until 2007 12/1

JUPITER CHALLENGING
1938 2/9 – 4/29
1938 8/15 – 12/18
1940 7/17 – 10/23

1941 3/5 – 5/18
1946 11/20 – until 1947 10/14
1950 1/24 – 4/5
1950 10/8 – 11/8
1952 6/21 – 12/11
1953 1/29 – 5/1
1958 11/4 – until 1959 1/25
1959 5/11 – 9/24
1962 1/7 – 3/17
1964 6/2 – until 1965 4/13
1970 10/19 – until 1971 1/3
1971 6/23 – 8/24
1973 5/22 – 6/7
1973 12/20 – until 1974 2/28
1976 5/16 – 8/5
1976 11/4 – until 1977 3/24
1982 10/3 – 12/16
1985 4/7 – 8/4
1985 11/29 – until 1986 2/12
1988 4/30 – 7/11
1988 12/17 – until 1989 2/23
1994 1/17 – 4/12
1994 9/14 – 11/30
1997 3/16 – until 1998 1/27
2000 4/13 – 6/21
2005 12/24 – until 2006 5/20
2006 8/21 – 11/15
2009 2/26 – until 2010 1/8
2012 3/26 – 6/3

SATURN CHALLENGING
1940 6/30 – 10/26
1941 3/20 – 8/17
1941 10/5 – until 1942 4/22
1954 11/4 – until 1955 12/23
1956 6/10 – 9/17
1963 1/19 – until 1964 3/6
1970 5/2 – until 1971 6/2
1983 12/11 – until 1984 5/17
1984 9/5 – until 1985 2/24
1985 3/18 – 10/31
1992 2/22 – 10/1
1992 10/30 – until 1993 4/16
1993 8/5 – until 1994 1/11
1999 6/9 – 11/28
2000 2/24 – 7/14
2000 11/13 – until 2001 4/3

URANUS CHALLENGING
1938 4/4 – until 1942 4/8
1977 11/3 – until 1981 10/13
1998 4/5 – until 2003 2/4

NEPTUNE CHALLENGING
1961 11/30 – until 1969 11/9
2003 3/9 – until 2011 2/7

PLUTO CHALLENGING
1988 1/1 – until 1995 9/4

JUPITER SPECIAL
1943 8/24 – until 1944 7/16
1955 8/8 – 10/31
1956 2/4 – 6/26
1967 7/23 – 10/8
1968 3/14 – 5/30
1979 7/7 – 9/19
1990 10/29 – 12/31
1991 6/18 – 9/3
2002 9/30 – until 2003 2/10
2003 5/26 – 8/18

SATURN SPECIAL
1947 8/2 – until 1948 9/3
1976 9/11 – until 1977 2/20
1977 5/30 – 10/18
1978 2/5 – 7/8
2006 7/16 – until 2007 8/17

URANUS SPECIAL
1958 8/5 – until 1962 7/5

PLUTO SPECIAL
1946 8/25 – until 1957 5/28

August 14

SUN: LEO · DECANATE: ARIES/MARS · DEGREE: 21°–22° LEO · MODE: FIXED · ELEMENT: FIRE

Your Personal Powers

Active, motivated, and dramatic, you appear as a confident and capable person. Often well-informed, you can empower yourself through the pursuit of knowledge or by improving your executive skills. Your ruler, the Sun, grants you a sense of the dramatic, an idealistic nature and confidence. With an inquiring mind you gain power when you apply logic to your intuition and set high standards for yourself. With your unique and fresh approach to problem solving, you can enlighten others. Capable and hardworking, you can impress superiors with your diligence and creativity. Although you are determined to achieve on a material level, your need for self-expression or mental stimulation implies that money and work alone may not be enough to help you achieve personal satisfaction. You lose some of your power when you allow boredom, doubt, or skepticism to undermine your highly receptive mind. Nevertheless, once set on a course of action, your strong sense of purpose confirms that little can stand in the way of your success.

Your Powers of Attraction in Relationships

Dramatic and affectionate, you have a wonderful way of uplifting other people's spirits with your quick wit and positive ideas. Usually your practical instincts and intuition suggest that you can also quickly assess people's moods. Although you are usually decisive and purposeful, you sometimes have a tendency to be emotionally uncertain in your relationships. When you have a change of heart you can become restless, stubborn, and refuse to compromise. Usually you prefer intelligent or enterprising individuals who are ambitious and versatile. Being affectionate and generous, you need to be appreciated and respected, not taken for granted. In your close relationship you want a smart partner who is supportive but liberal enough to give you the freedom to express yourself.

Your attractive qualities: intelligent, confident, decisive, head for business, productive, kind, independent, creative, imaginative, dramatic, entertaining, direct, generous, persuasive, witty sociable, pragmatic, hardworking, receptive, common sense, sympathetic, good listener, loyal

Your less attractive qualities: impatient, intolerant, restless, interfering, stubborn, unsure, melodramatic, too sensitive or emotional, too proud, overambitious, pretentious, too cautious or too impulsive, thoughtless, bossy, irritable

Your Venus Power

The planet Venus has a great deal of influence on your powers of attraction. Below are four possible Venus types for women and men. To find your Venus you need to go to page 771, where you will find the Venus table and extra information. The planet Mars also affects your powers of attraction. To find your Mars table and interpretation go to page 761.

WOMEN WITH VENUS IN CANCER: Possessing a soft femininity, you have tender and sensitive emotions. Sympathetic and caring, you often mother those in your care by making sure they are comfortable and have plenty to eat. When you feel hurt or insecure in relationships you are likely to cover your feelings by being defensive or appearing tough on the outside while on the inside you are feeling vulnerable. Affectionate and romantic, you make a faithful and devoted partner.

MEN WITH VENUS IN CANCER: Being emotionally receptive, you can make a sensitive lover. With your desire to care for and protect others, you are likely to have strong family connections. Love is often tied in with being attentive to the needs of others and you may find yourself attracted to individuals who have sympathetic or maternal qualities. Security conscious, you need a loyal partner who can offer you support and ideally be a good cook and homemaker.

WOMEN WITH VENUS IN LEO: Your friendly and sunny personality often makes you stand out in a crowd. Generous and giving, you know how to make your partner feel special. As you often expect loyalty and devotion from your partners in return, you can become easily offended if they ignore you or behave in an inconsiderate manner. Charming and kind, when you are in love you can be romantic, dramatic, and passionate.

MEN WITH VENUS IN LEO: Generous, animated, and pleasure-seeking, you can be very entertaining and fun to be with. You are usually attracted to extroverted and benevolent individuals with sunny personalities. If ambitious, you are drawn to a partner who shows leadership qualities or one who is highly motivated. Your less attractive qualities are your tendencies to be bossy or vain. With a sense of the dramatic, however, you can be the life and soul of the party and inspire those around you.

WOMEN WITH VENUS IN VIRGO: Articulate and straight-forward in your relationships, you attract others with your genuine concern for their well-being. By being understanding and a good listener, you are able to show your love and friendship. With your analytical approach to relationships, however, you may have to be careful of becoming too matter-of-fact. You often display your concern for the welfare of others by your willingness to offer practical help and assistance. You usually seek a partner who is willing to work as hard on relationships as you are.

MEN WITH VENUS IN VIRGO: Although you are constantly analyzing your relationships in order to understand and improve them, you may nevertheless need to refrain from continuously mulling over issues that can cause anxiety. You are happiest when you are able to help your loved ones in practical ways and forget yourself in your willingness to be of service to others. You seek a partner who has high standards and can be as pragmatic and hardworking as yourself. Ideally they should also be impeccably dressed with a fine analytical mind.

WOMEN WITH VENUS IN LIBRA: A natural romantic with good social skills, you love to entertain or put people at ease by projecting a warm and gracious manner. Elegant and fair with a touch of glamour, you are also adept at dealing with people in delicate situations or conflicts. You seek refinement and will go out of your way to achieve harmony and keep the peace. For you, relationships are so important you may need to guard against becoming dependent on others for approval. With your friendly personality and inherent charm, however, you will always be popular and loved.

MEN WITH VENUS IN LIBRA: You are such good company, people are naturally drawn to you and especially appreciate your talent for making them feel special. You find status in your social contacts and place importance on your relationships. Being clever and a charming companion, you will go out of your way to keep situations peaceful and harmonious. In relationships, however, be careful of indecision or compromising too much. Nevertheless, others are attracted by your natural refinement and good taste, which is reflected in your sense of style.

To read all about your Outer Planets and work out how to use your personalized timetable, go to Section Three, page 789.

To read all about your Outer Planets and work out how to use your personalized timetable, go to Section Three, page 789.

Your Personalized Timetable

JUPITER BENEFICIAL
1940 3/5 – 5/11
1941 8/10 – 12/11
1942 4/1 – 5/23
1945 11/8 – until 1946 1/12
1946 3/13 – 9/4
1947 12/22 – until 1948 11/10
1951 7/8 – 8/31
1952 2/14 – 4/24
1953 7/19 – 9/27
1953 11/1 – until 1954 5/4
1957 10/23 – 12/14
1958 4/23 – 8/13
1959 12/6 – until 1960 2/23
1960 6/18 – 10/19
1963 6/3 – 10/19
1964 1/20 – 4/8
1965 7/1 – 8/20
1965 12/20 – until 1966 4/12
1969 10/7 – 11/24
1971 11/20 – until 1972 2/1
1972 8/7 – 9/11
1975 5/13 – until 1976 3/21
1977 6/14 – 7/30
1981 9/22 – 11/7
1983 11/3 – until 1984 1/14
1987 4/26 – 7/29
1987 9/10 – until 1988 3/3
1989 5/29 – 7/12
1993 9/5 – 10/22
1995 2/20 – 5/12
1995 10/16 – 12/29
1999 4/9 – 6/22
1999 10/30 – until 2000 2/8
2001 5/12 – 6/25
2004 12/20 – until 2005 3/18
2005 8/17 – 10/7
2007 1/26 – 6/21
2007 9/21 – 12/14
2011 3/23 – 5/30
2012 9/18 – 10/19

SATURN BENEFICIAL
1938 5/10 – 10/30
1939 1/28 – 6/22
1939 10/7 – until 1940 3/11
1943 6/7 – 9/13
1943 11/5 – until 1944 5/19
1952 9/25 – 12/28
1953 3/17 – 9/18
1957 2/11 – 5/4
1957 11/6 – until 1958 12/27
1968 3/17 – until 1969 4/21
1972 7/19 – 12/23
1973 4/5 – 6/29
1981 11/1 – until 1982 5/25
1982 7/12 – 10/25
1986 12/11 – until 1988 2/2
1988 6/24 – 11/1
1997 4/21 – until 1998 5/30
1998 11/8 – until 1999 2/17
2002 5/21 – 8/12
2002 12/13 – until 2003 4/30
2010 12/19 – until 2011 3/5
2011 9/8 – 12/3
2012 4/18 – 8/29

URANUS BENEFICIAL
1945 7/24 – until 1948 6/11
1971 11/10 – until 1974 9/16
1984 2/10 – until 1988 11/13

NEPTUNE BENEFICIAL
1949 11/6 – until 1955 8/20
1976 1/14 – until 1984 10/14

PLUTO BENEFICIAL
1977 11/30 – until 1982 9/28
2000 12/10 – until 2008 10/22

JUPITER CHALLENGING
1938 2/14 – 5/6
1938 8/7 – 12/24

1940 7/25 – 10/16
1941 3/10 – 5/22
1946 11/24 – until 1947 10/19
1950 1/28 – 4/9
1950 9/25 – 11/22
1952 6/26 – 12/1
1953 2/8 – 5/5
1958 11/9 – until 1959 2/1
1959 5/3 – 9/29
1962 1/12 – 3/21
1964 6/6 – until 1965 4/17
1970 10/24 – until 1971 1/8
1971 6/14 – 9/3
1973 12/25 – until 1974 3/4
1976 5/20 – 8/13
1976 10/27 – until 1977 3/29
1982 10/7 – 12/21
1985 4/14 – 7/28
1985 12/4 – until 1986 2/16
1988 5/4 – 7/16
1988 12/8 – until 1989 3/3
1994 1/26 – 4/2
1994 9/19 – 12/4
1997 3/21 – 9/15
1997 10/31 – until 1998 1/31
2000 4/17 – 6/25
2005 12/30 – until 2006 5/12
2006 8/29 – 11/19
2009 3/2 – until 2010 1/13
2012 3/30 – 6/7

SATURN CHALLENGING
1940 7/12 – 10/13
1941 3/29 – until 1942 4/30
1954 11/12 – until 1956 1/1
1956 5/28 – 9/29
1963 1/27 – until 1964 3/14
1964 10/5 – 11/28
1970 5/9 – until 1971 6/10
1983 12/21 – until 1984 5/4
1984 9/17 – until 1985 11/8
1992 3/2 – 9/7
1992 11/22 – until 1993 4/30
1993 7/22 – until 1994 1/19
1999 6/18 – 11/15
2000 3/7 – 7/26
2000 10/31 – until 2001 4/12

URANUS CHALLENGING
1938 4/22 – until 1942 4/27
1977 11/18 – until 1981 10/30
1999 2/5 – until 2003 11/21

NEPTUNE CHALLENGING
1962 1/1 – until 1970 10/6
2003 4/18 – until 2012 1/4

PLUTO CHALLENGING
1988 11/16 – until 1995 10/13

JUPITER SPECIAL
1943 8/29 – until 1944 7/20
1955 8/12 – 11/7
1956 1/27 – 7/2
1967 7/28 – 10/13
1968 3/6 – 6/7
1979 7/11 – 9/24
1990 11/10 – 12/19
1991 6/23 – 9/7
2002 10/6 – until 2003 2/3
2003 6/2 – 8/22

SATURN SPECIAL
1947 8/9 – until 1948 9/10
1976 9/20 – until 1977 2/8
1977 6/10 – 10/30
1978 1/23 – 7/17
2006 7/23 – until 2007 8/25

URANUS SPECIAL
1958 8/21 – until 1962 7/23

PLUTO SPECIAL
1946 10/4 – until 1957 7/17

℺

305

August 15

Your Personal Powers

Creative and charismatic, you are an enthusiastic and intelligent individual full of energy and determination. Youthful and friendly, you are likely to seek ways to express your beliefs and ideas. Having vitality and confidence, you gain power from the combination of your reasoning abilities and practical skills. Usually your self-esteem and assertiveness increase when you concentrate on improving your knowledge or accumulating information. Your pride or a stubborn streak also implies that you like your independence and resent being confined by too many rules or restrictions. Although with your intuitive powers you are able recognize opportunities when they arise, if you are reluctant to take responsibility for your actions you can lose some of your power and appear immature or impulsive. Idealistic yet enterprising, your need for material security implies that you can be hardworking and keen on making money. With your foresight, organizational skills, and business acumen, you can make long-term commitments that will ensure your prosperity and success.

Your Powers of Attraction in Relationships

Charming and gregarious, your friendly personality ensures your popularity, providing you with many friends and romantic possibilities. Other people are attracted to your spontaneous and enthusiastic nature. Usually you are drawn to intelligent individuals you feel have a distinct bond with you. A tendency to fluctuate between being cooperative and committed and being stubborn and uncompromising warns against the stress of becoming involved in power struggles. You may look for a special or almost spiritual link with partners or become involved in clandestine relationships. Being romantic, you can be a daring and passionate lover. Although you may be looking for the ideal love or partnership, you also need to maintain your independence.

Your attractive qualities: clever, quick learner, youthful, independent thinker, creative ideas, dynamic, determined, ambitious, compassionate, sensitive, witty, generous, responsible, kind, cooperative, idealistic, entertaining, practical, sparkling individuality, flair for writing

Your less attractive qualities: proud, arrogant, materialistic, fluctuating finances, restless, impatient, stubborn, disruptive, ir-

responsible, self-centered, fear of change, skeptical, extravagant, nonconformist, unsettled

Your Venus Power

The planet Venus has a great deal of influence on your powers of attraction. Below are four possible Venus types for women and men. To find your Venus you need to go to page 771, where you will find the Venus table and extra information. The planet Mars also affects your powers of attraction. To find your Mars table and interpretation go to page 761.

WOMEN WITH VENUS IN CANCER: Gentle and tender, you are romantic by nature. You possess a strong need for security and usually help others feel safe and protected. This preservation is especially centered in the home, which is your haven from life's storm. Although your maternal instincts are strong, avoid making sacrifices for others at your own expense. Nevertheless, affectionate and caring, once committed to a relationship, your loyalty and devotion to your partner is very strong.

MEN WITH VENUS IN CANCER: You seek a partner who is sympathetic, caring, and protective. Able to be forgiving and compassionate, you want a secure emotional bond in your close relationships. You are usually drawn to partners who are maternal, unselfish, or demonstrative with their feelings. Although you can sometimes appear to others as impressionable, you have powerful emotions and inner strength.

WOMEN WITH VENUS IN LEO: As a person who wants to radiate in her own right, you are likely to desire partners you can be proud of. Usually you are attracted to fun-loving, warm, and generous individuals. If self-expression is important to you, you will probably seek the company of creative people such as artists, musicians, or those with a flair for acting. Alternatively, you may be drawn to people who are dignified, regal, or have already achieved success.

MEN WITH VENUS IN LEO: Generous, animated, and pleasure-seeking, you can be very entertaining and fun to be with. You are usually attracted to extroverted and benevolent individuals with sunny personalities. If ambitious, you are drawn to a partner who shows leadership qualities or one who is highly motivated. Your less attractive qualities are your tendencies to be bossy or vain. With a sense of the dramatic, how-

ever, you can be the life and soul of the party and inspire those around you.

WOMEN WITH VENUS IN VIRGO: Intelligent and discriminating, you are usually drawn to polite and refined individuals. As a perfectionist, you may be keen to analyze and criticize yourself but be careful of continually going over your partner's shortcomings. By focusing on how you can make positive improvements in yourself and in your relationships, you avoid becoming skeptical or confused. You empower yourself when you display kind and caring concern for the well-being of loved ones and spontaneously offer your practical assistance.

MEN WITH VENUS IN VIRGO: A love of order usually indicates that you are attracted to refined individuals with analytical or practical abilities. You and your partner may be working together or serving similar causes. As you constantly analyze partnerships in order to improve them, you are likely to use former relationships as a point of reference and compare them to your present partner. As you are helpful and kind, others usually rely on your good judgment and often turn to you for advice or practical assistance.

WOMEN WITH VENUS IN LIBRA: Usually you are attractive and sociable with an easygoing manner. Your love of beauty, harmony, and pleasure implies that you are a romantic with a desire for love and affection. Once in a relationship you need to learn to negotiate your position rather than adapt to the wishes of others and compromise just to keep the peace. Nevertheless, your advanced social skills and strong sense of fair play can help you succeed in any social or romantic situation.

MEN WITH VENUS IN LIBRA: Courteous and refined, you are attracted to beautiful and elegant people. You are looking for a partner who can share your natural good taste and enjoy an intellectual conversation. Disliking conflict, you may have to be careful not to go along with others just to keep the peace. Your ideal partner will appreciate beauty and the little luxuries of life as well as possess good social skills. You have a strong sense of social etiquette yourself so you need an intelligent and sophisticated partner.

To read all about your Outer Planets and work out how to use your personalized timetable, go to Section Three, page 789.

♌

Your Personalized Timetable

JUPITER BENEFICIAL
1940 3/9 – 5/16
1941 8/16 – 12/4
1942 4/7 – 5/27
1945 11/13 – until 1946 1/26
1946 2/27 – 9/9
1947 12/26 – until 1948 11/15
1951 7/23 – 8/16
1952 2/19 – 4/28
1953 7/24 – until 1954 1/24
1954 2/27 – 5/9
1957 10/28 – 12/20
1958 4/16 – 8/20
1959 12/10 – until 1960 3/1
1960 6/10 – 10/25
1963 6/9 – 10/12
1964 1/26 – 4/12
1965 7/5 – 8/27
1965 12/13 – until 1966 4/18
1969 10/12 – 11/29
1970 5/30 – 7/17
1971 11/24 – until 1972 2/6
1972 7/25 – 9/24
1975 5/17 – until 1976 3/26
1977 6/18 – 8/3
1978 1/28 – 3/15
1981 9/26 – 11/12
1983 11/8 – until 1984 1/19
1987 4/30 – until 1988 3/8
1989 6/2 – 7/16
1993 9/10 – 10/27
1995 3/1 – 5/2
1995 10/21 – until 1996 1/3
1999 4/13 – 6/28
1999 10/23 – until 2000 2/14
2001 5/16 – 6/29
2004 12/28 – until 2005 3/9
2005 8/23 – 10/12
2007 1/31 – 6/13
2007 9/28 – 12/18
2011 3/27 – 6/4

SATURN BENEFICIAL
1938 5/19 – 10/17
1939 2/8 – 7/5
1939 9/23 – until 1940 3/19
1943 6/14 – until 1944 5/27
1952 10/3 – until 1953 1/16
1953 2/25 – 9/26
1957 3/3 – 4/14
1968 3/24 – until 1969 4/29
1972 7/28 – 12/11
1973 4/16 – 7/7
1981 11/9 – until 1982 5/6
1982 7/30 – 11/2
1986 12/19 – until 1988 2/13
1988 6/11 – 11/11
1997 4/30 – 11/25
1998 1/6 – 6/8
1998 10/26 – until 1999 2/28
2002 5/28 – 8/23
2002 12/1 – until 2003 5/9
2011 1/8 – 2/13
2011 9/16 – 12/14
2012 4/5 – 9/8

URANUS BENEFICIAL
1945 8/19 – until 1949 4/5
1971 11/28 – until 1974 10/2
1984 12/8 – until 1988 12/1

NEPTUNE BENEFICIAL
1949 12/11 – until 1955 9/23
1976 3/4 – until 1984 11/19

PLUTO BENEFICIAL
1978 10/18 – until 1983 8/4
2001 1/5 – until 2008 11/25

JUPITER CHALLENGING
1938 2/18 – 5/13
1938 7/30 – 12/29
1940 8/2 – 10/7

1941 3/15 – 5/26
1946 11/29 – until 1947 10/23
1950 2/1 – 4/15
1950 9/15 – 12/1
1952 7/2 – 11/23
1953 2/17 – 5/9
1958 11/13 – until 1959 2/10
1959 4/25 – 10/5
1962 1/16 – 3/25
1964 6/11 – until 1965 4/22
1970 10/28 – until 1971 1/14
1971 6/5 – 9/11
1973 12/29 – until 1974 3/8
1976 5/24 – 8/22
1976 10/17 – until 1977 4/3
1982 10/12 – 12/25
1985 4/21 – 7/20
1985 12/10 – until 1986 2/20
1988 5/8 – 7/21
1988 12/1 – until 1989 3/10
1994 2/7 – 3/22
1994 9/25 – 12/9
1997 3/26 – 9/4
1997 11/11 – until 1998 2/4
2000 4/21 – 6/30
2006 1/5 – 5/5
2006 9/4 – 11/23
2009 3/6 – until 2010 1/17
2012 4/3 – 6/11

SATURN CHALLENGING
1940 7/27 – 9/27
1941 4/6 – until 1942 5/8
1954 11/20 – until 1956 1/12
1956 5/15 – 10/9
1963 2/4 – until 1964 3/23
1964 9/18 – 12/15
1970 5/17 – until 1971 6/18
1972 1/12 – 2/19
1984 1/1 – 4/21
1984 9/27 – until 1985 11/16
1992 3/11 – 8/23
1992 12/6 – until 1993 5/19
1993 7/2 – until 1994 1/28
1999 6/28 – 11/3
2000 3/17 – 8/9
2000 10/17 – until 2001 4/20

URANUS CHALLENGING
1938 5/9 – until 1942 5/14
1977 12/4 – until 1981 11/15
1999 2/22 – until 2003 12/28

NEPTUNE CHALLENGING
1962 11/25 – until 1970 11/4
2004 3/2 – until 2012 2/2

PLUTO CHALLENGING
1988 12/11 – until 1995 11/9

JUPITER SPECIAL
1943 9/2 – until 1944 7/25
1955 8/17 – 11/16
1956 1/18 – 7/7
1967 8/1 – 10/19
1968 2/27 – 6/15
1979 7/16 – 9/29
1991 6/28 – 9/11
2002 10/12 – until 2003 1/27
2003 6/8 – 8/27

SATURN SPECIAL
1947 8/17 – until 1948 9/18
1949 4/4 – 5/27
1976 9/30 – until 1977 1/27
1977 6/20 – 11/15
1978 1/6 – 7/25
2006 7/31 – until 2007 9/2

URANUS SPECIAL
1958 9/6 – until 1962 8/9

PLUTO SPECIAL
1947 9/8 – until 1958 6/5

August 16

Your Personal Powers

Intuitive yet discriminating, you are an intelligent and mentally creative individual who is usually rational and thoughtful. You often succeed by combining your confidence, executive abilities, and creativity. Although you are usually self-assured and determined, inwardly you are sensitive and imaginative. You achieve more when you learn to trust your innate intuition. Curious about what motivates others, you like to delve into the minds of those you interact with. Although you are proud and tenacious, by compromising and creating harmony, you can ensure the approval of others and achieve personal satisfaction. You can lose some of your power through being stubborn, dissatisfied, or dominating. As you are likely to grasp information and ideas quickly, you usually prefer to make up your own mind and are not easily swayed by others. You gain power, however, when you resist being too opinionated. As you are enthusiastic and spontaneous about ideas that capture your imagination, your creativity can make you someone special. Your self-mastery comes through being decisive and disciplined.

Your Powers of Attraction in Relationships

Magnetic and friendly, you attract other people with your forceful personality. Clever and intuitive, you are able to quickly assess people, frequently recognizing their special qualities and weaknesses. Although you can be cautious and serious, your generosity and sense of the dramatic usually win you many friends and admirers. Learning to express your inner doubts or feelings can help you alleviate some of your emotional frustrations or dissatisfaction. Although you can be very loving and supportive, a tendency to be moody suggests that you can be prone to periods of discontentment. Often you are attracted to independent and enterprising people or individuals who are forceful and masterful. Alternatively, you may be drawn to persuasive people who are knowledgeable and idealistic.

Your attractive qualities: independent, knowledgeable, analytical, business sense, insightful, determined, forceful, persuasive, authoritative, pragmatic, helpful, intuitive, generous, modest, ambitious, disciplined, perceptive, discriminative, responsible, love of learning, hardworking

Your less attractive qualities: cold, demanding, detached, unsympathetic, moody, pessimistic, interfering, controlling, arrogant, easily bored, impulsive, vain, irresponsible, self-promoting, opinionated, skeptical, irritable

Your Venus Power

The planet Venus has a great deal of influence on your powers of attraction. Below are four possible Venus types for women and men. To find your Venus you need to go to page 771, where you will find the Venus table and extra information. The planet Mars also affects your powers of attraction. To find your Mars table and interpretation go to page 761.

WOMEN WITH VENUS IN CANCER: Possessing a soft femininity, you have tender and sensitive emotions. Sympathetic and caring, you often mother those in your care by making sure they are comfortable and have plenty to eat. When you feel hurt or insecure in relationships, you are likely to cover your feelings by being defensive or appearing tough on the outside while on the inside you are feeling vulnerable. Affectionate and romantic, you make a faithful and devoted partner.

MEN WITH VENUS IN CANCER: Being emotionally receptive, you can make a sensitive lover. With your desire to care for and protect others, you are likely to have strong family connections. Love is often tied in with being attentive to the needs of others and you may find yourself attracted to individuals who have sympathetic or maternal qualities. Security conscious, you need a loyal partner who can offer you support and ideally be a good cook and homemaker.

WOMEN WITH VENUS IN LEO: Warm and playful with a touch of the dramatic, you enjoy the company of generous or strong individuals who can share your sense of fun. Although there are advantages to your being strong-willed, in your relationships you need to resist being bossy as it can cause resentment. With your wonderful mixture of regal authority and childlike wonder, you love to keep others entertained and amused.

MEN WITH VENUS IN LEO: Sociable and outgoing, you are kind and generous with those you love. Looking for a relationship that can be fun and entertaining, you need a playmate who can share your enthusiasm and high spirits. Your pride, however, often stops you from associating with lovers or partners you see as beneath you. As you desire someone who

can appreciate your sense of the dramatic, you are often attracted to people with strong personalities.

WOMEN WITH VENUS IN VIRGO: In relationships you can be modest and unassuming but desire perfection. You usually analyze your partnerships until you feel you have understood them to the last little detail in order to improve them. A problem usually arises when you become too critical either of partners or yourself and indulge in being skeptical or faultfinding. As you are modest, others may not be aware of the strong sensuality beneath your well-groomed exterior.

MEN WITH VENUS IN VIRGO: Industrious and well-ordered, you relate to others in a considerate and down-to-earth way. You enjoy giving practical advice and being of service to those you love, even in small ways. Being a perfectionist you are drawn to partners with high morals or a strong work ethic. Partners who have strong analytical minds are very attractive to you, particularly if they are also clean and meticulously dressed.

WOMEN WITH VENUS IN LIBRA: A natural romantic with good social skills, you love to entertain or put people at ease by projecting a warm and gracious manner. Elegant and fair with a touch of glamour, you are also adept at dealing with people in delicate situations or conflicts. You seek refinement and will go out of your way to achieve harmony and keep the peace. For you, relationships are so important that you may need to guard against becoming dependent on others for approval. With your friendly personality and inherent charm, however, you will always be popular and loved.

MEN WITH VENUS IN LIBRA: As a sociable and friendly individual with an eye for beauty, you are amorous and charming. You are a natural gentleman and your ideal partner usually has an elegant appearance, artistic appreciation, and good taste. Your relationships benefit when you resist the temptation to take the easy way out or put too much emphasis on vanity and high living. Intellectual and naturally refined, you seek a loving partner who can share your romantic and sophisticated aspirations.

To read all about your Outer Planets and work out how to use your personalized timetable, go to Section Three, page 789.

Your Personalized Timetable

JUPITER BENEFICIAL
1940 3/13 – 5/20
1941 8/23 – 11/27
1942 4/12 – 6/1
1945 11/18 – until 1946 5/28
1946 7/2 – 9/14
1947 12/30 – until 1948 11/19
1952 2/24 – 5/2
1953 7/28 – until 1954 1/11
1954 3/12 – 5/14
1957 11/1 – 12/26
1958 4/8 – 8/26
1959 12/14 – until 1960 3/8
1960 6/2 – 10/31
1963 6/15 – 10/5
1964 2/1 – 4/16
1965 7/9 – 9/2
1965 12/5 – until 1966 4/24
1969 10/16 – 12/4
1970 5/18 – 7/29
1971 11/28 – until 1972 2/11
1972 7/15 – 10/4
1975 5/22 – 12/1
1975 12/19 – until 1976 3/30
1977 6/22 – 8/8
1978 1/17 – 3/25
1981 10/1 – 11/16
1983 11/12 – until 1984 1/23
1987 5/4 – until 1988 3/12
1989 6/6 – 7/21
1993 9/14 – 10/31
1995 3/14 – 4/19
1995 10/26 – until 1996 1/7
1999 4/17 – 7/4
1999 10/16 – until 2000 2/20
2001 5/21 – 7/3
2005 1/8 – 2/26
2005 8/28 – 10/16
2007 2/6 – 6/6
2007 10/5 – 12/22
2011 3/31 – 6/9
2011 12/8 – until 2012 1/12

SATURN BENEFICIAL
1938 5/29 – 10/4
1939 2/18 – 7/24
1939 9/3 – until 1940 3/27
1943 6/22 – until 1944 6/4
1952 10/10 – until 1953 10/5
1957 11/23 – until 1959 1/13
1959 8/12 – 9/28
1968 4/1 – until 1969 5/7
1972 8/7 – 11/29
1973 4/25 – 7/15
1974 2/17 – 3/10
1981 11/18 – until 1982 4/22
1982 8/12 – 11/10
1983 6/17 – 7/15
1986 12/27 – until 1987 7/29
1987 9/9 – until 1988 2/25
1988 5/28 – 11/21
1997 5/8 – 11/6
1998 1/24 – 6/18
1998 10/14 – until 1999 3/9
2002 6/5 – 9/5
2002 11/17 – until 2003 5/17
2011 9/25 – 12/26
2012 3/23 – 9/17

URANUS BENEFICIAL
1946 6/14 – until 1949 5/1
1971 12/24 – until 1974 10/18
1984 12/23 – until 1988 12/17

NEPTUNE BENEFICIAL
1950 11/1 – until 1956 8/8
1977 1/8 – until 1985 9/25

PLUTO BENEFICIAL
1978 11/13 – until 1983 9/12
2001 2/9 – until 2009 10/11

JUPITER CHALLENGING
1938 2/22 – 5/23

1938 7/21 – until 1939 1/3
1940 8/13 – 9/26
1941 3/20 – 5/30
1946 12/3 – until 1947 10/28
1950 2/5 – 4/20
1950 9/7 – 12/8
1952 7/7 – 11/15
1953 2/23 – 5/13
1958 11/17 – until 1959 2/20
1959 4/14 – 10/10
1962 1/20 – 3/30
1964 6/15 – until 1965 4/26
1970 11/2 – until 1971 1/19
1971 5/28 – 9/18
1974 1/3 – 3/12
1976 5/28 – 9/6
1976 10/3 – until 1977 4/8
1982 10/17 – 12/30
1985 4/29 – 7/11
1985 12/15 – until 1986 2/24
1988 5/12 – 7/27
1988 11/24 – until 1989 3/17
1994 9/30 – 12/13
1997 3/31 – 8/26
1997 11/19 – until 1998 2/8
2000 4/25 – 7/4
2006 1/11 – 4/27
2006 9/10 – 11/28
2009 3/11 – until 2010 1/22
2012 4/8 – 6/15

SATURN CHALLENGING
1941 4/14 – until 1942 5/15
1954 11/28 – until 1955 6/27
1955 8/10 – until 1956 1/23
1956 5/1 – 10/19
1963 2/12 – until 1964 4/1
1964 9/4 – 12/27
1970 5/24 – until 1971 6/26
1971 12/24 – until 1972 3/9
1984 1/13 – 4/7
1984 10/6 – until 1985 11/24
1992 3/20 – 8/10
1992 12/17 – until 1994 2/5
1999 7/8 – 10/22
2000 3/26 – 9/3
2000 9/21 – until 2001 4/28

URANUS CHALLENGING
1938 5/26 – until 1943 3/6
1977 12/22 – until 1982 9/5
1999 3/12 – until 2004 1/18

NEPTUNE CHALLENGING
1962 12/25 – until 1971 9/28
2004 4/4 – until 2012 12/25

PLUTO CHALLENGING
1989 1/16 – until 1996 9/24

JUPITER SPECIAL
1943 9/7 – until 1944 7/30
1955 8/21 – 11/28
1956 1/6 – 7/12
1967 8/5 – 10/25
1968 2/20 – 6/21
1979 7/20 – 10/4
1980 4/6 – 5/16
1991 7/3 – 9/16
2002 10/19 – until 2003 1/19
2003 6/14 – 8/31

SATURN SPECIAL
1947 8/25 – until 1948 9/26
1949 3/18 – 6/13
1976 10/11 – until 1977 1/14
1977 6/29 – until 1978 8/3
2006 8/7 – until 2007 9/9

URANUS SPECIAL
1958 9/25 – until 1962 8/24

PLUTO SPECIAL
1947 11/1 – until 1958 7/21

♌

August 17

Your Personal Powers

Shrewd and imaginative, you have the ability to understand concepts intuitively and instantly. Clever, with a wealth of wonderful ideas and powerful desires, you usually feel inspired to be hardworking and productive. You may, however, lose some of that power and undermine your capabilities by becoming restless and stubborn. Nevertheless, your ruler, the Sun, grants you confidence, a sense of the dramatic, and creativity. Since you are eager to express your ideas or talents, you gain power through self-discipline or by obtaining the type of education that can lead you to freely express yourself. A tendency to vacillate between being reserved and serious and being enthusiastic or spontaneous implies that by staying objective and positive you can overcome feelings of frustration or apprehension. You are capable and independent, and your good sense of values suggests that your natural business sense or management capabilities can really help you succeed in life.

Your Powers of Attraction in Relationships

Your warmth, kindness, generosity, and sense of fun indicate that you are sociable and friendly. Being instinctive with analytical abilities, you can be very persuasive and charismatic when you are in a positive frame of mind. Other people admire your inventiveness and creative ideas. Quick at repartee, you enjoy communicating or being witty. Willing to lend a helping hand, you are often supportive and encouraging to those you love or admire. In close relationships, however, you may need to resist being bossy or too demanding. Your many ideas imply that usually you are attracted to loyal and enterprising partners who can keep up with your imaginative thoughts. Alternatively, you need a partner who offers emotional support. Although a good parent and a loyal and sympathetic partner, you need to make sure there is equal give and take in your relationships.

Your attractive qualities: intuitive, imaginative, objective, optimistic outlook, creative, talent for writing, bright, cheerful, productive, tolerant, loyal, caring, generous, broad-minded, dramatic, rational, intelligent, loving nature, thoughtful, skilled, communicative, astute

Your less attractive qualities: critical, impulsive, emotional inhibitions, impetuous, discontented, melodramatic, depressed, frustrated, stuck in a rut, extravagant, dogmatic, uncommunicative, moody, stubborn, carelessness, sensitive to criticism, worried, suspicious, anxious

Your Venus Power

The planet Venus has a great deal of influence on your powers of attraction. Below are four possible Venus types for women and men. To find your Venus you need to go to page 771, where you will find the Venus table and extra information. The planet Mars also affects your powers of attraction. To find your Mars table and interpretation go to page 761.

WOMEN WITH VENUS IN CANCER: Possessing a soft femininity, you have tender and sensitive emotions. Sympathetic and caring, you often mother those in your care by making sure they are comfortable and have plenty to eat. When you feel hurt or insecure in relationships you are likely to cover your feelings by being defensive or appearing tough on the outside while on the inside you are feeling vulnerable. Affectionate and romantic, you make a faithful and devoted partner.

MEN WITH VENUS IN CANCER: You seek a partner who is sympathetic, caring, and protective. Able to be forgiving and compassionate, you want a secure emotional bond in your close relationships. Usually you are drawn to partners who are maternal, unselfish, or demonstrative with their feelings. Although you can sometimes appear to others as impressionable, you have powerful emotions and inner strength.

WOMEN WITH VENUS IN LEO: As a person who wants to radiate in her own right, you are likely to desire partners you can be proud of. Usually you are attracted to fun-loving, warm, and generous individuals. If self-expression is important to you, you will probably seek the company of creative people such as artists, musicians, or those with a flair for acting. Alternatively, you may be drawn to people who are dignified, regal, or have already achieved success.

MEN WITH VENUS IN LEO: A childlike nature suggests that you are versatile and keen on games or being entertained. You are usually attracted to vivacious partners with a benevolent nature. As an extrovert you enjoy being involved in all types of activities where you can assert yourself and show your talents and abilities. Others may recognize your inborn tendencies to lead but are also aware of your vanity or pride. Nevertheless, generous and caring, you often show more compassion to those less fortunate than yourself.

WOMEN WITH VENUS IN VIRGO: Polite, refined, and organized, you are attracted to articulate and intelligent people. Since you are caring, concerned, and want to be of practical help to others, you can be an asset to any partnership. By being too analytical, exacting, or faultfinding, however, a doubting element can creep into your relationships. By expressing your feelings in a positive way you can become more decisive and improve on how you relate to your loved ones.

MEN WITH VENUS IN VIRGO: Industrious and well-ordered, you relate to others in a considerate and down-to-earth way. You enjoy giving practical advice and being of service to those you love, even in small ways. Being a perfectionist you are drawn to partners with high morals or a strong work ethic. Partners who have strong analytical minds are very attractive to you, particularly if they are also clean and meticulously dressed.

WOMEN WITH VENUS IN LIBRA: Gracious, charming, and sociable with a sense of style, you have no trouble in drawing admirers. With your natural diplomatic skills and desire for harmony you usually like to keep the peace and avoid confrontations, but be careful of failing to make a stand when it is necessary. Romantic and easygoing yourself, you are attracted to affectionate and refined individuals who share your love of peace, justice, and fair play.

MEN WITH VENUS IN LIBRA: You are such good company, people are naturally drawn to you and especially appreciate your talent for making them feel special. You find status in your social contacts and place importance on your relationships. Being clever and a charming companion, you will go out of your way to keep situations peaceful and harmonious. In relationships, however, be careful of indecision or compromising too much. Nevertheless, others are attracted by your natural refinement and good taste, which is reflected in your sense of style.

To read all about your Outer Planets and work out how to use your personalized timetable, go to Section Three, page 789.

go to Section Three, page 789.

Your Personalized Timetable

JUPITER BENEFICIAL
1940 3/17 – 5/24
1941 8/30 – 11/19
1942 4/18 – 6/5
1945 11/23 – until 1946 5/14
1946 7/15 – 9/19
1948 1/4 – 11/24
1952 2/28 – 5/6
1953 8/3 – until 1954 1/2
1954 3/21 – 5/18
1957 11/6 – until 1958 1/3
1958 3/31 – 8/31
1959 12/19 – until 1960 3/17
1960 5/24 – 11/5
1963 6/22 – 9/27
1964 2/7 – 4/20
1965 7/14 – 9/10
1965 11/28 – until 1966 4/29
1969 10/21 – 12/10
1970 5/9 – 8/6
1971 12/3 – until 1972 2/17
1972 7/7 – 10/11
1975 5/27 – 11/15
1976 1/4 – 4/3
1977 6/27 – 8/14
1978 1/9 – 4/3
1981 10/5 – 11/21
1983 11/17 – until 1984 1/28
1987 5/8 – until 1988 3/17
1989 6/10 – 7/25
1993 9/19 – 11/5
1995 10/31 – until 1996 1/11
1999 4/21 – 7/11
1999 10/9 – until 2000 2/25
2001 5/25 – 7/7
2005 2/1 – 2/2
2005 9/2 – 10/20
2007 2/13 – 5/29
2007 10/11 – 12/26
2011 4/4 – 6/13
2011 11/26 – until 2012 1/24

SATURN BENEFICIAL
1938 6/9 – 9/22
1939 2/28 – until 1940 4/4
1943 6/29 – until 1944 6/11
1952 10/18 – until 1953 10/13
1957 12/1 – until 1959 1/22
1959 7/23 – 10/16
1968 4/9 – until 1969 5/14
1972 8/19 – 11/16
1973 5/4 – 7/23
1974 1/24 – 4/3
1981 11/28 – until 1982 4/9
1982 8/23 – 11/19
1983 5/24 – 8/8
1987 1/5 – 7/8
1987 9/29 – until 1988 3/13
1988 5/10 – 11/29
1997 5/17 – 10/23
1998 2/6 – 6/30
1998 10/1 – until 1999 3/18
2002 6/12 – 9/26
2002 10/27 – until 2003 5/25
2011 10/3 – until 2012 1/11
2012 3/6 – 9/25

URANUS BENEFICIAL
1946 7/1 – until 1949 5/21
1972 10/14 – until 1975 8/10
1985 1/9 – until 1989 10/15

NEPTUNE BENEFICIAL
1950 12/2 – until 1956 9/16
1977 2/14 – until 1985 11/13

PLUTO BENEFICIAL
1978 12/17 – until 1983 10/8
2001 12/27 – until 2009 11/20

JUPITER CHALLENGING
1938 2/26 – 6/6
1938 7/7 – until 1939 1/8

1941 3/25 – 6/3
1946 12/8 – until 1947 11/1
1950 2/9 – 4/26
1950 8/31 – 12/15
1952 7/13 – 11/8
1953 3/2 – 5/17
1958 11/22 – until 1959 3/9
1959 3/27 – 10/15
1962 1/24 – 4/3
1964 6/20 – until 1965 4/30
1970 11/6 – until 1971 1/25
1971 5/21 – 9/24
1974 1/7 – 3/16
1976 6/1 – until 1977 4/12
1982 10/21 – until 1983 1/4
1983 7/6 – 8/20
1985 5/9 – 7/1
1985 12/20 – until 1986 2/28
1988 5/16 – 8/2
1988 11/17 – until 1989 3/22
1994 10/5 – 12/18
1997 4/5 – 8/18
1997 11/26 – until 1998 2/12
2000 4/29 – 7/9
2001 1/5 – 2/14
2006 1/18 – 4/19
2006 9/16 – 12/2
2009 3/15 – until 2010 1/26
2012 4/12 – 6/20

SATURN CHALLENGING
1941 4/22 – until 1942 5/23
1954 12/7 – until 1955 6/7
1955 8/29 – until 1956 2/7
1956 4/15 – 10/28
1963 2/20 – until 1964 4/11
1964 8/22 – until 1965 1/7
1970 6/1 – until 1971 1/4
1971 1/30 – 7/4
1971 12/10 – until 1972 3/21
1984 1/30 – 3/20
1984 10/14 – until 1985 12/2
1992 3/31 – 7/28
1992 12/27 – until 1994 2/13
1999 7/21 – 10/8
2000 4/4 – until 2001 5/6

URANUS CHALLENGING
1938 6/13 – until 1943 4/4
1978 1/16 – until 1982 10/3
1999 4/3 – until 2004 2/5

NEPTUNE CHALLENGING
1963 11/21 – until 1971 10/30
2005 2/24 – Continues

PLUTO CHALLENGING
1989 11/26 – until 1996 10/26

JUPITER SPECIAL
1943 9/12 – until 1944 8/4
1955 8/26 – until 1956 7/17
1967 8/10 – 10/31
1968 2/13 – 6/27
1979 7/25 – 10/9
1980 3/24 – 5/29
1991 7/8 – 9/21
2002 10/27 – until 2003 1/11
2003 6/19 – 9/4

SATURN SPECIAL
1947 9/1 – until 1948 4/6
1948 4/27 – 10/5
1949 3/5 – 6/25
1976 10/25 – 12/31
1977 7/7 – until 1978 8/10
2006 8/15 – until 2007 9/17
2008 4/19 – 5/16

URANUS SPECIAL
1958 10/20 – until 1963 6/18

PLUTO SPECIAL
1948 9/22 – until 1959 6/10

August 18

SUN: LEO • DECANATE: ARIES/MARS • DEGREE: 24°45–26° LEO • MODE: FIXED • ELEMENT: FIRE

Your Personal Powers

Motivated by inspired ideals, you are a mentally sharp individual with foresight and natural strategic skills. Your ruler, the Sun, grants you vitality and confidence. You gain power when you combine your sense of purpose with your innate intuition or imagination. Although you want to improve yourself through wisdom and knowledge, you may lose some of your energy by engaging in ego conflicts or by resorting to stubborn behavior. As a practical visionary you are usually industrious and active but you empower yourself by also learning to be composed and relaxed. Broad-minded, you are likely to possess a philanthropic approach to life but still have much potential for achievement and financial reward. It may be to your advantage, however, to avoid overexerting yourself with work if you want to find inner peace of mind. Inspired by knowledge and quick at grasping new information, you gain power by learning to structure large concepts down to the finest detail. You work well with others but also need to maintain your own independence.

Your Powers of Attraction in Relationships

Friendly and kind, you are a warmhearted individual who has a full social life. Other people admire your sympathetic approach and good organizational skills. Although you can be generous, you appear less attractive when you feel dissatisfied or become involved in mental power games. In close relationships you seek stability and a comfortable lifestyle. You are usually attracted to generous and charming individuals who are practical and hardworking or who possess a good business sense. Alternatively, you may be attracted to emotionally dynamic partners who give sound advice and solve other people's problems. Mentally quick and highly intuitive, you want a relationship with someone who is communicative and direct. With courage and strong convictions, you can inspire others with your insight and imagination.

Your attractive qualities: intelligent, vitality, realistic aspirations, mentally quick, imaginative, efficient, disciplined, focused, communicative, compassionate, good debater, progressive, inquisitive, courageous, enterprising, strategist, intuitive, assertive, resolute, visionary, idealistic, willpower

Your less attractive qualities: irritable, lack of motivation, unrealistic dreams, escapist, restless, inner tension, argumentative, lack of planing, impatient, lazy, lack of order, skeptical, unfinished work or project, moody, discontented, manipulative

Your Venus Power

The planet Venus has a great deal of influence on your powers of attraction. Below are four possible Venus types for women and men. To find your Venus you need to go to page 771, where you will find the Venus table and extra information. The planet Mars also affects your powers of attraction. To find your Mars table and interpretation go to page 761.

WOMEN WITH VENUS IN CANCER: Good-natured and romantic, you have a highly developed sense of touch that particularly responds to massage, hugs, and all things physical. Being friendly, you enjoy socializing and are able to put others at their ease. With your natural sense of beauty and harmony, your natural charm can attract others. Although you can be lavish toward your partner you may have to be careful that you do not overdo things.

MEN WITH VENUS IN CANCER: Being emotionally receptive, you can make a sensitive lover. With your desire to care for and protect others, you are likely to have strong family connections. Love is often tied in with being attentive to the needs of others and you may find yourself attracted to individuals who have sympathetic or maternal qualities. Security conscious, you need a loyal partner who can offer you support and ideally be a good cook and homemaker.

WOMEN WITH VENUS IN LEO: Your friendly and sunny personality often makes you stand out in a crowd. Generous and giving, you know how to make your partner feel special. As you often expect loyalty and devotion from your partners in return, you can become easily offended if they ignore you or behave in an inconsiderate manner. Charming and kind, when you are in love, you can be romantic, dramatic, and passionate.

MEN WITH VENUS IN LEO: Warm and playful with a touch of the dramatic, you enjoy the company of generous or strong individuals who can share your sense of fun. Although there are advantages to your being strong-willed, in your relationships you need to resist being bossy as it can cause resentment. With your wonderful mixture of regal authority and childlike wonder, you love to keep others entertained and amused.

WOMEN WITH VENUS IN VIRGO: In relationships you can

be modest and unassuming but desire perfection. You usually analyze your partnerships until you feel you have understood them to the last little detail in order to improve them. A problem usually arises when you become too critical either of partners or yourself and indulge in being skeptical or faultfinding. As you are modest, others may not be aware of the strong sensuality beneath your well-groomed exterior.

MEN WITH VENUS IN VIRGO: Practical, idealistic, and a perfectionist, you seek a relationship with an intelligent and hardworking partner who can inspire you to be more industrious and well-ordered. At times you can come across as a sympathetic and caring person and at other times you may appear pragmatic and very businesslike. This may sometimes lead to unclear communication between you and your partner. Usually helpful and caring, however, you like to analyze the faults in your relationships and then work methodically to improve them.

WOMEN WITH VENUS IN LIBRA: Attractive, refined, and conscious of the needs of others, you usually desire harmonious relationships. As a peacemaker with good negotiating skills, you can smooth out difficulties with others but your dislike of confrontation may sometimes leave you refusing to take a stand or compromising too many of your own needs. Courteous, stylish, and charming with polished social skills, you are an expert at relating to others in a gracious and civilized manner.

MEN WITH VENUS IN LIBRA: Courteous and refined, you are attracted to beautiful and elegant people. You are looking for a partner who can share your natural good taste and enjoy an intellectual conversation. Disliking conflict, you may have to be careful not to go along with others just to keep the peace. Your ideal partner will appreciate beauty and the little luxuries of life as well as possess good social skills. You have a strong sense of social etiquette yourself so you need an intelligent and sophisticated partner.

To read all about your Outer Planets and work out how to use your personalized timetable, go to Section Three, page 789.

To read all about your Outer Planets and work out how to use your personalized timetable, go to Section Three, page 789.

Your Personalized Timetable

JUPITER BENEFICIAL
1940 3/22 – 5/28
1941 9/8 – 11/10
1942 4/23 – 6/9
1945 11/29 – until 1946 5/5
1946 7/25 – 9/24
1948 1/8 – 11/28
1952 3/4 – 5/10
1953 8/8 – 12/25
1954 3/29 – 5/23
1957 11/10 – until 1958 1/11
1958 3/22 – 9/6
1959 12/23 – until 1960 3/28
1960 5/12 – 11/10
1963 6/29 – 9/20
1964 2/12 – 4/24
1965 7/18 – 9/19
1965 11/18 – until 1966 5/4
1969 10/25 – 12/15
1970 5/1 – 8/14
1971 12/7 – until 1972 2/22
1972 6/29 – 10/18
1975 6/1 – 11/5
1976 1/14 – 4/7
1977 7/1 – 8/19
1978 1/1 – 4/10
1981 10/9 – 11/26
1983 11/21 – until 1984 2/2
1987 5/12 – until 1988 3/21
1989 6/15 – 7/30
1993 9/24 – 11/9
1995 11/4 – until 1996 1/15
1999 4/25 – 7/19
1999 9/30 – until 2000 3/1
2001 5/29 – 7/12
2005 9/7 – 10/25
2007 2/20 – 5/21
2007 10/17 – 12/31
2011 4/8 – 6/19
2011 11/17 – until 2012 2/2

SATURN BENEFICIAL
1938 6/22 – 9/7
1939 3/8 – until 1940 4/12
1943 7/7 – until 1944 2/8
1944 3/3 – 6/18
1952 10/26 – until 1953 10/21
1957 12/9 – until 1959 1/31
1959 7/9 – 10/30
1968 4/16 – until 1969 5/23
1969 12/5 – until 1970 2/1
1972 9/3 – 11/1
1973 5/12 – 7/31
1974 1/10 – 4/16
1981 12/8 – until 1982 3/28
1982 9/2 – 11/27
1983 5/9 – 8/22
1987 1/14 – 6/23
1987 10/12 – until 1988 12/8
1997 5/26 – 10/11
1998 2/16 – 7/16
1998 9/15 – until 1999 3/26
2002 6/20 – until 2003 6/2
2011 10/10 – until 2012 10/4

URANUS BENEFICIAL
1946 7/19 – until 1949 6/7
1972 10/29 – until 1975 9/4
1985 1/29 – until 1989 11/9

NEPTUNE BENEFICIAL
1951 10/28 – until 1956 10/14
1978 1/3 – until 1985 12/11

PLUTO BENEFICIAL
1979 10/30 – until 1984 8/20
2002 1/25 – until 2010 9/24

JUPITER CHALLENGING
1938 3/2 – until 1939 1/12
1941 3/30 – 6/7

1946 12/13 – until 1947 11/6
1950 2/13 – 5/2
1950 8/23 – 12/21
1952 7/19 – 11/1
1953 3/7 – 5/21
1958 11/26 – until 1959 10/20
1962 1/28 – 4/8
1964 6/25 – 12/21
1965 1/30 – 5/5
1970 11/10 – until 1971 2/1
1971 5/13 – 9/30
1974 1/11 – 3/20
1976 6/6 – until 1977 4/17
1982 10/26 – until 1983 1/9
1983 6/24 – 9/1
1985 5/26 – 6/13
1985 12/25 – until 1986 3/4
1988 5/20 – 8/9
1988 11/9 – until 1989 3/28
1994 10/9 – 12/22
1997 4/11 – 8/11
1997 12/2 – until 1998 2/16
2000 5/3 – 7/14
2000 12/25 – until 2001 2/25
2006 1/27 – 4/10
2006 9/21 – 12/6
2009 3/20 – until 2010 1/30
2012 4/16 – 6/24

SATURN CHALLENGING
1941 4/29 – until 1942 5/30
1954 12/16 – until 1955 5/23
1955 9/12 – until 1956 11/6
1963 2/28 – 9/30
1963 11/11 – until 1964 4/23
1964 8/9 – until 1965 1/16
1970 6/9 – 12/13
1971 2/21 – 7/14
1971 11/28 – until 1972 4/1
1984 10/23 – until 1985 12/10
1992 4/12 – 7/14
1993 1/5 – until 1994 2/21
1999 8/9 – 9/19
2000 4/12 – until 2001 5/13

URANUS CHALLENGING
1938 7/5 – until 1943 4/24
1978 11/11 – until 1982 10/23
2000 2/6 – until 2004 2/22

NEPTUNE CHALLENGING
1963 12/19 – until 1972 9/18
2005 3/26 – Continues

PLUTO CHALLENGING
1989 12/23 – until 1996 11/20

JUPITER SPECIAL
1943 9/17 – until 1944 8/8
1955 8/30 – until 1956 7/22
1967 8/14 – 11/7
1968 2/5 – 7/3
1979 7/29 – 10/14
1980 3/15 – 6/7
1991 7/13 – 9/25
2002 11/6 – until 2003 1/1
2003 6/25 – 9/9

SATURN SPECIAL
1947 9/9 – until 1948 3/13
1948 5/21 – 10/14
1949 2/21 – 7/6
1976 11/20 – 12/5
1977 7/15 – until 1978 8/18
2006 8/22 – until 2007 9/25
2008 3/27 – 6/8

URANUS SPECIAL
1959 8/12 – until 1963 7/11

PLUTO SPECIAL
1949 8/30 – until 1959 7/24

♌

August 19

SUN: LEO • DECANATE: ARIES/MARS • DEGREE: 25°45–27° LEO • MODE: FIXED • ELEMENT: FIRE

Your Personal Powers

You are energetic and ambitious, and your strong determination reveals that you are a bright and enterprising individual. Your ruler, the Sun, grants you a creative nature, executive abilities, and self-confidence. Although your pride suggests that you want to be respected or admired, you gain power by developing your tolerance and patience toward others. Highly intuitive with a finely tuned mind, you need to stay focused and overcome stress or worry in order to achieve success. When you develop your inner faith and free yourself from doubt, you have the ability to persuasively present your innovative ideas to others and win them over. Inspired by knowledge and wisdom, you like to be well-informed and often have the ability to assess other people's strengths and weaknesses. You can achieve a great deal by staying mentally positive and objective. Being spontaneous, enterprising, and hardworking, you have a natural business sense that allows you to succeed admirably, especially concerning the general public.

Your Powers of Attraction in Relationships

Other people admire your resourcefulness and sense of fun. Being friendly, you enjoy being part of a crowd yet you can act independently. Since you like to have things your own way, you may need to develop more patience and tolerance toward others. Although you can assess people with canny accuracy, avoid being too skeptical. Being highly intuitive and sensitive suggests that although you can be sociable, generous, and affectionate, you can also be withdrawn or moody. Usually you are attracted to ambitious and hardworking individuals who are practical and confident. When in love you need time to accept your partner and develop your relationship. You also admire those who act independently and live by their principles. Romantic and dramatic, you usually enjoy creative partners who can inspire you to express yourself.

Your attractive qualities: shrewd, energetic, confident, determined, inspired, youthful, intuitive, creative, inquisitive, informed, ambitious, analytical, business acumen, progressive, optimistic, generous, competitive, gregarious, sensitive, resourceful, executive skills, decisive, charismatic

Your less attractive qualities: restless mind, self-doubt, too competitive, anxious, indulgent, selfish, stubborn, materialistic, indecisive, argumentative, depressive, fearful, mistrust-

ing, impatient, moody, withdrawn, bossy, unsympathetic, lack of faith

Your Venus Power

The planet Venus has a great deal of influence on your powers of attraction. Below are four possible Venus types for women and men. To find your Venus you need to go to page 771, where you will find the Venus table and extra information. The planet Mars also affects your powers of attraction. To find your Mars table and interpretation go to page 761.

WOMEN WITH VENUS IN CANCER: Possessing a soft femininity, you have tender and sensitive emotions. Sympathetic and caring, you often mother those in your care by making sure they are comfortable and have plenty to eat. When you feel hurt or insecure in relationships you are likely to cover your feelings by being defensive or appearing tough on the outside while on the inside you are feeling vulnerable. Affectionate and romantic, you make a faithful and devoted partner.

MEN WITH VENUS IN CANCER: Being caring and sensitive, you probably seek a nurturing partner who could provide you with emotional security and a sense of belonging in a loving and safe environment. Receptive to others, at times you find it hard to be direct or confrontational in relationships. You are affectionate and caring with loved ones; home and family are especially important to you.

WOMEN WITH VENUS IN LEO: Warm and playful with a touch of the dramatic, you enjoy the company of generous or strong individuals who can share your sense of fun. Although there are advantages to your being strong-willed, in your relationships you need to resist being bossy as it can cause resentment. With your wonderful mixture of regal authority and childlike wonder, you love to keep others entertained and amused.

MEN WITH VENUS IN LEO: Sociable and outgoing, you are kind and generous with those you love. Looking for a relationship that can be fun and entertaining, you need a playmate who can share your enthusiasm and high spirits. Your pride, however, often stops you from associating with lovers or partners you see as beneath you. As you desire someone who can appreciate your sense of the dramatic, you are often attracted to people with strong personalities.

WOMEN WITH VENUS IN VIRGO: Intelligent and dis-

criminating, you are usually drawn to polite and refined individuals. As a perfectionist, you may be keen to analyze and criticize yourself but be careful of continually going over your partner's shortcomings. By focusing on how you can make positive improvements in yourself and in your relationships, you avoid becoming skeptical or confused. You empower yourself when you display kind and caring concern for the well-being of loved ones and spontaneously offer your practical assistance.

MEN WITH VENUS IN VIRGO: A love of order usually indicates that you are attracted to refined individuals with analytical or practical abilities. You and your partner may be working together or serving similar causes. As you constantly analyze partnerships in order to improve them, you are likely to use former relationships as a point of reference and compare them to your present partner. As you are helpful and kind, others usually rely on your good judgment and often turn to you for advice or practical assistance.

WOMEN WITH VENUS IN LIBRA: A natural romantic with good social skills, you love to entertain or put people at ease by projecting a warm and gracious manner. Elegant and fair with a touch of glamour, you are also adept at dealing with people in delicate situations or conflicts. You seek refinement and will go out of your way to achieve harmony and keep the peace. For you, relationships are so important you may need to guard against becoming dependent on others for approval. With your friendly personality and inherent charm, however, you will always be popular and loved.

MEN WITH VENUS IN LIBRA: As a sociable and friendly individual with an eye for beauty, you are amorous and charming. You are a natural gentleman and your ideal partner usually has an elegant appearance, artistic appreciation, and good taste. Your relationships benefit when you resist the temptation to take the easy way out or put too much emphasis on vanity and high living. Intellectual and naturally refined, you seek a loving partner who can share your romantic and sophisticated aspirations.

To read all about your Outer Planets and work out how to use your personalized timetable, go to Section Three, page 789.

Your Personalized Timetable

JUPITER BENEFICIAL
1940 3/26 – 6/2
1941 9/20 – 10/30
1942 4/28 – 6/13
1945 12/4 – until 1946 4/26
1946 8/2 – 9/29
1948 1/13 – 12/3
1952 3/8 – 5/14
1953 8/14 – 12/18
1954 4/5 – 5/27
1957 11/15 – until 1958 1/22
1958 3/11 – 9/11
1959 12/27 – until 1960 11/15
1963 7/7 – 9/11
1964 2/17 – 4/28
1965 7/23 – 10/2
1965 11/6 – until 1966 5/9
1969 10/30 – 12/21
1970 4/24 – 8/21
1971 12/11 – until 1972 2/29
1972 6/22 – 10/25
1975 6/6 – 10/27
1976 1/22 – 4/11
1977 7/5 – 8/25
1977 12/25 – until 1978 4/17
1981 10/14 – 12/1
1982 6/13 – 7/12
1983 11/26 – until 1984 2/7
1984 8/9 – 9/19
1987 5/17 – until 1988 3/26
1989 6/19 – 8/3
1993 9/28 – 11/14
1995 11/9 – until 1996 1/20
1999 4/29 – 7/28
1999 9/21 – until 2000 3/6
2001 6/2 – 7/16
2005 9/12 – 10/29
2007 2/28 – 5/12
2007 10/22 – until 2008 1/4
2011 4/12 – 6/24
2011 11/9 – until 2012 2/9

SATURN BENEFICIAL
1938 7/13 – 8/17
1939 3/16 – until 1940 4/20
1943 7/15 – until 1944 1/16
1944 3/26 – 6/26
1952 11/3 – until 1953 6/7
1953 7/10 – 10/29
1957 12/17 – until 1959 2/10
1959 6/26 – 11/10
1968 4/24 – until 1969 5/31
1969 11/20 – until 1970 2/16
1973 5/20 – 8/9
1973 12/29 – until 1974 4/27
1981 12/21 – until 1982 3/14
1982 9/11 – 12/7
1983 4/26 – 9/2
1987 1/24 – 6/10
1987 10/23 – until 1988 12/16
1997 6/6 – 9/29
1998 2/26 – until 1999 4/3
2002 6/27 – until 2003 6/10
2011 10/18 – until 2012 10/12

URANUS BENEFICIAL
1946 8/9 – until 1949 6/23
1972 11/15 – until 1975 9/23
1985 3/1 – until 1989 11/28

NEPTUNE BENEFICIAL
1951 11/26 – until 1957 9/11
1978 2/4 – until 1986 11/6

PLUTO BENEFICIAL
1979 11/26 – until 1984 9/22
2002 12/18 – until 2010 11/16

JUPITER CHALLENGING
1938 3/6 – until 1939 1/17
1941 4/3 – 6/11
1946 12/18 – until 1947 7/8

1947 7/23 – 11/10
1950 2/17 – 5/8
1950 8/16 – 12/27
1952 7/26 – 10/25
1953 3/13 – 5/25
1958 12/1 – until 1959 10/25
1962 2/1 – 4/13
1962 10/5 – 11/22
1964 6/30 – 12/9
1965 2/11 – 5/9
1970 11/15 – until 1971 2/9
1971 5/5 – 10/6
1974 1/16 – 3/24
1976 6/10 – until 1977 4/22
1982 10/30 – until 1983 1/15
1983 6/15 – 9/10
1985 12/29 – until 1986 3/8
1988 5/24 – 8/17
1988 11/1 – until 1989 4/2
1994 10/14 – 12/27
1997 4/18 – 8/3
1997 12/8 – until 1998 2/20
2000 5/7 – 7/19
2000 12/16 – until 2001 3/6
2006 2/6 – 3/31
2006 9/27 – 12/11
2009 3/25 – 9/24
2009 11/1 – until 2010 2/3
2012 4/20 – 6/28

SATURN CHALLENGING
1941 5/7 – until 1942 6/7
1954 12/26 – until 1955 5/10
1955 9/23 – until 1956 11/14
1963 3/9 – 9/10
1963 11/30 – until 1964 5/6
1964 7/25 – until 1965 1/25
1970 6/18 – 11/29
1971 3/6 – 7/24
1971 11/16 – until 1972 4/10
1984 10/31 – until 1985 12/19
1986 7/7 – 9/5
1992 4/29 – 6/27
1993 1/14 – until 1994 3/1
2000 4/19 – until 2001 5/21

URANUS CHALLENGING
1938 8/15 – until 1943 5/11
1978 11/26 – until 1982 11/9
2000 2/23 – until 2004 12/28

NEPTUNE CHALLENGING
1964 2/4 – until 1972 10/24
2006 2/19 – Continues

PLUTO CHALLENGING
1990 2/15 – until 1997 10/12

JUPITER SPECIAL
1943 9/21 – until 1944 3/22
1944 5/5 – 8/13
1955 9/4 – until 1956 7/27
1967 8/19 – 11/15
1968 1/27 – 7/9
1979 8/13 – 10/20
1980 3/7 – 6/15
1991 7/17 – 9/30
2002 11/20 – 12/18
2003 6/30 – 9/13

SATURN SPECIAL
1947 9/18 – until 1948 2/27
1948 6/4 – 10/25
1949 2/9 – 7/15
1977 7/23 – until 1978 8/26
2006 8/30 – until 2007 10/4
2008 3/13 – 6/22

URANUS SPECIAL
1959 8/27 – until 1963 7/29

PLUTO SPECIAL
1949 10/8 – until 1960 6/11

August 20

SUN: LEO • DECANATE: ARIES/ MARS • DEGREE: 26°45–28° LEO • MODE: FIXED • ELEMENT: FIRE

Your Personal Powers

Proud yet receptive, you are a friendly and mentally smart individual who likes to be well-informed. Your ruler, the Sun, grants you creativity, determination, and confidence. Although you can be hardworking and dedicated, you may at times criticize yourself for not doing enough. You find peace of mind, however, when you become self-disciplined and stay open-minded. You empower yourself by combining your strong intuition and practical skills or by blending your aspirations and ideas with hard work and dedication. Being sensitive, you also need a congenial environment around you. Yet without real motivation you can easily resort to taking it too easy, being caught in inertia or the pursuit of material pleasures. Fortunately, your pride and desire for recognition suggest that you possess the courage and stamina needed to succeed, especially if the rewards include prestige and financial gains. By combining your diplomacy and persuasive charm with your determination and drive, you can achieve outstanding success.

Your Powers of Attraction in Relationships

You are sociable and generous, and other people admire your idealistic nature and sense of the dramatic. Although you are loyal and generous, guard against becoming too intense or stubborn. Usually compassionate or sensitive, you do not mind helping as long as you feel appreciated by others. Although you have a confident manner, you can take things to heart or get offended. Security-conscious, you consider your close relationship with a pragmatic outlook. You are often drawn to creative or idealistic partners or individuals who are knowledgeable and easy to talk to. As you are also romantic, you may be attracted to sensitive partners who are affectionate and loving. If things do not work the way you planned, you gain more by staying lighthearted than by taking emotional issues too seriously.

Your attractive qualities: sociable, generous, gentle, intuitive, determined, insightful, charming, ambitious, proud, share knowledge or ideas, dramatic, creative, responsible, tactful, entertaining, cooperative, enthusiastic, considerate, harmonious, business sense, enduring

Your less attractive qualities: too opinionated, controlling, inertia, lack stamina, manipulative, unmotivated, anxious, worried, easily hurt, suspicious, over- or underconfident, selfish, codependent, uncompromising, prone to flattery, easily hurt, impatient, overindulgent

Your Venus Power

The planet Venus has a great deal of influence on your powers of attraction. Below are four possible Venus types for women and men. To find your Venus you need to go to page 771, where you will find the Venus table and extra information. The planet Mars also affects your powers of attraction. To find your Mars table and interpretation go to page 761.

WOMEN WITH VENUS IN CANCER: Gentle and tender, you are romantic by nature. You possess a strong need for security and usually help others feel safe and protected. This preservation is especially centered in the home, which is your haven from life's storm. Although your maternal instincts are strong, avoid making sacrifices for others at your own expense. Nevertheless, affectionate and caring, once committed to a relationship, your loyalty and devotion to your partner is very strong.

MEN WITH VENUS IN CANCER: Affectionate with a strong sensitive streak, you can love very deeply. You may find yourself drawn to sympathetic partners who can tune into your moods and feelings as well as be reassuring and supportive. Family links are especially important to you and the more positive these relationships are, the more confident and safe you feel.

WOMEN WITH VENUS IN LEO: As a person who wants to radiate in her own right, you are likely to desire partners you can be proud of. You are usually attracted to fun-loving, warm, and generous individuals. If self-expression is important to you, you will probably seek the company of creative people such as artists, musicians, or those with a flair for acting. Alternatively, you may be drawn to people who are dignified, regal, or have already achieved success.

MEN WITH VENUS IN LEO: Generous, animated, and pleasure-seeking, you can be very entertaining and fun to be with. Usually you are attracted to extroverted and benevolent individuals with sunny personalities. If ambitious, you are drawn to a partner who shows leadership qualities or one who is highly motivated. Your less attractive qualities are your ten-

dencies to be bossy or vain. With a sense of the dramatic, however, you can be the life and soul of the party and inspire those around you.

Women with Venus in Virgo: Polite, refined, and organized, you are attracted to articulate and intelligent people. Since you are caring, concerned, and want to be of practical help to others, you can be an asset to any partnership. By being too analytical, exacting, or faultfinding, however, a doubting element can creep into your relationships. Through expressing your feelings in a positive way you can become more decisive and improve on how you relate to your loved ones.

Men with Venus in Virgo: Practical, idealistic, and a perfectionist, you seek a relationship with an intelligent and hardworking partner who can inspire you to be more industrious and well-ordered. At times you can come across as a sympathetic and caring person and at other times you may appear pragmatic and very businesslike. This may sometimes lead to unclear communication between you and your partner. Usually helpful and caring, however, you like to analyze the faults in your relationships and then work methodically to improve them.

Women with Venus in Libra: A natural romantic with good social skills, you love to entertain or put people at ease by projecting a warm and gracious manner. Elegant and fair with a touch of glamour, you are also adept at dealing with people in delicate situations or conflicts. You seek refinement and will go out of your way to achieve harmony and keep the peace. For you, relationships are so important you may need to guard against becoming dependent on others for approval. With your friendly personality and inherent charm, however, you will always be popular and loved.

Men with Venus in Libra: Courteous and refined, you are attracted to beautiful and elegant people. You are looking for a partner who can share your natural good taste and enjoy an intellectual conversation. Disliking conflict, you may have to be careful not to go along with others just to keep the peace. Your ideal partner will appreciate beauty and the little luxuries of life as well as possess good social skills. You have a strong sense of social etiquette yourself, so you need an intelligent and sophisticated partner.

To read all about your Outer Planets and work out how to use your personalized timetable, go to Section Three, page 789.

Your Personalized Timetable

Jupiter Beneficial
1940 3/30 – 6/6
1942 5/3 – 6/18
1945 12/10 – until **1946** 4/18
1946 8/9 – 10/3
1948 1/18 – 12/7
1952 3/12 – 5/19
1953 8/20 – 12/11
1954 4/11 – 6/1
1957 11/20 – until **1958** 9/16
1960 1/1 – 11/20
1963 7/19 – 8/30
1964 2/22 – 5/2
1965 7/28 – until **1966** 1/29
1966 3/4 – 5/14
1969 11/3 – 12/27
1970 4/16 – 8/27
1971 12/15 – until **1972** 3/6
1972 6/14 – 10/30
1975 6/12 – 10/20
1976 1/29 – 4/15
1977 7/9 – 8/31
1977 12/18 – until **1978** 4/23
1981 10/18 – 12/6
1982 5/29 – 7/27
1983 11/30 – until **1984** 2/12
1984 7/28 – 10/1
1987 5/21 – until **1988** 3/30
1989 6/23 – 8/8
1990 2/1 – 3/20
1993 10/3 – 11/18
1995 11/14 – until **1996** 1/24
1999 5/3 – 8/13
1999 9/5 – until **2000** 3/11
2001 6/6 – 7/20
2005 9/17 – 11/3
2007 3/11 – 5/2
2007 10/27 – until **2008** 1/8
2011 4/16 – 6/29
2011 11/2 – until **2012** 2/16

Saturn Beneficial
1939 3/24 – until **1940** 4/27
1943 7/24 – until **1944** 1/2
1944 4/8 – 7/3
1952 11/12 – until **1953** 5/16
1953 8/1 – 11/6
1957 12/25 – until **1959** 2/21
1959 6/12 – 11/20
1968 5/2 – 12/15
1968 12/27 – until **1969** 6/9
1969 11/7 – until **1970** 2/28
1973 5/28 – 8/19
1973 12/17 – until **1974** 5/7
1982 1/7 – 2/24
1982 9/20 – 12/17
1983 4/13 – 9/12
1987 2/4 – 5/28
1987 11/2 – until **1988** 12/24
1997 6/18 – 9/15
1998 3/6 – until **1999** 4/11
2002 7/5 – until **2003** 6/17
2011 10/26 – until **2012** 10/20

Uranus Beneficial
1946 9/16 – until **1950** 4/21
1972 12/4 – until **1975** 10/9
1985 12/19 – until **1989** 12/15

Neptune Beneficial
1952 10/22 – until **1957** 10/9
1978 12/29 – until **1986** 12/6

Pluto Beneficial
1980 1/14 – until **1984** 10/17
2003 1/14 – until **2010** 12/15

Jupiter Challenging
1938 3/11 – until **1939** 1/21
1941 4/7 – 6/15
1946 12/23 – until **1947** 6/19
1947 8/11 – 11/15
1950 2/22 – 5/15
1950 8/8 – until **1951** 1/1
1952 8/3 – 10/17
1953 3/18 – 5/29
1958 12/5 – until **1959** 10/29
1962 2/5 – 4/18
1962 9/24 – 12/2
1964 7/5 – 12/1
1965 2/19 – 5/13
1970 11/19 – until **1971** 2/17
1971 4/26 – 10/11
1974 1/20 – 3/29
1976 6/14 – until **1977** 4/26
1982 11/3 – until **1983** 1/20
1983 6/7 – 9/18
1986 1/3 – 3/12
1988 5/28 – 8/26
1988 10/23 – until **1989** 4/7
1994 10/19 – until **1995** 1/1
1997 4/25 – 7/26
1997 12/14 – until **1998** 2/24
2000 5/11 – 7/24
2000 12/8 – until **2001** 3/13
2006 2/24 – 3/13
2006 10/2 – 12/15
2009 3/30 – 9/11
2009 11/13 – until **2010** 2/7
2012 4/24 – 7/3

Saturn Challenging
1941 5/14 – until **1942** 6/14
1955 1/5 – 4/27
1955 10/3 – until **1956** 11/22
1963 3/18 – 8/27
1963 12/13 – until **1964** 5/27
1964 7/4 – until **1965** 2/2
1970 6/27 – 11/16
1971 3/17 – 8/4
1971 11/4 – until **1972** 4/19
1984 11/8 – until **1985** 12/28
1986 6/20 – 9/22
1993 1/22 – until **1994** 3/9
2000 4/27 – until **2001** 5/28

Uranus Challenging
1939 5/25 – until **1943** 5/28
1978 12/13 – until **1982** 11/25
2000 3/12 – until **2005** 1/19

Neptune Challenging
1964 12/12 – until **1973** 9/1
2006 3/19 – 7/30
2007 1/19 – Continues

Pluto Challenging
1990 12/6 – until **1997** 11/8

Jupiter Special
1943 9/27 – until **1944** 3/10
1944 5/17 – 8/17
1955 9/8 – until **1956** 8/1
1967 8/23 – 11/26
1968 1/17 – 7/14
1979 8/7 – 10/25
1980 2/28 – 6/22
1991 7/22 – 10/5
1992 4/22 – 5/8
2003 7/5 – 9/18

Saturn Special
1947 9/27 – until **1948** 2/15
1948 6/16 – 11/6
1949 1/27 – 7/24
1977 7/31 – until **1978** 9/2
2006 9/7 – until **2007** 3/25
2007 5/15 – 10/13
2008 2/29 – 7/3

Uranus Special
1959 9/13 – until **1963** 8/14

Pluto Special
1950 9/10 – until **1960** 7/25

August 21

Your Personal Powers

Gregarious and resourceful, you are a discerning individual with a receptive mind and quick comprehension. Your ruler, the Sun, grants you vitality, agility, an idealistic nature, and self-esteem. Usually proud and enterprising, with an optimistic outlook and a conviction that success is within your grasp, you usually project a confident and assured front. Yet without advance planning, your great potential for success can be undermined. You gain power by taking the time to develop your natural gifts and mental aptitude, especially through education and learning new skills. You lose some of your power by being overly eager to achieve and by letting restlessness or boredom disperse your energy in too many directions. With your inborn common sense and natural flair for strategy, you can become methodical and focused. It is often when you feel inspired and creative that you show your dedication and true capabilities. Nevertheless, your enthusiasm and outgoing personality imply that you are curious and likely to experience many adventures in life.

Your Powers of Attraction in Relationships

Mentally quick, you thrive in the company of intellectually bright people who are creative and enterprising. You are also attracted to imaginative and idealistic partners who have an alluring side to their nature. A good conversationalist and full of ideas, you need to keep busy; otherwise you may become bored and restless. Usually affectionate and sociable, you do not have difficulties in attracting many friends. Your generosity and sense of fun suggest that you can be witty and amusing. If, however, you become skeptical and uncommunicative, you can be reluctant to speak openly about your true feelings. Your relationships may also suffer from your unwillingness to become fully committed. If inspired by other individuals, you need to be careful not to get carried away with their plans by staying practical and focused.

Your attractive qualities: intuitive, enthusiastic, common sense, sociable, intelligent, mentally quick, optimistic, strategist, enterprising, practical, generous, compassionate, enduring, frank, direct, honorable, charming, well-informed, determined, friendly, creative, strong instincts, witty

Your less attractive qualities: restless, impatient, careless, easily bored, cynical, arrogant, self-righteous, nervous, emotionally insecure, too proud, willful, controlling, lack of vision, dissatisfied, too outspoken, inflexible, impractical

Your Venus Power

The planet Venus has a great deal of influence on your powers of attraction. Below are four possible Venus types for women and men. To find your Venus you need to go to page 771, where you will find the Venus table and extra information. The planet Mars also affects your powers of attraction. To find your Mars table and interpretation go to page 761.

WOMEN WITH VENUS IN CANCER: Gentle and tender, you are romantic by nature. You possess a strong need for security and usually help others feel safe and protected. This preservation is especially centered in the home, which is you haven from life's storm. Although your maternal instincts are strong, avoid making sacrifices for others at your own expense. Nevertheless, affectionate and caring, once committed to a relationship, your loyalty and devotion to your partner is very strong.

MEN WITH VENUS IN CANCER: Being emotionally receptive, you can make a sensitive lover. With your desire to care for and protect others, you are likely to have strong family connections. Love is often tied in with being attentive to the needs of others and you may find yourself attracted to individuals who have sympathetic or maternal qualities. Security conscious, you need a loyal partner who can offer you support and ideally be a good cook and homemaker.

WOMEN WITH VENUS IN LEO: As a person who wants to radiate in her own right, you are likely to desire partners you can be proud of. You are usually attracted to fun-loving, warm, and generous individuals. If self-expression is important to you, you will probably seek the company of creative people such as artists, musicians, or those with a flair for acting. Alternatively, you may be drawn to people who are dignified, regal, or have already achieved success.

MEN WITH VENUS IN LEO: Generous, animated, and pleasure-seeking, you can be very entertaining and fun to be with. Usually you are attracted to extroverted and benevolent individuals with sunny personalities. If ambitious, you are drawn to a partner who shows leadership qualities or one who is highly motivated. Your less attractive qualities are your tendencies to be bossy or vain. With a sense of the dramatic, however, you can be the life and soul of the party and inspire those around you.

WOMEN WITH VENUS IN VIRGO: Intelligent and discriminating, you are usually drawn to polite and refined individuals. As a perfectionist, you may be keen to analyze and criticize yourself but be careful of continually going over your partner's shortcomings. By focusing on how you can make positive improvements in yourself and in your relationships, you avoid becoming skeptical or confused. You empower yourself when you display kind and caring concern for the well-being of loved ones and spontaneously offer your practical assistance.

MEN WITH VENUS IN VIRGO: A love of order usually indicates that you are attracted to refined individuals with analytical or practical abilities. You and your partner may be working together or serving similar causes. As you constantly analyze partnerships in order to improve them, you are likely to use former relationships as a point of reference and compare them to your present partner. As you are helpful and kind, others usually rely on your good judgment and often turn to you for advice or practical assistance.

WOMEN WITH VENUS IN LIBRA: Attractive, refined, and conscious of the needs of others, you usually desire harmonious relationships. As a peacemaker with good negotiating skills, you can smooth out difficulties with others but your dislike of confrontation may sometimes leave you refusing to make a stand or compromising too many of your own needs. Courteous, stylish, and charming with polished social skills, you are an expert at relating to others in a gracious and civilized manner.

MEN WITH VENUS IN LIBRA: Your good social skills, charming personality, and refined manner usually make you attractive to the opposite sex. Equally, you desire a sophisticated partner with grace, elegance, and a strong sense of style. Although you have the ability to be persuasive and irresistible to others, avoid manipulative love games. Nevertheless, your natural diplomacy and sense of fair play help you to relate to people in all social situations. With your love for balance and harmony, you seek a partner who is also moderate, easygoing, and loving.

To read all about your Outer Planets and work out how to use your personalized timetable, go to Section Three, page 789.

To read all about your Outer Planets and work out how to use your personalized timetable, go to Section Three, page 789.

Your Personalized Timetable

JUPITER BENEFICIAL
1940 4/3 – 6/11
1940 12/28 – until **1941** 1/2
1942 5/8 – 6/22
1945 12/16 – until **1946** 4/11
1946 8/16 – 10/8
1948 1/23 – 7/27
1948 9/4 – 12/11
1952 3/16 – 5/23
1953 8/26 – 12/4
1954 4/16 – 6/5
1957 11/25 – until **1958** 5/24
1958 7/14 – 9/21
1960 1/5 – 11/24
1964 2/27 – 5/6
1965 8/2 – until **1966** 1/16
1966 3/17 – 5/19
1969 11/8 – until **1970** 1/3
1970 4/8 – 9/2
1971 12/20 – until **1972** 3/14
1972 6/6 – 11/5
1975 6/18 – 10/13
1976 2/4 – 4/19
1977 7/14 – 9/7
1977 12/10 – until **1978** 4/29
1981 10/23 – 12/11
1982 5/18 – 8/6
1983 12/4 – until **1984** 2/17
1984 7/19 – 10/10
1987 5/26 – until **1988** 4/3
1989 6/27 – 8/13
1990 1/21 – 3/31
1993 10/7 – 11/23
1995 11/18 – until **1996** 1/29
1999 5/7 – until **2000** 3/16
2001 6/11 – 7/25
2005 9/22 – 11/7
2007 3/31 – 4/12
2007 11/1 – until **2008** 1/12
2011 4/20 – 7/5
2011 10/26 – until **2012** 2/22

SATURN BENEFICIAL
1939 4/1 – until **1940** 5/5
1943 8/2 – 12/21
1944 4/19 – 7/11
1952 11/20 – until **1953** 5/1
1953 8/14 – 11/14
1954 6/28 – 7/14
1958 1/3 – 7/27
1958 9/20 – until **1959** 3/6
1959 5/28 – 11/29
1968 5/10 – 11/17
1969 1/23 – 6/19
1969 10/26 – until **1970** 3/10
1973 6/4 – 8/30
1973 12/5 – until **1974** 5/16
1982 9/28 – 12/29
1983 3/31 – 9/22
1987 2/16 – 5/13
1987 11/12 – until **1989** 1/1
1997 7/5 – 8/29
1998 3/15 – until **1999** 4/19
2002 7/13 – until **2003** 1/28
2003 3/19 – 6/25
2011 11/3 – until **2012** 10/28

URANUS BENEFICIAL
1947 6/27 – until **1950** 5/14
1972 12/30 – until **1975** 10/25
1986 1/4 – until **1990** 9/30

NEPTUNE BENEFICIAL
1952 11/19 – until **1958** 9/4
1979 1/28 – until **1987** 10/29

PLUTO BENEFICIAL
1980 11/9 – until **1985** 9/3
2003 2/21 – until **2011** 11/12

JUPITER CHALLENGING
1938 3/15 – until **1939** 1/26
1941 4/12 – 6/20
1946 12/28 – until **1947** 6/8

1947 8/22 – 11/19
1950 2/26 – 5/24
1950 7/30 – until **1951** 1/6
1952 8/12 – 10/7
1953 3/23 – 6/3
1958 12/10 – until **1959** 11/3
1962 2/9 – 4/23
1962 9/16 – 12/10
1964 7/10 – 11/23
1965 2/26 – 5/17
1970 11/24 – until **1971** 3/1
1971 4/14 – 10/16
1974 1/24 – 4/2
1976 6/19 – until **1977** 4/30
1982 11/8 – until **1983** 1/26
1983 5/30 – 9/24
1986 1/7 – 3/16
1988 6/1 – 9/8
1988 10/10 – until **1989** 4/12
1994 10/23 – until **1995** 1/5
1995 7/23 – 8/12
1997 5/2 – 7/18
1997 12/19 – until **1998** 2/28
2000 5/15 – 7/30
2000 12/1 – until **2001** 3/20
2006 10/7 – 12/20
2009 4/4 – 9/2
2009 11/21 – until **2010** 2/11
2012 4/28 – 7/7

SATURN CHALLENGING
1941 5/22 – until **1942** 6/22
1943 1/26 – 2/17
1955 1/18 – 4/13
1955 10/12 – until **1956** 11/30
1963 3/28 – 8/14
1963 12/24 – until **1965** 2/10
1970 7/7 – 11/4
1971 3/27 – 8/19
1971 10/19 – until **1972** 4/27
1984 11/16 – until **1986** 1/6
1986 6/6 – 10/4
1993 1/30 – until **1994** 3/17
1994 11/5 – 11/13
2000 5/5 – until **2001** 6/4

URANUS CHALLENGING
1939 6/11 – until **1944** 3/28
1979 1/1 – until **1983** 9/21
2000 4/2 – until **2005** 2/6

NEPTUNE CHALLENGING
1965 1/18 – until **1973** 10/19
2006 5/2 – Continues

PLUTO CHALLENGING
1991 1/5 – until **1998** 9/23

JUPITER SPECIAL
1943 10/2 – until **1944** 3/1
1944 5/25 – 8/22
1955 9/13 – until **1956** 8/5
1967 8/27 – 12/13
1967 12/30 – until **1968** 7/19
1979 8/11 – 11/1
1980 2/21 – 6/28
1991 7/26 – 10/10
1992 4/4 – 5/27
2003 7/10 – 9/23

SATURN SPECIAL
1947 10/6 – until **1948** 2/3
1948 6/26 – 8 11/23
1949 1/9 – 8/2
1977 8/7 – until **1978** 9/10
2006 9/15 – until **2007** 3/8
2007 6/1 – 10/23
2008 2/17 – 7/13

URANUS SPECIAL
1959 10/2 – until **1963** 8/30

PLUTO SPECIAL
1950 10/27 – until **1961** 6/11

August 22

SUN: LEO/VIRGO CUSP · DECANATE: ARIES/MARS · DEGREE: 28°5 LEO–29°5 · MODE: FIXED · ELEMENT: FIRE

Your Personal Powers

Your idealism and pragmatism indicate that you are a creative thinker with many ideas and a talent for problem solving. Your ruler, the Sun, grants you self-esteem, executive abilities, and creativity. Your confidence increases through acquiring knowledge and being well-informed. Yet you gain power when you learn to trust your strong instincts about people and situations, resisting a tendency to worry or be anxious. Being aware of your responsibilities implies that although you appear lighthearted and amusing, you are inwardly security-conscious, serious, and hardworking. Having strong convictions or opinions suggests that you are not usually afraid to speak your mind and stand for what you believe in. By learning to convey your ideas with gentleness and diplomacy you can be persuasive and inspire others. Although proud and direct, you lose some of your power when you become arrogant. Some of your challenges may focus on humility and patience. Your many enterprising plans and your desire for truth help you in your quest for success.

Your Powers of Attraction in Relationships

Persuasive and dramatic, your optimistic outlook suggests that you can usually get your way by enchanting others with your charismatic character. Caring and sympathetic, you make a loyal partner and a good friend. You are usually drawn to purposeful or influential people with an enterprising personality or different background. Although you are, by nature, gregarious and enthusiastic with a friendly manner, you do not suffer fools gladly. By developing your tolerance and an inner desire for peace and harmony you can enhance your relationships with others. Often you prefer an intelligent or creative partner who can keep you youthful and feeling playful. Nevertheless, you do not fall deeply in love often. Although you want a loving relationship and believe in loyalty and devotion, you like your independence.

Your attractive qualities: persuasive, pragmatic, peaceful mind, harmonious, fighting spirit, strong convictions, intuitive, enthusiastic, good strategist, responsible, affectionate, generous, decisive, inner wisdom, idealistic, success through education, enterprising, ambitious, honorable, creative

Your less attractive qualities: mentally restless, impatient, critical, domineering, interfering, rebellious, easily bored, too sensitive, arrogant, materialistic, self-promoting, impractical, indulgent, anxious, selfish, dissatisfied

Your Venus Power

The planet Venus has a great deal of influence on your powers of attraction. Below are four possible Venus types for women and men. To find your Venus you need to go to page 771, where you will find the Venus table and extra information. The planet Mars also affects your powers of attraction. To find your Mars table and interpretation go to page 761.

WOMEN WITH VENUS IN CANCER: Possessing a soft femininity, you have tender and sensitive emotions. Sympathetic and caring, you often mother those in your care by making sure they are comfortable and have plenty to eat. When you feel hurt or insecure in relationships you are likely to cover your feelings by being defensive or appearing tough on the outside while on the inside you are feeling vulnerable. Affectionate and romantic, you make a faithful and devoted partner.

MEN WITH VENUS IN CANCER: You seek a partner who is sympathetic, caring, and protective. Able to be forgiving and compassionate, you want a secure emotional bond in your close relationships. You are usually drawn to partners who are maternal, unselfish, or demonstrative with their feelings. Although you can sometimes appear to others as impressionable, you have powerful emotions and inner strength.

WOMEN WITH VENUS IN LEO: You possess the wonderful ability to project your warm and sunny personality and keep others happily entertained. Loving attention yourself, you seek a partner who can appreciate you and be supportive and give you positive feedback. Proud, with a natural regal air, you expect respect from your partners but are willing to be loyal and supportive in exchange. Although sometimes a little self-centered, you know how to make your partner feel special.

MEN WITH VENUS IN LEO: A childlike nature suggests that you are versatile and keen on games or being entertained. You are usually attracted to vivacious partners with a benevolent nature. As an extrovert you enjoy being involved in all types of activities where you can assert yourself and show your talents and abilities. Others may recognize your inborn tendencies to lead but are also aware of your vanity or pride. Nevertheless, generous and caring, you often show more compassion to those less fortunate than yourself.

WOMEN WITH VENUS IN VIRGO: In relationships you can be modest and unassuming but desire perfection. You usually analyze your partnerships until you feel you have understood them to the last little detail in order to improve them. A problem usually arises when you become too critical either of partners or yourself and indulge in being skeptical or fault-finding. As you are modest, others may not be aware of the strong sensuality beneath your well-groomed exterior.

MEN WITH VENUS IN VIRGO: Industrious and well-ordered, you relate to others in a considerate and down-to-earth way. You enjoy giving practical advice and being of service to those you love even in small ways. Being a perfectionist you are drawn to partners with high morals or a strong work ethic. Partners who have strong analytical minds are very attractive to you, particularly if they are also clean and meticulously dressed.

WOMEN WITH VENUS IN LIBRA: Usually you are attractive and sociable with an easygoing manner. Your love of beauty, harmony, and pleasure implies that you are a romantic with a desire for love and affection. Once in a relationship you need to learn to negotiate your position rather than adapt to the wishes of others and compromise just to keep the peace. Nevertheless, your advanced social skills and strong sense of fair play can help you succeed in any social or romantic situation.

MEN WITH VENUS IN LIBRA: You are such good company, people are naturally drawn to you and especially appreciate your talent for making them feel special. You find status in your social contacts and place importance on your relationships. Being clever and a charming companion, you will go out of your way to keep situations peaceful and harmonious. In relationships, however, be careful of indecision or compromising too much. Nevertheless, others are attracted by your natural refinement and good taste, which is reflected in your sense of style.

To read all about your Outer Planets and work out how to use your personalized timetable, go to Section Three, page 789.

Your Personalized Timetable

JUPITER BENEFICIAL
1940 4/7 – 6/16
1940 12/7 – until **1941** 1/24
1942 5/12 – 6/26
1945 12/23 – until **1946** 4/3
1946 8/22 – 10/12
1948 1/28 – 7/14
1948 9/17 – 12/15
1952 3/20 – 5/27
1953 9/2 – 11/26
1954 4/22 – 6/9
1957 11/30 – until **1958** 5/13
1958 7/25 – 9/26
1960 1/10 – 11/29
1964 3/2 – 5/10
1965 8/7 – until **1966** 1/7
1966 3/26 – 5/23
1969 11/12 – until **1970** 1/11
1970 3/31 – 9/7
1971 12/24 – until **1972** 3/23
1972 5/28 – 11/10
1975 6/24 – 10/6
1976 2/10 – 4/23
1977 7/18 – 9/14
1977 12/2 – until **1978** 5/4
1981 10/27 – 12/16
1982 5/10 – 8/14
1983 12/8 – until **1984** 2/22
1984 7/10 – 10/17
1987 5/31 – 11/22
1988 1/7 – 4/7
1989 7/1 – 8/19
1990 1/13 – 4/8
1993 10/12 – 11/28
1995 11/23 – until **1996** 2/3
1999 5/11 – until **2000** 3/20
2001 6/15 – 7/30
2005 9/26 – 11/12
2007 11/6 – until **2008** 1/17
2011 4/24 – 7/12
2011 10/18 – until **2012** 2/27

SATURN BENEFICIAL
1939 4/9 – until **1940** 5/12
1943 8/11 – 12/9
1944 4/29 – 7/18
1952 11/30 – until **1953** 4/18
1953 8/26 – 11/22
1954 5/31 – 8/11
1958 1/12 – 7/9
1958 10/7 – until **1959** 3/25
1959 5/8 – 12/8
1968 5/19 – 11/2
1969 2/6 – 6/29
1969 10/13 – until **1970** 3/19
1973 6/11 – 9/12
1973 11/21 – until **1974** 5/24
1982 10/6 – until **1983** 1/13
1983 3/14 – 9/30
1987 3/7 – 4/24
1987 11/20 – until **1989** 1/10
1998 3/23 – until **1999** 4/26
2002 7/21 – until **2003** 1/11
2003 4/4 – 7/2
2011 11/12 – until **2012** 5/22
2012 7/28 – 11/5

URANUS BENEFICIAL
1947 7/14 – until **1950** 6/1
1973 10/20 – until **1976** 8/18
1986 1/22 – until **1990** 11/4

NEPTUNE BENEFICIAL
1952 12/28 – until **1958** 10/5
1979 12/25 – until **1987** 12/1

PLUTO BENEFICIAL
1980 12/9 – until **1985** 10/2
2004 1/5 – until **2011** 12/13

JUPITER CHALLENGING
1938 3/20 – until **1939** 1/30

1941 4/16 – 6/24
1947 1/2 – 5/30
1947 8/30 – 11/23
1950 3/2 – 6/4
1950 7/19 – until **1951** 1/11
1952 8/26 – 9/23
1953 3/28 – 6/7
1958 12/15 – until **1959** 11/7
1962 2/13 – 4/28
1962 9/8 – 12/17
1964 7/16 – 11/16
1965 3/5 – 5/21
1970 11/28 – until **1971** 10/21
1974 1/28 – 4/7
1976 6/23 – until **1977** 5/5
1982 11/12 – until **1983** 2/1
1983 5/23 – 9/30
1986 1/12 – 3/20
1988 6/6 – until **1989** 4/17
1994 10/28 – until **1995** 1/10
1995 7/6 – 8/30
1997 5/12 – 7/8
1997 12/24 – until **1998** 3/4
2000 5/19 – 8/5
2000 11/24 – until **2001** 3/26
2006 10/12 – 12/24
2009 4/9 – 8/25
2009 11/29 – until **2010** 2/15
2012 5/2 – 7/12

SATURN CHALLENGING
1941 5/29 – until **1942** 6/30
1943 1/2 – 3/12
1955 2/5 – 3/25
1955 10/21 – until **1956** 12/8
1963 4/8 – 7/31
1964 1/3 – until **1965** 2/18
1970 7/18 – 10/23
1971 4/5 – until **1972** 5/5
1984 11/24 – until **1986** 1/16
1986 5/24 – 10/15
1993 2/7 – until **1994** 3/26
1994 10/5 – 12/13
2000 5/12 – until **2001** 6/12

URANUS CHALLENGING
1939 7/2 – until **1944** 4/19
1979 1/28 – until **1983** 10/15
2000 5/6 – until **2005** 2/23

NEPTUNE CHALLENGING
1965 12/7 – until **1973** 11/16
2007 3/12 – Continues

PLUTO CHALLENGING
1991 11/22 – until **1998** 10/28

JUPITER SPECIAL
1943 10/7 – until **1944** 2/22
1944 6/2 – 8/26
1955 9/18 – until **1956** 8/10
1967 9/1 – until **1968** 7/24
1979 8/16 – 11/7
1980 2/14 – 7/4
1991 7/31 – 10/15
1992 3/24 – 6/7
2003 7/14 – 9/27

SATURN SPECIAL
1947 10/18 – until **1948** 1/22
1948 7/5 – until **1949** 8/10
1977 8/15 – until **1978** 9/18
2006 9/24 – until **2007** 2/23
2007 6/13 – 11/3
2008 2/5 – 7/22

URANUS SPECIAL
1959 10/28 – until **1964** 6/24

PLUTO SPECIAL
1951 9/22 – until **1961** 7/26

♌

321

Leo Timetable
X-Special · X-Beneficial · X-Challenging

July 23
URANUS X-BENEFICIAL
2010 4/10 – until 2012 2/4

July 24
URANUS X-BENEFICIAL
2010 4/29 – until 2012 2/24

July 25
URANUS X-BENEFICIAL
2010 5/22 – until 2012 3/12

July 26
URANUS X-BENEFICIAL
2011 3/25 – until 2013 1/1

July 27
URANUS X-BENEFICIAL
2011 4/11 – until 2013 2/3

July 28
URANUS X-BENEFICIAL
2011 4/30 – until 2013 2/24

July 29
URANUS X-BENEFICIAL
2011 5/22 – until 2013 3/14

July 30
URANUS X-BENEFICIAL
2012 3/26 – until 2013 12/21

NEPTUNE X-CHALLENGING
2000 2/20 – until 2002 11/27

July 31
URANUS X-BENEFICIAL
2012 4/12 – until 2013 4/16

NEPTUNE X-CHALLENGING
2001 1/7 – until 2002 12/31

August 1
URANUS X-BENEFICIAL
2012 4/30 – until 2013 5/5

NEPTUNE X-CHALLENGING
2001 2/1 – until 2003 11/11

August 2
URANUS X-BENEFICIAL
2012 5/21 – Continues

NEPTUNE X-CHALLENGING
2001 2/28 – until 2003 12/25

August 3
URANUS X-BENEFICIAL
2012 6/26 – until 2013 7/2

NEPTUNE X-CHALLENGING
2001 4/5 – until 2004 1/21

August 4
NEPTUNE X-CHALLENGING
2002 2/22 – until 2004 12/16

August 5
NEPTUNE X-CHALLENGING
2002 3/25 – until 2005 1/15

PLUTO X-BENEFICIAL
2000 6/23 – until 2001 11/17

August 6
NEPTUNE X-CHALLENGING
2003 2/16 – until 2005 12/7

PLUTO X-BENEFICIAL
2000 10/17 – until 2002 10/3

August 7
NEPTUNE X-CHALLENGING
2003 3/17 – until 2006 1/9

PLUTO X-BENEFICIAL
2001 1/15 – until 2002 11/7

August 8
NEPTUNE X-CHALLENGING
2004 2/11 – 2006 11/23

PLUTO X-BENEFICIAL
2000 12/12 – 2002 12/3

August 9
NEPTUNE X-CHALLENGING
2004 3/9 – until 2007 1/2

PLUTO X-BENEFICIAL
2001 1/13 – until 2003 10/28

August 10
NEPTUNE X-CHALLENGING
2004 4/16 – until 2007 1/30

PLUTO X-BENEFICIAL
2001 2/23 – until 2003 11/25

August 11
NEPTUNE X-CHALLENGING
2005 3/3 – until 2007 12/26

PLUTO X-BENEFICIAL
2002 1/2 – until 2004 10/15

August 12
NEPTUNE X-CHALLENGING
2005 4/4 – until 2008 1/24

PLUTO X-BENEFICIAL
2002 2/3 – until 2004 11/16

August 13
NEPTUNE X-CHALLENGING
2006 2/25 – until 2008 12/16

PLUTO X-BENEFICIAL
2002 12/24 – until 2005 9/28

August 14
URANUS X-CHALLENGING
2001 1/7 – until 2002 1/11

NEPTUNE X-CHALLENGING
2006 3/27 – until 2009 1/17

PLUTO X-BENEFICIAL
2003 1/21 – until 2005 11/8

August 15
URANUS X-CHALLENGING
2001 1/25 – until 2002 1/29

NEPTUNE X-CHALLENGING
2007 2/20 – until 2009 12/4

PLUTO X-BENEFICIAL
2003 3/16 – until 2005 12/6

August 16
URANUS X-CHALLENGING
2001 2/10 – until 2002 2/15

NEPTUNE X-CHALLENGING
2007 3/19 – until 2010 1/11

PLUTO X-BENEFICIAL
2004 1/12 – until 2006 10/31

August 17
URANUS X-CHALLENGING
2001 2/27 – until 2002 12/22

NEPTUNE X-CHALLENGING
2007 4/29 – until 2010 2/7

PLUTO X-BENEFICIAL
2004 2/16 – until 2006 11/30

August 18
URANUS X-CHALLENGING
2001 3/17 – until 2003 1/12

NEPTUNE X-CHALLENGING
2008 3/12 – until 2011 1/3

PLUTO X-BENEFICIAL
2005 1/3 – until 2007 10/22

August 19
URANUS X-CHALLENGING
2001 4/8 – until 2003 1/30

NEPTUNE X-CHALLENGING
2008 4/14 – until 2011 2/1

PLUTO X-BENEFICIAL
2005 2/2 – until 2007 11/24

August 20
URANUS X-CHALLENGING
2001 5/14 – until 2003 2/16

NEPTUNE X-CHALLENGING
2009 3/6 – until 2011 12/26

PLUTO X-BENEFICIAL
2005 12/28 – until 2008 10/9

August 21
URANUS X-CHALLENGING
2002 3/1 – until 2003 12/22

NEPTUNE X-CHALLENGING
2009 4/5 – until 2012 1/26

PLUTO X-BENEFICIAL
2006 1/25 – until 2008 11/18

August 22
URANUS X-CHALLENGING
2002 3/18 – until 2004 1/14

NEPTUNE X-CHALLENGING
2010 2/28 – until 2012 12/14

PLUTO X-BENEFICIAL
2006 3/12 – until 2009 9/17

Virgo

August 23–September 22

August 23

SUN: VIRGO/LEO CUSP · DECANATE: VIRGO/MERCURY · DEGREE: 29°5 LEO–0°5 VIRGO · MODE: MUTABLE · ELEMENT: EARTH

Your Personal Powers

Verbally creative and intelligent, you make a good first impression. Being analytical and precise, you like to know where you stand. As a versatile and imaginative individual you are able to see different points of view in every situation. Your ruling planet, Mercury, endows you with practical skills, a need for order, and patience with details. Being a proud perfectionist, you dislike making mistakes. By being diplomatic, lighthearted, and less nervous or intense, you can use your wit and create harmony or resolve difficult situations. Although you are keen on accumulating information and deepening your awareness, you gain more power when you act decisively and develop your foresight or ability to view the whole. Having a good business sense indicates that you can succeed admirably when you invest time and effort in projects and are not put off by obstacles. Nevertheless, as a sensitive and intuitive individual who has the ability to quickly evaluate people, you are a good psychologist and an excellent communicator.

Your Powers of Attraction in Relationships

Being attracted by different ideas, you are drawn to versatile and mentally creative people who can keep your interest. As you are often a keen collaborator, you enjoy working with others, especially if it can further your knowledge. As you are kind and willing to lend a hand, other people are drawn to your friendly and generous nature. Although you have a warm heart and a way with people, mental restlessness implies that you are prone to fluctuating moods and a tendency to change your mind. If you overanalyze your close relationships, however, you can also end up being unsure about how you feel. Nevertheless, when in love, you can be compassionate, caring, and make sacrifices, putting your partner's needs before your own.

Your attractive qualities: articulate, precise, cautious, decisive, enterprising, hardworking, friendly, versatile, persevering, inner faith, confident, business sense, intellectual, determined, shrewd, practical, multitalented, loyal, compassionate, responsible, communicative, intuitive

Your less attractive qualities: easily bored, restlessness, extravagant, impatient, indecisive, selfish, uncertain, materialistic, too critical, cynical, irritable, scattered, moody, selfish, insecure, stubborn, uncompromising, unhelpful, boastful, too fastidious, unsympathetic

Your Venus Power

The planet Venus has a great deal of influence on your powers of attraction. Below are four possible Venus types for women and men. To find your Venus you need to go to page 771, where you will find the Venus table and extra information. The planet Mars also affects your powers of attraction. To find your Mars table and interpretation go to page 761.

WOMEN WITH VENUS IN CANCER: Gentle and tender, you are romantic by nature. You possess a strong need for security and usually help others feel safe and protected. This preservation is especially centered round the home, which is your haven from life's storm. Although your maternal instincts are strong, avoid making too many sacrifices for others at your own expense. Nevertheless, affectionate and caring, once committed to a relationship, your loyalty and devotion to your partner is very strong.

MEN WITH VENUS IN CANCER: Affectionate with a strong, sensitive streak, you can love very deeply. You may find yourself drawn to sympathetic partners who can tune into your moods and feelings as well as be reassuring and supportive. Family links are especially important to you and the more positive these relationships are, the more confident and safe you feel.

WOMEN WITH VENUS IN LEO: You possess the wonderful ability to project your warm and sunny personality and keep others happily entertained. Loving attention yourself, you seek a partner who can appreciate you, be supportive, and give you positive feedback. Proud, with a natural regal air, you expect respect from your partners but are willing to be loyal and supportive in exchange. Although sometimes a little self-centered, you know how to make your partner feel special.

MEN WITH VENUS IN LEO: Enthusiastic, playful, and kind, you can be benevolent with those you love. Warm, romantic, and self-expressive, you adore the drama of love or having fun with your friends. Usually you are attracted to partners with a warm and generous nature. Although you can be a confident and charismatic partner, you may need to develop humility in order to stop pride or arrogance from marring your relationships.

WOMEN WITH VENUS IN VIRGO: Intelligent and discriminating, you are usually drawn to polite and refined individuals. As a perfectionist you may be keen to analyze and criticize yourself but be careful of continually going over your partner's shortcomings. By focusing on how you can make positive improvements in yourself and in your relationships, you avoid becoming skeptical or confused. You empower yourself when you display your kind and caring concern for the well-being of loved ones and spontaneously offer your practical assistance.

MEN WITH VENUS IN VIRGO: A love of order usually indicates that you are attracted to refined individuals with analytical or practical abilities. You and your partner may be working together or serving similar causes. As you constantly analyze partnerships in order to improve them, you are likely to use former relationships as a point of reference and compare them to your present partner. As you are helpful and kind, others usually rely on your good judgment and often turn to you for advice or practical assistance.

WOMEN WITH VENUS IN LIBRA: Attractive, refined, and conscious of the needs of others, you usually desire harmonious relationships. As a peacemaker with good negotiating skills, you can smooth out difficulties with others but your dislike of confrontation may sometimes leave you refusing to take a stand or compromising too many of your own needs. Courteous, stylish, and charming with polished social skills, you are an expert at relating to others in a gracious and civilized manner.

MEN WITH VENUS IN LIBRA: As a sociable and friendly individual with an eye for beauty, you are amorous and charming. You are a natural gentleman and your ideal partner usually has an elegant appearance, artistic appreciation, and good taste. Your relationships benefit when you resist the temptation to take the easy way out or put too much emphasis on vanity and high living. Intellectual and naturally refined, you seek a loving partner who can share your romantic and sophisticated aspirations.

To read all about your Outer Planets and work out how to use your personalized timetable, go to Section Three, page 789.

Your Personalized Timetable

JUPITER BENEFICIAL
1940 4/10 – 6/21
1940 11/27 – until 1941 2/2
1942 5/16 – 6/30
1945 12/30 – until 1946 3/27
1946 8/27 – 10/17
1948 2/2 – 7/5
1948 9/25 – 12/19
1952 3/24 – 5/31
1953 9/10 – 11/18
1954 4/27 – 6/13
1957 12/5 – until 1958 5/5
1958 8/2 – 9/30
1960 1/14 – 12/3
1964 3/6 – 5/14
1965 8/12 – 12/31
1966 4/2 – 5/28
1969 11/17 – until 1970 1/20
1970 3/22 – 9/12
1971 12/28 – until 1972 4/3
1972 5/17 – 11/15
1975 6/30 – 9/29
1976 2/15 – 4/27
1977 7/23 – 9/23
1977 11/24 – until 1978 5/9
1981 10/31 – 12/22
1982 5/3 – 8/21
1983 12/12 – until 1984 2/28
1984 7/3 – 10/24
1987 6/5 – 11/12
1988 1/17 – 4/11
1989 7/5 – 8/24
1990 1/5 – 4/15
1993 10/16 – 12/2
1995 11/27 – until 1996 2/7
1999 5/15 – until 2000 3/24
2001 6/19 – 8/3
2005 10/1 – 11/16
2007 11/10 – until 2008 1/21
2011 4/27 – 7/19
2011 10/11 – until 2012 3/3

SATURN BENEFICIAL
1939 4/16 – until 1940 5/20
1943 8/22 – 11/28
1944 5/7 – 7/26
1945 2/5 – 4/3
1952 12/9 – until 1953 4/6
1953 9/4 – 11/30
1954 5/16 – 8/25
1958 1/20 – 6/25
1958 10/19 – until 1959 12/15
1968 5/27 – 10/21
1969 2/17 – 7/12
1969 9/30 – until 1970 3/27
1973 6/18 – 10/3
1973 10/31 – until 1974 6/1
1982 10/14 – until 1983 10/8
1987 11/28 – until 1989 1/18
1989 8/24 – 9/29
1998 3/30 – until 1999 5/3
2002 7/29 – 12/30
2003 4/15 – 7/9
2011 11/20 – until 2012 5/7
2012 8/12 – 11/13

URANUS BENEFICIAL
1947 7/31 – until 1950 6/17
1973 11/4 – until 1976 9/10
1986 2/12 – until 1990 11/24

NEPTUNE BENEFICIAL
1953 11/12 – until 1959 8/23
1980 1/20 – until 1988 10/12

PLUTO BENEFICIAL
1981 10/25 – until 1986 7/26
2004 2/3 – until 2012 11/6

JUPITER CHALLENGING
1938 3/24 – until 1939 2/3

1941 4/20 – 6/28
1947 1/8 – 5/23
1947 9/6 – 11/27
1950 3/6 – until 1951 1/15
1953 4/1 – 6/11
1958 12/19 – until 1959 11/12
1962 2/17 – 5/4
1962 9/1 – 12/23
1964 7/21 – 11/9
1965 3/11 – 5/25
1970 12/2 – until 1971 10/25
1974 2/1 – 4/11
1976 08-07 – 12/31
1977 1/30 – 5/9
1982 11/16 – until 1983 2/8
1983 5/15 – 10/6
1986 1/16 – 3/24
1988 6/10 – until 1989 4/21
1994 11/1 – until 1995 1/15
1995 6/26 – 9/8
1997 5/26 – 6/25
1997 12/28 – until 1998 3/8
2000 5/23 – 8/11
2000 11/17 – until 2001 3/31
2006 10/16 – 12/29
2009 4/15 – 8/18
2009 12/5 – until 2010 2/19
2012 5/6 – 7/17

SATURN CHALLENGING
1941 6/6 – until 1942 7/8
1942 12/20 – until 1943 3/25
1955 10/29 – until 1956 12/16
1963 4/20 – 7/18
1964 1/11 – until 1965 2/26
1970 8/1 – 10/9
1971 4/12 – until 1972 5/12
1984 12/2 – until 1985 7/14
1985 8/6 – until 1986 1/27
1986 5/12 – 10/24
1993 2/15 – until 1994 4/3
1994 9/21 – 12/26
2000 5/19 – until 2001 6/19

URANUS CHALLENGING
1939 7/28 – until 1944 5/7
1979 11/18 – until 1983 11/2
2001 2/22 – until 2005 12/27

NEPTUNE CHALLENGING
1966 1/6 – until 1974 10/10
2007 4/13 – Continues

PLUTO CHALLENGING
1991 12/16 – until 1998 11/21

JUPITER SPECIAL
1943 10/13 – until 1944 2/15
1944 6/9 – 8/30
1955 9/22 – until 1956 4/10
1956 4/24 – 8/14
1967 9/5 – until 1968 7/29
1979 8/20 – 11/14
1980 2/6 – 7/10
1991 8/4 – 10/20
1992 3/16 – 6/15
2003 7/19 – 10/2

SATURN SPECIAL
1947 10/30 – until 1948 1/8
1948 7/13 – until 1949 8/17
1977 8/22 – until 1978 9/25
1979 4/15 – 6/2
2006 10/3 – until 2007 2/11
2007 6/23 – 11/16
2008 1/22 – 7/30

URANUS SPECIAL
1960 8/16 – until 1964 7/15

PLUTO SPECIAL
1952 8/26 – until 1962 6/2

August 24

SUN: VIRGO • DECANATE: VIRGO/MERCURY • DEGREE: 0°5–1°5 VIRGO • MODE: MUTABLE • ELEMENT: EARTH

Your Personal Powers

Intuitive and astute, your determination and motivation indicate that you can be direct and resourceful. Your ruling planet, Mercury, endows you with love of order, practical skills, and analytical abilities. You can succeed by balancing your intuition, common sense, and pragmatism. Although your penetrating intellect suggests that you are observant, your tendency to pay attention to the smallest detail or be too self-analytical implies that you cannot afford to indulge in worry and self-doubt. You therefore empower yourself by staying objective or taking a step back and viewing the whole. As you are often well-informed or hold strong opinions, you also empower yourself when you use tact and diplomacy rather than insisting that you know best. When positive and happy, you not only display your protective and compassionate nature but also show others how witty and interesting you can be. When you feel unhappy or dissatisfied, however, you can be cynical or uncommunicative. In order to create inner balance and the harmony you desire, you may have to learn to communicate your deeper feelings.

Your Powers of Attraction in Relationships

Other people are attracted to your friendly and compassionate nature. Your flair for dealing with others is often linked to your personal touch. When you are positive and optimistic, your charming wit and lighthearted manner can inspire others. Although you are often willing to advise those who ask for your opinions, guard against being bossy or patronizing. You are usually drawn to enterprising individuals who know how to utilize their knowledge. A talent for mixing business with friendship also suggests that you can profit from partnerships or establish long-term relationships with business partners. Keen on establishing harmony and a solid foundation for yourself, you will often do your utmost to keep your home in order. Although you like to present yourself in a dignified way, underneath you are serious and sensitive.

Your attractive qualities: mentally sharp, self-assured, direct, persuasive, logical, hardworking, persistent, witty, warmhearted, discriminative, inventive, well-informed, quick learner, progressive, methodical, organized, energetic, tidy, idealistic, practical, communicative, determined

Your less attractive qualities: discontented, overconfident, critical, anxious, too sensitive, too fastidious or lazy, irritable, argumentative, skeptical, materialistic, too economical, extremist, bossy, stubborn, anxious, worried, moody

Your Venus Power

The planet Venus has a great deal of influence on your powers of attraction. Below are four possible Venus types for women and men. To find your Venus you need to go to page 771, where you will find the Venus table and extra information. The planet Mars also affects your powers of attraction. To find your Mars table and interpretation go to page 761.

WOMEN WITH VENUS IN CANCER: Possessing a soft femininity, you have tender and sensitive emotions. Sympathetic and caring, you often mother those in your care by making sure they are comfortable and have plenty to eat. When you feel hurt or insecure in relationships, you are likely to cover your feelings by being defensive or appearing tough on the outside while on the inside you are feeling vulnerable. Affectionate and romantic, you make a faithful and devoted partner.

MEN WITH VENUS IN CANCER: Being emotionally receptive, you can make a sensitive lover. With your desire to care for and protect others, you are likely to have strong family connections. Love is often tied in with being attentive to the needs of others and you may find yourself attracted to individuals who have sympathetic or maternal qualities. Security conscious, you need a loyal partner who can offer you support and ideally be a good cook and homemaker.

WOMEN WITH VENUS IN LEO: Warm and playful with a touch of the dramatic, you enjoy the company of generous or strong individuals who can share your sense of fun. Although there are advantages to your being strong-willed, in your relationships you need to resist being bossy as it can cause resentment. With your wonderful mixture of regal authority and childlike wonder, you love to keep others entertained and amused.

MEN WITH VENUS IN LEO: Sociable and outgoing, you are kind and generous with those you love. Looking for a relationship that can be fun and entertaining, you need a playmate who can share your enthusiasm and high spirits. Your pride, however, often stops you from associating with lovers or partners you see as beneath you. As you desire someone who can appreciate your sense of the dramatic, you are often attracted to people with strong personalities.

WOMEN WITH VENUS IN VIRGO: Intelligent and discriminating, you are usually drawn to polite and refined individuals. As a perfectionist, you may be keen to analyze and criticize yourself but be careful of continually going over your partner's shortcomings. By focusing on how you can make positive improvements in yourself and in your relationships, you avoid becoming skeptical or confused. You empower yourself when you display your kind and caring concern for the well-being of loved ones and spontaneously offer your practical assistance.

MEN WITH VENUS IN VIRGO: A love of order usually indicates that you are attracted to refined individuals with analytical or practical abilities. You and your partner may be working together or serving similar causes. As you constantly analyze partnerships in order to improve them, you are likely to use former relationships as a point of reference and compare them to your present partner. As you are helpful and kind, others usually rely on your good judgment and often turn to you for advice or practical assistance.

WOMEN WITH VENUS IN LIBRA: Usually you are attractive and sociable with an easygoing manner. Your love of beauty, harmony, and pleasure implies that you are a romantic with a desire for love and affection. Once in a relationship, you need to learn to negotiate your position rather than adapt to the wishes of others and compromise just to keep the peace. Nevertheless, your advanced social skills and strong sense of fair play can help you succeed in any social or romantic situation.

MEN WITH VENUS IN LIBRA: Your good social skills, charming personality, and refined manner usually make you attractive to the opposite sex. Equally, you desire a sophisticated partner with grace, elegance, and a strong sense of style. Although you have the ability to be persuasive and irresistible to others, avoid manipulative love games. Nevertheless, your natural diplomacy and sense of fair play help you to relate to people in all social situations. With your love for balance and harmony, you seek a partner who is also moderate, easygoing, and loving.

To read all about your Outer Planets and work out how to use your personalized timetable, go to Section Three, page 789.

♍

Your Personalized Timetable

JUPITER BENEFICIAL
1940 4/15 – 6/26
1940 11/18 – until 1941 2/11
1942 5/21 – 7/5
1946 1/8 – 3/17
1946 9/2 – 10/21
1948 2/8 – 6/27
1948 10/3 – 12/24
1952 3/29 – 6/5
1953 9/21 – 11/7
1954 5/2 – 6/18
1957 12/11 – until 1958 4/26
1958 8/10 – 10/5
1960 1/19 – 12/7
1964 3/11 – 5/18
1965 8/18 – 12/23
1966 4/9 – 6/1
1969 11/22 – until 1970 2/4
1970 3/7 – 9/18
1972 1/2 – 11/20
1975 7/9 – 9/20
1976 2/20 – 5/1
1977 7/28 – 10/6
1977 11/11 – until 1978 5/14
1981 11/5 – 12/28
1982 4/24 – 8/28
1983 12/17 – until 1984 3/5
1984 6/25 – 10/30
1987 6/10 – 11/3
1988 1/25 – 4/15
1989 7/10 – 8/30
1989 12/29 – until 1990 4/22
1993 10/20 – 12/7
1994 6/8 – 7/25
1995 12/1 – until 1996 2/12
1996 8/12 – 9/25
1999 5/20 – until 2000 3/29
2001 6/23 – 8/8
2005 10/5 – 11/21
2007 11/15 – until 2008 1/25
2011 5/2 – 7/28
2011 10/2 – until 2012 3/9

SATURN BENEFICIAL
1939 4/24 – until 1940 5/28
1940 12/12 – until 1941 2/5
1943 9/5 – 11/12
1944 5/16 – 8/4
1945 1/19 – 4/19
1952 12/22 – until 1953 3/23
1953 9/14 – 12/10
1954 5/2 – 9/6
1958 1/31 – 6/11
1958 10/31 – until 1959 12/24
1968 6/7 – 10/9
1969 2/27 – 8/1
1969 9/10 – until 1970 4/4
1973 6/26 – until 1974 6/9
1982 10/22 – until 1983 10/17
1987 12/7 – until 1989 1/27
1989 8/1 – 10/21
1998 4/7 – until 1999 5/11
2002 8/8 – 12/17
2003 4/26 – 7/17
2011 11/29 – until 2012 4/23
2012 8/24 – 11/21

URANUS BENEFICIAL
1947 8/26 – until 1951 4/4
1973 11/21 – until 1976 9/29
1986 12/15 – until 1990 12/12

NEPTUNE BENEFICIAL
1953 12/17 – until 1959 9/30
1980 3/8 – until 1988 11/25

PLUTO BENEFICIAL
1981 11/21 – until 1986 9/15
2004 12/28 – until 2012 12/11

JUPITER CHALLENGING
1938 3/29 – 10/8
1938 10/29 – until 1939 2/7
1941 4/25 – 7/3

1947 1/14 – 5/15
1947 9/13 – 12/2
1950 3/10 – until 1951 1/20
1953 4/6 – 6/15
1958 12/24 – until 1959 7/3
1959 8/6 – 11/16
1962 2/21 – 5/11
1962 8/24 – 12/29
1964 7/28 – 11/1
1965 3/16 – 5/30
1970 12/7 – until 1971 10/30
1974 2/5 – 4/16
1974 10/15 – 11/22
1976 7/3 – 12/17
1977 2/13 – 5/13
1982 11/21 – until 1983 2/16
1983 5/6 – 10/12
1986 1/20 – 3/29
1988 6/14 – until 1989 4/26
1994 11/5 – until 1995 1/21
1995 6/17 – 9/17
1998 1/2 – 3/12
2000 5/28 – 8/19
2000 11/9 – until 2001 4/6
2006 10/21 – until 2007 1/3
2009 4/21 – 8/10
2009 12/11 – until 2010 2/23
2012 5/11 – 7/22

SATURN CHALLENGING
1941 6/14 – 12/21
1942 2/24 – 7/18
1942 12/7 – until 1943 4/6
1955 11/6 – until 1956 12/25
1957 7/8 – 9/14
1963 5/9 – 6/28
1964 1/21 – until 1965 3/6
1970 8/30 – 9/9
1971 4/21 – until 1972 5/20
1984 12/11 – until 1985 6/17
1985 9/1 – until 1986 2/10
1986 4/25 – 11/3
1993 2/23 – until 1994 4/13
1994 9/7 – until 1995 1/7
2000 5/27 – until 2001 6/28
2002 1/14 – 3/4

URANUS CHALLENGING
1940 5/23 – until 1944 5/24
1979 12/5 – until 1983 11/19
2001 3/13 – until 2006 1/21

NEPTUNE CHALLENGING
1966 12/3 – until 1974 11/11
2008 3/5 – Continues

PLUTO CHALLENGING
1992 1/20 – until 1999 10/14

JUPITER SPECIAL
1943 10/19 – until 1944 2/8
1944 6/15 – 9/4
1955 9/28 – until 1956 3/21
1956 5/14 – 8/19
1967 9/10 – until 1968 8/3
1979 8/25 – 11/24
1980 1/28 – 7/15
1991 8/9 – 10/26
1992 3/8 – 6/23
2003 7/24 – 10/7

SATURN SPECIAL
1947 11/25 – 12/13
1948 7/21 – until 1949 8/25
1977 8/30 – until 1978 10/4
1979 3/27 – 6/21
2006 10/14 – until 2007 1/29
2007 7/3 – until 2008 8/8

URANUS SPECIAL
1960 9/2 – until 1964 8/3

PLUTO SPECIAL
1952 10/1 – until 1962 7/26

327

August 25

Your Personal Powers

Observant, intuitive, and mentally sharp, you grasp ideas quickly and are always keen on learning something new or gathering more information. Your ruling planet, Mercury, endows you with graceful expression, practical skills, and analytical abilities. Being curious and alert with a love of order, you benefit by keeping yourself intellectually stimulated. You gain power when you see knowledge as your ticket to success or when you apply your discrimination and methodology to refining and improving existing projects or ideas. You can also succeed and achieve by initiating new concepts or being creative, especially through writing. You lose power when you drift from one interest to another and act on impulse. Although you may appear independent and resourceful, inwardly you possess intense emotions and are keener on working with others than doing things alone. Your success is often linked to education, research, and promoting new concepts that can be of benefit to others. As a good team player you like to collaborate with others and often show a willingness to help good causes.

Your Powers of Attraction in Relationships

Charismatic and gregarious, you enjoy socializing and mixing with people who share your interests. With your charm and diplomacy, you can attract many friends. Sensitive to friction, you need to surround yourself with congenial people who are honest, easygoing, and supportive. Ambitious and intelligent, you usually admire determined and enterprising individuals who are daring and success-oriented. As a devoted and loving individual, you are probably willing to make great sacrifices for your partner or those you love. If your expectations of others are too high, however, you may find out that your partners cannot give you all the attention you want. To achieve emotional equilibrium you need to resist a tendency to vacillate between being too bossy and being overdependent. Nevertheless, you make an excellent friend, devoted parent, and loyal partner.

Your attractive qualities: instinctive, alert, good judgment, independent, enthusiastic, daring, courageous, devoted, highly intuitive, perfectionist, perceptive, creative, good people skills, high ideals, imaginative, precise, decisive, charming, leadership, diplomatic, active, initiative, knowledgeable

Your less attractive qualities: restless, impulsive, impatient, inconsistent, too emotional, jealous, secretive, too critical, moody, nervous, intense emotions, easily bored, negligent with small details, overanalytical, bossy, disorganized, unsympathetic

Your Venus Power

The planet Venus has a great deal of influence on your powers of attraction. Below are four possible Venus types for women and men. To find your Venus you need to go to page 771, where you will find the Venus table and extra information. The planet Mars also affects your powers of attraction. To find your Mars table and interpretation go to page 761.

WOMEN WITH VENUS IN CANCER: Possessing a soft femininity, you have tender and sensitive emotions. Sympathetic and caring, you often mother those in your care by making sure they are comfortable and have plenty to eat. When you feel hurt or insecure in relationships, you are likely to cover your feelings by being defensive or appearing tough on the outside while on the inside you are feeling vulnerable. Affectionate and romantic, you make a faithful and devoted partner.

MEN WITH VENUS IN CANCER: Being emotionally receptive, you can make a sensitive lover. With your desire to care for and protect others, you are likely to have strong family connections. Love is often tied in with being attentive to the needs of others and you may find yourself attracted to individuals who have sympathetic or maternal qualities. Security conscious, you need a loyal partner who can offer you support and ideally be a good cook and homemaker.

WOMEN WITH VENUS IN LEO: Your friendly and sunny personality often makes you stand out in a crowd. Generous and giving, you know how to make your partner feel special. As you often expect loyalty and devotion from your partners in return, you can become easily offended if they ignore you or behave in an inconsiderate manner. Charming and kind, when you are in love, you can be romantic, dramatic, and passionate.

MEN WITH VENUS IN LEO: A childlike nature suggests that you are versatile and keen on games or being entertained. You are usually attracted to vivacious partners with a benevolent nature. As an extrovert you enjoy being involved in all types of activities where you can assert yourself and show

your talents and abilities. Others may recognize your inborn tendencies to lead but are also aware of your vanity or pride. Nevertheless, generous, kind, and caring, you often show compassion to those less fortunate than yourself.

WOMEN WITH VENUS IN VIRGO: Articulate and straightforward in your relationships, you attract others with your genuine concern for their well-being. By being understanding and a good listener, you are able to show your love and friendship. With your analytical approach to relationships, however, you may have to be careful of becoming too matter-of-fact. You often display your concern for the welfare of others by your willingness to offer practical help and assistance. You usually seek a partner who is willing to work as hard on relationships as you are.

MEN WITH VENUS IN VIRGO: Although you are constantly analyzing your relationships in order to understand and improve them, you may nevertheless need to refrain from continuously mulling over issues that can cause anxiety. You are happiest when you are able to help your loved ones in practical ways and forget yourself in your willingness to be of service to others. You seek a partner who has high standards and can be as pragmatic and hardworking as yourself. Ideally they should also be impeccably dressed with a fine analytical mind.

WOMEN WITH VENUS IN LIBRA: Gracious, charming, and sociable with a sense of style, you have no trouble attracting admirers. With your natural diplomatic skills and desire for harmony you usually like to keep the peace and avoid confrontations, but be careful of failing to take a stand when it is necessary. Romantic and easygoing yourself, you are attracted to affectionate and refined individuals who share your love of peace, justice, and fair play.

MEN WITH VENUS IN LIBRA: Courteous and refined, you are attracted to beautiful and elegant people. You are looking for a partner who can share your natural good taste and enjoy an intellectual conversation. Disliking conflict, you may have to be careful not to go along with others just to keep the peace. Your ideal partner will appreciate beauty and the little luxuries of life as well as possess good social skills. You have a strong sense of social etiquette yourself so you need an intelligent and sophisticated partner.

To read all about your Outer Planets and work out how to use your personalized timetable, go to Section Three, page 789.

Your Personalized Timetable

JUPITER BENEFICIAL
1940 4/19 – 7/2
1940 11/11 – until 1941 2/18
1942 5/26 – 7/9
1946 1/19 – 3/6
1946 9/7 – 10/26
1948 2/13 – 6/19
1948 10/10 – 12/28
1952 4/2 – 6/9
1954 5/7 – 6/22
1957 12/17 – until 1958 4/19
1958 8/17 – 10/10
1960 1/24 – 12/12
1964 3/15 – 5/22
1965 8/24 – 12/16
1966 4/16 – 6/6
1969 11/27 – until 1970 6/5
1970 7/11 – 9/23
1972 1/6 – 11/24
1975 7/19 – 9/10
1976 2/25 – 5/5
1977 8/1 – until 1978 2/3
1978 3/9 – 5/19
1981 11/10 – until 1982 1/4
1982 4/17 – 9/3
1983 12/21 – until 1984 3/12
1984 6/17 – 11/5
1987 6/16 – 10/26
1988 2/1 – 4/19
1989 7/14 – 9/5
1989 12/22 – until 1990 4/28
1993 10/25 – 12/13
1994 5/28 – 8/6
1995 12/6 – until 1996 2/17
1996 7/31 – 10/7
1999 5/25 – until 2000 4/2
2001 6/27 – 8/13
2002 2/5 – 3/25
2005 10/10 – 11/25
2007 11/20 – until 2008 1/30
2011 5/6 – 8/8
2011 9/21 – until 2012 3/14

SATURN BENEFICIAL
1939 5/2 – until 1940 6/6
1940 11/26 – until 1941 2/21
1943 10/1 – 10/18
1944 5/24 – 8/12
1945 1/7 – 4/30
1953 1/7 – 3/6
1953 9/23 – 12/20
1954 4/20 – 9/17
1958 2/11 – 5/29
1958 11/10 – until 1960 1/1
1968 6/18 – 9/26
1969 3/8 – until 1970 4/12
1973 7/4 – until 1974 6/16
1982 10/30 – until 1983 10/25
1987 12/15 – until 1989 2/5
1989 7/17 – 11/3
1998 4/15 – until 1999 5/19
2002 8/18 – 12/5
2003 5/6 – 7/25
2004 2/19 – 3/24
2011 12/9 – until 2012 4/10
2012 9/4 – 11/30

URANUS BENEFICIAL
1948 6/21 – until 1951 5/5
1973 12/11 – until 1976 10/16
1986 12/31 – until 1990 12/29

NEPTUNE BENEFICIAL
1954 11/9 – until 1960 8/14
1981 1/15 – until 1988 12/22

PLUTO BENEFICIAL
1981 12/25 – until 1986 10/12
2005 1/25 – Continues

JUPITER CHALLENGING
1938 4/3 – 9/22
1938 11/14 – until 1939 2/11

1941 4/29 – 7/7
1947 1/20 – 5/7
1947 9/19 – 12/6
1950 3/15 – until 1951 1/24
1953 4/11 – 6/19
1958 12/29 – until 1959 6/19
1959 8/20 – 11/21
1962 2/25 – 5/18
1962 8/17 – until 1963 1/4
1964 8/5 – 10/25
1965 3/22 – 6/3
1970 12/11 – until 1971 11/4
1974 2/9 – 4/21
1974 10/3 – 12/4
1976 7/8 – 12/8
1977 2/22 – 5/17
1982 11/25 – until 1983 2/26
1983 4/27 – 10/17
1986 1/24 – 4/2
1988 6/19 – until 1989 5/1
1994 11/10 – until 1995 1/27
1995 6/9 – until 1995 9/24
1998 1/7 – 3/16
2000 6/1 – 8/28
2000 10/31 – until 2001 4/11
2006 10/25 – until 2007 1/7
2009 4/28 – 8/3
2009 12/17 – until 2010 2/27
2012 5/15 – 7/28

SATURN CHALLENGING
1941 6/23 – 12/7
1942 3/10 – 7/27
1942 11/25 – until 1943 4/15
1955 11/14 – until 1957 1/3
1957 6/22 – 9/30
1964 1/29 – until 1965 3/14
1971 4/29 – until 1972 5/28
1984 12/20 – until 1985 6/2
1985 9/15 – until 1986 3/6
1986 4/1 – 11/12
1993 3/3 – until 1994 4/23
1994 8/25 – until 1995 1/17
2000 6/4 – until 2001 7/6
2001 12/28 – until 2002 3/21

URANUS CHALLENGING
1940 6/9 – until 1945 3/20
1979 12/22 – until 1984 8/25
2001 4/2 – until 2006 2/8

NEPTUNE CHALLENGING
1967 1/1 – until 1975 10/5
2008 4/5 – Continues

PLUTO CHALLENGING
1992 12/2 – until 1999 11/12

JUPITER SPECIAL
1943 10/26 – until 1944 1/31
1944 6/21 – 9/8
1955 10/3 – until 1956 3/11
1956 5/25 – 8/24
1967 9/15 – until 1968 8/8
1979 8/29 – 12/6
1980 1/16 – 7/21
1991 8/13 – 11/1
1992 3/1 – 6/29
2003 7/28 – 10/12
2004 4/14 – 5/25

SATURN SPECIAL
1948 7/29 – until 1949 9/2
1977 9/7 – until 1978 10/13
1979 3/14 – until 1979 7/3
2006 10/26 – until 2007 1/16
2007 7/12 – until 2008 8/16

URANUS SPECIAL
1960 9/19 – until 1964 8/19

PLUTO SPECIAL
1953 9/5 – until 1963 5/30

August 26

Your Personal Powers

Idealistic and passionate, you are a highly motivated individual with practical abilities and discriminative powers. Often proud, confident, and dignified, you empower yourself by using your deeply felt emotions to uplift and inspire other people. Your ruling planet, Mercury, endows you with practical thinking, a love of order, and analytical abilities. Hardworking and kind, you usually get a great deal of satisfaction from being in command and leading other people. You lose power by overindulging yourself and letting your strong desires get the better of you. Nevertheless, your idealism and principles of fair play imply that you are a fighter for truth and your sympathy usually lies with those who are being treated badly or unfairly. A flair for business, organizational abilities, and a natural gift for dealing with people indicate that you can be charming, persuasive, and enterprising. Although you are usually sociable and lighthearted, at times you can become critical or too serious, especially when you feel that your hard efforts are not being appreciated. Nonetheless, your strong will and determination can help you in your climb to success.

Your Powers of Attraction in Relationships

Friendly and enthusiastic, you enjoy meeting people and being sociable. You are usually drawn to creative or dynamic people who can express themselves forcefully. Caring and thoughtful, your generosity implies that are usually willing to support friends and relatives who may turn to you in time of need. Frequently you are a tower of strength for people around you. Although you are loyal and caring, your pride and ability to endure indicate that you may find it hard to express your pain and disappointment. When you share your deep feelings or misgivings with those you love and clear the air, you can restore your emotional equilibrium. Although you can make sacrifices in order to keep your relationships, you need to learn to be less bossy. Nevertheless, you attract others with your natural nobility and warm heart.

Your attractive qualities: magnanimous, intelligent, dramatic, generous, friendly, sociable, witty, helpful, creative, inspiring, supportive, confident, optimistic, efficient, hardworking, caring, enthusiastic, dedicated, idealistic, responsible, courageous, managerial skills, fair, honorable, benevolent, practical

Your less attractive qualities: stubborn, willful, self-doubting, selfish, too proud, indulgent, controlling, too sentimental, critical, mistrusting, pessimistic, rebellious, manipulative, unenthusiastic, lack of persistence, love of ease, materialistic, extravagant

Your Venus Power

The planet Venus has a great deal of influence on your powers of attraction. Below are four possible Venus types for women and men. To find your Venus you need to go to page 771, where you will find the Venus table and extra information. The planet Mars also affects your powers of attraction. To find your Mars table and interpretation go to page 761.

WOMEN WITH VENUS IN CANCER: Sensitive and understanding, you are sympathetic to other people's emotions and needs. Protective toward those you love, close relationships with your partner, relatives, and friends are important to your sense of well-being. Aware of how easy it is to hurt other people's feelings, you are often indirect and approach delicate issues in a roundabout way. Nevertheless, learning to face facts and not allowing others to exploit your good nature is a lesson just as valuable.

MEN WITH VENUS IN CANCER: You seek a partner who is sympathetic, caring, and protective. Able to be forgiving and compassionate, you want a secure emotional bond in your close relationships. Usually you are drawn to partners who are maternal, unselfish, or demonstrative with their feelings. Although you can sometimes appear to others as impressionable, you have powerful emotions and inner strength.

WOMEN WITH VENUS IN LEO: Your friendly and sunny personality often makes you stand out in a crowd. Generous and giving, you know how to make your partner feel special. As you often expect loyalty and devotion from your partners in return, you can become easily offended if they ignore you or behave in an inconsiderate manner. Charming and kind, when you are in love, you can be romantic, dramatic, and passionate.

MEN WITH VENUS IN LEO: As an extrovert you enjoy being involved in all types of activities where you can assert yourself and show your talents and abilities. A childlike nature suggests that you are versatile and keen on games or being entertained. You are usually attracted to vivacious partners with a benevolent nature. Others may recognize your inborn ten-

dencies to lead but are also aware of your vanity or pride. Nevertheless, generous, kind, and caring, you often show compassion to those less fortunate than yourself.

WOMEN WITH VENUS IN VIRGO: In relationships, you can be modest and unassuming but desire perfection. You usually analyze your partnerships until you feel you have understood them to the last little detail in order to improve them. A problem usually arises when you become too critical either of partners or yourself and indulge in being skeptical or faultfinding. As you are modest, others may not be aware of the strong sensuality beneath your well-groomed exterior.

MEN WITH VENUS IN VIRGO: Industrious and well-ordered, you relate to others in a considerate and down-to-earth way. You enjoy giving practical advice and being of service to those you love even in small ways. Being a perfectionist, you are drawn to partners with high morals or a strong work ethic. Partners who have strong analytical minds are very attractive to you, particularly if they are also clean and meticulously dressed.

WOMEN WITH VENUS IN LIBRA: Gracious, charming, and sociable with a sense of style, you have no trouble attracting admirers. With your natural diplomatic skills and desire for harmony you usually like to keep the peace and avoid confrontations, but be careful of failing to make a stand when it is necessary. Romantic and easygoing yourself, you are attracted to affectionate and refined individuals who share your love of peace, justice, and fair play.

MEN WITH VENUS IN LIBRA: Courteous and refined, you are attracted to beautiful and elegant people. You are looking for a partner who can share your natural good taste and enjoy an intellectual conversation. Disliking conflict, you may have to be careful not to go along with others just to keep the peace. Your ideal partner will appreciate beauty and the little luxuries of life as well as possess good social skills. You have a strong sense of social etiquette yourself so you need an intelligent and sophisticated partner.

To read all about your Outer Planets and work out how to use your personalized timetable, go to Section Three, page 789.

go to Section Three, page 789.

♍

Your Personalized Timetable

JUPITER BENEFICIAL
1940 4/23 – 7/7
1940 11/3 – until 1941 2/24
1942 5/30 – 7/13
1946 9/12 – 10/30
1948 2/20 – 6/11
1948 10/16 – until 1949 1/1
1952 4/6 – 6/14
1954 5/12 – 6/27
1957 12/24 – until 1958 4/11
1958 8/23 – 10/14
1960 1/28 – 7/29
1960 9/11 – 12/16
1964 3/20 – 5/26
1965 8/31 – 12/8
1966 4/21 – 6/10
1969 12/2 – until 1970 5/23
1970 7/24 – 9/28
1972 1/10 – 11/29
1975 8/4 – 8/24
1976 3/1 – 5/9
1977 8/6 – until 1978 1/21
1978 3/22 – 5/24
1981 11/14 – until 1982 1/11
1982 4/9 – 9/9
1983 12/25 – until 1984 3/20
1984 6/9 – 11/10
1987 6/21 – 10/19
1988 2/8 – 4/23
1989 7/19 – 9/12
1989 12/14 – until 1990 5/4
1993 10/29 – 12/18
1994 5/18 – 8/15
1995 12/10 – until 1996 2/23
1996 7/22 – 10/15
1999 5/29 – until 2000 4/6
2001 7/2 – 8/18
2002 1/26 – 4/5
2005 10/14 – 11/30
2007 11/24 – until 2008 2/3
2011 5/10 – until 2012 3/18

SATURN BENEFICIAL
1939 5/10 – 12/17
1940 1/7 – 6/15
1940 11/13 – until 1941 3/5
1944 6/1 – 8/22
1944 12/26 – until 1945 5/10
1953 10/1 – until 1954 1/1
1954 4/6 – 9/26
1958 2/25 – 5/14
1958 11/19 – until 1960 1/10
1968 7/3 – 9/11
1969 3/17 – until 1970 4/20
1973 7/12 – until 1974 6/24
1982 11/7 – until 1983 11/2
1987 12/23 – until 1989 2/15
1989 7/3 – 11/15
1998 4/22 – until 1999 5/27
1999 12/27 – until 2000 1/27
2002 8/30 – 11/22
2003 5/14 – 8/2
2004 1/30 – 4/13
2011 12/21 – until 2012 3/28
2012 9/13 – 12/9

URANUS BENEFICIAL
1938 1/1 – 3/2
1948 7/8 – until 1951 5/25
1974 1/8 – until 1976 10/31
1987 1/17 – until 1991 10/29

NEPTUNE BENEFICIAL
1954 12/9 – until 1960 9/24
1981 2/20 – until 1989 11/19

PLUTO BENEFICIAL
1982 11/6 – until 1987 8/23
2005 12/22 – Continues

JUPITER CHALLENGING
1938 4/8 – 9/12
1938 11/24 – until 1939 2/15
1941 5/3 – 7/12

JUPITER BENEFICIAL (continued)
1947 1/28 – 4/29
1947 9/25 – 12/11
1950 3/19 – until 1951 1/29
1953 4/15 – 6/23
1959 1/4 – 6/9
1959 8/30 – 11/25
1962 3/1 – 5/26
1962 8/8 – until 1963 1/9
1964 8/14 – 10/16
1965 3/27 – 6/7
1970 12/16 – until 1971 11/9
1974 2/13 – 4/26
1974 9/24 – 12/12
1976 7/14 – 11/30
1977 3/2 – 5/21
1982 11/30 – until 1983 3/12
1983 4/13 – 10/22
1986 1/28 – 4/7
1988 6/23 – until 1989 5/5
1994 11/14 – until 1995 2/2
1995 6/1 – 10/1
1998 1/11 – 3/20
2000 6/5 – 9/9
2000 10/20 – until 2001 4/16
2006 10/30 – until 2007 1/12
2007 7/18 – 8/26
2009 5/5 – 7/26
2009 12/22 – until 2010 3/3
2012 5/19 – 8/2

SATURN CHALLENGING
1941 7/2 – 11/24
1942 3/21 – 8/8
1942 11/13 – until 1943 4/24
1955 11/23 – until 1957 1/12
1957 6/8 – 10/12
1964 2/6 – until 1965 3/22
1965 11/8 – 11/19
1971 5/6 – until 1972 6/4
1984 12/29 – until 1985 5/19
1985 9/27 – until 1986 11/20
1993 3/12 – 9/25
1993 11/29 – until 1994 5/5
1994 8/12 – until 1995 1/27
2000 6/12 – until 2001 1/2
2001 2/16 – 7/15
2001 12/15 – until 2002 4/2

URANUS CHALLENGING
1940 6/28 – until 1945 4/15
1980 1/11 – until 1984 10/5
2001 5/1 – until 2006 2/26

NEPTUNE CHALLENGING
1967 11/28 – until 1975 11/7
2009 2/28 – Continues

PLUTO CHALLENGING
1992 12/29 – until 2000 9/26

JUPITER SPECIAL
1943 11/3 – until 1944 1/23
1944 6/27 – 9/13
1955 10/8 – until 1956 3/3
1956 6/2 – 8/28
1967 9/19 – until 1968 8/12
1979 9/3 – until 1980 7/26
1991 8/18 – 11/8
1992 2/22 – 7/6
2003 8/2 – 10/17
2004 4/2 – 6/7

SATURN SPECIAL
1948 8/6 – until 1949 9/10
1977 9/15 – until 1978 3/24
1978 5/27 – 10/22
1979 3/2 – 7/14
2006 11/12 – 12/30
2007 7/20 – until 2008 8/24

URANUS SPECIAL
1960 10/8 – until 1964 9/4

PLUTO SPECIAL
1953 10/12 – until 1963 7/24

331

August 27

Your Personal Powers

Intuitive, passionate, and sensitive, you are a highly receptive individual with an idealistic nature and deep feelings. Often serious and responsible, your dedication indicates that you are hardworking and reliable. Your ruling planet, Mercury, endows you with creative ideas, a love of order, and analytical abilities. You lose some of your power when you feel emotionally insecure or when you resort to being manipulative or domineering. Although you are impressionable and thoughtful, your need for self-expression is usually the force behind your motivation and mental creativity. Highly idealistic, you need to be truly inspired by something or someone in order to feel motivated and enthusiastic. You also empower yourself when you act with confidence or show others how talented you really are. As you are often ambitious and proud, you like to have an important role to play. You display your capabilities and determination by being enthusiastic, positive, and optimistic. Nevertheless, you can also empower yourself by showing your compassion and sensitivity toward others.

Your Powers of Attraction in Relationships

Your powerful love expression indicates that underneath your charming exterior lies a passionate and emotionally sensitive individual. Caring and loyal, you can be a devoted friend and partner. You are usually attracted to determined and ambitious persons. Although you can be romantic and affectionate, your need for stability and security implies that you should be patient and cautious in your choice of partners. Since emotional satisfaction can also be realized through your own creativity, you thrive on collaborating with people who are optimistic and enthusiastic. If you become engaged in an ego battle or indulge in negative thinking, you can end up feeling vulnerable, suspicious, or even depressed. In relationships, by being patient and tolerant, you can overcome a tendency to feel frustrated when things don't go according to plan. When positive and inspired, you really show your desire to be of practical help to your loved ones.

Your attractive qualities: intuitive, shrewd, visionary, determined, disciplined, hardworking, quick comprehension, charismatic, inspired, idealistic, generous, sense of duty, compassionate, caring, sympathetic, witty, entertaining, creative, imaginative, thorough, methodical, talented

Your less attractive qualities: critical, too emotional, envious, impatient, dissatisfied, intolerant, frustrated, worried, discontented, too dramatic, calculating, miserly, restless, controlling, domineering, easily discouraged, lack of planning, interfering

Your Venus Power

The planet Venus has a great deal of influence on your powers of attraction. Below are four possible Venus types for women and men. To find your Venus you need to go to page 771, where you will find the Venus table and extra information. The planet Mars also affects your powers of attraction. To find your Mars table and interpretation go to page 761.

WOMEN WITH VENUS IN CANCER: With your intuitive abilities and sympathetic nature, you are usually supportive to those you love. Impressionable and intuitive, your receptivity allows you to quickly pick up on the moods of others, making you especially aware of the emotional changes in your partner. As you often display true maternal tendencies toward those you know, you want a partner who is considerate and sensitive.

MEN WITH VENUS IN CANCER: Being caring and sensitive, you probably seek a nurturing partner who could provide you with emotional security and a sense of belonging in a loving and safe environment. Receptive to others, at times you find it hard to be direct or confrontational in relationships. Usually you deal indirectly with what is causing you concern, and although you are willing to make sacrifices for dear ones, resist the temptation to be exploited by those you love.

WOMEN WITH VENUS IN LEO: You possess the wonderful ability to project your warm and sunny personality and keep others happily entertained. Loving attention yourself, you seek a partner who can appreciate you, be supportive, and give you positive feedback. Proud, with a natural regal air, you expect respect from your partners but are willing to be loyal and supportive in exchange. Although sometimes a little self-centered, you know how to make your partner feel special.

MEN WITH VENUS IN LEO: Enthusiastic, playful, and kind, you can be benevolent with those you love. Warm, romantic, and self-expressive, you adore the drama of love or having fun with your friends. Usually you are attracted to partners with a warm and generous nature. Although you can be a confident and charismatic partner, you may need to de-

velop humility in order to stop pride or arrogance from marring your relationships.

WOMEN WITH VENUS IN VIRGO: Intelligent and discriminating, you are usually drawn to polite and refined individuals. As a perfectionist, you may be keen to analyze and criticize yourself, but be careful of continually going over your partner's shortcomings. By focusing on how you can make positive improvements in yourself and in your relationships, you avoid becoming skeptical or confused. You empower yourself when you display kind and caring concern for the well-being of loved ones and spontaneously offer your practical assistance.

MEN WITH VENUS IN VIRGO: A love of order usually indicates that you are attracted to refined individuals with analytical or practical abilities. You and your partner may be working together or serving similar causes. As you constantly analyze partnerships in order to improve them, you are likely to use former relationships as a point of reference and compare them to your present partner. As you are helpful and kind, others usually rely on your good judgment and often turn to you for advice or practical assistance.

WOMEN WITH VENUS IN LIBRA: Attractive, refined, and conscious of the needs of others, you usually desire harmonious relationships. As a peacemaker with good negotiating skills, you can smooth out difficulties with others but your dislike of confrontation may sometimes leave you refusing to take a stand or compromising too many of your own needs. Courteous, stylish, and charming with polished social skills, you are an expert at relating to others in a gracious and civilized manner.

MEN WITH VENUS IN LIBRA: As a sociable and friendly individual with an eye for beauty, you are amorous and charming. You are a natural gentleman and your ideal partner usually has an elegant appearance, artistic appreciation, and good taste. Your relationships benefit when you resist the temptation to take the easy way out or put too much emphasis on vanity and high living. Intellectual and naturally refined, you seek a loving partner who can share your romantic and sophisticated aspirations.

To read all about your Outer Planets and work out how to use your personalized timetable, go to Section Three, page 789.

♍

Your Personalized Timetable

JUPITER BENEFICIAL
1940 4/27 – 7/14
1940 10/27 – until **1941** 3/2
1942 6/3 – 7/17
1946 9/17 – 11/4
1948 2/27 – 6/3
1948 10/22 – until **1949** 1/5
1952 4/10 – 6/19
1952 12/19 – until **1953** 1/22
1954 5/17 – 7/1
1957 12/31 – until **1958** 4/3
1958 8/29 – 10/19
1960 2/3 – 7/17
1960 9/23 – 12/20
1964 3/24 – 5/31
1965 9/7 – 12/1
1966 4/27 – 6/15
1969 12/7 – until **1970** 5/13
1970 8/3 – 10/3
1972 1/15 – 12/4
1976 3/6 – 5/13
1977 8/12 – until **1978** 1/12
1978 3/31 – 5/29
1981 11/19 – until **1982** 1/20
1982 3/31 – 9/14
1983 12/30 – until **1984** 3/29
1984 5/30 – 11/15
1987 6/28 – 10/12
1988 2/14 – 4/28
1989 7/23 – 9/20
1989 12/6 – until **1990** 5/9
1993 11/3 – 12/24
1994 5/10 – 8/22
1995 12/14 – until **1996** 2/28
1996 7/14 – 10/23
1999 6/3 – 12/4
2000 1/6 – 4/11
2001 7/6 – 8/23
2002 1/17 – 4/13
2005 10/19 – 12/5
2007 11/28 – until **2008** 2/8
2011 5/14 – until **2012** 3/23

SATURN BENEFICIAL
1939 5/18 – 11/23
1940 1/31 – 6/24
1940 11/1 – until **1941** 3/15
1944 6/8 – 9/2
1944 12/14 – until **1945** 5/20
1953 10/10 – until **1954** 1/16
1954 3/21 – 10/5
1958 3/19 – 4/21
1958 11/27 – until **1960** 1/18
1968 7/29 – 8/15
1969 3/25 – until **1970** 4/28
1973 7/19 – until **1974** 1/31
1974 3/27 – 7/1
1982 11/15 – until **1983** 5/31
1983 8/1 – 11/10
1988 1/1 – until **1989** 2/26
1989 6/20 – 11/25
1998 4/30 – until **1999** 6/4
1999 12/6 – until **2000** 2/17
2002 9/16 – 11/6
2003 5/22 – 8/10
2004 1/16 – 4/26
2012 1/4 – 3/13
2012 9/22 – 12/19

URANUS BENEFICIAL
1938 1/1 – 3/25
1948 7/25 – until **1951** 6/12
1974 10/27 – until **1977** 8/28
1987 2/6 – until **1991** 11/22

NEPTUNE BENEFICIAL
1955 11/4 – until **1960** 10/22
1982 1/10 – until **1989** 12/17

PLUTO BENEFICIAL
1982 12/3 – until **1987** 9/27
2006 1/18 – Continues

JUPITER CHALLENGING
1938 4/13 – 9/4

1938 12/2 – until **1939** 2/19
1941 5/7 – 7/17
1942 1/29 – 2/12
1947 2/5 – 4/20
1947 9/30 – 12/15
1950 3/23 – until **1951** 2/2
1953 4/19 – 6/28
1959 1/9 – 6/1
1959 9/6 – 11/29
1962 3/5 – 6/4
1962 7/29 – until **1963** 1/14
1964 8/26 – 10/4
1965 4/1 – 6/11
1970 12/21 – until **1971** 11/13
1974 2/17 – 5/2
1974 9/16 – 12/20
1976 7/19 – 11/23
1977 3/8 – 5/26
1982 12/4 – until **1983** 10/27
1986 2/1 – 4/11
1988 6/28 – until **1989** 5/9
1994 11/19 – until **1995** 2/8
1995 5/24 – 10/7
1998 1/15 – 3/24
2000 6/9 – until **2001** 4/21
2006 11/3 – until **2007** 1/17
2007 7/5 – 9/8
2009 5/15 – 7/16
2009 12/27 – until **2010** 3/7
2012 5/23 – 8/8

SATURN CHALLENGING
1941 7/12 – 11/12
1942 3/31 – 8/22
1942 10/29 – until **1943** 5/2
1955 12/1 – until **1957** 1/23
1957 5/26 – 10/22
1964 2/14 – until **1965** 3/31
1965 10/10 – 12/17
1971 5/14 – until **1972** 6/12
1985 1/9 – 5/6
1985 10/7 – until **1986** 11/28
1993 3/21 – 9/9
1993 12/14 – until **1994** 5/20
1994 7/27 – until **1995** 2/4
2000 6/20 – 12/15
2001 3/5 – 7/24
2001 12/3 – 4/12

URANUS CHALLENGING
1940 7/23 – until **1945** 5/4
1980 2/16 – until **1984** 10/26
2002 2/25 – until **2006** 12/30

NEPTUNE CHALLENGING
1967 12/26 – until **1976** 9/24
2009 3/28 – Continues

PLUTO CHALLENGING
1993 2/16 – until **2000** 10/31

JUPITER SPECIAL
1943 11/12 – until **1944** 1/14
1944 7/2 – 9/17
1955 10/14 – until **1956** 2/24
1956 6/9 – 9/1
1967 9/24 – until **1968** 8/17
1979 9/7 – until **1980** 7/31
1991 8/22 – 11/15
1992 2/14 – 7/11
2003 8/6 – 10/22
2004 3/24 – 6/16

SATURN SPECIAL
1948 8/14 – until **1949** 9/17
1977 9/23 – until **1978** 3/9
1978 6/11 – 11/1
1979 2/17 – 7/23
2007 7/28 – until **2008** 8/31

URANUS SPECIAL
1960 11/5 – until **1965** 6/30

PLUTO SPECIAL
1954 9/13 – until **1963** 8/24

August 28

Your Personal Powers

Practical, determined, yet receptive, your strong instincts and vitality indicate that you are a dynamic individual with sensitive emotions. Quietly determined and hardworking, you are usually modest and enjoy being of service to others. As an articulate and observant individual you are usually well-informed and like to do a job well. Your ruling planet, Mercury, endows you with analytical ability, a love of knowledge, and organizational skills. Being generous and emotionally motivated implies that when you are inspired, you are often warmhearted and energized. Showing a responsible attitude, you empower yourself when you are mindful, discriminating, and helpful. Sociable, enthusiastic, and enterprising, you can particularly succeed in all types of people-related careers. If things do not work out the way you planned, resist taking things too seriously or wasting your emotional energy. By developing a detached perspective, you can make impartial judgments more easily and avoid being hurt by others. Although independent, you work well with others, often displaying your potential for achievement and financial reward.

Your Powers of Attraction in Relationships

Other people are drawn to your youthful charm. Helpful and capable, you gain emotional satisfaction from making kind gestures. Although you like to be generous and spontaneous, being too intense at times implies that you can become bossy or too serious. Usually friendly and polite, however, you can easily attract partners or friends. Being very sociable, you enjoy having fun and interacting with people. You can also be compassionate and concerned for others. Generous, enthusiastic, and giving, when in love you can be affectionate and giving. You are usually attracted to creative or intelligent people who are optimistic and full of ideas. Alternatively, you may be drawn to charismatic people who are inventive and alluring. When with your ideal partner, you can be romantic and loving.

Your attractive qualities: clever, hardworking, understanding, good listener, progressive, daring, artistic, compassionate, romantic, idealistic, creative, ambitious, enterprising, helpful, analytical, strong-willed, generous, friendly, kind, charismatic, youthful, sensitive, sociable, compassionate

Your less attractive qualities: anxious, unrealistic, rest-less, too sensitive, bossy, hasty judgment, critical, selfish, impatient, impulsive, easily hurt, unmotivated, lack of compassion, possessive, lack of confidence, codependent, skeptical, mistrusting

Your Venus Power

The planet Venus has a great deal of influence on your powers of attraction. Below are four possible Venus types for women and men. To find your Venus you need to go to page 771, where you will find the Venus table and extra information. The planet Mars also affects your powers of attraction. To find your Mars table and interpretation go to page 761.

WOMEN WITH VENUS IN CANCER: Possessing a soft femininity, you have tender and sensitive emotions. Sympathetic and caring, you often mother those in your care by making sure they are comfortable and have plenty to eat. When you feel hurt or insecure in relationships you are likely to cover your feelings by being defensive or appearing tough on the outside while on the inside you are feeling vulnerable. Affectionate and romantic, you make a faithful and devoted partner.

MEN WITH VENUS IN CANCER: Being emotionally receptive, you can make a sensitive lover. With your desire to care for and protect others, you are likely to have strong family connections. Love is often tied in with being attentive to the needs of others and you may find yourself attracted to individuals who have sympathetic or maternal qualities. Security conscious, you need a loyal partner who can offer you support and ideally be a good cook and homemaker.

WOMEN WITH VENUS IN LEO: Warm and playful with a touch of the dramatic, you enjoy the company of generous or strong individuals who can share your sense of fun. Although there are advantages to your being strong-willed, in your relationships you need to resist being bossy as it can cause resentment. With your wonderful mixture of regal authority and childlike wonder, you love to keep others entertained and amused.

MEN WITH VENUS IN LEO: Sociable and outgoing, you are kind and generous with those you love. Looking for a relationship that can be fun and entertaining, you need a playmate who can share your enthusiasm and high spirits. Your pride, however, often stops you from associating with lovers or partners you see as beneath you. As you desire someone who

can appreciate your sense of the dramatic, you are often attracted to people with strong personalities.

WOMEN WITH VENUS IN VIRGO: Intelligent and discriminating, you are usually drawn to polite and refined individuals. As a perfectionist, you may be keen to analyze and criticize yourself, but be careful of continually going over your partner's shortcomings. By focusing on how you can make positive improvements in yourself and in your relationships, you avoid becoming skeptical or confused. You empower yourself when you display your kind and caring concern for the well-being of your loved ones and spontaneously offer your practical assistance.

MEN WITH VENUS IN VIRGO: A love of order usually indicates that you are attracted to refined individuals with analytical or practical abilities. You and your partner may be working together or serving similar causes. As you constantly analyze partnerships in order to improve them, you are likely to use former relationships as a point of reference and compare them to your present partner. As you are helpful and kind, others usually rely on your good judgment and often turn to you for advice or practical assistance.

WOMEN WITH VENUS IN LIBRA: You are usually attractive and sociable with an easygoing manner. Your love of beauty, harmony, and pleasure implies that you are a romantic with a desire for love and affection. Once in a relationship you need to learn to negotiate your position rather than adapt to the wishes of others and compromise just to keep the peace. Nevertheless, your advanced social skills and strong sense of fair play can help you succeed in any social or romantic situation.

MEN WITH VENUS IN LIBRA: Your good social skills, charming personality, and refined manner usually make you attractive to the opposite sex. Equally, you desire a sophisticated partner with grace, elegance, and a strong sense of style. Although you have the ability to be persuasive and irresistible to others, avoid manipulative love games. Nevertheless, your natural diplomacy and sense of fair play help you to relate to people in all social situations. With your love for balance and harmony, you seek a partner who is also moderate, easygoing, and loving.

To read all about your Outer Planets and work out how to use your personalized timetable, go to Section Three, page 789.

♍

Your Personalized Timetable

JUPITER BENEFICIAL
1940 5/1 – 7/21
1940 10/20 – until 1941 3/7
1942 6/8 – 7/22
1946 9/22 – 11/8
1948 3/5 – 5/26
1948 10/28 – until 1949 1/10
1952 4/14 – 6/24
1952 12/6 – until 1953 2/4
1954 5/21 – 7/5
1958 1/8 – 3/26
1958 9/4 – 10/23
1960 2/8 – 7/8
1960 10/1 – 12/24
1964 3/28 – 6/4
1965 9/15 – 11/22
1966 5/2 – 6/19
1969 12/13 – until 1970 5/4
1970 8/11 – 10/7
1972 1/20 – 12/8
1976 3/10 – 5/18
1977 8/17 – until 1978 1/4
1978 4/8 – 6/2
1981 11/24 – until 1982 1/31
1982 3/19 – 9/20
1984 1/3 – 4/11
1984 5/17 – 11/20
1987 7/4 – 10/5
1988 2/19 – 5/2
1989 7/28 – 9/29
1989 11/27 – until 1990 5/15
1993 11/7 – 12/30
1994 5/3 – 8/29
1995 12/18 – until 1996 3/5
1996 7/6 – 10/29
1999 6/8 – 11/21
2000 1/18 – 4/15
2001 7/10 – 8/29
2002 1/10 – 4/21
2005 10/23 – 12/10
2006 6/18 – 7/24
2007 12/3 – until 2008 2/13
2011 5/19 – until 2012 3/28

SATURN BENEFICIAL
1939 5/27 – 11/8
1940 2/14 – 7/5
1940 10/20 – until 1941 3/24
1944 6/16 – 9/14
1944 12/1 – until 1945 5/28
1953 10/18 – until 1954 10/13
1958 12/6 – until 1960 1/26
1960 8/18 – 10/13
1969 4/1 – until 1970 5/5
1973 7/28 – until 1974 1/15
1974 4/11 – 7/9
1982 11/24 – until 1983 5/14
1983 8/17 – 11/18
1988 1/9 – 8/4
1988 9/24 – until 1989 3/11
1989 6/6 – 12/4
1998 5/8 – until 1999 6/13
1999 11/22 – until 2000 3/1
2003 5/30 – 8/19
2004 1/4 – 5/7
2012 1/31 – 2/15
2012 10/1 – 12/30

URANUS BENEFICIAL
1938 1/1 – 4/13
1948 8/15 – until 1951 6/28
1974 11/12 – until 1977 9/20
1987 3/7 – until 1991 12/10

NEPTUNE BENEFICIAL
1955 12/3 – until 1961 9/18
1982 2/11 – until 1990 11/12

PLUTO BENEFICIAL
1983 1/16 – until 1987 10/22
2006 2/24 – Continues

JUPITER CHALLENGING
1938 4/19 – 8/27
1938 12/9 – until 1939 2/23

1941 5/11 – 7/22
1942 1/11 – 3/2
1947 2/15 – 4/10
1947 10/6 – 12/19
1950 3/28 – until 1951 2/6
1953 4/24 – 7/2
1959 1/15 – 5/24
1959 9/14 – 12/3
1962 3/10 – 6/20
1962 7/13 – until 1963 1/18
1965 4/6 – 6/15
1970 12/26 – until 1971 11/17
1974 2/21 – 5/7
1974 9/9 – 12/26
1976 7/25 – 11/15
1977 3/15 – 5/30
1982 12/9 – until 1983 11/1
1986 2/5 – 4/16
1988 7/3 – until 1989 1/6
1989 2/3 – until 1989 5/14
1994 11/23 – until 1995 2/16
1995 5/16 – 10/13
1998 1/20 – 3/28
2000 6/14 – until 2001 4/26
2006 11/8 – until 2007 1/23
2007 6/26 – 9/17
2009 5/27 – 7/3
2010 1/1 – 3/11
2012 5/27 – 8/14
2012 11/24 – Continues

SATURN CHALLENGING
1941 7/23 – 10/31
1942 4/9 – 9/17
1942 10/3 – until 1943 5/10
1955 12/9 – until 1956 7/11
1956 8/18 – until 1957 2/4
1957 5/12 – 11/1
1964 2/22 – until 1965 4/9
1965 9/25 – until 1966 1/1
1971 5/21 – until 1972 6/19
1985 1/21 – 4/23
1985 10/16 – until 1986 12/6
1993 3/30 – 8/26
1993 12/26 – until 1995 2/13
2000 6/29 – 12/2
2001 3/17 – 8/3
2001 11/21 – until 2002 4/21

URANUS CHALLENGING
1941 5/22 – until 1945 5/22
1980 11/27 – until 1984 11/13
2002 3/14 – until 2007 1/23

NEPTUNE CHALLENGING
1968 2/11 – until 1976 11/1
2009 5/20 – Continues

PLUTO CHALLENGING
1993 12/14 – until 2000 11/27

JUPITER SPECIAL
1943 11/24 – until 1944 1/2
1944 7/8 – 9/22
1955 10/20 – until 1956 2/16
1956 6/16 – 9/6
1967 9/29 – until 1968 4/1
1968 5/12 – 8/21
1979 9/12 – until 1980 8/5
1991 8/26 – 11/23
1992 2/6 – 7/17
2003 8/11 – 10/28
2004 3/15 – 6/24

SATURN SPECIAL
1948 8/21 – until 1949 9/25
1977 10/2 – until 1978 2/24
1978 6/22 – 11/14
1979 2/4 – 8/1
2007 8/5 – until 2008 9/8

URANUS SPECIAL
1961 8/24 – until 1965 7/22

PLUTO SPECIAL
1954 10/22 – until 1964 7/21

August 29

SUN: VIRGO • DECANATE: VIRGO/MERCURY • DEGREE: 5°5–6°5 VIRGO • MODE: MUTABLE • ELEMENT: EARTH

Your Personal Powers

Passionate and inspired yet analytical and thoughtful, you are usually motivated by your desire to achieve emotional fulfillment. With your fine analytical mind, you can be discriminating with many creative ideas. Although often success-oriented with big plans, an inner restlessness indicates that unless you apply self-discipline and determination, you can become discouraged or bored. You lose power by being impulsive or becoming easily distracted by other people. You gain power when you develop an objective outlook and resist the temptation to be totally ruled by your emotions. Optimistic and spirited by nature, you can be enterprising and enthusiastic. As a clever and talented individual, you gain power by being well-informed and finding ways to express yourself creatively. You also empower yourself when you utilize your natural warmth and kindness, attracting admirers and influencing others. When you present yourself as a responsible and capable individual you are given respect or put in positions of trust. Although you are usually confident and resolute, in order to succeed it is important for you to be methodical and plan your actions.

Your Powers of Attraction in Relationships

You are charismatic and dynamic, and people are attracted to your idealism and charming manner. Usually friendly, you enjoy working with others and like to be part of a team. As you are persuasive, other people are often taken by your wonderful ideas. You may be drawn to hardworking and ambitious partners who are likely to achieve positions of power and authority, but try to avoid clashes of will. Security-conscious, you like to take your time or feel in control, and can be drawn to relationships that can offer you stability. You admire those who are not afraid to take on challenges or risks. Although you can be compassionate and humanitarian, you usually want to find emotional satisfaction and are not willing to settle for second best.

Your attractive qualities: dynamic, charismatic, expressive, sociable, generous, ambitious, keen intellect, strong desires, perfectionist, disciplined, intuitive, idealistic, enthusiastic, caring, inspired, creative, imaginative, compassionate, inner faith, focused, will-power, inspirational

Your less attractive qualities: carried away by emotions, anxious, controlling, too sensitive, insecure, unfocused, moody, stubborn, argumentative, skeptical, mistrusting, extremist, inconsiderate, too demanding, overindulgent or extravagant, arrogant

Your Venus Power

The planet Venus has a great deal of influence on your powers of attraction. Below are four possible Venus types for women and men. To find your Venus you need to go to page 771, where you will find the Venus table and extra information. The planet Mars also affects your powers of attraction. To find your Mars table and interpretation go to page 761.

WOMEN WITH VENUS IN CANCER: Sensitive and understanding, you are sympathetic to other people's emotions and needs. You are protective toward those you love, and close relationships with your partner, relatives, and friends are important to your sense of well-being. Aware of how easy it is to hurt other people's feelings, you are often indirect and approach delicate issues in a roundabout way. Nevertheless, learning to face facts and not allowing others to exploit your good nature is a lesson just as valuable.

MEN WITH VENUS IN CANCER: You seek a partner who is sympathetic, caring, and protective. Able to be forgiving and compassionate, you want a secure emotional bond in your close relationships. Usually you are drawn to partners who are maternal, unselfish, or demonstrative with their feelings. Although you can sometimes appear to others as shy or impressionable, you have powerful emotions and inner strength.

WOMEN WITH VENUS IN LEO: Your friendly and sunny personality often makes you stand out in a crowd. Generous and giving, you know how to make your partner feel special. As you often expect loyalty and devotion from your partners in return, you can become easily offended if they ignore you or behave in an inconsiderate manner. Charming and kind, when you're in love you can be romantic, dramatic, and passionate.

MEN WITH VENUS IN LEO: A childlike nature suggests that you are versatile and keen on games or being entertained. You are usually attracted to vivacious partners with a benevolent nature. As an extrovert you enjoy being involved in all types of activities where you can assert yourself and show

your talents and abilities. Others may recognize your inborn tendencies to lead but are also aware of your vanity or pride. Nevertheless, generous, kind, and caring, you often show compassion to those less fortunate than yourself.

WOMEN WITH VENUS IN VIRGO: In relationships you can be modest and unassuming but desire perfection. You usually analyze your partnerships until you feel you have understood them to the last little detail in order to improve them. A problem usually arises when you become too critical either of partners or yourself and indulge in being skeptical or fault-finding. As you are modest, others may not be aware of the strong sensuality beneath your well-groomed exterior.

MEN WITH VENUS IN VIRGO: Industrious and well-ordered, you relate to others in a considerate and down-to-earth way. You enjoy giving practical advice and being of service to those you love, even in small ways. Being a perfectionist, you are drawn to partners with high morals or a strong work ethic. Partners who have strong analytical minds are very attractive to you, particularly if they are also clean and meticulously dressed.

WOMEN WITH VENUS IN LIBRA: Gracious, charming, and sociable with a sense of style, you have no trouble in drawing admirers. With your natural diplomatic skills and desire for harmony you usually like to keep the peace and avoid confrontations, but be careful of failing to take a stand when it is necessary. Romantic and easygoing yourself, you are attracted to affectionate and refined individuals who share your love of peace, justice, and fair play.

MEN WITH VENUS IN LIBRA: Courteous and refined, you are attracted to beautiful and elegant people. You are looking for a partner who can share your natural good taste and enjoy an intellectual conversation. Disliking conflict, you may have to be careful not to go along with others just to keep the peace. Your ideal partner will appreciate beauty and the little luxuries of life as well as possess good social skills. You have a strong sense of social etiquette yourself so you need an intelligent and sophisticated partner.

To read all about your Outer Planets and work out how to use your personalized timetable, go to Section Three, page 789.

To read all about your Outer Planets and work out how to use your personalized timetable, go to Section Three, page 789.

Your Personalized Timetable

JUPITER BENEFICIAL
1940 5/5 – 7/28
1940 10/12 – until 1941 3/13
1942 6/12 – 7/26
1946 9/27 – 11/12
1948 3/14 – 5/17
1948 11/2 – until 1949 1/14
1952 4/18 – 6/29
1952 11/27 – until 1953 2/12
1954 5/26 – 7/9
1958 1/18 – 3/15
1958 9/9 – 10/28
1960 2/13 – 6/30
1960 10/9 – 12/29
1964 4/1 – 6/8
1965 9/26 – 11/11
1966 5/7 – 6/23
1969 12/19 – until 1970 4/26
1970 8/18 – 10/12
1972 1/24 – 12/12
1976 3/15 – 5/22
1977 8/23 – 12/27
1978 4/14 – 6/7
1981 11/29 – until 1982 9/25
1984 1/7 – 11/25
1987 7/12 – 9/27
1988 2/24 – 5/6
1989 8/2 – 10/12
1989 11/14 – until 1990 5/20
1993 11/12 – until 1994 1/5
1994 4/25 – 9/4
1995 12/22 – until 1996 3/11
1996 6/29 – 11/4
1999 6/13 – 11/12
2000 1/27 – 4/19
2001 7/14 – 9/3
2002 1/2 – 4/27
2005 10/28 – 12/15
2006 6/5 – 8/6
2007 12/7 – until 2008 2/18
2008 8/15 – 10/1
2011 5/23 – until 2012 4/1

SATURN BENEFICIAL
1939 6/5 – 10/27
1940 2/25 – 7/18
1940 10/6 – until 1941 4/2
1944 6/23 – 10/3
1944 11/11 – until 1945 6/5
1953 10/26 – until 1954 10/22
1958 12/14 – until 1960 2/4
1960 7/31 – 10/30
1969 4/9 – until 1970 5/13
1973 8/5 – until 1974 1/2
1974 4/23 – 7/16
1982 12/3 – until 1983 5/1
1983 8/29 – 11/27
1984 6/13 – 8/12
1988 1/18 – 7/16
1988 10/12 – until 1989 3/29
1989 5/18 – 12/13
1998 5/16 – 12/2
1999 1/25 – 6/22
1999 11/10 – until 2000 3/12
2003 6/7 – 8/29
2003 12/23 – until 2004 5/17
2012 10/9 – Continues

URANUS BENEFICIAL
1938 1/1 – 4/30
1948 9/17 – until 1952 4/21
1974 11/29 – until 1977 10/7
1987 12/27 – until 1991 12/27

NEPTUNE BENEFICIAL
1956 10/30 – until 1961 10/17
1983 1/5 – until 1990 12/13

PLUTO BENEFICIAL
1983 11/16 – until 1988 9/6
2007 1/12 – until 1938 1/1

JUPITER CHALLENGING
1938 4/25 – 8/20

1938 12/15 – until 1939 2/27
1941 5/15 – 7/27
1942 1/1 – 3/12
1947 3/5 – 3/23
1947 10/11 – 12/24
1950 4/2 – until 1951 2/10
1953 4/28 – 7/7
1959 1/21 – 5/16
1959 9/20 – 12/8
1962 3/14 – until 1963 1/23
1965 4/10 – 6/19
1970 12/31 – until 1971 7/1
1971 8/17 – 11/22
1974 2/25 – 5/14
1974 9/1 – until 1975 1/1
1976 8/1 – 11/8
1977 3/20 – 6/3
1982 12/13 – until 1983 11/5
1986 2/9 – 4/21
1986 10/23 – 11/24
1988 7/7 – 12/23
1989 2/17 – 5/18
1994 11/27 – until 1995 2/24
1995 5/7 – 10/18
1998 1/24 – 4/2
2000 6/18 – until 2001 4/30
2006 11/12 – until 2007 1/28
2007 6/17 – 9/25
2010 1/6 – 3/15
2012 5/31 – 8/21
2012 11/16 – Continues

SATURN CHALLENGING
1941 8/5 – 10/16
1942 4/17 – until 1943 5/18
1955 12/18 – until 1956 6/20
1956 9/8 – until 1957 2/19
1957 4/26 – 11/10
1964 3/1 – until 1965 4/18
1965 9/11 – until 1966 1/12
1971 5/29 – until 1972 6/27
1985 2/6 – 4/5
1985 10/25 – until 1986 12/14
1993 4/9 – 8/13
1994 1/5 – until 1995 2/21
2000 7/8 – 11/20
2001 3/28 – 8/16
2001 11/8 – until 2002 4/30

URANUS CHALLENGING
1941 6/8 – until 1946 2/24
1980 12/13 – until 1984 11/29
2002 4/3 – until 2007 2/11

NEPTUNE CHALLENGING
1968 12/20 – until 1977 9/7
2010 3/21 – Continues

PLUTO CHALLENGING
1994 1/13 – until 2001 10/20

JUPITER SPECIAL
1944 7/13 – 9/26
1955 10/26 – until 1956 2/9
1956 6/22 – 9/10
1967 10/4 – until 1968 3/20
1968 5/24 – 8/26
1979 9/16 – until 1980 8/9
1991 8/31 – 12/3
1992 1/27 – 7/22
2003 8/15 – 11/3
2004 3/8 – 7/1

SATURN SPECIAL
1948 8/29 – until 1949 10/3
1950 4/13 – 6/15
1977 10/12 – until 1978 2/12
1978 7/2 – 12/1
1979 1/17 – 8/10
2007 8/13 – until 2008 9/16

URANUS SPECIAL
1961 9/9 – until 1965 8/9

PLUTO SPECIAL
1955 9/19 – until 1964 8/21

♍

August 30

Your Personal Powers

Although logical and modest, your powerful feelings and sensitivity indicate that you are an idealistic and creative individual with a discriminating mind. A strong sense of duty indicates that you can be serious and hardworking. Your ruling planet, Mercury, endows you with analytical abilities and creative ideas. Having good business ideas, you can succeed if you stay optimistic yet realistic. Finding emotional satisfaction through self-expression and creative activities usually motivates you and brings you financial rewards. You gain power when you learn to trust your intuition and express yourself with confidence. You lose power when you let skepticism and worry cause you to doubt yourself or mistrust others. Often inspired by knowledge, you can dedicate a great deal of time and effort to your projects. Often self-aware and observant, you like to pay attention to small details. Being concerned with order and efficiency, you are usually organized and methodical. Although you often prefer a routine, if you become too rigid you can lose your spark and spontaneity.

Your Powers of Attraction in Relationships

Sociable and sympathetic, you are romantic and impressionable by nature. Often you are attracted to intelligent and independent individuals who are youthful or young at heart. With your ability to be both soft and loving yet firm and critical, you can experience conflicting emotions. Even though you enjoy being generous and sympathetic, your pragmatic view calls you to act cautiously. Although you are willing to make sacrifices for those you love, avoid letting others undermine your efforts or self-esteem. You may be enthusiastic at the beginning of the relationship, but reality soon sets in and challenges your idyllic attitude. Nevertheless, you enjoy showing your affection by being of practical help to others. By staying objective, lighthearted, and resisting a temptation to be too serious, you can gain more enjoyment from your close relationships.

Your attractive qualities: caring, hardworking, dramatic, intuitive, inspired, practical, happy, disciplined, articulate, good concentration, dedicated, sociable, charming, fun-loving, loyal, friendly, good conversationalist, creative, good-natured, persuasive, gregarious, spontaneous

Your less attractive qualities: oversensitive, worried, tough, critical, high expectations, disappointed in others, too perfectionist, martyr, overindulgent, obstinate, erratic, insecure, impatient, scattered, too serious, withdrawn, inhibited

Your Venus Power

The planet Venus has a great deal of influence on your powers of attraction. Below are four possible Venus types for women and men. To find your Venus you need to go to page 771, where you will find the Venus table and extra information. The planet Mars also affects your powers of attraction. To find your Mars table and interpretation go to page 761.

WOMEN WITH VENUS IN CANCER: Sensitive and understanding, you are sympathetic to other people's emotions and needs. Protective toward those you love, close relationships with your partner, relatives, and friends are important to your sense of well-being. Aware of how easy it is to hurt other people's feelings, you are often indirect and approach delicate issues in a roundabout way. Nevertheless, learning to face facts and not allowing others to exploit your good nature is a lesson just as valuable.

MEN WITH VENUS IN CANCER: You seek a partner who is sympathetic, caring, and protective. Able to be forgiving and compassionate, you want a secure emotional bond in your close relationships. You are usually drawn to partners who are maternal, unselfish, or demonstrative with their feelings. Although you can sometimes appear to others as impressionable, you have powerful emotions and inner strength.

WOMEN WITH VENUS IN LEO: Your friendly and sunny personality often makes you stand out in a crowd. Generous and giving, you know how to make your partner feel special. As you often expect loyalty and devotion from your partners in return, you can become easily offended if they ignore you or behave in an inconsiderate manner. Charming and kind, when you are in love, you can be romantic, dramatic, and passionate.

MEN WITH VENUS IN LEO: As an extrovert you enjoy being involved in all types of activities where you can assert yourself and show your talents and abilities. A childlike nature suggests that you are versatile and keen on games or being entertained. You are usually attracted to vivacious partners with a benevolent nature. Others may recognize your inborn tendencies to lead but are also aware of your vanity or pride. Nevertheless, generous, kind, and caring, you often show compassion to those less fortunate than yourself.

WOMEN WITH VENUS IN VIRGO: In relationships you can be modest and unassuming but desire perfection. You usually analyze your partnerships until you feel you have understood them to the last little detail in order to improve them. A problem usually arises when you become too critical either of partners or yourself and indulge in being skeptical or fault-finding. As you are modest, others may not be aware of the strong sensuality beneath your well-groomed exterior.

MEN WITH VENUS IN VIRGO: Industrious and well-ordered, you relate to others in a considerate and down-to-earth way. You enjoy giving practical advice and being of service to those you love even in small ways. Being a perfectionist, you are drawn to partners with high morals or a strong work ethic. Partners who have strong analytical minds are very attractive to you, particularly if they are also clean and meticulously dressed.

WOMEN WITH VENUS IN LIBRA: Gracious, charming, and sociable with a sense of style, you have no trouble attracting admirers. With your natural diplomatic skills and desire for harmony you usually like to keep the peace and avoid confrontations, but be careful of failing to take a stand when it is necessary. Romantic and easygoing yourself, you are attracted to affectionate and refined individuals who share your love of peace, justice, and fair play.

MEN WITH VENUS IN LIBRA: Courteous and refined, you are attracted to beautiful and elegant people. You are looking for a partner who can share your natural good taste and enjoy an intellectual conversation. Disliking conflict, you may have to be careful not to go along with others just to keep the peace. Your ideal partner will appreciate beauty and the little luxuries of life as well as possess good social skills. You have a strong sense of social etiquette yourself so you need an intelligent and sophisticated partner.

To read all about your Outer Planets and work out how to use your personalized timetable, go to Section Three, page 789.

♍

Your Personalized Timetable

JUPITER BENEFICIAL
1940 5/9 – 8/7
1940 10/2 – until 1941 3/18
1942 6/16 – 7/31
1946 10/2 – 11/17
1948 3/27 – 5/4
1948 11/7 – until 1949 1/18
1952 4/22 – 7/4
1952 11/19 – until 1953 2/20
1954 5/30 – 7/14
1958 2/2 – 2/28
1958 9/14 – 11/1
1960 2/19 – 6/22
1960 10/16 – until 1961 1/2
1964 4/5 – 6/13
1966 5/12 – 6/28
1969 12/25 – until 1970 4/19
1970 8/25 – 10/16
1972 1/29 – 12/17
1976 3/19 – 5/26
1977 8/29 – 12/20
1978 4/21 – 6/11
1981 12/4 – until 1982 6/2
1982 7/23 – 9/30
1984 1/12 – 11/30
1987 7/21 – 9/7
1988 2/29 – 5/10
1989 8/6 – until 1990 2/6
1990 3/15 – 5/24
1993 11/16 – until 1994 1/12
1994 4/17 – 9/10
1995 12/27 – until 1996 3/18
1996 6/21 – 11/10
1999 6/18 – 11/4
2000 2/4 – 4/23
2001 7/19 – 9/10
2001 12/26 – until 2002 5/3
2005 11/1 – 12/20
2006 5/26 – 8/16
2007 12/11 – until 2008 2/23
2008 8/4 – 10/12
2011 5/27 – until 2012 4/5

SATURN BENEFICIAL
1939 6/15 – 10/14
1940 3/5 – 8/6
1940 9/17 – until 1941 4/10
1944 7/1 – until 1945 6/13
1953 11/3 – until 1954 10/30
1958 12/22 – until 1960 2/14
1960 7/17 – 11/12
1969 4/17 – until 1970 5/20
1973 8/15 – 12/21
1974 5/3 – 7/24
1982 12/13 – until 1983 4/18
1983 9/9 – 12/5
1984 5/27 – 8/28
1988 1/27 – 7/2
1988 10/25 – until 1989 12/21
1998 5/24 – 11/16
1999 2/10 – 7/2
1999 10/29 – until 2000 3/21
2003 6/14 – 9/10
2003 12/11 – until 2004 5/25
2012 10/17 – Continues

URANUS BENEFICIAL
1938 1/1 – until 1939 2/27
1949 7/3 – until 1952 5/16
1974 12/18 – until 1977 10/24
1988 1/13 – until 1992 10/21

NEPTUNE BENEFICIAL
1956 11/27 – until 1962 9/12
1983 2/4 – until 1991 11/3

PLUTO BENEFICIAL
1983 12/15 – until 1988 10/7
2007 2/13 – Continues

JUPITER CHALLENGING
1938 5/1 – 8/12
1938 12/20 – until 1939 3/3

1941 5/19 – 8/1
1941 12/23 – until 1942 3/21
1947 10/16 – 12/28
1950 4/6 – 10/2
1950 11/15 – until 1951 2/15
1953 5/2 – 7/11
1959 1/28 – 5/8
1959 9/26 – 12/12
1962 3/18 – until 1963 1/28
1965 4/15 – 6/24
1971 1/5 – 6/19
1971 8/28 – 11/26
1974 3/1 – 5/20
1974 8/25 – until 1975 1/7
1976 8/8 – 11/1
1977 3/26 – 6/7
1982 12/18 – until 1983 11/10
1986 2/13 – 4/25
1986 10/10 – 12/7
1988 7/13 – 12/13
1989 2/26 – 5/22
1994 12/2 – until 1995 3/7
1995 4/26 – 10/23
1998 1/28 – 4/6
2000 6/22 – until 2001 5/5
2006 11/16 – until 2007 2/3
2007 6/10 – 10/2
2010 1/10 – 3/19
2012 6/4 – 8/30
2012 11/8 – Continues

SATURN CHALLENGING
1941 8/28 – 9/24
1942 4/25 – until 1943 5/26
1955 12/27 – until 1956 6/5
1956 9/22 – until 1957 11/18
1964 3/9 – 10/26
1964 11/8 – until 1965 4/28
1965 8/30 – until 1966 1/22
1971 6/5 – until 1972 7/5
1973 1/16 – 3/14
1985 11/3 – until 1986 12/23
1993 4/21 – 7/31
1994 1/14 – until 1995 3/1
2000 7/19 – 11/8
2001 4/6 – 9/1
2001 10/22 – until 2002 5/8

URANUS CHALLENGING
1941 6/26 – until 1946 4/9
1980 12/31 – until 1985 9/23
2002 4/30 – until 2007 2/28

NEPTUNE CHALLENGING
1969 1/26 – until 1977 10/27
2010 4/27 – Continues

PLUTO CHALLENGING
1994 12/1 – until 2001 11/18

JUPITER SPECIAL
1944 7/18 – 10/1
1955 11/2 – until 1956 2/1
1956 6/28 – 9/15
1967 10/10 – until 1968 3/11
1968 6/2 – 8/30
1979 9/21 – until 1980 8/14
1991 9/4 – 12/18
1992 1/11 – 7/28
2003 8/20 – 11/9
2004 2/29 – 7/7

SATURN SPECIAL
1948 9/6 – until 1949 10/12
1950 3/29 – 7/1
1977 10/23 – until 1978 1/31
1978 7/12 – until 1979 8/18
2007 8/20 – until 2008 9/23

URANUS SPECIAL
1961 9/25 – until 1965 8/25

PLUTO SPECIAL
1955 11/1 – until 1965 7/17

August 31

Your Personal Powers

Your personal magnetism and idealism indicate that you are an altruistic individual with charm and a persuasive manner. Your ruling planet, Mercury, endows you with discriminative abilities, sharp perception, and good communication skills. You gain power when you combine your analytical skills, powerful imagination, and flair for business to create something concrete and long lasting. You are idealistic, kind-hearted, and compassionate and are often inspired to be truthful and honorable. Although you can be charming and easygoing, at times you can also dig your heels in and be stubborn. Purposeful and resourceful, you can be hardworking and focused, especially if you have faith in what you do. Resolved to achieve excellence, you have an eye for detail and can refine and improve existing commercial projects or ideas. You lose some of your power, however, when your quest for perfection turns you into a critical and uncompromising person. Nevertheless, being able to uplift the spirit of others with your positive outlook, you gain power when you inspire people with your enthusiasm and goodwill.

Your Powers of Attraction in Relationships

Your personal charisma and charm indicate that you can easily win people's affections. Usually you are attracted to sensitive and imaginative partners who can inspire you with their unique ideas or independent views. Alternatively, a need for stability indicates that you take into consideration the practical aspects of your close relationships. You may therefore be drawn to a security-conscious partner who can give you a strong home base and make you feel protected. As you are usually modest, loyal, and intelligent, you take your relationships seriously. While you make every effort to establish a long-lasting relationship, unless you are willing to reveal your inner insecurities or fears you may experience frustration and moodiness. Nevertheless, as you usually desire harmony, you often sacrifice or compromise in order to keep the peace.

Your attractive qualities: articulate, inspiring, balanced, harmonious, analytical, charismatic, helpful, spiritual potential, discreet, methodical, honorable, confident, idealistic, kind, creative, sociable, contented, generous, original, constructive, persistent, practical, responsible, organized

Your less attractive qualities: critical, stubborn, nervous, too demanding, restless, self-righteous, inner conflicts, selfish, insecure, bossy, suspicious, easily discouraged, lack of ambition, overly generous, lose faith, dissatisfied, argumentative, indecisive

Your Venus Power

The planet Venus has a great deal of influence on your powers of attraction. Below are four possible Venus types for women and men. To find your Venus you need to go to page 771, where you will find the Venus table and extra information. The planet Mars also affects your powers of attraction. To find your Mars table and interpretation go to page 761.

WOMEN WITH VENUS IN CANCER: Sensitive and understanding, you are sympathetic to other people's emotions and needs. Protective toward those you love, close relationships with your partner, relatives, and friends are important to your sense of well-being. Aware of how easy it is to hurt other people's feelings, you are often indirect and approach delicate issues in a roundabout way. Nevertheless, learning to face facts and not allowing others to exploit your good nature is a lesson just as valuable.

MEN WITH VENUS IN CANCER: You seek a partner who is sympathetic, caring, and protective. Able to be forgiving and compassionate, you want a secure emotional bond in your close relationships. Usually you are drawn to partners who are maternal, unselfish, or demonstrative with their feelings. Although you can sometimes appear to others as impressionable, you have powerful emotions and inner strength.

WOMEN WITH VENUS IN LEO: You possess the wonderful ability to project your warm and sunny personality and keep others happily entertained. Loving attention yourself, you seek a partner who can appreciate you, be supportive, and give you positive feedback. Proud, with a natural regal air, you expect respect from your partners but are willing to be loyal and supportive in exchange. Although sometimes a little self-centered, you know how to make your partner feel special.

MEN WITH VENUS IN LEO: Enthusiastic, playful, and kind, you can be benevolent with those you love. Warm, romantic, and self-expressive, you adore the drama of love or having fun with your friends. You are usually attracted to partners with a warm and generous nature. Although you can be a

confident and charismatic partner, you may need to develop humility in order to stop pride or arrogance from marring your relationships.

WOMEN WITH VENUS IN VIRGO: Intelligent and discriminating, you are usually drawn to polite and refined individuals. As a perfectionist, you may be keen to analyze and criticize yourself, but be careful of continually going over your partner's shortcomings. By focusing on how you can make positive improvements in yourself and in your relationships, you avoid becoming skeptical or confused. You empower yourself when you display kind and caring concern for the well-being of loved ones and spontaneously offer your practical assistance.

MEN WITH VENUS IN VIRGO: A love of order usually indicates that you are attracted to refined individuals with analytical or practical abilities. You and your partner may be working together or serving similar causes. As you constantly analyze partnerships in order to improve them, you are likely to use former relationships as a point of reference and compare them to your present partner. As you are helpful and kind, others usually rely on your good judgment and often turn to you for advice or practical assistance.

WOMEN WITH VENUS IN LIBRA: Attractive, refined, and conscious of the needs of others, you usually desire harmonious relationships. As a peacemaker with good negotiating skills, you can smooth out difficulties with others, but your dislike of confrontation may sometimes leave you refusing to take a stand or compromising too many of your own needs. Courteous, stylish, and charming with polished social skills, you are an expert at relating to others in a gracious and civilized manner.

MEN WITH VENUS IN LIBRA: As a sociable and friendly individual with an eye for beauty, you are amorous and charming. You are a natural gentleman and your ideal partner usually has an elegant appearance, artistic appreciation, and good taste. Your relationships benefit when you resist the temptation to take the easy way out or put too much emphasis on vanity and high living. Intellectual and naturally refined, you seek a loving partner who can share your romantic and sophisticated aspirations.

To read all about your Outer Planets and work out how to use your personalized timetable, go to Section Three, page 789.

To read all about your Outer Planets and work out how to use your personalized timetable, go to Section Three, page 789.

♍

Your Personalized Timetable

JUPITER BENEFICIAL
1940 5/13 – 8/21
1940 9/18 – until 1941 3/22
1942 6/20 – 8/4
1946 10/6 – 11/21
1948 11/12 – until 1949 1/22
1952 4/26 – 7/10
1952 11/12 – until 1953 2/26
1954 6/4 – 7/18
1958 9/19 – 11/6
1960 2/26 – 6/15
1960 10/22 – until 1961 1/6
1964 4/9 – 6/17
1966 5/17 – 7/2
1970 1/1 – 4/11
1970 8/31 – 10/21
1972 2/3 – 8/1
1972 9/17 – 12/21
1976 3/23 – 5/30
1977 9/4 – 12/13
1978 4/26 – 6/16
1981 12/9 – until 1982 5/22
1982 8/3 – 10/4
1984 1/16 – 12/4
1987 8/4 – 9/3
1988 3/5 – 5/14
1989 8/11 – until 1990 1/25
1990 3/27 – 5/29
1993 11/21 – until 1994 1/20
1994 4/9 – 9/16
1995 12/31 – until 1996 3/26
1996 6/13 – 11/15
1999 6/24 – 10/28
2000 2/10 – 4/27
2001 7/23 – 9/17
2001 12/19 – until 2002 5/9
2005 11/6 – 12/26
2006 5/17 – 8/24
2007 12/16 – until 2008 2/28
2008 7/26 – 10/21
2011 6/1 – until 2012 4/10

SATURN BENEFICIAL
1939 6/27 – 10/1
1940 3/14 – until 1941 4/18
1944 7/8 – until 1945 6/21
1953 11/11 – until 1954 11/7
1958 12/31 – until 1960 2/24
1960 7/4 – 11/23
1969 4/24 – until 1970 5/28
1973 8/25 – 12/9
1974 5/13 – 8/1
1975 2/21 – 4/4
1982 12/24 – until 1983 4/5
1983 9/18 – 12/15
1984 5/13 – 9/10
1988 2/6 – 6/19
1988 11/5 – until 1989 12/29
1998 6/2 – 11/3
1999 2/22 – 7/14
1999 10/16 – until 2000 3/30
2003 6/22 – 9/24
2003 11/26 – until 2004 6/3
2012 10/25 – Continues

URANUS BENEFICIAL
1938 1/1 – until 1939 3/24
1949 7/20 – until 1952 6/4
1975 1/21 – until 1978 7/30
1988 1/31 – until 1992 11/18

NEPTUNE BENEFICIAL
1957 1/4 – until 1962 10/13
1984 1/1 – until 1991 12/8

PLUTO BENEFICIAL
1984 11/1 – until 1988 10/31
2008 1/7 – Continues

JUPITER CHALLENGING
1938 5/9 – 8/4
1938 12/26 – until 1939 3/7

1941 5/23 – 8/6
1941 12/16 – until 1942 3/28
1947 10/21 – until 1948 1/2
1950 4/11 – 9/21
1950 11/25 – until 1951 2/19
1953 5/6 – 7/16
1959 2/4 – 4/30
1959 10/1 – 12/16
1962 3/23 – until 1963 2/1
1965 4/19 – 6/28
1971 1/10 – 6/10
1971 9/6 – 11/30
1974 3/5 – 5/28
1974 8/17 – until 1975 1/12
1976 8/16 – 10/23
1977 3/31 – 6/11
1982 12/22 – until 1983 11/15
1986 2/18 – 5/1
1986 9/30 – 12/16
1988 7/18 – 12/5
1989 3/6 – 5/26
1994 12/6 – until 1995 3/28
1995 4/5 – 10/28
1998 2/1 – 4/10
2000 6/27 – until 2001 5/9
2006 11/21 – until 2007 2/9
2007 6/2 – 10/8
2010 1/15 – 3/23
2012 6/8 – 9/9
2012 10/29 – Continues

SATURN CHALLENGING
1942 5/3 – until 1943 6/2
1956 1/5 – 5/22
1956 10/3 – until 1957 11/27
1964 3/18 – 9/27
1964 12/6 – until 1965 5/10
1965 8/16 – until 1966 1/31
1971 6/13 – until 1972 7/13
1972 12/31 – until 1973 3/29
1985 11/11 – until 1986 12/31
1987 7/18 – 9/20
1993 5/6 – 7/15
1994 1/23 – until 1995 3/8
2000 7/31 – 10/26
2001 4/15 – until 2002 5/16

URANUS CHALLENGING
1941 7/18 – until 1946 4/30
1981 1/22 – until 1985 10/20
2003 2/27 – until 2007 12/31

NEPTUNE CHALLENGING
1969 12/15 – until 1977 11/24
2011 3/15 – Continues

PLUTO CHALLENGING
1994 12/26 – until 2002 10/6

JUPITER SPECIAL
1944 7/22 – 10/6
1955 11/11 – until 1956 1/24
1956 7/4 – 9/19
1967 10/15 – until 1968 3/3
1968 6/10 – 9/4
1979 9/26 – until 1980 8/19
1991 9/9 – until 1992 8/2
2003 8/24 – 11/16
2004 2/22 – 7/13

SATURN SPECIAL
1948 9/13 – until 1949 4/25
1949 5/7 – 10/21
1950 3/16 – 7/13
1977 11/5 – until 1978 1/17
1978 7/20 – until 1979 8/26
2007 8/28 – until 2008 10/1
2009 4/24 – 6/8

URANUS SPECIAL
1961 10/15 – until 1965 9/10

PLUTO SPECIAL
1956 9/24 – until 1965 8/18

September 1

SUN: VIRGO • DECANATE: VIRGO/MERCURY • DEGREE: 8°–9°25 VIRGO • MODE: MUTABLE • ELEMENT: EARTH

Your Personal Powers

As an ambitious and intelligent individual, you possess an optimistic outlook and are usually motivated by your need to expand and prosper. Often determined and practical, your ruling planet, Mercury, endows you with quick comprehension, shrewd perception, discriminative abilities, and creative ideas. Being independent suggests that you gain power when you trust your common sense and combine your resourcefulness with the ability to structure your big plans. Fortunately, you have an inventive mind and the necessary foresight to see new opportunities. By utilizing the information at your disposal in an innovative way you can turn your ideas into successful or profitable ventures. You lose power when you get carried away with grandiose schemes that are unrealistic or hard to accomplish. Nevertheless, articulate and enterprising with natural leadership ability, you can achieve admirably if you are consistent and determined to succeed. Mentally creative, you also find satisfaction through intellectual pursuits. Although you may seek material success, inwardly you are a sensitive individual who needs to feel inspired.

Your Powers of Attraction in Relationships

Other people are attracted to your optimistic and enthusiastic nature. Sociable and generous, you can be a loyal and supportive friend. You are usually drawn to intelligent and dynamic people who are idealistic and bright. Alternatively, you may find enterprising individuals with foresight or business skills very appealing. You may choose to be in relationships that can offer you freedom or enough space to feel free or unconstrained. Although you can be very generous, do not let doubts or selfishness creep into your close relationships. On occasion you can be impulsive so you may need to be realistic when you think about long-term relationships. A dislike for restriction or criticism indicates that at times you can vacillate between your strong needs for love and affection and your desire for freedom.

Your attractive qualities: ambitious, practical, optimistic, inspired ideas, idealistic, confident, forceful, gregarious, enthusiastic, innovative, independent, purposeful, foresight, intuitive, kind, enterprising, accomplished, keen intellect, precise, articulate, independent, creative, determined

Your less attractive qualities: dislike restrictions, critical, impatient, intolerant, materialistic, easily bored, emotional ups and downs, too sensitive, overbearing, selfish, self-centered, temperamental, restless, worried, nervous, indecisive, lack of faith

Your Venus Power

The planet Venus has a great deal of influence on your powers of attraction. Below are four possible Venus types for women and men. To find your Venus you need to go to page 771, where you will find the Venus table and extra information. The planet Mars also affects your powers of attraction. To find your Mars table and interpretation go to page 761.

WOMEN WITH VENUS IN CANCER: Possessing a soft femininity, you have tender and sensitive emotions. Sympathetic and caring, you often mother those in your care by making sure they are comfortable and have plenty to eat. When you feel hurt or insecure in relationships, you are likely to cover your feelings by being defensive or appearing tough on the outside while on the inside you are feeling vulnerable. Affectionate and romantic, you make a faithful and devoted partner.

MEN WITH VENUS IN CANCER: Being emotionally receptive, you can make a sensitive lover. With your desire to care for and protect others, you are likely to have strong family connections. Love is often tied in with being attentive to the needs of others and you may find yourself attracted to individuals who have sympathetic or maternal qualities. Security conscious, you need a loyal partner who can offer you support and ideally be a good cook and homemaker.

WOMEN WITH VENUS IN LEO: Warm and playful with a touch of the dramatic, you enjoy the company of generous or strong individuals who can share your sense of fun. Although there are advantages to your being strong-willed, in your relationships you need to resist being bossy as it can cause resentment. With your wonderful mixture of regal authority and childlike wonder, you love to keep others entertained and amused.

MEN WITH VENUS IN LEO: Sociable and outgoing, you are kind and generous with those you love. Looking for a relationship that can be fun and entertaining, you need a playmate who can share your enthusiasm and high spirits. Your pride, however, often stops you from associating with lovers or partners you see as beneath you. As you desire someone who

can appreciate your sense of the dramatic, you are often attracted to people with strong personalities.

WOMEN WITH VENUS IN VIRGO: Intelligent and discriminating, you are usually drawn to polite and refined individuals. As a perfectionist, you may be keen to analyze and criticize yourself, but be careful of continually going over your partner's shortcomings. By focusing on how you can make positive improvements in yourself and in your relationships, you avoid becoming skeptical or confused. You empower yourself when you display your kind and caring concern for the well-being of loved ones and spontaneously offer your practical assistance.

MEN WITH VENUS IN VIRGO: A love of order usually indicates that you are attracted to refined individuals with analytical or practical abilities. You and your partner may be working together or serving similar causes. As you constantly analyze partnerships in order to improve them, you are likely to use former relationships as a point of reference and compare them to your present partner. As you are helpful and kind, others usually rely on your good judgment and often turn to you for advice or practical assistance.

WOMEN WITH VENUS IN LIBRA: Usually you are attractive and sociable with an easygoing manner. Your love of beauty, harmony, and pleasure implies that you are a romantic with a desire for love and affection. Once in a relationship you need to learn to negotiate your position rather than adapt to the wishes of others and compromise just to keep the peace. Nevertheless, your advanced social skills and strong sense of fair play can help you succeed in any social or romantic situation.

MEN WITH VENUS IN LIBRA: Your good social skills, charming personality, and refined manner usually make you attractive to the opposite sex. Equally, you desire a sophisticated partner with grace, elegance, and a strong sense of style. Although you have the ability to be persuasive and irresistible to others, avoid manipulative love games. Nevertheless, your natural diplomacy and sense of fair play help you to relate to people in all social situations. With your love for balance and harmony, you seek a partner who is also moderate, easygoing, and loving.

To read all about your Outer Planets and work out how to use your personalized timetable, go to Section Three, page 789.

♍

Your Personalized Timetable

JUPITER BENEFICIAL
1940 5/17 – until 1941 3/27
1942 6/25 – 8/9
1946 10/11 – 11/26
1948 11/17 – until 1949 1/26
1952 4/30 – 7/16
1952 11/5 – until 1953 3/5
1954 6/8 – 7/22
1958 9/24 – 11/10
1960 3/4 – 6/7
1960 10/27 – until 1961 1/10
1964 4/13 – 6/22
1964 12/30 – until 1965 1/21
1966 5/22 – 7/6
1970 1/8 – 4/3
1970 9/5 – 10/25
1972 2/8 – 7/21
1972 9/28 – 12/25
1976 3/27 – 6/3
1977 9/11 – 12/5
1978 5/2 – 6/20
1981 12/14 – until 1982 5/13
1982 8/11 – 10/9
1984 1/21 – 12/9
1988 3/10 – 5/18
1989 8/17 – until 1990 1/15
1990 4/5 – 6/3
1993 11/26 – until 1994 1/30
1994 3/30 – 9/21
1996 1/4 – 4/5
1996 6/3 – 11/20
1999 6/30 – 10/20
2000 2/16 – 5/1
2001 7/28 – 9/24
2001 12/11 – until 2002 5/15
2005 11/10 – until 2006 1/1
2006 5/9 – 8/31
2007 12/20 – until 2008 3/5
2008 7/18 – 10/28
2011 6/6 – until 2012 4/14

SATURN BENEFICIAL
1939 7/11 – 9/16
1940 3/23 – until 1941 4/25
1944 7/16 – until 1945 6/28
1953 11/19 – until 1954 6/7
1954 8/4 – 11/15
1959 1/8 – until 1960 3/6
1960 6/20 – 12/2
1969 5/2 – until 1970 6/5
1970 12/22 – until 1971 2/12
1973 9/7 – 11/26
1974 5/21 – 8/9
1975 2/2 – 4/22
1983 1/7 – 3/21
1983 9/27 – 12/25
1984 4/30 – 9/20
1988 2/18 – 6/5
1988 11/15 – until 1990 1/7
1998 6/12 – 10/21
1999 3/4 – 7/29
1999 9/30 – until 2000 4/8
2003 6/29 – until 2004 6/11
2012 11/2 – Continues

URANUS BENEFICIAL
1938 1/1 – until 1939 4/12
1949 8/7 – until 1952 6/21
1975 11/3 – until 1978 9/8
1988 2/23 – until 1992 12/8

NEPTUNE BENEFICIAL
1957 11/22 – until 1963 9/4
1984 1/28 – until 1992 10/20

PLUTO BENEFICIAL
1984 11/26 – until 1989 9/20
2008 2/6 – Continues

JUPITER CHALLENGING
1938 5/17 – 7/27
1938 12/31 – until 1939 3/11
1941 5/27 – 8/12

1941 12/9 – until 1942 4/3
1947 10/25 – until 1948 1/6
1950 4/17 – 9/12
1950 12/4 – until 1951 2/23
1953 5/11 – 7/20
1959 2/13 – 4/21
1959 10/7 – 12/21
1962 3/27 – until 1963 2/5
1965 4/24 – 7/2
1971 1/16 – 6/2
1971 9/14 – 12/5
1974 3/9 – 6/6
1974 8/7 – until 1975 1/17
1976 8/27 – 10/12
1977 4/5 – 6/15
1982 12/27 – until 1983 11/19
1986 2/22 – 5/6
1986 9/22 – 12/24
1988 7/23 – 11/28
1989 3/13 – 5/30
1994 12/10 – until 1995 11/2
1998 2/5 – 4/15
2000 7/1 – until 2001 5/14
2006 11/25 – until 2007 2/16
2007 5/25 – 10/14
2010 1/19 – 3/28
2012 6/13 – 9/29
2012 10/10 – Continues

SATURN CHALLENGING
1942 5/11 – until 1943 6/10
1956 1/16 – 5/9
1956 10/13 – until 1957 12/5
1964 3/27 – 9/12
1964 12/20 – until 1965 5/26
1965 7/31 – until 1966 2/9
1971 6/21 – until 1972 1/3
1972 2/28 – 7/22
1972 12/18 – until 1973 4/9
1985 11/19 – until 1987 1/9
1987 7/1 – 10/6
1993 6/8 – 6/9
1994 1/31 – until 1995 3/16
2000 8/16 – 10/9
2001 4/23 – until 2002 5/23

URANUS CHALLENGING
1941 8/28 – until 1946 5/18
1981 11/21 – until 1985 11/8
2003 3/16 – until 2008 1/25

NEPTUNE CHALLENGING
1970 1/17 – until 1978 10/21
2011 4/16 – Continues

PLUTO CHALLENGING
1995 2/1 – until 2002 11/9

JUPITER SPECIAL
1944 7/27 – 10/11
1955 11/20 – until 1956 1/14
1956 7/9 – 9/24
1967 10/21 – until 1968 2/24
1968 6/17 – 9/8
1979 10/1 – until 1980 4/20
1980 5/2 – 8/23
1991 9/13 – until 1992 8/7
2003 8/28 – 11/23
2004 2/14 – 7/19

SATURN SPECIAL
1948 9/21 – until 1949 3/28
1949 6/4 – 10/30
1950 3/3 – 7/23
1977 11/26 – 12/27
1978 7/29 – until 1979 9/3
2007 9/5 – until 2008 10/10
2009 4/5 – 6/27

URANUS SPECIAL
1961 11/14 – until 1966 7/6

PLUTO SPECIAL
1956 11/9 – until 1966 7/11

September 2

SUN: VIRGO · DECANATE: VIRGO/ MERCURY · DEGREE: 9°–10° VIRGO · MODE: MUTABLE · ELEMENT: EARTH

Your Personal Powers

Inquisitive, sensitive, and inventive, you are an intuitive individual with practical abilities and sharp awareness. Your ruling planet, Mercury, endows you with powers of perception, discriminative abilities, and imaginative ideas. Usually friendly and considerate with an enthusiastic manner, you can inspire others with your plans and ideas. As an astute person with business acumen, you gain power when you are cautiously optimistic about your future prospects. You lose power when you become impatient and restless or when you feel frustrated by obstacles and delays. You may therefore need to overcome a tendency to become disappointed by people or situations. Nevertheless, you are usually sympathetic and caring, with the ability to be diplomatic and persuasive. Well-informed and methodical, you like to pay attention to details and your quest for knowledge can inspire you to perfect your skills. Although you carefully analyze situations, do not let a tendency to be mistrusting or skeptical undermine your excellent objectivity.

Your Powers of Attraction in Relationships

Usually generous, helpful, and charming, you win people over with your keen intellect, spontaneity, and wonderful sense of humor. Although you are keen on partnerships and interacting with others, an inclination to act independently implies that you do not like to be restricted. Since at times you may appear cool or detached and at others times you can be helpful and caring, it is important to keep a sense of balance in your relationships. You are usually attracted to witty or clever individuals who can keep up with your discriminating mind and need for mental stimulation. In your close relationships it is vital that you accept your partner's little faults and refrain from being too critical or argumentative. Nevertheless, caring and compassionate, you can always turn things around by seeing the funny side of a situation or by saying something comforting and positive.

Your attractive qualities: enterprising, methodical, practical, informed, resourceful, generous, humanitarian, broadminded, visionary, inventive, quick responses, charming, friendly, helpful, sympathetic, calculated risks, adaptable, cooperative, considerate, gentle, tactful, diplomatic

Your less attractive qualities: extremist, nervous, compulsive, materialistic, extravagant, skeptical, fluctuating finances, restless, impatient, risk taking, codependent, hasty, strong reactions, suspicious, lack of confidence

Your Venus Power

The planet Venus has a great deal of influence on your powers of attraction. Below are four possible Venus types for women and men. To find your Venus you need to go to page 771, where you will find the Venus table and extra information. The planet Mars also affects your powers of attraction. To find your Mars table and interpretation go to page 761.

WOMEN WITH VENUS IN CANCER: Sensitive and understanding, you are sympathetic to other people's emotions and needs. Protective toward those you love, close relationships with your partner, relatives, and friends are important to your sense of well-being. Aware of how easy it is to hurt other people's feelings, you are often indirect and approach delicate issues in a roundabout way. Nevertheless, learning to face facts and not allowing others to exploit your good nature is a lesson just as valuable.

MEN WITH VENUS IN CANCER: You seek a partner who is sympathetic, caring, and protective. Able to be forgiving and compassionate, you want a secure emotional bond in your close relationships. You are usually drawn to partners who are maternal, unselfish, or demonstrative with their feelings. Although you can sometimes appear to others as impressionable, you have powerful emotions and inner strength.

WOMEN WITH VENUS IN LEO: Your friendly and sunny personality often makes you stand out in a crowd. Generous and giving, you know how to make your partners feel special. As you often expect loyalty and devotion from your partner in return, you can become easily offended if they ignore you or behave in an inconsiderate manner. Charming and kind, when you are in love you can be romantic, dramatic, and passionate.

MEN WITH VENUS IN LEO: As an extrovert you enjoy being involved in all types of activities where you can assert yourself and show your talents and abilities. A childlike nature suggests that you are versatile and keen on games or being entertained. You are usually attracted to vivacious partners with a benevolent nature. Others may recognize your inborn tendencies to lead but are also aware of your vanity or pride. Nevertheless, generous, kind, and caring, you often show compassion to those less fortunate than yourself.

WOMEN WITH VENUS IN VIRGO: In relationships you can

be modest and unassuming but desire perfection. You usually analyze your partnerships until you feel you have understood them to the last little detail in order to improve them. A problem usually arises when you become too critical either of partners or yourself and indulge in being skeptical or fault-finding. As you are modest, others may not be aware of the strong sensuality beneath your well-groomed exterior.

MEN WITH VENUS IN VIRGO: Industrious and well-ordered, you relate to others in a considerate and down-to-earth way. You enjoy giving practical advice and being of service to those you love even in small ways. Being a perfectionist, you are drawn to partners with high morals or a strong work ethic. Partners who have strong analytical minds are very attractive to you, particularly if they are also clean and meticulously dressed.

WOMEN WITH VENUS IN LIBRA: Gracious, charming, and sociable with a sense of style, you have no trouble attracting admirers. With your natural diplomatic skills and desire for harmony you usually like to keep the peace and avoid confrontations, but be careful of failing to take a stand when it is necessary. Romantic and easygoing yourself, you are attracted to affectionate and refined individuals who share your love of peace, justice, and fair play.

MEN WITH VENUS IN LIBRA: Courteous and refined, you are attracted to beautiful and elegant people. You are looking for a partner who can share your natural good taste and enjoy an intellectual conversation. Disliking conflict, you may have to be careful not to go along with others just to keep the peace. Your ideal partner will appreciate beauty and the little luxuries of life as well as possess good social skills. You have a strong sense of social etiquette yourself so you need an intelligent and sophisticated partner.

To read all about your Outer Planets and work out how to use your personalized timetable, go to Section Three, page 789.

To read all about your Outer Planets and work out how to use your personalized timetable, go to Section Three, page 789.

Your Personalized Timetable

JUPITER BENEFICIAL
1940 5/22 – until 1941 4/1
1942 6/29 – 8/13
1946 10/15 – 12/1
1948 11/21 – until 1949 1/31
1952 5/4 – 7/22
1952 10/29 – until 1953 3/10
1954 6/12 – 7/27
1958 9/29 – 11/15
1960 3/12 – 5/29
1960 11/2 – until 1961 1/14
1964 4/17 – 6/27
1964 12/15 – until 1965 2/5
1966 5/26 – 7/10
1970 1/17 – 3/25
1970 9/11 – 10/30
1972 2/13 – 7/12
1972 10/7 – 12/29
1976 4/1 – 6/8
1977 9/20 – 11/27
1978 5/7 – 6/24
1981 12/20 – until 1982 5/5
1982 8/19 – 10/14
1984 1/25 – 12/13
1988 3/14 – 5/22
1989 8/22 – until 1990 1/8
1990 4/13 – 6/8
1993 12/1 – until 1994 2/13
1994 3/15 – 9/26
1996 1/9 – 4/19
1996 5/19 – 11/25
1999 7/7 – 10/13
2000 2/22 – 5/5
2001 8/2 – 10/4
2001 12/1 – until 2002 5/20
2005 11/15 – until 2006 1/7
2006 5/2 – 9/6
2007 12/24 – until 2008 3/11
2008 7/10 – 11/3
2011 6/11 – 12/2
2012 1/18 – 4/18

SATURN BENEFICIAL
1940 3/31 – until 1941 5/3
1944 7/24 – until 1945 2/11
1945 3/28 – 7/6
1953 11/28 – until 1954 5/21
1954 8/21 – 11/23
1959 1/16 – 8/3
1959 10/7 – until 1960 3/21
1960 6/5 – 12/11
1969 5/10 – until 1970 6/13
1970 12/5 – until 1971 2/28
1973 9/24 – 11/8
1974 5/29 – 8/17
1975 1/20 – 5/5
1983 1/30 – 2/25
1983 10/6 – until 1984 1/5
1984 4/17 – 9/30
1988 3/2 – 5/21
1988 11/24 – until 1990 1/15
1998 6/23 – 10/9
1999 3/13 – until 2000 4/16
2003 7/7 – until 2004 6/18
2012 11/10 – Continues

URANUS BENEFICIAL
1938 1/1 – until 1939 4/30
1949 8/31 – until 1952 7/7
1975 11/19 – until 1978 9/29
1988 12/24 – until 1992 12/25

NEPTUNE BENEFICIAL
1957 12/25 – until 1963 10/9
1984 3/11 – until 1992 12/1

PLUTO BENEFICIAL
1984 12/28 – until 1989 10/17
2009 1/1 – Continues

JUPITER CHALLENGING
1938 5/28 – 7/16

1939 1/5 – 3/15
1941 6/1 – 8/19
1941 12/2 – until 1942 4/9
1947 10/30 – until 1948 1/11
1950 4/22 – 9/4
1950 12/11 – until 1951 2/27
1953 5/15 – 7/25
1954 1/18 – 3/5
1959 2/25 – 4/9
1959 10/12 – 12/25
1962 4/1 – until 1963 2/10
1965 4/28 – 7/7
1971 1/22 – 5/25
1971 9/20 – 12/9
1974 3/14 – 6/18
1974 7/26 – until 1975 1/22
1977 4/10 – 6/20
1983 1/1 – 7/17
1983 8/10 – 11/23
1986 2/26 – 5/12
1986 9/15 – 12/30
1988 7/29 – 11/21
1989 3/19 – 6/4
1994 12/15 – until 1995 11/7
1998 2/9 – 4/19
2000 7/6 – until 2001 1/18
2001 2/1 – 5/18
2006 11/30 – until 2007 2/24
2007 5/17 – 10/19
2010 1/23 – 4/1
2012 6/17 – Continues

SATURN CHALLENGING
1942 5/18 – until 1943 6/17
1956 1/29 – 4/25
1956 10/23 – until 1957 12/13
1964 4/5 – 8/29
1964 12/31 – until 1966 2/17
1971 6/29 – 12/18
1972 3/14 – 8/1
1972 12/6 – until 1973 4/19
1985 11/27 – until 1987 1/19
1987 6/17 – 10/18
1994 2/8 – until 1995 3/24
2001 5/1 – until 2002 5/31

URANUS CHALLENGING
1942 6/6 – until 1946 6/4
1981 12/7 – until 1985 11/25
2003 4/5 – until 2008 2/13

NEPTUNE CHALLENGING
1970 12/11 – until 1978 11/20
2012 3/9 – Continues

PLUTO CHALLENGING
1995 12/13 – until 2003 9/11

JUPITER SPECIAL
1944 8/1 – 10/15
1955 12/6 – 12/29
1956 7/14 – 9/28
1967 10/27 – until 1968 2/17
1968 6/24 – 9/13
1979 10/6 – until 1980 3/31
1980 5/22 – 8/28
1991 9/18 – until 1992 8/11
2003 9/2 – 12/2
2004 2/5 – 7/25

SATURN SPECIAL
1948 9/30 – until 1949 3/13
1949 6/18 – 11/10
1950 2/19 – 8/1
1978 8/6 – until 1979 9/10
2007 9/12 – until 2008 10/18
2009 3/22 – 7/10

URANUS SPECIAL
1962 8/30 – until 1966 7/28

PLUTO SPECIAL
1957 9/29 – until 1966 8/14

♍

September 3

Your Personal Powers

Although you are ambitious, strong-willed, and determined, your assertive and confident personality often hides your sensitivity or nervous inner tension. Your ruling planet, Mercury, endows you with powers of perception, common sense, foresight, and depth of thought. Your discriminative abilities and a pragmatic outlook indicate that you gain power when you utilize your natural organizational skills. You lose some of your power by being skeptical or allowing fear to undermine your resolute nature. By trusting your strong intuition and having channels for your natural creativity, you can overcome a tendency to be anxious or mull over issues in great detail. Nevertheless, capable and intelligent with a good business sense, you are hardworking and competitive. When you find something that truly captures your imagination you feel inspired and motivated. Your inner faith gives you the courage to be daring, quick, and spontaneous. You can succeed when you utilize your keen insight and embrace opportunities for advancement.

Your Powers of Attraction in Relationships

Although you are usually hardworking you enjoy having fun and socializing. Other people admire your modesty and your ability to tackle problems and overcome challenges. Although you are intelligent with good reasoning powers, at times you can come across as too serious. Your indecision regarding affairs of the heart can cause delays in forming close relationships. Alternatively, being sociable, career-oriented, and dynamic, too many choices for romance can make it hard for you to pick the right partner. Usually you are attracted to sensitive or creative individuals who can be loving and comforting. If you feel discontented or dissatisfied, however, you may come across as cold and unfeeling. Nevertheless, once you fall in love you are loving and helpful with the ability to show total devotion.

Your attractive qualities: determined, informed, business acumen, friendly, creative, reliable, loving, self-assured, organized, discriminative, optimistic, practical, helpful, innate wisdom, methodical, strategist, analytical, insightful, helpful, productive, ambitious, strong willpower, articulate, focused

Your less attractive qualities: doubting, skeptical, controlling, bossy, critical, faultfinding, insecure, worried, mental stress, too proud, too ambitious, indecisive, irritable, frustrated, easily bored, vain, exaggerate, boastful, extravagant, self-indulgent, impatient

Your Venus Power

The planet Venus has a great deal of influence on your powers of attraction. Below are four possible Venus types for women and men. To find your Venus you need to go to page 771, where you will find the Venus table and extra information. The planet Mars also affects your powers of attraction. To find your Mars table and interpretation go to page 761.

WOMEN WITH VENUS IN CANCER: Sensitive and understanding, you are sympathetic to other people's emotions and needs. Protective toward those you love, close relationships with your partner, relatives, and friends are important to your sense of well-being. Aware of how easy it is to hurt other people's feelings, you are often indirect and approach delicate issues in a roundabout way. Nevertheless, learning to face facts and not allowing others to exploit your good nature is a lesson just as valuable.

MEN WITH VENUS IN CANCER: You seek a partner who is sympathetic, caring, and protective. Able to be forgiving and compassionate, you want a secure emotional bond in your close relationships. You are usually drawn to partners who are maternal, unselfish, or demonstrative with their feelings. Although you can sometimes appear to others as impressionable, you have powerful emotions and inner strength.

WOMEN WITH VENUS IN LEO: Your friendly and sunny personality often makes you stand out in a crowd. Generous and giving, you know how to make your partner feel special. As you often expect loyalty and devotion from your partners in return, you can become easily offended if they ignore you or behave in an inconsiderate manner. Charming and kind, when you are in love you can be romantic, dramatic, and passionate.

MEN WITH VENUS IN LEO: A childlike nature suggests that you are versatile and keen on games or being entertained. You are usually attracted to vivacious partners with a benevolent nature. As an extrovert you enjoy being involved in all types of activities where you can assert yourself and show your talents and abilities. Others may recognize your inborn tendencies to lead but are also aware of your vanity or pride. Nevertheless, generous, kind, and caring, you often show compassion to those less fortunate than yourself.

346

WOMEN WITH VENUS IN VIRGO: In relationships you can be modest and unassuming but desire perfection. You usually analyze your partnerships until you feel you have understood them to the last little detail in order to improve them. A problem usually arises when you become too critical either of partners or yourself and indulge in being skeptical or fault-finding. Being modest, others may not be aware of the strong sensuality beneath your well-groomed exterior.

MEN WITH VENUS IN VIRGO: Industrious and well-ordered, you relate to others in a considerate and down-to-earth way. You enjoy giving practical advice and being of service to those you love even in small ways. Being a perfectionist, you are drawn to partners with high morals or a strong work ethic. Partners who have strong analytical minds are very attractive to you, particularly if they are also clean and meticulously dressed.

WOMEN WITH VENUS IN LIBRA: Gracious, charming, and sociable with a sense of style, you have no trouble attracting admirers. With your natural diplomatic skills and desire for harmony you usually like to keep the peace and avoid confrontations, but be careful of failing to make a stand when it is necessary. Romantic and easygoing yourself, you are attracted to affectionate and refined individuals who share your love of peace, justice, and fair play.

MEN WITH VENUS IN LIBRA: Courteous and refined, you are attracted to beautiful and elegant people. You are looking for a partner who can share your natural good taste and enjoy an intellectual conversation. Disliking conflict, you may have to be careful not to go along with others just to keep the peace. Your ideal partner will appreciate beauty and the little luxuries of life as well as possess good social skills. You have a strong sense of social etiquette yourself so you need an intelligent and sophisticated partner.

To read all about your Outer Planets and work out how to use your personalized timetable, go to Section Three, page 789.

♍

Your Personalized Timetable

JUPITER BENEFICIAL
1940 5/26 – until 1941 4/5
1942 7/3 – 8/18
1943 3/5 – 3/18
1946 10/20 – 12/5
1948 11/26 – until 1949 2/4
1952 5/8 – 7/30
1952 10/21 – until 1953 3/16
1954 6/17 – 7/31
1958 10/4 – 11/19
1960 3/21 – 5/19
1960 11/7 – until 1961 1/18
1964 4/21 – 7/2
1964 12/5 – until 1965 2/15
1966 5/31 – 7/15
1970 1/29 – 3/13
1970 9/16 – 11/3
1972 2/19 – 7/4
1972 10/14 – until 1973 1/2
1976 4/5 – 6/12
1977 10/1 – 11/16
1978 5/12 – 6/29
1981 12/26 – until 1982 4/27
1982 8/26 – 10/18
1984 1/30 – 12/18
1988 3/19 – 5/26
1989 8/28 – 12/31
1990 4/20 – 6/12
1993 12/6 – until 1994 6/14
1994 7/20 – 10/1
1996 1/13 – 11/30
1999 7/14 – 10/5
2000 2/27 – 5/9
2001 8/6 – 10/17
2001 11/18 – until 2002 5/25
2005 11/19 – until 2006 1/14
2006 4/24 – 9/12
2007 12/28 – until 2008 3/17
2008 7/3 – 11/9
2011 6/16 – 11/22
2012 1/28 – 4/22

SATURN BENEFICIAL
1940 4/8 – until 1941 5/10
1944 8/1 – until 1945 1/24
1945 4/14 – 7/13
1953 12/7 – until 1954 5/7
1954 9/2 – 12/2
1955 6/18 – 8/18
1959 1/25 – 7/17
1959 10/22 – until 1960 4/13
1960 5/11 – 12/20
1969 5/18 – 12/20
1970 1/18 – 6/22
1970 11/22 – until 1971 3/12
1974 6/6 – 8/27
1975 1/8 – 5/15
1983 10/14 – until 1984 1/19
1984 4/1 – 10/9
1988 3/23 – 4/29
1988 12/3 – until 1990 1/23
1998 7/6 – 9/25
1999 3/22 – until 2000 4/23
2003 7/14 – until 2004 6/26
2012 11/18 – Continues

URANUS BENEFICIAL
1938 1/1 – until 1940 2/21
1950 6/28 – until 1953 5/5
1975 12/7 – until 1978 10/16
1989 1/9 – until 1993 10/5

NEPTUNE BENEFICIAL
1958 11/17 – until 1964 8/23
1985 1/22 – until 1992 12/29

PLUTO BENEFICIAL
1985 11/11 – until 1990 8/26
2009 1/30 – Continues

JUPITER CHALLENGING
1939 1/10 – 3/19

1941 6/5 – 8/26
1941 11/24 – until 1942 4/15
1947 11/3 – until 1948 1/16
1950 4/28 – 8/28
1950 12/17 – until 1951 3/3
1953 5/19 – 7/30
1954 1/7 – 3/16
1959 10/17 – 12/29
1962 4/5 – until 1963 2/14
1965 5/2 – 7/11
1971 1/28 – 5/18
1971 9/26 – 12/13
1974 3/18 – until 1975 1/26
1977 4/14 – 6/24
1983 1/6 – 7/1
1983 8/26 – 11/28
1986 3/2 – 5/18
1986 9/7 – until 1987 1/5
1988 8/5 – 11/14
1989 3/25 – 6/8
1994 12/20 – until 1995 11/11
1998 2/13 – 4/24
1998 11/6 – 11/20
2000 7/11 – 12/31
2001 2/19 – 5/22
2006 12/4 – until 2007 3/5
2007 5/7 – 10/24
2010 1/28 – 4/5
2012 6/21 – Continues

SATURN CHALLENGING
1942 5/26 – until 1943 6/25
1956 2/15 – 4/7
1956 11/1 – until 1957 12/21
1964 4/16 – 8/16
1965 1/11 – until 1966 2/25
1971 7/8 – 12/5
1972 3/26 – 8/11
1972 11/24 – until 1973 4/29
1985 12/6 – until 1987 1/29
1987 6/3 – 10/29
1994 2/16 – until 1995 4/2
1995 11/4 – 12/8
2001 5/9 – until 2002 6/8

URANUS CHALLENGING
1942 6/23 – until 1947 3/31
1981 12/24 – until 1985 12/11
2003 5/1 – until 2008 3/2

NEPTUNE CHALLENGING
1971 1/10 – until 1979 10/14
2012 4/7 – Continues

PLUTO CHALLENGING
1996 1/10 – until 2003 10/30

JUPITER SPECIAL
1944 8/5 – 10/20
1945 4/22 – 6/5
1956 7/19 – 10/3
1967 11/3 – until 1968 2/9
1968 6/30 – 9/17
1979 10/11 – until 1980 3/20
1980 6/2 – 9/1
1991 9/23 – until 1992 8/16
2003 9/6 – 12/15
2004 1/23 – 7/30

SATURN SPECIAL
1948 10/9 – until 1949 2/28
1949 6/30 – 11/24
1950 2/4 – 8/10
1978 8/14 – until 1979 9/18
2007 9/20 – until 2008 4/7
2008 5/28 – 10/28
2009 3/10 – 7/21

URANUS SPECIAL
1962 9/15 – until 1966 8/15

PLUTO SPECIAL
1957 11/18 – until 1967 7/1

347

September 4

Your Personal Powers

As a pragmatic and analytical individual, you usually rely on your common sense, practical skills, and strong sense of duty. Your ruling planet, Mercury, endows you with powers of perception, discriminative abilities, and an urge to think independently. Being serious and persistent, you possess the patience to work with meticulous precision. You gain power when you combine your idealism and practical outlook, using your intuitive mind to refine and perfect your ideas. Although your shrewd common sense indicates that you are methodical and dedicated, inwardly you can be highly sensitive. Tendencies to fluctuate between realism and idealism can cause you frustration. You may also lose some of your power when you put high demands on yourself and others, causing you to worry or repress your emotions. A good worker, however, you are usually conscientious, self-disciplined, and sincere. By creating a good balance between your own needs and your responsibilities toward others, you feel encouraged and can act spontaneously. Intelligent with an honest approach, you also gain power through learning to value yourself.

Your Powers of Attraction in Relationships

Your natural charm and sociability suggest that you can be romantic and idealistic about relationships. Usually you are drawn to individuals who are warmhearted and loving with attractive personalities. Being modest, caring, and considerate indicates that when you are in love you will go out of your way to make your partner happy. Although you are caring, avoid martyring yourself. Other people are drawn to your kind, thoughtful, and sympathetic nature. Your idealistic sensitivity may even draw you to help others through compassionate causes. While you can be charming and generous, when you feel unsure about your feelings or financial circumstances you can become soberly realistic or emotionally tight. Nevertheless, hardworking with an ability to endure challenges, you are usually faithful and loyal to your partner and friends.

Your attractive qualities: well-organized, analytical, persuasive, realistic, self-disciplined, business sense, steady, hardworking, productive, loyal, pragmatic, trusting, exact, compromising, generous, reliable, methodical, broad-minded, fair, just, sincere, security-conscious, intelligent, honest

Your less attractive qualities: critical, stubborn, uncommunicative, repressed, rigid, lazy, frustrated, too economical, bossy, resentful, strict, inner conflict between love and duty, discontented, prejudging, undemonstrative, selfish

Your Venus Power

The planet Venus has a great deal of influence on your powers of attraction. Below are four possible Venus types for women and men. To find your Venus you need to go to page 771, where you will find the Venus table and extra information. The planet Mars also affects your powers of attraction. To find your Mars table and interpretation go to page 761.

WOMEN WITH VENUS IN CANCER: With your intuitive abilities and sympathetic nature, you are usually supportive to those you love. Impressionable and intuitive, your receptivity allows you to quickly pick up on the moods of others, making you especially aware of the emotional changes in your partner. As you often display true maternal tendencies toward those you know, you want a partner who is considerate and sensitive.

MEN WITH VENUS IN CANCER: Being caring and sensitive, you probably seek a nurturing partner who could provide you with emotional security and a sense of belonging in a loving and safe environment. Receptive to others, at times you find it hard to be direct or confrontational in relationships. You are affectionate and caring, and family links are important to you.

WOMEN WITH VENUS IN LEO: You possess the wonderful ability to project your warm and sunny personality and keep others happily entertained. Loving attention yourself, you seek a partner who can appreciate you, be supportive, and give you positive feedback. Proud, with a natural regal air, you expect respect from your partners but are willing to be loyal and supportive in exchange. Although sometimes a little self-centered, you know how to make your partner feel special.

MEN WITH VENUS IN LEO: Enthusiastic, playful, and kind, you can be benevolent with those you love. Warm, romantic, and self-expressive, you adore the drama of love or having fun with your friends. Usually you are attracted to partners with a warm and generous nature. Although you can be a confident and charismatic partner, you may need to develop humility in order to stop pride or arrogance from marring your relationships.

WOMEN WITH VENUS IN VIRGO: Intelligent and dis-

criminating, you are usually drawn to polite and refined individuals. As a perfectionist, you may be keen to analyze and criticize yourself, but be careful of continually going over your partner's shortcomings. By focusing on how you can make positive improvements in yourself and in your relationships, you avoid becoming skeptical or confused. You empower yourself when you display kind and caring concern for the well-being of loved ones and spontaneously offer your practical assistance.

MEN WITH VENUS IN VIRGO: A love of order usually indicates that you are attracted to refined individuals with analytical or practical abilities. You and your partner may be working together or serving similar causes. As you constantly analyze partnerships in order to improve them, you are likely to use former relationships as a point of reference and compare them to your present partner. As you are helpful and kind, others usually rely on your good judgment and often turn to you for advice or practical assistance.

WOMEN WITH VENUS IN LIBRA: Attractive, refined, and conscious of the needs of others, you usually desire harmonious relationships. As a peacemaker with good negotiating skills, you can smooth out difficulties with others, but your dislike of confrontation may sometimes leave you refusing to take a stand or compromising too many of your own needs. Courteous, stylish, and charming with polished social skills, you are an expert at relating to others in a gracious and civilized manner.

MEN WITH VENUS IN LIBRA: As a sociable and friendly individual with an eye for beauty, you are amorous and charming. You are a natural gentleman and your ideal partner usually has an elegant appearance, artistic appreciation, and good taste. Your relationships benefit when you resist the temptation to take the easy way out or put too much emphasis on vanity and high living. Intellectual and naturally refined, you seek a loving partner who can share your romantic and sophisticated aspirations.

To read all about your Outer Planets and work out how to use your personalized timetable, go to Section Three, page 789.

♍

Your Personalized Timetable

JUPITER BENEFICIAL
1940 5/30 – until **1941** 4/10
1942 7/7 – 8/23
1943 2/14 – 4/7
1946 10/24 – 12/10
1948 11/30 – until **1949** 2/9
1952 5/12 – 8/7
1952 10/12 – until **1953** 3/21
1954 6/21 – 8/5
1958 10/8 – 11/23
1960 4/4 – 5/5
1960 11/12 – until **1961** 1/23
1964 4/25 – 7/7
1964 11/27 – until **1965** 2/23
1966 6/4 – 7/19
1970 9/21 – 11/8
1972 2/25 – 6/26
1972 10/21 – until **1973** 1/7
1976 4/9 – 6/17
1978 5/17 – 7/3
1982 1/2 – 4/20
1982 9/1 – 10/23
1984 2/4 – 8/22
1984 9/6 – 12/22
1988 3/23 – 5/30
1989 9/3 – 12/24
1990 4/26 – 6/17
1993 12/11 – until **1994** 5/31
1994 8/2 – 10/6
1996 1/17 – 12/5
1999 7/23 – 9/27
2000 3/3 – 5/13
2001 8/11 – until **2002** 2/10
2002 3/20 – 5/30
2005 11/24 – until **2006** 1/21
2006 4/16 – 9/18
2008 1/1 – 3/24
2008 6/25 – 11/15
2011 6/21 – 11/13
2012 2/5 – 4/26

SATURN BENEFICIAL
1940 4/15 – until **1941** 5/18
1944 8/9 – until **1945** 1/11
1945 4/27 – 7/21
1953 12/17 – until **1954** 4/24
1954 9/13 – 12/10
1955 6/1 – 9/4
1959 2/4 – 7/3
1959 11/4 – until **1960** 12/29
1969 5/26 – 11/28
1970 2/8 – 7/2
1970 11/10 – until **1971** 3/22
1974 6/14 – 9/6
1974 12/27 – until **1975** 5/25
1983 10/22 – until **1984** 2/11
1984 3/8 – 10/18
1988 12/11 – until **1990** 2/1
1990 8/28 – 10/18
1998 7/25 – 9/6
1999 3/30 – until **2000** 5/1
2003 7/22 – until **2004** 7/4
2012 11/27 – Continues

URANUS BENEFICIAL
1938 1/1 – until **1940** 3/21
1950 7/14 – until **1953** 5/27
1975 12/28 – until **1978** 11/1
1989 1/26 – until **1993** 11/15

NEPTUNE BENEFICIAL
1958 12/18 – until **1964** 10/3
1985 2/26 – until **1993** 11/25

PLUTO BENEFICIAL
1985 12/7 – until **1990** 10/2
2009 3/19 – Continues

JUPITER CHALLENGING
1939 1/14 – 3/23
1941 6/9 – 9/2
1941 11/16 – until **1942** 4/20
1947 11/8 – until **1948** 1/20

1948 8/7 – 8/24
1950 5/4 – 8/20
1950 12/23 – until **1951** 3/7
1953 5/23 – 8/5
1953 12/30 – until **1954** 3/24
1959 10/22 – until **1960** 1/3
1962 4/10 – 10/14
1962 11/13 – until **1963** 2/18
1965 5/6 – 7/16
1971 2/4 – 5/10
1971 10/2 – 12/18
1974 3/22 – until **1975** 1/31
1977 4/19 – 6/28
1983 1/11 – 6/20
1983 9/5 – 12/2
1986 3/6 – 5/24
1986 8/31 – until **1987** 1/11
1988 8/12 – 11/6
1989 3/30 – 6/12
1994 12/24 – until **1995** 11/16
1998 2/17 – 4/29
1998 10/19 – 12/8
2000 7/16 – 12/21
2001 3/1 – 5/26
2006 12/8 – until **2007** 3/18
2007 4/24 – 10/30
2010 2/1 – 4/9
2012 6/26 – Continues

SATURN CHALLENGING
1942 6/2 – until **1943** 7/2
1956 11/9 – until **1957** 12/30
1958 8/11 – 9/5
1964 4/28 – 8/3
1965 1/20 – until **1966** 3/5
1971 7/18 – 11/23
1972 4/5 – 8/24
1972 11/11 – until **1973** 5/7
1985 12/14 – until **1986** 7/24
1986 8/21 – until **1987** 2/10
1987 5/21 – 11/7
1994 2/24 – until **1995** 4/10
1995 10/14 – 12/29
2001 5/16 – until **2002** 6/15

URANUS CHALLENGING
1942 7/14 – until **1947** 4/25
1982 1/11 – until **1986** 10/12
2004 2/29 – until **2008** 12/31

NEPTUNE CHALLENGING
1971 12/7 – until **1979** 11/16

PLUTO CHALLENGING
1996 11/30 – until **2003** 11/28

JUPITER SPECIAL
1944 8/10 – 10/26
1945 4/10 – 6/17
1956 7/24 – 10/8
1967 11/11 – until **1968** 2/1
1968 7/6 – 9/22
1979 10/16 – until **1980** 3/11
1980 6/11 – 9/6
1991 9/27 – until **1992** 8/21
2003 9/11 – until **2004** 8/4

SATURN SPECIAL
1948 10/19 – until **1949** 2/16
1949 7/10 – 12/15
1950 1/14 – 8/18
1978 8/21 – until **1979** 9/26
2007 9/29 – until **2008** 3/21
2008 6/14 – 11/7
2009 2/26 – 7/30

URANUS SPECIAL
1962 10/2 – until **1966** 8/31

NEPTUNE SPECIAL
1938 3/31 – until **1938** 7/27

PLUTO SPECIAL
1958 10/2 – until **1967** 8/9

September 5

Your Personal Powers

Charismatic and imaginative, you are an intelligent individual with common sense and strong desires. Your ruling planet, Mercury, endows you with good perception, resourcefulness, discriminative abilities, and creative ideas. Multitalented and enterprising, you gain power when you combine your wealth of ideas and practical attitude with your optimism. You usually show a willingness to work hard for what you believe in. Although you seek perfection or feel strongly about your life and interests, a tendency to worry or be indecisive warns that inner doubts may cause inertia or setbacks. Therefore, in order to succeed, you need to stay focused, determined, and confident. You can lose some of your power if you become skeptical or impatient and give up too quickly, blocking your creativity from flowing. When inspired, however, you are positive, intuitive, and original, with a warm interest in people. Since your advancement in life often depends on your efforts and dedication, the more patient you are the more likely you are to succeed.

Your Powers of Attraction in Relationships

Other people admire your direct approach and sincerity. Being warmhearted and sociable, your kind nature and charismatic personality usually gain you many friends and admirers. Although you are usually willing to help and advise those who request your support, guard against becoming too caught up in other people's problems. Usually you are attracted to dynamic and enterprising individuals who can offer you love, devotion, and an active life full of experiences. Alternatively, you may be drawn to creative or dramatic partners who share your passions or interests. Although you are usually affectionate and caring, indecisiveness about your emotions can at times confuse you, especially if you are drawn to more than one relationship. Nevertheless, you are home-loving and ordinarily loyal to and protective of your partner.

Your attractive qualities: persevering, tenacious, feel secure, positive thinker, idealistic, creative, intelligent, versatile, adaptable, humanitarian, patience, adaptable, good business sense, productive, practical, foresight, progressive, home-loving, creative, hardworking, dramatic, magnetic, daring

Your less attractive qualities: impatient, frustrated, irritable, restless, unreliable, changeable, procrastinator, gives up easily, overconfident, headstrong, hasty, too sensitive, extravagant, demanding, critical, inertia

Your Venus Power

The planet Venus has a great deal of influence on your powers of attraction. Below are four possible Venus types for women and men. To find your Venus you need to go to page 771, where you will find the Venus table and extra information. The planet Mars also affects your powers of attraction. To find your Mars table and interpretation go to page 761.

WOMEN WITH VENUS IN CANCER: Possessing a soft femininity, you have tender and sensitive emotions. Sympathetic and caring, you often mother those in your care by making sure they are comfortable and have plenty to eat. When you feel hurt or insecure in relationships, you are likely to cover your feelings by being defensive or appearing tough on the outside while on the inside you are feeling vulnerable. Affectionate and romantic, you make a faithful and devoted partner.

MEN WITH VENUS IN CANCER: Being emotionally receptive, you can make a sensitive lover. With your desire to care for and protect others, you are likely to have strong family connections. Love is often tied in with being attentive to the needs of others and you may find yourself attracted to individuals who have sympathetic or maternal qualities. Security conscious, you need a loyal partner who can offer you support and ideally be a good cook and homemaker.

WOMEN WITH VENUS IN LEO: Warm and playful with a touch of the dramatic, you enjoy the company of generous or strong individuals who can share your sense of fun. Although there are advantages to your being strong-willed, in your relationships you need to resist being bossy as it can cause resentment. With your wonderful mixture of regal authority and childlike wonder, you love to keep others entertained and amused.

MEN WITH VENUS IN LEO: Sociable and outgoing, you are kind and generous with those you love. Looking for a relationship that can be fun and entertaining, you need a playmate who can share your enthusiasm and high spirits. Your pride, however, often stops you from associating with lovers or partners you see as beneath you. As you desire someone who can appreciate your sense of the dramatic, you are often attracted to people with strong personalities.

WOMEN WITH VENUS IN VIRGO: Intelligent and discriminating, you are usually drawn to polite and refined individuals. As a perfectionist, you may be keen to analyze and criticize yourself, but be careful of continually going over your partner's shortcomings. By focusing on how you can make positive improvements in yourself and in your relationships, you avoid becoming skeptical or confused. You empower yourself when you display kind and caring concern for the well-being of loved ones and spontaneously offer your practical assistance.

MEN WITH VENUS IN VIRGO: A love of order usually indicates that you are attracted to refined individuals with analytical or practical abilities. You and your partner may be working together or serving similar causes. As you constantly analyze partnerships in order to improve them, you are likely to use former relationships as a point of reference and compare them to your present partner. As you are helpful and kind, others usually rely on your good judgment and often turn to you for advice or practical assistance.

WOMEN WITH VENUS IN LIBRA: Usually you are attractive and sociable with an easygoing manner. Your love of beauty, harmony, and pleasure implies that you are a romantic with a desire for love and affection. Once in a relationship you need to learn to negotiate your position rather than adapt to the wishes of others and compromise just to keep the peace. Nevertheless, your advanced social skills and strong sense of fair play can help you succeed in any social or romantic situation.

MEN WITH VENUS IN LIBRA: Your good social skills, charming personality, and refined manner usually make you attractive to the opposite sex. Equally, you desire a sophisticated partner with grace, elegance, and a strong sense of style. Although you have the ability to be persuasive and irresistible to others, avoid manipulative love games. Nevertheless, your natural diplomacy and sense of fair play help you to relate to people in all social situations. With your love of balance and harmony, you seek a partner who is also moderate, easygoing, and loving.

To read all about your Outer Planets and work out how to use your personalized timetable, go to Section Three, page 789.

Your Personalized Timetable

JUPITER BENEFICIAL
1940 6/4 – until **1941** 4/14
1942 7/12 – 8/28
1943 2/4 – 4/17
1946 10/29 – 12/15
1948 12/5 – until **1949** 2/13
1952 5/16 – 8/18
1952 10/1 – until **1953** 3/26
1954 6/25 – 8/9
1958 10/13 – 11/28
1960 11/17 – until **1961** 1/27
1964 4/29 – 7/13
1964 11/19 – until **1965** 3/2
1966 6/9 – 7/23
1970 9/26 – 11/12
1972 3/2 – 6/18
1972 10/27 – until **1973** 1/11
1976 4/13 – 6/21
1978 5/22 – 7/7
1982 1/9 – 4/12
1982 9/7 – 10/27
1984 2/9 – 8/3
1984 9/25 – 12/26
1988 3/27 – 6/4
1989 9/10 – 12/17
1990 5/2 – 6/21
1993 12/16 – until **1994** 5/21
1994 8/12 – 10/11
1996 1/22 – 12/9
1999 8/3 – 9/15
2000 3/8 – 5/17
2001 8/16 – until **2002** 1/29
2002 4/2 – 6/4
2005 11/29 – until **2006** 1/30
2006 4/6 – 9/24
2008 1/6 – 4/1
2008 6/16 – 11/20
2011 6/26 – 11/6
2012 2/12 – 5/1

SATURN BENEFICIAL
1940 4/23 – until **1941** 5/26
1944 8/19 – 12/30
1945 5/7 – 7/28
1953 12/28 – until **1954** 4/11
1954 9/23 – 12/20
1955 5/18 – 9/16
1959 2/14 – 6/20
1959 11/14 – until **1961** 1/6
1969 6/4 – 11/14
1970 2/21 – 7/12
1970 10/29 – until **1971** 3/31
1974 6/21 – 9/17
1974 12/14 – until **1975** 6/3
1983 10/30 – until **1984** 10/26
1988 12/20 – until **1990** 2/9
1990 8/9 – 11/5
1999 4/7 – until **2000** 5/8
2003 7/30 – until **2004** 2/5
2004 4/8 – 7/11
2012 12/6 – Continues

URANUS BENEFICIAL
1938 1/1 – until **1940** 4/10
1950 8/1 – until **1953** 6/15
1976 10/26 – until **1979** 8/20
1989 2/16 – until **1993** 12/7

NEPTUNE BENEFICIAL
1959 11/13 – until **1964** 10/31
1986 1/17 – until **1993** 12/24

PLUTO BENEFICIAL
1986 1/16 – until **1990** 10/28
2010 1/26 – Continues

JUPITER CHALLENGING
1939 1/19 – 3/28
1941 6/13 – 9/12
1941 11/6 – until **1942** 4/25
1947 11/12 – until **1948** 1/25
1948 7/20 – 9/11

1950 5/11 – 8/12
1950 12/29 – until **1951** 3/11
1953 5/27 – 8/10
1953 12/22 – until **1954** 4/1
1959 10/27 – until **1960** 1/7
1962 4/15 – 9/30
1962 11/27 – until **1963** 2/22
1965 5/11 – 7/20
1971 2/12 – 5/1
1971 10/8 – 12/22
1974 3/26 – until **1975** 2/4
1977 4/23 – 7/2
1983 1/17 – 6/12
1983 9/13 – 12/6
1986 3/10 – 6/1
1986 8/23 – until **1987** 1/16
1988 8/20 – 10/29
1989 4/4 – 6/16
1994 12/29 – until **1995** 11/20
1998 2/22 – 5/4
1998 10/9 – 12/18
2000 7/21 – 12/12
2001 3/9 – 5/31
2006 12/13 – until **2007** 11/3
2010 2/5 – 4/14
2012 6/30 – Continues

SATURN CHALLENGING
1942 6/10 – until **1943** 7/10
1944 1/28 – 3/15
1956 11/17 – until **1958** 1/7
1958 7/17 – 9/30
1964 5/14 – 7/17
1965 1/28 – until **1966** 3/13
1971 7/28 – 11/11
1972 4/14 – 9/11
1972 10/23 – until **1973** 5/15
1985 12/23 – until **1986** 6/29
1986 9/13 – until **1987** 2/25
1987 5/5 – 11/16
1994 3/4 – until **1995** 4/19
1995 9/29 – until **1996** 1/11
2001 5/24 – until **2002** 6/22

URANUS CHALLENGING
1942 8/10 – until **1947** 5/14
1982 2/7 – until **1986** 11/3
2004 3/18 – until **2009** 1/26

NEPTUNE CHALLENGING
1972 1/4 – until **1980** 10/3

PLUTO CHALLENGING
1996 12/26 – until **2004** 10/19

JUPITER SPECIAL
1944 8/15 – 10/31
1945 4/1 – 6/27
1956 7/29 – 10/13
1967 11/20 – until **1968** 1/23
1968 7/11 – 9/26
1979 10/22 – until **1980** 3/4
1980 6/18 – 9/10
1991 10/2 – until **1992** 8/25
2003 9/15 – until **2004** 8/9

SATURN SPECIAL
1948 10/30 – until **1949** 2/3
1949 7/19 – until **1950** 8/27
1978 8/29 – until **1979** 10/4
1980 5/20 – 5/20
2007 10/8 – until **2008** 3/7
2008 6/27 – 11/19
2009 2/12 – 8/8

URANUS SPECIAL
1962 10/22 – until **1966** 9/16

NEPTUNE SPECIAL
1938 2/23 – 8/26

PLUTO SPECIAL
1958 11/25 – until **1968** 6/9

♍

September 6

Your Personal Powers

Creative and intuitive, you are an intelligent and receptive individual with a desire to expand your knowledge or deepen your awareness. Your ruling planet, Mercury, endows you with powers of perception, discriminative abilities, imaginative ideas, and an urge to think independently. Although your keen insight and analytical abilities indicate that you can be observant and resourceful, you gain power when you learn to persevere and develop your endurance. Even though you are likely to enjoy new opportunities and lucky breaks throughout your life, you may experience some fluctuations in your financial circumstances. Therefore you gain power when you develop a long-range strategy for securing your future through saving and being cautious. As a multitalented person, you are versatile and adaptable with the ability to see new possibilities. You can also be highly focused when something captures your imagination and makes you feel enterprising. Being both practical and idealistic also implies that you need to be mentally stimulated and active in order to avoid becoming restless or bored.

Your Powers of Attraction in Relationships

You are thoughtful and rational, and other people admire your modesty, dry humor, and practical approach. Usually you are drawn to intelligent and sensitive partners with whom you can communicate or share ideas. Alternatively, you may become involved with a partner who shares your sense of adventure and inspires you to be enterprising. Your youthfulness and natural charm indicate that you can be idealistic and romantic. As you often want serious relationships, you are willing to support or sacrifice a great deal for those you love. You may need to be careful, however, not to martyr yourself to someone before you know his or her true character. Your kindness and understanding also suggest that you are naturally sympathetic; however, if hurt, you may withdraw and become uncommunicative.

Your attractive qualities: instinctive, adventurous, educated, well-informed, hardworking, focused, persevering, humanitarian, idealistic, sociable, creative ideas, intuitive, entertaining, sense of humor, progressive, youthful, good image, friendly, compassionate, dependable, poised

Your less attractive qualities: anxiety about money, restless, impatient, stuck in rut, easily discouraged, too materialistic, lack of self-confidence, irresponsible, discontented, stubborn, uncompromising, domineering, selfish, suspicious, cynical

Your Venus Power

The planet Venus has a great deal of influence on your powers of attraction. Below are four possible Venus types for women and men. To find your Venus you need to go to page 771, where you will find the Venus table and extra information. The planet Mars also affects your powers of attraction. To find your Mars table and interpretation go to page 761.

WOMEN WITH VENUS IN CANCER: Sensitive and understanding, you are sympathetic to other people's emotions and needs. Protective toward those you love, close relationships with your partner, relatives, and friends are important to your sense of well-being. Aware of how easy it is to hurt other people's feelings, you are often indirect and approach delicate issues in a roundabout way. Nevertheless, learning to face facts and not allowing others to exploit your good nature is a lesson just as valuable.

MEN WITH VENUS IN CANCER: You seek a partner who is sympathetic, caring, and protective. Able to be forgiving and compassionate, you want a secure emotional bond in your close relationships. Usually you are drawn to partners who are maternal, unselfish, or demonstrative with their feelings. Although you can sometimes appear to others as impressionable, you have powerful emotions and inner strength.

WOMEN WITH VENUS IN LEO: Your friendly and sunny personality often makes you stand out in a crowd. Generous and giving, you know how to make your partner feel special. As you often expect loyalty and devotion from your partners in return, you can become easily offended if they ignore you or behave in an inconsiderate manner. Charming and kind, when you are in love, you can be romantic, dramatic, and passionate.

MEN WITH VENUS IN LEO: A childlike nature suggests that you are versatile and keen on games or being entertained. You are usually attracted to vivacious partners with a benevolent nature. As an extrovert you enjoy being involved in all types of activities where you can assert yourself and show your talents and abilities. Others may recognize your inborn tendencies to lead but are also aware of your vanity or pride.

Nevertheless, generous, kind, and caring, you often show compassion to those less fortunate than yourself.

WOMEN WITH VENUS IN VIRGO: In relationships you can be modest and unassuming but desire perfection. You usually analyze your partnerships until you feel you have understood them to the last little detail in order to improve them. A problem usually arises when you become too critical either of partners or yourself and indulge in being skeptical or fault-finding. As you are modest, others may not be aware of the strong sensuality beneath your well-groomed exterior.

MEN WITH VENUS IN VIRGO: Industrious and well-ordered, you relate to others in a considerate and down-to-earth way. You enjoy giving practical advice and being of service to those you love even in small ways. Being a perfectionist you are drawn to partners with high morals or a strong work ethic. Partners who have strong analytical minds are very attractive to you, particularly if they are also clean and meticulously dressed.

WOMEN WITH VENUS IN LIBRA: Gracious, charming, and sociable with a sense of style, you have no trouble attracting admirers. With your natural diplomatic skills and desire for harmony you usually like to keep the peace and avoid confrontations, but be careful of failing to make a stand when it is necessary. Romantic and easygoing yourself, you are attracted to affectionate and refined individuals who share your love of peace, justice, and fair play.

MEN WITH VENUS IN LIBRA: Courteous and refined, you are attracted to beautiful and elegant people. You are looking for a partner who can share your natural good taste and enjoy an intellectual conversation. Disliking conflict, you may have to be careful not to go along with others just to keep the peace. Your ideal partner will appreciate beauty and the little luxuries of life as well as possess good social skills. You have a strong sense of social etiquette yourself so you need an intelligent and sophisticated partner.

To read all about your Outer Planets and work out how to use your personalized timetable, go to Section Three, page 789.

Your Personalized Timetable

JUPITER BENEFICIAL
1940 6/9 – until 1941 4/18
1942 7/16 – 9/3
1943 1/26 – 4/25
1946 11/2 – 12/20
1947 6/28 – 8/2
1948 12/9 – until 1949 2/18
1952 5/20 – until 1953 3/30
1954 6/29 – 8/14
1958 10/17 – 12/2
1960 11/22 – until 1961 1/31
1964 5/3 – 7/19
1964 11/12 – until 1965 3/8
1966 6/13 – 7/28
1970 10/1 – 11/17
1972 3/10 – 6/11
1972 11/2 – until 1973 1/15
1976 4/17 – 6/26
1978 5/27 – 7/12
1982 1/17 – 4/3
1982 9/13 – 11/1
1984 2/14 – 7/24
1984 10/5 – 12/30
1988 4/1 – 6/8
1989 9/17 – 12/9
1990 5/8 – 6/25
1993 12/22 – until 1994 5/13
1994 8/20 – 10/16
1996 1/26 – 12/14
2000 3/13 – 5/22
2001 8/21 – until 2002 1/20
2002 4/11 – 6/8
2005 12/3 – until 2006 2/11
2006 3/25 – 9/29
2008 1/10 – 4/11
2008 6/6 – 11/25
2011 7/2 – 10/29
2012 2/19 – 5/5

SATURN BENEFICIAL
1940 4/30 – until 1941 6/2
1944 8/29 – 12/18
1945 5/17 – 8/5
1946 3/5 – 4/4
1954 1/11 – 3/27
1954 10/2 – 12/30
1955 5/5 – 9/27
1959 2/26 – 6/6
1959 11/24 – until 1961 1/14
1969 6/13 – 11/1
1970 3/4 – 7/25
1970 10/16 – until 1971 4/9
1974 6/29 – 10/3
1974 11/28 – until 1975 6/11
1983 11/8 – until 1984 11/3
1988 12/28 – until 1990 2/19
1990 7/26 – 11/18
1999 4/15 – until 2000 5/16
2003 8/8 – until 2004 1/21
2004 4/22 – 7/19

URANUS BENEFICIAL
1938 1/1 – until 1940 4/28
1950 8/20 – until 1953 7/1
1976 11/10 – until 1979 9/19
1989 3/20 – until 1993 12/24

NEPTUNE BENEFICIAL
1959 12/12 – until 1965 9/28
1986 2/17 – until 1994 11/18

PLUTO BENEFICIAL
1986 11/22 – until 1991 9/13
2010 3/7 – Continues

JUPITER CHALLENGING
1939 1/23 – 4/1
1941 6/17 – 9/27
1941 10/22 – until 1942 4/30
1947 11/17 – until 1948 1/31

1948 7/9 – 9/22
1950 5/19 – 8/4
1951 1/3 – 3/15
1953 5/31 – 8/16
1953 12/15 – until 1954 4/7
1959 10/31 – until 1960 1/12
1962 4/20 – 9/21
1962 12/6 – until 1963 2/26
1965 5/15 – 7/25
1971 2/22 – 4/21
1971 10/13 – 12/26
1974 3/31 – until 1975 2/9
1977 4/28 – 7/7
1983 1/23 – 6/4
1983 9/21 – 12/11
1986 3/14 – 6/9
1986 8/14 – until 1987 1/21
1988 8/31 – 10/18
1989 4/9 – 6/20
1995 1/3 – 11/25
1998 2/26 – 5/9
1998 9/30 – 12/26
2000 7/27 – 12/5
2001 3/16 – 6/4
2006 12/17 – until 2007 11/8
2010 2/9 – 4/18
2012 7/5 – Continues

SATURN CHALLENGING
1942 6/18 – until 1943 7/19
1944 1/10 – 3/31
1956 11/26 – until 1958 1/16
1958 7/1 – 10/14
1965 2/6 – until 1966 3/21
1971 8/10 – 10/28
1972 4/23 – until 1973 5/23
1986 1/1 – 6/14
1986 9/28 – until 1987 11/25
1994 3/13 – until 1995 4/29
1995 9/16 – until 1996 1/22
2001 5/31 – until 2002 6/30

URANUS CHALLENGING
1943 6/4 – until 1947 6/1
1982 12/2 – until 1986 11/21
2004 4/6 – until 2009 2/15

NEPTUNE CHALLENGING
1972 2/18 – until 1980 11/10

PLUTO CHALLENGING
1997 1/28 – until 2004 11/20

JUPITER SPECIAL
1944 8/19 – 11/6
1945 3/24 – 7/4
1956 8/3 – 10/17
1967 12/2 – until 1968 1/11
1968 7/16 – 10/1
1979 10/28 – until 1980 2/25
1980 6/25 – 9/15
1991 10/7 – until 1992 4/12
1992 5/19 – 8/30
2003 9/20 – until 2004 8/14

SATURN SPECIAL
1948 11/13 – until 1949 1/20
1949 7/28 – until 1950 9/3
1978 9/6 – until 1979 10/12
1980 4/18 – 6/25
2007 10/17 – until 2008 2/24
2008 7/8 – 12/6
2009 1/26 – 8/17

URANUS SPECIAL
1962 11/24 – until 1967 7/13

NEPTUNE SPECIAL
1938 1/1 – until 1939 7/20

PLUTO SPECIAL
1959 10/5 – until 1968 8/2

♍

September 7

Your Personal Powers

Perceptive, analytical, and mentally sharp, your personal powers include a shrewd practicality combined with a reserved sensitivity. Your ruling planet, Mercury, imparts a rational and reflective approach to life, a good sense of values, and good communication skills, whether through conversation or writing. With common sense and latent organizational abilities you empower yourself by being liberal, intuitive, and methodical. Since you benefit from the practical application of your knowledge, your work is particularly important to you. Often a perfectionist, you enjoy performing a job well, and being sensible can help you achieve your big dreams. Usually you prefer to be honest and direct with others, but if you become too self-absorbed you are in danger of losing some of your power to emotional misunderstandings or being stubborn. Trusting your very strong intuition can help you overcome skepticism. Pragmatic, thoughtful, and sincere, with a strong imagination, you can be a determined visionary who can recognize and make the most of opportunities for success.

Your Powers of Attraction in Relationships

Your straightforward approach and thoughtful manner draw others to you. Although you can attract admirers by being charming and sociable, you also have a private side that is reticent at exposing your deep sensitivity. Being emotionally impressionable, you are very sensitive to what is going on around you. Attracted to strong-willed individuals with big ambitions, you have a lot of love to give. With your powerful emotions you need positive channels of self-expression. Buildups of repressed emotions may cause you to become dissatisfied, restless, or sulk. In your relationships it may be important to learn patience and how to communicate your inner doubts or feelings. Nonetheless, you often show your love for others by being supportive or practical and your magnetic charm can always help you win friends and influence people.

Your attractive qualities: hardworking, sensitive, practical, meticulous, idealistic, clever, honest, trusting, psychic, scientific, rational, reflective, perfectionist, communication skills, loving, responsible, creative, methodical, diligent, common sense, sense of duty, imaginative

Your less attractive qualities: rebellious, stubborn, critical, disharmonious, selfish, secretive, skeptical, misunderstood, withdrawn, moody, concealing, confused, detached, too serious, escapism

Your Venus Power

The planet Venus has a great deal of influence on your powers of attraction. Below are four possible Venus types for women and men. To find your Venus you need to go to page 771, where you will find the Venus table and extra information. The planet Mars also affects your powers of attraction. To find your Mars table and interpretation go to page 761.

WOMEN WITH VENUS IN CANCER: Sensitive and understanding, you are sympathetic to other people's emotions and needs. Protective toward those you love, close relationships with your partner, relatives, and friends are important to your sense of well-being. Aware of how easy it is to hurt other people's feelings, you are often indirect and approach delicate issues in a roundabout way. Nevertheless, learning to face facts and not allowing others to exploit your good nature is a lesson just as valuable.

MEN WITH VENUS IN CANCER: You seek a partner who is sympathetic, caring, and protective. Able to be forgiving and compassionate, you want a secure emotional bond in your close relationships. Usually you are drawn to partners who are maternal, unselfish, or demonstrative with their feelings. Although you can sometimes appear to others as impressionable, you have powerful emotions and inner strength.

WOMEN WITH VENUS IN LEO: Your friendly and sunny personality often makes you stand out in a crowd. Generous and giving, you know how to make your partner feel special. As you often expect loyalty and devotion from your partners in return, you can become easily offended if they ignore you or behave in an inconsiderate manner. Charming and kind, when you are in love, you can be romantic, dramatic, and passionate.

MEN WITH VENUS IN LEO: A childlike nature suggests that you are versatile and keen on games or being entertained. You are usually attracted to vivacious partners with a benevolent nature. As an extrovert you enjoy being involved in all types of activities where you can assert yourself and show your talents and abilities. Others may recognize your inborn tendencies to lead but are also aware of your vanity or pride. Nevertheless, generous, kind, and caring, you often show compassion to those less fortunate than yourself.

WOMEN WITH VENUS IN VIRGO: In relationships you can be modest and unassuming but desire perfection. You usually analyze your partnerships until you feel you have understood them to the last little detail in order to improve them. A problem usually arises when you become too critical either of partners or yourself and indulge in being skeptical or fault-finding. As you are modest, others may not be aware of the strong sensuality beneath your well-groomed exterior.

MEN WITH VENUS IN VIRGO: Industrious and well-ordered, you relate to others in a considerate and down-to-earth way. You enjoy giving practical advice and being of service to those you love even in small ways. Being a perfectionist, you are drawn to partners with high morals or a strong work ethic. Partners who have strong analytical minds are very attractive to you, particularly if they are also clean and meticulously dressed.

WOMEN WITH VENUS IN LIBRA: Gracious, charming, and sociable with a sense of style, you have no trouble attracting admirers. With your natural diplomatic skills and desire for harmony you usually like to keep the peace and avoid confrontations, but be careful of failing to take a stand when it is necessary. Romantic and easygoing yourself, you are attracted to affectionate and refined individuals who share your love of peace, justice, and fair play.

MEN WITH VENUS IN LIBRA: Courteous and refined, you are attracted to beautiful and elegant people. You are looking for a partner who can share your natural good taste and enjoy an intellectual conversation. Disliking conflict, you may have to be careful not to go along with others just to keep the peace. Your ideal partner will appreciate beauty and the little luxuries of life as well as possess good social skills. You have a strong sense of social etiquette yourself so you need an intelligent and sophisticated partner.

To read all about your Outer Planets and work out how to use your personalized timetable, go to Section Three, page 789.

Your Personalized Timetable

JUPITER BENEFICIAL
1940 6/13 – 12/15
1941 1/16 – 4/23
1942 7/20 – 9/8
1943 1/19 – 5/2
1946 11/7 – 12/25
1947 6/14 – 8/16
1948 12/13 – until **1949** 2/23
1952 5/25 – until **1953** 4/4
1954 7/4 – 8/19
1958 10/22 – 12/7
1960 11/26 – until **1961** 2/5
1964 5/7 – until **1964** 7/25
1964 11/5 – until **1965** 3/14
1966 6/18 – 8/1
1970 10/6 – 11/21
1972 3/18 – 6/2
1972 11/7 – until **1973** 1/19
1976 4/21 – 7/1
1976 12/22 – until **1977** 2/8
1978 6/1 – 7/16
1982 1/27 – 3/24
1982 9/18 – 11/5
1984 2/19 – 7/15
1984 10/13 – until **1985** 1/3
1988 4/5 – 6/12
1989 9/26 – 11/30
1990 5/13 – 6/30
1993 12/28 – until **1994** 5/5
1994 8/27 – 10/20
1996 1/31 – 12/18
2000 3/18 – 5/26
2001 8/27 – until **2002** 1/12
2002 4/18 – 6/13
2005 12/8 – until **2006** 6/26
2006 7/16 – 10/4
2008 1/14 – 4/27
2008 5/21 – 11/30
2011 7/8 – 10/22
2012 2/24 – 5/9

SATURN BENEFICIAL
1940 5/8 – until **1941** 6/10
1941 12/31 – until **1942** 2/15
1944 9/10 – 12/5
1945 5/25 – 8/13
1946 2/11 – 4/25
1954 2/1 – 3/4
1954 10/11 – until **1955** 1/10
1955 4/22 – 10/7
1959 3/14 – 5/21
1959 12/3 – until **1961** 1/22
1969 6/23 – 10/20
1970 3/14 – 8/12
1970 9/27 – until **1971** 4/17
1974 7/6 – until **1975** 6/19
1983 11/16 – until **1984** 11/11
1989 1/5 – until **1990** 3/1
1990 7/13 – 11/29
1999 4/22 – until **2000** 5/24
2003 8/16 – until **2004** 1/8
2004 5/4 – 7/26

URANUS BENEFICIAL
1938 1/1 – until **1940** 5/15
1950 9/17 – until **1954** 4/14
1976 11/26 – until **1979** 10/8
1990 1/7 – until **1994** 1/10

NEPTUNE BENEFICIAL
1960 2/9 – until **1965** 10/27
1987 1/13 – until **1994** 12/20

PLUTO BENEFICIAL
1986 12/20 – until **1991** 10/14
2011 1/24 – Continues

JUPITER CHALLENGING
1939 1/27 – 4/5
1941 6/22 – until **1942** 5/5
1947 11/21 – until **1948** 2/5
1948 6/30 – 9/30

1950 5/29 – 7/25
1951 1/8 – 3/19
1953 6/4 – 8/22
1953 12/8 – until **1954** 4/13
1959 11/5 – until **1960** 1/17
1962 4/25 – 9/12
1962 12/13 – until **1963** 3/2
1965 5/19 – 7/30
1966 1/23 – 3/10
1971 3/9 – 4/6
1971 10/18 – 12/31
1974 4/4 – until **1975** 2/13
1977 5/2 – 7/11
1983 1/29 – 5/27
1983 9/27 – 12/15
1986 3/18 – 6/21
1986 8/2 – until **1987** 1/26
1989 4/14 – 6/25
1995 1/8 – 7/13
1995 8/22 – 11/29
1998 3/2 – 5/15
1998 9/23 – until **1999** 1/2
2000 8/2 – 11/28
2001 3/23 – 6/8
2006 12/22 – until **2007** 11/13
2010 2/13 – 4/23
2012 7/10 – Continues

SATURN CHALLENGING
1942 6/26 – until **1943** 1/12
1943 3/2 – 7/27
1943 12/28 – until **1944** 4/13
1956 12/4 – until **1958** 1/26
1958 6/17 – 10/26
1965 2/14 – until **1966** 3/29
1971 8/29 – 10/9
1972 5/1 – until **1973** 5/31
1986 1/10 – 5/31
1986 10/9 – until **1987** 12/3
1994 3/21 – 10/17
1994 12/2 – until **1995** 5/9
1995 9/4 – until **1996** 2/1
2001 6/8 – until **2002** 7/8

URANUS CHALLENGING
1943 6/21 – until **1948** 3/8
1982 12/18 – until **1986** 12/7
2004 5/1 – until **2009** 3/4

NEPTUNE CHALLENGING
1972 12/29 – until **1981** 9/16

PLUTO CHALLENGING
1997 12/14 – until **2005** 10/6

JUPITER SPECIAL
1944 8/24 – 11/12
1945 3/16 – 7/11
1956 8/7 – 10/22
1957 5/5 – 6/1
1968 7/21 – 10/5
1979 11/4 – until **1980** 2/18
1980 7/1 – 9/19
1991 10/12 – until **1992** 3/30
1992 6/1 – 9/4
2003 9/25 – until **2004** 8/19

SATURN SPECIAL
1948 12/9 – 12/24
1949 8/5 – until **1950** 9/11
1978 9/13 – until **1979** 10/21
1980 4/2 – 7/10
2007 10/27 – until **2008** 2/12
2008 7/17 – until **2009** 8/25

URANUS SPECIAL
1963 9/6 – until **1967** 8/3

NEPTUNE SPECIAL
2015 1/1 – until **1939** 8/22

PLUTO SPECIAL
1959 11/28 – until **1968** 8/31

♍

September 8

Your Personal Powers

A shrewd business sense, quick wit, and a creative approach to life are among your many personal powers. Your ruling planet, Mercury, bestows on you a keen intelligence and a strong need to express your original ideas either orally, in writing, or through research. Ambitious and innovative, you gain power from your genial manner and enterprising nature. Although you are usually lighthearted, you possess a more serious side that can lead you to the exploration or academic study of deeper subjects. Although you can be hardworking and meticulous, if you take life too seriously, you may lose some of your power through anxiety or worry. Often pragmatic and concerned about material security, you are usually responsible and take pride in your work. Although sometimes rebellious, you possess an inner need for peace and harmony that emphasizes the importance of your home. Alternatively, you may be inspired to develop artistic or musical gifts. Bright and articulate, with intuitive insight and a unique point of view, you have the potential for outstanding success.

Your Powers of Attraction in Relationships

Friendly, clever, and charming, you can attract others with your original ideas, individualism, and ability to adapt to different social situations. Being a natural psychologist you can understand intuitively what motivates others. At your best when you are spontaneous and creative, you enjoy company and a chance to shine. Although being a perfectionist implies that you are idealistic, in love it may be hard for others to live up to your high expectations. If so, you may have to learn how to implement your sense of fairness to avoid sometimes appearing too cold, critical, or domineering. When positive and dynamic, however, you can be liberal and free in the expression of your love. Usually dependable and confident, you seek a partner who will understand your need for security and match your intelligence.

Your attractive qualities: leadership, friendly, creative, humorous, sociable, thoroughness, determined, hardworking, sharp mind, humanitarian, authoritative, responsible, problem solver, business sense, protective, good judge of values, individuality

Your less attractive qualities: impatient, wasteful, worry, rebellious, intolerant, indecision, restless, power plays, too critical, domineering, too serious, easily discouraged, lack of planning, controlling behavior

Your Venus Power

The planet Venus has a great deal of influence on your powers of attraction. Below are four possible Venus types for women and men. To find your Venus you need to go to page 771, where you will find the Venus table and extra information. The planet Mars also affects your powers of attraction. To find your Mars table and interpretation go to page 761.

WOMEN WITH VENUS IN LEO: You possess the wonderful ability to project your warm and sunny personality and keep others happily entertained. Loving attention yourself, you seek a partner who can appreciate you, be supportive, and give you positive feedback. Proud, with a natural regal air, you expect respect from your partners but are willing to be loyal and supportive in exchange. Although sometimes a little self-centered, you know how to make your partner feel special.

MEN WITH VENUS IN LEO: Enthusiastic, playful, and kind, you can be benevolent with those you love. Warm, romantic, and self-expressive, you adore the drama of love or having fun with your friends. Usually you are attracted to partners with a warm and generous nature. Although you can be a confident and charismatic partner, you may need to develop humility in order to stop pride or arrogance from marring your relationships.

WOMEN WITH VENUS IN VIRGO: Intelligent and discriminating, you are usually drawn to polite and refined individuals. As a perfectionist, you may be keen to analyze and criticize yourself but be careful of continually going over your partner's shortcomings. By focusing on how you can make positive improvements in yourself and in your relationships, you avoid becoming skeptical or confused. You empower yourself when you display kind and caring concern for the well-being of loved ones and spontaneously offer your practical assistance.

MEN WITH VENUS IN VIRGO: A love of order usually indicates that you are attracted to refined individuals with analytical or practical abilities. You and your partner may be working together or serving similar causes. As you constantly analyze partnerships in order to improve them, you are likely to use former relationships as a point of reference and compare them to your present partner. As you are helpful and

kind, others usually rely on your good judgment and often turn to you for advice or practical assistance.

WOMEN WITH VENUS IN LIBRA: Attractive, refined, and conscious of the needs of others, you usually desire harmonious relationships. As a peacemaker with good negotiating skills, you can smooth out difficulties with others but your dislike of confrontation may sometimes leave you refusing to take a stand or compromising too many of your own needs. Courteous, stylish, and charming with polished social skills, you are an expert at relating to others in a gracious and civilized manner.

MEN WITH VENUS IN LIBRA: As a sociable and friendly individual with an eye for beauty, you are amorous and charming. You are a natural gentleman, and your ideal partner usually has an elegant appearance, artistic appreciation, and good taste. Your relationships benefit when you resist the temptation to take the easy way out or put too much emphasis on vanity and high living. Intellectual and naturally refined, you seek a loving partner who can share your romantic and sophisticated aspirations.

WOMEN WITH VENUS IN SCORPIO: Your strength and power is in your ability to love both deeply and sensitively. For you, love and desire go hand in hand. As you feel so deeply, you often keep your sensitivity or vulnerability hidden from others in order to keep some control in your relationships. You are more likely to prefer a few very close loyal friends than many superficial acquaintances. In relationships your sensual nature and magnetic intensity can easily attract others.

MEN WITH VENUS IN SCORPIO: You are attracted to partners with deep and powerful emotions or individuals you find intriguing. Your gift for creating smoke screens to maintain secrecy around your feelings can conceal your inner sensitivity and vulnerability. Nevertheless, you are looking for a partner who can pierce your defenses and understand you at a very deep level. Needing a relationship with a powerful sexual connection, you thrive on emotional intensity.

To read all about your Outer Planets and work out how to use your personalized timetable, go to Section Three, page 789.

Your Personalized Timetable

JUPITER BENEFICIAL
1940 6/18 – 12/2
1941 1/29 – 4/27
1942 7/25 – 9/14
1943 1/11 – 5/9
1946 11/11 – 12/30
1947 6/4 – 8/25
1948 12/17 – until 1949 2/27
1949 8/27 – 10/10
1952 5/29 – until 1953 4/9
1954 7/8 – 8/23
1955 3/5 – 3/28
1958 10/26 – 12/12
1960 12/1 – until 1961 2/9
1964 5/12 – 8/1
1964 10/28 – until 1965 3/19
1966 6/22 – 8/6
1970 10/10 – 11/25
1972 3/27 – 5/23
1972 11/12 – until 1973 1/23
1976 4/25 – 7/6
1976 12/12 – until 1977 2/18
1978 6/5 – 7/20
1982 2/12 – 3/7
1982 9/23 – 11/10
1984 2/25 – 7/7
1984 10/20 – until 1985 1/8
1988 4/9 – 6/17
1989 10/7 – 11/19
1990 5/18 – 7/4
1994 1/3 – 4/27
1994 9/2 – 10/25
1996 2/5 – 12/23
2000 3/22 – 5/30
2001 9/2 – until 2002 1/5
2002 4/25 – 6/18
2005 12/13 – until 2006 6/8
2006 8/3 – 10/9
2008 1/19 – 12/5
2011 7/15 – 10/15
2012 3/1 – 5/13

SATURN BENEFICIAL
1940 5/16 – until 1941 6/19
1941 12/13 – until 1942 3/4
1944 9/26 – 11/19
1945 6/3 – 8/22
1946 1/28 – 5/9
1954 10/19 – until 1955 1/24
1955 4/6 – 10/16
1959 12/11 – until 1961 1/31
1969 7/5 – 10/7
1970 3/23 – until 1971 4/25
1974 7/14 – until 1975 6/27
1983 11/24 – until 1984 6/20
1984 8/4 – 11/20
1989 1/14 – until 1990 3/12
1990 6/29 – 12/8
1999 4/30 – until 2000 5/31
2003 8/26 – 12/27
2004 5/14 – 8/3

URANUS BENEFICIAL
1938 1/1 – until 1941 3/18
1951 7/9 – until 1954 5/17
1976 12/14 – until 1979 10/25
1990 1/24 – until 1994 11/12

NEPTUNE BENEFICIAL
1960 12/5 – until 1966 9/22
1987 2/11 – until 1995 11/8

PLUTO BENEFICIAL
1987 11/8 – until 1991 11/8
2011 3/1 – Continues

JUPITER CHALLENGING
1939 2/1 – 4/9
1941 6/26 – until 1942 5/10
1947 11/25 – until 1948 2/11
1948 6/22 – 10/7

1950 6/12 – 7/11
1951 1/13 – 3/23
1953 6/9 – 8/29
1953 11/30 – until 1954 4/19
1959 11/9 – until 1960 1/21
1962 5/1 – 9/5
1962 12/20 – until 1963 3/6
1965 5/23 – 8/4
1966 1/12 – 3/21
1971 10/23 – until 1972 1/4
1974 4/9 – until 1975 2/17
1977 5/7 – 7/16
1983 2/4 – 5/19
1983 10/3 – 12/19
1986 3/22 – until 1987 1/31
1989 4/19 – 6/29
1995 1/13 – 7/1
1995 9/4 – 12/4
1998 3/6 – 5/21
1998 9/15 – until 1999 1/8
2000 8/8 – 11/21
2001 3/29 – 6/12
2006 12/26 – until 2007 11/18
2010 2/17 – 4/27
2012 7/14 – Continues

SATURN CHALLENGING
1942 7/4 – 12/26
1943 3/19 – 8/6
1943 12/16 – until 1944 4/23
1956 12/12 – until 1958 2/6
1958 6/4 – 11/5
1965 2/22 – until 1966 4/6
1966 11/12 – 12/11
1972 5/9 – until 1973 6/7
1986 1/21 – 5/18
1986 10/20 – until 1987 12/12
1994 3/30 – 9/28
1994 12/20 – until 1995 5/22
1995 8/21 – until 1996 2/10
2001 6/16 – until 2002 7/16
2003 1/20 – 3/26

URANUS CHALLENGING
1943 7/10 – until 1948 4/17
1983 1/4 – until 1987 10/1
2005 3/3 – until 2010 1/1

NEPTUNE CHALLENGING
1973 2/3 – until 1981 11/5

PLUTO CHALLENGING
1998 1/11 – until 2005 11/12

JUPITER SPECIAL
1944 8/28 – 11/18
1945 3/9 – 7/18
1956 8/12 – 10/27
1957 4/20 – 6/17
1968 7/26 – 10/10
1979 11/11 – until 1980 2/10
1980 7/7 – 9/24
1991 10/18 – until 1992 3/20
1992 6/11 – 9/8
2003 9/29 – until 2004 8/23

SATURN SPECIAL
1949 8/13 – until 1950 9/19
1978 9/21 – until 1979 5/4
1979 5/15 – 10/30
1980 3/20 – 7/22
2007 11/9 – until 2008 1/29
2008 7/26 – until 2009 9/2

URANUS SPECIAL
1963 9/22 – until 1967 8/21

NEPTUNE SPECIAL
1938 11/28 – until 1940 7/11

PLUTO SPECIAL
1960 10/6 – until 1969 7/24

♍

September 9

Your Personal Powers

Analytical, determined, and smart, you are a friendly and articulate individual with enterprising ideas. Your ruling planet, Mercury, bestows you with intelligence and excellent communication skills. You gain power from the combination of your active imagination, shrewd practicality, and determination to succeed. As a good strategist when inspired, you possess the energy and drive necessary to achieve your objectives. Equally, you also have an intuitive sensitivity that can lead you to explore humanitarian principles and encourage a generosity of spirit. It is important therefore to have a well-balanced outlook, as your desire for material security or recognition may be as strong as your desire for truth and high ideals. Be careful not to lose some of your power in the pursuit of material achievement or escape into unrealistic fantasies. Fortunately, you possess an innate modesty, diplomacy, and a gift for making contacts that can help you connect or work with others to ensure your success. When motivated and focused, you gain power and prosperity from your enthusiasm, sociability, and active single-mindedness.

Your Powers of Attraction in Relationships

Being gregarious, friendly, and aware, you attract popularity. Idealistic and giving, you can also be romantic and generous with those you love. You are drawn to people with intelligence and determination or those of power and influence. Although at times you can be extremely sensitive to the feelings of others, on other occasions you are very assertive, strong-willed, and businesslike. Although compassionate, creative, and imaginative, if you do not use your natural discriminative powers your idealism may lead to self-deception. By maintaining a balanced attitude and learning to stay detached, you become more philosophical and improve your relationships. Since you need recognition, it is important that, although you are loyal and concerned for the welfare of others, your partners do not take you for granted. A good friend and companion, you are loyal and concerned for the welfare of others.

Your attractive qualities: idealistic, humanitarian, creative, sensitive, responsible, focused, magnetic, writing potential, giving, realistic, modest, detached, business sense, good contacts, lucky, popular, benevolence, compassionate, perfectionist, intelligent, hardworking

Your less attractive qualities: frustrated, nervous, rebellious, insecure, worry, selfish, bossy, impractical, stubborn, ungrounded fears about money, self-delusion, disappointed

Your Venus Power

The planet Venus has a great deal of influence on your powers of attraction. Below are four possible Venus types for women and men. To find your Venus you need to go to page 771, where you will find the Venus table and extra information. The planet Mars also affects your powers of attraction. To find your Mars table and interpretation go to page 761.

WOMEN WITH VENUS IN LEO: Warm and playful with a touch of the dramatic, you enjoy the company of generous or strong individuals who can share your sense of fun. Although there are advantages to your being strong-willed, in your relationships you need to resist being bossy as it can cause resentment. With your wonderful mixture of regal authority and childlike wonder, you love to keep others entertained and amused.

MEN WITH VENUS IN LEO: Sociable and outgoing, you are kind and generous with those you love. Looking for a relationship that can be fun and entertaining, you need a playmate who can share your enthusiasm and high spirits. Your pride, however, often stops you from associating with lovers or partners you see as beneath you. As you desire someone who can appreciate your sense of the dramatic, you are often attracted to people with strong personalities.

WOMEN WITH VENUS IN VIRGO: Intelligent and discriminating, you are usually drawn to polite and refined individuals. As a perfectionist, you may be keen to analyze and criticize yourself but be careful of continually going over your partner's shortcomings. By focusing on how you can make positive improvements in yourself and in your relationships, you avoid becoming skeptical or confused. You empower yourself when you display kind and caring concern for the well-being of loved ones and spontaneously offer your practical assistance.

MEN WITH VENUS IN VIRGO: A love of order usually means you are attracted to refined individuals with analytical or practical abilities. You and your partner may be working together or serving similar causes. As you constantly analyze partnerships in order to improve them, you are likely to use former relationships as a point of reference and compare

them to your present partner. As you are helpful and kind, others usually rely on your good judgment and often turn to you for advice or practical assistance.

WOMEN WITH VENUS IN LIBRA: Usually you are attractive and sociable with an easygoing manner. Your love of beauty, harmony, and pleasure implies that you are a romantic with a desire for love and affection. Once in a relationship you need to learn to negotiate your position rather than adapt to the wishes of others and compromise just to keep the peace. Nevertheless, your advanced social skills and strong sense of fair play can help you succeed in any social or romantic situation.

MEN WITH VENUS IN LIBRA: Your good social skills, charming personality, and refined manner usually make you attractive to the opposite sex. Equally, you desire a sophisticated partner with grace, elegance, and a strong sense of style. Although you have the ability to be persuasive and irresistible to others, avoid manipulative love games. Nevertheless, your natural diplomacy and sense of fair play help you to relate to people in all social situations. With your love of balance and harmony, you seek a partner who is also moderate, easygoing, and loving.

WOMEN WITH VENUS IN SCORPIO: With a natural psychic gift for penetrating the feelings of others, you can often help partners transform emotional challenges or sexual difficulties. When you fall in love your strong feelings of determination give you a potent force that others find attractive and seductive. Although you know what really turns people on, your most profound desire is usually for the deepness and closeness of real love and intimacy in an enduring relationship.

MEN WITH VENUS IN SCORPIO: In relationships you possess a sensitive understanding of your partner's deeper nature. Although you are strongly attached to those you love, you may have to be careful that your feelings do not turn into jealousy or possessiveness. When you fall in love it is often with power and an emotional intensity. You are attracted to partners who can share your passion and display strong feelings of sexuality like your own.

To read all about your Outer Planets and work out how to use your personalized timetable, go to Section Three, page 789.

♍

Your Personalized Timetable

JUPITER BENEFICIAL
1940 6/23 – 11/22
1941 2/7 – 5/1
1942 7/29 – 9/21
1943 1/4 – 5/15
1946 11/15 – until 1947 1/5
1947 5/27 – 9/2
1948 12/22 – until 1949 3/5
1949 8/16 – 10/21
1952 6/2 – until 1953 4/13
1954 7/12 – 8/28
1955 2/17 – 4/13
1958 10/31 – 12/17
1960 12/5 – until 1961 2/13
1964 5/16 – 8/10
1964 10/20 – until 1965 3/25
1966 6/26 – 8/10
1970 10/15 – 11/30
1972 4/12 – 5/7
1972 11/17 – until 1973 1/27
1976 4/29 – 7/11
1976 12/3 – until 1977 2/26
1978 6/10 – 7/25
1982 9/28 – 11/14
1984 3/2 – 6/29
1984 10/27 – until 1985 1/12
1988 4/13 – 6/21
1990 5/23 – 7/8
1994 1/10 – 4/20
1994 9/9 – 10/29
1996 2/10 – 8/22
1996 9/16 – 12/27
2000 3/27 – 6/3
2001 9/8 – 12/28
2002 5/1 – 6/22
2005 12/19 – until 2006 5/29
2006 8/13 – 10/14
2008 1/23 – 12/10
2011 7/23 – 10/7
2012 3/6 – 5/17

SATURN BENEFICIAL
1940 5/24 – 12/26
1941 1/23 – 6/28
1941 11/30 – until 1942 3/16
1945 6/11 – 8/31
1946 1/16 – 5/20
1954 10/27 – until 1955 2/19
1955 3/11 – 10/24
1959 12/20 – until 1961 2/8
1961 8/26 – 10/29
1969 7/20 – 9/22
1970 3/31 – until 1971 5/3
1974 7/21 – until 1975 7/4
1983 12/3 – until 1984 5/31
1984 8/23 – 11/28
1989 1/22 – 8/10
1989 10/12 – until 1990 3/26
1990 6/14 – 12/18
1999 5/7 – until 2000 6/8
2001 1/21 – 1/28
2003 9/6 – 12/15
2004 5/23 – 8/11
2005 2/22 – 4/18

URANUS BENEFICIAL
1938 1/1 – until 1941 4/9
1951 7/25 – until 1954 6/7
1977 1/6 – until 1979 11/10
1990 2/12 – until 1994 12/6

NEPTUNE BENEFICIAL
1961 1/13 – until 1966 10/23
1988 1/8 – until 1995 12/15

PLUTO BENEFICIAL
1987 12/2 – until 1992 9/27
2012 1/22 – Continues

JUPITER CHALLENGING
1939 2/5 – 4/13
1941 6/30 – until 1942 5/14
1947 11/30 – until 1948 2/17
1948 6/15 – 10/14

1951 1/18 – 3/27
1953 6/13 – 9/6
1953 11/22 – until 1954 4/24
1959 11/14 – until 1960 1/26
1960 8/7 – 9/3
1962 5/7 – 8/28
1962 12/26 – until 1963 3/10
1965 5/27 – 8/9
1966 1/3 – 3/29
1971 10/28 – until 1972 1/8
1974 4/14 – 10/27
1974 11/10 – until 1975 2/21
1977 5/11 – 7/20
1983 2/12 – 5/11
1983 10/9 – 12/23
1986 3/27 – until 1987 2/4
1989 4/24 – 7/3
1995 1/18 – 6/21
1995 9/13 – 12/8
1998 3/10 – 5/27
1998 9/8 – until 1999 1/14
2000 8/15 – 11/13
2001 4/3 – 6/17
2006 12/31 – until 2007 11/22
2010 2/21 – 5/2
2010 10/31 – 12/7
2012 7/19 – 12/29

SATURN CHALLENGING
1942 7/13 – 12/13
1943 3/31 – 8/16
1943 12/4 – until 1944 5/3
1956 12/21 – until 1957 7/20
1957 9/3 – until 1958 2/18
1958 5/21 – 11/15
1965 3/2 – until 1966 4/15
1966 10/20 – until 1967 1/2
1972 5/16 – until 1973 6/15
1986 2/2 – 5/4
1986 10/29 – until 1987 12/20
1994 4/8 – 9/14
1995 1/2 – 6/8
1995 8/3 – until 1996 2/18
2001 6/23 – until 2002 2/1
2002 2/14 – 7/24
2003 1/5 – 4/9

URANUS CHALLENGING
1943 8/2 – until 1948 5/9
1983 1/25 – until 1987 10/29
2005 3/20 – until 2010 1/29

NEPTUNE CHALLENGING
1973 12/24 – until 1981 12/3

PLUTO CHALLENGING
1998 12/4 – until 2006 9/7

JUPITER SPECIAL
1944 9/2 – 11/25
1945 3/1 – 7/24
1956 8/17 – 11/2
1957 4/9 – 6/27
1968 7/31 – 10/15
1979 11/19 – until 1980 2/2
1980 7/13 – 9/28
1991 10/23 – until 1992 3/12
1992 6/19 – 9/13
2003 10/4 – until 2004 8/28

SATURN SPECIAL
1949 8/21 – until 1950 9/27
1978 9/29 – until 1979 4/5
1979 6/12 – 11/9
1980 3/8 – 8/1
2007 11/26 – until 2008 1/11
2008 8/3 – until 2009 9/10

URANUS SPECIAL
1963 10/9 – until 1967 9/6

NEPTUNE SPECIAL
1938 1/1 – until 1940 8/16

PLUTO SPECIAL
1960 11/26 – until 1969 8/25

September 10

Your Personal Powers

Independent and strong-willed, your personal powers include natural leadership ability and strong determination. Your ruling planet, Mercury, bestows on you good analytical skills and persuasive speech. As a practical visionary you gain power by combining your idealism, shrewd practicality, and strategic skills. Although you possess a natural sense of authority, you lose some of your power if you become impatient, obstinate, or critical. On the other extreme, you can be very generous and understanding with those you choose to assist or encourage. Bold and committed when interested in a project, you gain power from your ability to be decisive, hardworking, and insightful. Being ambitious, with a pioneering spirit and able to utilize opportunities, you can be enthusiastic in promoting your favorite people or ideas. Your strong motivation and determination can certainly help you manifest your desires, but you may find yourself happiest when you include others in your plans or vision for the future. You can be highly persuasive while being modest yet purposeful.

Your Powers of Attraction in Relationships

Your strong will and determination can attract and influence others. With your potent desires and emotions you may need to resist rushing into romantic situations you may later question. Often mentally quick on the uptake yet restless, you prefer a partner who recognizes your desire for action, mental stimulation, and changing moods. Being independent, you may be attracted to a partner who is liberal and thoughtful. As you are very practical, material considerations may also influence your choice of partner. By developing patience and tolerance with your loved ones you can combine your idealism and pragmatism to create good relationships. An interest in people gives you a deeper insight into others and helps you channel your strong feelings into positive and beneficial situations for those around you.

Your attractive qualities: leadership, creative, progressive, forceful, optimistic, strong convictions, responsible, writing potential, confident, people skills, competitive, independent, gregarious, intuitive, sensitive, proud, business sense, courageous, resourceful

Your less attractive qualities: domineering, jealous, too proud, antagonistic, lack of restraint, arrogant, selfish, inner tensions, emotionally changeable, rebellious, impatient, critical

Your Venus Power

The planet Venus has a great deal of influence on your powers of attraction. Below are four possible Venus types for women and men. To find your Venus you need to go to page 771, where you will find the Venus table and extra information. The planet Mars also affects your powers of attraction. To find your Mars table and interpretation go to page 761.

WOMEN WITH VENUS IN LEO: Your friendly and sunny personality often makes you stand out in a crowd. Generous and giving, you know how to make your partner feel special. As you often expect loyalty and devotion from your partners in return, you can become easily offended if they ignore you or behave in an inconsiderate manner. Charming and kind, when you are in love you can be romantic, dramatic, and passionate.

MEN WITH VENUS IN LEO: A childlike nature suggests that you are versatile and keen on games or being entertained. You are usually attracted to vivacious partners with a benevolent nature. As an extrovert you enjoy being involved in all types of activities where you can assert yourself and show your talents and abilities. Others may recognize your inborn tendencies to lead but are also aware of your vanity or pride. Nevertheless, generous, kind, and caring, you often show compassion to those less fortunate than yourself.

WOMEN WITH VENUS IN VIRGO: Articulate and straightforward in your relationships, you attract others with your genuine concern for their well-being. By being understanding and a good listener, you are able to show your love and friendship. With your analytical approach to relationships, however, you may have to be careful of becoming too matter-of-fact. You often display your concern for the welfare of others by your willingness to offer practical help and assistance. You usually seek a partner who is willing to work as hard on relationships as you are.

MEN WITH VENUS IN VIRGO: Although you are constantly analyzing your relationships in order to understand and improve them, you may nevertheless need to refrain from continuously mulling over issues that can cause anxiety. You are happiest when you are able to help your loved ones in practical ways and forget yourself in your willingness to be

of service to others. You seek a partner who has high standards and can be as pragmatic and hardworking as yourself. Ideally they should also be impeccably dressed with a fine analytical mind.

WOMEN WITH VENUS IN LIBRA: Gracious, charming, and sociable with a sense of style, you have no trouble attracting admirers. With your natural diplomatic skills and desire for harmony you usually like to keep the peace and avoid confrontations, but be careful of failing to take a stand when it is necessary. Romantic and easygoing yourself, you are attracted to affectionate and refined individuals who share your love of peace, justice, and fair play.

MEN WITH VENUS IN LIBRA: Courteous and refined, you are attracted to beautiful and elegant people. You are looking for a partner who can share your natural good taste and enjoy an intellectual conversation. Disliking conflict, you may have to be careful not to go along with others just to keep the peace. Your ideal partner will appreciate beauty and the little luxuries of life as well as possess good social skills. You have a strong sense of social etiquette yourself so you need an intelligent and sophisticated partner.

WOMEN WITH VENUS IN SCORPIO: Loving and passionate, you are often sensitive with deep feelings and strong powers of attraction. A love for the truth coupled with a tendency to be suspicious can be an influence that motivates you to delve deep into the activities of your partner. When in love or in a relationship that matters, you will often bend over backward to cooperate. Although loyal, guard against losing sight of your own needs and desires.

MEN WITH VENUS IN SCORPIO: As you are emotionally intense and passionate, personal relationships are probably a major factor in your own transformation. Being sensitive yet loyal, you are usually attracted to forceful partners who can express themselves intimately but intensely. Rather than seek easy and simple relationships, you are drawn to partners who act as a catalyst for your own internal changes. Through your relationships with your partners you can unravel your own motives and understand your deep-seated feelings or emotional insecurities.

To read all about your Outer Planets and work out how to use your personalized timetable, go to Section Three, page 789.

Your Personalized Timetable

JUPITER BENEFICIAL
1940 6/29 – 11/14
1941 2/14 – 5/5
1942 8/3 – 9/28
1942 12/28 – until 1943 5/21
1946 11/20 – until 1947 1/11
1947 5/19 – 9/9
1948 12/26 – until 1949 3/10
1949 8/7 – 10/30
1952 6/7 – until 1953 4/18
1954 7/17 – 9/3
1955 2/7 – 4/23
1958 11/4 – 12/21
1960 12/10 – until 1961 2/18
1964 5/20 – 8/20
1964 10/10 – until 1965 3/30
1966 7/1 – 8/15
1970 10/20 – 12/4
1972 11/22 – until 1973 2/1
1976 5/3 – 7/17
1976 11/26 – until 1977 3/5
1978 6/14 – 7/29
1982 10/3 – 11/18
1984 3/9 – 6/22
1984 11/2 – until 1985 1/16
1988 4/17 – 6/26
1990 5/28 – 7/13
1994 1/17 – 4/11
1994 9/14 – 11/3
1996 2/15 – 8/6
1996 10/1 – 12/31
2000 3/31 – 6/7
2001 9/14 – 12/21
2002 5/7 – 6/26
2005 12/24 – until 2006 5/20
2006 8/22 – 10/18
2008 1/28 – 12/14
2011 8/2 – 9/27
2012 3/11 – 5/21

SATURN BENEFICIAL
1940 6/1 – 12/4
1941 2/14 – 7/7
1941 11/17 – until 1942 3/27
1945 6/18 – 9/10
1946 1/4 – 5/29
1954 11/4 – until 1955 11/2
1959 12/28 – until 1961 2/17
1961 8/9 – 11/14
1970 4/8 – until 1971 5/10
1974 7/29 – until 1975 3/3
1975 3/25 – 7/12
1983 12/12 – until 1984 5/17
1984 9/6 – 12/6
1985 6/28 – 8/21
1989 1/31 – 7/24
1989 10/28 – until 1990 4/16
1990 5/23 – 12/26
1999 5/15 – until 2000 6/16
2000 12/23 – until 2001 2/26
2003 9/19 – 12/1
2004 5/31 – 8/19
2005 2/6 – 5/4

URANUS BENEFICIAL
1938 1/1 – until 1941 4/27
1951 8/12 – until 1954 6/24
1977 11/3 – until 1980 9/4
1990 3/9 – until 1994 12/24

NEPTUNE BENEFICIAL
1961 12/1 – until 1967 9/14
1988 2/5 – until 1996 10/23

PLUTO BENEFICIAL
1988 1/3 – until 1992 10/25
2012 2/26 – Continues

JUPITER CHALLENGING
1939 2/9 – 4/18
1941 7/5 – until 1942 5/19
1947 12/4 – until 1948 2/23
1948 6/7 – 10/20

1951 1/22 – 3/31
1953 6/17 – 9/15
1953 11/13 – until 1954 4/29
1959 11/18 – until 1960 1/31
1960 7/22 – 9/18
1962 5/14 – 8/21
1963 1/1 – 3/14
1965 6/1 – 8/15
1965 12/27 – until 1966 4/6
1971 11/2 – until 1972 1/13
1974 4/19 – 10/9
1974 11/28 – until 1975 2/26
1977 5/15 – 7/25
1983 2/20 – 5/2
1983 10/14 – 12/28
1986 3/31 – until 1987 2/9
1989 4/28 – 7/8
1995 1/24 – 6/13
1995 9/21 – 12/12
1998 3/14 – 6/3
1998 8/31 – until 1999 1/19
2000 8/23 – 11/5
2001 4/8 – 6/21
2007 1/5 – 11/26
2010 2/25 – 5/7
2010 10/19 – 12/19
2012 7/25 – 12/20

SATURN CHALLENGING
1942 7/22 – 12/1
1943 4/10 – 8/28
1943 11/21 – until 1944 5/11
1956 12/29 – until 1957 6/30
1957 9/22 – until 1958 3/7
1958 5/3 – 11/24
1965 3/10 – until 1966 4/24
1966 10/5 – until 1967 1/15
1972 5/24 – until 1973 6/22
1986 2/19 – 4/16
1986 11/7 – until 1987 12/28
1994 4/18 – 9/1
1995 1/12 – until 1996 2/27
2001 7/1 – until 2002 1/5
2002 3/13 – 8/2
2002 12/24 – until 2003 4/21

URANUS CHALLENGING
1944 6/1 – until 1948 5/27
1983 3/3 – until 1987 11/17
2005 4/8 – until 2010 2/18

NEPTUNE CHALLENGING
1974 1/25 – until 1982 10/30

PLUTO CHALLENGING
1998 12/30 – until 2006 11/5

JUPITER SPECIAL
1944 9/6 – 12/3
1945 2/21 – 7/30
1956 8/21 – 11/7
1957 4/1 – 7/6
1968 8/5 – 10/20
1979 11/29 – until 1980 1/23
1980 7/18 – 10/3
1991 10/29 – until 1992 3/4
1992 6/26 – 9/17
2003 10/9 – until 2004 4/26
2004 5/14 – 9/2

SATURN SPECIAL
1949 8/29 – until 1950 10/5
1978 10/8 – until 1979 3/21
1979 6/27 – 11/20
1980 2/24 – 8/10
2008 8/12 – until 2009 9/18

URANUS SPECIAL
1963 10/29 – until 1967 9/22

NEPTUNE SPECIAL
1938 1/1 – until 1941 6/28

PLUTO SPECIAL
1961 10/7 – until 1970 7/12

September 11

SUN: VIRGO · DECANATE: CAPRICORN/SATURN · DEGREE: 17°45′–19° VIRGO · MODE: MUTABLE · ELEMENT: EARTH

Your Personal Powers

Strong will and determination, combined with intelligence and organizational skills, are just some of your personal powers. Your ruling planet, Mercury, provides you with sharp analytical abilities as well as good communication skills, making you articulate and precise. You gain power from the combination of your rationality, practical approach, and intuitive sensitivity. Although you are often regarded as a realist, you possess sensitivity and high ideals. Resourceful and hardworking with natural leadership ability, you prefer to be in charge or work independently. Although you usually appear to others as self-confident, you can sometimes lose some of your power to insecurity and self-doubt or skepticism. On other occasions, however, you can go to the other extreme and become domineering. Nevertheless, receptive and broad-minded, a latent humanitarian streak can give you satisfaction from giving practical help and assistance to others. Although observant and pragmatic, you also possess an unconventional side to your nature. The combination of your ingenuity and inner strength can bring you success.

Your Powers of Attraction in Relationships

Naturally dramatic, others are attracted to your sharp intelligence and creativity. Observant, you can utilize your mental agility to be witty and entertaining. You often enjoy debates, solving problems, and friendly mental rivalry. Although you are strong-willed and independent, you realize the advantages of being in a partnership or team situation, so your relationships are especially important to you. You are attracted to sensible, stable, and honest people who are responsible and affectionate. Being pragmatic and straightforward, you enjoy being of practical help to those you love. As hidden doubts may sometimes affect your relationships, you benefit from communicating your deeper feelings rather than just your opinions. Security-conscious, you usually like the stability of a long-term relationship and can be a loyal, loving, and dependable partner.

Your attractive qualities: focused, objective, clever, leadership ability, analytical, confident, enthusiastic, inspirational, good communication skills, broad-minded, idealistic, intuitive, healing ability, visionary, practical, writing potential, humanitarian, psychic

Your less attractive qualities: superiority complex, dishonest, aimless, too emotional, easily hurt, selfish, too critical, lack of clarity, overanxious, hidden fears, dominating, impractical, high-strung

Your Venus Power

The planet Venus has a great deal of influence on your powers of attraction. Below are four possible Venus types for women and men. To find your Venus you need to go to page 771, where you will find the Venus table and extra information. The planet Mars also affects your powers of attraction. To find your Mars table and interpretation go to page 761.

WOMEN WITH VENUS IN LEO: Your friendly and sunny personality often makes you stand out in a crowd. Generous and giving, you know how to make your partner feel special. As you often expect loyalty and devotion from your partners in return, you can become easily offended if they ignore you or behave in an inconsiderate manner. Charming and kind, when you are in love you can be romantic, dramatic, and passionate.

MEN WITH VENUS IN LEO: A childlike nature suggests that you are versatile and keen on games or being entertained. You are usually attracted to vivacious partners with a benevolent nature. As an extrovert you enjoy being involved in all types of activities where you can assert yourself and show your talents and abilities. Others may recognize your inborn tendencies to lead but are also aware of your vanity or pride. Nevertheless, generous, kind, and caring, you often show compassion to those less fortunate than yourself.

WOMEN WITH VENUS IN VIRGO: In relationships you can be modest and unassuming but desire perfection. You usually analyze your partnerships until you feel you have understood them to the last little detail in order to improve them. A problem usually arises when you become too critical either of partners or yourself and indulge in being skeptical or faultfinding. As you are modest, others may not be aware of the strong sensuality beneath your well-groomed exterior.

MEN WITH VENUS IN VIRGO: Industrious and well-ordered, you relate to others in a considerate and down-to-earth way. You enjoy giving practical advice and being of service to those you love even in small ways. Being a perfectionist, you are drawn to partners with high morals or a strong work ethic. Partners who have strong analytical minds are

very attractive to you, particularly if they are also clean and meticulously dressed.

WOMEN WITH VENUS IN LIBRA: Gracious, charming, and sociable with a sense of style, you have no trouble attracting admirers. With your natural diplomatic skills and desire for harmony you usually like to keep the peace and avoid confrontations, but be careful of failing to take a stand when it is necessary. Romantic and easygoing yourself, you are attracted to affectionate and refined individuals who share your love of peace, justice, and fair play.

MEN WITH VENUS IN LIBRA: Courteous and refined, you are attracted to beautiful and elegant people. You are looking for a partner who can share your natural good taste and enjoy an intellectual conversation. Disliking conflict, you may have to be careful not to go along with others just to keep the peace. Your ideal partner will appreciate beauty and the little luxuries of life as well as possess good social skills. You have a strong sense of social etiquette yourself so you need an intelligent and sophisticated partner.

WOMEN WITH VENUS IN SCORPIO: You are usually drawn to partners who are sensual in appearance with a strong character. As you are emotionally intense and passionate, personal relationships are probably a major factor in your life. Since you like to be in control you can at times exhibit some of your less attractive qualities by being willful or dominating. Although you need to feel established and in command in your relationships, you are constantly searching for some higher truth that can bring significant transformation.

MEN WITH VENUS IN SCORPIO: Usually you are attracted to sensual and passionate partners who have a strong character. You are often intense with deep feelings and magnetic powers of attraction. As a cautious yet devoted and ardent lover, you are likely to seek experiences that are more sexual in their nature. You display your less attractive qualities when you project your negative thoughts and resort to being suspicious or possessive. Nevertheless, loyal and loving, you are a sensitive lover.

To read all about your Outer Planets and work out how to use your personalized timetable, go to Section Three, page 789.

Your Personalized Timetable

JUPITER BENEFICIAL
1940 7/4 – 11/7
1941 2/21 – 5/9
1942 8/7 – 10/6
1942 12/19 – until 1943 5/26
1946 11/25 – until 1947 1/17
1947 5/11 – 9/16
1948 12/30 – until 1949 3/15
1949 7/30 – 11/6
1952 6/12 – until 1953 4/22
1954 7/21 – 9/8
1955 1/30 – 5/1
1958 11/9 – 12/27
1959 6/26 – 8/13
1960 12/14 – until 1961 2/22
1964 5/24 – 9/7
1964 9/22 – until 1965 4/3
1966 7/5 – 8/20
1970 10/24 – 12/9
1972 11/27 – until 1973 2/5
1976 5/7 – 7/22
1976 11/19 – until 1977 3/12
1978 6/19 – 8/2
1982 10/8 – 11/23
1984 3/16 – 6/13
1984 11/7 – until 1985 1/20
1988 4/21 – 6/30
1990 6/2 – 7/17
1994 1/26 – 4/2
1994 9/20 – 11/7
1996 2/20 – 7/27
1996 10/11 – until 1997 1/4
2000 4/4 – 6/12
2001 9/22 – 12/13
2002 5/13 – 7/1
2005 12/30 – until 2006 5/12
2006 8/29 – 10/23
2008 2/1 – 12/19
2011 8/16 – 9/13
2012 3/16 – 5/25

SATURN BENEFICIAL
1940 6/10 – 11/20
1941 2/27 – 7/18
1941 11/5 – until 1942 4/5
1945 6/26 – 9/21
1945 12/23 – until 1946 6/7
1954 11/12 – until 1955 11/10
1960 1/5 – until 1961 2/27
1961 7/26 – 11/26
1970 4/16 – until 1971 5/18
1974 8/6 – until 1975 2/7
1975 4/17 – 7/19
1983 12/21 – until 1984 5/4
1984 9/17 – 12/15
1985 6/10 – 9/8
1989 2/10 – 7/10
1989 11/9 – until 1991 1/4
1999 5/23 – until 2000 6/25
2000 12/8 – until 2001 3/12
2003 10/11 – 11/9
2004 6/8 – 8/28
2005 1/24 – 5/16

URANUS BENEFICIAL
1938 2/13 – until 1941 5/14
1951 9/3 – until 1954 7/11
1977 11/19 – until 1980 9/29
1991 1/5 – until 1995 1/10

NEPTUNE BENEFICIAL
1962 1/4 – until 1967 10/19
1988 3/18 – until 1996 12/8

PLUTO BENEFICIAL
1988 11/17 – until 1993 9/4

JUPITER CHALLENGING
1939 2/13 – 4/22
1941 7/10 – until 1942 5/23
1947 12/8 – until 1948 3/2
1948 5/30 – 10/25
1951 1/26 – 4/4

1953 6/21 – 9/28
1953 10/31 – until 1954 5/4
1959 11/23 – until 1960 2/5
1960 7/12 – 9/28
1962 5/21 – 8/13
1963 1/6 – 3/18
1965 6/5 – 8/21
1965 12/20 – until 1966 4/12
1971 11/6 – until 1972 1/18
1974 4/24 – 9/29
1974 12/8 – until 1975 3/2
1977 5/19 – 7/30
1983 3/4 – 4/21
1983 10/19 – until 1984 1/1
1986 4/4 – until 1987 2/13
1989 5/3 – 7/12
1995 1/30 – 6/5
1995 9/28 – 12/16
1998 3/18 – 6/12
1998 8/23 – until 1999 1/24
2000 9/2 – 10/26
2001 4/14 – 6/25
2007 1/10 – 7/30
2007 8/14 – 12/1
2010 3/1 – 5/12
2010 10/10 – 12/27
2012 7/30 – 12/12

SATURN CHALLENGING
1942 8/2 – 11/19
1943 4/20 – 9/14
1943 11/4 – until 1944 5/20
1957 1/7 – 6/15
1957 10/6 – until 1958 12/2
1965 3/18 – until 1966 5/3
1966 9/22 – until 1967 1/26
1972 5/31 – until 1973 6/30
1986 11/16 – until 1988 1/5
1988 8/20 – 9/9
1994 4/29 – 8/19
1995 1/22 – until 1996 3/6
2001 7/10 – 12/21
2002 3/27 – 8/12
2002 12/12 – until 2003 5/1

URANUS CHALLENGING
1944 6/18 – until 1948 6/12
1983 12/13 – until 1987 12/4
2005 5/2 – until 2010 3/7

NEPTUNE CHALLENGING
1974 12/20 – until 1982 11/29

PLUTO CHALLENGING
1999 2/1 – until 2006 12/4

JUPITER SPECIAL
1944 9/10 – 12/12
1945 2/11 – 8/4
1956 8/26 – 11/13
1957 3/24 – 7/13
1968 8/10 – 10/25
1979 12/15 – until 1980 1/6
1980 7/23 – 10/8
1991 11/4 – until 1992 2/26
1992 7/2 – 9/22
2003 10/14 – until 2004 4/8
2004 6/1 – 9/6

SATURN SPECIAL
1949 9/6 – until 1950 10/13
1951 5/5 – 6/21
1978 10/17 – until 1979 3/8
1979 7/9 – 12/4
1980 2/9 – 8/19
2008 8/20 – until 2009 9/26

URANUS SPECIAL
1963 12/7 – until 1968 7/19

NEPTUNE SPECIAL
1938 1/1 – until 1941 8/11

PLUTO SPECIAL
1961 11/22 – until 1970 8/18

September 12

SUN: VIRGO · DECANATE: CAPRICORN/SATURN · DEGREE: 18°45–20° VIRGO · MODE: MUTABLE · ELEMENT: EARTH

Your Personal Powers

Mentally sharp and imaginative, you are a friendly individual with a progressive outlook. Mercury, your ruler, grants you excellent analytical skills, a sharp intellect, and a talent with words. As a disciplinarian you gain power from the combination of your direct approach, common sense, and developed social skills. Usually you are hardworking and conscientious with an innate business acumen. With your flair for dealing with people and your organizational skills, you often rise to leadership positions. Being proud and dignified, you appear to others as confident and self-assured, but you lose some of your power if you allow worry, insecurity, or nervous tension to undermine your remarkable potential. With a strong desire to express yourself you can be very creative and witty. Although you usually speak your mind, by developing tolerance and patience you can inspire rather than manage others. Fortunately, you can also be modest, sensitive, and intuitive and gain power from your generosity and diplomatic skills.

Your Powers of Attraction in Relationships

Being friendly and sociable, you can easily attract admirers. Sensitive and intuitive yet mentally quick, you want a partner who can share your goals or need for variety and mental stimulation; otherwise you can become bored. You will, however, be wise to resist losing your charm to emotional worry or indecision in your close relationships. Although you enjoy socializing and meeting different people, you often prefer the company of intelligent individuals who possess a wealth of knowledge and ideas or an enterprising nature. A skilled commentator, you may act as the liaison between different groups. Generous when in love, you are often willing to make sacrifices, but avoid playing the martyr. Although very independent, once committed to a relationship you can be affectionate, loyal, and understanding.

Your attractive qualities: intelligent, creative, intuitive, friendly, innovative, sensitive, ambitious, initiative, generous, responsible, easygoing, common sense, disciplinarian, inventive, assertive, talent with words, positive thinker, organizer, confident

Your less attractive qualities: intolerant, impatient, martyr, irresponsible, uncooperative, worry, indecisive, materi-

alistic, suspicious, too sensitive, lack of self-esteem, scattered, self-doubt

Your Venus Power

The planet Venus has a great deal of influence on your powers of attraction. Below are four possible Venus types for women and men. To find your Venus you need to go to page 771, where you will find the Venus table and extra information. The planet Mars also affects your powers of attraction. To find your Mars table and interpretation go to page 761.

WOMEN WITH VENUS IN LEO: You possess the wonderful ability to project your warm and sunny personality and keep others happily entertained. Loving attention yourself, you seek a partner who can appreciate you, be supportive, and give you positive feedback. Proud, with a natural regal air, you expect respect from your partners but are willing to be loyal and supportive in exchange. Although sometimes a little self-centered, you know how to make your partner feel special.

MEN WITH VENUS IN LEO: Enthusiastic, playful, and kind, you can be benevolent with those you love. Warm, romantic, and self-expressive, you adore the drama of love and having fun with your friends. You are usually attracted to partners with warm and generous natures. Although you can be a confident and charismatic partner, you may need to develop humility in order to stop pride or arrogance from marring your relationships.

WOMEN WITH VENUS IN VIRGO: Intelligent and discriminating, you are usually drawn to polite and refined individuals. As a perfectionist, you may be keen to analyze and criticize yourself but be careful of continually going over your partner's shortcomings. By focusing on how you can make positive improvements in yourself and in your relationships, you avoid becoming skeptical or confused. You empower yourself when you display kind and caring concern for the well-being of loved ones and spontaneously offer your practical assistance.

MEN WITH VENUS IN VIRGO: A love of order usually indicates that you are attracted to refined individuals with analytical or practical abilities. You and your partner may be working together or serving similar causes. As you constantly analyze partnerships in order to improve them, you are likely to use former relationships as a point of reference and com-

pare them to your present partner. As you are helpful and kind, others usually rely on your good judgment and often turn to you for advice or practical assistance.

WOMEN WITH VENUS IN LIBRA: Attractive, refined, and conscious of the needs of others, you usually desire harmonious relationships. As a peacemaker with good negotiating skills you can smooth out difficulties with others, but your dislike of confrontation may sometimes leave you refusing to take a stand or compromising too many of your own needs. Courteous, stylish, and charming with polished social skills, you are an expert in relating to others in a gracious and civilized manner.

MEN WITH VENUS IN LIBRA: As a sociable and friendly individual with an eye for beauty, you are amorous and charming. You are a natural gentleman and your ideal partner usually has an elegant appearance and artistic appreciation, and good taste. Your relationships benefit when you resist the temptation to take the easy way out or put too much emphasis on vanity and high living. Intellectual and naturally refined, you seek a loving partner who can share your romantic and sophisticated aspirations.

WOMEN WITH VENUS IN SCORPIO: Your strength and power is in your ability to love both deeply and sensitively. For you, love and desire go hand in hand. As you feel so deeply, you often keep your sensitivity or vulnerability hidden from others in order to keep some control in your relationships. You are more likely to prefer a few very close loyal friends than many superficial acquaintances. In relationships your sensual nature and magnetic intensity can easily attract others.

MEN WITH VENUS IN SCORPIO: You are attracted to partners with deep and powerful emotions or individuals who you find intriguing. Your gift for creating smoke screens to maintain secrecy around your feelings can conceal your inner sensitivity and vulnerability. Nevertheless, you are looking for a partner who can pierce your defenses and understand you at a very deep level. Needing a relationship with a powerful sexual connection, you thrive on emotional intensity.

To read all about your Outer Planets and work out how to use your personalized timetable, go to Section Three, page 789.

♍

Your Personalized Timetable

JUPITER BENEFICIAL
1940 7/10 – 10/31
1941 2/27 – 5/13
1942 8/12 – 10/16
1942 12/10 – until 1943 6/1
1946 11/29 – until 1947 1/24
1947 5/3 – 9/22
1949 1/3 – 3/21
1949 7/22 – 11/13
1952 6/16 – until 1953 1/4
1953 1/7 – 4/26
1954 7/25 – 9/14
1955 1/22 – 5/8
1958 11/13 – until 1959 1/1
1959 6/14 – 8/25
1960 12/18 – until 1961 2/27
1964 5/28 – until 1965 4/8
1966 7/9 – 8/24
1970 10/29 – 12/14
1972 12/1 – until 1973 2/9
1976 5/11 – 7/29
1976 11/11 – until 1977 3/18
1978 6/23 – 8/7
1982 10/12 – 11/27
1984 3/24 – 6/5
1984 11/13 – until 1985 1/24
1988 4/25 – 7/5
1988 12/28 – until 1989 2/12
1990 6/6 – 7/22
1994 2/8 – 3/21
1994 9/25 – 11/12
1996 2/25 – 7/18
1996 10/19 – until 1997 1/8
2000 4/9 – 6/16
2001 10/1 – 12/4
2002 5/18 – 7/5
2006 1/5 – 5/4
2006 9/5 – 10/27
2008 2/6 – 12/23
2012 3/21 – 5/29

SATURN BENEFICIAL
1940 6/19 – 11/7
1941 3/10 – 7/30
1941 10/23 – until 1942 4/14
1945 7/3 – 10/6
1945 12/8 – until 1946 6/16
1954 11/21 – until 1955 11/18
1960 1/14 – until 1961 3/9
1961 7/13 – 12/6
1970 4/24 – until 1971 5/25
1974 8/15 – until 1975 1/24
1975 5/1 – 7/27
1984 1/1 – 4/21
1984 9/27 – 12/24
1985 5/27 – 9/21
1989 2/20 – 6/27
1989 11/20 – until 1991 1/12
1999 5/31 – 12/15
2000 2/8 – 7/4
2000 11/25 – until 2001 3/23
2004 6/16 – 9/6
2005 1/12 – 5/26

URANUS BENEFICIAL
1938 3/14 – until 1942 3/14
1952 7/2 – until 1955 5/1
1977 12/5 – until 1980 10/18
1991 1/22 – until 1995 11/8

NEPTUNE BENEFICIAL
1962 11/27 – until 1968 9/3
1989 1/30 – until 1997 1/5

PLUTO BENEFICIAL
1988 12/13 – until 1993 10/11

JUPITER CHALLENGING
1939 2/17 – 4/27
1941 7/14 – until 1942 5/28
1947 12/13 – until 1948 3/10
1948 5/21 – 10/31
1951 1/31 – 4/8

1953 6/26 – until 1954 5/9
1959 11/27 – until 1960 2/11
1960 7/4 – 10/6
1962 5/30 – 8/4
1963 1/11 – 3/22
1965 6/9 – 8/27
1965 12/12 – until 1966 4/18
1971 11/11 – until 1972 1/22
1974 4/29 – 9/20
1974 12/16 – until 1975 3/6
1977 5/24 – 8/4
1978 1/27 – 3/15
1983 10/25 – until 1984 1/5
1986 4/9 – until 1987 2/17
1989 5/7 – 7/16
1995 2/5 – 5/28
1995 10/4 – 12/21
1998 3/22 – 6/22
1998 8/12 – until 1999 1/29
2000 9/18 – 10/11
2001 4/18 – 6/29
2007 1/15 – 7/11
2007 9/2 – 12/5
2010 3/5 – 5/18
2010 10/2 – until 2011 1/4
2012 8/5 – 12/5

SATURN CHALLENGING
1942 8/14 – 11/6
1943 4/28 – until 1944 5/27
1957 1/17 – 6/2
1957 10/17 – until 1958 12/11
1965 3/26 – 10/20
1965 12/8 – until 1966 5/14
1966 9/10 – until 1967 2/5
1972 6/8 – until 1973 7/7
1986 11/24 – until 1988 1/14
1988 7/24 – 10/5
1994 5/12 – 8/4
1995 1/31 – until 1996 3/14
2001 7/19 – 12/9
2002 4/7 – 8/23
2002 11/30 – until 2003 5/10

URANUS CHALLENGING
1944 7/6 – until 1949 4/7
1983 12/29 – until 1987 12/21
2006 3/6 – until 2011 1/2

NEPTUNE CHALLENGING
1975 1/19 – until 1983 10/22

PLUTO CHALLENGING
1999 12/20 – until 2007 10/29

JUPITER SPECIAL
1944 9/15 – 12/25
1945 1/29 – 8/9
1956 8/30 – 11/19
1957 3/16 – 7/19
1968 8/14 – 10/30
1969 4/29 – 6/17
1980 7/28 – 10/12
1991 11/11 – until 1992 2/18
1992 7/8 – 9/26
2003 10/20 – until 2004 3/28
2004 6/12 – 9/11

SATURN SPECIAL
1949 9/13 – until 1950 10/21
1951 4/16 – 7/10
1978 10/27 – until 1979 2/24
1979 7/19 – until 1980 1/3
1980 1/10 – 8/27
2008 8/27 – until 2009 10/3

URANUS SPECIAL
1964 9/11 – until 1968 8/9

NEPTUNE SPECIAL
1938 1/1 – until 1941 9/9

PLUTO SPECIAL
1962 10/7 – until 1971 6/15

September 13

SUN: VIRGO • DECANATE: TAURUS/VENUS • DEGREE: 19°45–20°45 VIRGO • MODE: MUTABLE • ELEMENT: EARTH

Your Personal Powers

Idealistic and optimistic with keen intelligence, you are blessed with creative ideas and a youthful charm. Your ruling planet, Mercury, grants you good analytical skills and a talent for communication whether through spoken words or writing. You gain power from your captivating and competent manner and ability to deal with people from all walks of life. A certain dynamism and ability to stay focused can also make you an excellent information disseminator or fighter for an ideal cause. You may lose some of your power, however, if you allow nervous tension or anxiety to undermine your many talents through worry, particularly about material concerns. Fortunately, being a creative thinker with a good sense of fun, you do not lose your enthusiasm. Although you can also be pragmatic with good organizational skills, you benefit most when your work involves personal contacts, variety, and possibly travel. Enterprising when you find projects you love, you enjoy sharing your knowledge with others but prefer to be in positions of control rather than taking orders.

Your Powers of Attraction in Relationships

With your caring concern and flair for dealing with people, you have no trouble attracting admirers. Although you can be eager, you may sometimes repress your emotions. Your enthusiasm and friendly personality suggest, however, that you are gregarious and popular. Idealistic, you may seek a spiritual link with your partner. Alternatively, you may be drawn to intelligent people or partners with innate wisdom. Although you can be caring and willing to give much of yourself, you have to accept that people are not always able to reciprocate on your level. When positive and inspired, you can be spontaneous and funny, but if you lose faith you may feel withdrawn. Practical yet compassionate, you can be a loyal and helpful partner.

Your attractive qualities: ambitious, intelligent, creative, humorous, freedom-loving, self-expressive, leader, independent, inventive, fun, responsible, initiative, generous, controlled, youthful, hardworking, organizational skills, talent with words, loving, enthusiastic, practical

Your less attractive qualities: stubborn, impulsive, indecisive, bossy, impatient, materialistic, nervous tension, critical, unemotional, overzealous, rebellious, rash, take on too much, stressed, worry, skeptical

Your Venus Power

The planet Venus has a great deal of influence on your powers of attraction. Below are four possible Venus types for women and men. To find your Venus you need to go to page 771, where you will find the Venus table and extra information. The planet Mars also affects your powers of attraction. To find your Mars table and interpretation go to page 761.

WOMEN WITH VENUS IN LEO: Warm and playful with a touch of the dramatic, you enjoy the company of generous or strong individuals who can share your sense of fun. Although there are advantages to your being strong-willed, in your relationships you need to resist being bossy as it can cause resentment. With your wonderful mixture of regal authority and childlike wonder, you love to keep others entertained and amused.

MEN WITH VENUS IN LEO: Sociable and outgoing, you are kind and generous with those you love. Looking for a relationship that can be fun and entertaining, you need a playmate who can share your enthusiasm and high spirits. Your pride, however, often stops you from associating with lovers or partners you see as beneath you. As you desire someone who can appreciate your sense of the dramatic, you are often attracted to people with strong personalities.

WOMEN WITH VENUS IN VIRGO: Intelligent and discriminating, you are usually drawn to polite and refined individuals. As a perfectionist, you may be keen to analyze and criticize yourself but be careful of continually going over your partner's shortcomings. By focusing on how you can make positive improvements in yourself and in your relationships, you avoid becoming skeptical or confused. You empower yourself when you display kind and caring concern for the well-being of loved ones and spontaneously offer your practical assistance.

MEN WITH VENUS IN VIRGO: A love of order usually indicates that you are attracted to refined individuals with analytical or practical abilities. You and your partner may be working together or serving similar causes. As you constantly analyze partnerships in order to improve them, you are likely to use former relationships as a point of reference and com-

pare them to your present partner. As you are helpful and kind, others usually rely on your good judgment and often turn to you for advice or practical assistance.

WOMEN WITH VENUS IN LIBRA: Usually you are attractive and sociable with an easygoing manner. Your love of beauty, harmony, and pleasure implies that you are a romantic with a desire for love and affection. Once in a relationship you need to learn to negotiate your position rather than adapt to the wishes of others and compromise just to keep the peace. Nevertheless, your advanced social skills and strong sense of fair play can help you succeed in any social or romantic situation.

MEN WITH VENUS IN LIBRA: Your good social skills, charming personality, and refined manner usually make you attractive to the opposite sex. Equally, you desire a sophisticated partner with grace, elegance, and a strong sense of style. Although you have the ability to be persuasive and irresistible to others, avoid manipulative love games. Nevertheless, your natural diplomacy and sense of fair play help you to relate to people in all social situations. With your love of balance and harmony, you seek a partner who is also moderate, easygoing, and loving.

WOMEN WITH VENUS IN SCORPIO: With a natural psychic gift for penetrating the feelings of others, you can often help partners transform emotional challenges or sexual difficulties. When you fall in love, your strong feelings of determination give you a potent force that others find attractive and seductive. Although you know what really turns people on, your most profound desire is usually for the deepness and closeness of real love and intimacy in an enduring relationship.

MEN WITH VENUS IN SCORPIO: In relationships you possess a sensitive understanding of your partner's deeper nature. Although you are strongly attached to those you love, you may have to be careful that your feelings do not turn into jealousy or possessiveness. When you fall in love it is often with power and an emotional intensity. You are attracted to partners who can share your passion and display strong feelings of sexuality like your own.

To read all about your Outer Planets and work out how to use your personalized timetable, go to Section Three, page 789.

♍

Your Personalized Timetable

JUPITER BENEFICIAL
1940 7/17 – 10/24
1941 3/5 – 5/17
1942 8/17 – 10/31
1942 11/25 – until 1943 6/6
1946 12/4 – until 1947 1/31
1947 4/25 – 9/28
1949 1/7 – 3/28
1949 7/14 – 11/19
1952 6/21 – 12/12
1953 1/29 – 4/30
1954 7/30 – 9/20
1955 1/15 – 5/15
1958 11/18 – until 1959 1/6
1959 6/5 – 9/2
1960 12/22 – until 1961 3/4
1961 9/3 – 10/13
1964 6/2 – until 1965 4/13
1966 7/13 – 8/29
1967 3/3 – 4/8
1970 11/2 – 12/18
1972 12/6 – until 1973 2/14
1976 5/16 – 8/5
1976 11/4 – until 1977 3/23
1978 6/27 – 8/11
1982 10/17 – 12/2
1984 4/4 – 5/25
1984 11/18 – until 1985 1/28
1988 4/30 – 7/10
1988 12/17 – until 1989 2/23
1990 6/11 – 7/26
1994 9/30 – 11/16
1996 3/2 – 7/10
1996 10/26 – until 1997 1/13
2000 4/13 – 6/20
2001 10/12 – 11/23
2002 5/23 – 7/10
2006 1/12 – 4/26
2006 9/11 – 11/1
2008 2/10 – 12/27
2012 3/25 – 6/2

SATURN BENEFICIAL
1940 6/29 – 10/26
1941 3/20 – 8/16
1941 10/6 – until 1942 4/22
1945 7/11 – until 1946 6/24
1954 11/29 – until 1955 6/25
1955 8/12 – 11/26
1960 1/22 – 9/2
1960 9/29 – until 1961 3/21
1961 6/29 – 12/16
1970 5/1 – until 1971 6/2
1974 8/24 – until 1975 1/12
1975 5/12 – 8/3
1984 1/14 – 4/6
1984 10/6 – until 1985 1/3
1985 5/13 – 10/2
1989 3/4 – 6/13
1989 11/29 – until 1991 1/20
1999 6/9 – 11/29
2000 2/24 – 7/14
2000 11/13 – until 2001 4/2
2004 6/24 – 9/17
2004 12/31 – until 2005 6/5

URANUS BENEFICIAL
1938 4/4 – until 1942 4/7
1952 7/19 – until 1955 5/28
1977 12/24 – until 1980 11/3
1991 2/9 – until 1995 12/5

NEPTUNE BENEFICIAL
1962 12/28 – until 1968 10/13
1989 3/6 – until 1997 12/2

PLUTO BENEFICIAL
1989 1/20 – until 1993 11/6

JUPITER CHALLENGING
1939 2/21 – 5/1
1941 7/19 – until 1942 1/18
1942 2/24 – 6/1
1947 12/17 – until 1948 3/21

1948 5/10 – 11/5
1951 2/4 – 4/12
1953 6/30 – until 1954 5/14
1959 12/1 – until 1960 2/17
1960 6/26 – 10/13
1962 6/11 – 7/23
1963 1/16 – 3/26
1965 6/13 – 9/3
1965 12/5 – until 1966 4/24
1971 11/15 – until 1972 1/27
1974 5/5 – 9/12
1974 12/23 – until 1975 3/10
1977 5/28 – 8/9
1978 1/16 – 3/26
1983 10/29 – until 1984 1/10
1986 4/13 – until 1987 2/22
1989 5/11 – 7/21
1995 2/12 – 5/20
1995 10/10 – 12/25
1998 3/26 – 7/11
1998 7/24 – until 1999 2/3
2001 4/23 – 7/4
2007 1/20 – 6/30
2007 9/13 – 12/9
2010 3/9 – 5/23
2010 9/24 – until 2011 1/10
2012 8/11 – 11/28

SATURN CHALLENGING
1942 8/31 – 10/20
1943 5/6 – until 1944 6/4
1957 1/28 – 5/19
1957 10/27 – until 1958 12/19
1965 4/4 – 10/2
1965 12/25 – until 1966 5/26
1966 8/27 – until 1967 2/14
1972 6/15 – until 1973 7/15
1974 2/14 – 3/13
1986 12/2 – until 1988 1/23
1988 7/8 – 10/20
1994 5/31 – 7/16
1995 2/8 – until 1996 3/21
2001 7/29 – 11/27
2002 4/17 – 9/6
2002 11/15 – until 2003 5/18

URANUS CHALLENGING
1944 7/27 – until 1949 5/3
1984 1/16 – until 1988 10/22
2006 3/23 – until 2011 1/31

NEPTUNE CHALLENGING
1975 12/16 – until 1983 11/24

PLUTO CHALLENGING
2000 1/17 – until 2007 11/29

JUPITER SPECIAL
1944 9/20 – until 1945 8/15
1956 9/4 – 11/26
1957 3/9 – 7/26
1968 8/19 – 11/4
1969 4/17 – 6/28
1980 8/2 – 10/17
1991 11/19 – until 1992 2/10
1992 7/14 – 10/1
2003 10/25 – until 2004 3/20
2004 6/20 – 9/15

SATURN SPECIAL
1949 9/21 – until 1950 10/30
1951 4/2 – 7/23
1978 11/7 – until 1979 2/11
1979 7/28 – until 1980 9/4
2008 9/4 – until 2009 10/12
2010 5/18 – 6/12

URANUS SPECIAL
1964 9/27 – until 1968 8/26

NEPTUNE SPECIAL
1938 1/1 – until 1942 8/6

PLUTO SPECIAL
1962 11/18 – until 1971 8/9

September 14

Your Personal Powers

Honest and direct with natural leadership ability, you are an intelligent and purposeful individual with a down-to-earth approach. Although intellectually bright and insightful, you usually prefer to back your expertise with practical experience. Independent and strong-willed, you are often ready to fight for your ideals or enthusiastically protect what you think. Success-oriented, you gain power from the combination of your communication skills, common sense, and natural charm. Although you are clever and assertive with a commanding nature, you can lose some of your power if you become bossy, stubborn, or argumentative. Fortunately, your keen awareness and sensitivity suggest that you know how far you can push others. Being hardworking and highly persuasive, your strong drive also makes you ambitious and determined. The only essential requirement for your success is your genuine enthusiasm for what you are doing. You empower yourself when you stay optimistic and focused on your course of action while letting your original ideas and adventurous nature lead you to success.

Your Powers of Attraction in Relationships

You are independent and confident, and people are attracted to your quick intelligence, strong convictions, and ability to work well with others. Being friendly and persuasive, you value your relationships and enjoy meeting people. Although you can be generous, loving, and modest, guard against occasionally being arrogant or opinionated in your interaction with others. You are attracted to partners who are smart and hardworking or those with a natural sense of power and command. Alternatively, you can be stimulated or inspired into action by creative people. In your close relationships you may have to be less skeptical and more decisive if you want trust and loyalty from your partner. Being strong-willed with a sense of the dramatic, you need an enthusiastic partner who will not let you be dominant.

Your attractive qualities: strong-willed, common sense, ambitious, enthusiastic, success-oriented, honest, independent, quick intelligence, versatile, intuitive, direct, practical, friendly, optimistic, generous, analytical, sixth sense, modest, charming, sociable

Your less attractive qualities: stubborn, manipulative, opinionated, arrogance or lacking in self-confidence, critical, over-indulgence, impulsive, anger, anxiety, argumentative, impatient, bossy, bored, nervous, restless

Your Venus Power

The planet Venus has a great deal of influence on your powers of attraction. Below are four possible Venus types for women and men. To find your Venus you need to go to page 771, where you will find the Venus table and extra information. The planet Mars also affects your powers of attraction. To find your Mars table and interpretation go to page 761.

WOMEN WITH VENUS IN LEO: Your friendly and sunny personality often makes you stand out in a crowd. Generous and giving, you know how to make your partner feel special. As you often expect loyalty and devotion from your partners in return, you can become easily offended if they ignore you or behave in an inconsiderate manner. Charming and kind, when you are in love you can be romantic, dramatic, and passionate.

MEN WITH VENUS IN LEO: A childlike nature suggests that you are versatile and keen on games or being entertained. You are usually attracted to vivacious partners with a benevolent nature. As an extrovert you enjoy being involved in all types of activities where you can assert yourself and show your talents and abilities. Others may recognize your inborn tendencies to lead but are also aware of your vanity or pride. Nevertheless, generous, kind, and caring, you often show compassion to those less fortunate than yourself.

WOMEN WITH VENUS IN VIRGO: Articulate and straightforward in your relationships, you attract others with your genuine concern for their well-being. By being understanding and a good listener, you are able to show your love and friendship. With your analytical approach to relationships, however, you may have to be careful of becoming too matter-of-fact. You often display your concern for the welfare of others by your willingness to offer practical help and assistance. You usually seek a partner who is willing to work as hard on relationships as you are.

MEN WITH VENUS IN VIRGO: Although you are constantly analyzing your relationships in order to understand and improve them, you may nevertheless need to refrain from continuously mulling over issues that can cause anxiety. You are happiest when you are able to help your loved ones in practical ways and forget yourself in your willingness to be

of service to others. You seek a partner who has high standards and can be as pragmatic and hardworking as yourself. Ideally they should also be impeccably dressed with a fine analytical mind.

WOMEN WITH VENUS IN LIBRA: Gracious, charming, and sociable with a sense of style, you have no trouble attracting admirers. With your natural diplomatic skills and desire for harmony you usually like to keep the peace and avoid confrontations, but be careful of failing to make a stand when it is necessary. Romantic and easygoing yourself, you are attracted to affectionate and refined individuals who share your love of peace, justice, and fair play.

MEN WITH VENUS IN LIBRA: Courteous and refined, you are attracted to beautiful and elegant people. You are looking for a partner who can share your natural good taste and enjoy an intellectual conversation. Disliking conflict, you may have to be careful not to go along with others just to keep the peace. Your ideal partner will appreciate beauty and the little luxuries of life as well as possess good social skills. You have a strong sense of social etiquette yourself so you need an intelligent and sophisticated partner.

WOMEN WITH VENUS IN SCORPIO: Loving and passionate, you are often sensitive with deep feelings and strong powers of attraction. A love for the truth coupled with a tendency to be suspicious can be an influence that motivates you to delve deep into the activities of your partner. When in love or in a relationship that matters, you will often bend over backward to cooperate. Although loyal, guard against losing sight of your own needs and desires.

MEN WITH VENUS IN SCORPIO: As you are emotionally intense and passionate, personal relationships are probably a major factor in your own transformation. Being sensitive yet loyal, you are usually attracted to forceful partners who can express themselves intimately but intensely. Rather than seek easy and simple relationships, you are drawn to partners who act as a catalyst for your own internal changes. Through your relationships with your partners you can unravel your own motives and understand your deep-seated feelings or emotional insecurities.

To read all about your Outer Planets and work out how to use your personalized timetable, go to Section Three, page 789.

Your Personalized Timetable

JUPITER BENEFICIAL
1940 7/24 – 10/16
1941 3/10 – 5/22
1942 8/22 – until 1943 2/18
1943 4/2 – 6/11
1946 12/9 – until 1947 2/9
1947 4/16 – 10/3
1949 1/12 – 4/4
1949 7/7 – 11/25
1952 6/26 – 12/1
1953 2/8 – 5/5
1954 8/3 – 9/26
1955 1/8 – 5/21
1958 11/22 – until 1959 1/12
1959 5/28 – 9/10
1960 12/27 – until 1961 3/9
1961 8/22 – 10/25
1964 6/6 – until 1965 4/17
1966 7/18 – 9/3
1967 2/18 – 4/21
1970 11/6 – 12/23
1972 12/10 – until 1973 2/18
1976 5/20 – 8/13
1976 10/27 – until 1977 3/29
1978 7/2 – 8/16
1982 10/22 – 12/6
1984 4/29 – 5/2
1984 11/23 – until 1985 2/2
1988 5/4 – 7/16
1988 12/9 – until 1989 3/3
1990 6/15 – 7/30
1994 10/5 – 11/21
1996 3/8 – 7/3
1996 11/1 – until 1997 1/17
2000 4/17 – 6/25
2002 5/28 – 7/14
2006 1/19 – 4/18
2006 9/16 – 11/5
2008 2/15 – 8/23
2008 9/24 – until 2009 1/1
2012 3/30 – 6/7

SATURN BENEFICIAL
1940 7/11 – 10/13
1941 3/28 – until 1942 4/30
1945 7/19 – until 1946 7/2
1954 12/8 – until 1955 6/5
1955 8/31 – 12/5
1960 1/31 – 8/8
1960 10/23 – until 1961 4/6
1961 6/13 – 12/25
1970 5/9 – until 1971 6/10
1974 9/3 – 12/31
1975 5/22 – 8/11
1984 2/2 – 3/18
1984 10/15 – until 1985 1/14
1985 4/30 – 10/12
1989 3/19 – 5/28
1989 12/8 – until 1991 1/28
1999 6/18 – 11/16
2000 3/7 – 7/25
2000 11/1 – until 2001 4/11
2004 7/1 – 9/30
2004 12/17 – until 2005 6/13

URANUS BENEFICIAL
1938 4/21 – until 1942 4/26
1952 8/4 – until 1955 6/17
1978 1/18 – until 1980 11/19
1991 3/3 – until 1995 12/24

NEPTUNE BENEFICIAL
1963 11/23 – until 1969 8/10
1990 1/25 – until 1998 1/1

PLUTO BENEFICIAL
1989 11/28 – until 1994 9/23

JUPITER CHALLENGING
1939 2/25 – 5/6
1939 11/19 – 11/30
1941 7/24 – until 1942 1/5

1942 3/8 – 6/5
1947 12/21 – until 1948 11/10
1951 2/8 – 4/17
1953 7/4 – until 1954 5/19
1959 12/6 – until 1960 2/23
1960 6/18 – 10/19
1963 1/21 – 3/30
1965 6/17 – 9/11
1965 11/27 – until 1966 4/29
1971 11/20 – until 1972 2/1
1972 8/8 – 9/11
1974 5/11 – 9/5
1974 12/29 – until 1975 3/14
1977 6/1 – 8/14
1978 1/8 – 4/4
1983 11/3 – until 1984 1/14
1986 4/18 – until 1987 2/26
1989 5/16 – 7/25
1995 2/20 – 5/12
1995 10/15 – 12/29
1998 3/30 – until 1999 2/8
2001 4/28 – 7/8
2007 1/25 – 6/21
2007 9/21 – 12/14
2010 3/13 – 5/30
2010 9/17 – until 2011 1/16
2012 8/18 – 11/20

SATURN CHALLENGING
1943 5/14 – until 1944 6/12
1957 2/11 – 5/5
1957 11/5 – until 1958 12/27
1965 4/13 – 9/18
1966 1/7 – 6/11
1966 8/10 – until 1967 2/23
1972 6/23 – until 1973 7/23
1974 1/23 – 4/4
1986 12/10 – until 1988 2/2
1988 6/24 – 11/1
1995 2/17 – until 1996 3/29
2001 8/9 – 11/15
2002 4/26 – 9/29
2002 10/23 – until 2003 5/26

URANUS CHALLENGING
1944 8/28 – until 1949 5/22
1984 2/9 – until 1988 11/13
2006 4/11 – until 2011 2/20

NEPTUNE CHALLENGING
1976 1/13 – until 1984 10/12

PLUTO CHALLENGING
2000 12/10 – until 2008 10/20

JUPITER SPECIAL
1944 9/24 – until 1945 8/19
1956 9/8 – 12/3
1957 3/1 – 8/1
1968 8/24 – 11/9
1969 4/8 – 7/7
1980 8/7 – 10/22
1991 11/28 – until 1992 2/1
1992 7/20 – 10/5
2003 10/31 – until 2004 3/12
2004 6/28 – 9/20

SATURN SPECIAL
1949 9/29 – until 1950 4/24
1950 6/4 – 11/9
1951 3/21 – 8/3
1978 11/21 – until 1979 1/27
1979 8/6 – until 1980 9/12
2008 9/12 – until 2009 10/20
2010 4/23 – 7/6

URANUS SPECIAL
1964 10/15 – until 1968 9/11

NEPTUNE SPECIAL
1938 1/1 – until 1942 9/5

PLUTO SPECIAL
1963 10/5 – until 1971 9/7

♍

September 15

Your Personal Powers

Resourceful and quick-witted, you are a friendly individual with strong instincts and powers of perception. Often intuitive and clear thinking, your ruling planet, Mercury, indicates that among your personal powers are pragmatic rationality and determination. Usually conscientious and aware of your responsibilities, you gain power from your ability to quickly recognize opportunities or assess situations. You also possess a gift for finding help and support from others when you need it. Although you are verbally direct with fast responses, be careful not to lose some of your power to impatience or restlessness. Generally you are optimistic and purposeful, with a constant desire to update your knowledge. Be careful not to lose your power to disappointment and frustration if people or plans do not live up to your high ideals or standards. Benevolent and generous with your resources, you are willing to help others. Your inner creativity or sensitivity implies that in order to express yourself and succeed, you need to utilize your ingenuity, courage, and intuition.

Your Powers of Attraction in Relationships

Intelligent and kind, you enjoy associating with people who are mentally stimulating and enterprising. Security-conscious, you possess a strong need for a stable home base as well as love and affection. Although you can be romantic and idealistic when single, once you have settled down you are usually reliable and responsible. Even though partners who can provide you with emotional and financial support usually attract you, avoid dependent situations. When you have a positive philosophy in life, your relationships are more balanced and rewarding. You may need to resist being dissatisfied or too critical in order to avoid friction. With your inner sensitivity, however, you have a warm heart and can be affectionate. Loving and generous with those you love, you also possess a strong sense of duty or obligation.

Your attractive qualities: willing, intelligent, generous, fast responses, responsible, kind, inventive, cooperative, conscientious, worldly, philosophical, kindhearted, courage, practical, appreciative, responsible, creative ideas, interest in people, intuitive, optimistic, home-loving

Your less attractive qualities: negative thinking, restless, disappointment, self-centered, frustration, critical, fear of change, worry, indecisive, irresponsible, rash, too economical, impatient, opinionated

Your Venus Power

The planet Venus has a great deal of influence on your powers of attraction. Below are four possible Venus types for women and men. To find your Venus you need to go to page 771, where you will find the Venus table and extra information. The planet Mars also affects your powers of attraction. To find your Mars table and interpretation go to page 761.

WOMEN WITH VENUS IN LEO: Your friendly and sunny personality often makes you stand out in a crowd. Generous and giving, you know how to make your partner feel special. As you often expect loyalty and devotion from your partners in return, you can become easily offended if they ignore you or behave in an inconsiderate manner. Charming and kind, when you are in love you can be romantic, dramatic, and passionate.

MEN WITH VENUS IN LEO: A childlike nature suggests that you are versatile and keen on games or being entertained. You are usually attracted to vivacious partners with a benevolent nature. As an extrovert you enjoy being involved in all types of activities where you can assert yourself and show your talents and abilities. Others may recognize your inborn tendencies to lead but are also aware of your vanity or pride. Nevertheless, generous, kind, and caring, you often show compassion to those less fortunate than yourself.

WOMEN WITH VENUS IN VIRGO: In relationships you can be modest and unassuming but desire perfection. You usually analyze your partnerships until you feel you have understood them to the last little detail in order to improve them. A problem usually arises when you become too critical either of partners or yourself and indulge in being skeptical or fault-finding. As you are modest, others may not be aware of the strong sensuality beneath your well-groomed exterior.

MEN WITH VENUS IN VIRGO: Industrious and well-ordered, you relate to others in a considerate and down-to-earth way. You enjoy giving practical advice and being of service to those you love, even in small ways. Being a perfectionist, you are drawn to partners with high morals or a strong work ethic. Partners who have strong analytical minds are very attractive to you, particularly if they are also clean and meticulously dressed.

WOMEN WITH VENUS IN LIBRA: Gracious, charming, and sociable with a sense of style, you have no trouble attracting admirers. With your natural diplomatic skills and desire for harmony you usually like to keep the peace and avoid confrontations, but be careful of failing to take a stand when it is necessary. Romantic and easygoing yourself, you are attracted to affectionate and refined individuals who share your love of peace, justice, and fair play.

MEN WITH VENUS IN LIBRA: Courteous and refined, you are attracted to beautiful and elegant people. You are looking for a partner who can share your natural good taste and enjoy an intellectual conversation. Disliking conflict, you may have to be careful not to go along with others just to keep the peace. Your ideal partner will appreciate beauty and the little luxuries of life as well as possess good social skills. You have a strong sense of social etiquette yourself so you need an intelligent and sophisticated partner.

WOMEN WITH VENUS IN SCORPIO: You are usually drawn to partners who are sensual in appearance with a strong character. As you are emotionally intense and passionate, personal relationships are probably a major factor in your life. Since you like to be in control, you can at times exhibit some of your less attractive qualities by being willful or domineering. Although you need to feel established and in command in your relationships, you are constantly searching for some higher truth that can bring significant transformation.

MEN WITH VENUS IN SCORPIO: Usually you are attracted to sensual and passionate partners who have a strong character. You are often intense with deep feelings and magnetic powers of attraction. As a cautious yet devoted and ardent lover, you are likely to seek experiences that are more sexual in their nature. You display your less attractive qualities when you project your negative thoughts and resort to being suspicious or possessive. Nevertheless, loyal and loving, you are a sensitive lover.

To read all about your Outer Planets and work out how to use your personalized timetable, go to Section Three, page 789.

♍

Your Personalized Timetable

JUPITER BENEFICIAL
1940 8/2 – 10/7
1941 3/15 – 5/26
1942 8/27 – until 1943 2/7
1943 4/14 – 6/16
1946 12/13 – until 1947 2/22
1947 4/3 – 10/8
1949 1/16 – 4/12
1949 6/28 – 11/30
1952 7/1 – 11/23
1953 2/16 – 5/9
1954 8/8 – 10/3
1954 12/31 – until 1955 5/27
1958 11/27 – until 1959 1/18
1959 5/20 – 9/17
1960 12/31 – until 1961 3/14
1961 8/13 – 11/3
1964 6/11 – until 1965 4/22
1966 7/22 – 9/9
1967 2/9 – 5/1
1970 11/11 – 12/28
1971 7/10 – 8/8
1972 12/15 – until 1973 2/23
1976 5/24 – 8/22
1976 10/17 – until 1977 4/3
1978 7/6 – 8/21
1982 10/26 – 12/11
1984 11/28 – until 1985 2/6
1988 5/8 – 7/21
1988 12/1 – until 1989 3/10
1990 6/20 – 8/4
1994 10/10 – 11/25
1996 3/15 – 6/25
1996 11/7 – until 1997 1/21
2000 4/21 – 6/29
2002 6/2 – 7/18
2006 1/28 – 4/9
2006 9/22 – 11/10
2008 2/20 – 8/9
2008 10/7 – until 2009 1/5
2012 4/3 – 6/11

SATURN BENEFICIAL
1940 7/26 – 9/27
1941 4/6 – until 1942 5/8
1945 7/26 – until 1946 7/9
1954 12/17 – until 1955 5/22
1955 9/13 – 12/13
1956 6/29 – 8/30
1960 2/9 – 7/24
1960 11/6 – until 1962 1/3
1970 5/17 – until 1971 6/18
1972 1/12 – 2/19
1974 9/14 – 12/18
1975 5/31 – 8/19
1976 2/25 – 4/28
1984 10/24 – until 1985 1/28
1985 4/15 – 10/21
1989 4/23 – 4/25
1989 12/17 – until 1991 2/6
1999 6/27 – 11/3
2000 3/17 – 8/8
2000 10/17 – until 2001 4/20
2004 7/9 – 10/18
2004 11/29 – until 2005 6/22

URANUS BENEFICIAL
1938 5/8 – until 1942 5/13
1952 8/23 – until 1955 7/4
1978 11/12 – until 1981 9/18
1992 1/5 – until 1996 1/10

NEPTUNE BENEFICIAL
1963 12/22 – until 1969 10/8
1990 2/26 – until 1998 11/24

PLUTO BENEFICIAL
1989 12/26 – until 1994 10/24

JUPITER CHALLENGING
1939 3/1 – 5/11
1939 10/31 – 12/19
1941 7/29 – 12/27

1942 3/17 – 6/10
1947 12/26 – until 1948 11/15
1951 2/13 – 4/21
1953 7/9 – until 1954 5/23
1959 12/10 – until 1960 3/1
1960 6/10 – 10/25
1963 1/25 – 4/3
1965 6/22 – 9/20
1965 11/17 – until 1966 5/5
1971 11/24 – until 1972 2/6
1972 7/25 – 9/24
1974 5/17 – 8/28
1975 1/4 – 3/18
1977 6/5 – 8/20
1977 12/31 – until 1978 4/11
1983 11/8 – until 1984 1/19
1986 4/23 – 10/15
1986 12/2 – until 1987 3/2
1989 5/20 – 7/30
1995 3/1 – 5/2
1995 10/21 – until 1996 1/2
1998 4/4 – until 1999 2/12
2001 5/3 – 7/12
2007 1/31 – 6/13
2007 9/28 – 12/18
2010 3/17 – 6/5
2010 9/9 – until 2011 1/22
2012 8/26 – 11/12

SATURN CHALLENGING
1943 5/22 – until 1944 6/19
1957 3/2 – 4/14
1957 11/14 – until 1959 1/4
1965 4/23 – 9/5
1966 1/18 – until 1967 3/3
1972 7/1 – until 1973 1/27
1973 3/2 – 8/1
1974 1/8 – 4/17
1986 12/19 – until 1988 2/13
1988 6/11 – 11/11
1995 2/25 – until 1996 4/6
2001 8/23 – 10/31
2002 5/4 – until 2003 6/3

URANUS CHALLENGING
1945 6/16 – until 1949 6/8
1984 12/7 – until 1988 12/1
2006 5/5 – until 2011 3/10

NEPTUNE CHALLENGING
1976 3/2 – until 1984 11/19

PLUTO CHALLENGING
2001 1/5 – until 2008 11/24

JUPITER SPECIAL
1944 9/29 – until 1945 8/24
1956 9/13 – 12/12
1957 2/20 – 8/6
1968 8/28 – 11/15
1969 3/31 – 7/14
1980 8/12 – 10/27
1991 12/9 – until 1992 1/20
1992 7/25 – 10/10
2003 11/6 – until 2004 3/4
2004 7/4 – 9/24

SATURN SPECIAL
1949 10/7 – until 1950 4/5
1950 6/24 – 11/19
1951 3/8 – 8/12
1978 12/21 – 12/28
1979 8/14 – until 1980 9/20
2008 9/20 – until 2009 10/29
2010 4/9 – until 2010 7/20

URANUS SPECIAL
1964 11/5 – until 1969 6/17

NEPTUNE SPECIAL
1938 10/13 – until 1943 7/30

PLUTO SPECIAL
1963 11/13 – until 1972 7/27

September 16

Your Personal Powers

Observant and shrewd, you possess many personal powers, including articulate speech, analytical understanding, and a desire to learn. Intuitive and imaginative, you gain power from the combination of your natural business sense and visionary ability. Being both sensitive and practical has many advantages and can provide you with times of perceptive insight and inspiration. Blending your sixth sense with foresight can help you to creatively channel your emotions and stop you from losing power to delusion or escapism. Resourceful and methodical, you have the advantage of a wide range of personal powers to help you in life. Since you already possess good intellect, people skills, common sense, and imagination, avoid becoming involved in power tactics or games. Although you seek perfection and have many ambitious dreams, there is another part of you that is content just to seek peace and comfort in harmonious surroundings. Being mentally smart, however, you are constantly looking for ways to improve yourself or your circumstances.

Your Powers of Attraction in Relationships

Others are attracted to your fine mind and original approach to life. Even though you need time alone to reflect, being extremely sensitive, love and affection are likely to be especially important to you. Attracted to intelligent and engaging people, you can be inspired by knowledge and success. You are also drawn to forthright individuals with common sense and plans for the future. You need a partner who can share your enjoyment of the good things in life, but you may experience inner tension if you fail to acknowledge your idealism and responsibilities. Although others admire your imagination and pragmatism, guard against a stubborn streak or an inclination to get carried away with your fantasies. As you are impressionable and caring, your family, a secure home, and inner peace are usually very high among your priorities.

Your attractive qualities: clever, business sense, responsible, integrity, caring, visionary, subtle, analytical, drive, intuitive, sociable, mystical potential, cooperative, generous, vision, compassionate, insightful, perfectionist, original, home-loving, independent, sensitive

Your less attractive qualities: worry, self-centered, irresponsible, manipulative, opinionated, critical, skeptical, power games, rash, fussy, overconfident, insecure, escapist, moody, stubborn

Your Venus Power

The planet Venus has a great deal of influence on your powers of attraction. Below are four possible Venus types for women and men. To find your Venus you need to go to page 771, where you will find the Venus table and extra information. The planet Mars also affects your powers of attraction. To find your Mars table and interpretation go to page 761.

WOMEN WITH VENUS IN LEO: You possess the wonderful ability to project your warm and sunny personality and keep others happily entertained. Loving attention yourself, you seek a partner who can appreciate you, be supportive, and give you positive feedback. Proud, with a natural regal air, you expect respect from your partners but are willing to be loyal and supportive in exchange. Although sometimes a little self-centered, you know how to make your partner feel special.

MEN WITH VENUS IN LEO: Enthusiastic, playful, and kind, you can be benevolent with those you love. Warm, romantic, and self-expressive, you adore the drama of love or having fun with your friends. Usually you are attracted to partners with a warm and generous nature. Although you can be a confident and charismatic partner, you may need to develop humility in order to stop pride or arrogance from marring your relationships.

WOMEN WITH VENUS IN VIRGO: Intelligent and discriminating, you are usually drawn to polite and refined individuals. As a perfectionist, you may be keen to analyze and criticize yourself, but be careful of continually going over your partner's shortcomings. By focusing on how you can make positive improvements in yourself and in your relationships, you avoid becoming skeptical or confused. You empower yourself when you display kind and caring concern for the well-being of loved ones and spontaneously offer your practical assistance.

MEN WITH VENUS IN VIRGO: A love of order usually indicates that you are attracted to refined individuals with analytical or practical abilities. You and your partner may be working together or serving similar causes. As you constantly analyze partnerships in order to improve them, you are likely to use former relationships as a point of reference and compare them to your present partner. As you are helpful and

kind, others usually rely on your good judgment and often turn to you for advice or practical assistance.

WOMEN WITH VENUS IN LIBRA: Attractive, refined, and conscious of the needs of others, you usually desire harmonious relationships. As a peacemaker with good negotiating skills, you can smooth out difficulties with others, but your dislike of confrontation may sometimes leave you refusing to take a stand or compromising too many of your own needs. Courteous, stylish, and charming with polished social skills, you are an expert at relating to others in a gracious and civilized manner.

MEN WITH VENUS IN LIBRA: As a sociable and friendly individual with an eye for beauty, you are amorous and charming. You are a natural gentleman and your ideal partner usually has an elegant appearance, artistic appreciation, and good taste. Your relationships benefit when you resist the temptation to take the easy way out or put too much emphasis on vanity and high living. Intellectual and naturally refined, you seek a loving partner who can share your romantic and sophisticated aspirations.

WOMEN WITH VENUS IN SCORPIO: Your strength and power is in your ability to love both deeply and sensitively. For you, love and desire go hand in hand. As you feel so deeply, you often keep your sensitivity or vulnerability hidden from others in order to keep some control in your relationships. You are more likely to prefer a few very close loyal friends than many superficial acquaintances. In relationships your sensual nature and magnetic intensity can easily attract others.

MEN WITH VENUS IN SCORPIO: You are attracted to partners with deep and powerful emotions or individuals whom you find intriguing. Your gift for creating smoke screens to maintain secrecy around your feelings can conceal your inner sensitivity and vulnerability. Nevertheless, you are looking for a partner who can pierce your defenses and understand you at a very deep level. Needing a relationship with a powerful sexual connection, you thrive on emotional intensity.

To read all about your Outer Planets and work out how to use your personalized timetable, go to Section Three, page 789.

♍

Your Personalized Timetable

JUPITER BENEFICIAL
1940 8/13 – 9/26
1941 3/20 – 5/30
1942 9/1 – until 1943 1/29
1943 4/23 – 6/20
1946 12/18 – until 1947 7/5
1947 7/27 – 10/13
1949 1/20 – 4/22
1949 6/18 – 12/5
1952 7/7 – 11/15
1953 2/23 – 5/13
1954 8/12 – 10/12
1954 12/22 – until 1955 6/1
1958 12/1 – until 1959 1/24
1959 5/12 – 9/23
1961 1/4 – 3/20
1961 8/5 – 11/10
1964 6/15 – until 1965 4/26
1966 7/27 – 9/14
1967 2/1 – 5/9
1970 11/15 – until 1971 1/2
1971 6/25 – 8/23
1972 12/19 – until 1973 2/27
1976 5/28 – 9/6
1976 10/3 – until 1977 4/8
1978 7/10 – 8/25
1982 10/31 – 12/15
1984 12/2 – until 1985 2/10
1988 5/12 – 7/27
1988 11/24 – until 1989 3/16
1990 6/24 – 8/8
1994 10/14 – 11/29
1996 3/22 – 6/17
1996 11/13 – until 1997 1/25
2000 4/25 – 7/4
2002 6/7 – 7/23
2006 2/7 – 3/29
2006 9/27 – 11/14
2008 2/26 – 7/30
2008 10/17 – until 2009 1/9
2012 4/8 – 6/15

SATURN BENEFICIAL
1941 4/14 – until 1942 5/15
1945 8/3 – until 1946 7/17
1954 12/27 – until 1955 5/9
1955 9/24 – 12/22
1956 6/12 – 9/15
1960 2/19 – 7/10
1960 11/18 – until 1962 1/11
1970 5/24 – until 1971 6/26
1971 12/24 – until 1972 3/9
1974 9/28 – 12/4
1975 6/9 – 8/28
1976 2/10 – 5/13
1984 11/1 – until 1985 2/19
1985 3/23 – 10/30
1989 12/26 – until 1991 2/14
1991 9/5 – 11/3
1999 7/8 – 10/22
2000 3/26 – 9/3
2000 9/21 – until 2001 4/28
2004 7/16 – until 2005 6/29

URANUS BENEFICIAL
1938 5/25 – until 1943 3/6
1952 9/16 – until 1955 7/20
1978 11/28 – until 1981 10/10
1992 1/21 – until 1996 11/3

NEPTUNE BENEFICIAL
1964 11/18 – until 1969 11/6
1991 1/21 – until 1998 12/27

PLUTO BENEFICIAL
1938 3/27 – 6/22
1990 12/10 – until 1995 8/24

JUPITER CHALLENGING
1939 3/5 – 5/16
1939 10/20 – 12/29
1941 8/4 – 12/19
1942 3/24 – 6/14
1947 12/30 – until 1948 11/19

1951 2/17 – 4/25
1953 7/13 – until 1954 5/28
1959 12/14 – until 1960 3/8
1960 6/2 – 10/31
1963 1/30 – 4/7
1965 6/26 – 10/4
1965 11/4 – until 1966 5/10
1971 11/28 – until 1972 2/11
1972 7/15 – 10/4
1974 5/24 – 8/21
1975 1/9 – 3/22
1977 6/9 – 8/26
1977 12/24 – until 1978 4/18
1983 11/12 – until 1984 1/23
1986 4/28 – 10/5
1986 12/12 – until 1987 3/6
1989 5/24 – 8/4
1990 2/18 – 3/3
1995 3/14 – 4/19
1995 10/26 – until 1996 1/7
1998 4/8 – until 1999 2/17
2001 5/7 – 7/17
2007 2/6 – 6/6
2007 10/5 – 12/22
2010 3/21 – 6/13
2010 9/1 – until 2011 1/27
2012 9/4 – 11/3

SATURN CHALLENGING
1938 1/1 – 1/25
1943 5/30 – until 1944 6/27
1957 11/23 – until 1959 1/13
1959 8/12 – 9/28
1965 5/4 – 8/23
1966 1/27 – until 1967 3/11
1972 7/9 – until 1973 1/7
1973 3/22 – 8/10
1973 12/27 – until 1974 4/28
1986 12/27 – until 1987 7/29
1987 9/9 – until 1988 2/25
1988 5/28 – 11/21
1995 3/5 – until 1996 4/14
1996 11/15 – 12/20
2001 9/18 – 10/5
2002 5/12 – until 2003 6/11

URANUS CHALLENGING
1945 7/3 – until 1949 6/25
1984 12/23 – until 1988 12/17
2007 3/9 – until 2012 1/3

NEPTUNE CHALLENGING
1977 1/8 – until 1985 9/25

PLUTO CHALLENGING
2001 2/9 – until 2009 10/11

JUPITER SPECIAL
1944 10/3 – until 1945 8/29
1956 9/17 – 12/23
1957 2/9 – 8/12
1968 9/2 – 11/21
1969 3/23 – 7/21
1980 8/17 – 11/1
1981 5/10 – 6/13
1992 7/30 – 10/14
2003 11/12 – until 2004 2/26
2004 7/11 – 9/29

SATURN SPECIAL
1949 10/16 – until 1950 3/22
1950 7/7 – 12/2
1951 2/22 – 8/22
1979 8/22 – until 1980 9/28
2008 9/28 – until 2009 11/7
2010 3/27 – 8/1

URANUS SPECIAL
1965 9/2 – until 1969 7/26

NEPTUNE SPECIAL
1938 1/1 – until 1943 8/31

PLUTO SPECIAL
1964 10/2 – until 1972 8/28

September 17

SUN: VIRGO • DECANATE: TAURUS/VENUS • DEGREE: 23°45–25°45 VIRGO • MODE: MUTABLE • ELEMENT: EARTH

Your Personal Powers

Thoughtful and intelligent, your common sense and quick receptivity indicate that you are both observant and independent. Quick on the uptake, you gain power when you combine your articulate speech with your analytical skills and ability to pay attention to details. Methodical and hardworking, you have quick responses and are also capable of concentrating on lengthy and exacting tasks. A natural business sense and a talent for responding well to a competitive challenge can also add to your assets and success. With your assured attitude and natural executive ability, you have the potential to handle large projects. Although usually gifted in the area of communication, at times you may lose some of your power to self-doubt by becoming cynical and suspicious. Since this can also cause anxiety or mental blocks, it is necessary to maintain a positive outlook by building up your inner faith and spontaneity. Fortunately, when you go with the flow, you are confident with a strong inner determination.

Your Powers of Attraction in Relationships

Although reserved by nature, you can attract others with your fine intellect and friendly manner. Sociable yet sensitive, your contemplative nature implies that you need to be alone from time to time to rest or reflect. Helpful and discreet, you can be a good and loyal friend. In close relationships you are drawn to hardworking partners with a strong sense of self-identity or those with sharp insight. Shrewd and independent, you usually enjoy putting your points across to others but avoid being contentious or stubborn. Although perceptive, you may sometimes repress some of your feelings so it is important to talk things through with your partners. Although your love life can be a dramatic area for you, when you do give of yourself you can be very generous, loving, and magnetic.

Your attractive qualities: intelligent, good planner, practical, thoughtful, dependable, precise, organizational abilities, progressive, writing potential, charming, sociable, creative, original, spiritual potential, helpful, scientific, determined, modest, efficient

Your less attractive qualities: skeptical, isolated, moody, cold, too sensitive, lonely, materialistic, narrow-minded, lack of drive, irritable, overanalytical, vain, critical, stubborn, worry, suspicious

Your Venus Power

The planet Venus has a great deal of influence on your powers of attraction. Below are four possible Venus types for women and men. To find your Venus you need to go to page 771, where you will find the Venus table and extra information. The planet Mars also affects your powers of attraction. To find your Mars table and interpretation go to page 761.

WOMEN WITH VENUS IN LEO: Warm and playful with a touch of the dramatic, you enjoy the company of generous or strong individuals who can share your sense of fun. Although there are advantages to your being strong-willed, in your relationships you need to resist being bossy as it can cause resentment. With your wonderful mixture of regal authority and childlike wonder, you love to keep others entertained and amused.

MEN WITH VENUS IN LEO: Sociable and outgoing, you are kind and generous with those you love. Looking for a relationship that can be fun and entertaining, you need a playmate who can share your enthusiasm and high spirits. Your pride, however, often stops you from associating with lovers or partners you see as beneath you. As you desire someone who can appreciate your sense of the dramatic, you are often attracted to people with strong personalities.

WOMEN WITH VENUS IN VIRGO: Intelligent and discriminating, you are usually drawn to polite and refined individuals. As a perfectionist, you may be keen to analyze and criticize yourself, but be careful of continually going over your partner's shortcomings. By focusing on how you can make positive improvements in yourself and in your relationships, you avoid becoming skeptical or confused. You empower yourself when you display kind and caring concern for the well-being of loved ones and spontaneously offer your practical assistance.

MEN WITH VENUS IN VIRGO: A love of order usually indicates that you are attracted to refined individuals with analytical or practical abilities. You and your partner may be working together or serving similar causes. As you constantly analyze partnerships in order to improve them, you are likely to use former relationships as a point of reference and compare them to your present partner. As you are helpful and kind, others usually rely on your good judgment and often turn to you for advice or practical assistance.

WOMEN WITH VENUS IN LIBRA: Usually you are attractive and sociable with an easygoing manner. Your love of

beauty, harmony, and pleasure implies that you are a romantic with a desire for love and affection. Once in a relationship you need to learn to negotiate your position rather than adapt to the wishes of others and compromise just to keep the peace. Nevertheless, your advanced social skills and strong sense of fair play can help you succeed in any social or romantic situation.

MEN WITH VENUS IN LIBRA: Your good social skills, charming personality, and refined manner usually make you attractive to the opposite sex. Equally, you desire a sophisticated partner with grace, elegance, and a strong sense of style. Although you have the ability to be persuasive and irresistible to others, avoid manipulative love games. Nevertheless, your natural diplomacy and sense of fair play help you to relate to people in all social situations. With your love for balance and harmony, you seek a partner who is also moderate, easygoing, and loving.

WOMEN WITH VENUS IN SCORPIO: With a natural psychic gift for penetrating the feelings of others, you can often help partners transform emotional challenges or sexual difficulties. When you fall in love, your strong feelings and determination give you a potent force that others find attractive and seductive. Although you know what really turns people on, your most profound desire is usually for the deepness and closeness of real love and intimacy in an enduring relationship.

MEN WITH VENUS IN SCORPIO: In relationships you possess a sensitive understanding of your partner's deeper nature. Although you are strongly attached to those you love, you may have to be careful that your feelings do not turn into jealousy or possessiveness. When you fall in love it is often with power and an emotional intensity. You are attracted to partners who can share your passion and display strong feelings of sexuality like your own.

To read all about your Outer Planets and work out how to use your personalized timetable, go to Section Three, page 789.

Your Personalized Timetable

JUPITER BENEFICIAL
1941 3/25 – 6/3
1942 9/7 – until 1943 1/21
1943 5/1 – 6/25
1946 12/23 – until 1947 6/17
1947 8/13 – 10/18
1949 1/24 – 5/7
1949 6/3 – 12/10
1952 7/13 – 11/8
1953 3/2 – 5/17
1954 8/17 – 10/22
1954 12/12 – until 1955 6/7
1958 12/6 – until 1959 2/1
1959 5/4 – 9/29
1961 1/8 – 3/26
1961 7/28 – 11/17
1964 6/20 – until 1965 4/30
1966 7/31 – 9/20
1967 1/24 – 5/15
1970 11/20 – until 1971 1/8
1971 6/15 – 9/2
1972 12/23 – until 1973 3/4
1976 6/1 – until 1977 4/12
1978 7/15 – 8/30
1982 11/4 – 12/20
1984 12/7 – until 1985 2/14
1988 5/16 – 8/2
1988 11/17 – until 1989 3/22
1990 6/29 – 8/13
1994 10/19 – 12/4
1996 3/31 – 6/8
1996 11/18 – until 1997 1/29
2000 4/29 – 7/9
2001 1/5 – 2/14
2002 6/12 – 7/27
2006 10/2 – 11/19
2008 3/2 – 7/22
2008 10/25 – until 2009 1/13
2012 4/12 – 6/20

SATURN BENEFICIAL
1941 4/22 – until 1942 5/23
1945 8/11 – until 1946 2/16
1946 4/21 – 7/24
1955 1/7 – 4/25
1955 10/4 – 12/31
1956 5/29 – 9/28
1960 3/1 – 6/27
1960 11/28 – until 1962 1/19
1970 6/1 – until 1971 1/4
1971 1/30 – 7/4
1971 12/10 – until 1972 3/22
1974 10/26 – 11/6
1975 6/17 – 9/5
1976 1/28 – 5/24
1984 11/9 – until 1985 11/7
1990 1/3 – until 1991 2/23
1991 8/19 – 11/19
1999 7/22 – 10/8
2000 4/4 – until 2001 5/6
2004 7/24 – until 2005 7/7

URANUS BENEFICIAL
1938 6/13 – until 1943 4/4
1953 7/13 – until 1956 5/13
1978 12/15 – until 1981 10/28
1992 2/8 – until 1996 12/3

NEPTUNE BENEFICIAL
1964 12/16 – until 1970 10/2
1991 2/19 – until 1999 11/14

PLUTO BENEFICIAL
1938 1/25 – 6/22
1990 12/10 – until 1995 10/10

JUPITER CHALLENGING
1939 3/10 – 5/21
1939 10/12 – until 1940 1/6
1941 8/10 – 12/12
1942 3/31 – 6/18

1948 1/4 – 11/24
1951 2/21 – 4/30
1953 7/18 – until 1954 6/1
1959 12/19 – until 1960 3/17
1960 5/24 – 11/5
1963 2/3 – 4/12
1965 6/30 – until 1966 5/15
1971 12/3 – until 1972 2/17
1972 7/7 – 10/12
1974 6/1 – 8/12
1975 1/15 – 3/26
1977 6/14 – 9/1
1977 12/17 – until 1978 4/24
1983 11/17 – until 1984 1/28
1986 5/3 – 9/26
1986 12/20 – until 1987 3/10
1989 5/29 – 8/9
1990 1/30 – 3/22
1995 10/31 – until 1996 1/11
1998 4/13 – until 1999 2/21
2001 5/11 – 7/21
2007 2/13 – 5/29
2007 10/11 – 12/27
2010 3/26 – 6/22
2010 8/23 – until 2011 2/1
2012 9/17 – 10/21

SATURN CHALLENGING
1938 1/1 – 2/4
1943 6/6 – until 1944 7/4
1957 12/1 – until 1959 1/22
1959 7/23 – 10/17
1965 5/18 – 8/8
1966 2/5 – until 1967 3/19
1972 7/18 – 12/24
1973 4/4 – 8/20
1973 12/15 – until 1974 5/8
1987 1/5 – 7/8
1987 9/29 – until 1988 3/13
1988 5/10 – 11/30
1995 3/13 – until 1996 4/23
1996 10/26 – until 1997 1/10
2002 5/20 – until 2003 6/18

URANUS CHALLENGING
1945 7/22 – until 1950 4/25
1985 1/10 – until 1989 10/15
2007 3/26 – until 2012 2/2

NEPTUNE CHALLENGING
1977 2/14 – until 1985 11/13

PLUTO CHALLENGING
2001 12/27 – until 2009 11/20

JUPITER SPECIAL
1944 10/8 – until 1945 9/3
1956 9/22 – until 1957 8/17
1968 9/6 – 11/28
1969 3/16 – 7/28
1980 8/21 – 11/6
1981 4/26 – 6/27
1992 8/4 – 10/19
2003 11/20 – until 2004 2/18
2004 7/16 – 10/3

SATURN SPECIAL
1949 10/26 – until 1950 3/9
1950 7/18 – 12/19
1951 2/4 – 8/30
1979 8/30 – until 1980 10/6
2008 10/6 – until 2009 4/13
2009 6/19 – 11/17
2010 3/14 – 8/11

URANUS SPECIAL
1965 9/18 – until 1969 8/16

NEPTUNE SPECIAL
1938 1/1 – until 1944 7/21

PLUTO SPECIAL
1964 11/7 – until 1973 7/8

♍

September 18

SUN: VIRGO · DECANATE: TAURUS/VENUS · DEGREE: 24°45–25°45 VIRGO · MODE: MUTABLE · ELEMENT: EARTH

Your Personal Powers

Determined and strong-willed, you possess good strategic skills, mental acumen, and a practical yet caring nature. Generally, you love acquiring knowledge and sharing it with others. Your high standards and natural organizational skills can ensure that when you do a job you like to be efficient, dedicated, and hardworking. You may lose some of your power, however, if you become overanxious or involved in avoidance and escapism. You empower yourself when you combine your charm and cooperative skill with your strong inner desire to achieve results. Although you are generally motivated or self-driven, you can also experience periods of passivity and indolence. When you remain positive and focused, however, you can overcome your challenges. As you also need recognition for your efforts, you thrive on encouragement and support. Although you do not mind working behind the scenes, you like to be in control. You may even take a humanistic or philanthropic approach in business situations. Imaginative and intuitive, as long as you have a clear vision you can be successful.

Your Powers of Attraction in Relationships

Your good mind and determination attract others. Although independent, you have a skill for dealing with people and an ability to make the right contacts. Aware of the advantages of cooperative efforts, you may even have a working partnership with your spouse. Usually you are attracted to sensitive and intelligent people with charm and magnetism. Caring and romantic in close personal relationships, love and affection are very important to you. If your love life goes wrong, however, you may become manipulative, demanding, or temperamental. Fortunately, once committed, you are likely to take your responsibilities seriously, but as a perfectionist, you may have to avoid being hard on yourself. Desiring security and a harmonious environment, you need a partner who understands the importance of home and family.

Your attractive qualities: determined, progressive, assertive, business sense, organizational skills, assertive, friendly, intuitive, strategist, independent, dynamic, practical, dramatic, home-loving, courageous, resolute, ambitious, efficient, imaginative, advisory skills

Your less attractive qualities: bossy, lazy, lack of order, nervous, overtax yourself or inertia, selfish, power challenges, moody, worry, escapist, intolerant, underachiever, manipulative, anxious, avoidance, interfering

Your Venus Power

The planet Venus has a great deal of influence on your powers of attraction. Below are four possible Venus types for women and men. To find your Venus you need to go to page 771, where you will find the Venus table and extra information. The planet Mars also affects your powers of attraction. To find your Mars table and interpretation go to page 761.

WOMEN WITH VENUS IN LEO: Your friendly and sunny personality often makes you stand out in a crowd. Generous and giving, you know how to make your partner feel special. As you often expect loyalty and devotion from your partners in return, you can become easily offended if they ignore you or behave in an inconsiderate manner. Charming and kind, when you are in love you can be romantic, dramatic, and passionate.

MEN WITH VENUS IN LEO: A childlike nature suggests that you are versatile and keen on games or being entertained. You are usually attracted to vivacious partners with a benevolent nature. As an extrovert you enjoy being involved in all types of activities where you can assert yourself and show your talents and abilities. Others may recognize your inborn tendencies to lead but are also aware of your vanity or pride. Nevertheless, generous, kind, and caring, you often show compassion to those less fortunate than yourself.

WOMEN WITH VENUS IN VIRGO: Articulate and straightforward in your relationships, you attract others with your genuine concern for their well-being. By being understanding and a good listener, you are able to show your love and friendship. With your analytical approach to relationships, however, you may have to be careful of becoming too matter-of-fact. You often display your concern for the welfare of others by your willingness to offer practical help and assistance. You usually seek a partner who is willing to work as hard on relationships as you are.

MEN WITH VENUS IN VIRGO: Although you are constantly analyzing your relationships in order to understand and improve them, you may nevertheless need to refrain from continuously mulling over issues that can cause anxiety. You are happiest when you are able to help your loved ones in practical ways and forget yourself in your willingness to be of service to others. You seek a partner who has high stan-

dards and can be as pragmatic and hardworking as yourself. Ideally they should also be impeccably dressed with a fine analytical mind.

WOMEN WITH VENUS IN LIBRA: Gracious, charming, and sociable with a sense of style, you have no trouble attracting admirers. With your natural diplomatic skills and desire for harmony you usually like to keep the peace and avoid confrontations, but be careful of failing to take a stand when it is necessary. Romantic and easygoing yourself, you are attracted to affectionate and refined individuals who share your love of peace, justice, and fair play.

MEN WITH VENUS IN LIBRA: Courteous and refined, you are attracted to beautiful and elegant people. You are looking for a partner who can share your natural good taste and enjoy an intellectual conversation. Disliking conflict, you may have to be careful not to go along with others just to keep the peace. Your ideal partner will appreciate beauty and the little luxuries of life as well as possess good social skills. You have a strong sense of social etiquette yourself so you need an intelligent and sophisticated partner.

WOMEN WITH VENUS IN SCORPIO: Loving and passionate, you are often sensitive with deep feelings and strong powers of attraction. A love for the truth coupled with a tendency to be suspicious can be an influence that motivates you to delve deep into the activities of your partner. When in love or in a relationship that matters, you will often bend over backward to cooperate. Although loyal, guard against losing sight of your own needs and desires.

MEN WITH VENUS IN SCORPIO: As you are emotionally intense and passionate, personal relationships are probably a major factor in your own transformation. Being sensitive yet loyal, you are usually attracted to forceful partners who can express themselves intimately but intensely. Rather than seek easy and simple relationships, you are drawn to partners who act as a catalyst for your own internal changes. Through your relationships with your partners you can unravel your own motives and understand your deep-seated feelings or emotional insecurities.

To read all about your Outer Planets and work out how to use your personalized timetable, go to Section Three, page 789.

Your Personalized Timetable

JUPITER BENEFICIAL
1941   3/30 – 6/7
1942   9/13 – until **1943** 1/13
1943   5/7 – 6/30
1946   12/29 – until **1947** 6/7
1947   8/23 – 10/23
1949   1/29 – 12/15
1952   7/19 – 11/1
1953   3/8 – 5/21
1954   8/22 – 11/9
1954   11/24 – until **1955** 6/12
1958   12/10 – until **1959** 2/9
1959   4/26 – 10/4
1961   1/12 – 4/1
1961   7/20 – 11/23
1964   6/25 – 12/20
1965   1/31 – 5/5
1966   8/4 – 9/26
1967   1/17 – until **1967** 5/22
1970   11/24 – until **1971** 1/13
1971   6/6 – 9/10
1972   12/27 – until **1973** 3/9
1973   9/10 – 10/16
1976   6/6 – until **1977** 4/17
1978   7/19 – 9/4
1979   3/3 – 4/18
1982   11/8 – 12/25
1984   12/11 – until **1985** 2/19
1988   5/20 – 8/9
1988   11/9 – until **1989** 3/28
1990   7/3 – 8/17
1994   10/24 – 12/8
1996   4/11 – 5/27
1996   11/23 – until **1997** 2/2
2000   5/3 – 7/14
2000   12/24 – until **2001** 2/26
2002   6/16 – 8/1
2006   10/7 – 11/23
2008   3/8 – 7/14
2008   10/31 – until **2009** 1/17
2012   4/16 – 6/24

SATURN BENEFICIAL
1941   4/29 – until **1942** 5/30
1945   8/19 – until **1946** 2/1
1946   5/5 – 8/1
1955   1/20 – 4/11
1955   10/13 – until **1956** 1/11
1956   5/16 – 10/9
1960   3/14 – 6/12
1960   12/7 – until **1962** 1/27
1970   6/9 – 12/12
1971   2/21 – 7/14
1971   11/28 – until **1972** 4/1
1975   6/24 – 9/15
1976   1/16 – 6/3
1984   11/17 – until **1985** 11/15
1990   1/11 – until **1991** 3/5
1991   8/5 – 12/1
1999   8/10 – 9/18
2000   4/12 – until **2001** 5/13
2004   8/1 – until **2005** 7/15

URANUS BENEFICIAL
1938   7/5 – until **1943** 4/24
1953   7/29 – until **1956** 6/6
1979   1/4 – until **1981** 11/13
1992   2/28 – until **1996** 12/24

NEPTUNE BENEFICIAL
1965   1/27 – until **1970** 11/2
1992   1/17 – until **1999** 12/22

PLUTO BENEFICIAL
1938   1/1 – until **1939** 6/7
1991   1/10 – until **1995** 11/6

JUPITER CHALLENGING
1939   3/14 – 5/27
1939   10/4 – until **1940** 1/13
1941   8/16 – 12/5

1942   4/6 – 6/22
1948   1/9 – 11/28
1951   2/25 – 5/4
1953   7/23 – until **1954** 1/25
1954   2/26 – 6/6
1959   12/23 – until **1960** 3/28
1960   5/12 – 11/10
1963   2/8 – 4/16
1965   7/5 – until **1966** 5/19
1971   12/7 – until **1972** 2/23
1972   6/29 – 10/18
1974   6/12 – 8/1
1975   1/20 – 3/30
1977   6/18 – 9/8
1977   12/9 – until **1978** 4/29
1983   11/21 – until **1984** 2/2
1986   5/9 – 9/18
1986   12/27 – until **1987** 3/14
1989   6/2 – 8/14
1990   1/20 – 4/1
1995   11/5 – until **1996** 1/16
1998   4/17 – until **1999** 2/25
2001   5/16 – 7/26
2007   2/20 – 5/21
2007   10/17 – 12/31
2010   3/30 – 7/5
2010   8/10 – until **2011** 2/6

SATURN CHALLENGING
1938   1/1 – 2/14
1943   6/14 – until **1944** 7/12
1957   12/9 – until **1959** 1/31
1959   7/8 – 10/30
1965   6/7 – 7/19
1966   2/13 – until **1967** 3/26
1972   7/27 – 12/12
1973   4/15 – 8/31
1973   12/3 – until **1974** 5/17
1987   1/14 – 6/23
1987   10/13 – until **1988** 12/8
1995   3/21 – until **1996** 5/2
1996   10/11 – until **1997** 1/23
2002   5/28 – until **2003** 6/26

URANUS CHALLENGING
1945   8/16 – until **1950** 5/17
1985   1/30 – until **1989** 11/9
2007   4/14 – until **2012** 2/23

NEPTUNE CHALLENGING
1978   1/3 – until **1985** 12/12

PLUTO CHALLENGING
2002   1/26 – until **2010** 9/28

JUPITER SPECIAL
1944   10/13 – until **1945** 9/8
1956   9/26 – until **1957** 8/22
1968   9/11 – 12/5
1969   3/8 – 8/3
1980   8/26 – 11/11
1981   4/16 – 7/7
1992   8/9 – 10/24
2003   11/28 – until **2004** 2/9
2004   7/22 – 10/8

SATURN SPECIAL
1949   11/5 – until **1950** 2/25
1950   7/28 – until **1951** 9/7
1979   9/7 – until **1980** 10/14
2008   10/14 – until **2009** 3/28
2009   7/4 – 11/29
2010   3/1 – 8/20

URANUS SPECIAL
1965   10/4 – until **1969** 9/2

NEPTUNE SPECIAL
1938   1/1 – until **1944** 8/26

PLUTO SPECIAL
1965   9/30 – until **1973** 8/18

♍

377

September 19

SUN: VIRGO • DECANATE: TAURUS/VENUS • DEGREE: 25°45–26°5 VIRGO • MODE: MUTABLE • ELEMENT: EARTH

Your Personal Powers

Confident, practical, and quick-witted, you are an instinctive and sensitive individual with sharp awareness. You gain power from your desire to seek new experiences that keep your spirit young and active. Your ruling planet, Mercury, grants you fast responses, keen intelligence, and emphasizes your enjoyment at adding to your wide store of knowledge and information. Being both ambitious and perceptive, you can appear to others as strong-willed, competitive, and gregarious. Independent with natural executive skills, you also make a good leader. As you become bored easily, however, be careful not to lose some of your power to restlessness and impatience. You empower yourself when you combine your foresight with your sense of adventure and the ability to adapt to new situations. You are usually at your best when working productively to deadlines or on new and stimulating projects. At these times you are able to utilize your good mental concentration and skill at problem solving to enhance your enterprising spirit and achieve success.

Your Powers of Attraction in Relationships

Others are drawn to your progressive personality, creativity, and ability to mix with people on all levels. Besides being sociable you have a latent humanitarian streak that can concern you with the welfare of others. Although you usually appear confident, you are very sensitive inside, which may sometimes cause you emotional highs and lows. Highly perceptive, you can be an entertaining friend and companion, attracting others with your quick repartee. Although private about your romantic life, resist letting restlessness lure you to secrecy or hidden affairs. Although you may be challenged in early relationships, the more you find your life purpose, the better you respond to others. Generally you are attracted to a partner with strong determination or natural leadership ability. Alternatively, you may seek those who resonate with your inner desire for deeper insight in life.

Your attractive qualities: dynamic, creative, intuitive, universal, leadership, progressive, optimistic, strong convictions, confident, keen intelligence, adventurous, practical, ambitious, quick responses, humanitarian, idealistic, competitive, gregarious, independent

Your less attractive qualities: self-centered, worry, escapist, materialistic, bored, impatient, restless, cynical, frustrated, inner tensions, disappointed, self-doubt, too serious, critical

Your Venus Power

The planet Venus has a great deal of influence on your powers of attraction. Below are four possible Venus types for women and men. To find your Venus you need to go to page 771, where you will find the Venus table and extra information. The planet Mars also affects your powers of attraction. To find your Mars table and interpretation go to page 761.

WOMEN WITH VENUS IN LEO: Your friendly and sunny personality often makes you stand out in a crowd. Generous and giving, you know how to make your partner feel special. As you often expect loyalty and devotion from your partners in return, you can become easily offended if they ignore you or behave in an inconsiderate manner. Charming and kind, when you are in love you can be romantic, dramatic, and passionate.

MEN WITH VENUS IN LEO: A childlike nature suggests that you are versatile and keen on games or being entertained. You are usually attracted to vivacious partners with a benevolent nature. As an extrovert you enjoy being involved in all types of activities where you can assert yourself and show your talents and abilities. Others may recognize your inborn tendencies to lead but are also aware of your vanity or pride. Nevertheless, generous, kind, and caring, you often show compassion to those less fortunate than yourself.

WOMEN WITH VENUS IN VIRGO: In relationships you can be modest and unassuming but desire perfection. You usually analyze your partnerships until you feel you have understood them to the last little detail in order to improve them. A problem usually arises when you become too critical either of partners or yourself and indulge in being skeptical or fault-finding. As you are modest, others may not be aware of the strong sensuality beneath your well-groomed exterior.

MEN WITH VENUS IN VIRGO: Industrious and well-ordered, you relate to others in a considerate and down-to-earth way. You enjoy giving practical advice and being of service to those you love even in small ways. Being a perfectionist, you are drawn to partners with high morals or a strong work ethic. Partners who have strong analytical minds are very attractive to you, particularly if they are also clean and meticulously dressed.

WOMEN WITH VENUS IN LIBRA: Gracious, charming, and sociable with a sense of style, you have no trouble attracting admirers. With your natural diplomatic skills and desire for harmony you usually like to keep the peace and avoid confrontations, but be careful of failing to take a stand when it is necessary. Romantic and easygoing yourself, you are attracted to affectionate and refined individuals who share your love of peace, justice, and fair play.

MEN WITH VENUS IN LIBRA: Courteous and refined, you are attracted to beautiful and elegant people. You are looking for a partner who can share your natural good taste and enjoy an intellectual conversation. Disliking conflict, you may have to be careful not to go along with others just to keep the peace. Your ideal partner will appreciate beauty and the little luxuries of life as well as possess good social skills. You have a strong sense of social etiquette yourself so you need an intelligent and sophisticated partner.

WOMEN WITH VENUS IN SCORPIO: Usually you are drawn to partners who are sensual in appearance with a strong character. As you are emotionally intense and passionate, personal relationships are probably a major factor in your life. Since you like to be in control, you can at times exhibit some of your less attractive qualities by being willful or domineering. Although you need to feel established and in command in your relationships, you are constantly searching for some higher truth that can bring significant transformation.

MEN WITH VENUS IN SCORPIO: Usually you are attracted to sensual and passionate partners who have a strong character. You are often intense with deep feelings and magnetic powers of attraction. As a cautious yet devoted and ardent lover, you are likely to seek experiences that are more sexual in their nature. You display your less attractive qualities when you project your negative thoughts and resort to being suspicious or possessive. Nevertheless, loyal and loving, you are a sensitive lover.

To read about your Outer Planets and to work out how to use your personalized timetable, go to Section Three, page 789.

Your Personalized Timetable

JUPITER BENEFICIAL
1941 4/3 – 6/11
1942 9/19 – until **1943** 1/6
1943 5/14 – 7/4
1947 1/3 – 5/29
1947 8/31 – 10/28
1949 2/2 – 12/19
1952 7/26 – 10/24
1953 3/13 – 5/25
1954 8/27 – until **1955** 2/20
1955 4/10 – 6/17
1958 12/15 – until **1959** 2/19
1959 4/15 – 10/10
1961 1/17 – 4/8
1961 7/12 – 11/29
1964 6/30 – 12/9
1965 2/11 – 5/9
1966 8/9 – 10/3
1967 1/9 – 5/28
1970 11/29 – until **1971** 1/19
1971 5/29 – 9/17
1973 1/1 – 3/14
1973 8/28 – 10/29
1976 6/10 – until **1977** 4/22
1978 7/23 – 9/9
1979 2/19 – 4/29
1982 11/13 – 12/30
1984 12/16 – until **1985** 2/23
1988 5/24 – 8/17
1988 11/1 – until **1989** 4/2
1990 7/7 – 8/22
1994 10/28 – 12/13
1996 11/28 – until **1997** 2/6
2000 5/7 – 7/19
2000 12/16 – until **2001** 3/6
2002 6/21 – 8/5
2006 10/12 – 11/27
2008 3/14 – 7/6
2008 11/7 – until **2009** 1/21
2012 4/20 – 6/29

SATURN BENEFICIAL
1941 5/7 – until **1942** 6/7
1945 8/28 – until **1946** 1/19
1946 5/17 – 8/9
1955 2/8 – 3/21
1955 10/22 – until **1956** 1/22
1956 5/2 – 10/18
1960 3/31 – 5/25
1960 12/16 – until **1962** 2/5
1970 6/18 – 11/28
1971 3/7 – 7/24
1971 11/16 – until **1972** 4/11
1975 7/2 – 9/26
1976 1/4 – 6/12
1984 11/26 – until **1985** 11/24
1990 1/19 – until **1991** 3/15
1991 7/22 – 12/12
2000 4/20 – until **2001** 5/21
2004 8/9 – until **2005** 2/28
2005 4/12 – 7/22

URANUS BENEFICIAL
1939 5/9 – until **1943** 5/12
1953 8/15 – until **1956** 6/25
1979 2/4 – until **1982** 9/2
1992 3/31 – until **1997** 1/10

NEPTUNE BENEFICIAL
1965 12/12 – until **1971** 9/25
1992 2/14 – until **2000** 10/25

PLUTO BENEFICIAL
1938 1/1 – until **1940** 5/14
1991 11/26 – until **1996** 9/21

JUPITER CHALLENGING
1939 3/18 – 6/2
1939 9/27 – until **1940** 1/19
1941 8/22 – 11/28

1942 4/12 – 6/27
1948 1/13 – 12/3
1951 3/1 – 5/9
1953 7/28 – until **1954** 1/12
1954 3/11 – 6/10
1959 12/27 – until **1960** 11/15
1963 2/12 – 4/20
1965 7/9 – until **1966** 5/24
1971 12/11 – until **1972** 2/29
1972 6/21 – 10/25
1974 7/2 – 7/11
1975 1/24 – 4/3
1977 6/22 – 9/16
1977 12/1 – until **1978** 5/5
1983 11/26 – until **1984** 2/7
1984 8/9 – 9/19
1986 5/15 – 9/11
1987 1/2 – 3/18
1989 6/6 – 8/19
1990 1/11 – 4/10
1995 11/9 – until **1996** 1/20
1998 4/22 – until **1999** 3/1
2001 5/20 – 7/30
2007 3/1 – 5/12
2007 10/22 – until **2008** 1/4
2010 4/3 – until **2011** 2/11

SATURN CHALLENGING
1938 1/1 – 2/23
1943 6/21 – until **1944** 7/20
1957 12/18 – until **1959** 2/10
1959 6/25 – 11/10
1966 2/22 – until **1967** 4/3
1972 8/6 – 11/30
1973 4/25 – 9/15
1973 11/18 – until **1974** 5/25
1987 1/24 – 6/9
1987 10/24 – until **1988** 12/17
1995 3/29 – until **1996** 5/12
1996 9/28 – until **1997** 2/3
2002 6/4 – until **2003** 7/3

URANUS CHALLENGING
1946 6/13 – until **1950** 6/4
1985 3/3 – until **1989** 11/29
2007 5/7 – until **2012** 3/12

NEPTUNE CHALLENGING
1978 2/6 – until **1986** 11/7

PLUTO CHALLENGING
2002 12/19 – until **2010** 11/17

JUPITER SPECIAL
1944 10/18 – until **1945** 4/30
1945 5/28 – 9/12
1956 10/1 – until **1957** 8/27
1968 9/15 – 12/13
1969 2/28 – 8/8
1980 8/30 – 11/17
1981 4/8 – 7/15
1992 8/14 – 10/29
2003 12/8 – until **2004** 1/30
2004 7/28 – 10/12

SATURN SPECIAL
1949 11/17 – until **1950** 2/11
1950 8/6 – until **1951** 9/16
1979 9/15 – until **1980** 10/22
1981 5/4 – 7/6
2008 10/23 – until **2009** 3/15
2009 7/16 – 12/14
2010 2/13 – 8/29

URANUS SPECIAL
1965 10/21 – until **1969** 9/18

NEPTUNE SPECIAL
1938 1/1 – until **1945** 7/9

PLUTO SPECIAL
1965 11/1 – until **1973** 9/15

September 20

SUN: VIRGO · DECANATE: TAURUS/VENUS · DEGREE: 26°45–27°5 VIRGO · MODE: MUTABLE · ELEMENT: EARTH

Your Personal Powers

Practical yet sensitive, you are a strong character with natural diplomatic skills and inspired ideas. Courteous and friendly, you gain power from your idealistic vision and enterprising nature. Your ruler, Mercury, grants you quick understanding, fluent speech, and keen perceptions. You empower yourself by combining your ability to plan with your ingenuity and foresight. Although you prefer to be honest and direct, you can also charm others with a gracious and persuasive manner. As you have fast responses and are likely to be constantly seeking mental stimulation, be careful not to lose some of your power to restlessness, impatience, or becoming overly critical. Often highly sensitive, you can integrate your intuitive impressionability with your organizational skills in order to accomplish your goals in life. Although you enjoy learning and are quick to see opportunities, you also possess a strong need for peace and harmonious surroundings. This may place an extra emphasis on your home and family responsibilities as a secure base from which to carry out your many plans for success.

Your Powers of Attraction in Relationships

Others are attracted to your sociable and friendly manner. You can be considerate and courteous but still maintain your sincerity. Modest and persuasive, you usually enjoy cooperative activities where you can relate intellectually to others. Being astute and straightforward, you are often drawn to individuals who inspire you to gain wider knowledge. Although you may be drawn to more unusual relationships, you want a partner who is wise yet entertaining. Extremely sensitive to the feelings of others, you usually need to maintain the balance of give and take in your partnerships in order to avoid dependent situations. Intuitive and shrewd, you can be affectionate and understanding as well as practical and realistic. Your relationships thrive when you and your partner share the same goals or ideals.

Your attractive qualities: idealistic, practical, intuitive, frank, planner, diplomatic, intelligent, receptive, intuitive, honest, good partnerships, considerate, harmonious, receptive, decisiveness, agreeable, amicable, clever, sensitive, individualist, productive, optimistic

Your less attractive qualities: suspicious, critical, impatient, lack of confidence, deceptive, shy, too sensitive, selfish, restlessness, easily hurt, martyr, intolerant, stubborn

Your Venus Power

The planet Venus has a great deal of influence on your powers of attraction. Below are four possible Venus types for women and men. To find your Venus you need to go to page 771, where you will find the Venus table and extra information. The planet Mars also affects your powers of attraction. To find your Mars table and interpretation go to page 761.

WOMEN WITH VENUS IN LEO: You possess the wonderful ability to project your warm and sunny personality and keep others happily entertained. Loving attention yourself, you seek a partner who can appreciate you, be supportive, and give you positive feedback. Proud, with a natural regal air, you expect respect from your partners but are willing to be loyal and supportive in exchange. Although sometimes a little self-centered, you know how to make your partner feel special.

MEN WITH VENUS IN LEO: Enthusiastic, playful, and kind, you can be benevolent with those you love. Warm, romantic, and self-expressive, you adore the drama of love or having fun with your friends. Usually you are attracted to partners with a warm and generous nature. Although you can be a confident and charismatic partner, you may need to develop humility in order to stop pride or arrogance from marring your relationships.

WOMEN WITH VENUS IN VIRGO: Intelligent and discriminating, you are usually drawn to polite and refined individuals. As a perfectionist, you may be keen to analyze and criticize yourself but be careful of continually going over your partner's shortcomings. By focusing on how you can make positive improvements in yourself and in your relationships, you avoid becoming skeptical or confused. You empower yourself when you display kind and caring concern for the well-being of loved ones and spontaneously offer your practical assistance.

MEN WITH VENUS IN VIRGO: A love of order usually indicates that you are attracted to refined individuals with analytical or practical abilities. You and your partner may be working together or serving similar causes. As you constantly analyze partnerships in order to improve them, you are likely to use former relationships as a point of reference and com-

pare them to your present partner. As you are helpful and kind, others usually rely on your good judgment and often turn to you for advice or practical assistance.

WOMEN WITH VENUS IN LIBRA: Attractive, refined, and conscious of the needs of others, you usually desire harmonious relationships. As a peacemaker with good negotiating skills, you can smooth out difficulties with others but your dislike of confrontation may sometimes leave you refusing to take a stand or compromising too many of your own needs. Courteous, stylish, and charming with polished social skills, you are an expert at relating to others in a gracious and civilized manner.

MEN WITH VENUS IN LIBRA: As a sociable and friendly individual with an eye for beauty, you are amorous and charming. You are a natural gentleman and your ideal partner usually has an elegant appearance, artistic appreciation, and good taste. Your relationships benefit when you resist the temptation to take the easy way out or put too much emphasis on vanity and high living. Intellectual and naturally refined, you seek a loving partner who can share your romantic and sophisticated aspirations.

WOMEN WITH VENUS IN SCORPIO: Your strength and power is in your ability to love both deeply and sensitively. For you, love and desire go hand in hand. As you feel so deeply, you often keep your sensitivity or vulnerability hidden from others in order to keep some control in your relationships. You are more likely to prefer a few very close loyal friends than many superficial acquaintances. In relationships your sensual nature and magnetic intensity can easily attract others.

MEN WITH VENUS IN SCORPIO: You are attracted to partners with deep and powerful emotions or individuals whom you find intriguing. Your gift for creating smoke screens to maintain secrecy around your feelings can conceal your inner sensitivity and vulnerability. Nevertheless, you are looking for a partner who can pierce your defenses and understand you at a very deep level. Needing a relationship with a powerful sexual connection, you thrive on emotional intensity.

To read all about your Outer Planets and work out how to use your personalized timetable, go to Section Three, page 789.

♍

Your Personalized Timetable

JUPITER BENEFICIAL
1941 4/8 – 6/16
1942 9/26 – 12/30
1943 5/19 – 7/9
1947 1/9 – 5/21
1947 9/8 – 11/1
1949 2/7 – 12/24
1952 8/3 – 10/16
1953 3/18 – 5/30
1954 9/1 – until 1955 2/10
1955 4/21 – 6/22
1958 12/20 – until 1959 3/8
1959 3/29 – 10/15
1961 1/21 – 4/16
1961 7/4 – 12/4
1964 7/5 – 11/30
1965 2/20 – 5/13
1966 8/14 – 10/10
1967 1/2 – 6/3
1970 12/3 – until 1971 1/25
1971 5/21 – 9/24
1973 1/5 – 3/19
1973 8/19 – 11/7
1976 6/15 – until 1977 4/26
1978 7/28 – 9/15
1979 2/11 – 5/8
1982 11/17 – until 1983 1/4
1983 7/7 – 8/20
1984 12/20 – until 1985 2/28
1988 5/28 – 8/27
1988 10/22 – until 1989 4/8
1990 7/12 – 8/26
1994 11/2 – 12/17
1996 12/3 – until 1997 2/11
2000 5/12 – 7/25
2000 12/8 – until 2001 3/14
2002 6/25 – 8/9
2006 10/17 – 12/2
2008 3/21 – 6/28
2008 11/13 – until 2009 1/26
2012 4/25 – 7/3

SATURN BENEFICIAL
1941 5/15 – until 1942 6/15
1945 9/7 – until 1946 1/7
1946 5/27 – 8/16
1955 10/31 – until 1956 2/6
1956 4/16 – 10/27
1960 12/25 – until 1962 2/13
1962 10/3 – 10/15
1970 6/27 – 11/16
1971 3/18 – 8/5
1971 11/3 – until 1972 4/20
1975 7/10 – 10/10
1975 12/21 – until 1976 6/21
1984 12/4 – until 1985 7/5
1985 8/14 – 12/2
1990 1/28 – 9/13
1990 10/3 – until 1991 3/27
1991 7/9 – 12/22
2000 4/28 – until 2001 5/28
2004 8/17 – until 2005 2/10
2005 4/30 – 7/30

URANUS BENEFICIAL
1939 5/26 – until 1943 5/29
1953 9/4 – until 1956 7/12
1979 11/22 – until 1982 10/2
1993 1/20 – until 1997 10/25

NEPTUNE BENEFICIAL
1966 1/16 – until 1971 10/29
1992 3/27 – until 2000 12/15

PLUTO BENEFICIAL
1938 1/1 – until 1940 6/30
1991 12/22 – until 1996 10/24

JUPITER CHALLENGING
1939 3/22 – 6/8
1939 9/20 – until 1940 1/25
1941 8/30 – 11/20

1942 4/18 – 7/1
1948 1/18 – 12/7
1951 3/5 – 5/14
1951 11/12 – 12/18
1953 8/2 – until 1954 1/3
1954 3/21 – 6/14
1960 1/1 – 11/20
1963 2/16 – 4/24
1965 7/14 – until 1966 5/29
1971 12/16 – until 1972 3/7
1972 6/14 – 10/31
1975 1/29 – 4/7
1977 6/26 – 9/25
1977 11/22 – until 1978 5/10
1983 11/30 – until 1984 2/12
1984 7/27 – 10/1
1986 5/21 – 9/3
1987 1/8 – 3/22
1989 6/10 – 8/25
1990 1/4 – 4/17
1995 11/14 – until 1996 1/25
1998 4/27 – 10/25
1998 12/2 – until 1999 3/6
2001 5/25 – 8/4
2007 3/11 – 5/1
2007 10/27 – until 2008 1/8
2010 4/7 – until 2011 2/15

SATURN CHALLENGING
1938 1/1 – 3/3
1943 6/29 – until 1944 7/28
1945 2/1 – 4/7
1957 12/26 – until 1959 2/22
1959 6/11 – 11/20
1966 3/2 – until 1967 4/11
1972 8/18 – 11/17
1973 5/3 – until 1974 6/2
1987 2/4 – 5/27
1987 11/3 – until 1988 12/25
1995 4/6 – 10/22
1995 12/21 – until 1996 5/22
1996 9/16 – until 1997 2/13
2002 6/12 – until 2003 7/11

URANUS CHALLENGING
1946 6/30 – until 1950 6/20
1985 12/20 – until 1989 12/16
2008 3/11 – Continues

NEPTUNE CHALLENGING
1978 12/31 – until 1986 12/8

PLUTO CHALLENGING
2003 1/16 – until 2010 12/17

JUPITER SPECIAL
1944 10/23 – until 1945 4/15
1945 6/13 – 9/17
1956 10/6 – until 1957 9/1
1968 9/20 – 12/23
1969 2/18 – 8/14
1980 9/4 – 11/23
1981 3/31 – 7/23
1992 8/19 – 11/3
1993 5/28 – 6/4
2003 12/27 – until 2004 1/11
2004 8/2 – 10/17

SATURN SPECIAL
1949 12/3 – until 1950 1/25
1950 8/15 – until 1951 9/23
1979 9/22 – until 1980 10/31
1981 4/18 – 7/22
2008 11/2 – until 2009 3/3
2009 7/26 – until 2010 9/6

URANUS SPECIAL
1965 11/12 – until 1970 6/30

NEPTUNE SPECIAL
1938 1/1 – until 1945 8/21

PLUTO SPECIAL
1966 9/26 – until 1974 8/6

381

September 21

SUN: VIRGO • DECANATE: TAURUS/VENUS • DEGREE: 27°45–28°45 VIRGO • MODE: MUTABLE • ELEMENT: EARTH

Your Personal Powers

Friendly with sharp intelligence and a quick wit, you are a determined and versatile individualist. With your sharp analytical mind you also possess creative talents or a gift with words. You gain power from your enthusiastic approach to life and your fast responses, but you may have to guard against losing some of your power to nervousness or anxiety if you become scattered. Practical and articulate, you are likely to be rational yet imaginative with a need for self-expression. Although you can be amusing and charming, you also possess the ability to go straight to the heart of a matter. With a desire for knowledge and a natural business sense, you have the ability to turn your many inspired ideas into reality. Even though you are intellectually bright, skepticism or a tendency to worry can undermine your efforts. Nevertheless, developing your patience, inner faith, and natural intuition can help you in your quest for happiness. You are a good psychologist and often utilize your people skills in your quest for success.

Your Powers of Attraction in Relationships

Independent and socially inclined, you can attract others with your intelligence, imagination, and creative reasoning. Although you can be pragmatic, your captivating manner enhances your charm. You are likely to possess a wide circle of friends and can work well with others. A good conversationalist, you can attract people with your originality and ability to express yourself. Although you are romantic with deep emotions, in your love life you may occasionally encounter indecision or emotional highs and lows. You are usually drawn to clever people or those you feel will emotionally understand you. Although you are usually optimistic, when you become critical or overly serious you can cause tension in your relationships. By being loving yet philosophical or more detached, you can magnetize good relationships into your life.

Your attractive qualities: friendly, mentally quick, inspired, honest, direct, sociable, fun-loving, talent with words, independent, expressive, loving, organizational skills, creative, charming, fast responses, sensitive, broad-minded, imaginative, just, receptive, visionary

Your less attractive qualities: dependency, nervous, scattered, worry, insecure, disappointed, too critical, impulsive, indecisive, fear of change, bored, anxious, indecisive, rash

Your Venus Power

The planet Venus has a great deal of influence on your powers of attraction. Below are four possible Venus types for women and men. To find your Venus you need to go to page 771, where you will find the Venus table and extra information. The planet Mars also affects your powers of attraction. To find your Mars table and interpretation go to page 761.

WOMEN WITH VENUS IN LEO: Your friendly and sunny personality often makes you stand out in a crowd. Generous and giving, you know how to make your partner feel special. As you often expect loyalty and devotion from your partners in return, you can become easily offended if they ignore you or behave in an inconsiderate manner. Charming and kind, when you are in love, you can be romantic, dramatic, and passionate.

MEN WITH VENUS IN LEO: A childlike nature suggests that you are versatile and keen on games or being entertained. You are usually attracted to vivacious partners with a benevolent nature. As an extrovert you enjoy being involved in all types of activities where you can assert yourself and show your talents and abilities. Others may recognize your inborn tendencies to lead but are also aware of your vanity or pride. Nevertheless, generous, kind, and caring, you often show compassion to those less fortunate than yourself.

WOMEN WITH VENUS IN VIRGO: Articulate and straightforward in your relationships, you attract others with your genuine concern for their well-being. By being understanding and a good listener, you are able to show your love and friendship. With your analytical approach to relationships, however, you may have to be careful of becoming too matter-of-fact. You often display your concern for the welfare of others by your willingness to offer practical help and assistance. You usually seek a partner who is willing to work as hard on relationships as you are.

MEN WITH VENUS IN VIRGO: A love of order usually means you are attracted to refined individuals with analytical or practical abilities. You and your partner may be working together or serving similar causes. As you constantly analyze partnerships in order to improve them, you are likely to use former relationships as a point of reference and compare

them to your present partner. As you are helpful and kind, others usually rely on your good judgment and often turn to you for advice or practical assistance.

WOMEN WITH VENUS IN LIBRA: Usually you are attractive and sociable with an easygoing manner. Your love of beauty, harmony, and pleasure implies that you are a romantic with a desire for love and affection. Once in a relationship you need to learn to negotiate your position rather than adapt to the wishes of others and compromise just to keep the peace. Nevertheless, your advanced social skills and strong sense of fair play can help you succeed in any social or romantic situation.

MEN WITH VENUS IN LIBRA: Your good social skills, charming personality, and refined manner usually make you attractive to the opposite sex. Equally, you desire a sophisticated partner with grace, elegance, and a strong sense of style. Although you have the ability to be persuasive and irresistible to others, avoid manipulative love games. Nevertheless, your natural diplomacy and sense of fair play help you to relate to people in all social situations. With your love of balance and harmony, you seek a partner who is also moderate, easygoing, and loving.

WOMEN WITH VENUS IN SCORPIO: With a natural psychic gift for penetrating the feelings of others, you can often help partners transform emotional challenges or sexual difficulties. When you fall in love, your strong feelings and determination give you a potent force that others find attractive and seductive. Although you know what really turns people on, your most profound desire is usually for the deepness and closeness of real love and intimacy in an enduring relationship.

MEN WITH VENUS IN SCORPIO: In relationships you possess a sensitive understanding of your partner's deeper nature. Although you are strongly attached to those you love, you may have to be careful that your feelings do not turn into jealousy or possessiveness. When you fall in love it is often with power and an emotional intensity. You are attracted to partners who can share your passion and display strong feelings of sexuality like your own.

To read all about your Outer Planets and work out how to use your personalized timetable, go to Section Three, page 789.

♍

Your Personalized Timetable

JUPITER BENEFICIAL
1938 1/1 – 1/14
1941 4/12 – 6/20
1942 10/3 – 12/22
1943 5/25 – 7/13
1947 1/15 – 5/13
1947 9/14 – 11/6
1949 2/11 – 12/28
1952 8/13 – 10/6
1953 3/24 – 6/3
1954 9/7 – until 1955 2/1
1955 4/29 – 6/26
1958 12/25 – until 1959 6/29
1959 8/10 – 10/20
1961 1/25 – 4/25
1961 6/24 – 12/9
1964 7/11 – 11/22
1965 2/27 – 5/17
1966 8/18 – 10/19
1966 12/24 – until 1967 6/8
1970 12/8 – until 1971 2/1
1971 5/14 – 9/30
1973 1/9 – 3/25
1973 8/10 – 11/14
1976 6/19 – until 1977 5/1
1978 8/1 – 9/20
1979 2/3 – 5/15
1982 11/22 – until 1983 1/9
1983 6/25 – 9/1
1984 12/24 – until 1985 3/4
1988 6/2 – 9/10
1988 10/8 – until 1989 4/13
1990 7/16 – 8/31
1994 11/6 – 12/22
1996 12/7 – until 1997 2/15
2000 5/16 – 7/31
2000 11/30 – until 2001 3/20
2002 6/30 – 8/14
2006 10/22 – 12/6
2008 3/29 – 6/20
2008 11/18 – until 2009 1/30
2012 4/29 – 7/8

SATURN BENEFICIAL
1941 5/22 – until 1942 6/23
1943 1/23 – 2/20
1945 9/18 – 12/26
1946 6/5 – 8/24
1947 3/4 – 5/4
1955 11/8 – until 1956 3/5
1956 3/18 – 11/5
1961 1/2 – until 1962 2/22
1962 9/3 – 11/13
1970 7/8 – 11/3
1971 3/27 – 8/21
1971 10/18 – until 1972 4/28
1975 7/17 – 10/31
1975 11/29 – until 1976 6/29
1984 12/13 – until 1985 6/14
1985 9/4 – 12/10
1990 2/6 – 8/17
1990 10/29 – until 1991 4/10
1991 6/23 – 12/31
2000 5/5 – until 2001 6/5
2004 8/26 – until 2005 1/27
2005 5/13 – 8/7

URANUS BENEFICIAL
1939 6/13 – until 1944 3/30
1953 10/2 – until 1956 7/28
1979 12/8 – until 1982 10/22
1993 2/6 – until 1997 12/3

NEPTUNE BENEFICIAL
1966 12/8 – until 1972 9/15
1993 2/8 – until 2001 1/13

PLUTO BENEFICIAL
1938 1/1 – until 1941 6/14
1992 1/31 – until 1996 11/19

JUPITER CHALLENGING
1939 3/26 – 6/15
1939 9/12 – until 1940 1/31

1941 9/8 – 11/11
1942 4/23 – 7/5
1948 1/23 – 7/26
1948 9/5 – 12/12
1951 3/9 – 5/19
1951 10/31 – 12/30
1953 8/8 – 12/25
1954 3/28 – 6/19
1960 1/5 – 11/25
1963 2/20 – 4/29
1965 7/18 – until 1966 6/2
1971 12/20 – until 1972 3/14
1972 6/5 – 11/5
1975 2/3 – 4/11
1977 7/1 – 10/9
1977 11/8 – until 1978 5/15
1983 12/4 – until 1984 2/17
1984 7/18 – 10/10
1986 5/28 – 8/27
1987 1/14 – 3/26
1989 6/14 – 8/31
1989 12/27 – until 1990 4/23
1995 11/18 – until 1996 1/29
1998 5/2 – 10/13
1998 12/14 – until 1999 3/10
2001 5/29 – 8/9
2002 2/20 – 3/10
2007 11/1 – until 2008 1/13
2010 4/12 – until 2011 2/20

SATURN CHALLENGING
1938 1/1 – 3/11
1943 7/7 – until 1944 2/11
1944 3/1 – 8/5
1945 1/17 – 4/21
1958 1/4 – 7/25
1958 9/22 – until 1959 3/7
1959 5/27 – 11/29
1966 3/10 – until 1967 4/19
1967 11/27 – 12/20
1972 9/2 – 11/1
1973 5/12 – until 1974 6/10
1987 2/17 – 5/12
1987 11/12 – until 1989 1/2
1995 4/15 – 10/5
1996 1/6 – 6/4
1996 9/2 – until 1997 2/21
2002 6/19 – until 2003 7/19

URANUS CHALLENGING
1946 7/18 – until 1951 4/12
1986 1/5 – until 1990 10/4
2008 3/28 – Continues

NEPTUNE CHALLENGING
1979 1/30 – until 1987 11/1

PLUTO CHALLENGING
2003 2/26 – until 2011 11/15

JUPITER SPECIAL
1944 10/29 – until 1945 4/5
1945 6/23 – 9/21
1956 10/10 – until 1957 9/5
1968 9/24 – until 1969 1/7
1969 2/2 – 8/19
1980 9/8 – 11/29
1981 3/24 – 7/29
1992 8/23 – 11/8
1993 5/6 – 6/27
2004 8/7 – 10/22

SATURN SPECIAL
1950 8/23 – until 1951 10/1
1979 9/30 – until 1980 11/9
1981 4/4 – 8/3
2008 11/14 – until 2009 2/18
2009 8/4 – until 2010 9/14

URANUS SPECIAL
1966 9/9 – until 1970 8/2

NEPTUNE SPECIAL
1938 1/1 – until 1945 9/18

PLUTO SPECIAL
1966 10/26 – until 1974 9/5

September 22

SUN: VIRGO/LIBRA CUSP • DECANATE: TAURUS/VENUS • DEGREE: 28°45–29°45 VIRGO • MODE: MUTABLE • ELEMENT: EARTH

Your Personal Powers

Practical yet sensitive, you are an astute individual with sharp intelligence and a good understanding of people. Being born on the cusp of Virgo and Libra shows you to be articulate and shrewd with a skillful and diplomatic approach to communication. Ambitious and competitive, you gain power from your people skills and the application of your original ideas but may lose some of your power if you become too obstinate or provocative. Proud with personal charisma, your natural leadership ability often attracts help and support from others. Skepticism or nervous tension, on the other hand, can undermine your efforts and cause you unnecessary stress. You also lose some of your power by being irritable or moody. Fortunately, you have a wonderful sense of humor that can help alleviate life's problems and put them in perspective. You usually gain power when following your extra strong intuition and working cooperatively with others. Your determination, organizational skills, and insight, when combined, can produce outstanding results.

Your Powers of Attraction in Relationships

Others admire your insight, keen perceptions, and inner strength. Your diplomatic skills ensure that you realize the advantages of working in unison with others. You are attracted to creative people or those who know how to enjoy themselves. Your youthfulness implies that you have the ability to be entertaining, but it is when you are responsible that you impress others. When positive, you can be generous and good company. Although on occasion you can be selfish, you are capable of showing your sensitivity to other's feelings. An idealistic streak suggests that you may get more satisfaction from being of practical help to others. You respond well to love and affection and need a partner who can keep up with your fast mental responses and unorthodox approach to life.

Your attractive qualities: intelligent, ambitious, highly intuitive, observant, practical, universal, skillful, sympathetic, meticulous, perceptive, builder, humorous, organizer, realist, problem solver, honest, achiever, good critic, persistent, precise

Your less attractive qualities: nervous, provocative, inferiority complex, bossy, materialistic, impatience, too sensitive, worry, selfish, get-rich-quick schemes, moody, too critical, lazy, egotistical, argumentative, sarcastic

Your Venus Power

The planet Venus has a great deal of influence on your powers of attraction. Below are four possible Venus types for women and men. To find your Venus you need to go to page 771, where you will find the Venus table and extra information. The planet Mars also affects your powers of attraction. To find your Mars table and interpretation go to page 761.

WOMEN WITH VENUS IN LEO: Your friendly and sunny personality often makes you stand out in a crowd. Generous and giving, you know how to make your partner feel special. As you often expect loyalty and devotion from your partners in return, you can become easily offended if they ignore you or behave in an inconsiderate manner. Charming and kind, when you are in love you can be romantic, dramatic, and passionate.

MEN WITH VENUS IN LEO: A childlike nature suggests that you are versatile and keen on games or being entertained. You are usually attracted to vivacious partners with a benevolent nature. As an extrovert you enjoy being involved in all types of activities where you can assert yourself and show your talents and abilities. Others may recognize your inborn tendencies to lead but are also aware of your vanity or pride. Nevertheless, generous, kind, and caring, you often show compassion to those less fortunate than yourself.

WOMEN WITH VENUS IN VIRGO: Articulate and straightforward in your relationships, you attract others with your genuine concern for their well-being. By being understanding and a good listener you are able to show your love and friendship. With your analytical approach to relationships, however, you may have to be careful of becoming too matter-of-fact. You often display your concern for the welfare of others by your willingness to offer practical help and assistance. You usually seek a partner who is willing to work as hard on relationships as you are.

MEN WITH VENUS IN VIRGO: Although you are constantly analyzing your relationships in order to understand and improve them, you may nevertheless need to refrain from continuously mulling over issues that can cause anxiety. You are happiest when you are able to help your loved ones in practical ways and forget yourself in your willingness to be

of service to others. You seek a partner who has high standards and can be as pragmatic and hardworking as yourself. Ideally they should also be impeccably dressed with a fine analytical mind.

WOMEN WITH VENUS IN LIBRA: Attractive, refined, and conscious of the needs of others, you usually desire harmonious relationships. As a peacemaker with good negotiating skills, you can smooth out difficulties with others, but your dislike of confrontation may sometimes leave you refusing to take a stand or compromising too many of your own needs. Courteous, stylish, and charming with polished social skills, you are an expert at relating to others in a gracious and civilized manner.

MEN WITH VENUS IN LIBRA: As a sociable and friendly individual with an eye for beauty, you are amorous and charming. You are a natural gentleman and your ideal partner usually has an elegant appearance, artistic appreciation, and good taste. Your relationships benefit when you resist the temptation to take the easy way out or put too much emphasis on vanity and high living. Intellectual and naturally refined, you seek a loving partner who can share your romantic and sophisticated aspirations.

WOMEN WITH VENUS IN SCORPIO: With a natural psychic gift for penetrating the feelings of others, you can often help partners transform emotional challenges or sexual difficulties. When you fall in love, your strong feelings and determination give you a potent force that others find attractive and seductive. Although you know what really turns people on, your most profound desire is usually for the deepness and closeness of real love and intimacy in an enduring relationship.

MEN WITH VENUS IN SCORPIO: In relationships you possess a sensitive understanding of your partner's deeper nature. Although you are strongly attached to those you love, you may have to be careful that your feelings do not turn into jealousy or possessiveness. When you fall in love, it is often with emotional intensity and power. You are attracted to partners who can share your passion and display strong feelings of sexuality like your own.

To read all about your Outer Planets and work out how to use your personalized timetable, go to Section Three, page 789.

♍

Your Personalized Timetable

JUPITER BENEFICIAL
1938 1/1 – 1/18
1941 4/16 – 6/24
1942 10/13 – 12/12
1943 5/30 – 7/18
1947 1/22 – 5/6
1947 9/20 – 11/10
1949 2/16 – until 1950 1/2
1952 8/29 – 9/21
1953 3/28 – 6/7
1954 9/12 – until 1955 1/24
1955 5/7 – 7/1
1958 12/30 – until 1959 6/17
1959 8/22 – 10/24
1961 1/29 – 5/9
1961 6/10 – 12/14
1964 7/16 – 11/15
1965 3/5 – 5/22
1966 8/23 – 10/31
1966 12/12 – until 1967 6/13
1970 12/12 – until 1971 2/8
1971 5/5 – 10/5
1973 1/13 – 3/30
1973 8/3 – 11/21
1976 6/24 – until 1977 5/5
1978 8/6 – 9/26
1979 1/26 – 5/22
1982 11/26 – until 1983 1/14
1983 6/15 – 9/10
1984 12/28 – until 1985 3/9
1988 6/6 – until 1989 4/17
1990 7/20 – 9/5
1991 3/19 – 4/10
1994 11/11 – 12/27
1996 12/12 – until 1997 2/19
2000 5/20 – 8/6
2000 11/23 – until 2001 3/26
2002 7/4 – 8/18
2006 10/26 – 12/11
2008 4/7 – 6/11
2008 11/23 – until 2009 2/3
2012 5/3 – 7/13

SATURN BENEFICIAL
1941 5/30 – until 1942 7/1
1943 1/1 – 3/13
1945 10/2 – 12/12
1946 6/14 – 9/2
1947 2/16 – 5/19
1955 11/16 – until 1956 11/14
1961 1/10 – until 1962 3/3
1962 8/19 – 11/28
1970 7/19 – 10/22
1971 4/5 – until 1972 5/6
1975 7/25 – until 1976 7/7
1984 12/22 – until 1985 5/30
1985 9/18 – 12/19
1986 7/8 – 9/5
1990 2/15 – 8/1
1990 11/12 – until 1991 5/6
1991 5/27 – until 1992 1/8
2000 5/13 – until 2001 6/13
2004 9/4 – until 2005 1/15
2005 5/24 – 8/14

URANUS BENEFICIAL
1939 7/4 – until 1944 4/21
1954 7/22 – until 1957 5/25
1979 12/26 – until 1982 11/8
1993 2/25 – until 1997 12/24

NEPTUNE BENEFICIAL
1967 1/9 – until 1972 10/23
1993 3/15 – until 2001 12/9

PLUTO BENEFICIAL
1938 1/1 – until 1942 5/22
1992 12/7 – until 1997 10/11

JUPITER CHALLENGING
1939 3/30 – 6/23
1939 9/3 – until 1940 2/5
1941 9/20 – 10/30

1942 4/28 – 7/10
1948 1/28 – 7/13
1948 9/18 – 12/16
1951 3/13 – 5/24
1951 10/21 – until 1952 1/8
1953 8/13 – 12/18
1954 4/4 – 6/23
1960 1/10 – 11/29
1963 2/24 – 5/3
1965 7/23 – until 1966 6/7
1971 12/24 – until 1972 3/24
1972 5/27 – 11/10
1975 2/7 – 4/15
1977 7/5 – until 1978 5/20
1983 12/9 – until 1984 2/23
1984 7/10 – 10/18
1986 6/6 – 8/18
1987 1/19 – 3/30
1989 6/19 – 9/6
1989 12/20 – until 1990 4/29
1995 11/23 – until 1996 2/3
1998 5/7 – 10/4
1998 12/23 – until 1999 3/14
2001 6/2 – 8/14
2002 2/3 – 3/28
2007 11/6 – until 2008 1/17
2010 4/16 – until 2011 2/24

SATURN CHALLENGING
1938 1/1 – 3/19
1943 7/15 – until 1944 1/17
1944 3/25 – 8/14
1945 1/4 – 5/3
1958 1/12 – 7/7
1958 10/8 – until 1959 3/28
1959 5/6 – 12/8
1966 3/18 – until 1967 4/28
1967 11/3 – until 1968 1/13
1973 5/20 – until 1974 6/18
1987 3/9 – 4/22
1987 11/21 – until 1989 1/10
1995 4/24 – 9/22
1996 1/18 – 6/21
1996 8/15 – 3/2
2002 6/27 – until 2003 7/26
2004 2/14 – 3/30

URANUS CHALLENGING
1946 8/8 – until 1951 5/10
1986 1/24 – until 1990 11/6
2008 4/16 – Continues

NEPTUNE CHALLENGING
1979 12/27 – until 1987 12/3

PLUTO CHALLENGING
2004 1/8 – until 2011 12/15

JUPITER SPECIAL
1944 11/3 – until 1945 3/27
1945 7/1 – 9/26
1956 10/15 – until 1957 9/10
1968 9/29 – until 1969 8/24
1980 9/13 – 12/6
1981 3/16 – 8/4
1992 8/28 – 11/13
1993 4/25 – 7/8
2004 8/12 – 10/27

SATURN SPECIAL
1950 8/31 – until 1951 10/9
1979 10/9 – until 1980 4/27
1980 6/17 – 11/19
1981 3/23 – 8/14
2008 11/28 – until 2009 2/3
2009 8/13 – until 2010 9/23

URANUS SPECIAL
1966 9/24 – until 1970 8/23

NEPTUNE SPECIAL
1938 1/31 – until 1946 8/16

PLUTO SPECIAL
1967 9/22 – until 1975 7/18

Virgo Timetable
X-Special · X-Beneficial · X-Challenging

August 23
URANUS X-CHALLENGING
2002 4/7 – until **2004** 1/31

NEPTUNE X-CHALLENGING
2010 3/26 – Continues

PLUTO X-BENEFICIAL
2007 1/16 – until **2009** 11/11

August 24
URANUS X-CHALLENGING
2002 5/9 – until **2004** 2/18

NEPTUNE X-CHALLENGING
2010 5/12 – Continues

PLUTO X-BENEFICIAL
2007 2/22 – until **2009** 12/12

August 25
URANUS X-CHALLENGING
2003 3/3 – until **2004** 12/22

NEPTUNE X-CHALLENGING
2011 3/21 – Continues

PLUTO X-BENEFICIAL
2008 1/12 – until **2010** 11/8

August 26
URANUS X-CHALLENGING
2003 3/20 – until **2005** 1/15

NEPTUNE X-CHALLENGING
2011 4/25 – Continues

PLUTO X-BENEFICIAL
2008 2/13 – until **2010** 12/9

August 27
URANUS X-CHALLENGING
2003 4/9 – until **2005** 2/2

NEPTUNE X-CHALLENGING
2012 3/14 – Continues

PLUTO X-BENEFICIAL
2009 1/7 – until **2011** 11/4

August 28
URANUS X-CHALLENGING
2003 5/8 – until **2005** 2/20

NEPTUNE X-CHALLENGING
2012 4/14 – Continues

PLUTO X-BENEFICIAL
2009 2/6 – until **2011** 12/7

August 29
URANUS X-CHALLENGING
2004 3/4 – until **2005** 12/23

PLUTO X-BENEFICIAL
2010 1/4 – Continues

August 30
URANUS X-CHALLENGING
2004 3/21 – until **2006** 1/16

PLUTO X-BENEFICIAL
2010 2/2 – until **2012** 12/4

August 31
URANUS X-CHALLENGING
2004 4/10 – until **2006** 2/5

PLUTO X-BENEFICIAL
2010 3/22 – until **2013** 10/28

September 1
URANUS X-CHALLENGING
2004 5/7 – until **2006** 2/22

PLUTO X-BENEFICIAL
2011 1/30 – Continues

September 2
URANUS X-CHALLENGING
2005 3/6 – until **2006** 12/23

PLUTO X-BENEFICIAL
2011 3/11 – Continues

September 3
URANUS X-CHALLENGING
2005 3/24 – until **2007** 1/19

PLUTO X-BENEFICIAL
2012 1/28 – Continues

September 4
URANUS X-CHALLENGING
2005 4/12 – until **2007** 2/7

PLUTO X-CHALLENGING
2001 7/1 – 10/13

PLUTO X-BENEFICIAL
2012 3/5 – until **2013** 8/20

September 5
URANUS X-CHALLENGING
2005 5/8 – until **2007** 2/25

PLUTO X-CHALLENGING
1999 11/26 – until **2001** 11/13

September 6
URANUS X-CHALLENGING
2006 3/9 – until **2007** 12/24

September 7
URANUS X-CHALLENGING
2006 3/26 – until **2008** 1/21

PLUTO X-CHALLENGING
2000 1/20 – until **2002** 11/3

September 8
URANUS X-CHALLENGING
2006 4/15 – until **2008** 2/10

PLUTO X-CHALLENGING
2000 12/12 – until **2002** 12/1

September 9
URANUS X-CHALLENGING
2006 5/10 – until **2008** 2/28

PLUTO X-CHALLENGING
2001 1/10 – until **2003** 10/24

September 10
URANUS X-CHALLENGING
2007 3/12 – until **2008** 12/24

PLUTO X-CHALLENGING
2001 2/18 – until **2003** 11/23

September 11
URANUS X-CHALLENGING
2007 3/29 – until **2009** 1/22

PLUTO X-CHALLENGING
2001 12/31 – until **2004** 10/12

September 12
URANUS X-CHALLENGING
2007 4/17 – until **2009** 2/12

PLUTO X-CHALLENGING
2002 1/31 – until **2004** 11/15

September 13
URANUS X-CHALLENGING
2007 5/12 – until **2009** 3/1

PLUTO X-CHALLENGING
2002 12/23 – until **2005** 9/25

September 14
URANUS X-CHALLENGING
2008 3/14 – until **2009** 12/25

PLUTO X-CHALLENGING
2003 1/20 – until **2005** 11/7

PLUTO X-CHALLENGING
1999 12/20 – until **2002** 9/26

September 15
URANUS X-CHALLENGING
2008 3/31 – until **2010** 1/25

PLUTO X-CHALLENGING
2003 3/12 – until **2005** 12/5

September 16
URANUS X-CHALLENGING
2008 3/31 – until **2010** 1/25

PLUTO X-CHALLENGING
2003 3/12 – until **2005** 12/5

September 17
URANUS X-CHALLENGING
2008 5/13 – until **2010** 3/4

PLUTO X-CHALLENGING
2004 2/16 – until **2006** 11/30

September 18
URANUS X-CHALLENGING
2009 3/17 – until **2010** 12/25

PLUTO X-CHALLENGING
2005 1/4 – until **2007** 10/23

September 19
URANUS X-CHALLENGING
2009 4/3 – until **2011** 1/27

PLUTO X-CHALLENGING
2005 2/4 – until **2007** 11/25

September 20
URANUS X-CHALLENGING
2009 4/22 – until **2011** 2/17

PLUTO X-CHALLENGING
2005 12/29 – until **2008** 10/12

September 21
URANUS X-CHALLENGING
2009 5/15 – until **2011** 3/8

PLUTO X-CHALLENGING
2006 1/27 – until **2008** 11/20

September 22
URANUS X-CHALLENGING
2010 3/20 – until **2011** 12/25

PLUTO X-CHALLENGING
2006 3/27 – until **2009** 9/30

Libra

September 23–October 22

September 23

Your Personal Powers

Quick thinking, emotional sensitivity, charm, and strong will are among your many personal powers. Being born on the cusp grants you an astute mind, creativity, and the ability to deal with people in a friendly and diplomatic manner. You gain power from the combination of your amiable approach, persistence, and professional manner. Ambitious with strong opinions, you may find yourself naturally gravitating to positions of leadership. Although you are usually keen to work or collaborate with others, you may lose some of your power if you become bossy, impatient, or uncompromising. Your pioneering thoughts and idealism suggest, however, that you enjoy presenting new ideas, initiating projects, or fighting for just causes. Being mentally sharp and having an adventurous nature also implies that you like to keep yourself mentally motivated. You gain power when you blend your acquired knowledge and theories with personal experiences and practical skills. Your grace, intelligence, and ability to be verbally persuasive indicate that when you are disciplined you have the attributes to take you to the top.

Your Powers of Attraction in Relationships

Clever and sociable with a creative streak and personal charisma, you can always attract friends and admirers. You work very well with others and are usually an entertaining and delightful companion. Even though you appear independent and self-assured to your partners, you need the security of a close relationship. Looking for the perfect love, you may attract many admirers before you find the right partner. You are drawn to individuals with an aura of success, strong self-identity, or those who are willing to work hard to achieve their objectives. Being sensitive to others' feelings, you can be an affectionate lover, but a restless side to your nature may occasionally make you impatient or bossy. Idealistic, you should always make sure your relationships are based on an equal footing.

Your attractive qualities: intelligent, loyal, responsible, adventurous, friendly, intuitive, creative, quick thinker, sensitive, communicative, artistic talent, perfectionist, passionate, intuitive, creative, drive, courageous, versatile, trustworthy, independent

Your less attractive qualities: restless, selfish, easily bored, insecure, stubborn, withdrawn, uncompromising, faultfinding, vain, codependent, bossy, self-indulgent, prejudiced

Your Venus Power

The planet Venus has a great deal of influence on your powers of attraction. Below are four possible Venus types for women and men. To find your Venus you need to go to page 771, where you will find the Venus table and extra information. The planet Mars also affects your powers of attraction. To find your Mars table and interpretation go to page 761.

WOMEN WITH VENUS IN LEO: You possess the wonderful ability to project your warm and sunny personality and keep others happily entertained. Loving attention yourself, you seek a partner who can appreciate you, be supportive, and give you positive feedback. Proud, with a natural regal air, you expect respect from your partners but are willing to be loyal and supportive in exchange. Although sometimes a little self-centered, you know how to make your partner feel special.

MEN WITH VENUS IN LEO: Enthusiastic, playful, and kind, you can be benevolent with those you love. Warm, romantic, and self-expressive, you adore the drama of love or having fun with your friends. You are usually attracted to partners with a warm and generous nature. Although you can be a confident and charismatic partner, you may need to develop humility in order to stop pride or arrogance from marring your relationships.

WOMEN WITH VENUS IN VIRGO: Intelligent and discriminating, you are usually drawn to polite and refined individuals. As a perfectionist, you may be keen to analyze and criticize yourself, but be careful of continually going over your partner's shortcomings. By focusing on how you can make positive improvements in yourself and your relationships, you avoid becoming skeptical or confused. You empower yourself when you display kind and caring concern for the well-being of loved ones and spontaneously offer your practical assistance.

MEN WITH VENUS IN VIRGO: A love of order usually means that you are attracted to refined individuals with analytical or practical abilities. You and your partner may be working together or serving similar causes. As you constantly analyze partnerships in order to improve them, you are likely to use former relationships as a point of reference and compare them to your present partner. As you are helpful and

kind, others usually rely on your good judgment and often turn to you for advice or practical assistance.

WOMEN WITH VENUS IN LIBRA: Attractive, refined, and conscious of the needs of others, you usually desire harmonious relationships. As a peacemaker with good negotiating skills, you can smooth out difficulties with others, but your dislike of confrontation may sometimes leave you refusing to take a stand or compromising too many of your own needs. Courteous, stylish, and charming with polished social skills, you are an expert at relating to others in a gracious and civilized manner.

MEN WITH VENUS IN LIBRA: As a sociable and friendly individual with an eye for beauty, you are amorous and charming. You are a natural gentleman and your ideal partner usually has an elegant appearance, artistic appreciation, and good taste. Your relationships benefit when you resist the temptation to take the easy way out or put too much emphasis on vanity and high living. Intellectual and naturally refined, you seek a loving partner who can share your romantic and sophisticated aspirations.

WOMEN WITH VENUS IN SCORPIO: Your strength and power is in your ability to love both deeply and sensitively. For you, love and desire go hand in hand. As you feel so deeply, you often keep your sensitivity or vulnerability hidden from others in order to keep some control in your relationships. You are more likely to prefer a few very close loyal friends than many superficial acquaintances. In relationships your sensual nature and magnetic intensity can easily attract others.

MEN WITH VENUS IN SCORPIO: You are attracted to individuals with deep and powerful emotions or whom you find intriguing. Your gift for creating smoke screens to maintain secrecy around your feelings can conceal your inner sensitivity and vulnerability. Nevertheless, you are looking for a partner who can pierce your defenses and understand you at a very deep level. Needing a relationship with a powerful sexual connection, you thrive on emotional intensity.

To read all about your Outer Planets and work out how to use your personalized timetable, go to Section Three, page 789.

To read all about your Outer Planets and work out how to use your personalized timetable, go to Section Three, page 789.

Your Personalized Timetable

JUPITER BENEFICIAL
1941 4/21 – 6/29
1942 10/26 – 11/29
1943 6/5 – 7/22
1947 1/29 – 4/27
1947 9/26 – 11/15
1949 2/21 – until 1950 1/6
1953 4/2 – 6/11
1954 9/18 – until 1955 1/17
1955 5/13 – 7/6
1959 1/5 – 6/7
1959 8/31 – 10/29
1961 2/3 – 12/19
1964 7/23 – 11/8
1965 3/11 – 5/26
1966 8/28 – until 1967 3/7
1967 4/4 – 6/18
1970 12/17 – until 1971 2/17
1971 4/26 – 10/11
1973 1/17 – 4/6
1973 7/26 – 11/27
1976 6/29 – 12/28
1977 2/2 – 5/9
1978 8/10 – 10/2
1979 1/19 – 5/29
1982 12/1 – until 1983 1/20
1983 6/7 – 9/17
1985 1/2 – 3/14
1985 9/14 – 10/22
1988 6/10 – until 1989 4/22
1990 7/25 – 9/10
1991 3/3 – 4/27
1994 11/15 – until 1995 1/1
1996 12/16 – until 1997 2/24
2000 5/24 – 8/13
2000 11/16 – until 2001 4/1
2002 7/9 – 8/23
2006 10/31 – 12/15
2008 4/19 – 5/29
2008 11/28 – until 2009 2/7
2012 5/7 – Continues

SATURN BENEFICIAL
1941 6/7 – until 1942 1/13
1942 2/1 – 7/10
1942 12/18 – until 1943 3/27
1945 10/24 – 11/20
1946 6/22 – 9/11
1947 2/3 – 5/31
1955 11/24 – until 1956 11/22
1961 1/19 – until 1962 3/13
1962 8/5 – 12/10
1970 8/3 – 10/6
1971 4/14 – until 1972 5/14
1975 8/1 – until 1976 7/15
1985 1/1 – 5/17
1985 9/29 – 12/28
1986 6/20 – 9/22
1990 2/24 – 7/18
1990 11/24 – until 1992 1/17
2000 5/20 – until 2001 6/20
2004 9/14 – until 2005 1/3
2005 6/2 – 8/22
2006 3/17 – 4/25

URANUS BENEFICIAL
1939 8/4 – until 1944 5/9
1954 8/8 – until 1957 6/16
1980 1/16 – until 1982 11/24
1993 3/24 – until 1998 1/12

NEPTUNE BENEFICIAL
1967 12/4 – until 1973 8/31
1994 2/4 – until 2002 1/9

PLUTO BENEFICIAL
1938 1/1 – until 1942 7/6
1993 1/5 – until 1997 11/8

JUPITER CHALLENGING
1939 4/3 – 7/4
1939 8/24 – until 1940 2/10

1942 5/3 – 7/14
1948 2/3 – 7/4
1948 9/27 – 12/20
1951 3/17 – 5/29
1951 10/13 – until 1952 1/15
1953 8/19 – 12/11
1954 4/11 – 6/27
1960 1/15 – 12/4
1963 2/28 – 5/8
1965 7/28 – until 1966 1/29
1966 3/4 – 6/11
1971 12/29 – until 1972 4/5
1972 5/14 – 11/15
1975 2/11 – 4/20
1977 7/9 – until 1978 5/25
1983 12/13 – until 1984 2/29
1984 7/2 – 10/25
1986 6/16 – 8/8
1987 1/24 – 4/3
1989 6/23 – 9/13
1989 12/13 – until 1990 5/5
1995 11/27 – until 1996 2/8
1998 5/12 – 9/26
1998 12/30 – until 1999 3/18
2001 6/6 – 8/19
2002 1/24 – 4/7
2007 11/11 – until 2008 1/21
2010 4/21 – until 2011 2/28

SATURN CHALLENGING
1938 1/1 – 3/27
1943 7/24 – until 1944 1/2
1944 4/8 – 8/24
1944 12/24 – until 1945 5/12
1958 1/22 – 6/23
1958 10/21 – until 1959 12/17
1966 3/26 – until 1967 5/7
1967 10/19 – until 1968 1/27
1973 5/27 – until 1974 6/25
1987 11/30 – until 1989 1/19
1989 8/19 – 10/4
1995 5/5 – 9/9
1996 1/28 – until 1997 3/10
2002 7/5 – until 2003 8/4
2004 1/27 – 4/16

URANUS CHALLENGING
1946 9/15 – until 1951 5/29
1986 2/17 – until 1990 11/27
2008 5/9 – Continues

NEPTUNE CHALLENGING
1980 1/25 – until 1988 10/22

PLUTO CHALLENGING
2004 2/10 – until 2012 11/12

JUPITER SPECIAL
1944 11/9 – until 1945 3/20
1945 7/9 – 9/30
1956 10/20 – until 1957 9/15
1968 10/3 – until 1969 8/29
1980 9/17 – 12/13
1981 3/8 – 8/10
1992 9/2 – 11/19
1993 4/16 – 7/17
2004 8/17 – 10/31

SATURN SPECIAL
1950 9/8 – until 1951 10/17
1979 10/17 – until 1980 4/8
1980 7/4 – 11/30
1981 3/10 – 8/23
2008 12/26 – until 2009 1/6
2009 8/22 – until 2010 9/30

URANUS SPECIAL
1966 10/11 – until 1970 9/9

NEPTUNE SPECIAL
1938 10/7 – until 1946 9/15

PLUTO SPECIAL
1967 10/21 – until 1975 8/25

389

September 24

SUN: LIBRA • DECANATE: LIBRA/VENUS • DEGREE: 0°5–1°5 LIBRA • MODE: CARDINAL • ELEMENT: AIR

Your Personal Powers

Generous, kind, and decisive, you are usually a dynamic individual with great charm and a direct approach. Your personal powers also include a warm and dignified heart and natural honesty. With a strong need for self-expression, you have a dynamic and resolute nature. If you sometimes encounter setbacks, do not let these disappointments create emotional blocks or frustration as these obstacles can show your true determination. Nevertheless, you empower yourself by using your compelling personality to lead or inspire others and by resisting your bossy and stubborn tendencies. With inspired ideas you may wish to develop your innate creative talents. You gain power from the unique combination of your sensitivity, common sense, and personal charisma. Being an astute judge of character can help you increase your awareness or love of humanity. Often hardworking with a strong desire for fair play, you like to project a practical but caring persona. Although you are usually diplomatic and gracious, you also possess a rebellious streak and powerful emotions that may stimulate you to fight for social reforms.

Your Powers of Attraction in Relationships

Sociable and kind, you can be popular and attract admirers by your ability to mix with people from different walks of life. As you are romantic and idealistic, your relationships are particularly important to you. When you channel your powerful emotions in a positive manner, you can be a devoted friend, lover, or parent. Although you can be very dramatic, an inner desire for peace, harmony, and security highlights the importance that home and family play in your life. Usually you are drawn to responsible individuals or those who can emotionally empathize with your needs. Often willing to make sacrifices for those you love, you can be sympathetic and supportive, but you can also be frank and straightforward. If a woman, you may prefer to take a more active role rather than being passive or retiring.

Your attractive qualities: idealistic, friendly, emotionally sensitive, creative, generous, good organizer, imaginative, kind, good friend, practical skills, strong determination, socialite, honest, frank, fair, generous, love of home, energetic, responsible, leadership, talented

Your less attractive qualities: materialistic, unsettled, undemonstrative, frustrated, dislike routine, discontented, lazy, unfaithful, bossy, domineering, stubborn

Your Venus Power

The planet Venus has a great deal of influence on your powers of attraction. Below are four possible Venus types for women and men. To find your Venus you need to go to page 771, where you will find the Venus table and extra information. The planet Mars also affects your powers of attraction. To find your Mars table and interpretation go to page 761.

WOMEN WITH VENUS IN LEO: Warm and playful with a touch of the dramatic, you enjoy the company of generous or strong individuals who can share your sense of fun. Although there are advantages to your being strong-willed, in your relationships you need to resist being bossy as it can cause resentment. With your wonderful mixture of regal authority and childlike wonder, you love to keep others entertained and amused.

MEN WITH VENUS IN LEO: Sociable and outgoing, you are kind and generous with those you love. Looking for a relationship that can be fun and entertaining, you need a playmate who can share your enthusiasm and high spirits. Your pride, however, often stops you from associating with lovers or partners you see as beneath you. As you desire someone who can appreciate your sense of the dramatic, you are often attracted to people with strong personalities.

WOMEN WITH VENUS IN VIRGO: Intelligent and discriminating, you are usually drawn to polite and refined individuals. As a perfectionist, you may be keen to analyze and criticize yourself, but be careful of continually going over your partner's shortcomings. By focusing on how you can make positive improvements in yourself and in your relationships you avoid becoming skeptical or confused. You empower yourself when you display kind and caring concern for the well-being of loved ones and spontaneously offer your practical assistance.

MEN WITH VENUS IN VIRGO: A love of order usually means that you are attracted to refined individuals with analytical or practical abilities. You and your partner may be working together or serving similar causes. As you constantly analyze partnerships in order to improve them, you are likely

to use former relationships as a point of reference and compare them to your present partner. As you are helpful and kind, others usually rely on your good judgment and often turn to you for advice or practical assistance.

WOMEN WITH VENUS IN LIBRA: Usually you are attractive and sociable with an easygoing manner. Your love of beauty, harmony, and pleasure implies that you are a romantic with a desire for love and affection. Once in a relationship you need to learn to negotiate your position rather than adapt to the wishes of others and compromise just to keep the peace. Nevertheless, your advanced social skills and strong sense of fair play can help you succeed in any social or romantic situation.

MEN WITH VENUS IN LIBRA: Your good social skills, charming personality, and refined manner usually make you attractive to the opposite sex. Equally, you desire a sophisticated partner with grace, elegance, and a strong sense of style. Although you have the ability to be persuasive and irresistible to others, avoid manipulative love games. Nevertheless, your natural diplomacy and sense of fair play help you to relate to people in all social situations. With your love for balance and harmony you seek a partner who is also moderate, easygoing, and loving.

WOMEN WITH VENUS IN SCORPIO: With a natural psychic gift for penetrating the feelings of others, you can often help partners transform emotional challenges or sexual difficulties. When you fall in love, your strong feelings and determination give you a potent force that others find attractive and seductive. Although you know what really turns people on, your most profound desire is usually for the deepness and closeness of real love and intimacy in an enduring relationship.

MEN WITH VENUS IN SCORPIO: In relationships you possess a sensitive understanding of your partner's deeper nature. Although you are strongly attached to those you love, you may have to be careful that your feelings do not turn into jealousy or possessiveness. When you fall in love it is often with power and an emotional intensity. You are attracted to partners who can share your passion and display strong feelings of sexuality like your own.

To read all about your Outer Planets and work out how to use your personalized timetable, go to Section Three, page 789.

To read all about your Outer Planets and work out how to use your personalized timetable, go to Section Three, page 789.

Your Personalized Timetable

JUPITER BENEFICIAL
1941 4/25 – 7/3
1943 6/10 – 7/27
1947 2/7 – 4/18
1947 10/2 – 11/19
1949 2/25 – 9/3
1949 10/3 – until 1950 1/10
1953 4/7 – 6/15
1954 9/25 – until 1955 1/9
1955 5/20 – 7/10
1959 1/10 – 5/30
1959 9/8 – 11/3
1961 2/7 – 12/23
1964 7/29 – 10/31
1965 3/17 – 5/30
1966 9/2 – until 1967 2/21
1967 4/19 – 6/23
1970 12/22 – until 1971 3/1
1971 4/14 – 10/16
1973 1/22 – 4/13
1973 7/18 – 12/3
1976 7/4 – 12/16
1977 2/14 – 5/14
1978 8/15 – 10/9
1979 1/11 – 6/3
1982 12/5 – until 1983 1/26
1983 5/30 – 9/24
1985 1/6 – 3/19
1985 9/1 – 11/3
1988 6/15 – until 1989 4/27
1990 7/29 – 9/15
1991 2/21 – 5/7
1994 11/19 – until 1995 1/6
1995 7/23 – 8/13
1996 12/21 – until 1997 2/28
2000 5/28 – 8/20
2000 11/8 – until 2001 4/7
2002 7/13 – 8/28
2006 11/4 – 12/20
2008 12/3 – until 2009 2/11
2012 5/11 – Continues

SATURN BENEFICIAL
1941 6/15 – 12/19
1942 2/26 – 7/19
1942 12/5 – until 1943 4/7
1946 6/30 – 9/20
1947 1/22 – 6/10
1955 12/3 – until 1956 11/30
1961 1/27 – until 1962 3/23
1962 7/23 – 12/20
1971 4/22 – until 1972 5/21
1975 8/9 – until 1976 7/23
1985 1/12 – 5/3
1985 10/9 – until 1986 1/6
1986 6/6 – 10/4
1990 3/7 – 7/5
1990 12/4 – until 1992 1/25
2000 5/28 – until 2001 6/29
2002 1/12 – 3/6
2004 9/26 – 12/21
2005 6/11 – 8/31
2006 2/25 – 5/14

URANUS BENEFICIAL
1940 5/25 – until 1944 5/26
1954 8/26 – until 1957 7/4
1980 11/15 – until 1983 9/22
1994 1/20 – until 1998 1/28

NEPTUNE BENEFICIAL
1968 1/3 – until 1973 10/19
1994 3/7 – until 2002 12/2

PLUTO BENEFICIAL
1938 1/1 – until 1943 6/18
1993 11/24 – until 1998 9/23

JUPITER CHALLENGING
1939 4/7 – 7/23
1939 8/5 – until 1940 2/14
1942 5/8 – 7/18
1948 2/8 – 6/26

1948 10/4 – 12/24
1951 3/21 – 6/4
1951 10/6 – until 1952 1/22
1953 8/26 – 12/3
1954 4/16 – 7/2
1960 1/19 – 12/8
1963 3/4 – 5/12
1965 8/2 – until 1966 1/16
1966 3/17 – 6/16
1972 1/2 – 11/20
1975 2/16 – 4/24
1977 7/14 – until 1978 5/30
1983 12/17 – until 1984 3/6
1984 6/24 – 10/31
1986 7/3 – 7/22
1987 1/29 – 4/7
1989 6/27 – 9/22
1989 12/4 – until 1990 5/11
1995 12/2 – until 1996 2/13
1996 8/10 – 9/27
1998 5/18 – 9/18
1999 1/6 – 3/22
2001 6/11 – 8/24
2002 1/15 – 4/15
2007 11/16 – until 2008 1/26
2010 4/25 – until 2011 3/5

SATURN CHALLENGING
1938 1/1 – 4/4
1943 8/2 – 12/21
1944 4/19 – 9/4
1944 12/11 – until 1945 5/22
1958 2/1 – 6/10
1958 11/1 – until 1959 12/25
1966 4/3 – until 1967 5/16
1967 10/6 – until 1968 2/7
1973 6/4 – until 1974 7/3
1987 12/8 – until 1989 1/28
1989 7/30 – 10/23
1995 5/16 – 8/27
1996 2/6 – until 1997 3/18
2002 7/13 – until 2003 1/28
2003 3/19 – 8/12
2004 1/13 – 4/29

URANUS CHALLENGING
1947 6/27 – until 1951 6/16
1986 12/17 – until 1990 12/14
2009 3/14 – Continues

NEPTUNE CHALLENGING
1980 12/22 – until 1988 11/28

PLUTO CHALLENGING
2004 12/31 – until 2012 12/14

JUPITER SPECIAL
1944 11/15 – until 1945 3/12
1945 7/15 – 10/5
1956 10/25 – until 1957 4/25
1957 6/12 – 9/19
1968 10/8 – until 1969 9/3
1980 9/22 – 12/22
1981 2/26 – 8/16
1992 9/6 – 11/24
1993 4/8 – 7/24
2004 8/21 – 11/5

SATURN SPECIAL
1950 9/16 – until 1951 10/26
1952 5/16 – 7/5
1979 10/26 – until 1980 3/26
1980 7/17 – 12/14
1981 2/23 – 9/1
2009 8/30 – until 2010 10/8

URANUS SPECIAL
1966 10/28 – until 1970 9/25

NEPTUNE SPECIAL
1938 11/8 – until 1947 8/10

PLUTO SPECIAL
1967 12/3 – until 1975 9/22

September 25

SUN: LIBRA • DECANATE: LIBRA/VENUS • DEGREE: 1°5–2°5 LIBRA • MODE: CARDINAL • ELEMENT: AIR

Your Personal Powers

Friendly and optimistic, you possess a kind heart and special charisma. You gain power from the blend of your emotional sensitivity, strong imagination, and good people skills. By radiating a warm and loving personality, you can enchant others and be popular, but be careful that your desire for pleasure does not cause you to lose some of your power to overindulgence. As you possess a natural business sense and are quick to see opportunities for success, you can continually improve or change your circumstances. Your desire for perfection may stimulate you to be productive, and when you apply the necessary discipline, you can achieve remarkable results. Being impressionable with dynamic emotions implies that you also possess powerful intuition. By trusting this strong sixth sense and developing your faith and patience, you can add to your chances for achieving success. You may need to guard against becoming too self-absorbed, however, or losing your power to oversensitivity. With your innate charm and strong mental and emotional energies, you have the potential needed to achieve outstanding results in life.

Your Powers of Attraction in Relationships

Charming, sensitive, and astute, you have no problem attracting others. With your strong emotions you feel deeply, so relationships are especially important to you. Being romantic and idealistic, you can be supportive to those you love. Although usually caring, a more stubborn or skeptical side to your personality may sometimes cause you to become tough or moody. Equally, the extremes of your nature could have you going from being disciplined and dutiful to being lazy or preoccupied with pleasure. You are usually attracted to determined individuals or partners with power and financial influence. Being sociable and generous, you know how to make people feel special, and with your quick wit can be very entertaining. Quite dramatic and sometimes headstrong, you usually work hard to create harmony in your partnerships.

Your attractive qualities: highly intuitive, charming, astute, idealistic, perfectionist, perceptive, creative, social skills, quick reactions, talented, charismatic, imaginative, leadership skills, visionary, clever, sensitive, friendly, good organizer

Your less attractive qualities: impulsive, impatient, irresponsible, too emotional, bossy, lazy, frustration, self-indulgent, too serious, temperamental, indecisive, skeptical, self-doubt, critical, moody, nervous

Your Venus Power

The planet Venus has a great deal of influence on your powers of attraction. Below are four possible Venus types for women and men. To find your Venus you need to go to page 771, where you will find the Venus table and extra information. The planet Mars also affects your powers of attraction. To find your Mars table and interpretation go to page 761.

WOMEN WITH VENUS IN LEO: Your friendly and sunny personality often makes you stand out in a crowd. Generous and giving, you know how to make your partner feel special. As you often expect loyalty and devotion from your partners in return, you can easily become offended if they ignore you or behave in an inconsiderate manner. Charming and kind, when you're in love you can be romantic, dramatic, and passionate.

MEN WITH VENUS IN LEO: A childlike nature suggests that you are versatile and keen on games or being entertained. You are usually attracted to vivacious partners with a benevolent nature. As an extrovert you enjoy being involved in all types of activities where you can assert yourself and show your talents and abilities. Others may recognize your inborn tendencies to lead but are also aware of your vanity or pride. Nevertheless, generous, kind, and caring, you often show compassion to those less fortunate than yourself.

WOMEN WITH VENUS IN VIRGO: Articulate and straightforward in your relationships, you attract others with your genuine concern for their well-being. By being understanding and a good listener you are able to show your love and friendship. With your analytical approach to relationships, however, you may have to be careful of becoming too matter-of-fact. You often display your concern for the welfare of others by your willingness to offer practical help and assistance. You usually seek a partner who is willing to work as hard on relationships as you are.

MEN WITH VENUS IN VIRGO: Although you are constantly analyzing your relationships in order to understand and improve them, you may nevertheless need to refrain from continuously mulling over issues that can cause anxiety. You are happiest when you are able to help your loved ones in practical ways and forget yourself in your willingness to be of service to others. You seek a partner who has high standards

and can be as pragmatic and hardworking as you. Ideally they should also be impeccably dressed with a fine analytical mind.

WOMEN WITH VENUS IN LIBRA: Gracious, charming, and sociable with a sense of style, you have no trouble attracting admirers. With your natural diplomatic skills and desire for harmony you usually like to keep the peace and avoid confrontations, but be careful of failing to take a stand when it is necessary. Romantic and easygoing yourself, you are attracted to affectionate and refined individuals who share your love of peace, justice, and fair play.

MEN WITH VENUS IN LIBRA: Courteous and refined, you are attracted to beautiful and elegant people. You are looking for a partner who can share your natural good taste and enjoy an intellectual conversation. Disliking conflict, you may have to be careful not to go along with others just to keep the peace. Your ideal partner will appreciate beauty and the little luxuries of life as well as possess good social skills. You have a strong sense of social etiquette so you need an intelligent and sophisticated partner.

WOMEN WITH VENUS IN SCORPIO: Loving and passionate, you are often sensitive with deep feelings and strong powers of attraction. A love for the truth coupled with a tendency to be suspicious can be an influence that motivates you to delve deep into the activities of your partner. When in love or in a relationship that matters, you will often bend over backward to cooperate. Although loyal, guard against losing sight of your own needs and desires.

MEN WITH VENUS IN SCORPIO: As you are emotionally intense and passionate, personal relationships are probably a major factor in your own transformation. Being sensitive yet loyal, you are usually attracted to forceful partners who can express themselves intimately but intensely. Rather than seek easy and simple relationships, you are drawn to partners who act as a catalyst for your own internal changes. Through your relationships with your partners you can unravel your own motives and understand your deep-seated feelings or emotional insecurities.

To read all about your Outer Planets and work out how to use your personalized timetable, go to Section Three, page 789.

Your Personalized Timetable

JUPITER BENEFICIAL
1941 4/29 – 7/8
1943 6/15 – 7/31
1947 2/18 – 4/7
1947 10/7 – 11/23
1949 3/2 – 8/20
1949 10/17 – until 1950 1/14
1953 4/11 – 6/20
1954 10/2 – until 1955 1/2
1955 5/26 – 7/15
1959 1/16 – 5/22
1959 9/15 – 11/7
1961 2/12 – 12/28
1964 8/6 – 10/23
1965 3/22 – 6/3
1966 9/7 – until 1967 2/11
1967 4/29 – 6/28
1970 12/27 – until 1971 7/17
1971 7/31 – 10/21
1973 1/26 – 4/20
1973 7/10 – 12/8
1976 7/9 – 12/7
1977 2/23 – 5/18
1978 8/19 – 10/17
1979 1/3 – 6/9
1982 12/10 – until 1983 2/1
1983 5/22 – 10/1
1985 1/10 – 3/24
1985 8/23 – 11/12
1988 6/19 – until 1989 5/1
1990 8/3 – 9/21
1991 2/12 – 5/15
1994 11/24 – until 1995 1/11
1995 7/6 – 8/30
1996 12/25 – until 1997 3/5
2000 6/1 – 8/29
2000 10/30 – until 2001 4/12
2002 7/17 – 9/1
2006 11/9 – 12/24
2008 12/8 – until 2009 2/15
2012 5/15 – Continues

SATURN BENEFICIAL
1941 6/24 – 12/5
1942 3/12 – 7/29
1942 11/23 – until 1943 4/16
1946 7/7 – 10/1
1947 1/10 – 6/19
1955 12/11 – until 1956 7/5
1956 8/25 – 12/8
1961 2/5 – 9/4
1961 10/20 – until 1962 4/5
1962 7/8 – 12/29
1971 4/30 – until 1972 5/29
1975 8/17 – until 1976 2/29
1976 4/23 – 7/30
1985 1/25 – 4/19
1985 10/19 – until 1986 1/16
1986 5/24 – 10/15
1990 3/20 – 6/21
1990 12/14 – until 1992 2/2
2000 6/5 – until 2001 7/7
2001 12/26 – until 2002 3/22
2004 10/12 – 12/4
2005 6/20 – 9/8
2006 2/11 – 5/27

URANUS BENEFICIAL
1940 6/11 – until 1945 3/24
1954 9/16 – until 1957 7/21
1980 12/1 – until 1983 10/16
1994 2/6 – until 1998 12/3

NEPTUNE BENEFICIAL
1968 11/30 – until 1973 11/16
1995 1/30 – until 2003 1/4

PLUTO BENEFICIAL
1938 1/1 – until 1944 5/24
1993 12/20 – until 1998 10/28

JUPITER CHALLENGING
1939 4/12 – until 1940 2/19
1942 5/12 – 7/23
1948 2/14 – 6/18

1948 10/11 – 12/29
1951 3/25 – 6/10
1951 9/29 – until 1952 1/28
1953 9/2 – 11/26
1954 4/22 – 7/6
1960 1/24 – 12/12
1963 3/9 – 5/17
1963 11/26 – 12/14
1965 8/7 – until 1966 1/7
1966 3/26 – 6/20
1972 1/7 – 11/25
1975 2/20 – 4/28
1977 7/18 – until 1978 6/3
1983 12/22 – until 1984 3/13
1984 6/16 – 11/6
1987 2/2 – 4/12
1989 7/1 – 10/2
1989 11/24 – until 1990 5/16
1995 12/6 – until 1996 2/18
1996 7/30 – 10/8
1998 5/25 – 9/11
1999 1/12 – 3/26
2001 6/15 – 8/30
2002 1/8 – 4/22
2007 11/20 – until 2008 1/30
2010 4/30 – 11/8
2010 11/28 – until 2011 3/9

SATURN CHALLENGING
1938 1/1 – 4/12
1943 8/12 – 12/9
1944 4/29 – 9/18
1944 11/27 – until 1945 5/30
1958 2/13 – 5/27
1958 11/11 – until 1960 1/3
1966 4/11 – 10/27
1966 12/26 – until 1967 5/27
1967 9/24 – until 1968 2/17
1973 6/12 – until 1974 7/11
1987 12/16 – until 1989 2/6
1989 7/15 – 11/5
1995 5/31 – 8/11
1996 2/15 – until 1997 3/26
2002 7/21 – until 2003 1/11
2003 4/4 – 8/22
2004 1/1 – 5/9

URANUS CHALLENGING
1947 7/14 – until 1951 7/2
1987 1/2 – until 1990 12/31
2009 4/1 – Continues

NEPTUNE CHALLENGING
1981 1/19 – until 1989 10/7

PLUTO CHALLENGING
2005 1/30 – Continues

JUPITER SPECIAL
1944 11/22 – until 1945 3/4
1945 7/21 – 10/9
1956 10/31 – until 1957 4/13
1957 6/23 – 9/24
1968 10/13 – until 1969 9/8
1980 9/27 – until 1981 1/3
1981 2/14 – 8/21
1992 9/11 – 11/30
1993 3/31 – 7/31
2004 8/26 – 11/10
2005 5/14 – 6/27

SATURN SPECIAL
1950 9/24 – until 1951 11/3
1952 4/28 – 7/23
1979 11/5 – until 1980 3/13
1980 7/28 – until 1981 1/8
1981 1/28 – 9/10
2009 9/7 – until 2010 10/16

URANUS SPECIAL
1966 11/20 – until 1971 7/11

NEPTUNE SPECIAL
1939 10/3 – until 1947 9/11

PLUTO SPECIAL
1968 10/14 – until 1976 8/11

September 26

SUN: LIBRA • DECANATE: LIBRA/VENUS • DEGREE: 2°5–3°5 LIBRA • MODE: CARDINAL • ELEMENT: AIR

Your Personal Powers

Proud, sensitive, and entertaining, when you apply self-discipline to your talents you possess outstanding potential for success. Your ruling planet, Venus, provides you with creativity, a loving nature, and a gracious manner. Stylish, you also appreciate beauty and have a natural aesthetic sense. Naturally empathetic and an idealist, you gain power from your natural charm and ability to deal with people on a personal level. With your wonderful ability to make contacts, you also have a knack for combining business and pleasure. You gain power when you develop order or take control of your life. Be careful, however, not to lose some of your power to idleness, your love of luxury, or overindulgence. When you are willing to persevere and work hard to develop your innate creativity, money will flow; hence you need to show your dedication in order to manifest your remarkable gifts. With your natural diplomatic skills and interest in people, you possess outstanding potential for success. You often gain more satisfaction if your work can benefit others.

Your Powers of Attraction in Relationships

Sociable and friendly, your courteous personality attracts others. Proud and dramatic, you can be a romantic lover and a caring partner. Due to your extreme sensitivity, however in close partnerships it is necessary that you stay detached; otherwise you may care too much and encounter disappointment or frustration when people let you down. Being sympathetic and a good listener, you may also find people turning to you for advice or help. Usually playful and entertaining, you can attract people with your agreeable manner. Although you possess an inner nobility and a generous nature, do not let your powerful need for love lead you into situations where you compromise your ideals. Youthful and gregarious, you enjoy group activities yet you can also be competitive or take the lead.

Your attractive qualities: creative, practical, caring, good business sense, responsible, mentally keen, stylish, responsible, imaginative, charming, magnetic, refined, kind, loving, supportive, intuitive, proud, refined, idealist, enthusiasm, charismatic, courageous, inspired

Your less attractive qualities: stubborn, rebellious, unstable relationships, unenthusiastic, lack of persistence, vanity, materialistic, secretive, controlling, indecisive, overindulgent, lazy, lack of drive or discipline

Your Venus Power

The planet Venus has a great deal of influence on your powers of attraction. Below are four possible Venus types for women and men. To find your Venus you need to go to page 771, where you will find the Venus table and extra information. The planet Mars also affects your powers of attraction. To find your Mars table and interpretation go to page 761.

WOMEN WITH VENUS IN LEO: Warm and playful with a touch of the dramatic, you enjoy the company of generous or strong individuals who can share your sense of fun. Although there are advantages to your being strong-willed, in your relationships you need to resist being bossy as it can cause resentment. With your wonderful mixture of regal authority and childlike wonder, you love to keep others entertained and amused.

MEN WITH VENUS IN LEO: Sociable and outgoing, you are kind and generous with those you love. Looking for a relationship that can be fun and entertaining, you need a playmate who can share your enthusiasm and high spirits. Your pride, however, often stops you from associating with lovers or partners you see as beneath you. As you desire someone who can appreciate your sense of the dramatic, you are often attracted to people with strong personalities.

WOMEN WITH VENUS IN VIRGO: Intelligent and discriminating, you are usually drawn to polite and refined individuals. As a perfectionist, you may be keen to analyze and criticize yourself, but be careful of continually going over your partner's shortcomings. By focusing on how you can make positive improvements in yourself and in your relationships, you avoid becoming skeptical or confused. You empower yourself when you display kind and caring concern for the well-being of loved ones and spontaneously offer your practical assistance.

MEN WITH VENUS IN VIRGO: A love of order usually indicates that you are attracted to refined individuals with analytical or practical abilities. You and your partner may be working together or serving similar causes. As you constantly analyze partnerships in order to improve them, you are likely to use former relationships as a point of reference and compare them to your present partner. You are helpful and kind,

and others usually rely on your good judgment and often turn to you for advice or practical assistance.

WOMEN WITH VENUS IN LIBRA: Usually you are attractive and sociable with an easygoing manner. Your love of beauty, harmony, and pleasure implies that you are a romantic with a desire for love and affection. Once in a relationship you need to learn to negotiate your position rather than adapt to the wishes of others and compromise just to keep the peace. Nevertheless, your advanced social skills and strong sense of fair play can help you succeed in any social or romantic situation.

MEN WITH VENUS IN LIBRA: Your good social skills, charming personality, and refined manner usually make you attractive to the opposite sex. Equally, you desire a sophisticated partner with grace, elegance, and a strong sense of style. Although you have the ability to be persuasive and irresistible to others, avoid manipulative love games. Nevertheless, your natural diplomacy and sense of fair play help you to relate to people in all social situations. With your love for balance and harmony, you seek a partner who is also moderate, easygoing, and loving.

WOMEN WITH VENUS IN SCORPIO: With a natural psychic gift for penetrating the feelings of others, you can often help partners transform emotional challenges or sexual difficulties. When you fall in love, your strong feelings and determination give you a potent force that others find attractive and seductive. Although you know what really turns people on, your most profound desire is usually for the deepness and closeness of real love and intimacy in an enduring relationship.

MEN WITH VENUS IN SCORPIO: In relationships you possess a sensitive understanding of your partner's deeper nature. Although you are strongly attached to those you love, you may have to be careful that your feelings do not turn into jealousy or possessiveness. When you fall in love it is often with power and an emotional intensity. You are attracted to partners who can share your passion and display strong feelings of sexuality like your own.

To read all about your Outer Planets and work out how to use your personalized timetable, go to Section Three, page 789.

To read all about your Outer Planets and work out how to use your personalized timetable, go to Section Three, page 789.

Your Personalized Timetable

JUPITER BENEFICIAL
1938 1/1 – 2/4
1941 5/3 – 7/13
1943 6/19 – 8/4
1947 10/12 – 11/28
1949 3/8 – 8/10
1949 10/27 – until 1950 1/19
1953 4/16 – 6/24
1954 10/10 – 12/25
1955 5/31 – 7/19
1959 1/23 – 5/14
1959 9/22 – 11/12
1961 2/16 – until 1962 1/1
1964 8/15 – 10/14
1965 3/28 – 6/7
1966 9/13 – until 1967 2/2
1967 5/7 – 7/3
1971 1/1 – 6/28
1971 8/20 – 10/26
1973 1/30 – 4/30
1973 6/30 – 12/13
1976 7/14 – 11/29
1977 3/3 – 5/22
1978 8/24 – 10/27
1978 12/25 – until 1979 6/14
1982 12/14 – until 1983 2/9
1983 5/15 – 10/6
1985 1/14 – 3/30
1985 8/15 – 11/20
1988 6/24 – until 1989 5/6
1990 8/7 – 9/27
1991 2/4 – 5/23
1994 11/28 – until 1995 1/16
1995 6/25 – 9/9
1996 12/29 – until 1997 3/9
2000 6/6 – 9/11
2000 10/17 – until 2001 4/17
2002 7/22 – 9/6
2006 11/13 – 12/29
2008 12/12 – until 2009 2/20
2012 5/19 – Continues

SATURN BENEFICIAL
1941 7/3 – 11/22
1942 3/23 – 8/10
1942 11/11 – until 1943 4/25
1946 7/15 – 10/15
1946 12/27 – until 1947 6/28
1955 12/20 – until 1956 6/16
1956 9/12 – 12/17
1961 2/14 – 8/15
1961 11/8 – until 1962 4/22
1962 6/21 – until 1963 1/7
1971 5/7 – until 1972 6/5
1975 8/26 – until 1976 2/13
1976 5/9 – 8/7
1985 2/12 – 3/30
1985 10/28 – until 1986 1/28
1986 5/10 – 10/25
1990 4/6 – 6/3
1990 12/23 – until 1992 2/10
2000 6/13 – 12/30
2001 2/19 – 7/16
2001 12/13 – until 2002 4/3
2005 6/28 – 9/17
2006 1/30 – 6/7

URANUS BENEFICIAL
1940 7/1 – until 1945 4/18
1954 10/25 – until 1958 5/2
1980 12/18 – until 1983 11/3
1994 2/25 – until 1998 12/26

NEPTUNE BENEFICIAL
1968 12/28 – until 1974 10/14
1995 3/1 – until 2003 11/22

PLUTO BENEFICIAL
1938 1/1 – until 1944 7/8
1994 1/23 – until 1998 11/23

JUPITER CHALLENGING
1939 4/16 – until 1940 2/24
1942 5/17 – 7/27
1948 2/21 – 6/10

1948 10/17 – until 1949 1/2
1951 3/29 – 6/17
1951 9/21 – until 1952 2/2
1953 9/11 – 11/17
1954 4/27 – 7/10
1960 1/29 – 7/27
1960 9/13 – 12/17
1963 3/13 – 5/22
1963 11/9 – 12/31
1965 8/13 – 12/30
1966 4/3 – 6/24
1972 1/11 – 11/30
1975 2/24 – 5/2
1977 7/23 – until 1978 6/8
1983 12/26 – until 1984 3/21
1984 6/8 – 11/11
1987 2/7 – 4/16
1989 7/6 – 10/17
1989 11/8 – until 1990 5/21
1995 12/10 – until 1996 2/23
1996 7/21 – 10/16
1998 5/31 – 9/3
1999 1/17 – 3/30
2001 6/19 – 9/5
2002 1/1 – 4/29
2007 11/25 – until 2008 2/4
2010 5/5 – 10/23
2010 12/15 – until 2011 3/13

SATURN CHALLENGING
1938 1/1 – 4/20
1943 8/23 – 11/26
1944 5/8 – 10/12
1944 11/3 – until 1945 6/7
1958 2/28 – 5/11
1958 11/20 – until 1960 1/11
1966 4/20 – 10/11
1967 1/10 – 6/8
1967 9/10 – until 1968 2/26
1973 6/19 – until 1974 7/18
1987 12/25 – until 1989 2/16
1989 7/1 – 11/16
1995 6/26 – 7/15
1996 2/23 – until 1997 4/3
2002 7/30 – 12/29
2003 4/16 – 9/1
2003 12/20 – until 2004 5/19

URANUS CHALLENGING
1947 8/2 – until 1952 4/29
1987 1/20 – until 1991 11/2
2009 4/19 – Continues

NEPTUNE CHALLENGING
1981 3/1 – until 1989 11/23

PLUTO CHALLENGING
2005 12/26 – Continues

JUPITER SPECIAL
1944 11/29 – until 1945 2/24
1945 7/27 – 10/14
1956 11/5 – until 1957 4/4
1957 7/2 – 9/28
1968 10/18 – until 1969 9/13
1980 10/1 – until 1981 8/26
1992 9/15 – 12/7
1993 3/23 – 8/6
2004 8/31 – 11/16
2005 5/1 – 7/9

SATURN SPECIAL
1950 10/2 – until 1951 11/12
1952 4/14 – 8/5
1979 11/15 – until 1980 3/1
1980 8/7 – until 1981 9/18
2009 9/15 – until 2010 10/25
2011 5/28 – 6/29

URANUS SPECIAL
1967 9/16 – until 1971 8/10

NEPTUNE SPECIAL
1939 11/2 – until 1948 8/1

PLUTO SPECIAL
1968 11/17 – until 1976 9/10

September 27

SUN: LIBRA · DECANATE: LIBRA/VENUS · DEGREE: 3°5–4°5 LIBRA · MODE: CARDINAL · ELEMENT: AIR

Your Personal Powers

Emotionally warm and magnetic, with the ability to uplift the spirit of others, you enjoy sharing and making people feel at ease. Your ruling planet, Venus, grants you personal charm, natural diplomatic skills, and an ability to mix with people from all walks of life. Although this influence can also attract you to beauty, luxury, and the good things of life, it also warns against overindulgence. You gain power from the unique blend of your people skills, enterprising spirit, and organizational ability. Although sensitive and imaginative, with your fine intellect and adventurous nature you also have many opportunities to succeed in business. With your strong emotions, however, you can lose power if you do not put in the persistence and discipline needed to make the most of your natural talents or if you allow changing moods to lead you to escapism or self-doubts. Nevertheless, honest and direct as well as compassionate and understanding, you possess an interesting blend of ambition and idealism.

Your Powers of Attraction in Relationships

With your kind nature and charming personality, you can be an excellent friend and easily attract others. Courteous, sensitive, and able to mix well, you gain much success through your social contacts. You are receptive to others' needs and your relationships are highly important to you. With your need to express your strong feelings, dramatic situations are likely to occur in your relationships. To avoid feeling oversensitive or disappointed, you may need to balance your suspicious tendencies with your more objective outlook. As you often hold the upper hand, avoid becoming involved in power struggles with partners. You are attracted to determined individuals as well as those with influence or material strength. A humanitarian side to your personality can bring out your compassionate nature. Generous and broad-minded, when committed you can make a loyal and loving partner.

Your attractive qualities: versatile, intelligent, kind, imaginative, creative, brave, understanding, loving, idealistic, generous, humanitarian, friendly, sensitive, compassionate, persuasive, visionary, refined, spiritual, loves harmony, inventive

Your less attractive qualities: disagreeable, stubborn, self-pity, argumentative, restless, nervous, vanity, lazy, overindulgent, mistrusting, lack of drive, overemotional, secretive, inner tensions

Your Venus Power

The planet Venus has a great deal of influence on your powers of attraction. Below are four possible Venus types for women and men. To find your Venus you need to go to page 771, where you will find the Venus table and extra information. The planet Mars also affects your powers of attraction. To find your Mars table and interpretation go to page 761.

WOMEN WITH VENUS IN LEO: Your friendly and sunny personality often makes you stand out in a crowd. Generous and giving, you know how to make your partner feel special. As you often expect loyalty and devotion from your partners in return, you can become easily offended if they ignore you or behave in an inconsiderate manner. Charming and kind, when you're in love you can be romantic, dramatic, and passionate.

MEN WITH VENUS IN LEO: A childlike nature suggests that you are versatile and keen on games or being entertained. You are usually attracted to vivacious partners with a benevolent nature. As an extrovert, you enjoy being involved in all types of activities where you can assert yourself and show your talents and abilities. Others may recognize your inborn tendencies to lead but are also aware of your vanity or pride. Nevertheless, generous, kind, and caring, you often show compassion to those less fortunate than yourself.

WOMEN WITH VENUS IN VIRGO: In relationships you can be modest and unassuming but desire perfection. You usually analyze your partnerships until you feel you have understood them to the last little detail in order to improve them. A problem usually arises when you become too critical either of partners or yourself and indulge in being skeptical or fault-finding. As you are modest, others may not be aware of the strong sensuality beneath your well-groomed exterior.

MEN WITH VENUS IN VIRGO: Industrious and well-ordered, you relate to others in a considerate and down-to-earth way. You enjoy giving practical advice and being of service to those you love, even in small ways. Being a perfectionist, you are drawn to partners with high morals or a strong work ethic. Partners who have strong analytical minds are very attractive to you, particularly if they are also clean and meticulously dressed.

WOMEN WITH VENUS IN LIBRA: Gracious, charming,

and sociable with a sense of style, you have no trouble attracting admirers. With your natural diplomatic skills and desire for harmony you usually like to keep the peace and avoid confrontations, but be careful of failing to take a stand when it is necessary. Romantic and easygoing yourself, you are attracted to affectionate and refined individuals who share your love of peace, justice, and fair play.

MEN WITH VENUS IN LIBRA: Courteous and refined, you are attracted to beautiful and elegant people. You are looking for a partner who can share your natural good taste and enjoy an intellectual conversation. Disliking conflict, you may have to be careful not to go along with others just to keep the peace. Your ideal partner will appreciate beauty and the little luxuries of life as well as possess good social skills. You have a strong sense of social etiquette yourself so you need an intelligent and sophisticated partner.

WOMEN WITH VENUS IN SCORPIO: Your strength and power is in your ability to love both deeply and sensitively. For you, love and desire go hand in hand. As you feel so deeply, you often keep your sensitivity or vulnerability hidden from others in order to keep some control in your relationships. You are more likely to prefer a few very close loyal friends than many superficial acquaintances. In relationships your sensual nature and magnetic intensity can easily attract others.

MEN WITH VENUS IN SCORPIO: You are attracted to partners with deep and powerful emotions or individuals whom you find intriguing. Your gift for creating smoke screens to maintain secrecy around your feelings can conceal your inner sensitivity and vulnerability. Nevertheless, you are looking for a partner who can pierce your defenses and understand you at a very deep level. Needing a relationship with a powerful sexual connection, you thrive on emotional intensity.

To read all about your Outer Planets and work out how to use your personalized timetable, go to Section Three, page 789.

Your Personalized Timetable

JUPITER BENEFICIAL
1938 1/1 – 2/8
1941 5/8 – 7/18
1942 1/24 – 2/17
1943 6/24 – 8/9
1947 10/17 – 12/2
1949 3/13 – 8/2
1949 11/4 – until 1950 1/23
1953 4/20 – 6/28
1954 10/19 – 12/15
1955 6/5 – 7/24
1959 1/30 – 5/6
1959 9/27 – 11/16
1961 2/21 – until 1962 1/6
1964 8/29 – 10/1
1965 4/2 – 6/12
1966 9/19 – until 1967 1/26
1967 5/14 – 7/8
1971 1/6 – 6/17
1971 8/31 – 10/31
1973 2/3 – 5/13
1973 6/17 – 12/18
1976 7/20 – 11/21
1977 3/9 – 5/26
1978 8/29 – 11/10
1978 12/11 – until 1979 6/20
1982 12/19 – until 1983 2/17
1983 5/6 – 10/12
1985 1/18 – 4/5
1985 8/7 – 11/26
1988 6/29 – until 1989 5/10
1990 8/12 – 10/3
1991 1/28 – 5/29
1994 12/3 – until 1995 1/21
1995 6/16 – 9/18
1997 1/3 – 3/14
2000 6/10 – until 2001 4/22
2002 7/26 – 9/11
2003 3/16 – 4/23
2006 11/18 – until 2007 1/3
2008 12/17 – until 2009 2/24
2012 5/24 – Continues

SATURN BENEFICIAL
1941 7/13 – 11/10
1942 4/2 – 8/25
1942 10/26 – until 1943 5/4
1946 7/23 – 11/4
1946 12/6 – until 1947 7/6
1955 12/29 – until 1956 6/1
1956 9/25 – 12/26
1957 7/7 – 9/15
1961 2/23 – 7/31
1961 11/22 – until 1963 1/16
1971 5/15 – until 1972 6/13
1975 9/3 – until 1976 1/31
1976 5/22 – 8/14
1985 11/5 – until 1986 2/11
1986 4/24 – 11/3
1990 12/31 – until 1992 2/19
2000 6/22 – 12/13
2001 3/7 – 7/26
2001 12/1 – until 2002 4/14
2005 7/5 – 9/28
2006 1/18 – 6/17

URANUS BENEFICIAL
1940 7/28 – until 1945 5/7
1955 8/1 – until 1958 6/5
1981 1/5 – until 1983 11/20
1994 3/21 – until 1999 1/13

NEPTUNE BENEFICIAL
1969 2/14 – until 1974 11/13
1996 1/26 – until 2003 12/30

PLUTO BENEFICIAL
1938 1/1 – until 1945 6/19
1994 12/7 – until 1999 10/16

JUPITER CHALLENGING
1939 4/20 – until 1940 2/28
1942 5/21 – 8/1
1948 2/28 – 6/2

1948 10/23 – until 1949 1/6
1951 4/2 – 6/25
1951 9/13 – until 1952 2/7
1953 9/22 – 11/6
1954 5/3 – 7/15
1960 2/3 – 7/16
1960 9/24 – 12/21
1963 3/17 – 5/27
1963 10/30 – until 1964 1/9
1965 8/18 – 12/22
1966 4/10 – 6/29
1972 1/16 – 12/4
1975 2/28 – 5/7
1977 7/28 – until 1978 6/12
1983 12/30 – until 1984 3/31
1984 5/29 – 11/16
1987 2/11 – 4/20
1989 7/10 – until 1990 5/26
1995 12/15 – until 1996 2/29
1996 7/13 – 10/24
1998 6/8 – 8/26
1999 1/22 – 4/3
2001 6/23 – 9/12
2001 12/24 – until 2002 5/5
2007 11/29 – until 2008 2/9
2010 5/10 – 10/13
2010 12/24 – until 2011 3/17

SATURN CHALLENGING
1938 1/1 – 4/28
1938 11/23 – until 1939 1/5
1943 9/6 – 11/11
1944 5/16 – until 1945 6/15
1958 3/28 – 4/12
1958 11/29 – until 1960 1/19
1966 4/29 – 9/27
1967 1/22 – 6/24
1967 8/25 – until 1968 3/5
1973 6/27 – until 1974 7/26
1988 1/2 – until 1989 2/28
1989 6/18 – 11/26
1996 3/3 – until 1997 4/11
2002 8/8 – 12/17
2003 4/27 – 9/13
2003 12/7 – until 2004 5/28

URANUS CHALLENGING
1947 8/28 – until 1952 5/22
1987 2/9 – until 1991 11/25
2009 5/12 – Continues

NEPTUNE CHALLENGING
1982 1/15 – until 1989 12/22

PLUTO CHALLENGING
2006 1/23 – Continues

JUPITER SPECIAL
1944 12/8 – until 1945 2/15
1945 8/2 – 10/19
1956 11/11 – until 1957 3/27
1957 7/10 – 10/3
1968 10/23 – until 1969 9/17
1980 10/6 – until 1981 8/31
1992 9/20 – 12/14
1993 3/15 – 8/12
2004 9/4 – 11/21
2005 4/22 – 7/19

SATURN SPECIAL
1950 10/10 – until 1951 5/18
1951 6/8 – 11/22
1952 4/1 – 8/16
1979 11/28 – until 1980 2/15
1980 8/16 – until 1981 9/26
2009 9/23 – until 2010 11/2
2011 5/5 – 7/21

URANUS SPECIAL
1967 10/1 – until 1971 8/30

NEPTUNE SPECIAL
1940 9/29 – until 1948 9/6

PLUTO SPECIAL
1969 10/7 – until 1977 7/21

September 28

SUN: LIBRA • DECANATE: LIBRA/VENUS • DEGREE: 4°5–5°5 LIBRA • MODE: CARDINAL • ELEMENT: AIR

Your Personal Powers

Gracious and friendly, your personal powers include keen perception, intelligence, and a compassionate and caring nature. Aware of image and beauty, you possess a touch of glamour and enjoy dressing stylishly or making your environment harmonious or attractive. You gain power from the special blend of your refined social skills and shrewd practicality. Being ambitious and responsible often spurs you on to utilize your natural business talents and work hard. Nevertheless, if you stop listening to your powerful sixth sense or become rigid in your work habits, you can lose some of your power. This can result in taking your responsibilities too seriously or forgetting how to enjoy life and be spontaneous. When you are optimistic and focused, everyone gains power from your enthusiasm and loving understanding. With your imaginative ideas and strong emotions, you particularly benefit from developing your self-expression, whether through your innate creativity, artistic ability, or your idealistic support of a cause. Whatever you do, your natural vivacity and enterprising nature can inspire others to follow your lead.

Your Powers of Attraction in Relationships

You are sensitive and idealistic, and your courteous manner and natural charm attract others. As you possess a depth of feeling, the demonstration of love and affection is especially important to you. With your interest in people, you can project a warm sympathy for the feelings of others. In your desire to love and be loved, however, do not compromise too much of your true self. When you are indecisive or worried, your sensitive emotions can cause you to withdraw or appear melancholic. You are often attracted to active individuals who can stimulate or share your sense of adventure. Although you are romantic and loving, you may need to be more patient with your partners. Your love life greatly improves when you learn the importance of valuing your feelings.

Your attractive qualities: compassionate, progressive, daring, artistic, idealistic, ambitious, hardworking, stable home life, detached, responsible, spontaneous, leadership ability, enthusiasm, humanitarian streak, enterprising, dutiful, strong-willed, kind, discerning

Your less attractive qualities: unmotivated, lack of confidence, too proud, unrealistic, lack of judgment, withdrawn, skeptical, too enthusiastic or serious, intolerant, indecisive, too dependent on others, workaholic, impatient, bossy

Your Venus Power

The planet Venus has a great deal of influence on your powers of attraction. Below are four possible Venus types for women and men. To find your Venus you need to go to page 771, where you will find the Venus table and extra information. The planet Mars also affects your powers of attraction. To find your Mars table and interpretation go to page 761.

WOMEN WITH VENUS IN LEO: Warm and playful with a touch of the dramatic, you enjoy the company of generous or strong individuals who can share your sense of fun. Although there are advantages to your being strong-willed, in your relationships you need to resist being bossy as it can cause resentment. With your wonderful mixture of regal authority and childlike wonder, you love to keep others entertained and amused.

MEN WITH VENUS IN LEO: Sociable and outgoing, you are kind and generous with those you love. Looking for a relationship that can be fun and entertaining, you need a playmate who can share your enthusiasm and high spirits. Your pride, however, often stops you from associating with lovers or partners you see as beneath you. As you desire someone who can appreciate your sense of the dramatic, you are often attracted to people with strong personalities.

WOMEN WITH VENUS IN VIRGO: Intelligent and discriminating, you are usually drawn to polite and refined individuals. As a perfectionist, you may be keen to analyze and criticize yourself, but be careful of continually going over your partner's shortcomings. By focusing on how you can make positive improvements in yourself and in your relationships, you avoid becoming skeptical or confused. You empower yourself when you display kind and caring concern for the well-being of loved ones and spontaneously offer your practical assistance.

MEN WITH VENUS IN VIRGO: A love of order usually indicates that you are attracted to refined individuals with analytical or practical abilities. You and your partner may be working together or serving similar causes. As you constantly analyze partnerships in order to improve them, you are likely to use former relationships as a point of reference and compare them to your present partner. As you are helpful and

kind, and others usually rely on your good judgment and often turn to you for advice or practical assistance.

WOMEN WITH VENUS IN LIBRA: Usually you are attractive and sociable with an easygoing manner. Your love of beauty, harmony, and pleasure implies that you are a romantic with a desire for love and affection. Once in a relationship you need to learn to negotiate your position rather than adapt to the wishes of others and compromise just to keep the peace. Nevertheless, your advanced social skills and strong sense of fair play can help you succeed in any social or romantic situation.

MEN WITH VENUS IN LIBRA: Your good social skills, charming personality, and refined manner usually make you attractive to the opposite sex. Equally, you desire a sophisticated partner with grace, elegance, and a strong sense of style. Although you have the ability to be persuasive and irresistible to others, avoid manipulative love games. Nevertheless, your natural diplomacy and sense of fair play help you to relate to people in all social situations. With your love for balance and harmony, you seek a partner who is also moderate, easygoing, and loving.

WOMEN WITH VENUS IN SCORPIO: With a natural psychic gift for penetrating the feelings of others, you can often help partners transform emotional challenges or sexual difficulties. When you fall in love, your strong feelings and determination give you a potent force that others find attractive and seductive. Although you know what really turns people on, your most profound desire is usually for the deepness and closeness of real love and intimacy in an enduring relationship.

MEN WITH VENUS IN SCORPIO: In relationships you possess a sensitive understanding of your partner's deeper nature. Although you are strongly attached to those you love, you may have to be careful that your feelings do not turn into jealousy or possessiveness. When you fall in love it is often with power and an emotional intensity. You are attracted to partners who can share your passion and display strong feelings of sexuality like your own.

To read all about your Outer Planets and work out how to use your personalized timetable, go to Section Three, page 789.

Your Personalized Timetable

JUPITER BENEFICIAL
1938 1/1 – 2/12
1941 5/12 – 7/22
1942 1/9 – 3/4
1943 6/29 – 8/13
1947 10/22 – 12/7
1949 3/19 – 7/25
1949 11/11 – until 1950 1/27
1953 4/25 – 7/3
1954 11/3 – 11/30
1955 6/11 – 7/28
1959 2/7 – 4/28
1959 10/3 – 11/21
1961 2/25 – until 1962 1/10
1965 4/6 – 6/16
1966 9/25 – until 1967 1/18
1967 5/20 – 7/12
1971 1/12 – 6/8
1971 9/8 – 11/4
1973 2/8 – 12/23
1976 7/26 – 11/14
1977 3/16 – 5/31
1978 9/3 – until 1979 3/6
1979 4/14 – 6/25
1982 12/24 – until 1983 2/27
1983 4/26 – 10/17
1985 1/23 – 4/11
1985 7/30 – 12/2
1988 7/3 – until 1989 1/2
1989 2/7 – 5/14
1990 8/16 – 10/9
1991 1/21 – 6/4
1994 12/7 – until 1995 1/27
1995 6/8 – until 1995 9/25
1997 1/7 – 3/19
1997 9/20 – 10/26
2000 6/14 – until 2001 4/26
2002 7/31 – 9/17
2003 3/3 – 5/6
2006 11/22 – until 2007 1/8
2008 12/21 – until 2009 2/28
2012 5/28 – Continues

SATURN BENEFICIAL
1941 7/25 – 10/28
1942 4/11 – until 1943 5/12
1946 7/30 – until 1947 7/14
1956 1/8 – 5/19
1956 10/6 – until 1957 1/4
1957 6/21 – 10/1
1961 3/5 – 7/18
1961 12/3 – until 1963 1/24
1971 5/22 – until 1972 6/21
1975 9/13 – until 1976 1/19
1976 6/1 – 8/22
1985 11/14 – until 1986 3/10
1986 3/28 – 11/12
1991 1/9 – until 1992 2/27
1992 9/14 – 11/16
2000 6/30 – 11/30
2001 3/20 – 8/5
2001 11/19 – until 2002 4/23
2005 7/13 – 10/10
2006 1/5 – 6/26

URANUS BENEFICIAL
1941 5/25 – until 1945 5/25
1955 8/18 – until 1958 6/25
1981 1/31 – until 1984 9/1
1995 1/20 – until 1999 1/30

NEPTUNE BENEFICIAL
1969 12/24 – until 1975 10/8
1996 2/23 – until 2004 11/2

PLUTO BENEFICIAL
1938 7/21 – until 1946 5/21
1995 1/4 – until 1999 11/14

JUPITER CHALLENGING
1939 4/25 – until 1940 3/4
1942 5/26 – 8/5
1948 3/7 – 5/25
1948 10/29 – until 1949 1/10
1951 4/7 – 7/4

1951 9/4 – until 1952 2/13
1954 5/7 – 7/19
1960 2/9 – 7/7
1960 10/3 – 12/25
1963 3/21 – 6/1
1963 10/22 – until 1964 1/17
1965 8/24 – 12/15
1966 4/16 – 7/3
1972 1/20 – 12/9
1975 3/4 – 5/11
1977 8/2 – until 1978 2/2
1978 3/10 – 6/17
1984 1/4 – 4/15
1984 5/14 – 11/21
1987 2/16 – 4/24
1989 7/15 – until 1990 5/31
1995 12/19 – until 1996 3/6
1996 7/5 – 10/30
1998 6/18 – 8/16
1999 1/27 – 4/7
2001 6/28 – 9/19
2001 12/17 – until 2002 5/11
2007 12/4 – until 2008 2/14
2008 8/31 – 9/15
2010 5/16 – 10/5
2011 1/1 – 3/21

SATURN CHALLENGING
1938 1/1 – 5/7
1938 11/4 – until 1939 1/23
1944 5/24 – until 1945 6/23
1958 12/7 – until 1960 1/28
1960 8/14 – 10/17
1966 5/10 – 9/14
1967 2/1 – until 1968 3/14
1973 7/4 – until 1974 8/3
1975 2/15 – 4/10
1988 1/11 – 7/31
1988 9/28 – until 1989 3/13
1989 6/3 – 12/6
1996 3/11 – until 1997 4/19
2002 8/19 – 12/5
2003 5/6 – 9/30
2003 11/20 – until 2004 6/5

URANUS CHALLENGING
1948 6/23 – until 1952 6/9
1987 3/17 – until 1991 12/14
2010 3/18 – Continues

NEPTUNE CHALLENGING
1982 2/19 – until 1990 11/18

PLUTO CHALLENGING
2006 3/8 – Continues

JUPITER SPECIAL
1944 12/19 – until 1945 2/4
1945 8/7 – 10/23
1956 11/17 – until 1957 3/19
1957 7/17 – 10/7
1968 10/28 – until 1969 5/4
1969 6/11 – 9/22
1980 10/10 – until 1981 9/5
1992 9/24 – 12/23
1993 3/6 – 8/18
2004 9/9 – 11/27
2005 4/14 – 7/27

SATURN SPECIAL
1950 10/18 – until 1951 4/22
1951 7/4 – 12/3
1952 3/19 – 8/26
1979 12/17 – until 1980 1/27
1980 8/24 – until 1981 10/4
2009 10/1 – until 2010 11/11
2011 4/20 – 8/4

URANUS SPECIAL
1967 10/17 – until 1971 9/16

NEPTUNE SPECIAL
1940 10/27 – until 1949 7/23

PLUTO SPECIAL
1969 11/7 – until 1977 8/29

399

September 29

SUN: LIBRA • DECANATE: LIBRA/VENUS • DEGREE: 5°5–6°5 LIBRA • MODE: CARDINAL • ELEMENT: AIR

Your Personal Powers

You are generous, kind, and entertaining, and among your many personal powers are determination, strong emotional expression, and an innate business sense. Because of the influence of your ruling planet, Venus, both love and affection are important to you. Although you like to aim high with your expectations, beware of losing some of your power to disappointment or discontentment. You gain power, however, from the combination of your friendly manner, strong imagination, and natural creativity. If developed, this creativity may find expression through art, design, music, writing, or drama. As a strong and determined individual who enjoys being surrounded by luxuries and beauty, you are usually willing to work hard to achieve your goals. Fortunately, you are often able to combine your charm and people skills with a talent for negotiating a hard bargain. As well as possessing business acumen, you are also sensitive and idealistic, but be careful that this does not lead to escapism. Nevertheless, forceful when you need to be, you possess a charisma that is particularly dynamic when uplifting or enriching the lives of others.

Your Powers of Attraction in Relationships

Sociable and friendly, you can attract others with your generous and kindhearted personality. With your desire for harmony and security, you seek a responsible partner who can understand or share the importance you place on home and family. Although you can be lighthearted and compassionate, repressed emotions can cause you to be moody or obstinate. Your frustration with others may also result in your forfeiting the inspired and joyful side of your personality to emotional power struggles. Romantic and idealistic, however, you possess a richness of feelings and a determination to make your relationships work. You are often willing to give more than you receive in partnerships. With the combination of your sensitivity and fighting spirit, if you believe in someone, you are ardently loyal and supportive.

Your attractive qualities: generous, kind, warm, entertaining, business sense, creative, inspired, mentally keen, artistic, determination, compassionate, intuitive, powerful dreams, worldly, faithful, fighting spirit, spontaneous, enthusiastic, dynamic, imaginative

Your less attractive qualities: moody, insecure, dreamer, nervous, unfocused, difficult, secretive, extremist, lazy, power games, overindulgent, inconsiderate, discontented, isolated, too sensitive

Your Venus Power

The planet Venus has a great deal of influence on your powers of attraction. Below are four possible Venus types for women and men. To find your Venus you need to go to page 771, where you will find the Venus table and extra information. The planet Mars also affects your powers of attraction. To find your Mars table and interpretation go to page 761.

WOMEN WITH VENUS IN LEO: You possess the wonderful ability to project your warm and sunny personality and keep others happily entertained. Loving attention yourself, you seek a partner who can appreciate you, be supportive, and give you positive feedback. Proud, with a natural regal air, you expect respect from your partners but are willing to be loyal and supportive in exchange. Although sometimes a little self-centered, you know how to make your partner feel special.

MEN WITH VENUS IN LEO: Enthusiastic, playful, and kind, you can be benevolent with those you love. Warm, romantic, and self-expressive, you adore the drama of love or having fun with your friends. You are usually attracted to partners with warm and generous natures. Although you can be a confident and charismatic partner, you may need to develop humility in order to stop pride or arrogance from marring your relationships.

WOMEN WITH VENUS IN VIRGO: Intelligent and discriminating, you are usually drawn to polite and refined individuals. As a perfectionist you may be keen to analyze and criticize yourself, but be careful of continually going over your partner's shortcomings. By focusing on how you can make positive improvements in yourself and in your relationships, you avoid becoming skeptical or confused. You empower yourself when you display kind and caring concern for the well-being of loved ones and spontaneously offer your practical assistance.

MEN WITH VENUS IN VIRGO: A love of order usually indicates that you are attracted to refined individuals with analytical or practical abilities. You and your partner may be working together or serving similar causes. As you constantly analyze partnerships in order to improve them, you are likely to use former relationships as a point of reference and com-

pare them to your present partner. As you are helpful and kind, others usually rely on your good judgment and often turn to you for advice or practical assistance.

WOMEN WITH VENUS IN LIBRA: Attractive, refined, and conscious of the needs of others, you usually desire harmonious relationships. As a peacemaker with good negotiating skills, you can smooth out difficulties with others but your dislike of confrontation may sometimes leave you refusing to take a stand or compromising too many of your own needs. Courteous, stylish, and charming with polished social skills, you are an expert at relating to others in a gracious and civilized manner.

MEN WITH VENUS IN LIBRA: As a sociable and friendly individual with an eye for beauty, you are amorous and charming. You are a natural gentleman and your ideal partner usually has an elegant appearance, artistic appreciation, and good taste. Your relationships benefit when you resist the temptation to take the easy way out or put too much emphasis on vanity and high living. Intellectual and naturally refined, you seek a loving partner who can share your romantic and sophisticated aspirations.

WOMEN WITH VENUS IN SCORPIO: Your strength and power is in your ability to love both deeply and sensitively. For you, love and desire go hand in hand. As you feel so deeply, you often keep your sensitivity or vulnerability hidden from others in order to keep some control in your relationships. You are more likely to prefer a few very close loyal friends than many superficial acquaintances. In relationships your sensual nature and magnetic intensity can easily attract others.

MEN WITH VENUS IN SCORPIO: You are attracted to partners with deep and powerful emotions or individuals you find intriguing. Your gift for creating smoke screens to maintain secrecy around your feelings can conceal your inner sensitivity and vulnerability. Nevertheless, you are looking for a partner who can pierce your defenses and understand you at a very deep level. Needing a relationship with a powerful sexual connection, you thrive on emotional intensity.

To read all about your Outer Planets and work out how to use your personalized timetable, go to Section Three, page 789.

♎

Your Personalized Timetable

JUPITER BENEFICIAL
1938 1/1 – 2/16
1941 5/16 – 7/28
1941 12/30 – until **1942** 3/14
1943 7/3 – 8/18
1947 10/27 – 12/11
1949 3/25 – 7/17
1949 11/17 – until **1950** 1/31
1953 4/29 – 7/7
1955 6/16 – 8/2
1959 2/16 – 4/18
1959 10/8 – 11/25
1961 3/2 – 9/10
1961 10/6 – until **1962** 1/14
1965 4/11 – 6/20
1966 10/1 – until **1967** 1/11
1967 5/27 – 7/17
1971 1/18 – 5/31
1971 9/16 – 11/9
1973 2/12 – 12/28
1976 8/2 – 11/7
1977 3/21 – 6/4
1978 9/8 – until **1979** 2/22
1979 4/27 – 6/30
1982 12/29 – until **1983** 3/14
1983 4/10 – 10/23
1985 1/27 – 4/18
1985 7/23 – 12/8
1988 7/8 – 12/21
1989 2/19 – 5/19
1990 8/21 – 10/17
1991 1/13 – 6/10
1994 12/12 – until **1995** 2/2
1995 5/31 – 10/1
1997 1/11 – 3/24
1997 9/7 – 11/7
2000 6/19 – until **2001** 5/1
2002 8/4 – 9/22
2003 2/22 – 5/15
2006 11/26 – until **2007** 1/13
2007 7/16 – 8/28
2008 12/26 – until **2009** 3/5
2012 6/1 – Continues

SATURN BENEFICIAL
1941 8/9 – 10/13
1942 4/19 – until **1943** 5/20
1946 8/7 – until **1947** 7/22
1956 1/20 – 5/5
1956 10/16 – until **1957** 1/13
1957 6/7 – 10/13
1961 3/17 – 7/4
1961 12/13 – until **1963** 2/1
1971 5/30 – until **1972** 6/29
1975 9/24 – until **1976** 1/6
1976 6/10 – 8/30
1977 3/15 – 5/8
1985 11/22 – until **1986** 11/21
1991 1/17 – until **1992** 3/7
1992 8/28 – 12/1
2000 7/10 – 11/18
2001 3/30 – 8/18
2001 11/5 – until **2002** 5/1
2005 7/21 – 10/25
2005 12/20 – until **2006** 7/4

URANUS BENEFICIAL
1941 6/11 – until **1946** 3/13
1955 9/5 – until **1958** 7/13
1981 11/26 – until **1984** 10/8
1995 2/6 – until **1999** 12/4

NEPTUNE BENEFICIAL
1970 1/31 – until **1975** 11/9
1996 4/7 – until **2004** 12/24

PLUTO BENEFICIAL
1938 8/27 – until **1946** 7/7
1995 11/26 – until **2000** 9/30

JUPITER CHALLENGING
1939 4/29 – until **1940** 3/8
1942 5/30 – 8/10
1948 3/16 – 5/14

1948 11/3 – until **1949** 1/15
1951 4/11 – 7/16
1951 8/22 – until **1952** 2/17
1954 5/12 – 7/24
1960 2/15 – 6/29
1960 10/10 – 12/29
1963 3/25 – 6/7
1963 10/14 – until **1964** 1/24
1965 8/31 – 12/8
1966 4/22 – 7/7
1972 1/25 – 12/13
1975 3/8 – 5/16
1977 8/7 – until **1978** 1/20
1978 3/23 – 6/21
1984 1/8 – 11/26
1987 2/20 – 4/28
1989 7/19 – until **1990** 6/4
1995 12/23 – until **1996** 3/13
1996 6/27 – 11/5
1998 7/1 – 8/3
1999 2/1 – 4/11
2001 7/2 – 9/27
2001 12/8 – until **2002** 5/16
2007 12/8 – until **2008** 2/19
2008 8/12 – 10/4
2010 5/21 – 9/27
2011 1/8 – 3/25

SATURN CHALLENGING
1938 1/1 – 5/16
1938 10/21 – until **1939** 2/5
1944 6/1 – until **1945** 7/1
1958 12/16 – until **1960** 2/6
1960 7/28 – 11/2
1966 5/21 – 9/1
1967 2/11 – until **1968** 3/22
1973 7/12 – until **1974** 8/11
1975 1/29 – 4/26
1988 1/20 – 7/13
1988 10/15 – until **1989** 4/3
1989 5/12 – 12/14
1996 3/18 – until **1997** 4/27
1997 12/7 – 12/25
2002 8/31 – 11/21
2003 5/15 – until **2004** 6/13

URANUS CHALLENGING
1948 7/9 – until **1952** 6/26
1987 12/31 – until **1991** 12/30
2010 4/4 – Continues

NEPTUNE CHALLENGING
1983 1/11 – until **1990** 12/18

PLUTO CHALLENGING
2007 1/17 – Continues

JUPITER SPECIAL
1945 8/13 – 10/28
1956 11/23 – until **1957** 3/12
1957 7/24 – 10/12
1968 11/2 – until **1969** 4/21
1969 6/24 – 9/26
1980 10/15 – until **1981** 9/10
1992 9/29 – until **1993** 1/2
1993 2/24 – 8/23
2004 9/14 – 12/3
2005 4/6 – 8/3

SATURN SPECIAL
1950 10/27 – until **1951** 4/7
1951 7/18 – 12/16
1952 3/5 – 9/4
1980 9/2 – until **1981** 10/12
2009 10/9 – until **2010** 11/20
2011 4/7 – 8/16

URANUS SPECIAL
1967 11/5 – until **1971** 10/2

NEPTUNE SPECIAL
1940 12/13 – until **1949** 9/1

PLUTO SPECIAL
1970 10/1 – until **1977** 9/25

September 30

SUN: LIBRA · DECANATE: LIBRA/VENUS · DEGREE: 6°5–7°5 LIBRA · MODE: CARDINAL · ELEMENT: AIR

Your Personal Powers

You are a charismatic, intelligent, and creative individual. Imaginative and sensitive, you can also be astute and analytical. These extremes of your nature can work in your favor when you are feeling positive and spontaneous, making you witty and able to put your ideas across in an interesting and dramatic way. You can lose some of your power, however, if you allow indecisiveness, worry, and skepticism to cloud your judgment and cause you to withdraw. You gain power through your refined social skills, ability to think pragmatically, and progressive ideas. You may wish to develop your natural creativity and affinity for the arts through a form of artistic expression such as music, design, art, or drama. Alternatively, you may use your appreciation of beauty by surrounding yourself with luxury. Refined and gracious, you are likely to have an attractive speaking voice and a talent with words. Keeping yourself creatively challenged and finding time for quiet contemplation can bring out the best of your many talents.

Your Powers of Attraction in Relationships

Intelligent yet sensitive, you can attract others with your agreeable manner and natural charm. As a progressive thinker with a desire for knowledge, you need partners who will keep you mentally stimulated and connected to your need for change and new ideas. Although you can have a captivating quality, your powerful inner emotions need an avenue of expression or you may withdraw and become insecure or moody. Although you can be ambitious and businesslike, your idealistic side may attract you to people or projects that involve self-awareness or higher knowledge. Love and affection are high on your agenda, but your partner will have to understand that you also need periods alone for reflection or self-analysis. When positive or inspired, you can be very loving and spontaneous and possess a charismatic quality.

Your attractive qualities: creative, analytical abilities, loyal, idealistic, friendly, fun-loving, good synthesizer, talent with words, imaginative, intuitive, intelligent, dramatic, progressive, ambitious, charismatic, critical skills, warm heart, generosity, charm, lighthearted, sensitive

Your less attractive qualities: skeptical, too self-absorbed, lazy, obstinate, erratic, impatient, jealous, bad-tempered, bored, worried, insecure, suspicious, indifferent, overindulgent, escapist, scattered

Your Venus Power

The planet Venus has a great deal of influence on your powers of attraction. Below are four possible Venus types for women and men. To find your Venus you need to go to page 771, where you will find the Venus table and extra information. The planet Mars also affects your powers of attraction. To find your Mars table and interpretation go to page 761.

WOMEN WITH VENUS IN LEO: Your friendly and sunny personality often makes you stand out in a crowd. Generous and giving, you know how to make your partner feel special. As you often expect loyalty and devotion from your partners in return, you can become easily offended if they ignore you or behave in an inconsiderate manner. Charming and kind, when you're in love you can be romantic, dramatic, and passionate.

MEN WITH VENUS IN LEO: A childlike nature suggests that you are versatile and keen on games or being entertained. You are usually attracted to vivacious partners with a benevolent nature. As an extrovert you enjoy being involved in all types of activities where you can assert yourself and show your talents and abilities. Others may recognize your inborn tendencies to lead but are also aware of your vanity or pride. Nevertheless, generous, kind, and caring, you often show compassion to those less fortunate than yourself.

WOMEN WITH VENUS IN VIRGO: Articulate and straightforward in your relationships, you attract others with your genuine concern for their well-being. By being understanding and a good listener you are able to show your love and friendship. With your analytical approach to relationships, however, you may have to be careful of becoming too matter-of-fact. You often display your concern for the welfare of others by your willingness to offer practical help and assistance. You usually seek a partner who is willing to work as hard on relationships as you are.

MEN WITH VENUS IN VIRGO: Although you are constantly analyzing your relationships in order to understand and improve them, you may nevertheless need to refrain from continuously mulling over issues that can cause anxiety. You are happiest when you are able to help your loved ones in practical ways and forget yourself in your willingness to be

of service to others. You seek a partner who has high standards and can be as pragmatic and hardworking as yourself. Ideally they should also be impeccably dressed with a fine analytical mind.

WOMEN WITH VENUS IN LIBRA: Gracious, charming, and sociable with a sense of style, you have no trouble attracting admirers. With your natural diplomatic skills and desire for harmony you usually like to keep the peace and avoid confrontations, but be careful of failing to take a stand when it is necessary. Romantic and easygoing yourself, you are attracted to affectionate and refined individuals who share your love of peace, justice, and fair play.

MEN WITH VENUS IN LIBRA: Courteous and refined, you are attracted to beautiful and elegant people. You are looking for a partner who can share your natural good taste and enjoy an intellectual conversation. Disliking conflict, you may have to be careful not to go along with others just to keep the peace. Your ideal partner will appreciate beauty and the little luxuries of life as well as possess good social skills. You have a strong sense of social etiquette yourself so you need an intelligent and sophisticated partner.

WOMEN WITH VENUS IN SCORPIO: Loving and passionate, you are often sensitive with deep feelings and strong powers of attraction. A love for the truth coupled with a tendency to be suspicious can be an influence that motivates you to delve deep into the activities of your partner. When in love or in a relationship that matters, you will often bend over backward to cooperate. Although loyal, guard against losing sight of your own needs and desires.

MEN WITH VENUS IN SCORPIO: As you are emotionally intense and passionate, personal relationships are probably a major factor in your own transformation. Being sensitive yet loyal, you are usually attracted to forceful partners who can express themselves intimately but intensely. Rather than seek easy and simple relationships you are drawn to partners who act as a catalyst for your own internal changes. Through your relationships with your partners you can unravel your own motives and understand your deep-seated feelings or emotional insecurities.

To read all about your Outer Planets and work out how to use your personalized timetable, go to Section Three, page 789.

Your Personalized Timetable

JUPITER BENEFICIAL
1938 1/18 – 2/20
1941 5/20 – 8/2
1941 12/22 – until 1942 3/22
1943 7/8 – 8/22
1947 10/31 – 12/15
1949 4/1 – 7/9
1949 11/23 – until 1950 2/4
1953 5/3 – 7/12
1955 6/21 – 8/6
1959 3/3 – 4/3
1959 10/14 – 11/30
1961 3/7 – 8/26
1961 10/21 – until 1962 1/19
1965 4/16 – 6/25
1966 10/9 – until 1967 1/3
1967 6/1 – 7/21
1971 1/24 – 5/23
1971 9/22 – 11/14
1973 2/16 – until 1974 1/1
1976 8/10 – 10/30
1977 3/27 – 6/8
1978 9/14 – until 1979 2/12
1979 5/6 – 7/5
1983 1/3 – 7/10
1983 8/16 – 10/28
1985 1/31 – 4/26
1985 7/14 – 12/13
1988 7/14 – 12/12
1989 2/28 – 5/23
1990 8/25 – 10/25
1991 1/4 – 6/16
1994 12/16 – until 1995 2/9
1995 5/23 – 10/8
1997 1/15 – 3/29
1997 8/28 – 11/16
2000 6/23 – until 2001 5/6
2002 8/9 – 9/27
2003 2/13 – 5/23
2006 12/1 – until 2007 1/18
2007 7/4 – 9/9
2008 12/30 – until 2009 3/9
2012 6/5 – Continues

SATURN BENEFICIAL
1942 4/27 – until 1943 5/27
1946 8/15 – until 1947 7/30
1956 2/3 – 4/20
1956 10/26 – until 1957 1/24
1957 5/25 – 10/23
1961 3/31 – 6/19
1961 12/22 – until 1963 2/9
1971 6/7 – until 1972 7/7
1973 1/12 – 3/17
1975 10/6 – 12/24
1976 6/19 – 9/8
1977 2/26 – 5/24
1985 11/30 – until 1986 11/29
1991 1/25 – until 1992 3/17
1992 8/14 – 12/13
2000 7/21 – 11/5
2001 4/8 – 9/6
2001 10/17 – until 2002 5/10
2005 7/28 – until 2006 7/12

URANUS BENEFICIAL
1941 6/30 – until 1946 4/14
1955 9/28 – until 1958 7/29
1981 12/12 – until 1984 10/29
1995 2/25 – until 1999 12/28

NEPTUNE BENEFICIAL
1970 12/20 – until 1976 9/30
1997 2/17 – until 2005 1/22

PLUTO BENEFICIAL
1939 8/12 – until 1947 6/16
1995 12/21 – until 2000 11/4

JUPITER CHALLENGING
1939 5/4 – until 1940 3/12
1942 6/4 – 8/15
1948 3/31 – 4/29

1948 11/8 – until 1949 1/19
1951 4/15 – until 1952 2/22
1954 5/17 – 7/28
1960 2/21 – 6/21
1960 10/17 – until 1961 1/3
1963 3/29 – 6/13
1963 10/7 – until 1964 1/30
1965 9/8 – 11/30
1966 4/28 – 7/12
1972 1/30 – 8/17
1972 9/1 – 12/18
1975 3/12 – 5/21
1977 8/12 – until 1978 1/11
1978 4/1 – 6/26
1984 1/13 – 12/1
1987 2/24 – 5/3
1989 7/24 – until 1990 6/9
1995 12/28 – until 1996 3/20
1996 6/19 – 11/11
1999 2/6 – 4/15
2001 7/6 – 10/7
2001 11/28 – until 2002 5/21
2007 12/12 – until 2008 2/24
2008 8/2 – 10/14
2010 5/27 – 9/19
2011 1/14 – 3/29

SATURN CHALLENGING
1938 1/1 – 5/25
1938 10/8 – until 1939 2/15
1944 6/9 – until 1945 7/8
1958 12/24 – until 1960 2/16
1960 7/14 – 11/14
1966 6/5 – 8/17
1967 2/20 – until 1968 3/30
1973 7/20 – until 1974 1/29
1974 3/29 – 8/20
1975 1/16 – 5/8
1988 1/29 – 6/29
1988 10/28 – until 1989 12/23
1996 3/26 – until 1997 5/5
1997 11/11 – until 1998 1/19
2002 9/18 – 11/3
2003 5/23 – until 2004 6/21

URANUS CHALLENGING
1948 7/27 – until 1953 4/10
1988 1/17 – until 1992 10/29
2010 4/23 – Continues

NEPTUNE CHALLENGING
1983 2/11 – until 1991 11/12

PLUTO CHALLENGING
2007 2/23 – Continues

JUPITER SPECIAL
1945 8/18 – 11/2
1956 12/1 – until 1957 3/4
1957 7/30 – 10/17
1968 11/7 – until 1969 4/11
1969 7/4 – 10/1
1980 10/20 – until 1981 9/15
1992 10/4 – until 1993 1/21
1993 2/5 – 8/29
2004 9/18 – 12/9
2005 3/29 – 8/9

SATURN SPECIAL
1950 11/5 – until 1951 3/25
1951 7/30 – until 1952 1/4
1952 2/14 – 9/13
1980 9/10 – until 1981 10/20
2009 10/17 – until 2010 4/30
2010 6/29 – 12/1
2011 3/25 – 1 8/26

URANUS SPECIAL
1967 11/28 – until 1972 7/21

NEPTUNE SPECIAL
1941 10/23 – until 1950 7/4

PLUTO SPECIAL
1970 10/29 – until 1978 8/13

October 1

Your Personal Powers

Charming but determined, you possess a strong will and an independent spirit. Your ruling planet, Venus, ensures that you have the warmth and social skills to get your way most of the time. You gain power from your enthusiasm, creative ideas, and quick wit. You enjoy power and when you are set on a goal you can be forceful and inspired, often aiming toward leadership positions. Although you are dramatic and ambitious with a drive for accomplishment and recognition, you lose some of your power if you become too self-oriented, impatient, or overbearing. Fortunately, a natural business sense and a desire to please can often guarantee your success with people and the commercial world, as long as you apply the necessary persistence and discipline. Although you are usually active and productive, on your way to the top you may have to overcome a tendency to be skeptical or obstinate. Dramatic and creative with sharp intelligence and the ability to think big, your strength lies in your originality and resolve to achieve your goals.

Your Powers of Attraction in Relationships

With your flair for people and your refined awareness, you have no trouble attracting admirers. Friendly and amiable, you aim to please and be popular. Although usually agreeable, at times you must guard against being bossy or opinionated. Even though you can be daring and determined, you can also be emotionally indecisive, which sometimes blocks the expression of your more intimate feelings. With your strong views and resolute nature, however, you are usually willing to give much support to those you love. You are proud and dramatic, and a demonstration of loyalty can be especially important to you. Your career sense and ability to put others at ease translates into a gift for mixing business and pleasure. You are usually drawn to individuals who stimulate your innate creativity and make you feel joyful.

Your attractive qualities: leadership, charming, creative, friendly, progressive, clever, social skills, forceful, artistic, amiable, organizational skills, optimistic, strong convictions, business sense, competitive, independent, pioneering, gregarious, diplomatic, talented, quick-witted

Your less attractive qualities: overbearing, jealous, egotistical, obstinate, too proud, domineering, indecisive, antagonistic, bossy, worry, lack of restraint, selfish, weak, restless, impatient

Your Venus Power

The planet Venus has a great deal of influence on your powers of attraction. Below are four possible Venus types for women and men. To find your Venus you need to go to page 771, where you will find the Venus table and extra information. The planet Mars also affects your powers of attraction. To find your Mars table and interpretation go to page 761.

WOMEN WITH VENUS IN LEO: As someone who wants to radiate in her own right, you are likely to desire partners you can be proud of. You are usually attracted to fun-loving, warm, and generous individuals. If self-expression is important to you, you will probably seek the company of creative people such as artists, musicians, or those with a flair for acting. Romantic and dignified, with a regal air, you can project confidence and success to attract others.

MEN WITH VENUS IN LEO: Generous, animated, and pleasure-seeking, you can be very entertaining and fun to be with. You are usually attracted to extroverted and benevolent individuals with sunny personalities. If ambitious, you are drawn to a partner who shows leadership qualities or one who is highly motivated. Your less attractive qualities are your tendencies to be bossy or vain. With a sense of the dramatic, however, you can be the life and soul of the party and inspire those around you.

WOMEN WITH VENUS IN VIRGO: Articulate and straightforward in your relationships, you attract others with your genuine concern for their well-being. By being understanding and a good listener you are able to show your love and friendship. With your analytical approach to relationships, however, you may have to be careful of becoming too matter-of-fact. You often display your concern for the welfare of others by your willingness to offer practical help and assistance. You usually seek a partner who is willing to work as hard on relationships as you are.

MEN WITH VENUS IN VIRGO: Although you are constantly analyzing your relationships in order to understand and improve them, you may nevertheless need to refrain from continuously mulling over issues that can cause anxiety. You are happiest when you are able to help your loved ones in

practical ways and forget yourself in your willingness to be of service to others. You seek a partner who has high standards and can be as pragmatic and hardworking as yourself.

WOMEN WITH VENUS IN LIBRA: A natural romantic with good social skills, you love to entertain and can put people at ease with your warm and gracious manner. Elegant and fair with a touch of glamour, you are also adept at dealing with people in delicate situations or conflicts. You seek refinement and will go out of your way to achieve harmony and keep the peace. Relationships are so important to you that you may need to guard against becoming dependent on others for approval. With your friendly personality and inherent charm, however, you will always be popular and loved.

MEN WITH VENUS IN LIBRA: As you are good company, people are drawn to you and especially appreciate your talent for making them feel special. You find status in your social contacts and place importance on your relationships. Being a clever and charming companion, you will go out of your way to keep situations peaceful and harmonious. In relationships, however, be careful of indecision or compromising too much. Nevertheless, others are attracted by your natural refinement and good taste, which is reflected in your sense of style.

WOMEN WITH VENUS IN SCORPIO: With a natural psychic gift for penetrating the feelings of others, you can often help partners transform emotional challenges or sexual difficulties. When you fall in love, your strong feelings and determination give you a potent force that others find attractive and seductive. Although you know what really turns people on, your most profound desire is usually for the deepness and closeness of real love and intimacy in an enduring relationship.

MEN WITH VENUS IN SCORPIO: In relationships you possess a sensitive understanding of your partner's deeper nature. Although you are strongly attached to those you love, you may have to be careful that your feelings do not turn into jealousy or possessiveness. When you fall in love it is often with power and emotional intensity. You are attracted to partners who can share your passion and display strong feelings of sexuality like your own.

To read all about your Outer Planets and work out how to use your personalized timetable, go to Section Three, page 789.

⎯⎯

Your Personalized Timetable

JUPITER BENEFICIAL
1938 1/1 – 2/25
1941 5/24 – 8/8
1941 12/14 – until 1942 3/29
1943 7/12 – 8/27
1947 11/5 – 12/20
1949 4/9 – 7/1
1949 11/28 – until 1950 2/8
1953 5/7 – 7/17
1955 6/25 – 8/11
1959 10/19 – 12/4
1961 3/13 – 8/16
1961 10/31 – until 1962 1/23
1965 4/20 – 6/29
1966 10/17 – 12/26
1967 6/7 – 7/26
1971 1/30 – 5/15
1971 9/28 – 11/18
1973 2/21 – until 1974 1/6
1976 8/19 – 10/21
1977 4/1 – 6/12
1978 9/19 – until 1979 2/4
1979 5/14 – 7/9
1983 1/8 – 6/27
1983 8/30 – 11/1
1985 2/4 – 5/6
1985 7/4 – 12/18
1988 7/19 – 12/4
1989 3/8 – 5/27
1990 8/30 – 11/5
1990 12/25 – until 1991 6/21
1994 12/21 – until 1995 2/17
1995 5/15 – 10/13
1997 1/19 – 4/4
1997 8/20 – 11/24
2000 6/28 – until 2001 5/10
2002 8/13 – 10/3
2003 2/6 – 5/30
2006 12/5 – until 2007 1/23
2007 6/25 – 9/18
2009 1/3 – 3/14
2012 6/9 – Continues

SATURN BENEFICIAL
1942 5/5 – until 1943 6/4
1946 8/23 – until 1947 3/8
1947 4/30 – 8/6
1956 2/24 – 3/28
1956 11/3 – until 1957 2/5
1957 5/10 – 11/2
1961 4/21 – 5/28
1961 12/31 – until 1963 2/18
1971 6/15 – until 1972 7/15
1972 12/28 – until 1973 4/1
1975 10/25 – 12/5
1976 6/28 – 9/17
1977 2/13 – 6/6
1985 12/8 – until 1986 12/7
1991 2/3 – until 1992 3/28
1992 8/1 – 12/24
2000 8/3 – 10/22
2001 4/17 – until 2002 5/18
2005 8/5 – until 2006 7/20

URANUS BENEFICIAL
1941 7/24 – until 1946 5/5
1956 7/24 – until 1959 5/18
1981 12/29 – until 1984 11/15
1995 3/19 – until 2000 1/16

NEPTUNE BENEFICIAL
1971 1/22 – until 1976 11/5
1997 3/25 – until 2005 12/18

PLUTO BENEFICIAL
1939 9/25 – until 1947 7/23
1948 4/14 – 5/5
1996 1/22 – until 2001 9/4

JUPITER CHALLENGING
1939 5/9 – 11/4
1939 12/15 – until 1940 3/16
1942 6/8 – 8/20

1943 2/24 – 3/27
1948 11/13 – until 1949 1/23
1951 4/19 – until 1952 2/27
1954 5/22 – 8/2
1960 2/27 – 6/13
1960 10/23 – until 1961 1/7
1963 4/2 – 6/20
1963 9/29 – until 1964 2/5
1965 9/16 – 11/21
1966 5/3 – 7/16
1972 2/4 – 7/29
1972 9/20 – 12/22
1975 3/16 – 5/26
1975 11/18 – until 1976 1/1
1977 8/18 – until 1978 1/3
1978 4/8 – 6/30
1984 1/17 – 12/5
1987 3/1 – 5/7
1989 7/29 – until 1990 6/14
1996 1/1 – 3/28
1996 6/11 – 11/16
1999 2/11 – 4/20
2001 7/11 – 10/26
2001 11/10 – until 2002 5/27
2007 12/17 – until 2008 2/29
2008 7/24 – 10/22
2010 6/3 – 9/12
2011 1/20 – 4/3

SATURN CHALLENGING
1938 1/8 – 6/5
1938 9/25 – until 1939 2/25
1944 6/17 – until 1945 7/16
1959 1/1 – until 1960 2/26
1960 7/1 – 11/25
1966 6/30 – 7/22
1967 2/28 – until 1968 4/6
1973 7/29 – until 1974 1/13
1974 4/13 – 8/30
1975 1/4 – 5/18
1988 2/9 – 6/16
1988 11/8 – until 1989 12/31
1996 4/3 – until 1997 5/14
1997 10/27 – until 1998 2/2
2003 5/31 – until 2004 6/29

URANUS CHALLENGING
1948 8/18 – until 1953 5/13
1988 2/5 – until 1992 11/23
2010 5/15 – Continues

NEPTUNE CHALLENGING
1984 1/7 – until 1991 12/14

PLUTO CHALLENGING
2008 1/13 – Continues

JUPITER SPECIAL
1945 8/23 – 11/6
1956 12/9 – until 1957 2/23
1957 8/4 – 10/21
1968 11/13 – until 1969 4/3
1969 7/12 – 10/6
1980 10/25 – until 1981 9/20
1992 10/8 – until 1993 9/3
2004 9/23 – 12/17
2005 3/21 – 8/15

SATURN SPECIAL
1950 11/15 – until 1951 3/13
1951 8/9 – until 1952 9/21
1980 9/18 – until 1981 10/28
1982 6/8 – 6/27
2009 10/25 – until 2010 4/13
2010 7/16 – 12/13
2011 3/12 – 9/4

URANUS SPECIAL
1968 9/22 – until 1972 8/18

NEPTUNE SPECIAL
1941 11/30 – until 1950 8/28

PLUTO SPECIAL
1970 12/12 – until 1978 9/13

October 2

SUN: LIBRA • DECANATE: LIBRA/VENUS • DEGREE: 8°5–9°5 LIBRA • MODE: CARDINAL • ELEMENT: AIR

Your Personal Powers

You are idealistic and sensitive with practical common sense, and your personal powers include sharp intelligence, emotional awareness, and a magnetic personality. Aware of image, you often look attractive, stylish, or have a touch of glamour. A need for self-expression may draw you to music and singing or the arts and drama. You gain power from your polite and charming manner and refined social skills that ensure your success with people. A person of extremes, you may lose some of your power when you lose the right balance between your need to control, work, and be serious and your need for love, affection, and spontaneity. With natural diplomatic skills and an interest in people, your idealism may draw you to work cooperatively with others or support humanitarian causes. You often enjoy group endeavors and can give generously of your time and energy. Although highly intuitive, resist worry and indecision. You are creative and ambitious, and inspiration can be a vital key to unlocking your greatest potential for success.

Your Powers of Attraction in Relationships

Charming and intelligent, you attract others with your unique ideas and ability to care. You are romantic and idealistic and can be kind and fun-loving; at the other extreme, however, you may sometimes take things too seriously and experience insecurity or isolation. To get the balance right in your relationships, fair play or give and take is essential. Equally important, valuing yourself and staying detached stops you trying too hard to please others. Sympathetic and giving, you can be a supportive partner or devoted parent, however, in relationships avoid martyring yourself or being too stubborn. When all is working well in your relationships you are trusting, diplomatic, and sensitive to others. An idealistic side to your nature may be also drawn to a more humanitarian or unconditional type of love.

Your attractive qualities: refined, intelligent, creative, good partnerships, gentle, tactful, receptive, reserved, intuitive, agile, considerate, harmonious, friendly, ambassadors of goodwill, good taste, business sense, humanitarian, hardworking, idealistic, sensitive

Your less attractive qualities: stubborn, controlling, suspicious, lack of confidence, worry, subservient, too sensitive, moody, martyr, selfish, easily hurt, doubting, cold, too serious, manipulative

Your Venus Power

The planet Venus has a great deal of influence on your powers of attraction. Below are four possible Venus types for women and men. To find your Venus you need to go to page 771, where you will find the Venus table and extra information. The planet Mars also affects your powers of attraction. To find your Mars table and interpretation go to page 761.

WOMEN WITH VENUS IN LEO: Warm and playful with a touch of the dramatic, you enjoy the company of generous or strong individuals who can share your sense of fun. Although there are advantages to your being strong-willed, in your relationships you need to resist being bossy as it can cause resentment. With your wonderful mixture of regal authority and childlike wonder you love to keep others entertained and amused.

MEN WITH VENUS IN LEO: Sociable and outgoing, you are kind and generous with those you love. Looking for a relationship that can be fun and entertaining, you need a playmate who can share your enthusiasm and high spirits. Your pride, however, often stops you from associating with lovers or partners you see as beneath you. As you desire someone who can appreciate your sense of the dramatic, you are often attracted to people with strong personalities.

WOMEN WITH VENUS IN VIRGO: Intelligent and discriminating, you are usually drawn to polite and refined individuals. As a perfectionist you may be keen to analyze and criticize yourself, but be careful of continually going over your partner's shortcomings. By focusing on how you can make positive improvements in yourself and in your relationships, you avoid becoming skeptical or confused. You empower yourself when you display kind and caring concern for the well-being of loved ones and spontaneously offer your practical assistance.

MEN WITH VENUS IN VIRGO: A love of order usually indicates that you are attracted to refined individuals with analytical or practical abilities. You and your partner may be working together or serving similar causes. As you constantly analyze partnerships in order to improve them, you are likely to use former relationships as a point of reference and com-

pare them to your present partner. As you are helpful and kind, others usually rely on your good judgment and often turn to you for advice or practical assistance.

WOMEN WITH VENUS IN LIBRA: Usually you are attractive and sociable with an easygoing manner. Your love of beauty, harmony, and pleasure implies that you are a romantic with a desire for love and affection. Once in a relationship you need to learn to negotiate your position rather than adapt to the wishes of others and compromise just to keep the peace. Nevertheless, your advanced social skills and strong sense of fair play can help you succeed in any social or romantic situation.

MEN WITH VENUS IN LIBRA: Your good social skills, charming personality, and refined manner usually make you attractive to the opposite sex. Equally, you desire a sophisticated partner with grace, elegance, and a strong sense of style. Although you have the ability to be persuasive and irresistible to others, avoid manipulative love games. Nevertheless, your natural diplomacy and sense of fair play help you to relate to people in all social situations. With your love of balance and harmony you seek a partner who is also moderate, easygoing, and loving.

WOMEN WITH VENUS IN SCORPIO: With a natural psychic gift for penetrating the feelings of others, you can often help partners transform emotional challenges or sexual difficulties. When you fall in love, your strong feelings and determination give you a potent force that others find attractive and seductive. Although you know what really turns people on, your most profound desire is usually for the deepness and closeness of real love and intimacy in an enduring relationship.

MEN WITH VENUS IN SCORPIO: In relationships you possess a sensitive understanding of your partner's deeper nature. Although you are strongly attached to those you love, you may have to be careful that your feelings do not turn into jealousy or possessiveness. When you fall in love it is often with power and an emotional intensity. You are attracted to partners who can share your passion and display strong feelings of sexuality like your own.

To read all about your Outer Planets and work out how to use your personalized timetable, go to Section Three, page 789.

⚖

Your Personalized Timetable

JUPITER BENEFICIAL
1938 1/1 – 3/1
1941 5/28 – 8/14
1941 12/7 – until 1942 4/5
1943 7/17 – 9/1
1947 11/9 – 12/24
1949 4/18 – 6/22
1949 12/3 – until 1950 2/12
1953 5/12 – 7/22
1954 2/1 – 2/19
1955 6/30 – 8/15
1959 10/24 – 12/8
1961 3/18 – 8/7
1961 11/8 – until 1962 1/27
1965 4/25 – 7/3
1966 10/28 – 12/15
1967 6/12 – 7/30
1971 2/7 – 5/7
1971 10/4 – 11/22
1973 2/26 – until 1974 1/10
1976 8/31 – 10/9
1977 4/6 – 6/17
1978 9/25 – until 1979 1/28
1979 5/21 – 7/14
1983 1/13 – 6/17
1983 9/8 – 11/6
1985 2/9 – 5/20
1985 6/20 – 12/23
1988 7/25 – 11/26
1989 3/14 – 6/1
1990 9/4 – 11/26
1990 12/4 – until 1991 4/2
1991 4/2 – 6/26
1994 12/26 – until 1995 2/25
1995 5/6 – 10/19
1997 1/24 – 4/10
1997 8/12 – 12/1
2000 7/3 – until 2001 5/15
2002 8/18 – 10/10
2003 1/29 – 6/6
2006 12/10 – until 2007 1/29
2007 6/16 – 9/26
2009 1/8 – 3/19
2012 6/14 – Continues

SATURN BENEFICIAL
1942 5/13 – until 1943 6/12
1946 8/31 – until 1947 2/19
1947 5/16 – 8/14
1956 11/12 – until 1957 2/22
1957 4/23 – 11/11
1962 1/8 – until 1963 2/26
1963 10/10 – 11/1
1971 6/23 – 12/29
1972 3/3 – 7/24
1972 12/15 – until 1973 4/12
1976 7/6 – 9/26
1977 1/31 – 6/16
1985 12/17 – until 1986 7/13
1986 8/31 – 12/16
1991 2/11 – 9/14
1991 10/25 – until 1992 4/9
1992 7/18 – until 1993 1/2
2000 8/22 – 10/4
2001 4/25 – until 2002 5/25
2005 8/13 – until 2006 7/28

URANUS BENEFICIAL
1942 5/24 – until 1946 5/23
1956 8/10 – until 1959 6/15
1982 1/19 – until 1984 12/2
1996 1/21 – until 2000 2/2

NEPTUNE BENEFICIAL
1971 12/16 – until 1977 9/21
1998 2/13 – until 2006 1/17

PLUTO BENEFICIAL
1940 9/4 – until 1948 7/3
1996 12/9 – until 2001 10/25

JUPITER CHALLENGING
1939 5/14 – 10/24
1939 12/26 – until 1940 3/20

1942 6/12 – 8/25
1943 2/10 – 4/10
1948 11/18 – until 1949 1/28
1951 4/24 – until 1952 3/2
1954 5/26 – 8/6
1960 3/5 – 6/5
1960 10/29 – until 1961 1/11
1963 4/6 – 6/27
1963 9/22 – until 1964 2/11
1965 9/28 – 11/10
1966 5/8 – 7/21
1972 2/9 – 7/19
1972 10/1 – 12/26
1975 3/21 – 5/31
1975 11/7 – until 1976 1/12
1977 8/23 – 12/26
1978 4/15 – 7/4
1984 1/22 – 12/10
1987 3/5 – 5/11
1989 8/2 – until 1990 6/18
1996 1/5 – 4/8
1996 5/31 – 11/22
1999 2/15 – 4/24
2001 7/15 – until 2002 5/31
2007 12/21 – until 2008 3/6
2008 7/16 – 10/30
2010 6/10 – 9/4
2011 1/25 – 4/7

SATURN CHALLENGING
1938 1/21 – 6/18
1938 9/11 – until 1939 3/6
1944 6/24 – until 1945 7/23
1959 1/10 – 8/24
1959 9/16 – until 1960 3/10
1960 6/17 – 12/5
1967 3/8 – until 1968 4/14
1973 8/7 – 12/31
1974 4/25 – 9/9
1974 12/23 – until 1975 5/28
1988 2/21 – 6/2
1988 11/17 – until 1990 1/9
1996 4/12 – until 1997 5/24
1997 10/14 – until 1998 2/13
2003 6/8 – until 2004 7/6

URANUS CHALLENGING
1948 10/1 – until 1953 6/3
1988 3/2 – until 1992 12/12
2010 6/27 – Continues

NEPTUNE CHALLENGING
1984 2/5 – until 1992 11/4

PLUTO CHALLENGING
2008 2/15 – Continues

JUPITER SPECIAL
1945 8/28 – 11/11
1956 12/19 – until 1957 2/13
1957 8/10 – 10/26
1968 11/19 – until 1969 3/26
1969 7/19 – 10/10
1980 10/30 – until 1981 5/19
1981 6/4 – 9/24
1992 10/13 – until 1993 9/8
2004 9/27 – 12/25
2005 3/13 – 8/21

SATURN SPECIAL
1950 11/27 – until 1951 2/27
1951 8/18 – until 1952 9/29
1980 9/26 – until 1981 11/6
1982 5/13 – 7/24
2009 11/4 – until 2010 3/31
2010 7/28 – 12/30
2011 2/22 – 9/13

URANUS SPECIAL
1968 10/7 – until 1972 9/6

NEPTUNE SPECIAL
1942 10/19 – until 1950 9/26

PLUTO SPECIAL
1971 10/20 – until 1979 7/19

October 3

SUN: LIBRA · DECANATE: LIBRA/VENUS · DEGREE: 9°5–10°5 LIBRA · MODE: CARDINAL · ELEMENT: AIR

Your Personal Powers

Magnetic and refined, your personal powers include a gracious and kind personality with advanced social skills. Your ruling planet, Venus, grants you artistic and creative talent or appreciation and a desire for beauty and luxury. You gain power from your honest and direct approach delivered with charm, diplomacy, and good manners. Although you are clever, talented, and an expert at putting people at ease, you lose some of your power if you dwell on your emotional insecurities, since they often cause indecision or unnecessary worry. You gain power from building your self-esteem and finding ways to express yourself. Although you can be easygoing and sometimes content to relax in a comfortable routine, you can equally be very determined and purposeful when set on a course of action. A desire for the good things in life is also likely to help motivate you to achieve. Guard against losing power to stubbornness or irritability. You empower yourself when you combine your common sense with your fine intelligence, generosity, and liberal attitude.

Your Powers of Attraction in Relationships

Friendly, loyal, and broad-minded, you can attract people from all walks of life. A good conversationalist, you love entertaining and social affairs where you can express your ideas and sense of fun. Magnetic and charming, you like to identify with success and often seek a confident partner who can keep you mentally stimulated and motivated. You are romantic, with the ability to powerfully project love, and your partners needs to equal your level of giving or fulfill your strong need for affection. Rather than becoming frustrated or disappointed if others do not live up to your high expectations, you are better building up your own talents and inner peace and security. The more assertive and independent you are, the more positive you become about your relationships.

Your attractive qualities: friendly, productive, humorous, creative, happy, artistic, freedom-loving, a talent with words, charming, determined, clever, artistic, good taste, home-loving, refined, honest, expressive, responsible, sociable, social skills

Your less attractive qualities: easily bored, insecure, vain, too imaginative, indecisive, extravagant, exaggerates, worry, boastful, self-indulgent, inertia, scattered, lazy, stubborn, irritable

Your Venus Power

The planet Venus has a great deal of influence on your powers of attraction. Below are four possible Venus types for women and men. To find your Venus you need to go to page 771, where you will find the Venus table and extra information. The planet Mars also affects your powers of attraction. To find your Mars table and interpretation go to page 761.

WOMEN WITH VENUS IN LEO: You possess the wonderful ability to project your warm and sunny personality and keep others happily entertained. Loving attention yourself, you seek a partner who can appreciate you, be supportive, and give you positive feedback. Proud, with a natural regal air, you expect respect from your partners but are willing to be loyal and supportive in exchange. Although sometimes a little self-centered, you know how to make your partner feel special.

MEN WITH VENUS IN LEO: Enthusiastic, playful, and kind, you can be benevolent with those you love. Warm, romantic, and self-expressive, you adore the drama of love or having fun with your friends. Usually you are attracted to partners with a warm and generous nature. Although you can be a confident and charismatic partner, you may need to develop humility in order to stop pride or arrogance from marring your relationships.

WOMEN WITH VENUS IN VIRGO: Intelligent and discriminating, you are usually drawn to polite and refined individuals. As a perfectionist you may be keen to analyze and criticize yourself, but be careful of continually going over your partner's shortcomings. By focusing on how you can make positive improvements in yourself and in your relationships, you avoid becoming skeptical or confused. You empower yourself when you display kind and caring concern for the well-being of loved ones and spontaneously offer your practical assistance.

MEN WITH VENUS IN VIRGO: A love of order usually indicates that you are attracted to refined individuals with analytical or practical abilities. You and your partner may be working together or serving similar causes. As you constantly analyze partnerships in order to improve them, you are likely to use former relationships as a point of reference and compare them to your present partner. As you are helpful and kind, others usually rely on your good judgment and often turn to you for advice or practical assistance.

WOMEN WITH VENUS IN LIBRA: Attractive, refined, and conscious of the needs of others, you usually desire harmo-

nious relationships. As a peacemaker with good negotiating skills, you can smooth out difficulties with others, but your dislike of confrontation may sometimes leave you refusing to take a stand or compromising too many of your own needs. Courteous, stylish, and charming with polished social skills, you are an expert at relating to others in a gracious and civilized manner.

MEN WITH VENUS IN LIBRA: As a sociable and friendly individual with an eye for beauty, you are amorous and charming. You are a natural gentleman and your ideal partner usually has an elegant appearance, artistic appreciation, and good taste. Your relationships benefit when you resist the temptation to take the easy way out or put too much emphasis on vanity and high living. Intellectual and naturally refined, you seek a loving partner who can share your romantic and sophisticated aspirations.

WOMEN WITH VENUS IN SCORPIO: Loving and passionate, you are often sensitive with deep feelings and strong powers of attraction. A love for the truth coupled with a tendency to be suspicious can be an influence that motivates you to delve deep into the activities of your partner. When in love or in a relationship that matters, you will often bend over backward to cooperate. Although loyal, guard against losing sight of your own needs and desires.

MEN WITH VENUS IN SCORPIO: As you are emotionally intense and passionate, personal relationships are probably a major factor in your own transformation. Being sensitive yet loyal, you are usually attracted to forceful partners who can express themselves intimately but intensely. Rather than seek easy and simple relationships you are drawn to partners who act as a catalyst for your own internal changes. Through your relationships with your partners you can unravel your own motives and understand your deep-seated feelings or emotional insecurities.

To read all about your Outer Planets and work out how to use your personalized timetable, go to Section Three, page 789.

Your Personalized Timetable

JUPITER BENEFICIAL
1938 1/1 – 3/5
1941 6/2 – 8/20
1941 11/30 – until 1942 4/10
1943 7/21 – 9/5
1947 11/14 – 12/29
1949 4/30 – 6/9
1949 12/8 – until 1950 2/16
1953 5/16 – 7/27
1954 1/15 – 3/8
1955 7/5 – 8/20
1959 10/28 – 12/13
1961 3/24 – 7/30
1961 11/15 – until 1962 1/31
1965 4/29 – 7/8
1967 6/17 – 8/4
1971 2/15 – 4/28
1971 10/10 – 11/27
1973 3/2 – until 1974 1/15
1977 4/11 – 6/21
1978 10/1 – until 1979 1/20
1979 5/27 – 7/19
1983 1/19 – 6/9
1983 9/16 – 11/11
1985 2/13 – 12/28
1988 7/31 – 11/19
1989 3/21 – 6/5
1990 9/9 – until 1991 3/5
1991 4/24 – 7/1
1994 12/31 – until 1995 3/9
1995 4/24 – 10/24
1997 1/28 – 4/16
1997 8/5 – 12/7
2000 7/7 – until 2001 1/11
2001 2/8 – 5/19
2002 8/22 – 10/17
2003 1/22 – 6/12
2006 12/14 – until 2007 2/4
2007 6/8 – 10/3
2009 1/12 – 3/24
2009 9/28 – 10/28
2012 6/18 – Continues

SATURN BENEFICIAL
1942 5/20 – until 1943 6/19
1946 9/9 – until 1947 2/6
1947 5/29 – 8/22
1956 11/20 – until 1957 11/20
1962 1/17 – until 1963 3/7
1963 9/14 – 11/26
1971 7/2 – 12/14
1972 3/18 – 8/3
1972 12/3 – until 1973 4/22
1976 7/13 – 10/7
1977 1/19 – 6/26
1985 12/26 – until 1986 6/23
1986 9/19 – 12/24
1987 8/16 – 8/21
1991 2/20 – 8/24
1991 11/14 – until 1992 4/24
1992 7/2 – until 1993 1/12
2001 5/3 – until 2002 6/2
2005 8/21 – until 2006 3/23
2006 4/19 – 8/5

URANUS BENEFICIAL
1942 6/10 – until 1946 6/8
1956 8/27 – until 1959 7/5
1982 2/24 – until 1985 9/29
1996 2/7 – until 2000 12/5

NEPTUNE BENEFICIAL
1972 1/16 – until 1977 11/1
1998 3/17 – until 2006 12/11

PLUTO BENEFICIAL
1941 8/19 – until 1949 6/7
1997 1/5 – until 2001 11/22

JUPITER CHALLENGING
1939 5/19 – 10/15
1940 1/4 – 3/25
1942 6/17 – 8/30
1943 2/1 – 4/20

1948 11/22 – until 1949 2/1
1951 4/28 – until 1952 3/7
1954 5/31 – 8/11
1960 3/14 – 5/27
1960 11/3 – until 1961 1/15
1963 4/10 – 7/5
1963 9/13 – until 1964 2/16
1966 5/13 – 7/25
1972 2/15 – 7/10
1972 10/9 – 12/30
1975 3/25 – 6/5
1975 10/29 – until 1976 1/20
1977 8/30 – 12/19
1978 4/22 – 7/9
1984 1/27 – 12/14
1987 3/9 – 5/16
1989 8/7 – until 1990 2/3
1990 3/17 – 6/23
1996 1/10 – 4/27
1996 5/12 – 11/27
1999 2/20 – 4/28
2001 7/20 – until 2002 6/5
2007 12/25 – until 2008 3/12
2008 7/8 – 11/5
2010 6/19 – 8/26
2011 1/30 – 4/11

SATURN CHALLENGING
1938 2/1 – 7/6
1938 8/24 – until 1939 3/14
1944 7/2 – until 1945 7/31
1959 1/19 – 7/29
1959 10/11 – until 1960 3/25
1960 5/31 – 12/14
1967 3/16 – until 1968 4/22
1973 8/16 – 12/19
1974 5/5 – 9/22
1974 12/9 – until 1975 6/6
1988 3/7 – 5/17
1988 11/27 – until 1990 1/17
1996 4/20 – 10/31
1997 1/4 – 6/3
1997 10/2 – until 1998 2/23
2003 6/16 – until 2004 7/14

URANUS CHALLENGING
1949 7/6 – until 1953 6/21
1988 12/28 – until 1992 12/29
2011 4/8 – Continues

NEPTUNE CHALLENGING
1985 1/2 – until 1992 12/9

PLUTO CHALLENGING
2009 1/9 – Continues

JUPITER SPECIAL
1945 9/1 – 11/16
1946 6/7 – 6/21
1957 1/4 – 1/28
1957 8/15 – 10/30
1968 11/25 – until 1969 3/18
1969 7/26 – 10/15
1980 11/4 – until 1981 4/30
1981 6/24 – 9/29
1992 10/18 – until 1993 9/13
2004 10/2 – until 2005 1/3
2005 3/3 – 8/26

SATURN SPECIAL
1950 12/12 – until 1951 2/11
1951 8/27 – until 1952 10/8
1980 10/3 – until 1981 11/15
1982 4/27 – 8/8
2009 11/14 – until 2010 3/18
2010 8/8 – until 2011 9/22

URANUS SPECIAL
1968 10/24 – until 1972 9/23

NEPTUNE SPECIAL
1942 11/22 – until 1951 8/23

PLUTO SPECIAL
1971 11/23 – until 1979 8/31

October 4

Your Personal Powers

Ambitious, creative, and versatile, you need the freedom to explore a wide variety of experiences in life. You gain power by combining your pragmatic approach with your direct, charming, and friendly manner. You are imaginative and aware of image, and your strong visual sense can enhance your appearance and help you achieve success. Being naturally refined, you also have a love of beauty and luxury. Although opportunities for progress may involve change or travel, be careful that you do not lose power to restlessness or impatience. Your quick comprehension and innate psychological awareness can aid your methods of persuasion and overall empowerment. Although you possess strong determination when you have a goal in mind, guard against losing some of your power to stubbornness or bossy behavior. Being security-conscious, you gain power from having a plan of action and a strong base from which to work. Fortunately, your more practical and down-to-earth side endows you with the business sense to carry through your many creative ideas.

Your Powers of Attraction in Relationships

Sociable and aware, you can attract others with your innate understanding of people. An entertaining companion, you enjoy socializing. The display of affection from others is important to you, especially as you can sometimes repress your true feelings. Although you possess a pleasing manner, you prefer an honest and direct approach. Ideally, you want a partner with whom you can share your ideas and adventurous spirit. This person will have to understand that you need to broaden your horizon by mixing with different people through study or travel. You are particularly drawn to creative individuals or those who can be witty and amusing. Although you want a secure and solid base in your life, your restless streak may cause delays in settling down. Once committed to a relationship, however, you are a romantic and caring partner.

Your attractive qualities: practical, imaginative, good taste, creative, friendly, self-disciplined, steady, hardworking, refined, organized, business sense, ambitious, adventurous, sensitive, visionary, humanitarian, intuitive, fair, direct, sincere

Your less attractive qualities: impatient, indecisive, lazy, unfeeling, frustrating, bossy, critical, indecisive, procrastinator, restlessness, too economical or extravagant, stubborn

Your Venus Power

The planet Venus has a great deal of influence on your powers of attraction. Below are four possible Venus types for women and men. To find your Venus you need to go to page 771, where you will find the Venus table and extra information. The planet Mars also affects your powers of attraction. To find your Mars table and interpretation go to page 761.

WOMEN WITH VENUS IN LEO: Your friendly and sunny personality often makes you stand out in a crowd. Generous and giving, you know how to make your partners feel special. As you often expect loyalty and devotion from your partners in return, you can become easily offended if they ignore you or behave in an inconsiderate manner. Charming and kind, when you are in love you can be romantic, dramatic, and passionate.

MEN WITH VENUS IN LEO: A childlike nature suggests that you are versatile and keen on games or being entertained. You are usually attracted to vivacious partners with a benevolent nature. As an extrovert you enjoy being involved in all types of activities where you can assert yourself and show your talents and abilities. Others may recognize your inborn tendencies to lead but are also aware of your vanity or pride. Nevertheless, generous, kind, and caring, you often show compassion to those less fortunate than yourself.

WOMEN WITH VENUS IN VIRGO: Articulate and straightforward in your relationships, you attract others with your genuine concern for their well-being. By being understanding and a good listener, you are able to show your love and friendship. With your analytical approach to relationships, however, you may have to be careful of becoming too matter-of-fact. You often display your concern for the welfare of others by your willingness to offer practical help and assistance. You usually seek a partner who is willing to work as hard on relationships as you are.

MEN WITH VENUS IN VIRGO: Although you are constantly analyzing your relationships in order to understand and improve them, you may nevertheless need to refrain from continuously mulling over issues that can cause anxiety. You are happiest when you are able to help your loved ones in practical ways and forget yourself in your willingness to be of service to others. You seek a partner who has high standards and can be as pragmatic and hardworking as you. Ideally they should also be impeccably dressed with a fine analytical mind.

WOMEN WITH VENUS IN LIBRA: Gracious, charming, and sociable with a sense of style, you have no trouble attract-

ing admirers. With your natural diplomatic skills and desire for harmony you usually like to keep the peace and avoid confrontations, but be careful of failing to take a stand when it is necessary. Romantic and easygoing yourself, you are attracted to affectionate and refined individuals who share your love of peace, justice, and fair play.

MEN WITH VENUS IN LIBRA: Courteous and refined, you are attracted to beautiful and elegant people. You are looking for a partner who can share your natural good taste and enjoy an intellectual conversation. Disliking conflict, you may have to be careful not to go along with others just to keep the peace. Your ideal partner will appreciate beauty and the little luxuries of life as well as possess good social skills. You have a strong sense of social etiquette yourself so you need an intelligent and sophisticated partner.

WOMEN WITH VENUS IN SCORPIO: Loving and passionate, you are often sensitive with deep feelings and strong powers of attraction. A love for the truth coupled with a tendency to be suspicious can be an influence that motivates you to delve deep into the activities of your partner. When in love or in a relationship that matters, you will often bend over backward to cooperate. Although loyal, guard against losing sight of your own needs and desires.

MEN WITH VENUS IN SCORPIO: As you are emotionally intense and passionate, personal relationships are probably a major factor in your own transformation. Being sensitive yet loyal, you are usually attracted to forceful partners who can express themselves intimately but intensely. Rather than seek easy and simple relationships, you are drawn to partners who act as a catalyst for your own internal changes. Through your relationships with your partners you can unravel your own motives and understand your deep-seated feelings or emotional insecurities.

To read all about your Outer Planets and work out how to use your personalized timetable, go to Section Three, page 789.

Your Personalized Timetable

JUPITER BENEFICIAL
1938 1/1 – 3/10	**1943** 1/23 – 4/28
1941 6/6 – 8/28	**1948** 11/27 – until **1949** 2/5
1941 11/22 – until **1942** 4/16	**1951** 5/3 – until **1952** 3/11
1943 7/26 – 9/10	**1954** 6/4 – 8/16
1947 11/18 – until **1948** 1/2	**1960** 3/24 – 5/16
1949 12/13 – until **1950** 2/21	**1960** 11/9 – until **1961** 1/20
1953 5/20 – 8/1	**1963** 4/14 – 7/16
1954 1/5 – 3/18	**1963** 9/2 – until **1964** 2/21
1955 7/9 – 8/24	**1966** 5/18 – 7/29
1959 11/2 – 12/17	**1972** 2/21 – 7/2
1961 3/30 – 7/23	**1972** 10/16 – until **1973** 1/4
1961 11/21 – until **1962** 2/4	**1975** 3/29 – 6/10
1965 5/3 – 7/12	**1975** 10/22 – until **1976** 1/27
1967 6/22 – 8/8	**1977** 9/5 – 12/12
1971 2/27 – 4/16	**1978** 4/28 – 7/13
1971 10/15 – 12/1	**1984** 1/31 – 12/19
1973 3/7 – 9/16	**1987** 3/13 – 5/20
1973 10/10 – until **1974** 1/19	**1989** 8/12 – until **1990** 1/23
1977 4/16 – 6/25	**1990** 3/29 – 6/27
1978 10/8 – until **1979** 1/13	**1996** 1/14 – 12/1
1979 6/2 – 7/23	**1999** 2/24 – 5/2
1983 1/25 – 6/1	**2001** 7/24 – until **2002** 6/10
1983 9/23 – 11/15	**2007** 12/29 – until **2008** 3/19
1985 2/17 – until **1986** 1/2	**2008** 7/1 – 11/11
1988 8/7 – 11/12	**2010** 6/30 – 8/15
1989 3/26 – 6/9	**2011** 2/4 – 4/15
1990 9/15 – until **1991** 2/22	
1991 5/5 – 7/6	**SATURN CHALLENGING**
1995 1/5 – 10/29	**1938** 2/11 – until **1939** 3/23
1997 2/1 – 7 4/23	**1944** 7/9 – until **1945** 8/8
1997 7/28 – 12/12	**1946** 2/23 – 4/14
2000 7/12 – 12/28	**1959** 1/28 – 7/13
2001 2/22 – 5/23	**1959** 10/26 – until **1960** 12/22
2002 8/27 – 10/24	**1967** 3/24 – until **1968** 4/30
2003 1/14 – 6/17	**1973** 8/27 – 12/7
2006 12/19 – until **2007** 2/10	**1974** 5/14 – 10/11
2007 6/1 – 10/9	**1974** 11/20 – until **1975** 6/14
2009 1/16 – 3/29	**1988** 4/6 – 4/14
2009 9/14 – 11/11	**1988** 12/5 – until **1990** 1/25
2012 6/23 – Continues	**1996** 4/29 – 10/15
	1997 1/19 – 6/15
SATURN BENEFICIAL	**1997** 9/18 – until **1998** 3/4
1942 5/28 – until **1943** 6/27	**2003** 6/23 – until **2004** 7/21
1946 9/19 – until **1947** 1/25	
1947 6/8 – 8/30	**URANUS CHALLENGING**
1956 11/29 – until **1957** 11/28	**1949** 7/23 – until **1953** 7/7
1962 1/25 – until **1963** 3/16	**1989** 1/14 – until **1993** 10/24
1963 8/30 – 12/11	**2011** 4/27 – Continues
1971 7/11 – 12/2	
1972 3/29 – 8/15	**NEPTUNE CHALLENGING**
1972 11/21 – until **1973** 5/1	**1985** 1/30 – until **1993** 10/23
1976 7/21 – 10/20	
1977 1/5 – 7/4	**PLUTO CHALLENGING**
1986 1/4 – 6/9	**2009** 2/9 – Continues
1986 10/2 – until **1987** 1/2	
1987 7/14 – 9/23	**JUPITER SPECIAL**
1991 3/2 – 8/9	**1945** 9/6 – 11/22
1991 11/28 – until **1993** 1/20	**1946** 5/18 – 7/11
2001 5/11 – until **2002** 6/10	**1957** 8/20 – 11/4
2005 8/29 – until **2006** 2/28	**1968** 12/2 – until **1969** 3/11
2006 5/11 – 8/12	**1969** 8/1 – 10/19
	1980 11/9 – until **1981** 4/19
URANUS BENEFICIAL	**1981** 7/4 – 10/3
1942 6/29 – until **1947** 4/8	**1992** 10/22 – until **1993** 9/17
1956 9/14 – until **1959** 7/22	**2004** 10/6 – until **2005** 1/18
1982 12/7 – until **1985** 10/24	**2005** 2/16 – 9/1
1996 2/25 – until **2000** 12/29	
	SATURN SPECIAL
NEPTUNE BENEFICIAL	**1951** 9/5 – until **1952** 10/16
1972 12/11 – until **1977** 11/29	**1980** 10/12 – until **1981** 11/24
1999 2/9 – until **2007** 1/13	**1982** 4/14 – 8/20
	2009 11/25 – until **2010** 3/5
PLUTO BENEFICIAL	**2010** 8/17 – until **2011** 9/30
1941 10/3 – until **1949** 7/18	
1997 2/21 – until **2002** 10/14	**URANUS SPECIAL**
	1968 11/11 – until **1972** 10/9
JUPITER CHALLENGING	
1939 5/25 – 10/7	**NEPTUNE SPECIAL**
1940 1/11 – 3/29	**1943** 10/15 – until **1951** 9/23
1942 6/21 – 9/5	
	PLUTO SPECIAL
	1972 10/11 – until **1979** 9/27

411

October 5

SUN: LIBRA · DECANATE: AQUARIUS/URANUS · DEGREE: 11°5–2°45 · MODE: CARDINAL · ELEMENT: AIR

Your Personal Powers

Intelligent yet charismatic, you are a pragmatist with an inventive mind and dynamic energy. Your ruling planet, Venus, bestows you with refined taste, artistic talents, or an affinity for art and beauty. You empower yourself when you combine your creative and productive ideas with your innate sense of form and design. Alternatively, you may wish to develop your creativity by pursuing music, art, writing, dance, or drama. Your interest in people also gives you a natural understanding of the public. Although you like to be honest and direct with others, you also possess intuition and diplomatic skills that can enhance your natural business sense. You lose some of your power, however, if your quick instincts cause you to become restless and impatient. An ability to attract opportunities implies that you need to utilize your organizational skills, maintain order, and handle your finances wisely in order to achieve success. Your work is likely to be extra important to you. A practical visionary with inner sensitivity and an adventurous streak, you usually thrive on new experiences and opportunities that expand your horizons.

Your Powers of Attraction in Relationships

Your flair for people and your charismatic warmth often attract admirers. Clever, versatile, and active, you are a delightful and enthusiastic companion. An interesting blend of pragmatism, charm, and verve, you enjoy socializing and have a knack for combining business and pleasure. At times a restless streak may pull you in different directions and cause you some challenges within a relationship. Despite having a practical approach, you can also be emotionally sensitive, though you often keep this hidden. Although you are drawn to strong-willed individuals, beware that they do not turn out to be too bossy or demanding. Although you can sometimes be stubborn, moody, or impatient, when you love you are generous, loyal, and affectionate. Since you usually want order and structure in your life, you need a secure partnership.

Your attractive qualities: versatile, enterprising, progressive, strong instincts, daring, creative, visionary, determination, ambitious, adventurous, practical, imaginative, organizational skills, honest, charismatic, freedom-loving, quick-witted, mystical, sensitivity, sociable

Your less attractive qualities: stubborn, changeable, procrastinator, inconsistent, overindulgent, frustrated, restless, critical, bored, irritable, bossy, demanding, overconfident, unpredictable, headstrong

Your Venus Power

The planet Venus has a great deal of influence on your powers of attraction. Below are four possible Venus types for women and men. To find your Venus you need to go to page 771, where you will find the Venus table and extra information. The planet Mars also affects your powers of attraction. To find your Mars table and interpretation go to page 761.

WOMEN WITH VENUS IN LEO: Your friendly and sunny personality often makes you stand out in a crowd. Generous and giving, you know how to make your partner feel special. As you often expect loyalty and devotion from your partners in return, you can become easily offended if they ignore you or behave in an inconsiderate manner. Charming and kind, when you are in love you can be romantic, dramatic, and passionate.

MEN WITH VENUS IN LEO: A childlike nature suggests that you are versatile and keen on games or being entertained. You are usually attracted to vivacious partners with a benevolent nature. As an extrovert you enjoy being involved in all types of activities where you can assert yourself and show your talents and abilities. Others may recognize your inborn tendencies to lead but are also aware of your vanity or pride. Nevertheless, generous, kind, and caring, you often show compassion to those less fortunate than yourself.

WOMEN WITH VENUS IN VIRGO: In relationships you can be modest and unassuming but desire perfection. You usually analyze your partnerships until you feel you have understood them to the last little detail in order to improve them. A problem usually arises when you become too critical either of your partners or yourself and indulge in being skeptical or fault-finding. As you are modest, others may not be aware of the strong sensuality beneath your well-groomed exterior.

MEN WITH VENUS IN VIRGO: Industrious and well-ordered, you relate to others in a considerate and down-to-earth way. You enjoy giving practical advice and being of service to those you love even in small ways. Being a perfectionist you are drawn to partners with high morals or a strong work ethic. Partners who have strong analytical minds are very attractive to you, particularly if they are also clean and meticulously dressed.

WOMEN WITH VENUS IN LIBRA: Gracious, charming, and sociable with a sense of style, you have no trouble attracting admirers. With your natural diplomatic skills and desire for harmony you usually like to keep the peace and avoid confrontations, but be careful of failing to take a stand when it is necessary. Romantic and easygoing yourself, you are attracted to affectionate and refined individuals who share your love of peace, justice, and fair play.

MEN WITH VENUS IN LIBRA: Courteous and refined, you are attracted to beautiful and elegant people. You are looking for a partner who can share your natural good taste and enjoy an intellectual conversation. Disliking conflict, you may have to be careful not to go along with others just to keep the peace. Your ideal partner will appreciate beauty and the little luxuries of life as well as possess good social skills. You have a strong sense of social etiquette yourself so you need an intelligent and sophisticated partner.

WOMEN WITH VENUS IN SCORPIO: Loving and passionate, you are often sensitive with deep feelings and strong powers of attraction. A love for the truth coupled with a tendency to be suspicious can be an influence that motivates you to delve deep into the activities of your partner. When in love or in a relationship that matters, you will often bend over backward to cooperate. Although loyal, guard against losing sight of your own needs and desires.

MEN WITH VENUS IN SCORPIO: As you are emotionally intense and passionate, personal relationships are probably a major factor in your own transformation. Being sensitive yet loyal, you are usually attracted to forceful partners who can express themselves intimately but intensely. Rather than seek easy and simple relationships, you are drawn to partners who act as a catalyst for your own internal changes. Through your relationships with your partners you can unravel your own motives and understand your deep-seated feelings or emotional insecurities.

To read all about your Outer Planets and work out how to use your personalized timetable, go to Section Three, page 789.

Your Personalized Timetable

JUPITER BENEFICIAL
1938 1/4 – 3/14
1941 6/10 – 9/5
1941 11/13 – until 1942 4/21
1943 7/30 – 9/15
1947 11/23 – until 1948 1/7
1949 12/18 – until 1950 2/25
1953 5/24 – 8/6
1953 12/27 – until 1954 3/26
1955 7/14 – 8/29
1959 11/7 – 12/22
1961 4/6 – 7/15
1961 11/27 – until 1962 2/8
1965 5/8 – 7/17
1967 6/27 – 8/13
1971 10/20 – 12/6
1973 3/12 – 8/31
1973 10/26 – until 1974 1/23
1977 4/20 – 6/29
1978 10/16 – until 1979 1/5
1979 6/8 – 7/28
1983 1/31 – 5/24
1983 9/30 – 11/20
1985 2/22 – until 1986 1/6
1988 8/14 – 11/4
1989 4/1 – 6/13
1990 9/20 – until 1991 2/14
1991 5/14 – 7/11
1995 1/10 – 7/8
1995 8/28 – 11/3
1997 2/5 – 5/1
1997 7/20 – 12/18
2000 7/18 – 12/18
2001 3/4 – 5/28
2002 9/1 – 11/2
2003 1/4 – 6/23
2006 12/24 – until 2007 2/18
2007 5/24 – 10/15
2009 1/20 – 4/3
2009 9/4 – 11/20
2012 6/27 – Continues

SATURN BENEFICIAL
1942 6/5 – until 1943 7/5
1946 9/29 – until 1947 1/12
1947 6/18 – 9/7
1948 3/18 – 5/16
1956 12/7 – until 1957 12/7
1962 2/2 – until 1963 3/26
1963 8/16 – 12/22
1971 7/21 – 11/19
1972 4/8 – 8/28
1972 11/6 – until 1973 5/10
1976 7/29 – 11/8
1976 12/17 – until 1977 7/13
1986 1/14 – 5/26
1986 10/14 – until 1987 1/11
1987 6/28 – 10/8
1991 3/12 – 7/26
1991 12/9 – until 1993 1/28
2001 5/19 – until 2002 6/17
2005 9/7 – until 2006 2/13
2006 5/25 – 8/20

URANUS BENEFICIAL
1942 7/21 – until 1947 5/1
1956 10/11 – until 1959 8/7
1982 12/24 – until 1985 11/12
1996 3/18 – until 2001 1/17

NEPTUNE BENEFICIAL
1973 1/10 – until 1978 10/28
1999 3/11 – until 2007 12/1

PLUTO BENEFICIAL
1942 9/10 – until 1950 6/26
1997 12/25 – until 2002 11/14

JUPITER CHALLENGING
1939 5/31 – 9/29
1940 1/17 – 4/2

1942 6/25 – 9/11
1943 1/16 – 5/5
1948 12/1 – until 1949 2/10
1951 5/7 – until 1952 3/15
1954 6/9 – 8/20
1960 4/12 – 4/27
1960 11/14 – until 1961 1/24
1963 4/19 – until 1964 2/26
1966 5/23 – 8/3
1972 2/27 – 6/24
1972 10/23 – until 1973 1/8
1975 4/2 – 6/16
1975 10/14 – until 1976 2/3
1977 9/13 – 12/4
1978 5/3 – 7/18
1984 2/5 – 8/14
1984 9/14 – 12/23
1987 3/17 – 5/25
1989 8/18 – until 1990 1/14
1990 4/7 – 7/2
1996 1/19 – 12/6
1999 2/28 – 5/6
2001 7/29 – until 2002 6/15
2008 1/3 – 3/26
2008 6/22 – 11/17
2011 2/9 – 4/19

SATURN CHALLENGING
1938 2/20 – until 1939 3/30
1944 7/17 – until 1945 8/17
1946 2/5 – 5/1
1959 2/7 – 6/29
1959 11/7 – until 1960 12/31
1967 4/1 – until 1968 5/9
1968 11/21 – until 1969 1/20
1973 9/10 – 11/23
1974 5/23 – until 1975 6/22
1988 12/14 – until 1990 2/3
1990 8/22 – 10/24
1996 5/9 – 10/2
1997 1/31 – 7/1
1997 9/2 – until 1998 3/13
2003 7/1 – until 2004 7/29

URANUS CHALLENGING
1949 8/11 – until 1954 4/30
1989 2/1 – until 1993 11/22
2011 5/19 – Continues

NEPTUNE CHALLENGING
1985 3/17 – until 1993 12/5

PLUTO CHALLENGING
2010 1/6 – Continues

JUPITER SPECIAL
1945 9/11 – 11/27
1946 5/7 – 7/22
1957 8/25 – 11/9
1968 12/10 – until 1969 3/2
1969 8/7 – 10/24
1980 11/15 – until 1981 4/11
1981 7/13 – 10/8
1992 10/27 – until 1993 9/22
2004 10/11 – until 2005 9/6

SATURN SPECIAL
1951 9/13 – until 1952 10/24
1980 10/20 – until 1981 5/11
1981 6/30 – 12/5
1982 4/1 – 8/30
2009 12/8 – until 2010 2/18
2010 8/26 – until 2011 10/8

URANUS SPECIAL
1968 12/7 – until 1973 8/2

NEPTUNE SPECIAL
1943 11/15 – until 1952 8/16

PLUTO SPECIAL
1972 11/9 – until 1980 8/12

October 6

SUN: LIBRA · DECANATE: AQUARIUS/URANUS · DEGREE: 12°5–13°5 LIBRA · MODE: CARDINAL · ELEMENT: AIR

Your Personal Powers

Friendly and intelligent, among your many personal powers are a sense of refinement and a clear objective mind. Your ruling planet, Venus, ensures that you have charm, warmth, and an agreeable manner as well as good taste and an appreciation for beauty and luxury. Independent and easygoing, you gain power from your polished social skills and ability to make contacts. You can lose some power, however, if you allow anxiety, worry, or indecision, particularly about monetary matters, to block your usual bright and cheerful personality. Usually responsible and caring, you often end up advising others and have a strong interest in home and family. Although you may sometimes interfere or appear bossy, your desire for peace enables you to create a harmonious environment around you. With an inner sense of the dramatic, you have a need for self-expression whether through your many inventive ideas, creative projects, or socializing. Behind your gentle appeal and elegance is a strong mind with unique thoughts and strong individuality.

Your Powers of Attraction in Relationships

Friendly and sociable, you can always attract others with your natural charm and keen intelligence. You are also able to utilize your natural psychological understanding of others in all your relationships. Although you like to be honest and straightforward, you can also argue your point in a refined and diplomatic manner. You prefer a partner who can share your strong need for security and harmony. Equally, you desire an intelligent partner who can give you positive feedback on your many creative ideas. Although you value freedom, you are romantic, and your relationships are particularly important to you. In your search for an ideal love, resist feeling lonely or abandoned. By using your ingenuity, graciousness, and affectionate nature you can establish close relationships and work well with your partner.

Your attractive qualities: worldly, friendly, intelligent, responsible, artistic, dependable, understanding, sympathetic, caring, persistent, idealistic, home-loving, charming, popular, enterprising, creative, humanitarian, poised, good business sense, balanced

Your less attractive qualities: discontented, indecisive, interfering, anxious, unreasonable, stubborn, outspoken, dis-harmonious, selfish, domineering, critical, worry, selfish, suspicious

Your Venus Power

The planet Venus has a great deal of influence on your powers of attraction. Below are four possible Venus types for women and men. To find your Venus you need to go to page 771, where you will find the Venus table and extra information. The planet Mars also affects your powers of attraction. To find your Mars table and interpretation go to page 761.

WOMEN WITH VENUS IN LEO: Warm and playful with a touch of the dramatic, you enjoy the company of generous or strong individuals who can share your sense of fun. Although there are advantages to your being strong-willed, in your relationships you need to resist being bossy as it can cause resentment. With your wonderful mixture of regal authority and childlike wonder, you love to keep others entertained and amused.

MEN WITH VENUS IN LEO: Sociable and outgoing, you are kind and generous with those you love. Looking for a relationship that can be fun and entertaining, you need a playmate who can share your enthusiasm and high spirits. Your pride, however, often stops you from associating with lovers or partners you see as beneath you. As you desire someone who can appreciate your sense of the dramatic, you are often attracted to people with strong personalities.

WOMEN WITH VENUS IN VIRGO: Intelligent and discriminating, you are usually drawn to polite and refined individuals. As a perfectionist you may be keen to analyze and criticize yourself, but be careful of continually going over your partner's shortcomings. By focusing on how you can make positive improvements in yourself and in your relationships, you avoid becoming skeptical or confused. You empower yourself when you display kind and caring concern for the well-being of loved ones and spontaneously offer your practical assistance.

MEN WITH VENUS IN VIRGO: A love of order usually indicates that you are attracted to refined individuals with analytical or practical abilities. You and your partner may be working together or serving similar causes. As you constantly analyze partnerships in order to improve them, you are likely to use former relationships as a point of reference and compare them to your present partner. As you are helpful and

kind, others usually rely on your good judgment and often turn to you for advice or practical assistance.

WOMEN WITH VENUS IN LIBRA: Usually you are attractive and sociable with an easygoing manner. Your love of beauty, harmony, and pleasure implies that you are a romantic with a desire for love and affection. Once in a relationship you need to learn to negotiate your position rather than adapt to the wishes of others and compromise just to keep the peace. Nevertheless, your advanced social skills and strong sense of fair play can help you succeed in any social or romantic situation.

MEN WITH VENUS IN LIBRA: Your good social skills, charming personality, and refined manner usually make you attractive to the opposite sex. Equally, you desire a sophisticated partner with grace, elegance, and a strong sense of style. Although you have the ability to be persuasive and irresistible to others, avoid manipulative love games. Nevertheless, your natural diplomacy and sense of fair play help you to relate to people in all social situations. With your love for balance and harmony you seek a partner who is also moderate, easygoing, and loving.

WOMEN WITH VENUS IN SCORPIO: With a natural psychic gift for penetrating the feelings of others, you can often help partners transform emotional challenges or sexual difficulties. When you fall in love, your strong feelings and determination give you a potent force that others find attractive and seductive. Although you know what really turns people on, your most profound desire is usually for the deepness and closeness of real love and intimacy in an enduring relationship.

MEN WITH VENUS IN SCORPIO: When in a relationship you possess a sensitive understanding of your partner's deeper nature. Although you are strongly attached to those you love, you may have to be careful that your feelings do not turn into jealousy or possessiveness. When you fall in love it is often with power and an emotional intensity. You are attracted to partners who can share your passion and display strong feelings of sexuality like your own.

To read all about your Outer Planets and work out how to use your personalized timetable, go to Section Three, page 789.

Your Personalized Timetable

JUPITER BENEFICIAL
1938 1/9 – 3/19
1941 6/14 – 9/16
1941 11/3 – until 1942 4/27
1943 8/4 – 9/20
1944 3/27 – 4/30
1947 11/27 – until 1948 1/12
1949 12/22 – until 1950 3/1
1953 5/28 – 8/12
1953 12/20 – until 1954 4/3
1955 7/19 – 9/2
1959 11/11 – 12/26
1961 4/14 – 7/7
1961 12/2 – until 1962 2/12
1965 5/12 – 7/22
1967 7/2 – 8/17
1971 10/25 – 12/10
1973 3/18 – 8/21
1973 11/4 – until 1974 1/27
1977 4/25 – 7/4
1978 10/25 – 12/27
1979 6/14 – 8/1
1983 2/7 – 5/16
1983 10/6 – 11/24
1985 2/26 – until 1986 1/11
1988 8/23 – 10/26
1989 4/6 – 6/18
1990 9/26 – until 1991 2/6
1991 5/21 – 7/16
1995 1/15 – 6/26
1995 9/8 – 11/8
1997 2/9 – 5/10
1997 7/10 – 12/23
2000 7/23 – 12/10
2001 3/12 – 6/1
2002 9/6 – 11/15
2002 12/23 – until 2003 6/28
2006 12/28 – until 2007 2/26
2007 5/15 – 10/20
2009 1/24 – 4/8
2009 8/26 – 11/28
2012 7/2 – Continues

SATURN BENEFICIAL
1942 6/12 – until 1943 7/13
1944 1/21 – 3/21
1946 10/12 – 12/30
1947 6/26 – 9/15
1948 3/2 – 6/1
1956 12/15 – until 1957 12/15
1962 2/11 – until 1963 4/6
1963 8/3 – until 1964 1/1
1971 8/1 – 11/7
1972 4/17 – 9/23
1972 10/12 – until 1973 5/18
1976 8/6 – until 1977 7/21
1986 1/26 – 5/13
1986 10/24 – until 1987 1/21
1987 6/14 – 10/20
1991 3/23 – 7/13
1991 12/19 – until 1993 2/6
2001 5/26 – until 2002 6/25
2005 9/16 – until 2006 2/1
2006 6/5 – 8/28

URANUS BENEFICIAL
1942 8/27 – until 1947 5/20
1957 8/3 – until 1960 5/30
1983 1/12 – until 1985 11/28
1996 4/25 – until 2001 2/4

NEPTUNE BENEFICIAL
1973 12/8 – until 1978 11/26
2000 2/5 – until 2008 1/8

PLUTO BENEFICIAL
1943 8/23 – until 1951 5/19
1998 1/26 – until 2003 9/29

JUPITER CHALLENGING
1939 6/6 – 9/22
1940 1/23 – 4/6
1942 6/30 – 9/17

1943 1/9 – 5/12
1948 12/6 – until 1949 2/15
1951 5/12 – 11/18
1951 12/12 – until 1952 3/20
1954 6/13 – 8/25
1955 2/25 – 4/5
1960 11/18 – until 1961 1/28
1963 4/23 – until 1964 3/1
1966 5/27 – 8/8
1972 3/5 – 6/16
1972 10/29 – until 1973 1/12
1975 4/6 – 6/23
1975 10/7 – until 1976 2/9
1977 9/22 – 11/25
1978 5/9 – 7/22
1984 2/10 – 7/30
1984 9/28 – 12/27
1987 3/21 – 5/30
1987 11/24 – until 1988 1/5
1989 8/23 – until 1990 1/6
1990 4/15 – 7/6
1996 1/23 – 12/11
1999 3/4 – 5/11
2001 8/3 – until 2002 6/19
2008 1/7 – 4/4
2008 6/13 – 11/22
2011 2/14 – 4/23

SATURN CHALLENGING
1938 3/1 – until 1939 4/7
1944 7/25 – until 1945 2/6
1945 4/1 – 8/25
1946 1/23 – 5/13
1959 2/18 – 6/16
1959 11/17 – until 1961 1/8
1967 4/9 – until 1968 5/17
1968 11/5 – until 1969 2/4
1973 10/1 – 11/2
1974 5/31 – until 1975 6/30
1988 12/22 – until 1990 2/12
1990 8/5 – 11/9
1996 5/19 – 9/19
1997 2/10 – until 1998 3/21
2003 7/8 – until 2004 8/6
2005 3/11 – 4/1

URANUS CHALLENGING
1949 9/6 – until 1954 5/26
1989 2/24 – until 1993 12/12
2011 6/27 – Continues

NEPTUNE CHALLENGING
1986 1/26 – until 1994 1/2

PLUTO CHALLENGING
2010 2/6 – Continues

JUPITER SPECIAL
1945 9/15 – 12/2
1946 4/29 – 7/31
1957 8/30 – 11/14
1968 12/19 – until 1969 2/21
1969 8/12 – 10/28
1980 11/21 – until 1981 4/2
1981 7/21 – 10/13
1992 11/1 – until 1993 9/27
2004 10/16 – until 2005 9/11

SATURN SPECIAL
1951 9/21 – until 1952 11/1
1980 10/28 – until 1981 4/22
1981 7/18 – 12/17
1982 3/18 – 9/8
2010 1/1 – 1/26
2010 9/4 – until 2011 10/16

URANUS SPECIAL
1969 9/29 – until 1973 8/27

NEPTUNE SPECIAL
1944 10/11 – until 1952 9/18

PLUTO SPECIAL
1973 10/3 – until 1980 9/13

415

October 7

SUN: LIBRA • DECANATE: AQUARIUS/URANUS • DEGREE: 13°5–14°5 LIBRA • MODE: CARDINAL • ELEMENT: AIR

Your Personal Powers

Friendly, thoughtful, and mentally sharp, you are a determined and enterprising individual with excellent social skills. You gain power from your original and broad-minded ideas as well as your keen insight into human nature. Your ruling planet, Venus, accents your sociability and your capacity to mix with people from all walks of life. Although ambitious and independent, you also realize the importance of working cooperatively with others. A keen business sense indicates that you can be benevolent, materially astute, and talented at making useful contacts. When you are focused on a goal, you can be persistent and utilize your strategic skills; however, you may lose some power by becoming skeptical, too materialistic, or too tough. Your need for recognition and status often motivates you to achieve, yet your idealism can inspire you to be generous, supportive, and compassionate to humanitarian causes. Usually analyzing your situations to improve and refine them, you gain power from your ability to quickly discern opportunities when they arise.

Your Powers of Attraction in Relationships

You can attract others with your charm and thoughtful approach to life. Your innate gift for making contacts implies that many of the opportunities you've had in life revolve around your relationships. You usually seek partners and friends who have determination and powerful intellects. Although you also enjoy being with those who are strong-willed and ambitious, avoid ego struggles in your close relationships. Although people are important to you and you can be generous to those you care for, you need time alone for self-analysis or reflection. With two sides to your personality, in your relationships you sometimes alternate between being idealistic and cynical. Nevertheless, since you are very supportive of the people you love, you usually have loyal friends and admirers.

Your attractive qualities: friendly, persistent, ambitious, analytical, enterprising, idealistic, popular, entertaining, hardworking, determined, honest, creative, generous, humanitarian, scientific, rational, reflective, perfectionist, good business sense, intuitive

Your less attractive qualities: skeptical, self-absorbed, materialistic, unfriendly, cold, escapist, too tough, cynical, fears about money, confused, impatient, withdrawn, critical

Your Venus Power

The planet Venus has a great deal of influence on your powers of attraction. Below are four possible Venus types for women and men. To find your Venus you need to go to page 771, where you will find the Venus table and extra information. The planet Mars also affects your powers of attraction. To find your Mars table and interpretation go to page 761.

WOMEN WITH VENUS IN LEO: You possess the wonderful ability to project your warm and sunny personality and keep others happily entertained. Loving attention yourself, you seek a partner who can appreciate you, be supportive, and give you positive feedback. Proud, with a natural regal air, you expect respect from your partners but are willing to be loyal and supportive in exchange. Although sometimes a little self-centered, you know how to make your partner feel special.

MEN WITH VENUS IN LEO: Enthusiastic, playful, and kind, you can be benevolent with those you love. Warm, romantic, and self-expressive, you adore the drama of love or having fun with your friends. You are usually attracted to partners with a warm and generous nature. Although you can be a confident and charismatic partner, you may need to develop humility in order to stop pride or arrogance from marring your relationships.

WOMEN WITH VENUS IN VIRGO: Intelligent and discriminating, you are usually drawn to polite and refined individuals. As a perfectionist you may be keen to analyze and criticize yourself, but be careful of continually going over your partner's shortcomings. By focusing on how you can make positive improvements in yourself and in your relationships, you avoid becoming skeptical or confused. You empower yourself when you display kind and caring concern for the well-being of loved ones and spontaneously offer your practical assistance.

MEN WITH VENUS IN VIRGO: A love of order usually indicates that you are attracted to refined individuals with analytical or practical abilities. You and your partner may be working together or serving similar causes. As you constantly analyze partnerships in order to improve them, you are likely to use former relationships as a point of reference and compare them to your present partner. As you are helpful and kind, others usually rely on your good judgment and often turn to you for advice or practical assistance.

WOMEN WITH VENUS IN LIBRA: Attractive, refined, and conscious of the needs of others, you usually desire harmo-

nious relationships. As a peacemaker with good negotiating skills, you can smooth out difficulties with others, but your dislike of confrontation may sometimes leave you refusing to take a stand or compromising too many of your own needs. Courteous, stylish, and charming with polished social skills, you are an expert at relating to others in a gracious and civilized manner.

MEN WITH VENUS IN LIBRA: As a sociable and friendly individual with an eye for beauty, you are amorous and charming. You are a natural gentleman and your ideal partner usually has an elegant appearance, artistic appreciation, and good taste. Your relationships benefit when you resist the temptation to take the easy way out or put too much emphasis on vanity and high living. Intellectual and naturally refined, you seek a loving partner who can share your romantic and sophisticated aspirations.

WOMEN WITH VENUS IN SCORPIO: Loving and passionate, you are often sensitive with deep feelings and strong powers of attraction. A love for the truth coupled with a tendency to be suspicious can be an influence that motivates you to delve deep into the activities of your partner. When in love or in a relationship that matters, you will often bend over backward to cooperate. Although loyal, guard against losing sight of your own needs and desires.

MEN WITH VENUS IN SCORPIO: As you are emotionally intense and passionate, personal relationships are probably a major factor in your own transformation. Being sensitive yet loyal, you are usually attracted to forceful partners who can express themselves intimately but intensely. Rather than seek easy and simple relationships you are drawn to partners who act as a catalyst for your own internal changes. Through your relationships with your partners you can unravel your own motives and understand your deep-seated feelings or emotional insecurities.

To read all about your Outer Planets and work out how to use your personalized timetable, go to Section Three, page 789.

Your Personalized Timetable

JUPITER BENEFICIAL
1938 1/13 – 3/24
1941 6/19 – until 1942 5/2
1943 8/8 – 9/25
1944 3/13 – 5/14
1947 12/2 – until 1948 1/17
1949 12/27 – until 1950 3/5
1953 6/2 – 8/18
1953 12/13 – until 1954 4/9
1955 7/23 – 9/7
1959 11/16 – 12/30
1961 4/23 – 6/27
1961 12/8 – until 1962 2/17
1965 5/16 – 7/27
1966 2/3 – 2/26
1967 7/7 – 8/22
1971 10/30 – 12/14
1973 3/23 – 8/13
1973 11/12 – until 1974 1/31
1977 4/29 – 7/8
1978 11/7 – 12/14
1979 6/19 – 8/6
1983 2/15 – 5/7
1983 10/11 – 11/29
1985 3/3 – until 1986 1/15
1988 9/5 – 10/13
1989 4/11 – 6/22
1990 10/2 – until 1991 1/29
1991 5/28 – 7/21
1995 1/21 – 6/17
1995 9/16 – 11/12
1997 2/14 – 5/24
1997 6/26 – 12/28
2000 7/29 – 12/3
2001 3/18 – 6/5
2002 9/11 – until 2003 3/18
2003 4/20 – 7/3
2007 1/2 – 3/8
2007 5/5 – 10/26
2009 1/29 – 4/14
2009 8/19 – 12/4
2012 7/6 – Continues

SATURN BENEFICIAL
1942 6/20 – until 1943 7/21
1944 1/6 – 4/5
1946 10/31 – 12/11
1947 7/5 – 9/24
1948 2/18 – 6/13
1956 12/24 – until 1957 7/10
1957 9/12 – 12/23
1962 2/19 – 9/9
1962 11/8 – until 1963 4/19
1963 7/19 – until 1964 1/11
1971 8/15 – 10/23
1972 4/26 – until 1973 5/26
1976 8/13 – until 1977 7/29
1986 2/9 – 4/27
1986 11/2 – until 1987 2/1
1987 5/31 – 10/31
1991 4/6 – 6/28
1991 12/28 – until 1993 2/14
2001 6/3 – until 2002 7/3
2005 9/26 – until 2006 1/20
2006 6/15 – 9/5
2007 3/31 – 5/9

URANUS BENEFICIAL
1943 6/10 – until 1947 6/6
1957 8/19 – until 1960 6/24
1983 2/5 – until 1986 9/14
1997 2/8 – until 2001 12/7

NEPTUNE BENEFICIAL
1974 1/5 – until 1979 10/23
2000 3/5 – until 2008 11/11

PLUTO BENEFICIAL
1943 10/7 – until 1951 7/10
1998 12/15 – until 2003 11/7

JUPITER CHALLENGING
1939 6/13 – 9/14
1940 1/29 – 4/10

1942 7/4 – 9/24
1943 1/1 – 5/18
1948 12/10 – until 1949 2/19
1951 5/17 – 11/3
1951 12/27 – until 1952 3/24
1954 6/18 – 8/31
1955 2/13 – 4/18
1960 11/23 – until 1961 2/2
1963 4/27 – until 1964 3/6
1966 6/1 – 8/12
1972 3/12 – 6/8
1972 11/4 – until 1973 1/16
1975 4/10 – 6/30
1975 9/29 – until 1976 2/14
1977 10/4 – 11/13
1978 5/14 – 7/26
1984 2/16 – 7/21
1984 10/8 – until 1985 1/1
1987 3/25 – 6/4
1987 11/13 – until 1988 1/16
1989 8/29 – 12/30
1990 4/21 – 7/10
1996 1/28 – 12/15
1999 3/9 – 5/15
2001 8/7 – until 2002 6/24
2008 1/11 – 4/15
2008 6/2 – 11/27
2011 2/18 – 4/27

SATURN CHALLENGING
1938 3/9 – until 1939 4/15
1944 8/3 – until 1945 1/21
1945 4/18 – 9/4
1946 1/11 – 5/24
1959 3/3 – 6/1
1959 11/27 – until 1961 1/17
1967 4/17 – until 1968 5/27
1968 10/22 – until 1969 2/16
1974 6/8 – until 1975 7/7
1988 12/31 – until 1990 2/22
1990 7/21 – 11/21
1996 5/31 – 9/6
1997 2/19 – until 1998 3/29
2003 7/16 – until 2004 8/14
2005 2/15 – 4/26

URANUS CHALLENGING
1950 7/2 – until 1954 6/14
1989 12/27 – until 1993 12/30
2012 4/11 – Continues

NEPTUNE CHALLENGING
1986 3/4 – until 1994 11/30

PLUTO CHALLENGING
2011 1/5 – Continues

JUPITER SPECIAL
1945 9/20 – 12/8
1946 4/20 – 8/8
1957 9/4 – 11/19
1969 1/1 – 2/8
1969 8/18 – 11/2
1980 11/27 – until 1981 3/26
1981 7/27 – 10/17
1992 11/6 – until 1993 5/10
1993 6/23 – 10/1
2004 10/20 – until 2005 9/16

SATURN SPECIAL
1951 9/29 – until 1952 11/9
1953 5/20 – 7/27
1980 11/6 – until 1981 4/8
1981 7/31 – until 1982 1/2
1982 3/1 – 9/17
2010 9/12 – until 2011 10/24

URANUS SPECIAL
1969 10/15 – until 1973 9/15

NEPTUNE SPECIAL
1944 11/9 – until 1953 8/9

PLUTO SPECIAL
1973 10/30 – until 1980 10/9

417

October 8

SUN: LIBRA · DECANATE: AQUARIUS/URANUS · DEGREE: 14°5–15°5 LIBRA · MODE: CARDINAL · ELEMENT: AIR

Your Personal Powers

Although you have excellent social skills and a charming and friendly personality, you are a strong-willed and forceful individual. A desire for personal accomplishment suggests that you are also ambitious and determined. Your ruling planet, Venus, grants you grace and a love of beauty. When you recognize the strength of your emotional power, you can inspire and encourage people. You gain power when you balance your need for financial security or status with your need for emotional fulfillment. Even though you like to be in control, you can lose some of your power by being too domineering. Nevertheless, charismatic and idealistic, you can accomplish much if you believe in your aims or aspirations. Being a practical visionary, your foresight and originality can assist you in the business world, especially when you learn to trust your instincts. Ambitious and self-confident, you are goal-oriented and efficient with the capabilities to handle large projects.

Your Powers of Attraction in Relationships

People admire your liberal, gracious, and generous nature. Being cooperative, you are often keen to help and encourage those you like or respect. You are usually drawn to dynamic and creative people with style and strong values. Enthusiastic yet practical, you enjoy being active and mixing with new people or trying different experiences. Although you can be relaxed and tactful, a tendency to be indecisive implies that you can become anxious, bossy, or restless. A strong desire for stability indicates that even though you are usually very security-conscious, you need a relationship that can offer you variety and excitement to keep you from becoming bored. Your ideal partner therefore, would be someone loving and understanding who is able to keep you interested.

Your attractive qualities: enterprising, impartial, liberal, adventurous, idealistic, generous, powerful emotions, persuasive, methodical, hardworking, authoritative, protective, good judge of values, fortunate ideas, artistic, intuitive, charismatic, determined, direct, cooperative

Your less attractive qualities: impatient, intolerant, restless, workaholic, power struggles, risk taking, daring, domineering, easily discouraged, lack of planning, bossy, dissatisfied, critical, overindulgent, too materialistic, too emotional, insecure, controlling, speculative

Your Venus Power

The planet Venus has a great deal of influence on your powers of attraction. Below are four possible Venus types for women and men. To find your Venus you need to go to page 771, where you will find the Venus table and extra information. The planet Mars also affects your powers of attraction. To find your Mars table and interpretation go to page 761.

WOMEN WITH VENUS IN VIRGO: Articulate and straightforward in your relationships, you attract others with your genuine concern for their well-being. By being understanding and a good listener you are able to show your love and friendship. With your analytical approach to relationships, you may have to be careful of becoming too matter-of-fact. You often display your concern for the welfare of others by your willingness to offer practical help and assistance. You usually seek a partner who is willing to work as hard on relationships as you are.

MEN WITH VENUS IN VIRGO: Although you are constantly analyzing your relationships in order to understand and improve them, you may nevertheless need to refrain from continuously mulling over issues that can cause anxiety. You are happiest when you are able to help loved ones in practical ways and forget yourself in your willingness to be of service to others. You seek a partner who has high standards and can be as pragmatic and hardworking as yourself. Ideally they should also be impeccably dressed with a fine analytical mind.

WOMEN WITH VENUS IN LIBRA: Gracious, charming, and sociable with a sense of style, you have no trouble attracting admirers. With your natural diplomatic skills and desire for harmony you usually like to keep the peace and avoid confrontations, but be careful of failing to take a stand when it is necessary. Romantic and easygoing yourself, you are attracted to affectionate and refined individuals who share your love of peace, justice, and fair play.

MEN WITH VENUS IN LIBRA: Courteous and refined, you are attracted to beautiful and elegant people. You are looking for a partner who can share your natural good taste and enjoy an intellectual conversation. Disliking conflict, you may have to be careful not to go along with others just to keep the peace. Your ideal partner will appreciate beauty and the little luxuries of life as well as possess good social skills. You have a strong sense of social etiquette yourself so you need an intelligent and sophisticated partner.

WOMEN WITH VENUS IN SCORPIO: Loving and pas-

sionate, you are often sensitive with deep feelings and strong powers of attraction. A love for the truth coupled with a tendency to be suspicious can be an influence that motivates you to delve deep into the activities of your partner. When in love or in a relationship that matters, you will often bend over backward to cooperate. Although loyal, guard against losing sight of your own needs and desires.

MEN WITH VENUS IN SCORPIO: As you are emotionally intense and passionate, personal relationships are probably a major factor in your own transformation. Being sensitive yet loyal, you are usually attracted to forceful partners who can express themselves intimately but intensely. Rather than seek easy and simple relationships, you are drawn to partners who act as a catalyst for your own internal changes. Through your relationships with your partners you can unravel your own motives and understand your deep-seated feelings or emotional insecurities.

WOMEN WITH VENUS IN SAGITTARIUS: Sociable, warm, and friendly, you possess an honest and frank style in your relationships. Being naturally gregarious, you want others to share your enthusiasm and enjoy encouraging the people you love. You fare better when you have a sense of personal freedom within a relationship and are usually generous with the faults of others. You need a partner who can share your need to explore and take risks whether through travel, education, or recreation.

MEN WITH VENUS IN SAGITTARIUS: When in love you are open and friendly, with a need for a partner who can share your adventurous spirit and sense of fun. Be careful, however, that your desire for freedom does not cause you to avoid commitment. You prefer your partners to be positive, direct, and generous in spirit. Being outspoken as well as an idealist, you usually enjoy a partner with whom you can share your strong opinions. Alternatively, you may wish to explore life together whether through travel, education, or by having fun.

To read all about your Outer Planets and work out how to use your personalized timetable, go to Section Three, page 789.

♎

Your Personalized Timetable

JUPITER BENEFICIAL
1938 1/17 – 3/28
1938 10/12 – 10/26
1941 6/23 – until 1942 5/6
1943 8/13 – 10/1
1944 3/3 – 5/24
1947 12/6 – until 1948 1/22
1948 7/31 – 8/31
1949 12/31 – until 1950 3/10
1953 6/6 – 8/24
1953 12/5 – until 1954 4/15
1955 7/28 – 9/12
1959 11/20 – until 1960 1/4
1961 5/5 – 6/15
1961 12/13 – until 1962 2/21
1965 5/21 – 8/1
1966 1/19 – 3/14
1967 7/12 – 8/26
1971 11/4 – 12/19
1973 3/29 – 8/5
1973 11/19 – until 1974 2/4
1977 5/4 – 7/13
1979 6/24 – 8/10
1983 2/25 – 4/27
1983 10/17 – 12/3
1985 3/8 – until 1986 1/19
1989 4/16 – 6/26
1990 10/8 – until 1991 1/22
1991 6/4 – 7/25
1995 1/26 – 6/9
1995 9/24 – 11/17
1997 2/18 – until 1998 1/2
2000 8/4 – 11/25
2001 3/25 – 6/10
2002 9/16 – until 2003 3/5
2003 5/4 – 7/8
2007 1/7 – 3/23
2007 4/19 – 10/31
2009 2/2 – 4/20
2009 8/11 – 12/11
2012 7/11 – Continues

SATURN BENEFICIAL
1942 6/29 – until 1943 1/6
1943 3/9 – 7/30
1943 12/24 – until 1944 4/17
1947 7/13 – 10/4
1948 2/6 – 6/23
1957 1/2 – 6/23
1957 9/28 – until 1958 1/1
1958 8/2 – 9/14
1962 2/28 – 8/23
1962 11/24 – until 1963 5/6
1963 7/1 – until 1964 1/20
1971 9/12 – 9/25
1972 5/4 – until 1973 6/2
1976 8/21 – until 1977 8/6
1986 3/3 – 4/4
1986 11/11 – until 1987 2/13
1987 5/17 – 11/10
1991 4/26 – 6/7
1992 1/6 – until 1993 2/22
2001 6/11 – until 2002 7/11
2003 2/3 – 3/13
2005 10/8 – until 2006 1/7
2006 6/24 – 9/13
2007 3/11 – 5/29

URANUS BENEFICIAL
1943 6/28 – until 1948 3/29
1957 9/5 – until 1960 7/13
1983 12/4 – until 1986 10/18
1997 2/26 – until 2002 1/1

NEPTUNE BENEFICIAL
1974 2/17 – until 1979 11/23
2000 4/20 – until 2009 1/2

PLUTO BENEFICIAL
1944 9/11 – until 1952 6/11
1999 1/12 – until 2003 12/4

JUPITER CHALLENGING
1939 6/21 – 9/6
1940 2/3 – 4/14

1942 7/8 – 10/1
1942 12/24 – until 1943 5/23
1948 12/15 – until 1949 2/24
1949 9/10 – 9/27
1951 5/22 – 10/24
1952 1/5 – 3/28
1954 6/22 – 9/5
1955 2/3 – 4/27
1960 11/28 – until 1961 2/6
1963 5/2 – until 1964 3/11
1966 6/6 – 8/17
1972 3/21 – 5/30
1972 11/9 – until 1973 1/21
1975 4/14 – 7/8
1975 9/21 – until 1976 2/20
1978 5/19 – 7/31
1984 2/21 – 7/12
1984 10/16 – until 1985 1/5
1987 3/29 – 6/9
1987 11/4 – until 1988 1/25
1989 9/5 – 12/22
1990 4/28 – 7/15
1996 2/2 – 12/20
1999 3/13 – 5/20
2001 8/12 – until 2002 2/7
2002 3/24 – 6/28
2008 1/16 – 12/2
2011 2/23 – 5/5

SATURN CHALLENGING
1938 3/17 – until 1939 4/23
1944 8/12 – until 1945 1/8
1945 4/30 – 9/15
1945 12/30 – until 1946 6/2
1959 3/21 – 5/13
1959 12/6 – until 1961 1/25
1967 4/25 – 11/8
1968 1/8 – 6/6
1968 10/10 – until 1969 2/26
1974 6/16 – until 1975 7/15
1989 1/8 – until 1990 3/5
1990 7/8 – 12/2
1996 6/15 – 8/21
1997 2/28 – until 1998 4/6
2003 7/24 – until 2004 2/22
2004 3/21 – 8/23
2005 1/31 – 5/10

URANUS CHALLENGING
1950 7/19 – until 1954 7/1
1990 1/13 – until 1994 10/16
2012 4/29 – Continues

NEPTUNE CHALLENGING
1987 1/22 – until 1994 12/29

PLUTO CHALLENGING
2011 2/4 – Continues

JUPITER SPECIAL
1945 9/25 – 12/15
1946 4/13 – 8/14
1957 9/9 – 11/24
1958 5/28 – 7/11
1969 8/23 – 11/7
1980 12/4 – until 1981 3/18
1981 8/3 – 10/22
1992 11/12 – until 1993 4/27
1993 7/5 – 10/6
2004 10/25 – until 2005 9/21

SATURN SPECIAL
1951 10/7 – until 1952 11/18
1953 5/4 – 8/12
1980 11/16 – until 1981 3/26
1981 8/11 – until 1982 9/26
2010 9/20 – until 2011 11/1

URANUS SPECIAL
1969 10/31 – until 1973 10/1

NEPTUNE SPECIAL
1945 10/7 – until 1953 9/15

PLUTO SPECIAL
1973 12/5 – until 1981 8/29

October 9

SUN: LIBRA • DECANATE: LIBRA/AQUARIUS/VENUS/URANUS • DEGREE: 15°5–16°5 LIBRA • MODE: CARDINAL • ELEMENT: AIR

Your Personal Powers

Charming, sociable, and intuitive, you are a discerning individual with keen perceptions and a particular interest in people. Your ruling planet, Venus, endows you with an aesthetic sense, innate artistic or creative talents, and a love of beauty. Articulate, you gain power when you utilize your talent for communication or through improving your knowledge. Your original ideas and quick comprehension also indicate that you are observant and receptive. Although you appear self-assured, inner insecurities indicate that you can lose some of your power through self-doubts or being indecisive. Although you may outwardly be a pragmatist or a traditionalist, your vision and sense of justice indicate that you can be a radical thinker or an advocate for progress and reform, especially for human rights. When an idea or a person inspires your idealistic nature you can be highly supportive. Yet when you oppose someone or something, you are not afraid to speak up. With your strong willpower, foresight, and compassion, you can achieve a great deal, especially when you follow your ideals.

Your Powers of Attraction in Relationships

People admire your good mind and generous nature, suggesting you usually have many friends. Since you possess special talents, working with others and showing a willingness to cooperate usually bring recognition or favorable results. With your quick responses you are able to stand up for yourself and even enjoy a little friendly banter. A tendency to be stubborn or domineering implies that if you want others to turn to you for support and advice, you may need to refrain from being too critical. Generally, you are drawn to tolerant and kind individuals who are intelligent and practical. Although you can be a charming extrovert, underneath you are sensitive. This indicates that in order to establish a close personal relationship you may need to overcome a tendency for emotional ups and downs.

Your attractive qualities: creative, sensitive, generous, magnetic, independent, popular, witty, good debater, intuitive, loyal, inner strength, tenacious, artistic, original, hardworking, humanitarian, determined, persevering, confident, shrewd, imaginative, intelligent, progressive

Your less attractive qualities: controlling, self-doubt, temperamental, arrogant, skeptical, uncompromising, intolerant, frustrated, rebellious, worried, argumentative, sarcastic, tense, competitive, discontented, domineering, overindulgent

Your Venus Power

The planet Venus has a great deal of influence on your powers of attraction. Below are four possible Venus types for women and men. To find your Venus you need to go to page 771, where you will find the Venus table and extra information. The planet Mars also affects your powers of attraction. To find your Mars table and interpretation go to page 761.

WOMEN WITH VENUS IN VIRGO: In relationships you can be modest and unassuming but desire perfection. You usually analyze partnerships until you feel you understand them to the last little detail in order to improve them. A problem usually arises when you become too critical either of partners or yourself and indulge in being skeptical or faultfinding. As you are modest, others may not be aware of the strong sensuality beneath your well-groomed exterior.

MEN WITH VENUS IN VIRGO: Industrious and well-ordered, you relate to others in a considerate and down-to-earth way. You enjoy giving practical advice and being of service to those you love even in small ways. Being a perfectionist you are drawn to partners with high morals or a strong work ethic. Partners who have strong analytical minds are very attractive to you, particularly if they are also clean and meticulously dressed.

WOMEN WITH VENUS IN LIBRA: Gracious, charming, and sociable with a sense of style, you have no trouble attracting admirers. With your natural diplomatic skills and desire for harmony you usually like to keep the peace and avoid confrontations, but be careful of failing to take a stand when it is necessary. Romantic and easygoing yourself, you are attracted to affectionate and refined individuals who share your love of peace, justice, and fair play.

MEN WITH VENUS IN LIBRA: Courteous and refined, you are attracted to beautiful and elegant people. You are looking for a partner who can share your natural good taste and enjoy an intellectual conversation. Disliking conflict, you may have to be careful not to go along with others just to keep the peace. Your ideal partner will appreciate beauty and the little luxuries of life as well as possess good social skills. You have a strong sense of social etiquette yourself so you need an intelligent and sophisticated partner.

WOMEN WITH VENUS IN SCORPIO: Loving and passionate, you are often sensitive with deep feelings and strong powers of attraction. A love for the truth coupled with a tendency to be suspicious can be an influence that motivates you to delve deep into the activities of your partner. When in love or in a relationship that matters, you will often bend over backward to cooperate. Although loyal, guard against losing sight of your own needs and desires.

MEN WITH VENUS IN SCORPIO: As you are emotionally intense and passionate, personal relationships are probably a major factor in your own transformation. Being sensitive yet loyal, you are usually attracted to forceful partners who can express themselves intimately but intensely. Rather than seek easy and simple relationships you are drawn to partners who act as a catalyst for your own internal changes. Through your relationships with your partners you can unravel your own motives and understand your deep-seated feelings or emotional insecurities.

WOMEN WITH VENUS IN SAGITTARIUS: When you feel generous you can make others feel more optimistic about life. You may be interested in higher learning and seek partners who are scholarly or broad-minded. You are outspoken and direct and sometimes say things that you later regret. Curious and versatile, you can adjust quickly to new situations, and a foreign influence implies that you love to travel or may have a partner who comes from a different culture.

MEN WITH VENUS IN SAGITTARIUS: Your enthusiasm and straightforward conduct usually appeal to others and imply that you are approachable and easygoing. Being open to ideas and willing to believe that life has a great deal to offer suggests that you are generous, broad-minded, and show an eagerness to cooperate with others. A love of travel and an interest in other cultures also imply that your partner may come from a foreign country.

To read all about your Outer Planets and work out how to use your personalized timetable, go to Section Three, page 789.

Your Personalized Timetable

JUPITER BENEFICIAL
1938 1/21 – 4/2
1938 9/23 – 11/13
1941 6/28 – until 1942 5/11
1943 8/17 – 10/6
1944 2/24 – 6/1
1947 12/10 – until 1948 1/27
1948 7/17 – 9/15
1950 1/5 – 3/14
1953 6/10 – 9/1
1953 11/28 – until 1954 4/21
1955 1/9 – 9/17
1959 11/25 – until 1960 1/9
1961 12/18 – until 1962 2/25
1965 5/25 – 8/6
1966 1/9 – 3/24
1967 7/16 – 8/31
1971 11/8 – 12/23
1973 4/4 – 7/28
1973 11/26 – until 1974 2/9
1977 5/8 – 7/17
1979 6/29 – 8/15
1983 3/11 – 4/14
1983 10/22 – 12/8
1985 3/13 – 9/19
1985 10/17 – until 1986 1/24
1989 4/21 – 6/30
1990 10/15 – until 1991 1/14
1991 6/9 – 7/30
1995 2/1 – 6/1
1995 10/1 – 11/22
1997 2/22 – until 1998 1/6
2000 8/11 – 11/18
2001 3/31 – 6/14
2002 9/21 – until 2003 2/23
2003 5/14 – 7/13
2007 1/12 – 7/19
2007 8/25 – 11/5
2009 2/6 – 4/27
2009 8/3 – 12/16
2012 7/16 – Continues

SATURN BENEFICIAL
1942 7/7 – 12/21
1943 3/24 – 8/9
1943 12/12 – until 1944 4/27
1947 7/21 – 10/15
1948 1/24 – 7/3
1957 1/12 – 6/9
1957 10/11 – until 1958 1/10
1958 7/12 – 10/4
1962 3/10 – 8/8
1962 12/7 – until 1964 1/28
1972 5/12 – until 1973 6/10
1976 8/29 – until 1977 3/18
1977 5/5 – 8/13
1986 11/19 – until 1987 3/2
1987 4/29 – 11/19
1992 1/15 – until 1993 3/2
2001 6/18 – until 2002 7/19
2003 1/14 – 4/1
2005 10/23 – 12/22
2006 7/3 – 9/22
2007 2/25 – 6/11

URANUS BENEFICIAL
1943 7/18 – until 1948 4/26
1957 9/27 – until 1960 7/29
1983 12/20 – until 1986 11/8
1997 3/19 – until 2002 1/20

NEPTUNE BENEFICIAL
1975 1/2 – until 1980 10/16
2001 2/28 – until 2009 1/31

PLUTO BENEFICIAL
1945 8/23 – until 1952 7/21
1999 3/3 – until 2004 10/29

JUPITER CHALLENGING
1939 7/1 – 8/27
1940 2/8 – 4/18
1942 7/13 – 10/10
1942 12/15 – until 1943 5/29

1948 12/19 – until 1949 3/1
1949 8/23 – 10/15
1951 5/28 – 10/15
1952 1/13 – 4/1
1954 6/26 – 9/11
1955 1/26 – 5/5
1960 12/2 – until 1961 2/11
1963 5/6 – until 1964 3/15
1966 6/10 – 8/22
1972 4/1 – 5/18
1972 11/14 – until 1973 1/25
1975 4/18 – 7/18
1975 9/11 – until 1976 2/25
1978 5/24 – 8/4
1984 2/27 – 7/4
1984 10/23 – until 1985 1/9
1987 4/2 – 6/15
1987 10/27 – until 1988 2/1
1989 9/11 – 12/15
1990 5/4 – 7/19
1996 2/6 – 12/24
1999 3/17 – 5/24
2001 8/18 – until 2002 1/26
2002 4/4 – 7/3
2008 1/20 – 12/7
2011 2/27 – 5/14

SATURN CHALLENGING
1938 3/25 – until 1939 5/1
1944 8/21 – 12/27
1945 5/10 – 9/27
1945 12/16 – until 1946 6/11
1959 12/15 – until 1961 2/3
1961 9/11 – 10/14
1967 5/4 – 10/23
1968 1/24 – 6/17
1968 9/27 – until 1969 3/7
1974 6/23 – until 1975 7/23
1989 1/17 – 8/28
1989 9/25 – until 1990 3/17
1990 6/24 – 12/12
1997 3/8 – until 1998 4/14
2003 8/1 – until 2004 1/31
2004 4/12 – 9/1
2005 1/19 – 5/21

URANUS CHALLENGING
1950 8/6 – until 1954 7/18
1990 1/30 – until 1994 11/22
2012 5/21 – Continues

NEPTUNE CHALLENGING
1987 2/24 – until 1995 11/24

PLUTO CHALLENGING
2011 3/28 – Continues

JUPITER SPECIAL
1945 9/29 – 12/21
1946 4/5 – 8/21
1957 9/13 – 11/29
1958 5/15 – 7/23
1969 8/28 – 11/11
1980 12/11 – until 1981 3/10
1981 8/9 – 10/26
1992 11/17 – until 1993 4/18
1993 7/14 – 10/11
2004 10/30 – until 2005 9/25

SATURN SPECIAL
1951 10/15 – until 1952 11/28
1953 4/20 – 8/24
1980 11/27 – until 1981 3/13
1981 8/21 – until 1982 10/4
2010 9/28 – until 2011 11/10
2012 5/26 – 7/24

URANUS SPECIAL
1969 11/20 – until 1973 10/17

NEPTUNE SPECIAL
1945 11/5 – until 1954 7/31

PLUTO SPECIAL
1974 10/20 – until 1981 9/27

October 10

SUN: LIBRA • DECANATE: AQUARIUS/URANUS • DEGREE: 16°5–17°5 LIBRA • MODE: CARDINAL • ELEMENT: AIR

Your Personal Powers

Ambitious, independent, and idealistic, you are a resourceful individual with resolute character and determination. With your practical skills and strong personality, you often aim high and rise to positions of authority. Although you show a confident front, underneath you may feel sensitive or vulnerable. Your ruling planet, Venus, grants you good social skills and innate artistic, creative, or musical talents you may wish to develop. As an enterprising and creative person, you usually want to display your individuality. You gain more power when you stay open-minded and listen in a detached manner to the opinions of people even when they seem too critical. You lose power if you become selfish or overreact. Nevertheless, usually optimistic and resourceful, you empower yourself by being self-disciplined and showing a willingness to work hard for your ideals. As a determined person who wants to achieve a great deal, guard against rushing into commitments too quickly or overestimating your abilities. Through perseverance and inner faith, you can improve your intuitive skills and overcome any obstacles in your way.

Your Powers of Attraction in Relationships

You are quietly ambitious, and people admire your subtle charm and natural generosity. You are gregarious and friendly but also forceful and persuasive. Although independent and freedom-loving, your need to be in a loving and supportive relationship implies that you are sensitive and affectionate to partners. If challenged in relationships, however, avoid being resentful or letting people take advantage of your kindness. You are often drawn to confident and intelligent people who can stimulate your mind and offer you variety and excitement. Alternatively, you may be attracted to enterprising individuals who are clever at business and share your ambitions or goals. A tendency to be easily bored implies that you prefer the company of people who can appreciate your quick wit and sharp intellect.

Your attractive qualities: astute, enterprising, authoritative, progressive, forceful, optimistic, independent, gregarious, knowledgeable, confident, entertaining, easygoing, sharp, observant, organized, charming, selfless, creative, multitalented, liberal, friendly, generous

Your less attractive qualities: stubborn, jealous, egotistical, too proud, easily hurt, overbearing, moody, indecisive, impatient, materialistic, unexpressed deep feelings, doubting or too competitive, critical, overindulgent, willful, too emotional

Your Venus Power

The planet Venus has a great deal of influence on your powers of attraction. Below are four possible Venus types for women and men. To find your Venus you need to go to page 771, where you will find the Venus table and extra information. The planet Mars also affects your powers of attraction. To find your Mars table and interpretation go to page 761.

WOMEN WITH VENUS IN VIRGO: Intelligent and discriminating, you are usually drawn to polite and refined individuals. As a perfectionist you may be keen to analyze and criticize yourself, but be careful of continually going over your partner's shortcomings. By focusing on how you can make positive improvements in yourself and in your relationships you avoid becoming skeptical or confused. You empower yourself when you display kind and caring concern for the well-being of loved ones and spontaneously offer your practical assistance.

MEN WITH VENUS IN VIRGO: A love of order usually means that you are attracted to refined individuals with analytical or practical abilities. You and your partner may be working together or serving similar causes. As you constantly analyze partnerships in order to improve them, you are likely to use former relationships as a point of reference and compare them to your present partner. As you are helpful and kind, others usually rely on your good judgment and often turn to you for advice or practical assistance.

WOMEN WITH VENUS IN LIBRA: Usually you are attractive and sociable with an easygoing manner. Your love of beauty, harmony, and pleasure implies that you are a romantic with a desire for love and affection. Once in a relationship you need to learn to negotiate your position rather than adapt to the wishes of others and compromise just to keep the peace. Nevertheless, your advanced social skills and strong sense of fair play can help you succeed in any social or romantic situation.

MEN WITH VENUS IN LIBRA: Your good social skills, charming personality, and refined manner usually make you attractive to the opposite sex. Equally, you desire a sophisticated partner with grace, elegance, and a strong sense of style.

Although you have the ability to be persuasive and irresistible to others, avoid manipulative love games. Nevertheless, your natural diplomacy and sense of fair play help you to relate to people in all social situations. With your love of balance and harmony you seek a partner who is also moderate, easygoing, and loving.

WOMEN WITH VENUS IN SCORPIO: With a natural psychic gift for penetrating the feelings of others, you can often help partners transform emotional challenges or sexual difficulties. When you fall in love, your strong feelings and determination give you a potent force that others find attractive and seductive. Although you know what really turns people on, your most profound desire is usually for the deepness and closeness of real love and intimacy in an enduring relationship.

MEN WITH VENUS IN SCORPIO: In relationships you possess a sensitive understanding of your partner's deeper nature. Although you are strongly attached to those you love, you may have to be careful that your feelings do not turn into jealousy or possessiveness. When you fall in love it is often with power and an emotional intensity. You are attracted to partners who can share your passion and display strong feelings of sexuality like your own.

WOMEN WITH VENUS IN SAGITTARIUS: Optimistic and fun-loving, you love adventure and seek a partner who can expand your horizons. Being truthful and direct, you often say what you think, and at times you may be naively tactless. A need for expansion and prosperity suggests that you may enjoy traveling with your friends or partner. Being lighthearted and idealistic, once you have given your heart to someone you will stay honorable and loyal.

MEN WITH VENUS IN SAGITTARIUS: You are usually attracted to partners who are knowledgeable or well-traveled. Enthusiastic and optimistic, you often respond quickly to love offers and enter relationships with enthusiasm. Generally you seek to expand your social circle, and meeting people from all walks of life can bring the variety and fun that you seek in life. Although you are generous and honest, your partners may sometimes accuse you of being overly optimistic or too blunt.

To read all about your Outer Planets and work out how to use your personalized timetable, go to Section Three, page 789.

Your Personalized Timetable

JUPITER BENEFICIAL
1938 1/25 – 4/8
1938 9/13 – 11/23
1941 7/2 – until **1942** 5/16
1943 8/22 – 10/12
1944 2/16 – 6/8
1947 12/15 – until **1948** 2/1
1948 7/6 – 9/24
1950 1/9 – 3/19
1953 6/14 – 9/9
1953 11/19 – until **1954** 4/26
1955 8/5 – 9/22
1959 11/29 – until **1960** 1/13
1961 12/22 – until **1962** 3/1
1965 5/29 – 8/11
1965 12/31 – until **1966** 4/1
1967 7/21 – 9/5
1971 11/13 – 12/28
1973 4/11 – 7/20
1973 12/1 – until **1974** 2/13
1977 5/12 – 7/22
1979 7/4 – 8/19
1983 10/27 – 12/12
1985 3/18 – 9/4
1985 10/31 – until **1986** 1/28
1989 4/25 – 7/5
1990 10/24 – until **1991** 1/6
1991 6/15 – 8/3
1995 2/8 – 5/25
1995 10/7 – 11/26
1997 2/27 – until **1998** 1/11
2000 8/18 – 11/10
2001 4/5 – 6/18
2002 9/27 – until **2003** 2/15
2003 5/22 – 7/18
2007 1/17 – 7/6
2007 9/7 – 11/10
2009 2/10 – 5/5
2009 7/26 – 12/22
2012 7/21 – Continues

SATURN BENEFICIAL
1942 7/16 – 12/9
1943 4/4 – 8/20
1943 11/29 – until **1944** 5/6
1947 7/29 – 10/28
1948 1/10 – 7/12
1957 1/22 – 5/26
1957 10/22 – until **1958** 1/19
1958 6/27 – 10/18
1962 3/20 – 7/26
1962 12/17 – until **1964** 2/5
1972 5/19 – until **1973** 6/18
1976 9/7 – until **1977** 2/28
1977 5/22 – 8/21
1986 11/28 – until **1987** 11/27
1992 1/23 – until **1993** 3/11
1993 9/26 – 11/28
2001 6/26 – until **2002** 1/18
2002 3/1 – 7/28
2002 12/31 – until **2003** 4/14
2006 7/11 – 10/1
2007 2/13 – 6/22

URANUS BENEFICIAL
1943 8/15 – until **1948** 5/16
1957 10/27 – until **1960** 8/14
1984 1/6 – until **1986** 11/26
1997 4/20 – until **2002** 2/7

NEPTUNE BENEFICIAL
1975 2/7 – until **1980** 11/18
2001 4/6 – until **2009** 12/27

PLUTO BENEFICIAL
1945 10/4 – until **1953** 6/25
2000 1/1 – until **2004** 11/27

JUPITER CHALLENGING
1939 7/15 – 8/12
1940 2/13 – 4/22
1942 7/17 – 10/21
1942 12/4 – until **1943** 6/3
1948 12/23 – until **1949** 3/7
1949 8/12 – 10/25

1951 6/3 – 10/8
1952 1/20 – 4/5
1954 7/1 – 9/16
1955 1/19 – 5/12
1960 12/7 – until **1961** 2/15
1963 5/11 – until **1964** 3/19
1966 6/15 – 8/27
1967 3/18 – 3/24
1972 11/19 – until **1973** 1/29
1975 4/23 – 8/2
1975 8/27 – until **1976** 3/1
1978 5/28 – 8/9
1984 3/5 – 6/26
1984 10/29 – until **1985** 1/13
1987 4/6 – 6/21
1987 10/20 – until **1988** 2/7
1989 9/19 – 12/7
1990 5/9 – 7/24
1996 2/11 – 8/14
1996 9/23 – 12/28
1999 3/21 – 5/29
2001 8/23 – until **2002** 1/18
2002 4/13 – 7/7
2008 1/25 – 12/11
2011 3/4 – 5/14

SATURN CHALLENGING
1938 4/2 – until **1939** 5/9
1939 12/22 – until **1940** 1/3
1944 9/1 – 12/15
1945 5/19 – 10/15
1945 11/28 – until **1946** 6/20
1959 12/23 – until **1961** 2/12
1961 8/19 – 11/5
1967 5/14 – 10/10
1968 2/4 – 7/2
1968 9/12 – until **1969** 3/16
1974 7/1 – until **1975** 7/30
1989 1/25 – 8/3
1989 10/19 – until **1990** 4/2
1990 6/7 – 12/21
1997 3/16 – until **1998** 4/22
2003 8/10 – until **2004** 1/17
2004 4/26 – 9/11
2005 1/6 – 5/31

URANUS CHALLENGING
1950 8/27 – until **1955** 5/16
1990 2/20 – until **1994** 12/13
2012 6/29 – Continues

NEPTUNE CHALLENGING
1988 1/18 – until **1995** 12/25

PLUTO CHALLENGING
2012 2/3 – Continues

JUPITER SPECIAL
1945 10/4 – 12/29
1946 3/28 – 8/27
1957 9/18 – 12/5
1958 5/6 – 8/1
1969 9/2 – 11/16
1980 12/20 – until **1981** 3/1
1981 8/14 – 10/31
1992 11/23 – until **1993** 4/10
1993 7/22 – 10/15
2004 11/4 – until **2005** 9/30

SATURN SPECIAL
1951 10/23 – until **1952** 5/24
1952 6/27 – 12/8
1953 4/7 – 9/3
1980 12/10 – until **1981** 2/27
1981 8/30 – until **1982** 10/13
2010 10/6 – until **2011** 11/19
2012 5/9 – 8/10

URANUS SPECIAL
1969 12/17 – until **1974** 8/14

NEPTUNE SPECIAL
1945 12/17 – until **1954** 9/11

PLUTO SPECIAL
1974 11/19 – until **1982** 8/8

October 11

SUN: LIBRA · DECANATE: AQUARIUS/URANUS · DEGREE: 17°5–18°5 LIBRA · MODE: AIR · ELEMENT: MUTABLE

Your Personal Powers

Sociable and friendly, you are an enthusiastic and intelligent individual with an engaging manner and good communication skills. Your ruling plant, Venus, grants you refined taste, a love of beauty, and a charismatic personality. As you often learn new subjects with relative ease, you gain power when you invest time in improving your knowledge and skills. Although you enjoy being part of a team, by nature you are an independent individual with strong beliefs. By letting your mental creativity flow, you can also display how inventive and original you are. Your love of freedom suggests that you are idealistic, enterprising, and keen on adventure. Young at heart, you enjoy spontaneity and therefore dislike being ordered or restricted. Being multitalented and articulate, you can also be very persuasive. When you are inspired by something new, your positive outlook and high spirits indicate that you can accomplish a great deal, yet your success often depends on self-empowerment through self-discipline, purposefulness, and responsibility.

Your Powers of Attraction in Relationships

You are charismatic and sociable, and people are usually drawn to your charming and enthusiastic manner. Friendly by nature, you have a sense of style and liberal attitude that attracts partners with relative ease. Although you may be clever and intuitive, sometimes you can attract unsuitable partners. Usually honest and direct, you enjoy sharing your many interests with others and can be an excellent companion. Although you can be serious about your close relationships, your spontaneous and idealistic nature suggests that you also need to maintain some freedom or independence. You may, however, have to be careful not to appear too detached and self-reliant as others may interpret your behavior as nonchalant or too aloof. Nevertheless, when you find a spiritual bond with your partner, you can be very romantic, loyal, and loving.

Your attractive qualities: balanced, charming, focused, objective, enthusiastic, inspired, intelligent, friendly, inventive, humanitarian, articulate, witty, intelligent, intuitive, idealistic, personal magnetism, youthful, independent thinker, enterprising, persuasive, diplomatic

Your less attractive qualities: materialistic, disinterested, impatient, restless, easily hurt, lazy, anxious, manipulative, love of luxury, stressed, extremist, take the easy route, overconfident, impractical, codependent

Your Venus Power

The planet Venus has a great deal of influence on your powers of attraction. Below are four possible Venus types for women and men. To find your Venus you need to go to page 771, where you will find the Venus table and extra information. The planet Mars also affects your powers of attraction. To find your Mars table and interpretation go to page 761.

WOMEN WITH VENUS IN VIRGO: In relationships you can be modest and unassuming but desire perfection. You usually analyze your partnerships until you feel you understand them to the last little detail in order to improve them. A problem usually arises when you become too critical either of partners or yourself and indulge in being skeptical or faultfinding. As you are modest, others may not be aware of the strong sensuality beneath your well-groomed exterior.

MEN WITH VENUS IN VIRGO: A love of order usually indicates that you are attracted to refined individuals with analytical or practical abilities. You and your partner may be working together or serving similar causes. As you constantly analyze partnerships in order to improve them, you are likely to use former relationships as a point of reference and compare them to your present partner. As you are helpful and kind, others usually rely on your good judgment and often turn to you for advice or practical assistance.

WOMEN WITH VENUS IN LIBRA: Attractive, refined, and conscious of the needs of others, you usually desire harmonious relationships. As a peacemaker with good negotiating skills you can smooth out difficulties with others, but your dislike of confrontation may sometimes leave you refusing to take a stand or compromising too many of your own needs. Courteous, stylish, and charming with polished social skills, you are an expert at relating to others in a gracious and civilized manner.

MEN WITH VENUS IN LIBRA: As a sociable and friendly individual with an eye for beauty, you are amorous and charming. You are a natural gentleman and your ideal partner usually has an elegant appearance, artistic appreciation, and good taste. Your relationships benefit when you resist the temptation to take the easy way out or put too much emphasis on vanity and high living. Intellectual and naturally refined,

you seek a loving partner who can share your romantic and sophisticated aspirations.

WOMEN WITH VENUS IN SCORPIO: Loving and passionate, you are often sensitive with deep feelings and strong powers of attraction. A love for the truth coupled with a tendency to be suspicious can be an influence that motivates you to delve deep into the activities of your partner. When in love or in a relationship that matters, you will often bend over backward to cooperate. Although loyal, guard against losing sight of your own needs and desires.

MEN WITH VENUS IN SCORPIO: As you are emotionally intense and passionate, personal relationships are probably a major factor in your own transformation. Being sensitive yet loyal, you are usually attracted to forceful partners who can express themselves intimately but intensely. Rather than seek easy and simple relationships you are drawn to partners who act as a catalyst for your own internal changes. Through your relationships with your partners you can unravel your own motives and understand your deep-seated feelings or emotional insecurities.

WOMEN WITH VENUS IN SAGITTARIUS: Optimistic and fun-loving, you love adventure and seek a partner who can expand your horizons. Being truthful and direct, you often say what you think, and at times you may be naively tactless. A need for expansion and prosperity suggests that you may enjoy traveling with your friends or partner. Being lighthearted and idealistic, once you have given your heart to someone you will stay honorable and loyal.

MEN WITH VENUS IN SAGITTARIUS: You are usually attracted to partners who are knowledgeable or well-traveled. Enthusiastic and optimistic, you often respond quickly to love offers and enter relationships with enthusiasm. Generally you seek to expand your social circle, and meeting people from all walks of life can bring the variety and fun that you seek in life. Although you are generous and honest, your partners may sometimes accuse you of being overly optimistic or too blunt.

To read all about your Outer Planets and work out how to use your personalized timetable, go to Section Three, page 789.

Your Personalized Timetable

JUPITER BENEFICIAL
1938 1/30 – 4/13
1938 9/4 – 12/1
1941 7/7 – until **1942** 5/20
1943 8/26 – 10/18
1944 2/9 – 6/14
1947 12/19 – until **1948** 2/7
1948 6/28 – 10/2
1950 1/13 – 3/23
1953 6/19 – 9/20
1953 11/9 – until **1954** 5/1
1955 8/10 – 9/27
1956 3/23 – 5/12
1959 12/3 – until **1960** 1/18
1961 12/27 – until **1962** 3/5
1965 6/2 – 8/17
1965 12/24 – until **1966** 4/8
1967 7/25 – 9/9
1971 11/17 – until **1972** 1/1
1973 4/18 – 7/12
1973 12/7 – until **1974** 2/17
1977 5/17 – 7/27
1979 7/9 – 8/24
1983 11/1 – 12/16
1985 3/23 – 8/25
1985 11/10 – until **1986** 2/1
1989 4/30 – 7/9
1990 11/3 – 12/26
1991 6/20 – 8/8
1995 2/16 – 5/16
1995 10/13 – 12/1
1997 3/4 – until **1998** 1/15
2000 8/27 – 11/1
2001 4/11 – 6/22
2002 10/3 – until **2003** 2/7
2003 5/29 – 7/23
2007 1/23 – 6/26
2007 9/17 – 11/14
2009 2/14 – 5/14
2009 7/17 – 12/27
2012 7/27 – Continues

SATURN BENEFICIAL
1942 7/26 – 11/26
1943 4/14 – 9/3
1943 11/15 – until **1944** 5/15
1947 8/5 – 11/18
1947 12/19 – until **1948** 7/20
1957 2/4 – 5/12
1957 11/1 – until **1958** 1/29
1958 6/13 – 10/29
1962 4/2 – 7/12
1962 12/27 – until **1964** 2/14
1972 5/27 – until **1973** 6/25
1976 9/15 – until **1977** 2/14
1977 6/4 – 8/29
1986 12/6 – until **1987** 12/6
1992 1/31 – until **1993** 3/20
1993 9/9 – 12/13
2001 7/5 – 12/30
2002 3/19 – 8/6
2002 12/19 – until **2003** 4/25
2006 7/19 – 10/12
2007 1/31 – 7/2

URANUS BENEFICIAL
1944 6/8 – until **1948** 6/2
1958 8/12 – until **1961** 6/10
1984 1/27 – until **1986** 12/12
1998 2/10 – until **2002** 12/9

NEPTUNE BENEFICIAL
1975 12/29 – until **1981** 10/9
2002 2/24 – until **2010** 1/26

PLUTO BENEFICIAL
1946 9/10 – until **1953** 7/31
2000 2/4 – until **2005** 10/20

JUPITER CHALLENGING
1940 2/18 – 4/26
1942 7/22 – until **1943** 6/8
1948 12/28 – until **1949** 3/12

1949 8/3 – 11/2
1951 6/9 – 9/30
1952 1/26 – 4/9
1954 7/5 – 9/23
1955 1/11 – 5/18
1960 12/11 – until **1961** 2/20
1963 5/16 – until **1964** 3/24
1966 6/19 – 9/1
1967 2/24 – 4/15
1972 11/24 – until **1973** 2/2
1975 4/27 – until **1976** 3/5
1978 6/2 – 8/13
1984 3/11 – 6/18
1984 11/4 – until **1985** 1/18
1987 4/11 – 6/27
1987 10/12 – until **1988** 2/13
1989 9/29 – 11/27
1990 5/15 – 7/28
1996 2/17 – 8/2
1996 10/5 – until **1997** 1/2
1999 3/25 – 6/3
1999 12/5 – until **2000** 1/5
2001 8/29 – until **2002** 1/10
2002 4/21 – 7/12
2008 1/29 – 12/16
2011 3/8 – 5/14

SATURN CHALLENGING
1938 4/10 – until **1939** 5/17
1939 11/24 – until **1940** 1/30
1944 9/14 – 12/1
1945 5/28 – until **1946** 6/28
1959 12/31 – until **1961** 2/21
1961 8/3 – 11/19
1967 5/24 – 9/27
1968 2/14 – 7/27
1968 8/17 – until **1969** 3/24
1974 7/9 – until **1975** 8/7
1989 2/4 – 7/18
1989 11/2 – until **1990** 12/30
1997 3/24 – until **1998** 4/30
2003 8/19 – until **2004** 1/4
2004 5/7 – 9/23
2004 12/25 – until **2005** 6/9

URANUS CHALLENGING
1950 10/6 – until **1955** 6/7
1990 3/26 – until **1994** 12/31

NEPTUNE CHALLENGING
1988 2/18 – until **1996** 11/16

PLUTO CHALLENGING
2012 3/20 – Continues

JUPITER SPECIAL
1945 10/8 – until **1946** 1/6
1946 3/19 – 9/1
1957 9/23 – 12/10
1958 4/28 – 8/9
1969 9/7 – 11/21
1980 12/31 – until **1981** 2/18
1981 8/20 – 11/4
1992 11/29 – until **1993** 4/2
1993 7/29 – 10/20
2004 11/9 – until **2005** 5/17
2005 6/23 – 10/5

SATURN SPECIAL
1951 11/1 – until **1952** 5/2
1952 7/19 – 12/20
1953 3/25 – 9/13
1980 12/30 – until **1981** 2/7
1981 9/8 – until **1982** 10/21
2010 10/14 – until **2011** 11/28
2012 4/25 – 8/23

URANUS SPECIAL
1970 10/6 – until **1974** 9/5

NEPTUNE SPECIAL
1946 11/1 – until **1954** 10/10

PLUTO SPECIAL
1975 10/11 – until **1982** 9/13

October 12

Your Personal Powers

Your friendly manner and social skills often conceal the fact that you are a highly intelligent individual with an astute mind and inspired ideas. As an independent thinker with analytical abilities, you gain power by using your mind creatively and letting your imagination flow. Your ruling planet, Venus, grants you refined or artistic taste and an interest in social affairs. Naturally ambitious, charming, and persuasive, you can succeed admirably when you use your diplomacy to deal with people on a personal level. Your talent for leadership implies that you also gain power when you think as part of a team and resist the temptation to be too demanding or critical. With your need for personal self-expression, you can also be creative or possess a talent with words. You lose some of your power, however, when you let worry or indecision undermine your great potential for success. By focusing on your inner faith and strength, you empower yourself to become more disciplined and achieve success.

Your Powers of Attraction in Relationships

You are captivating and strong-willed, and people admire your inventive mind and daring nature. While you have a strong need for recognition, you can attract others more easily by being friendly and charming. You are usually drawn to forceful and independent individuals who are shrewd and confident. Alternatively, you can be attracted to hardworking people who show dedication and strong self-discipline. Although being intuitive and sensitive indicates that you are able to see your partners for who they really are, resist the temptation to be critical or faultfinding. Even though you can be faithful and loving, when you are bored or uncertain about how you truly feel you may become confrontational and cause tension. Sharing new ideas with your partner or being enterprising usually brings a breath of fresh air into your relationships.

Your attractive qualities: clever, intuitive, intelligent, attractive, independent, disciplined, confident, productive, tactful, original, cooperative, charming, enthusiastic, sociable, hardworking, creative, shrewd, self-assured, articulate, witty, motivated, pragmatic, determined

Your less attractive qualities: stubborn, imposing, arrogant, pessimistic, too reserved, selfish, uncooperative, humorless, too sensitive, lack of self-esteem, insecure, restless, too serious, manipulative, demanding, tactless

Your Venus Power

The planet Venus has a great deal of influence on your powers of attraction. Below are four possible Venus types for women and men. To find your Venus you need to go to page 771, where you will find the Venus table and extra information. The planet Mars also affects your powers of attraction. To find your Mars table and interpretation go to page 761.

WOMEN WITH VENUS IN VIRGO: Articulate and straightforward in your relationships, you attract others with your genuine concern for their well-being. By being understanding and a good listener you are able to show your love and friendship. With your analytical approach to relationships, however, you may have to be careful of becoming too matter-of-fact. You often display your concern for the welfare of others by your willingness to offer practical help and assistance. You usually seek a partner who is willing to work as hard on relationships as you are.

MEN WITH VENUS IN VIRGO: Although you are constantly analyzing your relationships in order to understand and improve them, you may nevertheless need to refrain from continuously mulling over issues that can cause anxiety. You are happiest when you are able to help loved ones in practical ways and forget yourself in your willingness to be of service to others. You seek a partner who has high standards and can be as pragmatic and hardworking as you. Ideally they should also be impeccably dressed with a fine analytical mind.

WOMEN WITH VENUS IN LIBRA: Gracious, charming, and sociable with a sense of style, you have no trouble attracting admirers. With your natural diplomatic skills and desire for harmony you usually like to keep the peace and avoid confrontations, but be careful of failing to take a stand when it is necessary. Romantic and easygoing yourself, you are attracted to affectionate and refined individuals who share your love of peace, justice, and fair play.

MEN WITH VENUS IN LIBRA: Courteous and refined, you are attracted to beautiful and elegant people. You are looking for a partner who can share your natural good taste and enjoy an intellectual conversation. Disliking conflict, you may have to be careful not to go along with others just to keep the peace.

Your ideal partner will appreciate beauty and the little luxuries of life as well as possess good social skills. You have a strong sense of social etiquette yourself so you need an intelligent and sophisticated partner.

WOMEN WITH VENUS IN SCORPIO: Loving and passionate, you are often sensitive with deep feelings and strong powers of attraction. A love for the truth coupled with a tendency to be suspicious can be an influence that motivates you to delve deep into the activities of your partner. When in love or in a relationship that matters, you will often bend over backward to cooperate. Although loyal, guard against losing sight of your own needs and desires.

MEN WITH VENUS IN SCORPIO: As you are emotionally intense and passionate, personal relationships are probably a major factor in your own transformation. Being sensitive yet loyal, you are usually attracted to forceful partners who can express themselves intimately but intensely. Rather than seek easy and simple relationships you are drawn to partners who act as a catalyst for your own internal changes. Through your relationships with your partners you can unravel your own motives and understand your deep-seated feelings or emotional insecurities.

WOMEN WITH VENUS IN SAGITTARIUS: Sociable, warm, and friendly, you possess an honest and frank style in your relationships. Being naturally gregarious, you want others to share your enthusiasm and enjoy encouraging the people you love. You fare better when you have a sense of personal freedom within a relationship and are usually generous with the faults of others. You need a partner who can share your need to explore and take risks whether through travel, education, or recreation.

MEN WITH VENUS IN SAGITTARIUS: When in love you are open and friendly with a need for a partner who can share your adventurous spirit and sense of fun. Be careful, however, that your desire for freedom does not cause you to avoid commitment. You prefer your partners to be positive, direct, and generous in spirit. Being outspoken as well as an idealist, you usually enjoy a partner with whom you can share your strong opinions. Alternatively, you may wish to explore life together whether through travel, education, or by having fun.

To read all about your Outer Planets and work out how to use your personalized timetable, go to Section Three, page 789.

Your Personalized Timetable

JUPITER BENEFICIAL
1938 2/3 – 4/19
1938 8/27 – 12/8
1941 7/12 – until 1942 5/25
1943 8/31 – 10/25
1944 2/1 – 6/21
1947 12/24 – until 1948 2/13
1948 6/20 – 10/9
1950 1/18 – 3/28
1953 6/23 – 10/11
1953 10/20 – until 1954 5/6
1955 8/14 – 10/2
1956 3/12 – 5/23
1959 12/8 – until 1960 1/23
1961 12/31 – until 1962 3/10
1965 6/6 – 8/23
1965 12/17 – until 1966 4/15
1967 7/30 – 9/14
1971 11/22 – until 1972 1/5
1973 4/27 – 7/3
1973 12/12 – until 1974 2/21
1977 5/21 – 8/1
1978 2/5 – 3/6
1979 7/13 – 8/28
1983 11/5 – 12/21
1985 3/29 – 8/17
1985 11/18 – until 1986 2/5
1989 5/5 – 7/14
1990 11/20 – 12/9
1991 6/26 – 8/13
1995 2/24 – 5/7
1995 10/18 – 12/5
1997 3/8 – until 1998 1/20
2000 9/7 – 10/21
2001 4/16 – 6/27
2002 10/9 – until 2003 1/30
2003 6/5 – 7/28
2007 1/28 – 6/17
2007 9/25 – 11/19
2009 2/19 – until 2010 1/1
2012 8/2 – Continues

SATURN BENEFICIAL
1942 8/7 – 11/14
1943 4/23 – 9/25
1943 10/24 – until 1944 5/23
1947 8/13 – until 1948 7/28
1957 2/19 – 4/26
1957 11/10 – until 1958 2/10
1958 5/31 – 11/8
1962 4/17 – 6/26
1963 1/5 – until 1964 2/22
1972 6/4 – until 1973 7/3
1976 9/25 – until 1977 2/2
1977 6/15 – 9/6
1986 12/15 – until 1987 12/14
1992 2/8 – until 1993 3/30
1993 8/26 – 12/25
2001 7/14 – 12/16
2002 4/1 – 8/17
2002 12/7 – until 2003 5/4
2006 7/27 – 10/24
2007 1/18 – 7/11

URANUS BENEFICIAL
1944 6/25 – until 1948 6/19
1958 8/28 – until 1961 7/3
1984 3/1 – until 1987 10/12
1998 2/28 – until 2003 1/4

NEPTUNE BENEFICIAL
1976 1/31 – until 1981 11/15
2002 3/29 – until 2010 12/20

PLUTO BENEFICIAL
1947 8/21 – until 1954 7/7
2000 12/22 – until 2005 11/22

JUPITER CHALLENGING
1940 2/23 – 5/1
1942 7/26 – until 1943 6/13
1949 1/1 – 3/18

1949 7/26 – 11/9
1951 6/15 – 9/23
1952 2/1 – 4/14
1954 7/9 – 9/30
1955 1/4 – 5/24
1960 12/16 – until 1961 2/24
1963 5/21 – 11/12
1963 12/28 – until 1964 3/28
1966 6/23 – 9/6
1967 2/13 – 4/26
1972 11/29 – until 1973 2/7
1975 5/1 – until 1976 3/10
1978 6/7 – 8/18
1984 3/19 – 6/10
1984 11/10 – until 1985 1/22
1987 4/15 – 7/4
1987 10/5 – until 1988 2/19
1989 10/12 – 11/14
1990 5/20 – 8/1
1996 2/22 – 7/23
1996 10/15 – until 1997 1/6
1999 3/29 – 6/8
1999 11/21 – until 2000 1/18
2001 9/4 – until 2002 1/2
2002 4/27 – 7/16
2008 2/3 – 12/21
2011 3/12 – 5/19

SATURN CHALLENGING
1938 4/18 – until 1939 5/26
1939 11/8 – until 1940 2/13
1944 10/3 – 11/11
1945 6/5 – until 1946 7/5
1960 1/9 – until 1961 3/3
1961 7/20 – 11/30
1967 6/5 – 9/14
1968 2/24 – until 1969 4/1
1974 7/16 – until 1975 8/15
1976 3/6 – 4/17
1989 2/14 – 7/5
1989 11/14 – until 1991 1/7
1997 4/1 – until 1998 5/8
2003 8/30 – 12/23
2004 5/17 – 10/7
2004 12/9 – until 2005 6/17

URANUS CHALLENGING
1951 7/14 – until 1955 6/25
1991 1/12 – until 1995 1/17

NEPTUNE CHALLENGING
1989 1/14 – until 1996 12/20

JUPITER SPECIAL
1945 10/13 – until 1946 1/18
1946 3/7 – 9/7
1957 9/27 – 12/16
1958 4/20 – 8/16
1969 9/11 – 11/26
1970 6/8 – 7/8
1981 8/25 – 11/9
1992 12/5 – until 1993 3/25
1993 8/5 – 10/24
2004 11/14 – until 2005 5/4
2005 7/7 – 10/9

SATURN SPECIAL
1951 11/10 – until 1952 4/17
1952 8/2 – until 1953 1/4
1953 3/9 – 9/22
1981 9/16 – until 1982 10/29
2010 10/23 – until 2011 12/8
2012 4/12 – 9/2

URANUS SPECIAL
1970 10/22 – until 1974 9/24

NEPTUNE SPECIAL
1946 12/7 – until 1955 9/7

PLUTO SPECIAL
1975 11/7 – until 1982 10/9

October 13

SUN: LIBRA • DECANATE: AQUARIUS/URANUS • DEGREE: 19°5–20°5 LIBRA • MODE: MUTABLE • ELEMENT: AIR

Your Personal Powers

Creative, witty, and ambitious, your charming and gregarious personality often disguises your powerful emotions and dramatic nature. Your ruling planet, Venus, endows you with a love of beauty, artistic talents, and refined taste. Being intuitive and mentally sharp implies that you can comprehend ideas and concepts quickly or be creative and imaginative. You gain power by using your detached or analytical approach when dealing with people or situations. By being stubborn or bossy you can overwhelm others and lose some of your personal charm. Nevertheless, resourceful and ambitious, your determination to succeed indicates that you are hardworking and responsible. Since knowledge often boosts your self-confidence and improves your mental self-discipline, you empower yourself through any form of education or higher learning. You are at your happiest, however, when you can be creative or when you receive recognition for your talents. Alternatively, as an enterprising idealist with passionate beliefs, you may be involved in campaigns for social reforms.

Your Powers of Attraction in Relationships

Romantic and loving, you dislike being alone, so your need for a close relationship is usually very strong. You are friendly and outgoing, and people admire your gracious manner, spontaneity, and enthusiasm. Often affectionate and generous, you are an excellent host and an entertaining companion. Your cool exterior, however, can frequently hide your sensitivity or anxiety. Nevertheless, you should resist losing self-esteem by being too dependent on others. Although showing your compassion and benevolence can impress others, guard against being extravagant or excessive. You are usually attracted to people who are sociable and have a refined style. Alternatively, you may be drawn to individuals with a strong dramatic sense. A need for encouragement or acknowledgment indicates that you feel happier when you have a supportive partner.

Your attractive qualities: ambitious, knowledgeable, focused, creative, loving, self-expressive, enterprising, optimistic, independent, cooperative, persuasive, practical, gregarious, charming, diplomatic, tolerant, responsible, disciplined, productive, enthusiastic, compassionate, generous

Your less attractive qualities: stubborn, frustrated, impulsive, indecisive, worried, bossy, too sensitive, domineering, restless, unrealistic, tense, insecure, negative thinking, rebellious, melodramatic, manipulative, moody

Your Venus Power

The planet Venus has a great deal of influence on your powers of attraction. Below are four possible Venus types for women and men. To find your Venus you need to go to page 771, where you will find the Venus table and extra information. The planet Mars also affects your powers of attraction. To find your Mars table and interpretation go to page 761.

WOMEN WITH VENUS IN VIRGO: In relationships you can be modest and unassuming but desire perfection. You usually analyze your partnerships until you feel you understand them to the last little detail in order to improve them. A problem usually arises when you become too critical either of partners or yourself and indulge in being skeptical or faultfinding. As you are modest, others may not be aware of the strong sensuality beneath your well-groomed exterior.

MEN WITH VENUS IN VIRGO: Industrious and well-ordered, you relate to others in a considerate and down-to-earth way. You enjoy giving practical advice and being of service to those you love, even in small ways. Being a perfectionist you are drawn to partners with high morals or a strong work ethic. Partners who have strong analytical minds are very attractive to you, particularly if they are also clean and meticulously dressed.

WOMEN WITH VENUS IN LIBRA: Gracious, charming, and sociable with a sense of style, you have no trouble attracting admirers. With your natural diplomatic skills and desire for harmony you usually like to keep the peace and avoid confrontations, but be careful of failing to take a stand when it is necessary. Romantic and easygoing yourself, you are attracted to affectionate and refined individuals who share your love of peace, justice, and fair play.

MEN WITH VENUS IN LIBRA: Courteous and refined, you are attracted to beautiful and elegant people. You are looking for a partner who can share your natural good taste and enjoy an intellectual conversation. Disliking conflict, you may have to be careful not to go along with others just to keep the peace. Your ideal partner will appreciate beauty and the little luxuries

of life as well as possess good social skills. You have a strong sense of social etiquette yourself so you need an intelligent and sophisticated partner.

WOMEN WITH VENUS IN SCORPIO: With a natural psychic gift for penetrating the feelings of others, you can often help partners transform emotional challenges or sexual difficulties. When you fall in love, your strong feelings and determination give you a potent force that others find attractive and seductive. Although you know what really turns people on, your most profound desire is usually for the deepness and closeness of real love and intimacy in an enduring relationship.

MEN WITH VENUS IN SCORPIO: In relationships you possess a sensitive understanding of your partner's deeper nature. Although you are strongly attached to those you love, you may have to be careful that your feelings do not turn into jealousy or possessiveness. When you fall in love, it is often with emotional intensity and power. You are attracted to partners who can share your passion and display strong feelings of sexuality like your own.

WOMEN WITH VENUS IN SAGITTARIUS: Optimistic and fun-loving, you love adventure and seek a partner who can expand your horizons. Being truthful and direct you often say what you think, and at times you may be naively tactless. A need for expansion and prosperity suggests that you may enjoy traveling with your friends or partner. Being lighthearted and idealistic, once you have given your heart to someone you will stay honorable and loyal.

MEN WITH VENUS IN SAGITTARIUS: Usually you are attracted to partners who are knowledgeable or well-traveled. Enthusiastic and optimistic, you often respond quickly to love offers and enter relationships with enthusiasm. Generally you seek to expand your social circle, and meeting people from all walks of life can bring the variety and fun that you seek in life. Although you are generous and honest, your partners may sometimes accuse you of being overly optimistic or too blunt.

To read all about your Outer Planets and work out how to use your personalized timetable, go to Section Three, page 789.

To read all about your Outer Planets and work out how to use your personalized timetable, go to Section Three, page 789.

Your Personalized Timetable

JUPITER BENEFICIAL
1938 2/7 – 4/25
1938 8/20 – 12/15
1941 7/16 – until 1942 2/1
1942 2/9 – 5/29
1943 9/5 – 11/2
1944 1/24 – 6/26
1947 12/28 – until 1948 2/19
1948 6/12 – 10/16
1950 1/22 – 4/2
1953 6/27 – until 1954 5/11
1955 8/19 – 10/8
1956 3/3 – 6/1
1959 12/12 – until 1960 1/28
1960 7/31 – until 1960 9/9
1962 1/5 – until 1962 3/14
1965 6/11 – until 1965 8/30
1965 12/9 – until 1966 4/21
1967 8/3 – 9/19
1971 11/26 – until 1972 1/10
1973 5/9 – 6/21
1973 12/17 – until 1974 2/25
1977 5/25 – 8/6
1978 1/22 – 3/21
1979 7/18 – 9/2
1983 11/10 – 12/25
1985 4/3 – 8/9
1985 11/25 – until 1986 2/9
1989 5/9 – 7/18
1991 7/1 – 8/17
1995 3/7 – 4/26
1995 10/23 – 12/9
1997 3/13 – until 1998 1/24
2001 4/21 – 7/1
2002 10/16 – until 2003 1/23
2003 6/11 – 8/1
2007 2/3 – 6/9
2007 10/2 – 11/24
2009 2/23 – until 2010 1/6
2012 8/8 – Continues

SATURN BENEFICIAL
1942 8/21 – 10/30
1943 5/2 – until 1944 5/31
1947 8/21 – until 1948 8/5
1957 11/19 – until 1958 2/24
1958 5/15 – 11/18
1963 1/14 – until 1964 3/1
1972 6/11 – until 1973 7/11
1976 10/5 – until 1977 1/21
1977 6/24 – 9/14
1978 3/26 – 5/25
1986 12/23 – until 1987 12/23
1992 2/17 – until 1993 4/9
1993 8/13 – until 1994 1/5
2001 7/23 – 12/4
2002 4/11 – 8/29
2002 11/24 – until 2003 5/13
2006 8/4 – 11/9
2007 1/1 – 7/19

URANUS BENEFICIAL
1944 7/14 – until 1949 4/20
1958 9/15 – until 1961 7/21
1984 12/16 – until 1987 11/5
1998 3/20 – until 2003 1/24

NEPTUNE BENEFICIAL
1976 12/25 – until 1982 9/29
2003 2/20 – until 2011 1/22

PLUTO BENEFICIAL
1947 9/29 – until 1955 5/29
2001 1/21 – until 2006 10/11

JUPITER CHALLENGING
1940 2/27 – 5/5
1942 7/31 – until 1943 6/18
1949 1/5 – 3/24
1949 7/19 – 11/16

1951 6/23 – 9/15
1952 2/6 – 4/18
1954 7/14 – 10/7
1954 12/27 – until 1955 5/30
1960 12/20 – until 1961 3/1
1961 9/16 – 9/30
1963 5/26 – 11/1
1964 1/7 – 4/1
1966 6/28 – 9/11
1967 2/4 – 5/5
1972 12/3 – until 1973 2/11
1975 5/6 – until 1976 3/15
1978 6/11 – 8/23
1984 3/29 – 5/31
1984 11/15 – until 1985 1/26
1987 4/19 – 7/12
1987 9/27 – until 1988 2/24
1990 5/25 – 8/6
1996 2/28 – 7/15
1996 10/22 – until 1997 1/10
1999 4/2 – 6/13
1999 11/12 – until 2000 1/27
2001 9/10 – 12/26
2002 5/4 – 7/21
2008 2/8 – 12/25
2011 3/16 – 5/23

SATURN CHALLENGING
1938 4/26 – 11/30
1938 12/29 – until 1939 6/5
1939 10/26 – until 1940 2/25
1945 6/13 – until 1946 7/13
1960 1/17 – until 1961 3/14
1961 7/7 – 12/11
1967 6/19 – 8/29
1968 3/4 – until 1969 4/9
1974 7/24 – until 1975 8/23
1976 2/16 – 5/6
1989 2/25 – 6/21
1989 11/24 – until 1991 1/15
1997 4/9 – until 1998 5/16
1998 12/2 – until 1999 1/25
2003 9/10 – 12/10
2004 5/26 – until 2005 6/26

URANUS CHALLENGING
1951 8/1 – until 1955 7/12
1991 1/30 – until 1995 11/21

NEPTUNE CHALLENGING
1989 2/12 – until 1997 11/7

JUPITER SPECIAL
1945 10/18 – until 1946 9/12
1957 10/2 – 12/23
1958 4/12 – 8/23
1969 9/16 – 12/2
1970 5/24 – 7/23
1981 8/30 – 11/14
1992 12/13 – until 1993 3/17
1993 8/11 – 10/29
2004 11/20 – until 2005 4/24
2005 7/17 – 10/14

SATURN SPECIAL
1951 11/20 – until 1952 4/4
1952 8/14 – until 1953 10/1
1981 9/24 – until 1982 11/6
2010 10/31 – until 2011 5/9
2011 7/17 – 12/19
2012 3/30 – 9/12

URANUS SPECIAL
1970 11/8 – until 1974 10/10

NEPTUNE SPECIAL
1947 10/28 – until 1955 10/7

PLUTO SPECIAL
1975 12/14 – until 1983 8/27

October 14

SUN: LIBRA · DECANATE: GEMINI/MERCURY · DEGREE: 20°5–21°5 LIBRA · MODE: CARDINAL · ELEMENT: AIR

Your Personal Powers

Although you appear friendly and unassuming, you are a mentally astute individual with strong instincts and inspired imagination. Your ruling planet, Venus, grants you a romantic nature, refined or aesthetic taste, and good social skills. Although being imaginative and hopeful aids your inspiration, you lose some of your power if you are not disciplined enough. Exercising the right balance between being realistic and idealistic usually leads to successful achievement. You lose power, however, if you become restless or stubborn. Talented and versatile, you have a desire for variety that can lead you to seek new experiences or provide an interest in travel. You gain power when you combine your practical skills with your creative ideas. Intuitive and mentally sharp, you can be both charming and persuasive, but try to avoid losing power to being manipulative. Since you are usually good at presenting your point of view, you benefit from all types education where you can sharpen your intellect and improve your skills.

Your Powers of Attraction in Relationships

Usually sociable and friendly, you can gain popularity easily. Your charm and idealism indicate that you are romantic and sensitive to your surroundings and usually do not have problems attracting a partner or a lover. Disharmonious and tense situations caused by power struggles, however, can affect your well-being or produce anxiety. Although diplomatic, in relationships you generally like to be direct, so honesty and loyalty are very important to you. Capable of being affectionate and loving, you are attracted to optimistic and stylish individuals who are alluring or charismatic. Alternatively, you may seek a forceful partner who can reassure and protect you financially and emotionally. As you dislike being restricted, however, resist a temptation to give too much of yourself away. Although you need a congenial environment, in the pursuit of fun and happiness you may need to guard against overindulging.

Your attractive qualities: decisive, focused, knowledgeable, inspired, meticulous, hardworking, creative, pragmatic, imaginative, industrious, visionary, inner faith, sensitive, intuitive, diplomatic, understanding, loves harmony, adaptable, versatile, articulate, charismatic

Your less attractive qualities: impulsive, unsettled, thoughtless, stubborn, self-deceptive, dissatisfied, manipulative, stressed, lack of purpose, overindulgent, worried, tactless, mental power games, frustrated, escapist, restless, speculative, emotionally tense

Your Venus Power

The planet Venus has a great deal of influence on your powers of attraction. Below are four possible Venus types for women and men. To find your Venus you need to go to page 771, where you will find the Venus table and extra information. The planet Mars also affects your powers of attraction. To find your Mars table and interpretation go to page 761.

WOMEN WITH VENUS IN VIRGO: Intelligent and discriminating, you are usually drawn to polite and refined individuals. As a perfectionist you may be keen to analyze and criticize yourself, but be careful of continually going over your partner's shortcomings. By focusing on how you can make positive improvements in yourself and in your relationships you avoid becoming skeptical or confused. You empower yourself when you display kind and caring concern for the well-being of loved ones and spontaneously offer your practical assistance.

MEN WITH VENUS IN VIRGO: A love of order usually indicates that you are attracted to refined individuals with analytical or practical abilities. You and your partner may be working together or serving similar causes. As you constantly analyze partnerships in order to improve them, you are likely to use former relationships as a point of reference and compare them to your present partner. As you are helpful and kind, others usually rely on your good judgment and often turn to you for advice or practical assistance.

WOMEN WITH VENUS IN LIBRA: Usually you are attractive and sociable with an easygoing manner. Your love of beauty, harmony, and pleasure implies that you are a romantic with a desire for love and affection. Once in a relationship you need to learn to negotiate your position rather than adapt to the wishes of others and compromise just to keep the peace. Nevertheless, your advanced social skills and strong sense of fair play can help you succeed in any social or romantic situation.

MEN WITH VENUS IN LIBRA: Your good social skills, charming personality, and refined manner usually make you attractive to the opposite sex. Equally, you desire a sophisticated partner with grace, elegance, and a strong sense of style.

Although you have the ability to be persuasive and irresistible to others, avoid manipulative love games. Nevertheless, your natural diplomacy and sense of fair play help you to relate to people in all social situations. With your love for balance and harmony, you seek a partner who is also moderate, easygoing, and loving.

WOMEN WITH VENUS IN SCORPIO: With a natural psychic gift for penetrating the feelings of others, you can often help partners transform emotional challenges or sexual difficulties. When you fall in love, your strong feelings and determination give you a potent force that others find attractive and seductive. Although you know what really turns people on, your most profound desire is usually for the deepness and closeness of real love and intimacy in an enduring relationship.

MEN WITH VENUS IN SCORPIO: In relationships you possess a sensitive understanding of your partner's deeper nature. Although you are strongly attached to those you love, you may have to be careful that your feelings do not turn into jealousy or possessiveness. When you fall in love it is often with power and an emotional intensity. You are attracted to partners who can share your passion and display strong feelings of sexuality like your own.

WOMEN WITH VENUS IN SAGITTARIUS: When you feel generous, you can make others feel more optimistic about life. You may be interested in higher learning and seek partners who are scholarly or broad-minded. You are outspoken and direct and sometimes say things that you later regret. Curious and versatile, you can adjust quickly to new situations, and a foreign influence implies that you love to travel or may have a partner who comes from a different culture.

MEN WITH VENUS IN SAGITTARIUS: Your enthusiasm and straightforward conduct usually appeal to others and imply that you are approachable and easygoing. Being open to ideas and willing to believe that life has a great deal to offer suggests that you are generous, broad-minded, and show eagerness to cooperate with others. A love of travel and an interest in other cultures also imply that your partner may come from a foreign country.

To read about your Outer Planets and work out how to use your personalized timetable, go to Section Three, page 789.

Your Personalized Timetable

JUPITER BENEFICIAL
1938 2/11 – 5/2
1938 8/12 – 12/21
1941 7/21 – until 1942 1/11
1942 3/2 – 6/3
1943 9/10 – 11/11
1944 1/15 – 7/2
1948 1/2 – 2/26
1948 6/4 – 10/22
1950 1/26 – 4/7
1950 10/2 – 11/15
1953 7/2 – until 1954 5/16
1955 8/24 – 10/13
1956 2/24 – 6/9
1959 12/17 – until 1960 2/2
1960 7/18 – 9/22
1962 1/9 – 3/18
1965 6/15 – 9/6
1965 12/1 – until 1966 4/27
1967 8/8 – 9/24
1971 12/1 – until 1972 1/15
1973 12/22 – until 1974 3/1
1977 5/30 – 8/11
1978 1/12 – 3/30
1979 7/23 – 9/7
1983 11/15 – 12/29
1985 4/10 – 8/1
1985 12/1 – until 1986 2/14
1989 5/13 – 7/23
1991 7/6 – 8/22
1995 10/28 – 12/14
1997 3/18 – 9/24
1997 10/22 – until 1998 1/28
2001 4/25 – 7/5
2002 10/23 – until 2003 1/15
2003 6/17 – 8/6
2007 2/10 – 6/2
2007 10/8 – 11/28
2009 2/27 – until 2010 1/10
2012 8/14 – Continues

SATURN BENEFICIAL
1942 9/14 – 10/6
1943 5/10 – until 1944 6/8
1947 8/29 – until 1948 8/13
1957 11/27 – until 1958 3/17
1958 4/23 – 11/27
1963 1/22 – until 1964 3/10
1964 10/24 – 11/10
1972 6/19 – until 1973 7/19
1974 2/2 – 3/25
1976 10/18 – until 1977 1/7
1977 7/3 – 9/23
1978 3/10 – 6/9
1987 1/1 – 7/16
1987 9/21 – 12/31
1992 2/26 – 9/19
1992 11/11 – until 1993 4/22
1993 7/30 – until 1994 1/14
2001 8/3 – 11/22
2002 4/21 – 9/14
2002 11/7 – until 2003 5/22
2006 8/11 – until 2007 7/28

URANUS BENEFICIAL
1944 8/7 – until 1949 5/12
1958 10/7 – until 1961 8/7
1985 1/1 – until 1987 11/24
1998 4/19 – until 2003 2/11

NEPTUNE BENEFICIAL
1977 1/25 – until 1982 11/11
2003 3/22 – until 2011 12/10

PLUTO BENEFICIAL
1948 9/5 – until 1955 7/16
2001 12/15 – until 2006 11/17

JUPITER CHALLENGING
1940 3/3 – 5/9
1942 8/4 – until 1943 6/23
1949 1/9 – 3/31
1949 7/11 – 11/22
1951 7/2 – 9/6

1952 2/11 – 4/22
1954 7/18 – 10/17
1954 12/17 – until 1955 6/4
1960 12/24 – until 1961 3/6
1961 8/28 – 10/19
1963 5/31 – 10/24
1964 1/16 – 4/5
1966 7/2 – 9/17
1967 1/28 – 5/12
1972 12/8 – until 1973 2/16
1975 5/10 – until 1976 3/19
1978 6/16 – 8/28
1984 4/11 – 5/18
1984 11/20 – until 1985 1/30
1987 4/23 – 7/22
1987 9/17 – until 1988 2/29
1990 5/30 – 8/10
1996 3/5 – 7/7
1996 10/29 – until 1997 1/14
1999 4/6 – 6/19
1999 11/4 – until 2000 2/4
2001 9/17 – 12/18
2002 5/9 – 7/25
2008 2/13 – 12/29
2011 3/20 – 5/28

SATURN CHALLENGING
1938 5/5 – 11/7
1939 1/20 – 6/15
1939 10/14 – until 1940 3/6
1945 6/21 – until 1946 7/21
1960 1/26 – 8/19
1960 10/12 – until 1961 3/28
1961 6/22 – 12/20
1967 7/17 – 8/1
1968 3/12 – until 1969 4/17
1974 8/1 – until 1975 2/19
1975 4/5 – 9/1
1976 2/3 – 5/19
1989 3/10 – 6/6
1989 12/4 – until 1991 1/24
1997 4/17 – until 1998 5/25
1998 11/15 – until 1999 2/10
2003 9/26 – 11/25
2004 6/3 – until 2005 7/4

URANUS CHALLENGING
1951 8/20 – until 1956 4/26
1991 2/18 – until 1995 12/14

NEPTUNE CHALLENGING
1990 1/11 – until 1997 12/16

PLUTO CHALLENGING
1938 2/16 – 6/2

JUPITER SPECIAL
1945 10/22 – until 1946 9/17
1957 10/6 – 12/30
1958 4/4 – 8/29
1969 9/21 – 12/7
1970 5/13 – 8/2
1981 9/4 – 11/19
1992 12/21 – until 1993 3/9
1993 8/17 – 11/2
2004 11/26 – until 2005 4/16
2005 7/25 – 10/18

SATURN SPECIAL
1951 11/30 – until 1952 3/22
1952 8/24 – until 1953 10/9
1981 10/2 – until 1982 11/15
1983 6/2 – 7/30
2010 11/9 – until 2011 4/23
2011 8/1 – until 2012 1/3
2012 3/14 – 9/21

URANUS SPECIAL
1970 11/28 – until 1975 7/17

NEPTUNE SPECIAL
1947 11/30 – until 1956 9/1

PLUTO SPECIAL
1976 10/25 – until 1983 9/26

431

October 15

SUN: LIBRA • DECANATE: GEMINI/MERCURY • DEGREE: 21°5–22°5 LIBRA • MODE: CARDINAL • ELEMENT: AIR

Your Personal Powers

Charming yet shrewd, although you may appear modest or receptive, you have an astute mind and strong instincts indicating that you can quickly comprehend what motivates people. You are quietly determined, and your ruling planet, Venus, endows you with a love of beauty, refined taste, and a friendly manner. Feeling confident when you are completely sure about what you feel or believe in, you gain power by investing time in furthering your knowledge or skills. An inclination to worry too much about people's opinions implies that you also gain power when you stay detached and do not let others undermine your positive outlook or inspired ideas. Usually determined and hardworking, you can achieve great success by combining your business acumen with your natural flair for dealing with people. Since you have an inner need to express yourself creatively, you may also benefit from pursuing and developing your artistic or creative talents. You empower yourself when you utilize your natural sixth sense and apply the necessary self-discipline needed to accomplish your ambitious plans.

Your Powers of Attraction in Relationships

People are attracted to your good mind and friendly nature. You are socially inclined, and your spontaneous or generous gestures can also make you popular. Even though you can be high-spirited and fun-loving, the more sensitive or introspective side to your nature needs time to reflect and relax in quiet surroundings. Usually you admire hardworking and determined individuals with a strong sense of purpose. Alternatively, you may be drawn to creative or artistic partners who can inspire you with their bright ideas. Highly intuitive yet anxious, your ability to sense what others are thinking or feeling implies that you should not take things too seriously. Although you can find yourself suddenly in love, in order to establish close relationships, you need to be able to trust your partner.

Your attractive qualities: astute, instinctive, generous, sociable, responsible, cooperative, creative, assured, inner faith, inspired, genuine, helpful, purposeful, business acumen, harmonious, productive, articulate, quick wit, versatile, analytical, spontaneous, enthusiastic

Your less attractive qualities: skeptical, argumentative, restless, easily bored, irresponsible, self-centered, lack of faith, worried, indecisive, too competitive, irritable, obstinate, nervous, too serious, tense, insecure, risk taking, withdrawn

Your Venus Power

The planet Venus has a great deal of influence on your powers of attraction. Below are four possible Venus types for women and men. To find your Venus you need to go to page 771, where you will find the Venus table and extra information. The planet Mars also affects your powers of attraction. To find your Mars table and interpretation go to page 761.

WOMEN WITH VENUS IN VIRGO: Polite, refined, and organized, you are attracted to articulate and intelligent people. Since you are caring, concerned, and want to be of practical help to others, you can be an asset to any partnership. By being too analytical, exacting, or faultfinding, however, a doubting element can creep into your relationships. Through expressing your feelings in a positive way you can become more decisive and improve how you relate to loved ones.

MEN WITH VENUS IN VIRGO: Practical, idealistic, and perfectionist, you seek a relationship with an intelligent and hardworking partner who can inspire you to be more industrious and well-ordered. At times you can come across as a sympathetic and caring person and at other times you may appear pragmatic and very businesslike. This may sometimes lead to unclear communication between you and your partner. Usually helpful and caring, you like to analyze the faults in your relationships and then work methodically to improve them.

WOMEN WITH VENUS IN LIBRA: Attractive, refined, and conscious of the needs of others, you usually desire harmonious relationships. As a peacemaker with good negotiating skills, you can smooth out difficulties with others, but your dislike of confrontation may sometimes leave you refusing to take a stand or compromising too many of your own needs. Courteous, stylish, and charming with polished social skills, you are an expert at relating to others in a gracious and civilized manner.

MEN WITH VENUS IN LIBRA: As a sociable and friendly individual with an eye for beauty, you are amorous and charming. You are a natural gentleman and your ideal partner

usually has an elegant appearance, artistic appreciation, and good taste. Your relationships benefit when you resist the temptation to take the easy way out or put too much emphasis on vanity and high living. Intellectual and naturally refined, you seek a loving partner who can share your romantic and sophisticated aspirations.

WOMEN WITH VENUS IN SCORPIO: You are usually drawn to partners who are sensual in appearance with a strong character. As you are emotionally intense and passionate, personal relationships are probably a major factor in your life. Since you like to be in control you can at times exhibit some of your less attractive qualities by being willful or domineering. Although you need to feel established and in command in your relationships, you are constantly searching for some higher truth that can bring about a significant transformation.

MEN WITH VENUS IN SCORPIO: You are usually attracted to sensual and passionate partners with strong character. You are often private with deep feelings and magnetic powers of attraction. As a cautious yet devoted and ardent lover, you are likely to seek experiences that are more sexual in their nature. You display your less attractive qualities when you project your negative thoughts and resort to being suspicious or possessive. Nevertheless, loyal and loving, you are a sensitive lover.

WOMEN WITH VENUS IN SAGITTARIUS: At your best when being optimistic and generous, you possess a mischievous sense of fun. In relationships your open-minded approach to people and places may attract you to those of a different culture or make you tolerant of the foibles of others. Although warm and enthusiastic when in love, your natural honesty and idealism may inspire you to look for a partner who shares your love of freedom.

MEN WITH VENUS IN SAGITTARIUS: Forward-thinking rather than dwelling on the past, you are looking for a partner who can share your future plans. You enjoy exploring life whether through travel and mental pursuits or sports and games. Idealistic, you usually prefer the company of a partner who is optimistic and shares your beliefs. In your desire for honesty in relationships, however, be careful not to become tactless. Nevertheless, you are attracted to honest, direct, and fun-loving partners who have a sense of humor like your own.

To read all about your Outer Planets and work out how to use your personalized timetable, go to Section Three, page 789.

⎯⎯

Your Personalized Timetable

JUPITER BENEFICIAL
1938 2/15 – 5/9
1938 8/4 – 12/26
1941 7/27 – until 1942 1/1
1942 3/12 – 6/7
1943 9/14 – 11/23
1944 1/2 – 7/7
1948 1/6 – 3/5
1948 5/27 – 10/27
1950 1/30 – 4/12
1950 9/20 – 11/26
1953 7/6 – until 1954 5/21
1955 8/28 – 10/19
1956 2/17 – 6/16
1959 12/21 – until 1960 2/8
1960 7/9 – 10/1
1962 1/13 – 3/23
1965 6/19 – 9/15
1965 11/23 – until 1966 5/2
1967 8/12 – 9/29
1968 4/2 – 5/11
1971 12/5 – until 1972 1/19
1973 12/27 – until 1974 3/5
1977 6/3 – 8/17
1978 1/4 – 4/7
1979 7/27 – 9/11
1983 11/19 – until 1984 1/3
1985 4/17 – 7/24
1985 12/7 – until 1986 2/18
1989 5/18 – 7/28
1991 7/11 – 8/26
1995 11/2 – 12/18
1997 3/23 – 9/9
1997 11/5 – until 1998 2/1
2001 4/30 – 7/10
2002 11/1 – until 2003 1/6
2003 6/22 – 8/10
2007 2/17 – 5/25
2007 10/14 – 12/3
2009 3/4 – until 2010 1/15
2012 8/21 – Continues

SATURN BENEFICIAL
1943 5/18 – until 1944 6/15
1947 9/6 – until 1948 3/21
1948 5/14 – 8/21
1957 12/6 – until 1958 12/5
1963 1/30 – until 1964 3/18
1964 9/26 – 12/7
1972 6/27 – until 1973 7/27
1974 1/16 – 4/11
1976 11/5 – 12/20
1977 7/12 – 10/2
1978 2/25 – 6/22
1987 1/10 – 6/29
1987 10/7 – until 1988 1/9
1988 8/6 – 9/23
1992 3/6 – 8/31
1992 11/28 – until 1993 5/7
1993 7/14 – until 1994 1/23
2001 8/15 – 11/8
2002 4/30 – until 2003 5/30
2006 8/19 – until 2007 8/5

URANUS BENEFICIAL
1945 6/7 – until 1962 5/8
1985 1/20 – until 1987 12/11
1999 2/13 – until 2003 12/13

NEPTUNE BENEFICIAL
1977 12/22 – until 1982 12/9
2004 2/16 – until 2012 1/17

PLUTO BENEFICIAL
1948 10/22 – until 1956 6/12
2002 1/11 – until 2007 9/26

JUPITER CHALLENGING
1940 3/7 – 5/13
1942 8/9 – until 1943 6/28
1949 1/14 – 4/7
1949 7/3 – 11/27
1951 7/13 – 8/25

JUPITER BENEFICIAL *(continued)*
1952 2/16 – 4/26
1954 7/23 – 10/30
1954 12/4 – until 1955 6/9
1960 12/29 – until 1961 3/12
1961 8/17 – 10/29
1963 6/6 – 10/16
1964 1/23 – 4/9
1966 7/6 – 9/23
1967 1/20 – 5/19
1972 12/12 – until 1973 2/20
1975 5/15 – until 1976 3/23
1978 6/20 – 9/2
1979 3/10 – 4/10
1984 11/25 – until 1985 2/4
1987 4/27 – 8/6
1987 9/2 – until 1988 3/5
1990 6/3 – 8/15
1996 3/11 – 6/29
1996 11/4 – until 1997 1/19
1999 4/10 – 6/24
1999 10/27 – until 2000 2/11
2001 9/25 – 12/10
2002 5/15 – 7/30
2008 2/18 – 8/15
2008 10/1 – until 2009 1/3
2011 3/25 – 6/1

SATURN CHALLENGING
1938 5/14 – 10/24
1939 2/2 – 6/27
1939 10/1 – until 1940 3/15
1945 6/29 – until 1946 7/29
1960 2/4 – 7/31
1960 10/30 – until 1961 4/16
1961 6/2 – 12/29
1968 3/20 – until 1969 4/25
1974 8/10 – until 1975 2/1
1975 4/23 – 9/11
1976 1/21 – 5/30
1989 3/28 – 5/18
1989 12/13 – until 1991 2/1
1997 4/25 – until 1998 6/3
1998 11/2 – until 1999 2/22
2004 6/11 – until 2005 7/11

URANUS CHALLENGING
1951 9/14 – until 1956 5/28
1991 3/18 – until 1996 1/1

NEPTUNE CHALLENGING
1990 2/8 – until 1998 10/19

PLUTO CHALLENGING
1938 1/1 – until 1939 5/11

JUPITER SPECIAL
1945 10/27 – until 1946 9/22
1957 10/11 – until 1958 1/7
1958 3/26 – 9/4
1969 9/25 – 12/13
1970 5/5 – 8/11
1981 9/9 – 11/24
1992 12/31 – until 1993 2/26
1993 8/22 – 11/7
2004 12/2 – until 2005 4/8
2005 8/1 – 10/23

SATURN SPECIAL
1951 12/13 – until 1952 3/8
1952 9/2 – until 1953 10/17
1981 10/10 – until 1982 11/23
1983 5/15 – 8/16
2010 11/18 – until 2011 4/10
2011 8/13 – until 2012 1/28
2012 2/18 – 9/30

URANUS SPECIAL
1970 12/30 – until 1975 8/25

NEPTUNE SPECIAL
1948 10/24 – until 1956 10/3

PLUTO SPECIAL
1976 11/24 – until 1984 7/26

433

October 16

Your Personal Powers

As an idealistic and friendly individual with strong opinions and determination, you can be both charming and persuasive. A love of learning suggests that you can be inspired by new ideas and your enthusiasm for progress can usually motivate you to initiate new enterprises. Although being responsible suggests that you are well aware of your duties, resist being bossy or critical. Your ruling planet, Venus, grants you mental creativity, charm, and good social skills. Being diplomatic yet independent implies that although you are a good team player you still want to play an important role within the group. You gain power through compromising with others in order to achieve the group's aims. You lose some of your power when you feel uninspired, and a tendency to worry or feel insecure may undermine your progress or bring inertia. Nevertheless, being security-conscious, you do not stay idle for long. In fact, as a tireless worker, you can be very dedicated when you feel inspired. Alternatively, you may become an eager campaigner for social reforms or human rights.

Your Powers of Attraction in Relationships

Charismatic and sociable, you enjoy meeting people who are intelligent and share your pursuits or creative interests. Keen on communicating and willing to exchange ideas or information, you attract people with your friendly and fun-loving personality. An excellent networker, you can make important contacts with people who matter and further your career through socializing. Although you can be romantic and affectionate, your practical nature implies that you also take into consideration issues of security and stability when you enter into a relationship. Often gregarious, you love meeting people who can fire your imagination. Being dramatic warns against a tendency to be too emotional or too demanding. Nevertheless, when you believe in something or someone, you can be very passionate and supportive.

Your attractive qualities: confident, ambitious, intuitive, business acumen, inquisitive, liberal, perceptive, creative, many ideas, dignified, love of knowledge, loyal, peacemaker, harmonious, humanitarian, compromising, loyal, dedicated, diplomatic, motivated, analytical, purposeful, sociable

Your less attractive qualities: doubtful, insecure, inner tensions, irresponsible, self-obsessed, too emotional, bossy, interfering, controlling, indecisive, inertia, excessive, withdrawn, escapism, overindulgent, too proud, self-righteous, anxious, worried

Your Venus Power

The planet Venus has a great deal of influence on your powers of attraction. Below are four possible Venus types for women and men. To find your Venus you need to go to page 771, where you will find the Venus table and extra information. The planet Mars also affects your powers of attraction. To find your Mars table and interpretation go to page 761.

WOMEN WITH VENUS IN VIRGO: Articulate and straightforward in your relationships, you attract others with your genuine concern for their well-being. By being understanding and a good listener, you are able to show your love and friendship. With your analytical approach to relationships, however, you may have to be careful of becoming too matter-of-fact. You often display your concern for the welfare of others by your willingness to offer practical help and assistance. You usually seek a partner who is willing to work as hard on relationships as you are.

MEN WITH VENUS IN VIRGO: Although you are constantly analyzing your relationships in order to understand and improve them, you may nevertheless need to refrain from continuously mulling over issues that can cause anxiety. You are happiest when you are able to help loved ones in practical ways and forget yourself in your willingness to be of service to others. You seek a partner who has high standards and can be as pragmatic and hardworking as you. Ideally they should also be impeccably dressed with a fine analytical mind.

WOMEN WITH VENUS IN LIBRA: Gracious, charming, and sociable with a sense of style, you have no trouble attracting admirers. With your natural diplomatic skills and desire for harmony you usually like to keep the peace and avoid confrontations, but be careful of failing to take a stand when it is necessary. Romantic and easygoing yourself, you are attracted to affectionate and refined individuals who share your love of peace, justice, and fair play.

MEN WITH VENUS IN LIBRA: Courteous and refined, you are attracted to beautiful and elegant people. You are looking for a partner who can share your natural good taste and enjoy an intellectual conversation. Disliking conflict, you may have to be careful not to go along with others just to keep the peace.

Your ideal partner will appreciate beauty and the little luxuries of life as well as possess good social skills. You have a strong sense of social etiquette yourself so you need an intelligent and sophisticated partner.

WOMEN WITH VENUS IN SCORPIO: Loving and passionate, you are often sensitive with deep feelings and strong powers of attraction. A love for the truth coupled with a tendency to be suspicious can be an influence that motivates you to delve deep into the activities of your partner. When in love or in a relationship that matters, you will often bend over backward to cooperate. Although loyal, guard against losing sight of your own needs and desires.

MEN WITH VENUS IN SCORPIO: As you are emotionally intense and passionate, personal relationships are probably a major factor in your own transformation. Being sensitive yet loyal, you are usually attracted to forceful partners who can express themselves intimately but intensely. Rather than seek easy and simple relationships you are drawn to partners who act as a catalyst for your own internal changes. Through your relationships with your partners you can unravel your own motives and understand your deep-seated feelings or emotional insecurities.

WOMEN WITH VENUS IN SAGITTARIUS: Sociable, warm, and friendly, you possess an honest and frank style in your relationships. Being naturally gregarious, you want others to share your enthusiasm and enjoy encouraging the people you love. You do better when you have a sense of personal freedom within a relationship and are usually generous with the faults of others. You need a partner who can share your need to explore and take risks, whether through travel, education, or recreation.

MEN WITH VENUS IN SAGITTARIUS: When in love, you are open and friendly with a need for a partner who can share your adventurous spirit and sense of fun. Be careful, however, that your desire for freedom does not cause you to avoid commitment. You prefer your partners to be positive, direct, and generous in spirit. Being outspoken as well as an idealist, you usually enjoy a partner with whom you can share your strong opinions. Alternatively, you may wish to explore life together through travel, education, or by having fun.

To read all about your Outer Planets and work out how to use your personalized timetable, go to Section Three, page 789.

Your Personalized Timetable

JUPITER BENEFICIAL
1938 2/20 – 5/18
1938 7/26 – 12/31
1941 8/1 – 12/23
1942 3/21 – 6/12
1943 9/19 – until 1944 3/29
1944 4/28 – 7/12
1948 1/11 – 3/14
1948 5/17 – 11/2
1950 2/3 – 4/17
1950 9/11 – 12/5
1953 7/11 – until 1954 5/26
1955 9/2 – 10/26
1956 2/9 – 6/22
1959 12/25 – until 1960 2/13
1960 6/30 – 10/9
1962 1/18 – 3/27
1965 6/24 – 9/26
1965 11/12 – until 1966 5/7
1967 8/17 – 10/4
1968 3/20 – 5/24
1971 12/10 – until 1972 1/24
1973 12/31 – until 1974 3/10
1977 6/7 – 8/22
1977 12/28 – until 1978 4/14
1979 8/1 – 9/16
1983 11/24 – until 1984 1/7
1985 4/24 – 7/16
1985 12/12 – until 1986 2/22
1989 5/22 – 8/1
1991 7/15 – 8/31
1995 11/7 – 12/22
1997 3/28 – 8/30
1997 11/15 – until 1998 2/6
2001 5/5 – 7/14
2002 11/13 – 12/25
2003 6/28 – 8/15
2007 2/25 – 5/16
2007 10/20 – 12/7
2009 3/8 – until 2010 1/19
2012 8/30 – Continues

SATURN BENEFICIAL
1943 5/26 – until 1944 6/23
1947 9/14 – until 1948 3/4
1948 5/30 – 8/29
1957 12/14 – until 1958 12/14
1963 2/8 – until 1964 3/27
1964 9/11 – 12/21
1972 7/5 – until 1973 1/15
1973 3/14 – 8/5
1974 1/2 – 4/23
1977 7/20 – 10/11
1978 2/12 – 7/2
1987 1/20 – 6/15
1987 10/19 – until 1988 1/18
1988 7/17 – 10/12
1992 3/15 – 8/17
1992 12/11 – until 1994 2/1
2001 9/1 – 10/22
2002 5/8 – until 2003 6/7
2006 8/27 – until 2007 8/13

URANUS BENEFICIAL
1945 6/24 – until 1949 6/16
1959 8/21 – until 1962 6/21
1985 2/14 – until 1988 10/4
1999 3/2 – until 2004 1/8

NEPTUNE BENEFICIAL
1978 1/21 – until 1983 11/6
2004 3/16 – until 2012 11/21

PLUTO BENEFICIAL
1949 9/20 – until 1956 7/24
2002 2/19 – until 2007 11/12

JUPITER CHALLENGING
1940 3/11 – 5/18
1942 8/14 – until 1943 7/2
1949 1/18 – 4/16

1949 6/23 – 12/2
1952 2/21 – 4/30
1954 7/27 – until 1955 6/15
1961 1/2 – 3/17
1961 8/9 – 11/7
1963 6/12 – 10/8
1964 1/29 – 4/13
1966 7/11 – 9/30
1967 1/13 – 5/25
1972 12/17 – until 1973 2/25
1975 5/20 – until 1976 3/28
1978 6/25 – 9/7
1979 2/24 – 4/25
1984 11/30 – until 1985 2/8
1987 5/2 – until 1988 3/10
1990 6/8 – 8/20
1996 3/18 – 6/21
1996 11/10 – until 1997 1/23
1999 4/15 – 7/1
1999 10/20 – until 2000 2/17
2001 10/5 – 11/30
2002 5/20 – 8/3
2008 2/23 – 8/4
2008 10/12 – until 2009 1/7
2011 3/29 – 6/6
2011 12/23 – 12/28

SATURN CHALLENGING
1938 5/23 – 10/11
1939 2/13 – 7/13
1939 9/15 – until 1940 3/23
1945 7/7 – until 1946 8/5
1960 2/14 – 7/17
1960 11/12 – until 1962 1/7
1968 3/28 – until 1969 5/3
1974 8/18 – until 1975 1/19
1975 5/6 – 9/21
1976 1/9 – 6/8
1989 12/21 – until 1991 2/10
1991 9/19 – 10/20
1997 5/3 – 11/15
1998 1/16 – 6/13
1998 10/20 – until 1999 3/5
2004 6/19 – until 2005 7/19

URANUS CHALLENGING
1952 7/9 – until 1956 6/17
1992 1/12 – until 1996 1/19

NEPTUNE CHALLENGING
1990 3/22 – until 1998 12/12

PLUTO CHALLENGING
1938 1/1 – until 1939 6/30

JUPITER SPECIAL
1945 11/1 – until 1946 9/27
1957 10/16 – until 1958 1/18
1958 3/16 – 9/9
1969 9/30 – 12/19
1970 4/27 – 8/18
1981 9/14 – 11/29
1993 1/15 – 2/11
1993 8/28 – 11/12
2004 12/8 – until 2005 3/31
2005 8/8 – 10/27

SATURN SPECIAL
1951 12/30 – until 1952 2/19
1952 9/11 – until 1953 10/25
1981 10/18 – until 1982 12/3
1983 5/1 – 8/29
2010 11/29 – until 2011 3/28
2011 8/24 – until 2012 10/9

URANUS SPECIAL
1971 10/14 – until 1975 9/15

NEPTUNE SPECIAL
1948 11/23 – until 1957 8/27

PLUTO SPECIAL
1977 10/15 – until 1984 9/10

October 17

SUN: LIBRA • DECANATE: GEMINI/MERCURY • DEGREE: 23°5–24°5 LIBRA • MODE: MUTABLE • ELEMENT: AIR

Your Personal Powers

Friendly yet independent, you are a sociable individual with an astute mind and quick perceptions. Your ruling planet, Venus, endows you with mental creativity, charm, and refined taste. Talented and original, you are able to think creatively and be articulate. Being clever and multitalented also implies that you are keen to explore different subjects and widen your interests. Usually enthusiastic about making progress, you value action and experience. A tendency to worry about money or career moves indicates that you can empower yourself by developing inner faith and establishing a philosophy that you truly believe in. You also gain power when you can overcome your fears or skepticism. Although you need to be mentally stimulated and move at a fast pace, your success often depends on your common sense and analytic abilities. You gain power by being cautious, methodical, or persevering. By combining your thirst for knowledge with your pragmatic approach, you can be decisive and focused.

Your Powers of Attraction in Relationships

People are attracted to your enthusiastic nature, friendly manner, and witty charm. Being self-reliant, however, implies that although you may be romantic and easygoing, you need a certain amount of independence in your close relationships. As you like new opportunities or fresh beginnings, you are drawn to people who can fire your imagination or offer you something exciting that can inspire you to achieve. Usually you need to be cautious about involving your friends or lovers with business. Since you like to keep things close to your chest, there is a danger of your being secretive. Yet in order to grow and develop you need to be open and honest about how you feel and think. By developing your patience and being discriminating you can also learn to be more trusting.

Your attractive qualities: shrewd, business sense, thorough, enterprising, constructive, patient, tolerant, persevering, intuitive, inner wisdom, desire for truth, philosophical, idealistic, versatile, sociable, inquisitive, magnetic, entertaining, logical, articulate, diplomatic, faithful, witty

Your less attractive qualities: impulsive, easily bored, stubborn, careless, moody, sensitive, easily led, critical, mentally restless, indulgent, calculating, secretive, indecisive, skeptical, suspicious, hasty actions

Your Venus Power

The planet Venus has a great deal of influence on your powers of attraction. Below are four possible Venus types for women and men. To find your Venus you need to go to page 771, where you will find the Venus table and extra information. The planet Mars also affects your powers of attraction. To find your Mars table and interpretation go to page 761.

WOMEN WITH VENUS IN VIRGO: In relationships you can be modest and unassuming but desire perfection. You usually analyze your partnerships until you feel you understand them to the last little detail in order to improve them. A problem usually arises when you become too critical either of partners or yourself and indulge in being skeptical or faultfinding. As you are modest, others may not be aware of the strong sensuality beneath your well-groomed exterior.

MEN WITH VENUS IN VIRGO: Industrious and well-ordered, you relate to others in a considerate and down-to-earth way. You enjoy giving practical advice and being of service to those you love even in small ways. Being a perfectionist, you are drawn to partners with high morals or a strong work ethic. Partners who have strong analytical minds are very attractive to you, particularly if they are also clean and meticulously dressed.

WOMEN WITH VENUS IN LIBRA: Gracious, charming, and sociable with a sense of style, you have no trouble attracting admirers. With your natural diplomatic skills and desire for harmony you usually like to keep the peace and avoid confrontations, but be careful of failing to take a stand when it is necessary. Romantic and easygoing yourself, you are attracted to affectionate and refined individuals who share your love of peace, justice, and fair play.

MEN WITH VENUS IN LIBRA: Courteous and refined, you are attracted to beautiful and elegant people. You are looking for a partner who can share your natural good taste and enjoy an intellectual conversation. Disliking conflict, you may have to be careful not to go along with others just to keep the peace. Your ideal partner will appreciate beauty and the little luxuries of life as well as possess good social skills. You have a strong sense of social etiquette yourself so you need an intelligent and sophisticated partner.

WOMEN WITH VENUS IN SCORPIO: With a natural psychic gift for penetrating the feelings of others, you can often help partners transform emotional challenges or sexual difficulties. When you fall in love, your strong feelings and determination

give you a potent force that others find attractive and seductive. Although you know what really turns people on, your most profound desire is usually for the deepness and closeness of real love and intimacy in an enduring relationship.

MEN WITH VENUS IN SCORPIO: In relationships you possess a sensitive understanding of your partner's deeper nature. Although you are strongly attached to those you love, you may have to be careful that your feelings do not turn into jealousy or possessiveness. When you fall in love, it is often with emotional intensity and power. You are attracted to partners who can share your passion and display strong feelings of sexuality like your own.

WOMEN WITH VENUS IN SAGITTARIUS: Optimistic and fun-loving, you love adventure and seek a partner who can expand your horizons. Being truthful and direct you often say what you think, and at times you may be naively tactless. A need for expansion and prosperity suggests that you may enjoy traveling with your friends or partner. Being lighthearted and idealistic, once you have given your heart to someone you will stay honorable and loyal.

MEN WITH VENUS IN SAGITTARIUS: Usually you are attracted to partners who are knowledgeable or well-traveled. Enthusiastic and optimistic, you often respond quickly to love offers and enter relationships with enthusiasm. Generally you seek to expand your social circle, and meeting people from all walks of life can bring you the variety and fun that you seek in life. Although you are generous and honest, your partners may sometimes accuse you of being overly optimistic or too blunt.

To read all about your Outer Planets and work out how to use your personalized timetable, go to Section Three, page 789.

To read all about your Outer Planets and work out how to use your personalized timetable, go to Section Three, page 789.

Your Personalized Timetable

JUPITER BENEFICIAL
1938 2/24 – 5/29
1938 7/14 – until 1939 1/5
1941 8/7 – 12/16
1942 3/28 – 6/16
1943 9/25 – until 1944 3/14
1944 5/12 – 7/18
1948 1/16 – 3/27
1948 5/4 – 11/7
1950 2/7 – 4/23
1950 9/3 – 12/12
1953 7/16 – until 1954 5/30
1955 9/7 – 11/2
1956 2/1 – 6/28
1959 12/30 – until 1960 2/19
1960 6/22 – 10/16
1962 1/22 – 4/1
1965 6/28 – until 1966 5/12
1967 8/21 – 10/10
1968 3/11 – 6/2
1971 12/14 – until 1972 1/29
1974 1/5 – 3/14
1977 6/11 – 8/29
1977 12/20 – until 1978 4/21
1979 8/5 – 9/21
1983 11/28 – until 1984 1/12
1985 5/4 – 7/6
1985 12/17 – until 1986 2/26
1989 5/26 – 8/6
1990 2/6 – 3/15
1991 7/20 – 9/4
1995 11/12 – 12/27
1997 4/3 – 8/22
1997 11/22 – until 1998 2/10
2001 5/9 – 7/19
2003 7/3 – 8/20
2007 3/6 – 5/6
2007 10/25 – 12/11
2009 3/13 – until 2010 1/24
2012 9/9 – Continues

SATURN BENEFICIAL
1943 6/2 – until 1944 7/1
1947 9/23 – until 1948 2/19
1948 6/12 – 9/6
1957 12/22 – until 1958 12/22
1963 2/16 – until 1964 4/6
1964 8/28 – until 1965 1/2
1972 7/14 – 12/30
1973 3/29 – 8/15
1973 12/21 – until 1974 5/3
1977 7/28 – 10/23
1978 1/31 – 7/12
1987 1/30 – 6/2
1987 10/30 – until 1988 1/27
1988 7/2 – 10/25
1992 3/25 – 8/4
1992 12/22 – until 1994 2/9
2002 5/16 – until 2003 6/14
2006 9/4 – until 2007 4/4
2007 5/5 – 8/20

URANUS BENEFICIAL
1945 7/12 – until 1950 4/10
1959 9/7 – until 1962 7/12
1985 3/11 – until 1988 11/1
1999 3/23 – until 2004 1/28

NEPTUNE BENEFICIAL
1978 12/19 – until 1983 12/6
2004 5/12 – Continues

PLUTO BENEFICIAL
1950 8/29 – until 1957 6/22
2003 1/4 – until 2007 12/11

JUPITER CHALLENGING
1940 3/15 – 5/22
1942 8/19 – until 1943 3/1
1943 3/23 – 7/7
1949 1/22 – 4/28

1949 6/11 – 12/8
1952 2/26 – 5/4
1954 8/1 – until 1955 6/20
1961 1/6 – 3/23
1961 8/1 – 11/14
1963 6/18 – 10/1
1964 2/4 – 4/18
1966 7/15 – 10/7
1967 1/5 – 5/31
1972 12/21 – until 1973 3/2
1975 5/25 – 11/21
1975 12/29 – until 1976 4/1
1978 6/29 – 9/12
1979 2/14 – 5/4
1984 12/4 – until 1985 2/12
1987 5/6 – until 1988 3/15
1990 6/13 – 8/24
1996 3/26 – 6/12
1996 11/15 – until 1997 1/27
1999 4/19 – 7/7
1999 10/12 – until 2000 2/23
2001 10/20 – 11/15
2002 5/26 – 8/8
2008 2/28 – 7/26
2008 10/21 – until 2009 1/11
2011 4/2 – 6/11
2011 12/1 – until 2012 1/19

SATURN CHALLENGING
1938 6/3 – 8 9/28
1939 2/23 – until 1940 4/1
1945 7/14 – until 1946 8/13
1960 2/24 – 7/3
1960 11/23 – until 1962 1/15
1968 4/5 – until 1969 5/11
1974 8/28 – until 1975 1/6
1975 5/17 – 10/3
1975 12/27 – until 1976 6/17
1989 12/30 – until 1991 2/19
1991 8/27 – 11/12
1997 5/12 – 10/30
1998 1/31 – 6/24
1998 10/8 – until 1999 3/14
2004 6/27 – until 2005 7/27

URANUS CHALLENGING
1952 7/26 – until 1956 7/5
1992 1/30 – until 1996 11/21

NEPTUNE CHALLENGING
1991 2/4 – until 1999 1/9

PLUTO CHALLENGING
1938 1/1 – until 1940 6/14

JUPITER SPECIAL
1945 11/5 – until 1946 10/2
1957 10/20 – until 1958 2/2
1958 2/28 – 9/14
1969 10/5 – 12/25
1970 4/19 – 8/25
1981 9/19 – 12/4
1982 6/2 – 7/23
1993 9/2 – 11/16
2004 12/15 – until 2005 3/23
2005 8/14 – 11/1

SATURN SPECIAL
1952 9/20 – until 1953 11/3
1981 10/27 – until 1982 12/13
1983 4/18 – 9/9
2010 12/11 – until 2011 3/14
2011 9/2 – until 2012 10/17

URANUS SPECIAL
1971 10/31 – until 1975 10/3

NEPTUNE SPECIAL
1949 10/21 – until 1957 9/29

PLUTO SPECIAL
1977 11/11 – until 1984 10/8

October 18

SUN: LIBRA • DECANATE: GEMINI/MERCURY • DEGREE: 24°5–25°5 LIBRA • MODE: CARDINAL • ELEMENT: AIR

Your Personal Powers

Determined and ambitious, you are a talented individual with creative and progressive ideas. Usually you prefer to promote discussions before you make up your mind. Your ruling planet, Venus, grants you charm, elegance, and aesthetic sense. You gain power when you are engaged in some type of mental pursuit that can challenge you intellectually. Although you possess good planning skills and common sense, your success often depends on whether you find something inspiring that captures your imagination. You lose some of your power if you let boredom and dissatisfaction undermine your great potential. As a rational and pragmatic individual you enjoy solving problems, but you do not like to be told what to do. By being confident and utilizing the knowledge at your disposal, you can express your views calmly. A deep desire for harmony and simplicity also indicates that in order to achieve peace of mind and establish material or emotional security, you need to concentrate on self-mastery rather than attempt to control situations or people's lives.

Your Powers of Attraction in Relationships

You are mentally quick, tactful, and enterprising, and people are drawn to your enthusiastic and optimistic nature. At times your career or responsibilities may interfere with your close relationships. In your close personal partnerships you may sometimes find it difficult to express your emotions as easily as your thoughts. Ideally, therefore, you need a partner who can help you to get in touch with your deeper feelings and preferably share your ideals and interests. Usually you are attracted to strong individuals who are independent and intelligent. Alternatively, you can be drawn to artistic people who hold strong opinions or are success-oriented. By nature you dislike being restrained so are not likely to yield to others unless persuaded by logic. Protective toward those you love and care for, you can be loyal and loving.

Your attractive qualities: relaxed, pragmatic, knowledgeable, adaptable, efficient, diplomatic, instinctive, negotiator, idealistic, patient, tolerant, astute, well-informed, assertive, artistic, intelligent, amusing, witty, persuasive, enthusiastic, focused, progressive, intuitive, resolute

Your less attractive qualities: intolerant, anxious, highly sensitive, lazy, lack of order, failure to complete work or projects, bossy, easily bored, too critical, selfish, controlling, insecure, lack of faith, obstinate, overindulgent, restless, interfering

Your Venus Power

The planet Venus has a great deal of influence on your powers of attraction. Below are four possible Venus types for women and men. To find your Venus you need to go to page 771, where you will find the Venus table and extra information. The planet Mars also affects your powers of attraction. To find your Mars table and interpretation go to page 761.

WOMEN WITH VENUS IN VIRGO: Intelligent and discriminating, you are usually drawn to polite and refined individuals. As a perfectionist, you may be keen to analyze and criticize yourself, but be careful of continually going over your partner's shortcomings. By focusing on how you can make positive improvements in yourself and in your relationships, you avoid becoming skeptical or confused. You empower yourself when you display kind and caring concern for the well-being of loved ones and spontaneously offer your practical assistance.

MEN WITH VENUS IN VIRGO: A love of order usually indicates that you are attracted to refined individuals with analytical or practical abilities. You and your partner may be working together or serving similar causes. As you constantly analyze partnerships in order to improve them, you are likely to use former relationships as a point of reference and compare them to your present partner. As you are helpful and kind, others usually rely on your good judgment and often turn to you for advice or practical assistance.

WOMEN WITH VENUS IN LIBRA: Usually you are attractive and sociable with an easygoing manner. Your love of beauty, harmony, and pleasure implies that you are a romantic with a desire for love and affection. Once in a relationship you need to learn to negotiate your position rather than adapt to the wishes of others and compromise just to keep the peace. Nevertheless, your advanced social skills and strong sense of fair play can help you succeed in any social or romantic situation.

MEN WITH VENUS IN LIBRA: Your good social skills, charming personality, and refined manner usually make you attractive to the opposite sex. Equally, you desire a sophisticated partner with grace, elegance, and a strong sense of style.

Although you have the ability to be persuasive and irresistible to others, avoid manipulative love games. Nevertheless, your natural diplomacy and sense of fair play help you to relate to people in all social situations. With your love for balance and harmony you seek a partner who is also moderate, easygoing, and loving.

WOMEN WITH VENUS IN SCORPIO: With a natural psychic gift for penetrating the feelings of others, you can often help partners transform emotional challenges or sexual difficulties. When you fall in love, your strong feelings and determination give you a potent force that others find attractive and seductive. Although you know what really turns people on, your most profound desire is usually for the deepness and closeness of real love and intimacy in an enduring relationship.

MEN WITH VENUS IN SCORPIO: In relationships you possess a sensitive understanding of your partner's deeper nature. Although you are strongly attached to those you love, you may have to be careful that your feelings do not turn into jealousy or possessiveness. When you fall in love it is often with power and an emotional intensity. You are attracted to partners who can share your passion and display strong feelings of sexuality like your own.

WOMEN WITH VENUS IN SAGITTARIUS: Optimistic and fun-loving, you love adventure and seek a partner who can expand your horizons. Being truthful and direct, you often say what you think, and at times you may be naively tactless. A need for expansion and prosperity suggests that you may enjoy traveling with your friends or partner. Being lighthearted and idealistic, once you have given your heart to someone you will stay honorable and loyal.

MEN WITH VENUS IN SAGITTARIUS: You are usually attracted to partners who are knowledgeable or well-traveled. Enthusiastic and optimistic, you often respond quickly to love offers and enter relationships with enthusiasm. Generally you seek to expand your social circle, and meeting people from all walks of life can bring the variety and fun that you seek in life. Although you are generous and honest, your partners may sometimes accuse you of being overly optimistic or too blunt.

To read about your Outer Planets and work out how to use your personalized timetable, go to Section Three, page 789.

Your Personalized Timetable

JUPITER BENEFICIAL
1938 2/28 – until 1939 1/10
1941 8/13 – 12/8
1942 4/3 – 6/20
1943 9/30 – until 1944 3/4
1944 5/23 – 7/22
1948 1/21 – 8/2
1948 8/29 – 11/12
1950 2/12 – 4/29
1950 8/27 – 12/18
1953 7/21 – until 1954 6/4
1955 9/11 – 11/11
1956 1/24 – 7/4
1960 1/3 – 2/26
1960 6/15 – 10/22
1962 1/26 – 4/6
1965 7/2 – until 1966 5/17
1967 8/26 – 10/15
1968 3/3 – 6/11
1971 12/18 – until 1972 2/3
1972 8/1 – 9/18
1974 1/9 – 3/18
1977 6/16 – 9/4
1977 12/13 – until 1978 4/27
1979 8/10 – 9/26
1983 12/3 – until 1984 1/16
1985 5/16 – 6/24
1985 12/22 – until 1986 3/2
1989 5/31 – 8/12
1990 1/24 – 3/28
1991 7/25 – 9/9
1995 11/17 – 12/31
1997 4/9 – 8/14
1997 11/29 – until 1998 2/14
2001 5/14 – 7/23
2003 7/8 – 8/24
2007 3/21 – 4/21
2007 10/30 – 12/16
2009 3/18 – until 2010 1/28

SATURN BENEFICIAL
1943 6/10 – until 1944 7/8
1947 10/3 – until 1948 2/7
1948 6/22 – 9/14
1949 4/23 – 5/9
1957 12/31 – until 1958 8/5
1958 9/11 – 12/31
1963 2/25 – until 1964 4/17
1964 8/15 – until 1965 1/12
1972 7/23 – 12/17
1973 4/10 – 8/26
1973 12/9 – until 1974 5/13
1977 8/5 – 11/5
1978 1/16 – 7/21
1987 2/12 – 5/19
1987 11/9 – until 1988 2/7
1988 6/18 – 11/5
1992 4/6 – 7/21
1993 1/1 – until 1994 2/17
2002 5/24 – until 2003 6/22
2006 9/12 – until 2007 3/13
2007 5/27 – 8/28

URANUS BENEFICIAL
1945 8/3 – until 1950 5/7
1959 9/25 – until 1962 7/30
1985 12/29 – until 1988 11/21
1999 4/20 – until 2004 2/15

NEPTUNE BENEFICIAL
1979 1/17 – until 1984 10/31
2005 3/11 – Continues

PLUTO BENEFICIAL
1950 10/7 – until 1957 7/30
2003 2/5 – until 2008 11/7

JUPITER CHALLENGING
1940 3/20 – 5/26
1942 8/24 – until 1943 2/12
1943 4/8 – 7/11
1949 1/27 – 12/12

1952 3/1 – 5/8
1954 8/5 – until 1955 6/24
1961 1/10 – 3/29
1961 7/24 – 11/20
1963 6/25 – 9/23
1964 2/10 – 4/22
1966 7/20 – 10/15
1966 12/27 – until 1967 6/6
1972 12/25 – until 1973 3/6
1973 9/22 – 10/5
1975 5/30 – 11/9
1976 1/10 – 4/5
1978 7/4 – 9/18
1979 2/6 – 5/12
1984 12/9 – until 1985 2/17
1987 5/10 – until 1988 3/19
1990 6/17 – 8/29
1996 4/5 – 6/2
1996 11/21 – until 1997 1/31
1999 4/23 – 7/15
1999 10/4 – until 2000 2/28
2002 5/31 – 8/12
2008 3/5 – 7/17
2008 10/28 – until 2009 1/15
2011 4/6 – 6/16
2011 11/21 – until 2012 1/29

SATURN CHALLENGING
1938 6/16 – 9/14
1939 3/4 – until 1940 4/9
1945 7/22 – until 1946 8/21
1947 3/13 – 4/25
1960 3/7 – 6/19
1960 12/3 – until 1962 1/23
1968 4/13 – until 1969 5/19
1969 12/16 – until 1970 1/22
1974 9/7 – 12/25
1975 5/26 – 10/20
1975 12/10 – until 1976 6/26
1990 1/7 – until 1991 2/28
1991 8/11 – 11/26
1997 5/22 – 10/16
1998 2/11 – 7/8
1998 9/23 – until 1999 3/23
2004 7/5 – until 2005 8/4

URANUS CHALLENGING
1952 8/12 – until 1956 7/21
1992 2/18 – until 1996 12/14

NEPTUNE CHALLENGING
1991 3/12 – until 1999 12/7

PLUTO CHALLENGING
1938 1/1 – until 1941 5/25

JUPITER SPECIAL
1945 11/10 – until 1946 10/6
1957 10/25 – until 1958 9/19
1969 10/9 – until 1970 1/1
1970 4/11 – 8/31
1981 9/23 – 12/9
1982 5/22 – 8/3
1993 9/7 – 11/21
2004 12/23 – until 2005 3/15
2005 8/20 – 11/6

SATURN SPECIAL
1952 9/28 – until 1953 11/11
1981 11/4 – until 1982 5/16
1982 7/21 – 12/25
1983 4/4 – 9/19
2010 12/26 – until 2011 2/26
2011 9/11 – until 2012 10/25

URANUS SPECIAL
1971 11/17 – until 1975 10/19

NEPTUNE SPECIAL
1949 11/19 – until 1958 8/20

PLUTO SPECIAL
1977 12/17 – until 1985 8/21

October 19

SUN: LIBRA • DECANATE: GEMINI/MERCURY • DEGREE: 25°5–26°5 LIBRA • MODE: CARDINAL • ELEMENT: AIR

Your Personal Powers

Sociable and versatile, you are a sensitive and creative individual who can achieve admirably by being decisive, focused, and optimistic. Your ruling planet, Venus, grants you good social skills, artistic appreciation or talent, and charm. Even though you need to find different ways to express yourself or be inventive, resist losing power by scattering your energies or being indecisive. As a pragmatic person with a good sense of values, however, you can intuitively evaluate people or recognize new opportunities. Although you are usually witty, easygoing, and sympathetic, being prone to mood swings indicates that you can also be self-centered or insensitive. Fortunately, you are articulate and a good conversationalist who can use persuasive charm to put your point across. In order to avoid sending out conflicting messages, you need to stay detached yet friendly. Being both receptive and imaginative implies that you are also visionary and adaptable. Ambitious and strong-willed, you gain power by developing your confidence and allowing your ingenuity and mental creativity to flow freely.

Your Powers of Attraction in Relationships

Gregarious and friendly, you attract people with your spontaneity and lighthearted nature. Inwardly sensitive and idealistic, you are charming and romantic with a compassionate heart. A tendency to hold back hurt or a failure to communicate your feelings in a mature way means that you may be prone to emotional outbursts. You seek a partner who is sensitive and encouraging or who has faith in your abilities. Generous with loved ones, you are sometimes willing to make sacrifices for your partner, but guard against resenting it later. With your charm and entertaining wit, you usually find it easy to attract others. If unsettled or worried, however, you can become anxious or indecisive about how you truly feel in close relationships. By developing inner faith in your own abilities, you become less vulnerable and more self-reliant or loving.

Your attractive qualities: dynamic, creative, focused, popular, creative, progressive, optimistic, independent, gregarious, altruistic, multitalented, quick, eloquent, entertaining, refined, decisive, articulate, resilient, knowledgeable, charismatic, pioneering, persevering, visionary, intuitive

Your less attractive qualities: selfish, temperamental, impatient, extravagant, overindulgent, argumentative, lack of faith, too proud, insecure, restless, easily bored, feel restricted, changeable, codependent, sarcastic, indecisive

Your Venus Power

The planet Venus has a great deal of influence on your powers of attraction. Below are four possible Venus types for women and men. To find your Venus you need to go to page 771, where you will find the Venus table and extra information. The planet Mars also affects your powers of attraction. To find your Mars table and interpretation go to page 761.

WOMEN WITH VENUS IN VIRGO: Intelligent and discriminating, you are usually drawn to polite and refined individuals. As a perfectionist you may be keen to analyze and criticize yourself, but be careful of continually going over your partner's shortcomings. By focusing on how you can make positive improvements in yourself and in your relationships, you avoid becoming skeptical or confused. You empower yourself when you display kind and caring concern for the well-being of loved ones and spontaneously offer your practical assistance.

MEN WITH VENUS IN VIRGO: A love of order usually indicates that you are attracted to refined individuals with analytical or practical abilities. You and your partner may be working together or serving similar causes. As you constantly analyze partnerships in order to improve them, you are likely to use former relationships as a point of reference and compare them to your present partner. As you are helpful and kind, others usually rely on your good judgment and often turn to you for advice or practical assistance.

WOMEN WITH VENUS IN LIBRA: Usually you are attractive and sociable with an easygoing manner. Your love of beauty, harmony, and pleasure implies that you are a romantic with a desire for love and affection. Once in a relationship you need to learn to negotiate your position rather than adapt to the wishes of others and compromise just to keep the peace. Nevertheless, your advanced social skills and strong sense of fair play can help you succeed in any social or romantic situation.

MEN WITH VENUS IN LIBRA: Your good social skills, charming personality, and refined manner usually make you attractive to the opposite sex. Equally, you desire a sophisticated partner with grace, elegance, and a strong sense of style. Although you have the ability to be persuasive and irresistible

to others, avoid manipulative love games. Nevertheless, your natural diplomacy and sense of fair play help you to relate to people in all social situations. With your love of balance and harmony you seek a partner who is also moderate, easygoing, and loving.

WOMEN WITH VENUS IN SCORPIO: With a natural psychic gift for penetrating the feelings of others, you can often help partners transform emotional challenges or sexual difficulties. When you fall in love, your strong feelings and determination give you a potent force that others find attractive and seductive. Although you know what really turns people on, your most profound desire is usually for the deepness and closeness of real love and intimacy in an enduring relationship.

MEN WITH VENUS IN SCORPIO: In relationships you possess a sensitive understanding of your partner's deeper nature. Although you are strongly attached to those you love, you may have to be careful that your feelings do not turn into jealousy or possessiveness. When you fall in love it is often with power and an emotional intensity. You are attracted to partners who can share your passion and display strong feelings of sexuality like your own.

WOMEN WITH VENUS IN SAGITTARIUS: Sociable, warm, and friendly, you possess an honest and frank style in your relationships. Being naturally gregarious, you want others to share your enthusiasm and enjoy encouraging the people you love. You do better when you have a sense of personal freedom within a relationship and are usually generous with the faults of others. You need a partner who can share your need to explore and take risks, whether through travel, education, or recreation.

MEN WITH VENUS IN SAGITTARIUS: When in love you are open and friendly with a need for a partner who can share your adventurous spirit and sense of fun. Be careful, however, that your desire for freedom does not cause you to avoid commitment. You prefer your partners to be positive, direct, and generous in spirit. Being outspoken as well as an idealist, you usually enjoy a partner with whom you can share your strong opinions. Alternatively, you may wish to explore life together, whether through travel, education, or by having fun.

To read all about your Outer Planets and work out how to use your personalized timetable, go to Section Three, page 789.

Your Personalized Timetable

JUPITER BENEFICIAL
1938 3/5 – until 1939 1/15
1941 8/19 – 12/1
1942 4/9 – 6/25
1943 10/6 – until 1944 2/25
1944 5/31 – 7/27
1948 1/26 – 7/18
1948 9/13 – 11/17
1950 2/16 – 5/5
1950 8/19 – 12/24
1953 7/26 – until 1954 1/17
1954 3/6 – 6/8
1955 9/16 – 11/21
1956 1/13 – 7/9
1960 1/8 – 3/4
1960 6/7 – 10/28
1962 1/30 – 4/11
1962 10/11 – 11/16
1965 7/7 – until 1966 5/22
1967 8/31 – 10/21
1968 2/24 – 6/18
1971 12/23 – until 1972 2/8
1972 7/20 – 9/29
1974 1/14 – 3/23
1977 6/20 – 9/12
1977 12/5 – until 1978 5/2
1979 8/14 – 10/1
1980 4/17 – 5/5
1983 12/7 – until 1984 1/21
1985 12/27 – until 1986 3/6
1989 6/4 – 8/17
1990 1/15 – 4/6
1991 7/29 – 9/14
1995 11/21 – until 1996 1/4
1997 4/15 – 8/6
1997 12/6 – until 1998 2/18
2001 5/18 – 7/28
2003 7/13 – 8/29
2007 11/4 – 12/20
2009 3/23 – 10/2
2009 10/23 – until 2010 2/1

SATURN BENEFICIAL
1943 6/18 – until 1944 7/16
1947 10/14 – until 1948 1/26
1948 7/2 – 9/22
1949 3/27 – 6/5
1958 1/9 – 7/14
1958 10/3 – until 1959 1/8
1963 3/5 – 9/17
1963 11/23 – until 1964 4/30
1964 8/1 – until 1965 1/21
1972 8/1 – 12/5
1973 4/20 – 9/8
1973 11/25 – until 1974 5/22
1977 8/13 – 11/28
1977 12/25 – until 1978 7/29
1987 2/28 – 5/1
1987 11/18 – until 1988 2/18
1988 6/4 – 11/16
1992 4/21 – 7/5
1993 1/10 – until 1994 2/26
2002 6/1 – until 2003 6/30
2006 9/21 – until 2007 2/26
2007 6/10 – 9/5

URANUS BENEFICIAL
1945 9/9 – until 1950 5/27
1959 10/18 – until 1962 8/16
1986 1/16 – until 1988 12/8
2000 2/16 – until 2004 12/16

NEPTUNE BENEFICIAL
1979 3/2 – until 1984 12/2
2005 4/20 – Continues

PLUTO BENEFICIAL
1951 9/11 – until 1958 6/30
2003 12/28 – until 2008 12/7

JUPITER CHALLENGING
1940 3/24 – 5/31
1942 8/29 – until 1943 2/2

1943 4/18 – 7/16
1949 1/31 – 12/17
1952 3/6 – 5/13
1954 8/10 – until 1955 6/29
1961 1/15 – 4/5
1961 7/16 – 11/26
1963 7/4 – 9/15
1964 2/15 – 4/26
1966 7/24 – 10/26
1966 12/17 – until 1967 6/11
1972 12/30 – until 1973 3/12
1973 9/2 – 10/24
1975 6/4 – 10/31
1976 1/19 – 4/9
1978 7/8 – 9/24
1979 1/29 – 5/20
1984 12/14 – until 1985 2/21
1987 5/15 – until 1988 3/24
1990 6/22 – 9/3
1996 4/21 – 5/17
1996 11/26 – until 1997 2/5
1999 4/27 – 7/24
1999 9/25 – until 2000 3/4
2002 6/4 – 8/17
2008 3/11 – 7/10
2008 11/4 – until 2009 1/20
2011 4/10 – 6/22
2011 11/12 – until 2012 2/6

SATURN CHALLENGING
1938 7/2 – 8/28
1939 3/13 – until 1940 4/16
1945 7/30 – until 1946 8/30
1947 2/22 – 5/14
1960 3/22 – 6/3
1960 12/12 – until 1962 2/1
1968 4/21 – until 1969 5/27
1969 11/26 – until 1970 2/10
1974 9/20 – 12/12
1975 6/4 – until 1976 7/4
1990 1/16 – until 1991 3/10
1991 7/28 – 12/7
1997 6/1 – 10/4
1998 2/22 – 7/29
1998 9/1 – until 1999 3/31
2004 7/12 – until 2005 8/11

URANUS CHALLENGING
1952 9/2 – until 1957 5/14
1992 3/13 – until 1997 1/2

NEPTUNE CHALLENGING
1992 2/1 – until 2000 1/6

PLUTO CHALLENGING
1938 1/1 – until 1941 7/8

JUPITER SPECIAL
1945 11/15 – until 1946 10/11
1957 10/30 – until 1958 9/25
1969 10/14 – until 1970 1/9
1970 4/3 – 9/6
1981 9/28 – 12/15
1982 5/12 – 8/12
1993 9/12 – 11/26
2005 1/2 – 3/5
2005 8/25 – 11/10

SATURN SPECIAL
1952 10/6 – until 1953 11/20
1954 6/6 – 8/5
1981 11/13 – until 1982 4/30
1982 8/5 – until 1983 1/8
1983 3/20 – 9/28
2011 9/20 – until 2012 11/2

URANUS SPECIAL
1971 12/8 – until 1976 8/7

NEPTUNE SPECIAL
1950 10/18 – until 1958 9/26

PLUTO SPECIAL
1978 10/30 – until 1985 9/24

441

October 20

Your Personal Powers

Receptive and communicative, you are a versatile, independent, yet sensitive individual with strong instincts and powers of endurance. Your ruling planet, Venus, grants you charm, creative thoughts, and artistic appreciation or talents. Keen on the personal touch, you prefer an open and sincere approach when dealing with others. With an ability to grasp ideas quickly, you are fast at intuitively evaluating people's character. Persuasive and astute, you gain power when you develop your inner faith and combine it with your determination and willpower to succeed. When you feel tense or threatened, however, you can become confrontational and thus lose some of your personal charm. A need to find ways to express your powerful feelings indicates that you want recognition for your individuality. Being proud and dignified, you can claim center stage when you use your charm and excellent people skills. Nevertheless, without a touch of humility, you run the risk of appearing provocative or difficult. As you have a strong emphasis on collaboration, you can often achieve far more in partnership or by being part of a team.

Your Powers of Attraction in Relationships

Sociable yet independent, you enjoy group activities or mixing with people who share your objectives and interests. A touch of arrogance or sarcasm warns that when you have nothing nice to say, you are better off saying nothing and thus avoiding disputes. Being proud and gallant, you rarely take your confident mask off and reveal your inner doubts or insecurities, yet people often prefer your sincerity, even though this involves showing your vulnerability. Affectionate, fun-loving, and altruistic, you know how to entertain others and be amusing. You are usually attracted to those with a youthful or playful side who can also be clever and entrepreneurial. Being persuasive, you know how to attract others to your way of thinking.

Your attractive qualities: cooperative, gracious, diplomatic, strategist, adaptable, creative, understanding, good partnerships, tactful, receptive, intuitive, considerate, harmonious, stylish, balanced, independent, mediator, entertaining, charismatic, dedicated, hardworking, original

Your less attractive qualities: suspicious, lack of confidence, manipulative, too sensitive, selfish, easily hurt, too proud, sarcastic, lazy, indulgent, argumentative, nervous, irritable, self-doubting, tactless, arrogant, stressed

Your Venus Power

The planet Venus has a great deal of influence on your powers of attraction. Below are four possible Venus types for women and men. To find your Venus you need to go to page 771, where you will find the Venus table and extra information. The planet Mars also affects your powers of attraction. To find your Mars table and interpretation go to page 761.

WOMEN WITH VENUS IN VIRGO: Articulate and straightforward in your relationships, you attract others with your genuine concern for their well-being. By being understanding and a good listener you are able to show your love and friendship. With your analytical approach to relationships, however, you may have to be careful of becoming too matter-of-fact. You often display your concern for the welfare of others by your willingness to offer practical help and assistance. You usually seek a partner who is willing to work as hard on relationships as you are.

MEN WITH VENUS IN VIRGO: Although you are constantly analyzing your relationships in order to understand and improve them, you may nevertheless need to refrain from continuously mulling over issues that can cause anxiety. You are happiest when you are able to help loved ones in practical ways and forget yourself in your willingness to be of service to others. You seek a partner who has high standards and can be as pragmatic and hardworking as you. Ideally they should also be impeccably dressed with a fine analytical mind.

WOMEN WITH VENUS IN LIBRA: Gracious, charming, and sociable with a sense of style, you have no trouble attracting admirers. With your natural diplomatic skills and desire for harmony you usually like to keep the peace and avoid confrontations, but be careful of failing to take a stand when it is necessary. Romantic and easygoing yourself, you are attracted to affectionate and refined individuals who share your love of peace, justice, and fair play.

MEN WITH VENUS IN LIBRA: Courteous and refined, you are attracted to beautiful and elegant people. You are looking for a partner who can share your natural good taste and enjoy an intellectual conversation. Disliking conflict, you may have to be careful not to go along with others just to keep the peace. Your ideal partner will appreciate beauty and the little luxuries

of life as well as possess good social skills. You have a strong sense of social etiquette yourself so you need an intelligent and sophisticated partner.

WOMEN WITH VENUS IN SCORPIO: Loving and passionate, you are often sensitive with deep feelings and strong powers of attraction. A love for the truth coupled with a tendency to be suspicious can be the impetus that motivates you to delve deep into the activities of your partner. When in love or in a relationship that matters, you will often bend over backward to cooperate. Although loyal, guard against losing sight of your own needs and desires.

MEN WITH VENUS IN SCORPIO: As you are emotionally intense and passionate, personal relationships are probably a major factor in your own transformation. Being sensitive yet loyal, you are usually attracted to forceful partners who can express themselves intimately but intensely. Rather than seek easy and simple relationships you are drawn to partners who act as a catalyst for your own internal changes. Through your relationships with your partners you can unravel your own motives and understand your deep-seated feelings or emotional insecurities.

WOMEN WITH VENUS IN SAGITTARIUS: Sociable, warm, and friendly, you possess an honest and frank style in your relationships. Being naturally gregarious, you want others to share your enthusiasm and so you enjoy encouraging the people you love. You do better when you have a sense of personal freedom within a relationship and are usually generous with the faults of others. You need a partner who can share your need to explore and take risks, whether through travel, education, or recreation.

MEN WITH VENUS IN SAGITTARIUS: When in love you are open and friendly with a need for a partner who can share your adventurous spirit and sense of fun. Be careful, however, that your desire for freedom does not cause you to avoid commitment. You prefer your partners to be positive, direct, and generous in spirit. Being outspoken as well as an idealist, you usually enjoy a partner with whom you can share your strong opinions. Alternatively, you may wish to explore life together, whether through travel, education, or by having fun.

To read all about your Outer Planets and work out how to use your personalized timetable, go to Section Three, page 789.

≏

Your Personalized Timetable

JUPITER BENEFICIAL
1938 3/9 – until 1939 1/20
1941 8/26 – 11/23
1942 4/15 – 6/29
1943 10/12 – until 1944 2/17
1944 6/7 – 8/1
1948 2/1 – 7/7
1948 9/23 – 11/21
1950 2/20 – 5/13
1950 8/11 – 12/30
1953 7/31 – until 1954 1/6
1954 3/17 – 6/13
1955 9/21 – 12/9
1955 12/27 – until 1956 7/15
1960 1/13 – 3/12
1960 5/29 – 11/2
1962 2/3 – 4/16
1962 9/28 – 11/28
1965 7/12 – until 1966 5/27
1967 9/4 – 10/28
1968 2/16 – 6/24
1971 12/27 – until 1972 2/14
1972 7/11 – 10/8
1974 1/18 – 3/27
1977 6/24 – 9/21
1977 11/26 – until 1978 5/8
1979 8/19 – 10/6
1980 3/30 – 5/23
1983 12/11 – until 1984 1/26
1986 1/1 – 3/10
1989 6/8 – 8/22
1990 1/7 – 4/14
1991 8/3 – 9/18
1995 11/26 – until 1996 1/9
1997 4/22 – 7/30
1997 12/11 – until 1998 2/22
2001 5/23 – 8/2
2003 7/18 – 9/2
2007 11/9 – 12/24
2009 3/28 – 9/16
2009 11/9 – until 2010 2/6

SATURN BENEFICIAL
1943 6/26 – until 1944 7/24
1945 2/10 – 3/29
1947 10/27 – until 1948 1/11
1948 7/11 – 10/1
1949 3/12 – 6/19
1958 1/18 – 6/28
1958 10/17 – until 1959 1/17
1959 8/1 – 10/8
1963 3/15 – 9/1
1963 12/8 – until 1964 5/17
1964 7/14 – until 1965 1/30
1972 8/13 – 11/23
1973 4/29 – 9/26
1973 11/6 – until 1974 5/30
1977 8/20 – until 1978 8/6
1987 11/27 – until 1988 3/3
1988 5/20 – 11/25
1992 5/16 – 6/9
1993 1/19 – until 1994 3/6
2002 6/8 – until 2003 7/7
2006 10/1 – until 2007 2/14
2007 6/21 – 9/13

URANUS BENEFICIAL
1946 6/22 – until 1950 6/13
1960 8/13 – until 1963 5/31
1986 2/7 – until 1989 9/17
2000 3/5 – until 2005 1/11

NEPTUNE BENEFICIAL
1980 1/13 – until 1985 10/26
2006 3/7 – Continues

PLUTO BENEFICIAL
1951 10/27 – until 1958 8/5
2004 1/27 – until 2009 11/3

JUPITER CHALLENGING
1940 3/28 – 6/5
1942 9/4 – until 1943 1/25

1943 4/27 – 7/20
1949 2/5 – 12/22
1952 3/10 – 5/17
1954 8/15 – until 1955 7/4
1961 1/19 – 4/12
1961 7/8 – 12/2
1963 7/14 – 9/4
1964 2/20 – 4/30
1966 7/29 – 11/13
1966 11/29 – until 1967 6/16
1973 1/3 – 3/17
1973 8/23 – 11/3
1975 6/9 – 10/23
1976 1/26 – 4/14
1978 7/12 – 9/30
1979 1/22 – 5/26
1984 12/18 – until 1985 2/26
1987 5/20 – until 1988 3/28
1990 6/26 – 9/8
1991 3/8 – 4/22
1996 12/1 – until 1997 2/9
1999 5/1 – 8/5
1999 9/13 – until 2000 3/9
2002 6/9 – 8/21
2008 3/18 – 7/2
2008 11/10 – until 2009 1/24
2011 4/14 – 6/27
2011 11/4 – until 2012 2/13

SATURN CHALLENGING
1939 3/21 – until 1940 4/24
1945 8/7 – until 1946 2/27
1946 4/10 – 9/7
1947 2/8 – 5/27
1960 4/18 – 5/5
1960 12/21 – until 1962 2/9
1968 4/29 – until 1969 6/5
1969 11/12 – until 1970 2/23
1974 10/7 – 11/24
1975 6/12 – until 1976 7/12
1990 1/24 – until 1991 3/21
1991 7/15 – 12/18
1997 6/13 – 9/21
1998 3/3 – until 1999 4/8
2004 7/20 – until 2005 8/19

URANUS CHALLENGING
1952 10/5 – until 1957 6/9
1993 1/12 – until 1997 1/20

NEPTUNE CHALLENGING
1992 3/4 – until 2000 11/30

PLUTO CHALLENGING
1938 1/1 – until 1942 6/22

JUPITER SPECIAL
1945 11/21 – until 1946 5/21
1946 7/9 – 10/16
1957 11/3 – until 1958 9/29
1969 10/18 – until 1970 1/18
1970 3/24 – 9/11
1981 10/3 – 12/21
1982 5/4 – 8/20
1993 9/17 – 12/1
2005 1/15 – 2/19
2005 8/31 – 11/15

SATURN SPECIAL
1952 10/14 – until 1953 11/28
1954 5/20 – 8/22
1981 11/23 – until 1982 4/16
1982 8/18 – until 1983 2/4
1983 2/21 – 10/7
2011 9/28 – until 2012 11/11

URANUS SPECIAL
1972 10/6 – until 1976 9/5

NEPTUNE SPECIAL
1950 11/15 – until 1959 8/11

PLUTO SPECIAL
1978 11/28 – until 1985 10/20

October 21

SUN: LIBRA • DECANATE: GEMINI/MERCURY • DEGREE: 27°5–28°5 LIBRA • MODE: CARDINAL • ELEMENT: AIR

Your Personal Powers

Gregarious, receptive, and mentally quick, you are usually a determined individual with a charming manner and an inquiring intellect. Your ruling planet, Venus, can grant you charm, good social skills, and refined taste. Although you are enthusiastic and creative, a need to be purposeful or mentally stimulated indicates that you achieve more by staying focused and progressive. Keen on communicating with others, you gain power by expressing yourself articulately and enthusiastically. You lose power, however, if you worry or become indecisive. Nevertheless, since you like to be knowledgeable on many subjects, you are usually well-informed. Exploring new ideas, studying, or reading can also inspire your imagination and give you confidence. Although you are daring, ambitious, and determined to achieve, you gain power when you overcome a tendency to be impatient or restless. Nevertheless, adaptable and multitalented, you are a practical idealist, willing to work hard for what you believe in. Since you also like to work with others, often much of your success depends on your collaborative efforts and close partnerships.

Your Powers of Attraction in Relationships

Even though you appear confident and independent, you like to be a part of a partnership. People are usually drawn to your alluring charm and friendly personality. Although being responsive to people's needs suggests that you are willing to go out of your way for those you love, it may be vital for your sense of self-worth to maintain the balance of give and take in close relationships. You are usually attracted to optimistic individuals who are full of ideas or the determination to succeed. You also admire hardworking people who are self-made and have the stamina to overcome challenges. Being romantic and loyal, in close relationships you want a partner who can show you undying love and devotion.

Your attractive qualities: diplomatic, articulate, inspired, creative, cooperative, enthusiastic, practical, idealistic, sociable, magnetic charm, adaptable, versatile, inquisitive, dedicated, loyal, direct, talented, friendly, daring, love of knowledge, easygoing, assertive, disciplined

Your less attractive qualities: codependent, nervous, too sensitive, resentful, possessive, manipulative, lack of purpose, vain, fear of change, easily bored, afraid of being alone, bossy, suspicious, controlling, indulgent

Your Venus Power

The planet Venus has a great deal of influence on your powers of attraction. Below are four possible Venus types for women and men. To find your Venus you need to go to page 771, where you will find the Venus table and extra information. The planet Mars also affects your powers of attraction. To find your Mars table and interpretation go to page 761.

WOMEN WITH VENUS IN VIRGO: Polite, refined, and organized, you are attracted to articulate and intelligent people. Since you are caring, concerned, and want to be of practical help to others, you can be an asset to any partnership. By being too analytical, exacting, or faultfinding, however, a doubting element can creep into your relationships. By expressing your feelings in a positive way you can become more decisive and improve how you relate to loved ones.

MEN WITH VENUS IN VIRGO: Practical, idealistic, and a perfectionist, you seek a relationship with an intelligent and hardworking partner who can inspire you to be more industrious and well-ordered. At times you can come across as a sympathetic and caring person and at other times you may appear pragmatic and very businesslike. This may sometimes lead to unclear communication between you and your partner. Usually helpful and caring, however, you like to analyze the faults in your relationships and then work methodically to improve them.

WOMEN WITH VENUS IN LIBRA: Usually you are attractive and sociable with an easygoing manner. Your love of beauty, harmony, and pleasure implies that you are a romantic with a desire for love and affection. Once in a relationship you need to learn to negotiate your position rather than adapt to the wishes of others and compromise just to keep the peace. Nevertheless, your advanced social skills and strong sense of fair play can help you succeed in any social or romantic situation.

MEN WITH VENUS IN LIBRA: Your good social skills, charming personality, and refined manner usually make you attractive to the opposite sex. Equally, you desire a sophisticated partner with grace, elegance, and a strong sense of style. Although you have the ability to be persuasive and irresistible

to others, avoid manipulative love games. Nevertheless, your natural diplomacy and sense of fair play help you to relate to people in all social situations. With your love of balance and harmony you seek a partner who is also moderate, easygoing, and loving.

WOMEN WITH VENUS IN SCORPIO: Your strength and power is in your ability to love both deeply and sensitively. For you, love and desire go hand in hand. As you feel so deeply, you often keep your sensitivity or vulnerability hidden from others in order to keep some control in your relationships. You are more likely to prefer a few very close loyal friends than many superficial acquaintances. In relationships your sensual nature and magnetic intensity can easily attract others.

MEN WITH VENUS IN SCORPIO: You are attracted to partners with deep and powerful emotions or individuals you find intriguing. Your gift for creating smoke screens to maintain secrecy around your feelings can conceal your inner sensitivity and vulnerability. Nevertheless, you are looking for a partner who can pierce your defenses and understand you at a very deep level. Needing a relationship with a powerful sexual connection, you thrive on emotional intensity.

WOMEN WITH VENUS IN SAGITTARIUS: At your best when being optimistic and generous, you possess a mischievous sense of fun. In relationships your open-minded approach to people and places may attract you to those of a different culture or make you tolerant of the foibles of others. Although warm and enthusiastic when in love, your natural honesty and idealism may inspire you to look for a partner who shares your love of freedom.

MEN WITH VENUS IN SAGITTARIUS: Forward-thinking rather than dwelling on the past, you are looking for a partner who can share your future plans. You enjoy exploring life whether through travel and mental pursuits or sports and games. Idealistic, you usually prefer the company of a partner who is optimistic and shares your beliefs. In your desire for honesty in relationships, however, be careful not to become tactless. Nevertheless, you are attracted to honest, direct, and fun-loving partners who have a sense of humor like your own.

To read all about your Outer Planets and work out how to use your personalized timetable, go to Section Three, page 789.

Your Personalized Timetable

JUPITER BENEFICIAL
1938 3/14 – until 1939 1/24
1941 9/4 – 11/15
1942 4/21 – 7/4
1943 10/18 – until 1944 2/9
1944 6/14 – 8/6
1948 2/6 – 6/29
1948 10/2 – 11/26
1950 2/24 – 5/21
1950 8/2 – until 1951 1/4
1953 8/5 – 12/29
1954 3/25 – 6/17
1955 9/26 – until 1956 3/25
1956 5/11 – 7/20
1960 1/18 – 3/22
1960 5/18 – 11/8
1962 2/8 – 4/21
1962 9/19 – 12/7
1965 7/16 – until 1966 5/31
1967 9/9 – 11/4
1968 2/9 – 6/30
1972 1/1 – 2/20
1972 7/3 – 10/15
1974 1/22 – 4/1
1977 6/29 – 10/2
1977 11/15 – until 1978 5/13
1979 8/24 – 10/11
1980 3/19 – 6/3
1983 12/16 – until 1984 1/30
1986 1/6 – 3/15
1989 6/13 – 8/28
1989 12/31 – until 1990 4/21
1991 8/8 – 9/23
1995 11/30 – until 1996 1/13
1997 4/29 – 7/21
1997 12/17 – until 1998 2/26
2001 5/27 – 8/7
2003 7/22 – 9/7
2007 11/14 – 12/29
2009 4/2 – 9/5
2009 11/19 – until 2010 2/10

SATURN BENEFICIAL
1943 7/3 – until 1944 8/2
1945 1/23 – 4/16
1947 11/16 – 12/22
1948 7/19 – 10/10
1949 2/27 – 7/1
1958 1/28 – 6/14
1958 10/28 – until 1959 1/26
1959 7/16 – 10/24
1963 3/24 – 8/18
1963 12/20 – until 1965 2/7
1972 8/26 – 11/9
1973 5/8 – until 1974 6/7
1977 8/28 – until 1978 8/14
1987 12/5 – until 1988 3/27
1988 4/26 – 12/4
1993 1/27 – until 1994 3/14
2002 6/16 – until 2003 7/15
2006 10/11 – until 2007 2/1
2007 7/1 – 9/21
2008 4/5 – 5/30

URANUS BENEFICIAL
1946 7/10 – until 1950 6/30
1960 8/29 – until 1963 7/1
1986 3/22 – until 1989 10/29
2000 3/25 – until 2005 1/31

NEPTUNE BENEFICIAL
1980 2/19 – until 1985 11/28
2006 4/11 – Continues

PLUTO BENEFICIAL
1952 9/22 – until 1959 7/6
2004 12/22 – until 2009 12/5

JUPITER CHALLENGING
1940 4/1 – 6/9
1942 9/10 – until 1943 1/17

1943 5/4 – 7/25
1949 2/9 – 12/26
1952 3/15 – 5/21
1954 8/20 – until 1955 7/9
1961 1/23 – 4/21
1961 6/29 – 12/7
1963 8/1 – 8/17
1964 2/25 – 5/4
1966 8/2 – until 1967 6/22
1973 1/7 – 3/22
1973 8/14 – 11/11
1975 6/15 – 10/15
1976 2/2 – 4/18
1978 7/17 – 10/7
1979 1/14 – 6/1
1984 12/22 – until 1985 3/2
1987 5/24 – until 1988 4/1
1990 7/1 – 9/14
1991 2/24 – 5/4
1996 12/5 – until 1997 2/13
1999 5/6 – until 2000 3/14
2002 6/14 – 8/26
2008 3/25 – 6/24
2008 11/16 – until 2009 1/28
2011 4/18 – 7/3
2011 10/28 – until 2012 2/20

SATURN CHALLENGING
1939 3/29 – until 1940 5/2
1945 8/15 – until 1946 2/8
1946 4/29 – 9/17
1947 1/27 – 6/6
1960 12/30 – until 1962 2/18
1962 9/12 – 11/5
1968 5/7 – 11/24
1969 1/17 – 6/15
1969 10/30 – until 1970 3/6
1975 6/21 – until 1976 7/20
1990 2/2 – 8/25
1990 10/21 – until 1991 4/4
1991 6/30 – 12/27
1997 6/28 – 9/5
1998 3/12 – until 1999 4/16
2004 7/28 – until 2005 8/28
2006 3/3 – 5/8

URANUS CHALLENGING
1953 7/21 – until 1957 6/28
1993 1/29 – until 1997 11/21

NEPTUNE CHALLENGING
1993 1/27 – until 2001 1/1

PLUTO CHALLENGING
1938 1/1 – until 1943 6/2

JUPITER SPECIAL
1945 11/26 – until 1946 5/9
1946 7/21 – 10/20
1957 11/8 – until 1958 10/4
1969 10/23 – until 1970 1/31
1970 3/11 – 9/17
1981 10/7 – 12/27
1982 4/26 – 8/26
1993 9/21 – 12/6
1994 6/12 – 7/21
2005 9/5 – 11/20

SATURN SPECIAL
1952 10/22 – until 1953 12/8
1954 5/5 – 9/4
1981 12/3 – until 1982 4/3
1982 8/28 – until 1983 10/15
2011 10/7 – until 2012 11/19

URANUS SPECIAL
1972 10/22 – until 1976 9/25

NEPTUNE SPECIAL
1950 12/27 – until 1959 9/23

PLUTO SPECIAL
1979 10/18 – until 1986 9/7

445

October 22

SUN: LIBRA · DECANATE: GEMINI/MERCURY · DEGREE: 28°5–29°5 LIBRA · MODE: CARDINAL · ELEMENT: AIR

Your Personal Powers

Proud and dignified, you generally possess a charismatic personality and a persuasive charm. Being born on the cusp of Libra and Scorpio suggests that although you can be agreeable and loving, you can also be resolute, intense, and passionate. Shrewd and pragmatic by nature, you are able to judge a situation or a person with relative ease. Being also decisive, you act with competence and prefer to be in positions of authority. You gain power by combining your excellent diplomatic skills with your spirit of enterprise. Although you are usually hardworking and forceful, a tendency to be stubborn or too serious indicates that you may experience setbacks or periods of frustration. Your unyielding determination, however, usually guarantees your success. Even though you may be tense or anxious, you are able to conceal your sensitivity by projecting a determined and confident front. You gain power when you find your inner strength through being creative and expressing yourself in a dramatic and original way.

Your Powers of Attraction in Relationships

You are dynamic and affectionate, and people are attracted to your generous and sincere nature. As you are generally compassionate, sociable, and diplomatic, people often ask for your advice or seek your company. Romantic and idealistic, you have a great deal of love to give if you express yourself honestly. Usually you are attracted to dynamic individuals with an idealistic nature and a tender heart or those who can offer you emotional security. Being persuasive suggests that you can impress people with your quick repartee, creative ideas, and enterprising schemes. A tendency to be rash, willful, or stubborn, however, means that you need to refrain from becoming bossy or embroiled in controversial issues and disputes. By being liberal and using your excellent communication skills, you can charm others and turn your opponents to friends.

Your attractive qualities: pragmatic, organized, dynamic, idealistic, sociable, loving, generous, confident, proud, charismatic, intuitive, instinctive, creative, magnetic, enterprising, diplomatic, social skills, honorable, persuasive, shrewd, easygoing, amusing, elegant, friendly, disciplined

Your less attractive qualities: too proud, arrogant, bossy, materialistic, lack of vision, lazy, egotistical, self-promoting, indecisive, overindulgent, feeling vulnerable, selfish, moody, overemotional, frustrated

Your Venus Power

The planet Venus has a great deal of influence on your powers of attraction. Below are four possible Venus types for women and men. To find your Venus you need to go to page 771, where you will find the Venus table and extra information. The planet Mars also affects your powers of attraction. To find your Mars table and interpretation go to page 761.

WOMEN WITH VENUS IN VIRGO: Intelligent and discriminating, you are usually drawn to polite and refined individuals. As a perfectionist you may be keen to analyze and criticize yourself, but be careful of continually going over your partner's shortcomings. By focusing on how you can make positive improvements in yourself and in your relationships you avoid becoming skeptical or confused. You empower yourself when you display kind and caring concern for the well-being of loved ones and spontaneously offer your practical assistance.

MEN WITH VENUS IN VIRGO: A love of order usually indicates that you are attracted to refined individuals with analytical or practical abilities. You and your partner may be working together or serving similar causes. As you constantly analyze partnerships in order to improve them, you are likely to use former relationships as a point of reference and compare them to your present partner. As you are helpful and kind, others usually rely on your good judgment and often turn to you for advice or practical assistance.

WOMEN WITH VENUS IN LIBRA: Usually you are attractive and sociable with an easygoing manner. Your love of beauty, harmony, and pleasure implies that you are a romantic with a desire for love and affection. Once in a relationship you need to learn to negotiate your position rather than adapt to the wishes of others and compromise just to keep the peace. Nevertheless, your advanced social skills and strong sense of fair play can help you succeed in any social or romantic situation.

MEN WITH VENUS IN LIBRA: Your good social skills, charming personality, and refined manner usually make you attractive to the opposite sex. Equally, you desire a sophisticated partner with grace, elegance, and a strong sense of style.

Although you have the ability to be persuasive and irresistible to others, avoid manipulative love games. Nevertheless, your natural diplomacy and sense of fair play help you to relate to people in all social situations. With your love of balance and harmony you seek a partner who is also moderate, easygoing, and loving.

WOMEN WITH VENUS IN SCORPIO: With a natural psychic gift for penetrating the feelings of others, you can often help partners transform emotional challenges or sexual difficulties. When you fall in love, your strong feelings and determination give you a potent force that others find attractive and seductive. Although you know what really turns people on, your most profound desire is usually for the deepness and closeness of real love and intimacy in an enduring relationship.

MEN WITH VENUS IN SCORPIO: In relationships you possess a sensitive understanding of your partner's deeper nature. Although you are strongly attached to those you love, you may have to be careful that your feelings do not turn into jealousy or possessiveness. When you fall in love it is often with power and an emotional intensity. You are attracted to partners who can share your passion and display strong feelings of sexuality like your own.

WOMEN WITH VENUS IN SAGITTARIUS: Optimistic and fun-loving, you love adventure and seek a partner who can expand your horizons. Being truthful and direct, you often say what you think, and at times you may be naively tactless. A need for expansion and prosperity suggests that you may enjoy traveling with your friends or partner. Being lighthearted and idealistic, once you have given your heart to someone you will stay honorable and loyal.

MEN WITH VENUS IN SAGITTARIUS: You are usually attracted to partners who are knowledgeable or well-traveled. Enthusiastic and optimistic, you often respond quickly to love offers and enter relationships with enthusiasm. Generally you seek to expand your social circle, and meeting people from all walks of life can bring the variety and fun that you seek in life. Although you are generous and honest, your partners may sometimes accuse you of being overly optimistic or too blunt.

To read all about your Outer Planets and work out how to use your personalized timetable, go to Section Three, page 789.

Your Personalized Timetable

JUPITER BENEFICIAL
1938 3/18 – until 1939 1/28
1941 9/14 – 11/5
1942 4/26 – 7/8
1943 10/25 – until 1944 2/2
1944 6/20 – 8/11
1948 2/12 – 6/20
1948 10/9 – 12/1
1950 2/28 – 5/31
1950 7/23 – until 1951 1/9
1953 8/11 – 12/21
1954 4/2 – 6/21
1955 10/2 – until 1956 3/13
1956 5/23 – 7/25
1960 1/23 – 4/7
1960 5/3 – 11/13
1962 2/12 – 4/27
1962 9/11 – 12/15
1965 7/21 – until 1966 6/5
1967 9/14 – 11/12
1968 1/31 – 7/6
1972 1/5 – 2/26
1972 6/25 – 10/22
1974 1/27 – 4/5
1977 7/3 – until 1978 5/18
1979 8/28 – 10/17
1980 3/10 – 6/12
1983 12/20 – until 1984 2/4
1984 8/18 – 9/10
1986 1/10 – 3/19
1989 6/17 – 9/4
1989 12/23 – until 1990 4/27
1991 8/12 – 9/28
1995 12/5 – until 1996 1/18
1997 5/9 – 7/12
1997 12/22 – until 1998 3/2
2001 5/31 – 8/12
2002 2/8 – 3/22
2003 7/27 – 9/11
2007 11/19 – until 2008 1/2
2009 4/7 – 8/28
2009 11/26 – until 2010 2/14

SATURN BENEFICIAL
1943 7/12 – until 1944 1/24
1944 3/18 – 8/11
1945 1/9 – 4/28
1948 7/28 – 10/20
1949 2/14 – 7/11
1958 2/9 – 6/1
1958 11/8 – until 1959 2/5
1959 7/1 – 11/5
1963 4/4 – 8/5
1963 12/31 – until 1965 2/16
1972 9/16 – 10/18
1973 5/16 – until 1974 6/15
1977 9/5 – until 1978 8/22
1987 12/14 – until 1988 12/13
1993 2/4 – until 1994 3/23
1994 10/12 – 12/7
2002 6/24 – until 2003 7/23
2004 2/28 – 3/15
2006 10/23 – until 2007 1/19
2007 7/10 – 9/30
2008 3/19 – 6/16

URANUS BENEFICIAL
1946 7/30 – until 1951 4/30
1960 9/15 – until 1963 7/22
1986 12/27 – until 1989 11/20
2000 4/21 – until 2005 2/18

NEPTUNE BENEFICIAL
1981 1/9 – until 1986 10/18
2007 3/3 – Continues

PLUTO BENEFICIAL
1953 8/29 – until 1959 8/10
2005 1/19 – until 2010 10/31

JUPITER CHALLENGING
1940 4/5 – 6/14

1940 12/11 – until 1941 1/19
1942 9/16 – until 1943 1/10
1943 5/11 – 7/29
1949 2/14 – 12/31
1952 3/19 – 5/26
1954 8/25 – until 1955 2/28
1955 4/2 – 7/13
1961 1/28 – 5/3
1961 6/17 – 12/12
1964 3/1 – 5/8
1966 8/7 – until 1967 6/26
1973 1/11 – 3/28
1973 8/6 – 11/18
1975 6/22 – 10/8
1976 2/8 – 4/22
1978 7/21 – 10/15
1979 1/6 – 6/7
1984 12/27 – until 1985 3/7
1987 5/29 – 11/27
1988 1/2 – 4/6
1990 7/5 – 9/19
1991 2/15 – 5/13
1996 12/10 – until 1997 2/18
1999 5/10 – until 2000 3/19
2002 6/19 – 8/31
2008 4/3 – 6/15
2008 11/21 – until 2009 2/1
2011 4/22 – 7/10
2011 10/21 – until 2012 2/26

SATURN CHALLENGING
1939 4/6 – until 1940 5/10
1945 8/24 – until 1946 1/25
1946 5/12 – 9/27
1947 1/15 – 6/16
1961 1/7 – until 1962 2/27
1962 8/25 – 11/22
1968 5/16 – 11/7
1969 2/2 – 6/26
1969 10/17 – until 1970 3/16
1975 6/28 – until 1976 7/28
1990 2/11 – 8/7
1990 11/7 – until 1991 4/22
1991 6/11 – until 1992 1/5
1998 3/20 – until 1999 4/24
2004 8/5 – until 2005 9/5
2006 2/16 – 5/23

URANUS CHALLENGING
1953 8/7 – until 1957 7/15
1993 2/17 – until 1997 12/16

NEPTUNE CHALLENGING
1993 2/27 – until 2001 11/22

PLUTO CHALLENGING
1938 1/1 – until 1943 7/13

JUPITER SPECIAL
1945 12/2 – until 1946 4/30
1946 7/30 – 10/25
1957 11/13 – until 1958 10/9
1969 10/28 – until 1970 9/22
1981 10/12 – until 1982 1/3
1982 4/19 – 9/2
1993 9/26 – 12/12
1994 5/30 – 8/4
2005 9/10 – 11/24

SATURN SPECIAL
1952 10/31 – until 1953 12/18
1954 4/22 – 9/14
1981 12/15 – until 1982 3/20
1982 9/7 – until 1983 10/23
2011 10/15 – until 2012 11/28

URANUS SPECIAL
1972 11/7 – until 1976 10/12

NEPTUNE SPECIAL
1951 11/12 – until 1959 10/21

PLUTO SPECIAL
1979 11/13 – until 1986 10/7

♎

447

Libra Timetable
X-Special · X-Beneficial · X-Challenging

September 23
URANUS X-CHALLENGING
2010 4/26 – until 2011 12/24

PLUTO X-CHALLENGING
2007 1/21 – until 2009 11/16

September 24
URANUS X-CHALLENGING
2010 5/19 – until 2012 1/30
2007 3/1 – until 2009 12/15

September 25
URANUS X-CHALLENGING
2010 5/19 – until 2012 1/30

PLUTO X-CHALLENGING
2007 3/1 – until 2009 12/15

September 26
URANUS X-CHALLENGING
2011 3/22 – until 2012 12/13

PLUTO X-CHALLENGING
2007 3/1 – until 2009 12/15

September 27
URANUS X-CHALLENGING
2011 4/29 – until 2012 12/22

PLUTO X-CHALLENGING
2009 1/12 – until 2011 11/10

September 28
URANUS X-CHALLENGING
2011 5/22 – until 2013 2/1

NEPTUNE X-BENEFICIAL
2001 1/1 – 12/5

PLUTO X-CHALLENGING
2009 2/13 – until 2011 12/12

September 29
URANUS X-CHALLENGING
2012 3/26 – Continues

NEPTUNE X-BENEFICIAL
2001 1/1 – until 2002 1/5

PLUTO X-CHALLENGING
2010 1/9 – until 2012 11/8

September 30
URANUS X-CHALLENGING
2012 4/13 – Continues

NEPTUNE X-BENEFICIAL
2001 1/1 – until 2002 11/27

PLUTO X-CHALLENGING
2010 2/9 – until 2012 12/11

October 1
URANUS X-CHALLENGING
2012 5/1 – Continues

NEPTUNE X-BENEFICIAL
2001 1/8 – until 2003 1/1

PLUTO X-CHALLENGING
2011 1/7 – until 2013 11/8

October 2
URANUS X-CHALLENGING
2012 5/24 – Continues

NEPTUNE X-BENEFICIAL
2001 2/3 – until 2003 11/15

PLUTO X-CHALLENGING
2011 2/7 – Continues

October 3
NEPTUNE X-BENEFICIAL
2001 3/2 – until 2003 12/27

PLUTO X-CHALLENGING
2012 1/7 – Continues

October 4
NEPTUNE X-BENEFICIAL
2001 4/11 – until 2004 1/24

PLUTO X-CHALLENGING
2012 2/6 – Continues

October 5
NEPTUNE X-BENEFICIAL
2002 2/26 – until 2004 12/21

PLUTO X-CHALLENGING
2012 3/28 – Continues

October 6
NEPTUNE X-BENEFICIAL
2002 4/1 – until 2005 1/19

October 7
NEPTUNE X-BENEFICIAL
2003 2/22 – until 2005 12/15

PLUTO X-BENEFICIAL
2001 1/1 – until 2002 10/12

October 8
NEPTUNE X-BENEFICIAL
2003 3/25 – until 2006 1/15

PLUTO X-BENEFICIAL
2001 1/1 – until 2002 11/13

October 9
NEPTUNE X-BENEFICIAL
2004 2/18 – until 2006 12/7

PLUTO X-BENEFICIAL
2001 1/1 – until 2003 9/27

October 10
NEPTUNE X-BENEFICIAL
2004 3/18 – until 2007 1/11

PLUTO X-BENEFICIAL
2001 1/22 – until 2003 11/6

October 11
NEPTUNE X-BENEFICIAL
2005 2/13 – until 2007 11/26

PLUTO X-BENEFICIAL
2001 12/16 – until 2003 12/3

October 12
NEPTUNE X-BENEFICIAL
2005 4/3 – until 2008 1/6

PLUTO X-BENEFICIAL
2002 1/12 – until 2004 10/28

October 13
NEPTUNE X-BENEFICIAL
2005 4/24 – until 2008 2/3

PLUTO X-BENEFICIAL
2002 2/21 – until 2004 11/27

October 14
NEPTUNE X-BENEFICIAL
2006 3/9 – until 2008 12/31

PLUTO X-BENEFICIAL
2003 1/4 – until 2005 10/19

October 15
URANUS X-BENEFICIAL
2001 1/15 – until 2002 1/19

NEPTUNE X-BENEFICIAL
2006 4/13 – until 2009 1/29

PLUTO X-BENEFICIAL
2003 2/6 – until 2005 11/21

October 16
URANUS X-BENEFICIAL
2001 2/2 – until 2002 2/6

NEPTUNE X-BENEFICIAL
2007 3/4 – until 2009 12/25

PLUTO X-BENEFICIAL
2003 12/29 – until 2006 10/9

October 17
URANUS X-BENEFICIAL
2001 2/19 – until 2002 12/7

NEPTUNE X-BENEFICIAL
2007 4/5 – until 2010 1/25

PLUTO X-BENEFICIAL
2004 1/28 – until 2006 11/16

October 18
URANUS X-BENEFICIAL
2001 3/9 – until 2003 1/3

NEPTUNE X-BENEFICIAL
2008 2/28 – until 2010 12/17

PLUTO X-BENEFICIAL
2004 12/22 – until 2007 9/24

October 19
URANUS X-BENEFICIAL
2001 3/29 – until 2003 1/23

NEPTUNE X-BENEFICIAL
2008 3/29 – until 2011 1/21

PLUTO X-BENEFICIAL
2005 1/19 – until 2007 11/11

October 20
URANUS X-BENEFICIAL
2001 4/25 – until 2003 2/10

NEPTUNE X-BENEFICIAL
2009 2/23 – until 2011 12/7

PLUTO X-BENEFICIAL
2005 3/3 – until 2007 12/10

October 21
URANUS X-BENEFICIAL
2002 2/23 – until 2003 12/11

NEPTUNE X-BENEFICIAL
2009 3/24 – until 2012 1/16

PLUTO X-BENEFICIAL
2006 1/14 – until 2008 11/6

October 22
URANUS X-BENEFICIAL
2002 3/12 – until 2004 1/7

NEPTUNE X-BENEFICIAL
2009 5/7 – until 2012 2/13

PLUTO X-BENEFICIAL
2006 2/19 – until 2008 12/7

♏

Scorpio

October 23–November 21

October 23

SUN: SCORPIO/LIBRA CUSP • DECANATE: SCORPIO/PLUTO • DEGREE: 29°5 LIBRA–0°5 SCORPIO • MODE: FIXED • ELEMENT: WATER

Your Personal Powers

Sensitive and alert, you are a dynamic and insightful individual with strong emotions. Being born on the cusp of Libra and Scorpio implies that, although you can be charming and sympathetic with an idealistic nature, you are also tenacious, determined, and enterprising, especially when inspired. As a dramatic and imaginative person, you need to find ways to express yourself, whether through your creativity or idealism. You gain power by disciplining yourself to stay positive and focused. Since you usually respond to people or situations according to how you feel, you empower yourself by remaining calm or unruffled. Your deep sensitivity or vulnerability suggests you may lose power to worry and anxiety if you let your emotional restlessness control you. As a quick thinker with a professional attitude, you are often progressive, versatile, and full of inventive ideas. You can project the identity of someone who is pleasing and impressionable, but underneath you possess great inner strength and your true mastery often only surfaces if you feel challenged.

Your Powers of Attraction in Relationships

Your warm and friendly approach enchants other people. In time of adversity, however, you can be bold and intense. A tendency to be willful or uncompromising warns that if you clash with others, you may end up feeling despondent. Emotionally sensitive and compassionate, however, you are protective of those you love and at times of crisis a tower of strength to those around you. In love, you can be fiercely loyal to your partner and stand by him or her regardless of the difficulties. Although your sensitivity implies that you are aware of other people's feelings, you can also be brutally frank. Usually you are attracted to enterprising and determined individuals who are hardworking and independent. Fond of socializing, you enjoy yourself when you let your hair down and have fun.

Your attractive qualities: idealistic, imaginative, dynamic, powerful emotions, loyal, responsible, enthusiastic, disciplined, willpower, hardworking, affectionate, communicative, intuitive, creative, charismatic, versatile, pragmatic, trustworthy, direct, daring, generous, perceptive

Your less attractive qualities: self-centered, temperamental, demanding, frustrated, impetuous, restless, insecure, impatient, moody, discontented, stubborn, controlling, faultfinding, possessive, jealous, too competitive

Your Venus Power

The planet Venus has a great deal of influence on your powers of attraction. Below are four possible Venus types for women and men. To find your Venus you need to go to page 771, where you will find the Venus table and extra information. The planet Mars also affects your powers of attraction. To find your Mars table and interpretation go to page 761.

WOMEN WITH VENUS IN VIRGO: Polite, refined, and organized, you are attracted to articulate and intelligent people. Since you are caring, concerned, and want to be of practical help to others, you can be an asset to any partnership. By being too analytical, exacting, or faultfinding, however, a doubting element can creep into your relationships. By expressing your feelings in a positive way you can become more decisive and improve on how you relate to your loved ones.

MEN WITH VENUS IN VIRGO: A love of order usually indicates that you are attracted to refined individuals with analytical or practical abilities. You and your partner may be working together or serving similar causes. As you constantly analyze partnerships in order to improve them, you are likely to use former relationships as a point of reference and compare them to your present partner. As you are helpful and kind, others usually rely on your good judgment and often turn to you for advice or practical assistance.

WOMEN WITH VENUS IN LIBRA: Gracious, charming, and sociable with a sense of style, you have no trouble attracting admirers. With your natural diplomatic skills and desire for harmony you usually like to keep the peace and avoid confrontations, but be careful of failing to take a stand when it is necessary. Romantic and easygoing yourself, you are attracted to affectionate and refined individuals who share your love of peace, justice, and fair play.

MEN WITH VENUS IN LIBRA: You are such good company, people are naturally drawn to you and especially appreciate your talent for making them feel special. You find status in your social contacts and place importance on your relationships. Being clever and a charming companion, you will go out of your way to keep situations peaceful and harmonious. In relationships, however, be careful of indecision or of com-

promising too much. Nevertheless, others are attracted by your natural refinement and good taste, which is reflected in your sense of style.

WOMEN WITH VENUS IN SCORPIO: Your strength and power is in your ability to love both deeply and sensitively. For you, love and desire go hand in hand. As you feel so deeply, you often keep your sensitivity or vulnerability hidden from others in order to keep some control in your relationships. You are more likely to prefer a few very close loyal friends than many superficial acquaintances. In relationships your sensual nature and magnetic intensity can easily attract others.

MEN WITH VENUS IN SCORPIO: You are attracted to partners with deep and powerful emotions or individuals you find intriguing. Your gift for creating smoke screens to maintain secrecy around your feelings can conceal your inner sensitivity and vulnerability. Nevertheless, you are looking for a partner who can pierce your defenses and understand you at a very deep level. Needing a relationship with a powerful sexual connection, you thrive on emotional intensity.

WOMEN WITH VENUS IN SAGITTARIUS: When you feel generous, you can make others feel more optimistic about life. You may be interested in higher learning and seek partners who are scholarly or broad-minded. You are outspoken and direct and sometimes say things that you later regret. Curious and versatile, you can adjust quickly to new situations and a foreign influence implies that you love to travel or may have a partner who comes from a different culture.

MEN WITH VENUS IN SAGITTARIUS: Your enthusiasm and straightforward conduct usually appeal to others and imply that you are approachable and easygoing. Being open to ideas and willing to believe that life has a great deal to offer suggests that you are generous, broad-minded, and show eagerness to cooperate with others. A love of travel and an interest in other cultures imply that your partner may come from a foreign country.

To read all about your Outer Planets and work out how to use your personalized timetable, go to Section Three, page 789.

♏

Your Personalized Timetable

JUPITER BENEFICIAL
1938 3/23 – until 1939 2/2
1941 10/3 – 10/17
1942 5/1 – 7/12
1943 11/1 – until 1944 1/25
1944 6/26 – 8/15
1948 2/19 – 6/13
1948 10/15 – 12/5
1950 3/5 – 6/19
1950 7/4 – until 1951 1/14
1953 8/17 – 12/14
1954 4/8 – 6/26
1955 10/7 – until 1956 3/4
1956 6/1 – 7/30
1960 1/28 – 8/1
1960 9/8 – 11/18
1962 2/16 – 5/3
1962 9/3 – 12/22
1965 7/26 – until 1966 2/7
1966 2/22 – 6/10
1967 9/19 – 11/21
1968 1/22 – 7/12
1972 1/10 – 3/3
1972 6/17 – 10/28
1974 1/31 – 4/10
1977 7/8 – until 1978 5/23
1979 9/2 – 10/23
1980 3/3 – 6/19
1983 12/25 – until 1984 2/10
1984 8/1 – 9/26
1986 1/15 – 3/23
1989 6/21 – 9/11
1989 12/16 – until 1990 5/3
1991 8/17 – 10/3
1995 12/9 – until 1996 1/22
1997 5/21 – 6/29
1997 12/27 – until 1998 3/7
2001 6/5 – 8/17
2002 1/28 – 4/3
2003 8/1 – 9/16
2007 11/23 – until 2008 1/6
2009 4/13 – 8/20
2009 12/3 – until 2010 2/18

SATURN BENEFICIAL
1943 7/20 – until 1944 1/8
1944 4/3 – 8/20
1944 12/28 – until 1945 5/9
1948 8/5 – 11/1
1949 2/1 – 7/21
1958 2/22 – 5/16
1958 11/17 – until 1959 2/16
1959 6/18 – 11/16
1963 4/17 – 7/22
1964 1/9 – until 1965 2/24
1973 5/24 – until 1974 6/23
1977 9/13 – until 1978 3/28
1978 5/23 – 8/30
1987 12/22 – until 1988 12/21
1993 2/13 – until 1994 4/1
1994 9/24 – 12/23
2002 7/2 – until 2003 7/31
2004 2/2 – 4/10
2006 11/8 – until 2007 1/3
2007 7/19 – 10/9
2008 3/5 – 6/29

URANUS BENEFICIAL
1946 8/26 – until 1951 5/22
1960 10/4 – until 1963 8/8
1987 1/14 – until 1989 12/8
2001 2/18 – until 2005 12/20

NEPTUNE BENEFICIAL
1981 2/12 – until 1986 11/25
2007 4/4 – Continues

PLUTO BENEFICIAL
1953 10/4 – until 1960 7/10
2005 3/2 – until 2010 12/4

JUPITER CHALLENGING
1938 1/1 – 1/21
1940 4/9 – 6/19

1940 11/29 – until 1941 1/31
1942 9/22 – until 1943 1/2
1943 5/17 – 8/3
1949 2/19 – until 1950 1/4
1952 3/23 – 5/30
1954 8/30 – until 1955 2/14
1955 4/16 – 7/18
1961 2/1 – 12/17
1964 3/5 – 5/13
1966 8/11 – until 1967 7/1
1973 1/16 – 4/3
1973 7/29 – 11/25
1975 6/29 – 9/30
1976 2/14 – 4/26
1978 7/26 – 10/23
1978 12/28 – until 1979 6/13
1984 12/31 – until 1985 3/12
1985 9/22 – 10/14
1987 6/3 – 11/14
1988 1/15 – 4/10
1990 7/10 – 9/25
1991 2/7 – 5/20
1996 12/15 – until 1997 2/22
1999 5/14 – until 2000 3/23
2002 6/23 – 9/5
2008 4/14 – 6/4
2008 11/26 – until 2009 2/5
2011 4/27 – 7/17
2011 10/13 – until 2012 3/2

SATURN CHALLENGING
1939 4/14 – until 1940 5/18
1945 9/2 – until 1946 1/13
1946 5/22 – 10/10
1947 1/1 – 6/25
1961 1/15 – until 1962 3/9
1962 8/10 – 12/5
1968 5/25 – 10/24
1969 2/14 – 7/8
1969 10/4 – until 1970 3/25
1975 7/6 – until 1976 8/4
1990 2/21 – 7/23
1990 11/20 – until 1992 1/14
1998 3/28 – until 1999 5/2
2004 8/13 – until 2005 2/17
2005 4/23 – 9/14
2006 2/3 – 6/4

URANUS CHALLENGING
1953 8/25 – until 1957 7/31
1993 3/12 – until 1998 1/5

NEPTUNE CHALLENGING
1994 1/24 – until 2001 12/29

PLUTO CHALLENGING
1938 1/3 – until 1944 6/25

JUPITER SPECIAL
1945 12/7 – until 1946 4/22
1946 8/6 – 10/29
1957 11/18 – until 1958 10/14
1969 11/1 – until 1970 9/27
1981 10/16 – until 1982 1/10
1982 4/10 – 9/8
1993 10/1 – 12/17
1994 5/20 – 8/13
2005 9/15 – 11/29

SATURN SPECIAL
1952 11/8 – until 1953 5/23
1953 7/24 – 12/30
1954 4/9 – 9/24
1981 12/30 – until 1982 3/4
1982 9/16 – until 1983 11/1
2011 10/23 – until 2012 12/7

URANUS SPECIAL
1972 11/25 – until 1976 10/28

NEPTUNE SPECIAL
1951 12/18 – until 1960 9/18

PLUTO SPECIAL
1979 12/17 – until 1987 8/13

October 24

Your Personal Powers

Sociable, idealistic, and imaginative, you have a graceful manner and charismatic personality. Although you possess a friendly character, your ruling planet, Pluto, indicates that you can be a tenacious, determined, and hardworking individual. Although evasive and secretive, when you do speak your mind you can be critical and forthright. As a responsible and efficient person, you possess executive skills and leadership abilities, yet a tendency to worry warns against becoming too serious. Being generous and sympathetic, you gain power when you use your dynamic emotions to uplift people or inspire them to rise above the mundane problems of life. If you fail to take notice of other people's feelings and act irresponsibly, you can lose some of your charm and popularity. By staying self-disciplined, modest, and sincere rather than arrogant or stubborn, you can empower yourself and create the harmonious and loving environment you so wish for. A desire to find emotional fulfillment suggests that you need to be purposeful, yet stay idealistic.

Your Powers of Attraction in Relationships

You are capable of being loving and giving, and your loyalty gains you friends who will stand by you when times are hard. Your innate understanding of human nature implies that you are a shrewd judge of character and, if in the limelight, you can gain popularity with the masses. You are usually attracted to compassionate partners who can be romantic and sensitive or those with a playful spirit. Although you keep your thoughts and feelings close to your chest, in intimate relationships you can be passionate. When positive, you are fun-loving and entertaining, yet your frustration or displeasure can also be reflected in your moods. In close relationships, guard against martyring yourself or controlling behavior. Nevertheless, liable to make magnanimous gestures of generosity, you are a caring friend and loving partner.

Your attractive qualities: people skills, graceful, creative, youthful, disciplined, idealist, determined, frank, generous, glamorous, home-loving, popular, subtle, inquisitive, responsible, inspired, dramatic, direct, daring, bold, tenacious, understanding, compassionate

Your less attractive qualities: unsympathetic, materialistic, martyr, ruthless, lazy, self-pity, critical, domineering, stubborn, revengeful, jealous, secretive, controlling, too sensitive, easily offended, overindulgent

Your Venus Power

The planet Venus has a great deal of influence on your powers of attraction. Below are four possible Venus types for women and men. To find your Venus you need to go to page 771, where you will find the Venus table and extra information. The planet Mars also affects your powers of attraction. To find your Mars table and interpretation go to page 761.

WOMEN WITH VENUS IN VIRGO: Articulate and straightforward in your relationships, you attract others with your genuine concern for their well being. By being understanding and a good listener you are able to show your love and friendship. With your analytical approach to relationships, however, you may have to be careful of becoming too matter-of-fact. You often display your concern for the welfare of others by your willingness to offer practical help and assistance. You usually seek a partner who is willing to work as hard on relationships as you are.

MEN WITH VENUS IN VIRGO: Industrious and well-ordered, you relate to others in a considerate and down-to-earth way. You enjoy giving practical advice and being of service to those you love even in small ways. Being a perfectionist you are drawn to partners with high morals or a strong work ethic. Partners who have strong analytical minds are very attractive to you, particularly if they are also clean and meticulously dressed.

WOMEN WITH VENUS IN LIBRA: Attractive, refined, and conscious of the needs of others, you usually desire harmonious relationships. As a peacemaker with good negotiating skills, you can smooth out difficulties with others, but your dislike of confrontation may sometimes leave you refusing to take a stand or compromising too many of your own needs. Courteous, stylish, and charming with polished social skills, you are an expert at relating to others in a gracious and civilized manner.

MEN WITH VENUS IN LIBRA: Courteous and refined, you are attracted to beautiful and elegant people. You are looking for a partner who can share your natural good taste and enjoy an intellectual conversation. Disliking conflict, you may have to be careful not to go along with others just to keep the peace. Your ideal partner will appreciate beauty and the little luxuries

of life as well as possess good social skills. You have a strong sense of social etiquette yourself so you need an intelligent and sophisticated partner.

WOMEN WITH VENUS IN SCORPIO: With a natural psychic gift for penetrating the feelings of others, you can often help partners transform emotional challenges or sexual difficulties. When you fall in love, your strong feelings and sense of determination give you a potent force that others find attractive and seductive. Although you know what really turns people on, your most profound desire is usually for the deepness and closeness of real love and intimacy in an enduring relationship.

MEN WITH VENUS IN SCORPIO: In relationships you possess a sensitive understanding of your partner's deeper nature. Although you are strongly attached to those you love, you may have to be careful that your feelings do not turn into jealousy or possessiveness. When you fall in love it is often with an emotional intensity that helps you to get in touch with your deep feelings. You are attracted to partners who can share your passion and display strong feelings of sexuality like your own.

WOMEN WITH VENUS IN SAGITTARIUS: Optimistic and fun-loving, you love adventure and seek a partner who can expand your horizons. Being truthful and direct, you often say what you think. At times you may be naively tactless. A need for expansion and prosperity suggests that you may enjoy traveling with your friends or partner. Being both lighthearted and idealistic, however, indicates that once you have given your heart to someone you will stay honorable and loyal.

MEN WITH VENUS IN SAGITTARIUS: Usually you are attracted to partners who are knowledgeable or well-traveled. Enthusiastic and optimistic, you often respond quickly to love offers and enter relationships with enthusiasm. Usually you seek to expand your social circle and meeting people from all walks of life can bring you the variety and fun you seek in life. Although you are generous and honest, your partners may accuse you of being overly optimistic or too blunt.

To read all about your Outer Planets and work out how to use your personalized timetable, go to Section Three, page 789.

♏

Your Personalized Timetable

JUPITER BENEFICIAL
1938 3/28 – until 1939 2/6
1942 5/6 – 7/17
1943 11/10 – until 1944 1/15
1944 7/1 – 8/20
1948 2/25 – 6/5
1948 10/21 – 12/10
1950 3/9 – until 1951 1/19
1953 8/24 – 12/6
1954 4/14 – 6/30
1955 10/13 – until 1956 2/25
1956 6/8 – 8/4
1960 2/2 – 7/19
1960 9/21 – 11/22
1962 2/20 – 5/9
1962 8/26 – 12/28
1965 7/31 – until 1966 1/20
1966 3/13 – 6/14
1967 9/24 – 12/4
1968 1/8 – 7/17
1972 1/14 – 3/11
1972 6/9 – 11/3
1974 2/4 – 4/15
1974 10/20 – 11/17
1977 7/12 – until 1978 5/28
1979 9/6 – 10/29
1980 2/24 – 6/26
1983 12/29 – until 1984 2/15
1984 7/22 – 10/7
1986 1/19 – 3/28
1989 6/26 – 9/18
1989 12/8 – until 1990 5/9
1991 8/21 – 10/8
1992 4/9 – 5/22
1995 12/13 – until 1996 1/27
1998 1/1 – 3/11
2001 6/9 – 8/22
2002 1/18 – 4/12
2003 8/6 – 9/21
2007 11/28 – until 2008 1/11
2009 4/19 – 8/12
2009 12/10 – until 2010 2/22

SATURN BENEFICIAL
1943 7/29 – 12/25
1944 4/15 – 8/31
1944 12/16 – until 1945 5/18
1948 8/12 – 11/16
1949 1/16 – 7/29
1958 3/15 – 4/25
1958 11/26 – until 1959 3/1
1959 6/3 – 11/25
1963 5/3 – 7/4
1964 1/18 – until 1965 3/4
1973 6/1 – until 1974 6/30
1977 9/22 – until 1978 3/11
1978 6/9 – 9/7
1987 12/31 – until 1988 12/29
1993 2/21 – until 1994 4/10
1994 9/10 – until 1995 1/5
2002 7/10 – until 2003 2/7
2003 3/8 – 8/9
2004 1/18 – 4/24
2007 7/27 – 10/19
2008 2/22 – 7/9

URANUS BENEFICIAL
1947 6/20 – until 1951 6/9
1960 10/30 – until 1963 8/24
1987 2/2 – until 1989 12/25
2001 3/8 – until 2006 1/16

NEPTUNE BENEFICIAL
1982 1/6 – until 1987 10/7
2008 2/27 – Continues

PLUTO BENEFICIAL
1954 9/8 – until 1960 8/13
2006 1/13 – until 2011 10/28

JUPITER CHALLENGING
1938 1/1 – 1/25
1940 4/14 – 6/25
1940 11/20 – until 1941 2/9

1942 9/30 – 12/25
1943 5/23 – 8/7
1949 2/24 – until 1950 1/9
1952 3/27 – 6/4
1954 9/4 – until 1955 2/5
1955 4/26 – 7/22
1961 2/5 – 12/22
1964 3/10 – 5/17
1966 8/16 – until 1967 7/6
1973 1/20 – 4/10
1973 7/21 – 12/1
1975 7/7 – 9/22
1976 2/19 – 4/30
1978 7/30 – 11/5
1978 12/16 – until 1979 6/18
1985 1/4 – 3/17
1985 9/5 – 10/30
1987 6/9 – 11/5
1988 1/23 – 4/14
1990 7/14 – 10/1
1991 1/30 – 5/27
1996 12/19 – until 1997 2/26
1999 5/19 – until 2000 3/28
2002 6/28 – 9/10
2003 3/22 – 4/17
2008 5/5 – 5/13
2008 12/1 – until 2009 2/10
2011 5/1 – 7/25
2011 10/4 – until 2012 3/8

SATURN CHALLENGING
1939 4/22 – until 1940 5/26
1940 12/18 – until 1941 1/31
1945 9/13 – until 1946 1/1
1946 6/1 – 10/27
1946 12/14 – until 1947 7/4
1961 1/24 – until 1962 3/19
1962 7/28 – 12/16
1968 6/4 – 10/12
1969 2/25 – 7/26
1969 9/16 – until 1970 4/2
1975 7/14 – until 1976 8/12
1990 3/3 – 7/10
1990 12/1 – until 1992 1/22
1998 4/5 – until 1999 5/9
2004 8/22 – until 2005 2/2
2005 5/8 – 9/24
2006 1/22 – 6/14

URANUS CHALLENGING
1953 9/18 – until 1958 5/28
1994 1/13 – until 1998 1/22

NEPTUNE CHALLENGING
1994 2/22 – until 2002 11/12

PLUTO CHALLENGING
1938 8/16 – until 1945 6/4

JUPITER SPECIAL
1945 12/14 – until 1946 4/14
1946 8/13 – 11/3
1957 11/23 – until 1958 5/30
1958 7/9 – 10/18
1969 11/6 – until 1970 10/2
1981 10/21 – until 1982 1/19
1982 4/1 – 9/14
1993 10/5 – 12/23
1994 5/11 – 8/21
2005 9/20 – 12/4

SATURN SPECIAL
1952 11/17 – until 1953 5/6
1953 8/10 – until 1954 1/14
1954 3/24 – 10/4
1982 9/25 – until 1983 11/9
2011 10/31 – until 2012 12/18

URANUS SPECIAL
1972 12/18 – until 1977 8/24

NEPTUNE SPECIAL
1952 11/8 – until 1960 10/18

PLUTO SPECIAL
1980 10/31 – until 1987 9/22

October 25

Your Personal Powers

Independent and optimistic, you are an enterprising and enthusiastic individual with energy and powerful emotions. Your ruling planet, Pluto, grants you irrepressible drive and the determination to overcome obstacles. You gain power when you let your actions be guided by your imagination, creativity, and idealism. Although you can be ambitious and daring, being impatient implies that you can lose some of your power if you act on impulse or attempt to take on more than you can master. Being rebellious or obstinate can also undermine your wonderful potential for success. Nevertheless, a desire for excellence urges you to work hard and be productive. Your enthusiasm implies that by combining inspiration and intuition with a good strategy, you can discipline yourself and succeed admirably. You also empower yourself when you take control over your emotions and learn to deal with your frustrations in a calm and detached way. Your spontaneity, spirit of adventure, and passionate idealism can also transform the way you approach everyday life.

Your Powers of Attraction in Relationships

Optimistic by nature, you can attract people with your generosity and positive outlook. Compelling and tenacious, you are often drawn to powerful people who are patient and industrious or individuals who are sincere and present themselves with confidence. You also admire people who are audacious and authoritative. You may need to be careful, however, not to get involved in personality clashes when issues of control may surface in close relationships. Other people admire your determination and persuasive approach. Loyal by nature, you are usually keen on keeping your home and personal relationships harmonious. Your emotional restlessness, however, warns that without some excitement in your life you may become bored or unsettled. You need a partner who can keep you on your toes or one who can maintain an air of mystery and thrill.

Your attractive qualities: intuitive, charismatic, perfectionist, perceptive, quick creative mind, analytical, persuasive, optimistic, graceful, popular, enthusiastic, independent, enterprising, sympathetic, resolute, understanding, adventurous, captivating manner, focused, organized, worker

Your less attractive qualities: impulsive, demanding, irresponsible, frustrated, overemotional, controlling, jealous, secretive, critical, moody, restless, possessive, impatient, dissatisfied, easily bored, temperamental, mistrusting

Your Venus Power

The planet Venus has a great deal of influence on your powers of attraction. Below are four possible Venus types for women and men. To find your Venus you need to go to page 771, where you will find the Venus table and extra information. The planet Mars also affects your powers of attraction. To find your Mars table and interpretation go to page 761.

WOMEN WITH VENUS IN LIBRA: A natural romantic, with good social skills, you love to entertain or put people at ease by projecting a warm and gracious manner. Elegant and fair with a touch of glamour, you are also adept at dealing with people in delicate situations or conflicts. You seek refinement and will go out of your way to achieve harmony and keep the peace. For you, relationships are so important you may need to guard against becoming dependent on approval from others. With your friendly personality and inherent charm, however, you will always be popular and loved.

MEN WITH VENUS IN LIBRA: As a sociable and friendly individual with an eye for beauty, you are amorous and charming. You are a natural gentleman, and your ideal partner usually has an elegant appearance, artistic appreciation, and good taste. Your relationships benefit when you resist the temptation to take the easy route or put too much emphasis on vanity and high living. Intellectual and naturally refined, you seek a loving partner who can share your romantic and sophisticated aspirations.

WOMEN WITH VENUS IN VIRGO: In relationships you can be modest and unassuming but desire perfection. You usually analyze your partnerships until you feel you have understood them to the last little detail in order to improve them. A problem usually arises when you become too critical either of partners or yourself and indulge in being skeptical or faultfinding. As you are modest, others may not be aware of the strong sensuality beneath your well-groomed exterior.

MEN WITH VENUS IN VIRGO: Although you are constantly analyzing your relationships in order to understand and improve them, you may nevertheless need to refrain from continuously mulling over issues that can cause anxiety. You are happiest when you are able to help your loved ones in practical ways and forget yourself in your willingness to be of service to others. You seek a partner who has high standards and can be as pragmatic and hardworking as yourself. Ideally they should also be impeccably dressed with a fine analytical mind.

WOMEN WITH VENUS IN LIBRA: Usually you are attractive and sociable with an easygoing manner. Your love of

beauty, harmony, and pleasure implies that you are a romantic with a desire for love and affection. Once in a relationship you need to learn to negotiate your position rather than adapt to the wishes of others and compromise just to keep the peace. Nevertheless, your advanced social skills and strong sense of fair play can help you succeed in any social or romantic situation.

MEN WITH VENUS IN LIBRA: As a sociable and friendly individual with an eye for beauty, you are amorous and charming. You are a natural gentleman and your ideal partner usually has an elegant appearance, artistic appreciation, and good taste. Your relationships benefit when you resist the temptation to take the easy way out or put too much emphasis on vanity and high living. Intellectual and naturally refined, you seek a loving partner who can share your romantic and sophisticated aspirations.

WOMEN WITH VENUS IN SCORPIO: Loving and passionate, you are often sensitive with deep feelings and strong powers of attraction. A love for the truth coupled with a tendency to be suspicious can be an influence that motivates you to delve deep into the activities of your partner. When in love or in a relationship that matters, you will often bend over backward to cooperate. Although loyal, guard against losing sight of your own needs and desires.

MEN WITH VENUS IN SCORPIO: As you are emotionally intense and passionate, personal relationships are probably a major factor in your own transformation. Being sensitive yet loyal, you are usually attracted to forceful partners who can express themselves intimately but intensely. Rather than seek easy and simple relationships, you are drawn to partners who act as a catalyst for your own internal changes. Through your relationships with your partners you can unravel your own motives and understand your deep-seated feelings or emotional insecurities.

WOMEN WITH VENUS IN SAGITTARIUS: Sociable, warm, and friendly, you possess an honest and frank style in your relationships. Being naturally gregarious, you want others to share your enthusiasm and enjoy encouraging the people you love. You fare better when you have a sense of personal freedom within a relationship and are usually generous with the faults of others. You need a partner who can share your need to explore and take risks, whether through travel, education, or recreation.

MEN WITH VENUS IN SAGITTARIUS: When in love, you are open and friendly with a need for a partner who can share your adventurous spirit and sense of fun. Be careful, however, that your desire for freedom does not cause you to avoid commitment. You prefer your partners to be positive, direct, and generous in spirit. Being outspoken as well as an idealist, you usually enjoy a partner with whom you can share your strong opinions. Alternatively, you may wish to explore life together, whether through travel, education, or having fun.

To read all about your Outer Planets and work out how to use your personalized timetable, go to Section Three, page 789.

To read all about your Outer Planets and work out how to use your personalized timetable, go to Section Three, page 789.

Your Personalized Timetable

JUPITER BENEFICIAL
1938 4/2 – 9/25
1938 11/11 – until 1939 2/10
1942 5/11 – 7/21
1943 11/22 – until 1944 1/4
1944 7/7 – 8/24
1948 3/4 – 5/27
1948 10/27 – 12/14
1950 3/14 – until 1951 1/23
1953 8/31 – 11/29
1954 4/20 – 7/5
1955 10/19 – until 1956 2/17
1956 6/15 – 8/8
1960 2/7 – 7/9
1960 10/1 – 11/27
1962 2/24 – 5/16
1962 8/19 – until 1963 1/2
1965 8/5 – until 1966 1/10
1966 3/23 – 6/18
1967 9/29 – until 1968 4/4
1968 5/10 – 7/22
1972 1/19 – 3/19
1972 5/31 – 11/8
1974 2/8 – 4/20
1974 10/6 – 12/1
1977 7/17 – until 1978 6/2
1979 9/11 – 11/5
1980 2/16 – 7/2
1984 1/2 – 2/21
1984 7/13 – 10/15
1986 1/23 – 4/1
1989 6/30 – 9/28
1989 11/28 – until 1990 5/14
1991 8/26 – 10/13
1992 3/28 – 6/3
1995 12/18 – until 1996 2/1
1998 1/6 – 3/15
2001 6/13 – 8/28
2002 1/11 – 4/20
2003 8/10 – 9/26
2007 12/2 – until 2008 1/15
2009 4/26 – 8/4
2009 12/16 – until 2010 2/26

SATURN BENEFICIAL
1943 8/8 – 12/13
1944 4/26 – 9/13
1944 12/2 – until 1945 5/27
1948 8/20 – until 1949 8/7
1958 12/5 – until 1959 3/17
1959 5/16 – 12/5
1964 1/27 – until 1965 3/12
1973 6/9 – until 1974 7/8
1977 10/1 – until 1978 2/26
1978 6/21 – 9/15
1988 1/8 – 8/7
1988 9/21 – until 1989 1/7
1993 3/1 – until 1994 4/21
1994 8/28 – until 1995 1/15
2002 7/18 – until 2003 1/16
2003 3/30 – 8/18
2004 1/6 – 5/6
2007 8/4 – 10/30
2008 2/9 – 7/19

URANUS BENEFICIAL
1947 7/8 – until 1951 6/26
1961 8/22 – until 1964 6/13
1987 3/2 – until 1990 10/26
2001 3/28 – until 2006 2/4

NEPTUNE BENEFICIAL
1982 2/6 – until 1987 11/21
2008 3/28 – Continues

PLUTO BENEFICIAL
1955 8/16 – until 1961 7/14
2006 2/18 – until 2011 12/3

JUPITER CHALLENGING
1938 1/1 – 1/29
1940 4/18 – 6/30
1940 11/12 – until 1941 2/16
1942 10/9 – 12/17

1943 5/28 – 8/12
1949 3/1 – 8/24
1949 10/13 – until 1950 1/13
1952 4/1 – 6/8
1954 9/10 – until 1955 1/27
1955 5/4 – 7/27
1961 2/10 – 12/26
1964 3/14 – 5/21
1966 8/21 – until 1967 7/11
1973 1/24 – 4/17
1973 7/13 – 12/6
1975 7/16 – 9/12
1976 2/24 – 5/4
1978 8/4 – until 1979 6/23
1985 1/9 – 3/23
1985 8/26 – 11/9
1987 6/14 – 10/28
1988 1/31 – 4/18
1990 7/19 – 10/7
1991 1/23 – 6/3
1996 12/24 – until 1997 3/3
1999 5/24 – until 2000 4/1
2002 7/2 – 9/15
2003 3/6 – 5/2
2008 12/6 – until 2009 2/14
2011 5/5 – 8/5
2011 9/24 – until 2012 3/13

SATURN CHALLENGING
1939 4/30 – until 1940 6/4
1940 11/29 – until 1941 2/18
1945 9/25 – 12/18
1946 6/10 – until 1947 7/12
1961 2/2 – 9/17
1961 10/8 – until 1962 3/31
1962 7/14 – 12/26
1968 6/16 – 9/29
1969 3/6 – until 1970 4/11
1975 7/22 – until 1976 8/20
1990 3/15 – 6/26
1990 12/11 – until 1992 1/30
1998 4/13 – until 1999 5/17
2004 8/31 – until 2005 1/20
2005 5/19 – 10/6
2006 1/9 – 6/23

URANUS CHALLENGING
1954 7/16 – until 1958 6/20
1994 1/31 – until 1998 11/23

NEPTUNE CHALLENGING
1994 4/19 – until 2002 12/25

PLUTO CHALLENGING
1938 10/5 – until 1945 7/15

JUPITER SPECIAL
1945 12/20 – until 1946 4/6
1946 8/20 – 11/7
1957 11/29 – until 1958 5/17
1958 7/22 – 10/23
1969 11/11 – until 1970 10/7
1981 10/26 – until 1982 1/30
1982 3/21 – 9/19
1993 10/10 – 12/29
1994 5/3 – 8/28
2005 9/25 – 12/9
2006 6/20 – 7/21

SATURN SPECIAL
1952 11/27 – until 1953 4/22
1953 8/22 – until 1954 2/14
1954 2/19 – 10/12
1982 10/3 – until 1983 11/17
2011 11/9 – until 2012 5/29
2012 7/21 – 12/29

URANUS SPECIAL
1973 10/15 – until 1977 9/17

NEPTUNE SPECIAL
1952 12/11 – until 1961 9/14

PLUTO SPECIAL
1980 11/28 – until 1987 10/19

455

October 26

Your Personal Powers

Your powerful emotions, determination, and sensitivity indicate that you are hardworking and resourceful. Your ruling planet, Pluto, grants you shrewd perception, intuitive powers, and tenacity. Being idealistic and imaginative, you need to find ways to express your powerful feelings. As an enterprising person with a strong sense of duty, you gain power when you utilize your intense emotions and determination to transform difficult situations. When you abandon your cautiousness and surrender to your desires, you can lose some of your power by acting impulsively. Nevertheless, you are resolute and security-conscious, and your fighting spirit indicates that you can always revitalize yourself and overcome obstacles. Although your pragmatic approach suggests that you can have inborn business acumen, your humanitarian side implies that you can also be a campaigner for just causes or come to the aid of those who need your help. Emotional satisfaction can also come from unexpected sources and you can be very lucky when you least expect it.

Your Powers of Attraction in Relationships

Other people are attracted to your romantic and caring personality. Although you are courteous and sociable, you can sometimes act flamboyantly to hide your sensitivity. If you are constantly facing frustrating circumstances in your personal life, you may need to learn to let go of relationships that cease to be harmonious or beneficial. By staying detached and realizing that you don't have to close your heart even if you need to move on in order to progress, a new beginning can become a key to transforming your life. Often a tower of strength for others, you are willing to support loved ones who turn to you in difficult times. Intense and sensitive, you may need to resist being overly serious, especially since money issues and love can clash. Usually you are attracted to enterprising and dynamic individuals who are highly motivated.

Your attractive qualities: idealistic, ambitious, charming, imaginative, romantic, shrewd, calm, business sense, creative, practical, caring, responsible, enthusiastic, courageous, tolerant, self-esteem, humanitarian, magnanimous, receptive, resolute, fighting spirit, dynamic will

Your less attractive qualities: stubborn, rebellious, intense relationships, unenthusiastic, self-indulgent, reserved, melancholic, inflexible, too serious, tough, skeptical, frustrated, materialistic, dissatisfied, self-critical, moody

Your Venus Power

The planet Venus has a great deal of influence on your powers of attraction. Below are four possible Venus types for women and men. To find your Venus you need to go to page 771, where you will find the Venus table and extra information. The planet Mars also affects your powers of attraction. To find your Mars table and interpretation go to page 761.

WOMEN WITH VENUS IN VIRGO: Intelligent and discriminating, you are usually drawn to polite and refined individuals. As a perfectionist, you may be keen to analyze and criticize yourself but be careful of continually going over your partner's shortcomings. By focusing on how you can make positive improvements in yourself and in your relationships, you avoid becoming skeptical or confused. You empower yourself when you display kind and caring concern for the well-being of loved ones and spontaneously offer your practical assistance.

MEN WITH VENUS IN VIRGO: A love of order usually indicates that you are attracted to refined individuals with analytical or practical abilities. You and your partner may be working together or serving similar causes. As you constantly analyze partnerships in order to improve them, you are likely to use former relationships as a point of reference and compare them to your present partner. As you are helpful and kind, others usually rely on your good judgment and often turn to you for advice or practical assistance.

WOMEN WITH VENUS IN LIBRA: Usually you are attractive and sociable with an easygoing manner. Your love of beauty, harmony, and pleasure implies that you are a romantic with a desire for love and affection. Once in a relationship you need to learn to negotiate your position rather than adapt to the wishes of others and compromise just to keep the peace. Nevertheless, your advanced social skills and strong sense of fair play can help you succeed in any social or romantic situation.

MEN WITH VENUS IN LIBRA: Courteous and refined, you are attracted to beautiful and elegant people. You are looking for a partner who can share your natural good taste and enjoy an intellectual conversation. Disliking conflict, you may have to be careful not to go along with others just to keep the peace.

Your ideal partner will appreciate beauty and the little luxuries of life as well as possess good social skills. You have a strong sense of social etiquette yourself so you need an intelligent and sophisticated partner.

WOMEN WITH VENUS IN SCORPIO: Usually you are drawn to partners who are sensual in appearance with a strong character. As you are emotionally intense and passionate, personal relationships are probably a major factor in your life. Since you like to be in control, you can at times exhibit some of your less attractive qualities by being willful or domineering. Although you need to feel established and in command in your relationships, you are constantly searching for some higher truth that can bring about a significant transformation.

MEN WITH VENUS IN SCORPIO: Usually you are attracted to sensual and passionate partners with strong character. You are often intense with deep feelings and magnetic powers of attraction. As a cautious yet devoted and ardent lover, you are likely to seek experiences that are more sexual in their nature. You display your less attractive qualities when you project your negative thoughts and resort to being suspicious or possessive. Nevertheless, loyal and loving, you are a sensitive lover.

WOMEN WITH VENUS IN SAGITTARIUS: At your best when being optimistic and generous, you possess a mischievous sense of fun. In relationships your open-minded approach to people and places may attract you to those of a different culture or make you tolerant of the foibles of others. Although warm and enthusiastic when in love, your natural honesty and idealism may inspire you to look for a partner who shares your love of freedom.

MEN WITH VENUS IN SAGITTARIUS: Forward-thinking rather than dwelling on the past, you are looking for a partner who can share your future plans. You enjoy exploring life whether through travel and mental pursuits or sports and games. Idealistic, you usually prefer the company of a partner who is optimistic and shares your beliefs. In your desire for honesty in relationships, however, be careful not to become tactless. Nevertheless, you are attracted to honest, direct, and fun-loving partners who have a sense of humor like your own.

To read all about your Outer Planets and work out how to use your personalized timetable, go to Section Three, page 789.

♏

Your Personalized Timetable

JUPITER BENEFICIAL
1938 4/7 – 9/14
1938 11/22 – until 1939 2/15
1942 5/15 – 7/26
1944 7/12 – 8/29
1948 3/14 – 5/18
1948 11/1 – 12/18
1950 3/18 – until 1951 1/28
1953 9/8 – 11/20
1954 4/26 – 7/9
1955 10/26 – until 1956 2/10
1956 6/22 – 8/13
1960 2/13 – 7/1
1960 10/8 – 12/2
1962 3/1 – 5/24
1962 8/10 – until 1963 1/8
1965 8/11 – until 1966 1/1
1966 3/31 – 6/23
1967 10/4 – until 1968 3/21
1968 5/23 – 7/28
1972 1/24 – 3/30
1972 5/20 – 11/13
1974 2/12 – 4/25
1974 9/26 – 12/11
1977 7/22 – until 1978 6/6
1979 9/16 – 11/12
1980 2/8 – 7/8
1984 1/7 – 2/26
1984 7/5 – 10/22
1986 1/27 – 4/6
1989 7/4 – 10/10
1989 11/15 – until 1990 5/19
1991 8/30 – 10/19
1992 3/18 – 6/13
1995 12/22 – until 1996 2/6
1998 1/10 – 3/19
2001 6/18 – 9/3
2002 1/3 – 4/27
2003 8/15 – 10/1
2007 12/7 – until 2008 1/20
2009 5/4 – 7/27
2009 12/21 – until 2010 3/2

SATURN BENEFICIAL
1943 8/19 – 12/1
1944 5/5 – 10/1
1944 11/14 – until 1945 6/5
1948 8/28 – until 1949 8/15
1958 12/13 – until 1959 12/13
1964 2/4 – until 1965 3/21
1973 6/17 – until 1974 7/16
1977 10/11 – until 1978 2/13
1978 7/2 – 9/23
1979 4/22 – 5/26
1988 1/17 – 7/18
1988 10/11 – until 1989 1/16
1989 9/4 – 9/17
1993 3/10 – 9/29
1993 11/25 – until 1994 5/3
1994 8/14 – until 1995 1/25
2002 7/27 – until 2003 1/2
2003 4/13 – 8/29
2003 12/24 – until 2004 5/16
2007 8/12 – 11/12
2008 1/26 – 7/28

URANUS BENEFICIAL
1947 7/26 – until 1952 4/18
1961 9/7 – until 1964 7/10
1987 12/26 – until 1990 11/19
2001 4/24 – until 2006 2/22

NEPTUNE BENEFICIAL
1983 1/3 – until 1987 12/20
2009 2/23 – Continues

PLUTO BENEFICIAL
1955 9/16 – until 1961 8/16
2007 1/9 – until 2012 10/26

JUPITER CHALLENGING
1938 1/1 – 2/2
1940 4/22 – 7/6
1940 11/5 – until 1941 2/23
1942 10/20 – 12/5

1943 6/3 – 8/17
1949 3/6 – 8/13
1949 10/24 – until 1950 1/17
1952 4/5 – 6/13
1954 9/16 – until 1955 1/20
1955 5/11 – 7/31
1961 2/15 – 12/31
1964 3/19 – 5/25
1966 8/26 – until 1967 7/16
1973 1/29 – 4/26
1973 7/4 – 12/12
1975 7/31 – 8/29
1976 2/29 – 5/9
1978 8/8 – until 1979 6/28
1985 1/13 – 3/28
1985 8/17 – 11/17
1987 6/20 – 10/21
1988 2/7 – 4/23
1990 7/23 – 10/15
1991 1/15 – 6/9
1996 12/28 – until 1997 3/8
1999 5/28 – until 2000 4/6
2002 7/7 – 9/20
2003 2/24 – 5/13
2008 12/11 – until 2009 2/18
2011 5/9 – 8/28
2011 9/1 – until 2012 3/18

SATURN CHALLENGING
1939 5/8 – until 1940 6/13
1940 11/16 – until 1941 3/3
1945 10/13 – 12/1
1946 6/19 – until 1947 7/20
1961 2/11 – 8/21
1961 11/3 – until 1962 4/15
1962 6/28 – until 1963 1/4
1968 6/30 – 9/14
1969 3/15 – until 1970 4/19
1975 7/29 – until 1976 8/28
1977 3/21 – 5/1
1990 3/30 – 6/9
1990 12/20 – until 1992 2/8
1998 4/21 – until 1999 5/26
2000 1/5 – 1/19
2004 9/10 – until 2005 1/8
2005 5/30 – 10/20
2005 12/25 – until 2006 7/2

URANUS CHALLENGING
1938 1/1 – 2/25
1954 8/1 – until 1958 7/8
1994 2/18 – until 1998 12/19

NEPTUNE CHALLENGING
1995 2/18 – until 2003 1/22

PLUTO CHALLENGING
1938 1/1 – until 1946 6/27

JUPITER SPECIAL
1945 12/28 – until 1946 3/29
1946 8/26 – 11/12
1957 12/4 – until 1958 5/7
1958 7/31 – 10/27
1969 11/16 – until 1970 10/12
1981 10/30 – until 1982 9/24
1993 10/15 – until 1994 1/4
1994 4/26 – 9/4
2005 9/29 – 12/15
2006 6/5 – 8/5

SATURN SPECIAL
1952 12/7 – until 1953 4/9
1953 9/2 – until 1954 10/21
1982 10/12 – until 1983 11/26
1984 6/15 – 8/10
2011 11/18 – until 2012 5/11
2012 8/8 – Continues

URANUS SPECIAL
1973 10/31 – until 1977 10/6

NEPTUNE SPECIAL
1953 11/5 – until 1961 10/15

PLUTO SPECIAL
1981 1/21 – until 1988 9/3

October 27

Your Personal Powers

Dynamic and imaginative, you are a sensitive individual with deep feelings and idealistic notions. You also possess intuitive abilities and a strong will. You gain power when you let your powerful emotions motivate you to be determined, purposeful, and productive yet realistic. As you possess magnetic charm and excellent social skills, you can succeed in all types of people-related businesses. Although you are usually benevolent and warmhearted, you can at times become stubbornly intense or moody, especially when you refuse to communicate or express yourself honestly. Usually you feel more secure when you keep your thoughts and feelings to yourself. You may lose some of your power, however, by being worried, inflexible, or too serious. You usually empower yourself through gaining knowledge and being forward-looking. Usually your inner strength and willpower can help you stay calm and collected even when situations become turbulent. By letting go of emotional baggage and resisting any form of controlling behavior, you can realize the power of love and achieve contentment.

Your Powers of Attraction in Relationships

Friendly and sociable, you attract people with your charismatic personality and purposeful nature. By being more open or less secretive, you can gain other people's trust and support, thereby charming and impressing them with your generosity and sincerity. If your partner fails to interpret your changing moods, you may end up feeling frustrated or misunderstood. You can also express your fears by being possessive and jealous. When you feel inspired, however, you become enthusiastic, cheering others with your warmth and love. Usually you are attracted to hardworking and responsible partners who can be loyal and enduring. Since you like to maintain the peace and are easily disturbed by conflict, resist becoming involved in power struggles that can cause you anxiety. Security-conscious, you are usually very protective of those you love.

Your attractive qualities: versatile, purposeful, sensitive, friendly, supportive, imaginative, strong instincts and willpower, flair for people, creative, resolute, brave, calm, detached, spiritual, good understanding, tolerant, dedicated, inventive, mental strength, productive, industrious, fiercely loyal, independent

Your less attractive qualities: disagreeable, quarrelsome, easily offended, restless, nervous, mistrusting, overemotional, tense, stubborn, controlling, reserved, possessive, jealous, uncommunicative, moody, secretive

Your Venus Power

The planet Venus has a great deal of influence on your powers of attraction. Below are four possible Venus types for women and men. To find your Venus you need to go to page 771, where you will find the Venus table and extra information. The planet Mars also affects your powers of attraction. To find your Mars table and interpretation go to page 761.

WOMEN WITH VENUS IN VIRGO: Polite, refined, and organized, you are attracted to articulate and intelligent people. Since you are caring, concerned, and want to be of practical help to others, you can be an asset to any partnership. By being too analytical, exacting, or faultfinding, however, a doubting element can creep into your relationships. By expressing your feelings in a positive way you can become more decisive and improve on how you relate to loved ones.

MEN WITH VENUS IN VIRGO: Industrious and well-ordered, you relate to others in a considerate and down-to-earth way. You enjoy giving practical advice and being of service to those you love even in small ways. Being a perfectionist, you are drawn to partners with high morals or a strong work ethic. Partners who have strong analytical minds are very attractive to you, particularly if they are also clean and meticulously dressed.

WOMEN WITH VENUS IN LIBRA: Gracious, charming, and sociable with a sense of style, you have no trouble attracting admirers. With your natural diplomatic skills and desire for harmony you usually like to keep the peace and avoid confrontations, but be careful of failing to take a stand when it is necessary. Romantic and easygoing yourself, you are attracted to affectionate and refined individuals who share your love of peace, justice, and fair play.

MEN WITH VENUS IN LIBRA: You are such good company, people are naturally drawn to you and especially appreciate your talent for making them feel special. You find status in your social contacts and place importance on your relationships. Being clever and a charming companion, you will go out of your way to keep situations peaceful and harmonious. In relationships, however, be careful of indecision or compro-

mising too much. Nevertheless, others are attracted by your natural refinement and good taste, which is reflected in your sense of style.

WOMEN WITH VENUS IN SCORPIO: Loving and passionate, you are often sensitive with deep feelings and strong powers of attraction. A love for the truth coupled with a tendency to be suspicious can be an influence that motivates you to delve deep into the activities of your partner. When in love or in a relationship that matters, you will often bend over backward to cooperate. Although loyal, guard against losing sight of your own needs and desires.

MEN WITH VENUS IN SCORPIO: You are usually attracted to sensual and passionate partners with strong character. You are often intense with deep feelings and magnetic powers of attraction. As a cautious yet devoted and ardent lover you are likely to seek experiences that are more sexual in their nature. You display your less attractive qualities when you project your negative thoughts and resort to being suspicious or possessive. Nevertheless, loyal and loving, you are a sensitive lover.

WOMEN WITH VENUS IN SAGITTARIUS: Sociable, warm, and friendly, you possess an honest and frank style in your relationships. Being naturally gregarious, you want others to share your enthusiasm and enjoy encouraging the people you love. You fare better when you have a sense of personal freedom within a relationship and are usually generous with the faults of others. You need a partner who can share your need to explore and take risks, whether through travel, education, or recreation.

MEN WITH VENUS IN SAGITTARIUS: Usually you are attracted to partners who are knowledgeable or well traveled. Enthusiastic and optimistic, you often respond quickly to love offers and enter relationships with enthusiasm. Usually you seek to expand your social circle and meeting people from all walks of life can bring you the variety and fun you seek in life. Although you are generous and honest, your partners may accuse you of being overly optimistic or too blunt.

To read all about your Outer Planets and work out how to use your personalized timetable, go to Section Three, page 789.

Your Personalized Timetable

JUPITER BENEFICIAL
1938 4/12 – 9/5
1938 12/1 – until 1939 2/19
1942 5/20 – 7/30
1944 7/17 – 9/3
1948 3/26 – 5/5
1948 11/7 – 12/23
1950 3/23 – until 1951 2/1
1953 9/18 – 11/10
1954 5/1 – 7/13
1955 11/2 – until 1956 2/2
1956 6/28 – 8/18
1960 2/19 – 6/23
1960 10/15 – 12/6
1962 3/5 – 6/3
1962 7/31 – until 1963 1/13
1965 8/16 – 12/25
1966 4/8 – 6/27
1967 10/9 – until 1968 3/11
1968 6/2 – 8/2
1972 1/29 – 11/18
1974 2/16 – 5/1
1974 9/17 – 12/19
1977 7/26 – until 1978 6/11
1979 9/21 – 11/21
1980 1/30 – 7/14
1984 1/11 – 3/4
1984 6/27 – 10/28
1986 2/1 – 4/10
1989 7/9 – until 1990 5/24
1991 9/4 – 10/25
1992 3/10 – 6/21
1995 12/27 – until 1996 2/11
1996 8/16 – 9/21
1998 1/15 – 3/23
2001 6/22 – 9/9
2001 12/27 – until 2002 5/3
2003 8/19 – 10/6
2007 12/11 – until 2008 1/24
2009 5/13 – 7/18
2009 12/26 – until 2010 3/7

SATURN BENEFICIAL
1943 9/1 – 11/17
1944 5/14 – until 1945 6/13
1948 9/5 – until 1949 8/23
1958 12/22 – until 1959 12/22
1964 2/13 – until 1965 3/29
1965 10/13 – 12/15
1973 6/24 – until 1974 7/23
1977 10/22 – until 1978 2/1
1978 7/11 – 10/2
1979 3/31 – 6/17
1988 1/27 – 7/3
1988 10/25 – until 1989 1/24
1989 8/5 – 10/17
1993 3/19 – 9/11
1993 12/12 – until 1994 5/17
1994 7/29 – until 1995 2/3
2002 8/5 – 12/20
2003 4/24 – 9/9
2003 12/12 – until 2004 5/25
2007 8/20 – 12/3
2008 1/4 – 8/6

URANUS BENEFICIAL
1947 8/19 – until 1952 5/15
1961 9/24 – until 1964 7/30
1988 1/12 – until 1990 12/8
2002 2/22 – until 2006 12/25

NEPTUNE BENEFICIAL
1983 2/2 – until 1988 11/16
2009 3/23 – Continues

PLUTO BENEFICIAL
1955 10/28 – until 1962 7/16
2007 2/11 – until 2012 12/3

JUPITER CHALLENGING
1938 1/1 – 2/7
1940 4/26 – 7/13
1940 10/28 – until 1941 3/1
1943 6/8 – 8/21

1949 3/11 – 8/4
1949 11/1 – until 1950 1/21
1952 4/9 – 6/18
1952 12/22 – until 1953 1/19
1954 9/22 – until 1955 1/12
1955 5/17 – 8/5
1961 2/19 – until 1962 1/4
1964 3/23 – 5/30
1966 8/31 – until 1967 2/25
1967 4/14 – 7/20
1973 2/2 – 5/8
1973 6/22 – 12/17
1976 3/5 – 5/13
1978 8/13 – until 1979 7/3
1985 1/17 – 4/3
1985 8/9 – 11/24
1987 6/27 – 10/13
1988 2/13 – 4/27
1990 7/27 – 10/23
1991 1/7 – 6/14
1997 1/1 – 3/13
1999 6/2 – 12/7
2000 1/3 – 4/10
2002 7/11 – 9/26
2003 2/16 – 5/21
2008 12/16 – until 2009 2/23
2011 5/14 – until 2012 3/22

SATURN CHALLENGING
1939 5/17 – 11/26
1940 1/28 – 6/23
1940 11/3 – until 1941 3/13
1946 6/27 – until 1947 7/28
1961 2/20 – 8/5
1961 11/18 – until 1962 5/13
1962 5/30 – until 1963 1/13
1968 7/22 – 8/22
1969 3/23 – until 1970 4/26
1975 8/6 – until 1976 9/5
1977 3/2 – 5/20
1990 12/29 – until 1992 2/16
1998 4/29 – until 1999 6/3
1999 12/9 – until 2000 2/15
2004 9/21 – 12/26
2005 6/8 – until 2006 7/10

URANUS CHALLENGING
1938 1/1 – 3/22
1954 8/19 – until 1958 7/25
1994 3/12 – until 1999 1/8

NEPTUNE CHALLENGING
1995 3/31 – until 2003 12/20

PLUTO CHALLENGING
1938 1/1 – until 1947 6/2

JUPITER SPECIAL
1946 1/5 – 3/20
1946 9/1 – 11/17
1957 12/10 – until 1958 4/28
1958 8/8 – 11/1
1969 11/21 – until 1970 10/16
1981 11/4 – until 1982 9/29
1993 10/19 – until 1994 1/12
1994 4/18 – 9/10
2005 10/4 – 12/20
2006 5/26 – 8/15

SATURN SPECIAL
1952 12/19 – until 1953 3/26
1953 9/12 – until 1954 10/29
1982 10/20 – until 1983 12/5
1984 5/27 – 8/27
2011 11/27 – until 2012 4/26
2012 8/21 – Continues

URANUS SPECIAL
1973 11/17 – until 1977 10/23

NEPTUNE SPECIAL
1953 12/7 – until 1962 9/9

PLUTO SPECIAL
1981 11/14 – until 1988 10/5

♏

459

October 28

SUN: SCORPIO • DECANATE: CANCER • DEGREE: 4°5–5°5 SCORPIO • MODE: FIXED • ELEMENT: WATER

Your Personal Powers

Idealistic and independent, you are a determined individual with an imaginative mind and charismatic personality. Your ruling planet, Pluto, endows you with perseverance, endurance to overcome obstacles, and tenacity to begin again stronger and more confident. A tendency to be overly serious warns that you need to learn to detach yourself from inner fears and insecurities. You lose some of your power when you become vain and disagreeable or behave in an egotistical way. You gain power when you use your dynamic emotions, creativity, and charm to convey your inspired plans, thoughts, and ideas. Being a perfectionist indicates that when you accept or work within the limitations of your circumstances, you realize that the learning process has a greater value than the end result. Self-acceptance is also essential if you want to empower yourself and be a force for good. Usually agreeable and sensitive with deep awareness, you can be highly persuasive when you use your excellent people skills, wit, and captivating manner.

Your Powers of Attraction in Relationships

Other people admire your stamina and determined nature. You are clever and enterprising, and your strong sense of purpose suggests that although you can accomplish much by yourself, you benefit greatly from collaborating or interacting with others. A tendency to vacillate between being giving and loving and being bossy or too demanding implies that you may need to find a balance between being independent or part of a team. Usually you are attracted to charismatic and generous people who are warmhearted, youthful, and romantic. When you are positive you can be witty and entertaining. If you feel insecure, issues of control or personality clashes can damage your close relationships. By remaining detached yet compassionate, you can appear more compromising. Nevertheless, loyal and courageous, you are capable of making great sacrifices for those you love.

Your attractive qualities: ambitious, strong-willed, daring, inner faith, determined, persevering, calm, autonomous, tenacious, analytical, compassionate, progressive, creative, imaginative, idealistic, hardworking, charismatic, enthusiastic, persuasive, noble ideals, integrity, perfectionist, responsible

Your less attractive qualities: arrogant, controlling, restless, moody, impatient, intolerant, too dependent on others, daydreamer, unmotivated, unrealistic, bossy, impulsive, aggressive, lack of confidence or pride, withdrawn

Your Venus Power

The planet Venus has a great deal of influence on your powers of attraction. Below are four possible Venus types for women and men. To find your Venus you need to go to page 771, where you will find the Venus table and extra information. The planet Mars also affects your powers of attraction. To find your Mars table and interpretation go to page 761.

WOMEN WITH VENUS IN VIRGO: In relationships, you can be modest and unassuming but desire perfection. You usually analyze your partnerships until you feel you have understood them to the last little detail in order to improve them. A problem usually arises when you become too critical either of partners or yourself and indulge in being skeptical or faultfinding. You are modest, and others may not be aware of the strong sensuality beneath your well-groomed exterior.

MEN WITH VENUS IN VIRGO: Practical, idealistic, and a perfectionist, you seek a relationship with an intelligent and hardworking partner who can inspire you to be more industrious and well-ordered. At times you can come across as a sympathetic and caring person and at other times you may appear pragmatic and very businesslike. This may sometimes lead to unclear communication between you and your partner. Usually helpful and caring, however, you like to analyze the faults in your relationships and then work methodically to improve them.

WOMEN WITH VENUS IN LIBRA: Attractive, refined, and conscious of the needs of others, you usually desire harmonious relationships. As a peacemaker with good negotiating skills, you can smooth out difficulties with others, but your dislike of confrontation may sometimes leave you refusing to take a stand or compromising too many of your own needs. Courteous, stylish, and charming with polished social skills, you are an expert at relating to others in a gracious and civilized manner.

MEN WITH VENUS IN LIBRA: Courteous and refined, you are attracted to beautiful and elegant people. You are looking for a partner who can share your natural good taste and enjoy an intellectual conversation. Disliking conflict, you may have to be careful not to go along with others just to keep the peace.

Your ideal partner will appreciate beauty and the little luxuries of life as well as possess good social skills. You have a strong sense of social etiquette yourself so you need an intelligent and sophisticated partner.

WOMEN WITH VENUS IN SCORPIO: You are usually drawn to partners who are sensual in appearance with a strong character. As you are emotionally intense and passionate, personal relationships are probably a major factor in your life. Since you like to be in control you can at times exhibit some of your less attractive qualities by being willful or domineering. Although you need to feel established and in command in your relationships you are constantly searching for some higher truth that can bring about a significant transformation.

MEN WITH VENUS IN SCORPIO: As you are emotionally intense and passionate, personal relationships are probably a major factor in your own transformation. Being sensitive yet loyal, you are usually attracted to forceful partners who can express themselves intimately but intensely. Rather than seek easy and simple relationships, you are drawn to partners who act as a catalyst for your own internal changes. Through your relationships with your partners you can unravel your own motives and understand your deep-seated feelings or emotional insecurities.

WOMEN WITH VENUS IN SAGITTARIUS: Optimistic and fun-loving, you love adventure and seek a partner who can expand your horizons. Being truthful and direct, you often say what you think. At times you may be naively tactless. A need for expansion and prosperity suggests that you may enjoy traveling with your friends or partner. Being both lighthearted and idealistic, however, indicates that once you have given your heart to someone you will stay honorable and loyal.

MEN WITH VENUS IN SAGITTARIUS: When in love, you are open and friendly, with a need for a partner who can share your adventurous spirit and sense of fun. Be careful, however, that your desire for freedom does not cause you to avoid commitment. You prefer your partners to be positive, direct, and generous in spirit. Being outspoken as well as an idealist, you usually enjoy a partner with whom you can share your strong opinions. Alternatively, you may wish to explore life together, whether through travel education or having fun.

To read all about your Outer Planets and work out how to use your personalized timetable, go to Section Three, page 789.

To read all about your Outer Planets and work out how to use your personalized timetable, go to Section Three, page 789.

Your Personalized Timetable

JUPITER BENEFICIAL
1938 4/18 – 8/28
1938 12/8 – until 1939 2/23
1942 5/25 – 8/4
1944 7/22 – 9/7
1948 11/12 – 12/27
1950 3/27 – until 1951 2/6
1953 10/6 – 10/23
1954 5/6 – 7/18
1955 11/10 – until 1956 1/24
1956 7/4 – 8/22
1960 2/25 – 6/15
1960 10/22 – 12/11
1962 3/9 – 6/17
1962 7/17 – until 1963 1/18
1965 8/23 – 12/17
1966 4/14 – 7/2
1967 10/15 – until 1968 3/3
1968 6/10 – 8/6
1972 2/3 – 8/2
1972 9/17 – 11/23
1974 2/21 – 5/7
1974 9/10 – 12/25
1977 7/31 – until 1978 2/7
1978 3/4 – 6/15
1979 9/26 – 12/2
1980 1/19 – 7/20
1984 1/16 – 3/11
1984 6/19 – 11/3
1986 2/5 – 4/15
1989 7/13 – until 1990 5/29
1991 9/9 – 10/31
1992 3/2 – 6/28
1995 12/31 – until 1996 2/16
1996 8/3 – 10/4
1998 1/19 – 3/28
2001 6/26 – 9/16
2001 12/19 – until 2002 5/9
2003 8/24 – 10/11
2004 4/18 – 5/21
2007 12/15 – until 2008 1/29
2009 5/25 – 7/5
2009 12/31 – until 2010 3/11

SATURN BENEFICIAL
1943 9/21 – 10/27
1944 5/22 – until 1945 6/21
1948 9/13 – until 1949 4/26
1949 5/5 – 8/31
1958 12/30 – until 1959 12/30
1964 2/21 – until 1965 4/8
1965 9/26 – 12/30
1973 7/2 – until 1974 8/1
1975 2/22 – 4/3
1977 11/5 – until 1978 1/17
1978 7/20 – 10/10
1979 3/17 – 6/30
1988 2/6 – 6/19
1988 11/5 – until 1989 2/3
1989 7/20 – 11/1
1993 3/29 – 8/28
1993 12/24 – until 1994 6/14
1994 7/1 – until 1995 2/11
2002 8/16 – 12/8
2003 5/3 – 9/24
2003 11/26 – until 2004 6/3
2007 8/28 – until 2008 8/14

URANUS BENEFICIAL
1948 6/18 – until 1952 6/4
1961 10/15 – until 1964 8/16
1988 1/31 – until 1990 12/25
2002 3/12 – until 2007 1/20

NEPTUNE BENEFICIAL
1983 12/31 – until 1988 12/16
2009 5/6 – Continues

PLUTO BENEFICIAL
1956 9/23 – until 1962 8/18
2008 1/6 – Continues

JUPITER CHALLENGING
1938 1/1 – 2/11
1940 4/30 – 7/20
1940 10/21 – until 1941 3/7

1943 6/13 – 8/26
1949 3/17 – 7/27
1949 11/9 – until 1950 1/26
1952 4/13 – 6/23
1952 12/8 – until 1953 2/2
1954 9/29 – until 1955 1/5
1955 5/23 – 8/9
1961 2/24 – until 1962 1/9
1964 3/27 – 6/3
1966 9/5 – until 1967 2/14
1967 4/25 – 7/25
1973 2/6 – 12/22
1976 3/10 – 5/17
1978 8/18 – until 1979 7/8
1985 1/21 – 4/9
1985 8/2 – 11/30
1987 7/4 – 10/6
1988 2/18 – 5/1
1990 8/1 – 11/2
1990 12/28 – until 1991 6/20
1997 1/6 – 3/17
1997 9/26 – 10/19
1999 6/7 – 11/22
2000 1/17 – 4/14
2002 7/16 – 10/2
2003 2/8 – 5/28
2008 12/20 – until 2009 2/27
2011 5/18 – until 2012 3/27

SATURN CHALLENGING
1939 5/25 – 11/10
1940 2/12 – 7/4
1940 10/21 – until 1941 3/23
1946 7/5 – until 1947 8/4
1961 3/2 – 7/22
1961 11/29 – until 1963 1/22
1969 3/31 – until 1970 5/4
1975 8/14 – until 1976 3/9
1976 4/14 – 9/14
1977 2/16 – 6/3
1991 1/6 – until 1992 2/25
1992 9/21 – 11/9
1998 5/7 – until 1999 6/12
1999 11/24 – until 2000 2/29
2004 10/6 – 12/11
2005 6/17 – until 2006 7/18

URANUS CHALLENGING
1938 1/1 – 4/10
1954 9/7 – until 1959 5/5
1994 4/26 – until 1999 1/25

NEPTUNE CHALLENGING
1996 2/14 – until 2004 1/19

PLUTO CHALLENGING
1940 10/31 – until 1947 7/15

JUPITER SPECIAL
1946 1/16 – 3/9
1946 9/6 – 11/21
1957 12/16 – until 1958 4/20
1958 8/16 – 11/6
1969 11/26 – until 1970 6/10
1970 7/6 – 10/21
1981 11/9 – until 1982 10/4
1993 10/24 – until 1994 1/20
1994 4/9 – 9/16
2005 10/9 – 12/26
2006 5/17 – 8/24

SATURN SPECIAL
1953 1/2 – 3/11
1953 9/21 – until 1954 11/7
1982 10/28 – until 1983 12/14
1984 5/13 – 9/9
2011 12/7 – until 2012 4/13
2012 9/1 – Continues

URANUS SPECIAL
1973 12/6 – until 1978 7/27

NEPTUNE SPECIAL
1954 11/3 – until 1962 10/12

PLUTO SPECIAL
1981 12/15 – until 1988 10/31

♏

461

October 29

SUN: SCORPIO • DECANATE: SCORPIO • DEGREE: 5°5–6°5 SCORPIO • MODE: FIXED • ELEMENT: WATER

Your Personal Powers

Intuitive and warmhearted, you are a dynamic individual with strong intellect and high ideals. Receptive and mentally quick, you also empower yourself when you create harmony and peace around you or feel contented from within. Personal satisfaction often comes from trusting your strong instincts, finding the truth, and living up to your high ideals. Although you are often easygoing and sociable, your heightened sensitivity implies that when you lose your inner equilibrium you can become intense and let your emotions take control. Do not let suspicion or inner doubts cause you stress, frustration, or worry. As a multitalented and inspired individual, you possess many qualities that need to be expressed, yet without a clear course of action you may find it hard to manifest your wonderful dreams. In order to succeed, you may need to develop your patience, faith, and strategic skills. Luckily, you are an astute and discriminating person who is not afraid to confront challenges and transform the way you think and feel.

Your Powers of Attraction in Relationships

With your caring and attentive manner and sociable personality, you can make a good impression and gain friends. Although often dynamic, you have a tender side to your nature that can be very appealing. You are generally drawn to persuasive individuals with good social skills and an enterprising nature. In love, you can be generous and supportive toward your partners. A strong desire for peace and harmony implies that you are easygoing, yet at times you can also be uncompromising with a need to delve beneath the surface in order to find out the truth about others. Although your intentions are often good, an inclination to interfere indicates that on occasion you can be too critical. Nevertheless, as a considerate and loving person, you can be loyal and sympathetic with a compassionate heart.

Your attractive qualities: truthful, direct, problem solver, shrewd, pragmatic, inspired, balanced, inner peace, generous, successful, creative, intuitive, mystical, powerful dreams, caring, sensitive, charitable, responsible, cooperative, quick wit, highly intuitive, independent, enthusiastic

Your less attractive qualities: unfocused, dreamer, moody, insecure, nervous, selfish, arrogant, extremist, isolated, too sensitive, critical, indecisive, inertia, frustrated, controlling, stubborn, resentful, anxious

Your Venus Power

The planet Venus has a great deal of influence on your powers of attraction. Below are four possible Venus types for women and men. To find your Venus you need to go to page 771, where you will find the Venus table and extra information. The planet Mars also affects your powers of attraction. To find your Mars table and interpretation go to page 761.

WOMEN WITH VENUS IN VIRGO: Intelligent and discriminating, you are usually drawn to polite and refined individuals. As a perfectionist, you may be keen to analyze and criticize yourself but be careful of continually going over your partner's shortcomings. By focusing on how you can make positive improvements in yourself and in your relationships, you avoid becoming skeptical or confused. You empower yourself when you display kind and caring concern for the well-being of loved ones and spontaneously offer your practical assistance.

MEN WITH VENUS IN VIRGO: A love of order usually indicates that you are attracted to refined individuals with analytical or practical abilities. You and your partner may be working together or serving similar causes. As you constantly analyze partnerships in order to improve them, you are likely to use former relationships as a point of reference and compare them to your present partner. As you are helpful and kind, others usually rely on your good judgment and often turn to you for advice or practical assistance.

WOMEN WITH VENUS IN LIBRA: A natural romantic with good social skills, you love to entertain or put people at ease by projecting a warm and gracious manner. Elegant and fair with a touch of glamour, you are also adept at dealing with people in delicate situations or conflicts. You seek refinement and will go out of your way to achieve harmony and keep the peace. For you, relationships are so important that you may need to guard against becoming dependent on others for approval. With your friendly personality and inherent charm, however, you will always be popular and loved.

MEN WITH VENUS IN LIBRA: As a sociable and friendly individual with an eye for beauty, you are amorous and charming. You are a natural gentleman and your ideal partner

usually has an elegant appearance, artistic appreciation, and good taste. Your relationships benefit when you resist the temptation to take the easy way out or put too much emphasis on vanity and high living. Intellectual and naturally refined, you seek a loving partner who can share your romantic and sophisticated aspirations.

WOMEN WITH VENUS IN SCORPIO: With a natural psychic gift for penetrating the feelings of others, you can often help partners transform emotional challenges or sexual difficulties. When you fall in love, your strong feelings and determination give you a potent force that others find attractive and seductive. Although you know what really turns people on, your most profound desire is usually for the deepness and closeness of real love and intimacy in an enduring relationship.

MEN WITH VENUS IN SCORPIO: In relationships you possess a sensitive understanding of your partner's deeper nature. Although you are strongly attached to those you love, you may have to be careful that your feelings do not turn into jealousy or possessiveness. When you fall in love, it is often with an emotional intensity that helps you get in touch with your deep feelings. You are attracted to partners who can share your passion and display strong feelings of sexuality like your own.

WOMEN WITH VENUS IN SAGITTARIUS: At your best when being optimistic and generous, you possess a mischievous sense of fun. In relationships your open-minded approach to people and places may attract you to those of a different culture or make you tolerant of the foibles of others. Although warm and enthusiastic when in love, your natural honesty and idealism may inspire you to look for a partner who shares your love of freedom.

MEN WITH VENUS IN SAGITTARIUS: Forward-thinking rather than dwelling on the past, you are looking for a partner who can share your future plans. You enjoy exploring life whether through travel and mental pursuits or sports and games. Idealistic, you usually prefer the company of a partner who is optimistic and shares your beliefs. In your desire for honesty in relationships, however, be careful not to become tactless. Nevertheless, you are attracted to honest, direct, and fun-loving partners who have a sense of humor like your own.

To read all about your Outer Planets and work out how to use your personalized timetable, go to Section Three, page 789.

♏

Your Personalized Timetable

JUPITER BENEFICIAL
1938 4/24 – 8/20
1938 12/14 – until 1939 2/27
1942 5/29 – 8/9
1944 7/27 – 9/12
1948 11/17 – 12/31
1950 4/1 – until 1951 2/10
1954 5/11 – 7/22
1955 11/21 – until 1956 1/14
1956 7/9 – 8/27
1960 3/4 – 6/7
1960 10/28 – 12/15
1962 3/13 – until 1963 1/23
1965 8/29 – 12/10
1966 4/20 – 7/6
1967 10/21 – until 1968 2/24
1968 6/17 – 8/11
1972 2/8 – 7/21
1972 9/29 – 11/28
1974 2/25 – 5/13
1974 9/2 – until 1975 1/1
1977 8/5 – until 1978 1/23
1978 3/19 – 6/20
1979 10/1 – until 1980 4/19
1980 5/3 – 7/25
1984 1/21 – 3/18
1984 6/11 – 11/9
1986 2/9 – 4/20
1986 10/25 – 11/22
1989 7/18 – until 1990 6/3
1991 9/13 – 11/6
1992 2/24 – 7/4
1996 1/4 – 2/21
1996 7/24 – 10/14
1998 1/24 – 4/1
2001 7/1 – 9/24
2001 12/11 – until 2002 5/15
2003 8/28 – 10/16
2004 4/4 – 6/5
2007 12/20 – until 2008 2/3
2010 1/5 – 3/15

SATURN BENEFICIAL
1944 5/30 – until 1945 6/28
1948 9/22 – until 1949 3/27
1949 6/4 – 9/8
1959 1/8 – until 1960 1/8
1964 2/29 – until 1965 4/17
1965 9/13 – until 1966 1/11
1973 7/10 – until 1974 8/9
1975 2/2 – 4/22
1977 11/26 – 12/26
1978 7/29 – 10/20
1979 3/4 – 7/12
1988 2/18 – 6/5
1988 11/15 – until 1989 2/13
1989 7/6 – 11/13
1993 4/8 – 8/14
1994 1/4 – until 1995 2/20
2002 8/28 – 11/25
2003 5/13 – until 2004 6/11
2007 9/5 – until 2008 8/22

URANUS BENEFICIAL
1948 7/4 – until 1952 6/21
1961 11/14 – until 1964 9/1
1988 2/23 – until 1991 10/23
2002 4/1 – until 2007 2/9

NEPTUNE BENEFICIAL
1984 1/29 – until 1989 11/12
2010 3/19 – Continues

PLUTO BENEFICIAL
1956 11/10 – until 1963 7/17
2008 2/6 – until 2011 10/28

JUPITER CHALLENGING
1938 1/1 – 2/15
1940 5/4 – 7/28
1940 10/12 – until 1941 3/12
1943 6/18 – 8/30
1949 3/23 – 7/19
1949 11/15 – until 1950 1/30

1952 4/17 – 6/28
1952 11/28 – until 1953 2/12
1954 10/7 – 12/28
1955 5/29 – 8/14
1961 3/1 – 9/26
1961 9/26 – until 1962 1/13
1964 4/1 – 6/8
1966 9/11 – until 1967 2/5
1967 5/4 – 7/29
1973 2/11 – 12/27
1976 3/14 – 5/21
1978 8/23 – until 1979 7/13
1985 1/26 – 4/16
1985 7/25 – 12/6
1987 7/11 – 9/27
1988 2/24 – 5/5
1990 8/6 – 11/17
1990 12/12 – until 1991 6/25
1997 1/10 – 3/23
1997 9/10 – 11/4
1999 6/13 – 11/13
2000 1/27 – 4/19
2002 7/20 – 10/8
2003 1/31 – 6/4
2008 12/25 – until 2009 3/3
2011 5/23 – until 2012 4/1

SATURN CHALLENGING
1939 6/4 – 10/28
1940 2/24 – 7/17
1940 10/7 – until 1941 4/1
1946 7/12 – until 1947 8/12
1961 3/13 – 7/8
1961 12/10 – until 1963 1/30
1969 4/8 – until 1970 5/12
1975 8/23 – until 1976 2/18
1976 5/5 – 9/24
1977 2/3 – 6/14
1991 1/15 – until 1992 3/5
1992 9/1 – 11/27
1998 5/15 – 12/4
1999 1/23 – 6/21
1999 11/11 – until 2000 3/11
2004 11/7 – 11/10
2005 6/25 – until 2006 7/26

URANUS CHALLENGING
1938 1/1 – 4/28
1954 10/5 – until 1959 6/10
1995 2/1 – until 1999 11/25

NEPTUNE CHALLENGING
1996 3/21 – until 2004 12/14

PLUTO CHALLENGING
1938 1/1 – until 1948 6/24

JUPITER SPECIAL
1946 2/8 – 2/14
1946 9/11 – 11/26
1957 12/22 – until 1958 4/13
1958 8/22 – 11/10
1969 12/1 – until 1970 5/25
1970 7/22 – 10/25
1981 11/13 – until 1982 10/9
1993 10/28 – until 1994 1/30
1994 3/30 – 9/21
2005 10/13 – until 2006 1/1
2006 5/9 – 8/31

SATURN SPECIAL
1953 9/30 – until 1954 11/15
1982 11/5 – until 1983 12/25
1984 4/30 – 9/20
2011 12/18 – until 2012 3/31
2012 9/11 – Continues

URANUS SPECIAL
1974 1/1 – until 1978 9/8

NEPTUNE SPECIAL
1954 12/3 – until 1963 9/4

PLUTO SPECIAL
1982 11/1 – until 1989 9/20

October 30

SUN: SCORPIO • DECANATE: SCORPIO/PLUTO • DEGREE: 6°5–7°5 SCORPIO • MODE: FIXED • ELEMENT: WATER

Your Personal Powers

Sensitive and versatile, you are a receptive and adventurous individual who responds to life according to how you feel. Your ruling planet, Pluto, grants you tenacity and an unyielding willpower. Alternating between being pragmatic and decisive and being emotionally uncertain or hesitant, you gain power when you become detached and find a way to calm your restless heart. You lose some of your power when you fail to find a compromise between wanting to be independent and free and committing yourself to the responsibility needed for something long lasting. You empower yourself by finding inner satisfaction and by staying focused and purposeful. Creative expression can also elevate your enthusiasm and restrain you from making dramatic changes for no apparent reason other than boredom. Nevertheless, enterprising and versatile, once you have found something truly inspirational, you can be determined and commit yourself wholeheartedly. Mentally quick with a keen eye for business, you are usually enthusiastic about acquiring material wealth or expressing and communicating some of your wonderful ideas.

Your Powers of Attraction in Relationships

As you are mentally quick with a direct approach, others see you as an exciting and stimulating companion. Your enthusiasm, persuasive speech, and friendly nature usually captivate other people. Being indecisive about your feelings, you need to take your time before you commit to long-term relationships. A tendency to be secretive also suggests that you like to keep your emotions under control. Nevertheless, when you fall in love you can be passionate and loving. Although you are entertaining and witty, your comments or criticism can at times be sharp as well as amusing. Usually you are attracted to creative and versatile individuals who can offer you alternative points of view or different styles of living. You also admire individuals who are ambitious, enterprising, and resolute. As your quest for emotional fulfillment is strong, you benefit from being lighthearted and spontaneous.

Your attractive qualities: versatile, charming, friendly, adaptable, adventurous, freedom-loving, loyal, friendly, good synthesizer, talent with words, creative, expressive, lively, dramatic, loyal, charismatic, affectionate, tenacious, dutiful, compassionate, pragmatist, resolute, focused, ambitious

Your less attractive qualities: secretive, easily bored, restless, dissatisfied, obstinate, impatient, bad-tempered, insecure, scattered energy, moody, irresponsible, disillusioned, escapist, overindulgent, jealous

Your Venus Power

The planet Venus has a great deal of influence on your powers of attraction. Below are four possible Venus types for women and men. To find your Venus you need to go to page 771, where you will find the Venus table and extra information. The planet Mars also affects your powers of attraction. To find your Mars table and interpretation go to page 761.

WOMEN WITH VENUS IN VIRGO: Articulate and straightforward in your relationships, you attract others with your genuine concern for their well-being. By being understanding and a good listener, you are able to show your love and friendship. With your analytical approach to relationships, however, you may have to be careful of becoming too matter-of-fact. You often display your concern for the welfare of others by your willingness to offer practical help and assistance. You usually seek a partner who is willing to work as hard on relationships as you are.

MEN WITH VENUS IN VIRGO: Although you are constantly analyzing your relationships in order to understand and improve them, you may nevertheless need to refrain from continuously mulling over issues that can cause anxiety. You are happiest when you are able to help your loved ones in practical ways and forget yourself in your willingness to be of service to others. You seek a partner who has high standards and can be as pragmatic and hardworking as yourself. Ideally they should also be impeccably dressed with a fine analytical mind.

WOMEN WITH VENUS IN LIBRA: A natural romantic with good social skills, you love to entertain or put people at ease by projecting a warm and gracious manner. Elegant and fair with a touch of glamour, you are also adept at dealing with people in delicate situations or conflicts. You seek refinement and will go out of your way to achieve harmony and keep the peace. For you, relationships are so important that you may need to guard against becoming dependent on others for approval. With your friendly personality and inherent charm, however, you will always be popular and loved.

MEN WITH VENUS IN LIBRA: You are such good com-

pany, people are naturally drawn to you and especially appreciate your talent for making them feel special. You find status in your social contacts and place importance on your relationships. Being clever and a charming companion, you will go out of your way to keep situations peaceful and harmonious. In relationships, however, be careful of indecision or compromising too much. Nevertheless, others are attracted by your natural refinement and good taste, which is reflected in your sense of style.

WOMEN WITH VENUS IN SCORPIO: With a natural psychic gift for penetrating the feelings of others, you can often help partners transform emotional challenges or sexual difficulties. When you fall in love, your strong feelings and determination give you a potent force that others find attractive and seductive. Although you know what really turns people on, your most profound desire is usually for the deepness and closeness of real love and intimacy in an enduring relationship.

MEN WITH VENUS IN SCORPIO: As you are emotionally intense and passionate, personal relationships are probably a major factor in your own transformation. Being sensitive yet loyal, you are usually attracted to forceful partners who can express themselves intimately but intensely. Rather than seek easy and simple relationships, you are drawn to partners who act as a catalyst for your own internal changes. Through your relationships with your partners you can unravel your own motives and understand your deep-seated feelings or emotional insecurities.

WOMEN WITH VENUS IN SAGITTARIUS: When you feel generous, you can make others feel more optimistic about life. You may be interested in higher learning and seek partners who are scholarly or broad-minded. You are outspoken and direct and sometimes say things that you later regret. Curious and versatile, you can adjust quickly to new situations; a foreign influence implies that you love to travel or may have a partner who comes from a different culture.

MEN WITH VENUS IN SAGITTARIUS: Your enthusiasm and straightforward conduct usually appeal to others and imply that you are approachable and easygoing. Being open to ideas and willing to believe that life has a great deal to offer suggests that you are generous, broad-minded, and eager to cooperate with others. A love of travel and an interest in other cultures imply that your partner may come from a foreign country.

To read all about your Outer Planets and work out how to use your personalized timetable, go to Section Three, page 789.

To read all about your Outer Planets and work out how to use your personalized timetable, go to Section Three, page 789.

♏

Your Personalized Timetable

JUPITER BENEFICIAL
1938 5/1 – 8/13
1938 12/20 – until 1939 3/3
1942 6/3 – 8/14
1944 8/1 – 9/17
1948 11/21 – until 1949 1/5
1950 4/6 – 10/3
1950 11/14 – until 1951 2/14
1954 5/16 – 7/27
1955 12/8 – 12/28
1956 7/14 – 9/1
1960 3/12 – 5/29
1960 11/2 – 12/20
1962 3/18 – until 1963 1/27
1965 9/6 – 12/2
1966 4/26 – 7/11
1967 10/28 – until 1968 2/17
1968 6/24 – 8/16
1972 2/14 – 7/12
1972 10/7 – 12/3
1974 3/1 – 5/20
1974 8/25 – until 1975 1/6
1977 8/11 – until 1978 1/13
1978 3/29 – 6/24
1979 10/6 – until 1980 3/30
1980 5/23 – 7/30
1984 1/26 – 3/28
1984 6/1 – 11/14
1986 2/13 – 4/25
1986 10/10 – 12/6
1989 7/23 – until 1990 6/8
1991 9/18 – 11/14
1992 2/16 – 7/10
1996 1/9 – 2/27
1996 7/15 – 10/22
1998 1/28 – 4/6
2001 7/5 – 10/4
2001 12/1 – until 2002 5/20
2003 9/2 – 10/21
2004 3/25 – 6/15
2007 12/24 – until 2008 2/7
2010 1/10 – 3/19

SATURN BENEFICIAL
1944 6/7 – until 1945 7/6
1948 9/30 – until 1949 3/12
1949 6/19 – 9/16
1959 1/17 – 8/2
1959 10/7 – until 1960 1/17
1964 3/9 – until 1965 4/28
1965 8/31 – until 1966 1/22
1973 7/18 – until 1974 2/3
1974 3/24 – 8/18
1975 1/19 – 5/5
1978 8/6 – 10/31
1979 2/19 – 7/22
1988 3/3 – 5/20
1988 11/25 – until 1989 2/24
1989 6/22 – 11/23
1993 4/20 – 8/1
1994 1/14 – until 1995 2/28
2002 9/12 – 11/9
2003 5/21 – until 2004 6/19
2007 9/13 – until 2008 8/30

URANUS BENEFICIAL
1948 7/22 – until 1952 7/8
1962 8/31 – until 1965 6/25
1988 12/25 – until 1991 11/19
2002 4/28 – until 2007 2/27

NEPTUNE BENEFICIAL
1984 3/15 – until 1989 12/13
2010 4/24 – Continues

PLUTO BENEFICIAL
1957 9/30 – until 1963 8/19
2009 1/3 – Continues

JUPITER CHALLENGING
1938 1/1 – 2/19
1940 5/9 – 8/6
1940 10/3 – until 1941 3/17
1943 6/23 – 9/4

1949 3/30 – 7/12
1949 11/21 – until 1950 2/3
1952 4/21 – 7/4
1952 11/20 – until 1953 2/19
1954 10/16 – 12/18
1955 6/4 – 8/19
1961 3/6 – 8/29
1961 10/18 – until 1962 1/17
1964 4/5 – 6/13
1966 9/17 – until 1967 1/28
1967 5/12 – 8/3
1973 2/15 – 12/31
1976 3/19 – 5/26
1978 8/27 – until 1979 7/18
1985 1/30 – 4/24
1985 7/17 – 12/12
1987 7/21 – 9/18
1988 2/29 – 5/9
1990 8/10 – until 1991 6/30
1997 1/14 – 3/28
1997 8/31 – 11/14
1999 6/18 – 11/4
2000 2/3 – 4/23
2002 7/25 – 10/15
2003 1/24 – 6/10
2008 12/29 – until 2009 3/8
2011 5/27 – until 2012 4/5

SATURN CHALLENGING
1939 6/14 – 10/15
1940 3/5 – 8/4
1940 9/18 – until 1941 4/9
1946 7/20 – until 1947 8/20
1961 3/26 – 6/23
1961 12/19 – until 1963 2/7
1969 4/16 – until 1970 5/20
1975 8/31 – until 1976 2/4
1976 5/18 – 10/4
1977 1/22 – 6/24
1991 1/23 – until 1992 3/14
1992 8/18 – 12/10
1998 5/24 – 11/17
1999 2/9 – 7/2
1999 10/29 – until 2000 3/21
2005 7/3 – until 2006 8/3

URANUS CHALLENGING
1938 1/1 – until 1939 2/25
1955 7/27 – until 1959 7/1
1995 2/19 – until 1999 12/22

NEPTUNE CHALLENGING
1997 2/10 – until 2005 1/14

PLUTO CHALLENGING
1938 2/20 – until 1949 5/24

JUPITER SPECIAL
1946 9/17 – 12/1
1957 12/30 – until 1958 4/5
1958 8/28 – 11/15
1969 12/7 – until 1970 5/14
1970 8/2 – 10/30
1981 11/18 – until 1982 10/14
1993 11/2 – until 1994 2/14
1994 3/14 – 9/27
2005 10/18 – until 2006 1/7
2006 5/2 – 9/7

SATURN SPECIAL
1953 10/8 – until 1954 11/23
1982 11/14 – until 1983 6/4
1983 7/28 – until 1984 1/5
1984 4/16 – 9/30
2012 1/1 – 3/16
2012 9/21 – Continues

URANUS SPECIAL
1974 10/25 – until 1978 9/29

NEPTUNE SPECIAL
1955 10/31 – until 1963 10/10

PLUTO SPECIAL
1982 11/28 – until 1989 10/19

October 31

Your Personal Powers

Idealistic and imaginative with an optimistic yet practical outlook, you are an inspired individual who seeks inner contentment or emotional fulfillment. Since your ruling planet, Pluto, grants you tenacity, a resolute nature, and powerful feelings, you can succeed admirably when you remain relaxed or emotionally unruffled. An ability to intuitively assess people and situations indicates that you can succeed in all types of people-related activities. Being hardworking and practical also implies that you have an excellent head for business and a good sense of values. You gain power when you use your persuasive charm and share your enthusiasm and ideas with others. Although you can be self-reliant and determined, a tendency to fluctuate between being too confident and self-doubting suggests that you can lose some of your power when you become willful or anxious. By learning to be less controlling and more giving, you can gain the balance and harmony you so desire. Nevertheless, security-conscious and reliable, you empower yourself by developing your inner faith and foresight.

Your Powers of Attraction in Relationships

Usually you want to maintain the status quo and keep everyone happy. An emphasis on collaborating with others indicates that you prefer to be in partnerships. Other people are attracted to your friendly and warmhearted personality. When you are challenged or deceived, however, your compassionate nature can turn very cold and be unforgiving. A tendency to be controlling or harbor inner fears warns that stubbornness may be one of your less attractive qualities. Usually you are drawn to individuals who possess quick instincts and sharp wit. In close relationships you want an honest partner who understands your moods and can offer you reassurance or emotional security. Although you may choose to present yourself in a lighthearted way, inwardly you are tenacious and strong.

Your attractive qualities: productive, contented, bold, pragmatic, philanthropic, charming, friendly, good mind, strong sense of justice, responsible, collaborative, practical, persistent, discriminating, intuitive, creative, original, constructive, relentless, good conversationalist, sincere, hard worker

Your less attractive qualities: stubborn, insecure, too rigid, controlling, overstretch your resources, fixed views, anxious, periods of inertia, manipulative, too dependent, restless, impatient, suspicious, easily discouraged

Your Venus Power

The planet Venus has a great deal of influence on your powers of attraction. Below are four possible Venus types for women and men. To find your Venus you need to go to page 771, where you will find the Venus table and extra information. The planet Mars also affects your powers of attraction. To find your Mars table and interpretation go to page 761.

WOMEN WITH VENUS IN VIRGO: In relationships you can be modest and unassuming but desire perfection. You usually analyze your partnerships until you feel you have understood them to the last little detail in order to improve them. A problem usually arises when you become too critical either of partners or yourself and indulge in being skeptical or fault-finding. As you are modest, others may not be aware of the strong sensuality beneath your well-groomed exterior.

MEN WITH VENUS IN VIRGO: Industrious and well-ordered, you relate to others in a considerate and down-to-earth way. You enjoy giving practical advice and being of service to those you love even in small ways. Being a perfectionist, you are drawn to partners with high morals or a strong work ethic. Partners who have strong analytical minds are very attractive to you, particularly if they are also clean and meticulously dressed.

WOMEN WITH VENUS IN LIBRA: A natural romantic with good social skills, you love to entertain or put people at ease by projecting a warm and gracious manner. Elegant and fair with a touch of glamour, you are also adept at dealing with people in delicate situations or conflicts. You seek refinement and will go out of your way to achieve harmony and keep the peace. For you, relationships are so important that you may need to guard against becoming dependent on others for approval. With your friendly personality and inherent charm, however, you will always be popular and loved.

MEN WITH VENUS IN LIBRA: As a sociable and friendly individual with an eye for beauty, you are amorous and charming. You are a natural gentleman and your ideal partner usually has an elegant appearance, artistic appreciation, and good taste. Your relationships benefit when you resist the temptation to take the easy way out or put too much emphasis on vanity and high living. Intellectual and naturally refined, you

seek a loving partner who can share your romantic and sophisticated aspirations.

WOMEN WITH VENUS IN SCORPIO: Usually you are drawn to partners who are sensual in appearance with a strong character. As you are emotionally intense and passionate, personal relationships are probably a major factor in your life. Since you like to be in control, you can at times exhibit some of your less attractive qualities by being willful or domineering. Although you need to feel established and in command in your relationships, you are constantly searching for some higher truth that can bring about a significant transformation.

MEN WITH VENUS IN SCORPIO: As you are emotionally intense and passionate, personal relationships are probably a major factor in your own transformation. Being sensitive yet loyal, you are usually attracted to forceful partners who can express themselves intimately but intensely. Rather than seek easy and simple relationships you are drawn to partners who act as a catalyst for your own internal changes. Through your relationships with your partners you can unravel your own motives and understand your deep-seated feelings or emotional insecurities.

WOMEN WITH VENUS IN SAGITTARIUS: At your best when being optimistic and generous, you possess a mischievous sense of fun. In relationships your open-minded approach to people and places may attract you to those of a different culture or make you tolerant of the foibles of others. Although warm and enthusiastic when in love, your natural honesty and idealism may inspire you to look for a partner who shares your love of freedom.

MEN WITH VENUS IN SAGITTARIUS: Forward-thinking rather than dwelling on the past, you are looking for a partner who can share your future plans. You enjoy exploring life whether through travel and mental pursuits or sports and games. Idealistic, you usually prefer the company of a partner who is optimistic and shares your beliefs. In your desire for honesty in relationships, however, be careful not to become tactless. Nevertheless, you are attracted to honest, direct, and fun-loving partners who have a sense of humor like your own.

To read all about your Outer Planets and work out how to use your personalized timetable, go to Section Three, page 789.

Your Personalized Timetable

JUPITER BENEFICIAL
1938 5/8 – 8/4
1938 12/26 – until 1939 3/7
1942 6/7 – 8/19
1943 3/2 – 3/21
1944 8/6 – 9/21
1948 11/26 – until 1949 1/9
1950 4/11 – 9/21
1950 11/25 – until 1951 2/18
1954 5/21 – 7/31
1956 7/20 – 9/5
1960 3/22 – 5/19
1960 11/8 – 12/24
1962 3/22 – until 1963 2/1
1965 9/14 – 11/23
1966 5/2 – 7/15
1967 11/4 – until 1968 2/9
1968 6/30 – 8/21
1972 2/19 – 7/3
1972 10/15 – 12/7
1974 3/5 – 5/28
1974 8/17 – until 1975 1/12
1977 8/16 – until 1978 1/5
1978 4/7 – 6/29
1979 10/11 – until 1980 3/20
1980 6/3 – 8/4
1984 1/30 – 4/9
1984 5/19 – 11/20
1986 2/17 – 4/30
1986 10/1 – 12/16
1989 7/27 – until 1990 6/12
1991 9/23 – 11/22
1992 2/7 – 7/16
1996 1/13 – 3/4
1996 7/7 – 10/28
1998 2/1 – 4/10
2001 7/10 – 10/19
2001 11/16 – until 2002 5/25
2003 9/7 – 10/27
2004 3/16 – 6/23
2007 12/29 – until 2008 2/12
2010 1/15 – 3/23

SATURN BENEFICIAL
1944 6/15 – until 1945 7/14
1948 10/10 – until 1949 2/27
1949 7/1 – 9/24
1959 1/26 – 7/16
1959 10/23 – until 1960 1/25
1960 8/21 – 10/10
1964 3/18 – 9/28
1964 12/5 – until 1965 5/10
1965 8/17 – until 1966 1/31
1973 7/27 – until 1974 1/17
1974 4/10 – 8/27
1975 1/7 – 5/16
1978 8/14 – 11/12
1979 2/6 – 7/31
1988 3/26 – 4/27
1988 12/4 – until 1989 3/9
1989 6/8 – 12/3
1993 5/6 – 7/15
1994 1/23 – until 1995 3/8
2003 12/9 – until 2004 6/27
2007 9/21 – until 2008 4/5
2008 5/30 – 9/7

URANUS BENEFICIAL
1948 8/12 – until 1953 5/7
1962 9/16 – until 1965 7/20
1989 1/10 – until 1991 12/8
2003 2/27 – until 2007 12/30

NEPTUNE BENEFICIAL
1985 1/24 – until 1990 11/7
2011 3/15 – Continues

PLUTO BENEFICIAL
1958 9/3 – until 1964 7/16
2009 2/2 – Continues

JUPITER CHALLENGING
1938 1/1 – 2/24
1940 5/13 – 8/21
1940 9/18 – until 1941 3/22

1943 6/27 – 9/9
1949 4/7 – 7/3
1949 11/27 – until 1950 2/7
1952 4/26 – 7/10
1952 11/12 – until 1953 2/26
1954 10/29 – 12/6
1955 6/9 – 8/23
1961 3/11 – 8/18
1961 10/29 – until 1962 1/22
1964 4/9 – 6/17
1966 9/23 – until 1967 1/21
1967 5/19 – 8/7
1973 2/20 – until 1974 1/5
1976 3/23 – 5/30
1978 9/1 – until 1979 3/12
1979 4/9 – 7/22
1985 2/3 – 5/3
1985 7/7 – 12/17
1987 8/4 – 9/4
1988 3/5 – 5/14
1990 8/15 – until 1991 7/5
1997 1/18 – 4/2
1997 8/22 – 11/22
1999 6/24 – 10/28
2000 2/10 – 4/27
2002 7/29 – 10/23
2003 1/16 – 6/16
2009 1/2 – 3/13
2011 6/1 – until 2012 4/10

SATURN CHALLENGING
1939 6/26 – 10/2
1940 3/14 – until 1941 4/17
1946 7/28 – until 1947 8/28
1961 4/14 – 6/4
1961 12/28 – until 1963 2/16
1969 4/24 – until 1970 5/28
1975 9/10 – until 1976 1/22
1976 5/29 – 10/17
1977 1/8 – 7/3
1991 2/1 – until 1992 3/25
1992 8/4 – 12/21
1998 6/2 – 11/3
1999 2/21 – 7/14
1999 10/16 – until 2000 3/30
2005 7/11 – until 2006 8/11

URANUS CHALLENGING
1938 1/1 – until 1939 3/23
1955 8/13 – until 1959 7/18
1995 3/13 – until 2000 1/11

NEPTUNE CHALLENGING
1997 3/14 – until 2005 12/8

PLUTO CHALLENGING
1938 1/1 – until 1939 3/20
1939 5/5 – until 1949 7/11

JUPITER SPECIAL
1946 9/22 – 12/6
1958 1/7 – 3/27
1958 9/3 – 11/19
1969 12/12 – until 1970 5/5
1970 8/10 – 11/4
1981 11/23 – until 1982 10/19
1993 11/7 – until 1994 10/2
2005 10/23 – until 2006 1/14
2006 4/23 – 9/13

SATURN SPECIAL
1953 10/17 – until 1954 12/2
1955 6/16 – 8/20
1982 11/23 – until 1983 5/16
1983 8/15 – until 1984 1/20
1984 3/31 – 10/10
2012 1/24 – 2/21
2012 9/30 – Continues

URANUS SPECIAL
1974 11/10 – until 1978 10/17

NEPTUNE SPECIAL
1955 11/29 – until 1964 8/27

PLUTO SPECIAL
1983 1/6 – until 1990 8/30

♏

November 1

SUN: SCORPIO • DECANATE: SCORPIO/PLUTO • DEGREE: 8°5–9°5 SCORPIO • MODE: FIXED • ELEMENT: WATER

Your Personal Powers

Idealistic and independent, you are a determined individual with strong desires and deep emotions. Your ruling planet, Pluto, endows you with tenacity, aspirations, and the power to overcome obstacles. You gain power when you stay focused and purposeful while showing your compassion and sensitivity toward others. Although you can be lighthearted and charming, a need for personal growth implies that you are ambitious and enterprising. Dwelling on negative thoughts can deplete your energy and cause you frustration or inertia, while positive or inspired ideas can invigorate and empower you. By staying resolute in the face of adversity rather than letting worry cloud your judgment, you can achieve admirable results. Although you are usually gentle and inoffensive, you can show the fearless and ruthless side to your nature if you are confronted with threats or danger. As an advocate for truth and fairness, you often campaign for just causes; with your purposeful nature you can inspire others to fight for equality and freedom.

Your Powers of Attraction in Relationships

Friendly and gregarious, you like to socialize with friends and have an active life. Usually you prefer people who are success-oriented or sincere, honest, and direct. Security-conscious, you can also be attracted by partners who can help you fulfill your need for a secure and comfortable home. Other people are enchanted by your charismatic and affectionate personality, and being attractive to the opposite sex, you can have many admirers. Your need for personal freedom or your indecisiveness may make it difficult for you to chose a partner. Being prone to emotional fluctuations indicates that harboring frustration or resentment can harm your popularity. Nevertheless, being sympathetic and caring, you can project much love and magnetism to others. Sensitive to others, you usually do not like to hurt anyone's feelings.

Your attractive qualities: creative, intuitive, altruistic, persistent, persuasive, idealistic, optimistic, understanding, strong sense of justice, strong convictions, imaginative, gregarious, inquisitive, determined, tenacious, responsible, considerate, progressive, independent, forceful, focused

Your less attractive qualities: self-centered, frustrated, disappointed, overbearing, jealous, egotistical, too proud, antagonistic, scattered, overindulgent, moody, impatient, inertia, codependent

Your Venus Power

The planet Venus has a great deal of influence on your powers of attraction. Below are four possible Venus types for women and men. To find your Venus you need to go to page 771, where you will find the Venus table and extra information. The planet Mars also affects your powers of attraction. To find your Mars table and interpretation go to page 761.

WOMEN WITH VENUS IN VIRGO: Polite, refined, and organized, you are attracted to articulate and intelligent people. Since you are caring, concerned, and want to be of practical help to others, you can be an asset to any partnership. By being too analytical, exacting, or faultfinding, however, a doubting element can creep into your relationships. By expressing your feelings in a positive way, you can become more decisive and improve on how you relate to your loved ones.

MEN WITH VENUS IN VIRGO: Industrious and well ordered, you relate to others in a considerate and down-to-earth way. You enjoy giving practical advice and being of service to those you love even in small ways. Being a perfectionist, you are drawn to partners with high morals or a strong work ethic. Partners who have strong analytical minds are very attractive to you, particularly if they are also clean and meticulously dressed.

WOMEN WITH VENUS IN LIBRA: Gracious, charming, and sociable with a sense of style, you have no trouble attracting admirers. With your natural diplomatic skills and desire for harmony, you usually like to keep the peace and avoid confrontations, but be careful of failing to take a stand when it is necessary. Romantic and easygoing yourself, you are attracted to affectionate and refined individuals who share your love of peace, justice, and fair play.

MEN WITH VENUS IN LIBRA: You are such good company, people are naturally drawn to you and especially appreciate your talent for making them feel special. You find status in your social contacts and place importance on your relationships. Being clever and a charming companion, you will go out of your way to keep situations peaceful and harmonious. In relationships, however, be careful of indecision or compro-

mising too much. Nevertheless, others are attracted by your natural refinement and good taste, which is reflected in your sense of style.

WOMEN WITH VENUS IN SCORPIO: Loving and passionate, you are often sensitive with deep feelings and strong powers of attraction. A love for the truth coupled with a tendency to be suspicious can be an influence that motivates you to delve deep into the activities of your partner. When in love or in a relationship that matters, you will often bend over backward to cooperate. Although loyal, guard against losing sight of your own needs and desires.

MEN WITH VENUS IN SCORPIO: Usually you are attracted to sensual and passionate partners with strong character. You are often intense with deep feelings and magnetic powers of attraction. As a cautious yet devoted and ardent lover you are likely to seek experiences that are more sexual in nature. You display your less attractive qualities when you project your negative thoughts and resort to being suspicious or possessive. Nevertheless, loyal and loving, you are a sensitive lover.

WOMEN WITH VENUS IN SAGITTARIUS: Optimistic and fun-loving, you love adventure and seek a partner who can expand your horizons. Being truthful and direct, you often say what you think. At times you may be naively tactless. A need for expansion and prosperity suggests that you may enjoy traveling with your friends or partner. Being both lighthearted and idealistic, however, indicates that once you have given your heart to someone you will stay honorable and loyal.

MEN WITH VENUS IN SAGITTARIUS: Usually you are attracted to partners who are knowledgeable or well-traveled. Enthusiastic and optimistic, you often respond quickly to love offers and enter relationships with enthusiasm. Usually you seek to expand your social circle and meeting people from all walks of life can bring you the variety and fun you seek in life. Although you are generous and honest, your partners may accuse you of being overoptimistic or too blunt.

To read all about your Outer Planets and work out how to use your personalized timetable, go to Section Three, page 789.

♏

Your Personalized Timetable

JUPITER BENEFICIAL
1938 5/17 – 7/27
1938 12/31 – until **1939** 3/11
1942 6/11 – 8/24
1943 2/13 – 4/8
1944 8/11 – 9/26
1948 12/1 – until **1949** 1/13
1950 4/17 – 9/12
1950 12/4 – until **1951** 2/23
1954 5/25 – 8/5
1956 7/25 – 9/10
1960 4/7 – 5/3
1960 11/13 – 12/28
1962 3/27 – until **1963** 2/5
1965 9/25 – 11/13
1966 5/7 – 7/20
1967 11/12 – until **1968** 1/31
1968 7/6 – 8/25
1972 2/26 – 6/25
1972 10/22 – 12/12
1974 3/9 – 6/6
1974 8/7 – until **1975** 1/17
1977 8/22 – 12/28
1978 4/14 – 7/3
1979 10/17 – until **1980** 3/11
1980 6/11 – 8/9
1984 2/4 – 8/19
1984 9/10 – 11/25
1986 2/22 – 5/6
1986 9/22 – 12/24
1989 8/1 – until **1990** 6/17
1991 9/28 – 12/2
1992 1/28 – 7/22
1996 1/18 – 3/11
1996 6/30 – 11/4
1998 2/5 – 4/15
2001 7/14 – until **2002** 5/30
2003 9/11 – 11/2
2004 3/9 – 6/30
2008 1/2 – 2/17
2008 8/16 – 9/30
2010 1/19 – 3/28

SATURN BENEFICIAL
1944 6/22 – until **1945** 7/22
1948 10/20 – until **1949** 2/15
1949 7/11 – 10/2
1950 4/15 – 6/14
1959 2/5 – 7/2
1959 11/5 – until **1960** 2/3
1960 8/2 – 10/29
1964 3/27 – 9/12
1964 12/20 – until **1965** 5/26
1965 7/31 – until **1966** 2/9
1973 8/5 – until **1974** 1/3
1974 4/22 – 9/7
1974 12/26 – until **1975** 5/26
1978 8/22 – 11/29
1979 1/19 – 8/9
1988 12/12 – until **1989** 3/27
1989 5/20 – 12/12
1994 1/31 – until **1995** 3/16
2003 6/6 – until **2004** 7/4
2007 9/30 – until **2008** 3/19
2008 6/16 – 9/15

URANUS BENEFICIAL
1948 9/12 – until **1953** 5/29
1962 10/4 – until **1965** 8/7
1989 1/28 – until **1991** 12/26
2003 3/17 – until **2008** 1/25

NEPTUNE BENEFICIAL
1985 3/4 – until **1990** 12/10
2011 4/17 – Continues

PLUTO BENEFICIAL
1958 10/6 – until **1964** 8/18
2010 1/1 – Continues

JUPITER CHALLENGING
1938 1/1 – 2/28
1940 5/17 – until **1941** 3/27
1943 7/2 – 9/14

1949 4/16 – 6/24
1949 12/2 – until **1950** 2/11
1952 4/30 – 7/16
1952 11/5 – until **1953** 3/5
1955 6/14 – 8/28
1961 3/17 – 8/9
1961 11/6 – until **1962** 1/26
1964 4/13 – 6/22
1964 12/30 – until **1965** 1/21
1966 9/29 – until **1967** 1/13
1967 5/25 – 8/12
1973 2/25 – until **1974** 1/9
1976 3/27 – 6/3
1978 9/7 – until **1979** 2/25
1979 4/24 – 7/27
1985 2/8 – 5/16
1985 6/24 – 12/22
1988 3/10 – 5/18
1990 8/19 – until **1991** 7/10
1997 1/23 – 4/8
1997 8/14 – 11/29
1999 6/30 – 10/20
2000 2/16 – 5/1
2002 8/3 – 11/1
2003 1/6 – 6/22
2009 1/7 – 3/18
2011 6/6 – until **2012** 4/14

SATURN CHALLENGING
1939 7/11 – 9/16
1940 3/23 – until **1941** 4/25
1946 8/5 – until **1947** 9/5
1948 3/22 – 5/12
1962 1/6 – until **1963** 2/24
1969 5/2 – until **1970** 6/5
1970 12/22 – until **1971** 2/12
1975 9/20 – until **1976** 1/10
1976 6/8 – 11/3
1976 12/22 – until **1977** 7/11
1991 2/9 – 9/22
1991 10/17 – until **1992** 4/6
1992 7/22 – 12/31
1998 6/12 – 10/21
1999 3/4 – 7/29
1999 9/30 – until **2000** 4/8
2005 7/19 – until **2006** 8/19

URANUS CHALLENGING
1938 1/1 – until **1939** 4/12
1955 8/31 – until **1959** 8/4
1995 4/17 – until **2000** 1/29

NEPTUNE CHALLENGING
1998 2/7 – until **2006** 1/11

PLUTO CHALLENGING
1938 8/16 – until **1950** 6/17

JUPITER SPECIAL
1946 9/27 – 12/10
1958 1/17 – 3/17
1958 9/9 – 11/24
1969 12/18 – until **1970** 4/27
1970 8/18 – 11/8
1981 11/28 – until **1982** 10/23
1993 11/11 – until **1994** 10/7
2005 10/27 – until **2006** 1/22
2006 4/15 – 9/19

SATURN SPECIAL
1953 10/25 – until **1954** 12/11
1955 5/30 – 9/5
1982 12/2 – until **1983** 5/2
1983 8/28 – until **1984** 2/17
1984 3/2 – 10/19
2012 10/8 – until **1938** 1/1

URANUS SPECIAL
1974 11/27 – until **1978** 11/3

NEPTUNE SPECIAL
1956 1/15 – until **1964** 10/6

PLUTO SPECIAL
1983 11/14 – until **1990** 10/5

469

November 2

Your Personal Powers

Receptive and mentally quick, you are a sensitive individual with strong determination and an investigative nature. Your ruling planet, Pluto, endows you with psychological insight and encourages you to explore different possibilities. You gain power when you develop your patience and perseverance and resist the innate restlessness that causes your instability. Although you have good business acumen and opportunities to be entrepreneurial, you need to stay cautious when you manage your own finances. By having a definite plan of action, you can overcome obstacles in life and achieve prosperity. A need for variety implies that you may lose some of your power if you become stuck in monotonous situations that cause you frustration or boredom. Being enterprising, friendly, and generous indicates that your success often comes from your collaborative efforts or from people-related careers. Alternatively, by stimulating your mind with knowledge or new experiences you can achieve the diversity that keeps you optimistic and alert.

Your Powers of Attraction in Relationships

People-oriented, you enjoy all kinds of social activities. Since your awareness and personal growth is often linked to what you learn from others, you benefit from mixing with different types of people. Capable of being entertaining and witty, you have a friendly personality that often attracts friends and admirers. Sympathetic and loyal by nature, you are usually attracted to intelligent individuals who can inspire you and keep you mentally stimulated. Your sensitivity implies that if you feel insecure you may run the risk of feeling vulnerable or become overly dependent. By developing your self-esteem, you can overcome a tendency to take things too seriously. An inclination to be secretive suggests that sometimes you are unwilling to share your thoughts and true feelings with your partner. In close relationships it is vital to maintain honesty.

Your attractive qualities: hardworking, collaborative, tactful, receptive, intuitive, considerate, harmonious, agreeable, versatile, sensitive, observant, aware, intelligent, gregarious, tenacious, determined, gentle, receptive, open-minded, optimistic, generous, resourceful, sincere

Your less attractive qualities: codependent, suspicious, sarcastic, secretive, extravagant, frustrated, self-doubting, insecure, critical, easily bored, subservient, emotional, stuck in a rut, easily hurt, moody, restless

Your Venus Power

The planet Venus has a great deal of influence on your powers of attraction. Below are four possible Venus types for women and men. To find your Venus you need to go to page 771, where you will find the Venus table and extra information. The planet Mars also affects your powers of attraction. To find your Mars table and interpretation go to page 761.

WOMEN WITH VENUS IN VIRGO: In relationships you can be modest and unassuming but desire perfection. You usually analyze your partnerships until you feel you have understood them to the last little detail in order to improve them. A problem usually arises when you become too critical either of partners or yourself and indulge in being skeptical or faultfinding. As you are modest, others may not be aware of the strong sensuality beneath your well-groomed exterior.

MEN WITH VENUS IN VIRGO: Practical, idealistic, and a perfectionist, you seek a relationship with an intelligent and hardworking partner who can inspire you to be more industrious and well ordered. At times you can come across as a sympathetic and caring person and at other times you may appear pragmatic and very businesslike. This may sometimes lead to unclear communication between you and your partner. Usually helpful and caring, you like to analyze the faults in your relationships and then work methodically to improve them.

WOMEN WITH VENUS IN LIBRA: Attractive, refined, and conscious of the needs of others, you usually desire harmonious relationships. As a peacemaker with good negotiating skills, you can smooth out difficulties with others, but your dislike of confrontation may sometimes leave you refusing to take a stand or compromising too many of your own needs. Courteous, stylish, and charming with polished social skills you are an expert at relating to others in a gracious and civilized manner.

MEN WITH VENUS IN LIBRA: Courteous and refined, you are attracted to beautiful and elegant people. You are looking for a partner who can share your natural good taste and enjoy an intellectual conversation. Disliking conflict, you may have to be careful not to go along with others just to keep the peace. Your ideal partner will appreciate beauty and the little luxuries

of life as well as possess good social skills. You have a strong sense of social etiquette yourself so you need an intelligent and sophisticated partner.

WOMEN WITH VENUS IN SCORPIO: Loving and passionate, you are often sensitive with deep feelings and strong powers of attraction. A love for the truth coupled with a tendency to be suspicious can be an influence that motivates you to delve deep into the activities of your partner. When in love or in a relationship that matters, you will often bend over backward to cooperate. Although loyal, guard against losing sight of your own needs and desires.

MEN WITH VENUS IN SCORPIO: You are usually attracted to sensual and passionate partners with strong character. You are often intense with deep feelings and magnetic powers of attraction. As a cautious yet devoted and ardent lover, you are likely to seek experiences that are more sexual in their nature. You display your less attractive qualities when you project your negative thoughts and resort to being suspicious or possessive. Nevertheless, loyal and loving, you are a sensitive lover.

WOMEN WITH VENUS IN SAGITTARIUS: Sociable, warm, and friendly, you possess an honest and frank style in your relationships. Being naturally gregarious, you want others to share your enthusiasm and you enjoy encouraging the people you love. You fare better when you have a sense of personal freedom within a relationship and are usually generous with the faults of others. You need a partner who can share your need to explore and take risks; whether through travel, education, or recreation.

MEN WITH VENUS IN SAGITTARIUS: You are usually attracted to partners who are knowledgeable or well traveled. Enthusiastic and optimistic, you often respond quickly to love offers and enter relationships with enthusiasm. Usually you seek to expand your social circle, and meeting people from all walks of life can bring you the variety and fun to you seek in life. Although you are generous and honest, your partners may accuse you of being overly optimistic or too blunt.

To read all about your Outer Planets and work out how to use your personalized timetable, go to Section Three, page 789.

To read all about your Outer Planets and work out how to use your personalized timetable, go to Section Three, page 789.

Your Personalized Timetable

JUPITER BENEFICIAL
1938 5/28 – 7/15
1939 1/5 – 3/16
1942 6/16 – 8/29
1943 2/3 – 4/18
1944 8/15 – 10/1
1948 12/5 – until 1949 1/18
1950 4/22 – 9/4
1950 12/11 – until 1951 2/27
1954 5/30 – 8/10
1956 7/30 – 9/15
1960 11/18 – until 1961 1/2
1962 4/1 – until 1963 2/10
1966 5/12 – 7/24
1967 11/21 – until 1968 1/22
1968 7/12 – 8/30
1972 3/3 – 6/17
1972 10/28 – 12/16
1974 3/14 – 6/19
1974 7/25 – until 1975 1/22
1977 8/28 – 12/21
1978 4/20 – 7/8
1979 10/23 – until 1980 3/3
1980 6/19 – 8/14
1984 2/10 – 8/2
1984 9/26 – 11/30
1986 2/26 – 5/12
1986 9/14 – 12/30
1989 8/6 – until 1990 2/7
1990 3/14 – 6/22
1991 10/3 – 12/17
1992 1/13 – 7/27
1996 1/22 – 3/18
1996 6/21 – 11/10
1998 2/10 – 4/20
2001 7/19 – until 2002 6/4
2003 9/16 – 11/9
2004 3/1 – 7/7
2008 1/6 – 2/23
2008 8/4 – 10/12
2010 1/24 – 4/1

SATURN BENEFICIAL
1944 6/30 – until 1945 7/29
1948 11/1 – until 1949 2/1
1949 7/21 – 10/11
1950 3/29 – 6/30
1959 2/16 – 6/18
1959 11/16 – until 1960 2/13
1960 7/18 – 11/11
1964 4/6 – 8/29
1965 1/1 – until 1966 2/18
1973 8/14 – 12/22
1974 5/3 – 9/19
1974 12/12 – until 1975 6/4
1978 8/30 – until 1979 8/18
1988 12/21 – until 1989 12/21
1994 2/9 – until 1995 3/25
2003 6/14 – until 2004 7/12
2007 10/9 – until 2008 3/5
2008 6/28 – 9/23

URANUS BENEFICIAL
1949 7/2 – until 1953 6/17
1962 10/26 – until 1965 8/24
1989 2/19 – until 1992 10/18
2003 4/6 – until 2008 2/14

NEPTUNE BENEFICIAL
1986 1/21 – until 1991 10/31
2012 3/10 – Continues

PLUTO BENEFICIAL
1959 9/8 – until 1965 7/15
2010 1/31 – Continues

JUPITER CHALLENGING
1938 1/1 – 3/4
1940 5/22 – until 1941 4/1
1943 7/7 – 9/19
1944 3/30 – 4/26
1949 4/27 – 6/12

JUPITER BENEFICIAL (continued)
1949 12/7 – until 1950 2/16
1952 5/4 – 7/23
1952 10/28 – until 1953 3/10
1955 6/19 – 9/2
1961 3/23 – 8/1
1961 11/13 – until 1962 1/30
1964 4/17 – 6/27
1964 12/14 – until 1965 2/6
1966 10/7 – until 1967 1/5
1967 5/31 – 8/17
1973 3/1 – until 1974 1/14
1976 4/1 – 6/8
1978 9/12 – until 1979 2/15
1979 5/4 – 8/1
1985 2/12 – 12/27
1988 3/14 – 5/22
1990 8/24 – until 1991 7/15
1997 1/27 – 4/15
1997 8/7 – 12/5
1999 7/7 – 10/13
2000 2/22 – 5/5
2002 8/7 – 11/12
2002 12/26 – until 2003 6/27
2009 1/11 – 3/22
2009 10/3 – 10/22
2011 6/11 – 12/2
2012 1/18 – 4/18

SATURN CHALLENGING
1940 3/31 – until 1941 5/3
1946 8/13 – until 1947 9/14
1948 3/5 – 5/29
1962 1/15 – until 1963 3/5
1963 9/18 – 11/22
1969 5/10 – until 1970 6/14
1970 12/5 – until 1971 2/28
1975 10/3 – 12/28
1976 6/17 – until 1977 7/20
1991 2/18 – 8/28
1991 11/11 – until 1992 4/20
1992 7/6 – until 1993 1/10
1998 6/24 – 10/8
1999 3/13 – until 2000 4/16
2005 7/26 – until 2006 8/27

URANUS CHALLENGING
1938 1/1 – until 1939 4/30
1955 9/21 – until 1960 5/24
1996 2/4 – until 2000 11/27

NEPTUNE CHALLENGING
1998 3/9 – until 2006 12/1

PLUTO CHALLENGING
1938 10/4 – until 1950 7/25

JUPITER SPECIAL
1946 10/1 – 12/15
1958 2/1 – 3/1
1958 9/14 – 11/29
1969 12/25 – until 1970 4/19
1970 8/24 – 11/13
1981 12/4 – until 1982 6/3
1982 7/22 – 10/28
1993 11/16 – until 1994 10/12
2005 11/1 – until 2006 2/1
2006 4/5 – 9/24

SATURN SPECIAL
1953 11/2 – until 1954 12/21
1955 5/16 – 9/18
1982 12/12 – until 1983 4/19
1983 9/8 – until 1984 10/27
2012 10/17 – Continues

URANUS SPECIAL
1974 12/17 – until 1979 8/26

NEPTUNE SPECIAL
1956 11/25 – until 1965 8/18

PLUTO SPECIAL
1983 12/13 – until 1990 11/1

♏

November 3

SUN: SCORPIO · DECANATE: PISCES/NEPTUNE · DEGREE: 10°5–11°5 SCORPIO · MODE: FIXED · ELEMENT: WATER

Your Personal Powers

Romantic and idealistic, you are a sensitive individual with quick perception and intense emotions. Your ruling planet, Pluto, grants you intuitive abilities and a probing mind that can help you assess people and situations with cunning accuracy. Having a natural flair for commerce indicates that you gain power when you combine your determination, creativity, and intuition with your practical skills. In order to be enterprising, successful, and enjoy the many opportunities life presents to you, you also need to be dedicated and hardworking. Although at times sudden flights of fancy may carry you away, a need for material security implies that you usually keep your feet firmly on the ground. Being a perfectionist suggests that you take pride in your work or gain particular satisfaction from it. Since you also possess a need for self-expression, it is good for you to find projects or work that can be inspiring or mentally stimulating.

Your Powers of Attraction in Relationships

Intuitive, receptive, and friendly, you often attract many friends. You are loyal, generous, and idealistic, and people admire your special charm. When you want to put your views across, you achieve more with your witty repartee or by being subtle and observant. Being sociable, you enjoy meeting people and can mix business with pleasure. Making contacts is useful as partnerships often suit you more than working independently. A need to be in control, however, can bring tension into relationships. Although being passionate indicates that you can be affectionate and loving, you expect a great deal of love in return. In order to feel secure in close relationships, resist emotional clashes, power games, and refrain from sulking. Nevertheless, devoted and romantic with an altruistic nature, you have a lot to offer others.

Your attractive qualities: talented, charming, astute, business acumen, idealistic, contented, loyal, persevering, inner vision, instinctive, psychic abilities, witty, good economic circumstances, humorous, happy, friendly, productive, creative, freedom-loving, enthusiastic, imaginative

Your less attractive qualities: stubborn, inner doubts, indecisive, easily bored, overimaginative, exaggerates, extravagant, self-indulgent, emotional, worried, indecisive, dissatisfied, restlessness impatient, unrealistic, secretive

Your Venus Power

The planet Venus has a great deal of influence on your powers of attraction. Below are four possible Venus types for women and men. To find your Venus you need to go to page 771, where you will find the Venus table and extra information. The planet Mars also affects your powers of attraction. To find your Mars table and interpretation go to page 761.

WOMEN WITH VENUS IN VIRGO: Intelligent and discriminating, you are usually drawn to polite and refined individuals. As a perfectionist, you may be keen to analyze and criticize yourself, but be careful of continually going over your partner's shortcomings. By focusing on how you can make positive improvements in yourself and your relationships you avoid becoming skeptical or confused. You empower yourself when you display kind and caring concern for the well-being of loved ones and spontaneously offer your practical assistance.

MEN WITH VENUS IN VIRGO: A love of order usually indicates that you are attracted to refined individuals with analytical or practical abilities. You and your partner may be working together or serving similar causes. As you constantly analyze partnerships in order to improve them, you are likely to use former relationships as a point of reference and compare them to your present partner. As you are helpful and kind, others usually rely on your good judgment and often turn to you for advice or practical assistance.

WOMEN WITH VENUS IN LIBRA: A natural romantic with good social skills, you love to entertain or put people at ease by projecting a warm and gracious manner. Elegant and fair with a touch of glamour, you are also adept at dealing with people in delicate situations or conflicts. You seek refinement and will go out of your way to achieve harmony and keep the peace. For you, relationships are so important that you may need to guard against becoming dependent on others for approval. With your friendly personality and inherent charm, however, you will always be popular and loved.

MEN WITH VENUS IN LIBRA: As a sociable and friendly individual with an eye for beauty, you are amorous and charming. You are a natural gentleman and your ideal partner usually has an elegant appearance, artistic appreciation, and good taste. Your relationships benefit when you resist the temptation to take the easy way out or put too much emphasis on vanity and high living. Intellectual and naturally refined,

you seek a loving partner who can share your romantic and sophisticated aspirations.

WOMEN WITH VENUS IN SCORPIO: Loving and passionate, you are often sensitive with deep feelings and strong powers of attraction. A love for the truth coupled with a tendency to be suspicious can be an influence that motivates you to delve deep into the activities of your partner. When in love or in a relationship that matters, you will often bend over backward to cooperate. Although loyal, guard against losing sight of your own needs and desires.

MEN WITH VENUS IN SCORPIO: In relationships you possess a sensitive understanding of your partner's deeper nature. Although you are strongly attached to those you love, you may have to be careful that your feelings do not turn into jealousy or possessiveness. When you fall in love, it is often with an emotional intensity that helps you get in touch with your deep feelings. You are attracted to partners who can share your passion and display strong feelings of sexuality like your own.

WOMEN WITH VENUS IN SAGITTARIUS: At your best when being optimistic and generous, you possess a mischievous sense of fun. In relationships your open-minded approach to people and places may attract you to those of a different culture or make you tolerant of the foibles of others. Although warm and enthusiastic when in love, your natural honesty and idealism may inspire you to look for a partner who shares your love of freedom.

MEN WITH VENUS IN SAGITTARIUS: When in love you are open and friendly with a need for a partner who can share your adventurous spirit and sense of fun. Be careful, however, that your desire for freedom does not cause you to avoid commitment. You prefer your partners to be positive, direct, and generous in spirit. Being outspoken as well as an idealist, you usually enjoy a partner with whom you can share your strong opinions. Alternatively, you may wish to explore life together, whether through travel, education, or having fun.

To read all about your Outer Planets and work out how to use your personalized timetable, go to Section Three, page 789.

♏

Your Personalized Timetable

JUPITER BENEFICIAL
1939 1/10 – 3/20
1942 6/20 – 9/4
1943 1/25 – 4/27
1944 8/20 – 10/6
1948 12/10 – until **1949** 1/22
1950 4/29 – 8/27
1950 12/18 – until **1951** 3/3
1954 6/3 – 8/15
1956 8/4 – 9/19
1960 11/22 – until **1961** 1/6
1962 4/6 – until **1963** 2/14
1966 5/17 – 7/29
1967 12/4 – until **1968** 1/9
1968 7/17 – 9/4
1972 3/11 – 6/9
1972 11/3 – 12/21
1974 3/18 – until **1975** 1/27
1977 9/4 – 12/13
1978 4/26 – 7/12
1979 10/29 – until **1980** 2/24
1980 6/26 – 8/19
1984 2/15 – 7/22
1984 10/6 – 12/4
1986 3/2 – 5/18
1986 9/7 – until **1987** 1/6
1989 8/11 – until **1990** 1/25
1990 3/27 – 6/26
1991 10/8 – until **1992** 4/9
1992 5/22 – 8/2
1996 1/27 – 3/26
1996 6/13 – 11/15
1998 2/14 – 4/24
1998 11/3 – 11/23
2001 7/23 – until **2002** 6/9
2003 9/21 – 11/16
2004 2/22 – 7/13
2008 1/11 – 2/28
2008 7/26 – 10/21
2010 1/28 – 4/5

SATURN BENEFICIAL
1944 7/8 – until **1945** 8/7
1946 2/28 – 4/9
1948 11/16 – until **1949** 1/17
1949 7/29 – 10/20
1950 3/16 – 7/12
1959 3/1 – 6/3
1959 11/25 – until **1960** 2/24
1960 7/4 – 11/22
1964 4/17 – 8/15
1965 1/11 – until **1966** 2/26
1973 8/25 – 12/10
1974 5/12 – 10/6
1974 11/25 – until **1975** 6/12
1978 9/7 – until **1979** 8/26
1988 12/29 – until **1989** 12/29
1994 2/17 – until **1995** 4/2
1995 11/2 – 12/11
2003 6/22 – until **2004** 7/20
2007 10/19 – until **2008** 2/22
2008 7/9 – 10/1
2009 4/25 – 6/8

URANUS BENEFICIAL
1949 7/19 – until **1953** 7/4
1963 8/24 – until **1965** 9/9
1989 12/25 – until **1992** 11/18
2003 5/3 – until **2008** 3/3

NEPTUNE BENEFICIAL
1986 2/24 – until **1991** 12/7
2012 4/10 – Continues

PLUTO BENEFICIAL
1959 10/11 – until **1965** 8/18
2010 3/20 – Continues

JUPITER CHALLENGING
1938 1/1 – 3/9
1940 5/26 – until **1941** 4/6
1943 7/11 – 9/24
1944 3/15 – 5/12
1949 12/12 – until **1950** 2/20

1952 5/8 – 7/30
1952 10/20 – until **1953** 3/16
1955 6/24 – 9/6
1961 3/29 – 7/24
1961 11/20 – until **1962** 2/3
1964 4/22 – 7/3
1964 12/4 – until **1965** 2/16
1966 10/15 – 12/28
1967 6/6 – 8/21
1973 3/6 – 9/24
1973 10/3 – until **1974** 1/18
1976 4/5 – 6/12
1978 9/18 – until **1979** 2/6
1979 5/12 – 8/5
1985 2/17 – until **1986** 1/1
1988 3/19 – 5/26
1990 8/29 – until **1991** 7/20
1997 1/31 – 4/21
1997 7/30 – 12/11
1999 7/15 – 10/5
2000 2/28 – 5/10
2002 8/12 – until **2003** 7/3
2009 1/15 – 3/28
2009 9/16 – 11/8
2011 6/16 – 11/21
2012 1/29 – 4/23

SATURN CHALLENGING
1940 4/8 – until **1941** 5/11
1946 8/21 – until **1947** 3/14
1947 4/24 – 9/23
1948 2/20 – 6/11
1962 1/23 – until **1963** 3/14
1963 9/1 – 12/8
1969 5/18 – 12/17
1970 1/21 – 6/23
1970 11/21 – until **1971** 3/13
1975 10/19 – 12/11
1976 6/26 – until **1977** 7/28
1991 2/28 – 8/12
1991 11/25 – until **1992** 5/15
1992 6/11 – until **1993** 1/18
1998 7/7 – 9/24
1999 3/22 – until **2000** 4/24
2005 8/3 – until **2006** 9/4
2007 4/6 – 5/3

URANUS CHALLENGING
1938 1/1 – until **1940** 2/24
1955 11/7 – until **1960** 6/20
1996 2/22 – until **2000** 12/25

NEPTUNE CHALLENGING
1999 2/4 – until **2007** 1/7

PLUTO CHALLENGING
1939 9/12 – until **1951** 7/4

JUPITER SPECIAL
1946 10/6 – 12/21
1947 6/25 – 8/5
1958 9/19 – 12/3
1970 1/1 – 4/11
1970 8/31 – 11/17
1981 12/9 – until **1982** 5/22
1982 8/3 – 11/2
1993 11/21 – until **1994** 10/17
2005 11/5 – until **2006** 2/14
2006 3/23 – 9/30

SATURN SPECIAL
1953 11/11 – until **1955** 1/1
1955 5/3 – 9/29
1982 12/24 – until **1983** 4/5
1983 9/18 – until **1984** 11/5
2012 10/25 – Continues

URANUS SPECIAL
1975 1/19 – until **1979** 9/22

NEPTUNE SPECIAL
1957 1/3 – until **1965** 10/3

PLUTO SPECIAL
1984 10/31 – until **1991** 9/19

473

November 4

Your Personal Powers

Mentally alert and determined, you are an astute individual with a strong personality. With an innate business sense, courage, and psychological insight, you can solve problems and turn challenging situations to your advantage. You gain power when you use your strong instincts and analytical skills in an original and constructive way. You also empower yourself by presenting your point of view or radical ideas in a clever and simplistic way. Although you can be witty and entertaining, you lose some of your power by being controlling and using sarcasm to criticize or undermine others. Although you are usually confident and forceful, an inclination to vacillate between being self-assured and doubtful or worried implies that you may need to resist taking too much on. Since apprehension and tension often center around money matters, avoid becoming involved in enterprises that lead you to scatter your energies and resources. Nevertheless, pragmatic and inventive, you can always find a solution to your problems when you create inner peace and listen to your powerful intuition.

Your Powers of Attraction in Relationships

You are romantic and spontaneous, and other people admire your idealism, enterprising spirit, and honesty. Usually you are drawn to dynamic or purposeful individuals who can offer you new opportunities. Your sensitivity suggests that you also seek relationships that offer harmony, security, and affection. Although you can be responsible, sincere, and faithful, some people are not necessarily what they appear to be; therefore you may need to be cautious before you give away your affections or trust. Keen on establishing a stable relationship, you are often willing to go to a great deal of trouble in order to help loved ones. If you become overly idealistic, you can go to extremes by martyring yourself. You may experience dissatisfaction in your close relationships if you set standards that are too high for yourself and your partner.

Your attractive qualities: organized, resolute, disciplined, steady, hardworking, organized, honest, pragmatic, trusting, exact, affectionate, idealistic, spontaneous, cautious, reliant, inventive, astute, creative, determined, business acumen, versatile, insightful, receptive, imaginative, forgiving

Your less attractive qualities: worry, repressed, rigid, withdrawn, unfeeling, indecisive, bossy, secretive, resentful, too strict, pessimistic, scattered, hasty, stubborn, domineering, materialistic

Your Venus Power

The planet Venus has a great deal of influence on your powers of attraction. Below are four possible Venus types for women and men. To find your Venus you need to go to page 771, where you will find the Venus table and extra information. The planet Mars also affects your powers of attraction. To find your Mars table and interpretation go to page 761.

WOMEN WITH VENUS IN VIRGO: Polite, refined, and organized, you are attracted to articulate and intelligent people. Since you are caring, concerned, and want to be of practical help to others, you can be an asset to any partnership. By being too analytical, exacting, or faultfinding, however, a doubting element can creep into your relationships. By expressing your feelings in a positive way, you can become more decisive and improve on how you relate to loved ones.

MEN WITH VENUS IN VIRGO: Practical, idealistic, and a perfectionist, you seek a relationship with an intelligent and hardworking partner who can inspire you to be more industrious and well ordered. At times you can come across as a sympathetic and caring person and at other times you may appear pragmatic and very businesslike. This may sometimes lead to unclear communication between you and your partner. Usually helpful and caring, however, you like to analyze the faults in your relationships and then work methodically to improve them.

WOMEN WITH VENUS IN LIBRA: A natural romantic with good social skills, you love to entertain or put people at ease by projecting a warm and gracious manner. Elegant and fair with a touch of glamour, you are also adept at dealing with people in delicate situations or conflicts. You seek refinement and will go out of your way to achieve harmony and keep the peace. For you, relationships are so important that you may need to guard against becoming dependent on others for approval. With your friendly personality and inherent charm, however, you will always be popular and loved.

MEN WITH VENUS IN LIBRA: Courteous and refined, you are attracted to beautiful and elegant people. You are looking for a partner who can share your natural good taste and enjoy an intellectual conversation. Disliking conflict, you may have to be careful not to go along with others just to keep the peace.

Your ideal partner will appreciate beauty and the little luxuries of life as well as possess good social skills. You have a strong sense of social etiquette yourself so you need an intelligent and sophisticated partner.

WOMEN WITH VENUS IN SCORPIO: With a natural psychic gift for penetrating the feelings of others, you can often help partners transform emotional challenges or sexual difficulties. When you fall in love, your strong feelings and determination give you a potent force that others find attractive and seductive. Although you know what really turns people on, your most profound desire is usually for the deepness and closeness of real love and intimacy in an enduring relationship.

MEN WITH VENUS IN SCORPIO: In relationships you possess a sensitive understanding of your partner's deeper nature. Although you are strongly attached to those you love, you may have to be careful that your feelings do not turn into jealousy or possessiveness. When you fall in love, it is often with an emotional intensity that helps you get in touch with your deep feelings. You are attracted to partners who can share your passion and display strong feelings of sexuality like your own.

WOMEN WITH VENUS IN SAGITTARIUS: Sociable, warm, and friendly, you possess an honest and frank style in your relationships. Being naturally gregarious, you want others to share your enthusiasm and enjoy encouraging the people you love. You fare better when you have a sense of personal freedom within a relationship and are usually generous with the faults of others. You need a partner who can share your need to explore and take risks, whether through travel, education, or recreation.

MEN WITH VENUS IN SAGITTARIUS: Your enthusiasm and straightforward conduct usually appeal to others and imply that you are approachable and easygoing. Being open to ideas and willing to believe that life has a great deal to offer suggests that you are generous, broad-minded, and show eagerness to cooperate with others. A love of travel and an interest in other cultures imply that your partner may come from a foreign country.

To read all about your Outer Planets and work out how to use your personalized timetable, go to Section Three, page 789.

Your Personalized Timetable

JUPITER BENEFICIAL
1939 1/15 – 3/24
1942 6/25 – 9/9
1943 1/17 – 5/4
1944 8/24 – 10/11
1948 12/14 – until 1949 1/27
1950 5/5 – 8/19
1950 12/24 – until 1951 3/7
1954 6/8 – 8/20
1956 8/8 – 9/24
1960 11/27 – until 1961 1/10
1962 4/10 – 10/12
1962 11/15 – until 1963 2/18
1966 5/22 – 8/2
1968 7/22 – 9/8
1972 3/19 – 5/31
1972 11/8 – 12/25
1974 3/23 – until 1975 2/1
1977 9/12 – 12/5
1978 5/2 – 7/17
1979 11/5 – until 1980 2/16
1980 7/2 – 8/23
1984 2/21 – 7/13
1984 10/15 – 12/9
1986 3/6 – 5/25
1986 8/30 – until 1987 1/11
1989 8/17 – until 1990 1/15
1990 4/6 – 7/1
1991 10/13 – until 1992 3/28
1992 6/3 – 8/7
1996 2/1 – 4/5
1996 6/2 – 11/21
1998 2/18 – 4/30
1998 10/18 – 12/9
2001 7/28 – until 2002 6/14
2003 9/26 – 11/23
2004 2/14 – 7/19
2008 1/15 – 3/5
2008 7/18 – 10/28
2010 2/1 – 4/10

SATURN BENEFICIAL
1944 7/16 – until 1945 8/15
1946 2/8 – 4/28
1949 8/7 – 10/30
1950 3/3 – 7/23
1959 3/17 – 5/16
1959 12/5 – until 1960 3/7
1960 6/20 – 12/2
1964 4/30 – 8/1
1965 1/21 – until 1966 3/6
1973 9/7 – 11/26
1974 5/21 – until 1975 6/20
1978 9/15 – until 1979 9/3
1989 1/7 – until 1990 1/7
1994 2/25 – until 1995 4/11
1995 10/12 – 12/31
2003 6/29 – until 2004 7/28
2007 10/30 – until 2008 2/9
2008 7/19 – 10/10
2009 4/5 – 6/27

URANUS BENEFICIAL
1949 8/8 – until 1954 4/24
1963 9/9 – until 1966 7/7
1990 1/10 – until 1992 12/8
2004 3/2 – until 2009 1/4

NEPTUNE BENEFICIAL
1987 1/18 – until 1992 10/21

PLUTO BENEFICIAL
1960 9/11 – until 1966 7/12
2011 1/30 – Continues

JUPITER CHALLENGING
1938 1/4 – 3/13
1940 5/31 – until 1941 4/10
1943 7/16 – 9/30
1944 3/5 – 5/22
1949 12/17 – until 1950 2/24

1952 5/13 – 8/8
1952 10/11 – until 1953 3/21
1955 6/29 – 9/11
1961 4/5 – 7/16
1961 11/26 – until 1962 2/8
1964 4/26 – 7/8
1964 11/26 – until 1965 2/24
1966 10/25 – 12/17
1967 6/11 – 8/26
1973 3/11 – 9/3
1973 10/24 – until 1974 1/22
1976 4/9 – 6/17
1978 9/24 – until 1979 1/29
1979 5/19 – 8/10
1985 2/21 – until 1986 1/6
1988 3/24 – 5/31
1990 9/3 – until 1991 7/25
1997 2/4 – 4/29
1997 7/21 – 12/17
1999 7/24 – 9/25
2000 3/4 – 5/14
2002 8/17 – until 2003 7/8
2009 1/19 – 4/2
2009 9/6 – 11/18
2011 6/21 – 11/12
2012 2/6 – 4/27

SATURN CHALLENGING
1940 4/16 – until 1941 5/19
1946 8/29 – until 1947 2/22
1947 5/13 – 10/3
1948 2/7 – 6/22
1962 2/1 – until 1963 3/24
1963 8/18 – 12/20
1969 5/27 – 11/26
1970 2/10 – 7/3
1970 11/9 – until 1971 3/23
1976 7/4 – until 1977 8/5
1991 3/10 – 7/29
1991 12/7 – until 1993 1/27
1998 7/28 – 9/2
1999 3/31 – until 2000 5/2
2005 8/11 – until 2006 9/12
2007 3/13 – 5/26

URANUS CHALLENGING
1938 1/1 – until 1940 3/24
1956 8/6 – until 1960 7/10
1996 3/14 – until 2001 1/14

NEPTUNE CHALLENGING
1999 3/5 – until 2007 11/18

PLUTO CHALLENGING
1940 8/26 – until 1952 6/2

JUPITER SPECIAL
1946 10/11 – 12/26
1947 6/12 – 8/18
1958 9/24 – 12/8
1970 1/9 – 4/3
1970 9/6 – 11/22
1981 12/15 – until 1982 5/13
1982 8/12 – 11/6
1993 11/26 – until 1994 10/21
2005 11/10 – until 2006 10/5

SATURN SPECIAL
1953 11/19 – until 1954 6/7
1954 8/4 – until 1955 1/13
1955 4/19 – 10/8
1983 1/7 – 3/20
1983 9/28 – until 1984 11/13
2012 11/2 – Continues

URANUS SPECIAL
1975 11/4 – until 1979 10/12

NEPTUNE SPECIAL
1957 11/22 – until 1965 11/1

PLUTO SPECIAL
1984 11/26 – until 1991 10/19

♏

November 5

SUN: SCORPIO · DECANATE: PISCES/NEPTUNE · DEGREE: 12°5–13°5 SCORPIO · MODE: FIXED · ELEMENT: WATER

Your Personal Powers

Instinctive and enterprising, you are an idealistic and sensitive individual with good strategies and strong determination. Since you are often caught between an urge to be financially successful and a desire to be altruistic, you may lose some of your power if you experience inner conflicts about which direction you should take. Your ruling planet, Pluto, endows you with insight and strong convictions. Although diplomatic and good at presenting ideas, you may need to learn to balance your emotions or resist an inclination to be intense. You gain power when you embrace change and show a willingness to transform your fixed views or outlook on life. Your dynamic unconscious and strong principles indicate that you can be very resolute when inspired. Although you are perceptive, your direct approach or biting comments can lead to clashes of power, especially if you are too forceful. You empower yourself by developing your natural talents and broadening your horizons through new experiences.

Your Powers of Attraction in Relationships

Other people admire your tenacity and spirit of enterprise. Sociable, generous, and people-oriented, you are an excellent networker who knows how to mix business with pleasure. Strong-willed and determined when inspired, you work well in cooperative efforts, particularly gaining from partnerships or through teamwork. Although you have many interests and love your freedom, you are searching for a soul mate who can share your passion and love. You want a partner who is not afraid to challenge you intellectually. An inclination to be argumentative, however, implies that you may need to resist being stubborn. As you admire loyalty and faithfulness, you seek a partner who is reliable and honest. If you feel doubtful about your partnerships, you may experience intense moods. When you are appreciative and collaborative, you usually enjoy popularity and prosperity.

Your attractive qualities: adaptable, intelligent, progressive, enthusiastic, instinctive, magnetic, disciplined, daring, witty, gentle, independent, resolute, forceful, persistent, sensitive, able to concentrate, quick comprehension, perceptive, faithful, sociable, idealistic, strategist, instinctive

Your less attractive qualities: stubborn, inconsistent, restless, impulsive, too daring, materialistic, headstrong, intense emotions, sarcastic, critical, excessive, skeptical, secretive, controlling, moody

Your Venus Power

The planet Venus has a great deal of influence on your powers of attraction. Below are four possible Venus types for women and men. To find your Venus you need to go to page 771, where you will find the Venus table and extra information. The planet Mars also affects your powers of attraction. To find your Mars table and interpretation go to page 761.

WOMEN WITH VENUS IN VIRGO: Polite, refined, and organized, you are attracted to articulate and intelligent people. Since you are caring, concerned, and want to be of practical help to others you can be an asset to any partnership. By being too analytical, exacting, or faultfinding, however, a doubting element can creep into your relationships. By expressing your feelings in a positive way you can become more decisive and improve on how you relate to loved ones.

MEN WITH VENUS IN VIRGO: A love of order usually indicates that you are attracted to refined individuals with analytical or practical abilities. You and your partner may be working together or serving similar causes. As you constantly analyze partnerships in order to improve them, you are likely to use former relationships as a point of reference and compare them to your present partner. As you are helpful and kind, others usually rely on your good judgment and often turn to you for advice or practical assistance.

WOMEN WITH VENUS IN LIBRA: Gracious, charming, and sociable with a sense of style, you have no trouble attracting admirers. With your natural diplomatic skills and desire for harmony you usually like to keep the peace and avoid confrontations, but be careful of failing to take a stand when it is necessary. Romantic and easygoing yourself, you are attracted to affectionate and refined individuals who share your love of peace, justice, and fair play.

MEN WITH VENUS IN LIBRA: You are such good company, people are naturally drawn to you and especially appreciate your talent for making them feel special. You find status in your social contacts and place importance on your relationships. Being clever and a charming companion you will go out of your way to keep situations peaceful and harmonious. In relationships, however, be careful of indecision or compromising too much. Nevertheless, others are attracted by your

natural refinement and good taste, which is reflected in your sense of style.

WOMEN WITH VENUS IN SCORPIO: Your strength and power is in your ability to love both deeply and sensitively. For you, love and desire go hand in hand. As you feel so deeply, you often keep your sensitivity or vulnerability hidden from others in order to keep some control in your relationships. You are more likely to prefer a few very close loyal friends than many superficial acquaintances. In relationships your sensual nature and magnetic intensity can easily attract others.

MEN WITH VENUS IN SCORPIO: You are attracted to partners with deep and powerful emotions or individuals whom you find intriguing. Your gift for creating smoke screens to maintain secrecy around your feelings can conceal your inner sensitivity and vulnerability. Nevertheless, you are looking for a partner who can pierce your defenses and understand you at a very deep level. Needing a relationship with a powerful sexual connection, you thrive on emotional intensity.

WOMEN WITH VENUS IN SAGITTARIUS: When you feel generous, you can make others feel more optimistic about life. You may be interested in higher learning and seek partners who are scholarly or broad-minded. You are outspoken and direct and sometimes say things that you later regret. Curious and versatile, you can adjust quickly to new situations, and a foreign influence implies that you love to travel or may have a partner who comes from a different culture.

MEN WITH VENUS IN SAGITTARIUS: Your enthusiasm and straightforward conduct usually appeal to others and imply that you are approachable and easygoing. Being open to ideas and willing to believe that life has a great deal to offer suggest that you are generous, broad-minded, and show eagerness to cooperate with others. A love of travel and an interest in other cultures imply that your partner may come from a foreign country.

To read all about your Outer Planets and work out how to use your personalized timetable, go to Section Three, page 789.

♏

Your Personalized Timetable

JUPITER BENEFICIAL
1939 1/19 – 3/28
1942 6/29 – 9/16
1943 1/10 – 5/11
1944 8/29 – 10/16
1948 12/18 – until **1949** 1/31
1950 5/12 – 8/11
1950 12/30 – until **1951** 3/11
1954 6/12 – 8/25
1955 2/28 – 4/2
1956 8/13 – 9/29
1960 12/2 – until **1961** 1/15
1962 4/16 – 9/29
1962 11/28 – until **1963** 2/23
1966 5/27 – 8/7
1968 7/28 – 9/13
1972 3/31 – 5/20
1972 11/13 – 12/29
1974 3/27 – until **1975** 2/5
1977 9/20 – 11/26
1978 5/8 – 7/21
1979 11/12 – until **1980** 2/8
1980 7/8 – 8/28
1984 2/26 – 7/5
1984 10/22 – 12/13
1986 3/10 – 6/2
1986 8/22 – until **1987** 1/17
1989 8/22 – until **1990** 1/7
1990 4/13 – 7/5
1991 10/19 – until **1992** 3/18
1992 6/13 – 8/12
1996 2/6 – 4/20
1996 5/18 – 11/26
1998 2/22 – 5/5
1998 10/7 – 12/19
2001 8/2 – until **2002** 6/19
2003 10/1 – 12/3
2004 2/4 – 7/25
2008 1/20 – 3/11
2008 7/10 – 11/4
2010 2/5 – 4/14

SATURN BENEFICIAL
1944 7/24 – until **1945** 2/10
1945 3/29 – 8/24
1946 1/25 – 5/11
1949 8/15 – 11/11
1950 2/18 – 8/2
1959 12/13 – until **1960** 3/21
1960 6/4 – 12/12
1964 5/17 – 7/14
1965 1/30 – until **1966** 3/14
1973 9/26 – 11/7
1974 5/30 – until **1975** 6/28
1978 9/23 – until **1979** 4/22
1979 5/26 – 9/11
1989 1/16 – 9/4
1989 9/17 – until **1990** 1/15
1994 3/6 – until **1995** 4/20
1995 9/27 – until **1996** 1/13
2003 7/7 – until **2004** 8/5
2007 11/12 – until **2008** 1/25
2008 7/28 – 10/19
2009 3/22 – 7/10

URANUS BENEFICIAL
1949 9/1 – until **1954** 5/23
1963 9/26 – until **1966** 7/29
1990 1/28 – until **1992** 12/26
2004 3/20 – until **2009** 1/29

NEPTUNE BENEFICIAL
1987 2/19 – until **1992** 12/3

PLUTO BENEFICIAL
1960 10/14 – until **1966** 8/16
2011 3/15 – Continues

JUPITER CHALLENGING
1938 1/8 – 3/18
1940 6/5 – until **1941** 4/15
1943 7/20 – 10/5
1944 2/25 – 5/31

1949 12/22 – until **1950** 2/28
1952 5/17 – 8/21
1952 9/29 – until **1953** 3/26
1955 7/4 – 9/16
1961 4/12 – 7/8
1961 12/2 – until **1962** 2/12
1964 4/30 – 7/14
1964 11/18 – until **1965** 3/3
1966 11/12 – 11/30
1967 6/16 – 8/30
1973 3/17 – 8/23
1973 11/3 – until **1974** 1/26
1976 4/13 – 6/22
1978 9/30 – until **1979** 1/22
1979 5/26 – 8/14
1985 2/26 – until **1986** 1/10
1988 3/28 – 6/4
1990 9/8 – until **1991** 3/8
1991 4/22 – 7/29
1997 2/9 – 5/9
1997 7/12 – 12/22
1999 8/5 – 9/13
2000 3/9 – 5/18
2002 8/21 – until **2003** 7/13
2009 1/24 – 4/7
2009 8/28 – 11/26
2011 6/27 – 11/5
2012 2/13 – 5/1

SATURN CHALLENGING
1940 4/24 – until **1941** 5/27
1946 9/7 – until **1947** 2/8
1947 5/26 – 10/14
1948 1/26 – 7/2
1962 2/9 – until **1963** 4/4
1963 8/5 – 12/31
1969 6/5 – 11/12
1970 2/23 – 7/14
1970 10/27 – until **1971** 4/2
1976 7/12 – until **1977** 8/12
1991 3/21 – 7/15
1991 12/17 – until **1993** 2/4
1999 4/8 – until **2000** 5/10
2005 8/19 – until **2006** 9/21
2007 2/27 – 6/9

URANUS CHALLENGING
1938 1/1 – until **1940** 4/13
1956 8/23 – until **1960** 7/27
1996 4/14 – until **2001** 2/1

NEPTUNE CHALLENGING
1999 4/26 – until **2008** 1/3

PLUTO CHALLENGING
1940 11/5 – until **1952** 7/17

JUPITER SPECIAL
1946 10/16 – 12/31
1947 6/2 – 8/27
1958 9/29 – 12/13
1970 1/18 – 3/24
1970 9/11 – 11/26
1981 12/20 – until **1982** 5/4
1982 8/19 – 11/11
1993 12/1 – until **1994** 10/26
2005 11/15 – until **2006** 10/10

SATURN SPECIAL
1953 11/28 – until **1954** 5/20
1954 8/21 – until **1955** 1/29
1955 4/2 – 10/18
1983 2/2 – 2/22
1983 10/6 – until **1984** 11/21
2012 11/11 – Continues

URANUS SPECIAL
1975 11/20 – until **1979** 10/29

NEPTUNE SPECIAL
1957 12/27 – until **1966** 9/30

PLUTO SPECIAL
1984 12/31 – until **1992** 8/25

477

November 6

SUN: SCORPIO · DECANATE: PISCES/NEPTUNE · DEGREE: 13°5–14°5 SCORPIO · MODE: FIXED · ELEMENT: WATER

Your Personal Powers

Determined and ambitious with sound judgment, you are an idealistic individual with strong motivation. Your ruling plant, Pluto, grants you tenacity, sharp instincts, and intuition. Action-oriented, you gain power when you combine your practical skills and penetrating mind with your inner vision. Honest and direct, you work best when you believe in your projects and are full of enthusiasm. Inner restlessness and anxiety, however, may undermine your purposeful nature and cause you discontent. Although you are often keen to take the initiative, you empower yourself when you use your tact and diplomacy in dealing with others to create unity and harmony. With your foresight and innate understanding of people, you can also succeed admirably when you promote new ideas and ventures that can inspire others. As a responsible individual you can be hardworking and a perfectionist, yet you lose some of your power if you become overly critical or bossy. Nevertheless, being supportive and caring, you can achieve a great deal when you are focused and inspired.

Your Powers of Attraction in Relationships

You are often friendly and sincere, and others admire your loyalty and enthusiasm. Caring by nature, you will protect with passion those you love and admire. Usually you are attracted to dynamic individuals who are talented and creative. Alternatively, you may be drawn to enterprising and ambitious people who know how to promote their ideas and utilize their business acumen. In close relationships you want a partner who is loyal and proud of his or her home and devoted to family. A tendency to become restless warns that if you become dissatisfied, you may act impulsively and throw caution to the wind. Nevertheless, being responsible and practical assures that you put material security on your list of priorities and carefully weigh all your options. When in love, you will do your utmost to support your partner and loved ones.

Your attractive qualities: adaptable, dependable, home-loving, intelligent, progressive, enthusiastic, instinctive, magnetic, disciplined, balanced, daring, witty, gentle, independent, resolute, forceful, persistent, sympathetic, sensitive, able to concentrate, quick comprehension, perceptive, faithful, sociable, idealistic, strategist

Your less attractive qualities: secretive, bossy, anxious, unreasonable, stubborn, outspoken, disharmonious, moody, inconsistent, impulsive, cynical, suspicious, materialistic, headstrong, intense, sarcastic, critical, excessive, skeptical

Your Venus Power

The planet Venus has a great deal of influence on your powers of attraction. Below are four possible Venus types for women and men. To find your Venus you need to go to page 771, where you will find the Venus table and extra information. The planet Mars also affects your powers of attraction. To find your Mars table and interpretation go to page 761.

WOMEN WITH VENUS IN VIRGO: Intelligent and discriminating, you are usually drawn to polite and refined individuals. As a perfectionist, you may be keen to analyze and criticize yourself, but be careful of continually going over your partner's shortcomings. By focusing on how you can make positive improvements in yourself and in your relationships you avoid becoming skeptical or confused. You empower yourself when you display kind and caring concern for the well-being of loved ones and spontaneously offer your practical assistance.

MEN WITH VENUS IN VIRGO: A love of order usually indicates that you are attracted to refined individuals with analytical or practical abilities. You and your partner may be working together or serving similar causes. As you constantly analyze partnerships in order to improve them, you are likely to use former relationships as a point of reference and compare them to your present partner. You are helpful and kind, and others usually rely on your good judgment and often turn to you for advice or practical assistance.

WOMEN WITH VENUS IN LIBRA: A natural romantic with good social skills, you love to entertain or put people at ease by projecting a warm and gracious manner. Elegant and fair with a touch of glamour, you are also adept at dealing with people in delicate situations or conflicts. You seek refinement and will go out of your way to achieve harmony and keep the peace. For you, relationships are so important that you may need to guard against becoming dependent on others for approval. With your friendly personality and inherent charm, however, you will always be popular and loved.

MEN WITH VENUS IN LIBRA: Courteous and refined, you are attracted to beautiful and elegant people. You are looking for a partner who can share your natural good taste and enjoy

an intellectual conversation. Disliking conflict, you may have to be careful not to go along with others just to keep the peace. Your ideal partner will appreciate beauty and the little luxuries of life as well as possess good social skills. You have a strong sense of social etiquette yourself so you need an intelligent and sophisticated partner.

WOMEN WITH VENUS IN SCORPIO: Loving and passionate, you are often sensitive with deep feelings and strong powers of attraction. A love for the truth coupled with a tendency to be suspicious can be an influence that motivates you to delve deep into the activities of your partner. When in love or in a relationship that matters, you will often bend over backward to cooperate. Although loyal, guard against losing sight of your own needs and desires.

MEN WITH VENUS IN SCORPIO: You are usually attracted to sensual and passionate partners with strong character. You are often sensitive with deep feelings and magnetic powers of attraction. As a cautious yet devoted and ardent lover, you are likely to seek experiences that are more sexual in nature. You display your less attractive qualities when you project your negative thoughts and resort to being suspicious or possessive. Nevertheless, loyal and loving, you are a sensitive lover.

WOMEN WITH VENUS IN SAGITTARIUS: Sociable, warm, and friendly, you possess an honest and frank style in your relationships. Being naturally gregarious, you want others to share your enthusiasm and enjoy encouraging the people you love. You fare better when you have a sense of personal freedom within a relationship and are usually generous with the faults of others. You need a partner who can share your need to explore and take risks, whether through travel, education, or recreation.

MEN WITH VENUS IN SAGITTARIUS: You are usually attracted to partners who are knowledgeable or well-traveled. Enthusiastic and optimistic, you often respond quickly to love offers and enter relationships with enthusiasm. Usually you seek to expand your social circle and meeting people from all walks of life can bring you the variety and fun you seek in life. Although you are generous and honest, your partners may accuse you of being overly optimistic or too blunt.

To read all about your Outer Planets and work out how to use your personalized timetable, go to Section Three, page 789.

To read all about your Outer Planets and work out how to use your personalized timetable, go to Section Three, page 789.

Your Personalized Timetable

JUPITER BENEFICIAL
1939 1/24 – 4/1
1942 7/3 – 9/22
1943 1/2 – 5/17
1944 9/3 – 10/21
1945 4/21 – 6/7
1948 12/23 – until **1949** 2/5
1950 5/21 – 8/3
1951 1/4 – 3/15
1954 6/17 – 8/30
1955 2/14 – 4/16
1956 8/18 – 10/3
1960 12/6 – until **1961** 1/19
1962 4/21 – 9/19
1962 12/7 – until **1963** 2/27
1966 5/31 – 8/11
1968 8/2 – 9/18
1972 11/19 – until **1973** 1/3
1974 4/1 – until **1975** 2/10
1977 10/2 – 11/15
1978 5/13 – 7/26
1979 11/21 – until **1980** 1/30
1980 7/14 – 9/2
1984 3/4 – 6/27
1984 10/28 – 12/18
1986 3/15 – 6/11
1986 8/12 – until **1987** 1/22
1989 8/28 – 12/31
1990 4/20 – 7/10
1991 10/25 – until **1992** 3/10
1992 6/21 – 8/17
1996 2/11 – 8/16
1996 9/21 – 12/1
1998 2/26 – 5/10
1998 9/29 – 12/27
2001 8/7 – until **2002** 6/23
2003 10/6 – 12/16
2004 1/22 – 7/30
2008 1/24 – 3/18
2008 7/2 – 11/10
2010 2/10 – 4/19

SATURN BENEFICIAL
1944 8/1 – until **1945** 1/23
1945 4/15 – 9/2
1946 1/13 – 5/22
1949 8/23 – 11/25
1950 2/3 – 8/11
1959 12/22 – until **1960** 4/17
1960 5/7 – 12/21
1965 2/7 – until **1966** 3/22
1974 6/7 – until **1975** 7/6
1978 10/2 – until **1979** 3/31
1979 6/17 – 9/19
1989 1/24 – 8/5
1989 10/17 – until **1990** 1/24
1994 3/14 – until **1995** 5/1
1995 9/14 – until **1996** 1/24
2003 7/15 – until **2004** 8/13
2005 2/17 – 4/23
2007 12/4 – until **2008** 1/3
2008 8/6 – 10/29
2009 3/9 – 7/21

URANUS BENEFICIAL
1950 6/29 – until **1954** 6/12
1963 10/14 – until **1966** 8/16
1990 2/18 – until **1993** 10/13
2004 4/10 – until **2009** 2/18

NEPTUNE BENEFICIAL
1988 1/15 – until **1992** 12/31

PLUTO BENEFICIAL
1961 9/14 – until **1967** 7/6
2012 1/30 – Continues

JUPITER CHALLENGING
1938 1/12 – 3/23
1940 6/9 – until **1941** 4/19
1943 7/25 – 10/11
1944 2/17 – 6/7

1949 12/26 – until **1950** 3/5
1952 5/21 – until **1953** 3/31
1955 7/9 – 9/21
1961 4/21 – 6/29
1961 12/7 – until **1962** 2/16
1964 5/4 – 7/20
1964 11/11 – until **1965** 3/9
1967 6/21 – 9/4
1973 3/22 – 8/14
1973 11/11 – until **1974** 1/31
1976 4/18 – 6/27
1977 1/6 – 1/25
1978 10/7 – until **1979** 1/14
1979 6/1 – 8/19
1985 3/2 – until **1986** 1/15
1988 4/1 – 6/9
1990 9/14 – until **1991** 2/24
1991 5/3 – 8/3
1997 2/13 – 5/21
1997 6/29 – 12/27
2000 3/14 – 5/22
2002 8/26 – until **2003** 7/18
2009 1/28 – 4/13
2009 8/20 – 12/3
2011 7/3 – 10/28
2012 2/20 – 5/5

SATURN CHALLENGING
1940 5/2 – until **1941** 6/4
1946 9/17 – until **1947** 1/27
1947 6/6 – 10/27
1948 1/12 – 7/11
1962 2/18 – 9/13
1962 11/5 – until **1963** 4/17
1963 7/22 – until **1964** 1/9
1969 6/15 – 10/30
1970 3/6 – 7/28
1970 10/13 – until **1971** 4/10
1976 7/20 – until **1977** 8/20
1991 4/3 – 6/30
1991 12/27 – until **1993** 2/13
1999 4/16 – until **2000** 5/17
2005 8/27 – until **2006** 3/3
2006 5/8 – 9/30
2007 2/14 – 6/21

URANUS CHALLENGING
1938 1/1 – until **1940** 5/1
1956 9/11 – until **1960** 8/13
1997 2/5 – until **2001** 12/1

NEPTUNE CHALLENGING
2000 2/29 – until **2008** 2/1

PLUTO CHALLENGING
1941 9/22 – until **1953** 6/20

JUPITER SPECIAL
1946 10/20 – until **1947** 1/6
1947 5/25 – 9/4
1958 10/4 – 12/18
1970 1/31 – 3/11
1970 9/17 – 12/1
1981 12/27 – until **1982** 4/26
1982 8/26 – 11/15
1993 12/6 – until **1994** 6/12
1994 7/21 – 10/31
2005 11/20 – until **2006** 10/15

SATURN SPECIAL
1953 12/8 – until **1954** 5/6
1954 9/3 – until **1955** 10/27
1983 10/15 – until **1984** 11/30
2012 11/19 – Continues

URANUS SPECIAL
1975 12/8 – until **1979** 11/14

NEPTUNE SPECIAL
1958 11/20 – until **1966** 10/30

PLUTO SPECIAL
1985 11/13 – until **1992** 10/5

♏

November 7

SUN: SCORPIO · DECANATE: PISCES/NEPTUNE · DEGREE: 14°5–15°5 SCORPIO · MODE: FIXED · ELEMENT: WATER

Your Personal Powers

With your keen intelligence and ability to lead, you are an independent and responsible individual. You gain power from the combination of your sensitivity, imagination, and analytical thinking. Resourceful and perceptive, you also possess insight into the motives of others. If you are cynical or skeptical, however, you can lose some of your persuasive power. You are usually more successful when playing the role of an idealist who wants to fight injustice and make the world a better place. Being well-informed, you are usually educated in your favorite areas of interest. You are likely to have a natural sense of authority and usually enjoy being in control. If you become bossy or demanding, you are likely to lose some of your power. If female, you tend to stand up for your principles and play a strong rather than passive role. Your reliability and capacity for hard work indicate that you are pragmatic and determined, yet intuitive and visionary with unique ideas.

Your Powers of Attraction in Relationships

People are attracted to your fine mind and strong sense of self-identity. Underneath your bold façade, however, you are more sensitive than you may care to show. This often emphasizes your need for an emotionally supportive and understanding partner. Although independent, you value your partnerships and can be equally sympathetic to others. With your perfectionist streak and analytical skills, you may find yourself reevaluating your relationships in order to improve them. You are drawn to sincere and straightforward people and those with practical common sense. Being clever and autonomous, you also need people who can match your intelligence and respect your freedom. As you often are strong-willed, you may have to get the balance of power right, knowing when to take charge and when to comply with your partner.

Your attractive qualities: sensitive, leadership, intelligent, meticulous, talent for writing, idealistic, honest, thoughtful, imaginative, intuitive, creative, knowledgeable, scientific, just, rational, reflective, humanitarian, determined, responsible, introspective

Your less attractive qualities: concealing, bossy, deceitful, skeptical, cold, confused, inner fears, secretive, controlling, revenge, vacillate between overconfident or self-doubt

Your Venus Power

The planet Venus has a great deal of influence on your powers of attraction. Below are four possible Venus types for women and men. To find your Venus you need to go to page 771, where you will find the Venus table and extra information. The planet Mars also affects your powers of attraction. To find your Mars table and interpretation go to page 761.

WOMEN WITH VENUS IN LIBRA: A natural romantic with good social skills, you love to entertain or put people at ease by projecting a warm and gracious manner. Elegant and fair with a touch of glamour, you are also adept at dealing with people in delicate situations or conflicts. You seek refinement and will go out of your way to achieve harmony and keep the peace. For you, relationships are so important that you may need to guard against becoming dependent on others for approval. With your friendly personality and inherent charm, however, you will always be popular and loved.

MEN WITH VENUS IN LIBRA: You are such good company, people are naturally drawn to you and especially appreciate your talent for making them feel special. You find status in your social contacts and place importance on your relationships. Being clever and a charming companion, you will go out of your way to keep situations peaceful and harmonious. In relationships, however, be careful of indecision or compromising too much. Nevertheless, others are attracted by your natural refinement and good taste, which is reflected in your sense of style.

WOMEN WITH VENUS IN SCORPIO: Loving and passionate, you are often sensitive with deep feelings and strong powers of attraction. A love for the truth coupled with a tendency to be suspicious can be an influence that motivates you to delve deep into the activities of your partner. When in love or in a relationship that matters, you will often bend over backward to cooperate. Although loyal, guard against losing sight of your own needs and desires.

MEN WITH VENUS IN SCORPIO: You are usually attracted to sensual and passionate partners with strong character. You are often sensitive with deep feelings and magnetic powers of attraction. As a cautious yet devoted and ardent lover, you are likely to seek experiences that are more sexual in nature. You display your less attractive qualities when you project your negative thoughts and resort to being suspicious or possessive. Nevertheless, loyal and loving, you are a sensitive lover.

WOMEN WITH VENUS IN SAGITTARIUS: Sociable, warm, and friendly, you possess an honest and frank style in your relationships. Being naturally gregarious, you want others to share your enthusiasm and enjoy encouraging the people you love. You fare better when you have a sense of personal freedom within a relationship and are usually generous with the faults of others. You need a partner who can share your need to explore and take risks, whether through travel, education, or recreation.

MEN WITH VENUS IN SAGITTARIUS: Usually you are attracted to partners who are knowledgeable or well-traveled. Enthusiastic and optimistic, you often respond quickly to love offers and enter relationships with enthusiasm. Usually you seek to expand your social circle and meeting people from all walks of life can bring you the variety and fun you seek in life. Although you are generous and honest, your partners may accuse you of being overly optimistic or too blunt.

WOMEN WITH VENUS IN CAPRICORN: As you possess natural caution in romantic affairs, you often appear reserved and controlled. You may be shy, but try to be more forward, especially if you want to be noticed. When you care about people, however, you are usually willing to put in extra time and energy to preserve the relationship. You are practical and dependable, and a sense of duty can often play a large part in the affairs of your heart. With elegant simplicity you can attract others through your well-cut clothes and refined manners.

MEN WITH VENUS IN CAPRICORN: In relationships you take love seriously and can be a strong and practical support for friends or partners. You are usually attracted to partners who are as hardworking as yourself. As you tend not to express your feelings until you feel really secure in a relationship, you may be drawn to those who seem loyal, faithful, and not likely to let you down. As you respect the wisdom of experience you may be drawn to mature partners or, alternatively, you may act as an authority figure for someone younger.

To read all about your Outer Planets and work out how to use your personalized timetable, go to Section Three, page 789.

♍

Your Personalized Timetable

JUPITER BENEFICIAL
1939 1/28 – 4/6
1942 7/8 – 9/30
1942 12/25 – until 1943 5/23
1944 9/7 – 10/26
1945 4/9 – 6/19
1948 12/27 – until 1949 2/9
1950 5/31 – 7/23
1951 1/9 – 3/20
1954 6/21 – 9/4
1955 2/5 – 4/26
1956 8/23 – 10/8
1960 12/11 – until 1961 1/23
1962 4/27 – 9/11
1962 12/15 – until 1963 3/3
1966 6/5 – 8/16
1968 8/7 – 9/22
1972 11/23 – until 1973 1/7
1974 4/5 – until 1975 2/14
1978 5/18 – 7/30
1979 12/3 – until 1980 1/19
1980 7/20 – 9/6
1984 3/11 – 6/19
1984 11/4 – 12/22
1986 3/19 – 6/25
1986 7/30 – until 1987 1/27
1989 9/4 – 12/23
1990 4/27 – 7/14
1991 10/31 – until 1992 3/2
1992 6/28 – 8/21
1996 2/16 – 8/3
1996 10/4 – 12/5
1998 3/2 – 5/16
1998 9/21 – until 1999 1/3
2001 8/12 – until 2002 2/8
2002 3/22 – 6/28
2003 10/11 – until 2004 4/18
2004 5/21 – 8/5
2008 1/29 – 3/25
2008 6/24 – 11/16
2010 2/14 – 4/24

SATURN BENEFICIAL
1944 8/10 – until 1945 1/9
1945 4/28 – 9/13
1946 1/1 – 6/1
1949 8/31 – 12/20
1950 1/8 – 8/19
1959 12/31 – until 1960 12/30
1965 2/16 – until 1966 3/31
1974 6/15 – until 1975 7/14
1978 10/11 – until 1979 3/17
1979 7/1 – 9/27
1989 2/3 – 7/20
1989 11/1 – until 1990 2/2
1990 8/25 – 10/21
1994 3/23 – 10/12
1994 12/7 – until 1995 5/12
1995 9/1 – until 1996 2/3
2003 7/23 – until 2004 2/29
2004 3/15 – 8/22
2005 2/2 – 5/8
2008 8/14 – 11/9
2009 2/24 – 7/31

URANUS BENEFICIAL
1950 7/16 – until 1954 6/29
1963 11/6 – until 1966 9/2
1990 3/21 – until 1993 11/18
2004 5/8 – until 2009 3/8

NEPTUNE BENEFICIAL
1938 3/27 – 7/31
1988 2/15 – until 1993 11/29

PLUTO BENEFICIAL
1961 10/17 – until 1967 8/13
2012 3/12 – Continues

JUPITER CHALLENGING
1938 1/17 – 3/28
1940 6/14 – 12/11
1941 1/19 – 4/23
1943 7/29 – 10/18

1944 2/9 – 6/14
1949 12/31 – until 1950 3/9
1952 5/26 – until 1953 4/5
1955 7/13 – 9/26
1956 3/25 – 5/11
1961 5/3 – 6/17
1961 12/12 – until 1962 2/20
1964 5/8 – 7/27
1964 11/3 – until 1965 3/15
1967 6/26 – 9/9
1973 3/28 – 8/6
1973 11/18 – until 1974 2/4
1976 4/22 – 7/2
1976 12/20 – until 1977 2/10
1978 10/15 – until 1979 1/6
1979 6/7 – 8/23
1985 3/7 – until 1986 1/19
1988 4/6 – 6/13
1990 9/19 – until 1991 2/15
1991 5/13 – 8/8
1997 2/17 – until 1998 1/1
2000 3/19 – 5/27
2002 8/31 – until 2003 7/22
2009 2/1 – 4/20
2009 8/12 – 12/10
2011 7/10 – 10/21
2012 2/26 – 5/10

SATURN CHALLENGING
1940 5/10 – until 1941 6/12
1941 12/26 – until 1942 2/19
1946 9/27 – until 1947 1/15
1947 6/16 – 11/15
1947 12/23 – until 1948 7/19
1962 2/27 – 8/25
1962 11/22 – until 1963 5/3
1963 7/4 – until 1964 1/18
1969 6/26 – 10/17
1970 3/16 – 8/18
1970 9/22 – until 1971 4/19
1976 7/28 – until 1977 8/28
1991 4/22 – 6/11
1992 1/5 – until 1993 2/21
1999 4/24 – until 2000 5/25
2005 9/5 – until 2006 2/16
2006 5/23 – 10/11
2007 2/2 – 7/1

URANUS CHALLENGING
1938 1/1 – until 1941 2/20
1956 10/5 – until 1961 6/8
1997 2/23 – until 2001 12/29

NEPTUNE CHALLENGING
2000 4/9 – until 2008 12/29

PLUTO CHALLENGING
1942 9/3 – until 1953 7/28

JUPITER SPECIAL
1946 10/25 – until 1947 1/12
1947 5/17 – 9/11
1958 10/9 – 12/23
1959 7/8 – 8/1
1970 9/22 – 12/6
1982 1/3 – 4/19
1982 9/2 – 11/20
1993 12/12 – until 1994 5/30
1994 8/4 – 11/4
2005 11/24 – until 2006 10/20

SATURN SPECIAL
1953 12/18 – until 1954 4/22
1954 9/14 – until 1955 11/4
1983 10/23 – until 1984 12/9
1985 6/22 – 8/28
2012 11/28 – Continues

URANUS SPECIAL
1975 12/31 – until 1980 9/13

NEPTUNE SPECIAL
1958 12/22 – until 1967 9/26

PLUTO SPECIAL
1985 12/11 – until 1992 11/1

481

November 8

SUN: SCORPIO • DECANATE: PISCES/NEPTUNE • DEGREE: 15°5–16°5 SCORPIO • MODE: FIXED • ELEMENT: WATER

Your Personal Powers

Ambitious and assured, among your many personal powers are quick intelligence and strong determination. With your deep sensitivity and probing mind, you can often think like a psychologist or a detective. Although you gain power from your tenacity, resolve, and astute mind, you may need to apply self-discipline and exercise patience. With your natural leadership ability, you can utilize your organizational or executive skills to further your success or work to put your inspired ideas into form. Although you can be purposeful, resist losing some of your power by being too domineering or stubborn. When you let doubt and indecision undermine your positive outlook you may become discouraged and feel sorry for yourself. Nevertheless, usually optimistic, kind, and courageous, you can be very resourceful and intuitive. Being productive with a natural business sense, you are often responsible and hardworking. You can achieve success and gain power from handling your own material affairs and using your innate common sense.

Your Powers of Attraction in Relationships

You are proud and dramatic, and others are attracted to your good mind, generosity, and confident personality. As an enterprising person, you can often act as a link between different social groups. With your realistic stand in life, you need relationships that can provide you with material as well as emotional security. Drawn to those who can outsmart you in intelligence or at least keep up, you need mental stimulation to stop you from becoming disinterested or impatient. In love you are loyal and supportive as long as you receive respect and are treated as an equal. Do not let jealousy, suspicion, or stubbornness undermine your relationships. Sensitive and intuitive, you may not place your feelings in the open but you can be generous and kind with those you love and care for.

Your attractive qualities: intelligent, leadership, thoroughness, hardworking, perceptive, sensitive, leadership ability, productive, quick-witted, determined, strong-willed, inspired ideas, organizational skills, business sense, determined, good judge of values, generous

Your less attractive qualities: impatient, intolerant, workaholic, power struggles, unforgiving, domineering, escapist, easily discouraged, lack of planning, stubborn, controlling behavior, manipulative

Your Venus Power

The planet Venus has a great deal of influence on your powers of attraction. Below are four possible Venus types for women and men. To find your Venus you need to go to page 771, where you will find the Venus table and extra information. The planet Mars also affects your powers of attraction. To find your Mars table and interpretation go to page 761.

WOMEN WITH VENUS IN LIBRA: Gracious, charming, and sociable with a sense of style, you have no trouble attracting admirers. With your natural diplomatic skills and desire for harmony you usually like to keep the peace and avoid confrontations, but be careful of failing to take a stand when it is necessary. Romantic and easygoing yourself, you are attracted to affectionate and refined individuals who share your love of peace, justice, and fair play.

MEN WITH VENUS IN LIBRA: You are such good company, people are naturally drawn to you and especially appreciate your talent for making them feel special. You find status in your social contacts and place importance on your relationships. Being clever and a charming companion, you will go out of your way to keep situations peaceful and harmonious. In relationships, however, be careful of indecision or compromising too much. Nevertheless, others are attracted by your natural refinement and good taste, which is reflected in your sense of style.

WOMEN WITH VENUS IN SCORPIO: Your strength and power is in your ability to love both deeply and sensitively. For you, love and desire go hand in hand. As you feel so deeply, you often keep your sensitivity or vulnerability hidden from others in order to keep some control in your relationships. You are more likely to prefer a few very close loyal friends than many superficial acquaintances. In relationships your sensual nature and magnetic intensity can easily attract others.

MEN WITH VENUS IN SCORPIO: You are attracted to partners with deep and powerful emotions or individuals whom you find intriguing. Your gift for creating smoke screens to maintain secrecy around your feelings can conceal your inner sensitivity and vulnerability. Nevertheless, you are looking for a partner who can pierce your defenses and understand you at

a very deep level. Needing a relationship with a powerful sexual connection, you thrive on emotional intensity.

WOMEN WITH VENUS IN SAGITTARIUS: When you feel generous you can make others feel more optimistic about life. You may be interested in higher learning and seek partners who are scholarly or broad-minded. You are outspoken and direct and sometimes say things that you later regret. Curious and versatile, you can adjust quickly to new situations; a foreign influence implies that you love to travel or may have a partner who comes from a different culture.

MEN WITH VENUS IN SAGITTARIUS: Your enthusiasm and straightforward conduct usually appeal to others and imply that you are approachable and easygoing. Being open to ideas and willing to believe that life can have a great deal to offer suggests that you are generous, broad-minded, and show eagerness to cooperate with others. A love of travel and an interest in other cultures imply that your partner may come from a foreign country.

WOMEN WITH VENUS IN CAPRICORN: Loyal and responsible, you are attracted to dignified and reserved individuals. Being practical and security-conscious, you prefer hardworking partners who are resourceful and enterprising. Work may even be a factor in many of your associations and partnerships. For you, family and faithfulness can be especially important, so you are usually willing to work hard or make sacrifices in order to build a strong relationship.

MEN WITH VENUS IN CAPRICORN: In relationships you take love seriously and can be a strong and practical support for friends or partners. You are usually attracted to partners who are as hardworking as yourself. As you tend not to express your feelings until you feel really secure in a relationship, you may be drawn to those who seem loyal, faithful, and not likely to let you down. As you respect the wisdom of experience you may be drawn to mature partners or, alternatively, you may act as an authority figure for someone younger.

To read all about your Outer Planets and work out how to use your personalized timetable, go to Section Three, page 789.

♏

Your Personalized Timetable

JUPITER BENEFICIAL
1939 2/2 – 4/10
1942 7/12 – 10/9
1942 12/16 – until **1943** 5/28
1944 9/12 – 11/1
1945 3/31 – 6/28
1948 12/31 – until **1949** 2/14
1950 6/19 – 7/4
1951 1/14 – 3/24
1954 6/26 – 9/10
1955 1/27 – 5/4
1956 8/27 – 10/13
1960 12/15 – until **1961** 1/28
1962 5/3 – 9/3
1962 12/22 – until **1963** 3/7
1966 6/10 – 8/21
1968 8/11 – 9/27
1972 11/28 – until **1973** 1/11
1974 4/10 – until **1975** 2/18
1978 5/23 – 8/4
1980 7/25 – 9/11
1984 3/19 – 6/11
1984 11/9 – 12/27
1986 3/23 – until **1987** 2/1
1989 9/11 – 12/16
1990 5/3 – 7/19
1991 11/6 – until **1992** 2/23
1992 7/4 – 8/26
1996 2/22 – 7/24
1996 10/14 – 12/10
1998 3/7 – 5/22
1998 9/13 – until **1999** 1/9
2001 8/17 – until **2002** 1/27
2002 4/3 – 7/2
2003 10/16 – until **2004** 4/4
2004 6/5 – 8/10
2008 2/3 – 4/3
2008 6/15 – 11/21
2010 2/18 – 4/28

SATURN BENEFICIAL
1944 8/20 – 12/28
1945 5/9 – 9/26
1945 12/18 – until **1946** 6/10
1949 9/8 – until **1950** 8/28
1960 1/8 – until **1961** 1/7
1965 2/24 – until **1966** 4/8
1966 11/4 – 12/18
1974 6/23 – until **1975** 7/22
1978 10/20 – until **1979** 3/4
1979 7/12 – 10/5
1980 5/9 – 6/4
1989 2/13 – 7/6
1989 11/13 – until **1990** 2/11
1990 8/7 – 11/7
1994 4/1 – 9/24
1994 12/23 – until **1995** 5/25
1995 8/17 – until **1996** 2/12
2003 7/31 – until **2004** 2/2
2004 4/10 – 8/31
2005 1/20 – 5/20
2008 8/22 – 11/22
2009 2/10 – 8/10

URANUS BENEFICIAL
1950 8/4 – until **1954** 7/16
1964 9/1 – until **1967** 6/10
1991 1/11 – until **1993** 12/9
2005 3/7 – until **2010** 1/9

NEPTUNE BENEFICIAL
1938 2/17 – until **1938** 8/30
1989 1/12 – until **1993** 12/29

PLUTO BENEFICIAL
1962 9/17 – until **1968** 6/26

JUPITER CHALLENGING
1938 1/21 – 4/2
1938 9/25 – 11/12
1940 6/20 – 11/29
1941 1/31 – 4/28

1943 8/3 – 10/25
1944 2/2 – 6/20
1950 1/4 – 3/14
1952 5/30 – until **1953** 4/10
1955 7/18 – 10/2
1956 3/13 – 5/23
1961 12/17 – until **1962** 2/24
1964 5/13 – 8/3
1964 10/26 – until **1965** 3/21
1967 7/1 – 9/14
1973 4/3 – 7/29
1973 11/25 – until **1974** 2/8
1976 4/26 – 7/7
1976 12/10 – until **1977** 2/20
1978 10/23 – 12/28
1979 6/13 – 8/28
1985 3/12 – 9/22
1985 10/15 – until **1986** 1/23
1988 4/10 – 6/18
1990 9/25 – until **1991** 2/7
1991 5/20 – 8/12
1997 2/22 – until **1998** 1/6
2000 3/23 – 5/31
2002 9/5 – until **2003** 7/27
2009 2/5 – 4/26
2009 8/4 – 12/16
2011 7/17 – 10/13
2012 3/2 – 5/14

SATURN CHALLENGING
1940 5/18 – until **1941** 6/21
1941 12/9 – until **1942** 3/7
1946 10/10 – until **1947** 1/1
1947 6/25 – until **1948** 7/28
1962 3/9 – 8/10
1962 12/5 – until **1964** 1/27
1969 7/8 – 10/4
1970 3/25 – until **1971** 4/27
1976 8/4 – until **1977** 9/5
1992 1/14 – until **1993** 3/2
1999 5/2 – until **2000** 6/2
2005 9/14 – until **2006** 2/3
2006 6/4 – 10/23
2007 1/19 – 7/10

URANUS CHALLENGING
1938 1/1 – until **1941** 3/24
1957 7/31 – until **1961** 7/2
1997 3/16 – until **2002** 1/18

NEPTUNE CHALLENGING
2001 2/24 – until **2009** 1/27

PLUTO CHALLENGING
1943 8/17 – until **1954** 7/4

JUPITER SPECIAL
1946 10/29 – until **1947** 1/19
1947 5/9 – 9/18
1958 10/14 – 12/28
1959 6/21 – 8/18
1970 9/27 – 12/11
1982 1/10 – 4/10
1982 9/8 – 11/24
1993 12/17 – until **1994** 5/20
1994 8/13 – 11/9
2005 11/29 – until **2006** 10/24

SATURN SPECIAL
1953 12/30 – until **1954** 4/9
1954 9/24 – until **1955** 11/13
1983 11/1 – until **1984** 12/18
1985 6/5 – 9/12
2012 12/8 – Continues

URANUS SPECIAL
1976 10/28 – until **1980** 10/5

NEPTUNE SPECIAL
1959 11/17 – until **1967** 10/28

PLUTO SPECIAL
1986 2/3 – until **1993** 9/19

November 9

SUN: SCORPIO • DECANATE: CANCER/MOON • DEGREE: 16°5–17°5 SCORPIO • MODE: FIXED • ELEMENT: WATER

Your Personal Powers

Clever and entertaining, your personal powers include an enterprising and idealistic nature. Your ruling planet, Pluto, indicates that you possess deep feelings and at times can be emotionally intense. You gain power through your love of knowledge, generosity, and desire to improve or transform your circumstances. As you are also strong-willed and ambitious, you may find yourself naturally gravitating to leading positions. Intuitive and sensitive, you lose some power if you forfeit your detachment and become frustrated or disappointed with others. Usually very engaging and persuasive, you are able to mix with people from different social circles. Your unique outlook implies that you relay information in interesting ways. With an ability to inspire others, you are usually action-oriented and motivated. Although you can be enthusiastic, direct, and dynamic, you can also be secretive and struggle with inner anxieties, particularly regarding material security. Nevertheless, being keen, sociable, intelligent, and success-oriented, you have only to apply the necessary discipline to achieve outstanding attainment in life.

Your Powers of Attraction in Relationships

Broad-minded and smart, you attract others with your independent spirit. Sensitive to the feelings of others, you also possess a generous, caring, and sentimental nature. Equally, your youthfulness emphasizes your enthusiasm and entertaining manner in social situations. Being sensitive with high ideals and strong passions, you often seek a perfect partner. Alternatively, you may be attracted to people with innate wisdom and self-awareness. In order to improve your relationships, you may have to resist being cynical, suspicious, or feeling lonely and isolated. By making sure that you maintain your inner faith and spontaneity, you can project a warm and powerful love and affection to others and enhance your relationships. A compassionate side to your nature often helps you to empathize with others.

Your attractive qualities: intelligent, broad-minded, idealistic, creative, persevering, sensitive, generous, entertaining, youthful, giving, magnetic, charitable, humanitarian, detached, popular, leadership, imaginative, receptive, intuitive, impressionable, independent, psychic

Your less attractive qualities: frustrated, nervous, selfish, impractical, bitter, inferiority complex, isolated, too excitable, secretive, immature, escapist, unforgiving, fearful, cold, disappointing, resentful, worry

Your Venus Power

The planet Venus has a great deal of influence on your powers of attraction. Below are four possible Venus types for women and men. To find your Venus you need to go to page 771, where you will find the Venus table and extra information. The planet Mars also affects your powers of attraction. To find your Mars table and interpretation go to page 761.

WOMEN WITH VENUS IN LIBRA: You are usually attractive and sociable with an easygoing manner. Your love of beauty, harmony, and pleasure implies that you are a romantic with a desire for love and affection. Once in a relationship you need to learn to negotiate your position rather than adapt to the wishes of others and compromise just to keep the peace. Nevertheless, your advanced social skills and strong sense of fair play can help you succeed in any social or romantic situation.

MEN WITH VENUS IN LIBRA: As a sociable and friendly individual with an eye for beauty, you are amorous and charming. You are a natural gentleman and your ideal partner usually has an elegant appearance, artistic appreciation, and good taste. Your relationships benefit when you resist the temptation to take the easy way out or put too much emphasis on vanity and high living. Intellectual and naturally refined, you seek a loving partner who can share your romantic and sophisticated aspirations.

WOMEN WITH VENUS IN SCORPIO: With a natural psychic gift for penetrating the feelings of others, you can often help partners transform emotional challenges or sexual difficulties. When you fall in love, your strong feelings of determination give you a potent force that others find attractive and seductive. Although you know what really turns people on, your most profound desire is usually for the deepness and closeness of real love and intimacy in an enduring relationship.

MEN WITH VENUS IN SCORPIO: In relationships you possess a sensitive understanding of your partner's deeper nature. Although you are strongly attached to those you love, you may have to be careful that your feelings do not turn into jealousy or possessiveness. When you fall in love it is often with an emotional intensity that helps you get in touch with your deep

feelings. You are attracted to partners who can share your passion and display strong feelings of sexuality like your own.

WOMEN WITH VENUS IN SAGITTARIUS: Optimistic and fun-loving, you love adventure and seek a partner who can expand your horizons. Being truthful and direct, you often say what you think. At times you may be naively tactless. A need for expansion and prosperity suggests that you may enjoy traveling with your friends or partner. Being both lighthearted and idealistic, however, indicates that once you have given your heart to someone you will stay honorable and loyal.

MEN WITH VENUS IN SAGITTARIUS: Usually you are attracted to partners who are knowledgeable or well-traveled. Enthusiastic and optimistic, you often respond quickly to love offers and enter relationships with enthusiasm. Usually you seek to expand your social circle and meeting people from all walks of life can bring you the variety and fun to you seek in life. Although you are generous and honest, your partners may accuse you of being overly optimistic or too blunt.

WOMEN WITH VENUS IN CAPRICORN: As you possess natural caution in romantic affairs, you often appear reserved and controlled. You may be shy, but try to be more forward, especially if you want to be noticed by others. When you care about people, however, you are usually willing to put in extra time and energy to preserve the relationship. You are practical and dependable, and a sense of duty can often play a large part in the affairs of your heart. With elegant simplicity you can attract others through your well-cut clothes and refined manners.

MEN WITH VENUS IN CAPRICORN: As you admire loyal, hardworking, and dedicated individuals, you probably want a partner who can share your vocational interests or who can provide you with the security you need. You could even find yourself with a partner who is of a different age group or maturity. Guard against denying your true emotional needs or focusing on your career at the expense of your relationship. You are drawn to reserved partners who display self-control.

To read all about your Outer Planets and work out how to use your personalized timetable, go to Section Three, page 789.

♏

Your Personalized Timetable

JUPITER BENEFICIAL
1939 2/6 – 4/14
1942 7/17 – 10/20
1942 12/5 – until 1943 6/3
1944 9/17 – 11/7
1945 3/23 – 7/6
1949 1/5 – 2/19
1951 1/19 – 3/28
1954 6/30 – 9/16
1955 1/20 – 5/11
1956 9/1 – 10/18
1960 12/20 – until 1961 2/1
1962 5/9 – 8/26
1962 12/28 – until 1963 3/11
1966 6/14 – 8/26
1968 8/16 – 10/2
1972 12/3 – until 1973 1/16
1974 4/15 – 10/20
1974 11/18 – until 1975 2/23
1978 5/28 – 8/8
1980 7/30 – 9/16
1984 3/28 – 6/1
1984 11/15 – 12/31
1986 3/28 – until 1987 2/5
1989 9/18 – 12/7
1990 5/9 – 7/23
1991 11/14 – until 1992 2/15
1992 7/11 – 8/31
1996 2/27 – 7/15
1996 10/22 – 12/15
1998 3/11 – 5/29
1998 9/6 – until 1999 1/15
2001 8/22 – until 2002 1/18
2002 4/12 – 7/7
2003 10/22 – until 2004 3/25
2004 6/15 – 8/15
2008 2/7 – 4/14
2008 6/4 – 11/26
2010 2/22 – 5/3
2010 10/27 – 12/11

SATURN BENEFICIAL
1944 8/31 – 12/16
1945 5/18 – 10/13
1945 11/30 – until 1946 6/19
1949 9/16 – until 1950 9/5
1960 1/17 – until 1961 1/16
1965 3/4 – until 1966 4/17
1966 10/16 – until 1967 1/6
1974 6/30 – until 1975 7/30
1978 10/31 – until 1979 2/19
1979 7/22 – 10/14
1980 4/14 – 6/28
1989 2/24 – 6/22
1989 11/23 – until 1990 2/21
1990 7/23 – 11/20
1994 4/10 – 9/10
1995 1/5 – 6/14
1995 7/28 – until 1996 2/21
2003 8/9 – until 2004 1/18
2004 4/25 – 9/10
2005 1/8 – 5/30
2008 8/30 – 12/10
2009 1/22 – 8/19

URANUS BENEFICIAL
1950 8/25 – until 1955 5/13
1964 9/17 – until 1967 7/18
1991 1/28 – until 1993 12/28
2005 3/25 – until 2010 2/4

NEPTUNE BENEFICIAL
1938 1/1 – until 1939 7/28
1989 2/10 – until 1994 11/25

PLUTO BENEFICIAL
1962 10/19 – until 1968 8/8

JUPITER CHALLENGING
1938 1/25 – 4/7
1938 9/14 – 11/22
1940 6/25 – 11/20
1941 2/9 – 5/2
1943 8/8 – 11/1
1944 1/25 – 6/26

1950 1/9 – 3/18
1952 6/4 – until 1953 4/14
1955 7/22 – 10/7
1956 3/4 – 6/1
1961 12/22 – until 1962 3/1
1964 5/17 – 8/12
1964 10/17 – until 1965 3/26
1967 7/6 – 9/19
1973 4/10 – 7/21
1973 12/1 – until 1974 2/12
1976 4/30 – 7/13
1976 12/1 – until 1977 3/1
1978 11/5 – 12/16
1979 6/18 – 9/2
1985 3/17 – 9/5
1985 10/30 – until 1986 1/28
1988 4/14 – 6/22
1990 10/1 – until 1991 1/30
1991 5/27 – 8/17
1997 2/27 – until 1998 1/10
2000 3/28 – 6/4
2002 9/10 – until 2003 3/22
2003 4/17 – 8/1
2009 2/10 – 5/4
2009 7/27 – 12/21
2011 7/25 – 10/4
2012 3/8 – 5/18

SATURN CHALLENGING
1940 5/26 – 12/18
1941 1/31 – 6/30
1941 11/26 – until 1942 3/19
1946 10/27 – 12/14
1947 7/4 – until 1948 8/5
1962 3/19 – 7/27
1962 12/16 – until 1964 2/5
1969 7/26 – 9/16
1970 4/2 – until 1971 5/5
1976 8/12 – until 1977 9/13
1978 3/28 – 5/23
1992 1/22 – until 1993 3/10
1993 9/28 – 11/26
1999 5/10 – until 2000 6/10
2001 1/7 – 2/11
2005 9/25 – until 2006 1/21
2006 6/14 – 11/8
2007 1/3 – 7/19

URANUS CHALLENGING
1938 1/1 – until 1941 4/14
1957 8/17 – until 1961 7/20
1997 4/15 – until 2002 2/5

NEPTUNE CHALLENGING
2001 4/1 – until 2009 12/23

PLUTO CHALLENGING
1943 9/28 – until 1955 5/21

JUPITER SPECIAL
1946 11/3 – until 1947 1/26
1947 5/1 – 9/24
1958 10/18 – until 1959 1/3
1959 6/11 – 8/28
1970 10/2 – 12/15
1982 1/19 – 4/1
1982 9/14 – 11/29
1993 12/23 – until 1994 5/11
1994 8/21 – 11/13
2005 12/4 – until 2006 10/29

SATURN SPECIAL
1954 1/14 – 3/24
1954 10/4 – until 1955 11/21
1983 11/9 – until 1984 12/28
1985 5/22 – 9/25
2012 12/18 – Continues

URANUS SPECIAL
1976 11/13 – until 1980 10/24

NEPTUNE SPECIAL
1959 12/18 – until 1968 9/21

PLUTO SPECIAL
1986 11/26 – until 1993 10/21

485

November 10

SUN: SCORPIO • DECANATE: PISCES/NEPTUNE • DEGREE: 17°5–18°5 SCORPIO • MODE: FIXED • ELEMENT: WATER

Your Personal Powers

Success-oriented with strong convictions, you are a determined and intelligent individual. With the influence of your ruling planet, Pluto, you also possess powerful emotions and an independent but competitive nature. You gain power from the combination of your pioneering spirit and natural courage, which can often lead you to positions of prominence and responsibility. Being forceful, however, implies that you can lose some of your power by being obstinate or argumentative. In order to utilize your powerful vision, you need to synthesize your intuition, creativity, original ideas, and imagination. You need only apply hard work and self-discipline to make your dreams a reality. Although a vital key in your success is true enthusiasm, it is not something you are able to fake. Being proud of your achievements or work is likely to play a major role in your life success. The more freedom you have personally and professionally, the happier you are. Although usually ambitious and confident, you empower yourself by staying humble and using your innate wisdom and common sense.

Your Powers of Attraction in Relationships

You are usually talented and entertaining, and your magnetism attracts others and makes you popular. Clever, generous, and kind, you can impress others with your intelligence and ability to stay focused and exercise power. Although you like to take charge or lead, resist a tendency to be dictatorial with your partners. You are attracted to individuals who are leaders in their own right or strong-willed people who will not be intimidated by your forceful nature and intelligence. Equally, you respect hardworking individuals with realistic insight and common sense. Sensitive with strong and passionate emotions, you can be proud and dramatic in your love life. With your compelling manner, energy, and creative ideas, your original approach is very appealing to the opposite sex, although you should be careful of jealousy and indecision.

Your attractive qualities: intelligent, leadership, sensitive, creative, entertaining, progressive, forceful, optimistic, strong convictions, witty, original, talented, independent, gregarious, executive abilities, pioneering, magnetic, strong-willed, honest

Your less attractive qualities: overbearing, jealous, egotistical, too proud, obsessive, selfish, provocative, argumentative, weak, stubborn, restless, bossy, impatient

Your Venus Power

The planet Venus has a great deal of influence on your powers of attraction. Below are four possible Venus types for women and men. To find your Venus you need to go to page 771, where you will find the Venus table and extra information. The planet Mars also affects your powers of attraction. To find your Mars table and interpretation go to page 761.

WOMEN WITH VENUS IN LIBRA: Attractive, refined, and conscious of the needs of others, you usually desire harmonious relationships. As a peacemaker with good negotiating skills, you can smooth out difficulties with others but your dislike of confrontation may sometimes leave you refusing to take a stand or compromising too many of your own needs. Courteous, stylish, and charming with polished social skills, you are an expert at relating to others in a gracious and civilized manner.

MEN WITH VENUS IN LIBRA: Your good social skills, charming personality, and refined manner usually make you attractive to the opposite sex. Equally, you desire a sophisticated partner with grace, elegance, and a strong sense of style. Although you have the ability to be persuasive and irresistible to others, avoid manipulative love games. Nevertheless, your natural diplomacy and sense of fair play help you to relate to people in all social situations. With your love of balance and harmony, you seek a partner who is also moderate, easygoing, and loving.

WOMEN WITH VENUS IN SCORPIO: Loving and passionate, you are often sensitive with deep feelings and strong powers of attraction. A love for the truth coupled with a tendency to be suspicious can be an influence that motivates you to delve deep into the activities of your partner. When in love or in a relationship that matters, you will often bend over backward to cooperate. Although loyal, guard against losing sight of your own needs and desires.

MEN WITH VENUS IN SCORPIO: Usually you are attracted to sensual and passionate partners with strong character. You are often intense with deep feelings and magnetic powers of attraction. As a cautious yet devoted and ardent lover, you are likely to seek experiences that are more sexual in nature. You display your less attractive qualities when you project your negative thoughts and resort to being suspicious or possessive. Nevertheless, loyal and loving, you are a sensitive lover.

WOMEN WITH VENUS IN SAGITTARIUS: Optimistic and fun-loving, you love adventure and seek a partner who can ex-

pand your horizons. Being truthful and direct, you often say what you think. At times you may be naively tactless. A need for expansion and prosperity suggests that you may enjoy traveling with your friends or partner. Being both lighthearted and idealistic, however, indicates that once you have given your heart to someone you will stay honorable and loyal.

MEN WITH VENUS IN SAGITTARIUS: You are usually attracted to partners who are knowledgeable or well-traveled. Enthusiastic and optimistic, you often respond quickly to love offers and enter relationships with enthusiasm. Usually you seek to expand your social circle and meeting people from all walks of life can bring you the variety and fun to you seek in life. Although you are generous and honest, your partners may accuse you of being overly optimistic or too blunt.

WOMEN WITH VENUS IN CAPRICORN: As you possess natural caution in romantic affairs, you often appear reserved and controlled. You may be shy but try to be more forward, especially if you want to be noticed by others. When you care about people, however, you are usually willing to put in extra time and energy to preserve the relationship. You are practical and dependable, and a sense of duty can often play a large part in the affairs of your heart. With elegant simplicity, you can attract others through your well-cut clothes and refined manners.

MEN WITH VENUS IN CAPRICORN: As you do not display your deeper emotions freely, you are usually dignified and controlled in your relationships with others. Practical and down-to-earth partners are particularly attractive to you, especially those who do not rush into expressing their feelings but seem to possess natural class and reserve. You need a partner who is loyal and dependable and willing to take your relationship seriously.

To read all about your Outer Planets and work out how to use your personalized timetable, go to Section Three, page 789.

Your Personalized Timetable

JUPITER BENEFICIAL
1939 2/10 – 4/19
1942 7/21 – until 1943 6/8
1944 9/21 – 11/13
1945 3/15 – 7/13
1949 1/9 – 2/24
1949 9/17 – 9/21
1951 1/23 – 4/1
1954 7/5 – 9/22
1955 1/12 – 5/18
1956 9/5 – 10/23
1957 4/30 – 6/6
1960 12/24 – until 1961 2/6
1962 5/16 – 8/18
1963 1/2 – 3/15
1966 6/19 – 8/31
1967 2/25 – 4/14
1968 8/21 – 10/6
1972 12/8 – until 1973 1/20
1974 4/20 – 10/5
1974 12/2 – until 1975 2/27
1978 6/2 – 8/13
1980 8/4 – 9/20
1984 4/10 – 5/19
1984 11/20 – until 1985 1/4
1986 4/1 – until 1987 2/10
1989 9/28 – 11/28
1990 5/14 – 7/28
1991 11/22 – until 1992 2/7
1992 7/16 – 9/5
1996 3/4 – 7/7
1996 10/29 – 12/19
1998 3/15 – 6/6
1998 8/29 – until 1999 1/21
2001 8/28 – until 2002 1/10
2002 4/20 – 7/11
2003 10/27 – until 2004 3/16
2004 6/23 – 8/20
2008 2/12 – 12/1
2010 2/26 – 5/9
2010 10/16 – 12/22

SATURN BENEFICIAL
1944 9/13 – 12/2
1945 5/27 – until 1946 6/27
1949 9/24 – until 1950 9/13
1960 1/26 – 8/21
1960 10/11 – until 1961 1/24
1965 3/13 – until 1966 4/27
1966 10/1 – until 1967 1/19
1974 7/8 – until 1975 8/6
1978 11/12 – until 1979 2/5
1979 8/1 – 10/23
1980 3/30 – 7/13
1989 3/9 – 6/7
1989 12/3 – until 1990 3/3
1990 7/10 – 12/1
1994 4/21 – 8/28
1995 1/15 – until 1996 2/29
2003 8/19 – until 2004 1/5
2004 5/6 – 9/22
2004 12/26 – until 2005 6/8
2008 9/7 – until 2009 8/27

URANUS BENEFICIAL
1950 9/29 – until 1955 6/5
1964 10/4 – until 1967 8/8
1991 2/17 – until 1994 1/14
2005 4/15 – until 2010 2/23

NEPTUNE BENEFICIAL
1938 1/1 – until 1939 8/28
1989 4/4 – until 1994 12/26

PLUTO BENEFICIAL
1963 9/18 – until 1968 9/7

JUPITER CHALLENGING
1938 1/29 – 4/13
1938 9/5 – 12/1
1940 6/30 – 11/12
1941 2/16 – 5/6

1943 8/12 – 11/11
1944 1/15 – 7/2
1950 1/13 – 3/23
1952 6/8 – until 1953 4/19
1955 7/27 – 10/13
1956 2/25 – 6/8
1961 12/27 – until 1962 3/5
1964 5/21 – 8/24
1964 10/6 – until 1965 3/31
1967 7/11 – 9/24
1973 4/18 – 7/13
1973 12/7 – until 1974 2/17
1976 5/4 – 7/18
1976 11/24 – until 1977 3/8
1979 6/23 – 9/6
1985 3/23 – 8/26
1985 11/9 – until 1986 2/1
1988 4/19 – 6/27
1990 10/7 – until 1991 1/23
1991 6/3 – 8/21
1997 3/3 – until 1998 1/15
2000 4/1 – 6/9
2002 9/15 – until 2003 3/6
2003 5/3 – 8/6
2009 2/14 – 5/13
2009 7/17 – 12/26
2011 8/5 – 9/23
2012 3/13 – 5/22

SATURN CHALLENGING
1940 6/4 – 11/29
1941 2/18 – 7/10
1941 11/14 – until 1942 3/30
1947 7/12 – until 1948 8/13
1962 4/1 – 7/13
1962 12/26 – until 1964 2/13
1970 4/11 – until 1971 5/13
1976 8/20 – until 1977 9/22
1978 3/11 – 6/9
1992 1/30 – until 1993 3/19
1993 9/11 – 12/12
1999 5/18 – until 2000 6/19
2000 12/17 – until 2001 3/3
2005 10/6 – until 2006 1/9
2006 6/23 – until 2007 7/27

URANUS CHALLENGING
1938 1/1 – until 1941 5/3
1957 9/3 – until 1961 8/6
1998 2/9 – until 2002 12/6

NEPTUNE CHALLENGING
2002 2/21 – until 2010 1/24

PLUTO CHALLENGING
1944 9/6 – until 1955 7/15

JUPITER SPECIAL
1946 11/8 – until 1947 2/4
1947 4/22 – 9/30
1958 10/23 – until 1959 1/8
1959 6/2 – 9/5
1970 10/7 – 12/20
1982 1/30 – 3/21
1982 9/19 – 12/4
1993 12/29 – until 1994 5/3
1994 8/29 – 11/18
2005 12/9 – until 2006 6/20
2006 7/21 – 11/3

SATURN SPECIAL
1954 10/13 – until 1955 11/30
1983 11/18 – until 1985 1/7
1985 5/8 – 10/6
2012 12/29 – Continues

URANUS SPECIAL
1976 11/30 – until 1980 11/10

NEPTUNE SPECIAL
1960 11/14 – until 1968 10/25

PLUTO SPECIAL
1986 12/28 – until 1994 8/22

♏

November 11

SUN: SCORPIO · DECANATE: PISCES/NEPTUNE · DEGREE: 18°5–19°5 SCORPIO · MODE: FIXED · ELEMENT: WATER

Your Personal Powers

Tough yet sensitive and idealistic, you are able to feel things deeply. Although you may not always find it easy to communicate those feelings, there are many sides to your personality. Your ruling planet, Pluto, gives you endurance, tenacity, and strong passions. You gain power by combining your determination and foresight with your emotional sensitivity. With an inner sense of the dramatic, you usually show a confident front to the world and aim for leadership positions. Hidden fears or negative thinking can sometimes undermine your outstanding potential or cause you to lose direction. When you are optimistic, however, you can be very generous with your resources. You gain power through your awareness of your obligations, liberal approach, and ability to stand up for your ideals. Although you are independent and freedom-loving, enterprises that involve collaboration or partnership can play an important role in your learning curve. These efforts stop you from losing power by becoming too self-absorbed. When focused, your inspiration and dedication also work well to bring out your remarkable potential.

Your Powers of Attraction in Relationships

With your warm heart and ability to deal with people, you have no trouble attracting friends and admirers. You particularly gain from partnerships and team efforts. Although you appear self-assured, underneath you are sensitive and easily hurt. Idealistic in love, you are usually romantic, caring, and aware of your duties and responsibilities. You need a partner who understands your need for a secure and harmonious home base. Although having a close relationship is important to you, be careful of becoming too dependent on your partners. With your strong emotions, it is important to stay balanced or you may become too serious or intense. Nevertheless, persuasive, generous, and loving, you can be a passionate partner.

Your attractive qualities: sensitive, intelligent, confident, receptive, intuitive, inspired, optimistic, charm, enthusiastic, humanitarian, focused, objective, outgoing, artistic, common sense, psychic, broad-minded, sensitive, inventive, responsible, leadership abilities, unique style of work

Your less attractive qualities: frustrating, superiority complex or self-doubt, deceptive, overemotional, conceit, extremist, high-strung, disappointing, depressed, stubborn, selfish, arrogant, worry

Your Venus Power

The planet Venus has a great deal of influence on your powers of attraction. Below are four possible Venus types for women and men. To find your Venus you need to go to page 771, where you will find the Venus table and extra information. The planet Mars also affects your powers of attraction. To find your Mars table and interpretation go to page 761.

WOMEN WITH VENUS IN LIBRA: A natural romantic with good social skills, you love to entertain or put people at ease by projecting a warm and gracious manner. Elegant and fair with a touch of glamour, you are also adept at dealing with people in delicate situations or conflicts. You seek refinement and will go out of your way to achieve harmony and keep the peace. For you, relationships are so important that you may need to guard against becoming dependent on others for approval. With your friendly personality and inherent charm, however, you will always be popular and loved.

MEN WITH VENUS IN LIBRA: Courteous and refined, you are attracted to beautiful and elegant people. You are looking for a partner who can share your natural good taste and enjoy an intellectual conversation. Disliking conflict, you may have to be careful not to go along with others just to keep the peace. Your ideal partner will appreciate beauty and the little luxuries of life as well as possess good social skills. You have a strong sense of social etiquette yourself so you need an intelligent and sophisticated partner.

WOMEN WITH VENUS IN SCORPIO: With a natural psychic gift for penetrating the feelings of others, you can often help partners transform emotional challenges or sexual difficulties. When you fall in love your strong feelings of determination give you a potent force that others find attractive and seductive. Although you know what really turns people on, your most profound desire is usually for the deepness and closeness of real love and intimacy in an enduring relationship.

MEN WITH VENUS IN SCORPIO: In relationships you possess a sensitive understanding of your partner's deeper nature. Although you are strongly attached to those you love, you may have to be careful that your feelings do not turn into jealousy or possessiveness. When you fall in love it is often with an emotional intensity that helps you get in touch with your deep

feelings. You are attracted to partners who can share your passion and display strong feelings of sexuality like your own.

WOMEN WITH VENUS IN SAGITTARIUS: Optimistic and fun-loving, you love adventure and seek a partner who can expand your horizons. Being truthful and direct, you often say what you think. At times you may be naively tactless. A need for expansion and prosperity suggests that you may enjoy traveling with your friends or partner. Being both lighthearted and idealistic, however, indicates that once you have given your heart to someone you will stay honorable and loyal.

MEN WITH VENUS IN SAGITTARIUS: You are usually attracted to partners who are knowledgeable or well traveled. Enthusiastic and optimistic, you often respond quickly to love offers and enter relationships with enthusiasm. Usually you seek to expand your social circle and meeting people from all walks of life can bring you the variety and fun you seek in life. Although you are generous and honest, your partners may accuse you of being overly optimistic or too blunt.

WOMEN WITH VENUS IN CAPRICORN: Romantically, you do not give your heart easily but hide behind a cool reserve until you feel free to express your emotions. As you take your relationships seriously, you may find yourself drawn to people who are businesslike, resourceful, and practical, or those who can act as teachers or mentors. Work or career may also be a factor in many of your associations and partnerships. As security can play an important role in your relationships, you are often attracted to partners who are loyal and hardworking,

MEN WITH VENUS IN CAPRICORN: In relationships you take love seriously and can be a strong and practical support for friends or partners. You are usually attracted to partners who are as hardworking as yourself. As you tend not to express your feelings until you feel really secure in a relationship, you may be drawn to those who seem loyal, faithful, and not likely to let you down. As you respect the wisdom of experience, you may be drawn to mature partners or, alternatively, you may act as an authority figure for someone younger.

To read all about your Outer Planets and work out how to use your personalized timetable, go to Section Three, page 789.

go to Section Three, page 789.

♏

Your Personalized Timetable

JUPITER BENEFICIAL	
1939 2/15 – 4/24	1943 8/17 – 11/23
1942 7/26 – until 1943 6/13	1944 1/3 – 7/7
1944 9/26 – 11/20	1950 1/17 – 3/28
1945 3/7 – 7/19	1952 6/13 – until 1953 4/23
1949 1/13 – 3/1	1955 8/1 – 10/19
1949 8/24 – 10/13	1956 2/17 – 6/15
1951 1/28 – 4/5	1961 12/31 – until 1962 3/9
1954 7/9 – 9/29	1964 5/26 – until 1965 4/5
1955 1/4 – 5/24	1967 7/16 – 9/29
1956 9/10 – 10/29	1968 4/3 – 5/10
1957 4/17 – 6/20	1973 4/27 – 7/3
1960 12/28 – until 1961 2/10	1973 12/12 – until 1974 2/21
1962 5/24 – 8/10	1976 5/9 – 7/25
1963 1/8 – 3/20	1976 11/16 – until 1977 3/14
1966 6/23 – 9/6	1979 6/28 – 9/11
1967 2/14 – 4/26	1985 3/28 – 8/17
1968 8/26 – 10/11	1985 11/17 – until 1986 2/5
1972 12/12 – until 1973 1/24	1988 4/23 – 7/2
1974 4/25 – 9/25	1989 1/8 – 2/1
1974 12/11 – until 1975 3/3	1990 10/15 – until 1991 1/15
1978 6/6 – 8/18	1991 6/9 – 8/26
1980 8/9 – 9/25	1997 3/8 – until 1998 1/19
1984 11/25 – until 1985 1/9	2000 4/6 – 6/13
1986 4/6 – until 1987 2/15	2002 9/21 – until 2003 2/24
1989 10/11 – 11/15	2003 5/13 – 8/10
1990 5/19 – 8/1	2009 2/18 – 5/26
1991 12/2 – until 1992 1/28	2009 7/5 – until 2010 1/1
1992 7/22 – 9/9	2012 3/18 – 5/27
1996 3/11 – 6/29	
1996 11/4 – 12/24	SATURN CHALLENGING
1998 3/19 – 6/15	1940 6/13 – 11/15
1998 8/19 – until 1999 1/26	1941 3/3 – 7/22
2001 9/3 – until 2002 1/3	1941 11/1 – until 1942 4/8
2002 4/27 – 7/16	1947 7/20 – until 1948 8/21
2003 11/2 – until 2004 3/8	1962 4/16 – 6/27
2004 7/1 – 8/25	1963 1/4 – until 1964 2/21
2008 2/18 – 8/16	1970 4/19 – until 1971 5/20
2008 10/1 – 12/6	1976 8/28 – until 1977 3/20
2010 3/3 – 5/14	1977 5/2 – 10/1
2010 10/7 – 12/30	1978 2/25 – 6/21
	1992 2/8 – until 1993 3/29
SATURN BENEFICIAL	1993 8/27 – 12/25
1944 10/2 – 11/13	1999 5/26 – until 2000 1/3
1945 6/5 – until 1946 7/5	2000 1/20 – 6/28
1949 10/3 – until 1950 4/15	2000 12/3 – until 2001 3/16
1950 6/14 – 9/21	2005 10/21 – 12/24
1960 2/4 – 8/1	2006 7/2 – until 2007 8/4
1960 10/29 – until 1961 2/2	
1961 9/15 – 10/10	URANUS CHALLENGING
1965 3/21 – until 1966 5/7	1938 2/26 – until 1942 2/8
1966 9/18 – until 1967 1/30	1957 9/23 – until 1961 8/22
1974 7/16 – until 1975 8/15	1998 2/27 – until 2003 1/3
1976 3/8 – 4/15	
1978 11/30 – until 1979 1/18	NEPTUNE CHALLENGING
1979 8/9 – 11/1	2002 3/26 – until 2010 12/17
1980 3/17 – 7/24	
1989 3/27 – 5/19	PLUTO CHALLENGING
1989 12/12 – until 1990 3/16	1945 8/19 – until 1956 6/10
1990 6/26 – 12/11	
1994 5/3 – 8/14	JUPITER SPECIAL
1995 1/25 – until 1996 3/8	1946 11/12 – until 1947 2/14
2003 8/29 – 12/24	1947 4/11 – 10/5
2004 5/16 – 10/6	1958 10/28 – until 1959 1/14
2004 12/11 – until 2005 6/17	1959 5/24 – 9/13
2008 9/15 – until 2009 9/4	1970 10/12 – 12/25
	1982 9/24 – 12/8
URANUS BENEFICIAL	1994 1/5 – 4/25
1951 7/13 – until 1955 6/24	1994 9/4 – 11/22
1964 10/23 – until 1967 8/25	2005 12/15 – until 2006 6/5
1991 3/17 – until 1994 11/19	2006 8/6 – 11/7
2005 5/14 – until 2010 3/13	
	SATURN SPECIAL
NEPTUNE BENEFICIAL	1954 10/21 – until 1955 12/8
1938 1/1 – until 1940 7/23	1956 7/15 – 8/15
1990 2/7 – until 1995 11/20	1983 11/26 – until 1984 6/14
	1984 8/10 – until 1985 1/20
PLUTO BENEFICIAL	1985 4/24 – 10/16
1963 10/20 – 1969 8/3	
	URANUS SPECIAL
JUPITER CHALLENGING	1976 12/20 – until 1981 8/31
1938 2/2 – 4/18	
1938 8/28 – 12/8	NEPTUNE SPECIAL
1940 7/6 – 11/4	1960 12/14 – until 1969 9/16
1941 2/23 – 5/11	
	PLUTO SPECIAL
	1987 11/14 – until 1994 10/8

November 12

Your Personal Powers

Mentally sharp but subtle and sensitive, you possess deep and powerful emotions yet are good at assessing the motives of others. Highly intuitive, you gain power from your originality and strong sense of vision. When combined with your natural business acumen and strategic talents, you have the ability to put your inspired ideas into a concrete structure. With a gift for people and an easygoing manner, you can turn on the charm and be verbally persuasive. Although you enjoy a mental challenge or a little friendly rivalry, be careful not to lose energy to manipulative power games. Imaginative and intuitive, you have a strong need for inspiration and emotional expression. You can successfully channel this need through creative enterprises if you are willing to put in the necessary discipline. Usually friendly and peace loving, you need a secure or harmonious environment. With your acute sensitivity, however, avoid losing power to escapism through fantasy or indulgence. With your drive, keen mental awareness, and innate talents, you have an outstanding potential for success.

Your Powers of Attraction in Relationships

With your fine mind and sociable manner, you can work well with others and attract friends and partners. In relationships, although your strong emotions can make you passionate, you can be equally tender and caring. Being sensitive and idealistic, you can also be romantic with your partner; equality in close relationships plays an integral part in your happiness. You need a smart partner who can match your intelligence. You are also drawn to sincere, candid, and straightforward individuals. In close relationships, you may encounter some tension between your own need for self-expression and your innate disposition to be supportive of others. It is beneficial to find someone who is like-minded and with whom you can communicate or share the same level of understanding.

Your attractive qualities: mentally sharp, sensitive, creative, highly intuitive, imaginative, business sense, tactful, friendly, initiative, idealistic, drive, persuasive, wise, people skills, confident, optimistic, innovative, talent with words, independent, visionary, understanding

Your less attractive qualities: stubborn, too sensitive, materialistic, evasive, lack of self-esteem or arrogance, opinionated, obsessive, escapist, worry, indecision, manipulative

Your Venus Power

The planet Venus has a great deal of influence on your powers of attraction. Below are four possible Venus types for women and men. To find your Venus you need to go to page 771, where you will find the Venus table and extra information. The planet Mars also affects your powers of attraction. To find your Mars table and interpretation go to page 761.

WOMEN WITH VENUS IN LIBRA: A natural romantic with good social skills, you love to entertain or put people at ease by projecting a warm and gracious manner. Elegant and fair with a touch of glamour, you are also adept at dealing with people in delicate situations or conflicts. You seek refinement and will go out of your way to achieve harmony and keep the peace. For you, relationships are so important that you may need to guard against becoming dependent on others for approval. With your friendly personality and inherent charm, however, you will always be popular and loved.

MEN WITH VENUS IN LIBRA: You are such good company, people are naturally drawn to you and especially appreciate your talent for making them feel special. You find status in your social contacts and place importance on your relationships. Being clever and a charming companion, you will go out of your way to keep situations peaceful and harmonious. In relationships, however, be careful of indecision or compromising too much. Nevertheless, others are attracted by your natural refinement and good taste, which is reflected in your sense of style.

WOMEN WITH VENUS IN SCORPIO: With a natural psychic gift for penetrating the feelings of others, you can often help partners transform emotional challenges or sexual difficulties. When you fall in love, your strong feelings and determination give you a potent force that others find attractive and seductive. Although you know what really turns people on, your most profound desire is usually for the deepness and closeness of real love and intimacy in an enduring relationship.

MEN WITH VENUS IN SCORPIO: In relationships you possess a sensitive understanding of your partner's deeper nature. Although you are strongly attached to those you love, you may have to be careful that your feelings do not turn into jealousy or possessiveness. When you fall in love it is often with an emotional intensity that helps you get in touch with your deep feelings. You are attracted to partners who can share your passion and display strong feelings of sexuality like your own.

WOMEN WITH VENUS IN SAGITTARIUS: At your best

when being optimistic and generous, you possess a mischievous sense of fun. In relationships your open-minded approach to people and places may attract you to those of a different culture or make you tolerant of the foibles of others. Warm and enthusiastic when in love, your natural honesty and idealism may inspire you to look for a partner who shares your love of freedom.

MEN WITH VENUS IN SAGITTARIUS: Forward-thinking rather than dwelling on the past, you are looking for a partner who can share your future plans. You enjoy exploring life whether through travel and mental pursuits or sports and games. Idealistic, you usually prefer the company of a partner who is optimistic and shares your beliefs. In your desire for honesty in relationships, however, be careful not to become tactless. Nevertheless, you are attracted to honest, direct, and fun-loving partners who have a sense of humor like your own.

WOMEN WITH VENUS IN CAPRICORN: Loyal and responsible, you are attracted to dignified and reserved individuals. Being practical and security-conscious, you prefer hardworking partners who are resourceful and enterprising. Work may even be a factor in many of your associations and partnerships. For you, family and faithfulness can be especially important, so you are usually willing to work hard or make sacrifices in order to build a strong relationship.

MEN WITH VENUS IN CAPRICORN: In relationships you take love seriously and can be a strong and practical support for friends or partners. You are usually attracted to partners who are as hardworking as yourself. As you tend not to express your feelings until you feel really secure in a relationship, you may be drawn to those who seem loyal, faithful, and not likely to let you down. As you respect the wisdom of experience, you may be drawn to mature partners or, alternatively, you may act as an authority figure for someone younger.

To read all about your Outer Planets and work out how to use your personalized timetable, go to Section Three, page 789.

To read all about your Outer Planets and work out how to use your personalized timetable, go to Section Three, page 789.

Your Personalized Timetable

JUPITER BENEFICIAL
1939 2/19 – 4/28
1942 7/31 – until 1943 6/18
1944 10/1 – 11/27
1945 2/27 – 7/26
1949 1/18 – 3/6
1949 8/13 – 10/24
1951 2/1 – 4/10
1954 7/14 – 10/7
1954 12/27 – until 1955 5/29
1956 9/15 – 11/3
1957 4/7 – 6/30
1961 1/2 – 2/15
1962 6/3 – 7/31
1963 1/13 – 3/24
1966 6/28 – 9/11
1967 2/5 – 5/4
1968 8/30 – 10/16
1972 12/17 – until 1973 1/29
1974 5/1 – 9/17
1974 12/19 – until 1975 3/7
1978 6/11 – 8/23
1980 8/14 – 9/30
1984 11/30 – until 1985 1/13
1986 4/11 – until 1987 2/19
1990 5/24 – 8/6
1991 12/18 – until 1992 1/12
1992 7/28 – 9/14
1996 3/18 – 6/21
1996 11/10 – 12/28
1998 3/24 – 6/27
1998 8/7 – until 1999 1/31
2001 9/10 – 12/26
2002 5/3 – 7/20
2003 11/9 – until 2004 3/1
2004 7/7 – 8/29
2008 2/23 – 8/4
2008 10/12 – 12/11
2010 3/7 – 5/20
2010 9/29 – until 2011 1/6

SATURN BENEFICIAL
1945 6/13 – until 1946 7/13
1949 10/11 – until 1950 3/29
1950 6/30 – 9/29
1960 2/13 – 7/17
1960 11/12 – until 1961 2/11
1961 8/20 – 11/4
1965 3/30 – 10/12
1965 12/15 – until 1966 5/18
1966 9/5 – until 1967 2/9
1974 7/24 – until 1975 8/23
1976 2/17 – 5/5
1979 8/18 – 11/12
1980 3/4 – 8/4
1989 12/21 – until 1990 3/31
1990 6/9 – 12/20
1994 5/18 – 7/29
1995 2/3 – until 1996 3/17
2003 9/10 – 12/11
2004 5/25 – until 2005 6/25
2008 9/23 – until 2009 9/12

URANUS BENEFICIAL
1951 7/31 – until 1955 7/11
1964 11/18 – until 1967 9/11
1992 1/12 – until 1994 12/11
2006 3/12 – until 2011 1/15

NEPTUNE BENEFICIAL
1938 1/1 – until 1940 8/25
1990 3/20 – until 1995 12/23

PLUTO BENEFICIAL
1964 9/17 – until 1969 9/2

JUPITER CHALLENGING
1938 2/7 – 4/25
1938 8/20 – 12/14
1940 7/13 – 10/28
1941 3/1 – 5/15
1943 8/21 – until 1944 7/12

1950 1/22 – 4/1
1952 6/18 – 12/21
1953 1/20 – 4/28
1955 8/5 – 10/26
1956 2/9 – 6/22
1962 1/5 – 3/14
1964 5/30 – until 1965 4/10
1967 7/20 – 10/4
1968 3/21 – 5/24
1973 5/9 – 6/21
1973 12/17 – until 1974 2/25
1976 5/13 – 7/31
1976 11/9 – until 1977 3/20
1979 7/3 – 9/16
1985 4/3 – 8/9
1985 11/24 – until 1986 2/9
1988 4/27 – 7/7
1988 12/23 – until 1989 2/16
1990 10/23 – until 1991 1/6
1991 6/15 – 8/31
1997 3/13 – until 1998 1/24
2000 4/10 – 6/18
2002 9/26 – until 2003 2/15
2003 5/21 – 8/15
2009 2/23 – until 2010 1/5
2012 3/23 – 5/31

SATURN CHALLENGING
1940 6/23 – 11/3
1941 3/14 – 8/5
1941 10/17 – until 1942 4/17
1947 7/28 – until 1948 8/28
1962 5/16 – 5/26
1963 1/13 – until 1964 3/1
1970 4/27 – until 1971 5/28
1976 9/6 – until 1977 3/1
1977 5/21 – 10/11
1978 2/13 – 7/2
1992 2/16 – until 1993 4/9
1993 8/14 – until 1994 1/4
1999 6/3 – 12/8
2000 2/15 – 7/8
2000 11/21 – until 2001 3/27
2006 7/10 – until 2007 8/12

URANUS CHALLENGING
1938 3/23 – until 1942 3/24
1957 10/22 – until 1962 6/20
1998 3/19 – until 2003 1/23

NEPTUNE CHALLENGING
2003 2/18 – until 2011 1/21

PLUTO CHALLENGING
1945 9/29 – until 1956 7/23

JUPITER SPECIAL
1946 11/17 – until 1947 3/3
1947 3/25 – 10/11
1958 11/1 – until 1959 1/21
1959 5/16 – 9/20
1970 10/16 – 12/30
1971 7/2 – 8/16
1982 9/30 – 12/13
1994 1/12 – 4/17
1994 9/10 – 11/27
2005 12/20 – until 2006 5/26
2006 8/16 – 11/12

SATURN SPECIAL
1954 10/30 – until 1955 12/17
1956 6/21 – 9/7
1983 12/5 – until 1984 5/27
1984 8/28 – until 1985 2/5
1985 4/6 – 10/25

URANUS SPECIAL
1977 1/15 – until 1981 9/29

NEPTUNE SPECIAL
1961 11/12 – until 1969 10/22

PLUTO SPECIAL
1987 12/11 – until 1994 11/5

♏

491

November 13

SUN: SCORPIO • DECANATE: CANCER/MOON • DEGREE: 20°5–21°5 SCORPIO • MODE: FIXED • ELEMENT: WATER

Your Personal Powers

Your astute awareness and determined nature indicate that you are a sincere individual with strong instincts and responses. A good organizer, you like to take the lead or to be in charge. You possess strong emotions and a mind that likes to investigate the motivations of others or delve into the heart of the matter. Although you can be open and charming, you can also be secretive and stubborn. You gain power from the combination of your resolve, creative approach, and inspired ideas. You can pick up very quickly on what is happening around you, yet this sensitivity also implies that you can experience worry, anxiety, or inner tensions. When positive, you can utilize this receptivity to be more daring and give yourself a competitive edge in your activities. If you lose faith and become skeptical, however, you forfeit your natural spontaneity and tenacious spirit by being controlling or headstrong. Original and motivated, you empower yourself by being productive, and your natural talent for making money can aid your remarkable potential.

Your Powers of Attraction in Relationships

An independent thinker, you can attract others with your charm and unique approach. Since at times you can be very sociable and fun-loving and at other times you need time for reflection or self-analysis, you need a partner who understands the extremes of your nature. If you become secretive, cynical, or doubting in your close relationships, you may also feel insecure or withdraw. You are attracted to hardworking and successful people or those with a strong sense of self-identity. By expressing your feelings sincerely you can release repressed emotions. Although you can be romantic and charming, keeping a balance between being passive or strong-willed can enhance your relationships. Capable of being loyal and passionate, you are at your best when you are spontaneous, generous, and trusting.

Your attractive qualities: thoughtful, astute, ambitious, determined, highly intuitive, creative, fun-loving, mentally sharp, hardworking, independent, freedom-loving, original, sincere, humanitarian, dependable, enduring, self-expressive, initiative, enthusiasm, inspired

Your less attractive qualities: impulsive, skeptical, self-doubt, too intense, indecisive, bossy, insecure, cold, self-absorbed, withdrawn, manipulative, too material, unemotional, cynical, rebellious

Your Venus Power

The planet Venus has a great deal of influence on your powers of attraction. Below are four possible Venus types for women and men. To find your Venus you need to go to page 771, where you will find the Venus table and extra information. The planet Mars also affects your powers of attraction. To find your Mars table and interpretation go to page 761.

WOMEN WITH VENUS IN LIBRA: A natural romantic with good social skills, you love to entertain or put people at ease by projecting a warm and gracious manner. Elegant and fair with a touch of glamour, you are also adept at dealing with people in delicate situations or conflicts. You seek refinement and will go out of your way to achieve harmony and keep the peace. For you, relationships are so important that you may need to guard against becoming dependent on others for approval. With your friendly personality and inherent charm, however, you will always be popular and loved.

MEN WITH VENUS IN LIBRA: Courteous and refined, you are attracted to beautiful and elegant people. You are looking for a partner who can share your natural good taste and enjoy an intellectual conversation. Disliking conflict, you may have to be careful not to go along with others just to keep the peace. Your ideal partner will appreciate beauty and the little luxuries of life as well as possess good social skills. You have a strong sense of social etiquette yourself so you need an intelligent and sophisticated partner.

WOMEN WITH VENUS IN SCORPIO: With a natural psychic gift for penetrating the feelings of others, you can often help partners transform emotional challenges or sexual difficulties. When you fall in love, your strong feelings and determination give you a potent force that others find attractive and seductive. Although you know what really turns people on, your most profound desire is usually for the deepness and closeness of real love and intimacy in an enduring relationship.

MEN WITH VENUS IN SCORPIO: In relationships you possess a sensitive understanding of your partner's deeper nature. Although you are strongly attached to those you love, you may have to be careful that your feelings do not turn into jealousy or possessiveness. When you fall in love it is often with an emotional intensity that helps you get in touch with your deep

feelings. You are attracted to partners who can share your passion and display strong feelings of sexuality like your own.

WOMEN WITH VENUS IN SAGITTARIUS: Optimistic and fun-loving, you love adventure and seek a partner who can expand your horizons. Being truthful and direct, you often say what you think. At times you may be naively tactless. A need for expansion and prosperity suggests that you may enjoy traveling with your friends or partner. Being both lighthearted and idealistic, however, indicates that once you have given your heart to someone you will stay honorable and loyal.

MEN WITH VENUS IN SAGITTARIUS: Usually you are attracted to partners who are knowledgeable or well-traveled. Enthusiastic and optimistic, you often respond quickly to love offers and enter relationships with enthusiasm. Usually you seek to expand your social circle and meeting people from all walks of life can bring you the variety and fun to you seek in life. Although you are generous and honest, your partners may accuse you of being overly optimistic or too blunt.

WOMEN WITH VENUS IN CAPRICORN: Romantically, you do not give your heart easily but hide behind a cool reserve until you feel free to express your emotions. As you take your relationships seriously, you may find yourself drawn to people who are businesslike, resourceful, and practical, or those who can act as teachers or mentors. Work or career may also be a factor in many of your associations and partnerships. As security can play an important role in your relationships, you are often attracted to partners who are loyal and hardworking.

MEN WITH VENUS IN CAPRICORN: As you do not display your deeper emotions freely, you are usually dignified and controlled in your relationships with others. Practical and down-to-earth partners are particularly attractive to you, especially those who do not rush into expressing their feelings but seem to possess natural class and reserve. You need a partner who is loyal and dependable and willing to take your relationship seriously.

To read all about your Outer Planets and work out how to use your personalized timetable, go to Section Three, page 789.

Your Personalized Timetable

JUPITER BENEFICIAL
1939 2/23 – 5/3
1942 8/4 – until **1943** 6/23
1944 10/6 – 12/5
1945 2/18 – 7/31
1949 1/22 – 3/12
1949 8/4 – 11/2
1951 2/6 – 4/14
1954 7/18 – 10/16
1954 12/18 – until **1955** 6/4
1956 9/19 – 11/9
1957 3/29 – 7/8
1961 1/6 – 2/19
1962 6/18 – 7/16
1963 1/18 – 3/28
1966 7/2 – 9/17
1967 1/28 – 5/12
1968 9/4 – 10/21
1972 12/21 – until **1973** 2/2
1974 5/7 – 9/9
1974 12/26 – until **1975** 3/12
1978 6/16 – 8/28
1980 8/19 – 10/4
1984 12/4 – until **1985** 1/17
1986 4/15 – until **1987** 2/23
1990 5/29 – 8/10
1992 8/2 – 9/19
1996 3/26 – 6/12
1996 11/15 – until **1997** 1/1
1998 3/28 – until **1999** 2/5
2001 9/17 – 12/19
2002 5/9 – 7/25
2003 11/16 – until **2004** 2/22
2004 7/14 – 9/3
2008 2/28 – 7/26
2008 10/21 – 12/16
2010 3/11 – 5/26
2010 9/21 – until **2011** 1/13

SATURN BENEFICIAL
1945 6/21 – until **1946** 7/21
1949 10/21 – until **1950** 3/15
1950 7/13 – 10/8
1960 2/24 – 7/3
1960 11/23 – until **1961** 2/20
1961 8/4 – 11/18
1965 4/8 – 9/26
1965 12/31 – until **1966** 6/1
1966 8/21 – until **1967** 2/18
1974 8/1 – until **1975** 2/20
1975 4/4 – 9/1
1976 2/3 – 5/19
1979 8/26 – 11/24
1980 2/20 – 8/13
1989 12/30 – until **1990** 12/29
1994 6/18 – 6/28
1995 2/12 – until **1996** 3/25
2003 9/25 – 11/25
2004 6/3 – until **2005** 7/3
2008 10/2 – until **2009** 4/23
2009 6/9 – 9/20

URANUS BENEFICIAL
1951 8/19 – until **1956** 4/24
1965 9/10 – until **1968** 6/28
1992 1/29 – until **1994** 12/30
2006 3/31 – until **2011** 2/9

NEPTUNE BENEFICIAL
1938 1/1 – until **1941** 7/18
1991 2/4 – until **1996** 11/13

PLUTO BENEFICIAL
1938 2/18 – until **1938** 6/1
1964 10/18 – until **1970** 7/27

JUPITER CHALLENGING
1938 2/11 – 5/1
1938 8/12 – 12/20
1940 7/20 – 10/20
1941 3/7 – 5/19
1943 8/26 – until **1944** 7/18

1950 1/26 – 4/6
1950 10/2 – 11/14
1952 6/23 – 12/7
1953 2/3 – 5/2
1955 8/10 – 11/2
1956 2/1 – 6/28
1962 1/9 – 3/18
1964 6/4 – until **1965** 4/15
1967 7/25 – 10/10
1968 3/11 – 6/2
1973 12/22 – until **1974** 3/1
1976 5/17 – 8/8
1976 11/1 – until **1977** 3/26
1979 7/8 – 9/21
1985 4/9 – 8/1
1985 12/1 – until **1986** 2/13
1988 5/1 – 7/12
1988 12/13 – until **1989** 2/26
1990 11/2 – 12/27
1991 6/20 – 9/4
1997 3/18 – 9/25
1997 10/21 – until **1998** 1/28
2000 4/14 – 6/22
2002 10/2 – until **2003** 2/7
2003 5/29 – 8/19
2009 2/27 – until **2010** 1/10
2012 3/27 – 6/4

SATURN CHALLENGING
1940 7/4 – 10/21
1941 3/23 – 8/28
1941 9/24 – until **1942** 4/25
1947 8/5 – until **1948** 9/5
1963 1/22 – until **1964** 3/9
1964 10/26 – 11/6
1970 5/4 – until **1971** 6/5
1976 9/15 – until **1977** 2/15
1977 6/3 – 10/23
1978 1/31 – 7/12
1992 2/25 – 9/20
1992 11/10 – until **1993** 4/21
1993 7/31 – until **1994** 1/14
1999 6/12 – 11/23
2000 2/29 – 7/18
2000 11/8 – until **2001** 4/6
2006 7/19 – until **2007** 8/20

URANUS CHALLENGING
1938 4/11 – until **1942** 4/15
1958 8/11 – until **1962** 7/12
1998 4/17 – until **2003** 2/10

NEPTUNE CHALLENGING
2003 3/21 – until **2011** 12/8

PLUTO CHALLENGING
1946 9/7 – until **1957** 6/22

JUPITER SPECIAL
1946 11/21 – until **1947** 10/16
1958 11/6 – until **1959** 1/28
1959 5/8 – 9/26
1970 10/21 – until **1971** 1/5
1971 6/20 – 8/28
1982 10/5 – 12/18
1994 1/20 – 4/8
1994 9/16 – 12/2
2005 12/26 – until **2006** 5/17
2006 8/24 – 11/16

SATURN SPECIAL
1954 11/7 – until **1955** 12/27
1956 6/5 – 9/22
1983 12/15 – until **1984** 5/12
1984 9/10 – until **1985** 11/3

URANUS SPECIAL
1977 11/8 – until **1981** 10/20

NEPTUNE SPECIAL
1961 12/11 – until **1970** 9/9

PLUTO SPECIAL
1988 1/19 – until **1995** 9/22

♍

November 14

Your Personal Powers

Your many personal powers include dignity, determination, a friendly but levelheaded manner, and keen intelligence. With your deep and powerful emotions, you also possess inner strength and tenacity. You are persuasive and purposeful, and your social skills often help you to make important contacts that further your success. Persistent, when set on a course of action you can be focused and resolute. Although you can be quietly forceful, resist losing some of your power by becoming stubborn or bossy. You gain power by combining your ambition, natural business sense, and good strategic skills. These enable you to achieve outstanding results, particularly if you make the necessary effort in your work. You usually prefer to be honest and direct with others but may at times suffer from avoidance or escapism when dealing with difficulties. Practical yet dramatic, you empower yourself when you use your clear vision and original ideas. A love of knowledge means you improve your chances when you establish a solid philosophy upon which you can build.

Your Powers of Attraction in Relationships

Clever and talented, you can use your talents and sociability to win friends and admirers. Although you possess innate leadership skills, you understand the advantages of teamwork or partnership. You are attracted to clever and entertaining partners who can stimulate your own ability to be witty and amusing. You also need a partner who is strong enough to match you if you become impatient or temperamental. Although you are progressive and charming, your intense emotions imply that your love life is likely to be dramatic. On one hand you seek security and a strong home base, but another side of your personality seeks freedom and adventure. Although you enjoy power, be careful to keep a balance between your needs, your work, and the needs of your partner.

Your attractive qualities: clever, common sense, idealistic, original, determined, hardworking, assertive, creative, pragmatic, popular, visionary, open-minded, ambitious, imaginative, considerate, endurance, responsible, sensitive, homeloving, sociable

Your less attractive qualities: stubborn, restless, rebellious, indiscreet, overly cautious or impulsive, overindulgent, inertia, bossy, too serious, anxious, unsettled, too outspoken, skeptical, avoidance

Your Venus Power

The planet Venus has a great deal of influence on your powers of attraction. Below are four possible Venus types for women and men. To find your Venus you need to go to page 771, where you will find the Venus table and extra information. The planet Mars also affects your powers of attraction. To find your Mars table and interpretation go to page 761.

WOMEN WITH VENUS IN LIBRA: Attractive, refined, and conscious of the needs of others, you usually desire harmonious relationships. As a peacemaker with good negotiating skills, you can smooth out difficulties with others but your dislike of confrontation may sometimes leave you refusing to take a stand or compromising too many of your own needs. Courteous, stylish, and charming with polished social skills, you are an expert at relating to others in a gracious and civilized manner.

MEN WITH VENUS IN LIBRA: Your good social skills, charming personality, and refined manner usually make you attractive to the opposite sex. Equally, you desire a sophisticated partner with grace, elegance, and a strong sense of style. Although you have the ability to be persuasive and irresistible to others, avoid manipulative love games. Nevertheless, your natural diplomacy and sense of fair play help you to relate to people in all social situations. With your love of balance and harmony you seek a partner who is also moderate, easygoing, and loving.

WOMEN WITH VENUS IN SCORPIO: You are usually drawn to partners who are sensual in appearance with a strong character. As you are emotionally intense and passionate, personal relationships are probably a major factor in your life. Since you like to be in control you can at times exhibit some of your less attractive qualities by being willful or domineering. Although you need to feel established and in command in your relationships, you are constantly searching for some higher truth that can bring about a significant transformation.

MEN WITH VENUS IN SCORPIO: As you are emotionally intense and passionate, personal relationships are probably a major factor in your own transformation. Being sensitive yet loyal, you are usually attracted to forceful partners who can

express themselves intimately but intensely. Rather than seek easy and simple relationships you are drawn to partners who act as a catalyst for your own internal changes. Through your relationships with your partners you can unravel your own motives and understand your deep-seated feelings or emotional insecurities.

WOMEN WITH VENUS IN SAGITTARIUS: At your best when being optimistic and generous, you possess a mischievous sense of fun. In relationships your open-minded approach to people and places may attract you to those of a different culture or make you tolerant of the foibles of others. Although warm and enthusiastic when in love, your natural honesty and idealism may inspire you to look for a partner who shares your love of freedom.

MEN WITH VENUS IN SAGITTARIUS: Forward-thinking rather than dwelling on the past, you are looking for a partner who can share your future plans. You enjoy exploring life whether through travel and mental pursuits or sports and games. Idealistic, you usually prefer the company of a partner who is optimistic and shares your beliefs. In your desire for honesty in relationships, however, be careful not to become tactless. Nevertheless, you are attracted to honest, direct, and fun-loving partners who have a sense of humor like your own.

WOMEN WITH VENUS IN CAPRICORN: With your natural caution in romantic affairs, you often appear reserved and controlled. You may be shy, but try to be more forward, especially if you want to be noticed by others. When you care about people, however, you are usually willing to put in extra time and energy to preserve the relationship. You are practical and dependable, and a sense of duty can often play a large role in the affairs of your heart. With elegant simplicity, you can attract others through your well-cut clothes and refined manners.

MEN WITH VENUS IN CAPRICORN: In relationships you take love seriously and can be a strong and practical support for friends or partners. You are usually attracted to partners who are as hardworking as yourself. As you tend not to express your feelings until you feel really secure in a relationship, you may be drawn to those who seem loyal, faithful, and not likely to let you down. As you respect the wisdom of experience, you may be drawn to mature partners or, alternatively, you may act as an authority figure for someone younger.

To read all about your Outer Planets and work out how to use your personalized timetable, go to Section Three, page 789.

To read all about your Outer Planets and work out how to use your personalized timetable, go to Section Three, page 789.

♏

Your Personalized Timetable

JUPITER BENEFICIAL
1939 2/27 – 5/8
1939 11/7 – 12/12
1942 8/9 – until 1943 6/28
1944 10/11 – 12/16
1945 2/7 – 8/6
1949 1/27 – 3/18
1949 7/27 – 11/9
1951 2/10 – 4/18
1954 7/23 – 10/29
1954 12/5 – until 1955 6/9
1956 9/24 – 11/15
1957 3/21 – 7/15
1961 1/10 – 2/24
1963 1/23 – 4/1
1966 7/6 – 9/23
1967 1/20 – 5/19
1968 9/9 – 10/26
1969 5/10 – 6/5
1972 12/25 – until 1973 2/6
1974 5/13 – 9/2
1975 1/1 – 3/16
1978 6/20 – 9/2
1979 3/11 – 4/10
1980 8/24 – 10/9
1984 12/9 – until 1985 1/22
1986 4/20 – 10/24
1986 11/23 – until 1987 2/28
1990 6/3 – 8/15
1992 8/7 – 9/23
1996 4/6 – 6/2
1996 11/21 – until 1997 1/6
1998 4/1 – until 1999 2/10
2001 9/25 – 12/10
2002 5/15 – 7/29
2003 11/24 – until 2004 2/13
2004 7/20 – 9/8
2008 3/5 – 7/17
2008 10/28 – 12/20
2010 3/15 – 6/1
2010 9/14 – until 2011 1/19

SATURN BENEFICIAL
1945 6/29 – until 1946 7/28
1949 10/31 – until 1950 3/3
1950 7/23 – 10/16
1951 4/27 – 6/29
1960 3/7 – 6/19
1960 12/3 – until 1961 3/2
1961 7/21 – 11/30
1965 4/18 – 9/12
1966 1/12 – 6/22
1966 7/30 – until 1967 2/26
1974 8/9 – until 1975 2/2
1975 4/23 – 9/10
1976 1/22 – 5/30
1979 9/3 – 12/11
1980 2/2 – 8/22
1990 1/7 – until 1991 1/7
1995 2/20 – until 1996 4/2
2004 6/11 – until 2005 7/11
2008 10/10 – until 2009 4/4
2009 6/28 – 9/28

URANUS BENEFICIAL
1951 9/13 – until 1956 5/27
1965 9/26 – until 1968 7/27
1992 2/18 – until 1995 1/16
2006 4/21 – until 2011 2/28

NEPTUNE BENEFICIAL
1938 1/1 – until 1941 8/22
1991 3/12 – until 1996 12/19

PLUTO BENEFICIAL
1938 1/2 – until 1939 5/10
1965 9/16 – until 1970 8/28

JUPITER CHALLENGING
1938 2/15 – 5/9
1938 8/4 – 12/26
1940 7/28 – 10/12
1941 3/12 – 5/23

1943 8/31 – until 1944 7/23
1950 1/30 – 4/12
1950 9/20 – 11/26
1952 6/29 – 11/28
1953 2/12 – 5/7
1955 8/14 – 11/11
1956 1/24 – 7/4
1962 1/13 – 3/23
1964 6/8 – until 1965 4/19
1967 7/30 – 10/15
1968 3/3 – 6/11
1973 12/27 – until 1974 3/5
1976 5/22 – 8/17
1976 10/23 – until 1977 3/31
1979 7/13 – 9/26
1985 4/16 – 7/24
1985 12/7 – until 1986 2/18
1988 5/5 – 7/18
1988 12/5 – until 1989 3/6
1990 11/19 – 12/11
1991 6/25 – 9/9
1997 3/23 – 9/9
1997 11/5 – until 1998 2/1
2000 4/19 – 6/27
2002 10/8 – until 2003 1/31
2003 6/4 – 8/24
2009 3/4 – until 2010 1/15
2012 4/1 – 6/9

SATURN CHALLENGING
1940 7/17 – 10/7
1941 4/1 – until 1942 5/3
1947 8/13 – until 1948 9/14
1949 4/23 – 5/10
1963 1/30 – until 1964 3/18
1964 9/27 – 12/6
1970 5/12 – until 1971 6/13
1976 9/24 – until 1977 2/3
1977 6/14 – 11/5
1978 1/16 – 7/21
1992 3/5 – 9/1
1992 11/28 – until 1993 5/7
1993 7/14 – until 1994 1/23
1999 6/22 – 11/10
2000 3/11 – 7/31
2000 10/25 – until 2001 4/15
2006 7/27 – until 2007 8/28

URANUS CHALLENGING
1938 4/29 – until 1942 5/4
1958 8/27 – until 1962 7/30
1999 2/12 – until 2003 12/12

NEPTUNE CHALLENGING
2004 2/16 – until 2012 1/17

PLUTO CHALLENGING
1947 8/19 – until 1957 7/30

JUPITER SPECIAL
1946 11/26 – until 1947 10/21
1958 11/10 – until 1959 2/5
1959 4/30 – 10/2
1970 10/26 – until 1971 1/10
1971 6/10 – 9/6
1982 10/9 – 12/23
1994 1/30 – 3/29
1994 9/22 – 12/6
2006 1/1 – 5/9
2006 8/31 – 11/21

SATURN SPECIAL
1954 11/15 – until 1956 1/6
1956 5/22 – 10/4
1983 12/25 – until 1984 4/29
1984 9/21 – until 1985 11/11

URANUS SPECIAL
1977 11/25 – until 1981 11/6

NEPTUNE SPECIAL
1962 1/25 – until 1970 10/19

PLUTO SPECIAL
1988 11/26 – until 1995 10/25

495

November 15

SUN: SCORPIO · DECANATE: CANCER/MOON · DEGREE: 22°5–23°5 SCORPIO · MODE: FIXED · ELEMENT: WATER

Your Personal Powers

Mentally sharp with strong instincts and an adventurous spirit, you are a determined individual with deep feelings. Intense and forceful, you usually do not do things by half measures. You gain power from your charismatic personality and ability to mix with different people. As you comprehend matters very quickly, you need activities that can keep you interested; otherwise you tend to lose some of your power to restlessness or escapism. Although you have an innate ability to assess people and situations instinctively, if you are bored you may become provocative or impatient. Very sensitive and perceptive, however, you make major gains from trusting your powerful intuition when making decisions. Preferring to combine practice with theory, you have a gift for attracting money and often earn as you are learning new skills. Versatile with a need for variety, you may also be drawn to activities that involve travel. Being ambitious, with a need for recognition, your enthusiasm often inspires others and you are quick to recognize opportunities or turning situations to your advantage.

Your Powers of Attraction in Relationships

With your ability to be witty and entertaining, you can be popular. Having a penetrating mind and good psychological skills, you are akin to a detective. You therefore need partners who can match your sharp intelligence. With your powerful emotions and strong character you have the ability to come straight to the heart of a matter, yet you may mask your own inner sensitivity to protect your vulnerability. Although you can be secretive, you usually enjoy a mental challenge and like to test your wits against others. Sympathetic and understanding, you can be a devoted spouse or parent. Do not allow restlessness or overindulgence to mar your relationships. You are attracted to strong-willed and insightful individuals who can see through the smoke screen you create around your emotions and motivations.

Your attractive qualities: intelligent, quick responses, willing, generous, determined, popular, responsible, kind, strong-willed, versatile, highly intuitive, endurance, assertive, good morals, cooperative, problem solver, deep insight, psychic, creative ideas, ambitious

Your less attractive qualities: disruptive, stubborn, rebel-lious, irresponsible, self-centered, loss of faith, indecisive, lack of honor, escapist, overindulgent, impulsive, materialistic, ruthless streak, restless

Your Venus Power

The planet Venus has a great deal of influence on your powers of attraction. Below are four possible Venus types for women and men. To find your Venus you need to go to page 771, where you will find the Venus table and extra information. The planet Mars also affects your powers of attraction. To find your Mars table and interpretation go to page 761.

WOMEN WITH VENUS IN LIBRA: Usually you are attractive and sociable with an easygoing manner. Your love of beauty, harmony, and pleasure implies that you are a romantic with a desire for love and affection. Once in a relationship you need to learn to negotiate your position rather than adapt to the wishes of others and compromise just to keep the peace. Nevertheless, your advanced social skills and strong sense of fair play can help you succeed in any social or romantic situation.

MEN WITH VENUS IN LIBRA: You are such good company, people are naturally drawn to you and especially appreciate your talent for making them feel special. You find status in your social contacts and place importance on your relationships. Being clever and a charming companion, you will go out of your way to keep situations peaceful and harmonious. In relationships, however, be careful of indecision or compromising too much. Nevertheless, others are attracted by your natural refinement and good taste, which is reflected in your sense of style.

WOMEN WITH VENUS IN SCORPIO: Loving and passionate, you are often sensitive with deep feelings and strong powers of attraction. A love for the truth coupled with a tendency to be suspicious can be an influence that motivates you to delve deep into the activities of your partner. When in love or in a relationship that matters you will often bend over backward to cooperate. Although loyal, guard against losing sight of your own needs and desires.

MEN WITH VENUS IN SCORPIO: Usually you are attracted to sensual and passionate partners with strong character. You are often intense with deep feelings and magnetic powers of attraction. As a cautious yet devoted and ardent lover you are likely to seek experiences that are more sexual in their nature.

You display your less attractive qualities when you project your negative thoughts and resort to being suspicious or possessive. Nevertheless, loyal and loving, you are a sensitive lover.

WOMEN WITH VENUS IN SAGITTARIUS: Optimistic and fun-loving, you love adventure and seek a partner who can expand your horizons. Being truthful and direct, you often say what you think. At times you may be naively tactless. A need for expansion and prosperity suggests that you may enjoy traveling with your friends or partner. Being both lighthearted and idealistic, however, indicates that once you have given your heart to someone you will stay honorable and loyal.

MEN WITH VENUS IN SAGITTARIUS: You are usually attracted to partners who are knowledgeable or well-traveled. Enthusiastic and optimistic, you often respond quickly to love offers and enter relationships with enthusiasm. Usually you seek to expand your social circle and meeting people from all walks of life can bring you the variety and fun you seek in life. Although you are generous and honest, your partners may accuse you of being overly optimistic or too blunt.

WOMEN WITH VENUS IN CAPRICORN: Loyal and responsible, you are attracted to dignified and reserved individuals. Being practical and security-conscious, you prefer hardworking partners who are resourceful and enterprising. Work may even be a factor in many of your associations and partnerships. For you, family and faithfulness can be especially important, so you are usually willing to work hard or make sacrifices in order to build up a strong relationship.

MEN WITH VENUS IN CAPRICORN: As you admire loyal, hardworking, and dedicated individuals, you probably want a partner who can share your vocational interests or who can provide you with the security you need. You could even find yourself with a partner who is of a different age group or maturity. Guard against denying your true emotional needs or focusing on your career at the expense of your relationship. You are drawn to reserved partners who display self-control.

To read all about your Outer Planets and work out how to use your personalized timetable, go to Section Three, page 789.

Your Personalized Timetable

JUPITER BENEFICIAL
1939 3/3 – 5/13
1939 10/25 – 12/24
1942 8/14 – until **1943** 7/2
1944 10/16 – until **1945** 1/4
1945 1/19 – 8/11
1949 1/31 – 3/24
1949 7/19 – 11/15
1951 2/15 – 4/23
1954 7/27 – until **1955** 6/15
1956 9/29 – 11/22
1957 3/13 – 7/22
1961 1/15 – 3/1
1961 9/17 – 9/29
1963 1/28 – 4/5
1966 7/11 – 9/30
1967 1/13 – 5/25
1968 9/13 – 11/1
1969 4/24 – 6/21
1972 12/30 – until **1973** 2/11
1974 5/20 – 8/25
1975 1/7 – 3/20
1978 6/25 – 9/7
1979 2/24 – 4/25
1980 8/28 – 10/14
1984 12/14 – until **1985** 1/26
1986 4/25 – 10/10
1986 12/7 – until **1987** 3/4
1990 6/8 – 8/20
1992 8/12 – 9/28
1996 4/21 – 5/17
1996 11/26 – until **1997** 1/10
1998 4/6 – until **1999** 2/14
2001 10/5 – 11/30
2002 5/20 – 8/3
2003 12/3 – until **2004** 2/4
2004 7/25 – 9/13
2008 3/11 – 7/10
2008 11/4 – 12/25
2010 3/19 – 6/9
2010 9/6 – until **2011** 1/24

SATURN BENEFICIAL
1938 1/1 – 1/19
1945 7/6 – until **1946** 8/5
1949 11/11 – until **1950** 2/17
1950 8/2 – 10/25
1951 4/10 – 7/15
1960 3/22 – 6/3
1960 12/12 – until **1961** 3/14
1961 7/7 – 12/10
1965 4/29 – 8/30
1966 1/22 – until **1967** 3/7
1974 8/18 – until **1975** 1/19
1975 5/6 – 9/21
1976 1/9 – 6/8
1979 9/11 – until **1980** 8/31
1990 1/16 – until **1991** 1/15
1995 3/1 – until **1996** 4/10
2004 6/19 – until **2005** 7/19
2008 10/19 – until **2009** 3/21
2009 7/11 – 10/7

URANUS BENEFICIAL
1952 7/9 – until **1956** 6/17
1965 10/13 – until **1968** 8/16
1992 3/14 – until **1995** 11/21
2006 5/21 – until **2011** 3/18

NEPTUNE BENEFICIAL
1938 1/1 – until **1942** 7/11
1992 2/1 – until **1997** 11/5

PLUTO BENEFICIAL
1938 1/1 – until **1939** 6/30
1965 10/17 – until **1971** 7/16

JUPITER CHALLENGING
1938 2/20 – 5/18
1938 7/26 – 12/31
1940 8/7 – 10/2
1941 3/18 – 5/28
1943 9/5 – until **1944** 7/27

1950 2/3 – 4/17
1950 9/11 – 12/4
1952 7/4 – 11/19
1953 2/20 – 5/11
1955 8/19 – 11/21
1956 1/13 – 7/9
1962 1/18 – 3/27
1964 6/13 – until **1965** 4/24
1967 8/3 – 10/21
1968 2/24 – 6/18
1973 12/31 – until **1974** 3/10
1976 5/26 – 8/28
1976 10/11 – until **1977** 4/5
1979 7/18 – 10/1
1980 4/17 – 5/6
1985 4/24 – 7/16
1985 12/12 – until **1986** 2/22
1988 5/10 – 7/24
1988 11/28 – until **1989** 3/13
1991 7/1 – 9/14
1997 3/28 – 8/30
1997 11/15 – until **1998** 2/6
2000 4/23 – 7/2
2002 10/15 – until **2003** 1/23
2003 6/11 – 8/29
2009 3/8 – until **2010** 1/19
2012 4/5 – 6/13

SATURN CHALLENGING
1940 8/6 – 9/17
1941 4/10 – until **1942** 5/11
1947 8/21 – until **1948** 9/22
1949 3/26 – 6/5
1963 2/8 – until **1964** 3/27
1964 9/11 – 12/21
1970 5/20 – until **1971** 6/21
1972 1/1 – 2/29
1976 10/5 – until **1977** 1/21
1977 6/24 – 11/28
1977 12/24 – until **1978** 7/29
1992 3/15 – 8/17
1992 12/11 – until **1994** 2/1
1999 7/2 – 10/29
2000 3/21 – 8/17
2000 10/8 – until **2001** 4/24
2006 8/3 – until **2007** 9/5

URANUS CHALLENGING
1938 5/17 – until **1942** 5/21
1958 9/15 – until **1962** 8/16
1999 3/2 – until **2004** 1/8

NEPTUNE CHALLENGING
2004 3/16 – until **2012** 11/21

PLUTO CHALLENGING
1947 9/27 – until **1958** 7/1

JUPITER SPECIAL
1946 12/1 – until **1947** 10/26
1958 11/15 – until **1959** 2/14
1959 4/20 – 10/7
1970 10/30 – until **1971** 1/16
1971 6/1 – 9/14
1982 10/14 – 12/28
1994 2/15 – 3/13
1994 9/27 – 12/11
2006 1/8 – 5/1
2006 9/7 – 11/25

SATURN SPECIAL
1954 11/24 – until **1956** 1/17
1956 5/8 – 10/14
1984 1/6 – 4/15
1984 10/1 – until **1985** 11/20

URANUS SPECIAL
1977 12/12 – until **1981** 11/22

NEPTUNE SPECIAL
1962 12/8 – until **1971** 8/30

PLUTO SPECIAL
1988 12/26 – until **1996** 8/24

♏

497

November 16

SUN: SCORPIO • DECANATE: CANCER/MOON • DEGREE: 23°5–24°5 SCORPIO • MODE: FIXED • ELEMENT: WATER

Your Personal Powers

Practical and shrewd, you are an independent individual with good planning or organizational skills. Your ruling planet, Pluto, provides you with the ability to sense the emotions of others and project your inner strength. Although on the surface you appear determined, dramatic, and confident, inside you can be sensitive or inclined to worry. Being very self-reliant, however, you like the freedom to work in your own way. Imaginative with psychic abilities, you gain power from the combination of your common sense, idealism, and deeply felt emotions. With your unique and unusual approach to life, you enjoy learning and realize the importance of knowledge. You may possess excellent technical know-how or scientific skills. Alternatively, inspired by knowledge, you are interested in investigating spiritual or metaphysical subjects. Although you are usually active with a dynamic zest for life, you also gain power from leading a well-balanced life and staying relaxed or calm. Nevertheless, it is your adventurous spirit and creative ideas that usually stimulate you into action and enable you to manifest material success.

Your Powers of Attraction in Relationships

Thoughtful yet direct, you attract others by being sympathetic and friendly. You are often aware of the advantages of working cooperatively and may become involved in working partnerships. Sexual and magnetic, you are attracted to creative and sharp people but should avoid nonconformist individuals with dubious morals. Loving harmony, your home and family can be an especially important area of your life. You may, however, experience a pull between your own need for self-expression and your responsibilities to others. Extremely sensitive, you may have to work at learning to communicate your deeper feelings to your partner. Although you are independent and happy working alone, you may encounter times when you feel isolated. When you are enthusiastic and spontaneous, you are witty, entertaining, and fun to be with.

Your attractive qualities: direct, practical, responsible, intelligent, integrity, intuitive, sociable, caring, sincere, creative ideas, rational, cooperative, insightful, clever, determined, endurance, power to overcome, sensitive, confident, independent, dynamic, imaginative, strong sixth sense

Your less attractive qualities: impatient, intolerant, anxious, dissatisfied, irresponsible, self-absorbed, opinionated, aloof, skeptical, cynical, emotional extremes, critical, irritable, overconfident or insecure, unsympathetic

Your Venus Power

The planet Venus has a great deal of influence on your powers of attraction. Below are four possible Venus types for women and men. To find your Venus you need to go to page 771, where you will find the Venus table and extra information. The planet Mars also affects your powers of attraction. To find your Mars table and interpretation go to page 761.

WOMEN WITH VENUS IN LIBRA: A natural romantic with good social skills, you love to entertain and can put people at ease by projecting a warm and gracious manner. Elegant and fair with a touch of glamour, you are also adept at dealing with people in delicate situations or conflicts. You seek refinement and will go out of your way to achieve harmony and keep the peace. For you, relationships are so important that you may need to guard against becoming dependent on others for approval. With your friendly personality and inherent charm, however, you will always be popular and loved.

MEN WITH VENUS IN LIBRA: As a sociable and friendly individual with an eye for beauty, you are amorous and charming. You are a natural gentleman and your ideal partner usually has an elegant appearance, artistic appreciation, and good taste. Your relationships benefit when you resist the temptation to take the easy way out or put too much emphasis on vanity and high living. Intellectual and naturally refined, you seek a loving partner who can share your romantic and sophisticated aspirations.

WOMEN WITH VENUS IN SCORPIO: Usually you are drawn to partners who are sensual in appearance with a strong character. As you are emotionally intense and passionate, personal relationships are probably a major factor in your life. Since you like to be in control, you can at times exhibit some of your less attractive qualities by being willful or domineering. Although you need to feel established and in command in your relationships, you are constantly searching for some higher truth that can bring about a significant transformation.

MEN WITH VENUS IN SCORPIO: As you are emotionally intense and passionate, personal relationships are probably a major factor in your own transformation. Being sensitive yet loyal, you are usually attracted to forceful partners who can

express themselves intimately but intensely. Rather than seek easy and simple relationships you are drawn to partners who act as a catalyst for your own internal changes. Through your relationships with your partners you can unravel your own motives and understand your deep-seated feelings or emotional insecurities.

WOMEN WITH VENUS IN SAGITTARIUS: Optimistic and fun-loving, you love adventure and seek a partner who can expand your horizons. Being truthful and direct, you often say what you think. At times you may be naively tactless. A need for expansion and prosperity suggests that you may enjoy traveling with your friends or partner. Being both lighthearted and idealistic, however, means that once you have given your heart to someone you will stay honorable and loyal.

MEN WITH VENUS IN SAGITTARIUS: When in love you are open and friendly with a need for a partner who can share your adventurous spirit and sense of fun. Be careful, however, that your desire for freedom does not cause you to avoid commitment. You prefer your partners to be positive, direct, and generous in spirit. Being outspoken as well as an idealist, you usually enjoy a partner with whom you can share your strong opinions. Alternatively, you may wish to explore life together, whether through travel, education, or having fun.

WOMEN WITH VENUS IN CAPRICORN: With your natural caution in romantic affairs, you often appear reserved and controlled. You may be shy, but try to be more forward, especially if you want to be noticed. When you care about people, however, you are usually willing to put in extra time and energy to preserve the relationship. You are practical and dependable, and a sense of duty can often play a large role in the affairs of your heart. With elegant simplicity, you can attract others with your well-cut clothes and refined manners.

MEN WITH VENUS IN CAPRICORN: As you do not display your deeper emotions freely, you are usually dignified and controlled in your relationships with others. Practical and down-to-earth partners are particularly attractive to you, especially those who do not rush into expressing their feelings but seem to possess natural class and reserve. You need a partner who is loyal and dependable and willing to take your relationship seriously.

To read all about your Outer Planets and work out how to use your personalized timetable, go to Section Three, page 789.

go to Section Three, page 789.

♏

Your Personalized Timetable

JUPITER BENEFICIAL
1939 3/8 – 5/19
1939 10/16 – until 1940 1/3
1942 8/19 – until 1943 2/28
1943 3/23 – 7/7
1944 10/21 – until 1945 4/20
1945 6/7 – 8/17
1949 2/5 – 3/31
1949 7/11 – 11/21
1951 2/19 – 4/27
1954 8/1 – until 1955 6/20
1956 10/4 – 11/29
1957 3/5 – 7/28
1961 1/19 – 3/6
1961 8/28 – 10/19
1963 2/1 – 4/10
1966 7/15 – 10/7
1967 1/5 – 5/31
1968 9/18 – 11/6
1969 4/13 – 7/2
1973 1/3 – 2/16
1974 5/28 – 8/16
1975 1/12 – 3/24
1978 6/29 – 9/12
1979 2/14 – 5/4
1980 9/2 – 10/19
1984 12/18 – until 1985 1/30
1986 5/1 – 9/30
1986 12/16 – until 1987 3/8
1990 6/13 – 8/25
1992 8/17 – 10/3
1996 12/1 – until 1997 1/14
1998 4/11 – until 1999 2/19
2001 10/20 – 11/15
2002 5/26 – 8/8
2003 12/17 – until 2004 1/21
2004 7/31 – 9/17
2008 3/18 – 7/2
2008 11/10 – 12/29
2010 3/24 – 6/17
2010 8/28 – until 2011 1/30

SATURN BENEFICIAL
1938 1/1 – 1/31
1945 7/14 – until 1946 8/13
1949 11/26 – until 1950 2/2
1950 8/11 – 11/3
1951 3/28 – 7/28
1960 4/22 – 5/3
1960 12/21 – until 1961 3/27
1961 6/22 – 12/20
1965 5/11 – 8/16
1966 2/1 – until 1967 3/15
1974 8/28 – until 1975 1/6
1975 5/17 – 10/4
1975 12/27 – until 1976 6/18
1979 9/19 – until 1980 9/8
1990 1/24 – until 1991 1/24
1995 3/9 – until 1996 4/19
1996 11/3 – until 1997 1/2
2004 6/27 – until 2005 7/27
2008 10/29 – until 2009 3/8
2009 7/22 – 10/15
2010 5/4 – 6/25

URANUS BENEFICIAL
1952 7/26 – until 1956 7/5
1965 11/2 – until 1968 9/3
1993 1/13 – until 1995 12/14
2007 3/18 – until 2012 1/21

NEPTUNE BENEFICIAL
1938 1/1 – until 1942 8/20
1992 3/6 – until 1997 12/16

PLUTO BENEFICIAL
1938 1/1 – until 1940 6/14
1965 12/5 – until 1971 8/22

JUPITER CHALLENGING
1938 2/24 – 5/29
1938 7/14 – until 1939 1/5
1940 8/22 – 9/17

1941 3/23 – 6/1
1943 9/9 – until 1944 8/1
1950 2/7 – 4/23
1950 9/3 – 12/12
1952 7/10 – 11/12
1953 2/27 – 5/15
1955 8/23 – 12/10
1955 12/25 – until 1956 7/15
1962 1/22 – 4/1
1964 6/18 – until 1965 4/28
1967 8/8 – 10/28
1968 2/16 – 6/25
1974 1/5 – 3/14
1976 5/30 – until 1977 4/10
1979 7/23 – 10/6
1980 3/30 – 5/24
1985 5/4 – 7/6
1985 12/18 – until 1986 2/26
1988 5/14 – 7/30
1988 11/20 – until 1989 3/20
1991 7/6 – 9/18
1997 4/3 – 8/22
1997 11/23 – until 1998 2/10
2000 4/27 – 7/7
2001 1/14 – 2/5
2002 10/23 – until 2003 1/15
2003 6/17 – 9/2
2009 3/13 – until 2010 1/24
2012 4/10 – 6/17

SATURN CHALLENGING
1941 4/18 – until 1942 5/19
1947 8/29 – until 1948 10/1
1949 3/11 – 6/20
1963 2/16 – until 1964 4/6
1964 8/28 – until 1965 1/2
1970 5/28 – until 1971 6/30
1971 12/16 – until 1972 3/16
1976 10/18 – until 1977 1/7
1977 7/3 – until 1978 8/7
1992 3/26 – 8/3
1992 12/22 – until 1994 2/9
1999 7/15 – 10/15
2000 3/31 – until 2001 5/2
2006 8/11 – until 2007 9/13

URANUS CHALLENGING
1938 6/4 – until 1943 3/23
1958 10/6 – until 1963 6/1
1999 3/23 – until 2004 1/28

NEPTUNE CHALLENGING
2005 2/12 – until 2012 9/6

PLUTO CHALLENGING
1948 9/4 – until 1958 8/6

JUPITER SPECIAL
1946 12/6 – until 1947 10/30
1958 11/20 – until 1959 2/27
1959 4/7 – 10/13
1970 11/4 – until 1971 1/23
1971 5/24 – 9/21
1982 10/19 – until 1983 1/2
1983 7/15 – 8/12
1994 10/2 – 12/15
2006 1/15 – 4/23
2006 9/13 – 11/30

SATURN SPECIAL
1954 12/3 – until 1955 6/15
1955 8/21 – until 1956 1/30
1956 4/23 – 10/24
1984 1/21 – 3/30
1984 10/10 – until 1985 11/28

URANUS SPECIAL
1978 1/3 – until 1982 9/22

NEPTUNE SPECIAL
1963 1/16 – until 1971 10/17

PLUTO SPECIAL
1989 11/14 – until 1996 10/12

499

November 17

SUN: SCORPIO • DECANATE: CANCER/MOON • DEGREE: 24°5–25°5 SCORPIO • MODE: FIXED • ELEMENT: WATER

Your Personal Powers

Your strong individuality, original ideas, and sharp observation indicate that you are an astute individual with keen perception. Your personal powers also include good analytical abilities and a magnetic personal charm. Your ruler, Pluto, provides you with a more introspective nature than you care to admit. Your desire to uncover people's hidden motives makes you a good student of human nature. You gain power by combining your enthusiasm, social skills, and ability to commercialize your talents. Although usually witty and entertaining, you can at times lose power to self-doubt, worry, or indecision. By developing your faith and trusting your innate intuition, you become more confident in your capabilities. Whatever you do, you are likely to take a creative approach and use your communication skills. Success is almost guaranteed in all people-related activities as long as you stay liberal and optimistic. Being inventive, proud, and dramatic, you also possess original ideas and a need for self-expression. Being a good strategist, when decisive, you can be very focused and determined on achieving your goals.

Your Powers of Attraction in Relationships

Friendly, ambitious, and talented, you can always attract friends and admirers. Blessed with good people skills, you understand your partners and their motives. Confident and clever, you can turn on the charm when it is to your advantage. Possessing strong feelings, you need partners who can be both affectionate and loving yet strong and powerful enough to stand up to you. You may, however, sometimes encounter conflicts between your ambition and your relationships. Nevertheless, being proud and creative with a sense of the dramatic, you can be a good lover and project a magnetic presence. If you get angry with your partner there is a danger you may withdraw or become cold, critical, or stubborn. Usually, however, you attract others by being loving and dependable.

Your attractive qualities: creative ideas, ambitious, clever, social skills, talent with words, shrewd, specialist, strategist, natural business sense, individualist, good psychologist, assertive, charming, sensitive, skilled researcher, original, scientific, independent, determined

Your less attractive qualities: indecisive, too detached, withdrawn, stubborn, careless, worry, moody, scattered, too proud, overly sensitive, cynical, narrow-minded, secretive, critical, secretive, outspoken, suspicious

Your Venus Power

The planet Venus has a great deal of influence on your powers of attraction. Below are four possible Venus types for women and men. To find your Venus you need to go to page 771, where you will find the Venus table and extra information. The planet Mars also affects your powers of attraction. To find your Mars table and interpretation go to page 761.

WOMEN WITH VENUS IN LIBRA: Gracious, charming, and sociable with a sense of style, you have no trouble attracting admirers. With your natural diplomatic skills and desire for harmony you usually like to keep the peace and avoid confrontations, but be careful of failing to take a stand when it is necessary. Romantic and easygoing yourself, you are attracted to affectionate and refined individuals who share your love of peace, justice, and fair play.

MEN WITH VENUS IN LIBRA: You are such good company, people are naturally drawn to you and especially appreciate your talent for making them feel special. You find status in your social contacts and place importance on your relationships. Being clever and such a charming companion, you will go out of your way to keep situations peaceful and harmonious. In relationships, however, be careful of indecision or compromising too much. Nevertheless, others are attracted by your natural refinement and good taste, which is reflected in your sense of style.

WOMEN WITH VENUS IN SCORPIO: Loving and passionate, you are often sensitive with deep feelings and strong powers of attraction. A love for the truth coupled with a tendency to be suspicious can be an influence that motivates you to delve deep into the activities of your partner. When in love or in a relationship that matters, you will often bend over backward to cooperate. Although loyal, guard against losing sight of your own needs and desires.

MEN WITH VENUS IN SCORPIO: You are usually attracted to sensual and passionate partners with strong character. You are often intense with deep feelings and magnetic powers of attraction. As a cautious yet devoted and ardent lover, you are likely to seek experiences that are more sexual in their nature.

You display your less attractive qualities when you project your negative thoughts and resort to being suspicious or possessive. Nevertheless, loyal and loving, you are a sensitive lover.

WOMEN WITH VENUS IN SAGITTARIUS: Optimistic and fun-loving, you love adventure and seek a partner who can expand your horizons. Being truthful and direct, you often say what you think. At times you may be naively tactless. A need for expansion and prosperity suggests that you may enjoy traveling with your friends or partner. Being both lighthearted and idealistic, however, means that once you have given your heart to someone you will stay honorable and loyal.

MEN WITH VENUS IN SAGITTARIUS: You are usually attracted to partners who are knowledgeable or well-traveled. Enthusiastic and optimistic, you often respond quickly to love offers and enter relationships with enthusiasm. Usually you seek to expand your social circle and meeting people from all walks of life can bring you the variety and fun you seek in life. Although you are generous and honest, your partners may accuse you of being overly optimistic or too blunt.

WOMEN WITH VENUS IN CAPRICORN: With your natural caution in romantic affairs, you often appear reserved and controlled. You may be shy, but try to be more forward, especially if you want to be noticed. When you care about people, however, you are usually willing to put in extra time and energy to preserve the relationship. You are practical and dependable, and a sense of duty can often play a large role in the affairs of your heart. With elegant simplicity, you can attract others with your well-cut clothes and refined manners.

MEN WITH VENUS IN CAPRICORN: As you admire loyal, hardworking, and dedicated individuals, you probably want a partner who can share your vocational interests or provide you with the sense of security you need. You could even find yourself with a partner of a different age group or maturity. Guard against denying your true emotional needs or focusing on your career at the expense of your relationship. You are drawn to reserved partners who display self-control.

To read all about your Outer Planets and work out how to use your personalized timetable, go to Section Three, page 789.

℔

JUPITER BENEFICIAL
1939 3/12 – 5/24
1939 10/8 – until 1940 1/10
1942 8/24 – until 1943 2/12
1943 4/9 – 7/12
1944 10/27 – until 1945 4/9
1945 6/19 – 8/22
1949 2/9 – 4/7
1949 7/3 – 11/27
1951 2/23 – 5/2
1954 8/5 – until 1955 6/25
1956 10/9 – 12/7
1957 2/25 – 8/3
1961 1/23 – 3/12
1961 8/17 – 10/29
1963 2/6 – 4/14
1966 7/20 – 10/16
1966 12/27 – until 1967 6/6
1968 9/23 – 11/12
1969 4/4 – 7/10
1973 1/7 – 2/20
1974 6/7 – 8/7
1975 1/17 – 3/28
1978 7/4 – 9/18
1979 2/6 – 5/13
1980 9/7 – 10/24
1984 12/23 – until 1985 2/4
1986 5/6 – 9/22
1986 12/24 – until 1987 3/12
1990 6/17 – 8/29
1992 8/22 – 10/7
1996 12/6 – until 1997 1/19
1998 4/15 – until 1999 2/23
2002 5/31 – 8/12
2004 8/5 – 9/22
2008 3/26 – 6/23
2008 11/16 – until 2009 1/3
2010 3/28 – 6/28
2010 8/17 – until 2011 2/4

SATURN BENEFICIAL
1938 1/1 – 2/10
1945 7/22 – until 1946 8/21
1947 3/12 – 4/26
1949 12/24 – until 1950 1/4
1950 8/20 – 11/14
1951 3/15 – 8/7
1960 12/30 – until 1961 4/16
1961 6/2 – 12/29
1965 5/27 – 7/30
1966 2/10 – until 1967 3/23
1974 9/8 – 12/25
1975 5/26 – 10/21
1975 12/9 – until 1976 6/26
1979 9/27 – until 1980 9/16
1990 2/2 – 8/24
1990 10/22 – until 1991 2/1
1995 3/17 – until 1996 4/28
1996 10/17 – until 1997 1/17
2004 7/5 – until 2005 8/4
2008 11/9 – until 2009 2/23
2009 8/1 – 10/24
2010 4/16 – 7/13

URANUS BENEFICIAL
1952 8/13 – until 1956 7/22
1965 12/3 – until 1968 9/19
1993 1/30 – until 1996 1/1
2007 4/5 – Continues

NEPTUNE BENEFICIAL
1938 1/1 – until 1943 7/2
1993 1/29 – until 1998 10/19

PLUTO BENEFICIAL
1938 1/1 – until 1941 5/27
1966 10/14 – until 1972 6/27

JUPITER CHALLENGING
1938 2/28 – until 1939 1/10
1941 3/28 – 6/5
1943 9/14 – until 1944 8/6

1950 2/12 – 4/29
1950 8/26 – 12/18
1952 7/16 – 11/4
1953 3/5 – 5/19
1955 8/28 – until 1956 7/20
1962 1/26 – 4/6
1964 6/23 – 12/28
1965 1/23 – 5/3
1967 8/12 – 11/4
1968 2/8 – 7/1
1974 1/9 – 3/18
1976 6/4 – until 1977 4/15
1979 7/27 – 10/12
1980 3/19 – 6/4
1985 5/17 – 6/23
1985 12/23 – until 1986 3/2
1988 5/18 – 8/6
1988 11/13 – until 1989 3/26
1991 7/11 – 9/23
1997 4/9 – 8/14
1997 11/30 – until 1998 2/14
2000 5/2 – 7/12
2000 12/29 – until 2001 2/21
2002 11/1 – until 2003 1/6
2003 6/22 – 9/7
2009 3/18 – until 2010 1/28
2012 4/14 – 6/22

SATURN CHALLENGING
1941 4/26 – until 1942 5/27
1947 9/6 – until 1948 3/21
1948 5/14 – 10/10
1949 2/26 – 7/2
1963 2/25 – until 1964 4/18
1964 8/14 – until 1965 1/12
1970 6/6 – 12/20
1971 2/13 – 7/10
1971 12/3 – until 1972 3/28
1976 11/5 – 12/20
1977 7/12 – until 1978 8/15
1992 4/7 – 7/21
1993 1/1 – until 1994 2/18
1999 7/31 – 9/29
2000 4/8 – until 2001 5/10
2006 8/19 – until 2007 9/22
2008 4/4 – 5/31

URANUS CHALLENGING
1938 6/25 – until 1943 4/16
1959 8/5 – until 1963 7/2
1999 4/21 – until 2004 2/15

NEPTUNE CHALLENGING
2005 3/12 – Continues

PLUTO CHALLENGING
1948 10/22 – until 1959 7/8

JUPITER SPECIAL
1946 12/11 – until 1947 11/4
1958 11/24 – until 1959 10/18
1970 11/9 – until 1971 1/29
1971 5/16 – 9/27
1982 10/24 – until 1983 1/7
1983 6/29 – 8/28
1994 10/7 – 12/20
2006 1/23 – 4/14
2006 9/19 – 12/5

SATURN SPECIAL
1954 12/12 – until 1955 5/29
1955 9/6 – until 1956 2/19
1956 4/3 – 11/2
1984 10/19 – until 1985 12/7

URANUS SPECIAL
1978 2/20 – until 1982 10/15

NEPTUNE SPECIAL
1963 12/6 – until 1971 11/15

PLUTO SPECIAL
1989 12/10 – until 1996 11/9

November 18

Your Personal Powers

Strong-willed and mentally sharp, you have an assertive and determined personality as well as deep and powerful emotions. With your strong convictions, you gain power from your daring, courageous, and pragmatic approach to life. The extremes of your personality, however, imply that you may lose power if you alternate between being friendly and obliging and being moody or impatient. Through working on self-awareness, you are able to stay well-balanced and use your humor, insight, and vision to achieve great success for yourself, as well as help others. Proud, dramatic, and sociable, you enjoy taking center stage. With your fast mind and responses, you often hide your emotional sensitivity. Usually resolute and hardworking, once set on a course of action, you have strong endurance and an ability to lead others. If you push people too far, however, you may lose power to being provocative or domineering. Possessing immense inner power, you can rise to a challenge and rarely admit defeat.

Your Powers of Attraction in Relationships

Clever, independent, and quick-witted, you can turn on the charm to influence and attract others. Dramatic and sociable, you enjoy entertaining and can be a witty and amusing companion. Be careful, when you become negative, that you do not let your moods and stubbornness spoil your relationships. At times you may show your less attractive qualities of being self-centered and inflexible, but this is more than compensated for by your generosity and broad-minded attitude. Although your feelings are usually openly expressed, hidden emotional insecuritites may lead to power struggles, especially if you unconsciously want to get even. Fortunately you realize the importance of working cooperatively and use your diplomatic skills instead. You are attracted to individuals with a strong sense of identity.

Your attractive qualities: strong-willed, daring, quick intelligence, good psychologist, proud, capable, insightful, assertive, multitalented, natural business sense, determined, ambitious, intuitive, courageous, resolute, entertaining, charming, generous, humorous, efficient

Your less attractive qualities: provocative, stubborn, uncontrolled emotions, selfish, opinionated, dark moods, calous, failure to complete projects, unruly, arrogant, irritable, sarcastic, secretive, impatient, temperamental

Your Venus Power

The planet Venus has a great deal of influence on your powers of attraction. Below are four possible Venus types for women and men. To find your Venus you need to go to page 771, where you will find the Venus table and extra information. The planet Mars also affects your powers of attraction. To find your Mars table and interpretation go to page 761.

WOMEN WITH VENUS IN LIBRA: Attractive, refined, and conscious of the needs of others, you usually desire harmonious relationships. As a peacemaker with good negotiating skills, you can smooth out difficulties with others, but your dislike of confrontation may sometimes leave you refusing to take a stand or compromising too many of your own needs. Courteous, stylish, and charming with polished social skills, you are an expert at relating to others in a gracious and civilized manner.

MEN WITH VENUS IN LIBRA: Courteous and refined, you are attracted to beautiful and elegant people. You are looking for a partner who can share your natural good taste and enjoy an intellectual conversation. Disliking conflict, you may have to be careful not to go along with others just to keep the peace. Your ideal partner will appreciate beauty and the little luxuries of life as well as possess good social skills. You have a strong sense of social etiquette yourself so you need an intelligent and sophisticated partner.

WOMEN WITH VENUS IN SCORPIO: With a natural psychic gift for penetrating the feelings of others, you can often help partners transform emotional challenges or sexual difficulties. When you fall in love your strong feelings of determination give you a potent force that others find attractive and seductive. Although you know what really turns people on, your most profound desire is usually for the deepness and closeness of real love and intimacy in an enduring relationship.

MEN WITH VENUS IN SCORPIO: In relationships you possess a sensitive understanding of your partner's deeper nature. Although you are strongly attached to those you love, you may have to be careful that your feelings do not turn into jealousy or possessiveness. When you fall in love it is often with an emotional intensity that helps you get in touch with your deep

feelings. You are attracted to partners who can share your passion and display strong feelings of sexuality like your own.

WOMEN WITH VENUS IN SAGITTARIUS: Sociable, warm, and friendly, you possess an honest and frank style in your relationships. Being naturally gregarious, you want others to share your enthusiasm and you enjoy encouraging the people you love. You fare better when you have a sense of personal freedom within a relationship and are usually generous with the faults of others. You need a partner who can share your need to explore and take risks, whether through travel, education, or recreation.

MEN WITH VENUS IN SAGITTARIUS: Your enthusiasm and straightforward conduct usually appeal to others and imply that you are approachable and easygoing. Being open to ideas and willing to believe that life has a great deal to offer suggests that you are generous, broad-minded, and eager to cooperate with others. A love of travel and an interest in other cultures imply that your partner may come from a foreign country.

WOMEN WITH VENUS IN CAPRICORN: With your natural caution in romantic affairs, you often appear reserved and controlled. You may be shy, but try to be more forward, especially if you want to be noticed. When you care about people, however, you are usually willing to put in extra time and energy to preserve the relationship. You are practical and dependable, and a sense of duty can often play a large role in the affairs of your heart. With elegant simplicity, you can attract others with your well-cut clothes and refined manners.

MEN WITH VENUS IN CAPRICORN: In relationships you take love seriously and can be a strong and practical support for friends or partners. You are usually attracted to partners who are as hardworking as yourself. As you tend not to express your feelings until you feel really secure in a relationship, you may be drawn to those who seem loyal, faithful, and not likely to let you down. As you respect the wisdom of experience, you may be drawn to mature partners or, alternatively, you may act as an authority figure for someone younger.

To read all about your Outer Planets and work out how to use your personalized timetable, go to Section Three, page 789.

go to Section Three, page 789.

Your Personalized Timetable

JUPITER BENEFICIAL
1939 3/16 – 5/30
1939 9/30 – until 1940 1/17
1942 8/30 – until 1943 2/2
1943 4/19 – 7/16
1944 11/1 – until 1945 3/30
1945 6/28 – 8/27
1949 2/14 – 4/16
1949 6/23 – 12/3
1951 2/27 – 5/7
1954 8/10 – until 1955 6/29
1956 10/14 – 12/17
1957 2/15 – 8/9
1961 1/28 – 3/17
1961 8/8 – 11/7
1963 2/10 – 4/18
1966 7/24 – 10/26
1966 12/16 – until 1967 6/11
1968 9/27 – 11/18
1969 3/27 – 7/18
1973 1/12 – 2/25
1974 6/21 – 7/24
1975 1/22 – 4/1
1978 7/8 – 9/24
1979 1/29 – 5/20
1980 9/11 – 10/29
1984 12/27 – until 1985 2/8
1986 5/12 – 9/14
1986 12/31 – until 1987 3/17
1990 6/22 – 9/3
1992 8/26 – 10/12
1996 12/10 – until 1997 1/23
1998 4/20 – until 1999 2/28
2002 6/5 – 8/17
2004 8/10 – 9/27
2008 4/3 – 6/14
2008 11/21 – until 2009 1/7
2010 4/1 – until 2011 2/9

SATURN BENEFICIAL
1938 1/1 – 2/19
1945 7/30 – until 1946 8/30
1947 2/21 – 5/14
1950 8/28 – 11/25
1951 3/1 – 8/17
1961 1/8 – until 1962 1/7
1966 2/18 – until 1967 3/31
1974 9/20 – 12/11
1975 6/4 – until 1976 7/4
1979 10/6 – until 1980 5/6
1980 6/7 – 9/24
1990 2/11 – 8/6
1990 11/8 – until 1991 2/10
1991 9/19 – 10/21
1995 3/25 – until 1996 5/7
1996 10/3 – until 1997 1/29
2004 7/13 – until 2005 8/12
2008 11/22 – until 2009 2/9
2009 8/10 – 11/2
2010 4/2 – 7/26

URANUS BENEFICIAL
1952 9/3 – until 1957 5/15
1966 9/19 – until 1969 7/12
1993 2/18 – until 1996 1/19
2007 4/27 – until 2012 3/5

NEPTUNE BENEFICIAL
1938 1/1 – until 1943 8/17
1993 3/1 – until 1998 12/12

PLUTO BENEFICIAL
1938 1/1 – until 1941 7/9
1966 11/24 – until 1972 8/13

JUPITER CHALLENGING
1938 3/5 – until 1939 1/15
1941 4/1 – 6/10
1943 9/20 – until 1944 3/28
1944 4/28 – 8/11
1950 2/16 – 5/6

1950 8/19 – 12/24
1952 7/23 – 10/28
1953 3/11 – 5/24
1955 9/2 – until 1956 7/25
1962 1/31 – 4/11
1962 10/10 – 11/16
1964 6/28 – 12/13
1965 2/7 – 5/7
1967 8/17 – 11/12
1968 1/31 – 7/7
1974 1/14 – 3/23
1976 6/8 – until 1977 4/20
1979 8/1 – 10/17
1980 3/10 – 6/12
1985 12/28 – until 1986 3/6
1988 5/22 – 8/14
1988 11/5 – until 1989 3/31
1991 7/16 – 9/28
1997 4/15 – 8/6
1997 12/6 – until 1998 2/18
2000 5/6 – 7/17
2000 12/19 – until 2001 3/3
2002 11/13 – 12/25
2003 6/28 – 9/12
2009 3/23 – 10/1
2009 10/24 – until 2010 2/2
2012 4/19 – 6/27

SATURN CHALLENGING
1941 5/4 – until 1942 6/4
1947 9/15 – until 1948 3/3
1948 5/31 – 10/21
1949 2/14 – 7/12
1963 3/6 – 9/17
1963 11/24 – until 1964 5/1
1964 7/31 – until 1965 1/21
1970 6/14 – 12/4
1971 3/2 – 7/20
1971 11/21 – until 1972 4/7
1977 7/20 – until 1978 8/23
1992 4/22 – 7/4
1993 1/10 – until 1994 2/26
2000 4/17 – until 2001 5/18
2006 8/27 – until 2007 9/30
2008 3/18 – 6/17

URANUS CHALLENGING
1938 7/23 – until 1943 5/5
1959 8/21 – until 1963 7/23
2000 2/16 – until 2004 12/17

NEPTUNE CHALLENGING
2005 4/23 – Continues

PLUTO CHALLENGING
1949 9/21 – until 1959 8/12

JUPITER SPECIAL
1946 12/16 – until 1947 11/9
1958 11/29 – until 1959 10/23
1970 11/13 – until 1971 2/6
1971 5/8 – 10/3
1982 10/28 – until 1983 1/12
1983 6/18 – 9/7
1994 10/12 – 12/25
2006 2/2 – 4/4
2006 9/25 – 12/9

SATURN SPECIAL
1954 12/22 – until 1955 5/15
1955 9/19 – until 1956 11/11
1984 10/28 – until 1985 12/16
1986 7/17 – 8/27

URANUS SPECIAL
1978 11/20 – until 1982 11/3

NEPTUNE SPECIAL
1964 1/10 – until 1972 10/12

PLUTO SPECIAL
1990 1/14 – until 1997 9/28

♏

November 19

Your Personal Powers

Clever, intuitive, and independent with strong will, you project a confident personality. Your ruling planet, Pluto, ensures that you feel deeply and passionately about your favorite interests. You gain power by combining your endurance and superior mental capabilities with the ability to face up to challenges or take the lead in difficult situations. Alternatively, you can play the diplomat and work cooperatively with others. If you become bored or too stressed, you may lose some of your power by becoming stubborn, domineering, or scattering your energies. Nevertheless, you can be sensitive, charming, and progressive, with creative and innovative ideas or a strong sense of vision. With your desire for knowledge, you may also find yourself developing your communication skills and gaining from disseminating information to others. You are dynamic yet idealistic, and self-awareness can help you balance the emotional extremes of your nature. As an innovative and dramatic individual, your remarkable potential comes forth when you are enthusiastic or initiating new activities.

Your Powers of Attraction in Relationships

Charismatic and intelligent, you attract people with your forceful personality. Although you seem very independent, your relationships are in fact especially important to you. A secret longing for love may have you searching for the ideal partner. If you do not insist on equality in your relationships, however, you may compromise too much of your spirit and feel frustrated or disappointed. You admire strong-willed individuals, especially those who live more by experience than by theory. As you usually like to keep busy yourself, you need a partner who is also ambitious and not afraid of hard work. As well as attracting others with your originality and sharp mind, you can be sensitive and loving. Once committed to a relationship, you can be a loyal and caring partner.

Your attractive qualities: confident, dynamic, intelligent, dramatic, creative, leader, charm, progressive, visionary, humanitarian, optimistic, strong convictions, too competitive, idealistic, sensitive, independent, sociable, compassionate, resourceful, imaginative sixth sense

Your less attractive qualities: self-centered, dependent, depressive, worry, fear of rejection, extreme, bossy, stubborn, too intense, inner doubts, materialistic, temperamental, jealous, impatient, careless, critical

Your Venus Power

The planet Venus has a great deal of influence on your powers of attraction. Below are four possible Venus types for women and men. To find your Venus you need to go to page 771, where you will find the Venus table and extra information. The planet Mars also affects your powers of attraction. To find your Mars table and interpretation go to page 761.

WOMEN WITH VENUS IN SCORPIO: With a natural psychic gift for penetrating the feelings of others, you can often help partners transform emotional challenges or sexual difficulties. When you fall in love your strong feelings of determination give you a potent force that others find attractive and seductive. Although you know what really turns people on, your most profound desire is usually for the deepness and closeness of real love and intimacy in an enduring relationship.

MEN WITH VENUS IN SCORPIO: As you are emotionally intense and passionate, personal relationships are probably a major factor in your own transformation. Being sensitive yet loyal, you are usually attracted to forceful partners who can express themselves intimately but intensely. Rather than seek easy and simple relationships you are drawn to partners who act as a catalyst for your own internal changes. Through your relationships with your partners you can unravel your own motives and understand your deep-seated feelings or emotional insecurities.

WOMEN WITH VENUS IN SAGITTARIUS: When you feel generous, you can make others feel more optimistic about life. You may be interested in higher learning and seek partners who are scholarly or broad-minded. You are outspoken and direct and sometimes say things that you later regret. Curious and versatile, you can adjust quickly to new situations and a foreign influence implies that you love to travel or may have a partner who comes from a different culture.

MEN WITH VENUS IN SAGITTARIUS: Your enthusiasm and straightforward conduct usually appeal to others and imply that you are approachable and easygoing. Being open to ideas and willing to believe that life has a great deal to offer suggests that you are generous, broad-minded, and eager to cooperate with others. A love of travel and an interest in other

cultures imply that your partner may come from a foreign country.

WOMEN WITH VENUS IN CAPRICORN: Romantically, you do not give your heart easily but hide behind a cool reserve until you feel free to express your emotions. As you take your relationships seriously, you may find yourself drawn to people who are businesslike, resourceful, and practical, or who can act as teachers or mentors. Work or career may also be a factor in many of your associations and partnerships. As security can play an important role in your relationships, you are often attracted to partners who are loyal and hardworking.

MEN WITH VENUS IN CAPRICORN: As you do not display your deeper emotions freely, you are usually dignified and controlled in your relationships with others. Practical and down-to-earth partners are particularly attractive to you, especially those who do not rush into expressing their feelings but seem to possess natural class and reserve. You need a partner who is loyal and dependable and willing to take your relationship seriously.

To read all about your Outer Planets and work out how to use your personalized timetable, go to Section Three, page 789.

♍

Your Personalized Timetable

JUPITER BENEFICIAL
1939 3/20 – 6/5
1939 9/22 – until 1940 1/23
1942 9/4 – until 1943 1/24
1943 4/27 – 7/21
1944 11/7 – until 1945 3/22
1945 7/6 – 9/1
1949 2/19 – 4/28
1949 6/11 – 12/8
1951 3/3 – 5/12
1951 11/20 – 12/9
1954 8/15 – until 1955 7/4
1956 10/19 – until 1957 1/1
1957 1/31 – 8/14
1961 2/1 – 3/23
1961 7/31 – 11/14
1963 2/14 – 4/23
1966 7/29 – 11/15
1966 11/26 – until 1967 6/17
1968 10/2 – 11/25
1969 3/19 – 7/25
1973 1/16 – 3/2
1975 1/27 – 4/6
1978 7/13 – 9/30
1979 1/21 – 5/27
1980 9/16 – 11/3
1981 5/2 – 6/22
1984 12/31 – until 1985 2/12
1986 5/19 – 9/6
1987 1/6 – 3/21
1990 6/27 – 9/9
1991 3/7 – 4/23
1992 8/31 – 10/17
1996 12/15 – until 1997 1/27
1998 4/25 – 11/1
1998 11/25 – until 1999 3/4
2002 6/10 – 8/22
2004 8/15 – 10/1
2008 4/14 – 6/3
2008 11/27 – until 2009 1/11
2010 4/6 – until 2011 2/13

SATURN BENEFICIAL
1938 1/1 – 2/28
1945 8/7 – until 1946 2/25
1946 4/11 – 9/8
1947 2/7 – 5/27
1950 9/6 – 12/10
1951 2/14 – 8/26
1961 1/16 – until 1962 1/15
1966 2/27 – until 1967 4/8
1974 10/8 – 11/23
1975 6/13 – until 1976 7/13
1979 10/14 – until 1980 4/13
1980 6/29 – 10/2
1990 2/21 – 7/22
1990 11/21 – until 1991 2/19
1991 8/26 – 11/12
1995 4/3 – 10/30
1995 12/13 – until 1996 5/18
1996 9/20 – until 1997 2/9
2004 7/21 – until 2005 8/20
2006 3/30 – 4/12
2008 12/12 – until 2009 1/20
2009 8/19 – 11/12
2010 3/20 – 8/6

URANUS BENEFICIAL
1952 10/9 – until 1957 6/10
1966 10/5 – until 1969 8/7
1993 3/14 – until 1996 11/22
2007 5/28 – until 2012 3/23

NEPTUNE BENEFICIAL
1938 9/28 – until 1943 9/15
1994 1/26 – until 1999 1/10

PLUTO BENEFICIAL
1938 1/1 – until 1942 6/24
1967 10/11 – until 1972 9/12

JUPITER CHALLENGING
1938 3/9 – until 1939 1/20
1941 4/6 – 6/14

1943 9/25 – until 1944 3/14
1944 5/13 – 8/16
1950 2/20 – 5/13
1950 8/11 – 12/30
1952 7/31 – 10/20
1953 3/16 – 5/28
1955 9/7 – until 1956 7/30
1962 2/4 – 4/16
1962 9/28 – 11/29
1964 7/3 – 12/3
1965 2/17 – 5/12
1967 8/22 – 11/22
1968 1/21 – 7/12
1974 1/18 – 3/27
1976 6/13 – until 1977 4/24
1979 8/6 – 10/23
1980 3/2 – 6/20
1986 1/1 – 3/11
1988 5/27 – 8/22
1988 10/26 – until 1989 4/6
1991 7/20 – 10/3
1997 4/22 – 7/29
1997 12/12 – until 1998 2/22
2000 5/10 – 7/23
2000 12/11 – until 2001 3/11
2003 7/3 – 9/16
2009 3/28 – 9/15
2009 11/9 – until 2010 2/6
2012 4/23 – 7/1

SATURN CHALLENGING
1941 5/12 – until 1942 6/12
1947 9/24 – until 1948 2/19
1948 6/12 – 11/2
1949 1/31 – 7/21
1963 3/15 – 8/31
1963 12/9 – until 1964 5/18
1964 7/12 – until 1965 1/30
1970 6/24 – 11/20
1971 3/14 – 7/31
1971 11/8 – until 1972 4/16
1977 7/28 – until 1978 8/31
1992 5/19 – 6/6
1993 1/19 – until 1994 3/6
2000 4/25 – until 2001 5/26
2006 9/4 – until 2007 4/2
2007 5/6 – 10/10
2008 3/4 – 6/29

URANUS CHALLENGING
1939 5/19 – until 1943 5/22
1959 9/7 – until 1963 8/9
2000 3/6 – until 2005 1/12

NEPTUNE CHALLENGING
2006 3/9 – Continues

PLUTO CHALLENGING
1950 8/30 – until 1960 7/13

JUPITER SPECIAL
1946 12/21 – until 1947 6/23
1947 8/6 – 11/13
1958 12/4 – until 1959 10/28
1970 11/18 – until 1971 2/14
1971 4/29 – 10/9
1982 11/2 – until 1983 1/18
1983 6/10 – 9/15
1994 10/17 – 12/30
2006 2/16 – 3/21
2006 9/30 – 12/14

SATURN SPECIAL
1955 1/2 – 5/2
1955 9/29 – until 1956 11/19
1984 11/5 – until 1985 12/25
1986 6/25 – 9/17

URANUS SPECIAL
1978 12/7 – until 1982 11/19

NEPTUNE SPECIAL
1964 12/3 – until 1972 11/12

PLUTO SPECIAL
1990 11/28 – until 1997 10/31

505

November 20

Your Personal Powers

Self-assured with good social skills, you present a considerate and amiable personality to the world. Your ruling planet, Pluto, implies that underneath your friendly exterior lie deep feelings and emotional sensitivity. Ambitious and dramatic, you gain power from your dynamic approach and warm generosity. Balance is a vital key to your self-development as the extremes of your nature may sometimes lead you to stubborn or selfish behavior. Usually charming, gracious, and an expert at social contacts, you can mix with people from all walks of life. Although you possess natural leadership skills, you may find that your greatest successes come through partnerships or team effort. Some of your major tests, however, may involve the ability to let go and stay detached. With your quick responses and astute perception, success can be achieved with just the minimum amount of self-discipline. Although indulgence in luxury and sensuality may sometimes cause you to lose power, you fortunately also possess strong intuition that can guide you to outstanding achievement.

Your Powers of Attraction in Relationships

Your shrewd judgment and strong sensitivity can help you in all your relationships. People are attracted to your individuality, and your social skills enable you to entertain others or make useful contacts. Naturally dramatic and strong-willed yet kind and aware of the feelings of others, you possess a wide emotional range. Affectionate and loving and often unhappy alone, you seek partners who can give you emotional support and/or security. Although you can be considerate and generous, you may sometimes become moody or bossy. Nevertheless, you are usually popular and enjoy cooperative activities where you can interact, share experiences, or learn from others. Partners and friends are especially important to you. To decide whether to compromise or assert yourself in your relationships, let your strong sixth sense guide you.

Your attractive qualities: magnetic, leadership, tactful, receptive, intuitive, considerate, confident, humanitarian, harmonious, charm, hardworking, sensitive, friendly, entertaining, confident, agreeable, sociable, diplomatic, gregarious, imaginative, humorous

Your less attractive qualities: stubborn, suspicious, arrogance or lack of confidence, subservient, disappointment, overindulgent, lack of discipline, frustration, too sensitive, secretive, selfish, easily hurt, evasive

Your Venus Power

The planet Venus has a great deal of influence on your powers of attraction. Below are four possible Venus types for women and men. To find your Venus you need to go to page 771, where you will find the Venus table and extra information. The planet Mars also affects your powers of attraction. To find your Mars table and interpretation go to page 761.

WOMEN WITH VENUS IN LIBRA: A natural romantic with good social skills, you love to entertain or put people at ease by projecting a warm and gracious manner. Elegant and fair with a touch of glamour, you are also adept at dealing with people in delicate situations or conflicts. You seek refinement and will go out of your way to achieve harmony and keep the peace. For you, relationships are so important that you may need to guard against becoming dependent on others for approval. With your friendly personality and inherent charm, however, you will always be popular and loved.

MEN WITH VENUS IN LIBRA: You are such good company, people are naturally drawn to you and especially appreciate your talent for making them feel special. You find status in your social contacts and place importance on your relationships. Being clever and a charming companion, you will go out of your way to keep situations peaceful and harmonious. In relationships, however, be careful of indecision or compromising too much. Nevertheless, others are attracted by your natural refinement and good taste, which is reflected in your sense of style.

WOMEN WITH VENUS IN SCORPIO: Loving and passionate, you are often sensitive with deep feelings and strong powers of attraction. A love for the truth coupled with a tendency to be suspicious can be an influence that motivates you to delve deep into the activities of your partner. When in love or in a relationship that matters, you will often bend over backward to cooperate. Although loyal, guard against losing sight of your own needs and desires.

MEN WITH VENUS IN SCORPIO: In relationships you possess a sensitive understanding of your partner's deeper nature. Although you are strongly attached to those you love, you may have to be careful that your feelings do not turn into jealousy or possessiveness. When you fall in love it is often with an

emotional intensity that helps you get in touch with your deep feelings. You are attracted to partners who can share your passion and display strong feelings of sexuality like your own.

Women with Venus in Sagittarius: At your best when being optimistic and generous, you possess a mischievous sense of fun. In relationships your open-minded approach to people and places may attract you to those of a different culture or make you tolerant of the foibles of others. Although warm and enthusiastic when in love, your natural honesty and idealism may inspire you to look for a partner who shares your love of freedom.

Men with Venus in Sagittarius: When in love you are open and friendly with a need for a partner who can share your adventurous spirit and sense of fun. Be careful, however, that your desire for freedom does not cause you to avoid commitment. You prefer your partners to be positive, direct, and generous in spirit. Being outspoken as well as an idealist, you usually enjoy a partner with whom you can share your strong opinions. Alternatively, you may wish to explore life together, whether through travel, education, or having fun.

Women with Venus in Capricorn: Loyal and responsible, you are attracted to dignified and reserved individuals. Being practical and security-conscious, you prefer hardworking partners who are resourceful and enterprising. Work may even be a factor in many of your associations and partnerships. For you, family and faithfulness can be especially important, so you are usually willing to work hard or make sacrifices in order to build up a strong relationship.

Men with Venus in Capricorn: As you admire loyal, hardworking, and dedicated individuals, you probably want a partner who can share your vocational interests or who can provide you with the security you need. You could even find yourself with a partner who is of a different age group or maturity. Guard against denying your true emotional needs or focusing on your career at the expense of your relationship. You are drawn to reserved partners who display self-control.

To read all about your Outer Planets and work out how to use your personalized timetable, go to Section Three, page 789.

Your Personalized Timetable

Jupiter Beneficial

1939 3/24 – 6/13
1939 9/15 – until **1940** 1/29
1942 9/10 – until **1943** 1/17
1943 5/5 – 7/25
1944 11/13 – until **1945** 3/14
1945 7/13 – 9/6
1949 2/24 – 9/11
1949 9/25 – 12/13
1951 3/8 – 5/17
1951 11/3 – 12/26
1954 8/20 – until **1955** 7/9
1956 10/24 – until **1957** 4/29
1957 6/7 – 8/20
1961 2/6 – 3/29
1961 7/23 – 11/21
1963 2/19 – 4/27
1966 8/3 – until **1967** 6/22
1968 10/7 – 12/2
1969 3/11 – 7/31
1973 1/20 – 3/7
1973 9/19 – 10/7
1975 2/1 – 4/10
1978 7/17 – 10/7
1979 1/14 – 6/2
1980 9/21 – 11/9
1981 4/20 – 7/3
1985 1/5 – 2/17
1986 5/26 – 8/29
1987 1/12 – 3/25
1990 7/1 – 9/14
1991 2/23 – 5/4
1992 9/5 – 10/22
1996 12/20 – until **1997** 2/1
1998 4/30 – 10/17
1998 12/10 – until **1999** 3/8
2002 6/14 – 8/26
2004 8/20 – 10/6
2008 12/2 – until **2009** 1/16
2010 4/10 – until **2011** 2/18

Saturn Beneficial

1938 1/1 – 3/8
1945 8/16 – until **1946** 2/7
1946 4/30 – 9/18
1947 1/26 – 6/7
1950 9/14 – until **1951** 9/4
1961 1/25 – until **1962** 1/24
1966 3/7 – until **1967** 4/17
1975 6/21 – until **1976** 7/20
1979 10/23 – until **1980** 3/29
1980 7/14 – 10/11
1990 3/4 – 7/9
1990 12/2 – until **1991** 3/1
1991 8/10 – 11/26
1995 4/12 – 10/11
1996 1/1 – 5/30
1996 9/7 – until **1997** 2/18
2004 7/28 – until **2005** 8/28
2006 3/2 – 5/10
2009 8/28 – 11/23
2010 3/7 – 8/16

Uranus Beneficial

1953 7/22 – until **1957** 6/29
1966 10/23 – until **1969** 8/26
1994 1/15 – until **1996** 12/15
2008 3/22 – Continues

Neptune Beneficial

1938 10/29 – until **1944** 8/13
1994 2/25 – until **1999** 12/8

Pluto Beneficial

1938 1/1 – until **1943** 6/6
1967 11/16 – until **1973** 8/4

Jupiter Challenging

1938 3/14 – until **1939** 1/24
1941 4/11 – 6/19
1943 9/30 – until **1944** 3/4
1944 5/23 – 8/20
1950 2/24 – 5/21
1950 8/2 – until **1951** 1/4
1952 8/9 – 10/10
1953 3/22 – 6/1
1955 9/12 – until **1956** 8/4
1962 2/8 – 4/21
1962 9/18 – 12/8
1964 7/9 – 11/25
1965 2/24 – 5/16
1967 8/26 – 12/6
1968 1/7 – 7/18
1974 1/23 – 4/1
1976 6/18 – until **1977** 4/29
1979 8/10 – 10/30
1980 2/23 – 6/27
1986 1/6 – 3/15
1988 5/31 – 9/4
1988 10/14 – until **1989** 4/11
1991 7/25 – 10/9
1992 4/8 – 5/23
1997 4/30 – 7/21
1997 12/17 – until **1998** 2/27
2000 5/14 – 7/28
2000 12/3 – until **2001** 3/18
2003 7/8 – 9/21
2009 4/2 – 9/5
2009 11/19 – until **2010** 2/10
2012 4/27 – 7/6

Saturn Challenging

1941 5/20 – until **1942** 6/20
1947 10/4 – until **1948** 2/6
1948 6/23 – 11/18
1949 1/15 – 7/30
1963 3/25 – 8/17
1963 12/21 – until **1965** 2/8
1970 7/4 – 11/8
1971 3/24 – 8/15
1971 10/24 – until **1972** 4/25
1977 8/5 – until **1978** 9/8
1993 1/28 – until **1994** 3/15
2000 5/3 – until **2001** 6/2
2006 9/13 – until **2007** 3/12
2007 5/28 – 10/20
2008 2/21 – 7/10

Uranus Challenging

1939 6/6 – until **1944** 3/20
1959 9/26 – until **1963** 8/26
2000 3/26 – until **2005** 2/1

Neptune Challenging

2006 4/14 – Continues

Pluto Challenging

1950 10/9 – until **1960** 8/15

Jupiter Special

1946 12/26 – until **1947** 6/11
1947 8/19 – 11/18
1958 12/8 – until **1959** 11/2
1970 11/22 – until **1971** 2/25
1971 4/18 – 10/15
1982 11/7 – until **1983** 1/24
1983 6/1 – 9/22
1994 10/22 – until **1995** 1/4
2006 10/5 – 12/18

Saturn Special

1955 1/14 – 4/17
1955 10/9 – until **1956** 11/28
1984 11/14 – until **1986** 1/3
1986 6/10 – 10/1

Uranus Special

1978 12/26 – until **1983** 9/12

Neptune Special

1965 1/5 – until **1973** 10/9

Pluto Special

1990 12/26 – until **1998** 9/7

November 21

Your Personal Powers

Friendly, charming, yet determined, you are a strong-willed and talented individual. Born on the cusp, you possess the emotional sensitivity and passion of Scorpio and the warm sociability of Sagittarius. You gain power by combining your strong imagination with your creativity and intuition. When your sense of vision is creatively employed, you often achieve remarkable results. Avoid losing some of your power to your intense emotions or to escapism. With your magnetic personality and charm, you can be kind and inspiring, yet you also have the ability to be a disciplinarian when required. Being dramatic with a natural sense of command, when you display your dependability and capacity for hard work you invariably rise to positions of power. Your wide emotional range and desire for self-expression ensures that you can play any role on life's stage, from tough leader to caring and compassionate friend. With your strong emotions, however, you need to avoid being melodramatic or losing power to worry, indecision, or being scattered. Nevertheless, you are usually astute and discriminating with a strong sixth sense that can help guide you successfully through life.

Your Powers of Attraction in Relationships

Others are attracted to your friendly and caring personality. Able to express a wide range of emotions, others find you alluring and tender yet strong-willed and resolute. You are usually attracted to determined individuals with power and influence. Your prospective partners need to be financially capable; otherwise you may end up bossing them around. When committed to a relationship, however, you can be very loyal and protective. Being idealistic also suggests that you are willing to go to great lengths to preserve your close relationships. With your strong desires, however, be careful that insecurity does not lead to suspicion or jealousy. You can build your confidence by acknowledging positive qualities and loyalty to partners. You can attract others with your emotional magnetism and affectionate and loving nature.

Your attractive qualities: original, sociable, creative, inspired, loving, subtle, leadership ability, sensitive, friendly, loyal, hardworking, visionary, self-reliant, generous, popular, charm, dependable, talented, confident, resolute, idealistic, enterprising, gift with words

Your less attractive qualities: stubborn, melodramatic, worry, insecure, indecisive, confused, too dependent, scattered, escapist, extreme reactions, nervous, inflexible, over-emotional, temperamental

Your Venus Power

The planet Venus has a great deal of influence on your powers of attraction. Below are four possible Venus types for women and men. To find your Venus you need to go to page 771, where you will find the Venus table and extra information. The planet Mars also affects your powers of attraction. To find your Mars table and interpretation go to page 761.

WOMEN WITH VENUS IN LIBRA: A natural romantic with good social skills, you love to entertain or put people at ease by projecting a warm and gracious manner. Elegant and fair with a touch of glamour, you are also adept at dealing with people in delicate situations or conflicts. You seek refinement and will go out of your way to achieve harmony and keep the peace. For you, relationships are so important that you may need to guard against becoming dependent on others for approval. With your friendly personality and inherent charm, however, you will always be popular and loved.

MEN WITH VENUS IN LIBRA: You are such good company, people are naturally drawn to you and especially appreciate your talent for making them feel special. You find status in your social contacts and place importance on your relationships. Being clever and a charming companion, you will go out of your way to keep situations peaceful and harmonious. In relationships, however, be careful of indecision or compromising too much. Nevertheless, others are attracted by your natural refinement and good taste, which is reflected in your sense of style.

WOMEN WITH VENUS IN SCORPIO: You are usually drawn to partners who are sensual in appearance with a strong character. As you are emotionally intense and passionate, personal relationships are probably a major factor in your life. Since you like to be in control, you can at times exhibit some of your less attractive qualities by being willful or domineering. Although you need to feel established and in command in your relationships, you are constantly searching for some higher truth that can bring about a significant transformation.

MEN WITH VENUS IN SCORPIO: As you are emotionally intense and passionate, personal relationships are probably a

major factor in your own transformation. Being sensitive yet loyal, you are usually attracted to forceful partners who can express themselves intimately but intensely. Rather than seek easy and simple relationships you are drawn to partners who act as a catalyst for your own internal changes. Through your relationships with your partners you can unravel your own motives and understand your deep-seated feelings or emotional insecurities.

WOMEN WITH VENUS IN SAGITTARIUS: Optimistic and fun-loving, you love adventure and seek a partner who can expand your horizons. Being truthful and direct, you often say what you think. At times you may be naively tactless. A need for expansion and prosperity suggests that you may enjoy traveling with your friends or partner. Being both lighthearted and idealistic, however, means that once you have given your heart to someone you will stay honorable and loyal.

MEN WITH VENUS IN SAGITTARIUS: When in love you are open and friendly with a need for a partner who can share your adventurous spirit and sense of fun. Be careful, however, that your desire for freedom does not cause you to avoid commitment. You prefer your partners to be positive, direct, and generous in spirit. Being outspoken as well as an idealist, you usually enjoy a partner with whom you can share your strong opinions. Alternatively, you may wish to explore life together, whether through travel, education, or having fun.

WOMEN WITH VENUS IN CAPRICORN: Proud and refined, you attract others with your composed dignity. Needing to display a strong front and disliking vulnerability, you usually need to feel safe before you can express your feelings. In relationships, if you feel insecure or inadequate, this may motivate you to become manipulative in order to regain control. Nevertheless, you can project an attractive sense of self-assurance and are capable of displaying loyalty and a wonderful dry sense of humor.

MEN WITH VENUS IN CAPRICORN: Hardworking and ambitious, you are usually attracted to determined, focused, and ambitious partners who have a strong sense of duty. You want them to take relationships as seriously as you do, so loyalty and faithfulness are high on your agenda. Since you may display a natural reserve about expressing your feelings in an intimate relationship, you need a partner who shares your need for emotional security.

To read all about your Outer Planets and work out how to use your personalized timetable, go to Section Three, page 789.

To read all about your Outer Planets and work out how to use your personalized timetable, go to Section Three, page 789.

♏

Your Personalized Timetable

JUPITER BENEFICIAL
1939 3/29 – 6/21
1939 9/6 – until 1940 2/3
1942 9/16 – until 1943 1/9
1943 5/11 – 7/30
1944 11/20 – until 1945 3/6
1945 7/20 – 9/10
1949 3/1 – 8/23
1949 10/14 – 12/18
1951 3/12 – 5/22
1951 10/24 – until 1952 1/5
1954 8/25 – until 1955 2/26
1955 4/4 – 7/14
1956 10/29 – until 1957 4/16
1957 6/21 – 8/25
1961 2/10 – 4/5
1961 7/16 – 11/27
1963 2/23 – 5/2
1966 8/7 – until 1967 6/27
1968 10/12 – 12/9
1969 3/3 – 8/6
1973 1/25 – 3/12
1973 9/1 – 10/25
1975 2/6 – 4/14
1978 7/22 – 10/15
1979 1/5 – 6/8
1980 9/25 – 11/15
1981 4/11 – 7/12
1985 1/9 – 2/22
1986 6/3 – 8/21
1987 1/17 – 3/29
1990 7/6 – 9/20
1991 2/14 – 5/13
1992 9/10 – 10/27
1996 12/24 – until 1997 2/5
1998 5/5 – 10/6
1998 12/20 – until 1999 3/13
2002 6/19 – 8/31
2004 8/25 – 10/11
2008 12/7 – until 2009 1/20
2010 4/15 – until 2011 2/23

SATURN BENEFICIAL
1938 1/1 – 3/17
1945 8/25 – until 1946 1/24
1946 5/13 – 9/28
1947 1/13 – 6/17
1950 9/22 – until 1951 9/12
1961 2/2 – 9/12
1961 10/13 – until 1962 2/1
1966 3/15 – until 1967 4/25
1967 11/9 – until 1968 1/8
1975 6/29 – until 1976 7/28
1979 11/2 – until 1980 3/16
1980 7/25 – 10/19
1981 5/13 – 6/27
1990 3/17 – 6/24
1990 12/12 – until 1991 3/11
1991 7/27 – 12/8
1995 4/21 – 9/26
1996 1/14 – 6/15
1996 8/22 – until 1997 2/27
2004 8/6 – until 2005 3/15
2005 3/28 – 9/6
2006 2/14 – 5/24
2009 9/5 – 12/7
2010 2/20 – 8/26

URANUS BENEFICIAL
1953 8/8 – until 1957 7/16
1966 11/13 – until 1969 9/12
1994 2/1 – until 1997 1/4
2008 4/10 – Continues

NEPTUNE BENEFICIAL
1939 9/26 – until 1944 9/12
1995 1/24 – until 2000 1/8

PLUTO BENEFICIAL
1938 1/1 – until 1944 5/1
1968 10/6 – until 1973 9/5

JUPITER CHALLENGING
1938 3/19 – until 1939 1/29

1941 4/15 – 6/23
1943 10/6 – until 1944 2/24
1944 5/31 – 8/25
1950 3/1 – 6/1
1950 7/22 – until 1951 1/10
1952 8/22 – 9/27
1953 3/27 – 6/6
1955 9/17 – until 1956 8/9
1962 2/12 – 4/27
1962 9/10 – 12/16
1964 7/14 – 11/17
1965 3/3 – 5/20
1967 8/31 – until 1968 7/23
1974 1/27 – 4/6
1976 6/22 – until 1977 5/4
1979 8/15 – 11/6
1980 2/15 – 7/3
1986 1/11 – 3/19
1988 6/5 – until 1989 4/16
1991 7/30 – 10/14
1992 3/27 – 6/4
1997 5/10 – 7/11
1997 12/23 – until 1998 3/3
2000 5/19 – 8/4
2000 11/26 – until 2001 3/25
2003 7/13 – 9/26
2009 4/8 – 8/27
2009 11/27 – until 2010 2/14
2012 5/2 – 7/11

SATURN CHALLENGING
1941 5/28 – until 1942 6/28
1943 1/6 – 3/8
1947 10/15 – until 1948 1/25
1948 7/3 – until 1949 8/8
1963 4/5 – 8/4
1964 1/1 – until 1965 2/16
1970 7/15 – 10/26
1971 4/2 – 9/9
1971 9/28 – until 1972 5/3
1977 8/13 – until 1978 9/16
1993 2/5 – until 1994 3/24
1994 10/10 – 12/8
2000 5/10 – until 2001 6/10
2006 9/22 – until 2007 2/25
2007 6/10 – 10/31
2008 2/8 – 7/20

URANUS CHALLENGING
1939 6/27 – until 1944 4/15
1959 10/20 – until 1964 6/17
2000 4/24 – until 2005 2/19

NEPTUNE CHALLENGING
2007 3/6 – Continues

PLUTO CHALLENGING
1951 9/13 – until 1961 7/18

JUPITER SPECIAL
1947 1/1 – 6/1
1947 8/28 – 11/22
1958 12/13 – until 1959 11/6
1970 11/27 – until 1971 3/21
1971 3/25 – 10/20
1982 11/11 – until 1983 1/31
1983 5/24 – 9/29
1994 10/27 – until 1995 1/9
1995 7/9 – 8/27
2006 10/10 – 12/23

SATURN SPECIAL
1955 1/30 – 3/31
1955 10/19 – until 1956 12/6
1984 11/22 – until 1986 1/13
1986 5/27 – 10/13

URANUS SPECIAL
1979 1/20 – until 1983 10/10

NEPTUNE SPECIAL
1965 12/1 – until 1973 11/10

PLUTO SPECIAL
1991 11/16 – until 1998 10/21

509

Scorpio Timetable
X-Special · X-Beneficial · X-Challenging

October 23
URANUS X-BENEFICIAL
2002 4/2 – until 2004 1/27

NEPTUNE X-BENEFICIAL
2010 3/19 – until 2013 1/10

PLUTO X-BENEFICIAL
2007 1/10 – until 2009 11/2

October 24
URANUS X-BENEFICIAL
2002 4/29 – until 2004 2/14

NEPTUNE X-BENEFICIAL
2010 4/25 – until 2013 2/8

PLUTO X-BENEFICIAL
2007 2/11 – until 2009 12/5

October 25
URANUS X-BENEFICIAL
2003 2/27 – until 2004 12/14

NEPTUNE X-BENEFICIAL
2011 3/15 – until 2013 9/19

PLUTO X-BENEFICIAL
2008 1/6 – until 2010 10/30

October 26
URANUS X-BENEFICIAL
2003 3/17 – until 2005 1/10

NEPTUNE X-BENEFICIAL
2011 4/17 – until 2013 8/13

PLUTO X-BENEFICIAL
2008 2/6 – until 2010 12/3

October 27
URANUS X-BENEFICIAL
2003 4/6 – until 2005 1/31

NEPTUNE X-BENEFICIAL
2012 3/10 – until 2013 9/19

PLUTO X-BENEFICIAL
2009 1/3 – until 2011 10/28

October 28
URANUS X-BENEFICIAL
2003 5/3 – until 2005 2/17

NEPTUNE X-CHALLENGING
2001 9/12 – 11/21

PLUTO X-BENEFICIAL
2009 2/2 – until 2011 12/3

October 29
URANUS X-BENEFICIAL
2004 3/2 – until 2005 12/19

NEPTUNE X-CHALLENGING
2001 1/1 – 12/28

PLUTO X-BENEFICIAL
2010 1/1 – until 2012 10/26

October 30
URANUS X-BENEFICIAL
2004 3/20 – until 2006 1/15

NEPTUNE X-CHALLENGING
2001 1/1 – until 2002 11/11

PLUTO X-BENEFICIAL
2010 1/31 – until 2012 12/3

October 31
URANUS X-BENEFICIAL
2004 4/10 – until 2006 2/4

NEPTUNE X-CHALLENGING
2001 1/1 – until 2002 12/24

PLUTO X-BENEFICIAL
2010 3/19 – until 2013 10/27

November 1
URANUS X-BENEFICIAL
2004 5/7 – until 2006 2/22

NEPTUNE X-CHALLENGING
2001 1/28 – until 2003 1/22

PLUTO X-BENEFICIAL
2011 1/30 – until 2013 12/4

November 2
URANUS X-BENEFICIAL
2005 3/7 – until 2006 12/25

NEPTUNE X-CHALLENGING
2001 2/24 – until 2003 12/20

PLUTO X-BENEFICIAL
2011 3/14 – Continues

November 3
URANUS X-BENEFICIAL
2005 3/25 – until 2007 1/20

NEPTUNE X-CHALLENGING
2001 3/31 – until 2004 1/19

PLUTO X-BENEFICIAL
2012 1/30 – Continues

November 4
URANUS X-BENEFICIAL
2005 4/15 – until 2007 2/9

NEPTUNE X-CHALLENGING
2002 2/21 – until 2004 12/15

PLUTO X-BENEFICIAL
2012 3/12 – Continues

November 5
URANUS X-BENEFICIAL
2005 5/13 – until 2007 2/27

NEPTUNE X-CHALLENGING
2002 3/25 – until 2005 1/15

November 6
URANUS X-BENEFICIAL
2006 3/12 – until 2007 12/31

NEPTUNE X-CHALLENGING
2003 2/18 – until 2005 12/9

November 7
URANUS X-BENEFICIAL
2006 3/30 – until 2008 1/26

NEPTUNE X-CHALLENGING
2003 3/20 – until 2006 1/11

November 8
URANUS X-BENEFICIAL
2006 4/20 – until 2008 2/14

NEPTUNE X-CHALLENGING
2004 2/15 – until 2006 12/2

November 9
URANUS X-BENEFICIAL
2006 5/19 – until 2008 3/3

NEPTUNE X-CHALLENGING
2004 3/15 – until 2007 1/8

November 10
URANUS X-BENEFICIAL
2007 3/17 – until 2009 1/4

NEPTUNE X-CHALLENGING
2004 5/6 – until 2007 11/20

November 11
URANUS X-BENEFICIAL
2007 4/5 – until 2009 1/30

NEPTUNE X-CHALLENGING
2005 3/11 – until 2008 1/4

November 12
URANUS X-CHALLENGING
2001 1/14 – 12/2

URANUS X-BENEFICIAL
2007 4/26 – until 2009 2/19

NEPTUNE X-CHALLENGING
2005 4/20 – until 2008 2/1

November 13
URANUS X-CHALLENGING
2001 1/1 – 12/30

URANUS X-BENEFICIAL
2007 5/26 – until 2009 3/9

NEPTUNE X-CHALLENGING
2006 3/7 – until 2008 12/30

November 14
URANUS X-CHALLENGING
2001 1/15 – until 2002 1/19

URANUS X-BENEFICIAL
2008 3/21 – until 2010 1/10

NEPTUNE X-CHALLENGING
2006 4/12 – until 2009 1/28

November 15
URANUS X-CHALLENGING
2001 2/2 – until 2002 2/6

URANUS X-BENEFICIAL
2008 4/9 – until 2010 2/4

NEPTUNE X-CHALLENGING
2007 3/4 – until 2009 12/25

November 16
URANUS X-CHALLENGING
2001 2/19 – until 2002 12/8

URANUS X-BENEFICIAL
2008 4/30 – until 2010 2/24

NEPTUNE X-CHALLENGING
2007 4/6 – until 2010 1/25

November 17
URANUS X-CHALLENGING
2001 3/9 – until 2003 1/4

URANUS X-BENEFICIAL
2008 6/2 – until 2010 3/14

NEPTUNE X-CHALLENGING
2008 2/29 – until 2010 12/19

November 18
URANUS X-CHALLENGING
2001 3/30 – until 2003 1/24

URANUS X-BENEFICIAL
2009 3/27 – until 2011 1/17

NEPTUNE X-CHALLENGING
2008 3/31 – until 2011 1/22

November 19
URANUS X-CHALLENGING
2001 4/27 – until 2003 2/11

URANUS X-BENEFICIAL
2009 4/15 – until 2011 2/10

NEPTUNE X-CHALLENGING
2009 2/25 – until 2011 12/11

November 20
URANUS X-CHALLENGING
2002 2/24 – until 2003 12/14

URANUS X-BENEFICIAL
2009 5/6 – until 2011 3/1

NEPTUNE X-CHALLENGING
2009 3/26 – until 2012 1/18

November 21
URANUS X-CHALLENGING
2002 3/14 – until 2004 1/9

URANUS X-BENEFICIAL
2009 6/10 – until 2011 3/19

NEPTUNE X-CHALLENGING
2009 5/17 – until 2012 11/27

Sagittarius

November 22–December 21

November 22

Your Personal Powers

Proud, dramatic, and warmhearted, with a sense of inner nobility, you can be both pragmatic and idealistic. Born on the cusp, you have the passion and deep emotions of Scorpio and the optimism of Sagittarius. Although you have a playful nature, you are also strong-willed and realistic. You gain power from your advanced people skills and willingness to collaborate with others, especially in teamwork activities and partnerships. With good organizational skills and a competitive streak, you have a flair for business and naturally gravitate to leadership positions. Although you are generous, with your love of luxury and the good life, avoid losing power to self-indulgence. Equally, you may also lose power if you allow negative emotions to turn into self-doubts. Nevertheless, success is usually yours with just the necessary self-discipline. Generally friendly and magnanimous, your popularity aids you in your climb up the ladder of success. Highly intuitive, you usually find inspiration and your greatest fulfillment in being helpful to others.

Your Powers of Attraction in Relationships

Idealistic and sincere, you attract others with your inner strength, charisma, and practical common sense. Sociable, caring, and loving, though sometimes undemonstrative, you can entertain and captivate others with your honest and straightforward style. In love, you are sensitive and can give a lot of yourself, yet you may have to develop detachment to avoid martyring yourself or being hurt by people less idealistic or benevolent than you. Developing your innate humanitarian streak will help you to put your love life into perspective. With an inner youthful quality you also attract many admirers. You are often drawn to those with a universal outlook with whom you can share your desire to work for the good of all. You are a generous lover or friend who often shows responsible and protective concern for those you love.

Your attractive qualities: optimistic, direct, highly intuitive, pragmatic, practical, skillful, friendly, playful, competitive, good organizer, realist, dramatic, sensitive, loving, idealistic, problem solver, universal achiever, generous, enthusiastic, sociable

Your less attractive qualities: nervous, insecure, bossy, materialistic, overindulgent, get-rich-quick schemes, escapist, lazy, discontentment, critical, egotistical, self-promoting

Your Venus Power

The planet Venus has a great deal of influence on your powers of attraction. Below are four possible Venus types for women and men. To find your Venus you need to go to page 771, where you will find the Venus table and extra information. The planet Mars also affects your powers of attraction. To find your Mars table and interpretation go to page 761.

WOMEN WITH VENUS IN LIBRA: Gracious, charming, and sociable with a sense of style, you have no trouble attracting admirers. With your natural diplomatic skills and desire for harmony you usually like to keep the peace and avoid confrontations, but be careful of failing to take a stand when it is necessary. Romantic and easygoing yourself, you are attracted to affectionate and refined individuals who share your love of peace, justice, and fair play.

MEN WITH VENUS IN LIBRA: You are such good company, people are naturally drawn to you and especially appreciate your talent for making them feel special. You find status in your social contacts and place importance on your relationships. Being clever and a charming companion, you will go out of your way to keep situations peaceful and harmonious. In relationships, however, be careful of indecision or compromising too much. Nevertheless, others are attracted by your natural refinement and good taste, which is reflected in your sense of style.

WOMEN WITH VENUS IN SCORPIO: Your strength and power is in your ability to love both deeply and sensitively. For you, love and desire go hand in hand. As you feel so deeply, you often keep your sensitivity or vulnerability hidden from others in order to keep some control in your relationships. You are more likely to prefer a few very close loyal friends than many superficial acquaintances. In relationships your sensual nature and magnetic intensity can easily attract others.

MEN WITH VENUS IN SCORPIO: You are attracted to partners who have deep and powerful emotions or individuals whom you find intriguing. Your gift for creating smoke screens to maintain secrecy around your feelings can conceal your inner sensitivity and vulnerability. Nevertheless, you are looking for a partner who can pierce your defenses and understand

you at a very deep level. Needing a relationship with a powerful sexual connection, you thrive on emotional intensity.

WOMEN WITH VENUS IN SAGITTARIUS: When you feel generous, you can make others feel more optimistic about life. You may be interested in higher learning and seek partners who are scholarly or broad-minded. You are outspoken and direct and sometimes say things that you later regret. Curious and versatile, you can adjust quickly to new situations and a foreign influence implies that you love to travel or may have a partner who comes from a different culture.

MEN WITH VENUS IN SAGITTARIUS: Your enthusiasm and straightforward conduct usually appeal to others and imply that you are approachable and easygoing. Being open to ideas and willing to believe that life has a great deal to offer suggests that you are generous, broad-minded, and show eagerness to cooperate with others. A love of travel and an interest in other cultures imply that your partner may come from a foreign country.

WOMEN WITH VENUS IN CAPRICORN: Proud and refined, you attract others with your composed dignity. Disliking vulnerability and needing to feel safe before you can express your feelings, you usually put up a strong front. Feeling insecure or inadequate in relationships may force you to become manipulative in order to regain control. Nevertheless, you can project an attractive sense of self-assurance and be capable of displaying loyalty and a wonderful dry sense of humor.

MEN WITH VENUS IN CAPRICORN: As you do not display your deeper emotions freely, you are usually dignified and controlled in your relationships with others. Practical and down-to-earth partners are particularly attractive to you, especially those who do not rush into expressing their feelings but seem to possess natural class and reserve. You need a partner who is loyal, dependable, and willing to take your relationship seriously.

To read all about your Outer Planets and work out how to use your personalized timetable, go to Section Three, page 789.

♐

Your Personalized Timetable

JUPITER BENEFICIAL
1939 4/3 – 7/4
1939 8/24 – until 1940 2/10
1942 9/25 – 12/30
1943 5/19 – 8/5
1944 11/30 – until 1945 2/24
1945 7/28 – 9/16
1949 3/8 – 8/10
1949 10/27 – 12/23
1951 3/17 – 5/29
1951 10/13 – until 1952 1/15
1954 9/1 – until 1955 2/10
1955 4/20 – 7/20
1956 11/5 – until 1957 4/4
1957 7/3 – 8/31
1961 2/16 – 4/15
1961 7/5 – 12/4
1963 2/28 – 5/8
1966 8/13 – until 1967 7/3
1968 10/18 – 12/22
1969 2/18 – 8/13
1973 1/30 – 3/19
1973 8/19 – 11/6
1975 2/11 – 4/20
1978 7/27 – 10/28
1978 12/24 – until 1979 6/15
1980 10/1 – 11/22
1981 4/1 – 7/22
1985 1/15 – 2/27
1986 6/16 – 8/8
1987 1/24 – 4/3
1990 7/11 – 9/27
1991 2/4 – 5/23
1992 9/16 – 11/2
1996 12/30 – until 1997 2/10
1998 5/12 – 9/26
1998 12/30 – until 1999 3/18
2002 6/25 – 9/7
2004 8/31 – 10/17
2008 12/13 – until 2009 1/25
2010 4/21 – until 2011 2/28

SATURN BENEFICIAL
1938 1/1 – 3/27
1945 9/6 – until 1946 1/8
1946 5/26 – 10/15
1946 12/26 – until 1947 6/28
1950 10/2 – until 1951 9/23
1961 2/14 – 8/14
1961 11/9 – until 1962 2/12
1966 3/26 – until 1967 5/7
1967 10/19 – until 1968 1/27
1975 7/9 – until 1976 8/7
1979 11/16 – until 1980 2/29
1980 8/7 – 10/30
1981 4/19 – 7/21
1990 4/7 – 6/1
1990 12/23 – until 1991 3/26
1991 7/10 – 12/21
1995 5/5 – 9/9
1996 1/28 – until 1997 3/10
2004 8/16 – until 2005 2/11
2005 4/29 – 9/18
2006 1/29 – 6/8
2009 9/15 – until 2010 9/6

URANUS BENEFICIAL
1953 9/2 – until 1958 5/6
1967 9/16 – until 1970 6/24
1994 2/26 – until 1997 1/26
2008 5/9 – Continues

NEPTUNE BENEFICIAL
1939 11/4 – until 1945 8/19
1995 3/3 – until 2000 12/13

PLUTO BENEFICIAL
1938 1/1 – until 1944 7/10
1968 11/20 – until 1974 8/3

JUPITER CHALLENGING
1938 3/25 – until 1939 2/3
1941 4/21 – 6/29

1943 10/14 – until 1944 2/14
1944 6/10 – 8/31
1950 3/6 – until 1951 1/16
1953 4/2 – 6/11
1955 9/23 – until 1956 4/5
1956 4/29 – 8/15
1962 2/18 – 5/5
1962 8/31 – 12/24
1964 7/23 – 11/8
1965 3/11 – 5/26
1967 9/6 – until 1968 7/30
1974 2/1 – 4/12
1976 6/29 – 12/28
1977 2/2 – 5/9
1979 8/21 – 11/16
1980 2/5 – 7/11
1986 1/16 – 3/25
1988 6/10 – until 1989 4/22
1991 8/5 – 10/21
1992 3/15 – 6/16
1997 5/29 – 6/21
1997 12/29 – until 1998 3/8
2000 5/24 – 8/12
2000 11/16 – until 2001 4/1
2003 7/19 – 10/2
2009 4/16 – 8/17
2009 12/6 – until 2010 2/20
2012 5/7 – 7/18

SATURN CHALLENGING
1941 6/7 – until 1942 1/13
1942 2/1 – 7/9
1942 12/18 – until 1943 3/27
1947 11/2 – until 1948 1/5
1948 7/14 – until 1949 8/18
1963 4/22 – 7/16
1964 1/13 – until 1965 2/27
1970 8/3 – 10/6
1971 4/14 – until 1972 5/14
1977 8/23 – until 1978 9/26
1979 4/12 – 6/6
1993 2/16 – until 1994 4/4
1994 9/19 – 12/28
2000 5/20 – until 2001 6/20
2006 10/4 – until 2007 2/9
2007 6/25 – 11/19
2008 1/19 – 7/31

URANUS CHALLENGING
1939 8/4 – until 1944 5/9
1960 8/19 – until 1964 7/18
2001 2/25 – until 2006 1/1

NEPTUNE CHALLENGING
2007 4/21 – Continues

PLUTO CHALLENGING
1952 8/31 – until 1962 6/16

JUPITER SPECIAL
1947 1/9 – 5/22
1947 9/7 – 11/28
1958 12/20 – until 1959 11/12
1970 12/3 – until 1971 10/26
1982 11/17 – until 1983 2/9
1983 5/14 – 10/7
1994 11/1 – until 1995 1/16
1995 6/24 – 9/10
2006 10/17 – 12/29

SATURN SPECIAL
1955 10/30 – until 1956 12/17
1957 8/5 – 8/18
1984 12/3 – until 1985 7/8
1985 8/12 – until 1986 1/29
1986 5/9 – 10/26

URANUS SPECIAL
1979 11/21 – until 1983 11/4

NEPTUNE SPECIAL
1966 1/13 – until 1974 10/16

PLUTO SPECIAL
1991 12/20 – until 1998 11/25

November 23

SUN: SAGITTARIUS • DECANATE: SAGITTARIUS/JUPITER • DEGREE: 0°5–1°5 SAGITTARIUS • MODE: MUTABLE • ELEMENT: FIRE

Your Personal Powers

Active and gregarious, you are an idealistic individual with powerful emotions and a warm heart. You gain power by combining your direct approach and openness with your ability to see the big picture of life's experiences. Having an adventurous nature, you may also possess an interest in travel or foreign cultures. Although you admire truth and honesty, you should resist being outspoken to the point of tactlessness. Your charismatic attraction and keen intellect indicate that you may find yourself naturally gravitating to positions of leadership. Although you possess many talents, in order to achieve your remarkable potential, you must apply the necessary persistence and self-discipline. You can lose some of your power if, due to boredom, you take too many risks or act impulsively without proper planning. Nevertheless, being a quick thinker, you can have an adaptable and inventive approach to life, often preferring practice to theory. Passionate with a persuasive manner, when inspired you can be spontaneous, dramatic, and creative, utilizing your emotional power to aid your success.

Your Powers of Attraction in Relationships

Highly receptive to the feelings of others, you can attract friends and partners by being understanding, compassionate, and charming. Very sociable, you are often entertaining, amusing, and a delightful companion. Your love of freedom indicates that a restless streak may be the one obstacle to your settling down with one person. You are usually attracted to partners who are forceful and determined. In order to create harmony in your relationships, you may need to resist becoming entangled in power struggles. Nevertheless, your quick intelligence and captivating manner can help you in all your relationships. Warmhearted and idealistic, you admire those with intelligence and foresight. If they also love new experiences or travel then so much the better. If not, you want space in your relationship for exploration and adventure.

Your attractive qualities: friendly, emotionally sensitive, loyal, responsible, popular, focused, loving, creative, communicative, intuitive, ambitious, persuasive, versatile, common sense, dramatic, compassionate, adventurous, trustworthy, thoughtful, idealistic

Your less attractive qualities: restless, selfish, bored, inse-cure, tactless, prejudiced, stubborn, uncompromising, fault-finding, withdrawn, too outspoken, rash, impulsive, tense

Your Venus Power

The planet Venus has a great deal of influence on your powers of attraction. Below are four possible Venus types for women and men. To find your Venus you need to go to page 771, where you will find the Venus table and extra information. The planet Mars also affects your powers of attraction. To find your Mars table and interpretation go to page 761.

WOMEN WITH VENUS IN LIBRA: You are usually attractive and sociable with an easygoing manner. Your love of beauty, harmony, and pleasure implies that you are a romantic with a desire for love and affection. Once in a relationship you need to learn to negotiate your position rather than adapt to the wishes of others and compromise just to keep the peace. Nevertheless, your advanced social skills and strong sense of fair play can help you succeed in any social or romantic situation.

MEN WITH VENUS IN LIBRA: As a sociable and friendly individual with an eye for beauty, you are amorous and charming. You are a natural gentleman and your ideal partner usually has an elegant appearance, artistic appreciation, and good taste. Your relationships benefit when you resist the temptation to take the easy way out or put too much emphasis on vanity and high living. Intellectual and naturally refined, you seek a loving partner who can share your romantic and sophisticated aspirations.

WOMEN WITH VENUS IN SCORPIO: With a natural psychic gift for penetrating the feelings of others, you can often help partners transform emotional challenges or sexual difficulties. When you fall in love, your strong feelings and determination give you a potent force that others find attractive and seductive. Although you know what really turns people on, your most profound desire is usually for the deepness and closeness of real love and intimacy in an enduring relationship.

MEN WITH VENUS IN SCORPIO: In relationships you possess a sensitive understanding of your partner's deeper nature. Although you are strongly attached to those you love, you may have to be careful that your feelings do not turn into jealousy or possessiveness. When you fall in love it is often with an emotional intensity that helps you get in touch with your deep

feelings. You are attracted to partners who can share your passion and display strong feelings of sexuality like your own.

WOMEN WITH VENUS IN SAGITTARIUS: Optimistic and fun-loving, you love adventure and seek a partner who can expand your horizons. Being truthful and direct, you often say what you think, and at times you may be naively tactless. A need for expansion and prosperity suggests that you may enjoy traveling with your friends or partner. Being both lighthearted and idealistic, however, indicates that once you have given your heart to someone you will stay honorable and loyal.

MEN WITH VENUS IN SAGITTARIUS: You are usually attracted to partners who are knowledgeable or well-traveled. Enthusiastic and optimistic, you often respond quickly to love offers and enter relationships with enthusiasm. Usually you seek to expand your social circle and meeting people from all walks of life can bring you the variety and fun to you seek in life. Although you are generous and honest, your partners may accuse you of being overly optimistic or too blunt.

WOMEN WITH VENUS IN CAPRICORN: With your natural caution in romantic affairs, you often appear reserved and controlled. You may be shy, but try to be more forward, especially if you want to be noticed. When you care about people, however, you are usually willing to put in extra time and energy to preserve the relationship. You are practical and dependable, and a sense of duty can often play a large role in the affairs of your heart. With elegant simplicity you can attract others with your well-cut clothes and refined manners.

MEN WITH VENUS IN CAPRICORN: In relationships you take love seriously and can be a strong and practical support for friends or partners. You are usually attracted to partners who are as hardworking as you. As you tend not to express your feelings until you feel really secure in a relationship, you may be drawn to those who seem loyal, faithful, and not likely to let you down. As you respect the wisdom of experience, you may be drawn to mature partners or, alternatively, you may act as an authority figure for someone younger.

To read all about your Outer Planets and work out how to use your personalized timetable, go to Section Three, page 789.

Your Personalized Timetable

JUPITER BENEFICIAL
1939 4/7 – 7/24
1939 8/3 – until 1940 2/15
1942 10/3 – 12/22
1943 5/25 – 8/9
1944 12/9 – until 1945 2/14
1945 8/2 – 9/21
1949 3/14 – 8/1
1949 11/4 – 12/28
1951 3/21 – 6/4
1951 10/6 – until 1952 1/22
1954 9/6 – until 1955 2/1
1955 4/29 – 7/24
1956 11/11 – until 1957 3/26
1957 7/11 – 9/5
1961 2/21 – 4/25
1961 6/25 – 12/9
1963 3/5 – 5/12
1966 8/18 – until 1967 7/8
1968 10/23 – until 1969 1/6
1969 2/3 – 8/19
1973 2/4 – 3/24
1973 8/11 – 11/14
1975 2/16 – 4/24
1978 8/1 – 11/12
1978 12/9 – until 1979 6/20
1980 10/6 – 11/29
1981 3/24 – 7/29
1985 1/19 – 3/4
1986 7/4 – 7/20
1987 1/29 – 4/8
1990 7/16 – 10/3
1991 1/27 – 5/30
1992 9/20 – 11/8
1993 5/6 – 6/26
1997 1/3 – 2/15
1998 5/18 – 9/18
1999 1/6 – 3/22
2002 6/30 – 9/12
2003 3/14 – 4/24
2004 9/5 – 10/22
2008 12/17 – until 2009 1/30
2010 4/25 – until 2011 3/5

SATURN BENEFICIAL
1938 1/1 – 4/4
1945 9/18 – 12/27
1946 6/5 – 11/8
1946 12/3 – until 1947 7/7
1950 10/11 – until 1951 5/14
1951 6/13 – 10/1
1961 2/24 – 7/30
1961 11/23 – until 1962 2/21
1962 9/4 – 11/13
1966 4/3 – until 1967 5/17
1967 10/6 – until 1968 2/7
1975 7/17 – until 1976 8/15
1979 11/30 – until 1980 2/14
1980 8/16 – 11/9
1981 4/5 – 8/3
1991 1/1 – 4/10
1991 6/24 – 12/30
1995 5/17 – 8/26
1996 2/7 – until 1997 3/18
2004 8/25 – until 2005 1/28
2005 5/13 – 9/29
2006 1/17 – 6/18
2009 9/23 – until 2010 9/14

URANUS BENEFICIAL
1953 10/1 – until 1958 6/7
1967 10/3 – until 1970 8/1
1994 3/23 – until 1997 12/2
2009 3/15 – Continues

NEPTUNE BENEFICIAL
1940 10/1 – until 1945 9/17
1996 1/29 – until 2001 1/12

PLUTO BENEFICIAL
1938 1/1 – until 1945 6/22
1969 10/10 – until 1974 9/4

JUPITER CHALLENGING
1938 3/30 – 10/4

1938 11/2 – until 1939 2/8
1941 4/25 – 7/4
1943 10/20 – until 1944 2/6
1944 6/16 – 9/5
1950 3/11 – until 1951 1/21
1953 4/7 – 6/16
1955 9/28 – until 1956 3/20
1956 5/16 – 8/20
1962 2/22 – 5/12
1962 8/23 – 12/30
1964 7/30 – 10/31
1965 3/17 – 5/30
1967 9/11 – until 1968 8/4
1974 2/6 – 4/17
1974 10/13 – 11/24
1976 7/4 – 12/16
1977 2/15 – 5/14
1979 8/25 – 11/25
1980 1/26 – 7/16
1986 1/21 – 3/29
1988 6/15 – until 1989 4/27
1991 8/9 – 10/27
1992 3/7 – 6/24
1998 1/3 – 3/12
2000 5/28 – 8/20
2000 11/8 – until 2001 4/7
2003 7/24 – 10/8
2009 4/22 – 8/9
2009 12/12 – until 2010 2/24
2012 5/11 – Continues

SATURN CHALLENGING
1941 6/15 – 12/19
1942 2/26 – 7/19
1942 12/5 – until 1943 4/7
1948 7/23 – until 1949 8/26
1963 5/13 – 6/25
1964 1/22 – until 1965 3/7
1971 4/22 – until 1972 5/21
1977 8/31 – until 1978 10/5
1979 3/25 – 6/23
1993 2/24 – until 1994 4/14
1994 9/5 – until 1995 1/9
2000 5/28 – until 2001 6/29
2002 1/11 – 3/7
2006 10/15 – until 2007 1/28
2007 7/4 – until 2008 8/9

URANUS CHALLENGING
1940 5/25 – until 1944 5/27
1960 9/4 – until 1964 8/6
2001 3/16 – until 2006 1/24

NEPTUNE CHALLENGING
2008 3/9 – Continues

PLUTO CHALLENGING
1952 10/8 – until 1962 7/30

JUPITER SPECIAL
1947 1/15 – 5/14
1947 9/14 – 12/3
1958 12/25 – until 1959 6/30
1959 8/9 – 11/17
1970 12/8 – until 1971 10/31
1982 11/22 – until 1983 2/17
1983 5/5 – 10/13
1994 11/6 – until 1995 1/22
1995 6/15 – 9/18
2006 10/22 – until 2007 1/3

SATURN SPECIAL
1955 11/8 – until 1956 12/26
1957 7/5 – 9/17
1984 12/12 – until 1985 6/15
1985 9/3 – until 1986 2/13
1986 4/23 – 11/4

URANUS SPECIAL
1979 12/7 – until 1983 11/22

NEPTUNE SPECIAL
1966 12/7 – until 1974 11/15

PLUTO SPECIAL
1992 1/28 – until 1999 10/19

November 24

SUN: SAGITTARIUS • DECANATE: SAGITTARIUS/JUPITER • DEGREE: 1°5–2°5 SAGITTARIUS • MODE: MUTABLE • ELEMENT: FIRE

Your Personal Powers

Your sharp intellect and good communication skills are just some of your personal powers. Your ruling planet, Jupiter, ensures that you are ambitious with big plans and a magnetic charm. You gain power from the mixture of your good social skills and original ideas; your capacity for hard work often aids your success. A taste for the good life can also stimulate your ambition. Although you are determined, resist being rigid in your plans or letting stubbornness undermine your great efforts. You usually fare better in life when you are sincere, direct, or maintain your freedom. The extremes of your nature imply that sometimes you can be sensitive, caring, and compassionate and other times you can be bossy or too tough. Fortunately, your idealism and honesty usually help you to let go of frustration when you become too serious. The combination of your generosity, genuine interest in people, and pragmatic approach to life blend well to help you overcome obstacles and achieve prosperity and emotional satisfaction.

Your Powers of Attraction in Relationships

As an idealist with deep feelings, you need some form of emotional expression, so love and relationships are especially important to you. You can attract others with your sincerity, natural charm, and sociability. You seek a partner with whom you can share adventures or someone who can be sensitive yet active and dynamic. Although you want to be responsible and establish a secure home base, another part of you becomes bored and restless if a relationship becomes too fixed and predictable. By valuing yourself and acting spontaneously, your confidence increases and your relationships become more successful. Being sensitive, you need to express your inner feelings and communicate your needs. Generous, kind, and giving, you are likely to have a large circle of friends and be a devoted spouse and parent.

Your attractive qualities: idealist, practical skills, ambitious, hardworking, popular, determined, endurance, generous, fair, faithful, frank, love of home, focused, active, energetic, natural business sense, creative, ability to overcome obstacles, loving

Your less attractive qualities: materialistic, restless, too strict, too outspoken, inertia, moody, disappointed, too serious, frustrated, too verbose, domineering, too opportunistic, stubborn

Your Venus Power

The planet Venus has a great deal of influence on your powers of attraction. Below are four possible Venus types for women and men. To find your Venus you need to go to page 771, where you will find the Venus table and extra information. The planet Mars also affects your powers of attraction. To find your Mars table and interpretation go to page 761.

WOMEN WITH VENUS IN LIBRA: A natural romantic with good social skills, you love to entertain and can put people at ease by projecting a warm and gracious manner. Elegant and fair with a touch of glamour, you are also adept at dealing with people in delicate situations or conflicts. You seek refinement and will go out of your way to achieve harmony and keep the peace. Relationships are so important to you that you may need to guard against becoming dependent on others for approval. With your friendly personality and inherent charm, however, you will always be popular and loved.

MEN WITH VENUS IN LIBRA: You are such good company, people are naturally drawn to you and especially appreciate your talent for making them feel special. You find status in your social contacts and place importance on your relationships. Being clever and a charming companion, you will go out of your way to keep situations peaceful and harmonious. In relationships, however, be careful of indecision or compromising too much. Nevertheless, others are attracted by your natural refinement and good taste, which is reflected in your sense of style.

WOMEN WITH VENUS IN SCORPIO: Loving and passionate, you are often sensitive with deep feelings and strong powers of attraction. A love for the truth coupled with a tendency to be suspicious can be an influence that motivates you to delve deep into the activities of your partner. When in love or in a relationship that matters, you will often bend over backward to cooperate. Although loyal, guard against losing sight of your own needs and desires

MEN WITH VENUS IN SCORPIO: As you are emotionally intense and passionate, personal relationships are probably a major factor in your own transformation. Being sensitive yet loyal, you are usually attracted to forceful partners who can express themselves intimately but intensely. Rather than seek easy and simple relationships, you are drawn to partners who act as a catalyst for your own internal changes. Through your relationships with your partners you can unravel your own motives and understand your deep-seated feelings or emotional insecurities.

WOMEN WITH VENUS IN SAGITTARIUS: Sociable, warm, and friendly, you possess an honest and frank style in your relationships. Being naturally gregarious, you want others to share your enthusiasm and enjoy encouraging the people you love. You fare better when you have a sense of personal freedom within a relationship and are usually generous with the faults of others. You need a partner who can share your need to explore and take risks whether through travel, education, or recreation.

MEN WITH VENUS IN SAGITTARIUS: When in love you are open and friendly with a need for a partner who can share your adventurous spirit and sense of fun. Be careful, however, that your desire for freedom does not cause you to avoid commitment. You prefer your partners to be positive, direct, and generous in spirit. Being outspoken as well as an idealist, you usually enjoy a partner with whom you can share your strong opinions. Alternatively, you may wish to explore life together, whether through travel, education, or having fun.

WOMEN WITH VENUS IN CAPRICORN: Loyal and responsible, you are attracted to dignified and reserved individuals. Being practical and security-conscious, you prefer hardworking partners who are resourceful and enterprising. Work may even be a factor in many of your associations and partnerships. For you, family and faithfulness can be especially important, so you are usually willing to work hard or make sacrifices in order to build a strong relationship.

MEN WITH VENUS IN CAPRICORN: You take love seriously and can be a strong and practical support for friends or partners. You are usually attracted to people who are as hardworking as yourself. As you tend not to express your feelings until you feel really secure in a relationship, you may be drawn to those who seem loyal, faithful, and not likely to let you down. As you respect the wisdom of experience, you may be drawn to mature partners or, alternatively, you may act as an authority figure for someone younger.

To read all about your Outer Planets and work out how to use your personalized timetable, go to Section Three, page 789.

♐

Your Personalized Timetable

JUPITER BENEFICIAL
1939 4/12 – until 1940 2/19
1942 10/13 – 12/12
1943 5/30 – 8/14
1944 12/21 – until 1945 2/2
1945 8/8 – 9/26
1949 3/20 – 7/24
1949 11/11 – until 1950 1/2
1951 3/25 – 6/11
1951 9/28 – until 1952 1/28
1954 9/12 – until 1955 1/24
1955 5/7 – 7/29
1956 11/18 – until 1957 3/18
1957 7/18 – 9/10
1961 2/26 – 5/9
1961 6/10 – 12/14
1963 3/9 – 5/17
1963 11/24 – 12/16
1966 8/23 – until 1967 7/13
1968 10/28 – until 1969 5/2
1969 6/13 – 8/24
1973 2/8 – 3/30
1973 8/3 – 11/21
1975 2/20 – 4/28
1978 8/6 – until 1979 6/25
1980 10/11 – 12/6
1981 3/16 – 8/4
1985 1/23 – 3/9
1987 2/3 – 4/12
1990 7/20 – 10/10
1991 1/20 – 6/5
1992 9/25 – 11/13
1993 4/25 – 7/8
1997 1/7 – 2/19
1998 5/25 – 9/10
1999 1/12 – 3/26
2002 7/4 – 9/17
2003 3/2 – 5/7
2004 9/10 – 10/27
2008 12/22 – until 2009 2/3
2010 4/30 – 11/7
2010 11/30 – until 2011 3/9

SATURN BENEFICIAL
1938 1/1 – 4/12
1945 10/1 – 12/12
1946 6/14 – until 1947 7/15
1950 10/19 – until 1951 4/20
1951 7/6 – 10/9
1961 3/6 – 7/16
1961 12/4 – until 1962 3/3
1962 8/19 – 11/28
1966 4/12 – 10/26
1966 12/27 – until 1967 5/27
1967 9/23 – until 1968 2/17
1975 7/25 – until 1976 8/23
1979 12/21 – until 1980 1/24
1980 8/25 – 11/19
1981 3/23 – 8/13
1991 1/10 – 5/6
1991 5/27 – until 1992 1/8
1995 6/1 – 8/10
1996 2/16 – until 1997 3/26
2004 9/4 – until 2005 1/15
2005 5/24 – 10/11
2006 1/3 – 6/27
2009 10/1 – until 2010 9/22

URANUS BENEFICIAL
1954 7/22 – until 1958 6/28
1967 10/20 – until 1970 8/23
1995 1/22 – until 1997 12/24
2009 4/2 – Continues

NEPTUNE BENEFICIAL
1940 10/31 – until 1946 8/16
1996 2/27 – until 2001 12/9

PLUTO BENEFICIAL
1938 1/1 – until 1946 5/30
1969 11/11 – until 1975 7/18

JUPITER CHALLENGING
1938 4/4 – 9/20
1938 11/16 – until 1939 2/12

1941 4/29 – 7/8
1943 10/28 – until 1944 1/30
1944 6/22 – 9/9
1950 3/15 – until 1951 1/25
1953 4/12 – 6/20
1955 10/4 – until 1956 3/9
1956 5/26 – 8/24
1962 2/26 – 5/19
1962 8/15 – until 1963 1/5
1964 8/7 – 10/23
1965 3/23 – 6/4
1967 9/16 – until 1968 8/8
1974 2/10 – 4/22
1974 10/1 – 12/6
1976 7/9 – 12/6
1977 2/24 – 5/18
1979 8/30 – 12/9
1980 1/12 – 7/22
1986 1/25 – 4/3
1988 6/20 – until 1989 5/1
1991 8/14 – 11/2
1992 2/28 – 7/1
1998 1/8 – 3/17
2000 6/2 – 8/30
2000 10/29 – until 2001 4/12
2003 7/29 – 10/13
2004 4/11 – 5/28
2009 4/29 – 8/1
2009 12/18 – until 2010 2/28
2012 5/16 – Continues

SATURN CHALLENGING
1941 6/24 – 12/4
1942 3/12 – 7/30
1942 11/23 – until 1943 4/17
1948 7/31 – until 1949 9/3
1964 1/30 – until 1965 3/16
1971 4/30 – until 1972 5/29
1977 9/8 – until 1978 4/15
1978 5/5 – 10/14
1979 3/11 – 7/5
1993 3/5 – 10/17
1993 11/8 – until 1994 4/25
1994 8/22 – until 1995 1/19
2000 6/5 – until 2001 7/8
2001 12/25 – until 2002 3/23
2006 10/29 – until 2007 1/13
2007 7/14 – until 2008 8/17

URANUS CHALLENGING
1940 6/13 – until 1945 3/26
1960 9/22 – until 1964 8/22
2001 4/7 – until 2006 2/12

NEPTUNE CHALLENGING
2008 4/13 – Continues

PLUTO CHALLENGING
1953 9/11 – until 1963 6/19

JUPITER SPECIAL
1947 1/22 – 5/6
1947 9/20 – 12/7
1958 12/30 – until 1959 6/17
1959 8/22 – 11/21
1970 12/12 – until 1971 11/5
1982 11/26 – until 1983 2/28
1983 4/24 – 10/18
1994 11/11 – until 1995 1/28
1995 6/7 – 9/26
2006 10/26 – until 2007 1/8

SATURN SPECIAL
1955 11/16 – until 1957 1/5
1957 6/19 – 10/2
1984 12/22 – until 1985 5/30
1985 9/18 – until 1986 11/13

URANUS SPECIAL
1979 12/26 – until 1984 9/9

NEPTUNE SPECIAL
1967 1/9 – until 1975 10/13

PLUTO SPECIAL
1992 12/7 – until 1999 11/17

November 25

SUN: SAGITTARIUS • DECANATE: SAGITTARIUS/ JUPITER • DEGREE: 2°5–3°5 SAGITTARIUS • MODE: MUTABLE • ELEMENT: FIRE

Your Personal Powers

Proud with strong convictions, you are an individual with dynamic energy, strong instincts, and endurance. Your ruling planet, Jupiter, grants you organizational skills and the ability to think broadly. You gain power by combining your determination, natural business sense, and good social skills. Honest and direct, your interesting mixture of skepticism and sincerity implies that you can be outspoken, but avoid losing power by becoming tactless or critical. With a flair for the dramatic, it is important that you channel your powerful emotions into some creative endeavors. Your natural idealism or moral sense often seeks, sometimes unconsciously, higher inspiration. Being sociable, you need people as an appreciative audience and you can achieve much by using your persuasive charm. Although you are usually practical and down-to-earth with a friendly personality, you can lose some of your power to lack of inner faith or by appearing cold and withdrawn. Naturally philanthropic and idealistic, you excel when you fight to support a cause or protect others.

Your Powers of Attraction in Relationships

You can attract others with your emotional power and strong individuality. Being sensitive and intuitive, you can be kind and thoughtful, but prospective partners need to understand that you also need time for yourself to rest and reflect. Possessing both practical and social skills, you have the ability to combine business with pleasure. You are attracted to hardworking individuals who can provide you with the security and the peace that you desire. In relationships you may go from being quiet and introspective to being spontaneous, entertaining, and extroverted. If you express your deep feelings and resist moodiness or power plays with partners, you can channel your strong emotions into inspiring them. Nevertheless, your fighting spirit and strong loyalty ensure that you stand by your loved ones.

Your attractive qualities: proud, strong-willed, idealistic, honest, good social skills, highly intuitive, dedicated, frank, high aims, perfectionist, visionary, perceptive, creative mind, daring, determined, popular, focused, endurance, sincere, spiritual potential, hardworking

Your less attractive qualities: impulsive, impatient, irresponsible, too emotional, jealous, secretive, too competitive, materialistic, too outspoken, critical, moody

Your Venus Power

The planet Venus has a great deal of influence on your powers of attraction. Below are four possible Venus types for women and men. To find your Venus you need to go to page 771, where you will find the Venus table and extra information. The planet Mars also affects your powers of attraction. To find your Mars table and interpretation go to page 761.

WOMEN WITH VENUS IN LIBRA: A natural romantic with good social skills, you love to entertain and can put people at ease by projecting a warm and gracious manner. Elegant and fair with a touch of glamour, you are also adept at dealing with people in delicate situations or conflicts. You seek refinement and will go out of your way to achieve harmony and keep the peace. Relationships are so important to you that you may need to guard against becoming dependent on others for approval. With your friendly personality and inherent charm, however, you will always be popular and loved.

MEN WITH VENUS IN LIBRA: As a sociable and friendly individual with an eye for beauty, you are amorous and charming. You are a natural gentleman and your ideal partner usually has an elegant appearance, artistic appreciation, and good taste. Your relationships benefit when you resist the temptation to take the easy way out or put too much emphasis on vanity and high living. Intellectual and naturally refined, you seek a loving partner who can share your romantic and sophisticated aspirations.

WOMEN WITH VENUS IN SCORPIO: You are usually drawn to partners who are sensual in appearance with a strong character. As you are emotionally intense and passionate, personal relationships are probably a major factor in your life. Since you like to be in control, you can at times exhibit some of your less attractive qualities by being willful or domineering. Although you need to feel established and in command in your relationships, you are constantly searching for some higher truth that can bring significant transformation.

MEN WITH VENUS IN SCORPIO: You are usually attracted to sensual and passionate partners with strong character. You are often sensitive with deep feelings and magnetic powers of attraction. As a cautious yet devoted and ardent lover, you are likely to seek experiences that are more sexual in their nature. You display your less attractive qualities when you project negative thoughts and resort to being suspicious or possessive. Nevertheless, loyal and loving, you are a sensitive lover.

WOMEN WITH VENUS IN SAGITTARIUS: At your best

when being optimistic and generous, you possess a mischievous sense of fun. In relationships your open-minded approach to people and places may attract you to those of a different culture or make you tolerant of the foibles of others. Although warm and enthusiastic when in love, your natural honesty and idealism may inspire you to look for a partner who shares your love of freedom.

MEN WITH VENUS IN SAGITTARIUS: Forward-thinking rather than dwelling on the past, you are looking for a partner who can share your future plans. You enjoy exploring life whether through travel and mental pursuits or sports and games. Idealistic, you usually prefer the company of a partner who is optimistic and shares your beliefs. In your desire for honesty in relationships, however, be careful not to become tactless. Nevertheless, you are attracted to honest, direct, and fun-loving partners who have a sense of humor like your own.

WOMEN WITH VENUS IN CAPRICORN: With your natural caution in romantic affairs, you often appear reserved and controlled. If shy, try to be more forward, especially if you want to be noticed. When you care about people, however, you are usually willing to put in extra time and energy to preserve the relationship. You are practical and dependable, and a sense of duty can often play a large role in the affairs of your heart. With elegant simplicity, you can attract others with your well-cut clothes and refined manners.

MEN WITH VENUS IN CAPRICORN: As you admire loyal, hardworking, and dedicated individuals, you probably want a partner who can share your vocational interests or who can provide you with the sense of security you need. You could even find yourself with a partner who is of a different age group or maturity. Guard against denying your true emotional needs or focusing on your career at the expense of your relationship. You are drawn to reserved partners who display self-control.

To read all about your Outer Planets and work out how to use your personalized timetable, go to Section Three, page 789.

Your Personalized Timetable

JUPITER BENEFICIAL
1938 1/1 – until 1940 2/24
1942 10/26 – 11/29
1943 6/5 – 8/19
1945 8/13 – 10/1
1949 3/26 – 7/16
1949 11/18 – until 1950 1/6
1951 3/30 – 6/18
1951 9/20 – until 1952 2/3
1954 9/18 – until 1955 1/16
1955 5/14 – 8/2
1956 11/24 – until 1957 3/10
1957 7/24 – 9/15
1961 3/3 – 9/7
1961 10/10 – 12/19
1963 3/13 – 5/22
1963 11/8 – until 1964 1/1
1966 8/28 – until 1967 3/7
1967 4/4 – 7/17
1968 11/3 – until 1969 4/19
1969 6/26 – 8/29
1973 2/13 – 4/6
1973 7/26 – 11/27
1975 2/24 – 5/3
1978 8/10 – until 1979 6/30
1980 10/16 – 12/14
1981 3/7 – 8/10
1985 1/28 – 3/14
1985 9/13 – 10/23
1987 2/7 – 4/16
1990 7/25 – 10/18
1991 1/12 – 6/11
1992 9/30 – 11/19
1993 4/15 – 7/17
1997 1/12 – 2/24
1998 6/1 – 9/3
1999 1/18 – 3/30
2002 7/9 – 9/23
2003 2/20 – 5/16
2004 9/14 – 11/1
2008 12/26 – until 2009 2/7
2010 5/6 – 10/22
2010 12/16 – until 2011 3/13

SATURN BENEFICIAL
1938 1/1 – 4/20
1945 10/25 – 11/18
1946 6/22 – until 1947 7/23
1950 10/28 – until 1951 4/5
1951 7/20 – 10/18
1961 3/19 – 7/2
1961 12/14 – until 1962 3/13
1962 8/4 – 12/10
1966 4/21 – 10/9
1967 1/11 – 6/9
1967 9/9 – until 1968 2/27
1975 8/2 – until 1976 9/1
1977 3/12 – 5/11
1980 9/3 – 12/1
1981 3/9 – 8/23
1991 1/18 – until 1992 1/17
1996 2/24 – until 1997 4/4
2004 9/14 – until 2005 1/3
2005 6/3 – 10/29
2005 12/16 – until 2006 7/5
2009 10/10 – until 2010 10/1

URANUS BENEFICIAL
1954 8/8 – until 1958 7/15
1967 11/8 – until 1970 9/9
1995 2/9 – until 1998 1/12
2009 4/21 – Continues

NEPTUNE BENEFICIAL
1941 9/29 – until 1946 9/15
1997 1/25 – until 2002 1/9

PLUTO BENEFICIAL
1938 1/1 – until 1946 7/13
1970 10/5 – until 1975 8/26

JUPITER CHALLENGING
1938 4/9 – 9/10
1938 11/26 – until 1939 2/16
1941 5/4 – 7/13

1943 11/5 – until 1944 1/21
1944 6/28 – 9/14
1950 3/20 – until 1951 1/30
1953 4/16 – 6/25
1955 10/10 – until 1956 3/1
1956 6/4 – 8/29
1962 3/2 – 5/28
1962 8/6 – until 1963 1/10
1964 8/16 – 10/13
1965 3/28 – 6/8
1967 9/21 – until 1968 8/13
1974 2/14 – 4/28
1974 9/22 – 12/14
1976 7/15 – 11/28
1977 3/3 – 5/23
1979 9/4 – until 1980 7/27
1986 1/29 – 4/8
1988 6/24 – until 1989 5/6
1991 8/19 – 11/9
1992 2/20 – 7/7
1998 1/12 – 3/21
2000 6/6 – 9/12
2000 10/16 – until 2001 4/17
2003 8/3 – 10/18
2004 3/30 – 6/9
2009 5/8 – 7/23
2009 12/23 – until 2010 3/4
2012 5/20 – Continues

SATURN CHALLENGING
1941 7/4 – 11/21
1942 3/24 – 8/11
1942 11/9 – until 1943 4/26
1948 8/8 – until 1949 9/11
1964 2/8 – until 1965 3/24
1965 10/27 – 12/1
1971 5/8 – until 1972 6/6
1977 9/17 – until 1978 3/20
1978 5/31 – 10/24
1979 2/27 – 7/16
1993 3/14 – 9/20
1993 12/3 – until 1994 5/8
1994 8/8 – until 1995 1/29
2000 6/14 – 12/28
2001 2/21 – 7/17
2001 12/12 – until 2002 4/4
2006 11/18 – 12/24
2007 7/22 – until 2008 8/25

URANUS CHALLENGING
1940 7/3 – until 1945 4/20
1960 10/14 – until 1965 5/30
2001 5/16 – until 2006 3/2

NEPTUNE CHALLENGING
2009 3/6 – Continues

PLUTO CHALLENGING
1953 10/25 – until 1963 8/1

JUPITER SPECIAL
1947 1/30 – 4/27
1947 9/26 – 12/12
1959 1/5 – 6/7
1959 9/1 – 11/26
1970 12/17 – until 1971 11/10
1982 12/1 – until 1983 3/18
1983 4/6 – 10/23
1994 11/15 – until 1995 2/3
1995 5/30 – 10/2
2006 10/31 – until 2007 1/13
2007 7/14 – 8/30

SATURN SPECIAL
1955 11/25 – until 1957 1/15
1957 6/5 – 10/14
1985 1/1 – 5/16
1985 9/29 – until 1986 11/22

URANUS SPECIAL
1980 1/17 – until 1984 10/11

NEPTUNE SPECIAL
1967 12/5 – until 1975 11/14

PLUTO SPECIAL
1993 1/6 – until 2000 10/7

519

November 26

SUN: SAGITTARIUS • DECANATE: SAGITTARIUS/JUPITER • DEGREE: 3°5–4°5 SAGITTARIUS • MODE: MUTABLE • ELEMENT: FIRE

Your Personal Powers

Possessing a keen analytical mind and strong imagination, you are a creative thinker with a pragmatic approach to life. Your ruling planet, Jupiter, ensures that you have an enterprising nature and a desire for honesty. You gain power when you utilize your problem-solving skills in business and display your natural executive ability. Alternatively, with your sense of responsibility and love of home, you may be an adviser and support for family and friends. In your desire to help, however, be careful of losing power by interfering or being too bossy. Nevertheless, you are also sensitive and intuitive, and benefit most when you have enough faith in your own abilities to be truly spontaneous. By keeping a positive perspective, you are able to direct your powerful emotions and resist being skeptical or withdrawn. You can particularly benefit from initiating new projects, seeking spiritual inspiration, or expanding your mental horizons. Being a person with high ideals means that if you channel your creativity, you can easily inspire others with your special talents.

Your Powers of Attraction in Relationships

Clever and imaginative, you can attract others with your charming manner and sociable personality. Others appreciate your inner power and unique approach to life. You are usually attracted to quick-thinking individuals who stimulate your sense of adventure and your enjoyment of new experiences. Nevertheless, in relationships, you may have to deal with issues concerning restlessness and impatience or feelings of isolation. Your partners have to understand that you may need periods alone for contemplation and self-analysis. With your special blend of idealism and skepticism, you can be generous, affectionate, and loving yet reserved. Usually dependable and responsible, you need a partner who can share your desire for a secure home but who also enjoys freedom, whether in the mind or through travel.

Your attractive qualities: creative, intelligent, sensitive, practical, charming, idealistic, caring, supportive, ambitious, spontaneous, faithful, inspired, humanitarian, responsible, loyal, family-oriented, business sense, honorable, sincere, enthusiastic, determined, courageous

Your less attractive qualities: stubborn, rebellious, skeptical, materialistic, controlling, critical, bored, cold, lonely, lack of faith, bossy, interfering, too perfectionist, unenthusiastic, moody, self-doubt, suspicious

Your Venus Power

The planet Venus has a great deal of influence on your powers of attraction. Below are four possible Venus types for women and men. To find your Venus you need to go to page 771, where you will find the Venus table and extra information. The planet Mars also affects your powers of attraction. To find your Mars table and interpretation go to page 761.

WOMEN WITH VENUS IN LIBRA: Gracious, charming, and sociable with a sense of style, you have no trouble drawing admirers. With your natural diplomatic skills and desire for harmony you usually like to keep the peace and avoid confrontations, but be careful of failing to take a stand when it is necessary. Romantic and easygoing yourself, you are attracted to affectionate and refined individuals who share your love of peace, justice, and fair play.

MEN WITH VENUS IN LIBRA: You are such good company, people are naturally drawn to you and especially appreciate your talent for making them feel special. You find status in your social contacts and place importance on your relationships. Being clever and a charming companion, you will go out of your way to keep situations peaceful and harmonious. In relationships, however, be careful of indecision or compromising too much. Nevertheless, others are attracted by your natural refinement and good taste, which is reflected in your sense of style.

WOMEN WITH VENUS IN SCORPIO: Loving and passionate, you are often sensitive with deep feelings and strong powers of attraction. A love for the truth coupled with a tendency to be suspicious can be an influence that motivates you to delve deep into the activities of your partner. When in love or in a relationship that matters, you will often bend over backward to cooperate. Although loyal, guard against losing sight of your own needs and desires.

MEN WITH VENUS IN SCORPIO: You are usually attracted to sensual and passionate partners with strong character. You are often sensitive with deep feelings and magnetic powers of attraction. As a cautious yet devoted and ardent lover, you are likely to seek experiences that are more sexual in their nature. You display your less attractive qualities when you project your negative thoughts and resort to being suspicious or

possessive. Nevertheless, loyal and loving, you are a sensitive lover.

WOMEN WITH VENUS IN SAGITTARIUS: Sociable, warm, and friendly, you possess an honest and frank style in your relationships. Being naturally gregarious, you want others to share your enthusiasm and enjoy encouraging the people you love. You fare better when you have a sense of personal freedom within a relationship and are usually generous with the faults of others. You need a partner who can share your need to explore and take risks, whether through travel, education, or recreation.

MEN WITH VENUS IN SAGITTARIUS: You are usually attracted to partners who are knowledgeable or well-traveled. Enthusiastic and optimistic, you often respond quickly to love offers and enter relationships with enthusiasm. Usually you seek to expand your social circle and meeting people from all walks of life can bring you the variety and fun you seek in life. Although you are generous and honest, your partners may accuse you of being overly optimistic or too blunt.

WOMEN WITH VENUS IN CAPRICORN: With your natural caution in romantic affairs, you often appear reserved and controlled. If shy, try to be more forward, especially if you want to be noticed. When you care about people, however, you are usually willing to put in extra time and energy to preserve the relationship. You are practical and dependable, and a sense of duty can often play a large role in the affairs of your heart. With elegant simplicity, you can attract others with your well-cut clothes and refined manners.

MEN WITH VENUS IN CAPRICORN: As you do not display your deeper emotions freely, you are usually dignified and controlled in your relationships with others. Practical and down-to-earth partners are particularly attractive to you, especially those who do not rush into expressing their feelings but seem to possess natural class and reserve. You need a partner who is loyal and dependable and willing to take your relationship seriously.

To read all about your Outer Planets and work out how to use your personalized timetable, go to Section Three, page 789.

Your Personalized Timetable

JUPITER BENEFICIAL
1938 1/1 – 1/27
1939 4/21 – until **1940** 2/29
1943 6/10 – 8/23
1945 8/19 – 10/5
1949 4/2 – 7/8
1949 11/24 – until **1950** 1/10
1951 4/3 – 6/26
1951 9/12 – until **1952** 2/8
1954 9/25 – until **1955** 1/9
1955 5/20 – 8/7
1956 12/2 – until **1957** 3/2
1957 7/31 – 9/20
1961 3/8 – 8/24
1961 10/23 – 12/24
1963 3/17 – 5/28
1963 10/29 – until **1964** 1/10
1966 9/2 – until **1967** 2/20
1967 4/19 – 7/22
1968 11/8 – until **1969** 4/10
1969 7/5 – 9/3
1973 2/17 – 4/13
1973 7/18 – 12/3
1975 3/1 – 5/7
1978 8/15 – until **1979** 7/5
1980 10/21 – 12/23
1981 2/26 – 8/16
1985 2/1 – 3/19
1985 9/1 – 11/4
1987 2/12 – 4/20
1990 7/29 – 10/27
1991 1/3 – 6/17
1992 10/4 – 11/25
1993 4/7 – 7/25
1997 1/16 – 2/28
1998 6/9 – 8/25
1999 1/23 – 4/4
2002 7/13 – 9/29
2003 2/12 – 5/24
2004 9/19 – 11/6
2008 12/31 – until **2009** 2/11
2010 5/11 – 10/12
2010 12/25 – until **2011** 3/18

SATURN BENEFICIAL
1938 1/1 – 4/29
1938 11/20 – until **1939** 1/8
1946 6/30 – until **1947** 7/31
1950 11/7 – until **1951** 3/23
1951 8/1 – 10/26
1952 5/15 – 7/6
1961 4/3 – 6/16
1961 12/23 – until **1962** 3/24
1962 7/22 – 12/20
1966 5/1 – 9/26
1967 1/23 – 6/26
1967 8/23 – until **1968** 3/7
1975 8/10 – until **1976** 9/9
1977 2/23 – 5/27
1980 9/11 – 12/15
1981 2/22 – 9/2
1991 1/27 – until **1992** 1/26
1996 3/4 – until **1997** 4/12
2004 9/27 – 12/20
2005 6/12 – until **2006** 7/14
2009 10/18 – until **2010** 4/27
2010 7/3 – 10/9

URANUS BENEFICIAL
1954 8/27 – until **1958** 8/1
1967 12/4 – until **1970** 9/26
1995 2/28 – until **1998** 1/30
2009 5/15 – Continues

NEPTUNE BENEFICIAL
1941 10/28 – until **1947** 8/12
1997 2/23 – until **2002** 12/5

PLUTO BENEFICIAL
1938 1/1 – until **1947** 6/24
1970 11/4 – until **1975** 9/23

JUPITER CHALLENGING
1938 4/15 – 9/1
1938 12/4 – until **1939** 2/21

1941 5/8 – 7/18
1942 1/21 – 2/20
1943 11/15 – until **1944** 1/11
1944 7/4 – 9/19
1950 3/25 – until **1951** 2/3
1953 4/21 – 6/29
1955 10/16 – until **1956** 2/22
1956 6/11 – 9/3
1962 3/7 – 6/8
1962 7/26 – until **1963** 1/15
1964 8/31 – 9/29
1965 4/2 – 6/12
1967 9/26 – until **1968** 8/18
1974 2/18 – 5/3
1974 9/14 – 12/22
1976 7/21 – 11/20
1977 3/10 – 5/27
1979 9/8 – until **1980** 8/1
1986 2/3 – 4/12
1988 6/29 – until **1989** 5/11
1991 8/23 – 11/17
1992 2/12 – 7/13
1998 1/17 – 3/25
2000 6/10 – until **2001** 4/22
2003 8/8 – 10/24
2004 3/21 – 6/18
2009 5/18 – 7/13
2009 12/29 – until **2010** 3/8
2012 5/24 – Continues

SATURN CHALLENGING
1941 7/15 – 11/9
1942 4/3 – 8/27
1942 10/24 – until **1943** 5/5
1948 8/16 – until **1949** 9/20
1964 2/16 – until **1965** 4/2
1965 10/5 – 12/22
1971 5/16 – until **1972** 6/14
1977 9/26 – until **1978** 3/5
1978 6/14 – 11/5
1979 2/14 – 7/26
1993 3/23 – 9/5
1993 12/17 – until **1994** 5/26
1994 7/21 – until **1995** 2/7
2000 6/23 – 12/11
2001 3/9 – 7/27
2001 11/30 – until **2002** 4/15
2007 7/31 – until **2008** 9/2

URANUS CHALLENGING
1940 8/2 – until **1945** 5/10
1960 11/22 – until **1965** 7/7
2002 3/2 – until **2007** 1/7

NEPTUNE CHALLENGING
2009 4/7 – Continues

PLUTO CHALLENGING
1954 9/22 – until **1964** 6/18

JUPITER SPECIAL
1947 2/8 – 4/18
1947 10/2 – 12/16
1959 1/11 – 5/29
1959 9/9 – 11/30
1970 12/22 – until **1971** 11/14
1982 12/5 – until **1983** 10/28
1994 11/20 – until **1995** 2/10
1995 5/22 – 10/9
2006 11/5 – until **2007** 1/19
2007 7/2 – 9/11

SATURN SPECIAL
1955 12/3 – until **1957** 1/26
1957 5/22 – 10/25
1985 1/12 – 5/3
1985 10/10 – until **1986** 12/1

URANUS SPECIAL
1980 11/16 – until **1984** 11/1

NEPTUNE SPECIAL
1968 1/5 – until **1976** 10/8

PLUTO SPECIAL
1993 11/26 – until **2000** 11/9

November 27

SUN: SAGITTARIUS • DECANATE: SAGITTARIUS/JUPITER • DEGREE: 4°5–5°5 SAGITTARIUS • MODE: MUTABLE • ELEMENT: FIRE

Your Personal Powers

Intelligent and idealistic, you are a friendly and charming individual with an engaging personality. Honest and direct, you possess a strong enterprising streak. Although you are usually ruled by your feelings, your fast mind is constantly thinking new and original thoughts. You gain power by combining your strong intuition, good communication skills, and common sense. Usually full of ideas and plans, you like to keep active and communicate with others. Nevertheless there is a part of you that yearns for peace and tranquillity. This side of your personality emphasizes the importance of finding time alone for reflection and of having a harmonious home environment. Although your inventive mind can assimilate information very quickly, you lose some of your power if you become impatient with or intolerant of those less able. Working cooperatively with others in a team or in a working partnership, however, may prove particularly beneficial for you. Through disciple and self-expression you can successfully manifest your many wonderful creative ideas.

Your Powers of Attraction in Relationships

Sociable and idealistic, you can attract others with your generosity and liberal approach. Equally, your original ideas and ability to give to others in the way of love and friendship can draw friends and admirers. You work well with people and usually find that your natural skill for making contacts can help your overall success. You need a partner who understands the two sides to your nature: on one hand you seek peace, harmony, and a secure environment, while on the other, you seek change and adventure. Extremely sensitive to the emotions and needs of others, you possess true compassion and deep feelings. In close relationships, you may need to resist dramatic situations. Nevertheless, you usually fare better in partnerships or in team situations than you do on your own.

Your attractive qualities: versatile, original, imaginative, affectionate, creative, resolute, brave, good understanding, idealistic, charismatic, talented, sensitive, fine mind, spiritual aspirations, inventive, mental strength, endurance, hardworking, dedication, kindhearted

Your less attractive qualities: impatient, disagreeable, argumentative, restless, inner tensions, materialistic, intolerant, nervous, too outspoken, critical, mistrusting, interfering, bossy, inertia, overemotional, restless

Your Venus Power

The planet Venus has a great deal of influence on your powers of attraction. Below are four possible Venus types for women and men. To find your Venus you need to go to page 771, where you will find the Venus table and extra information. The planet Mars also affects your powers of attraction. To find your Mars table and interpretation go to page 761.

WOMEN WITH VENUS IN LIBRA: A natural romantic with good social skills, you love to entertain and can put people at ease by projecting a warm and gracious manner. Elegant and fair with a touch of glamour, you are also adept at dealing with people in delicate situations or conflicts. You seek refinement and will go out of your way to achieve harmony and keep the peace. For you, relationships are so important that you may need to guard against becoming dependent on others for approval. With your friendly personality and inherent charm, however, you will always be popular and loved.

MEN WITH VENUS IN LIBRA: As a sociable and friendly individual with an eye for beauty, you are amorous and charming. You are a natural gentleman, and your ideal partner usually has an elegant appearance, artistic appreciation, and good taste. Your relationships benefit when you resist the temptation to take the easy way out or put too much emphasis on vanity and high living. Intellectual and naturally refined, you seek a loving partner who can share your romantic and sophisticated aspirations.

WOMEN WITH VENUS IN SCORPIO: You are usually drawn to partners who are sensual in appearance with a strong character. As you are emotionally intense and passionate, personal relationships are probably a major factor in your life. Since you like to be in control, you can at times exhibit some of your less attractive qualities by being willful or domineering. Although you need to feel established and in command in your relationships, you are constantly searching for some higher truth that can bring about a significant transformation.

MEN WITH VENUS IN SCORPIO: As you are emotionally intense and passionate, personal relationships are probably a major factor in your own transformation. Being sensitive yet loyal, you are usually attracted to forceful partners who can express themselves intimately but intensely. Rather than seek easy

and simple relationships, you are drawn to partners who act as a catalyst for your own internal changes. Through your relationships with your partners you can unravel your own motives and understand your deep-seated feelings or emotional insecurities.

WOMEN WITH VENUS IN SAGITTARIUS: Optimistic and fun-loving, you love adventure and seek a partner who can expand your horizons. Being truthful and direct, you often say what you think, and at times you may be naively tactless. A need for expansion and prosperity suggests that you may enjoy traveling with your friends or partner. Being both light-hearted and idealistic means that once you have given your heart to someone, you will stay honorable and loyal.

MEN WITH VENUS IN SAGITTARIUS: When in love you are open and friendly with a need for a partner who can share your adventurous spirit and sense of fun. Be careful, however, that your desire for freedom does not cause you to avoid commitment. You prefer your partners to be positive, direct, and generous in spirit. Being outspoken as well as an idealist, you usually enjoy a partner with whom you can share your strong opinions. Alternatively, you may wish to explore life together, whether through travel, education, or having fun.

WOMEN WITH VENUS IN CAPRICORN: Proud and refined, you attract others with your composed dignity. Disliking vulnerability and needing to feel safe before you can express your feelings, you usually display a strong front. Feeling insecure or inadequate in relationships may force you to become manipulative in order to regain control. Nevertheless, you can project an attractive sense of self-assurance and are capable of displaying loyalty and a wonderful dry sense of humor.

MEN WITH VENUS IN CAPRICORN: Hardworking and ambitious, you are usually attracted to determined, focused, and ambitious partners with a strong sense of duty. You want them to take relationships as seriously as you do, so loyalty and faithfulness are high on your agenda. Since you may display a natural reserve about expressing your feelings in an intimate relationship, you need a partner who shares your need for emotional security.

To read all about your Outer Planets and work out how to use your personalized timetable, go to Section Three, page 789.

♐

Your Personalized Timetable

JUPITER BENEFICIAL
1938 1/1 – 1/31
1939 4/26 – until 1940 3/4
1943 6/15 – 8/28
1945 8/24 – 10/10
1949 4/11 – 6/29
1949 11/29 – until 1950 1/15
1951 4/7 – 7/5
1951 9/2 – until 1952 2/13
1954 10/2 – until 1955 1/1
1955 5/26 – 8/12
1956 12/11 – until 1957 2/21
1957 8/5 – 9/24
1961 3/14 – 8/14
1961 11/2 – 12/28
1963 3/21 – 6/2
1963 10/21 – until 1964 1/18
1966 9/8 – until 1967 2/10
1967 4/29 – 7/27
1968 11/14 – until 1969 4/1
1969 7/13 – 9/8
1973 2/22 – 4/21
1973 7/9 – 12/9
1975 3/5 – 5/12
1978 8/20 – until 1979 7/10
1980 10/26 – until 1981 1/5
1981 2/13 – 8/22
1985 2/5 – 3/25
1985 8/22 – 11/13
1987 2/16 – 4/25
1990 8/3 – 11/7
1990 12/22 – until 1991 6/22
1992 10/9 – 12/1
1993 3/30 – 8/1
1997 1/20 – 3/5
1998 6/19 – 8/15
1999 1/28 – 4/8
2002 7/18 – 10/5
2003 2/4 – 6/1
2004 9/24 – 11/11
2005 5/12 – 6/29
2009 1/4 – 2/16
2010 5/16 – 10/3
2011 1/2 – 3/22

SATURN BENEFICIAL
1938 1/1 – 5/8
1938 11/1 – until 1939 1/25
1946 7/8 – until 1947 8/8
1950 11/18 – until 1951 3/10
1951 8/11 – 11/4
1952 4/26 – 7/24
1961 4/30 – 5/18
1962 1/1 – 4/6
1962 7/7 – 12/30
1966 5/11 – 9/12
1967 2/3 – until 1968 3/15
1975 8/18 – until 1976 2/27
1976 4/25 – 9/19
1977 2/10 – 6/8
1980 9/19 – until 1981 9/10
1991 2/4 – until 1992 2/3
1996 3/12 – until 1997 4/20
2004 10/14 – 12/2
2005 6/20 – until 2006 7/22
2009 10/27 – until 2010 4/10
2010 7/18 – 10/17

URANUS BENEFICIAL
1954 9/18 – until 1959 5/25
1968 9/25 – until 1971 7/15
1995 3/25 – until 1998 12/6
2010 3/21 – Continues

NEPTUNE BENEFICIAL
1941 12/14 – until 1947 9/13
1997 4/7 – until 2003 1/7

PLUTO BENEFICIAL
1938 1/1 – until 1948 5/26
1971 9/29 – until 1976 8/14

JUPITER CHALLENGING
1938 4/21 – 8/24
1938 12/11 – until 1939 2/25

1941 5/12 – 7/23
1942 1/7 – 3/6
1943 11/30 – 12/26
1944 7/9 – 9/23
1950 3/30 – until 1951 2/8
1953 4/25 – 7/4
1955 10/22 – until 1956 2/14
1956 6/18 – 9/7
1962 3/11 – until 1963 1/20
1965 4/7 – 6/17
1967 10/1 – until 1968 3/28
1968 5/17 – 8/23
1974 2/22 – 5/10
1974 9/6 – 12/28
1976 7/27 – 11/13
1977 3/17 – 5/31
1979 9/13 – until 1980 8/6
1986 2/7 – 4/17
1988 7/4 – 12/31
1989 2/9 – 5/15
1991 8/28 – 11/26
1992 2/3 – 7/19
1998 1/21 – 3/30
2000 6/15 – until 2001 4/27
2003 8/12 – 10/30
2004 3/13 – 6/26
2009 6/3 – 6/26
2010 1/3 – 3/13
2012 5/28 – Continues

SATURN CHALLENGING
1941 7/27 – 10/26
1942 4/12 – until 1943 5/13
1948 8/24 – until 1949 9/28
1950 4/30 – 5/30
1964 2/25 – until 1965 4/12
1965 9/20 – until 1966 1/5
1971 5/24 – until 1972 6/22
1977 10/5 – until 1978 2/20
1978 6/26 – 11/19
1979 1/30 – 8/4
1993 4/2 – 8/22
1993 12/29 – until 1995 2/15
2000 7/2 – 11/28
2001 3/21 – 8/7
2001 11/17 – until 2002 4/24
2007 8/8 – until 2008 9/11

URANUS CHALLENGING
1941 5/27 – until 1945 5/27
1961 8/29 – until 1965 7/29
2002 3/21 – until 2007 1/30

NEPTUNE CHALLENGING
2010 3/3 – Continues

PLUTO CHALLENGING
1954 11/21 – until 1964 8/1

JUPITER SPECIAL
1947 2/20 – 4/5
1947 10/7 – 12/21
1959 1/17 – 5/21
1959 9/16 – 12/5
1970 12/27 – until 1971 7/13
1971 8/4 – 11/19
1982 12/10 – until 1983 11/2
1994 11/24 – until 1995 2/18
1995 5/13 – 10/14
2006 11/9 – until 2007 1/24
2007 6/23 – 9/20

SATURN SPECIAL
1955 12/12 – until 1956 7/2
1956 8/27 – until 1957 2/8
1957 5/7 – 11/4
1985 1/26 – 4/17
1985 10/20 – until 1986 12/9

URANUS SPECIAL
1980 12/3 – until 1984 11/19

NEPTUNE SPECIAL
1968 12/2 – until 1976 11/11

PLUTO SPECIAL
1993 12/23 – until 2001 9/22

523

November 28

Your Personal Powers

Among your many personal powers are generosity, intelligence, and quick perception as well as honesty, directness, and inspiration. Your ruling planet, Jupiter, implies that you have grand dreams and an expansive personality. You gain power from the display of your warmth, benevolence, and good social skills. With your strong convictions and desire for truth, you may sometimes be accused of being too outspoken. Although you possess a strong desire for new experiences, be careful that you do not lose power by becoming bored, restless, or impatient. Your gregarious and congenial personality, however, makes you a witty and entertaining companion. Being adventurous, you are likely to constantly look for exciting interests to keep your active mind positively focused. As an ambitious person, you usually aim high, yet wanting the best can cause you to be dissatisfied with what you already have. With your philosophical attitude to life, inspiration, and your desire for knowledge, you can explore metaphysical subjects or search for creative self-expression, truth, and noble aspirations.

Your Powers of Attraction in Relationships

Adaptable and cooperative, you attract others with your friendliness. Being creative and imaginative, you can be sensitive and affectionate. If you repress your feelings, however, you become frustrated or dissatisfied. Romantic and idealistic, you are attracted to creative and sociable individuals. Astute and with quick instincts, you are also drawn to intelligent people with knowledge and insight. If you become emotionally insecure, you can stabilize your relationships by avoiding indecision or jealousy. When your strong emotions are channeled positively, you are happy and entertaining with an ability to lift the spirits of others. Avoid restlessness in your relationships by ensuring that you have plenty of variety in your life—plan weekend breaks or exciting adventures with your partner. Although you are independent, you gain from partnerships or teamwork situations.

Your attractive qualities: compassion, enthusiasm, adventurous, progressive, daring, artistic, creative, idealistic, independent, kindhearted, ambitious, hardworking, stable home life, leadership potential, strong-willed, original approach, sensitive

Your less attractive qualities: rash, escapist, restless, un-motivated, lack of compassion, pride, unrealistic, bossy, lack of judgment, intolerant, aggressive, lack of confidence, too dependent on others, discontented

Your Venus Power

The planet Venus has a great deal of influence on your powers of attraction. Below are four possible Venus types for women and men. To find your Venus you need to go to page 771, where you will find the Venus table and extra information. The planet Mars also affects your powers of attraction. To find your Mars table and interpretation go to page 761.

WOMEN WITH VENUS IN LIBRA: A natural romantic with good social skills, you love to entertain and can put people at ease by projecting a warm and gracious manner. Elegant and fair with a touch of glamour, you are also adept at dealing with people in delicate situations or conflicts. You seek refinement and will go out of your way to achieve harmony and keep the peace. Relationships are so important to you that you may need to guard against becoming dependent on others for approval. With your friendly personality and inherent charm, however, you will always be popular and loved.

MEN WITH VENUS IN LIBRA: Courteous and refined, you are attracted to beautiful and elegant people. You are looking for a partner who can share your natural good taste and enjoy an intellectual conversation. Disliking conflict, you may have to be careful not to go along with others just to keep the peace. Your ideal partner will appreciate beauty and the little luxuries of life as well as possess good social skills. You have a strong sense of social etiquette yourself so you need an intelligent and sophisticated partner.

WOMEN WITH VENUS IN SCORPIO: With a natural psychic gift for penetrating the feelings of others, you can often help partners transform emotional challenges or sexual difficulties. When you fall in love, your strong feelings of determination give you a potent force that others find attractive and seductive. Although you know what really turns people on, your most profound desire is usually for the deepness and closeness of real love and intimacy in an enduring relationship.

MEN WITH VENUS IN SCORPIO: In relationships you possess a sensitive understanding of your partner's deeper nature. Although you are strongly attached to those you love, you may have to be careful that your feelings do not turn into jealousy or possessiveness. When you fall in love it is often with an

emotional intensity that helps you get in touch with your deep feelings. You are attracted to partners who can share your passion and display strong feelings of sexuality like your own.

WOMEN WITH VENUS IN SAGITTARIUS: At your best when being optimistic and generous, you possess a mischievous sense of fun. In relationships your open-minded approach to people and places may attract you to those of a different culture or make you tolerant of the foibles of others. Although warm and enthusiastic when in love, your natural honesty and idealism may inspire you to look for a partner who shares your love of freedom.

MEN WITH VENUS IN SAGITTARIUS: Forward-thinking rather than dwelling on the past, you are looking for a partner who can share your future plans. You enjoy exploring life whether through travel and mental pursuits or sports and games. Idealistic, you usually prefer the company of a partner who is optimistic and shares your beliefs. In your desire for honesty in relationships, however, be careful not to become tactless. Nevertheless, you are attracted to honest, direct, and fun-loving partners who have a sense of humor like your own.

WOMEN WITH VENUS IN CAPRICORN: With your natural caution in romantic affairs, you often appear reserved and controlled. If shy, try to be more forward, especially if you want to be noticed. When you care about people, however, you are usually willing to put in extra time and energy to preserve the relationship. You are practical and dependable, and a sense of duty can often play a large role in the affairs of your heart. With elegant simplicity, you can attract others with your well-cut clothes and refined manners.

MEN WITH VENUS IN CAPRICORN: As you do not display your deeper emotions freely, you are usually dignified and controlled in your relationships with others. Practical and down-to-earth partners are particularly attractive to you, especially those who do not rush into expressing their feelings but seem to possess natural class and reserve. You need a partner who is loyal and dependable and willing to take your relationship seriously.

To read all about your Outer Planets and work out how to use your personalized timetable, go to Section Three, page 789.

Your Personalized Timetable

JUPITER BENEFICIAL
1938 1/1 – 2/4
1939 4/30 – until 1940 3/9
1943 6/20 – 9/2
1945 8/29 – 10/15
1949 4/20 – 6/19
1949 12/5 – until 1950 1/19
1951 4/12 – 7/20
1951 8/19 – until 1952 2/18
1954 10/11 – 12/23
1955 6/1 – 8/16
1956 12/22 – until 1957 2/10
1957 8/11 – 9/29
1961 3/19 – 8/5
1961 11/10 – until 1962 1/2
1963 3/26 – 6/8
1963 10/13 – until 1964 1/25
1966 9/14 – until 1967 2/1
1967 5/8 – 7/31
1968 11/20 – until 1969 3/24
1969 7/21 – 9/13
1973 2/27 – 5/1
1973 6/29 – 12/14
1975 3/9 – 5/17
1978 8/25 – until 1979 7/15
1980 10/31 – until 1981 5/12
1981 6/11 – 8/27
1985 2/10 – 3/31
1985 8/14 – 11/20
1987 2/21 – 4/29
1990 8/8 – until 1991 6/28
1992 10/14 – 12/8
1993 3/22 – 8/7
1997 1/25 – 3/10
1998 7/5 – 7/30
1999 2/2 – 4/12
2002 7/22 – 10/11
2003 1/28 – 6/7
2004 9/28 – 11/16
2005 4/30 – 7/11
2009 1/9 – 2/20
2010 5/22 – 9/25
2011 1/9 – 3/26

SATURN BENEFICIAL
1938 1/1 – 5/17
1938 10/18 – until 1939 2/7
1946 7/16 – until 1947 8/16
1950 12/1 – until 1951 2/24
1951 8/21 – 11/13
1952 4/12 – 8/7
1962 1/10 – 4/24
1962 6/18 – until 1963 1/8
1966 5/24 – 8/30
1967 2/12 – until 1968 3/23
1975 8/27 – until 1976 2/11
1976 5/11 – 9/29
1977 1/29 – 6/18
1980 9/27 – until 1981 9/19
1991 2/13 – 9/7
1991 10/31 – until 1992 2/12
1996 3/20 – until 1997 4/28
1997 11/29 – until 1998 1/2
2005 6/29 – until 2006 7/30
2009 11/6 – until 2010 3/28
2010 7/31 – 10/26
2011 5/23 – 7/3

URANUS BENEFICIAL
1955 7/18 – until 1959 6/20
1968 10/11 – until 1971 8/13
1996 1/25 – until 1998 12/28
2010 4/8 – Continues

NEPTUNE BENEFICIAL
1942 10/26 – until 1948 8/7
1998 2/20 – until 2003 11/29

PLUTO BENEFICIAL
1938 1/1 – until 1948 7/12
1971 10/27 – until 1976 9/13

JUPITER CHALLENGING
1938 4/27 – 8/17
1938 12/17 – until 1939 3/1

1941 5/17 – 7/29
1941 12/28 – until 1942 3/16
1944 7/15 – 9/28
1950 4/3 – 10/13
1950 11/3 – until 1951 2/12
1953 4/30 – 7/8
1955 10/29 – until 1956 2/6
1956 6/25 – 9/12
1962 3/16 – until 1963 1/25
1965 4/12 – 6/21
1967 10/6 – until 1968 3/16
1968 5/28 – 8/28
1974 2/27 – 5/16
1974 8/29 – until 1975 1/3
1976 8/3 – 11/5
1977 3/22 – 6/5
1979 9/18 – until 1980 8/11
1986 2/11 – 4/22
1986 10/17 – 11/30
1988 7/9 – 12/19
1989 2/21 – 5/19
1991 9/2 – 12/8
1992 1/22 – 7/24
1998 1/26 – 4/3
2000 6/20 – until 2001 5/2
2003 8/17 – 11/5
2004 3/5 – 7/3
2010 1/7 – 3/17
2012 6/2 – Continues

SATURN CHALLENGING
1941 8/12 – 10/9
1942 4/21 – until 1943 5/21
1948 9/1 – until 1949 10/6
1950 4/7 – 6/22
1964 3/4 – until 1965 4/22
1965 9/7 – until 1966 1/16
1971 6/1 – until 1972 6/30
1973 1/31 – 2/26
1977 10/16 – until 1978 2/7
1978 7/6 – 12/12
1979 1/5 – 8/13
1993 4/14 – 8/8
1994 1/9 – until 1995 2/24
2000 7/12 – 11/15
2001 4/1 – 8/21
2001 11/2 – until 2002 5/3
2007 8/16 – until 2008 9/19

URANUS CHALLENGING
1941 6/14 – until 1946 3/22
1961 9/15 – until 1965 8/15
2002 4/12 – until 2007 2/18

NEPTUNE CHALLENGING
2010 4/2 – Continues

PLUTO CHALLENGING
1955 10/3 – until 1965 6/15

JUPITER SPECIAL
1947 10/13 – 12/25
1959 1/24 – 5/13
1959 9/22 – 12/9
1971 1/2 – 6/26
1971 8/22 – 11/24
1982 12/15 – until 1983 11/7
1994 11/29 – until 1995 2/28
1995 5/3 – 10/20
2006 11/14 – until 2007 1/30
2007 6/14 – 9/27

SATURN SPECIAL
1955 12/21 – until 1956 6/13
1956 9/14 – until 1957 2/27
1957 4/18 – 11/13
1985 2/16 – 3/27
1985 10/29 – until 1986 12/18

URANUS SPECIAL
1980 12/20 – until 1984 12/5

NEPTUNE SPECIAL
1969 1/1 – until 1977 10/4

PLUTO SPECIAL
1994 1/30 – until 2001 11/1

November 29

SUN: SAGITTARIUS · DECANATE: SAGITTARIUS/JUPITER · DEGREE: 6°5–7°5 SAGITTARIUS · MODE: MUTABLE · ELEMENT: FIRE

Your Personal Powers

With your optimism and shrewd pragmatism, you are an idealist with common sense and a gift for seeing opportunities. Your ruling planet, Jupiter, suggests that you enjoy working on large projects and appreciate the good things in life. Although practical and a good organizer, your strong emotions suggest that you need inspiration to bring out your best qualities. Perceptive and resourceful, you gain power from your quick intelligence and determination to achieve your objectives. Success-oriented, you possess strong convictions and opinions but you may have to resist being self-righteous. Although you possess remarkable potential, the two sides of your nature may cause you to alternate in mood from bossy and outspoken to self-doubting and reserved. By balancing these extremes, you can achieve inner peace and contentment. You are likely to get real satisfaction from being of service or inspiring others. Usually generous, kind, and enterprising, your adventurous spirit and straightforward manner suggests that with perseverance you can find success.

Your Powers of Attraction in Relationships

Being sociable and direct, you can attract people with your gregarious personality. Cooperative and insightful, you benefit from collaborating with others. Although you can give much love and friendship, nervous tension may sometimes cause you to become stubborn or highly emotional. You are able, however, to hide your feelings behind a pragmatic front. Issues of power in your relationships indicate that if you do go to extremes you can occasionally become involved in dramatic situations. By displaying the idealistic and affectionate side of your nature, you can avoid becoming anxious or controlling. Honest and sincere, you want to establish security and harmony, and usually you are kind and devoted to your family or loved ones. By staying independent while still being caring and loyal, you can keep your adventurous spirit alive.

Your attractive qualities: direct, practical, inspirational, sensitive, inner peace, generous, successful, creative, determined, humanitarian, adventurous, honest, idealistic, strong opinions, intuitive, mystical potential, worldly, frank, loving, organizational skills, loyal

Your less attractive qualities: too outspoken, rigid, insecure, nervous, moody, selfish, vain, arrogant, tactless, bossy, difficult, extremist, too opinionated, anxious, too sensitive, self-indulgent, too intense

Your Venus Power

The planet Venus has a great deal of influence on your powers of attraction. Below are four possible Venus types for women and men. To find your Venus you need to go to page 771, where you will find the Venus table and extra information. The planet Mars also affects your powers of attraction. To find your Mars table and interpretation go to page 761.

WOMEN WITH VENUS IN LIBRA: Gracious, charming, and sociable with a sense of style, you have no trouble attracting admirers. With your natural diplomatic skills and desire for harmony you usually like to keep the peace and avoid confrontations, but be careful of failing to take a stand when it is necessary. Romantic and easygoing yourself, you are attracted to affectionate and refined individuals who share your love of peace, justice, and fair play.

MEN WITH VENUS IN LIBRA: You are such good company, people are naturally drawn to you and especially appreciate your talent for making them feel special. You find status in your social contacts and place importance on your relationships. Being clever and a charming companion, you will go out of your way to keep situations peaceful and harmonious. In relationships, however, be careful of indecision or compromising too much. Nevertheless, others are attracted by your natural refinement and good taste, which is reflected in your sense of style.

WOMEN WITH VENUS IN SCORPIO: Loving and passionate, you are often sensitive with deep feelings and strong powers of attraction. A love for the truth coupled with a tendency to be suspicious can be an influence that motivates you to delve deep into the activities of your partner. When in love or in a relationship that matters, you will often bend over backward to cooperate. Although loyal, guard against losing sight of your own needs and desires.

MEN WITH VENUS IN SCORPIO: You are usually attracted to sensual and passionate partners with strong character. You are often sensitive with deep feelings and magnetic powers of attraction. As a cautious yet devoted and ardent lover, you are likely to seek experiences that are more sexual in their nature. You display your less attractive qualities when you project your negative thoughts and resort to being suspicious or

possessive. Nevertheless, loyal and loving, you are a sensitive lover.

WOMEN WITH VENUS IN SAGITTARIUS: Optimistic and fun-loving, you love adventure and seek a partner who can expand your horizons. Being truthful and direct, you often say what you think, and at times you may be naively tactless. A need for expansion and prosperity suggest that you may enjoy traveling with your friends or partner. Being both lighthearted and idealistic, however, means that once you have given your heart to someone you will stay honorable and loyal.

MEN WITH VENUS IN SAGITTARIUS: You are usually attracted to partners who are knowledgeable or well-traveled. Enthusiastic and optimistic, you often respond quickly to love offers and enter relationships with enthusiasm. Usually you seek to expand your social circle and meeting people from all walks of life can bring you the variety and fun you seek in life. Although you are generous and honest, your partners may accuse you of being overly optimistic or too blunt.

WOMEN WITH VENUS IN CAPRICORN: With your natural caution in romantic affairs, you often appear reserved and controlled. If shy, try to be more forward, especially if you want to be noticed. When you care about people, however, you are usually willing to put in extra time and energy to preserve the relationship. You are practical and dependable, and a sense of duty can often play a large role in the affairs of your heart. With elegant simplicity, you can attract others with your well-cut clothes and refined manners.

MEN WITH VENUS IN CAPRICORN: As you do not display your deeper emotions freely, you are usually dignified and controlled in your relationships with others. Practical and down-to-earth partners are particularly attractive to you, especially those who do not rush into expressing their feelings but seem to possess natural class and reserve. You need a partner who is loyal and dependable and willing to take your relationship seriously.

To read all about your Outer Planets and work out how to use your personalized timetable, go to Section Three, page 789.

Your Personalized Timetable

JUPITER BENEFICIAL
1938 1/1 – 2/9
1939 5/5 – until 1940 3/13
1943 6/25 – 9/7
1945 9/3 – 10/19
1949 5/5 – 6/4
1949 12/10 – until 1950 1/23
1951 4/16 – until 1952 2/23
1954 10/21 – 12/13
1955 6/6 – 8/21
1957 8/16 – 10/4
1961 3/26 – 7/28
1961 11/17 – until 1962 1/7
1963 3/30 – 6/14
1963 10/5 – until 1964 2/1
1966 9/20 – until 1967 1/25
1967 5/15 – 8/5
1968 11/27 – until 1969 3/16
1969 7/27 – 9/18
1973 3/4 – 5/17
1973 6/13 – 12/19
1975 3/13 – 5/22
1975 12/5 – 12/16
1978 8/30 – until 1979 7/20
1980 11/5 – until 1981 4/27
1981 6/27 – 9/1
1985 2/14 – 4/6
1985 8/6 – 11/27
1987 2/25 – 5/3
1990 8/12 – until 1991 7/3
1992 10/19 – 12/16
1993 3/14 – 8/13
1997 1/29 – 3/15
1999 2/7 – 4/16
2002 7/27 – 10/19
2003 1/20 – 6/13
2004 10/3 – 11/22
2005 4/21 – 7/20
2009 1/13 – 2/25
2010 5/29 – 9/18
2011 1/15 – 3/30

SATURN BENEFICIAL
1938 1/1 – 5/28
1938 10/5 – until 1939 2/18
1946 7/24 – until 1947 8/24
1950 12/18 – until 1951 2/6
1951 8/30 – 11/24
1952 3/30 – 8/18
1962 1/19 – until 1963 1/17
1966 6/9 – 8/13
1967 2/21 – until 1968 3/31
1975 9/5 – until 1976 1/29
1976 5/23 – 10/10
1977 1/16 – 6/28
1980 10/6 – until 1981 9/27
1991 2/23 – 8/20
1991 11/18 – until 1992 2/20
1996 3/28 – until 1997 5/7
1997 11/8 – until 1998 1/23
2005 7/7 – until 2006 8/7
2009 11/16 – until 2010 3/15
2010 8/10 – 11/4
2011 5/2 – 7/24

URANUS BENEFICIAL
1955 8/4 – until 1959 7/9
1968 10/28 – until 1971 9/2
1996 2/12 – until 1999 1/16
2010 4/27 – Continues

NEPTUNE BENEFICIAL
1942 12/5 – until 1948 9/10
1998 3/29 – until 2004 1/4

PLUTO BENEFICIAL
1938 1/1 – until 1949 6/20
1971 12/6 – until 1977 7/30

JUPITER CHALLENGING
1938 5/4 – 8/9
1938 12/23 – until 1939 3/5

1941 5/21 – 8/3
1941 12/20 – until 1942 3/24
1944 7/20 – 10/3
1950 4/9 – 9/27
1950 11/20 – until 1951 2/16
1953 5/4 – 7/13
1955 11/6 – until 1956 1/29
1956 7/1 – 9/17
1962 3/20 – until 1963 1/29
1965 4/17 – 6/25
1967 10/12 – until 1968 3/7
1968 6/6 – 9/1
1974 3/3 – 5/24
1974 8/21 – until 1975 1/9
1976 8/11 – 10/28
1977 3/28 – 6/9
1979 9/23 – until 1980 8/16
1986 2/15 – 4/28
1986 10/5 – 12/11
1988 7/15 – 12/10
1989 3/2 – 5/24
1991 9/6 – until 1992 7/30
1998 1/30 – 4/8
2000 6/24 – until 2001 5/7
2003 8/21 – 11/12
2004 2/26 – 7/10
2010 1/12 – 3/21
2012 6/6 – Continues

SATURN CHALLENGING
1942 4/29 – until 1943 5/29
1948 9/9 – until 1949 10/15
1950 3/23 – 7/6
1964 3/13 – 10/9
1964 11/25 – until 1965 5/3
1965 8/24 – until 1966 1/26
1971 6/9 – until 1972 7/9
1973 1/8 – 3/21
1977 10/28 – until 1978 1/25
1978 7/16 – until 1979 8/21
1993 4/27 – 7/24
1994 1/18 – until 1995 3/4
2000 7/24 – 11/2
2001 4/10 – 9/14
2001 10/10 – until 2002 5/11
2007 8/24 – until 2008 9/27

URANUS CHALLENGING
1941 7/5 – until 1946 4/19
1961 10/3 – until 1965 9/1
2002 5/26 – until 2007 12/3

NEPTUNE CHALLENGING
2011 2/28 – Continues

PLUTO CHALLENGING
1956 9/6 – until 1965 8/1

JUPITER SPECIAL
1947 10/18 – 12/30
1959 1/31 – 5/5
1959 9/28 – 12/14
1971 1/7 – 6/15
1971 9/1 – 11/28
1982 12/20 – until 1983 11/12
1994 12/4 – until 1995 3/13
1995 4/20 – 10/25
2006 11/18 – until 2007 2/6
2007 6/6 – 10/4

SATURN SPECIAL
1955 12/31 – until 1956 5/30
1956 9/27 – until 1957 11/22
1985 11/7 – until 1986 12/26
1987 8/1 – 9/6

URANUS SPECIAL
1981 1/9 – until 1985 10/6

NEPTUNE SPECIAL
1969 11/30 – until 1977 11/9

PLUTO SPECIAL
1994 12/11 – until 2001 11/29

November 30

Your Personal Powers

Mentally sharp with quick responses, your personal powers include superior communication skills and a love of the dramatic. Your ruling planet, Jupiter, endows you with an adventurous spirit and a desire to see the broader picture. You gain power from your amiable personality and ability to articulate yourself in a persuasive and often entertaining manner. Although you can alternate between charm and fast verbal retorts, you can lose power if you become irritable, argumentative, or too outspoken. Nevertheless, your need to express yourself intellectually and emotionally points to your outstanding creative potential. Ambitious and enterprising, your quick comprehension suggests that you thrive on variety and mental stimulation. With your powerful emotions it is important that you stay focused and avoid an inclination to be indecisive, worried, or too self-involved. Nevertheless, optimistic and idealistic, you usually bounce right back from difficulties. Usually you enjoy an element of risk that can bring you excitement and opportunities. With your strong willpower, bright ideas, and convincing speech, you have the potential to achieve remarkable success.

Your Powers of Attraction in Relationships

You attract others with your superior communication skills and ability to express yourself. Although you possess deep feelings, your strong need for love may not always be obvious to others. Usually you are attracted to clever and witty individuals who have a sense of the dramatic. Sometimes you are drawn to idealistic individuals with a capricious side who may not want to make a commitment. Alternatively, your own indecisive streak may send conflicting messages to others. You can avoid insecurity in your relationships by keeping your inner faith and being spontaneous. With your strong need for self-expression, however, you are likely to be sociable, and you have a gift for attracting love and friends. Trust your instincts and innate common sense, when you are making decisions about love and relationships.

Your attractive qualities: sociable, articulate, quick intelligence, adventurous, communication skills, intuitive, resourceful, dynamic, friendly, creative, sensitive, talent with words, loyal, expressive, inspirational, generous, kind, enthusiastic

Your less attractive qualities: worry, insecure, indecisive, jealous, scattered, argumentative, stubborn, too outspoken, lazy, impatient, bored, overindulgent, irritable, indifferent, restlessness

Your Venus Power

The planet Venus has a great deal of influence on your powers of attraction. Below are four possible Venus types for women and men. To find your Venus you need to go to page 771, where you will find the Venus table and extra information. The planet Mars also affects your powers of attraction. To find your Mars table and interpretation go to page 761.

WOMEN WITH VENUS IN LIBRA: Attractive, refined, and conscious of the needs of others, you usually desire harmonious relationships. As a peacemaker with good negotiating skills, you can smooth out difficulties with others, but your dislike of confrontation may sometimes leave you refusing to take a stand or compromising too many of your own needs. Courteous, stylish, and charming with polished social skills, you are an expert at relating to others in a gracious and civilized manner.

MEN WITH VENUS IN LIBRA: Your good social skills, charming personality, and refined manner usually make you attractive to the opposite sex. Equally, you desire a sophisticated partner with grace, elegance, and a strong sense of style. Although you have the ability to be persuasive and irresistible to others, avoid manipulative love games. Nevertheless, your natural diplomacy and sense of fair play help you to relate to people in all social situations. With your love of balance and harmony, you seek a partner who is also moderate, easygoing, and loving.

WOMEN WITH VENUS IN SCORPIO: With a natural psychic gift for penetrating the feelings of others, you can often help partners transform emotional challenges or sexual difficulties. When you fall in love, your strong feelings of determination give you a potent force that others find attractive and seductive. Although you know what really turns people on, your most profound desire is usually for the deepness and closeness of real love and intimacy in an enduring relationship.

MEN WITH VENUS IN SCORPIO: As you are emotionally intense and passionate, personal relationships are probably a major factor in your own transformation. Being sensitive yet loyal, you are usually attracted to forceful partners who can

express themselves intimately but intensely. Rather than seek easy and simple relationships, you are drawn to partners who act as a catalyst for your own internal changes. Through your relationships with your partners you can unravel your own motives and understand your deep-seated feelings or emotional insecurities.

WOMEN WITH VENUS IN SAGITTARIUS: When you feel generous, you can make others feel more optimistic about life. You may be interested in higher learning and seek partners who are scholarly or broad-minded. You are outspoken and direct, and sometimes say things that you later regret. Curious and versatile, you can adjust quickly to new situations, and a foreign influence implies that you love to travel or may have a partner who comes from a different culture.

MEN WITH VENUS IN SAGITTARIUS: Your enthusiasm and straightforward conduct usually appeal to others and imply that you are approachable and easygoing. Being open to ideas and willing to believe that life has a great deal to offer suggests that you are generous, broad-minded, and show eagerness to cooperate with others. A love of travel and an interest in other cultures imply that your partner may come from a foreign country.

WOMEN WITH VENUS IN CAPRICORN: With your natural caution in romantic affairs, you often appear reserved and controlled. If shy, try to be more forward, especially if you want to be noticed. When you care about people, however, you are usually willing to put in extra time and energy to preserve the relationship. You are practical and dependable, and a sense of duty can often play a large role in the affairs of your heart. With elegant simplicity, you can attract others with your well-cut clothes and refined manners.

MEN WITH VENUS IN CAPRICORN: As you do not display your deeper emotions freely, you are usually dignified and controlled in your relationships with others. Practical and down-to-earth partners are particularly attractive to you, especially those who do not rush into expressing their feelings but seem to possess natural class and reserve. You need a partner who is loyal and dependable and willing to take your relationship seriously.

To read all about your Outer Planets and work out how to use your personalized timetable, go to Section Three, page 789.

To read all about your Outer Planets and work out how to use your personalized timetable, go to Section Three, page 789.

Your Personalized Timetable

JUPITER BENEFICIAL
1938 1/1 – 2/13
1939 5/10 – 11/1
1939 12/18 – until **1940** 3/17
1943 6/30 – 9/12
1945 9/7 – 10/24
1949 12/15 – until **1950** 1/28
1951 4/20 – until **1952** 2/28
1954 11/8 – 11/25
1955 6/12 – 8/25
1957 8/22 – 10/8
1961 4/1 – 7/20
1961 11/23 – until **1962** 1/11
1963 4/3 – 6/21
1963 9/28 – until **1964** 2/7
1966 9/26 – until **1967** 1/17
1967 5/22 – 8/10
1968 12/5 – until **1969** 3/8
1969 8/3 – 9/23
1973 3/9 – 9/10
1973 10/16 – 12/24
1975 3/18 – 5/27
1975 11/15 – until **1976** 1/4
1978 9/4 – until **1979** 3/3
1979 4/17 – 7/25
1980 11/11 – until **1981** 4/17
1981 7/7 – 9/6
1985 2/19 – 4/13
1985 7/29 – 12/3
1987 3/2 – 5/8
1990 8/17 – until **1991** 7/8
1992 10/24 – 12/25
1993 3/5 – 8/19
1997 2/2 – 3/20
1997 9/17 – 10/29
1999 2/12 – 4/21
2002 7/31 – 10/27
2003 1/11 – 6/19
2004 10/8 – 11/28
2005 4/12 – 7/28
2009 1/17 – 3/1
2010 6/5 – 9/10
2011 1/21 – 4/4

SATURN BENEFICIAL
1938 1/11 – 6/8
1938 9/22 – until **1939** 2/27
1946 8/1 – until **1947** 9/1
1948 4/9 – 4/25
1951 9/7 – 12/5
1952 3/16 – 8/28
1962 1/27 – until **1963** 1/26
1967 3/2 – until **1968** 4/8
1975 9/15 – until **1976** 1/16
1976 6/3 – 10/24
1976 12/31 – until **1977** 7/7
1980 10/14 – until **1981** 10/6
1991 3/4 – 8/5
1991 12/1 – until **1992** 2/29
1992 9/10 – 11/19
1996 4/5 – until **1997** 5/16
1997 10/24 – until **1998** 2/5
2005 7/15 – until **2006** 8/15
2009 11/28 – until **2010** 3/1
2010 8/20 – 11/13
2011 4/17 – 8/7

URANUS BENEFICIAL
1955 8/21 – until **1959** 7/27
1968 11/18 – until **1971** 9/19
1996 3/2 – until **1999** 2/3
2010 5/22 – Continues

NEPTUNE BENEFICIAL
1943 10/24 – until **1949** 8/3
1999 2/17 – until **2004** 11/21

PLUTO BENEFICIAL
1938 7/28 – until **1950** 5/13
1972 10/19 – until **1977** 9/4

JUPITER CHALLENGING
1938 5/12 – 7/31
1938 12/28 – until **1939** 3/9

1941 5/25 – 8/9
1941 12/12 – until **1942** 3/31
1944 7/25 – 10/8
1950 4/14 – 9/16
1950 11/30 – until **1951** 2/21
1953 5/8 – 7/18
1955 11/15 – until **1956** 1/19
1956 7/6 – 9/22
1962 3/25 – until **1963** 2/3
1965 4/21 – 6/30
1967 10/18 – until **1968** 2/28
1968 6/14 – 9/6
1974 3/7 – 6/1
1974 8/12 – until **1975** 1/14
1976 8/21 – 10/18
1977 4/2 – 6/13
1979 9/28 – until **1980** 8/21
1986 2/19 – 5/3
1986 9/26 – 12/20
1988 7/21 – 12/2
1989 3/9 – 5/28
1991 9/11 – until **1992** 8/4
1998 2/3 – 4/12
2000 6/29 – until **2001** 5/11
2003 8/26 – 11/19
2004 2/18 – 7/16
2010 1/17 – 3/25
2012 6/11 – 9/16
2012 10/22 – Continues

SATURN CHALLENGING
1942 5/7 – until **1943** 6/6
1948 9/17 – until **1949** 4/7
1949 5/25 – 10/25
1950 3/10 – 7/18
1964 3/22 – 9/19
1964 12/13 – until **1965** 5/17
1965 8/9 – until **1966** 2/5
1971 6/17 – until **1972** 1/15
1972 2/16 – 7/17
1972 12/24 – until **1973** 4/4
1977 11/13 – until **1978** 1/8
1978 7/25 – until **1979** 8/30
1993 5/16 – 7/5
1994 1/27 – until **1995** 3/12
2000 8/7 – 10/19
2001 4/19 – until **2002** 5/20
2007 9/1 – until **2008** 10/5
2009 4/14 – 6/18

URANUS CHALLENGING
1941 8/1 – until **1946** 5/9
1961 10/27 – until **1966** 6/20
2003 3/7 – until **2008** 1/13

NEPTUNE CHALLENGING
2011 3/29 – Continues

PLUTO CHALLENGING
1956 10/12 – until **1966** 6/3

JUPITER SPECIAL
1947 10/23 – until **1948** 1/4
1959 2/9 – 4/26
1959 10/4 – 12/18
1971 1/13 – 6/6
1971 9/10 – 12/3
1982 12/25 – until **1983** 11/17
1994 12/8 – until **1995** 10/31
2006 11/23 – until **2007** 2/12
2007 5/29 – 10/11

SATURN SPECIAL
1956 1/10 – 5/16
1956 10/8 – until **1957** 12/1
1985 11/15 – until **1987** 1/5
1987 7/9 – 9/28

URANUS SPECIAL
1981 2/8 – until **1985** 10/30

NEPTUNE SPECIAL
1969 12/30 – until **1978** 9/28

PLUTO SPECIAL
1995 1/10 – until **2002** 10/24

♐

December 1

SUN: SAGITTARIUS · DECANATE: SAGITTARIUS/JUPITER · DEGREE: 8°5–9°5 SAGITTARIUS · MODE: MUTABLE · ELEMENT: FIRE

Your Personal Powers

Friendly and straightforward, you are a strong-willed individual with powerful imagination and polished common sense. You gain power from the combination of your dynamic emotions, personal charm, and organizational skills. With honesty high on your list of priorities, you like to know where you stand. With your strong opinions and direct approach, you usually achieve good results, but be careful not to lose your power to tactless or overbearing behavior. Independent and innovative with natural executive or leadership abilities, you usually enjoy initiating projects or improving existing ones. Ambitious and idealistic, your work is likely to be especially important in your need to build a strong foundation in life. Nevertheless, as you are sociable and desire change, you also need activities that involve people and variety. Being purposeful and determined to get things done, you may need to resist being impatient or stubborn. Possessing plenty of energy, dynamic emotions, and original ideas, once set on a course of action, you can be very focused in achieving success.

Your Powers of Attraction in Relationships

With your charismatic warmth and talent for dealing with people, you can easily attract admirers. Active and sociable, you are a delightful companion, inspiring others with your enthusiasm. Your sensitivity provides you with a strong visionary sense and the ability to put yourself in someone else's position. On these occasions, you show your caring and compassionate nature. In love, you are attracted to other strong-willed individuals, but be careful of becoming involved in power struggles. Loyal and dependable when committed, you want a reliable partner who also appreciates a harmonious or secure home base. Preferring to do things your own way, you may need to develop a more flexible and less fixed attitude with your loved ones. Idealistic and kind, you can be a generous lover and friend.

Your attractive qualities: honest, pragmatic, friendly, leadership ability, creative, progressive, forceful, optimistic, administrative skills, productive, kind, strong-willed, idealistic, common sense, daring, determined, independent, adventurous, charm, compassionate, sociable, enthusiastic

Your less attractive qualities: stubborn, bossy, restless, overbearing, impatient, bored, self-centered, scattered energies, too proud, antagonistic, overzealous

Your Venus Power

The planet Venus has a great deal of influence on your powers of attraction. Below are four possible Venus types for women and men. To find your Venus you need to go to page 771, where you will find the Venus table and extra information. The planet Mars also affects your powers of attraction. To find your Mars table and interpretation go to page 761.

WOMEN WITH VENUS IN LIBRA: A natural romantic with good social skills, you love to entertain and can put people at ease by projecting a warm and gracious manner. Elegant and fair with a touch of glamour, you are also adept at dealing with people in delicate situations or conflicts. You seek refinement and will go out of your way to achieve harmony and keep the peace. Relationships are so important to you that you may need to guard against becoming dependent on others for approval. With your friendly personality and inherent charm, however, you will always be popular and loved.

MEN WITH VENUS IN LIBRA: You are such good company, people are naturally drawn to you and especially appreciate your talent for making them feel special. You find status in your social contacts and place importance on your relationships. Being a clever and charming companion, you will go out of your way to keep situations peaceful and harmonious. In relationships, however, be careful of indecision or compromising too much. Nevertheless, others are attracted by your natural refinement and good taste, which is reflected in your sense of style.

WOMEN WITH VENUS IN SCORPIO: With a natural psychic gift for penetrating the feelings of others you can often help partners transform emotional challenges or sexual difficulties. When you fall in love, your strong feelings of determination give you a potent force that others find attractive and seductive. Although you know what really turns people on, your most profound desire is usually for the deepness and closeness of real love and intimacy in an enduring relationship.

MEN WITH VENUS IN SCORPIO: In relationships you possess a sensitive understanding of your partner's deeper nature. Although you are strongly attached to those you love, you may have to be careful that your feelings do not turn into jealousy

or possessiveness. When you fall in love it is often with an emotional intensity that helps you get in touch with your deep feelings. You are attracted to partners who can share your passion and display strong feelings of sexuality like your own.

WOMEN WITH VENUS IN SAGITTARIUS: At your best when being optimistic and generous, you possess a mischievous sense of fun. In relationships, your open-minded approach to people and places may attract you to those of a different culture or make you tolerant of the foibles of others. Although warm and enthusiastic when in love, your natural honesty and idealism may inspire you to look for a partner who shares your love of freedom.

MEN WITH VENUS IN SAGITTARIUS: Forward-thinking rather than dwelling on the past, you are looking for a partner who can share your future plans. You enjoy exploring life whether through travel and mental pursuits or sports and games. Idealistic, you usually prefer the company of a partner who is optimistic and shares your beliefs. In your desire for honesty in relationships, however, be careful not to become tactless. Nevertheless, you are attracted to honest, direct, and fun-loving partners who have a sense of humor like your own.

WOMEN WITH VENUS IN CAPRICORN: Loyal and responsible, you are attracted to dignified and reserved individuals. Being practical and security-conscious, you prefer hardworking partners who are resourceful and enterprising. Work may even be a factor in many of your associations and partnerships. For you, family and faithfulness can be especially important, so you are usually willing to work hard or make sacrifices in order to build a strong relationship.

MEN WITH VENUS IN CAPRICORN: As you do not display your deeper emotions freely, you are usually dignified and controlled in your relationships with others. Practical and down-to-earth partners are particularly attractive to you, especially those who do not rush into expressing their feelings but seem to possess natural class and reserve. You need a partner who is loyal and dependable and willing to take your relationship seriously.

To read all about your Outer Planets and work out how to use your personalized timetable, go to Section Three, page 789.

Your Personalized Timetable

JUPITER BENEFICIAL
1938 1/6 – 2/17
1939 5/16 – 10/21
1939 12/29 – until **1940** 3/22
1943 7/4 – 9/17
1945 9/12 – 10/29
1949 12/19 – until **1950** 2/1
1951 4/25 – until **1952** 3/4
1955 6/17 – 8/30
1957 8/27 – 10/13
1961 4/8 – 7/12
1961 11/29 – until **1962** 1/15
1963 4/7 – 6/29
1963 9/19 – until **1964** 2/12
1966 10/3 – until **1967** 1/9
1967 5/28 – 8/14
1968 12/13 – until **1969** 2/27
1969 8/8 – 9/28
1973 3/14 – 8/28
1973 10/29 – 12/29
1975 3/22 – 6/1
1975 11/4 – until **1976** 1/14
1978 9/9 – until **1979** 2/19
1979 4/29 – 7/29
1980 11/17 – until **1981** 4/8
1981 7/16 – 9/11
1985 2/23 – 4/20
1985 7/21 – 12/9
1987 3/6 – 5/13
1990 8/22 – until **1991** 7/13
1992 10/29 – until **1993** 1/5
1993 2/21 – 8/25
1997 2/7 – 3/25
1997 9/5 – 11/10
1999 2/16 – 4/25
2002 8/5 – 11/6
2003 1/1 – 6/25
2004 10/13 – 12/4
2005 4/4 – 8/4
2009 1/22 – 3/6
2010 6/12 – 9/2
2011 1/27 – 4/8

SATURN BENEFICIAL
1938 1/24 – 6/23
1938 9/7 – until **1939** 3/8
1946 8/9 – until **1947** 9/10
1948 3/12 – 5/22
1951 9/16 – 12/19
1952 3/1 – 9/6
1962 2/5 – until **1963** 2/3
1967 3/10 – until **1968** 4/16
1975 9/26 – until **1976** 1/3
1976 6/13 – 11/21
1976 12/3 – until **1977** 7/15
1980 10/23 – until **1981** 5/4
1981 7/6 – 10/14
1991 3/15 – 7/22
1991 12/12 – until **1992** 3/10
1992 8/25 – 12/4
1996 4/14 – 11/17
1996 12/19 – until **1997** 5/26
1997 10/11 – until **1998** 2/16
2005 7/23 – until **2006** 8/23
2009 12/14 – until **2010** 2/13
2010 8/29 – 11/23
2011 4/4 – 8/18

URANUS BENEFICIAL
1955 9/10 – until **1959** 8/12
1968 12/20 – until **1971** 10/6
1996 3/27 – until **1999** 12/10
2011 3/26 – Continues

NEPTUNE BENEFICIAL
1943 11/29 – until **1949** 9/8
1999 3/23 – until **2004** 12/31

PLUTO BENEFICIAL
1938 9/6 – until **1950** 7/8
1972 11/21 – until **1977** 10/1

JUPITER CHALLENGING
1938 5/22 – 7/21

1939 1/3 – 3/14
1941 5/30 – 8/16
1941 12/5 – until **1942** 4/6
1944 7/30 – 10/13
1950 4/20 – 9/8
1950 12/8 – until **1951** 2/25
1953 5/13 – 7/23
1954 1/25 – 2/26
1955 11/27 – until **1956** 1/7
1956 7/12 – 9/26
1962 3/29 – until **1963** 2/8
1965 4/26 – 7/5
1967 10/24 – until **1968** 2/20
1968 6/21 – 9/11
1974 3/12 – 6/12
1974 8/1 – until **1975** 1/20
1976 9/5 – 10/4
1977 4/7 – 6/18
1979 10/3 – until **1980** 4/6
1980 5/16 – 8/26
1986 2/24 – 5/9
1986 9/18 – 12/27
1988 7/27 – 11/24
1989 3/16 – 6/2
1991 9/16 – until **1992** 8/9
1998 2/8 – 4/17
2000 7/4 – until **2001** 5/16
2003 8/31 – 11/28
2004 2/9 – 7/22
2010 1/21 – 3/30
2012 6/15 – Continues

SATURN CHALLENGING
1942 5/15 – until **1943** 6/14
1948 9/26 – until **1949** 3/19
1949 6/12 – 11/5
1950 2/25 – 7/28
1964 4/1 – 9/4
1964 12/26 – until **1965** 6/6
1965 7/19 – until **1966** 2/13
1971 6/25 – 12/25
1972 3/8 – 7/27
1972 12/12 – until **1973** 4/15
1978 8/2 – until **1979** 9/7
1994 2/5 – until **1995** 3/21
2000 8/31 – 9/24
2001 4/27 – until **2002** 5/28
2007 9/9 – until **2008** 10/14
2009 3/29 – 7/4

URANUS CHALLENGING
1942 5/29 – until **1946** 5/27
1962 8/23 – until **1966** 7/19
2003 3/26 – until **2008** 2/5

NEPTUNE CHALLENGING
2011 5/16 – Continues

PLUTO CHALLENGING
1957 9/13 – until **1966** 7/31

JUPITER SPECIAL
1947 10/28 – until **1948** 1/9
1959 2/19 – 4/15
1959 10/10 – 12/23
1971 1/19 – 5/29
1971 9/17 – 12/7
1982 12/30 – until **1983** 11/21
1994 12/13 – until **1995** 11/5
2006 11/28 – until **2007** 2/20
2007 5/21 – 10/17

SATURN SPECIAL
1956 1/23 – 5/2
1956 10/18 – until **1957** 12/9
1985 11/24 – until **1987** 1/14
1987 6/23 – 10/12

URANUS SPECIAL
1981 11/30 – until **1985** 11/17

NEPTUNE SPECIAL
1970 2/17 – until **1978** 11/7

PLUTO SPECIAL
1995 12/1 – until **2002** 11/23

December 2

SUN: SAGITTARIUS • DECANATE: SAGITTARIUS/JUPITER • DEGREE: 9°5–10°5 SAGITTARIUS • MODE: MUTABLE • ELEMENT: FIRE

Your Personal Powers

Frank and direct, you are a friendly and sociable individual with many original and creative ideas. Usually optimistic and philosophical about life, you gain power from your ability to go straight to the heart of a matter, displaying your ingenuity, insight, and ability to solve problems creatively. Dramatic with sharp intelligence, you greatly benefit from finding ways to express yourself both intellectually and emotionally. Although open and assertive in your stand for honesty, be careful not to lose some of your power by being too outspoken or verbally cutting. Inner doubts and insecurities can also undermine your efforts. Proud and purposeful, you dislike being in subservient positions, yet you can benefit greatly from cooperative efforts. Competitive and a good strategist, you are quick to recognize opportunities, although you are at your best when you feel inspired. Your bold personality can often hide your inner sensitivity and powerful intuition. By trusting this strong inner voice and applying the necessary work needed, you have the potential to achieve outstanding success.

Your Powers of Attraction in Relationships

Your friendly, diplomatic yet direct, optimistic, and courteous manner often attracts admirers. You are likely to prefer partnerships or team efforts to working alone. Very sensitive to people's feelings and possessing high ideals, you seek an almost spiritual link with your partner. If they are unable to reach your high expectations, then you may encounter setbacks or experience occasional disappointments. Avoid becoming cynical about relationships, however, or you may feel down or isolated. Nonetheless, caring and responsible with a strong need for love and affection, you are often willing to work hard to create harmony in your relationships. When inspired, you have enormous faith, making you very loving and spontaneous. When you add your gift with words, you can be sensitive and persuasive as well as adaptable.

Your attractive qualities: keen mentality, adventurous, optimistic, kind, idealistic, daring, friendly, receptive, intuitive, strong convictions, business sense, considerate, broadminded, harmonious, responsible, diplomatic, strong insight, committed, humanitarian, sociable

Your less attractive qualities: rebellious, lack of confidence, suspicious, subservient, too sensitive, secretive, rash, too detached, selfish, hot tempered, obstinate, self-denial, moody, too outspoken

Your Venus Power

The planet Venus has a great deal of influence on your powers of attraction. Below are four possible Venus types for women and men. To find your Venus you need to go to page 771, where you will find the Venus table and extra information. The planet Mars also affects your powers of attraction. To find your Mars table and interpretation go to page 761.

WOMEN WITH VENUS IN LIBRA: You are usually attractive and sociable with an easygoing manner. Your love of beauty, harmony, and pleasure implies that you are a romantic with a desire for love and affection. Once in a relationship you need to learn to negotiate your position rather than adapt to the wishes of others and compromise just to keep the peace. Nevertheless, your advanced social skills and strong sense of fair play can help you succeed in any social or romantic situation.

MEN WITH VENUS IN LIBRA: You are such good company, people are naturally drawn to you and especially appreciate your talent for making them feel special. You find status in your social contacts and place importance on your relationships. Being clever and a charming companion, you will go out of your way to keep situations peaceful and harmonious. In relationships, however, be careful of indecision or compromising too much. Nevertheless, others are attracted by your natural refinement and good taste, which is reflected in your sense of style.

WOMEN WITH VENUS IN SCORPIO: Loving and passionate, you are often sensitive with deep feelings and strong powers of attraction. A love for the truth coupled with a tendency to be suspicious can be an influence that motivates you to delve deep into the activities of your partner. When in love or in a relationship that matters, you will often bend over backward to cooperate. Although loyal, guard against losing sight of your own needs and desires.

MEN WITH VENUS IN SCORPIO: In relationships you possess a sensitive understanding of your partner's deeper nature. Although you are strongly attached to those you love, you may have to be careful that your feelings do not turn into jealousy or possessiveness. When you fall in love it is often with an emotional intensity that helps you get in touch with your deep

feelings. You are attracted to partners who can share your passion and display strong feelings of sexuality like your own.

WOMEN WITH VENUS IN SAGITTARIUS: At your best when being optimistic and generous, you possess a mischievous sense of fun. In relationships your open-minded approach to people and places may attract you to those of a different culture or make you tolerant of the foibles of others. Although warm and enthusiastic when in love, your natural honesty and idealism may inspire you to look for a partner who shares your love of freedom.

MEN WITH VENUS IN SAGITTARIUS: When in love you are open and friendly with a need for a partner who can share your adventurous spirit and sense of fun. Be careful, however, that your desire for freedom does not cause you to avoid commitment. You prefer your partners to be positive, direct, and generous in spirit. Being outspoken as well as an idealist, you usually enjoy a partner with whom you can share your strong opinions. Alternatively, you may wish to explore life together, whether through travel, education, or having fun.

WOMEN WITH VENUS IN CAPRICORN: Loyal and responsible, you are attracted to dignified and reserved individuals. Being practical and security-conscious, you prefer hardworking partners who are resourceful and enterprising. Work may even be a factor in many of your associations and partnerships. For you, family and faithfulness can be especially important, so you are usually willing to work hard or make sacrifices in order to build a strong relationship.

MEN WITH VENUS IN CAPRICORN: In relationships you take love seriously and can be a strong and practical support for friends or partners. You are usually attracted to partners who are as hardworking as yourself. As you tend not to express your feelings until you feel really secure in a relationship, you may be drawn to those who seem loyal, faithful, and not likely to let you down. As you respect the wisdom of experience, you may be drawn to mature partners or, alternatively, you may act as an authority figure for someone younger.

To read all about your Outer Planets and work out how to use your personalized timetable, go to Section Three, page 789.

To read all about your Outer Planets and work out how to use your personalized timetable, go to Section Three, page 789.

♐

Your Personalized Timetable

JUPITER BENEFICIAL
1938 1/10 – 2/22
1939 5/21 – 10/12
1940 1/6 – 3/26
1943 7/9 – 9/22
1944 3/21 – 5/6
1945 9/17 – 11/3
1949 12/24 – until **1950** 2/5
1951 4/30 – until **1952** 3/8
1955 6/22 – 9/4
1957 9/1 – 10/18
1961 4/16 – 7/4
1961 12/4 – until **1962** 1/20
1963 4/12 – 7/8
1963 9/10 – until **1964** 2/18
1966 10/11 – until **1967** 1/1
1967 6/3 – 8/19
1968 12/23 – until **1969** 2/17
1969 8/14 – 10/2
1973 3/19 – 8/18
1973 11/7 – until **1974** 1/3
1975 3/26 – 6/7
1975 10/27 – until **1976** 1/23
1978 9/15 – until **1979** 2/10
1979 5/8 – 8/3
1980 11/23 – until **1981** 3/31
1981 7/23 – 9/16
1985 2/28 – 4/28
1985 7/12 – 12/15
1987 3/10 – 5/17
1990 8/27 – until **1991** 7/18
1992 11/3 – until **1993** 5/24
1993 6/8 – 8/30
1997 2/11 – 3/31
1997 8/26 – 11/18
1999 2/21 – 4/29
2002 8/10 – 11/22
2002 12/16 – until **2003** 6/30
2004 10/17 – 12/11
2005 3/27 – 8/11
2009 1/26 – 3/10
2010 6/22 – 8/23
2011 2/1 – 4/12

SATURN BENEFICIAL
1938 2/4 – 7/16
1938 8/14 – until **1939** 3/17
1946 8/17 – until **1947** 9/18
1948 2/26 – 6/5
1951 9/24 – until **1952** 1/13
1952 2/5 – 9/15
1962 2/14 – 9/29
1962 10/19 – until **1963** 2/12
1967 3/18 – until **1968** 4/25
1975 10/10 – 12/20
1976 6/22 – until **1977** 7/24
1980 11/1 – until **1981** 4/17
1981 7/23 – 10/22
1991 3/27 – 7/8
1991 12/22 – until **1992** 3/20
1992 8/11 – 12/16
1996 4/23 – 10/26
1997 1/9 – 6/7
1997 9/28 – until **1998** 2/26
2005 7/30 – until **2006** 8/31
2010 9/7 – 12/4
2011 3/22 – 8/28

URANUS BENEFICIAL
1955 10/6 – until **1960** 6/9
1969 10/4 – until **1972** 7/30
1997 1/28 – until **2000** 1/2
2011 4/13 – Continues

NEPTUNE BENEFICIAL
1944 10/21 – until **1950** 7/28
2000 2/15 – until **2005** 11/6

PLUTO BENEFICIAL
1939 8/22 – until **1951** 6/13
1973 10/12 – until **1978** 8/23

JUPITER CHALLENGING
1938 6/6 – 7/7

1939 1/8 – 3/18
1941 6/3 – 8/23
1941 11/27 – until **1942** 4/12
1944 8/4 – 10/18
1945 4/30 – 5/29
1950 4/26 – 8/31
1950 12/15 – until **1951** 3/1
1953 5/17 – 7/28
1954 1/11 – 3/12
1956 7/17 – 10/1
1962 4/3 – until **1963** 2/12
1965 4/30 – 7/9
1967 10/31 – until **1968** 2/13
1968 6/27 – 9/15
1974 3/16 – 7/7
1974 7/10 – until **1975** 1/24
1977 4/12 – 6/22
1979 10/9 – until **1980** 3/24
1980 5/29 – 8/30
1986 2/28 – 5/15
1986 9/11 – until **1987** 1/3
1988 8/2 – 11/17
1989 3/22 – 6/6
1991 9/21 – until **1992** 8/14
1998 2/12 – 4/22
2000 7/9 – until **2001** 1/5
2001 2/14 – 5/20
2003 9/4 – 12/9
2004 1/29 – 7/28
2010 1/26 – 4/3
2012 6/19 – Continues

SATURN CHALLENGING
1942 5/23 – until **1943** 6/22
1948 10/5 – until **1949** 3/5
1949 6/25 – 11/18
1950 2/11 – 8/6
1964 4/11 – 8/22
1965 1/6 – until **1966** 2/22
1971 7/4 – 12/10
1972 3/21 – 8/7
1972 11/29 – until **1973** 4/25
1978 8/10 – until **1979** 9/15
1994 2/13 – until **1995** 3/29
2001 5/6 – until **2002** 6/4
2007 9/17 – until **2008** 4/19
2008 5/16 – 10/24
2009 3/15 – 7/16

URANUS CHALLENGING
1942 6/16 – until **1947** 3/12
1962 9/8 – until **1966** 8/8
2003 4/18 – until **2008** 2/23

NEPTUNE CHALLENGING
2012 3/25 – Continues

PLUTO CHALLENGING
1957 10/21 – until **1966** 8/31

JUPITER SPECIAL
1947 11/1 – until **1948** 1/13
1959 3/9 – 3/27
1959 10/15 – 12/28
1971 1/25 – 5/21
1971 9/24 – 12/12
1983 1/4 – 7/6
1983 8/20 – 11/26
1994 12/18 – until **1995** 11/9
2006 12/2 – until **2007** 3/1
2007 5/11 – 10/22

SATURN SPECIAL
1956 2/7 – 4/15
1956 10/28 – until **1957** 12/18
1985 12/2 – until **1987** 1/24
1987 6/9 – 10/24

URANUS SPECIAL
1981 12/16 – until **1985** 12/4

NEPTUNE SPECIAL
1970 12/27 – until **1979** 9/21

PLUTO SPECIAL
1995 12/29 – until **2003** 10/16

December 3

SUN: SAGITTARIUS · DECANATE: ARIES/MARS · DEGREE: 10°5–11°5 SAGITTARIUS · MODE: MUTABLE · ELEMENT: FIRE

Your Personal Powers

Friendly, sociable, and determined, you have strong convictions and a talent for making contacts. You gain power by combining your creative ideas and original self-expression with your determination and persistence. Once you have decided on a course of action, you can be both enthusiastic and focused. On occasions, however, indecision or anxiety may be the reason why you feel powerless. Your gift with people and your ability to be hardworking, however, ensure that you are usually optimistic, cheerful, and productive. Being also assertive and adventurous, you are often willing to take risks in your quest for opportunities. Nevertheless, try not to lose power by being too direct or impulsive. Although you possess strong ambition and a need for recognition, you also desire harmony and balance. Therefore you may need to take time out to restore your inner peace. This also emphasizes the importance of a tranquil environment or secure home. By uniting realistic goals with your strong ideals and people skills, you can achieve success.

Your Powers of Attraction in Relationships

Sociable and kind, you attract others with your friendly enthusiasm. Usually generous and supportive with those you love, you have loyal friends and admirers. With your strong need for self-expression, you can be entertaining and fun to be with. Often romantic, you are drawn to individuals with power and influence or people with exceptional intelligence. In love it is very important for you to keep a balance between your need for independence and your need for a relationship to avoid codependent partnerships. Although you are attracted to mentally determined and purposeful individuals, as a strong individual, you need to resist power clashes with partners. Nevertheless, possessing a gift of gab and a need for action, you will always attract others. With your warm ardor you can be an exciting lover or friend.

Your attractive qualities: optimistic, sociable, happy, determined, strong convictions, humorous, friendly, courageous, productive, creative, artistic, freedom-loving, talent with words, good contacts, hardworking, assertive, generous, honest, fighting spirit, versatile, enthusiastic

Your less attractive qualities: vain, insecure, tactless, exaggerates, selfish, worry, rash, self-deception, overindulgent, stubborn, rebellious, anxious, inertia, fear over money, scattered

Your Venus Power

The planet Venus has a great deal of influence on your powers of attraction. Below are four possible Venus types for women and men. To find your Venus you need to go to page 771, where you will find the Venus table and extra information. The planet Mars also affects your powers of attraction. To find your Mars table and interpretation go to page 761.

WOMEN WITH VENUS IN LIBRA: A natural romantic with good social skills, you love to entertain and can put people at ease by projecting a warm and gracious manner. Elegant and fair with a touch of glamour, you are also adept at dealing with people in delicate situations or conflicts. You seek refinement and will go out of your way to achieve harmony and keep the peace. Relationships are so important to you that you may need to guard against becoming dependent on others for approval. With your friendly personality and inherent charm, however, you will always be popular and loved.

MEN WITH VENUS IN LIBRA: Courteous and refined, you are attracted to beautiful and elegant people. You are looking for a partner who can share your natural good taste and enjoy an intellectual conversation. Disliking conflict, you may have to be careful not to go along with others just to keep the peace. Your ideal partner will appreciate beauty and the little luxuries of life as well as possess good social skills. You have a strong sense of social etiquette yourself so need an intelligent and sophisticated partner.

WOMEN WITH VENUS IN SCORPIO: With a natural psychic gift for penetrating the feelings of others, you can often help partners transform emotional challenges or sexual difficulties. When you fall in love, your strong feelings of determination give you a potent force that others find attractive and seductive. Although you know what really turns people on, your most profound desire is usually for the deepness and closeness of real love and intimacy in an enduring relationship.

MEN WITH VENUS IN SCORPIO: In relationships you possess a sensitive understanding of your partner's deeper nature. Although you are strongly attached to those you love, you may have to be careful that your feelings do not turn into jealousy or possessiveness. When you fall in love it is often with an emotional intensity that helps you get in touch with your deep

feelings. You are attracted to partners who can share your passion and display strong feelings of sexuality like your own.

WOMEN WITH VENUS IN SAGITTARIUS: Optimistic and fun-loving, you love adventure and seek a partner who can expand your horizons. Being truthful and direct, you often say what you think. At times you may be naively tactless. A need for expansion and prosperity suggests that you may enjoy traveling with your friends or partner. Being both lighthearted and idealistic, however, means that once you have given your heart to someone you will stay honorable and loyal.

MEN WITH VENUS IN SAGITTARIUS: You are usually attracted to partners who are knowledgeable or well-traveled. Enthusiastic and optimistic, you often respond quickly to love offers and enter relationships with enthusiasm. Usually you seek to expand your social circle and meeting people from all walks of life can bring you the variety and fun you seek in life. Although you are generous and honest, your partners may accuse you of being overly optimistic or too blunt.

WOMEN WITH VENUS IN CAPRICORN: Proud and refined, you attract others with your composed dignity. Disliking vulnerability and needing to feel safe before you can express your feelings, you usually display a strong front. Feeling insecure or inadequate in relationships may force you to become manipulative in order to regain control. Nevertheless, you can project an attractive sense of self-assurance and are capable of displaying loyalty and a wonderful dry sense of humor.

MEN WITH VENUS IN CAPRICORN: As you do not display your deeper emotions freely, you are usually dignified and controlled in your relationships with others. Practical and down-to-earth partners are particularly attractive to you, especially those who do not rush into expressing their feelings but seem to possess natural class and reserve. You need a partner who is loyal and dependable and willing to take your relationship seriously.

To read all about your Outer Planets and work out how to use your personalized timetable, go to Section Three, page 789.

To read all about your Outer Planets and work out how to use your personalized timetable, go to Section Three, page 789.

♐

Your Personalized Timetable

JUPITER BENEFICIAL
1938 1/14 – 2/26
1939 5/27 – 10/4
1940 1/13 – 3/30
1943 7/14 – 9/27
1944 3/9 – 5/18
1945 9/22 – 11/8
1949 12/29 – until **1950** 2/9
1951 5/4 – until **1952** 3/13
1955 6/27 – 9/9
1957 9/6 – 10/22
1961 4/27 – 6/23
1961 12/10 – until **1962** 1/24
1963 4/16 – 7/21
1963 8/28 – until **1964** 2/23
1966 10/20 – 12/23
1967 6/8 – 8/24
1969 1/10 – 1/30
1969 8/20 – 10/7
1973 3/25 – 8/10
1973 11/15 – until **1974** 1/7
1975 3/30 – 6/12
1975 10/19 – until **1976** 1/30
1978 9/21 – until **1979** 2/2
1979 5/16 – 8/8
1980 11/30 – until **1981** 3/23
1981 7/30 – 9/21
1985 3/5 – 5/9
1985 7/1 – 12/20
1987 3/14 – 5/22
1990 9/1 – until **1991** 7/22
1992 11/8 – until **1993** 5/4
1993 6/28 – 9/4
1997 2/15 – 4/6
1997 8/18 – 11/26
1999 2/25 – 5/4
2002 8/14 – until **2003** 7/5
2004 10/22 – 12/19
2005 3/19 – 8/17
2009 1/30 – 3/15
2010 7/5 – 8/10
2011 2/6 – 4/16

SATURN BENEFICIAL
1938 2/14 – until **1939** 3/25
1946 8/25 – until **1947** 3/2
1947 5/5 – 9/28
1948 2/13 – 6/17
1951 10/2 – until **1952** 9/24
1962 2/23 – 9/2
1962 11/15 – until **1963** 2/20
1967 3/27 – until **1968** 5/3
1968 12/8 – until **1969** 1/3
1975 11/4 – 11/25
1976 6/30 – until **1977** 8/1
1980 11/10 – until **1981** 4/3
1981 8/4 – 10/31
1982 5/28 – 7/9
1991 4/12 – 6/21
1992 1/1 – 3/31
1992 7/28 – 12/27
1996 5/2 – 10/11
1997 1/23 – 6/20
1997 9/13 – until **1998** 3/7
2005 8/7 – until **2006** 9/8
2007 3/22 – 5/18
2010 9/15 – 12/17
2011 3/7 – 9/7

URANUS BENEFICIAL
1956 7/29 – until **1960** 7/1
1969 10/21 – until **1972** 8/24
1997 2/15 – until **2000** 1/21
2011 5/3 – Continues

NEPTUNE BENEFICIAL
1944 11/23 – until **1950** 9/6
2000 3/18 – until **2005** 12/28

PLUTO BENEFICIAL
1939 10/20 – until **1951** 7/23
1973 11/11 – until **1978** 9/21

JUPITER CHALLENGING
1939 1/13 – 3/22

1941 6/7 – 8/30
1941 11/19 – until **1942** 4/18
1944 8/8 – 10/24
1945 4/14 – 6/14
1950 5/2 – 8/23
1950 12/21 – until **1951** 3/5
1953 5/21 – 8/3
1954 1/2 – 3/21
1956 7/22 – 10/6
1962 4/8 – 10/24
1962 11/2 – until **1963** 2/16
1965 5/5 – 7/14
1967 11/8 – until **1968** 2/4
1968 7/3 – 9/20
1974 3/20 – until **1975** 1/29
1977 4/17 – 6/27
1979 10/14 – until **1980** 3/15
1980 6/8 – 9/4
1986 3/4 – 5/22
1986 9/3 – until **1987** 1/9
1988 8/9 – 11/9
1989 3/28 – 6/10
1991 9/26 – until **1992** 8/19
1998 2/16 – 4/27
1998 10/24 – 12/3
2000 7/14 – 12/24
2001 2/26 – 5/25
2003 9/9 – 12/30
2004 1/7 – 8/2
2010 1/30 – 4/8
2012 6/24 – Continues

SATURN CHALLENGING
1942 5/31 – until **1943** 6/29
1948 10/15 – until **1949** 2/20
1949 7/6 – 12/5
1950 1/24 – 8/15
1964 4/23 – 8/8
1965 1/16 – until **1966** 3/2
1971 7/14 – 11/27
1972 4/1 – 8/19
1972 11/16 – until **1973** 5/4
1978 8/18 – until **1979** 9/23
1994 2/21 – until **1995** 4/7
1995 10/20 – 12/23
2001 5/13 – until **2002** 6/12
2007 9/26 – until **2008** 3/26
2008 6/9 – 11/3
2009 3/2 – 7/27

URANUS CHALLENGING
1942 7/6 – until **1947** 4/17
1962 9/26 – until **1966** 8/25
2004 2/23 – until **2008** 12/14

NEPTUNE CHALLENGING
1938 4/15 – 7/13
2012 5/3 – Continues

PLUTO CHALLENGING
1958 9/20 – until **1967** 7/28

JUPITER SPECIAL
1947 11/6 – until **1948** 1/19
1959 10/20 – until **1960** 1/1
1971 2/1 – 5/13
1971 9/30 – 12/16
1983 1/9 – 6/24
1983 9/2 – 11/30
1994 12/22 – until **1995** 11/14
2006 12/7 – until **2007** 3/12
2007 4/30 – 10/28

SATURN SPECIAL
1956 11/6 – until **1957** 12/27
1985 12/11 – until **1987** 2/5
1987 5/26 – 11/4

URANUS SPECIAL
1982 1/4 – until **1986** 10/1

NEPTUNE SPECIAL
1971 2/6 – until **1979** 11/5

PLUTO SPECIAL
1996 2/5 – until **2003** 11/18

December 4

SUN: SAGITTARIUS • DECANATE: ARIES/MARS • DEGREE: 11°5–12°5 SAGITTARIUS • MODE: MUTABLE • ELEMENT: FIRE

Your Personal Powers

Idealistic, dynamic, and enterprising, you are often a dramatic individual with a pragmatic outlook and strong willpower. Your ruling planet, Jupiter, highlights your desire for honesty and your preference for freedom and adventure. You gain power from your determination, loyalty, and candor; this also suggests that you can speak your mind with conviction. Liking order, you prefer to be well organized and will work very hard when you have a project in mind. Although you can be forceful and persevering, beware of losing some of your power by being too dogmatic or domineering. If you feel restricted, you can easily become restless and dissatisfied. Ambitious and daring, however, you are usually willing to take risks and are quick to see opportunities for success. Alternatively, you may decide to utilize your assertiveness in competitive situations or executive and leadership positions. Independent with strong desires and quick intelligence, you possess a talent for manifesting your ideals with extraordinary results and can do so if you only apply the necessary self-discipline and focus.

Your Powers of Attraction in Relationships

You can attract others with your honesty and direct approach. Being protective, you are usually willing to fight for those in your care. Although loyal and sincere, you should avoid becoming impatient, stubborn, or bossy with loved ones. Frank and fair, however, you can be kind and generous and a dynamic force in helping others. While you possess powerful feelings, you are also very aware of the practical considerations involved in your partnerships. Your ideal partner would be someone who is as adventurous and as dynamic as you are. A restless streak implies, however, that if you ignore your usual pragmatic approach and rush into a relationship, you may encounter setbacks or disappointments. Nevertheless, once committed, your relationships can be important to you, suggesting that you usually give much to make them work.

Your attractive qualities: strong-willed, organized, leadership ability, generous, courageous, direct, loyal, business sense, idealistic, daring, disciplined, hardworking, organized, ambitious, patient, assertive, endurance, practical, strong convictions, determined, strategist, foresight

Your less attractive qualities: bossy, repressed, too rigid, lazy, unfeeling, rebellious, too outspoken, lack of drive, procrastinator, too frugal or overindulgent, resentful, stubborn

Your Venus Power

The planet Venus has a great deal of influence on your powers of attraction. Below are four possible Venus types for women and men. To find your Venus you need to go to page 771, where you will find the Venus table and extra information. The planet Mars also affects your powers of attraction. To find your Mars table and interpretation go to page 761.

WOMEN WITH VENUS IN LIBRA: A natural romantic with good social skills, you love to entertain and can put people at ease by projecting a warm and gracious manner. Elegant and fair with a touch of glamour, you are also adept at dealing with people in delicate situations or conflicts. You seek refinement and will go out of your way to achieve harmony and keep the peace. Relationships are so important to you that you may need to guard against becoming dependent on others for approval. With your friendly personality and inherent charm, however, you will always be popular and loved.

MEN WITH VENUS IN LIBRA: You are such good company, people are naturally drawn to you and especially appreciate your talent for making them feel special. You find status in your social contacts and place importance on your relationships. Being clever and a charming companion, you will go out of your way to keep situations peaceful and harmonious. In relationships, however, be careful of indecision or compromising too much. Nevertheless, others are attracted by your natural refinement and good taste, which is reflected in your sense of style.

WOMEN WITH VENUS IN SCORPIO: You are usually drawn to partners who are sensual in appearance with a strong character. As you are emotionally intense and passionate, personal relationships are probably a major factor in your life. Since you like to be in control, you can at times exhibit some of your less attractive qualities by being willful or domineering. Although you need to feel established and in command in your relationships, you are constantly searching for some higher truth that can bring about a significant transformation.

MEN WITH VENUS IN SCORPIO: As you are emotionally intense and passionate, personal relationships are probably a major factor in your own transformation. Being sensitive yet

loyal, you are usually attracted to forceful partners who can express themselves intimately but intensely. Rather than seek easy and simple relationships, you are drawn to partners who act as a catalyst for your own internal changes. Through your relationships with your partners you can unravel your own motives and understand your deep-seated feelings or emotional insecurities.

Women with Venus in Sagittarius: Optimistic and fun-loving, you love adventure and seek a partner who can expand your horizons. Being truthful and direct, you often say what you think and at times are naively tactless. A need for expansion and prosperity suggests that you may enjoy traveling with your friends or partner. Being both lighthearted and idealistic, however, means that once you have given your heart to someone you will stay honorable and loyal.

Men with Venus in Sagittarius: When in love you are open and friendly with a need for a partner who can share your adventurous spirit and sense of fun. Be careful however, that your desire for freedom does not cause you to avoid commitment. You prefer your partners to be positive, direct, and generous in spirit. Being outspoken as well as an idealist, you usually enjoy a partner with whom you can share your strong opinions. Alternatively, you may wish to explore life together, whether through travel, education, or having fun.

Women with Venus in Capricorn: Proud and refined, you attract others with your composed dignity. Disliking vulnerability and needing to feel safe before you can express your feelings, you usually display a strong front. Feeling insecure or inadequate in relationships may force you to become manipulative in order to regain control. Nevertheless, you can project an attractive sense of self-assurance and are capable of displaying loyalty and a wonderful dry sense of humor.

Men with Venus in Capricorn: Hardworking and ambitious, you are usually attracted to determined, focused, and ambitious partners who have a strong sense of duty. You want them to take relationships as seriously as you do, so loyalty and faithfulness are high on your agenda. Since you may display a natural reserve about expressing your feelings in an intimate relationship, you need a partner who shares your need for emotional security.

To read all about your Outer Planets and work out how to use your personalized timetable, go to Section Three, page 789.

Your Personalized Timetable

Jupiter Beneficial
1938 1/19 – 3/2
1939 6/2 – 9/26
1940 1/20 – 4/3
1943 7/18 – 10/3
1944 2/29 – 5/27
1945 9/26 – 11/13
1950 1/2 – 2/14
1951 5/9 – until **1952** 3/17
1955 7/2 – 9/14
1957 9/11 – 10/27
1961 5/13 – 6/7
1961 12/15 – until **1962** 1/28
1963 4/20 – until **1964** 2/27
1966 11/2 – 12/10
1967 6/14 – 8/28
1969 8/25 – 10/12
1973 3/31 – 8/2
1973 11/22 – until **1974** 1/12
1975 4/3 – 6/19
1975 10/11 – until **1976** 2/5
1978 9/27 – until **1979** 1/25
1979 5/23 – 8/12
1980 12/7 – until **1981** 3/15
1981 8/5 – 9/26
1985 3/10 – 5/28
1985 6/11 – 12/25
1987 3/19 – 5/27
1987 12/7 – 12/23
1990 9/6 – until **1991** 3/16
1991 4/13 – 7/27
1992 11/14 – until **1993** 4/23
1993 7/9 – 9/9
1997 2/20 – 4/12
1997 8/10 – 12/3
1999 3/2 – 5/8
2002 8/19 – until **2003** 7/10
2004 10/27 – 12/28
2005 3/10 – 8/23
2009 2/3 – 3/20
2011 2/11 – 4/20

Saturn Beneficial
1938 2/23 – until **1939** 4/2
1946 9/3 – until **1947** 2/15
1947 5/21 – 10/8
1948 2/1 – 6/27
1951 10/10 – until **1952** 10/2
1962 3/4 – 8/17
1962 11/29 – until **1963** 3/1
1963 9/29 – 11/13
1967 4/4 – until **1968** 5/12
1968 11/14 – until **1969** 1/26
1976 7/8 – until **1977** 8/9
1980 11/21 – until **1981** 3/21
1981 8/15 – 11/9
1982 5/7 – 7/29
1992 1/10 – 4/13
1992 7/13 – until **1993** 1/5
1996 5/12 – 9/27
1997 2/3 – 7/9
1997 8/25 – until **1998** 3/16
2005 8/15 – until **2006** 9/17
2007 3/5 – 6/3
2010 9/24 – until **2011** 1/6
2011 2/14 – 9/16

Uranus Beneficial
1956 8/15 – until **1960** 7/20
1969 11/8 – until **1972** 9/12
1997 3/6 – until **2000** 2/7
2011 5/29 – Continues

Neptune Beneficial
1945 10/19 – until **1951** 7/20
2001 2/11 – until **2006** 1/26

Pluto Beneficial
1940 9/19 – until **1952** 6/29
1974 10/5 – until **1979** 8/6

Jupiter Challenging
1939 1/17 – 3/26
1941 6/12 – 9/9
1941 11/10 – until **1942** 4/23
1944 8/13 – 10/29
1945 4/4 – 6/24
1950 5/9 – 8/15
1950 12/27 – until **1951** 3/9
1953 5/26 – 8/8
1953 12/25 – until **1954** 3/29
1956 7/27 – 10/11
1962 4/13 – 10/4
1962 11/23 – until **1963** 2/21
1965 5/9 – 7/19
1967 11/16 – until **1968** 1/26
1968 7/9 – 9/25
1974 3/25 – until **1975** 2/3
1977 4/22 – 7/1
1979 10/20 – until **1980** 3/6
1980 6/16 – 9/9
1986 3/8 – 5/29
1986 8/26 – until **1987** 1/14
1988 8/18 – 11/1
1989 4/3 – 6/15
1991 10/1 – until **1992** 8/24
1998 2/20 – 5/2
1998 10/12 – 12/15
2000 7/20 – 12/15
2001 3/7 – 5/29
2003 9/14 – until **2004** 8/7
2010 2/4 – 4/12
2012 6/29 – Continues

Saturn Challenging
1942 6/8 – until **1943** 7/8
1944 2/6 – 3/5
1948 10/26 – until **1949** 2/8
1949 7/16 – until **1950** 8/24
1964 5/8 – 7/23
1965 1/26 – until **1966** 3/11
1971 7/25 – 11/15
1972 4/11 – 9/4
1972 10/30 – until **1973** 5/13
1978 8/26 – until **1979** 10/1
1994 3/2 – until **1995** 4/16
1995 10/4 – until **1996** 1/7
2001 5/21 – until **2002** 6/20
2007 10/5 – until **2008** 3/11
2008 6/23 – 11/15
2009 2/17 – 8/5

Uranus Challenging
1942 7/31 – until **1947** 5/9
1962 10/15 – until **1966** 9/11
2004 3/12 – until **2009** 1/19

Neptune Challenging
1938 1/1 – 8/17

Pluto Challenging
1958 10/30 – until **1967** 8/29

Jupiter Special
1947 11/11 – until **1948** 1/24
1948 7/24 – 9/7
1959 10/25 – until **1960** 1/6
1971 2/9 – 5/4
1971 10/6 – 12/21
1983 1/15 – 6/14
1983 9/11 – 12/5
1994 12/27 – until **1995** 11/19
2006 12/11 – until **2007** 11/2

Saturn Special
1956 11/15 – until **1958** 1/5
1958 7/23 – 9/24
1985 12/20 – until **1986** 7/5
1986 9/8 – until **1987** 2/19
1987 5/10 – 11/13

Uranus Special
1982 1/27 – until **1986** 10/28

Neptune Special
1971 12/25 – until **1979** 12/4

Pluto Special
1996 12/17 – until **2004** 10/5

December 5

SUN: SAGITTARIUS • DECANATE: ARIES/MARS • DEGREE: 12°5–13°5 SAGITTARIUS • MODE: MUTABLE • ELEMENT: FIRE

Your Personal Powers

Your keen intelligence, quick mental responses, and broad-minded outlook indicate that you are an instinctive individual with strong determination. You gain power from your knowledgeable and authoritative manner and responsible attitude. Usually you gravitate to positions of leadership. Your ruling planet, Jupiter, ensures that you value honesty even though it may sometimes cause you to be outspoken. You can lose some of your power, however, if you are too critical or tactless. Nevertheless, your honorable and confident manner often impresses people. Being proud, adventurous, and optimistic, you need the freedom to express yourself or to explore different interests. Although you are usually resolute, at times you can experience inner doubts and insecurities that may threaten your self-confidence. Often hardworking and persevering, however, you can focus on your goals with uncompromising determination. Your desire for growth suggests that you may find travel or education particularly good for expanding your horizons. With self-discipline you have all the ingredients for attaining prosperity and success.

Your Powers of Attraction in Relationships

People are impressed by your intelligence and independent personality. Being sociable, you enjoy friendly activities where you can share your knowledge and experiences with others. You are often drawn to reliable, straightforward individuals with common sense. If your partner can share your desire for new experiences or travel then so much the better. Being practical, you like to build strong life foundations, which include making a safe and secure home for you and your loved ones. You are freedom loving and independent, and if you become overly dependent on your partner, however, you may resent it in the long run. Responsible and idealistic, you are caring and protective, yet you achieve more by using your diplomacy than by trying to force issues with your strong will. You ideally also need a partner who enjoys your zany sense of humor.

Your attractive qualities: keen mentality, versatile, leadership ability, broad-minded, adaptable, adventurous, traveled, progressive, quick instincts, pragmatic, daring, optimistic, freedom-loving, curious, sociable, strong convictions, endurance, responsible, determination

Your less attractive qualities: obstinate, impatient, too outspoken, rebellious, inconsistent, destructive behavior, lack of drive, tense, undependable, overconfident or insecure, headstrong, too tough

Your Venus Power

The planet Venus has a great deal of influence on your powers of attraction. Below are four possible Venus types for women and men. To find your Venus you need to go to page 771, where you will find the Venus table and extra information. The planet Mars also affects your powers of attraction. To find your Mars table and interpretation go to page 761.

WOMEN WITH VENUS IN LIBRA: A natural romantic with good social skills, you love to entertain and can put people at ease by projecting a warm and gracious manner. Elegant and fair with a touch of glamour, you are also adept at dealing with people in delicate situations or conflicts. You seek refinement and will go out of your way to achieve harmony and keep the peace. Relationships are so important to you that you may need to guard against becoming dependent on others for approval. With your friendly personality and inherent charm, however, you will always be popular and loved.

MEN WITH VENUS IN LIBRA: As a sociable and friendly individual with an eye for beauty, you are amorous and charming. You are a natural gentleman, and your ideal partner usually has an elegant appearance, artistic appreciation, and good taste. Your relationships benefit when you resist the temptation to take the easy way out or put too much emphasis on vanity and high living. Intellectual and naturally refined, you seek a loving partner who can share your romantic and sophisticated aspirations.

WOMEN WITH VENUS IN SCORPIO: You are usually drawn to partners who are sensual in appearance with a strong character. As you are emotionally intense and passionate, personal relationships are probably a major factor in your life. Since you like to be in control, you can at times exhibit some of your less attractive qualities by being willful or domineering. Although you need to feel established and in command in your relationships, you are constantly searching for some higher truth that can bring about a significant transformation.

MEN WITH VENUS IN SCORPIO: As you are emotionally intense and passionate, personal relationships are probably a major factor in your own transformation. Being sensitive yet

loyal, you are usually attracted to forceful partners who can express themselves intimately but intensely. Rather than seek easy and simple relationships, you are drawn to partners who act as a catalyst for your own internal changes. Through your relationships with your partners you can unravel your own motives and understand your deep-seated feelings or emotional insecurities.

WOMEN WITH VENUS IN SAGITTARIUS: Optimistic and fun-loving, you love adventure and seek a partner who can expand your horizons. Being truthful and direct, you often say what you think, and at times you may be naively tactless. A need for expansion and prosperity suggests that you may enjoy traveling with your friends or partner. Being both lighthearted and idealistic, however, means that once you have given your heart to someone you will stay honorable and loyal.

MEN WITH VENUS IN SAGITTARIUS: When in love you are open and friendly with a need for a partner who can share your adventurous spirit and sense of fun. Be careful, however, that your desire for freedom does not cause you to avoid commitment. You prefer your partners to be positive, direct, and generous in spirit. Being outspoken as well as an idealist, you usually enjoy a partner with whom you can share your strong opinions. Alternatively, you may wish to explore life together, whether through travel, education, or having fun.

WOMEN WITH VENUS IN CAPRICORN: With your natural caution in romantic affairs, you often appear reserved and controlled. If shy, try to be more forward, especially if you want to be noticed. When you care about people, however, you are usually willing to put in extra time and energy to preserve the relationship. You are practical and dependable, and a sense of duty can often play a large role in the affairs of your heart. With elegant simplicity, you can attract others with your well-cut clothes and refined manners.

MEN WITH VENUS IN CAPRICORN: As you admire loyal, hardworking, and dedicated individuals, you probably want a partner who can share your vocational interests or who can provide you with the sense of security you need. You could even find yourself with a partner who is of a different age group or maturity. Guard against denying your true emotional needs or focusing on your career at the expense of your relationship. You are drawn to reserved partners who display self-control.

To read all about your Outer Planets and work out how to use your personalized timetable, go to Section Three, page 789.

go to Section Three, page 789.

Your Personalized Timetable

JUPITER BENEFICIAL
1938 1/23 – 3/7
1939 6/9 – 9/19
1940 1/26 – 4/8
1943 7/23 – 10/9
1944 2/21 – 6/4
1945 10/1 – 11/18
1946 5/28 – 7/2
1950 1/7 – 2/18
1951 5/14 – 11/11
1951 12/19 – until **1952** 3/21
1955 7/6 – 9/19
1957 9/15 – 11/1
1961 12/20 – until **1962** 2/2
1963 4/25 – until **1964** 3/3
1967 6/19 – 9/2
1969 8/30 – 10/16
1973 4/7 – 7/25
1973 11/28 – until **1974** 1/16
1975 4/8 – 6/25
1975 10/4 – until **1976** 2/11
1978 10/4 – until **1979** 1/18
1979 5/30 – 8/17
1980 12/15 – until **1981** 3/6
1981 8/11 – 10/1
1985 3/15 – 9/11
1985 10/24 – 12/30
1987 3/23 – 6/1
1987 11/19 – until **1988** 1/10
1990 9/11 – until **1991** 3/1
1991 4/29 – 8/1
1992 11/20 – until **1993** 4/14
1993 7/18 – 9/14
1997 2/24 – 4/18
1997 8/2 – 12/9
1999 3/6 – 5/12
2002 8/24 – until **2003** 7/15
2004 11/1 – until **2005** 1/8
2005 2/26 – 8/28
2009 2/8 – 3/25
2009 9/22 – 11/3
2011 2/16 – 4/25

SATURN BENEFICIAL
1938 3/4 – until **1939** 4/10
1946 9/12 – until **1947** 2/1
1947 6/1 – 10/20
1948 1/18 – 7/7
1951 10/19 – until **1952** 10/10
1962 3/14 – 8/3
1962 12/11 – until **1963** 3/10
1963 9/8 – 12/2
1967 4/12 – until **1968** 5/21
1968 10/30 – until **1969** 2/9
1976 7/16 – until **1977** 8/17
1980 12/3 – until **1981** 3/7
1981 8/25 – 11/18
1982 4/22 – 8/12
1992 1/18 – 5/1
1992 6/24 – until **1993** 1/15
1996 5/24 – 9/14
1997 2/13 – until **1998** 3/25
2005 8/24 – until **2006** 3/12
2006 4/29 – 9/26
2007 2/20 – 6/16
2010 10/2 – until **2011** 9/25

URANUS BENEFICIAL
1956 9/2 – until **1960** 8/5
1969 11/30 – until **1972** 9/29
1997 3/30 – until **2000** 12/14
2012 3/31 – Continues

NEPTUNE BENEFICIAL
1945 11/19 – until **1951** 9/4
2001 3/14 – until **2006** 12/24

PLUTO BENEFICIAL
1941 9/1 – until **1953** 5/23
1974 11/1 – until **1979** 9/10

JUPITER CHALLENGING
1939 1/22 – 3/31
1941 6/16 – 9/22

1941 10/28 – until **1942** 4/29
1944 8/18 – 11/4
1945 3/26 – 7/2
1950 5/17 – 8/7
1951 1/2 – 3/14
1953 5/30 – 8/14
1953 12/17 – until **1954** 4/5
1956 8/1 – 10/16
1962 4/19 – 9/23
1962 12/4 – until **1963** 2/25
1965 5/14 – 7/24
1967 11/28 – until **1968** 1/15
1968 7/15 – 9/30
1974 3/30 – until **1975** 2/8
1977 4/27 – 7/6
1979 10/26 – until **1980** 2/27
1980 6/23 – 9/14
1986 3/13 – 6/7
1986 8/17 – until **1987** 1/20
1988 8/28 – 10/21
1989 4/8 – 6/19
1991 10/6 – until **1992** 4/18
1992 5/13 – 8/29
1998 2/24 – 5/8
1998 10/3 – 12/24
2000 7/25 – 12/7
2001 3/14 – 6/3
2003 9/19 – until **2004** 8/13
2010 2/8 – 4/17
2012 7/4 – Continues

SATURN CHALLENGING
1942 6/16 – until **1943** 7/16
1944 1/14 – 3/28
1948 11/8 – until **1949** 1/24
1949 7/26 – until **1950** 9/1
1964 6/2 – 6/27
1965 2/4 – until **1966** 3/19
1971 8/6 – 11/1
1972 4/20 – until **1973** 5/21
1978 9/3 – until **1979** 10/10
1980 4/23 – 6/20
1994 3/10 – until **1995** 4/26
1995 9/20 – until **1996** 1/19
2001 5/29 – until **2002** 6/28
2007 10/14 – until **2008** 2/27
2008 7/5 – 11/30
2009 2/1 – 8/15

URANUS CHALLENGING
1943 5/30 – until **1947** 5/27
1962 11/11 – until **1967** 7/5
2004 3/31 – until **2009** 2/10

NEPTUNE CHALLENGING
1938 1/23 – until **1939** 7/8

PLUTO CHALLENGING
1959 9/26 – until **1968** 7/23

JUPITER SPECIAL
1947 11/15 – until **1948** 1/29
1948 7/12 – 9/19
1959 10/30 – until **1960** 1/11
1971 2/19 – 4/24
1971 10/12 – 12/25
1983 1/21 – 6/6
1983 9/19 – 12/9
1995 1/1 – 11/24
2006 12/16 – until **2007** 11/7

SATURN SPECIAL
1956 11/23 – until **1958** 1/14
1958 7/5 – 10/10
1985 12/29 – until **1986** 6/18
1986 9/24 – until **1987** 3/13
1987 4/17 – 11/22

URANUS SPECIAL
1982 11/27 – until **1986** 11/16

NEPTUNE SPECIAL
1972 1/31 – until **1980** 11/1

PLUTO SPECIAL
1997 1/17 – until **2004** 11/12

♐

December 6

SUN: SAGITTARIUS · DECANATE: ARIES/MARS · DEGREE: 13°5–14°5 SAGITTARIUS · MODE: MUTABLE · ELEMENT: FIRE

Your Personal Powers

You are clever and enterprising, and your personal powers also include sharp intelligence, foresight, and an ability to see new opportunities or the advantages in any given situation. Your ruling planet, Jupiter, implies that you are broad-minded with an aptitude for continually updating your knowledge or overseeing large projects. With your leadership abilities, you generally do not like to be subordinate to anyone less capable than yourself. Being inventive and quick-witted, you usually enjoy a challenge but inspiration can be a strong factor in your success. Although you possess good business acumen and can reap monetary rewards, usually your greatest satisfaction comes from fulfilling some of your high ideals. You often benefit from expanding your horizons through education or travel, although home and family are likely to play an especially important role in your learning process. Generous and caring, by accepting your responsibilities, you are usually able to avoid losing power to anxiety, worry, or indecision. With your special insight, convincing speech, and organizational skills, you can have many fortunate openings for success.

Your Powers of Attraction in Relationships

Others are attracted to your sociable, friendly, and caring personality. With your quick intelligence, you need a partner who is as sharp and witty as you are. A tendency to become restless suggests, however, that without mental stimulation you can easily become bored. You therefore need a daring partner with whom you can share your views and ideals or your spirit of adventure and optimism. Although you are independent and freedom-loving, you also value the importance of a harmonious and secure home base from which to reach out to the world. With your warm heart, you can be affectionate and kind, but if you become negative you may appear obstinate, intolerant, or discontented. Nevertheless, resourceful, clever, and creative, you can be a loyal partner and a sympathetic and responsible friend.

Your attractive qualities: intelligent, kind, generous, compassionate, dependable, caring, understanding, worldly, sympathetic, creative, idealistic, leadership ability, home-loving, endurance, humanitarian, artistic, pragmatic, organizational skills, business sense, honest

Your less attractive qualities: anxious, tactless, unreasonable, stubborn, outspoken, shy, perfectionist, domineering, rebellious, lack of responsibility, self-pity, lack of drive, suspicious, bossy, obstinate, self-centered

Your Venus Power

The planet Venus has a great deal of influence on your powers of attraction. Below are four possible Venus types for women and men. To find your Venus you need to go to page 771, where you will find the Venus table and extra information. The planet Mars also affects your powers of attraction. To find your Mars table and interpretation go to page 761.

WOMEN WITH VENUS IN LIBRA: Usually you are attractive and sociable with an easygoing manner. Your love of beauty, harmony, and pleasure implies that you are a romantic with a desire for love and affection. Once in a relationship you need to learn to negotiate your position rather than adapt to the wishes of others and compromise just to keep the peace. Nevertheless, your advanced social skills and strong sense of fair play can help you succeed in any social or romantic situation.

MEN WITH VENUS IN LIBRA: As a sociable and friendly individual with an eye for beauty, you are amorous and charming. You are a natural gentleman, and your ideal partner usually has an elegant appearance, artistic appreciation, and good taste. Your relationships benefit when you resist the temptation to take the easy way out or put too much emphasis on vanity and high living. Intellectual and naturally refined, you seek a loving partner who can share your romantic and sophisticated aspirations.

WOMEN WITH VENUS IN SCORPIO: With a natural psychic gift for penetrating the feelings of others, you can often help partners transform emotional challenges or sexual difficulties. When you fall in love, your strong feelings and determination give you a potent force that others find attractive and seductive. Although you know what really turns people on, your most profound desire is usually for the deepness and closeness of real love and intimacy in an enduring relationship.

MEN WITH VENUS IN SCORPIO: In relationships you possess a sensitive understanding of your partner's deeper nature. Although you are strongly attached to those you love, you may have to be careful that your feelings do not turn into jealousy or possessiveness. When you fall in love it is often with an emotional intensity that helps you get in touch with your deep

feelings. You are attracted to partners who can share your passion and display strong feelings of sexuality like your own.

WOMEN WITH VENUS IN SAGITTARIUS: Sociable, warm, and friendly, you possess an honest and frank style in your relationships. Being naturally gregarious, you want others to share your enthusiasm and enjoy encouraging the people you love. You fare better when you have a sense of personal freedom within a relationship and are usually generous with the faults of others. You need a partner who can share your need to explore and take risks, whether through travel, education, or recreation.

MEN WITH VENUS IN SAGITTARIUS: Your enthusiasm and straightforward conduct usually appeal to others and imply that you are approachable and easygoing. Being open to ideas and willing to believe that life has a great deal to offer suggests that you are generous, broad-minded, and show eagerness to cooperate with others. A love of travel and an interest in other cultures also imply that your partner may come from a foreign country.

WOMEN WITH VENUS IN CAPRICORN: With your natural caution in romantic affairs, you often appear reserved and controlled. If shy, try to be more forward, especially if you want to be noticed. When you care about people, however, you are usually willing to put in extra time and energy to preserve the relationship. You are practical and dependable, and a sense of duty can often play a large role in the affairs of your heart. With elegant simplicity, you can attract others with your well-cut clothes and refined manners.

MEN WITH VENUS IN CAPRICORN: As you do not display your deeper emotions freely, you are usually dignified and controlled in your relationships with others. Practical and down-to-earth partners are particularly attractive to you, especially those who do not rush into expressing their feelings but seem to possess natural class and reserve. You need a partner who is loyal and dependable and willing to take your relationship seriously.

To read all about your Outer Planets and work out how to use your personalized timetable, go to Section Three, page 789.

go to Section Three, page 789.

Your Personalized Timetable

JUPITER BENEFICIAL
1938 1/27 – 3/11
1939 6/16 – 9/11
1940 1/31 – 4/12
1943 7/27 – 10/15
1944 2/13 – 6/11
1945 10/6 – 11/24
1946 5/14 – 7/16
1950 1/11 – 2/22
1951 5/19 – 10/29
1951 12/31 – until 1952 3/26
1955 7/11 – 9/24
1956 4/1 – 5/3
1957 9/20 – 11/6
1961 12/24 – until 1962 2/6
1963 4/29 – until 1964 3/8
1967 6/24 – 9/7
1969 9/4 – 10/21
1973 4/14 – 7/17
1973 12/4 – until 1974 1/20
1975 4/12 – 7/3
1975 9/26 – until 1976 2/17
1978 10/11 – until 1979 1/10
1979 6/5 – 8/21
1980 12/24 – until 1981 2/24
1981 8/17 – 10/5
1985 3/20 – 8/30
1985 11/5 – until 1986 1/4
1987 3/27 – 6/6
1987 11/9 – until 1988 1/20
1990 9/17 – until 1991 2/19
1991 5/9 – 8/6
1992 11/26 – until 1993 4/6
1993 7/26 – 9/19
1997 3/1 – 4/26
1997 7/25 – 12/14
1999 3/10 – 5/17
2002 8/29 – until 2003 7/20
2004 11/6 – until 2005 9/3
2009 2/12 – 3/31
2009 9/10 – 11/14
2011 2/20 – 4/29

SATURN BENEFICIAL
1938 3/12 – until 1939 4/18
1946 9/23 – until 1947 1/20
1947 6/12 – 11/5
1948 1/2 – 7/16
1951 10/27 – until 1952 5/12
1952 7/9 – 10/19
1962 3/26 – 7/20
1962 12/22 – until 1963 3/20
1963 8/24 – 12/15
1967 4/21 – 11/22
1967 12/26 – until 1968 5/31
1968 10/17 – until 1969 2/20
1976 7/24 – until 1977 8/25
1980 12/18 – until 1981 2/19
1981 9/3 – 11/28
1982 4/9 – 8/24
1992 1/27 – until 1993 1/23
1996 6/6 – 8/31
1997 2/23 – until 1998 4/2
2005 9/1 – until 2006 2/22
2006 5/17 – 10/6
2007 2/7 – 6/27
2010 10/10 – until 2011 10/3

URANUS BENEFICIAL
1956 9/23 – until 1961 5/23
1970 9/28 – until 1972 10/15
1998 2/1 – until 2001 1/6
2012 4/18 – Continues

NEPTUNE BENEFICIAL
1946 10/17 – until 1951 10/3
2002 2/9 – until 2007 1/24

PLUTO BENEFICIAL
1942 8/17 – until 1953 7/13
1974 12/8 – until 1979 10/7

JUPITER CHALLENGING
1939 1/26 – 4/4
1941 6/21 – until 1942 5/4

1944 8/23 – 11/10
1945 3/18 – 7/10
1950 5/26 – 7/28
1951 1/7 – 3/18
1953 6/3 – 8/21
1953 12/9 – until 1954 4/12
1956 8/6 – 10/21
1957 5/12 – 5/25
1962 4/24 – 9/14
1962 12/12 – until 1963 3/1
1965 5/18 – 7/29
1966 1/26 – 3/7
1968 7/20 – 10/4
1974 4/3 – until 1975 2/12
1977 5/1 – 7/10
1979 11/2 – until 1980 2/20
1980 6/30 – 9/18
1986 3/17 – 6/18
1986 8/6 – until 1987 1/25
1988 9/13 – 10/5
1989 4/13 – 6/24
1991 10/11 – until 1992 4/1
1992 5/30 – 9/3
1998 3/1 – 5/14
1998 9/24 – 12/31
2000 7/31 – 11/29
2001 3/21 – 6/7
2003 9/24 – until 2004 8/18
2010 2/12 – 4/22
2012 7/8 – Continues

SATURN CHALLENGING
1942 6/24 – until 1943 1/18
1943 2/24 – 7/25
1943 12/31 – until 1944 4/10
1948 11/29 – until 1949 1/3
1949 8/3 – until 1950 9/9
1965 2/12 – until 1966 3/27
1971 8/23 – 10/15
1972 4/29 – until 1973 5/29
1978 9/12 – until 1979 10/19
1980 4/6 – 7/7
1994 3/19 – 10/24
1994 11/25 – until 1995 5/7
1995 9/7 – until 1996 1/30
2001 6/6 – until 2002 7/6
2007 10/25 – until 2008 2/15
2008 7/15 – until 2009 8/23

URANUS CHALLENGING
1943 6/17 – until 1947 6/13
1963 9/2 – until 1967 7/30
2004 4/24 – until 2009 2/28

NEPTUNE CHALLENGING
1938 1/1 – until 1939 8/15

PLUTO CHALLENGING
1959 11/7 – until 1968 8/25

JUPITER SPECIAL
1947 11/20 – until 1948 2/4
1948 7/2 – 9/28
1959 11/4 – until 1960 1/15
1971 3/5 – 4/10
1971 10/17 – 12/30
1983 1/27 – 5/29
1983 9/26 – 12/14
1995 1/7 – 7/18
1995 8/18 – 11/28
2006 12/21 – until 2007 11/12

SATURN SPECIAL
1956 12/2 – until 1958 1/24
1958 6/20 – 10/23
1986 1/8 – 6/3
1986 10/7 – until 1987 12/1

URANUS SPECIAL
1982 12/14 – until 1986 12/4

NEPTUNE SPECIAL
1972 12/22 – until 1980 12/1

PLUTO SPECIAL
1997 12/8 – until 2005 9/20

541

December 7

Your Personal Powers

Intelligent yet unconventional, you are a self-reliant individual with an independent nature and good communication skills. Your ruling planet, Jupiter, grants you enthusiasm, optimism, and a desire to explore and expand your horizons. You gain power when you combine your determination, practical skills, and cerebral powers in the pursuit of knowledge and self-awareness. Your natural leadership skills may even place you in positions of authority. Alternatively, as a restless, inquisitive, and daring person, you may chose to experiment with a more adventurous lifestyle that can offer you opportunities for travel or new challenges. Being mentally quick implies that you can also be witty and enterprising, but you may lose power if you become too frank or critical. Although you are a friendly individual with the ability to assimilate information fast and act upon it spontaneously, you like to make up your own mind. With your impulsive or impatient streak, you may need to learn to be more self-disciplined or methodical so as to channel your strong will and original ideas in a constructive way.

Your Powers of Attraction in Relationships

People are attracted to your natural charm, quick wit, and broad-minded attitude. Although you are spontaneous and youthful, you can at times be reserved and appear detached. Since you like to question people's ideas or opinions, you may sometimes seem skeptical. You are usually drawn to intelligent, enterprising, and freedom-loving individuals. In personal relationships you are often intuitive and sensitive, yet you can also be intense and passionate. As a nonconformist you usually adhere to your own principles. Since you are idealistic, and attractive to others, you may have to exercise discrimination to avoid involvement in secret or unsuitable relationships. Ideally, you may be looking for a partner with whom you can establish an almost spiritual bond, someone who can still be faithful and loving.

Your attractive qualities: enthusiastic, educated, philosophical, intelligent, optimistic, sociable, meticulous, idealistic, spiritual potential, creative thinker, reflective, inspired, communicator, progressive, generous, direct, carefree, shrewd, diplomatic, independent, intuitive

Your less attractive qualities: restless, unfriendly, skeptical, unfeeling, eccentric, impulsive, rebellious, materialistic, too opinionated, critical, tend to overrationalize, secretive, tactless, moody, provocative, too idealistic, uncommunicative

Your Venus Power

The planet Venus has a great deal of influence on your powers of attraction. Below are four possible Venus types for women and men. To find your Venus you need to go to page 771, where you will find the Venus table and extra information. The planet Mars also affects your powers of attraction. To find your Mars table and interpretation go to page 761.

WOMEN WITH VENUS IN SCORPIO: With a natural psychic gift for penetrating the feelings of others, you can often help partners transform emotional challenges or sexual difficulties. When you fall in love, your strong feelings and determination give you a potent force that others find attractive and seductive. Although you know what really turns people on, your most profound desire is usually for the deepness and closeness of real love and intimacy in an enduring relationship.

MEN WITH VENUS IN SCORPIO: As you are emotionally intense and passionate, personal relationships are probably a major factor in your own transformation. Being sensitive yet loyal, you are usually attracted to forceful partners who can express themselves intimately but intensely. Rather than seek easy and simple relationships, you are drawn to partners who act as a catalyst for your own internal changes. Through your relationships with your partners you can unravel your own motives and understand your deep-seated feelings or emotional insecurities.

WOMEN WITH VENUS IN SAGITTARIUS: When you feel generous you can make others feel more optimistic about life. You may be interested in higher learning and seek partners who are scholarly or broad-minded. You are outspoken and direct and sometimes say things that you later regret. Curious and versatile, you can adjust quickly to new situations, and a foreign influence implies that you love to travel or may have a partner who comes from a different culture.

MEN WITH VENUS IN SAGITTARIUS: Your enthusiasm and straightforward conduct usually appeal to others and imply that you are approachable and easygoing. Being open to ideas and willing to believe that life has a great deal to offer suggests that you are generous, broad-minded, and show eagerness to

cooperate with others. A love of travel and an interest in other cultures also imply that your partner may come from a foreign country.

Women with Venus in Capricorn: Proud and refined, you attract others with your composed dignity. Disliking vulnerability and needing to feel safe before you can express your feelings, you usually display a strong front. Feeling insecure or inadequate in relationships may force you to become manipulative in order to regain control. Nevertheless, you can project an attractive sense of self-assurance and are capable of displaying loyalty and a wonderful dry sense of humor.

Men with Venus in Capricorn: As you do not display your deeper emotions freely, you are usually dignified and controlled in your relationships with others. Practical and down-to-earth partners are particularly attractive to you, especially those who do not rush into expressing their feelings but seem to possess natural class and reserve. You need a partner who is loyal and dependable and willing to take your relationship seriously.

Women with Venus in Aquarius: You attract and impress others with your friendly approach and progressive ideas. As you are usually independent and easygoing, you value freedom within a relationship. A good companion, with a sense of your own person, you enjoy socializing, especially with people who are original, cosmopolitan, and have a strong sense of individuality. Although being friendly and detached usually serves you well, avoid losing touch with your emotions. You usually prefer the company of those who have innovative or progressive views.

Men with Venus in Aquarius: Friendly and honest, you attract people with your broad-minded approach to life. You usually possess an objective and slightly detached attitude to affairs of the heart. If you are too removed, however, others can misinterpret your behavior as uncaring. It is often more important to you that your love relationships are based on friendship and honesty rather than intense passion. As you are generally tolerant and liberal, you may be drawn to less conventional relationships.

To read all about your Outer Planets and work out how to use your personalized timetable, go to Section Three, page 789.

Your Personalized Timetable

Jupiter Beneficial
1938 2/1 – 3/16
1939 6/25 – 9/2
1940 2/6 – 4/16
1943 8/1 – 10/22
1944 2/5 – 6/17
1945 10/11 – 11/29
1946 5/4 – 7/26
1950 1/15 – 2/27
1951 5/25 – 10/20
1952 1/9 – 3/30
1955 7/16 – 9/29
1956 3/18 – 5/18
1957 9/25 – 11/11
1961 12/29 – until **1962** 2/10
1963 5/4 – until **1964** 3/13
1967 6/29 – 9/12
1969 9/9 – 10/26
1973 4/23 – 7/8
1973 12/10 – until **1974** 1/25
1975 4/16 – 7/12
1975 9/17 – until **1976** 2/22
1978 10/20 – until **1979** 1/1
1979 6/10 – 8/26
1981 1/7 – 2/10
1981 8/22 – 10/10
1985 3/26 – 8/21
1985 11/14 – until **1986** 1/8
1987 3/31 – 6/12
1987 10/31 – until **1988** 1/28
1990 9/22 – until **1991** 2/10
1991 5/17 – 8/10
1992 12/2 – until **1993** 3/29
1993 8/2 – 9/24
1997 3/6 – 5/4
1997 7/16 – 12/20
1999 3/15 – 5/22
2002 9/3 – until **2003** 7/25
2004 11/12 – until **2005** 5/10
2005 7/1 – 9/8
2009 2/16 – 4/5
2009 8/31 – 11/23
2011 2/25 – 5/3

Saturn Beneficial
1938 3/21 – until **1939** 4/27
1946 10/4 – until **1947** 1/7
1947 6/21 – until **1948** 7/24
1951 11/5 – until **1952** 4/24
1952 7/26 – 10/27
1962 4/8 – 7/5
1962 12/31 – until **1963** 3/30
1963 8/11 – 12/27
1967 4/29 – 10/31
1968 1/16 – 6/11
1968 10/4 – until **1969** 3/2
1976 8/1 – until **1977** 9/2
1981 9/12 – 12/9
1982 3/26 – 9/3
1992 2/4 – until **1993** 2/1
1996 6/25 – 8/11
1997 3/3 – until **1998** 4/10
2005 9/10 – until **2006** 2/8
2006 5/30 – 10/17
2007 1/25 – 7/6
2010 10/18 – until **2011** 10/11

Uranus Beneficial
1956 11/1 – until **1961** 6/22
1970 10/14 – until **1973** 8/14
1998 2/19 – until **2001** 1/25
2012 5/9 – Continues

Neptune Beneficial
1946 11/16 – until **1952** 9/1
2002 3/10 – until **2007** 12/20

Pluto Beneficial
1942 9/30 – until **1954** 6/15
1975 10/23 – until **1980** 8/27

Jupiter Challenging
1939 1/31 – 4/8
1941 6/25 – until **1942** 5/9
1944 8/27 – 11/17
1945 3/10 – 7/17
1950 6/9 – 7/14
1951 1/12 – 3/22
1953 6/8 – 8/28
1953 12/2 – until **1954** 4/18
1956 8/11 – 10/27
1957 4/22 – 6/15
1962 4/30 – 9/6
1962 12/19 – until **1963** 3/5
1965 5/22 – 8/3
1966 1/14 – 3/19
1968 7/25 – 10/9
1974 4/8 – until **1975** 2/17
1977 5/6 – 7/15
1979 11/9 – until **1980** 2/12
1980 7/6 – 9/23
1986 3/22 – until **1987** 1/30
1989 4/18 – 6/28
1991 10/17 – until **1992** 3/22
1992 6/9 – 9/7
1998 3/5 – 5/20
1998 9/17 – until **1999** 1/7
2000 8/7 – 11/22
2001 3/28 – 6/12
2003 9/29 – until **2004** 8/23
2010 2/16 – 4/26
2012 7/14 – Continues

Saturn Challenging
1942 7/2 – 12/29
1943 3/16 – 8/4
1943 12/18 – until **1944** 4/21
1949 8/12 – until **1950** 9/18
1965 2/20 – until **1966** 4/5
1966 11/23 – 11/30
1972 5/7 – until **1973** 6/6
1978 9/20 – until **1979** 10/28
1980 3/23 – 7/19
1994 3/28 – 10/1
1994 12/17 – until **1995** 5/19
1995 8/24 – until **1996** 2/8
2001 6/14 – until **2002** 7/14
2003 1/24 – 3/23
2007 11/6 – until **2008** 2/1
2008 7/24 – until **2009** 9/1

Uranus Challenging
1943 7/6 – until **1948** 4/13
1963 9/19 – until **1967** 8/18
2005 2/28 – until **2009** 12/24

Neptune Challenging
1938 1/1 – until **1940** 6/30

Pluto Challenging
1960 9/30 – until **1969** 7/17

Jupiter Special
1947 11/25 – until **1948** 2/10
1948 6/24 – 10/6
1959 11/9 – until **1960** 1/20
1971 10/22 – until **1972** 1/3
1983 2/3 – 5/21
1983 10/2 – 12/18
1995 1/12 – 7/3
1995 9/2 – 12/3
2006 12/25 – until **2007** 11/17

Saturn Special
1956 12/11 – until **1958** 2/4
1958 6/7 – 11/3
1986 1/19 – 5/21
1986 10/18 – until **1987** 12/10

Uranus Special
1983 1/1 – until **1987** 9/23

Neptune Special
1973 1/25 – until **1981** 10/29

Pluto Special
1998 1/5 – until **2005** 11/7

December 8

SUN: SAGITTARIUS • DECANATE: ARIES/MARS • DEGREE: 15°5–16°5 SAGITTARIUS • MODE: MUTABLE • ELEMENT: FIRE

Your Personal Powers

Forceful and ambitious, you are a determined individual with intellectual capabilities and sensitive emotions. Your ruling planet, Jupiter, endows you with confidence, organizational skills, and enthusiasm. You empower yourself when you realize that self-mastery and emotional satisfaction can be achieved through gaining knowledge and integrating your intuition with your analytical abilities. Often hardworking, you can impress others with your talents and skills. Being enterprising and practical with a shrewd mind, you like to take charge or be in a position of power. Even though you are likely to be energetic with a forceful mind and strong determination, your emotional sensitivity implies that if you are restless or too intense you can lose some of your personal charm. Not afraid to voice your opinions, at times you can lose power by being too outspoken and obstinate. You may need to learn that although honesty and being direct are important, tact and diplomacy are just as meaningful. Fortunately, being idealistic, you can often compensate for your shortcomings with kindness and generosity.

Your Powers of Attraction in Relationships

Sharp and determined, you impress people with your purposeful nature. Inspired by wisdom, you are drawn to intelligent or accomplished individuals who possess knowledge, insight, and experience. Alternatively, you may seek the company of persuasive people with authoritative qualities and innate power. Although you can be generous and understanding, in close relationships you may need to resist being too demanding or overly serious. Lack of activity or boredom can often cause you to be restless and irritable. Inspired by new ideas and projects you show your enthusiasm when you can find something exciting to learn or share with your partner. A need for mental stimulation indicates that if your relationship is dull or monotonous, the prospects of travel or an adventure can often revive your interests.

Your attractive qualities: idealistic, dynamic, philosophical, hardworking, authoritative, good judge of values, intelligent, ambitious, hardworking, generous, natural business sense, intuitive, independent, disciplined, love of learning, enthusiastic, direct, honest

Your less attractive qualities: self-centered, emotionally restless, insecure or too opinionated, easily bored, argumentative, impatient, intolerant, workaholic, domineering, easily discouraged, lack of planning, controlling

Your Venus Power

The planet Venus has a great deal of influence on your powers of attraction. Below are four possible Venus types for women and men. To find your Venus you need to go to page 771, where you will find the Venus table and extra information. The planet Mars also affects your powers of attraction. To find your Mars table and interpretation go to page 761.

WOMEN WITH VENUS IN SCORPIO: Loving and passionate, you are often sensitive with deep feelings and strong powers of attraction. A love for the truth coupled with a tendency to be suspicious can be an influence that motivates you to delve deep into the activities of your partner. When in love or in a relationship that matters, you will often bend over backward to cooperate. Although loyal, guard against losing sight of your own needs and desires.

MEN WITH VENUS IN SCORPIO: In relationships you possess a sensitive understanding of your partner's deeper nature. Although you are strongly attached to those you love, you may have to be careful that your feelings do not turn into jealousy or possessiveness. When you fall in love it is often with an emotional intensity that helps you get in touch with your deep feelings. You are attracted to partners who can share your passion and display strong feelings of sexuality like your own.

WOMEN WITH VENUS IN SAGITTARIUS: At your best when being optimistic and generous, you possess a mischievous sense of fun. In relationships your open-minded approach to people and places may attract you to those of a different culture or make you tolerant of the foibles of others. Although warm and enthusiastic when in love, your natural honesty and idealism may inspire you to look for a partner who shares your love of freedom.

MEN WITH VENUS IN SAGITTARIUS: When in love, you are open and friendly with a need for a partner who can share your adventurous spirit and sense of fun. Be careful, however, that your desire for freedom does not cause you to avoid commitment. You prefer your partners to be positive, direct, and generous in spirit. Being outspoken as well as an idealist, you usually enjoy a partner with whom you can share your strong

opinions. Alternatively, you may wish to explore life together, whether through travel, education, or having fun.

WOMEN WITH VENUS IN CAPRICORN: Loyal and responsible, you are attracted to dignified and reserved individuals. Being practical and security-conscious, you prefer hardworking partners who are resourceful and enterprising. Work may even be a factor in many of your associations and partnerships. For you, family and faithfulness can be especially important, so you are usually willing to work hard and make sacrifices in order to build up a strong relationship.

MEN WITH VENUS IN CAPRICORN: As you do not display your deeper emotions freely, you are usually dignified and controlled in your relationships with others. Practical and down-to-earth partners are particularly attractive to you, especially those who do not rush into expressing their feelings but seem to possess natural class and reserve. You need a partner who is loyal and dependable and willing to take your relationship seriously.

WOMEN WITH VENUS IN AQUARIUS: When it comes to relationships, others are attracted to your honest, friendly, and easygoing approach. You enjoy social interaction and have a genuine concern for others. In fact, sometimes your friends may be just as important as your partner. Usually you put up a tolerant and reasonable front in love situations and attempt to view your relationships objectively. If partners become too demanding, however, you can become stubborn or awkward. Nevertheless, inventive and progressive, you enjoy the company of like-minded people who can share your original ideas.

MEN WITH VENUS IN AQUARIUS: You are sociable and open-minded, and people are attracted by your friendly and easygoing style. Being independent, you value freedom-loving partners who give you the space to be yourself. People sometimes interpret your detachment as being emotionally cool, but they admire your objectivity and humanitarian inclinations. You are attracted to intelligent individuals who are as truthful and direct as you are, but above all they must be true friends. Ideally, your partner shares your liberal views on life and possesses a strong sense of individuality.

To read all about your Outer Planets and work out how to use your personalized timetable, go to Section Three, page 789.

↗

Your Personalized Timetable

JUPITER BENEFICIAL
1938 2/5 – 3/21
1939 7/7 – 8/21
1940 2/11 – 4/20
1943 8/6 – 10/29
1944 1/28 – 6/24
1945 10/15 – 12/5
1946 4/25 – 8/3
1950 1/20 – 3/3
1951 5/31 – 10/12
1952 1/16 – 4/3
1955 7/21 – 10/5
1956 3/7 – 5/28
1957 9/30 – 11/16
1962 1/3 – 2/14
1963 5/9 – until **1964** 3/17
1967 7/4 – 9/17
1969 9/14 – 10/30
1973 5/3 – 6/27
1973 12/15 – until **1974** 1/29
1975 4/20 – 7/24
1975 9/5 – until **1976** 2/27
1978 10/30 – 12/21
1979 6/16 – 8/31
1981 8/28 – 10/15
1985 4/1 – 8/12
1985 11/21 – until **1986** 1/13
1987 4/4 – 6/18
1987 10/24 – until **1988** 2/4
1990 9/28 – until **1991** 2/2
1991 5/25 – 8/15
1992 12/9 – until **1993** 3/21
1993 8/8 – 9/29
1997 3/11 – 5/16
1997 7/5 – 12/25
1999 3/19 – 5/26
2002 9/8 – until **2003** 7/30
2004 11/17 – until **2005** 4/29
2005 7/12 – 9/13
2009 2/21 – 4/11
2009 8/23 – 12/1
2011 3/1 – 5/8

SATURN BENEFICIAL
1938 3/29 – until **1939** 5/5
1946 10/19 – 12/22
1947 6/30 – until **1948** 8/1
1951 11/15 – until **1952** 4/10
1952 8/8 – 11/5
1953 6/1 – 7/15
1962 4/28 – 6/14
1963 1/10 – 4/11
1963 7/28 – until **1964** 1/6
1967 5/9 – 10/16
1968 1/29 – 6/24
1968 9/20 – until **1969** 3/12
1976 8/9 – until **1977** 9/10
1978 4/7 – 5/13
1981 9/20 – 12/23
1982 3/11 – 9/13
1992 2/13 – until **1993** 2/9
1997 3/12 – until **1998** 4/18
2005 9/20 – until **2006** 1/27
2006 6/10 – 11/1
2007 1/10 – 7/15
2010 10/27 – until **2011** 5/19
2011 7/7 – 10/20

URANUS BENEFICIAL
1957 8/10 – until **1961** 7/13
1970 10/31 – until **1973** 9/5
1998 3/10 – until **2001** 11/8
2012 6/4 – Continues

NEPTUNE BENEFICIAL
1947 10/15 – until **1952** 10/1
2002 5/2 – until **2008** 1/21

PLUTO BENEFICIAL
1943 9/9 – until **1954** 7/25
1975 11/23 – until **1980** 9/25

JUPITER CHALLENGING
1939 2/4 – 4/13
1941 6/30 – until **1942** 5/13

1944 9/1 – 11/24
1945 3/2 – 7/23
1951 1/17 – 3/26
1953 6/12 – 9/5
1953 11/24 – until **1954** 4/23
1956 8/16 – 11/1
1957 4/11 – 6/26
1962 5/6 – 8/29
1962 12/25 – until **1963** 3/10
1965 5/27 – 8/9
1966 1/5 – 3/28
1968 7/31 – 10/14
1974 4/13 – until **1975** 2/21
1977 5/10 – 7/20
1979 11/18 – until **1980** 2/3
1980 7/12 – 9/28
1986 3/26 – until **1987** 2/4
1989 4/23 – 7/3
1991 10/22 – until **1992** 3/13
1992 6/18 – 9/12
1998 3/9 – 5/26
1998 9/9 – until **1999** 1/13
2000 8/14 – 11/14
2001 4/2 – 6/16
2003 10/4 – until **2004** 8/27
2010 2/21 – 5/1
2010 11/2 – 12/4
2012 7/19 – 12/30

SATURN CHALLENGING
1942 7/11 – 12/15
1943 3/29 – 8/14
1943 12/6 – until **1944** 5/1
1949 8/20 – until **1950** 9/26
1965 3/1 – until **1966** 4/13
1966 10/22 – 12/30
1972 5/15 – until **1973** 6/14
1978 9/28 – until **1979** 4/7
1979 6/10 – 11/7
1980 3/10 – 7/30
1994 4/6 – 9/16
1994 12/31 – until **1995** 6/5
1995 8/6 – until **1996** 2/17
2001 6/22 – until **2002** 7/23
2003 1/7 – 4/8
2007 11/23 – until **2008** 1/14
2008 8/2 – until **2009** 9/9

URANUS CHALLENGING
1943 7/30 – until **1948** 5/6
1963 10/6 – until **1967** 9/4
2005 3/18 – until **2010** 1/25

NEPTUNE CHALLENGING
1938 1/1 – until **1940** 8/12

PLUTO CHALLENGING
1960 11/13 – until **1969** 8/21

JUPITER SPECIAL
1947 11/29 – until **1948** 2/16
1948 6/16 – 10/13
1959 11/13 – until **1960** 1/25
1960 8/10 – 8/30
1971 10/27 – until **1972** 1/8
1983 2/11 – 5/12
1983 10/8 – 12/23
1995 1/17 – 6/22
1995 9/12 – 12/7
2006 12/30 – until **2007** 11/21

SATURN SPECIAL
1956 12/19 – until **1957** 7/25
1957 8/29 – until **1958** 2/16
1958 5/23 – 11/13
1986 2/1 – 5/6
1986 10/28 – until **1987** 12/19

URANUS SPECIAL
1983 1/21 – until **1987** 10/26

NEPTUNE SPECIAL
1973 12/20 – until **1981** 11/29

PLUTO SPECIAL
1998 2/19 – until **2005** 12/6

December 9

SUN: SAGITTARIUS · DECANATE: ARIES/MARS · DEGREE: 16°5–17°5 SAGITTARIUS · MODE: MUTABLE · ELEMENT: FIRE

Your Personal Powers

Versatile and intuitive, you are an idealistic and enthusiastic individual with a sharp intellect and emotional sensitivity. Your ruling planet, Jupiter, grants you a wealth of imaginative ideas, optimism, and compassion. Since a great deal depends on how contented or confident you feel, the more knowledgeable, self-assured, and creative you are, the more productive and successful you become. A desire to expand your horizons suggests that you benefit from exploring spirituality or philosophy. Although you are often gifted and enterprising, a tendency to be frustrated or impulsive indicates that it is through perseverance and hard work that you can achieve your goals. You gain power when you stay calm and resist being anxious when you are faced with challenges or delays. When you remain composed and stop worrying about all the small details in favor of the big picture, you can also express yourself freely. Your thoughtfulness, generosity, and universal understanding can also inspire you to stand by your ideals or uplift others.

Your Powers of Attraction in Relationships

Benevolent and clever, you attract people with your congenial personality. Your quick wit and emotional magnetism indicate that you are fun to be with. Although you have a warm heart and generous nature, a tendency to be critical or too demanding indicates that you can sometimes be impatient with others. It may be more beneficial for you to show people your more tolerant and detached viewpoint. Keen on collaborating with others, however, you make a good partner or team player. You are usually attracted to dynamic individuals who are sharp and decisive yet generous and warm. Although your need for a close loving relationship or a partner is strong, maintaining the balance of power can guarantee that you do not become codependent and lose your independence.

Your attractive qualities: Intuitive, gregarious, benevolent, patient, persevering, responsible, tolerant, generous, liberal, independent, idealistic, creative, sensitive, magnetic, detached, popular, imaginative, strong convictions, affectionate, considerate, love of freedom or travel

Your less attractive qualities: sentimental, irritable, emotional ups and downs, unrealistic, frustrated, nervous, unsure, selfish, impractical, restricted, restless, extravagant, irresponsible, worry, too dependent, discontented

Your Venus Power

The planet Venus has a great deal of influence on your powers of attraction. Below are four possible Venus types for women and men. To find your Venus you need to go to page 771, where you will find the Venus table and extra information. The planet Mars also affects your powers of attraction. To find your Mars table and interpretation go to page 761.

WOMEN WITH VENUS IN SCORPIO: With a natural psychic gift for penetrating the feelings of others, you can often help partners transform emotional challenges or sexual difficulties. When you fall in love, your strong feelings and determination give you a potent force that others find attractive and seductive. Although you know what really turns people on, your most profound desire is usually for the deepness and closeness of real love and intimacy in an enduring relationship.

MEN WITH VENUS IN SCORPIO: In relationships you possess a sensitive understanding of your partner's deeper nature. Although you are strongly attached to those you love, you may have to be careful that your feelings do not turn into jealousy or possessiveness. When you fall in love, it is often with an emotional intensity that helps you get in touch with your deep feelings. You are attracted to partners who can share your passion and display strong feelings of sexuality like your own.

WOMEN WITH VENUS IN SAGITTARIUS: Optimistic and fun-loving, you love adventure and seek a partner who can expand your horizons. Being truthful and direct, you often say what you think, and at times you may be naively tactless. A need for expansion and prosperity suggests that you may enjoy traveling with your friends or partner. Being lighthearted and idealistic, once you have given your heart to someone you will stay honorable and loyal.

MEN WITH VENUS IN SAGITTARIUS: You are usually attracted to partners who are knowledgeable or well-traveled. Enthusiastic and optimistic, you often respond quickly to love offers and enter relationships with enthusiasm. Usually you seek to expand your social circle; meeting people from all walks of life can bring you the variety and fun you seek in life. Although you are generous and honest, your partners may accuse you of being overly optimistic or too blunt.

WOMEN WITH VENUS IN CAPRICORN: Romantically, you do not give your heart easily but hide behind a cool reserve until you feel free to express your emotions. As you take your relationships seriously, you may find yourself drawn to people who are businesslike, resourceful, and practical, or those who

can act as teachers or mentors. Work or career may also be a factor in many of your associations and partnerships. As security can play an important role in your relationships, you are often attracted to partners who are loyal and hardworking,

MEN WITH VENUS IN CAPRICORN: In relationships you take love seriously and can be a strong and practical support for friends or partners. You are usually attracted to partners who are as hardworking as yourself. As you tend not to express your feelings until you feel really secure in a relationship, you may be drawn to those who seem loyal, faithful, and not likely to let you down. As you respect the wisdom of experience, you may be drawn to mature partners or, alternatively, you may act as an authority figure for someone younger.

WOMEN WITH VENUS IN AQUARIUS: Sociable and gracious, you are usually sincere and are capable of showing attributes of real tolerance and liberalism. Although you are keen on forming relationships, you also like to have freedom and act independently. Your intimate partnerships need to be founded on true friendships. Full of bright and progressive ideas, you can express yourself better when you are free and unrestricted. An ability to think in a dispassionate way suggests that you can stay detached. Your love of freedom also implies that, without smothering your partner, you can be loving and loyal.

MEN WITH VENUS IN AQUARIUS: Although independent, you often enjoy being part of a group. The partners you frequently attract are themselves nonconformists or free spirits. As an individual you may not find it easy to settle into a routine or an entirely mundane type of relationship. You may have some unconventional views on the traditional marriage or your partner may hold such views. It is usually important to you that your love relationships are based on friendship.

To read all about your Outer Planets and work out how to use your personalized timetable, go to Section Three, page 789.

♐

Your Personalized Timetable

JUPITER BENEFICIAL
1938 2/9 – 3/26
1940 2/16 – 4/24
1943 8/10 – 11/7
1944 1/19 – 6/29
1945 10/20 – 12/11
1946 4/17 – 8/11
1950 1/24 – 3/7
1951 6/6 – 10/4
1952 1/23 – 4/7
1955 7/25 – 10/11
1956 2/28 – 6/6
1957 10/4 – 11/21
1958 6/7 – 6/30
1962 1/7 – 2/19
1963 5/13 – until 1964 3/21
1967 7/9 – 9/22
1969 9/19 – 11/4
1973 5/21 – 6/9
1973 12/20 – until 1974 2/2
1975 4/25 – until 1976 3/3
1978 11/18 – 12/2
1979 6/21 – 9/5
1981 9/2 – 10/19
1985 4/7 – 8/5
1985 11/28 – until 1986 1/17
1987 4/9 – 6/24
1987 10/16 – until 1988 2/10
1990 10/5 – until 1991 1/26
1991 5/31 – 8/20
1992 12/17 – until 1993 3/13
1993 8/14 – 10/4
1997 3/16 – 12/30
1999 3/23 – 5/31
2002 9/13 – until 2003 3/11
2003 4/28 – 8/4
2004 11/23 – until 2005 4/19
2005 7/21 – 9/18
2009 2/25 – 4/17
2009 8/15 – 12/7
2011 3/6 – 5/12

SATURN BENEFICIAL
1938 4/6 – until 1939 5/13
1939 12/3 – until 1940 1/21
1947 7/9 – until 1948 8/9
1951 11/25 – until 1952 3/28
1952 8/19 – 11/14
1953 5/12 – 8/4
1963 1/18 – 4/26
1963 7/12 – until 1964 1/15
1967 5/19 – 10/3
1968 2/10 – 7/11
1968 9/2 – until 1969 3/20
1976 8/17 – until 1977 9/19
1978 3/17 – 6/3
1981 9/29 – until 1982 1/13
1982 2/18 – 9/22
1992 2/22 – 10/3
1992 10/28 – until 1993 2/18
1997 3/20 – until 1998 4/26
2005 10/1 – until 2006 1/14
2006 6/20 – 11/25
2006 12/16 – until 2007 7/24
2010 11/5 – until 2011 4/30
2011 7/26 – 10/28

URANUS BENEFICIAL
1957 8/27 – until 1961 7/31
1970 11/19 – until 1973 9/23
1998 4/3 – until 2001 12/20

NEPTUNE BENEFICIAL
1947 11/14 – until 1953 8/29
2003 3/7 – until 2008 12/14

PLUTO BENEFICIAL
1944 8/22 – until 1955 6/29
1976 10/14 – until 1981 8/9

JUPITER CHALLENGING
1939 2/9 – 4/17
1941 7/5 – until 1942 5/18
1944 9/6 – 12/2

1945 2/22 – 7/29
1951 1/22 – 3/30
1953 6/17 – 9/14
1953 11/14 – until 1954 4/29
1956 8/21 – 11/7
1957 4/2 – 7/5
1962 5/13 – 8/22
1962 12/31 – until 1963 3/14
1965 5/31 – 8/14
1965 12/27 – until 1966 4/5
1968 8/5 – 10/19
1974 4/18 – 10/10
1974 11/27 – until 1975 2/25
1977 5/15 – 7/25
1979 11/28 – until 1980 1/24
1980 7/17 – 10/2
1986 3/30 – until 1987 2/8
1989 4/28 – 7/7
1991 10/28 – until 1992 3/5
1992 6/25 – 9/17
1998 3/13 – 6/3
1998 9/1 – until 1999 1/19
2000 8/22 – 11/6
2001 4/8 – 6/20
2003 10/9 – until 2004 5/1
2004 5/9 – 9/1
2010 2/25 – 5/7
2010 10/20 – 12/18
2012 7/24 – Continues

SATURN CHALLENGING
1942 7/21 – 12/2
1943 4/9 – 8/27
1943 11/22 – until 1944 5/10
1949 8/28 – until 1950 10/4
1965 3/9 – until 1966 4/23
1966 10/7 – until 1967 1/14
1972 5/23 – until 1973 6/21
1978 10/7 – until 1979 3/22
1979 6/26 – 11/19
1980 2/26 – 8/9
1994 4/17 – 9/2
1995 1/11 – until 1996 2/26
2001 7/1 – until 2002 1/7
2002 3/11 – 8/1
2002 12/25 – until 2003 4/20
2008 8/11 – until 2009 9/17

URANUS CHALLENGING
1944 5/31 – until 1948 5/25
1963 10/27 – until 1967 9/20
2005 4/6 – until 2010 2/16

NEPTUNE CHALLENGING
1938 1/1 – until 1941 6/19

PLUTO CHALLENGING
1961 10/4 – until 1970 7/7

JUPITER SPECIAL
1947 12/4 – until 1948 2/23
1948 6/8 – 10/19
1959 11/18 – until 1960 1/31
1960 7/23 – 9/17
1971 11/1 – until 1972 1/13
1983 2/20 – 5/3
1983 10/14 – 12/27
1995 1/23 – 6/13
1995 9/20 – 12/12
2007 1/4 – 11/26

SATURN SPECIAL
1956 12/28 – until 1957 7/1
1957 9/21 – until 1958 3/5
1958 5/5 – 11/23
1986 2/17 – 4/18
1986 11/6 – until 1987 12/27

URANUS SPECIAL
1983 2/24 – until 1987 11/16

NEPTUNE SPECIAL
1974 1/22 – until 1982 10/26

PLUTO SPECIAL
1998 12/27 – until 2006 11/2

December 10

Your Personal Powers

Broad-minded and intuitive, your daring personality indicates that you are a practical visionary with high ideals. Naturally independent and spirited, you are usually determined to expand your horizons and take advantage of new opportunities. Often optimistic, you possess a love of truth and an imaginative nature. You gain power when you combine your inspired thoughts with your strategic skills and business acumen. Although when interested in a project you can be highly motivated, being idealistic indicates that you need to keep your feet firmly on the ground and have faith in what you do. You can lose some of your power, however, if you get too involved in fantasy or escapism. As you are likely to show a bold front to others, you hide your sensitivity and delicate nervous system very well. You nevertheless need to resist a tendency to become involved in power struggles and provocation by being more tactful and diplomatic. By utilizing your powerful intellect and natural leadership ability, you are able to display your true power and outstanding potential for success.

Your Powers of Attraction in Relationships

Others admire your imaginative ideas, adventurous nature, and enterprising personality. Preferring to take the initiative, you do not usually enjoy being in subordinate positions or taking orders from others. Frank and mentally quick, you prefer people who are intelligent and inspired. Alternatively, you may be drawn to ambitious and hardworking people who are practical or resourceful. Although you can be a sensitive and tender lover, avoid manipulating partners by giving them what you think they want to get your own way. In close relationships you can create stability by being honest, discreet, and compromising. Usually you are loyal and supportive of your partners, but you may need to keep your emotions in check and resist being too impulsive or stubborn. Friendly and sociable, you will always attract admirers.

Your attractive qualities: ambitious, original, pioneering, enterprising, independent, talented, daring, forceful, optimistic, strong convictions, competitive, gregarious, idealistic, sensitive, humanitarian, resourceful, spiritual, visionary, disciplined, responsible, practical, adventurous, clever

Your less attractive qualities: manipulative, restless, stubborn, overbearing, moody, impatient, opinionated, tactless, rebellious, controlling, too proud, lack of restraint, hypocritical, self-centered, escapist, overindulgent

Your Venus Power

The planet Venus has a great deal of influence on your powers of attraction. Below are four possible Venus types for women and men. To find your Venus you need to go to page 771, where you will find the Venus table and extra information. The planet Mars also affects your powers of attraction. To find your Mars table and interpretation go to page 761.

WOMEN WITH VENUS IN SCORPIO: With a natural psychic gift for penetrating the feelings of others, you can often help partners transform emotional challenges or sexual difficulties. When you fall in love, your strong feelings and determination give you a potent force that others find attractive and seductive. Although you know what really turns people on, your most profound desire is usually for the deepness and closeness of real love and intimacy in an enduring relationship.

MEN WITH VENUS IN SCORPIO: In relationships you possess a sensitive understanding of your partner's deeper nature. Although you are strongly attached to those you love, you may have to be careful that your feelings do not turn into jealousy or possessiveness. When you fall in love it is often with an emotional intensity that helps you get in touch with your deep feelings. You are attracted to partners who can share your passion and display strong feelings of sexuality like your own.

WOMEN WITH VENUS IN SAGITTARIUS: At your best when being optimistic and generous, you possess a mischievous sense of fun. In relationships your open-minded approach to people and places may attract you to those of a different culture or make you tolerant of the foibles of others. Although warm and enthusiastic when in love, your natural honesty and idealism may inspire you to look for a partner who shares your love of freedom.

MEN WITH VENUS IN SAGITTARIUS: Forward-thinking rather than dwelling on the past, you are looking for a partner who can share your future plans. You enjoy exploring life whether through travel and mental pursuits or sports and games. Idealistic, you usually prefer the company of a partner who is optimistic and shares your beliefs. In your desire for honesty in relationships, however, be careful not to become tactless. Nevertheless, you are attracted to honest, direct, and fun-loving partners who have a sense of humor like your own.

WOMEN WITH VENUS IN CAPRICORN: Loyal and responsible, you are attracted to dignified and reserved individuals. Being practical and security-conscious, you prefer hardworking partners who are resourceful and enterprising. Work may even be a factor in many of your associations and partnerships. For you, family and faithfulness can be especially important, so you are usually willing to work hard or make sacrifices in order to build up a strong relationship.

MEN WITH VENUS IN CAPRICORN: In relationships you take love seriously and can be a strong and practical support for friends or partners. You are usually attracted to partners who are as hardworking as yourself. As you tend not to express your feelings until you feel really secure in a relationship, you may be drawn to those who seem loyal, faithful, and not likely to let you down. As you respect the wisdom of experience you may be drawn to mature partners or, alternatively, you may act as an authority figure for someone younger.

WOMEN WITH VENUS IN AQUARIUS: Usually you have a modern outlook on love and are open to new or current lifestyles. Your intuitive abilities, communal sense, and people skills often allow you to see deeper into human intentions and read telepathically other people's thoughts. Although you are usually group-oriented, you are drawn to strong individuals within the group who are independent and self-motivated. You are more inclined to choose a partner who is unconventional or freedom-loving. Conscious of your social standing, however, you want someone who can relate well to your friends.

MEN WITH VENUS IN AQUARIUS: You are sociable and open-minded, and people are attracted by your friendly and relaxed style. Being independent, you value freedom-loving partners who give you the space to be yourself. Others sometimes interpret your detachment as being emotionally cool, but they may not understand your progressive views on relationships. Friendship can sometimes be even more important than earthly passion. Ideally, your partners can share your ideas on life and possess as strong a sense of originality as your own. Not easily ruffled, you can deal well with difficult situations or moody partners.

To read all about your Outer Planets and work out how to use your personalized timetable, go to Section Three, page 789.

To read all about your Outer Planets and work out how to use your personalized timetable, go to Section Three, page 789.

↗

Your Personalized Timetable

JUPITER BENEFICIAL
1938 2/14 – 3/31
1938 9/30 – 11/6
1940 2/21 – 4/29
1943 8/15 – 11/17
1944 1/8 – 7/5
1945 10/25 – 12/18
1946 4/9 – 8/18
1950 1/28 – 3/12
1951 6/12 – 9/27
1952 1/29 – 4/12
1955 7/30 – 10/17
1956 2/20 – 6/13
1957 10/9 – 11/27
1958 5/21 – 7/17
1962 1/12 – 2/23
1963 5/18 – 11/19
1963 12/21 – until 1964 3/26
1967 7/14 – 9/27
1968 4/12 – 5/1
1969 9/24 – 11/9
1973 12/25 – until 1974 2/7
1975 4/29 – until 1976 3/8
1979 6/27 – 9/9
1981 9/7 – 10/24
1985 4/14 – 7/28
1985 12/4 – until 1986 1/22
1987 4/13 – 7/1
1987 10/8 – until 1988 2/16
1990 10/12 – until 1991 1/18
1991 6/7 – 8/24
1992 12/26 – until 1993 3/3
1993 8/20 – 10/8
1997 3/21 – 9/15
1997 10/31 – until 1998 1/4
1999 3/27 – 6/5
1999 11/27 – until 2000 1/13
2002 9/18 – until 2003 2/27
2003 5/9 – 8/8
2004 11/29 – until 2005 4/11
2005 7/29 – 9/23
2009 3/2 – 4/24
2009 8/7 – 12/14
2011 3/10 – 5/16

SATURN BENEFICIAL
1938 4/14 – until 1939 5/22
1939 11/15 – until 1940 2/7
1947 7/17 – until 1948 8/17
1951 12/7 – until 1952 3/14
1952 8/29 – 11/23
1953 4/27 – 8/18
1963 1/27 – 5/21
1963 6/15 – until 1964 1/24
1967 5/30 – 9/20
1968 2/20 – until 1969 3/29
1976 8/25 – until 1977 4/7
1977 4/15 – 9/28
1978 3/2 – 6/17
1981 10/7 – until 1982 9/30
1992 3/2 – 9/7
1992 11/22 – until 1993 2/26
1997 3/28 – until 1998 5/4
2005 10/15 – 12/31
2006 6/29 – until 2007 8/1
2010 11/14 – until 2011 4/15
2011 8/8 – 11/6
2012 6/9 – 7/11

URANUS BENEFICIAL
1957 9/15 – until 1961 8/16
1970 12/13 – until 1973 10/9
1999 2/5 – until 2002 1/11

NEPTUNE BENEFICIAL
1948 1/7 – until 1953 9/29
2003 4/18 – until 2009 1/17

PLUTO BENEFICIAL
1944 10/6 – until 1955 8/4
1976 11/10 – until 1981 9/14

JUPITER CHALLENGING
1939 2/13 – 4/22
1941 7/9 – until 1942 5/23
1944 9/10 – 12/11

1945 2/12 – 8/4
1951 1/26 – 4/4
1953 6/21 – 9/27
1953 11/1 – until 1954 5/4
1956 8/25 – 11/13
1957 3/24 – 7/12
1962 5/21 – 8/13
1963 1/6 – 3/18
1965 6/4 – 8/20
1965 12/20 – until 1966 4/12
1968 8/10 – 10/24
1974 4/23 – 9/29
1974 12/8 – until 1975 3/2
1977 5/19 – 7/30
1979 12/14 – until 1980 1/8
1980 7/23 – 10/7
1986 4/4 – until 1987 2/13
1989 5/2 – 7/12
1991 11/4 – until 1992 2/26
1992 7/2 – 9/21
1998 3/18 – 6/11
1998 8/23 – until 1999 1/24
2000 9/1 – 10/27
2001 4/13 – 6/25
2003 10/14 – until 2004 4/8
2004 5/31 – 9/6
2010 3/1 – 5/12
2010 10/10 – 12/27
2012 7/30 – Continues

SATURN CHALLENGING
1942 8/1 – 11/20
1943 4/19 – 9/13
1943 11/5 – until 1944 5/19
1949 9/5 – until 1950 10/13
1951 5/6 – 6/20
1965 3/18 – until 1966 5/3
1966 9/23 – until 1967 1/26
1972 5/31 – until 1973 6/29
1978 10/17 – until 1979 3/8
1979 7/8 – 12/3
1980 2/10 – 8/19
1994 4/28 – 8/19
1995 1/21 – until 1996 3/5
2001 7/10 – 12/22
2002 3/26 – 8/12
2002 12/13 – until 2003 4/30
2008 8/19 – until 2009 9/25

URANUS CHALLENGING
1944 6/17 – until 1948 6/12
1963 12/2 – until 1968 7/17
2005 5/1 – until 2010 3/6

NEPTUNE CHALLENGING
1938 1/1 – until 1941 8/10

PLUTO CHALLENGING
1961 11/18 – until 1970 8/16

JUPITER SPECIAL
1947 12/8 – until 1948 3/1
1948 5/30 – 10/25
1959 11/22 – until 1960 2/5
1960 7/13 – 9/27
1971 11/6 – until 1972 1/17
1983 3/3 – 4/21
1983 10/19 – until 1984 1/1
1995 1/29 – 6/5
1995 9/27 – 12/16
2007 1/9 – 8/2
2007 8/11 – 12/1

SATURN SPECIAL
1957 1/7 – 6/16
1957 10/5 – until 1958 12/2
1986 11/15 – until 1988 1/5
1988 8/23 – 9/6

URANUS SPECIAL
1983 12/12 – until 1987 12/3

NEPTUNE SPECIAL
1974 12/19 – until 1982 11/27

PLUTO SPECIAL
1999 1/30 – until 2006 12/3

549

December 11

Your Personal Powers

Friendly and enterprising, you are an ambitious individual who likes adventure but is capable of hard work and being purposeful. Your ruling planet, Jupiter, grants you an optimistic outlook and a love of freedom. With the tenacity to overcome obstacles, you gain power when you learn to use your inborn intuition and enthusiasm, and not let apprehension or self-doubts undermine your inner faith. You empower yourself when you realize that your belief system is the foundation of your inner peace, and that the more self-assured you are, the more positive your outlook is. With the knowledge that good fortune is usually on your side, you can triumph over adversity by staying focused. Although you are shrewd with good business acumen, money alone rarely brings you the personal satisfaction that you seek. In order to find emotional fulfillment you often need to find ways to expand your knowledge or express your creativity. Once inspired, you can be spontaneous and impress others with your talents or ideas.

Your Powers of Attraction in Relationships

Affectionate and fun-loving, your friendly nature can make you popular. You often enjoy socializing and mix business with pleasure. Although you may appear innocent to others, underneath you are shrewd and instinctive. Mentally sharp, you enjoy exploring new ideas and sharing knowledge and information. Group activities that include learning are highly suitable for you. Usually you are drawn to optimistic, strong-willed, and hardworking individuals. Alternatively, you may be drawn to intuitive and insightful people with unusual gifts or talents. Although you may appear bright, an ability to conceal your stress indicates that inwardly you can experience mental tension or worry. So, even if you have a partner and are in a loving relationship, you may need to have time alone to relax and unwind.

Your attractive qualities: focused, objective, enthusiastic, spiritual, intuitive, intelligent, outgoing, inventive, artistic, humanitarian, psychic, idealistic, adventurous, inspired, innovative, modest, energetic, enterprising, freedom-loving, productive, hardworking, youthful, generous

Your less attractive qualities: anxious, impractical, suspicious, restless, nervous, aimless, overemotional, easily hurt, high-strung, self-centered, materialistic, lack of clarity, mean, worried, skeptical, impulsive, tactless, cynical

Your Venus Power

The planet Venus has a great deal of influence on your powers of attraction. Below are four possible Venus types for women and men. To find your Venus you need to go to page 771, where you will find the Venus table and extra information. The planet Mars also affects your powers of attraction. To find your Mars table and interpretation go to page 761.

WOMEN WITH VENUS IN SCORPIO: With a natural psychic gift for penetrating the feelings of others, you can often help partners transform emotional challenges or sexual difficulties. When you fall in love, your strong feelings and determination give you a potent force that others find attractive and seductive. Although you know what really turns people on, your most profound desire is usually for the deepness and closeness of real love and intimacy in an enduring relationship.

MEN WITH VENUS IN SCORPIO: In relationships you possess a sensitive understanding of your partner's deeper nature. Although you are strongly attached to those you love, you may have to be careful that your feelings do not turn into jealousy or possessiveness. When you fall in love, it is often with an emotional intensity that helps you get in touch with your deep feelings. You are attracted to partners who can share your passion and display strong feelings of sexuality like your own.

WOMEN WITH VENUS IN SAGITTARIUS: Sociable, warm, and friendly, you possess an honest and frank style in your relationships. Being naturally gregarious, you want others to share your enthusiasm and enjoy encouraging the people you love. You fare better when you have a sense of personal freedom within a relationship and are usually generous with the faults of others. You need a partner who can share your need to explore and take risks, whether through travel, education, or recreation.

MEN WITH VENUS IN SAGITTARIUS: Your enthusiasm and straightforward conduct usually appeal to others and imply that you are approachable and easygoing. Being open to ideas and willing to believe that life has a great deal to offer suggests that you are generous, broad-minded, and show eagerness to cooperate with others. A love of travel and an interest in other cultures also imply that your partner may come from a foreign country.

WOMEN WITH VENUS IN CAPRICORN: With your natural caution in romantic affairs, you often appear reserved and controlled. If shy, try to be more forward, especially if you want to be noticed. When you care about people, however, you are usually willing to put in extra time and energy to preserve the relationship. You are practical and dependable, and a sense of duty can often play a large role in the affairs of your heart. With elegant simplicity, you can attract others with your well-cut clothes and refined manners.

MEN WITH VENUS IN CAPRICORN: In relationships you take love seriously and can be a strong and practical support for friends or partners. You are usually attracted to partners who are as hardworking as yourself. As you tend not to express your feelings until you feel really secure in a relationship, you may be drawn to those who seem loyal, faithful, and not likely to let you down. As you respect the wisdom of experience, you may be drawn to mature partners or, alternatively, you may act as an authority figure for someone younger.

WOMEN WITH VENUS IN AQUARIUS: When it comes to relationships others are attracted to your honest, friendly, and easygoing approach. You really enjoy social interaction with others and may develop a genuine concern for humanity. Usually you present a tolerant and reasonable front in love situations and attempt to view your relationships objectively. However, if partners become too demanding you can become stubborn and fixed. Friendship may be even more important for you than sexual compatibility.

MEN WITH VENUS IN AQUARIUS: Ideally, in your relationships your lover is also your best friend. Since freedom of expression is a prerequisite to your well-being, you fare better when left alone to do your own thing. You also need a partner who recognizes and appreciates your need for independence. Although usually friendly, at times you can be stubborn or your cool detachment can appear to others as distant or impersonal. Very sociable, however, you particularly enjoy the company of those who share your original, fair-minded, and progressive views.

To read all about your Outer Planets and work out how to use your personalized timetable, go to Section Three, page 789.

Your Personalized Timetable

JUPITER BENEFICIAL
1938 2/18 – 4/5
1938 9/17 – 11/19
1940 2/25 – 5/3
1943 8/20 – 12/7
1943 12/19 – until 1944 7/10
1945 10/30 – 12/25
1946 4/1 – 8/24
1950 2/2 – 3/16
1951 6/19 – 9/19
1952 2/4 – 4/16
1955 8/3 – 10/23
1956 2/12 – 6/20
1957 10/14 – 12/2
1958 5/10 – 7/28
1962 1/16 – 2/27
1963 5/24 – 11/6
1964 1/3 – 3/30
1967 7/19 – 10/2
1968 3/25 – 5/19
1969 9/28 – 11/14
1973 12/30 – until 1974 2/11
1975 5/4 – until 1976 3/13
1979 7/2 – 9/14
1981 9/12 – 10/29
1985 4/21 – 7/19
1985 12/10 – until 1986 1/26
1987 4/17 – 7/9
1987 9/30 – until 1988 2/22
1990 10/20 – until 1991 1/10
1991 6/12 – 8/29
1993 1/8 – 2/18
1993 8/25 – 10/13
1997 3/26 – 9/3
1997 11/11 – until 1998 1/9
1999 3/31 – 6/11
1999 11/16 – until 2000 1/24
2002 9/24 – until 2003 2/18
2003 5/18 – 8/13
2004 12/5 – until 2005 4/3
2005 8/5 – 9/28
2009 3/7 – 5/1
2009 7/30 – 12/19
2011 3/14 – 5/21

SATURN BENEFICIAL
1938 4/22 – until 1939 6/1
1939 11/1 – until 1940 2/20
1947 7/25 – until 1948 8/25
1951 12/22 – until 1952 2/27
1952 9/8 – 12/3
1953 4/13 – 8/29
1963 2/4 – until 1964 2/2
1967 6/12 – 9/6
1968 2/29 – until 1969 4/6
1976 9/3 – until 1977 3/7
1977 5/15 – 10/7
1978 2/17 – 6/28
1981 10/15 – until 1982 10/9
1992 3/11 – 8/23
1992 12/6 – until 1993 3/7
1993 10/7 – 11/17
1997 4/5 – until 1998 5/12
1998 12/14 – until 1999 1/14
2005 11/4 – 12/10
2006 7/7 – until 2007 8/9
2010 11/24 – until 2011 4/2
2011 8/20 – 11/14
2012 5/16 – 8/3

URANUS BENEFICIAL
1957 10/9 – until 1962 6/10
1971 10/8 – until 1974 7/29
1999 2/23 – until 2002 1/30

NEPTUNE BENEFICIAL
1948 11/10 – until 1954 8/26
2004 3/4 – until 2009 12/7

PLUTO BENEFICIAL
1945 9/12 – until 1956 7/9
1976 12/21 – until 1981 10/10

JUPITER CHALLENGING
1939 2/17 – 4/26
1941 7/14 – until 1942 5/28

1944 9/15 – 12/25
1945 1/29 – 8/9
1951 1/31 – 4/8
1953 6/26 – until 1954 5/9
1956 8/30 – 11/19
1957 3/16 – 7/19
1962 5/30 – 8/4
1963 1/11 – 3/22
1965 6/9 – 8/27
1965 12/12 – until 1966 4/18
1968 8/14 – 10/30
1969 4/29 – 6/16
1974 4/29 – 9/20
1974 12/16 – until 1975 3/6
1977 5/24 – 8/4
1978 1/27 – 3/15
1980 7/28 – 10/12
1986 4/9 – until 1987 2/17
1989 5/7 – 7/16
1991 11/11 – until 1992 2/18
1992 7/8 – 9/26
1998 3/22 – 6/22
1998 8/12 – until 1999 1/29
2000 9/17 – 10/11
2001 4/18 – 6/29
2003 10/20 – until 2004 3/28
2004 6/11 – 9/11
2010 3/5 – 5/18
2010 10/2 – until 2011 1/4
2012 8/5 – Continues

SATURN CHALLENGING
1942 8/14 – 11/6
1943 4/28 – until 1944 5/27
1949 9/13 – until 1950 10/21
1951 4/16 – 7/10
1965 3/26 – 10/21
1965 12/8 – until 1966 5/14
1966 9/10 – until 1967 2/5
1972 6/8 – until 1973 7/7
1978 10/27 – until 1979 2/24
1979 7/19 – until 1980 1/1
1980 1/11 – 8/27
1994 5/12 – 8/4
1995 1/31 – until 1996 3/13
2001 7/19 – 12/9
2002 4/7 – 8/23
2002 11/30 – until 2003 5/10
2008 8/27 – until 2009 10/3

URANUS CHALLENGING
1944 7/6 – until 1949 4/7
1964 9/11 – until 1968 8/9
2006 3/6 – until 2011 1/2

NEPTUNE CHALLENGING
1938 1/1 – until 1941 9/8

PLUTO CHALLENGING
1962 10/6 – until 1971 6/13

JUPITER SPECIAL
1947 12/13 – until 1948 3/10
1948 5/21 – 10/31
1959 11/27 – until 1960 2/11
1960 7/4 – 10/6
1971 11/11 – until 1972 1/22
1983 10/24 – until 1984 1/5
1995 2/5 – 5/28
1995 10/4 – 12/21
2007 1/15 – 7/11
2007 9/2 – 12/5

SATURN SPECIAL
1957 1/17 – 6/2
1957 10/17 – until 1958 12/10
1986 11/24 – until 1988 1/14
1988 7/24 – 10/5

URANUS SPECIAL
1983 12/29 – until 1987 12/20

NEPTUNE SPECIAL
1975 1/19 – until 1983 10/22

PLUTO SPECIAL
1999 12/19 – until 2007 10/29

551

December 12

SUN: SAGITTARIUS • DECANATE: ARIES/MARS • DEGREE: 19°5–20°5 SAGITTARIUS • MODE: MUTABLE • ELEMENT: FIRE

Your Personal Powers

Intuitive and friendly, you are a sociable individual with bright ideas and an enterprising spirit. Your ruling planet, Jupiter, grants you a love of truth, optimism, and a desire to learn. Interested in broadening your horizons, you gain power when you explore or establish a philosophy of life that you can truly embrace. You lose power if you overindulge in worry or escape from your responsibilities. Being mentally quick and inquisitive, you are usually talented and versatile with many interests or hobbies. You can lose some of your power, however, if you fail to concentrate on your goals and scatter your mental energies in too many directions. A tendency to be apprehensive when you do not have clear and definite goals suggests that you empower yourself when you have a set plan and long-term strategy. Fortunately, your determination to succeed implies that you are hardworking, and once you find an aim or purpose, you are able to succeed by showing your astuteness, creative flair, and dedication.

Your Powers of Attraction in Relationships

People are usually attracted to your friendly and affectionate nature. Naturally warmhearted and gregarious, you enjoy mixing with people and making contacts. A tendency to have strong opinions suggests that, if you are too fixed, you may come across as bossy. As you possess a strong need to express yourself, you are drawn to dynamic and creative people who have a sense of the dramatic. By keeping a balance between needing others and pursuing your own interests, you are able to make the best of both worlds. It is important, however, that in your close relations you do not become too demanding or intense. Nevertheless, mentally quick and curious, you can be charming and persuasive. Having powerful emotions also implies that when you fall in love you can be passionate and loving.

Your attractive qualities: creative, attractive, enterprising, persuasive, idealistic, ambitious, cooperative, intuitive, keen on learning, spiritual potential, philosophical, hardworking, determined, enthusiastic, meticulous, helpful, friendly, clever, tactful, cooperative, confident

Your less attractive qualities: too sensitive, lack of self-esteem, easily discouraged, lack of purpose, inner tension, discontented, dogmatic, too serious, overindulgent, worry, inertia, materialistic, domineering, escapism, inertia

Your Venus Power

The planet Venus has a great deal of influence on your powers of attraction. Below are four possible Venus types for women and men. To find your Venus you need to go to page 771, where you will find the Venus table and extra information. The planet Mars also affects your powers of attraction. To find your Mars table and interpretation go to page 761.

WOMEN WITH VENUS IN SCORPIO: Loving and passionate, you are often sensitive with deep feelings and strong powers of attraction. A love for the truth coupled with a tendency to be suspicious can be an influence that motivates you to delve deep into the activities of your partner. When in love or in a relationship that matters, you will often bend over backward to cooperate. Although loyal, guard against losing sight of your own needs and desires.

MEN WITH VENUS IN SCORPIO: In relationships you possess a sensitive understanding of your partner's deeper nature. Although you are strongly attached to those you love, you may have to be careful that your feelings do not turn into jealousy or possessiveness. When you fall in love it is often with an emotional intensity that helps you get in touch with your deep feelings. You are attracted to partners who can share your passion and display strong feelings of sexuality like your own.

WOMEN WITH VENUS IN SAGITTARIUS: At your best when being optimistic and generous, you possess a mischievous sense of fun. In relationships your open-minded approach to people and places may attract you to those of a different culture or make you tolerant of the foibles of others. Although warm and enthusiastic when in love, your natural honesty and idealism may inspire you to look for a partner who shares your love of freedom.

MEN WITH VENUS IN SAGITTARIUS: When in love you are open and friendly. You are best matched with a partner who can share your adventurous spirit and sense of fun. Be careful, however, that your desire for freedom does not cause you to avoid commitment. You prefer your partners to be positive, direct, and generous in spirit. Being outspoken as well as an idealist, you usually enjoy a partner with whom you can share your strong opinions. Alternatively, you may wish to explore

life together, whether through travel, education, or just having fun.

WOMEN WITH VENUS IN CAPRICORN: Proud and refined, you attract others with your composed dignity. Disliking vulnerability and needing to feel safe before you can express your feelings, you usually display a strong front. Feeling insecure or inadequate in relationships may force you to become manipulative in order to regain control. Nevertheless, you can project an attractive sense of self-assurance and are capable of displaying loyalty and a wonderful dry sense of humor

MEN WITH VENUS IN CAPRICORN: As you do not display your deeper emotions freely, you are usually dignified and controlled in your relationships with others. Practical and down-to-earth partners are particularly attractive to you, especially those who do not rush into expressing their feelings but seem to possess natural class and reserve. You need a partner who is loyal and dependable and willing to take your relationship seriously.

WOMEN WITH VENUS IN AQUARIUS: Sociable and gracious, you are usually sincere and are capable of showing attributes of real tolerance and liberalism. Although you are keen on forming relationships you also like to have freedom and act independently. Your intimate partnerships need to be founded on true friendships. Full of bright and progressive ideas, you can express yourself better when you are free and unrestricted. An ability to think in a dispassionate way suggests that you can stay detached. Your love of freedom also implies that, without smothering your partner, you can be loving and loyal.

MEN WITH VENUS IN AQUARIUS: Ideally, in relationships your lover is also your best friend. Since freedom of expression is a prerequisite to your well-being, you do better when left alone to do your own thing. You also need a partner who recognizes and appreciates your need for independence. Although usually friendly, at times you can be stubborn or your cool detachment can appear to others as distant or impersonal. Being very sociable, however, you particularly enjoy the company of those who share your original, fair-minded, and progressive views.

To read all about your Outer Planets and work out how to use your personalized timetable, go to Section Three, page 789.

go to Section Three, page 789.

♐

Your Personalized Timetable

JUPITER BENEFICIAL
1938 2/22 – 4/11
1938 9/8 – 11/28
1940 3/1 – 5/7
1943 8/24 – until 1944 7/16
1945 11/4 – until 1946 1/2
1946 3/23 – 8/30
1950 2/6 – 3/21
1951 6/28 – 9/10
1952 2/9 – 4/20
1955 8/8 – 10/30
1956 2/4 – 6/26
1957 10/18 – 12/8
1958 5/1 – 8/6
1962 1/20 – 3/3
1963 5/29 – 10/27
1964 1/13 – 4/3
1967 7/23 – 10/8
1968 3/14 – 5/30
1969 10/3 – 11/19
1974 1/3 – 2/15
1975 5/8 – until 1976 3/17
1979 7/7 – 9/19
1981 9/17 – 11/2
1985 4/30 – 7/10
1985 12/16 – until 1986 1/30
1987 4/21 – 7/18
1987 9/21 – until 1988 2/27
1990 10/29 – 12/31
1991 6/18 – 9/3
1993 8/31 – 10/18
1997 4/1 – 8/25
1997 11/20 – until 1998 1/13
1999 4/5 – 6/16
1999 11/7 – until 2000 2/1
2002 9/30 – until 2003 2/10
2003 5/26 – 8/18
2004 12/12 – until 2005 3/26
2005 8/12 – 10/3
2009 3/11 – 5/10
2009 7/21 – 12/25
2011 3/19 – 5/26

SATURN BENEFICIAL
1938 5/1 – 11/15
1939 1/13 – 6/11
1939 10/19 – until 1940 3/2
1947 8/2 – until 1948 9/3
1952 9/16 – 12/15
1953 3/31 – 9/9
1963 2/13 – until 1964 2/10
1967 7/2 – 8/17
1968 3/9 – until 1969 4/14
1976 9/11 – until 1977 2/20
1977 5/30 – 10/18
1978 2/5 – 7/8
1981 10/24 – until 1982 10/17
1992 3/21 – 8/9
1992 12/18 – until 1993 3/16
1993 9/16 – 12/7
1997 4/14 – until 1998 5/21
1998 11/22 – until 1999 2/4
2006 7/16 – until 2007 8/17
2010 12/6 – until 2011 3/20
2011 8/30 – 11/24
2012 5/1 – 8/17

URANUS BENEFICIAL
1958 8/5 – until 1962 7/5
1971 10/24 – until 1974 8/27
1999 3/15 – until 2002 11/19

NEPTUNE BENEFICIAL
1948 12/23 – until 1954 9/28
2004 4/9 – until 2010 1/14

PLUTO BENEFICIAL
1946 8/24 – until 1957 5/28
1977 10/31 – until 1982 8/30

JUPITER CHALLENGING
1939 2/22 – 5/1
1941 7/19 – until 1942 1/17
1942 2/24 – 6/1

JUPITER BENEFICIAL (continued)
1944 9/20 – until 1945 8/15
1951 2/4 – 4/12
1953 6/30 – until 1954 5/14
1956 9/4 – 11/26
1957 3/9 – 7/26
1962 6/11 – 7/22
1963 1/16 – 3/26
1965 6/13 – 9/3
1965 12/5 – until 1966 4/24
1968 8/19 – 11/4
1969 4/17 – 6/28
1974 5/5 – 9/12
1974 12/23 – until 1975 3/10
1977 5/28 – 8/9
1978 1/16 – 3/27
1980 8/2 – 10/17
1986 4/14 – until 1987 2/22
1989 5/12 – 7/21
1991 11/19 – until 1992 2/10
1992 7/14 – 10/1
1998 3/26 – 7/13
1998 7/22 – until 1999 2/3
2001 4/23 – 7/4
2003 10/25 – until 2004 3/19
2004 6/20 – 9/15
2010 3/9 – 5/24
2010 9/24 – until 2011 1/10
2012 8/11 – Continues

SATURN CHALLENGING
1942 9/1 – 10/19
1943 5/7 – until 1944 6/4
1949 9/21 – until 1950 10/31
1951 4/2 – 7/23
1965 4/4 – 10/1
1965 12/26 – until 1966 5/27
1966 8/26 – until 1967 2/14
1972 6/16 – until 1973 7/15
1974 2/12 – 3/15
1978 11/8 – until 1979 2/10
1979 7/28 – until 1980 9/5
1994 6/1 – 7/14
1995 2/9 – until 1996 3/22
2001 7/29 – 11/27
2002 4/17 – 9/7
2002 11/15 – until 2003 5/18
2008 9/4 – until 2009 10/12
2010 5/16 – 6/13

URANUS CHALLENGING
1944 7/28 – until 1949 5/4
1964 9/28 – until 1968 8/27
2006 3/24 – until 2011 2/1

NEPTUNE CHALLENGING
1938 1/1 – until 1942 8/7

PLUTO CHALLENGING
1962 11/20 – until 1971 8/10

JUPITER SPECIAL
1947 12/17 – until 1948 3/21
1948 5/9 – 11/5
1959 12/1 – until 1960 2/17
1960 6/25 – 10/13
1971 11/15 – until 1972 1/27
1983 10/30 – until 1984 1/10
1995 2/12 – 5/20
1995 10/10 – 12/25
2007 1/20 – 6/30
2007 9/13 – 12/10

SATURN SPECIAL
1957 1/29 – 5/19
1957 10/27 – until 1958 12/19
1986 12/3 – until 1988 1/24
1988 7/7 – 10/20

URANUS SPECIAL
1984 1/17 – until 1988 10/23

NEPTUNE SPECIAL
1975 12/17 – until 1983 11/25

PLUTO SPECIAL
2000 1/18 – until 2007 12/1

December 13

SUN: SAGITTARIUS • DECANATE: LEO/SUN • DEGREE: 20°5–21°5 SAGITTARIUS • MODE: MUTABLE • ELEMENT: FIRE

Your Personal Powers

Independent and spirited, you are a shrewd individual with foresight and practical skills. Your ruling planet, Jupiter, grants you optimism, integrity, an adventurous nature, and the enthusiasm to embrace life's possibilities. Discriminating and intuitive with quick comprehension, you can often benefit from expanding your knowledge. As a methodical and broad-minded individual, you can be resourceful and enterprising. Although you have high ideals, you may need to guard against being too serious or opinionated. Being multitalented yet pragmatic implies that you enjoy exploring different ideas and often excel at more than one subject. Being impatient or dissatisfied with a restrictive or dull environment suggests that you empower yourself through mental challenges. By synthesizing the talents and knowledge at your disposal into one main objective, you usually achieve success. Although variety, mental stimulation, and constant progress are vital to your well-being, your conflicting needs can at times pull you in different directions. Nevertheless, being practical and security-conscious also urges you to establish a firm and stable foundation in life.

Your Powers of Attraction in Relationships

Your natural gift for dealing with people indicates that you are considerate, warmhearted, and affectionate. Although you can be frank about your opinions, a tendency to keep your feelings to yourself implies that you can sometimes hold back your deeper emotions. People admire your earnest personality, quick comprehension, and liberal outlook. Although you can be idealistic, your shrewd understanding and common sense suggest that you can assess people's character with cunning accuracy. Usually you are drawn to ambitious individuals who may appear modest but are clever and enterprising. Although you can be devoted, generous, and loving, your enthusiasm often emerges when you and your partner are initiating new projects or an adventure that can offer you new opportunities.

Your attractive qualities: Inspired, focused, ambitious, confident, astute, enterprising, creative thinker, pragmatic, rational, quick, alert, optimistic, scientific, freedom-loving, self-expressive, initiative, adventurous, witty, idealistic, humanitarian, noble ideas, philosophical, organizational ability, original

Your less attractive qualities: impulsive, restless, indecisive, bossy, unemotional, rebellious, self-righteous, risk taker, scattered, opinionated, secretive, self-centered, tactless, disorganized, self-indulgent, too materialistic

Your Venus Power

The planet Venus has a great deal of influence on your powers of attraction. Below are four possible Venus types for women and men. To find your Venus you need to go to page 771, where you will find the Venus table and extra information. The planet Mars also affects your powers of attraction. To find your Mars table and interpretation go to page 761.

WOMEN WITH VENUS IN SCORPIO: With a natural psychic gift for penetrating the feelings of others, you can often help partners transform emotional challenges or sexual difficulties. When you fall in love, your strong feelings and determination give you a potent force that others find attractive and seductive. Although you know what really turns people on, your most profound desire is usually for the deepness and closeness of real love and intimacy in an enduring relationship.

MEN WITH VENUS IN SCORPIO: As you are emotionally intense and passionate, personal relationships are probably a major factor in your own transformation. Being sensitive yet loyal, you are usually attracted to forceful partners who can express themselves intimately but intensely. Rather than seek easy and simple relationships you are drawn to partners who act as a catalyst for your own internal changes. Through your relationships with your partners you can unravel your own motives and understand your deep-seated feelings or emotional insecurities.

WOMEN WITH VENUS IN SAGITTARIUS: When you feel generous you can make others feel more optimistic about life. You may be interested in higher learning and seek partners who are scholarly or broad-minded. You are outspoken and direct and sometimes say things that you later regret. Curious and versatile, you can adjust quickly to new situations, and a foreign influence implies that you love to travel or may have a partner who comes from a different culture.

MEN WITH VENUS IN SAGITTARIUS: Your enthusiasm and straightforward conduct usually appeal to others and imply that you are approachable and easygoing. Being open to ideas and willing to believe that life has a great deal to offer suggests that you are generous, broad-minded, and show eagerness to

cooperate with others. A love of travel and an interest in other cultures also imply that your partner may come from a foreign country.

WOMEN WITH VENUS IN CAPRICORN: Romantically, you do not give your heart easily but hide behind a cool reserve until you feel free to express your emotions. As you take your relationships seriously, you may find yourself drawn to people who are businesslike, resourceful, and practical, or those who can act as teachers or mentors. Work or career may also be a factor in many of your associations and partnerships. As security can play an important role in your relationships you are often attracted to partners who are loyal and hardworking,

MEN WITH VENUS IN CAPRICORN: As you do not display your deeper emotions freely, you are usually dignified and controlled in your relationships with others. Practical and down-to-earth partners are particularly attractive to you, especially those who do not rush into expressing their feelings but seem to possess natural class and reserve. You need a partner who is loyal and dependable and willing to take your relationship seriously.

WOMEN WITH VENUS IN AQUARIUS: When it comes to relationships, others are attracted to your honest, friendly, and easygoing approach. You really enjoy social interaction with others and may develop a genuine concern for humanity. Usually you present a tolerant and reasonable front in love situations and attempt to view your relationships objectively. If partners become too demanding, however, you can become stubborn and fixed. Friendship may be even more important for you than sexual compatibility.

MEN WITH VENUS IN AQUARIUS: Although independent, you often enjoy being part of a group. The partners you frequently attract are themselves nonconformists or free spirits. As an individual you may not find it easy to settle into a routine or an entirely mundane type of relationship. You may have some unconventional views on the traditional marriage or your partner may hold such views. It is usually important to you that your love relationships are based on friendship.

To read all about your Outer Planets and work out how to use your personalized timetable, go to Section Three, page 789.

Your Personalized Timetable

JUPITER BENEFICIAL
1938 2/27 – 4/16
1938 8/30 – 12/6
1940 3/5 – 5/12
1943 8/29 – until 1944 7/21
1945 11/9 – until 1946 1/12
1946 3/12 – 9/4
1950 2/10 – 3/26
1951 7/8 – 8/30
1952 2/15 – 4/24
1955 8/13 – 11/8
1956 1/27 – 7/2
1957 10/23 – 12/14
1958 4/23 – 8/13
1962 1/25 – 3/8
1963 6/4 – 10/19
1964 1/20 – 4/8
1967 7/28 – 10/13
1968 3/5 – 6/8
1969 10/8 – 11/24
1974 1/8 – 2/19
1975 5/13 – until 1976 3/22
1979 7/11 – 9/24
1981 9/22 – 11/7
1985 5/11 – 6/29
1985 12/21 – until 1986 2/4
1987 4/26 – 7/30
1987 9/9 – until 1988 3/3
1990 11/11 – 12/18
1991 6/24 – 9/7
1993 9/5 – 10/22
1997 4/6 – 8/17
1997 11/27 – until 1998 1/18
1999 4/9 – 6/22
1999 10/30 – until 2000 2/8
2002 10/6 – until 2003 2/2
2003 6/2 – 8/22
2004 12/20 – until 2005 3/18
2005 8/18 – 10/7
2009 3/16 – 5/21
2009 7/10 – 12/30
2011 3/23 – 5/30

SATURN BENEFICIAL
1938 5/10 – 10/29
1939 1/28 – 6/22
1939 10/6 – until 1940 3/11
1947 8/10 – until 1948 9/11
1952 9/25 – 12/28
1953 3/16 – 9/18
1963 2/22 – until 1964 2/18
1968 3/17 – until 1969 4/22
1976 9/21 – until 1977 2/7
1977 6/10 – 10/31
1978 1/22 – 7/18
1981 11/1 – until 1982 5/24
1982 7/13 – 10/25
1992 4/2 – 7/26
1992 12/28 – until 1993 3/26
1993 9/1 – 12/21
1997 4/22 – until 1998 5/30
1998 11/7 – until 1999 2/18
2006 7/24 – until 2007 8/25
2010 12/20 – until 2011 3/4
2011 9/8 – 12/4
2012 4/17 – 8/29

URANUS BENEFICIAL
1958 8/21 – until 1962 7/24
1971 11/11 – until 1974 9/16
1999 4/8 – until 2002 12/26

NEPTUNE BENEFICIAL
1949 11/8 – until 1955 8/23
2005 3/1 – until 2010 11/26

PLUTO BENEFICIAL
1946 10/7 – until 1957 7/18
1977 12/1 – until 1982 9/29

JUPITER CHALLENGING
1939 2/26 – 5/6
1939 11/15 – 12/3
1941 7/25 – until 1942 1/5

1942 3/9 – 6/6
1944 9/25 – until 1945 8/20
1951 2/9 – 4/17
1953 7/5 – until 1954 5/19
1956 9/9 – 12/4
1957 2/28 – 8/1
1963 1/21 – 3/31
1965 6/18 – 9/11
1965 11/26 – until 1966 4/30
1968 8/24 – 11/10
1969 4/7 – 7/7
1974 5/11 – 9/4
1974 12/30 – until 1975 3/14
1977 6/1 – 8/15
1978 1/7 – 4/4
1980 8/7 – 10/22
1986 4/19 – 11/3
1986 11/13 – until 1987 2/26
1989 5/16 – 7/26
1991 11/28 – until 1992 1/31
1992 7/20 – 10/6
1998 3/31 – until 1999 2/8
2001 4/28 – 7/8
2003 10/31 – until 2004 3/11
2004 6/28 – 9/20
2010 3/14 – 5/30
2010 9/16 – until 2011 1/17
2012 8/19 – Continues

SATURN CHALLENGING
1943 5/15 – until 1944 6/12
1949 9/30 – until 1950 4/22
1950 6/7 – 11/10
1951 3/20 – 8/3
1965 4/14 – 9/17
1966 1/8 – 6/13
1966 8/9 – until 1967 2/23
1972 6/24 – until 1973 7/24
1974 1/21 – 4/5
1978 11/23 – until 1979 1/25
1979 8/6 – until 1980 9/13
1995 2/17 – until 1996 3/30
2001 8/10 – 11/14
2002 4/26 – 10/4
2002 10/18 – until 2003 5/27
2008 9/12 – until 2009 10/21
2010 4/22 – 7/7

URANUS CHALLENGING
1944 9/2 – until 1949 5/24
1964 10/16 – until 1968 9/13
2006 4/13 – until 2011 2/22

NEPTUNE CHALLENGING
1938 1/1 – until 1942 9/7

PLUTO CHALLENGING
1963 10/8 – until 1971 9/9

JUPITER SPECIAL
1947 12/22 – until 1948 11/10
1959 12/6 – until 1960 2/23
1960 6/17 – 10/20
1971 11/20 – until 1972 2/1
1972 8/6 – 9/12
1983 11/4 – until 1984 1/15
1995 2/20 – 5/11
1995 10/16 – 12/30
2007 1/26 – 6/21
2007 9/22 – 12/14

SATURN SPECIAL
1957 2/12 – 5/3
1957 11/6 – until 1958 12/28
1986 12/11 – until 1988 2/3
1988 6/23 – 11/2

URANUS SPECIAL
1984 2/12 – until 1988 11/14

NEPTUNE SPECIAL
1976 1/16 – until 1984 10/16

PLUTO SPECIAL
2000 12/12 – until 2008 10/24

↗

December 14

SUN: SAGITTARIUS • DECANATE: LEO/SUN • DEGREE: 21°5–22°5 SAGITTARIUS • MODE: MUTABLE • ELEMENT: FIRE

Your Personal Powers

Astute and pragmatic, your common sense indicates that you are also a capable individual with a positive outlook and a purposeful nature. You usually enjoy expanding your horizons through gaining knowledge and being adventurous. Bold, daring, and resourceful, you are likely to be an independent thinker with original ideas. Being capable of seeing the many layers of a concept enables you to think on a grand scale as well as be creative. As you are full of profitable ideas, success is often guaranteed if you invest time in establishing a strong foundation to your education and skills. Having strong opinions and convictions also indicates that you can be persuasive and forceful. Although you are often direct and matter-of-fact, you can lose some of your charm when you rush into a situation that demands tact and diplomacy and are too candid or blunt. Your emotional restlessness and need for mental stimulation imply that you need to find a satisfying plan or vocation that can keep you busy and allow you to express your enthusiasm and idealism.

Your Powers of Attraction in Relationships

People admire your friendly, determined, and decisive nature. Preferring to be in the company of those who share your interests, you often respect intelligent people who have a mind of their own. Therefore you seek a partner who is independent, clever, and original. Alternatively, you may be attracted to shrewd businesspeople who are persuasive and successful. You may make links with people of a difficult culture or meet your partner through travel. As you are likely to have strong opinions, resist imposing your philosophical views on others or being stubborn. Not shy in speaking your mind, you can be direct and critical even though you do not mean to hurt or offend loved ones. Being sensitive to those around you can often get you out of arguments and confrontations.

Your attractive qualities: honest, diplomatic, intelligent, instinctive, intuitive, decisive, common sense, idealistic, hardworking, creative, optimistic, observant, pragmatic, cautious, imaginative, philosophical, home-loving, responsible, charitable, enterprising

Your less attractive qualities: restless, rebellious, overly cautious or impulsive, bossy, tactless, easily bored, opinionated, thoughtless, stubborn, extravagant, exaggerate, materialistic, dissatisfied, critical

Your Venus Power

The planet Venus has a great deal of influence on your powers of attraction. Below are four possible Venus types for women and men. To find your Venus you need to go to page 771, where you will find the Venus table and extra information. The planet Mars also affects your powers of attraction. To find your Mars table and interpretation go to page 761.

WOMEN WITH VENUS IN SCORPIO: With a natural psychic gift for penetrating the feelings of others, you can often help partners transform emotional challenges or sexual difficulties. When you fall in love, your strong feelings and determination give you a potent force that others find attractive and seductive. Although you know what really turns people on, your most profound desire is usually for the deepness and closeness of real love and intimacy in an enduring relationship.

MEN WITH VENUS IN SCORPIO: In relationships you possess a sensitive understanding of your partner's deeper nature. Although you are strongly attached to those you love, you may have to be careful that your feelings do not turn into jealousy or possessiveness. When you fall in love it is often with an emotional intensity that helps you get in touch with your deep feelings. You are attracted to partners who can share your passion and display strong feelings of sexuality like your own.

WOMEN WITH VENUS IN SAGITTARIUS: At your best when being optimistic and generous, you possess a mischievous sense of fun. In relationships your open-minded approach to people and places may attract you to those of a different culture or make you tolerant of the foibles of others. Warm and enthusiastic when in love, your natural honesty and idealism inspire you to look for a partner who shares your love of freedom.

MEN WITH VENUS IN SAGITTARIUS: Forward-thinking rather than dwelling on the past, you are looking for a partner who can share your future plans. You enjoy exploring life whether through travel and mental pursuits or sports and games. Idealistic, you usually prefer the company of a partner who is optimistic and shares your beliefs. In your desire for honesty in relationships however, be careful not to become tactless. Nevertheless, you are attracted to honest, direct, and fun-loving partners who have a sense of humor like your own.

WOMEN WITH VENUS IN CAPRICORN: With your natural caution in romantic affairs, you often appear reserved and controlled. If shy, try to be more forward, especially if you

want to be noticed. When you care about people, however, you are usually willing to put in extra time and energy to preserve the relationship. You are practical and dependable, and a sense of duty can often play a large role in the affairs of your heart. With elegant simplicity, you can attract others with your well-cut clothes and refined manners.

MEN WITH VENUS IN CAPRICORN: As you do not display your deeper emotions freely, you are usually dignified and controlled in your relationships with others. Practical and down-to-earth partners are particularly attractive to you, especially those who do not rush into expressing their feelings but seem to possess natural class and reserve. You need a partner who is loyal and dependable and willing to take your relationship seriously.

WOMEN WITH VENUS IN AQUARIUS: When it comes to relationships, others are attracted to your honest, friendly, and easygoing approach. You really enjoy social interaction with others and may develop a genuine concern for humanity. Usually you present a tolerant and reasonable front in love situations and attempt to view your relationships objectively. If partners become too demanding, however, you can become stubborn and fixed. Friendship may be even more important for you than sexual compatibility.

MEN WITH VENUS IN AQUARIUS: You are sociable and open-minded, and people are attracted by your friendly and easygoing style. Being independent, you value freedom-loving partners who give you the space to be yourself. People can sometimes interpret your detachment as being emotionally cool but they admire your objectivity and humanitarian inclinations. You are attracted to intelligent individuals who are as truthful and direct as you but who, above all, must be true friends. Ideally, your partner shares your liberal views on life and possesses a strong sense of individuality.

To read all about your Outer Planets and work out how to use your personalized timetable, go to Section Three, page 789.

Your Personalized Timetable

JUPITER BENEFICIAL
1938 3/3 – 4/22
1938 8/22 – 12/12
1940 3/10 – 5/16
1943 9/3 – until **1944** 7/26
1945 11/14 – until **1946** 1/28
1946 2/25 – 9/10
1950 2/14 – 3/31
1951 7/26 – 8/13
1952 2/20 – 4/29
1955 8/17 – 11/17
1956 1/17 – 7/8
1957 10/28 – 12/21
1958 4/15 – 8/20
1962 1/29 – 3/12
1963 6/10 – 10/11
1964 1/27 – 4/12
1967 8/2 – 10/19
1968 2/26 – 6/15
1969 10/12 – 11/30
1970 5/29 – 7/18
1974 1/12 – 2/24
1975 5/18 – until **1976** 3/26
1979 7/16 – 9/29
1981 9/27 – 11/12
1985 12/26 – until **1986** 2/8
1987 4/30 – until **1988** 3/8
1991 6/29 – 9/12
1993 9/10 – 10/27
1997 4/13 – 8/9
1997 12/4 – until **1998** 1/22
1999 4/13 – 6/28
1999 10/22 – until **2000** 2/15
2002 10/13 – until **2003** 1/26
2003 6/9 – 8/27
2004 12/29 – until **2005** 3/8
2005 8/24 – 10/12
2009 3/21 – until **2010** 1/4
2011 3/27 – 6/4

SATURN BENEFICIAL
1938 5/20 – 10/15
1939 2/10 – 7/7
1939 9/21 – until **1940** 3/20
1947 8/18 – until **1948** 9/19
1949 4/2 – 5/30
1952 10/3 – until **1953** 1/19
1953 2/21 – 9/27
1963 3/2 – 9/24
1963 11/17 – until **1964** 2/27
1968 3/25 – until **1969** 4/30
1976 10/1 – until **1977** 1/26
1977 6/21 – 11/18
1978 1/4 – 7/26
1981 11/10 – until **1982** 5/4
1982 8/1 – 11/3
1992 4/16 – 7/11
1993 1/7 – 4/5
1993 8/18 – until **1994** 1/1
1997 4/30 – 11/22
1998 1/8 – 6/9
1998 10/25 – until **1999** 3/1
2006 8/1 – until **2007** 9/2
2011 1/12 – 2/9
2011 9/17 – 12/15
2012 4/4 – 9/9

URANUS BENEFICIAL
1958 9/8 – until **1962** 8/10
1971 11/30 – until **1974** 10/4
2000 2/10 – until **2003** 1/17

NEPTUNE BENEFICIAL
1949 12/16 – until **1955** 9/26
2005 4/4 – until **2011** 1/11

PLUTO BENEFICIAL
1947 9/12 – until **1958** 6/13
1978 10/21 – until **1983** 8/10

JUPITER CHALLENGING
1939 3/2 – 5/11
1939 10/29 – 12/21

1941 7/30 – 12/26
1942 3/18 – 6/10
1944 9/29 – until **1945** 8/25
1951 2/13 – 4/21
1953 7/9 – until **1954** 5/24
1956 9/13 – 12/13
1957 2/19 – 8/7
1963 1/26 – 4/4
1965 6/22 – 9/21
1965 11/16 – until **1966** 5/5
1968 8/29 – 11/16
1969 3/30 – 7/15
1974 5/18 – 8/28
1975 1/5 – 3/18
1977 6/6 – 8/20
1977 12/30 – until **1978** 4/12
1980 8/12 – 10/27
1986 4/24 – 10/14
1986 12/3 – until **1987** 3/2
1989 5/21 – 7/31
1991 12/11 – until **1992** 1/18
1992 7/26 – 10/10
1998 4/4 – until **1999** 2/13
2001 5/3 – 7/13
2003 11/7 – until **2004** 3/3
2004 7/5 – 9/25
2010 3/18 – 6/6
2010 9/8 – until **2011** 1/22
2012 8/27 – 11/11

SATURN CHALLENGING
1943 5/23 – until **1944** 6/20
1949 10/9 – until **1950** 4/3
1950 6/26 – 11/21
1951 3/6 – 8/14
1965 4/25 – 9/3
1966 1/19 – until **1967** 3/4
1972 7/2 – until **1973** 1/23
1973 3/6 – 8/2
1974 1/7 – 4/19
1979 8/15 – until **1980** 9/21
1995 2/26 – until **1996** 4/7
2001 8/25 – 10/29
2002 5/5 – until **2003** 6/4
2008 9/21 – until **2009** 10/30
2010 4/7 – 7/22

URANUS CHALLENGING
1945 6/18 – until **1949** 6/10
1964 11/8 – until **1969** 6/26
2006 5/8 – until **2011** 3/12

NEPTUNE CHALLENGING
1938 1/1 – until **1943** 8/4

PLUTO CHALLENGING
1963 11/21 – until **1972** 8/1

JUPITER SPECIAL
1947 12/26 – until **1948** 11/15
1959 12/10 – until **1960** 3/1
1960 6/9 – 10/26
1971 11/25 – until **1972** 2/7
1972 7/24 – 9/26
1983 11/8 – until **1984** 1/19
1995 3/3 – 5/1
1995 10/21 – until **1996** 1/3
2007 2/1 – 6/12
2007 9/29 – 12/19

SATURN SPECIAL
1957 3/6 – 4/10
1957 11/15 – until **1959** 1/5
1986 12/20 – until **1988** 2/14
1988 6/9 – 11/12

URANUS SPECIAL
1984 12/9 – until **1988** 12/3

NEPTUNE SPECIAL
1976 12/15 – until **1984** 11/22

PLUTO SPECIAL
2001 1/9 – until **2008** 11/28

December 15

SUN: SAGITTARIUS • DECANATE: LEO/SUN • DEGREE: 22°5–23°5 SAGITTARIUS • MODE: MUTABLE • ELEMENT: FIRE

Your Personal Powers

Instinctive and versatile, you are a mentally creative and imaginative individual with many ideas and an energetic nature. Your ruling planet, Jupiter, inspires you to explore different themes and be adventurous. Intellectually bright and daring, you can comprehend information quickly. Inspired by knowledge, you benefit from expanding your horizons or exploring philosophy and spirituality. Travel can also inspire your imagination. Although you are inquisitive and talented and have many wonderful plans, you can lose some of your power by failing to have a long-term strategy and a clear purpose or vision. It is often your inner restlessness or dissatisfaction that causes you to be bored or unsure about your aspirations. Having a good sense of values and being insightful indicate, however, that you can quickly recognize opportunities when they arise. Being active and determined with a talent for business, you gain power when you examine the broader picture and then act decisively. By resolutely focusing on a particular course of action you can achieve your desired objective.

Your Powers of Attraction in Relationships

Sociable, charming, and engaging, you can be very witty and entertaining. People are drawn to your bright and idealistic nature and are often impressed with your many ideas. When you meet a new partner, you usually display eagerness and your passionate side, but you can also lose interest and become quickly bored with the relationship. Being proud, you do not like to appear weak and usually you are reluctant to rely on people. Although you enjoy collaborating with others, your independent nature implies that you want to have a great deal of personal freedom, especially when you see new opportunities. You are usually attracted to romantic and idealistic individuals who are affectionate and caring. Although you may have strong convictions, you are sensitive and intuitive enough to sense tension and act tactfully when necessary.

Your attractive qualities: witty, optimistic, enterprising, entertaining, confident, versatile, generous, responsible, kind, cooperative, appreciative, creative, compassionate, charming, communicative, well-informed, spiritual potential, philosophical, decisive, mentally quick

Your less attractive qualities: materialistic, uncaring, irresponsible, self-centered, fear of change, moody, inner doubts, worried, indecisive, cold, restless, fluctuating finances or uncertainty about money

Your Venus Power

The planet Venus has a great deal of influence on your powers of attraction. Below are four possible Venus types for women and men. To find your Venus you need to go to page 771, where you will find the Venus table and extra information. The planet Mars also affects your powers of attraction. To find your Mars table and interpretation go to page 761.

WOMEN WITH VENUS IN SCORPIO: Usually you are drawn to partners who are sensual in appearance with strong character. As you are emotionally intense and passionate, personal relationships are probably a major factor in your life. Since you like to be in control, you can at times exhibit some of your less attractive qualities by being willful or domineering. Although you need to feel established and in command in your relationships, you are constantly searching for some higher truth that can bring about a significant transformation.

MEN WITH VENUS IN SCORPIO: As you are emotionally intense and passionate, personal relationships are probably a major factor in your own transformation. Being sensitive yet loyal, you are usually attracted to forceful partners who can express themselves intimately but intensely. Rather than seek easy and simple relationships, you are drawn to partners who act as a catalyst for your own internal changes. Through your relationships with your partners you can unravel your own motives and understand your deep-seated feelings or emotional insecurities.

WOMEN WITH VENUS IN SAGITTARIUS: Optimistic and fun-loving, you love adventure and seek a partner who can expand your horizons. Being truthful and direct, you often say what you think, and at times you may be naively tactless. A need for expansion and prosperity suggests that you may enjoy traveling with your friends or partner. Being lighthearted and idealistic, once you have given your heart to someone you will stay honorable and loyal.

MEN WITH VENUS IN SAGITTARIUS: When in love you are open and friendly, but you need a a partner who can share your adventurous spirit and sense of fun. Be careful, however, that your desire for freedom does not cause you to avoid commitment. You prefer your partners to be positive, direct, and

generous in spirit. Being outspoken as well as an idealist, you usually enjoy a partner with whom you can share your strong opinions. Alternatively, you may wish to explore life together, whether through travel, education, or by having fun.

WOMEN WITH VENUS IN CAPRICORN: Proud and refined, you attract others with your composed dignity. Disliking vulnerability and needing to feel safe before you can express your feelings, you usually display a strong front. Feeling insecure or inadequate in relationships may force you to become manipulative in order to regain control. Nevertheless, you can project an attractive sense of self-assurance and are capable of displaying loyalty and a wonderful dry sense of humor.

MEN WITH VENUS IN CAPRICORN: As you admire loyal, hardworking, and dedicated individuals, you probably want a partner who can share your vocational interests or provide you with the sense of security that you need. You could even find yourself with a partner who is of a different age group or maturity. Guard against denying your true emotional needs or focusing on your career at the expense of your relationship. You are drawn to reserved partners who display self-control.

WOMEN WITH VENUS IN AQUARIUS: Usually you have a modern outlook on love and are open to new or current lifestyles. Your intuitive abilities, communal sense, and people skills often allow you to see deeper into human intentions and sense other people's thoughts telepathically. Although you are usually group-oriented, you are drawn to strong individuals within the group who are independent and self-motivated. You are more inclined to choose a partner who is unconventional or freedom-loving. Conscious of your social standing, however, you want someone who can relate well to your friends.

MEN WITH VENUS IN AQUARIUS: When it comes to relationships, others are attracted to your honest, friendly, and easygoing approach. You really enjoy social interaction with others and may develop a genuine concern for humanity. Usually you present a tolerant and reasonable front in love situations and attempt to view your relationships objectively. If partners become too demanding, however, you can become stubborn and fixed. Friendship may be even more important for you than sexual compatibility.

To read all about your Outer Planets and work out how to use your personalized timetable, go to Section Three, page 789.

Your Personalized Timetable

JUPITER BENEFICIAL
1938 3/8 – 4/29
1938 8/15 – 12/19
1940 3/14 – 5/21
1943 9/8 – until 1944 7/31
1945 11/19 – until 1946 5/25
1946 7/4 – 9/15
1950 2/19 – 4/5
1950 10/7 – 11/9
1952 2/24 – 5/3
1955 8/22 – 12/1
1956 1/3 – 7/13
1957 11/2 – 12/28
1958 4/7 – 8/27
1962 2/2 – 3/17
1963 6/16 – 10/3
1964 2/2 – 4/16
1967 8/6 – 10/26
1968 2/19 – 6/22
1969 10/17 – 12/5
1970 5/17 – 7/30
1974 1/17 – 4 2/28
1975 5/23 – 11/27
1975 12/23 – until 1976 3/31
1979 7/21 – 10/4
1980 4/3 – 5/19
1981 10/1 – 11/17
1985 12/31 – until 1986 2/12
1987 5/5 – until 1988 3/13
1991 7/4 – 9/17
1993 9/15 – 11/1
1997 4/20 – 8/1
1997 12/10 – until 1998 1/27
1999 4/17 – 7/5
1999 10/15 – until 2000 2/21
2002 10/20 – until 2003 1/18
2003 6/15 – 9/1
2005 1/10 – 2/24
2005 8/29 – 10/17
2009 3/26 – 9/20
2009 11/5 – until 2010 1/9
2011 3/31 – 6/9
2011 12/5 – 1/14

SATURN BENEFICIAL
1938 5/30 – 10/2
1939 2/20 – 7/29
1939 8/29 – until 1940 3/29
1947 8/26 – until 1948 9/28
1949 3/16 – 6/15
1952 10/12 – until 1953 10/6
1963 3/12 – 9/6
1963 12/4 – until 1964 3/7
1968 4/2 – until 1969 5/8
1976 10/13 – until 1977 1/12
1977 6/30 – until 1978 8/4
1981 11/20 – until 1982 4/20
1982 8/14 – 11/12
1983 6/11 – 7/21
1992 5/5 – 6/20
1993 1/16 – 4/17
1993 8/5 – until 1994 1/11
1997 5/9 – 11/4
1998 1/26 – 6/20
1998 10/12 – until 1999 3/11
2006 8/9 – until 2007 9/11
2011 9/26 – 12/28
2012 3/20 – 9/18

URANUS BENEFICIAL
1958 9/28 – until 1962 8/27
1971 12/30 – until 1974 10/20
2000 2/28 – until 2003 2/4

NEPTUNE BENEFICIAL
1950 11/6 – until 1956 8/17
2006 2/26 – until 2011 2/8

PLUTO BENEFICIAL
1948 8/23 – until 1958 7/26
1978 11/18 – until 1983 9/16

JUPITER CHALLENGING
1939 3/6 – 5/17
1939 10/19 – 12/31

1941 8/5 – 12/18
1942 3/26 – 6/15
1944 10/4 – until 1945 8/30
1951 2/17 – 4/26
1953 7/14 – until 1954 5/29
1956 9/18 – 12/25
1957 2/6 – 8/12
1963 1/31 – 4/8
1965 6/27 – 10/7
1965 10/31 – until 1966 5/11
1968 9/2 – 11/22
1969 3/22 – 7/22
1974 5/25 – 8/19
1975 1/10 – 3/23
1977 6/10 – 8/27
1977 12/23 – until 1978 4/19
1980 8/17 – 11/1
1981 5/7 – 6/17
1986 4/29 – 10/3
1986 12/13 – until 1987 3/7
1989 5/25 – 8/5
1990 2/12 – 3/8
1992 7/31 – 10/15
1998 4/9 – until 1999 2/17
2001 5/8 – 7/17
2003 11/14 – until 2004 2/24
2004 7/12 – 9/30
2010 3/22 – 6/14
2010 8/31 – until 2011 1/28
2012 9/6 – Continues

SATURN CHALLENGING
1943 5/31 – until 1944 6/28
1949 10/18 – until 1950 3/19
1950 7/9 – 12/4
1951 2/20 – 8/23
1965 5/7 – 8/21
1966 1/29 – until 1967 3/12
1972 7/11 – until 1973 1/4
1973 3/25 – 8/12
1973 12/25 – until 1974 4/30
1979 8/23 – until 1980 9/30
1995 3/6 – until 1996 4/16
1996 11/11 – 12/25
2002 5/13 – until 2003 6/12
2008 9/29 – until 2009 5/4
2009 5/29 – 11/8
2010 3/24 – 8/2

URANUS CHALLENGING
1945 7/6 – until 1950 3/25
1965 9/5 – until 1969 7/30
2007 3/12 – until 2012 1/10

NEPTUNE CHALLENGING
1938 1/1 – until 1943 9/5

PLUTO CHALLENGING
1964 10/8 – until 1972 9/2

JUPITER SPECIAL
1947 12/31 – until 1948 11/20
1959 12/15 – until 1960 3/9
1960 6/1 – 11/1
1971 11/29 – until 1972 2/12
1972 7/14 – 10/5
1983 11/13 – until 1984 1/24
1995 3/18 – 4/15
1995 10/27 – until 1996 1/8
2007 2/7 – 6/4
2007 10/6 – 12/23

SATURN SPECIAL
1957 11/24 – until 1959 1/14
1959 8/8 – 10/2
1986 12/29 – until 1987 7/24
1987 9/13 – until 1988 2/28
1988 5/25 – 11/22

URANUS SPECIAL
1984 12/26 – until 1988 12/20

NEPTUNE SPECIAL
1977 1/13 – until 1985 10/10

PLUTO SPECIAL
2001 2/18 – until 2009 10/20

December 16

SUN: SAGITTARIUS · DECANATE: LEO/SUN · DEGREE: 23°5–24°5 SAGITTARIUS · MODE: MUTABLE · ELEMENT: FIRE

Your Personal Powers

Mentally quick and determined, you are a proud and strong-willed individual. Daring, capable, and progressive, your ruling planet, Jupiter, grants you optimism, good opportunities, and confidence. As an enterprising and sympathetic person, you excel at initiating new projects that you feel passionate about. Travel may also inspire you to explore different philosophies or styles of living. You gain power when you use your sharp intellect, persuasive charm, and discussion skills to win others over to your way of thinking. Often your success also depends on your cooperative efforts or willingness to be of service to a higher cause or goal. While your astute perception grants you the ability to be insightful and direct, your tendency to be overconfident implies that you can also be unintentionally arrogant and critical. An urge to be free implies that you can rebel against restrictive circumstances by being provocative. Nevertheless, intelligent and inquisitive, you enjoy interacting with others and your witty remarks can be both entertaining and perceptive.

Your Powers of Attraction in Relationships

Being spontaneous, gregarious, and generous, you enjoy being sociable, often making a good impression on others with your humor, smart image, or sense of the dramatic. As a natural psychologist and communicator, you have excellent insight into people. With your engaging manner you also have a natural flair for dealing with individuals on a one-to-one basis. Able to offer the right incentives, you can be quietly persuasive. Although sociable, you also need regular time alone to renew your energies. Kind and friendly when you are in a positive frame of mind, you need to beware of being bossy or cynical when you feel insecure. Often you are attracted to successful or enterprising people with good social connections. Keeping the balance of power in your close partnerships is vital to your well-being.

Your attractive qualities: direct, frank, responsible, good integrity, intuitive, social, cooperative, insightful, optimistic, sense of the dramatic, witty, entertaining, self-aware, philosophical, compassionate, independent, gregarious, fun-loving, diplomatic, confident, generous

Your less attractive qualities: worry, irresponsible, self-promoting, opinionated, skeptical, cynical, irritable, frustrated, too proud, moody, extravagant, snobbish, dissatisfied, opportunist, codependent

Your Venus Power

The planet Venus has a great deal of influence on your powers of attraction. Below are four possible Venus types for women and men. To find your Venus you need to go to page 771, where you will find the Venus table and extra information. The planet Mars also affects your powers of attraction. To find your Mars table and interpretation go to page 761.

WOMEN WITH VENUS IN SCORPIO: With a natural psychic gift for penetrating the feelings of others, you can often help partners transform emotional challenges or sexual difficulties. When you fall in love, your strong feelings and determination give you a potent force that others find attractive and seductive. Although you know what really turns people on, your most profound desire is usually for the deepness and closeness of real love and intimacy in an enduring relationship.

MEN WITH VENUS IN SCORPIO: As you are emotionally intense and passionate, personal relationships are probably a major factor in your own transformation. Being sensitive yet loyal, you are usually attracted to forceful partners who can express themselves intimately but intensely. Rather than seek easy and simple relationships you are drawn to partners who act as a catalyst for your own internal changes. Through your relationships with your partners you can unravel your own motives and understand your deep-seated feelings or emotional insecurities.

WOMEN WITH VENUS IN SAGITTARIUS: When you feel generous, you can make others feel more optimistic about life. You may be interested in higher learning and seek partners who are scholarly or broad-minded. You are outspoken and direct and sometimes say things that you later regret. Curious and versatile, you can adjust quickly to new situations and a foreign influence implies that you love to travel or may have a partner who comes from a different culture.

MEN WITH VENUS IN SAGITTARIUS: Your enthusiasm and straightforward conduct usually appeal to others and imply that you are approachable and easygoing. Being open to ideas and willing to believe that life has a great deal to offer suggests that you are generous, broad-minded, and show eagerness to cooperate with others. A love of travel and an interest in other

cultures also imply that your partner may come from a foreign country.

WOMEN WITH VENUS IN CAPRICORN: Proud and refined, you attract others with your composed dignity. Disliking vulnerability and needing to feel safe before you can express your feelings, you usually display a strong front. Feeling insecure or inadequate in relationships may force you to become manipulative in order to regain control. Nevertheless, you can project an attractive sense of self-assurance and are capable of displaying loyalty and a wonderful dry sense of humor.

MEN WITH VENUS IN CAPRICORN: As you do not display your deeper emotions freely, you are usually dignified and controlled in your relationships with others. Practical and down-to-earth partners are particularly attractive to you, especially those who do not rush into expressing their feelings but seem to possess natural class and reserve. You need a partner who is loyal and dependable and willing to take your relationship seriously.

WOMEN WITH VENUS IN AQUARIUS: You attract and impress others with your friendly approach and progressive ideas. As you are usually independent and easygoing, you value freedom within a relationship. A good companion with a sense of your own person, you enjoy socializing, especially with people who are original, cosmopolitan, and have a strong sense of individuality. Although being friendly and detached usually serves you well, avoid losing touch with your emotions. You usually prefer the company of those who have innovative or progressive views.

MEN WITH VENUS IN AQUARIUS: Friendly and honest, you attract people are attracted with your broad-minded approach to life. You usually possess an objective and slightly detached attitude to affairs of the heart. If you are too removed, however, others can misinterpret your behavior as uncaring. It is often more important to you that your love relationships are based on friendship and honesty rather than intense passion. As you are generally tolerant and liberal, you may be drawn to less conventional relationships.

To read all about your Outer Planets and work out how to use your personalized timetable, go to Section Three, page 789.

Your Personalized Timetable

JUPITER BENEFICIAL
1938 3/12 – 5/6
1938 8/7 – 12/24
1940 3/18 – 5/25
1943 9/13 – until **1944** 8/5
1945 11/24 – until **1946** 5/12
1946 7/18 – 9/20
1950 2/23 – 4/10
1950 9/24 – 11/23
1952 2/29 – 5/7
1955 8/27 – until **1956** 7/18
1957 11/7 – until **1958** 1/5
1958 3/29 – 9/2
1962 2/6 – 3/21
1963 6/23 – 9/26
1964 2/8 – 4/20
1967 8/11 – 11/2
1968 2/11 – 6/29
1969 10/22 – 12/11
1970 5/8 – 8/8
1974 1/21 – 3/4
1975 5/28 – 11/12
1976 1/7 – 4/4
1979 7/26 – 10/10
1980 3/22 – 5/31
1981 10/6 – 11/22
1986 1/4 – 2/16
1987 5/9 – until **1988** 3/18
1991 7/9 – 9/22
1993 9/20 – 11/6
1997 4/27 – 7/24
1997 12/15 – until **1998** 1/31
1999 4/22 – 7/12
1999 10/7 – until **2000** 2/26
2002 10/29 – until **2003** 1/9
2003 6/20 – 9/6
2005 9/3 – 10/21
2009 3/31 – 9/8
2009 11/16 – until **2010** 1/13
2011 4/5 – 6/15
2011 11/24 – until **2012** 1/26

SATURN BENEFICIAL
1938 6/12 – 9/19
1939 3/2 – until **1940** 4/6
1947 9/3 – until **1948** 3/29
1948 5/5 – 10/7
1949 3/2 – 6/28
1952 10/20 – until **1953** 10/15
1963 3/22 – 8/22
1963 12/17 – until **1964** 3/15
1964 10/3 – 12/1
1968 4/10 – until **1969** 5/16
1969 12/30 – until **1970** 1/7
1976 10/29 – 12/27
1977 7/9 – until **1978** 8/12
1981 11/30 – until **1982** 4/7
1982 8/25 – 11/20
1983 5/20 – 8/11
1993 1/25 – 5/1
1993 7/20 – until **1994** 1/20
1997 5/19 – 10/20
1998 2/8 – 7/3
1998 9/28 – until **1999** 3/20
2006 8/17 – until **2007** 9/19
2008 4/12 – 5/24
2011 10/4 – until **2012** 1/16
2012 2/29 – 9/27

URANUS BENEFICIAL
1958 10/28 – until **1963** 6/24
1972 10/17 – until **1975** 8/17
2000 3/19 – until **2003** 11/28

NEPTUNE BENEFICIAL
1950 12/11 – until **1956** 9/23
2006 3/30 – until **2012** 1/7

PLUTO BENEFICIAL
1948 10/2 – until **1959** 6/23
1978 12/30 – until **1983** 10/13

JUPITER CHALLENGING
1939 3/10 – 5/22

1939 10/10 – until **1940** 1/8
1941 8/11 – 12/11
1942 4/1 – 6/19
1944 10/9 – until **1945** 9/4
1951 2/22 – 5/1
1953 7/19 – until **1954** 6/2
1956 9/23 – until **1957** 8/18
1963 2/4 – 4/12
1965 7/1 – until **1966** 5/16
1968 9/7 – 11/29
1969 3/14 – 7/29
1974 6/3 – 8/10
1975 1/16 – 3/27
1977 6/14 – 9/2
1977 12/15 – until **1978** 4/25
1980 8/22 – 11/7
1981 4/24 – 6/30
1986 5/5 – 9/24
1986 12/22 – until **1987** 3/11
1989 5/29 – 8/10
1990 1/28 – 3/24
1992 8/5 – 10/20
1998 4/14 – until **1999** 2/22
2001 5/12 – 7/22
2003 11/21 – until **2004** 2/16
2004 7/18 – 10/4
2010 3/27 – 6/24
2010 8/21 – until **2011** 2/2
2012 9/21 – Continues

SATURN CHALLENGING
1943 6/8 – until **1944** 7/6
1949 10/28 – until **1950** 3/6
1950 7/20 – 12/25
1951 1/29 – 9/1
1965 5/21 – 8/5
1966 2/7 – until **1967** 3/20
1972 7/20 – 12/21
1973 4/7 – 8/22
1973 12/13 – until **1974** 5/10
1979 9/1 – until **1980** 10/8
1995 3/14 – until **1996** 4/25
1996 10/22 – until **1997** 1/13
2002 5/22 – until **2003** 6/20
2008 10/8 – until **2009** 4/9
2009 6/23 – 11/19
2010 3/11 – 8/13

URANUS CHALLENGING
1945 7/27 – until **1950** 4/30
1965 9/21 – until **1969** 8/19
2007 3/30 – until **2012** 2/7

NEPTUNE CHALLENGING
1938 1/1 – until **1944** 7/30

PLUTO CHALLENGING
1964 11/18 – until **1973** 7/20

JUPITER SPECIAL
1948 1/5 – 11/25
1959 12/20 – until **1960** 3/19
1960 5/22 – 11/6
1971 12/4 – until **1972** 2/18
1972 7/5 – 10/13
1983 11/18 – until **1984** 1/29
1995 11/1 – until **1996** 1/12
2007 2/14 – 5/27
2007 10/12 – 12/27

SATURN SPECIAL
1957 12/3 – until **1959** 1/24
1959 7/20 – 10/20
1987 1/7 – 7/4
1987 10/2 – until **1988** 3/18
1988 5/5 – 12/1

URANUS SPECIAL
1985 1/14 – until **1989** 10/21

NEPTUNE SPECIAL
1977 3/2 – until **1985** 11/20

PLUTO SPECIAL
2002 1/2 – until **2009** 11/27

December 17

Your Personal Powers

Shrewd, dignified, and discriminating, you are an astute individual with quick perceptions and a forceful and determined personality. Usually broad-minded and inquisitive, you like to be well informed and to arrive at your own conclusions. As an independent thinker, you are usually inspired by original ideas and are capable of quickly comprehending new concepts. Your ruling planet, Jupiter, grants you integrity, a love of truth, and enthusiasm. With big plans, determination, and an innate business sense, you have excellent prospects for material success. Energetic and curious, you are constantly searching for new and exciting themes to explore. Although you can be elegant and charming, a tendency to be skeptical or impulsive can undermine your progress and potential for success. Nevertheless, decisive and forceful, you can be persuasive and commanding. You lose some of your power, however, by projecting your strong beliefs onto others. A need to be intellectually stimulated indicates that you gain power from your knowledge and many productive ideas.

Your Powers of Attraction in Relationships

Being charming, friendly, and stimulating company, you possess a natural gift for dealing with people. Others admire your daring and determined personality. Usually you are attracted to strong individuals who are ambitious and thrive on challenges and hard work. Alternatively, you seek a partner who is honest and shares your strong beliefs or morals. With your good communication skills or charismatic and agreeable manner, you can make a good impression on people. A need for intimacy and love indicates that you look for a soul mate or a partner in order to feel whole. Being affectionate and caring, you enjoy cooperating and helping those you love. Even though you like supporting others, it is vital that you stay independent in your personal relationships. By keeping a healthy balance, you avoid becoming too dependent on your partner.

Your attractive qualities: thoughtful, good planner, business sense, love of learning, shrewd, individual thinker, methodical, accurate, scientific, self-confident, independent, organized, enterprising, practical, discriminating, progressive, writing talent, investigative, retrospective

Your less attractive qualities: too detached, stubborn, careless, moody, critical, worried, suspicious, indecisive, skeptical, insecure, sentimental, secretive, scattered, restless, bossy, overindulgent, easily bored, impatient

Your Venus Power

The planet Venus has a great deal of influence on your powers of attraction. Below are four possible Venus types for women and men. To find your Venus you need to go to page 771, where you will find the Venus table and extra information. The planet Mars also affects your powers of attraction. To find your Mars table and interpretation go to page 761.

WOMEN WITH VENUS IN SCORPIO: With a natural psychic gift for penetrating the feelings of others, you can often help partners transform emotional challenges or sexual difficulties. When you fall in love, your strong feelings and determination give you a potent force that others find attractive and seductive. Although you know what really turns people on, your most profound desire is usually for the deepness and closeness of real love and intimacy in an enduring relationship.

MEN WITH VENUS IN SCORPIO: In relationships you possess a sensitive understanding of your partner's deeper nature. Although you are strongly attached to those you love, you may have to be careful that your feelings do not turn into jealousy or possessiveness. When you fall in love it is often with an emotional intensity that helps you get in touch with your deep feelings. You are attracted to partners who can share your passion and display strong feelings of sexuality like your own.

WOMEN WITH VENUS IN SAGITTARIUS: Sociable, warm, and friendly, you possess an honest and frank style in your relationships. Being naturally gregarious, you want others to share your enthusiasm and enjoy encouraging the people you love. You fare better when you have a sense of personal freedom within a relationship and are usually generous with the faults of others. You need a partner who can share your need to explore and take risks, whether through travel, education, or recreation.

MEN WITH VENUS IN SAGITTARIUS: Your enthusiasm and straightforward conduct usually appeal to others and imply that you are approachable and easygoing. Being open to ideas and willing to believe that life has a great deal to offer suggests that you are generous, broad-minded, and show eagerness to cooperate with others. A love of travel and an interest in other

cultures also imply that your partner may come from a foreign country.

WOMEN WITH VENUS IN CAPRICORN: Romantically, you do not give your heart easily but hide behind a cool reserve until you feel free to express your emotions. As you take your relationships seriously, you may find yourself drawn to people who are businesslike, resourceful, and practical or who can act as teachers or mentors. Work or career may also be a factor in many of your associations and partnerships. As security can play an important role in your relationships, you are often attracted to partners who are loyal and hardworking,

MEN WITH VENUS IN CAPRICORN: In relationships you take love seriously and can be a strong and practical support for friends or partners. You are usually attracted to partners who are as hardworking as you. As you tend not to express your feelings until you feel really secure in a relationship, you may be drawn to those who seem loyal, faithful, and not likely to let you down. As you respect the wisdom of experience, you may be drawn to mature partners or, alternatively, you may act as an authority figure for someone younger.

WOMEN WITH VENUS IN AQUARIUS: Sociable and gracious, you are usually sincere and are capable of showing attributes of real tolerance and liberalism. Although you are keen on forming relationships, you also like to have freedom and act independently. Your intimate partnerships need to be founded on true friendships. Full of bright and progressive ideas, you can express yourself better when you are free and unrestricted. An ability to think in a dispassionate way suggests that you can stay detached. Your love of freedom also implies that you can be loving and loyal without smothering your partner.

MEN WITH VENUS IN AQUARIUS: Although independent, you often enjoy being part of a group. The partners you frequently attract are themselves nonconformists or free spirits. As an individual you may not find it easy to settle into a routine or an entirely mundane type of relationship. You may have some unconventional views on traditional marriage or your partner may hold such views. It is usually important to you that your love relationships are based on friendship.

To read all about your Outer Planets and work out how to use your personalized timetable, go to Section Three, page 789.

Your Personalized Timetable

JUPITER BENEFICIAL
1938 3/17 – 5/15
1938 7/29 – 12/30
1940 3/23 – 5/30
1943 9/18 – until 1944 4/8
1944 4/19 – 8/9
1945 11/30 – until 1946 5/2
1946 7/28 – 9/25
1950 2/27 – 4/15
1950 9/14 – 12/2
1952 3/5 – 5/11
1955 8/31 – until 1956 7/24
1957 11/12 – until 1958 1/14
1958 3/19 – 9/7
1962 2/11 – 3/26
1963 7/1 – 9/17
1964 2/14 – 4/25
1967 8/15 – 11/10
1968 2/2 – 7/5
1969 10/26 – 12/17
1970 4/29 – 8/16
1974 1/25 – 3/8
1975 6/2 – 11/2
1976 1/17 – 4/8
1979 7/30 – 10/16
1980 3/13 – 6/10
1981 10/11 – 11/27
1986 1/9 – 2/21
1987 5/14 – until 1988 3/23
1991 7/14 – 9/27
1993 9/25 – 11/10
1997 5/6 – 7/14
1997 12/21 – until 1998 2/4
1999 4/26 – 7/21
1999 9/28 – until 2000 3/3
2002 11/9 – 12/29
2003 6/26 – 9/10
2005 9/9 – 10/26
2009 4/6 – 8/30
2009 11/25 – until 2010 1/18
2011 4/9 – 6/20
2011 11/14 – until 2012 2/4

SATURN BENEFICIAL
1938 6/27 – 9/2
1939 3/11 – until 1940 4/14
1947 9/12 – until 1948 3/8
1948 5/26 – 10/17
1949 2/18 – 7/9
1952 10/29 – until 1953 10/23
1963 4/1 – 8/8
1963 12/28 – until 1964 3/25
1964 9/15 – 12/17
1968 4/18 – until 1969 5/25
1969 11/30 – until 1970 2/6
1977 7/18 – until 1978 8/20
1981 12/11 – until 1982 3/24
1982 9/5 – 11/30
1983 5/5 – 8/25
1993 2/2 – 5/24
1993 6/26 – until 1994 1/29
1997 5/29 – 10/7
1998 2/19 – 7/21
1998 9/9 – until 1999 3/29
2006 8/25 – until 2007 9/28
2008 3/23 – 6/12
2011 10/13 – until 2012 10/6

URANUS BENEFICIAL
1959 8/16 – until 1963 7/17
1972 11/3 – until 1975 9/10
2000 4/12 – until 2004 1/1

NEPTUNE BENEFICIAL
1951 11/4 – until 1957 8/12
2007 2/24 – until 2012 2/6

PLUTO BENEFICIAL
1949 9/9 – until 1959 8/2
1979 11/6 – until 1984 8/31

JUPITER CHALLENGING
1939 3/15 – 5/28

1939 10/2 – until 1940 1/15
1941 8/17 – 12/3
1942 4/8 – 6/24
1944 10/14 – until 1945 9/9
1951 2/26 – 5/5
1953 7/24 – until 1954 1/21
1954 3/2 – 6/7
1956 9/28 – until 1957 8/23
1963 2/9 – 4/17
1965 7/6 – until 1966 5/21
1968 9/12 – 12/7
1969 3/6 – 8/4
1974 6/15 – 7/29
1975 1/21 – 3/31
1977 6/19 – 9/10
1977 12/7 – until 1978 5/1
1980 8/27 – 11/13
1981 4/14 – 7/10
1986 5/10 – 9/16
1986 12/29 – until 1987 3/15
1989 6/3 – 8/15
1990 1/17 – 4/4
1992 8/10 – 10/25
1998 4/18 – until 1999 2/26
2001 5/17 – 7/27
2003 11/30 – until 2004 2/7
2004 7/24 – 10/9
2010 3/31 – 7/10
2010 8/5 – until 2011 2/7

SATURN CHALLENGING
1943 6/16 – until 1944 7/14
1949 11/8 – until 1950 2/21
1950 7/30 – until 1951 9/10
1965 6/15 – 7/10
1966 2/16 – until 1967 3/28
1972 7/30 – 12/9
1973 4/17 – 9/4
1973 11/29 – until 1974 5/19
1979 9/9 – until 1980 10/16
1981 5/25 – 6/15
1995 3/23 – until 1996 5/4
1996 10/8 – until 1997 1/26
2002 5/30 – until 2003 6/28
2008 10/17 – until 2009 3/25
2009 7/7 – 12/2
2010 2/25 – 8/22

URANUS CHALLENGING
1945 8/25 – until 1950 5/21
1965 10/8 – until 1969 9/6
2007 4/19 – until 2012 2/28

NEPTUNE CHALLENGING
1938 1/1 – until 1944 9/2

PLUTO CHALLENGING
1965 10/7 – until 1973 8/26

JUPITER SPECIAL
1948 1/10 – 11/30
1959 12/24 – until 1960 4/2
1960 5/8 – 11/11
1971 12/8 – until 1972 2/24
1972 6/27 – 10/20
1983 11/22 – until 1984 2/3
1995 11/6 – until 1996 1/17
2007 2/22 – 5/19
2007 10/18 – until 2008 1/1

SATURN SPECIAL
1957 12/11 – until 1959 2/3
1959 7/5 – 11/2
1987 1/17 – 6/19
1987 10/16 – until 1988 12/10

URANUS SPECIAL
1985 2/5 – until 1989 11/15

NEPTUNE SPECIAL
1978 1/11 – until 1986 9/28

PLUTO SPECIAL
2002 2/4 – until 2010 10/18

December 18

SUN: SAGITTARIUS · DECANATE: LEO/SUN · DEGREE: 25°5–26°5 SAGITTARIUS · MODE: MUTABLE · ELEMENT: FIRE

Your Personal Powers

Enthusiastic and determined, you are a charismatic and idealistic individual with an astute mind and deep-seated emotions. Your ruling planet, Jupiter, endows you with natural leadership, humor, and the ability to think big. Dignified and proud, your commanding personality can be highly productive if you use your sound judgment and discriminative mind. Although you can be frank and outspoken, you empower yourself by combining your penetrating intellect and powers of persuasion with tact and charm. You lose some of your grace when you become too demanding, intense, or critical. Being enterprising and hardworking, you act decisively, yet in order to achieve success you need to develop the necessary self-discipline and resist acting impulsively. Being idealistic with strong desires emphasizes the importance in your life of sincerity, creativity, and peace of mind rather than indulging in an expensive lifestyle. Nevertheless, in order to maintain a high standard or enjoy material luxuries, you are usually willing to work hard. Partnerships or cooperative efforts can prove to be especially fortunate for you. With your keen mind and many talents, you have remarkable potential for success.

Your Powers of Attraction in Relationships

People are attracted to your magnetic and competent personality. Often generous and sociable, you can be loyal and supportive to those you love. You can endure setbacks and challenges in close relationships even though you sometimes find it difficult to express your true feelings. Usually you are attracted to passionate and caring individuals who can show compassion and have a strong sense of responsibility. Alternatively, you are drawn to determined and enthusiastic individuals who can be purposeful, direct, and frank. Although you are friendly, you can sometimes appear too proud or arrogant. On other occasions your detached or independent attitude can separate you from those close to you. Opening your heart and communicating your inner feelings usually helps you to get closer to your partner.

Your attractive qualities: assertive, optimistic, kind, progressive, charming, confident, ambitious, intuitive, courageous, resolute, efficient, advisory skills, diplomatic, charismatic, sociable, humanitarian, tremendous drive, endurance, leadership, clever

Your less attractive qualities: stubborn, arrogant, moody, bossy, overindulgent, lazy, impulsive, selfish, callous, secretive, controlling, overreacting, provocative, frustrated, depressed, too serious, sarcastic

Your Venus Power

The planet Venus has a great deal of influence on your powers of attraction. Below are four possible Venus types for women and men. To find your Venus you need to go to page 771, where you will find the Venus table and extra information. The planet Mars also affects your powers of attraction. To find your Mars table and interpretation go to page 761.

WOMEN WITH VENUS IN SCORPIO: Loving and passionate, you are often sensitive with deep feelings and strong powers of attraction. A love for the truth coupled with a tendency to be suspicious can be an influence that motivates you to delve deep into the activities of your partner. When in love or in a relationship that matters, you will often bend over backward to cooperate. Although loyal, guard against losing sight of your own needs and desires.

MEN WITH VENUS IN SCORPIO: You are usually attracted to sensual and passionate partners with strong character. You are often sensitive with deep feelings and magnetic powers of attraction. As a cautious yet devoted and ardent lover, you are likely to seek experiences that are more sexual in nature. You display your less attractive qualities when you project negative thoughts and resort to being suspicious or possessive. Nevertheless, loyal and loving, you are a sensitive lover.

WOMEN WITH VENUS IN SAGITTARIUS: Optimistic and fun-loving, you love adventure and seek a partner who can expand your horizons. Being truthful and direct, you often say what you think, and at times you may be naively tactless. A need for expansion and prosperity suggests that you may enjoy traveling with your friends or partner. Being lighthearted and idealistic, once you have given your heart to someone you will stay honorable and loyal.

MEN WITH VENUS IN SAGITTARIUS: You are usually attracted to partners who are knowledgeable or well-traveled. Enthusiastic and optimistic, you often respond quickly to love offers and enter relationships with enthusiasm. Usually you seek to expand your social circle, and meeting people from all walks of life can bring you the variety and fun you seek in life. Although you are generous and honest, your partners may accuse you of being overly optimistic or too blunt.

WOMEN WITH VENUS IN CAPRICORN: Loyal and responsible, you are attracted to dignified and reserved individuals. Being practical and security-conscious, you prefer hardworking partners who are resourceful and enterprising. Work may even be a factor in many of your associations and partnerships. For you, family and faithfulness can be especially important, so you are usually willing to work hard or make sacrifices in order to build a strong relationship.

MEN WITH VENUS IN CAPRICORN: As you do not display your deeper emotions freely, you are usually dignified and controlled in your relationships with others. Practical and down-to-earth partners are particularly attractive to you, especially those who do not rush into expressing their feelings but seem to possess natural class and reserve. You need a partner who is loyal and dependable and willing to take your relationship seriously.

WOMEN WITH VENUS IN AQUARIUS: Others are attracted to your honest, friendly, and easygoing attitude. You enjoy social interaction and have a genuine concern for others. In fact, at times your friends may be just as important as your partner. Usually you present a tolerant and reasonable front in love situations and attempt to view your relationships objectively. If partners become too demanding, however, you can become stubborn or awkward. Nevertheless, inventive and progressive, you enjoy the company of like-minded people who can share your original ideas.

MEN WITH VENUS IN AQUARIUS: You are sociable and liberal, and people are attracted by your friendly and easygoing style. Being independent, you value freedom-loving partners who give you the space to be yourself. People can sometimes interpret your detachment as being emotionally cool, but they admire your objectivity and humanitarian inclinations. You are attracted to intelligent individuals who are as truthful and direct as you, but above all they must be true friends. Ideally, your partner shares your liberal views on life and possesses a strong sense of individuality.

To read all about your Outer Planets and work out how to use your personalized timetable, go to Section Three, page 789.

Your Personalized Timetable

JUPITER BENEFICIAL
1938 3/22 – 5/25
1938 7/18 – until 1939 1/4
1940 3/27 – 6/3
1943 9/23 – until 1944 3/17
1944 5/9 – 8/14
1945 12/6 – until 1946 4/23
1946 8/5 – 9/30
1950 3/4 – 4/21
1950 9/5 – 12/10
1952 3/9 – 5/16
1955 9/5 – until 1956 7/29
1957 11/17 – until 1958 1/27
1958 3/6 – 9/13
1962 2/15 – 3/31
1963 7/11 – 9/7
1964 2/19 – 4/29
1967 8/20 – 11/19
1968 1/24 – 7/11
1969 10/31 – 12/23
1970 4/21 – 8/23
1974 1/30 – 3/13
1975 6/8 – 10/25
1976 1/24 – 4/13
1979 8/4 – 10/21
1980 3/4 – 6/17
1981 10/15 – 12/2
1982 6/6 – 7/19
1986 1/14 – 2/25
1987 5/18 – until 1988 3/27
1991 7/19 – 10/2
1993 9/30 – 11/15
1997 5/18 – 7/2
1997 12/26 – until 1998 2/9
1999 4/30 – 8/2
1999 9/16 – until 2000 3/8
2003 7/1 – 9/15
2005 9/14 – 10/31
2009 4/12 – 8/22
2009 12/2 – until 2010 1/23
2011 4/13 – 6/26
2011 11/6 – until 2012 2/12

SATURN BENEFICIAL
1939 3/19 – until 1940 4/22
1947 9/21 – until 1948 2/23
1948 6/9 – 10/29
1949 2/4 – 7/19
1952 11/6 – until 1953 5/28
1953 7/19 – 10/31
1963 4/14 – 7/25
1964 1/7 – 4/4
1964 9/1 – 12/30
1968 4/27 – until 1969 6/3
1969 11/15 – until 1970 2/20
1977 7/26 – until 1978 8/28
1981 12/26 – until 1982 3/9
1982 9/14 – 12/10
1983 4/22 – 9/6
1993 2/11 – until 1994 2/7
1997 6/10 – 9/24
1998 3/1 – until 1999 4/6
2006 9/2 – until 2007 10/7
2008 3/8 – 6/26
2011 10/21 – until 2012 10/15

URANUS BENEFICIAL
1959 9/2 – until 1963 8/4
1972 11/21 – until 1975 9/28
2001 2/14 – until 2004 1/23

NEPTUNE BENEFICIAL
1951 12/8 – until 1957 9/21
2007 3/26 – Continues

PLUTO BENEFICIAL
1949 10/31 – until 1960 6/30
1979 12/8 – until 1984 10/1

JUPITER CHALLENGING
1939 3/19 – 6/4
1939 9/25 – until 1940 1/21

JUPITER BENEFICIAL (continued, right column top)
1941 8/24 – 11/25
1942 4/14 – 6/28
1944 10/20 – until 1945 4/25
1945 6/3 – 9/14
1951 3/2 – 5/10
1953 7/30 – until 1954 1/9
1954 3/14 – 6/11
1956 10/2 – until 1957 8/28
1963 2/13 – 4/21
1965 7/10 – until 1966 5/26
1968 9/17 – 12/15
1969 2/25 – 8/10
1975 1/26 – 4/4
1977 6/23 – 9/18
1977 11/29 – until 1978 5/6
1980 9/1 – 11/18
1981 4/6 – 7/18
1986 5/17 – 9/9
1987 1/4 – 3/19
1989 6/7 – 8/21
1990 1/9 – 4/12
1992 8/15 – 10/30
1998 4/23 – until 1999 3/3
2001 5/22 – 8/1
2003 12/12 – until 2004 1/26
2004 7/29 – 10/14
2010 4/4 – until 2011 2/12

SATURN CHALLENGING
1943 6/24 – until 1944 7/22
1945 2/16 – 3/22
1949 11/21 – until 1950 2/7
1950 8/9 – until 1951 9/18
1966 2/24 – until 1967 4/6
1972 8/9 – 11/26
1973 4/27 – 9/20
1973 11/12 – until 1974 5/28
1979 9/17 – until 1980 10/25
1981 4/29 – 7/11
1995 3/31 – 11/10
1995 12/2 – until 1996 5/15
1996 9/24 – until 1997 2/6
2002 6/6 – until 2003 7/5
2008 10/26 – until 2009 3/12
2009 7/19 – 12/20
2010 2/7 – 8/31

URANUS CHALLENGING
1946 6/18 – until 1950 6/9
1965 10/27 – until 1969 9/23
2007 5/16 – until 2012 3/17

NEPTUNE CHALLENGING
1938 1/1 – until 1945 7/26

PLUTO CHALLENGING
1965 11/14 – until 1974 6/27

JUPITER SPECIAL
1948 1/15 – 12/4
1959 12/29 – until 1960 11/17
1971 12/13 – until 1972 3/2
1972 6/19 – 10/26
1983 11/27 – until 1984 2/8
1984 8/4 – 9/24
1995 11/11 – until 1996 1/21
2007 3/4 – 5/9
2007 10/24 – until 2008 1/5

SATURN SPECIAL
1957 12/20 – until 1959 2/13
1959 6/21 – 11/13
1987 1/27 – 6/6
1987 10/27 – until 1988 12/19

URANUS SPECIAL
1985 12/8 – until 1989 12/4

NEPTUNE SPECIAL
1978 2/21 – until 1986 11/17

PLUTO SPECIAL
2002 12/27 – until 2010 11/27

December 19

SUN: SAGITTARIUS • DECANATE: LEO/SUN • DEGREE: 26°5–27°5 SAGITTARIUS • MODE: MUTABLE • ELEMENT: FIRE

Your Personal Powers

Dynamic and sensitive, you are an intuitive and imaginative individual with depth of feeling and an idealistic nature. Your ruling planet, Jupiter, grants you self-confidence, receptivity, and an optimistic outlook. Although you can be charismatic and dramatic, when you become emotionally discontented you lose some of your charm and power by thinking negatively. Being too opinionated or critical can also undermine your chances of achievement. By remaining detached and liberal-minded, you learn to resist a tendency to overreact to situations and people. You gain power when you let inspiration and benevolence guide you in your quest for emotional fulfillment, whether personal or vocational. Being decisive and resourceful, you possess a commanding personality that demands the attention of others. Although you can be determined, hardworking, sociable, and people-oriented, your interests are often focused on human relationships. As an intelligent person who seeks mental stimulation, you also benefit from sharing your knowledge and experiences with others.

Your Powers of Attraction in Relationships

You are strong-willed but receptive, and people admire your thoughtfulness and caring nature. Your broad range of emotions suggests that you usually base your judgment on how you feel. Often loving and giving with a sense of the dramatic, you can make a strong impression on people. You are usually attracted to enterprising, ambitious, and intelligent individuals with power and resolve. The more determined you are about your own plans for the future, the more confident you become, building better relationships in the process. Although you are romantic and blessed with an active and imaginative mind, you may need to stay realistic and resist a temptation to delude yourself. Since at times you can be demanding, in your close relationships you achieve more through compromise and cooperation.

Your attractive qualities: dynamic, positive thinker, centered, creative, passionate, idealistic, generous, humanitarian, progressive, persevering, dutiful, purposeful, faithful, honest, optimistic, kind, friendly, competitive, independent, gregarious, resolute, direct, inner vision

Your less attractive qualities: self-centered, restless, temperamental, frustrated, dissatisfied, easily bored, depressive, worry, fear of rejection, too materialistic, impatient, frustrated, bossy, possessive, insecure, controlling, melodramatic, nervous

Your Venus Power

The planet Venus has a great deal of influence on your powers of attraction. Below are four possible Venus types for women and men. To find your Venus you need to go to page 771, where you will find the Venus table and extra information. The planet Mars also affects your powers of attraction. To find your Mars table and interpretation go to page 761.

WOMEN WITH VENUS IN SCORPIO: You are usually drawn to partners who are sensual in appearance with a strong character. As you are emotionally intense and passionate, personal relationships are probably a major factor in your life. Since you like to be in control, you can at times exhibit some of your less attractive qualities by being willful or domineering. Although you need to feel established and in command in your relationships, you are constantly searching for some higher truth that can bring about a significant transformation.

MEN WITH VENUS IN SCORPIO: As you are emotionally intense and passionate, personal relationships are probably a major factor in your own transformation. Being sensitive yet loyal, you are usually attracted to forceful partners who can express themselves intimately but intensely. Rather than seek easy and simple relationships, you are drawn to partners who act as a catalyst for your own internal changes. Through your relationships with your partners you can unravel your own motives and understand your deep-seated feelings or emotional insecurities.

WOMEN WITH VENUS IN SAGITTARIUS: Optimistic and fun-loving, you love adventure and seek a partner who can expand your horizons. Being truthful and direct, you often say what you think, and at times you may be naively tactless. A need for expansion and prosperity suggests that you may enjoy traveling with your friends or partner. Being lighthearted and idealistic, once you have given your heart to someone you will stay honorable and loyal.

MEN WITH VENUS IN SAGITTARIUS: When in love you are open and friendly, but you need a partner who can share your adventurous spirit and sense of fun. Be careful, however, that your desire for freedom does not cause you to avoid commit-

ment. You prefer your partners to be positive, direct, and generous in spirit. Being outspoken as well as an idealist, you usually enjoy a partner with whom you can share your strong opinions. Alternatively, you may wish to explore life together, whether through travel, education, or by having fun.

WOMEN WITH VENUS IN CAPRICORN: Romantically, you do not give your heart easily but hide behind a cool reserve until you feel free to express your emotions. As you take your relationships seriously, you may find yourself drawn to people who are businesslike, resourceful, and practical, or who can act as teachers or mentors. Work or career may also be a factor in many of your associations and partnerships. As security can play an important role in your relationships, you are often attracted to partners who are loyal and hardworking,

MEN WITH VENUS IN CAPRICORN: In relationships you take love seriously and can be a strong and practical support for friends or partners. You are usually attracted to partners who are as hardworking as yourself. As you tend not to express your feelings until you feel really secure in a relationship, you may be drawn to those who seem to be loyal, faithful, and not likely to let you down. As you respect the wisdom of experience, you may be drawn to mature partners or, alternatively, you may act as an authority figure for someone younger.

WOMEN WITH VENUS IN AQUARIUS: Sociable and gracious, you are usually sincere and capable of showing attributes of real tolerance and liberalism. Although you are keen on forming relationships, you also like to have your freedom and act independently. Your intimate partnerships need to be founded on true friendships. Full of bright and progressive ideas, you can express yourself better when you are free and unrestricted. An ability to think in a dispassionate way suggests that you can stay detached. Your love of freedom also implies that you can be loving and loyal without smothering your partner.

MEN WITH VENUS IN AQUARIUS: Although independent, you often enjoy being part of a group. The partners you frequently attract are themselves nonconformists or free spirits. As an individual you may not find it easy to settle into a routine or an entirely mundane type of relationship. You may have some unconventional views on traditional marriage or your partner may hold such views. As a nonconformist you may also be interested in alternative lifestyles such as collective living.

To read all about your Outer Planets and work out how to use your personalized timetable, go to Section Three, page 789.

Your Personalized Timetable

JUPITER BENEFICIAL
1938 3/27 – 6/13
1938 6/29 – until 1939 1/9
1940 3/31 – 6/8
1943 9/29 – until 1944 3/6
1944 5/20 – 8/19
1945 12/12 – until 1946 4/15
1946 8/12 – 10/5
1950 3/8 – 4/27
1950 8/29 – 12/17
1952 3/14 – 5/20
1955 9/10 – until 1956 8/3
1957 11/22 – until 1958 6/3
1958 7/4 – 9/18
1962 2/19 – 4/5
1963 7/26 – 8/23
1964 2/24 – 5/3
1967 8/25 – 12/1
1968 1/12 – 7/16
1969 11/5 – 12/30
1970 4/13 – 8/29
1974 2/3 – 3/17
1975 6/14 – 10/17
1976 1/31 – 4/17
1979 8/9 – 10/28
1980 2/26 – 6/25
1981 10/20 – 12/8
1982 5/24 – 7/31
1986 1/18 – 3/1
1987 5/23 – until 1988 3/31
1991 7/24 – 10/7
1992 4/13 – 5/18
1993 10/4 – 11/20
1997 12/31 – until 1998 2/13
1999 5/5 – until 2000 3/13
2003 7/7 – 9/20
2005 9/19 – 11/4
2009 4/18 – 8/14
2009 12/8 – until 2010 1/27
2011 4/17 – 7/2
2011 10/30 – until 2012 2/18

SATURN BENEFICIAL
1939 3/27 – until 1940 4/30
1947 9/30 – until 1948 2/10
1948 6/20 – 11/12
1949 1/20 – 7/28
1952 11/15 – until 1953 5/9
1953 8/7 – 11/9
1963 4/29 – 7/9
1964 1/16 – 4/14
1964 8/18 – until 1965 1/9
1968 5/5 – 11/29
1969 1/12 – 6/13
1969 11/2 – until 1970 3/4
1977 8/3 – until 1978 9/5
1982 1/19 – 2/11
1982 9/23 – 12/21
1983 4/8 – 9/16
1993 2/19 – until 1994 2/15
1997 6/24 – 9/9
1998 3/10 – until 1999 4/14
2006 9/10 – until 2007 3/17
2007 5/23 – 10/17
2008 2/24 – 7/7
2011 10/29 – until 2012 10/23

URANUS BENEFICIAL
1959 9/20 – until 1963 8/21
1972 12/13 – until 1975 10/15
2001 3/4 – until 2004 2/10

NEPTUNE BENEFICIAL
1952 11/2 – until 1958 8/4
2008 2/22 – Continues

PLUTO BENEFICIAL
1950 9/25 – until 1960 8/6
1980 10/25 – until 1985 8/8

JUPITER CHALLENGING
1939 3/23 – 6/10
1939 9/17 – until 1940 1/27

1941 9/2 – 11/17
1942 4/19 – 7/2
1944 10/25 – until 1945 4/11
1945 6/16 – 9/18
1951 3/6 – 5/15
1951 11/7 – 12/22
1953 8/4 – 12/31
1954 3/23 – 6/16
1956 10/7 – until 1957 9/2
1963 2/17 – 4/26
1965 7/15 – until 1966 5/30
1968 9/21 – 12/27
1969 2/13 – 8/16
1975 1/31 – 4/9
1977 6/28 – 9/29
1977 11/18 – until 1978 5/12
1980 9/5 – 11/25
1981 3/29 – 7/25
1986 5/24 – 9/1
1987 1/10 – 3/24
1989 6/12 – 8/27
1990 1/1 – 4/19
1992 8/20 – 11/4
1993 5/16 – 6/16
1998 4/28 – 10/20
1998 12/7 – until 1999 3/7
2001 5/26 – 8/6
2004 8/4 – 10/19
2010 4/9 – until 2011 2/17

SATURN CHALLENGING
1943 7/2 – until 1944 7/31
1945 1/26 – 4/12
1949 12/12 – until 1950 1/17
1950 8/18 – until 1951 9/26
1966 3/4 – until 1967 4/14
1972 8/22 – 11/12
1973 5/6 – until 1974 6/5
1979 9/25 – until 1980 11/3
1981 4/13 – 7/26
1995 4/9 – 10/16
1995 12/27 – until 1996 5/26
1996 9/11 – until 1997 2/16
2002 6/14 – until 2003 7/13
2008 11/6 – until 2009 2/27
2009 7/29 – until 2010 9/9

URANUS CHALLENGING
1946 7/6 – until 1950 6/26
1965 11/22 – until 1970 7/15
2008 3/17 – Continues

NEPTUNE CHALLENGING
1938 7/23 – until 1945 8/31

PLUTO CHALLENGING
1966 10/6 – until 1974 8/17

JUPITER SPECIAL
1948 1/20 – 8/13
1948 8/19 – 12/9
1960 1/2 – 11/21
1971 12/17 – until 1972 3/9
1972 6/11 – 11/1
1983 12/2 – until 1984 2/14
1984 7/24 – 10/5
1995 11/15 – until 1996 1/26
2007 3/16 – 4/26
2007 10/29 – until 2008 1/10

SATURN SPECIAL
1957 12/29 – until 1958 8/18
1958 8/29 – until 1959 2/26
1959 6/7 – 11/23
1987 2/8 – 5/22
1987 11/6 – until 1988 12/28

URANUS SPECIAL
1985 12/25 – until 1989 12/21

NEPTUNE SPECIAL
1979 1/9 – until 1986 12/17

PLUTO SPECIAL
2003 1/27 – until 2011 10/17

December 20

Your Personal Powers

You are idealistic and receptive, and your natural charm and gregarious manner indicate that you are a people person. Your ruling planet, Jupiter, grants you optimism, big plans, and a sense of justice. Refined with a good sense of values, you can succeed by being cooperative and enterprising. Intuitive and understanding, you also benefit from trusting your strong instincts, with your assessment of people and their motives being cunningly accurate. If developed, an interest in higher learning or spirituality can bring you emotional satisfaction and inner peace. As you often see yourself as part of a larger group, you gain power when you use your diplomatic skills and charm rather than being emotionally frustrated or controlling. Since your professional progress and personal development very much depend on your relationship with people, you empower yourself when you are confident, independent, adaptable, and easygoing. With your dynamic emotions and natural compassion, you have the ability to inspire others and spread a great deal of warmth and love.

Your Powers of Attraction in Relationships

Emotionally magnetic, you are admired for your charm and relaxed manner. Sociable and romantic, you are usually drawn to creative and artistic individuals who are idealistic and imaginative. Alternatively, you may be attracted to sensitive people who are hardworking and have a strong sense of duty. Being generous and sympathetic, you usually offer emotional support and practical advice to those who you befriend. Fluctuating between wanting personal advancement and sacrificing your personal wishes for the sake of others, you may have to balance your needs with demands made by loved ones. By staying detached and resisting a tendency to become overly serious, you can enjoy the pleasurable and less demanding aspect of your relationships. Luckily, adaptable and understanding, you enjoy activities where you can interact with others and feel appreciated.

Your attractive qualities: receptive, romantic, deep feelings, good partnerships, self-confident, hopeful, optimistic, diplomatic, broad-minded, astute, determined, patient, philosophical, gentle, tactful, receptive, intuitive, considerate, harmonious, agreeable

Your less attractive qualities: suspicious, frustrated, jealous, possessive, impulsive, lack of confidence, subservient, oversensitive, selfish, easily hurt, insincere, possessive, insecure, critical, extravagance, overindulgence

Your Venus Power

The planet Venus has a great deal of influence on your powers of attraction. Below are four possible Venus types for women and men. To find your Venus you need to go to page 771, where you will find the Venus table and extra information. The planet Mars also affects your powers of attraction. To find your Mars table and interpretation go to page 761.

WOMEN WITH VENUS IN SCORPIO: Loving and passionate, you are often sensitive with deep feelings and strong powers of attraction. A love for the truth coupled with a tendency to be suspicious can be an influence that motivates you to delve deep into the activities of your partner. When in love or in a relationship that matters, you will often bend over backward to cooperate. Although loyal, guard against losing sight of your own needs and desires.

MEN WITH VENUS IN SCORPIO: In relationships you possess a sensitive understanding of your partner's deeper nature. Although you are strongly attached to those you love, you may have to be careful that your feelings do not turn into jealousy or possessiveness. When you fall in love it is often with an emotional intensity that helps you get in touch with your deep feelings. You are attracted to partners who can share your passion and display strong feelings of sexuality like your own.

WOMEN WITH VENUS IN SAGITTARIUS: At your best when you are optimistic and generous, you possess a mischievous sense of fun. In relationships, your open-minded approach to people and places may attract you to those of a different culture or make you tolerant of the foibles of others. Although warm and enthusiastic when in love, your natural honesty and idealism may inspire you to look for a partner who shares your love of freedom.

MEN WITH VENUS IN SAGITTARIUS: When in love you are open and friendly, but you need a partner who can share your adventurous spirit and sense of fun. Be careful, however, that your desire for freedom does not cause you to avoid commitment. You prefer your partners to be positive, direct, and generous in spirit. Being outspoken as well as an idealist, you

usually enjoy a partner with whom you can share your strong opinions. Alternatively, you may wish to explore life together whether through travel, education, or by having fun.

WOMEN WITH VENUS IN CAPRICORN: Romantically, you do not give your heart easily but hide behind a cool reserve until you feel free to express your emotions. As you take your relationships seriously, you may find yourself drawn to people who are businesslike, resourceful, and practical, or who can act as teachers or mentors. Work or career may also be a factor in many of your associations and partnerships. As security can play an important role in your relationships, you are often attracted to partners who are loyal and hardworking,

MEN WITH VENUS IN CAPRICORN: In relationships you take love seriously and can be a strong and practical support for friends or partners. You are usually attracted to partners who are as hardworking as you. As you tend not to express your feelings until you feel really secure in a relationship, you may be drawn to those who seem loyal, faithful, and not likely to let you down. As you respect the wisdom of experience, you may be drawn to mature partners or, alternatively, you may act as an authority figure for someone younger.

WOMEN WITH VENUS IN AQUARIUS: Sociable and gracious, you are usually sincere and are capable of showing attributes of real tolerance and liberalism. Although you are keen on forming relationships, you also like to have your freedom and act independently. Your intimate partnerships need to be founded on true friendships. Full of bright and progressive ideas, you can express yourself better when you are free and unrestricted. An ability to think in a dispassionate way suggests that you can stay detached. Your love of freedom also implies that you can be loving and loyal without smothering your partner.

MEN WITH VENUS IN AQUARIUS: Ideally, in your relationships your lover is also your best friend. Since freedom of expression is a prerequisite to your well-being, you do better when left alone to do your own thing. You also need a partner who recognizes and appreciates your need for independence. Although usually friendly, at times you can be stubborn or your cool detachment can appear to others as distant or impersonal. Very sociable, however, you particularly enjoy the company of those who share your original, fair-minded, and progressive views.

To read all about your Outer Planets and work out how to use your personalized timetable, go to Section Three, page 789.

To read all about your Outer Planets and work out how to use your personalized timetable, go to Section Three, page 789.

Your Personalized Timetable

JUPITER BENEFICIAL
1938 4/1 – 9/27
1938 11/9 – until 1939 1/14
1940 4/4 – 6/13
1940 12/14 – until 1941 1/16
1943 10/4 – until 1944 2/27
1944 5/29 – 8/24
1945 12/19 – until 1946 4/7
1946 8/19 – 10/10
1950 3/13 – 5/4
1950 8/21 – 12/23
1952 3/18 – 5/25
1955 9/15 – until 1956 8/7
1957 11/27 – until 1958 5/19
1958 7/19 – 9/23
1962 2/24 – 4/10
1962 10/15 – 11/12
1964 2/29 – 5/8
1967 8/29 – until 1968 7/21
1969 11/10 – until 1970 1/7
1970 4/5 – 9/4
1974 2/7 – 3/22
1975 6/20 – 10/9
1976 2/7 – 4/21
1979 8/13 – 11/4
1980 2/18 – 7/1
1981 10/25 – 12/13
1982 5/14 – 8/10
1986 1/22 – 3/5
1987 5/28 – 11/30
1987 12/30 – until 1988 4/5
1991 7/28 – 10/12
1992 3/30 – 6/1
1993 10/9 – 11/25
1998 1/5 – 2/17
1999 5/9 – until 2000 3/18
2003 7/12 – 9/25
2005 9/24 – 11/9
2009 4/25 – 8/6
2009 12/15 – until 2010 1/31
2011 4/21 – 7/8
2011 10/22 – until 2012 2/24

SATURN BENEFICIAL
1939 4/4 – until 1940 5/8
1947 10/11 – until 1948 1/28
1948 6/30 – 12/9
1948 12/24 – until 1949 8/5
1952 11/25 – until 1953 4/25
1953 8/20 – 11/18
1954 6/11 – 7/31
1964 1/25 – 4/27
1964 8/4 – until 1965 1/19
1968 5/14 – 11/10
1969 1/30 – 6/23
1969 10/20 – until 1970 3/14
1977 8/11 – until 1978 9/13
1982 10/2 – until 1983 1/4
1983 3/24 – 9/26
1993 2/28 – until 1994 2/24
1997 7/17 – 8/17
1998 3/18 – until 1999 4/22
2006 9/19 – until 2007 3/1
2007 6/7 – 10/28
2008 2/12 – 7/17
2011 11/7 – until 2012 6/3
2012 7/16 – 11/1

URANUS BENEFICIAL
1959 10/12 – until 1964 6/5
1973 10/12 – until 1976 7/27
2001 3/24 – until 2004 12/7

NEPTUNE BENEFICIAL
1952 12/4 – until 1958 9/19
2008 3/22 – Continues

PLUTO BENEFICIAL
1951 9/3 – until 1961 7/6
1980 11/22 – until 1985 9/17

JUPITER CHALLENGING
1939 3/27 – 6/18

1939 9/9 – until 1940 2/2
1941 9/12 – 11/7
1942 4/25 – 7/7
1944 10/31 – until 1945 4/2
1945 6/26 – 9/23
1951 3/10 – 5/21
1951 10/27 – until 1952 1/2
1953 8/10 – 12/23
1954 3/31 – 6/20
1956 10/12 – until 1957 9/7
1963 2/22 – 4/30
1965 7/20 – until 1966 6/4
1968 9/26 – until 1969 8/21
1975 2/4 – 4/13
1977 7/2 – until 1978 5/17
1980 9/10 – 12/1
1981 3/21 – 8/1
1986 5/31 – 8/23
1987 1/16 – 3/28
1989 6/16 – 9/2
1989 12/25 – until 1990 4/26
1992 8/25 – 11/10
1993 5/1 – 7/1
1998 5/4 – 10/9
1998 12/18 – until 1999 3/11
2001 5/30 – 8/11
2002 2/11 – 3/19
2004 8/9 – 10/24
2010 4/13 – until 2011 2/21

SATURN CHALLENGING
1943 7/10 – until 1944 1/29
1944 3/13 – 8/9
1945 1/12 – 4/26
1950 8/26 – until 1951 10/4
1966 3/13 – until 1967 4/23
1967 11/15 – until 1968 1/1
1972 9/10 – 10/24
1973 5/15 – until 1974 6/13
1979 10/3 – until 1980 11/13
1981 3/30 – 8/7
1995 4/19 – 9/30
1996 1/11 – 6/9
1996 8/27 – until 1997 2/25
2002 6/22 – until 2003 7/22
2008 11/19 – until 2009 2/13
2009 8/8 – until 2010 9/18

URANUS CHALLENGING
1946 7/25 – until 1951 4/24
1966 9/15 – until 1970 8/11
2008 4/4 – Continues

NEPTUNE CHALLENGING
1938 1/1 – until 1946 7/21

PLUTO CHALLENGING
1966 11/10 – until 1974 9/15

JUPITER SPECIAL
1948 1/25 – 7/20
1948 9/11 – 12/13
1960 1/7 – 11/26
1971 12/22 – until 1972 3/18
1972 6/2 – 11/7
1983 12/6 – until 1984 2/19
1984 7/15 – 10/13
1995 11/20 – until 1996 1/31
2007 11/3 – until 2008 1/14

SATURN SPECIAL
1958 1/7 – 7/18
1958 9/29 – until 1959 3/14
1959 5/20 – 12/3
1987 2/24 – 5/6
1987 11/16 – until 1989 1/5

URANUS SPECIAL
1986 1/12 – until 1990 10/20

NEPTUNE SPECIAL
1979 2/15 – until 1987 11/15

PLUTO SPECIAL
2003 12/22 – until 2011 11/27

December 21

SUN: SAGITTARIUS • DECANATE: LEO/SUN • DEGREE: 28°5–29°5 SAGITTARIUS • MODE: MUTABLE • ELEMENT: FIRE

Your Personal Powers

Being sociable and optimistic yet practical, you are a capable and enthusiastic individual with an ambitious attitude and strong desires. Being born on the cusp of Sagittarius and Capricorn implies that you can be hardworking, disciplined, and highly motivated when you believe in your goals. You may need to learn to persevere and be patient if you want to manifest your splendid ideas and plans. You gain emotional strength and power by combining your enthusiasm, sense of duty, and determination to succeed, especially if you stay resolute and optimistic. Often keen to learn, your quick comprehension can assist you to advance and make progress. Inner tensions and a tendency to feel irritable, however, imply that although self-confidence is vital to your overall success, a tendency to be overly ambitious or rash can cause discontentment with yourself and others. Nevertheless, usually direct and honest with strong personal magnetism, you can be diplomatic and persuasive, especially when you are inspired by high ideals.

Your Powers of Attraction in Relationships

People are attracted to your charismatic and charming personality. Courteous and sympathetic, you have the ability to mix with people from all walks of life. With your tactful manner you can easily make others feel at ease. When you are full of vitality, you can inspire others with your spirit of enterprise. Although you can be inclined to cooperative relationships or marriage, you also want to be acknowledged for your own talents and abilities. Usually you are attracted to dynamic and forceful individuals who are ambitious, self-confident, and commanding. Although drawn to relationships that can offer security and stability, a need for emotional fulfillment indicates that if your relationships become monotonous or boring you may become restless and look for stimulation elsewhere. You therefore need a partner who can continually keep your interest.

Your attractive qualities: inspired, gregarious, tolerant, creative, friendly, charming, spontaneous, youthful, gracious, multitalented, persuasive, confident, charismatic, dynamic, powerful emotions, enthusiastic, realistic, practical, honest, idealistic, generous

Your less attractive qualities: codependent, easily influ-enced, nervous, temperamental, lack of vision, dissatisfied, unrealistic expectations, fear of change, restless, impatient, selfish, arrogant, lofty ideas, waste of emotional power

Your Venus Power

The planet Venus has a great deal of influence on your powers of attraction. Below are four possible Venus types for women and men. To find your Venus you need to go to page 771, where you will find the Venus table and extra information. The planet Mars also affects your powers of attraction. To find your Mars table and interpretation go to page 761.

WOMEN WITH VENUS IN SCORPIO: With a natural psychic gift for penetrating the feelings of others, you can often help partners transform emotional challenges or sexual difficulties. When you fall in love, your strong feelings and determination give you a potent force that others find attractive and seductive. Although you know what really turns people on, your most profound desire is usually for the deepness and closeness of real love and intimacy in an enduring relationship.

MEN WITH VENUS IN SCORPIO: In relationships you possess a sensitive understanding of your partner's deeper nature. Although you are strongly attached to those you love, you may have to be careful that your feelings do not turn into jealousy or possessiveness. When you fall in love it is often with an emotional intensity that helps you get in touch with your deep feelings. You are attracted to partners who can share your passion and display strong feelings of sexuality like your own.

WOMEN WITH VENUS IN SAGITTARIUS: Sociable, warm, and friendly, you possess an honest and frank style in your relationships. Being naturally gregarious, you want others to share your enthusiasm and enjoy encouraging the people you love. You do better when you have a sense of personal freedom within a relationship and are usually generous with the faults of others. You need a partner who can share your need to explore and take risks, whether through travel, education, or recreation.

MEN WITH VENUS IN SAGITTARIUS: Your enthusiasm and straightforward conduct usually appeal to others and imply that you are approachable and easygoing. Being open to ideas and willing to believe that life has a great deal to offer suggests that you are generous, broad-minded, and show eagerness to cooperate with others. A love of travel and an interest in other

cultures also imply that your partner may come from a foreign country.

WOMEN WITH VENUS IN CAPRICORN: Proud and refined, you attract others with your composed dignity. Disliking vulnerability and needing to feel safe before you can express your feelings, you usually display a strong front. Feeling insecure or inadequate in relationships may force you to become manipulative in order to regain control. Nevertheless, you can project an attractive sense of self-assurance and are capable of displaying loyalty and a wonderful dry sense of humor.

MEN WITH VENUS IN CAPRICORN: As you do not display your deeper emotions freely, you are usually dignified and controlled in your relationships with others. Practical and down-to-earth partners are particularly attractive to you, especially those who do not rush into expressing their feelings but seem to possess natural class and reserve. You need a partner who is loyal and dependable and willing to take your relationship seriously.

WOMEN WITH VENUS IN AQUARIUS: Sociable and gracious, you are usually sincere and are capable of showing attributes of real tolerance and liberalism. Although you are keen on forming relationships you also like to have freedom and act independently. Your intimate partnerships need to be founded on true friendships. Full of bright and progressive ideas, you can express yourself better when you are free and unrestricted. An ability to think in a dispassionate way suggests that you can stay detached. Your love of freedom also implies that you can be loving and loyal without smothering your partner.

MEN WITH VENUS IN AQUARIUS: Ideally, in your relationships your lover is also your best friend. Since freedom of expression is a prerequisite to your well-being, you do better when left alone to do your own thing. You also need a partner who recognizes and appreciates your need for independence. Although usually friendly, at times you can be stubborn or your cool detachment can appear to others as distant or impersonal. Very sociable, however, you particularly enjoy the company of those who share your original, fair-minded, and progressive views.

To read all about your Outer Planets and work out how to use your personalized timetable, go to Section Three, page 789.

To read all about your Outer Planets and work out how to use your personalized timetable, go to Section Three, page 789.

Your Personalized Timetable

JUPITER BENEFICIAL
1938 4/6 – 9/16
1938 11/21 – until 1939 1/19
1940 4/9 – 6/19
1940 12/1 – until 1941 1/29
1943 10/10 – until 1944 2/18
1944 6/6 – 8/28
1945 12/26 – until 1946 3/30
1946 8/25 – 10/15
1950 3/17 – 5/11
1950 8/13 – 12/29
1952 3/22 – 5/29
1955 9/20 – until 1956 8/12
1957 12/3 – until 1958 5/9
1958 7/30 – 9/28
1962 2/28 – 4/15
1962 9/30 – 11/26
1964 3/5 – 5/12
1967 9/3 – until 1968 7/27
1969 11/15 – until 1970 1/16
1970 3/26 – 9/10
1974 2/12 – 3/26
1975 6/27 – 10/2
1976 2/13 – 4/25
1979 8/18 – 11/11
1980 2/10 – 7/7
1981 10/30 – 12/19
1982 5/6 – 8/18
1986 1/27 – 3/10
1987 6/2 – 11/16
1988 1/13 – 4/9
1991 8/2 – 10/18
1992 3/20 – 6/11
1993 10/14 – 11/30
1998 1/9 – 2/21
1999 5/14 – until 2000 3/22
2003 7/17 – 9/30
2005 9/29 – 11/14
2009 5/3 – 7/29
2009 12/20 – until 2010 2/5
2011 4/26 – 7/16
2011 10/14 – until 2012 3/1

SATURN BENEFICIAL
1939 4/13 – until 1940 5/16
1947 10/24 – until 1948 1/15
1948 7/9 – until 1949 8/14
1952 12/5 – until 1953 4/11
1953 8/31 – 11/27
1954 5/23 – 8/19
1964 2/3 – 5/13
1964 7/18 – until 1965 1/28
1968 5/23 – 10/27
1969 2/12 – 7/6
1969 10/6 – until 1970 3/23
1977 8/19 – until 1978 9/22
1979 4/29 – 5/19
1982 10/10 – until 1983 1/25
1983 3/2 – 10/5
1993 3/9 – 10/3
1993 11/21 – until 1994 3/4
1998 3/27 – until 1999 4/30
2006 9/29 – until 2007 2/16
2007 6/19 – 11/10
2008 1/28 – 7/26
2011 11/16 – until 2012 5/13
2012 8/6 – 11/9

URANUS BENEFICIAL
1960 8/10 – until 1964 7/6
1973 10/28 – until 1976 9/1
2001 4/18 – until 2005 1/7

NEPTUNE BENEFICIAL
1953 10/31 – until 1958 10/19
2008 5/8 – Continues

PLUTO BENEFICIAL
1951 10/14 – until 1961 8/11
1981 1/2 – until 1985 10/15

JUPITER CHALLENGING
1939 4/1 – 6/27

1939 8/30 – until 1940 2/7
1941 9/27 – 10/22
1942 4/30 – 7/11
1944 11/6 – until 1945 3/24
1945 7/4 – 9/28
1951 3/15 – 5/26
1951 10/18 – until 1952 1/11
1953 8/16 – 12/15
1954 4/7 – 6/25
1956 10/17 – until 1957 9/12
1963 2/26 – 5/5
1965 7/25 – until 1966 6/9
1968 10/1 – until 1969 8/26
1975 2/9 – 4/17
1977 7/7 – until 1978 5/22
1980 9/15 – 12/9
1981 3/12 – 8/7
1986 6/9 – 8/14
1987 1/21 – 4/1
1989 6/20 – 9/9
1989 12/17 – until 1990 5/2
1992 8/30 – 11/15
1993 4/21 – 7/12
1998 5/9 – 9/30
1998 12/26 – until 1999 3/16
2001 6/4 – 8/16
2002 1/29 – 4/1
2004 8/14 – 10/29
2010 4/18 – until 2011 2/26

SATURN CHALLENGING
1938 1/1 – 3/22
1943 7/19 – until 1944 1/10
1944 3/31 – 8/18
1944 12/30 – until 1945 5/7
1950 9/3 – until 1951 10/13
1966 3/21 – until 1967 5/2
1967 10/28 – until 1968 1/19
1973 5/23 – until 1974 6/21
1979 10/12 – until 1980 4/18
1980 6/25 – 11/24
1981 3/17 – 8/18
1995 4/29 – 9/16
1996 1/22 – 7/2
1996 8/4 – until 1997 3/5
2002 6/30 – until 2003 7/30
2004 2/5 – 4/7
2008 12/6 – until 2009 1/26
2009 8/17 – until 2010 9/26

URANUS CHALLENGING
1946 8/20 – until 1951 5/18
1966 10/1 – until 1970 8/30
2008 4/25 – Continues

NEPTUNE CHALLENGING
1938 9/21 – until 1946 8/29

PLUTO CHALLENGING
1967 10/4 – until 1975 8/6

JUPITER SPECIAL
1948 1/31 – 7/9
1948 9/22 – 12/18
1960 1/12 – 12/1
1971 12/26 – until 1972 3/28
1972 5/22 – 11/13
1983 12/11 – until 1984 2/25
1984 7/6 – 10/21
1995 11/25 – until 1996 2/5
2007 11/8 – until 2008 1/19

SATURN SPECIAL
1958 1/16 – 7/1
1958 10/14 – until 1959 12/12
1987 11/25 – until 1989 1/14

URANUS SPECIAL
1986 2/2 – until 1990 11/15

NEPTUNE SPECIAL
1980 1/7 – until 1987 12/15

PLUTO SPECIAL
2004 1/20 – until 2012 10/16

♐

571

Sagittarius Timetable
X-Special · X-Beneficial · X-Challenging

November 22
URANUS X-CHALLENGING
2002 4/10 – until **2004** 2/3
URANUS X-BENEFICIAL
2010 4/6 – until **2012** 1/30
NEPTUNE X-CHALLENGING
2010 3/31 – until **2013** 1/22

November 23
URANUS X-CHALLENGING
2002 5/18 – until **2004** 2/21
URANUS X-BENEFICIAL
2010 4/26 – until **2012** 2/21
NEPTUNE X-CHALLENGING
2011 2/26 – Continues

November 24
URANUS X-CHALLENGING
2003 3/6 – until **2004** 12/27
URANUS X-BENEFICIAL
2010 5/20 – until **2012** 3/11
NEPTUNE X-CHALLENGING
2011 3/27 – Continues

November 25
URANUS X-CHALLENGING
2003 3/25 – until **2005** 1/19
URANUS X-BENEFICIAL
2011 3/25 – until **2012** 12/31
NEPTUNE X-CHALLENGING
2011 5/9 – Continues

November 26
URANUS X-CHALLENGING
2003 4/16 – until **2005** 2/8
URANUS X-BENEFICIAL
2011 4/12 – until **2013** 2/4
NEPTUNE X-CHALLENGING
2012 3/22 – Continues

November 27
URANUS X-CHALLENGING
2003 5/29 – until **2005** 2/25
URANUS X-BENEFICIAL
2011 5/2 – until **2013** 2/26
NEPTUNE X-BENEFICIAL
2001 8/22 – 12/11
NEPTUNE X-CHALLENGING
2012 4/29 – Continues

November 28
URANUS X-CHALLENGING
2004 3/10 – until **2006** 1/2
URANUS X-BENEFICIAL
2011 5/26 – Continues
NEPTUNE X-BENEFICIAL
2001 7/14 – until **2002** 1/10

November 29
URANUS X-CHALLENGING
2004 3/30 – until **2006** 1/25
URANUS X-BENEFICIAL
2012 3/30 – Continues

November 30
URANUS X-CHALLENGING
2004 4/22 – until **2006** 2/13
URANUS X-BENEFICIAL
2012 4/17 – Continues
NEPTUNE X-BENEFICIAL
2001 1/14 – until **2003** 1/8

December 1
URANUS X-CHALLENGING
2005 2/26 – until **2006** 11/27
URANUS X-BENEFICIAL
2012 5/7 – Continues
NEPTUNE X-BENEFICIAL
2001 2/10 – until **2003** 12/1

December 2
URANUS X-CHALLENGING
2005 3/16 – until **2007** 1/9
URANUS X-BENEFICIAL
2012 6/1 – Continues
NEPTUNE X-BENEFICIAL
2001 3/12 – until **2004** 1/5

December 3
URANUS X-CHALLENGING
2005 4/5 – until **2007** 1/31
NEPTUNE X-BENEFICIAL
2002 2/8 – until **2004** 11/23
NEPTUNE X-BENEFICIAL
2001 7/19 – until **2001** 9/27

December 4
URANUS X-CHALLENGING
2005 4/28 – until **2007** 2/19
NEPTUNE X-BENEFICIAL
2002 3/9 – until **2005** 1/2

December 5
URANUS X-CHALLENGING
2005 4/28 – until **2007** 2/19
NEPTUNE X-BENEFICIAL
2002 3/9 – until **2005** 1/2

December 6
URANUS X-CHALLENGING
2006 3/22 – until **2008** 1/16
NEPTUNE X-BENEFICIAL
2003 3/6 – until **2005** 12/29
PLUTO X-SPECIAL
2001 1/1 – until **2002** 10/27

December 7
URANUS X-CHALLENGING
2006 4/11 – until **2008** 2/6
NEPTUNE X-BENEFICIAL
2003 4/15 – until **2006** 1/27
PLUTO X-SPECIAL
2001 1/1 – until **2002** 11/26

December 8
URANUS X-CHALLENGING
2006 5/5 – until **2008** 2/25

NEPTUNE X-BENEFICIAL
2004 3/2 – until **2006** 12/26
PLUTO X-SPECIAL
2001 1/6 – until **2003** 10/19

December 9
URANUS X-CHALLENGING
2007 3/10 – until **2008** 12/20
NEPTUNE X-BENEFICIAL
2004 4/7 – until **2007** 1/25
PLUTO X-SPECIAL
2001 2/12 – until **2003** 11/20

December 10
URANUS X-CHALLENGING
2007 3/28 – until **2009** 1/21
NEPTUNE X-BENEFICIAL
2005 2/28 – until **2007** 12/22
PLUTO X-SPECIAL
2001 12/30 – until **2004** 10/9

December 11
URANUS X-CHALLENGING
2007 4/17 – until **2009** 2/12
NEPTUNE X-BENEFICIAL
2005 4/2 – until **2008** 1/22
PLUTO X-SPECIAL
2002 1/31 – until **2004** 11/14

December 12
URANUS X-CHALLENGING
2007 5/13 – until **2009** 3/2
NEPTUNE X-BENEFICIAL
2006 2/25 – until **2008** 12/16
PLUTO X-SPECIAL
2002 12/24 – until **2005** 9/28

December 13
URANUS X-BENEFICIAL
2001 1/8 – until **2002** 1/12
URANUS X-CHALLENGING
2008 3/15 – until **2009** 12/29
NEPTUNE X-BENEFICIAL
2006 3/28 – until **2009** 1/18
PLUTO X-SPECIAL
2003 1/23 – until **2005** 11/10

December 14
URANUS X-BENEFICIAL
2001 1/27 – until **2002** 1/31
URANUS X-CHALLENGING
2008 4/2 – until **2010** 1/28
NEPTUNE X-BENEFICIAL
2007 2/23 – until **2009** 12/10
PLUTO X-SPECIAL
2003 12/19 – until **2005** 12/9

December 15
URANUS X-BENEFICIAL
2001 2/13 – until **2002** 11/22
URANUS X-CHALLENGING
2008 4/23 – until **2010** 2/18
NEPTUNE X-BENEFICIAL
2007 3/24 – until **2010** 1/15

PLUTO X-SPECIAL
2004 1/17 – until **2006** 11/6

December 16
URANUS X-BENEFICIAL
2001 2/13 – until **2002** 11/22
URANUS X-CHALLENGING
2008 4/23 – until **2010** 2/18
NEPTUNE X-BENEFICIAL
2007 3/24 – until **2010** 1/15
PLUTO X-SPECIAL
2004 1/17 – until **2006** 11/6

December 17
URANUS X-BENEFICIAL
2001 3/23 – until **2003** 1/18
URANUS X-CHALLENGING
2009 3/21 – until **2011** 1/6
NEPTUNE X-BENEFICIAL
2008 3/20 – until **2011** 1/12
PLUTO X-SPECIAL
2005 1/11 – until **2007** 11/2

December 18
URANUS X-BENEFICIAL
2001 4/17 – until **2003** 2/5
URANUS X-CHALLENGING
2009 4/9 – until **2011** 2/3
NEPTUNE X-BENEFICIAL
2008 5/3 – until **2011** 2/10
PLUTO X-SPECIAL
2005 2/16 – until **2007** 12/3

December 19
URANUS X-BENEFICIAL
2002 2/19 – until **2003** 12/1
URANUS X-CHALLENGING
2009 4/29 – until **2011** 2/24
NEPTUNE X-BENEFICIAL
2009 3/17 – until **2012** 1/9
PLUTO X-SPECIAL
2006 1/7 – until **2008** 10/28

December 20
URANUS X-BENEFICIAL
2002 3/9 – until **2004** 1/2
URANUS X-CHALLENGING
2009 5/27 – until **2011** 3/14
NEPTUNE X-BENEFICIAL
2009 4/24 – until **2012** 2/7
PLUTO X-SPECIAL
2006 2/9 – until **2008** 12/1

December 21
URANUS X-BENEFICIAL
2002 3/29 – until **2004** 1/24
URANUS X-CHALLENGING
2010 3/27 – until **2012** 1/14
NEPTUNE X-BENEFICIAL
2010 3/14 – until **2013** 1/4
PLUTO X-SPECIAL
2007 1/4 – until **2009** 10/25

Capricorn

December 22–January 20

December 22

SUN: CAPRICORN/SAGITTARIUS CUSP • DECANATE: CAPRICORN/SATURN • DEGREE: 29°5–0°5 CAPRICORN • MODE: CARDINAL • ELEMENT: EARTH

Your Personal Powers

You are sensitive and sincere, and your intuition and cautious approach indicate that you are a serious individual with powerful feelings and a practical attitude. Your ruling planet, Saturn, endows you with determination, endurance, and a strong sense of duty. Capable of tolerating great challenges, you gain power when you persevere with your grand plans. Although you are usually courteous and receptive to others, you can, at times, bury yourself in work and appear indifferent or too matter-of-fact. Often inspired by high ideals and creativity, you need to find an avenue to express your powerful emotions. Although you may be ambitious and concerned with material success, a more visionary side to your nature indicates that personal satisfaction rarely comes just from your financial accomplishments. You can lose some of your power when you behave in a controlling manner or vacillate from being warm and friendly to being stubborn or uncaring. You empower yourself by establishing the right balance between your need for accomplishment and material security, and your need for emotional fulfillment.

Your Powers of Attraction in Relationships

Other people admire your idealism and sincerity. Generous and kind, you have an innate ability to inspire others. Often intuitive and receptive to people's needs, you can feel the moods of those close to you. Being enthusiastic, reliable, and idealistic suggests that you can also be a loyal and supportive partner or friend. You benefit, however, from practicing a cautious or patient approach when forming new relationships. Finding it hard to offend anyone, you can at times suffer in silence, and decision making about close relationship can then become challenging or complex. You therefore cannot afford to be taken for granted or be overly romantic. Nevertheless, by agreeing on basic principles and maintaining a balance of give and take in close relationships you can often succeed. Women often play an important role in your life.

Your attractive qualities: pragmatic, dutiful, disciplined, sincere, idealistic, optimistic, ambitious, compassionate, highly intuitive, loyal, spontaneous, skillful, good organizer, realist, problem solver, strategist, hardworking, achiever, creative, generous, positive thinker, affectionate, warm

Your less attractive qualities: materialistic, undemonstrative, skeptical, anxious, doubting, thrifty, too sensitive, insecure, bossy, cynical, lack of vision, lazy, self-absorbed, denial, manipulative, restless

Your Venus Power

The planet Venus has a great deal of influence on your powers of attraction. Below are four possible Venus types for women and men. To find your Venus you need to go to page 771, where you will find the Venus table and extra information. The planet Mars also affects your powers of attraction. To find your Mars table and interpretation go to page 761.

WOMEN WITH VENUS IN SCORPIO: Your strength and power is in your ability to love both deeply and sensitively. For you, love and desire go hand in hand. As you feel so deeply, you often keep your sensitivity or vulnerability hidden from others in order to keep some control in your relationships. You are more likely to prefer a few very close loyal friends than many superficial acquaintances. In relationships your sensual nature and magnetic intensity can easily attract others.

MEN WITH VENUS IN SCORPIO: You are attracted to partners who have deep and powerful emotions or individuals you find intriguing. Your gift for creating smoke screens to maintain secrecy around your feelings can conceal your inner sensitivity and vulnerability. Nevertheless, you are looking for a partner who can pierce your defenses and understand you at a very deep level. Needing a relationship with a powerful sexual connection, you thrive on emotional intensity.

WOMEN WITH VENUS IN SAGITTARIUS: When you feel generous, you can make others feel more optimistic about life. You may be interested in higher learning and seek partners who are scholarly or broad-minded. You are outspoken and direct, and you sometimes say things that you later regret. Curious and versatile, you can adjust quickly to new situations, and a foreign influence implies that you love to travel or may have a partner who comes from a different culture.

MEN WITH VENUS IN SAGITTARIUS: Optimistic and fun-loving, you love adventure and seek a partner who can expand your horizons. Being truthful and direct you often say what you think, and at times you may be naively tactless. A need for expansion and prosperity suggest that you may enjoy traveling with your friends or partner. Being lighthearted and idealistic,

once you have given your heart to someone you will stay honorable and loyal.

WOMEN WITH VENUS IN CAPRICORN: Proud and refined, you attract others with your composed dignity. Disliking vulnerability and needing to feel safe before you can express your feelings, you display a strong front. Feeling insecure or inadequate in relationships may force you to become manipulative in order to regain control. Nevertheless, you can project an attractive sense of self-assurance and are capable of displaying loyalty and a wonderful dry sense of humor.

MEN WITH VENUS IN CAPRICORN: As you do not display your deeper emotions freely, you are usually dignified and controlled in your relationships with others. Practical and down-to-earth partners are particularly attractive to you, especially those who do not rush into expressing their feelings but seem to possess natural class and reserve. You need a partner who is loyal and dependable and willing to take your relationship seriously.

WOMEN WITH VENUS IN AQUARIUS: Usually you have a modern outlook on love and are open to new or current lifestyles. Your intuitive abilities, communal sense, and people skills often allow you to see deeper into human intentions and read people's thoughts telepathically. You are usually group-oriented and are drawn to the individuals within the group who are independent and self-motivated. You are more inclined to choose a partner who is unconventional or freedom-loving. Conscious of your social standing, however, you want someone who can relate well to your friends.

MEN WITH VENUS IN AQUARIUS: Although independent, you often enjoy being part of a group. The partners you frequently attract are themselves nonconformists or free spirits. As an individual, you may not find it easy to settle into a routine or an entirely mundane type of relationship. You may have some unconventional views on traditional marriage or your partner may hold such views. It is usually important to you that your love relationships are based on friendship.

To read all about your Outer Planets and work out how to use your personalized timetable, go to Section Three, page 789.

go to Section Three, page 789.

Your Personalized Timetable

JUPITER BENEFICIAL
1938 4/10 – until 1939 1/22
1940 4/11 – 6/22
1940 11/24 – until 1941 2/5
1943 10/15 – until 1944 8/31
1946 1/1 – 10/18
1950 3/20 – until 1951 1/1
1952 3/25 – 6/1
1955 9/24 – until 1956 8/15
1957 12/7 – until 1958 10/2
1962 3/3 – 4/18
1962 9/24 – 12/3
1964 3/8 – 5/15
1967 9/6 – until 1968 7/30
1969 11/18 – until 1970 1/23
1970 3/19 – 9/14
1974 2/14 – 3/29
1975 7/2 – 9/26
1976 2/16 – 4/28
1979 8/21 – 11/17
1980 2/4 – 7/11
1981 11/2 – 12/24
1982 4/30 – 8/23
1986 1/30 – 3/13
1987 6/6 – 11/10
1988 1/19 – 4/12
1991 8/5 – 10/22
1992 3/14 – 6/17
1993 10/17 – 12/4
1994 6/26 – 7/8
1998 1/13 – 2/24
1999 5/17 – until 2000 3/26
2003 7/20 – 10/3
2005 10/2 – 11/17
2009 5/8 – until 2010 2/8
2011 4/29 – until 2012 3/5

SATURN BENEFICIAL
1939 4/18 – until 1940 5/22
1947 11/4 – until 1948 1/3
1948 7/15 – until 1949 8/19
1952 12/12 – until 1953 4/2
1953 9/7 – 12/3
1954 5/13 – 8/28
1964 2/9 – 5/30
1964 6/30 – until 1965 2/3
1968 5/30 – 10/18
1969 2/20 – 7/16
1969 9/26 – until 1970 3/29
1977 8/24 – until 1978 9/27
1979 4/9 – 6/8
1982 10/16 – until 1983 10/11
1993 3/15 – 9/19
1993 12/4 – until 1994 3/10
1998 4/1 – until 1999 5/5
2006 10/5 – until 2007 2/8
2007 6/26 – 11/21
2008 1/17 – 8/1
2011 11/22 – until 2012 5/3
2012 8/15 – 11/15

URANUS BENEFICIAL
1960 8/21 – until 1964 7/20
1973 11/8 – until 1976 9/15
2001 5/28 – until 2005 1/21

NEPTUNE BENEFICIAL
1953 11/20 – until 1959 9/4
2009 3/8 – Continues

PLUTO BENEFICIAL
1952 9/3 – until 1962 6/23
1981 10/31 – until 1986 8/16

JUPITER CHALLENGING
1939 4/4 – until 1940 2/10
1942 5/3 – 7/14
1944 11/10 – until 1945 10/1
1951 3/17 – until 1952 1/16
1953 8/20 – 12/10
1954 4/11 – 6/28
1956 10/21 – until 1957 9/15
1963 3/1 – 5/8
1965 7/28 – until 1966 6/12
1968 10/4 – until 1969 8/30
1975 2/12 – 4/20
1977 7/10 – until 1978 5/25
1980 9/18 – 12/14
1981 3/7 – 8/11
1986 6/17 – 8/6
1987 1/24 – 4/4
1989 6/23 – until 1990 5/6
1992 9/2 – 11/19
1993 4/15 – 7/17
1998 5/13 – until 1999 3/18
2001 6/7 – 8/20
2002 1/23 – 4/8
2004 8/17 – 11/1
2010 4/21 – until 2011 3/1

SATURN CHALLENGING
1938 1/1 – 3/28
1943 7/24 – until 1944 1/1
1944 4/9 – 8/25
1944 12/22 – until 1945 5/14
1950 9/9 – until 1951 10/18
1966 3/26 – until 1968 1/28
1973 5/28 – until 1974 6/26
1979 10/18 – until 1980 4/7
1980 7/6 – 12/2
1981 3/8 – 8/24
1995 5/6 – 9/8
1996 1/29 – until 1997 3/11
2002 7/5 – until 2003 8/5
2004 1/25 – 4/18
2009 8/23 – until 2010 10/1

URANUS CHALLENGING
1947 6/12 – until 1951 5/31
1966 10/12 – until 1970 9/11
2008 5/12 – Continues

NEPTUNE CHALLENGING
1938 10/10 – until 1946 9/17

PLUTO CHALLENGING
1967 10/24 – until 1975 8/29

JUPITER SPECIAL
1948 2/3 – 12/21
1960 1/15 – 12/4
1971 12/29 – until 1972 11/16
1983 12/14 – until 1984 10/25
1995 11/28 – until 1996 9/4
2007 11/12 – until 2008 1/22

SATURN SPECIAL
1958 1/23 – until 1959 12/18
1987 12/1 – until 1989 1/20
1989 8/16 – 10/6

URANUS SPECIAL
1986 2/20 – until 1990 11/29

NEPTUNE SPECIAL
1980 1/28 – until 1988 10/27

PLUTO SPECIAL
2004 2/15 – until 2012 11/16

♑

December 23

SUN: CAPRICORN • DECANATE: CAPRICORN • DEGREE: 0°5–1°5 CAPRICORN • MODE: CARDINAL • ELEMENT: EARTH

Your Personal Powers

Charming and purposeful, you are an altruistic and persuasive individual with foresight and determination. Being instinctive implies that you can assess people and situations with your innate intuitive skills. Your ruling planet, Saturn, grants you endurance, ambition, and a realistic outlook on life. You gain power by being imaginative, generous, yet realistic and industrious. Although you may experience some setbacks, you succeed by staying focused on plans that can bring you both emotional satisfaction and material rewards. Being self-reliant and capable may strengthen your character but a stubborn streak indicates that you can lose some of your power by being controlling or too proud. You therefore empower yourself by being cooperative and sensitive to others, rather than insisting on doing things in a particular way. Nevertheless, convincing and forceful, with a desire to achieve stability and security, you can influence people and rise above mundane challenges to really succeed in life.

Your Powers of Attraction in Relationships

People admire your determination, drive, and persistence. Having a sense of duty, you are often attracted to strong individuals who are idealistic, hardworking, and security-conscious. Alternatively, you may be drawn to mystical and caring people who show their compassion by taking care of you and others. Usually you are sociable and entertaining with a need for security and stability in your close relationships. A tendency to have high hopes means that you need to stay pragmatic about your close partners. Thinking pessimistically, however, may lead to isolation and sometimes leave you feeling withdrawn or moody. Since you possess powerful emotions, you win other people's affections by being sympathetic, caring, and generous. By sharing your vision and using your dynamic energy and charm, you can easily impress people and attract admirers.

Your attractive qualities: loyal, compassionate, responsible, communicative, intuitive, creative, versatile, trustworthy, determined, ambitious, hardworking, persistent, courteous, friendly, charming, generous, disciplined, resourceful, persuasive

Your less attractive qualities: selfish, insecure, stubborn, uncompromising, faultfinding, controlling, withdrawn, prejudiced, repressed emotions, restless, emotionally sensitive, materialistic, unsympathetic, calculating, too demanding

Your Venus Power

The planet Venus has a great deal of influence on your powers of attraction. Below are four possible Venus types for women and men. To find your Venus you need to go to page 771, where you will find the Venus table and extra information. The planet Mars also affects your powers of attraction. To find your Mars table and interpretation go to page 761.

WOMEN WITH VENUS IN SCORPIO: With a natural psychic gift for penetrating the feelings of others, you can often help partners transform emotional challenges or sexual difficulties. When you fall in love, your strong feelings and determination give you a potent force that others find attractive and seductive. Although you know what really turns people on, your most profound desire is usually for the deepness and closeness of real love and intimacy in an enduring relationship.

MEN WITH VENUS IN SCORPIO: In relationships you possess a sensitive understanding of your partner's deeper nature. Although you are strongly attached to those you love, you may have to be careful that your feelings do not turn into jealousy or possessiveness. When you fall in love it is often with emotional intensity and power. You are attracted to partners who can share your passion and display strong feelings of sexuality like your own.

WOMEN WITH VENUS IN SAGITTARIUS: Optimistic and fun-loving, you love adventure and seek a partner who can expand your horizons. Being truthful and direct, you often say what you think, and at times you may be naively tactless. A need for expansion and prosperity suggests that you may enjoy traveling with your friends or partner. Being lighthearted and idealistic, once you have given your heart to someone you will stay honorable and loyal.

MEN WITH VENUS IN SAGITTARIUS: You are usually attracted to partners who are knowledgeable or well-traveled. Enthusiastic and optimistic, you often respond quickly to love offers and enter relationships with enthusiasm. Generally you seek to expand your social circle, and meeting people from all walks of life can bring you the variety and fun that you seek in life. You are generous and honest, but your partners may sometimes accuse you of being overly optimistic or too blunt.

WOMEN WITH VENUS IN CAPRICORN: With your natural caution in romantic affairs, you often appear reserved and controlled. If shy, try to be more forward, especially if you want to be noticed. When you care about people, however, you are usually willing to put in extra time and energy to preserve

the relationship. You are practical and dependable, and a sense of duty can often play a large role in the affairs of your heart. With elegant simplicity, you can attract others with your well-cut clothes and refined manners.

MEN WITH VENUS IN CAPRICORN: In relationships you take love seriously and can be a strong and practical support for friends or partners. You are usually attracted to partners who are as hardworking as you. As you tend not to express your feelings until you feel really secure in a relationship, you may be drawn to those who seem loyal, faithful, and not likely to let you down. Since you respect the wisdom of experience, you may be drawn to mature partners or, alternatively, you may act as an authority figure for someone younger.

WOMEN WITH VENUS IN AQUARIUS: You attract and impress others with your friendly approach and progressive ideas. As you are usually independent and easygoing you value freedom within a relationship. A good companion with a sense of your own person, you enjoy socializing, especially with people who are original, cosmopolitan, and have a strong sense of individuality. Although being friendly and detached usually serves you well, avoid losing touch with your emotions. You usually prefer the company of those who have innovative or progressive views.

MEN WITH VENUS IN AQUARIUS: You are sociable and open-minded, and people are attracted by your friendly and easygoing style. Being independent, you value freedom-loving partners who give you the space to be yourself. People can sometimes interpret your detachment as being emotionally cool, but they admire your objectivity and humanitarian inclinations. You are attracted to intelligent individuals who are as truthful and direct as you but who, above all, must be true friends. Ideally your partner shares your liberal views on life and possesses a strong sense of individuality.

To read all about your Outer Planets and work out how to use your personalized timetable, go to Section Three, page 789.

Your Personalized Timetable

JUPITER BENEFICIAL
1938 4/15 – until **1939** 1/26
1940 4/16 – until **1941** 2/13
1943 10/21 – until **1944** 9/5
1946 1/11 – 10/23
1950 3/25 – until **1951** 1/7
1952 3/30 – 6/6
1955 9/29 – until **1956** 8/20
1957 12/13 – until **1958** 10/7
1962 3/7 – 12/11
1964 3/12 – 5/19
1967 9/11 – until **1968** 8/4
1969 11/23 – until **1970** 9/19
1974 2/19 – 4/3
1975 7/11 – 9/17
1976 2/22 – 5/2
1979 8/26 – 11/26
1980 1/25 – 7/17
1981 11/6 – 12/30
1982 4/22 – 8/30
1986 2/3 – 3/17
1987 6/12 – 11/1
1988 1/27 – 4/16
1991 8/10 – 10/28
1992 3/6 – 6/24
1993 10/22 – 12/9
1994 6/5 – 7/29
1998 1/17 – 2/28
1999 5/21 – until **2000** 3/30
2003 7/25 – 10/8
2005 10/7 – 11/22
2009 5/19 – until **2010** 2/12
2011 5/3 – until **2012** 3/10

SATURN BENEFICIAL
1939 4/26 – until **1940** 5/30
1940 12/7 – until **1941** 2/10
1948 7/24 – until **1949** 8/27
1952 12/26 – until **1953** 12/13
1954 4/29 – 9/9
1964 2/17 – until **1965** 2/12
1968 6/10 – 10/5
1969 3/2 – until **1970** 4/7
1977 9/1 – until **1978** 10/6
1979 3/23 – 6/24
1982 10/24 – until **1983** 10/19
1993 3/24 – until **1994** 3/18
1994 10/26 – 11/23
1998 4/9 – until **1999** 5/14
2006 10/17 – until **2007** 1/26
2007 7/6 – until **2008** 8/10
2011 12/2 – until **2012** 11/24

URANUS BENEFICIAL
1960 9/6 – until **1964** 8/8
1973 11/26 – until **1976** 10/4
2002 3/3 – until **2005** 2/9

NEPTUNE BENEFICIAL
1953 12/31 – until **1959** 10/7
2009 4/10 – Continues

PLUTO BENEFICIAL
1952 10/14 – until **1962** 8/3
1981 11/29 – until **1986** 9/23

JUPITER CHALLENGING
1939 4/8 – until **1940** 2/15
1942 5/8 – 7/19

1944 11/16 – until **1945** 10/6
1951 3/22 – until **1952** 1/22
1953 8/27 – 12/2
1954 4/17 – 7/2
1956 10/26 – until **1957** 9/20
1963 3/5 – 5/13
1965 8/3 – until **1966** 6/16
1968 10/9 – until **1969** 9/4
1975 2/16 – 4/24
1977 7/15 – until **1978** 5/30
1980 9/23 – until **1981** 8/17
1987 1/29 – 4/8
1989 6/28 – until **1990** 5/11
1992 9/7 – 11/25
1993 4/6 – 7/25
1998 5/19 – until **1999** 3/23
2001 6/11 – 8/25
2002 1/14 – 4/16
2004 8/22 – 11/6
2010 4/26 – until **2011** 3/5

SATURN CHALLENGING
1938 1/1 – 4/5
1943 8/3 – 12/19
1944 4/21 – until **1945** 5/23
1950 9/17 – until **1951** 10/27
1952 5/13 – 7/8
1966 4/4 – until **1968** 2/9
1973 6/5 – until **1974** 7/4
1979 10/27 – until **1980** 12/17
1981 2/20 – 9/2
1995 5/18 – 8/25
1996 2/8 – until **1997** 3/19
2002 7/14 – until **2003** 8/14
2004 1/12 – 4/30
2009 8/31 – until **2010** 10/10

URANUS CHALLENGING
1947 6/29 – until **1951** 6/18
1966 10/31 – until **1970** 9/27
2009 3/17 – Continues

NEPTUNE CHALLENGING
1938 11/14 – until **1947** 8/15

PLUTO CHALLENGING
1967 12/22 – until **1975** 9/25

JUPITER SPECIAL
1948 2/9 – 6/24
1948 10/5 – 12/25
1960 1/20 – 12/9
1972 1/3 – 11/21
1983 12/18 – until **1984** 11/1
1995 12/2 – until **1996** 2/14
1996 8/8 – 9/29
2007 11/16 – until **2008** 1/27

SATURN SPECIAL
1958 2/3 – until **1959** 12/26
1987 12/9 – until **1989** 10/25

URANUS SPECIAL
1986 12/19 – until **1990** 12/17

NEPTUNE SPECIAL
1980 12/26 – until **1988** 12/2

PLUTO SPECIAL
2005 1/4 – until **2012** 12/18

♑

December 24

SUN: CAPRICORN • DECANATE: CAPRICORN/SATURN • DEGREE: 1°5–2°5 CAPRICORN • MODE: CARDINAL • ELEMENT: EARTH

Your Personal Powers

As a perfectionist with high ideals, you are a rational yet sensitive individual with determination and the power to persevere. Through your emotional strength you have the potential to charm, inspire, or uplift others. An ability to visualize, structure, and plan indicates that you can be observant, paying attention to the smallest detail. Your ruling planet, Saturn, endows you with an ambitious nature, a strong sense of responsibility, and a realistic approach to life. Usually you have the stamina to endure and overcome difficulties or advance slowly toward your target goal. Yet at times, you lose some of your power by being too stubborn or critical. Since you are likely to be refined and imaginative, you gain power by being spontaneous and combining your inborn pragmatism with your high standards. You lose power, however, when you let dispassionate caution turn to fear and pessimism, as it can restrain you from initiating new plans or projects. Nevertheless, you achieve success by staying open-minded, optimistic, and true to your faith and principles.

Your Powers of Attraction in Relationships

Courteous and friendly, you are usually thoughtful and loyal. Although you can be sympathetic and caring, a tendency to be frustrated or hurt implies that at times you take matters too much to heart. You are usually attracted to dynamic and purposeful individuals who can be creative and enterprising. A need to be active and a love of variety suggest that you like to be spontaneous and preferably share this with your partner. Issues of trust and money, however, need to be approached with caution if you do not want to be let down by others. Although you can be an idealistic individual with firm ideas, if you offer pragmatic advice without sympathy to your partner you could create tension. Nevertheless, being dutiful and devoted suggests that you are capable of making great sacrifices for those you love.

Your attractive qualities: idealistic, inspired, energetic, careful, receptive, practical skills, strong determination, tolerant, faithful, frank, fair, highly intuitive, generous, love of home, active, spontaneous, optimistic, dry sense of humor, reliable, introspective, perfectionist, innate wisdom

Your less attractive qualities: critical, skeptical, materialistic, jealous, inertia, anxious, undemonstrative, domineering, stubborn, melancholy, mistrusting, insecure, fear of being alone or abandoned, too demanding, too high expectations

Your Venus Power

The planet Venus has a great deal of influence on your powers of attraction. Below are four possible Venus types for women and men. To find your Venus you need to go to page 771, where you will find the Venus table and extra information. The planet Mars also affects your powers of attraction. To find your Mars table and interpretation go to page 761.

WOMEN WITH VENUS IN SCORPIO: You are usually drawn to partners who are sensual in appearance with strong character. As you are emotionally intense and passionate, personal relationships are probably a major factor in your life. Since you like to be in control, you can at times exhibit some of your less attractive qualities by being willful or domineering. Although you need to feel established and in command in your relationships, you are constantly searching for some higher truth that can bring about a significant transformation.

MEN WITH VENUS IN SCORPIO: You are usually attracted to sensual and passionate partners with strong character. You are often sensitive with deep feelings and magnetic powers of attraction. As a cautious yet devoted and ardent lover, you are likely to seek experiences that are more sexual in nature. You display your less attractive qualities when you project your negative thoughts and resort to being suspicious or possessive. Nevertheless, loyal and loving, you are a sensitive lover.

WOMEN WITH VENUS IN SAGITTARIUS: At your best when being optimistic and generous, you possess a mischievous sense of fun. In relationships your open-minded approach to people and places may attract you to those of a different culture or make you tolerant of the foibles of others. Although warm and enthusiastic when in love, your natural honesty and idealism may inspire you to look for a partner who shares your love of freedom.

MEN WITH VENUS IN SAGITTARIUS: Forward-thinking rather than dwelling on the past, you are looking for a partner who can share your future plans. You enjoy exploring life whether through travel and mental pursuits or sports and games. Idealistic, you usually prefer the company of a partner who is optimistic and shares your beliefs. In your desire for

honesty in relationships, however, be careful not to become tactless. Nevertheless, you are attracted to honest, direct, and fun-loving partners who have a sense of humor like your own.

WOMEN WITH VENUS IN CAPRICORN: With your natural caution in romantic affairs, you often appear reserved and controlled. You may be shy but try to be more forward, especially if you want to be noticed. When you care about people, however, you are usually willing to put in extra time and energy to preserve the relationship. You are practical and dependable, and a sense of duty can often play a large role in the affairs of your heart. With elegant simplicity, you can attract others with your well-cut clothes and refined manners.

MEN WITH VENUS IN CAPRICORN: In relationships you take love seriously and can be a strong and practical support for friends or partners. You are usually attracted to partners who are as hardworking as you. As you tend not to express your feelings until you feel really secure in a relationship, you may be drawn to those who seem loyal, faithful, and not likely to let you down. As you respect the wisdom of experience, you may be drawn to mature partners or, alternatively, you may act as an authority figure for someone younger.

WOMEN WITH VENUS IN AQUARIUS: When it comes to relationships, others are attracted to your honest, friendly, and easygoing attitude. You really enjoy social interaction with others and may develop a genuine concern for humanity. Usually you present a tolerant and reasonable front in love situations and attempt to view your relationships objectively. If partners become too demanding, however, you can become stubborn and fixed. Friendship may be even more important for you than sexual compatibility.

MEN WITH VENUS IN AQUARIUS: You are sociable and open-minded, and people are attracted by your friendly and relaxed style. Being independent, you value freedom-loving partners who give you the space to be yourself. Others sometimes interpret your detachment as being emotionally cool, but they may not understand your progressive views on relationships. Friendship can sometimes be even more important than earthly passion. Ideally, your partner shares your ideas on life and possesses as strong a sense of originality as you. Not easily ruffled, you can deal well with difficult situations or moody partners.

To read all about your Outer Planets and work out how to use your personalized timetable, go to Section Three, page 789.

To read all about your Outer Planets and work out how to use your personalized timetable, go to Section Three, page 789.

♑

Your Personalized Timetable

JUPITER BENEFICIAL
1938 4/21 – until 1939 1/31
1940 4/20 – 7/3
1940 11/8 – until 1941 2/20
1943 10/29 – until 1944 9/10
1946 1/24 – 2/28
1946 9/9 – 10/27
1950 3/30 – until 1951 1/12
1952 4/3 – 6/11
1955 10/4 – until 1956 8/25
1957 12/19 – until 1958 4/16
1958 8/19 – 10/11
1962 3/11 – 4/30
1962 9/7 – 12/19
1964 3/17 – 5/23
1967 9/16 – until 1968 8/9
1969 11/29 – until 1970 5/31
1970 7/16 – 9/25
1974 2/23 – 4/8
1975 7/23 – 9/6
1976 2/27 – 5/7
1979 8/31 – 12/11
1980 1/10 – 7/22
1981 11/11 – until 1982 1/6
1982 4/14 – 9/5
1986 2/7 – 3/21
1987 6/17 – 10/24
1988 2/4 – 4/21
1991 8/15 – 11/3
1992 2/27 – 7/1
1993 10/26 – 12/14
1994 5/24 – 8/9
1998 1/22 – 3/5
1999 5/26 – until 2000 4/4
2003 7/30 – 10/13
2004 4/10 – 5/30
2005 10/11 – 11/27
2009 6/6 – 6/24
2010 1/3 – 2/16
2011 5/7 – 8/13
2011 9/16 – until 2012 3/15

SATURN BENEFICIAL
1939 5/4 – until 1940 6/8
1940 11/22 – until 1941 2/25
1948 8/1 – until 1949 9/4
1953 1/14 – 2/27
1953 9/26 – 12/24
1954 4/15 – 9/20
1964 2/25 – until 1965 2/20
1968 6/23 – 9/21
1969 3/11 – until 1970 4/15
1977 9/9 – until 1978 4/10
1978 5/11 – 10/16
1979 3/10 – 7/7
1982 11/2 – until 1983 10/28
1993 4/3 – 8/21
1993 12/30 – until 1994 3/27
1994 10/2 – 12/16
1998 4/17 – until 1999 5/22
2006 10/30 – until 2007 1/11
2007 7/15 – until 2008 8/18
2011 12/13 – until 2012 4/6
2012 9/7 – 12/3

URANUS BENEFICIAL
1938 1/1 – 2/5
1960 10/17 – until 1964 8/24
1973 12/18 – until 1976 10/21
2002 3/23 – until 2005 11/23

NEPTUNE BENEFICIAL
1954 11/18 – until 1960 8/31
2010 3/6 – Continues

PLUTO BENEFICIAL
1953 9/16 – until 1963 6/27
1982 1/15 – until 1986 10/20

JUPITER CHALLENGING
1939 4/12 – until 1940 2/20
1942 5/13 – 7/24
1944 11/23 – until 1945 3/3
1945 7/23 – 10/10

1951 3/26 – 6/11
1951 9/27 – until 1952 1/29
1953 9/4 – 11/24
1954 4/23 – 7/7
1956 11/1 – until 1957 4/11
1957 6/25 – 9/25
1963 3/9 – 5/18
1963 11/21 – 12/19
1965 8/8 – until 1966 1/5
1966 3/28 – 6/21
1968 10/14 – until 1969 9/9
1975 2/21 – 4/29
1977 7/19 – until 1978 6/4
1980 9/27 – until 1981 1/6
1981 2/11 – 8/22
1987 2/3 – 4/12
1989 7/2 – 10/4
1989 11/22 – until 1990 5/17
1992 9/12 – 12/2
1993 3/29 – 8/1
1998 5/26 – 9/9
1999 1/13 – 3/27
2001 6/16 – 8/31
2002 1/6 – 4/24
2004 8/27 – 11/11
2005 5/11 – 6/30
2010 5/1 – 11/4
2010 12/3 – until 2011 3/10

SATURN CHALLENGING
1938 1/1 – 4/13
1943 8/14 – 12/7
1944 5/1 – 9/21
1944 11/23 – until 1945 6/1
1950 9/25 – until 1951 11/5
1952 4/25 – 7/26
1966 4/13 – 10/24
1966 12/29 – until 1967 5/29
1967 9/21 – until 1968 2/19
1973 6/13 – until 1974 7/12
1979 11/6 – until 1980 3/11
1980 7/30 – until 1981 9/11
1995 6/3 – 8/8
1996 2/17 – until 1997 3/27
2002 7/23 – until 2003 1/8
2003 4/7 – 8/24
2003 12/30 – until 2004 5/11
2009 9/8 – until 2010 10/18

URANUS CHALLENGING
1947 7/17 – until 1951 7/5
1966 11/26 – until 1971 7/19
2009 4/4 – Continues

NEPTUNE CHALLENGING
1939 10/9 – until 1947 9/16

PLUTO CHALLENGING
1968 10/19 – until 1976 8/17

JUPITER SPECIAL
1948 2/15 – 6/16
1948 10/12 – 12/29
1960 1/25 – 12/13
1972 1/7 – 11/26
1983 12/23 – until 1984 3/15
1984 6/15 – 11/7
1995 12/7 – until 1996 2/19
1996 7/28 – 10/10
2007 11/21 – until 2008 1/31

SATURN SPECIAL
1958 2/16 – 5/24
1958 11/13 – until 1960 1/4
1987 12/18 – until 1989 2/8
1989 7/12 – 11/7

URANUS SPECIAL
1987 1/5 – until 1991 9/28

NEPTUNE SPECIAL
1981 1/25 – until 1989 10/22

PLUTO SPECIAL
2005 2/6 – Continues

December 25

SUN: CAPRICORN • DECANATE: CAPRICORN/SATURN • DEGREE: 2°5–3°5 CAPRICORN • MODE: CARDINAL • ELEMENT: EARTH

Your Personal Powers

Being astute with an inventive mind and practical abilities implies that you are a self-reliant and versatile individual with common sense. Your ruling planet, Saturn, grants you endurance and powers of concentration and tenacity. Although your conduct shows that you are a realist with keen perceptions, your idealism suggests that you possess a benevolent nature and a sincere regard for others. Full of good intentions, you can lose some of your power if you get carried away and become domineering, critical, or interfering. You gain power when you use your persuasive charm and enthusiasm to promote your inspired ideas. Being imaginative and a good networker, you also empower yourself when you combine your originality, strategic skills, and innate business sense to succeed. You also excel at work that demands dedication and fortitude. Your search for equilibrium and harmony often impels you to structure your belief system, explore spirituality, or place extra importance on your home. You usually achieve peace of mind by staying calm and dispassionate yet inspired and imaginative.

Your Powers of Attraction in Relationships

Sociable and friendly, you can be both enterprising and affectionate. You are charismatic and strong, and people are drawn to your idealistic nature, practical approach, and determination. Although you attract many admirers, it is important to pick your partners carefully. You are usually attracted to clever people who are motivated, have bright ideas, good business acumen, and a tactful manner. Although you have a strong need for harmony, love, inner peace, and security, you often prefer to act independently. If your inborn restlessness is too strong, you may encounter opposition from others. Your success in relationships often depends on your ability to keep a good balance of power. You benefit from partnerships or team efforts by being charming and cooperative. As a good collaborator with social contacts, you enjoy making connections that can also lead to business opportunities.

Your attractive qualities: modest, tolerant, optimistic, highly intuitive, keen intellect, perfectionist, creative, skillful negotiator, idealistic, broad-minded, practical, inventive ideas, common sense, good communicator, trustworthy, dependable, responsible, humanitarian, honest, direct, enterprising

Your less attractive qualities: impulsive, impatient, irresponsible, too emotional, jealous, secretive, critical, moody, nervous, indecisive, worried, self-centered, withdrawn, restless, frustrated, skeptical, materialistic

Your Venus Power

The planet Venus has a great deal of influence on your powers of attraction. Below are four possible Venus types for women and men. To find your Venus you need to go to page 771, where you will find the Venus table and extra information. The planet Mars also affects your powers of attraction. To find your Mars table and interpretation go to page 761.

WOMEN WITH VENUS IN SCORPIO: Loving and passionate, you are often sensitive with deep feelings and strong powers of attraction. A love for the truth coupled with a tendency to be suspicious can be an influence that motivates you to delve deep into the activities of your partner. When in love or in a relationship that matters, you will often bend over backward to cooperate. Although loyal, guard against losing sight of your own needs and desires.

MEN WITH VENUS IN SCORPIO: As you are emotionally intense and passionate, personal relationships are probably a major factor in your own transformation. Being sensitive yet loyal, you are usually attracted to forceful partners who can express themselves intimately but intensely. Rather than seek easy and simple relationships you are drawn to partners who act as a catalyst for your own internal changes. Through your relationships with your partners you can unravel your own motives and understand your deep-seated feelings or emotional insecurities.

WOMEN WITH VENUS IN SAGITTARIUS: Sociable, warm, and friendly, you possess an honest and frank style in your relationships. Being naturally gregarious, you want others to share your enthusiasm, and you enjoy encouraging the people you love. You do better when you have a sense of personal freedom within a relationship and are usually generous with the faults of others. You need a partner who can share your need to explore and take risks, whether through travel, education, or recreation.

MEN WITH VENUS IN SAGITTARIUS: When in love you are open and friendly with a need for a partner who can share your adventurous spirit and sense of fun. Be careful, however, that your desire for freedom does not cause you to avoid com-

mitment. You prefer your partners to be positive, direct, and generous in spirit. Being outspoken as well as an idealist, you usually enjoy a partner with whom you can share your strong opinions. Alternatively, you may wish to explore life together, whether through travel, education, or by having fun.

WOMEN WITH VENUS IN CAPRICORN: Romantically, you do not give your heart easily but hide behind a cool reserve until you feel free to express your emotions. As you take your relationships seriously, you may find yourself drawn to people who are businesslike, resourceful, and practical or who can act as teachers or mentors. Work or career may also be a factor in many of your associations and partnerships. As security can play an important role in your relationships, you are often attracted to partners who are loyal and hardworking.

MEN WITH VENUS IN CAPRICORN: As you admire loyal, hardworking, and dedicated individuals, you probably want a partner who can share your vocational interests or provide you with the sense of security you need. You could even find yourself with a partner who is of a different age group or maturity. Guard against denying your true emotional needs or focusing on your career at the expense of your relationship. You are drawn to reserved partners who display self-control.

WOMEN WITH VENUS IN AQUARIUS: When it comes to relationships, others are attracted to your honest, friendly, and easygoing attitude. You enjoy social interaction and have a genuine concern for others. In fact, at times your friends may be just as important as your partner. You usually present a tolerant and reasonable front in love situations and attempt to view your relationships objectively. If partners become too demanding, however, you can become stubborn or awkward. Nevertheless, inventive and progressive, you enjoy the company of like-minded people who can share your original ideas.

MEN WITH VENUS IN AQUARIUS: Friendly and honest, you attract people with your broad-minded approach to life. You usually possess an objective and slightly detached attitude to affairs of the heart. If you are too removed, however, others can misinterpret your behavior as uncaring. It is often more important to you that your love relationships are based on friendship and honesty than intense passion. As you are generally tolerant and liberal, you may be drawn to less conventional relationships.

To read all about your Outer Planets and work out how to use your personalized timetable, go to Section Three, page 789.

Your Personalized Timetable

JUPITER BENEFICIAL
1938 4/28 – 8/16
1938 12/18 – until 1939 2/4
1940 4/24 – 7/10
1940 11/1 – until 1941 2/26
1943 11/6 – until 1944 1/20
1944 6/29 – 9/15
1946 9/14 – 11/1
1950 4/4 – 10/11
1950 11/6 – until 1951 1/17
1952 4/7 – 6/16
1955 10/10 – until 1956 2/28
1956 6/5 – 8/30
1957 12/26 – until 1958 4/8
1958 8/26 – 10/16
1962 3/16 – 5/6
1962 8/30 – 12/25
1964 3/21 – 5/28
1967 9/21 – until 1968 8/14
1969 12/4 – until 1970 5/18
1970 7/28 – 9/30
1974 2/27 – 4/13
1976 3/3 – 5/11
1979 9/4 – until 1980 7/28
1981 11/16 – until 1982 1/15
1982 4/6 – 9/11
1986 2/11 – 3/26
1987 6/24 – 10/17
1988 2/10 – 4/25
1991 8/19 – 11/10
1992 2/19 – 7/8
1993 10/31 – 12/20
1994 5/15 – 8/18
1998 1/26 – 3/9
1999 5/31 – until 2000 4/8
2003 8/3 – 10/19
2004 3/29 – 6/11
2005 10/16 – 12/2
2010 1/8 – 2/20
2011 5/12 – until 2012 3/20

SATURN BENEFICIAL
1939 5/13 – 12/5
1940 1/19 – 6/18
1940 11/9 – until 1941 3/9
1948 8/9 – until 1949 9/12
1953 10/5 – until 1954 1/6
1954 3/31 – 9/29
1964 3/5 – until 1965 2/28
1968 7/10 – 9/4
1969 3/20 – until 1970 4/23
1977 9/18 – until 1978 3/18
1978 6/2 – 10/26
1979 2/25 – 7/18
1982 11/10 – until 1983 6/17
1983 7/15 – 11/5
1993 4/15 – 8/7
1994 1/9 – 4/6
1994 9/16 – 12/30
1998 4/25 – until 1999 5/30
1999 12/17 – until 2000 2/6
2006 11/22 – 12/19
2007 7/23 – until 2008 8/26
2011 12/26 – until 2012 3/23
2012 9/17 – 12/13

URANUS BENEFICIAL
1938 1/1 – 3/12
1960 10/17 – until 1965 6/8
1974 10/18 – until 1977 8/6
2002 4/15 – until 2006 1/5

NEPTUNE BENEFICIAL
1954 12/25 – until 1960 10/5
2010 4/6 – Continues

PLUTO BENEFICIAL
1953 11/4 – until 1963 8/6
1982 11/15 – until 1987 9/8

JUPITER CHALLENGING
1939 4/17 – until 1940 2/25
1942 5/18 – 7/28

1944 12/1 – until 1945 2/22
1945 7/29 – 10/15
1951 3/30 – 6/19
1951 9/19 – until 1952 2/3
1953 9/13 – 11/15
1954 4/29 – 7/11
1956 11/6 – until 1957 4/2
1957 7/4 – 9/29
1963 3/14 – 5/23
1963 11/7 – until 1964 1/2
1965 8/14 – 12/28
1966 4/5 – 6/25
1968 10/19 – until 1969 9/14
1975 2/25 – 5/3
1977 7/24 – until 1978 6/9
1980 10/2 – until 1981 8/28
1987 2/8 – 4/17
1989 7/7 – until 1990 5/22
1992 9/16 – 12/9
1993 3/21 – 8/8
1998 6/2 – 9/2
1999 1/18 – 3/31
2001 6/20 – 9/7
2001 12/30 – until 2002 4/30
2004 9/1 – 11/17
2005 4/29 – 7/12
2010 5/6 – 10/20
2010 12/17 – until 2011 3/14

SATURN CHALLENGING
1938 1/1 – 4/22
1943 8/26 – 11/23
1944 5/10 – until 1945 6/9
1950 10/3 – until 1951 11/14
1952 4/11 – 8/8
1966 4/22 – 10/8
1967 1/13 – 6/11
1967 9/7 – until 1968 2/28
1973 6/21 – until 1974 7/20
1979 11/18 – until 1980 2/27
1980 8/9 – until 1981 9/20
1996 2/25 – until 1997 4/5
2002 8/1 – 12/26
2003 4/19 – 9/4
2003 12/17 – until 2004 5/21
2009 9/16 – until 2010 10/27
2011 5/21 – 7/6

URANUS CHALLENGING
1947 8/7 – until 1952 5/5
1967 9/19 – until 1971 8/15
2009 4/24 – Continues

NEPTUNE CHALLENGING
1939 11/11 – until 1948 8/11

PLUTO CHALLENGING
1968 11/30 – until 1976 9/16

JUPITER SPECIAL
1948 2/22 – 6/8
1948 10/19 – until 1949 1/3
1960 1/30 – 12/18
1972 1/12 – 12/1
1983 12/27 – until 1984 3/23
1984 6/6 – 11/12
1995 12/11 – until 1996 2/25
1996 7/19 – 10/18
2007 11/26 – until 2008 2/5

SATURN SPECIAL
1958 3/4 – 5/7
1958 11/22 – until 1960 1/13
1987 12/27 – until 1989 2/19
1989 6/28 – 11/19

URANUS SPECIAL
1987 1/24 – until 1991 11/8

NEPTUNE SPECIAL
1981 12/25 – until 1989 11/30

PLUTO SPECIAL
2006 1/1 – Continues

VS

December 26

SUN: CAPRICORN • DECANATE: CAPRICORN/SATURN • DEGREE: 3°5–4°5 CAPRICORN • MODE: CARDINAL • ELEMENT: EARTH

Your Personal Powers

Determined yet intuitive and sensitive, you are an instinctive individual with strong feelings and a serious outlook on life. Caught between a firm sense of duty and a desire for self-expression, you may at times vacillate and feel emotionally restless. Your ruling planet, Saturn, endows you with resolve, endurance, and common sense. Although you can be security-conscious, your spirit of enterprise often urges you to make changes in order to improve your circumstances. However, you may need to learn to take one step at a time and resist the temptation to rush into situations or be hardheaded and stubborn. You gain power when you develop patience and learn to persevere even when you are feeling emotionally unsettled. Nevertheless, your spontaneity and need for action or adventure indicate that you do not fare well in a restrictive environment. By finding a goal that can inspire your creativity and excite your imagination, you can discard your inhibitions and liberate yourself as well as satisfy your energetic spirit.

Your Powers of Attraction in Relationships

Other people admire your spontaneity, enthusiasm, and friendly nature. Being intuitive and sympathetic, you have a natural gift for dealing with people. You are usually drawn to enterprising and purposeful individuals with creative intellect and good organizational skills. Alternatively, you may find people with mystical inclinations very appealing. Although you can be very enthusiastic when you meet new people, a tendency to become bored or be indecisive can cause tension in close relationships. You may need to take your time before settling into permanent partnerships. At times you can be highly idealistic and take your personal relationships very seriously. You can achieve more harmony if you stay detached and less critical about your partner. The more open and communicative you are about your feelings, the closer you get to your loved ones.

Your attractive qualities: practical, strong instincts, versatile, persistent, optimistic, creative, caring, meticulous, idealistic, enterprising, hardworking, honest, responsible, enthusiastic, courageous, intelligent, purposeful, self-reliant, efficient, gregarious, sound judgment

Your less attractive qualities: stubborn, indecisive, lack of consistency, materialistic, dissatisfied, easily bored, escapist, impatient, rebellious, restless, unenthusiastic, lack of persistence, running hot and cold emotionally, unforgiving

Your Venus Power

The planet Venus has a great deal of influence on your powers of attraction. Below are four possible Venus types for women and men. To find your Venus you need to go to page 771, where you will find the Venus table and extra information. The planet Mars also affects your powers of attraction. To find your Mars table and interpretation go to page 761.

WOMEN WITH VENUS IN SCORPIO: Your strength and power is in your ability to love both deeply and sensitively. For you, love and desire go hand in hand. As you feel so deeply, you often keep your sensitivity or vulnerability hidden from others in order to keep some control in your relationships. You are more likely to prefer a few very close loyal friends than many superficial acquaintances. In relationships your sensual nature and magnetic intensity can easily attract others.

MEN WITH VENUS IN SCORPIO: You are attracted to partners who have deep and powerful emotions or individuals you find intriguing. Your gift for creating smoke screens to maintain secrecy around your feelings can conceal your inner sensitivity and vulnerability. Nevertheless, you are looking for a partner who can pierce your defenses and understand you at a very deep level. Needing a relationship with a powerful sexual connection, you thrive on emotional intensity.

WOMEN WITH VENUS IN SAGITTARIUS: When you feel generous, you can make others feel more optimistic about life. You may be interested in higher learning and seek partners who are scholarly or broad-minded. You are outspoken and direct, and you sometimes say things that you later regret. Curious and versatile, you can adjust quickly to new situations, and a foreign influence implies that you love to travel or may have a partner who comes from a different culture.

WOMEN WITH VENUS IN SAGITTARIUS: Optimistic and fun-loving, you love adventure and seek a partner who can expand your horizons. Being truthful and direct, you often say what you think, and at times you may be naively tactless. A need for expansion and prosperity suggests that you may enjoy traveling with your friends or partner. Being lighthearted and idealistic, once you have given your heart to someone you will stay honorable and loyal.

WOMEN WITH VENUS IN CAPRICORN: Proud and refined, you attract others with your composed dignity. Disliking vulnerability and needing to feel safe before you can express your feelings, you display a strong front. Feeling insecure or inadequate in a relationship forces you to become manipulative in order to regain control. Nevertheless, you can project an attractive sense of self-assurance and are capable of displaying loyalty and a wonderful dry sense of humor.

MEN WITH VENUS IN CAPRICORN: As you do not display your deeper emotions freely, you are usually dignified and controlled in your relationships with others. Practical and down-to-earth partners are particularly attractive to you, especially those who do not rush into expressing their feelings but seem to possess natural class and reserve. You need a partner who is loyal and dependable and willing to take your relationship seriously.

WOMEN WITH VENUS IN AQUARIUS: Usually you have a modern outlook on love and are open to new or current lifestyles. Your intuitive abilities, communal sense, and people skills often allow you to see deeper into human intentions and to read people's thoughts telepathically. You are usually group-oriented and are drawn to the individuals within the group who are independent and self-motivated. You are more inclined to choose a partner who is unconventional or freedom-loving. Conscious of your social standing, however, you want someone who can relate well to your friends.

MEN WITH VENUS IN AQUARIUS: Although independent, you often enjoy being part of a group. The partners you frequently attract are themselves nonconformists or free spirits. As an individual you may not find it easy to settle into a routine or an entirely mundane type of relationship. You may have some unconventional views on the traditional marriage or your partner may hold such views. It is usually important to you that your love relationships are based on friendship.

To read all about your Outer Planets and work out how to use your personalized timetable, go to Section Three, page 789.

♑

Your Personalized Timetable

JUPITER BENEFICIAL
1938 5/5 – 8/8
1938 12/23 – until 1939 2/8
1940 4/28 – 7/17
1940 10/24 – until 1941 3/4
1943 11/17 – until 1944 1/9
1944 7/5 – 9/19
1946 9/20 – 11/6
1950 4/9 – 9/25
1950 11/21 – until 1951 1/21
1952 4/11 – 6/21
1952 12/13 – until 1953 1/28
1955 10/16 – until 1956 2/20
1956 6/12 – 9/3
1958 1/3 – 3/31
1958 9/1 – 10/21
1962 3/21 – 5/13
1962 8/22 – 12/31
1964 3/26 – 6/1
1967 9/26 – until 1968 4/15
1968 4/28 – 8/19
1969 12/10 – until 1970 5/9
1970 8/7 – 10/5
1974 3/3 – 4/18
1974 10/11 – 11/26
1976 3/8 – 5/15
1979 9/9 – until 1980 8/2
1981 11/21 – until 1982 1/24
1982 3/26 – 9/17
1986 2/16 – 3/30
1987 6/30 – 10/9
1988 2/16 – 4/29
1991 8/24 – 11/18
1992 2/11 – 7/14
1993 11/5 – 12/26
1994 5/7 – 8/25
1998 1/30 – 3/13
1999 6/5 – 11/27
2000 1/12 – 4/12
2003 8/8 – 10/25
2004 3/20 – 6/20
2005 10/21 – 12/7
2010 1/13 – 2/25
2011 5/16 – until 2012 3/25

SATURN BENEFICIAL
1939 5/22 – 11/16
1940 2/6 – 6/29
1940 10/27 – until 1941 3/19
1948 8/17 – until 1949 9/21
1953 10/13 – until 1954 1/25
1954 3/11 – 10/9
1964 3/14 – 10/6
1964 11/27 – until 1965 3/9
1969 3/28 – until 1970 5/1
1977 9/27 – until 1978 3/3
1978 6/16 – 11/6
1979 2/12 – 7/27
1982 11/19 – until 1983 5/23
1983 8/8 – 11/14
1993 4/29 – 7/23
1994 1/19 – 4/16
1994 9/3 – until 1995 1/11
1998 5/3 – until 1999 6/8
1999 11/29 – until 2000 2/23
2007 8/1 – until 2008 9/4
2012 1/12 – 3/4
2012 9/26 – 12/24

URANUS BENEFICIAL
1938 1/1 – 4/2
1961 8/15 – until 1965 7/10
1974 11/3 – until 1977 9/8
2003 2/19 – until 2006 1/27

NEPTUNE BENEFICIAL
1955 11/16 – until 1961 8/26
2011 3/3 – Continues

PLUTO BENEFICIAL
1954 9/28 – until 1964 6/27
1982 12/17 – until 1987 10/8

JUPITER CHALLENGING
1939 4/21 – until 1940 2/29
1942 5/23 – 8/2

1944 12/11 – until 1945 2/13
1945 8/3 – 10/20
1951 4/3 – 6/27
1951 9/11 – until 1952 2/9
1953 9/26 – 11/2
1954 5/4 – 7/16
1956 11/12 – until 1957 3/25
1957 7/12 – 10/4
1963 3/18 – 5/28
1963 10/28 – until 1964 1/12
1965 8/20 – 12/20
1966 4/12 – 6/30
1968 10/24 – until 1969 9/18
1975 3/1 – 5/8
1977 7/29 – until 1978 6/14
1980 10/7 – until 1981 9/2
1987 2/13 – 4/21
1989 7/11 – until 1990 5/27
1992 9/21 – 12/16
1993 3/13 – 8/14
1998 6/11 – 8/24
1999 1/24 – 4/4
2001 6/24 – 9/13
2001 12/22 – until 2002 5/7
2004 9/6 – 11/23
2005 4/20 – 7/21
2010 5/12 – 10/11
2010 12/26 – 3/18

SATURN CHALLENGING
1938 1/1 – 4/30
1938 11/17 – until 1939 1/11
1943 9/11 – 11/6
1944 5/19 – until 1945 6/17
1950 10/12 – until 1951 5/8
1951 6/18 – 11/25
1952 3/28 – 8/19
1966 5/2 – 9/24
1967 1/25 – 6/29
1967 8/19 – until 1968 3/8
1973 6/29 – until 1974 7/28
1979 12/2 – until 1980 2/11
1980 8/18 – until 1981 9/28
1996 3/5 – until 1997 4/13
2002 8/11 – 12/13
2003 4/29 – 9/17
2003 12/3 – until 2004 5/30
2009 9/25 – until 2010 11/4
2011 5/1 – 7/25

URANUS CHALLENGING
1947 9/8 – until 1952 5/27
1967 10/5 – until 1971 9/4
2009 5/19 – Continues

NEPTUNE CHALLENGING
1940 10/6 – until 1948 9/13

PLUTO CHALLENGING
1969 10/15 – until 1977 8/3

JUPITER SPECIAL
1948 3/1 – 5/31
1948 10/25 – until 1949 1/7
1960 2/5 – 7/13
1960 9/27 – 12/22
1972 1/17 – 12/6
1984 1/1 – 11/17
1995 12/16 – until 1996 3/2
1996 7/11 – 10/26
2007 11/30 – until 2008 2/10

SATURN SPECIAL
1958 12/1 – until 1960 1/22
1960 9/5 – 9/26
1988 1/4 – until 1989 3/3
1989 6/14 – 11/29

URANUS SPECIAL
1987 2/16 – until 1991 11/30

NEPTUNE SPECIAL
1982 1/23 – until 1990 10/13

PLUTO SPECIAL
2006 2/1 – Continues

December 27

SUN: CAPRICORN • DECANATE: CAPRICORN/SATURN • DEGREE: 4°5–5°5 CAPRICORN • MODE: CARDINAL • ELEMENT: EARTH

Your Personal Powers

Usually easygoing and hardworking with a pragmatic nature, you are an intuitive visionary who needs to feel emotionally secure. Your practical common sense and motivation can help you succeed but your creative side also gives you a unique approach. Willing to invest time and effort in your ideas and plans, you gain power when you act with confidence upon what inspires you or fires your imagination. You also empower yourself when you use your sixth sense and imagination to comprehend the subtle messages you receive in order to create inner peace. A desire to find the ideal or perfect situation and feel emotionally assured imply that you lose some of your powers when a conflict of interests causes you to be indecisive. You may also need to resist a temptation to let lack of clarity or unrealistic plans lead you to self-deception. Nevertheless, being imaginative, optimistic, and practical, you usually have many fortunate ideas. You can achieve success by being forward-thinking and having a good, structured plan to work with.

Your Powers of Attraction in Relationships

People like your easygoing manner, fairness, and warmhearted personality. Being charming and sympathetic with an ability to listen to others, you have no problems attracting friends. You are usually drawn to determined and intelligent individuals who know how to relate well to others. Although you can be very supportive and loving, a tendency to sulk or be stubborn can lead to tension in your personal relationships. Willing to share your knowledge and acumen, you benefit from being involved in group activities that encourage you to broaden your horizons. Since partnerships and being collaborative can further your career and bring success, you benefit from all types of joint ventures. It is important, however, to maintain a good balance of power and not succumb to being overly dependent on people.

Your attractive qualities: confident, broad-minded, shrewd, hardworking, purposeful, strategist, witty, tolerant, contented, persevering, ambitious, direct, creative, idealistic, enterprising, imaginative, intuitive, diplomatic, humanitarian, charming, romantic, common sense, independent

Your less attractive qualities: stubborn, restless, workaholic, secretive, dissatisfied, emotional excesses, easily discour-

aged, moody, lack of purpose, controlling, overconfident, preoccupied with self-fulfillment, self-indulgent, skeptical

Your Venus Power

The planet Venus has a great deal of influence on your powers of attraction. Below are four possible Venus types for women and men. To find your Venus you need to go to page 771, where you will find the Venus table and extra information. The planet Mars also affects your powers of attraction. To find your Mars table and interpretation go to page 761.

WOMEN WITH VENUS IN SCORPIO: Usually you are drawn to partners who are sensual in appearance with strong character. As you are emotionally intense and passionate, personal relationships are probably a major factor in your life. Since you like to be in control, you can at times exhibit some of your less attractive qualities by being willful or domineering. Although you need to feel established and in command in your relationships, you are constantly searching for some higher truth that can bring about a significant transformation.

MEN WITH VENUS IN SCORPIO: You are usually attracted to sensual and passionate partners with strong character. You are often sensitive with deep feelings and magnetic powers of attraction. As a cautious yet devoted and ardent lover, you are likely to seek experiences that are more sexual in nature. You display your less attractive qualities when you project your negative thoughts and resort to being suspicious or possessive. Nevertheless, loyal and loving, you are a sensitive lover.

WOMEN WITH VENUS IN SAGITTARIUS: At your best when being optimistic and generous, you possess a mischievous sense of fun. In relationships your open-minded approach to people and places may attract you to those of a different culture or make you tolerant of the foibles of others. Although warm and enthusiastic when in love, your natural honesty and idealism may inspire you to look for a partner who shares your love of freedom.

MEN WITH VENUS IN SAGITTARIUS: Forward-thinking rather than dwelling on the past, you are looking for a partner who can share your future plans. You enjoy exploring life, whether through travel and mental pursuits or sports and games. Idealistic, you usually prefer the company of a partner who is optimistic and shares your beliefs. In your desire for honesty in relationships, however, be careful not to become tactless. Nevertheless, you are attracted to honest, direct,

and fun-loving partners who have a sense of humor like your own.

WOMEN WITH VENUS IN CAPRICORN: With your natural caution in romantic affairs, you often appear reserved and controlled. You may be shy but try to be more forward, especially if you want to be noticed. When you care about people, however, you are usually willing to put in extra time and energy to preserve the relationship. You are practical and dependable, and a sense of duty can often play a large role in the affairs of your heart. With elegant simplicity, you can attract others with your well-cut clothes and refined manners.

MEN WITH VENUS IN CAPRICORN: In relationships you take love seriously and can be a strong and practical support for friends or partners. You are usually attracted to partners who are as hardworking as you. As you tend not to express your feelings until you feel really secure in a relationship, you may be drawn to those who seem loyal, faithful, and not likely to let you down. As you respect the wisdom of experience, you may be drawn to mature partners or, alternatively, you may act as an authority figure for someone younger.

WOMEN WITH VENUS IN AQUARIUS: When it comes to relationships, others are attracted to your honest, friendly, and easygoing attitude. You really enjoy social interaction with others and may develop a genuine concern for humanity. Usually you present a tolerant and reasonable front in love situations and attempt to view your relationships objectively. If partners become too demanding, however, you can become stubborn and fixed. Friendship may be even more important for you than sexual compatibility.

MEN WITH VENUS IN AQUARIUS: You are sociable and open-minded, and people are attracted by your friendly and relaxed style. Being independent, you value freedom-loving partners who give you the space to be yourself. Others sometimes interpret your detachment as being emotionally cool, but they may not understand your progressive views on relationships. Friendship can sometimes be even more important than earthly passion. Ideally, your partners share your ideas on life and possess the same strong sense of originality as you. Not easily ruffled, you can deal well with difficult situation or moody partners.

To read all about your Outer Planets and work out how to use your personalized timetable, go to Section Three, page 789.

go to Section Three, page 789.

♑

Your Personalized Timetable

JUPITER BENEFICIAL
1938 5/14 – 7/30
1938 12/29 – until 1939 2/13
1940 5/3 – 7/25
1940 10/15 – until 1941 3/10
1943 12/7 – 12/19
1944 7/10 – 9/24
1946 9/25 – 11/11
1950 4/15 – 9/15
1950 12/1 – until 1951 1/26
1952 4/16 – 6/26
1952 12/1 – until 1953 2/9
1955 10/23 – until 1956 2/12
1956 6/20 – 9/8
1958 1/13 – 3/20
1958 9/7 – 10/26
1962 3/25 – 5/21
1962 8/13 – until 1963 1/6
1964 3/30 – 6/6
1967 10/2 – until 1968 3/25
1968 5/19 – 8/24
1969 12/16 – until 1970 4/30
1970 8/15 – 10/10
1974 3/8 – 4/23
1974 9/29 – 12/8
1976 3/13 – 5/20
1979 9/14 – until 1980 8/7
1981 11/27 – until 1982 2/9
1982 3/10 – 9/22
1986 2/20 – 4/4
1987 7/9 – 9/30
1988 2/22 – 5/4
1991 8/29 – 11/28
1992 2/1 – 7/20
1993 11/10 – until 1994 1/2
1994 4/28 – 9/2
1998 2/4 – 3/18
1999 6/11 – 11/16
2000 1/24 – 4/17
2003 8/13 – 10/31
2004 3/11 – 6/28
2005 10/26 – 12/13
2006 6/10 – 8/1
2010 1/18 – 3/1
2011 5/21 – until 2012 3/30

SATURN BENEFICIAL
1939 6/1 – 11/1
1940 2/20 – 7/12
1940 10/12 – until 1941 3/29
1948 8/26 – until 1949 9/30
1950 4/23 – 6/6
1953 10/22 – until 1954 10/18
1964 3/24 – 9/17
1964 12/16 – until 1965 3/18
1969 4/6 – until 1970 5/9
1977 10/7 – until 1978 2/17
1978 6/28 – 11/22
1979 1/26 – 8/6
1982 11/29 – until 1983 5/6
1983 8/24 – 11/23
1984 6/24 – 8/1
1993 5/21 – 6/30
1994 1/28 – 4/28
1994 8/19 – until 1995 1/22
1998 5/12 – 12/14
1999 1/14 – 6/18
1999 11/15 – until 2000 3/7
2007 8/9 – until 2008 9/12
2012 10/5 – Continues

URANUS BENEFICIAL
1938 1/1 – 4/22
1961 9/2 – until 1965 8/2
1974 11/21 – until 1977 9/30
2003 3/10 – until 2006 2/16

NEPTUNE BENEFICIAL
1955 12/24 – until 1961 10/5
2011 4/4 – Continues

PLUTO BENEFICIAL
1955 9/5 – until 1964 8/8
1983 11/5 – until 1988 8/18

JUPITER CHALLENGING
1939 4/27 – until 1940 3/5

1942 5/28 – 8/7
1944 12/25 – until 1945 1/29
1945 8/9 – 10/25
1951 4/8 – 7/8
1951 8/31 – until 1952 2/14
1954 5/9 – 7/21
1956 11/19 – until 1957 3/16
1957 7/19 – 10/9
1963 3/22 – 6/3
1963 10/19 – until 1964 1/20
1965 8/27 – 12/12
1966 4/18 – 7/5
1968 10/30 – until 1969 4/29
1969 6/17 – 9/24
1975 3/6 – 5/13
1977 8/4 – until 1978 1/27
1978 3/15 – 6/18
1980 10/12 – until 1981 9/7
1987 2/17 – 4/26
1989 7/16 – until 1990 6/1
1992 9/26 – 12/26
1993 3/3 – 8/20
1998 6/22 – 8/12
1999 1/29 – 4/9
2001 6/29 – 9/22
2001 12/14 – until 2002 5/13
2004 9/11 – 11/29
2005 4/11 – 7/29
2010 5/18 – 10/2
2011 1/4 – 3/23

SATURN CHALLENGING
1938 1/1 – 5/10
1938 10/29 – until 1939 1/28
1944 5/27 – until 1945 6/26
1950 10/21 – until 1951 4/16
1951 7/10 – 12/7
1952 3/14 – 8/29
1966 5/14 – 9/10
1967 2/5 – until 1968 3/17
1973 7/7 – until 1974 8/6
1975 2/8 – 4/17
1980 1/3 – 1/10
1980 8/27 – until 1981 10/7
1996 3/14 – until 1997 4/22
2002 8/23 – 11/30
2003 5/10 – 10/10
2003 11/11 – until 2004 6/8
2009 10/3 – until 2010 11/14
2011 4/15 – 8/9

URANUS CHALLENGING
1948 6/29 – until 1952 6/16
1967 10/24 – until 1971 9/22
2010 3/24 – Continues

NEPTUNE CHALLENGING
1940 11/9 – until 1949 8/10

PLUTO CHALLENGING
1969 11/22 – until 1977 9/9

JUPITER SPECIAL
1948 3/10 – 5/21
1948 10/31 – until 1949 1/12
1960 2/11 – 12/27
1972 1/22 – 12/10
1984 1/5 – 11/23
1995 12/21 – until 1996 3/8
1996 7/2 – 11/2
2007 12/5 – until 2008 2/16
2008 8/22 – 9/25

SATURN SPECIAL
1958 12/11 – until 1960 1/31
1960 8/7 – 10/24
1988 1/14 – 7/24
1988 10/5 – until 1989 3/20
1989 5/27 – 12/9

URANUS SPECIAL
1987 12/21 – until 1991 12/20

NEPTUNE SPECIAL
1982 3/17 – until 1990 11/30

PLUTO SPECIAL
2006 12/31 – Continues

December 28

Your Personal Powers

Idealistic and purposeful, you are a dynamic individual with sharp perception and a tendency to take life seriously. Ambitious and determined, you have the power to endure. You gain inner strength when you use your concentration and problem-solving skills to quickly grasp ideas and assess situations. Although you are shrewd, you lose some of your power when you allow your mind to rule your heart or be too pragmatic. A tendency to be restless, nervous, or discontented indicates that you can at times also lose some of your power through anxiety and worry. Nevertheless, versatile and imaginative with the ability to lead others, you empower yourself when you combine your enthusiasm and resourceful nature with your creativity. It is vital, however, that you maintain your resolve and stay focused. You can lose some of your power if you allow indecision or lack of faith to undermine your otherwise practical and well-structured mind. You also empower yourself when you succeed by your own merit or when you find a creative outlet for your sensitivity and deep feelings.

Your Powers of Attraction in Relationships

With your charm, dramatic sense, and persuasive speech, you can make a strong impression on others. Sociable, you enjoy mixing with intelligent people who can communicate and exchange information and ideas. Versatile and multitalented, you usually benefit from joining groups that can offer you variety and adventure. Although you possess deep feelings, your strong need for love and self-expression may not always be obvious from the outside. If you become involved in verbal power struggles, you may win the argument but lose the affection you truly want. Although charismatic and friendly, a tendency to be unsettled or indecisive about long-term commitments suggests that you may rationalize your emotions too much. By being spontaneous and learning to trust your feelings or intuition, you can better enjoy your close relationships.

Your attractive qualities: Ambitious, independent, enterprising, progressive, intuitive, daring, creative, sensitive, loyal, compassionate, idealistic, hardworking, single-minded, intelligent, multitalented, well-informed, witty, communication skills, common sense, persuasive, friendly

Your less attractive qualities: uncertain, too reserved, worry, daydreamer, melancholy, bossy, unmotivated, lack of compassion, unrealistic, too forceful, too dependent on others, too serious, self-centered, isolated, too sensitive

Your Venus Power

The planet Venus has a great deal of influence on your powers of attraction. Below are four possible Venus types for women and men. To find your Venus you need to go to page 771, where you will find the Venus table and extra information. The planet Mars also affects your powers of attraction. To find your Mars table and interpretation go to page 761.

WOMEN WITH VENUS IN SCORPIO: Loving and passionate, you are often sensitive with deep feelings and strong powers of attraction. A love for the truth coupled with a tendency to be suspicious can be an influence that motivates you to delve deep into the activities of your partner. When in love or in a relationship that matters, you will often bend over backward to cooperate. Although loyal, guard against losing sight of your own needs and desires.

MEN WITH VENUS IN SCORPIO: As you are emotionally intense and passionate, personal relationships are probably a major factor in your own transformation. Being sensitive yet loyal, you are usually attracted to forceful partners who can express themselves intimately but intensely. Rather than seek easy and simple relationships you are drawn to partners who act as a catalyst for your own internal changes. Through your relationships with your partners you can unravel your own motives and understand your deep-seated feelings or emotional insecurities.

WOMEN WITH VENUS IN SAGITTARIUS: Sociable, warm, and friendly, you possess an honest and frank style in your relationships. Being naturally gregarious, you want others to share your enthusiasm and enjoy encouraging the people you love. You do better when you have a sense of personal freedom within a relationship and are usually generous with the faults of others. You need a partner who can share your need to explore and take risks, whether through travel, education, or recreation.

MEN WITH VENUS IN SAGITTARIUS: When in love you are open and friendly with a need for a partner who can share your adventurous spirit and sense of fun. Be careful, however, that your desire for freedom does not cause you to avoid commitment. You prefer your partners to be positive, direct, and generous in spirit. Being outspoken as well as an idealist, you

usually enjoy a partner with whom you can share your strong opinions. Alternatively, you may wish to explore life together, whether through travel, education, or by having fun.

WOMEN WITH VENUS IN CAPRICORN: Romantically, you do not give your heart easily but hide behind a cool reserve until you feel free to express your emotions. As you take your relationships seriously, you may find yourself drawn to people who are businesslike, resourceful, and practical or who can act as teachers or mentors. Work or career may also be a factor in many of your associations and partnerships. As security can play an important role in your relationships, you are often attracted to partners who are loyal and hardworking.

MEN WITH VENUS IN CAPRICORN: As you admire loyal, hardworking, and dedicated individuals, you probably want a partner who can share your vocational interests or provide you with the sense of security you need. You could even find yourself with a partner who is of a different age group or maturity. Guard against denying your true emotional needs or focusing on your career at the expense of your relationship. You are drawn to reserved partners who display self-control.

WOMEN WITH VENUS IN AQUARIUS: When it comes to relationships, others are attracted to your honest, friendly, and easygoing attitude. You enjoy social interaction and have a genuine concern for others. In fact, at times, your friends may be just as important as your partner. Usually you present a tolerant and reasonable front in love situations and attempt to view your relationships objectively. If partners become too demanding, however, you can become stubborn or awkward. Nevertheless, inventive and progressive, you enjoy the company of like-minded people who can share your original ideas.

MEN WITH VENUS IN AQUARIUS: Friendly and honest, you attract people with your broad-minded approach to life. You usually possess an objective and slightly detached attitude toward affairs of the heart. If you are too removed, however, others can misinterpret your behavior as uncaring. It is often more important to you that your love relationships are based on friendship and honesty than intense passion. As you are generally tolerant and liberal, you may be drawn to less conventional relationships.

To read all about your Outer Planets and work out how to use your personalized timetable, go to Section Three, page 789.

VS

Your Personalized Timetable

JUPITER BENEFICIAL
1938 5/24 – 7/19
1939 1/4 – 2/17
1940 5/7 – 8/3
1940 10/6 – until **1941** 3/16
1944 7/16 – 9/29
1946 9/30 – 11/15
1950 4/21 – 9/6
1950 12/9 – until **1951** 1/31
1952 4/20 – 7/2
1952 11/22 – until **1953** 2/17
1955 10/31 – until **1956** 2/4
1956 6/26 – 9/13
1958 1/26 – 3/7
1958 9/12 – 10/31
1962 3/30 – 5/30
1962 8/4 – until **1963** 1/11
1964 4/4 – 6/11
1967 10/8 – until **1968** 3/14
1968 5/30 – 8/29
1969 12/23 – until **1970** 4/22
1970 8/22 – 10/15
1974 3/12 – 4/29
1974 9/20 – 12/16
1976 3/17 – 5/24
1979 9/19 – until **1980** 8/12
1981 12/2 – until **1982** 6/8
1982 7/17 – 9/28
1986 2/24 – 4/9
1987 7/18 – 9/21
1988 2/27 – 5/8
1991 9/3 – 12/11
1992 1/19 – 7/26
1993 11/15 – until **1994** 1/9
1994 4/20 – 9/8
1998 2/8 – 3/22
1999 6/16 – 11/7
2000 2/1 – 4/21
2003 8/18 – 11/7
2004 3/3 – 7/5
2005 10/30 – 12/18
2006 5/29 – 8/12
2010 1/22 – 3/5
2011 5/26 – until **2012** 4/4

SATURN BENEFICIAL
1939 6/11 – 10/19
1940 3/2 – 7/28
1940 9/26 – until **1941** 4/7
1948 9/3 – until **1949** 10/8
1950 4/3 – 6/25
1953 10/31 – until **1954** 10/27
1964 4/3 – 9/2
1964 12/28 – until **1965** 3/27
1965 10/20 – 12/8
1969 4/14 – until **1970** 5/17
1977 10/18 – until **1978** 2/5
1978 7/8 – until **1979** 8/15
1982 12/9 – until **1983** 4/23
1983 9/5 – 12/2
1984 6/1 – 8/22
1994 2/6 – 5/12
1994 8/4 – until **1995** 1/31
1998 5/21 – 11/21
1999 2/4 – 6/28
1999 11/2 – until **2000** 3/18
2007 8/17 – until **2008** 9/20
2012 10/14 – Continues

URANUS BENEFICIAL
1938 1/1 – until **1939** 2/11
1961 9/19 – until **1965** 8/19
1974 12/10 – until **1977** 10/17
2003 3/30 – until **2006** 12/12

NEPTUNE BENEFICIAL
1956 11/16 – until **1962** 8/25
2012 3/1 – Continues

PLUTO BENEFICIAL
1955 10/12 – until **1965** 6/30
1983 12/3 – until **1988** 9/26

JUPITER CHALLENGING
1939 5/1 – until **1940** 3/10
1942 6/1 – 8/12

1945 8/15 – 10/30
1951 4/12 – 7/25
1951 8/14 – until **1952** 2/19
1954 5/14 – 7/25
1956 11/26 – until **1957** 3/8
1957 7/26 – 10/14
1963 3/26 – 6/9
1963 10/11 – until **1964** 1/27
1965 9/3 – 12/5
1966 4/24 – 7/9
1968 11/4 – until **1969** 4/17
1969 6/28 – 9/28
1975 3/10 – 5/18
1977 8/9 – until **1978** 1/16
1978 3/27 – 6/23
1980 10/17 – until **1981** 9/12
1987 2/22 – 4/30
1989 7/21 – until **1990** 6/6
1992 10/1 – until **1993** 1/8
1993 2/18 – 8/26
1998 7/13 – 7/22
1999 2/3 – 4/13
2001 7/4 – 10/1
2001 12/4 – until **2002** 5/18
2004 9/16 – 12/6
2005 4/3 – 8/5
2010 5/24 – 9/24
2011 1/11 – 3/27

SATURN CHALLENGING
1938 1/1 – 5/20
1938 10/16 – until **1939** 2/9
1944 6/5 – until **1945** 7/4
1950 10/31 – until **1951** 4/2
1951 7/23 – 12/22
1952 2/27 – 9/8
1966 5/27 – 8/26
1967 2/14 – until **1968** 3/25
1973 7/16 – until **1974** 2/12
1974 3/15 – 8/15
1975 1/24 – 5/1
1980 9/5 – until **1981** 10/15
1996 3/22 – until **1997** 4/30
1997 11/23 – until **1998** 1/8
2002 9/7 – 11/15
2003 5/18 – until **2004** 6/16
2009 10/12 – until **2010** 5/16
2010 6/14 – 11/25
2011 4/2 – 8/20

URANUS CHALLENGING
1948 7/17 – until **1952** 7/3
1967 11/13 – until **1971** 10/8
2010 4/12 – Continues

NEPTUNE CHALLENGING
1941 10/6 – until **1949** 9/13

PLUTO CHALLENGING
1970 10/12 – until **1978** 7/14

JUPITER SPECIAL
1948 3/22 – 5/9
1948 11/5 – until **1949** 1/16
1960 2/17 – 6/25
1960 10/13 – 12/31
1972 1/27 – 12/15
1984 1/10 – 11/28
1995 12/25 – until **1996** 3/16
1996 6/24 – 11/8
2007 12/10 – until **2008** 2/21
2008 8/8 – 10/8

SATURN SPECIAL
1958 12/19 – until **1960** 2/10
1960 7/22 – 11/7
1988 1/24 – 7/7
1988 10/21 – until **1989** 12/18

URANUS SPECIAL
1988 1/7 – until **1992** 1/6

NEPTUNE SPECIAL
1983 1/23 – until **1991** 10/5

PLUTO SPECIAL
2007 1/30 – Continues

December 29

SUN: CAPRICORN • DECANATE: CAPRICORN/SATURN • DEGREE: 6°5–7°5 CAPRICORN • MODE: CARDINAL • ELEMENT: EARTH

Your Personal Powers

Imaginative and charming, you are a sensitive and intuitive individual with an idealistic nature and romantic inclinations. Your ruler, Saturn, grants you determination, practical abilities, and endurance. As an imaginative and smart person you can grasp ideas quickly, especially when they inspire you to be creative and expressive. Although you are shrewd and independent, being aware of others' needs implies that you are a charming and persuasive strategist with an understanding of how to market or promote ideas. When you are faced with challenges, however, you need to balance your idealism with a realistic attitude and resist an inclination toward pessimism or negative thinking. You lose some of your power when you become critical or skeptical about your situation. Rather than resort to moodiness, you empower yourself when you use your natural tact and communicate your thoughts. Since you are usually easygoing and agreeable, you can create harmony around you and show willingness to cooperate with others. The combination of your pragmatism, keen intellegence, and excellent communication skills can bring you success.

Your Powers of Attraction in Relationships

People are attracted to your charismatic personality and admire your modest and naturally refined nature. Having a pleasant voice and a nice appearance often adds to your attractive qualities. You are usually drawn to strong-willed, dramatic, and mentally quick individuals who show their intelligence and knowledge. Alternatively, you may be attracted to enterprising and clever people who have a good head for business and bright ideas. Since you do not feel whole and secure when alone, you usually prefer to be in a relationship or partnership. In order to establish happy relations with others, you may need to overcome an inclination to be cynical or doubtful. Nevertheless, loyal and idealistic by nature, once you commit yourself to your partner, you will stand firmly by him or her and make sure that your relationship is safe and secure.

Your attractive qualities: charismatic, friendly, gracious, agreeable, communicative, idealistic, romantic, balanced, creative, inspired, intuitive, attention to detail, faithful, graceful, diplomatic, well-informed, imaginative, humanitarian, independent, trusting, conscientious, hardworking, considerate

Your less attractive qualities: unfocused, uncertain, too sensitive, stubborn, opinionated, mistrusting, jealous, moody, shy, lack of balance, nervous, dependent, inner fears, secretive

Your Venus Power

The planet Venus has a great deal of influence on your powers of attraction. Below are four possible Venus types for women and men. To find your Venus you need to go to page 771, where you will find the Venus table and extra information. The planet Mars also affects your powers of attraction. To find your Mars table and interpretation go to page 761.

WOMEN WITH VENUS IN SCORPIO: Loving and passionate, you are often sensitive with deep feelings and strong powers of attraction. A love for the truth coupled with a tendency to be suspicious can be an influence that motivates you to delve deep into the activities of your partner. When in love or in a relationship that matters, you will often bend over backward to cooperate. Although loyal, guard against losing sight of your own needs and desires.

MEN WITH VENUS IN SCORPIO: As you are emotionally intense and passionate, personal relationships are probably a major factor in your own transformation. Being sensitive yet loyal, you are usually attracted to forceful partners who can express themselves intimately but intensely. Rather than seek easy and simple relationships you are drawn to partners who act as a catalyst for your own internal changes. Through your relationships with your partners you can unravel your own motives and understand your deep-seated feelings or emotional insecurities.

WOMEN WITH VENUS IN SAGITTARIUS: Sociable, warm, and friendly, you possess an honest and frank style in your relationships. Being naturally gregarious, you want others to share your enthusiasm and enjoy encouraging the people you love. You do better when you have a sense of personal freedom within a relationship and are usually generous with the faults of others. You need a partner who can share your need to explore and take risks, whether through travel, education, or recreation.

MEN WITH VENUS IN SAGITTARIUS: When in love, you are open and friendly with a need for a partner who can share your adventurous spirit and sense of fun. Be careful, however, that your desire for freedom does not cause you to avoid com-

mitment. You prefer your partners to be positive, direct, and generous in spirit. Being outspoken as well as an idealist, you usually enjoy a partner with whom you can share your strong opinions. Alternatively, you may wish to explore life together whether through travel, education, or by having fun.

WOMEN WITH VENUS IN CAPRICORN: Romantically, you do not give your heart easily but hide behind a cool reserve until you feel free to express your emotions. As you take your relationships seriously, you may find yourself drawn to people who are businesslike, resourceful, and practical or can act as teachers or mentors. Work or career may also be a factor in many of your associations and partnerships. As security can play an important role in your relationships, you are often attracted to partners who are loyal and hardworking.

MEN WITH VENUS IN CAPRICORN: As you admire loyal, hardworking, and dedicated individuals, you probably want a partner who can share your vocational interests or provide you with the sense of security you need. You could even find yourself with a partner who is of a different age group or maturity. Guard against denying your true emotional needs or focusing on your career at the expense of your relationship. You are drawn to reserved partners who display self-control.

WOMEN WITH VENUS IN AQUARIUS: When it comes to relationships, others are attracted to your honest, friendly, and easygoing attitude. You enjoy social interaction and have a genuine concern for others. In fact, at times, your friends may be just as important as your partner. You usually present a tolerant and reasonable front in love situations and attempt to view your relationships objectively. If partners become too demanding, however, you can become stubborn or awkward. Nevertheless, inventive and progressive, you enjoy the company of like-minded people who can share your original ideas.

MEN WITH VENUS IN AQUARIUS: Friendly and honest, you attract people with your broad-minded approach to life. You usually possess an objective and slightly detached attitude to affairs of the heart. If you are too removed, however, others can misinterpret your behavior as uncaring. It is often more important to you that your love relationships are based on friendship and honesty rather than intense passion. As you are generally tolerant and liberal, you may be drawn to less conventional relationships.

To read all about your Outer Planets and work out how to use your personalized timetable, go to Section Three, page 789.

VŞ

Your Personalized Timetable

JUPITER BENEFICIAL
1938 6/11 – 7/1
1939 1/9 – 2/22
1940 5/12 – 8/16
1940 9/23 – until 1941 3/21
1944 7/21 – 10/4
1946 10/5 – 11/20
1950 4/27 – 8/29
1950 12/16 – until 1951 2/5
1952 4/25 – 7/8
1952 11/14 – until 1953 2/25
1955 11/8 – until 1956 1/26
1956 7/2 – 9/18
1958 9/18 – 11/4
1962 4/4 – 6/12
1962 7/21 – until 1963 1/17
1964 4/8 – 6/16
1967 10/14 – until 1968 3/5
1968 6/8 – 9/2
1969 12/30 – until 1970 4/13
1970 8/29 – 10/20
1974 3/17 – 5/5
1974 9/11 – 12/24
1976 3/22 – 5/29
1979 9/24 – until 1980 8/17
1981 12/8 – until 1982 5/25
1982 7/31 – 10/3
1986 3/1 – 4/14
1987 7/31 – 9/8
1988 3/4 – 5/13
1991 9/7 – until 1992 7/31
1993 11/20 – until 1994 1/18
1994 4/11 – 9/14
1998 2/13 – 3/27
1999 6/22 – 10/30
2000 2/9 – 4/26
2003 8/23 – 11/14
2004 2/24 – 7/12
2005 11/4 – 12/24
2006 5/20 – 8/22
2010 1/27 – 3/10
2011 5/31 – until 2012 4/8

SATURN BENEFICIAL
1939 6/23 – 10/5
1940 3/12 – until 1941 4/15
1948 9/11 – until 1949 10/18
1950 3/19 – 7/9
1953 11/8 – until 1954 11/5
1964 4/14 – 8/19
1965 1/9 – 4/5
1965 9/30 – 12/27
1969 6/22 – until 1970 5/26
1977 11/1 – until 1978 1/21
1978 7/18 – until 1979 8/24
1982 12/21 – until 1983 4/9
1983 9/16 – 12/12
1984 5/16 – 9/6
1994 2/15 – 6/3
1994 7/13 – until 1995 2/9
1998 5/31 – 11/6
1999 2/18 – 7/11
1999 10/19 – until 2000 3/28
2007 8/26 – until 2008 9/29
2009 5/3 – 5/30
2012 10/23 – Continues

URANUS BENEFICIAL
1938 1/1 – until 1939 3/18
1961 10/9 – until 1965 9/5
1975 1/7 – until 1977 11/4
2003 4/25 – until 2007 1/15

NEPTUNE BENEFICIAL
1956 12/21 – until 1962 10/5
2012 4/1 – Continues

PLUTO BENEFICIAL
1956 9/15 – until 1965 8/10
1984 1/21 – until 1988 10/25

JUPITER CHALLENGING
1939 5/6 – 11/14

1939 12/5 – until 1940 3/14
1942 6/6 – 8/17
1945 8/20 – 11/4
1951 4/17 – until 1952 2/24
1954 5/19 – 7/30
1956 12/4 – until 1957 2/28
1957 8/1 – 10/19
1963 3/31 – 6/16
1963 10/3 – until 1964 2/2
1965 9/12 – 11/26
1966 4/30 – 7/14
1968 11/10 – until 1969 4/7
1969 7/8 – 10/3
1975 3/14 – 5/23
1975 11/26 – 12/24
1977 8/15 – until 1978 1/7
1978 4/5 – 6/28
1980 10/22 – until 1981 9/17
1987 2/26 – 5/5
1989 7/26 – until 1990 6/11
1992 10/6 – until 1993 8/31
1999 2/8 – 4/17
2001 7/8 – 10/14
2001 11/21 – until 2002 5/24
2004 9/20 – 12/13
2005 3/25 – 8/12
2010 5/30 – 9/16
2011 1/17 – 3/31

SATURN CHALLENGING
1938 1/1 – 5/30
1938 10/2 – until 1939 2/20
1944 6/13 – until 1945 7/12
1950 11/10 – until 1951 3/19
1951 8/4 – until 1952 9/17
1966 6/14 – 8/7
1967 2/24 – until 1968 4/2
1973 7/24 – until 1974 1/20
1974 4/6 – 8/25
1975 1/10 – 5/13
1980 9/14 – until 1981 10/24
1996 3/30 – until 1997 5/10
1997 11/3 – until 1998 1/27
2003 5/27 – until 2004 6/25
2009 10/21 – until 2010 4/7
2010 7/8 – 12/7
2011 3/19 – 8/31

URANUS CHALLENGING
1948 8/6 – until 1953 4/30
1967 12/18 – until 1972 8/6
2010 5/3 – Continues

NEPTUNE CHALLENGING
1941 11/8 – until 1950 8/9

PLUTO CHALLENGING
1970 11/15 – until 1978 8/30

JUPITER SPECIAL
1948 11/10 – until 1949 1/21
1960 2/24 – 6/17
1960 10/20 – until 1961 1/5
1972 2/2 – 8/6
1972 9/13 – 12/20
1984 1/15 – 12/3
1995 12/30 – until 1996 3/24
1996 6/15 – 11/14
2007 12/14 – until 2008 2/27
2008 7/28 – 10/18

SATURN SPECIAL
1958 12/28 – until 1960 2/21
1960 7/7 – 11/20
1988 2/3 – 6/22
1988 11/2 – until 1989 12/27

URANUS SPECIAL
1988 1/26 – until 1992 11/11

NEPTUNE SPECIAL
1983 3/8 – until 1991 11/29

PLUTO SPECIAL
2007 12/30 – Continues

December 30

SUN: CAPRICORN • DECANATE: CAPRICORN/SATURN • DEGREE: 7°5–8°5 CAPRICORN • MODE: CARDINAL • ELEMENT: EARTH

Your Personal Powers

Energetic, idealistic, and sensitive, you are a bright and motivated individual with an affectionate nature and strong desires. Although you are often independent and hold unconventional views, in order to achieve material success and status you need to remain dispassionate and detached, diplomatic rather than controversial. Your ruling planet, Saturn, grants you toughness, the determination to succeed, and the power to overcome challenges. Your unique outlook, keen perception, and quick mental abilities indicate that you have foresight and the ability to synthesis ideas as well as think creatively. Keen on progress or initiating new projects, you gain power when you utilize your fortunate ideas. Although you have the strength to follow your convictions, once you have made up your mind, a tendency to worry or be unsure warns that you can miss good opportunities if you are indecisive or scattered. You therefore empower yourself by following your strong instincts and staying focused. As your actions can encourage or inspire others, you also gain power when you feel exuberant and reveal your loving and affectionate nature.

Your Powers of Attraction in Relationships

People admire your charismatic and dynamic personality. When you feel inspired, you generate a great deal of warmth with your enthusiasm. As a charming and tactful individual, you are often an excellent networker who enjoys socializing and who is capable of mixing business with pleasure. With your foresight and ability to see financial opportunities, you are usually attracted to enterprising and determined individuals with good business acumen and executive abilities. Alternatively, you may be drawn to creative and idealistic partners who share your views and beliefs. Although to others you may sometimes appear restless or reserved, you possess powerful inner feelings and desires. When these deep emotions are directed into selfless love and helping others, your vision and high ideals can prove to be a remarkable force for good.

Your attractive qualities: practical, astute, strong-willed, loyal, friendly, well-informed, good conversationalist, hardworking, empathy, creative, amusing or witty, intuitive, fun-loving, clever, independent, gregarious, harmonious, sharing, trusting, engaging, diplomatic

Your less attractive qualities: indecisive, obstinate, restless, moody, skeptical, self-centered, impatient, worried, temperamental, jealous, confusion, scattered, insecure, indifferent, overindulgent

Your Venus Power

The planet Venus has a great deal of influence on your powers of attraction. Below are four possible Venus types for women and men. To find your Venus you need to go to page 771, where you will find the Venus table and extra information. The planet Mars also affects your powers of attraction. To find your Mars table and interpretation go to page 761.

WOMEN WITH VENUS IN SCORPIO: You are usually drawn to partners who are sensual in appearance with a strong character. As you are emotionally intense and passionate, personal relationships are probably a major factor in your life. Since you like to be in control, you can at times exhibit some of your less attractive qualities by being willful or domineering. Although you need to feel established and in command in your relationships, you are constantly searching for some higher truth that can bring about a significant transformation.

MEN WITH VENUS IN SCORPIO: Usually you are attracted to sensual and passionate partners with strong character. You are often sensitive with deep feelings and magnetic powers of attraction. As a cautious yet devoted and ardent lover, you are likely to seek experiences that are more sexual in nature. You display your less attractive qualities when you project your negative thoughts and resort to being suspicious or possessive. Nevertheless, loyal and loving, you are a sensitive lover.

WOMEN WITH VENUS IN SAGITTARIUS: At your best when being optimistic and generous, you possess a mischievous sense of fun. In relationships your open-minded approach to people and places may attract you to those of a different culture or make you tolerant of the foibles of others. Although warm and enthusiastic when in love, your natural honesty and idealism may inspire you to look for a partner who shares your love of freedom.

MEN WITH VENUS IN SAGITTARIUS: Forward-thinking rather than dwelling on the past, you are looking for a partner who can share your future plans. You enjoy exploring life whether through travel and mental pursuits or sports and games. Idealistic, you usually prefer the company of a partner who is optimistic and shares your beliefs. In your desire for honesty in relationships, however, be careful not to become

tactless. Nevertheless, you are attracted to honest, direct, and fun-loving partners with a sense of humor like your own.

WOMEN WITH VENUS IN CAPRICORN: Proud and refined, you attract others with your composed dignity. Disliking vulnerability and needing to feel safe before you can express your feelings, you display a strong front. Feeling insecure or inadequate in relationships may force you to become manipulative in order to regain control. Nevertheless, you can project an attractive sense of self-assurance and are capable of displaying loyalty and a wonderful dry sense of humor.

MEN WITH VENUS IN CAPRICORN: As you do not display your deeper emotions freely, you are usually dignified and controlled in your relationships with others. Practical and down-to-earth partners are particularly attractive to you, especially those who do not rush into expressing their feelings but seem to possess natural class and reserve. You need a partner who is loyal and dependable and willing to take your relationship seriously.

WOMEN WITH VENUS IN AQUARIUS: Usually you have a modern outlook on love and are open to new or current lifestyles. Your intuitive abilities, communal sense, and people skills often allow you to see deeper into human intentions and to read people's thoughts telepathically. You are usually group-oriented and are drawn to individuals within the group who are independent and self-motivated. You are more inclined to choose a partner who is unconventional or freedom-loving. Conscious of your social standing, however, you want someone who can relate well to your friends.

MEN WITH VENUS IN AQUARIUS: Although independent, you often enjoy being part of a group. The partners you frequently attract are themselves nonconformists or free spirits. As an individual you may not find it easy to settle into a routine or an entirely mundane type of relationship. You may have some unconventional views on traditional marriage or your partner may hold such views. It is usually important to you that your love relationships are based on friendship.

To read all about your Outer Planets and work out how to use your personalized timetable, go to Section Three, page 789.

♍

Your Personalized Timetable

JUPITER BENEFICIAL
1939 1/14 – 2/26
1940 5/16 – until 1941 3/26
1944 7/26 – 10/9
1946 10/10 – 11/25
1950 5/3 – 8/21
1950 12/22 – until 1951 2/9
1952 4/29 – 7/14
1952 11/7 – until 1953 3/3
1955 11/18 – until 1956 1/16
1956 7/8 – 9/23
1958 9/23 – 11/9
1962 4/9 – 10/16
1962 11/10 – until 1963 1/21
1964 4/12 – 6/21
1967 10/20 – until 1968 2/26
1968 6/16 – 9/7
1970 1/6 – 4/5
1970 9/4 – 10/24
1974 3/21 – 5/11
1974 9/4 – 12/30
1976 3/26 – 6/2
1979 9/29 – until 1980 8/22
1981 12/13 – until 1982 5/15
1982 8/10 – 10/8
1986 3/5 – 4/19
1986 10/31 – 11/16
1988 3/9 – 5/17
1991 9/12 – until 1992 8/5
1993 11/25 – until 1994 1/27
1994 4/1 – 9/20
1998 2/17 – 3/31
1999 6/29 – 10/22
2000 2/15 – 4/30
2003 8/27 – 11/21
2004 2/16 – 7/18
2005 11/9 – 12/30
2006 5/11 – 8/29
2010 1/31 – 3/14
2011 6/5 – until 2012 4/13

SATURN BENEFICIAL
1939 7/7 – 9/20
1940 3/21 – until 1941 4/24
1948 9/20 – until 1949 4/1
1949 5/31 – 10/28
1950 3/6 – 7/21
1953 11/17 – until 1954 6/13
1954 7/30 – 11/13
1964 4/26 – 8/5
1965 1/19 – 4/15
1965 9/16 – until 1966 1/9
1969 4/30 – until 1970 6/3
1970 12/27 – until 1971 2/6
1977 11/19 – until 1978 1/2
1978 7/27 – until 1979 9/1
1983 1/3 – 3/24
1983 9/25 – 12/22
1984 5/3 – 9/18
1994 2/23 – until 1995 2/18
1998 6/10 – 10/24
1999 3/2 – 7/25
1999 10/4 – until 2000 4/6
2007 9/3 – until 2008 10/8
2009 4/9 – 6/23
2012 10/31 – Continues

URANUS BENEFICIAL
1938 1/1 – until 1939 4/8
1961 11/5 – until 1966 6/30
1975 10/31 – until 1978 9/2
2004 2/27 – until 2007 2/5

NEPTUNE BENEFICIAL
1957 11/15 – until 1963 8/22
2012 5/22 – Continues

PLUTO BENEFICIAL
1956 10/25 – until 1966 6/30
1984 11/20 – until 1989 9/12

JUPITER CHALLENGING
1939 5/12 – 10/29

1939 12/21 – until 1940 3/18
1942 6/10 – 8/23
1943 2/16 – 4/5
1945 8/25 – 11/9
1951 4/22 – until 1952 2/29
1954 5/24 – 8/4
1956 12/14 – until 1957 2/18
1957 8/7 – 10/24
1963 4/4 – 6/23
1963 9/25 – until 1964 2/8
1965 9/22 – 11/15
1966 5/6 – 7/18
1968 11/16 – until 1969 3/30
1969 7/16 – 10/8
1975 3/19 – 5/28
1975 11/12 – until 1976 1/7
1977 8/21 – 12/30
1978 4/12 – 7/2
1980 10/27 – until 1981 9/22
1987 3/3 – 5/9
1989 7/31 – until 1990 6/16
1992 10/11 – until 1993 9/5
1999 2/13 – 4/22
2001 7/13 – until 2002 5/29
2004 9/25 – 12/21
2005 3/17 – 8/18
2010 6/7 – 9/8
2011 1/23 – 4/5

SATURN CHALLENGING
1938 1/15 – 6/12
1938 9/18 – until 1939 3/2
1944 6/21 – until 1945 7/20
1950 11/21 – until 1951 3/6
1951 8/14 – until 1952 9/26
1967 3/4 – until 1968 4/10
1973 8/2 – until 1974 1/6
1974 4/20 – 9/4
1974 12/29 – until 1975 5/23
1980 9/22 – until 1981 11/2
1982 5/22 – 7/15
1996 4/8 – until 1997 5/19
1997 10/20 – until 1998 2/8
2003 6/4 – until 2004 7/3
2009 10/30 – until 2010 4/6
2010 7/22 – 12/21
2011 3/3 – 9/9

URANUS CHALLENGING
1948 9/3 – until 1953 5/25
1968 9/30 – until 1972 8/28
2010 5/31 – Continues

NEPTUNE CHALLENGING
1942 10/6 – until 1950 9/13

PLUTO CHALLENGING
1971 10/7 – until 1978 9/27

JUPITER SPECIAL
1948 11/15 – until 1949 1/25
1960 3/2 – 6/9
1960 10/26 – until 1961 1/9
1972 2/7 – 7/23
1972 9/26 – 12/24
1984 1/20 – 12/8
1996 1/3 – 4/2
1996 6/5 – 11/19
2007 12/19 – until 2008 3/3
2008 7/20 – 10/26

SATURN SPECIAL
1959 1/6 – until 1960 3/4
1960 6/23 – 11/30
1988 2/15 – 6/8
1988 11/13 – until 1990 1/5

URANUS SPECIAL
1988 2/17 – until 1992 12/4

NEPTUNE SPECIAL
1984 1/22 – until 1991 12/28

PLUTO SPECIAL
2008 1/29 – Continues

591

December 31

Your Personal Powers

Independent and talented, you are a determined individual with an imaginative mind, strong instincts, and the potential for inner wisdom. Usually practical and hardworking, you can be extremely persistent in pursuing your objectives. Your patience and concentrated effort therefore usually guarantee success. You lose some of your power, however, if you let a lack of faith make you feel insecure or indecisive. Your ruling planet, Saturn, grants you determination and puts accomplishment high on your list of priorities. By combining your tenacity with modesty and sincerity, you can achieve a great deal. With your powerful projection and strong opinions, you can also be persuasive and inspire or impress others. You gain power by resisting a tendency to vacillate between being mercenary or profoundly idealistic. Naturally dramatic, you can lose some of your charm when you take issues too seriously or overreact to situations. Nevertheless, resourceful and self-reliant, you empower yourself when you practice self-discipline. When you focus your strong willpower and inner drive on success, you can achieve remarkable results.

Your Powers of Attraction in Relationships

Highly intuitive, you have a natural ability to assess people's moods and feelings. Although your compelling charm and natural dramatic sense can help you captivate an audience or make you stand out in a crowd, your modesty and concern for others makes you popular. Usually you are attracted to strong individuals who share your enthusiasm and ideals. Inspired by knowledge and wisdom, you often seek the company of intelligent people who can inspire you with their ideas or further your development. Although you may sometimes experience anxiety or become too self-centered, you are usually a warm, reliable, and affectionate partner and a devoted friend. When centered on your own goals, you can be single-minded and quite demanding, expecting others to support your ideas or projects. You will always attract many friends and admirers.

Your attractive qualities: charismatic, original, independent, constructive, persistent, practical, willpower, conversationalist, reliable, hardworking, ambitious, dramatic, leadership, organized, dedicated, self-disciplined, imaginative, optimistic, enterprising, patient, multitalented, engaging

Your less attractive qualities: insecure, impatient, suspicious, selfish, stubborn, anxious, insecure, indecisive, selfish, too sensitive, pessimistic, mercenary, too serious, emotionally blocked, melodramatic

Your Venus Power

The planet Venus has a great deal of influence on your powers of attraction. Below are four possible Venus types for women and men. To find your Venus you need to go to page 771, where you will find the Venus table and extra information. The planet Mars also affects your powers of attraction. To find your Mars table and interpretation go to page 761.

WOMEN WITH VENUS IN SCORPIO: You are usually drawn to partners who are sensual in appearance with a strong character. As you are emotionally intense and passionate, personal relationships are probably a major factor in your life. Since you like to be in control, you can at times exhibit some of your less attractive qualities by being willful or domineering. Although you need to feel established and in command in your relationships, you are constantly searching for some higher truth that can bring about a significant transformation.

MEN WITH VENUS IN SCORPIO: You are usually attracted to sensual and passionate partners with strong character. You are often sensitive with deep feelings and magnetic powers of attraction. As a cautious yet devoted and ardent lover, you are likely to seek experiences that are more sexual in nature. You display your less attractive qualities when you project your negative thoughts and resort to being suspicious or possessive. Nevertheless, loyal and loving, you are a sensitive lover.

WOMEN WITH VENUS IN SAGITTARIUS: At your best when being optimistic and generous, you possess a mischievous sense of fun. In relationships your open-minded approach to people and places may attract you to those of a different culture or make you tolerant of the foibles of others. Warm and enthusiastic when in love, your natural honesty and idealism may inspire you to look for a partner who shares your love of freedom.

MEN WITH VENUS IN SAGITTARIUS: Forward-thinking rather than dwelling on the past, you are looking for a partner who can share your future plans. You enjoy exploring life whether through travel and mental pursuits or sports and games. Idealistic, you usually prefer the company of a partner who is optimistic and shares your beliefs. In your desire for

honesty in relationships, however, be careful not to become tactless. Nevertheless, you are attracted to honest, direct, and fun-loving partners with sense of humor like your own.

WOMEN WITH VENUS IN CAPRICORN: With your natural caution in romantic affairs, you often appear reserved and controlled. If shy, try to be more forward, especially if you want to be noticed. When you care about people, however, you are usually willing to put in extra time and energy to preserve the relationship. Being practical and dependable, a sense of duty can often play a large role in affairs of your heart. With elegant simplicity, you can attract others with your well-cut clothes and refined manners.

MEN WITH VENUS IN CAPRICORN: In relationships you take love seriously and can be a strong and practical support for friends or partners. You are usually attracted to partners who are as hardworking as you. As you tend not to express your feelings until you feel really secure in a relationship, you may be drawn to those who seem loyal, faithful, and not likely to let you down. As you respect the wisdom of experience, you may be drawn to mature partners or, alternatively, you may act as an authority figure for someone younger.

WOMEN WITH VENUS IN AQUARIUS: When it comes to relationships, others are attracted to your honest, friendly, and easygoing attitude. You really enjoy social interaction with others and may develop a genuine concern for humanity. Usually you present a tolerant and reasonable front in love situations and attempt to view your relationships objectively. If partners become too demanding, however, you can become stubborn and fixed. Friendship may be even more important for you than sexual compatibility.

MEN WITH VENUS IN AQUARIUS: You are sociable and open-minded, and people are attracted by your friendly and relaxed style. Being independent, you value freedom-loving partners who give you the space to be yourself. Others sometimes interpret your detachment as being emotionally cool, but they may not understand your progressive views on relationships. Friendship can sometimes be even more important than earthly passion. Ideally, your partners share your ideas on life and possess the same strong sense of originality as you. Not easily ruffled, you can deal well with difficult situation or moody partners.

To read all about your Outer Planets and work out how to use your personalized timetable, go to Section Three, page 789.

♍

Your Personalized Timetable

JUPITER BENEFICIAL
1939 1/18 – 3/2
1940 5/21 – until 1941 3/31
1944 7/31 – 10/15
1946 10/15 – 11/30
1950 5/11 – 8/13
1950 12/28 – until 1951 2/13
1952 5/3 – 7/21
1952 10/30 – until 1953 3/9
1955 12/3 – until 1956 1/2
1956 7/13 – 9/28
1958 9/28 – 11/14
1962 4/14 – 10/1
1962 11/26 – until 1963 1/26
1964 4/16 – 6/26
1964 12/17 – until 1965 2/3
1967 10/26 – until 1968 2/18
1968 6/23 – 9/12
1970 1/16 – 3/26
1970 9/10 – 10/29
1974 3/26 – 5/18
1974 8/27 – until 1975 1/5
1976 3/31 – 6/7
1979 10/5 – until 1980 4/2
1980 5/20 – 8/27
1981 12/19 – until 1982 5/6
1982 8/18 – 10/13
1986 3/9 – 4/24
1986 10/13 – 12/4
1988 3/13 – 5/21
1991 9/17 – until 1992 8/11
1993 11/30 – until 1994 2/10
1994 3/18 – 9/26
1998 2/21 – 4/5
1999 7/5 – 10/14
2000 2/21 – 5/4
2003 9/1 – 12/1
2004 2/6 – 7/24
2005 11/14 – until 2006 1/6
2006 5/3 – 9/5
2010 2/5 – 3/18
2011 6/10 – 12/5
2012 1/15 – 4/17

SATURN BENEFICIAL
1939 7/31 – 8/26
1940 3/29 – until 1941 5/2
1948 9/28 – until 1949 3/15
1949 6/16 – 11/8
1950 2/21 – 7/31
1953 11/26 – until 1954 5/23
1954 8/18 – 11/22
1964 5/12 – 7/19
1965 1/28 – 4/25
1965 9/2 – until 1966 1/19
1969 5/8 – until 1970 6/12
1970 12/8 – until 1971 2/25
1978 8/4 – until 1979 9/9
1983 1/24 – 3/3
1983 10/4 – until 1984 1/3
1984 4/19 – 9/28
1994 3/4 – until 1995 2/26
1998 6/21 – 10/11
1999 3/11 – 8/22
1999 9/7 – until 2000 4/14
2007 9/11 – until 2008 10/17
2009 3/25 – 7/8
2012 11/9 – Continues

URANUS BENEFICIAL
1938 1/1 – until 1939 4/27
1962 8/28 – until 1966 7/25
1975 11/16 – until 1978 9/25
2004 3/16 – until 2007 2/23

NEPTUNE BENEFICIAL
1957 12/18 – until 1963 10/3

PLUTO BENEFICIAL
1957 9/23 – until 1966 8/9
1984 12/21 – until 1989 10/13

JUPITER CHALLENGING
1939 5/17 – 10/18
1939 12/31 – until 1940 3/23
1942 6/15 – 8/28

1943 2/5 – 4/16
1945 8/30 – 11/14
1951 4/26 – until 1952 3/5
1954 5/29 – 8/9
1956 12/26 – until 1957 2/6
1957 8/13 – 10/28
1963 4/8 – 7/1
1963 9/17 – until 1964 2/14
1965 10/9 – 10/30
1966 5/11 – 7/23
1968 11/23 – until 1969 3/22
1969 7/23 – 10/13
1975 3/23 – 6/3
1975 11/2 – until 1976 1/17
1977 8/27 – 12/22
1978 4/19 – 7/7
1980 11/2 – until 1981 5/6
1981 6/17 – 9/27
1987 3/7 – 5/14
1989 8/5 – until 1990 2/11
1990 3/10 – 6/21
1992 10/15 – until 1993 9/11
1999 2/18 – 4/26
2001 7/18 – until 2002 6/3
2004 9/30 – 12/30
2005 3/7 – 8/24
2010 6/15 – 8/30
2011 1/28 – 4/9

SATURN CHALLENGING
1938 1/28 – 6/27
1938 9/2 – until 1939 3/11
1944 6/28 – until 1945 7/28
1950 12/5 – until 1951 2/19
1951 8/24 – until 1952 10/4
1967 3/13 – until 1968 4/19
1973 8/12 – 12/24
1974 5/1 – 9/16
1974 12/15 – until 1975 6/2
1980 9/30 – until 1981 11/11
1982 5/3 – 8/2
1996 4/16 – 11/9
1996 12/27 – until 1997 5/29
1997 10/7 – until 1998 2/19
2003 6/12 – until 2004 7/10
2009 11/9 – until 2010 3/24
2010 8/3 – until 2011 1/15
2011 2/5 – 9/18

URANUS CHALLENGING
1949 6/28 – until 1953 6/13
1968 10/16 – until 1972 9/16
2011 3/31 – Continues

NEPTUNE CHALLENGING
1942 11/5 – until 1951 8/4

PLUTO CHALLENGING
1971 11/7 – until 1979 8/16

JUPITER SPECIAL
1948 11/20 – until 1949 1/30
1960 3/10 – 5/31
1960 11/1 – until 1961 1/14
1972 2/12 – 7/13
1972 10/6 – 12/28
1984 1/24 – 12/12
1996 1/8 – 4/16
1996 5/22 – 11/24
2007 12/23 – until 2008 3/10
2008 7/12 – 11/2

SATURN SPECIAL
1959 1/15 – 8/7
1959 10/3 – until 1960 3/18
1960 6/8 – 12/10
1988 2/28 – 5/24
1988 11/23 – until 1990 1/13

URANUS SPECIAL
1988 12/21 – until 1992 12/22

NEPTUNE SPECIAL
1984 2/29 – until 1992 11/26

PLUTO SPECIAL
2008 3/23 – Continues

January 1

Your Personal Powers

Strong-willed and determined yet sensitive, you are usually an independent individual with initiative and stamina. Capable of taking the lead, you often gravitate to positions of power and prefer being in charge of situations. Your ruling planet, Saturn, endows you with an ambitious and industrious nature, strong sense of realism, and power to overcome challenges. Prone to restlessness and discontent, however, you lose some of your power by being impulsive, headstrong, or uncompromising. A tendency to be too serious also warns that you cannot afford to indulge in pessimism or negative thoughts as they sap your energy and enthusiasm. You gain power when you have a definite goal or purpose and combine your ingenuity and perseverance with self-discipline. Perceptive and visionary, you show your strength by using your foresight, facing up to your responsibilities and expressing what you know is right. Self-mastery can be achieved when you integrate your innovative ideas with your practical skills and act upon your powerful insight.

Your Powers of Attraction in Relationships

Idealistic about relationships, people recognize your unique qualities and admire your inner strength. You can be loyal, spontaneous, and romantic, and a tendency to be dignified or formal suggests that you often seem serious. Usually you are attracted to mentally quick individuals who are intelligent and well-informed. Alternatively, you may be attracted to charming and friendly individuals with good social skills and an easygoing manner. Often single-minded, you can at times be stubborn and refuse to back down. With your patience and subtle inner powers you can inspire others but resist being controlling. If you find it hard to express your thoughts and feelings, you may shy away from situations or appear too detached. Being considerate and showing a willingness to collaborate and compromise bring you closer to your partner.

Your attractive qualities: courageous, self-confident, pioneering, shrewd, decisive, authoritative, enthusiastic, rational, intuitive, inspired, resolute, forceful, creative, humanitarian, progressive, optimistic, strong convictions, competitive, ambitious, independent, gregarious, practical

Your less attractive qualities: controlling, mistrusting, too demanding, overbearing, antagonistic, too dependent, weak, un-caring, materialistic, bossy, impatient, too serious, egotistical, stubborn, negative thoughts, feel defeated, uncompromising

Your Venus Power

The planet Venus has a great deal of influence on your powers of attraction. Below are four possible Venus types for women and men. To find your Venus you need to go to page 771, where you will find the Venus table and extra information. The planet Mars also affects your powers of attraction. To find your Mars table and interpretation go to page 761.

WOMEN WITH VENUS IN SCORPIO: Loving and passionate, you are often sensitive with deep feelings and strong powers of attraction. A love for the truth coupled with a tendency to be suspicious can be an influence that motivates you to delve deep into the activities of your partner. When in love or in a relationship that matters, you will often bend over backward to cooperate. Although loyal, guard against losing sight of your own needs and desires.

MEN WITH VENUS IN SCORPIO: As you are emotionally intense and passionate, personal relationships are probably a major factor in your own transformation. Being sensitive yet loyal, you are usually attracted to forceful partners who can express themselves intimately but intensely. Rather than seek easy and simple relationships, you are drawn to partners who act as a catalyst for your own internal changes. Through your relationships with your partners you can unravel your own motives and understand your deep-seated feelings or emotional insecurities.

WOMEN WITH VENUS IN SAGITTARIUS: Sociable, warm, and friendly, you possess an honest and frank style in your relationships. Being naturally gregarious, you want others to share your enthusiasm and enjoy encouraging the people you love. You do better when you have a sense of personal freedom within a relationship and are usually generous with the faults of others. You need a partner who can share your need to explore and take risks, whether through travel, education, or recreation.

MEN WITH VENUS IN SAGITTARIUS: When in love you are open and friendly with a need for a partner who can share your adventurous spirit and sense of fun. Be careful, however, that your desire for freedom does not cause you to avoid commitment. You prefer your partners to be positive, direct, and generous in spirit. Being outspoken as well as an idealist, you

usually enjoy a partner with whom you can share your strong opinions. Alternatively, you may wish to explore life together, whether through travel, education, or by having fun.

WOMEN WITH VENUS IN CAPRICORN: Romantically, you do not give your heart easily but hide behind a cool reserve until you feel free to express your emotions. As you take your relationships seriously, you may find yourself drawn to people who are businesslike, resourceful, and practical or who can act as teachers or mentors. Work or career may also be a factor in many of your associations and partnerships. As security can play an important role in your relationships, you are often attracted to partners who are loyal and hardworking.

MEN WITH VENUS IN CAPRICORN: As you admire loyal, hardworking, and dedicated individuals, you probably want a partner who can share your vocational interests or can provide you with the sense of security you need. You could even find yourself with a partner who is of a different age group or maturity. Guard against denying your true emotional needs or focusing on your career at the expense of your relationship. You are drawn to reserved partners who display self-control.

WOMEN WITH VENUS IN AQUARIUS: When it comes to relationships, others are attracted to your honest, friendly, and easygoing attitude. You enjoy social interaction and have a genuine concern for others. In fact, at times, your friends may be just as important as your partner. Usually you present a tolerant and reasonable front in love situations and attempt to view your relationships objectively. If partners become too demanding, however, you can become stubborn or awkward. Nevertheless, inventive and progressive, you enjoy the company of like-minded people who share your original ideas.

MEN WITH VENUS IN AQUARIUS: Friendly and honest, you attract people with your broad-minded approach to life. You usually possess an objective and slightly detached attitude to affairs of the heart. If you are too removed, however, others can misinterpret your behavior as uncaring. It is often more important to you that your love relationships are based on friendship and honesty than intense passion. As you are generally tolerant and liberal, you may be drawn to less conventional relationships.

To read all about your Outer Planets and work out how to use your personalized timetable, go to Section Three, page 789.

♑

Your Personalized Timetable

JUPITER BENEFICIAL
1939 1/23 – 3/6
1940 5/25 – until 1941 4/5
1944 8/5 – 10/20
1945 4/24 – 6/3
1946 10/19 – 12/5
1950 5/19 – 8/4
1951 1/3 – 2/18
1952 5/7 – 7/29
1952 10/22 – until 1953 3/15
1956 7/19 – 10/2
1958 10/3 – 11/18
1962 4/20 – 9/21
1962 12/6 – until 1963 1/31
1964 4/21 – 7/1
1964 12/6 – until 1965 2/14
1967 11/2 – until 1968 2/10
1968 6/29 – 9/17
1970 1/27 – 3/14
1970 9/16 – 11/3
1974 3/31 – 5/26
1974 8/19 – until 1975 1/11
1976 4/4 – 6/12
1979 10/10 – until 1980 3/21
1980 6/1 – 9/1
1981 12/25 – until 1982 4/28
1982 8/25 – 10/18
1986 3/14 – 4/29
1986 10/2 – 12/14
1988 3/18 – 5/26
1991 9/22 – until 1992 8/16
1993 12/5 – until 1994 6/16
1994 7/17 – 10/1
1998 2/25 – 4/9
1999 7/13 – 10/6
2000 2/27 – 5/9
2003 9/6 – 12/13
2004 1/25 – 7/29
2005 11/19 – until 2006 1/13
2006 4/25 – 9/12
2010 2/9 – 3/22
2011 6/15 – 11/23
2012 1/27 – 4/22

SATURN BENEFICIAL
1940 4/7 – until 1941 5/9
1948 10/8 – until 1949 3/1
1949 6/29 – 11/22
1950 2/6 – 8/9
1953 12/6 – until 1954 5/8
1954 9/1 – 11/30
1955 6/20 – 8/16
1965 2/6 – 5/8
1965 8/19 – until 1966 1/29
1969 5/17 – 12/25
1970 1/13 – 6/21
1970 11/24 – until 1971 3/10
1978 8/13 – until 1979 9/17
1983 10/13 – until 1984 1/17
1984 4/3 – 10/8
1994 3/12 – until 1995 3/7
1998 7/4 – 9/27
1999 3/21 – until 2000 4/22
2007 9/19 – until 2008 4/10
2008 5/25 – 10/27
2009 3/11 – 7/19
2012 11/17 – Continues

URANUS BENEFICIAL
1938 1/1 – until 1940 2/14
1962 9/13 – until 1966 8/13
1975 12/4 – until 1978 10/14
2004 4/5 – until 2007 12/23

NEPTUNE BENEFICIAL
1958 11/14 – until 1964 8/13

PLUTO BENEFICIAL
1957 11/7 – until 1967 6/23
1985 11/8 – until 1990 8/19

JUPITER CHALLENGING
1939 5/23 – 10/10
1940 1/8 – 3/27

1942 6/19 – 9/3
1943 1/27 – 4/25
1945 9/4 – 11/19
1946 5/24 – 7/6
1951 5/1 – until 1952 3/9
1954 6/3 – 8/14
1957 8/18 – 11/2
1963 4/13 – 7/11
1963 9/7 – until 1964 2/19
1966 5/16 – 7/28
1968 11/29 – until 1969 3/14
1969 7/29 – 10/17
1975 3/27 – 6/8
1975 10/25 – until 1976 1/25
1977 9/3 – 12/15
1978 4/25 – 7/11
1980 11/7 – until 1981 4/23
1981 7/1 – 10/2
1987 3/11 – 5/19
1989 8/10 – until 1990 1/27
1990 3/25 – 6/25
1992 10/20 – until 1993 9/16
1999 2/22 – 4/30
2001 7/22 – until 2002 6/8
2004 10/5 – until 2005 1/11
2005 2/23 – 8/30
2010 6/25 – 8/20
2011 2/2 – 4/13

SATURN CHALLENGING
1938 2/7 – until 1939 3/19
1944 7/6 – until 1945 8/5
1946 3/6 – 4/3
1950 12/27 – until 1951 1/27
1951 9/1 – until 1952 10/12
1967 3/21 – until 1968 4/27
1973 8/23 – 12/12
1974 5/11 – 10/2
1974 11/29 – until 1975 6/11
1980 10/8 – until 1981 11/20
1982 4/19 – 8/15
1996 4/25 – 10/21
1997 1/14 – 6/10
1997 9/24 – until 1998 3/1
2003 6/20 – until 2004 7/18
2009 11/20 – until 2010 3/11
2010 8/13 – until 2011 9/27

URANUS CHALLENGING
1949 7/16 – until 1953 7/1
1968 11/3 – until 1972 10/2
2011 4/19 – Continues

NEPTUNE CHALLENGING
1943 10/4 – until 1951 9/11

PLUTO CHALLENGING
1972 10/1 – until 1979 9/17

JUPITER SPECIAL
1948 11/25 – until 1949 2/4
1960 3/20 – 5/21
1960 11/6 – until 1961 1/18
1972 2/18 – 7/5
1972 10/13 – until 1973 1/2
1984 1/29 – 12/17
1996 1/12 – 11/30
2007 12/28 – until 2008 3/16
2008 7/4 – 11/9

SATURN SPECIAL
1959 1/24 – 7/19
1959 10/21 – until 1960 4/9
1960 5/16 – 12/19
1988 3/19 – 5/3
1988 12/2 – until 1990 1/22

URANUS SPECIAL
1989 1/7 – until 1993 1/8

NEPTUNE SPECIAL
1985 1/19 – until 1992 12/26

PLUTO SPECIAL
2009 1/26 – Continues

595

January 2

Your Personal Powers

Insightful and receptive, you are a purposeful and shrewd individual with a pragmatic outlook and strong determination. Your ruling planet, Saturn, endows you with endurance and an ability to work hard. Having common sense, an enterprising spirit, and sound judgment indicates that you possess excellent business acumen and usually know how to capitalize on situations. Although you are likely to be a practical and down-to-earth individual, your astute mind and sharp perceptions also suggest that you are highly sensitive and intuitive. Since you have a strong need to interact with others, you gain power when you establish harmonious partnerships that are also beneficial professionally. Even though you are usually decisive, a tendency to worry implies that one of your challenges is establishing a positive attitude to money and long-term commitments. You lose some of your power if you indulge in skepticism and allow pessimism to cloud your otherwise clear perspective. By trusting your sixth sense, you can develop both your insight and self-esteem.

Your Powers of Attraction in Relationships

People admire your inner strength and tenacity. You show a willingness to support others and possess unique qualities and leadership skills. A stubborn streak warns that you need to avoid becoming resentful or frustrated with others. By being optimistic, understanding, and adaptable you usually gain the support and respect you want. Generous with the people you love, your popularity increases when you use your natural flair for dealing with people. You are usually attracted to enterprising and generous people, who can be spontaneous and affectionate. Alternatively, you may be drawn to benevolent and humanitarian individuals who are idealistic and independent. Although you may experience some challenges or setbacks early in life, you learn to become more detached and therefore improve your personal relationships.

Your attractive qualities: considerate, intuitive, hardworking, disciplined, enduring, diplomatic, gentle, tactful, modest, receptive, intuitive, harmonious, agreeable, authoritative, helpful, good judge of human nature, inner faith, idealistic, spiritual, insightful, determined, ambitious, sensitive

Your less attractive qualities: materialistic, reserved, suspicious, lack of confidence, subservient, lazy, too sensitive, self-centered, unsympathetic, mistrusting, manipulative, insecure, stubborn, indifferent, calculating, too demanding

Your Venus Power

The planet Venus has a great deal of influence on your powers of attraction. Below are four possible Venus types for women and men. To find your Venus you need to go to page 771, where you will find the Venus table and extra information. The planet Mars also affects your powers of attraction. To find your Mars table and interpretation go to page 761.

WOMEN WITH VENUS IN SCORPIO: Loving and passionate, you are often sensitive with deep feelings and strong powers of attraction. A love for the truth coupled with a tendency to be suspicious can be an influence that motivates you to delve deep into the activities of your partner. When in love or in a relationship that matters, you will often bend over backward to cooperate. Although loyal, guard against losing sight of your own needs and desires.

MEN WITH VENUS IN SCORPIO: As you are emotionally intense and passionate, personal relationships are probably a major factor in your own transformation. Being sensitive yet loyal, you are usually attracted to forceful partners who can express themselves intimately but intensely. Rather than seek easy and simple relationships, you are drawn to partners who act as a catalyst for your own internal changes. Through your relationships with your partners you can unravel your own motives and understand your deep-seated feelings or emotional insecurities.

WOMEN WITH VENUS IN SAGITTARIUS: At your best when being optimistic and generous, you possess a mischievous sense of fun. In relationships your open-minded approach to people and places may attract you to those of a different culture or make you tolerant of the foibles of others. Although warm and enthusiastic when in love, your natural honesty and idealism may inspire you to look for a partner who shares your love of freedom.

MEN WITH VENUS IN SAGITTARIUS: Forward-thinking rather than dwelling on the past, you are looking for a partner who can share your future plans. You enjoy exploring life whether through travel and mental pursuits or sports and games. Idealistic, you usually prefer the company of a partner who is optimistic and shares your beliefs. In your desire for honesty in relationships, however, be careful not to become

tactless. Nevertheless, you are attracted to honest, direct, and fun-loving partners with a sense of humor like your own.

WOMEN WITH VENUS IN CAPRICORN: Proud and refined, you attract others with your composed dignity. Disliking vulnerability and needing to feel safe before you can express your feelings, you display a strong front. Feeling insecure or inadequate in relationships may force you to become manipulative in order to regain control. Nevertheless, you can project an attractive sense of self-assurance and are capable of displaying loyalty and a wonderful dry sense of humor.

MEN WITH VENUS IN CAPRICORN: As you do not display your deeper emotions freely, you are usually dignified and controlled in your relationships with others. Practical and down-to-earth partners are particularly attractive to you, especially those who do not rush into expressing their feelings but seem to possess natural class and reserve. You need a partner who is loyal and dependable and willing to take your relationship seriously.

WOMEN WITH VENUS IN AQUARIUS: Usually you have a modern outlook on love and are open to new or current lifestyles. Your intuitive abilities, communal sense, and people skills often allow you to see deeper into human intentions and read people's thoughts telepathically. You are usually group-oriented and are drawn to individuals within the group who are independent and self-motivated. You are more inclined to choose a partner who is unconventional or freedom-loving. Conscious of your social standing, however, you want someone who can relate well to your friends.

MEN WITH VENUS IN AQUARIUS: Although independent, you often enjoy being part of a group. The partners you frequently attract are themselves nonconformists or free spirits. As an individual you may not find it easy to settle into a routine or an entirely mundane type of relationship. You may have some unconventional views on traditional marriage or your partner may hold such views. It is usually important to you that your love relationships are based on friendship.

To read all about your Outer Planets and work out how to use your personalized timetable, go to Section Three, page 789.

♑

Your Personalized Timetable

JUPITER BENEFICIAL
1939 1/28 – 3/11
1940 5/30 – until 1941 4/9
1944 8/10 – 10/25
1945 4/11 – 6/17
1946 10/24 – 12/10
1950 5/29 – 7/25
1951 1/8 – 2/22
1952 5/12 – 8/6
1952 10/13 – until 1953 3/20
1956 7/24 – 10/7
1958 10/8 – 11/23
1962 4/25 – 9/12
1962 12/13 – until 1963 2/5
1964 4/25 – 7/7
1964 11/27 – until 1965 2/22
1967 11/10 – until 1968 2/2
1968 7/5 – 9/21
1970 9/21 – 11/7
1974 4/4 – 6/4
1974 8/9 – until 1975 1/16
1976 4/8 – 6/16
1979 10/16 – until 1980 3/12
1980 6/10 – 9/6
1982 1/1 – 4/20
1982 9/1 – 10/23
1986 3/18 – 5/5
1986 9/24 – 12/22
1988 3/23 – 5/30
1991 9/27 – until 1992 8/20
1993 12/10 – until 1994 6/1
1994 8/1 – 10/6
1998 3/2 – 4/14
1999 7/22 – 9/27
2000 3/3 – 5/13
2003 9/10 – until 2004 8/4
2005 11/23 – until 2006 1/21
2006 4/16 – 9/18
2010 2/13 – 3/27
2011 6/20 – 11/14
2012 2/5 – 4/26

SATURN BENEFICIAL
1940 4/15 – until 1941 5/17
1948 10/18 – until 1949 2/17
1949 7/9 – 12/12
1950 1/16 – 8/18
1953 12/16 – until 1954 4/25
1954 9/12 – 12/10
1955 6/2 – 9/3
1965 2/14 – 5/23
1965 8/3 – until 1966 2/8
1969 5/25 – 11/29
1970 2/7 – 7/1
1970 11/11 – until 1971 3/21
1978 8/21 – until 1979 9/25
1983 10/22 – until 1984 2/8
1984 3/11 – 10/17
1994 3/21 – 10/16
1994 12/2 – until 1995 3/15
1998 7/23 – 9/8
1999 3/29 – until 2000 4/30
2007 9/28 – until 2008 3/22
2008 6/13 – 11/6
2009 2/26 – 7/30
2012 11/26 – Continues

URANUS BENEFICIAL
1938 1/1 – until 1940 3/19
1962 10/1 – until 1966 8/30
1975 12/26 – until 1978 10/31
2004 5/1 – until 2008 1/21

NEPTUNE BENEFICIAL
1938 4/3 – 7/25
1958 12/15 – until 1964 10/1

PLUTO BENEFICIAL
1958 9/30 – until 1967 8/7
1985 12/5 – until 1990 9/30

JUPITER CHALLENGING
1939 5/29 – 10/2

1940 1/15 – 3/31
1942 6/24 – 9/8
1943 1/19 – 5/3
1945 9/9 – 11/25
1946 5/11 – 7/19
1951 5/6 – until 1952 3/14
1954 6/7 – 8/19
1957 8/23 – 11/7
1963 4/17 – 7/26
1963 8/23 – until 1964 2/24
1966 5/21 – 8/1
1968 12/7 – until 1969 3/5
1969 8/5 – 10/22
1975 3/31 – 6/14
1975 10/17 – until 1976 2/1
1977 9/10 – 12/7
1978 5/1 – 7/16
1980 11/13 – until 1981 4/14
1981 7/10 – 10/6
1987 3/15 – 5/23
1989 8/16 – until 1990 1/17
1990 4/4 – 6/30
1992 10/25 – until 1993 9/20
1999 2/27 – 5/5
2001 7/27 – until 2002 6/13
2004 10/9 – until 2005 9/4
2010 7/11 – 8/4
2011 2/7 – 4/17

SATURN CHALLENGING
1938 2/17 – until 1939 3/28
1944 7/14 – until 1945 8/13
1946 2/11 – 4/25
1951 9/10 – until 1952 10/21
1967 3/29 – until 1968 5/5
1968 11/29 – until 1969 1/12
1973 9/4 – 11/28
1974 5/20 – until 1975 6/19
1980 10/17 – until 1981 5/22
1981 6/18 – 12/1
1982 4/5 – 8/26
1996 5/5 – 10/7
1997 1/27 – 6/24
1900 1/00 – until 1998 3/10
2003 6/28 – until 2004 7/26
2009 12/3 – until 2010 2/24
2010 8/23 – until 2011 10/5

URANUS CHALLENGING
1949 8/4 – until 1954 4/15
1968 11/26 – until 1973 7/19
2011 5/10 – Continues

NEPTUNE CHALLENGING
1943 11/3 – until 1952 7/29

PLUTO CHALLENGING
1972 10/29 – until 1980 7/24

JUPITER SPECIAL
1948 11/30 – until 1949 2/8
1960 4/3 – 5/6
1960 11/12 – until 1961 1/22
1972 2/25 – 6/27
1972 10/20 – until 1973 1/6
1984 2/3 – 8/26
1984 9/1 – 12/21
1996 1/17 – 12/4
2008 1/1 – 3/24
2008 6/25 – 11/15

SATURN SPECIAL
1959 2/3 – 7/4
1959 11/3 – until 1960 12/28
1988 12/11 – until 1990 1/31
1990 8/30 – 10/16

URANUS SPECIAL
1989 1/25 – until 1993 11/13

NEPTUNE SPECIAL
1985 2/23 – until 1993 11/23

PLUTO SPECIAL
2009 3/12 – Continues

January 3

Your Personal Powers

Quietly determined and astute, you are a resilient individual with unique ideas and a cautious outlook. As a thoughtful and determined person, you like to put your imaginative and enterprising thoughts to practical use. Your ruling planet, Saturn, endows you with a sense of duty, a composed manner, and the power to persevere. Usually inspired by knowledge and new ideas, you benefit greatly by applying the self-discipline and hard work needed to express yourself creatively and mentally. Although being cautious and realistic grants you practical abilities, being stubborn or a nonconformist can sap your vitality. As an independent thinker, however, you gain power by embracing progressive thoughts and campaigning for constructive change or reforms. You lose some of your power when you let anxiety or indecision undermine your strong instincts and foresight. Being idealistic and sensitive implies that, although you may appear modest and impartial, you possess an inner strength that allows you to be spontaneous and enterprising. You gain power when you combine your vision with inventiveness and utilize your communication skills to your advantage.

Your Powers of Attraction in Relationships

Although you may appear reserved, you are often witty and engaging with a good sense of humor. People also admire your purposeful nature and original ideas. Intuitive with a strong sense of values, you can assess people and situations easily. You are usually drawn to bright individuals who are full of creative ideas and a responsible attitude. Alternatively, you may be attracted to optimistic and benevolent people who are compassionate and supportive. Although often considerate and unassuming, you are not afraid to stand alone or speak out on issues you believe in. Security-conscious, an inclination to keep emotional matters close to your chest warns that you are prone to being suspicious or skeptical. Nevertheless, you have a great deal of love to give and are usually are generous and protective.

Your attractive qualities: enterprising, original, independent, idealistic, inventive, youthful, responsible, productive, authoritative, enthusiastic, expressive, charming, methodical, modest, spontaneous, humanitarian, industrious, creative, progressive, intuitive, optimistic, humorous

Your less attractive qualities: worry, pessimistic, easily bored, vain, exaggerates, extravagant, self-indulgent, lazy, manipulative, negative thinking, lack of purpose, indecisive, skeptical, cynical, risk taking, mercenary

Your Venus Power

The planet Venus has a great deal of influence on your powers of attraction. Below are four possible Venus types for women and men. To find your Venus you need to go to page 771, where you will find the Venus table and extra information. The planet Mars also affects your powers of attraction. To find your Mars table and interpretation go to page 761.

WOMEN WITH VENUS IN SCORPIO: Loving and passionate, you are often sensitive with deep feelings and strong powers of attraction. A love for the truth coupled with a tendency to be suspicious can be an influence that motivates you to delve deep into the activities of your partner. When in love or in a relationship that matters, you will often bend over backward to cooperate. Although loyal, guard against losing sight of your own needs and desires.

MEN WITH VENUS IN SCORPIO: As you are emotionally intense and passionate, personal relationships are probably a major factor in your own transformation. Being sensitive yet loyal, you are usually attracted to forceful partners who can express themselves intimately but intensely. Rather than seek easy and simple relationships you are drawn to partners who act as a catalyst for your own internal changes. Through your relationships with your partners you can unravel your own motives and understand your deep-seated feelings or emotional insecurities.

WOMEN WITH VENUS IN SAGITTARIUS: At your best when being optimistic and generous, you possess a mischievous sense of fun. In relationships your open-minded approach to people and places may attract you to those of a different culture or make you tolerant of the foibles of others. Although warm and enthusiastic when in love, your natural honesty and idealism may inspire you to look for a partner who shares your love of freedom.

MEN WITH VENUS IN SAGITTARIUS: Forward-thinking rather than dwelling on the past, you are looking for a partner who can share your future plans. You enjoy exploring life whether through travel and mental pursuits or sports and games. Idealistic, you usually prefer the company of a partner

who is optimistic and shares your beliefs. In your desire for honesty in relationships, however, be careful not to become tactless. Nevertheless, you are attracted to honest, direct, and fun-loving partners with a sense of humor like your own.

WOMEN WITH VENUS IN CAPRICORN: Proud and refined, you attract others with your composed dignity. Disliking vulnerability and needing to feel safe before you can express your feelings, you display a strong front. Feeling insecure or inadequate in relationships may force you to become manipulative in order to regain control. Nevertheless, you can project an attractive sense of self-assurance and are capable of displaying loyalty and a wonderful dry sense of humor.

MEN WITH VENUS IN CAPRICORN: As you do not display your deeper emotions freely, you are usually dignified and controlled in your relationships. Practical and down-to-earth partners are particularly attractive to you, especially those who do not rush into expressing their feelings but seem to possess natural class and reserve. You need a partner who is loyal and dependable and willing to take your relationship seriously.

WOMEN WITH VENUS IN AQUARIUS: Usually you have a modern outlook on love and are open to new or current lifestyles. Your intuitive abilities, communal sense, and people skills often allow you to see deeper into human intentions and to read people's thoughts telepathically. You are usually group-oriented and are drawn to individuals within the group who are independent and self-motivated. You are more inclined to choose a partner who is unconventional or freedom-loving. Conscious of your social standing, however, you want someone who can relate well to your friends.

MEN WITH VENUS IN AQUARIUS: Although independent, you often enjoy being part of a group. The partners you frequently attract are themselves nonconformists or free spirits. As an individual you may not find it easy to settle into a routine or an entirely mundane type of relationship. You may have some unconventional views on the traditional marriage or your partner may hold such views. As a nonconformist, you may also be interested in alternative lifestyles such as collective living.

To read all about your Outer Planets and work out how to use your personalized timetable, go to Section Three, page 789.

Your Personalized Timetable

JUPITER BENEFICIAL
1939 2/1 – 3/15
1940 6/4 – until 1941 4/14
1944 8/14 – 10/31
1945 4/1 – 6/26
1946 10/29 – 12/15
1950 6/14 – 7/9
1951 1/13 – 2/26
1952 5/16 – 8/18
1952 10/1 – until 1953 3/25
1956 7/29 – 10/12
1958 10/13 – 11/28
1962 5/1 – 9/4
1962 12/20 – until 1963 2/9
1964 4/29 – 7/13
1964 11/19 – until 1965 3/2
1967 11/19 – until 1968 1/23
1968 7/11 – 9/26
1970 9/26 – 11/12
1974 4/9 – 6/17
1974 7/28 – until 1975 1/21
1976 4/13 – 6/21
1979 10/22 – until 1980 3/4
1980 6/18 – 9/10
1982 1/9 – 4/12
1982 9/7 – 10/27
1986 3/23 – 5/11
1986 9/16 – 12/29
1988 3/27 – 6/3
1991 10/2 – until 1992 8/25
1993 12/16 – until 1994 5/21
1994 8/12 – 10/11
1998 3/6 – 4/19
1999 8/2 – 9/16
2000 3/8 – 5/17
2003 9/15 – until 2004 8/9
2005 11/28 – until 2006 1/30
2006 4/7 – 9/23
2010 2/17 – 3/31
2011 6/26 – 11/6
2012 2/12 – 4/30

SATURN BENEFICIAL
1940 4/23 – until 1941 5/25
1948 10/30 – until 1949 2/4
1949 7/19 – until 1950 8/26
1953 12/28 – until 1954 4/11
1954 9/23 – 12/19
1955 5/18 – 9/16
1965 2/23 – 6/21
1965 7/4 – until 1966 2/16
1969 6/3 – 11/14
1970 2/21 – 7/12
1970 10/29 – until 1971 3/31
1978 8/29 – until 1979 10/4
1983 10/30 – until 1984 10/26
1994 3/30 – 9/27
1994 12/21 – until 1995 3/23
1999 4/7 – until 2000 5/8
2007 10/7 – until 2008 3/7
2008 6/27 – 11/19
2009 2/12 – 8/8
2012 12/6 – Continues

URANUS BENEFICIAL
1938 1/1 – until 1940 4/10
1962 10/22 – until 1966 9/15
1976 10/25 – until 1979 8/19
2005 3/4 – until 2008 2/11

NEPTUNE BENEFICIAL
1938 2/24 – 8/26
1959 11/12 – until 1964 10/30

PLUTO BENEFICIAL
1958 11/22 – until 1968 6/4
1986 1/15 – until 1990 10/28

JUPITER CHALLENGING
1939 6/4 – 9/24
1940 1/21 – 4/5
1942 6/28 – 9/15

1943 1/11 – 5/9
1945 9/14 – 12/1
1946 5/1 – 7/28
1951 5/11 – until 1952 3/18
1954 6/12 – 8/24
1955 3/3 – 3/30
1957 8/28 – 11/12
1963 4/21 – until 1964 2/29
1966 5/26 – 8/6
1968 12/16 – until 1969 2/24
1969 8/10 – 10/27
1975 4/4 – 6/21
1975 10/9 – until 1976 2/7
1977 9/19 – 11/28
1978 5/7 – 7/20
1980 11/19 – until 1981 4/5
1981 7/18 – 10/11
1987 3/20 – 5/28
1987 11/30 – 12/30
1989 8/21 – until 1990 1/8
1990 4/12 – 7/4
1992 10/30 – until 1993 9/25
1999 3/3 – 5/9
2001 8/1 – until 2002 6/18
2004 10/14 – until 2005 9/9
2011 2/12 – 4/22

SATURN CHALLENGING
1938 2/26 – until 1939 4/5
1944 7/23 – until 1945 2/14
1945 3/24 – 8/22
1946 1/27 – 5/9
1951 9/18 – until 1952 10/29
1967 4/6 – until 1968 5/14
1968 11/9 – until 1969 1/31
1973 9/22 – 11/11
1974 5/28 – until 1975 6/27
1980 10/26 – until 1981 4/27
1981 7/12 – 12/12
1982 3/23 – 9/5
1996 5/15 – 9/24
1997 2/6 – 7/18
1997 8/15 – until 1998 3/19
2003 7/6 – until 2004 8/3
2009 12/21 – until 2010 2/5
2010 9/1 – until 2011 10/13

URANUS CHALLENGING
1949 8/27 – until 1954 5/19
1969 9/24 – until 1973 8/20
2011 6/9 – Continues

NEPTUNE CHALLENGING
1943 12/21 – until 1952 9/9

PLUTO CHALLENGING
1972 12/8 – until 1980 9/4

JUPITER SPECIAL
1948 12/4 – until 1949 2/13
1960 11/17 – until 1961 1/27
1972 3/2 – 6/19
1972 10/27 – until 1973 1/11
1984 2/9 – 8/4
1984 9/24 – 12/26
1996 1/22 – 12/9
2008 1/6 – 4/1
2008 6/16 – 11/20

SATURN SPECIAL
1959 2/14 – 6/20
1959 11/14 – until 1961 1/6
1988 12/20 – until 1990 2/9
1990 8/10 – 11/4

URANUS SPECIAL
1989 2/15 – until 1993 12/6

NEPTUNE SPECIAL
1986 1/17 – until 1993 12/24

PLUTO SPECIAL
2010 1/26 – Continues

♑

January 4

Your Personal Powers

Ambitious and intelligent with sound common sense, you are a determined individual with an enterprising nature and a direct approach. Being daring, you are not afraid to initiate large projects that demand a great deal of time and effort. So, in order to empower yourself, you need to blend your creativity and imagination with your visionary outlook and practical skills. Your ruling planet, Saturn, grants you willpower, a sense of duty, and the desire to build something enduring. You gain power when you combine your perseverance, positive outlook, and wealth of ideas with your business acumen to achieve your aims and objectives. Although when inspired you can focus on your goals with remarkable tenacity, you lose some of your power if you become too stubborn or egocentric. As you often appear self-reliant and assured, your outer personality often hides your sensitivity and idealistic nature. Success-oriented, you gain power when you apply self-discipline to your many talents.

Your Powers of Attraction in Relationships

Persuasive and dynamic, you can attract many friends and lead an active social life. People admire your sincere and direct approach. They also recognize your sharp mind and quick perception. Although you are often generous with those you love, a tendency to be indecisive about your feelings or to worry about money and security indicates that honesty and trust are vital in close relationships. Usually you are attracted to enterprising individuals who are independent, talented, and original. Alternatively, you may be drawn to people who are intelligent and well-informed with bright ideas and common sense. When you become less doubting of others, you can be more spontaneous or express your true feelings freely. Nevertheless, loyal and idealistic, you can be a loving and supportive partner.

Your attractive qualities: organized, pragmatic, creative thinker, problem solver, wealth of ideas, disciplined, steady, good conversationalist, hardworking, trusting, exact, ambitious, competitive, quick intellect, enthusiastic, optimistic, shrewd, common sense, sociable

Your less attractive qualities: procrastinator, moody, stubborn, pessimistic, arrogant, impatient, vain, uncommunicative, overconfident, repressed, rigid, self-indulgent, too economical, bossy, resentful, strict, lack of clarity

Your Venus Power

The planet Venus has a great deal of influence on your powers of attraction. Below are four possible Venus types for women and men. To find your Venus you need to go to page 771, where you will find the Venus table and extra information. The planet Mars also affects your powers of attraction. To find your Mars table and interpretation go to page 761.

WOMEN WITH VENUS IN SCORPIO: You are usually drawn to partners who are sensual in appearance with a strong character. As you are emotionally intense and passionate, personal relationships are probably a major factor in your life. Since you like to be in control, you can at times exhibit some of your less attractive qualities by being willful or domineering. Although you need to feel established and in command in your relationship, you are constantly searching for some higher truth that can bring about a significant transformation.

MEN WITH VENUS IN SCORPIO: You are usually attracted to sensual and passionate partners with strong character. You are often sensitive with deep feelings and magnetic powers of attraction. As a cautious yet devoted and ardent lover, you are likely to seek experiences that are more sexual in nature. You display your less attractive qualities when you project your negative thoughts and resort to being suspicious or possessive. Nevertheless, loyal and loving, you are a sensitive lover.

WOMEN WITH VENUS IN SAGITTARIUS: At your best when being optimistic and generous, you possess a mischievous sense of fun. In relationships your open-minded approach to people and places may attract you to those of a different culture or make you tolerant of the foibles of others. Although warm and enthusiastic when in love, your natural honesty and idealism may inspire you to look for a partner who shares your love of freedom.

MEN WITH VENUS IN SAGITTARIUS: Forward-thinking rather than dwelling on the past, you are looking for a partner who can share your future plans. You enjoy exploring life whether through travel and mental pursuits or sports and games. Idealistic, you usually prefer the company of a partner who is optimistic and shares your beliefs. In your desire for honesty in relationships, however, be careful not to become

tactless. Nevertheless, you are attracted to honest, direct, and fun-loving partners with a sense of humor like your own.

WOMEN WITH VENUS IN CAPRICORN: With your natural caution in romantic affairs, you often appear reserved and controlled. If shy, try to be more forward, especially if you want to be noticed. When you care about people, however, you are usually willing to put in extra time and energy to preserve the relationship. You are practical and dependable, and a sense of duty can often play a large role in affairs of your heart. With elegant simplicity, you can attract others with your well-cut clothes and refined manners.

MEN WITH VENUS IN CAPRICORN: In relationships you take love seriously and can be a strong and practical support for friends or partners. You are usually attracted to partners who are as hardworking as you. As you tend not to express your feelings until you feel really secure in a relationship, you may be drawn to those who seem loyal, faithful, and not likely to let you down. As you respect the wisdom of experience you may be drawn to mature partners or, alternatively, you may act as an authority figure for someone younger.

WOMEN WITH VENUS IN AQUARIUS: When it comes to relationships, others are attracted to your honest, friendly, and easygoing attitude. You really enjoy social interaction with others and may develop a genuine concern for humanity. Usually you present a tolerant and reasonable front in love situations and attempt to view your relationships objectively. If partners become too demanding, however, you can become stubborn and fixed. Friendship may be even more important for you than sexual compatibility.

MEN WITH VENUS IN AQUARIUS: You are sociable and open-minded, and people are attracted by your friendly and relaxed style. Being independent, you value freedom-loving partners who give you the space to be yourself. Others sometimes interpret your detachment as being emotionally cool, but they may not understand your progressive views on relationships. Friendship can sometimes be even more important than earthly passion. Ideally, your partners can share your ideas on life and possess a sense of originality as strong as your own. Not easily ruffled, you can deal well with difficult situations or moody partners.

To read all about your Outer Planets and work out how to use your personalized timetable, go to Section Three, page 789.

♍

Your Personalized Timetable

JUPITER BENEFICIAL
1939 2/5 – 3/19
1940 6/9 – until 1941 4/18
1944 8/19 – 11/6
1945 3/24 – 7/5
1946 11/2 – 12/20
1947 6/27 – 8/3
1951 1/18 – 3/2
1952 5/21 – until 1953 3/31
1956 8/3 – 10/17
1958 10/18 – 12/3
1962 5/8 – 8/27
1962 12/27 – until 1963 2/13
1964 5/3 – 7/19
1964 11/12 – until 1965 3/8
1967 12/2 – until 1968 1/11
1968 7/16 – 10/1
1970 10/1 – 11/17
1974 4/14 – 10/23
1974 11/14 – until 1975 1/26
1976 4/17 – 6/26
1977 1/13 – 1/18
1979 10/28 – until 1980 2/25
1980 6/25 – 9/15
1982 1/17 – 4/3
1982 9/13 – 11/1
1986 3/27 – 5/17
1986 9/8 – until 1987 1/5
1988 4/1 – 6/8
1991 10/7 – until 1992 4/11
1992 5/20 – 8/30
1993 12/22 – until 1994 5/13
1994 8/20 – 10/16
1998 3/10 – 4/24
1998 11/9 – 11/17
2000 3/13 – 5/22
2003 9/20 – until 2004 8/14
2005 12/3 – until 2006 2/12
2006 3/25 – 9/29
2010 2/22 – 4/5
2011 7/2 – 10/29
2012 2/19 – 5/5

SATURN BENEFICIAL
1940 5/1 – until 1941 6/3
1948 11/13 – until 1949 1/19
1949 7/28 – until 1950 9/4
1954 1/11 – 3/26
1954 10/2 – 12/30
1955 5/4 – 9/27
1965 3/3 – until 1966 2/25
1969 6/13 – 11/1
1970 3/5 – 7/26
1970 10/15 – until 1971 4/9
1978 9/6 – until 1979 10/12
1980 4/17 – 6/26
1983 11/8 – until 1984 11/3
1994 4/9 – 9/12
1995 1/3 – 4/1
1995 11/6 – 12/6
1999 4/15 – until 2000 5/16
2007 10/17 – until 2008 2/23
2008 7/8 – 12/6
2009 1/22 – 8/17
2012 12/16 – Continues

URANUS BENEFICIAL
1938 1/1 – until 1940 4/29
1962 11/26 – until 1967 7/13
1976 11/11 – until 1979 9/19
2005 3/22 – until 2008 3/1

NEPTUNE BENEFICIAL
1938 1/1 – until 1939 7/21
1959 12/13 – until 1965 9/29

PLUTO BENEFICIAL
1959 10/6 – until 1968 8/3
1986 11/22 – until 1991 9/14

JUPITER CHALLENGING
1939 6/11 – 9/16
1940 1/27 – 4/9

1942 7/3 – 9/21
1943 1/3 – 5/16
1945 9/19 – 12/6
1946 4/23 – 8/5
1951 5/16 – 11/6
1951 12/23 – until 1952 3/23
1954 6/16 – 8/29
1955 2/16 – 4/14
1957 9/2 – 11/17
1963 4/26 – until 1964 3/5
1966 5/31 – 8/11
1968 12/28 – until 1969 2/12
1969 8/16 – 11/1
1975 4/9 – 6/28
1975 10/1 – until 1976 2/13
1977 9/30 – 11/17
1978 5/12 – 7/25
1980 11/25 – until 1981 3/28
1981 7/25 – 10/16
1987 3/24 – 6/3
1987 11/16 – until 1988 1/13
1989 8/27 – until 1990 1/1
1990 4/19 – 7/9
1992 11/5 – until 1993 5/15
1993 6/17 – 9/30
1999 3/7 – 5/14
2001 8/6 – until 2002 6/23
2004 10/19 – until 2005 9/14
2011 2/17 – 4/26

SATURN CHALLENGING
1938 3/6 – until 1939 4/13
1944 7/31 – until 1945 1/25
1945 4/13 – 9/1
1946 1/15 – 5/21
1951 9/27 – until 1952 11/7
1953 5/26 – 7/21
1967 4/15 – until 1968 5/24
1968 10/26 – until 1969 2/13
1974 6/6 – until 1975 7/5
1980 11/4 – until 1981 4/12
1981 7/27 – 12/27
1982 3/7 – 9/15
1996 5/27 – 9/10
1997 2/16 – until 1998 3/27
2003 7/14 – until 2004 8/12
2005 2/20 – 4/20
2010 9/10 – until 2011 10/22

URANUS CHALLENGING
1950 6/27 – until 1954 6/9
1969 10/10 – until 1973 9/9
2012 4/5 – Continues

NEPTUNE CHALLENGING
1944 10/31 – until 1953 7/21

PLUTO CHALLENGING
1973 10/21 – until 1980 10/2

JUPITER SPECIAL
1948 12/9 – until 1949 2/18
1960 11/22 – until 1961 1/31
1972 3/10 – 6/10
1972 11/2 – until 1973 1/15
1984 2/14 – 7/23
1984 10/5 – 12/30
1996 1/26 – 12/14
2008 1/10 – 4/12
2008 6/5 – 11/26

SATURN SPECIAL
1959 2/27 – 6/6
1959 11/24 – until 1961 1/14
1988 12/28 – until 1990 2/19
1990 7/25 – 11/18

URANUS SPECIAL
1989 3/22 – until 1993 12/25

NEPTUNE SPECIAL
1986 2/19 – until 1994 11/19

PLUTO SPECIAL
2010 3/9 – Continues

January 5

Your Personal Powers

Determined and enduring, you are a tenacious yet deeply sensitive individual with inspired beliefs and a wealth of feelings. Your ruling planet, Saturn, grants you a strong sense of duty, a conservative outlook, and practical abilities. Proud yet altruistic, you can make a good impression on others by showing your tolerance and generosity. Usually hardworking and loyal, you gain power when you remain resolute, optimistic, and liberal. Often charismatic and ambitious, you empower yourself by combining your enthusiasm and idealism with perseverance and a sense of purpose. Since making real changes is part of your life lesson, the less stubborn you are about holding on to the past, the quicker you undergo the transformation that leads to your new success. Although you can show great patience and resilience, at times slow progress may cause you restlessness or frustration. With humanitarian or spiritual potential, you empower yourself by staying detached or by focusing on something that has more value than money and material achievements.

Your Powers of Attraction in Relationships

People are drawn to your caring and considerate nature. Having powerful feelings and being sensitive imply that you can be romantic or sentimental. Although you are hardworking, you enjoy meeting new people and socializing. You are gregarious, and your personal magnetism and friendly manner ensure that you have many friends. Kindhearted and well-mannered, you can also create a friendly working environment and congenial relations with coworkers. Although you are often modest and reserved, you need to express your passionate nature and let out some of your intense feelings. Usually you are attracted to dynamic, enterprising, creative, and generous individuals with a sense of the dramatic. Giving and loving, once you make a commitment to a partner, you can be loyal and faithful and do your utmost for your family.

Your attractive qualities: enthusiastic, ambitious, enduring, versatile, compassionate, focused, charming, friendly, sociable, leadership, strong-willed, sympathetic, adaptable, generous, progressive, magnetic, daring, freedom-loving, mentally quick, witty, curious, spiritual potential, optimistic

Your less attractive qualities: stubborn, headstrong, impatient, speculative, frustrated, rigid, too materialistic, overly serious, self-indulgent, lack of confidence, ruthless, disappointed, bossy, pessimistic

Your Venus Power

The planet Venus has a great deal of influence on your powers of attraction. Below are four possible Venus types for women and men. To find your Venus you need to go to page 771, where you will find the Venus table and extra information. The planet Mars also affects your powers of attraction. To find your Mars table and interpretation go to page 761.

WOMEN WITH VENUS IN SCORPIO: Loving and passionate, you are often sensitive with deep feelings and strong powers of attraction. A love for the truth coupled with a tendency to be suspicious can be an influence that motivates you to delve deep into the activities of your partner. When in love or in a relationship that matters, you will often bend over backward to cooperate. Although loyal, guard against losing sight of your own needs and desires.

MEN WITH VENUS IN SCORPIO: As you are emotionally intense and passionate, personal relationships are probably a major factor in your own transformation. Being sensitive yet loyal, you are usually attracted to forceful partners who can express themselves intimately but intensely. Rather than seek easy and simple relationships you are drawn to partners who act as a catalyst for your own internal changes. Through your relationships with your partners you can unravel your own motives and understand your deep-seated feelings or emotional insecurities.

WOMEN WITH VENUS IN SAGITTARIUS: Sociable, warm, and friendly, you possess an honest and frank style in your relationships. Being naturally gregarious, you want others to share your enthusiasm and enjoy encouraging the people you love. You do better when you have a sense of personal freedom within a relationship and are usually generous with the faults of others. You need a partner who can share your need to explore and take risks whether through travel, education, or recreation.

MEN WITH VENUS IN SAGITTARIUS: When in love, you are open and friendly with a need for a partner who can share your adventurous spirit and sense of fun. Be careful, however, that your desire for freedom does not cause you to avoid commitment. You prefer your partners to be positive, direct, and generous in spirit. Being outspoken as well as an idealist, you

usually enjoy a partner with whom you can share your strong opinions. Alternatively, you may wish to explore life together whether through travel, education, or by having fun.

WOMEN WITH VENUS IN CAPRICORN: Romantically, you do not give your heart easily but hide behind a cool reserve until you feel free to express your emotions. As you take your relationships seriously, you may find yourself drawn to people who are businesslike, resourceful, and practical or who can act as teachers or mentors. Work or career may also be a factor in many of your associations and partnerships. As security can play an important role in your relationships, you are often attracted to partners who are loyal and hardworking.

MEN WITH VENUS IN CAPRICORN: As you admire loyal, hardworking, and dedicated individuals, you probably want a partner who can share your vocational interests or can provide you with the security you need. You could even find yourself with a partner who is of a different age group or maturity. Guard against denying your true emotional needs or focusing on your career at the expense of your relationship. You are drawn to reserved partners who display self-control.

WOMEN WITH VENUS IN AQUARIUS: When it comes to relationships, others are attracted to your honest, friendly, and easygoing attitude. You enjoy social interaction and have a genuine concern for others. In fact, at times, your friends may be just as important as your partner. Usually you present a tolerant and reasonable front in love situations and attempt to view your relationships objectively. If partners become too demanding, however, you can become stubborn or awkward. Nevertheless, inventive and progressive, you enjoy the company of like-minded people who can share your original ideas.

MEN WITH VENUS IN AQUARIUS: Friendly and honest, you attract people with your broad-minded approach to life. You usually possess an objective and slightly detached attitude to affairs of the heart. If you are too removed, however, others can misinterpret your behavior as uncaring. It is often more important to you that your love relationships are based on friendship and honesty than intense passion. As you are generally tolerant and liberal, you may be drawn to less conventional relationships.

To read all about your Outer Planets and work out how to use your personalized timetable, go to Section Three, page 789.

go to Section Three, page 789.

VĨ

Your Personalized Timetable

JUPITER BENEFICIAL
1939 2/10 – 3/23
1940 6/14 – 12/13
1941 1/17 – 4/23
1944 8/24 – 11/12
1945 3/16 – 7/12
1946 11/7 – 12/25
1947 6/13 – 8/17
1951 1/23 – 3/7
1952 5/25 – until 1953 4/4
1956 8/8 – 10/23
1957 5/3 – 6/3
1958 10/22 – 12/7
1962 5/15 – 8/19
1963 1/2 – 2/18
1964 5/8 – 7/26
1964 11/4 – until 1965 3/14
1968 7/22 – 10/6
1970 10/6 – 11/21
1974 4/19 – 10/7
1974 11/30 – until 1975 1/31
1976 4/21 – 7/1
1976 12/21 – until 1977 2/9
1979 11/4 – until 1980 2/17
1980 7/2 – 9/20
1982 1/28 – 3/23
1982 9/18 – 11/6
1986 4/1 – 5/24
1986 8/31 – until 1987 1/11
1988 4/5 – 6/12
1991 10/13 – until 1992 3/29
1992 6/2 – 9/4
1993 12/28 – until 1994 5/4
1994 8/27 – 10/21
1998 3/14 – 4/29
1998 10/19 – 12/8
2000 3/18 – 5/26
2003 9/25 – until 2004 8/19
2005 12/9 – until 2006 6/24
2006 7/18 – 10/4
2010 2/26 – 4/9
2011 7/9 – 10/22
2012 2/25 – 5/9

SATURN BENEFICIAL
1940 5/9 – until 1941 6/11
1941 12/29 – until 1942 2/17
1949 8/6 – until 1950 9/12
1954 2/5 – 3/1
1954 10/11 – until 1955 1/11
1955 4/20 – 10/7
1965 3/11 – until 1966 3/5
1969 6/24 – 10/19
1970 3/15 – 8/14
1970 9/25 – until 1971 4/18
1978 9/14 – until 1979 10/21
1980 4/1 – 7/11
1983 11/16 – until 1984 11/12
1994 4/19 – 8/29
1995 1/14 – 4/10
1995 10/14 – 12/29
1999 4/23 – until 2000 5/24
2007 10/28 – until 2008 2/11
2008 7/18 – until 2009 8/26
2012 12/27 – Continues

URANUS BENEFICIAL
1938 1/1 – until 1941 2/11
1963 9/7 – until 1967 8/5
1976 11/28 – until 1979 10/10
2005 4/12 – until 2008 12/31

NEPTUNE BENEFICIAL
1938 1/1 – until 1939 8/24
1960 11/10 – until 1965 10/29

PLUTO BENEFICIAL
1960 9/8 – until 1968 9/3
1986 12/22 – until 1991 10/16

JUPITER CHALLENGING
1939 6/19 – 9/8
1940 2/2 – 4/13
1942 7/7 – 9/29

1942 12/26 – until 1943 5/22
1945 9/23 – 12/13
1946 4/15 – 8/13
1951 5/21 – 10/26
1952 1/3 – 3/27
1954 6/21 – 9/3
1955 2/6 – 4/25
1957 9/7 – 11/23
1958 6/1 – 7/6
1963 5/1 – until 1964 3/9
1966 6/4 – 8/16
1969 8/21 – 11/5
1975 4/13 – 7/6
1975 9/23 – until 1976 2/18
1978 5/17 – 7/30
1980 12/2 – until 1981 3/20
1981 8/1 – 10/20
1987 3/28 – 6/8
1987 11/6 – until 1988 1/22
1989 9/3 – 12/24
1990 4/26 – 7/14
1992 11/10 – until 1993 4/30
1993 7/2 – 10/5
1999 3/12 – 5/18
2001 8/11 – until 2002 2/10
2002 3/20 – 6/27
2004 10/24 – until 2005 9/19
2011 2/22 – 4/30

SATURN CHALLENGING
1938 3/15 – until 1939 4/21
1944 8/9 – until 1945 1/11
1945 4/27 – 9/12
1946 1/2 – 5/31
1951 10/5 – until 1952 11/16
1953 5/8 – 8/8
1967 4/23 – 11/14
1968 1/3 – 6/3
1968 10/13 – until 1969 2/23
1974 6/14 – until 1975 7/13
1980 11/14 – until 1981 3/30
1981 8/8 – until 1982 1/25
1982 2/5 – 9/24
1996 6/11 – 8/26
1997 2/25 – until 1998 4/4
2003 7/22 – until 2004 8/21
2005 2/4 – 5/6
2010 9/18 – until 2011 10/30

URANUS CHALLENGING
1950 7/14 – until 1954 6/27
1969 10/27 – until 1973 9/27
2012 4/24 – Continues

NEPTUNE CHALLENGING
1944 12/11 – until 1953 9/7

PLUTO CHALLENGING
1973 11/23 – until 1981 8/20

JUPITER SPECIAL
1948 12/13 – until 1949 2/23
1960 11/27 – until 1961 2/5
1972 3/18 – 6/1
1972 11/7 – until 1973 1/19
1984 2/20 – 7/14
1984 10/14 – until 1985 1/4
1996 1/31 – 12/19
2008 1/15 – 4/29
2008 5/18 – 12/1

SATURN SPECIAL
1959 3/15 – 5/19
1959 12/3 – until 1961 1/23
1989 1/6 – until 1990 3/2
1990 7/12 – 11/29

URANUS SPECIAL
1990 1/8 – until 1994 1/11

NEPTUNE SPECIAL
1987 1/15 – until 1994 12/22

PLUTO SPECIAL
2011 1/26 – Continues

January 6

Your Personal Powers

Pragmatic yet sensitive, you are a strong-willed individual with determination and drive. Your ruling planet, Saturn, implies that you can be hardworking, ambitious, and goal-oriented. You gain power from your special blend of imaginative ability and firmness of mind. With your multifaceted personality, you are also idealistic and intent on self-improvement, both emotionally and materially. Although you are often willing to make sacrifices to achieve your objectives, you will lose some of your power if you become too serious or anxious. Being sociable and creative, however, you also desire peace, harmony, and beauty. As a practical visionary with powerful intuition, you accomplish more when you are patient and have a clear image of what you want to achieve. You can then utilize your foresight and inner wisdom to reconfirm your choices and direction. With a desire for recognition and successes, you may find that much of your personal satisfaction comes through your work. You are responsible and persevering, and your executive skills can also play an important role in your overall achievement.

Your Powers of Attraction in Relationships

Magnetic and charming with strong character, you can impress others with your quick wit and insight. Proud and determined, you are attracted to strong and ambitious individuals. Being forceful and caring, you need to be careful that in your desire to help you do not become domineering. You may choose to work with your partner or begin new ventures together, especially if you both share the same ideals and ambitions. Although you can be very sensitive and in touch with the feelings of others, being practical means that you are also aware of the monetary considerations involved in your relationships. Loving your home, you can be an excellent parent or responsible and caring partner. You usually have more influence in your relationships when you act in a selfless way.

Your attractive qualities: determined, sensitive, hardworking, visionary, worldly, friendly, compassionate, practical, dependable, home-loving, imaginative, responsible, business sense, proud, understanding, idealistic, persevering, caring, leadership potential, creative, ambitious

Your less attractive qualities: anxious, bossy, unreasonable, stubborn, outspoken, domineering, workaholic, lacking responsibility, too willful, selfish, power struggles, suspicious, inertia, critical

Your Venus Power

The planet Venus has a great deal of influence on your powers of attraction. Below are four possible Venus types for women and men. To find your Venus you need to go to page 771, where you will find the Venus table and extra information. The planet Mars also affects your powers of attraction. To find your Mars table and interpretation go to page 761.

WOMEN WITH VENUS IN SCORPIO: Your strength and power is in your ability to love both deeply and sensitively. For you, love and desire go hand in hand. Because you feel so deeply, you often keep your sensitivity or vulnerability hidden in order to keep some control in your relationships. You are more likely to prefer a few very close loyal friends than many superficial acquaintances. In relationships your sensual nature and magnetic intensity can easily attract others.

MEN WITH VENUS IN SCORPIO: You are attracted to partners who have deep and powerful emotions or individuals you find intriguing. Your gift for creating smoke screens to maintain secrecy around your feelings can conceal your inner sensitivity and vulnerability. Nevertheless, you are looking for a partner who can pierce your defenses and understand you at a very deep level. Needing a relationship with a powerful sexual connection, you thrive on emotional intensity.

WOMEN WITH VENUS IN SAGITTARIUS: When you feel generous, you can make others feel more optimistic about life. You may be interested in higher learning and seek partners who are scholarly or broad-minded. You are outspoken and direct, and sometimes say things that you later regret. Curious and versatile, you can adjust quickly to new situations, and a foreign influence implies that you love to travel or may have a partner who comes from a different culture.

MEN WITH VENUS IN SAGITTARIUS: Optimistic and fun-loving, you love adventure and seek a partner who can expand your horizons. Being truthful and direct, you often say what you think, and at times you may be naively tactless. A need for expansion and prosperity suggests that you may enjoy traveling with your friends or partner. Being lighthearted and idealistic, once you have given your heart to someone you will stay honorable and loyal.

WOMEN WITH VENUS IN CAPRICORN: Proud and refined,

you attract others with your composed dignity. Disliking vulnerability and needing to feel safe before you can express your feelings, you display a strong front. Feeling insecure or inadequate in relationship may force you to become manipulative in order to regain control. Nevertheless, you can project an attractive sense of self-assurance and are capable of displaying loyalty and a wonderful dry sense of humor.

MEN WITH VENUS IN CAPRICORN: As you do not display your deeper emotions freely, you are usually dignified and controlled in your relationships. Practical and down-to-earth partners are particularly attractive to you, especially those who do not rush into expressing their feelings but seem to possess natural class and reserve. You need a partner who is loyal and dependable and willing to take your relationship seriously.

WOMEN WITH VENUS IN AQUARIUS: Usually you have a modern outlook on love and are open to new or current lifestyles. Your intuitive abilities, communal sense, and people skills often allow you to see deeper into human intentions and to read people's thoughts telepathically. You are usually group-oriented and drawn to individuals within the group who are independent and self-motivated. You are more inclined to choose a partner who is unconventional or freedom-loving. Conscious of your social standing, however, you want someone who can relate well to your friends.

MEN WITH VENUS IN AQUARIUS: Although independent, you often enjoy being part of a group. The partners you frequently attract are themselves nonconformists or free spirits. As an individual you may not find it easy to settle into a routine or an entirely mundane type of relationship. You may have some unconventional views on the traditional marriage or your partner may hold such views. It is usually important to you that your love relationships are based on friendship.

To read all about your Outer Planets and work out how to use your personalized timetable, go to Section Three, page 789.

VS

Your Personalized Timetable

JUPITER BENEFICIAL
1939 2/14 – 3/28
1940 6/19 – 11/30
1941 1/30 – 4/27
1944 8/29 – 11/19
1945 3/8 – 7/19
1946 11/12 – 12/31
1947 6/3 – 8/27
1951 1/27 – 3/11
1952 5/30 – until 1953 4/9
1956 8/13 – 10/28
1957 4/18 – 6/19
1958 10/27 – 12/12
1962 5/23 – 8/11
1963 1/7 – 2/22
1964 5/12 – 8/2
1964 10/27 – until 1965 3/20
1968 7/27 – 10/11
1970 10/11 – 11/26
1974 4/25 – 9/27
1974 12/10 – until 1975 2/5
1976 4/26 – 7/6
1976 12/11 – until 1977 2/19
1979 11/12 – until 1980 2/9
1980 7/8 – 9/24
1982 2/16 – 3/3
1982 9/24 – 11/10
1986 4/5 – 6/1
1986 8/23 – until 1987 1/16
1988 4/10 – 6/17
1991 10/18 – until 1992 3/19
1992 6/12 – 9/9
1994 1/4 – 4/26
1994 9/3 – 10/26
1998 3/19 – 5/4
1998 10/8 – 12/18
2000 3/23 – 5/30
2003 9/30 – until 2004 8/24
2005 12/14 – until 2006 6/7
2006 8/4 – 10/9
2010 3/2 – 4/14
2011 7/16 – 10/14
2012 3/2 – 5/13

SATURN BENEFICIAL
1940 5/17 – until 1941 6/20
1941 12/11 – until 1942 3/6
1949 8/14 – until 1950 9/20
1954 10/20 – until 1955 1/27
1955 4/4 – 10/17
1965 3/20 – until 1966 3/13
1969 7/7 – 10/5
1970 3/24 – until 1971 4/26
1978 9/22 – until 1979 4/26
1979 5/23 – 10/31
1980 3/19 – 7/23
1983 11/25 – until 1984 6/17
1984 8/7 – 11/21
1994 5/1 – 8/16
1995 1/24 – 4/19
1995 9/29 – until 1996 1/12
1999 5/1 – until 2000 6/1
2007 11/11 – until 2008 1/27
2008 7/27 – until 2009 9/3

URANUS BENEFICIAL
1938 1/1 – until 1941 3/21
1963 9/24 – until 1967 8/23
1976 12/17 – until 1979 10/27
2005 5/9 – until 2009 1/27

NEPTUNE BENEFICIAL
1938 1/1 – until 1940 7/17
1960 12/9 – until 1966 9/26

PLUTO BENEFICIAL
1960 10/10 – until 1969 7/29
1987 11/11 – until 1992 8/17

JUPITER CHALLENGING
1939 6/28 – 8/30
1940 2/7 – 4/17
1942 7/12 – 10/8

1942 12/17 – until 1943 5/28
1945 9/28 – 12/20
1946 4/7 – 8/19
1951 5/27 – 10/17
1952 1/11 – 3/31
1954 6/25 – 9/9
1955 1/28 – 5/3
1957 9/12 – 11/28
1958 5/18 – 7/20
1963 5/5 – until 1964 3/14
1966 6/9 – 8/21
1969 8/27 – 11/10
1975 4/17 – 7/15
1975 9/13 – until 1976 2/24
1978 5/22 – 8/3
1980 12/9 – until 1981 3/12
1981 8/7 – 10/25
1987 4/1 – 6/14
1987 10/29 – until 1988 1/30
1989 9/10 – 12/16
1990 5/2 – 7/18
1992 11/16 – until 1993 4/20
1993 7/12 – 10/10
1999 3/16 – 5/23
2001 8/16 – until 2002 1/29
2002 4/2 – 7/2
2004 10/29 – until 2005 9/24
2011 2/26 – 5/5

SATURN CHALLENGING
1938 3/23 – until 1939 4/29
1944 8/19 – 12/30
1945 5/8 – 9/24
1945 12/20 – until 1946 6/9
1951 10/13 – until 1952 11/25
1953 4/23 – 8/21
1967 5/2 – 10/26
1968 1/20 – 6/14
1968 9/30 – until 1969 3/5
1974 6/22 – until 1975 7/21
1980 11/24 – until 1981 3/16
1981 8/18 – until 1982 10/2
1996 7/5 – 8/1
1997 3/6 – until 1998 4/12
2003 7/30 – until 2004 2/4
2004 4/8 – 8/30
2005 1/21 – 5/18
2010 9/26 – until 2011 11/8
2012 6/1 – 7/19

URANUS CHALLENGING
1950 8/1 – until 1954 7/14
1969 11/15 – until 1973 10/13
2012 5/16 – Continues

URANUS CHALLENGING
1945 10/29 – until 1953 10/6

PLUTO CHALLENGING
1974 10/14 – until 1981 9/21

JUPITER SPECIAL
1948 12/18 – until 1949 2/28
1949 8/26 – 10/12
1960 12/1 – until 1961 2/9
1972 3/29 – 5/21
1972 11/13 – until 1973 1/24
1984 2/26 – 7/6
1984 10/21 – until 1985 1/8
1996 2/5 – 12/23
2008 1/19 – 12/6

SATURN SPECIAL
1959 12/13 – until 1961 2/1
1989 1/15 – until 1990 3/14
1990 6/27 – 12/10

URANUS SPECIAL
1990 1/26 – until 1994 11/16

NEPTUNE SPECIAL
1987 2/15 – until 1995 11/15

PLUTO SPECIAL
2011 3/8 – Continues

January 7

Your Personal Powers

Practical, intuitive, and mentally sharp, you are an interesting mixture of idealism and pragmatism. Usually hardworking, you are aware of your commitments and responsibilities. A natural psychologist, you gain power from your original and inventive ideas as well as from your shrewd insight into human nature. Possessing intelligence, you are usually open to new concepts and are keen on progress. When you have faith in your own abilities, you increase your resolve and find yourself naturally drawn to leadership positions. Although you are usually sociable, if you allow your sensitivity to affect your inner confidence, you can lose some of your power by withdrawing and isolating yourself. As a liberal and independent thinker as well as an idealist, you work best when you feel inspired and act decisively. Although you are often willing to fight for freedom, avoid losing power to a rebellious or contrary streak. Developing your natural sixth sense can aid your overall success. When positive, you can be spontaneous and uplift or enchant others with your many talents.

Your Powers of Attraction in Relationships

You can attract others with your thoughtful attitude and charming manner. You often seek friends and partners with a strong sense of self-identity who can match your intelligence. Although you can be quiet, reserved, and analytical, you can also be dramatic with good people skills. Being a perfectionist, you often analyze your relationships in order to improve them, but be careful of being too critical, cynical, or bossy with loved ones. You prefer a partner who will understand your need for time alone to reflect and revitalize your energies. Nevertheless, you gain from being open and communicative with loved ones, and your creative collaboration with others can be especially beneficial to you. You can also enhance your relationships by being altruistic or developing your humanitarian traits.

Your attractive qualities: spontaneous, intelligent, practical, highly intuitive, hardworking, meticulous, progressive, faithful, spiritual potential, idealistic, humanitarian, honest, inventive, analytical, original, psychic, trusting, psychological skills, discriminating, rational, reflective

Your less attractive qualities: worry, self-doubt, withdrawn, stubborn, contrary, cold, bossy, skeptical, pessimistic, too serious, self-absorbed, secretive, argumentative, confused, too detached

Your Venus Power

The planet Venus has a great deal of influence on your powers of attraction. Below are four possible Venus types for women and men. To find your Venus you need to go to page 771, where you will find the Venus table and extra information. The planet Mars also affects your powers of attraction. To find your Mars table and interpretation go to page 761.

WOMEN WITH VENUS IN SAGITTARIUS: Optimistic and fun-loving, you love adventure and seek a partner who can expand your horizons. Being truthful and direct, you often say what you think, and at times you may be naively tactless. A need for expansion and prosperity suggests that you may enjoy traveling with your friends or partner. Being lighthearted and idealistic, once you have given your heart to someone you will stay honorable and loyal.

MEN WITH VENUS IN SAGITTARIUS: You are usually attracted to partners who are knowledgeable or well-traveled. Enthusiastic and optimistic, you often respond quickly to love offers and enter relationships with enthusiasm. Generally you seek to expand your social circle, and meeting people from all walks of life can bring the variety and fun you seek in life. Although you are generous and honest, your partners may sometimes accuse you of being overly optimistic or too blunt.

WOMEN WITH VENUS IN CAPRICORN: Proud and refined, you attract others with your composed dignity. Disliking vulnerability and needing to feel safe before you can express your feelings, you display a strong front. Feeling insecure or inadequate in relationships may force you to become manipulative in order to regain control. Nevertheless, you can project an attractive sense of self-assurance and are capable of displaying loyalty and a wonderful dry sense of humor.

MEN WITH VENUS IN CAPRICORN: As you do not display your deeper emotions freely, you are usually dignified and controlled in your relationships with others. Practical and down-to-earth partners are particularly attractive to you, especially those who do not rush into expressing their feelings but seem to possess natural class and reserve. You need a partner who is loyal and dependable and willing to take your relationship seriously.

WOMEN WITH VENUS IN AQUARIUS: Usually you have a

modern outlook on love and are open to new or current lifestyles. Your intuitive abilities, communal sense, and people skills often allow you to see deeper into human intentions and to read people's thoughts telepathically. You are usually group-oriented and are drawn to individuals within the group who are independent and self-motivated. You are more inclined to choose a partner who is unconventional or freedom-loving. Conscious of your social standing, however, you want someone who can relate well to your friends.

MEN WITH VENUS IN AQUARIUS: Although independent, you often enjoy being part of a group. The partners you frequently attract are themselves nonconformists or free spirits. As an individual you may not find it easy to settle into a routine or an entirely mundane type of relationship. You may have some unconventional views on traditional marriage or your partner may hold such views. It is usually important to you that your love relationships are based on friendship.

WOMEN WITH VENUS IN PISCES: Idealistic and impressionable, in love you are romantic. Being sensitive to other people, you are receptive to their moods and feelings. This affinity indicates that although you can be selfless you may have to guard against being too sentimental or overly romantic, especially of those who can take advantage of your kindness. Nevertheless, alluring and seductive, your partners can be intrigued by your emotional magnetism, compassion, or mysterious nature.

MEN WITH VENUS IN PISCES: Being adaptable and sensitive, you are able to intuitively feel the moods of those you love. Although you are receptive to others, you can be ambiguous about your own feelings toward your partner. Romantic and kindhearted, you long to be loved but you need to be realistic about your relationships in order to avoid disappointments. When in love you may idealize your partners and fail to see any faults in their personalities.

To read all about your Outer Planets and work out how to use your personalized timetable, go to Section Three, page 789.

Your Personalized Timetable

JUPITER BENEFICIAL
1939 2/18 – 4/1
1940 6/24 – 11/21
1941 2/8 – 5/2
1944 9/2 – 11/26
1945 2/28 – 7/25
1946 11/16 – until 1947 1/6
1947 5/25 – 9/4
1951 2/1 – 3/15
1952 6/3 – until 1953 4/14
1956 8/17 – 11/3
1957 4/8 – 6/29
1958 11/1 – 12/17
1962 6/2 – 8/1
1963 1/12 – 2/26
1964 5/16 – 8/11
1964 10/18 – until 1965 3/25
1968 8/1 – 10/16
1970 10/16 – 12/1
1974 4/30 – 9/18
1974 12/18 – until 1975 2/9
1976 4/30 – 7/12
1976 12/2 – until 1977 2/28
1979 11/20 – until 1980 1/31
1980 7/14 – 9/29
1982 9/29 – 11/15
1986 4/10 – 6/10
1986 8/13 – until 1987 1/21
1988 4/14 – 6/22
1991 10/24 – until 1992 3/11
1992 6/20 – 9/13
1994 1/11 – 4/18
1994 9/10 – 10/30
1998 3/23 – 5/10
1998 9/29 – 12/27
2000 3/27 – 6/4
2003 10/5 – until 2004 8/29
2005 12/20 – until 2006 5/27
2006 8/15 – 10/14
2010 3/6 – 4/18
2011 7/25 – 10/5
2012 3/7 – 5/18

SATURN BENEFICIAL
1940 5/25 – 12/21
1941 1/29 – 6/29
1941 11/27 – until 1942 3/18
1949 8/22 – until 1950 9/28
1954 10/29 – until 1955 10/26
1965 3/29 – 10/15
1965 12/13 – until 1966 3/22
1969 7/24 – 9/18
1970 4/2 – until 1971 5/4
1978 10/1 – until 1979 4/2
1979 6/15 – 11/11
1980 3/6 – 8/2
1983 12/4 – until 1984 5/28
1984 8/26 – 11/29
1994 5/16 – 7/31
1995 2/2 – 4/30
1995 9/15 – until 1996 1/23
1999 5/9 – until 2000 6/10
2001 1/10 – 2/8
2007 12/1 – until 2008 1/6
2008 8/5 – until 2009 9/11

URANUS BENEFICIAL
1938 1/1 – until 1941 4/12
1963 10/12 – until 1967 9/9
1977 1/11 – until 1979 11/13
2006 3/10 – until 2009 2/16

NEPTUNE BENEFICIAL
1938 1/1 – until 1940 8/21
1961 1/28 – until 1966 10/28

PLUTO BENEFICIAL
1961 9/12 – until 1969 8/30
1987 12/7 – until 1992 10/2

JUPITER CHALLENGING
1939 7/11 – 8/16
1940 2/12 – 4/21
1942 7/16 – 10/19
1942 12/6 – until 1943 6/2

1945 10/3 – 12/27
1946 3/29 – 8/25
1951 6/1 – 10/9
1952 1/18 – 4/4
1954 6/30 – 9/15
1955 1/20 – 5/10
1957 9/17 – 12/3
1958 5/8 – 7/31
1963 5/10 – until 1964 3/18
1966 6/14 – 8/26
1969 9/1 – 11/15
1975 4/22 – 7/29
1975 8/30 – until 1976 2/29
1978 5/27 – 8/8
1980 12/18 – until 1981 3/3
1981 8/13 – 10/30
1987 4/6 – 6/20
1987 10/21 – until 1988 2/6
1989 9/18 – 12/8
1990 5/8 – 7/23
1992 11/22 – until 1993 4/11
1993 7/21 – 10/14
1999 3/20 – 5/28
2001 8/22 – until 2002 1/19
2002 4/11 – 7/6
2004 11/3 – until 2005 9/29
2011 3/3 – 5/9

SATURN CHALLENGING
1938 3/31 – until 1939 5/7
1944 8/30 – 12/17
1945 5/17 – 10/11
1945 12/2 – until 1946 6/18
1951 10/22 – until 1952 6/2
1952 6/18 – 12/6
1953 4/10 – 9/1
1967 5/12 – 10/12
1968 2/2 – 6/28
1968 9/15 – until 1969 3/14
1974 6/29 – until 1975 7/29
1980 12/7 – until 1981 3/2
1981 8/28 – until 1982 10/11
1997 3/14 – until 1998 4/20
2003 8/8 – until 2004 1/19
2004 4/23 – 9/9
2005 1/9 – 5/29
2010 10/5 – until 2011 11/17
2012 5/12 – 8/7

URANUS CHALLENGING
1950 8/22 – until 1955 5/10
1969 12/10 – until 1974 8/8
2012 6/16 – Continues

NEPTUNE CHALLENGING
1945 12/5 – until 1954 9/5

PLUTO CHALLENGING
1974 11/12 – until 1982 7/26

JUPITER SPECIAL
1948 12/22 – until 1949 3/5
1949 8/14 – 10/23
1960 12/6 – until 1961 2/14
1972 4/18 – 4/30
1972 11/18 – until 1973 1/28
1984 3/3 – 6/28
1984 10/28 – until 1985 1/12
1996 2/10 – 8/18
1996 9/19 – 12/28
2008 1/24 – 12/11

SATURN SPECIAL
1959 12/21 – until 1961 2/10
1961 8/22 – 11/2
1989 1/24 – 8/7
1989 10/15 – until 1990 3/29
1990 6/11 – 12/19

URANUS SPECIAL
1990 2/16 – until 1994 12/9

NEPTUNE SPECIAL
1988 1/13 – until 1995 12/20

PLUTO SPECIAL
2012 1/28 – Continues

♑

607

January 8

SUN: CAPRICORN • DECANATE: TAURUS/VENUS • DEGREE: 16°–18° CAPRICORN • MODE: CARDINAL • ELEMENT: EARTH

Your Personal Powers

Possessing personal charisma and a practical attitude, you are a determined individual with original ideas. If you stay focused, your ruling planet, Saturn, ensures that you have the ambition and perseverance to put your large plans into practice. You gain power from your strong awareness of image that you can use to envisage your future goals or create your personal style. While motivated by material success, indulgence in luxury and the good life may cause you to lose some of your power. Nevertheless, your excellent people skills and flair for the dramatic indicate that you benefit from working in partnerships or teamwork situations. Your work can be especially important in your life as a means of channeling your strong drive. In order to empower yourself and feel rejuvenated, however, you need to create harmony around you or take time off to relax. By developing inner detachment, you can avoid frustration and disappointment or a tendency to be too serious. Although pragmatic, you possess sensitivity and an intuitive comprehension that can greatly aid your overall success.

Your Powers of Attraction in Relationships

You attract others with your magnetic charm and strong personality. Although you are independent and resourceful, you understand the value of working cooperatively as a team. You are attracted to confident and enthusiastic individuals who can inspire your ambitious nature and desire for success. Equally, with your need for security, you want a reliable mate who can understand and share your love of home and family; however, avoid getting stuck in a comfortable rut. Romantic in love, you can be charming and caring in your intimate relationships. Although you can be full of enthusiasm when projecting your love, be careful that a desire for control and inner fears do not cause you to become domineering. Nevertheless, your self-confidence can attract many admirers and opportunities for personal relationships.

Your attractive qualities: practical, leadership, people skills, friendly, intuitive, thorough, sensitive, home-loving, hardworking, imaginative, authoritative, original, organizational skills, caring, business sense, determination, ambitious, subtle, love of harmony

Your less attractive qualities: impatient, intolerant, restlessness, power struggles, domineering, inertia, escapist, self-doubt, sensitive, nervous, confused, controlling, too serious

Your Venus Power

The planet Venus has a great deal of influence on your powers of attraction. Below are four possible Venus types for women and men. To find your Venus you need to go to page 771, where you will find the Venus table and extra information. The planet Mars also affects your powers of attraction. To find your Mars table and interpretation go to page 761.

WOMEN WITH VENUS IN SAGITTARIUS: When you feel generous, you can make others feel more optimistic about life. You may be interested in higher learning and seek partners who are scholarly or broad-minded. You are outspoken and direct, and sometimes say things that you later regret. Curious and versatile, you can adjust quickly to new situations, and a foreign influence implies that you love to travel or may have a partner who comes from a different culture.

MEN WITH VENUS IN SAGITTARIUS: Your enthusiasm and straightforward conduct usually appeal to others and imply that you are approachable and easygoing. Being open to ideas and willing to believe that life has a great deal to offer suggest that you are generous, broad-minded, and show eagerness to cooperate with others. A love of travel and an interest in other cultures also imply that your partner may come from a foreign country.

WOMEN WITH VENUS IN CAPRICORN: Proud and refined, you attract others with your composed dignity. Disliking vulnerability and needing to feel safe before you can express your feelings, you display a strong front. Feeling insecure or inadequate in relationships may force you to become manipulative in order to regain control. Nevertheless, you can project an attractive sense of self-assurance and are capable of displaying loyalty and a wonderful dry sense of humor.

MEN WITH VENUS IN CAPRICORN: As you do not display your deeper emotions freely, you are usually dignified and controlled in your relationships with others. Practical and down-to-earth partners are particularly attractive to you, especially those who do not rush into expressing their feelings but seem to possess natural class and reserve. You need a partner who is loyal and dependable and willing to take your relationship seriously.

WOMEN WITH VENUS IN AQUARIUS: Usually you have a

modern outlook on love and are open to new or current lifestyles. Your intuitive abilities, communal sense, and people skills often allow you to see deeper into human intentions and to telepathically read people's thoughts. You are usually group-oriented and are drawn to individuals within the group who are independent and self-motivated. You are more inclined to choose a partner who is unconventional or freedom-loving. Conscious of your social standing, however, you want someone who can relate well to your friends.

MEN WITH VENUS IN AQUARIUS: Although independent, you often enjoy being part of a group. The partners you frequently attract are themselves nonconformists or free spirits. As an individual you may not find it easy to settle into a routine or an entirely mundane type of relationship. You may have some unconventional views on traditional marriage or your partner may hold such views. It is usually important to you that your love relationships are based on friendship.

WOMEN WITH VENUS IN PISCES: Idealistic and impressionable, in love you are romantic. Being sensitive to people means you are receptive to their moods and feelings. This affinity indicates that although you can be selfless, you may have to guard against being too sentimental or overly romantic, especially of those who can take advantage of your kindness. Nevertheless, alluring and seductive, your partners can be intrigued by your poetic soul or mysterious nature.

MEN WITH VENUS IN PISCES: The combination of your emotional subtlety and charm can make you very alluring when dealing with affairs of the heart. Perceptive and impressionable, you have an easygoing style in your relationships, usually preferring to avoid ugly confrontation. You are drawn to partners who have a touch of glamour and are sensitive to the needs of others. Alternatively, they could be visionaries with rich imaginations who know how to keep you enchanted. With your insight you have the ability to observe the subtle moods of your partner.

To read all about your Outer Planets and work out how to use your personalized timetable, go to Section Three, page 789.

♍

Your Personalized Timetable

JUPITER BENEFICIAL
1939 2/23 – 4/5
1940 6/30 – 11/13
1941 2/16 – 5/6
1944 9/7 – 12/5
1945 2/19 – 7/31
1946 11/21 – until 1947 1/12
1947 5/17 – 9/11
1951 2/5 – 3/19
1952 6/8 – until 1953 4/18
1956 8/22 – 11/9
1957 3/30 – 7/7
1958 11/5 – 12/23
1959 7/11 – 7/29
1962 6/16 – 7/18
1963 1/17 – 3/3
1964 5/21 – 8/23
1964 10/7 – until 1965 3/31
1968 8/6 – 10/21
1970 10/21 – 12/5
1974 5/6 – 9/10
1974 12/25 – until 1975 2/14
1976 5/4 – 7/18
1976 11/24 – until 1977 3/7
1979 12/2 – until 1980 1/20
1980 7/19 – 10/4
1982 10/4 – 11/19
1986 4/15 – 6/23
1986 7/31 – until 1987 1/27
1988 4/18 – 6/27
1991 10/30 – until 1992 3/3
1992 6/27 – 9/18
1994 1/19 – 4/9
1994 9/15 – 11/4
1998 3/28 – 5/16
1998 9/22 – until 1999 1/3
2000 4/1 – 6/8
2003 10/10 – until 2004 4/19
2004 5/20 – 9/3
2005 12/25 – until 2006 5/18
2006 8/23 – 10/19
2010 3/10 – 4/23
2011 8/4 – 9/24
2012 3/12 – 5/22

SATURN BENEFICIAL
1940 6/3 – 11/30
1941 2/17 – 7/9
1941 11/15 – until 1942 3/29
1949 8/31 – until 1950 10/7
1954 11/6 – until 1955 11/4
1965 4/7 – 9/27
1965 12/29 – until 1966 3/30
1970 4/10 – until 1971 5/12
1978 10/10 – until 1979 3/18
1979 6/30 – 11/23
1980 2/21 – 8/12
1983 12/14 – until 1984 5/14
1984 9/9 – 12/8
1985 6/23 – 8/26
1994 6/11 – 7/5
1995 2/11 – 5/11
1995 9/2 – until 1996 2/2
1999 5/17 – until 2000 6/18
2000 12/19 – until 2001 3/2
2008 8/13 – until 2009 9/20

URANUS BENEFICIAL
1938 1/1 – until 1941 5/1
1963 11/4 – until 1968 6/23
1977 11/7 – until 1980 9/11
2006 3/29 – until 2009 3/7

NEPTUNE BENEFICIAL
1938 1/1 – until 1941 7/13
1961 12/7 – until 1967 9/24

PLUTO BENEFICIAL
1961 10/15 – until 1970 7/22
1988 1/13 – until 1992 10/31

JUPITER CHALLENGING
1940 2/17 – 4/26
1942 7/21 – until 1943 6/7
1945 10/7 – until 1946 1/5

1946 3/20 – 8/31
1951 6/8 – 10/2
1952 1/25 – 4/9
1954 7/4 – 9/22
1955 1/13 – 5/17
1957 9/22 – 12/9
1958 4/29 – 8/8
1963 5/15 – until 1964 3/23
1966 6/18 – 8/31
1967 2/26 – 4/13
1969 9/6 – 11/20
1975 4/26 – until 1976 3/5
1978 6/1 – 8/13
1980 12/29 – until 1981 2/20
1981 8/19 – 11/4
1987 4/10 – 6/26
1987 10/14 – until 1988 2/12
1989 9/27 – 11/29
1990 5/14 – 7/27
1992 11/28 – until 1993 4/3
1993 7/28 – 10/19
1999 3/24 – 6/2
1999 12/8 – until 2000 1/1
2001 8/28 – until 2002 1/11
2002 4/19 – 7/11
2004 11/8 – until 2005 5/21
2005 6/20 – 10/4
2011 3/7 – 5/13

SATURN CHALLENGING
1938 4/8 – until 1939 5/16
1939 11/27 – until 1940 1/27
1944 9/12 – 12/3
1945 5/27 – until 1946 6/26
1951 10/30 – until 1952 5/4
1952 7/16 – 12/18
1953 3/27 – 9/11
1967 5/22 – 9/29
1968 2/13 – 7/20
1968 8/24 – until 1969 3/23
1974 7/7 – until 1975 8/6
1980 12/26 – until 1981 2/11
1981 9/6 – until 1982 10/19
1997 3/23 – until 1998 4/28
2003 8/18 – until 2004 1/6
2004 5/5 – 9/20
2004 12/27 – until 2005 6/7
2010 10/13 – until 2011 11/26
2012 4/27 – 8/21

URANUS CHALLENGING
1950 9/24 – until 1955 6/4
1970 10/4 – until 1974 9/2

NEPTUNE CHALLENGING
1946 10/27 – until 1954 10/5

PLUTO CHALLENGING
1975 10/6 – until 1982 9/8

JUPITER SPECIAL
1948 12/27 – until 1949 3/11
1949 8/5 – 11/1
1960 12/10 – until 1961 2/19
1972 11/23 – until 1973 2/2
1984 3/10 – 6/20
1984 11/3 – until 1985 1/17
1996 2/16 – 8/3
1996 10/4 – until 1997 1/1
2008 1/29 – 12/15

SATURN SPECIAL
1959 12/30 – until 1961 2/19
1961 8/6 – 11/17
1989 2/2 – 7/21
1989 10/31 – until 1990 4/26
1990 5/13 – 12/28

URANUS SPECIAL
1990 3/17 – until 1994 12/28

NEPTUNE SPECIAL
1988 2/12 – until 1996 11/8

PLUTO SPECIAL
2012 3/8 – Continues

January 9

SUN: CAPRICORN • DECANATE: TAURUS/VENUS • DEGREE: 17°–19° CAPRICORN • MODE: CARDINAL • ELEMENT: EARTH

Your Personal Powers

Broad-minded and imaginative, your personal powers include a shrewd practicality combined with a desire for new experiences. Capable and discerning, you gain power from your desire for self-improvement and your ability to endure. Although usually hardworking, you can lose power if you become pessimistic or discouraged and do not put in the effort needed to bring out your remarkable potential. With your appreciation of beauty and luxury, you are likely to have creative talents and imaginative ideas. Your interest in people may manifest in sociable activities or humanitarian interests. Being security-conscious and diligent, you benefit from making long-term plans, yet a need for variety suggests that you are likely to seek many types of experience to enrich your life. Just be careful that impatience and restlessness do not cause you to lose some of your positive power. With your progressive approach, vision, and plain common sense, you can succeed admirably. Your perseverance and desire for action can also aid your accomplishments.

Your Powers of Attraction in Relationships

Others are attracted to your friendly down-to-earth manner. Your ability to work well with others ensures that you usually benefit from group collaboration. Although you love variety, you want security within a relationship. Often idealistic in love, you can be disappointed if partners do not live up to your expectations. Although you have a strong need for love and affection, avoid rushing into a relationship or taking on a partner who may turn out to be a burden on you. Being generous, however, you can be a rock of support for others, and once committed, you are usually loyal. You are often drawn to broad-minded and intelligent individuals. If you display your intense emotions, you may encounter some dramatic situations. Staying detached helps you overcome frustrations and develops the more compassionate side to your nature.

Your attractive qualities: kind, intelligent, ambitious, idealistic, humanitarian, adventurous, quick responses, creative, psychic, compassionate, sensitive, generous, magnetic, artistic, charitable, universal, giving, detached, enterprising, capable, wise, progressive, imaginative

Your less attractive qualities: frustrated, impatient, nervous, isolated, pessimistic, materialistic, escapist, inferiority complex, unrealistic dreams, disappointed, fearful, worry

Your Venus Power

The planet Venus has a great deal of influence on your powers of attraction. Below are four possible Venus types for women and men. To find your Venus you need to go to page 771, where you will find the Venus table and extra information. The planet Mars also affects your powers of attraction. To find your Mars table and interpretation go to page 761.

WOMEN WITH VENUS IN SAGITTARIUS: Sociable, warm, and friendly, you possess an honest and frank style in your relationships. Being naturally gregarious, you want others to share your enthusiasm and you enjoy encouraging the people you love. You do better when you have a sense of personal freedom within a relationship and are usually generous with the faults of others. You need a partner who can share your need to explore and take risks whether through travel, education, or recreation.

MEN WITH VENUS IN SAGITTARIUS: When in love, you are open and friendly with a need for a partner who can share your adventurous spirit and sense of fun. Be careful, however, that your desire for freedom does not cause you to avoid commitment. You prefer your partners to be positive, direct, and generous in spirit. Being outspoken as well as an idealist, you usually enjoy a partner with whom you can share your strong opinions. Alternatively, you may wish to explore life together, whether through travel, education, or by having fun.

WOMEN WITH VENUS IN CAPRICORN: Romantically, you do not give your heart easily but hide behind a cool reserve until you feel free to express your emotions. As you take your relationships seriously, you may find yourself drawn to people who are businesslike, resourceful, and practical or who can act as teachers or mentors. Work or career may also be a factor in many of your associations and partnerships. As security can play an important role in your relationships, you are often attracted to partners who are loyal and hardworking.

MEN WITH VENUS IN CAPRICORN: As you admire loyal, hardworking, and dedicated individuals, you probably want a partner who can share your vocational interests or can provide you with the security you need. You could even find yourself with a partner who is of a different age group or maturity. Guard against denying your true emotional needs or focusing

on your career at the expense of your relationship. You are drawn to reserved partners who display self-control.

WOMEN WITH VENUS IN AQUARIUS: When it comes to relationships, others are attracted to your honest, friendly, and easygoing attitude. You enjoy social interaction and have a genuine concern for others. In fact, at times, your friends may be just as important as your partner. Usually you present a tolerant and reasonable front in love situations and attempt to view your relationships objectively. If partners become too demanding, however, you can become stubborn or awkward. Nevertheless, inventive and progressive, you enjoy the company of like-minded people who can share your original ideas.

MEN WITH VENUS IN AQUARIUS: Friendly and honest, you attract people with your broad-minded approach to life. You usually possess an objective and slightly detached attitude to affairs of the heart. If you are too removed, however, others can misinterpret your behavior as uncaring. It is often more important to you that your love relationships are based on friendship and honesty than intense passion. As you are generally tolerant and liberal, you may be drawn to less conventional relationships.

WOMEN WITH VENUS IN PISCES: Idealistic and impressionable, in love you are romantic. Being sensitive to other people, you are receptive to their moods and feelings. This affinity means that although you can be selfless, you may have to guard against being too sentimental or overly romantic, especially of those who can take advantage of your kindness. Nevertheless, alluring and seductive, your partners can be intrigued by your emotional magnetism, compassion, or mysterious nature.

MEN WITH VENUS IN PISCES: Being adaptable and sensitive, you are able to intuitively feel the moods of those you love. Although you are receptive to others, you can be ambiguous about your own feelings toward your partner. Romantic and kindhearted, you long to be loved but you need to be realistic about your relationships in order to avoid disappointments. When in love you may idealize your partners and fail to see any faults in their personalities.

To read all about your Outer Planets and work out how to use your personalized timetable, go to Section Three, page 789.

♍

Your Personalized Timetable

JUPITER BENEFICIAL
1939 2/27 – 4/10
1940 7/6 – 11/5
1941 2/23 – 5/10
1944 9/12 – 12/15
1945 2/8 – 8/6
1946 11/26 – until 1947 1/19
1947 5/9 – 9/18
1951 2/10 – 3/23
1952 6/13 – until 1953 4/23
1956 8/27 – 11/15
1957 3/22 – 7/15
1958 11/10 – 12/28
1959 6/22 – 8/17
1963 1/22 – 3/7
1964 5/25 – until 1965 4/5
1968 8/11 – 10/26
1969 5/12 – 6/3
1970 10/25 – 12/10
1974 5/13 – 9/2
1974 12/31 – until 1975 2/18
1976 5/8 – 7/24
1976 11/17 – until 1977 3/14
1980 7/25 – 10/9
1982 10/9 – 11/24
1986 4/20 – 10/25
1986 11/21 – until 1987 1/31
1988 4/22 – 7/2
1989 1/9 – 1/31
1991 11/6 – until 1992 2/24
1992 7/4 – 9/23
1994 1/29 – 3/30
1994 9/21 – 11/9
1998 4/1 – 5/22
1998 9/14 – until 1999 1/9
2000 4/5 – 6/13
2003 10/16 – until 2004 4/4
2004 6/4 – 9/7
2006 1/1 – 5/10
2006 8/31 – 10/24
2010 3/15 – 4/28
2011 8/25 – 9/4
2012 3/17 – 5/26

SATURN BENEFICIAL
1940 6/12 – 11/16
1941 3/2 – 7/21
1941 11/2 – until 1942 4/8
1949 9/8 – until 1950 10/15
1951 4/29 – 6/27
1954 11/15 – until 1955 11/12
1965 4/17 – 9/13
1966 1/11 – 4/8
1966 11/6 – 12/17
1970 4/18 – until 1971 5/20
1978 10/20 – until 1979 3/4
1979 7/11 – 12/9
1980 2/4 – 8/21
1983 12/24 – until 1984 4/30
1984 9/20 – 12/17
1985 6/6 – 9/12
1995 2/20 – 5/25
1995 8/18 – until 1996 2/12
1999 5/25 – until 2000 1/10
2000 1/12 – 6/27
2000 12/4 – until 2001 3/16
2008 8/22 – until 2009 9/28

URANUS BENEFICIAL
1938 2/23 – until 1941 5/19
1964 8/31 – until 1968 7/25
1977 11/23 – until 1980 10/4
2006 4/19 – until 2010 1/8

NEPTUNE BENEFICIAL
1938 1/1 – until 1941 8/20
1962 1/18 – until 1967 10/26

PLUTO BENEFICIAL
1962 9/15 – until 1970 8/26
1988 11/24 – until 1993 9/17

JUPITER CHALLENGING
1940 2/22 – 4/30

1942 7/26 – until 1943 6/13
1945 10/12 – until 1946 1/16
1946 3/9 – 9/6
1951 6/14 – 9/24
1952 1/31 – 4/13
1954 7/9 – 9/29
1955 1/5 – 5/23
1957 9/27 – 12/16
1958 4/21 – 8/15
1963 5/20 – 11/14
1963 12/26 – until 1964 3/27
1966 6/23 – 9/5
1967 2/14 – 4/25
1969 9/11 – 11/26
1970 6/11 – 7/5
1975 5/1 – until 1976 3/9
1978 6/6 – 8/17
1981 1/17 – 1/31
1981 8/24 – 11/8
1987 4/14 – 7/3
1987 10/6 – until 1988 2/18
1989 10/10 – 11/16
1990 5/19 – 8/1
1992 12/4 – until 1993 3/26
1993 8/4 – 10/24
1999 3/29 – 6/7
1999 11/23 – until 2000 1/17
2001 9/3 – until 2002 1/3
2002 4/26 – 7/16
2004 11/14 – 5/5
2005 7/5 – 10/9
2011 3/11 – 5/18

SATURN CHALLENGING
1938 4/17 – until 1939 5/25
1939 11/10 – until 1940 2/11
1944 9/30 – 11/15
1945 6/4 – until 1946 7/4
1951 11/9 – until 1952 4/19
1952 7/31 – until 1953 1/2
1953 3/11 – 9/21
1967 6/3 – 9/16
1968 2/22 – until 1969 3/31
1974 7/15 – until 1975 8/14
1976 3/10 – 4/13
1981 9/15 – until 1982 10/28
1997 3/31 – until 1998 5/7
2003 8/28 – 12/25
2004 5/15 – 10/5
2004 12/12 – until 2005 6/16
2010 10/21 – until 2011 12/6
2012 4/14 – 9/1

URANUS CHALLENGING
1951 7/12 – until 1955 6/23
1970 10/20 – until 1974 9/21

NEPTUNE CHALLENGING
1946 11/30 – until 1955 9/2

PLUTO CHALLENGING
1975 11/2 – until 1982 10/6

JUPITER SPECIAL
1948 12/31 – until 1949 3/17
1949 7/27 – 11/8
1960 12/15 – until 1961 2/24
1972 11/28 – until 1973 2/6
1984 3/18 – 6/11
1984 11/9 – until 1985 1/21
1996 2/21 – 7/24
1996 10/13 – until 1997 1/5
2008 2/2 – 12/20

SATURN SPECIAL
1960 1/8 – until 1961 3/1
1961 7/22 – 11/29
1989 2/12 – 7/6
1989 11/12 – until 1991 1/6

URANUS SPECIAL
1991 1/10 – until 1995 1/15

NEPTUNE SPECIAL
1989 1/10 – until 1996 12/16

January 10

Your Personal Powers

Enterprising and mentally sharp, you are an independent individual with practical awareness and a strong drive for success. Your ruling planet, Saturn, ensures that you can be determined and hardworking in achieving your goals. You gain power from the combination of your ambition, organizational ability, and people skills. Persuasive, purposeful, and action-oriented, you may find yourself being drawn to leadership positions. Possessing natural artistic or creative tendencies, you also appreciate beauty and the good things of life. Be careful, however, not to lose power by becoming too indulgent or extravagant. Your desire for accomplishment or independence indicates that if you are not happy with your situation you may go it alone. Just be careful that in your desire for autonomy you do not lose some of your power by becoming too domineering, headstrong, or arrogant. Nevertheless, with your impressive manner, executive skills, inspired ideas, and enterprising nature, you can afford to be friendly and helpful and enhance your potential to succeed.

Your Powers of Attraction in Relationships

You are security-conscious, and people are attracted to your innovative and confident nature. Enhanced social skills and a warm and gregarious manner can help you make friends and ensure you work well with others. Being practical and rational on the outside, you usually find it hard to display your inner sensitivity or vulnerability. Generally, you are attracted to successful people and those with ambition and influence. You are also drawn to partners who stimulate your own potential for achievement. With your shrewd sense of values, you respect people with money, knowledge, and ingenuity. Although you can be generous with your partners and friends, be careful that a stubborn streak and bossy behavior does not mar your relationships. Being mentally keen with personal magnetism ensures you can always attract others.

Your attractive qualities: creative, mentally sharp, ambitious, enterprising, independent, leadership, progressive, practical, hardworking, forceful, artistic, strong-willed, optimistic, strong convictions, innovative, competitive, independent, original, gregarious

Your less attractive qualities: overbearing, materialistic, overindulgent, jealous, egotistical, impatient, rigid, too proud, antagonistic, too willful, lacks restraint, restless, stubborn

Your Venus Power

The planet Venus has a great deal of influence on your powers of attraction. Below are four possible Venus types for women and men. To find your Venus you need to go to page 771, where you will find the Venus table and extra information. The planet Mars also affects your powers of attraction. To find your Mars table and interpretation go to page 761.

WOMEN WITH VENUS IN SAGITTARIUS: Sociable, warm, and friendly, you possess an honest and frank style in your relationships. Being naturally gregarious, you want others to share your enthusiasm and enjoy encouraging the people you love. You do better when you have a sense of personal freedom within a relationship and are usually generous with the faults of others. You need a partner who can share your need to explore and take risks, whether through travel, education, or recreation.

MEN WITH VENUS IN SAGITTARIUS: When in love you are open and friendly with a need for a partner who can share your adventurous spirit and sense of fun. Be careful, however, that your desire for freedom does not cause you to avoid commitment. You prefer your partners to be positive, direct, and generous in spirit. Being outspoken as well as an idealist, you usually enjoy a partner with whom you can share your strong opinions. Alternatively, you may wish to explore life together, whether through travel, education, or by having fun.

WOMEN WITH VENUS IN CAPRICORN: Loyal and responsible, you are attracted to dignified and reserved individuals. Being practical and security-conscious, you prefer hardworking partners who are resourceful and enterprising. Work may even be a factor in many of your associations and partnerships. For you, family and faithfulness can be especially important, so you are usually willing to work hard or make sacrifices in order to build a strong relationship.

MEN WITH VENUS IN CAPRICORN: Hardworking and ambitious, you are usually attracted to determined, focused, and ambitious partners who have a strong sense of duty. You want them to take relationships as seriously as you do, so loyalty and faithfulness are high on your agenda. Since you may display a natural reserve about expressing your feelings in an

intimate relationship, you need a partner who shares your need for emotional security.

WOMEN WITH VENUS IN AQUARIUS: Usually you have a modern outlook on love and are open to new or current lifestyles. Your intuitive abilities, communal sense, and people skills often allow you to see deeper into human intentions and to read people's thoughts telepathically. You are usually group-oriented and are drawn to individuals within the group who are independent and self-motivated. You are more inclined to choose a partner who is unconventional or freedom-loving. Conscious of your social standing, however, you want someone who can relate well to your friends.

MEN WITH VENUS IN AQUARIUS: Although independent, you often enjoy being part of a group. The partners you frequently attract are themselves nonconformists or free spirits. As an individual you may not find it easy to settle into a routine or an entirely mundane type of relationship. You may have some unconventional views on traditional marriage or your partner may hold such views. It is usually important to you that your love relationships are based on friendship.

WOMEN WITH VENUS IN PISCES: Romantic and idealistic when in love, you can be a sensitive and responsive lover. With your affectionate and impressionable nature, you are often attracted to those who understand your sensitivity and share your vision. Being flexible with an impressionable nature helps you to adapt to the needs of others. In your desire to blend with those you love, guard against giving too much of yourself by not clearly defining your boundaries. Nevertheless, your benevolence and sacrifices in the right relationship make you a partner who is devoted and kind.

MEN WITH VENUS IN PISCES: The combination of your emotional subtlety and charm can make you very alluring when dealing with affairs of the heart. Perceptive and impressionable, you have an easygoing style in your relationships, usually preferring to avoid ugly confrontation. You are drawn to partners who have a touch of glamour and are sensitive to the needs of others. Alternatively, they could be visionaries with rich imaginations who know how to keep you enchanted. With your insight you have the ability to observe the subtle moods of your partner.

To read all about your Outer Planets and work out how to use your personalized timetable, go to Section Three, page 789.

♍

Your Personalized Timetable

JUPITER BENEFICIAL
1939 3/3 – 4/14
1940 7/13 – 10/28
1941 3/1 – 5/15
1944 9/16 – until 1945 1/1
1945 1/22 – 8/11
1946 12/1 – until 1947 1/26
1947 5/1 – 9/24
1951 2/14 – 3/28
1952 6/18 – 12/22
1953 1/19 – 4/28
1956 9/1 – 11/21
1957 3/14 – 7/22
1958 11/15 – until 1959 1/2
1959 6/11 – 8/28
1963 1/27 – 3/11
1964 5/30 – until 1965 4/10
1968 8/16 – 10/31
1969 4/25 – 6/20
1970 10/30 – 12/15
1974 5/20 – 8/25
1975 1/6 – 2/22
1976 5/13 – 7/31
1976 11/9 – until 1977 3/20
1980 7/30 – 10/14
1982 10/14 – 11/29
1986 4/25 – 10/11
1986 12/6 – until 1987 2/5
1988 4/27 – 7/7
1988 12/24 – until 1989 2/16
1991 11/13 – until 1992 2/16
1992 7/10 – 9/27
1994 2/13 – 3/15
1994 9/28 – 11/13
1998 4/6 – 5/29
1998 9/6 – until 1999 1/15
2000 4/10 – 6/17
2003 10/21 – until 2004 3/25
2004 6/15 – 9/12
2006 1/7 – 5/2
2006 9/6 – 10/29
2010 3/19 – 5/3
2010 10/27 – 12/10
2012 3/22 – 5/31

SATURN BENEFICIAL
1940 6/22 – 11/3
1941 3/13 – 8/4
1941 10/18 – until 1942 4/16
1949 9/16 – until 1950 10/24
1951 4/11 – 7/14
1954 11/23 – until 1955 11/21
1965 4/28 – 8/31
1966 1/21 – 4/17
1966 10/16 – until 1967 1/5
1970 4/26 – until 1971 5/28
1978 10/30 – until 1979 2/20
1979 7/22 – until 1980 8/30
1984 1/8 – 4/16
1984 9/30 – 12/27
1985 5/22 – 9/24
1995 2/28 – 6/13
1995 7/29 – until 1996 2/20
1999 6/3 – 12/9
2000 2/14 – 7/7
2000 11/21 – until 2001 3/27
2008 8/30 – until 2009 10/6

URANUS BENEFICIAL
1938 3/21 – until 1942 3/23
1964 9/16 – until 1968 8/15
1977 12/11 – until 1980 10/23
2006 5/18 – until 2010 2/3

NEPTUNE BENEFICIAL
1938 1/1 – until 1942 7/7
1962 12/6 – until 1968 9/19

PLUTO BENEFICIAL
1962 10/17 – until 1971 7/13
1988 12/23 – until 1993 10/20

JUPITER CHALLENGING
1940 2/27 – 5/4

1942 7/30 – until 1943 6/18
1945 10/17 – until 1946 2/5
1946 2/16 – 9/11
1951 6/22 – 9/16
1952 2/6 – 4/17
1954 7/13 – 10/6
1954 12/28 – until 1955 5/29
1957 10/1 – 12/22
1958 4/13 – 8/22
1963 5/25 – 11/2
1964 1/6 – 3/31
1966 6/27 – 9/11
1967 2/5 – 5/4
1969 9/16 – 12/1
1970 5/25 – 7/22
1975 5/5 – until 1976 3/14
1978 6/11 – 8/22
1981 8/30 – 11/13
1987 4/18 – 7/11
1987 9/27 – until 1988 2/24
1990 5/24 – 8/5
1992 12/12 – until 1993 3/18
1993 8/10 – 10/28
1999 4/2 – 6/12
1999 11/13 – until 2000 1/26
2001 9/9 – 12/27
2002 5/3 – 7/20
2004 11/19 – until 2005 4/25
2005 7/16 – 10/13
2011 3/16 – 5/22

SATURN CHALLENGING
1938 4/25 – 12/5
1938 12/23 – until 1939 6/4
1939 10/28 – until 1940 2/23
1945 6/12 – until 1946 7/12
1951 11/18 – until 1952 4/5
1952 8/12 – until 1953 9/30
1967 6/18 – 8/31
1968 3/3 – until 1969 4/8
1974 7/23 – until 1975 8/22
1976 2/18 – 5/4
1981 9/23 – until 1982 11/5
1997 4/8 – until 1998 5/15
1998 12/5 – until 1999 1/22
2003 9/9 – 12/12
2004 5/25 – 11/2
2004 11/12 – until 2005 6/25
2010 10/30 – until 2011 5/11
2011 7/15 – 12/18
2012 3/31 – 9/11

URANUS CHALLENGING
1951 7/30 – until 1955 7/10
1970 11/6 – until 1974 10/8

NEPTUNE CHALLENGING
1947 10/25 – until 1955 10/4

PLUTO CHALLENGING
1975 12/8 – until 1983 8/23

JUPITER SPECIAL
1949 1/5 – 3/23
1949 7/19 – 11/15
1960 12/19 – until 1961 3/1
1972 12/3 – until 1973 2/11
1984 3/27 – 6/1
1984 11/14 – until 1985 1/26
1996 2/27 – 7/15
1996 10/21 – until 1997 1/10
2008 2/7 – 12/24

SATURN SPECIAL
1960 1/16 – until 1961 3/13
1961 7/8 – 12/10
1989 2/24 – 6/23
1989 11/23 – until 1991 1/15

URANUS SPECIAL
1991 1/28 – until 1995 11/18

NEPTUNE SPECIAL
1989 2/9 – until 1997 10/30

January 11

SUN: CAPRICORN • DECANATE: VIRGO/MERCURY • DEGREE: 19°–21° CAPRICORN • MODE: CARDINAL • ELEMENT: EARTH

Your Personal Powers

Friendly, determined, and enterprising, you are a practical and creative individual with many interests. Being pragmatic and ambitious, you are often driven by a desire to find fulfilling work or something definite and inspiring to focus on. Being versatile and mentally alert can also help you in your overall climb to success, but beware of negative thoughts or worry and indecision. When interested in a project, you can show your ingenuity and willingness to work hard for what you believe in. Being idealistic emphasizes a need to stay enthusiastic and motivated if you want to achieve long-term success. By developing your highly creative energies and trusting your intuition, you can avoid frustration or discontent and produce outstanding results. Nevertheless, resist taking on too much too soon to avoid disappointment later. By developing your sense of responsibility, you can also evade financial burdens and lessons concerning money. Talented, quick-witted, and imaginative, you are certainly not boring and your original ideas can help you considerably in achieving success.

Your Powers of Attraction in Relationships

When confident, you possess an ability to win people over with your natural charm and persuasive speech. Sensitive and idealistic, you possess a strong romantic streak that emphasizes the importance of intimate relationships in your life. Sometimes you can seek an almost spiritual bond with a partner, but if you become disillusioned, you may occasionally withdraw and appear cold. You need a partner who is encouraging, intelligent, or positively challenging. Love and affection can be very important to you, even more so if you have issues concerning being let down in the past. Honesty is vital if you want your relationships to last. Dramatic and aware of image, you can be sociable and entertaining. By developing your innate talents and diplomatic skills, you can improve your relationships.

Your attractive qualities: determined, creative, practical, focused, objective, enthusiastic, inspirational, talented, confident, mentally quick, ambitious, mystical potential, idealistic, intuitive, hardworking, humanitarian, imaginative, psychic, entertaining, love of freedom

Your less attractive qualities: worry, indecision, superiority complex or insecure, scattered, overanxious, mean, aimless, too emotional, high-strung, selfish, lack of clarity

Your Venus Power

The planet Venus has a great deal of influence on your powers of attraction. Below are four possible Venus types for women and men. To find your Venus you need to go to page 771, where you will find the Venus table and extra information. The planet Mars also affects your powers of attraction. To find your Mars table and interpretation go to page 761.

WOMEN WITH VENUS IN SAGITTARIUS: Sociable, warm, and friendly, you possess an honest and frank style in your relationships. Being naturally gregarious, you want others to share your enthusiasm and enjoy encouraging the people you love. You do better when you have a sense of personal freedom within a relationship and are usually generous with the faults of others. You need a partner who can share your need to explore and take risks whether through travel, education, or recreation.

MEN WITH VENUS IN SAGITTARIUS: When in love, you are open and friendly with a need for a partner who can share your adventurous spirit and sense of fun. Be careful, however, that your desire for freedom does not cause you to avoid commitment. You prefer your partners to be positive, direct, and generous in spirit. Being outspoken as well as an idealist, you usually enjoy a partner with whom you can share your strong opinions. Alternatively, you may wish to explore life together whether through travel, education, or by having fun.

WOMEN WITH VENUS IN CAPRICORN: Romantically, you do not give your heart easily but hide behind a cool reserve until you feel free to express your emotions. As you take your relationships seriously, you may find yourself drawn to people who are businesslike, resourceful, and practical, or those who can act as teachers or mentors. Work or career may also be a factor in many of your associations and partnerships. As security can play an important role in your relationships, you are often attracted to partners who are loyal and hardworking.

MEN WITH VENUS IN CAPRICORN: As you admire loyal, hardworking, and dedicated individuals, you probably want a partner who can share your vocational interests or can provide you with the sense of security you need. You could even find yourself with a partner who is of a different age group or maturity. Guard against denying your true emotional needs or focusing on your career at the expense of your relationship. You are drawn to reserved partners who display self-control.

WOMEN WITH VENUS IN AQUARIUS: Usually you have a modern outlook on love and are open to new or current

lifestyles. Your intuitive abilities, communal sense, and people skills often allow you to see deeper into human intentions and to telepathically read people's thoughts. You are usually group-oriented and are drawn to individuals within the group who are independent and self-motivated. You are more inclined to choose a partner who is unconventional or freedom-loving. Conscious of your social standing, however, you want someone who can relate well to your friends.

MEN WITH VENUS IN AQUARIUS: Although independent, you often enjoy being part of a group. The partners you frequently attract are themselves nonconformists or free spirits. As an individual you may not find it easy to settle into a routine or an entirely mundane type of relationship. You may have some unconventional views on traditional marriage or your partner may hold such views. It is usually important to you that your love relationships are based on friendship.

WOMEN WITH VENUS IN PISCES: Idealistic and impressionable, in love you are romantic. Being sensitive to other people, you are receptive to their moods and feelings. This affinity indicates that, although you can be selfless, you may have to guard against being too sentimental or overly romantic, especially of those who can take advantage of your kindness. Nevertheless, you are alluring and seductive, and your partners may be intrigued by your emotional magnetism, compassion, or mysterious nature.

MEN WITH VENUS IN PISCES: Being adaptable and sensitive, you are able to intuitively feel the moods of those you love. Although you are receptive to others, you can be ambiguous about your own feelings to your partner. Romantic and kindhearted, you long to be loved but you need to be realistic about your relationships in order to avoid disappointments. When in love you may idealize your partners and fail to see any faults in their personalities.

To read all about your Outer Planets and work out how to use your personalized timetable, go to Section Three, page 789.

To read all about your Outer Planets and work out how to use your personalized timetable, go to Section Three, page 789.

♍

Your Personalized Timetable

JUPITER BENEFICIAL
1939 3/7 – 4/19
1940 7/20 – 10/21
1941 3/7 – 5/19
1944 9/21 – until 1945 8/16
1946 12/5 – until 1947 2/3
1947 4/22 – 9/30
1951 2/18 – 4/1
1952 6/23 – 12/8
1953 2/2 – 5/2
1956 9/5 – 11/29
1957 3/6 – 7/28
1958 11/19 – until 1959 1/8
1959 6/2 – 9/5
1963 2/1 – 3/15
1964 6/3 – until 1965 4/14
1968 8/21 – 11/6
1969 4/14 – 7/1
1970 11/4 – 12/20
1974 5/28 – 8/17
1975 1/12 – 2/27
1976 5/17 – 8/7
1976 11/1 – until 1977 3/25
1980 8/4 – 10/19
1982 10/19 – 12/3
1986 4/30 – 9/30
1986 12/16 – until 1987 2/10
1988 5/1 – 7/12
1988 12/14 – until 1989 2/26
1991 11/22 – until 1992 2/7
1992 7/16 – 10/2
1994 10/2 – 11/18
1998 4/10 – 6/6
1998 8/29 – until 1999 1/21
2000 4/14 – 6/22
2003 10/27 – until 2004 3/16
2004 6/23 – 9/17
2006 1/14 – 4/23
2006 9/13 – 11/3
2010 3/23 – 5/8
2010 10/16 – 12/21
2012 3/27 – 6/4

SATURN BENEFICIAL
1940 7/4 – 10/21
1941 3/23 – 8/26
1941 9/25 – until 1942 4/25
1949 9/24 – until 1950 11/3
1951 3/28 – 7/27
1954 12/2 – until 1955 6/16
1955 8/20 – 11/29
1965 5/10 – 8/17
1966 1/31 – 4/26
1966 10/1 – until 1967 1/18
1970 5/4 – until 1971 6/5
1978 11/12 – until 1979 2/6
1979 7/31 – until 1980 9/7
1984 1/20 – 3/31
1984 10/10 – until 1985 1/7
1985 5/9 – 10/5
1995 3/8 – until 1996 2/29
1999 6/12 – 11/24
2000 2/29 – 7/18
2000 11/9 – until 2001 4/6
2008 9/7 – until 2009 10/15
2010 5/6 – 6/23

URANUS BENEFICIAL
1938 4/10 – until 1942 4/14
1964 10/3 – until 1968 9/1
1978 1/1 – until 1980 11/9
2007 3/17 – until 2010 2/23

NEPTUNE BENEFICIAL
1938 1/1 – until 1942 8/18
1963 1/12 – until 1968 10/24

PLUTO BENEFICIAL
1963 9/17 – until 1971 8/20
1989 11/12 – until 1994 8/19

JUPITER CHALLENGING
1940 3/2 – 5/9
1942 8/4 – until 1943 6/22
1945 10/22 – until 1946 9/17

1951 7/1 – 9/7
1952 2/11 – 4/21
1954 7/18 – 10/16
1954 12/18 – until 1955 6/4
1957 10/6 – 12/30
1958 4/4 – 8/28
1963 5/31 – 10/24
1964 1/15 – 4/5
1966 7/2 – 9/17
1967 1/28 – 5/12
1969 9/20 – 12/7
1970 5/14 – 8/2
1975 5/10 – until 1976 3/19
1978 6/15 – 8/27
1981 9/4 – 11/18
1987 4/23 – 7/21
1987 9/18 – until 1988 2/29
1990 5/29 – 8/10
1992 12/20 – until 1993 3/9
1993 8/16 – 11/2
1999 4/6 – 6/18
1999 11/4 – until 2000 2/3
2001 9/16 – 12/19
2002 5/9 – 7/25
2004 11/25 – until 2005 4/16
2005 7/24 – 10/18
2011 3/20 – 5/27

SATURN CHALLENGING
1938 5/4 – 11/9
1939 1/18 – 6/14
1939 10/15 – until 1940 3/5
1945 6/21 – until 1946 7/20
1951 11/29 – until 1952 3/23
1952 8/23 – until 1953 10/8
1967 7/13 – 8/6
1968 3/11 – until 1969 4/16
1974 7/31 – until 1975 2/22
1975 4/3 – 8/31
1976 2/4 – 5/18
1981 10/2 – until 1982 11/14
1983 6/4 – 7/28
1997 4/16 – until 1998 5/24
1998 11/16 – until 1999 2/9
2003 9/24 – 11/26
2004 6/3 – until 2005 7/3
2010 11/8 – until 2011 4/24
2011 7/31 – until 2012 1/1
2012 3/16 – 9/21

URANUS CHALLENGING
1951 8/18 – until 1956 4/21
1970 11/27 – until 1974 10/24

NEPTUNE CHALLENGING
1947 11/27 – until 1956 8/29

PLUTO CHALLENGING
1938 2/20 – 5/29
1976 10/23 – until 1983 9/24

JUPITER SPECIAL
1949 1/9 – 3/30
1949 7/11 – 11/21
1960 12/24 – until 1961 3/6
1961 8/29 – 10/18
1972 12/7 – until 1973 2/15
1984 4/9 – 5/19
1984 11/20 – until 1985 1/30
1996 3/4 – 7/7
1996 10/28 – until 1997 1/14
2008 2/12 – 12/29

SATURN SPECIAL
1960 1/25 – 8/21
1960 10/10 – until 1961 3/26
1961 6/23 – 12/19
1989 3/9 – 6/8
1989 12/3 – until 1991 1/23

URANUS SPECIAL
1991 2/17 – until 1995 12/12

NEPTUNE SPECIAL
1989 3/31 – until 1997 12/14

January 12

Your Personal Powers

You are creative, friendly, and easygoing, and your personal powers also include good people skills and keen observations. Your ruling planet Saturn emphasizes the importance of having clear goals and suggests that your work can be highly significant in your life plan. A practical visionary, you gain power by combining your personal charm and shrewd pragmatism with your sensitivity and imagination. Being intelligent and presenting a confident front to the world, you often achieve leadership positions. You may lose power, however, if you become stubborn or allow self-doubt to cloud your judgment. A need for harmony may encourage you to develop skills in music and art or to emphasize a love of nature. Your strong intuition implies that you gain power when you balance your rational thinking with your gut feelings or when you trust your inner voice. Although clever and hardworking, your desire for a peaceful life can undermine your strength if you relax too much or avoid facing up to difficult situations. Fortunately, your ambition and need for personal expression drives you on to achievement and success.

Your Powers of Attraction in Relationships

You attract others with your personal charm and sharp intelligence. Your diplomatic skills ensure your ability to handle people successfully. You also work well in partnership or team situations. Although you are usually resourceful, you may have to get the balance right between your own desires and the needs of others in order to avoid codependent situations. Aware of your responsibilities, you seek a reassuring and supportive partner who can share your desire for harmony and security. If you experience inner tensions or fears, you may cut yourself off from your partner or escape into a world of your own. Nevertheless, your natural compassion draws you to help others. When positive, you can be an affectionate and sensitive lover or a delightful friend. With your dignity and inner strength, you can also inspire others.

Your attractive qualities: creative, friendly, ambitious, intelligent, sensitive, attractive, tactful, intuitive, initiative, disciplinarian, charm, independent, assertive, easygoing, confident, hardworking, supportive, diplomatic, visionary, practical, compassion, innovative

Your less attractive qualities: reclusive, too sensitive, lack of self-esteem, too detached, pessimistic, escapist, living in dream world, uncooperative, contrary, rebellious, codependent, suspicious, worry

Your Venus Power

The planet Venus has a great deal of influence on your powers of attraction. Below are four possible Venus types for women and men. To find your Venus you need to go to page 771, where you will find the Venus table and extra information. The planet Mars also affects your powers of attraction. To find your Mars table and interpretation go to page 761.

WOMEN WITH VENUS IN SAGITTARIUS: Sociable, warm, and friendly, you possess an honest and frank style in your relationships. Being naturally gregarious, you want others to share your enthusiasm and you enjoy encouraging the people you love. You do better when you have a sense of personal freedom within a relationship and are usually generous with the faults of others. You need a partner who can share your need to explore and take risks, whether through travel, education, or recreation.

MEN WITH VENUS IN SAGITTARIUS: When in love you are open and friendly with a need for a partner who can share your adventurous spirit and sense of fun. Be careful, however, that your desire for freedom does not cause you to avoid commitment. You prefer your partners to be positive, direct, and generous in spirit. Being outspoken as well as an idealist, you usually enjoy a partner with whom you can share your strong opinions. Alternatively, you may wish to explore life together whether through travel, education, or by having fun.

WOMEN WITH VENUS IN CAPRICORN: With your natural caution in romantic affairs, you often appear reserved and controlled. If shy, try to be more forward, especially if you want to be noticed. When you care about people, however, you are usually willing to put in extra time and energy to preserve the relationship. You are practical and dependable, and a sense of duty can often play a large role in affairs of your heart. With elegant simplicity, you can attract others with your well-cut clothes and refined manners.

MEN WITH VENUS IN CAPRICORN: In relationships you take love seriously and can be a strong and practical support for friends or partners. You are usually attracted to partners who are as hardworking as you. As you tend not to express your feelings until you feel really secure in a relationship, you

may be drawn to those who seem loyal, faithful, and not likely to let you down. As you respect the wisdom of experience, you may be drawn to mature partners or, alternatively, you may act as an authority figure for someone younger.

WOMEN WITH VENUS IN AQUARIUS: When it comes to relationships, others are attracted to your honest, friendly, and easygoing attitude. You enjoy social interaction and have a genuine concern for others. In fact, at times, your friends may be just as important as your partner. Usually you present a tolerant and reasonable front in love situations and attempt to view your relationships objectively. If partners become too demanding, however, you can become stubborn or awkward. Nevertheless, inventive and progressive, you enjoy the company of like-minded people who can share your original ideas.

MEN WITH VENUS IN AQUARIUS: Friendly and honest, you attract people with your broad-minded approach to life. You usually possess an objective and slightly detached attitude to affairs of the heart. If you are too removed, however, others can misinterpret your behavior as uncaring. It is often more important to you that your love relationships are based on friendship and honesty than intense passion. As you are generally tolerant and liberal, you may be drawn to less conventional relationships.

WOMEN WITH VENUS IN PISCES: Romantic and idealistic when in love, you can be a sensitive and responsive lover. With your affectionate and impressionable nature you are often attracted to those who understand your sensitivity and share your vision. Being flexible with an impressionable nature helps you to adapt to the needs of others. In your desire to blend with those you love, guard against giving too much of yourself by not clearly defining your boundaries. Nevertheless, your benevolence and sacrifices in the right relationship make you a partner who is devoted and kind.

MEN WITH VENUS IN PISCES: The combination of your emotional subtlety and charm can make you very alluring when dealing with affairs of the heart. Perceptive and impressionable, you have an easygoing style in your relationships, usually preferring to avoid ugly confrontation. You are drawn to partners who have a touch of glamour and are sensitive to the needs of others. Alternatively, they could be visionaries with rich imaginations who know how to keep you enchanted. With your insight you have the ability to observe the subtle moods of your partner.

To read all about your Outer Planets and work out how to use your personalized timetable, go to Section Three, page 789.

♍

Your Personalized Timetable

JUPITER BENEFICIAL
1939 3/11 – 4/23
1940 7/28 – 10/12
1941 3/12 – 5/23
1944 9/26 – until **1945** 8/22
1946 12/10 – until **1947** 2/14
1947 4/11 – 10/5
1951 2/23 – 4/5
1952 6/28 – 11/28
1953 2/12 – 5/6
1956 9/10 – 12/7
1957 2/25 – 8/3
1958 11/24 – until **1959** 1/14
1959 5/24 – 9/13
1963 2/5 – 3/19
1964 6/8 – until **1965** 4/19
1968 8/25 – 11/12
1969 4/5 – 7/10
1970 11/8 – 12/25
1974 6/6 – 8/7
1975 1/17 – 3/3
1976 5/21 – 8/16
1976 10/23 – until **1977** 3/31
1980 8/9 – 10/24
1982 10/23 – 12/8
1986 5/6 – 9/22
1986 12/24 – until **1987** 2/14
1988 5/5 – 7/18
1988 12/5 – until **1989** 3/6
1991 12/2 – until **1992** 1/28
1992 7/22 – 10/7
1994 10/7 – 11/22
1998 4/15 – 6/15
1998 8/19 – until **1999** 1/26
2000 4/19 – 6/27
2003 11/2 – until **2004** 3/8
2004 6/30 – 9/22
2006 1/22 – 4/15
2006 9/19 – 11/7
2010 3/28 – 5/14
2010 10/7 – 12/30
2012 4/1 – 6/8

SATURN BENEFICIAL
1940 7/17 – 10/7
1941 4/1 – until **1942** 5/3
1949 10/3 – until **1950** 4/15
1950 6/14 – 11/13
1951 3/15 – 8/7
1954 12/11 – until **1955** 5/30
1955 9/5 – 12/8
1956 7/15 – 8/14
1965 5/26 – 7/31
1966 2/9 – 5/7
1966 9/18 – until **1967** 1/30
1970 5/12 – until **1971** 6/13
1978 11/29 – until **1979** 1/19
1979 8/9 – until **1980** 9/16
1984 2/19 – 3/1
1984 10/19 – until **1985** 1/20
1985 4/24 – 10/15
1995 3/17 – until **1996** 3/8
1999 6/21 – 11/10
2000 3/11 – 7/31
2000 10/26 – until **2001** 4/15
2008 9/15 – until **2009** 10/23
2010 4/17 – 7/12

URANUS BENEFICIAL
1938 4/28 – until **1942** 5/3
1964 10/23 – until **1968** 9/18
1978 2/8 – until **1981** 8/30
2007 4/4 – until **2010** 3/13

NEPTUNE BENEFICIAL
1938 1/1 – until **1943** 6/27
1963 12/4 – until **1969** 9/15

PLUTO BENEFICIAL
1963 10/19 – until **1972** 6/21
1989 12/9 – until **1994** 10/7

JUPITER CHALLENGING
1940 3/7 – 5/13
1942 8/9 – until **1943** 6/27

1945 10/27 – until **1946** 9/22
1951 7/12 – 8/26
1952 2/16 – 4/26
1954 7/22 – 10/29
1954 12/5 – until **1955** 6/9
1957 10/11 – until **1958** 1/7
1958 3/27 – 9/3
1963 6/5 – 10/16
1964 1/22 – 4/9
1966 7/6 – 9/23
1967 1/21 – 5/19
1969 9/25 – 12/12
1970 5/5 – 8/10
1975 5/15 – until **1976** 3/23
1978 6/20 – 9/2
1979 3/11 – 4/9
1981 9/9 – 11/23
1987 4/27 – 8/4
1987 9/3 – until **1988** 3/5
1990 6/3 – 8/15
1992 12/30 – until **1993** 2/27
1993 8/22 – 11/7
1999 4/10 – 6/24
1999 10/28 – until **2000** 2/10
2001 9/25 – 12/11
2002 5/15 – 7/29
2004 12/1 – until **2005** 4/8
2005 8/1 – 10/23
2011 3/24 – 6/1

SATURN CHALLENGING
1938 5/13 – 10/24
1939 2/2 – 6/26
1939 10/1 – until **1940** 3/14
1945 6/28 – until **1946** 7/28
1951 12/12 – until **1952** 3/9
1952 9/2 – until **1953** 10/17
1968 3/20 – until **1969** 4/24
1974 8/9 – until **1975** 2/2
1975 4/22 – 9/10
1976 1/22 – 5/29
1981 10/10 – until **1982** 11/23
1983 5/16 – 8/15
1997 4/25 – until **1998** 6/2
1998 11/3 – until **1999** 2/22
2004 6/11 – until **2005** 7/11
2010 11/18 – until **2011** 4/10
2011 8/13 – until **2012** 1/25
2012 2/20 – 9/30

URANUS CHALLENGING
1951 9/12 – until **1956** 5/26
1970 12/28 – until **1975** 8/24

NEPTUNE CHALLENGING
1948 10/22 – until **1956** 10/1

PLUTO CHALLENGING
1938 1/3 – until **1939** 5/7
1976 11/22 – until **1984** 7/20

JUPITER SPECIAL
1949 1/13 – 4/7
1949 7/3 – 11/27
1960 12/28 – until **1961** 3/11
1961 8/18 – 10/29
1972 12/12 – until **1973** 2/20
1984 11/25 – until **1985** 2/3
1996 3/11 – 6/29
1996 11/4 – until **1997** 1/18
2008 2/17 – 8/16
2008 9/30 – until **2009** 1/2

SATURN SPECIAL
1960 2/4 – 8/1
1960 10/29 – until **1961** 4/14
1961 6/3 – 12/29
1989 3/27 – 5/19
1989 12/12 – until **1991** 2/1

URANUS SPECIAL
1991 3/16 – until **1995** 12/31

NEPTUNE SPECIAL
1990 2/6 – until **1998** 1/11

617

January 13

Your Personal Powers

Independent and strong-willed, you are a mentally sharp individual with practical awareness. Being determined, you possess perseverance, and when set on a course of action will work hard to achieve your goals. Although a shrewd realist, you also possess an idealistic side to your nature that seeks outlets for your sensitive emotions and strong imagination. You gain power from the combination of your resolve, keen insight, and ability to turn on the charm when it is in your own interests. With your heightened sensitivity, however, if you become too self-absorbed, you can lose power to inner frustration or even depression. Nevertheless, with your talent for self-analysis and your natural psychological skills, you can help yourself and others. Refined, with inspired thoughts or artistic ability, you profit from creative self-expression. With your original ideas and preference for giving orders rather than taking them, you may find success through leadership positions or working for yourself.

Your Powers of Attraction in Relationships

People are attracted to your determination and fine mind. Although you seem independent and pragmatic, the display of affection is very important to you. Respecting knowledge, you are attracted to intelligent or wise individuals. Having a strong awareness of work and duty, you may sometimes find a pull between your responsibilities and your desire for a relationship. Although you can be enthusiastic and assured, avoid being stubborn or trying to force your opinions on others. Nevertheless, with your emotional sensitivity, you can be spontaneous and loving when you trust that life will take care of your needs. If you dwell on the negative, you can become cynical or skeptical. By developing your faith and a more detached viewpoint, you are able to feel more relaxed about your relationships and express the deep love and loyalty you possess.

Your attractive qualities: ambitious, intelligent, determined, practical, hardworking, highly intuitive, black humor, leadership potential, creative, initiative, perfectionist, sensitive, independent, mystical potential, charming, pioneering, wise, original, expressive, realist, hardworking

Your less attractive qualities: too serious, indecisive, negative thinking, critical, rebellious, obstinate, self-deception, egocentric, impulsive, cynical, withdrawn, too willful, overbearing, worried, stubborn

Your Venus Power

The planet Venus has a great deal of influence on your powers of attraction. Below are four possible Venus types for women and men. To find your Venus you need to go to page 771, where you will find the Venus table and extra information. The planet Mars also affects your powers of attraction. To find your Mars table and interpretation go to page 761.

WOMEN WITH VENUS IN SAGITTARIUS: Sociable, warm, and friendly, you possess an honest and frank style in your relationships. Being naturally gregarious, you want others to share your enthusiasm and you enjoy encouraging the people you love. You do better when you have a sense of personal freedom within a relationship and you are usually generous with the faults of others. You need a partner who can share your need to explore and take risks, whether through travel, education, or recreation.

MEN WITH VENUS IN SAGITTARIUS: When in love you are open and friendly with a need for a partner who can share your adventurous spirit and sense of fun. Be careful, however, that your desire for freedom does not cause you to avoid commitment. You prefer your partners to be positive, direct, and generous in spirit. Being outspoken as well as an idealist, you usually enjoy a partner with whom you can share your strong opinions. Alternatively, you may wish to explore life together whether through travel, education, or by having fun.

WOMEN WITH VENUS IN CAPRICORN: Romantically, you do not give your heart easily but hide behind a cool reserve until you feel free to express your emotions. As you take your relationships seriously, you may find yourself drawn to people who are businesslike, resourceful, and practical or who can act as teachers or mentors. Work or career may also be a factor in many of your associations and partnerships. As security can play an important role in your relationships, you are often attracted to partners who are loyal and hardworking.

MEN WITH VENUS IN CAPRICORN: As you admire loyal, hardworking, and dedicated individuals, you probably want a partner who can share your vocational interests or can provide you with the security you need. You could even find yourself with a partner who is of a different age group or maturity.

Guard against denying your true emotional needs or focusing on your career at the expense of your relationship. You are drawn to reserved partners who display self-control.

WOMEN WITH VENUS IN AQUARIUS: When it comes to relationships, others are attracted to your honest, friendly, and easygoing attitude. You enjoy social interaction and have a genuine concern for others. In fact, at times, your friends may be just as important as your partner. Usually you present a tolerant and reasonable front in love situations and attempt to view your relationships objectively. If partners become too demanding, however, you can become stubborn or awkward. Nevertheless, inventive and progressive, you enjoy the company of like-minded people who can share your original ideas.

MEN WITH VENUS IN AQUARIUS: Friendly and honest, you attract people with your broad-minded approach to life. You usually possess an objective and slightly detached attitude to affairs of the heart. If you are too removed, however, others can misinterpret your behavior as uncaring. It is often more important to you that your love relationships are based on friendship and honesty than intense passion. As you are generally tolerant and liberal, you may be drawn to less conventional relationships.

WOMEN WITH VENUS IN PISCES: Idealistic and impressionable, in love you are romantic. Being sensitive to other people, you are receptive to their moods and feelings. This affinity indicates that although you can be selfless you may have to guard against being too sentimental or overly romantic, especially of those who can take advantage of your kindness. Nevertheless, alluring and seductive, your partners can be intrigued by your emotional magnetism, compassion, or mysterious nature.

MEN WITH VENUS IN PISCES: Being adaptable and sensitive, you are able to intuitively feel the moods of those you love. Although you are receptive to others you can be ambiguous about your feelings toward your partner. Romantic and kindhearted, you long to be loved but you need to be realistic about your relationships in order to avoid disappointments. When in love you may idealize your partners and fail to see any faults in their personality.

To read all about your Outer Planets and work out how to use your personalized timetable, go to Section Three, page 789.

♍

Your Personalized Timetable

JUPITER BENEFICIAL
1939 3/16 – 4/28
1940 8/7 – 10/2
1941 3/17 – 5/28
1944 10/1 – until 1945 8/27
1946 12/16 – until 1947 3/3
1947 3/25 – 10/10
1951 2/27 – 4/10
1952 7/4 – 11/19
1953 2/20 – 5/11
1956 9/15 – 12/17
1957 2/15 – 8/9
1958 11/29 – until 1959 1/21
1959 5/16 – 9/20
1963 2/10 – 3/24
1964 6/13 – until 1965 4/24
1968 8/30 – 11/18
1969 3/28 – 7/18
1970 11/13 – 12/30
1971 7/2 – 8/16
1974 6/20 – 7/25
1975 1/22 – 3/7
1976 5/26 – 8/28
1976 10/12 – until 1977 4/5
1980 8/14 – 10/29
1982 10/28 – 12/13
1986 5/12 – 9/14
1986 12/31 – until 1987 2/19
1988 5/10 – 7/24
1988 11/28 – until 1989 3/13
1991 12/18 – until 1992 1/12
1992 7/27 – 10/12
1994 10/12 – 11/27
1998 4/20 – 6/27
1998 8/7 – until 1999 1/31
2000 4/23 – 7/2
2003 11/9 – until 2004 3/1
2004 7/7 – 9/26
2006 2/1 – 4/5
2006 9/24 – 11/12
2010 4/1 – 5/20
2010 9/29 – until 2011 1/6
2012 4/5 – 6/13

SATURN BENEFICIAL
1940 8/5 – 9/17
1941 4/10 – until 1942 5/11
1949 10/11 – until 1950 3/29
1950 6/30 – 11/25
1951 3/2 – 8/17
1954 12/21 – until 1955 5/16
1955 9/18 – 12/17
1956 6/21 – 9/7
1966 2/18 – 5/18
1966 9/5 – until 1967 2/8
1970 5/20 – until 1971 6/21
1972 1/2 – 2/29
1979 8/18 – until 1980 9/24
1984 10/27 – until 1985 2/5
1985 4/6 – 10/25
1995 3/25 – until 1996 3/16
1999 7/2 – 10/29
2000 3/21 – 8/17
2000 10/8 – until 2001 4/23
2008 9/23 – until 2009 11/2
2010 4/2 – 7/26

URANUS BENEFICIAL
1938 5/16 – until 1942 5/21
1964 11/18 – until 1969 7/10
1978 11/19 – until 1981 9/29
2007 4/26 – until 2011 1/15

NEPTUNE BENEFICIAL
1938 1/1 – until 1943 8/15
1964 1/8 – until 1969 10/22

PLUTO BENEFICIAL
1964 9/17 – until 1972 8/12
1990 1/12 – until 1994 11/5

JUPITER CHALLENGING
1940 3/11 – 5/17

1942 8/14 – until 1943 7/2
1945 10/31 – until 1946 9/27
1952 2/21 – 4/30
1954 7/27 – until 1955 6/14
1957 10/15 – until 1958 1/17
1958 3/16 – 9/9
1963 6/12 – 10/8
1964 1/29 – 4/13
1966 7/11 – 9/30
1967 1/13 – 5/25
1969 9/30 – 12/18
1970 4/27 – 8/18
1975 5/20 – until 1976 3/28
1978 6/25 – 9/7
1979 2/24 – 4/24
1981 9/14 – 11/29
1987 5/2 – until 1988 3/10
1990 6/8 – 8/20
1993 1/14 – 2/11
1993 8/27 – 11/12
1999 4/14 – 6/30
1999 10/20 – until 2000 2/17
2001 10/5 – 11/30
2002 5/20 – 8/3
2004 12/8 – until 2005 3/31
2005 8/8 – 10/27
2011 3/28 – 6/6
2011 12/27 – 12/27

SATURN CHALLENGING
1938 5/23 – 10/11
1939 2/13 – 7/12
1939 9/15 – until 1940 3/23
1945 7/6 – until 1946 8/5
1951 12/29 – until 1952 2/20
1952 9/11 – until 1953 10/25
1968 3/28 – until 1969 5/2
1974 8/18 – until 1975 1/19
1975 5/6 – 9/21
1976 1/9 – 6/8
1981 10/18 – until 1982 12/3
1983 5/1 – 8/28
1997 5/3 – 11/15
1998 1/15 – 6/13
1998 10/21 – until 1999 3/4
2004 6/19 – until 2005 7/19
2010 11/28 – until 2011 3/28
2011 8/24 – until 2012 10/8

URANUS CHALLENGING
1952 7/9 – until 1956 6/17
1971 10/14 – until 1975 9/15

NEPTUNE CHALLENGING
1948 11/23 – until 1957 8/26

PLUTO CHALLENGING
1938 1/1 – until 1939 6/29
1977 10/14 – until 1984 9/9

JUPITER SPECIAL
1949 1/18 – 4/16
1949 6/24 – 12/2
1961 1/2 – 3/17
1961 8/9 – 11/6
1972 12/16 – until 1973 2/25
1984 11/30 – until 1985 2/8
1996 3/18 – 6/21
1996 11/10 – until 1997 1/23
2008 2/23 – 8/4
2008 10/12 – until 2009 1/7

SATURN SPECIAL
1960 2/13 – 7/17
1960 11/12 – until 1962 1/6
1989 12/21 – until 1991 2/10
1991 9/20 – 10/19

URANUS SPECIAL
1992 1/12 – until 1996 1/18

NEPTUNE SPECIAL
1990 3/20 – until 1998 12/11

January 14

Your Personal Powers

Your personal powers include keen intelligence, good common sense, and an ambitious drive to succeed. With endurance and determination, you possess the ability to persist despite all obstacles. You gain power from your psychological insights into the motivation of others and from your pragmatic approach to problem solving. With a creative flair to your thinking, you can also be inspired and enthusiastic. Although at times you possess natural caution or reserve, be careful not to lose power to worry or self-doubt. Fortunately, you are usually friendly and helpful with good communication skills and the ability to go straight to the heart of a matter. Clever and original, your natural executive skills often place you in positions of leadership. Talented and versatile, you are usually willing to work hard to achieve your aims and objectives. Your need for creative self-expression can also be developed to obtain outstanding results. By applying faith and purpose to your life, you can achieve remarkable success.

Your Powers of Attraction in Relationships

You can attract others with your friendly manner and bright intelligence. With your people skills, you understand the advantages of working cooperatively with others and are a good team player. Being security-conscious, you are attracted to honest and direct individuals who can provide you with stability or a secure home base. Equally, you need a partner who can match your quick mental responses, otherwise you may become bored and impatient. As you like to make plans for the future, ideally your partner needs to be supportive. You are loyal and hardworking, but your partner or loved ones will have to understand that you also need some space for yourself. Independent and strong-willed, you may need to avoid becoming too stubborn or bossy with your partners. Sociable and enthusiastic, however, you can be an entertaining and amusing companion.

Your attractive qualities: practical, good judge of values, determined, hardworking, loyal, creative, people skills, pragmatic, imaginative, original ideas, humanitarian potential, industrious, decisive actions, leadership, clever, communication skills, friendly, enterprising

Your less attractive qualities: worry, indecision, overly cautious or impulsive, impatient, unsettled, materialistic, overindulgent, bossy, thoughtless, stubborn

Your Venus Power

The planet Venus has a great deal of influence on your powers of attraction. Below are four possible Venus types for women and men. To find your Venus you need to go to page 771, where you will find the Venus table and extra information. The planet Mars also affects your powers of attraction. To find your Mars table and interpretation go to page 761.

WOMEN WITH VENUS IN SAGITTARIUS: Sociable, warm, and friendly, you possess an honest and frank style in your relationships. Being naturally gregarious, you want others to share your enthusiasm and you enjoy encouraging the people you love. You do better when you have a sense of personal freedom within a relationship and are usually generous with the faults of others. You need a partner who can share your need to explore and take risks, whether through travel, education, or recreation.

MEN WITH VENUS IN SAGITTARIUS: When in love you are open and friendly with a need for a partner who can share your adventurous spirit and sense of fun. Be careful, however, that your desire for freedom does not cause you to avoid commitment. You prefer your partners to be positive, direct, and generous in spirit. Being outspoken as well as an idealist, you usually enjoy a partner with whom you can share your strong opinions. Alternatively, you may wish to explore life together whether through travel, education, or by having fun.

WOMEN WITH VENUS IN CAPRICORN: Loyal and responsible, you are attracted to dignified and reserved individuals. Being practical and security-conscious you prefer hardworking partners who are resourceful and enterprising. Work may even be a factor in many of your associations and partnerships. For you, family and faithfulness can be especially important, so you are usually willing to work hard or make sacrifices in order to build a strong relationship.

MEN WITH VENUS IN CAPRICORN: Hardworking and ambitious, you are usually attracted to determined, focused, and ambitious partners with a strong sense of duty. You want them to take relationships as seriously as you do, so loyalty and faithfulness are high on your agenda. Since you may display a natural reserve about expressing your feelings in an in-

timate relationship, you need a partner who shares your need for emotional security.

WOMEN WITH VENUS IN AQUARIUS: When it comes to relationships, others are attracted to your honest, friendly, and easygoing attitude. You really enjoy social interaction with others and may develop a genuine concern for humanity. Usually you present a tolerant and reasonable front in love situations and attempt to view your relationships objectively. If partners become too demanding, however, you can become stubborn and fixed. Friendship may be even more important for you than sexual compatibility.

MEN WITH VENUS IN AQUARIUS: You are sociable and open-minded, and people are attracted by your friendly and relaxed style. Being independent, you value freedom-loving partners who give you the space to be yourself. Others sometimes interpret your detachment as being emotionally cool, but they may not understand your progressive views on relationships. Friendship can sometimes be even more important than earthly passion. Ideally, your partners share your ideas on life and possess a sense of originality as strong your own. Not easily ruffled, you can deal well with difficult situation or moody partners.

WOMEN WITH VENUS IN PISCES: Romantic and idealistic when in love, you can be a sensitive and responsive lover. With your affectionate and impressionable nature you are often attracted to those who understand your sensitivity and share your vision. Being flexible with an impressionable nature helps you to adapt to the needs of others. In your desire to blend with those you love, guard against giving too much of yourself by not defining your boundaries clearly. Nevertheless, your benevolence and sacrifices in the right relationship make you a partner who is devoted and kind.

MEN WITH VENUS IN PISCES: The combination of your emotional subtlety and charm can make you very alluring when dealing with affairs of the heart. Perceptive and impressionable, you have an easygoing style in your relationships, usually preferring to avoid ugly confrontation. You are drawn to partners who have a touch of glamour and are sensitive to the needs of others. Alternatively, they could be visionaries with rich imaginations who know how to keep you enchanted. With your insight you have the ability to observe the subtle moods of your partner.

To read all about your Outer Planets and work out how to use your personalized timetable, go to Section Three, page 789.

♍

Your Personalized Timetable

JUPITER BENEFICIAL
1939 3/20 – 5/3
1940 8/22 – 9/17
1941 3/23 – 6/1
1944 10/6 – until 1945 9/1
1946 12/21 – until 1947 6/24
1947 8/6 – 10/16
1951 3/3 – 4/14
1952 7/10 – 11/12
1953 2/27 – 5/15
1956 9/19 – 12/31
1957 2/1 – 8/14
1958 12/3 – until 1959 1/28
1959 5/8 – 9/26
1963 2/14 – 3/28
1964 6/18 – until 1965 4/28
1968 9/4 – 11/24
1969 3/20 – 7/25
1970 11/17 – until 1971 1/5
1971 6/19 – 8/28
1975 1/27 – 3/12
1976 5/30 – until 1977 4/10
1980 8/19 – 11/3
1981 5/2 – 6/21
1982 11/2 – 12/18
1986 5/19 – 9/6
1987 1/6 – 2/23
1988 5/14 – 7/30
1988 11/20 – until 1989 3/20
1992 8/2 – 10/17
1994 10/17 – 12/2
1998 4/25 – 11/2
1998 11/24 – until 1999 2/5
2000 4/27 – 7/7
2001 1/14 – 2/4
2003 11/16 – until 2004 2/22
2004 7/14 – 10/1
2006 2/15 – 3/22
2006 9/30 – 11/16
2010 4/5 – 5/26
2010 9/21 – until 2011 1/13
2012 4/10 – 6/17

SATURN BENEFICIAL
1941 4/18 – until 1942 5/19
1949 10/21 – until 1950 3/15
1950 7/13 – 12/10
1951 2/14 – 8/26
1955 1/1 – 5/2
1955 9/29 – 12/27
1956 6/5 – 9/22
1966 2/26 – 6/1
1966 8/20 – until 1967 2/18
1970 5/28 – until 1971 6/30
1971 12/16 – until 1972 3/16
1979 8/26 – until 1980 10/2
1984 11/5 – until 1985 11/3
1995 4/3 – 10/31
1995 12/12 – until 1996 3/25
1999 7/15 – 10/15
2000 3/30 – until 2001 5/2
2008 10/2 – until 2009 4/23
2009 6/9 – 11/12
2010 3/20 – 8/6

URANUS BENEFICIAL
1938 6/4 – until 1943 3/23
1965 9/10 – until 1969 8/6
1978 12/6 – until 1981 10/20
2007 5/27 – until 2011 2/9

NEPTUNE BENEFICIAL
1938 1/1 – until 1943 9/14
1964 12/2 – until 1970 9/10

PLUTO BENEFICIAL
1964 10/18 – until 1972 9/11
1990 11/27 – until 1995 9/23

JUPITER CHALLENGING
1940 3/15 – 5/22
1942 8/19 – until 1943 3/1

1943 3/23 – 7/7
1945 11/5 – until 1946 10/2
1952 2/26 – 5/4
1954 8/1 – until 1955 6/19
1957 10/20 – until 1958 2/2
1958 2/28 – 9/14
1963 6/18 – 10/1
1964 2/4 – 4/18
1966 7/15 – 10/7
1967 1/5 – 5/31
1969 10/5 – 12/25
1970 4/19 – 8/25
1975 5/25 – 11/21
1975 12/29 – until 1976 4/1
1978 6/29 – 9/12
1979 2/14 – 5/4
1981 9/19 – 12/4
1982 6/2 – 7/23
1987 5/6 – until 1988 3/15
1990 6/13 – 8/24
1993 9/2 – 11/16
1999 4/19 – 7/7
1999 10/12 – until 2000 2/23
2001 10/20 – 11/15
2002 5/25 – 8/8
2004 12/15 – until 2005 3/23
2005 8/14 – 11/1
2011 4/2 – 6/11
2011 12/1 – until 2012 1/19

SATURN CHALLENGING
1938 6/3 – 9/28
1939 2/23 – until 1940 3/31
1945 7/14 – until 1946 8/13
1952 9/20 – until 1953 11/3
1968 4/5 – until 1969 5/11
1974 8/28 – until 1975 1/6
1975 5/17 – 10/3
1975 12/27 – until 1976 6/17
1981 10/27 – until 1982 12/13
1983 4/18 – 9/9
1997 5/12 – 10/30
1998 1/31 – 6/24
1998 10/8 – until 1999 3/14
2004 6/27 – until 2005 7/27
2010 12/11 – until 2011 3/14
2011 9/2 – until 2012 10/17

URANUS CHALLENGING
1952 7/26 – until 1956 7/5
1971 10/31 – until 1975 10/3

NEPTUNE CHALLENGING
1949 10/21 – until 1957 9/29

PLUTO CHALLENGING
1938 1/1 – until 1940 6/14
1977 11/11 – until 1984 10/8

JUPITER SPECIAL
1949 1/22 – 4/28
1949 6/11 – 12/7
1961 1/6 – 3/23
1961 8/1 – 11/14
1972 12/21 – until 1973 3/2
1984 12/4 – until 1985 2/12
1996 3/26 – 6/12
1996 11/15 – until 1997 1/27
2008 2/28 – 7/26
2008 10/21 – until 2009 1/11

SATURN SPECIAL
1960 2/24 – 7/3
1960 11/23 – until 1962 1/15
1989 12/30 – until 1991 2/19
1991 8/26 – 11/12

URANUS SPECIAL
1992 1/30 – until 1996 11/21

NEPTUNE SPECIAL
1991 2/4 – until 1999 1/9

January 15

SUN: CAPRICORN • DECANATE: VIRGO/MERCURY • DEGREE: 23°–25° CAPRICORN • MODE: CARDINAL • ELEMENT: EARTH

Your Personal Powers

Independent, instinctive, and assured, you are a resourceful and astute individual. Your ruling planet, Saturn, grants you determination and a good sense of structure. Being a realist with insight, you gain power from your ability to quickly evaluate people and situations. Ambitious, with innate leadership skills, you possess a talent for attracting money or receiving help and support from others. Just be careful that your desire for material security is balanced with your need to broaden your horizons. Fortunately, you comprehend ideas quickly and with your good mental focus, you have the capacity for deep thought. As a persuasive communicator who likes to keep busy, you work hard toward your objectives. With your natural business sense and an enterprising spirit, you usually learn better through practice than through theory. You are also likely to value personal freedom. This may even extend to fighting for the rights of others. Reserved but dramatic, with your creative ideas and ability to inspire others, you can achieve remarkable success in life through self-discipline.

Your Powers of Attraction in Relationships

People are attracted to your willpower and shrewd insight. With your inventive ideas and ability to turn on the charm, you can be witty and entertaining in social situations. Although aware of your responsibilities, you also seek to be independent. Caring and understanding of those you love, you can be a devoted spouse and parent. You are usually attracted to other sociable individuals with creative ideas. However, if you allow a pessimistic streak in your nature to rule, you may encounter some worry or indecision in the area of your relationships. By being adaptable rather than stubborn, you can restore harmony to your partnerships. Nevertheless, your generosity and ability to support others suggest that you are loyal, caring, and security-conscious, especially about your home and family.

Your attractive qualities: ambitious, determined, clever, creative, organizational skills, hardworking, quick responses, logical, practical, persistent, business sense, generous, responsible, fighter, kind, artistic, cooperative, appreciative, good judgment, humanitarian, strong instincts

Your less attractive qualities: restlessness, negative thinking, too reserved, self-centered, fear of change, uncommunicative, critical, indecisive, loss of faith, worry, verbally caustic, too materialistic

Your Venus Power

The planet Venus has a great deal of influence on your powers of attraction. Below are four possible Venus types for women and men. To find your Venus you need to go to page 771, where you will find the Venus table and extra information. The planet Mars also affects your powers of attraction. To find your Mars table and interpretation go to page 761.

WOMEN WITH VENUS IN SAGITTARIUS: At your best when being optimistic and generous, you possess a mischievous sense of fun. In relationships, your open-minded approach to people and places may attract you to those of a different culture or make you tolerant of the foibles of others. Although warm and enthusiastic when in love, your natural honesty and idealism may inspire you to look for a partner who shares your love of freedom.

MEN WITH VENUS IN SAGITTARIUS: Forward-thinking rather than dwelling on the past, you are looking for a partner who can share your future plans. You enjoy exploring life whether through travel and mental pursuits or sports and games. Idealistic, you usually prefer the company of a partner who is optimistic and shares your beliefs. In your desire for honesty in relationships, however, be careful not to become tactless. Nevertheless, you are attracted to honest, direct, and fun-loving partners with a sense of humor like your own.

WOMEN WITH VENUS IN CAPRICORN: Proud and refined, you attract others with your composed dignity. Disliking vulnerability and needing to feel safe before you can express your feelings, you display a strong front. Feeling insecure or inadequate in relationships may force you to become manipulative in order to regain control. Nevertheless, you can project an attractive sense of self-assurance and are capable of displaying loyalty and a wonderful dry sense of humor.

MEN WITH VENUS IN CAPRICORN: As you do not display your deeper emotions freely, you are usually dignified and controlled in your relationships. Practical and down-to-earth partners are particularly attractive to you, especially those who do not rush into expressing their feelings but seem to possess natural class and reserve. You need a partner who is loyal and dependable and willing to take your relationship seriously.

WOMEN WITH VENUS IN AQUARIUS: Usually you have a modern outlook on love and are open to new or current lifestyles. Your intuitive abilities, communal sense, and people skills often allow you to see deeper into human intentions and to read people's thoughts telepathically. You are usually group-oriented and are drawn to individuals within the group who are independent and self-motivated. You are more inclined to choose a partner who is unconventional or freedom-loving. Conscious of your social standing, however, you want someone who can relate well to your friends.

MEN WITH VENUS IN AQUARIUS: Although independent, you often enjoy being part of a group. The partners you frequently attract are themselves nonconformists or free spirits. As an individual you may not find it easy to settle into a routine or an entirely mundane type of relationship. You may have some unconventional views on traditional marriage or your partner may hold such views. It is usually important to you that your love relationships are based on friendship.

WOMEN WITH VENUS IN PISCES: Idealistic and impressionable, in love you are romantic. Being sensitive to other people, you are receptive to their moods and feelings. This affinity indicates that although you can be selfless, you may have to guard against being too sentimental or overly romantic, especially of those who can take advantage of your kindness. Nevertheless, you are alluring and seductive, and your partners may be intrigued by your emotional magnetism, compassion, or mysterious nature.

MEN WITH VENUS IN PISCES: Being adaptable and sensitive, you are able to intuitively feel the moods of those you love. Although you are receptive to others, you can be ambiguous about your own feelings toward your partner. Romantic and kindhearted, you long to be loved but you need to be realistic about your relationships in order to avoid disappointments. When in love you may idealize your partners and fail to see any faults in their personality.

To read all about your Outer Planets and work out how to use your personalized timetable, go to Section Three, page 789.

Your Personalized Timetable

JUPITER BENEFICIAL
1939 3/24 – 5/8
1939 11/7 – 12/12
1941 3/28 – 6/5
1944 10/11 – until 1945 9/5
1946 12/26 – until 1947 6/11
1947 8/19 – 10/21
1951 3/7 – 4/19
1952 7/16 – 11/4
1953 3/5 – 5/19
1956 9/24 – until 1957 8/19
1958 12/8 – until 1959 2/5
1959 4/30 – 10/2
1963 2/19 – 4/1
1964 6/23 – 12/28
1965 1/23 – 5/3
1968 9/9 – 12/1
1969 3/12 – 7/31
1970 11/22 – until 1971 1/10
1971 6/10 – 9/6
1975 2/1 – 3/16
1976 6/4 – until 1977 4/15
1980 8/24 – 11/9
1981 4/21 – 7/3
1982 11/6 – 12/23
1986 5/26 – 8/30
1987 1/12 – 2/28
1988 5/18 – 8/6
1988 11/13 – until 1989 3/26
1992 8/7 – 10/22
1994 10/22 – 12/6
1998 4/30 – 10/17
1998 12/10 – until 1999 2/10
2000 5/1 – 7/12
2000 12/29 – until 2001 2/21
2003 11/24 – until 2004 2/13
2004 7/20 – 10/6
2006 10/5 – 11/21
2010 4/10 – 6/2
2010 9/13 – until 2011 1/19
2012 4/14 – 6/22

SATURN BENEFICIAL
1941 4/26 – until 1942 5/27
1949 10/31 – until 1950 3/2
1950 7/24 – until 1951 9/4
1955 1/14 – 4/18
1955 10/9 – until 1956 1/6
1956 5/22 – 10/4
1966 3/7 – 6/23
1966 7/29 – until 1967 2/26
1970 6/6 – 12/20
1971 2/13 – 7/9
1971 12/3 – until 1972 3/28
1979 9/3 – until 1980 10/10
1984 11/14 – until 1985 11/12
1995 4/12 – 10/11
1996 1/1 – 4/2
1999 7/31 – 9/28
2000 4/8 – until 2001 5/10
2008 10/10 – until 2009 4/4
2009 6/28 – 11/23
2010 3/7 – 8/16

URANUS BENEFICIAL
1938 6/25 – until 1943 4/16
1965 9/26 – until 1969 8/25
1978 12/25 – until 1981 11/6
2008 3/22 – until 2011 3/1

NEPTUNE BENEFICIAL
1938 1/1 – until 1944 8/12
1965 1/4 – until 1970 10/20

PLUTO BENEFICIAL
1965 9/17 – until 1973 8/3
1990 12/25 – until 1995 10/26

JUPITER CHALLENGING
1940 3/20 – 5/27
1942 8/24 – until 1943 2/12
1943 4/8 – 7/12

1945 11/10 – until 1946 10/6
1952 3/2 – 5/9
1954 8/5 – until 1955 6/24
1957 10/25 – until 1958 9/20
1963 6/25 – 9/23
1964 2/10 – 4/22
1966 7/20 – 10/16
1966 12/27 – until 1967 6/6
1969 10/9 – until 1970 1/1
1970 4/11 – 8/31
1975 5/30 – 11/9
1976 1/10 – 4/5
1978 7/4 – 9/18
1979 2/6 – 5/13
1981 9/24 – 12/9
1982 5/21 – 8/3
1987 5/11 – until 1988 3/19
1990 6/17 – 8/29
1993 9/7 – 11/21
1999 4/23 – 7/15
1999 10/4 – until 2000 2/28
2002 5/31 – 8/12
2004 12/23 – until 2005 3/14
2005 8/20 – 11/6
2011 4/6 – 6/16
2011 11/20 – until 2012 1/29

SATURN CHALLENGING
1938 6/16 – 9/14
1939 3/5 – until 1940 4/9
1945 7/22 – until 1946 8/21
1947 3/12 – 4/26
1952 9/28 – until 1953 11/11
1968 4/13 – until 1969 5/19
1969 12/15 – until 1970 1/23
1974 9/8 – 12/25
1975 5/26 – 10/21
1975 12/9 – until 1976 6/26
1981 11/4 – until 1982 5/15
1982 7/21 – 12/25
1983 4/4 – 9/19
1997 5/22 – 10/16
1998 2/12 – 7/8
1998 9/23 – until 1999 3/23
2004 7/5 – until 2005 8/4
2010 12/26 – until 2011 2/26
2011 9/12 – until 2012 10/25

URANUS CHALLENGING
1952 8/13 – until 1956 7/22
1971 11/17 – until 1975 10/20

NEPTUNE CHALLENGING
1949 11/20 – until 1958 8/22

PLUTO SPECIAL
1938 1/1 – until 1941 5/27
1977 12/18 – until 1985 8/22

JUPITER SPECIAL
1949 1/27 – 12/13
1961 1/10 – 3/29
1961 7/24 – 11/20
1972 12/25 – until 1973 3/7
1973 9/20 – 10/6
1984 12/9 – until 1985 2/17
1996 4/6 – 6/2
1996 11/21 – until 1997 1/31
2008 3/5 – 7/17
2008 10/29 – until 2009 1/15

SATURN SPECIAL
1960 3/7 – 6/19
1960 12/3 – until 1962 1/24
1990 1/7 – until 1991 2/28
1991 8/11 – 11/26

URANUS SPECIAL
1992 2/18 – until 1996 12/15

NEPTUNE SPECIAL
1991 3/13 – until 1999 12/8

♍

January 16

SUN: CAPRICORN • DECANATE: VIRGO/MERCURY • DEGREE: 24°–26° CAPRICORN • MODE: CARDINAL • ELEMENT: EARTH

Your Personal Powers

Slightly reserved yet friendly and sociable, you can express yourself well. As a determined individual with a strong sense of identity, you usually have a rational and balanced outlook. Your ruling planet, Saturn, suggests that you are also shrewd and practical. Being purposeful implies that you can be very focused when set on a course of action. A perfectionist streak suggests that you can be hardworking and meticulous by paying attention to details. You gain power from your sharp and quick mental responses and your personal charisma, ensuring that you can befriend people from all walks of life. Although you can be proud and dignified, you also possess a youthful and playful side to your nature. If you indulge in worry and negativity, however, you can lose some power by being too serious or too concerned with material security. Nevertheless, when inspired, you often enchant others with your original and innovative ideas. Equally with your vision and sense of beauty, you usually possess an awareness of image or style. With your many talents you need only apply the necessary self-discipline to access your outstanding potential.

Your Powers of Attraction in Relationships

You attract others with your magnetism and social gifts. Very persuasive, you can use your quick replies and communication skills to entertain others. Be careful, however, of a self-centered or stubborn streak that can harm your close relationships. Although you love freedom, you have a strong need for security and usually you want a partner who can offer you practical help and support. You may prefer someone pragmatic with a good sense of order and structure. Although you can be sensitive and idealistic on an inner level and feel deeply, you sometimes repress your emotions. It is often vital for you to balance your individual needs with those of your partner or family. With your natural charm and creativity, however, you will always be popular.

Your attractive qualities: clever, creative, friendly, pragmatic, responsible, home-loving, honest, intuitive, sociable, imaginative, original, dignified, youthful, cooperative, idealistic, communication skills, personal magnetism, humanitarian, dutiful, business sense

Your less attractive qualities: too materialistic, worry, overconfident or insecure, too tough, dissatisfied, too security-conscious, skeptical, selfish, negative thinking, manipulative

Your Venus Power

The planet Venus has a great deal of influence on your powers of attraction. Below are four possible Venus types for women and men. To find your Venus you need to go to page 771, where you will find the Venus table and extra information. The planet Mars also affects your powers of attraction. To find your Mars table and interpretation go to page 761.

WOMEN WITH VENUS IN SAGITTARIUS: At your best when being optimistic and generous, you possess a mischievous sense of fun. In relationships your open-minded approach to people and places may attract you to those of a different culture or make you tolerant of the foibles of others. Although warm and enthusiastic when in love, your natural honesty and idealism may inspire you to look for a partner who shares your love of freedom.

MEN WITH VENUS IN SAGITTARIUS: Forward-thinking rather than dwelling on the past, you are looking for a partner who can share your future plans. You enjoy exploring life whether through travel and mental pursuits or sports and games. Idealistic, you usually prefer the company of a partner who is optimistic and shares your beliefs. In your desire for honesty in relationships, however, be careful not to become tactless. Nevertheless, you are attracted to honest, direct, and fun-loving partners who have a sense of humor like your own.

WOMEN WITH VENUS IN CAPRICORN: With your natural caution in romantic affairs, you often appear reserved and controlled. If shy, try to be more forward, especially if you want to be noticed. When you care about people, however, you are usually willing to put in extra time and energy to preserve the relationship. You are practical and dependable, and a sense of duty can often play a large role in affairs of your heart. With elegant simplicity, you can attract others through your well-cut clothes and refined manners.

MEN WITH VENUS IN CAPRICORN: In relationships, you take love seriously and can be a strong and practical support for friends or partners. You are usually attracted to partners who are as hardworking as yourself. As you tend not to express your feelings until you feel really secure in a relationship, you may be drawn to those who seem loyal, faithful, and not likely to let you down. As you respect the wisdom of experience, you

may be drawn to mature partners or, alternatively, you may act as an authority figure for someone younger.

WOMEN WITH VENUS IN AQUARIUS: When it comes to relationships, others are attracted to your honest, friendly, and easygoing attitude. You really enjoy social interaction with others and may develop a genuine concern for humanity. Usually you present a tolerant and reasonable front in love situations and attempt to view your relationships objectively. If partners become too demanding, however, you can become stubborn and fixed. Friendship may be even more important for you than sexual compatibility.

MEN WITH VENUS IN AQUARIUS: You are sociable and open-minded, and people are attracted by your friendly and relaxed style. Being independent, you value freedom-loving partners who give you the space to be yourself. Others sometimes interpret your detachment as being emotionally cool, but they may not understand your progressive views on relationships. Friendship can sometimes be even more important than earthly passion. Ideally, your partner shares your ideas on life and possesses as strong a sense of originality as your own. Not easily ruffled, you can deal well with difficult situations or moody partners.

WOMEN WITH VENUS IN PISCES: As a romantic and idealistic individual, you can be both loving and giving. In relationships you may need to balance the practical with the charitable. While making allowances and sacrifices is understandable in a loving relationship, playing the martyr is often a state of romantic illusion that can lead to self-deception. Your benevolence and sacrifices in the right relationship nonetheless make you a partner who is devoted, kind, and compassionate. Subtle, sensitive, and alluring, you make a sensual and caring partner.

MEN WITH VENUS IN PISCES: Romantic and idealistic when in love, you can be a sensitive and responsive lover. Being pliant and flexible with an impressionable nature helps you to adapt to the needs of others. In your desire to blend with those you love, however, guard against not clearly defining your own boundaries. With your affectionate and sentimental nature, you are often attracted to those who understand your sensitivity and share your vision.

To read all about your Outer Planets and work out how to use your personalized timetable, go to Section Three, page 789.

Your Personalized Timetable

JUPITER BENEFICIAL
1939 3/28 – 5/13
1939 10/25 – 12/25
1941 4/1 – 6/10
1944 10/16 – until 1945 9/10
1947 1/1 – 6/1
1947 8/28 – 10/26
1951 3/12 – 4/23
1952 7/23 – 10/28
1953 3/11 – 5/24
1956 9/29 – until 1957 8/25
1958 12/13 – until 1959 2/14
1959 4/20 – 10/7
1963 2/23 – 4/5
1964 6/28 – 12/13
1965 2/7 – 5/7
1968 9/13 – 12/9
1969 3/3 – 8/6
1970 11/27 – until 1971 1/16
1971 6/1 – 9/14
1975 2/5 – 3/20
1976 6/8 – until 1977 4/20
1980 8/28 – 11/14
1981 4/11 – 7/12
1982 11/11 – 12/28
1986 6/3 – 8/21
1987 1/17 – 3/4
1988 5/22 – 8/14
1988 11/4 – until 1989 3/31
1992 8/12 – 10/27
1994 10/26 – 12/11
1998 5/5 – 10/7
1998 12/20 – until 1999 2/14
2000 5/6 – 7/17
2000 12/19 – until 2001 3/3
2003 12/4 – until 2004 2/3
2004 7/25 – 10/11
2006 10/10 – 11/26
2010 4/15 – 6/9
2010 9/5 – until 2011 1/25
2012 4/19 – 6/27

1943 4/19 – 7/16
1945 11/16 – until 1946 10/11
1952 3/6 – 5/13
1954 8/10 – until 1955 6/29
1957 10/30 – until 1958 9/25
1963 7/4 – 9/14
1964 2/15 – 4/26
1966 7/24 – 10/26
1966 12/16 – until 1967 6/11
1969 10/14 – until 1970 1/9
1970 4/2 – 9/6
1975 6/4 – 10/30
1976 1/19 – 4/10
1978 7/8 – 9/24
1979 1/29 – 5/20
1981 9/28 – 12/15
1982 5/12 – 8/12
1987 5/15 – until 1988 3/24
1990 6/22 – 9/3
1993 9/12 – 11/26
1999 4/27 – 7/24
1999 9/25 – until 2000 3/4
2002 6/5 – 8/17
2005 1/2 – 3/4
2005 8/26 – 11/10
2011 4/10 – 6/22
2011 11/12 – until 2012 2/7

SATURN CHALLENGING
1938 7/3 – 8/27
1939 3/13 – until 1940 4/17
1945 7/30 – until 1946 8/30
1947 2/21 – 5/14
1952 10/7 – until 1953 11/20
1954 6/5 – 8/6
1968 4/21 – until 1969 5/28
1969 11/25 – until 1970 2/11
1974 9/21 – 12/11
1975 6/4 – until 1976 7/4
1981 11/14 – until 1982 4/29
1982 8/6 – until 1983 1/9
1983 3/19 – 9/28
1997 6/2 – 10/3
1998 2/22 – 7/31
1998 8/30 – until 1999 3/31
2004 7/13 – until 2005 8/12
2011 9/20 – until 2012 11/3

URANUS CHALLENGING
1952 9/3 – until 1957 5/15
1971 12/10 – until 1976 8/10

NEPTUNE CHALLENGING
1950 10/19 – until 1958 9/28

PLUTO CHALLENGING
1938 1/1 – until 1941 7/10
1978 10/31 – until 1985 9/25

JUPITER SPECIAL
1949 1/31 – 12/17
1961 1/15 – 4/5
1961 7/16 – 11/26
1972 12/30 – until 1973 3/12
1973 9/2 – 10/24
1984 12/14 – until 1985 2/21
1996 4/22 – 5/16
1996 11/26 – until 1997 2/5
2008 3/11 – 7/9
2008 11/4 – until 2009 1/20

SATURN BENEFICIAL
1938 1/1 – 1/19
1941 5/4 – until 1942 6/4
1949 11/12 – until 1950 2/17
1950 8/2 – until 1951 9/12
1955 1/30 – 3/31
1955 10/18 – until 1956 1/17
1956 5/8 – 10/14
1966 3/15 – until 1967 3/7
1970 6/15 – 12/3
1971 3/2 – 7/20
1971 11/21 – until 1972 4/7
1979 9/11 – until 1980 10/19
1981 5/13 – 6/27
1984 11/22 – until 1985 11/20
1995 4/21 – 9/26
1996 1/14 – 4/10
2000 4/17 – until 2001 5/18
2008 10/20 – until 2009 3/21
2009 7/11 – 12/7
2010 2/20 – 8/25

URANUS BENEFICIAL
1938 7/24 – until 1943 5/5
1965 10/14 – until 1969 9/12
1979 1/19 – until 1981 11/23
2008 4/10 – until 2011 3/19

NEPTUNE BENEFICIAL
1938 1/1 – until 1944 9/11
1965 11/30 – until 1971 9/2

PLUTO BENEFICIAL
1965 10/18 – until 1973 9/4
1991 11/16 – until 1996 8/28

JUPITER CHALLENGING
1940 3/24 – 5/31
1942 8/30 – until 1943 2/2

SATURN SPECIAL
1960 3/23 – 6/2
1960 12/13 – until 1962 2/1
1990 1/16 – until 1991 3/11
1991 7/28 – 12/8

URANUS SPECIAL
1992 3/15 – until 1997 1/3

NEPTUNE SPECIAL
1992 2/2 – until 2000 1/7

♑

January 17

SUN: CAPRICORN • DECANATE: VIRGO/MERCURY • DEGREE: 25°–27° CAPRICORN • MODE: CARDINAL • ELEMENT: EARTH

Your Personal Powers

Proud, clever, and determined, you are a thoughtful individual with the potential to attract money. Success-oriented, you gain power from the combination of your fast mental responses, high standards, and ability to concentrate on large projects. You also possess practical sensibility and endurance. When positive, you can be confident and optimistic, with the ability to think in broad terms. Enjoying power and having a natural business sense, you can achieve wealth and success if you apply the necessary self-discipline. Although you may have strong material desires, you can lose power if you sacrifice your personal satisfaction or your creativity. Nevertheless, being generous and a good planner, you usually find your greatest rewards come from helping others. You are enthusiastic and circumspect, and your ability to see opportunities and market your ideas indicates that your talent for self-promotion can greatly aid your climb to the top. Although your path may not always be easy, great achievement and success is often brought about through your knowledge and perseverance.

Your Powers of Attraction in Relationships

You attract others with your self-confidence and strong sense of purpose. Usually generous and sociable, you can mix in different social groups. Proud and dramatic yet introspective, the opposites within your nature suggest that you can be both practical and realistic. You also possess a sensitivity that you may not always find easy to express. When you do open up, however, you can project a strong and powerful love that often involves protecting your loved ones. Nevertheless, be careful of a selfish streak that can emerge and affect your relationships. You can be friendly yet also project a serious and thoughtful attitude that others find appealing.

Your attractive qualities: endurance, intuitiveness, thinks big, good planner, business sense, generous, thoughtful, success-oriented, courageous, accurate, good talker, quick responses, ambitious, determined, analytical, leadership ability, executive, attracts money, perfectionist

Your less attractive qualities: stubborn, selfish, too detached, lonely, carelessness, moody, too sensitive, overindulgent, overconfident or worried, intolerant, abuse of power, critical, demanding, suspicious

Your Venus Power

The planet Venus has a great deal of influence on your powers of attraction. Below are four possible Venus types for women and men. To find your Venus you need to go to page 771, where you will find the Venus table and extra information. The planet Mars also affects your powers of attraction. To find your Mars table and interpretation go to page 761.

WOMEN WITH VENUS IN SAGITTARIUS: Sociable, warm, and friendly, you possess an honest and frank style in your relationships. Being naturally gregarious, you want others to share your enthusiasm and enjoy encouraging the people you love. You do better when you have a sense of personal freedom within a relationship and you are usually generous with the faults of others. You need a partner who can share your need to explore and take risks whether through travel, education, or recreation.

MEN WITH VENUS IN SAGITTARIUS: When in love you are open and friendly with a need for a partner who can share your adventurous spirit and sense of fun. Be careful, however, that your desire for freedom does not cause you to avoid commitment. You prefer your partners to be positive, direct, and generous in spirit. Being outspoken as well as an idealist, you usually enjoy a partner with whom you can share your strong opinions. Alternatively, you may wish to explore life together whether through travel, education, or by having fun.

WOMEN WITH VENUS IN CAPRICORN: Romantically, you do not give your heart easily but hide behind a cool reserve until you feel free to express your emotions. As you take your relationships seriously, you may find yourself drawn to people who are businesslike, resourceful, and practical or who can act as teachers or mentors. Work or career may also be a factor in many of your associations and partnerships. As security can play an important role in your relationships, you are often attracted to partners who are loyal and hardworking.

MEN WITH VENUS IN CAPRICORN: As you admire loyal, hardworking, and dedicated individuals, you probably want a partner who can share your vocational interests or provide you with the sense of security you need. You could even find yourself with a partner who is of a different age group or maturity. Guard against denying your true emotional needs or focusing on your career at the expense of your relationship. You are drawn to reserved partners who display self-control.

WOMEN WITH VENUS IN AQUARIUS: When it comes to relationships, others are attracted to your honest, friendly, and

easygoing attitude. You enjoy social interaction and have a genuine concern for others. In fact, at times, your friends may be just as important as your partner. Usually you present a tolerant and reasonable front in love situations and attempt to view your relationships objectively. If partners become too demanding, however, you can become stubborn or awkward. Nevertheless, inventive and progressive, you enjoy the company of like-minded people who can share your original ideas.

MEN WITH VENUS IN AQUARIUS: Friendly and honest, you attract people with your broad-minded approach to life. You usually possess an objective and slightly detached attitude to affairs of the heart. If you are too removed, however, others can misinterpret your behavior as uncaring. It is often more important to you that your love relationships are based on friendship and honesty than intense passion. As you are generally tolerant and liberal, you may be drawn to less conventional relationships.

WOMEN WITH VENUS IN PISCES: Idealistic and impressionable, in love you are romantic. Being sensitive to other people, you are receptive to their moods and feelings. This affinity indicates that, although you can be selfless, you may have to guard against being too sentimental or overly romantic, especially of those who can take advantage of your kindness. Nevertheless, you are alluring and seductive, and your partners may be intrigued by your emotional magnetism, compassion, or mysterious nature.

MEN WITH VENUS IN PISCES: Being adaptable and sensitive, you are able to intuitively feel the moods of those you love. Although you are receptive to others, you can be ambiguous about your own feelings toward your partner. Romantic and kindhearted, you long to be loved but you need to be realistic about your relationships in order to avoid disappointments. When in love you may idealize your partners and fail to see any faults in their personality.

To read all about your Outer Planets and work out how to use your personalized timetable, go to Section Three, page 789.

Your Personalized Timetable

JUPITER BENEFICIAL
1939 4/2 – 5/19
1939 10/15 – until 1940 1/3
1941 4/6 – 6/14
1944 10/21 – until 1945 4/20
1945 6/8 – 9/15
1947 1/7 – 5/24
1947 9/5 – 10/30
1951 3/16 – 4/28
1952 7/31 – 10/19
1953 3/17 – 5/28
1956 10/4 – until 1957 8/30
1958 12/18 – until 1959 2/28
1959 4/6 – 10/13
1963 2/27 – 4/10
1964 7/3 – 12/3
1965 2/17 – 5/12
1968 9/18 – 12/19
1969 2/21 – 8/12
1970 12/1 – until 1971 1/23
1971 5/24 – 9/21
1975 2/10 – 3/24
1976 6/13 – until 1977 4/25
1980 9/2 – 11/20
1981 4/3 – 7/20
1982 11/16 – until 1983 1/2
1983 7/13 – 8/13
1986 6/12 – 8/11
1987 1/22 – 3/8
1988 5/27 – 8/23
1988 10/26 – until 1989 4/6
1992 8/17 – 11/1
1994 10/31 – 12/16
1998 5/11 – 9/28
1998 12/28 – until 1999 2/19
2000 5/10 – 7/23
2000 12/10 – until 2001 3/11
2003 12/18 – until 2004 1/20
2004 7/31 – 10/15
2006 10/15 – 11/30
2010 4/19 – 6/18
2010 8/27 – until 2011 1/30
2012 4/23 – 7/1

SATURN BENEFICIAL
1938 1/1 – 1/31
1941 5/12 – until 1942 6/12
1949 11/27 – until 1950 2/1
1950 8/12 – until 1951 9/21
1955 10/27 – until 1956 1/31
1956 4/23 – 10/24
1966 3/23 – until 1967 3/15
1970 6/24 – 11/20
1971 3/14 – 7/31
1971 11/8 – until 1972 4/16
1979 9/20 – until 1980 10/28
1981 4/23 – 7/17
1984 12/1 – until 1985 11/29
1995 5/1 – 9/13
1996 1/25 – 4/19
1996 11/2 – until 1997 1/2
2000 4/25 – until 2001 5/26
2008 10/30 – until 2009 3/8
2009 7/22 – 12/29
2010 1/28 – 9/3

URANUS BENEFICIAL
1939 5/19 – until 1943 5/23
1965 11/3 – until 1969 9/28
1979 11/16 – until 1982 9/23
2008 5/2 – until 2012 1/22

NEPTUNE BENEFICIAL
1938 1/1 – until 1945 8/9
1966 1/1 – until 1971 10/18

PLUTO BENEFICIAL
1965 12/11 – until 1974 7/21
1991 12/12 – until 1996 10/14

JUPITER CHALLENGING
1940 3/28 – 6/5

1942 9/4 – until 1943 1/24
1943 4/27 – 7/21
1945 11/21 – until 1946 5/20
1946 7/10 – 10/16
1952 3/11 – 5/17
1954 8/15 – until 1955 7/4
1957 11/4 – until 1958 9/30
1963 7/15 – 9/3
1964 2/20 – 4/30
1966 7/29 – 11/17
1966 11/25 – until 1967 6/17
1969 10/19 – until 1970 1/19
1970 3/23 – 9/12
1975 6/10 – 10/22
1976 1/27 – 4/14
1978 7/13 – 10/1
1979 1/21 – 5/27
1981 10/3 – 12/21
1982 5/4 – 8/20
1987 5/20 – until 1988 3/28
1990 6/27 – 9/9
1991 3/6 – 4/23
1993 9/17 – 12/2
1999 5/2 – 8/7
1999 9/11 – until 2000 3/9
2002 6/10 – 8/22
2005 1/16 – 2/18
2005 8/31 – 11/15
2011 4/14 – 6/28
2011 11/4 – 2/14

SATURN CHALLENGING
1939 3/22 – until 1940 4/25
1945 8/7 – until 1946 2/25
1946 4/12 – 9/8
1947 2/7 – 5/27
1952 10/15 – until 1953 11/29
1954 5/18 – 8/23
1968 4/29 – until 1969 6/6
1969 11/10 – until 1970 2/24
1974 10/9 – 11/22
1975 6/13 – until 1976 7/13
1981 11/23 – until 1982 4/15
1982 8/19 – until 1983 10/7
1997 6/14 – 9/19
1998 3/4 – until 1999 4/9
2004 7/21 – until 2005 8/20
2006 3/28 – 4/13
2011 9/29 – until 2012 11/11

URANUS CHALLENGING
1952 10/10 – until 1957 6/10
1972 10/7 – until 1976 9/7

NEPTUNE CHALLENGING
1950 11/18 – until 1959 8/16

PLUTO CHALLENGING
1938 1/1 – until 1942 6/25
1978 11/30 – until 1985 10/22

JUPITER SPECIAL
1938 1/8 – until 1949 12/22
1961 1/19 – 4/13
1961 7/7 – 12/2
1973 1/3 – 3/17
1973 8/22 – 11/4
1984 12/18 – until 1985 2/26
1996 12/1 – until 1997 2/9
2008 3/18 – 7/1
2008 11/10 – until 2009 1/24

SATURN SPECIAL
1960 12/22 – until 1962 2/10
1990 1/25 – until 1991 3/22
1991 7/14 – 12/18

URANUS SPECIAL
1993 1/14 – until 1997 1/21

NEPTUNE SPECIAL
1992 3/7 – until 2000 12/3

♍

January 18

SUN: CAPRICORN • DECANATE: VIRGO/MERCURY • DEGREE: 26°–28° CAPRICORN • MODE: CARDINAL • ELEMENT: EARTH

Your Personal Powers

Broad-minded and shrewd, you are an individual with a keen intellect and good communication skills. Your ruling planet, Saturn, grants you natural authority and good concentration. You gain power from the combination of your detached viewpoint and strong determination. Once committed, you can be very hardworking in achieving your goals. Being practical and ambitious with innate evaluation skills, you usually prefer to take the lead. Be careful, however, that you do not lose power to being bossy or to a need for material security at all costs. Nevertheless, with vision, unique ideas, and a resolved attitude, whatever you do, you are likely to possess an original approach and a commanding manner. Although pragmatic, an idealistic or humanitarian side to your nature may arise from your astute observations of human behavior. With your special blend of universal awareness and common sense, you enjoy helping others or fighting for a cause or ideal. With your dynamic sensitivity you also have the ability to inspire others.

Your Powers of Attraction in Relationships

Others are attracted to your intelligence, generosity, and insight. Friendly, with fast responses, you can keep others entertained. You are attracted to those who can match your wit or fine mind and enjoy friendly quips or smart replies. In your relationships a lighthearted or detached approach can also help you to overcome frustrations or disappointments. Although you can give much in the way of affection and friendship, inhibitions or hidden fears may cause you to repress some of your feelings. Lessons in relationships often involve being able to let go. Nevertheless, your sense of responsibility to others suggests that you may prefer the security of a more conventional relationship. Although you like to retain some independence, you are generous and giving to those you love.

Your attractive qualities: progressive, assertive, intuitive, courageous, resolute, efficient, advisory skills, humanitarian, ambitious, business sense, creative ideas, determination, sensitive, dynamic, enthusiastic, imaginative, sympathetic, idealistic, original, generous

Your less attractive qualities: frustrated, lazy, lack of order, unchecked emotions, selfishness, failure to complete work or projects, critical, misunderstood, disappointed

Your Venus Power

The planet Venus has a great deal of influence on your powers of attraction. Below are four possible Venus types for women and men. To find your Venus you need to go to page 771, where you will find the Venus table and extra information. The planet Mars also affects your powers of attraction. To find your Mars table and interpretation go to page 761.

WOMEN WITH VENUS IN SAGITTARIUS: Sociable, warm, and friendly, you possess an honest and frank style in your relationships. Being naturally gregarious, you want others to share your enthusiasm and you enjoy encouraging the people you love. You do better when you have a sense of personal freedom within a relationship and are usually generous with the faults of others. You need a partner who can share your need to explore and take risks, whether through travel, education, or recreation.

MEN WITH VENUS IN SAGITTARIUS: When in love you are open and friendly with a need for a partner who can share your adventurous spirit and sense of fun. Be careful, however, that your desire for freedom does not cause you to avoid commitment. You prefer your partners to be positive, direct, and generous in spirit. Being outspoken as well as an idealist, you usually enjoy a partner with whom you can share your strong opinions. Alternatively, you may wish to explore life together whether through travel, education, or by having fun.

WOMEN WITH VENUS IN CAPRICORN: With your natural caution in romantic affairs, you often appear reserved and controlled. If shy, try to be more forward, especially if you want to be noticed. When you care about people, however, you are usually willing to put in extra time and energy to preserve the relationship. You are practical and dependable, and a sense of duty can often play a large role in affairs of the heart. With elegant simplicity, you can attract others with your well-cut clothes and refined manners.

MEN WITH VENUS IN CAPRICORN: In relationships you take love seriously and can be a strong and practical support for friends or partners. You are usually attracted to partners who are as hardworking as you. As you tend not to express your feelings until you feel really secure in a relationship, you may be drawn to those who seem loyal, faithful, and not likely to let you down. As you respect the wisdom of experience, you may be drawn to mature partners or, alternatively, you may act as an authority figure for someone younger.

WOMEN WITH VENUS IN AQUARIUS: When it comes to relationships, others are attracted to your honest, friendly, and easygoing attitude. You really enjoy social interaction with others and may develop a genuine concern for humanity. Usually you present a tolerant and reasonable front in love situations and attempt to view your relationships objectively. If partners become too demanding, however, you can become stubborn and fixed. Friendship may be even more important for you than sexual compatibility.

MEN WITH VENUS IN AQUARIUS: You are sociable and open-minded, and people are attracted by your friendly and relaxed style. Being independent, you value freedom-loving partners who give you the space to be yourself. Others sometimes interpret your detachment as being emotionally cool, but they may not understand your progressive views on relationships. Friendship can sometimes be even more important than earthly passion. Ideally, your partners can share your ideas on life and possess a sense of originality as strong as your own. Not easily ruffled, you can deal well with difficult situations or moody partners.

WOMEN WITH VENUS IN PISCES: Romantic and idealistic when in love, you can be a sensitive and responsive lover. With your affectionate and impressionable nature you are often attracted to those who understand your sensitivity and share your vision. Being flexible with an impressionable nature helps you to adapt to the needs of others. In your desire to blend with those you love, guard against giving too much of yourself by not defining your boundaries clearly. Nevertheless, your benevolence and sacrifices in the right relationship make you a devoted and kind partner.

MEN WITH VENUS IN PISCES: The combination of your emotional subtlety and charm can make you very alluring when dealing with affairs of the heart. Perceptive and impressionable, you have an easygoing style in your relationships, usually preferring to avoid ugly confrontation. You are drawn to partners who have a touch of glamour and are sensitive to the needs of others. Alternatively, they could be visionaries with rich imaginations who know how to keep you enchanted. With your insight you have the ability to observe the subtle moods of your partner.

To read all about your Outer Planets and work out how to use your personalized timetable, go to Section Three, page 789.

♍

Your Personalized Timetable

JUPITER BENEFICIAL
1939 4/6 – 5/24
1939 10/7 – until 1940 1/10
1941 4/11 – 6/19
1944 10/27 – until 1945 4/8
1945 6/20 – 9/20
1947 1/13 – 5/16
1947 9/12 – 11/4
1951 3/20 – 5/2
1952 8/10 – 10/10
1953 3/22 – 6/1
1956 10/9 – until 1957 9/4
1958 12/23 – until 1959 7/5
1959 8/4 – 10/18
1963 3/3 – 4/14
1964 7/9 – 11/25
1965 2/25 – 5/16
1968 9/23 – until 1969 1/1
1969 2/8 – 8/17
1970 12/6 – until 1971 1/30
1971 5/16 – 9/28
1975 2/14 – 3/28
1976 6/18 – until 1977 4/29
1980 9/7 – 11/27
1981 3/26 – 7/27
1982 11/20 – until 1983 1/7
1983 6/28 – 8/28
1986 6/27 – 7/28
1987 1/27 – 3/13
1988 5/31 – 9/4
1988 10/14 – until 1989 4/11
1992 8/22 – 11/6
1993 5/10 – 6/22
1994 11/5 – 12/20
1998 5/17 – 9/20
1999 1/4 – 2/24
2000 5/14 – 7/29
2000 12/3 – until 2001 3/18
2004 8/5 – 10/20
2006 10/20 – 12/5
2010 4/24 – 6/29
2010 8/16 – until 2011 2/4
2012 4/27 – 7/6

SATURN BENEFICIAL
1938 1/1 – 2/10
1941 5/20 – until 1942 6/20
1950 8/20 – until 1951 9/29
1955 11/5 – until 1956 2/20
1956 4/1 – 11/2
1966 4/1 – until 1967 3/23
1970 7/4 – 11/7
1971 3/24 – 8/15
1971 10/23 – until 1972 4/25
1979 9/28 – until 1980 11/6
1981 4/8 – 7/30
1984 12/10 – until 1985 6/20
1985 8/29 – 12/7
1995 5/13 – 8/30
1996 2/4 – 4/28
1996 10/16 – until 1997 1/18
2000 5/3 – until 2001 6/3
2008 11/10 – until 2009 2/23
2009 8/1 – until 2010 9/12

URANUS BENEFICIAL
1939 6/7 – until 1944 3/21
1965 12/6 – until 1970 7/25
1979 12/3 – until 1982 10/16
2008 6/5 – until 2012 2/15

NEPTUNE BENEFICIAL
1938 1/1 – until 1945 9/10
1966 11/29 – until 1971 11/16

PLUTO BENEFICIAL
1966 10/16 – until 1974 8/27
1992 1/14 – until 1996 11/11

JUPITER CHALLENGING
1940 4/2 – 6/10

1942 9/10 – until 1943 1/16
1943 5/5 – 7/25
1945 11/26 – until 1946 5/8
1946 7/22 – 10/21
1952 3/15 – 5/22
1954 8/20 – until 1955 7/9
1957 11/9 – until 1958 10/5
1963 8/6 – 8/11
1964 2/25 – 5/5
1966 8/3 – until 1967 6/22
1969 10/23 – until 1970 2/2
1970 3/9 – 9/17
1975 6/16 – 10/15
1976 2/3 – 4/18
1978 7/17 – 10/8
1979 1/13 – 6/2
1981 10/8 – 12/27
1982 4/26 – 8/27
1987 5/25 – until 1988 4/2
1990 7/1 – 9/14
1991 2/23 – 5/5
1993 9/22 – 12/7
1994 6/10 – 7/23
1999 5/6 – until 2000 3/14
2002 6/14 – 8/26
2005 9/5 – 11/20
2011 4/19 – 7/4
2011 10/27 – until 2012 2/20

SATURN CHALLENGING
1939 3/30 – until 1940 5/3
1945 8/16 – until 1946 2/6
1946 4/30 – 9/18
1947 1/25 – 6/7
1952 10/23 – until 1953 12/9
1954 5/4 – 9/5
1968 5/8 – 11/22
1969 1/19 – 6/16
1969 10/29 – until 1970 3/7
1975 6/21 – until 1976 7/21
1981 12/4 – until 1982 4/2
1982 8/29 – until 1983 10/16
1997 6/30 – 9/3
1998 3/13 – until 1999 4/17
2004 7/29 – until 2005 8/28
2006 3/1 – 5/10
2011 10/7 – until 2012 11/20

URANUS CHALLENGING
1953 7/22 – until 1957 6/30
1972 10/23 – until 1976 9/27

NEPTUNE CHALLENGING
1951 1/5 – until 1959 9/26

PLUTO CHALLENGING
1938 1/1 – until 1943 6/7
1979 10/21 – until 1986 9/11

JUPITER SPECIAL
1938 1/1 – until 1949 12/27
1961 1/24 – 4/22
1961 6/28 – 12/7
1973 1/8 – 3/29
1973 8/13 – 11/12
1984 12/23 – until 1985 3/3
1996 12/6 – until 1997 2/14
2008 3/26 – 6/23
2008 11/16 – until 2009 1/28

SATURN SPECIAL
1960 12/30 – until 1962 2/19
1962 9/10 – 11/7
1990 2/3 – 8/23
1990 10/23 – until 1991 4/5
1991 6/28 – 12/28

URANUS SPECIAL
1993 1/31 – until 1997 11/25

NEPTUNE SPECIAL
1993 1/30 – until 2001 1/4

January 19

SUN: CAPRICORN · DECANATE: VIRGO/MERCURY · DEGREE: 27°–29° CAPRICORN · MODE: CARDINAL · ELEMENT: EARTH

Your Personal Powers

Practical and ambitious, you are a strong-willed individual with ambition and determination. Being goal-oriented, you possess a particular need for material security. You gain power from the special blend of your communication skills, original approach, and sharp intelligence. With your strong convictions, you can often influence others, just be careful not to lose power by being too self-centered or bossy. If you are willing to apply the necessary discipline to your inspired or creative ideas, your innate business sense means that you can achieve successful results. At times, however, you may become skeptical and lose faith in yourself or others. This cynical attitude may discourage your competitive spirit or dampen your enthusiasm. By channeling your sensitivity and dynamic will, you can achieve remarkable results. Developing the more impersonal side to your nature can also help you overcome obstacles. Usually innovative in your approach, you enjoy power and with natural executive abilities, you usually prefer to initiate new projects and be independent.

Your Powers of Attraction in Relationships

Others are attracted to your determination and creativity. Ambitious and sociable, you are likely to be popular. Unless someone inspires you, you usually do not like to take orders from others. Nevertheless, with your ability to turn on the charm, you can win friends and influence people. You are attracted to individuals who can express themselves emotionally or with creative ideas. Although you appear very confident on the outside, you need partners you can trust enough to expose your inner vulnerability. Proud and independent, by collaborating in joint or team efforts, you can improve your relationships. Developing patience also aids your success with others. Once you believe in someone, you can be extremely loyal and supportive even to the point of making sacrifices.

Your attractive qualities: dynamic, strong-willed, determined, creative, leadership, progressive, optimistic, daring, original, sensitive, structured, business sense, strong convictions, competitive, productive, independent, efficient, talented, gregarious

Your less attractive qualities: self-centered, depressed, worry, fear of rejection, materialistic, egotistical, codependent, bossy, headstrong, impatient

Your Venus Power

The planet Venus has a great deal of influence on your powers of attraction. Below are four possible Venus types for women and men. To find your Venus, you need to go to page 771, where you will find the Venus table and extra information. The planet Mars also affects your powers of attraction. To find your Mars table and interpretation go to page 761.

WOMEN WITH VENUS IN SAGITTARIUS: At your best when being optimistic and generous, you possess a mischievous sense of fun. In relationships your open-minded approach to people and places may attract you to people of a different culture or make you tolerant of the foibles of others. Although warm and enthusiastic when in love, your natural honesty and idealism may inspire you to look for a partner who shares your love of freedom.

MEN WITH VENUS IN SAGITTARIUS: Forward-thinking rather than dwelling on the past, you are looking for a partner who can share your future plans. You enjoy exploring life whether through travel and mental pursuits or sports and games. Idealistic, you usually prefer the company of a partner who is optimistic and shares your beliefs. In your desire for honesty in relationships, however, be careful not to become tactless. Nevertheless, you are attracted to honest, direct, and fun-loving partners who have a sense of humor like your own.

WOMEN WITH VENUS IN CAPRICORN: Loyal and responsible, you are attracted to dignified and reserved individuals. Being practical and security-conscious, you prefer hardworking partners who are resourceful and enterprising. Work may even be a factor in many of your associations and partnerships. For you, family and faithfulness can be especially important, so you are usually willing to work hard or make sacrifices in order to build a strong relationship.

MEN WITH VENUS IN CAPRICORN: Hardworking and ambitious, you are usually attracted to determined, focused, and ambitious partners with a strong sense of duty. You want them to take relationships as seriously as you do, so loyalty and faithfulness are high on your agenda. Since you may display a natural reserve about expressing your feelings in an intimate relationship, you need a partner who shares your need for emotional security.

WOMEN WITH VENUS IN AQUARIUS: Usually you have a modern outlook on love and are open to new or current lifestyles. Your intuitive abilities, communal sense, and people skills often allow you to see deeper into human intentions and

to telepathically read people's thoughts. You are usually group-oriented and are drawn to individuals within the group who are independent and self-motivated. You are more inclined to choose a partner who is unconventional or freedom-loving. Conscious of your social standing, however, you want someone who can relate well to your friends.

MEN WITH VENUS IN AQUARIUS: Although independent, you often enjoy being part of a group. The partners you frequently attract are themselves nonconformists or free spirits. As an individual you may not find it easy to settle into a routine or an entirely mundane type of relationship. You may have some unconventional views on traditional marriage or your partner may hold such views. It is usually important to you that your love relationships are based on friendship.

WOMEN WITH VENUS IN PISCES: Idealistic and impressionable, in love you are romantic. Being sensitive to other people, you are receptive to their moods and feelings. This affinity indicates that although you can be selfless, you may have to guard against being too sentimental or overly romantic, especially of those who can take advantage of your kindness. Nevertheless, you are alluring and seductive, and your partners may be intrigued by your emotional magnetism, compassion, or mysterious nature.

MEN WITH VENUS IN PISCES: Being adaptable and sensitive, you are able to intuitively feel the moods of those you love. Although you are receptive to others, you can be ambiguous about your own feelings toward your partner. Romantic and kindhearted, you long to be loved but you need to be realistic about your relationships in order to avoid disappointments. When in love you may idealize your partners and fail to see any faults in their personality.

To read all about your Outer Planets and work out how to use your personalized timetable, go to Section Three, page 789.

Your Personalized Timetable

JUPITER BENEFICIAL
1939 4/11 – 5/30
1939 9/29 – until 1940 1/17
1941 4/15 – 6/23
1944 11/2 – until 1945 3/30
1945 6/29 – 9/25
1947 1/20 – 5/8
1947 9/19 – 11/9
1951 3/24 – 5/7
1952 8/23 – 9/26
1953 3/27 – 6/6
1956 10/14 – until 1957 9/9
1958 12/29 – until 1959 6/20
1959 8/19 – 10/23
1963 3/8 – 4/18
1964 7/15 – 11/17
1965 3/4 – 5/20
1968 9/28 – until 1969 8/23
1970 12/11 – until 1971 2/6
1971 5/8 – 10/4
1975 2/19 – 4/2
1976 6/23 – until 1977 5/4
1980 9/12 – 12/4
1981 3/18 – 8/3
1982 11/25 – until 1983 1/13
1983 6/18 – 9/7
1987 2/1 – 3/17
1988 6/5 – until 1989 4/16
1992 8/27 – 11/12
1993 4/27 – 7/5
1994 11/9 – 12/25
1998 5/23 – 9/12
1999 1/10 – 2/28
2000 5/19 – 8/4
2000 11/25 – until 2001 3/25
2004 8/10 – 10/25
2006 10/25 – 12/9
2010 4/29 – until 2011 2/9
2012 5/2 – 7/11

SATURN BENEFICIAL
1938 1/1 – 2/20
1941 5/28 – until 1942 6/29
1943 1/6 – 3/9
1950 8/29 – until 1951 10/7
1955 11/14 – until 1956 11/11
1966 4/9 – 11/1
1966 12/21 – until 1967 4/1
1970 7/16 – 10/25
1971 4/3 – 9/12
1971 9/25 – until 1972 5/4
1979 10/6 – until 1980 5/4
1980 6/9 – 11/16
1981 3/26 – 8/11
1984 12/19 – until 1985 6/3
1985 9/14 – 12/16
1986 7/15 – 8/29
1995 5/27 – 8/15
1996 2/13 – 5/8
1996 10/3 – until 1997 1/30
2000 5/11 – until 2001 6/10
2008 11/23 – until 2009 2/8
2009 8/11 – until 2010 9/20

URANUS BENEFICIAL
1939 6/27 – until 1944 4/15
1966 9/20 – until 1970 8/17
1979 12/20 – until 1982 11/4
2009 3/28 – until 2012 3/6

NEPTUNE BENEFICIAL
1938 1/1 – until 1946 8/5
1966 12/30 – until 1972 10/15

PLUTO BENEFICIAL
1966 11/28 – until 1974 9/24
1992 11/30 – until 1997 10/1

JUPITER CHALLENGING
1940 4/6 – 6/15
1940 12/9 – until 1941 1/21

1942 9/17 – until 1943 1/9
1943 5/11 – 7/30
1945 12/2 – until 1946 4/29
1946 7/31 – 10/25
1952 3/20 – 5/26
1954 8/25 – until 1955 2/25
1955 4/5 – 7/14
1957 11/14 – until 1958 10/10
1964 3/1 – 5/9
1966 8/7 – until 1967 6/27
1969 10/28 – until 1970 9/23
1975 6/23 – 10/7
1976 2/9 – 4/22
1978 7/22 – 10/16
1979 1/5 – 6/8
1981 10/12 – until 1982 1/3
1982 4/17 – 9/3
1987 5/30 – 11/25
1988 1/4 – 4/6
1990 7/6 – 9/20
1991 2/14 – 5/14
1993 9/27 – 12/12
1994 5/28 – 8/5
1999 5/11 – until 2000 3/19
2002 6/19 – 8/31
2005 9/11 – 11/25
2011 4/23 – 7/11
2011 10/20 – until 2012 2/26

SATURN CHALLENGING
1939 4/7 – until 1940 5/11
1945 8/25 – until 1946 1/24
1946 5/13 – 9/29
1947 1/13 – 6/17
1952 11/1 – until 1953 12/20
1954 4/21 – 9/16
1968 5/17 – 11/5
1969 2/4 – 6/27
1969 10/16 – until 1970 3/17
1975 6/29 – until 1976 7/29
1981 12/16 – until 1982 3/19
1982 9/8 – until 1983 10/24
1998 3/21 – until 1999 4/25
2004 8/6 – until 2005 3/13
2005 3/31 – 9/6
2006 2/14 – 5/24
2011 10/16 – until 2012 11/29

URANUS CHALLENGING
1953 8/9 – until 1957 7/17
1972 11/9 – until 1976 10/14

NEPTUNE CHALLENGING
1951 11/16 – until 1960 8/7

PLUTO CHALLENGING
1938 1/1 – until 1944 5/6
1979 11/17 – until 1986 10/10

JUPITER SPECIAL
1938 1/1 – until 1949 12/31
1961 1/28 – 5/5
1961 6/15 – 12/13
1973 1/12 – 3/29
1973 8/5 – 11/19
1984 12/27 – until 1985 3/8
1996 12/11 – until 1997 2/18
2008 4/4 – 6/13
2008 11/22 – until 2009 2/2

SATURN SPECIAL
1961 1/8 – until 1962 2/28
1962 8/23 – 11/24
1990 2/12 – 8/5
1990 11/9 – until 1991 4/26
1991 6/7 – until 1992 1/6

URANUS SPECIAL
1993 2/19 – until 1997 12/19

NEPTUNE SPECIAL
1993 3/3 – until 2001 11/28

♍

January 20

SUN: CAPRICORN • DECANATE: VIRGO/MERCURY • DEGREE: 28° CAPRICORN–00° AQUARIUS • MODE: CARDINAL • ELEMENT: EARTH

Your Personal Powers

Disciplined and discerning with a gracious manner and a practical approach, you are a charming and meticulous individual. Born on the cusp, you possess both the determination of Capricorn and the friendly side of Aquarius. You gain power from your amicable manner, diplomatic skills, and ability to mix with people from all walks of life. Although usually pragmatic, you also possess very sensitive emotions. You do best when you can balance your need to express your feelings and natural spontaneity with your responsibilities and sense of duty. If you neglect to maintain this balance you can lose power by becoming too serious or controlling on the one hand and too sensitive on the other. Nevertheless, you possess the ability to work hard, so you can persevere even in difficult situations. When you learn to have faith in your abilities and trust your intuition, you can also successfully market your creative talents. Persuasive and observant, you need only apply your natural persistence and tenacity to really succeed.

Your Powers of Attraction in Relationships

You can attract others with your friendly and responsible manner. Naturally sociable and generous, you can be a good team player and usually enjoy entertaining others. Although you can be tough and clear about your boundaries, you can also be very supportive, loving, and giving. Even though your relationships are especially important to you, avoid becoming too dependent on partners. The more confident and spontaneous you become, the less time you waste on misplaced sympathy. You are attracted to people with a youthful spirit or those who can give you the loyalty and affection you crave. Sensitive to the feelings of others, your desire to help may extend to humanitarian or compassionate causes. By learning unconditional love, you can fully express your romantic and idealistic traits or show your devotion.

Your attractive qualities: receptive, tactful, intuitive, loving, artistic, gentle, considerate, harmonious, amicable, gracious, diplomatic, perfectionist, methodical, sensitive, dutiful, loyal, spontaneous, responsible, persuasive, communication skills, supportive, caring, original

Your less attractive qualities: too serious, suspicious, lack of confidence, codependent, too reserved, critical, too rigid, overly sensitive, too tough, manipulative, depressive, controlling, stubborn

Your Venus Power

The planet Venus has a great deal of influence on your powers of attraction. Below are four possible Venus types for women and men. To find your Venus you need to go to page 771, where you will find the Venus table and extra information. The planet Mars also affects your powers of attraction. To find your Mars table and interpretation go to page 761.

WOMEN WITH VENUS IN SAGITTARIUS: Sociable, warm, and friendly, you possess an honest and frank style in your relationships. Being naturally gregarious, you want others to share your enthusiasm and enjoy encouraging the people you love. You do better when you have a sense of personal freedom within a relationship and are usually generous with the faults of others. You need a partner who can share your need to explore and take risks whether through travel, education, or recreation.

MEN WITH VENUS IN SAGITTARIUS: When in love you are open and friendly with a need for a partner who can share your adventurous spirit and sense of fun. Be careful, however, that your desire for freedom does not cause you to avoid commitment. You prefer your partners to be positive, direct, and generous in spirit. Being outspoken as well as an idealist, you usually enjoy a partner with whom you can share your strong opinions. Alternatively, you may wish to explore life together whether through travel, education, or by having fun.

WOMEN WITH VENUS IN CAPRICORN: Romantically, you do not give your heart easily but hide behind a cool reserve until you feel free to express your emotions. As you take your relationships seriously, you may find yourself drawn to people who are businesslike, resourceful, and practical or who can act as teachers or mentors. Work or career may also be a factor in many of your associations and partnerships. As security can play an important role in your relationships, you are often attracted to partners who are loyal and hardworking.

MEN WITH VENUS IN CAPRICORN: As you admire loyal, hardworking, and dedicated individuals, you probably want a partner who can share your vocational interests or who can provide you with the security you need. You could even find yourself with a partner who is of a different age group or ma-

turity. Guard against denying your true emotional needs or focusing on your career at the expense of your relationship. You are drawn to reserved partners who display self-control.

WOMEN WITH VENUS IN AQUARIUS: Usually you have a modern outlook on love and are open to new or current lifestyles. Your intuitive abilities, communal sense, and people skills often allow you to see deeper into human intentions and to read people's thoughts telepathically. You are usually group-oriented and are drawn to individuals within the group who are independent and self-motivated. You are more inclined to choose a partner who is unconventional or freedom-loving. Conscious of your social standing, however, you want someone who can relate well to your friends.

MEN WITH VENUS IN AQUARIUS: Although independent, you often enjoy being part of a group. The partners you frequently attract are themselves nonconformists or free spirits. As an individual you may not find it easy to settle into a routine or an entirely mundane type of relationship. You may have some unconventional views on traditional marriage or your partner may hold such views. It is usually important to you that your love relationships are based on friendship.

WOMEN WITH VENUS IN PISCES: Romantic and idealistic when in love, you can be a sensitive and responsive lover. With your affectionate and impressionable nature you are often attracted to those who understand your sensitivity and share your vision. Being flexible with an impressionable nature helps you to adapt to the needs of others. In your desire to blend with those you love, guard against giving too much of yourself by not clearly defining your boundaries. Nevertheless, your benevolence and sacrifices in the right relationship make you a devoted and kind partner.

MEN WITH VENUS IN PISCES: The combination of your emotional subtlety and charm can make you very alluring when dealing with affairs of the heart. Perceptive and impressionable, you have an easygoing style in your relationships and usually prefer avoiding ugly confrontation. You are drawn to partners who have a touch of glamour and are sensitive to the needs of others. Alternatively, they could be visionaries with rich imaginations who know how to keep you enchanted. With your insight you have the ability to observe the subtle moods of your partner.

To read all about your Outer Planets and work out how to use your personalized timetable, go to Section Three, page 789.

♍

Your Personalized Timetable

JUPITER BENEFICIAL
1939 4/15 – 6/6
1939 9/22 – until 1940 1/23
1941 4/20 – 6/28
1944 11/8 – until 1945 3/21
1945 7/7 – 9/29
1947 1/27 – 4/29
1947 9/25 – 11/14
1951 3/28 – 5/12
1951 11/18 – 12/12
1953 4/1 – 6/10
1956 10/19 – until 1957 9/14
1959 1/3 – 6/9
1959 8/29 – 10/28
1963 3/12 – 4/23
1964 7/21 – 11/10
1965 3/10 – 5/25
1968 10/2 – until 1969 8/28
1970 12/16 – until 1971 2/15
1971 4/28 – 10/9
1975 2/23 – 4/6
1976 6/28 – until 1977 1/2
1977 1/28 – 5/8
1980 9/16 – 12/11
1981 3/10 – 8/9
1982 11/30 – until 1983 1/19
1983 6/9 – 9/16
1987 2/6 – 3/21
1988 6/9 – until 1989 4/21
1992 9/1 – 11/17
1993 4/18 – 7/15
1994 11/14 – 12/30
1998 5/30 – 9/5
1999 1/16 – 3/4
2000 5/23 – 8/11
2000 11/18 – until 2001 3/31
2004 8/15 – 10/30
2006 10/30 – 12/14
2010 5/4 – 10/25
2010 12/12 – until 2011 2/14
2012 5/6 – 7/16

SATURN BENEFICIAL
1938 1/1 – 3/1
1941 6/5 – until 1942 7/7
1942 12/21 – until 1943 3/24
1950 9/6 – until 1951 10/15
1955 11/22 – until 1956 11/20
1966 4/18 – 10/13
1967 1/8 – 4/9
1970 7/30 – 10/10
1971 4/12 – until 1972 5/12
1979 10/15 – until 1980 4/12
1980 7/1 – 11/28
1981 3/13 – 8/21
1984 12/29 – until 1985 5/20
1985 9/26 – 12/25
1986 6/24 – 9/18
1995 6/19 – 7/23
1996 2/22 – 5/19
1996 9/19 – until 1997 2/10
2000 5/19 – until 2001 6/19
2008 12/14 – until 2009 1/17
2009 8/20 – until 2010 9/29

URANUS BENEFICIAL
1939 7/25 – until 1944 5/5
1966 10/7 – until 1970 9/5
1980 1/11 – until 1982 11/21
2009 4/16 – until 2012 3/24

NEPTUNE BENEFICIAL
1938 10/1 – until 1946 9/8
1967 11/28 – until 1972 11/14

PLUTO BENEFICIAL
1967 10/13 – until 1975 8/18
1992 12/28 – until 1997 11/2

JUPITER CHALLENGING
1940 4/10 – 6/20
1940 11/28 – until 1941 2/1

1942 9/23 – until 1943 1/1
1943 5/18 – 8/4
1945 12/8 – until 1946 4/20
1946 8/7 – 10/30
1952 3/24 – 5/31
1954 8/31 – until 1955 2/13
1955 4/18 – 7/18
1957 11/19 – until 1958 10/14
1964 3/6 – 5/13
1966 8/12 – until 1967 7/2
1969 11/2 – until 1970 9/28
1975 6/30 – 9/29
1976 2/14 – 4/27
1978 7/26 – 10/25
1978 12/27 – until 1979 6/14
1981 10/17 – until 1982 1/11
1982 4/9 – 9/9
1987 6/4 – 11/13
1988 1/16 – 4/11
1990 7/10 – 9/26
1991 2/6 – 5/21
1993 10/1 – 12/18
1994 5/19 – 8/14
1999 5/15 – until 2000 3/24
2002 6/24 – 9/5
2005 9/16 – 11/30
2011 4/27 – 7/18
2011 10/12 – until 2012 3/3

SATURN CHALLENGING
1939 4/15 – until 1940 5/19
1945 9/4 – until 1946 1/11
1946 5/24 – 10/12
1946 12/30 – until 1947 6/26
1952 11/9 – until 1953 5/20
1953 7/27 – until 1954 1/1
1954 4/6 – 9/26
1968 5/27 – 10/22
1969 2/16 – 7/10
1969 10/2 – until 1970 3/26
1975 7/7 – until 1976 8/5
1982 1/2 – 3/1
1982 9/17 – until 1983 11/2
1998 3/29 – until 1999 5/3
2004 8/14 – until 2005 2/14
2005 4/26 – 9/16
2006 2/1 – 6/5
2011 10/24 – until 2012 12/9

URANUS CHALLENGING
1953 8/28 – until 1957 8/3
1972 11/28 – until 1976 10/31

NEPTUNE CHALLENGING
1951 12/27 – until 1960 9/23

PLUTO CHALLENGING
1938 1/1 – until 1944 7/1
1979 12/25 – until 1987 8/22

JUPITER SPECIAL
1938 1/1 – until 1950 1/5
1961 2/2 – 12/18
1973 1/16 – 4/4
1973 7/28 – 11/26
1985 1/1 – 3/13
1985 9/18 – 10/18
1996 12/15 – until 1997 2/23
2008 4/15 – 6/2
2008 11/27 – until 2009 2/6

SATURN SPECIAL
1961 1/17 – until 1962 3/10
1962 8/8 – 12/7
1990 2/22 – 7/21
1990 11/21 – until 1992 1/15

URANUS SPECIAL
1993 3/16 – until 1998 1/7

NEPTUNE SPECIAL
1994 1/28 – until 2002 1/2

Capricorn Timetable
X-Special · X-Beneficial · X-Challenging

December 22
URANUS X-BENEFICIAL
2002 4/13 – until 2004 2/5
URANUS X-CHALLENGING
2010 4/8 – until 2012 2/2
NEPTUNE X-BENEFICIAL
2010 4/4 – until 2013 1/25
PLUTO X-SPECIAL
2007 1/24 – until 2009 11/19

December 23
URANUS X-BENEFICIAL
2003 2/18 – until 2004 2/23
URANUS X-CHALLENGING
2010 4/28 – until 2012 2/23
NEPTUNE X-BENEFICIAL
2011 3/1 – until 2012 5/2
PLUTO X-SPECIAL
2007 3/11 – until 2010 9/29

December 24
URANUS X-BENEFICIAL
2003 3/8 – until 2004 12/31
URANUS X-CHALLENGING
2010 5/24 – until 2012 3/13
NEPTUNE X-BENEFICIAL
2011 3/31 – until 2013 3/21
PLUTO X-SPECIAL
2008 1/22 – until 2010 11/19

December 25
URANUS X-BENEFICIAL
2003 3/27 – until 2005 1/22
URANUS X-CHALLENGING
2011 3/27 – until 2013 1/7
NEPTUNE X-BENEFICIAL
2011 5/23 – until 2013 4/25
PLUTO X-SPECIAL
2008 3/2 – until 2011 9/18

December 26
URANUS X-BENEFICIAL
2003 4/20 – until 2005 2/10
URANUS X-CHALLENGING
2011 4/15 – until 2013 2/7

NEPTUNE X-BENEFICIAL
2012 3/27 – Continues
PLUTO X-SPECIAL
2009 1/19 – until 2011 11/20

December 27
URANUS X-BENEFICIAL
2004 2/25 – until 2005 12/4
URANUS X-CHALLENGING
2011 5/6 – until 2013 3/2
NEPTUNE X-BENEFICIAL
2012 5/12 – Continues
PLUTO X-SPECIAL
2009 3/2 – until 2012 9/30

December 28
URANUS X-BENEFICIAL
2004 3/14 – until 2006 1/8
URANUS X-CHALLENGING
2011 6/3 – Continues
PLUTO X-SPECIAL
2010 1/21 – Continues

December 29
URANUS X-BENEFICIAL
2004 4/4 – until 2006 1/30
URANUS X-CHALLENGING
2012 4/3 – Continues
PLUTO X-SPECIAL
2010 3/2 – Continues

December 30
URANUS X-BENEFICIAL
2004 4/29 – until 2006 2/18
URANUS X-CHALLENGING
2012 4/22 – Continues
PLUTO X-SPECIAL
2011 1/23 – Continues

December 31
URANUS X-BENEFICIAL
2005 3/3 – until 2006 12/17
URANUS X-CHALLENGING
2012 5/13 – Continues

PLUTO X-SPECIAL
2011 3/1 – Continues

January 1
URANUS X-BENEFICIAL
2005 3/21 – until 2007 1/16
URANUS X-CHALLENGING
2012 6/11 – Continues
PLUTO X-SPECIAL
2012 1/24 – Continues

January 2
URANUS X-BENEFICIAL
2005 4/11 – until 2007 2/6
PLUTO X-SPECIAL
2012 3/2 – Continues

January 3
URANUS X-BENEFICIAL
2005 5/7 – until 2007 2/24

January 4
URANUS X-BENEFICIAL
2006 3/9 – until 2007 12/25

January 5
URANUS X-BENEFICIAL
2006 3/28 – until 2008 1/23

January 6
URANUS X-BENEFICIAL
2006 4/17 – until 2008 2/12

January 7
URANUS X-BENEFICIAL
2006 5/16 – until 2008 3/2

January 8
URANUS X-BENEFICIAL
2007 3/16 – until 2009 1/2

January 9
URANUS X-BENEFICIAL
2007 4/3 – until 2009 1/28

January 10
URANUS X-BENEFICIAL
2007 4/24 – until 2009 2/18

January 11
URANUS X-BENEFICIAL
2007 5/24 – until 2009 3/8

January 12
URANUS X-BENEFICIAL
2008 3/21 – until 2010 1/9

January 13
URANUS X-BENEFICIAL
2008 4/9 – until 2010 2/4

January 14
URANUS X-BENEFICIAL
2008 4/30 – until 2010 2/24

January 15
URANUS X-BENEFICIAL
2008 6/2 – until 2010 3/14

January 16
URANUS X-BENEFICIAL
2009 3/27 – until 2011 1/17

January 17
URANUS X-BENEFICIAL
2009 4/15 – until 2011 2/10

January 18
URANUS X-BENEFICIAL
2009 5/7 – until 2011 3/2

January 19
URANUS X-BENEFICIAL
2009 6/12 – until 2011 3/20

January 20
URANUS X-BENEFICIAL
2010 4/2 – until 2012 1/24

Aquarius

January 21–February 19

January 21

Your Personal Powers

Friendly and direct, you possess warmth, a charismatic personality, and a sharp mind. Being born on the cusp, you are an individual with the shrewd practicality of Capricorn and the humanitarian understanding of Aquarius. You gain power from your creative and original ideas, people skills, and astute insights. Although easygoing by nature, you can lose power if you become worried or irritable. Nevertheless, sociable and a good conversationalist, you usually work well with others. Being imaginative with strong feelings you need a form of self-expression, particularly one that brings out your innate creative or artistic talents. With your quick intelligence you often have many interests, but resist scattering your energies. You can lose your power, however, if your sense of security has you resting in a comfortable rut or falling into inertia. Nevertheless, with a desire for prestige and your innate business sense, you can achieve high levels of material accomplishment. Clever and inventive, you can also be an inspired thinker who is ahead of your time.

Your Powers of Attraction in Relationships

Affectionate and loving, you can attract others with your friendly manner and good social skills. Very sensitive, you can be caring and put yourself in the place of others. You are usually able to utilize your natural charm to make yourself popular. In love you can be romantic with strong emotions. By developing your confidence and self-esteem, you project more of your powerful love and share it with others. Often attracted to enterprising and creative individuals, you want a partner you can be proud of. By concentrating on your own natural creativity and self-expression, you can avoid feelings of insecurity and uplift others, rather than help them at your own expense. A natural adviser, you usually take your responsibilities seriously. You have a strong desire for peace and security and place importance on generosity, loyalty, and devotion.

Your attractive qualities: original, inspiring, clever, creative, love unions, communication skills, good mental abilities, charm, optimistic, fun-loving, sensitive, loving, inventive, home-loving, sympathetic, individual, humanitarian, responsible, caring

Your less attractive qualities: indecisive, worried, rebel-lious, bossy, frustrated, nervous, scattered, disappointment, too frank, dependent, irritable, anxious, inertia, stubborn

Your Venus Power

The planet Venus has a great deal of influence on your powers of attraction. Below are four possible Venus types for women and men. To find your Venus you need to go to page 771, where you will find the Venus table and extra information. The planet Mars also affects your powers of attraction. To find your Mars table and interpretation go to page 761.

WOMEN WITH VENUS IN SAGITTARIUS: When you feel generous, you can make others feel more optimistic about life. You may be interested in higher learning and seek partners who are scholarly or broad-minded. You are outspoken and direct and sometimes say things that you later regret. Curious and versatile, you can adjust quickly to new situations, and a foreign influence implies that you love to travel or may have a partner who comes from a different culture.

MEN WITH VENUS IN SAGITTARIUS: Your enthusiasm and straightforward conduct usually appeal to others and imply that you are approachable and easygoing. Being open to ideas and willing to believe that life has a great deal to offer suggest that you are generous, broad-minded, and eager to cooperate with others. A love of travel and an interest in other cultures imply that your partner may come from a foreign country.

WOMEN WITH VENUS IN CAPRICORN: Proud and refined, you attract others with your composed dignity. Disliking vulnerability and needing to feel safe before you can express your feelings, you display a strong front. Feeling insecure or inadequate in relationships may force you to become manipulative in order to regain control. Nevertheless, you can project an attractive sense of self-assurance and are capable of displaying loyalty and a wonderful dry sense of humor.

MEN WITH VENUS IN CAPRICORN: As you do not display your deeper emotions freely, you are usually dignified and controlled in your relationships with others. Practical and down-to-earth partners are particularly attractive to you, especially those who do not rush into expressing their feelings but seem to possess natural class and reserve. You need a partner who is loyal and dependable and willing to take your relationship seriously.

WOMEN WITH VENUS IN AQUARIUS: Usually you have a modern outlook on love and are open to new or current

lifestyles. Your intuitive abilities, communal sense, and people skills often allow you to see deeper into human intentions and to read people's thoughts telepathically. You are usually group-oriented and are drawn to individuals within the group who are independent and self-motivated. You are more inclined to choose a partner who is unconventional or freedom-loving. Conscious of your social standing, however, you want someone who can relate well to your friends.

MEN WITH VENUS IN AQUARIUS: Although independent, you often enjoy being part of a group. The partners you frequently attract are often nonconformists or free spirits. As an individual you may not find it easy to settle into a routine or an entirely mundane type of relationship. You may have some unconventional views on traditional marriage or your partner may hold such views. You value your freedom and can sometimes be cool and detached. Friendship is important to you as you enjoy sharing your progressive ideas.

WOMEN WITH VENUS IN PISCES: In love you are sensitive, tender, and affectionate, experiences your partner's feelings almost as strongly as your own. You are imaginative and a visionary and possess the ability to develop deep compassion for others. As you are idealistic when in love, you usually prefer to see only your partner's good points, but be careful that your high expectations do not bring disappointment if you avoid being realistic. Nevertheless, in your relationships with others, you can be devoted, loving, and positively enchanting.

MEN WITH VENUS IN PISCES: The combination of your emotional subtlety and charm can make you very alluring when dealing with affairs of the heart. Perceptive and impressionable, you have an easygoing style in your relationships, usually preferring to avoid ugly confrontation. You are drawn to a woman who has a touch of glamour and is sensitive to the needs of others. Alternatively, she can be a visionary with a rich imagination who can keep you enchanted.

To read all about your Outer Planets and work out how to use your personalized timetable, go to Section Three, page 789.

≈

Your Personalized Timetable

JUPITER BENEFICIAL
1939 4/19 – 6/13
1939 9/14 – until 1940 1/29
1941 4/24 – 7/2
1944 11/14 – until 1945 3/14
1945 7/14 – 10/4
1947 2/5 – 4/21
1947 9/30 – 11/18
1951 4/2 – 5/17
1951 11/3 – 12/26
1953 4/6 – 6/14
1956 10/24 – until 1957 4/28
1957 6/8 – 9/18
1959 1/9 – 6/1
1959 9/6 – 11/2
1963 3/16 – 4/27
1964 7/28 – 11/2
1965 3/16 – 5/29
1968 10/7 – until 1969 9/2
1970 12/21 – until 1971 2/26
1971 4/17 – 10/15
1975 2/27 – 4/10
1976 7/3 – 12/18
1977 2/12 – 5/13
1980 9/21 – 12/20
1981 3/1 – 8/14
1982 12/4 – until 1983 1/24
1983 6/1 – 9/23
1987 2/11 – 3/25
1988 6/14 – until 1989 4/26
1992 9/5 – 11/23
1993 4/10 – 7/22
1994 11/18 – until 1995 1/4
1998 6/7 – 8/28
1999 1/21 – 3/8
2000 5/27 – 8/18
2000 11/10 – until 2001 4/5
2004 8/20 – 11/4
2006 11/3 – 12/19
2010 5/9 – 10/15
2010 12/23 – until 2011 2/18
2012 5/10 – Continues

SATURN BENEFICIAL
1938 1/1 – 3/9
1941 6/13 – 12/24
1942 2/22 – 7/16
1942 12/8 – until 1943 4/4
1950 9/14 – until 1951 10/24
1952 5/23 – 6/28
1955 12/1 – until 1956 11/28
1966 4/28 – 9/30
1967 1/20 – 4/17
1970 8/23 – 9/17
1971 4/20 – until 1972 5/19
1979 10/24 – until 1980 3/29
1980 7/14 – 12/11
1981 2/27 – 8/30
1985 1/9 – 5/7
1985 10/7 – until 1986 1/4
1986 6/9 – 10/2
1996 3/1 – 5/31
1996 9/6 – until 1997 2/19
2000 5/26 – until 2001 6/27
2002 1/17 – 3/1
2009 8/28 – until 2010 10/6

URANUS BENEFICIAL
1940 5/21 – until 1944 5/22
1966 10/24 – until 1970 9/21
1980 2/14 – until 1983 9/13
2009 5/7 – Continues

NEPTUNE BENEFICIAL
1938 10/30 – until 1947 7/30
1967 12/26 – until 1973 10/11

PLUTO BENEFICIAL
1967 11/18 – until 1975 9/15
1993 2/13 – until 1998 9/10

JUPITER CHALLENGING
1940 4/14 – 6/25
1940 11/19 – until 1941 2/10

1942 10/1 – 12/24
1943 5/23 – 8/8
1945 12/14 – until 1946 4/13
1946 8/14 – 11/4
1952 3/28 – 6/4
1954 9/5 – until 1955 2/3
1955 4/27 – 7/23
1957 11/24 – until 1958 5/28
1958 7/10 – 10/19
1964 3/10 – 5/17
1966 8/17 – until 1967 7/7
1969 11/7 – until 1970 10/3
1975 7/8 – 9/21
1976 2/20 – 5/1
1978 7/31 – 11/6
1978 12/14 – until 1979 6/19
1981 10/22 – until 1982 1/20
1982 3/31 – 9/14
1987 6/9 – 11/4
1988 1/24 – 4/15
1990 7/15 – 10/2
1991 1/29 – 5/28
1993 10/6 – 12/24
1994 5/10 – 8/22
1999 5/20 – until 2000 3/28
2002 6/28 – 9/10
2003 3/19 – 4/20
2005 9/21 – 12/5
2011 5/1 – 7/27
2011 10/3 – until 2012 3/8

SATURN CHALLENGING
1939 4/23 – until 1940 5/27
1940 12/15 – until 1941 2/3
1945 9/15 – 12/30
1946 6/2 – 10/30
1946 12/11 – until 1947 7/5
1952 11/18 – until 1953 5/4
1953 8/11 – until 1954 1/16
1954 3/21 – 10/5
1968 6/6 – 10/10
1969 2/26 – 7/28
1969 9/13 – until 1970 4/3
1975 7/15 – until 1976 8/13
1982 9/26 – until 1983 11/10
1998 4/6 – until 1999 5/10
2004 8/23 – until 2005 1/31
2005 5/9 – 9/26
2006 1/20 – 6/15
2011 11/1 – until 2012 12/19

URANUS CHALLENGING
1953 9/21 – until 1958 5/31
1972 12/22 – until 1977 8/28

NEPTUNE CHALLENGING
1952 11/12 – until 1960 10/21

PLUTO CHALLENGING
1938 1/1 – until 1945 6/10
1980 11/3 – until 1987 10/23

JUPITER SPECIAL
1949 2/24 – 9/10
1949 9/27 – until 1950 1/9
1961 2/6 – 12/22
1973 1/20 – 4/11
1973 7/20 – 12/2
1985 1/5 – 3/18
1985 9/4 – 11/1
1996 12/20 – until 1997 2/27
2008 12/2 – until 2009 2/10

SATURN SPECIAL
1961 1/25 – until 1962 3/21
1962 7/26 – 12/17
1990 3/5 – 7/8
1990 12/2 – until 1992 1/23

URANUS SPECIAL
1994 1/16 – until 1998 1/24

NEPTUNE SPECIAL
1994 2/26 – until 2002 11/20

January 22

SUN: AQUARIUS • DECANATE: AQUARIUS/URANUS • DEGREE: 1°–2° AQUARIUS • MODE: FIXED • ELEMENT: AIR

Your Personal Powers

Honest and direct, with your fast responses and astute observations you possess great potential. A universal approach to life indicates that you possess a natural insight into human nature. You gain power from your inner strength, original approach, and ability to lead. Usually positive and hardworking, you have the capacity to combine your exceptional imagination and keen business sense to create success. Beware of nervous tension, impatience, or restlessness as they often undermine your power. Nevertheless, often charismatic, you benefit from excellent people skills and a broad-minded attitude. Being also idealistic, you often have a desire to work for the good of all. Your inventive ideas and objective intellect suggest that you can lead others in new directions. However, if you are unable to harness your natural power, you may experience feelings of inferiority or a stubborn streak may cause you to rebel. Nonetheless, with practical and intuitive insight and the ability to think big, you have the potential to achieve outstanding results in life.

Your Powers of Attraction in Relationships

Friendly and broad-minded, you can attract people with your straightforward approach and concern for others. While you can attract others with your many talents, it is important for you to be totally honest with your partners. With your ingenuity you can be witty and entertaining and enjoy the company of those who are playful and intelligent. Although very sensitive and diplomatic, at times you may be undemonstrative about your deeper feelings. People-oriented, you are aware of image and like to make a good impression. You are an original thinker, and others are often drawn to your unusual perceptions, but a restless streak and a strong need for freedom may cause you to delay commitment. Nevertheless, loving and affectionate, you can be a romantic and loyal lover.

Your attractive qualities: practical, universal, objective thinker, leader, ambitious, thinks big, creative, good people skills, humanitarian, inventive, good organizer, sensitive, visionary, adventurous, independent, achiever, highly intuitive, inventive

Your less attractive qualities: nervous, impatient, restlessness, inferiority complex, bossy, materialistic, lazy, egotistical, stubborn, escapism, get-rich-quick schemes, antagonistic, deceptive, impulsive

Your Venus Power

The planet Venus has a great deal of influence on your powers of attraction. Below are four possible Venus types for women and men. To find your Venus you need to go to page 771, where you will find the Venus table and extra information. The planet Mars also affects your powers of attraction. To find your Mars table and interpretation go to page 761.

WOMEN WITH VENUS IN SAGITTARIUS: Optimistic and fun-loving, you love adventure and seek a partner who can expand your horizons. Being truthful and direct, you often say what you think, and at times you may be naively tactless. A need for expansion and prosperity suggests that you may enjoy traveling with your friends or partner. Being lighthearted and idealistic, once you have given your heart to someone you will stay honorable and loyal.

MEN WITH VENUS IN SAGITTARIUS: You are usually attracted to partners who are knowledgeable or well-traveled. Enthusiastic and optimistic, you often respond quickly to love offers and enter relationships with enthusiasm. Generally you seek to expand your social circle, and meeting people from all walks of life can bring the variety and fun that you seek in life. Although you are generous and honest, your partners may sometimes accuse you of being overly optimistic or too blunt.

WOMEN WITH VENUS IN CAPRICORN: With your natural caution in romantic affairs, you often appear reserved and controlled. You may be shy but try to be more forward, especially if you want to be noticed. When you care about people, however, you are usually willing to put in extra time and energy to preserve the relationship. You are practical and dependable, and a sense of duty can often play a large role in affairs of your heart. With elegant simplicity, you can attract others with your well-cut clothes and refined manners.

MEN WITH VENUS IN CAPRICORN: In relationships you take love seriously and can be a strong and practical support for friends or partners. You are usually attracted to partners who are as hardworking as you. As you tend not to express your feelings until you feel really secure in a relationship, you may be drawn to those who seem loyal, faithful, and not likely to let you down. As you respect the wisdom of experience, you

may be drawn to mature partners or, alternatively, you may act as an authority figure for someone younger.

WOMEN WITH VENUS IN AQUARIUS: You attract and impress others with your friendly approach and progressive ideas. As you are usually independent and easygoing, you value freedom within a relationship. A good companion with a sense of your own person, you enjoy socializing, especially with people who are original, cosmopolitan, and have a strong sense of individuality. Although being friendly and detached usually serves you well, avoid losing touch with your emotions. You usually prefer the company of those who have innovative or progressive views.

MEN WITH VENUS IN AQUARIUS: You are sociable and open-minded, and people are attracted by your friendly and easygoing style. Being independent, you value freedom-loving partners who give you the space to be yourself. People can sometimes interpret your detachment as being emotionally cool but they admire your objectivity and humanitarian inclinations. You are attracted to intelligent individuals who are as truthful and direct as you are, but above all they must be true friends. Ideally your partner shares your liberal views on life and possesses a strong sense of individuality.

WOMEN WITH VENUS IN PISCES: As a romantic and idealistic individual, you can be both loving and giving. In relationships you may need to balance the practical with the charitable. While making allowances and sacrifices is understandable in a loving relationship, playing the martyr is often a state of romantic illusion that can lead to self-deception. Your benevolence and sacrifices in the right relationship nonetheless make you a partner who is devoted, kind, and compassionate. Subtle, sensitive, and alluring, you make a sensual and caring partner.

MEN WITH VENUS IN PISCES: Romantic and idealistic when in love, you can be a sensitive and responsive lover. The fact that you are pliant, flexible, and have an impressionable nature helps you adapt to the needs of others. In your desire to blend with those you love, however, guard against not clearly defining your own boundaries. With your affectionate and sentimental nature you are often attracted to those who understand your sensitivity and share your vision.

To read all about your Outer Planets and work out how to use your personalized timetable, go to Section Three, page 789.

≋

Your Personalized Timetable

JUPITER BENEFICIAL
1939 4/24 – 6/21
1939 9/6 – until 1940 2/3
1941 4/28 – 7/7
1944 11/20 – until 1945 3/6
1945 7/20 – 10/9
1947 2/16 – 4/9
1947 10/6 – 11/23
1951 4/6 – 5/22
1951 10/24 – until 1952 1/5
1953 4/10 – 6/19
1956 10/29 – until 1957 4/15
1957 6/21 – 9/23
1959 1/15 – 5/23
1959 9/14 – 11/6
1963 3/20 – 5/2
1964 8/4 – 10/25
1965 3/21 – 6/2
1968 10/12 – until 1969 9/7
1970 12/26 – until 1971 10/20
1975 3/4 – 4/14
1976 7/8 – 12/8
1977 2/22 – 5/17
1980 9/26 – 12/31
1981 2/17 – 8/20
1982 12/9 – until 1983 1/31
1983 5/24 – 9/29
1987 2/15 – 3/29
1988 6/18 – until 1989 4/30
1992 9/10 – 11/29
1993 4/1 – 7/30
1994 11/23 – until 1995 1/10
1995 7/8 – 8/27
1998 6/16 – 8/18
1999 1/27 – 3/13
2000 6/1 – 8/27
2000 11/1 – until 2001 4/11
2004 8/25 – 11/9
2005 5/17 – 6/24
2006 11/8 – 12/23
2010 5/15 – 10/6
2010 12/31 – until 2011 2/23
2012 5/14 – Continues

SATURN BENEFICIAL
1938 1/1 – 3/17
1941 6/22 – 12/7
1942 3/9 – until 1943 4/15
1950 9/22 – until 1951 11/1
1952 5/1 – 7/20
1955 12/9 – until 1956 7/10
1956 8/19 – 12/7
1966 5/8 – 9/16
1967 1/31 – 4/26
1967 11/8 – until 1968 1/9
1971 4/28 – until 1972 5/27
1979 11/3 – until 1980 3/16
1980 7/26 – 12/31
1981 2/5 – 9/8
1985 1/22 – 4/22
1985 10/17 – until 1986 1/14
1986 5/27 – 10/13
1996 3/9 – 6/15
1996 8/21 – until 1997 2/28
2000 6/3 – until 2001 7/5
2001 12/29 – until 2002 3/20
2009 9/5 – until 2010 10/15

URANUS BENEFICIAL
1940 6/8 – until 1945 3/17
1966 11/15 – until 1971 6/28
1980 11/28 – until 1983 10/12
2009 6/13 – Continues

NEPTUNE BENEFICIAL
1939 9/28 – until 1947 9/5
1968 2/15 – until 1973 11/11

PLUTO BENEFICIAL
1968 10/8 – until 1976 8/3
1993 12/14 – until 1998 10/22

JUPITER CHALLENGING
1940 4/18 – 7/1

1940 11/11 – until 1941 2/17
1942 10/10 – 12/15
1943 5/29 – 8/13
1945 12/21 – until 1946 4/5
1946 8/21 – 11/8
1952 4/1 – 6/9
1954 9/11 – until 1955 1/26
1955 5/5 – 7/28
1957 11/29 – until 1958 5/15
1958 7/23 – 10/24
1964 3/15 – 5/22
1966 8/22 – until 1967 7/12
1969 11/12 – until 1970 10/7
1975 7/18 – 9/11
1976 2/25 – 5/5
1978 8/4 – until 1979 6/24
1981 10/26 – until 1982 2/1
1982 3/19 – 9/20
1987 6/15 – 10/27
1988 2/1 – 4/19
1990 7/19 – 10/8
1991 1/22 – 6/4
1993 10/11 – 12/30
1994 5/2 – 8/29
1999 5/24 – until 2000 4/2
2002 7/3 – 9/16
2003 3/4 – 5/4
2005 9/25 – 12/10
2006 6/18 – 7/24
2011 5/6 – 8/7
2011 9/22 – until 2012 3/13

SATURN CHALLENGING
1939 5/1 – until 1940 6/5
1940 11/27 – until 1941 2/20
1945 9/28 – 12/16
1946 6/11 – until 1947 7/13
1952 11/28 – until 1953 4/20
1953 8/24 – until 1954 10/14
1968 6/18 – 9/27
1969 3/7 – until 1970 4/12
1975 7/23 – until 1976 8/21
1982 10/5 – until 1983 11/19
1998 4/14 – until 1999 5/19
2004 9/1 – until 2005 1/18
2005 5/21 – 10/8
2006 1/7 – 6/24
2011 11/10 – until 2012 5/26
2012 7/25 – 12/31

URANUS CHALLENGING
1954 7/18 – until 1958 6/23
1973 10/17 – until 1977 9/20

NEPTUNE CHALLENGING
1952 12/18 – until 1961 9/19

PLUTO CHALLENGING
1938 1/1 – until 1946 5/7
1980 12/3 – until 1987 10/23

JUPITER SPECIAL
1949 3/1 – 8/22
1949 10/15 – until 1950 1/14
1961 2/11 – 12/27
1973 1/25 – 4/19
1973 7/12 – 12/7
1985 1/9 – 3/23
1985 8/25 – 11/10
1996 12/24 – until 1997 3/4
2008 12/7 – until 2009 2/15

SATURN SPECIAL
1961 2/3 – 9/10
1961 10/14 – until 1962 4/2
1962 7/12 – 12/27
1990 3/17 – 6/24
1990 12/12 – until 1992 2/1

URANUS SPECIAL
1994 2/2 – until 1998 11/28

NEPTUNE SPECIAL
1995 1/25 – until 2002 12/29

January 23

Your Personal Powers

Friendly and mentally astute, you are a trustworthy and versatile individual with many personal talents. Interested in people, you possess a keen insight into human nature. You gain power from the combination of your practical common sense and inventive approach. Being organized, you like to have a plan of action and are usually methodical and hardworking. Although pragmatic, you are also proud and sensitive with strong intuition, powerful feelings, and an active imagination. Being mentally smart you are resourceful and good at solving problems, yet you lose some of your power if you become stubborn or obstinate. As a practical idealist you often place a strong emphasis on your work and responsibilities. An ability to comprehend new subjects quickly implies that you usually prefer practice to theory. Although reliable by nature, you need change and new experiences in your life, otherwise you may become restless or impatient. Nevertheless, sociable and kind, you usually succeed when using your advanced people skills and progressive ideas in a practical way.

Your Powers of Attraction in Relationships

Others are attracted to your friendly and generous personality. With your special talent for understanding people, you benefit from team endeavors. Although you can be sensitive to the feelings of others, you must still resist being critical or moody. As a humanitarian and objective thinker you enjoy the company of intelligent people or those with whom you can enjoy your imaginative jaunts and entertaining ways. A restless streak suggests that you enjoy going out and meeting friends. Your need for order and structure indicates that you usually feel happier in a secure relationship with a strong home base. You are attracted to determined, ambitious, and strong individuals but be mindful of becoming involved in power struggles. Once committed, you can be a loyal and dependable partner.

Your attractive qualities: friendly, responsible, quick thinker, emotionally sensitive, creative, independent, reformist, honest, practical, methodical, loyal, original, inventive, trustworthy, hardworking, dedicated, popular, persevering, diligent, humanitarian, intuitive, sociable

Your less attractive qualities: selfish, insecure, stubborn, uncompromising, antagonistic, restlessness, withdrawn, mistrusting, inflexible, moody, impatient, rebelliousness

Your Venus Power

The planet Venus has a great deal of influence on your powers of attraction. Below are four possible Venus types for women and men. To find your Venus you need to go to page 771, where you will find the Venus table and extra information. The planet Mars also affects your powers of attraction. To find your Mars table and interpretation go to page 761.

WOMEN WITH VENUS IN SAGITTARIUS: Sociable, warm, and friendly, you possess an honest and frank style in your relationships. Being naturally gregarious, you want others to share your enthusiasm and enjoy encouraging the people you love. You do better when you have a sense of personal freedom within a relationship and are usually generous with the faults of others. You need a partner who can share your need to explore and take risks, whether through travel, education, or recreation.

MEN WITH VENUS IN SAGITTARIUS: When in love you are open and friendly with a need for a partner who can share your adventurous spirit and sense of fun. Be careful, however, that your desire for freedom does not cause you to avoid commitment. You prefer partners who are positive, direct, and generous in spirit. Being outspoken as well as an idealist, you usually enjoy a partner with whom you can share your strong opinions. Alternatively, you may wish to explore life together, whether through travel, education, or by having fun.

WOMEN WITH VENUS IN CAPRICORN: Romantically, you do not give your heart easily but hide behind a cool reserve until you feel free to express your emotions. As you take your relationships seriously, you may find yourself drawn to people who are businesslike, resourceful, and practical or those who can act as teachers or mentors. Work or career may also be a factor in many of your associations and partnerships. As security can play an important role in your relationships, you are often attracted to partners who are loyal and hardworking.

MEN WITH VENUS IN CAPRICORN: As you admire loyal, hardworking, and dedicated individuals, you probably want a partner who can share your vocational interests or provide you with the sense of security you need. You could even find yourself with a partner who is of a different age group or ma-

turity. Guard against denying your true emotional needs or focusing on your career at the expense of your relationship. You are drawn to reserved partners who display self-control.

WOMEN WITH VENUS IN AQUARIUS: When it comes to relationships, others are attracted to your honest, friendly, and easygoing attitude. You enjoy social interaction and have a genuine concern for others. In fact, at times, your friends may be just as important as your partner. Usually you present a tolerant and reasonable front in love situations and attempt to view your relationships objectively. If partners become too demanding, however, you can become stubborn or awkward. Nevertheless, inventive and progressive, you enjoy the company of like-minded people who can share your original ideas.

MEN WITH VENUS IN AQUARIUS: Friendly and honest, you attract people with your broad-minded approach to life. You usually possess an objective and slightly detached attitude to affairs of the heart. If you are too removed, however, others can misinterpret your behavior as uncaring. It is often more important to you that your love relationships are based on friendship and honesty than intense passion. As you are generally tolerant and liberal, you may be drawn to less conventional relationships.

WOMEN WITH VENUS IN PISCES: As a romantic and idealistic individual, you can be both loving and giving. In relationships you may need to balance the practical with the charitable. While making allowances and sacrifices is understandable in a loving relationship, playing the martyr is often a state of romantic illusion that can lead to self-deception. Your benevolence and sacrifices in the right relationship nonetheless make you a partner who is devoted, kind, and compassionate. Subtle, sensitive, and alluring, you make a sensual and caring partner.

MEN WITH VENUS IN PISCES: Romantic and idealistic when in love, you can be a sensitive and responsive lover. Being pliant and flexible with an impressionable nature helps you to adapt to the needs of others. In your desire to blend with those you love, however, guard against not clearly defining your own boundaries. With your affectionate and sentimental nature, you are often attracted to those who understand your sensitivity and share your vision.

To read all about your Outer Planets and work out how to use your personalized timetable, go to Section Three, page 789.

≋

Your Personalized Timetable

JUPITER BENEFICIAL
1939 4/29 – 7/1
1939 8/27 – until 1940 2/9
1941 5/3 – 7/12
1944 11/28 – until 1945 2/26
1945 7/26 – 10/13
1947 3/9 – 3/19
1947 10/11 – 11/27
1951 4/10 – 5/28
1951 10/15 – until 1952 1/13
1953 4/15 – 6/23
1956 11/4 – until 1957 4/6
1957 7/1 – 9/28
1959 1/22 – 5/15
1959 9/20 – 11/11
1963 3/24 – 5/7
1964 8/14 – 10/16
1965 3/27 – 6/7
1968 10/17 – until 1969 9/12
1970 12/31 – until 1971 6/30
1971 8/18 – 10/25
1975 3/8 – 4/19
1976 7/13 – 11/30
1977 3/2 – 5/21
1980 9/30 – until 1981 8/26
1982 12/14 – until 1983 2/7
1983 5/16 – 10/6
1987 2/20 – 4/3
1988 6/23 – until 1989 5/5
1992 9/15 – 12/6
1993 3/25 – 8/5
1994 11/28 – until 1995 1/15
1995 6/26 – 9/8
1998 6/29 – 8/5
1999 2/1 – 3/17
2000 6/5 – 9/8
2000 10/20 – until 2001 4/16
2004 8/30 – 11/15
2005 5/3 – 7/8
2006 11/13 – 12/28
2010 5/21 – 9/28
2011 1/7 – 2/27
2012 5/19 – Continues

SATURN BENEFICIAL
1938 1/1 – 3/25
1941 7/2 – 11/24
1942 3/21 – until 1943 4/24
1950 9/30 – until 1951 11/11
1952 4/16 – 8/3
1955 12/18 – until 1956 12/16
1966 5/20 – 9/3
1967 2/10 – 5/5
1967 10/22 – until 1968 1/24
1971 5/6 – until 1972 6/4
1979 11/13 – until 1980 3/3
1980 8/5 – until 1981 9/17
1985 2/8 – 4/3
1985 10/26 – until 1986 1/26
1986 5/13 – 10/24
1996 3/18 – until 1997 3/8
2000 6/12 – until 2001 1/3
2001 2/15 – 7/14
2001 12/15 – until 2002 4/1
2009 9/13 – until 2010 10/23
2011 6/5 – 6/21

URANUS BENEFICIAL
1940 6/28 – until 1945 4/14
1967 9/13 – until 1971 8/6
1980 12/15 – until 1983 11/1
2010 4/2 – Continues

NEPTUNE BENEFICIAL
1939 10/28 – until 1948 7/24
1968 12/23 – until 1974 10/8

PLUTO BENEFICIAL
1968 11/10 – until 1976 9/5
1994 1/16 – until 1998 11/19

JUPITER CHALLENGING
1940 4/23 – 7/7
1940 11/3 – until 1941 2/24

1942 10/22 – 12/3
1943 6/3 – 8/17
1945 12/29 – until 1946 3/27
1946 8/27 – 11/13
1952 4/6 – 6/14
1954 9/17 – until 1955 1/18
1955 5/12 – 8/1
1957 12/5 – until 1958 5/5
1958 8/2 – 10/28
1964 3/19 – 5/26
1966 8/27 – until 1967 3/14
1967 3/28 – 7/16
1969 11/17 – until 1970 10/12
1975 8/4 – 8/25
1976 3/1 – 5/9
1978 8/9 – until 1979 6/29
1981 10/31 – until 1982 9/25
1987 6/21 – 10/19
1988 2/8 – 4/23
1990 7/24 – 10/16
1991 1/14 – 6/10
1993 10/15 – until 1994 1/6
1994 4/24 – 9/5
1999 5/29 – until 2000 4/6
2002 7/8 – 9/21
2003 2/23 – 5/14
2005 9/30 – 12/16
2006 6/4 – 8/7
2011 5/10 – until 2012 3/18

SATURN CHALLENGING
1939 5/9 – 12/18
1940 1/6 – 6/14
1940 11/13 – until 1941 3/5
1945 10/16 – 11/27
1946 6/20 – until 1947 7/21
1952 12/9 – until 1953 4/7
1953 9/4 – until 1954 10/22
1968 7/2 – 9/11
1969 3/16 – until 1970 4/20
1975 7/31 – until 1976 8/29
1977 3/17 – 5/5
1982 10/13 – until 1983 11/27
1984 6/11 – 8/13
1998 4/22 – until 1999 5/27
1999 12/28 – until 2000 1/27
2004 9/12 – until 2005 1/6
2005 5/31 – 10/23
2005 12/22 – until 2006 7/3
2011 11/19 – Continues

URANUS CHALLENGING
1954 8/4 – until 1958 7/11
1973 11/3 – until 1977 10/9

NEPTUNE CHALLENGING
1953 11/10 – until 1961 10/20

PLUTO CHALLENGING
1938 1/1 – until 1946 7/3
1981 10/23 – until 1988 9/10

JUPITER SPECIAL
1949 3/7 – 8/12
1949 10/26 – until 1950 1/18
1961 2/15 – until 1962 1/1
1973 1/29 – 4/28
1973 7/2 – 12/13
1985 1/14 – 3/29
1985 8/16 – 11/18
1996 12/29 – until 1997 3/9
2008 12/12 – until 2009 2/19

SATURN SPECIAL
1961 2/12 – 8/18
1961 11/6 – until 1962 4/18
1962 6/24 – until 1963 1/6
1990 4/2 – 6/6
1990 12/21 – until 1992 2/9

URANUS SPECIAL
1994 2/21 – until 1998 12/23

NEPTUNE SPECIAL
1995 2/23 – until 2003 11/11

January 24

SUN: AQUARIUS · DECANATE: AQUARIUS/URANUS · DEGREE: 3°–4° AQUARIUS · MODE: FIXED · ELEMENT: AIR

Your Personal Powers

Responsible and conscientious, you are an energetic individual with an amiable nature and an inventive mind. Interested in people, you can mix easily in any social group with your honest and direct style. Although you can be very mentally focused, you lose power if you dislike routine or become too stubborn. Usually, however, you are receptive and caring. A humanitarian streak means that although you prefer to be independent you can also work with others for a good cause. Possessing advisory skills, a good sense of values, and desire for peace, you know how to arbitrate or negotiate with others. Your strong desire for self-expression indicates that you have creative or artistic potential. With excellent mental capabilities, you have an original approach and shrewd insight into others that can greatly aid your overall success. Your clear and objective thinking can also stop you from losing power to worry or indecision, particularly about money. You empower yourself when you combine your ingenuity and insight with self-discipline.

Your Powers of Attraction in Relationships

Friendly and independent, you attract others with your sociable personality. Freedom is important to you but your need for love and security emphasizes the importance of home and family. Clever, analytical, or wise people attract you. You may also be drawn to those who have a perfectionist streak or high ideals like yourself. Sympathetic and kind, you can be helpful and caring with loved ones. Nevertheless, you may have issues about being isolated or lonely. If too detached, you may sometimes appear cold. By finding a higher form of love through your ideals, you avoid many of your personal frustrations. With your quick mental responses you are often witty and amusing, enjoying the company of others. When in love you can be sensitive and affectionate as well as a devoted spouse or parent.

Your attractive qualities: energetic, idealist, hardworking, practical, creative, frank, fair, strong determination, honest, creative, cooperative, kind, persevering, generous, home-loving, active, social, inventive, courageous, responsible, ambitious, caring

Your less attractive qualities: stubborn, materialistic, too frugal, cold, worry, indecisive, too security conscious, escapist, lazy, withdrawn, interfering, rebellious, uncaring, bossy, too serious

Your Venus Power

The planet Venus has a great deal of influence on your powers of attraction. Below are four possible Venus types for women and men. To find your Venus you need to go to page 771, where you will find the Venus table and extra information. The planet Mars also affects your powers of attraction. To find your Mars table and interpretation go to page 761.

WOMEN WITH VENUS IN SAGITTARIUS: At your best when being optimistic and generous, you possess a mischievous sense of fun. In relationships your open-minded approach to people and places may attract you to different cultures or make you tolerant of the foibles of others. Although warm and enthusiastic when in love, your natural honesty and idealism may inspire you to look for a partner who shares your love of freedom.

MEN WITH VENUS IN SAGITTARIUS: Forward-thinking rather than dwelling on the past, you are looking for a partner who can share your future plans. You enjoy exploring life whether through travel and mental pursuits or sports and games. Idealistic, you usually prefer the company of a partner who is optimistic and shares your beliefs. In your desire for honesty in relationships, however, be careful not to become tactless. Nevertheless, you are attracted to honest, direct, and fun-loving partners who have a sense of humor like your own.

WOMEN WITH VENUS IN CAPRICORN: Loyal and responsible, you are attracted to dignified and reserved individuals. Being practical and security-conscious, you prefer hardworking partners who are resourceful and enterprising. Work may even be a factor in many of your associations and partnerships. For you, family and faithfulness can be especially important, so you are usually willing to work hard or make sacrifices in order to build a strong relationship.

MEN WITH VENUS IN CAPRICORN: Hardworking and ambitious, you are usually attracted to determined, focused, and ambitious partners with a strong sense of duty. You want them to take relationships as seriously as you do, so loyalty and faithfulness are high on your agenda. Since you may display a natural reserve about expressing your feelings in an intimate relationship, you need a partner who shares your need for emotional security.

WOMEN WITH VENUS IN AQUARIUS: When it comes to relationships, others are attracted to your honest, friendly, and easygoing attitude. You really enjoy social interaction with others and may develop a genuine concern for humanity. Usually you present a tolerant and reasonable front in love situations and attempt to view your relationships objectively. If partners become too demanding, however, you can become stubborn and fixed. Friendship may be even more important for you than sexual compatibility.

MEN WITH VENUS IN AQUARIUS: You are sociable and open-minded, and people are attracted by your friendly and relaxed style. Being independent, you value freedom-loving partners who give you the space to be yourself. Others sometimes interpret your detachment as being emotionally cool, but they may not understand your progressive views on relationships. Friendship can sometimes be even more important than earthly passion. Ideally, your partner shares your ideas on life and possesses as strong a sense of originality as you. Not easily ruffled, you can deal well with difficult situations or moody partners.

WOMEN WITH VENUS IN PISCES: Idealistic and impressionable, in love you are romantic. Being sensitive to people, you are receptive to their moods and feelings. This affinity indicates that although you can be selfless, you may have to guard against being too sentimental or overly romantic, especially with those who can take advantage of your kindness. Nevertheless, alluring and seductive, your partners can be intrigued by your poetic soul or mysterious nature.

MEN WITH VENUS IN PISCES: Being adaptable and sensitive you are able to intuitively feel the moods of those you love. Although you are receptive to others, you can be ambiguous about your own feelings toward your partner. Romantic and kindhearted, you long to be loved but you need to be realistic about your relationships in order to avoid disappointments. When in love you may idealize your partners and fail to see any faults in their personality.

To read all about your Outer Planets and work out how to use your personalized timetable, go to Section Three, page 789.

To read all about your Outer Planets and work out how to use your personalized timetable, go to Section Three, page 789.

Your Personalized Timetable

JUPITER BENEFICIAL
1939 5/4 – 7/17
1939 8/11 – until 1940 2/14
1941 5/7 – 7/17
1942 1/27 – 2/13
1944 12/7 – until 1945 2/17
1945 8/1 – 10/18
1947 10/16 – 12/2
1951 4/15 – 6/3
1951 10/7 – until 1952 1/20
1953 4/20 – 6/28
1956 11/10 – until 1957 3/28
1957 7/9 – 10/2
1959 1/29 – 5/7
1959 9/27 – 11/16
1963 3/29 – 5/11
1964 8/26 – 10/3
1965 4/1 – 6/11
1968 10/22 – until 1969 9/17
1971 1/6 – 6/18
1971 8/30 – 10/30
1975 3/12 – 4/23
1976 7/19 – 11/22
1977 3/9 – 5/26
1980 10/5 – until 1981 8/31
1982 12/18 – until 1983 2/15
1983 5/7 – 10/11
1987 2/24 – 4/7
1988 6/28 – until 1989 5/9
1992 9/19 – 12/13
1993 3/16 – 8/12
1994 12/2 – until 1995 1/21
1995 6/17 – 9/17
1999 2/6 – 3/21
2000 6/9 – until 2001 4/21
2004 9/4 – 11/20
2005 4/23 – 7/18
2006 11/17 – until 2007 1/2
2010 5/27 – 9/20
2011 1/14 – 3/4
2012 5/23 – Continues

SATURN BENEFICIAL
1938 1/1 – 4/2
1941 7/12 – 11/12
1942 3/31 – 8/22
1942 10/28 – until 1943 5/3
1950 10/9 – until 1951 11/21
1952 4/2 – 8/15
1955 12/28 – until 1956 6/3
1956 9/24 – 12/24
1957 7/10 – 9/13
1966 6/4 – 8/18
1967 2/19 – 5/14
1967 10/9 – until 1968 2/5
1971 5/14 – until 1972 6/12
1979 11/26 – until 1980 2/17
1980 8/14 – until 1981 9/25
1985 11/4 – until 1986 2/9
1986 4/27 – 11/2
1996 3/26 – until 1997 3/17
2000 6/20 – 12/15
2001 3/6 – 7/24
2001 12/3 – until 2002 4/12
2009 9/22 – until 2010 11/1
2011 5/7 – 7/19

URANUS BENEFICIAL
1940 7/24 – until 1945 5/5
1967 9/29 – until 1971 8/28
1981 1/3 – until 1983 11/18
2010 4/21 – Continues

NEPTUNE BENEFICIAL
1940 9/25 – until 1948 9/2
1969 2/3 – until 1974 11/9

PLUTO BENEFICIAL
1969 10/4 – until 1977 7/12
1994 12/4 – until 1999 10/12

JUPITER CHALLENGING
1940 4/27 – 7/14

1940 10/27 – until 1941 3/2
1943 6/9 – 8/22
1946 1/7 – 3/18
1946 9/2 – 11/18
1952 4/10 – 6/19
1952 12/18 – until 1953 1/22
1954 9/23 – until 1955 1/11
1955 5/19 – 8/6
1957 12/11 – until 1958 4/27
1958 8/10 – 11/2
1964 3/24 – 5/31
1966 9/1 – until 1967 2/23
1967 4/16 – 7/21
1969 11/22 – until 1970 10/17
1976 3/6 – 5/14
1978 8/14 – until 1979 7/4
1981 11/5 – until 1982 9/30
1987 6/28 – 10/12
1988 2/14 – 4/28
1990 7/28 – 10/24
1991 1/5 – 6/15
1993 10/20 – until 1994 1/13
1994 4/16 – 9/11
1999 6/3 – 12/3
2000 1/6 – 4/11
2002 7/12 – 9/27
2003 2/14 – 5/23
2005 10/5 – 12/21
2006 5/25 – 8/17
2011 5/14 – until 2012 3/23

SATURN CHALLENGING
1939 5/18 – 11/22
1940 1/31 – 6/25
1940 11/1 – until 1941 3/15
1946 6/28 – until 1947 7/29
1952 12/21 – until 1953 3/24
1953 9/14 – until 1954 10/31
1968 8/2 – 8/12
1969 3/25 – until 1970 4/28
1975 8/8 – until 1976 9/7
1977 2/27 – 5/23
1982 10/21 – until 1983 12/7
1984 5/24 – 8/30
1998 4/30 – until 1999 6/5
1999 12/5 – until 2000 2/17
2004 9/24 – 12/24
2005 6/10 – until 2006 7/12
2011 11/29 – Continues

URANUS CHALLENGING
1954 8/22 – until 1958 7/28
1973 11/20 – until 1977 10/26

NEPTUNE CHALLENGING
1953 12/14 – until 1962 9/17

PLUTO CHALLENGING
1938 1/1 – until 1947 6/12
1981 11/19 – until 1988 10/10

JUPITER SPECIAL
1938 1/1 – 2/7
1949 3/13 – 8/3
1949 11/3 – until 1950 1/22
1961 2/20 – until 1962 1/5
1973 2/3 – 5/11
1973 6/19 – 12/18
1985 1/18 – 4/4
1985 8/8 – 11/25
1997 1/2 – 3/13
2008 12/16 – until 2009 2/23

SATURN SPECIAL
1961 2/22 – 8/2
1961 11/20 – until 1963 1/15
1990 12/30 – until 1992 2/18

URANUS SPECIAL
1994 3/17 – until 1999 1/11

NEPTUNE SPECIAL
1995 4/18 – until 2003 12/26

January 25

SUN: AQUARIUS • DECANATE: AQUARIUS/URANUS • DEGREE: 4°–5° AQUARIUS • MODE: FIXED • ELEMENT: AIR

Your Personal Powers

You are a mentally sharp individual with fast responses and deep thoughts. When positive, you are versatile and resolute with original and creative ideas. Your ruling planet, Uranus, indicates that you possess an interest in people and a unique approach to solving life's problems. Friendly and cooperative, you also have an ability to make helpful contacts. Once set on a course of action you gain power from your resourceful personality and determination to accomplish your goals. Be careful, however, that in your desire to achieve you do not become too obstinate or domineering. Although you can be very tough and focused when interested in a project, you also have a softer, sensitive, and more idealistic side to your personality. The combination of your logical and objective mind with your intuitive sensitivity can bring you success. An unwarranted fear about lack of money implies that you can lose power to anxiety and worry. Being a practical visionary with drive and original ideas, you have everything you need to really succeed.

Your Powers of Attraction in Relationships

Thoughtful and friendly, you enjoy meeting people and can attract others. Although you are generous and kind to your partner, occasionally you may become too self-absorbed. Although being extremely sensitive suggests that at times you may withdraw to protect yourself, your partners may interpret your detachment as coldness. Usually good with people on a one-to-one basis, you are able to realistically evaluate others. Ideally, your partner will understand your strong need for a harmonious and secure home. Attracted to intelligent and powerful individuals, you may have to avoid power struggles with partners. You have strong convictions and can be loyal and magnanimous to those you love. By balancing your love of freedom with your need for partnership, you are able to create harmonious relationships.

Your attractive qualities: friendly, hardworking, fine mind, perfectionist, ambitious, perceptive, rational, sensitive, confident, inventive, generous, creative mind, people skills, highly intuitive, talented, good strategist, imaginative, introspective, spiritual potential

Your less attractive qualities: stubborn, critical, impulsive, impatient, irresponsible, too emotional, moody, tough, bossy, inertia, anxious, nervous, inflexible

Your Venus Power

The planet Venus has a great deal of influence on your powers of attraction. Below are four possible Venus types for women and men. To find your Venus you need to go to page 771, where you will find the Venus table and extra information. The planet Mars also affects your powers of attraction. To find your Mars table and interpretation go to page 761.

WOMEN WITH VENUS IN SAGITTARIUS: When you feel generous, you can make others feel more optimistic about life. You may be interested in higher learning and seek partners who are scholarly or broad-minded. You are outspoken and direct and sometimes say things that you later regret. Curious and versatile, you can adjust quickly to new situations, and a foreign influence implies that you love to travel or may have a partner who comes from a different culture.

MEN WITH VENUS IN SAGITTARIUS: Your enthusiasm and straightforward conduct usually appeal to others and imply that you are approachable and easygoing. Being open to ideas and willing to believe that life has a great deal to offer suggest that you are generous, broad-minded, and eager to cooperate with others. A love of travel and an interest in other cultures imply that your partner may come from a foreign country.

WOMEN WITH VENUS IN CAPRICORN: Proud and refined, you attract others with your composed dignity. Disliking vulnerability and needing to feel safe before you can express your feelings, you display a strong front. Feeling insecure or inadequate in relationships may force you to become manipulative in order to regain control. Nevertheless, you can project an attractive sense of self-assurance and are capable of displaying loyalty and a wonderful dry sense of humor.

MEN WITH VENUS IN CAPRICORN: As you do not display your deeper emotions freely, you are usually dignified and controlled in your relationships. Practical and down-to-earth partners are particularly attractive to you, especially those who do not rush into expressing their feelings but seem to possess natural class and reserve. You need a partner who is loyal and dependable and willing to take your relationship seriously.

WOMEN WITH VENUS IN AQUARIUS: Usually you have a modern outlook on love and are open to new or current lifestyles. Your intuitive abilities, communal sense, and people skills often allow you to see deeper into human intentions and to telepathically read people's thoughts. You are usually group-oriented and are drawn to individuals within the group who

are independent and self-motivated. You are more inclined to choose a partner who is unconventional or freedom-loving. Conscious of your social standing, however, you want someone who can relate well to your friends.

MEN WITH VENUS IN AQUARIUS: Although independent, you often enjoy being part of a group. The partners you frequently attract are themselves nonconformists or free spirits. As an individual you may not find it easy to settle into a routine or an entirely mundane type of relationship. You may have some unconventional views on traditional marriage or your partner may hold such views. As a nonconformist you may also be interested in alternative lifestyles such as collective living.

WOMEN WITH VENUS IN PISCES: In love you are sensitive, tender, and affectionate, experiences your partner's feelings almost as strongly as your own. Being imaginative and a visionary, you possess the ability to develop your creative gifts as well as a deep compassion for others. As you are idealistic when in love, you usually prefer to see only your partner's good points, but be careful that your high expectations do not bring disappointment if you avoid being realistic. Nevertheless, in your relationships with others you can be devoted, loving, and positively enchanting.

MEN WITH VENUS IN PISCES: As a romantic and generous person you are attracted to imaginative or artistic partners who can be sensitive and generous. While you are willing to make allowances for loved ones, playing the martyr in relationships can lead to allowing others to take advantage of your kind nature. Nevertheless, giving and loving, you are usually willing to forgive your partner's shortcomings.

To read all about your Outer Planets and work out how to use your personalized timetable, go to Section Three, page 789.

≈

Your Personalized Timetable

JUPITER BENEFICIAL
1939 5/9 – 11/5
1939 12/14 – until 1940 2/18
1941 5/11 – 7/22
1942 1/10 – 3/3
1944 12/18 – until 1945 2/5
1945 8/7 – 10/23
1947 10/21 – 12/6
1951 4/19 – 6/9
1951 9/30 – until 1952 1/27
1953 4/24 – 7/3
1956 11/16 – until 1957 3/20
1957 7/16 – 10/7
1959 2/6 – 4/28
1959 10/3 – 11/20
1963 4/2 – 5/16
1965 4/6 – 6/16
1968 10/27 – until 1969 5/6
1969 6/9 – 9/21
1971 1/11 – 6/9
1971 9/8 – 11/4
1975 3/16 – 4/27
1976 7/26 – 11/15
1977 3/15 – 5/30
1980 10/10 – until 1981 9/5
1982 12/23 – until 1983 2/26
1983 4/27 – 10/17
1987 2/28 – 4/11
1988 7/3 – until 1989 1/4
1989 2/5 – 5/14
1992 9/24 – 12/22
1993 3/7 – 8/17
1994 12/7 – until 1995 1/27
1995 6/9 – 9/24
1999 2/10 – 3/25
2000 6/14 – until 2001 4/26
2004 9/9 – 11/26
2005 4/15 – 7/26
2006 11/22 – until 2007 1/7
2010 6/3 – 9/12
2011 1/20 – 3/8
2012 5/27 – Continues

SATURN BENEFICIAL
1938 1/7 – 4/10
1941 7/24 – 10/30
1942 4/10 – until 1943 5/11
1950 10/17 – until 1951 4/24
1951 7/2 – 12/2
1952 3/20 – 8/25
1956 1/7 – 5/20
1956 10/5 – until 1957 1/3
1957 6/22 – 9/29
1966 6/28 – 7/24
1967 2/28 – 5/25
1967 9/26 – until 1968 2/15
1971 5/22 – until 1972 6/20
1979 12/15 – until 1980 1/30
1980 8/23 – until 1981 10/3
1985 11/13 – until 1986 3/5
1986 4/2 – 11/11
1996 4/3 – until 1997 3/25
2000 6/30 – 12/1
2001 3/18 – 8/4
2001 11/20 – until 2002 4/22
2009 9/30 – until 2010 11/10
2011 4/21 – 8/3

URANUS BENEFICIAL
1941 5/23 – until 1945 5/23
1967 10/16 – until 1971 9/15
1981 4/28 – until 1984 8/21
2010 5/14 – Continues

NEPTUNE BENEFICIAL
1940 10/24 – until 1949 7/16
1969 12/21 – until 1975 10/4

PLUTO BENEFICIAL
1969 11/4 – until 1977 8/26
1995 1/1 – until 1999 11/12

JUPITER CHALLENGING
1940 5/1 – 7/21
1940 10/19 – until 1941 3/8

1943 6/14 – 8/27
1946 1/19 – 3/6
1946 9/7 – 11/22
1952 4/14 – 6/24
1952 12/5 – until 1953 2/4
1954 9/30 – until 1955 1/3
1955 5/25 – 8/10
1957 12/17 – until 1958 4/19
1958 8/17 – 11/7
1964 3/28 – 6/4
1966 9/7 – until 1967 2/12
1967 4/27 – 7/26
1969 11/27 – until 1970 6/6
1970 7/10 – 10/22
1976 3/10 – 5/18
1978 8/19 – until 1979 7/9
1981 11/10 – until 1982 10/5
1987 7/5 – 10/4
1988 2/20 – 5/2
1990 8/2 – 11/4
1990 12/25 – until 1991 6/21
1993 10/25 – until 1994 1/22
1994 4/7 – 9/17
1999 6/8 – 11/20
2000 1/19 – 4/15
2002 7/17 – 10/3
2003 2/6 – 5/30
2005 10/10 – 12/27
2006 5/16 – 8/25
2011 5/19 – until 2012 3/28

SATURN CHALLENGING
1939 5/27 – 11/7
1940 2/15 – 7/6
1940 10/19 – until 1941 3/25
1946 7/6 – until 1947 8/6
1953 1/6 – 3/6
1953 9/23 – until 1954 11/8
1969 4/2 – until 1970 5/6
1975 8/16 – until 1976 3/4
1976 4/20 – 9/16
1977 2/13 – 6/5
1982 10/30 – until 1983 12/16
1984 5/10 – 9/12
1998 5/9 – until 1999 6/14
1999 11/21 – until 2000 3/2
2004 10/9 – 12/8
2005 6/18 – until 2006 7/20
2011 12/9 – until 2012 4/11
2012 9/4 – Continues

URANUS CHALLENGING
1954 9/12 – until 1959 5/16
1973 12/10 – until 1978 8/12

NEPTUNE CHALLENGING
1954 11/8 – until 1962 10/18

PLUTO CHALLENGING
1938 1/1 – until 1947 7/22
1981 12/24 – until 1989 8/16

JUPITER SPECIAL
1938 1/1 – 2/12
1949 3/19 – 7/25
1949 11/10 – until 1950 1/26
1961 2/25 – until 1962 1/10
1973 2/7 – 12/23
1985 1/22 – 4/11
1985 7/31 – 12/2
1997 1/6 – 3/18
1997 9/21 – 10/24
2008 12/21 – until 2009 2/28

SATURN SPECIAL
1961 3/4 – 7/19
1961 12/2 – until 1963 1/23
1991 1/8 – until 1992 2/27
1992 9/16 – 11/14

URANUS SPECIAL
1995 1/19 – until 1999 1/29

NEPTUNE SPECIAL
1996 2/20 – until 2004 1/24

January 26

SUN: AQUARIUS • DECANATE: AQUARIUS/URANUS • DEGREE: 5°–6° AQUARIUS • MODE: FIXED • ELEMENT: AIR

Your Personal Powers

Friendly and direct, you are an intuitive individual with original ideas and strong willpower. You benefit from the combination of your personal drive, ambition, and ability to work hard. Action-oriented, you do not like to waste time, preferring to be at the cutting edge of new trends. Although your assertive personality serves you well in the achievement of your goals or in leadership positions, you may lose power if you become too bossy or obstinate. Nevertheless, with your natural people skills, innate understanding, and good sense of values, you are quick to take advantage of opportunities. An idealistic streak suggests you also enjoy projects that can help others. Your need for stability and material security may find expression in your desire for financial rewards or an attractive home. With good taste and an appreciation of luxury, you possess a refined aesthetic sense and creative gifts. Success-oriented with a straightforward approach, you need to persist and to stay focused to manifest your remarkable potential.

Your Powers of Attraction in Relationships

You attract others with your confident and friendly manner. Although pragmatic about your love life, your powerful inner desire for love and affection or high ideals inspire you to be altruistic toward your partner. Generous with strong convictions and a sense of responsibility, you are ready to make sacrifices for family members and those you love. Nevertheless, avoid becoming controlling with your loved ones by developing patience and your powers of persuasion. Desiring freedom and independence, you need your own space even within a relationship. You may even attract partners who are not around all the time. With your desire for action and new experiences you often seek diversity in your relationships to keep yourself from becoming bored or changing your mind. You may find yourself attracted to partners who are enterprising and enjoy their freedom. With your strength of will and conviction, you can be a strong support for others.

Your attractive qualities: good mind, leadership ability, original ideas, creative, hardworking, ambitious, executive ability, practical, caring, broad-minded, intuitive, independent, responsible, proud, loving, courageous, supportive, enterprising, people skills, determined

Your less attractive qualities: stubborn, rebellious, too serious, unstable relationships, materialistic, unenthusiastic, impatient, bossy, lack of persistence, controlling, willful

Your Venus Power

The planet Venus has a great deal of influence on your powers of attraction. Below are four possible Venus types for women and men. To find your Venus you need to go to page 771, where you will find the Venus table and extra information. The planet Mars also affects your powers of attraction. To find your Mars table and interpretation go to page 761.

WOMEN WITH VENUS IN SAGITTARIUS: Optimistic and fun-loving, you love adventure and seek a partner who can expand your horizons. Being truthful and direct, you often say what you think, and at times you may be naively tactless. A need for expansion and prosperity suggests that you may enjoy traveling with your friends or partner. Being lighthearted and idealistic, once you have given your heart to someone you will stay honorable and loyal.

MEN WITH VENUS IN SAGITTARIUS: You are usually attracted to partners who are knowledgeable or well-traveled. Enthusiastic and optimistic, you often respond quickly to love offers and enter relationships with enthusiasm. Generally you seek to expand your social circle, and meeting people from all walks of life can bring the variety and fun that you seek in life. Although you are generous and honest, your partners may sometimes accuse you of being overly optimistic or too blunt.

WOMEN WITH VENUS IN CAPRICORN: With your natural caution in romantic affairs, you often appear reserved and controlled. You may be shy but try to be more forward, especially if you want to be noticed. When you care about people, however, you are usually willing to put in extra time and energy to preserve the relationship. You are practical and dependable, and a sense of duty can often play a large role in affairs of your heart. With elegant simplicity, you can attract others with your well-cut clothes and refined manners.

MEN WITH VENUS IN CAPRICORN: In relationships you take love seriously and can be a strong and practical support for friends or partners. You are usually attracted to partners who are as hardworking as you. As you tend not to express your feelings until you feel really secure in a relationship, you may be drawn to those who seem loyal, faithful, and not likely

to let you down. As you respect the wisdom of experience, you may be drawn to mature partners or, alternatively, you may act as an authority figure for someone younger.

WOMEN WITH VENUS IN AQUARIUS: You attract and impress others with your friendly approach and progressive ideas. As you are usually independent and easygoing, you value freedom within a relationship. A good companion with a sense of your own person, you enjoy socializing, especially with people who are original, cosmopolitan, and have a strong sense of individuality. Although being friendly and detached usually serves you well, avoid losing touch with your emotions. You usually prefer the company of those who have innovative or progressive views.

MEN WITH VENUS IN AQUARIUS: You are sociable and open-minded, and people are attracted by your friendly and easygoing style. Being independent, you value freedom-loving partners who give you the space to be yourself. People can sometimes interpret your detachment as being emotionally cool, but they admire your objectivity and humanitarian inclinations. You are attracted to intelligent individuals who are as truthful and direct as you are, but above all they must be true friends. Ideally, your partner shares your liberal views on life and possesses a strong sense of individuality.

WOMEN WITH VENUS IN PISCES: In love you are sensitive, tender, and affectionate, experiences your partner's feelings almost as strongly as your own. Being imaginative and a visionary, you possess the ability to develop creative gifts as well as a deep compassion for others. As you are idealistic when in love, you usually prefer to see only your partner's good points, but be careful that your high expectations do not bring disappointment if you avoid being realistic. Nevertheless, in your relationships with others, you can be devoted, loving, and positively enchanting.

MEN WITH VENUS IN PISCES: As a romantic and generous person, you are attracted to imaginative or artistic partners who can be sensitive and generous. While you are willing to make allowances for your loved ones, playing the martyr in relationships can lead to allowing others to take advantage of your kind nature. Nevertheless, giving and loving, you are usually willing to forgive your partner's shortcomings.

To read all about your Outer Planets and work out how to use your personalized timetable, go to Section Three, page 789.

≈

Your Personalized Timetable

JUPITER BENEFICIAL
1939 5/14 – 10/24
1939 12/26 – until 1940 2/23
1941 5/16 – 7/27
1941 12/30 – until 1942 3/14
1945 8/12 – 10/28
1947 10/26 – 12/11
1951 4/24 – 6/16
1951 9/22 – until 1952 2/2
1953 4/29 – 7/7
1956 11/23 – until 1957 3/12
1957 7/23 – 10/12
1959 2/16 – 4/18
1959 10/8 – 11/25
1963 4/6 – 5/21
1963 11/11 – 12/29
1965 4/11 – 6/20
1968 11/2 – until 1969 4/22
1969 6/24 – 9/26
1971 1/17 – 5/31
1971 9/15 – 11/9
1975 3/21 – 5/2
1976 8/2 – 11/7
1977 3/21 – 6/4
1980 10/15 – until 1981 9/10
1982 12/28 – until 1983 3/13
1983 4/12 – 10/22
1987 3/5 – 4/15
1988 7/8 – 12/21
1989 2/18 – 5/18
1992 9/29 – until 1993 1/2
1993 2/25 – 8/23
1994 12/12 – until 1995 2/2
1995 6/1 – 10/1
1999 2/15 – 3/30
2000 6/18 – until 2001 5/1
2004 9/13 – 12/3
2005 4/6 – 8/2
2006 11/26 – until 2007 1/12
2007 7/17 – 8/27
2010 6/10 – 9/4
2011 1/25 – 3/13
2012 6/1 – Continues

SATURN BENEFICIAL
1938 1/21 – 4/19
1941 8/8 – 10/14
1942 4/19 – until 1943 5/19
1950 10/26 – until 1951 4/8
1951 7/18 – 12/15
1952 3/6 – 9/4
1956 1/19 – 5/6
1956 10/16 – until 1957 1/13
1957 6/8 – 10/12
1967 3/8 – 6/6
1967 9/12 – until 1968 2/25
1971 5/30 – until 1972 6/28
1980 9/1 – until 1981 10/12
1985 11/21 – until 1986 11/20
1996 4/12 – until 1997 4/2
2000 7/10 – 11/18
2001 3/29 – 8/18
2001 11/6 – until 2002 5/1
2009 10/8 – until 2010 11/20
2011 4/8 – 8/15

URANUS BENEFICIAL
1941 6/10 – until 1946 3/10
1967 11/4 – until 1971 10/1
1981 11/25 – until 1984 10/6
2010 6/27 – Continues

NEPTUNE BENEFICIAL
1940 12/8 – until 1949 8/31
1970 1/27 – until 1975 11/8

PLUTO BENEFICIAL
1970 9/29 – until 1977 9/23
1995 2/19 – until 2000 9/28

JUPITER CHALLENGING
1940 5/5 – 7/30
1940 10/10 – until 1941 3/13

1943 6/19 – 9/1
1946 9/13 – 11/27
1952 4/18 – 6/29
1952 11/26 – until 1953 2/13
1954 10/9 – 12/26
1955 5/30 – 8/15
1957 12/24 – until 1958 4/11
1958 8/24 – 11/11
1964 4/2 – 6/9
1966 9/12 – until 1967 2/3
1967 5/6 – 7/30
1969 12/2 – until 1970 5/22
1970 7/25 – 10/27
1976 3/15 – 5/22
1978 8/24 – until 1979 7/14
1981 11/15 – until 1982 10/10
1987 7/13 – 9/25
1988 2/25 – 5/6
1990 8/7 – 11/26
1990 12/4 – until 1991 6/26
1993 10/30 – until 1994 2/1
1994 3/27 – 9/23
1999 6/14 – 11/11
2000 1/28 – 4/20
2002 7/21 – 10/10
2003 1/30 – 6/6
2005 10/14 – until 2006 1/2
2006 5/8 – 9/2
2011 5/24 – until 2012 4/2

SATURN CHALLENGING
1939 6/6 – 10/25
1940 2/26 – 7/20
1940 10/4 – until 1941 4/3
1946 7/14 – until 1947 8/14
1953 10/2 – until 1954 11/17
1969 4/10 – until 1970 5/14
1975 8/25 – until 1976 2/14
1976 5/8 – 9/26
1977 1/31 – 6/16
1982 11/7 – until 1983 12/27
1984 4/27 – 9/23
1998 5/17 – 11/30
1999 1/27 – 6/24
1999 11/8 – until 2000 3/13
2005 6/27 – until 2006 7/28
2011 12/21 – until 2012 3/28
2012 9/14 – Continues

URANUS CHALLENGING
1954 10/16 – until 1959 6/15
1974 1/10 – until 1978 9/13

NEPTUNE CHALLENGING
1954 12/11 – until 1963 9/14

PLUTO CHALLENGING
1938 1/1 – until 1948 7/3
1982 11/7 – until 1989 9/27

JUPITER SPECIAL
1938 1/1 – 2/16
1949 3/25 – 7/18
1949 11/16 – until 1950 1/31
1961 3/2 – 9/11
1961 10/5 – until 1962 1/14
1973 2/12 – 12/28
1985 1/27 – 4/18
1985 7/23 – 12/8
1997 1/11 – 3/24
1997 9/8 – 11/7
2008 12/26 – until 2009 3/5

SATURN SPECIAL
1961 3/16 – 7/5
1961 12/12 – until 1963 2/1
1991 1/17 – until 1992 3/7
1992 8/29 – 12/1

URANUS SPECIAL
1995 2/5 – until 1999 12/2

NEPTUNE SPECIAL
1996 4/2 – until 2004 12/22

January 27

SUN: AQUARIUS • DECANATE: AQUARIUS/URANUS • DEGREE: 6°–7° AQUARIUS • MODE: FIXED • ELEMENT: AIR

Your Personal Powers

With keen intelligence and an active mind full of ideas, you are an ambitious character with outstanding potential. With a strong interest in human nature, you have a sociable approach to life. Inventive and hardworking, you gain power from your innovative thoughts and ability to take your work or responsibilities seriously. Although determined and steadfast in achieving your goals, avoid losing power by becoming stubborn or rebellious. Your straightforward personality suggests that you can be outspoken and your progressive views are often ahead of their time. You usually enjoy power, value freedom, and like to be in control. As an individualist with natural authority, you often gravitate to leadership positions. Women born on this day prefer an active and direct role in life rather than a passive one. An objective thinker who needs mental stimulation, you enjoy matching wits with others in friendly debate. Possessing natural organizational skills, communication abilities, and consecutive ideas, you need only apply patience and perseverance to achieve outstanding success.

Your Powers of Attraction in Relationships

Broad-minded and sociable, you attract friends and admirers. Although you appear confident and resilient, underneath you can be very sensitive. With your natural humanitarian streak you can work well with others, benefitting from partnerships or group endeavors. Although independence and freedom is important to you, you need the stability of a secure home and relationship. Honest and straightforward individuals who are loyal and reliable attract you. Being intelligent, you need a partner with whom you can share your ideas. As hidden fears can sometimes undermine your faith or cause you to be disagreeable or bossy, it is important that you contact and express your feelings. Valuing loyalty, you can give much in the way of affection and support to others.

Your attractive qualities: broad-minded, sociable, keen intelligence, leadership, idealistic, creative, imaginative, brave, good understanding, spiritual potential, humanitarian, generous, inventive, mental strength, sympathetic, cooperative, sensitive, persuasive

Your less attractive qualities: self-centered, argumentative, restlessness, nervous, inner tension, mistrusting, power tactics, intolerant, rebellious, stubborn, too outspoken, too sensitive, high-strung, obstinate

Your Venus Power

The planet Venus has a great deal of influence on your powers of attraction. Below are four possible Venus types for women and men. To find your Venus you need to go to page 771, where you will find the Venus table and extra information. The planet Mars also affects your powers of attraction. To find your Mars table and interpretation go to page 761.

WOMEN WITH VENUS IN SAGITTARIUS: Sociable, warm, and friendly, you possess an honest and frank style in your relationships. Being naturally gregarious, you want others to share your enthusiasm and enjoy encouraging the people you love. You do better when you have a sense of personal freedom within a relationship and are usually generous with the faults of others. You need a partner who can share your need to explore and take risks, whether through travel, education, or recreation.

MEN WITH VENUS IN SAGITTARIUS: When in love you are open and friendly with a need for a partner who can share your adventurous spirit and sense of fun. Be careful, however, that your desire for freedom does not cause you to avoid commitment. You prefer your partners to be positive, direct, and generous in spirit. Being outspoken as well as an idealist, you usually enjoy a partner with whom you can share your strong opinions. Alternatively, you may wish to explore life together whether through travel, education, or by having fun.

WOMEN WITH VENUS IN CAPRICORN: Proud and refined, you attract others with your composed dignity. Disliking vulnerability and needing to feel safe before you can express your feelings, you display a strong front. Feeling insecure or inadequate in relationships may force you to become manipulative in order to regain control. Nevertheless, you can project an attractive sense of self-assurance and are capable of displaying loyalty and a wonderful dry sense of humor.

MEN WITH VENUS IN CAPRICORN: As you do not display your deeper emotions freely, you are usually dignified and controlled in your relationships with others. Practical and down-to-earth partners are particularly attractive to you, especially those who do not rush into expressing their feelings but seem to possess natural class and reserve. You need a part-

ner who is loyal and dependable and willing to take your relationship seriously.

WOMEN WITH VENUS IN AQUARIUS: You attract and impress others with your friendly approach and progressive ideas. As you are usually independent and easygoing, you value freedom within a relationship. A good companion with a sense of your own person, you enjoy socializing, especially with people who are original, cosmopolitan, and have a strong sense of individuality. Although being friendly and detached usually serves you well, avoid losing touch with your emotions. You usually prefer the company of those who have innovative or progressive views.

MEN WITH VENUS IN AQUARIUS: You are sociable and open-minded, and people are attracted by your friendly and easygoing style. Being independent, you value freedom-loving partners who give you the space to be yourself. People can sometimes interpret your detachment as being emotionally cool, but they admire your objectivity and humanitarian inclinations. You are attracted to intelligent individuals who are as truthful and direct as you, but above all they must be true friends. Ideally, your partner shares your liberal views on life and possesses a strong sense of individuality.

WOMEN WITH VENUS IN PISCES: Romantic and idealistic when in love, you can be a sensitive and responsive lover. With your affectionate and impressionable nature you are often attracted to those who understand your sensitivity and share your vision. Being flexible with an impressionable nature helps you to adapt to the needs of others. In your desire to blend with those you love, guard against giving too much of yourself by not defining your boundaries clearly.

MEN WITH VENUS IN PISCES: The combination of your emotional subtlety and charm can make you very alluring when dealing with affairs of the heart. Perceptive and impressionable, you have an easygoing style in your relationships, usually preferring to avoid ugly confrontation. You are drawn to partners who have a touch of glamour and are sensitive to the needs of others. Alternatively, they could be visionaries with rich imaginations who know how to keep you enchanted. With your insight you have the ability to observe the subtle moods of your partner.

To read all about your Outer Planets and work out how to use your personalized timetable, go to Section Three, page 789.

≈≈≈

Your Personalized Timetable

JUPITER BENEFICIAL
1939 5/20 – 10/14
1940 1/4 – 2/28
1941 5/20 – 8/2
1941 12/22 – until 1942 3/22
1945 8/18 – 11/2
1947 10/31 – 12/15
1951 4/28 – 6/24
1951 9/14 – until 1952 2/7
1953 5/3 – 7/12
1956 11/30 – until 1957 3/4
1957 7/29 – 10/16
1959 3/2 – 4/3
1959 10/14 – 11/30
1963 4/10 – 5/27
1963 10/31 – until 1964 1/9
1965 4/16 – 6/24
1968 11/7 – until 1969 4/12
1969 7/4 – 10/1
1971 1/24 – 5/23
1971 9/22 – 11/13
1975 3/25 – 5/6
1976 8/9 – 10/30
1977 3/27 – 6/8
1980 10/20 – until 1981 9/15
1983 1/3 – 7/11
1983 8/16 – 10/27
1987 3/9 – 4/20
1988 7/14 – 12/12
1989 2/28 – 5/23
1992 10/3 – until 1993 1/20
1993 2/6 – 8/29
1994 12/16 – until 1995 2/9
1995 5/24 – 10/7
1999 2/20 – 4/3
2000 6/23 – until 2001 5/6
2004 9/18 – 12/9
2005 3/29 – 8/9
2006 12/1 – until 2007 1/18
2007 7/4 – 9/9
2010 6/19 – 8/26
2011 1/31 – 3/17
2012 6/5 – Continues

SATURN BENEFICIAL
1938 2/2 – 4/27
1938 11/25 – until 1939 1/3
1942 4/27 – until 1943 5/27
1950 11/5 – until 1951 3/25
1951 7/30 – until 1952 1/3
1952 2/14 – 9/13
1956 2/2 – 4/20
1956 10/25 – until 1957 1/24
1957 5/25 – 10/23
1967 3/16 – 6/22
1967 8/26 – until 1968 3/5
1971 6/7 – until 1972 7/7
1973 1/12 – 3/17
1980 9/9 – until 1981 10/20
1985 11/30 – until 1986 11/29
1996 4/20 – 10/31
1997 1/5 – 4/10
2000 7/21 – 11/6
2001 4/8 – 9/6
2001 10/17 – until 2002 5/9
2009 10/17 – until 2010 5/1
2010 6/29 – 12/1
2011 3/26 – 8/26

URANUS BENEFICIAL
1941 6/30 – until 1946 4/13
1967 11/28 – until 1972 7/21
1981 12/12 – until 1984 10/28
2011 4/8 – Continues

NEPTUNE BENEFICIAL
1941 10/22 – until 1949 9/29
1970 12/19 – until 1976 9/29

PLUTO BENEFICIAL
1970 10/28 – until 1978 8/13
1995 12/21 – until 2000 11/3

JUPITER CHALLENGING
1940 5/10 – 8/9
1940 9/30 – until 1941 3/19

1943 6/24 – 9/5
1946 9/18 – 12/2
1952 4/22 – 7/5
1952 11/18 – until 1953 2/21
1954 10/18 – 12/16
1955 6/5 – 8/20
1957 12/31 – until 1958 4/3
1958 8/30 – 11/16
1964 4/6 – 6/14
1966 9/18 – until 1967 1/26
1967 5/13 – 8/4
1969 12/8 – until 1970 5/12
1970 8/4 – 10/31
1976 3/20 – 5/27
1978 8/29 – until 1979 7/19
1981 11/20 – until 1982 10/15
1987 7/24 – 9/15
1988 3/1 – 5/10
1990 8/11 – until 1991 7/2
1993 11/3 – until 1994 2/21
1994 3/7 – 9/28
1999 6/19 – 11/2
2000 2/5 – 4/24
2002 7/26 – 10/17
2003 1/22 – 6/12
2005 10/19 – until 2006 1/9
2006 4/30 – 9/8
2011 5/28 – until 2012 4/6

SATURN CHALLENGING
1939 6/17 – 10/12
1940 3/7 – 8/12
1940 9/11 – until 1941 4/11
1946 7/22 – until 1947 8/22
1953 10/10 – until 1954 11/26
1955 7/10 – 7/28
1969 4/18 – until 1970 5/22
1975 9/3 – until 1976 2/1
1976 5/21 – 10/7
1977 1/19 – 6/26
1982 11/16 – until 1983 5/29
1983 8/2 – until 1984 1/9
1984 4/12 – 10/3
1998 5/26 – 11/13
1999 2/12 – 7/5
1999 10/26 – until 2000 3/23
2005 7/5 – until 2006 8/5
2012 1/5 – 3/11
2012 9/23 – Continues

URANUS CHALLENGING
1938 1/1 – until 1939 3/5
1955 7/31 – until 1959 7/5
1974 10/28 – until 1978 10/4

NEPTUNE CHALLENGING
1955 11/7 – until 1963 10/17

PLUTO CHALLENGING
1938 1/1 – until 1949 6/9
1982 12/5 – until 1989 10/25

JUPITER SPECIAL
1938 1/1 – 2/20
1949 4/1 – 7/10
1949 11/23 – until 1950 2/4
1961 3/7 – 8/26
1961 10/21 – until 1962 1/19
1973 2/16 – until 1974 1/1
1985 1/31 – 4/26
1985 7/14 – 12/13
1997 1/15 – 3/29
1997 8/29 – 11/16
2008 12/30 – until 2009 3/9

SATURN SPECIAL
1961 3/30 – 6/19
1961 12/22 – until 1963 2/9
1991 1/25 – until 1992 3/17
1992 8/15 – 12/13

URANUS SPECIAL
1995 2/24 – until 1999 12/27

NEPTUNE SPECIAL
1997 2/17 – until 2005 1/21

January 28

SUN: AQUARIUS • DECANATE: AQUARIUS/URANUS • DEGREE: 7°–8° AQUARIUS • MODE: FIXED • ELEMENT: AIR

Your Personal Powers

Socially aware with strong instincts or fast responses, you are a bright and intelligent individual with unconventional views. You gain power from your decisive actions, assertive manner, and ability to evaluate people and situations in a flash. Astute and shrewd, you also have a gift for witticisms or smart replies. Your keen insight into human nature suggests that you are a liberal-minded humanitarian. Ambitious, with organizational skills or leadership ability, you prefer to think on a large scale. Innovative and enterprising, you are daring enough to pioneer new and exciting projects or ideas. Developing your innate diplomatic skills will keep you from losing power to impatience or being stubborn. Naturally dramatic, you have a need for self-expression that could manifest as creative and productive endeavors. Although you often have big plans and enjoy friendly competition, avoid losing power to a material streak. You often seek new and exciting knowledge or pursuits to keep you mentally stimulated. Your ability to quickly spot opportunities can particularly aid your overall success.

Your Powers of Attraction in Relationships

Idealistic and spirited, you can attract others with your resourceful and friendly nature. Team efforts can prove especially beneficial to you, but you may encounter a pull between working in partnerships and wanting to work alone. As you dislike being bored, you need a partner who can keep up with your fast mind and quick wit. Being dramatic and creative, you are a good friend or partner. Nevertheless, your love of freedom may cause you to be indecisive about commitment. Your relationships are still very important to you as you enjoy socializing and meeting new people. Very independent, if people tell you what to do, you may become sarcastic or difficult. Alternatively, being sensitive and generous, you can be very loving and give much of yourself, but avoid going too far at your expense. Your kindness and support can nevertheless be a source of inspiration for others.

Your attractive qualities: quick intelligence, leadership, good organizer, communication skills, good psychologist, compassionate, progressive, daring, artistic, independent, creative, idealistic, ambitious, hardworking, strong-willed, innovative

Your less attractive qualities: unmotivated, dreamer, unrealistic, bossy, self-pity, impatient, self-centered, aggressive, lack of confidence, sarcastic, irritable, intolerant, too dependent on others, too proud

Your Venus Power

The planet Venus has a great deal of influence on your powers of attraction. Below are four possible Venus types for women and men. To find your Venus you need to go to page 771, where you will find the Venus table and extra information. The planet Mars also affects your powers of attraction. To find your Mars table and interpretation go to page 761.

WOMEN WITH VENUS IN SAGITTARIUS: At your best when being optimistic and generous, you possess a mischievous sense of fun. In relationships, your open-minded approach to people and places may attract you to different cultures or make you tolerant of the foibles of others. Although warm and enthusiastic when in love, your natural honesty and idealism may inspire you to look for a partner who shares your love of freedom.

MEN WITH VENUS IN SAGITTARIUS: Forward-thinking rather than dwelling on the past, you are looking for a partner who can share your future plans. You enjoy exploring life whether through travel and mental pursuits or sports and games. Idealistic, you usually prefer the company of a partner who is optimistic and shares your beliefs. In your desire for honesty in relationships, however, be careful not to become tactless. Nevertheless, you are attracted to honest, direct, and fun-loving partners with a sense of humor like your own.

WOMEN WITH VENUS IN CAPRICORN: Loyal and responsible, you are attracted to dignified and reserved individuals. Being practical and security-conscious, you prefer hardworking partners who are resourceful and enterprising. Work may even be a factor in many of your associations and partnerships. For you, family and faithfulness can be especially important, so you are usually willing to work hard or make sacrifices in order to build a strong relationship.

MEN WITH VENUS IN CAPRICORN: Hardworking and ambitious, you are usually attracted to determined, focused, and ambitious partners with a strong sense of duty. You want them to take relationships as seriously as you do, so loyalty and faithfulness are high on your agenda. Since you may display a natural reserve about expressing your feelings in an intimate relationship, you need a partner who shares your need for emotional security.

WOMEN WITH VENUS IN AQUARIUS: When it comes to relationships others are attracted to your honest, friendly, and easygoing attitude. You really enjoy social interaction with others and may develop a genuine concern for humanity. Usually you present a tolerant and reasonable front in love situations and attempt to view your relationships objectively. If partners become too demanding, however, you can become stubborn and fixed. Friendship may be even more important for you than sexual compatibility.

MEN WITH VENUS IN AQUARIUS: You are sociable and open-minded, and people are attracted by your friendly and relaxed style. Being independent, you value freedom-loving partners who give you the space to be yourself. Others sometimes interpret your detachment as being emotionally cool, but they may not understand your progressive views on relationships. Friendship can sometimes be even more important than earthly passion. Ideally, your partners share your ideas on life and possess as strong a sense of originality as your own. Not easily ruffled, you can deal well with difficult situations or moody partners.

WOMEN WITH VENUS IN PISCES: Being sensitive to affairs of the heart, when you care for someone you can feel their emotions and sense their every mood. Their goals can even become as important as your own. This empathy indicates that you can love on an unselfish level, but you may have to guard against giving too much, especially to those who do not reciprocate. You are seductive and captivating, and partners may be fascinated by your subtle charms and attracted by your caring and affectionate nature.

MEN WITH VENUS IN PISCES: In love you are sensitive, tender, and affectionate, experiences your partner's feelings almost as strongly as your own. Being imaginative and a visionary, you possess the ability to develop a deep compassion for others. As you are idealistic when in love, you usually prefer to see only your partner's good points, but be careful that your high expectations do not bring disappointment if you avoid harsh reality. Nevertheless, in your relationships with others, you can be devoted, loving, and positively enchanting.

To read all about your Outer Planets and work out how to use your personalized timetable, go to Section Three, page 789.

≈≈≈

Your Personalized Timetable

JUPITER BENEFICIAL
1939 5/25 – 10/6
1940 1/11 – 3/3
1941 5/24 – 8/8
1941 12/14 – until 1942 3/29
1945 8/23 – 11/6
1947 11/5 – 12/20
1951 5/3 – 7/3
1951 9/4 – until 1952 2/12
1953 5/7 – 7/17
1956 12/9 – until 1957 2/23
1957 8/4 – 10/21
1959 10/19 – 12/4
1963 4/15 – 6/1
1963 10/22 – until 1964 1/17
1965 4/20 – 6/29
1968 11/13 – until 1969 4/3
1969 7/12 – 10/6
1971 1/31 – 5/15
1971 9/29 – 11/18
1975 3/29 – 5/11
1976 8/19 – 10/21
1977 4/1 – 6/12
1980 10/25 – until 1981 9/20
1983 1/8 – 6/27
1983 8/30 – 11/1
1987 3/13 – 4/24
1988 7/19 – 12/4
1989 3/8 – 5/27
1992 10/8 – until 1993 9/3
1994 12/21 – until 1995 2/17
1995 5/15 – 10/13
1999 2/24 – 4/7
2000 6/28 – until 2001 5/10
2004 9/23 – 12/17
2005 3/21 – 8/15
2006 12/5 – until 2007 1/23
2007 6/24 – 9/18
2010 7/1 – 8/14
2011 2/5 – 3/21
2012 6/9 – Continues

SATURN BENEFICIAL
1938 2/12 – 5/6
1938 11/4 – until 1939 1/22
1942 5/5 – until 1943 6/4
1950 11/16 – until 1951 3/12
1951 8/9 – until 1952 9/21
1956 2/25 – 3/28
1956 11/4 – until 1957 2/6
1957 5/10 – 11/2
1967 3/24 – until 1968 3/13
1971 6/15 – until 1972 1/30
1972 2/2 – 7/15
1972 12/28 – until 1973 4/1
1980 9/18 – until 1981 10/28
1982 6/8 – 6/28
1985 12/9 – until 1986 12/7
1996 4/30 – 10/15
1997 1/20 – 4/18
2000 8/3 – 10/22
2001 4/17 – until 2002 5/18
2009 10/26 – until 2010 4/13
2010 7/16 – 12/13
2011 3/11 – 9/4

URANUS BENEFICIAL
1941 7/24 – until 1946 5/5
1968 9/22 – until 1972 8/18
1981 12/30 – until 1984 11/15
2011 4/28 – Continues

NEPTUNE BENEFICIAL
1941 11/30 – until 1950 8/28
1971 1/23 – until 1976 11/5

PLUTO BENEFICIAL
1970 12/13 – until 1978 9/14
1996 1/23 – until 2001 9/6

JUPITER CHALLENGING
1940 5/14 – 8/28
1940 9/11 – until 1941 3/24
1943 6/29 – 9/10
1946 9/23 – 12/7
1952 4/27 – 7/11
1952 11/10 – until 1953 2/28
1954 11/2 – 12/1
1955 6/10 – 8/24
1958 1/9 – 3/24
1958 9/5 – 11/20
1964 4/10 – 6/19
1966 9/24 – until 1967 1/19
1967 5/20 – 8/9
1969 12/14 – until 1970 5/3
1970 8/12 – 11/5
1976 3/24 – 5/31
1978 9/3 – until 1979 3/7
1979 4/14 – 7/24
1981 11/25 – until 1982 10/20
1987 8/10 – 8/28
1988 3/6 – 5/15
1990 8/16 – until 1991 7/7
1993 11/8 – until 1994 10/3
1999 6/25 – 10/26
2000 2/12 – 4/28
2002 7/30 – 10/25
2003 1/13 – 6/18
2005 10/24 – until 2006 1/16
2006 4/21 – 9/14
2011 6/2 – until 2012 4/11

SATURN CHALLENGING
1939 6/30 – 9/28
1940 3/16 – until 1941 4/20
1946 7/30 – until 1947 8/30
1953 10/19 – until 1954 12/5
1955 6/11 – 8/25
1969 4/26 – until 1970 5/30
1975 9/13 – until 1976 1/19
1976 6/1 – 10/21
1977 1/4 – 7/5
1982 11/25 – until 1983 5/12
1983 8/19 – until 1984 1/25
1984 3/26 – 10/12
1998 6/5 – 10/31
1999 2/24 – 7/17
1999 10/12 – until 2000 4/1
2005 7/13 – until 2006 8/13
2012 10/2 – Continues

URANUS CHALLENGING
1938 1/1 – until 1939 3/29
1955 8/17 – until 1959 7/23
1974 11/14 – until 1978 10/22

NEPTUNE CHALLENGING
1955 12/8 – until 1964 9/10

PLUTO CHALLENGING
1938 7/20 – until 1949 7/20
1983 10/26 – until 1990 9/11

JUPITER SPECIAL
1938 1/1 – 2/25
1949 4/9 – 7/1
1949 11/28 – until 1950 2/8
1961 3/13 – 8/16
1961 10/31 – until 1962 1/23
1973 2/21 – until 1974 1/6
1985 2/4 – 5/6
1985 7/4 – 12/19
1997 1/19 – 4/4
1997 8/20 – 11/24
2009 1/3 – 3/14

SATURN SPECIAL
1961 4/22 – 5/27
1961 12/31 – until 1963 2/18
1991 2/3 – until 1992 3/28
1992 8/1 – 12/24

URANUS SPECIAL
1995 3/19 – until 2000 1/16

NEPTUNE SPECIAL
1997 3/26 – until 2005 12/19

January 29

Your Personal Powers

Forceful and creative with keen intelligence, you are a friendly and liberal individual with intuitive sensitivity. With a strong love of freedom, you are usually interested in the rights of others. You gain power from your ability to communicate your ideas in an entertaining and enlightening way. With your astute understanding of human nature, you can quickly assess others and mix easily with people from different social circles. Avoid losing power to inner tension and stress as they can often make you moody or stubborn. Usually thoughtful, however, you are an interesting blend of idealism and shrewd practicality. Very persuasive, you have a natural gift for the spoken or written word. A youthful quality can stay with you throughout life and suggests that you can see things from a broader perspective. Although you possess strong feelings and a need for self-expression, you may have to avoid going to extremes or acting too much on impulse. Nevertheless, when you find true inspiration, you are willing to work hard to achieve results and inspire others.

Your Powers of Attraction in Relationships

You attract people with your original approach, personal magnetism, and creative talents. Sociable and progressive, you usually enjoy the company of interesting and entertaining individuals, especially those who enjoy exploring new ideas. You also need a partner who can share your love of the beauty and luxuries of life. With all your sensitivity and idealism, you seek an almost perfect relationship and can give much in the way of love and affection. If your partner cannot live up to your high standards or expectations, you may encounter old insecurities or become withdrawn. Nevertheless, you usually have faith and can attract others with your positive enthusiasm and desire to help. Being independent, however, you need freedom within a relationship. You can be devoted and loyal to partners and a good companion.

Your attractive qualities: keen intelligence, idealistic, sensitive, analytical, inner peace, generous, faith, persuasive, people skills, successful, creative, inspirational, much spiritual potential, worldly, sociable, freedom fighter, progressive ideas, enterprising, honest

Your less attractive qualities: unfocused, insecure, nervous tension, moody, rebellious, cold, doubtful, argumenta-

tive, extremist, anxious, dreamer, too outspoken, stubborn, too sensitive

Your Venus Power

The planet Venus has a great deal of influence on your powers of attraction. Below are four possible Venus types for women and men. To find your Venus you need to go to page 771, where you will find the Venus table and extra information. The planet Mars also affects your powers of attraction. To find your Mars table and interpretation go to page 761.

WOMEN WITH VENUS IN SAGITTARIUS: When you feel generous, you can make others feel more optimistic about life. You may be interested in higher learning and seek partners who are scholarly or broad-minded. You are outspoken and direct and sometimes say things that you later regret. Curious and versatile, you can adjust quickly to new situations, and a foreign influence implies that you love to travel or may have a partner who comes from a different culture.

MEN WITH VENUS IN SAGITTARIUS: Your enthusiasm and straightforward conduct usually appeal to others and imply that you are approachable and easygoing. Being open to ideas and willing to believe that life has a great deal to offer suggest that you are generous, broad-minded, and eager to cooperate with others. A love of travel and an interest in other cultures imply that your partner may come from a foreign country.

WOMEN WITH VENUS IN CAPRICORN: Proud and refined, you attract others with your composed dignity. Disliking vulnerability and needing to feel safe before you can express your feelings, you display a strong front. Feeling insecure or inadequate in relationships may force you to become manipulative in order to regain control. Nevertheless, you can project an attractive sense of self-assurance and are capable of displaying loyalty and a wonderful dry sense of humor.

MEN WITH VENUS IN CAPRICORN: As you do not display your deeper emotions freely, you are usually dignified and controlled in your relationships. Practical and down-to-earth partners are particularly attractive to you, especially those who do not rush into expressing their feelings but seem to possess natural class and reserve. You need a partner who is loyal and dependable and willing to take your relationship seriously.

WOMEN WITH VENUS IN AQUARIUS: Usually you have a modern outlook on love and are open to new or current

lifestyles. Your intuitive abilities, communal sense, and people skills often allow you to see deeper into human intentions and to telepathically read people's thoughts. You are usually group-oriented and are drawn to individuals within the group who are independent and self-motivated. You are more inclined to choose a partner who is unconventional or freedom-loving. Conscious of your social standing, however, you want someone who can relate well to your friends.

Men with Venus in Aquarius: Although independent, you often enjoy being part of a group. The partners you frequently attract are often nonconformists or free spirits. As an individual you may not find it easy to settle into a routine or an entirely mundane type of relationship. You may have some unconventional views on traditional marriage or your partner may hold such views. Friendship is important to you as you enjoy sharing your progressive ideas.

Women with Venus in Pisces: Romantic and idealistic when in love, you can be a sensitive and responsive lover. With your affectionate and impressionable nature you are often attracted to those who understand your sensitivity and share your vision. Being flexible with an impressionable nature helps you to adapt to the needs of others. In your desire to blend with those you love, guard against giving too much of yourself by not clearly defining your boundaries.

Men with Venus in Pisces: The combination of your emotional subtlety and charm can make you very alluring when dealing with affairs of the heart. Perceptive and impressionable, you have an easygoing style in your relationships, usually preferring to avoid ugly confrontation. You are drawn to partners who have a touch of glamour and are sensitive to the needs of others. Alternatively, they can be visionaries with rich imaginations who can keep you enchanted.

To read all about your Outer Planets and work out how to use your personalized timetable, go to Section Three, page 789.

≈

Your Personalized Timetable

Jupiter Beneficial
1939 5/31 – 9/29
1940 1/18 – 3/8
1941 5/29 – 8/14
1941 12/7 – until **1942** 4/5
1945 8/28 – 11/12
1947 11/10 – 12/24
1951 5/8 – 7/16
1951 8/22 – until **1952** 2/17
1953 5/12 – 7/22
1954 1/31 – 2/20
1956 12/19 – until **1957** 2/13
1957 8/10 – 10/26
1959 10/24 – 12/9
1963 4/19 – 6/7
1963 10/14 – until **1964** 1/24
1965 4/25 – 7/4
1968 11/19 – until **1969** 3/26
1969 7/19 – 10/10
1971 2/7 – 5/6
1971 10/5 – 11/23
1975 4/2 – 5/16
1976 8/31 – 10/8
1977 4/6 – 6/17
1980 10/30 – until **1981** 5/17
1981 6/6 – 9/25
1983 1/14 – 6/17
1983 9/9 – 11/6
1987 3/17 – 4/28
1988 7/25 – 11/26
1989 3/15 – 6/1
1992 10/13 – until **1993** 9/8
1994 12/26 – until **1995** 2/26
1995 5/5 – 10/19
1999 3/1 – 4/11
2000 7/3 – until **2001** 5/15
2004 9/27 – 12/25
2005 3/12 – 8/21
2006 12/10 – until **2007** 1/29
2007 6/16 – 9/26
2011 2/10 – 3/25
2012 6/14 – Continues

Saturn Beneficial
1938 2/21 – 5/16
1938 10/21 – until **1939** 2/5
1942 5/13 – until **1943** 6/12
1950 11/28 – until **1951** 2/27
1951 8/19 – until **1952** 9/30
1956 11/12 – until **1957** 2/23
1957 4/22 – 11/11
1967 4/2 – until **1968** 3/22
1971 6/23 – 12/28
1972 3/4 – 7/25
1972 12/15 – until **1973** 4/12
1980 9/26 – until **1981** 11/6
1982 5/12 – 7/25
1985 12/17 – until **1986** 7/12
1986 9/2 – 12/16
1996 5/9 – 10/1
1997 2/1 – 4/27
1997 12/8 – 12/24
2000 8/23 – 10/2
2001 4/25 – until **2002** 5/26
2009 11/4 – until **2010** 3/30
2010 7/28 – 12/31
2011 2/21 – 9/13

Uranus Beneficial
1942 5/25 – until **1946** 5/23
1968 10/8 – until **1972** 9/7
1982 1/20 – until **1984** 12/2
2011 5/21 – Continues

Neptune Beneficial
1942 10/20 – until **1950** 9/27
1971 12/17 – until **1977** 9/23

Pluto Beneficial
1971 10/22 – until **1979** 7/22
1996 12/10 – until **2001** 10/26

Jupiter Challenging
1940 5/19 – until **1941** 3/29
1943 7/3 – 9/15
1946 9/28 – 12/12
1952 5/1 – 7/18
1952 11/3 – until **1953** 3/6
1955 6/16 – 8/29
1958 1/20 – 3/13
1958 9/10 – 11/25
1964 4/14 – 6/24
1964 12/24 – until **1965** 1/27
1966 10/1 – until **1967** 1/11
1967 5/27 – 8/13
1969 12/20 – until **1970** 4/25
1970 8/20 – 11/9
1976 3/29 – 6/5
1978 9/8 – until **1979** 2/22
1979 4/27 – 7/28
1981 11/30 – until **1982** 6/17
1982 7/8 – 10/25
1988 3/11 – 5/19
1990 8/21 – until **1991** 7/12
1993 11/13 – until **1994** 10/8
1999 7/2 – 10/18
2000 2/18 – 5/2
2002 8/4 – 11/3
2003 1/4 – 6/23
2005 10/28 – until **2006** 1/25
2006 4/12 – 9/20
2011 6/7 – 12/14
2012 1/6 – 4/15

Saturn Challenging
1939 7/17 – 9/10
1940 3/25 – until **1941** 4/28
1946 8/7 – until **1947** 9/8
1948 3/17 – 5/18
1953 10/27 – until **1954** 12/14
1955 5/26 – 9/9
1969 5/4 – until **1970** 6/7
1970 12/16 – until **1971** 2/17
1975 9/24 – until **1976** 1/6
1976 6/10 – 11/11
1976 12/14 – until **1977** 7/14
1982 12/5 – until **1983** 4/28
1983 8/31 – until **1984** 10/21
1998 6/15 – 10/18
1999 3/7 – 8/4
1999 9/24 – until **2000** 4/10
2005 7/21 – until **2006** 8/21
2012 10/11 – Continues

Uranus Challenging
1938 1/1 – until **1939** 4/17
1955 9/5 – until **1959** 8/8
1974 12/2 – until **1978** 11/7

Neptune Challenging
1956 11/4 – until **1964** 10/14

Pluto Challenging
1938 8/27 – until **1950** 6/29
1983 11/21 – until **1990** 10/13

Jupiter Special
1938 1/1 – 3/1
1949 4/18 – 6/21
1949 12/4 – until **1950** 2/13
1961 3/18 – 8/7
1961 11/8 – until **1962** 1/27
1973 2/26 – until **1974** 1/10
1985 2/9 – 5/21
1985 6/19 – 12/24
1997 1/24 – 4/10
1997 8/12 – 12/1
2009 1/8 – 3/19

Saturn Special
1962 1/9 – until **1963** 2/27
1963 10/8 – 11/4
1991 2/12 – 9/12
1991 10/27 – until **1992** 4/9
1992 7/18 – until **1993** 1/3

Uranus Special
1996 1/22 – until **2000** 2/3

Neptune Special
1998 2/14 – until **2006** 1/19

January 30

SUN: AQUARIUS • DECANATE: AQUARIUS/URANUS • DEGREE: 9°–10° AQUARIUS • MODE: FIXED • ELEMENT: AIR

Your Personal Powers

Independent, confident, and friendly, you are an original thinker with developed social skills. Your interest in people indicates that you possess an astute insight into human nature. You gain power from your enthusiasm, creativity, and ability to project success. Your innovative ideas can also bring you material rewards. Although you have innate leadership ability and can inspire others with your spirited approach, be careful that your rebel streak does not cause you to lose power to stubbornness or impatience. Nevertheless, you are usually sociable and insightful with ideas ahead of your time. Although your sharp intelligence ensures your quick comprehension, decision-making may not always be as easy. Be careful not to lose power to worry or boredom. Usually you have a genuine commitment to your work and are ambitious and determined. When you combine your strong intuition and ability to recognize new trends with your organizational and people skills, you have the potential to succeed in a big way.

Your Powers of Attraction in Relationships

You attract others with your quick intelligence, confidence, and friendly personality. Gregarious and fun-loving, you enjoy socializing. You are independent but you need a partner you can look admire and respect. Your dynamic mental approach to life suggests that your career or work can sometimes be more important than devoting yourself to a partner. Nevertheless, you are attracted to ambitious and hardworking individuals or those with power and influence. In your relationships you may need to be careful that your strong will does not lead you to become bossy or controlling. Usually optimistic and enthusiastic, you can be an amusing and uplifting friend or lover as well as an excellent parent. The more you develop your self-esteem, the more positive and decisive you become about your relationships.

Your attractive qualities: clever, sociable, leadership potential, loyal, friendly, artistic, good conversationalist, fun-loving, confident, creative, talent with words, idealistic, strong feelings, gregarious, entertaining, optimistic, affectionate, ambitious, enthusiastic

Your less attractive qualities: worry, insecure, lazy, obstinate, erratic, impatient, easily bored, temperamental, jealous, overindulgent, indecisive, lazy, critical, indifferent, scattered

Your Venus Power

The planet Venus has a great deal of influence on your powers of attraction. Below are four possible Venus types for women and men. To find your Venus you need to go to page 771, where you will find the Venus table and extra information. The planet Mars also affects your powers of attraction. To find your Mars table and interpretation go to page 761.

WOMEN WITH VENUS IN SAGITTARIUS: Optimistic and fun-loving, you love adventure and seek a partner who can expand your horizons. Being truthful and direct, you often say what you think, and at times you may be naively tactless. A need for expansion and prosperity suggests that you may enjoy traveling with your friends or partner. Being lighthearted and idealistic, once you have given your heart to someone you will stay honorable and loyal.

MEN WITH VENUS IN SAGITTARIUS: You are usually attracted to partners who are knowledgeable or well-traveled. Enthusiastic and optimistic, you often respond quickly to love offers and enter relationships with enthusiasm. Generally you seek to expand your social circle, and meeting people from all walks of life can bring the variety and fun that you seek in life. Although you are generous and honest, your partners may sometimes accuse you of being overly optimistic or too blunt.

WOMEN WITH VENUS IN CAPRICORN: With your natural caution in romantic affairs, you often appear reserved and controlled. You may be shy but try to be more forward, especially if you want to be noticed. When you care about people, however, you are usually willing to put in extra time and energy to preserve the relationship. You are practical and dependable, and a sense of duty can often play a large role in affairs of your heart. With elegant simplicity you can attract others with your well-cut clothes and refined manners.

MEN WITH VENUS IN CAPRICORN: In relationships you take love seriously and can be a strong and practical support for friends or partners. You are usually attracted to partners who are as hardworking as you. As you tend not to express your feelings until you feel really secure in a relationship, you may be drawn to those who seem loyal, faithful, and not likely to let you down. As you respect the wisdom of experience, you may be drawn to mature partners or, alternatively, you may act as an authority figure for someone younger.

WOMEN WITH VENUS IN AQUARIUS: You attract and impress others with your friendly approach and progressive ideas. As you are usually independent and easygoing, you value free-

dom within a relationship. A good companion with a sense of your own person, you enjoy socializing, especially with people who are original, cosmopolitan, and have a strong sense of individuality. Although being friendly and detached usually serves you well, avoid losing touch with your emotions. You usually prefer the company of those who have innovative or progressive views.

MEN WITH VENUS IN AQUARIUS: You are sociable and open-minded, and people are attracted by your friendly and easygoing style. Being independent, you value freedom-loving partners who give you the space to be yourself. People can sometimes interpret your detachment as being emotionally cool, but they admire your objectivity and humanitarian inclinations. You are attracted to intelligent individuals who are as truthful and direct as you are, but above all they must be true friends. Ideally, your partner shares your liberal views on life and possesses a strong sense of individuality.

WOMEN WITH VENUS IN PISCES: Romantic and idealistic when in love, you can be a sensitive and responsive lover. With your affectionate and impressionable nature you are often attracted to those who understand your sensitivity and share your vision. Being flexible with an impressionable nature helps you to adapt to the needs of others. In your desire to blend with those you love, guard against giving too much of yourself by not defining your boundaries clearly.

MEN WITH VENUS IN PISCES: The combination of your emotional subtlety and charm can make you very alluring when dealing with affairs of the heart. Perceptive and impressionable, you have an easygoing style in your relationships, usually preferring to avoid ugly confrontation. You are drawn to a woman who has a touch of glamour and is sensitive to the needs of others. Alternatively, she can be a visionary with a rich imagination who can keep you enchanted.

To read all about your Outer Planets and work out how to use your personalized timetable, go to Section Three, page 789.

Your Personalized Timetable

JUPITER BENEFICIAL
1939 6/7 – until 1940 3/12
1941 6/2 – 8/21
1941 11/29 – until 1942 4/11
1945 9/2 – 11/17
1946 6/4 – 6/25
1947 11/14 – 12/29
1951 5/13 – 11/15
1951 12/14 – until 1952 2/22
1953 5/16 – 7/27
1954 1/14 – 3/9
1957 1/6 – 1/26
1957 8/15 – 10/31
1959 10/29 – 12/13
1963 4/23 – 6/13
1963 10/7 – until 1964 1/31
1965 4/29 – 7/8
1968 11/26 – until 1969 3/18
1969 7/26 – 10/15
1971 2/16 – 4/27
1971 10/10 – 11/27
1975 4/6 – 5/21
1977 4/11 – 6/21
1980 11/4 – until 1981 4/29
1981 6/25 – 9/29
1983 1/19 – 6/8
1983 9/17 – 11/11
1987 3/22 – 5/3
1988 8/1 – 11/18
1989 3/21 – 6/5
1992 10/18 – until 1993 9/13
1994 12/31 – until 1995 3/10
1995 4/23 – 10/24
1999 3/5 – 4/16
2000 7/8 – until 2001 1/9
2001 2/10 – 5/19
2004 10/2 – until 2005 1/4
2005 3/2 – 8/27
2006 12/15 – until 2007 2/4
2007 6/8 – 10/3
2011 2/14 – 3/30
2012 6/18 – Continues

SATURN BENEFICIAL
1938 3/2 – until 1939 2/16
1942 5/21 – until 1943 6/20
1950 12/14 – until 1951 2/10
1951 8/28 – until 1952 10/8
1956 11/21 – until 1957 11/20
1967 4/10 – until 1968 3/30
1971 7/2 – 12/13
1972 3/19 – 8/4
1972 12/2 – until 1973 4/23
1980 10/4 – until 1981 11/15
1982 4/26 – 8/9
1985 12/27 – until 1986 6/22
1986 9/20 – 12/25
1987 8/9 – 8/29
1996 5/20 – 9/18
1997 2/11 – 5/5
1997 11/11 – until 1998 1/20
2001 5/4 – until 2002 6/3
2009 11/14 – until 2010 3/17
2010 8/8 – until 2011 9/22

URANUS BENEFICIAL
1942 6/12 – until 1946 6/10
1968 10/25 – until 1972 9/24
1982 3/8 – until 1985 10/1
2012 3/26 – Continues

NEPTUNE BENEFICIAL
1942 11/25 – until 1951 8/26
1972 1/19 – until 1977 11/3

PLUTO BENEFICIAL
1971 11/26 – until 1979 9/2
1997 1/8 – until 2001 11/24

JUPITER CHALLENGING
1940 5/23 – until 1941 4/2
1943 7/8 – 9/21

1944 3/24 – 5/2
1946 10/3 – 12/17
1952 5/5 – 7/25
1952 10/26 – until 1953 3/12
1955 6/21 – 9/3
1958 2/10 – 2/19
1958 9/16 – 11/30
1964 4/19 – 6/29
1964 12/11 – until 1965 2/9
1966 10/9 – until 1967 1/3
1967 6/2 – 8/18
1969 12/27 – until 1970 4/17
1970 8/26 – 11/14
1976 4/2 – 6/9
1978 9/14 – until 1979 2/12
1979 5/6 – 8/2
1981 12/5 – until 1982 5/30
1982 7/26 – 10/29
1988 3/16 – 5/23
1990 8/26 – until 1991 7/17
1993 11/18 – until 1994 10/13
1999 7/9 – 10/11
2000 2/24 – 5/7
2002 8/9 – 11/17
2002 12/21 – until 2003 6/29
2005 11/2 – until 2006 2/4
2006 4/2 – 9/26
2011 6/12 – 11/28
2012 1/22 – 4/20

SATURN CHALLENGING
1940 4/2 – until 1941 5/5
1946 8/15 – until 1947 9/16
1948 2/29 – 6/2
1953 11/5 – until 1954 12/24
1955 5/12 – 9/21
1969 5/13 – until 1970 6/16
1970 12/1 – until 1971 3/4
1975 10/7 – 12/23
1976 6/20 – until 1977 7/22
1982 12/16 – until 1983 4/15
1983 9/11 – until 1984 10/30
1998 6/27 – 10/4
1999 3/16 – until 2000 4/18
2005 7/29 – until 2006 8/29

URANUS CHALLENGING
1938 1/1 – until 1939 5/5
1955 9/29 – until 1960 6/3
1974 12/24 – until 1979 9/5

NEPTUNE CHALLENGING
1956 12/4 – until 1965 9/6

PLUTO CHALLENGING
1939 8/14 – until 1951 5/30
1983 12/24 – until 1991 8/12

JUPITER SPECIAL
1938 1/1 – 3/6
1949 5/2 – until 1950 2/17
1961 3/24 – 7/30
1961 11/15 – until 1962 1/31
1973 3/3 – until 1974 1/15
1985 2/13 – 12/29
1997 1/28 – 4/16
1997 8/4 – 12/7
2009 1/12 – 3/24
2009 9/26 – 10/29

SATURN SPECIAL
1962 1/17 – until 1963 3/8
1963 9/13 – 11/28
1991 2/21 – 8/23
1991 11/15 – until 1992 4/26
1992 6/30 – until 1993 1/12

URANUS SPECIAL
1996 2/9 – until 2000 12/7

NEPTUNE SPECIAL
1998 3/20 – until 2006 12/14

January 31

SUN: AQUARIUS • DECANATE: GEMINI/MERCURY • DEGREE: 10°–11° AQUARIUS • MODE: FIXED • ELEMENT: AIR

Your Personal Powers

Mentally sharp with an independent manner, you are an energetic individual with progressive views. Inventive and freedom-loving, you possess a gift for penetrating the psychology of others as well as dealing with your own insecurities. Preferring to be direct, you gain power from your quick mental responses and talent for communication. A natural predilection for business combined with good organizational skills is likely to aid you in your climb to success. Although you possess a fast mind, by developing patience and tolerance, you avoid losing power by being rebellious, stubborn, or bored. Nevertheless, dramatic and often ahead of your time, you have a strong need to express your idealism and creativity. If you apply the necessary discipline and positive mental focus, your strong willpower and determination can help you put your ideas into a practical form. Allowing yourself to be negatively focused is likely to drain you of power through frustration or disappointment. However, you are usually untiring and open-minded with a generous spirit and the potential to achieve remarkable results.

Your Powers of Attraction in Relationships

Naturally friendly, you have no trouble attracting friends and admirers. Generous and giving to loved ones, you are attracted to people who can match your loyalty and intelligence. At times, you can doubt yourself, so you need a supportive partner who understands your emotional fears or uncertainty. Being creative in your approach to life, you want encouragement to bring out the best of your talents. Once in a long-term relationship, your sense of duty or responsibility can match your high ideals of romance and encourage you to take your relationships much more seriously. For you, it is important to get the balance right between being independent and needing others. It really benefits your relationships when you discuss and clearly communicate your feelings to your partner.

Your attractive qualities: good mind, creative, hardworking, original, practical, good organizer, business sense, fun-loving, sincere, willpower, constructive, friendly, persistent, practical, persevering, responsible, good conversationalist, freedom-loving, determined, generous

Your less attractive qualities: disappointing, insecure, frustrated, impatient, suspicious, easily discouraged, too security-conscious, obstinate, lack of ambition, rigid, impatient, selfish, stubborn

Your Venus Power

The planet Venus has a great deal of influence on your powers of attraction. Below are four possible Venus types for women and men. To find your Venus you need to go to page 771, where you will find the Venus table and extra information. The planet Mars also affects your powers of attraction. To find your Mars table and interpretation go to page 761.

WOMEN WITH VENUS IN SAGITTARIUS: At your best when being optimistic and generous, you possess a mischievous sense of fun. In relationships, your open-minded approach to people and places may attract you to different cultures or make you tolerant of the foibles of others. Although warm and enthusiastic when in love, your natural honesty and idealism may inspire you to look for a partner who shares your love of freedom.

MEN WITH VENUS IN SAGITTARIUS: Forward-thinking rather than dwelling on the past, you are looking for a partner who can share your future plans. You enjoy exploring life whether through travel and mental pursuits or sports and games. Idealistic, you usually prefer the company of a partner who is optimistic and shares your beliefs. In your desire for honesty in relationships, however, be careful not to become tactless. Nevertheless, you are attracted to honest, direct, and fun-loving partners with a sense of humor like your own.

WOMEN WITH VENUS IN CAPRICORN: With your natural caution in romantic affairs, you often appear reserved and controlled. You may be shy but try to be more forward, especially if you want to be noticed. When you care about people, however, you are usually willing to put in extra time and energy to preserve the relationship. You are practical and dependable, and a sense of duty can often play a large role in affairs of your heart. With elegant simplicity, you can attract others with your well-cut clothes and refined manners.

MEN WITH VENUS IN CAPRICORN: In relationships you take love seriously and can be a strong and practical support for friends or partners. You are usually attracted to partners who are as hardworking as you. As you tend not to express your feelings until you feel really secure in a relationship, you

may be drawn to those who seem loyal, faithful, and not likely to let you down. As you respect the wisdom of experience, you may be drawn to mature partners or, alternatively, you may act as an authority figure for someone younger.

WOMEN WITH VENUS IN AQUARIUS: When it comes to relationships others are attracted to your honest, friendly, and easygoing attitude. You really enjoy social interaction with others and may develop a genuine concern for humanity. Usually you present a tolerant and reasonable front in love situations and attempt to view your relationships objectively. If partners become too demanding, however, you can become stubborn and fixed. Friendship may be even more important for you than sexual compatibility.

MEN WITH VENUS IN AQUARIUS: Sociable and open-minded, you attract people with your friendly and relaxed style. Being independent, you value freedom-loving partners who give you the space to be yourself. Others sometimes interpret your detachment as being emotionally cool, but they may not understand your progressive views on relationships. Friendship can sometimes be even more important than earthly passion. Ideally, your partners share your ideas on life and possess a sense of originality as strong as your own. Not easily ruffled, you can deal well with difficult situations or moody partners.

WOMEN WITH VENUS IN PISCES: As a romantic and idealistic individual you can be both loving and giving. In relationships you may need to balance the practical with the charitable. While making allowances and sacrifices is understandable in a loving relationship, playing the martyr is often a state of romantic illusion that can lead to self-deception. Your benevolence and sacrifices in the right relationship nonetheless make you a partner who is devoted, kind, and compassionate. Subtle, sensitive, and alluring, you make a sensual and caring partner.

MEN WITH VENUS IN PISCES: Romantic and idealistic when in love, you can be a sensitive and responsive lover. Being pliant and flexible with an impressionable nature helps you to adapt to the needs of others. In your desire to blend with those you love, however, guard against not clearly defining your own boundaries. With your affectionate and sentimental nature you are often attracted to those who understand your sensitivity and share your vision.

To read all about your Outer Planets and work out how to use your personalized timetable, go to Section Three, page 789.

≈

Your Personalized Timetable

JUPITER BENEFICIAL
1939 6/14 – until 1940 3/17
1941 6/6 – 8/29
1941 11/21 – until 1942 4/17
1945 9/7 – 11/22
1946 5/17 – 7/13
1947 11/19 – until 1948 1/3
1951 5/18 – 11/1
1951 12/28 – until 1952 2/27
1953 5/20 – 8/1
1954 1/4 – 3/19
1957 8/21 – 11/5
1959 11/3 – 12/18
1963 4/28 – 6/20
1963 9/29 – until 1964 2/6
1965 5/4 – 7/13
1968 12/3 – until 1969 3/10
1969 8/1 – 10/20
1971 2/28 – 4/15
1971 10/16 – 12/2
1975 4/11 – 5/26
1975 11/17 – until 1976 1/2
1977 4/16 – 6/26
1980 11/10 – until 1981 4/18
1981 7/5 – 10/4
1983 1/26 – 5/31
1983 9/24 – 11/16
1987 3/26 – 5/7
1988 8/8 – 11/11
1989 3/27 – 6/9
1992 10/23 – until 1993 9/18
1995 1/5 – 7/25
1995 8/10 – 10/30
1999 3/9 – 4/20
2000 7/13 – 12/26
2001 2/23 – 5/24
2004 10/7 – until 2005 1/21
2005 2/13 – 9/1
2006 12/19 – until 2007 2/11
2007 5/31 – 10/10
2011 2/19 – 4/3
2012 6/23 – Continues

SATURN BENEFICIAL
1938 3/10 – 6/6
1938 9/25 – until 1939 2/26
1942 5/29 – until 1943 6/28
1951 9/6 – until 1952 10/16
1956 11/30 – until 1957 11/29
1967 4/18 – until 1968 4/7
1971 7/12 – 11/30
1972 3/30 – 8/16
1972 11/19 – until 1973 5/2
1980 10/12 – until 1981 11/25
1982 4/12 – 8/21
1986 1/5 – 6/7
1986 10/4 – until 1987 1/3
1987 7/12 – 9/25
1996 6/2 – 9/4
1997 2/20 – 5/15
1997 10/26 – until 1998 2/3
2001 5/12 – until 2002 6/10
2009 11/26 – until 2010 3/4
2010 8/18 – until 2011 10/1

URANUS BENEFICIAL
1942 7/1 – until 1947 4/11
1968 11/14 – until 1972 10/10
1982 5/14 – until 1985 10/26
2012 4/13 – Continues

NEPTUNE BENEFICIAL
1943 10/18 – until 1951 9/26
1972 12/14 – until 1978 9/15

PLUTO BENEFICIAL
1972 10/14 – until 1979 9/30
1997 12/2 – until 2002 10/18

JUPITER CHALLENGING
1940 5/28 – until 1941 4/7
1943 7/13 – 9/26
1944 3/11 – 5/15

1946 10/8 – 12/22
1947 6/20 – 8/10
1952 5/10 – 8/2
1952 10/18 – until 1953 3/18
1955 6/26 – 9/8
1958 9/21 – 12/5
1964 4/23 – 7/4
1964 12/1 – until 1965 2/18
1966 10/18 – 12/25
1967 6/7 – 8/23
1970 1/3 – 4/9
1970 9/2 – 11/19
1976 4/6 – 6/14
1978 9/19 – until 1979 2/4
1979 5/14 – 8/7
1981 12/11 – until 1982 5/19
1982 8/5 – 11/3
1988 3/20 – 5/28
1990 8/31 – until 1991 7/21
1993 11/23 – until 1994 10/18
1999 7/17 – 10/2
2000 2/29 – 5/11
2002 8/13 – until 2003 7/4
2005 11/7 – until 2006 2/21
2006 3/16 – 10/1
2011 6/18 – 11/18
2012 1/31 – 4/24

SATURN CHALLENGING
1940 4/11 – until 1941 5/13
1946 8/23 – until 1947 3/7
1947 5/1 – 9/26
1948 2/16 – 6/15
1953 11/13 – until 1955 1/4
1955 4/29 – 10/2
1969 5/21 – 12/9
1970 1/28 – 6/26
1970 11/18 – until 1971 3/16
1975 10/27 – 12/3
1976 6/28 – until 1977 7/30
1982 12/28 – until 1983 4/1
1983 9/21 – until 1984 11/7
1998 7/12 – 9/18
1999 3/25 – until 2000 4/26
2005 8/6 – until 2006 9/6
2007 3/27 – 5/13

URANUS CHALLENGING
1938 1/1 – until 1940 3/6
1956 7/25 – until 1960 6/27
1975 10/23 – until 1979 9/29

NEPTUNE CHALLENGING
1957 11/3 – until 1965 10/13

PLUTO CHALLENGING
1939 9/29 – until 1951 7/15
1984 11/8 – until 1991 9/30

JUPITER SPECIAL
1938 1/1 – 3/10
1949 12/14 – until 1950 2/21
1961 3/31 – 7/22
1961 11/22 – until 1962 2/5
1973 3/8 – 9/14
1973 10/12 – until 1974 1/19
1985 2/18 – until 1986 1/2
1997 2/1 – 4/24
1997 7/27 – 12/13
2009 1/16 – 3/29
2009 9/13 – 11/12

SATURN SPECIAL
1962 1/26 – until 1963 3/17
1963 8/28 – 12/12
1991 3/3 – 8/7
1991 11/29 – until 1993 1/21

URANUS SPECIAL
1996 2/28 – until 2000 12/31

NEPTUNE SPECIAL
1999 2/12 – until 2007 1/16

February 1

SUN: AQUARIUS · DECANATE: GEMINI/MERCURY · DEGREE: 11°–12° AQUARIUS · MODE: FIXED · ELEMENT: AIR

Your Personal Powers

Independent with an alert mind, you are an innovative individual with the ability to impress others. With your strong individuality you can accomplish much doing things your way. You gain power from your insight into human nature, compelling speech, fast responses, and desire to keep improving your knowledge. You may, however, lose power if you become involved in opportunism or have too much self-interest. Usually you enjoy a mental challenge and your pioneering spirit often encourages you to stand up for new ideas or take the lead. The ambitious yet humanitarian side to your nature likes to advance people by inspiring them to take positive action or become involved in social reforms. Although you can be strong-willed and dislike constraint of any kind, avoid losing power through dominating or contentious behavior. You may particularly achieve power through your work, as it helps you to develop self-discipline and perseverance. When inspired, you possess mental dynamism, daring, and an inner vitality that can help you win success.

Your Powers of Attraction in Relationships

You can attract others with your originality, progressive ideas, and sociability. Very independent, you need a partner who will give you freedom within a relationship. Although you may not show it, underneath your determined and self-confident front you can be sensitive. You are attracted to those who are caring or easygoing. Partners who can provide you with a sense of security or a harmonious home environment can also seem very attractive. In relationships you will always retain a playful, youthful charm, but you also need to stay flexible and display integrity in all your dealings. With your sense of the dramatic you can be romantic and idealistic, but to keep your loved ones happy remember to stay in touch with their needs and emotions.

Your attractive qualities: leadership, creative, progressive, common sense, forceful, optimistic, persuasive speech, strong convictions, competitive, independent, gregarious, originality, courageous, individuality, inspirational, pioneering, original ideas, inventiveness

Your less attractive qualities: self-centered, stubborn, too proud, antagonistic, lack of restraint, mental tension, dictatorial, contentious, jealous, selfish, impatient, insecure, argumentative, inner restlessness

Your Venus Power

The planet Venus has a great deal of influence on your powers of attraction. Below are four possible Venus types for women and men. To find your Venus you need to go to page 771, where you will find the Venus table and extra information. The planet Mars also affects your powers of attraction. To find your Mars table and interpretation go to page 761.

WOMEN WITH VENUS IN SAGITTARIUS: Optimistic and fun-loving, you love adventure and seek a partner who can expand your horizons. Being truthful and direct, you often say what you think, and at times you may be naively tactless. A need for expansion and prosperity suggests that you may enjoy traveling with your friends or partner. Being lighthearted and idealistic, once you have given your heart to someone you will stay honorable and loyal.

MEN WITH VENUS IN SAGITTARIUS: You are usually attracted to partners who are knowledgeable or well-traveled. Enthusiastic and optimistic, you often respond quickly to love offers and enter relationships with enthusiasm. Generally you seek to expand your social circle, and meeting people from all walks of life can bring the variety and fun that you seek in life. Although you are generous and honest, your partners may sometimes accuse you of being overly optimistic or too blunt.

WOMEN WITH VENUS IN CAPRICORN: Loyal and responsible, you are attracted to dignified and reserved individuals. Being practical and security-conscious, you prefer hardworking partners who are resourceful and enterprising. Work may even be a factor in many of your associations and partnerships. For you, family and faithfulness can be especially important, so you are usually willing to work hard or make sacrifices in order to build a strong relationship.

MEN WITH VENUS IN CAPRICORN: Hardworking and ambitious, you are usually attracted to determined, focused, and ambitious partners with a strong sense of duty. You want them to take relationships as seriously as you do, so loyalty and faithfulness are high on your agenda. Since you may display a natural reserve about expressing your feelings in an intimate relationship, you need a partner who shares your need for emotional security.

WOMEN WITH VENUS IN AQUARIUS: When it comes to relationships, others are attracted to your honest, friendly, and easygoing attitude. You really enjoy social interaction with others and may develop a genuine concern for humanity. Usually you present a tolerant and reasonable front in love situations and attempt to view your relationships objectively. If partners become too demanding, however, you can become stubborn and fixed. Friendship may be even more important for you than sexual compatibility.

MEN WITH VENUS IN AQUARIUS: You are sociable and open-minded, and people are attracted by your friendly and relaxed style. Being independent, you value freedom-loving partners who give you the space to be yourself. Others sometimes interpret your detachment as being emotionally cool, but they may not understand your progressive views on relationships. Friendship can sometimes be even more important than earthly passion. Ideally, friends can share your ideas on life and possess a sense of originality as strong as your own. Not easily ruffled, you can deal well with difficult situations or moody partners.

WOMEN WITH VENUS IN PISCES: Being sensitive to affairs of the heart, when you care for someone, you can feel their emotions and sense their every mood. Their goals can even become as important as your own. This empathy indicates that you can love on an unselfish level, but you may have to guard against giving too much, especially to those who do not reciprocate. You are seductive and captivating, and partners can be fascinated by your subtle charms and attracted by your caring and affectionate nature.

MEN WITH VENUS IN PISCES: Being adaptable and sensitive, you are able to intuitively feel the moods of those you love. Although you are receptive to others, you can be ambiguous about your own feelings toward your partner. Romantic and kindhearted, you long to be loved but you need to be realistic about your relationships in order to avoid disappointments. When in love you may idealize your partners and fail to see any faults in their personality.

To read all about your Outer Planets and work out how to use your personalized timetable, go to Section Three, page 789.

≋

Your Personalized Timetable

JUPITER BENEFICIAL	**1944** 3/2 – 5/25
1939 6/23 – 9/4	**1946** 10/12 – 12/28
1940 2/4 – 3/21	**1947** 6/9 – 8/21
1941 6/11 – 9/6	**1952** 5/14 – 8/12
1941 11/12 – until **1942** 4/22	**1952** 10/8 – until **1953** 3/23
1945 9/11 – 11/28	**1955** 7/1 – 9/13
1946 5/6 – 7/24	**1958** 9/26 – 12/10
1947 11/23 – until **1948** 1/8	**1964** 4/27 – 7/10
1951 5/23 – 10/22	**1964** 11/23 – until **1965** 2/26
1952 1/7 – 3/3	**1966** 10/30 – 12/13
1953 5/25 – 8/7	**1967** 6/13 – 8/27
1953 12/26 – until **1954** 3/28	**1970** 1/11 – 3/31
1957 8/26 – 11/10	**1970** 9/7 – 11/23
1959 11/7 – 12/22	**1976** 4/11 – 6/19
1963 5/3 – 6/28	**1978** 9/26 – until **1979** 1/27
1963 9/21 – until **1964** 2/11	**1979** 5/22 – 8/11
1965 5/8 – 7/18	**1981** 12/16 – until **1982** 5/10
1968 12/11 – until **1969** 3/1	**1982** 8/14 – 11/8
1969 8/7 – 10/24	**1988** 3/25 – 6/1
1971 10/21 – 12/6	**1990** 9/5 – until **1991** 3/23
1975 4/15 – 5/31	**1991** 4/7 – 7/26
1975 11/6 – until **1976** 1/13	**1993** 11/28 – until **1994** 10/23
1977 4/21 – 6/30	**1999** 7/27 – 9/22
1980 11/16 – until **1981** 4/9	**2000** 3/6 – 5/15
1981 7/14 – 10/9	**2002** 8/18 – until **2003** 7/9
1983 2/1 – 5/23	**2005** 11/12 – until **2006** 10/6
1983 9/30 – 11/20	**2011** 6/23 – 11/10
1987 3/30 – 5/12	**2012** 2/8 – 4/28
1988 8/16 – 11/3	
1989 4/2 – 6/14	**SATURN CHALLENGING**
1992 10/28 – until **1993** 9/23	**1940** 4/19 – until **1941** 5/21
1995 1/10 – 7/6	**1946** 9/1 – until **1947** 2/18
1995 8/30 – 11/4	**1947** 5/18 – 10/6
1999 3/13 – 4/24	**1948** 2/4 – 6/25
2000 7/18 – 12/17	**1953** 11/22 – until **1954** 5/31
2001 3/5 – 5/28	**1954** 8/11 – until **1955** 1/17
2004 10/12 – until **2005** 9/7	**1955** 4/14 – 10/12
2006 12/24 – until **2007** 2/19	**1969** 5/30 – 11/21
2007 5/22 – 10/16	**1970** 2/14 – 7/6
2011 2/24 – 4/7	**1970** 11/5 – until **1971** 3/26
2012 6/28 – Continues	**1976** 7/6 – until **1977** 8/7
	1983 1/13 – 3/15
SATURN BENEFICIAL	**1983** 9/30 – until **1984** 11/16
1938 3/18 – 6/20	**1999** 4/2 – until **2000** 5/4
1938 9/10 – until **1939** 3/7	**2005** 8/14 – until **2006** 9/15
1942 6/6 – until **1943** 7/6	**2007** 3/8 – 5/31
1951 9/14 – until **1952** 10/25	
1956 12/8 – until **1957** 12/8	**URANUS CHALLENGING**
1967 4/27 – 11/5	**1938** 1/1 – until **1940** 3/31
1968 1/11 – 4/15	**1956** 8/11 – until **1960** 7/16
1971 7/22 – 11/18	**1975** 11/9 – until **1979** 10/18
1972 4/9 – 8/31	
1972 11/4 – until **1973** 5/11	**NEPTUNE CHALLENGING**
1980 10/21 – until **1981** 5/8	**1957** 12/2 – until **1966** 8/31
1981 7/3 – 12/6	
1982 3/30 – 8/31	**PLUTO CHALLENGING**
1986 1/16 – 5/24	**1940** 9/8 – until **1952** 6/19
1986 10/15 – until **1987** 1/12	**1984** 12/6 – until **1991** 10/28
1987 6/26 – 10/10	
1996 6/19 – 8/17	**JUPITER SPECIAL**
1997 3/1 – 5/25	**1938** 1/5 – 3/15
1997 10/13 – until **1998** 2/14	**1949** 12/19 – until **1950** 2/25
2001 5/20 – until **2002** 6/18	**1961** 4/7 – 7/14
2009 12/11 – until **2010** 2/16	**1961** 11/28 – until **1962** 2/9
2010 8/27 – until **2011** 10/9	**1973** 3/13 – 8/30
	1973 10/27 – until **1974** 1/24
URANUS BENEFICIAL	**1985** 2/23 – until **1986** 1/7
1942 7/24 – until **1947** 5/4	**1997** 2/6 – 5/2
1968 12/12 – until **1973** 8/6	**1997** 7/18 – 12/18
1982 12/27 – until **1985** 11/14	**2009** 1/21 – 4/4
2012 5/3 – Continues	**2009** 9/3 – 11/21
NEPTUNE BENEFICIAL	**SATURN SPECIAL**
1943 11/21 – until **1952** 8/22	**1962** 2/3 – until **1963** 3/27
1973 1/14 – until **1978** 11/1	**1963** 8/14 – 12/24
	1991 3/13 – 7/25
PLUTO BENEFICIAL	**1991** 12/10 – until **1993** 1/30
1972 11/14 – until **1980** 8/17	
1997 12/28 – until **2002** 11/18	**URANUS SPECIAL**
	1996 3/22 – until **2001** 1/20
JUPITER CHALLENGING	
1940 6/1 – until **1941** 4/12	**NEPTUNE SPECIAL**
1943 7/17 – 10/2	**1999** 3/16 – until **2007** 12/8

February 2

SUN: AQUARIUS · DECANATE: GEMINI/MERCURY · DEGREE: 12°–13° AQUARIUS · MODE: FIXED · ELEMENT: AIR

Your Personal Powers

Quick receptivity, good communication skills, and the ability to assess people accurately are among your personal strengths. You gain power from the combination of your original ideas, natural talent with words, and your strong imagination. Being success-oriented, you are usually willing to work hard to achieve your objectives. Although generally a fast, objective thinker who loves new experiences, avoid losing power by becoming impatient or so detached you appear indifferent. Nevertheless, you are generally friendly and sociable with a liberal outlook and a direct and honest approach. The special blend of your intuitive mind and emotional sensitivity create a strong sixth sense that can aid your overall success. An independent thinker, you may wish to channel your innate talents through art, music, writing, drama, or by developing your spiritual potential. If you decide to take the path of escapism, however, you will lose your self-confidence and power. Fortunately, your innate pragmatism also confers you with a natural business sense and the determination to market your inspired ideas.

Your Powers of Attraction in Relationships

Friendly and sociable, you can attract others with your courteous manner and original approach. Although you value your independence you also enjoy being able to interact with others. Witty and amusing, you can be very persuasive and a clever conversationalist. However, do not allow concerns about money to affect your close relationships. You are attracted to creative and enterprising individuals who can amuse or mentally stimulate you. If you become indecisive about your love life, you need to stay focused on your own creative ideas rather than worry. With an inner sense of the dramatic you enjoy the romantic part of a relationship but you also highly value friendship. Ambitious and security conscious, you may have to balance your inspired objectives with your need for relationship.

Your attractive qualities: success-oriented, friendly, good communication skills, diplomatic, tactful, good partnerships or group member, sociable, visionary, leadership potential, inner sensitivity, common sense, imaginative, humanitarian, intuitive, clever, considerate, honest

Your less attractive qualities: inner tension, stubborn, suspicious, lack of confidence, dependent, irritable, too sensitive, addictive tendencies, discontent, selfish, impatient, deceptive, too proud, escapist, moody

Your Venus Power

The planet Venus has a great deal of influence on your powers of attraction. Below are four possible Venus types for women and men. To find your Venus you need to go to page 771, where you will find the Venus table and extra information. The planet Mars also affects your powers of attraction. To find your Mars table and interpretation go to page 761.

WOMEN WITH VENUS IN SAGITTARIUS: When you feel generous, you can make others feel more optimistic about life. You may be interested in higher learning and seek partners who are scholarly or broad-minded. You are outspoken and direct and sometimes say things that you later regret. Curious and versatile, you can adjust quickly to new situations, and a foreign influence implies that you love to travel or may have a partner who comes from a different culture.

MEN WITH VENUS IN SAGITTARIUS: Your enthusiasm and straightforward conduct usually appeal to others and imply that you are approachable and easygoing. Being open to ideas and willing to believe that life has a great deal to offer suggests that you are generous, broad-minded, and eager to cooperate with others. A love of travel and an interest in other cultures imply that your partner may come from a foreign country.

WOMEN WITH VENUS IN CAPRICORN: Proud and refined, you attract others with your composed dignity. Disliking vulnerability and needing to feel safe before you can express your feelings, you display a strong front. Feeling insecure or inadequate in relationships may force you to become manipulative in order to regain control. Nevertheless, you can project an attractive sense of self-assurance and are capable of displaying loyalty and a wonderful dry sense of humor.

MEN WITH VENUS IN CAPRICORN: As you do not display your deeper emotions freely, you are usually dignified and controlled in your relationships. Practical and down-to-earth partners are particularly attractive to you, especially those who do not rush into expressing their feelings but seem to possess natural class and reserve. You need a partner who is loyal and dependable and willing to take your relationship seriously.

WOMEN WITH VENUS IN AQUARIUS: Usually you have a

modern outlook on love and are open to new or current lifestyles. Your intuitive abilities, communal sense, and people skills often allow you to see deeper into human intentions and to read people's thoughts telepathically. You are usually group-oriented and are drawn to individuals within the group who are independent and self-motivated. You are more inclined to choose a partner who is unconventional or freedom-loving. Conscious of your social standing, however, you want someone who can relate well to your friends.

MEN WITH VENUS IN AQUARIUS: Although independent, you often enjoy being part of a group. The partners you frequently attract are themselves nonconformists or free spirits. As an individual you may not find it easy to settle into a routine or an entirely mundane type of relationship. You may have some unconventional views on traditional marriage or your partner may hold such views. Friendship, even within a relationship, is as important to you as your freedom.

WOMEN WITH VENUS IN PISCES: Idealistic and impressionable, in love you are romantic. Being sensitive to people, you are receptive to their moods and feelings. This affinity indicates that although you can be selfless, you may have to guard against being too sentimental or overly romantic, especially of those who can take advantage of your kindness. Nevertheless, alluring and seductive, your partners can be intrigued by your poetic soul or mysterious nature.

MEN WITH VENUS IN PISCES: The combination of your emotional subtlety and charm can make you very alluring when dealing with affairs of the heart. Perceptive and impressionable, you have an easygoing style in your relationships, usually preferring to avoid ugly confrontation. You are drawn to partners who have a touch of glamour and are sensitive to the needs of others. Alternatively, they could be visionaries with rich imaginations who know how to keep you enchanted. With your insight you have the ability to observe the subtle moods of your partner.

To read all about your Outer Planets and work out how to use your personalized timetable, go to Section Three, page 789.

To read all about your Outer Planets and work out how to use your personalized timetable, go to Section Three, page 789.

Your Personalized Timetable

JUPITER BENEFICIAL
1939 7/3 – 8/25
1940 2/9 – 3/25
1941 6/15 – 9/18
1941 10/31 – until 1942 4/27
1945 9/16 – 12/3
1946 4/27 – 8/1
1947 11/28 – until 1948 1/13
1951 5/29 – 10/14
1952 1/15 – 3/7
1953 5/29 – 8/13
1953 12/19 – until 1954 4/4
1957 8/31 – 11/15
1959 11/12 – 12/27
1963 5/7 – 7/6
1963 9/12 – until 1964 2/17
1965 5/13 – 7/23
1968 12/21 – until 1969 2/19
1969 8/13 – 10/29
1971 10/26 – 12/11
1975 4/19 – 6/6
1975 10/28 – until 1976 1/21
1977 4/26 – 7/5
1980 11/22 – until 1981 4/1
1981 7/22 – 10/13
1983 2/9 – 5/15
1983 10/6 – 11/25
1987 4/3 – 5/16
1988 8/25 – 10/24
1989 4/7 – 6/18
1992 11/2 – until 1993 9/28
1995 1/16 – 6/25
1995 9/9 – 11/9
1999 3/18 – 4/28
2000 7/24 – 12/9
2001 3/13 – 6/2
2004 10/17 – until 2005 9/12
2006 12/29 – until 2007 2/27
2007 5/13 – 10/21
2011 2/28 – 4/11
2012 7/2 – Continues

SATURN BENEFICIAL
1938 3/27 – 7/10
1938 8/20 – until 1939 3/15
1942 6/14 – until 1943 7/14
1944 1/18 – 3/24
1951 9/22 – until 1952 11/2
1953 6/12 – 7/5
1956 12/17 – until 1957 12/16
1967 5/6 – 10/20
1968 1/26 – 4/23
1971 8/3 – 11/5
1972 4/18 – until 1973 5/19
1980 10/30 – until 1981 4/20
1981 7/20 – 12/19
1982 3/16 – 9/10
1986 1/28 – 5/10
1986 10/25 – until 1987 1/23
1987 6/11 – 10/22
1997 3/10 – 6/4
1997 9/30 – until 1998 2/25
2001 5/27 – until 2002 6/26
2010 9/5 – until 2011 10/17

URANUS BENEFICIAL
1943 5/27 – until 1947 5/23
1969 10/1 – until 1973 8/30
1983 1/15 – until 1985 12/1
2012 5/27 – Continues

NEPTUNE BENEFICIAL
1944 10/15 – until 1952 9/23
1973 12/13 – until 1978 11/30

PLUTO BENEFICIAL
1973 10/7 – until 1980 9/18
1998 2/2 – until 2003 10/8

JUPITER CHALLENGING
1940 6/6 – until 1941 4/16
1943 7/22 – 10/7

1944 2/22 – 6/2
1946 10/17 – until 1947 1/2
1947 5/30 – 8/30
1952 5/18 – 8/27
1952 9/23 – until 1953 3/28
1955 7/5 – 9/18
1958 10/1 – 12/15
1964 5/1 – 7/16
1964 11/16 – until 1965 3/5
1967 6/18 – 9/1
1970 1/21 – 3/20
1970 9/13 – 11/28
1976 4/15 – 6/23
1978 10/2 – until 1979 1/19
1979 5/28 – 8/16
1981 12/22 – until 1982 5/2
1982 8/22 – 11/12
1988 3/29 – 6/6
1990 9/10 – until 1991 3/4
1991 4/26 – 7/31
1993 12/3 – until 1994 10/28
1999 8/11 – 9/7
2000 3/11 – 5/19
2002 8/23 – until 2003 7/14
2005 11/16 – until 2006 10/12
2011 6/29 – 11/2
2012 2/15 – 5/3

SATURN CHALLENGING
1940 4/27 – until 1941 5/29
1946 9/10 – until 1947 2/4
1947 5/30 – 10/18
1948 1/22 – 7/5
1953 12/1 – until 1954 5/15
1954 8/26 – until 1955 2/5
1955 3/25 – 10/21
1969 6/8 – 11/8
1970 2/27 – 7/18
1970 10/23 – until 1971 4/5
1976 7/14 – until 1977 8/15
1983 10/9 – until 1984 11/24
1999 4/11 – until 2000 5/12
2005 8/22 – until 2006 3/18
2006 4/23 – 9/24
2007 2/22 – Continues

URANUS CHALLENGING
1938 1/1 – until 1940 4/19
1956 8/29 – until 1960 8/2
1975 11/26 – until 1979 11/4

NEPTUNE CHALLENGING
1958 1/16 – until 1966 10/11

PLUTO CHALLENGING
1941 8/23 – until 1952 7/28
1985 1/21 – until 1992 9/12

JUPITER SPECIAL
1938 1/9 – 3/20
1949 12/23 – until 1950 3/2
1961 4/15 – 7/5
1961 12/3 – until 1962 2/13
1973 3/18 – 8/20
1973 11/6 – until 1974 1/28
1985 2/27 – until 1986 1/12
1997 2/10 – 5/12
1997 7/8 – 12/24
2009 1/25 – 4/9
2009 8/25 – 11/29

SATURN SPECIAL
1962 2/12 – until 1963 4/8
1963 7/31 – until 1964 1/3
1991 3/25 – 7/11
1991 12/21 – until 1993 2/7

URANUS SPECIAL
1997 1/25 – until 2001 2/7

NEPTUNE SPECIAL
2000 2/10 – until 2008 1/13

February 3

SUN: AQUARIUS • DECANATE: GEMINI/MERCURY • DEGREE: 13°–14° AQUARIUS • MODE: FIXED • ELEMENT: AIR

Your Personal Powers

Charming and determined, you are a friendly individual with an ability to relate to people from all walks of life. You gain power from your many creative ideas and subtle sensitivity. Intelligent and aware of image, you can be engaging and impress others with your diplomatic manner. Generous, you possess a genuine interest in people and enjoy working in collaboration with others. You can lose some of your power by allowing insecurity or misgivings to undermine your efforts. If you start to worry you can become overly serious or react in an extreme manner. With your direct approach and innovative ideas, you enjoy learning and are often ahead of your time. Possessing a strong desire to express yourself, you may be particularly drawn to creative pursuits and have a gift for music, art, or writing. Self-expression helps keep you happy and stops you from holding on to disappointments from the past. It is through the manifestation of your unique perspective and originality that you can particularly achieve success.

Your Powers of Attraction in Relationships

Others are attracted to your natural magnetism and sociable nature. A good companion, you enjoy social activities and are likely to have many interests. Being independent, you value your freedom, so you need some space within a relationship. With your natural dramatic sense, you usually enjoy romance and can be a loving partner. The more you develop the universal and detached side to your personality, the less frustrated and more tolerant you become. Although usually affectionate, if you are overworked or become too detached you can appear cold and remote or uncommunicative to your partner. Nevertheless, a good conversationalist, you can attract others with your subtle sensitivity and entertaining personality. A more humanitarian approach to relationships implies that you may accept a more unconventional partner.

Your attractive qualities: friendly, productive, creative, idealistic, freedom-loving, a gift with words, expressive, compassion, original, humanitarian, artistic, diplomatic, spiritual potential, sociable, generous, kind, charming, intelligent, universal, communication skills, kind

Your less attractive qualities: insecure, easily bored, disappointing, stubborn, worried, vain, too imaginative, eccentric, irritable, too serious, self-indulgent, confused, escapist, scattered, indecisive

Your Venus Power

The planet Venus has a great deal of influence on your powers of attraction. Below are four possible Venus types for women and men. To find your Venus you need to go to page 771, where you will find the Venus table and extra information. The planet Mars also affects your powers of attraction. To find your Mars table and interpretation go to page 761.

WOMEN WITH VENUS IN SAGITTARIUS: Optimistic and fun-loving, you love adventure and seek a partner who can expand your horizons. Being truthful and direct, you often say what you think, and at times you may be naively tactless. A need for expansion and prosperity suggests that you may enjoy traveling with your friends or partner. Being lighthearted and idealistic, once you have given your heart to someone you will stay honorable and loyal.

MEN WITH VENUS IN SAGITTARIUS: You are usually attracted to partners who are knowledgeable or well-traveled. Enthusiastic and optimistic, you often respond quickly to love offers and enter relationships with enthusiasm. Generally you seek to expand your social circle, and meeting people from all walks of life can bring the variety and fun that you seek in life. Although you are generous and honest, your partners may sometimes accuse you of being overly optimistic or too blunt.

WOMEN WITH VENUS IN CAPRICORN: With your natural caution in romantic affairs, you often appear reserved and controlled. You may be shy but try to be more forward, especially if you want to be noticed. When you care about people, however, you are usually willing to put in extra time and energy to preserve the relationship. You are practical and dependable, and a sense of duty can often play a large role in affairs of your heart. With elegant simplicity you can attract others with your well-cut clothes and refined manners.

MEN WITH VENUS IN CAPRICORN: In relationships, you take love seriously and can be a strong and practical support for friends or partners. You are usually attracted to partners who are as hardworking as you. As you tend not to express your feelings until you feel really secure in a relationship, you may be drawn to people who seem loyal, faithful, and not

likely to let you down. As you respect the wisdom of experience, you may be drawn to mature partners or, alternatively, you may act as an authority figure for someone younger.

WOMEN WITH VENUS IN AQUARIUS: You attract and impress others with your friendly approach and progressive ideas. As you are usually independent and easygoing, you value freedom within a relationship. A good companion with a sense of your own person, you enjoy socializing, especially with people who are original, cosmopolitan, and have a strong sense of individuality. Although being friendly and detached usually serves you well, avoid losing touch with your emotions. You usually prefer the company of those who have innovative or progressive views.

MEN WITH VENUS IN AQUARIUS: You are sociable and open-minded, and people are attracted by your friendly and easygoing style. Being independent, you value freedom-loving partners who give you the space to be yourself. People can sometimes interpret your detachment as being emotionally cool, but they admire your objectivity and humanitarian inclinations. You are attracted to intelligent individuals who are as truthful and direct as you are, but above all they must be true friends. Ideally your partner shares your liberal views on life and possesses a strong sense of individuality.

WOMEN WITH VENUS IN PISCES: Romantic and impressionable, you are a caring and loving individual with a dreamy nature. In relationships you are often attracted to idealistic, compassionate, or sympathetic individuals who have imaginations or a strong romantic sense. A tendency to be sensitive to others suggests that you are intuitive and aware of people's inner feelings. Be careful therefore not to get caught in other people's dramas or play the rescuer too often.

MEN WITH VENUS IN PISCES: In love you are sensitive, tender, and affectionate, experiences your partner's feelings almost as strongly as your own. Being also imaginative and visionary, you possess the capability to develop deep compassion for others. As you are idealistic when in love, you usually prefer to see only your partner's good points, but be careful that your high expectations do not bring disappointment if you avoid harsh reality. Nevertheless, in your relationships with others, you can be devoted, loving, and positively enchanting.

To read all about your Outer Planets and work out how to use your personalized timetable, go to Section Three, page 789.

≈

Your Personalized Timetable

JUPITER BENEFICIAL
1939 7/22 – 8/6
1940 2/14 – 3/29
1941 6/20 – until 1942 5/3
1945 9/21 – 12/9
1946 4/19 – 8/9
1947 12/2 – until 1948 1/18
1951 6/4 – 10/6
1952 1/21 – 3/12
1953 6/2 – 8/19
1953 12/11 – until 1954 4/10
1957 9/5 – 11/20
1959 11/17 – 12/31
1963 5/12 – 7/18
1963 8/31 – until 1964 2/22
1965 5/17 – 7/28
1966 1/30 – 3/3
1969 1/5 – 2/4
1969 8/19 – 11/3
1971 10/31 – 12/15
1975 4/24 – 6/11
1975 10/20 – until 1976 1/28
1977 4/30 – 7/9
1980 11/28 – until 1981 3/24
1981 7/29 – 10/18
1983 2/17 – 5/6
1983 10/12 – 11/30
1987 4/7 – 5/21
1988 9/8 – 10/10
1989 4/12 – 6/23
1992 11/7 – until 1993 5/7
1993 6/26 – 10/2
1995 1/22 – 6/16
1995 9/18 – 11/13
1999 3/22 – 5/3
2000 7/30 – 12/1
2001 3/20 – 6/6
2004 10/21 – until 2005 9/17
2007 1/3 – 3/10
2007 5/2 – 10/27
2011 3/5 – 4/15
2012 7/7 – Continues

SATURN BENEFICIAL
1938 4/4 – until 1939 3/24
1942 6/22 – until 1943 1/27
1943 2/16 – 7/23
1944 1/3 – 4/7
1951 10/1 – until 1952 11/11
1953 5/17 – 7/31
1956 12/26 – until 1957 7/6
1957 9/16 – 12/25
1967 5/16 – 10/7
1968 2/7 – 5/1
1971 8/19 – 10/20
1972 4/27 – until 1973 5/27
1980 11/8 – until 1981 4/5
1981 8/2 – until 1982 1/6
1982 2/25 – 9/19
1986 2/12 – 4/24
1986 11/4 – until 1987 2/3
1987 5/29 – 11/2
1997 3/18 – 6/17
1997 9/16 – until 1998 3/6
2001 6/4 – until 2002 7/4
2010 9/14 – until 2011 10/26

URANUS BENEFICIAL
1943 6/13 – until 1947 6/9
1969 10/18 – until 1973 9/18
1983 2/11 – until 1986 9/24

NEPTUNE BENEFICIAL
1944 11/16 – until 1953 8/18
1974 1/12 – until 1979 10/30

PLUTO BENEFICIAL
1973 11/5 – until 1981 7/24
1998 12/20 – until 2003 11/13

JUPITER CHALLENGING
1940 6/11 – 12/30
1941 1/1 – 4/21
1943 7/26 – 10/14

1944 2/14 – 6/9
1946 10/22 – until 1947 1/8
1947 5/22 – 9/7
1952 5/23 – until 1953 4/2
1955 7/10 – 9/23
1956 4/6 – 4/28
1958 10/6 – 12/20
1964 5/6 – 7/22
1964 11/8 – until 1965 3/11
1967 6/23 – 9/6
1970 2/6 – 3/5
1970 9/18 – 12/3
1976 4/19 – 6/28
1976 12/29 – until 1977 2/1
1978 10/9 – until 1979 1/12
1979 6/3 – 8/20
1981 12/29 – until 1982 4/24
1982 8/29 – 11/17
1988 4/3 – 6/10
1990 9/15 – until 1991 2/21
1991 5/7 – 8/5
1993 12/8 – until 1994 6/7
1994 7/27 – 11/1
2000 3/16 – 5/24
2002 8/28 – until 2003 7/19
2005 11/21 – until 2006 10/16
2011 7/5 – 10/26
2012 2/22 – 5/7

SATURN CHALLENGING
1940 5/5 – until 1941 6/7
1942 1/16 – 1/29
1946 9/20 – until 1947 1/23
1947 6/10 – 11/1
1948 1/6 – 7/14
1953 12/11 – until 1954 5/1
1954 9/7 – until 1955 10/30
1969 6/18 – 10/26
1970 3/10 – 8/2
1970 10/7 – until 1971 4/13
1976 7/22 – until 1977 8/23
1983 10/18 – until 1984 12/3
1985 7/9 – 8/10
1999 4/19 – until 2000 5/20
2005 8/30 – until 2006 2/25
2006 5/14 – 10/4
2007 2/10 – 6/24

URANUS CHALLENGING
1938 1/1 – until 1940 5/7
1956 9/18 – until 1961 5/6
1975 12/15 – until 1980 8/20

NEPTUNE CHALLENGING
1958 11/30 – until 1967 8/23

PLUTO CHALLENGING
1941 10/16 – until 1953 7/5
1985 11/22 – until 1992 10/15

JUPITER SPECIAL
1938 1/14 – 3/25
1949 12/28 – until 1950 3/6
1961 4/24 – 6/25
1961 12/9 – until 1962 2/17
1973 3/24 – 8/11
1973 11/14 – until 1974 2/1
1985 3/4 – until 1986 1/16
1997 2/15 – 5/28
1997 6/22 – 12/29
2009 1/29 – 4/15
2009 8/17 – 12/6

SATURN SPECIAL
1962 2/21 – 9/5
1962 11/12 – until 1963 4/22
1963 7/16 – until 1964 1/13
1991 4/9 – 6/25
1991 12/30 – until 1993 2/15

URANUS SPECIAL
1997 2/11 – until 2001 12/13

NEPTUNE SPECIAL
2000 3/11 – until 2008 11/29

February 4

SUN: AQUARIUS • DECANATE: GEMINI/MERCURY • DEGREE: 14°–15° AQUARIUS • MODE: FIXED • ELEMENT: AIR

Your Personal Powers

Mentally sharp with quick responses and original ideas, you are a resourceful individual with determination. Independent and freedom-loving, you have a need to do things in your own unique way. You gain power by combining your sincerity, shrewd practicality, and sheer tenacity. You also possess the organizational skills to bring your big ideas to fruition. Be careful, however, that with your strong will and resolve you do not lose power by being too forceful or stubborn. Nonetheless, normally energetic, assertive, and enterprising, you can be ambitious and hardworking in achieving your goals. Being industrious may be necessary if you want to fulfill your need for luxury, beauty, and the good things of life. As you are a quick learner, you are constantly updating yourself with the latest information on your favorite subjects. You possess innovative ideas, a businesslike approach, and a gift for communicating in a dynamic and convincing way. All this suggests that you have the potential for outstanding success if you only apply the necessary self-discipline.

Your Powers of Attraction in Relationships

Being sociable, generous, and energetic, you can always attract admirers. You value friendship and like to help people in a practical way. You possess a desire for power, money, and prestige and are especially attracted to self-made and successful people. Valuing knowledge, you respect those who possess wisdom and are well-informed. Although you can project power and confidence and often get your way, resist being overbearing or critical with your partners. Equally, your rebellious streak may sometimes land you in trouble. Underneath your strong front you can possess sensitive emotions that emphasize the importance of loved ones in your life. Your practical qualities and desire for a harmonious and secure home environment can make you a good provider and solid family member.

Your attractive qualities: direct, well-organized, self-disciplined, steady, hardworking, determined, ambitious, business sense, humanitarian, communication skills, frank, honest, idealistic, pragmatism, sociable, generous, kind, intelligent, original, proud

Your less attractive qualities: bossy, stubborn, lazy, unfeeling, too security conscious, procrastinator, too economical, self-indulgent, resentful, too tough, impatient, self-willed

Your Venus Power

The planet Venus has a great deal of influence on your powers of attraction. Below are four possible Venus types for women and men. To find your Venus you need to go to page 771, where you will find the Venus table and extra information. The planet Mars also affects your powers of attraction. To find your Mars table and interpretation go to page 761.

WOMEN WITH VENUS IN SAGITTARIUS: Optimistic and fun-loving, you love adventure and seek a partner who can expand your horizons. Being truthful and direct, you often say what you think, and at times you may be naively tactless. A need for expansion and prosperity suggests that you may enjoy traveling with your friends or partner. Being lighthearted and idealistic, once you have given your heart to someone you will stay honorable and loyal.

MEN WITH VENUS IN SAGITTARIUS: You are usually attracted to partners who are knowledgeable or well-traveled. Enthusiastic and optimistic, you often respond quickly to love offers and enter relationships with enthusiasm. Generally you seek to expand your social circle, and meeting people from all walks of life can bring the variety and fun that you seek in life. Although you are generous and honest, your partners may sometimes accuse you of being overly optimistic or too blunt.

WOMEN WITH VENUS IN CAPRICORN: Loyal and responsible, you are attracted to dignified and reserved individuals. Being practical and security-conscious, you prefer hardworking partners who are resourceful and enterprising; work may even be a factor in many of your associations and partnerships. For you, family and faithfulness can be especially important, so you are usually willing to work hard or make sacrifices in order to build a strong relationship.

MEN WITH VENUS IN CAPRICORN: Hardworking and ambitious, you are usually attracted to determined, focused, and ambitious partners with a strong sense of duty. You want them to take relationships as seriously as you do, so loyalty and faithfulness are high on your agenda. Since you may display a natural reserve about expressing your feelings in an intimate relationship, you need a partner who shares your need for emotional security.

WOMEN WITH VENUS IN AQUARIUS: When it comes to relationships, others are attracted to your honest, friendly, and easygoing attitude. You really enjoy social interaction with others and may develop a genuine concern for humanity. Usually you present a tolerant and reasonable front in love situations and attempt to view your relationships objectively. If partners become too demanding, however, you can become stubborn and fixed. Friendship may be even more important for you than sexual compatibility.

MEN WITH VENUS IN AQUARIUS: You are sociable and open-minded, and people are attracted by your friendly and relaxed style. Being independent, you value freedom-loving partners who give you the space to be yourself. Others sometimes interpret your detachment as being emotionally cool, but they may not understand your progressive views on relationships. Friendship can sometimes be even more important than earthly passion. Ideally, friends can share your ideas on life and possess a sense of originality as strong as your own. Not easily ruffled, you can deal well with difficult situations or moody partners.

WOMEN WITH VENUS IN PISCES: In love you are sensitive, tender, and affectionate, experiences your partner's feelings almost as strongly as your own. Being also imaginative and visionary, you possess the ability to develop creative gifts and a deep compassion for others. As you are idealistic when in love, you usually prefer to see only your partner's good points, but be careful that your high expectations do not bring disappointment if you avoid being realistic. Nevertheless, in your relationships with others, you can be devoted, loving, and positively enchanting.

MEN WITH VENUS IN PISCES: The combination of your emotional subtlety and charm can make you very alluring when dealing with affairs of the heart. Perceptive and impressionable, you have an easygoing style in your relationships, usually preferring to avoid ugly confrontation. You are drawn to a woman who has a touch of glamour and is sensitive to the needs of others. Alternatively, she can be a visionary with a rich imagination who can keep you enchanted.

To read all about your Outer Planets and work out how to use your personalized timetable, go to Section Three, page 789.

To read all about your Outer Planets and work out how to use your personalized timetable, go to Section Three, page 789.

≈

Your Personalized Timetable

JUPITER BENEFICIAL
1940 2/19 – 4/3
1941 6/24 – until 1942 5/8
1945 9/26 – 12/16
1946 4/11 – 8/16
1947 12/7 – until 1948 1/23
1948 7/27 – 9/4
1951 6/10 – 9/29
1952 1/28 – 3/16
1953 6/7 – 8/26
1953 12/4 – until 1954 4/16
1957 9/10 – 11/25
1958 5/25 – 7/14
1959 11/21 – until 1960 1/5
1963 5/17 – 11/25
1963 12/14 – until 1964 2/27
1965 5/21 – 8/2
1966 1/16 – 3/17
1969 8/24 – 11/8
1971 11/5 – 12/20
1975 4/28 – 6/17
1975 10/13 – until 1976 2/4
1977 5/5 – 7/14
1980 12/5 – until 1981 3/16
1981 8/4 – 10/23
1983 2/27 – 4/25
1983 10/18 – 12/4
1987 4/12 – 5/26
1989 4/17 – 6/27
1992 11/13 – until 1993 4/25
1993 7/7 – 10/7
1995 1/28 – 6/7
1995 9/25 – 11/18
1999 3/26 – 5/7
2000 8/5 – 11/24
2001 3/26 – 6/11
2004 10/26 – until 2005 9/22
2007 1/8 – 3/30
2007 4/12 – 11/1
2011 3/9 – 4/20
2012 7/12 – Continues

SATURN BENEFICIAL
1938 4/12 – until 1939 4/1
1942 6/30 – until 1943 1/2
1943 3/13 – 8/2
1943 12/21 – until 1944 4/19
1951 10/9 – until 1952 11/20
1953 5/1 – 8/14
1957 1/4 – 6/20
1957 10/1 – until 1958 1/3
1958 7/27 – 9/20
1967 5/27 – 9/24
1968 2/17 – 5/10
1968 11/17 – until 1969 1/23
1972 5/5 – until 1973 6/4
1980 11/19 – until 1981 3/23
1981 8/13 – until 1982 9/28
1986 3/17 – 3/19
1986 11/13 – until 1987 2/16
1987 5/14 – 11/12
1997 3/26 – 7/4
1997 8/29 – until 1998 3/15
2001 6/12 – until 2002 7/13
2003 1/28 – 3/18
2010 9/22 – until 2011 11/3

URANUS BENEFICIAL
1943 7/2 – until 1948 4/6
1969 11/4 – until 1973 10/5
1983 12/7 – until 1986 10/23

NEPTUNE BENEFICIAL
1945 10/13 – until 1953 9/21
1974 12/11 – until 1979 11/29

PLUTO BENEFICIAL
1973 12/19 – until 1981 9/5
1999 1/19 – until 2004 9/23

JUPITER CHALLENGING
1940 6/16 – 12/6
1941 1/24 – 4/25

1943 7/31 – 10/20
1944 2/7 – 6/16
1946 10/26 – until 1947 1/15
1947 5/14 – 9/14
1952 5/27 – until 1953 4/7
1955 7/15 – 9/28
1956 3/20 – 5/16
1958 10/11 – 12/25
1959 6/30 – 8/8
1964 5/10 – 7/29
1964 11/1 – until 1965 3/17
1967 6/28 – 9/11
1970 9/24 – 12/7
1976 4/23 – 7/4
1976 12/16 – until 1977 2/14
1978 10/17 – until 1979 1/3
1979 6/9 – 8/25
1982 1/5 – 4/16
1982 9/4 – 11/21
1988 4/7 – 6/15
1990 9/21 – until 1991 2/12
1991 5/15 – 8/9
1993 12/13 – until 1994 5/26
1994 8/7 – 11/6
2000 3/20 – 5/28
2002 9/2 – until 2003 7/24
2005 11/26 – until 2006 10/21
2011 7/12 – 10/18
2012 2/28 – 5/11

SATURN CHALLENGING
1940 5/13 – until 1941 6/15
1941 12/20 – until 1942 2/26
1946 10/1 – until 1947 1/10
1947 6/19 – until 1948 7/22
1953 12/22 – until 1954 4/18
1954 9/18 – until 1955 11/7
1969 6/30 – 10/13
1970 3/19 – until 1971 4/22
1976 7/30 – until 1977 8/31
1983 10/26 – until 1984 12/12
1985 6/15 – 9/3
1999 4/27 – until 2000 5/28
2005 9/8 – until 2006 2/11
2006 5/27 – 10/15
2007 1/28 – 7/4

URANUS CHALLENGING
1938 1/1 – until 1941 3/6
1956 10/18 – until 1961 6/17
1976 1/11 – until 1980 9/22

NEPTUNE CHALLENGING
1959 1/8 – until 1967 10/9

PLUTO CHALLENGING
1942 9/18 – until 1954 5/31
1985 12/23 – until 1992 11/10

JUPITER SPECIAL
1938 1/18 – 3/29
1938 10/6 – 11/1
1950 1/1 – 3/11
1961 5/8 – 6/11
1961 12/14 – until 1962 2/22
1973 3/30 – 8/3
1973 11/21 – until 1974 2/5
1985 3/9 – until 1986 1/20
1997 2/19 – until 1998 1/3
2009 2/3 – 4/22
2009 8/9 – 12/12

SATURN SPECIAL
1962 3/2 – 8/19
1962 11/27 – until 1963 5/12
1963 6/26 – until 1964 1/22
1991 5/4 – 5/30
1992 1/8 – until 1993 2/24

URANUS SPECIAL
1997 3/2 – until 2002 1/6

NEPTUNE SPECIAL
2001 2/6 – until 2009 1/9

665

February 5

Your Personal Powers

Discerning and receptive, you are an innovative individual with high ideals and quick perception. With keen insight into human nature, you possess an original outlook on life. Often an intuitive thinker, you gain power when you combine your foresight and creativity with your progressive ideas. Although your strong views can make you stubborn or confrontational, your innate sense of values implies that you often turn situations to your advantage. Since you are likely to be multitalented yet meticulous, you enjoy challenging undertakings or initiating new projects. As there are probably wonderful opportunities for you to achieve success, you may need to stay more focused on your goals rather than be impatient or skeptical. You lose some of your power when you let anxiety or impatience undermine your sense of purpose. You become more persuasive and influential when you deal with situations in a dispassionate way. Independent and freedom-loving, you often work better as your own boss. You also empower yourself by developing inner faith in your abilities and knowing your true self-worth.

Your Powers of Attraction in Relationships

Keenly aware, friendly, and diplomatic, you are sensitive to people's feelings. As a good team player you are willing to participate in group activities and share experiences with others. Being intelligent, you are attracted to intellectual or clever people who are confident and decisive. Usually you seek a partner with whom you can share your thoughts, sense of humor, and beliefs. People admire your progressive ideas and persuasive personality. Although you possess a natural gift for dealing with people, inclinations to be argumentative or bossy may bring tension to partnerships and close relationships. Although sociable, you need time alone to rest or meditate. As your life is likely to be exciting and full of opportunities, you usually need to balance your close relationships with commitments and career.

Your attractive qualities: versatile, mentally sharp, adaptable, intuitive, original ideas, progressive, independent, magnetic, daring, freedom-loving, quick wit, spiritual potential, sociable, disciplined, inner faith, inspired, generous, humanitarian, values knowledge, friendly, sensitive, objective

Your less attractive qualities: reserved, mistrusting, indecisive, extravagant, cynical, restlessness, stubborn, frustrated, self-absorbed, overconfident or self-doubt, headstrong, argumentative, impatient, moody, discontented, irritable

Your Venus Power

The planet Venus has a great deal of influence on your powers of attraction. Below are four possible Venus types for women and men. To find your Venus you need to go to page 771, where you will find the Venus table and extra information. The planet Mars also affects your powers of attraction. To find your Mars table and interpretation go to page 761.

WOMEN WITH VENUS IN SAGITTARIUS: Sociable, warm, and friendly, you possess an honest and frank style in your relationships. Being naturally gregarious, you want others to share your enthusiasm and enjoy encouraging the people you love. You do better when you have a sense of personal freedom within a relationship and are usually generous with the faults of others. You need a partner who can share your need to explore and take risks whether through travel, education, or recreation.

MEN WITH VENUS IN SAGITTARIUS: When in love you are open and friendly with a need for a partner who can share your adventurous spirit and sense of fun. Be careful, however, that your desire for freedom does not cause you to avoid commitment. You prefer your partners to be positive, direct, and generous in spirit. Being outspoken as well as an idealist, you usually enjoy a partner with whom you can share your strong opinions. Alternatively, you may wish to explore life together whether through travel, education, or by having fun.

WOMEN WITH VENUS IN CAPRICORN: With your natural caution in romantic affairs, you often appear reserved and controlled. You may be shy but try to be more forward, especially if you want to be noticed. When you care about people, however, you are usually willing to put in extra time and energy to preserve the relationship. You are practical and dependable, and a sense of duty can often play a large role in affairs of your heart. With elegant simplicity you can attract others with your well-cut clothes and refined manners.

MEN WITH VENUS IN CAPRICORN: In relationships you take love seriously and can be a strong and practical support for friends or partners. You are usually attracted to people who are as hardworking as you. As you tend not to express your feelings until you feel really secure in a relationship, you

may be drawn to those who seem loyal, faithful, and not likely to let you down. As you respect the wisdom of experience, you may be drawn to mature partners or, alternatively, you may act as an authority figure for someone younger.

WOMEN WITH VENUS IN AQUARIUS: When it comes to relationships, others are attracted to your honest, friendly, and easygoing attitude. You really enjoy social interaction with others and may develop a genuine concern for humanity. Usually you present a tolerant and reasonable front in love situations and attempt to view your relationships objectively. If partners become too demanding, however, you can become stubborn and fixed. Friendship may be even more important for you than sexual compatibility.

MEN WITH VENUS IN AQUARIUS: You are sociable and open-minded, and people are attracted by your friendly and relaxed style. Being independent, you value freedom-loving partners who give you the space to be yourself. Others sometimes interpret your detachment as being emotionally cool, but they may not understand your progressive views on relationships. Friendship can sometimes be even more important than earthly passion. Ideally, friends can share your ideas on life and possess a sense of originality as strong as your own. Not easily ruffled, you can deal well with difficult situations or moody partners.

WOMEN WITH VENUS IN PISCES: Being sensitive to affairs of the heart, when you care for someone you can feel their emotions and sense their every mood. Their goals can even become as important as your own. This empathy indicates that you can love on an unselfish level, but you may have to guard against giving too much, especially to those who do not reciprocate. As you are seductive and captivating, partners can be fascinated by your subtle charms and attracted by your caring and affectionate nature.

MEN WITH VENUS IN PISCES: Romantic and idealistic when in love, you can be a sensitive and responsive lover. Being pliant and flexible with an impressionable nature helps you to adapt to the needs of others. In your desire to blend with those you love, however, guard against not clearly defining your own boundaries. With your affectionate and sentimental nature you are often attracted to those who understand your sensitivity and share your vision.

To read all about your Outer Planets and work out how to use your personalized timetable, go to Section Three, page 789.

To read all about your Outer Planets and work out how to use your personalized timetable, go to Section Three, page 789.

Your Personalized Timetable

JUPITER BENEFICIAL
1940 2/24 – 4/7
1941 6/29 – until 1942 5/12
1945 9/30 – 12/23
1946 4/3 – 8/22
1947 12/11 – until 1948 1/28
1948 7/14 – 9/17
1951 6/17 – 9/21
1952 2/2 – 3/21
1953 6/11 – 9/3
1953 11/26 – until 1954 4/22
1957 9/15 – 12/1
1958 5/13 – 7/25
1959 11/26 – until 1960 1/10
1963 5/22 – 11/9
1963 12/31 – until 1964 3/2
1965 5/26 – 8/7
1966 1/7 – 3/26
1969 8/29 – 11/13
1971 11/10 – 12/24
1975 5/3 – 6/24
1975 10/5 – until 1976 2/10
1977 5/9 – 7/19
1980 12/13 – until 1981 3/8
1981 8/10 – 10/27
1983 3/16 – 4/8
1983 10/23 – 12/9
1987 4/16 – 5/31
1987 11/22 – until 1988 1/7
1989 4/22 – 7/2
1992 11/18 – until 1993 4/16
1993 7/16 – 10/12
1995 2/3 – 5/30
1995 10/2 – 11/23
1999 3/30 – 5/12
2000 8/12 – 11/16
2001 4/1 – 6/15
2004 10/31 – until 2005 9/26
2007 1/13 – 7/15
2007 8/29 – 11/6
2011 3/13 – 4/24
2012 7/18 – Continues

SATURN BENEFICIAL
1938 4/20 – until 1939 4/9
1942 7/9 – 12/18
1943 3/27 – 8/12
1943 12/9 – until 1944 4/29
1951 10/17 – until 1952 11/30
1953 4/17 – 8/26
1957 1/14 – 6/6
1957 10/14 – until 1958 1/12
1958 7/8 – 10/8
1967 6/9 – 9/10
1968 2/26 – 5/19
1968 11/2 – until 1969 2/7
1972 5/13 – until 1973 6/12
1980 11/30 – until 1981 3/10
1981 8/23 – until 1982 10/6
1986 11/22 – until 1987 3/8
1987 4/23 – 11/21
1997 4/3 – until 1998 3/23
2001 6/20 – until 2002 7/21
2003 1/11 – 4/5
2010 9/30 – until 2011 11/12
2012 5/21 – 7/29

URANUS BENEFICIAL
1943 7/24 – until 1948 5/1
1969 11/25 – until 1974 7/12
1983 12/24 – until 1986 11/13

NEPTUNE BENEFICIAL
1945 11/13 – until 1954 8/14
1975 1/9 – until 1980 10/26

PLUTO BENEFICIAL
1974 10/27 – until 1981 10/3
1999 12/12 – until 2004 11/6

JUPITER CHALLENGING
1940 6/21 – 11/26
1941 2/4 – 4/29

1943 8/5 – 10/27
1944 1/30 – 6/22
1946 10/31 – until 1947 1/22
1947 5/6 – 9/20
1952 6/1 – until 1953 4/11
1955 7/19 – 10/4
1956 3/10 – 5/26
1958 10/15 – 12/30
1959 6/17 – 8/22
1964 5/14 – 8/6
1964 10/23 – until 1965 3/23
1967 7/3 – 9/15
1970 9/29 – 12/12
1976 4/28 – 7/9
1976 12/6 – until 1977 2/23
1978 10/27 – 12/24
1979 6/15 – 8/30
1982 1/13 – 4/7
1982 9/10 – 11/26
1988 4/12 – 6/19
1990 9/27 – until 1991 2/4
1991 5/23 – 8/14
1993 12/19 – until 1994 5/17
1994 8/16 – 11/10
2000 3/25 – 6/1
2002 9/7 – until 2003 7/29
2005 12/1 – until 2006 10/26
2011 7/20 – 10/10
2012 3/4 – 5/15

SATURN CHALLENGING
1940 5/21 – until 1941 6/24
1941 12/4 – until 1942 3/12
1946 10/15 – 12/26
1947 6/28 – until 1948 7/31
1954 1/4 – 4/3
1954 9/28 – until 1955 11/16
1969 7/14 – 9/28
1970 3/28 – until 1971 4/30
1976 8/7 – until 1977 9/8
1978 4/17 – 5/3
1983 11/4 – until 1984 12/21
1985 5/31 – 9/17
1999 5/5 – until 2000 6/5
2005 9/18 – until 2006 1/29
2006 6/7 – 10/28
2007 1/14 – 7/13

URANUS CHALLENGING
1938 1/1 – until 1941 4/2
1957 8/6 – until 1961 7/9
1976 11/3 – until 1980 10/12

NEPTUNE CHALLENGING
1959 11/27 – until 1967 11/7

PLUTO CHALLENGING
1943 8/31 – until 1954 7/17
1986 11/10 – until 1993 10/2

JUPITER SPECIAL
1938 1/22 – 4/4
1938 9/20 – 11/16
1950 1/6 – 3/15
1961 12/19 – until 1962 2/26
1973 4/6 – 7/26
1973 11/27 – until 1974 2/10
1985 3/14 – 9/14
1985 10/22 – until 1986 1/25
1997 2/24 – until 1998 1/7
2009 2/7 – 4/29
2009 8/1 – 12/18

SATURN SPECIAL
1962 3/12 – 8/5
1962 12/9 – until 1964 1/30
1992 1/17 – until 1993 3/5
1993 10/18 – 11/6

URANUS SPECIAL
1997 3/25 – until 2002 1/25

NEPTUNE SPECIAL
2001 3/8 – until 2009 11/13

February 6

Your Personal Powers

Intuitive and sensitive, you are a gregarious and inventive individual with original views and a need for stability. Your ruling planet, Uranus, endows you with an understanding of human nature and an innovative mind. Although you are hardworking and determined, when your beliefs or objectives become vague or confused you may feel blocked and frustrated, losing some of your stamina. Although you dislike restriction and value your independence, many of your life lessons focus on endurance, fortitude, and responsibilities. Fortunately, you are idealistic with good reasoning powers and strong self-will. You gain power when you combine your interest in people or social reform with your insight, sense of purpose, and practical skills. Inspired by knowledge and wisdom, you empower yourself when you avoid inertia and apply self-discipline to your resolute nature and objective ideas. As you often seek to establish a strong foundation upon which to work, you benefit from being persevering and methodical. You also empower yourself when you use your determination and charm without appearing too stubborn.

Your Powers of Attraction in Relationships

As you are usually good at relating to others on a personal level, you can be courteous and understanding. You are usually attracted to dynamic or creative people who can be entertaining and mentally stimulating. Alternatively, you may be drawn to charismatic and dramatic individuals who are enthusiastic and enterprising. Although you are usually friendly and socially inclined, you can also be stubborn or too serious. Nevertheless, in close personal relationships you usually show your support and willingness to share your good fortune with loved ones. Others admire your sense of purpose, dramatic self-expression, and discerning mind. You are caring, and home, family, or partnerships are likely to play an important role in your life. Sharing or collaborating with others can also be a vital key to your success.

Your attractive qualities: caring, objective, persuasive, inventive, responsible, worldly, original, friendly, artistic, compassionate, dependable, intelligent, loving, idealistic, sympathetic, home-loving, kind, humanitarian, creative, loves harmony, good judgment, diplomatic

Your less attractive qualities: discontented, inertia, anxious, unreasonable, stubborn, outspoken, disharmonious, stuck in rut, perfectionist, domineering, lack of responsibility, selfish, suspicious, cynical, self-centered, interfering

Your Venus Power

The planet Venus has a great deal of influence on your powers of attraction. Below are four possible Venus types for women and men. To find your Venus you need to go to page 771, where you will find the Venus table and extra information. The planet Mars also affects your powers of attraction. To find your Mars table and interpretation go to page 761.

WOMEN WITH VENUS IN CAPRICORN: Proud and refined, you attract others with your composed dignity. Disliking vulnerability and needing to feel safe before you can express your feelings, you display a strong front. Feeling insecure or inadequate in relationships may force you to become manipulative in order to regain control. Nevertheless, you can project an attractive sense of self-assurance and are capable of displaying loyalty and a wonderful dry sense of humor.

MEN WITH VENUS IN CAPRICORN: As you do not display your deeper emotions freely, you are usually dignified and controlled in your relationships. Practical and down-to-earth partners are particularly attractive to you, especially those who do not rush into expressing their feelings but seem to possess natural class and reserve. You need a partner who is loyal and dependable and willing to take your relationship seriously.

WOMEN WITH VENUS IN AQUARIUS: Usually you have a modern outlook on love and are open to new or current lifestyles. Your intuitive abilities, communal sense, and people skills often allow you to see deeper into human intentions and to telepathically read people's thoughts. You are usually group-oriented and are drawn to individuals within the group who are independent and self-motivated. You are more inclined to choose a partner who is unconventional or freedom-loving. Conscious of your social standing, however, you want someone who can relate well to your friends.

MEN WITH VENUS IN AQUARIUS: Although independent, you often enjoy being part of a group. The partners you frequently attract are themselves nonconformists or free spirits. As an individual you may not find it easy to settle into a routine or an entirely mundane type of relationship. You may have some unconventional views on traditional marriage or

your partner may hold such views. You value your freedom and can sometimes be cool and detached. Friendship is important to you as you enjoy sharing your progressive ideas.

WOMEN WITH VENUS IN PISCES: Romantic and impressionable, you are a caring and loving individual with a dreamy nature. In relationships you are often attracted to idealistic, compassionate, or sympathetic individuals with imagination or a strong romantic sense. A tendency to be sensitive to others suggests that you are intuitive and aware of people's inner feelings. Be careful, therefore, not to get caught in people's dramas or play the rescuer too often.

MEN WITH VENUS IN PISCES: As a romantic and generous person, you are attracted to imaginative or artistic partners who can be sensitive and generous. While you are willing to make allowances for loved ones, playing the martyr in relationships can lead to allowing others to take advantage of your kind nature. Nevertheless, giving and loving, you are usually willing to forgive your partner's shortcomings.

WOMEN WITH VENUS IN ARIES: You gain power from your strong individuality, energy, and enthusiasm. Your young-at-heart and spirited approach to relationships adds to your appeal. If you become too impatient or self-absorbed, however, your partnerships are likely to suffer. Nevertheless, you can be creative, sharp, and quick, especially when you are able to share new and exciting projects with your partners. Mischievous, with a love of action, you may even incite them to a playful fight.

MEN WITH VENUS IN ARIES: As you often have the courage and strength to initiate situations, you like to take the lead. With your unconscious desire for conquest you may also have to beware of being competitive with your partners. Nevertheless, you are drawn to direct and strong-willed women who can share your love of action and enthusiasm for life. When you are feeling good you can be charming and enthusiastic in romantic situations with an entertaining and spontaneous spirit.

To read all about your Outer Planets and work out how to use your personalized timetable, go to Section Three, page 789.

≈

Your Personalized Timetable

JUPITER BENEFICIAL
1940 2/28 – 4/11
1941 7/3 – until **1942** 5/17
1945 10/5 – 12/31
1946 3/25 – 8/28
1947 12/16 – until **1948** 2/3
1948 7/4 – 9/27
1951 6/25 – 9/12
1952 2/8 – 3/25
1953 6/16 – 9/12
1953 11/16 – until **1954** 4/28
1957 9/19 – 12/6
1958 5/4 – 8/4
1959 11/30 – until **1960** 1/15
1963 5/27 – 10/29
1964 1/10 – 3/7
1965 5/30 – 8/13
1965 12/29 – until **1966** 4/3
1969 9/3 – 11/18
1971 11/14 – 12/29
1975 5/7 – 7/2
1975 9/27 – until **1976** 2/16
1977 5/14 – 7/23
1980 12/22 – until **1981** 2/26
1981 8/16 – 11/1
1983 10/28 – 12/13
1987 4/20 – 6/5
1987 11/11 – until **1988** 1/18
1989 4/27 – 7/6
1992 11/24 – until **1993** 4/7
1993 7/24 – 10/16
1995 2/10 – 5/22
1995 10/8 – 11/27
1999 4/3 – 5/16
2000 8/20 – 11/8
2001 4/7 – 6/19
2004 11/5 – until **2005** 10/1
2007 1/19 – 7/3
2007 9/10 – 11/11
2011 3/18 – 4/28
2012 7/23 – 12/23

SATURN BENEFICIAL
1938 4/29 – 11/21
1939 1/7 – 4/17
1942 7/19 – 12/5
1943 4/7 – 8/24
1943 11/26 – until **1944** 5/8
1951 10/26 – until **1952** 5/16
1952 7/5 – 12/11
1953 4/4 – 9/6
1957 1/26 – 5/23
1957 10/25 – until **1958** 1/22
1958 6/23 – 10/21
1967 6/25 – 8/23
1968 3/6 – 5/29
1968 10/19 – until **1969** 2/18
1972 5/21 – until **1973** 6/20
1980 12/15 – until **1981** 2/22
1981 9/1 – until **1982** 10/15
1986 11/30 – until **1987** 11/30
1997 4/11 – until **1998** 3/31
2001 6/29 – until **2002** 1/11
2002 3/7 – 7/30
2002 12/28 – until **2003** 4/17
2010 10/9 – until **2011** 11/21
2012 5/5 – 8/14

URANUS BENEFICIAL
1943 8/29 – until **1948** 5/21
1970 1/2 – until **1974** 8/21
1984 1/12 – until **1986** 12/1

NEPTUNE BENEFICIAL
1946 10/12 – until **1954** 9/20
1975 2/27 – until **1980** 11/26

PLUTO BENEFICIAL
1974 11/29 – until **1982** 8/20
2000 1/9 – until **2004** 12/5

JUPITER CHALLENGING
1940 6/27 – 11/17
1941 2/12 – 5/4
1943 8/9 – 11/5

1944 1/21 – 6/28
1946 11/5 – until **1947** 1/29
1947 4/27 – 9/26
1952 6/5 – until **1953** 4/16
1955 7/24 – 10/9
1956 3/1 – 6/4
1958 10/20 – until **1959** 1/5
1959 6/7 – 8/31
1964 5/18 – 8/16
1964 10/14 – until **1965** 3/28
1967 7/8 – 9/20
1970 10/4 – 12/17
1976 5/2 – 7/15
1976 11/28 – until **1977** 3/3
1978 11/11 – 12/9
1979 6/20 – 9/3
1982 1/23 – 3/28
1982 9/16 – 12/1
1988 4/16 – 6/24
1990 10/3 – until **1991** 1/27
1991 5/30 – 8/18
1993 12/25 – until **1994** 5/8
1994 8/24 – 11/15
2000 3/30 – 6/6
2002 9/12 – until **2003** 3/14
2003 4/24 – 8/3
2005 12/6 – until **2006** 10/31
2011 7/29 – 10/1
2012 3/10 – 5/20

SATURN CHALLENGING
1940 5/29 – 12/10
1941 2/8 – 7/4
1941 11/21 – until **1942** 3/23
1946 11/7 – 12/3
1947 7/7 – until **1948** 8/8
1954 1/21 – 3/16
1954 10/7 – until **1955** 11/24
1969 8/5 – 9/5
1970 4/6 – until **1971** 5/8
1976 8/15 – until **1977** 9/17
1978 3/21 – 5/30
1983 11/12 – until **1985** 1/1
1985 5/17 – 9/29
1999 5/13 – until **2000** 6/14
2000 12/29 – until **2001** 2/20
2005 9/29 – until **2006** 1/17
2006 6/17 – 11/17
2006 12/25 – until **2007** 7/22

URANUS CHALLENGING
1938 1/1 – until **1941** 4/21
1957 8/23 – until **1961** 7/27
1976 11/19 – until **1980** 10/30

NEPTUNE CHALLENGING
1960 1/2 – until **1968** 10/5

PLUTO CHALLENGING
1943 10/31 – until **1955** 6/18
1986 12/7 – until **1993** 10/31

JUPITER SPECIAL
1938 1/27 – 4/9
1938 9/10 – 11/26
1950 1/10 – 3/20
1961 12/24 – until **1962** 3/2
1973 4/13 – 7/18
1973 12/3 – until **1974** 2/14
1985 3/19 – 9/1
1985 11/3 – until **1986** 1/29
1997 2/28 – until **1998** 1/12
2009 2/11 – 5/7
2009 7/24 – 12/23

SATURN SPECIAL
1962 3/24 – 7/22
1962 12/20 – until **1964** 2/8
1992 1/25 – until **1993** 3/14
1993 9/21 – 12/2

URANUS SPECIAL
1998 1/29 – until **2002** 2/12

NEPTUNE SPECIAL
2001 4/27 – until **2010** 1/5

669

February 7

SUN: AQUARIUS • DECANATE: GEMINI/MERCURY • DEGREE: 17°–18° AQUARIUS • MODE: FIXED • ELEMENT: AIR

Your Personal Powers

Instinctive and sensitive, you are an astute and charismatic individual with strong incentives and a circumspect manner. Although you are often rational and practical, as an independent thinker you want to have the freedom to make your own decisions and mistakes. Your foresight and deep awareness often encourage you to initiate new enterprises. Methodical and industrious, you usually prefer to be active and productive. Your ruling planet, Uranus, grants you intuitive powers, original ideas, and keen mental abilities. You are inventive and enthusiastic, which implies that you usually seek experiences that can stimulate your mind and fulfill your need for change or excitement. Although you can be versatile, you lose some of your power if you let skepticism or stubbornness undermine your determination and fine talents. With a constant need for greater self-awareness you can empower yourself by developing your analytical abilities or innate humanitarian qualities and becoming more thoughtful and patient. You gain power when you combine your flair for networking with your spirit of enterprise and a need to be mentally creative.

Your Powers of Attraction in Relationships

Usually polite and sociable, you possess an amiable nature and the ability to make people feel at ease. People admire your quick perception, broad-minded attitude, and direct approach. In close relationships guard against being uncommunicative, critical, or moody. You are usually attracted to intelligent and intuitive yet determined individuals who are full of ideas. Alternatively, you may be drawn to creative and enthusiastic people who are hardworking and quietly ambitious. When you make a commitment to someone you love, you are loyal and supportive even in times of hardship. Although you can be inwardly anxious or frustrated, you can appear to others as aloof and dispassionate. Being cooperative and working in partnerships or in a team rather than independently can bring unexpected benefits, often leading to greater success.

Your attractive qualities: knowledgeable, sensitive, diplomatic, creative, original, trusting, meticulous, idealistic, intuitive, scientific, rational, reflective, enterprising, independent, honest, lively expression, persevering, progressive, liberal, shrewd, warmhearted, spiritual potential, cooperative

Your less attractive qualities: stubborn, restlessness, impulsive, skeptical, argumentative, indecisive, detached, withdrawn, prone to emotional dramas, tend to over rationalize, isolated, high-strung, misunderstood, impatient, frustrated

Your Venus Power

The planet Venus has a great deal of influence on your powers of attraction. Below are four possible Venus types for women and men. To find your Venus you need to go to page 771, where you will find the Venus table and extra information. The planet Mars also affects your powers of attraction. To find your Mars table and interpretation go to page 761.

WOMEN WITH VENUS IN CAPRICORN: With your natural caution in romantic affairs, you often appear reserved and controlled. You may be shy but try to be more forward, especially if you want to be noticed. When you care about people, however, you are usually willing to put in extra time and energy to preserve the relationship. You are practical and dependable, and a sense of duty can often play a large role in the affairs of your heart. With elegant simplicity you can attract others with your well-cut clothes and refined manners.

MEN WITH VENUS IN CAPRICORN: In relationships you take love seriously and can be a strong and practical support for friends or partners. You are usually attracted to people who are as hardworking as you. As you tend not to express your feelings until you feel really secure in a relationship, you may be drawn to those who seem loyal, faithful, and not likely to let you down. As you respect the wisdom of experience, you may be drawn to mature partners or, alternatively, you may act as an authority figure for someone younger.

WOMEN WITH VENUS IN AQUARIUS: You attract and impress others with your friendly approach and progressive ideas. As you are usually independent and easygoing, you value freedom within a relationship. A good companion with a sense of your own person, you enjoy socializing, especially with people who are original, cosmopolitan, and have a strong sense of individuality. Although being friendly and detached usually serves you well, avoid losing touch with your emotions. You usually prefer the company of those who have innovative or progressive views.

MEN WITH VENUS IN AQUARIUS: You are sociable and open-minded, and people are attracted by your friendly and easygoing style. Being independent, you value freedom-loving partners who give you the space to be yourself. People can

sometimes interpret your detachment as being emotionally cool, but they admire your objectivity and humanitarian inclinations. You are attracted to intelligent individuals who are as truthful and direct as you are, but above all they must be true friends. Ideally, your partner shares your liberal views on life and possesses a strong sense of individuality.

WOMEN WITH VENUS IN PISCES: Romantic and idealistic when in love, you can be a sensitive and responsive lover. With your affectionate and impressionable nature, you are often attracted to those who understand your sensitivity and share your vision. Your flexible, impressionable nature helps you to adapt to the needs of others. In your desire to blend with those you love, guard against giving too much of yourself by not clearly defining your boundaries.

MEN WITH VENUS IN PISCES: The combination of your emotional subtlety and charm can make you very alluring when dealing with affairs of the heart. Perceptive and impressionable, you have an easygoing style in your relationships, usually preferring to avoid ugly confrontation. You are drawn to partners who have a touch of glamour and are sensitive to the needs of others. Alternatively, they could be visionaries with rich imaginations who know how to keep you enchanted. With your insight you have the ability to observe the subtle moods of your partner.

WOMEN WITH VENUS IN ARIES: With your strong desires and enthusiastic nature you can be a passionate lover. Although idealistic and single-minded, you need to be more patient and less headstrong to avoid unnecessary conflicts in your relationships. Although at times others can accuse you of being bossy or impulsive, you possess a great deal of warmth and charm. When necessary you can disarm others by making them feel important.

MEN WITH VENUS IN ARIES: You are usually inclined to seek a partner who is active, goal-oriented, or decisive. Not known for your patience, you probably seek relationships early in life. You may find that you are attracted more to women who have a daring or adventurous spirit, but in your close relationships you may encounter rivalry or find that both you and your partner want to lead or be the boss. Although you may act rashly, you possess a great deal of magnetism and are capable of demonstrating your love and affection.

To read all about your Outer Planets and work out how to use your personalized timetable, go to Section Three, page 789.

≈≈≈

Your Personalized Timetable

JUPITER BENEFICIAL
1940 3/4 – 4/15
1941 7/8 – until 1942 5/22
1945 10/10 – until 1946 1/9
1946 3/16 – 9/3
1947 12/21 – until 1948 2/8
1948 6/25 – 10/5
1951 7/5 – 9/3
1952 2/13 – 3/29
1953 6/20 – 9/24
1953 11/5 – until 1954 5/3
1957 9/24 – 12/12
1958 4/25 – 8/11
1959 12/5 – until 1960 1/19
1963 6/2 – 10/21
1964 1/18 – 3/12
1965 6/3 – 8/19
1965 12/22 – until 1966 4/10
1969 9/8 – 11/23
1971 11/19 – until 1972 1/2
1975 5/12 – 7/10
1975 9/18 – until 1976 2/21
1977 5/18 – 7/28
1981 1/4 – 2/13
1981 8/21 – 11/6
1983 11/2 – 12/18
1987 4/24 – 6/11
1987 11/2 – until 1988 1/27
1989 5/1 – 7/11
1992 12/1 – until 1993 3/30
1993 7/31 – 10/21
1995 2/18 – 5/14
1995 10/14 – 12/2
1999 4/8 – 5/21
2000 8/30 – 10/29
2001 4/12 – 6/24
2004 11/11 – until 2005 5/13
2005 6/28 – 10/6
2007 1/24 – 6/23
2007 9/19 – 11/16
2011 3/22 – 5/2
2012 7/29 – 12/14

SATURN BENEFICIAL
1938 5/8 – 11/2
1939 1/25 – 4/25
1942 7/29 – 11/23
1943 4/17 – 9/8
1943 11/10 – until 1944 5/17
1951 11/4 – until 1952 4/27
1952 7/24 – 12/24
1953 3/20 – 9/16
1957 2/8 – 5/8
1957 11/3 – until 1958 2/2
1958 6/9 – 11/1
1968 3/15 – 6/9
1968 10/7 – until 1969 3/1
1972 5/29 – until 1973 6/27
1981 1/12 – 1/24
1981 9/10 – until 1982 10/23
1986 12/9 – until 1987 12/8
1997 4/20 – until 1998 4/8
2001 7/7 – 12/25
2002 3/23 – 8/9
2002 12/16 – until 2003 4/28
2010 10/17 – until 2011 12/1
2012 4/21 – 8/26

URANUS BENEFICIAL
1944 6/13 – until 1948 6/8
1970 10/11 – until 1974 9/11
1984 2/3 – until 1987 9/8

NEPTUNE BENEFICIAL
1946 11/10 – until 1955 8/9
1976 1/7 – until 1981 10/22

PLUTO BENEFICIAL
1975 10/18 – until 1982 9/21
2000 2/20 – until 2005 11/1

JUPITER CHALLENGING
1940 7/3 – 11/9
1941 2/19 – 5/8

1943 8/14 – 11/15
1944 1/11 – 7/4
1946 11/9 – until 1947 2/7
1947 4/18 – 10/2
1952 6/10 – until 1953 4/21
1955 7/29 – 10/15
1956 2/22 – 6/11
1958 10/25 – until 1959 1/11
1959 5/29 – 9/8
1964 5/23 – 8/30
1964 9/30 – until 1965 4/2
1967 7/13 – 9/26
1970 10/9 – 12/22
1976 5/6 – 7/21
1976 11/21 – until 1977 3/10
1979 6/25 – 9/8
1982 2/5 – 3/15
1982 9/21 – 12/5
1988 4/20 – 6/29
1990 10/10 – until 1991 1/20
1991 6/5 – 8/23
1993 12/31 – until 1994 4/30
1994 8/31 – 11/20
2000 4/3 – 6/10
2002 9/17 – until 2003 3/2
2003 5/7 – 8/7
2005 12/11 – until 2006 6/13
2006 7/28 – 11/4
2011 8/11 – 9/18
2012 3/15 – 5/24

SATURN CHALLENGING
1940 6/7 – 11/24
1941 2/23 – 7/14
1941 11/9 – until 1942 4/2
1947 7/15 – until 1948 8/16
1954 10/16 – until 1955 12/3
1970 4/14 – until 1971 5/16
1976 8/23 – until 1977 9/26
1978 3/5 – 6/14
1983 11/21 – until 1984 7/7
1984 7/19 – until 1985 1/12
1985 5/3 – 10/10
1999 5/21 – until 2000 6/22
2000 12/12 – until 2001 3/9
2005 10/11 – until 2006 1/3
2006 6/27 – until 2007 7/30

URANUS CHALLENGING
1938 1/1 – until 1941 5/9
1957 9/10 – until 1961 8/12
1976 12/7 – until 1980 11/16

NEPTUNE CHALLENGING
1960 11/25 – until 1968 11/4

PLUTO CHALLENGING
1944 9/23 – until 1955 7/28
1987 1/14 – until 1994 9/15

JUPITER SPECIAL
1938 1/31 – 4/15
1938 9/2 – 12/4
1950 1/15 – 3/25
1961 12/28 – until 1962 3/7
1973 4/21 – 7/9
1973 12/9 – until 1974 2/18
1985 3/25 – 8/22
1985 11/13 – until 1986 2/2
1997 3/5 – until 1998 1/17
2009 2/16 – 5/17
2009 7/13 – 12/28

SATURN SPECIAL
1962 4/6 – 7/8
1962 12/30 – until 1964 2/16
1992 2/3 – until 1993 3/23
1993 9/5 – 12/17

URANUS SPECIAL
1998 2/15 – until 2002 12/18

NEPTUNE SPECIAL
2002 3/4 – until 2010 2/3

February 8

SUN: AQUARIUS · DECANATE: GEMINI/MERCURY · DEGREE: 18°–19°5 AQUARIUS · MODE: FIXED · ELEMENT: AIR

Your Personal Powers

Purposeful and optimistic, you are a determined individual with a charismatic manner and sociable nature. Usually benevolent and intelligent, your generosity and positive outlook indicate that you can be practical and enterprising. You are usually ambitious, and your ruling planet, Uranus, endows you with a persuasive manner, sudden opportunities, and the capacity to become popular. You lose power, however, if you get carried away or succumb to wastefulness and extravagance. Although you are usually sociable and friendly, your desire for accomplishment indicates that you gain power by developing your self-discipline and practical skills. Capable of outstanding success, with your self-assured attitude you can make things happen. Nevertheless, you empower yourself by being modest and considerate rather than too confident or arrogant. Often inventive or progressive, you can intuitively recognize the commercial potential of new ideas. Along with the ability to plan ahead and quickly spot opportunities, you can think big and project success. Mentally inspired and exuberant, you can also express yourself creatively or put your talent to some practical use.

Your Powers of Attraction in Relationships

Charming and sociable, you know how to enjoy yourself and be entertaining. Usually you are drawn to successful people who are generous or glamorous. Alternatively, you may be attracted to those who have an enterprising and altruistic nature. You also admire those who work hard and have gained prestigious positions. You are capable of making magnanimous gestures of generosity, and people admire your spontaneity and benevolent nature. Although you can be warmhearted, at times you can be bossy, stubborn, or overbearing. In close relationships you achieve more by compromising and being cooperative or by using your engaging charm. Although money is an important factor in relationships, you need to resist an inclination to be materialistic. Nevertheless, when you are in love you can be helpful, supportive, and loyal.

Your attractive qualities: practical, friendly, self-reliant, thorough, hardworking, progressive, protective, power to heal, common sense, confident, ambitious, enthusiastic, motivated, astute, enterprising, determination, quick to see opportunities, business acumen, strong sense of values

Your less attractive qualities: impatient, wasteful, intolerant, miserly, restlessness, domineering, lack of planning, controlling behavior, overindulgent, contrary, stubborn, arrogant, critical

Your Venus Power

The planet Venus has a great deal of influence on your powers of attraction. Below are four possible Venus types for women and men. To find your Venus you need to go to page 771, where you will find the Venus table and extra information. The planet Mars also affects your powers of attraction. To find your Mars table and interpretation go to page 761.

WOMEN WITH VENUS IN CAPRICORN: Loyal and responsible, you are attracted to dignified and reserved individuals. Being practical and security-conscious, you prefer hardworking partners who are resourceful and enterprising. Work may even be a factor in many of your associations and partnerships. For you, family and faithfulness can be especially important, so you are usually willing to work hard or make sacrifices in order to build a strong relationship.

MEN WITH VENUS IN CAPRICORN: Hardworking and ambitious, you are usually attracted to determined, focused, and ambitious partners with a strong sense of duty. You want them to take relationships as seriously as you do, so loyalty and faithfulness are high on your agenda. Since you may display a natural reserve about expressing your feelings in an intimate relationship, you need a partner who shares your need for emotional security.

WOMEN WITH VENUS IN AQUARIUS: When it comes to relationships, others are attracted to your honest, friendly, and easygoing attitude. You really enjoy social interaction with others and may develop a genuine concern for humanity. Usually you present a tolerant and reasonable front in love situations and attempt to view your relationships objectively. If partners become too demanding, however, you can become stubborn and fixed. Friendship may be even more important for you than sexual compatibility.

MEN WITH VENUS IN AQUARIUS: You are sociable and open-minded, and people are attracted by your friendly and relaxed style. Being independent, you value freedom-loving partners who give you the space to be yourself. Others sometimes interpret your detachment as being emotionally cool, but they may not understand your progressive views on rela-

tionships. Friendship can sometimes be even more important than earthly passion. Ideally, friends can share your ideas on life and possess a sense of originality as strong as your own. Not easily ruffled, you can deal well with difficult situations or moody partners.

WOMEN WITH VENUS IN PISCES: As a romantic and idealistic individual, you can be both loving and giving. In relationships you may need to balance the practical with the charitable. While making allowances and sacrifices is understandable in a loving relationship, playing the martyr is often a state of romantic illusion that can lead to self-deception. Your benevolence and sacrifices in the right relationship nonetheless make you a partner who is devoted, kind, and compassionate. Subtle, sensitive, and alluring, you make a sensual and caring partner.

MEN WITH VENUS IN PISCES: In love you are sensitive, tender, and affectionate, experiencing your partner's feelings almost as strongly as your own. Being also imaginative and visionary, you possess the ability to develop a deep compassion for others. As you are idealistic when in love, you usually prefer to see only your partner's good points, but be careful that your high expectations do not bring disappointment if you avoid harsh reality. Nevertheless, in your relationships with others, you can be devoted, loving, and positively enchanting.

WOMEN WITH VENUS IN ARIES: With your strong desires and enthusiastic nature you can be a passionate lover. Although idealistic and single-minded, you need to be more patient and less headstrong to avoid unnecessary conflicts in your relationships. Although at times others can accuse you of being bossy or impulsive, you possess a great deal of warmth and charm. When necessary you can disarm others by making them feel important.

MEN WITH VENUS IN ARIES: You are usually inclined to seek a partner who is active, goal-oriented, or decisive. Not known for your patience, you probably seek relationships early in life. You may find that you are attracted more to women who have a daring or adventurous spirit, but in your close relationships you may encounter rivalry or find that both you and your partner want to lead or be the boss. Although you may act rashly, you possess a great deal of magnetism and are capable of demonstrating your love and affection.

To read all about your Outer Planets and work out how to use your personalized timetable, go to Section Three, page 789.

≈

Your Personalized Timetable

JUPITER BENEFICIAL
1940 3/8 – 4/19
1941 7/13 – until 1942 5/26
1945 10/14 – until 1946 1/22
1946 3/2 – 9/8
1947 12/25 – until 1948 2/15
1948 6/17 – 10/12
1951 7/19 – 8/20
1952 2/18 – 4/2
1953 6/24 – until 1954 5/8
1957 9/29 – 12/19
1958 4/17 – 8/18
1959 12/9 – until 1960 1/25
1963 6/8 – 10/13
1964 1/25 – 3/16
1965 6/8 – 8/25
1965 12/14 – until 1966 4/17
1969 9/13 – 11/28
1970 6/2 – 7/14
1971 11/23 – until 1972 1/7
1975 5/17 – 7/21
1975 9/7 – until 1976 2/26
1977 5/22 – 8/2
1978 1/30 – 3/12
1981 8/27 – 11/11
1983 11/7 – 12/22
1987 4/29 – 6/17
1987 10/25 – until 1988 2/3
1989 5/6 – 7/15
1992 12/8 – until 1993 3/23
1993 8/7 – 10/26
1995 2/27 – 5/4
1995 10/20 – 12/6
1999 4/12 – 5/26
2000 9/12 – 10/16
2001 4/17 – 6/28
2004 11/16 – until 2005 5/1
2005 7/10 – 10/11
2007 1/30 – 6/15
2007 9/27 – 11/21
2011 3/26 – 5/7
2012 8/3 – 12/7

SATURN BENEFICIAL
1938 5/17 – 10/19
1939 2/6 – 5/3
1942 8/11 – 2 11/9
1943 4/26 – until 1944 5/25
1951 11/13 – until 1952 4/12
1952 8/6 – until 1953 1/11
1953 3/2 – 9/25
1957 2/26 – 4/19
1957 11/13 – until 1958 2/14
1958 5/26 – 11/12
1968 3/23 – 6/21
1968 9/23 – until 1969 3/10
1972 6/6 – until 1973 7/5
1981 9/19 – until 1982 11/1
1986 12/17 – until 1987 12/17
1997 4/28 – 12/1
1997 12/31 – until 1998 4/16
2001 7/17 – 12/12
2002 4/4 – 8/20
2002 12/3 – until 2003 5/7
2010 10/25 – until 2011 5/25
2011 7/2 – 12/12
2012 4/8 – 9/6

URANUS BENEFICIAL
1944 7/1 – until 1949 3/28
1970 10/28 – until 1974 9/29
1984 12/5 – until 1987 10/21

NEPTUNE BENEFICIAL
1946 12/30 – until 1955 9/17
1976 2/17 – until 1981 11/24

PLUTO BENEFICIAL
1975 11/17 – until 1983 7/19
2000 12/31 – until 2005 12/1

JUPITER CHALLENGING
1940 7/9 – 11/2
1941 2/26 – 5/12
1943 8/18 – 11/30
1943 12/27 – until 1944 7/9

1946 11/14 – until 1947 2/19
1947 4/6 – 10/7
1952 6/15 – until 1953 4/25
1955 8/2 – 10/22
1956 2/14 – 6/18
1958 10/29 – until 1959 1/17
1959 5/21 – 9/16
1964 5/27 – until 1965 4/7
1967 7/17 – 10/1
1968 3/28 – 5/16
1970 10/14 – 12/27
1971 7/15 – 8/3
1976 5/10 – 7/27
1976 11/13 – until 1977 3/16
1979 6/30 – 9/13
1982 9/26 – 12/10
1988 4/24 – 7/4
1988 12/31 – until 1989 2/8
1990 10/18 – until 1991 1/12
1991 6/11 – 8/28
1994 1/7 – 4/22
1994 9/7 – 11/24
2000 4/7 – 6/15
2002 9/23 – until 2003 2/20
2003 5/16 – 8/12
2005 12/17 – until 2006 6/1
2006 8/10 – 11/9
2012 3/20 – 5/28

SATURN CHALLENGING
1940 6/17 – 11/10
1941 3/7 – 7/27
1941 10/27 – until 1942 4/12
1947 7/23 – until 1948 8/24
1954 10/24 – until 1955 12/12
1956 7/3 – 8/26
1970 4/22 – until 1971 5/23
1976 9/1 – until 1977 3/12
1977 5/11 – 10/5
1978 2/20 – 6/26
1983 11/30 – until 1984 6/6
1984 8/18 – until 1985 1/26
1985 4/18 – 10/19
1999 5/29 – 12/20
2000 2/3 – 7/2
2000 11/28 – until 2001 3/21
2005 10/29 – 12/16
2006 7/5 – until 2007 8/8

URANUS CHALLENGING
1938 3/8 – until 1942 3/5
1957 10/3 – until 1962 6/1
1976 12/28 – until 1981 9/14

NEPTUNE CHALLENGING
1960 12/28 – until 1969 10/2

PLUTO CHALLENGING
1945 9/2 – until 1956 6/30
1987 11/24 – until 1994 10/19

JUPITER SPECIAL
1938 2/4 – 4/21
1938 8/25 – 12/10
1950 1/19 – 3/29
1962 1/2 – 3/11
1973 5/1 – 6/29
1973 12/14 – until 1974 2/22
1985 3/30 – 8/14
1985 11/20 – until 1986 2/7
1997 3/10 – until 1998 1/21
2009 2/20 – 6/2
2009 6/27 – until 2010 1/2

SATURN SPECIAL
1962 4/23 – 6/19
1963 1/8 – until 1964 2/24
1992 2/11 – until 1993 4/2
1993 8/22 – 12/29

URANUS SPECIAL
1998 3/6 – until 2003 1/11

NEPTUNE SPECIAL
2002 4/14 – until 2011 1/1

February 9

SUN: AQUARIUS · DECANATE: GEMINI/MERCURY · DEGREE: 19°5–20°5 AQUARIUS · MODE: FIXED · ELEMENT: AIR

Your Personal Powers

Intuitive and sensitive, you are a practical idealist with progressive ideas and humanitarian inclinations. Your ruling planet, Uranus, endows you with a friendly nature and original or creative ideas. Although at times your thoughts can be unconventional, you are sometimes blessed with flashes of inspiration. Mentally quick and receptive, you gain power by using your practical skills, inner wisdom, and versatility. You are often multitalented with diverse interests, and you empower yourself when you combine your natural creativity and inspiration with self-discipline. Staying focused on your goals and learning to persevere can help you refrain from making impulsive decisions. You lose some of your power when you let worry or indecisiveness sap your enthusiasm or energy. Since you may encounter times of great inspiration and periods of frustration, the key to your success is often patience, detachment, and constancy. Once you have found something that captures your imagination, you need to develop the willpower necessary in order to make real use of your unique gifts.

Your Powers of Attraction in Relationships

People are drawn to your friendly manner and often admire your creative ideas or talents. Compassionate by nature, your personal charisma is likely to be one of your attractive qualities. With your altruistic personality you have no problems attracting friends and lovers. You are usually drawn to clever individuals who have original ideas or unconventional lifestyles. Although you can be very gregarious and sociable, at times you can appear to others distant or disinterested. Needing freedom, you do not like to be restricted by demanding partners. If you fail to communicate or be open about your feelings, your partners may assume that you are keeping secrets or be uncertain about your relationship. Nevertheless, sentimental and loving, you can be very generous with those you love.

Your attractive qualities: idealistic, tolerant, liberal, spontaneous, humanitarian, original, creative, sensitive, generous, magnetic, charismatic, friendly, charitable, detached, popular, inventive, good at solving problems, focused, purposeful, persuasive, people-oriented, intuitive, hardworking

Your less attractive qualities: stubborn, indecisive, suspicious, frustrated, nervous, anxious, unconventional, rebellious, scattered, unsure, selfish, impractical, bitter, argumentative, worry about money, moody

Your Venus Power

The planet Venus has a great deal of influence on your powers of attraction. Below are four possible Venus types for women and men. To find your Venus you need to go to page 771, where you will find the Venus table and extra information. The planet Mars also affects your powers of attraction. To find your Mars table and interpretation go to page 761.

WOMEN WITH VENUS IN CAPRICORN: With your natural caution in romantic affairs, you often appear reserved and controlled. You may be shy but try to be more forward, especially if you want to be noticed. When you care about people, however, you are usually willing to put in extra time and energy to preserve the relationship. You are practical and dependable, and a sense of duty can often play a large role in affairs of your heart. With elegant simplicity you can attract others with your well-cut clothes and refined manners.

MEN WITH VENUS IN CAPRICORN: In relationships you take love seriously and can be a strong and practical support for friends or partners. You are usually attracted to partners who are as hardworking as you. As you tend not to express your feelings until you feel really secure in a relationship, you may be drawn to those who seem loyal, faithful, and not likely to let you down. As you respect the wisdom of experience, you may be drawn to mature partners or, alternatively, you may act as an authority figure for someone younger.

WOMEN WITH VENUS IN AQUARIUS: When it comes to relationships, others are attracted to your honest, friendly, and easygoing approach. You really enjoy social interaction with others and may develop a genuine concern for humanity. Usually you present a tolerant and reasonable front in love situations and attempt to view your relationships objectively. If partners become too demanding, however, you can become stubborn and fixed. Friendship may be even more important for you than sexual compatibility.

MEN WITH VENUS IN AQUARIUS: You are sociable and open-minded, and people are attracted by your friendly and relaxed style. Being independent, you value freedom-loving partners who give you the space to be yourself. Others sometimes interpret your detachment as being emotionally cool, but they may not understand your progressive views on rela-

tionships. Friendship can sometimes be even more important than earthly passion. Ideally, friends can share your ideas on life and possess a sense of originality as strong as your own. Not easily ruffled, you can deal well with difficult situations or moody partners.

WOMEN WITH VENUS IN PISCES: Idealistic and impressionable, in love you are romantic. Being sensitive to people, you are receptive to their moods and feelings. This affinity indicates that although you can be selfless, you may have to guard against being too sentimental or overly romantic, especially with those who can take advantage of your kindness. Nevertheless, as you are alluring and seductive, your partners can be intrigued by your poetic soul or mysterious nature.

MEN WITH VENUS IN PISCES: The combination of your emotional subtlety and charm can make you very alluring when dealing with affairs of the heart. Perceptive and impressionable, you have an easygoing style in your relationships, usually preferring to avoid ugly confrontation. You are drawn to a partner who has a touch of glamour and is sensitive to the needs of others. Alternatively, your partner can be a visionary with a rich imagination who can keep you enchanted.

WOMEN WITH VENUS IN ARIES: Self-reliant and strong, you usually want things your own way. This can present problems if you refuse to compromise with your partners. Your life lessons in love and relationships often involve patience and learning to trust. When you project the full power of your Venus, however, you can radiate a charismatic and captivating energy and make a strong impression on others. Independence is often high on your relationship agenda.

MEN WITH VENUS IN ARIES: You are drawn to strong, independent women who can stand up to you. Although you can enthusiastically follow the object of your desire, you may lose power if you allow your forceful emotions to become too dominant. Warm and passionate, you have a side to your nature that longs for new adventures. Romantic and chivalrous, you really enjoy the excitement of the initial chase, but unless you keep the enthusiasm alive and avoid falling into a rut you may become easily bored.

To read all about your Outer Planets and work out how to use your personalized timetable, go to Section Three, page 789.

≈

Your Personalized Timetable

JUPITER BENEFICIAL
1940 3/13 – 4/24
1941 7/18 – until 1942 1/21
1942 2/20 – 5/31
1945 10/19 – until 1946 9/14
1947 12/30 – until 1948 2/21
1948 6/9 – 10/18
1952 2/23 – 4/7
1953 6/29 – until 1954 5/13
1957 10/3 – 12/25
1958 4/9 – 8/25
1959 12/14 – until 1960 1/30
1960 7/26 – 9/14
1963 6/14 – 10/6
1964 1/31 – 3/21
1965 6/12 – 9/1
1965 12/7 – until 1966 4/23
1969 9/18 – 12/3
1970 5/20 – 7/27
1971 11/28 – until 1972 1/12
1975 5/22 – 12/8
1975 12/11 – until 1976 3/2
1977 5/27 – 8/8
1978 1/18 – 3/24
1981 9/1 – 11/16
1983 11/12 – 12/26
1987 5/3 – 6/23
1987 10/17 – until 1988 2/9
1989 5/11 – 7/20
1992 12/15 – until 1993 3/14
1993 8/13 – 10/30
1995 3/12 – 4/21
1995 10/25 – 12/11
1999 4/16 – 5/30
2001 4/22 – 7/3
2004 11/22 – until 2005 4/21
2005 7/20 – 10/15
2007 2/5 – 6/7
2007 10/4 – 11/25
2011 3/30 – 5/11
2012 8/10 – 11/29

SATURN BENEFICIAL
1938 5/27 – 10/6
1939 2/17 – 5/12
1939 12/8 – until 1940 1/16
1942 8/27 – 10/24
1943 5/5 – until 1944 6/3
1951 11/23 – until 1952 3/30
1952 8/17 – until 1953 10/4
1957 11/22 – until 1958 3/2
1958 5/9 – 11/21
1968 3/31 – 7/7
1968 9/6 – until 1969 3/19
1972 6/14 – until 1973 7/13
1981 9/27 – until 1982 11/9
1983 6/25 – 7/7
1986 12/26 – until 1987 8/2
1987 9/4 – 12/26
1997 5/7 – 11/8
1998 1/22 – 4/24
2001 7/27 – 11/30
2002 4/15 – 9/3
2002 11/19 – until 2003 5/16
2010 11/3 – until 2011 5/3
2011 7/23 – 12/24
2012 3/25 – 9/16

URANUS BENEFICIAL
1944 7/22 – until 1949 4/28
1970 11/15 – until 1974 10/16
1984 12/21 – until 1987 11/12

NEPTUNE BENEFICIAL
1947 11/7 – until 1956 7/30
1977 1/4 – until 1982 10/18

PLUTO BENEFICIAL
1976 10/9 – until 1983 9/8
2001 2/3 – until 2006 10/26

JUPITER CHALLENGING
1940 7/16 – 10/25
1941 3/4 – 5/17
1943 8/23 – until 1944 7/14
1946 11/19 – until 1947 10/13

1952 6/20 – 12/15
1953 1/26 – 4/30
1955 8/7 – 10/29
1956 2/6 – 6/24
1958 11/3 – until 1959 1/24
1959 5/13 – 9/22
1964 6/1 – until 1965 4/12
1967 7/22 – 10/6
1968 3/17 – 5/28
1970 10/18 – until 1971 1/2
1971 6/26 – 8/21
1976 5/15 – 8/3
1976 11/6 – until 1977 3/22
1979 7/5 – 9/18
1982 10/2 – 12/15
1988 4/29 – 7/9
1988 12/19 – until 1989 2/21
1990 10/27 – until 1991 1/3
1991 6/17 – 9/1
1994 1/15 – 4/14
1994 9/13 – 11/29
2000 4/12 – 6/19
2002 9/28 – until 2003 2/12
2003 5/24 – 8/17
2005 12/22 – until 2006 5/22
2006 8/19 – 11/14
2012 3/24 – 6/2

SATURN CHALLENGING
1940 6/27 – 10/29
1941 3/18 – 8/11
1941 10/10 – until 1942 4/20
1947 7/31 – until 1948 9/1
1954 11/2 – until 1955 12/21
1956 6/14 – 9/13
1970 4/30 – until 1971 5/31
1976 9/9 – until 1977 2/23
1977 5/27 – 10/15
1978 2/8 – 7/6
1983 12/9 – until 1984 5/21
1984 9/2 – until 1985 2/15
1985 3/28 – 10/28
1999 6/7 – 12/2
2000 2/21 – 7/12
2000 11/16 – until 2001 3/31
2006 7/14 – until 2007 8/16

URANUS CHALLENGING
1938 3/31 – until 1942 4/3
1958 8/1 – until 1962 6/30
1977 2/8 – until 1981 10/8

NEPTUNE CHALLENGING
1961 11/23 – until 1969 11/2

PLUTO CHALLENGING
1945 10/30 – 11/26
1946 8/16 – until 1947 2/20
1947 6/23 – until 1955 10/2
1956 2/1 – 8/5
1987 12/23 – until 1988 4/10
1988 10/17 – until 1994 1/28
1994 4/3 – 11/15

JUPITER SPECIAL
1938 2/8 – 4/27
1938 8/17 – 12/17
1950 1/23 – 4/3
1950 10/14 – 11/3
1962 1/6 – 3/15
1973 5/15 – 6/14
1973 12/19 – until 1974 2/27
1985 4/6 – 8/6
1985 11/27 – until 1986 2/11
1997 3/15 – until 1998 1/25
2009 2/24 – until 2010 1/7

SATURN SPECIAL
1963 1/17 – until 1964 3/4
1992 2/20 – until 1993 4/13
1993 8/9 – until 1994 1/8

URANUS SPECIAL
1998 3/29 – until 2003 1/30

NEPTUNE SPECIAL
2003 3/2 – until 2011 2/1

675

February 10

SUN: AQUARIUS • DECANATE: LIBRA/VENUS • DEGREE: 20°–21°5 AQUARIUS • MODE: FIXED • ELEMENT: AIR

Your Personal Powers

Ambitious and determined, you are a strong-willed individual with a powerful mind and inventive ideas. Your ruling planet, Uranus, endows you with inspired and progressive thoughts and a love of freedom. Mentally quick, you have good powers of perception and are usually excellent at business or problem solving. Although you can be hardworking and practical, you gain power when you balance your need to operate alone with the necessity to be cooperative in teamwork situations. By using your people skills, charm, and diplomacy you can usually negotiate amicable agreements. You lose some of your power by being stubborn, single-minded, or too domineering. Although you value your independence and prefer to make up your own mind, you may need to develop your tolerance and patience. If restricted by periods of doubt or insecurity, you have to learn to trust your strong intuition and your instincts about people. You usually empower yourself by combining your common sense, natural leadership skills, and vision to create successful results.

Your Powers of Attraction in Relationships

Caring and aware, your insight into human nature indicates that you can attract many admirers. Socializing and exchanging ideas with your friends or partner usually uplifts your sense of well-being. Since sharing and collaborating with others also aid your success, you benefit from business partnerships and teamwork. You also benefit from joining groups that are concerned with reforms. You are usually attracted to intelligent people who are well-informed and show a willingness to share their knowledge. As you are highly intuitive and sensitive to others' moods, you may be prone to fluctuating moods yourself. Since keeping the balance of power is a key factor in your close relationships, you show your strength by remaining calm and composed or by creating a harmonious atmosphere around you.

Your attractive qualities: kindhearted, well-balanced, common sense, quick perception, hardworking, ambitious, determined, enterprising, strong initiative, creative, progressive, strong-willed and forceful, optimistic, competitive, shrewd, strong convictions, independent, intuitive, gregarious

Your less attractive qualities: overbearing, jealous, manipulative, bossy, escapism, stubborn, antagonistic, lack of restraint, selfish, irritable, impatient, dependent on others, restlessness, moody, too sensitive, inner doubts, tense

Your Venus Power

The planet Venus has a great deal of influence on your powers of attraction. Below are four possible Venus types for women and men. To find your Venus you need to go to page 771, where you will find the Venus table and extra information. The planet Mars also affects your powers of attraction. To find your Mars table and interpretation go to page 761.

WOMEN WITH VENUS IN CAPRICORN: Proud and refined, you attract others with your composed dignity. Disliking vulnerability and needing to feel safe before you can express your feelings, you display a strong front. Feeling insecure or inadequate in relationships may force you to become manipulative in order to regain control. Nevertheless, you can project an attractive sense of self-assurance and are capable of displaying loyalty and a wonderful dry sense of humor.

MEN WITH VENUS IN CAPRICORN: As you do not display your deeper emotions freely, you are usually dignified and controlled in your relationships. Practical and down-to-earth partners are particularly attractive to you, especially those who do not rush into expressing their feelings but seem to possess natural class and reserve. You need a partner who is loyal and dependable and willing to take your relationship seriously.

WOMEN WITH VENUS IN AQUARIUS: Usually you have a modern outlook on love and are open to new or current lifestyles. Your intuitive abilities, communal sense, and people skills often allow you to see deeper into human intentions and to telepathically read people's thoughts. You are usually group-oriented and are drawn to individuals within the group who are independent and self-motivated. You are more inclined to choose a partner who is unconventional or freedom-loving. Conscious of your social standing, however, you want someone who can relate well to your friends.

MEN WITH VENUS IN AQUARIUS: Although independent, you often enjoy being part of a group. The partners you frequently attract are themselves nonconformists or free spirits. As an individual you may not find it easy to settle into a routine or an entirely mundane type of relationship. You may have some unconventional views on traditional marriage or your partner may hold such views. Friendship can be as important to you as your freedom.

WOMEN WITH VENUS IN PISCES: Romantic and idealistic when in love, you can be a sensitive and responsive lover. With your affectionate and impressionable nature you are often attracted to those who understand your sensitivity and share your vision. Your flexibility and impressionable nature help you adapt to the needs of others. In your desire to blend with those you love, guard against giving too much of yourself by not clearly defining your boundaries.

MEN WITH VENUS IN PISCES: Romantic and idealistic when in love, you can be a sensitive and responsive lover. Being pliant and flexible with an impressionable nature helps you to adapt to the needs of others. In your desire to blend with those you love, however, guard against not clearly defining your own boundaries. With your affectionate and sentimental nature, you are often attracted to those who understand your sensitivity and share your vision.

WOMEN WITH VENUS IN ARIES: You gain power from your strong individuality, energy, and enthusiasm. Your young-at-heart and spirited approach to relationships adds to your appeal. However, if you become too impatient or self-absorbed your partnerships are likely to suffer. Nevertheless, you can be creative, sharp, and quick, especially when you are able to share new and exciting projects with your partners. Mischievous with a love of action, you may even incite them to a playful fight.

MEN WITH VENUS IN ARIES: As you often have the courage and strength to initiate situations, you like to take the lead. With your unconscious desire for conquest you may also have to beware of being competitive with your partners. Nevertheless, you are drawn to direct and strong-willed women who can share your love of action and enthusiasm for life. When you are feeling good you can be charming and enthusiastic in romantic situations with an entertaining and spontaneous spirit.

To read all about your Outer Planets and work out how to use your personalized timetable, go to Section Three, page 789.

≈

JUPITER BENEFICIAL
1940 3/17 – 4/28
1941 7/23 – until 1942 1/7
1942 3/6 – 6/5
1945 10/24 – until 1946 9/19
1948 1/4 – 2/29
1948 6/1 – 10/24
1952 2/28 – 4/11
1953 7/4 – until 1954 5/18
1957 10/8 – until 1958 1/2
1958 4/1 – 8/31
1959 12/18 – until 1960 2/4
1960 7/15 – 9/26
1963 6/21 – 9/28
1964 2/6 – 3/25
1965 6/17 – 9/9
1965 11/28 – until 1966 4/29
1969 9/23 – 12/9
1970 5/10 – 8/6
1971 12/2 – until 1972 1/16
1975 5/27 – 11/16
1976 1/3 – 3/7
1977 5/31 – 8/13
1978 1/9 – 4/2
1981 9/6 – 11/21
1983 11/16 – 12/31
1987 5/8 – 6/29
1987 10/10 – until 1988 2/15
1989 5/15 – 7/25
1992 12/24 – until 1993 3/5
1993 8/19 – 11/4
1995 10/30 – 12/15
1999 4/20 – 6/4
1999 11/29 – until 2000 1/10
2001 4/27 – 7/7
2004 11/28 – until 2005 4/13
2005 7/28 – 10/20
2007 2/12 – 5/30
2007 10/10 – 11/30
2011 4/3 – 5/16
2012 8/17 – 11/22

SATURN BENEFICIAL
1938 6/8 – 9/23
1939 2/27 – 5/20
1939 11/18 – until 1940 2/4
1943 5/13 – until 1944 6/10
1951 12/5 – until 1952 3/17
1952 8/27 – until 1953 10/12
1957 11/30 – until 1958 11/30
1968 4/8 – until 1969 3/27
1972 6/22 – until 1973 7/22
1974 1/25 – 4/1
1981 10/5 – until 1982 11/18
1983 5/25 – 8/6
1987 1/4 – 7/9
1987 9/27 – until 1988 1/3
1997 5/16 – 10/24
1998 2/5 – 5/2
2001 8/7 – 11/17
2002 4/24 – 9/23
2002 10/29 – until 2003 5/25
2010 11/12 – until 2011 4/18
2011 8/6 – until 2012 1/9
2012 3/7 – 9/25

URANUS BENEFICIAL
1944 8/20 – until 1949 5/19
1970 12/8 – until 1975 8/7
1985 1/8 – until 1987 11/30

NEPTUNE BENEFICIAL
1947 12/18 – until 1956 9/14
1977 2/10 – until 1982 11/22

PLUTO BENEFICIAL
1976 11/5 – until 1983 10/6
2001 12/24 – until 2006 11/28

JUPITER CHALLENGING
1940 7/23 – 10/17
1941 3/9 – 5/21
1943 8/28 – until 1944 7/20

1946 11/23 – until 1947 10/18
1952 6/25 – 12/3
1953 2/7 – 5/4
1955 8/11 – 11/6
1956 1/29 – 6/30
1958 11/8 – until 1959 1/31
1959 5/5 – 9/28
1964 6/5 – until 1965 4/17
1967 7/27 – 10/12
1968 3/8 – 6/6
1970 10/23 – until 1971 1/7
1971 6/15 – 9/1
1976 5/19 – 8/11
1976 10/28 – until 1977 3/28
1979 7/10 – 9/23
1982 10/7 – 12/20
1988 5/3 – 7/15
1988 12/10 – until 1989 3/2
1990 11/7 – 12/22
1991 6/22 – 9/6
1994 1/24 – 4/5
1994 9/18 – 12/3
2000 4/16 – 6/24
2002 10/5 – until 2003 2/4
2003 5/31 – 8/21
2005 12/28 – until 2006 5/14
2006 8/27 – 11/18
2012 3/29 – 6/6

SATURN CHALLENGING
1940 7/9 – 10/16
1941 3/27 – until 1942 4/29
1947 8/8 – until 1948 9/9
1954 11/10 – until 1955 12/30
1956 5/30 – 9/27
1970 5/8 – until 1971 6/8
1976 9/19 – until 1977 2/10
1977 6/8 – 10/28
1978 1/25 – 7/15
1983 12/19 – until 1984 5/7
1984 9/14 – until 1985 11/6
1999 6/16 – 11/18
2000 3/5 – 7/23
2000 11/3 – until 2001 4/10
2006 7/22 – until 2007 8/23

URANUS CHALLENGING
1938 4/18 – until 1942 4/23
1958 8/17 – until 1962 7/20
1977 11/15 – until 1981 10/27

NEPTUNE CHALLENGING
1961 12/24 – until 1970 9/29

PLUTO CHALLENGING
1946 9/24 – until 1957 7/9
1988 11/11 – until 1995 10/7

JUPITER SPECIAL
1938 2/13 – 5/4
1938 8/9 – 12/23
1950 1/27 – 4/8
1950 9/27 – 11/19
1962 1/11 – 3/20
1973 12/24 – until 1974 3/3
1985 4/12 – 7/29
1985 12/3 – until 1986 2/15
1997 3/20 – 9/17
1997 10/28 – until 1998 1/30
2009 3/1 – until 2010 1/12

SATURN SPECIAL
1963 1/25 – until 1964 3/13
1964 10/10 – 11/24
1992 2/29 – 9/11
1992 11/18 – until 1993 4/27
1993 7/25 – until 1994 1/18

URANUS SPECIAL
1999 2/2 – until 2003 2/17

NEPTUNE SPECIAL
2003 4/7 – until 2011 12/27

February 11

SUN: AQUARIUS • DECANATE: LIBRA/VENUS • DEGREE: 21°–22°5 AQUARIUS • MODE: FIXED • ELEMENT: AIR

Your Personal Powers

Intuitive and highly sensitive, you are a determined individual with strong willpower and the capacity to endure. Your ruling planet, Uranus, grants you original ways of self-expression and an idealistic nature. You gain power when you develop your practical skills and do not let limitations or frustrations undermine your resolute mind. Although you value your independence, being group-oriented suggests that you benefit from interacting with people who share your vision or aspirations. As you may sometimes be ahead of your time, your foresight and inner faith can be keys to your success. Even though you can be highly motivated, a tendency to vacillate emotionally implies that you need to remain focused on your objectives even though you feel frustrated when your high ideals seem unreachable. In your eagerness to bring about progress remember that patience can be one of your most powerful tools. By letting your spontaneity and humanitarian inclinations help you to stay detached or unconcerned, you can overcome your inner fears and express your thoughts or powerful emotions. When you have a definite goal in mind, you will work hard to achieve success.

Your Powers of Attraction in Relationships

Your gregarious personality often has a great deal of personal magnetism. With an ability to mix with all types of people, you can be sociable and altruistic. You enjoy the company of friends and acquaintances and can be fun and entertaining. Usually you are drawn to individuals with strong principles or partners who are hardworking and possess business acumen. Alternatively, your progressive outlook and love of freedom may draw you to idealistic individuals who are nonconformist. You may also possess creative talents and have an original approach to your relationships. Although you can be loyal and compassionate with a deep need for intimacy, when you feel inhibited you may become aloof or too self-absorbed. This may be overcome by finding a partner who shares your high ideals and aspirations.

Your attractive qualities: independent, focused, objective, enthusiastic, inspirational, idealistic, intuitive, intelligent, outgoing, inventive, healing potential, humanitarian, psychic, witty, hardworking, sharp insight, progressive, persevering, disciplined, calm, problem solving, adaptable, strong-willed

Your less attractive qualities: provocative, stubborn, aimless, too emotional, high-strung, selfish, doubtful, cynical, unfeeling, domineering, mean, impractical, overanxious, mistrusting, rebellious, materialistic, moody, unrealistic, too willful

Your Venus Power

The planet Venus has a great deal of influence on your powers of attraction. Below are four possible Venus types for women and men. To find your Venus you need to go to page 771, where you will find the Venus table and extra information. The planet Mars also affects your powers of attraction. To find your Mars table and interpretation go to page 761.

WOMEN WITH VENUS IN CAPRICORN: With your natural caution in romantic affairs, you often appear reserved and controlled. You may be shy but try to be more forward, especially if you want to be noticed. When you care about people, however, you are usually willing to put in extra time and energy to preserve the relationship. You are practical and dependable, and a sense of duty can often play a large role in affairs of your heart. With elegant simplicity you can attract others with your well-cut clothes and refined manners.

MEN WITH VENUS IN CAPRICORN: In relationships you take love seriously and can be a strong and practical support for friends or partners. You are usually attracted to partners who are as hardworking as you. As you tend not to express your feelings until you feel really secure in a relationship, you may be drawn to those who seem loyal, faithful, and not likely to let you down. As you respect the wisdom of experience, you may be drawn to mature partners or, alternatively, you may act as an authority figure for someone younger.

WOMEN WITH VENUS IN AQUARIUS: You attract and impress others with your friendly approach and progressive ideas. As you are usually independent and easygoing, you value freedom within a relationship. A good companion with a sense of your own person, you enjoy socializing, especially with people who are original, cosmopolitan, and have a strong sense of individuality. Although being friendly and detached usually serves you well, avoid losing touch with your emotions. You usually prefer the company of those who have innovative or progressive views.

MEN WITH VENUS IN AQUARIUS: You are sociable and open-minded, and people are attracted by your friendly and easygoing style. Being independent, you value freedom-loving

partners who give you the space to be yourself. People can sometimes interpret your detachment as being emotionally cool, but they admire your objectivity and humanitarian inclinations. You are attracted to intelligent individuals who are as truthful and direct as you are, but above all they must be true friends. Ideally your partner shares your liberal views on life and possesses a strong sense of individuality.

WOMEN WITH VENUS IN PISCES: In love you are sensitive, tender, and affectionate, experiencing your partner's feelings almost as strongly as your own. Being imaginative and a visionary, you possess the ability to develop creative gifts and a deep compassion for others. As you are idealistic when in love, you usually prefer to see only your partner's good points, but be careful that your high expectations do not bring disappointment if you avoid being realistic. Nevertheless, in your relationships with others, you can be devoted, loving, and positively enchanting.

MEN WITH VENUS IN PISCES: Being adaptable and sensitive, you are able to intuitively feel the moods of those you love. Although you are receptive to others, you can be ambiguous about your own feelings toward your partner. Romantic and kindhearted, you long to be loved but you need to be realistic about your relationships in order to avoid disappointments. When in love you may idealize your partners and fail to see any faults in their personality.

WOMEN WITH VENUS IN ARIES: With your strong desires and enthusiastic nature, you can be a passionate lover. Although idealistic and single-minded, you need to be more patient and less headstrong to avoid unnecessary conflicts in your relationships. Although at times others can accuse you of being bossy or impulsive, you possess a great deal of warmth and charm. When necessary you can disarm others by making them feel important.

MEN WITH VENUS IN ARIES: You are usually drawn to courageous or assertive women who possess strong personal magnetism. You might therefore find those who seem to be independent or action-oriented very attractive. Your own eagerness and need for activity suggest that you start relationships with great enthusiasm, especially if they offer you excitement or adventures. The challenge is often to maintain relationships and not get bored too easily.

To read all about your Outer Planets and work out how to use your personalized timetable, go to Section Three, page 789.

≈

Your Personalized Timetable

JUPITER BENEFICIAL
1940 3/21 – 5/2
1941 7/29 – 12/28
1942 3/16 – 6/9
1945 10/29 – until 1946 9/24
1948 1/8 – 3/8
1948 5/23 – 10/29
1952 3/3 – 4/15
1953 7/8 – until 1954 5/23
1957 10/13 – until 1958 1/11
1958 3/22 – 9/6
1959 12/23 – until 1960 2/10
1960 7/5 – 10/4
1963 6/29 – 9/20
1964 2/12 – 3/29
1965 6/21 – 9/19
1965 11/19 – until 1966 5/4
1969 9/27 – 12/15
1970 5/2 – 8/14
1971 12/7 – until 1972 1/21
1975 6/1 – 11/5
1976 1/14 – 3/12
1977 6/5 – 8/19
1978 1/1 – 4/10
1981 9/11 – 11/26
1983 11/21 – until 1984 1/4
1987 5/12 – 7/7
1987 10/2 – until 1988 2/21
1989 5/19 – 7/30
1993 1/4 – 2/21
1993 8/24 – 11/9
1995 11/4 – 12/20
1999 4/25 – 6/10
1999 11/18 – until 2000 1/22
2001 5/2 – 7/12
2004 12/4 – until 2005 4/5
2005 8/4 – 10/25
2007 2/20 – 5/21
2007 10/16 – 12/4
2011 4/8 – 5/20
2012 8/25 – 2 11/13

SATURN BENEFICIAL
1938 6/22 – 9/8
1939 3/8 – 5/30
1939 11/4 – until 1940 2/18
1943 5/21 – until 1944 6/18
1951 12/18 – until 1952 3/2
1952 9/6 – until 1953 10/20
1957 12/9 – until 1958 12/9
1968 4/16 – until 1969 4/4
1972 6/30 – until 1973 2/1
1973 2/26 – 7/31
1974 1/10 – 4/16
1981 10/14 – until 1982 11/27
1983 5/9 – 8/21
1987 1/14 – 6/24
1987 10/12 – until 1988 1/12
1988 7/28 – 10/2
1997 5/26 – 10/11
1998 2/16 – 5/11
1998 12/26 – until 1999 1/1
2001 8/21 – 11/2
2002 5/3 – until 2003 6/2
2010 11/22 – until 2011 4/5
2011 8/18 – until 2012 10/4

URANUS BENEFICIAL
1945 6/13 – until 1949 6/6
1971 10/5 – until 1975 9/3
1985 1/29 – until 1987 12/17

NEPTUNE BENEFICIAL
1948 11/4 – until 1956 10/13
1978 1/2 – until 1983 10/12

PLUTO BENEFICIAL
1976 12/10 – until 1984 8/19
2002 1/24 – until 2007 10/20

JUPITER CHALLENGING
1940 8/1 – 10/8
1941 3/15 – 5/25
1943 9/2 – until 1944 7/25

1946 11/28 – until 1947 10/23
1952 7/1 – 11/24
1953 2/15 – 5/8
1955 8/16 – 11/15
1956 1/20 – 7/6
1958 11/12 – until 1959 2/8
1959 4/26 – 10/4
1964 6/10 – until 1965 4/21
1967 7/31 – 10/18
1968 2/28 – 6/14
1970 10/28 – until 1971 1/13
1971 6/6 – 9/9
1976 5/23 – 8/21
1976 10/19 – until 1977 4/2
1979 7/15 – 9/28
1982 10/11 – 12/25
1988 5/7 – 7/20
1988 12/2 – until 1989 3/9
1991 6/28 – 9/11
1994 2/5 – 3/24
1994 9/24 – 12/8
2000 4/20 – 6/29
2002 10/11 – until 2003 1/28
2003 6/7 – 8/26
2006 1/4 – 5/6
2006 9/3 – 11/23
2012 4/3 – 6/10

SATURN CHALLENGING
1940 7/24 – 9/30
1941 4/5 – until 1942 5/7
1947 8/16 – until 1948 9/17
1949 4/8 – 5/24
1954 11/19 – until 1956 1/10
1956 5/17 – 10/8
1970 5/16 – until 1971 6/16
1972 1/16 – 2/15
1976 9/29 – until 1977 1/29
1977 6/18 – 11/12
1978 1/9 – 7/24
1983 12/30 – until 1984 4/23
1984 9/25 – until 1985 11/15
1999 6/26 – 11/5
2000 3/16 – 8/6
2000 10/19 – until 2001 4/19
2006 7/30 – until 2007 8/31

URANUS CHALLENGING
1938 5/6 – until 1942 5/11
1958 9/4 – until 1962 8/6
1977 12/2 – until 1981 11/13

NEPTUNE CHALLENGING
1962 11/21 – until 1970 10/31

PLUTO CHALLENGING
1947 9/3 – until 1958 5/15
1988 12/7 – until 1995 11/5

JUPITER SPECIAL
1938 2/17 – 5/12
1938 8/1 – 12/28
1950 2/1 – 4/14
1950 9/17 – 11/29
1962 1/15 – 3/25
1973 12/29 – until 1974 3/7
1985 4/20 – 7/21
1985 12/9 – until 1986 2/19
1997 3/25 – 9/5
1997 11/9 – until 1998 2/3
2009 3/6 – until 2010 1/17

SATURN SPECIAL
1963 2/3 – until 1964 3/22
1964 9/20 – 12/13
1992 3/9 – 8/26
1992 12/4 – until 1993 5/15
1993 7/6 – until 1994 1/27

URANUS SPECIAL
1999 2/19 – until 2003 12/24

NEPTUNE SPECIAL
2004 2/27 – Continues

February 12

SUN: AQUARIUS • DECANATE: LIBRA/VENUS • DEGREE: 22°–23°5 AQUARIUS • MODE: FIXED • ELEMENT: AIR

Your Personal Powers

Creative and versatile, you are an independent individual with bright ideas and good social skills. Possessing common sense, you gain power by combining your objectivity and good sense of values with your intuition and ability to quickly assess people. With your progressive outlook, you have quick perception and a love of freedom. You can also succeed admirably when you combine your diplomacy and social skills with your inventive ideas, knowledge, and talents. Although you are often ambitious and clever with leadership potential, a tendency to be impatient or indecisive implies that you may need to learn to utilize your talents more efficiently. By disciplining yourself to stay focused and purposeful you can achieve success. A tendency to worry about your financial resources means that if you focus too much on money you may fail to realize your true potential as an innovator and reformer. Since you are both idealistic and shrewd when it comes to business or cutting a good deal, you empower yourself when you believe in what you do, sell, or promote.

Your Powers of Attraction in Relationships

Naturally understanding and sensitive, you know how to be tactful and cooperative. An ability to make the right contacts implies that you can combine your business and social activities. Usually charming and sociable, you are attracted to intelligent, loyal, and determined individuals with common sense and bright ideas. Since you are often interested in education or self-awareness, you also admire people with insight who are working on themselves. You may prefer, however, to communicate your thoughts with your partner rather than demonstrate your feelings. Sometimes others may interpret your assertiveness as stubbornness. Although you can occasionally appear offhand, you often mask your sensitivity and need for approval behind a self-assured front. In relationships honesty, freedom, and feeling safe enough to express your love are especially important to you.

Your attractive qualities: mentally sharp, independent, creative, initiative, disciplinarian, promoter, objective, humanitarian, leadership, intuitive, friendly, innovative, confident, diplomatic, wit, inner faith, calm, detached, good sense of values, enthusiastic, good with words, dynamic, unique style

Your less attractive qualities: stubborn, worried, rebellious, uncooperative, lack of self-esteem, too easily discouraged, insecure, indecisive, bossy, anxious, impatient, mentally restless, undermined by others, overindulgent

Your Venus Power

The planet Venus has a great deal of influence on your powers of attraction. Below are four possible Venus types for women and men. To find your Venus you need to go to page 771, where you will find the Venus table and extra information. The planet Mars also affects your powers of attraction. To find your Mars table and interpretation go to page 761.

WOMEN WITH VENUS IN CAPRICORN: With your natural caution in romantic affairs, you often appear reserved and controlled. You may be shy but try to be more forward, especially if you want to be noticed. When you care about people, however, you are usually willing to put in extra time and energy to preserve the relationship. You are practical and dependable, and a sense of duty can often play a large role in affairs of your heart. With elegant simplicity you can attract others with your well-cut clothes and refined manners.

MEN WITH VENUS IN CAPRICORN: In relationships you take love seriously and can be a strong and practical support for friends or partners. You are usually attracted to partners who are as hardworking as you. As you tend not to express your feelings until you feel really secure in a relationship, you may be drawn to those who seem loyal, faithful, and not likely to let you down. As you respect the wisdom of experience, you may be drawn to mature partners or, alternatively, you may act as an authority figure for someone younger.

WOMEN WITH VENUS IN AQUARIUS: When it comes to relationships, others are attracted to your honest, friendly, and easygoing attitude. You really enjoy social interaction with others and may develop a genuine concern for humanity. Usually you present a tolerant and reasonable front in love situations and attempt to view your relationships objectively. If partners become too demanding, however, you can become stubborn and fixed. Friendship may be even more important for you than sexual compatibility.

MEN WITH VENUS IN AQUARIUS: You are sociable and open-minded, and people are attracted by your friendly and relaxed style. Being independent, you value freedom-loving partners who give you the space to be yourself. Others sometimes interpret your detachment as being emotionally cool,

but they may not understand your progressive views on relationships. Friendship can sometimes be even more important than earthly passion. Ideally, friends can share your ideas on life and possess a sense of originality as strong as your own. Not easily ruffled, you can deal well with difficult situations or moody partners.

WOMEN WITH VENUS IN PISCES: As a romantic and idealistic individual, you can be both loving and giving. In relationships you may need to balance the practical with the charitable. While making allowances and sacrifices is understandable in a loving relationship, playing the martyr is often a state of romantic illusion that can lead to self-deception. Your benevolence and sacrifices in the right relationship nonetheless make you a partner who is devoted, kind, and compassionate. Subtle, sensitive, and alluring, you make a sensual and caring partner.

MEN WITH VENUS IN PISCES: As a romantic and generous person, you are attracted to imaginative or artistic partners who can be sensitive and generous. While you are willing to make allowances for loved ones, playing the martyr in relationships can lead to allowing others to take advantage of your kind nature. Nevertheless, giving and loving, you are usually willing to forgive your partner's shortcomings.

WOMEN WITH VENUS IN ARIES: You gain power from your strong individuality, energy, and enthusiasm. Your young-at-heart and spirited approach to relationships adds to your appeal. If you become too impatient or self-absorbed, however, your partnerships are likely to suffer. Nevertheless, you can be creative, sharp, and quick, especially when you are able to share new and exciting projects with your partners. Mischievous with a love of action, you may even incite them to a playful fight.

MEN WITH VENUS IN ARIES: You are drawn to strong, independent women who can stand up to you. Although you can enthusiastically follow the object of your desire, you may lose power if you allow your forceful emotions to become too dominant. Warm and passionate, you have a side to your nature that longs for new adventures. Romantic and chivalrous, you really enjoy the excitement of the initial chase, but unless you keep the enthusiasm alive and avoid falling into a rut you may become easily bored.

To read all about your Outer Planets and work out how to use your personalized timetable, go to Section Three, page 789.

≋

To read all about your Outer Planets and work out how to use your personalized timetable, go to Section Three, page 789.

Your Personalized Timetable

JUPITER BENEFICIAL
1940 3/26 – 5/6	1943 9/7 – until 1944 7/29
1941 8/3 – 12/20	1946 12/3 – until 1947 10/27
1942 3/24 – 6/14	1952 7/6 – 11/16
1945 11/3 – until 1946 9/29	1953 2/23 – 5/13
1948 1/13 – 3/19	1955 8/21 – 11/27
1948 5/12 – 11/4	1956 1/7 – 7/12
1952 3/8 – 4/19	1958 11/17 – until 1959 2/19
1953 7/13 – until 1954 5/7	1959 4/15 – 10/9
1957 10/18 – until 1958 1/23	1964 6/15 – until 1965 4/26
1958 3/11 – 9/11	1967 8/5 – 10/24
1959 12/27 – until 1960 2/16	1968 2/21 – 6/21
1960 6/27 – 10/12	1970 11/1 – until 1971 1/19
1963 7/8 – 9/11	1971 5/29 – 9/17
1964 2/17 – 4/3	1976 5/28 – 9/4
1965 6/25 – 10/2	1976 10/5 – until 1977 4/7
1965 11/6 – until 1966 5/9	1979 7/20 – 10/3
1969 10/2 – 12/21	1980 4/7 – 5/15
1970 4/24 – 8/21	1982 10/16 – 12/30
1971 12/11 – until 1972 1/26	1988 5/11 – 7/26
1975 6/6 – 10/27	1988 11/24 – until 1989 3/16
1976 1/22 – 3/16	1991 7/3 – 9/16
1977 6/9 – 8/25	1994 9/29 – 12/13
1977 12/25 – until 1978 4/17	2000 4/25 – 7/4
1981 9/16 – 12/1	2002 10/18 – until 2003 1/20
1982 6/12 – 7/13	2003 6/13 – 8/31
1983 11/26 – until 1984 1/9	2006 1/10 – 4/28
1987 5/17 – 7/16	2006 9/10 – 11/27
1987 9/23 – until 1988 2/26	2012 4/7 – 6/15
1989 5/24 – 8/4	
1993 8/30 – 11/14	
1995 11/9 – 12/24	
1999 4/29 – 6/15	
1999 11/9 – until 2000 1/30	
2001 5/7 – 7/16	
2004 12/11 – until 2005 3/28	
2005 8/10 – 10/29	
2007 2/28 – 5/12	
2007 10/22 – 12/9	
2011 4/12 – 5/25	
2012 9/3 – 11/4	

SATURN CHALLENGING
1941 4/13 – until 1942 5/15
1947 8/24 – until 1948 9/26
1949 3/20 – 6/12
1954 11/28 – until 1955 6/30
1955 8/7 – until 1956 1/22
1956 5/2 – 10/18
1970 5/24 – until 1971 6/25
1971 12/25 – until 1972 3/7
1976 10/10 – until 1977 1/16
1977 6/28 – until 1978 8/2
1984 1/12 – 4/9
1984 10/5 – until 1985 11/23
1999 7/7 – 10/23
2000 3/25 – 8/29
2000 9/26 – until 2001 4/27
2006 8/7 – until 2007 9/9

SATURN BENEFICIAL
1938 7/14 – 8/17
1939 3/17 – 6/9
1939 10/22 – until 1940 2/29
1943 5/29 – until 1944 6/26
1952 1/11 – 2/7
1952 9/15 – until 1953 10/29
1957 12/17 – until 1958 12/17
1968 4/24 – until 1969 4/12
1972 7/8 – until 1973 1/8
1973 3/21 – 8/9
1973 12/28 – until 1974 4/27
1981 10/22 – until 1982 12/7
1983 4/26 – 9/2
1987 1/24 – 6/10
1987 10/24 – until 1988 1/22
1988 7/10 – 10/18
1997 6/6 – 9/28
1998 2/26 – 5/19
1998 11/25 – until 1999 2/1
2001 9/13 – 10/10
2002 5/11 – until 2003 6/10
2010 12/3 – until 2011 3/23
2011 8/28 – until 2012 10/12

URANUS CHALLENGING
1938 5/24 – until 1943 3/2
1958 9/23 – until 1962 8/22
1977 12/20 – until 1982 9/1

NEPTUNE CHALLENGING
1962 12/21 – until 1971 9/24

PLUTO CHALLENGING
1947 10/22 – until 1958 7/17
1989 1/11 – until 1996 9/20

JUPITER SPECIAL
1938 2/21 – 5/22
1938 7/22 – until 1939 1/2
1950 2/5 – 4/19
1950 9/8 – 12/8
1962 1/19 – 3/29
1974 1/2 – 3/11
1985 4/28 – 7/12
1985 12/14 – until 1986 2/24
1997 3/30 – 8/27
1997 11/18 – until 1998 2/7
2009 3/10 – until 2010 1/21

URANUS BENEFICIAL
1945 7/1 – until 1949 6/23
1971 10/21 – until 1975 9/23
1985 3/2 – until 1988 10/17

NEPTUNE BENEFICIAL
1948 12/11 – until 1957 9/11
1978 2/5 – until 1983 11/19

SATURN SPECIAL
1963 2/11 – until 1964 3/31
1964 9/5 – 12/26
1992 3/19 – 8/11
1992 12/16 – until 1994 2/4

PLUTO BENEFICIAL
1977 10/25 – until 1984 9/22
2002 12/19 – until 2007 11/25

URANUS SPECIAL
1999 3/10 – until 2004 1/16

JUPITER CHALLENGING
1940 8/12 – 9/27
1941 3/20 – 5/29

NEPTUNE SPECIAL
2004 3/31 – Continues

February 13

Your Personal Powers

Mentally quick and determined, your strong sense of values and practical approach imply that you are a talented individual with an enterprising spirit. Often creative and articulate, you can express yourself quite forcefully and impress others. Your ruling planet, Uranus, grants you quick perception, ingenuity, and originality. As a strong character who is usually freedom-loving, hardworking, and proud, you do not enjoy taking orders or being in subservient positions. Although you are by nature friendly and obliging, your excellent negotiating skills can help you to rise to positions of authority and assist in your overall success. You gain power when you combine your business acumen and inventiveness with your people skills and diplomacy. Even though you are often objective in your views, you have a tendency to be stubborn or argumentative. You lose some of your power when you display arrogance and become involved in disputes. Since you empower yourself by being both resourceful and humanitarian, a great deal of your success depends on how adaptable and cooperative you are when dealing with others.

Your Powers of Attraction in Relationships

People admire your enterprising nature, quick mind, and business acumen. With your progressive ideas and spirit of adventure you can inspire others to follow your lead. As a gregarious person you enjoy being sociable and meeting people. Well-informed and witty, you welcome discussions, serious debates, and friendly banter with people around you. Although you like to express your opinions, avoid repressing your emotions; use tact and persuasion instead of being confrontational. You are usually drawn to enthusiastic people who are versatile, mentally creative, or intelligent. Although outwardly detached, your emotional sensitivity indicates that you possess a strong need for love and affection. Since you can be extremely generous or make sacrifices for those you love, you need to use a discriminating approach when it comes to trusting others.

Your attractive qualities: diligent, courageous, dependable, analytical, mentally quick, precise, shrewd, business sense, ambitious, articulate, original, creative, freedom-loving, self-expressive, initiative, sociable, charming, philanthropic, idealistic, forthright, generous, broad-minded, reformer

Your less attractive qualities: impulsive, indecisive, obstinate, rebellious, argumentative, self-centered, stubborn, materialistic, bossy, unemotional, extravagant, worried, frustrated

Your Venus Power

The planet Venus has a great deal of influence on your powers of attraction. Below are four possible Venus types for women and men. To find your Venus you need to go to page 771, where you will find the Venus table and extra information. The planet Mars also affects your powers of attraction. To find your Mars table and interpretation go to page 761.

WOMEN WITH VENUS IN CAPRICORN: With your natural caution in romantic affairs, you often appear reserved and controlled. You may be shy but try to be more forward, especially if you want to be noticed. When you care about people, however, you are usually willing to put in extra time and energy to preserve the relationship. You are practical and dependable, and a sense of duty can often play a large role in affairs of your heart. With elegant simplicity you can attract others with your well-cut clothes and refined manners.

MEN WITH VENUS IN CAPRICORN: In relationships you take love seriously and can be a strong and practical support for friends or partners. You are usually attracted to partners who are as hardworking as you. As you tend not to express your feelings until you feel really secure in a relationship, you may be drawn to those who seem loyal, faithful, and not likely to let you down. As you respect the wisdom of experience, you may be drawn to mature partners or, alternatively, you may act as an authority figure for someone younger.

WOMEN WITH VENUS IN AQUARIUS: You attract and impress others with your friendly approach and progressive ideas. As you are usually independent and easygoing, you value freedom within a relationship. A good companion with a sense of your own person, you enjoy socializing, especially with people who are original, cosmopolitan, and have a strong sense of individuality. Although being friendly and detached usually serves you well, avoid losing touch with your emotions. You usually prefer the company of those who have innovative or progressive views.

MEN WITH VENUS IN AQUARIUS: You are sociable and open-minded, and people are attracted by your friendly and easygoing style. Being independent, you value freedom-loving partners who give you the space to be yourself. People can

sometimes interpret your detachment as being emotionally cool, but they admire your objectivity and humanitarian inclinations. You are attracted to intelligent individuals who are as truthful and direct as you are, but above all they must be true friends. Ideally your partner shares your liberal views on life and possesses a strong sense of individuality.

WOMEN WITH VENUS IN PISCES: Being sensitive to affairs of the heart, when you care for someone you can feel their emotions and sense their every mood. Their goals can even become as important as your own. This empathy indicates that you can love on an unselfish level, but you may have to guard against giving too much, especially to those who do not reciprocate. As you are seductive and captivating, partners can be fascinated by your subtle charms and attracted by your caring and affectionate nature.

MEN WITH VENUS IN PISCES: The combination of your emotional subtlety and charm can make you very alluring when dealing with affairs of the heart. Perceptive and impressionable, you have an easygoing style in your relationships, usually preferring to avoid ugly confrontation. You are drawn to partners who have a touch of glamour and are sensitive to the needs of others. Alternatively, they could be visionaries with rich imagination who know how to keep you enchanted. With your insight you have the ability to observe the subtle moods of your partner.

WOMEN WITH VENUS IN ARIES: You gain power from your strong individuality, energy, and enthusiasm. Your young-at-heart and spirited approach to relationships adds to your appeal. If you become too impatient or self-absorbed, however, your partnerships are likely to suffer. Nevertheless, you can be creative, sharp, and quick, especially when you are able to share new and exciting projects with your partners. Mischievous with a love of action, you may even incite them to a playful fight.

MEN WITH VENUS IN ARIES: You are drawn to strong, independent women who can stand up to you. Although you can enthusiastically follow the object of your desire, you may lose power if you allow your forceful emotions to become too dominant. Warm and passionate, you have a side to your nature that longs for new adventures. Romantic and chivalrous, you really enjoy the excitement of the initial chase, but unless you keep the enthusiasm alive and avoid falling into a rut you may become easily bored.

To read all about your Outer Planets and work out how to use your personalized timetable, go to Section Three, page 789.

≈

Your Personalized Timetable

JUPITER BENEFICIAL
1940 3/30 – 5/11
1941 8/9 – 12/12
1942 3/31 – 6/18
1945 11/8 – until **1946** 10/4
1948 1/18 – 4/6
1948 4/23 – 11/9
1952 3/12 – 4/23
1953 7/18 – until **1954** 6/1
1957 10/22 – until **1958** 9/17
1960 1/1 – 2/22
1960 6/19 – 10/18
1963 7/20 – 8/29
1964 2/22 – 4/7
1965 6/30 – until **1966** 5/14
1969 10/7 – 12/28
1970 4/16 – 8/27
1971 12/16 – until **1972** 1/31
1972 8/11 – 9/8
1975 6/12 – 10/19
1976 1/29 – 3/21
1977 6/13 – 8/31
1977 12/17 – until **1978** 4/23
1981 9/21 – 12/6
1982 5/28 – 7/28
1983 11/30 – until **1984** 1/14
1987 5/22 – 7/27
1987 9/12 – until **1988** 3/2
1989 5/28 – 8/9
1990 1/31 – 3/21
1993 9/4 – 11/19
1995 11/14 – 12/29
1999 5/3 – 6/21
1999 11/1 – until **2000** 2/7
2001 5/11 – 7/21
2004 12/18 – until **2005** 3/19
2005 8/16 – 11/3
2007 3/12 – 5/1
2007 10/27 – 12/13
2011 4/16 – 5/29
2012 9/16 – 10/22

SATURN BENEFICIAL
1939 3/25 – 6/20
1939 10/9 – until **1940** 3/9
1943 6/6 – until **1944** 7/4
1952 9/23 – until **1953** 11/6
1957 12/26 – until **1958** 12/26
1968 5/3 – 12/10
1969 1/1 – 4/20
1972 7/17 – 12/25
1973 4/4 – 8/19
1973 12/16 – until **1974** 5/8
1981 10/30 – until **1982** 5/30
1982 7/7 – 12/18
1983 4/12 – 9/13
1987 2/4 – 5/27
1987 11/3 – until **1988** 2/1
1988 6/26 – 10/30
1997 6/19 – 9/14
1998 3/7 – 5/28
1998 11/10 – until **1999** 2/15
2002 5/19 – until **2003** 6/18
2010 12/17 – until **2011** 3/8
2011 9/6 – until **2012** 10/21

URANUS BENEFICIAL
1945 7/21 – until **1950** 4/23
1971 11/7 – until **1975** 10/10
1985 12/20 – until **1988** 11/10

NEPTUNE BENEFICIAL
1949 11/2 – until **1957** 10/11
1978 12/31 – until **1984** 10/3

PLUTO BENEFICIAL
1977 11/24 – until **1984** 10/18
2003 1/16 – until **2008** 10/13

JUPITER CHALLENGING
1941 3/25 – 6/3
1943 9/12 – until **1944** 8/3
1946 12/8 – until **1947** 11/1

1952 7/13 – 11/9
1953 3/1 – 5/17
1955 8/25 – until **1956** 7/17
1958 11/21 – until **1959** 3/8
1959 3/29 – 10/15
1964 6/20 – until **1965** 4/30
1967 8/10 – 10/31
1968 2/13 – 6/27
1970 11/6 – until **1971** 1/25
1971 5/21 – 9/24
1976 6/1 – until **1977** 4/12
1979 7/25 – 10/8
1980 3/25 – 5/28
1982 10/21 – until **1983** 1/4
1983 7/7 – 8/20
1988 5/16 – 8/2
1988 11/17 – until **1989** 3/22
1991 7/8 – 9/20
1994 10/4 – 12/17
2000 4/29 – 7/9
2001 1/6 – 2/13
2002 10/27 – until **2003** 1/11
2003 6/19 – 9/4
2006 1/18 – 4/19
2006 9/16 – 12/2
2012 4/12 – 6/19

SATURN CHALLENGING
1941 4/21 – until **1942** 5/22
1947 9/1 – until **1948** 4/10
1948 4/24 – 10/5
1949 3/6 – 6/25
1954 12/6 – until **1955** 6/7
1955 8/28 – until **1956** 2/6
1956 4/16 – 10/28
1970 6/1 – until **1971** 1/6
1971 1/28 – 7/4
1971 12/11 – until **1972** 3/21
1976 10/24 – until **1977** 1/1
1977 7/7 – until **1978** 8/10
1984 1/29 – 3/21
1984 10/14 – until **1985** 12/2
1999 7/21 – 10/9
2000 4/3 – until **2001** 5/5
2006 8/15 – until **2007** 9/17
2008 4/21 – 5/14

URANUS CHALLENGING
1938 6/12 – until **1943** 4/3
1958 10/18 – until **1963** 6/17
1978 1/14 – until **1982** 10/2

NEPTUNE CHALLENGING
1963 11/19 – until **1971** 10/29

PLUTO CHALLENGING
1948 9/20 – until **1959** 6/6
1989 11/25 – until **1996** 10/25

JUPITER SPECIAL
1938 2/26 – 6/5
1938 7/7 – until **1939** 1/7
1950 2/9 – 4/25
1950 8/31 – 12/15
1962 1/24 – 4/3
1974 1/7 – 3/16
1985 5/8 – 7/2
1985 12/20 – until **1986** 2/28
1997 4/5 – 8/18
1997 11/26 – until **1998** 2/12
2009 3/15 – until **2010** 1/26

SATURN SPECIAL
1963 2/20 – until **1964** 4/11
1964 8/22 – until **1965** 1/6
1992 3/30 – 7/29
1992 12/26 – until **1994** 2/13

URANUS SPECIAL
1999 4/2 – until **2004** 2/5

NEPTUNE SPECIAL
2005 2/23 – Continues

683

February 14

SUN: AQUARIUS • DECANATE: LIBRA/VENUS • DEGREE: 24°–25°5 AQUARIUS • MODE: FIXED • ELEMENT: AIR

Your Personal Powers

Friendly and independent with charm and common sense, you have a good mind and an enterprising nature. Your ruling planet, Uranus, grants you intuitive powers, quick perception, liberal views, and objectivity. With your people skills you are usually able to make a positive impression on others and are good at presenting ideas. Although you can be determined and hardworking, a dislike for restriction implies that you may be reluctant to take orders. You gain power when you combine your many talents with self-discipline. Although material security is highly important to your sense of achievement, your bright ideas and desire for self-expression suggest that you need to channel your vitality and restlessness through some type of creative pursuit. You lose some of your powers if you fall into a monotonous routine or let indecision and worries about money undermine your resolution to succeed. A need for mental stimulation indicates that you usually feel enthusiastic and youthful when you broaden your horizons, especially through travel or when gaining new knowledge and skills.

Your Powers of Attraction in Relationships

Your natural charm, quick mind, and sociable personality can help you make friends easily. Talented and versatile, you work well with others. Usually you are attracted to people who are enterprising, straightforward, and hardworking or those who can provide you with a sense of security. You are independent and generous, and others are drawn to your easygoing manner. Be careful, however, that a restless streak does not prompt you at times to shirk your responsibilities or cause problems in your relationships. Being humanitarian and naturally helpful, however, implies that you enjoy being cooperative or mixing with different types of people. More confident when you are financially established, you enjoy mixing business and pleasure and entertaining friends or business associates. Able to talk your way out of the most difficult situations, you can be amusing and persuasive.

Your attractive qualities: independent, responsible, mentally quick, decisive, hardworking, friendly, charming, social skills, kind, talented, creative, pragmatic, imaginative, intuitive, self-aware, clever, direct, entertaining, bright personality, youthful, sociable, original

Your less attractive qualities: stubborn, worry about money or security, indecisive, lack of self-discipline, overindulgent, anxious, rebellious, irresponsible, too detached, restless, critical, self-absorbed, dissatisfied

Your Venus Power

The planet Venus has a great deal of influence on your powers of attraction. Below are four possible Venus types for women and men. To find your Venus you need to go to page 771, where you will find the Venus table and extra information. The planet Mars also affects your powers of attraction. To find your Mars table and interpretation go to page 761.

WOMEN WITH VENUS IN CAPRICORN: Proud and refined, you attract others with your composed dignity. Disliking vulnerability and needing to feel safe before you can express your feelings, you display a strong front. Feeling insecure or inadequate in relationships may force you to become manipulative in order to regain control. Nevertheless, you can project an attractive sense of self-assurance and are capable of displaying loyalty and a wonderful dry sense of humor.

MEN WITH VENUS IN CAPRICORN: As you do not display your deeper emotions freely, you are usually dignified and controlled in your relationships. Practical and down-to-earth partners are particularly attractive to you, especially those who do not rush into expressing their feelings but seem to possess natural class and reserve. You need a partner who is loyal and dependable and willing to take your relationship seriously.

WOMEN WITH VENUS IN AQUARIUS: Usually you have a modern outlook on love and are open to new or current lifestyles. Your intuitive abilities, communal sense, and people skills often allow you to see deeper into human intentions and to telepathically read people's thoughts. You are usually group-oriented and drawn to individuals within the group who are independent and self-motivated. You are more inclined to choose a partner who is unconventional or freedom-loving. Conscious of your social standing, however, you want someone who can relate well to your friends.

MEN WITH VENUS IN AQUARIUS: Although independent, you often enjoy being part of a group. The partners you frequently attract are themselves nonconformists or free spirits. As an individual you may not find it easy to settle into a routine or an entirely mundane type of relationship. You may

have some unconventional views on traditional marriage or your partner may hold such views. You value your freedom and can sometimes be cool and detached. Friendship is important to you as you enjoy sharing your progressive ideas.

WOMEN WITH VENUS IN PISCES: Romantic and impressionable, you are a caring and loving individual with a dreamy nature. In relationships you are often attracted to idealistic, compassionate, or sympathetic individuals who have imagination or a strong romantic sense. A tendency to be sensitive to others suggests that you are intuitive and aware of people's inner feelings. Be careful, therefore, not to get caught in other people's dramas or play the rescuer too often.

MEN WITH VENUS IN PISCES: In love you are sensitive, tender, and affectionate, experiencing your partner's feelings almost as strongly as your own. Being imaginative and visionary, you possess the ability to develop a deep compassion for others. As you are idealistic when in love, you usually prefer to see only your partner's good points, but be careful that your high expectations do not bring disappointment if you avoid harsh reality. Nevertheless, in your relationships with others you can be devoted, loving, and positively enchanting.

WOMEN WITH VENUS IN ARIES: Idealistic, passionate, and adventurous, you are direct in your dealings with others. When you are attracted to a person you usually take the initiative and use your people skills to make things happen. In close relationships you are not afraid to confront your other half. This self-assertiveness is positive if differences can be brought into the open through diplomacy and compromise. Independent and spirited, you enjoy your freedom.

MEN WITH VENUS IN ARIES: As you often have the courage and strength to initiate situations, you like to take the lead. With your unconscious desire for conquest you may also have to beware of being competitive with your partners. Nevertheless, you are drawn to direct and strong-willed women who can share your love of action and enthusiasm for life. When you are feeling good, you can be charming and enthusiastic in romantic situations with an entertaining and spontaneous spirit.

To read all about your Outer Planets and work out how to use your personalized timetable, go to Section Three, page 789.

To read all about your Outer Planets and work out how to use your personalized timetable, go to Section Three, page 789.

Your Personalized Timetable

JUPITER BENEFICIAL
1940 4/3 – 5/15
1941 8/16 – 12/5
1942 4/6 – 6/22
1945 11/13 – until 1946 10/8
1948 1/23 – 7/25
1948 9/6 – 11/14
1952 3/17 – 4/28
1953 7/23 – until 1954 1/26
1954 2/25 – 6/6
1957 10/27 – until 1958 9/22
1960 1/6 – 2/29
1960 6/11 – 10/25
1964 2/27 – 4/11
1965 7/4 – until 1966 5/19
1969 10/11 – until 1970 1/4
1970 4/7 – 9/3
1971 12/20 – until 1972 2/5
1972 7/26 – 9/23
1975 6/18 – 10/12
1976 2/5 – 3/25
1977 6/18 – 9/8
1977 12/9 – until 1978 4/29
1981 9/26 – 12/12
1982 5/17 – 8/7
1983 12/5 – until 1984 1/18
1987 12/7 – 12/10
1987 12/20 – until 1988 3/7
1989 6/2 – 8/14
1990 1/20 – 4/1
1993 9/9 – 11/23
1995 11/19 – until 1996 1/2
1999 5/8 – 6/27
1999 10/24 – until 2000 2/13
2001 5/16 – 7/26
2004 12/27 – until 2005 3/10
2005 8/22 – 11/8
2007 11/2 – 12/18
2011 4/20 – 6/3

SATURN BENEFICIAL
1939 4/2 – 7/3
1939 9/25 – until 1940 3/18
1943 6/14 – until 1944 7/12
1952 10/2 – until 1953 11/15
1954 6/22 – 7/21
1958 1/4 – 7/24
1958 9/23 – until 1959 1/4
1968 5/11 – 11/15
1969 1/25 – 4/28
1972 7/27 – 12/12
1973 4/15 – 8/31
1973 12/3 – until 1974 5/17
1981 11/8 – until 1982 5/8
1982 7/28 – 12/31
1983 3/29 – 9/23
1987 2/18 – 5/12
1987 11/13 – until 1988 2/12
1988 6/12 – 11/10
1997 7/7 – 8/26
1998 3/16 – 6/7
1998 10/28 – until 1999 2/27
2002 5/27 – until 2003 6/25
2011 1/5 – 2/16
2011 9/15 – until 2012 10/29

URANUS BENEFICIAL
1945 8/15 – until 1950 5/16
1971 11/26 – until 1975 10/26
1986 1/6 – until 1988 11/29

NEPTUNE BENEFICIAL
1949 12/6 – until 1958 9/8
1979 2/1 – until 1984 11/16

PLUTO BENEFICIAL
1978 10/15 – until 1985 9/7
2003 3/1 – until 2008 11/21

JUPITER CHALLENGING
1941 3/30 – 6/7
1943 9/17 – until 1944 8/8

1946 12/13 – until 1947 11/6
1952 7/19 – 11/1
1953 3/7 – 5/21
1955 8/30 – until 1956 7/22
1958 11/26 – until 1959 10/20
1964 6/25 – 12/21
1965 1/30 – 5/5
1967 8/14 – 11/7
1968 2/5 – 7/3
1970 11/10 – until 1971 2/1
1971 5/13 – 9/30
1976 6/6 – until 1977 4/17
1979 7/29 – 10/14
1980 3/15 – 6/7
1982 10/26 – until 1983 1/9
1983 6/24 – 9/1
1988 5/20 – 8/9
1988 11/9 – until 1989 3/28
1991 7/13 – 9/25
1994 10/9 – 12/22
2000 5/3 – 7/14
2000 12/25 – until 2001 2/25
2002 11/6 – until 2003 1/1
2003 6/25 – 9/9
2006 1/27 – 4/10
2006 9/21 – 12/6
2012 4/16 – 6/24

SATURN CHALLENGING
1941 4/29 – until 1942 5/30
1947 9/9 – until 1948 3/13
1948 5/22 – 10/15
1949 2/21 – 7/6
1954 12/16 – until 1955 5/23
1955 9/12 – until 1956 11/6
1970 6/9 – 12/13
1971 2/21 – 7/14
1971 11/28 – until 1972 4/1
1976 11/20 – 12/4
1977 7/15 – until 1978 8/18
1984 10/23 – until 1985 12/10
1999 8/9 – 9/19
2000 4/12 – until 2001 5/13
2006 8/22 – until 2007 9/25
2008 3/27 – 6/8

URANUS CHALLENGING
1938 7/5 – until 1943 4/24
1959 8/12 – until 1963 7/11
1978 11/11 – until 1982 10/23

NEPTUNE CHALLENGING
1963 12/19 – until 1972 9/18

PLUTO CHALLENGING
1949 8/30 – until 1959 7/24
1989 12/23 – until 1996 11/20

JUPITER SPECIAL
1938 3/2 – until 1939 1/12
1950 2/13 – 5/2
1950 8/23 – 12/21
1962 1/28 – 4/8
1962 10/30 – 10/30
1974 1/11 – 3/20
1985 5/26 – 6/13
1985 12/25 – until 1986 3/4
1997 4/11 – 8/10
1997 12/2 – until 1998 2/16
2009 3/20 – until 2010 1/30

SATURN SPECIAL
1963 2/28 – 9/30
1963 11/11 – until 1964 4/23
1964 8/9 – until 1965 1/16
1992 4/12 – 7/14
1993 1/5 – until 1994 2/21

URANUS SPECIAL
2000 2/6 – until 2004 2/22

NEPTUNE SPECIAL
2005 3/26 – Continues

≈

February 15

SUN: AQUARIUS · DECANATE: LIBRA/VENUS · DEGREE: 25°–26°5 AQUARIUS · MODE: FIXED · ELEMENT: AIR

Your Personal Powers

With original ideas and quick perception, you are an enterprising and enthusiastic individual. Your ruling planet, Uranus, endows you with a love of freedom, ingenuity, and foresight. Although you love ease, with your willpower and ability to think big, you have the courage to take on challenging projects. Although your strong character can make an impact and influence people, you lose power if you become overly preoccupied with material success in the pursuit of your goals. A rebellious or stubborn side to your nature may not help your cause. As you possess many talents, you gain power when you learn that only through self-discipline and patience can you achieve your objectives or grand plans. By applying a methodology or a strategy to your plans you can accomplish much. You empower yourself by acquiring knowledge and combining your inborn intuition and business acumen with your original ideas. Sociable and dramatic, you also possess a humanitarian side to your nature that helps you make contacts or influence people.

Your Powers of Attraction in Relationships

Your captivating charm is likely to increase your chances for romantic and social success. Often generous with your time and money, you can make a good impression on others. Mentally quick and dynamic, your independent and assertive nature indicates that you can be fascinating and witty. Usually you are attracted to dynamic and idealistic people who are clever and versatile. Alternatively you may be drawn to creative or success-oriented individuals who know how to promote their talents or ideas. Your need for freedom suggests that you may prefer to be in relationships that can allow you to feel unrestricted. You may also need to take your time where love is concerned and not rush or make spur-of-the-moment commitments. When you direct your strong personal desire toward giving to others, you enhance your powers of attraction.

Your attractive qualities: generous, practical, disciplined, cooperative, appreciative, creative ideas, meticulous, attention to detail, responsible, home-loving, helpful, enthusiastic, generous, charismatic, business sense, quick at evaluating situations, sees opportunities, confident

Your less attractive qualities: self-centered, restless, materialistic, critical, self-absorbed, worry, stubborn, dissatisfied, disruptive, restless, irresponsible, fear of change, loss of faith, indecision, contrary, overindulgent

Your Venus Power

The planet Venus has a great deal of influence on your powers of attraction. Below are four possible Venus types for women and men. To find your Venus you need to go to page 771, where you will find the Venus table and extra information. The planet Mars also affects your powers of attraction. To find your Mars table and interpretation go to page 761.

WOMEN WITH VENUS IN CAPRICORN: With your natural caution in romantic affairs, you often appear reserved and controlled. You may be shy but try to be more forward, especially if you want to be noticed. When you care about people, however, you are usually willing to put in extra time and energy to preserve the relationship. You are practical and dependable, and a sense of duty can often play a large role in affairs of your heart. With elegant simplicity you can attract others with your well-cut clothes and refined manners.

MEN WITH VENUS IN CAPRICORN: In relationships you take love seriously and can be a strong and practical support for friends or partners. You are usually attracted to partners who are as hardworking as you. As you tend not to express your feelings until you feel really secure in a relationship, you may be drawn to those who seem loyal, faithful, and not likely to let you down. As you respect the wisdom of experience, you may be drawn to mature partners or, alternatively, you may act as an authority figure for someone younger.

WOMEN WITH VENUS IN AQUARIUS: You attract and impress others with your friendly approach and progressive ideas. As you are usually independent and easygoing, you value freedom within a relationship. A good companion with a sense of your own person, you enjoy socializing, especially with people who are original, cosmopolitan, and have a strong sense of individuality. Although being friendly and detached usually serves you well, avoid losing touch with your emotions. You usually prefer the company of those who have innovative or progressive views.

MEN WITH VENUS IN AQUARIUS: You are sociable and open-minded, and people are attracted by your friendly and easygoing style. Being independent, you value freedom-loving partners who give you the space to be yourself. Other people

can sometimes interpret your detachment as being emotionally cool, but they admire your objectivity and humanitarian inclinations. You are attracted to intelligent individuals who are as truthful and direct as you are, but above all they must be true friends. Ideally, your partner shares your liberal views on life and possesses a strong sense of individuality.

WOMEN WITH VENUS IN PISCES: Romantic and idealistic when in love, you can be a sensitive and responsive lover. With your affectionate and impressionable nature, you are often attracted to those who understand your sensitivity and share your vision. Being flexible with an impressionable nature helps you to adapt to the needs of others. In your desire to blend with those you love, guard against giving too much of yourself by not clearly defining your boundaries.

MEN WITH VENUS IN PISCES: The combination of your emotional subtlety and charm can make you very alluring when dealing with affairs of the heart. Perceptive and impressionable, you have an easygoing style in your relationships, usually preferring to avoid ugly confrontation. You are drawn to a partner who has a touch of glamour and is sensitive to the needs of others. Alternatively, your partner can be a visionary with a rich imagination who can keep you enchanted.

WOMEN WITH VENUS IN ARIES: Idealistic, passionate, and adventurous, you are direct in your dealings with others. When you are attracted to a person you usually take the initiative and use your people skills to make things happen. In close relationships you are not afraid to confront your other half. This self-assertiveness is positive if differences can be brought into the open through diplomacy and compromise. Independent and spirited, you enjoy your freedom.

MEN WITH VENUS IN ARIES: As you often have the courage and strength to initiate situations, you like to take the lead. With your unconscious desire for conquest you may also have to beware of being competitive with your partners. Nevertheless, you are drawn to direct and strong-willed women who can share your love of action and enthusiasm for life. When you are feeling good, you can be charming and enthusiastic in romantic situations with an entertaining and spontaneous spirit.

To read all about your Outer Planets and work out how to use your personalized timetable, go to Section Three, page 789.

To read all about your Outer Planets and work out how to use your personalized timetable, go to Section Three, page 789.

≋

Your Personalized Timetable

JUPITER BENEFICIAL
1940 4/7 – 5/20
1941 8/22 – 11/27
1942 4/12 – 6/27
1945 11/18 – until 1946 5/30
1946 6/30 – 10/13
1948 1/29 – 7/13
1948 9/18 – 11/19
1952 3/21 – 5/2
1953 7/28 – until 1954 1/12
1954 3/11 – 6/10
1957 11/1 – until 1958 9/27
1960 1/10 – 3/8
1960 6/3 – 10/30
1964 3/3 – 4/15
1965 7/9 – until 1966 5/24
1969 10/16 – until 1970 1/13
1970 3/29 – 9/8
1971 12/25 – until 1972 2/11
1972 7/16 – 10/3
1975 6/25 – 10/4
1976 2/11 – 3/30
1977 6/22 – 9/16
1977 12/1 – until 1978 5/5
1981 9/30 – 12/17
1982 5/9 – 8/16
1983 12/9 – until 1984 1/23
1987 6/1 – 11/20
1988 1/9 – 3/12
1989 6/6 – 8/20
1990 1/11 – 4/10
1993 9/14 – 11/28
1995 11/23 – until 1996 1/7
1999 5/12 – 7/3
1999 10/17 – until 2000 2/19
2001 5/20 – 7/30
2005 1/7 – 2/27
2005 8/28 – 11/12
2007 11/7 – 12/22
2011 4/24 – 6/8
2011 12/9 – until 2012 1/11

SATURN BENEFICIAL
1939 4/10 – 7/22
1939 9/5 – until 1940 3/27
1943 6/21 – until 1944 7/20
1952 10/10 – until 1953 11/24
1954 5/28 – 8/14
1958 1/13 – 7/6
1958 10/10 – until 1959 1/12
1959 8/14 – 9/26
1968 5/20 – 10/31
1969 2/8 – 5/6
1972 8/6 – 11/30
1973 4/25 – 9/15
1973 11/18 – until 1974 5/25
1981 11/17 – until 1982 4/23
1982 8/11 – until 1983 1/17
1983 3/11 – 10/2
1987 3/11 – 4/20
1987 11/22 – until 1988 2/24
1988 5/29 – 11/20
1998 3/24 – 6/18
1998 10/15 – until 1999 3/9
2002 6/4 – until 2003 7/3
2011 9/24 – until 2012 11/6

URANUS BENEFICIAL
1946 6/13 – until 1950 6/4
1971 12/21 – until 1976 8/23
1986 1/26 – until 1988 12/16

NEPTUNE BENEFICIAL
1950 10/31 – until 1958 10/9
1979 12/29 – until 1984 12/14

PLUTO BENEFICIAL
1978 11/11 – until 1985 10/6
2004 1/10 – until 2009 10/7

JUPITER CHALLENGING
1941 4/3 – 6/12
1943 9/22 – until 1944 3/21

1944 5/5 – 8/13
1946 12/18 – until 1947 7/6
1947 7/24 – 11/11
1952 7/26 – 10/24
1953 3/13 – 5/26
1955 9/4 – until 1956 7/27
1958 12/1 – until 1959 10/25
1964 6/30 – 12/9
1965 2/11 – 5/9
1967 8/19 – 11/16
1968 1/27 – 7/9
1970 11/15 – until 1971 2/9
1971 5/5 – 10/6
1976 6/10 – until 1977 4/22
1979 8/3 – 10/20
1980 3/7 – 6/15
1982 10/30 – until 1983 1/15
1983 6/15 – 9/10
1988 5/24 – 8/17
1988 11/1 – until 1989 4/3
1991 7/18 – 9/30
1994 10/14 – 12/27
2000 5/8 – 7/19
2000 12/15 – until 2001 3/6
2002 11/22 – 12/17
2003 6/30 – 9/14
2006 2/6 – 3/30
2006 9/27 – 12/11
2012 4/20 – 6/29

SATURN CHALLENGING
1941 5/7 – until 1942 6/7
1947 9/18 – until 1948 2/27
1948 6/5 – 10/25
1949 2/8 – 7/16
1954 12/26 – until 1955 5/9
1955 9/23 – until 1956 11/14
1970 6/18 – 11/28
1971 3/7 – 7/24
1971 11/16 – until 1972 4/11
1977 7/24 – until 1978 8/26
1984 10/31 – until 1985 12/19
1986 7/6 – 9/7
2000 4/20 – until 2001 5/21
2006 8/31 – until 2007 10/4
2008 3/12 – 6/22

URANUS CHALLENGING
1939 5/9 – until 1943 5/12
1959 8/28 – until 1963 7/30
1978 11/27 – until 1982 11/10

NEPTUNE CHALLENGING
1964 2/15 – until 1972 10/26

PLUTO CHALLENGING
1949 10/10 – until 1960 6/15
1990 11/13 – until 1997 10/13

JUPITER SPECIAL
1938 3/7 – until 1939 1/17
1950 2/18 – 5/8
1950 8/15 – 12/27
1962 2/1 – 4/13
1962 10/4 – 11/22
1974 1/16 – 3/25
1985 12/30 – until 1986 3/8
1997 4/18 – 8/3
1997 12/8 – until 1998 2/20
2009 3/25 – 9/23
2009 11/2 – until 2010 2/3

SATURN SPECIAL
1963 3/10 – 9/9
1963 12/1 – until 1964 5/7
1964 7/24 – until 1965 1/25
1992 4/30 – 6/26
1993 1/14 – until 1994 3/1

URANUS SPECIAL
2000 2/24 – until 2004 12/29

NEPTUNE SPECIAL
2006 2/20 – Continues

February 16

Your Personal Powers

Instinctive and intelligent, you are a friendly individual with a good mind and strong ideals. Although you often gauge situations with emotional detachment, you can be sensitive and introspective. You gain power when you generally act with less haste, even though you can be spontaneous with quick perceptions. Your inventive mind and exceptional skills indicate that you can achieve success by being resourceful and productive. Dissatisfaction with changing financial circumstances or lack of planning can leave you fluctuating between being extravagant and being thrifty and implies that you empower yourself by learning to persevere and budget long term. Although you usually possess courage and determination, you lose some of your power through being obstinate. Your leadership abilities, natural business acumen, and people skills suggest that even though you value your independence, you are willing to work as part of a team, especially if you share the same beliefs. Nevertheless, it is your fine mind, keen intuition, and unique approach that often help you attain your goals.

Your Powers of Attraction in Relationships

A natural flair for dealing with people implies that you are a thoughtful individual and a good communicator. Strong-willed and opinionated, you can be persuasive and forceful. You may often seem cool and unemotional, but underneath you are sensitive with a caring and compassionate heart. Often witty, diplomatic, and good at relating to others on a one-to-one basis, you impress others with your ability to make people feel at ease. Attracted by intelligent individuals, you can often sense what your partner is thinking or feeling. If you feel insecure or negative, however, you may become argumentative, stubborn, or skeptical and spoil the harmonious relationships you have created. When socializing with people with whom you share some type of intellectual activity, you come into your own and display your powers of observation and humor.

Your attractive qualities: witty, practical, responsible, principled, intuitive, quick reactions, humanitarian, cooperative, unique ideas, well-informed, insightful, sociable, good communication skills, analytical, sensitive, friendly, flashes of inspiration, creative

Your less attractive qualities: disappointed, worry, impulsive, stubborn, dissatisfied, skeptical, confrontational, irresponsible, opinionated, irritable, frustrated, selfish, unsympathetic, bored easily, inner tensions, doubting

Your Venus Power

The planet Venus has a great deal of influence on your powers of attraction. Below are four possible Venus types for women and men. To find your Venus you need to go to page 771, where you will find the Venus table and extra information. The planet Mars also affects your powers of attraction. To find your Mars table and interpretation go to page 761.

WOMEN WITH VENUS IN CAPRICORN: With your natural caution in romantic affairs, you often appear reserved and controlled. You may be shy but try to be more forward, especially if you want to be noticed. When you care about people, however, you are usually willing to put in extra time and energy to preserve the relationship. You are practical and dependable, and a sense of duty can often play a large role in the affairs of your heart. With elegant simplicity you can attract others with your well-cut clothes and refined manners.

MEN WITH VENUS IN CAPRICORN: In relationships you take love seriously and can be a strong and practical support for friends or partners. You are usually attracted to partners who are as hardworking as you. As you tend not to express your feelings until you feel really secure in a relationship, you may be drawn to those who seem loyal, faithful, and not likely to let you down. As you respect the wisdom of experience, you may be drawn to mature partners or, alternatively, you may act as an authority figure for someone younger.

WOMEN WITH VENUS IN AQUARIUS: You attract and impress others with your friendly approach and progressive ideas. As you are usually independent and easygoing, you value freedom within a relationship. A good companion with a sense of your own person, you enjoy socializing, especially with people who are original, cosmopolitan, and have a strong sense of individuality. Although being friendly and detached usually serves you well, avoid losing touch with your emotions. You usually prefer the company of those who have innovative or progressive views.

MEN WITH VENUS IN AQUARIUS: You are sociable and open-minded, and people are attracted by your friendly and easygoing style. Being independent, you value freedom-loving partners who give you the space to be yourself. Other people can sometimes interpret your detachment as being emotion-

ally cool, but they admire your objectivity and humanitarian inclinations. You are attracted to intelligent individuals who are as truthful and direct as you are, but above all they must be true friends. Ideally your partner shares your liberal views on life and possesses a strong sense of individuality.

WOMEN WITH VENUS IN PISCES: As a romantic and idealistic individual, you can be both loving and giving. In relationships you may need to balance the practical with the charitable. While making allowances and sacrifices is understandable in a loving relationship, playing the martyr is often a state of romantic illusion that can lead to self-deception. Your benevolence and sacrifices in the right relationship nonetheless make you a partner who is devoted, kind, and compassionate. Subtle, sensitive, and alluring, you make a sensual and caring partner.

MEN WITH VENUS IN PISCES: The combination of your emotional subtlety and charm can make you very alluring when dealing with affairs of the heart. Perceptive and impressionable, you have an easygoing style in your relationships, usually preferring to avoid ugly confrontation. You are drawn to partners who have a touch of glamour and are sensitive to the needs of others. Alternatively, they could be visionaries with rich imaginations who know how to keep you enchanted. With your insight you have the ability to observe the subtle moods of your partner.

WOMEN WITH VENUS IN ARIES: Idealistic, passionate, and adventurous, you are direct in your dealings with others. When you are attracted to a person you usually take the initiative and use your people skills to make things happen. In close relationships you are not afraid to confront your other half. This self-assertiveness is positive if differences can be brought into the open through diplomacy and compromise. Independent and spirited, you enjoy your freedom.

MEN WITH VENUS IN ARIES: As you often have the courage and strength to initiate situations, you like to take the lead. With your unconscious desire for conquest you may also have to beware of being competitive with your partners. Nevertheless, you are drawn to direct and strong-willed women who can share your love of action and enthusiasm for life. When you are feeling good, you can be charming and enthusiastic in romantic situations with an entertaining and spontaneous spirit.

To read all about your Outer Planets and work out how to use your personalized timetable, go to Section Three, page 789.

≈

Your Personalized Timetable

JUPITER BENEFICIAL
1940 4/11 – 5/24
1941 8/30 – 11/19
1942 4/18 – 7/1
1945 11/23 – until 1946 5/15
1946 7/15 – 10/18
1948 2/3 – 7/3
1948 9/28 – 11/24
1952 3/25 – 5/6
1953 8/3 – until 1954 1/2
1954 3/21 – 6/15
1957 11/6 – until 1958 10/2
1960 1/15 – 3/17
1960 5/24 – 11/5
1964 3/8 – 4/20
1965 7/14 – until 1966 5/29
1969 10/21 – until 1970 1/24
1970 3/18 – 9/14
1971 12/29 – until 1972 2/17
1972 7/7 – 10/11
1975 7/2 – 9/26
1976 2/16 – 4/3
1977 6/26 – 9/26
1977 11/21 – until 1978 5/10
1981 10/5 – 12/24
1982 4/30 – 8/23
1983 12/14 – until 1984 1/28
1987 6/6 – 11/10
1988 1/19 – 3/17
1989 6/10 – 8/25
1990 1/3 – 4/17
1993 9/19 – 12/4
1994 6/26 – 7/8
1995 11/28 – until 1996 1/11
1999 5/17 – 7/11
1999 10/9 – until 2000 2/25
2001 5/25 – 8/4
2005 1/30 – 2/3
2005 9/2 – 11/17
2007 11/12 – 12/26
2011 4/29 – 6/13
2011 11/26 – until 2012 1/24

SATURN BENEFICIAL
1939 4/18 – until 1940 4/4
1943 6/29 – until 1944 7/28
1945 1/31 – 4/8
1952 10/18 – until 1953 12/3
1954 5/13 – 8/28
1958 1/23 – 6/21
1958 10/22 – until 1959 1/22
1959 7/24 – 10/16
1968 5/30 – 10/18
1969 2/20 – 5/14
1972 8/19 – 11/16
1973 5/4 – until 1974 6/3
1981 11/27 – until 1982 4/10
1982 8/23 – until 1983 10/11
1987 12/1 – until 1988 3/12
1988 5/11 – 11/29
1998 4/1 – 6/30
1998 10/1 – until 1999 3/18
2002 6/12 – until 2003 7/11
2011 10/2 – until 2012 11/15

URANUS BENEFICIAL
1946 7/1 – until 1950 6/21
1972 10/14 – until 1976 9/15
1986 2/20 – until 1989 10/14

NEPTUNE BENEFICIAL
1950 12/2 – until 1959 9/4
1980 1/29 – until 1985 11/13

PLUTO BENEFICIAL
1978 12/16 – until 1986 8/16
2004 2/15 – until 2009 11/19

JUPITER CHALLENGING
1941 4/8 – 6/16
1943 9/27 – until 1944 3/9
1944 5/17 – 8/18

JUPITER BENEFICIAL (right column)
1946 12/23 – until 1947 6/18
1947 8/12 – 11/15
1952 8/4 – 10/16
1953 3/19 – 5/30
1955 9/9 – until 1956 8/1
1958 12/6 – until 1959 10/30
1964 7/5 – 11/30
1965 2/20 – 5/13
1967 8/23 – 11/27
1968 1/16 – 7/15
1970 11/20 – until 1971 2/19
1971 4/25 – 10/11
1976 6/15 – until 1977 4/26
1979 8/7 – 10/26
1980 2/28 – 6/23
1982 11/4 – until 1983 1/21
1983 6/6 – 9/18
1988 5/29 – 8/27
1988 10/22 – until 1989 4/8
1991 7/22 – 10/6
1992 4/19 – 5/12
1994 10/19 – until 1995 1/1
2000 5/12 – 7/25
2000 12/7 – until 2001 3/14
2003 7/5 – 9/18
2006 3/3 – 3/7
2006 10/2 – 12/16
2012 4/25 – 7/3

SATURN CHALLENGING
1941 5/15 – until 1942 6/15
1947 9/28 – until 1948 2/14
1948 6/17 – 11/8
1949 1/25 – 7/25
1955 1/6 – 4/26
1955 10/4 – until 1956 11/23
1970 6/28 – 11/15
1971 3/18 – 8/6
1971 11/2 – until 1972 4/20
1977 8/1 – until 1978 9/3
1984 11/9 – until 1985 12/29
1986 6/19 – 9/23
2000 4/28 – until 2001 5/29
2006 9/8 – until 2007 3/23
2007 5/17 – 10/14
2008 2/28 – 7/4

URANUS CHALLENGING
1939 5/27 – until 1944 2/17
1959 9/15 – until 1963 8/16
1978 12/15 – until 1982 11/26

NEPTUNE CHALLENGING
1964 12/15 – until 1973 9/10

PLUTO CHALLENGING
1950 9/14 – until 1960 7/28
1990 12/9 – until 1997 11/11

JUPITER SPECIAL
1938 3/11 – until 1939 1/22
1950 2/22 – 5/16
1950 8/7 – until 1951 1/1
1962 2/5 – 4/18
1962 9/24 – 12/3
1974 1/20 – 3/29
1986 1/3 – 3/13
1997 4/25 – 7/26
1997 12/14 – until 1998 2/24
2009 3/30 – 9/10
2009 11/14 – until 2010 2/8

SATURN SPECIAL
1963 3/19 – 8/25
1963 12/14 – until 1964 5/31
1964 6/30 – until 1965 2/3
1993 1/23 – until 1994 3/10

URANUS SPECIAL
2000 3/14 – until 2005 1/21

NEPTUNE SPECIAL
2006 3/22 – Continues

February 17

SUN: AQUARIUS • DECANATE: GEMINI/MERCURY • DEGREE: 27°–28°5 AQUARIUS • MODE: FIXED • ELEMENT: AIR

Your Personal Powers

Independent, proud, and ambitious, you are a perceptive individual with inner sensitivity and determination. Your ruling planet, Uranus, grants you intuitive powers, inspired thoughts, and a love of freedom. Usually mentally quick and resourceful, you gain power by being productive and shrewd, particularly at business. Although you can be spontaneous and discerning, a tendency to be skeptical or doubting means that without inner faith you can become anxious or easily stressed. You also lose some of your power when you work too hard or take on more than you can handle. As a self-reliant individual you like to make up your own mind. You benefit, however, from utilizing your quick insight, improving your knowledge, or specializing in a particular skill. You also empower yourself by being more liberal and sympathetic and less critical or aloof. Nevertheless, keen on progress, you possess the stamina to overcome obstacles and learn quickly from past experiences. Although you usually take your work seriously, another side to your nature implies that you can be witty and creative.

Your Powers of Attraction in Relationships

You are sociable and friendly, and people are attracted to your determined and dynamic personality. When you are optimistic and spontaneous you follow your heart and do things on impulse. Although you can be sympathetic, loving, and loyal, indecision about your inner feelings implies that you can sometimes be uncertain about how you truly feel or can become stubborn and upset with partners. Nevertheless, you often want a meaningful or serious relationship with someone you can trust and communicate with. Your inner sensitivity is often in contrast to your confident and strong-willed personality. Often you are attracted to bright, emotionally powerful, or creative individuals. Alternatively, you may be attracted to sensitive and alluring individuals who know how to express their deeper feelings.

Your attractive qualities: hardworking, enduring, insightful, inner faith, thoughtful, ambitious, optimistic, focused, common sense, good planner, business acumen, attracts money, independent thinker, cautious, analytical, direct, accurate, skilled, strong-willed, sensitive, patient, enterprising

Your less attractive qualities: materialistic, bossy, too detached, worried, irritable, stubborn, moody, oversensitive, narrow-minded, critical, too proud, suspicious, patronizing, self-willed, unfeeling, irresponsible

Your Venus Power

The planet Venus has a great deal of influence on your powers of attraction. Below are four possible Venus types for women and men. To find your Venus you need to go to page 771, where you will find the Venus table and extra information. The planet Mars also affects your powers of attraction. To find your Mars table and interpretation go to page 761.

WOMEN WITH VENUS IN CAPRICORN: Proud and refined, you attract others with your composed dignity. Disliking vulnerability and needing to feel safe before you can express your feelings, you display a strong front. Feeling insecure or inadequate in relationships may force you to become manipulative in order to regain control. Nevertheless, you can project an attractive sense of self-assurance and are capable of displaying loyalty and a wonderful dry sense of humor.

MEN WITH VENUS IN CAPRICORN: As you do not display your deeper emotions freely, you are usually dignified and controlled in your relationships. Practical and down-to-earth partners are particularly attractive to you, especially those who do not rush into expressing their feelings but seem to possess natural class and reserve. You need a partner who is loyal and dependable and willing to take your relationship seriously.

WOMEN WITH VENUS IN AQUARIUS: You attract and impress others with your friendly approach and progressive ideas. As you are usually independent and easygoing, you value freedom within a relationship. A good companion with a sense of your own person, you enjoy socializing, especially with people who are original, cosmopolitan, and have a strong sense of individuality. Although being friendly and detached usually serves you well, avoid losing touch with your emotions. You usually prefer the company of those who have innovative or progressive views.

MEN WITH VENUS IN AQUARIUS: You are sociable and open-minded, and people are attracted by your friendly and easygoing style. Being independent, you value freedom-loving partners who give you the space to be yourself. People can

sometimes interpret your detachment as being emotionally cool, but they admire your objectivity and humanitarian inclinations. You are attracted to intelligent individuals who are as truthful and direct as you are, but above all they must be true friends. Ideally your partner shares your liberal views on life and possesses a strong sense of individuality.

WOMEN WITH VENUS IN PISCES: Idealistic and impressionable, in love you are romantic. Being sensitive to people, you are receptive to their moods and feelings. This affinity indicates that although you can be selfless you may have to guard against being too sentimental or overly romantic, especially with those who can take advantage of your kindness. Nevertheless, as you are alluring and seductive, your partners can be intrigued by your poetic soul or mysterious nature.

MEN WITH VENUS IN PISCES: The combination of your emotional subtlety and charm can make you very alluring when dealing with affairs of the heart. Perceptive and impressionable, you have an easygoing style in your relationships, usually preferring to avoid ugly confrontation. You are drawn to a partner who has a touch of glamour and is sensitive to the needs of others. Alternatively, your partner can be a visionary with a rich imagination who can keep you enchanted.

WOMEN WITH VENUS IN ARIES: Idealistic, passionate, and adventurous, you are direct in your dealings with others. When you are attracted to a person, you usually take the initiative and use your people skills to make things happen. In close relationships you are not afraid to confront your other half. This self-assertiveness is positive if differences can be brought into the open through diplomacy and compromise. Independent and spirited, you enjoy your freedom.

MEN WITH VENUS IN ARIES: As you often have the courage and strength to initiate situations, you like to take the lead. With your unconscious desire for conquest you may also have to beware of being competitive with your partners. Nevertheless, you are drawn to direct and strong-willed women who can share your love of action and enthusiasm for life. When you are feeling good you can be charming and enthusiastic in romantic situations with an entertaining and spontaneous spirit.

To read all about your Outer Planets and work out how to use your personalized timetable, go to Section Three, page 789.

Your Personalized Timetable

JUPITER BENEFICIAL
1940 4/16 – 5/29
1941 9/8 – 11/10
1942 4/23 – 7/6
1945 11/29 – until 1946 5/4
1946 7/25 – 10/23
1948 2/9 – 6/24
1948 10/5 – 11/28
1952 3/30 – 5/10
1953 8/8 – 12/25
1954 3/29 – 6/19
1957 11/11 – until 1958 10/7
1960 1/20 – 3/29
1960 5/12 – 11/10
1964 3/12 – 4/24
1965 7/19 – until 1966 6/3
1969 10/25 – until 1970 2/11
1970 2/27 – 9/19
1972 1/3 – 2/23
1972 6/29 – 10/18
1975 7/11 – 9/17
1976 2/22 – 4/7
1977 7/1 – 10/11
1977 11/6 – until 1978 5/16
1981 10/10 – 12/30
1982 4/22 – 8/30
1983 12/18 – until 1984 2/2
1987 6/12 – 11/1
1988 1/27 – 3/21
1989 6/15 – 8/31
1989 12/27 – until 1990 4/24
1993 9/24 – 12/9
1994 6/5 – 7/29
1995 12/2 – until 1996 1/16
1999 5/21 – 7/19
1999 9/30 – until 2000 3/1
2001 5/29 – 8/9
2002 2/18 – 3/13
2005 9/8 – 11/22
2007 11/16 – 12/31
2011 5/3 – 6/19
2011 11/17 – until 2012 2/2

SATURN BENEFICIAL
1939 4/26 – until 1940 4/12
1943 7/7 – until 1944 2/7
1944 3/4 – 8/6
1945 1/16 – 4/22
1952 10/26 – until 1953 12/13
1954 4/29 – 9/9
1958 2/3 – 6/8
1958 11/3 – until 1959 1/31
1959 7/8 – 10/30
1968 6/10 – 10/5
1969 3/2 – 5/23
1969 12/5 – until 1970 2/2
1972 9/4 – 10/31
1973 5/12 – until 1974 6/11
1981 12/8 – until 1982 3/27
1982 9/2 – until 1983 10/19
1987 12/9 – until 1988 12/8
1998 4/9 – 7/16
1998 9/15 – until 1999 3/27
2002 6/20 – until 2003 7/19
2011 10/11 – until 2012 11/24

URANUS BENEFICIAL
1946 7/19 – until 1951 4/15
1972 10/30 – until 1976 10/4
1986 12/19 – until 1989 11/10

NEPTUNE BENEFICIAL
1951 10/29 – until 1959 10/7
1980 12/26 – until 1985 12/12

PLUTO BENEFICIAL
1979 10/31 – until 1986 9/23
2005 1/4 – until 2010 9/29

JUPITER CHALLENGING
1941 4/12 – 6/20
1943 10/3 – until 1944 2/29
1944 5/27 – 8/22

JUPITER BENEFICIAL (continued)
1946 12/29 – until 1947 6/7
1947 8/23 – 11/20
1952 8/14 – 10/5
1953 3/24 – 6/3
1955 9/14 – until 1956 8/6
1958 12/11 – until 1959 11/4
1964 7/11 – 11/22
1965 2/27 – 5/18
1967 8/28 – until 1968 7/20
1970 11/24 – until 1971 3/3
1971 4/12 – 10/17
1976 6/20 – until 1977 5/1
1979 8/12 – 11/2
1980 2/20 – 6/29
1982 11/9 – until 1983 1/27
1983 5/29 – 9/25
1988 6/2 – 9/11
1988 10/7 – until 1989 4/13
1991 7/27 – 10/11
1992 4/2 – 5/29
1994 10/24 – until 1995 1/6
1995 7/19 – 8/16
2000 5/16 – 7/31
2000 11/30 – until 2001 3/21
2003 7/10 – 9/23
2006 10/7 – 12/20
2012 4/29 – 7/8

SATURN CHALLENGING
1941 5/23 – until 1942 6/23
1943 1/20 – 2/23
1947 10/8 – until 1948 2/1
1948 6/27 – 11/27
1949 1/5 – 8/3
1955 1/20 – 4/11
1955 10/13 – until 1956 12/1
1970 7/8 – 11/3
1971 3/28 – 8/22
1971 10/16 – until 1972 4/28
1977 8/9 – until 1978 9/11
1984 11/17 – until 1986 1/7
1986 6/4 – 10/6
2000 5/6 – until 2001 6/6
2006 9/17 – until 2007 3/6
2007 6/3 – 10/24
2008 2/15 – 7/14

URANUS CHALLENGING
1939 6/14 – until 1944 4/1
1959 10/5 – until 1963 9/1
1979 1/4 – until 1983 9/26

NEPTUNE CHALLENGING
1965 1/27 – until 1973 10/23

PLUTO CHALLENGING
1950 11/15 – until 1961 6/21
1991 1/10 – until 1998 9/30

JUPITER SPECIAL
1938 3/16 – until 1939 1/26
1950 2/26 – 5/26
1950 7/28 – until 1951 1/7
1962 2/10 – 4/24
1962 9/15 – 12/11
1974 1/24 – 4/3
1986 1/8 – 3/17
1997 5/4 – 7/17
1997 12/19 – until 1998 2/28
2009 4/5 – 9/1
2009 11/23 – until 2010 2/12

SATURN SPECIAL
1963 3/30 – 8/12
1963 12/26 – until 1965 2/12
1993 1/31 – until 1994 3/18
1994 10/26 – 11/23

URANUS SPECIAL
2000 4/5 – until 2005 2/9

NEPTUNE SPECIAL
2007 2/17 – Continues

February 18

SUN: AQUARIUS • DECANATE: LIBRA/VENUS • DEGREE: 28°–29°5 AQUARIUS • MODE: FIXED • ELEMENT: AIR

Your Personal Powers

Idealistic yet pragmatic, you are an ambitious individual with a strong personality and liberal or original views. Your ruling planet, Uranus, grants you a love of freedom, independence, and humanitarian beliefs. Capable, hardworking, and responsible with a need for a challenge, you are an achiever who likes to be purposeful or active. You gain power when you learn to compromise and be less stubborn or single-minded. You are caught between your ideals and a need to be practical or in control so that at times you can be sensitive and supportive and at other times detached or matter-of-fact. You empower yourself when you apply your high principles to yourself or become less critical of others. When you feel positive you can be extremely generous and compassionate. Opportunities for progress and a willingness to work hard indicate that you gain power when you combine your ingenuity and practical skills. Although you possess natural business sense, you also benefit from trusting your intuition and developing inner faith in your talents.

Your Powers of Attraction in Relationships

People-oriented and sociable, you are a sensitive yet tough individual. Others admire your quick mind, optimism, and enthusiasm. Seeing issues in black and white suggests that people find you both definite and strong-willed. One of your main challenges may be to keep a balance between your material values or work and your intimate relationships. You are usually attracted to charismatic and successful people or those who have a playful side to their personality. Alternatively, you may be drawn to those who have charm and a generous nature. Although you usually seek serious relationships, you may need to develop a more pragmatic and less romantic or idealistic attitude to love in order to minimize your disappointments. Nevertheless, your ability to make sacrifices in your relationships means that you can be supportive and loyal.

Your attractive qualities: progressive, humanitarian, assertive, intuitive, courageous, business sense, organizational skills, resolute, healing ability, efficient, advisory skills, intuitive, creative, inspirational, original, practical, receptive, determined, ambitious, persuasive, spontaneous

Your less attractive qualities: controlled emotions, overly sensitive, negative thinking, self-pity, manipulative, cold, lazy, selfish, too demanding, materialistic, unsympathetic, too detached

Your Venus Power

The planet Venus has a great deal of influence on your powers of attraction. Below are four possible Venus types for women and men. To find your Venus you need to go to page 771, where you will find the Venus table and extra information. The planet Mars also affects your powers of attraction. To find your Mars table and interpretation go to page 761.

WOMEN WITH VENUS IN CAPRICORN: Loyal and responsible, you are attracted to dignified and reserved individuals. Being practical and security-conscious, you prefer hardworking partners who are resourceful and enterprising. Work may even be a factor in many of your associations and partnerships. For you, family and faithfulness can be especially important, so you are usually willing to work hard or make sacrifices in order to build a strong relationship.

MEN WITH VENUS IN CAPRICORN: Hardworking and ambitious, you are usually attracted to determined, focused, and ambitious partners with a strong sense of duty. You want them to take relationships as seriously as you do, so loyalty and faithfulness are high on your agenda. Since you may display a natural reserve about expressing your feelings in an intimate relationship, you need a partner who shares your need for emotional security.

WOMEN WITH VENUS IN AQUARIUS: Usually you have a modern outlook on love and are open to new or current lifestyles. Your intuitive abilities, communal sense, and people skills often allow you to see deeper into human intentions and to telepathically read people's thoughts. You are usually group-oriented and are drawn to individuals within the group who are independent and self-motivated. You are more inclined to choose a partner who is unconventional or freedom-loving. Conscious of your social standing, however, you want someone who can relate well to your friends.

MEN WITH VENUS IN AQUARIUS: Although independent, you often enjoy being part of a group. The partners you frequently attract are themselves nonconformists or free spirits. As an individual you may not find it easy to settle into a routine or an entirely mundane type of relationship. You may have some unconventional views on traditional marriage or

your partner may hold such views. Friendship within a relationship can be as important to you as your freedom.

WOMEN WITH VENUS IN PISCES: Romantic and idealistic when in love, you can be a sensitive and responsive lover. With your affectionate and impressionable nature you are often attracted to those who understand your sensitivity and share your vision. Being flexible with an impressionable nature helps you to adapt to the needs of others. In your desire to blend with those you love, guard against giving too much of yourself by not clearly defining your boundaries.

MEN WITH VENUS IN PISCES: Romantic and idealistic when in love, you can be a sensitive and responsive lover. Being pliant and flexible with an impressionable nature helps you to adapt to the needs of others. In your desire to blend with those you love, however, guard against not clearly defining your boundaries. With your affectionate and sentimental nature, you are often attracted to those who understand your sensitivity and share your vision.

WOMEN WITH VENUS IN ARIES: Self-reliant and strong, you usually want things your own way. This can present problems if you refuse to compromise with your partners. Your life lessons in love and relationships often involve patience and learning to trust. When you project the full power of your Venus you can radiate a charismatic and captivating energy and make a strong impression on others. Independence is often high on your relationship agenda.

MEN WITH VENUS IN ARIES: Usually you are inclined to seek a partner who is active, goal-oriented, or decisive. Not known for your patience, you probably seek relationships early in life. You may find that you are attracted to women with a daring or adventurous spirit, but in your close relationships you may encounter rivalry or find that both you and your partner want to lead or be the boss. Although you may act rashly, you possess a great deal of magnetism and are capable of demonstrating your love and affection.

To read all about your Outer Planets and work out how to use your personalized timetable, go to Section Three, page 789.

Your Personalized Timetable

JUPITER BENEFICIAL
1940 4/20 – 6/2
1941 9/21 – 10/29
1942 4/28 – 7/10
1945 12/4 – until 1946 4/26
1946 8/3 – 10/27
1948 2/15 – 6/16
1948 10/12 – 12/3
1952 4/3 – 5/15
1953 8/14 – 12/17
1954 4/5 – 6/24
1957 11/16 – until 1958 10/11
1960 1/25 – 8/14
1960 8/27 – 11/15
1964 3/17 – 4/28
1965 7/24 – until 1966 6/7
1969 10/30 – until 1970 9/25
1972 1/7 – 2/29
1972 6/21 – 10/25
1975 7/23 – 9/6
1976 2/27 – 4/11
1977 7/5 – until 1978 5/21
1981 10/14 – until 1982 1/6
1982 4/14 – 9/5
1983 12/22 – until 1984 2/7
1984 8/8 – 9/20
1987 6/17 – 10/24
1988 2/3 – 3/26
1989 6/19 – 9/7
1989 12/19 – until 1990 4/30
1993 9/29 – 12/14
1994 5/24 – 8/9
1995 12/7 – until 1996 1/20
1999 5/26 – 7/29
1999 9/20 – until 2000 3/7
2001 6/3 – 8/14
2002 2/2 – 3/29
2005 9/13 – 11/27
2007 11/21 – until 2008 1/4
2011 5/7 – 6/24
2011 11/8 – until 2012 2/10

SATURN BENEFICIAL
1939 5/4 – until 1940 4/20
1943 7/16 – until 1944 1/15
1944 3/27 – 8/15
1945 1/3 – 5/4
1952 11/4 – until 1953 6/4
1953 7/12 – 12/24
1954 4/15 – 9/20
1958 2/15 – 5/24
1958 11/13 – until 1959 2/11
1959 6/24 – 11/11
1968 6/23 – 9/21
1969 3/11 – 6/1
1969 11/18 – until 1970 2/17
1973 5/21 – until 1974 6/19
1981 12/22 – until 1982 3/13
1982 9/12 – until 1983 10/28
1987 12/18 – until 1988 12/17
1998 4/17 – until 1999 4/4
2002 6/28 – until 2003 7/27
2004 2/11 – 4/1
2011 10/19 – until 2012 12/3

URANUS BENEFICIAL
1946 8/11 – until 1951 5/12
1972 11/16 – until 1976 10/20
1987 1/5 – until 1989 11/29

NEPTUNE BENEFICIAL
1951 11/28 – until 1960 8/30
1981 1/24 – until 1986 11/9

PLUTO BENEFICIAL
1979 11/29 – until 1986 10/20
2005 2/5 – until 2010 11/19

JUPITER CHALLENGING
1941 4/17 – 6/25

1943 10/9 – until 1944 2/21
1944 6/3 – 8/27
1947 1/3 – 5/29
1947 9/1 – 11/24
1952 9/1 – 9/18
1953 3/29 – 6/7
1955 9/19 – until 1956 8/11
1958 12/15 – until 1959 11/8
1964 7/17 – 11/14
1965 3/6 – 5/22
1967 9/2 – until 1968 7/25
1970 11/29 – until 1971 10/22
1976 6/24 – until 1977 5/5
1979 8/17 – 11/9
1980 2/12 – 7/5
1982 11/13 – until 1983 2/3
1983 5/21 – 10/2
1988 6/6 – until 1989 4/18
1991 8/1 – 10/16
1992 3/23 – 6/9
1994 10/28 – until 1995 1/12
1995 7/3 – 9/1
2000 5/20 – 8/6
2000 11/22 – until 2001 3/27
2003 7/15 – 9/28
2006 10/12 – 12/25
2012 5/3 – 7/13

SATURN CHALLENGING
1941 5/31 – until 1942 7/2
1942 12/30 – until 1943 3/15
1947 10/20 – until 1948 1/19
1948 7/6 – until 1949 8/11
1955 2/10 – 3/20
1955 10/22 – until 1956 12/10
1970 7/21 – 10/20
1971 4/6 – until 1972 5/7
1977 8/16 – until 1978 9/19
1984 11/26 – until 1986 1/18
1986 5/22 – 10/17
2000 5/14 – until 2001 6/14
2006 9/26 – until 2007 2/20
2007 6/15 – 11/5
2008 2/2 – 7/24

URANUS CHALLENGING
1939 7/6 – until 1944 4/23
1959 11/5 – until 1964 6/29
1979 2/6 – until 1983 10/19

NEPTUNE CHALLENGING
1965 12/13 – until 1974 8/25

PLUTO CHALLENGING
1951 9/29 – until 1961 8/1
1991 11/27 – until 1998 11/2

JUPITER SPECIAL
1938 3/21 – until 1939 1/31
1950 3/3 – 6/7
1950 7/16 – until 1951 1/12
1962 2/14 – 4/30
1962 9/7 – 12/18
1974 1/29 – 4/8
1986 1/12 – 3/21
1997 5/14 – 7/6
1997 12/25 – until 1998 3/5
2009 4/10 – 8/24
2009 11/30 – until 2010 2/16

SATURN SPECIAL
1963 4/10 – 7/29
1964 1/5 – until 1965 2/20
1993 2/9 – until 1994 3/27
1994 10/2 – 12/16

URANUS SPECIAL
2001 2/10 – until 2005 11/21

NEPTUNE SPECIAL
2007 3/18 – Continues

February 19

SUN: AQUARIUS/PISCES CUSP • DECANATE: LIBRA/VENUS TO NEPTUNE/PISCES • DEGREE: 29°5 AQUARIUS–0°5 PISCES • MODE: FIXED/MUTABLE • ELEMENT: AIR/WATER

Your Personal Powers

Determined yet sensitive, you are a direct and idealistic individual with a keen mentality and compassionate heart. Born on the cusp of Aquarius and Pisces, you are independent, inventive, and imaginative. Although you are usually optimistic, with high expectations, a tendency to become easily discouraged or frustrated suggests you may experience disappointments that come from impatience, or feeling stuck in a rut. You gain power when you learn to plan ahead, be organized, and persevere. When you articulate your inspired thoughts or unique ideas calmly, you can succeed admirably. With your sense of fair play and goodwill you often show a willingness to lend a helping hand and support others. Since you need to find ways to express your emotions and vitality, you empower yourself by being spontaneous and using your dynamic creativity and innovative ideas in a constructive way. Dramatic and impressionable, you thrive on positive feedback. Although caring and sociable, you gain power when you discipline yourself to be methodical and self-reliant.

Your Powers of Attraction in Relationships

Your charismatic appeal and gregarious nature imply that you have a gift for dealing with people. Others are attracted to your warmhearted nature. Usually you are drawn to purposeful, charismatic, and enterprising individuals who are full of self-confidence. A need to be appreciated suggests that you are willing to make sacrifices for those you love, yet you need much love and acknowledgment for your efforts. If your expectations for your close relationships are not met, you can become restless and dissatisfied with yourself and others. Although you are friendly and a team player, you may need time alone to achieve your goals or ambitions. With the power to attract people from all walks of life, you will always be popular.

Your attractive qualities: kindhearted, warm, compassionate, ambitious, intelligent, humanitarian, courteous, persevering, romantic, creative, depth of vision, imaginative, idealistic, decisive, resourceful, optimistic, resilient, intuitive, considerate, home-loving, friendly, sociable, unique ideas

Your less attractive qualities: easily influenced, dreamer, inner tensions, moody, restless, discontented, arrogant, impatient, negative thinker, fear of failure, inertia, anxious, overindulgent, indecisive, materialistic, frustrated, escapist

Your Venus Power

The planet Venus has a great deal of influence on your powers of attraction. Below are four possible Venus types for women and men. To find your Venus you need to go to page 771, where you will find the Venus table and extra information. The planet Mars also affects your powers of attraction. To find your Mars table and interpretation go to page 761.

WOMEN WITH VENUS IN CAPRICORN: With your natural caution in romantic affairs, you often appear reserved and controlled. You may be shy but try to be more forward, especially if you want to be noticed. When you care about people, however, you are usually willing to put in extra time and energy to preserve the relationship. You are practical and dependable, and a sense of duty can often play a large role in affairs of your heart. With elegant simplicity you can attract others with your well-cut clothes and refined manners.

MEN WITH VENUS IN CAPRICORN: In relationships you take love seriously and can be a strong and practical support for friends or partners. You are usually attracted to partners who are as hardworking as you. As you tend not to express your feelings until you feel really secure in a relationship, you may be drawn to those who seem loyal, faithful, and not likely to let you down. As you respect the wisdom of experience, you may be drawn to mature partners or, alternatively, you may act as an authority figure for someone younger.

WOMEN WITH VENUS IN AQUARIUS: You attract and impress others with your friendly approach and progressive ideas. As you are usually independent and easygoing, you value freedom within a relationship. A good companion with a sense of your own person, you enjoy socializing, especially with people who are original, cosmopolitan, and have a strong sense of individuality. Although being friendly and detached usually serves you well, avoid losing touch with your emotions. You usually prefer the company of those who have innovative or progressive views.

MEN WITH VENUS IN AQUARIUS: You are sociable and open-minded, and people are attracted by your friendly and easygoing style. Being independent you value freedom-loving partners who give you the space to be yourself. People can

sometimes interpret your detachment as being emotionally cool, but they admire your objectivity and humanitarian inclinations. You are attracted to intelligent individuals who are as truthful and direct as you are, but above all they must be true friends. Ideally, your partner shares your liberal views on life and possesses a strong sense of individuality.

WOMEN WITH VENUS IN PISCES: Romantic and impressionable, you are a caring and loving individual with a dreamy nature. In relationships you are often attracted to idealistic, compassionate, or sympathetic individuals who are imaginative or have a strong romantic sense. A tendency to be sensitive to others suggests that you are intuitive and aware of people's inner feelings. Be careful, therefore, not to get caught in other people's dramas or play the rescuer too often.

MEN WITH VENUS IN PISCES: In love you are sensitive, tender, and affectionate, experiencing your partner's feelings almost as strongly as your own. Being imaginative and visionary, you possess the ability to develop a deep compassion for others. As you are idealistic when in love, you usually prefer to see only your partner's good points, but be careful that your high expectations do not bring disappointment if you avoid harsh reality. Nevertheless, in your relationships with others you can be devoted, loving, and positively enchanting.

WOMEN WITH VENUS IN ARIES: Idealistic, passionate, and adventurous, you are direct in your dealings with others. When you are attracted to a person you usually take the initiative and use your people skills to make things happen. In close relationships you are not afraid to confront your other half. This self-assertiveness is positive if differences can be brought into the open through diplomacy and compromise. Independent and spirited, you enjoy your freedom.

MEN WITH VENUS IN ARIES: As you often have the courage and strength to initiate situations, you like to take the lead. With your unconscious desire for conquest you may also have to beware of being competitive with your partners. Nevertheless, you are drawn to direct and strong-willed women who can share your love of action and enthusiasm for life. When you are feeling good, you can be charming and enthusiastic in romantic situations with an entertaining and spontaneous spirit.

To read all about your Outer Planets and work out how to use your personalized timetable, go to Section Three, page 789.

Your Personalized Timetable

JUPITER BENEFICIAL
1940 4/24 – 6/7
1942 5/3 – 7/15
1945 12/11 – until 1946 4/17
1946 8/10 – 11/1
1948 2/22 – 6/9
1948 10/19 – 12/8
1952 4/7 – 5/19
1953 8/20 – 12/10
1954 4/11 – 6/28
1957 11/21 – until 1958 6/10
1958 6/27 – 10/16
1960 1/30 – 7/25
1960 9/16 – 11/20
1964 3/21 – 5/2
1965 7/29 – until 1966 1/27
1966 3/6 – 6/12
1969 11/4 – until 1970 9/30
1972 1/12 – 3/7
1972 6/13 – 10/31
1976 3/3 – 4/16
1977 7/10 – until 1978 5/26
1981 10/19 – until 1982 1/14
1982 4/6 – 9/11
1983 12/27 – until 1984 2/12
1984 7/27 – 10/2
1987 6/23 – 10/17
1988 2/10 – 3/30
1989 6/23 – 9/15
1989 12/12 – until 1990 5/6
1993 10/3 – 12/20
1994 5/15 – 8/18
1995 12/11 – until 1996 1/25
1999 5/31 – 8/16
1999 9/2 – until 2000 3/12
2001 6/7 – 8/20
2002 1/23 – 4/8
2005 9/18 – 12/2
2007 11/26 – until 2008 1/9
2011 5/12 – 6/30
2011 11/1 – until 2012 2/17

SATURN BENEFICIAL
1939 5/13 – 12/5
1940 1/19 – 4/28
1943 7/25 – 12/31
1944 4/10 – 8/26
1944 12/22 – until 1945 5/14
1952 11/13 – until 1953 5/13
1953 8/3 – until 1954 1/6
1954 4/1 – 9/29
1958 3/3 – 5/7
1958 11/22 – until 1959 2/22
1959 6/10 – 11/21
1968 7/9 – 9/4
1969 3/19 – 6/10
1969 11/5 – until 1970 3/1
1973 5/29 – until 1974 6/27
1982 1/10 – 2/20
1982 9/21 – until 1983 11/5
1987 12/26 – until 1988 12/25
1998 4/25 – until 1999 4/12
2002 7/6 – until 2003 8/5
2004 1/25 – 4/18
2011 10/27 – until 2012 12/13

URANUS BENEFICIAL
1947 6/12 – until 1951 6/1
1972 12/6 – until 1977 8/5
1987 1/23 – until 1989 12/17

NEPTUNE BENEFICIAL
1952 10/26 – until 1960 10/4
1981 12/24 – until 1986 12/10

PLUTO BENEFICIAL
1980 10/19 – until 1987 9/7
2005 12/31 – until 2010 12/19

JUPITER CHALLENGING
1941 4/21 – 6/29
1943 10/15 – until 1944 2/13

1944 6/11 – 9/1
1947 1/9 – 5/20
1947 9/8 – 11/29
1953 4/3 – 6/12
1955 9/24 – until 1956 4/2
1956 5/3 – 8/16
1958 12/21 – until 1959 11/13
1964 7/23 – 11/7
1965 3/12 – 5/26
1967 9/7 – until 1968 7/30
1970 12/4 – until 1971 10/27
1976 6/29 – 12/26
1977 2/4 – 5/10
1979 8/21 – 11/17
1980 2/4 – 7/11
1982 11/18 – until 1983 2/10
1983 5/13 – 10/8
1988 6/11 – until 1989 4/23
1991 8/5 – 10/22
1992 3/14 – 6/17
1994 11/2 – until 1995 1/17
1995 6/23 – 9/11
2000 5/25 – 8/14
2000 11/15 – until 2001 4/2
2003 7/20 – 10/3
2006 10/17 – 12/30
2012 5/8 – Continues

SATURN CHALLENGING
1941 6/8 – until 1942 1/7
1942 2/7 – 7/11
1942 12/16 – until 1943 3/28
1947 11/4 – until 1948 1/3
1948 7/15 – until 1949 8/19
1955 10/31 – until 1956 12/19
1957 7/28 – 8/27
1970 8/6 – 10/3
1971 4/15 – until 1972 5/15
1977 8/24 – until 1978 9/28
1979 4/9 – 6/8
1984 12/5 – until 1985 7/3
1985 8/16 – until 1986 1/31
1986 5/7 – 10/27
2000 5/21 – until 2001 6/22
2006 10/6 – until 2007 2/8
2007 6/26 – 11/22
2008 1/16 – 8/2

URANUS CHALLENGING
1939 8/13 – until 1944 5/12
1960 8/21 – until 1964 7/21
1979 11/23 – until 1983 11/7

NEPTUNE CHALLENGING
1966 1/20 – until 1974 10/21

PLUTO CHALLENGING
1952 9/4 – until 1962 6/25
1991 12/24 – until 1999 9/9

JUPITER SPECIAL
1938 3/25 – until 1939 2/4
1950 3/7 – until 1951 1/17
1962 2/18 – 5/6
1962 8/30 – 12/25
1974 2/2 – 4/13
1986 1/17 – 3/26
1997 6/3 – 6/16
1997 12/30 – until 1998 3/9
2009 4/16 – 8/16
2009 12/7 – until 2010 2/20

SATURN SPECIAL
1963 4/25 – 7/13
1964 1/14 – until 1965 2/28
1993 2/17 – until 1994 4/6
1994 9/17 – 12/30

URANUS SPECIAL
2001 2/27 – until 2006 1/4

NEPTUNE SPECIAL
2007 4/30 – Continues

Aquarius Timetable
X-Special · X-Beneficial · X-Challenging

January 21
URANUS X-BENEFICIAL
2010 4/20 – until **2012** 2/16

January 22
URANUS X-BENEFICIAL
2010 5/13 – until **2012** 3/6

January 23
URANUS X-BENEFICIAL
2010 6/21 – until **2012** 3/24

January 24
URANUS X-BENEFICIAL
2011 4/7 – until **2013** 1/29

January 25
URANUS X-BENEFICIAL
2011 4/27 – until **2013** 2/21

January 26
URANUS X-BENEFICIAL
2011 5/20 – until **2013** 3/12
NEPTUNE X-SPECIAL
2001 1/1 – until **2002** 1/4

January 27
URANUS X-BENEFICIAL
2012 3/25 – until **2013** 3/30
NEPTUNE X-SPECIAL
2001 1/1 – until **2002** 11/26

January 28
URANUS X-BENEFICIAL
2012 4/12 – until **2013** 10/27
NEPTUNE X-SPECIAL
2001 1/8 – until **2003** 1/1

January 29
URANUS X-BENEFICIAL
2012 5/2 – until **2013** 12/23
NEPTUNE X-SPECIAL
2001 2/4 – until **2003** 11/19

January 30
URANUS X-BENEFICIAL
2012 5/26 – until **2013** 10/27

NEPTUNE X-SPECIAL
2001 3/5 – until **2003** 12/30

January 31
NEPTUNE X-SPECIAL
2001 4/18 – until **2004** 11/4

February 1
NEPTUNE X-SPECIAL
2002 3/2 – until **2001** 10/28

February 2
NEPTUNE X-SPECIAL
2002 4/9 – until **2005** 1/24

February 3
NEPTUNE X-SPECIAL
2003 2/27 – until **2005** 12/22
PLUTO X-BENEFICIAL
2001 1/1 – until **2002** 10/19

February 4
NEPTUNE X-SPECIAL
2003 4/3 – until **2006** 1/21
PLUTO X-BENEFICIAL
2001 1/1 – until **2002** 11/19

February 5
NEPTUNE X-SPECIAL
2004 2/25 – until **2006** 12/18
PLUTO X-BENEFICIAL
2001 1/1 – until **2003** 10/10

February 6
NEPTUNE X-SPECIAL
2004 3/28 – until **2007** 1/19
PLUTO X-BENEFICIAL
2001 2/1 – until **2003** 11/14

February 7
NEPTUNE X-SPECIAL
2005 2/21 – until **2007** 12/12
PLUTO X-BENEFICIAL
2001 12/23 – until **2004** 9/26

February 8
NEPTUNE X-SPECIAL
2005 3/24 – until **2008** 1/16
PLUTO X-BENEFICIAL
2002 1/22 – until **2004** 11/7

February 9
NEPTUNE X-SPECIAL
2006 2/19 – until **2008** 12/4
PLUTO X-BENEFICIAL
2002 12/18 – until **2004** 12/6

February 10
URANUS X-SPECIAL
2001 1/3 – until **2002** 1/7
NEPTUNE X-SPECIAL
2006 3/20 – until **2009** 1/11
PLUTO X-BENEFICIAL
2003 1/15 – until **2005** 11/2

February 11
URANUS X-SPECIAL
2001 1/22 – until **2002** 1/26
NEPTUNE X-SPECIAL
2006 5/12 – until **2009** 11/23
PLUTO X-BENEFICIAL
2003 2/27 – until **2005** 12/2

February 12
URANUS X-SPECIAL
2001 2/9 – until **2002** 2/13
NEPTUNE X-SPECIAL
2007 3/16 – until **2010** 1/8
PLUTO X-BENEFICIAL
2004 1/9 – until **2006** 10/27

February 13
URANUS X-SPECIAL
2001 2/26 – until **2002** 12/20
NEPTUNE X-SPECIAL
2007 4/26 – until **2010** 2/5
PLUTO X-BENEFICIAL
2004 2/13 – until **2006** 11/28

February 14
URANUS X-SPECIAL
2001 3/17 – until **2003** 1/12

NEPTUNE X-SPECIAL
2008 3/12 – until **2011** 1/3
PLUTO X-BENEFICIAL
2005 1/3 – until **2007** 10/22

February 15
URANUS X-SPECIAL
2001 4/9 – until **2003** 1/31
NEPTUNE X-SPECIAL
2008 4/17 – until **2011** 2/2
PLUTO X-BENEFICIAL
2005 2/4 – until **2007** 11/25

February 16
URANUS X-SPECIAL
2002 2/14 – until **2003** 2/18
NEPTUNE X-SPECIAL
2009 3/8 – until **2011** 12/30
PLUTO X-BENEFICIAL
2005 12/30 – until **2008** 10/15

February 17
URANUS X-SPECIAL
2002 3/3 – until **2003** 12/26
NEPTUNE X-SPECIAL
2009 4/10 – until **2012** 1/30
PLUTO X-BENEFICIAL
2006 1/30 – until **2008** 11/22

February 18
URANUS X-SPECIAL
2002 3/22 – until **2004** 1/18
NEPTUNE X-SPECIAL
2010 3/5 – until **2012** 12/23
PLUTO X-BENEFICIAL
2006 12/27 – until **2009** 10/9

February 19
URANUS X-SPECIAL
2002 4/14 – until **2004** 2/6
NEPTUNE X-SPECIAL
2010 4/5 – until **2013** 1/26
PLUTO X-BENEFICIAL
2007 1/25 – until **2009** 11/20

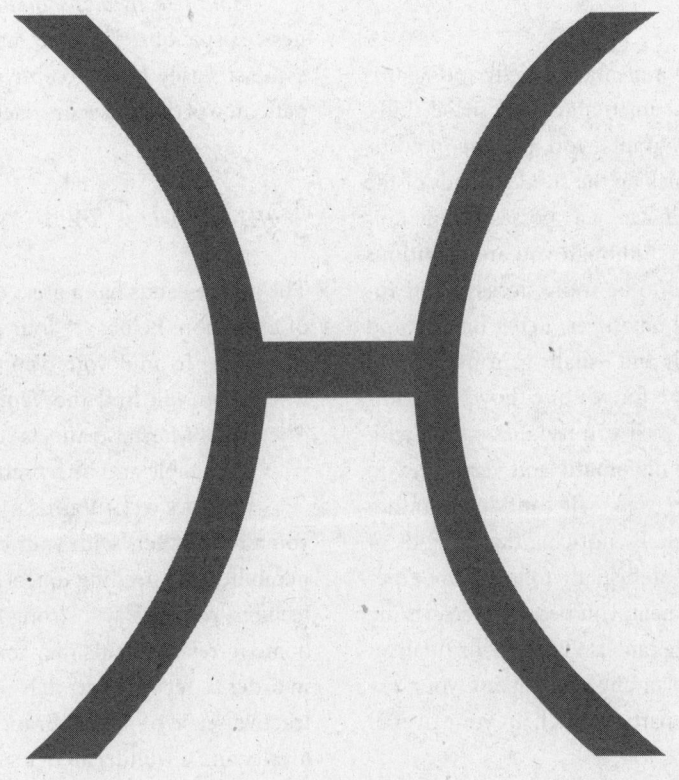

Pisces

February 20–March 20

February 20

SUN: PISCES · DECANATE: PISCES/NEPTUNE · DEGREE: 0°–1°5 PISCES · MODE: MUTABLE · ELEMENT: WATER

Your Personal Powers

Sensitive but dynamic, you are a mentally bright and adaptable individual with business acumen and good social skills. Your ruling planet, Neptune, grants you psychic powers, imagination, and an ability to pick up the subtle moods of the people around you. Aware of image, you possess many creative ideas and a desire to learn. Although you are ambitious and determined, you may need to be more decisive and focused on your future goals and objectives. Being flexible and intelligent, you can learn quickly and usually gain from travel or new experiences. Your dislike for routine, however, indicates that you can become restless if you feel dissatisfied with your circumstances. As you are diplomatic and versatile, you gain power when you develop your self-confidence rather than letting others influence you. By noticing that periods of achievement and advancement are usually followed by a period of inactivity or slow movement, you become persevering and steadier. Since this influence can also affect your finances it will be wiser to budget or plan ahead. Utilizing your exceptional intuitive abilities can particularly help your overall success.

Your Powers of Attraction in Relationships

You are keen on being part of a team, and other people are attracted to your youthful and easygoing nature. The fact that you are receptive and progressive and your ability to mix with different types of people suggest that socializing is important to you. Often enthusiastic about new learning experiences, you can be influenced or inspired by those who can further your knowledge and skills. Being enterprising, you admire mentally quick or intelligent people who are well-informed or proficient. When you feel confident and relaxed your natural charm and good sense of humor can entertain others. When you feel insecure, however, you can be moody and uncommunicative. You need to be able to relate to your partner with ease or share common interests if you want your relationships to last.

Your attractive qualities: intelligent, cooperative, friendly, diplomatic, adaptable, considerate, practical, gentle, tactful, receptive, intuitive, harmonious, patient, decisive, instinctive, assertive, witty, observant, flair for people, persevering, charming, creative, versatile, inspired, quick insight, visionary

Your less attractive qualities: lack of confidence, restlessness, suspicious, isolated, subservient, too sensitive, selfish, escapist, easily hurt, deceptive, codependent, self-doubts, impatient, worried, insecure, lack of direction, irritable

Your Venus Power

The planet Venus has a great deal of influence on your powers of attraction. Below are four possible Venus types for women and men. To find your Venus you need to go to page 771, where you will find the Venus table and extra information. The planet Mars also affects your powers of attraction. To find your Mars table and interpretation go to page 761.

WOMEN WITH VENUS IN CAPRICORN: Proud and refined, you attract others with your composed dignity. Disliking vulnerability and needing to feel safe before you can express your feelings, you display a strong front. Feeling insecure or inadequate in relationships may force you to become manipulative in order to regain control. Nevertheless, you can project an attractive sense of self-assurance and are capable of displaying loyalty and a wonderful dry sense of humor.

MEN WITH VENUS IN CAPRICORN: As you do not display your deeper emotions freely, you are usually dignified and controlled in your relationships. Practical and down-to-earth partners are particularly attractive to you, especially those who do not rush into expressing their feelings but seem to possess natural class and reserve. You need a partner who is loyal and dependable and willing to take your relationship seriously.

WOMEN WITH VENUS IN AQUARIUS: You attract and impress others with your friendly approach and progressive ideas. As you are usually independent and easygoing, you value freedom within a relationship. A good companion with a sense of your own person, you enjoy socializing, especially with people who are original, cosmopolitan, and have a strong sense of individuality. Although being friendly and detached usually serves you well, avoid losing touch with your emotions. You usually prefer the company of those with innovative or progressive views.

MEN WITH VENUS IN AQUARIUS: Friendly and honest, you attract people with your broad-minded approach to life. You usually possess an objective and slightly detached attitude to affairs of the heart. If you are too removed, however, others can misinterpret your behavior as uncaring. It is often more

important to you that your love relationships are based on friendship and honesty rather than intense passion. As you are generally tolerant and liberal, you may be drawn to less conventional relationships.

WOMEN WITH VENUS IN PISCES: Being sensitive to affairs of the heart, when you care for someone you can feel their emotions and sense their every mood. This empathy indicates that you can love on an unselfish level, but you may have to guard against giving too much, especially to those who do not reciprocate. As you are seductive and captivating, partners can be fascinated by your subtle charms and attracted by your caring and affectionate nature.

MEN WITH VENUS IN PISCES: The combination of your emotional subtlety and charm can make you very alluring when dealing with affairs of the heart. Perceptive and impressionable, you have an easygoing style in your relationships, usually preferring to avoid ugly confrontation. You are drawn to a partner who has a touch of glamour and is sensitive to the needs of others. Alternatively, your partner can be a visionary with a rich imagination who can keep you enchanted.

WOMEN WITH VENUS IN ARIES: You gain power from your strong individuality, energy, and enthusiasm. Your young-at-heart and spirited approach to relationships adds to your appeal. If you become too impatient or self-absorbed, however, your partnerships are likely to suffer. Nevertheless, you can be creative, sharp, and quick, especially when you are able to share new and exciting projects with your partners. Mischievous with a love of action, you may even incite them to a playful fight.

MEN WITH VENUS IN ARIES: You are drawn to strong, independent women who can stand up to you. Although you can enthusiastically follow the object of your desire, you may lose power if you allow your forceful emotions to become too dominant. Warm and passionate, you have a side to your nature that longs for new adventures. Romantic and chivalrous, you really enjoy the excitement of the initial chase, but unless you keep the enthusiasm alive and avoid falling into a rut you may become easily bored.

To read all about your Outer Planets and work out how to use your personalized timetable, go to Section Three, page 789.

Your Personalized Timetable

JUPITER BENEFICIAL
1940 4/30 – 6/14
1940 12/12 – until 1941 1/18
1942 5/10 – 7/21
1945 12/20 – until 1946 11/7
1948 3/4 – 5/28
1948 10/27 – 12/14
1952 4/13 – 5/25
1953 8/30 – 11/29
1954 4/20 – 7/4
1957 11/28 – until 1958 10/23
1960 2/7 – 11/27
1964 3/27 – 5/8
1965 8/5 – until 1966 6/18
1969 11/11 – until 1970 10/6
1972 1/19 – 11/8
1976 3/9 – 4/22
1977 7/17 – until 1978 6/1
1981 10/25 – until 1982 9/19
1984 1/2 – 2/20
1984 7/14 – 10/14
1987 7/3 – 10/6
1988 2/18 – 4/5
1989 6/30 – until 1990 5/14
1993 10/10 – 12/28
1994 5/4 – 8/28
1995 12/17 – until 1996 2/1
1999 6/7 – until 2000 3/18
2001 6/13 – 8/28
2002 1/11 – 4/19
2005 9/24 – 12/9
2006 6/22 – 7/20
2007 12/2 – until 2008 1/15
2011 5/18 – until 2012 2/25

SATURN BENEFICIAL
1939 5/25 – 11/11
1940 2/11 – 5/9
1943 8/7 – 12/14
1944 4/25 – 9/12
1944 12/3 – until 1945 5/27
1952 11/26 – until 1953 4/23
1953 8/21 – until 1954 2/8
1954 2/26 – 10/12
1958 12/4 – until 1959 3/16
1959 5/18 – 12/4
1969 3/31 – 6/25
1969 10/18 – until 1970 3/15
1973 6/8 – until 1974 7/7
1982 10/3 – until 1983 11/17
1988 1/8 – 8/9
1988 9/19 – until 1989 1/6
1998 5/6 – until 1999 4/23
2002 7/17 – until 2003 1/17
2003 3/29 – 8/18
2004 1/6 – 5/5
2011 11/8 – until 2012 5/31
2012 7/20 – 12/28

URANUS BENEFICIAL
1947 7/6 – until 1951 6/25
1973 10/14 – until 1977 9/16
1987 2/28 – until 1990 10/24

NEPTUNE BENEFICIAL
1952 12/8 – until 1961 9/11
1982 2/4 – until 1987 11/19

PLUTO BENEFICIAL
1980 11/26 – until 1987 10/18
2006 2/15 – until 2011 12/1

JUPITER CHALLENGING
1941 4/27 – 7/6

1943 10/24 – until 1944 9/7
1947 1/19 – 12/5
1953 4/9 – 6/18
1955 10/1 – until 1956 8/22
1958 12/28 – until 1959 11/19
1964 8/3 – 10/27
1965 3/20 – 6/1
1967 9/13 – until 1968 8/6
1970 12/10 – until 1971 11/3
1976 7/7 – 12/10
1977 2/20 – 5/16
1979 8/28 – until 1980 7/19
1982 11/24 – until 1983 10/15
1988 6/17 – until 1989 4/29
1991 8/12 – 10/30
1992 3/3 – 6/27
1994 11/8 – until 1995 1/25
1995 6/11 – 9/22
2000 5/31 – until 2001 4/10
2003 7/27 – 10/10
2004 4/19 – 5/20
2006 10/24 – until 2007 1/6
2012 5/13 – 7/26

SATURN CHALLENGING
1941 6/20 – 12/11
1942 3/6 – 7/24
1942 11/28 – until 1943 4/12
1948 7/27 – until 1949 8/31
1955 11/12 – until 1956 12/31
1957 6/26 – 9/26
1971 4/26 – until 1972 5/26
1977 9/5 – until 1978 10/10
1979 3/18 – 6/30
1984 12/17 – until 1985 6/6
1985 9/11 – until 1986 2/24
1986 4/11 – 11/9
2000 6/2 – until 2001 7/3
2002 1/1 – 3/16
2006 10/22 – until 2007 1/20
2007 7/9 – until 2008 8/13

URANUS CHALLENGING
1940 6/4 – until 1945 3/7
1960 9/14 – until 1964 8/15
1979 12/17 – until 1983 11/30

NEPTUNE CHALLENGING
1966 12/23 – until 1975 9/20

PLUTO CHALLENGING
1953 8/27 – until 1962 8/16
1992 11/25 – until 1999 11/4

JUPITER SPECIAL
1938 4/1 – until 1939 2/10
1950 3/13 – until 1951 1/23
1962 2/24 – until 1963 1/2
1974 2/8 – 4/20
1974 10/6 – 12/1
1986 1/23 – 4/1
1998 1/5 – 3/15
2009 4/26 – 8/5
2009 12/15 – until 2010 2/26

SATURN SPECIAL
1964 1/26 – until 1965 3/12
1993 3/1 – until 1994 4/20
1994 8/29 – until 1995 1/15

URANUS SPECIAL
2001 3/27 – until 2006 2/3

NEPTUNE SPECIAL
2008 3/26 – Continues

♓

February 21

SUN: PISCES · DECANATE: PISCES/NEPTUNE · DEGREE: 1°5–2°5 PISCES · MODE: MUTABLE · ELEMENT: WATER

Your Personal Powers

Receptive and friendly, you are an idealistic individual with common sense and an alluring charm. Usually active and enterprising, you often seek a varied and eventful life. Your ruling planet, Neptune, grants you imaginative ideas and intuitive powers, enabling you to absorb the subtle moods of those around you. You gain power when you learn to take advantage of opportunities by combining your strong practicality and innate psychic awareness. As a visionary with good organizational skills, you need to express your creativity and enterprising nature in a constructive way. Sometimes a worrier, you may have to develop your decisiveness and keep your feet firmly on the ground if you want your plans to succeed. Although your imaginative ideas can bring financial rewards, guard against taking risks and becoming involved in get-rich-quick schemes. Nevertheless, a strong sense of values and a need to fulfill your inspired ideas imply that once you make a commitment you can be hardworking and take pride in your work.

Your Powers of Attraction in Relationships

Sociable and charming, you are a gregarious individual who enjoys being around people. Usually you want friendships with those whom you can trust or feel secure with. Loyal and idealistic, you can particularly benefit from partnerships that are based on equality, caring, and sharing. People admire your pragmatic approach, common sense, and good negotiation skills. Romantic and sensitive, love is important to you. If your intense emotions do not have positive outlets for expression, you can be subject to moods, frustration, or become involved in emotional power struggles. Being sensitive and impressionable, you usually look for a strong but devoted partner and have high expectations in love. Your inner restlessness can surface if you become too restricted, so having a partner who can give you a great deal of freedom is a prerequisite to happiness and emotional satisfaction.

Your attractive qualities: inspired, pragmatic, optimistic, productive, imaginative, creative, stable, charming, business sense, kind, visionary, warmhearted, attention to details, idealistic, focused, sociable, friendly, rhythmic, gregarious, adaptable, methodical, versatile, enthusiastic, talented

Your less attractive qualities: restlessness, dependent, stubborn, discontented, fear of change, escapist, moody, secretive, worried, indecisive, pessimistic, impatient, shy and reserved, too impressionable

Your Venus Power

The planet Venus has a great deal of influence on your powers of attraction. Below are four possible Venus types for women and men. To find your Venus you need to go to page 771, where you will find the Venus table and extra information. The planet Mars also affects your powers of attraction. To find your Mars table and interpretation go to page 761.

WOMEN WITH VENUS IN CAPRICORN: Proud and refined, you attract others with your composed dignity. Disliking vulnerability and needing to feel safe before you can express your feelings, you display a strong front. Feeling insecure or inadequate in relationships may force you to become manipulative in order to regain control. Nevertheless, you can project an attractive sense of self-assurance and are capable of displaying loyalty and a wonderful dry sense of humor.

MEN WITH VENUS IN CAPRICORN: As you do not display your deeper emotions freely, you are usually dignified and controlled in your relationships. Practical and down-to-earth partners are particularly attractive to you, especially those who do not rush into expressing their feelings but seem to possess natural class and reserve. You need a partner who is loyal and dependable and willing to take your relationship seriously.

WOMEN WITH VENUS IN AQUARIUS: You attract and impress others with your friendly approach and progressive ideas. As you are usually independent and easygoing, you value freedom within a relationship. A good companion with a sense of your own person, you enjoy socializing, especially with people who are original, cosmopolitan, and have a strong sense of individuality. Although being friendly and detached usually serves you well, avoid losing touch with your emotions. You usually prefer the company of those who have innovative or progressive views.

MEN WITH VENUS IN AQUARIUS: Friendly and honest, you attract people with your broad-minded approach to life. You usually possess an objective and slightly detached attitude to affairs of the heart. If you are too removed, however, others can misinterpret your behavior as uncaring. It is often more important to you that your love relationships are based on

friendship and honesty rather than intense passion. As you are generally tolerant and liberal, you may be drawn to less conventional relationships.

WOMEN WITH VENUS IN PISCES: As a romantic and idealistic individual, you can be both loving and giving. While making allowances and sacrifices is understandable in a loving relationship, avoid playing the martyr. In relationships you may need to balance the practical with the charitable. Nevertheless, your benevolence and sacrifices in the right relationship make you a partner who is devoted and kind. Subtle, sensitive, and alluring, you can be sensual and caring.

MEN WITH VENUS IN PISCES: Romantic and idealistic when in love, you can be a sensitive and responsive lover. Being pliant and flexible with an impressionable nature helps you to adapt to the needs of others. In your desire to blend with those you love, however, guard against not clearly defining your own boundaries. With your affectionate and sentimental nature you are often attracted to those who understand your sensitivity and share your vision.

WOMEN WITH VENUS IN ARIES: Idealistic, passionate, and adventurous, you are direct in your dealings with others. When you are attracted to a person you usually take the initiative and use your people skills to make things happen. In close relationships you are not afraid to confront your other half. This self-assertiveness is positive if differences can be brought into the open through diplomacy and compromise.

MEN WITH VENUS IN ARIES: As you often have the courage and strength to initiate situations, you like to take the lead. With your unconscious desire for conquest you may also have to beware of being competitive with your partners. Nevertheless, you are drawn to direct and strong-willed partners who share your love of action and enthusiasm for life. When you are feeling good you can be charming and enthusiastic in romantic situations with an entertaining and spontaneous spirit.

To read all about your Outer Planets and work out how to use your personalized timetable, go to Section Three, page 789.

Your Personalized Timetable

JUPITER BENEFICIAL
1940 5/4 – 6/19
1940 11/29 – until 1941 1/31
1942 5/15 – 7/26
1945 12/28 – until 1946 3/29
1946 8/26 – 11/12
1948 3/14 – 5/18
1948 11/1 – 12/18
1952 4/17 – 5/30
1953 9/8 – 11/20
1954 4/26 – 7/9
1957 12/4 – until 1958 10/27
1960 2/13 – 12/2
1964 4/1 – 5/13
1965 8/11 – until 1966 6/23
1969 11/16 – until 1970 10/12
1972 1/24 – 11/13
1976 3/14 – 4/26
1977 7/22 – until 1978 6/6
1981 10/30 – until 1982 9/24
1984 1/7 – 2/26
1984 7/5 – 10/22
1987 7/11 – 9/27
1988 2/24 – 4/10
1989 7/4 – until 1990 5/19
1993 10/15 – until 1994 9/4
1995 12/22 – until 1996 2/6
1999 6/13 – until 2000 3/23
2001 6/18 – 9/3
2002 1/3 – 4/27
2005 9/29 – 12/15
2006 6/5 – 8/5
2007 12/7 – until 2008 1/20
2011 5/23 – until 2012 3/2

SATURN BENEFICIAL
1939 6/4 – 10/28
1940 2/24 – 5/18
1943 8/19 – 12/1
1944 5/5 – 10/1
1944 11/14 – until 1945 6/5
1952 12/7 – until 1953 4/9
1953 9/2 – until 1954 10/21
1958 12/13 – until 1959 12/13
1969 4/9 – 7/8
1969 10/4 – until 1970 3/25
1973 6/17 – until 1974 7/16
1982 10/12 – until 1983 11/26
1984 6/15 – 8/10
1988 1/17 – 7/18
1988 10/11 – until 1989 1/16
1989 9/4 – 9/17
1998 5/15 – until 1999 5/2
2002 7/27 – until 2003 8/29
2003 12/24 – until 2004 5/16
2011 11/18 – until 2012 5/11
2012 8/8 – Continues

URANUS BENEFICIAL
1947 7/27 – until 1952 4/18
1973 10/31 – until 1977 10/6
1987 12/26 – until 1990 11/19

NEPTUNE BENEFICIAL
1953 11/5 – until 1961 10/15
1983 1/3 – until 1987 12/20

PLUTO BENEFICIAL
1981 1/22 – until 1988 9/3
2007 1/9 – Continues

JUPITER CHALLENGING
1941 5/2 – 7/11
1943 11/1 – until 1944 1/25

1944 6/26 – 9/12
1947 1/26 – 12/10
1953 4/14 – 6/23
1955 10/7 – until 1956 8/27
1959 1/3 – 11/24
1964 8/12 – 10/17
1965 3/26 – 6/6
1967 9/18 – until 1968 8/11
1970 12/15 – until 1971 11/8
1976 7/13 – 12/1
1977 2/28 – 5/21
1979 9/2 – until 1980 7/25
1982 11/29 – until 1983 10/21
1988 6/22 – until 1989 5/4
1991 8/17 – until 1992 7/4
1994 11/13 – until 1995 2/1
1995 6/2 – 9/30
2000 6/4 – until 2001 4/15
2003 8/1 – 10/16
2004 4/4 – 6/5
2006 10/29 – until 2007 1/11
2007 7/22 – 8/23
2012 5/18 – 8/1
2012 12/10 – Continues

SATURN CHALLENGING
1941 6/30 – 11/26
1942 3/19 – until 1943 4/22
1948 8/5 – until 1949 9/8
1955 11/21 – until 1957 1/11
1957 6/11 – 10/9
1971 5/5 – until 1972 6/3
1977 9/13 – until 1978 10/20
1979 3/4 – 7/12
1984 12/28 – until 1985 5/22
1985 9/25 – until 1986 11/18
2000 6/10 – until 2001 7/13
2001 12/17 – until 2002 3/30
2006 11/8 – until 2007 1/3
2007 7/19 – until 2008 8/22

URANUS CHALLENGING
1940 6/24 – until 1945 4/11
1960 10/4 – until 1964 9/1
1980 1/7 – until 1984 9/30

NEPTUNE CHALLENGING
1967 2/18 – until 1975 11/1

PLUTO CHALLENGING
1953 10/4 – until 1963 7/18
1992 12/23 – until 2000 9/15

JUPITER SPECIAL
1938 4/7 – until 1939 2/15
1950 3/18 – until 1951 1/28
1962 3/1 – until 1963 1/8
1974 2/12 – 4/25
1974 9/26 – 12/11
1986 1/27 – 4/6
1998 1/10 – 3/19
2009 5/4 – 7/27
2009 12/21 – until 2010 3/2

SATURN SPECIAL
1964 2/4 – until 1965 3/21
1993 3/10 – until 1994 5/3
1994 8/14 – until 1995 1/25

URANUS SPECIAL
2001 4/24 – until 2006 2/22

NEPTUNE SPECIAL
2009 2/23 – Continues

♓

February 22

SUN: PISCES • DECANATE: PISCES/NEPTUNE • DEGREE: 2°5–3°5 PISCES • MODE: MUTABLE • ELEMENT: WATER

Your Personal Powers

Sensitive but mentally sharp, you are an astute and resourceful individual with a sense of responsibility and good communication skills. Your ruling planet, Neptune, grants you intuitive powers, imagination, and an ability to pick up the moods and feelings of others. Although you can maintain a certain light-hearted attitude toward life, a tendency to worry about your financial security implies that a more serious side to your nature emerges when money matters are on the agenda. Nevertheless, resourceful and observant with a natural business sense, you have a good understanding of values and are often persuasive in negotiation. Having high ideals, charm, and an enterprising spirit suggests that you can succeed in all types of activities related to the public. Although you are often willing to make allowances for others, you benefit from being decisive and focused and not burdening yourself with too many commitments. Intelligent and creative with an inventive mind, you empower yourself when you use your ingenuity to structure ideas or solve problems.

Your Powers of Attraction in Relationships

With your charismatic personality you do not have any problems attracting partners. Although your intuitive powers can be strong and accurate, when love is concerned you sometimes choose to ignore them. Frequently generous and giving, you are often willing to assist others or give useful advice. Although you are often idealistic and sensitive to others, guard against feeling insecure or putting up walls of defense in your close relationships. Usually you are attracted to intelligent people with integrity and independent views. By being confident and self-disciplined, you can enjoy loving relationships. Although sociable, you still need some time alone for reflection and renewal. Usually you want a partner who is loyal and able to recognize your wonderful potential.

Your attractive qualities: responsible, talent with words, inventive, highly intuitive, pragmatic, skillful, problem solver, organized, business acumen, ambitious, proud, dramatic, enterprising, quick to learn, adaptable, receptive, versatile, friendly, diplomatic, sympathetic, decisive, clever

Your less attractive qualities: nervous, escapist, too sensitive, indecisive, scattered, unpredictable, pessimistic, worried about money, bossy, materialistic, lazy, egotistical, self-promoting, lacks direction

Your Venus Power

The planet Venus has a great deal of influence on your powers of attraction. Below are four possible Venus types for women and men. To find your Venus you need to go to page 771, where you will find the Venus table and extra information. The planet Mars also affects your powers of attraction. To find your Mars table and interpretation go to page 761.

WOMEN WITH VENUS IN CAPRICORN: Loyal and responsible, you are attracted to dignified and reserved individuals. Being practical and security-conscious, you prefer hardworking partners who are resourceful and enterprising. Work may even be a factor in many of your associations and partnerships. For you, family and faithfulness can be especially important, so you are usually willing to work hard or make sacrifices in order to build a strong relationship.

MEN WITH VENUS IN CAPRICORN: As you do not display your deeper emotions freely, you are usually dignified and controlled in your relationships. Practical and down-to-earth partners are particularly attractive to you, especially those who do not rush into expressing their feelings but seem to possess natural class and reserve. You need a partner who is loyal and dependable and willing to take your relationship seriously.

WOMEN WITH VENUS IN AQUARIUS: When it comes to relationships, others are attracted to your honest, friendly, and easygoing attitude. You enjoy social interaction and have a genuine concern for others. In fact, at times your friends may be just as important as your partner. Usually you present a tolerant and reasonable front in love situations and attempt to view your relationships objectively. If partners become too demanding, however, you can become stubborn or awkward. Nevertheless, inventive and progressive, you enjoy the company of like-minded people who can share your original ideas.

MEN WITH VENUS IN AQUARIUS: You are sociable and open-minded, and people are attracted by your friendly and easygoing style. Being independent, you value freedom-loving partners who give you the space to be yourself. People can sometimes interpret your detachment as being emotionally cool, but they admire your objectivity and humanitarian incli-

nations. You are attracted to intelligent individuals who are as truthful and direct as you, but above all they must be true friends. Ideally, your partner shares your liberal views on life and possesses a strong sense of individuality.

WOMEN WITH VENUS IN PISCES: Being sensitive to affairs of the heart, when you care for someone you can feel their emotions and sense their every mood. This empathy indicates that you can love on an unselfish level, but you may have to guard against giving too much, especially to those who do not reciprocate. As you are seductive and captivating, partners can be fascinated by your subtle charms and attracted by your caring and affectionate nature.

MEN WITH VENUS IN PISCES: Romantic and idealistic when in love, you can be a sensitive and responsive lover. Being pliant and flexible with an impressionable nature helps you to adapt to the needs of others. In your desire to blend with those you love, however, guard against not clearly defining your own boundaries. With your affectionate and sentimental nature you are often attracted to those who understand your sensitivity and share your vision.

WOMEN WITH VENUS IN ARIES: Idealistic, passionate, and adventurous, you are direct in your dealings with others. When you are attracted to a person, you usually take the initiative and use your people skills to make things happen. In close relationships you are not afraid to confront your other half. This self-assertiveness is positive if differences can be brought into the open through diplomacy and compromise.

MEN WITH VENUS IN ARIES: As you often have the courage and strength to initiate situations, you like to take the lead. With your unconscious desire for conquest you may also have to beware of being competitive with your partners. Nevertheless, you are drawn to direct and strong-willed partners who can share your love of action and enthusiasm for life. When you are feeling good you can be charming and enthusiastic in romantic situations with an entertaining and spontaneous spirit.

To read all about your Outer Planets and work out how to use your personalized timetable, go to Section Three, page 789.

Your Personalized Timetable

JUPITER BENEFICIAL
1940 5/9 – 6/25
1940 11/20 – until 1941 2/9
1942 5/20 – 7/30.
1946 1/5 – 3/20
1946 9/1 – 11/17
1948 3/27 – 5/4
1948 11/7 – 12/23
1952 4/22 – 6/4
1953 9/18 – 11/10
1954 5/1 – 7/13
1957 12/10 – until 1958 4/28
1958 8/8 – 11/1
1960 2/19 – 6/23
1960 10/15 – 12/6
1964 4/5 – 5/17
1965 8/17 – 12/25
1966 4/8 – 6/27
1969 11/21 – until 1970 10/16
1972 1/29 – 11/19
1976 3/19 – 4/30
1977 7/26 – until 1978 6/11
1981 11/4 – until 1982 9/29
1984 1/12 – 10/28
1987 7/21 – 9/17
1988 2/29 – 4/14
1989 7/9 – until 1990 5/24
1993 10/19 – until 1994 9/10
1995 12/27 – until 1996 2/11
1996 8/16 – 9/21
1999 6/18 – until 2000 3/28
2001 6/22 – 9/9
2001 12/27 – until 2002 5/3
2005 10/4 – 12/20
2006 5/26 – 8/16
2007 12/11 – until 2008 1/24
2011 5/27 – until 2012 3/8

SATURN BENEFICIAL
1939 6/14 – 10/15
1940 3/5 – 5/26
1940 12/18 – until 1941 1/31
1943 9/1 – 11/17
1944 5/14 – until 1945 6/13
1952 12/19 – until 1953 3/26
1953 9/12 – until 1954 10/29
1958 12/22 – until 1959 12/22
1969 4/16 – 7/26
1969 9/16 – until 1970 4/2
1973 6/24 – until 1974 7/24
1982 10/20 – until 1983 12/5
1984 5/27 – 8/27
1988 1/27 – 7/2
1988 10/25 – until 1989 1/24
1989 8/5 – 10/17
1998 5/24 – 11/16
1999 2/9 – 5/10
2002 8/5 – 12/20
2003 4/24 – 9/9
2003 12/11 – until 2004 5/25
2011 11/27 – until 2012 4/26
2012 8/21 – Continues

URANUS BENEFICIAL
1947 8/19 – until 1952 5/15
1973 11/17 – until 1977 10/23
1988 1/12 – until 1990 12/8

NEPTUNE BENEFICIAL
1953 12/7 – until 1962 9/10
1983 2/2 – until 1988 11/17

PLUTO BENEFICIAL
1981 11/14 – until 1988 10/6
2007 2/11 – Continues

JUPITER CHALLENGING
1941 5/6 – 7/16

1943 11/10 – until 1944 1/15
1944 7/2 – 9/17
1947 2/4 – 4/22
1947 9/30 – 12/14
1953 4/19 – 6/27
1955 10/13 – until 1956 9/1
1959 1/8 – 11/28
1964 8/24 – 10/6
1965 3/31 – 6/10
1967 9/24 – until 1968 8/16
1970 12/20 – until 1971 11/12
1976 7/18 – 11/24
1977 3/7 – 5/25
1979 9/6 – until 1980 7/30
1982 12/4 – until 1983 10/26
1988 6/27 – until 1989 5/9
1991 8/21 – 11/14
1992 2/16 – 7/11
1994 11/18 – until 1995 10/6
2000 6/9 – until 2001 4/20
2003 8/6 – 10/21
2004 3/25 – 6/15
2006 11/3 – until 2007 1/17
2007 7/7 – 9/6
2012 5/22 – Continues

SATURN CHALLENGING
1941 7/10 – 11/14
1942 3/30 – 8/19
1942 10/31 – until 1943 5/1
1948 8/13 – until 1949 9/16
1955 11/29 – until 1957 1/21
1957 5/28 – 10/21
1971 5/12 – until 1972 6/11
1977 9/22 – until 1978 10/31
1979 2/19 – 7/22
1985 1/7 – 5/8
1985 10/6 – until 1986 11/27
2000 6/19 – 12/18
2001 3/3 – 7/22
2001 12/5 – until 2002 4/10
2007 7/27 – until 2008 8/30

URANUS CHALLENGING
1940 7/18 – until 1945 5/2
1960 10/30 – until 1965 6/26
1980 2/7 – until 1984 10/24

NEPTUNE CHALLENGING
1967 12/22 – until 1976 9/15

PLUTO CHALLENGING
1954 9/8 – until 1963 8/20
1993 2/2 – until 2000 10/27

JUPITER SPECIAL
1938 4/12 – until 1939 2/19
1950 3/23 – until 1951 2/1
1962 3/5 – until 1963 1/13
1974 2/16 – 12/19
1986 2/1 – 4/10
1998 1/15 – 3/24
2009 5/13 – 7/18
2009 12/26 – until 2010 3/7

SATURN SPECIAL
1964 2/13 – until 1965 3/30
1965 10/13 – 12/15
1993 3/19 – until 1994 5/18
1994 7/29 – until 1995 2/3

URANUS SPECIAL
2002 2/22 – until 2006 12/25

NEPTUNE SPECIAL
2009 3/23 – Continues

February 23

SUN: PISCES • DECANATE: PISCES/NEPTUNE • DEGREE: 3°5–4°5 PISCES • MODE: MUTABLE • ELEMENT: WATER

Your Personal Powers

Gregarious and instinctive, you are a dynamic individual with high ideals and strong determination. Although you can be romantic and idealistic, a desire for power implies that status or prestige is equally important to you. Your ruling planet, Neptune, grants you receptivity, intuitive powers, and an ability to relate to other people's emotional needs. Resolute to succeed yet imaginative and sensitive by nature, you gain power when you combine your versatility and innovative ideas with your people skills and talent for business. Able to tune into the collective need of society, you can also initiate or promote new projects. Although you are usually charismatic and energetic, a tendency to vacillate from being confident to impressionable suggests that you can lose some of your power if you become moody or apprehensive about your capabilities. Nevertheless, through sharing your inspired vision with others you can build successful partnerships or be involved in projects that can be both financially beneficial and emotionally satisfying.

Your Powers of Attraction in Relationships

Keen on interacting with others, you are a friendly yet independent individual who enjoys a busy social life. Determined and versatile, your ability to associate and network suggests that you can mix business with pleasure. People admire your spontaneity, negotiation skills, and charming manner. Your strong convictions indicate, however, that you can sometimes be unyielding. When you sense that things are amiss, you usually want to confront situations and clear the air. As you like to stand your ground, you may be inclined to test your wits against others; if you overstep the mark, however, you may become involved in power struggles. Usually you are attracted to dynamic individuals who are enterprising and success-oriented. Alternatively, you may be drawn to idealistic people who are original, honest, and direct.

Your attractive qualities: Visionary, intuitive, quick instincts, idealistic, loyal, witty, dynamic, inspired, responsible, communicative, receptive, creative, self-expressive, versatile, trustworthy, good business acumen, ambitious, motivated, methodical, sympathetic, compassionate, caring

Your less attractive qualities: insecure, moody, stubborn, restlessness, discontented, uncompromising, faultfinding, withdrawn, impatient, easily bored, unreliable, codependent, secretive, fear about money, escapist

Your Venus Power

The planet Venus has a great deal of influence on your powers of attraction. Below are four possible Venus types for women and men. To find your Venus you need to go to page 771, where you will find the Venus table and extra information. The planet Mars also affects your powers of attraction. To find your Mars table and interpretation go to page 761.

WOMEN WITH VENUS IN CAPRICORN: Romantically, you do not give your heart easily but hide behind a cool reserve until you feel free to express your emotions. As you take your relationships seriously, you may find yourself drawn to people who are businesslike, resourceful, and practical or those who can act as teachers or mentors. Work or career may also be a factor in many of your associations and partnerships. As security can play an important role in your relationships you are often attracted to partners who are loyal and hardworking,

MEN WITH VENUS IN CAPRICORN: In relationships you take love seriously and can be a strong and practical support for friends or partners. You are usually attracted to partners who are as hardworking as you. As you tend not to express your feelings until you feel really secure in a relationship, you may be drawn to those who seem loyal, faithful, and not likely to let you down. As you respect the wisdom of experience, you may be drawn to mature partners or, alternatively, you may act as an authority figure for someone younger.

WOMEN WITH VENUS IN AQUARIUS: Sociable and gracious, you are usually sincere and are capable of showing attributes of real tolerance and liberalism. Although you are keen on forming relationships, you also like to have freedom and act independently. Your intimate partnerships need to be founded on true friendships. Full of bright and progressive ideas, you can express yourself better when you are free and unrestricted. An ability to think in a dispassionate way suggests that you can stay detached. Your love of freedom also implies that without smothering your partner you can be loving and loyal.

MEN WITH VENUS IN AQUARIUS: Although independent, you often enjoy being part of a group. The partners you frequently attract are themselves nonconformists or free spirits. As an individual you may not find it easy to settle into a rou-

tine or an entirely mundane type of relationship. You may have some unconventional views on traditional marriage or your partner may hold such views. As a nonconformist, you may also be interested in alternative lifestyles such as collective living.

WOMEN WITH VENUS IN PISCES: In love you are sensitive, tender, and affectionate, experiencing your partner's feelings almost as strongly as your own. Being also imaginative and visionary, you possess the ability to develop creative gifts and a deep compassion for others. As you are idealistic when in love you usually prefer to see only your partner's good points, but be careful that your high expectations do not bring disappointment if you avoid being realistic. Nevertheless, in your relationships with others, you can be devoted, loving, and positively enchanting.

MEN WITH VENUS IN PISCES: The combination of your emotional subtlety and charm can make you very alluring when dealing with affairs of the heart. Perceptive and impressionable, you have an easygoing style in your relationships, usually preferring to avoid ugly confrontation. You are drawn to a partner who has a touch of glamour and is sensitive to the needs of others. Alternatively, your partner can be a visionary with a rich imagination who can keep you enchanted.

WOMEN WITH VENUS IN ARIES: With your strong desires and enthusiastic nature you can be a passionate lover. Although idealistic and single-minded, you need to avoid unnecessary conflicts in your relationships by being more patient and less headstrong. Although at times others can accuse you of being bossy or impulsive, you possess a great deal of warmth and charm. When necessary you can disarm others by making them feel important.

MEN WITH VENUS IN ARIES: You are drawn to strong, independent women who can stand up to you. Although you can enthusiastically follow the object of your desire, you may lose power if you allow your forceful emotions to become too dominant. Warm and passionate, you have a side to your nature that longs for new adventures. Romantic and chivalrous, you really enjoy the excitement of the initial chase, but unless you keep the enthusiasm alive and avoid falling into a rut you may become easily bored.

To read all about your Outer Planets and work out how to use your personalized timetable, go to Section Three, page 789.

Your Personalized Timetable

JUPITER BENEFICIAL
1940 5/11 – 6/28
1940 11/16 – until 1941 2/13
1942 5/23 – 8/2
1946 1/11 – 11/19
1948 4/11 – 4/20
1948 11/10 – 12/25
1952 4/24 – 6/6
1953 9/26 – 11/2
1954 5/4 – 7/16
1957 12/13 – until 1958 11/4
1960 2/23 – 6/18
1960 10/19 – 12/9
1964 4/7 – 5/19
1965 8/20 – 12/20
1966 4/11 – 6/30
1969 11/24 – until 1970 10/19
1972 2/1 – 11/21
1976 3/21 – 5/3
1977 7/29 – until 1978 6/13
1981 11/7 – until 1982 10/2
1984 1/14 – 11/1
1987 7/28 – 9/11
1988 3/3 – 4/17
1989 7/11 – until 1990 5/27
1993 10/22 – until 1994 9/13
1995 12/29 – until 1996 2/14
1996 8/8 – 9/29
1999 6/21 – 10/31
2000 2/7 – 3/30
2001 6/24 – until 2002 5/6
2005 10/7 – 12/23
2006 5/21 – 8/20
2007 12/14 – until 2008 1/27
2011 5/30 – until 2012 3/10

SATURN BENEFICIAL
1939 6/21 – 10/8
1940 3/10 – 5/31
1940 12/7 – until 1941 2/11
1943 9/11 – 11/7
1944 5/18 – until 1945 6/17
1952 12/26 – until 1953 3/18
1953 9/17 – until 1954 11/3
1958 12/27 – until 1959 12/27
1969 4/21 – 8/14
1969 8/28 – until 1970 4/7
1973 6/29 – until 1974 7/28
1982 10/24 – until 1983 12/10
1984 5/19 – 9/4
1988 2/1 – 6/25
1988 10/31 – until 1989 1/30
1989 7/27 – 10/26
1998 5/29 – 11/9
1999 2/16 – 5/14
2002 8/11 – 12/14
2003 4/29 – 9/17
2003 12/3 – until 2004 5/30
2011 12/2 – until 2012 4/19
2012 8/28 – Continues

URANUS BENEFICIAL
1947 9/7 – until 1952 5/27
1973 11/27 – until 1977 11/1
1988 1/22 – until 1990 12/18

NEPTUNE BENEFICIAL
1954 1/3 – until 1962 9/29
1983 2/25 – until 1988 12/4

PLUTO BENEFICIAL
1981 11/30 – until 1988 10/20
2007 3/16 – Continues

JUPITER CHALLENGING
1941 5/9 – 7/19
1942 1/19 – 2/22

1943 11/16 – until 1944 1/9
1944 7/5 – 9/19
1947 2/9 – 4/16
1947 10/3 – 12/17
1953 4/21 – 6/30
1955 10/16 – until 1956 9/3
1959 1/12 – 12/1
1964 9/3 – 9/26
1965 4/3 – 6/13
1967 9/26 – until 1968 8/19
1970 12/23 – until 1971 11/15
1976 7/22 – 11/20
1977 3/11 – 5/27
1979 9/9 – until 1980 8/2
1982 12/6 – until 1983 10/29
1988 6/30 – until 1989 5/11
1991 8/24 – until 1992 7/14
1994 11/20 – until 1995 10/9
2000 6/11 – until 2001 4/23
2003 8/8 – 10/25
2004 3/20 – 6/20
2006 11/5 – until 2007 1/20
2007 7/1 – 9/12
2012 5/25 – Continues

SATURN CHALLENGING
1941 7/16 – 11/7
1942 4/4 – 8/30
1942 10/21 – until 1943 5/6
1948 8/17 – until 1949 9/21
1955 12/4 – until 1957 1/28
1957 5/20 – 10/26
1971 5/17 – until 1972 6/15
1977 9/27 – until 1978 3/3
1978 6/16 – 11/6
1979 2/12 – 7/27
1985 1/14 – 5/1
1985 10/11 – until 1986 12/2
2000 6/24 – 12/9
2001 3/11 – 7/28
2001 11/28 – until 2002 4/16
2007 8/1 – until 2008 9/3

URANUS CHALLENGING
1940 8/7 – until 1945 5/12
1961 8/15 – until 1965 7/10
1980 11/18 – until 1984 11/3

NEPTUNE CHALLENGING
1968 1/10 – until 1976 10/13

PLUTO CHALLENGING
1954 9/27 – until 1964 6/26
1993 11/29 – until 2000 11/12

JUPITER SPECIAL
1938 4/16 – until 1939 2/21
1950 3/25 – until 1951 2/4
1962 3/7 – until 1963 1/16
1974 2/19 – 12/23
1986 2/3 – 4/13
1998 1/17 – 3/26
2009 5/19 – 7/11
2009 12/29 – until 2010 3/9

SATURN SPECIAL
1964 2/17 – until 1965 4/3
1965 10/3 – 12/24
1993 3/25 – 9/3
1993 12/19 – until 1994 5/29
1994 7/18 – until 1995 2/8

URANUS SPECIAL
2002 3/4 – until 2007 1/10

NEPTUNE SPECIAL
2009 4/12 – Continues

February 24

SUN: PISCES · DECANATE: PISCES/NEPTUNE · DEGREE: 4°5–5°5 PISCES · MODE: MUTABLE · ELEMENT: WATER

Your Personal Powers

Being dynamic and ambitious with many goals, you are an energetic individual full of imaginative ideas and good business acumen. Resourceful and determined, you can be a strong-willed individual. Your ruling planet, Neptune, grants you receptivity, vision, intuitive powers, and emotional sensitivity. Although by nature you are idealistic with strong convictions, you gain power when you combine your enthusiasm and tenacity with your worthy objectives. Since much of your success often depends on your collaborative efforts, your success is often assured when you learn to differentiate between taking the lead and being bossy. Fortunately you are able to assess people and situations with uncanny accuracy. A tendency to feel restless means that you can lose some of your power when you are confined in restrictive circumstances. Since you enjoy initiating new ideas or projects, you empower yourself when you have a clear plan of action or goal in mind. This can also imply that by overcoming an inclination to waver or be impatient you can use your good mind and pragmatic approach to spot financial opportunities.

Your Powers of Attraction in Relationships

Energetic and motivated, you like to keep busy and usually enjoy an active social life. At times, however, you may rush into relationships and later change your mind. Issues of trust and good communication play an important role in your close ties with others. Enthusiastic and honest, you are often open about your feelings. Tension in relationships can accrue when you behave in a domineering manner; nevertheless, people admire your lively personality. You are usually attracted to charismatic and successful individuals who are generous and practical with a good sense of values. Being sensitive and caring, you are willing to support those you love and admire. Your ideal partner would be someone who is animated and dynamic, keeping you constantly curious and enchanted.

Your attractive qualities: idealistic, energetic, purposeful, charming, cooperative, home-loving, practical, determined, honest, frank, fair, charismatic, generous, business acumen, visionary, networker, imaginative, good strategist, dynamic, intuitive, good negotiator, pragmatic, motivated

Your less attractive qualities: restless, impatient, materialistic, insecure, dislikes routine, lazy, domineering, stubborn, bossy, stuck in a rut, escapist, impulsive, stubborn, moody, argumentative

Your Venus Power

The planet Venus has a great deal of influence on your powers of attraction. Below are four possible Venus types for women and men. To find your Venus you need to go to page 771, where you will find the Venus table and extra information. The planet Mars also affects your powers of attraction. To find your Mars table and interpretation go to page 761.

WOMEN WITH VENUS IN CAPRICORN: Loyal and responsible, you are attracted to dignified and reserved individuals. Being practical and security-conscious, you prefer hardworking partners who are resourceful and enterprising. Work may even be a factor in many of your associations and partnerships. For you, family and faithfulness can be especially important, so you are usually willing to work hard or make sacrifices in order to build a strong relationship.

MEN WITH VENUS IN CAPRICORN: In relationships you take love seriously and can be a strong and practical support for friends or partners. You are usually attracted to partners who are as hardworking as you. As you tend not to express your feelings until you feel really secure in a relationship, you may be drawn to those who seem loyal, faithful, and not likely to let you down. As you respect the wisdom of experience, you may be drawn to mature partners or, alternatively, you may act as an authority figure for someone younger.

WOMEN WITH VENUS IN AQUARIUS: Usually you have a modern outlook on love and are open to new or current lifestyles. Your intuitive abilities, communal sense, and people skills often allow you to see deeper into human intentions and to telepathically read people's thoughts. You are usually group-oriented and are drawn to individuals within the group who are independent and self-motivated. You are more inclined to choose a partner who is unconventional or freedom-loving. Conscious of your social standing, however, you want someone who can relate well to your friends.

MEN WITH VENUS IN AQUARIUS: You are sociable and open-minded, and people are attracted by your friendly and relaxed style. Being independent you value freedom-loving partners who give you the space to be yourself. Others sometimes interpret your detachment as being emotionally cool, but they may not understand your progressive views on rela-

tionships. Friendship can sometimes be even more important than earthly passion. Ideally, your partners share your ideas on life and possess a sense of originality as strong as your own. Not easily ruffled, you can deal well with difficult situations or moody partners.

WOMEN WITH VENUS IN PISCES: As a romantic and idealistic individual, you can be both loving and giving. While making allowances and sacrifices is understandable in a loving relationship, avoid playing the martyr. In relationships you may need to balance the practical with the charitable. Nevertheless your benevolence and sacrifices in the right relationship make you a partner who is devoted, kind, and compassionate. Subtle, sensitive, and alluring, you can be sensual and caring.

MEN WITH VENUS IN PISCES: The combination of your emotional subtlety and charm can make you very alluring when dealing with affairs of the heart. Perceptive and impressionable, you have an easygoing style in your relationships, usually preferring to avoid ugly confrontation. You are drawn to a partner who has a touch of glamour and is sensitive to the needs of others. Alternatively, your partner can be a visionary with a rich imagination who can keep you enchanted.

WOMEN WITH VENUS IN ARIES: With your strong desires and enthusiastic nature, you can be a passionate lover. Although idealistic and single-minded, you need to avoid unnecessary conflicts in your relationships by being more patient and less headstrong. Although at times others can accuse you of being bossy or impulsive, you possess a great deal of warmth and charm. When necessary you can disarm others by making them feel important.

MEN WITH VENUS IN ARIES: As you often have the courage and strength to initiate situations, you like to take the lead. With your unconscious desire for conquest you may also have to beware of being competitive with your partners. Nevertheless you are drawn to direct and strong-willed partners who can share your love of action and enthusiasm for life. When you are feeling good you can be charming and enthusiastic in romantic situations with an entertaining and spontaneous spirit.

To read all about your Outer Planets and work out how to use your personalized timetable, go to Section Three, page 789.

Your Personalized Timetable

JUPITER BENEFICIAL
1940 5/15 – 7/4
1940 11/8 – until **1941** 2/20
1942 5/27 – 8/7
1946 1/25 – 2/28
1946 9/9 – 11/24
1948 11/14 – 12/30
1952 4/28 – 6/11
1954 5/9 – 7/20
1957 12/20 – until **1958** 11/8
1960 2/29 – 6/10
1960 10/25 – 12/13
1964 4/11 – 5/24
1965 8/26 – 12/13
1966 4/18 – 7/4
1969 11/29 – until **1970** 10/24
1972 2/6 – 11/26
1976 3/26 – 5/7
1977 8/3 – until **1978** 6/18
1981 11/11 – until **1982** 10/7
1984 1/19 – 11/7
1988 3/8 – 4/21
1989 7/16 – until **1990** 6/1
1993 10/26 – until **1994** 9/19
1996 1/2 – 2/19
1996 7/28 – 10/10
1999 6/27 – 10/23
2000 2/14 – 4/4
2001 6/29 – 9/21
2001 12/14 – until **2002** 5/12
2005 10/11 – 12/29
2006 5/13 – 8/28
2007 12/18 – until **2008** 2/1
2011 6/4 – until **2012** 3/15

SATURN BENEFICIAL
1939 7/4 – 9/23
1940 3/19 – 6/9
1940 11/21 – until **1941** 2/26
1944 5/27 – until **1945** 6/25
1953 1/15 – 2/26
1953 9/26 – until **1954** 11/11
1959 1/4 – until **1960** 1/4
1969 4/29 – until **1970** 4/15
1973 7/7 – until **1974** 8/5
1975 2/9 – 4/15
1982 11/2 – until **1983** 12/20
1984 5/5 – 9/16
1988 2/12 – 6/11
1988 11/11 – until **1989** 2/8
1989 7/12 – 11/8
1998 6/8 – 10/27
1999 2/28 – 5/22
2002 8/22 – 12/1
2003 5/9 – 10/7
2003 11/13 – until **2004** 6/7
2011 12/13 – Continues

URANUS BENEFICIAL
1938 1/1 – 2/8
1948 6/27 – until **1952** 6/14
1973 12/19 – until **1978** 8/27
1988 2/12 – until **1991** 10/2

NEPTUNE BENEFICIAL
1954 11/19 – until **1963** 8/1
1984 1/16 – until **1989** 10/24

PLUTO BENEFICIAL
1982 1/20 – until **1989** 9/4
2008 1/23 – Continues

JUPITER CHALLENGING
1941 5/13 – 7/24
1942 1/6 – 3/7
1943 12/4 – 12/23

JUPITER BENEFICIAL (continued)
1944 7/10 – 9/24
1947 2/22 – 4/3
1947 10/8 – 12/21
1953 4/26 – 7/4
1955 10/23 – until **1956** 9/8
1959 1/18 – 12/5
1965 4/8 – 6/17
1967 10/2 – until **1968** 8/23
1970 12/28 – until **1971** 11/20
1976 7/28 – 11/12
1977 3/17 – 6/1
1979 9/14 – until **1980** 8/7
1982 12/11 – until **1983** 11/3
1988 7/5 – 12/29
1989 2/11 – 5/16
1991 8/28 – 11/27
1992 2/2 – 7/20
1994 11/25 – until **1995** 10/15
2000 6/16 – until **2001** 4/28
2003 8/13 – 10/31
2004 3/12 – 6/27
2006 11/10 – until **2007** 1/25
2007 6/22 – 9/21
2012 5/29 – Continues

SATURN CHALLENGING
1941 7/29 – 10/24
1942 4/13 – until **1943** 5/14
1948 8/25 – until **1949** 9/29
1950 4/26 – 6/3
1955 12/13 – until **1957** 11/5
1971 5/25 – until **1972** 6/23
1977 10/7 – until **1978** 2/19
1978 6/27 – 11/21
1979 1/28 – 8/5
1985 1/28 – 4/15
1985 10/21 – until **1986** 12/10
2000 7/3 – 11/26
2001 3/22 – 8/9
2001 11/15 – until **2002** 4/25
2007 8/9 – until **2008** 9/11

URANUS CHALLENGING
1941 5/29 – until **1945** 5/29
1961 8/31 – until **1965** 7/31
1980 12/5 – until **1984** 11/21

NEPTUNE CHALLENGING
1968 12/5 – until **1976** 11/14

PLUTO CHALLENGING
1955 9/2 – until **1964** 8/5
1993 12/26 – until **2001** 9/29

JUPITER SPECIAL
1938 4/22 – 8/24
1938 12/11 – until **1939** 2/25
1950 3/30 – until **1951** 2/8
1962 3/12 – until **1963** 1/21
1974 2/23 – 5/10
1974 9/5 – 12/29
1986 2/7 – 4/18
1998 1/22 – 3/30
2009 6/7 – 6/23
2010 1/3 – 3/13

SATURN SPECIAL
1964 2/26 – until **1965** 4/13
1965 9/18 – until **1966** 1/6
1993 4/4 – 8/20
1993 12/30 – until **1995** 2/16

URANUS SPECIAL
2002 3/23 – until **2007** 2/1

NEPTUNE SPECIAL
2010 3/6 – Continues

♓

February 25

Your Personal Powers

Sensitive and impressionable yet discriminating and analytical, you are a receptive individual with practical skills and a responsible nature. Your ruling planet, Neptune, grants you intuitive or psychic abilities, inspired thoughts, and a humanitarian outlook. You gain power when you combine your inner vision with your methodical and pragmatic approach, increasing your depth of understanding. Usually determined and hardworking or productive, you have a desire to perfect your skills and expertise or rise to positions of prominence. Although you are often caring and compassionate you lose power when you become too critical or domineering. A tendency to vacillate between being confident and independent and being doubtful and insecure implies that, in order to utilize your persuasive abilities, you need to maintain a dignified yet relaxed manner. Although you are an independent thinker with progressive views or strong opinions, your idealism suggests that you are a practical humanitarian who needs a cause or an ideal that can inspire you to be creative.

Your Powers of Attraction in Relationships

Thoughtful and perceptive, your relationships are usually an area where you can learn and develop. Wanting sincerity and stability from partners, you are security-conscious about your emotional needs. Although you are sensitive, at times your forceful manner may be interpreted as bossy behavior. Your tensions or anxiety can often be eliminated through clearing the air or talking issues through. Supportive and protective of those you love, you can inspire others with your wisdom, profound views, and knowledge. People admire your honesty and idealism. You are usually attracted to astute, direct, and imaginative people who can pick up on the subtleties of situations. Alternatively, you may be drawn to compassionate and sympathetic partners who can reassure you and show you love and understanding.

Your attractive qualities: highly intuitive, intelligent, idealistic, rational, observant, thoughtful, perfectionist, perceptive, creative mind, authoritative, productive, common sense, strong instincts, optimistic, imaginative, discriminating, confident, conscientious, knowledgeable, skillful

Your less attractive qualities: impulsive, indecisive, impatient, stubborn, inner fears, critical, materialistic, too emotional, jealous, secretive, pessimistic, insecure, doubting, moody, nervous, controlling

Your Venus Power

The planet Venus has a great deal of influence on your powers of attraction. Below are four possible Venus types for women and men. To find your Venus you need to go to page 771, where you will find the Venus table and extra information. The planet Mars also affects your powers of attraction. To find your Mars table and interpretation go to page 761.

WOMEN WITH VENUS IN CAPRICORN: With your natural caution in romantic affairs, you often appear reserved and controlled. You may be shy but try to be more forward, especially if you want to be noticed. When you care about people, however, you are usually willing to put in extra time and energy to preserve the relationship. You are practical and dependable, and a sense of duty can often play a large role in affairs of your heart. With elegant simplicity you can attract others with your well-cut clothes and refined manners.

MEN WITH VENUS IN CAPRICORN: In relationships you take love seriously and can be a strong and practical support for friends or partners. You are usually attracted to partners who are as hardworking as you. As you tend not to express your feelings until you feel really secure in a relationship, you may be drawn to those who seem loyal, faithful, and not likely to let you down. As you respect the wisdom of experience, you may be drawn to mature partners or, alternatively, you may act as an authority figure for someone younger.

WOMEN WITH VENUS IN AQUARIUS: When it comes to relationships, others are attracted to your honest, friendly, and easygoing attitude. You really enjoy social interaction with others and may develop a genuine concern for humanity. Usually you present a tolerant and reasonable front in love situations and attempt to view your relationships objectively. If partners become too demanding, however, you can become stubborn and fixed. Friendship may be even more important for you than sexual compatibility.

MEN WITH VENUS IN AQUARIUS: Ideally in your relationships your lover is also your best friend. Since freedom of expression is a prerequisite to your well-being, you do better when left alone to do your own thing. You also need a partner who recognizes and appreciates your need for independence. Although usually friendly, at times you can be stubborn or

your cool detachment can appear to others as distant or impersonal. Very sociable, however, you particularly enjoy the company of those who share your original, fair-minded, and progressive views.

WOMEN WITH VENUS IN PISCES: Romantic and impressionable, you are a caring and loving individual with a dreamy nature. In relationships you are often attracted to idealistic, compassionate, or sympathetic individuals who have imagination or a strong romantic sense. A tendency to be sensitive to others suggests that you are intuitive and aware of people's inner feelings. Be careful, therefore, not to get caught in other people's dramas or play the rescuer too often.

MEN WITH VENUS IN PISCES: As a romantic and generous person, you are attracted to imaginative or artistic partners who can be sensitive and generous. While you are willing to make allowances for your loved ones, playing the martyr in relationships can lead to others taking advantage of your kind nature. Nevertheless, giving and loving, you are usually willing to forgive your partner's shortcomings.

WOMEN WITH VENUS IN ARIES: You gain power from your strong individuality, energy, and enthusiasm. Your young-at-heart and spirited approach to relationships adds to your appeal. If you become too impatient or self-absorbed, however, your partnerships are likely to suffer. Nevertheless, you can be creative, sharp, and quick, especially when you are able to share new and exciting projects with your partners. Mischievous with a love of action, you may even incite them to a playful fight.

MEN WITH VENUS IN ARIES: You are drawn to strong, independent women who can stand up to you. Although you can enthusiastically follow the object of your desire, you may lose power if you allow your forceful emotions to become too dominant. Warm and passionate, you have a side to your nature that longs for new adventures. Romantic and chivalrous, you really enjoy the excitement of the initial chase, but unless you keep the enthusiasm alive and avoid falling into a rut you may become easily bored.

To read all about your Outer Planets and work out how to use your personalized timetable, go to Section Three, page 789.

Your Personalized Timetable

JUPITER BENEFICIAL
1940 5/20 – until 1941 2/26
1942 6/1 – 8/12
1946 9/14 – 11/29
1948 11/19 – until 1949 1/3
1952 5/2 – 6/16
1954 5/14 – 7/25
1957 12/27 – until 1958 4/8
1958 8/26 – 11/13
1960 3/8 – 6/2
1960 10/31 – 12/18
1964 4/16 – 5/28
1965 9/2 – 12/5
1966 4/24 – 7/9
1969 12/4 – until 1970 10/28
1972 2/11 – 12/1
1976 3/30 – 5/11
1977 8/8 – until 1978 6/23
1981 11/16 – until 1982 10/12
1984 1/23 – 11/12
1988 3/12 – 4/25
1989 7/21 – until 1990 6/6
1993 10/31 – until 1994 9/24
1996 1/7 – 2/25
1996 7/19 – 10/18
1999 7/4 – 10/16
2000 2/20 – 4/8
2001 7/3 – until 2002 5/18
2005 10/16 – until 2006 1/4
2006 5/5 – 9/4
2007 12/22 – until 2008 2/5
2011 6/9 – until 2012 3/20

SATURN BENEFICIAL
1939 7/24 – 9/3
1940 3/28 – 6/18
1940 11/8 – until 1941 3/9
1944 6/4 – until 1945 7/3
1953 10/5 – until 1954 11/20
1959 1/13 – 8/12
1959 9/28 – until 1960 1/13
1969 5/7 – until 1970 4/23
1973 7/15 – until 1974 2/16
1974 3/11 – 8/14
1975 1/25 – 4/30
1982 11/10 – until 1983 6/16
1983 7/16 – 12/31
1984 4/22 – 9/26
1988 2/25 – 5/27
1988 11/21 – until 1989 2/19
1989 6/28 – 11/19
1998 6/19 – 10/14
1999 3/10 – 5/30
1999 12/17 – until 2000 2/7
2002 9/5 – 11/16
2003 5/18 – until 2004 6/15
2011 12/26 – Continues

URANUS BENEFICIAL
1938 1/1 – 3/12
1948 7/15 – until 1952 7/1
1974 10/18 – until 1978 9/21
1988 3/18 – until 1991 11/9

NEPTUNE BENEFICIAL
1954 12/26 – until 1963 9/27
1984 2/19 – until 1989 12/1

PLUTO BENEFICIAL
1982 11/16 – until 1989 10/7
2008 3/3 – Continues

JUPITER CHALLENGING
1941 5/17 – 7/29
1941 12/27 – until 1942 3/17
1944 7/15 – 9/29
1947 10/13 – 12/26

1953 4/30 – 7/9
1955 10/30 – until 1956 2/5
1956 6/25 – 9/13
1959 1/25 – 5/12
1959 9/23 – 12/10
1965 4/13 – 6/22
1967 10/7 – until 1968 8/28
1971 1/2 – 11/24
1976 8/4 – 11/4
1977 3/23 – 6/5
1979 9/19 – until 1980 8/12
1982 12/16 – until 1983 11/8
1988 7/10 – 12/18
1989 2/22 – 5/20
1991 9/2 – 12/9
1992 1/21 – 7/25
1994 11/29 – until 1995 10/21
2000 6/20 – until 2001 5/2
2003 8/17 – 11/6
2004 3/4 – 7/4
2006 11/14 – until 2007 1/31
2007 6/13 – 9/28
2012 6/2 – Continues

SATURN CHALLENGING
1941 8/15 – 10/7
1942 4/22 – until 1943 5/22
1948 9/2 – until 1949 10/7
1950 4/5 – 6/24
1955 12/22 – until 1956 6/12
1956 9/15 – until 1957 3/2
1957 4/14 – 11/14
1971 6/1 – until 1972 7/1
1973 1/27 – 3/2
1977 10/17 – until 1978 2/6
1978 7/7 – 12/19
1978 12/29 – until 1979 8/14
1985 2/19 – 3/23
1985 10/30 – until 1986 12/19
2000 7/13 – 11/14
2001 4/2 – 8/23
2001 10/31 – until 2002 5/4
2007 8/17 – until 2008 9/20

URANUS CHALLENGING
1941 6/17 – until 1946 3/26
1961 9/17 – until 1965 8/17
1980 12/22 – until 1984 12/7

NEPTUNE CHALLENGING
1969 1/5 – until 1977 10/9

PLUTO CHALLENGING
1955 10/7 – until 1965 6/24
1994 2/6 – until 2001 11/4

JUPITER SPECIAL
1938 4/28 – 8/16
1938 12/18 – until 1939 3/1
1950 4/4 – until 1951 2/12
1962 3/16 – until 1963 1/25
1974 2/27 – until 1975 1/4
1986 2/12 – 4/23
1986 10/15 – 12/2
1998 1/26 – 4/4
2010 1/8 – 3/17

SATURN SPECIAL
1964 3/5 – until 1965 4/23
1965 9/5 – until 1966 1/17
1993 4/15 – 8/7
1994 1/10 – until 1995 2/25

URANUS SPECIAL
2002 4/15 – until 2007 2/20

NEPTUNE SPECIAL
2010 4/6 – Continues

February 26

SUN: PISCES · DECANATE: PISCES/NEPTUNE · DEGREE: 6°5–7°5 PISCES · MODE: MUTABLE · ELEMENT: WATER

Your Personal Powers

Sensitive and intuitive, you are an intelligent individual with a fast mind and powers of discrimination. Your innate understanding enables you to reliably assess others. Although you are often socially inclined, your independent spirit means that you can be ambitious and determined. If material circumstances are a cause for concern, you lose some of your power by letting doubts and indecision undermine your sense of purpose or compromise your ideals. Your ruling planet, Neptune, endows you with quick perception, a sixth sense, and imaginative or inspired realizations. You gain power when you learn to trust your quick comprehension and premonitions. Although your generous and idealistic nature can be caring and compassionate, taking charge or rising to positions of prominence usually appeals to you more than obeying others. You therefore empower yourself by uniting your shrewd common sense and strong determination to succeed. Naturally creative and versatile, you are usually multitalented with an active mind that seeks mental stimulation or opportunities for individual self-expression.

Your Powers of Attraction in Relationships

Friendly and clever, you have charm and an engaging personality. Intelligent and articulate, you need to be around inspired, imaginative, and creative people. Highly intuitive yet mentally restless, you also like intellectually bright and accomplished individuals. While being purposeful makes you enterprising, you may have to overcome an inclination to be indecisive about your deeper personal feelings. Making choices and decisions about your relationships may be one of the challenges to your otherwise rational mind. Nevertheless, you can be happy with a partner who is mentally stimulating or can offer you excitement. You are also attracted to enterprising individuals with good business sense. In love, you are loyal and supportive as long as you receive your partner's respect and loyalty in return.

Your attractive qualities: intuitive, creative, quick comprehension, practical, witty, responsible, receptive, caring, intuitive, proud of family, enthusiastic, friendly, courageous, spiritual potential, shrewd, independent, business sense, enterprising, sociable, decisive, instinctive, perfectionist

Your less attractive qualities: uncertain, materialistic, stubborn, rebellious, unstable relationships, unenthusiastic, dependent on others, restlessness, impatient, indecisive, worried, too competitive, selfish, too proud, ambiguous

Your Venus Power

The planet Venus has a great deal of influence on your powers of attraction. Below are four possible Venus types for women and men. To find your Venus you need to go to page 771, where you will find the Venus table and extra information. The planet Mars also affects your powers of attraction. To find your Mars table and interpretation go to page 761.

WOMEN WITH VENUS IN CAPRICORN: Proud and refined, you attract others with your composed dignity. Disliking vulnerability and needing to feel safe before you can express your feelings, you display a strong front. Feeling insecure or inadequate in relationships may force you to become manipulative in order to regain control. Nevertheless, you can project an attractive sense of self-assurance and are capable of displaying loyalty and a wonderful dry sense of humor.

MEN WITH VENUS IN CAPRICORN: As you do not display your deeper emotions freely, you are usually dignified and controlled in your relationships. Practical and down-to-earth partners are particularly attractive to you, especially those who do not rush into expressing their feelings but seem to possess natural class and reserve. You need a partner who is loyal and dependable and willing to take your relationship seriously.

WOMEN WITH VENUS IN AQUARIUS: Sociable and gracious, you are usually sincere and are capable of showing attributes of real tolerance and liberalism. Although you are keen on forming relationships, you also like to have freedom and act independently. Your intimate partnerships need to be founded on true friendships. Full of bright and progressive ideas, you can express yourself better when you are free and unrestricted. An ability to think in a dispassionate way suggests that you can stay detached. Your love of freedom also implies that you can be loving and loyal without smothering your partner.

MEN WITH VENUS IN AQUARIUS: Ideally in your relationships your lover is also your best friend. Since freedom of expression is a prerequisite to your well-being, you do better when left alone to do your own thing. You also need a partner who recognizes and appreciates your need for independence.

Although usually friendly, at times you can be stubborn or your cool detachment can appear to others as distant or impersonal. Very sociable, however, you particularly enjoy the company of those who share your original, fair-minded, and progressive views.

WOMEN WITH VENUS IN PISCES: Being sensitive to other people, you are receptive to their moods and feelings. This affinity indicates that although you can be selfless, you may have to guard against being too sentimental or overly romantic, especially with those who can take advantage of your kindness. Nevertheless, as you are alluring and seductive, your partners can be intrigued by your poetic soul or mysterious nature.

MEN WITH VENUS IN PISCES: Being adaptable and sensitive, you are able to intuitively feel the moods of those you love. Although you are receptive to others you can be ambiguous about your own feelings toward your partner. Romantic and kindhearted, you long to be loved, but you need to be realistic about your relationships in order to avoid disappointments. When in love you may idealize your partners and fail to see any faults in their personality.

WOMEN WITH VENUS IN ARIES: Idealistic, passionate, and adventurous, you are direct in your dealings with others. When you are attracted to a person you usually take the initiative and use your people skills to make things happen. In close relationships you are not afraid to confront your other half. This self-assertiveness is positive if differences can be brought into the open through diplomacy and compromise.

MEN WITH VENUS IN ARIES: As you often have the courage and strength to initiate situations, you like to take the lead. With your unconscious desire for conquest you may also have to beware of being competitive with your partners. Nevertheless, you are drawn to direct and strong-willed partners who can share your love of action and enthusiasm for life. When you are feeling good you can be charming and enthusiastic in romantic situations with an entertaining and spontaneous spirit.

To read all about your Outer Planets and work out how to use your personalized timetable, go to Section Three, page 789.

Your Personalized Timetable

JUPITER BENEFICIAL
1940 5/24 – until **1941** 3/4
1942 6/5 – 8/17
1946 9/20 – 12/4
1948 11/24 – until **1949** 1/7
1952 5/6 – 6/21
1952 12/13 – until **1953** 1/28
1954 5/19 – 7/29
1958 1/3 – 3/31
1958 9/1 – 11/17
1960 3/17 – 5/23
1960 11/5 – 12/22
1964 4/20 – 6/1
1965 9/10 – 11/27
1966 4/29 – 7/13
1969 12/10 – until **1970** 11/2
1972 2/17 – 7/7
1972 10/12 – 12/6
1976 4/3 – 5/15
1977 8/14 – until **1978** 6/27
1981 11/21 – until **1982** 10/17
1984 1/28 – 11/18
1988 3/17 – 4/29
1989 7/25 – until **1990** 6/11
1993 11/5 – until **1994** 9/30
1996 1/11 – 3/2
1996 7/11 – 10/26
1999 7/11 – 10/8
2000 2/25 – 4/12
2001 7/8 – until **2002** 5/23
2005 10/21 – until **2006** 9/10
2007 12/27 – until **2008** 2/10
2011 6/14 – 11/25
2012 1/25 – 3/25

SATURN BENEFICIAL
1940 4/5 – 6/29
1940 10/27 – until **1941** 3/19
1944 6/12 – until **1945** 7/11
1953 10/13 – until **1954** 11/29
1955 6/26 – 8/10
1959 1/22 – until **1960** 1/22
1960 9/5 – 9/26
1969 5/15 – until **1970** 5/1
1973 7/23 – until **1974** 8/23
1975 1/12 – 5/12
1982 11/19 – until **1983** 5/23
1983 8/9 – until **1984** 10/6
1988 3/14 – 5/9
1988 11/30 – until **1989** 3/3
1989 6/14 – 11/29
1998 7/1 – 9/30
1999 3/19 – 6/8
1999 11/29 – until **2000** 2/23
2002 9/28 – 10/24
2003 5/26 – until **2004** 6/23
2012 1/12 – Continues

URANUS BENEFICIAL
1938 1/1 – 4/3
1948 8/3 – until **1953** 4/24
1974 11/3 – until **1978** 10/10
1989 1/3 – until **1991** 11/30

NEPTUNE BENEFICIAL
1955 11/16 – until **1963** 10/26
1985 1/12 – until **1990** 10/14

PLUTO BENEFICIAL
1982 12/17 – until **1989** 11/2
2009 1/19 – Continues

JUPITER CHALLENGING
1941 5/21 – 8/4
1941 12/19 – until **1942** 3/25
1944 7/20 – 10/4

1947 10/18 – 12/31
1953 5/5 – 7/14
1955 11/7 – until **1956** 1/28
1956 7/1 – 9/17
1959 2/1 – 5/4
1959 9/29 – 12/14
1965 4/17 – 6/26
1967 10/13 – until **1968** 9/2
1971 1/8 – 11/29
1976 8/12 – 10/27
1977 3/29 – 6/9
1979 9/24 – until **1980** 8/17
1982 12/20 – until **1983** 11/12
1988 7/15 – 12/9
1989 3/3 – 5/24
1991 9/7 – until **1992** 7/30
1994 12/4 – until **1995** 10/26
2000 6/25 – until **2001** 5/7
2003 8/22 – until **2004** 7/11
2006 11/19 – until **2007** 2/6
2007 6/5 – 10/5
2012 6/7 – Continues

SATURN CHALLENGING
1942 4/30 – until **1943** 5/30
1948 9/10 – until **1949** 10/16
1950 3/21 – 7/7
1956 1/1 – 5/28
1956 9/28 – until **1957** 11/23
1971 6/9 – until **1972** 7/9
1973 1/6 – 3/22
1977 10/29 – until **1978** 1/23
1978 7/17 – until **1979** 8/22
1985 11/7 – until **1986** 12/27
1987 7/28 – 9/10
2000 7/25 – 11/1
2001 4/11 – 9/20
2001 10/4 – until **2002** 5/12
2007 8/25 – until **2008** 9/28
2009 5/19 – 5/19

URANUS CHALLENGING
1941 7/7 – until **1946** 4/21
1961 10/6 – until **1965** 9/3
1981 1/11 – until **1985** 10/9

NEPTUNE CHALLENGING
1969 12/3 – until **1977** 11/12

PLUTO CHALLENGING
1956 9/9 – until **1965** 8/5
1994 12/14 – until **2002** 9/2

JUPITER SPECIAL
1938 5/5 – 8/8
1938 12/23 – until **1939** 3/6
1950 4/9 – until **1951** 2/17
1962 3/21 – until **1963** 1/30
1974 3/3 – until **1975** 1/10
1986 2/16 – 4/28
1986 10/4 – 12/12
1998 1/30 – 4/8
2010 1/13 – 3/22

SATURN SPECIAL
1964 3/14 – 10/6
1964 11/27 – until **1965** 5/5
1965 8/23 – until **1966** 1/27
1993 4/29 – 7/23
1994 1/19 – until **1995** 3/5

URANUS SPECIAL
2003 2/19 – until **2007** 12/12

NEPTUNE SPECIAL
2011 3/3 – Continues

February 27

SUN: PISCES • DECANATE: PISCES/NEPTUNE • DEGREE: 7°5–8°5 PISCES • MODE: MUTABLE • ELEMENT: WATER

Your Personal Powers

Intelligent, sensitive, and impressionable, you are an idealistic individual with a thoughtful nature and quick perception. Being sympathetic to others, you are charming, adaptable, and usually enjoy being part of a group. Although you can be enterprising and enthusiastic, when you expect quick results for your efforts you are often disappointed. You therefore empower yourself and enhance your potential for success by developing perseverance and by showing a responsible or mature attitude. Your ruling planet, Neptune, grants you imagination, intuitive abilities, and creative thoughts. You gain power when you apply your discriminative mental powers to your inspired ideas and find practical solutions to your problems. Investing in education or developing your analytical powers increases your confidence and proficiency. A secretive side to your nature implies that, although your feelings can run deep, at times you can be evasive or find it difficult to express yourself fully. By working with your communication skills in particular, you can become more persuasive and successful.

Your Powers of Attraction in Relationships

Charming, youthful, and witty, you should have no difficulty in attracting partners. In tune with your peer group and aware of appearances, you can usually make a good impression on others. People admire your quick perception and discerning powers. Although being sociable is important to you, at times you can be detached or even withdrawn about your thoughts and feelings. Normally communicative and well-informed, you often enjoy lighthearted banter but resist being cynical or confrontational with your partners. You are usually attracted to individuals who are strong and optimistic or idealistic. Or, you may be drawn to people who are sensitive and considerate with unusual talents. Although you want to maintain your independence, you are likely to succeed in partnerships based on mutual respect, good understanding, and equality.

Your attractive qualities: intuitive, optimistic, versatile, analytical, imaginative, creative, noble ideas, visionary, romantic, enthusiastic, resolute, observant, understanding, spiritual, inventive, patient, detail-oriented, humanitarian, persuasive, sympathetic, inquisitive, friendly

Your less attractive qualities: disagreeable, quarrelsome, easily offended, restlessness, secretive, nervous, mistrusting, too emotional, ambiguous, high-strung, tense, inner tensions, anxious, , impulsive, moody

Your Venus Power

The planet Venus has a great deal of influence on your powers of attraction. Below are four possible Venus types for women and men. To find your Venus you need to go to page 771, where you will find the Venus table and extra information. The planet Mars also affects your powers of attraction. To find your Mars table and interpretation go to page 761.

WOMEN WITH VENUS IN CAPRICORN: Romantically, you do not give your heart easily but hide behind a cool reserve until you feel free to express your emotions. As you take your relationships seriously, you may find yourself drawn to people who are businesslike, resourceful, and practical or those who can act as teachers or mentors. Work or career may also be a factor in many of your associations and partnerships. As security can play an important role in your relationships, you are often attracted to partners who are loyal and hardworking.

MEN WITH VENUS IN CAPRICORN: As you do not display your deeper emotions freely, you are usually dignified and controlled in your relationships. Practical and down-to-earth partners are particularly attractive to you, especially those who do not rush into expressing their feelings but seem to possess natural class and reserve. You need a partner who is loyal and dependable and willing to take your relationship seriously.

WOMEN WITH VENUS IN AQUARIUS: When it comes to relationships, others are attracted to your honest, friendly, and easygoing attitude. You really enjoy social interaction with others and may develop a genuine concern for humanity. Usually you present a tolerant and reasonable front in love situations and attempt to view your relationships objectively. If partners become too demanding, however, you can become stubborn and fixed. Friendship may be even more important for you than sexual compatibility.

MEN WITH VENUS IN AQUARIUS: Although independent, you often enjoy being part of a group. The partners you frequently attract are themselves nonconformists or free spirits. As an individual you may not find it easy to settle into a routine or an entirely mundane type of relationship. You may have some unconventional views on traditional marriage or

your partner may hold such views. It is usually important to you that your love relationships are based on friendship.

WOMEN WITH VENUS IN PISCES: Being sensitive to other people, you are receptive to their moods and feelings. This affinity indicates that although you can be selfless, you may have to guard against being too sentimental or overly romantic, especially with those who can take advantage of your kindness. Nevertheless, as you are alluring and seductive, your partners can be intrigued by your poetic soul or mysterious nature.

MEN WITH VENUS IN PISCES: Being adaptable and sensitive, you are able to intuitively feel the moods of those you love. Although you are receptive to others, you can be ambiguous about your own feelings toward your partner. Romantic and kindhearted, you long to be loved but you need to be realistic about your relationships in order to avoid disappointments. When in love you may idealize your partners and fail to see any faults in their personality.

WOMEN WITH VENUS IN ARIES: With your strong desires and enthusiastic nature you can be a passionate lover. Although idealistic and single-minded, you need to avoid unnecessary conflicts in your relationships by being more patient and less headstrong. Although at times others can accuse you of being bossy or impulsive, you possess a great deal of warmth and charm. When necessary you can disarm others by making them feel important.

MEN WITH VENUS IN ARIES: You are usually drawn to courageous or assertive women who possess strong personal magnetism. Therefore you find those who seem to be independent or action-oriented very attractive. Your own eagerness and need for activity suggest that you start relationships with great enthusiasm, especially if they offer excitement or adventures. The challenge is often to maintain relationships and not become bored too easily.

To read all about your Outer Planets and work out how to use your personalized timetable, go to Section Three, page 789.

Your Personalized Timetable

JUPITER BENEFICIAL
1940 5/29 – 7/24
1940 10/16 – until 1941 3/10
1942 6/10 – 8/22
1943 2/18 – 4/2
1946 9/25 – 12/8
1948 11/29 – until 1949 1/12
1952 5/11 – 6/26
1954 5/23 – 8/3
1958 1/12 – 3/21
1958 9/6 – 11/22
1960 3/30 – 5/11
1960 11/11 – 12/27
1964 4/24 – 6/6
1965 9/20 – 11/17
1966 5/5 – 7/18
1969 12/16 – until 1970 11/6
1972 2/23 – 6/29
1972 10/19 – 12/10
1976 4/8 – 5/20
1977 8/20 – 12/31
1978 4/11 – 7/2
1981 11/26 – until 1982 10/21
1984 2/2 – 11/23
1988 3/22 – 5/4
1989 7/30 – until 1990 6/15
1993 11/10 – until 1994 10/5
1996 1/16 – 11/1
1999 7/20 – 9/30
2000 3/2 – 4/17
2001 7/12 – until 2002 5/28
2005 10/25 – until 2006 9/16
2007 12/31 – until 2008 2/15
2008 8/23 – 9/23
2011 6/19 – until 2012 3/30

SATURN BENEFICIAL
1940 4/13 – 7/11
1940 10/13 – until 1941 3/28
1944 6/19 – until 1945 7/18
1953 10/22 – until 1954 12/7
1955 6/6 – 8/30
1959 2/1 – 7/7
1959 10/31 – until 1960 1/31
1960 8/9 – 10/22
1969 5/23 – 12/3
1970 2/3 – 5/9
1973 8/1 – until 1974 1/8
1974 4/17 – 9/2
1974 12/31 – until 1975 5/22
1982 11/28 – until 1983 5/7
1983 8/23 – until 1984 2/1
1984 3/18 – 10/15
1988 12/9 – until 1989 3/18
1989 5/28 – 12/8
1998 7/18 – 9/13
1999 3/27 – 6/17
1999 11/16 – until 2000 3/7
2003 6/3 – until 2004 7/1
2012 10/5 – Continues

URANUS BENEFICIAL
1938 1/1 – 4/21
1948 8/28 – until 1953 5/21
1974 11/20 – until 1978 10/27
1989 1/21 – until 1991 12/19

NEPTUNE BENEFICIAL
1955 12/21 – until 1964 9/23
1985 2/13 – until 1990 11/28

PLUTO BENEFICIAL
1983 11/3 – until 1990 9/23
2009 2/26 – Continues

JUPITER CHALLENGING
1941 5/26 – 8/10

1941 12/12 – until 1942 3/31
1944 7/25 – 10/9
1947 10/23 – until 1948 1/4
1953 5/9 – 7/19
1955 11/16 – until 1956 9/22
1959 2/9 – 4/25
1959 10/5 – 12/19
1965 4/22 – 6/30
1967 10/19 – until 1968 9/6
1971 1/13 – 12/3
1976 8/22 – 10/17
1977 4/3 – 6/14
1979 9/29 – until 1980 8/21
1982 12/25 – until 1983 11/17
1988 7/21 – 12/1
1989 3/10 – 5/29
1991 9/11 – until 1992 8/5
1994 12/9 – until 1995 10/31
2000 6/30 – until 2001 5/12
2003 8/27 – until 2004 7/17
2006 11/23 – until 2007 10/11
2012 6/11 – Continues

SATURN CHALLENGING
1942 5/8 – until 1943 6/7
1948 9/18 – until 1949 4/4
1949 5/27 – 10/26
1950 3/8 – 7/19
1956 1/12 – 5/15
1956 10/9 – until 1957 12/1
1971 6/18 – until 1972 1/12
1972 2/19 – 7/18
1972 12/23 – until 1973 4/5
1977 11/15 – until 1978 1/6
1978 7/25 – until 1979 8/30
1985 11/16 – until 1987 1/5
1987 7/7 – 9/30
2000 8/8 – 10/17
2001 4/20 – until 2002 5/20
2007 9/2 – until 2008 10/6
2009 4/12 – 6/20

URANUS CHALLENGING
1941 8/4 – until 1946 5/11
1961 10/30 – until 1966 6/24
1981 2/12 – until 1985 10/31

NEPTUNE CHALLENGING
1970 1/2 – until 1978 10/4

PLUTO CHALLENGING
1956 10/16 – until 1966 6/17
1995 1/14 – until 2002 10/28

JUPITER SPECIAL
1938 5/13 – 7/30
1938 12/29 – until 1939 3/10
1950 4/15 – until 1951 2/21
1962 3/25 – until 1963 2/3
1974 3/8 – until 1975 1/15
1986 2/20 – 12/20
1998 2/4 – 4/13
2010 1/17 – 3/26

SATURN SPECIAL
1964 3/23 – 9/18
1964 12/15 – until 1965 5/19
1965 8/7 – until 1966 2/5
1993 5/19 – 7/2
1994 1/28 – until 1995 3/13

URANUS SPECIAL
2003 3/9 – until 2008 1/16

NEPTUNE SPECIAL
2011 4/2 – Continues

♓

713

February 28

SUN: PISCES · DECANATE: PISCES/NEPTUNE · DEGREE: 8°5–9°5 PISCES · MODE: MUTABLE · ELEMENT: WATER

Your Personal Powers

As a sensitive and intuitive individual with discerning powers, you possess a shrewd mind and an ability to reliably assess other people. Your determination and decisive actions can often help you make progress and achieve success. Intelligent and articulate, you are usually observant and a good communicator. Your ruling planet, Neptune, grants you insight and deep awareness as well as inner vision. Although you are usually dignified, a call for self-discipline implies that the more honorable, optimistic, and persevering you are the more likely you are to rise in life. You empower yourself by living up to your high principles and aspirations. As you frequently know things instinctively, you also possess an ability to adapt to situations or take advantage of opportunities. Although assertive, you lose power if you become overbearing. Being enterprising and ambitious, your courage is often based on your inner faith and hard work. Nevertheless, independent and persuasive, you gain power by being cooperative, thoughtful, and using your people skills when collaborating with others.

Your Powers of Attraction in Relationships

Intelligent, you seek the company of clever or independent people. Others admire your determination, powers of perception, and ability to deal with challenging situations. In your relationships you need to be careful that indecision does not stop you from taking action. Usually you are drawn to dynamic individuals who are instinctive and resolute. Alternatively you may be attracted to serious, hardworking individuals who are sensitive and responsible. Usually you enjoy a challenge, but in your attempt to test your wits and aptitude you may become too forceful or argumentative. If you feel emotionally confident, secure, and content, you can be generous and supportive. A need for emotional and creative self-expression indicates that in your close relationships you ideally need a supportive and insightful partner who is keen on self-mastery.

Your attractive qualities: compassion, imagination, receptive, progressive, daring, creative, idealistic, ambitious, hardworking, stable home life, strong-willed, shrewd, sympathetic, good organizational skills, business sense, enterprising, strong convictions, independent, humanitarian

Your less attractive qualities: unmotivated, demanding, daydreamer, ambiguous, unrealistic, proud, bossy, weak judgment, lack of confidence, codependent, arrogant, indulgent, unsympathetic, argumentative, too sensitive, frustrated

Your Venus Power

The planet Venus has a great deal of influence on your powers of attraction. Below are four possible Venus types for women and men. To find your Venus you need to go to page 771, where you will find the Venus table and extra information. The planet Mars also affects your powers of attraction. To find your Mars table and interpretation go to page 761.

WOMEN WITH VENUS IN CAPRICORN: With your natural caution in romantic affairs, you often appear reserved and controlled. You may be shy but try to be more forward, especially if you want to be noticed. When you care about people, however, you are usually willing to put in extra time and energy to preserve the relationship. You are practical and dependable, and a sense of duty can often play a large role in affairs of your heart. With elegant simplicity you can attract others with your well-cut clothes and refined manners.

MEN WITH VENUS IN CAPRICORN: As you do not display your deeper emotions freely, you are usually dignified and controlled in your relationships. Practical and down-to-earth partners are particularly attractive to you, especially those who do not rush into expressing their feelings but seem to possess natural class and reserve. You need a partner who is loyal and dependable and willing to take your relationship seriously.

WOMEN WITH VENUS IN AQUARIUS: When it comes to relationships, others are attracted to your honest, friendly, and easygoing attitude. You really enjoy social interaction with others and may develop a genuine concern for humanity. Usually you present a tolerant and reasonable front in love situations and attempt to view your relationships objectively. If partners become too demanding, however, you can become stubborn and fixed. Friendship may be even more important for you than sexual compatibility.

MEN WITH VENUS IN AQUARIUS: You are sociable and open-minded, and people are attracted by your friendly and easygoing style. Being independent, you value freedom-loving partners who give you the space to be yourself. People can sometimes interpret your detachment as being emotionally cool, but they admire your objectivity and humanitarian inclinations. You are attracted to intelligent individuals who are as

truthful and direct as you, but above all they must be true friends. Ideally, your partner shares your liberal views on life and possesses a strong sense of individuality.

WOMEN WITH VENUS IN PISCES: As a romantic and idealistic individual, you can be both loving and giving. While making allowances and sacrifices is understandable in a loving relationship, avoid playing the martyr. In relationships you may need to balance the practical with the charitable. Nevertheless, your benevolence and sacrifices in the right relationship make you a devoted, kind, and compassionate partner. Subtle, sensitive, and alluring, you can be sensual and caring.

MEN WITH VENUS IN PISCES: The combination of your emotional subtlety and charm can make you very alluring when dealing with affairs of the heart. Perceptive and impressionable, you have an easygoing style in your relationships, usually preferring to avoid ugly confrontation. You are drawn to a partner who has a touch of glamour and is sensitive to the needs of others. Alternatively, your partner can be a visionary with a rich imagination who can keep you enchanted.

WOMEN WITH VENUS IN ARIES: Idealistic, passionate, and adventurous, you are direct in your dealings with others. When you are attracted to a person you usually take the initiative and use your people skills to make things happen. In close relationships you are not afraid to confront your other half. This self-assertiveness is positive if differences can be brought into the open through diplomacy and compromise.

MEN WITH VENUS IN ARIES: As you often have the courage and strength to initiate situations, you like to take the lead. With your unconscious desire for conquest you may also have to beware of being competitive with your partners. Nevertheless, you are drawn to direct and strong-willed partners who can share your love of action and enthusiasm for life. When you are feeling good, you can be charming and enthusiastic in romantic situations with an entertaining and spontaneous spirit.

To read all about your Outer Planets and work out how to use your personalized timetable, go to Section Three, page 789.

To read all about your Outer Planets and work out how to use your personalized timetable, go to Section Three, page 789.

Your Personalized Timetable

JUPITER BENEFICIAL
1940 6/3 – until 1941 3/15
1942 6/14 – 8/27
1943 2/7 – 4/14
1946 9/29 – 12/13
1948 12/3 – until 1949 1/16
1952 5/15 – 7/1
1952 11/23 – until 1953 2/16
1954 5/28 – 8/8
1958 1/25 – 3/9
1958 9/12 – 11/27
1960 11/16 – 12/31
1964 4/28 – 6/11
1965 10/4 – 11/3
1966 5/10 – 7/22
1969 12/22 – until 1970 11/11
1972 3/1 – 6/21
1972 10/25 – 12/15
1976 4/12 – 5/24
1977 8/26 – until 1978 7/6
1981 12/1 – until 1982 10/26
1984 2/7 – 11/28
1988 3/26 – 5/8
1989 8/4 – until 1990 6/20
1993 11/14 – until 1994 10/10
1996 1/21 – 11/7
1999 7/30 – 9/19
2000 3/7 – 4/21
2001 7/17 – until 2002 6/2
2005 10/30 – until 2006 9/22
2008 1/5 – 2/20
2008 8/9 – 10/8
2011 6/25 – 11/8
2012 2/10 – 4/3

SATURN BENEFICIAL
1940 4/21 – 7/27
1940 9/27 – until 1941 4/6
1944 6/27 – until 1945 7/26
1953 10/30 – until 1954 12/17
1955 5/22 – 9/13
1959 2/11 – 6/24
1959 11/11 – until 1960 2/9
1960 7/24 – 11/6
1969 6/1 – 11/17
1970 2/18 – 5/17
1973 8/10 – 12/27
1974 4/29 – 9/14
1974 12/18 – until 1975 5/31
1982 12/8 – until 1983 4/24
1983 9/4 – until 1984 10/24
1988 12/17 – until 1989 12/17
1999 4/5 – 6/27
1999 11/3 – until 2000 3/17
2003 6/11 – until 2004 7/9
2012 10/13 – Continues

URANUS BENEFICIAL
1938 1/1 – until 1939 2/5
1949 6/25 – until 1953 6/10
1974 12/8 – until 1979 7/28
1989 2/10 – until 1992 1/5

NEPTUNE BENEFICIAL
1956 11/13 – until 1964 10/23
1986 1/10 – until 1990 12/27

PLUTO BENEFICIAL
1983 11/30 – until 1990 10/21
2010 1/18 – Continues

JUPITER CHALLENGING
1941 5/30 – 8/16
1941 12/4 – until 1942 4/7
1944 7/30 – 10/14
1947 10/28 – until 1948 1/9
1953 5/13 – 7/24
1954 1/24 – 2/27
1955 11/29 – until 1956 1/5
1956 7/12 – 9/27
1959 2/20 – 4/14
1959 10/10 – 12/23
1965 4/26 – 7/5
1967 10/25 – until 1968 9/11
1971 1/20 – 12/7
1976 9/6 – 10/2
1977 4/8 – 6/18
1979 10/4 – until 1980 8/26
1982 12/30 – until 1983 11/22
1988 7/27 – 11/24
1989 3/17 – 6/2
1991 9/16 – until 1992 8/10
1994 12/13 – until 1995 11/5
2000 7/4 – until 2001 5/16
2003 8/31 – until 2004 7/23
2006 11/28 – until 2007 10/17
2012 6/15 – Continues

SATURN CHALLENGING
1942 5/16 – until 1943 6/14
1948 9/27 – until 1950 7/29
1956 1/24 – until 1957 12/10
1971 6/26 – until 1973 4/16
1978 8/3 – until 1979 9/8
1985 11/24 – until 1987 10/14
2000 9/5 – 9/19
2001 4/28 – until 2002 5/28
2007 9/10 – until 2009 7/5

URANUS CHALLENGING
1942 5/31 – until 1946 5/29
1962 8/25 – until 1966 7/21
1981 12/1 – until 1985 11/19

NEPTUNE CHALLENGING
1970 12/1 – until 1978 11/10

PLUTO CHALLENGING
1957 9/16 – until 1966 8/3
1995 12/4 – until 2002 11/26

JUPITER SPECIAL
1938 5/23 – 7/20
1939 1/3 – 3/14
1950 4/20 – until 1951 2/25
1962 3/30 – until 1963 2/8
1974 3/12 – until 1975 1/20
1986 2/24 – 12/28
1998 2/8 – 4/18
2010 1/22 – 3/30

SATURN SPECIAL
1964 4/2 – 9/3
1964 12/27 – until 1965 6/9
1965 7/16 – until 1966 2/14
1994 2/5 – until 1995 3/21

URANUS SPECIAL
2003 3/28 – until 2008 2/6

NEPTUNE SPECIAL
2012 2/28 – Continues

⊬

February 29

SUN: PISCES · DECANATE: PISCES/NEPTUNE · DEGREE: 9°–10° PISCES · MODE: MUTABLE · ELEMENT: WATER

Your Personal Powers

Idealistic with a determined character, you are an imaginative and compassionate yet forceful individual. Your ruling planet, Neptune, grants you a strong sixth sense, powerful emotions, artistic talents, and visionary ideas. Although you are inventive with many wonderful projects and plans, a tendency to be impatient or frustrated with limitations can weaken your resolve and inner faith. Since mental stimulation and positive thinking often inspire your finely tuned mind, you gain power when you resist feeling discouraged. You often achieve success and empower yourself when you combine your courage, determination, and responsible attitude with perseverance. Articulate and astute with a wealth of feelings, you are able to intuitively understand people. With your blend of persuasive charm and direct approach, you can also communicate with others on a personal level. Although your strong feelings indicate that you are warmhearted and kind, you can lose some of your power by letting your emotions run high. You therefore often benefit from finding a way to express your creativity or enterprising spirit.

Your Powers of Attraction in Relationships

Your warm personality and love of socializing suggest that you have many friends. Romantic and sensitive, having a partner or a soul mate is a prerequisite to your well-being. People admire your witty and quick mind, sympathetic nature, and compassionate heart. Although your close relationships are important to you, resist becoming overly dependent on your partners. A tendency to fluctuate emotionally warns that you can show many sides to your personality. People, however, prefer your generous, modest, and sympathetic nature. Being faithful and loving, you generally prefer a secure and lasting relationship with one person. You are usually attracted to straightforward partners with whom you have honest communication or good understanding. Alternatively, you may be drawn to emotional people who are strong-willed, generous, and purposeful.

Your attractive qualities: determined, imaginative, inspirational, generous, positive thinking, idealistic, sense of the dramatic, inner peace, generous, creative, intuitive, mystical, powerful dreams, faithful, compassionate, tolerant, realistic, receptive, worldly, broad-minded, successful

Your less attractive qualities: impulsive, frustrated, moody, bossy, emotionally restless, unfocused, insecure, nervous, worried, difficult, extremist, isolated, too sensitive, overindulgent, disappointed, escapist, power-games

Your Venus Power

The planet Venus has a great deal of influence on your powers of attraction. Below are four possible Venus types for women and men. To find your Venus you need to go to page 771, where you will find the Venus table and extra information. The planet Mars also affects your powers of attraction. To find your Mars table and interpretation go to page 761.

WOMEN WITH VENUS IN CAPRICORN: Romantically, you do not give your heart easily but hide behind a cool reserve until you feel free to express your emotions. As you take your relationships seriously, you may find yourself drawn to people who are businesslike, resourceful, and practical or those who can act as teachers or mentors. Work or career may also be a factor in many of your associations and partnerships. As security can play an important role in your relationships, you are often attracted to partners who are loyal and hardworking.

MEN WITH VENUS IN CAPRICORN: In relationships, you take love seriously and can be a strong and practical support for friends or partners. You are usually attracted to partners who are as hardworking as you. As you tend not to express your feelings until you feel really secure in a relationship, you may be drawn to those who seem loyal, faithful, and not likely to let you down. As you respect the wisdom of experience, you may be drawn to mature partners or, alternatively, you may act as an authority figure for someone younger.

WOMEN WITH VENUS IN AQUARIUS: Sociable and gracious, you are usually sincere and are capable of showing attributes of real tolerance and liberalism. Although you are keen on forming relationships, you also like to have freedom and act independently. Your intimate partnerships need to be founded on true friendships. Full of bright and progressive ideas, you can express yourself better when you are free and unrestricted. An ability to think in a dispassionate way suggests that you can stay detached. Your love of freedom also implies that you can be loving and loyal without smothering your partner.

MEN WITH VENUS IN AQUARIUS: Although independent, you often enjoy being part of a group. The partners you fre-

quently attract are themselves nonconformists or free spirits. As an individual you may not find it easy to settle into a routine or an entirely mundane type of relationship. You may have some unconventional views on traditional marriage or your partner may hold such views. It is usually important to you that your love relationships are based on friendship.

WOMEN WITH VENUS IN PISCES: In love you are sensitive, tender, and affectionate, experiencing your partner's feelings almost as strongly as your own. Being also imaginative and visionary, you possess the ability to develop creative gifts and a deep compassion for others. As you are idealistic when in love, you usually prefer to see only your partner's good points, but be careful that your high expectations do not bring disappointment if you avoid being realistic. Nevertheless, in your relationships with others, you can be devoted, loving, and positively enchanting.

MEN WITH VENUS IN PISCES: The combination of your emotional subtlety and charm can make you very alluring when dealing with affairs of the heart. Perceptive and impressionable, you have an easygoing style in your relationships, usually preferring to avoid ugly confrontation. You are drawn to a partner who has a touch of glamour and is sensitive to the needs of others. Alternatively, your partner can be a visionary with a rich imagination who can keep you enchanted.

WOMEN WITH VENUS IN ARIES: Idealistic, passionate, and adventurous, you are direct in your dealings with others. When you are attracted to a person you usually take the initiative and use your people skills to make things happen. In close relationships you are not afraid to confront your other half. This self-assertiveness is positive if differences can be brought into the open through diplomacy and compromise.

MEN WITH VENUS IN ARIES: As you often have the courage and strength to initiate situations, you like to take the lead. With your unconscious desire for conquest you may also have to beware of being competitive with your partners. Nevertheless, you are drawn to direct and strong-willed partners who can share your love of action and enthusiasm for life. When you are feeling good you can be charming and enthusiastic in romantic situations with an entertaining and spontaneous spirit.

To read all about your Outer Planets and work out how to use your personalized timetable, go to Section Three, page 789.

Your Personalized Timetable

JUPITER BENEFICIAL
1940 6/7 – until 1941 3/20
1942 6/18 – 9/1
1943 1/28 – 4/23
1946 10/4 – 12/19
1947 7/3 – 7/28
1948 12/8 – until 1949 1/20
1952 5/19 – 7/7
1952 11/15 – until 1953 2/24
1954 6/2 – 8/13
1958 9/17 – 12/1
1960 11/21 – until 1961 1/4
1964 5/2 – 6/15
1966 5/15 – 7/27
1969 12/29 – until 1970 11/15
1972 3/8 – 6/13
1972 10/31 – 12/19
1976 4/16 – 5/28
1977 9/1 – 12/16
1978 4/24 – 7/10
1981 12/7 – until 1982 10/31
1984 2/13 – 12/2
1988 3/31 – 5/12
1989 8/9 – until 1990 6/24
1993 11/19 – until 1994 10/15
1996 1/25 – 3/23
1996 6/16 – 11/13
1999 8/20 – 8/30
2000 3/12 – 4/25
2001 7/21 – until 2002 6/7
2005 11/4 – until 2006 9/28
2008 1/9 – 2/26
2008 7/30 – 10/17
2011 7/1 – 10/31
2012 2/17 – 4/8

SATURN BENEFICIAL
1940 4/29 – until 1941 4/14
1944 7/5 – until 1945 8/3
1953 11/7 – until 1954 12/27
1955 5/8 – 9/24
1959 2/23 – 6/10
1959 11/21 – until 1960 2/19
1960 7/9 – 11/18
1969 6/11 – 11/4
1970 3/2 – 5/25
1973 8/21 – 12/15
1974 5/9 – 9/29
1974 12/3 – until 1975 6/9
1982 12/19 – until 1983 4/11
1983 9/14 – until 1984 11/1
1988 12/26 – until 1989 12/26
1999 4/13 – 7/9
1999 10/21 – until 2000 3/26
2003 6/19 – until 2004 7/17
2012 10/22 – Continues

URANUS BENEFICIAL
1938 1/1 – until 1939 3/14
1949 7/12 – until 1953 6/27
1975 1/2 – until 1979 9/13
1989 3/9 – until 1992 11/8

NEPTUNE BENEFICIAL
1956 12/15 – until 1965 9/19
1986 2/9 – until 1991 11/24

PLUTO BENEFICIAL
1984 1/9 – until 1991 9/3
2010 2/22 – Continues

JUPITER CHALLENGING
1941 6/3 – until 1942 4/13
1944 8/4 – 10/19

1945 4/28 – 5/31
1947 11/2 – until 1948 1/14
1953 5/17 – 7/29
1954 1/11 – 3/12
1956 7/18 – 10/1
1959 3/13 – 3/24
1959 10/15 – 12/28
1965 5/1 – 7/10
1967 11/1 – until 1968 2/12
1968 6/28 – 9/16
1971 1/26 – 5/20
1971 9/24 – 12/12
1977 4/13 – 6/22
1979 10/9 – until 1980 8/31
1983 1/4 – 11/26
1988 8/3 – 11/16
1989 3/23 – 6/6
1991 9/21 – until 1992 8/15
1994 12/18 – until 1995 11/10
2000 7/9 – until 2001 5/21
2003 9/5 – until 2004 7/28
2006 12/2 – until 2007 10/23
2012 6/20 – Continues

SATURN CHALLENGING
1942 5/23 – until 1943 6/22
1948 10/6 – until 1949 3/4
1949 6/26 – 11/19
1950 2/10 – 8/7
1956 2/8 – 4/14
1956 10/29 – until 1957 12/19
1971 7/5 – 12/9
1972 3/22 – 8/7
1972 11/28 – until 1973 4/26
1978 8/11 – until 1979 9/16
1985 12/3 – until 1987 1/25
1987 6/8 – 10/25
2001 5/6 – until 2002 6/5
2007 9/18 – until 2008 4/16
2008 5/19 – 10/25
2009 3/14 – 7/17

URANUS CHALLENGING
1942 6/17 – until 1947 3/17
1962 9/10 – until 1966 8/9
1981 12/18 – until 1985 12/6

NEPTUNE CHALLENGING
1970 12/30 – until 1979 9/27

PLUTO CHALLENGING
1957 10/25 – until 1966 9/2
1995 12/31 – until 2003 10/19

JUPITER SPECIAL
1938 6/7 – 7/5
1939 1/8 – 3/18
1950 4/26 – until 1951 3/1
1962 4/4 – until 1963 2/12
1974 3/16 – until 1975 1/25
1986 2/28 – until 1987 1/3
1998 2/12 – 4/23
2010 1/26 – 4/4

SATURN SPECIAL
1964 4/12 – 8/21
1965 1/7 – until 1966 2/23
1994 2/14 – until 1995 3/30

URANUS SPECIAL
2003 4/21 – until 2008 2/25

NEPTUNE SPECIAL
2012 3/27 – Continues

♓

March 1

SUN: PISCES • DECANATE: PISCES/NEPTUNE • DEGREE: 9°5–10°5 PISCES • MODE: MUTABLE • ELEMENT: WATER

Your Personal Powers

Idealistic yet determined, you are a charismatic and sensitive individual with emotional strength. Your ruling planet, Neptune, endows you with intuitive abilities, foresight, and an impressionable nature. Your strong sense of vision or high aspirations often suggest that you possess an ambitious nature that inspires you to go it alone or follow your dreams. Although you can encounter challenges, your endurance and willingness to work hard indicate that you gain power when you stay resolute in the face of adversity. You also empower yourself when you apply intuition, creativity, and idealism to your ambitious plans and original ideas. Having a generous and charismatic personality means that you win people over by being kind and compassionate. Although your warmth and enthusiasm can be inspiring, a tendency to be stubborn or too righteous suggests that you lose some of your power by appearing too single-minded or egocentric. You empower yourself by being cooperative and objective or expressing your true feelings in a dispassionate manner.

Your Powers of Attraction in Relationships

Romantic and charismatic, you enjoy being with people and often you show your generosity when socializing. Your easygoing approach and ability to deal with people suggest that you can make others feel special. People are attracted to your enthusiastic nature, sincerity, and spontaneity or altruistic behavior. Often noble and loyal, you will make sacrifices for those you love. You are usually drawn to dynamic or dramatic people with persuasive charm and good manners. Alternatively, mentally quick, creative, and determined individuals often impress you. Although you are usually hardworking and responsible, a tendency to get frustrated or become impulsive indicates that you need an outlet for your powerful emotions. Being sentimental, you benefit from staying detached and learning to let go rather than taking life too seriously.

Your attractive qualities: leadership, imagination, compassionate, persevering, creative, progressive, forceful, optimistic, strong convictions, competitive, independent, gregarious, insightful, receptive, creative, original, self-assured, decisive, focused, hardworking

Your less attractive qualities: moody, pessimistic, intense emotions, selfish, unsympathetic, overbearing, egotistical, impulsive, too proud, antagonistic, lack of restraint, oversensitive, blocked emotions, impatient, restless, risk taking

Your Venus Power

The planet Venus has a great deal of influence on your powers of attraction. Below are four possible Venus types for women and men. To find your Venus you need to go to page 771, where you will find the Venus table and extra information. The planet Mars also affects your powers of attraction. To find your Mars table and interpretation go to page 761.

WOMEN WITH VENUS IN CAPRICORN: Proud and refined, you attract others with your composed dignity. Disliking vulnerability and needing to feel safe before you can express your feelings, you display a strong front. Feeling insecure or inadequate in relationships may force you to become manipulative in order to regain control. Nevertheless, you can project an attractive sense of self-assurance and are capable of displaying loyalty and a wonderful dry sense of humor.

MEN WITH VENUS IN CAPRICORN: As you admire loyal, hardworking, and dedicated individuals, you probably want a partner who can share your vocational interests or provide you with the sense of security you need. You could even find yourself with a partner who is of a different age group or maturity. Guard against denying your true emotional needs or focusing on your career at the expense of your relationship. You are drawn to reserved partners who display self-control.

WOMEN WITH VENUS IN AQUARIUS: Usually you have a modern outlook on love and are open to new or current lifestyles. Your intuitive abilities, communal sense, and people skills often allow you to see deeper into human intentions and to telepathically read people's thoughts. You are usually group-oriented and are drawn to individuals within the group who are independent and self-motivated. You are more inclined to choose a partner who is unconventional or freedom-loving. Conscious of your social standing, however, you want someone who can relate well to your friends.

MEN WITH VENUS IN AQUARIUS: When it comes to relationships, others are attracted to your honest, friendly, and easygoing attitude. You really enjoy social interaction with others and may develop a genuine concern for humanity. Usually you present a tolerant and reasonable front in love situations and attempt to view your relationships objectively. If partners become too demanding, however, you can become

stubborn and fixed. Friendship may be even more important for you than sexual compatibility.

WOMEN WITH VENUS IN PISCES: Being sensitive to affairs of the heart, when you care for someone you can feel their emotions and sense their every mood. This empathy indicates that you can love on an unselfish level, but you may have to guard against giving too much, especially to those who do not reciprocate. As you are seductive and captivating, partners can be fascinated by your subtle charms and attracted by your caring and affectionate nature.

MEN WITH VENUS IN PISCES: Romantic and idealistic when in love, you can be a sensitive and responsive lover. Being pliant and flexible with an impressionable nature helps you to adapt to the needs of others. In your desire to blend with those you love, however, guard against not clearly defining your own boundaries. With your affectionate and sentimental nature, you are often attracted to those who understand your sensitivity and share your vision.

WOMEN WITH VENUS IN ARIES: With your strong desires and enthusiastic nature, you can be a passionate lover. Although idealistic and single-minded, you need to avoid unnecessary conflicts in your relationships by being more patient and less headstrong. Although at times others can accuse you of being bossy or impulsive, you possess a great deal of warmth and charm. When necessary, you can disarm others by making them feel important.

MEN WITH VENUS IN ARIES: Usually you are inclined to seek a partner who is active, goal-oriented, or decisive. Not known for your patience, you probably seek relationships from youth. You may find that you are attracted more to women who have a daring or adventurous spirit, but in your close relationships you may encounter rivalry or find that both you and your partner want to lead or be the boss. Although you may act rashly, you possess a great deal of magnetism and are capable of demonstrating your love and affection.

To read all about your Outer Planets and work out how to use your personalized timetable, go to Section Three, page 789.

Your Personalized Timetable

JUPITER BENEFICIAL
1940 6/12 – 12/19
1941 1/11 – 3/25
1942 6/23 – 9/7
1943 1/20 – 5/1
1946 10/9 – 12/24
1947 6/16 – 8/13
1948 12/12 – until 1949 1/25
1952 5/24 – 7/13
1952 11/8 – until 1953 3/2
1954 6/6 – 8/17
1958 9/22 – 12/6
1960 11/25 – until 1961 1/8
1964 5/7 – 6/20
1966 5/20 – 7/31
1970 1/5 – 4/6
1970 9/3 – 11/20
1972 3/16 – 6/4
1972 11/6 – 12/23
1976 4/20 – 6/2
1977 9/8 – 12/8
1978 4/30 – 7/15
1981 12/12 – until 1982 11/4
1984 2/18 – 12/7
1988 4/4 – 5/16
1989 8/15 – until 1990 6/29
1993 11/24 – until 1994 10/19
1996 1/30 – 11/18
2000 3/17 – 4/30
2001 7/26 – until 2002 6/12
2005 11/8 – until 2006 10/3
2008 1/13 – 3/3
2008 7/21 – 10/25
2011 7/7 – 10/24
2012 2/23 – 4/12

SATURN BENEFICIAL
1940 5/7 – until 1941 4/22
1944 7/13 – until 1945 8/12
1946 2/15 – 4/22
1953 11/16 – until 1955 1/8
1955 4/24 – 10/5
1959 3/10 – 5/24
1959 12/1 – until 1960 3/1
1960 6/26 – 11/29
1969 6/21 – 10/23
1970 3/12 – 6/2
1971 1/1 – 2/2
1973 9/2 – 12/2
1974 5/18 – until 1975 6/17
1983 1/1 – 3/27
1983 9/24 – until 1984 11/10
1989 1/3 – until 1990 1/3
1999 4/21 – until 2000 4/4
2003 6/26 – until 2004 7/25
2012 10/30 – Continues

URANUS BENEFICIAL
1938 1/1 – until 1939 4/5
1949 7/31 – until 1953 7/14
1975 10/28 – until 1979 10/5
1990 1/4 – until 1992 11/30

NEPTUNE BENEFICIAL
1957 11/11 – until 1965 10/21
1987 1/7 – until 1991 12/24

PLUTO BENEFICIAL
1984 11/16 – until 1991 10/8
2011 1/18 – Continues

JUPITER CHALLENGING
1941 6/8 – until 1942 4/18
1944 8/9 – 10/24
1945 4/14 – 6/14
1947 11/6 – until 1948 1/19

1953 5/22 – 8/3
1954 1/1 – 3/22
1956 7/23 – 10/6
1959 10/20 – until 1960 1/1
1965 5/5 – 7/14
1967 11/8 – until 1968 2/4
1968 7/4 – 9/20
1971 2/2 – 5/12
1971 10/1 – 12/16
1977 4/18 – 6/27
1979 10/15 – until 1980 9/5
1983 1/10 – 12/1
1988 8/10 – 11/8
1989 3/29 – 6/11
1991 9/26 – until 1992 8/19
1994 12/23 – until 1995 11/15
2000 7/15 – 12/24
2001 2/27 – 5/25
2003 9/9 – until 2004 8/2
2006 12/7 – until 2007 10/28
2012 6/24 – Continues

SATURN CHALLENGING
1942 5/31 – until 1943 6/30
1948 10/16 – until 1949 2/20
1949 7/7 – 12/6
1950 1/22 – 8/16
1956 11/7 – until 1957 12/27
1971 7/15 – 11/27
1972 4/2 – 8/20
1972 11/15 – until 1973 5/5
1978 8/19 – until 1979 9/24
1985 12/11 – until 1987 2/6
1987 5/25 – 11/4
2001 5/14 – until 2002 6/13
2007 9/26 – until 2008 3/25
2008 6/10 – 11/4
2009 3/1 – 7/27

URANUS CHALLENGING
1942 7/7 – until 1947 4/19
1962 9/27 – until 1966 8/26
1982 1/5 – until 1986 10/3

NEPTUNE CHALLENGING
1938 4/12 – 7/16
1971 2/11 – until 1979 11/7

PLUTO CHALLENGING
1958 9/22 – until 1967 7/31
1996 2/10 – until 2003 11/20

JUPITER SPECIAL
1939 1/13 – 3/22
1950 5/2 – 8/22
1950 12/22 – until 1951 3/6
1962 4/8 – 10/21
1962 11/6 – until 1963 2/17
1974 3/21 – until 1975 1/30
1986 3/4 – 5/22
1986 9/2 – until 1987 1/9
1998 2/16 – 4/27
1998 10/23 – 12/4
2010 1/30 – 4/8

SATURN SPECIAL
1964 4/24 – 8/7
1965 1/17 – until 1966 3/3
1994 2/22 – until 1995 4/7
1995 10/19 – 12/24

URANUS SPECIAL
2004 2/24 – until 2008 12/18

NEPTUNE SPECIAL
2012 5/7 – Continues

♓

March 2

SUN: PISCES • DECANATE: CANCER/MOON • DEGREE: 10°5–11°5 PISCES • MODE: MUTABLE • ELEMENT: WATER

Your Personal Powers

Charismatic and receptive, you are an instinctive individual with an enthusiastic and determined personality. As a practical and enterprising individual you gain power when you combine your knowledge or expertise with your innate people skills. Your ruling planet, Neptune, grants you keen senses, imaginative ideas, and heightened sensitivity. A desire for power or material rewards, however, warns that if you are dissatisfied you need to resist taking risks or indulging in get-rich-quick schemes as a means of escapism. Your idealism and determination imply that even though you can be friendly and helpful, you are also ambitious and resourceful. Although you like to play a key role or be in charge, you lose power when you become involved in power struggles with people or colleagues whose support you need. You can therefore achieve far more by being cooperative and showing a willingness to collaborate. Keen to initiate large projects, you empower yourself when you combine your intuitive powers, endurance, and ability to concentrate on one particular goal.

Your Powers of Attraction in Relationships

You are persuasive and hardworking, and other people admire your responsible attitude or strong sense of duty. Security-conscious, you usually want serious and lasting relationships. A tendency to be commanding, however, implies that you may like to lay down the law in close relationships. Be careful of getting involved in difficult experiences with others concerning issues of influence and control as these can consume your positive energies. Usually you are attracted to dynamic and enterprising individuals who have business acumen and influence. Dynamic and passionate, you should not let your pride stop you from displaying your true feelings. Although you can be loyal and supportive, you do not like to be taken for granted. As a sympathetic individual, you show your caring nature by responding to the needs of others.

Your attractive qualities: idealistic, good with people, visionary, intelligent, objective, determined, good organizer, enterprising, ambitious, good partnerships, progressive, agreeable, compassionate, gentle, tactful, harmonious, intuitive, resolute, humanitarian, considerate, intuitive, receptive, agile

Your less attractive qualities: impatient, restlessness, unsympathetic, controlling, suspicious, lack of confidence, disagreeable, too sensitive, selfish, bossy, indulging, demanding, easily hurt, escapist, dissatisfied, bad partnerships, manipulative

Your Venus Power

The planet Venus has a great deal of influence on your powers of attraction. Below are four possible Venus types for women and men. To find your Venus you need to go to page 771, where you will find the Venus table and extra information. The planet Mars also affects your powers of attraction. To find your Mars table and interpretation go to page 761.

WOMEN WITH VENUS IN CAPRICORN: With your natural caution in romantic affairs, you often appear reserved and controlled. You may be reserved, but try to be more forward, especially if you want to be noticed. When you care about people, however, you are usually willing to put in extra time and energy to preserve the relationship. You are practical and dependable, and a sense of duty can often play a large role in affairs of the heart. With elegant simplicity you can attract others with your well-cut clothes and refined manners.

MEN WITH VENUS IN CAPRICORN: In relationships you take love seriously and can be a strong and practical support for friends or partners. You are usually attracted to partners who are as hardworking as yourself. As you tend not to express your feelings until you feel really secure in a relationship, you may be drawn to those who seem loyal, faithful, and not likely to let you down. As you respect the wisdom of experience, you may be drawn to mature partners or, alternatively, you may act as an authority figure for someone younger.

WOMEN WITH VENUS IN AQUARIUS: When it comes to relationships others are attracted to your honest, friendly, and easygoing attitude. You really enjoy social interaction with others and may develop a genuine concern for humanity. Usually you present a tolerant and reasonable front in love situations and attempt to view your relationships objectively. If partners become too demanding, however, you can become stubborn and fixed. Friendship may be even more important for you than sexual compatibility.

MEN WITH VENUS IN AQUARIUS: Ideally, in your relationships your lover is also your best friend. Since freedom of expression is a prerequisite to your well-being, you do better when left alone to do your own thing. You also need a partner who recognizes and appreciates your need for independence. Although usually friendly, at times you can be stubborn or

your cool detachment can appear to others as distant or impersonal. Very sociable, you particularly enjoy the company of those who share your original, fair-minded, and progressive views.

WOMEN WITH VENUS IN PISCES: As a romantic and idealistic individual you can be both loving and giving. While making allowances and sacrifices is understandable in a loving relationship, playing the martyr is often a state of romantic illusion. In relationships you may therefore need to balance the practical with the charitable. Nevertheless, your benevolence and sacrifices in the right relationship make you a partner who is devoted and kind. Subtle, sensitive, and alluring, you can be sensual and caring.

MEN WITH VENUS IN PISCES: Romantic and idealistic when in love, you can be a sensitive and responsive lover. Being pliant and flexible and having an impressionable nature help you to adapt to the needs of others. In your desire to blend with those you love, however, guard against not clearly defining your own boundaries. With your affectionate and sentimental nature, you are often attracted to those who understand your sensitivity and share your vision.

WOMEN WITH VENUS IN ARIES: You gain power from your strong individuality, energy, and enthusiasm. Your young-at-heart and spirited approach to relationships adds to your appeal. However, if you become too impatient or self-absorbed, your partnerships are likely to suffer. Nevertheless, you can be creative, sharp, and quick, especially when you are able to share new and exciting projects with your partners. Mischievous with a love of action, you may even incite them to a playful fight.

MEN WITH VENUS IN ARIES: You are drawn to strong, independent women who can stand up to you. Although you can enthusiastically follow the object of your desire, you may lose power if you allow your forceful emotions to become too dominant. Warm and passionate, you have a side to your nature that longs for new adventures. Romantic and chivalrous, you really enjoy the excitement of the initial chase, but unless you keep the enthusiasm alive and avoid falling into a rut you may become easily bored.

To read all about your Outer Planets and work out how to use your personalized timetable, go to Section Three, page 789.

Your Personalized Timetable

JUPITER BENEFICIAL
1940 6/17 – 12/3
1941 1/27 – 3/30
1942 6/27 – 9/13
1943 1/13 – 5/8
1946 10/14 – 12/29
1947 6/6 – 8/24
1948 12/17 – until 1949 1/29
1952 5/28 – 7/20
1952 10/31 – until 1953 3/8
1954 6/11 – 8/23
1955 3/12 – 3/22
1958 9/27 – 12/11
1960 11/30 – until 1961 1/13
1964 5/11 – 6/25
1964 12/19 – until 1965 2/1
1966 5/25 – 8/5
1970 1/14 – 3/28
1970 9/9 – 11/25
1972 3/26 – 5/25
1972 11/11 – 12/28
1976 4/24 – 6/6
1977 9/17 – 11/30
1978 5/5 – 7/19
1981 12/18 – until 1982 5/8
1982 8/16 – 11/9
1984 2/24 – 7/8
1984 10/19 – 12/12
1988 4/8 – 5/20
1989 8/20 – until 1990 1/10
1990 4/11 – 7/3
1993 11/29 – until 1994 10/24
1996 2/4 – 4/13
1996 5/25 – 11/24
2000 3/21 – 5/4
2001 7/31 – until 2002 6/17
2005 11/13 – until 2006 10/8
2008 1/18 – 3/9
2008 7/13 – 11/1
2011 7/14 – 10/16
2012 2/29 – 4/17

SATURN BENEFICIAL
1940 5/15 – until 1941 4/30
1944 7/21 – until 1945 2/23
1945 3/16 – 8/20
1946 1/31 – 5/7
1953 11/25 – until 1954 5/26
1954 8/15 – until 1955 1/22
1955 4/9 – 10/14
1959 4/4 – 4/29
1959 12/10 – until 1960 3/15
1960 6/11 – 12/8
1969 7/3 – 10/10
1970 3/21 – 6/10
1970 12/11 – until 1971 2/23
1973 9/17 – 11/16
1974 5/26 – until 1975 6/25
1983 1/19 – 3/8
1983 10/3 – until 1984 11/18
1989 1/12 – until 1990 1/12
1999 4/28 – 8/13
1999 9/15 – until 2000 4/13
2003 7/4 – until 2004 8/1
2012 11/7 – Continues

URANUS BENEFICIAL
1938 1/1 – until 1939 4/23
1949 8/21 – until 1954 5/13
1975 11/13 – until 1979 10/23
1990 1/21 – until 1992 12/19

NEPTUNE BENEFICIAL
1957 12/11 – until 1966 9/15
1987 2/5 – until 1992 11/19

PLUTO BENEFICIAL
1984 12/15 – until 1991 11/4
2011 2/21 – Continues

JUPITER CHALLENGING
1941 6/12 – 9/9

1941 11/9 – until 1942 4/24
1944 8/13 – 10/30
1945 4/3 – 6/24
1947 11/11 – until 1948 1/24
1948 7/23 – 9/8
1953 5/26 – 8/9
1953 12/24 – until 1954 3/30
1956 7/28 – 10/11
1959 10/25 – until 1960 1/6
1965 5/10 – 7/19
1967 11/17 – until 1968 1/26
1968 7/10 – 9/25
1971 2/10 – 5/4
1971 10/6 – 12/21
1977 4/22 – 7/1
1979 10/20 – until 1980 3/6
1980 6/16 – 9/9
1983 1/15 – 6/14
1983 9/11 – 12/5
1988 8/18 – 10/31
1989 4/3 – 6/15
1991 10/1 – until 1992 8/24
1994 12/28 – until 1995 11/19
2000 7/20 – 12/15
2001 3/7 – 5/30
2003 9/14 – until 2004 8/8
2006 12/12 – until 2007 11/2
2012 6/29 – Continues

SATURN CHALLENGING
1942 6/8 – until 1943 7/8
1944 2/4 – 3/8
1948 10/27 – until 1949 2/7
1949 7/17 – until 1950 8/24
1956 11/15 – until 1958 1/5
1958 7/22 – 9/25
1971 7/25 – 11/14
1972 4/12 – 9/5
1972 10/29 – until 1973 5/13
1978 8/27 – until 1979 10/2
1985 12/20 – until 1986 7/4
1986 9/9 – until 1987 2/20
1987 5/9 – 11/14
2001 5/22 – until 2002 6/20
2007 10/5 – until 2008 3/10
2008 6/24 – 11/16
2009 2/16 – 8/6

URANUS CHALLENGING
1942 8/1 – until 1947 5/10
1962 10/16 – until 1966 9/11
1982 1/29 – until 1986 10/29

NEPTUNE CHALLENGING
1938 3/5 – 8/19
1971 12/27 – until 1980 9/12

PLUTO CHALLENGING
1958 11/2 – until 1967 8/30
1996 12/19 – until 2004 10/8

JUPITER SPECIAL
1939 1/18 – 3/26
1950 5/9 – 8/15
1950 12/27 – until 1951 3/10
1962 4/14 – 10/3
1962 11/24 – until 1963 2/21
1974 3/25 – until 1975 2/3
1986 3/9 – 5/30
1986 8/25 – until 1987 1/15
1998 2/20 – 5/3
1998 10/11 – 12/16
2010 2/4 – 4/12

SATURN SPECIAL
1964 5/9 – 7/22
1965 1/26 – until 1966 3/11
1994 3/2 – until 1995 4/17
1995 10/3 – until 1996 1/8

URANUS SPECIAL
2004 3/13 – until 2009 1/20

♓

721

March 3

SUN: PISCES • DECANATE: CANCER/MOON • DEGREE: 11°5–12°5 PISCES • MODE: MUTABLE • ELEMENT: WATER

Your Personal Powers

Friendly and sociable, you are a receptive and sensitive individual with an idealistic yet determined nature. Your ruling planet, Neptune, grants you retentive memory, intuitive powers, imagination, and inspired ideas. Although you are intelligent and quick at grasping new concepts, a tendency to be proud with strong opinions indicates that you prefer to find things out in your own time rather than take advice from others. Your heightened perception and quick understanding often inspire you to be productive and creative. Since you are inventive, versatile, and talented, you empower yourself by focusing on or specializing in one particular field. You also gain power when you synthesize your love of learning with your business acumen, enterprising spirit, and pragmatic approach. Usually sociable, sympathetic, and compassionate, you show willingness to collaborate on creative endeavors and to help others. Inner doubts imply that you gain power when you recognize your true value and inner strength. Luckily, you have many opportunities to turn your fortunes around and succeed admirably.

Your Powers of Attraction in Relationships

Gregarious and spontaneous, you enjoy socializing and meeting people from all walks of life. Other people are attracted to your affectionate, friendly, and optimistic nature. Although your youthful manner is often daring or unconventional, you are a receptive and sensitive person. Keen on communicating and learning, you seek the company of intelligent people who can share your interests. Or, you may be drawn to creative or artistic people who are full of bright ideas. Your love of freedom and your independent spirit indicate that you need a partner who can offer you a great deal of space to express yourself. Idealistic yet forceful, you do better in relationships when you find someone versatile and dynamic who can stand up to you but shares your aspirations.

Your attractive qualities: enthusiastic, romantic, independent, confident, progressive, sensitive, curious, friendly, witty, happy, productive, creative, loving, generous, helpful, freedom-loving, good values, a talent with words, original ideas, determined, strong premonitions, purposeful

Your less attractive qualities: easily bored, possessive, lacks self-esteem, self-centered, impulsive, indecisive, unsym-

pathetic, vain, exaggerates, extravagant, self-indulgent, lazy, too proud, emotionally restless, lack of purpose or faith, worry

Your Venus Power

The planet Venus has a great deal of influence on your powers of attraction. Below are four possible Venus types for women and men. To find your Venus you need to go to page 771, where you will find the Venus table and extra information. The planet Mars also affects your powers of attraction. To find your Mars table and interpretation go to page 761.

WOMEN WITH VENUS IN CAPRICORN: Proud and refined, you attract others with your composed dignity. Disliking vulnerability and needing to feel safe before you can express your feelings, you display a strong front. Feeling insecure or inadequate in relationships may force you to become manipulative in order to regain control. Nevertheless, you can project an attractive sense of self-assurance and are capable of displaying loyalty and a wonderful dry sense of humor.

MEN WITH VENUS IN CAPRICORN: As you do not display your deeper emotions freely, you are usually dignified and controlled in your relationships. Practical and down-to-earth partners are particularly attractive to you, especially those who do not rush into expressing their feelings but seem to possess natural class and reserve. You need a partner who is loyal and dependable and willing to take your relationship seriously.

WOMEN WITH VENUS IN AQUARIUS: Sociable and gracious, you are usually sincere and capable of showing attributes of real tolerance and liberalism. Although you are keen on forming relationships, you also like to have freedom and act independently. Your intimate partnerships need to be founded on true friendship. Full of bright and progressive ideas, you can express yourself better when you are free and unrestricted. An ability to think in a dispassionate way suggests that you can stay detached. Your love of freedom also implies that you can be loving and loyal without smothering your partner.

MEN WITH VENUS IN AQUARIUS: Ideally, in your relationships your lover is also your best friend. Since freedom of expression is a prerequisite to your well-being, you do better when left alone to do your own thing. You also need a partner who recognizes and appreciates your need for independence. Although usually friendly, at times you can be stubborn or your cool detachment can appear to others as distant or im-

personal. Very sociable, you particularly enjoy the company of those who share your original, fair-minded, and progressive views.

WOMEN WITH VENUS IN PISCES: As a romantic and idealistic individual, you can be both loving and giving. While making allowances and sacrifices is understandable in a loving relationship, playing the martyr is often a state of romantic illusion. In relationships you may therefore need to balance the practical with the charitable. Nevertheless, your benevolence and sacrifices in the right relationship make you a devoted and kind partner. Subtle, sensitive, and alluring, you can be sensual and caring.

MEN WITH VENUS IN PISCES: Romantic and idealistic when in love, you can be a sensitive and responsive lover. Being pliant and flexible and having an impressionable nature help you to adapt to the needs of others. In your desire to blend with those you love, however, guard against not clearly defining your own boundaries. With your affectionate and sentimental nature you are often attracted to those who understand your sensitivity and share your vision.

WOMEN WITH VENUS IN ARIES: Idealistic, passionate, and adventurous, you are direct in your dealings with others. When you are attracted to a person you usually take the initiative and use your people skills to make things happen. In close relationships you are not afraid to confront your other half. This self-assertiveness is positive if differences can be brought into the open through diplomacy and compromise.

MEN WITH VENUS IN ARIES: As you often have the courage and strength to initiate situations, you like to take the lead. With your unconscious desire for conquest you may also have to beware of being competitive with your partners. Nevertheless, you are drawn to direct and strong-willed partners who can share your love of action and enthusiasm for life. When you are feeling good you can be charming and enthusiastic in romantic situations with an entertaining and spontaneous spirit.

To read all about your Outer Planets and work out how to use your personalized timetable, go to Section Three, page 789.

Your Personalized Timetable

JUPITER BENEFICIAL
1940 6/23 – 11/24
1941 2/6 – 4/4
1942 7/2 – 9/20
1943 1/5 – 5/14
1946 10/18 – until 1947 1/4
1947 5/28 – 9/1
1948 12/21 – until 1949 2/3
1952 6/2 – 7/27
1952 10/24 – until 1953 3/14
1954 6/15 – 8/28
1955 2/19 – 4/11
1958 10/2 – 12/16
1960 12/5 – until 1961 1/17
1964 5/15 – 6/30
1964 12/8 – until 1965 2/12
1966 5/29 – 8/10
1970 1/25 – 3/17
1970 9/15 – 11/29
1972 4/9 – 5/10
1972 11/16 – until 1973 1/1
1976 4/29 – 6/11
1977 9/27 – 11/20
1978 5/11 – 7/24
1981 12/24 – until 1982 4/30
1982 8/24 – 11/13
1984 3/1 – 6/30
1984 10/26 – 12/16
1988 4/13 – 5/25
1989 8/26 – until 1990 1/3
1990 4/18 – 7/8
1993 12/4 – until 1994 6/21
1994 7/12 – 10/29
1996 2/9 – 8/26
1996 9/11 – 11/29
2000 3/26 – 5/8
2001 8/5 – until 2002 6/21
2005 11/18 – until 2006 10/13
2008 1/22 – 3/15
2008 7/5 – 11/7
2011 7/22 – 10/8
2012 3/5 – 4/21

SATURN BENEFICIAL
1940 5/23 – until 1941 1/3
1941 1/16 – 5/8
1944 7/29 – until 1945 1/29
1945 4/9 – 8/30
1946 1/18 – 5/18
1953 12/4 – until 1954 5/11
1954 8/30 – until 1955 2/13
1955 3/17 – 10/23
1959 12/19 – until 1960 4/3
1960 5/22 – 12/17
1969 7/18 – 9/24
1970 3/30 – 6/19
1970 11/26 – until 1971 3/8
1974 6/4 – until 1975 7/3
1983 10/12 – until 1984 11/27
1989 1/21 – 8/13
1989 10/9 – until 1990 1/20
1999 5/6 – until 2000 4/21
2003 7/12 – until 2004 8/10
2005 2/25 – 4/15
2012 11/16 – Continues

URANUS BENEFICIAL
1938 1/1 – until 1939 5/11
1949 9/28 – until 1954 6/4
1975 12/1 – until 1979 11/8
1990 2/9 – until 1993 1/5

NEPTUNE BENEFICIAL
1958 11/8 – until 1966 10/19
1987 3/26 – until 1992 12/20

PLUTO BENEFICIAL
1985 11/3 – until 1992 9/22
2012 1/18 – Continues

JUPITER CHALLENGING
1941 6/16 – 9/22

1941 10/27 – until 1942 4/29
1944 8/18 – 11/4
1945 3/26 – 7/3
1947 11/16 – until 1948 1/29
1948 7/11 – 9/19
1953 5/30 – 8/15
1953 12/17 – until 1954 4/6
1956 8/2 – 10/16
1959 10/30 – until 1960 1/11
1965 5/14 – 7/24
1967 11/28 – until 1968 1/14
1968 7/15 – 9/30
1971 2/20 – 4/24
1971 10/12 – 12/25
1977 4/27 – 7/6
1979 10/27 – until 1980 2/27
1980 6/23 – 9/14
1983 1/21 – 6/5
1983 9/19 – 12/10
1988 8/28 – 10/21
1989 4/8 – 6/19
1991 10/6 – until 1992 4/17
1992 5/14 – 8/29
1995 1/2 – 11/24
2000 7/26 – 12/7
2001 3/15 – 6/3
2003 9/19 – until 2004 8/13
2006 12/16 – until 2007 11/7
2012 7/4 – Continues

SATURN CHALLENGING
1942 6/16 – until 1943 7/17
1944 1/14 – 3/28
1948 11/9 – until 1949 1/23
1949 7/26 – until 1950 9/2
1956 11/24 – until 1958 1/14
1958 7/4 – 10/11
1971 8/7 – 11/1
1972 4/21 – until 1973 5/21
1978 9/4 – until 1979 10/10
1980 4/22 – 6/21
1985 12/29 – until 1986 6/17
1986 9/25 – until 1987 3/15
1987 4/16 – 11/23
2001 5/30 – until 2002 6/28
2007 10/15 – until 2008 2/27
2008 7/5 – 12/1
2009 1/31 – 8/15

URANUS CHALLENGING
1943 5/31 – until 1947 5/28
1962 11/13 – until 1967 7/6
1982 11/28 – until 1986 11/17

NEPTUNE CHALLENGING
1938 1/20 – until 1939 7/10
1972 2/2 – until 1980 11/3

PLUTO CHALLENGING
1959 9/27 – until 1968 7/25
1997 1/19 – until 2004 11/13

JUPITER SPECIAL
1939 1/22 – 3/31
1950 5/17 – 8/6
1951 1/2 – 3/14
1962 4/19 – 9/23
1962 12/4 – until 1963 2/25
1974 3/30 – until 1975 2/8
1986 3/13 – 6/7
1986 8/16 – until 1987 1/20
1998 2/25 – 5/8
1998 10/2 – 12/24
2010 2/8 – 4/17

SATURN SPECIAL
1964 6/4 – 6/25
1965 2/4 – until 1966 3/19
1994 3/11 – until 1995 4/26
1995 9/19 – until 1996 1/20

URANUS SPECIAL
2004 4/1 – until 2009 2/11

♓

723

March 4

Your Personal Powers

Thoughtful and practical, you are a receptive individual with a strong determination and an idealistic nature. Your ruling planet, Neptune, endows you with intuitive abilities, quick comprehension, deep emotions, and imaginative ideas. Usually sensitive and compassionate, you try to keep people and situations harmonious. Although you can tune in to the emotions of others, guard against perceiving them as your own. Security-conscious, you empower yourself when you persevere and move gradually toward your objectives. When you feel inspired you are keen to express yourself and often work very hard in order to achieve your goals. You gain power when you combine your dedication, common sense, creativity, and visionary thoughts. Although you can be motivated and purposeful, your sensitivity and inclination to daydream warns that you can fluctuate from being industrious to being passive or inactive. Luckily, material incentives and a need to accomplish often turn you into an ambitious and resolute person.

Your Powers of Attraction in Relationships

Since partnerships are usually important to you, collaborating with others can bring great benefits. Naturally diplomatic and gregarious, in social situations you can easily deal with people. Sensitive to others, you can be an understanding and sympathetic individual. Being involved in group activities that offer mental stimulation and dramatic self-expression can further your chances for success and recognition. Although you can be passionate and loving, a tendency to overreact or be impulsive means that you need to develop your patience and resist being bossy. People admire your spontaneity, practical approach, and inner vision. By ensuring that you always keep the balance of power in your relationships, you can succeed in forming profitable partnerships with creative and dynamic people. You are usually attracted to mentally sharp or smart individuals who are energetic, assertive, or success-oriented. Alternatively, you may be drawn to ambitious and hardworking people with strong convictions or ideals.

Your attractive qualities: friendly, intelligent, pragmatic, creative, diplomatic, good negotiator, imaginative, cooperative, love learning, receptive, self-disciplined, steady, hardworking, organized, trusting, exact, inspired, self-confident, home-loving, subtle, intuitive, insight

Your less attractive qualities: impulsive, too sensitive, controlling, manipulative, stubborn, selfish, indecisive, worried, too serious, repressed, stuck in a rut, lazy, procrastinator, bossy, secretive, resentful, escapist, weak, vague

Your Venus Power

The planet Venus has a great deal of influence on your powers of attraction. Below are four possible Venus types for women and men. To find your Venus you need to go to page 771, where you will find the Venus table and extra information. The planet Mars also affects your powers of attraction. To find your Mars table and interpretation go to page 761.

WOMEN WITH VENUS IN CAPRICORN: Romantically, you do not give your heart easily but hide behind a cool reserve until you feel free to express your emotions. As you take your relationships seriously, you may find yourself drawn to people who are businesslike, resourceful, and practical or those who can act as teachers or mentors. Work or career may also be a factor in many of your associations and partnerships. As security can play an important role in your relationships, you are often attracted to partners who are loyal and hardworking.

MEN WITH VENUS IN CAPRICORN: As you do not display your deeper emotions freely, you are usually dignified and controlled in your relationships. Practical and down-to-earth partners are particularly attractive to you, especially those who do not rush into expressing their feelings but seem to possess natural class and reserve. You need a partner who is loyal and dependable and willing to take your relationship seriously.

WOMEN WITH VENUS IN AQUARIUS: When it comes to relationships, others are attracted to your honest, friendly, and easygoing attitude. You really enjoy social interaction with others and may develop a genuine concern for humanity. Usually you present a tolerant and reasonable front in love situations and attempt to view your relationships objectively. If partners become too demanding, however, you can become stubborn and fixed. Friendship may be even more important for you than sexual compatibility.

MEN WITH VENUS IN AQUARIUS: Although independent, you often enjoy being part of a group. The partners you frequently attract are themselves nonconformists or free spirits. As an individual you may not find it easy to settle into a routine or an entirely mundane type of relationship. You may

have some unconventional views on traditional marriage or your partner may hold such views. As a nonconformist, you may also be interested in alternative lifestyles such as collective living.

WOMEN WITH VENUS IN PISCES: Being sensitive to affairs of the heart, when you care for someone you can feel their emotions and sense their every mood. This empathy indicates that you can love on an unselfish level, but you may have to guard against giving too much, especially to those who do not reciprocate. As you are seductive and captivating, partners can be fascinated by your subtle charms and attracted by your caring and affectionate nature.

MEN WITH VENUS IN PISCES: The combination of your emotional subtlety and charm can make you very alluring when dealing with affairs of the heart. Perceptive and impressionable, you have an easygoing style in your relationships, usually preferring to avoid ugly confrontation. You are drawn to a partner who has a touch of glamour and is sensitive to the needs of others. Alternatively, your partner can be a visionary with a rich imagination who can keep you enchanted.

WOMEN WITH VENUS IN ARIES: With your strong desires and enthusiastic nature, you can be a passionate lover. Although idealistic and single-minded, you need to avoid unnecessary conflicts in your relationships by being more patient and less headstrong. Although at times others can accuse you of being bossy or impulsive, you possess a great deal of warmth and charm. When necessary, you can disarm others by making them feel important.

MEN WITH VENUS IN ARIES: You are usually inclined to seek a partner who is active, goal-oriented, or decisive. Not known for your patience, you probably seek relationships early in life. You may find that you are attracted more to women who have a daring or adventurous spirit, but in your close relationships you may encounter rivalry or find that both you and your partner want to lead or be the boss. Although you may act rashly, you possess a great deal of magnetism and are capable of demonstrating your love and affection.

To read all about your Outer Planets and work out how to use your personalized timetable, go to Section Three, page 789.

To read all about your Outer Planets and work out how to use your personalized timetable, go to Section Three, page 789.

Your Personalized Timetable

JUPITER BENEFICIAL
1940 6/28 – 11/15
1941 2/13 – 4/8
1942 7/6 – 9/27
1942 12/29 – until 1943 5/20
1946 10/23 – until 1947 1/10
1947 5/20 – 9/9
1948 12/25 – until 1949 2/7
1952 6/6 – 8/4
1952 10/15 – until 1953 3/19
1954 6/20 – 9/2
1955 2/8 – 4/22
1958 10/7 – 12/21
1960 12/9 – until 1961 1/21
1964 5/19 – 7/6
1964 11/29 – until 1965 2/21
1966 6/3 – 8/14
1970 2/16 – 2/22
1970 9/20 – 12/4
1972 11/22 – until 1973 1/5
1976 5/3 – 6/15
1977 10/14 – 11/3
1978 5/16 – 7/28
1981 12/31 – until 1982 4/22
1982 8/30 – 11/18
1984 3/8 – 6/22
1984 11/1 – 12/21
1988 4/17 – 5/29
1989 9/1 – 12/26
1990 4/24 – 7/12
1993 12/9 – until 1994 6/4
1994 7/30 – 11/2
1996 2/14 – 8/7
1996 9/30 – 12/3
2000 3/30 – 5/12
2001 8/10 – until 2002 2/16
2002 3/15 – 6/26
2005 11/22 – until 2006 10/18
2008 1/27 – 3/22
2008 6/27 – 11/13
2011 7/31 – 9/28
2012 3/11 – 4/25

SATURN BENEFICIAL
1940 5/31 – 12/6
1941 2/12 – 5/16
1944 8/7 – until 1945 1/15
1945 4/23 – 9/9
1946 1/6 – 5/28
1953 12/14 – until 1954 4/28
1954 9/10 – until 1955 11/1
1959 12/27 – until 1960 12/26
1969 8/19 – 8/19
1970 4/7 – 6/29
1970 11/14 – until 1971 3/19
1974 6/12 – until 1975 7/11
1983 10/20 – until 1984 12/5
1985 7/1 – 8/19
1989 1/30 – 7/26
1989 10/26 – until 1990 1/29
1990 9/6 – 10/10
1999 5/14 – until 2000 4/29
2003 7/20 – until 2004 8/18
2005 2/7 – 5/2
2012 11/24 – Continues

URANUS BENEFICIAL
1938 1/1 – until 1940 3/14
1950 7/10 – until 1954 6/22
1975 12/21 – until 1980 8/31
1990 3/5 – until 1993 11/7

NEPTUNE BENEFICIAL
1958 12/8 – until 1967 9/9
1988 2/2 – until 1993 11/14

PLUTO BENEFICIAL
1985 11/29 – until 1992 10/22
2012 2/21 – Continues

JUPITER CHALLENGING
1941 6/21 – until 1942 5/4

1944 8/23 – 11/10
1945 3/18 – 7/10
1947 11/20 – until 1948 2/4
1948 7/2 – 9/28
1953 6/4 – 8/21
1953 12/9 – until 1954 4/12
1956 8/7 – 10/21
1957 5/11 – 5/27
1959 11/4 – until 1960 1/16
1965 5/18 – 7/29
1966 1/25 – 3/7
1968 7/20 – 10/4
1971 3/5 – 4/10
1971 10/17 – 12/30
1977 5/1 – 7/10
1979 11/2 – until 1980 2/19
1980 6/30 – 9/18
1983 1/28 – 5/28
1983 9/26 – 12/14
1988 9/14 – 10/5
1989 4/13 – 6/24
1991 10/11 – until 1992 4/1
1992 5/30 – 9/3
1995 1/7 – 7/17
1995 8/18 – 11/28
2000 8/1 – 11/29
2001 3/21 – 6/7
2003 9/24 – until 2004 8/18
2006 12/21 – until 2007 11/12
2012 7/9 – Continues

SATURN CHALLENGING
1942 6/24 – until 1943 1/17
1943 2/25 – 7/25
1943 12/30 – until 1944 4/11
1948 11/30 – until 1949 1/2
1949 8/4 – until 1950 9/10
1956 12/2 – until 1958 1/24
1958 6/20 – 10/24
1971 8/24 – 10/14
1972 4/29 – until 1973 5/29
1978 9/12 – until 1979 10/19
1980 4/5 – 7/7
1986 1/8 – 6/3
1986 10/7 – 12/2
2001 6/6 – until 2002 7/6
2007 10/25 – until 2008 2/14
2008 7/15 – until 2009 8/23

URANUS CHALLENGING
1943 6/18 – until 1947 6/14
1963 9/3 – until 1967 7/31
1982 12/14 – until 1986 12/4

NEPTUNE CHALLENGING
1938 1/1 – until 1939 8/16
1972 12/23 – until 1980 12/2

PLUTO CHALLENGING
1959 11/9 – until 1968 8/26
1997 12/9 – until 2005 9/23

JUPITER SPECIAL
1939 1/27 – 4/4
1950 5/27 – 7/27
1951 1/7 – 3/18
1962 4/24 – 9/14
1962 12/12 – until 1963 3/1
1974 4/3 – until 1975 2/12
1986 3/17 – 6/18
1986 8/5 – until 1987 1/25
1998 3/1 – 5/14
1998 9/24 – 12/31
2010 2/12 – 4/22

SATURN SPECIAL
1965 2/12 – until 1966 3/27
1994 3/19 – 10/23
1994 11/26 – until 1995 5/7
1995 9/6 – until 1996 1/30

URANUS SPECIAL
2004 4/25 – until 2009 3/1

March 5

Your Personal Powers

Bright and spirited, you are a sensitive yet motivated individual with high hopes. Your ruling planet, Neptune, endows you with receptivity, intuitive abilities, and a vivid imagination. Your versatility, idealism, and strong instincts indicate that your quest for personal transformation can often be attributed to your courage and resolute nature. A more romantic, gentle, or softhearted side to your nature implies that you can also be caring and understanding. If you hang on to the past for sentimental reasons, however, you can lose some of your enthusiasm or power. Although your need for a challenge or excitement implies that you are keen on travel or pursuing a busy life, your practical nature indicates that you also want emotional security and stability. Nevertheless, you are spontaneous and multitalented, and your need for variety suggests that by staying innovative, focused, and purposeful, you can avoid getting stuck in monotonous situations. By combining your enterprising and astute mind with your ability to adapt easily to new circumstances, you can achieve success.

Your Powers of Attraction in Relationships

Friendly and playful, you enjoy socializing and being with people. People admire your youthful spirit, idealism, and kindness. Sensitive and expressive, relationships are important to you. A generous person, you sometimes act impulsively. If you are overly romantic about relationships and commit yourself too quickly to a partner, changing circumstance can leave you disenchanted. You are usually attracted to loyal and caring individuals who can make a lasting commitment to you. Alternatively, you enjoy the company of optimistic and intelligent people who are enthusiastic and have bright ideas. Having a strong sense of duty suggests that you can at times be too serious about your close relationships. Staying more detached and resisting emotional fluctuations can help you avoid stress. When in love, however, you love wholeheartedly.

Your attractive qualities: versatile, compassionate, adaptable, imaginative, progressive, strong instincts, magnetic, daring, freedom-loving, productive, witty, curious, adventurous, mystical, sociable, sixth sense, sympathetic, hardworking, intuitive, quick responses, natural business sense

Your less attractive qualities: too impressionable, unreliable, changeable, procrastinator, vague, dreamer, overconfi-

dent, headstrong, too tense or dramatic, too sensitive, easily discouraged, impractical, escapist, too idealistic

Your Venus Power

The planet Venus has a great deal of influence on your powers of attraction. Below are four possible Venus types for women and men. To find your Venus you need to go to page 771, where you will find the Venus table and extra information. The planet Mars also affects your powers of attraction. To find your Mars table and interpretation go to page 761.

WOMEN WITH VENUS IN CAPRICORN: With your natural caution in romantic affairs, you often appear reserved and controlled. You may be shy but try to be more forward, especially if you want to be noticed. When you care about people, however, you are usually willing to put in extra time and energy to preserve the relationship. You are practical and dependable, and a sense of duty can often play a large role in affairs of the heart. With elegant simplicity you can attract others with your well-cut clothes and refined manners.

MEN WITH VENUS IN CAPRICORN: As you do not display your deeper emotions freely, you are usually dignified and controlled in your relationships. Practical and down-to-earth partners are particularly attractive to you, especially those who do not rush into expressing their feelings but seem to possess natural class and reserve. You need a partner who is loyal and dependable and willing to take your relationship seriously.

WOMEN WITH VENUS IN AQUARIUS: When it comes to relationships, others are attracted to your honest, friendly, and easygoing attitude. You really enjoy social interaction with others and may develop a genuine concern for humanity. Usually you present a tolerant and reasonable front in love situations and attempt to view your relationships objectively. If partners become too demanding, however, you can become stubborn and fixed. Friendship may be even more important for you than sexual compatibility.

MEN WITH VENUS IN AQUARIUS: You are sociable and open-minded, and people are attracted by your friendly and easygoing style. Being independent, you value freedom-loving partners who give you the space to be yourself. People can sometimes interpret your detachment as being emotionally cool, but they admire your objectivity and humanitarian inclinations. You are attracted to intelligent individuals who are as

truthful and direct as you, but above all they must be true friends. Ideally, your partner shares your liberal views on life and possesses a strong sense of individuality.

WOMEN WITH VENUS IN PISCES: Being sensitive to affairs of the heart, when you care for someone you can feel their emotions and sense their every mood. This empathy indicates that you can love on an unselfish level, but you may have to guard against giving too much, especially to those who do not reciprocate. As you are seductive and captivating, partners can be fascinated by your subtle charms and attracted by your caring and affectionate nature.

MEN WITH VENUS IN PISCES: A romantic and generous person, you are attracted to imaginative or artistic partners who can be sensitive and generous. While you are willing to make allowances for loved ones, playing the martyr in relationships can lead to others taking advantage of your kind nature. Nevertheless, giving and loving, you are usually willing to forgive your partner's shortcomings.

WOMEN WITH VENUS IN ARIES: You gain power from your strong individuality, energy, and enthusiasm. Your young-at-heart and spirited approach to relationships adds to your appeal. If you become too impatient or self-absorbed, however, your partnerships are likely to suffer. Nevertheless, you can be creative, sharp, and quick, especially when you are able to share new and exciting projects with your partners. Mischievous with a love of action, you may even incite them to a playful fight.

MEN WITH VENUS IN ARIES: As you often have the courage and strength to initiate situations, you like to take the lead. With your unconscious desire for conquest you may also have to beware of being competitive with your partners. Nevertheless, you are drawn to direct and strong-willed partners who can share your love of action and enthusiasm for life. When you are feeling good you can be charming and enthusiastic in romantic situations with an entertaining and spontaneous spirit.

To read all about your Outer Planets and work out how to use your personalized timetable, go to Section Three, page 789.

Your Personalized Timetable

JUPITER BENEFICIAL
1940 7/4 – 11/8
1941 2/20 – 4/13
1942 7/11 – 10/5
1942 12/20 – until 1943 5/26
1946 10/28 – until 1947 1/16
1947 5/12 – 9/15
1948 12/30 – until 1949 2/12
1952 6/11 – 8/15
1952 10/4 – until 1953 3/24
1954 6/24 – 9/7
1955 1/30 – 5/1
1958 10/12 – 12/26
1959 6/27 – 8/12
1960 12/14 – until 1961 1/26
1964 5/24 – 7/12
1964 11/21 – until 1965 2/28
1966 6/8 – 8/19
1970 9/25 – 12/9
1972 11/26 – until 1973 1/10
1976 5/7 – 6/20
1978 5/21 – 8/2
1982 1/7 – 4/14
1982 9/5 – 11/23
1984 3/15 – 6/14
1984 11/7 – 12/25
1988 4/21 – 6/2
1989 9/8 – 12/19
1990 5/1 – 7/17
1993 12/15 – until 1994 5/24
1994 8/10 – 11/7
1996 2/19 – 7/28
1996 10/10 – 12/8
2000 4/4 – 5/16
2001 8/15 – until 2002 2/1
2002 3/30 – 7/1
2005 11/27 – until 2006 10/23
2008 2/1 – 3/30
2008 6/19 – 11/19
2011 8/14 – 9/14
2012 3/16 – 4/29

SATURN BENEFICIAL
1940 6/9 – 11/21
1941 2/26 – 5/24
1944 8/16 – until 1945 1/2
1945 5/5 – 9/20
1945 12/24 – until 1946 6/7
1953 12/25 – until 1954 4/14
1954 9/20 – until 1955 11/9
1960 1/5 – until 1961 1/4
1970 4/15 – 7/10
1970 11/1 – until 1971 3/29
1974 6/19 – until 1975 7/19
1983 10/28 – until 1984 12/14
1985 6/11 – 9/7
1989 2/9 – 7/11
1989 11/8 – until 1990 2/7
1990 8/14 – 11/1
1999 5/22 – until 2000 5/7
2003 7/28 – until 2004 2/9
2004 4/3 – 8/27
2005 1/25 – 5/15
2012 12/4 – Continues

URANUS BENEFICIAL
1938 2/10 – until 1940 4/6
1950 7/27 – until 1954 7/9
1976 1/21 – until 1980 9/27
1991 1/4 – until 1993 12/1

NEPTUNE BENEFICIAL
1959 2/1 – until 1967 10/16
1988 3/12 – until 1993 12/17

PLUTO BENEFICIAL
1986 1/2 – until 1993 8/31

JUPITER CHALLENGING
1941 6/25 – until 1942 5/9

1944 8/27 – 11/17
1945 3/10 – 7/17
1947 11/25 – until 1948 2/10
1948 6/24 – 10/6
1953 6/8 – 8/28
1953 12/2 – until 1954 4/18
1956 8/11 – 10/27
1957 4/22 – 6/15
1959 11/9 – until 1960 1/20
1965 5/23 – 8/3
1966 1/14 – 3/19
1968 7/26 – 10/9
1971 10/22 – until 1972 1/3
1977 5/6 – 7/15
1979 11/9 – until 1980 2/11
1980 7/6 – 9/23
1983 2/3 – 5/20
1983 10/2 – 12/18
1989 4/18 – 6/28
1991 10/17 – until 1992 3/22
1992 6/9 – 9/7
1995 1/12 – 7/2
1995 9/2 – 12/3
2000 8/7 – 11/22
2001 3/28 – 6/12
2003 9/29 – until 2004 8/23
2006 12/26 – until 2007 11/17
2012 7/14 – Continues

SATURN CHALLENGING
1942 7/3 – 12/29
1943 3/16 – 8/4
1943 12/18 – until 1944 4/22
1949 8/12 – until 1950 9/18
1956 12/11 – until 1958 2/4
1958 6/6 – 11/4
1972 5/7 – until 1973 6/6
1978 9/20 – until 1979 10/28
1980 3/23 – 7/20
1986 1/19 – 5/20
1986 10/18 – until 1987 12/10
2001 6/14 – until 2002 7/15
2003 1/23 – 3/23
2007 11/7 – until 2008 2/1
2008 7/25 – until 2009 9/1

URANUS CHALLENGING
1943 7/7 – until 1948 4/13
1963 9/19 – until 1967 8/18
1983 1/1 – until 1987 9/24

NEPTUNE CHALLENGING
1938 1/1 – until 1940 7/2
1973 1/26 – until 1981 10/30

PLUTO CHALLENGING
1960 9/30 – until 1969 7/18
1998 1/6 – until 2005 11/7

JUPITER SPECIAL
1939 1/31 – 4/8
1950 6/9 – 7/14
1951 1/12 – 3/22
1962 4/30 – 9/6
1962 12/19 – until 1963 3/5
1974 4/8 – until 1975 2/17
1986 3/22 – until 1987 1/30
1998 3/5 – 5/20
1998 9/16 – until 1999 1/7
2010 2/16 – 4/26

SATURN SPECIAL
1965 2/21 – until 1966 4/5
1966 11/21 – 12/1
1994 3/28 – 10/1
1994 12/17 – until 1995 5/20
1995 8/23 – until 1996 2/8

URANUS SPECIAL
2005 2/28 – until 2009 12/25

♓

March 6

SUN: PISCES · DECANATE: CANCER/MOON · DEGREE: 14°5–15°5 PISCES · MODE: MUTABLE · ELEMENT: WATER

Your Personal Powers

Warm and sociable, with vitality and drive, you are a sensitive and imaginative individual with a practical outlook. Having common sense and good organizational skills, you gain power by combining your determination, direct approach, and strong visionary sense. With your need for harmony and self-expression, you may be strongly attracted by artistic or creative pursuits, such as dance, music, drama, or writing. As you are strong-willed with a love of luxury and the good life, be careful not to lose some of your power by becoming too forceful or self-indulgent. With your high aspirations and ability to execute big projects or plans, you need only apply the necessary self-discipline to achieve outstanding results. Proud and ambitious, usually you have an optimistic outlook and your love of truth and justice indicate that you are honorable and direct. If you get carried away, however, you may appear conceited or too arrogant. Nevertheless, by applying your exceptional intuition and enterprising spirit to your practical and personal affairs, you can recognize many opportunities for success.

Your Powers of Attraction in Relationships

Your warmth, social skills, and generous nature attract others. Mentally keen, you are attracted to individuals with knowledge and insight. Equally, as you value success, you admire those who have achieved either materially or through expertise in their field. Nevertheless, do not let money matters interfere with your happiness. Being practical and caring, you desire security and a good foundation for yourself and your loved ones. Usually this involves a strong home base from which you can launch yourself into the world. Be careful, however, that others do not interpret your strong will and desire to help as overbearing or interfering behavior. Proud and determined, you generally like to be honest and direct with people. With your magnetic charm and social grace, you should find it easy to attract partners.

Your attractive qualities: friendly, optimistic, caring, generous, compassionate, dependable, sympathetic, idealistic, enterprising, visionary, strong-willed, worldly, direct, home-loving, humanitarian, artistic, optimistic, fun-loving, thinks big, idealistic, honest, people skills

Your less attractive qualities: self-indulgent, discontented, anxious, oversensitive, escapist, unreasonable, stubborn, outspoken, bossy, arrogant, suspicious, self-centered, interfering

Your Venus Power

The planet Venus has a great deal of influence on your powers of attraction. Below are four possible Venus types for women and men. To find your Venus you need to go to page 771, where you will find the Venus table and extra information. The planet Mars also affects your powers of attraction. To find your Mars table and interpretation go to page 761.

WOMEN WITH VENUS IN AQUARIUS: Usually you have a modern outlook on love and are open to new or current lifestyles. Your intuitive abilities, communal sense, and people skills often allow you to see deeper into human intentions and to telepathically read people's thoughts. You are usually group-oriented and are drawn to strong individuals within the group who are independent and self-motivated. You are more inclined to choose a partner who is unconventional or freedom-loving. Conscious of your social standing, however, you want someone who can relate well to your friends.

MEN WITH VENUS IN AQUARIUS: When it comes to relationships, others are attracted to your honest, friendly, and easygoing attitude. You really enjoy social interaction with others and may develop a genuine concern for humanity. Usually you present a tolerant and reasonable front in love situations and attempt to view your relationships objectively. If partners become too demanding, however, you can become stubborn and fixed. Friendship may be even more important for you than sexual compatibility.

WOMEN WITH VENUS IN PISCES: A romantic and idealistic individual, you can be both loving and giving. While making allowances and sacrifices is understandable in a loving relationship, playing the martyr is often a state of romantic illusion. In relationships you may therefore need to balance the practical with the charitable. Nevertheless, your benevolence and sacrifices in the right relationship make you a devoted and kind partner. Subtle, sensitive, and alluring, you can be sensual and caring.

MEN WITH VENUS IN PISCES: In love you are sensitive, tender, and affectionate, experiencing your partner's feelings

almost as strongly as your own. Being also imaginative and visionary, you possess the ability to develop deep compassion for others. As you are idealistic when in love, you usually prefer to see only your partner's good points, but be careful that your high expectations do not bring disappointment if you avoid harsh reality. Nevertheless, in your relationships with others, you can be devoted, loving, and positively enchanting.

WOMEN WITH VENUS IN ARIES: With your strong desires and enthusiastic nature you can be a passionate lover. Although idealistic and single-minded, you need to avoid unnecessary conflicts in your relationships by being more patient and less headstrong. Although at times others can accuse you of being bossy or impulsive, you possess a great deal of warmth and charm. When necessary, you can disarm others by making them feel important.

MEN WITH VENUS IN ARIES: As you often have the courage and strength to initiate situations, you like to take the lead. With your unconscious desire for conquest you may also have to beware of being competitive with your partners. Nevertheless, you are drawn to direct and strong-willed partners who can share your love of action and enthusiasm for life. When you are feeling good you can be charming and enthusiastic in romantic situations with an entertaining and spontaneous spirit.

WOMEN WITH VENUS IN TAURUS: Good-natured and romantic, you have a highly developed sense of touch that particularly responds to massage, hugs, and all things physical. Being friendly, you enjoy socializing and are able to put others at their ease. With your natural sense of beauty and harmony your natural charm can attract others. Although you can be lavish toward your partner, you may have to be careful that you do not overdo things.

MEN WITH VENUS IN TAURUS: Attractive and affectionate, in relationships you are often faithful with a conservative outlook. You are drawn to warmhearted partners with whom you can share a familiar routine as well as life's pleasures and comforts. Seeking a partner who is dependable or reassuring, you often put security high on your priority list when looking for love. Your sociability and friendliness usually make you popular and partners often admire your good sense of values and practical skills.

To read all about your Outer Planets and work out how to use your personalized timetable, go to Section Three, page 789.

Your Personalized Timetable

JUPITER BENEFICIAL
1940 7/10 – 10/31
1941 2/27 – 4/17
1942 7/15 – 10/15
1942 12/10 – until 1943 5/31
1946 11/1 – until 1947 1/23
1947 5/4 – 9/22
1949 1/3 – 2/17
1952 6/16 – 9/6
1952 9/13 – until 1953 3/29
1954 6/28 – 9/13
1955 1/23 – 5/8
1958 10/16 – 12/31
1959 6/15 – 8/24
1960 12/18 – until 1961 1/30
1964 5/28 – 7/18
1964 11/14 – until 1965 3/7
1966 6/12 – 8/24
1970 9/30 – 12/13
1972 12/1 – until 1973 1/14
1976 5/11 – 6/25
1978 5/26 – 8/7
1982 1/15 – 4/5
1982 9/11 – 11/27
1984 3/24 – 6/5
1984 11/12 – 12/29
1988 4/25 – 6/7
1989 9/15 – 12/11
1990 5/6 – 7/21
1993 12/20 – until 1994 5/15
1994 8/18 – 11/12
1996 2/25 – 7/19
1996 10/19 – 12/13
2000 4/8 – 5/21
2001 8/20 – until 2002 1/22
2002 4/9 – 7/5
2005 12/2 – until 2006 10/27
2008 2/5 – 4/9
2008 6/9 – 11/24
2012 3/21 – 5/4

SATURN BENEFICIAL
1940 6/19 – 11/8
1941 3/9 – 6/1
1944 8/26 – 12/21
1945 5/15 – 10/5
1945 12/8 – until 1946 6/15
1954 1/7 – 3/31
1954 9/30 – until 1955 11/18
1960 1/13 – until 1961 1/12
1970 4/23 – 7/22
1970 10/19 – until 1971 4/7
1974 6/27 – until 1975 7/26
1983 11/6 – until 1984 12/24
1985 5/27 – 9/20
1989 2/19 – 6/28
1989 11/19 – until 1990 2/17
1990 7/29 – 11/15
1999 5/31 – 12/16
2000 2/7 – 5/14
2003 8/6 – until 2004 1/24
2004 4/19 – 9/6
2005 1/13 – 5/26
2012 12/13 – Continues

URANUS BENEFICIAL
1938 3/13 – until 1940 4/24
1950 8/15 – until 1955 4/29
1976 11/7 – until 1980 10/17
1991 1/21 – until 1993 12/21

NEPTUNE BENEFICIAL
1959 12/4 – until 1968 8/31
1989 1/29 – until 1994 11/8

PLUTO BENEFICIAL
1986 11/16 – until 1993 10/9

JUPITER CHALLENGING
1941 6/30 – until 1942 5/14
1944 9/1 – 11/24

1945 3/2 – 7/23
1947 11/29 – until 1948 2/16
1948 6/16 – 10/13
1953 6/12 – 9/5
1953 11/24 – until 1954 4/23
1956 8/16 – 11/1
1957 4/11 – 6/26
1959 11/13 – until 1960 1/25
1960 8/10 – 8/31
1965 5/27 – 8/9
1966 1/5 – 3/28
1968 7/31 – 10/14
1971 10/27 – until 1972 1/8
1977 5/10 – 7/20
1979 11/18 – until 1980 2/3
1980 7/12 – 9/28
1983 2/11 – 5/12
1983 10/8 – 12/23
1989 4/23 – 7/3
1991 10/22 – until 1992 3/13
1992 6/18 – 9/12
1995 1/17 – 6/22
1995 9/12 – 12/7
2000 8/14 – 11/14
2001 4/2 – 6/16
2003 10/4 – until 2004 8/27
2006 12/30 – until 2007 11/21
2012 7/19 – 12/30

SATURN CHALLENGING
1942 7/12 – 12/15
1943 3/29 – 8/14
1943 12/6 – until 1944 5/1
1949 8/20 – until 1950 9/26
1956 12/19 – until 1957 7/24
1957 8/29 – until 1958 2/17
1958 5/23 – 11/13
1972 5/15 – until 1973 6/14
1978 9/28 – until 1979 4/7
1979 6/10 – 11/7
1980 3/10 – 7/30
1986 2/1 – 5/6
1986 10/28 – until 1987 12/19
2001 6/22 – until 2002 7/23
2003 1/7 – 4/8
2007 11/23 – until 2008 1/14
2008 8/2 – until 2009 9/9

URANUS CHALLENGING
1943 7/30 – until 1948 5/6
1963 10/6 – until 1967 9/4
1983 1/21 – until 1987 10/26

NEPTUNE CHALLENGING
1938 1/1 – until 1940 8/12
1973 12/20 – until 1981 11/29

PLUTO CHALLENGING
1960 11/13 – until 1969 8/21
1998 2/19 – until 2005 12/6

JUPITER SPECIAL
1939 2/4 – 4/13
1951 1/17 – 3/26
1962 5/6 – 8/29
1962 12/25 – until 1963 3/10
1974 4/13 – until 1975 2/21
1986 3/26 – until 1987 2/4
1998 3/9 – 5/26
1998 9/9 – until 1999 1/13
2010 2/21 – 5/1
2010 11/2 – 12/4

SATURN SPECIAL
1965 3/1 – until 1966 4/13
1966 10/22 – 12/30
1994 4/6 – 9/15
1994 12/31 – until 1995 6/5
1995 8/6 – until 1996 2/17

URANUS SPECIAL
2005 3/18 – until 2010 1/26

☓

March 7

SUN: PISCES · DECANATE: CANCER/MOON · DEGREE: 15°5–16°5 PISCES · MODE: MUTABLE · ELEMENT: WATER

Your Personal Powers

Thoughtful and sensitive, you are a clever and imaginative individual with inspired vision. Your ruling planet, Neptune, indicates that you can be caring and receptive to the feelings of others. You gain power from the combination of your analytical abilities, perfectionism, and strong impressionability. Although you can be resourceful and versatile, some of your challenges may involve worry or indecision, particularly about material matters. By focusing your keen mind on your strong need for self-expression and creativity, you have the potential to achieve excellent results. Alternating between being lighthearted and cheerful and being very serious and reflective, you gain power when you balance the extreme sides of your nature. Developing your inner faith can also help you to avoid losing power if you become prone to changing moods. Idealistic and highly intuitive, you possess high aspirations and subtle emotional awareness. Being multitalented, it is necessary for you to stay centered on your goals and not scatter your energies. You gain power and success, however, from your desire for knowledge and self-awareness.

Your Powers of Attraction in Relationships

Sensitive and idealistic, you can attract others with your charm and considerate manner. Aware of image, you often have an original style. Although you desire close personal relationships, you also want time alone to pursue your own interests or to reflect. Keen on self-analysis, be careful not to get too self-absorbed, as your sensitivity can turn inward and cause you to appear overemotional or cold. Usually you are attracted to intelligent individuals with special insight. Equally, you can be drawn to those who are enthusiastic and adventurous. With your strong imagination and sensitivity, avoid being evasive with your partners. Romantic, affectionate, and highly creative, you can be an ideal lover. By developing patience, confidence, and your communication skills, you can greatly improve all your relationships.

Your attractive qualities: high aspirations, generous, highly creative, imaginative, meticulous, idealistic, thinker, scientific, sensitive, perfectionist, spiritual potential, optimistic, expanded vision, psychic, analytical, versatile, artistic, reflective, analytical, thoughtful

Your less attractive qualities: escapist, worried, indecisive, concealing, frustrated, self-doubt, skeptical, confused, disappointed, insecure, critical, moody, too self-absorbed, cynical

Your Venus Power

The planet Venus has a great deal of influence on your powers of attraction. Below are four possible Venus types for women and men. To find your Venus you need to go to page 771, where you will find the Venus table and extra information. The planet Mars also affects your powers of attraction. To find your Mars table and interpretation go to page 761.

WOMEN WITH VENUS IN AQUARIUS: You attract and impress others with your friendly approach and progressive ideas. As you are usually independent and easygoing, you value freedom within a relationship. A good companion with a sense of your own person, you enjoy socializing, especially with people who are original, cosmopolitan, and have a strong sense of individuality. Although being friendly and detached usually serves you well, avoid losing touch with your emotions. You usually prefer the company of those who have innovative or progressive views.

MEN WITH VENUS IN AQUARIUS: Friendly and honest, you attract people with your broad-minded approach to life. You usually possess an objective and slightly detached attitude to affairs of the heart. If you are too removed, however, others can misinterpret your behavior as uncaring. It is often more important to you that your love relationships are based on friendship and honesty rather than intense passion. As you are generally tolerant and liberal, you may be drawn to less conventional relationships.

WOMEN WITH VENUS IN PISCES: Being sensitive to other people, you are receptive to their moods and feelings. This affinity indicates that although you can be selfless, you may have to guard against being too sentimental or overly romantic, especially with those who can take advantage of your kindness. Nevertheless, as you are alluring and seductive, your partners can be intrigued by your poetic soul or mysterious nature.

MEN WITH VENUS IN PISCES: Romantic and idealistic when in love, you can be a sensitive and responsive lover. Being pliant and flexible and having an impressionable nature help you to adapt to the needs of others. In your desire to

blend with those you love, however, guard against not clearly defining your own boundaries. With your affectionate and sentimental nature, you are often attracted to those who understand your sensitivity and share your vision.

WOMEN WITH VENUS IN ARIES: Idealistic, passionate, and adventurous, you are direct in your dealings with others. When you are attracted to a person you usually take the initiative and use your people skills to make things happen. In close relationships you are not afraid to confront your other half. This self-assertiveness is positive if differences can be brought into the open through diplomacy and compromise.

MEN WITH VENUS IN ARIES: You are drawn to strong, independent women who can stand up to you. Although you can enthusiastically follow the object of your desire, you may lose power if you allow your forceful emotions to become too dominant. Warm and passionate, you have a side to your nature that longs for new adventures. Romantic and chivalrous, you really enjoy the excitement of the initial chase, but unless you keep the enthusiasm alive and avoid falling into a rut you may become easily bored.

WOMEN WITH VENUS IN TAURUS: Being physically attractive, you can make a good impression on the opposite sex. As security and stability in relationships are very important to you, you want a partner who is not only attractive but also reliable and a good provider. Being sensual or tactile, you also need a lover who is affectionate, but beware that your love does not show signs of possessiveness or jealousy. Your own sense of style and love of beauty imply that you can be attracted to creative people, especially those in art and music.

MEN WITH VENUS IN TAURUS: Attractive and affectionate, in relationships you are often faithful with a conservative outlook. You are drawn to warmhearted partners with whom you can share a familiar routine as well as life's pleasures and comforts. Seeking a partner who is dependable or reassuring, you often put security high on your priority list when looking for love. Your sociability and friendliness usually make you popular, and partners often admire your good sense of values and practical skills.

To read all about your Outer Planets and work out how to use your personalized timetable, go to Section Three, page 789.

♓

Your Personalized Timetable

JUPITER BENEFICIAL
1940 7/17 – 10/24
1941 3/5 – 4/22
1942 7/19 – 10/30
1942 11/25 – until 1943 6/6
1946 11/6 – until 1947 1/31
1947 4/25 – 9/27
1949 1/7 – 2/22
1952 6/21 – 12/12
1953 1/29 – 4/3
1954 7/3 – 9/20
1955 1/15 – 5/15
1958 10/21 – until 1959 1/6
1959 6/5 – 9/2
1960 12/22 – until 1961 2/4
1964 6/2 – 7/24
1964 11/6 – until 1965 3/13
1966 6/17 – 8/29
1967 3/3 – 4/8
1970 10/5 – 12/18
1972 12/6 – until 1973 1/18
1976 5/15 – 6/30
1976 12/25 – until 1977 2/5
1978 5/31 – 8/11
1982 1/25 – 3/26
1982 9/17 – 12/2
1984 4/4 – 5/25
1984 11/18 – until 1985 1/3
1988 4/29 – 6/11
1989 9/24 – 12/2
1990 5/12 – 7/26
1993 12/26 – until 1994 5/7
1994 8/26 – 11/16
1996 3/2 – 7/10
1996 10/26 – 12/17
2000 4/13 – 5/25
2001 8/26 – until 2002 1/14
2002 4/17 – 7/10
2005 12/7 – until 2006 11/1
2008 2/10 – 4/23
2008 5/25 – 11/29
2012 3/25 – 5/8

SATURN BENEFICIAL
1940 6/29 – 10/26
1941 3/19 – 6/9
1942 1/5 – 2/10
1944 9/7 – 12/8
1945 5/24 – until 1946 6/24
1954 1/26 – 3/10
1954 10/9 – until 1955 11/26
1960 1/22 – 9/3
1960 9/28 – until 1961 1/21
1970 5/1 – 8/8
1970 10/2 – until 1971 4/15
1974 7/5 – until 1975 8/3
1983 11/14 – until 1985 1/3
1985 5/14 – 10/1
1989 3/4 – 6/14
1989 11/29 – until 1990 2/27
1990 7/15 – 11/27
1999 6/8 – 11/29
2000 2/24 – 5/22
2003 8/15 – until 2004 1/10
2004 5/2 – 9/17
2004 12/31 – until 2005 6/4

URANUS BENEFICIAL
1938 4/3 – until 1940 5/12
1950 9/10 – until 1955 5/28
1976 11/23 – until 1980 11/3
1991 2/9 – until 1994 1/7

NEPTUNE BENEFICIAL
1960 1/15 – until 1968 10/12
1989 3/5 – until 1994 12/14

PLUTO BENEFICIAL
1986 12/14 – until 1993 11/5

JUPITER CHALLENGING
1941 7/4 – until 1942 5/18
1944 9/6 – 12/2

1945 2/22 – 7/29
1947 12/4 – until 1948 2/23
1948 6/8 – 10/19
1953 6/17 – 9/14
1953 11/14 – until 1954 4/29
1956 8/21 – 11/7
1957 4/2 – 7/5
1959 11/18 – until 1960 1/31
1960 7/24 – 9/17
1965 5/31 – 8/14
1965 12/28 – until 1966 4/5
1968 8/5 – 10/19
1971 11/1 – until 1972 1/12
1977 5/15 – 7/24
1979 11/27 – until 1980 1/24
1980 7/17 – 10/2
1983 2/19 – 5/3
1983 10/14 – 12/27
1989 4/28 – 7/7
1991 10/28 – until 1992 3/5
1992 6/25 – 9/17
1995 1/23 – 6/14
1995 9/20 – 12/12
2000 8/22 – 11/6
2001 4/8 – 6/20
2003 10/9 – until 2004 5/1
2004 5/8 – 9/1
2007 1/4 – 11/26
2012 7/24 – 12/21

SATURN CHALLENGING
1942 7/21 – 12/2
1943 4/9 – 8/27
1943 11/22 – until 1944 5/10
1949 8/28 – until 1950 10/4
1956 12/28 – until 1957 7/2
1957 9/20 – until 1958 3/5
1958 5/5 – 11/23
1972 5/23 – until 1973 6/21
1978 10/7 – until 1979 3/22
1979 6/26 – 11/19
1980 2/26 – 8/9
1986 2/17 – 4/18
1986 11/6 – until 1987 12/27
2001 7/1 – until 2002 1/7
2002 3/11 – 8/1
2002 12/25 – until 2003 4/20
2008 8/11 – until 2009 9/17

URANUS CHALLENGING
1944 5/30 – until 1948 5/25
1963 10/27 – until 1967 9/20
1983 2/23 – until 1987 11/15

NEPTUNE CHALLENGING
1938 1/1 – until 1941 6/17
1974 1/21 – until 1982 10/26

PLUTO CHALLENGING
1961 10/3 – until 1970 7/7
1998 12/27 – until 2006 11/2

JUPITER SPECIAL
1939 2/9 – 4/17
1951 1/22 – 3/30
1962 5/13 – 8/22
1962 12/31 – until 1963 3/14
1974 4/18 – 10/10
1974 11/27 – until 1975 2/25
1986 3/30 – until 1987 2/8
1998 3/13 – 6/3
1998 9/1 – until 1999 1/19
2010 2/25 – 5/6
2010 10/20 – 12/17

SATURN SPECIAL
1965 3/9 – until 1966 4/23
1966 10/7 – until 1967 1/14
1994 4/17 – 9/2
1995 1/11 – until 1996 2/26

URANUS SPECIAL
2005 4/6 – until 2010 2/16

731

March 8

SUN: PISCES • DECANATE: CANCER/MOON • DEGREE: 16°5–17°5 PISCES • MODE: MUTABLE • ELEMENT: WATER

Your Personal Powers

You are sensitive, inspired, and forceful, and you also possess a lucid imagination and a strong sense of values. Receptive, you also have the ability to sense the feelings of others. Being ambitious, you gain power by developing your innate business sense and organizational abilities. You empower yourself by combining your determination and foresight with your dedication and natural diplomatic skills. Although with your pride and inner nobility you often gravitate to leadership positions, self-doubts can make you moody and undermine your ability to handle challenging situations. Nevertheless, you usually do well in activities that involve partnerships or team efforts. Determined and commanding, however, you can lose your vitality if you become involved in power struggles. By balancing your need for material security and long-term plans with your desire to find creative outlets for your emotional self-expression, you can accomplish much and succeed. Naturally psychic, intuitive, and productive, you can inspire others with your hard work and vision for a better future.

Your Powers of Attraction in Relationships

Friendly and helpful, you can attract others with your considerate nature. Although you can be dynamic, you can also be diplomatic and persuasive. You are attracted to partners who have power and influence or a sense of responsibility. Alternatively, with your sense of duty you want someone who makes you feel secure or inspired. Although kind and sensitive, you become less attractive to others if you allow issues of control to enter your relationships. Your partner should ideally share your interests or high ideals. A love of opulence, however, warns that you should avoid falling into a comfortable rut. Romantic and loyal, although you can sometimes be manipulative or moody, you can also provide much affection, support, and encouragement for loved ones.

Your attractive qualities: business sense, imagination, determined, thoroughness, leadership, optimistic, friendly, organizational skills, hardworking, authority, sensitive, diplomatic, intuitive, generous, patient, good evaluator, caring, ambitious, visionary

Your less attractive qualities: impatient, intolerant, moody, restless, workaholic, domineering, easily discouraged, too proud, untruthful, difficult, escapism, self-pity, insecure, anxiety

Your Venus Power

The planet Venus has a great deal of influence on your powers of attraction. Below are four possible Venus types for women and men. To find your Venus you need to go to page 771, where you will find the Venus table and extra information. The planet Mars also affects your powers of attraction. To find your Mars table and interpretation go to page 761.

WOMEN WITH VENUS IN AQUARIUS: Sociable and gracious, you are usually sincere and capable of showing attributes of real tolerance and liberalism. Although you are keen on forming relationships, you also like to have freedom and act independently. Your intimate partnerships need to be founded on true friendships. Full of bright and progressive ideas, you can express yourself better when you are free and unrestricted. An ability to think in a dispassionate way suggests that you can stay detached. Your love of freedom also implies that you can be loving and loyal without smothering your partner.

MEN WITH VENUS IN AQUARIUS: Although independent, you often enjoy being part of a group. The partners you frequently attract are themselves nonconformists or free spirits. As an individual you may not find it easy to settle into a routine or an entirely mundane type of relationship. You may have some unconventional views on traditional marriage or your partner may hold such views. It is usually important to you that your love relationships are based on friendship.

WOMEN WITH VENUS IN PISCES: Romantic and impressionable, you are a caring and loving individual with a dreamy nature. In relationships you are often attracted to idealistic, compassionate, or sympathetic individuals who are imaginative or have a strong romantic sense. A tendency to be sensitive to others suggests that you are intuitive and aware of people's inner feelings. Be careful, therefore, not to get caught in other people's dramas or play the rescuer too often.

MEN WITH VENUS IN PISCES: Romantic and idealistic when in love, you can be a sensitive and responsive lover. With your affectionate and impressionable nature, you are often attracted to those who understand your sensitivity and share your vision. Being flexible with an impressionable nature

helps you to adapt to the needs of others. In your desire to blend with those you love, guard against giving too much of yourself by not clearly defining your boundaries.

WOMEN WITH VENUS IN ARIES: You gain power from your strong individuality, energy, and enthusiasm. Your young-at-heart and spirited approach to relationships adds to your appeal. If you become too impatient or self-absorbed, however, your partnerships are likely to suffer. Nevertheless, you can be creative, sharp, and quick, especially when you are able to share new and exciting projects with your partners. Mischievous with a love of action, you may even incite them to a playful fight.

MEN WITH VENUS IN ARIES: As you often have the courage and strength to initiate situations, you like to take the lead. With your unconscious desire for conquest you may also have to beware of being competitive with your partners. Nevertheless, you are drawn to direct and strong-willed partners who can share your love of action and enthusiasm for life. When you are feeling good you can be charming and enthusiastic in romantic situations with an entertaining and spontaneous spirit.

WOMEN WITH VENUS IN TAURUS: For your ideal relationship you seek partners who are both financially secure and demonstrative with their affections. With these thoughts in mind, you are likely to want a partner who is refined yet pragmatic or someone concerned with safeguarding your future. A stubborn streak suggests that even when you know you are in the wrong, you are reluctant to give way. Attracted to people with a good sense of style, you can succeed in all kinds of business partnerships, especially those involving the arts, music, and luxury goods.

MEN WITH VENUS IN TAURUS: As well as attracting people with your warm personality, you also possess an innate sense of the value of material possessions. Keeping yourself stylish and having an attractive appearance can also be important to you. You are naturally attracted to practical yet sensual women who understand your need for comfort, security, and the pleasures and luxuries of life. Naturally affectionate, you enjoy socializing but can make a loyal and loving partner.

To read all about your Outer Planets and work out how to use your personalized timetable, go to Section Three, page 789.

To read all about your Outer Planets and work out how to use your personalized timetable, go to Section Three, page 789.

Your Personalized Timetable

JUPITER BENEFICIAL
1940 7/24 – 10/16
1941 3/10 – 4/26
1942 7/24 – until 1943 6/11
1946 11/10 – until 1947 2/9
1947 4/16 – 10/3
1949 1/12 – 2/27
1949 8/30 – 10/7
1952 6/26 – 12/1
1953 2/8 – 4/8
1954 7/7 – 9/26
1955 1/8 – 5/21
1958 10/26 – until 1959 1/12
1959 5/28 – 9/10
1960 12/27 – until 1961 2/8
1964 6/6 – 7/31
1964 10/30 – until 1965 3/18
1966 6/21 – 9/3
1967 2/18 – 4/21
1970 10/10 – 12/23
1972 12/10 – until 1973 1/23
1976 5/20 – 7/5
1976 12/13 – until 1977 2/17
1978 6/4 – 8/16
1982 2/8 – 3/11
1982 9/22 – 12/6
1984 4/29 – 5/2
1984 11/23 – until 1985 1/7
1988 5/4 – 6/16
1989 10/5 – 11/21
1990 5/17 – 7/30
1994 1/2 – 4/29
1994 9/1 – 11/21
1996 3/8 – 7/3
1996 11/1 – 12/22
2000 4/17 – 5/29
2001 9/1 – until 2002 1/6
2002 4/24 – 7/14
2005 12/13 – until 2006 6/10
2006 7/31 – 11/5
2008 2/15 – 8/23
2008 9/24 – 12/4
2012 3/30 – 5/12

SATURN BENEFICIAL
1940 7/11 – 10/13
1941 3/28 – 6/17
1941 12/15 – until 1942 3/2
1944 9/23 – 11/22
1945 6/1 – until 1946 7/2
1954 10/18 – until 1955 12/5
1960 1/31 – 8/8
1960 10/23 – until 1961 1/29
1970 5/9 – until 1971 4/24
1974 7/13 – until 1975 8/11
1983 11/23 – until 1984 6/25
1984 7/30 – until 1985 1/14
1985 4/30 – 10/12
1989 3/19 – 5/28
1989 12/8 – until 1990 3/10
1990 7/2 – 12/7
1999 6/18 – 11/16
2000 3/7 – 5/30
2003 8/24 – 12/29
2004 5/12 – 9/30
2004 12/17 – until 2005 6/13

URANUS BENEFICIAL
1938 4/21 – until 1941 3/14
1951 7/6 – until 1955 6/17
1976 12/11 – until 1980 11/19
1991 3/3 – until 1994 11/7

NEPTUNE BENEFICIAL
1960 12/1 – until 1969 8/12
1990 1/26 – until 1995 10/29

PLUTO BENEFICIAL
1987 2/2 – until 1994 9/24

JUPITER CHALLENGING
1941 7/9 – until 1942 5/23
1944 9/10 – 12/11

1945 2/12 – 8/4
1947 12/8 – until 1948 3/1
1948 5/31 – 10/25
1953 6/21 – 9/27
1953 11/1 – until 1954 5/4
1956 8/25 – 11/13
1957 3/25 – 7/12
1959 11/22 – until 1960 2/5
1960 7/13 – 9/27
1965 6/4 – 8/20
1965 12/20 – until 1966 4/12
1968 8/9 – 10/24
1971 11/6 – until 1972 1/17
1977 5/19 – 7/29
1979 12/13 – until 1980 1/9
1980 7/23 – 10/7
1983 3/2 – 4/22
1983 10/19 – until 1984 1/1
1989 5/2 – 7/12
1991 11/4 – until 1992 2/27
1992 7/2 – 9/21
1995 1/29 – 6/5
1995 9/27 – 12/16
2000 9/1 – 10/27
2001 4/13 – 6/25
2003 10/14 – until 2004 4/9
2004 5/31 – 9/6
2007 1/9 – 8/5
2007 8/8 – 11/30
2012 7/30 – 12/13

SATURN CHALLENGING
1942 8/1 – 11/20
1943 4/19 – 9/12
1943 11/6 – until 1944 5/19
1949 9/5 – until 1950 10/12
1951 5/7 – 6/20
1957 1/7 – 6/16
1957 10/5 – until 1958 12/2
1972 5/31 – until 1973 6/29
1978 10/16 – until 1979 3/9
1979 7/8 – 12/3
1980 2/11 – 8/18
1986 11/15 – until 1988 1/5
1988 8/27 – 9/2
2001 7/9 – 12/23
2002 3/26 – 8/11
2002 12/13 – until 2003 4/30
2008 8/19 – until 2009 9/25

URANUS CHALLENGING
1944 6/17 – until 1948 6/11
1963 11/30 – until 1968 7/17
1983 12/11 – until 1987 12/3

NEPTUNE CHALLENGING
1938 1/1 – until 1941 8/9
1974 12/18 – until 1982 11/27

PLUTO CHALLENGING
1961 11/16 – until 1970 8/15
1999 1/28 – until 2006 12/2

JUPITER SPECIAL
1939 2/13 – 4/22
1951 1/26 – 4/4
1962 5/21 – 8/14
1963 1/6 – 3/18
1974 4/23 – 9/29
1974 12/7 – until 1975 3/1
1986 4/4 – until 1987 2/13
1998 3/18 – 6/11
1998 8/23 – until 1999 1/24
2010 3/1 – 5/12
2010 10/10 – 12/27

SATURN SPECIAL
1965 3/17 – until 1966 5/2
1966 9/23 – until 1967 1/25
1994 4/28 – 8/20
1995 1/21 – until 1996 3/5

URANUS SPECIAL
2005 4/30 – until 2010 3/6

♓

March 9

SUN: PISCES • DECANT: CANCER/MOON • DEGREE: 17°5–18°5 PISCES • MODE: MUTABLE • ELEMENT: WATER

Your Personal Powers

Sensitive yet purposeful, you are a creative and intelligent individual with a fertile imagination and inner determination. Inspired by new beginnings, you gain power from your sharp intellect and ability to initiate new ventures. With your natural leadership skills, you feel confident when working on a project you truly believe in and support. Your enthusiasm can also motivate and influence others. Your sense of resoluteness and capacity for hard work point out that once you have set your mind on a goal, you can really advance in any field of endeavor. Although you are highly intuitive and imaginative, be careful not to lose power by being easily led or moody. You also possess a strong sense of vision that can be used for spiritual development, creative projects, or problem solving. With your special insight, the more you follow a path that involves helping others, the more happiness and satisfaction you find. As an intelligent perfectionist with high ideals, you need challenging work to bring out your best potential.

Your Powers of Attraction in Relationships

You can attract others with your sensitivity and determination. Romantic and idealistic about love, you seek an almost perfect union. If your expectations are too high, your partners may disappoint you. Sensitive to people's needs, you usually work well with others. At times reserved, you may need to express your feelings more openly. When you lose faith you may withdraw or become tough and suspicious. By developing faith in yourself, however, you can be very loving and giving without needing much in return. Equally, you can be generous and compassionate when you maintain a detached and universal approach to relationships. Although you may sometimes attract partners who emotionally blow hot and cold, you are attracted to individuals with special insight or to those of intelligence and inner wisdom.

Your attractive qualities: visionary, hardworking, humanitarian, creative, sensitive, strong-willed, generous, leadership ability, idealistic, magnetic, poetic, kind, psychic, spiritual potential, detached, tolerant, popular, liberal, highly intuitive, perceptive, intelligent

Your less attractive qualities: frustrated, self-centered, nervous, selfish, depressed, self-pity, impractical, stubborn, secretive, materialistic, intuitive, easily led, inferiority complex, escapist, worry

Your Venus Power

The planet Venus has a great deal of influence on your powers of attraction. Below are four possible Venus types for women and men. To find your Venus you need to go to page 771, where you will find the Venus table and extra information. The planet Mars also affects your powers of attraction. To find your Mars table and interpretation go to page 761.

WOMEN WITH VENUS IN AQUARIUS: Others are attracted to your honest, friendly, and easygoing attitude. You enjoy social interaction and have a genuine concern for others. In fact, at times your friends may be just as important as your partner. Usually you present a tolerant and reasonable front in love situations and attempt to view your relationships objectively. If partners become too demanding, however, you can become stubborn or awkward. Nevertheless, inventive and progressive, you enjoy the company of like-minded people who can share your original ideas.

MEN WITH VENUS IN AQUARIUS: You are sociable and liberal, and people are attracted by your friendly and easygoing style. Being independent, you value freedom-loving partners who give you the space to be yourself. People can sometimes interpret your detachment as being emotionally cool, but they admire your objectivity and humanitarian inclinations. You are attracted to intelligent individuals who are as truthful and direct as you, but above all they must be true friends. Ideally, your partner shares your liberal views on life and possesses a strong sense of individuality.

WOMEN WITH VENUS IN PISCES: A romantic and idealistic individual, you can be both loving and giving. While making allowances and sacrifices is understandable in a loving relationship, playing the martyr is often a state of romantic illusion. In relationships you may therefore need to balance the practical with the charitable. Nevertheless, your benevolence and sacrifices in the right relationship make you a devoted and kind partner. Subtle, sensitive, and alluring, you can be sensual and caring.

MEN WITH VENUS IN PISCES: In love, you are sensitive, tender, and affectionate, experiencing your partner's feelings almost as strongly as your own. Being also imaginative and vi-

sionary, you possess the ability to develop a deep compassion for others. As you are idealistic when in love, you usually prefer to see only your partner's good points, but be careful that your high expectations do not bring disappointment if you avoid harsh reality. Nevertheless, in your relationships with others you can be devoted, loving, and positively enchanting.

WOMEN WITH VENUS IN ARIES: With your strong desires and enthusiastic nature, you can be a passionate lover. Although idealistic and single-minded, you need to avoid unnecessary conflicts in your relationships by being more patient and less headstrong. Although at times others can accuse you of being bossy or impulsive, you possess a great deal of warmth and charm. When necessary you can disarm others by making them feel important.

MEN WITH VENUS IN ARIES: As you often have the courage and strength to initiate situations, you like to take the lead. With your unconscious desire for conquest you may also have to beware of being competitive with your partners. Nevertheless, you are drawn to direct and strong-willed partners who can share your love of action and enthusiasm for life. When you are feeling good you can be charming and enthusiastic in romantic situations with an entertaining and spontaneous spirit.

WOMEN WITH VENUS IN TAURUS: For your ideal relationship, you seek partners who are both financially secure and demonstrative with their affections. With these thoughts in mind, you are likely to want a partner who is refined yet pragmatic or someone concerned with safeguarding your future. Attracted to people with good sense of style, you can succeed in all kinds of business partnerships, especially those involving the arts, music, and luxury goods. A stubborn streak suggests that even when you know you are in the wrong, you are reluctant to give way

MEN WITH VENUS IN TAURUS: As you yourself may be attractive to the opposite sex, you desire a partner who is sensual and loving or possesses physical beauty. Needing stability, when faced with changes that are out of your control you may become insecure or worried about your future. Faithful or loyal, you usually hang on to relationships but may display controlling tendencies. Your own sense of style and your love of beauty imply that you can be attracted to creative people, especially those in art and music.

To read all about your Outer Planets and work out how to use your personalized timetable, go to Section Three, page 789.

♓

Your Personalized Timetable

JUPITER BENEFICIAL
1940 8/2 – 10/7
1941 3/15 – 4/30
1942 7/29 – until 1943 6/16
1946 11/15 – until 1947 2/22
1947 4/3 – 10/8
1949 1/16 – 3/4
1949 8/17 – 10/20
1952 7/2 – 11/23
1953 2/17 – 4/13
1954 7/12 – 10/4
1954 12/31 – until 1955 5/27
1958 10/30 – until 1959 1/18
1959 5/20 – 9/17
1960 12/31 – until 1961 2/13
1964 6/11 – 8/8
1964 10/21 – until 1965 3/24
1966 6/26 – 9/9
1967 2/8 – 5/1
1970 10/14 – 12/28
1971 7/10 – 8/8
1972 12/15 – until 1973 1/27
1976 5/24 – 7/10
1976 12/5 – until 1977 2/25
1978 6/9 – 8/21
1982 9/27 – 12/11
1984 11/28 – until 1985 1/11
1988 5/8 – 6/20
1990 5/22 – 8/4
1994 1/9 – 4/21
1994 9/8 – 11/25
1996 3/15 – 6/25
1996 11/7 – 12/26
2000 4/21 – 6/3
2001 9/7 – 12/29
2002 5/1 – 7/19
2005 12/18 – until 2006 5/30
2006 8/12 – 11/10
2008 2/21 – 8/9
2008 10/8 – 12/9
2012 4/3 – 5/16

SATURN BENEFICIAL
1940 7/27 – 9/27
1941 4/6 – 6/26
1941 12/1 – until 1942 3/15
1945 6/10 – until 1946 7/9
1954 10/26 – until 1955 12/13
1956 6/29 – 8/30
1960 2/9 – 7/23
1960 11/6 – until 1961 2/7
1961 8/28 – 10/27
1970 5/17 – until 1971 5/2
1974 7/20 – until 1975 8/19
1976 2/24 – 4/28
1983 12/1 – until 1984 6/3
1984 8/21 – until 1985 1/29
1985 4/15 – 10/21
1989 12/17 – until 1990 3/24
1990 6/16 – 12/16
1999 6/28 – 11/3
2000 3/17 – 6/7
2003 9/4 – 12/17
2004 5/21 – 10/18
2004 11/28 – until 2005 6/22

URANUS BENEFICIAL
1938 5/9 – until 1941 4/6
1951 7/23 – until 1955 7/4
1977 1/2 – until 1981 9/19
1992 1/5 – until 1994 12/3

NEPTUNE BENEFICIAL
1961 1/6 – until 1969 10/9
1990 2/27 – until 1995 12/11

PLUTO BENEFICIAL
1987 11/29 – until 1994 10/25

JUPITER CHALLENGING
1941 7/14 – until 1942 5/27
1944 9/15 – 12/24

1945 1/30 – 8/9
1947 12/12 – until 1948 3/10
1948 5/21 – 10/30
1953 6/25 – until 1954 5/9
1956 8/30 – 11/19
1957 3/17 – 7/19
1959 11/27 – until 1960 2/11
1960 7/4 – 10/5
1965 6/9 – 8/27
1965 12/13 – until 1966 4/18
1968 8/14 – 10/29
1969 4/29 – 6/16
1971 11/11 – until 1972 1/22
1977 5/23 – 8/3
1978 1/28 – 3/15
1980 7/28 – 10/12
1983 10/24 – until 1984 1/5
1989 5/7 – 7/16
1991 11/11 – until 1992 2/19
1992 7/8 – 9/26
1995 2/5 – 5/29
1995 10/4 – 12/20
2000 9/16 – 10/12
2001 4/18 – 6/29
2003 10/19 – until 2004 3/29
2004 6/11 – 9/11
2007 1/14 – 7/12
2007 9/1 – 12/5
2012 8/5 – Continues

SATURN CHALLENGING
1942 8/13 – 11/7
1943 4/28 – until 1944 5/27
1949 9/13 – until 1950 10/21
1951 4/17 – 7/9
1957 1/17 – 6/2
1957 10/16 – until 1958 12/10
1972 6/8 – until 1973 7/7
1978 10/26 – until 1979 2/24
1979 7/18 – 12/29
1980 1/15 – 8/27
1986 11/24 – until 1988 1/14
1988 7/25 – 10/5
2001 7/19 – 12/10
2002 4/6 – 8/23
2002 11/30 – until 2003 5/9
2008 8/27 – until 2009 10/3

URANUS CHALLENGING
1944 7/5 – until 1949 4/5
1964 9/10 – until 1968 8/8
1983 12/28 – until 1987 12/20

NEPTUNE CHALLENGING
1938 1/1 – until 1941 9/7
1975 1/17 – until 1983 10/20

PLUTO CHALLENGING
1962 10/5 – until 1970 9/13
1999 12/18 – until 2007 10/27

JUPITER SPECIAL
1939 2/17 – 4/26
1951 1/31 – 4/8
1962 5/30 – 8/4
1963 1/11 – 3/22
1974 4/29 – 9/20
1974 12/16 – until 1975 3/6
1986 4/9 – until 1987 2/17
1998 3/22 – 6/21
1998 8/13 – until 1999 1/29
2010 3/5 – 5/17
2010 10/2 – until 2011 1/3

SATURN SPECIAL
1965 3/26 – 10/22
1965 12/6 – until 1966 5/13
1966 9/10 – until 1967 2/4
1994 5/11 – 8/5
1995 1/30 – until 1996 3/13

URANUS SPECIAL
2006 3/5 – until 2010 12/31

March 10

Your Personal Powers

Sociable, bright, and adaptable, you are an individual with a powerful imagination and a friendly manner. Highly intuitive, you can be sympathetic and caring but equally, you are ambitious with a good sense of values and business acumen. You gain power from utilizing your many talents and disciplining yourself to stand on your own two feet or strike out on your own. Naturally dramatic, you often appear more self-confident than you really are, sometimes losing power to inner insecurity or worry. You empower yourself by combining your excellent people skills and original ideas with hard work and a willingness to persevere. You do not generally like to take orders and are better at utilizing your innate leadership skills to lead others. In your career, you lose some of your power if you are bossy or let a stubborn streak influence you to become dogmatic. The more you develop your humanitarian potential and work on your self-esteem, the greater satisfaction and success you achieve.

Your Powers of Attraction in Relationships

Kind, generous, and mentally quick, you should have no problem attracting friends and admirers. Being entertaining, you enjoy social activities. Although you usually prefer to lead, you can collaborate and work well in team situations. With your easy charm and natural psychological insight, you often try to keep the peace. At the other extreme, you can sometimes be bossy or critical with loved ones. You are attracted to ambitious individuals with definite plans for the future. Your ideal mate needs to be intelligent, enthusiastic, and preferably share your interests. You are drawn to straightforward and honest individuals who will tell you what they think. Although very sensitive, at times you can be emotionally inhibited. Amicable and friendly, however, you can be a charming companion and loyal friend or partner.

Your attractive qualities: sociable, leadership, intelligent, creative, pioneering, progressive, forceful, optimistic, imaginative, original, sensitive, intuitive, sympathetic, kind, talented, strong convictions, friendly, warm, competitive, independent, strong-willed, gregarious

Your less attractive qualities: overbearing, jealous, worry, egotistical, prideful, scattered, escapist, martyr, selfish, cold, weak, moody, unstable, impatient, insecure

Your Venus Power

The planet Venus has a great deal of influence on your powers of attraction. Below are four possible Venus types for women and men. To find your Venus you need to go to page 771, where you will find the Venus table and extra information. The planet Mars also affects your powers of attraction. To find your Mars table and interpretation go to page 761.

WOMEN WITH VENUS IN AQUARIUS: Sociable and gracious, you are usually sincere and are capable of showing attributes of real tolerance and liberalism. Although you are keen on forming relationships, you also like to have freedom and act independently. Your intimate partnerships need to be founded on true friendships. Full of bright and progressive ideas, you can express yourself better when you are free and unrestricted. An ability to think in a dispassionate way suggests that you can stay detached. Your love of freedom also implies that you can be loving and loyal without smothering your partner.

MEN WITH VENUS IN AQUARIUS: Although independent, you often enjoy being part of a group. The partners you frequently attract are themselves nonconformists or free spirits. As an individual you may not find it easy to settle into a routine or an entirely mundane type of relationship. You may have some unconventional views on traditional marriage or your partner may hold such views. It is usually important to you that your love relationships are based on friendship.

WOMEN WITH VENUS IN PISCES: In love, you are sensitive, tender, and affectionate, experiencing your partner's feelings almost as strongly as your own. Being also imaginative and visionary, you possess the ability to develop creative gifts and a deep compassion for others. As you are idealistic when in love, you usually prefer to see only your partner's good points, but be careful that your high expectations do not bring disappointment if you avoid being realistic. Nevertheless, in your relationships with others, you can be devoted, loving, and positively enchanting.

MEN WITH VENUS IN PISCES: The combination of your emotional subtlety and charm can make you very alluring when dealing with affairs of the heart. Perceptive and impressionable, you have an easygoing style in your relationships, usually preferring to avoid ugly confrontation. You are drawn to a partner who has a touch of glamour and is sensitive to the needs of others. Alternatively, your partner can be a visionary with a rich imagination who can keep you enchanted.

WOMEN WITH VENUS IN ARIES: Idealistic, passionate, and adventurous, you are direct in your dealings with others. When you are attracted to a person you usually take the initiative and use your people skills to make things happen. In close relationships you are not afraid to confront your other half. This self-assertiveness is positive if differences can be brought into the open through diplomacy and compromise.

MEN WITH VENUS IN ARIES: As you often have the courage and strength to initiate situations, you like to take the lead. With your unconscious desire for conquest you may also have to beware of being competitive with your partners. Nevertheless, you are drawn to direct and strong-willed partners who can share your love of action and enthusiasm for life. When you are feeling good you can be charming and enthusiastic in romantic situations with an entertaining and spontaneous spirit.

WOMEN WITH VENUS IN TAURUS: Good-natured and romantic, you have a highly developed sense of touch that particularly responds to massage, hugs, and all things physical. Being friendly, you enjoy socializing and are able to put others at their ease. With your natural sense of beauty and harmony, your charm can attract others. Although you can be lavish toward your partner you may have to be careful that you do not overdo things.

MEN WITH VENUS IN TAURUS: Attractive and affectionate, in relationships you are often faithful with a conservative outlook. You are drawn to warmhearted partners with whom you can share a familiar routine as well as life's pleasures and comforts. Seeking a partner who is dependable or reassuring, you often put security high on your priority list when looking for love. Your sociability and friendliness usually make you popular and partners often admire your good sense of values and practical skills.

To read all about your Outer Planets and work out how to use your personalized timetable, go to Section Three, page 789.

Your Personalized Timetable

JUPITER BENEFICIAL
1940 8/14 – 9/25
1941 3/20 – 5/5
1942 8/2 – until 1943 6/21
1946 11/19 – until 1947 10/13
1949 1/20 – 3/9
1949 8/8 – 10/29
1952 7/7 – 11/15
1953 2/24 – 4/17
1954 7/16 – 10/12
1954 12/22 – until 1955 6/2
1958 11/4 – until 1959 1/25
1959 5/12 – 9/23
1961 1/4 – 2/17
1964 6/15 – 8/18
1964 10/11 – until 1965 3/29
1966 6/30 – 9/14
1967 1/31 – 5/9
1970 10/19 – until 1971 1/3
1971 6/24 – 8/23
1972 12/19 – until 1973 1/31
1976 5/28 – 7/16
1976 11/27 – until 1977 3/5
1978 6/14 – 8/26
1982 10/2 – 12/16
1984 12/2 – until 1985 1/15
1988 5/12 – 6/25
1990 5/27 – 8/8
1994 1/16 – 4/12
1994 9/14 – 11/30
1996 3/23 – 6/16
1996 11/13 – 12/31
2000 4/25 – 6/7
2001 9/14 – 12/22
2002 5/7 – 7/23
2005 12/24 – until 2006 5/21
2006 8/21 – 11/14
2008 2/26 – 7/30
2008 10/17 – 12/14
2012 4/8 – 5/21

SATURN BENEFICIAL
1941 4/14 – 7/6
1941 11/19 – until 1942 3/26
1945 6/18 – until 1946 7/17
1954 11/3 – until 1955 12/22
1956 6/11 – 9/16
1960 2/19 – 7/9
1960 11/18 – until 1961 2/16
1961 8/11 – 11/12
1970 5/25 – until 1971 5/9
1974 7/28 – until 1975 8/28
1976 2/9 – 5/13
1983 12/11 – until 1984 5/18
1984 9/5 – until 1985 2/21
1985 3/21 – 10/30
1989 12/26 – until 1990 4/13
1990 5/27 – 12/25
1999 7/9 – 10/21
2000 3/27 – 6/15
2000 12/24 – until 2001 2/24
2003 9/18 – 12/3
2004 5/30 – until 2005 6/30

URANUS BENEFICIAL
1938 5/26 – until 1941 4/25
1951 8/10 – until 1955 7/21
1977 11/2 – until 1981 10/11
1992 1/22 – until 1994 12/22

NEPTUNE BENEFICIAL
1961 11/28 – until 1969 11/7
1991 1/23 – until 1996 1/8

PLUTO BENEFICIAL
1938 3/20 – 5/2
1987 12/30 – until 1995 8/30

JUPITER CHALLENGING
1941 7/19 – until 1942 1/18
1942 2/23 – 6/1
1944 9/19 – until 1945 8/14

(JUPITER BENEFICIAL continued)
1947 12/17 – until 1948 3/21
1948 5/10 – 11/5
1953 6/30 – until 1954 5/14
1956 9/4 – 11/26
1957 3/9 – 7/26
1959 12/1 – until 1960 2/17
1960 6/26 – 10/13
1965 6/13 – 9/3
1965 12/5 – until 1966 4/24
1968 8/19 – 11/4
1969 4/18 – 6/28
1971 11/15 – until 1972 1/27
1977 5/28 – 8/9
1978 1/17 – 3/26
1980 8/2 – 10/17
1983 10/29 – until 1984 1/10
1989 5/11 – 7/21
1991 11/18 – until 1992 2/11
1992 7/14 – 9/30
1995 2/12 – 5/21
1995 10/10 – 12/25
2001 4/23 – 7/3
2003 10/25 – until 2004 3/20
2004 6/20 – 9/15
2007 1/20 – 7/1
2007 9/12 – 12/9
2012 8/11 – 11/28

SATURN CHALLENGING
1942 8/31 – 10/20
1943 5/6 – until 1944 6/4
1949 9/21 – until 1950 10/30
1951 4/3 – 7/22
1957 1/28 – 5/20
1957 10/27 – until 1958 12/19
1972 6/15 – until 1973 7/15
1974 2/15 – 3/12
1978 11/7 – until 1979 2/11
1979 7/28 – until 1980 9/4
1986 12/2 – until 1988 1/23
1988 7/8 – 10/20
2001 7/29 – 11/27
2002 4/16 – 9/6
2002 11/16 – until 2003 5/18
2008 9/4 – until 2009 10/11
2010 5/19 – 6/10

URANUS CHALLENGING
1944 7/26 – until 1949 5/2
1964 9/27 – until 1968 8/26
1984 1/16 – until 1988 10/21

NEPTUNE CHALLENGING
1938 1/1 – until 1942 8/5
1975 12/15 – until 1983 11/24

PLUTO CHALLENGING
1962 11/16 – until 1971 8/8
2000 1/16 – until 2007 11/29

JUPITER SPECIAL
1939 2/21 – 5/1
1951 2/4 – 4/12
1962 6/10 – 7/23
1963 1/16 – 3/26
1974 5/4 – 9/13
1974 12/23 – until 1975 3/10
1986 4/13 – until 1987 2/22
1998 3/26 – 7/10
1998 7/25 – until 1999 2/3
2010 3/9 – 5/23
2010 9/24 – until 2011 1/10

SATURN SPECIAL
1965 4/4 – 10/2
1965 12/25 – until 1966 5/26
1966 8/27 – until 1967 2/14
1994 5/30 – 7/16
1995 2/8 – until 1996 3/21

URANUS SPECIAL
2006 3/23 – until 2011 1/30

♓

March 11

SUN: PISCES • DECANATE: CANCER/MOON • DEGREE: 19°5–20°5 • MODE: MUTABLE • ELEMENT: WATER

Your Personal Powers

Intuitive, intelligent, and receptive, you are an astute individual with inspired ideas, imagination, and quick responses. A natural visionary, you gain power by combining your excellent evaluation skills and sensitive awareness. Your potent sixth sense also provides you with an ability to make important decisions speedily and to quickly comprehend the opinions of others. An innate creativity can inspire you or encourage you to develop some definite form of self-expression. With your many original ideas, you usually like to be on the cutting edge of new projects or activities. Your executive abilities imply that you often achieve more in life when in positions of responsibility and authority. Enterprising with strong values and an innate understanding of finances, you nevertheless lose power if you become too security-conscious or materially minded. Being ambitious as well as sensitive and idealistic, you empower yourself when you are able to balance the two extremes of your nature. By displaying a special fighting spirit and developing your self-discipline, you are able to achieve outstanding success.

Your Powers of Attraction in Relationships

You attract others with your original approach and independent spirit. Sociable and aware of image, you can be witty and entertaining. Proud and self-reliant, you value freedom. Although you usually like to lead, you are aware of the advantages of working cooperatively with others. Do not let indecision, anxiety, or worry, particularly regarding financial issues, spoil or undermine your partnerships. Being inventive, you are attracted to intelligent or creative individuals who can stimulate your own talents. Although often sensitive and caring, particularly with your family, be careful that an inclination to be headstrong, easily hurt, or bossy does not create tension within your relationship. Generous and giving with loved ones, you can be very protective of those in your care.

Your attractive qualities: organizational skills, focused, imaginative, kind, objective, enthusiastic, inspirational, resourceful, idealistic, confident, intuitive, intelligent, outgoing, inventive, artistic, proud, humanitarian potential, generous, sociable

Your less attractive qualities: materialistic, superiority complex, deceptive, too emotional, easily hurt, selfish, extremist, lack of clarity, domineering, overindulgent, extravagant, critical, frustrated

Your Venus Power

The planet Venus has a great deal of influence on your powers of attraction. Below are four possible Venus types for women and men. To find your Venus you need to go to page 771, where you will find the Venus table and extra information. The planet Mars also affects your powers of attraction. To find your Mars table and interpretation go to page 761.

WOMEN WITH VENUS IN AQUARIUS: Sociable and gracious, you are usually sincere and are capable of showing attributes of real tolerance and liberalism. Although you are keen on forming relationships, you also like to have freedom and act independently. Your intimate partnerships need to be founded on true friendships. Full of bright and progressive ideas, you can express yourself better when you are free and unrestricted. An ability to think in a dispassionate way suggests that you can stay detached. Your love of freedom also implies that you can be loving and loyal without smothering your partner.

MEN WITH VENUS IN AQUARIUS: Ideally, in your relationships your lover is also your best friend. Since freedom of expression is a prerequisite to your well-being, you do better when left alone to do your own thing. You also need a partner who recognizes and appreciates your need for independence. Although usually friendly, at times you can be stubborn or your cool detachment can appear to others as distant or impersonal. Very sociable, however, you particularly enjoy the company of those who share your original, fair-minded, and progressive views.

WOMEN WITH VENUS IN PISCES: A romantic and idealistic individual, you can be both loving and giving. While making allowances and sacrifices is understandable in a loving relationship, playing the martyr is often a state of romantic illusion. In relationships you may therefore need to balance the practical with the charitable. Nevertheless, your benevolence and sacrifices in the right relationship make you a devoted and kind partner. Subtle, compassionate, and alluring, you can be sensual and caring.

MEN WITH VENUS IN PISCES: Romantic and idealistic when in love, you can be a sensitive and responsive lover. Being pliant and flexible with an impressionable nature helps

you to adapt to the needs of others. In your desire to blend with those you love, however, guard against not clearly defining your own boundaries. With your affectionate and sentimental nature, you are often attracted to those who understand your sensitivity and share your vision.

WOMEN WITH VENUS IN ARIES: You gain power from your strong individuality, energy, and enthusiasm. Your young-at-heart and spirited approach to relationships adds to your appeal. If you become too impatient or self-absorbed, however, your partnerships are likely to suffer. Nevertheless, you can be creative, sharp, and quick, especially when you are able to share new and exciting projects with your partners. Mischievous with a love of action, you may even incite them to a playful fight.

MEN WITH VENUS IN ARIES: You are drawn to strong, independent women who can stand up to you. Although you can enthusiastically follow the object of your desire, you may lose power if you allow your forceful emotions to become too dominant. Warm and passionate, you have a side to your nature that longs for new adventures. Romantic and chivalrous, you really enjoy the excitement of the initial chase, but unless you keep the enthusiasm alive and avoid falling into a rut you may become easily bored.

WOMEN WITH VENUS IN TAURUS: Good-natured and romantic, you have a highly developed sense of touch that particularly responds to massage, hugs, and all things physical. Being friendly, you enjoy socializing and are able to put others at their ease. With your natural sense of beauty and harmony, your charm can attract others. Although you can be lavish toward your partner, you may have to be careful that you do not overdo things.

MEN WITH VENUS IN TAURUS: As well as attracting people with your warm personality, you also possess an innate sense of the value of material possessions. Keeping yourself stylish and having an attractive appearance can also be important to you. You are naturally attracted to practical yet sensual women who understand your need for comfort, security, and the pleasures and luxuries of life. Naturally affectionate, you enjoy socializing but can make a loyal and loving partner.

To read all about your Outer Planets and work out how to use your personalized timetable, go to Section Three, page 789.

Your Personalized Timetable

JUPITER BENEFICIAL
1941 3/25 – 5/9
1942 8/7 – until 1943 6/25
1946 11/24 – until 1947 10/18
1949 1/25 – 3/15
1949 7/30 – 11/6
1952 7/13 – 11/8
1953 3/2 – 4/22
1954 7/21 – 10/23
1954 12/11 – until 1955 6/7
1958 11/8 – until 1959 2/1
1959 5/4 – 9/29
1961 1/9 – 2/22
1964 6/20 – 9/4
1964 9/24 – until 1965 4/3
1966 7/4 – 9/20
1967 1/24 – 5/16
1970 10/24 – until 1971 1/8
1971 6/14 – 9/2
1972 12/23 – until 1973 2/5
1976 6/2 – 7/22
1976 11/19 – until 1977 3/11
1978 6/18 – 8/30
1982 10/7 – 12/20
1984 12/7 – until 1985 1/20
1988 5/16 – 6/30
1990 6/1 – 8/13
1994 1/26 – 4/3
1994 9/19 – 12/4
1996 4/1 – 6/7
1996 11/18 – until 1997 1/4
2000 4/30 – 6/11
2001 9/21 – 12/14
2002 5/12 – 7/28
2005 12/29 – until 2006 5/12
2006 8/28 – 11/19
2008 3/3 – 7/21
2008 10/25 – 12/18
2012 4/12 – 5/25

SATURN BENEFICIAL
1941 4/22 – 7/17
1941 11/6 – until 1942 4/4
1945 6/25 – until 1946 7/25
1954 11/12 – until 1956 1/1
1956 5/28 – 9/29
1960 3/2 – 6/26
1960 11/29 – until 1961 2/26
1961 7/27 – 11/25
1970 6/2 – until 1971 1/1
1971 2/2 – 5/17
1974 8/6 – until 1975 2/9
1975 4/16 – 9/6
1976 1/27 – 5/25
1983 12/21 – until 1984 5/5
1984 9/16 – until 1985 11/8
1990 1/3 – until 1991 1/3
1999 7/23 – 10/7
2000 4/4 – 6/24
2000 12/9 – until 2001 3/11
2003 10/8 – 11/12
2004 6/8 – until 2005 7/8

URANUS BENEFICIAL
1938 6/15 – until 1941 5/13
1951 9/1 – until 1956 5/16
1977 11/18 – until 1981 10/30
1992 2/9 – until 1995 1/9

NEPTUNE BENEFICIAL
1961 12/31 – until 1970 10/5
1991 2/22 – until 1996 12/5

PLUTO BENEFICIAL
1938 1/22 – 6/25
1988 11/15 – until 1995 10/12

JUPITER CHALLENGING
1941 7/24 – until 1942 1/5
1942 3/8 – 6/5

1944 9/24 – until 1945 8/19
1947 12/21 – until 1948 11/10
1953 7/4 – until 1954 5/19
1956 9/8 – 12/3
1957 3/1 – 8/1
1959 12/6 – until 1960 2/23
1960 6/18 – 10/19
1965 6/17 – 9/11
1965 11/27 – until 1966 4/29
1968 8/24 – 11/9
1969 4/8 – 7/7
1971 11/20 – until 1972 2/1
1972 8/8 – 9/11
1977 6/1 – 8/14
1978 1/8 – 4/4
1980 8/7 – 10/22
1983 11/3 – until 1984 1/14
1989 5/16 – 7/25
1991 11/28 – until 1992 2/1
1992 7/20 – 10/5
1995 2/20 – 5/12
1995 10/15 – 12/29
2001 4/28 – 7/8
2003 10/31 – until 2004 3/12
2004 6/28 – 9/20
2007 1/25 – 6/21
2007 9/21 – 12/14
2012 8/18 – 11/20

SATURN CHALLENGING
1943 5/14 – until 1944 6/12
1949 9/29 – until 1950 4/24
1950 6/4 – 11/9
1951 3/21 – 8/3
1957 2/11 – 5/5
1957 11/5 – until 1958 12/27
1972 6/23 – until 1973 7/23
1974 1/23 – 4/4
1978 11/21 – until 1979 1/27
1979 8/6 – until 1980 9/12
1986 12/10 – until 1988 2/2
1988 6/24 – 11/1
2001 8/9 – 11/15
2002 4/26 – 9/29
2002 10/23 – until 2003 5/26
2008 9/12 – until 2009 10/20
2010 4/24 – 7/6

URANUS CHALLENGING
1944 8/28 – until 1949 5/22
1964 10/15 – until 1968 9/11
1984 2/9 – until 1988 11/13

NEPTUNE CHALLENGING
1938 1/1 – until 1942 9/5
1976 1/13 – until 1984 10/12

PLUTO CHALLENGING
1963 10/5 – until 1971 9/7
2000 12/10 – until 2008 10/20

JUPITER SPECIAL
1939 2/25 – 5/6
1939 11/19 – 11/30
1951 2/8 – 4/17
1963 1/21 – 3/30
1974 5/11 – 9/5
1974 12/29 – until 1975 3/14
1986 4/18 – until 1987 2/26
1998 3/30 – until 1999 2/8
2010 3/13 – 5/30
2010 9/17 – until 2011 1/16

SATURN SPECIAL
1965 4/13 – 9/18
1966 1/7 – 6/11
1966 8/10 – until 1967 2/23
1995 2/17 – until 1996 3/29

URANUS SPECIAL
2006 4/11 – until 2011 2/20

♓

March 12

SUN: PISCES · DECANATE: SCORPIO/PLUTO · DEGREE: 20°5–21°5 PISCES · MODE: MUTABLE · ELEMENT: WATER

Your Personal Powers

Friendly and helpful, you possess a versatile and enterprising personality with innate charm and social skills. Sensitive and imaginative, your deep feelings and natural intuition mean you can quickly comprehend another's moods. Being enthusiastic, you gain power from your creative ideas, diplomatic manner, and powers of self-expression. You may lose some of that power if you become insecure or discouraged by others. By developing your self-esteem, you are able to resist escapism and make the most of your outstanding natural talents. When you summon up the courage to be independent, you can also show your determined and ambitious nature. While you are often a visionary with inspired ideals, you also have a shrewd head for business and materialistic traits. Your youthful spirit implies that you are bright and animated, and your intelligence, when expressed through words and ideas, may help you creatively or financially. By staying focused and avoiding indecision, you can put in the necessary effort to perfect your work and achieve outstanding results.

Your Powers of Attraction in Relationships

Kind, witty, and entertaining, you attract friends and admirers. Although you can be a good partner or team player, you may need to find a balance between your own need for self-expression and your desire to be supportive of others. Very affectionate, your longing for love emphasizes the importance of your relationships. You are attracted to practical partners who are stable, loyal, and straightforward. Ideally, they can provide you with the security and support you need. You like to be direct with partners yourself but your stubborn streak may sometimes arise and cause you trouble. Being intelligent and aware of image, you need a partner you can be proud of. If this person can provide inspiration or a luxurious lifestyle, then so much the better.

Your attractive qualities: friendly, creative, people skills, sensitive, generous, entertaining, youthful, determined, imaginative, confident, business sense, visionary, charming, sociable, gift with words, dramatic, clever, talented, expressive, psychic, kindhearted

Your less attractive qualities: worry, indecisive, escapist, self-indulgent, insecure, avoid responsibility, escapism, over-indulgent, materialistic, scattered

Your Venus Power

The planet Venus has a great deal of influence on your powers of attraction. Below are four possible Venus types for women and men. To find your Venus you need to go to page 771, where you will find the Venus table and extra information. The planet Mars also affects your powers of attraction. To find your Mars table and interpretation go to page 761.

WOMEN WITH VENUS IN AQUARIUS: Sociable and gracious, you are usually sincere and capable of showing attributes of real tolerance and liberalism. Although you are keen on forming relationships, you also like to have freedom and act independently. Your intimate partnerships need to be founded on true friendships. Full of bright and progressive ideas, you can express yourself better when you are free and unrestricted. An ability to think in a dispassionate way suggests that you can stay detached. Your love of freedom also implies you can be loving and loyal without smothering your partner.

MEN WITH VENUS IN AQUARIUS: Ideally, in your relationships your lover is also your best friend. Since freedom of expression is a prerequisite to your well-being, you do better when left alone to do your own thing. You also need a partner who recognizes and appreciates your need for independence. Although usually friendly, at times you can be stubborn or your cool detachment can appear to others as distant or impersonal. Very sociable, however, you particularly enjoy the company of those who share your original, fair-minded, and progressive views.

WOMEN WITH VENUS IN PISCES: Being sensitive to affairs of the heart, when you care for someone you can feel their emotions and sense their every mood. This empathy indicates that you can love on an unselfish level, but you may have to guard against giving too much, especially to those who do not reciprocate. As you are seductive and captivating, partners can be fascinated by your subtle charms and attracted by your caring and affectionate nature.

MEN WITH VENUS IN PISCES: Romantic and idealistic when in love, you can be a sensitive and responsive lover. Being pliant and flexible with an impressionable nature helps you to adapt to the needs of others. In your desire to blend with those you love, however, guard against not clearly defining your own boundaries. With your affectionate and sentimental nature, you are often attracted to those who understand your sensitivity and share your vision.

WOMEN WITH VENUS IN ARIES: With your strong desires

and enthusiastic nature, you can be a passionate lover. Although idealistic and single-minded, you need to avoid unnecessary conflicts in your relationships by being more patient and less headstrong. Although at times others can accuse you of being bossy or impulsive, you possess a great deal of warmth and charm. When necessary, you can disarm others by making them feel important.

MEN WITH VENUS IN ARIES: Usually you are inclined to seek a partner who is active, goal-oriented, or decisive. Not known for your patience, you probably seek relationships from youth. You may find that you are more attracted to women who have a daring or adventurous spirit, but in your close relationships you may encounter rivalry or find that both you and your partner want to lead or be the boss. Although you may act rashly, you possess a great deal of magnetism and are capable of demonstrating your love and affection.

WOMEN WITH VENUS IN TAURUS: For your ideal relationship you seek partners who are both financially secure and demonstrative with their affections. With these thoughts in mind, you are likely to want a partner who is refined yet pragmatic or someone concerned with safeguarding your future. A stubborn streak suggests that even when you know you are in the wrong, you are reluctant to give way. Attracted to people with a good sense of style, you can succeed in all kinds of business partnerships, especially those involving the arts, music, and luxury goods.

MEN WITH VENUS IN TAURUS: Although usually you are drawn toward sensual and physically beautiful individuals, you want a partner who is reliable and loyal. When in love you enjoy buying your partner things of quality that will grow in value or useful things of a practical nature. You also love to socialize and entertain, especially in luxurious surroundings. Often you are attracted to creative people or those with artistic talents.

To read all about your Outer Planets and work out how to use your personalized timetable, go to Section Three, page 789.

Your Personalized Timetable

JUPITER BENEFICIAL
1941 3/30 – 5/13
1942 8/12 – until 1943 6/30
1946 11/29 – until 1947 10/23
1949 1/29 – 3/21
1949 7/22 – 11/13
1952 7/20 – 10/31
1953 3/8 – 4/26
1954 7/25 – 11/16
1954 11/16 – until 1955 6/12
1958 11/13 – until 1959 2/10
1959 4/25 – 10/5
1961 1/13 – 2/27
1964 6/25 – 12/19
1965 2/1 – 4/8
1966 7/9 – 9/27
1967 1/16 – 5/23
1970 10/28 – until 1971 1/14
1971 6/5 – 9/11
1972 12/28 – until 1973 2/9
1976 6/6 – 7/28
1976 11/12 – until 1977 3/17
1978 6/23 – 9/5
1979 3/2 – 4/19
1982 10/12 – 12/25
1984 12/12 – until 1985 1/24
1988 5/20 – 7/5
1988 12/29 – until 1989 2/11
1990 6/6 – 8/18
1994 2/7 – 3/22
1994 9/25 – 12/9
1996 4/13 – 5/25
1996 11/24 – until 1997 1/8
2000 5/4 – 6/16
2001 9/30 – 12/5
2002 5/18 – 8/1
2006 1/5 – 5/5
2006 9/4 – 11/23
2008 3/9 – 7/13
2008 11/1 – 12/23
2012 4/17 – 5/29

SATURN BENEFICIAL
1941 4/30 – 7/29
1941 10/24 – until 1942 4/13
1945 7/3 – until 1946 8/2
1954 11/20 – until 1956 1/12
1956 5/14 – 10/10
1960 3/15 – 6/11
1960 12/8 – until 1961 3/9
1961 7/14 – 12/6
1970 6/10 – 12/11
1971 2/23 – 5/25
1974 8/14 – until 1975 1/25
1975 4/30 – 9/16
1976 1/15 – 6/4
1984 1/1 – 4/21
1984 9/27 – until 1985 11/16
1990 1/12 – until 1991 1/11
1999 8/13 – 9/15
2000 4/13 – 7/3
2000 11/26 – until 2001 3/23
2004 6/16 – until 2005 7/16

URANUS BENEFICIAL
1938 7/8 – until 1942 3/12
1951 10/10 – until 1956 6/8
1977 12/4 – until 1981 11/15
1992 3/1 – until 1995 11/6

NEPTUNE BENEFICIAL
1962 11/25 – until 1970 11/5
1992 1/20 – until 1997 1/4

PLUTO BENEFICIAL
1938 1/1 – until 1939 6/11
1988 12/11 – until 1995 11/9

JUPITER CHALLENGING
1941 7/29 – 12/27
1942 3/17 – 6/10
1944 9/29 – until 1945 8/24
1947 12/26 – until 1948 11/15
1953 7/9 – until 1954 5/23
1956 9/13 – 12/12
1957 2/20 – 8/6
1959 12/10 – until 1960 3/1
1960 6/10 – 10/25
1965 6/22 – 9/20
1965 11/17 – until 1966 5/5
1968 8/28 – 11/15
1969 3/31 – 7/15
1971 11/24 – until 1972 2/6
1972 7/25 – 9/25
1977 6/5 – 8/20
1977 12/31 – until 1978 4/11
1980 8/12 – 10/27
1983 11/8 – until 1984 1/19
1989 5/20 – 7/30
1991 12/10 – until 1992 1/20
1992 7/25 – 10/10
1995 3/1 – 5/2
1995 10/21 – until 1996 1/3
2001 5/3 – 7/12
2003 11/6 – until 2004 3/4
2004 7/4 – 9/24
2007 1/31 – 6/13
2007 9/28 – 12/18
2012 8/26 – 11/12

SATURN CHALLENGING
1943 5/22 – until 1944 6/19
1949 10/8 – until 1950 4/4
1950 6/24 – 11/20
1951 3/8 – 8/13
1957 3/3 – 4/13
1957 11/14 – until 1959 1/5
1972 7/1 – until 1973 1/26
1973 3/3 – 8/1
1974 1/8 – 4/18
1979 8/14 – until 1980 9/21
1986 12/19 – until 1988 2/13
1988 6/11 – 11/11
2001 8/24 – 10/31
2002 5/4 – until 2003 6/3
2008 9/20 – until 2009 10/29
2010 4/8 – 7/20

URANUS CHALLENGING
1945 6/16 – until 1949 6/9
1964 11/5 – until 1969 6/19
1984 12/8 – until 1988 12/1

NEPTUNE CHALLENGING
1938 1/1 – until 1943 7/31
1976 3/6 – until 1984 11/19

PLUTO CHALLENGING
1963 11/14 – until 1972 7/28
2001 1/6 – until 2008 11/25

♓

March 13

SUN: PISCES · DECANT: SCORPIO/PLUTO · DEGREE: 21°5–22°5 PISCES · MODE: MUTABLE · ELEMENT: WATER

Your Personal Powers

Imaginative with a keen mind, you are a person who thinks in large terms and is success-oriented. Your ruling planet, Neptune, suggests that you also possess imagination, intuition, and strong feelings. You gain power from your communication skills, innate organizational abilities, and flair for dealing with people. Combined, these can often help you to commercialize your different talents. Nevertheless, avoid losing some of that power by compromising too much of yourself in your quest for material rewards. Usually generous, optimistic, and gregarious, you can network among many social groups. Being versatile, you usually have numerous ideas and plans for the future. Although usually easygoing, you enjoy taking the lead whether with friends or at work. Intelligent and sensitive, you can be persuasive or influence others, especially when you are enthusiastic. You can lose power, however, if you do not develop the necessary practical determination and perseverance to fulfill your large dreams. Since you value knowledge and have original ideas, your innovative approach can bring you much satisfaction and success.

Your Powers of Attraction in Relationships

Friendly and sensitive, you attract others with your sociable personality. When you turn on the charm you can make yourself popular. You are attracted to strong-willed individuals with powerful feelings. If your strong desires become too self-centered, however, they may reflect on your relationships and create tension. However, if you are able to channel your strong emotions into giving to others, you attract love without really trying. You are also drawn to successful or influential people who can motivate you with new ideas and opportunities. By developing your confidence and ability to express yourself, you can avoid having frustration or stubbornness affect your relationships. A good companion, you can be kind and generous and enjoy friendly interactions with others.

Your attractive qualities: ambitious, creative, fun-loving, charming, sincere, hardworking, success-oriented, business sense, sensitive, persuasive, honest, freedom-loving, expressive, initiative, enthusiastic, optimistic, thinks big, organizational abilities, intelligent

Your less attractive qualities: stubborn, impulsive, indecisive, materialistic, bossy, unemotional, rebellious, egotistical, skeptical, escapist, easily bored, prideful

Your Venus Power

The planet Venus has a great deal of influence on your powers of attraction. Below are four possible Venus types for women and men. To find your Venus you need to go to page 771, where you will find the Venus table and extra information. The planet Mars also affects your powers of attraction. To find your Mars table and interpretation go to page 761.

WOMEN WITH VENUS IN AQUARIUS: Sociable and gracious, you are usually sincere and capable of showing attributes of real tolerance and liberalism. Although you are keen on forming relationships, you also like to have freedom and act independently. Your intimate partnerships need to be founded on true friendships. Full of bright and progressive ideas, you can express yourself better when you are free and unrestricted. An ability to think in a dispassionate way suggests that you can stay detached. Your love of freedom also implies that you can be loving and loyal without smothering your partner.

MEN WITH VENUS IN AQUARIUS: Ideally, in your relationships your lover is also your best friend. Since freedom of expression is a prerequisite to your well-being, you do better when left alone to do your own thing. You also need a partner who recognizes and appreciates your need for independence. Although usually friendly, at times you can be stubborn or your cool detachment can appear to others as distant or impersonal. Very sociable, however, you particularly enjoy the company of those who share your original, fair-minded, and progressive views.

WOMEN WITH VENUS IN PISCES: A romantic and idealistic individual, you can be both loving and giving. While making allowances and sacrifices is understandable in a loving relationship, playing the martyr is often a state of romantic illusion. In relationships you may therefore need to balance the practical with the charitable. Nevertheless, your benevolence and sacrifices in the right relationship make you a devoted, kind, and compassionate partner. Subtle, sensitive, and alluring, you can be sensual and caring.

MEN WITH VENUS IN PISCES: The combination of your emotional subtlety and charm can make you very alluring

when dealing with affairs of the heart. Perceptive and impressionable, you have an easygoing style in your relationships, usually preferring to avoid ugly confrontation. You are drawn to a partner who has a touch of glamour and is sensitive to the needs of others. Alternatively, your partner can be a visionary with a rich imagination who can keep you enchanted.

WOMEN WITH VENUS IN ARIES: Idealistic, passionate, and adventurous, you are direct in your dealings with others. When you are attracted to a person you usually take the initiative and use your people skills to make things happen. In close relationships you are not afraid to confront your other half. This self-assertiveness is positive if differences can be brought into the open through diplomacy and compromise.

MEN WITH VENUS IN ARIES: As you often have the courage and strength to initiate situations, you like to take the lead. With your unconscious desire for conquest you may also have to beware of being competitive with your partners. Nevertheless, you are drawn to direct and strong-willed partners who can share your love of action and enthusiasm for life. When you are feeling good you can be charming and enthusiastic in romantic situations with an entertaining and spontaneous spirit.

WOMEN WITH VENUS IN TAURUS: Being physically attractive, you can make a good impression on the opposite sex. As security and stability in relationships are very important to you, you usually want a partner who is not only attractive but also reliable and a good provider. Being sensual or tactile, you also need a lover who is affectionate, but beware that your love does not show signs of possessiveness or jealousy. Your own sense of style and love of beauty implies that you can be attracted to creative people, especially those in art and music.

MEN WITH VENUS IN TAURUS: As you yourself may be attractive to the opposite sex, you desire a partner who is sensual and loving or possesses physical beauty. Needing stability, when faced with changes that are out of your control, you may become insecure or worried about your future. Faithful or loyal, you usually hang on to relationships but may display controlling tendencies. Your own sense of style and love of beauty imply that you can be attracted to creative people, especially those in art and music.

To read all about your Outer Planets and work out how to use your personalized timetable, go to Section Three, page 789.

ॐ

Your Personalized Timetable

JUPITER BENEFICIAL
1941 4/4 – 5/17
1942 8/17 – until 1943 7/5
1946 12/4 – until 1947 10/28
1949 2/3 – 3/27
1949 7/15 – 11/19
1952 7/27 – 10/24
1953 3/14 – 4/30
1954 7/30 – until 1955 6/17
1958 11/17 – until 1959 2/21
1959 4/14 – 10/10
1961 1/17 – 3/4
1961 9/4 – 10/13
1964 6/30 – 12/8
1965 2/12 – 4/13
1966 7/13 – 10/4
1967 1/9 – 5/29
1970 11/2 – until 1971 1/20
1971 5/28 – 9/18
1973 1/1 – 2/13
1976 6/11 – 8/4
1976 11/4 – until 1977 3/23
1978 6/27 – 9/10
1979 2/18 – 4/30
1982 10/17 – 12/30
1984 12/16 – until 1985 1/28
1988 5/25 – 7/10
1988 12/18 – until 1989 2/22
1990 6/11 – 8/22
1994 9/30 – 12/13
1996 11/29 – until 1997 1/12
2000 5/8 – 6/20
2001 10/12 – 11/23
2002 5/23 – 8/6
2006 1/11 – 4/27
2006 9/10 – 11/28
2008 3/15 – 7/5
2008 11/7 – 12/27
2012 4/21 – 6/2

SATURN BENEFICIAL
1941 5/8 – 8/15
1941 10/7 – until 1942 4/22
1945 7/11 – until 1946 8/10
1954 11/29 – until 1955 6/26
1955 8/11 – until 1956 1/24
1956 4/30 – 10/19
1960 4/3 – 5/22
1960 12/17 – until 1961 3/21
1961 6/29 – 12/16
1970 6/19 – 11/26
1971 3/8 – 6/2
1974 8/23 – until 1975 1/12
1975 5/12 – 9/28
1976 1/2 – 6/13
1984 1/14 – 4/7
1984 10/6 – until 1985 11/25
1990 1/20 – until 1991 1/20
2000 4/21 – 7/14
2000 11/14 – until 2001 4/2
2004 6/24 – until 2005 7/23

URANUS BENEFICIAL
1939 5/11 – until 1942 4/6
1952 7/18 – until 1956 6/27
1977 12/23 – until 1982 9/7
1992 4/8 – until 1995 12/4

NEPTUNE BENEFICIAL
1962 12/26 – until 1971 9/30
1992 2/18 – until 1997 12/1

PLUTO BENEFICIAL
1938 1/1 – until 1940 5/22
1989 1/18 – until 1996 9/26

JUPITER CHALLENGING
1941 8/4 – 12/19
1942 3/25 – 6/14
1944 10/4 – until 1945 8/29
1947 12/31 – until 1948 11/19
1953 7/14 – until 1954 5/28

1956 9/17 – 12/24
1957 2/8 – 8/12
1959 12/14 – until 1960 3/8
1960 6/2 – 10/31
1965 6/26 – 10/4
1965 11/3 – until 1966 5/10
1968 9/2 – 11/21
1969 3/23 – 7/22
1971 11/29 – until 1972 2/11
1972 7/15 – 10/4
1977 6/10 – 8/26
1977 12/24 – until 1978 4/18
1980 8/17 – 11/1
1981 5/9 – 6/14
1983 11/13 – until 1984 1/24
1989 5/24 – 8/4
1990 2/16 – 3/5
1992 7/30 – 10/15
1995 3/15 – 4/18
1995 10/26 – until 1996 1/7
2001 5/7 – 7/17
2003 11/13 – until 2004 2/25
2004 7/11 – 9/29
2007 2/6 – 6/5
2007 10/5 – 12/22
2012 9/4 – 11/3

SATURN CHALLENGING
1943 5/30 – until 1944 6/27
1949 10/17 – until 1950 3/21
1950 7/8 – 12/3
1951 2/22 – 8/22
1957 11/23 – until 1959 1/13
1959 8/11 – 9/29
1972 7/10 – until 1973 1/6
1973 3/23 – 8/10
1973 12/27 – until 1974 4/29
1979 8/23 – until 1980 9/29
1986 12/28 – until 1987 7/27
1987 9/10 – until 1988 2/26
1988 5/27 – 11/21
2001 9/22 – 10/2
2002 5/12 – until 2003 6/11
2008 9/28 – until 2009 5/11
2009 5/21 – 11/7
2010 3/26 – 8/1

URANUS CHALLENGING
1945 7/4 – until 1949 6/25
1965 9/3 – until 1969 7/27
1984 12/24 – until 1988 12/18

NEPTUNE CHALLENGING
1938 1/1 – until 1943 9/2
1977 1/9 – until 1985 9/30

PLUTO CHALLENGING
1964 10/4 – until 1972 8/29
2001 2/11 – until 2009 10/14

JUPITER SPECIAL
1939 3/6 – 5/16
1939 10/20 – 12/30
1951 2/17 – 4/25
1963 1/30 – 4/8
1974 5/25 – 8/20
1975 1/10 – 3/22
1986 4/28 – 10/4
1986 12/12 – until 1987 3/6
1998 4/8 – until 1999 2/17
2010 3/22 – 6/13
2010 9/1 – until 2011 1/27

SATURN SPECIAL
1938 1/1 – 1/26
1965 5/5 – 8/22
1966 1/27 – until 1967 3/11
1995 3/5 – until 1996 4/15
1996 11/14 – 12/22

URANUS SPECIAL
2007 3/10 – until 2012 1/5

743

March 14

SUN: PISCES • DECANATE: SCORPIO/PLUTO • DEGREE: 22°5–23°5 PISCES • MODE: MUTABLE • ELEMENT: WATER

Your Personal Powers

Intellectually bright with a strong imagination, you are a resourceful individual with quick responses and many ideas. You gain power from being dedicated to your work and your desire for honesty. As a versatile and industrious person, you are usually willing to explore different experiences to discover what really excites you. You may lose some of your power, however, if you become stubborn or overindulgent. Fortunately, you are helped in life by a unique sense of humor that enables you to release frustration. Receptive and sensitive with innate awareness, you can easily understand another's needs or feelings. Alternatively, your psychic abilities may lead you to explore metaphysical subjects. Although you grasp information very quickly, your need for variety and new experiences means that you can lose power to restlessness or impatience. When confident, you are proud and independent, with a broad-minded attitude. Able to take the initiative, your good evaluation skills and instinct for financial matters indicate that you only need the necessary self-discipline to achieve outstanding success.

Your Powers of Attraction in Relationships

Dramatic and mentally quick, you can be witty and entertaining. Energetic, you usually enjoy social activities. Although you like to be in charge, you enjoy working with others. Your close partnerships are an important area in your life, even if you do not always show it. Ideally, you need a partner who can match your astute mind and share your desire for new experiences. If you become bored, impatient, or experience inner fears in your relationships, you may become provocative or argumentative. When positive, however, you can be generous, giving, and helpful. Although you are sensitive, by developing a detached or philosophical viewpoint, you can avoid emotional tensions. Caring and protective toward your partner, you often improve your relationships when you both communicate well or share a passion for knowledge.

Your attractive qualities: intelligent, detached, decisive actions, hardworking, creative, pragmatic, imaginative, sincere, independent, determined, good evaluator, honest, idealist, objective, psychic, universal outlook, leadership potential, humorous, talented, versatile

Your less attractive qualities: easily bored, restless, thoughtless, frustrated, disappointed, stubborn, overly cautious or impulsive, inner tensions, irresponsible, overindulgent, extravagant

Your Venus Power

The planet Venus has a great deal of influence on your powers of attraction. Below are four possible Venus types for women and men. To find your Venus you need to go to page 771, where you will find the Venus table and extra information. The planet Mars also affects your powers of attraction. To find your Mars table and interpretation go to page 761.

WOMEN WITH VENUS IN AQUARIUS: Sociable and gracious, you are usually sincere and capable of showing attributes of real tolerance and liberalism. Although you are keen on forming relationships you also like to have freedom and act independently. Your intimate partnerships need to be founded on true friendships. Full of bright and progressive ideas, you can express yourself better when you are free and unrestricted. An ability to think in a dispassionate way suggests that you can stay detached. Your love of freedom also implies that you can be loving and loyal without smothering your partner.

MEN WITH VENUS IN AQUARIUS: Although independent, you often enjoy being part of a group. The partners you frequently attract are themselves nonconformists or free spirits. As an individual you may not find it easy to settle into a routine or an entirely mundane type of relationship. You may have some unconventional views on traditional marriage or your partner may hold such views. It is usually important to you that your love relationships are based on friendship.

WOMEN WITH VENUS IN PISCES: Being sensitive to other people, you are receptive to their moods and feelings. This affinity indicates that although you can be selfless, you may have to guard against being too sentimental or overly romantic, especially with those who can take advantage of your kindness. Nevertheless, alluring and seductive, your partners can be intrigued by your poetic soul or mysterious nature.

MEN WITH VENUS IN PISCES: Being adaptable and sensitive, you are able to intuitively feel the moods of those you love. Although you are receptive to others, you can be ambiguous about your own feelings toward your partner. Romantic and kindhearted, you long to be loved but you need to be realistic about your relationships in order to avoid disappoint-

ments. When in love you may idealize your partners and fail to see any faults in their personalities.

WOMEN WITH VENUS IN ARIES: With your strong desires and enthusiastic nature you can be a passionate lover. Although idealistic and single-minded, you need to avoid unnecessary conflicts in your relationships by being more patient and less headstrong. Although at times others can accuse you of being bossy or impulsive, you possess a great deal of warmth and charm. When necessary you can disarm others by making them feel important.

MEN WITH VENUS IN ARIES: Usually you are drawn to courageous or assertive women who possess strong personal magnetism. Therefore you find those who seem to be independent or action-oriented very attractive. Your own eagerness and need for activity suggest that you start relationships with great enthusiasm, especially if they offer you excitement or adventures. The challenge is often to maintain relationships and not become bored too easily.

WOMEN WITH VENUS IN TAURUS: Warm and affectionate, you are naturally tactile with a love of sensual pleasures. With a streak of the conventional, you love the simple pleasures of life, good food, close friends, and happy relationships. Having an inner strength, you can express genuine patience and are often a pillar of support for loved ones and friends. Although you possess endurance, be careful not to let this turn into plain stubbornness.

MEN WITH VENUS IN TAURUS: Although you are usually drawn to sensual and physically beautiful individuals, you want a partner who is reliable and loyal. When in love you enjoy buying your partner things of quality that will grow in value or useful things of a practical nature. You also love to socialize and entertain, especially in luxurious surroundings. Often you are attracted to creative people or those with artistic talents.

To read all about your Outer Planets and work out how to use your personalized timetable, go to Section Three, page 789.

Your Personalized Timetable

JUPITER BENEFICIAL
1941 4/8 – 5/22
1942 8/22 – until 1943 2/18
1943 4/2 – 7/9
1946 12/8 – until 1947 11/2
1949 2/7 – 4/4
1949 7/7 – 11/25
1952 8/4 – 10/15
1953 3/19 – 5/5
1954 8/3 – until 1955 6/22
1958 11/22 – until 1959 3/14
1959 3/24 – 10/15
1961 1/21 – 3/9
1961 8/22 – 10/25
1964 7/6 – 11/29
1965 2/21 – 4/17
1966 7/18 – 10/11
1966 12/31 – until 1967 6/3
1970 11/6 – until 1971 1/26
1971 5/20 – 9/24
1973 1/5 – 2/18
1976 6/15 – 8/13
1976 10/27 – until 1977 3/29
1978 7/2 – 9/15
1979 2/10 – 5/9
1982 10/22 – until 1983 1/4
1983 7/5 – 8/22
1984 12/21 – until 1985 2/2
1988 5/29 – 7/16
1988 12/9 – until 1989 3/3
1990 6/15 – 8/27
1994 10/5 – 12/18
1996 12/3 – until 1997 1/17
2000 5/12 – 6/25
2002 5/28 – 8/10
2006 1/19 – 4/18
2006 9/16 – 12/2
2008 3/22 – 6/27
2008 11/13 – until 2009 1/1
2012 4/25 – 6/7

SATURN BENEFICIAL
1941 5/16 – until 1942 4/30
1945 7/18 – until 1946 8/18
1954 12/8 – until 1955 6/5
1955 8/30 – until 1956 2/8
1956 4/14 – 10/29
1960 12/26 – until 1961 4/5
1961 6/13 – 12/25
1970 6/29 – 11/14
1971 3/19 – 6/10
1974 9/2 – 12/31
1975 5/22 – 10/12
1975 12/18 – until 1976 6/22
1984 2/1 – 3/18
1984 10/15 – until 1985 12/3
1990 1/29 – 9/6
1990 10/9 – until 1991 1/28
2000 4/29 – 7/25
2000 11/1 – until 2001 4/11
2004 7/1 – until 2005 7/31

URANUS BENEFICIAL
1939 5/28 – until 1942 4/26
1952 8/4 – until 1956 7/14
1978 1/18 – until 1982 10/5
1993 1/22 – until 1995 12/24

NEPTUNE BENEFICIAL
1963 11/23 – until 1971 11/2
1992 4/12 – until 1997 12/31

PLUTO BENEFICIAL
1938 1/1 – until 1940 7/6
1989 11/28 – until 1996 10/28

JUPITER CHALLENGING
1941 8/10 – 12/12
1942 4/1 – 6/18
1944 10/9 – until 1945 9/3

1948 1/4 – 11/24
1953 7/19 – until 1954 6/2
1956 9/22 – until 1957 8/17
1959 12/19 – until 1960 3/18
1960 5/23 – 11/5
1965 6/30 – until 1966 5/15
1968 9/6 – 11/28
1969 3/15 – 7/28
1971 12/3 – until 1972 2/17
1972 7/6 – 10/12
1977 6/14 – 9/1
1977 12/16 – until 1978 4/24
1980 8/21 – 11/6
1981 4/26 – 6/28
1983 11/17 – until 1984 1/28
1989 5/29 – 8/9
1990 1/29 – 3/23
1992 8/5 – 10/19
1995 10/31 – until 1996 1/11
2001 5/12 – 7/21
2003 11/20 – until 2004 2/17
2004 7/17 – 10/4
2007 2/13 – 5/28
2007 10/11 – 12/27
2012 9/18 – 10/20

SATURN CHALLENGING
1943 6/7 – until 1944 7/5
1949 10/26 – until 1950 3/8
1950 7/19 – 12/21
1951 2/2 – 8/31
1957 12/2 – until 1959 1/22
1959 7/22 – 10/18
1972 7/18 – 12/23
1973 4/5 – 8/21
1973 12/15 – until 1974 5/9
1979 8/31 – until 1980 10/7
1987 1/6 – 7/7
1987 9/30 – until 1988 3/14
1988 5/8 – 11/30
2002 5/20 – until 2003 6/19
2008 10/6 – until 2009 4/12
2009 6/20 – 11/18
2010 3/13 – 8/11

URANUS CHALLENGING
1945 7/23 – until 1950 4/27
1965 9/19 – until 1969 8/17
1985 1/11 – until 1989 10/17

NEPTUNE CHALLENGING
1938 1/1 – until 1944 7/24
1977 2/19 – until 1985 11/16

PLUTO CHALLENGING
1964 11/10 – until 1973 7/12
2001 12/29 – until 2009 11/22

JUPITER SPECIAL
1939 3/10 – 5/21
1939 10/11 – until 1940 1/7
1951 2/21 – 4/30
1963 2/4 – 4/12
1974 6/2 – 8/11
1975 1/15 – 3/26
1986 5/4 – 9/25
1986 12/21 – until 1987 3/10
1998 4/13 – until 1999 2/21
2010 3/26 – 6/23
2010 8/22 – until 2011 2/1

SATURN SPECIAL
1938 1/1 – 2/5
1965 5/19 – 8/7
1966 2/6 – until 1967 3/19
1995 3/13 – until 1996 4/24
1996 10/24 – until 1997 1/11

URANUS SPECIAL
2007 3/27 – Continues

♓

745

March 15

SUN: PISCES • DECANATE: SCORPIO/PLUTO • DEGREE: 23°5–24°5 PISCES • MODE: MUTABLE • ELEMENT: WATER

Your Personal Powers

Proud and dramatic with strong emotions, you are an individual with inner sensitivity and determination. Having a powerful imagination, you also possess innate psychic awareness. Very sensitive to your environment, you need to create a harmonious atmosphere both in your home or work. A tendency to become suspicious or too self-righteous means that you can lose power by being stubborn or disruptive. Nevertheless, determined, with a strong sense of values, once you have made your mind up, you push forward to your goals in a resolute manner. As someone who does not like to take orders, you may have to also guard against being too bossy or skeptical. Although independent and seemingly confident, by working on your self-esteem you can increase your faith and balance your fluctuating moods. Security-conscious, you prefer to build for a long-term future and, fortunately, you possess a gift for attracting money. You are highly intuitive, and your fast perceptive insight may lead you to the study of mystical subjects or help you overcome life's challenges to obtain success.

Your Powers of Attraction in Relationships

You can attract others with your friendly manner and determined character. Being sociable, you can be entertaining and generous. You are often drawn to sensitive and creative people with astute minds. Usually you prefer to work cooperatively with others. Although independent and self-reliant, your personal relationships are of major importance to you. Being receptive, you can easily pick up another's subtle moods. Yet it is equally important for you to express your own true feelings rather than be held back by doubt or indecision. Being sensitive, you value trust, security, and a peaceful home environment. By developing patience you can avoid becoming irritable or locked in power struggles. Romantic and loving, once committed to a relationship, you can be devoted, loyal, and supportive.

Your attractive qualities: friendly, imaginative, willing, generous, responsible, kind, sympathetic, psychic, entertaining, caring, inspired, idealistic, appreciative, perceptive, enthusiast, intuitive, home-loving, mystical, independent, creative, determined

Your less attractive qualities: moody, restlessness, bossy, mistrusting, impatient, fear of change, victim, self-doubt, arrogance, worry, escapist, indecisive, prideful, materialistic, misuses power, confused, stubborn, headstrong, opinionated

Your Venus Power

The planet Venus has a great deal of influence on your powers of attraction. Below are four possible Venus types for women and men. To find your Venus you need to go to page 771, where you will find the Venus table and extra information. The planet Mars also affects your powers of attraction. To find your Mars table and interpretation go to page 761.

WOMEN WITH VENUS IN AQUARIUS: Others are attracted to your honest, friendly, and easygoing attitude. You enjoy social interaction and have a genuine concern for others. In fact, at times your friends may be just as important as your partner. Usually you present a tolerant and reasonable front in love situations and attempt to view your relationships objectively. If partners become too demanding, however, you can become stubborn or awkward. Nevertheless, inventive and progressive, you enjoy the company of like-minded people who can share your original ideas.

MEN WITH VENUS IN AQUARIUS: You are sociable and liberal, and people are attracted by your friendly and easygoing style. Being independent, you value freedom-loving partners who give you the space to be yourself. Other people can sometimes interpret your detachment as being emotionally cool, but they admire your objectivity and humanitarian inclinations. You are attracted to intelligent individuals who are truthful and direct, but above all they must be true friends. Ideally, your partner shares your liberal views on life and possesses a strong sense of individuality.

WOMEN WITH VENUS IN PISCES: Being sensitive to other people, you are receptive to their moods and feelings. This affinity means that although you can be selfless, you may have to guard against being too sentimental or overly romantic, especially of those who can take advantage of your kindness. Nevertheless, as you are alluring and seductive, your partners can be intrigued by your poetic soul or mysterious nature.

MEN WITH VENUS IN PISCES: Being adaptable and sensitive, you are able to intuitively feel the moods of those you love. Although you are receptive to others, you can be ambiguous about your own feelings toward your partner. Romantic and kindhearted, you long to be loved but you need to be real-

istic about your relationships in order to avoid disappointments. When in love you may idealize your partners and fail to see any faults in their personality.

WOMEN WITH VENUS IN ARIES: Idealistic, passionate, and adventurous, you are direct in your dealings with others. When you are attracted to a person you usually take the initiative and use your people skills to make things happen. In close relationships you are not afraid to confront your other half. This self-assertiveness is positive if differences can be brought into the open through diplomacy and compromise.

MEN WITH VENUS IN ARIES: As you often have the courage and strength to initiate situations, you like to take the lead. With your unconscious desire for conquest you may also have to beware of being competitive with your partners. Nevertheless, you are drawn to direct and strong-willed partners who can share your love of action and enthusiasm for life. When you are feeling good you can be charming and enthusiastic in romantic situations with an entertaining and spontaneous spirit.

WOMEN WITH VENUS IN TAURUS: Good-natured and romantic, you have a highly developed sense of touch that particularly responds to massage, hugs, and all things physical. Being friendly, you enjoy socializing and are able to put others at their ease. With your natural sense of beauty and harmony, your charm can attract others. Although you can be lavish toward your partner, you may have to be careful that you do not overdo things.

MEN WITH VENUS IN TAURUS: As you yourself may be attractive to the opposite sex, you desire a partner who is sensual and loving or possesses physical beauty. Needing stability, when faced with changes that are out of your control you may become insecure or worried about your future. Faithful or loyal, you usually hang on to relationships but may display controlling tendencies. Your own sense of style and love of beauty imply that you can be attracted to creative people, especially those in art and music.

To read all about your Outer Planets and work out how to use your personalized timetable, go to Section Three, page 789.

Your Personalized Timetable

JUPITER BENEFICIAL
1941 4/13 – 5/26
1942 8/27 – until 1943 2/6
1943 4/14 – 7/14
1946 12/13 – until 1947 11/6
1949 2/12 – 4/12
1949 6/28 – 11/30
1952 8/15 – 10/4
1953 3/24 – 5/9
1954 8/8 – until 1955 6/27
1958 11/27 – until 1959 10/20
1961 1/26 – 3/15
1961 8/13 – 11/3
1964 7/11 – 11/21
1965 2/28 – 4/22
1966 7/22 – 10/21
1966 12/22 – until 1967 6/9
1970 11/11 – until 1971 2/2
1971 5/12 – 10/1
1973 1/10 – 2/23
1976 6/20 – 8/22
1976 10/17 – until 1977 4/3
1978 7/6 – 9/21
1979 2/2 – 5/17
1982 10/26 – until 1983 1/10
1983 6/23 – 9/2
1984 12/25 – until 1985 2/6
1988 6/2 – 7/21
1988 12/1 – until 1989 3/10
1990 6/20 – 9/1
1994 10/10 – 12/23
1996 12/8 – until 1997 1/21
2000 5/16 – 6/30
2002 6/2 – 8/15
2006 1/28 – 4/9
2006 9/22 – 12/7
2008 3/30 – 6/19
2008 11/19 – until 2009 1/5
2012 4/29 – 6/11

SATURN BENEFICIAL
1941 5/24 – until 1942 5/8
1945 7/26 – until 1946 8/26
1947 3/1 – 5/7
1954 12/17 – until 1955 5/22
1955 9/13 – until 1956 11/7
1961 1/3 – until 1962 1/3
1970 7/9 – 11/2
1971 3/29 – 6/18
1972 1/12 – 2/19
1974 9/14 – 12/18
1975 5/31 – 11/8
1975 11/20 – until 1976 7/1
1984 10/24 – until 1985 12/11
1990 2/7 – 8/14
1990 11/1 – until 1991 2/6
2000 5/6 – 8/8
2000 10/17 – until 2001 4/20
2004 7/9 – until 2005 8/8

URANUS BENEFICIAL
1939 6/16 – until 1942 5/14
1952 8/23 – until 1957 4/22
1978 11/12 – until 1982 10/25
1993 2/9 – until 1996 1/11

NEPTUNE BENEFICIAL
1963 12/22 – until 1972 9/23
1993 2/13 – until 1998 11/25

PLUTO BENEFICIAL
1938 1/1 – until 1941 6/21
1989 12/26 – until 1997 9/1

JUPITER CHALLENGING
1941 8/16 – 12/4
1942 4/7 – 6/23
1944 10/14 – until 1945 9/8

1948 1/9 – 11/29
1953 7/24 – until 1954 1/24
1954 2/27 – 6/6
1956 9/27 – until 1957 8/22
1959 12/23 – until 1960 3/30
1960 5/11 – 11/11
1965 7/5 – until 1966 5/20
1968 9/11 – 12/5
1969 3/7 – 8/3
1971 12/7 – until 1972 2/23
1972 6/28 – 10/19
1977 6/18 – 9/8
1977 12/9 – until 1978 4/30
1980 8/26 – 11/12
1981 4/16 – 7/8
1983 11/22 – until 1984 2/2
1989 6/2 – 8/15
1990 1/19 – 4/2
1992 8/10 – 10/24
1995 11/5 – until 1996 1/16
2001 5/16 – 7/26
2003 11/29 – until 2004 2/8
2004 7/23 – 10/8
2007 2/21 – 5/20
2007 10/17 – 12/31

SATURN CHALLENGING
1943 6/14 – until 1944 7/13
1949 11/6 – until 1950 2/24
1950 7/29 – until 1951 9/8
1957 12/10 – until 1959 2/1
1959 7/7 – 10/31
1972 7/28 – 12/11
1973 4/16 – 9/1
1973 12/2 – until 1974 5/18
1979 9/8 – until 1980 10/15
1987 1/15 – 6/22
1987 10/14 – until 1988 12/9
2002 5/28 – until 2003 6/26
2008 10/15 – until 2009 3/27
2009 7/5 – 11/30
2010 2/28 – 8/21

URANUS CHALLENGING
1945 8/19 – until 1950 5/18
1965 10/5 – until 1969 9/3
1985 2/1 – until 1989 11/11

NEPTUNE CHALLENGING
1938 1/1 – until 1944 8/28
1978 1/6 – until 1985 12/14

PLUTO CHALLENGING
1965 10/2 – until 1973 8/21
2002 1/29 – until 2010 10/7

JUPITER SPECIAL
1939 3/14 – 5/27
1939 10/4 – until 1940 1/14
1951 2/25 – 5/5
1963 2/8 – 4/16
1974 6/13 – 7/31
1975 1/20 – 3/30
1986 5/10 – 9/18
1986 12/28 – until 1987 3/15
1998 4/18 – until 1999 2/26
2010 3/30 – 7/6
2010 8/9 – until 2011 2/6

SATURN SPECIAL
1938 1/1 – 2/15
1965 6/9 – 7/16
1966 2/14 – until 1967 3/27
1995 3/21 – until 1996 5/3
1996 10/10 – until 1997 1/24

URANUS SPECIAL
2007 4/16 – until 2012 2/25

♓

747

March 16

Your Personal Powers

Friendly and thoughtful, you possess a caring nature and keen insight. Being sensitive, you are also receptive to the feelings of others. You gain power from your ability to combine both the analytical and imaginative sides of your nature. A tendency to become overly serious means that you can lose power if you allow skepticism or anxiety to override your natural spontaneity. Usually you possess a strong sense of responsibility, especially toward home and family, and a desire for greater knowledge or understanding. An innate comprehension of power structures and a willingness to work hard can usually bring you material success. Alternatively, you also possess loving, mystical, or compassionate qualities that need to be developed and expressed creatively. These innate capabilities may lead you to the arts, healing work, or psychic explorations. You empower yourself when you balance your inspired ideas with your responsibilities. Developing inner faith and helping others can also enhance your powers and help you to achieve remarkable results.

Your Powers of Attraction in Relationships

Your insight and thoughtful personality can attract others. Romantic and loving, you can be loyal to your partner and generous with loved ones. Be careful not to martyr yourself unless you receive love in equal measure. Nevertheless, your sensitive feelings indicate your potential for compassion and universal love. If you become negative, however, you may become too self-absorbed or feel sorry for yourself. The more you work on building your self-esteem or self-worth, the more balanced your relationships become. You are attracted to people with a youthful spirit or who have charm and style. Although receptive and idealistic, financial security and stability can also be a high priority. In your desire to make people happy you can be a caring and faithful partner or parent.

Your attractive qualities: sensitive, caring, responsible, home-loving, integrity, loving, intuitive, friendly, intelligent, cooperative, spiritual potential, spontaneous, thoughtful, charm, enterprising, insightful, idealistic, kind, youthful, devoted, romantic, artistic, compassionate

Your less attractive qualities: inner tensions, too serious, lonely, interfering, never satisfied, self-absorbed, escapist, opinionated, cold, skeptical, cynical, self-pity, worry, irritable, selfish

Your Venus Power

The planet Venus has a great deal of influence on your powers of attraction. Below are four possible Venus types for women and men. To find your Venus you need to go to page 771, where you will find the Venus table and extra information. The planet Mars also affects your powers of attraction. To find your Mars table and interpretation go to page 761.

WOMEN WITH VENUS IN AQUARIUS: Sociable and gracious, you are usually sincere and capable of showing attributes of real tolerance and liberalism. Although you are keen on forming relationships, you also like to have freedom and act independently. Your intimate partnerships need to be founded on true friendships. Full of bright and progressive ideas, you can express yourself better when you are free and unrestricted. An ability to think in a dispassionate way suggests that you can stay detached. Your love of freedom also implies that you can be loving and loyal without smothering your partner.

MEN WITH VENUS IN AQUARIUS: Although independent, you often enjoy being part of a group. The partners you frequently attract are themselves nonconformists or free spirits. As an individual, you may not find it easy to settle into a routine or an entirely mundane type of relationship. You may have some unconventional views on traditional marriage or your partner may hold such views. As a nonconformist, you may also be interested in alternative lifestyles such as collective living.

WOMEN WITH VENUS IN PISCES: Romantic and impressionable, you are a caring and loving individual with a dreamy nature. In relationships you are often attracted to idealistic, compassionate, or sympathetic individuals who have imagination or a strong romantic sense. A tendency to be sensitive to others suggests that you are intuitive and aware of people's inner feelings. Be careful, therefore, not to get caught in other people's dramas or play the rescuer too often.

MEN WITH VENUS IN PISCES: As a romantic and generous person, you are attracted to imaginative or artistic partners who can be sensitive and generous. While you are willing to make allowances for loved ones, playing the martyr in relationships can lead to others taking advantage of your kind na-

ture. Nevertheless, giving and loving, you are usually willing to forgive your partner's shortcomings.

WOMEN WITH VENUS IN ARIES: You gain power from your strong individuality, energy, and enthusiasm. Your young-at-heart and spirited approach to relationships adds to your appeal. If you become too impatient or self-absorbed, however, your partnerships are likely to suffer. Nevertheless, you can be creative, sharp, and quick, especially when you are able to share new and exciting projects with your partners. Mischievous with a love of action, you may even incite them to a playful fight.

MEN WITH VENUS IN ARIES: You are drawn to strong, independent women who can stand up to you. Although you can enthusiastically follow the object of your desire, you may lose power if you allow your forceful emotions to become too dominant. Warm and passionate, you have a side to your nature that longs for new adventures. Romantic and chivalrous, you really enjoy the excitement of the initial chase, but unless you keep the enthusiasm alive and avoid falling into a rut you may become easily bored.

WOMEN WITH VENUS IN TAURUS: For your ideal relationship you seek partners who are both financially secure and demonstrative with their affections. With these thoughts in mind, you are likely to want a partner who is refined yet pragmatic or someone concerned with safeguarding your future. A stubborn streak suggests that even when you know you are in the wrong, you are reluctant to give way. Attracted to people with a good sense of style, you can succeed in all kinds of business partnerships, especially those involving the arts, music, and luxury goods.

MEN WITH VENUS IN TAURUS: As well as attracting people with your warm personality, you also possess an innate sense of the value of material possessions. Keeping yourself stylish and having an attractive appearance can also be important to you. You are naturally attracted to practical yet sensual women who understand your need for comfort, security, and the pleasures and luxuries of life. Naturally affectionate, you enjoy socializing but can make a loyal and loving partner.

To read all about your Outer Planets and work out how to use your personalized timetable, go to Section Three, page 789.

Your Personalized Timetable

JUPITER BENEFICIAL
1941 4/17 – 5/30
1942 9/1 – until 1943 1/28
1943 4/23 – 7/19
1946 12/18 – until 1947 7/4
1947 7/28 – 11/11
1949 2/17 – 4/22
1949 6/17 – 12/5
1952 9/4 – 9/15
1953 3/29 – 5/13
1954 8/13 – until 1955 7/2
1958 12/1 – until 1959 10/25
1961 1/30 – 3/20
1961 8/4 – 11/11
1964 7/17 – 11/14
1965 3/7 – 4/26
1966 7/27 – 11/3
1966 12/9 – until 1967 6/14
1970 11/15 – until 1971 2/10
1971 5/4 – 10/6
1973 1/14 – 2/27
1976 6/25 – 9/6
1976 10/2 – until 1977 4/8
1978 7/10 – 9/27
1979 1/25 – 5/23
1982 10/31 – until 1983 1/15
1983 6/14 – 9/11
1984 12/29 – until 1985 2/10
1988 6/7 – 7/27
1988 11/24 – until 1989 3/17
1990 6/24 – 9/6
1991 3/15 – 4/14
1994 10/15 – 12/28
1996 12/13 – until 1997 1/25
2000 5/21 – 7/4
2002 6/7 – 8/19
2006 2/8 – 3/29
2006 9/27 – 12/11
2008 4/8 – 6/9
2008 11/24 – until 2009 1/9
2012 5/4 – 6/15

SATURN BENEFICIAL
1941 5/31 – until 1942 5/16
1945 8/3 – until 1946 9/3
1947 2/14 – 5/21
1954 12/27 – until 1955 5/8
1955 9/24 – until 1956 11/15
1961 1/12 – until 1962 1/11
1970 7/22 – 10/19
1971 4/7 – 6/26
1971 12/23 – until 1972 3/9
1974 9/28 – 12/3
1975 6/9 – until 1976 7/9
1984 11/1 – until 1985 12/20
1986 7/4 – 9/9
1990 2/16 – 7/29
1990 11/15 – until 1991 2/14
1991 9/5 – 11/3
2000 5/14 – 9/5
2000 9/19 – until 2001 4/28
2004 7/17 – until 2005 8/16

URANUS BENEFICIAL
1939 7/8 – until 1943 3/8
1952 9/17 – until 1957 5/30
1978 11/29 – until 1982 11/11
1993 3/1 – until 1996 11/4

NEPTUNE BENEFICIAL
1964 11/19 – until 1972 10/29
1993 3/25 – until 1998 12/28

PLUTO BENEFICIAL
1938 1/1 – until 1942 6/2
1990 11/15 – until 1997 10/16

JUPITER CHALLENGING
1941 8/23 – 11/27

1942 4/13 – 6/27
1944 10/19 – until 1945 4/28
1945 5/30 – 9/13
1948 1/14 – 12/3
1953 7/29 – until 1954 1/11
1954 3/12 – 6/11
1956 10/1 – until 1957 8/27
1959 12/28 – until 1960 11/16
1965 7/10 – until 1966 5/25
1968 9/16 – 12/14
1969 2/27 – 8/9
1971 12/12 – until 1972 3/1
1972 6/21 – 10/25
1977 6/22 – 9/17
1977 11/30 – until 1978 5/5
1980 8/31 – 11/17
1981 4/7 – 7/16
1983 11/26 – until 1984 2/7
1984 8/7 – 9/21
1989 6/6 – 8/20
1990 1/10 – 4/10
1992 8/15 – 10/29
1995 11/10 – until 1996 1/21
2001 5/21 – 7/31
2003 12/10 – until 2004 1/28
2004 7/28 – 10/13
2007 3/2 – 5/11
2007 10/23 – until 2008 1/5

SATURN CHALLENGING
1943 6/22 – until 1944 7/21
1945 2/24 – 3/15
1949 11/19 – until 1950 2/10
1950 8/7 – until 1951 9/16
1957 12/18 – until 1959 2/11
1959 6/24 – 11/11
1972 8/7 – 11/28
1973 4/25 – 9/17
1973 11/16 – until 1974 5/26
1979 9/15 – until 1980 10/23
1981 5/2 – 7/8
1987 1/25 – 6/8
1987 10/25 – until 1988 12/17
2002 6/5 – until 2003 7/4
2008 10/24 – until 2009 3/14
2009 7/17 – 12/16
2010 2/11 – 8/30

URANUS CHALLENGING
1946 6/15 – until 1950 6/6
1965 10/24 – until 1969 9/20
1985 3/11 – until 1989 11/30

NEPTUNE CHALLENGING
1938 1/1 – until 1945 7/16
1978 2/11 – until 1986 11/11

PLUTO CHALLENGING
1965 11/6 – until 1973 9/18
2002 12/22 – until 2010 11/21

JUPITER SPECIAL
1939 3/18 – 6/2
1939 9/26 – until 1940 1/20
1951 3/1 – 5/9
1963 2/12 – 4/20
1975 1/25 – 4/3
1986 5/16 – 9/10
1987 1/3 – 3/19
1998 4/22 – until 1999 3/2
2010 4/4 – until 2011 2/11

SATURN SPECIAL
1938 1/1 – 2/24
1966 2/23 – until 1967 4/4
1995 3/30 – until 1996 5/13
1996 9/27 – until 1997 2/4

URANUS SPECIAL
2007 5/10 – until 2012 3/14

March 17

SUN: PISCES • DECANATE: SCORPIO/PLUTO • DEGREE: 25°5–26°5 PISCES • MODE: MUTABLE • ELEMENT: WATER

Your Personal Powers

Sensitive, charming, and highly intuitive, you are an imaginative individual with a frank and honest approach. You gain power from your quick intelligence and thoughtful personality. Although sensitive, you can be mentally sharp, and pragmatic or enterprising in the business world. With your powerful emotions and inspired ideas you possess a strong need for self-expression. If you do not allow self-doubt or anxiety to deter you, your innate artistic or creative gifts can help you achieve success. As you also possess a desire for peace, harmony, and security, your home can be especially significant as a refuge from the world. Idealistic with strong opinions and a natural sense of fair play, you will usually fight for justice. Although you are often optimistic and enthusiastic, be careful not to lose power by allowing your frustrations or disappointments to make you critical or irritable. You empower yourself and attract success when you combine your imaginative ideas with your common sense and your diplomatic or negotiating skills.

Your Powers of Attraction in Relationships

Sociable and magnetic, you have a flair for people and can easily attract friends and admirers. A good companion with a friendly nature, you can be amusing and entertaining. Although you have the ability to charm or enchant others, you can also show compassion and stand up for the rights of others. With your powerful emotions you want a partner who can match your loyalty and intense feelings. Although you may have to be discriminating in your choice of partners, you are drawn to successful and confident individuals. Usually you are friendly and charismatic with a gift for making others feel special. Although you need to resist harming your partnerships by being stubborn, you can be very generous and supportive with loved ones or become an adviser for others.

Your attractive qualities: imaginative, sensitive, strong-willed, thoughtful, analytical, friendly, business sense, caring, attracts money, creative, intelligent, individualist, honest, precise, quick responses, artistic, scientific, determined, loves harmony, confident, charming, idealist

Your less attractive qualities: stubborn, carelessness, too detached, sensitive, escapist, moody, self-centered, lonely, critical, frustrated, disappointed, worried, suspicious, anxious

Your Venus Power

The planet Venus has a great deal of influence on your powers of attraction. Below are four possible Venus types for women and men. To find your Venus you need to go to page 771, where you will find the Venus table and extra information. The planet Mars also affects your powers of attraction. To find your Mars table and interpretation go to page 761.

WOMEN WITH VENUS IN AQUARIUS: You attract and impress others with your friendly approach and progressive ideas. As you are usually independent and easygoing, you value freedom within a relationship. A good companion with a sense of your own person, you enjoy socializing, especially with people who are original, cosmopolitan, and have a strong sense of individuality. Although being friendly and detached usually serves you well, avoid losing touch with your emotions. You usually prefer the company of those who have innovative or progressive views.

MEN WITH VENUS IN AQUARIUS: Friendly and honest, you attract people with your broad-minded approach to life. You usually possess an objective and slightly detached attitude toward affairs of the heart. If you are too removed, however, others can misinterpret your behavior as uncaring. It is often more important to you that your love relationships are based on friendship and honesty rather than intense passion. As you are generally tolerant and liberal, you may be drawn to less conventional relationships.

WOMEN WITH VENUS IN PISCES: As a romantic and idealist, you can be both loving and giving. While making allowances and sacrifices is understandable in a loving relationship, playing the martyr is often a state of romantic illusion. In relationships you may therefore need to balance the practical with the charitable. Nevertheless, your benevolence and sacrifices in the right relationship make you a devoted and kind partner. Subtle, sensitive, and alluring, you can be sensual and caring.

MEN WITH VENUS IN PISCES: The combination of your emotional subtlety and charm can make you very alluring when dealing with affairs of the heart. Perceptive and impressionable, you have an easygoing style in your relationships, usually preferring to avoid ugly confrontation. You are drawn to a partner who has a touch of glamour and is sensitive to the needs of others. Alternatively, your partner can be a visionary with a rich imagination who can keep you enchanted.

WOMEN WITH VENUS IN ARIES: With your strong desires

and enthusiastic nature, you can be a passionate lover. Although idealistic and single-minded, you need to avoid unnecessary conflicts in your relationships by being more patient and less headstrong. Although at times others can accuse you of being bossy or impulsive, you possess a great deal of warmth and charm. When necessary you can disarm others by making them feel important.

MEN WITH VENUS IN ARIES: As you often have the courage and strength to initiate situations, you like to take the lead. With your unconscious desire for conquest you may also have to beware of being competitive with your partners. Nevertheless, you are drawn to direct and strong-willed partners who can share your love of action and enthusiasm for life. When you are feeling good you can be charming and enthusiastic in romantic situations with an entertaining and spontaneous spirit.

WOMEN WITH VENUS IN TAURUS: For your ideal relationship you seek partners who are both financially secure and demonstrative with their affections. With these thoughts in mind, you are likely to want a partner who is refined yet pragmatic or someone concerned with safeguarding your future. A stubborn streak suggests that even when you know you are in the wrong you are reluctant to give way. Attracted to people with a good sense of style, you can succeed in all kinds of business partnerships, especially those involving the arts, music, and luxury goods.

MEN WITH VENUS IN TAURUS: Attractive and affectionate, in relationships you are often faithful with a conservative outlook. You are drawn to warmhearted partners with whom you can share a familiar routine as well as life's pleasures and comforts. Seeking a partner who is dependable or reassuring, you often put security high on your priority list when looking for love. Your sociability and friendliness usually make you popular and partners often admire your good sense of values and practical skills.

To read all about your Outer Planets and work out how to use your personalized timetable, go to Section Three, page 789.

Your Personalized Timetable

JUPITER BENEFICIAL
1941 4/22 – 6/3
1942 9/7 – until 1943 1/20
1943 5/1 – 7/23
1946 12/24 – until 1947 6/17
1947 8/13 – 11/16
1949 2/21 – 5/8
1949 6/1 – 12/10
1953 4/3 – 5/17
1954 8/17 – until 1955 7/7
1958 12/6 – until 1959 10/30
1961 2/4 – 3/26
1961 7/27 – 11/17
1964 7/24 – 11/6
1965 3/13 – 5/1
1966 7/31 – until 1967 6/19
1970 11/20 – until 1971 2/19
1971 4/24 – 10/12
1973 1/18 – until 1973 3/4
1976 6/30 – 12/25
1977 2/5 – 4/13
1978 7/15 – 10/4
1979 1/18 – 5/30
1982 11/4 – until 1983 1/21
1983 6/6 – 9/19
1985 1/3 – 2/15
1988 6/11 – 8/3
1988 11/16 – until 1989 3/23
1990 6/29 – 9/11
1991 3/1 – 4/29
1994 10/19 – until 1995 1/2
1996 12/17 – until 1997 1/29
2000 5/25 – 7/9
2001 1/4 – 2/15
2002 6/12 – 8/24
2006 10/3 – 12/16
2008 4/22 – 5/26
2008 11/29 – until 2009 1/13
2012 5/8 – 6/20

SATURN BENEFICIAL
1941 6/9 – until 1942 1/5
1942 2/9 – 5/23
1945 8/11 – until 1946 2/15
1946 4/22 – 9/13
1947 2/1 – 6/2
1955 1/7 – 4/25
1955 10/4 – until 1956 11/24
1961 1/20 – until 1962 1/20
1970 8/7 – 10/2
1971 4/15 – 7/5
1971 12/9 – until 1972 3/22
1975 6/17 – until 1976 7/16
1984 11/10 – until 1985 12/29
1986 6/17 – 9/24
1990 2/26 – 7/16
1990 11/26 – until 1991 2/24
1991 8/18 – 11/20
2000 5/22 – until 2001 5/6
2004 7/24 – until 2005 8/24
2006 3/12 – 4/30

URANUS BENEFICIAL
1939 8/18 – until 1943 4/5
1953 7/13 – until 1957 6/20
1978 12/16 – until 1982 11/28
1993 4/1 – until 1996 12/4

NEPTUNE BENEFICIAL
1964 12/18 – until 1973 9/16
1994 2/9 – until 1999 11/17

PLUTO BENEFICIAL
1938 1/1 – until 1942 7/13
1990 12/11 – until 1997 11/13

JUPITER CHALLENGING
1941 8/31 – 11/19
1942 4/18 – 7/2
1944 10/24 – until 1945 4/14

1945 6/14 – 9/17
1948 1/19 – 12/8
1953 8/3 – until 1954 1/1
1954 3/22 – 6/15
1956 10/6 – until 1957 9/1
1960 1/1 – 11/20
1965 7/14 – until 1966 5/29
1968 9/20 – 12/24
1969 2/16 – 8/14
1971 12/16 – until 1972 3/8
1972 6/13 – 10/31
1977 6/27 – 9/26
1977 11/20 – until 1978 5/11
1980 9/4 – 11/23
1981 3/30 – 7/24
1983 12/1 – until 1984 2/13
1984 7/26 – 10/3
1989 6/11 – 8/26
1990 1/3 – 4/18
1992 8/19 – 11/3
1993 5/22 – 6/11
1995 11/15 – until 1996 1/25
2001 5/25 – 8/5
2004 8/2 – 10/18
2007 3/13 – 4/29
2007 10/28 – until 2008 1/9

SATURN CHALLENGING
1943 6/30 – until 1944 7/29
1945 1/30 – 4/9
1949 12/6 – until 1950 1/23
1950 8/16 – until 1951 9/24
1957 12/27 – until 1959 2/23
1959 6/10 – 11/21
1972 8/20 – 11/15
1973 5/4 – until 1974 6/3
1979 9/23 – until 1980 11/1
1981 4/16 – 7/23
1987 2/6 – 5/25
1987 11/4 – until 1988 12/26
2002 6/13 – until 2003 7/12
2008 11/4 – until 2009 3/2
2009 7/27 – until 2010 9/7

URANUS CHALLENGING
1946 7/2 – until 1950 6/22
1965 11/16 – until 1970 7/6
1985 12/22 – until 1989 12/18

NEPTUNE CHALLENGING
1938 1/1 – until 1945 8/25
1979 1/3 – until 1986 12/11

PLUTO CHALLENGING
1966 9/30 – until 1974 8/10
2003 1/20 – until 2011 9/27

JUPITER SPECIAL
1939 3/22 – 6/9
1939 9/19 – until 1940 1/26
1951 3/5 – 5/14
1951 11/10 – 12/19
1963 2/17 – 4/25
1975 1/30 – 4/8
1986 5/22 – 9/2
1987 1/9 – 3/23
1998 4/27 – 10/23
1998 12/4 – until 1999 3/6
2010 4/8 – until 2011 2/16

SATURN SPECIAL
1938 1/1 – 3/4
1966 3/3 – until 1967 4/12
1995 4/7 – 10/19
1995 12/24 – until 1996 5/24
1996 9/14 – until 1997 2/14

URANUS SPECIAL
2008 3/13 – Continues

♓

March 18

SUN: PISCES • DECANATE: SCORPIO/PLUTO • DEGREE: 26°5–27°5 PISCES • MODE: MUTABLE • ELEMENT: WATER

Your Personal Powers

Sensitive yet determined, you are an intelligent individual with a strong imagination. You gain power when you unite the extremes of your personality, making you both ambitious and organized yet modest and progressive. With your emotional perceptiveness you do best when you act on instincts or trust your strong sixth sense. You lose power, however, if you allow restlessness or impatience to distract you from the discipline needed to fulfill your high potential. Nevertheless, you can use your astute insight to initiate positive change or to observe human nature. Some of your challenges may come linked to fluctuations in your money situation. By developing your perseverance and long-term vision, you can usually avoid this material insecurity. As a visionary and talented individual, you can achieve remarkable results if you develop patience and self-esteem. When positive and inspired, you can be generous and altruistic with a genuine desire to help others. If you are willing to put in the work necessary, you possess the potential for achievement and excellent financial reward.

Your Powers of Attraction in Relationships

Your quick intelligence and insight can attract others. Ideally, in relationships you need someone intelligent with whom you can discuss your ideas and interests. You are also attracted to individuals who can inspire you or bring out the light side of your personality. Aware of image, you like to make a good impression, and your interest in people suggests that you can quickly evaluate others. Although you are an idealist, a restless streak suggests that by developing a more mature and responsible attitude you can improve your relationships. With your sensitivity and intuitive feelings, you can be a tender and sympathetic lover. When displaying your clever and humanistic approach, you can be a positive force in helping others.

Your attractive qualities: sensitive, progressive, determined, intuitive, ambitious, courageous, assertive, resolute, thoughtful, daring, efficient, imaginative, astute insight, humanitarian, common sense, understanding, creative ideas, adventurous, enterprising, charming, reformer

Your less attractive qualities: obstinate, easily bored, lack of order, selfish, callous, escapist, frustration, laziness or workaholic, failure to complete projects, moody, worry, self-doubt, impatient, restless

Your Venus Power

The planet Venus has a great deal of influence on your powers of attraction. Below are four possible Venus types for women and men. To find your Venus you need to go to page 771, where you will find the Venus table and extra information. The planet Mars also affects your powers of attraction. To find your Mars table and interpretation go to page 761.

WOMEN WITH VENUS IN AQUARIUS: Usually you have a modern outlook on love and are open to new or current lifestyles. Your intuitive abilities, communal sense, and people skills often allow you to see deeper into human intentions and to read people's thoughts telepathically. You are usually group-oriented and are drawn to individuals within the group who are independent and self-motivated. You are more inclined to choose a partner who is unconventional or freedom-loving. Conscious of your social standing, however, you want someone who can relate well to your friends.

MEN WITH VENUS IN AQUARIUS: When it comes to relationships, others are attracted to your honest, friendly, and easygoing attitude. You really enjoy social interaction with others and may develop a genuine concern for humanity. Usually you present a tolerant and reasonable front in love situations and attempt to view your relationships objectively. If partners become too demanding, however, you can become stubborn and fixed. Friendship may be even more important for you than sexual compatibility.

WOMEN WITH VENUS IN PISCES: In love you are sensitive, tender, and affectionate, experiencing your partner's feelings almost as strongly as your own. Being also imaginative and visionary, you possess the ability to develop creative gifts and a deep compassion for others. As you are idealistic when in love, you usually prefer to see only your partner's good points, but be careful that your high expectations do not bring disappointment if you avoid being realistic. Nevertheless, in your relationships with others you can be devoted, loving, and positively enchanting.

MEN WITH VENUS IN PISCES: The combination of your emotional subtlety and charm can make you very alluring when dealing with affairs of the heart. Perceptive and impressionable, you have an easygoing style in your relationships, usually preferring to avoid ugly confrontation. You are drawn to a partner who has a touch of glamour and is sensitive to the needs of others. Alternatively, your partner can be a visionary with a rich imagination who can keep you enchanted.

WOMEN WITH VENUS IN ARIES: With your strong desires and enthusiastic nature, you can be a passionate lover. Although idealistic and single-minded, you need to avoid unnecessary conflicts in your relationships by being more patient and less headstrong. Although at times others can accuse you of being bossy or impulsive, you possess a great deal of warmth and charm. When necessary you can disarm others by making them feel important.

MEN WITH VENUS IN ARIES: You are drawn to strong, independent women who can stand up to you. Although you can enthusiastically follow the object of your desire, you may lose power if you allow your forceful emotions to become too dominant. Warm and passionate, you have a side to your nature that longs for new adventures. Romantic and chivalrous, you really enjoy the excitement of the initial chase, but unless you keep the enthusiasm alive and avoid falling into a rut you may become easily bored.

WOMEN WITH VENUS IN TAURUS: Good-natured and romantic, you have a highly developed sense of touch that particularly responds to massage, hugs, and all things physical. Being friendly, you enjoy socializing and are able to put others at their ease. With your natural sense of beauty and harmony, your charm can attract others. Although you can be lavish toward your partner, you may have to be careful that you do not overdo things.

MEN WITH VENUS IN TAURUS: As you yourself may be attractive to the opposite sex, you desire a partner who is sensual and loving or possesses physical beauty. Needing stability, when faced with changes that are out of your control you may become insecure or worried about your future. Faithful or loyal, you usually hang on to relationships but may display controlling tendencies. Your own sense of style and love of beauty imply that you can be attracted to creative people, especially those in art and music.

To read all about your Outer Planets and work out how to use your personalized timetable, go to Section Three, page 789.

Your Personalized Timetable

JUPITER BENEFICIAL
1941 4/26 – 6/8
1942 9/13 – until **1943** 1/13
1943 5/8 – 7/28
1946 12/29 – until **1947** 6/6
1947 8/24 – 11/20
1949 2/27 – 8/30
1949 10/7 – 12/15
1953 4/8 – 5/22
1954 8/22 – until **1955** 3/13
1955 3/20 – 7/11
1958 12/11 – until **1959** 11/4
1961 2/8 – 4/2
1961 7/20 – 11/23
1964 7/31 – 10/30
1965 3/18 – 5/5
1966 8/5 – until **1967** 6/24
1970 11/24 – until **1971** 3/5
1971 4/10 – 10/17
1973 1/22 – 3/9
1973 9/9 – 10/17
1976 7/5 – 12/14
1977 2/16 – 4/17
1978 7/19 – 10/11
1979 1/10 – 6/5
1982 11/9 – until **1983** 1/27
1983 5/29 – 9/26
1985 1/7 – 2/19
1988 6/16 – 8/10
1988 11/9 – until **1989** 3/29
1990 7/3 – 9/17
1991 2/19 – 5/9
1994 10/24 – until **1995** 1/7
1995 7/17 – 8/18
1996 12/22 – until **1997** 2/3
2000 5/29 – 7/14
2000 12/24 – until **2001** 2/26
2002 6/17 – 8/29
2006 10/8 – 12/21
2008 12/4 – until **2009** 1/18
2012 5/12 – 6/24

SATURN BENEFICIAL
1941 6/17 – 12/16
1942 3/1 – 5/31
1945 8/20 – until **1946** 1/31
1946 5/6 – 9/23
1947 1/20 – 6/12
1955 1/21 – 4/10
1955 10/14 – until **1956** 12/2
1961 1/29 – until **1962** 1/28
1971 4/23 – 7/15
1971 11/27 – until **1972** 4/2
1975 6/25 – until **1976** 7/24
1984 11/18 – until **1986** 1/8
1986 6/3 – 10/7
1990 3/10 – 7/2
1990 12/6 – until **1991** 3/5
1991 8/4 – 12/2
2000 5/30 – until **2001** 5/14
2004 8/1 – until **2005** 9/1
2006 2/22 – 5/17

URANUS BENEFICIAL
1940 5/28 – until **1943** 4/26
1953 7/30 – until **1957** 7/8
1979 1/6 – until **1983** 9/28
1994 1/23 – until **1996** 12/25

NEPTUNE BENEFICIAL
1965 2/2 – until **1973** 10/25
1994 3/16 – until **1999** 12/24

PLUTO BENEFICIAL
1938 1/1 – until **1943** 6/27
1991 1/13 – until **1998** 10/2

JUPITER CHALLENGING
1941 9/9 – 11/9
1942 4/24 – 7/6
1944 10/29 – until **1945** 4/4

1945 6/24 – 9/22
1948 1/24 – 7/24
1948 9/8 – 12/12
1953 8/9 – 12/24
1954 3/30 – 6/19
1956 10/11 – until **1957** 9/6
1960 1/6 – 11/25
1965 7/19 – until **1966** 6/3
1968 9/25 – until **1969** 1/11
1969 1/29 – 8/20
1971 12/21 – until **1972** 3/16
1972 6/4 – 11/6
1977 7/1 – 10/13
1977 11/4 – until **1978** 5/16
1980 9/9 – 11/30
1981 3/22 – 7/30
1983 12/5 – until **1984** 2/18
1984 7/17 – 10/11
1989 6/15 – 9/1
1989 12/26 – until **1990** 4/24
1992 8/24 – 11/9
1993 5/4 – 6/29
1995 11/19 – until **1996** 1/30
2001 5/29 – 8/10
2002 2/16 – 3/14
2004 8/8 – 10/23
2007 11/2 – until **2008** 1/13

SATURN CHALLENGING
1943 7/8 – until **1944** 2/5
1944 3/7 – 8/7
1945 1/15 – 4/23
1950 8/24 – until **1951** 10/3
1958 1/5 – 7/22
1958 9/24 – until **1959** 3/9
1959 5/25 – 12/1
1972 9/5 – 10/30
1973 5/13 – until **1974** 6/11
1979 10/2 – until **1980** 11/11
1981 4/2 – 8/5
1987 2/20 – 5/10
1987 11/14 – until **1989** 1/3
2002 6/20 – until **2003** 7/20
2008 11/16 – until **2009** 2/16
2009 8/6 – until **2010** 9/16

URANUS CHALLENGING
1946 7/21 – until **1951** 4/17
1966 9/11 – until **1970** 8/5
1986 1/8 – until **1990** 10/11

NEPTUNE CHALLENGING
1938 1/1 – until **1946** 7/3
1979 2/5 – until **1987** 11/6

PLUTO CHALLENGING
1966 11/1 – until **1974** 9/9
2003 3/11 – until **2011** 11/20

JUPITER SPECIAL
1939 3/26 – 6/16
1939 9/11 – until **1940** 1/31
1951 3/10 – 5/19
1951 10/29 – 12/31
1963 2/21 – 4/29
1975 2/3 – 4/12
1986 5/30 – 8/25
1987 1/14 – 3/27
1998 5/3 – 10/11
1998 12/15 – until **1999** 3/10
2010 4/12 – until **2011** 2/20

SATURN SPECIAL
1938 1/1 – 3/12
1966 3/11 – until **1967** 4/21
1967 11/22 – 12/26
1995 4/16 – 10/3
1996 1/8 – 6/6
1996 8/31 – until **1997** 2/23

URANUS SPECIAL
2008 3/31 – Continues

♓

March 19

SUN: PISCES • DECANATE: SCORPIO/PLUTO • DEGREE: 27°5–28°5 PISCES • MODE: MUTABLE • ELEMENT: WATER

Your Personal Powers

Ambitious, clever, yet sensitive, you are a versatile and resilient individual with a pragmatic approach. Highly imaginative, you also possess clear vision and strong intuition. You gain power from your strong will and natural organizational or administrative abilities. As you need to create a strong foundation or security for yourself, your work is likely to play an especially important role in your life. Although you usually take pride in doing a job well, you lose power if you become stubborn or allow inner tensions to hinder the perseverance needed to fulfill your high potential. Usually you possess an original view and your desire for action often stimulates your enthusiasm to initiate new ideas or projects. Your natural creativity and idealism also indicate that you may aspire to much more than material success. If you become bored or restless, however, you may lose power to escapism or overindulgence. Nevertheless, perceptive and resourceful, you can find success and opportunities for self-expression through enterprising ventures or being at the forefront of new activities.

Your Powers of Attraction in Relationships

Your confidence and ambition attract others. Action-oriented and friendly, you enjoy meeting people and socializing. Aware of image, you like to make a good impression. Your desire for security indicates that you seek a partner with whom you can share a stable and comfortable home. Although you can be independent, you are attracted to strong-willed individuals. In order to maintain a fair balance you need to resist power struggles. Often romantic, your potent feelings, ideals, and sensitivity imply that you have a strong inner need for affection and love. If your deep emotions become restricted, you can become dissatisfied and moody. As you can feel deeply, you are usually sympathetic and dependable. When committed to a relationship, you can be a generous and loving partner.

Your attractive qualities: ambitious, imaginative, psychic, creative, progressive, optimistic, sensitive, good leader, strong convictions, perceptive, dynamic, enterprising, competitive, independent, determined, committed, compassionate, loyal, idealistic, sociable, original

Your less attractive qualities: stubborn, worry, fear of rejection, materialistic, egotistical, escapist, restlessness, willful, inner tensions, critical, moody, obstinate, rash, impatient, bossy

Your Venus Power

The planet Venus has a great deal of influence on your powers of attraction. Below are four possible Venus types for women and men. To find your Venus you need to go to page 771, where you will find the Venus table and extra information. The planet Mars also affects your powers of attraction. To find your Mars table and interpretation go to page 761.

WOMEN WITH VENUS IN AQUARIUS: When it comes to relationships, others are attracted to your honest, friendly, and easygoing attitude. You really enjoy social interaction with others and may develop a genuine concern for humanity. Usually you present a tolerant and reasonable front in love situations and attempt to view your relationships objectively. If partners become too demanding, however, you can become stubborn and fixed. Friendship may be even more important for you than sexual compatibility.

MEN WITH VENUS IN AQUARIUS: You are sociable and open-minded, and people are attracted by your friendly and easygoing style. Being independent, you value freedom-loving partners who give you the space to be yourself. Other people can sometimes interpret your detachment as being emotionally cool, but they admire your objectivity and humanitarian inclinations. You are attracted to intelligent individuals who are as truthful and direct as you, but above all they must be true friends. Ideally, your partner shares your liberal views on life and possesses a strong sense of individuality.

WOMEN WITH VENUS IN PISCES: As a romantic and idealistic individual, you can be both loving and giving. While making allowances and sacrifices is understandable in a loving relationship, playing the martyr is often a state of romantic illusion. In relationships you may therefore need to balance the practical with the charitable. Nevertheless, your benevolence and sacrifices in the right relationship make you a devoted and kind partner. Subtle, sensitive, and alluring, you can be sensual and caring.

MEN WITH VENUS IN PISCES: Romantic and idealistic when in love, you can be a sensitive and responsive lover. Being pliant and flexible with an impressionable nature helps you to adapt to the needs of others. In your desire to blend with those you love, however, guard against not clearly defining your own boundaries. With your affectionate and sentimental nature, you are often attracted to those who understand your sensitivity and share your vision.

WOMEN WITH VENUS IN ARIES: Idealistic, passionate,

and adventurous, you are direct in your dealings with others. When you are attracted to a person you usually take the initiative and use your people skills to make things happen. In close relationships you are not afraid to confront your other half. This self-assertiveness is positive if differences can be brought into the open through diplomacy and compromise.

MEN WITH VENUS IN ARIES: As you often have the courage and strength to initiate situations, you like to take the lead. With your unconscious desire for conquest you may also have to beware of being competitive with your partners. Nevertheless, you are drawn to direct and strong-willed partners who can share your love of action and enthusiasm for life. When you are feeling good you can be charming and enthusiastic in romantic situations with an entertaining and spontaneous spirit.

WOMEN WITH VENUS IN TAURUS: Being physically attractive, you can make a good impression on the opposite sex. As security and stability in relationships is very important to you, you usually want a partner who is not only attractive but also reliable and a good provider. Being sensual or tactile, you also need a lover who is affectionate, but beware that your love does not show signs of possessiveness or jealousy. Your own sense of style and love of beauty imply that you can be attracted to creative people, especially those in art and music.

MEN WITH VENUS IN TAURUS: Warm and affectionate, you are naturally tactile with a love of sensual pleasures. With a streak of the conventional, you love the simple pleasures of life: good food, close friends, and happy relationships. Having an inner strength, you can express genuine patience and are often a pillar of support for loved ones and friends. Although you possess endurance be careful not to let this turn to plain stubbornness.

To read all about your Outer Planets and work out how to use your personalized timetable, go to Section Three, page 789.

Your Personalized Timetable

JUPITER BENEFICIAL
1941 4/30 – 6/12
1942 9/19 – until 1943 1/6
1943 5/14 – 8/1
1947 1/4 – 5/28
1947 9/1 – 11/24
1949 3/4 – 8/18
1949 10/20 – 12/20
1953 4/12 – 5/26
1954 8/27 – until 1955 2/19
1955 4/11 – 7/16
1958 12/16 – until 1959 11/8
1961 2/13 – 4/9
1961 7/12 – 11/29
1964 8/8 – 10/22
1965 3/24 – 5/9
1966 8/9 – until 1967 6/29
1970 11/29 – until 1971 10/22
1973 1/27 – 3/14
1973 8/27 – 10/30
1976 7/10 – 12/5
1977 2/25 – 4/22
1978 7/24 – 10/19
1979 1/1 – 6/10
1982 11/13 – until 1983 2/3
1983 5/21 – 10/2
1985 1/11 – 2/24
1988 6/20 – 8/18
1988 10/31 – until 1989 4/3
1990 7/8 – 9/22
1991 2/10 – 5/17
1994 10/29 – until 1995 1/12
1995 7/3 – 9/1
1996 12/26 – until 1997 2/7
2000 6/2 – 7/20
2000 12/15 – until 2001 3/7
2002 6/21 – 9/3
2006 10/13 – 12/25
2008 12/9 – until 2009 1/22
2012 5/16 – 6/29

SATURN BENEFICIAL
1941 6/26 – 12/2
1942 3/14 – 6/8
1945 8/29 – until 1946 1/18
1946 5/18 – until 1946 10/4
1947 1/7 – 6/21
1955 2/11 – 3/18
1955 10/23 – until 1956 12/10
1961 2/7 – 8/29
1961 10/26 – until 1962 2/5
1971 5/1 – 7/25
1971 11/15 – until 1972 4/12
1975 7/3 – until 1976 8/1
1984 11/26 – until 1986 1/19
1986 5/21 – 10/18
1990 3/23 – 6/17
1990 12/16 – until 1991 3/16
1991 7/21 – 12/13
2000 6/7 – until 2001 5/22
2004 8/9 – until 2005 2/26
2005 4/14 – 9/10
2006 2/8 – 5/30

URANUS BENEFICIAL
1940 6/16 – until 1943 5/14
1953 8/17 – until 1957 7/24
1979 2/10 – until 1983 10/20
1994 2/10 – until 1997 1/12

NEPTUNE BENEFICIAL
1965 12/14 – until 1974 9/3
1995 2/5 – until 2000 11/4

PLUTO BENEFICIAL
1938 1/1 – until 1944 6/6
1991 11/28 – until 1998 11/3

JUPITER CHALLENGING
1941 9/22 – 10/28
1942 4/29 – 7/10

1944 11/4 – until 1945 3/26
1945 7/3 – 9/27
1948 1/29 – 7/12
1948 9/19 – 12/17
1953 8/14 – 12/17
1954 4/5 – 6/24
1956 10/16 – until 1957 9/11
1960 1/11 – 11/30
1965 7/24 – until 1966 6/8
1968 9/30 – until 1969 8/25
1971 12/25 – until 1972 3/25
1972 5/25 – 11/11
1977 7/6 – until 1978 5/21
1980 9/14 – 12/7
1981 3/15 – 8/5
1983 12/9 – until 1984 2/24
1984 7/8 – 10/19
1989 6/19 – 9/8
1989 12/19 – until 1990 4/30
1992 8/29 – 11/14
1993 4/23 – 7/9
1995 11/24 – until 1996 2/4
2001 6/3 – 8/15
2002 2/1 – 3/29
2004 8/13 – 10/27
2007 11/7 – until 2008 1/18

SATURN CHALLENGING
1943 7/16 – until 1944 1/14
1944 3/28 – 8/16
1945 1/3 – 5/4
1950 9/1 – until 1951 10/11
1958 1/14 – 7/5
1958 10/11 – until 1959 4/3
1959 4/30 – 12/10
1973 5/21 – until 1974 6/19
1979 10/10 – until 1980 4/23
1980 6/20 – 11/21
1981 3/21 – 8/15
1987 3/14 – 4/17
1987 11/23 – until 1989 1/12
2002 6/28 – until 2003 7/28
2004 2/10 – 4/2
2008 12/1 – until 2009 1/31
2009 8/15 – until 2010 9/24

URANUS CHALLENGING
1946 8/12 – until 1951 5/13
1966 9/27 – until 1970 8/26
1986 1/27 – until 1990 11/10

NEPTUNE CHALLENGING
1938 1/1 – until 1946 8/21
1979 12/31 – until 1987 12/8

PLUTO CHALLENGING
1967 9/26 – until 1975 7/26
2004 1/12 – until 2011 12/20

JUPITER SPECIAL
1939 3/31 – 6/25
1939 9/2 – until 1940 2/6
1951 3/14 – 5/25
1951 10/20 – until 1952 1/9
1963 2/25 – 5/4
1975 2/8 – 4/16
1986 6/7 – 8/17
1987 1/20 – 3/31
1998 5/8 – 10/2
1998 12/24 – until 1999 3/15
2010 4/17 – until 2011 2/25

SATURN SPECIAL
1938 3/20 – 3/20
1966 3/19 – until 1967 4/29
1967 10/31 – until 1968 1/16
1995 4/26 – 9/20
1996 1/19 – 6/24
1996 8/12 – until 1997 3/3

URANUS SPECIAL
2008 4/19 – Continues

♓

March 20

SUN: PISCES/ARIES CUSP • DECANATE: SCORPIO/PLUTO/ARIES/MARS • DEGREE: 28°5–29°5 PISCES • MODE: MUTABLE • ELEMENT: WATER

Your Personal Powers

Born on the cusp, you possess both the sensitivity of Pisces and the fast mental response of Aries. You gain power from the combination of your inventive ideas and good communication skills. Intelligent and friendly with a persuasive manner, you have a flair for dealing with people and an ability to put yourself in the position of others. Although you are an independent thinker, you usually work best in partnership or teamwork situations where you are able to utilize your natural diplomacy. You still, however, possess a competitive streak that can help you in your climb to success. Although considerate and receptive, it is important that you keep developing your self-esteem as you may lose some of your power to insecurity or indecision. Quick and insightful, your understanding of people and situations can help you achieve materially or may inspire you to study subjects of a more spiritual nature. Generally confident, your strong desire for self-expression may successfully manifest through creative projects or through your many original ideas.

Your Powers of Attraction in Relationships

Your friendly and bright personality attracts others. A good companion, you know how to enjoy yourself. Being able to mix with people from all walks of life, you can often combine business with pleasure. Romantic and idealistic, you want true love and affection, yet you have a shrewd understanding of material values. Your ideal partner needs to be intelligent to bring out your natural spontaneity. In your search for perfection you may have to compromise, but be careful of overanalyzing your relationships. Nevertheless, usually you are loving, giving, and very affectionate. Charming and gracious, you are sensitive to the feelings of others and like to create a harmonious atmosphere. Since you blossom when in an encouraging relationship, it is important to be discriminating with your choice of partners.

Your attractive qualities: intelligent, creative, friendly, original ideas, persuasive, courteous, tactful, receptive, cooperative, charming, intuitive, affectionate, sensitive to others, considerate, diplomatic, agreeable, gracious, gift with words, amiable, determination

Your less attractive qualities: stubborn, suspicious, indecisive, difficult, lack of confidence, too sensitive, escapist, worry, codependent, depressive, moody, selfish, deceitful, easily hurt

Your Venus Power

The planet Venus has a great deal of influence on your powers of attraction. Below are four possible Venus types for women and men. To find your Venus you need to go to page 771, where you will find the Venus table and extra information. The planet Mars also affects your powers of attraction. To find your Mars table and interpretation go to page 761.

WOMEN WITH VENUS IN AQUARIUS: You attract and impress others with your friendly approach and progressive ideas. As you are usually independent and easygoing, you value freedom within a relationship. A good companion with a sense of your own person, you enjoy socializing, especially with people who are original, cosmopolitan, and have a strong sense of individuality. Although being friendly and detached usually serves you well, avoid losing touch with your emotions. You usually prefer the company of those who have innovative or progressive views.

MEN WITH VENUS IN AQUARIUS: Friendly and honest, you attract people with your broad-minded approach to life. You usually possess an objective and slightly detached attitude to affairs of the heart. If you are too removed, however, others can misinterpret your behavior as uncaring. It is often more important to you that your love relationships are based on friendship and honesty rather than intense passion. As you are generally tolerant and liberal, you may be drawn to less conventional relationships.

WOMEN WITH VENUS IN PISCES: Being sensitive to affairs of the heart, when you care for someone you can feel their emotions and sense their every mood. This empathy indicates that you can love on an unselfish level, but you may have to guard against giving too much, especially to those who do not reciprocate. As you are seductive and captivating, partners can be fascinated by your subtle charms and attracted by your caring and affectionate nature.

MEN WITH VENUS IN PISCES: The combination of your emotional subtlety and charm can make you very alluring when dealing with affairs of the heart. Perceptive and impressionable, you have an easygoing style in your relationships, usually preferring to avoid ugly confrontation. You are drawn to a partner who has a touch of glamour and is sensitive to the

needs of others. Alternatively, your partner can be a visionary with a rich imagination who can keep you enchanted.

WOMEN WITH VENUS IN ARIES: You gain power from your strong individuality, energy, and enthusiasm. Your young-at-heart and spirited approach to relationships adds to your appeal. If you become too impatient or self-absorbed, however, your partnerships are likely to suffer. Nevertheless, you can be creative, sharp, and quick, especially when you are able to share new and exciting projects with your partners. Mischievous with a love of action, you may even incite them to a playful fight.

MEN WITH VENUS IN ARIES: You are drawn to strong, independent women who can stand up to you. Although you can enthusiastically follow the object of your desire, you may lose power if you allow your forceful emotions to become too dominant. Warm and passionate, you have a side to your nature that longs for new adventures. Romantic and chivalrous, you really enjoy the excitement of the initial chase, but unless you keep the enthusiasm alive and avoid falling into a rut you may become easily bored.

WOMEN WITH VENUS IN TAURUS: Being physically attractive, you can make a good impression on the opposite sex. As security and stability in relationships are very important to you, you usually want a partner who is not only attractive but also reliable and a good provider. Being sensual or tactile, you also need a lover who is affectionate, but beware that your love does not show signs of possessiveness or jealousy. Your own sense of style and love of beauty imply that you can be attracted to creative people, especially those in art and music.

MEN WITH VENUS IN TAURUS: Attractive and affectionate, in relationships you are often faithful with a conservative outlook. You are drawn to warmhearted partners with whom you can share a familiar routine as well as life's pleasures and comforts. Seeking a partner who is dependable or reassuring, you often put security high on your priority list when looking for love. Your sociability and friendliness usually make you popular, and partners often admire your good sense of values and practical skills.

To read all about your Outer Planets and work out how to use your personalized timetable, go to Section Three, page 789.

Your Personalized Timetable

JUPITER BENEFICIAL
1941 5/4 – until 1941 6/16
1942 9/27 – 12/29
1943 5/20 – 8/5
1947 1/10 – 5/20
1947 9/8 – 11/29
1949 3/9 – 8/8
1949 10/29 – 12/24
1953 4/17 – 5/30
1954 9/2 – until 1955 2/8
1955 4/22 – 7/20
1958 12/21 – until 1959 11/13
1961 2/17 – 4/17
1961 7/3 – 12/5
1964 8/18 – 10/12
1965 3/29 – 5/14
1966 8/14 – until 1967 7/4
1970 12/4 – until 1971 10/27
1973 1/31 – 3/20
1973 8/18 – 11/8
1976 7/16 – 11/27
1977 3/4 – 4/27
1978 7/28 – 10/30
1978 12/22 – until 1979 6/16
1982 11/18 – until 1983 2/10
1983 5/13 – 10/8
1985 1/15 – 2/28
1988 6/25 – 8/28
1988 10/21 – until 1989 4/8
1990 7/12 – 9/28
1991 2/3 – 5/24
1994 11/2 – until 1995 1/17
1995 6/23 – 9/11
1996 12/30 – until 1997 2/11
2000 6/7 – 7/25
2000 12/7 – until 2001 3/14
2002 6/26 – 9/8
2006 10/18 – 12/30
2008 12/14 – until 2009 1/26
2012 5/20 – 7/4

SATURN BENEFICIAL
1941 7/5 – 11/19
1942 3/25 – 6/16
1945 9/8 – until 1946 1/6
1946 5/28 – 10/18
1946 12/23 – until 1947 6/30
1955 10/31 – until 1956 12/19
1957 7/26 – 8/28
1961 2/16 – 8/11
1961 11/12 – until 1962 2/14
1962 9/27 – 10/22
1971 5/9 – 8/7
1971 11/1 – until 1972 4/20
1975 7/11 – until 1976 8/9
1984 12/5 – until 1985 7/2
1985 8/17 – until 1986 1/31
1986 5/7 – 10/27
1990 4/12 – 5/28
1990 12/25 – until 1991 3/28
1991 7/7 – 12/23
2000 6/15 – 12/25
2001 2/24 – 5/29
2004 8/18 – until 2005 2/8
2005 5/2 – 9/20
2006 1/27 – 6/9

URANUS BENEFICIAL
1940 7/7 – until 1944 2/25
1953 9/6 – until 1958 5/14
1979 11/23 – until 1983 11/8
1994 3/2 – until 1997 11/3

NEPTUNE BENEFICIAL
1966 1/22 – until 1974 10/22
1995 3/9 – until 2000 12/19

PLUTO BENEFICIAL
1938 1/1 – until 1944 7/16
1991 12/26 – until 1999 9/12

JUPITER CHALLENGING
1942 5/4 – 7/15
1944 11/10 – until 1945 3/18
1945 7/10 – 10/1

1948 2/4 – 7/2
1948 9/28 – 12/21
1953 8/21 – 12/10
1954 4/12 – 6/28
1956 10/21 – until 1957 5/13
1957 5/24 – 9/15
1960 1/15 – 12/4
1965 7/29 – until 1966 1/26
1966 3/7 – 6/12
1968 10/4 – until 1969 8/30
1971 12/30 – until 1972 4/8
1972 5/11 – 11/16
1977 7/10 – until 1978 5/26
1980 9/18 – 12/15
1981 3/6 – 8/11
1983 12/14 – until 1984 3/1
1984 7/1 – 10/26
1989 6/24 – 9/15
1989 12/11 – until 1990 5/6
1992 9/2 – 11/20
1993 4/14 – 7/18
1995 11/28 – until 1996 2/9
1996 8/27 – 9/10
2001 6/7 – 8/20
2002 1/22 – 4/8
2004 8/18 – 11/1
2007 11/12 – until 2008 1/22

SATURN CHALLENGING
1943 7/25 – 12/31
1944 4/10 – 8/26
1944 12/21 – until 1945 5/14
1950 9/9 – until 1951 10/19
1958 1/24 – 6/21
1958 10/23 – until 1959 12/18
1973 5/29 – until 1974 6/27
1979 10/19 – until 1980 4/6
1980 7/7 – 12/3
1981 3/7 – 8/25
1987 12/1 – until 1989 1/21
1989 8/14 – 10/8
2002 7/6 – until 2003 8/5
2004 1/24 – 4/19
2009 8/23 – until 2010 10/2

URANUS CHALLENGING
1947 6/13 – until 1951 6/1
1966 10/14 – until 1970 9/12
1986 2/22 – until 1990 11/30

NEPTUNE CHALLENGING
1938 10/12 – until 1939 3/15
1939 8/15 – until 1945 11/20
1946 3/4 – 9/19
1980 1/31 – 5/20
1980 12/1 – until 1987 3/22
1987 4/29 – until 1988 1/4
1988 8/6 – 10/30

PLUTO CHALLENGING
1967 10/26 – until 1975 8/30
2004 2/18 – Continues

JUPITER SPECIAL
1939 4/4 – 7/6
1939 8/22 – until 1940 2/11
1951 3/18 – 5/30
1951 10/12 – until 1952 1/16
1963 3/1 – 5/8
1975 2/12 – 4/20
1986 6/18 – 8/6
1987 1/25 – 4/4
1998 5/14 – 9/24
1998 12/31 – until 1999 3/19
2010 4/21 – until 2011 3/1

SATURN SPECIAL
1938 1/1 – 3/28
1966 3/27 – until 1967 5/8
1967 10/17 – until 1968 1/29
1995 5/7 – until 1995 9/7
1996 1/30 – until 1997 3/12

URANUS SPECIAL
2008 5/14 – Continues

Pisces Timetable
X-Special · X-Beneficial · X-Challenging

February 20
URANUS X-SPECIAL
2003 2/26 – until **2004** 12/12
NEPTUNE X-SPECIAL
2011 3/13 – until **2013** 3/5
PLUTO X-BENEFICIAL
2008 1/4 – until **2010** 10/27

February 21
URANUS X-SPECIAL
2003 3/17 – until **2005** 1/11
NEPTUNE X-SPECIAL
2011 4/17 – until **2013** 4/5
PLUTO X-BENEFICIAL
2008 2/6 – until **2010** 12/3

February 22
URANUS X-SPECIAL
2003 4/6 – until **2005** 1/31
NEPTUNE X-SPECIAL
2012 3/10 – until **2013** 5/28
PLUTO X-BENEFICIAL
2009 1/3 – until **2011** 10/28

February 23
URANUS X-SPECIAL
2003 4/20 – until **2005** 2/10
NEPTUNE X-SPECIAL
2012 3/26 – Continues
PLUTO X-BENEFICIAL
2009 1/19 – until **2011** 11/19

February 24
URANUS X-SPECIAL
2004 2/24 – until **2005** 11/27
NEPTUNE X-SPECIAL
2012 5/5 – Continues
PLUTO X-BENEFICIAL
2009 2/25 – until **2011** 12/20

February 25
URANUS X-SPECIAL
2004 3/12 – until **2006** 1/5
PLUTO X-BENEFICIAL
2010 1/18 – until **2012** 11/19

February 26
URANUS X-SPECIAL
2004 4/1 – until **2006** 1/27

PLUTO X-BENEFICIAL
2010 2/22 – until **2012** 12/20

February 27
URANUS X-SPECIAL
2004 4/24 – until **2006** 2/15
PLUTO X-BENEFICIAL
2011 1/17 – until **2013** 11/21

February 28
URANUS X-SPECIAL
2005 2/28 – until **2006** 12/6
PLUTO X-BENEFICIAL
2011 2/21 – until **2013** 12/22

February 29
URANUS X-SPECIAL
2005 3/18 – until **2007** 1/11
PLUTO X-BENEFICIAL
2012 1/18 – Continues

March 1
URANUS X-SPECIAL
2005 4/6 – until **2007** 2/2
2001 7/15 – 9/30
PLUTO X-BENEFICIAL
2012 2/21 – Continues

March 2
URANUS X-SPECIAL
2005 4/30 – until **2007** 2/20
PLUTO X-CHALLENGING
1999 9/19 – until **2001** 11/5

March 3
URANUS X-SPECIAL
2006 3/5 – until **2007** 12/14
PLUTO X-CHALLENGING
1999 11/20 – until **2002** 9/7

March 4
URANUS X-SPECIAL
2006 3/23 – until **2008** 1/16
PLUTO X-CHALLENGING
1999 12/20 – until **2002** 10/28

March 5
URANUS X-SPECIAL
2006 4/11 – until **2008** 2/7

March 6
URANUS X-SPECIAL
2006 5/5 – until **2008** 2/25
PLUTO X-CHALLENGING
2001 1/6 – until **2003** 10/19

March 7
URANUS X-SPECIAL
2007 3/10 – until **2008** 12/19
PLUTO X-CHALLENGING
2001 2/11 – until **2003** 11/20

March 8
URANUS X-SPECIAL
2007 3/28 – until **2009** 1/21
PLUTO X-CHALLENGING
2001 12/29 – until **2004** 10/8

March 9
URANUS X-SPECIAL
2007 4/16 – until **2009** 2/11
PLUTO X-CHALLENGING
2002 1/29 – until **2004** 11/13

March 10
URANUS X-SPECIAL
2007 5/11 – until **2009** 3/1
PLUTO X-CHALLENGING
2002 12/23 – until **2005** 9/23

March 11
URANUS X-SPECIAL
2008 3/14 – until **2009** 12/25
PLUTO X-CHALLENGING
2003 1/20 – until **2005** 11/7

March 12
URANUS X-SPECIAL
2008 4/1 – until **2010** 1/25
PLUTO X-CHALLENGING
2003 3/18 – until **2005** 12/6

March 13
URANUS X-SPECIAL
2008 4/20 – until **2010** 2/15

PLUTO X-CHALLENGING
1999 12/20 – until **2002** 11/26

PLUTO X-CHALLENGING
2004 1/13 – until **2006** 11/1

March 14
URANUS X-SPECIAL
2008 5/15 – until **2010** 3/6
PLUTO X-CHALLENGING
2004 2/20 – until **2006** 12/2

March 15
URANUS X-SPECIAL
2009 3/18 – until **2010** 12/30
PLUTO X-CHALLENGING
2005 1/6 – until **2007** 10/26

March 16
URANUS X-SPECIAL
2009 4/5 – until **2011** 1/30
PLUTO X-CHALLENGING
2005 2/8 – until **2007** 11/28

March 17
URANUS X-SPECIAL
2009 4/25 – until **2011** 2/20
PLUTO X-CHALLENGING
2006 1/1 – until **2008** 10/19

March 18
URANUS X-SPECIAL
2009 5/20 – until **2011** 3/10
PLUTO X-CHALLENGING
2006 2/1 – until **2008** 11/24

March 19
URANUS X-SPECIAL
2010 3/23 – until **2012** 1/4
PLUTO X-CHALLENGING
2006 12/28 – until **2009** 10/12

March 20
URANUS X-SPECIAL
2010 4/10 – until **2012** 2/3
PLUTO X-CHALLENGING
2007 1/26 – until **2009** 11/21

Mars and Venus

Your Mars Power

In the female/male polarity, Mars represents the male side. The planet Mars governs your energy and vitality, your motivation, masculine sexuality, and powers of attraction. Mars also rules physical strength, ambition, desires, concentrated effort, and action. In a woman's astrological chart Mars depicts the drive behind her personality, her assertive side, and the type of man she is naturally attracted to. In a man's astrological chart Mars represents his physical drive, motivation, and sensuality. To use the Mars table below all you need to do is first go to your year of birth and find which sign Mars was in on your birthday. At the end of the Mars table you will find interpretations for both women and men. You can also use this table to check Mars's placement of your friends, loved ones, and partner.

Mars Table: 1938–2012

1938
Mars in Pisces: Jan 1–Jan 30
Mars in Aries: Jan 30–Mar 12
Mars in Taurus: Mar 12–Apr 23
Mars in Gemini: Apr 23–June 7
Mars in Cancer: June 7–July 22
Mars in Leo: July 22–Sept 7
Mars in Virgo: Sept 7–Oct 25
Mars in Libra: Oct 25–Nov 11
Mars in Scorpio: Nov 11–Dec 31

1939
Mars in Scorpio: Jan 1–Jan 29
Mars in Sagittarius: Jan 29–Mar 21
Mars in Capricorn: Mar 21–May 25
Mars in Aquarius: May 25–July 21
Mars in Capricorn: July 21–Sept 24
Mars in Aquarius: Sept 24–Nov 19
Mars in Pisces: Nov 19–Dec 31

1940
Mars in Pisces: Jan 1–Jan 4
Mars in Aries: Jan 4–Feb 17
Mars in Taurus: Feb 17–Apr 1
Mars in Gemini: Apr 1–May 17
Mars in Cancer: May 17–July 3
Mars in Leo: July 3–Aug 19
Mars in Virgo: Aug 19–Oct 5
Mars in Libra: Oct 5–Nov 20
Mars in Scorpio: Nov 20–Dec 31

1941
Mars in Scorpio: Jan 1–Jan 4

Mars in Sagittarius: Jan 4–Feb 17
Mars in Capricorn: Feb 17–Apr 2
Mars in Aquarius: Apr 2–May 16
Mars in Pisces: May 16–July 2
Mars in Aries: July 2–Dec 31

1942
Mars in Aries: Jan 4–Jan 11
Mars in Taurus: Jan 11–Mar 7
Mars in Gemini: Mar 7–Apr 26
Mars in Cancer: Apr 26–June 14
Mars in Leo: June 14–Aug 1
Mars in Virgo: Aug 1–Sept 17
Mars in Libra: Sept 17–Nov 1
Mars in Scorpio: Nov 1–Dec 15
Mars in Sagittarius: Dec 15–Dec 31

1943
Mars in Sagittarius: Jan 1–Jan 26
Mars in Aquarius: Jan 26–Mar 8
Mars in Capricorn: Mar 8–Apr 17
Mars in Pisces: Apr 17–May 27
Mars in Aries: May 27–July 7
Mars in Taurus: July 7–Aug 23
Mars in Gemini: Aug 23–Dec 31

1944
Mars in Gemini: Jan 1–Mar 7
Mars in Cancer: Mar 7–May 22
Mars in Leo: May 22–July 12
Mars in Virgo: July 12–Aug 29
Mars in Libra: Aug 29–Oct 13

Mars in Scorpio: Oct 13–Nov 25
Mars in Sagittarius: Nov 25–Dec 31

1945
Mars in Sagittarius: Jan 1–Jan 5
Mars in Capricorn: Jan 5–Feb 14
Mars in Aquarius: Feb 14–Mar 25
Mars in Pisces: Mar 25–May 2
Mars in Aries: May 2–June 11
Mars in Taurus: June 11–July 23
Mars in Gemini: July 23–Sept 7
Mars in Cancer: Sept 7–Nov 11
Mars in Leo: Nov 11–Dec 26
Mars in Cancer: Dec 26–Dec 31

1946
Mars in Cancer: Jan 1–Apr 22
Mars in Leo: Apr 22–June 20
Mars in Virgo: June 20–Aug 9
Mars in Libra: Aug 9–Sept 24
Mars in Scorpio: Sept 24–Nov 6
Mars in Sagittarius: Nov 6–Dec 17
Mars in Capricorn: Dec 17–Dec 31

1947
Mars in Capricorn: Jan 5–Jan 25
Mars in Aquarius: Jan 25–Mar 4
Mars in Pisces: Mar 4–Apr 11
Mars in Aries: Apr 11–May 21
Mars in Taurus: May 21–July 1
Mars in Gemini: July 1–Aug 13
Mars in Cancer: Aug 13–Oct 1

Mars in Leo: Oct 1–Dec 1
Mars in Virgo: Dec 1–Dec 31

1948
Mars in Virgo: Jan 1–Feb 12
Mars in Leo: Feb 12–May 18
Mars in Virgo: May 18–July 17
Mars in Libra: July 17–Sept 3
Mars in Scorpio: Sept 3–Oct 17
Mars in Sagittarius: Oct 17–Nov 26
Mars in Capricorn: Nov 26–Dec 31

1949
Mars in Capricorn: Jan 1–Jan 4
Mars in Aquarius: Jan 4–Feb 11
Mars in Pisces: Feb 11–Mar 21
Mars in Aries: Mar 21–Apr 30
Mars in Taurus: Apr 30–June 10
Mars in Gemini: June 10–July 23
Mars in Cancer: July 23–Sept 7
Mars in Leo: Sept 7–Oct 27
Mars in Virgo: Oct 27–Dec 26
Mars in Libra: Dec 26–Dec 31

1950
Mars in Libra: Jan 1–Mar 28
Mars in Virgo: Mar 28–June 11
Mars in Libra: June 11–Aug 10
Mars in Scorpio: Aug 10–Sept 25
Mars in Sagittarius: Sept 25–Nov 6
Mars in Capricorn: Nov 6–Dec 15
Mars in Aquarius: Dec 15–Dec 31

1951

Mars in Aquarius: Jan 1–Jan 22
Mars in Pisces: Jan 22–Mar 1
Mars in Aries: Mar 1–Apr 10
Mars in Taurus: Apr 10–May 21
Mars in Gemini: May 21–July 3
Mars in Cancer: July 3–Aug 18
Mars in Leo: Aug 18–Oct 5
Mars in Virgo: Oct 5–Nov 24
Mars in Libra: Nov 24–Dec 31

1952

Mars in Libra: Jan 1–Jan 20
Mars in Scorpio: Jan 20–Aug 27
Mars in Sagittarius: Aug 27–Oct 12
Mars in Capricorn: Oct 12–Nov 6
Mars in Aquarius: Nov 6–Dec 30
Mars in Pisces: Dec 30–Dec 31

1953

Mars in Pisces: Jan 1–Feb 8
Mars in Aries: Feb 8–Mar 20
Mars in Taurus: Mar 20–May 1
Mars in Gemini: May 1–June 14
Mars in Cancer: June 14–July 29
Mars in Leo: July 29–Sept 14
Mars in Virgo: Sept 14–Nov 21
Mars in Libra: Nov 21–Dec 20
Mars in Scorpio: Dec 20–Dec 31

1954

Mars in Scorpio: Jan 1–Feb 9
Mars in Sagittarius: Feb 9–Apr 12
Mars in Capricorn: Apr 12–July 3
Mars in Sagittarius: July 3–Aug 24
Mars in Capricorn: Aug 24–Oct 21
Mars in Aquarius: Oct 21–Dec 4
Mars in Pisces: Dec 4–Dec 31

1955

Mars in Pisces: Jan 1–Jan 15
Mars in Aries: Jan 15–Feb 26
Mars in Taurus: Feb 26–Apr 10
Mars in Gemini: Apr 10–May 26
Mars in Cancer: May 26–July 11
Mars in Leo: July 11–Aug 27
Mars in Virgo: Aug 27–Oct 13
Mars in Libra: Oct 13–Nov 29
Mars in Scorpio: Nov 29–Dec 31

1956

Mars in Scorpio: Jan 1–Jan 14

Mars in Sagittarius: Jan 14–Feb 28
Mars in Capricorn: Feb 28–Apr 14
Mars in Aquarius: Apr 14–June 3
Mars in Pisces: June 3–Dec 6
Mars in Aries: Dec 6–Dec 31

1957

Mars in Aries: Jan 1–Jan 28
Mars in Taurus: Jan 28–Mar 17
Mars in Gemini: Mar 17–May 4
Mars in Cancer: May 4–June 21
Mars in Leo: June 21–Aug 8
Mars in Virgo: Aug 8–Sept 24
Mars in Libra: Sept 24–Nov 8
Mars in Scorpio: Nov 8–Dec 23
Mars in Sagittarius: Dec 23–Dec 31

1958

Mars in Sagittarius: Jan 1–Feb 3
Mars in Capricorn: Feb 3–Mar 17
Mars in Aquarius: Mar 17–Apr 27
Mars in Pisces: Apr 27–June 7
Mars in Aries: June 7–July 21
Mars in Taurus: July 21–Sept 21
Mars in Gemini: Sept 21–Oct 29
Mars in Taurus: Oct 29–Dec 31

1959

Mars in Taurus: Jan 1–Feb 10
Mars in Gemini: Feb 10–Apr 10
Mars in Cancer: Apr 10–June 1
Mars in Leo: June 1–June 20
Mars in Virgo: June 20–Sept 5
Mars in Libra: Sept 5–Oct 21
Mars in Scorpio: Oct 21–Dec 3
Mars in Sagittarius: Dec 3–Dec 31

1960

Mars in Sagittarius: Jan 1–Jan 14
Mars in Capricorn: Jan 14–Feb 23
Mars in Aquarius: Feb 23–Apr 2
Mars in Pisces: Apr 2–May 11
Mars in Aries: May 11–June 20
Mars in Taurus: June 20–Aug 2
Mars in Gemini: Aug 2–Sept 21
Mars in Cancer: Sept 21–Dec 31

1961

Mars in Cancer: Jan 1–Feb 5
Mars in Gemini: Feb 5–Feb 7
Mars in Cancer: Feb 7–May 6
Mars in Leo: May 6–June 28

Mars in Virgo: June 28–Aug 17
Mars in Libra: Aug 17–Oct 1
Mars in Scorpio: Oct 1–Nov 13
Mars in Sagittarius: Nov 13–Dec 24
Mars in Capricorn: Dec 24–Dec 31

1962

Mars in Capricorn: Jan 1–Feb 1
Mars in Aquarius: Feb 1–Mar 12
Mars in Pisces: Mar 12–Apr 19
Mars in Aries: Apr 19–May 28
Mars in Taurus: May 28–July 9
Mars in Gemini: July 9–Aug 22
Mars in Cancer: Aug 22–Oct 11
Mars in Leo: Oct 11–Dec 26

1963

Mars in Leo: Jan 1–June 3
Mars in Virgo: June 3–July 27
Mars in Libra: July 27–Sept 12
Mars in Scorpio: Sept 12–Oct 25
Mars in Sagittarius: Oct 25–Dec 5
Mars in Capricorn: Dec 5–Dec 31

1964

Mars in Capricorn: Jan 1–Jan 13
Mars in Aquarius: Jan 13–Feb 20
Mars in Pisces: Feb 20–Mar 29
Mars in Aries: Mar 29–May 7
Mars in Taurus: May 7–June 17
Mars in Gemini: June 17–July 30
Mars in Cancer: July 30–Sept 15
Mars in Leo: Sept 15–Nov 6
Mars in Virgo: Nov 6–Dec 31

1965

Mars in Virgo: Jan 1–June 29
Mars in Libra: June 29–Aug 20
Mars in Scorpio: Aug 20–Oct 4
Mars in Sagittarius: Oct 4–Nov 14
Mars in Capricorn: Nov 14–Dec 23
Mars in Aquarius: Dec 23–Dec 31

1966

Mars in Aquarius: Jan 1–Jan 30
Mars in Pisces: Jan 30–Mar 9
Mars in Aries: Mar 9–Apr 17
Mars in Taurus: Apr 17–May 28
Mars in Gemini: May 28–July 11
Mars in Cancer: July 11–Aug 25
Mars in Leo: Aug 25–Oct 12

Mars in Virgo: Oct 12–Dec 4
Mars in Libra: Dec 4–Dec 31

1967

Mars in Libra: Jan 1–Feb 12
Mars in Scorpio: Feb 12–Mar 31
Mars in Libra: Mar 31–June 19
Mars in Scorpio: June 19–Sept 20
Mars in Sagittarius: Sept 20–Oct 23
Mars in Capricorn: Oct 23–Dec 1
Mars in Aquarius: Dec 1–Dec 31

1968

Mars in Aquarius: Jan 1–Jan 9
Mars in Pisces: Jan 9–Feb 17
Mars in Aries: Feb 17–Mar 27
Mars in Taurus: Mar 27–May 8
Mars in Gemini: May 8–June 21
Mars in Cancer: June 21–Aug 5
Mars in Leo: Aug 5–Sept 21
Mars in Virgo: Sept 21–Nov 9
Mars in Libra: Nov 9–Dec 29
Mars in Scorpio: Dec 29–Dec 31

1969

Mars in Scorpio: Jan 1–Feb 25
Mars in Sagittarius: Feb 25–Sept 21
Mars in Capricorn: Sept 21–Nov 4
Mars in Aquarius: Nov 4–Dec 15
Mars in Pisces: Dec 15–Dec 31

1970

Mars in Pisces: Jan 1–Jan 24
Mars in Aries: Jan 24–Mar 7
Mars in Taurus: Mar 7–Apr 18
Mars in Gemini: Apr 18–June 2
Mars in Cancer: June 2–July 18
Mars in Leo: July 18–Sept 3
Mars in Virgo: Sept 3–Oct 20
Mars in Libra: Oct 20–Nov 6
Mars in Scorpio: Nov 6–Dec 31

1971

Mars in Scorpio: Jan 1–Jan 23
Mars in Sagittarius: Jan 23–Mar 12
Mars in Capricorn: Mar 12–May 3
Mars in Aquarius: May 3–Nov 6
Mars in Pisces: Nov 6–Dec 26
Mars in Aries: Dec 26–Dec 31

1972

Mars in Aries: Jan 1–Feb 10

Mars in Taurus: Feb 10–Mar 27
Mars in Gemini: Mar 27–May 12
Mars in Cancer: May 12–June 28
Mars in Leo: June 28–Aug 15
Mars in Virgo: Aug 15–Sept 30
Mars in Libra: Sept 30–Nov 15
Mars in Scorpio: Nov 15–Dec 30
Mars in Sagittarius: Dec 30–Dec 31

1973

Mars in Sagittarius: Jan 1–Feb 12
Mars in Capricorn: Feb 12–Mar 26
Mars in Aquarius: Mar 26–May 8
Mars in Pisces: May 8–June 20
Mars in Aries: June 20–Aug 12
Mars in Taurus: Aug 12–Oct 29
Mars in Aries: Oct 29–Dec 24
Mars in Taurus: Dec 24–Dec 31

1974

Mars in Taurus: Jan 1–Feb 27
Mars in Gemini: Feb 27–Apr 20
Mars in Cancer: Apr 20–June 9
Mars in Leo: June 9–July 27
Mars in Virgo: July 27–Sept 12
Mars in Libra: Sept 12–Oct 28
Mars in Scorpio: Oct 28–Dec 10
Mars in Sagittarius: Dec 10–Dec 31

1975

Mars in Sagittarius: Jan 1–Jan 21
Mars in Capricorn: Jan 21–Mar 3
Mars in Aquarius: Mar 3–Apr 11
Mars in Pisces: Apr 11–May 21
Mars in Aries: May 21–July 1
Mars in Taurus: July 1–Aug 14
Mars in Gemini: Aug 14–Oct 17
Mars in Cancer: Oct 17–Nov 25
Mars in Gemini: Nov 25–Dec 31

1976

Mars in Gemini: Jan 1–Mar 18
Mars in Cancer: Mar 18–May 16
Mars in Leo: May 16–July 6
Mars in Virgo: July 6–Aug 24
Mars in Libra: Aug 24–Oct 8
Mars in Scorpio: Oct 8–Nov 20
Mars in Sagittarius: Nov 20–Dec 31

1977

Mars in Sagittarius: Jan 1
Mars in Capricorn: Jan 1–Feb 9

Mars in Aquarius: Feb 9–Mar 20
Mars in Pisces: Mar 20–Apr 27
Mars in Aries: Apr 27–June 6
Mars in Taurus: June 6–July 17
Mars in Gemini: July 17–Sept 1
Mars in Cancer: Sept 1–Oct 26
Mars in Leo: Oct 26–Dec 31

1978

Mars in Leo: Jan 1–Jan 26
Mars in Cancer: Jan 26–Apr 10
Mars in Leo: Apr 10–June 14
Mars in Virgo: June 14–Aug 4
Mars in Libra: Aug 4–Sept 19
Mars in Scorpio: Sept 19–Nov 2
Mars in Sagittarius: Nov 2–Dec 12
Mars in Capricorn: Dec 12–Dec 31

1979

Mars in Capricorn: Jan 1–Jan 20
Mars in Aquarius: Jan 20–Feb 27
Mars in Pisces: Feb 27–Apr 7
Mars in Aries: Apr 7–May 16
Mars in Taurus: May 16–June 26
Mars in Gemini: June 26–Aug 8
Mars in Cancer: Aug 8–Sept 24
Mars in Leo: Sept 24–Nov 19
Mars in Virgo: Nov 19–Dec 31

1980

Mars in Virgo: Jan 1–Mar 11
Mars in Leo: Mar 11–May 4
Mars in Virgo: May 4–July 10
Mars in Libra: July 10–Aug 29
Mars in Scorpio: Aug 29–Oct 12
Mars in Sagittarius: Oct 12–Nov 22
Mars in Capricorn: Nov 22–Dec 30
Mars in Aquarius: Dec 30–Dec 31

1981

Mars in Aquarius: Jan 1–Feb 6
Mars in Pisces: Feb 6–Mar 17
Mars in Aries: Mar 17–Apr 25
Mars in Taurus: Apr 25–June 5
Mars in Gemini: June 5–July 18
Mars in Cancer: July 18–Sept 2
Mars in Leo: Sept 2–Oct 21
Mars in Virgo: Oct 21–Dec 16
Mars in Libra: Dec 16–Dec 31

1982

Mars in Libra: Jan 1–Aug 3

Mars in Scorpio: Aug 3–Sept 20
Mars in Sagittarius: Sept 20–Oct 31
Mars in Capricorn: Oct 31–Dec 10
Mars in Aquarius: Dec 10–Dec 31

1983

Mars in Aquarius: Jan 1–Jan 17
Mars in Pisces: Jan 17–Feb 25
Mars in Aries: Feb 25–Apr 5
Mars in Taurus: Apr 5–May 16
Mars in Gemini: May 16–June 29
Mars in Cancer: June 29–Aug 13
Mars in Leo: Aug 13–Sept 30
Mars in Virgo: Sept 30–Nov 18
Mars in Libra: Nov 18–Dec 31

1984

Mars in Libra: Jan 1–Jan 11
Mars in Scorpio: Jan 11–Aug 17
Mars in Sagittarius: Aug 17–Oct 5
Mars in Capricorn: Oct 5–Nov 15
Mars in Aquarius: Nov 15–Dec 25
Mars in Pisces: Dec 25–Dec 31

1985

Mars in Pisces: Jan 1–Feb 2
Mars in Aries: Feb 2–Mar 15
Mars in Taurus: Mar 15–Apr 26
Mars in Gemini: Apr 26–June 9
Mars in Cancer: June 9–July 25
Mars in Leo: July 25–Sept 10
Mars in Virgo: Sept 10–Oct 27
Mars in Libra: Oct 27–Dec 14
Mars in Scorpio: Dec 14–Dec 31

1986

Mars in Scorpio: Jan 1–Feb 2
Mars in Sagittarius: Feb 2–Mar 28
Mars in Capricorn: Mar 28–Oct 9
Mars in Aquarius: Oct 9–Nov 26
Mars in Pisces: Nov 26–Dec 31

1987

Mars in Pisces: Jan 1–Jan 8
Mars in Aries: Jan 8–Feb 20
Mars in Taurus: Feb 20–Apr 5
Mars in Gemini: Apr 5–May 21
Mars in Cancer: May 21–July 6
Mars in Leo: July 6–Aug 22
Mars in Virgo: Aug 22–Oct 8
Mars in Libra: Oct 8–Nov 24
Mars in Scorpio: Nov 24–Dec 31

1988

Mars in Scorpio: Jan 1–Jan 8
Mars in Sagittarius: Jan 8–Feb 22
Mars in Capricorn: Feb 22–Apr 6
Mars in Aquarius: Apr 6–May 22
Mars in Pisces: May 22–July 13
Mars in Aries: July 13–Oct 23
Mars in Pisces: Oct 23–Nov 1
Mars in Aries: Nov 1–Dec 31

1989

Mars in Aries: Jan 1–Jan 19
Mars in Taurus: Jan 19–Mar 11
Mars in Gemini: Mar 11–Apr 29
Mars in Cancer: Apr 29–June 16
Mars in Leo: June 16–Aug 3
Mars in Virgo: Aug 3–Sept 19
Mars in Libra: Sept 19–Nov 4
Mars in Scorpio: Nov 4–Dec 18
Mars in Sagittarius: Dec 18–Dec 31

1990

Mars in Sagittarius: Jan 1–Jan 29
Mars in Capricorn: Jan 29–Mar 11
Mars in Aquarius: Mar 11–Apr 20
Mars in Pisces: Apr 20–May 31
Mars in Aries: May 31–July 12
Mars in Taurus: July 12–Aug 31
Mars in Gemini: Aug 31–Dec 14
Mars in Taurus: Dec 14–Dec 31

1991

Mars in Taurus: Jan 1–Jan 21
Mars in Gemini: Jan 21–Apr 3
Mars in Cancer: Apr 3–May 26
Mars in Leo: May 26–July 15
Mars in Virgo: July 15–Sept 1
Mars in Libra: Sept 1–Oct 16
Mars in Scorpio: Oct 16–Nov 29
Mars in Sagittarius: Nov 29–Dec 31

1992

Mars in Sagittarius: Jan 1–Jan 9
Mars in Capricorn: Jan 9–Feb 18
Mars in Aquarius: Feb 18–Mar 28
Mars in Pisces: Mar 28–May 5
Mars in Aries: May 5–June 14
Mars in Taurus: June 14–July 26
Mars in Gemini: July 26–Sept 12
Mars in Cancer: Sept 12–Dec 31

1993

Mars in Cancer: Jan 1–Apr 27

Mars in Leo: Apr 27–July 23

Mars in Virgo: July 23–Aug 12

Mars in Libra: Aug 12–Sept 27

Mars in Scorpio: Sept 27–Nov 9

Mars in Sagittarius: Nov 9–Dec 20

Mars in Capricorn: Dec 20–Dec 31

1994

Mars in Capricorn: Jan 1–Jan 28

Mars in Aquarius: Jan 28–Mar 7

Mars in Pisces: Mar 7–Apr 14

Mars in Aries: Apr 14–May 23

Mars in Taurus: May 23–July 3

Mars in Gemini: July 3–Aug 16

Mars in Cancer: Aug 16–Oct 4

Mars in Leo: Oct 4–Dec 12

Mars in Virgo: Dec 12–Dec 31

1995

Mars in Virgo: Jan 1–Jan 22

Mars in Leo: Jan 22–May 25

Mars in Virgo: May 25–July 21

Mars in Libra: July 21–Sept 7

Mars in Scorpio: Sept 7–Oct 20

Mars in Sagittarius: Oct 20–Nov 30

Mars in Capricorn: Nov 30–Dec 31

1996

Mars in Capricorn: Jan 1–Jan 8

Mars in Aquarius: Jan 8–Feb 15

Mars in Pisces: Feb 15–Mar 24

Mars in Aries: Mar 24–May 2

Mars in Taurus: May 2–June 12

Mars in Gemini: June 12–July 25

Mars in Cancer: July 25–Sept 9

Mars in Leo: Sept 9–Oct 30

Mars in Virgo: Oct 30–Dec 31

1997

Mars in Virgo: Jan 1–Jan 3

Mars in Libra: Jan 3–Mar 8

Mars in Virgo: Mar 8–June 19

Mars in Libra: June 19–Aug 14

Mars in Scorpio: Aug 14–Sept 28

Mars in Sagittarius: Sept 28–Nov 9

Mars in Capricorn: Nov 9–Dec 18

Mars in Aquarius: Dec 18–Dec 31

1998

Mars in Aquarius: Jan 1–Jan 25

Mars in Pisces: Jan 25–Mar 4

Mars in Aries: Mar 4–Apr 13

Mars in Taurus: Apr 13–May 24

Mars in Gemini: May 24–July 6

Mars in Cancer: July 6–Aug 20

Mars in Leo: Aug 20–Oct 7

Mars in Virgo: Oct 7–Nov 27

Mars in Libra: Nov 27–Dec 31

1999

Mars in Libra: Jan 1–Jan 26

Mars in Scorpio: Jan 26–May 5

Mars in Libra: May 5–July 5

Mars in Scorpio: July 5–Sept 2

Mars in Sagittarius: Sept 2–Oct 17

Mars in Capricorn: Oct 17–Nov 26

Mars in Aquarius: Nov 26–Dec 31

2000

Mars in Aquarius: Jan 1–Jan 4

Mars in Pisces: Jan 4–Feb 12

Mars in Aries: Feb 12–Mar 23

Mars in Taurus: Mar 23–May 3

Mars in Gemini: May 3–June 16

Mars in Cancer: June 16–Aug 1

Mars in Leo: Aug 1–Sept 17

Mars in Virgo: Sept 17–Nov 4

Mars in Libra: Nov 4–Dec 23

Mars in Scorpio: Dec 23–Dec 31

2001

Mars in Scorpio: Jan 1–Feb 14

Mars in Sagittarius: Feb 14–Sept 8

Mars in Capricorn: Sept 8–Oct 27

Mars in Aquarius: Oct 27–Dec 8

Mars in Pisces: Dec 8–Dec 31

2002

Mars in Pisces: Jan 1–Jan 18

Mars in Aries: Jan 18–Mar 1

Mars in Taurus: Mar 1–Apr 13

Mars in Gemini: Apr 13–May 28

Mars in Cancer: May 28–July 13

Mars in Leo: July 13–Aug 29

Mars in Virgo: Aug 29–Oct 15

Mars in Libra: Oct 15–Dec 1

Mars in Scorpio: Dec 1–Dec 31

2003

Mars in Scorpio: Jan 1–Jan 17

Mars in Sagittarius: Jan 17–Mar 4

Mars in Capricorn: Mar 4–Apr 21

Mars in Aquarius: Apr 21–June 17

Mars in Pisces: June 17–Dec 16

Mars in Aries: Dec 16–Dec 31

2004

Mars in Aries: Jan 1–Feb 3

Mars in Taurus: Feb 3–Mar 21

Mars in Gemini: Mar 21–May 7

Mars in Cancer: May 7–June 23

Mars in Leo: June 23–Aug 10

Mars in Virgo: Aug 10–Sept 26

Mars in Libra: Sept 26–Nov 11

Mars in Scorpio: Nov 11–Dec 25

Mars in Sagittarius: Dec 25–31

2005

Mars in Sagittarius: Jan 1–Feb 6

Mars in Capricorn: Feb 6–Mar 20

Mars in Aquarius: Mar 20–May 1

Mars in Pisces: May 1–June 12

Mars in Aries: June 12–July 28

Mars in Taurus: July 28–Dec 31

2006

Mars in Taurus: Jan 1–Feb 17

Mars in Gemini: Feb 17–Apr 14

Mars in Cancer: Apr 14–June 3

Mars in Leo: June 3–July 22

Mars in Virgo: July 22–Sept 8

Mars in Libra: Sept 8–Oct 23

Mars in Scorpio: Oct 23–Dec 6

Mars in Sagittarius: Dec 6–Dec 31

2007

Mars in Sagittarius: Jan 1–Jan 16

Mars in Capricorn: Jan 16–Feb 26

Mars in Aquarius: Feb 26–Apr 6

Mars in Pisces: Apr 6–May 15

Mars in Aries: May 15–June 24

Mars in Taurus: June 24–Aug 7

Mars in Gemini: Aug 7–Sept 28

Mars in Cancer: Sept 28–Dec 31

2008

Mars in Gemini: Jan 1–Mar 4

Mars in Cancer: Mar 4–May 9

Mars in Leo: May 9–July 1

Mars in Virgo: July 1–Aug 19

Mars in Libra: Aug 19–Oct 4

Mars in Scorpio: Oct 4–Nov 16

Mars in Sagittarius: Nov 16–Dec 28

Mars in Capricorn: Dec 28–Dec 31

2009

Mars in Capricorn: Jan 1–Feb 4

Mars in Aquarius: Feb 4–Mar 15

Mars in Pisces: Mar 15–Apr 22

Mars in Aries: Apr 22–May 31

Mars in Taurus: May 31–July 12

Mars in Gemini: July 12–Aug 25

Mars in Cancer: Aug 25–Oct 16

Mars in Leo: Oct 16–Dec 31

2010

Mars in Leo: Jan 1–June 7

Mars in Virgo: June 7–July 29

Mars in Libra: July 29–Sept 14

Mars in Scorpio: Sept 14–Oct 28

Mars in Sagittarius: Oct 28–Dec 7

Mars in Capricorn: Dec 7–Dec 31

2011

Mars in Capricorn: Jan 1–Jan 15

Mars in Aquarius: Jan 15–Feb 23

Mars in Pisces: Feb 23–Apr 2

Mars in Aries: Apr 2–May 11

Mars in Taurus: May 11–June 21

Mars in Gemini: June 21–Aug 3

Mars in Cancer: Aug 3–Sept 19

Mars in Leo: Sept 19–Nov 11

Mars in Virgo: Nov 11–Dec 31

2012

Mars in Virgo: Jan 1–July 3

Mars in Libra: July 3–Aug 23

Mars in Scorpio: Aug 23–Oct 7

Mars in Sagittarius: Oct 7–Nov 17

Mars in Capricorn: Nov 17–Dec 25

Mars in Aquarius: Dec 25–Dec 31

Mars in Aries

MEN WITH MARS IN ARIES: Daring and bold, you are often confident and energetic. Action-oriented, you like to take the lead or be direct. In affairs of the heart you often act spontaneously and with dynamic vigor. Not always a great diplomat, you can sometimes be too blunt or headstrong, yet underneath you possess a chivalrous and brave nature. Being straightforward, your actions usually reveal your thoughts and beliefs. Your independent streak often implies that you do not like to take orders from others, yet when you go after your heart's desire you can be amiable and agreeable. Nonetheless, people admire your fearless character and enterprising attitude. Full of male potency, you enjoy the chase in relationships, and an element of risk or adventure can bring you the excitement you desire.

WOMEN WITH MARS IN ARIES: Willful and determined, you have courage and a forceful nature. Your energetic manner indicates that you are also decisive and purposeful. Usually daring, if challenged you tend to show a bold front and not back down. Being assertive and passionate suggest that you are not afraid to go after your heart's desire. You are often attracted to strong and willful individuals who act out your masculine qualities. Since weak characters rarely appeal to you, you prefer a partner who is not scared to confront you. Usually you are drawn to confident and independent individuals who ooze testosterone and who have an enterprising spirit like your own. However, you may have to establish who is the boss in the relationship as both of you may want to lead or be in charge. If your sense of adventure or need for action does not appeal to your partner you may prefer to go it alone. Being boisterous, you are also drawn to partners who are good sports or competitive.

Your appealing attributes: adventurous, independent, quick responses, enthusiastic, bold, mischievous, charming, daring, honest, spirited, creative, pioneering, courageous, ambitious

Your unappealing attributes: quick-tempered, impatient, too competitive, argumentative, impulsive, tactless, bossy, too passionate, easily bored, intolerant, aggressive

Mars in Taurus

MEN WITH MARS IN TAURUS: Your strong sense of values and determination indicate that more often than not you are practical and down-to-earth. Usually you are patient and persistent, yet a stubborn streak indicates that once you have made up your mind it is hard to convince you otherwise. Security-conscious, you like to be financially established, and the more traditional side of your nature prefers the old and tested methods. An innate creativity and an eye for beauty and style suggest that you can usually recognize quality and craftsmanship. Knowing the values of your assets, you often grow attached to your possessions, achieving success when you are confident with a strong sense of self-worth. In relationships you want a partner who is dependable yet sensual and stylish. By nature you are tactile with a sex drive and a slow approach. Being reliable implies that once you make a commitment you are usually a consistent and loyal partner.

WOMEN WITH MARS IN TAURUS: Being security conscious and practical, you are usually a productive and determined individual with common sense. Being tactile, you are often natural and sensual, preferring the slow but sure approach. Although you have a persistent nature you can sometimes be stubborn and uncompromising. When you set your mind on a project or a relationship, however, you will continue tirelessly until you achieve results. Your pragmatic approach implies that you have a good sense of values and a head for commerce, especially regarding property or land. Willing to be patient, you are able to take advantage of opportunities. Although you often have expensive taste, you usually love a bargain. You are often attracted to pragmatic and stable individuals, or those with status who can act out your masculine qualities. Usually you are drawn to purposeful and dependable yet charming individuals with sex appeal. You also seek partners who can provide you with security, physical affection, and comfort. Alternatively, creative and artistic people may be very appealing to you as you generally appreciate art, music, beauty, or style.

Your appealing attributes: sensual, practical, executive abilities, persistent, materialistic, economical, determined, productive, steady, creative, sociable, magnetic, love of beauty, attractive voice, loyal, tactile, endurance

Your unappealing attributes: stubborn, selfish, too materialistic, too economical, too fixed, irritable, obstinate, selfish, overindulgent, possessive, too security conscious

Mars in Gemini

MEN WITH MARS IN GEMINI: Keen to improve your knowledge and skills, you enjoy learning. Usually mentally quick, you can impress others with your sharp wit and wealth of information. You often rely on your quick comprehension and ability to assess situations. Good at debating, you can be persuasive and articulate. You can also be a charming or excellent salesman, whether you are selling yourself or a product. Although communication is an area you can excel in, you may improve your competence and relations with others when you develop patience and your listening skills. Therefore, a tendency to be

argumentative or restless may undermine your efforts. Discerning and keen on problem solving, however, you enjoy a mental challenge. In relationships it is important for you to be able to talk to your partner in order to understand the dynamics of the relationship, but talking should also include your deeper feelings and not just your thoughts. In love you need a partner who can offer you variety and mental stimulation to stop you from becoming bored. For you intimacy and sensuality blend well with wit and conversation.

WOMEN WITH MARS IN GEMINI: A keen communicator with an active mind, you can express yourself forcefully. Your mental agility implies that you respond quickly to people or situations with your razor-sharp mind. When you believe in something, you can argue your point of view with enthusiasm. Humorous and witty, you enjoy friendly banter and can be turned on sexually by someone who is clever and knows just the right thing to say. Often your youthful nature is adaptable and versatile and you can adjust quickly to new situations. Bored easily, your mental restlessness indicates that you are nervous by nature, and if you are not using your mind constructively you can become anxious or worried. It is therefore important for you to focus on some type of project that can challenge you intellectually or one that includes learning new skills or problem solving. You are often attracted to clever and expressive individuals who act out your more masculine qualities. You are keen on lively discussions, and your partners must be able to communicate well, be knowledgeable or skillful, and keen on learning new subjects. If they are witty and enterprising, then so much the better.

Your appealing attributes: persuasive, mentally quick, witty, good critic, entertaining, literary, writing skills, mentally curious, gift of the gab, quick comprehension, self-expressive, cultured, articulate, versatile

Your unappealing attributes: argumentative, superficial, biting criticism, lazy, too talkative, easily bored, scattered energies, restlessness, impatient

Mars in Cancer

MEN WITH MARS IN CANCER: Although on the surface you appear strong and dynamic, underneath you are sensitive, with powerful emotions. By using the gentle but firm approach you can resist shying away from challenges. When you do not feel secure you may retreat rather than face opposition. You usually possess a strong attachment to family and can be sensitive to conflict. This should not always be seen as a sign of weakness as you often gather all your energy for a counterattack. When you become impatient you can act on impulse, but more often than not your instincts are spot on. Highly aware

and receptive, you empower yourself in your relationships when you express your feelings in an assertive way. Nevertheless, being sensitive and tender can make you an excellent lover. Security conscious, you can be very protective toward partners and loved ones. You often show your compassion and caring qualities when others ask for help. In order to create harmonious and secure relationships, you have to balance your need to be assertive with your desire to be caring and understanding.

WOMEN WITH MARS IN CANCER: As you often act on your feelings, you are likely to fluctuate in moods. Often caring and loving, your emotional bonds are important to you, especially if you have invested time and effort in them. Concerned with security, you have a high protective factor, especially toward family members and loved ones. Intuitive toward others, you also have strong gut feelings or a powerful sixth sense. Your tendency for changing moods, however, means that you need to express your feelings rather than suppress them. You are often attracted to emotionally sympathetic or protective individuals who can act out your masculine qualities. Usually you are drawn to sensitive individuals who are emotionally aware and have loyalty high on their list of priorities. If your partner is a good cook you will appreciate his efforts. As you are likely to possess strong maternal instincts, you may prefer a partner who is family-oriented.

Your appealing attributes: instinctive, intuitive, security conscious, intense emotions, bold, ambitious, parental instincts, sympathetic, protective, caring, artistic, romantic, kind, enterprising, sensitive

Your unappealing attributes: moody, restlessness, temperamental, shy, quarrelsome with family members, lack of persistence, irritable, interfering, impulsive, frustrated

Mars in Leo

MEN WITH MARS IN LEO: Your strong presence and dynamic drive ensures that you make a strong impression on others. Being creative and enterprising, you can approach life with enthusiasm, often gravitating to positions of leadership and power. Proud, with a touch of the dramatic, you can usually attract others with your self-confidence and determination. Avoid becoming overconfident or arrogant; you empower yourself when you develop humility, modesty, or listen to others. In relationships you can be a passionate, generous, and romantic lover. Since loyalty is important to you, if you suspect that your partner is unfaithful or disloyal you can become very stubborn or unforgiving. Nevertheless, a need for amusement and excitement implies that you are often spontaneous and bold enough to take risks or inspire others to have fun.

WOMEN WITH MARS IN LEO: Confident and proud, you can make a good impression on others. Being popular and well thought of is important to your self-esteem. Often generous and fun-loving, you can be an enthusiastic friend or team player. With your vitality and drive, you may naturally find yourself gravitating to leading positions. Wanting to express yourself, you can succeed by developing your innate creative talents. Although determined and purposeful, your dislike of taking orders implies that you are sometimes bossy or stubborn. You are often attracted to strong and self-willed individuals who can act out your masculine qualities. You may find yourself drawn to the natural actors or performers. When you fall in love, you are usually warm, kind, and generous. As well as creative individuals, you admire dynamic, independent, and enterprising people who are self-assured. Nobility and honor are also high on your list of priorities, therefore weak or disloyal people would make unsuitable partners.

Your appealing attributes: creative, ambitious, dramatic, playful, generous, dignified, honorable, sociable, entertaining, courageous, self-assured, speculative, gifted, enterprising, enthusiastic, dynamic

Your unappealing attributes: stubborn, vain, bossy, snobbish, arrogant, domineering, egocentric, risk taking, melodramatic, too proud

Mars in Virgo

MEN WITH MARS IN VIRGO: Often efficient and orderly, you like to be well organized. Capable of exploring the different angles of any situation, you like to examine all the facts before you approach a new project or relationship. Good at debates, you often have the power to reason and support your beliefs. Being shrewd and keen on improvements, you know how to exploit situations and take advantage of opportunities. Your sensuality suggests that you enjoy perfecting your lovemaking techniques. A tendency to be skeptical, however, suggests that you like to question others and test their knowledge. Often methodical and careful, with your ability to pay attention to detail you excel in jobs that require good concentration. When you are armed with information you are assertive and direct, but worry and mental stress can cause you anxiety and affect your relationships. Nevertheless, thoughtful and competent, you enjoy being of practical help to your partner and others.

WOMEN WITH MARS IN VIRGO: Intellectually bright and methodical, you are often a cautious individual with an eye for detail. With the desire to refine and improve on situations or systems, you usually do not mind spending time sorting or reorganizing to create order. Equally, hoping to improve your

relationships you generally like to analyze in detail your personal life and your partnerships. A neat and tidy factor indicates that you may focus too much on the small details and lose sight of the big picture. Being a perfectionist, a tendency to spot mistakes may also manifest through criticism. You are often attracted to practical and analytical individuals who act out your masculine qualities. With your down-to-earth sensuality, you can approach relationships in a practical way. You can also be drawn to smart yet modest people. Clean and well-presented individuals usually catch your eye. At your best you are helpful and supportive and your partner is ideally a practical and hardworking person who takes pride in his work.

Your appealing attributes: well-organized, methodical, businesslike, rational, scientific, intelligent, practical, adaptable, helpful, meticulous, dutiful, modest, discriminating, analytical, orderly, efficient, faithful, detail-oriented, earthy, discreet, astute

Your unappealing attributes: critical, anxious, irritable, compulsive organizer or cleaner, nervous, worried, skeptical, gets lost in the details, takes on too much, too perfectionist, inhibited, overanalyzes

Mars in Libra

MEN WITH MARS IN LIBRA: Usually you are a refined and sociable person who enjoys mixing with others. You may have to balance your ability to be charming and polite with your sense of aggression. Being diplomatic suggests that you have good negotiating skills and when developed they can help you excel in careers dealing with the public. Although you are often charming and intelligent, a tendency to be indecisive means that you like to weigh all your options before you take any action. When you are blunt or too frank, you lose some of your attractive qualities, yet when you need to impress others you can express yourself in a stylish manner or in a creative way. Your friendly approach and enthusiasm toward others usually aids your success. You may find it hard to assert yourself with partners if you are unhappy about your relationships; however, you need to confront people even if it creates unpleasant tension.

WOMEN WITH MARS IN LIBRA: People-oriented, you are usually keen to interact with others. Being charming and diplomatic can aid in your overall success and powers of attraction. Seeing the advantages in partnership or team efforts, you can easily get on with colleagues or friends. In order to assert yourself, however, you need to maintain, from the start, a balance of give and take in all your relationships. Although you are keen to create harmony and peace around you, issues

concerning fair play and justice can incite you to become more forceful or angry. Keen on objectivity, you like to see all points of view and often have a flair for playing the devil's advocate. You are often attracted to assertive yet refined individuals who act out your masculine qualities. Sociable and fair-minded people with networking skills and good manners also impress you. Ideally your partner is an even-tempered and intelligent individual with creative skills and a love of beauty.

Your appealing attributes: friendly, courteous, teamwork, tactful, sociable, polite, networker, gracious, harmonious, creative, romantic, sophisticated, considerate, cultured, diplomatic, entertaining, fair

Your unappealing attributes: vain, competitive, rivalry, lack of tact, indecisive, too frank, too confrontational or too passive, impulsive, unable to say no, dependent

Mars in Scorpio

MEN WITH MARS IN SCORPIO: Ambitious and determined, you can exert a great deal of effort in order to succeed. In fact your dedication and persistence is sometimes interpreted as obsessive behavior while others admire your tenacity. Your inner strength is reflected by your penetrating look. Although sensitive and private, you nevertheless seek power and security. You may reveal your more forceful character when you are threatened with challenging situations or when the stakes are high. Having a competitive nature, you do not usually like to lose. You can be unforgiving if a person crosses you, yet at the same time when someone shows their loyalty you will defend them with strength and dedication. Your powerful sensuality can prove attractive to others while your strong emotions and desires can make you a passionate lover or devoted companion.

WOMEN WITH MARS IN SCORPIO: Although you are a strong individual, your inner strength and determination is not always obvious. Often magnetic, fearless, and assertive, you do not need to expose your inner strength and confidence. Being sensitive, you often protect your vulnerability by being secretive so that others will not have control over you. Although not keen on revealing too much of yourself, you nevertheless feel matters very strongly. You are likely to have a great deal of vitality and drive or much energy at your disposal. If you put all that wonderful energy into something inspiring, you can achieve remarkable things. You may be attracted to strong and self-willed individuals who act out your masculine qualities. Although you are often drawn to dominant individuals or the silent type, you may have to watch out that power issues do not enter into your relationships, especially if you both become forceful or stubborn. Trust and loyalty are high on your

list of priorities, and if anyone crosses you, you may find it hard to forgive. Your strong sensuality endows you with personal magnetism.

Your appealing attributes: strong ambition, survival instincts, forceful, sexual energy, indestructible, irresistible, passionate, tenacious, focused, the power to transform, hardworking, practical, daring, determined, courageous, sensual, sensitive, resourceful

Your unappealing attributes: controlling, secretive, ruthless streak, jealous, possessive, critical, selfishness, withholds love, emotional extremes, destructive, getting even, too competitive, dominating, unforgiving

Mars in Sagittarius

MEN WITH MARS IN SAGITTARIUS: Your competitive nature usually enjoys a challenge. Keeping up with the latest trends, you like to be where the action is. Keen to broaden your horizons, you often love freedom, adventure, and travel. You may even enjoy a type of sport or relationship that involves danger or an element of risk as well as skill. Being frank and direct, you often approach life with enthusiasm. Spontaneous and optimistic, you may sometimes rush into situations without much thought and later regret it. Nevertheless, if you have the resources you can be generous and expansive. You may find your true strength when you develop your philosophical attitude and explore the bigger picture in life. Capable of being inspired by a cause, wisdom, or idealistic motives, you can act with passion to protect your beliefs. Just make sure you are fighting with honorable motives. With your love of freedom, in relationships you want a partner who will not restrict you. Your approach to relationships often reflects your philosophy on life.

WOMEN WITH MARS IN SAGITTARIUS: Often competitive by nature, you can be daring and adventurous. A love of freedom and an ability to act on impulse indicate that you prefer to be spontaneous, and with your strong convictions, you tend to have firmly held beliefs. In relationships, you are usually frank and direct; you do not like to beat around the bush when you have something to say. Trouble may arise, however, if you are thoughtless or too blunt. Nevertheless, your enthusiasm and sincerity indicate that you usually do not mean to offend. Being broad-minded, you might explore different philosophies until you find one that suits you. You are often attracted to daring and adventurous individuals who can act out your masculine qualities. You can also be drawn to optimistic and idealistic people who are keen to embrace life or those with a love of sports and games. Although these types may not always be suitable for a domesticated life, you both share a love

of fun, optimism, and adventure. Alternatively, you may be attracted to the more intellectual and spiritual types you could meet while expanding your horizons or traveling.

Your appealing attributes: persuasive, frank, love of sport, competitive, enthusiastic, direct, open-minded, freedom-loving, warm, daring, honorable, spontaneous, honest, adventurous, generous, humanitarian, idealistic, dignified

Your unappealing attributes: tactless, extravagant, impetuous, opinionated, hasty, restless, argumentative, social climber, frightened of commitment, self-righteous, blunt, overindulgent, risk taker, too opportunistic

Mars in Capricorn

MEN WITH MARS IN CAPRICORN: Determined and ambitious, you can be purposeful and practical with a down-to-earth approach. Self-disciplined and hardworking, with the right strategy you can achieve a great deal. Lack of motivation, however, can undermine your resolute nature. Usually you take your responsibilities seriously, and with your ability to achieve maximum results with as little effort as possible, you can also excel in long-term planning. This may extend to taking control of situations, whether in business or relationships, in order to maintain positions of power. In relationships, however, you are generally admired for your self-reliance and natural authority. If you are dealing with other strong individuals you may exhibit your practical and realistic outlook in creative problem solving. Your tendency to be reserved suggests that your strong sexuality is well controlled.

WOMEN WITH MARS IN CAPRICORN: Often determined yet restrained, you usually like to work with goals and a set structure. Being practical and responsible, you often take charge of situations. Usually you prefer the slow but sure approach, and with your innate determination and patience, in time you can achieve a great deal. With a desire for status and recognition you are willing to work hard and show dedication. At times, however, a tendency to be stubborn or calculating can undermine your great efforts. You are often attracted to determined and ambitious individuals who can act out your masculine qualities. A serious and pragmatic person with respectful manners may suit you best. As loyalty and security are high on your list of priorities, once you commit to a relationship you will do your utmost to maintain stability.

Your appealing attributes: ambitious, self-reliant, dignified, authoritative, self-controlled, disciplined, hardworking, committed, dutiful, sensual, loyal, self-assured, executive abilities, industrious, goal-oriented, enterprising, purposeful, bold, energetic, direct, pragmatic, efficient

Your unappealing attributes: lack of endurance, overconfident, pessimistic, materialistic, cold, stubborn, controlling, hesitant, selfish, too ambitious, defiant, calculating

Mars in Aquarius

MEN WITH MARS IN AQUARIUS: An independent individual, you are assertive and often act with deliberation. Inventive and inspired by flashes of genius, your advanced thinking can produce ideas that are unique and often ahead of their time. Being progressive, you prefer new working methods and often have an aptitude for technology. Although you are usually people-oriented and a good team player, you can at times be controversial and contradicting. You may argue against others just to be different or contrary. Nevertheless, a humanitarian streak also implies that you will fight for social reforms and injustice. Even though you can at times be so detached as to be almost indifferent, you will instinctively go to the aid of others. You do best in situations where everyone is equal and shares a common goal. In relationships it is important that you have the freedom to operate independently and not be tied down with clinging partners. Willing to experiment, you may also be open to unconventional partnerships.

WOMEN WITH MARS IN AQUARIUS: Often group-oriented and freedom-loving, you usually value your independence. Being original and innovative, you understand current trends and think progressively. Sometimes your ideas are so unique they are ahead of their time. When you are detached you are objective in your attitude, but if you believe in something strongly enough you will rebel against restriction or tradition. Usually you prefer the company of unconventional or sociable people. At times you may act differently or say something provocative just to be contrary or to get a reaction. You are often attracted to independent and original individuals who act out your masculine qualities. Dispassionate or impartial yet friendly, you are attracted to people who are not afraid to be different. Being cool and detached, you need enough room to be yourself and do not like to be smothered by a needy partner. Since friendship is as important to you as love, you want a partner who is also a friend and confidant.

Your appealing attributes: independent, clever, original, freedom-loving, honest, friendly, practical, teamwork, intelligent, progressive, reformer, humanitarian, inspired, sociable, inventive, objective

Your unappealing attributes: stubborn, inconsistent, contradicting, nonconformist, difficult, too serious, too detached, eccentric, awkward, rebellious

Mars in Pisces

MEN WITH MARS IN PISCES: You are often inspired to act by your sense of vision and imaginative aspirations. If you are constantly dreaming you may fail to find enough energy to put your thoughts into action. Nonetheless, when you believe in something or someone you become very devoted, focused, and dedicated. In relationships your sensitivity can make you a tender and subtle lover in tune with your partner's feelings. Easily influenced by your peers, you need to be in the company of positive, enthusiastic, and idealistic people who will not lead you astray. By learning to stay detached you can make up your own mind and adopt a philosophy best suited to your needs. Your compassionate side indicates that you get a great deal of satisfaction from helping others and developing your humanitarian traits. Even when in a relationship, it is important for you to have some time alone to contemplate and rejuvenate your energies.

WOMEN WITH MARS IN PISCES: Moved by your emotions, your actions are often based on your feelings and sixth sense. Imaginative and creative, you are often a dreamer with compassion. Artistic and sensitive, you quickly observe the atmosphere around you. Although you often receive accurate impressions, you still need to clarify issues rather than let your imagination work overtime. Nevertheless, you work well when you are inspired and use your foresight to produce something concrete. You are often attracted to romantic and emotionally sensitive men who can act out your masculine qualities. You are also drawn to idealistic individuals with creative talents or poetic and spiritual inclinations. Alternatively, you may be drawn to partners with big plans or fantasies. But if your partner is a man of action you can work well together to manifest your wonderful visions.

Your appealing attributes: imaginative, idealistic, creative, inspired, subtle, sympathetic, visionary, psychic, compassionate, sensitive, poetic, artistic, musical, interest in metaphysics, carefree spirit, caring

Your unappealing attributes: lazy, daydreamer, passive, evasive, martyr, feeling vulnerable, delusion, follower, weak, moody, lacks discrimination, escapist, impressionable, overemotional

Your Venus Power

The planet Venus governs love, creativity, artistic gifts or talents, feminine sexuality, and your powers of attraction. Venus also rules physical beauty and money. In the female/male polarity, this planet represents the feminine side. In women's astrological charts, Venus depicts the power you possess to attract others. In men's astrological charts, Venus represents your feminine side and the women you are therefore instinctively drawn to. To use the Venus table below all you need to do is go first to your year of birth and check in which sign Venus was located on your birth date. Once you check out which Venus is yours, return to your birthday profile page and read your Venus interpretation. You can also use the Venus table to check the Venus placements of your friends, loved ones, and partner. If you want more information about your Sun sign and your Venus combination, read the interpretations that follow this Venus timetable.

Since the planet Venus does not have a regular yearly cycle pattern, you may on occasion not find your Venus on your birthday page. In this rare instance you need to go a few pages backward or forward to find your Venus interpretation on another birthday profile.

Venus Table: 1938–2012

1938
Venus in Capricorn: Jan 1–Jan 23
Venus in Aquarius: Jan 23–Feb 16
Venus in Pisces: Feb 16–Mar 12
Venus in Aries: Mar 12–Apr 5
Venus in Taurus: Apr 5–Apr 29
Venus in Gemini: Apr 29–May 24
Venus in Cancer: May 24–June 18
Venus in Leo: June 18–July 14
Venus in Virgo: July 14–Aug 9
Venus in Libra: Aug 9–Sept 7
Venus in Scorpio: Sept 7–Oct 13
Venus in Sagittarius: Oct 13–Nov 15
Venus in Scorpio: Nov 15–Dec 31

1939
Venus in Scorpio: Jan 1–Jan 4
Venus in Sagittarius: Jan 4–Feb 6
Venus in Capricorn: Feb 6–Mar 5
Venus in Aquarius: Mar 5–Mar 31
Venus in Pisces: Mar 31–Apr 25
Venus in Aries: Apr 25–May 20
Venus in Taurus: May 20–June 14
Venus in Gemini: June 1–July 9
Venus in Cancer: July 9–Aug 2
Venus in Leo: Aug 2–Aug 26
Venus in Virgo: Aug 26–Sept 20
Venus in Libra: Sept 20–Oct 14
Venus in Scorpio: Oct 14–Nov 7

Venus in Sagittarius: Nov 7–Dec 1
Venus in Capricorn: Dec 1–Dec 25
Venus in Aquarius: Dec 25–Dec 31

1940
Venus in Aquarius: Jan 1–Jan 18
Venus in Pisces: Jan 18–Feb 12
Venus in Aries: Feb 12–Mar 8
Venus in Taurus: Mar 8–Apr 4
Venus in Gemini: Apr 4–May 6
Venus in Cancer: May 6–July 5
Venus in Gemini: July 5–Aug 1
Venus in Cancer: Aug 1–Sept 8
Venus in Leo: Sept 8–Oct 6
Venus in Virgo: Oct 6–Nov 1
Venus in Libra: Nov 1–Nov 26
Venus in Scorpio: Nov 26–Dec 20
Venus in Sagittarius: Dec 20–Dec 31

1941
Venus in Sagittarius: Jan 1–Jan 13
Venus in Capricorn: Jan 13–Feb 6
Venus in Aquarius: Feb 6–Mar 2
Venus in Pisces: Mar 2–Mar 27
Venus in Aries: Mar 27–Apr 20
Venus in Taurus: Apr 24–May 14
Venus in Gemini: May 14–June 7
Venus in Cancer: June 7–July 2

Venus in Leo: July 2–July 27
Venus in Virgo: July 27–Aug 21
Venus in Libra: Aug 21–Aug 15
Venus in Scorpio: Aug 15–Oct 10
Venus in Sagittarius: Oct 10–Nov 6
Venus in Capricorn: Nov 6–Dec 5
Venus in Aquarius: Dec 5–Dec 31

1942
Venus in Aquarius: Jan 1–Apr 6
Venus in Pisces: Apr 6–May 6
Venus in Aries: May 6–June 2
Venus in Taurus: June 2–June 27
Venus in Gemini: June 27–July 23
Venus in Cancer: July 23–Aug 17
Venus in Leo: Aug 17–Sept 10
Venus in Virgo: Sept 10–Oct 4
Venus in Libra: Oct 4–Oct 28
Venus in Scorpio: Oct 28–Nov 21
Venus in Sagittarius: Nov 21–Dec 15
Venus in Capricorn: Dec 15–Dec 31

1943
Venus in Aquarius: Jan 1–Jan 5
Venus in Pisces: Jan 5–Feb 2
Venus in Aries: Feb 2–June 5
Venus in Taurus: June 5–July 7
Venus in Gemini: July 7–Aug 3
Venus in Cancer: Aug 3–Aug 29

Venus in Leo: Aug 29–Sept 23
Venus in Virgo: Sept 23–Oct 18
Venus in Libra: Oct 18–Nov 18
Venus in Scorpio: Nov 18–Dec 5
Venus in Sagittarius: Dec 5–Dec 29
Venus in Capricorn: Dec 29–Dec 31

1944
Venus in Scorpio: Jan 1–Jan 3
Venus in Sagittarius: Jan 3–Jan 28
Venus in Capricorn: Jan 28–Feb 21
Venus in Aquarius: Feb 21–Mar 17
Venus in Pisces: Mar 17–Apr 10
Venus in Aries: Apr 10–May 4
Venus in Taurus: May 4–May 29
Venus in Gemini: May 29–June 22
Venus in Cancer: June 22–July 17
Venus in Leo: Jul 17–Aug 10
Venus in Virgo: Aug 10–Sept 3
Venus in Libra: Sept 3–Sept 28
Venus in Scorpio: Sept 28–Oct 22
Venus in Sagittarius: Oct 22–Nov 16
Venus in Capricorn: Nov 16–Dec 11
Venus in Aquarius: Dec 11–Dec 31

1945
Venus in Aquarius: Jan 1–Jan 5
Venus in Pisces: Jan 5–Feb 2
Venus in Aries: Feb 2–Mar 11

Venus in Taurus: Mar 11–Apr 7
Venus in Aries: Apr 7–June 4
Venus in Taurus June 4–July 7
Venus in Gemini: July 7–Aug 4
Venus in Cancer: Aug 4–Aug 30
Venus in Leo: Aug 30–Sept 24
Venus in Virgo: Sept 24–Oct 19
Venus in Libra: Oct 19–Nov 12
Venus in Scorpio: Nov 12–Dec 6
Venus in Sagittarius: Dec 6–Dec 30
Venus in Capricorn: Dec 30–Dec 31

1946

Venus in Capricorn: Jan 1–Jan 22
Venus in Aquarius: Jan 22–Feb 15
Venus in Pisces: Feb 15–Mar 11
Venus in Aries: Mar 11–Apr 5
Venus in Taurus: Apr 5–Apr 29
Venus in Gemini: Apr 29–May 24
Venus in Cancer: May 24–June 18
Venus in Leo: June 18–July 13
Venus in Virgo: July 13–Aug 9
Venus in Libra: Aug 9–Sept 7
Venus in Scorpio: Sept 7–Oct 16
Venus in Sagittarius: Oct 16–Nov 8
Venus in Scorpio: Nov 8–Dec 31

1947

Venus in Scorpio: Jan 1–Jan 5
Venus in Sagittarius: Jan 5–Feb 6
Venus in Capricorn: Feb 6–Mar 5
Venus in Aquarius: Mar 5–Mar 30
Venus in Pisces: Mar 30–Apr 25
Venus in Aries: Apr 25–May 20
Venus in Taurus: May 20–June 13
Venus in Gemini: June 13–July 8
Venus in Cancer: July 8–Aug 2
Venus in Leo: Aug 2–Aug 26
Venus in Virgo: Aug 26–Sept 19
Venus in Libra: Sept 19–Oct 13
Venus in Scorpio: Oct 13–Nov 6
Venus in Sagittarius: 6 Nov–Nov 30
Venus in Capricorn: 30 Nov–Dec 24
Venus in Aquarius: Dec 24–Dec 31

1948

Venus in Aquarius: Jan 1–Jan 18
Venus in Pisces: Jan 18–Feb 11
Venus in Aries: Feb 11–Mar 8
Venus in Taurus: Mar 8–Apr 4
Venus in Gemini: Apr 4–May 7
Venus in Cancer: May 7–June 29

Venus in Gemini: June 29–Aug 3
Venus in Cancer: Aug 3–Sept 8
Venus in Leo: Sept 8–Oct 6
Venus in Virgo: Oct 6–Nov 1
Venus in Libra: Nov 1–Nov 26
Venus in Scorpio: Nov 26–Dec 20
Venus in Sagittarius: Dec 20–Dec 31

1949

Venus in Sagittarius: Jan 1–Jan 13
Venus in Capricorn: Jan 13–Feb 6
Venus in Aquarius: Feb 6–Mar 2
Venus in Pisces: Mar 2–Mar 26
Venus in Aries: Mar 26–Apr 19
Venus in Taurus: Apr 19–May 14
Venus in Gemini: May 14–June 7
Venus in Cancer: June 7–July 1
Venus in Leo: July 1–July 27
Venus in Virgo: July 27–Aug 20
Venus in Libra: Aug 20–Sept 14
Venus in Scorpio: Sept 14–Oct 10
Venus in Sagittarius: Oct 10–Nov 6
Venus in Capricorn: Nov 6–Dec 6
Venus in Aquarius: Dec 6–Dec 31

1950

Venus in Aquarius: Jan 1–Apr 6
Venus in Pisces: Apr 6–May 5
Venus in Aries: May 5–June 1
Venus in Taurus: June 1–June 27
Venus in Gemini: June 27–July 22
Venus in Cancer: July 22–Aug 16
Venus in Leo: Aug 16–Sept 10
Venus in Virgo: Sept 10–Oct 4
Venus in Libra: Oct 4–Oct 28
Venus in Scorpio: Oct 28–Nov 21
Venus in Sagittarius: Nov 21–Dec 14
Venus in Capricorn: Dec 14–Dec 31

1951

Venus in Capricorn: Jan 1–Jan 7
Venus in Aquarius: Jan 7–Jan 31
Venus in Pisces: Jan 31–Feb 24
Venus in Aries: Feb 24–Mar 21
Venus in Taurus: Mar 21–Apr 15
Venus in Gemini: Apr 15–May 11
Venus in Cancer: May 11–June 7
Venus in Leo: June 7–July 8
Venus in Virgo: July 8–Nov 9
Venus in Libra: Nov 9–Dec 8
Venus in Scorpio: Dec 8–Dec 31

1952

Venus in Scorpio: Jan 1–Jan 2
Venus in Sagittarius: Jan 2–Jan 27
Venus in Capricorn: Jan 27–Feb 21
Venus in Aquarius: Feb 21–Mar 16
Venus in Pisces: Mar 16–Apr 9
Venus in Aries: Apr 9–May 4
Venus in Taurus: May 4–May 28
Venus in Gemini: May 28–June 22
Venus in Cancer: June 22–16 July
Venus in Leo: July 16–Aug 9
Venus in Virgo: Aug 9–Sept 3
Venus in Libra: Sept 3–Sept 27
Venus in Scorpio: Sept 27–Oct 22
Venus in Sagittarius: Oct 22–Nov 15
Venus in Capricorn: Nov 15–Dec 10
Venus in Aquarius: Dec 10–Dec 31

1953

Venus in Aquarius: Jan 1–Jan 5
Venus in Pisces: Jan 5–Feb 2
Venus in Aries: Feb 2–Mar 14
Venus in Taurus: Mar 14–Mar 31
Venus in Aries: Mar 31–June 5
Venus in Taurus June 5–July 7
Venus in Gemini: July 7–Aug 4
Venus in Cancer: Aug 4–Aug 30
Venus in Leo: Aug 30–Sept 24
Venus in Virgo: Sept 24–Oct 18
Venus in Libra: Oct 18–Nov 11
Venus in Scorpio: Nov 11–Dec 5
Venus in Sagittarius: Dec 5–Dec 29
Venus in Capricorn: Dec 29–Dec 31

1954

Venus in Capricorn: Jan 1–Jan 22
Venus in Aquarius: Jan 22–Feb 15
Venus in Pisces: Feb 15–Mar 11
Venus in Aries: Mar 11–Apr 4
Venus in Taurus: Apr 4–Apr 28
Venus in Gemini: Apr 28–May 23
Venus in Cancer: May 23–June 17
Venus in Leo: June 17–July 13
Venus in Virgo: July 13–Aug 9
Venus in Libra: Aug 9–Sept 6
Venus in Scorpio: Sept 6–Oct 23
Venus in Sagittarius: Oct 23–Oct 27
Venus in Scorpio: Oct 27–Dec 31

1955

Venus in Scorpio: Jan 1–Jan 6
Venus in Sagittarius: Jan 6–Feb 6

Venus in Capricorn: Feb 6–Mar 4
Venus in Aquarius: Mar 4–30 Mar
Venus in Pisces: Mar 30–Apr 24
Venus in Aries: Apr 24–May 19
Venus in Taurus: May 19–June 13
Venus in Gemini: June 13–July 8
Venus in Cancer: July 8–Aug 1
Venus in Leo: Aug 1–Aug 25
Venus in Virgo: Aug 25–Sept 18
Venus in Libra: Sept 18–Oct 13
Venus in Scorpio: Oct 13–Nov 6
Venus in Sagittarius: 6 Nov–Nov 30
Venus in Capricorn: 30 Nov–Dec 24
Venus in Aquarius: Dec 24–Dec 31

1956

Venus in Aquarius: Jan 1–Jan 17
Venus in Pisces: Jan 17–Feb 11
Venus in Aries: Feb 11–Mar 7
Venus in Taurus: Mar 7–Apr 4
Venus in Gemini: Apr 4–May 8
Venus in Cancer: May 8–Jun 23
Venus in Gemini: June 23–Aug 4
Venus in Cancer: Aug 4–Sept 8
Venus in Leo: Sept 8–Oct 6
Venus in Virgo: Oct 6–Nov 1
Venus in Libra: Nov 1–Nov 25
Venus in Scorpio: Nov 25–Dec 19
Venus in Sagittarius: Dec 19–Dec 31

1957

Venus in Sagittarius: Jan–Jan 12
Venus in Capricorn: Jan 12–Feb 5
Venus in Aquarius: Feb 5–Mar 1
Venus in Pisces: Mar 1–Mar 25
Venus in Aries: Mar 25–Apr 19
Venus in Taurus: Apr 19–May 13
Venus in Gemini: May 13–June 6
Venus in Cancer: June 6–July 1
Venus in Leo: July 1–July 26
Venus in Virgo: July 26–Aug 20
Venus in Libra: Aug 20–Sept 14
Venus in Scorpio: Sept 14–Oct 10
Venus in Sagittarius: Oct 10–Nov 5
Venus in Capricorn: Nov 5–Dec 6
Venus in Aquarius: Dec 6–Dec 31

1958

Venus in Aquarius: Jan 1–Apr 6
Venus in Pisces: Apr 6–May 5
Venus in Aries: May 5–June 1
Venus in Taurus: June 1–June 26

Venus in Gemini: June 26–July 22
Venus in Cancer: July 22–Aug 16
Venus in Leo: Aug 16–Sept 9
Venus in Virgo: Sept 9–Oct 3
Venus in Libra: Oct 3–Oct 27
Venus in Scorpio: Oct 27–Nov 20
Venus in Sagittarius: Nov 20–Dec 14
Venus in Capricorn: Dec 14–Dec 31

1959

Venus in Capricorn: Jan 1–Jan 7
Venus in Aquarius: Jan 7–Jan 31
Venus in Pisces: Jan 31–Feb 24
Venus in Aries: Feb 24–Mar 20
Venus in Taurus: Mar 20–Apr 14
Venus in Gemini: Apr 14–May 10
Venus in Cancer: May 10–June 6
Venus in Leo: June 6–July 8
Venus in Virgo: July 8–Sept 20
Venus in Leo: Sept 20–Sept 25
Venus in Virgo: Sept 25–Nov 9
Venus in Libra: Nov 9–Dec 7
Venus in Scorpio: Dec 7–Dec 31

1960

Venus in Scorpio: Jan 1–Jan 2
Venus in Sagittarius: Jan 2–Jan 27
Venus in Capricorn: Jan 27–Feb 20
Venus in Aquarius: Feb 20–Mar 16
Venus in Pisces: Mar 16–Apr 9
Venus in Aries: Apr 9–May 3
Venus in Taurus: May 3–May 28
Venus in Gemini: May 28–June 21
Venus in Cancer: June 21–July 16
Venus in Leo: July 16–Aug 9
Venus in Virgo: Aug 9–Sept 2
Venus in Libra: Sept 2–Sept 27
Venus in Scorpio: Sept 27–Oct 21
Venus in Sagittarius: Oct 21–Nov 15
Venus in Capricorn: Nov 15–Dec 10
Venus in Aquarius: Dec 10–Dec 31

1961

Venus in Aquarius: Jan 1–Jan 5
Venus in Pisces: Jan 5–Feb 2
Venus in Aries: Feb 2–June 5
Venus in Taurus: June 5–July 7
Venus in Gemini: July 7–Aug 3
Venus in Cancer: Aug 3–Aug 29
Venus in Leo: Aug 29–Sept 23
Venus in Virgo: Sept 23–Oct 18
Venus in Libra: Oct 18–Nov 18

Venus in Scorpio: Nov 18–Dec 5
Venus in Sagittarius: Dec 5–Dec 29
Venus in Capricorn: Dec 29–Dec 31

1962

Venus in Capricorn: Jan 1–Jan 21
Venus in Aquarius: Jan 21–Feb 14
Venus in Pisces: Feb 14–Mar 10
Venus in Aries: Mar 10–Apr 3
Venus in Taurus: Apr 3–Apr 28
Venus in Gemini: Apr 28–May 23
Venus in Cancer: May 23–June 17
Venus in Leo: June 17–July 12
Venus in Virgo: July 12–Aug 8
Venus in Libra: Aug 8–Sept 7
Venus in Scorpio: Sept 7–Dec 31

1963

Venus in Scorpio: Jan 1–Jan 6
Venus in Sagittarius: Jan 6–Feb 5
Venus in Capricorn: Feb 5–Mar 4
Venus in Aquarius: Mar 4–Mar 30
Venus in Pisces: Mar 30–Apr 24
Venus in Aries: Apr 24–May 19
Venus in Taurus: May 19–June 12
Venus in Gemini: June 12–July 7
Venus in Cancer: July 7–Aug 2
Venus in Leo: Aug 2–Aug 25
Venus in Virgo: Aug 25–Sept 18
Venus in Libra: Sept 18–Oct 12
Venus in Scorpio: Oct 12–Nov 5
Venus in Sagittarius: Nov 5–Nov 29
Venus in Capricorn: Nov 29–Dec 23
Venus in Aquarius: Dec 23–Dec 31

1964

Venus in Aquarius: Jan 1–Jan 17
Venus in Pisces: Jan 17–Feb 10
Venus in Aries: Feb 10–Mar 7
Venus in Taurus: Mar 7–Apr 4
Venus in Gemini: Apr 4–May 9
Venus in Cancer: May 9–June 17
Venus in Gemini: June 17–Aug 5
Venus in Cancer: Aug 5–Sept 8
Venus in Leo: Sept 8–Oct 5
Venus in Virgo: Oct 5–Oct 31
Venus in Libra: Oct 31–Nov 25
Venus in Scorpio: Nov 25–Dec 19
Venus in Sagittarius: Dec 19–Dec 31

1965

Venus in Sagittarius: Jan 1–Jan 12

Venus in Capricorn: Jan 12–Feb 5
Venus in Aquarius: Feb 5–Mar 1
Venus in Pisces: Mar 1–Mar 25
Venus in Aries: Mar 25–Apr 18
Venus in Taurus: Apr 18–May 12
Venus in Gemini: May 12–June 6
Venus in Cancer: June 6–June 30
Venus in Leo: June 30–July 25
Venus in Virgo: July 25–Aug 19
Venus in Libra: Aug 19–Sept 13
Venus in Scorpio: Sept 13–Oct 9
Venus in Sagittarius: Oct 9–Nov 5
Venus in Capricorn: Nov 5–Dec 7
Venus in Aquarius: Dec 7–Dec 31

1966

Venus in Aquarius: Jan 1–Feb 6
Venus in Pisces: Feb 6–Feb 25
Venus in Aries: Feb 25–Apr 6
Venus in Taurus: Apr 6–May 5
Venus in Aries: May 5–May 31
Venus in Taurus May 31–June 26
Venus in Gemini: June 26–July 21
Venus in Cancer: July 21–Aug 15
Venus in Leo: Aug 15–Sept 8
Venus in Virgo: Sept 8–Oct 3
Venus in Libra: Oct 3–Oct 27
Venus in Scorpio: Oct 27–Nov 20
Venus in Sagittarius: Nov 20–Dec 13
Venus in Capricorn: Dec 13–Dec 31

1967

Venus in Capricorn: Jan 1–Jan 6
Venus in Aquarius: Jan 6–Jan 30
Venus in Pisces: Jan 30–Feb 23
Venus in Aries: Feb 23–Mar 20
Venus in Taurus: Mar 20–Apr 14
Venus in Gemini: Apr 14–May 10
Venus in Cancer: May 10–June 6
Venus in Leo: June 6–July 8
Venus in Virgo: July 8–Sept 9
Venus in Leo: Sept 9–Oct 1
Venus in Virgo: Oct 1–Nov 9
Venus in Libra: Nov 9–Dec 7
Venus in Scorpio: Dec 7–Dec 31

1968

Venus in Scorpio: Jan 1
Venus in Sagittarius: Jan 1–Jan 26
Venus in Capricorn: Jan 26–Feb 20
Venus in Aquarius: Feb 20–Mar 15
Venus in Pisces: Mar 15–Apr 8

Venus in Aries: Apr 8–May 3
Venus in Taurus: May 3–May 27
Venus in Gemini: May 27–June 21
Venus in Cancer: June 21–July 15
Venus in Leo: July 15–Aug 8
Venus in Virgo: Aug 8–Sept 2
Venus in Libra: Sept 2–Sept 26
Venus in Scorpio: Sept 26–Oct 21
Venus in Sagittarius: Oct 21–Nov 14
Venus in Capricorn: Nov 14–Dec 9
Venus in Aquarius: Dec 9–Dec 31

1969

Venus in Aquarius: Jan 1–Jan 4
Venus in Pisces: Jan 4–Feb 2
Venus in Aries: Feb 2–June 6
Venus in Taurus: June 6–July 6
Venus in Gemini: July 6–Aug 3
Venus in Cancer: Aug 3–Aug 29
Venus in Leo: Aug 29–Sept 23
Venus in Virgo: Sept 23–Oct 17
Venus in Libra: Oct 17–Nov 10
Venus in Scorpio: Nov 10–Dec 4
Venus in Sagittarius: Dec 4–Dec 28
Venus in Capricorn: Dec 28–Dec 31

1970

Venus in Capricorn: Jan 1–Jan 21
Venus in Aquarius: Jan 21–Feb 14
Venus in Pisces: Feb 14–Mar 10
Venus in Aries: Mar 10–Apr 3
Venus in Taurus: Apr 3–Apr 27
Venus in Gemini: Apr 27–May 22
Venus in Cancer: May 22–June 16
Venus in Leo: June 16–July 12
Venus in Virgo: July 12–Aug 8
Venus in Libra: Aug 8–Sept 7
Venus in Scorpio: Sept 7–Dec 31

1971

Venus in Scorpio: Jan 1–Jan 7
Venus in Sagittarius: Jan 7–Feb 5
Venus in Capricorn: Feb 5–Mar 4
Venus in Aquarius: Mar 4–Mar 29
Venus in Pisces: Mar 29–Apr 23
Venus in Aries: Apr 23–May 28
Venus in Taurus: May 28–June 12
Venus in Gemini: June 12–July 6
Venus in Cancer: July 6–July 31
Venus in Leo: July 31–Aug 24
Venus in Virgo: Aug 24–Sept 17

Venus in Libra: Sept 17–Oct 11
Venus in Scorpio: Oct 11–Nov 5
Venus in Sagittarius: Nov 5–Nov 29
Venus in Capricorn: Nov 29–Dec 23
Venus in Aquarius: Dec 23–Dec 31

1972

Venus in Aquarius: Jan 1–Jan 16
Venus in Pisces: Jan 16–Feb 10
Venus in Aries: Feb 10–Mar 7
Venus in Taurus: Mar 7–Apr 3
Venus in Gemini: Apr 3–May 10
Venus in Cancer: May 10–June 11
Venus in Gemini: June 11–Aug 6
Venus in Cancer: Aug 6–Sept 7
Venus in Leo: Sept 7–Oct 5
Venus in Virgo: Oct 5–Oct 30
Venus in Libra: Oct 30–Nov 24
Venus in Scorpio: Nov 24–Dec 18
Venus in Sagittarius: Dec 18–Dec 31

1973

Venus in Sagittarius: Jan 1–Jan 11
Venus in Capricorn: Jan 11–Feb 4
Venus in Aquarius: Feb 4–Feb 28
Venus in Pisces: Feb 28–Mar 24
Venus in Aries: Mar 24–Apr 18
Venus in Taurus: Apr 18–May 12
Venus in Gemini: May 12–June 5
Venus in Cancer: June 5–June 10
Venus in Leo: June 10–July 25
Venus in Virgo: July 25–Aug 19
Venus in Libra: Aug 19–Aug 13
Venus in Scorpio: Aug 13–Oct 9
Venus in Sagittarius: Oct 9–Nov 5
Venus in Capricorn: Nov 5–Dec 7
Venus in Aquarius: Dec 7–Dec 31

1974

Venus in Aquarius: Jan 1–Jan 29
Venus in Capricorn: Jan 29–Feb 28
Venus in Aquarius: Feb 28–Apr 6
Venus in Pisces: Apr 6–May 4
Venus in Aries: May 4–May 31
Venus in Taurus: May 31–June 25
Venus in Gemini: June 25–July 21
Venus in Cancer: July 21–Aug 14
Venus in Leo: Aug 14–Sept 8
Venus in Virgo: Sept 8–Oct 2
Venus in Libra: Oct 2–Oct 26
Venus in Scorpio: Oct 26–Nov 19

Venus in Sagittarius: Nov 19–Dec 13
Venus in Capricorn: Dec 13–Dec 31

1975

Venus in Capricorn: Jan 1–Jan 6
Venus in Aquarius: Jan 6–Jan 30
Venus in Pisces: Jan 30–Feb 23
Venus in Aries: Feb 23–Mar 19
Venus in Taurus: Mar 19–Apr 13
Venus in Gemini: Apr 13–May 9
Venus in Cancer: May 9–June 6
Venus in Leo: June 6–July 9
Venus in Virgo: July 9–Sept 2
Venus in Leo: Sept 2–Oct 4
Venus in Virgo: Oct 4–Nov 9
Venus in Libra: Nov 9–Dec 7
Venus in Scorpio: Dec 7–Dec 31

1976

Venus in Scorpio: Jan 1
Venus in Sagittarius: Jan 1–Jan 26
Venus in Capricorn: Jan 26–Feb 19
Venus in Aquarius: Feb 19–Mar 15
Venus in Pisces: Mar 15–Apr 8
Venus in Aries: Apr 8–May 2
Venus in Taurus: May 2–May 27
Venus in Gemini: May 27–June 20
Venus in Cancer: June 20–July 14
Venus in Leo: July 14–Aug 8
Venus in Virgo: Aug 8–Sept 1
Venus in Libra: Sept 1–Sept 26
Venus in Scorpio: Sept 26–Oct 20
Venus in Sagittarius: Oct 20–Nov 14
Venus in Capricorn: Nov 14–Dec 9
Venus in Aquarius: Dec 9–Dec 31

1977

Venus in Aquarius: Jan 1–Jan 4
Venus in Pisces: Jan 4–Feb 2
Venus in Aries: Feb 2–June 6
Venus in Taurus: June 6–July 6
Venus in Gemini: July 6–Aug 2
Venus in Cancer: Aug 2–Aug 28
Venus in Leo: Aug 28–Sept 22
Venus in Virgo: Sept 22–Oct 17
Venus in Libra: Oct 17–Nov 10
Venus in Scorpio: Nov 10–Dec 4
Venus in Sagittarius: Dec 4–Dec 27
Venus in Capricorn: Dec 27–Dec 31

1978

Venus in Aquarius: Jan 1–Jan 20

Venus in Pisces: Jan 20–Feb 13
Venus in Aries: Feb 13–Mar 9
Venus in Taurus: Mar 9–Apr 27
Venus in Gemini: Apr 27–May 22
Venus in Cancer: May 22–June 16
Venus in Leo: June 16–July 12
Venus in Virgo: July 12–Aug 8
Venus in Libra: Aug 8–Sept 7
Venus in Scorpio: Sept 7–Dec 31

1979

Venus in Scorpio: Jan 1–Jan 7
Venus in Sagittarius: Jan 7–Feb 5
Venus in Capricorn: Feb 5–Mar 3
Venus in Aquarius: Mar 3–Mar 29
Venus in Pisces: Mar 29–Apr 23
Venus in Aries: Apr 23–May 18
Venus in Taurus: May 18–June 11
Venus in Gemini: June 11–July 6
Venus in Cancer: July 6–July 30
Venus in Leo: July 30–Aug 24
Venus in Virgo: Aug 24–Sept 17
Venus in Libra: Sept 17–Oct 11
Venus in Scorpio: Oct 11–Nov 4
Venus in Sagittarius: Nov 4–Nov 28
Venus in Capricorn: Nov 28–Dec 22
Venus in Aquarius: Dec 22–Dec 31

1980

Venus in Aquarius: Jan 1–Jan 16
Venus in Pisces: Jan 16–Feb 9
Venus in Aries: Feb 9–Mar 6
Venus in Taurus: Mar 6–Apr 3
Venus in Gemini: Apr 3–May 12
Venus in Cancer: May 12–June 5
Venus in Gemini: June 5–Aug 6
Venus in Cancer: Aug 6–Sept 7
Venus in Leo: Sept 7–Oct 4
Venus in Virgo: Oct 4–Oct 30
Venus in Libra: Oct 30–Nov 24
Venus in Scorpio: Nov 24–Dec 18
Venus in Sagittarius: Dec 18–Dec 31

1981

Venus in Sagittarius: Jan 1–Jan 11
Venus in Capricorn: Jan 11–Feb 4
Venus in Aquarius: Feb 4–Feb 28
Venus in Pisces: Feb 28–Mar 24
Venus in Aries: Mar 24–Apr 17
Venus in Taurus: Apr 17–May 11
Venus in Gemini: May 11–June 5
Venus in Cancer: June 5–June 29

Venus in Leo: June 29–July 24
Venus in Virgo: July 24–Aug 18
Venus in Libra: Aug 18–Sept 12
Venus in Scorpio: Sept 12–Oct 9
Venus in Sagittarius: Oct 9–Nov 5
Venus in Capricorn: Nov 5–Dec 8
Venus in Aquarius: Dec 8–Dec 31

1982

Venus in Aquarius: Jan 1–Jan 23
Venus in Capricorn: Jan 23–Mar 2
Venus in Aquarius: Mar 2–Apr 6
Venus in Pisces: Apr 6–May 4
Venus in Aries: May 4–May 30
Venus in Taurus: May 30–June 25
Venus in Gemini: June 25–July 20
Venus in Cancer: July 20–Aug 14
Venus in Leo: Aug 14–Sept 7
Venus in Virgo: Sept 7–Oct 2
Venus in Libra: Oct 2–Oct 26
Venus in Scorpio: Oct 26–Nov 18
Venus in Sagittarius: Nov 18–Dec 12
Venus in Capricorn: Dec 12–Dec 31

1983

Venus in Capricorn: Jan 1–Jan 5
Venus in Aquarius: Jan 5–Jan 29
Venus in Pisces: Jan 29–Feb 22
Venus in Aries: Feb 22–Mar 19
Venus in Taurus: Mar 19–Apr 13
Venus in Gemini: Apr 13–May 9
Venus in Cancer: May 9–June 6
Venus in Leo: June 6–July 10
Venus in Virgo: July 10–Aug 27
Venus in Leo: Aug 27–Oct 5
Venus in Virgo: Oct 5–Nov 9
Venus in Libra: Nov 9–Dec 7
Venus in Scorpio: Dec 7–Dec 31

1984

Venus in Scorpio: Jan 1
Venus in Sagittarius: Jan 1–Jan 25
Venus in Capricorn: Jan 25–Feb 19
Venus in Aquarius: Feb 19–Mar 14
Venus in Pisces: Mar 14–Apr 7
Venus in Aries: Apr 7–May 2
Venus in Taurus: May 2–May 26
Venus in Gemini: May 26–June 20
Venus in Cancer: June 20–July 14
Venus in Leo: July 14–Aug 7
Venus in Virgo: Aug 7–Sept 1
Venus in Libra: Sept 1–Sept 25

Venus in Scorpio: Sept 25–Oct 20
Venus in Sagittarius: Oct 20–Nov 13
Venus in Capricorn: Nov 13–Dec 9
Venus in Aquarius: Dec 9–Dec 31

1985

Venus in Aquarius: Jan 1–Jan 4
Venus in Pisces: Jan 4–Feb 2
Venus in Aries: Feb 2–June 6
Venus in Taurus: June 6–July 6
Venus in Gemini: July 6–Aug 2
Venus in Cancer: Aug 2–Aug 28
Venus in Leo: Aug 28–Sept 22
Venus in Virgo: Sept 22–Oct 16
Venus in Libra: Oct 16–Nov 9
Venus in Scorpio: Nov 9–Dec 3
Venus in Sagittarius: Dec 3–Dec 27
Venus in Capricorn: Dec 27–Dec 31

1986

Venus in Capricorn: Jan 1–Jan 20
Venus in Aquarius: Jan 20–Feb 13
Venus in Pisces: Feb 13–Mar 9
Venus in Aries: Mar 9–Apr 2
Venus in Taurus: Apr 2–Apr 26
Venus in Gemini: Apr 27–May 21
Venus in Cancer: May 21–June 15
Venus in Leo: June 15–July 11
Venus in Virgo: July 11–Aug 7
Venus in Libra: Aug 7–Sept 7
Venus in Scorpio: Sept 7–Dec 31

1987

Venus in Scorpio: Jan 1–Jan 7
Venus in Sagittarius: Jan 7–Feb 5
Venus in Capricorn: Feb 5–Mar 3
Venus in Aquarius: Mar 3–Mar 28
Venus in Pisces: Mar 28–Apr 22
Venus in Aries: Apr 22–May 17
Venus in Taurus: May 17–June 11
Venus in Gemini: June 11–July 5
Venus in Cancer: July 5–July 30
Venus in Leo: July 30–Aug 23
Venus in Virgo: Aug 23–Sept 16
Venus in Libra: Sept 16–Oct 10
Venus in Scorpio: Oct 10–Nov 3
Venus in Sagittarius: Nov 3–Nov 28
Venus in Capricorn: Nov 28–Dec 22
Venus in Aquarius: Dec 22–Dec 31

1988

Venus in Aquarius: Jan 1–Jan 15

Venus in Pisces: Jan 15–Feb 9
Venus in Aries: Feb 9–Mar 6
Venus in Taurus: Mar 6–Apr 3
Venus in Gemini: Apr 3–May 17
Venus in Cancer: May 17–May 27
Venus in Gemini: May 27–Aug 6
Venus in Cancer: Aug 6–Sept 7
Venus in Leo: Sept 7–Oct 4
Venus in Virgo: Oct 4–Oct 29
Venus in Libra: Oct 29–Nov 23
Venus in Scorpio: Nov 23–Dec 17
Venus in Sagittarius: Dec 17–Dec 31

1989

Venus in Sagittarius: Jan 1–Jan 10
Venus in Capricorn: Jan 10–Feb 3
Venus in Aquarius: Feb 3–Feb 27
Venus in Pisces: Feb 27–Mar 23
Venus in Aries: Mar 23–Apr 16
Venus in Taurus: Apr 16–May 11
Venus in Gemini: May 11–June 4
Venus in Cancer: June 4–June 29
Venus in Leo: June 29–July 24
Venus in Virgo: July 24–Aug 18
Venus in Libra: Aug 18–Aug 12
Venus in Scorpio: Aug 12–Oct 8
Venus in Sagittarius: Oct 8–Nov 5
Venus in Capricorn: Nov 5–Dec 10
Venus in Aquarius: Dec 10–Dec 31

1990

Venus in Aquarius: Jan 1–Jan 16
Venus in Capricorn: Jan 16–Mar 3
Venus in Aquarius: Mar 3–Apr 6
Venus in Pisces: Apr 6–May 4
Venus in Aries: May 4–May 30
Venus in Taurus: May 30–June 25
Venus in Gemini: June 25–July 20
Venus in Cancer: July 20–Aug 13
Venus in Leo: Aug 13–Sept 7
Venus in Virgo: Sept 7–Oct 1
Venus in Libra: Oct 1–Oct 25
Venus in Scorpio: Oct 25–Nov 18
Venus in Sagittarius: Nov 18–Dec 12
Venus in Capricorn: Dec 12–Dec 31

1991

Venus in Capricorn: Jan 1–Jan 5
Venus in Aquarius: Jan 5–Jan 29
Venus in Pisces: Jan 29–Feb 22
Venus in Aries: Feb 22–Mar 18
Venus in Taurus: Mar 18–Apr 13

Venus in Gemini: Apr 13–May 9
Venus in Cancer: May 9–June 6
Venus in Leo: June 6–July 11
Venus in Virgo: July 11–Aug 21
Venus in Leo: Aug 21–Oct 6
Venus in Virgo: Oct 6–Nov 9
Venus in Libra: Nov 9–Dec 6
Venus in Scorpio: Dec 6–Dec 31
Venus in Sagittarius: Dec 31

1992

Venus in Sagittarius: Jan 1–Jan 25
Venus in Capricorn: Jan 25–Feb 18
Venus in Aquarius: Feb 18–Mar 13
Venus in Pisces: Mar 13–Apr 7
Venus in Aries: Apr 7–May 1
Venus in Taurus: May 1–May 26
Venus in Gemini: May 26–June 19
Venus in Cancer: June 19–July 13
Venus in Leo: July 13–Aug 7
Venus in Virgo: Aug 7–Aug 31
Venus in Libra: Aug 31–Sept 25
Venus in Scorpio: Sept 25–Oct 19
Venus in Sagittarius: Oct 19–Nov 13
Venus in Capricorn: Nov 13–Dec 8
Venus in Aquarius: Dec 8–Dec 31

1993

Venus in Aquarius: Jan 1–Jan 3
Venus in Pisces: Jan 3–Feb 2
Venus in Aries: Feb 2–June 6
Venus in Taurus: June 6–July 6
Venus in Gemini: July 6–Aug 1
Venus in Cancer: Aug 1–Aug 27
Venus in Leo: Aug 27–Sept 21
Venus in Virgo: Sept 21–Oct 16
Venus in Libra: Oct 16–Nov 9
Venus in Scorpio: Nov 9–Dec 2
Venus in Sagittarius: Dec 2–Dec 26
Venus in Capricorn: Dec 26–Dec 31

1994

Venus in Capricorn: Jan 1–Jan 19
Venus in Aquarius: Jan 19–Feb 12
Venus in Pisces: Feb 12–Mar 8
Venus in Aries: Mar 8–Apr 1
Venus in Taurus: Apr 1–Apr 26
Venus in Gemini: Apr 26–May 21
Venus in Cancer: May 21–June 15
Venus in Leo: June 15–July 11
Venus in Virgo: July 11–Aug 7

Venus in Libra: Aug 7–Sept 7
Venus in Scorpio: Sept 7–Dec 31

1995

Venus in Scorpio: Jan 1–Jan 7
Venus in Sagittarius: Jan 7–Feb 4
Venus in Capricorn: Feb 4–Mar 2
Venus in Aquarius: Mar 2–Mar 28
Venus in Pisces: Mar 28–Apr 22
Venus in Aries: Apr 22–May 16
Venus in Taurus: May 16–June 10
Venus in Gemini: June 10–July 5
Venus in Cancer: July 5–July 29
Venus in Leo: July 29–Aug 23
Venus in Virgo: Aug 23–Sept 16
Venus in Libra: Sept 16–Oct 10
Venus in Scorpio: Oct 10–Nov 3
Venus in Sagittarius: Nov 3–Nov 27
Venus in Capricorn: Nov 27–Dec 21
Venus in Aquarius: Dec 21–Dec 31

1996

Venus in Aquarius: Jan 1–Jan 15
Venus in Pisces: Jan 15–Feb 9
Venus in Aries: Feb 9–Mar 6
Venus in Taurus: Mar 6–Apr 3
Venus in Gemini: Apr 3–Aug 7
Venus in Cancer: Aug 7–Sept 7
Venus in Leo: Sept 7–Oct 4
Venus in Virgo: Oct 4–Oct 29
Venus in Libra: Oct 29–Nov 23
Venus in Scorpio: Nov 23–Dec 17
Venus in Sagittarius: Dec 17–Dec 31

1997

Venus in Sagittarius: Jan 1–Jan 10
Venus in Capricorn: Jan 10–Feb 3
Venus in Aquarius: Feb 3–Feb 27
Venus in Pisces: Feb 27–Mar 23
Venus in Aries: Mar 23–Apr 16
Venus in Taurus: Apr 16–May 10
Venus in Gemini: May 10–June 4
Venus in Cancer: June 4–June 28
Venus in Leo: June 28–July 23
Venus in Virgo: July 23–Aug 17
Venus in Libra: Aug 17–Sept 12
Venus in Scorpio: Sept 12–Oct 8
Venus in Sagittarius: Oct 8–Nov 5
Venus in Capricorn: Nov 5–Dec 12
Venus in Aquarius: Dec 12–Dec 31

1998

Venus in Aquarius: Jan 1–Jan 9

Venus in Capricorn: Jan 9–Mar 4
Venus in Aquarius: Mar 4–Apr 6
Venus in Pisces: Apr 6–May 3
Venus in Aries: May 3–May 29
Venus in Taurus: May 29–June 24
Venus in Gemini: June 24–July 19
Venus in Cancer: July 19–Aug 13
Venus in Leo: Aug 13–Sept 6
Venus in Virgo: Sept 6–Sep 30
Venus in Libra: Sept 30–Oct 24
Venus in Scorpio: Oct 24–Nov 17
Venus in Sagittarius: Nov 17–Dec 11
Venus in Capricorn: Dec 11–Dec 31

1999

Venus in Capricorn: Jan 1–Jan 4
Venus in Aquarius: Jan 4–Jan 28
Venus in Pisces: Jan 28–Feb 21
Venus in Aries: Feb 21–Mar 18
Venus in Taurus: Mar 18–Apr 12
Venus in Gemini: Apr 12–May 8
Venus in Cancer: May 8–June 5
Venus in Leo: June 5–July 12
Venus in Virgo: July 12–Aug 15
Venus in Leo: Aug 15–Oct 7
Venus in Virgo: Oct 7–Nov 9
Venus in Libra: Nov 9–Dec 5
Venus in Scorpio: Dec 5–Dec 31
Venus in Sagittarius: Dec 31

2000

Venus in Sagittarius: Jan 1–Jan 24
Venus in Capricorn: Jan 24–Feb 18
Venus in Aquarius: Feb 18–Mar 13
Venus in Pisces: Mar 13–Apr 6
Venus in Aries: Apr 6–May 1
Venus in Taurus: May 1–May 25
Venus in Gemini: May 25–June 18
Venus in Cancer: June 18–July 13
Venus in Leo: July 13–Aug 6
Venus in Virgo: Aug 6–Aug 31
Venus in Libra: Aug 31–Sept 24
Venus in Scorpio: Sept 24–Oct 19
Venus in Sagittarius: Oct 19–Nov 13
Venus in Capricorn: Nov 13–Dec 8
Venus in Aquarius: Dec 8–Dec 31

2001

Venus in Aquarius: Jan 1–Jan 3
Venus in Pisces: Jan 3–Feb 2
Venus in Aries: Feb 2–June 6
Venus in Taurus: June 6–July 5

Venus in Gemini: July 5–Aug 1
Venus in Cancer: Aug 1–Aug 27
Venus in Leo: Aug 27–Sept 21
Venus in Virgo: Sept 21–Oct 15
Venus in Libra: Oct 15–Nov 8
Venus in Scorpio: Nov 8–Dec 2
Venus in Sagittarius: Dec 2–Dec 26
Venus in Capricorn: Dec 26–Dec 31

2002

Venus in Capricorn: Jan 1–Jan 19
Venus in Aquarius: Jan 19–Feb 12
Venus in Pisces: Feb 12–Mar 8
Venus in Aries: Mar 8–Apr 1
Venus in Taurus: Apr 1–Apr 25
Venus in Gemini: Apr 25–May 20
Venus in Cancer: May 20–June 14
Venus in Leo: June 14–July 10
Venus in Virgo: July 10–Aug 7
Venus in Libra: Aug 7–Sept 8
Venus in Scorpio: Sept 8–Dec 31

2003

Venus in Scorpio: Jan 1–Jan 7
Venus in Sagittarius: Jan 7–Feb 4
Venus in Capricorn: Feb 4–Mar 2
Venus in Aquarius: Mar 2–Mar 27
Venus in Pisces: Mar 27–Apr 21
Venus in Aries: Apr 21–May 16
Venus in Taurus: May 16–June 10
Venus in Gemini: June 10–July 4
Venus in Cancer: July 4–July 29
Venus in Leo: July 29–Aug 22
Venus in Virgo: Aug 22–Sept 15
Venus in Libra: Sept 15–Oct 9
Venus in Scorpio: Oct 9–Nov 2
Venus in Sagittarius: Nov 2–Nov 27
Venus in Capricorn: Nov 27–Dec 21
Venus in Aquarius: Dec 21–Dec 31

2004

Venus in Aquarius: Jan 1–Jan 14
Venus in Pisces: Jan 14–Feb 8
Venus in Aries: Feb 8–Mar 5
Venus in Taurus: Mar 5–Apr 3
Venus in Gemini: Apr 3–Aug 7
Venus in Cancer: Aug 7–Sept 6
Venus in Leo: Sept 6–Oct 3
Venus in Virgo: Oct 3–Oct 29
Venus in Libra: Oct 29–Nov 22
Venus in Scorpio: Nov 22–Dec 16
Venus in Sagittarius: Dec 16–Dec 31

2005

Venus in Sagittarius: Jan–Jan 9
Venus in Capricorn: Jan 9–Feb 3
Venus in Aquarius: Feb 3–Feb 26
Venus in Pisces: Feb 26–Mar 22
Venus in Aries: Mar 22–Apr 15
Venus in Taurus: Apr 15–May 10
Venus in Gemini: May 10–June 3
Venus in Cancer: June 3–June 28
Venus in Leo: June 28–July 23
Venus in Virgo: July 23–Aug 17
Venus in Libra: Aug 17–Sept 11
Venus in Scorpio: Sept 11–Oct 8
Venus in Sagittarius: Oct 8–Nov 5
Venus in Capricorn: Nov 5–Dec 15
Venus in Aquarius: Dec 15–Dec 31

2006

Venus in Capricorn: Jan 1–Mar 5
Venus in Aquarius: Mar 5–Apr 6
Venus in Pisces: Apr 6–May 3
Venus in Aries: May 3–May 29
Venus in Taurus: May 29–June 24
Venus in Gemini: June 24–July 19
Venus in Cancer: July 19–Aug 12
Venus in Leo: Aug 12–Sept 6
Venus in Virgo: Sept 6–Sept 30
Venus in Libra: Sept 30–Oct 24
Venus in Scorpio: Oct 24–Nov 17
Venus in Sagittarius: Nov 17–Dec 11
Venus in Capricorn: Dec 11–Dec 31

2007

Venus in Capricorn: Jan 1–Jan 4
Venus in Aquarius: Jan 4–Jan 28
Venus in Pisces: Jan 28–Feb 21
Venus in Aries: Feb 21–Mar 17
Venus in Taurus: Mar 17–Apr 12
Venus in Gemini: Apr 12–May 8
Venus in Cancer: May 8–June 5
Venus in Leo: June 5–July 14
Venus in Virgo: July 14–Aug 9
Venus in Leo: Aug 9–Oct 8
Venus in Virgo: Oct 8–Nov 8
Venus in Libra: Nov 8–Dec 5
Venus in Scorpio: Dec 5–Dec 30
Venus in Sagittarius: Dec 30–Dec 31

2008

Venus in Sagittarius: Jan 1–Jan 24
Venus in Capricorn: Jan 24–Feb 17

Venus in Aquarius: Feb 17–Mar 12
Venus in Pisces: Mar 12–Apr 6
Venus in Aries: Apr 6–Apr 30
Venus in Taurus: Apr 30–May 24
Venus in Gemini: May 24–June 18
Venus in Cancer: June 18–July 12
Venus in Leo: July 12–Aug 6
Venus in Virgo: Aug 6–Aug 30
Venus in Libra: Aug 30–Sept 24
Venus in Scorpio: Sept 24–Oct 18
Venus in Sagittarius: Oct 18–Nov 12
Venus in Capricorn: Nov 12–Dec 7
Venus in Aquarius: Dec 7–Dec 31

2009

Venus in Aquarius: Jan 1–Jan 3
Venus in Pisces: Jan 3–Feb 3
Venus in Aries: Feb 3–Apr 11
Venus in Pisces: Apr 11–Apr 24
Venus in Aries: Apr 24–June 6
Venus in Taurus: June 6–July 5
Venus in Gemini: July 5–Aug 1
Venus in Cancer: Aug 1–Aug 26
Venus in Leo: Aug 26–Sept 20
Venus in Virgo: Sept 20–Oct 14
Venus in Libra: Oct 14–Nov 8
Venus in Scorpio: Nov 8–Dec 1
Venus in Sagittarius: Dec 1–Dec 25
Venus in Capricorn: Dec 25–Dec 31

2010

Venus in Capricorn: Jan 1–Jan 18
Venus in Aquarius: Jan 18–Feb 11
Venus in Pisces: Feb 11–Mar 7
Venus in Aries: Mar 7–Mar 31
Venus in Taurus: Mar 31–Apr 25
Venus in Gemini: Apr 25–May 20
Venus in Cancer: May 20–June 14
Venus in Leo: June 14–July 10
Venus in Virgo: July 10–Aug 7
Venus in Libra: Aug 7–Sept 8
Venus in Scorpio: Sept 8–Nov 8
Venus in Libra: Nov 8–Nov 30
Venus in Scorpio: Nov 30–Dec 31

2011

Venus in Scorpio: Jan 1–Jan 7
Venus in Sagittarius: Jan 7–Feb 4
Venus in Capricorn: Feb 4–Mar 2
Venus in Aquarius: Mar 2–Mar 27

Venus in Aries

SUN IN AQUARIUS–VENUS IN ARIES

Friendly and gregarious, you need a relationship where you are given the freedom to be yourself. Idealistic and original, you do better when you are involved in relationships based on friendship or group activities that can stimulate your passions and sense of adventure. Being detached, progressive, and independent suggests that you are open to less conventional relationships.

Your appealing attributes: friendly, dynamic, adventurous, brave, free spirit, spontaneous, independent, enthusiastic, daring, idealistic, nonconformist, flirtatious, progressive, inspirational, creative, avant-garde, detached

Your unappealing attributes: self-centered, impatient, competitive, inconsiderate, too demanding, impetuous, run hot and cold with your feelings

SUN IN PISCES–VENUS IN ARIES

As a romantic dreamer you are usually idealistic about relationships. Although passionate by nature, beneath your bold front you can also be emotionally withdrawn or unsure about how you really feel. Sensitive and imaginative with powerful emotions, you can be sympathetic yet daring. Even though you care for others, your determination and strong will suggest that others cannot take you for granted.

Your appealing attributes: warm, sympathetic, strong, direct, adventurous, active, independent, dramatic, quick responses, idealistic, charismatic, dynamic, enthusiastic, daring, friendly, creative, imaginative, sensitive

Your unappealing attributes: selfish, impatient, too passionate, emotional highs and lows, tactless, hasty, self-centered, lack of vision, melodramatic, too sensitive, competitive, naive

SUN IN ARIES–VENUS IN ARIES

Enterprising and daring by nature, you are not the type to sit around waiting for other people to make the first move. Impatient and passionate, you may rush into relationships without first thinking them through. Once in a relationship you tend to take the lead or enjoy being the boss. Usually determined or single-minded, you possess a great deal of charisma, warmth, and charm that attracts others.

Your appealing attributes: daring, ardent, spirited, friendly, brave, strong, spontaneous, adventurous, enthusiastic, loves action, creative, quick, bold, expressive, flirtatious, generous, passionate, idealistic, chivalrous

Your unappealing attributes: too competitive, impetuous, domineering, tactless, irritable, easily bored, selfish, rash, impulsive, impatient, demanding, hot-headed

SUN IN TAURUS–VENUS IN ARIES

Friendly and sociable, you can become animated and easily aroused when involved with a person who is close to your heart. Honest and direct, you are the purposeful type and often attract others by knowing what you want and how to get it. Although you are faithful and take a pragmatic look at relationships, your sense of adventure implies that you can be mischievous and enjoy teasing others.

Your appealing attributes: daring, passionate, creative, adventurous, flirtatious, spirited, direct, generous, charismatic, enthusiastic, idealistic, warm, inspirational, sensual, magnetic

Your unappealing attributes: competitive, impatient, selfish, lustful, overindulgent, domineering, tactless, irritable, emotional highs and lows, instant gratification, impetuous

SUN IN GEMINI–VENUS IN ARIES

Since you love to talk about the subjects you feel passionate about, you really enjoy partners who can share your constant stream of ideas. Action-oriented, warm, and passionate, a side to your nature longs for an adventurous soul mate. Being mentally quick and animated, however, you may need to develop patience and tolerance or get in touch with your deeper feelings. Full of enthusiasm, you attract others with your quick intelligence and creative mind.

Your appealing attributes: warm, adventurous, independent, quick responses, generous, witty, enthusiastic, mischievous, charming, daring, honest, friendly, playful, spirited, creative, direct

Your unappealing attributes: selfish, competitive, argumentative, impulsive, impatient, tactless, bossy, too passionate, easily bored, intolerant

Venus in Taurus

SUN IN PISCES–VENUS IN TAURUS

Sensitive and sensual, you are a warm and tactile individual in tune with your partner's needs and feelings. Desiring comfort and luxuries, you want a partner who will share your enjoyment of the good things in life. Nevertheless, avoid an inclination to overindulge. Loyal and understanding, you are often willing to make sacrifices for those you love and can attract others with your natural style and affectionate nature.

Your appealing attributes: affectionate, warm, steady, creative, sensual, friendly, sociable, magnetic, imaginative, love of beauty, attractive voice, loyal, tactile, seductive

Your unappealing attributes: overindulgent, evasive, easily seduced, self-pity, too sentimental, stubborn, unstable, materialistic, possessive, escapist

SUN IN ARIES–VENUS IN TAURUS

Enthusiastic, active, and faithful, your adventurous nature and love of beauty make you a purposeful and attractive partner. You can be passionate and loving, but sometimes others may see you as stubborn or headstrong. Expressive and creative, you can attract others with your enthusiasm and refined taste. Once in love you can be committed, dynamic, and sensual and have a lot of fun socializing.

Your appealing attributes: sensual, affectionate, fascinating, warm, steady, creative, sociable, magnetic, love of beauty, attractive voice, loyal, tactile

Your unappealing attributes: stubborn, selfish, overindulgent, materialistic, too economical, possessive

SUN IN TAURUS–VENUS IN TAURUS

As you are sensual and enjoy beauty and luxuries, you are often attracted to rich, image-conscious, or creative individuals. Your love of ease and comfort, however, warns that you need to resist being overindulgent. Although you pride yourself on being faithful and affectionate, status and material security are just as important to make your relationships last.

Your appealing attributes: sensual, attractive, charming, warm, seductive, consistent, reliable, loyal, steady, supportive, stylish, alluring, sociable, artistic

Your unappealing attributes: obstinate, selfish, stubborn, too extravagant or economical, overindulgent, materialistic, possessive, too security-conscious, too fixed

SUN IN GEMINI–VENUS IN TAURUS

Versatile and artistic, you usually seek a partner who is practical yet mentally stimulating. Being lighthearted and charming, you can attract others with your agreeable manner and witty humor. Although you value good communication with others, you also need stability and security. You usually

enjoy a good social life but be careful of overindulging. When in love you can be affectionate and sensual.

Your appealing attributes: charming, persuasive, friendly, sensual, attractive, warm, consistent, reliable, loyal, understanding, good company, supportive, stylish, sociable, artistic

Your unappealing attributes: obstinate, selfish, stubborn, too extravagant or economical, overindulgent, materialistic, possessive, too security conscious, lazy

SUN IN CANCER–VENUS IN TAURUS

Affectionate and tactile, you need a relationship that can make you feel both protected and materially comfortable. Although you have a need for security in relationships, you may have to avoid becoming overly preoccupied with monetary concerns. Caring and loving, you are not usually keen on direct confrontation, but you nevertheless get your own by being patient. You can attract others with your sympathetic and affectionate nature and by showing your devotion to loved ones.

Your appealing attributes: affectionate, protective, supportive, charming, desirable, persuasive, friendly, sensual, attractive, home-loving, warm, consistent, reliable, loyal, understanding, good company, stylish, sociable, artistic, reliable, good with money

Your unappealing attributes: unyielding, possessive or jealous, stubborn, manipulative, too sentimental, clingy, smothering, lazy, overindulgent, too extravagant or too economical

Venus in Gemini

SUN IN ARIES–VENUS IN GEMINI

Since you are action-oriented, you may be impulsive and enter into relationships too quickly. Although you show great enthusiasm at the beginning of a love affair, unless your partner keeps the romance alive, you can become bored easily. Your ideal partner is probably someone who is adventurous, youthful, and witty. Attracted to those who can stimulate you mentally, you like to be well-informed or well-versed. In relationships you need a partner who can keep you mentally stimulated and is not too emotionally demanding.

Your appealing attributes: persuasive, lighthearted, entertaining, charming, sociable, agreeable, refined, graceful, literary, artistic expression, cultured, articulate, well-informed, expressive

Your unappealing attributes: vain, conceited, superficial, lazy, too talkative, easily bored, pretentious

SUN IN TAURUS–VENUS IN GEMINI

Your ideal partner is probably someone who is affectionate, sociable, and willing to listen to your many ideas.

Although part of you wants stability and security in a relationship, your versatility suggests that you attract people with your lively mind and youthful manner. Mentally curious and charming, you enjoy flirting and socializing. Although you can at times be stubborn, your ability to adapt quickly to situations indicates that you have a flair for communication.

Your appealing attributes: persuasive, lighthearted, entertaining, charming, sociable, agreeable, love of beauty and luxury, artistic, mentally curious, expressive, pleasure-loving, articulate, sociable, knowledgeable

Your unappealing attributes: vain, conceited, superficial, extravagant, lazy, too talkative, easily bored, overindulgent

SUN IN GEMINI–VENUS IN GEMINI

Friendly and outgoing, you are a gregarious and talkative individual who enjoys meeting people and socializing. You often prefer to analyze your feelings and rationalize your needs, but learn to recognize your deeper emotions. You enjoy good conversation and usually want a partner who can respond readily to your thoughts and ideas.

Your appealing attributes: persuasive, lighthearted, entertaining, charming, sociable, agreeable, lively, youthful, artistic, mentally curious, gift of the gab, expressive, cultured, articulate, love learning, well-informed, adaptable, versatile

Your unappealing attributes: conceit, easily bored, inconsistent, restless, too flirtatious, superficial, lazy, too talkative, vain, scattered

SUN IN CANCER–VENUS IN GEMINI

Being caring and understanding, you are usually affectionate and feel protective toward your partners. Your love of communication indicates that sharing your philosophy or opinions with loved ones often stimulates and excites you. Your mental curiosity implies that you are interested in how your partner thinks and often analyze his or her motives and actions.

Your appealing attributes: persuasive, affectionate, sympathetic, lighthearted, entertaining, charming, sociable, agreeable, knowledgeable, artistic, articulate, mentally curious, gift of the gab, expressive, communication skills, good listener

Your unappealing attributes: clingy, manipulate, superficial, lazy, hypocritical, easily bored, pretentious, too talkative

SUN IN LEO–VENUS IN GEMINI

Gregarious, fun-loving, and creative, you enjoy communicating with others and meeting people sociably. Although you are lighthearted, generous, and entertaining, your pride and need for love suggest that you desire an intelligent partner who will make you feel special and appreciated. You are naturally enthusiastic and have persuasive charm; you can always attract others with your bright ideas.

Your appealing attributes: persuasive, lighthearted, en-

tertaining, charming, sociable, agreeable, literary, artistic, mentally curious, talkative, expressive, cultured, articulate, communication skills, versatile, enthusiastic, warm

Your unappealing attributes: conceited, prideful, superficial, lazy, too talkative, hypocritical, arrogant, easily bored, pretentious

Venus in Cancer

SUN IN TAURUS–VENUS IN CANCER

Your strong sense of values and parental instincts suggest that in relationships the important factor is often self-protection and preservation of the family. Faithful and reliable with a caring nature, you are usually supportive and nurturing to loved ones. Although affectionate and sympathetic, if unappreciated by others you can become moody or resentful that you have taken on more responsibilities than anyone else. Nevertheless, sensitive and kind, you can be a loving and devoted partner.

Your appealing attributes: sympathetic, tender, protective, caring, affectionate, artistic, romantic, kind, maternal or paternal, devoted, sensual, faithful, sentimental

Your unappealing attributes: overindulgent, interfering, overprotective, stubborn, interfering, shy, moody

SUN IN GEMINI–VENUS IN CANCER

Highly aware of other people's feelings, you are often an intuitive psychologist who is interested in people. Being caring and understanding, you can be sympathetic to others. You attract people by making them feel at ease or comfortable and keeping them entertained with witty conversation. Once you make a commitment, you are usually willing to make great sacrifices for the good of the family.

Your appealing attributes: sympathetic, tender, protective, intelligent, caring, affectionate, artistic, romantic, mentally sharp, kind, maternal or paternal, devoted

Your unappealing attributes: overindulgent, shy, too talkative, interfering, overprotective, misplaced sympathies, clingy, moody, too sensitive

SUN IN CANCER–VENUS IN CANCER

Intuitive, you pick up the changing moods of those around you. As a caring and sympathetic individual, you are able to put other people's needs before your own. You show your love by being affectionate and dedicated. Although you want to help, guard against smothering others with your good intentions. Usually you want a partner who can be supportive and reassuring, especially if you feel insecure.

Your appealing attributes: sympathetic, tender, protective, caring, affectionate, artistic, romantic, kind, maternal, devoted

Your unappealing attributes: overindulgent, interfering, overprotective, moody, too sensitive, manipulative, shy, clingy

SUN IN LEO–VENUS IN CANCER

Some of your most attractive attributes are your generosity, and considerate, affectionate nature. In your desire to help, however, avoid being bossy or interfering. Being aware of people's feelings suggests that you can be sympathetic and understanding and uplift others with your confident and entertaining personality. However, you want others to acknowledge your efforts, your dedication, and your hard work. Dramatic and caring, you can make others feel at ease.

Your appealing attributes: sympathetic, tender, protective, caring, affectionate, artistic, romantic, kind, maternal, devoted, entertaining, amusing, warm

Your unappealing attributes: overindulgent, interfering, stubborn, overprotective, interfering, moody

SUN IN VIRGO–VENUS IN CANCER

Being sensitive and protective, you are a caring individual who is aware of your loved ones' needs and moods. Among some of your most attractive attributes are practicality, modesty, and the ability to be helpful and supportive. Although you are usually sensitive to the feelings of those around you, you display your less attractive qualities when you become critical, manipulative, or too sensitive. Nevertheless, you can be sympathetic and caring and show partners your affectionate and protective nature.

Your appealing attributes: sympathetic, tender, protective, helpful, caring, affectionate, artistic, romantic, kind, maternal or paternal, modest, devoted, sensitive

Your unappealing attributes: overindulgent, critical, interfering, shy, stubborn, overprotective, interfering, moody

Venus in Leo

SUN IN GEMINI–VENUS IN LEO

Fun-loving, clever, and witty, you like to express your sense of the dramatic in an entertaining way. Enthusiastic and generous, you benefit from all types of creative partnerships. You are often attracted to intelligent individuals with generous natures and sunny personalities. Warmhearted and loyal, you can be a caring and supportive friend. Your self-assurance and confidence usually rise as a result of being appreciated and admired by your partner or loved ones.

Your appealing attributes: kindhearted, communication skills, generous, loyal friend, dignified, honorable, playful, generous, sociable, entertaining, good conversationalist

Your unappealing attributes: vain, too proud, arrogant,

too talkative, easily flattered, selfish, egocentric, scattered, melodramatic

SUN IN CANCER–VENUS IN LEO

Kind and encouraging, you are a loyal and devoted partner or friend. You seek a partner who can show you understanding or who is sensitive and generous. You like to entertain at home and are usually good at creating a warm and caring atmosphere. Although you can be animated and enthusiastic with a dramatic personality, you may sometimes appear overconfident or bossy when dealing with others. Nonetheless, with a strong family link, you can be caring and supportive of loved ones.

Your appealing attributes: kindhearted, generous, loyal friend, dignified, honorable, playful, generous, sociable, good parent, entertaining, sympathetic, home-loving

Your unappealing attributes: too sensitive, vain, too proud, arrogant, bossy, selfish, melodramatic, manipulative, easily flattered, overprotective

SUN IN LEO–VENUS IN LEO

Noble and confident, you want a partner you can be proud of, or one who can provide you with a luxurious lifestyle. Humorous and affectionate, you enjoy performing or being playful, something that adds to your overall attractive qualities. Avoid being bossy with loved ones, however. Nevertheless, usually warm, generous, and dramatic, you enjoy socializing and are often attracted to individuals who stand out in a crowd. You also admire those who can act out their dreams and aspirations with confidence and determination.

Your appealing attributes: kindhearted, generous, loyal friend, dignified, brave, honorable, playful, generous, sociable, entertaining, dramatic, leadership potential, fun-loving

Your unappealing attributes: stubborn, vain, bossy, melodramatic, too proud, snobbish, arrogant, easily flattered, selfish, egocentric

SUN IN VIRGO–VENUS IN LEO

Dignified and expressive, you like to present yourself and your partner in the right light. Although proud, you are often modest; yet, being popular or appreciated can still be important to your well-being. One of the challenges that you may experience in relationships is being accused of arrogance or stubbornness. Warm and affectionate, however, your kind heart and desire to be of practical help can make you very attractive to others.

Your appealing attributes: Kindhearted, generous, modest, loyal friend, practical, helpful, discriminating, dignified, honorable, playful, sociable, entertaining

Your unappealing attributes: stubborn, critical, vain, too proud, melodramatic, opinionated, interfering, easily flattered, selfish, self-centered, bossy

SUN IN LIBRA–VENUS IN LEO

Kind, generous, and loving, you have charm and a sunny personality. Intelligent and friendly, you usually make contacts easily and know how to impress people. Although you need to be popular, do not fear periods of solitude as these are useful for focusing on your creative goals and personal ambitions. Although your love life can often be a dramatic area for you, relationships are very high on your priority list. Your ability to be sociable and entertaining ensures that you can always have many friends.

Your appealing attributes: kindhearted, generous, refined, loyal friend, artistic, dignified, honorable, entertaining, diplomatic, playful, sociable, good networker, warm, gracious

Your unappealing attributes: stubborn, vain, too proud, egocentric, indecisive, trouble saying no, bossy, easily flattered, selfish, conceited, melodramatic

Venus in Virgo

SUN IN CANCER–VENUS IN VIRGO

Sympathetic yet down-to-earth, you can be a good adviser and pillar of strength for those you love. Although you can be caring and helpful, your love of order can sometimes turn you into too much of a perfectionist. You may find yourself particularly attracted to clever and hardworking individuals who can add to your sense of security. Others are attracted by your ability to pay attention to their needs and make them feel at ease.

Your appealing attributes: well-organized, caring, intelligent, like to give practical help, clean, fastidiously dressed, sensual, dutiful, modest, discriminating, analytical, down-to-earth, neat, efficient, faithful, attention to detail, earthy, discreet, self-contained

Your unappealing attributes: critical, anxious, overanalyze, worried, fussy, too perfectionist, take on too much, inhibited, cynical

SUN IN LEO–VENUS IN VIRGO

Warm, outgoing, and playful, you can be a caring and considerate partner. Expecting high standards from your partner, you enjoy offering practical support to your loved ones but need love and admiration in return. Usually meticulously dressed and aware of style, you attract others with your generous and confident personality. Although intelligent and warmhearted, you may alternate between being modest and unassuming and being somewhat self-centered. Nonetheless, people are attracted by your genuine concern for others.

Your appealing attributes: well-organized, caring, intelligent, like to give practical help, well-groomed, sensual, dutiful, modest, fastidious, discriminating, analytical, down-to-earth, neat, efficient, faithful, attention to detail, earthy, discreet, confident, self-contained

Your unappealing attributes: critical, vain, anxious, overanalyze, perfectionist, inhibited, worried, arrogant, faultfinding

SUN IN VIRGO–VENUS IN VIRGO

Thoughtful, practical, and modest, you usually like to analyze your relationships and talk through your problems to find positive solutions. You are usually attracted to pragmatic and caring individuals who are willing to work on their relationships like you are. Being a perfectionist, however, if you become too critical of your own faults, you will not place a high enough value on your own needs. Yet your genuine concern, practical ability, and willingness to assist others more than compensates for any of your shortcomings.

Your appealing attributes: well-organized, caring, intelligent, helpful, neat, sensual, dutiful, modest, fastidious, discriminating, analytical, down-to-earth, efficient, faithful, attention to detail, earthy, discreet, self-contained, helpful

Your unappealing attributes: critical, anxious, get lost in the details, perfectionist, inhibited, overanalyze, fussy, worried

SUN IN LIBRA–VENUS IN VIRGO

Refined and intellectual with a strong need to relate to others, you seek the idealized or perfect love. As this is hard to find, you may become unsure of your own beliefs when it comes to relationships. By using your natural analytical skills to sharpen your discrimination and improve your self-worth, you are able to get the balance right between giving love to others and feeling good about yourself. Helpful and discriminating, you attract others with your charm, gracious manner, and ability to pay attention to other people's needs.

Your appealing attributes: well-organized, caring, intelligent, like to give practical help, well-groomed, sensual, dutiful, modest, fastidious, discriminating, analytical, down-to-earth, neat, efficient, faithful, attention to detail, discreet, moral sense, self-contained

Your unappealing attributes: anxious, get lost in the details, too perfectionist, inhibited, overanalyze, worried, faultfinding

SUN IN SCORPIO–VENUS IN VIRGO

Although you are passionate, you can also be thoughtful and practical. You do not usually make a big display of your emotions even though you feel deeply and secretly seek perfection. On an inner level you tend to constantly analyze your relationships in great detail in order to improve them. As long as you do not become too skeptical or critical of your partner, once committed, you are devoted, caring, and often willing to work hard to make your relationships successful.

Your appealing attributes: sensitive, well-organized, caring, intelligent, like to give practical help, sensual, modest, passionate, meticulous, discriminating, analytical, down-to-earth, neat, efficient, faithful, moral sense, attention to detail, discreet, self-contained

Your unappealing attributes: anxious, critical, controlling, get lost in the details, perfectionist, inhibited, overanalyze, worried, too extremist, faultfinding

Venus in Libra

SUN IN LEO–VENUS IN LIBRA

Confident and sociable, you have a persuasive charm that draws others to you. Very aware of image, ideally you need an attractive and stylish partner with whom you can share your many social engagements. Generous and loving to those who win your heart, your romantic soul often seeks fulfillment through relationships. Dramatic and creative, ideally you can form a partnership that enhances your self-expression. Sociable and kindhearted, you can attract others with your warm and loving personality as well as your courteous and polite manner.

Your appealing attributes: dignified, fair, tactful, friendly, artistic, good taste, just, refined, agreeable, elegant, fun-loving, courteous, sociable, polite, stylish, gracious, harmonious, creative, romantic, gentle, sophisticated, considerate, peaceful, cultured, diplomatic, intelligent, entertaining

Your unappealing attributes: vain, overindulgent, lazy, egocentric, insincere, nonconfrontational, indecisive, too proud, superficial, lack integrity

SUN IN VIRGO–VENUS IN LIBRA

A practical romantic, you long for someone to support you in the same way you are willing to help others. Modest yet sophisticated in your taste, you want things to be just right, even your relationships. This practical perfectionism can make you discriminating in your choice of partners or skeptical that they even exist. Your gracious manner and genuine concern for others, however, can make you popular and appreciated.

Your appealing attributes: polite, modest, fair, diplomatic tactful, friendly, artistic, good taste, just, refined, agreeable, elegant, courteous, sociable, stylish, gracious, harmonious, creative, romantic, gentle, sophisticated, considerate, peaceful, practical, cultured

Your unappealing attributes: overanalytical, indulgent, vain, critical, cold, indecisive, dependent, avoidance, superficial, lacks integrity, insincere, indecisive

SUN IN LIBRA–VENUS IN LIBRA

With a double measure of charm, you are a natural romantic with a desire to please. Often in love with being in love, harmonious relationships are very important to your well-being. Although you possess a strong need to be popular, you may need to learn to be more confrontational or decisive

with others. Nevertheless, your appreciation of art, beauty, and luxury is often reflected in your good taste and stylish appearance, making you attractive to the opposite sex and increasing the opportunities for romance.

Your appealing attributes: fair, intellectual, tactful, friendly, artistic, good taste, just, refined, agreeable, elegant, courteous, sociable, polite, stylish, gracious, harmonious, creative, romantic, gentle, sophisticated, considerate, peaceful, cultured, diplomatic, entertaining

Your unappealing attributes: overindulgent, lazy, vain, dishonest with feelings, too passive, insincere, indecisive, superficial

SUN IN SCORPIO–VENUS IN LIBRA

Passionate and intense but also refined and diplomatic, you seek attractive, gracious, and intelligent partners with whom you can share romantic dates and good conversation. When it comes to partnerships, indecision could leave you trying to decide whether to emotionally jump in the deep end or stay friendly and detached. Wherever you go, your entertaining manner and polished social skills ensure you are loved and wanted.

Your appealing attributes: friendly, sensitive, fair, tactful, artistic, courteous, good taste, just, refined, agreeable, elegant, courteous, sociable, polite, stylish, gracious, entertaining, harmonious, passionate, creative, romantic, gentle, sophisticated, considerate, peaceful, cultured, diplomatic

Your unappealing attributes: vain, overindulgent, dishonest, too concerned with status, insincere, lack integrity, superficial, indecisive

SUN IN SAGITTARIUS–VENUS IN LIBRA

Very friendly and sociable, you have a warm and gracious manner and an idealistic approach to relationships. You need partners who share your love of life and adventure, but they also need to be sophisticated, cultured, and affectionate. Just be careful that with your love of ease and pleasure, you do not get carried away and overindulge in the luxuries of life. Considerate and warm, you attract people with your expert social skills and expansive personality.

Your appealing attributes: good taste, friendly, artistic, fair, honest, fun-loving, just, refined, agreeable, elegant, courteous, sociable, polite, stylish, gracious, harmonious, creative, romantic, gentle, sophisticated, considerate, peaceful, cultured, diplomatic, entertaining

Your unappealing attributes: vain, overindulgent, lazy, lacks integrity, dishonest, indecisive, superficial, escape from necessary conflict, insincere, social climber

Venus in Scorpio

SUN IN VIRGO–VENUS IN SCORPIO

Analytical and seductive, you have a way with words and an ability to articulate your feelings. People are attracted to your common sense and faithful nature. You are likely to be a thoughtful partner and you usually take relationships seriously. Being sensitive with a keen insight into what makes people tick suggests that you know how to draw people out of their shell. If you suffer from insecurities or repressed emotions, however, you may resort to cynicism or mistrust. People find you reliable, loyal, trustworthy, and practical.

Your appealing attributes: persuasive, charming, helpful, loyal, supportive, sympathetic, serious, inquisitive, sensual, professional, determined, organized, passionate, seductive

Your unappealing attributes: critical, suspicious, self-doubting, moody, obsessive, jealous, possessive, overanalyze

SUN IN LIBRA–VENUS IN SCORPIO

Friendly and passionate, you are a sociable and well-mannered individual who can express feelings in a dynamic way. You are often refined with deep feelings but may display your intense emotions if you are suspicious or jealous. The fact that you want to fall madly in love with someone implies that you are willing to go to great lengths in order to protect or please your partner. Sociable and charming, you attract others with your charismatic personality and sexual magnetism.

Your appealing attributes: loyal, alluring charming, passionate, sociable, caring, diplomatic, gracious, seductive, sensitive, charismatic, loving, protective, sensual

Your unappealing attributes: possessive, controlling, over-indulgent, secretive, infatuations, jealous, manipulative, vain

SUN IN SCORPIO–VENUS IN SCORPIO

As you are passionate and romantic and rarely do things by half measures, you want to fall in love wholeheartedly. Although you can love very deeply, you may need to guard against becoming too intense or serious. Very sensitive, you usually protect your inner vulnerability by being secretive. When your loyalty is tested, however, you will stand by your partner through thick and thin. Other people are fascinated by your alluring charm and sexual magnetism.

Your appealing attributes: strong attractions, passionate, loyal, tenacious, hardworking, practical, daring, seductive, determined, loving, sensual, magnetic, sensitive

Your unappealing attributes: controlling, jealous, possessive, obsessive, secretive, withholds love, gets even, emotional extremes

SUN IN SAGITTARIUS–VENUS IN SCORPIO

Your optimism and keen insight into what motivates people suggest that you know how to inspire or draw them out of their shell. As an idealistic and loyal individual, you are a loving and committed partner. Naturally intense, your sensitivity and depth of feeling indicate that you need to channel your emotions positively, otherwise you can be caught in power games. Your need for freedom or new opportunities implies that you do not want to be restricted. Rather than seek easy and simple relationships, you are often drawn to partners who act as a catalyst for your own transformation.

Your appealing attributes: romantic, quick responses, generous, loyal, idealistic, charming, daring, strong beliefs, passionate, love of travel, adventurous, seductive, sensitive, deep feelings

Your unappealing attributes: intense emotions, jealous, social climbing, gets even, opinionated, suspicious, restless, controlling

SUN IN CAPRICORN–VENUS IN SCORPIO

Motivated and resourceful, you possess emotional depth and determination. Responsible and sensitive, your strength and power lies in your ability to love both deeply and unconditionally. In your relationships you need to avoid negative emotions such as withholding love or possessiveness, which usually stem from your own insecurities. Nevertheless, your sense of duty means that you are a devoted individual with a strong sense of commitment. Other people admire your loyalty and inner strength.

Your appealing attributes: loyal, tenacious, hardworking, practical, daring, determined, seductive, passionate, self-control, strong-willed, strong attractions, protective, responsible, sensitive

Your unappealing attributes: controlling, jealous, possessive, emotional extremes, gets even, denial, secretive, stubborn, too restrained

Venus in Sagittarius

SUN IN LIBRA–VENUS IN SAGITTARIUS

Friendly and charismatic, you attract other people with your refined nature. Naturally gregarious and direct, you have a flair for dealing with people. You know how to utilize opportunities and impress others with your charming manner. Usually idealistic and helpful, you can be generous with those you like and support causes that are dear to your heart. With your diplomatic skills and sense of adventure you can be a good companion, but should avoid overindulging in the good things of life.

Your appealing attributes: diplomatic, honest, intelligent, direct, open-minded, idealistic, warm, sociable, freedom-loving, love of travel, romantic, enthusiastic, honest, good taste, adventurous, generous, refined social skills, well-mannered

Your unappealing attributes: overindulgent, extravagant, snobbish, opinionated, tactless, risk taker, social climber, indecisive

SUN IN SCORPIO–VENUS IN SAGITTARIUS

Forceful yet charming, in relationships you can be reserved yet honest and direct. You can easily make a comment that may be truthful but also affects others more deeply than you may realize. A tendency to fluctuate between extremes suggests that at times you can be idealistic and generous and at other times you can be controlling and stubborn. Being resourceful, you are often lucky to receive help from others just at the right time. Usually, people find you lively and seductive.

Your appealing attributes: open-minded, seductive, freedom-loving, warm, enthusiastic, honest, adventurous, love of travel, generous, sensitive, frank

Your unappealing attributes: manipulative, blunt, conceit, materialistic, selfish, too intense, gets carried away, tactless, opinionated, overindulgent, risk taker

SUN IN SAGITTARIUS–VENUS IN SAGITTARIUS

Being frank and direct, you say what you think and often wear your heart on your sleeve. Open-minded and freedom-loving, you can adjust quickly to new situations. A foreign influence implies that you may enjoy traveling or your partner may come from a different culture. You also admire those who are honorable or just and are more likely to seek a partner who shares your moral values, opinions, or sense of humor. Your independent nature suggests you may be reluctant to make a lasting commitment in relationships. Nevertheless, people are drawn to your optimistic nature and natural spontaneity.

Your appealing attributes: frank, direct, open-minded, freedom-loving, warm, enthusiastic, honest, adventurous, philosophical, generous, idealistic, humanitarian, idealistic

Your unappealing attributes: tactless, gullible, too opinionated, extravagant, naive, overindulgent, afraid of commitment, risk taker

SUN IN CAPRICORN–VENUS IN SAGITTARIUS

That you are both sincere and idealistic implies that in relationships you are loyal and honorable. Although you are usually sensible and take your responsibilities seriously, your love of freedom means that occasionally you need to break your usual routine and bring some excitement or inspiration into your partnerships. In relationships, you may need to create the right balance between leisure and your work or duties. People are attracted to your sincerity and determination.

Your appealing attributes: direct, open-minded, frank, hardworking, determined, freedom-loving, warm, philosophical potential, responsible, practical, love of learning, enthusiastic, honest, adventurous, generous, idealistic, sociable

Your unappealing attributes: overindulgent, tactless, bossy, risk taker, opinionated, snobbish, extravagant, restless, social climber

SUN IN AQUARIUS–VENUS IN SAGITTARIUS

Being enthusiastic and optimistic, you enjoy encouraging the people you love. Sociable and gregarious, you want to be where the action is. A tendency to keep your options open indicates that you do not like to feel restricted. Although you can often make beneficial contacts, you may at times neglect paying attention to your close partner. Nevertheless, you can be in a committed relationship as long as your partner understands your love of freedom. People are attracted to your friendly spontaneity and generosity.

Your appealing attributes: frank, direct, open-minded, independent, friendly, freedom-loving, warm, enthusiastic, honest, humanitarian, philosophical, friendly, competitive, adventurous, like to take a gamble, generous

Your unappealing attributes: blunt, opinionated, social climber, overindulgent, risk taker

Venus in Capricorn

SUN IN SCORPIO–VENUS IN CAPRICORN

Strong-willed and passionate behind a cool exterior, you do not show your deeper emotions until you feel safe and secure. Although you are pragmatic, avoid being too materially minded when it comes to your relationships or you could end up feeling unsatisfied. Once committed, however, you are usually willing to work hard to achieve a good relationship. You are reliable and trustworthy, and people admire your sense of responsibility and purposeful nature.

Your appealing attributes: dignified, proud, passionate, sensitive, well-mannered, self-controlled, disciplined, hardworking, committed, loyal, self-assured, classy, refined, faithful

Your unappealing attributes: manipulative, too reserved, shy, controlling, materialistic, insecure, pessimistic, ulterior motives

SUN IN SAGITTARIUS–VENUS IN CAPRICORN

You are ambitious, enthusiastic, and goal-oriented, and people are attracted to your practical nature and strong sense of loyalty. In relationships you can be security-conscious and seek partners who share your aims and ideals. Although you love freedom and adventure, for you, family and faithfulness can be especially important, so you are usually willing to work hard or make sacrifices in order to keep your relationships secure.

Your appealing attributes: dignified, proud, well-mannered, self-controlled, disciplined, truthful, sincere, generous, compassionate, hardworking, committed, philosophical, humorous, sensual, loyal, self-assured, classy

Your unappealing attributes: ulterior motives, manipulative, shy, authoritative, materialistic, insecure, controlling, pessimistic

SUN IN CAPRICORN–VENUS IN CAPRICORN

Projecting a dignified persona, you attract people with your reserved self-control. Possessing a very practical approach to your love life, you will certainly want to know your partner's prospects before you consider settling down. Loyal and reliable, you tend to take your relationships seriously as you hate to make a fool of yourself and want to be treated with respect. Other people are attracted by your modesty and inner strength. Persevering, you can be loyal and enduring even in time of challenges.

Your appealing attributes: dignified, proud, well-mannered, self-controlled, disciplined, hardworking, committed, dutiful, classy, sensual, loyal, self-assured

Your unappealing attributes: manipulative, shy, materialistic, insecure, cold, pessimistic, emotional inhibitions, controlling, lacks self-confidence, hesitant, ulterior motives

SUN IN AQUARIUS–VENUS IN CAPRICORN

Friendly but reserved, in relationships your natural detachment suggests that to avoid frustration you may need to work on spontaneously expressing your love and affection. By building your self-worth, you are able to display your wonderful strength, wisdom, and dry sense of humor. Sociable and group-oriented, you often show your loyalty to others through your willingness to give practical support.

Others are attracted to your original approach and down-to-earth common sense.

Your appealing attributes: dignified, proud, well-mannered, humor, self-controlled, disciplined, humanitarian, common sense, enduring, hardworking, classy, committed, sensual, loyal, self-assured

Your unappealing attributes: manipulative, stubborn, too shy, too detached, materialistic, insecure, cold, pessimistic, emotional inhibitions, controlling, hesitant, ulterior motives

SUN IN PISCES–VENUS IN CAPRICORN

Practical yet receptive, you have a pragmatic but caring nature and a subtle mystique. Not always openly demonstrative, you can hide your sensitive feelings behind a dignified exterior. To help you avoid self-doubt, you need a partner who can be a reliable and solid pillar of support. Once committed to a relationship, you can be loyal and devoted. Although willing to make sacrifices, guard against letting others take advantage of your good nature. Alternatively, you can be looking for a hardworking individual who will look after you and protect you. Others are attracted to your sympathetic and unassuming character.

Your appealing attributes: dignified, proud, well-

mannered, self-controlled, disciplined, hardworking, committed, sensual, classy, modest, loyal, self-assured, responsible

Your unappealing attributes: too reserved, manipulative, shy, compromise for material security, insecure, calculating, pessimistic, emotional inhibitions, materialistic, hesitant, ulterior motives

Venus in Aquarius

SUN IN SAGITTARIUS–VENUS IN AQUARIUS

Honest and direct, you are drawn to sociable individuals who can introduce you to new experiences. As an idealistic and independent person, you want partners who are energetic and adventurous with progressive views. Although you seek a loving relationship, your gregarious personality and desire for freedom imply that you value your independence. Before you commit yourself to a serious or long-lasting relationship you will probably want to experience many different types of friendships.

Your appealing attributes: philosophical, friendly, generous, spontaneous, love of freedom, independent, charming, people skills, social contacts, adventurous, philanthropic, progressive, idealistic

Your unappealing attributes: risk taking, overindulgent, impressionable, undisciplined, fear of commitment, stubborn, lacks integrity, social climber, headstrong, too direct, tactless, rebellious

SUN IN CAPRICORN–VENUS IN AQUARIUS

People are attracted to your determined character, strong principles, and liberal views. Although you are often practical with fixed views and ideas, you probably have an unconventional approach to love and relationships. Usually you value friendship, seeking a partner who can be a good companion and share some of your more unusual interests. Others can sometimes misinterpret your objective and slightly detached approach to affairs of the heart as cold and unfeeling. Realistic and intelligent, you want a partner who is independent yet loyal with good social skills. People often admire your sincerity, original ideas, and pragmatic approach.

Your appealing attributes: progressive, independent, friendly, rational, practical, loyal, keen on reforms at work, collaborative, work associations, loyal, group-oriented, humanitarian, self-control

Your unappealing attributes: stubborn, unfriendly, reserved, impressionable, too independent, awkward, rebellious

SUN IN AQUARIUS–VENUS IN AQUARIUS

Your intimate partnerships need to be founded on true friendship. Original and a freethinker, you are usually easygoing in your relationships. Detached with a friendly personality, you are usually tolerant and objective toward your

partners unless they infringe on your freedom. Although you behave in a reasonable manner most of the time, you can also be awkward and stubborn and refuse to listen to those who love you. In relationships you seek a partner who offers you opportunities for renewal or change.

Your appealing attributes: friendly, practical, independent, freedom-loving, honest, intelligent, progressive, reformer, group-oriented, sociable, original

Your unappealing attributes: stubborn, difficult, too serious, awkward, too detached, eccentric, nonconformist, rebellious

SUN IN PISCES–VENUS IN AQUARIUS

Friendly and impressionable, you need to interact with your peer group and have a sense of belonging. Open to new ideas, you are drawn to independent or unconventional individuals. Although you are friendly and sociable, your free spirit does not like partners who are too demanding or restrictive. Since you are receptive to those around you, you can easily pick up on the moods and feelings of others. Valuing friendship, you want your partner to also be your best buddy.

Your appealing attributes: friendly, independent, freedom-loving, honest, intelligent, sociable, original, progressive, creative, appreciation of progressive ideas, artistic, idealistic, caring, humanitarian, visionary, inspired, poetic, inventive, group-oriented

Your unappealing attributes: stubborn, secretive, rebellious, too impressionable, escapist, awkward, indulgent

Venus in Pisces

SUN IN CAPRICORN–VENUS IN PISCES

Although you are usually very practical, when it comes to love, you are sensitive and giving. A natural romantic when it comes to affairs of the heart, you are responsive and idealistic. Fortunately your sense of realism can help balance your tendency to lose yourself in your partner's needs. Usually you want a partner who is reliable yet tender with a compassionate heart. Others are attracted to your loyal and understanding nature.

Your appealing attributes: caring, unselfish, responsive, considerate, idealistic, easygoing, subtle, sensitive, devoted, sympathetic, imaginative, compassionate, generous

Your unappealing attributes: escapist, moody, evasive, lacking discrimination, weak, avoidance, martyr, delusion

SUN IN AQUARIUS–VENUS IN PISCES

Although you are independent, you can also be romantic and loving. You have a genuine concern for others, and

your partners gain from your easygoing yet subtle approach to relationships. Although you possess natural detachment in other areas of your life, in relationships, because of your sensitive and compassionate nature, be careful that you don't give too much of yourself in your desire to please. Sociable and group-oriented, you attract others with your humanitarian approach and friendly personality.

Your appealing attributes: caring, unselfish, responsive, considerate, idealistic, easygoing, subtle, sensitive, devoted, sympathetic, imaginative, compassionate

Your unappealing attributes: escapist, moody, evasive, self-pity, lacks discrimination, weak, avoidance, martyr, delusional

SUN IN PISCES–VENUS IN PISCES

As a romantic dreamer, you are idealistic about relationships. Generous and giving you are usually sympathetic to those who ask for your help. Quick to pick up on the moods of others, you have a natural flair for dealing with people. Subtle and charming, you can impress others without much effort. When in love you are affectionate and often willing to make sacrifices to keep the peace. However, resist making too many allowances or losing sight of your own goals. By learning to take responsibility for yourself you can boost your self-esteem. Your alluring qualities, gentleness, and creative gifts attract others.

Your appealing attributes: subtle, intuitive, sympathetic, imaginative, compassionate, sensitivity, entertaining, artistic or musical, vision, poetic, creative gifts, psychic, create an illusion, idealistic, kind, caring, humanitarian, versatile, adaptable, enchanting

Your unappealing attributes: evasive, martyr, feeling vulnerable, escapism, deceptive, easily led, weak, too impressionable, moody, lacks discrimination, self-pity

SUN IN ARIES–VENUS IN PISCES

You are chivalrous and dashing with an idealistic nature, and when you fall in love it is often with all your heart. Impulsive and enthusiastic, you may even rush into a relationship. Although you can appear daring and confident, you can also be romantic, sensitive, and impressionable. Sometimes you may want to help or rescue your partner, but do not martyr yourself if your partner keeps failing you. Friendly and caring, you enjoy socializing and entertaining others. People are attracted by your natural creativity and generous nature.

Your appealing attributes: idealistic, creative, imaginative, enthusiastic, compassionate, romantic, chivalrous, generous, receptive, warm, kind, loving, sensitive, visionary, subtle, caring

Your unappealing attributes: subject to highs and lows, moody, impressionable, evasive, impulsive, martyr, self-pity, escapist

SUN IN TAURUS–VENUS IN PISCES

As a romantic and charitable person, you are attracted to alluring or artistic individuals who can be sympathetic and compassionate. You may draw a partner who has an imaginative or poetic side to their nature like you. In love you are sensitive, tactile, and giving, with an ability to sense your partner's feelings as deeply as your own. If you are unhappy about your relationships or unwilling to face facts, avoid a tendency to escape through overindulgence. Nevertheless, your ability to be creative and responsive can make you a sensitive and tender lover and a caring companion.

Your appealing attributes: caring, unselfish, responsive, intuitive, adaptable, versatile, alluring, considerate, sympathetic, imaginative, tender, affectionate, subtle, talented, psychic, tactile, loves beauty, artistic or musical

Your unappealing attributes: escapist, overindulgent, moody, evasive, lacks discrimination, self-pity, vague, deceptive, weak, evasive, stubborn

Empowerment and the Outer Planets

A Guide to Your Personalized Timetable and a Step-by-Step Example

In this section are the interpretations of the Outer Planets in relation to your Sun's degree. You can use these interpretations to find out:

- In Chapter 1: What are the Outer Planets saying about you?
- In Chapter 2: What type of relationships are the Outer Planets attracting into your life? Are they challenging, beneficial, or special?
- In Chapter 3: When are you likely to encounter periods of challenge and when are you likely to encounter periods of opportunity and success?

How to Use Your Personalized Timetable

Each birthday has a Sun degree and a personalized timetable that begins in 1938 and continues until 2012. The timetable provides information on the positions of the Outer Planets Jupiter, Saturn, Uranus, Neptune, and Pluto. As these planets move they form different relationships with your Sun's degree.

By interpreting the effects of these planets, you will be able to understand in greater depth what you are attracting into your life. You will be able to discover:

- How your Sun interacts with the Outer Planets.
- How your Sun interacts with the Outer Planets of other people.
- How to use your Sun's interaction with the Outer Planets to predict the future.

What Are the Outer Planets Saying About You?

STEP 1. Look at the personal timetable on the pages for your birthday.

STEP 2. Look up your year of birth and see if it appears under any of the planets listed. Then check to see if your full date of birth appears within the time periods listed under each planet.

STEP 3. The timetable provides three different types of

influence for each planet; these come under the categories of beneficial, challenging, and special. If your birth date appears in any of these categories, note the name of the planet and type of influence. For example, if you were born on May 28, 1961, you will find that your birthday appears under the heading "Saturn Beneficial."

SATURN BENEFICIAL
1961 3/28 – 6/22

To find the interpretation for this influence, go to Chapter 1, "What Are the Outer Planets Saying About You?"

Your Relationships with Others

STEP 1. First ascertain the exact birth date of the other person. Then check to see if his or her birthday appears anywhere in your personalized timetable.

STEP 2. Note if it appears in any of the three categories listed under each planet. For example, if you are born on May 28, 1961, and you wish to know how you would get along with someone born on April 10, 1977, you will find his or her date of birth listed in your personalized timetable under "Saturn Beneficial."

SATURN BENEFICIAL
1977 2/28 – 5/22

To find the interpretation for this influence, you then go to Chapter 2, "Your Relationships with Others."

Predicting the Future

As your personalized timetable extends to the year 2012, you can check future trends to see when you are likely to encounter periods of opportunity, challenge, or success.

STEP 1. First determine the time period you wish to examine. According to your timetable you can discover if a planet is affecting you at that particular time.

STEP 2. Note if the date appears in any of the three categories listed under each planet. Is it beneficial, challenging, or special? For example, if your birthday is May 28 and you want to know what kind of influences you can expect on March 3,

2003, you can find this date in your timetable listed under "Neptune Beneficial."

NEPTUNE BENEFICIAL
1997 2/13 – until **2005** 1/17

As Uranus, Neptune, and Pluto have a longer period of influence, you can discover the time this influence is strongest by looking under your date of birth in the extra timetable at the end of your zodiac sign.

NEPTUNE X-BENEFICIAL
2000 2/20 – until **2002** 11/18

STEP 3. To find the interpretation for these influences, you now go to Chapter 3, "Predicting the Future," where you can find this influence under "Times of Neptune Beneficial."

Example of a Reader Using The Power of Attraction

The following is a step-by-step example of a reader we'll call Judy who was born on May 28, 1979. First, Judy turns to her own two pages of May 28. In the first part, "Your Personal Powers," Judy reads about herself and how to improve her potential for success. In the second part, "Your Powers of Attraction in Relationships," Judy reads about the Venus and Mars influences associated with her day, May 28. Here she can also find the attractive and less attractive qualities linked to her birthday.

Judy's Venus Power

On the entry for her birthday, May 28, Judy sees a number of Venus possibilities under the title "Your Power." To find out in which astrological sign Venus was positioned in her year of birth, Judy goes to Section Two of the book and looks up her Venus Year Table (see page 774).

Judy checks her year, 1979, and finds out that on her birthday Venus was in Taurus.

1979
Venus in Scorpio: Jan 1–Jan 7
Venus in Sagittarius: Jan 7–Feb 5
Venus in Capricorn: Feb 5–Mar 3
Venus in Aquarius: Mar 3–Mar 29
Venus in Pisces: Mar 29–Apr 23
Venus in Aries: Apr 23–May 18
→ Venus in Taurus: May 18–June 11
Venus in Gemini: June 11–July 6

Venus in Cancer: July 6–July 30
Venus in Leo: July 30–Aug 24
Venus in Virgo: Aug 24–Sept 17
Venus in Libra: Sept 17–Oct 11
Venus in Scorpio: Oct 11–Nov 4
Venus in Sagittarius: Nov 4–Nov 28
Venus in Capricorn: Nov 28–Dec 22
Venus in Aquarius: Dec 22–Dec 31

Judy discovers further information about herself in Section Two, after the Venus Year table. Under the heading "Sun in Gemini—Venus in Taurus" Judy reads about her Sun/Venus combination. Judy has a Gemini Sun with Venus in Taurus.

Judy's Mars Power

In Section Two of the book Judy can also discover her Mars power. First she finds her year of birth, 1979, in the Mars Year Table (page 763). She learns that in 1979, Mars was in Taurus on May 28.

1979
Mars in Capricorn: Jan 1–Jan 20
Mars in Aquarius: Jan 20–Feb 27
Mars in Pisces: Feb 27–Apr 7
Mars in Aries: Apr 7–May 16
→ Mars in Taurus: May 16–June 26
Mars in Gemini: June 26–Aug 8
Mars in Cancer: Aug 8–Sept 24
Mars in Leo: Sept 24–Nov 19
Mars in Virgo: Nov 19–Dec 31

Judy's interpretations of her personal Mars Power appear after the Mars Year Table. She reads the interpretation for both the women and the men. The women's part indicates her Mars qualities and the men's part describes the type of person she often finds attractive. In Judy's case she is attracted to men with Mars in Taurus qualities.

In the case of a male reader, however, the Mars and Venus interpretations have different meanings. The Mars interpretations describe men's motivation and drive and the way they act in relationships. The Venus interpretations on their main two-page birthday spread describe their Venus qualities and the type of partners they are most attracted to.

Now that Judy knows about her Venus and Mars powers she is ready to use her personalized table.

How Judy Uses Her Personalized Timetable

Judy's personalized timetable is the key to unlock the three chapters of interpretation in Section Three. These chapters contain very different information, yet the same personalized

timetable is used for all of them. To access this information Judy returns to her timetable on her birthday page for May 28.

HOW TO USE CHAPTER 1, "WHAT ARE THE OUTER PLANETS SAYING ABOUT YOU?"

First Judy examines the overall layout of her personalized timetable and sees many columns of dates under different categories—for example, Jupiter Beneficial, Saturn Beneficial, Neptune Challenging, Pluto Challenging.

Initially, Judy wants to find out about herself. Using her full date of birth—1979 5/28—she looks for her birth date in each column. Judy finds that it appears under the category "Jupiter Beneficial." Her birth date falls between the dates as they appear below:

1979 5/5 – 7/4

JUPITER BENEFICIAL
1973 2/16 – until **1974** 1/1
1975 3/24 – 5/6
1978 9/13 – until **1979** 2/14
→ **1979** 5/5 – 7/4
1980 10/19 – until **1981** 9/14

In Chapter 1, Judy finds the general interpretation for Jupiter Beneficial, which reads:

JUPITER BENEFICIAL
By nature you are honest and optimistic and are able to attract others with your natural enthusiasm. With the confidence to think big, you often see the right opportunity in order to improve yourself or your circumstances. With your need for expansion, you usually explore new ways of thinking and search for different experiences to enrich your life and bring success. You have an active mind and may be interested in a wide range of subjects, particularly education, religion, law, or philosophy. Alternatively, being lucky and enterprising, you may have an entrepreneurial spirit and go into business. Your relationship with your father benefited you by allowing you to be confident or enterprising. Travel is especially beneficial for you as it fits wells with your interest in other cultures and your desire to expand your knowledge.

Underneath this main interpretation Judy finds an added interpretation specific for her Sun in Gemini.

SUN IN GEMINI WITH JUPITER BENEFICIAL: As you have good communication skills and the ability to make quick decisions, you are often eager to learn. You enjoy mixing with others and benefit from exploring new and innovative ideas or working in collaboration with others.

Judy has to repeat this process every time she finds her date of birth in one of the columns in her personalized timetable. For example, Judy also finds that her birth date appears in her timetable under the category "Saturn Challenging." Her date of birth falls between the dates as they appear below:

1978 7/12 – until **1979** 8/18

Again in Chapter 1, Judy finds both interpretations for "Saturn Challenging."

HOW TO USE CHAPTER 2, "YOUR RELATIONSHIPS WITH OTHERS"

Now Judy wants to know what type of relationship she is attracting into her life. She looks up her boyfriend Bill's birthday, September 1, 1976, on her own personalized timetable. Judy finds Bill's date of birth under four different categories and notes these down.

First Judy finds Bill's birth date in the column of dates under the category "Saturn Beneficial" as below:

1976 6/18 – 9/6

SATURN BENEFICIAL
1961 3/28 – 6/22
1961 12/20 – until **1963** 2/8
1967 3/15 – 6/20
1967 8/29 – until **1968** 3/4
1975 10/4 – 12/26
→ **1976** 6/18 – 9/6
1977 2/28 – 5/22
1980 9/8 – until **1981** 10/19

This time Judy turns to Chapter 2, "Your Relationships with Others," to discover how the interpretation of "Saturn Beneficial in Relationships" describes her relationship with Bill. She reads the main interpretation first and then the added interpretation specific to her "Saturn Beneficial to Your Gemini Sun in Relationships." Next Judy finds that Bill's date of birth also appears under the category "Pluto Beneficial" in her personalized table. His date of birth falls between the dates as they appear below:

1970 10/24 – until **1978** 8/7

In this chapter Judy finds the interpretation for "Pluto Beneficial in Relationships" in the category "Beneficial Relationships."

Now Judy finds the other two categories in which Bill's birthday appears in her personalized timetable under the headings "Neptune Challenging" and "Jupiter Special." Judy first goes to the category "Challenging Relationships" and discovers the interpretation of "Neptune Challenging in Relationships" and reads how this interpretation describes her relationship with Bill. In the case of "Jupiter Special," Judy finds the interpretation in the category "Special Relationships" under "Jupiter Special in Relationships."

Using the same methods she checks all her friends, coworkers, and relatives.

How to Use Chapter 3, "Predicting the Future"

Judy wants to find out what the future has in store for her and when she is likely to experience important periods and attract success. Again she goes back to her own personalized birthday timetable of May 28.

Looking at the bottom of the columns Judy sees that the timetable extends past the year 2002 until 2012. In the "Saturn Special" category of her personalized timetable, Judy can see that she has a "Saturn Special" influence that runs from: **2001** 10/21 to **2002** 5/8.

In this chapter, under "Times of Saturn Special," Judy finds the interpretation of this period. Next Judy finds that she also has an influence of "Neptune Beneficial" from **1997** 2/13 to **2005** 1/17

Still in Chapter 3, Judy finds the interpretation of this planetary influence in "Times of Neptune Beneficial." By using the knowledge of all these interpretations, Judy can see what energies she will be attracting into her life over the next few years. She can therefore have more insight to make objective decisions and empower herself. Judy can also use Bill's timetable to see what future influences are likely to affect him and their relationship together. After a number of tries Judy uses her personalized table with relative ease and is ready to proceed to next stage.

More Advanced Methods of Using the Personalized Timetable

A planet reaches a peak as it encounters a Sun degree and its influence slowly lessens as it leaves. Important events often occur when the influence is at its most powerful. Each planet applies an influence to the Sun degree for different lengths of time. Jupiter and Saturn only spend a few weeks or months influencing the Sun degree, while Uranus, Neptune, and Pluto spend a number of years.

Judy notices that the two larger tables belong to Jupiter and Saturn. She can see that the tables of Uranus, Neptune, and Pluto are small and cover a longer period of time, some up to ten years. If Judy wants to know when a planet's influence is at its strongest and most noticeable she can look in the extra table at the end of her zodiac Sun sun under May 28. There she will find dates followed by an "X." These dates are extra special periods pinpointing the most important times when the Outer Planets connect exactly to her Sun degree.

Neptune X-Beneficial
2000 2/20 – until **2002** 11/18

A different way to calculate these extra special periods is by subtracting the end year of the period from the beginning year. For example, if the influence of Neptune to her Sun degree is during the following period

1997 2/13 – until **2005** 1/17

all Judy has to do is subtract 1997 from 2005, which is 8 years. She then divides 8 years by 2, which will give her 4 years. Judy now adds 4 years to 1997 and realizes that in 2001–2, Neptune's influence is at its greatest and therefore closest to her Sun degree. In other words, during the years: 1997, 1998, 1999, Neptune moves toward Judy's Sun; in 2000, 2001, 2002, Neptune is directly linked to her Sun degree; and in 2003 and 2004 it weakens until its influence is diminished is 2005.

By using these methods Judy can calculate how the influences of the Outer Planets Uranus, Neptune, and Pluto will affect her life in the future.

How to Use Other People's Personalized Timetables

After using her personalized timetable Judy can go to her boyfriend Bill's timetable to find her birthday and year of birth. By using the same method she used on her own timetable, she can gain more insight into the people she knows and her relationships with them as well as important periods in their lives.

Chapter 1: What Are the Outer Planets Saying About You?

Beneficial Planets

Jupiter Beneficial

By nature you are honest and optimistic and are able to attract others with your natural enthusiasm. With the confidence to think big, you often see the right opportunity in order to improve yourself or your circumstances. With your need for expansion, you usually explore new ways of thinking and search for different experiences to enrich your life and bring success. You have an active mind and may be interested in a wide range of subjects, particularly education, religion, law, or philosophy. Alternatively, being lucky and enterprising, you may have an entrepreneurial spirit and go into business. Your relationship with your father benefited you by allowing you to be confident or enterprising. Travel is especially beneficial for you as it can stimulate interest in other cultures and your desire to expand your horizons.

SUN IN ARIES WITH JUPITER BENEFICIAL: Enthusiastic and action-oriented, when you find projects of interest you like to take the initiative. You can have many fortunate or creative ideas that will bring you success. Usually bold and confident, you like to take the lead.

SUN IN TAURUS WITH JUPITER BENEFICIAL: Willing to work hard and with an optimistic outlook, you know how to use your knowledge in business. You usually have the desire to be productive as you enjoy life's luxuries.

SUN IN GEMINI WITH JUPITER BENEFICIAL: As you have good communication skills and the ability to make quick decisions, you are often eager to learn. You enjoy mixing or collaborating with others and benefit from friendships or exploring new and innovative ideas.

SUN IN CANCER WITH JUPITER BENEFICIAL: Generous and sensitive, with a wealth of feelings, you often can rely on family and friends for support. Highly imaginative, you work best when you trust your positive vision for the future.

SUN IN LEO WITH JUPITER BENEFICIAL: You are likely to have natural leadership skills and be able to see the positive side to any difficult situation. Enjoying the drama of life, you can positively encourage others with your warmth and benevolence.

SUN IN VIRGO WITH JUPITER BENEFICIAL: Versatile, dexterous, and articulate, you have a knack for solving problems and are a good organizer. Hardworking, you can be determined and productive.

SUN IN LIBRA WITH JUPITER BENEFICIAL: Diplomatic and sociable, you can be an enchanting and uplifting conversationalist. Usually you benefit from working in a group environment. With a mind that is particularly aware of balance, you possess a strong sense of justice and fair play.

SUN IN SCORPIO WITH JUPITER BENEFICIAL: You have the ability to seize opportunities or receive support from people or family members. With your persuasive manner and generous nature, you can also be caring and considerate. Your imagination or insight suggests that you have a dynamic unconscious or clairvoyant ability.

SUN IN SAGITTARIUS WITH JUPITER BENEFICIAL: With your big plans and natural dynamic character you can inspire others to action. Alternatively, as you enjoy socializing and have a sense of fun, people can be drawn to your generous personality.

SUN IN CAPRICORN WITH JUPITER BENEFICIAL: Hardworking with a wealth of knowledge or good business sense, you can succeed in achieving your goals and ambitions through your pragmatism and determination.

SUN IN AQUARIUS WITH JUPITER BENEFICIAL: You are an inventive person who is open to new ideas and can think success. You are likely to gain from widening your knowledge through study and travel, or benefit from your social contacts and group activities. You can also be fair and just.

SUN IN PISCES WITH JUPITER BENEFICIAL. With your abundance of feelings and imagination, you possess good perception and a positive outlook on life. You can benefit from your family links and ability to take advantage of the right opportunities.

Saturn Beneficial

Honorable and loyal, you can be hardworking, determined, and goal-oriented. Patient, persevering, and good at problem solving, once you commit yourself to a project you can be diligent and industrious. You are therefore likely to achieve success by being steady and persistent even though you may have to learn to overcome challenges. Ambitious and aware of

responsibility, you are likely to have good relationships with authority figures. In your youth, you probably enjoyed a good relationship with an older person, such as your father or grandfather. You usually show respect for people who are more mature or experienced than you. Although sometimes cautious, you have a good sense of timing and probably prefer to progress slowly but surely rather than hurry things along. Your sense of duty implies that people reward your dedication and often put you in positions of trust.

SUN IN ARIES WITH SATURN BENEFICIAL: Ambitious and purposeful, your ability to focus and endure indicates that you are not afraid to take on challenges, even if they can mean slow but steady progress and a great deal of hard work. The more effort you put in the more you are likely to succeed.

SUN IN TAURUS WITH SATURN BENEFICIAL: Loyal and reliable, you are a good strategist with a more conservative view. Usually you take your responsibilities seriously, especially when it concerns money and work.

SUN IN GEMINI WITH SATURN BENEFICIAL: Intelligent and hardworking with quiet determination, you are able to synthesize new ideas with respected traditions. You learn quickly yet have responsible attitudes toward getting things done.

SUN IN CANCER WITH SATURN BENEFICIAL: With your natural receptivity you are caring and sensitive yet resolute. You can be sympathetic to other people's needs and usually are a steady rock for those you love.

SUN IN LEO WITH SATURN BENEFICIAL: Proud and loyal, you are dignified and sincere. Usually you have a strong identity or respect for authority. Through your ability to work hard you can rise to positions of influence.

SUN IN VIRGO WITH SATURN BENEFICIAL: Ambitious, disciplined, and diligent, you do not shy away from hard work. Analytical and methodical, you are also able to evaluate situations or people by being cautious and patient.

SUN IN LIBRA WITH SATURN BENEFICIAL: Logical yet thoughtful, your strong sense of right and wrong in relation to others suggests that you know how to deal with people in a fair and dispassionate manner.

SUN IN SAGITTARIUS WITH SATURN BENEFICIAL: Honorable and righteous, you have strong beliefs and a clear code of conduct. Your determination indicates that you are not afraid to take on challenges even if they involve a great deal of effort on your part.

SUN IN CAPRICORN WITH SATURN BENEFICIAL: Ambitious and hardworking, you possess strong willpower and the determination to achieve your goals even if these involve slow advancement. You are a good evaluator and are able to make long-term investments.

SUN IN AQUARIUS WITH SATURN BENEFICIAL: You are a humanitarian with a strong sense of justice and duty. Faithful to a cause or to a group of people, you have skills and impressive speech that can often make you an idealist with practical abilities.

SUN IN PISCES WITH SATURN BENEFICIAL: Your vision, resolve, and insight imply that you have clear and definite goals. Although attainment of success may be slow, your faith and determination can bring you success.

Uranus Beneficial

You are inventive with personal magnetism, and your alert mind often looks for exciting ways to keep you interested and entertained. Honest and direct, you generally work well in a group or team situation. That you are an objective thinker and interested in people gives you insight into the motives and personality of others. Resourceful and freedom-loving, you have an interest in the future and a love of variety that keep you youthful. Your confidence especially increases when you are able to express yourself in a detached and universal way. Original and often ahead of your time, you may have unorthodox ideas that you present in a fresh or innovative way to inspire people. With your innate psychological skills you can provide an objective viewpoint for others thereby helping them to stay impartial. An interest in freedom and reform may draw you to protect the underdog or fight for humanitarian causes and ideals. Opportunities often come from unexpected sources.

SUN IN ARIES WITH URANUS BENEFICIAL: When you add your inventive ideas to your drive and enthusiasm you are able to approach projects from a different angle or initiate new schemes that have not been tried before. This often gives you a competitive edge.

SUN IN TAURUS WITH URANUS BENEFICIAL: Your down-to-earth practicality can help you put your more unusual or unorthodox ideas into practice, encouraging you to be more experimental. You can make money from unusual sources or by applying your unique skills.

SUN IN GEMINI WITH URANUS BENEFICIAL: You enjoy interests that keep your fast mind stimulated and prefer not to be tied down to routine. With your quick wit, you like social situations and possess an original approach to life. Often liberal, you are a progressive thinker.

SUN IN CANCER WITH URANUS BENEFICIAL: Although sensitive, you can also be objective and detached. Highly intuitive, you are likely to have psychic links with others. Some members of your family are individualists like yourself. Although caring, you still have a need for freedom.

SUN IN LEO WITH URANUS BENEFICIAL: Your confidence is linked to your unique self-expression. Your ability to see situations from an unbiased and dispassionate point of view suggests that you can be both an actor on life's stage and a detached observer in the audience. That you are creative and original with ideas and insight into people indicates that you can be entertaining and different.

SUN IN VIRGO WITH URANUS BENEFICIAL: Your analytical skills and ability to pay attention to details works well with your impartial outlook and original ideas. Very clever yet practical, you can come up with ideas that have not been tried before. That you are shrewd about people and have a humanitarian streak suggests that you enjoy helping others with your special insight and knowledge.

SUN IN LIBRA WITH URANUS BENEFICIAL: Your strong needs to socialize and to express something different and original could lead you to become interested in artistic or creative pursuits. Possessing personal magnetism, you have a way with people who appreciate your diplomatic and original approach.

SUN IN SAGITTARIUS WITH URANUS BENEFICIAL: Open-minded and philosophical in outlook, you can be magnanimous and tolerant toward others. Inspired by new experiences and places, you have an optimistic and innovative approach to life situations. A natural humanitarian side to your personality could attract you to educating, inspiring, or uplifting others.

SUN IN CAPRICORN WITH URANUS BENEFICIAL: Your innovative outlook suggests that you are capable of seeing new ways of approaching situations or altering old methods. You possess an interesting blend of conservatism and radical thinking that can make you responsible yet open to new ideas.

SUN IN AQUARIUS WITH URANUS BENEFICIAL: Mentally curious, you are progressive and future-oriented. Having a strong sense of individuality you prefer to be different and not follow the herd. Your friends and social groups are particularly important to you.

SUN IN PISCES WITH URANUS BENEFICIAL: You are sensitive yet inventive, and your open-mindedness to new experiences can set you apart from the crowd or put you ahead of your time. Being highly intuitive, you possess an ability to quickly assess the moods and personality of others.

Neptune Beneficial

Your imagination and intuition is usually excellent, and when inspired by something you have the ability to clearly visualize your aspirations and dreams. With your sensitivity and refined feelings you are receptive to the subtle moods of others. Your father may have been sensitive, artistic, or idealistic and had a positive influence on you. Impressionable and aware of cultural trends, you can use your insight to promote your ideas, often tuning in to what the public wants. Idealistic and astute, you are frequently drawn to creative and artistic people who can inspire you. You are usually a tolerant, receptive, and adaptable person. With your compassion and understanding you are often able to put yourself in other people's shoes and accept them for who they are. When seeking inspiration, you benefit from long journeys or from learning about metaphysi-

cal subjects, philosophy, and spirituality. Alternatively, your Neptune powers may direct you to the healing professions or your sense of vision could be used in practical or business situations.

SUN IN ARIES WITH NEPTUNE BENEFICIAL: Idealistic and enthusiastic, you can achieve a great deal if you are inspired and believe in what you want to accomplish. You may benefit from your creative endeavors or travel to distant lands. A poet or a pioneer, you are daring enough to live out your dream.

SUN IN TAURUS WITH NEPTUNE BENEFICIAL: Your intuitive understanding works in harmony with your practical abilities to help you plan and endure. If you are not drawn to service or the healing professions, perhaps you are able to put your astuteness and imagination to good use through creative self-expression or business enterprises.

SUN IN GEMINI WITH NEPTUNE BENEFICIAL: You are an imaginative communicator, and are original, articulate, and inquisitive with a high degree of intuition. Versatile and charming yet sensitive, you usually believe in people's good nature and are able to sympathize with others.

SUN IN CANCER WITH NEPTUNE BENEFICIAL: Sensitive and receptive, you have a natural ability to pick up other people's moods and feelings. Usually you are sympathetic to those who need help. Naturally psychic, your intuition is good and your inner vision can inspire you to be creative. Dreams can be of great use to you since some of them can be vivid and powerful.

SUN IN LEO WITH NEPTUNE BENEFICIAL: Creative and imaginative, you are receptive to all types of self-expression. You may be keen to travel to foreign lands. Able to draw upon your imagination and dreams, you can be original and artistic. When you feel inspired by an idea or a philosophical concept you can embrace it with enthusiasm. Inner faith and idealism can make you purposeful and generous.

SUN IN VIRGO WITH NEPTUNE BENEFICIAL: You are thoughtful, and your intuitive thinking allows you to be receptive to the subtlest interchanges between people. Your depth of vision and sensitivity open doors to the realms of the imagination. Usually you can remember small details from the past. Being understanding and intuitive, you can be sympathetic toward others.

SUN IN LIBRA WITH NEPTUNE BENEFICIAL: You can be quite charming and easygoing. Your being idealistic about relationships and love suggests that, as an understanding individual with a romantic nature, you can easily attract other people and be sympathetic to their needs.

SUN IN SCORPIO WITH NEPTUNE BENEFICIAL: As your receptivity to others blends well with your determination and willpower, you can be caring and a force for good for those around you. Being psychic and imaginative, you can sense the subtle undertones of situations or express your inner vision with clarity.

Sun in Sagittarius with Neptune Beneficial: Your idealism and hopeful outlook indicate that you express yourself in positive ways. Usually generous and imaginative, you enjoy creating and shaping ideas or large concepts. Your positive vision can also uplift others.

Sun in Capricorn with Neptune Beneficial: Your foresight and determination indicate that you can be trustworthy and a practical visionary. You usually succeed in attaining your goals by being methodical and cautious yet intuitive and idealistic.

Sun in Aquarius with Neptune Beneficial: An imaginative individualist, you enjoy the company of other idealists or are attracted to original, artistic, or refined people. Often inventive and inspired, your unique thoughts are usually in tune with your feelings.

Sun in Pisces with Neptune Beneficial: Compassionate, understanding, and tolerant toward others, you can be imaginative and receptive with psychic abilities. Subtle and sensitive, you pick up on emotional undercurrents or changes in social trends.

Pluto Beneficial

Your personal magnetism and willpower imply that you can be very focused when decided on a course of action. With your foresight, you are able to advance through interaction with others or by convincing them that change is the way forward. Highly instinctive, you are good at assessing people or situations quickly. You can enjoy popularity with the masses through your gift for making good first impressions. With your capacity for taking on challenges and comprehending the deeper complexities of life, you are not afraid to face difficult situations. You are usually confident with impressive ideas and have the power to influence social change. You also have the ability to see the irony in life or the humor in even the darkest moments. You have an enjoyment of the transformation process, and Pluto beneficial gives you the strength to be powerful and intense at the right time. You may be interested in therapy, changing society, or spirituality. Possessing courage and fast intuitive perceptions, you are often willing to take an all-or-nothing stance in your desire to transform challenging situations.

Sun in Aries with Pluto Beneficial: Once you have decided upon a course of action you can become focused, forceful, and persuasive, showing determination to achieve your goals. You instinctively know when to push ahead by tuning in to the responses of others.

Sun in Taurus with Pluto Beneficial: Although pragmatic, you possess an instinctive ability to judge the reactions of others. A desire to influence people or transform social situations can manifest through positions of power and authority. Your determination often allows you to push your otherwise cautious nature into more daring all-or-nothing situations.

Sun in Gemini with Pluto Beneficial: Communicative and keen to learn, you benefit from your relationships with others. Adaptable, you can see the other person's point of view and adjust to new situations. You are versatile and articulate with an inquisitive mind and persuasive manner. At times direct, you are able to ask penetrating questions that enable you to judge situations from the reactions of others.

Sun in Cancer with Pluto Beneficial: As you are highly intuitive, it is usually best for you to judge people or situations from your first reactions, as they are nearly always accurate. You are able to rise to positions of power; your confidence comes from not being afraid to tackle more challenging situations.

Sun in Leo with Pluto Beneficial: Courageous and able to handle power well, you often rise to leadership positions. Willing to go out on a limb if you believe that you are right, you often dare to face adverse reactions from others.

Sun in Virgo with Pluto Beneficial: Although practical and modest, you can still confidently express your power and will, especially if you are in a position of leadership or authority. You often have instinctive gut feelings about people or situations, then later analyze them in great detail. You are good at assessing people and their behavior.

Sun in Libra with Pluto Beneficial: Your awareness of human relations is intensified with this influence. Always conscious of the reactions of others, you can judge instinctively when to push forward your views or beliefs. You empower yourself through your ability to be a diplomat in difficult situations.

Sun in Scorpio with Pluto Beneficial: Not afraid to face adverse situations, you usually thrive on a challenge. You enjoy power and are resourceful and enterprising. Highly intuitive, you often rely on your excellent quick insights into situations or people.

Sun in Sagittarius with Pluto Beneficial: People are impressed by your confident personality. You can rise to positions of leadership due to your will, quick reactions, and ability to handle power. You can combine enthusiasm and insight with a desire to get a job done.

Sun in Capricorn with Pluto Beneficial: You are able to act with power and authority in order to change situations for the better. Practical and straightforward, you can combine your willpower, concentration, and intuitive insight to achieve positive results.

Sun in Aquarius with Pluto Beneficial: Original and strong-willed, you usually prefer to be given free rein to express yourself in your own way. Whether at work or at home, you are willing to give projects your full concentration if they hold your interest.

SUN IN PISCES WITH PLUTO BENEFICIAL: Highly intuitive, your quick instincts can save you from difficult situations or help you to get ahead in life. You usually prefer to involve yourself in projects wholeheartedly. Your quick insight into others often gives you an edge in personal or career situations.

Challenging Planets

Jupiter Challenging

Often appearing confident, you are an optimistic individual who prefers to show an assured front even though you can be inwardly uncertain. Your high hopes and wishful thinking about grand plans or ambitious ideas need to be accompanied by hard work. Without detailed planning and dedication your eagerness may be short-lived. Keen to push your boundaries beyond their limitations, you may need to watch out that your enthusiasm does not develop into overconfidence. However, if you feel you are not progressing or expanding fast enough, you may become restless or dissatisfied. Usually your moral sense and generosity imply that you have good intentions toward others, but situations can backfire if you appear arrogant or condescending. Although you often believe that luck is on your side and nothing can harm you, by resisting being careless or wasteful you can enhance your success rate. Although you can be generous, a tendency to be expansive and a desire for the good life suggest that you may also be overindulgent. You may need to learn that patience pays in the long run and not take things for granted. You achieve more by being cautious rather than being impulsive. Do not lose heart if things went wrong in the past but try again, as giving up too easily is unwise. With determination and learning to deal with setbacks, you can achieve a great deal.

SUN IN ARIES WITH JUPITER CHALLENGING: Your desire for action or progress may at times make you impatient or restless. Being more careful and less impulsive can work to your advantage. Paying more attention to your responsibilities or to those around you can win you the respect and admiration you desire.

SUN IN TAURUS WITH JUPITER CHALLENGING: Your need for stability and security indicates that you benefit from being cautious and less wasteful with your finances. Your desire for comfort and good living, however, may at times cause you to be indulgent. If your liberal and philanthropic aspirations are balanced by practical considerations you can plan your projects carefully and succeed admirably.

SUN IN GEMINI WITH JUPITER CHALLENGING: Capable of assimilating a great deal of information, you have a wealth of ideas or business abilities. Your broad-mindedness, curiosity, and eagerness can expand your horizons but your inconsistency can undermine your efforts. Discriminating awareness is needed in order to achieve long-term plans and success. Alternatively, by developing more efficient methods of work and staying focused, you can improve your skills or process the information that you collect.

SUN IN CANCER WITH JUPITER CHALLENGING: In order to achieve emotional stability or security you need to be even-tempered, adaptable, and sympathetic. Your family or home issues need to be balanced against your personal goals or aspirations. Emotional restlessness may make big demands on your time and resources. Although you can be friendly, constant expansion of your social circle may interfere with your domestic life.

SUN IN LEO WITH JUPITER CHALLENGING: Usually you can achieve more when your pride and confidence are balanced by congeniality and a liberal outlook. If you are too speculative or wasteful you may find it eventually costly. You can achieve success or influence others easily if you are subtle and less dramatic with your plans or ideas. Nevertheless, you can be generous and make magnanimous gestures toward those you love.

SUN IN VIRGO WITH JUPITER CHALLENGING: Your desire to be informed and your analytical abilities indicate that you are mentally quick and keen to achieve a great deal. Your preoccupation with methods and details needs to be balanced with your understanding of the whole. If you act in haste you can easily overlook important matters. Alternatively, your practical considerations and idealism suggest that you can be helpful and compassionate.

SUN IN LIBRA WITH JUPITER CHALLENGING: Although usually gregarious and friendly, you may need to find a balance between your commitments to your family or close partners and your friends. Alternatively, you may find that work and obligations do not blend well with your personal time. You can benefit from being patient and tolerant with others. With your love of luxuries, be careful not to overextend your finances.

SUN IN SCORPIO WITH JUPITER CHALLENGING: You are able to make great advances or gains in your attempt to change your fortunes. Your goal to secure power needs to remain realistic. You improve your chances by being cautious and resisting unnecessary risks. Avoid being exploitive, wasteful, or morally righteous if you want to succeed or influence others.

SUN IN SAGITTARIUS WITH JUPITER CHALLENGING: Your noble aspirations or good intentions need to be balanced by exactness and skillful communication. You achieve more if you are tolerant than if you are self-righteous. You may not be aware that your blunt honesty can offend people. You benefit if you plan ahead and resist rushing into projects without due preparation.

SUN IN CAPRICORN WITH JUPITER CHALLENGING: With

perseverance you are able to achieve a great deal. Your long-term plans need to be supported by consistency, optimism, and inner faith. Your discontent and frustration can undermine your desire to make quick progress. You benefit from being responsible and establishing a good structure. Slow and steady progress usually yields the best results.

SUN IN AQUARIUS WITH JUPITER CHALLENGING: Although you hold liberal views and you love your independence, your desire for material success or recognition implies that you can sometimes be materialistic. You benefit from being diplomatic rather than being too blunt and saying what you think.

SUN IN PISCES WITH JUPITER CHALLENGING: Imaginative and optimistic, you need to balance your idealism and high expectations with the actuality of a given situation. You are likely to succeed if you pay more attention to details and resist the temptation to speculate. Although you may be mentally quick and full of wonderful ideas, you could spread yourself too thinly in your attempt to know everything.

Saturn Challenging

By being determined, self-disciplined, and focused on your goals you are able build your confidence and sense of self-identity. You may have to overcome a tendency to take life too seriously and be self-critical. Growing up you may have experienced a strict parent or your father may not have been that available to you for whatever reason. You may not have felt like you got the full emotional support you needed. Your work and potential for self-mastery is important to you in overcoming self-doubt or building your self-esteem. You may need to keep a balance between work and being responsible, and having fun. Alternatively, you may have to resist alternating between overconfidence and anxiety. An inner fear of failure or a tendency to avoid your responsibilities may manifest as stress. Nevertheless, although you may face periods of frustration or creative block, your past lessons have already proven to you that you have the power to endure and overcome. Life gets better once you realize that your challenges are your best experiences for gaining wisdom and inner strength. You discover that you can achieve success and gain confidence through perseverance and being resolute. Life gets better as you get older, as you take your difficulties less personally and develop a wonderful dry sense of humor.

SUN IN ARIES WITH SATURN CHALLENGING: Even though you usually like quick results, you may have to be prepared to be patient in achieving your goals. Be careful of taking your personal frustrations out on others if life does not move fast enough for you. Nevertheless, you are proud and self-willed, and your personal drive and enthusiasm can give you the determination to persevere and succeed.

SUN IN TAURUS WITH SATURN CHALLENGING: If insecure or fearful, you are likely to become stubborn and resist change of any type. Alternatively, you may decide to indulge yourself, hoping that all your problems will go away. By facing your challenges directly your natural persistence and endurance can help you surmount difficulties and achieve outstanding results.

SUN IN GEMINI WITH SATURN CHALLENGING: Although a sharp observer, you may need to overcome tendencies to worry or to be too sensitive to criticism. By staying focused and resisting scattering your mental energies in too many directions, you can reduce your stress level and find peace of mind.

SUN IN CANCER WITH SATURN CHALLENGING: Being sensitive and security-conscious implies that you are likely to have a vulnerable side and strong defenses. It is important for you to reveal your deeper fears or emotions with someone you trust rather than keeping them inside, and instead acting with bravado. By expressing your true self you can increase your self-esteem.

SUN IN LEO WITH SATURN CHALLENGING: Fearing that you are not being noticed or that you are unloved, you may seek recognition. If you do not rely too heavily on another's approval, however, you can build your inner strength and self-confidence through your achievements.

SUN IN VIRGO WITH SATURN CHALLENGING: Although you are diligent and hardworking, there can be times in your quest for perfection when you are too hard on yourself. This may result in stress or worry, especially about your work or your health. Positive thinking and a healthy regime can enhance your vitality.

SUN IN LIBRA WITH SATURN CHALLENGING: Challenging times can cause you to alternate between being indecisive and being overly confident. A lack of action is likely to frustrate you. By acting, even though you may be fearful, you build your courage, initiative, and personal satisfaction.

SUN IN SAGITTARIUS WITH SATURN CHALLENGING: You may be torn between your desire for freedom and your responsibilities at home and at work. Although usually optimistic, self-doubts or inner fears can arise to cause indecision. By persevering and getting the right balance between your duties and your need to expand your horizons, you are able to achieve positive results.

SUN IN CAPRICORN WITH SATURN CHALLENGING: Knowing how to deal with authority figures is likely to be important to your success. Although you may experience some challenges in achieving your goals, it is vital that you do not give up but concentrate on your objectives and use your innate determination to achieve your goals.

SUN IN AQUARIUS WITH SATURN CHALLENGING: Do not let a fear of the unknown undermine your desire to experiment with new experiences that can help you progress. Your original approach to life suggests that you can manifest your

outstanding potential by concentrating on your positive and unique qualities and disciplining yourself.

SUN IN PISCES WITH SATURN CHALLENGING: Sensitive and impressionable, you need to develop perseverance and determination to avoid becoming frustrated when faced with a challenge. To overcome feelings of inferiority and achieve success, you need to remain resolute and build up your confidence. You can reach your goals by staying focused until you achieve results.

Uranus Challenging

Your independent nature implies that you may be stubborn and willful. At times you may have a strong need to be different or unconventional, yet this unconformity is often challenged by your desire to adapt. Although you want to belong, you may experience situations where you feel like an outsider or at odds with others. In life you probably experienced sudden and important changes that were outside your control. Wanting to put your own ideas or thoughts across, you may appear contradictory if you are not careful. Your original outlook, however, can work to your advantage if you accept that others may see situations in a different light and you learn to compromise. By listening objectively to others and showing tolerance, you can achieve cooperation. If you rebel or insist on doing things your own way, you can often encounter opposition. When you act, or say what you want without appearing stubborn or too frank, others will appreciate your honesty and respect your behavior. A tendency to become bored and change direction suddenly indicates that you benefit from some type of routine.

SUN IN ARIES WITH URANUS CHALLENGING: Wanting to take the lead or be in charge often meets with opposition if you show intolerance. An inclination to contradict others also implies that you can sometimes create tension by refusing to compromise. You benefit from being patient and tolerant with others.

SUN IN TAURUS WITH URANUS CHALLENGING: A need for stability may be challenged by a desire to be independent or free. If you go to extremes you are more inclined to obstinate behavior. Inner restlessness can also create inner tension. Strong-willed, you are not afraid to be different or to express yourself in an original way.

SUN IN GEMINI WITH URANUS CHALLENGING: Often direct, you can be outspoken. An inclination to have too many interests indicates that you can often be inconsistent. A tendency to become bored quickly means that you benefit from being focused and persevering. Nevertheless, you have original ideas and an unusual and innovative way of problem solving, which can give you an edge or advantage.

SUN IN CANCER WITH URANUS CHALLENGING: You may be susceptible to emotional tension and excitability by being impulsive. Constant changes in your routine may cause mood swings. Although you may sometimes feel sensitive in the company of others you have strong instincts and an ability to judge people and situations.

SUN IN LEO WITH URANUS CHALLENGING: Your strong ego or an inclination to be stubborn suggests that you can be contradictory at times just for the heck of it. This can cause tension and bring about conflicts with others. Unexpected circumstances teach you that nothing stays the same and you benefit from learning to adjust to new situations.

SUN IN VIRGO WITH URANUS CHALLENGING: Although you are practical, restlessness or a need for mental stimulation can entice you to suddenly change direction. An inclination to get bored quickly implies that you may find it hard to settle into a routine or be methodical. Nevertheless, new circumstances may often bring luck or changes in your working environment.

SUN IN LIBRA WITH URANUS CHALLENGING: You are genial and sociable and enjoy meeting different people; however, you are likely to be inconsistent with your feelings toward others. You may be too independent or reluctant to conform. Although you seek close relationships you also want to maintain your freedom.

SUN IN SCORPIO WITH URANUS CHALLENGING: Keen on renewal and progress, you may be an advocate for reform and innovation. Forceful by nature, you need to guard against forcing your will on others. By developing your patience and tolerance and resisting being disruptive, you can create more harmony.

SUN IN SAGITTARIUS WITH URANUS CHALLENGING: Your optimistic nature and need for expansion indicate that you dislike restriction and love freedom. Inner tension also implies that you are prone to restlessness or boredom. At times your open and frank approach can be interpreted as tactlessness. You can benefit from sudden opportunities that can alter your life situation.

SUN IN CAPRICORN WITH URANUS CHALLENGING: If you are stubborn by nature, you can be prone to stress or inner discontent. If you are not careful you can distance yourself from those you love or experience unrest in your close relationships because you're being stubborn. Although you dislike routine and restrictions you benefit from being more cooperative.

SUN IN AQUARIUS WITH URANUS CHALLENGING: Independent by nature, you may also be stubborn. Life can be smoother and more pleasant if you resist being confrontational. By cultivating the humanitarian and helpful side of your nature you can overcome a tendency to be willful.

SUN IN PISCES WITH URANUS CHALLENGING: Intuitive and receptive, you need to stay clear and objective if you want to avoid being misunderstood. At times you can have mystical experiences, but you may need to resist appearing too unconventional to others.

Neptune Challenging

With this influence you may be tempted to lose touch with the harsher realities of life. Your sensitivity suggests that you are open to more subtle emotional experiences than the average person. This sensitivity can leave you open to hurt or confusion if you are not aware or do not protect yourself. With your strong imagination and impressionability you often want the world to be a more beautiful place. If you project your ideals onto people or situations, you may later find yourself disappointed if they fail to meet your expectations. It is important to have a sense of boundaries between your feelings and the feelings of others. It is usually through problem solving and confronting difficulties that you learn, but you may have a block that keeps you from facing your responsibilities. This often involves escaping into a world of your own making, which may even possibly involve alcohol or drugs. Alternatively, with your sensitivity often comes a compassion that leads you to help others. If you put people on pedestals, however, or take on too much of other people's problems you may martyr yourself or lose some of your own drive to accomplish. Nevertheless, you possess a strong inner need for recognition and importance. You may also vacillate between being overly confident and feeling insecure. In order not to give way to discouragement, you may have to learn to push toward your goals with strength and determination and not give up. Equally, your sensitivity can be used constructively through the arts, healing, or mystical experiences, although you will have to balance your big dreams with self-discipline and common sense.

SUN IN ARIES WITH NEPTUNE CHALLENGING: Your desire for action and recognition may cause you to act impulsively, charging ahead with great expectations that later turn out to be disappointing. You gain from having a positive vision, but you also need clear boundaries and an acceptance of reality. You benefit from consolidating your actions with your vision.

SUN IN TAURUS WITH NEPTUNE CHALLENGING: Although you can be practical, down-to-earth, and security-conscious, another part of you yearns for high, almost unrealistic ideals. As your emotional sensitivity can cause you confusion, you need to build a secure foundation of solid values that can enhance your confidence and keep you from evading issues you would rather not face. You benefit from combining your imagination with your pragmatic approach.

SUN IN GEMINI WITH NEPTUNE CHALLENGING: Being clever can sometimes work against you if you end up utilizing your quick mind and strong imagination to outsmart yourself. It is really important for you to be very clear, honest, and direct in all your dealings to establish straightforward communication.

SUN IN CANCER WITH NEPTUNE CHALLENGING: Your strong sensitivity suggests that you can be easily hurt, so you need to protect yourself by being very clear about your feelings and boundaries, especially with partners and family.

SUN IN LEO WITH NEPTUNE CHALLENGING: Proud and dignified, you still need to feel special. Depending too much on others for admiration can weaken you and not allow you to build up your inner strength. Power comes from developing confidence in your self-identity.

SUN IN VIRGO WITH NEPTUNE CHALLENGING: Although part of you is practical, rational, and down-to-earth, another part can be idealistic and imaginative. By balancing these two extremes of your nature you can be both creative and methodical.

SUN IN LIBRA WITH NEPTUNE CHALLENGING: You are a romantic with high expectations when it comes to relationships. However, you may have to develop a more realistic outlook in your partnerships and stay grounded in the present. By accepting people as they are you can establish more satisfying relationships.

SUN IN SAGITTARIUS WITH NEPTUNE CHALLENGING: With your desire to increase your opportunities, you may have to resist schemes that are too ambitious or impractical. By establishing a definite set of beliefs you can increase your confidence and eliminate your self-doubts.

SUN IN CAPRICORN WITH NEPTUNE CHALLENGING: You benefit from combining your practical skills with your imagination. If you envisage the worst or lack faith, you may undermine your opportunities for improvement. By staying cautious but positive, you can make steady progress.

SUN IN AQUARIUS WITH NEPTUNE CHALLENGING: Even though you often seem detached and not that emotionally affected by situations, you still possess an inner idealism and sensitivity that can leave you open to disappointments. Make sure you express yourself clearly to avoid any confusion.

SUN IN PISCES WITH NEPTUNE CHALLENGING: Being extra sensitive, you may sometimes find it hard to separate yourself from your environment or your experiences with others. To avoid dissatisfaction you need to be very discriminating with your time and energy.

Pluto Challenging

At times you use your strong will to create positive dynamic change around you. At other times, however, you can direct your intense energy into creating difficulties for yourself or power challenges for others. For you, it is important to learn how to react in certain situations, especially those that involve your pride and need for recognition. If you underreact it appears that you do not care at all, but you may still be holding a grudge or a desire to get even. At the other extreme, you can overreact and shock others with the intensity of your responses. Sometimes this is the effect that you want to create,

but it is ultimately self-defeating as people gradually build up a resistance or aversion to your behavior. Although your quick instincts can be very effective, compromise usually yields better results. If you consider that a person challenging you is wasting your time, you need to be able to take a good objective look at what is involved and then walk away. The intensity of your reaction, coupled with a possible difficulty with forgiveness, does not make this easy. As you grew up you may have encountered some tension or challenges with your father or other authority figures. By learning to let go and forgive, you release yourself from situations that only sap your energy, and recover your power. Humor, especially seeing the ridiculous side of dark situations, can help to remove you from extreme reactions or situations.

SUN IN ARIES WITH PLUTO CHALLENGING: With your dynamic energy you are good at getting your own way. Just be careful that you do not push people too far or react too extremely. Channel any self-destructive energy into dramatic self-transformation and impress others with your positive drive and personal accomplishments.

SUN IN TAURUS WITH PLUTO CHALLENGING: Being tenacious and having a tendency to be stubborn can sometimes cause you to hold on to difficult situations for far too long. Utilize your purposeful nature to focus on transforming challenging areas of your life into opportunities to show just how determined and successful you can be.

SUN IN GEMINI WITH PLUTO CHALLENGING: Being a communicator with a tendency to go to extremes suggests that at times you can talk too much rather than be calm and listen. With your delicate nervous system you benefit from staying detached and impartial.

SUN IN CANCER WITH PLUTO CHALLENGING: Sensitive and impressionable, you feel things very keenly, but sometimes your intense emotions can act like a time bomb. To avoid overreacting, you may need to let go of past resentments and express yourself calmly. You benefit from channeling your powerful emotions into positive personal transformation.

SUN IN LEO WITH PLUTO CHALLENGING: Strong-willed and determined, you are able to take on challenges and achieve results. Be careful, however, not to let your pride or a tendency to overreact intimidate people. Exercise your innate generosity to forgive and help others.

SUN IN VIRGO WITH PLUTO CHALLENGING: In your desire to achieve perfection be careful not to overanalyze situations and get lost in the detail. At times you may get carried away and waste your energy by desiring to prove others wrong. Transform the intensity of your actions and thoughts to being of practical help to yourself and others.

SUN IN LIBRA WITH PLUTO CHALLENGING: Usually attracted to dynamic or intense people, your experiences with others may sometimes draw you into power struggles. You need to examine your own actions and responses to relationships in order to discover why other people react the way they do toward you.

SUN IN SCORPIO WITH PLUTO CHALLENGING: If you are willful or stubborn, you may provoke others to respond to you in a similar manner. By forcing confrontation you will only create tension and unrest. Your tenacity and willpower, if managed correctly, can be a force for change for the better.

SUN IN SAGITTARIUS WITH PLUTO CHALLENGING: Your thirst for knowledge enables you to undertake large projects or acquire a great deal of information. Although you have strong opinions or beliefs, you may need to resist being an extremist or argumentative. Taking big or unnecessary risks may not always bring you the desired results. You benefit from being flexible and tolerant.

SUN IN CAPRICORN WITH PLUTO CHALLENGING: Although your ambition and determination are strong, you may overwhelm others with your actions or behavior. Resisting change or being stubborn may lead to unnecessary confrontations. By being flexible and easygoing you often get better results. Knowing when to persist and when to give up is often the key to your success.

SUN IN AQUARIUS WITH PLUTO CHALLENGING: Although your independent and original views may be different from those around you, resist the temptation to be subversive or act in a compulsive manner. Impulsive actions can scatter your energies or inner tensions and impatient acts may cause unnecessary anxiety. You benefit from being tolerant and charitable with others.

SUN IN PISCES WITH PLUTO CHALLENGING: If you feel too strongly about your ideals you may run the risk of becoming obsessed with some of them. Be clear and detached about your views before you jump the gun and say something you later regret. You benefit from staying open and honest in your dealings with others.

Special Planets

Jupiter Special

Usually self-assured, enthusiastic, and gregarious, you are an optimistic individual with opportunities and creative ideas. With this special configuration you are often ambitious, daring, and outwardly confident. Your relationship with your father benefited you in some way by allowing you to be more self-assured or enterprising. Your friendly and cheerful personality can attract many friends. Often speculative and philanthropic, you have periods of luck that allow you to develop or progress. Your creative power indicates that you have many ideas and plans as well as scope to better your circumstances. When hard work, detailed planning, and dedication follow your grand plans, you have the capacity to be a prolific worker

and perform record achievements. Your enthusiasm and eagerness usually inspire others, and often you get the help you need to fulfill your ambitions. A strong desire to constantly expand implies that you may sometimes experience discontentment. You may also have to resist the temptation of having too many active projects or being impatient. Usually your generosity and kindness toward others implies that you have good intentions, but if you appear smug or boastful you may be perceived as arrogant or overbearing. With determination and perseverance you can achieve remarkable results in life.

SUN IN ARIES WITH JUPITER SPECIAL: Having a great deal of energy and a need to be active or enterprising indicates that you like to take the initiative. Your ability to focus on your goals makes you ambitious and single-minded. You may, however, need to avoid being impatient or impulsive in your actions. Nevertheless, quick at making decisions, you act with confidence and usually cope well with challenging situations.

SUN IN TAURUS WITH JUPITER SPECIAL: Sociable and generous, you can gain popularity with little effort. Material gains and opportunities to make money often present themselves and you usually live in comfortable surroundings. An inclination to enjoy the good things in life warns that you need to resist being indulgent or wasteful. You benefit from the combination of your endurance and positive plans for the future.

SUN IN GEMINI WITH JUPITER SPECIAL: Optimism and enthusiasm for mental pursuits suggest that you need to find projects that stimulate your inquisitive mind. Although you have wonderful ideas, you also benefit from learning to be patient and listen to others.

SUN IN CANCER WITH JUPITER SPECIAL: Often kindhearted and cheerful, you can uplift the spirits of those around you. There is a good chance that you come from a good background or your extended family is large. Your wealth of feelings and sympathetic nature indicate that you are caring, generous, and show a willingness to help others.

SUN IN LEO WITH JUPITER SPECIAL: Charismatic, generous, and fun-living, you are a creative and enterprising person. Usually you have the energy to perform and achieve a great deal by your sheer determination. You may, however, need to guard against having an inflated ego. Ambitious and proud, you seek recognition and can often succeed admirably.

SUN IN VIRGO WITH JUPITER SPECIAL: Knowledgeable and efficient, with the desire to learn, you can be analytical and orderly. That you are hardworking and thorough suggests that you are likely to be organized or good at research. Your ability to be discriminative or to pay attention to details also helps you to achieve excellent results. Practical yet ambitious, you benefit from your natural honesty.

SUN IN LIBRA WITH JUPITER SPECIAL: Blessed with good social skills, you can rely on others to give you good advice or lend a helping hand. You can benefit from working with the public and usually your amiable manner makes you popular. If you indulge in too much socializing, however, you may neglect your duties or responsibilities. Nevertheless, your natural faith and optimism protects you and can uplift others.

SUN IN SCORPIO WITH JUPITER SPECIAL: Being very resourceful you know how to utilize situations or take advantage of opportunities. An ambitious side to your nature implies that you may sometimes be subtly materialistic. Fearless, you can take on challenges that involve risk or change. You often benefit from legacies or from your partnerships and joint financial ventures.

SUN IN SAGITTARIUS WITH JUPITER SPECIAL: Usually optimistic and open-minded, you thrive on new opportunities to broaden your horizons. As your nature is expansive, you are inclined to take risks or be speculative. Your humanitarian side can also make you generous but at times also wasteful or indulgent. A need to explore new ideas may inspire you to seek spiritual enlightenment or travel to faraway places.

SUN IN CAPRICORN WITH JUPITER SPECIAL: Your strong willpower, determination, and ambitious nature indicate that you can be hardworking and focused. Although you possess a good business sense, guard against becoming overly concerned with materialistic issues. Being responsible and a natural organizer can elevate you to positions of power and authority.

SUN IN AQUARIUS WITH JUPITER SPECIAL: Your love of freedom and your independent nature make you liberal and progressive. Being humanitarian and people-oriented you can succeed by being philanthropic. Usually good-humored and congenial, you can receive help from others or have lucky breaks through prominent friends or social contacts.

SUN IN PISCES WITH JUPITER SPECIAL: Your compassion and tolerance indicate that you can be selfless, generous, and idealistic. You can even work in solitude for a cause that is dear to your heart. With your sensitivity, however, guard against overindulging in alcohol or drugs. When inspired, your creativity and imagination can bring you joy and contentment.

Saturn Special

Determined and willful, once set on a definite goal you can work toward it with persistence. By persevering despite adversity, you become self-reliant and succeed. In this way you develop confidence and an ability to express yourself without inhibitions. Since you are likely to take things seriously in your youth, life gets better as you get older. Authority figures are likely to have a strong influence on your life. You may have experienced a strict parent, parents who were always working, or even the lack of a father figure. Your confidence and self-esteem are often established through hard work and self-discipline. If you avoid your responsibilities, especially to yourself, you may find yourself with a lack of stamina or a

tendency to depression. Once you realize that everyone has inner fears or insecurities, you are likely to focus less on your failings and more on your achievements. Since respect is meaningful to you, being in positions of authority can be especially significant. Through dedication and patience and by making steady progress in life, you eventually gain the mastery and self-respect that you desire. Being a realist, your practical, down-to-earth wisdom is often delivered with a dry sense of humor. When positive, you can be responsible, unassuming, and hardworking.

SUN IN ARIES WITH SATURN SPECIAL: In your desire to take the lead you may have to overcome an inclination to be controlling. By keeping yourself constantly busy on projects that capture your enthusiasm you can avoid frustration. You enhance your confidence with slow, steady progress and achieving results.

SUN IN TAURUS WITH SATURN SPECIAL: With your good sense of values you usually realize that there is a price to pay for whatever you desire. In the majority of cases this is due to your productivity and hard work. You may have to overcome a fear of losing your possessions but your strength and endurance can ensure your ultimate success.

SUN IN GEMINI WITH SATURN SPECIAL: This influence challenges you to stay focused and have a definite goal in mind. You benefit when you resist worrying or becoming pessimistic. When you keep yourself occupied with projects that utilize your creativity and your ability to solve problems you can achieve outstanding results.

SUN IN CANCER WITH SATURN SPECIAL: Due to your intense sensitivity you may possess insecurities or an inner fear of rejection. With your tenacity, however, you can be self-reliant and build a solid support system. By persevering toward your goals you develop resolute determination and can achieve success.

SUN IN LEO WITH SATURN SPECIAL: As you are willful and proud, be careful that inhibitions, a fear of failure, or frustration does not cause you to become too domineering. Nevertheless, your inner strength ensures that you are able to lead and influence others with your determination and courage.

SUN IN VIRGO WITH SATURN SPECIAL: Even though you may possess a tendency to be self-critical, be careful not to take life too seriously as this can undermine your accomplishments. As a perfectionist you may develop a fear of failing. When you learn that it is your mistakes that prove to be your greatest lessons, you can become more positive in your attitude and achieve success.

SUN IN LIBRA WITH SATURN SPECIAL: Because your relationships are often the major factor of your life, you may possess a fear of being alone or becoming too dependent on others. When clear about your goals and objectives, however, you can be determined and businesslike yet still project enough charm to get your way.

SUN IN SCORPIO WITH SATURN SPECIAL: Stubborn and sometimes too serious, you may have to overcome a fear of others having control over you. Very focused and determined when set on a course of action, you achieve outstanding results when you display your tenacity.

SUN IN SAGITTARIUS WITH SATURN SPECIAL: As you are likely to take your opinions seriously, be careful of being too dogmatic. You may have to overcome a fear of being committed or of losing your freedom. Through hard work and patience, you can use your enterprising spirit to achieve success.

SUN IN CAPRICORN WITH SATURN SPECIAL: Even though you are a hardworking achiever who is capable of outstanding accomplishments, you may have to take your responsibilities less seriously. You may also have to overcome a fear of losing control or the respect of others. By valuing your abilities you can make great progress.

SUN IN AQUARIUS WITH SATURN SPECIAL: Although usually independent and self-sufficient, you may need to balance your desire for the conventional with some of your more progressive views. Once set on a course of action, however, your original ideas and determination can help you achieve outstanding results.

SUN IN PISCES WITH SATURN SPECIAL: At times you can be very determined and focused, yet at other times you become discouraged and give up too easily. By utilizing your natural vision and strong intuition you can achieve great results by persevering.

Uranus Special

An original thinker, you prefer to see yourself as an individualist. With the ability to get straight to the heart of a matter, you are also capable of sudden intuitive flashes or inspired thinking. Your need for freedom of expression implies that you become rebellious if others try to force you to do things against your will. Independent and clever, at times you can be quite detached, usually preferring to be different from the crowd. Your father's independence or progressive views could have had a strong influence on your way of thinking. A natural psychologist, you are likely to be interested in people, humanitarian ideals, or social reform. Alternatively, you can be good with technical matters such as computers or your objective approach may give you an interest in science. You are capable of tuning to high-frequency mental levels that give you powerful intuition or an interest in symbolism and metaphysical subjects. Others sometimes see you as unconventional, but they may misunderstand that with your touch of genius you are likely to be ahead of your time or interested in unusual subjects.

SUN IN ARIES WITH URANUS SPECIAL: You are an inventive pioneer always interested in exciting new ideas. Forward thinking, you usually have a plan of action that involves trying

out different ways of approaching situations. Be careful, however, of a tendency to act on impulse. An interest in people helps you to achieve satisfaction in your personal life and career.

SUN IN TAURUS WITH URANUS SPECIAL: Original, with common sense, you can make money with your inventive ideas. Be careful, however, of a stubborn streak. With your magnetic charm and interest in people you can be both loyal and independent.

SUN IN GEMINI WITH URANUS SPECIAL: Mentally curious and articulate, you are a bright and intelligent individual. Ahead of your time, you are likely to be particularly fortunate through the use of your excellent communication skills, original ideas, and quick grasp of people's character.

SUN IN CANCER WITH URANUS SPECIAL: Sensitive and aware, you can utilize your sharp intuition to understand others or achieve success by following your own unique path. Although you can be detached, you may also experience mood swings. Often influenced by family commitments you value your individuality and freedom.

SUN IN LEO WITH URANUS SPECIAL: Highly creative and sociable, you enjoy expressing your strong individuality, particularly with a group of friends. Sometimes stubborn, you usually do not like to take orders and often do better working for yourself or in a position where your original approach is valued.

SUN IN VIRGO WITH URANUS SPECIAL: Articulate and smart, you can use your analytical and detached viewpoint to clearly define situations for others or solve technical problems. Shrewd at assessing people's character, you can utilize your original ideas in business or for social reform.

SUN IN LIBRA WITH URANUS SPECIAL: Although intimacy and relationships are particularly important to you, you can also be objective in your desire for impartiality and justice. Valuing friendship, you have an ability to mix with people from all walks of life, which can really help you in your overall success.

SUN IN SCORPIO WITH URANUS SPECIAL: Strong-willed but sensitive, you possess powerful intuition and individuality. An interest in the deeper or more unorthodox side of life may attract you to unconventional pursuits or an interest in psychology.

SUN IN SAGITTARIUS WITH URANUS SPECIAL: You are friendly and optimistic, and a humanitarian streak suggests that when you feel good or learn something new, you like to uplift others or share your knowledge. You especially value freedom both for yourself and others.

SUN IN CAPRICORN WITH URANUS SPECIAL: Practical yet inventive, you are good at bringing change and new ideas to traditional systems or ways of thinking. By combining your pragmatic sensibility with your originality you can achieve success.

SUN IN AQUARIUS WITH URANUS SPECIAL: Independent, friendly, and a strong individualist, you are usually willing to be open-minded or experimental in your approach to life; however, you should avoid being too contrary. You are an objective thinker, and your original and inventive ideas can often bring you success and recognition.

SUN IN PISCES WITH URANUS SPECIAL: Imaginative and original, you have a unique approach to life. Highly intuitive with an innate ability to tap into the mass unconscious, you can combine sensitivity with objectivity and achieve remarkable results.

Neptune Special

You are imaginative and receptive, and your sensitivity and emotional awareness are highly refined. Being creative, poetic, or artistic, you benefit from expressing yourself and developing your unique gifts. Not always wanting to deal with the harsh reality of life, you enjoy escaping from the mundane restrictions of everyday living. If you have a goal or a vision, you can be inspired and motivated. Without a clear idea or purpose, however, you may experience inner doubts and confusion. Wanting to be special and less ordinary, you can use your sense of fantasy to create something unique, but you may need to stay realistic if you want to avoid self-deception. When you realize that not everything that glistens is gold, you become less susceptible to delusion. If you idealized or were disillusioned about your father, especially in your youth, you may need to reevaluate your relationship with him. As an adult this can help you to clarify misunderstandings or to find your own identity. Through this learning process you can also understand and establish better relationships with your current partners. As an adaptable and caring individual, however, you need to guard against losing yourself in other people's lives. Being mystical or psychic, you are able to pick up on the moods of the people around you. You may wish to use your sensitivity for healing as well as the arts. Your imaginative or clairvoyant powers suggest that you can gain from developing your extra-special talents.

SUN IN VIRGO WITH NEPTUNE SPECIAL: Often patient and discreet, you can be sensitive and intuitive. You may have healing powers or you may like to work in seclusion. Imaginative and thoughtful, you can express your thoughts and feelings in a subtle way, especially through writing. Make sure, however, that you communicate with others openly and clearly.

SUN IN LIBRA WITH NEPTUNE SPECIAL: Refined and artistic or receptive to others, you can be romantic, sympathetic, and loving. If you overidealize your partner, however, or seek idyllic relationships, you may encounter some disappointments. By staying kindhearted yet realistic you often achieve better results for yourself.

SUN IN SCORPIO WITH NEPTUNE SPECIAL: Your keen senses suggest that you are deeply intuitive and receptive. Usu-

ally you can pick up the undercurrents or moods of those around you. You may, however, need to guard against becoming involved in secretive or harmful fantasies. Nevertheless, you can gain a great deal from your sensitivity and imagination.

SUN IN SAGITTARIUS WITH NEPTUNE SPECIAL: As an optimistic visionary you are inclined to be idealistic with an altruistic nature. Being imaginative and compassionate, you are sensitive and often have strong premonitions or dreams. Although your idealism may draw you to mysticism and spirituality, you need to remain realistic and discriminative.

SUN IN CAPRICORN WITH NEPTUNE SPECIAL: As a practical visionary you are able to manifest your ideals. Although you are ambitious you can succeed when you combine your materialistic and idealistic tendencies. A desire to find something concrete to hold on to may eventually lead you to spirituality. Staying responsible can help you overcome a desire to escape from your duties and commitments.

SUN IN AQUARIUS WITH NEPTUNE SPECIAL: Idealistic and often group-oriented, you can easily tune in to the thoughts and feelings of others. A humanitarian streak and progressive outlook may lead you to an interest in social reform and a new vision for the future.

SUN IN PISCES WITH NEPTUNE SPECIAL: Your strong perceptions and psychic abilities indicate that you can develop your powers of telepathy and intuition. Being sensitive, you are able to pick up the moods and feelings of those around you. Highly imaginative, you can be very creative and inspire others with your unique vision.

Pluto Special

Strong-willed and ambitious, your determination to achieve something extraordinary gives you the vitality to continually strive and accomplish. Highly instinctive, you are good at assessing people and situations very quickly. Learning to deal with challenging or extreme situations can empower you and strengthen your character. Your willingness to work hard or concentrate on one particular area suggests that you will not allow obstacles or defeats to prevent you from achieving your aims. As Pluto usually represents transformation or regeneration and the Sun represents your ego, you may need to learn how to utilize Pluto's energies correctly. If you use Pluto's influence for selfish reasons you are likely to arouse opposition. The best results can be obtained if you focus on transforming yourself. By resisting a tendency to behave obsessively or get even, you can refrain from dominating people or creating difficult situations. As you are likely to have a great deal of energy, you need to exercise a certain amount of restraint if you do not want to overwhelm others with your personality. The

negative aspects of Sun/Pluto links are toughness and a desire for power. The noble influence of Sun/Pluto is the ability to positively transform yourself and others.

SUN IN CANCER WITH PLUTO SPECIAL: With this influence you can have strong feelings, especially toward family members. At times your powerful emotions can overwhelm others, especially if you become too intense. Nevertheless, you possess strong intuition about people and powerful instincts that are usually correct. You can be a strong force for positive change in others.

SUN IN LEO WITH PLUTO SPECIAL: Your self-expression and strong willpower indicate that you can be creative or achieve extraordinary results. You need to be less obsessive, however, if you want other people's support, help, or respect. Nevertheless, you understand people and can use your unique humor to entertain others.

SUN IN VIRGO WITH PLUTO SPECIAL: Your ability to accumulate information indicates that you have an inquisitive or scientific mind. You may, however, need to resist being hypercritical or overzealous in your communication or work. As a brilliant observer who can recognize the hidden faults within a detailed structure, you investigate or research difficult subjects with amazing results.

SUN IN LIBRA WITH PLUTO SPECIAL: Your personal magnetism and strong personality indicate that you can have a strong impact on people. Your partnerships are usually intense or purposeful. You can gain popularity very quickly but you need to learn to maintain harmony and equality in your dealings with others.

SUN IN SCORPIO WITH PLUTO SPECIAL: Your strong willpower and desire to accomplish record achievements indicate that you have extraordinary powers. If you fail to control your dynamic desires this amazing power can have a subversive effect or be destructive. When inspired, however, you can become influential and help bring about change and transformation.

SUN IN SAGITTARIUS WITH PLUTO SPECIAL: Your strong desire to gain knowledge and explore philosophical concepts may inspire you to study new theories or pioneer revolutionary ideas. You need to guard against becoming too intense in your beliefs or trying to impose them on others. Traveling to faraway places may change the way you view life and lead to personal transformation.

SUN IN CAPRICORN WITH PLUTO SPECIAL: Your ability to deal with challenging situations suggests that you can bring change and transformation to old or outdated structures that are no longer useful. With your immense willpower and ability to influence others, you can afford to be less rigid and more flexible.

Chapter 2: Your Relationships with Others

Beneficial Relationships

Jupiter Beneficial in Relationships

This person is likely to give you positive support in some area of your life, providing a solid basis for growth in your relationship. As this planet deals with expansion, this person can make you feel more optimistic about your abilities and opportunities. Since Jupiter governs ideals, philosophy, ethics, and religion, you may share the same social values or moral principles. When you are together, you both can project high levels of enthusiasm, although you occasionally have to be careful not to get carried away or be excessive. Nonetheless, together you are likely to feel more enterprising about achieving on a bigger scale or you can stimulate each other's idealism and future expectations. Although you can support each other, resist taking on more than you can handle. This planetary aspect is generally a happy one, and in retrospect you will find that this person has provided you with good fortune in some way or an opportunity to be productive.

JUPITER BENEFICIAL TO YOUR ARIES SUN IN RELATIONSHIPS: This person is likely to stimulate your enthusiasm or encourage you in your endeavors. You may make plans together, support each other, or work together on new projects. You are both likely to have an enterprising spirit and a strong sense of adventure. With your shared interests you are often willing to take a chance and initiate large or creative projects.

JUPITER BENEFICIAL TO YOUR TAURUS SUN IN RELATIONSHIPS: This person's influence can make you feel positive and secure in some way. There may be opportunities for financial rewards if you work together. Having a positive attitude, you can encourage each other to initiate creative endeavors. You are both likely to be ambitious and organized or hardworking. You usually share the same views and ethics on money and career. When you apply your practical skills and dedication to a project you can succeed admirably.

JUPITER BENEFICIAL TO YOUR GEMINI SUN IN RELATIONSHIPS: This person can provide a positive framework to help your flow of ideas and mental understanding. They may possibly provide you with help that makes you better able to express yourself or expand your social group. You can benefit from this person's encouragement and belief system.

JUPITER BENEFICIAL TO YOUR CANCER SUN IN RELATIONSHIPS: This person is able to expand the boundaries of your protective barriers and allow you to feel more relaxed and supported. They may compliment your views or philosophies. As you often tune in to each other's feelings, you can express generosity and understanding toward one another.

JUPITER BENEFICIAL TO YOUR LEO SUN IN RELATIONSHIPS: This person is likely to provide encouragement when you express yourself and your ideas. You respond particularly well to a positive and responsive audience, and they can help build your confidence. You are both likely to have an enterprising spirit and an adventurous nature. With your enthusiasm you are both willing to take a chance and initiate creative or large projects.

JUPITER BENEFICIAL TO YOUR VIRGO SUN IN RELATIONSHIPS: Although you can be fairly modest and unassuming, this relationship can bring positive and helpful influences, increasing your sense of adventure or enterprising spirit. Through this person you can have good opportunities or they may be especially helpful to your work and career.

JUPITER BENEFICIAL TO YOUR LIBRA SUN IN RELATIONSHIPS: Your charm and refined manners complement this person's social awareness. You can both enjoy shared interests, mentally stimulating activities, or a love for culture and the arts. You benefit from encouraging each other and being enterprising.

JUPITER BENEFICIAL TO YOUR SCORPIO SUN IN RELATIONSHIPS: In this relationship you are likely to support each other on an emotional level. This person can be reassuring and caring or their intuition and imagination can inspire you to transform yourself for the better. You can both be very enterprising and determined to achieve success.

JUPITER BENEFICIAL TO YOUR SAGITTARIUS SUN IN RELATIONSHIPS: In this relationship you both share an optimistic outlook and a love for adventure. Together you can be enterprising, creative, or daring. Good opportunities can bring you both advancement and success.

JUPITER BENEFICIAL TO YOUR CAPRICORN SUN IN RELATIONSHIPS: In this relationship both of you are ambitious and determined to achieve success. If you decide to work together you can complement each other with your practical abilities, good sense of value, or organizational skills. You can both

share the same aptitude for business or a willingness to work hard.

JUPITER BENEFICIAL TO YOUR AQUARIUS SUN IN RELATIONSHIPS: You can enjoy exploring new ideas or opportunities with this person. You may both share a love of socializing and freedom. Inventive and original, you both can communicate on the same level and support each other.

JUPITER BENEFICIAL TO YOUR PISCES SUN IN RELATIONSHIPS: In this relationship this person can provide you with emotional support and encouragement when you need it most. You are likely to share the same ideals or desire for improvement. You can feel more optimistic or generous when in the company of this person.

Saturn Beneficial in Relationships

This is a good sign for a long-term relationship with mutual respect. Since this relationship is based on some type of order or structure, you may stimulate each other to be productive or have similar views or objectives. This person is likely to provide you with loyalty and support when you need it most. You may both decide to work together or see the value of making a commitment to each other. This person can show you the benefits that come from discipline, perserverance, and taking responsibility. If there is an age gap between the two of you, one partner may act as a teacher or mentor for the other. You can complement each other by contributing different skills or points of view. There is mutual respect and sincerity in the relationship, and you both may appear loving, yet keep something in reserve. As this relationship often strengthens with time, you need not rush into making a commitment too quickly. Getting to know one another gradually can help the relationship to flourish.

SATURN BENEFICIAL TO YOUR ARIES SUN IN RELATIONSHIPS: Since you are both strong and determined, you are often willing to endure and therefore complement each other. This relationship can work well if you are both willing to work hard, compromise, and respect one another. If you are faced with challenges you will not give up easily. Steady progress and good strategies make this relationship successful.

SATURN BENEFICIAL TO YOUR TAURUS SUN IN RELATIONSHIPS: Since both of you are inclined to be loyal, practical, and productive, you have some common views concerning values and security. This relationship is often based on support, especially if money or other material assets are involved. Although you both may choose to be cautious, do not limit each other when new opportunities come along. It can be fortunate if you both work together.

SATURN BENEFICIAL TO YOUR GEMINI SUN IN RELATIONSHIPS: This relationship works well because you both show each other respect. Practical considerations may have brought you together from the start. This is a very good combination if you are in business together. Alternatively, you may share some common interests, study together, or learn from each other.

SATURN BENEFICIAL TO YOUR CANCER SUN IN RELATIONSHIPS: This is a good sign for a relationship based on endurance and emotional support. Tenacious and persistent, you are both able to overcome times of difficulties. This relationship may be based on dedication and loyalty. By not letting your partner become pessimistic you can build each other's confidence.

SATURN BENEFICIAL TO YOUR LEO SUN IN RELATIONSHIPS: Mutual respect and admiration for each other is the key to your relationship. If there is an age gap between you, one of you may be an authority figure. Since this relationship is often long lasting, it should grow in strength and outlast many other relationships.

SATURN BENEFICIAL TO YOUR VIRGO SUN IN RELATIONSHIPS: You probably both share a concern for the practical aspects of life. If you show respect for each other you can be more efficient or effective. This is a good relationship if you engage in problem solving or carry out detailed research together. Work or some type of educational pursuit may have brought you together.

SATURN BENEFICIAL TO YOUR LIBRA SUN IN RELATIONSHIPS: This relationship is not focused on pleasure or a glamorous lifestyle, and you complement each other in many ways. You may find it easy to talk to this person more than any one else because you trust and respect him or her. This person can inspire you to be more objective and disciplined.

SATURN BENEFICIAL TO YOUR SCORPIO SUN IN RELATIONSHIPS: As long as you both accept that change is an essential part of a long-lasting relationship, you can be a source of emotional strength for each other. By not getting into a rut you can bring new energy into the relationship. Not afraid to deal with responsibilities or challenges, you both have the staying power that is lacking in many fair-weather relationships.

SATURN BENEFICIAL TO YOUR SAGITTARIUS SUN IN RELATIONSHIPS: In this relationship you complement each other since one of you is optimistic and the other is more cautious or realistic. Often you are patient and generous with one another. When you consider doing something together, you usually like to plan ahead. A positive outlook, good timing, and perseverance make your relationship strong and lasting.

SATURN BENEFICIAL TO YOUR CAPRICORN SUN IN RELATIONSHIPS: Down-to-earth and practical, both of you are often ambitious and productive. You usually work well together and can show a willingness to take responsibility.

SATURN BENEFICIAL TO YOUR AQUARIUS SUN IN RELATIONSHIPS: In this relationship equality, fairness, and good communication are important. You can both be productive, and as long as both of you respect each other's freedom and

show a willingness to compromise, you can have a good and lasting relationship.

SATURN BENEFICIAL TO YOUR PISCES SUN IN RELATIONSHIPS: Through sharing the same ideals you grow to trust each other. This relationship can work well if you support each other and take your responsibilities seriously. You can pick up each other's subtle moods and therefore be understanding and loyal.

Uranus Beneficial in Relationships

This person's energy can help you be more objective about yourself and life situations. He or she is likely to offer you new ideas or experiences that can help you develop your self-awareness. This relationship is not likely to be boring and has the possibility of exciting times and opportunities for change. With this influence you can expect to feel youthful with an interest in the future. You may possibly be stimulated to explore progressive or alternative disciplines such as therapy, yoga, astrology, or other forms of spiritual insight. Alternatively, you may become involved in team or group situations that can benefit both of you. This person can empower your individuality and help you to feel more free and alive. Equally, this person may provide you with an alternate view of reality. Moneywise, this relationship can offer you surprises and unexpected opportunities. This person often encourages you to be more resourceful and independent. This is also a good friendship link.

URANUS BENEFICIAL TO YOUR ARIES SUN IN RELATIONSHIPS: Although you often rush into things, this relationship provides you with an opportunity to take a more objective view. You may share a friendship that emphasizes freedom and adventures rather than conventional or predictable situations.

URANUS BENEFICIAL TO YOUR TAURUS SUN IN RELATIONSHIPS: Through this relationship you may adopt a new set of values or see yourself in a new light. Both of you may be involved in doing something original and innovative together that can bring material rewards. This relationship encourages you to be more open-minded.

URANUS BENEFICIAL TO YOUR GEMINI SUN IN RELATIONSHIPS: This relationship can bring you benefits or material opportunities that come from knowledge or original and inspired ideas. Alternatively, you share a gregarious outlook that can aid your success. Often this can be a friendly or sociable connection.

URANUS BENEFICIAL TO YOUR CANCER SUN IN RELATIONSHIPS: Although you are sensitive or shy, this relationship can provide you with opportunities to be self-expressive and more experimental. Usually this person is in tune with your inner feelings and can understand you in ways that others cannot.

URANUS BENEFICIAL TO YOUR LEO SUN IN RELATIONSHIPS: Sociable and expressive, you may find that this person is friendly and able to offer you objective advice. He or she can also inspire you with unusual ideas that stimulate your creativity. This person's views or support can help you to feel more self-assured.

URANUS BENEFICIAL TO YOUR VIRGO SUN IN RELATIONSHIPS: Although practical and analytical, you may find that in this relationship you are more open to new ideas and methods of doing things. This person can offer you something different or bring you new interests.

URANUS BENEFICIAL TO YOUR LIBRA SUN IN RELATIONSHIPS: This person can provide you with original ideas, inspiration, or encourage you to be more experimental. Alternatively, he or she may introduce you to new types of people or different lifestyles. This may include humanitarian interests or learning experiences. Often this is a good sign for friendship.

URANUS BENEFICIAL TO YOUR SCORPIO SUN IN RELATIONSHIPS: Being very sensitive, you usually respond to this person's more unusual approach. He or she may help you to transform some of your views and encourage you to become more daring.

URANUS BENEFICIAL TO YOUR SAGITTARIUS SUN IN RELATIONSHIPS: With your far-reaching aims you already have a broad outlook on life, yet this person's influence may stimulate you to be more daring and original. Exchanging views with this person can also inspire you to explore unusual subjects or be more objective and philosophical.

URANUS BENEFICIAL TO YOUR CAPRICORN SUN IN RELATIONSHIPS: Although you are usually ambitious, goal-oriented, and somewhat traditional, you can gain from the more progressive and unusual ideas that this person can offer.

URANUS BENEFICIAL TO YOUR AQUARIUS SUN IN RELATIONSHIPS: This person's influence can extend your knowledge of human nature. You can respond well to this person's original and unconventional ways of approaching life. You may both be interested in reform or teamwork.

URANUS BENEFICIAL TO YOUR PISCES SUN IN RELATIONSHIPS: There is a strong likelihood that you may have a psychic link with this person. You can both be stimulated by new and exciting ideas and help each other see your overall life situations more clearly.

Neptune Beneficial in Relationships

You can feel close to this person because you share similar ideals or spiritual beliefs. Often this person will have a strong psychic or intuitive link with you as they can pick up on your moods and feelings easily. In this relationship you may be in tune with each other to such an extent that your communication is synchronized. When one of you begins to speak the other can be thinking similar thoughts. Since you are in sympathy with each other, you probably have a mutual appreciation for music and artistic or creative pursuits. You are likely

to have the same vision and therefore be willing to support or make sacrifices for each other. At times there can be a strong platonic link or you may inspire each other. In this relationship, you can develop mutual trust or a spiritual bond.

NEPTUNE BENEFICIAL TO YOUR ARIES SUN IN RELATIONSHIPS: Both of you often have shared ambitions, as long as you are both clear about what you want to do. Your actions and this person's vision work well together. If you take the lead, this person will support or encourage you to achieve your goals.

NEPTUNE BENEFICIAL TO YOUR TAURUS SUN IN RELATIONSHIPS: Both of you may share the same romantic attitude or you can admire and inspire each other. You may also share a love for music and art. Your practical abilities combined with the encouragement and support of this person helps your creativity or productivity.

NEPTUNE BENEFICIAL TO YOUR GEMINI SUN IN RELATIONSHIPS: Your mental agility is enhanced by this person's subtle receptivity. You may share the same ideals and therefore find it easier to talk about spiritual or sensitive issues. Your ideas work well with this person's imaginative or creative input.

NEPTUNE BENEFICIAL TO YOUR CANCER SUN IN RELATIONSHIPS: In this relationship you both have faith in one another. You are also very receptive to each other's moods. You can both be understanding and compassionate toward one another.

NEPTUNE BENEFICIAL TO YOUR LEO SUN IN RELATIONSHIPS: In this relationship you both make each other feel optimistic or idealistic. You can inspire each other to be creative and imaginative. This person may introduce you to new possibilities or encourage you to travel and explore spiritual or philosophical subjects.

NEPTUNE BENEFICIAL TO YOUR VIRGO SUN IN RELATIONSHIPS: Your analytical abilities are strengthened by this person's sensitive perception. You may both share the same objectives; therefore you find it easier to work together or talk about sensitive issues. Both of you can work well by combining your pragmatism with your imagination and intuition.

NEPTUNE BENEFICIAL TO YOUR LIBRA SUN IN RELATIONSHIPS: Being romantic or idealistic, you can either inspire each other creatively or share the same taste in music and art. You and your partner may intuitively understand each other's needs or feelings. You both can also talk freely about different subjects as you often see eye to eye on many issues.

NEPTUNE BENEFICIAL TO YOUR SCORPIO SUN IN RELATIONSHIPS: You both share some experiences that will help you to transform your life in a subtle way. Their behavior may also help you to make important realizations about your character. Often this person can inspire you or influence you indirectly by being more understanding or sympathetic.

NEPTUNE BENEFICIAL TO YOUR SAGITTARIUS SUN IN RELATIONSHIPS: You are likely to share similar views or ideals.

Both of you feel generous and compassionate toward each other. You can both create an atmosphere of happiness especially if you are studying or exploring spiritual or philosophical subjects. Traveling or experiences in foreign countries can also bring you closer together.

NEPTUNE BENEFICIAL TO YOUR CAPRICORN SUN IN RELATIONSHIPS: This person can inspire you to think about something other than work. Alternatively, you may share the same ideals or work together toward a common goal. This person can be sympathetic and understanding when you need it most.

NEPTUNE BENEFICIAL TO YOUR AQUARIUS SUN IN RELATIONSHIPS: In this relationship you can give each other emotional support and encouragement. This person can understand your need for freedom and let you be independent. Alternately, both of you can be drawn to idealistic people and enjoy being in the same type of social groups.

NEPTUNE BENEFICIAL TO YOUR PISCES SUN IN RELATIONSHIPS: As you are both likely to be sensitive and receptive, you understand each other's needs and moods. In this relationship you can be telepathic or intuitive and sense what the other person is thinking or feeling.

Pluto Beneficial in Relationships

This person's attitude can help you to strengthen your identity and his or her influence can have the effect of making you more powerful or daring. This can be a relationship that brings positive changes into your life by helping you react well to a challenge. This person can especially help you to see the light in a dark situation or you may both share the same sense of humor. The relationship is likely to be intense at times, but this can be channeled to produce positive results and may be a vehicle for self-regeneration. Being in the company of this person can make you more aware of your reactions to situations and provide you with deeper insight into yourself. Alternatively, this person may be in a position to advance you in some way or help you to rebuild or restructure your life. You can benefit from this relationship if you allow this person to transform the way you express yourself.

PLUTO BENEFICIAL TO YOUR ARIES SUN IN RELATIONSHIPS: Although already courageous, you may find that this relationship challenges you to be more daring. You may enjoy friendly competition with this person whether mentally or emotionally, as they know how to get a reaction from you.

PLUTO BENEFICIAL TO YOUR TAURUS SUN IN RELATIONSHIPS: Although you often resist change as it threatens your security, this person can bring positive transformation into your life by challenging you to alter your usual patterns or ways of thinking.

PLUTO BENEFICIAL TO YOUR GEMINI SUN IN RELATIONSHIPS: Although you share many ideas and enjoy discussing a

variety of subjects, this person can make you more conscious of your words and their impact.

PLUTO BENEFICIAL TO YOUR CANCER SUN IN RELATIONSHIPS: Although you are sensitive, this person is highly responsive to your moods and reactions. He or she can help you let go of the past and make way for new experiences.

PLUTO BENEFICIAL TO YOUR LEO SUN IN RELATIONSHIPS: This relationship can provide you with a chance to bring out the best in your personality if you rise to the challenge. As you both enjoy friendly rivalry, you often seek opportunity to test your strength and display your personal power.

PLUTO BENEFICIAL TO YOUR VIRGO SUN IN RELATIONSHIPS: Although you can be modest, this person can often dare you to be different or express yourself more dynamically. This person's influence can often enhance your personal power, and deepen your awareness.

PLUTO BENEFICIAL TO YOUR LIBRA SUN IN RELATIONSHIPS: You and your partner can influence each other positively to take on challenges. This person often recognizes your achievements or talents and can be attracted to what you say or do. As you are both dramatic, in a group environment, you both have an ability to shine due to your lively manner.

PLUTO BENEFICIAL TO YOUR SCORPIO SUN IN RELATIONSHIPS: In this relationship you have a strong emotional link or influence on one another. You may rely on this person for emotional security and support. He or she can help you express yourself well or get in touch with your deeper feelings.

PLUTO BENEFICIAL TO YOUR SAGITTARIUS SUN IN RELATIONSHIPS: In this relationship you can work well together especially if you share the same objectives. As you are both supportive, you are willing to help one another to transform or take advantage of new opportunities. If you are faced with challenges, you can often rely on each other for assistance and encouragement.

PLUTO BENEFICIAL TO YOUR CAPRICORN SUN IN RELATIONSHIPS: In this relationship you can achieve a great deal if you work together. One of you usually finds alternative methods for solving problems and you can usually make changes without a great deal of fuss. If faced with challenges, you encourage each other to hold on and not give up.

PLUTO BENEFICIAL TO YOUR AQUARIUS SUN IN RELATIONSHIPS: In this relationship you may both like to have a certain amount of freedom or independence and therefore respect each other's space. Your ability to understand the group dynamic indicates that you both relate well to other people. You can communicate well on a personal or intellectual level.

PLUTO BENEFICIAL TO YOUR PISCES SUN IN RELATIONSHIPS: In this relationship you both can experience intense emotions and therefore understand each other's moods. You may share an interest in mysticism or metaphysics. You can in-

fluence each other in a positive way and help one another in times of difficulties.

Challenging Relationships

Jupiter Challenging in Relationships

As Jupiter is the planet of expansion, it affects your relationship in a particular way, especially through excess. Perhaps the influence of this person causes you to become overly optimistic or to take on more than you can handle. Jupiter is a utopian planet, so excessive idealism may cause you to be naive or lose touch with harsh reality. Alternatively, you both may overindulge in the good things of life. Jupiter stimulates a desire for more and an appetite for the best. This may cause you both to be extravagant or too material. Nevertheless, by challenging your limitations, this person can inspire you to take a leap of faith and expand your horizons or offer you new and exciting opportunities. By staying realistic, patient, and disciplined you can avoid any possible problems.

JUPITER CHALLENGING TO YOUR ARIES SUN IN RELATIONSHIPS: Although usually direct and enthusiastic, this person's influence may cause you to act impulsively or take too many risks. Patience can be the vital key to success in this relationship.

JUPITER CHALLENGING TO YOUR TAURUS SUN IN RELATIONSHIPS: As you already possess a desire for the good things of life, be careful that this relationship does not stimulate you to overindulge or become too materialistic. This person may nevertheless inspire you to be more liberal and less fixed.

JUPITER CHALLENGING TO YOUR GEMINI SUN IN RELATIONSHIPS: Although you may be mentally quick and full of great ideas, this person may stimulate your enthusiasm even further, yet they may also cause you to spread yourself too thin. If you are selective you can benefit from this person's expansive influence but still stay focused.

JUPITER CHALLENGING TO YOUR CANCER SUN IN RELATIONSHIPS: This person's influence may sometimes cause you to emotionally overextend yourself. You need to be clear about your boundaries and stay realistic. Often from this relationship you can understand your own attitude to responsibilities for or other people.

JUPITER CHALLENGING TO YOUR LEO SUN IN RELATIONSHIPS: Be careful that this person does not inflate your ego, causing you to be too generous or extravagant. Still, this person can inspire you to express yourself in new and original ways if you can resist getting carried away.

JUPITER CHALLENGING TO YOUR VIRGO SUN IN RELATIONSHIPS: If this person's influence causes you to overextend yourself, you need to use your natural practicality and dis-

crimination to analyze the situation before you take any action. This person, however, can widen your horizons or encourage you to delve into new and exciting areas.

JUPITER CHALLENGING TO YOUR LIBRA SUN IN RELATIONSHIPS: This person may stimulate the side to your personality that loves quality and life's luxuries. But be careful not to exceed your boundaries or overindulge. Nevertheless, this person can also stimulate your sense of adventure.

JUPITER CHALLENGING TO YOUR SCORPIO SUN IN RELATIONSHIPS: At times this person may encourage you to extend yourself too far. Since you can be a creature of extremes, be careful to stay realistic and cautious. This person may nevertheless stimulate your desire for growth and freedom.

JUPITER CHALLENGING TO YOUR SAGITTARIUS SUN IN RELATIONSHIPS: Although you already desire to expand your horizons, this person may stimulate your enthusiasm further. Alternatively, you both may make spontaneous promises that you are unable to keep or take on more than you can handle. Nevertheless, this person can inspire you to see a different point of view.

JUPITER CHALLENGING TO YOUR CAPRICORN SUN IN RELATIONSHIPS: Your sense of realism may oppose this person's enthusiasm or desire to expand too fast. By persevering rather than becoming frustrated you can find a happy medium.

JUPITER CHALLENGING TO YOUR AQUARIUS SUN IN RELATIONSHIPS: Although you are usually objective and impartial, you and this person may not share the same ideals and ethics. Sometimes this person can make demands on you. Nevertheless, this person's values or self-expression can contribute to your creative flow or encourage you to be less fixed in your opinions.

JUPITER CHALLENGING TO YOUR PISCES SUN IN RELATIONSHIPS: This person may bring out your innate desire to escape from harsh reality. Although he or she may stimulate you to feel good, remember to keep your feet on the ground and pay attention to the practical details.

Saturn Challenging in Relationships

There may be restrictive circumstances involved in this relationship. You may experience a few challenging issues that you need to learn to work with. Although they may seem hard, you can benefit from them in the long run. In this relationship one of you often plays an authoritative role and this is good for a teacher/student relationship. Although this person may be a real taskmaster, he or she can force you to work hard in order to achieve excellence. Alternatively, you may think that you do not get recognized for your efforts and achievements. Therefore, you may not feel confident or important enough in the relationship. Rather than feel sorry for yourself, it is better to act sensibly and be mature or practical about the situation. On the positive side, you can learn a great deal from this person, since he or she usually picks your weakest points. For instance, if you are not organized in your thoughts and plans, this person will force you to become more focused and less scattered. If you feel anxious or unsure of yourself, in this relationship you can learn to assert yourself. You can become more responsible because this person may not always be able to help you due to a lack of time or resources. Whatever the reason, this person may expect you to do it yourself.

SATURN CHALLENGING TO YOUR ARIES SUN IN RELATIONSHIPS: In this relationship you need to make sure that you are not blocking the actions of this person. Alternatively, your responsibilities to your family, other people, or previous commitments may bring tension to the relationship. You can make better progress acting together rather than acting separately.

SATURN CHALLENGING TO YOUR TAURUS SUN IN RELATIONSHIPS: In this relationship you are reminded that you are unable to spend freely if you do not have the resources. If you both behave in a stubborn way you can reach a deadlock or become involved in power struggles. Being resourceful and resisting tension can make this relationship more productive.

SATURN CHALLENGING TO YOUR GEMINI SUN IN RELATIONSHIPS: In this relationship you may be reminded that although you are a quick thinker, you need to pay attention to details and be methodical. Your views may be challenged or considered too superficial. Misunderstandings and difficulties in communication may also occur in this relationship. You will have to be careful about what you say in case you hurt the feelings of this person. By talking through your problems you can clarify issues and gain better understanding.

SATURN CHALLENGING TO YOUR CANCER SUN IN RELATIONSHIPS: In this relationship you may not always receive the emotional support or reassurance you need to make you feel good about yourself. This person may work too hard or do things without consulting you, which makes you insecure. Alternatively, other people may cause you to feel unsure about them. By developing your confidence you can become more self-reliant and improve your relationships.

SATURN CHALLENGING TO YOUR LEO SUN IN RELATIONSHIPS: In this relationship you may both be very stubborn or seek to be in control. You may not get the devotion or compliments that you think you deserve and therefore at times you feel unappreciated. By compromising and being less proud you can work well together.

SATURN CHALLENGING TO YOUR VIRGO SUN IN RELATIONSHIPS: Your strong opinions or methods of doing things suggest that you and this person don't always see eye to eye. Either of you may be too critical. By improving your communication you can respond correctly or make the right judgments.

SATURN CHALLENGING TO YOUR LIBRA SUN IN RELATIONSHIPS: In this relationship one of you may be making too many emotional demands on the other. You or this person may put family or career issues above love or personal needs. By trying to share your responsibilities equally, you can improve this relationship.

SATURN CHALLENGING TO YOUR SCORPIO SUN IN RELATIONSHIPS: Your strong personalities may cause conflict in this relationship. If you both behave in a stubborn way, you can reach a deadlock or become involved in irresolvable conflicts. This relationship often benefits from compromise and flexibility.

SATURN CHALLENGING TO YOUR SAGITTARIUS SUN IN RELATIONSHIPS: In this relationship you and this person will need to learn to pace yourself and not be frustrated by limitations. When one of you is optimistic the other needs to stay realistic but not show pessimism. One of you may take things too seriously or complain of a lack of order. Perseverance and steady expansion often make this relationship work better.

SATURN CHALLENGING TO YOUR CAPRICORN SUN IN RELATIONSHIPS: In this relationship you both need to think about things other than work. Your partner or you may make too many demands on the other. Knowing how to divide your time and responsibilities may improve this relationship.

SATURN CHALLENGING TO YOUR AQUARIUS SUN IN RELATIONSHIPS: In this relationship your independence may be in some way restricted. One of you may be too proud or controlling. If both of you are self-willed you can reach a deadlock or become involved in power struggles. Being more flexible and less rigid can help this relationship.

SATURN CHALLENGING TO YOUR PISCES SUN IN RELATIONSHIPS: In this relationship you both need to be aware of each other's feelings. If the other person is too critical, opinionated, or does not listen you may feel vulnerable. Better understanding and greater tolerance can help this relationship.

Uranus Challenging in Relationships

With this person you may sometimes experience sudden change or situations that can make you feel uncomfortable. He or she may rebel against you when you least expect it or may not always see or share your views. This person may teach you to be more objective; therefore it is necessary for you to stay impartial and easygoing in this relationship. If you challenge this person head-on, you may fail to resolve your differences and end up arguing. The influence of this relationship may cause unexpected circumstances to change your course of direction. Alternatively, you may experience situations within this relationship where you feel you are suddenly on the outside and do not fit in. If you sometimes find yourself becoming too willful and stubborn in response to this person's actions, you may need to learn to adapt and stay detached. On occasion this influence also indicates that this person can suddenly appear in your life but may not necessarily stay for a long time. Positively, this person can bring out your strong independent spirit, encouraging you to express yourself. Equally, they can surprise you with their original ideas.

URANUS CHALLENGING TO YOUR ARIES SUN IN RELATIONSHIPS: Although you may share quick comprehension with this person, be careful that you do not stimulate each other to be impatient or stubborn. Developing tolerance, calm, and detachment can help you to inspire each other and create new and original ideas.

URANUS CHALLENGING TO YOUR TAURUS SUN IN RELATIONSHIPS: As you usually do not like change, the sudden and unexpected actions of this person can sometimes prove difficult for you. Although this person's influence may not be predictable, it can teach you to be self-reliant or independent.

URANUS CHALLENGING TO YOUR GEMINI SUN IN RELATIONSHIPS: Although this relationship can be mentally stimulating it can also be unpredictable. Fortunately, your versatility suggests that you can adapt quickly to unexpected situations. This person may transform the way you look at life, and at best encourage you to be original.

URANUS CHALLENGING TO YOUR CANCER SUN IN RELATIONSHIPS: There can be an unpredictable element to this relationship that can occasionally threaten your security. By retreating and staying open-minded, you can figure out exactly what is going on before you respond.

URANUS CHALLENGING TO YOUR LEO SUN IN RELATIONSHIPS: Within this relationship there may be times when issues of freedom or self-expression create some type of conflict. By showing tolerance and understanding you can stay positive and not feel offended. Nevertheless, this person encourages you to be original and less self-conscious.

URANUS CHALLENGING TO YOUR VIRGO SUN IN RELATIONSHIPS: In this relationship, even though you possess good comprehension and are practically resourceful in life, you may encounter some changes or disruptions. Avoid nervous tension by staying detached and establishing some type of a routine that can help both of you. Yet this person can surprise you with their original thoughts and methods of work.

URANUS CHALLENGING TO YOUR LIBRA SUN IN RELATIONSHIPS: Although you are not usually argumentative, this person's influence may cause disturbances to your otherwise harmonious nature. By utilizing your natural diplomatic skills you can keep the peace.

URANUS CHALLENGING TO YOUR SCORPIO SUN IN RELATIONSHIPS: At times you may encounter strong emotional tensions with this person. Guard against becoming stubborn in this relationship. You do better when you stay emotionally detached and unruffled.

URANUS CHALLENGING TO YOUR SAGITTARIUS SUN IN RELATIONSHIPS: You may encounter irrational behavior or arguments that can cause nervous tension in this relationship. By staying detached and patient, you can develop better understanding with this person. You can also utilize your natural philosophical outlook and goodwill to relieve any difficult situations.

URANUS CHALLENGING TO YOUR CAPRICORN SUN IN RELATIONSHIPS: Preferring to know where you stand and to have some control over your life, you may not like the unexpected element that can arise within this relationship. You can deal with any possible tension by being patient and more open to new concepts and experiences. This person can, however, help you to express your feelings more openly or to act less rigidly.

URANUS CHALLENGING TO YOUR AQUARIUS SUN IN RELATIONSHIPS: Although you have good powers of perception, this person can challenge some of your fixed views. If you do not allow your ego to get attached, problems can be resolved smoothly. This person can be more resourceful than you think.

URANUS CHALLENGING TO YOUR PISCES SUN IN RELATIONSHIPS: With this person you may encounter disagreement and therefore you may desire to rebel against their opinions. By staying detached, however, you can save your energy and not become too emotionally involved. Nevertheless, this person can offer you a totally different vision that sparks your imagination.

Neptune Challenging in Relationships

You may find it hard to define your roles clearly, as there is often an ambiguous quality to your relationship. There can often be something elusive that you cannot easily put into words. With this configuration there is always the danger that you are not entirely honest with each other. One of you may not be able to confront issues or problems head on. This person may say "can we talk about it some other time" or "I do not feel like talking about it right now." If you want to get through to this person, it is better to get them when they are receptive and open to you. Because of the receptivity and sensitivity this can be a contact where you both have an almost psychic link. There is a danger, however, that you can misunderstand the meaning of the message you receive from each other. If used positively, this contact can help you both reach deeper levels of awareness. It is important to stay grounded and realistic in this relationship to avoid possible disappointments that can arise from high expectations. If one of you idolizes the other and refuses to see his or her true character, you are sure to be disillusioned in the long run. In this relationship, however, you can gain greater insight into other people's sensitivity. This person can make you see what is missing in your life and inspire you to look for a new vision.

NEPTUNE CHALLENGING TO YOUR ARIES SUN IN RELATIONSHIPS: In this relationship you need to be clear about your plans and intentions. One of you may lead the other into a false sense of security. Alternatively, for one reason or another, one of you can make promises that he or she cannot keep. Nevertheless, this person can inspire you to seek a new direction.

NEPTUNE CHALLENGING TO YOUR TAURUS SUN IN RELATIONSHIPS: In this relationship you need to be honest about your resources and resist being secretive. If you want stability and security make sure you and your partner have the same values or ideals.

NEPTUNE CHALLENGING TO YOUR GEMINI SUN IN RELATIONSHIPS: In your communication, you may misunderstand this person or find them vague. Although this person may make good suggestions and inspire your imagination, make sure that what he or she says is realistic and practical. While the relationship may be good to begin with, you must judge this person more on what he or she does than on what is promised. This configuration demands honesty at all times.

NEPTUNE CHALLENGING TO YOUR CANCER SUN IN RELATIONSHIPS: Although this person appears idealistic or romantic, he or she may not be as security-conscious as you would like. You both need to be honest with each other about your feelings and know clearly what you want out of the relationship.

NEPTUNE CHALLENGING TO YOUR LEO SUN IN RELATIONSHIPS: In this relationship you may find that although this person may flatter you, he or she may not always mean it. You and your partner may not see eye to eye on issues regarding finances. In this relationship, you both need to be honest with each other and know clearly what you want out of the relationship.

NEPTUNE CHALLENGING TO YOUR VIRGO SUN IN RELATIONSHIPS: In this relationship you may find it hard to pinpoint your partner's thoughts. This person may use methods that are very different from yours. This person may be creative and imaginative but less organized or methodical than you. In this relationship your responsibilities should be shared equally and there should be clarity in your communication.

NEPTUNE CHALLENGING TO YOUR LIBRA SUN IN RELATIONSHIPS: If this is a romantic link, be realistic rather than fantasizing over this person. If you are overly romantic, you may find out later that this person cannot live up to your expectations or you have been refusing to see this person as he or she truly is. This person may inspire you to be more idealistic yet you both may want different things out of this relationship.

NEPTUNE CHALLENGING TO YOUR SCORPIO SUN IN RELATIONSHIPS: Often secretive, you may both want to hold on to your privacy and therefore find it hard to be open with one another. You may be less inclined to face the true nature of

your problems and avoid issues. You both benefit from being open and honest with each other.

NEPTUNE CHALLENGING TO YOUR SAGITTARIUS SUN IN RELATIONSHIPS: In this relationship you may need to be more pragmatic and less idealistic, otherwise you may both get carried away with your fantasies. As you may be overly imaginative or too optimistic together, you need to look at issues soberly in order to avoid being disillusioned. Be honest with your partner and do not promise what you cannot deliver.

NEPTUNE CHALLENGING TO YOUR CAPRICORN SUN IN RELATIONSHIPS: In this relationship you may both experience doubt or a lack of faith. Other people may come between you and confuse issues. Alternatively, you or your partner may not have enough confidence in each other's abilities. Your relationship can benefit from encouragement and solid support.

NEPTUNE CHALLENGING TO YOUR AQUARIUS SUN IN RELATIONSHIPS: You may be drawn to a more unconventional relationship with this person. Your values may conflict or you may both want to make changes at different times. If you are honest and clear about your long-term plans you may be able to compromise.

NEPTUNE CHALLENGING TO YOUR PISCES SUN IN RELATIONSHIPS: In this relationship your partner may not fully understand your idealism and sensitivity. You may even feel victimized by your partner's criticism or end up playing the martyr. You benefit from staying detached and not taking things to heart. By being clear about how you feel, you can improve your relationships.

Pluto Challenging in Relationships

Pluto deals with intensity and power; therefore your self-expression is likely to be challenged by this person in some way. You have a choice of using this challenge positively or negatively but you may not always like the way it is presented. This person has the ability to "get under your skin" or knows how to hit your weak spots and get you to react. You can overreact or use their energy positively to transform yourself and become more powerful. When handling this person's challenges, you need to quickly assess his or her behavior. It is often best for you to walk away from confrontations even though your ego may still be attached. In retrospect, you realize that if you had become involved in a power struggle, your resources would have become depleted and you would not have gained anything.

PLUTO CHALLENGING TO YOUR ARIES SUN IN RELATIONSHIPS: With your competitive spirit, you may find it hard to walk away from someone laying down the gauntlet in your direction. Resist having to prove that you are right or getting even with this person by staying focused on your positive goals.

PLUTO CHALLENGING TO YOUR TAURUS SUN IN RELATIONSHIPS: Although practical and down-to-earth, this relationship may sometimes cause you to deviate from your usual determined approach. By not overreacting or becoming too fixed, you can remain calm yet focused.

PLUTO CHALLENGING TO YOUR GEMINI SUN IN RELATIONSHIPS: This person's reactions and intensity can sometimes cause you nervous tension. By utilizing your good communication skills and adapting quickly, you can turn situations to your advantage.

PLUTO CHALLENGING TO YOUR CANCER SUN IN RELATIONSHIPS: This person's intensity may at times cause you to experience emotional ups and downs. To avoid power struggles, stay open and caring but do not let this person's dramas affect you.

PLUTO CHALLENGING TO YOUR LEO SUN IN RELATIONSHIPS: Often proud, you may find it hard to resist this person's challenge without becoming stubborn and melodramatic. Utilize your natural strength to avoid getting caught up in this person's need to control.

PLUTO CHALLENGING TO YOUR VIRGO SUN IN RELATIONSHIPS: Although you are pragmatic, this relationship may cause you to deviate from your usual efficient approach to life. By not overreacting or becoming anxious, you can stay focused and work with this person's intensity to transform the relationship.

PLUTO CHALLENGING TO YOUR LIBRA SUN IN RELATIONSHIPS: Issues of control may undermine your relationship. There may be tension if obsessive behavior patterns and personal ego deter you from compromising in difficult situations. You can transform this relationship if you stay detached and let go with good grace.

PLUTO CHALLENGING TO YOUR SCORPIO SUN IN RELATIONSHIPS: In this relationship your egos are strong and both of you usually want to be in control. If one of you insists on doing things one way, the other may stubbornly refuse to cooperate. In this relationship you need a great deal of autonomy to pursue your personal aims and objectives. Remembering that good relationships are based on encouragement and support, do not attempt to keep score of who is winning.

PLUTO CHALLENGING TO YOUR SAGITTARIUS SUN IN RELATIONSHIPS: Your ability to see the big picture can help you overcome any power challenges you may encounter in this relationship. Having a positive attitude can help you avoid getting stuck in any overly intense situations.

PLUTO CHALLENGING TO YOUR CAPRICORN SUN IN RELATIONSHIPS: In this relationship you can both become intense or stubborn. If one of you wants to instigate some new ideas the other may resist. If you are unable to compromise, you may reach a deadlock. Give and take is essential if this relationship is to work well.

PLUTO CHALLENGING TO YOUR AQUARIUS SUN IN RELATIONSHIPS: You may feel nervous or impatient in the company of one another and create tension in the relationship. Although you are usually detached, this person can cause you to lose your composure. If you both become stubborn or controlling, you can end up in a deadlock. Although you may hold different principles, you benefit from compromise.

PLUTO CHALLENGING TO YOUR PISCES SUN IN RELATIONSHIPS: In this relationship ignoring or concealing matters of importance may lead to emotional stress and worry. Avoid situations that lead to addictive behavior. By being clear and honest, you can avoid confusion or losses.

Special Relationships

Jupiter Special in Relationships

With this link you can enjoy a special relationship that makes both of you feel more optimistic or contented. You think positively together and therefore bring a feeling of success and expansion to the relationship. There is often an enthusiastic exchange of ideas that stimulates you to take on large or expansive projects either together or individually. This is a lucky combination, particularly as you will both motivate each other to be more honest, direct, and magnanimous. This person can lift your spirits when you are down, often using humor. You may travel together or be attracted to education, religion, or sport. Although you can both stimulate each other to be enterprising, you may, however, have to resist the temptation to take on too much in your desire to expand and prosper.

JUPITER SPECIAL TO YOUR ARIES SUN IN RELATIONSHIPS: In this relationship you are both enthusiastic and optimistic about your future plans. Generosity is often evident and you can inspire each other to be adventurous or daring. You enjoy doing things together and usually you succeed in your joint endeavors. You have a good sense of timing as long as you do not get carried away.

JUPITER SPECIAL TO YOUR TAURUS SUN IN RELATIONSHIPS: Whether this is a professional or a personal relationship you are likely to succeed in whatever you do together. You can be affectionate or loyal toward one another. Usually you have a similar approach to work or material values. If you are inclined to spend, you need to learn to budget, as you both enjoy indulging in the good things in life.

JUPITER SPECIAL TO YOUR GEMINI SUN IN RELATIONSHIPS: Together you appear cheerful and friendly. With this configuration there can be an enthusiastic exchange of ideas. You can enjoy a sociable time or have many contacts. You benefit from expanding your knowledge and going to lectures or other cultural events, as these activities often bring good opportunities. As you like to be well-informed and share many interests, you can be creative with some of your ideas bringing material success.

JUPITER SPECIAL TO YOUR CANCER SUN IN RELATIONSHIPS: Your wealth of feelings and goodwill indicate that usually you are kind to each other. Together you can feel relaxed and emotionally secure. You can be supportive of one another and cheer each other up. You may both share a love for family or prosper in business together.

JUPITER SPECIAL TO YOUR LEO SUN IN RELATIONSHIPS: In this relationship this person may stimulate the extrovert side to your personality. You can be lucky together, generous with each other, or encourage each other to be more buoyant. Together you can be dramatic and create an atmosphere of opulence. You may even want to be in the limelight and enjoy being popular. By being enthusiastic and optimistic, you can attract success.

JUPITER SPECIAL TO YOUR VIRGO SUN IN RELATIONSHIPS: In this relationship you are probably both career-oriented and organized. Usually you are keen on gathering knowledge and can show an eagerness to learn. You often share your responsibilities and generally try to be helpful to one another. You can be meticulous, and as you love paying attention to details you can be constantly perfecting each other.

JUPITER SPECIAL TO YOUR LIBRA SUN IN RELATIONSHIPS: In this relationship you both like to socialize or entertain. Usually you enjoy popularity by being well meaning and charitable. You can also be affectionate to each other, but guard against being too extravagant or self-indulgent. Usually you rely on one another and trust that this person will be there if you need help. You may have the same aesthetic taste in art or music. You can both succeed in work that involves the public.

JUPITER SPECIAL TO YOUR SCORPIO SUN IN RELATIONSHIPS: Together you can be very confident, determined, and successful. You know how to make the best of situations or turn circumstances to your advantage. Both of you have a strong influence over others and therefore you can make things happen. You usually have big plans and the tenacity to achieve them.

JUPITER SPECIAL TO YOUR SAGITTARIUS SUN IN RELATIONSHIPS: As both of you are naturally optimistic and expansive, you can encourage one another and feel contented. Together you often have fortunate ideas or noble aims and can be generous to one another. You can inspire each other to be more adventurous and traveling may be one of your main interests. Alternatively, you may be interested in spirituality and feel closer through your beliefs or ideals.

JUPITER SPECIAL TO YOUR CAPRICORN SUN IN RELATIONSHIPS: You both have a strong sense of responsibility.

Your determination and patience assure a slow but steady advancement. Together you can be industrious and hardworking with strong ambitions. Usually you are well-organized and constructive. Keen on furthering your careers, you will show respect and give support to each other.

JUPITER SPECIAL TO YOUR AQUARIUS SUN IN RELATIONSHIPS: You can be fortunate together and surprise one another with unexpected gifts or lucky breaks. As you are both independent and freedom-loving, you give each other room to be grow. Although you can be unconventional or progressive, you hold similar views, especially on humanitarian issues. Adventures and new opportunities may be needed to stimulate your relationship.

JUPITER SPECIAL TO YOUR PISCES SUN IN RELATIONSHIPS: You can be generous, tolerant, and compassionate to one another. You share the same ideals and together you can be imaginative and creative. Probably you share a love for the same type of music or style. Understanding and idealistic, you are often willing to make sacrifices for one another.

Saturn Special in Relationships

In this relationship there can be a restraining influence. Your Sun governs your confidence and ability to shine and expresses just who you are. Saturn prefers to take things more seriously and is more cautious and inhibited than fun-loving and flamboyant. This Saturn influence can therefore either repress your natural self-expression or bring stability and long-term security into the relationship. There can be an age difference in this relationship or one partner may appear as a teacher or authority figure. One of you may highlight the other's weaknesses. If you tend to act impulsively or rashly this person may help you by bringing a curbing influence to bear on the more impetuous side to your nature. Alternatively, you may feel this person's influence as blocking your spontaneity or discouraging you by adding extra responsibilities to your life. Either way, you will usually encounter this relationship as an important learning experience and gain insight into your responsibilities or self-discipline. Nevertheless, this bond is often strong and very important and you can both achieve much through steady progress.

SATURN SPECIAL TO YOUR ARIES SUN IN RELATIONSHIPS: You usually like to move fast but this person may slow you down and cause you to become frustrated. Nevertheless, if this person improves your perseverance and stops you from being impulsive or impatient then they can have a positive influence on you.

SATURN SPECIAL TO YOUR TAURUS SUN IN RELATIONSHIPS: As you are a person who needs warm and tactile gestures of affection, you may find this relationship to be a little too restraining. It may, however, provide security, something you may compromise for in the long term. This person can in-fluence you to be more self-disciplined and can also curb your overindulgence.

SATURN SPECIAL TO YOUR GEMINI SUN IN RELATIONSHIPS: Although you usually prefer to keep things light, this relationship may sometimes bring responsibilities or tests of patience. You may, however, find that this person's outlook is pessimistic yet practical. Nevertheless, this person can offer you more structure and discipline or you can both build for a long and secure future.

SATURN SPECIAL TO YOUR CANCER SUN IN RELATIONSHIPS: You usually like to do things when you feel in the mood, but this person may insist that you provide some sort of structure or definite outline for your plans. Positively, this can work to discipline you or, alternatively, you may find yourself always operating under the other person's terms.

SATURN SPECIAL TO YOUR LEO SUN IN RELATIONSHIPS: As you usually like to have fun, you may find this relationship a little too serious as it restrains your normal expressive self. Alternatively, this person may provide discipline and guidance in your life or be a solid support in times of difficulty.

SATURN SPECIAL TO YOUR VIRGO SUN IN RELATIONSHIPS: This person can highlight your sense of responsibility but also your tendency to be self-critical. You both may also stimulate each other's practical or organizational abilities and be dedicated to your work.

SATURN SPECIAL TO YOUR LIBRA SUN IN RELATIONSHIPS: As a sociable individual with a light and airy approach, you may find this person too serious. If you are committed to a long-term relationship, however, you may be willing to make this adjustment. Although there may be extra responsibilities involved with this person they are often fair and just.

SATURN SPECIAL TO YOUR SCORPIO SUN IN RELATIONSHIPS: Not one for being light and superficial, this relationship can cause you some serious thinking. In this relationship you may encounter some issues of power and control, but this person can also be loyal and tenacious when you both encounter outside difficulties.

SATURN SPECIAL TO YOUR SAGITTARIUS SUN IN RELATIONSHIPS: As you usually do not like to have your freedom curtailed, this relationship may challenge you by forcing you to make commitments or take some responsibilities. Nevertheless, you can both achieve much with a steady progress. This person can also cause you to reevaluate your principles and ideals.

SATURN SPECIAL TO YOUR CAPRICORN SUN IN RELATIONSHIPS: This person highlights your sense of work and responsibilities but avoids being overly materialistic or pessimistic. Pragmatic and ambitious, however, you may both be involved in making long-term plans and securing the future.

SATURN SPECIAL TO YOUR AQUARIUS SUN IN RELATIONSHIPS: Although you value your freedom and are keen on progress, you may find that this person's influence brings you

restrictions or responsibilities. There can be long-term advantages to this relationship if you both show respect for the other person's needs.

SATURN SPECIAL TO YOUR PISCES SUN IN RELATIONSHIPS: You may feel the structured and more serious influence of this relationship somewhat confining. Alternatively, if this person makes you more grounded and disciplined, you find it easier to develop your confidence and determination.

Uranus Special in Relationships

This is usually an unconventional, exciting, or powerful relationship. There is a dynamic yet restless energy between you both, and therefore you can easily become stimulated or agitated in each other's company. An unpredictable element indicates that your behavior may alter dramatically when you are together. One of you will constantly reintroduce new elements into the relationship, making it either changeable or exciting. This person may challenge you to be more adventurous, independent, or radical. If you are both on the same wavelength, you may find your partner inspiring and original. In this relationship you can both demand a great deal of freedom, and by making as few demands as possible, you can feel free and unrestricted. As you both feel the urge to be different from other people, you may decide to alter your old life patterns to such an extent that you will make dramatic changes in order to pursue your individual objectives. As long as you are both in agreement, you can gain from cooperative efforts. The main problem with this relationship is contrary behavior or a lack of collaboration if one of you insists on doing things in a particular way. Another problem may arise if one partner feels that by committing to the relationship this person somehow loses his or her freedom. A real test as to whether this is a long-lasting relationship is when one of you is faced with new opportunities. If you can work together, you will strengthen your relationship. This is an excellent influence for a relationship based on friendship, adventures, and initiating new ideas.

URANUS SPECIAL TO YOUR ARIES SUN IN RELATIONSHIPS: In this relationship you may find the other partner to be exciting and daring. This person may inspire you to be more adventurous and objective about yourself. There is a danger, however, that you both can act on impulse, without taking into consideration what the other person feels or thinks.

URANUS SPECIAL TO YOUR TAURUS SUN IN RELATIONSHIPS: This relationship may be fascinating and exciting in the short term, but in order for it to last, this person needs to respect your need for security and desire for stability. You have original ways of looking at issues or you may have unusual interests that link you together.

URANUS SPECIAL TO YOUR GEMINI SUN IN RELATIONSHIPS: You are both mentally quick and often attracted to each other by your sharp wit. Although to others you may appear unconventional, you often share similar beliefs. You may become bored quickly with one another if you do not have a common goal. You both like to think independently but you can work well as a team when you are engaged in problem solving, or initiating new enterprises.

URANUS SPECIAL TO YOUR CANCER SUN IN RELATIONSHIPS: Although you are quick to respond to one another's moods, you can both be very sensitive. Any problems you may encounter are often due to the fact that you can both be emotionally restless or unpredictable. Together you can be highly intuitive and sense each other's moods.

URANUS SPECIAL TO YOUR LEO SUN IN RELATIONSHIPS: In this relationship you are both strong and dynamic. The positive influence in this relationship means that one of you will encourage the other to be more enterprising or carefree. In each other's company, you will not be afraid to exhibit your more unconventional or unique qualities. Nevertheless, there can be ego clashes between the two of you, if one tries to dominate the other.

URANUS SPECIAL TO YOUR VIRGO SUN IN RELATIONSHIPS: You may share an interest in the same unusual line of work. Although both of you may be keen on refining and improving your methods, you are happier if you express your individuality. You may both be different in your way of looking at problems and together invent something original and useful. You can share a passion for something unique that keeps you together.

URANUS SPECIAL TO YOUR LIBRA SUN IN RELATIONSHIPS: There is a likelihood that you became attracted to one another very quickly. Although you are both sociable, one of you may hold unconventional views on love or relationships and inspire the other to be more adventurous. If you both share the same taste, you can enjoy a stimulating time looking for unusual forms of self-expression.

URANUS SPECIAL TO YOUR SCORPIO SUN IN RELATIONSHIPS: Although on occasions there could be some tension in this relationship, together you are fearless and daring. You have the power to transform one another and create new opportunities. This is a good combination if you put all your energies into something unique that will inspire your imagination and help you initiate or pioneer new enterprises.

URANUS SPECIAL TO YOUR SAGITTARIUS SUN IN RELATIONSHIPS: As both of you like to be free, in this relationship you need plenty of room to grow and develop. You may introduce advanced ideas or encourage one another to be more adventurous or experimental. You need to resist taking unnecessary risks together even though you can be very lucky at times.

URANUS SPECIAL TO YOUR CAPRICORN SUN IN RELATIONSHIPS: You need to understand one another's needs if you want this relationship to last. In this partnership one of you is

often traditional and loyal and the other progressive and free-thinking. If you are both willing to compromise, you can make real progress without causing tension and disruptions. An unusual career or ambition may bring you together and you can achieve much if you want to focus on reforms.

URANUS SPECIAL TO YOUR AQUARIUS SUN IN RELATIONSHIPS: In this relationship both of you are progressive and independent. You share the same interests or peculiar sense of humor. You respect each other's space and love of the unusual. Together you can be original and inventive. You must resist being stubborn or rebellious if you want to make things happen.

URANUS SPECIAL TO YOUR PISCES SUN IN RELATIONSHIPS: You can both be original and imaginative, with unusual talents and abilities yet unconventional in your behavior. You may have a telepathic link and read each other's mind. You may both be interested in metaphysics or have spiritual experiences.

Neptune Special in Relationships

In this relationship you are both sensitive to each other, often having a psychic link that enables you to feel each other's emotions as if they were your own. This relationship may stimulate your idealism with the result that you feel a special and almost spiritual link with this person. There can, however, be a shadow side to this influence if you delude yourself and project onto this person the ideal that you have created. If this is the case, ultimately this person will not live up to your expectations and you will be disappointed. Keep in mind the danger of placing this person on a pedestal and guard against trying to "save" him or her by martyring yourself. The subtle emotional sensitivity in this relationship can be used constructively, however, through compassion, music, healing, or the arts. There can also be a strong connection to mystical, spiritual, and intuitive influences. Nevertheless, it is vital that you stay grounded rather than become involved in unrealistic fantasies or escapism, especially through drugs and alcohol. To avoid confusion or any type of deception, you have to keep your special and sensitive link with this person open but also stay very realistic.

NEPTUNE SPECIAL TO YOUR VIRGO SUN IN RELATIONSHIPS: There are sensitive and subtle emotions that come into play in this relationship. You may rely on your intuition when dealing with this person, especially in unclear situations. They can also inspire you to be more compassionate or follow your ideals.

NEPTUNE SPECIAL TO YOUR LIBRA SUN IN RELATIONSHIPS: This person can enhance your sensitivity and share your appreciation of the refined and the beautiful. As this person can also stimulate your romanticism, be careful to keep

your feet very much on the ground. This can be a creative and sociable link.

NEPTUNE SPECIAL TO YOUR SCORPIO SUN IN RELATIONSHIPS: As this person can stimulate your imagination, make sure to stay in touch with the more practical and mundane side of life. This relationship can stimulate your natural sixth sense, so you may find yourself easily in tune with this person's emotions.

NEPTUNE SPECIAL TO YOUR SAGITTARIUS SUN IN RELATIONSHIPS: This relationship is likely to stimulate your idealism. Neptune is the planet of great dreams and usually you both like to look to the future. Back up any plans you make with this person with some solid common sense to achieve success.

NEPTUNE SPECIAL TO YOUR CAPRICORN SUN IN RELATIONSHIPS: This person can help you get in touch with your more subtle and sensitive emotions. Although you are practical this person can inspire you. If you are not careful this person can also cause you doubt or uncertainty. Nevertheless, their vision or imagination can add to your pragmatic outlook.

NEPTUNE SPECIAL TO YOUR AQUARIUS SUN IN RELATIONSHIPS: Although you can usually be dispassionate and mentally objective, this relationship is likely to bring out your more emotional side and enhance your sensitivity. By connecting to these more subtle feelings, you can learn much about yourself.

NEPTUNE SPECIAL TO YOUR PISCES SUN IN RELATIONSHIPS: You are likely to have a natural psychic link with this person. As you can be very sensitive to this person's feelings and vice versa, be careful to use this link for constructive or creative reasons and not get caught up in emotional dramas or fantasies. Honesty and pragmatism can enhance this relationship.

Pluto Special in Relationships

This relationship can bring strong change or transformation into your life. This person can stimulate you to react to situations more intensely than usual. If channeled constructively, this can make you feel more powerful and decisive. If channeled negatively, however, you can become involved in power struggles or desire to get even. If situations become too intense, you may need to detach yourself temporarily by walking away. When you regain your equilibrium, you can judge your reactions more clearly. On a subliminal level you can have a deep awareness of how this person responds and reacts. Since this person is also able to pick up on your weaknesses, it is important not to get too involved in issues of control or ego games. Nevertheless, you can share a sense of humor or enjoy exchanging friendly banter.

PLUTO SPECIAL TO YOUR CANCER SUN IN RELATIONSHIPS: This person can intensify your emotions, stimulating

deep changes and providing you with fresh insights into yourself. Although this person can intuitively understand your needs and desires, he or she can sometimes, even unintentionally, be forceful.

PLUTO SPECIAL TO YOUR LEO SUN IN RELATIONSHIPS: In this relationship, this person can enhance your drive and natural leadership skills by making you more aware of your personal power. This person may stimulate your self-expression or your drive for recognition and success.

PLUTO SPECIAL TO YOUR VIRGO SUN IN RELATIONSHIPS: This person may transform your routine or methods of work. Emotional and psychological changes can also be happening at a deep level due to this person's influence. By trusting your first impressions or natural instincts rather than your developed logic, you are likely to handle this person better.

PLUTO SPECIAL TO YOUR LIBRA SUN IN RELATIONSHIPS: Your partner may have a strong impact on your personality. If one of you becomes obsessive, the relationship can become too intense. Nevertheless, this person's views and emotions will transform the way you look at yourself and relationships in general.

PLUTO SPECIAL TO YOUR SCORPIO SUN IN RELATIONSHIPS: You and your partner can have a strong impact on each other. On the negative side, you may become overly sensitive and attempt to control one another emotionally. You need to resist jealousy or subversive behavior. On the positive side, you will help one another to transform or make real headway.

PLUTO SPECIAL TO YOUR SAGITTARIUS SUN IN RELATIONSHIPS: Your partner will have a strong impact on your beliefs and may transform your outlook on life. If this person is from a different culture, he or she may change your lifestyle or belief systems. Both of you need to guard against getting carried away or being too radical in your views.

PLUTO SPECIAL TO YOUR CAPRICORN SUN IN RELATIONSHIPS: This may not always be the easiest of relationships since both of you have different ideas or ways of doing things. On the one hand, this person may bring upheaval and force you to change direction. On the other hand, your partner may transform your rigid structure and help you to change your life if you let them. If you share the same goals, you can be a strong power for change and transformation for the better.

Chapter 3: Predicting the Future

Beneficial Times

Times of Jupiter Beneficial

This is a time when you are likely to be feeling more optimistic, enterprising, and forward thinking. Life can present you with a chance for growth, whether mental, physical, or spiritual. Jupiter is a planet that provides opportunities, so now is not a time to be overly cautious or turn down possible chances to expand your knowledge or experience. Your personal growth may involve taking a risk, looking at the bigger picture of your life, and daring to try new experiences. Perhaps you want to take that course that you have been putting off for some time. Alternatively, you may wish to travel while there is a window of opportunity, expand your home or business, or take on new projects. The less favorable aspect of this influence is that you may relax too much or do nothing to take advantage of the opportunities now available to you. Equally, you could become overconfident or take on too much. Nevertheless, this expansive influence suggests that the right opportunities will bring success. During this period you can advance yourself and add to your confidence by making definite plans for the future.

TIMES OF JUPITER BENEFICIAL TO YOUR SUN IN ARIES: At this time you are likely to feel more enthusiastic and in tune with your more creative and enterprising spirit. This is a good time to exert energy to improve your social, spiritual, or educational activities. Alternatively, you may want to initiate a new project, take up a new sport, or be adventurous.

TIMES OF JUPITER BENEFICIAL TO YOUR SUN IN TAURUS: Now is a time when there is a beneficial influence around your material resources. Although you often succeed through patience and steadiness of purpose, during this period you can also have an enterprising attitude and an ability to see the larger picture. Your sense of self-worth is on the increase.

TIMES OF JUPITER BENEFICIAL TO YOUR SUN IN GEMINI: During this period your desire for improvement is likely to open up new areas of communication for you either in your personal, social, or business life. Opportunities are also likely to come through new ideas and plans for the future. During this time, your outlook is more open or optimistic.

TIMES OF JUPITER BENEFICIAL TO YOUR SUN IN CANCER: At this time you may feel more generous toward others, especially toward your family members and new additions. During this period be careful that your love for food does not cause too much weight gain. Generally speaking, this is a lucky time for making plans, whether professional or personal, and improving your home.

TIMES OF JUPITER BENEFICIAL TO YOUR SUN IN LEO: Your general self-esteem is likely to be increased during this period. This may tempt you to take on too much or, alternatively, you will feel able to take risks now that you would not have had the confidence to take before. During this period you will also feel creative and full of ideas. With your positive outlook and enthusiasm you can attract others during this time.

TIMES OF JUPITER BENEFICIAL TO YOUR SUN IN VIRGO: There could be an expansion or new opportunity now, whether in your personal life or your work. Although you are good at being of practical help to others and are not usually into taking risks, now is a good time to do something for yourself or to take a chance. This is a good time to improve your skills and expertise.

TIMES OF JUPITER BENEFICIAL TO YOUR SUN IN LIBRA: You are likely to feel good at the moment or expand your social circle. Your usual diplomacy, artistic appreciation, or ability to charm others is heightened at the moment, so you have more opportunities to improve your situation at work or with friends and lovers. Teamwork will also bring benefits during this period.

TIMES OF JUPITER BENEFICIAL TO YOUR SUN IN SCORPIO: This is a time when there are opportunities for change and transformation that will improve your circumstances both materially and socially. This influence provides a form of protection so even though you may take a risk, you somehow end up in a good position.

TIMES OF JUPITER BENEFICIAL TO YOUR SUN IN SAGITTARIUS: You are likely to feel more optimistic than usual at this time or have an opportunity to travel, expand your learning, or discover business opportunities. As you are likely to feel more expansive, be careful not to take on too much or overindulge in the good things of life.

TIMES OF JUPITER BENEFICIAL TO YOUR SUN IN CAPRICORN: Although usually hardworking, you are not often one for being overly optimistic. During this period, however, you should increase your opportunities and with a positive attitude you can focus on the expansion of your resources. Rising to a higher position is also possible during this time.

TIMES OF JUPITER BENEFICIAL TO YOUR SUN IN AQUARIUS: This is a time when you may increase your circle of friends or

have fortunate opportunities, especially through group endeavors. Your natural broad-minded approach is stimulated now, so you may wish to expand your mental horizons through idealistic causes or original ideas.

TIMES OF JUPITER BENEFICIAL TO YOUR SUN IN PISCES: You are likely to be enterprising and optimistic during this period. As this is a fortunate influence, if you just back up your big plans and dreams with some hard work, you can make them a reality.

Times of Saturn Beneficial

During this period you are able to consolidate many personal or practical issues in your life. If you have made special efforts in a particular area, you will be able to enjoy the fruits of your labor. Although you are able to see some good results, this is not so much a period of luck as one of rewards for past activities. In this period, you will be able to get things done or make good yet steady progress. This is also a very important time to plan for the future. The more you achieve during this period, the better you will cope with challenges you may face in the future. This is a time when your superiors and those you work with will look upon you favorably. If you are looking for a promotion or want to impress others, use this period to your advantage. Alternatively, you may meet someone who is older or more experienced who will have a positive influence. This person may be able to help you or become a teacher and mentor. Even if this person is willing to support you, you will not get a free ride but will have to work and be responsible.

TIMES OF SATURN BENEFICIAL TO YOUR SUN IN ARIES: During this period you will be able to achieve a great deal due to your determination and hard work. Your plans will work well if you made the necessary preparations. Other people will admire your dedication and perseverance, so you will be able to impress others with your ideas. This is a good period for overcoming obstacles.

TIMES OF SATURN BENEFICIAL TO YOUR SUN IN TAURUS: Your sense of duty or responsible attitude indicates that during this period you will be able to see the rewards of your past efforts. This is a good time to make cautious long-term investments. You will be able to project yourself in the right light and gain other people's respect. Alternatively, during this period you can show people how valuable you really are.

TIMES OF SATURN BENEFICIAL TO YOUR SUN IN GEMINI: During this period you will be more focused and organized. You will approach matters in a logical or practical way. If you are facing problems, you will be able to solve them more easily. As your concentration should be good during this time, you will be able to undertake more challenging projects. Good results can be achieved during this period if you have been studying or writing.

TIMES OF SATURN BENEFICIAL TO YOUR SUN IN CANCER: During this period you may become emotionally more mature and as a result more secure within yourself. Your sense of duty toward your family will not be ignored during this period. Although you may have to make some sacrifices, you will do so willingly. You may consider making improvements in your home or undertaking repairs that will secure and increase the value of your house.

TIMES OF SATURN BENEFICIAL TO YOUR SUN IN LEO: During this period you will enjoy recognition for your hard work and past efforts. You may be promoted to a higher position that may include more responsibility. Your loyalty and reliable attitude will be rewarded. During this period you will be more focused and determined.

TIMES OF SATURN BENEFICIAL TO YOUR SUN IN VIRGO: During this period you will be rewarded for being pragmatic, organized, and productive. Your common sense, logic, and concentration will work well together. If you are involved in any type of work that demands problem solving or serious study you can achieve good results. This is also a good time for improving your health.

TIMES OF SATURN BENEFICIAL TO YOUR SUN IN LIBRA: During this period you may be rewarded for your loyalty, good deeds, or past efforts. You may also benefit from knowing people with a mature and responsible attitude. This is a good time to establish long and lasting partnerships that are based on trust and responsibility. Past activities concerning serious study or practical idealism often have a good outcome.

TIMES OF SATURN BENEFICIAL TO YOUR SUN IN SCORPIO: During this period you will be more self-disciplined and focused. You will be able to overcome past challenges and succeed in work that involves difficult undertakings. The foundations you are now building are long lasting or the changes that you are about to make will prove beneficial in the long term.

TIMES OF SATURN BENEFICIAL TO YOUR SUN IN SAGITTARIUS: During this period you will gain the approval of other people for your patience and perseverance. Your honesty, sense of duty, or strong beliefs will also be respected or honored by others. If you acted in the past with integrity and fairness, matters will be resolved in your favor. During this period, you can be more consistent, constructive, and determined.

TIMES OF SATURN BENEFICIAL TO YOUR SUN IN CAPRICORN: This is a good time to consolidate your past efforts. During this period you will be able to establish a more favorable situation for yourself due to your hard work and past contributions. This is also a good time to lay foundations for long-term projects. A possibility to rise to a higher position is favorable now.

TIMES OF SATURN BENEFICIAL TO YOUR SUN IN AQUARIUS: During this period you are more willing to make commitments without being concerned that they will restrict you.

This may also be a good time to put your original ideas into practice and establish a more firm foundation for yourself.

TIMES OF SATURN BENEFICIAL TO YOUR SUN IN PISCES: During this period your foresight and sense of purpose work well together. Rather than daydreaming, you will be keen to establish a firm foundation and apply practical solutions to your needs. Your sense of vision and positive attitude now will help you to manifest or concretize your ideals.

Times of Uranus Beneficial

This period is one where you gain by accepting new ideas and changes into your life. You may feel better able to express who you really are rather than what people expect of you. This influence affects your sense of freedom, so you will probably be more aware of your limitations and how you want to change them. You may decide on a new image or become more interested in subjects of an alternative nature that increase your self-awareness. The psychological changes you undergo during this period usually allow you to integrate new ideas fairly easily. Group endeavors, teamwork, or valuing friendship can all become more important at this time. You may become more interested in humanitarian projects or fight for the freedom of others. Alternatively, you will want to present yourself and your ideas in a more original way and learn to stand up for your individuality regardless of outside pressure. During this period, your intuitive flashes can aid your success. This can also be a very creative time in general.

TIMES OF URANUS BENEFICIAL TO YOUR SUN IN ARIES: This is a time when you may experience a strong drive for personal freedom or you may wish to experiment or go in a new direction. Friendships and group efforts may be emphasized now and you are likely to gain by being original or inventive.

TIMES OF URANUS BENEFICIAL TO YOUR SUN IN TAURUS: This is a time when you are more likely to break away from your usual routine and dare to be different. Although material security is important to you, by opening your mind and self-expression to the new and unknown, you can enhance the quality of your life and feel freer.

TIMES OF URANUS BENEFICIAL TO YOUR SUN IN GEMINI: Although you are usually quick and alert to current ideas, at this time you are more open to being experimental. During this period you may also be drawn to people who are interesting but unconventional. Always keen on learning, this is also a good time to mentally explore subjects such as astrology, psychology, or things of an alternative nature.

TIMES OF URANUS BENEFICIAL TO YOUR SUN IN CANCER: Although you love the comforts and security of home, during this period you may be more interested in exploring new and different ways of developing your self-expression. In the past your sensitivity may have sometimes held you back, but this influence allows you to be more free and open-minded. Your

intuition will be heightened during this period, and you can use it to your advantage.

TIMES OF URANUS BENEFICIAL TO YOUR SUN IN LEO: This is a period in your life when you are likely to have more creative ideas and particularly gain through teamwork or group efforts. Although you usually have a strong sense of self, this period can help you become more objective about the effect you have on those around you.

TIMES OF URANUS BENEFICIAL TO YOUR SUN IN VIRGO: At this time you can add to your practical resourcefulness with new and inventive ideas. Alternatively, you can improve your talent for business. Although normally analytical, you are likely to be more in tune with people's motivation, improving your powers of discrimination. You may now develop a new or greater interest in alternative health or unusual subjects.

TIMES OF URANUS BENEFICIAL TO YOUR SUN IN LIBRA: During this time you can improve your insight into human relationships. You are likely to add more impartiality to your natural diplomacy and sense of fair play, thereby developing greater equilibrium. You may be more interested in a new image or studying alternative subjects such as yoga, Pilates, healing, or aroma therapy. New people will enter your social life and increase your self-awareness.

TIMES OF URANUS BENEFICIAL TO YOUR SUN IN SCORPIO: At this time you can develop a strong determination to make changes. Alternatively, something out of the blue can capture your imagination and inspire you to take a new direction. You may have new ideas or experiences and meet new people. Your powerful emotions can now be tempered by taking a more unbiased and dispassionate attitude.

TIMES OF URANUS BENEFICIAL TO YOUR SUN IN SAGITTARIUS: Although you usually have a wide perspective, at this time you are likely to be more objective in the way you think. You will be more inspired or enthused by new and original ideas or opportunities may be presented to you unexpectedly.

TIMES OF URANUS BENEFICIAL TO YOUR SUN IN CAPRICORN: Your normal practical outlook is likely to be expanded at this time to include more radical or alternative views. You may be exposed to original ideas or something outside your usual belief system that proves beneficial for you.

TIMES OF URANUS BENEFICIAL TO YOUR SUN IN AQUARIUS: During this period you may find it easier to present your ideas to others, even though they may be progressive or unconventional. This period also provides you with a greater store of new ideas for problem solving and benefits can come from friends and group situations.

TIMES OF URANUS BENEFICIAL TO YOUR SUN IN PISCES: This influence can strengthen your natural intuition and provide you with sudden flashes of inspiration. This can help guide you in your personal life or career. This may also be a time when you may develop an interest in alternative matters such as meditation, astrology, yoga, dreams, or unusual subjects.

Times of Neptune Beneficial

This is a very idealistic time, and during this period, you may realize that you want more out of life. Therefore, you may be concerned more with your inner world or spiritual development. If in the past you had ideals or dreams that you never fulfilled or pursued, they may reemerge now, reminding you of what was important to you. As your approach to life changes, so will your priorities. More idealistic than before, your compassion toward others is likely to increase. You are more likely to be sympathetic, tolerant, and hopeful about people or situations and therefore less critical about your environment. During this period your sensitivity and receptivity will work well together, as will your self-expression and imagination. Although you are able to visualize your needs clearly, you will still have to actualize them by being determined and hardworking. During this period you may feel more optimistic about the future and therefore less worried or anxious. If this period does not inspire you to do something worthwhile, however, you can waste this time on daydreaming and wishful thinking. During this period you may also meet a person who will inspire you spiritually or who can match your vision and ideals.

TIMES OF NEPTUNE BENEFICIAL TO YOUR SUN IN ARIES: During this period you are likely to want to do only those things that interest or inspire you. If you do not believe in what you are doing, you can lose interest. During this period your vision and actions can work well together to bring you success.

TIMES OF NEPTUNE BENEFICIAL TO YOUR SUN IN TAURUS: During this period you are likely to feel more refined, romantic, or sensitive to art and music. Being more imaginative, you can be aware of your creative abilities. You may become involved in work that demands your artistic and writing skills or you may show a willingness to support others. Alternatively, your practical skills can work well with your vision during this time to create better financial opportunities.

TIMES OF NEPTUNE BENEFICIAL TO YOUR SUN IN GEMINI: During this period you will be able to communicate and relate to others on a more idealistic level. You may join groups in the pursuit of knowledge or meet people who share your ideals. Your sensitivity and understanding work well together and therefore you can pick up the subtle messages that other people are sending.

TIMES OF NEPTUNE BENEFICIAL TO YOUR SUN IN CANCER: Your receptivity and sensitivity during this period are heightened; therefore you should learn to trust your gut feelings. You can also feel sentimental, compassionate, and romantic. During this period you are willing to do selfless things in order to support those you love.

TIMES OF NEPTUNE BENEFICIAL TO YOUR SUN IN LEO: During this period you are likely to be more creative and imaginative. You may be inspired to travel or follow your dreams and aspirations. You may be inclined to express yourself in a subtler manner.

TIMES OF NEPTUNE BENEFICIAL TO YOUR SUN IN VIRGO: During this period your intuition may be stimulated and you will be more inclined to accept visionary ideas. You may be more inclined to pursue work or projects that involve helping others. During this period you are likely to trust your intuition more readily.

TIMES OF NEPTUNE BENEFICIAL TO YOUR SUN IN LIBRA: During this period you may be more receptive to others. You may feel more sensitive, imaginative, or creative. You may also meet people who share your ideals and vision. Alternatively, you may be inspired by new ideas, spirituality, or travel.

TIMES OF NEPTUNE BENEFICIAL TO YOUR SUN IN SCORPIO: Your willpower and sensitivity operate well during this period, therefore you can be subtly persuasive. You may deal with unusual issues now or you may uncover something that was hidden. Your hunches are usually very accurate during this time. You can also feel compassionate and romantic. During this period you may be willing to make selfless acts in order to support those you love.

TIMES OF NEPTUNE BENEFICIAL TO YOUR SUN IN SAGITTARIUS: During this period you may feel altruistic, romantic, and creative. You may yearn to travel to foreign places or be inspired to do something unusual. Your idealism and optimism are high during this period and you can attract opportunities. You may, however, need to resist being too speculative or indulgent.

TIMES OF NEPTUNE BENEFICIAL TO YOUR SUN IN CAPRICORN: Your sense of vision and pragmatic approach can work well together during this period. You may be inspired to follow your dreams and attempt to make them a reality rather than sticking to secure or rigid routines.

TIMES OF NEPTUNE BENEFICIAL TO YOUR SUN IN AQUARIUS: During this period you will be inclined to seek people who can inspire you. You may experience subtle emotions or become more sensitive to others. Alternatively, you may join a new group of people who share your visions and beliefs.

TIMES OF NEPTUNE BENEFICIAL TO YOUR SUN IN PISCES: You are even more receptive and sensitive during this period, your psychic abilities are enhanced, and you feel relaxed in the knowledge that you are able to pick up the subtle energies of different situations. You are in an idealistic and imaginative period and as long as you express yourself well you can be creative and productive.

Times of Pluto Beneficial

This is a time for progress and personal growth, especially if you look for opportunities to empower yourself and advance. In your work, you may have chances to change and reform

current projects and plans or be offered more power to influence others. You are also able, during this period, to be more effective if you work within a group to bring about change. Alternatively, you may go through one-on-one therapy and experience a powerful internal transformation. Equally, you could decide to transform yourself through a creative health program that involves exercise and losing weight. During this period you can meet people who can have long-lasting effects on your life. This can also be a time when you want to make definite headway in whatever you do, whether it is transforming your house and garden or using your work to make a strong statement of your beliefs. This is not a time for just fantasizing; Pluto's power can take you to a different level of achievement now if you decide to adopt an all-or-nothing approach.

TIMES OF PLUTO BENEFICIAL TO YOUR SUN IN ARIES: Now is a time to make new plans to transform old situations or bring improvements to previous systems. Once you have a definite course of action in mind, you can work passionately and energetically toward your goals.

TIMES OF PLUTO BENEFICIAL TO YOUR SUN IN TAURUS: Although you often prefer a comfortable routine, you will have more energy at this time to make positive changes in your life. Feeling more confident about yourself and your prospects, you are likely to have more drive to take on challenges and use them to your advantage.

TIMES OF PLUTO BENEFICIAL TO YOUR SUN IN GEMINI: Your energy to create change in your life is heightened by this influence. With your quick mind you will be better at problem solving as you become more focused and intense in your mental concentration. During this period you will be introduced to ideas or people who can have a strong impact on you.

TIMES OF PLUTO BENEFICIAL TO YOUR SUN IN CANCER: You are able to face more difficult situations during this time as you learn to express your feelings with increased power. Over this period you will be inclined to take on daring challenges or be more in touch with your deeper feelings. This can be a therapeutic influence or you may just want to use Pluto's energy to make changes around your home.

TIMES OF PLUTO BENEFICIAL TO YOUR SUN IN LEO: Even though you are normally strong-willed, during this period you can become more focused and determined to create positive change in your life. The influences you experience during this time can cause you to delve deeply into finding out about yourself. Alternatively, you may wish to investigate some area of study or express yourself more powerfully.

TIMES OF PLUTO BENEFICIAL TO YOUR SUN IN VIRGO: During this period you can increase your confidence and determination by taking on positive challenges and sticking with them until you have reached your goals. Your levels of intensity, focus, and personal power are likely to increase, bringing an end to outmoded viewpoints or ways of doing things.

TIMES OF PLUTO BENEFICIAL TO YOUR SUN IN LIBRA: During this period your relationships will have more meaning or become more dynamic. Other people will be drawn to your charm and vitality. You may begin new and meaningful relationships or strengthen old friendships. Your creativity and aesthetic sense may be reinforced.

TIMES OF PLUTO BENEFICIAL TO YOUR SUN IN SCORPIO: During this period your vitality and energy will increase. You will be able to achieve your objectives with more determination. Secure in the knowledge that you are doing the right thing, you can make changes or empower yourself as long you go with the flow and let events take place naturally.

TIMES OF PLUTO BENEFICIAL TO YOUR SUN IN SAGITTARIUS: During this period you will be able to expand your horizons and enjoy many new opportunities. This will be a good period to explore new ideas or pioneer new enterprises. Alternatively, you may want to express your creativity in different ways. Whatever you undertake now is likely to succeed if you stay focused and determined.

TIMES OF PLUTO BENEFICIAL TO YOUR SUN IN CAPRICORN: Your achievements during this period may bring financial success or a promotion at work. If you decide to change your career, you will find it easier to start something new and beneficial.

TIMES OF PLUTO BENEFICIAL TO YOUR SUN IN AQUARIUS: No matter how progressive and far-reaching your ideas or inventions, during this period they will be more readily accepted by others. Alternatively, you may meet new people or improve your social circle. If you decide to study, you will be able to learn new subjects with ease or refine your communication skills.

TIMES OF PLUTO BENEFICIAL TO YOUR SUN IN PISCES: During this period you will be able to utilize your imagination and drive to manifest some of your far-reaching goals. You will be able to leave behind aspects of your life that are no longer valid or useful in order to start afresh.

Challenging Times

Times of Jupiter Challenging

During this period you need to remain sensible yet open to new ideas or options. This can be a period for growth and new opportunities if you push your boundaries or attempt to do more with your life. Realizing that you have different alternatives will certainly encourage you to feel more optimistic and confident. In order to expand, however, you need to have a clear vision of where you want to go or what you want to do. As you are likely to be restless, you may want to do many things. If you attempt to do too much, you may scatter your energies or miss good chances. Rather than just get carried

away with ideas, you will be better off if you act cautiously and plan your moves; otherwise your optimism may turn to wishful thinking. Good timing and exercising a certain amount of restraint is essential during this period. Knowing when to move forward and when to pause will help you to recognize your limitations. If you rush into things without being prepared, your plans may hit obstacles or delays. Although your increased confidence will help you to progress, you need to avoid being arrogant or boastful. If you act in an overbearing manner during this period, others will resent your behavior and attempt to block your advance. Use common sense during this expansive period to avoid overindulgence.

TIMES OF JUPITER CHALLENGING TO YOUR SUN IN ARIES: During this period your assertiveness increases. Feeling energetic, you can be active and purposeful. Although you want to advance, you need to guard against being overly enthusiastic. If you are not careful, you may push yourself too far or work too hard, Being impatient or confrontational can undermine your success, therefore you need to stay composed and whenever possible compromise.

TIMES OF JUPITER CHALLENGING TO YOUR SUN IN TAURUS: Although during this period you may feel generous toward loved ones, you need to guard against stretching your resources to their limits. As you feel enterprising, resist making spontaneous investments that are costly or unnecessary. If you do not feel purposeful or productive, you may become more sociable yet self-indulgent.

TIMES OF JUPITER CHALLENGING TO YOUR SUN IN GEMINI: During this period you are likely to be more active mentally. You can increase your knowledge and improve your communication skills. Although you want to broaden your horizons or expand your ideas and interests, you need to remain focused and pay attention to the details. Resist being negligent, indiscreet, or arrogant. It is also important to listen carefully to what other people are saying as they may point out issues that you have not taken into consideration.

TIMES OF JUPITER CHALLENGING TO YOUR SUN IN CANCER: Matters relating to your relationships with others may be highlighted during this period. Guard against exaggerating or being self-righteous. Nevertheless, you are likely to feel more compassionate toward those less fortunate than you. Opportunities to further your career or meet new people may inspire you to be more adventurous. You may want to have more personal freedom, but you should give others the same amount.

TIMES OF JUPITER CHALLENGING TO YOUR SUN IN LEO: During this period your confidence will increase. Feeling good about yourself, you may be tempted to overindulge or be extravagant. If you act in an arrogant manner, you may upset other people. Others will praise your good qualities, however, if you express your kindness and generosity. This is a good time to expand your horizons as long as you apply common sense.

TIMES OF JUPITER CHALLENGING TO YOUR SUN IN VIRGO: During this period your need for freedom may challenge your otherwise dutiful nature. Alternatively, you may feel more ambitious about your achievements or work. Your urge to learn may also inspire you to take on new challenges. Although you are analytical, methodical, and organized, during this period you should resist being judgmental.

TIMES OF JUPITER CHALLENGING TO YOUR SUN IN LIBRA: During this period your relationships with others will do better if they are based on mutual give-and-take. If you form a new relationship during this time, take it slow. You may be concerned with personal progress or establishing your security right now, so you need to stay balanced and resist the temptation to overindulge.

TIMES OF JUPITER CHALLENGING TO YOUR SUN IN SCORPIO: During this period you will probably feel more determined and industrious. Although you will want to make progress or changes, guard against forcing issues to the extent that they will cause resentment or opposition. Your enthusiasm for expansion needs to be accompanied by discrimination and cautiousness if you do not want to get entangled in difficulties.

TIMES OF JUPITER CHALLENGING TO YOUR SUN IN SAGITTARIUS: During this period you will have new opportunities. However, if you do not exercise discrimination, you will take on too much, by being overly optimistic. If you behave in an excessive manner, you will have to pay for it later. Focusing on fewer projects or making cautious decisions will help you to avoid stretching your resources or making commitments that you cannot fulfill.

TIMES OF JUPITER CHALLENGING TO YOUR SUN IN CAPRICORN: During this period you will need to make some changes if you want to make progress. This can be at times rather frustrating, but in the long run very useful. You need to determine which areas in your life need improvement and which are unproductive or too demanding. Wavering between optimism and pragmatism, you need to avoid being swayed one way or the other.

TIMES OF JUPITER CHALLENGING TO YOUR SUN IN AQUARIUS: New opportunities and sudden changes can make this period exciting yet unsettled. Although you may be inclined to act impulsively, you will do better if you remain relaxed and unruffled. You may resent being restricted, but an overemphasis on freedom and change now may allow you a certain amount of independence for a short time but not in the long run.

TIMES OF JUPITER CHALLENGING TO YOUR SUN IN PISCES: Although you may feel more idealistic and generous than usual, you need to resist taking on other people's problems or scattering your energies. By staying realistic in your expectations or by being discriminating, you can find true fulfillment rather than being disappointed by false hopes.

Times of Saturn Challenging

This is a time when you may be tested in order to make yourself stronger and more self-reliant. Although delays and obstacles may seem to try your patience, it is important that you persevere at this time and become more determined to succeed. Great successes are not usually obtained without some trials along the way, and this period serves to strengthen your resolve. You may now be experiencing challenges with authority figures such as your father or government officials. If you are in a bad relationship this influence can cause you to cut your losses and move on. Saturn's influence over the bones and teeth can even have you making trips to the dentist. Since during this time your energy level may be lower than usual, it is important to look after your health. You may find yourself working extra hard, but Saturn ensures that all the effort you put in is repaid in the future. Equally, as Saturn rules the law of cause and effect, you may now be paying back any loans, whether financial or emotional. By realizing that this is only a temporary period, you can stay positive and focused on your future goals, rather than dwelling in disappointment or frustration. Often the decisions you make at this time are affected by limitation. In retrospect you will realize that by cutting down your options and clarifying your real needs, you have improved your situation in the long term.

TIMES OF SATURN CHALLENGING TO YOUR SUN IN ARIES: As you like to take life at a fast pace, it can be hard if this Saturn influence slows you down and forces you to be patient. Any blocks or limitations you encounter at this time will help you define your exact goals more clearly. Channel any possible frustration in your life by taking positive action.

TIMES OF SATURN CHALLENGING TO YOUR SUN IN TAURUS: The tests you encounter during this period may affect your sense of security or your finances. If you have any outstanding debts, material or emotional, you may now have to face your responsibilities. If you have been extravagant, you may now have to restructure your life. It is good to clarify your position and use the challenges during this period for simplifying your life and positive growth.

TIMES OF SATURN CHALLENGING TO YOUR SUN IN GEMINI: Although you usually like to keep life fairly light, at this time you may have extra work or responsibilities. This may affect your usually good communication skills, so remember to keep your sharp mind positively focused. During this period it is important to endure rather than give up.

TIMES OF SATURN CHALLENGING TO YOUR SUN IN CANCER: Now is a time when outside forces may cause you to feel more vulnerable, defensive, or oversensitive. By persevering and building strong boundaries or clearing emotional issues or misunderstandings with others, this period can make you stronger and more self-reliant.

TIMES OF SATURN CHALLENGING TO YOUR SUN IN LEO: During this time you may experience doubts and not be as confident as usual. Alternatively, you may have extra responsibilities or be working very hard. The challenge you face during this period is not to shut down your normal warm and spirited personality but to build strength and persevere toward long-term goals.

TIMES OF SATURN CHALLENGING TO YOUR SUN IN VIRGO: There may be an emphasis on duty or responsibility during this period but it is important for you to persevere. Overcoming adversity now can help you eliminate all that is unnecessary in your life. Avoid anxiety and look after your health.

TIMES OF SATURN CHALLENGING TO YOUR SUN IN LIBRA: During this period you may have to overcome opposition or feelings of discouragement. If you are experiencing challenges or delays, you may need to endure and be patient. You may have extra responsibilities or feel restricted by others. Balancing your needs can help you put everything in perspective.

TIMES OF SATURN CHALLENGING TO YOUR SUN IN SCORPIO: During this period you may need to develop patience and perseverance if things do not move as fast as you would like. Avoid power struggles during this period. You may have to work a bit harder now to achieve your goals or be more disciplined, but by the time this period ends you should have built up your stamina.

TIMES OF SATURN CHALLENGING TO YOUR SUN IN SAGITTARIUS: As you usually value your freedom, this period may be difficult if Saturn brings limitations or responsibilities. You may be torn between optimism or the desire to expand, and demands to fulfill your duties. Through patience and perseverance you can build better opportunities in the future.

TIMES OF SATURN CHALLENGING TO YOUR SUN IN CAPRICORN: As you already tend to take life seriously, during this period remember to keep a positive philosophy. Your determination to succeed despite all obstacles can bring you courage, strength of purpose, and greater success in the future. Resist being stubborn or too materialistic.

TIMES OF SATURN CHALLENGING TO YOUR SUN IN AQUARIUS: Although you usually have a detached approach to life, during this period you may experience challenges to your objectivity. People may oppose your plans or you can experience some delays. Nevertheless, this can be a good time for self-awareness that can bring you future success through learning, dedication, and patience.

TIMES OF SATURN CHALLENGING TO YOUR SUN IN PISCES: Outside challenges may seem to bring you delays or cause you emotional ups and downs now. By persevering and standing on your own two feet, you can strengthen your resolve and build up your self-esteem. Keep a positive attitude even if you feel despondent about your current situation as good things can ultimately come from these limitations.

As this period signifies change and unexpected events, you need to exercise caution and detachment. Some of the changes that you will encounter now are related to outside influences and others will be occurring internally. Some events may test your wits and ability to maintain your objectivity; therefore you will gain from adjusting to new circumstances during this period. Whatever you have done in the past may no longer be useful or workable. You may need to rethink what it is that you truly want to do next. Although you may want a greater amount of freedom, resist rebelling against others or upsetting people by making irresponsible or unpredictable moves. If you are holding on to situations out of fear, you will be forced to adjust to new circumstances. During this period it is always wise to examine your lifestyle and make the necessary changes in order to lead a healthier life. During this time, your ego or individuality may be tested by outside influences. If you are true to yourself, you will be able to withstand the challenges you are facing. If you are doubtful about your identity you will want to reinvent yourself.

TIMES OF URANUS CHALLENGING TO YOUR SUN IN ARIES: During this period you may become more self-willed or impulsive. In your desire for greater freedom guard against appearing bad tempered or impatient. Do not make hasty decisions as you may regret them later. Since you are more inclined to take risks, you need to be sure you are making the right moves. Entering into conflicts or disputes with others is not wise during this period as they can create more tension. This period can teach you to be cautious, patient, and discriminative.

TIMES OF URANUS CHALLENGING TO YOUR SUN IN TAURUS: During this period it is wiser to be flexible and less rigid or stubborn. You can lose more by being possessive. Your values may change and your priorities may alter. What was important to you in the past is not so important to you now. By discarding the nonessential items in your life, you can free yourself from burdensome situations.

TIMES OF URANUS CHALLENGING TO YOUR SUN IN GEMINI: This can be a very interesting yet unpredictable period if you are dealing with the unknown. During this period the more adaptable you are the less tense you will feel. Although you can learn a great deal, take time to assimilate all the information. By not rushing into situations too quickly, you can avoid making mistakes.

TIMES OF URANUS CHALLENGING TO YOUR SUN IN CANCER: During this period you may feel emotionally restless. Your relationships with other family members may suddenly become unsettled or different. Past tensions can come to the surface. You may want to change your residence or other family members may decide to leave. By staying emotionally detached you will be able to face any new circumstances.

TIMES OF URANUS CHALLENGING TO YOUR SUN IN LEO: During this period you are likely to want more personal freedom. If you act in a selfish or stubborn manner, you will only encounter opposition from others. During this period, however, you can be more daring and show your individuality.

TIMES OF URANUS CHALLENGING TO YOUR SUN IN VIRGO: If you are unwilling to accept the changes that occur during this period you may feel unsettled. Although you can learn a great deal of new information during this period, you need to take time to assimilate it. By not rushing into situations or jumping to conclusions too quickly, you can avoid making wrong judgments.

TIMES OF URANUS CHALLENGING TO YOUR SUN IN LIBRA: During this period you are likely to meet new people who will change your views or lifestyle. Since this period is one of change and transformation, your new relationships, while they may not necessarily be long lasting, will be essential for letting you see how different people live and express themselves.

TIMES OF URANUS CHALLENGING TO YOUR SUN IN SCORPIO: Although during this period you are able to make sweeping changes, you may not feel in control of your current situation. Your relationships with others may also alter during this period. Your financial circumstances may suddenly change. Although you may be involved with people who hold progressive views, resist being too radical.

TIMES OF URANUS CHALLENGING TO YOUR SUN IN SAGITTARIUS: During this period you may feel restless or unsettled. Although this period offers many opportunities for change and situations can alter suddenly, you benefit from being cautious and adaptable.

TIMES OF URANUS CHALLENGING TO YOUR SUN IN CAPRICORN: Although you usually feel dutiful and loyal, during this period you will be more concerned with freeing yourself from restrictions. If you feel restricted by others, you will want to separate from those to whom you no longer feel obligated. Alternatively, new situations or circumstances that may be forced upon you can alter your life in some way.

TIMES OF URANUS CHALLENGING TO YOUR SUN IN AQUARIUS: Although you may feel restless or unsettled by a situation outside your control, try to resist being rebellious or stubborn. During this period you may be able to free yourself from restrictions that you think are holding you back. Alternatively, your circumstances may suddenly change, allowing you to make a real breakthrough.

TIMES OF URANUS CHALLENGING TO YOUR SUN IN PISCES: During this period you may encounter situations that will force you to change your beliefs or ideals. You may experience unusual or extraordinary occurrences that will allow you to free your imagination or enhance your second insight. During this period you may meet or be drawn to an unusual person who will influence the way you look at life or yourself.

Times of Neptune Challenging

This is a time when you may experience a desire to change your direction or express yourself in different ways. During this period you may take on projects that do not always suit you or deal with people who do not really understand you. This can bring uncertainty into your life, so it is vital to stand true to yourself. It is also important to keep active now and not try to escape if things do not work out as planned. Don't be too hard on yourself, as your energy level may not be as high as when you are driven with enthusiasm. It may seem at times as though things are collapsing, but you cannot see the big picture yet. Remember that, in some sense, you may be walking through a period of uncertainty in your journey of life and it will not last forever. Avoid feeling sorry for yourself; this is an excellent time for searching for solutions. If you project your expectations onto others at this time, you may be disappointed if they do not act out the part you planned for them. Make sure the new people in your life are sincere and trustworthy. Avoid speculative ventures and an inclination to escape through drugs or alcohol. Your life decisions will become much clearer when this influence passes.

TIMES OF NEPTUNE CHALLENGING TO YOUR SUN IN ARIES: During this period your need for action could be compromised by confusion regarding your goals or sense of direction. You are also likely to become more impressionable to outside influences, so stay realistic and focused.

TIMES OF NEPTUNE CHALLENGING TO YOUR SUN IN TAURUS: Being pragmatic, you may find this period of confusion or uncertainty difficult as you like to know exactly where you stand in life. Avoid putting people on pedestals or deluding yourself during this time. Nevertheless, you can become more sensitive and emotionally aware during this period.

TIMES OF NEPTUNE CHALLENGING TO YOUR SUN IN GEMINI: Although you usually rely on your quick mental perceptions, you may now find that you experience some confusion in your communication or goals. You may find it difficult to understand the circumstances you are in or become too impressionable to the thoughts of others. Keep clear boundaries to protect yourself from unhelpful outside influences. Nevertheless, by staying honest and true to yourself, you can avoid confusion or misunderstandings.

TIMES OF NEPTUNE CHALLENGING TO YOUR SUN IN CANCER: You are usually emotionally impressionable, and at this time your sensitivity increases even more. To make sure that you do not take on too many of other people's problems, you need to be clear about where you stand. As your intuition will be heightened during this period, trust your sixth sense.

TIMES OF NEPTUNE CHALLENGING TO YOUR SUN IN LEO: Although during this period your sensitivity and idealism are increased, you may experience some uncertainty. Being a romantic, you may have to be careful that you do not delude yourself in affairs of the heart. Alternatively, be careful of speculative ventures. Dramatic and expressive, stay realistic when looking for new ways to express yourself.

TIMES OF NEPTUNE CHALLENGING TO YOUR SUN IN VIRGO: Your practical and analytical skills are tested during this period. By staying realistic or focusing on your ability to help others, you can avoid deluding yourself during this time. Your sensitivity and intuitive abilities, however, are heightened, so you should listen to your inner voice.

TIMES OF NEPTUNE CHALLENGING TO YOUR SUN IN LIBRA: During this period you are likely to be impressionable or experience uncertainty, especially with regard to relationships. Be careful of self-deception at this time as you may be more inclined to project your expectations onto others. Your creative senses may inspire you to express yourself in new and unusual ways.

TIMES OF NEPTUNE CHALLENGING TO YOUR SUN IN SCORPIO: As there may be some confusion during this period, you may have to be more aware of taking risks. Although your usual sensitivity and impressionability is enhanced, be careful to protect yourself from being oversensitive. By being discriminating and conscious of secrets, you can avoid any deception.

TIMES OF NEPTUNE CHALLENGING TO YOUR SUN IN SAGITTARIUS: At this time you need to avoid being too idealistic. As you are usually honest, you can be aware if you start to delude yourself during this period. By being discriminating with yourself and others you can make big yet realistic plans.

TIMES OF NEPTUNE CHALLENGING TO YOUR SUN IN CAPRICORN: As you prefer to be realistic and know precisely where you are, you can use this period to establish new priorities for yourself. Be careful of deception during this time, either from others or by fooling yourself.

TIMES OF NEPTUNE CHALLENGING TO YOUR SUN IN AQUARIUS: Although you are normally good at taking an impartial view of life, during this period you may find it harder to stay objective. During this period, you may be drawn to unusual people or have some extraordinary experiences.

TIMES OF NEPTUNE CHALLENGING TO YOUR SUN IN PISCES: During this period you need to be discriminating, but stay true to yourself to avoid possible confusion. This may involve making tricky decisions to let go of the past, but don't give things up due to discouragement. This is an excellent time to challenge yourself and creatively harness your imagination.

Times of Pluto Challenging

During this period you may experience a powerful yet subtle transformation that enables you to face the challenge of difficult situations. It is important to stay detached and not give your power away to people or circumstances, even though issues may become quite intense. You are learning to empower

yourself by adopting a new outlook on changing conditions around you. This can also be a time for letting go of the past and being born anew. There can be power factors involved at this time and you may be challenged to react in an extreme way. One of your lessons may be to judge whether or not to rise to a challenge. Now is not the time to support a cause that is not worth fighting for. Equally, as other people may project their power issues onto you, avoid being a scapegoat for others' negativity. These scenarios may happen at work or with people in authority. It is important to stay impartial and stand up for yourself. This period is one when you have to remember to keep your sense of humor no matter how surreal your life situations become. This is also a time that can accent healing and forgiveness. You often cannot control the circumstances that bring about these changes, but you can control your attitude toward them. In retrospect you will realize that this has been a valuable learning period for you that involves understanding your personal power.

TIMES OF PLUTO CHALLENGING TO YOUR SUN IN ARIES: During this period life may become more intense. There is a positive opportunity for change now, though you may not always like the form in which it is presented. You may experience power struggles that will force you to stand up for yourself.

TIMES OF PLUTO CHALLENGING TO YOUR SUN IN TAURUS: During this time you may experience challenges with regard to power that can test your personal strength. Although you do not usually enjoy change, you can use the transforming energy of this period for building new opportunities for growth.

TIMES OF PLUTO CHALLENGING TO YOUR SUN IN GEMINI: During this period transformation is likely to take place in your life. Whether you transform your home, career, or yourself, you will want to make changes. You may encounter power struggles during this time, but try to use these challenges as opportunities to learn. A need for clear and calm communication is emphasized now.

TIMES OF PLUTO CHALLENGING TO YOUR SUN IN CANCER: During this period you can experience some transformations. With your tendency to hang on to the past this period will challenge you to let go, transform, and move on. By handling these energies well, you can improve your self-knowledge and personal power.

TIMES OF PLUTO CHALLENGING TO YOUR SUN IN LEO: During this period you will be challenged with regard to your self-identity and your beliefs. As a natural leader you may encounter power struggles at work or in your personal life. How you face these can be a test of your self-control. Often this is a time when you have to take an all-or-nothing stance yet not become ruthless. The transformation that comes from this testing time can bring you positive opportunities and a greater ability to handle power.

TIMES OF PLUTO CHALLENGING TO YOUR SUN IN VIRGO: During this period you will experience changes that often mean ending one period in your life and beginning another. Although this can be an intense time, your attitude to these changes is a vital key to how they affect your life. Resist over-analyzing events by using your natural, practical skills to create new beginnings or transform old situations that are not working.

TIMES OF PLUTO CHALLENGING TO YOUR SUN IN LIBRA: During this period you will be able to reevaluate yourself and your relationships with others. If circumstances change, you will have to adapt to new situations. By staying detached you will be able to let go of the past, where you feel you are wasting emotional energy. By letting go of difficult relationships during this period you will make room for new ones. If you learn from the experiences you encounter, you will come out of this period a great deal wiser.

TIMES OF PLUTO CHALLENGING TO YOUR SUN IN SCORPIO: During this period you will be able to symbolically go through a death and rebirth situation. If you try to force your will on others you may encounter opposition. By calmly accepting the situations you are facing and concentrating on the future, you will reap great benefit from the changes that are taking place. Resist any involvement in power struggles.

TIMES OF PLUTO CHALLENGING TO YOUR SUN IN SAGITTARIUS: During this period you will be very determined to achieve your objectives. You will, however, need to resist being overly optimistic about what you can accomplish. You may also need to pay more attention to details or evaluate your methods of doing things. By being more liberal and less extreme with your opinions, you will be able to make real headway.

TIMES OF PLUTO CHALLENGING TO YOUR SUN IN CAPRICORN: Although you are often keen on establishing solid structures, during this period you will be facing changes that indicate a new chapter in your life. The more flexible and accepting you are the less difficult the process will be. Although you will feel on occasion that you are pressured, there is always a solution if you are willing to compromise.

TIMES OF PLUTO CHALLENGING TO YOUR SUN IN AQUARIUS: During this period you will experience transformation in your life. You may, however, need to guard against being too radical. Although these changes can alter your routine, they can also free you from restriction. After this period is over you may realize that you have been liberated in many ways.

TIMES OF PLUTO CHALLENGING TO YOUR SUN IN PISCES: During this period you will feel challenged by your ideals and beliefs. If in the past you let situations linger on and did nothing about them, now is the time to take action and stand for what you truly believe in. As some of the changes that are taking place now are inevitable, you can intuitively feel them and work with them. This is not a good time to be overly sentimental or feel regretful.

Times of Jupiter Special

During this period you are likely to be full of ideas and more confident than usual. With a chance for a lucky break, this can be a good time for concentrating on your ambitions and future plans. Opportunities are likely to be available now and it is best to make the most of them while they are there, although be careful of pushing your luck too far. You may wish to expand your knowledge or financial interests now and find yourself taking extra courses or becoming involved in new projects. Be careful, however, of not scattering your energies in too many directions or taking on more than you can handle. Equally, do not just sit back and let the opportunities afforded during this period pass you by. Sometimes the desire to expand and experience a broader perspective results in travel; alternatively, you may stay at home and make positive plans instead. People are more likely to help you now and you can feel more generous yourself. Incidentally, be careful of putting on weight during this expansive time.

TIMES OF JUPITER SPECIAL TO YOUR SUN IN ARIES: During this time your opportunities for beginning new ventures are likely to increase. Your creative and enterprising spirit can be stimulated now but be careful of becoming restless. You may also wish to increase your spiritual, social, or educational resources now.

TIMES OF JUPITER SPECIAL TO YOUR SUN IN TAURUS: During this period you can increase your resources. You can meet people who can have a positive influence on your life or you may wish to expand on your plans for the future. Even though this is a positive influence be careful of overindulgence if you relax and treat yourself too much.

TIMES OF JUPITER SPECIAL TO YOUR SUN IN GEMINI: During this period you are likely to increase your associations with people for the purpose of learning. This is an excellent time to take up new courses or learn new skills. You may also feel that you need to expand your social contacts, and may make new friends in your neighborhood who will be lucky for you.

TIMES OF JUPITER SPECIAL TO YOUR SUN IN CANCER: Now is the time to make positive plans for the future. You may wish to expand and organize your home in some way or be generous to family members. As you may feel optimistic, take advantage of any new opportunities.

TIMES OF JUPITER SPECIAL TO YOUR SUN IN LEO: During this period you are likely to feel more confident and be willing to take risks. You may wish to go for a promotion or you may decide to make positive changes in your personal life. Now is a good time for making new contacts that can help advance or improve your circumstances. You may wish to expand your horizons through travel or by planning for the future. However, be careful of extravagance.

TIMES OF JUPITER SPECIAL TO YOUR SUN IN VIRGO: Without losing your practical realism, this is a period when you may wish to take more chances to expand your opportunities. You will feel more optimistic about the future and may decide to be charitable to others. This is a time for writing down your positive plans for the future. Since your ability to see the big picture is heightened at this time, you can feel much more positive, but be careful of taking on too much.

TIMES OF JUPITER SPECIAL TO YOUR SUN IN LIBRA: As you are feeling sociable and friendly, this can be an excellent time for growth in your relationships. You are likely to meet people who can be of benefit to you. New friendships formed during this period can bring you prosperity. Feeling more generous toward others, you can sort out any problems with your positive attitude. You may, however, need to guard against overindulgence or taking life too leisurely. Your appreciation of beauty and your artistic interests are often enhanced during this period.

TIMES OF JUPITER SPECIAL TO YOUR SUN IN SCORPIO: More determined than ever to succeed, during this period you will do your utmost to make your mark. In your pursuit of power and success you can become single-minded. Although you are likely to achieve your objectives, forcing others to comply with your wishes can bring conflict. By being subtle and focusing on self-improvement, however, you are given a real opportunity to improve your life.

TIMES OF JUPITER SPECIAL TO YOUR SUN IN SAGITTARIUS: This is an important time for you. Although opportunities for expansion and progress are all within your grasp, be realistic and stay objective. However, avoid getting carried away with too many plans. By being selective you can make sure you are taking advantage of the right opportunities. People you meet now can inspire you spiritually or be fortunate for you. Opportunities for travel as well as expanding your knowledge need to be considered.

TIMES OF JUPITER SPECIAL TO YOUR SUN IN CAPRICORN: During this time you will be able to make progress if you overcome your reservations. If you feel restricted by duties and obligations this is a good time to review the situation and delegate responsibilities to others. In your eagerness to make progress be sure to plan your next move carefully. This is a good time to ask for a promotion or to invest in a business, if you have already done the necessary groundwork.

TIMES OF JUPITER SPECIAL TO YOUR SUN IN AQUARIUS: This is a time of opportunities and events can happen quite unexpectedly. A desire to expand your horizons may inspire you to take a break from your usual routine. If you have been waiting without much success for a project to take off, it is more likely to succeed during this period. You may be able to

travel quite unexpectedly. Stay optimistic but avoid taking unnecessary risks.

TIMES OF JUPITER SPECIAL TO YOUR SUN IN PISCES: As your receptivity is likely to increase during this period, you become more impressionable and open to others. Even though you may become more idealistic, resist living in a false reality. During this period your imagination can inspire you to be more creative and enterprising. You may want to explore mysticism, travel, or experience something spiritually rewarding.

Times of Saturn Special

During this period you may be more aware of your self-image. You will want to simplify your life by defining your goals and prioritizing your objectives. At this time you are likely to encounter obligations and have a more definite and serious outlook on your current situation. Although during your Saturn Special period you may encounter a few obstacles or delays, this is an excellent time to be purposeful and determined about your long-term plans. You may now obtain a promotion, but it is likely to involve extra work or duties. During this time you must resist overloading yourself since your energies may not be at full force. If you do not face up to your responsibilities and fears at this time, they may cause you to become worried or downhearted. Alternatively, you may meet someone who is older or more experienced who can give you useful advice or be a positive influence. During this period you may consolidate many of your practical issues, and achieve success through precision, concentration, and determination. This is a good time to reorganize your home and get rid of unecessary clutter.

TIMES OF SATURN SPECIAL TO YOUR SUN IN ARIES: During this period you are able to accomplish a great deal if you stay practical, disciplined, and determined. Avoid becoming irritable or frustrated by challenges. Do not waste your precious time or energy on trivial matters or become involved in power struggles. If you feel less energetic than usual or find yourself in restrictive situations, you need to persevere and be more focused.

TIMES OF SATURN SPECIAL TO YOUR SUN IN TAURUS: During this period you need to reevaluate yourself, your priorities, and your financial situation. By streamlining and simplifying your life, you can become more effective and therefore more productive. If in the past you indulged in an extravagant lifestyle, this is the time to minimize your expenses or be more cautious.

TIMES OF SATURN SPECIAL TO YOUR SUN IN GEMINI: Although during this period you are likely to view life more seriously, resist the temptation to be pessimistic in your outlook. If you take on a project during this time, your approach will be practical and often more focused and thorough. You may feel inhibited in your communication with others but what you say will have more impact. As you are likely to be more precise, guard against being critical with others, by positively defining your own position.

TIMES OF SATURN SPECIAL TO YOUR SUN IN CANCER: During this period you are likely to be more concerned with your security, family, and those you care for. If your attention is turned inward, you need to resist becoming more self-critical or self-doubting. Alternatively, you may find that other family members are now making more demands on your time and money.

TIMES OF SATURN SPECIAL TO YOUR SUN IN LEO: During this period you may be more aware of your image. Often proud and dignified, you can become more sensitive to criticism, especially if your self-esteem is low. You need to stay focused and build on your self-reliance and confidence. As your responsibilities may increase, resist taking on more than you can master.

TIMES OF SATURN SPECIAL TO YOUR SUN IN VIRGO: During this period you will be more concerned with your duties, and if you are not careful you will overload yourself with too many responsibilities. Seeking perfection, you need to resist being too exact or critical. This is a good time to study or undertake research. During this period, to gain more energy you may benefit from a positive health regime.

TIMES OF SATURN SPECIAL TO YOUR SUN IN LIBRA: During this period you are likely to be concentrating on achievement. This can bring hard work and extra responsibilities, but also successful completion and rewards for previous efforts. Although you may feel somewhat limited by this influence, you can now define what you want more clearly. Any areas that have not worked out previously, including relationships, can now be learned from, rebuilt, or left behind.

TIMES OF SATURN SPECIAL TO YOUR SUN IN SCORPIO: During this time you can experience challenges, but you can also overcome them. You are now likely to be very aware of your responsibilities at work and may have to exercise patience. Now is a time when you can be finalizing successful projects if you have worked hard in the past at achieving your goals. Alternatively, you may have to cut your losses and learn from your experiences. Your concentration can increase under this influence so if you focus on your positive goals now, you can achieve much.

TIMES OF SATURN SPECIAL TO YOUR SUN IN SAGITTARIUS: During this period you may need to create a balance between your desire to expand and demands to fulfill your responsibilities. By being patient and persevering, you can achieve better results. This is a time for work and staying focused on a few clearly defined goals rather than scattering your energies on too many projects.

TIMES OF SATURN SPECIAL TO YOUR SUN IN CAPRICORN: This is a good time to concentrate on your goals or lay foundations for long-term projects. During this period you may need to balance your serious outlook with a positive attitude. Your determination to succeed despite setbacks implies that you can achieve greater success by showing your resolve and sense of purpose.

TIMES OF SATURN SPECIAL TO YOUR SUN IN AQUARIUS: During this period you can restructure your life and set new goals for the future. As your sense of responsibility is likely to increase, you may be inclined to take on more commitments. Although you may encounter some obstacles, you will overcome them by being more flexible and patient.

TIMES OF SATURN SPECIAL TO YOUR SUN IN PISCES: During this period your sense of purpose is increased. By persevering and becoming self-reliant now you can strengthen your determination and build up your self-esteem. Although you may encounter some delays, do not be discouraged. By focusing on future goals, you can steadily work toward achieving your plans.

Times of Uranus Special

Your individuality or need for freedom will be unmistakable during this period. This is a good time to rethink your old ideas or find out about yourself. Unexpected events may also change the course of your life and the way you think. You are likely to have the opportunity to begin something new at this time and you may be inspired to step out of your usual routine. This may involve being daring enough to be yourself despite what others think. Alternatively, if you resist change and refuse to accept new circumstances or ways of looking at life, you may feel unsettled and restless. By staying detached and letting things settle before you commit yourself to new responsibilities, you can make the best of new opportunities that are available to you. During this period you can benefit from exploring unusual or alternative subjects. You may also be drawn to group activities or enjoy the company of unusual people.

TIMES OF URANUS SPECIAL TO YOUR SUN IN AQUARIUS: This special period is relevant until December 2003. During this period you will probably reevaluate your current situation in order to free yourself from past limitations. With the urge to feel freer, you may be inclined to seek more independence.

TIMES OF URANUS SPECIAL TO YOUR SUN IN PISCES: This special period begins in 2004 when Uranus enters your Sun sign and will remain there until 2010. During this period new ideas and flashes of creativity may inspire you. Unexpected events may cause you to change your direction or your goals. You may be more spontaneous and intuitive at this time.

TIMES OF URANUS SPECIAL TO YOUR SUN IN ARIES: This special period will begin in 2010 when Uranus enters your Sun sign. During this period you may be more aware of issues of freedom and the ability to fully express who you are. As this can also be a highly original influence, you can utilize this time to become more creative in your approach to life and build up your objectivity and sense of individuality.

Times of Neptune Special

During this period you are likely to become more impressionable and aware as your sensitivity is increased. You may pay more attention to your inner world or enhance your spiritual life. If you feel inspired by something or someone, you will want to follow your newfound ideals. If you do not have a clear goal or a realistic plan during this period, you may feel doubtful and vague about who you really are or what you really want. Therefore resist escaping through alcohol or drugs, as they can lead to confusion or misunderstandings. Since Neptune often dissolves boundaries and the Sun represents your ego, you may need to strengthen your sense of identity. By being receptive to both people and your environment, you are able to pick up the subtle moods of others. With this influence your idealism or compassion enters a new phase and you may increase your concern for others. Being very imaginative now, you benefit from pursuing some type of creative activity, or utilizing your vision for business purposes.

TIMES OF NEPTUNE SPECIAL TO YOUR SUN IN AQUARIUS: Neptune is transiting through Aquarius at present. It will remain in your Sun sign until 2011. During this period your vision and emotional sensitivity will increase and you may become inspired to achieve some of your ideals. You can become more sympathetic or in tune with others at this time.

TIMES OF NEPTUNE SPECIAL TO YOUR SUN IN PISCES: Neptune will enter your sign in 2011 and will remain there until 2025. During this period your sensitivity and imagination will increase. As your compassion and intuition is also heightened, you may become more interested in helping humanity or studying spiritual subjects. You will now be able to visualize your goals clearly, so by adding discipline and determination it is possible to manifest some of your emotional dreams or practical plans.

Times of Pluto Special

This is a once in a lifetime experience; therefore it is a very important period. You are likely to be energized and full of vitality or feel very strongly about issues. There is nothing superficial about you at this time, so the experiences that you are going through are forcing you to change old habits. During this time you are likely to be more determined than ever

and go after what you want. Since these changes are not always external, other people may not see what you are going through. Often with this influence you adopt the philosophy of "off with the old, on with the new." This is a good period for renewal, so it is wise to clear the decks and start something new or reorganize your life. Although your ego or ambition may be at its strongest, you need to watch out that you do not bring upheaval to others or try to be controlling. By focusing on your internal changes and deepening your understanding, you get the best out of what this period has to offer. If some of the changes that you are going through at this moment are difficult or challenging, you need to remember that they are often good for you in the long run. Pluto/Sun periods usually relate to your own mortality and remind you that nothing stays the same forever. As one door shuts another door opens and you can look to a period of renewal after this one is over.

TIMES OF PLUTO SPECIAL TO YOUR SUN IN SAGITTARIUS: Pluto is now passing through Sagittarius and will remain in this Sun sign until 2008. As you are likely to strengthen your enterprising spirit and idealism during this period, you can achieve success. Your need to expand your horizons may bring change and travel. You may also be inclined to transform your outlook and gain more self-awareness.

TIMES OF PLUTO SPECIAL TO YOUR SUN IN CAPRICORN: Pluto will enter your sign in 2008 and will remain there until 2023. You may be able to go through a real transformation if you allow change to reshape the old structures of your life. If you refuse to make the necessary alterations you may find this period more challenging. You will be well aware that some things in your life have passed their usefulness and in order to move forward, you need to let go.

Your Birthday Diary

Name	Date of Birth

Your Birthday Diary

Name	Date of Birth

Your Birthday Diary

Name	Date of Birth

Your Birthday Diary

Name	Date of Birth

Your Special Event Diary

Event	Date

Your Special Event Diary

Event	Date

About the Authors

SAFFI CRAWFORD, M.A., born May 28, is a professional numerologist and astrologer with thirteen years of experience. She runs a successful astrological counseling practice in London, teaches, and gives workshops in astrology and numerology. Her M.A. in social sciences combined the history and philosophy of Western civilization and included research into the history of astrology, hermeneutics, and reflexivity.

GERALDINE SULLIVAN, B.Sc., born June 4, is a professional astrologer with twenty years of experience. She is an international lecturer and has appeared on television talk shows in the United States. She runs a successful astrology practice, gives workshops, and teaches adult education classes in London. Her science degree combined astrology and psychology and included research into the unconscious, dreams, and mystical experience.